THE SPORT AMERICANA®

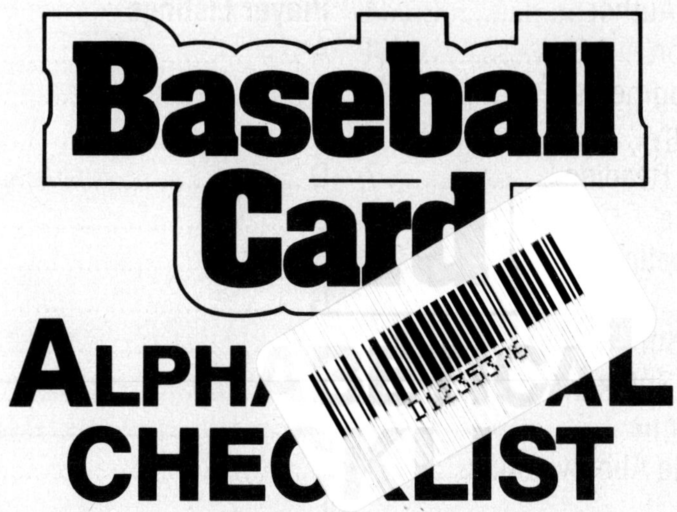

ALPHABETICAL CHECKLIST

NUMBER 6

By

DR. JAMES BECKETT

Published by Edgewater Book Co. Inc., Box 40238, Cleveland, OH 44140.

ISBN 0-937424-73-0

First Printing

The Sport Americana Baseball Card Alphabetical Checklist No. 6 Table of Contents

Index to Advertisers

Player Listings

About the Author

Jim Beckett, the leading authority on sport card values in the United States, maintains a wide range of activities in the world of sports. He possesses one of the finest collections of sports cards and autographs in the world, has made numerous appearances on radio and television, and has been frequently cited in many national publications. He was awarded the first "Special Achievement Award" for Contributions to the Hobby by the National Sports Collectors Convention in 1980, the "Jock-Jaspersen Award" for Hobby Dedication in 1983, and the "Buck Barker Spirit of the Hobby" Award in 1991.

Dr. Beckett is the author of *The Sport Americana Baseball Card Price Guide, The Official Price Guide to Baseball Cards, The Sport Americana Price Guide to Baseball Collectibles, The Sport Americana Baseball Memorabilia and Autograph Price Guide, The Sport Americana Football Card Price Guide, The Official Price Guide to Football Cards, The Sport Americana Hockey Card Price Guide, The Official Price Guide to Hockey Cards, The Sport Americana Basketball Card Price Guide and Alphabetical Checklist, The Official Price Guide to Basketball Cards,* and *The Sport Americana Baseball Card Alphabetical Checklist.* In addition, he is the founder, publisher, and editor of *Beckett Baseball Card Monthly, Beckett Basketball Monthly, Beckett Football Card Monthly, Beckett Hockey Monthly, Beckett Focus on Future Stars, Beckett Tribute:*, and *Beckett Racing Monthly* magazines.

Jim Beckett received his Ph.D. in Statistics from Southern Methodist University in 1975. Prior to starting Beckett Publications in 1984, Dr. Beckett served as an Associate Professor of Statistics at Bowling Green State University and as a vice president of a consulting firm in Dallas, Texas. He currently resides in Dallas with his wife, Patti, and their daughters, Christina, Rebecca, and Melissa.

Introduction

One of the many problems collectors of baseball cards face is the identification of the many, many thousands of different baseball cards that exist. The best method devised thus far is the checklist. This technique involves breaking down all cards into levels with identifiable characteristics. The most common system begins at the most general level and proceeds to more specific levels. These levels are:

MAKER (Topps, Bowman, Goudey, etc.);

YEAR OF ISSUE;

NUMBER ON CARD (beginning with #1 or the lowest card number and continuing in numerical order until the last or highest card number is reached);

PLAYER ON CARD (corresponding to the particular number on the card); listed alphabetically if the particular year's issue is unnumbered, in which case the NUMBER ON CARD level may not be listed.

The Sport Americana Baseball Card Price Guide, the parent book of this one, adds two additional categories to each card's description:

CONDITION (Mint, Very Good-Excellent, Fair-Good);

PRICE (Value of the card in a given condition grade).

The common checklist format is effective for many (possibly most) situations; however, it is not an all-purpose answer to the collector's needs. There are times when neither the common checklist nor the Price Guide provide the right tools for the collector. This alphabetical checklist is intended to fill the void when the common checklist will not suffice.

The theory behind the alphabetical checklist is quite simple: The four levels of the common checklist are reordered. Their hierarchy in the alphabetical checklist is as follows:

PLAYER ON CARD (players are listed alphabetically);

YEAR OF ISSUE;

MAKER (producer or manufacturer);

NUMBER ON CARD (not applicable to unnumbered cards).

Simple in design, this restructuring provides the collector with an easy-to-use cross-reference to his card collection.

Today's baseball card collecting hobby is no longer dominated by the complete-set collector. While obtaining all cards of all sets still remains the ultimate accomplishment, the sheer numbers, costs and time involved to obtain them has given rise to large numbers of card collecting specialists. Such specialists collect only cards of particular players or teams (see *The Sport Americana Baseball*

Card Team Checklist). The players may be stars, superstars, players from a particular team, players born in a particular place, players with surnames of a particular nationality, or even such ephemeral common denominators as players who are left-handed switch-hitters born east of the Mississippi below the Mason-Dixon line after 1933. As you can see, the possibilities are endless.

The Sport Americana Alphabetical Baseball Card Checklist presents all the cards issued for a particular player from virtually all baseball card sets, including Canadian and minor leagues, and a wide array of collectibles. No longer must a collector scan the entire 1957 Topps checklist to determine that the Brooks Robinson card of that year is #328. Nor must one go through four years of Bowman checklists to determine that the Bowman Rookie Card of Willie Mays is #305 in the 1951 series. The alphabetical checklist will show you without the necessity of having the actual card before you.

The concept of an alphabetical baseball card checklist is not new; however, we have attempted to make the current edition of *The Sport Americana Alphabetical Baseball Card Checklist* more complete, easier to use, and more attractive than any previous checklist of this kind. All of the cards of a particular player are listed consecutively below that player's name. There is no need to go to a second or third spot in the book to find that player's cards from another manufacturer or another time period.

Virtually all of the cards contained in any of the editions of *The Sport Americana Baseball Card Price Guide* and *The Sport Americana Baseball Collectibles Price Guide* are listed in this book. Many special cards are cross-referenced, as are checklist cards and team cards.

Acknowledgments

A great deal of hard work went into this volume, and it could not have been done without a considerable amount of help from many people. Our thanks are extended to each and every one of you.

Those who have worked closely with us on this and many other books have again proven themselves invaluable — Mike Aronstein, Chris Benjamin, Levi Bleam, Cartophilium (Andrew Pywowarczuk), Bill and Diane Dodge, Donruss/Leaf (Vince Nauss and Tracy Santiago), Doubleheaders, Fleer (Jeff Massien and Ted Taylor), Gervise Ford, Steve Freedman, Craig W. Friedemann, Larry and Jeff Fritsch, Tony Galovich, Georgia Music and Sports (Dick DeCourcy), Dick Goddard, Bill Goodwin (St. Louis Baseball Cards), Mike and Howard Gordon, George Grauer, Wayne Grove, Bill Haber, Don Harrison (Tenth Inning), Mike Hersh, Lew Lipset, Mark Macrae, Michael McDonald (The Sports Page), Don McPherson, Mid-Atlantic Sports Cards (Bill Bossert), Mike Mosier (Columbia City Collectibles Co.), B.A. Murry, Oldies and Goodies (Nigel Spill), Pacific Trading Cards (Mike and Marty Cramer), Pinnacle (Roy Whitehead), Jack Pollard, Jeff Prillaman, Gavin Riley, Alan Rosen (Mr. Mint), John Rumierz, San Diego Sport Collectibles (Bill Goepner and Nacho Arredondo), Kevin Savage (Sports Gallery), Gary Sawatski, Mike Schechter, Barry Sloate, John E. Spalding, Scoreboard (Ken Goldin and Phil Spector), Sports Collectors Store (Pat Quinn and Don Steinbach), Frank Steele, Murvin Sterling, Lee Temanson, Topps (Marty Appel, Sy Berger, and Bob Ibach), Treat (Harold Anderson), Ed Twombly (New England Bullpen), Upper Deck (Rich Bradley), Bill Wesslund (Portland Sports Card Co.), and Kit Young. Finally, we give a special acknowledgment to the late Dennis W. Eckes, "Mr. Sport Americana." The success of the Beckett Price Guides has always been the result of a team effort.

I believe this edition of the *The Sport Americana Alphabetical Baseball Card Checklist* is our best yet. For that, you can thank all of the contributors nationwide, as well as our staff here in Dallas. Our company now boasts a substantial Technical Services team, which has made (and will make) direct and important contributions to this work. Technical Services capably handled numerous technical details and provided able assistance in the preparation of this edition. That effort was directed by Technical Services manager Rich Olivieri. He was ably assisted by Technical Services assistant manager Mary Gregory and the Price Guide analysts: Jeff Allison, Terry Bloom, Theo Chen (Editorial Coordinator), Ben Ecklar, Dan Hitt (Market Information Coordinator), Mike Jaspersen (Product Information Coordinator), Rich Klein, Tom Layberger, Allan Muir, Grant Sandground (Pricing Coordinator), Dave Sliepka and Steve Smith. Also contributing to Technical Services functions were Jack Beaudry, Lynn Blackburn, Carlos Leal, Travis Raczynski and Gabriel Rangel. I want to especially thank Rich Klein and Ben Ecklar, who (incredibly) did most of the intensive proofing.

Granted, the production of any book is a total team effort. However, I owe special thanks to the members of our Book Team who demonstrated extraordinary contributions to this massive undertaking. Managing Editor Steve Wilson supervised a dedicated staff that continues to grow in expertise. He ensured deadlines were met, while looking for ways to improve our process and presentation throughout the cycle. Scott Layton, Assistant Manager of Special Projects, spearheaded the processing of information and the delegating of the myriad tasks involved in the production of this book. He was ably assisted by Julie Grove, Maria Neubauer, Judi Smalling, Peter Tepp and Ted Halbur.

Our computer experts, Rich Olivieri and Jack Beaudry, simplified the sorting and merging of thousands of card entries and ensured this would be our most comprehensive and accurate edition yet. Computer Services manager Airey Baringer, with help from Mary Gonzales-Davis and Matt Bowling, made sure the typesetting of the text went smoothly. Carrie Ehrhardt attended to the wishes of our dealer advertisers, and John Marshall turned those wishes into attractive advertisements.

Many other people have provided checklist verifications, errata, and/or background information. We would like to individually thank Ab D Cards (Dale Wesolewski), Jerry Adamic, Dennis Anderson, Chuck Baldree, Douglas Bell, Karen Bell, D. Bruce Brown, Ira Cetron, Mike Christianson, Brian DeCaussin, Ben Defibaugh, Donald Dietrich, Robert Duke, R.L. Dyke, Dana Eisenger, Doak Ewing, Linda Ferrigno, Russell Ferris, Michael Firkser, Shirley Fortin, Craig W. Friedemann, Cappy Gagnons, Daymond Gee, M.M. Gibson, Rob Grierson, John Grist, Hall's Nostalgia, Bill Henderson, William S. Herbert, Jim Hutchinson, Jack W. Kary, Frank J. Katen, David J. Kathman, Irv Lerner, Bill Ludlum, Rich Marquart, Andrew Menown, Mike Mezzardi, Joe Michalowicz, Tom Mohelnitzky, Mike O'Brien, Ronald Pashen, Tom Pfirrmann, Tom Reid, Michael Riordan, Bruce Rokos, Scott Rosen, David Rothlauf, Jack Rudley, Sandra Rufty, Garry Rust, Joe Sak, Mike Scholl, Randall L. Sheaffer, Jeffrey J. Swab, Mark W. Szczucinski, Vincent Tobin, Martha Toth, Randy Trierweiler, Walter Walbrick, Richard E. Walden, Dave Weber, Richard West, Brian Woolery, David Yoder, and Robert Zanze.

We have appreciated all of the help we have received over the years from collectors across the country and, indeed, throughout the world. Every year we make active solicitations to individuals and groups for input for a specific edition and we are particularly appreciative of the help (large and small) provided for this volume. While we receive many inquiries, comments and questions — and, in fact, each and every one is read and digested — time constraints prevent us from personally replying to all but a few such letters. We hope that the letters will continue, and that even though no reply is received, you will feel that you are making significant contributions to the hobby through your interest and comments.

In the years since this guide debuted, Beckett Publications has grown beyond any rational expectation. A great many talented and hard working individuals have been instrumental in this growth and success. Our whole team is to be congratulated for what we together have accomplished. Our Beckett Publications team is led by Associate Publisher Claire Backus, Vice Presidents Jeff Amano, Joe Galindo and Fred Reed, and Senior Managers Beth Harwell, Pepper Hastings and Reed Poole. They are ably assisted by Dana Alecknavage, Theresa Anderson, Alan Andrews, Jeff Anthony, Kelly Atkins, Kaye Ball, Marvin Bang, Barbara Barry, Nancy Bassi, James R. Beane, Therese Bellar, Christa Bencomo, Louise Bird, Wendy Bird, Cathryn Black, Terry Bloom, Diane Boudreaux, Amy Brougher, Anthony Brown, Bob Brown, Michael Brunelli, Janel Bush, Chris Calandro, Randy Calvert, Emily Camp, Mary Campana, Susan Catka, Tim Chamberlain, Jud Chappell, Albert Chavez, Evelyn Clark, Tommy Collins, Belinda Cross, Randy Cummings, Patrick Cunningham, Marlon DePaula, Gail Docekal, Alejandro Egusquiza, Paulo Egusquiza, Eric Evans, Dan Ferguson, Craig Ferris, Jorge Field, Sara Field, Jean Paul Figari, Jeany Finch, Kim Ford, Gayle Gasperin, Loretta Gibbs, Anita Gonzalez, Rosanna Gonzalez-Olaechea, Mary Gonzalez-Davis, Jeff Greer, Jenifer Grellhesl, Julie Grove, Susan Hamm, Susie Handleman, Jenny Harwell, Mark Harwell, Joanna Hayden, Chris Hellem, Barbara Hinkle, Tracy Hinton, Dan Hitt, Tim Jaksa, Deliese Jaspersen, Julia Jernigan, Jay Johnson, Paul Kerutis, Wendy Kizer, Rudy Klancnik, Frances Knight, Jane Ann Layton, Benedito Leme, Lori Lindsey, Stanley Lira, Sara Maneval, Louis Marroquin, John Marshall, Kaki Matheson, Mike McAllister, Patti

McCrary, Teri McGahey, Kirk McKinney, Omar Mediano, Lisa Monaghan, Sherry Monday, Robert Moore, Glen Morante, Mila Morante, Daniel Moscoso Jr., Mike Moss, Randy Mosty, Allan Muir, Hugh Murphy, Shawn Murphy, Steve Naughton, Lisa O'Neill, Stacy Olivieri, Mike Pagel, Wendy Pallugna, Laura Patterson, Mike Payne, Keith Pentico, Tim Polzer, Fran Poole, Cara Preuth, Travis Raczynski, Fred Reed IV, Shannon Remke, Bob Richardson, Tina Riojas, Gary Santaniello, Brett Setter, Janice Seydel, Elaine Simmons, Lynn Smith, Sheri Smith, Jeff Stanton, Laura Steele, Margaret Steele, Natalie Stephens, Marcia Stoesz, Cindy Struble, Doree Tate, Diane Taylor, Jim Tereschuk, Jana Threatt, Cindy Waisath, Carol Weaver, Robert Yearby and Mark Zeske. The whole Beckett Publications team has my thanks for jobs well done. Thank you, everyone.

I also thank my family, especially my wife, Patti, and daughters, Christina, Rebecca, and Melissa, for putting up with me again.

Terminology

Each hobby has its own language to describe its area of interest. The nomenclature traditionally used for trading cards is derived from the *American Card Catalog (ACC)*, published in 1960 by Nostalgia Press. That catalog, written by Jefferson Burdick (who is called the "Father of Card Collecting" for his pioneering work), uses letter and number designations for each separate set of cards. The letter used in the ACC designation refers to the generic type of card. While both sport and non-sport issues are classified in the ACC, we shall confine ourselves to the sport issues. The following list defines the letters and their meanings as used by the American Card Catalog.

(none) or **N** - 19th Century U.S. Tobacco
B - Blankets
D - Bakery Inserts Including Bread
E - Early Candy and Gum
F - Food Inserts
H - Advertising
M - Periodicals
PC - Postcards
R - Candy and Gum since 1930

Following the letter prefix and an optional hyphen are one-, two-, or three-digit numbers, R(-)999. These typically represent the company or entity issuing the cards. In several cases, the ACC number is extended by an additional hyphen and another one- or two-digit numerical suffix.

For example, the 1957 Topps regular-series baseball card issue carries an ACC designation of R414-11. The "R" indicates a Candy or Gum card produced since 1930. The "414" is the ACC designation for Topps Chewing Gum baseball card issues, and the "11" is the ACC designation for the 1957 regular issue (Topps' eleventh baseball set).

Like other traditional methods of identification, this system provides order to the process of cataloging cards; however, most serious collectors learn the ACC designation of the popular sets by repetition and familiarity, rather than by attempting to "figure out" what they might or should be. From 1948 forward, collectors and dealers commonly refer to all sets by their year, maker, type of issue and any other distinguishing characteristic. For example, such a characteristic could be an unusual issue or one of several regular issues put out by a specific maker in a single year. Regional issues are usually referred to by year, maker, and sometimes by title or theme of the set.

Additional Reading

With the increase in popularity of the hobby in recent years, there has been a corresponding increase in available literature. Below is a list of the books and periodicals that receive our highest recommendation and that we hope will further advance your knowledge and enjoyment of our great hobby.

The Sport Americana Baseball Card Price Guide by Dr. James Beckett (Sixteenth Edition, $16.95, released 1994, published by Edgewater Book Company) — the most comprehensive Price Guide and checklist ever issued on baseball cards.

The Official Price Guide to Baseball Cards by Dr. James Beckett (Fourteenth Edition, $6.99, released 1994, published by The House of Collectibles) — an abridgment of *The Sport Americana Price Guide* in a convenient and economical pocket-size format providing Dr. Beckett's pricing of the major baseball sets since 1948.

The Sport Americana Football Card Price Guide by Dr. James Beckett (Tenth Edition, $15.95, released 1993, published by Edgewater Book Company) — the most comprehensive Price Guide and checklist ever issued on football cards. No serious football card hobbyist should be without it.

The Official Price Guide to Football Cards by Dr. James Beckett (Thirteenth Edition, $6.99, released 1993, published by The House of Collectibles) — an abridgment of *The Sport Americana Price Guide* listed above in a convenient and economical pocket-size format providing Dr. Beckett's pricing of the major football sets since 1948.

The Sport Americana Hockey Card Price Guide by Dr. James Beckett (Third Edition, $14.95, released 1994, published by Edgewater Book Company) — the most comprehensive Price Guide and checklist ever issued on hockey cards.

The Official Price Guide to Hockey Cards by Dr. James Beckett (Third Edition, $6.99, released 1993, published by The House of Collectibles) — an abridgment of *The Sport Americana Price Guide* listed above in a convenient and economical pocket-size format providing Dr. Beckett's pricing of the major hockey sets since 1951.

The Sport Americana Basketball Card Price Guide and Alphabetical Checklist by Dr. James Beckett (Third Edition, $14.95, released 1993, published by Edgewater Book Company) — the most comprehensive combination Price Guide and alphabetical checklist ever issued on basketball cards.

The Official Price Guide to Basketball Cards by Dr. James Beckett (Third Edition, $6.99, released 1993, published by The House of Collectibles) — an abridgment of *The Sport Americana Price Guide* listed above in a convenient and economical pocket-size format providing Dr. Beckett's pricing of the major basketball sets since 1948.

The Sport Americana Price Guide to the Non-Sports Cards 1930-1960 by Christopher Benjamin (Second Edition, $14.95, released 1993, published by Edgewater Book Company) — the definitive guide to virtually all popular non-sports American tobacco and bubblegum cards issued between 1930 and 1960. In addition to cards, illustrations and prices for wrappers also are included.

The Sport Americana Price Guide to the Non-Sports Cards by Christopher Benjamin (Fourth Edition, $14.95, released 1992, published by Edgewater Book Company) — the definitive guide to all popular non-sports American cards. In addition to cards, illustrations and prices for wrappers also are included. This volume covers non-sports cards from 1961 to 1992.

The Sport Americana Baseball Address List by Jack Smalling (Seventh Edition, $12.95, released 1992, published by Edgewater Book Company) — the definitive guide for autograph hunters, giving addresses and deceased information for virtually all Major League Baseball players past and present.

The Sport Americana Team Baseball Card Checklist by Jeff Fritsch (Sixth Edition, $12.95, released 1992, published by Edgewater Book Company) — includes all Topps, Bowman, Donruss, Fleer, Score, Play Ball, Goudey, and Upper Deck cards, with the players portrayed on the cards listed with the teams for whom they played. The book is invaluable to the collector who specializes in an individual team because it is the most complete baseball card team checklist available.

The Sport Americana Team Football and Basketball Card Checklist by Jeff Fritsch and Jane Fritsch-Gavin (Second Edition, $12.95, released 1993, published by Edgewater Book Company) — the book is invaluable to the collector who specializes in an individual team because it is the most complete football and basketball card team checklist available.

Beckett Baseball Card Monthly, published and edited by Dr. James Beckett, contains the most extensive and accepted monthly Price Guide, collectible glossy superstar covers, colorful feature articles, "who's Hot and who's Cold" section, Convention Calendar, tips for beginners, "Readers Write" letters to and responses from the editor, information on errors and varieties, autograph collecting tips and profiles of the sport's Hottest stars. Published every month, *BBCM* is the hobby's largest paid circulation periodical. *Beckett Football Card Monthly*, *Beckett Basketball Monthly*, *Beckett Hockey Monthly*, *Beckett Focus on Future Stars®*, *Beckett Tribute:* and *Beckett Racing Monthly* were built on the success of *BBCM*.

Errata

While a great deal of effort has been made to avoid errors of any type, it seems inevitable that errors, misspellings, and inconsistencies may occur. Please inform the author of any you find, and corrections will be incorporated in the next edition. Send to: Dr. James Beckett, 15850 Dallas Parkway, Dallas, Texas 75248.

Advertising

Within this Price Guide you will find advertisements for sports memorabilia material, mail order, and retail sports collectibles establishments. All advertisements were accepted in good faith based on the reputation of the advertiser; however, neither the author, the publisher, the distributors, nor the other advertisers in this Price Guide accept any responsibility for any particular advertiser not complying with the terms of his or her ad.

How to Use the Alphabetical Checklist

This alphabetical index will prove to be an invaluable tool for seasoned and novice collectors alike. It has been designed to be user friendly. The set code abbreviations used throughout are easily identified and memorized. The format adopted for card identification is explained below. Because of the large number of different card sets contained in this volume, it is important that you familiarize yourself with the format and terminology used here. PLEASE READ THE FOLLOWING SECTION CAREFULLY BEFORE ATTEMPTING TO USE THE CHECKLIST.

The player cards are listed alphabetically by the player's current last name. Where appropriate, nicknames (e.g., "Babe" Ruth) and various shortened forms of the names (e.g., "Rich" for Richard) are given in parentheses on the second line of the entry. Different players with identical names are distinguished by additional information whenever possible. In the absence of such information, the players are distinguished by numbers (e.g., Anderson, Steve 1; Anderson, Steve 2 and Anderson, Steve 3). The codes following the players' names are indented and give the set names and numbers of the cards on which the players appeared. The set code abbreviations are designed so that each code is distinctive for a particular card set.

Depending on the particular card set, the set code abbreviations consist of from three to five different elements: a) Year of issue (listed in ascending chronological order); b) Producer or sponsor; c) Set code suffix (always after a slash); d) Number on card (always separated from the maker or set code suffix by a dash); e) Individual card descriptive suffixes.

Here is an example of a typical listing:

Ripken, Cal Jr.

92 D/Preview-10

Year: 1992, **Manufacturer:** Donruss, **Set Code Suffix:** Preview, **Card Number:** 10

In those rare instances where the year of issue extends beyond one calendar year (e.g., 1972-79 Dimanche/Derniere Heure *), an abbreviated form of the earliest date is given for the year of issue (i.e., 72 for 1972). Vintage sets are referred to not by their year of issue, but by their designations according to the *American Card Catalog* (e.g., C46 [1912 Imperial Tobacco]).

Minor league sets are referred to by year, the name of the city from which the team hails (or a shortened form thereof), and manufacturer or sponsor. For example, "88James/ProC-1920" refers to card number 1920 of the 1988 Jamestown Expos ProCards set.

When two different producers issued cards for a player in the same year, the cards are listed alphabetically according to the maker's name (e.g., 1990 Fleer Canadian precedes 1990 O-Pee-Chee).

The set code suffixes are necessary to distinguish two different sets produced or sponsored by the same company in the same year. In the following example, the set codes suffixes "/Fire" and "/Hit" distinguish two different insert sets featured in the 1994 Ultra baseball series:

Abbreviation	**Explanation**
94Ultra/Fire	1994 Ultra Firemen
94Ultra/Hit	1994 Ultra Hitting Machines

The use of two set code suffixes – indicated by two slashes in the set code abbreviation – was kept to a minimum but found necessary to identify accurately a small number of sets (e.g., 93BJ/D/WS is 1993 Blue Jays Donruss World Series).

The card number typically corresponds to the particular number on the card itself; in some instances, the card number also involves letter prefixes. For the most part, cards in unnumbered sets are usually entered alphabetically according to the player's last name and assigned a number arbitrarily. In sets in which all the cards are numbered, a single unnumbered card is marked either "x(x)" or "NNO" for "no number."

Although individual card suffixes are not necessary for unambiguous card identification, they do provide the reader with additional information about the card and the individual portrayed on it. These abbreviations usually mark subset cards (e.g., AS marks an "All-Star" card) or nonplayer cards (e.g., TR indicates a "trainer"), and they were added after the card number. The most common card suffix is "M," which indicates that the card is a multi-player card portraying two or more individuals. In those cases involving two possible letter suffixes, one of the card suffixes was dropped to avoid a cumbersome designation.

Lastly, the user of this checklist will notice that the cards of players from sports other than baseball (as well as subjects not even from the world of sports) are contained in this checklist. This circumstance arose because of the decision to include in this checklist multi-sport sets containing some baseball cards. In the checklist, these multi-sport card sets are typically indicated by an asterisk (*), which is placed after the set code suffix in the alphabetical checklist.

Organization of Codes

To facilitate easy reference, the codes used throughout this checklist have been organized into four categories:

1) Set Codes
2) Set Code Suffixes
3) Individual Card Suffix Codes
4) Minor League and College Abbreviations

Set Codes

Code	Example
A's	Oakland Athletics or A's
AlGrif	Alrak Griffey
AmTract	American Tract Society
AP	Action Packed
Armour	Armour Coins
Ast	Houston Astros
B	Bowman
BB	Bell Brand
BBBest	Baseball's Best
BBWit	Baseball Wit
BeeHive	Bee Hive Starch
Berg	David Berg
BestWest	Best Western
BF#	Felt Pennants
Bimbo	Bimbo Bread Discs
BJ	Toronto Blue Jays
BK	Burger King
BLChew	Big League Chew
Bleach	Bleachers
Bohem	Bohemian Padres
Bond	Bond Bread
BR	Berk Ross
Brave	Atlanta Braves
Brew	Milwaukee Brewers
Briggs	Briggs Hot Dogs
BU	Batter Up
BurgChef	Burger Chef Discs
Buster	Buster Brown Pins
Bz	Bazooka
Cadaco	Cadaco Ellis Game
Callahn	Callahan
Card	St. Louis Cardinals
CEA	Chicago Evening American
Centen	Centennial
ChefBoy	Chef Boyardee
CircK	Circle K
CityP	City Pride
CJ	Cracker Jack
ClBest	Classic Best
Clover	Cloverleaf Dairy
Coke	Coca-Cola
CokeK	Coke/Kroger
CollAB	Collect-A-Books
CounHrth	Country Hearth
Cram	Cramer
Crane	Crane Discs
Crunch	Cap'n Crunch (Topps)
Cub	Chicago Cubs
D	Donruss
D#	Bakery Inserts
DennyGS	Denny's Grand Slam
Det	Detroit
Detroit	Detroit News
Dexter	Dexter Press
DF	Darigold Farms
DG	Decade Greats
DH	Doubleheader
Diamond	Diamond Gum Pins
Dimanche	Dimanche/Derniere Heure
Dix	Dixie Lids
DL	Delong
DP	Double Play
DQ	Dairy Queen
DS	Diamond Stars
Dunkin	Dunkin Donuts
E#	Early Candy and Gum
EH	East Hills
EliteSenL	Elite Senior League
Eureka	Eureka Stamps
Exh	Exhibits
Expo	Montreal Expos
F	Fleer
FanSam	Fantastic Sam's Discs
FB	Fischer Baking Labels
FBI	FBI Discs
FleischBrd	Fleischmann Bread
Foil	Foil Best (Minor League cards)
FrBauer	French Bauer Caps
French	French Bray Orioles
FresnoSt	Fresno State
Fritsch	Fritsch
FrRow	Front Row
Fud's	Fud's Photography
FunFood	Fun Foods Pins
G	Goudey
Galasso	Galasso
Gard	Gardner
Gator	Gatorade
GenMills	General Mills
Giant	San Francisco Giants
Gol	Golden Braves Stamps
GoldEnt	Gold Entertainment
GP	Golden Press
Granny	Granny Goose
Grenada	Grenada Baseball Stamps
Griffey	Griffey Gazette

Hardee	Hardee's
Hawth	Hawthorne-Mellody Pins
HB	Hillerich/Bradsby
Helmar	Helmar Stamps
HenryH	Henry House Wieners
Highland	Highland Mint
Ho	Hostess
Homer	Homers Cookies
HomogBond	Homogenized Bond
HotPlay	Hottest 50 Players Stickers
HotRook	Hottest 50 Rookies Stickers
HRDerby	Home Run Derby
Hughes	Hughes Solons
HumDum	Humpty Dumpty
Hygrade	Hygrade Expos
Icee	Icee
Indian	Cleveland Indians
J	Jello
JB	Jack in the Box
JC	Johnston Cookies
JDean	Jimmy Dean
Jiffy	Jiffy Pop Discs
JP	Johnny Pro
K	Kelloggs
Kahn	Kahn's
Kaline	Kaline Story
KAS	KAS Cardinals Discs
Keller	Keller's
Kelly	Kelly Pins
KingB	King-B Discs
Kitty	Kitty Clover Discs
L	Leaf
L#	Leathers
Lake	Lake to Lake
LaPatrie	La Patrie
LaPizza	La Pizza Royale
LaPresse	La Presse
Laugh	Laughlin Great Feats
Laval	Laval Provinciale
LimeR	Lime Rock
LineD	Line Drive (Minor League cards)
LitSun	Little Sun
Lookout	Lookout Legends
LSU	Louisiana State University
M#	Periodical Issues
MajorLg	Major League Collector Pins
Maple	Toronto Maple Leafs
Mar	Seattle Mariners
Mara	Marathon
Marchant	Marchant Exhibits
Marlin	Florida Marlins
Master	Master Bread Discs
MB	Milton Bradley
McDon	McDonald's
MCI	MCI Ambassadors
MD	Milk Duds
MDA	MDA All-Stars
Mega	Megacards
Metallic	Metallic Images
Mets	New York Mets
MilSau	Milwaukee Sausage
MJB	MJB Holographics
MLBPA	MLBPA Baseball Pins
MooTown	MooTown Snackers
Morrell	Morrell Meats
Mother	Mother's Cookies
Motor	Motorola
MP	MP and Co.
MSA	Mike Schechter Associates
MTV	MTV Rock n' Jock
N#	19th Century
NatPhoto	National Photo (Royals)
NB	Northland Bread Labels
Negro	Negro League
Nes	Nestle
NTea	National Tea Labels
NTF	Nabisco Team Flakes
NuCard	Nu-Card Hi-Lites
NYJour	NY Journal American
OhHenry	Oh Henry
OldLond	Old London Coins
ONG	Our National Game pins
OPC	O-Pee-Chee
Orbit	Orbit Pins Unnumbered
Orio	Baltimore Orioles
Oscar	Oscar Mayers
P	Post
Pac	Pacific
PacBell	Packard Bell
PapaG	Papa Ginos Discs
Panini	Panini Stickers
Parade	Parade Sportive
Park	Parkhurst
PlayBall	Play Ball
PCL	Pacific Coast League
Pep	Pepsi
Peters	Peter's Meats
Perez	Perez-Steele
PermaGr	Perma-Graphic
Petro	Petro-Canada Standups
PG&E	Pacific Gas and Electric Giants
PhilBull	Philadelphia Bulletin
Phill	Philadelphia Phillies
Piedmont	Piedmont Stamps
Pinn	Pinnacle
Pirate	Pittsburgh Pirates
PM#	Pins
Pol	Police/Safety
Polar	Polaroid
Post	Post Cereal
ProStars	Pro Stars Postcards
PublInt	Publications International
Quaker	Quaker Oats
R#	1930s Gum Issues
Rainbow	Rainbow Foods
Rang	Texas Rangers
Rangers	Texas Rangers
Rawl	Rawling's
RedLob	Cubs Red Lobster
Reds	Cincinnati Reds
RedSox	Boston Red Sox
Rem	Rembrandt
Remar	Remar Bread
RFG	Robert F. Gould
RH	Red Heart
Rice	Rice Stix
Rini	Susan Rini postcards
RM	Red Man
Rodeo	Rodeo Meats
Royal	Royal Desserts
RoyRog	Roy Rogers Discs
S	Score
S#	Silks
Salada	Salada Coins
Salem	Salem Potato Chips
SanDiegoSt	San Diego State
Schnucks	Schnucks
Scrapps	Scrapps
Seattle	Seattle
Select	Select
Seven	SevenUp or Seven-Eleven
Sf	Sportflics

SFCallB	San Francisco Call-Bulletin
SFExam	San Francisco Examiner
Shakey	Shakey's
Sheraton	Sheraton
Sherlock	Mrs. Sherlock's Pins
Shirriff	Shirriff Coins
SigRook	Signature Rookies
SilverSt	SilverStar Holograms
SK	Sport Kings
Sky	SkyBox
SM	Stahl Meyer
Smok	Smokey Bear
SpicSpan	Spic and Span
Sqt	Squirt
StarCal	Star Cal Decals
Starshot	Starshots Pinback Badges
StCl	Stadium Club (Topps)
Stuart	Stuart Panels
Sugar	Sugardale
Sunflower	Sunflower Seeds
Sweet	Sweet Caporal Pins
Swell	Swell Sport Thrills
Swift	Swift Meats
T	Topps
Tast	Tastee Freeze Discs
TexGold	Texas Gold
ThomMc	Thom McAn Discs
Thorn	Thorn Apple Valley
Ticket	Ticketron
Tiger	Detroit Tigers or Tiger Wave
TipTop	TipTop Bread
T/M	T and M Sports Umpires
Tor	Toronto
ToysRUs	Toys "R" Us
Trans	Transogram
TripleP	Triple Play
TrueVal	True Value
TWill	Ted Williams
Twin	Minnesota Twins
T#	20th U.S. Tobacco
UD	Upper Deck
Union	Union Oil
USPlayC	U.S. Playing Cards
USPS	USPS Legends Stamp Cards
V#	Canada Candy
VFJuice	Very Fine Juice
W#	Strip Cards
Ward's	Ward's Sporties Pins
West	Doug West
WG#	Game Cards
WhatRyan	Whataburger Nolan Ryan
Wheat	Wheaties
WichSt	Wichita State Game Day
Wiffle	Wiffle Ball Discs
Wilson	Wilson Wieners
Windwlk	Windwalker Discs
WonderBrd	Wonder Bread
Woolwth	Woolworth
WSox	Chicago White Sox
Yank	New York Yankees
YellBase	Yellow Basepath Pins
Yueng	Yuenglings
Zeller	Zeller's

denotes a multi-sport set

Set Code Suffixes

Code	Example
/A	Type A (R303A)
/A	82OrlTw/A (Orlando after season)
/AAS	Action All-Stars
/AASingl	AA Singles
/AAASingl	AAA Singles
/Ace	Aces
/Aces	Baseball's Best Aces of the Mound
/Act	Action
/ActionSt	Action Stickers
/AGFA	MSA AGFA film
/AL	American League
/ALAS	AL All-Stars
/Alb	Stamp Albums
/AllLat	All-Latino
/AllRook	All-Rookies
/Am	Conlon American All-Stars
/Ames	Topps Ames (All-Stars, 20/20 Club)
/Amo	Amoco
/Angel(s)	California Angel(s)
/Ann	Anniversary '84
/Arc53	1991 Topps Archive 1953
/Arc54	1994 Topps Archive 1954
/Arco	Arco Oil
/Artist	Pinnacle Artist's Proof
/AS	All-Stars
/A's	Oakland A's or Athletics
/ASAL	All-Stars AL
/ASCMC	All-Stars CMC
/ASFan	Score All-Star Fanfest
/ASFF	All-Star FanFest
/ASG	All-Star Games
/ASGProto	Action Packed ASG Prototypes
/ASIns	Fleer All-Star Inserts
/ASNL	All-Stars NL
/ASP	All-Star Program
/ASRook	All-Star Rookies
/Ast(ros)	Houston Ast(ros)
/ATG	All Time Greats
/ATGHolo	ATG Holograms
/ATH	All-Time Heroes
/ATHPrev	All-Time Heroes Previews
/Atl	62Kahn/Atlanta
/Ault	Ault Foods
/AwardWin	Award Winners
/B	Type B (R303B)
/B	82OrlTw/B (Orlando before season)
/B	80Penin/B (Peninsula b&w set)
/Back	Topps Sticker Backs
/Bagwell	Jeff Bagwell
/Ball	Ballpark
/Banks	Ernie Banks
/BB	Blue Backs
/BB	1988 Fleer Baseball All-Stars
/BBGr	Baseball Greats
/BBMVP	Fleer Baseball MVP's
/BBonusC	Blue Bonus Cards
/BC	N172/BC (Brown's Champs) or Bonus Card
/Beisbol	Beisbol Amigos
/Ben	Ben's Super Pitchers Discs
/Bench	Bench/Morgan Heroes
/Berra	Yogi Berra
/Best	Best (Minor League cards)
/Best	1988 Donruss Baseball's Best
/BHN	Baseball Hobby News
/Big	Topps Big
/BJ	Blue Jays
/Bk	Donruss Team Book
/BK	Burger King
/Black	Laughlin Old Time Black Stars
/Blank	Meadow Gold Blank Back
/Bleach	Bleacher Bums
/BlkGold	Black Gold

/blue T213/blue (blue caption)
/BlueJ Toronto Blue Jays
/BlueS Blue Shield
/BlueTCL Blue Team Checklists
/Board 1887 Topps Board (Boardwalk & Baseball)
/Bob Bob's Camera (Minor League cards)
/Bomb Bomb Squad
/Bon The Bon (Minor League cards)
/Bonds 23K Barry Bonds
/Bonus Donruss Bonus MVP's
/Bonus Bonus Signatures
/Book Donruss Team Book
/Book Booklets
/Box Topps Sticker Boxes
/Box Box Scores (Minor League cards)
/BoxB Box Bottoms
/Boys Boys of Summer
/BPro Best/Pro (Minor League cards)
/Brave(s) Atlanta Braves
/Brew Milwaukee Brewers
/Brock Lou Brock
/brown T213/brown (brown caption)
/Bubble Bubble Yum
/bucks 1962 Topps Bucks (baseball bucks)
/Bumble Bumble Bee
/BW Black and White
/C 80Penin/C (Peninsula color set)
/Cal Cal League (Minor League cards)
/Can 1953 Exhibits Canadian or Post Canada
/Candl Candl Coin (Minor League cards)
/Card St. Louis Cardinals
/Career Career Achievement Awards
/Carl Carl's Jr. Restaurants
/Carlson Carlson Travel
/CAS Current All-Stars
/CB 1970 Topps (Comic) Story Booklets
/CBatL K-Mart Career Batting Leaders
/CC Perma-Graphics Credit Cards
/Cereal 1984 Topps Cereal
/Champs 1984 Donruss Champs
/Charter Charter Member
/ChasRook Chase Rookies
/ChasS Chase Stars
/Chong Chong (Minor League cards)
/CJMini Topps Cracker Jack Minis
/CL Carolina League
/Clark Clark Reggie Jackson
/Classic Homers Cookies Classics
/ClBest Classic Best (Minor League cards)
/Clean Clean-Up Crew
/Clemente Roberto Clemente
/Clemens Clemens Commemorative
/ClemIns Fleer Clemens Inserts
/Cloth Topps Test Cloth
/ClothSt Cloth Sticker
/Clown Laughlin Indianapolis Clowns
/Clutch Clutch Performers
/CM 1951 Topps Connie Mack All-Stars
/CMC Collectors Marketing Corp.
/Coin Coins
/Coins 1964 Topps coins
/Col 1953 Bowman Color
/CollC UD Collector's Choice
/CollCPr UD Collector's Choice Promo
/CollHolo College POY Holograms
/CollHR UD Collector's Choice Home Run All-Stars
/Comics 1973 Topps Comics
/ComRyan Score Commemorative Nolan Ryan
/Coop Kahn's Cooperstown
/Cooper Cooperstown
/CornAS Corn Flakes All-Stars
/Cr Crown Collection
/Cram Cramer (Minor League cards)
/CrCon Crown Contenders
/Crown Crown Oil
/CrPr Crown Collection Promos
/Crunch 1989 Topps Cap'n Crunch
/Cub Cubs
/CS 1977 Topps Cloth Stickers
/D Donruss
/Dandridge Ray Dandridge
/DC 1955 Spic and Span Die-Cut
/DColl Diamond Collection
/DE Deckle Edge
/DealP Sportflics Dealer Panels
/Dec Decade Greats
/decal Decals
/Demp Dempster's
/Detroit Detroit News
/DG Decade Greats
/DH Double Headers
/DHTest Topps Doubleheaders Test
/DI Donruss I
/Diam Diamond Gallery
/DiamD Diamond Dynamos
/DII Donruss II
/Dice 1961 Topps Dice Game
/DiMag Joe DiMaggio
/DiMagAU DiMaggio Autographs
/DIMD Diamond (Minor League cards)
/Disc Discs
/Dixon Phil Dixon
/DK (Super) Diamond Kings
/DKsuper 85D/DKsuper
/DM Diamond Marks
/DMArt Dimond Marks Art
/DMProto Diamond Marks Prototypes
/Dodg Los Angeles Dodgers
/DodgAngel Dodgers and Angels
/Dog Dog'n Shake
/Dome Dome Special
/DomI Dominators I
/DomII Dominators II
/DomPr Dominican Promos
/DP Draft Picks
/DPFoil Draft Picks Foil Bonus
/DPPr Draft Picks Promos
/DPPrev Draft Picks Previews
/DQ Dairy Queen
/DT Dream Team
/DTrib Diamond Tribute
/Dubuq Dubuque
/Dugout Dugout Dirt Comic Cards
/Dunkin Dunkin' Donuts
/Duques Duquesne
/Duri Durivage
/E Embossed
/Eck Dennis Eckersley
/EckComm Dennis Eckersley Commemorative
/ElecD Electric Diamond
/EliteDom Elite Dominators
/EliteUp Elite Update Supers
/Etch Etched in Stone
/Excit Fleer Exciting Stars
/Expan Expansion Opening Day
/ExpPick Expansion Picks
/Ext Extended
/Factory Factory Inserts
/FamFeat Famous Feats

/FamFun	Family Fun
/Fan	Fan Club
/Farmer	Farmer Jack
/Fast	Fasttrack
/FB	First Base
/Fig	Figures
/FFeat	Famous Feats
/Final (Ed)	Final Edition
/FinestASJ	Finest All-Star Jumbos
/FinestPr	Finest Promos
/FinestRef	Finest Refractors
/Fire	Fire Safety or (1994 Ultra) Firemen
/Fisher	Fisher Nuts
/FLAg	Florida Agriculture
/Floyd	Cliff Floyd
/Fold	Foldouts
/Ford	Whitey Ford
/FrAS	Frosted Flakes All-Stars
/FrBoxB	Frosted Flakes Box Back
/FriszP	Prisz Postcards
/Frit	Larry Fritsch (Minor league cards)
/FrSt	French Stickers
/Fruit	Fruit of the Loom
/Full	Full Shots
/FunPack	Fun Packs
/FunPackAS	Fun Packs All-Stars
/Fut	Futera
/G	Game Cards
/GAce	Gold Glow-In-The-Dark Acetates
/Gal	Gallery
/Gamer	Gamers
/GameWin	Game Winners
/Gardiner	Dan Gardiner Collection
/Gator	Gatorade
/GF	Great Feats
/Giant	Giants
/Glavine	Tom Glavine
/Glen	Glendale
/Gloss22	Gloss22 (All-Stars)
/Gloss40	83T/Gloss40 (Send In Glossy)
/Gloss60	86T/Gloss60 (Send In Glossy)
/GLP	Gold LPs
/GM	Greatest Moments
/Gold	Gold Inserts, Signature, or Prisms
/Gold	Golden Rainbow
/GoldAS	Gold All-Star
/GoldDT	Gold Dream Team
/GoldMom	Golden Moments
/GoldMI	Golden Moments I
/GoldMII	Golden Moments II
/GoldLP	Classic Best Gold No. 1 Pick LPs
/GoldPrev	Gold Previews
/GoldR	Gold Rush
/GoldS	Gold Stars
/GoldT	Gold Time Out Sports
/GoldWin	Gold Winners
/Gov	Governor's Cup
/GPromo	Gold Promo Sheet
/GPr	Gold Promos
/Granny	Granny Goose
/Great	Baseball Greats
/Greatest	Greatest Moments
/GreatMom	Great Moments
/Green	Tyler Green
/Griffey	Ken Griffey Jr.
/Griffey	23K Ken Griffey Jr.
/Griffey	Ken Griffey Jr. Oversized Card
/GriffeyClub	Griffey Club House
/GriffeyHolo	Griffey Holograms
/GriffyJ	Ken Griffey Jumbos
/GRook	Gold Rookies
/GS	Grand Slam
/GSlam	Grand Slammers
/Gwynn	Tony Gwynn
/HardC	Hardee's/Coke
/Head	Headliners
/Heading	Heading for the Hall
/Her	Heritage
/Hero	Heroes of Baseball
/HeroHL	Heroes Highlights
/Hill	1993 Topps Commanders of the Hill
/Hills	1989 Topps Hills Team MVP's
/HillsHM	1990 Topps Hills Hit Men
/Hit	Hit Machines
/HitM	Hit Men
/HL	Highlights
/HobSam	Hobby Samples
/Hocus	Hocus Focus
/HOF	Hall of Fame
/HOF	Hall of Fame Art Post Cards
/HolPrev	Holiday Previews
/Holsum	Holsum Discs
/HoSt	Hostess Stickers
/Hot	Hottest Prospects
/HotPros	Hot Prospects
/HotRook	Hottest 100 Rookies
/HotRook	Hot Rookies
/HotStar	Hottest 100 Stars
/Hottest	Hottest Stars
/HRC	Home Run Club
/HRH	Home Run Heroes
/HRK	Home Run Kings
/HSPros	High School Prospects
/HSProsG	High School Prospects Glossy
/HT	Home Team Supers
/Hygrade	Hygrade Meats
/II	Play II
/II	Champs Play II
/IICS	Play II Collector's Series
/IISingl	II Singles
/Impact	Impact Players
/Ind	Cleveland Indians
/Indian(s)	Cleveland Indians
/Ins	Inserts
/InsCL	Insert Checklists
/Iooss	Iooss Collection
/Irvin	Monte Irvin
/ISingl	I Singles
/Jackson	Upper Deck Reggie Jackson Heroes
/JAS	Jumbo All-Stars
/JITB	Jack in the Box
/JP	Jones Photo (Minor League cards)
/JR	Jackie Robinson
/Jub	Diamond Jubilee
/Jugador	Jugadores Calientes Prisms
/JumboR	Jumbo Rookies
/Justice	Bleachers 23K Dave Justice
/Kahn	Kahn's
/Karros	Eric Karros
/KC	Kansas City
/Keeb	Keebler
/KidGriff	Kid Griff Comic Holograms
/Kit	Mattingly Kit
/Knoblauch	Chuck Knoblauch
/Ko	Kodak
/L	1952 Star Cal Large
/LBC	Louisville Baseball Club
/Lead	K-Mart Leaders
/Leads	Leader Sheet
/Learning	Learning Series
/Lee	Paul Lee
/Leg	Legends

/Leonard	Buck Leonard
/Lewis	Ron Lewis
/Leyenda	Leyendas
/LgStand	League Standouts
/Lim	Limited Edition
/LineD	Line Drive (Minor League cards)
/Living	Living Legends
/LJN	Topps LJN Talking Cards
/LJS	Long John Silver
/LL	League Leaders
/Lock	Locklear Collection
/Locklear	Locklear Collection
/LongBall	Long Ball Leaders
/LS	Louisville Slugger
/Lumber	Lumber company
/L&U	Liberatore & Utter
/LykePerf	Lykes Perforated
/LykeStand	Lykes Standard
/M	Mini
/M	New York Mets
/Mag	Magazine
/MagRal	Magazine/Rally's Hamburgers
/MagUno	Magazine Unocal
/Mantle	Mickey Mantle's Long Shots
/MantleP	Mickey Mantle Promo
/Mar	Seattle Mariners
/Mara	Marathon Oil
/Marlin	Florida Marlins
/Mast	Score Scoremasters
/Master	Masters of the Game
/Master	Master Works
/MasterBW	Masters BW
/MasterCol	Masters Color
/Matting	Don Mattingly
/Mattingly	Don Mattingly
/Max	Maxwell House
/Mays	Willie Mays Heroes
/McDon	McDonald's
/McDonB	McDonald's Best
/McGwire	Mark McGwire
/Med	Medford
/Medal	Medalists
/Mem	Memories
/Member	Stadium Club Members Only
/Member#	Stadium Club Members Only (I, II, III, or IV)
/MerchB	Merchants Bank
/MetsY	New York Mets/New York Yankees
/MetYank	New York Mets/New York Yankees
/Mets	New York Mets Team Book
/Metz	Metz Baking
/Micro	Topps Micro Gold Insert or Micro Prism Inserts
/Milk	Meadow Gold Milk
/Milk	Milk Henneman
/MillB	Miller Brewing
/Milw	Milwaukee
/Mini	Mini
/Minn	Minnesota Twins
/Minor	Minor League Legends
/ML	Minor League
/MLAS	Minor League All-Stars
/MLG	Minor League Gold
/MLGPr	Minor League Gold Promos
/MLGPrev	Minor League Gold Previews
/MLP	Major League Prospects
/MLPI	Major League Prospects I
/MLPII	Major League Prospects II
/MM	Mickey Mantle
/Mont	Montreal
/Mov	Movers
/MPhoto	Master Photos
/MTV	MTV Rock n' Jock
/MurphyMP	Murphy Master Photos
/MurphyS	Murphy Special
/Museum	Museum Collection
/MVP	Most Valuable Player(s)
/MVPAL	Most Valuable Player American League
/MVPNL	Most Valuable Player National League
/MWilliam	Mother's Cookies Matt Williams
/Nat	Conlon National All-Stars
/Nation	Nationwide Insurance
/NBank	National Bank
/Neg	Conlon Negro All-Stars
/New	New Generation
/Nick	Nicknames
/NL	National League
/NLAS	NL All-Stars
/num	1932-34 Orbit Pins Numbered
/NWest	Score Nat West Yankees
/NWL	Northwest League
/OD	Opening Day
/OldStyle	Old Style
/OnBase	On-Base Leaders
/OneHour	One Hour Photo
/Orio	Baltimore Orioles
/P	Philadelphia Phillies
/Pac	Pacific
/Padres	San Diego Padres
/Palmer	Jim Palmer
/Pan	Panels
/PCL	Pacific Coast League
/PCPII	Play II
/Perf	Perforated or Performers
/Performer	The Performer
/Pep	Pepsi
/PGE	Pacific Gas and Electric
/Phill	Phillies
/PhillFinest	Phillies Finest
/Photo	Photographers
/PHR	Pitch, Hit, and Run
/PI	Paper Insert
/PII	Play II
/Pin	1909 Buster Brown Pins
/Pion	Fleer Pioneers
/Pirates	Pittsburgh Pirates
/POG	POG Cards
/Pol	Police/Safety Sets
/Pop	Popcorn
/PopUp	1986 Donruss Pop-Ups
/Post	Posters
/PostC	Postcards
/Power	Power Surge
/PowerPr	Power Surge Promo
/POY	Player of the Year
/PP	1967 Topps Test Pirates
/PPI	Power Players I
/PPII	Power Players II
/Pr	Promo(s)
/PreProd	Pre-Production (Samples)
/Prem	1949 Leaf Premiums
/Prev	Preview(s)
/ProC	ProCards (Minor League cards)
/Proctor	Proctor and Gamble
/Promo	Promo Sheet
/ProS	Pro Stars
/Proto	Prototypes
/Prov	Provigo
/ProV(F)	Fleer Pro-Visions (Factory)
/ProVI	Pro-Visions I

/ProVII	Pro-Visions II
/Pucko	Pucko (Minor League cards)
/Puzzle	Puzzle Back
/PW	Pizza World (Minor League cards)
/Quadra	Quadracard '53 Archives
/R	Texas Rangers
/Rang	Texas Rangers
/RB	Red Backs
/RBIK	RBI Kings
/RBonus	Red Bonus
/RD	Rub Downs
/Rec	For The Record
/RecBr	Baseball's Best Record Breakers
/RecSet	1987 Fleer Record Setters
/Red	Classic Red
/Redp	Redpath
/Reds	Cincinnati Reds
/RedSox	Boston Red Sox
/RedTCL	Red Team Checklists
/RetailSam	Retail Samples
/Retort	Retort Legends
/RetortII	Retort Legends II
/Revco	1988 Topps Revco
/Riley	Riley's (Minor League cards)
/RisSt	Rising Stars
/RiteAid	1988 Topps Rite-Aid
/Ritz	Topps Ritz Mattingly
/RO	Rub Offs
/Robinson	Brooks Robinson
/Rock	Rock's Dugout Wichita
/Rockie	Colorado Rockies
/Rodriguez	Frankie Rodriguez
/Rolaid	Rolaids
/Rook	Rookies
/Rook	Rookie Stars
/RookI	Rookie Idols
/RookPhen	Rookie Phenoms
/RookSen	Rookie Sensations
/RookSenI	Rookie Sensations I
/RookSenII	Rookie Sensations II
/RookSIns	Rookie Sensations Inserts
/RookSurg	Rookie Surge
/RookTP	Rookie Team Pinnacle
/RookTPinn	Rookie Team Pinnacle
/Royal(s)	Kansas City Royals
/RSox	Boston Red Sox
/Run	Run Creators
/Ruth	Babe Ruth
/RuthProto	Babe Ruth Prototypes
/Ryan	Nolan Ryan
/RyanCoke	Nolan Ryan Coke
/RyanF	Nolan Ryan Farewell
/RyanFar	Ryan Farewell McCormick
/RyanL&T	Nolan Ryan Life and Times
/RyanLtd	Ryan Limited
/RyanMag6	Ryan Magazine 6
/RyanPrism	Ryan Prism Inserts
/RyanSIns	Nolan Ryan Silver Inserts
/RyanTE	Nolan Ryan Texas Express
/RyanTExpII	Ryan Texas Express II
/Ryan7NH	Nolan Ryan 7th No-Hitter
/Ryan5	Nolan Ryan 5
/Ryan6	Nolan Ryan 6
/Ryan10	Nolan Ryan 10
/Ryan23	Nolan Ryan 23K
/Ryan27	Ryan 27th Season
/S	Seaver
/S	Supers or Giant Size
/Salmon	Tim Salmon
/Sam	Samples
/Sandberg	23K Ryne Sandberg
/SB	SkyBox
/SC	Street Clothes
/SchCd	Padres Schedule Cards
/Schmidt	Mike Schmidt
/ScoreB	Scorebook
/Scout	Scouting Report
/SDP	San Diego Padres
/Sea	84Moth/Sea (Seattle)
/SeasonHL	Season Highlights
/SeavPr	Seaver Promos
/Second	Second Year Standouts
/Sen	Sentry
/SenP	Senators Pink
/SenY	Senators Yellow
/Senator	Senators
/SenLg	Senior League
/Seven	7-Eleven
/SFG	San Francisco Giants
/Shak	Shakers
/Sil	Silhouettes
/SilSlug	Silver Sluggers
/Silv	Silver Prisms or Signature
/SilverT	Silver Time Out Sports
/Singl	Singles
/SIns6	Seaver Inserts 6
/Slug	Slugfest
/Slug	Sluggers vs. Pitchers
/Slide	Slide Show
/Sm	PM10 Small
/Smok	Smokey Bear
/Smoke	Smoke 'n Heat
/SO	Stick Ons, Scratch Offs
/SoarSt	Fleer Soaring Stars
/SoCal	Southern California
/Soda	MSA Soda Superstars
/SP	Sport Pro (Minor League cards)
/SpanishGold	Spanish Gold Estrellas
/SpanishP	Spanish Prism Inserts
/Special	Special Edition
/SpecOlym	Special Olympics
/Spirit	Spirit of the Game
/Sport	Sport Design
/Sport	Sporting News
/SportP	Sport Pro
/SPPlat	SP Platinum Power
/SS	Superstars
/ST	N172 Spotted Ties
/St	Stickers, Stamps
/Stand	Standard
/Star	Star (Minor League cards)
/Stargell	Willie Stargell
/StarP	Star Performers
/Stat	1986 Meadow Gold Stat Back
/StatL	Stat Leaders
/StatStand	Statistical Standouts
/StBk	Sticker Backs
/St	Stickers
/Strawb	Darryl Strawberry
/Strike	Strikeout Kings
/Stud	Studio
/StudPrev	Studio Preview
/StVar	Sticker Variations
/SU	Stand Ups
/SUI	Stand Ups I
/SUII	Stand Ups II
/Sum	Cape Cod Summer League
/SuperTC	Super Team Cards
/Sus	Sussman
/T	Team Cards, Test
/T	Detroit Tigers
/Taco	Taco Time (Minor League cards)

/TallT	Tallmadge Tire
/TastyK	Phillies Tastykake
/tatt	Tattoo
/TCL	Team Checklists
/TCMA	The Card and Memorabilia Associates
/TCr	Triple Crown
/TDP	Top Draft Picks
/Team	Team-issued Set
/TeamP	Team Pinnacle
/Test	Score Test Samples, Sportflics Test
/Test	1971 Bazooka Numbered Test
/TH	Triple Headers
/Then	Then and Now
/Thomas	Frank Thomas
/ThomasGold	Frank Thomas Gold
/Tiger	Tigers
/Tips	1982 Post Tips
/TL	Team Leaders
/TLAL	Team Leaders AL
/TLNL	Team Leaders NL
/TmLIns	Team Leaders Inserts
/TmMVPHolo	Team MVP Holograms
/TmPrev	Team Preview
/Tomb	Tombstone
/Tomorrow	Tomorrow's Heroes
/ToroBJ	Score Toronto Blue Jays
/TP	Team Pinnacle
/TPHolo	Top Prespect Holograms
/TPrev	Team Preview
/Tr	Traded
/Trade	Trade for Babe
/trans	transfers
/TrGold	Traded Gold
/Trib	Tribune or Tribute
/TripleP	Triple Play
/Tul	Tulsa Oilers
/TVAS	Topps TV All-Stars
/TVCard	Topps TV Cardinals
/TVYank	Topps TV Yankees
/TWillB	Ted Williams Best
/TWillH	Ted Williams Heroes
/TWillWB	Ted Williams Wax Boxes
/Twin	Minnesota Twins
/Twink	1975 Hostess Twinkies
/T202	Upper Deck All-Time Heroes of Baseball (T202 Reprints)
/UK	1988 Topps UK Minis
/Ultra(G)	Fleer Ultra (Gold)
/Ultra	Ultra-Pro
/un	1932-34 Orbit Pins Unnumbered
/Uno	Unocal
/Up	Update
/UpGoldAS	Update Gold All-Stars
/UpGRook	Update Gold Rookies
/UpHer	Update Herald-Sun
/UpThomasJ	Update Frank Thomas Jumbos
/USAB	USA Blue
/USAR	USA Red BDK
/Via	Viacom
/Vine	Vine Line
/WAS	WASSCA
/Wave	Wave of the Future
/Wave	Wave Postcards
/WaxBox	Wax Box Cards
/WBTV	Charlotte TV station
/WC	World Champions
/West	Weston
/Wiener	Wiener King
/Wild	Fleer Wildest Plays
/Winter	Winter Baseball
/WIZAS	WIZ Home Entertainment Centers All-Stars
/WIZ60	WIZ Home Entertainment Centers 60s
/WIZ70	WIZ Home Entertainment Centers 70s
/WIZ80	WIX Home Entertainment Centers 80s
/WS	Chicago White Sox or World Series
/WSHero	World Series Heroes
/WSox	Chicago White Sox
/WUAB	WUAB-TV
/Y	New York Yankees
/YB	Yearbook
/YG	Young Guns
/YMet	Yankees and Mets
/Yount	Robin Yount
/YS	Young Superstars
/1	1988 Conlon Series 1
/1stY	1st Year Phenoms
/1stDay	First Day Production
/1stDP	First Draft Picks
/4in1	Four-in-One
/5thAnn	Fifth Anniversary
/13Nat	13th National
/25Ann	Richmond Braves 25th Anniversary
/54	'54 Memories
/69Pr	'69 Spectrum Promos
/87	1987
/100Ris	1990 Score 100 Rising
/100RisSt	Score 100 Rising Stars
/100St	1990 Score 100 Stars
/100Stars	1990 Score 100 Stars
/200	Classic Game 200
/500	500 club
/24Taco	24 Taco Time
/3/4/500	1980 Laughlin 300/400/500 Club
/3D	1968 Topps 3-D (three-dimensional)
/4	1929-30 Exhibits 4-in-1
/8Men	1988 Pacific Eight Men Out
/2000Sam	2000 Samples

Individual Card Suffix Codes

AA	Awesome Action
ACO	Assistant Coach
ADM	Administrator
AGM	Assistant General Manager
ALCS	AL Championship Series
ANN	Announcer
AR	All-Rookie
AS	All-Star
ASA	All-Star Advice
ATHR	Author
AU	With Autograph
AW	Award Winner
bb	Batboy
BC	Bonus Card
BOX	Boxer
CA	Clubhouse Attendant
CAPT	Captain
CD	Clinic Director
CH	Community Heroes
CL	Checklist
CO	Coach
COMM	Commissioner
C/S	Cheerleader/Singer
CY	Cy Young
DC	Draft Choice
DD	Diamond Debut
DIR	Director
DK	Diamond King

DL	Division Leaders
DP	Draft Pick
DR	Doctor
DS	Diamond Skills
DT	Dream Team
EP	Elite Performer
EQMG	Equipment Manager
FB	Flashback
FDP	First Draft Pick
FF	Future Foundation
FOIL	Foil Embossed
FOLD	Foldouts
FRAN	Franchise
FS	Father and Son or Future Star
FT	Fantasy Team
FUN	Fun Cards
FUT	The Future is Now
GC	Ground Crew
GM	General Manager
GRIP	Grip
GS	Glow Stars
HERO	Upper Deck Heroes
HES	Headline Stars
HFA	Home Field Advantage
HH	Homerun Heroes
HL	Highlight
HOR	Horizontal Pose
HS	Hot Shots
I	Idol
IA	In Action
IF	Infielder
IN	Inside the Numbers
INS	Instructor
KM	K-Man
KP	Kid Picture (boyhood photo)
KS	Kid Stars
LCS	League Championship Series
LH	Little Hot Shots
LL	League Leader
M	Multi-player or miscellaneous card
MB	Master Blaster
MC	Members' Choice or Members' Club
MG	Manager
MLP	Major League Performance
MOY	Man of the Year
MVP	MVP Card
NH	No-hitter
NLCS	NL Championship Series
NT	Now and Then
OF	Outfielder
OLY	Olympics
org	Organist
OWN	Owner
P/CO	Player/Coach
PER	Office Personnel
PF	Pro-Files
P/MG	Player/Manager
PR(ES)	President
PV	Pro-vision
Pz	Puzzle
QS	Quick Starts
R	Rookie
RB	Record Breaker
RIF	Rifleman
ROY	Rookie of the Year
RP	Rookie Prospect
RR	Rated Rookie
RS	Rising Star or Record Setter
RT	Rookie Traded
SA	Super Action
SC	Scout
SH	Shades
SIDE	Sidelines
SLUG	Slugger
SOT	Stars of Tomorrow
SP	Single Print or Super Premium
SR	Star Rookie
SS	Shortstop or Score Supplemental
ST	Stat Twins
STA	Standouts
STAT	Statistician
SV	Super Veteran
SVR	Supervisor
T	Traded
TA	Tale 12 Players
TBC	Turn Back Clock
TC	Team Checklist
TECH	Technician
TL	Team Leader
TP	Top Prospect
TR	Trainer
TRI	Tribute
UDC	Upper Deck Classic
UMP	Umpire
UP	Up Close and Personal
USA	United States of America
VP	Vice President
WC	What's The Call?
WS	World Series
XGM	Ex-General Manager
35HR	35 Homeruns

Minor League and College Abbreviations

AAA	AAA All-Stars
AAASingl	AAA Singles
Adelaide	Adelaide Giants
AK	Arkansas
Alaska	Alaska Goldpanners (amateur)
Albany	Albany(-Colonie) A's/Yankees/ Polecats
Albuq	Albuquerque Dukes
AlexD	Alexandria Dukes
Amari	Amarillo Gold Sox
Anchora	Anchorage Glacier Pilots (amateur)
Ander	Anderson Braves/Rangers
AppFx	Appleton Foxes
ArkTr	Arkansas Travelers
Ashvl	Asheville Tourists
AubAs	Auburn Astros
Augusta	Augusta Pirates
AZ	Arizona
Bakers	Bakersfield Dodgers
Batavia	Batavia Clippers/Trojans
Baton	Baton Rouge Cougars
BBAmer	Baseball America All-Stars
BBAmAA	Baseball America AA Prospects
BBCity	Baseball City Royals
Beaum	Beaumont Golden Gators
Belling	Bellingham Mariners
Beloit	Beloit Brewers
Bend	Bend Bucks/Phillies/Rockies
Billings	Billings Mustangs
Bingham	Bingham Mets
BirmB	Birmingham Barons
Bluefld	Bluefield Orioles
Boise	Boise Hawks
Brisbane	Brisbane Bandits
Bristol	Bristol Red Sox/Tigers
BuffB	Buffalo Bisons
BurlAs	Burlington Astros

BurlB	Burlington Bees/Braves
BurlEx	Burlington Expos
BurlInd	Burlington Indians
BurlR	Burlington Rangers
Butte	Butte Copper Kings
BYU	Brigham Young University
Calgary	Calgary Cannons
CalLgAS	California League All-Stars
Canton	Canton-Akron Indians
CapeCod	Cape Cod Prospects
CaroMud	Carolina Mudcats
Cedar	Cedar Rapids Reds/Giants
Charl	Charleston Charlies
CharlK	Charlotte Knights
CharlR	Charlotte Rangers
CharlO	Charlotte O's
CharCh	Charleston Charlies
CharR	Charleston Royals
CharRain	Charleston Rainbows
CharWh	Charleston Wheelers
Chatt	Chattanooga Lookouts
CLAS	Carolina League All-Stars
ClBest	Classic Best
Clearw	Clearwater Phillies
Clinton	Clinton Dodgers/Giants
Clovis	Clovis HS
Clmbia	Columbia Mets
Cocoa	Cocoa Beach Astros
ColAst	Columbus Astros
ColClip	Columbus Clippers
ColInd	Columbus Indians
ColMud	Columbus Mudcats
ColRS	Columbus RedStixx
ColoSp	Colorado Springs Sky Sox
Colum	Columbus Clippers
ColumAst	Columbus Astros
ColumMet	Columbia Mets
ColumMud	Columbus Mudcats
Daikyo	Daikyo Dolphins
Danvl	Danville Suns
DayBe	Daytona Beach Astros
Denver	Denver Zephyrs
Dubuq	Dubuque Packers
Dunedin	Dunedin Blue Jays
Durham	Durham Bulls
EastLAS	Eastern League All-Stars
EastLDD	Eastern League Diamond Diplomacy
Edmon	Edmonton Trappers
Elizab	Elizabethton Twins
ElPaso	El Paso Diablos
Elmira	Elmira Pioneer Red Sox
Erie	Erie Cardinals/Orioles/Sailors
Eugene	Eugene Emeralds
Evansvl	Evansville Triplets
Everett	Everett Giants
Fayette	Fayetteville Generals
Freder	Frederick Keys
Fresno	Fresno Giants
FresonSt	Fresno State
FSLAS	Florida State League All-Stars
FtLaud	Ft. Lauderdale Yankees
FtMyr	Fort Myers Royals/Miracle
GA	Georgia College
Gaston	Gastonia Rangers
Gate	Gate City Pioneers
Geneva	Geneva Cubs
GlenF	Glen Falls White Sox
GreatF	Great Falls Dodgers
Green	Greenwood Braves
Greens	Greensboro Hornets
Greenvl	Greenville Braves

GulfCD	Gulf Coast Dodgers
GulfCM	Gulf Coast Mets
GulfCR	Gulf Coast Rangers
GulfCY	Gulf Coast Yankees
Hagers	Hagerstown Suns
Hamil	Hamilton Redbirds
Harris	Harrisburg Senators
Hawaii	Hawaii Islanders
Helena	Helena Brewers
HighD	High Desert Mavericks
Holyo	Holyoke Millers
Hunting	Huntington Cubs
Huntsvl	Huntsville Stars
Idaho	Idaho Falls Athletics/Braves/Gems
Indianap	Indianapolis Indians
IntLgAS	International League All-Stars
Iowa	Iowa Cubs
Jacks	Jackson Generals/Mets
James	Jamestown Expos
Jaxvl	Jacksonville Expos/Suns
Jesuit	Jesuit High School Alumni
Johnson	Johnson City Cardinals
Kane	Kane County Cougars
Kenosha	Kenosha Twins
Kingspt	Kingsport Mets
Kinston	Kinston Blue Jays/Eagles/Indians
Kissim	Kissimmee Dodgers
Knoxvl	Knoxville Blue Jays/Knox Sox/ Smokies
KS	Kansas
Lafay	Lafayette Drillers
Lakeland	Lakeland Tigers
LasVegas	Las Vegas Stars
Lipscomb	David Lipscomb University
LitFalls	Little Falls Mets
LitSun	Little Sun
LodiD	Lodi Dodgers
London	London Tigers
Louisvl	Louisville Redbirds
LSU	Louisiana State University
Lynch	Lynchburg Mets
LynchRS	Lynchburg Red Sox
LynnP	Lynn Pirates
LynnS	Lynn Sailors
Macon	Macon Braves/Pirates
Madis	Madison Muskies
Martins	Martinsville Phillies
Maine	Maine Guides
Medford	Medford Athletics
MedHat	Medicine Hat Blue Jays
Melbourne	Melbourne Bushrangers
Memphis	Memphis Chicks
Miami	Miami Marlins/Miracle/Orioles
MidldA	Midland Angels
MidldC	Midland Cubs
MidwLAS	Midwest League All-Stars
MissSt	Mississippi State
MN	Minnesota
Modesto	Modesto A's
Myrtle	Myrtle Beach Blue Jays/Hurricanes
Nashua	Nashua Angels
Nashvl	Nashville Sounds
NE	Nebraska
Newar	Newark Co-Pilots
NewBrit	New Britain Red Sox
Niagara	Niagara Falls Rapids
Ogden	Ogden A's
Ohio	Ohio
OK	Oklahoma
OkCty	Oklahoma City 89ers
OkSt	Oklahoma State

Omaha	Omaha Royals
Oneonta	Oneonta Yankees
OrlanSR	Orlando Sun Rays
OrlanTw	Orlando Twins
Osceola	Osceola Astros
Ottawa	Ottawa Lynx
PalmSp	Palm Springs Angels
Parramatta	Parramatta Patriots
Pawtu	Pawtucket Red Sox
Penin	Peninsula Pilots
Peoria	Peoria Chiefs
PeoriaCol	Peoria Collectors
Perth	Perth Heat
Phoenix	Phoenix Firebirds/Giants
Pittsfld	Pittsfield Cubs/Mets
Pocatel	Pocatello Giants/Pioneers
PortChar	Port Charlotte Rangers
Portl	Portland Beavers
PreRookPrev	Pre-Rookie Previews
Princet	Princeton Patriots/Pirates/Reds
ProC	ProCards
PrWill	Prince William Cannons/Pirates
Pulaski	Pulaski Braves
QuadC	Quad-City Cubs/Angels/River Bandits
Reading	Reading Phillies
RedFoley	Red Foley's
Redwd	Redwood Pioneers
Reno	Reno Silver Sox
Richm	Richmond Braves
River	Riverside Red Wave/Pilots
Rochester	Rochester
RochR	Rochester Red Wings
Rockford	Rockford Expos/Royals
RoyMont	Montreal Royals
Rowe	Rowe Exhibits
Sacra	Sacramento Solons
SALAS	South Atlantic League All-Stars
Salem	Salem Angels/Buccaneers/ Dodgers/Pirates
Salinas	Salinas Spurs
SanAn	San Antonio Brewers/Missions
SanBern	San Bernadino Spirit
SanJose	San Jose Bees/Giants/Missions
Saraso	Sarasota White Sox
Savan	Savannah Braves/Cardinals
SDSt	San Diego State
ScranWB	Scranton-Wilkes-Barre
Shrev	Shreveport Captains
SLAS	Southern League All-Stars
SLCity	Salt Lake City Gulls/Trappers
SoBend	South Bend White Sox
SoEastern	Southeastern
SoOreg	Southern Oregon A's
Spartan	Spartanburg Phillies
Spokane	Spokane Indians
SpokAT	Spokane All-Time Greats
Spring	Springfield Cardinals/Redbirds
StCath	St. Catharines Blue Jays
StLucie	St. Lucie Mets
Stockton	Stockton Ports
StPete	St. Petersburg Cardinals
Sumter	Sumter Braves
Sydney	Sydney Wave
Syrac	Syracuse Chiefs
Tacoma	Tacoma Tigers/Tugs/Twins
Tampa	Tampa Tarpons/Yankees
TexLgAS	Texas League All-Stars
Tidew	Tidewater Tides
Tigres	igres de Mexico
Toledo	Toledo Mud Hens
TNTech	Tennessee Tech
TriCit	Tri-Cities Triplets
TripleAAS	Triple A All-Stars
Tucson	Tucson Toros
Tulsa	Tulsa Drillers
TX	Texas
TxLgAS	Texas League All-Stars
Utica	Utica Blue Jays/Blue Sox
Vanco	Vancouver Canadians
Ventura	Ventura Gulls
Vermont	Vermont Reds
VeroB	Vero Beach Dodgers
Virgini	Virginia Generals
Visalia	Visalia Oaks
WA	Washington
Water	Waterbury Reds
Watertn	Watertown Indians/Pirates
Watlo	Waterloo Diamonds/Indians
Wausau	Wausau Mets/Timbers
Waverly	Waverly
Welland	Welland Pirates
WHave	West Haven A's/Yankees
Wichita	Wichita Aeros/Pilots/Wranglers
WichitaSt	Wichita State
WinHaven	Winter Haven Red Sox
WinSalem	Winston-Salem Spirits
Wisco	Wisconsin Rapids Twins
Wmsprt	Williamsport Bills/Tomahawks
WPalmB	West Palm Beach Expos
Wythe	Wytheville Cubs
Yakima	Yakima Bears

TEAM CARDS

Atlanta Braves
66T-326
66T/RO-115
67T-477
68T-221
69T/St/Alb-1
69T/T/Post-1
70OPC-472
70T-472
71OPC-652
71T-652
71T/tatt-5
72OPC-21
72T-21
73OPC-521
73OPC/BlueTCL-1
73T-521
73T/BlueTCL-1
74OPC-483
74OPC/RedTCL-1
74T-483
74T/RedTCL-1
74T/St/Alb-1
74T/TCL-1
75OPC-589
75T-589
75T/M-589
76OPC-631
76T-631
77T-442
78T-551
79T-302
80T-192
81T-675
83F/St-1B
87Sf/TPrev-24
90PublInt/St-628
90RedFoley/St-130
91T/TH-1
93UD-816TC
94StCl/SuperTC-1

Baltimore Orioles
56T-100
57T-251
58T-408
59T-48
60T-494
61T-159
61T/RO-85
62T-476
63T-377
64T-473
65T-572
66T-348
67T-302
68T-334
70OPC-387
70T-387
71OPC-1
71T-1
71T/tatt-10
72T-731
73OPC-278
73OPC/BlueTCL-2
73T-278
73T/BlueTCL-2
73T/BlueTCL-2
74OPC-16
74OPC/RedTCL-2
74T-16
74T/RedTCL-2
74T/TCL-2
75OPC-117
75T-117
75T/M-117
76OPC-73
76T-73
77T-546
78T-96
79T-689
80T-404
81T-661
83F/St-27
83F/St-7M
87Sf/TPrev-21
90PublInt/St-648
90RedFoley/St-108
91T/TH-1
93UD-827TC
94StCl/SuperTC-15
N690

Boston Braves
48Exh/T-1
T200

Boston Red Sox
51T
56T-111
57T-171
58T-312
59T-248
60T-537
60T/tatt-65
61T-373
61T/RO-5
62T-334
63T-202
64T-579
65T-403
66T-259
66T/RO-109
67T-604
69T/St/Alb-3
69T/T/Post-3
70T-563
71OPC-386
71T-386
71T/tatt-2
72OPC-328
72T-328
72T/Cloth-26
73OPC-596
73OPC/BlueTCL-3
73T-596
73T/BlueTCL-3
73T/BlueTCL-3
74OPC-567
74OPC/RedTCL-3
74T-567
74T/RedTCL-3
74T/St/Alb-3
74T/TCL-3
75OPC-172
75T-172
75T/M-172
76OPC-118
76T-118
77T-309
78T-424
79T-214
80T-689
81T-662
87Sf/TPrev-9
90PublInt/St-642
90RedFoley/St-109
91Panini/Top15-122
91Panini/Top15-125
91T/TH-2
93UD-832TC
94StCl/SuperTC-16
R309/2

Brooklyn Dodgers
48Exh/T-13
48Exh/T-15
48Exh/T-3
48Exh/T-9
49Exh/Team
51T
52Exh/Team
55Exh/Team
56Exh/Team
56T-166
57T-324
58T-71
T200

California Angels
61T/RO-6
62T-132
63T-39
64T-213
65T-293
66OPC-131
66T-131
66T/RO-79
67T-327
68T-252
69T/St/Alb-4
69T/T/Post-4
70OPC-522
70T-522
71OPC-442
71T-442
71T/tatt
72OPC-71
72T-71
73OPC-243
73T-243
74OPC-114
74T-114
74T/St/Alb-4
75OPC-236
75T-236
75T/M-236
76OPC-304
76T-304
77T-34
78T-214
79T-424
80T-214
81T-663
83F/St-1A
87Sf/TPrev-11
90PublInt/St-638
90RedFoley/St-120
91Panini/Top15-132
94StCl/SuperTC-17

Chicago Cubs
56T-11
57T-183
58T-327
59T-304
60T-513
60T/tatt-56
61T-122
61T/RO-17
62T-552
63T-222
64T-237
65OPC-91
65T-91
66T-204
66T/RO-97
67T-354
69T/St/Alb-5
69T/T/Post-5
70T-593
71OPC-502
71T-502
71T/tatt-6
72OPC-192
72T-192
73OPC-464
73OPC/BlueTCL-5
73T-464
73T/BlueTCL-5
74OPC-211
74OPC/RedTCL-5
74T-211
74T/RedTCL-5
74T/St/Alb-5
74T/TCL-5
75OPC-638
75T-638
75T/M-638
76OPC-277
76T-277
77T-518
78T-302
79T-551
80T-381
81T-676
87Sf/TPrev-22
90PublInt/St-632
90RedFoley/St-122
91Panini/Top15-120
91T/TH-2
93UD-819TC
94StCl/SuperTC-2
T200

Chicago White Sox
51T
56T-188
57T-329
58T-256
59T-94
60T-208
60T/tatt-66
61T-7
61T/RO-9
62T-113
63T-288
64T-496
65OPC-234
65T-234
66T-426
66T/RO-1
67T-573
68T-424
69T/St/Alb-6
69T/T/Post-6
70OPC-501
70T-501
71T-289
71T/tatt-8
72OPC-381
72T-381
73OPC-481
73OPC/BlueTCL-6
73T-481
73T/BlueTCL-6
73T/BlueTCL-6
74OPC-416
74OPC/RedTCL-6
74T-416
74T/RedTCL-6
74T/St/Alb-6
74T/TCL-6
75OPC-276
75T-276
75T/M-276
76OPC-656
76T-656
77T-418
78T-526
79T-404
80T-112
81T-664
87Sf/TPrev-26
90PublInt/St-639
90RedFoley/St-110
91Panini/Top15-136
91T/TH-4
91UD-617
93UD-838TC
94StCl/SuperTC-18
T200

Cincinnati Reds
51T
56T-90
57T-322
58T-428
59T-111
60T-164
60T/tatt-57
61T-249
61T/RO-15
62T-465
63T-288
64T-403
65T-316
66OPC-59
66T-59
66T/RO-91
67T-407
68T-574
69T/St/Alb-7
69T/T/Post-7
70OPC-544
70T-544
71OPC-357
71T-357
71T/tatt-6
72T-651
73OPC-641
73OPC/BlueTCL-7
73T-641
73T/BlueTCL-7
73T/BlueTCL-7
74OPC-459
74OPC/RedTCL-7
74T-459
74T/RedTCL-7
74T/St/Alb-7
74T/TCL-7
75OPC-531
75T-531
75T/M-531
76OPC-104
76T-104
77T-287
78T-526
79T-259
80T-606
81T-677
87Sf/TPrev-4
90PublInt/St-624
90RedFoley/St-107
91Panini/Top15-117
91Panini/Top15-128
91Panini/Top15-131
91T/TH-3
93UD-833TC
94StCl/SuperTC-3
T200
N690
W711/2

Cleveland Indians
48Exh/T-12
48Exh/T-2
48Exh/Team
54Exh/Team
56T-85
57T-275
58T-158
59T-476
60T-174
60T/tatt-67
61T-467
61T/RO-10
62T-537
63T-451
64T-172
65T-481
66T-303
66T/RO-67
67T-544
69T/St/Alb-8
69T/T/Post-8
70T-637
71OPC-584
71T-584
71T/tatt-7
72T-547
73OPC-629
73OPC/BlueTCL-8
73T-629
73T/BlueTCL-8
74OPC-541
74OPC/RedTCL-8
74T-541
74T/RedTCL-8
74T/St/Alb-8
74T/TCL-8
75OPC-331
75T-331
75T/M-331
76OPC-477
76T-477
77T-18
78T-689
79T-96
80T-451
81T-665
87Sf/TPrev-3
90PublInt/St-647
90RedFoley/St-105
91T/TH-5
93UD-823TC
94StCl/SuperTC-19
T200
R309/2

Colorado Rockies
92D/BC-BC7
93UD-834M
94S-650CL
94StCl/SuperTC-4

Detroit Tigers
56T-213
57T-198
58T-397
59T-329
60T-72
60T/tatt-68
61T-51
61T/RO-1
62T-24
63T-552
64T-67
65OPC-173
65T-173
66T-583
66T/RO-61
67T-378
68T-528
69T/St/Alb-9
69T/T/Post-9
70T-579
71OPC-336
71T-336
71T/tatt-9
72OPC-487
72T-487
73OPC-191
73OPC/BlueTCL-9
73T-191
73T/BlueTCL-9
73T/BlueTCL-9
74OPC-94
74OPC/RedTCL-9
74T-94
74T/RedTCL-9
74T/St/Alb-9
74T/TCL-9
75OPC-18
75T-18

75T/M-18
76OPC-361
76T-361
77T-621
78T-404
79T-66
80T-626
81Detroit-108
81Detroit-112
81Detroit-13
81Detroit-22
81Detroit-53
81Detroit-61
81Detroit-7
81Detroit-83
81Detroit-95
81Detroit-98
81T-666
81Tiger/Detroit-108
81Tiger/Detroit-112
81Tiger/Detroit-13
81Tiger/Detroit-22
81Tiger/Detroit-53
81Tiger/Detroit-61
81Tiger/Detroit-7
81Tiger/Detroit-83
81Tiger/Detroit-95
81Tiger/Detroit-98
87Sf/TPrev-15
88Negro/Duques-2
90PublInt/St-643
90RedFoley/St-112
91Panini/Top15-123
91T/TH-6
93UD-836TC
94StCl/SuperTC-20
T200
N690

Florida Marlins
92D/BC-BC8
93UD-825TC
94StCl/SuperTC-5

Houston Astros
63T-312
66T/RO-7
69T/St/Alb-10
69T/T/Post-10
70OPC-448
70T-448
71OPC-722
71T-722
71T/tatt-12
72OPC-282
72T-282
73OPC-158
73T-158
74OPC-154
74T-154
74T/St/Alb-10
75OPC-487
75T-487
75T/M-487
76OPC-147
76T-147
77T-327
78T-112
79T-381
80T-82
81T-678
87Sf/TPrev-8
90PublInt/St-627
90RedFoley/St-117
94StCl/SuperTC-6

Kansas City Athletics
56T-236
57T-204
58T-174
59T-172
60T-413
61T-297
61T/RO-7
62T-384
63T-397
64T-151
65OPC-151
65T-151
66T-492
66T/RO-103
67T-262
87Sf/TPrev-13
90PublInt/St-637
90RedFoley/St-126

Kansas City Royals
69T/St/Alb-11
69T/T/Post-11
70OPC-422
70T-422
71OPC-742
71T-742
71T/tatt-4
72T-617
73OPC-347
73OPC/BlueTCL-11
73T-347
73T/BlueTCL-11
73T/BlueTCL-11
74OPC-343
74OPC/RedTCL-11
74T-343
74T/RedTCL-11
74T/St/Alb-11
74T/TCL-11
75OPC-72
75T/M-72
76OPC-236
76T-236
76T-72
77T-371
78T-724
79T-451
80T-86
81T-667
91T/TH-7
93UD-835TC
94StCl/SuperTC-21

Los Angeles Dodgers
59T-457
60T-18
60T/tatt-58
61T-86
61T/RO-13
62T-43
63T-337
64T-531
65OPC-126
65T-126
66T-238
66T/RO-13
67T-503
68OPC-168
68T-168
69T/St/Alb-12
69T/T/Post-12
70OPC-411
70T-411
71OPC-402
71T-402
71T/tatt-5
72OPC-522
72T-522
73OPC-91
73OPC/BlueTCL-12
73OPC/BlueTCL-4
73T-91
73T/BlueTCL-12
73T/BlueTCL-12
73T/BlueTCL-4
73T/BlueTCL-4
74OPC-643
74OPC/RedTCL-12
74OPC/RedTCL-4
74T-643
74T/RedTCL-12
74T/RedTCL-4
74T/St/Alb-12
74T/TCL-12
74T/TCL-4
75OPC-361
75T-361
75T/M-361
76OPC-46
76T-46
77T-504
78T-259
79T-526
80T-302
81T-679
82T/St-255
82T/St-256
87Sf/TPrev-14
90PublInt/St-623
90RedFoley/St-111
91T/TH-3
91T/TH-5
93UD-812TC
93UD-820TC
94StCl/SuperTC-7

Milwaukee Braves
55Gol/Braves-32
56T-95
57T-114
58T-377
59T-419
60T-381
61T-426
61T/RO-18
62T-158
63T-503
64T-132
65T-426

Milwaukee Brewers
71OPC-698
71T-698
71T/tatt-7
72OPC-106
72T-106
73OPC-127
73OPC/BlueTCL-13
73T-127
73T/BlueTCL-13
74OPC-314
74OPC/RedTCL-13
74T-314
74T/RedTCL-13
74T/St/Alb-13
74T/TCL-13
75OPC-384
75T-384
75T/M-384
76OPC-606
76T-606
77T-51
78T-328
79T-577
80T-659
81T-668
87Pol/Brew-x
87Sf/TPrev-19
90PublInt/St-644
90RedFoley/St-123
91Panini/Top15-126
91T/TH-8
93UD-817TC
94StCl/SuperTC-22

Minnesota Twins
61T-542
61T/RO-3
62T-584
63T-162
64T-318
65OPC-24
65T-24
66T-526
66T/RO-49
67T-211
68OPC-137
68T-137
69T/St/Alb-13
69T/T/Post-13
70OPC-534
70T-534
71OPC-522
71T-522
71T/tatt-14
72OPC-156
72T-156
73OPC-654
73OPC/BlueTCL-14
73T-654
73T/BlueTCL-14
73T/BlueTCL-14
74OPC-74
74OPC/RedTCL-14
74T-74
74T/RedTCL-14
74T/St/Alb-14
74T/TCL-14
75OPC-443
75T-443
75T/M-443
76OPC-556
76T-556
77T-228
78T-451
79T-41
80T-328
81T-669
83Twin/Team-35
87Sf/TPrev-17
90PublInt/St-636
90RedFoley/St-124
91T/TH-9
93UD-837TC
94StCl/SuperTC-23

Montreal Expos
69T/St/Alb-14
69T/T/Post-14
70OPC-509
70T-509
71OPC-674
71T-674
71T/tatt-1
72T-582
73OPC-576
73OPC/BlueTCL-15
73T-576
73T/BlueTCL-15
74OPC-508
74OPC/RedTCL-15
74T-508
74T/RedTCL-15
74T/St/Alb-15
74T/TCL-15
75OPC-101
75T-101
75T/M-101
76OPC-216
76T-216
77T-647
78OPC-207
78T-244
79OPC-349
79T-606
80T-479
81T-680
86GenMills/Book-6
87GenMills/Book-4
87Sf/TPrev-20
90PublInt/St-631
90RedFoley/St-115
91Panini/Top15-121
91Panini/Top15-129
91T/TH-6
93UD-821TC

New York Yankees
49Exh/Team
50Exh/Team
51Exh/Team
52Exh/Team
55Exh/Team
56Exh/Team
56T-251
57T-97
58T-246
59T-510
60T-332
60T/tatt-70
61T-228
61T/RO-2
62T-251
63T-247
64T-433
65T-513
66OPC-92
66T-92
66T/RO-55
67OPC-131
67T-131
69T/St/Alb-16
69T/T/Post-16
70OPC-399
70T-399
71OPC-543
71T-543
71T/tatt-3
72OPC-237
72T-237
73OPC-556
73OPC/BlueTCL-17
73T-556
73T/BlueTCL-17
73T/BlueTCL-17
74OPC-363
74OPC/RedTCL-17
74T-363
74T/RedTCL-17
74T/St/Alb-17
74T/TCL-17
75OPC-611
75T-611
75T/M-611
76OPC-17
76T-17
77T-387
78SSPC/270-22
78T-282
79T-626
80T-424
81T-670
87Sf/TPrev-7
90PublInt/St-646
90RedFoley/St-121
91T/TH-10
93UD-839TC
94StCl/SuperTC-24
T200

New York Giants
51Exh/Team
51T
54Exh/Team
55Gol/Giants-8
56T-226
57T-317
58T-19
T200

New York Mets
63T-473
64T-27
65T-551
66OPC-172
66T-172
66T/RO-19
67OPC-42
67T-42
68T-401
69T/St/Alb-15
69T/T/Post-15
70OPC-1
70T-1
71OPC-641
71T-641
71T/tatt-2
72OPC-362
72T-362
73OPC-389
73OPC/BlueTCL-16
73T-389
73T/BlueTCL-16
73T/BlueTCL-16
74OPC-56
74OPC/RedTCL-16
74T-56
74T/RedTCL-16
74T/St/Alb-16
74T/TCL-16
75OPC-421
75T-421
75T/M-421
76OPC-531
76T-531
77T-259
78T-356
79T-82
80T-259
81T-681
87Sf/TPrev-2
90Kahn/Mets-x
90PublInt/St-629
90RedFoley/St-128
91Kahn/Mets-x
91Panini/Top15-118
91Panini/Top15-119
91Panini/Top15-130
91T/TH-7
92Mets/Kahn-NNO
93Mets/Kahn-NNO
93UD-826TC
94Mets/69-2
94StCl/SuperTC-9

New York Team
N690

Oakland A's
68T-554
69T/St/Alb-17
69T/T/Post-17
70T-631
71OPC-624
71T-624
71T/tatt-4
72OPC-454
72T-454
73OPC-500
73OPC/BlueTCL-18
73T-500
73T/BlueTCL-18
73T/BlueTCL-18
74OPC-246
74OPC/RedTCL-18
74T-246
74T/RedTCL-18
74T/St/Alb-18
74T/TCL-18
75OPC-561
75T-561
75T/M-561

76OPC-421
76T-421
77T-74
78T-577
79T-328
80T-96
81T-671
87Sf/TPrev-23
90PubIInt/St-635
91Panini/Top15-134
91Panini/Top15-135
91T/TH-11
93UD-814TC
94StCl/SuperTC-25

Oakland Oaks
46Remar
48Remar

Philadelphia Athletics
51T
T200

Philadelphia Phillies
50Exh/Team
51T
56T-72
57T-214
58T-134
59T-8
60T-302
60T/tatt-60
61T-491
61T/RO-14
62T-294
63T-13
64T-293
65T-338
66T-463
66T/RO-73
67OPC-102
67T-102
68T-477
69T/St/Alb-18
69T/T/Post-18
70OPC-436
70T-436
71OPC-268
71T-268
71T/tatt-3
72OPC-397
72T-397
73OPC-536
73OPC/BlueTCL-19
73T-536
73T/BlueTCL-19
73T/BlueTCL-19
74OPC-383
74OPC/RedTCL-19
74T-467
74T/RedTCL-19
74T/St/Alb-19
74T/TCL-19
75OPC-46
75T-46
75T/M-46
76OPC-384
76T-384
77T-467
78T-381
79T-112
80T-526
81T-682
84Phill/TastyK-2
85Phill/TastyK-47
86Phill/TastyK-x
87Phill/TastyK-x
87Sf/TPrev-6
88Phill/TastyK-28
90PubIInt/St-634
90RedFoley/St-129
91Panini/Top15-127
91T/TH-8
92Phill/Med-34
93UD-829TC
94StCl/SuperTC-10
T200

Philadelphia Team
N690

Pittsburgh Pirates
56T-121
57T-161
58T-341
59T-528
60T-484
60T/tatt-61
61T-554
61T/RO-11
62T-409
63T-151
64T-373
65OPC-209
65T-209
66T-404
66T/RO-43
67T-492
68T-308
69T/St/Alb-19
69T/T/Post-19
70T-608
71OPC-603
71T-603
71T/tatt-13
72OPC-1
72T-1
73OPC-26
73OPC/BlueTCL-20
73T-26
73T/BlueTCL-20
73T/BlueTCL-20
74OPC-626
74OPC/RedTCL-20
74T-626
74T/RedTCL-20
74T/St/Alb-20
74T/TCL-20
75OPC-304
75T-304
75T/M-304
76OPC-504
76T-504
77T-354
78T-606
79T-244
80T-551
81T-683
87Sf/TPrev-18
90PubIInt/St-630
90RedFoley/St-116
91T/TH-9
93UD-830TC
94StCl/SuperTC-11
T200

San Diego Padres
69T/St/Alb-21
69T/T/Post-21
70T-657
71OPC-482
71T-482
71T/tatt-8
72OPC-262
72T-262
73OPC-316
73OPC/BlueTCL-21
73T-316
73T/BlueTCL-21
73T/BlueTCL-21
74OPC-226
74OPC/RedTCL-21
74T-226
74T/RedTCL-21
74T/St/Alb-21
74T/TCL-21
75OPC-146
75T-146
75T/M-146
76OPC-331
76T-331
77T-135
78T-192
79T-479
80T-356
81T-685
87Sf/TPrev-16
90PubIInt/St-625
90RedFoley/St-119
91T/TH-10
93UD-828TC
94StCl/SuperTC-13

San Francisco Giants
59T-69
60T-151
60T/tatt-63
61T-167
61T/RO-12
62T-226
63T-417
64T-257
65T-379
66OPC-19
66T-19
66T/RO-25
67T-516
69T/St/Alb-22
69T/T/Post-22
70T-696
71OPC-563
71T-563
71T/tatt-1
72T-771
73OPC-434
73OPC/BlueTCL-22
73T-434
73T/BlueTCL-22
73T/BlueTCL-22
74OPC-281
74OPC/RedTCL-22
74T-281
74T/RedTCL-22
74T/St/Alb-22
74T/TCL-22
75OPC-216
75T-216
75T/M-216
76OPC-443
76T-443
77T-211
78T-82
79T-356
80T-499
81T-686
91T/TH-11
93UD-822TC
94StCl/SuperTC-14

Seattle Mariners
77T-597
78T-499
79T-659
80T-282
81T-672
87Sf/TPrev-25
90PubIInt/St-641
90RedFoley/St-113
91T/TH-12
93UD-824TC
94StCl/SuperTC-26

Seattle Pilots
69T/St/Alb-23
69T/T/Post-23
70T-713

St. Louis Browns
T200

St. Louis Cardinals
51T
56T-134
57T-243
58T-216
59T-223
60T-242
60T/tatt-62
61T-347
61T/RO-16
62T-61
63T-524
64T-87
65OPC-57
65T-57
66T-379
66T/RO-37
67OPC-173
67T-173
68T-497
69T/St/Alb-20
69T/T/Post-20
70T-549
71OPC-308
71T-308
71T/tatt-15
72T-688
73OPC-219
73OPC/BlueTCL-23
73T-219
73T/BlueTCL-23
73T/BlueTCL-23
74OPC-36
74OPC/RedTCL-23
74T-36
74T/RedTCL-23
74T/St/Alb-23
74T/TCL-23
75OPC 246
75T-246
75T/M-246
76OPC-581
77T-183
78T-479
79T-192
80T-244
81T-684
87Sf/TPrev-12
90PubIInt/St-633
90RedFoley/St-118
91T/TH-12
93UD-818TC
94StCl/SuperTC-12
T200

St. Louis Team
N690

Texas Rangers
72T-668
73OPC-7
73OPC/BlueTCL-24
73T-7
73T/BlueTCL-24
73T/BlueTCL-24
74OPC-184
74OPC/RedTCL-24
74T-184
74T/RedTCL-24
74T/St/Alb-24
74T/TCL-24
75OPC-511
75T-511
75T/M-511
76OPC-172
76T-172
77T-428
78T-659
79T-499
80T-41
81T-673
87Sf/TPrev-1
90PubIInt/St-640
90RedFoley/St-106
91T/TH-13
93UD-831TC
94StCl/SuperTC-27

Toronto Blue Jays
77T-113
78OPC-58
78T-626
79OPC-262
79T-282
80T-577
81T-674
86GenMills/Book-3
87GenMills/Book-1
87Sf/TPrev-5
90PubIInt/St-645
90RedFoley/St-114
91Panini/Top15-124
91Panini/Top15-133
91T/TH-14
92K/FrBoxB-1
92Nabisco-10
92Nabisco-22
93BJ/D/McDon-23
93UD-815TC
94StCl/SuperTC-28

Washington Nationals
51T
56T-146
57T-270
58T-44
59T-297
60T-43
60T/tatt-71
T200
R309/2

Washington Senators
61T/RO-4
62T-206
63T-131
64T-343
65OPC-267
65T-267
66OPC-194
66T-194
66T/RO-31
67T-437
69T/St/Alb-24
69T/T/Post-24
70T-676
71OPC-462
71T-462
71T/tatt-11

CHECKLISTS
56T-NNO
57T-NNO
58T-134
58T-158
58T-174
58T-19
58T-216
58T-246
58T-256
58T-312
58T-327
58T-341
58T-377
58T-397
58T-408
58T-428
58T-44
58T-475
58T-71
59T-111
59T-172
59T-223
59T-248
59T-304
59T-314
59T-329
59T-397
59T-412
59T-419
59T-457
59T-476
59T-48
59T-510
59T-528
59T-69
59T-8
59T-94
60T-151
60T-164
60T-174
60T-18
60T-208
60T-242
60T-302
60T-332
60T-381
60T-413
60T-43
60T-484
60T-494
60T-513
60T-537
60T-72
61F-1
61F-89
61T-17
61T-189
61T-273
61T-361
61T-437
61T-516
61T-98
62T-192
62T-22
62T-277
62T-367
62T-441
62T-516
62T-98
63F-NNO
63T-102
63T-191
63T-274
63T-362
63T-431
63T-509
63T-79
64T-102
64T-188
64T-274
64T-362
64T-438
64T-517
64T-76
65OPC-104
65OPC-189
65OPC-273
65OPC-79
65T-104
65T-189
65T-273
65T-361
65T-443
65T-508
65T-79
66OPC-101
66OPC-183
66OPC-34
66T-101
66T-183
66T-279

66T-34
66T-363
66T-444
66T-517
67OPC-103
67OPC-191
67OPC-62
67T-103
67T-191
67T-278
67T-361
67T-454
67T-531
67T-62
68OPC-107
68OPC-192
68OPC-67
68T-107
68T-192
68T-278
68T-356
68T-454
68T-518
68T-67
69OPC-107
69OPC-214
69OPC-57
69T-107
69T-214
69T-314
69T-412
69T-504
69T-57
69T-582
70OPC-128
70OPC-244
70OPC-343
70OPC-432
70OPC-542
70OPC-9
70T-128
70T-244
70T-343
70T-432
70T-542
70T 588
70T-9
71OPC-123
71OPC-206
71OPC-369
71OPC-499
71OPC-54
71OPC-619
71T-123
71T-161Coin
71T-206
71T-369
71T-499
71T-54
71T-619
72OPC-103
72OPC-251
72OPC-378
72OPC-4
72OPC-478
72ProStars/PostC-37
72T-103
72T-251
72T-378
72T-4
72T-478
72T-604
72T/Cloth-5
73OPC-264
73OPC-338
73OPC-453
73OPC-54
73OPC-588
73T-264
73T-338
73T-453
73T-54
73T-588
74OPC-126
74OPC-263
74OPC-273
74OPC-414
74OPC-637
74T-126
74T-263
74T-273
74T-414
74T-637
74T/Tr-NNO
75OPC-126
75OPC-257
75OPC-386
75OPC-517
75OPC-646
75Sheraton-NNO
75T-126
75T-257
75T-386
75T-517
75T-646
75T/M-126
75T/M-257
75T/M-386
75T/M-517
75T/M-646
76OPC-119
76OPC-262
76OPC-392
76OPC-526
76OPC-643
76SSPC-589--595
76T-119
76T-262
76T-392
76T-526
76T-643
76T/Tr
77Galasso-1353
77Galasso-1804
77Galasso-891
77Galasso-902
77OPC-124
77OPC-179
77T-208
77T-32
77T-356
77T-451
77T-562
77T/CS
78OPC-119
78OPC-183
78T-184
78T-289
78T-435
78T-535
78T 662
78T-74
78Twin/Frisz-25
78Twin/Frisz-50
79OPC-121
79OPC-242
79OPC-353
79T-121
79T-241
79T-353
79T-483
79T-602
79T-699
80OPC-128
80OPC-183
80OPC-249
80OPC-300
80OPC-67
80T-121
80T-241
80T-348
80T-484
80T-533
80T-646
81D-NNO
81F-641--644
81F-646--649
81F-651
81F-652
81F-654
81F-656
81F-658
81F-659
81OPC-241
81OPC-31
81OPC-331
81OPC-338
81T-241
81T-31
81T-338
81T-446
81T-562
81T-638
81T/Tr-858
82D-NNO
82F-647--660
82OPC-129
82OPC-226
82OPC-394
82T-129
82T-226
82T-394
82T-491
82T-634
82T-789
82T/Tr-132T
83D-NNO
83D/AAS-60
83D/HOF-44
83F-647--660
83F/St
83F/St-10M
83F/St-11M
83F/St-12ML
83F/St-14ML
83F/St-15M
83F/St-16M
83F/St-17M
83F/St-18M
83F/St-19AOM
83F/St-19BM
83F/St-20M
83F/St-21M
83F/St-22M
83F/St-23M
83F/St-24M
83F/St-25AM
83F/St-25BM
83F/St-26ML
83F/St-2M
83F/St-3M
83F/St-4M
83F/St-5M
83F/St-6M
83F/St-8M
83F/St-9M
83OPC-129
83OPC-249
83OPC-349
83T-129
83T-249
83T-349
83T-526
83T-642
83T-769
83Twin/Team-36
84Cram/PCL-194
84Cram/PCL-217
84D-NNO
84D/AAS-60
84D/Champs-60
84F-647--660
84F/X-U132
84Nes/792-114
84Nes/792-233
84Nes/792-379
84Nes/792-527
84Nes/792-646
84Nes/792-781
84Nestle/DT-23
84OPC-114
84OPC-233
84OPC-379
84Phill/TastyK-1
84T-114
84T-233
84T-379
84T-527
84T-646
84T-781
84T/Cereal-34
84T/Tr-132T
85D-NNO
85D/AAS-60
85D/DKsuper-27
85D/HL-56
85F-654--660
85F/Up-U132
85Leaf-260--263
85OPC-121
85OPC-261
85OPC-377
85Phill/TastyK-1
85T-121
85T-261
85T-377
85T-527
85T-659
85T-784
85T/Tr-132T
85Twin/Seven-NNO
85Twin/Team-36
86D-NNO
86D/AAS-60
86D/DKsuper-28
86D/HL-56
86D/Rook-56
86F-654--660
86F/Up-U132
86Leaf-261--264
86Negro/Frit-119
86OPC-131
86OPC-263
86OPC-396
86T-131
86T-263
86T-394
86T-527
86T-659
86T-791
86T/Mini-66
86T/Tr-132T
87D-100
87D-200
87D-27DK
87D-300
87D-400
87D-500
87D-600
87D/AAS-60
87D/DKsuper-27
87D/HL-56
87D/Rook-56
87F-654--660
87F/Up-U132
87Leaf-155
87Leaf-259
87Leaf-264
87Leaf-27
87OPC-128
87OPC-214
87OPC-264
87PanAm/USAB-NNO
87PanAm/USAR-NNO
87T-128
87T-264
87T-392
87T-522
87T-654
87T-792
87T/Mini-77
87T/Tr-132T
88D-100
88D-200
88D-27DK
88D-300
88D-400
88D-500
88D-600
88D/AS-32
88D/AS-64
88D/Best-288
88D/Best-329
88D/Best-336
88D/Rook-56
88F-654--660
88F/St-132
88F/Up-U132
88Leaf-209
88Leaf-261
88Leaf-264
88Leaf-27
88OPC-253
88OPC-373
88OPC-374
88T-121
88T-253
88T-373
88T-528
88T-646
88T-776
88T/Big-126
88T/Big-216
88T/Big-28
88T/Mini-77
88T/Tr-132T
88T/UK-88
88TM/Umpire-64
89B-481
89B-482
89B-483
89B-484
89D-100
89D-200
89D-27
89D-300
89D-400
89D-500
89D-600
89D/AS-32
89D/AS-64
89D/Best-300
89D/Best-329
89D/Best-332
89D/Rook-56
89D/Tr-56
89F-654--660
89F/Up-132
89OPC-118
89OPC-242
89OPC-247
89Pac/SenLg-187
89Pac/SenLg-218
89Swell-135
89T-118
89T-258
89T-378
89T-524
89T-619
89T-782
89T/Big-176
89T/Big-327
89T/Big-59
89T/LJN-164
89T/Mini-43
89T/SenLg-132
89T/St/Backs-67
89T/Tr-132T
89T/UK-88
89TM/SenLg-121
89UD-27
89UD-694--700
89UD/Ext-701
90B-525
90B-526
90B-527
90B-528
90D-100
90D-200
90D-27
90D-300
90D-400
90D-500
90D-600
90D-700
90D/BestAL-144
90D/BestAL-96
90D/BestNL-144
90D/BestNL-96
90D/Learning-55
90D/Rook-56
90F-654--660
90F/Can-654
90F/Can-655
90F/Can-656
90F/Can-657
90F/Can-658
90F/Can-659
90F/Can-660
90F/Up-132
90Leaf-174
90Leaf-264
90Leaf-364
90Leaf-444
90Leaf-528
90Leaf-84
90LitSun-1
90Mother/Giant-28
90OPC-128
90OPC-262
90OPC-376
90OPC-526
90OPC-646
90OPC-783
90Swell/Great-135
90T-128
90T-262
90T-376
90T-526
90T-646
90T-783
90T/89Debut-151
90T/89Debut-152
90T/Big-110
90T/Big-220
90T/Big-330
90T/Mini-45
90T/Tr-132T
90TeamUSA/87-26
90TM/Umpire-70
90UD-1
90UD-100
90UD-200
90UD-300
90UD-400

90UD-500
90UD-600
90UD-700
90UD/Ext-800
91B-699--704
91Conlon/Sport-328--330
91D-100
91D-200
91D-27
91D-300
91D-386
91D-500
91D-600
91D-700
91D-760
91D-770
91D/Rook-56
91F-714--720
91F/Ultra-397--400
91F/UltraUp-U120
91F/Up-U132
91Leaf-174
91Leaf-264
91Leaf-364
91Leaf-444
91Leaf-528
91Leaf-84
91Leaf/Stud-261--263
91OPC-131
91OPC-263
91OPC-366
91OPC-527
91OPC-656
91OPC-787
91OPC/Premier-132
91Perez/HOF-NNO
91Pol/Royal-27
91StCl-298--300
91StCl-598--600
91Swell/Great-150
91T-131
91T-263
91T-366
91T-527
91T-656
91T-787
91T/90Debut-170
91T/90Debut-171
91T/Arc53-335--337
91T/Tr-132T
91Tor/Fire-x
91UD-1
91UD-100
91UD-200
91UD-300
91UD-400
91UD-50
91UD-500
91UD-600
91UD-700
91UD/Ext-800
91UD/FinalEd-100F
91UD/FinalEd-1F
91UD/FinalEd-79F
91WIZMets-xx
92B-701
92B-702
92B-703
92B-704
92B-705
92BJ/Fire-36
92ClBest-395
92ClBest-396
92ClBest-398
92ClBest-399
92Conlon/Sport-658--660
92D-160
92D-240
92D-320
92D-396
92D-476
92D-556
92D-636
92D-716
92D-784
92D-80
92D/DK-DK27
92D/McDon-NNO
92D/Rook-131
92D/Rook-132
92Expo/D/Duri-NNO
92F-714--720
92F/Up-132U
92French-NNO
92FrRow/DP-100
92L-133
92L-199
92L-331
92L-397
92L-463
92L-67
92L/BlkGold-133
92L/BlkGold-199
92L/BlkGold-331
92L/BlkGold-397
92L/BlkGold-463
92L/BlkGold-67
92Mega/Ruth-164
92Mega/Ruth-165
92Mother/A's-28
92Mother/Ast-28
92Mother/Dodg-28
92Mother/Giant-28
92Mother/Mar-28
92Mother/Padre-28
92Mother/Rang-28
92OPC-131
92OPC-264
92OPC-366
92OPC-527
92OPC-658
92OPC-787
92OPC/Premier-399
92OPC/Premier-81
92Perez/Master-NNO
92Pol/Card-27
92ProC/Tomorrow-180
92ProC/Tomorrow-270
92ProC/Tomorrow-360
92ProC/Tomorrow-90
92StCl-298
92StCl-299
92StCl-300
92StCl-588
92StCl-589
92StCl-590
92StCl-898
92StCl-899
92StCl-900
92Studio-261
92Studio-262
92Studio-263
92T-131
92T-264
92T-366
92T-527
92T-658
92T-787
92T/91Debut-193
92T/91Debut-194
92T/Kids-132
92T/Tr-132T
92TripleP-132
92TripleP-198
92TripleP-264
92UD-1
92UD-100
92UD-200
92UD-300
92UD-400
92UD-500
92UD-600
92UD-640
92UD-700
92UD-800
92UD-99
92UD/Bench-45
92UD/ML-24
92UD/ML-25
92UD/ML-26
92UD/ML-27
92UD/ML-28
92UD/ML-29
92UD/ML-30
92UD/ML-31
92UD/ML-32
92UD/ML-33
92UD/ML-34
92UD/ML-35
92UD/ML-36
92UD/ML-37
92UD/ML-38
92UD/ML-39
92UD/ML-40
92UD/ML-41
92UD/ML-42
92UD/ML-43
92UD/ML-44
92UD/ML-45
92UD/ML-46
92UD/ML-47
92UD/ML-48
92UD/ML-49
92UD/ML-50M
92Ultra-298
92Ultra-299
92Ultra-300
92Ultra-598
92Ultra-599
92Ultra-600
93B-7051
93B-7062
93B-7073
93B-7084
93BJ/D/McDon-36
93BJ/Fire-36
93ClBest/MLG-217
93ClBest/MLG-218
93ClBest/MLG-220
93Colla/ASG-NNO
93Conlon/-988
93Conlon/-989
93Conlon/-990
93D-122
93D-132
93D-254
93D-264
93D-396
93D-518
93D-528
93D-650
93D-660
93D-715
93D/DK-31
93Expo/D/McDon-33
93F-358
93F-359
93F-360
93F-718
93F-719
93F-720
93F/Atlantic-25
93F/Final-298F
93F/Final-299F
93F/Final-300F
93F/Fruit-66
93FExcel/ML-248
93FExcel/ML-249
93FExcel/ML-250
93Flair-298
93Flair-299
93Flair-300
93HumDum/Can-51
93L-110
93L-120
93L-220
93L-330
93L-340
93L-440
93L-450
93Mother/A's-28
93Mother/Angel-28
93Mother/Ast-28
93Mother/Dodg-28
93Mother/Giant-28
93Mother/Mar-28
93Mother/Padre-28
93OPC-394
93OPC-395
93OPC-396
93OPC/Premier-132
93Pol/Card-26
93Rang/Keeb-442
93Rang/Keeb-443
93Rang/Keeb-444
93Rang/Keeb-445
93StCl-288
93StCl-289
93StCl-290
93StCl-588
93StCl-589
93StCl-590
93StCl-745
93StCl/1stDay-288
93StCl/1stDay-289
93StCl/1stDay-290
93StCl/1stDay-588
93StCl/1stDay-589
93StCl/1stDay-590
93StCl/1stDay-745
93Studio-120
93Studio-220
93T-394
93T-395
93T-396
93T-823
93T-824
93T-825
93T/Tr-132T
93TripleP-132
93TripleP-198
93TripleP-264
93TripleP-66
93TWill-115
93TWill-120
93TWill-130
93TWill-140
93TWill-150
93TWill-155
93TWill-160
93TWill-95
93TWill-96
93TWill/Locklear-10
93TWill/Mem-10M
93TWill/Mem-15M
93TWill/Mem-20M
93UD-105
93UD-210
93UD-315
93UD-420
93UD-471
93UD-525
93UD-630
93UD-735
93UD-840
93UD/Diam-NNO
93UDFutHero-63
93Ultra-298
93Ultra-299
93Ultra-300
93Ultra-648
93Ultra-649
94B-679
94B-680
94B-681
94B-682
94Conlon/-131
94Conlon/-1318
94Conlon/-1320
94D-110
94D-140
94D-220
94D-290
94D-440
94D-550
94D-600
94D-660
94D/DK-30
94Excel-298
94Excel-299
94Excel-300
94F-714
94F-715
94F-716
94F-717
94F-718
94F-719
94F-720
94FExcel-298
94FExcel-299
94FExcel-300
94Flair-248
94Flair-249
94Flair-250
94L-100
94L-150
94L-200
94L-330
94L-380
94L-440
94Mets/69-NNO
94OPC-269
94OPC-270
94S-317CL
94S-318CL
94S-319CL
94S-320CL
94S-321CL
94S-322CL
94S-323CL
94S-324CL
94S-325CL
94S-326CL
94S-327CL
94S-328CL
94S-329CL
94S-330CL
94S-647CL
94S-648CL
94S-649CL
94S-651CL
94S-653CL
94S-654CL
94S-655CL
94S-656CL
94S-657CL
94S-658CL
94S-659CL
94S-660CL
94S/GoldR-317CL
94S/GoldR-318CL
94S/GoldR-319CL
94S/GoldR-320CL
94S/GoldR-321CL
94S/GoldR-322CL
94S/GoldR-323CL
94S/GoldR-324CL
94S/GoldR-325CL
94S/GoldR-326CL
94S/GoldR-327CL
94S/GoldR-328CL
94S/GoldR-329CL
94S/GoldR-330CL
94Select-207
94Select-208
94Select-209
94Select-210
94StCl-269
94StCl-270
94StCl-539
94StCl-540
94StCl/1stDP-269
94StCl/1stDP-270
94StCl/1stDP-539
94StCl/1stDP-540
94StCl/Gold-269
94StCl/Gold-270
94StCl/Gold-539
94StCl/Gold-540
94Studio-219
94Studio-220
94T-395
94T-396
94T-791
94T-792
94TedW-117
94TedW-135
94TedW-144
94TedW-153
94TedW-162
94TedW-911
94TedW-922
94TedW-99
94TedW/500-9
94TedW/54-37
94TedW/Gardiner-9
94TedW/Lock-19
94TripleP-298
94TripleP-299
94TripleP-300
94UD/CollC-316
94UD/CollC-317
94UD/CollC-318
94UD/CollC-319
94UD/CollC-320
94UD/CollC/Gold-316
94UD/CollC/Gold-317
94UD/CollC/Gold-318
94UD/CollC/Gold-319
94UD/CollC/Gold-320
94UD/CollC/Silv-316
94UD/CollC/Silv-317
94UD/CollC/Silv-318
94UD/CollC/Silv-319
94UD/CollC/Silv-320
94UD/InsCL-1
94UD/InsCL-2
94UD/InsCL-3
94UD/InsCL-4
94Ultra-297
94Ultra-298
94Ultra-299
94Ultra-300
94Ultra-597
94Ultra-598
94Ultra-599
94Ultra-600

Aaron, Henry Louis
(Hank)
54JC-5
54SpicSpan/PostC-1
54T-128
55B-179
55Gol/Braves-1
55JC-44
55SpicSpan/DC-1
55T-47
55T/DH-105
56T-31
56T/Pin-16
56YellBase/Pin-1
57SpicSpan/4x5-1
57Swift-13
57T-20
58Hires-44
58T-30
58T-351M
58T-418M
58T-488AS
59Armour-1
59Bz
59HRDerby-1
59T-212M
59T-380
59T-467M
59T-561AS
60Armour-1A
60Armour-1B
60Bz-4
60Lake
60MacGregor-1
60NuCard-62
60SpicSpan-1
60T-300
60T-566AS
60T/tatt-1
61NuCard-462
61P-107
61T-415
61T-43LL
61T-484M
61T-577AS
61T/St-37
62Bz
62Exh
62J-149
62P-149
62P/Can-149
62Salada-180
62Shirriff-180
62T-320
62T-394AS
62T/St-143
62T/bucks
63Bz-9
63Exh
63J-152
63P-152
63Salada-24
63T-1LL
63T-242M
63T-390
63T-3LL
63T/SO
64Bz-9
64T-11LL
64T-300
64T-423M
64T-7LL
64T-9LL
64T/Coins-149AS
64T/Coins-83
64T/S-49
64T/SU
64T/St-84
64T/tatt
64Wheat/St-1
65Bz-9
65Kahn
65OPC-170
65OPC-2LL
65OldLond-1
65T-170
65T-2LL
65T/E-59
65T/trans-37
66Bz-30
66Kahn
66T-215LL
66T-500
66T/RO-1
66T/RO-117
67Bz-30
67CokeCap/AS-19
67CokeCap/Brave-3
67CokeCap/NLAS-19
67Kahn
67OPC/PI-15
67T-242LL
67T-244LL
67T-250
67T/PI-15
67T/Test/SU-20
68Bz-5
68CokeCap/Brave-3
68Dexter-1
68Kahn
68OPC-110
68OPC-3LL
68OPC-5LL
68T-110
68T-370AS
68T-3LL
68T-5LL
68T/ActionSt-10B
68T/ActionSt-16AM
68T/ActionSt-3AM
68T/G-4
68T/Post-14
69Citgo-16
69Kahn
69MB-1
69MLB/St-109
69MLBPA/Pin-31
69NTF
69OPC-100
69T-100
69T/S-34
69T/St-1
69T/decal
69Trans-53
70MB-1
70MLB/St-1
70OPC-462AS
70OPC-500
70OPC-65LL
70T-462AS
70T-500
70T-65LL
70T/S-24
70T/SO
70T/Super-24
70Trans-4
71Bz
71Bz/Test-23
71MD
71MLB/St-1
71MLB/St-553
71OPC-400
71T-400
71T/Coins-137
71T/S-44
71T/Super-44
71T/tatt-9
72Dimanche*-53
72MB-1
72OPC-299
72OPC-300IA
72OPC-87LL
72OPC-89LL
72ProStars/PostC-13
72T-299
72T-300A
72T-87LL
72T-89LL
72T/Cloth-1
72T/Post-9
73OPC-100
73OPC-1M
73OPC-473LL
73T-100
73T-1LL
73T-473LL
73T/Comics-1
73T/Lids-1
73T/PinUps-1
74Laugh/ASG-72
74OPC-1
74OPC-2M
74OPC-3M
74OPC-4M
74OPC-5M
74OPC-6M
74OPC-7M
74OPC-8M
74OPC-9M
74T-1
74T-2M
74T-332M
74T-3M
74T-4M
74T-5M
74T-6M
74T/DE-57
74T/Puzzles-1
74T/St-1
75Ho-130
75Ho/Twink-130
75OPC-195MVP
75OPC-1RB
75OPC-660
75SSPC/Puzzle-1
75SSPC/Sam-1
75T-195MVP
75T-1RB
75T-660
75T/M-195MVP
75T/M-1RB
75T/M-660
76A&P/Milw
76Crane-1
76Ho-94
76Laugh/Clown-34
76Laugh/Jub-8
76MSA/Disc
76OPC-1RB
76OPC-550
76SSPC-239
76T-1RB
76T-550
77Galasso-231
77Galasso-44
79T-412M
79T-413M
80Laugh/3/4/5-16
80Pac/Leg-7
80Perez/HOF-177
81Pol/Atl-44C
81TCMA-356
81Tiger/Detroit-54
82CJ-9
82KMart-43
83D/HOF-34
83MLBPA/Pin-19
83OPC/St-1FOIL
83T/St-1F
84D/Champs-8
85CircK-1
85D/HOF-7
85Woolwth-1
86BLChew-1
86D-602Pz
86D/AS/WaxBox-PUZ
86D/WaxBox-PUZ
86Leaf-259PUZ
86Sf/Dec-40
87KMart-1
87Leaf/SpecOlym-H7
87Nestle/DT-29
88Grenada-38
88Pac/Leg-1
89HOF/St-44
89Kenner/BBGr-1
89T-663TBC
89T/LJN-137
89T/LJN-161
90BBWit-6
90CollAB-22
90HOF/St-81
90MSA/AGFA-6
90Pac/Legend-1
90Perez/GreatMom-9
90Swell/Great-2
91K/3D-2
91K/SU-1A
91K/SU-1B
91Swell/Great-102
91T/Arc53-317
91UD/Aaron-Set
91UD/Ext-HH1
92Bz/Quadra-6
92FrRow/ATGHolo-1
92Ziploc-11
93Metallic-1
93UD/ATH-1
93UD/ATH-149
93UD/ATH-150M
94T-715
94T/Arc54-128
94T/Gold-715
94TedW/500-1
Exh47
PM10/Sm-1
TCMA78-290
WG10-24
WG9-26

Aaron, Tommie Lee
63T-46
64T-454
65T-567
68T-394
69OPC-128
69T-128
69T/4in1-3M
70OPC-278
70T-278
71MLB/St-2
71OPC-717
71Richm/Team-1
71T-717
72MB-2
78Richm
82Pol/Atl-23C
90Richm/25Ann-1MG

Aaron, Wil
75SanAn
76Wmsprt

Aase, Donald William
(Don)
76OPC-597R
76T-597R
77T-472R
78OPC-233
78T-12
79T-368
80OPC-126
80T-239
81D-411
81F-286
81T-601
82D-267
82F-450
82F/St-212
82OPC-199
82T-199
83D-38
83F-76
83T-599
84Smok/Cal-1
85D-255
85F-293
85F/Up-U1
85T-86
85T/Tr-1T
86D-392
86D/HL-12
86F-268
86T-288
87Classic-99
87D-231
87D/AAS-47
87F-461
87F-627M
87F/Excit-1
87F/Mini-1
87F/St-1
87OPC-207
87Seven-ME4
87Sf-165
87Sf-194M
87Sf/TPrev-21M
87T-766
87T/Mini-38
87T/St-228
88F-553
88French-41
88S-518
88T-467
89F/Up-100
89Kahn/Mets-49
89S-524
89T/Tr-1T
89UD-450
90F-196
90F/Can-196
90Mother/Dodg-27
90OPC-301
90S-377
90S/Tr-29T
90T-301
90UD-131
91Crown/Orio-1
91F-193
91S-289
91WIZMets-1

Abarbanel, Mickey
68T-287R

Abare, Bill
89StCath/ProC-2071
90Myrtle/ProC-2781
91Dunedin/ClBest-15
91Dunedin/ProC-212

Abbaticchio, Ed
12Sweet/Pin-65
D322-14
E254
E270/1
M116
T205
T206

Abbatiello, Pat
87Idaho-26

Abbe, Chris
92Yakima/ProC-3451
93FExcel/ML-51

Abbey, Bert Wood
90Target-1

Abbey, Charles S.
(Charlie)
N300/SC

Abbott, Frederick H.
(Fred)
E254
E270/1
T206

Abbott, Jim
87PanAm/USAB-25
87PanAm/USAR-25
88T/Tr-1T
89B-39
89Classic/Up/2-151
89D/Best-171
89D/Rook-16
89F/Up-11
89S/Tr-88
89T-573FDP
89T/Big-322
89T/HeadsUp-16
89T/Tr-2T
89UD/Ext-755
90B-288
90Bz-22
90Classic-40
90CollAB-27
90D-108
90D/Learning-44
90F-125
90F/Can-125
90F/SoarSt-10
90HotRook/St-1
90Kenner/Fig-1
90KingB/Discs-20
90Leaf-31
90MLBPA/Pins-95
90OPC-675
90Panini/St-34
90Post-13
90PublInt/St-362
90S-330
90S/100Ris-5
90S/YS/I-5
90Sf-99
90Smok/Angel-1
90T-675
90T/89Debut-1
90T/Big-329
90T/DH-1
90T/Gloss60-50
90T/HeadsUp-16
90T/JumboR-1
90T/St-172
90T/St-319FS
90TeamUSA/87-25
90ToysRUs-1
90UD-645
90WonderBrd-3
91B-200
91Classic/200-5
91Classic/III-T1
91D-78
91F-305
91Kenner-1
91Leaf-162
91Leaf/Stud-22
91MajorLg/Pins-23
91OPC-285

91Panini/FrSt-188
91Panini/St-140
91Post-20
91RedFoley/St-1
91S-105
91S/100SS-69
91Seven/3DCoin-1SC
91Smok/Angel-7
91StCl-124
91T-285
91UD-554
91Ultra-43
92B-185
92B-572FOIL
92CJ/DI-3
92Classic/Game200-109
92Classic/I-T1
92Classic/II-T1
92D-130
92F-50
92F/Smoke-S12
92JDean/18-1
92L-1
92L/BlkGold-1
92MrTurkey-1
92OPC-530
92OPC/Premier-140
92Panini-12
92Pinn-281I
92Pinn-539
92Pinn/RookI-2M
92Pinn/Team2000-42
92Pinn/TeamP-2
92Pol/Angel-1
92S-620
92S/100SS-19
92S/Impact-14
92Seven/Coin-22
92StCl-210
92Studio-141
92Studio/Prev-21
92Sunflower-11
92T-406AS
92T-530
92T/DQ-9
92T/Gold-406AS
92T/Gold-530
92T/GoldWin-406AS
92T/GoldWin-530
92T/Kids-97
92T/McDonB-20
92TripleP-204
92UD-325
92UD-642DS
92UD-78
92UD-86
92UD/TmMVPHolo-3
92USPlayC/Ace-4S
92Ultra-321
93B-131
93Classic/GameI-1
93D-35
93Duracel/PPII-16
93F-187
93F/Final-242
93Flair-244
93HumDum/Can-13
93Kraft-1
93L-253
93L/GoldAS-18
93MSA/Ben-18
93OPC-1
93OPC/Premier-130
93Pac/Spanish-551
93Pinn-11
93S-646
93Select-98
93Select/RookTr-30T
93StCl-615
93StCl/1stDay-615
93StCl/Y-2
93Studio-29
93T-780
93T/Finest-46
93T/FinestRef-46
93T/Gold-780
93T/Hill-4
93T/Tr-75T
93TripleP-258M
93TripleP/Gal-GS7
93UD-30M
93UD-31CH
93UD-451IN
93UD-53M
93UD-554
93UD/5thAnn-A4
93UD/FunPack-204GS
93UD/FunPack-205
93UD/OnDeck-D1
93UD/SP-262
93Ultra-590
94B-193
94D-357
94D/Special-357
94F-224
94F/GoldM-10M
94L-38
94OPC-211
94Oscar-1
94Pac/Cr-420
94Panini-98
94Pinn-110
94Pinn/Artist-110
94Pinn/Museum-110
94Pinn/Trib-2
94RedFoley-17M
94S-127
94S-626HL
94S/GoldR-127
94S/Tomb-16
94Select-78
94Sf/2000-138
94StCl-516
94StCl/1stDay-516
94StCl/Gold-516
94StCl/Team-184
94Studio-211
94T-350
94T/Finest-149
94T/Finest/PreProd-149
94T/FinestRef-149
94T/Gold-350
94TripleP-271
94UD-310
94UD/SP-195
94Ultra-397

Abbott, John
85Elmira-1
86Greens-1
88WinHaven/Star-1

Abbott, Kurt
89Medford/Best-27
90Madison/Best-3
90Madison/ProC-2274
90MidwLgAS/GS-1
91Huntsvl/Team-1
91Modesto/ClBest-1
91Modesto/ProC-3092
92Huntsvl/ProC-3954
92Huntsvl/SB-301
92Sky/AASingl-126
94B-534
94F/MLP-1
94Finest-431
94Flair-160
94Flair/Wave-1
94L-346
94Pinn-226
94Pinn/Artist-226
94Pinn/Museum-226
94Pinn/RookTPinn-5
94S-598
94S/Boys-53
94Select-187
94Sf/2000-153
94StCl/Team-86
94Studio-105
94UD-313
94UD/CollC-31
94UD/CollC/Gold-31
94UD/CollC/Silv-31
94Ultra-104
94Ultra-489
94Ultra/AllRook-1

Abbott, Kyle
89QuadC/GS-13
90B-287
90MidldA/GS-5
90OPC-444FDP
90S-673DC
90T-444
91AAA/LineD-151
91B-187
91Edmon/LineD-151
91Edmon/ProC-1507
91UD-51
92B-310
92Classic/Game200-198
92Classic/I-T2
92Classic/II-T57
92D-3RR
92D/Rook-1
92F-51
92L-495
92L/BlkGold-495
92OPC-763
92OPC/Premier-185
92Phill/Med-1
92Pinn-432
92Pinn/Team2000-75
92ProC/Tomorrow-27
92S-849
92S/Rook-2
92StCl-818
92T-763
92T/91Debut-1
92T/Gold-763
92T/GoldWin-763
92UD-754
92UD-8SR
93B-652
93D-676
93F-483
93Phill/Med-1
93Pinn-378
93S-403
93ScranWB/Team-1
93Select-332
93StCl-201
93StCl/1stDay-201
93StCl/Phill-3
93T-317
93T/Gold-317
93UD-300
93Ultra-82
94T-773
94T/Gold-773

Abbott, Leander F.
(Dan)
No Cards.

Abbott, Ody Cleon
No Cards.

Abbott, Paul
86Kenosha-1
87Kenosha-24
88Visalia/Cal-165
88Visalia/ProC-92
89OrlanTw/Best-7
89OrlanTw/ProC-1348
89SLAS-14
90AAASingl/ProC-238
90Portl/CMC-1
90Portl/ProC-168
90ProC/Singl-553
91AAA/LineD-401
91B-329
91D-639
91Portl/LineD-401
91Portl/ProC-1558
91S-363RP
91T/90Debut-1
91UD-487
92F-667
92OPC-781
92S-697
92StCl-567
92T-781
92T/Gold-781
92T/GoldWin-781
92USPlayC/Twin-2S
92USPlayC/Twin-3H

Abbott, Terry
78Green
89Augusta/ProC-515
90Cedar/Best-5CO
90Cedar/ProC-2338CO
90MidwLgAS/GS-53CO
92Billings/ProC-3374

Abbott, W. Glenn
(Glenn)
74OPC-602R
74T-602R
75OPC-591
75T-591
75T/M-591
76OPC-322
76SSPC-485
76T-322
77Ho-147
77Ho/Twink-147
77OPC-219
77T-207
78Ho-17
78OPC-92
78T-31
79OPC-263
79T-497
80OPC-92
80T-166
81D-47
81F-615
81OPC-174
81Pol/Mariners-3
81T-699
82D-302
82F-502
82T-336TL
82T-571
84F-74
84Nes/792-356
84OPC-356
84T-356
84Tiger/Wave-2
86Jacks/TCMA-25
87Jacks/Feder-20
88Jacks/GS-5
89Tidew/CMC-26
90Huntsvl/Best-25CO
91AAA/LineD-550CO
91Tacoma/LineD-550CO
91Tacoma/ProC-2322CO
92Tacoma/ProC-2518CO
92Tacoma/SB-550M

Abe, Keiji
90Gate/ProC-3362CO
90Gate/SportP-23CO

Abe, Osamu
83SanJose-8

Abel, Sid
51BR-C16

Abell, Scott
92Eugene/ClBest-4
92Eugene/ProC-3031

Aber, Albert Julius
(Al)
53T-233
54T-238
55B-24
56T-317
57T-141
91T/Arc53-233
94T/Arc54-238
D301

Abercrombie, John Jr.
91HighD/ClBest-14
91HighD/ProC-2397
92Watlo/ClBest-19
92Watlo/ProC-2146

Abernathie, William
(Bill)
No Cards.

Abernathy, Talmadge
No Cards.

Abernathy, Ted
57T-293
59T-169
60T-334
64T-64
65T-332
66OPC-2
66T-2
67T-597
68T-264
69MB-2
69T-483
69T/St-21
70T-562
71MLB/St-409
71OPC-187
71T-187
72MB-3
72OPC-519
72T-519
73OPC-22
73T-22
84Cub/Uno-9M
89Chatt/II/Team-1

Abernathy, Tom
V355-122

Abernathy, Virgil W.
(Woody)
No Cards.

Aberson, Clifford A.
(Cliff)
48L-136

Ables, Harry Terrell
No Cards.

Abner, Ben
86Macon-1
87Harris-26

Abner, Shawn
85Lynch-25
85T-282FDP
86Jacks/TCMA-19
87LasVegas-2
88D-33
88D/Best-21
88D/Rook-5
88F-576
88Leaf-33RR
88S-626
88Sf-223
88Smok/Padres-1
89D-323
89LasVegas/CMC-22
89LasVegas/ProC-21
89S-411
90Classic/III-20
90OPC-122
90S-352
90T-122
90UD-301
91D-561
91F-522
91Leaf-381
91OPC-697
91Padre/MagRal-8
91S-261
91StCl-291
91T-697
91UD/Ext-795
91Ultra-300
92D-736
92OPC-338
92S-616
92StCl-197
92T-338
92T/Gold-338
92T/GoldWin-338
92UD-502
92Vanco/SB-626
92WSox-45
93D-651
93F-579
93S-437
93StCl-403
93StCl/1stDay-403
93T-582
93T/Gold-582

Abone, Joseph
80Memphis-6
82Wichita-1

Abraham, Brian
77SanJose-23
79Ogden/TCMA-10
80Ogden-9
81WHave-18
82WHave-1

Abraham, Glenn
87Everett-10
87Pocatel/Bon-31

Abrams, Calvin Ross
(Cal)
51B-152
52B-86
52T-350
53B/Col-160
53NB
53T-98
54B-91
54Esskay
55B-55
55Esskay
89Rini/Dodg-34
90Target-2
91Crown/Orio-2
91T/Arc53-98

Abrams, George Allen
No Cards.

Abramvicius, Jason
93Welland/ProC-3346

Abrego, Johnny
86D-32
86Iowa-1

Abrell, Thomas
86Sumter/ProC-1
87CharWh-26

Abreu, Armand

77Spartan
Abreu, Bob
92Ashvl/ClBest-19
92ClBest-383
93ClBest/MLG-105
94FExcel-196
Abreu, Francisco
87DayBe-11
Abreu, Franklin
(Frank)
87Savan-20
88Spring/Best-21
89StPete/Star-1
90ArkTr/GS-4
91AA/LineD-26
91ArkTr/LineD-26
92StPete/ClBest-8
92StPete/ProC-2031
Abreu, Joseph L.
(Joe)
No Cards.
Abril, Ernest
(Odie)
85Greens-21
86FSLAS-1
86WinHaven-1
87WinHaven-15
88WinHaven/Star-2
89WinHaven/Star-1
90LynchRS/Team-14
Abshier, Lanny
87Salem/ProC-2438
Abstein, William H.
(Bill)
C46-86
E104
E254
T201
T206
Acker, James Austin
(Jim)
84D-146
84F-145
84Nes/792-359
84OPC-359
84T-359
84Tor/Fire 1
85F-96
85OPC-101
85T-101
85Tor/Fire-1
86BJ/Ault-1
86D-363
86F-50
86OPC-46
86T-569
86Tor/Fire-1
87D-659
87F-509
87Smok/Atl-10
87T-407
88F-531
88OPC-293
88S-576
88T-678
88T/St-43
89Brave/Dubuq-1
89T-244
89UD-52
90D-558
90OPC-728
90T-728
90Tor/BJ-34
91D-368
91F-167
91OPC-71
91S-122
91S/ToroBJ-21
91T-71
91Tor/Fire-34
91UD-670
92F-322
92Mother/Mar-23
92OPC-178
92S-63
92T-178
92T/Gold-178
92T/GoldWin-178
92TX-1
Acker, Larry
85Cram/PCL-55
86Tucson-1
87BirmB/Best-8
88Memphis/Best-7
Acker, Thomas James
(Tom)
57Kahn
57T-219
58T-149
59Kahn
59T-201
60T-274
Ackerman, John
84Everett/Cram-27
Ackley, Florian F.
(Fritz)
64T-368R
65T-477R
66Pep/Tul
78TCMA-27
Ackley, John
80Elmira-12
Acosta, Bert
78Newar
Acosta, Carlos
86Tampa-1
Acosta, Cecilio
73OPC-379
73T-379
74OPC-22
74T-22
75OPC-634
75T-634
75T/M-634
Acosta, Clemente
90PalmSp/Cal-226
90PalmSp/ProC-2569
90ProC/Singl-711
91AA/LineD-426
91MidldA/LineD-426
91MidldA/ProC-426
92MidldA/SB-451
Acosta, Ed
71OPC-343R
71T-343R
72OPC-123
72T-123
73OPC-244
73T-244
Acosta, Jose
87Watertn-17
88Augusta/ProC-371
89Augusta/ProC-492
Acosta, Oscar
89Gaston/ProC-1025
91AA/LineD-600M
91Tulsa/LineD-600CO
91Tulsa/ProC-2789CO
91Tulsa/Team-1CO
92OkCty/ProC-1930CO
92OkCty/SB-325M
Acre, Mark
92Reno/Cal-36
94B-332
94ClBest/Gold-97
94FExcel-116
94Ultra-405
Acta, Manuel
(Manny)
88Osceola/Star-1
89ColMud/Best-2
89ColMud/ProC-136
89ColMud/Star-1
90Osceola/Star-1
91BurlAs/ClBest-12
91BurlAs/ProC-2806
92Ashvl/ClBest-29
Adair, Bill
76Expo/Redp-1CO
Adair, James Aubrey
(Jimmy)
No Cards.
Adair, Kenneth Jerry
(Jerry)
60L-28
61T-71
62T-449
62T/St-2
63J-61
63P-61
63T-488
64T-22
65OPC-231
65T-231
66T-533
66T/RO-2
67CokeCap/WSox-2
67T-484
68CokeCap/RedSox-17
68Dexter-2
68T-346
69MB-3
69MLB/St-55
69OPC-159
69T-159
69T/4in1-1
69T/St-181
70MLB/St-217
70OPC-525
70T-525
72MB-4
73OPC-179CO
73T-179C
91Crown/Orio-3
Adair, Rick
81Wausau-14
82LynnS-1
83SLCity-8
84Chatt-23
87Watlo-29
89ColoSp/CMC-23
89ColoSp/ProC-247
90AAASingl/ProC-237CO
90ColoSp/CMC-19CO
90ColoSp/ProC-56CO
90ProC/Singl-471CO
91AAA/LineD-100M
91ColoSp/LineD-100CO
91ColoSp/ProC-2201CO
92Indian/McDon-30M
Adam, David
92SanBern/ClBest-18
92SanBern/ProC-
93River/Cal-3
Adamczak, Jim
86Jacks/TCMA-1
Adames, Hernan
88Tampa/Star-1
Adames, Juan
88Wythe/ProC-1997
89Peoria/Team-16
Adams, Ace Townsend
41DP-138
43PlayBall-43
88Conlon/3-1
Adams, Art
91Bristol/ClBest-29
91Bristol/ProC-3594
92Fayette/ClBest-16
Adams, Bob
77Evansvl/TCMA-1
Adams, Brian
90Spartan/Best-12
90Spartan/ProC-2493
90Spartan/Star-1
Adams, Bud
88BBCity/Star-1
Adams, Carl Ray
79Newar-15
Adams, Charles B.
(Babe)
11Diamond-1
16FleischBrd-1
21Exh-1
61F-90
80Laugh/FFeat-38
87Conlon/2-7
92Conlon/Sport-443
94Conlon-1245
D322-9
D329-1
D350/2-1
E104
E120
E121/120
E126
E220
E254
E90/1
E96
M101/4-1
M101/5-1
M116
V100
V61-91
W501-84
W514-54
W515-6
W516-18
W573
W575
Adams, Charles Dwight
(Red)
47Signal
49B/PCL-24
53Mother-53
73OPC-569CO
73T-569C
74OPC-144CO
74T-144C
Adams, Craig
77Watlo
81Chatt-20
82Chatt-22
Adams, Dan
75Lafay
Adams, Daniel Leslie
(Dan)
No Cards.
Adams, Daryl
80Penin/C-2
Adams, Dave
90QuadC/GS-12
90Spokane/SportP-8
91CharRain/ClBest-14
91CharRain/ProC-99
91QuadC/ClBest-1
91QuadC/ProC-2618
92MidldA/OneHour-1
92MidldA/ProC-4018
92MidldA/SB-452
92Sky/AASingl-191
92Watlo/ClBest-24
92Watlo/ProC-2147
Adams, Derek
91Bluefld/ClBest-12
91Bluefld/ProC-4132
92Kane/ClBest-21
92Kane/ProC-96
92Kane/Team-1
Adams, Earl John
(Sparky)
25Exh-17
26Exh-17
27Exh-9
29Exh/4-13
31Exh/4-15
33DH-1
33Exh/4-8
33G-213
34DS-24
35G-1H
35G-3F
35G-4F
35G-5F
93Conlon-695
Adams, Elvin Clark
(Buster)
No Cards.
Adams, Gary
90Gate/ProC-3352
90Gate/SportP-1
91Sumter/ClBest-22
91Sumter/ProC-2347
Adams, George
No Cards.
Adams, Gerald
84Newar-20
85Newar-9
Adams, Glenn Charles
76OPC-389
76SSPC-108
76T-389
78T-497
78Twin/FriszP-1
79T-193
79Twin/FriszP-1
80T-604
81D-566
81F-562
82D-431
82F-545
82Syrac-19
82Syrac/Team-1
82T-519
83OPC-374
83T-574
87Watlo-10MG
88CLAS/Star-21
Adams, Harold Douglas
(Doug)
No Cards.
Adams, Herbert Loren
(Herb)
No Cards.
Adams, James Irvin
(Willie)
No Cards.
Adams, James J.
(Jim)
No Cards.
Adams, Jason
90Kgsport/Star-30BB
Adams, John Bertram
(Bert)
11Helmar-153
14CJ-63
15CJ-63
T207
Adams, John
78BurlB
80Holyo-16
83ArkTr-10
84ArkTr-12
Adams, Joseph Edward
(Joe)
No Cards.
Adams, Karl Tutwiler
No Cards.
Adams, Ken
86Cram/NWL-46
88BBCity/Star-2
89BBCity/Star-1
Adams, Lionel
89Idaho/ProC-2012
89Sumter/ProC-1098
Adams, Mike
86Visalia-1
87Visalia-22
Adams, Moose
91Everett/ClBest-20
91Everett/ProC-3904
Adams, Morgan
90MedHat/Best-16
Adams, Pat
82AppFx/Frit-27
83AppFx/Frit-8
85Cram/PCL-186
87Phoenix-21
88WPalmB/Star-1
Adams, Ralph
84LitFalls-6
86Lynch-1
Adams, Richard Leroy
(Dick)
No Cards.
Adams, Ricky Lee
78DaytB
80ElPaso-21
81Holyo-7
82Holyo-13
84Cram/PCL-104
84D-85
84Nes/792-487
84T-487
85Cram/PCL-188
86Phoenix-1
86T-153
Adams, Robert Andrew
(Bob)
No Cards.
Adams, Robert Burdette
(Bob)
No Cards.
Adams, Robert Henry
(Bobby)
48L-54
49Eureka-76
51B-288
52B-166
52T-249
53B/Col-108
53RM-NL2
53T-152
54B-108
54T-123
55B-118
55T-178
56T-287
58T-99
59T-249
91Crown/Orio-4
91T/Arc53-152
94T/Arc54-123
Adams, Robert Melvin
(Bob)
No Cards.

Adams, Robert Michael
(Mike)
74OPC-573
74T-573
74Tacoma/Caruso-22
Adams, Rollo
81Clinton-26
Adams, Spencer Dewey
(Spencer)
No Cards.
Adams, Steve
86Watertn-1
87Macon-13
88Salem/Star-1
89EastLDD/ProC-DD27
89Harris/ProC-295
89Harris/Star-1
90EastLAS/ProC-EL30
90Harris/ProC-1185
90Harris/Star-1
91AA/LineD-101
91CaroMud/LineD-101
91CaroMud/ProC-1078
Adams, Terry 1
76Cedar
Adams, Terry 2
91Hunting/ClBest-1
91Hunting/ProC-3324
92ClBest-217
92Peoria/ClBest-19
92Peoria/Team-1
92StCl/Dome-1
Adams, Tommy
91Belling/ClBest-16
91Belling/ProC-3677
91ClBest/Singl-430
91Classic/DP-49
92AS/Cal-45
92ClBest-245
92SanBern/ClBest-1
92SanBern/ProC-
92StCl/Dome-2
92UD/ML-247
92UD/POY-PY13
93B-683
93ClBest/MLG-141
Adams, Willie
92T/Tr-1T
92T/TrGold-1T
93StCl/MurphyS-183
94B-632
Adamson, Joel
90Princet/DIMD-1
92ClBest-74
92Clearw/ClBest-14
92Clearw/ProC-2045
93T-613
93T/Gold-613
Adamson, John Michael
(Mike)
69OPC-66R
69T-66R
71OPC-362R
71T-362R
91Crown/Orio-5
Adamson, Tony
91Perth/Fut-18
Adamson, Wade
80OrlanTw-1
Adcock, Joseph Wilbur
(Joe)
51B-323
52B-69
52T-347
53B/Col-151
53JC-17
53SpicSpan/3x5-1
53SpicSpan/7x10-1
54B-96
54JC-9
54SpicSpan/PostC-2
55B-218
55Gol/Braves-2
55JC-9
55SpicSpan/DC-2
56T-320
56YellBase/Pin-2
57SpicSpan/4x5-2
57T-117
58T-325
58T-351M
59T-315
60Lake
60NuCard-33
60SpicSpan-2
60T-3
61NuCard-433
61P-104
61T-245
61T/St-38
62J-145
62P-145
62Salada-125
62Shirriff-125
62T-265
62T/St-144
62T/bucks
63F-46
63J-148
63P-148
63Sugar-4
63T-170
67T-563
72Laugh/GF-42
78TCMA-108
78TCMA-73
88Pac/Leg-31
89Swell-6
90HOF/St-50
90LSUGreat-12
91T/Arc53-285
92Bz/Quadra-1
94TedW-145
94TedW-40
Exh47
Adderly, Ken
87Miami-18
Addis, Robert Gorden
(Bob)
52T-259
53B/Col-94
53T-157
91T/Arc53-157
Adduci, James David
(Jim)
81Louisvl-19
82ArkTr-18
83Louisvl/Riley-19
84Louisvl-19
85Cram/PCL-206
86Vanco-1
87D-495
87Denver-16
88Pol/Brew-14
89F-176
89Phill/TastyK-37
89S-587
89T-338
90AAASingl/ProC-306
90ProC/Singl-238
90ScranWB/CMC-12
90ScranWB/ProC-604
Addy, Robert Edward
(Bob)
No Cards.
Aderholt, Morrie
90Target-888
Adkins, Adrian
89Princet/Star-1
Adkins, Grady Emmett
No Cards.
Adkins, John Dewey
(Dewey)
No Cards.
Adkins, Merle Theron
(Doc)
C46-18
E254
E270/2
T205
T206
Adkins, Richard Earl
(Dick)
No Cards.
Adkins, Rob
92Myrtle/ClBest-4
92StCath/ClBest-15
92StCath/ProC-3376
93ClBest/MLG-176
93MedHat/ProC-3729
93MedHat/SportP-11
Adkins, Steve
87FtLaud-22
87PrWill-20
88PrWill/Star-1
89BBAmAA/BPro-AA3
89EastLgAS/ProC-11
89FtLaud/Star-1
90AAASingl/ProC-317
90AlbanyDG/Best-28
90Classic/Up-T2
90ColClip/CMC-1
90ColClip/ProC-667
90Colum/Pol-17
90ProC/Singl-201
90T/TVYank-35
91AAA/LineD-101
91ColClip/LineD-101
91ColClip/ProC-588
91S-716
91S/Rook40-16
91T/90Debut-2
92Iowa/ProC-4044
92Iowa/SB-201
93Syrac/ProC-990
Adkins, Terry
85PrWill-6
Adkins, Tim
92LitSun/HSPros-20
93ClBest/MLG-171
93StCath/ClBest-2
93StCath/ProC-3965
Adkinson, Henry Magee
(Henry)
No Cards.
Adler, Marcus
88Fayette/ProC-1085
89Lakeland/Star-1
Adlesh, David George
(Dave)
67OPC-51R
67T-51R
68T-576
69T-341
Adriana, Sharnol
91StCath/ClBest-5
91StCath/ProC-3400
92Dunedin/ProC-2004
93Knoxvl/ProC-1255
Adriance, Dan
86Cram/NWL-190
87Beloit-23
88Beloit/GS-6
89Salinas/Cal-124
89Salinas/ProC-1818
Afenir, Troy
85Osceola/Team-13
86ColumAst-1
87ColAst/ProC-4
88ColAst/Best-23
89Huntsvl/Best-3
90AAASingl/ProC-142
90ProC/Singl-599
90Tacoma/CMC-22
90Tacoma/ProC-95
91AAA/LineD-526
91F-1
91S-745
91Tacoma/LineD-526
91Tacoma/ProC-2308
92B-509
92D/Rook-2
92F-248
92L-525
92L/BlkGold-525
92Nashvl/SB-276
92Reds/Kahn-38
92S-407
92StCl-613
Agado, David
89Batavia/ProC-1926
90Martins/ProC-3204
Agan, Tim
84Toledo-19
Agar, Jeff
86Lakeland-1
87GlenF-12
Agee, Tommie Lee
65OPC-166R
65T-166R
66OPC-164R
66T-164R
67Bz-2
67CokeCap/WSox-18
67OPC/PI-4
67T-455
67T/PI-4
68Bz-15
68Bz-6
68Kahn
68T-465
69MB-4
69MLB/St-163
69T-364
69T/St-61
70K-11
70MLB/St-73
70OPC-307WS
70OPC-50
70T-307WS
70T-50
70T/PI-13
70T/S-42
70T/Super-42
70Trans/M-23
71Bz
71Bz/Test-16
71K-46
71MLB/St-145
71OPC-310
71T-310
71T/Coins-91
71T/Super-36
71T/tatt-9
72MB-5
72OPC-245
72T-245
72T/S-36
73OPC-420
73T-420
74OPC-630
74T-630
74T/Tr-630T
81TCMA-315M
81TCMA-322M
90Pac/Legend-2
90Swell/Great-19
91LineD-30
91Swell/Great-1
91WIZMets-2
93UD/ATH-2
94Mets/69-5
94TedW-57
Agganis, Harry
55T-152
Agler, Joseph Abram
(Joe)
E254
Agnew, Samuel Lester
(Sam)
D328-1
D329-2
D350/2-2
E135-1
M101/4-2
M101/5-2
Agostinelli, Sal
84Savan-22
86StPete-1
87ArkTr-15
88Louisvl-5
88Louisvl/CMC-21
88Louisvl/ProC-424
89Reading/Best-22
89Reading/ProC-654
89Reading/Star-1
90ProC/Singl-237
90Reading/Best-13
90Reading/ProC-1222
90Reading/Star-1
90ScranWB/CMC-11
91AAA/LineD-476
91ScranWB/LineD-476
91ScranWB/ProC-2540
Agosto, Juan Roberto
82Edmon-12
84D-208
84F-50
84Nes/792-409
84T-409
84TrueVal/WS-1
85Coke/WS-50
85D-526
85F-506
85T-351
86Coke/WS-50
86D-488
86F-197
86T-657
87T-277
87Tucson-1
88F-437
88Mother/Ast-24
88Pol/Ast-1
88S-558
88T/Tr-2T
89B-321
89D-354
89F-348
89Lennox/Ast-17
89Mother/Ast-23
89Panini/St-81
89S-283
89T-559
89UD-251
90D-477
90F-220
90F/Can-220
90Lennox-1
90Mother/Ast-26
90OPC-181
90PublInt/St-85
90S-284
90T-181
90UD-450
91B-402
91D-531
91F-497
91Leaf-404
91OPC-703
91Pol/Card-49
91S-591
91StCl-570
91T-703
91T/Tr-1T
91UD-569
91UD/Ext-788
92D-37
92F-574
92OPC-421
92Pol/Card-1
92S-329
92T-421
92T/Gold-421
92T/GoldWin-421
92UD-693
92Ultra-562
Aguayo, Carmelo
82Tulsa-14
Aguayo, Luis
79OkCty
80OkCty
82D-622
82F-238
82T-449
83D-546
83Portl-1
83T-252
84Phill/TastyK-28
85D-503
85Phill/TastyK-11M
85Phill/TastyK-28
85T-663
86D-503
86F-433
86Phill/TastyK-16
86T-69
87F-169
87F-169
87OPC-18
87Phill/TastyK-16
87T-755
87T-755
88D-185
88F-297
88Phill/TastyK-1
88S-499
88T-356
88T/Big-226
89B-88
89D-551
89F-249
89S-436
89T-561
89UD-156
91AAA/LineD-351
91Pawtu/LineD-351
91Pawtu/ProC-43
92Pawtu/SB-351
92Yank/WIZ80-1
93Pawtu/Ball-25CO
Aguilar, Jose
85Tigres-14
Aguilar, Mark
88Stockton/Cal-191
88Stockton/ProC-723
89Madis/Star-1
Aguilera, Rick
85Tidew-11

86D-441
86F-74
86KayBee-1
86Leaf-216
86T-599
87Classic-79
87D-620
87F-1
87F/Excit-2
87Leaf-89
87OPC-103
87T-103
88D-446
88D/Mets/Bk-446
88F-127
88Kahn/Mets-15
88Leaf-231
88S-521
88S/YS/II-21
88T-434
89D-526
89D/Best-265
89F-27
89Kahn/Mets-38
89S-327
89T-257
89UD-563
90B-405
90D-391
90D/BestAL-79
90F-365
90F/Can-365
90Leaf-38
90OPC-711
90PublInt/St-127
90S-519
90T-711
90T/Big-284
90UD-11
91B-334
91BBBest/Aces-1
91D-172
91F-602
91Leaf-471
91Leaf/Stud-81
91OPC-318
91Panini/FrSt-308
91Panini/St-243
91RedFoley/St-2
91S-170
91S/100SS-67
91StCl-76
91T-318
91UD-542
91USPlayC/AS-7H
91Ultra-185
91WIZMets-3
92B-89
92D-95
92F-195
92L-34
92L/BlkGold-34
92OPC-44
92OPC/Premier-62
92Pinn-211
92S-42
92S/100SS-4
92StCl-726
92StCl/Dome-3
92Studio-201
92T-44
92T/Gold-44
92T/GoldWin-44
92T/Kids-114
92TripleP-65
92UD-130
92USPlayC/Twin-12H
92USPlayC/Twin-8C
92Ultra-88
93B-453
93D-19
93F-261
93Flair-233
93L-32
93OPC-25
93Pac/Spanish-168
93Pinn-386
93Pinn/TP-B11M
93S-64
93Select-206
93Select/StatL-68
93StCl-354
93StCl/1stDay-354
93StCl/MurphyS-122
93T-625
93T/Finest-22
93T/FinestRef-22
93T/Gold-625
93UD-303
93UD/SP-244
93Ultra-228
94B-132
94D-503
94F-198
94Finest-280
94L-45
94OPC-92
94Pinn-293
94RedFoley-21M
94S-129
94S/GoldR-129
94Select-160
94StCl-275
94StCl/1stDay-275
94StCl/Gold-275
94T-280
94T/Gold-280
94TripleP-251
94UD-141
94UD/ElecD-141
94UD/SP-182
94Ultra-384

Aguirre, Henry John
(Hank)
57T-96
58T-337
59T-36
60T-546
61T-324
61T/St-144
62T-407
63J-54
63P-54
63Salada-32
63T-257
63T-6LL
64Det/Lids-1
64T-39
64T/Coins-74
64T/SU
64T/St-38
64T/tatt
65T-522
66OPC-113
66T-113
67T-263
68T-553
69OPC-94
69T-94
70T-699
73OPC-81CO
73T-81C
74OPC-354CO
74T-354C
75Tucson-26
75Tucson/Caruso-21
75Tucson/Team-1
78TCMA-225
81Tiger/Detroit-122
90Target-3

Ahearn, Charles
(Charlie)
No Cards.

Ahearne, Pat
92Lakeland/ProC-2271

Ahern, Brian
88CapeCod/Sum-30
89Eugene/Best-23
90AppFox/Box-2
90AppFox/ProC-2086
90ProC/Singl-875
92Memphis/SB-426
92Omaha/ProC-2952
92Sky/AASingl-178

Ahern, Jeff
82Danvl/Frit-3
83Redwd-1

Ahr, Jeff
88Hagers/Star-1

Ahrens, Kelly
90Bend/Legoe-6
90Clinton/Best-3
90Clinton/ProC-2551

Aiello, Talbot
81Wisco-20

Aikens, Willie Mays
75QuadC
77SLCity
78Cr/PCL-20
78SSPC/270-201
80OPC-191
80T-368
81Coke
81D-220
81F-43
81OPC-23
81Pol/Royals-1
81T-524
81T/SO-27
81T/St-84
82D-412
82F-404
82F/St-206
82OPC-35
82T-35
82T/St-196
82T/StVar-196
83D-212
83F-104
83F/St-18M
83F/St-5M
83OPC-136
83Pol/Royals-1
83T-136
84D-155
84F-341
84F/X-1
84Nes/792-685
84OPC-137
84T-685
84T/St-276
84T/Tr-1
84Tor/Fire-2
85F-97
85OPC-147
85T-436
85Tor/Fire-2
89Pac/SenLg-147
89T/SenLg-57
89TM/SenLg-2
90ElPasoATG/Team-43
90EliteSenLg-107

Aikman, Troy
92StCl/MemberIV*-8

Ainge, Daniel Rae
(Danny)
78Syrac
79Syrac/Team-4
80Syrac-20
81D-569
81F-418
81T/Tr-727
82D-638
82F-608
82OPC-125
82T-125
92Syrac/TallT-1

Ainsmith, Edward W.
(Eddie)
90Target-4
D329-3
D350/2-3
E120
E286
M101/4-3
M101/5-3
T207
W572
W573

Ainsworth, Jeff
89MissSt-45M

Aitcheson, Kevin
83Knoxvl-15

Aitchison, Raleigh L.
90Target-889

Ake, John Leckie
(John)
No Cards.

Aker, Jack Delane
66T-287
67CokeCap/A's-7
67OPC-110
67T-110
68T-224
69MLB/St-91
69T-612
69T/St-221
70MLB/St-241
70OPC-43
70T-43
71MLB/St-481
71OPC-593
71T-593
72T-769
73OPC-262
73T-262
74OPC-562
74T-562
78TCMA-274
81Tidew-21MG
82Tidew-19MG
83BuffB-25MG
84BuffB-18MG
85Water-22MG
86OhHenry-CO
87Gator-CO
88BurlB/ProC-29MG
91WIZMets-4
92Yank/WIZ60-1
92Yank/WIZ70-1

Akerfelds, Darrel
84Madis/Pol-25
85Huntsvl/BK-32
86Tacoma-1
87Tacoma-2
88ColoSp/CMC-1
88ColoSp/ProC-1537
88S-632
88T-82
89OkCty/CMC-1
89OkCty/ProC-1532
89Smok/R-1
90F/Up-U41
90Leaf-526
90Phill/TastyK-1
90T/Tr-1T
91B-493
91D-110
91F-386
91OPC-524
91Phill/Medford-1
91S-223
91StCl-581
91T-524
91UD-619
92OkCty/SB-313
93Rang/Keeb-45
93Syrac/ProC-991

Akers, Albert Earl
(Jerry)
No Cards.

Akers, Howard
86Kinston-1

Akers, Thomas Earnest
(Bill)
No Cards.

Akimoto, Ratoo
87SanJose-14

Akins, Daron
86Lipscomb-1

Akins, Sid
85BurlR-12
85T-390OLY
87Durham-5
88Richm-16
88Richm/CMC-7
88Richm/ProC-14
89Greenvl/ProC-1151

Akins, Tom
88Indianap/ProC-525M
89Indianap/ProC-1216

Ako, Gerry
80Holyo-23
81ElPaso-9
81Vanco-22

Ala, Aurelio
52Laval-106

Alario, Dave
86Bakers-1

Alba, Gibson
85Syrac-1
86Syrac-1
87BuffB-14
88Louisvl-6
88Louisvl/CMC-6
88Louisvl/ProC-442
89Louisvl-7
89Louisvl/CMC-1
89Louisvl/ProC-1252
90AAASingl/ProC-507
90Louisvl/CMC-2
90Louisvl/LBC-5
90Louisvl/ProC-393
90ProC/Singl-102
90T/TVCard-37
91Richm/Bob-5
91Richm/ProC-2559
91Richm/Team-7

Albanese, Joseph P.
(Joe)
No Cards.

Alberro, Hector
87Beloit-20
90Johnson/Star-1

Alberro, Jose
91GulfC/SportP-2
92CharlR/ProC-2217
92Gaston/ClBest-6

Albert, August P.
(Gus)
N172

Albert, Richard
(Rick)
83Ander-2
85Greenvl/Team-1
86Greenvl/Team-1CO
87Richm/Crown-26CO
87Richm/TCMA-26
88Sumter/ProC-416

Albert, Tim
92Beloit/ClBest-15
92Beloit/ProC-416

Alberts, Francis Burt
(Butch)
77SLCity
78Syrac
79Syrac/Team-14
80Syrac-10
80Syrac/Team-1

Alberts, Frederick J.
(Cy)
No Cards.

Albertson, John
88Idaho/ProC-1839

Alborano, Pete
88CLAS/Star-22
88Virgini/Star-1
89BBCity/Star-2
89Star/Wax-62
90Memphis/Best-3
90Memphis/ProC-1020
90Memphis/Star-1
90Star/ISingl-82
91AA/LineD-401
91Memphis/LineD-401
91Memphis/ProC-665
92Reading/ProC-585
92Reading/SB-526

Albosta, Edward John
(Ed)
47Signal
90Target-5

Albrecht, Andrew
(Andy)
88CapeCod/Sum-159
91Oneonta/ProC-4164
92PrWill/ClBest-7
92PrWill/ProC-159

Albrecht, Edward A.
(Ed)
No Cards.

Albright, Dave
81CharR-9

Albright, Eric
89Niagara/Pucko-2
90Lakeland/Star-1
91ClBest/Singl-39
91Lakeland/ClBest-14
92Lakeland/ClBest-3

Albright, Gilbert
80Clinton-25

Albright, Harold John
(Jack)
No Cards.

Albro, Daryl
89MissSt-1
90MissSt-1
91MissSt-1
92MissSt-1
93MissSt-1

Albury, Allan
91Brisbane/Fut-2CO

Albury, Victor
(Vic)
72T-778R
74OPC-605R
74T-605R
75OPC-368
75T-368
75T/M-368

76OPC-336
76SSPC-205
76T-336
77T-536
82Watlo/B-27C
82Watlo/Frit-3CO
83Charl-20
83Watlo/Frit-27CO
84Maine-9

Alcala, Jesus
82Oneonta-12

Alcala, Julio
86FSLAS-2
86FtMyr-1
87Memphis-24
87Memphis/Best-5
89Memphis/Best-6
89Memphis/ProC-1183
89Memphis/Star-1

Alcala, Santo
76OPC-589R
76T-589R
77Pep-52
77T-636
78OPC-36
78T-321
81Portl-3

Alcantara, Francisco
90Niagara/Pucko-15
91Reno/Cal-20

Alcantara, Isreal
93BurlB/ClBest-2
93BurlB/ProC-163

Alcantara, Jose
75FtLaud/Sus-24

Alcaraz, Angel Luis
(Luis)
69T-437
90Target-6

Alcazar, Jorge
86Penin-1
88Vanco/CMC-23
88Vanco/ProC-772

Alcock, John Forbes
(Scotty)
No Cards.

Alder, Jimmy
90Bristol/ProC-3168
90Bristol/Star-1
91Fayette/ClBest-17
91Fayette/ProC-1176
92Lakeland/ClBest-11
92Lakeland/ProC-2284

Alderson, Dale L.
No Cards.

Aldred, Scott
87Fayette-11
88Lakeland/Star-1
89London/ProC-1368
90AAASingl/ProC-371
90B-344
90ProC/Singl-379
90Toledo/CMC-2
90Toledo/ProC-141
91AAA/LineD-576
91B-147
91D-422RR
91OPC-658
91S-740RP
91S/Rook40-3
91StCl-429
91T-658
91T/90Debut-3
91Toledo/LineD-576
91Toledo/ProC-1922
91UD-7
92Classic/Game200-147
92Classic/I-T3
92Classic/II-T75
92D-486
92F-127
92OPC-198
92Pinn-354
92ProC/Tomorrow-66
92S-729
92S/100RisSt-41
92StCl-762
92T-198
92T/Gold-198
92T/GoldWin-198
92USPlayC/Tiger-2S
92USPlayC/Tiger-7C
93D-733
93Pac/Spanish-419
93StCl-573
93StCl/1stDay-573
93StCl/Rockie-7
93T-463
93T/Gold-463
93USPlayC/Rockie-13H
93USPlayC/Rockie-4C
93Ultra-338

Aldrete, Mike
86F/Up-U1
86Phoenix-2
87D-450
87F-264
87Mother/SFG-24
87T-71
88D-362
88D/Best-191
88F-76
88Mother/Giants-5
88OPC-351
88Panini/St-426
88RedFoley/St-1
88S-556
88S/YS/I-35
88Sf-80
88T-602
88T/Big-119
88T/St-89
89B-368
89D-140
89D/Tr-25
89F-323
89F/Up-95
89OPC-9
89Panini/St-219
89S-82
89S/Tr-68
89T-158
89T/St-80
89UD-239
89UD/Ext-738
90OPC-589
90S-220
90T-589
90UD-415
91F-224
91OPC-483
91S-447
91T-483
92ColoSp/ProC-756
92ColoSp/SB-76
92D-621
92F-102
92OPC-256
92Panini-45
92S-351
92StCl-305
92T-256
92T/Gold-256
92T/GoldWin-256
94F-252
94S-277
94S/GoldR-277

Aldrete, Richard
87Everett-6
88CalLgAS-7
88SanJose/Cal-116
88SanJose/ProC-119
89Shrev/ProC-1847
90Shrev/ProC-1448
90Shrev/Star-1
91AAA/LineD-376
91Phoenix/LineD-376
91Phoenix/ProC-78
92ArkTr/SB-26

Aldrich, Jay
83Beloit/Frit-8
86ElPaso-1
87Denver-4
88D-460
88Denver/CMC-7
88Denver/ProC-1270
88F-155
88Pol/Brew-33
88S-578
88T-616
89Denver/CMC-1
89Denver/ProC-42
90AAASingl/ProC-452
90ProC/Singl-307
90RochR/CMC-6
90RochR/ProC-695
91Crown/Orio-6

Aldrich, Russell
80Water-20
81Water-18

Aldrich, Tom
88Bristol/ProC-1881
89London/ProC-1386
90London/ProC-1272

Aldridge, Vic
94Conlon-1114
E120
V61-74
W573

Alegre, Paul
90Salinas/Cal-133
90Salinas/ProC-2729

Aleno, Charles
(Chuck)
45Centen-1

Aleshire, Troy
86AubAs-1

Alesio, Chris
90Hamil/Best-22
90Hamil/Star-1

Alexander, Bob
52LaPatrie-1

Alexander, Charles
(Chuck)
88BurlInd/ProC-1785
89Watertn/Star-1

Alexander, Dave
89SLCity-22
90Miami/II/Star-1

Alexander, David Dale
(Dale)
29Exh/4-23
31Exh/4-23
32Orbit/num-27
32Orbit/un-1
33DH-2
33G-221
61F-91
81Tiger/Detroit-69
88Conlon/4-1
92Conlon/Sport-616
R300
R305
R308-181
R316

Alexander, Don
90AubAs/Best-23CO
90AubAs/ProC-3418CO
91AubAS/ClBest-25CO
91AubAS/ProC-4290CO

Alexander, Doyle L.
72T-579
73JP
73OPC-109
73T-109
74OPC-282
74T-282
75OPC-491
75T-491
75T/M-491
76OPC-638
76SSPC-374
76T-638
77Ho-140
77Ho/Twink-140
77T-254
78BK/R-4
78OPC-52
78SSPC/270-105
78T-146
79OPC-230
79T-442
80T-67
81D-448
81F-255
81T-708
81T/Tr-728
82D-96
82F-383
82T-364
82T/Tr-1T
83D-451
83T-512
84D-439
84F-146
84Nes/792-677
84OPC-112
84T-677
84Tor/Fire-3
85D-561
85F-98
85Leaf-134
85OPC-218
85OPC/Post-21
85SpokAT/Cram-1
85T-218
85T/St-365
85Tor/Fire-3
86BJ/Ault-2
86D-390
86F-51
86F/LimEd-1
86Leaf-182
86OPC-196
86Sf-133M
86T-196
86T/Mini-34
86Tor/Fire-2
87D-657
87D/HL-52
87F-510
87OPC-249
87T-686
88D-584
88D/Best-13
88F-51
88F/Mini-21
88F/St-23
88OPC-316
88Pep/T-19
88Pol/T-1
88S-610
88T-492
88T/Big-34
89B-94
89D-178
89D/AS-12
89D/Best-125
89F-128
89F/BBAS-1
89Mara/Tigers-19
89OPC-77
89Pol/Tigers-19
89RedFoley/St-1
89S-129
89Sf-211
89T-77
89T/Big-182
89T/St-274
89UD-298
90D-62
90F-599
90F/Can-599
90KayBee-1
90OPC-748
90PublInt/St-467
90S-237
90T-748
90Target-7
90UD-330
91Crown/Orio-8
92Yank/WIZ70-2
92Yank/WIZ80-2
93Rang/Keeb-46

Alexander, Eric
89Bluefld/Star-1
89Star/IISingl-113
91Bluefld/ClBest-11
91Bluefld/ProC-4138

Alexander, Gary Wayne
75Lafay
76Phoenix/Coke-1
77Phoenix
77T-476R
78OPC-72
78T-624
79Ho-57
79OPC-168
79T-332
80OPC-78
80T-141
81D-200
81F-398
81T-416
81T/Tr-729
82F-475
82T-11
89Pac/SenLg-141

Alexander, Gary
87AZ/Pol-1
88TexLgAS/GS-4
88Tulsa-12
89TexLAS/GS-31
89Tulsa/GS-5
89Tulsa/Team-1
90EastLAS/ProC-EL19
90Foil/Best-291
90Reading/Best-14
90Reading/ProC-1224
90Reading/Star-2
90Star/ISingl-79
91AAA/LineD-477
91ScranWB/LineD-477
91ScranWB/ProC-2542
92ScranWB/ProC-2451
92ScranWB/SB-476

Alexander, Gerald
90AAASingl/ProC-668
90CharlR/Star-1
90OkCty/ProC-422
91AAA/LineD-301
91Classic/III-11
91D-419RR
91F-278
91Mother/Rang-27
91OkCty/LineD-301
91OkCty/ProC-170
91S-733RP
91T/90Debut-4
91UD/FinalEd-72F
92D-578
92F-297
92OkCty/ProC-1905
92OkCty/SB-301
92S-163
92S/100RisSt-99
92StCl-185
93Rang/Keeb-47

Alexander, Grover C.
14CJ-37
15CJ-37
16FleischBrd-2
21Exh-2
24Sherlock-1
25Exh-18
27Exh-29
28Exh-29
29Exh/4-15
40PlayBall-119
48Exh/HOF
48Swell-11
49Leaf/Prem-1
50Call
50W576-1
51T/CM
60Exh/HOF-1
60F-5
61F-2
61GP-2
63Bz/ATG-29
69Bz-2
69Bz/Sm
72F/FFeat-13
72Laugh/GF-41
75Sheraton-16
76Motor-10
76Rowe-6M
76Shakey-14
77Galasso-153
77Shakey-5
80Laugh/3/4/5-8
80Laugh/FFeat-40
80Marchant/HOF-1
80Pac/Leg-124
80Perez/HOF-14
80SSPC/HOF
81Conlon-10
83D/HOF-23
85Woolwth-2
86Conlon/1-3
87Conlon/2-4
88Conlon/3-2
88Grenada-9
89HOF/St-72
90Perez/GreatMom-42
90Swell/Great-30
91Conlon/Sport-32
91Swell/Great-128
92Card/McDon/Pac-16
92Conlon/Col-15
92Conlon/Sport-534
92Conlon/Sport-630
92Cub/OldStyle-1
93AP/ASG-92
93AP/ASG24K-26G
93Conlon-932
93CrackJack-7
93Spectrum/HOFII-2

94Conlon-1223
BF2-81
D327
D328-2
D329-4
D350/2-4
E120
E121/120
E121/80
E122
E126-13
E135-2
E210-44
E220
L1-114
M101/4-4
M101/5-4
R332-19
R332-48
S81-89
T222
V100
V61-69
V89-18
W501-59
W502-44
W512-2
W514-65
W515-49
W516-9
W572
W573
W575
WG5-1
WG6-1

Alexander, Hugh
No Cards.

Alexander, Jon
88BBCity/Star-3
89BBCity/Star-3

Alexander, Manny
89Bluefld/Star-2
89Star/IISingl-114
90Foil/Best-241
90Wausau/Best-20
90Wausau/ProC-2135
91CLAS/ProC-CAR4
91ClBest/Singl-97
91Freder/ClBest-15
91Freder/ProC-2369
92B-41
92ClBest-119
92Hagers/ProC-2560
92Hagers/SB-251
92OPC-551M
92ProC/Tomorrow-9
92Sky/AASingl-104
92T-551M
92T/Gold-551M
92T/GoldWin-551M
93B-577
93D-11RR
93F/MLPI-4
93LimeR/Winter-145
93LimeR/Winter-49
93Pinn-244
93Pinn/RookTP-7M
93S-234
93Select-391
93T-587
93T/Gold-587
93UD-5SR
94B-215
94Pac/Cr-24
94Pinn-35
94Pinn/Artist-35
94Pinn/Museum-35
94StCl/Team-300

Alexander, Matt
92Lipscomb-1
93Lipscomb-1

Alexander, Matthew
(Matt)
73Wichita-1
76OPC-382
76SSPC-501
76T-382
77T-644
78T-102
81Portl-4
81T-68
82T-528

Alexander, P.
N172

Alexander, Pat
78Cedar
81Shrev-23

Alexander, Phil
91Adelaide/Fut-12CO

Alexander, Rob
88Madis-1
89Modesto/Cal-270
89Modesto/Chong-7

Alexander, Robert S.
(Bob)
52Park-63
53Exh/Can-34
55Esskay
91Crown/Orio-7

Alexander, Roberto
79Clinton/TCMA-4
82VeroB-1
84Cram/PCL-166

Alexander, Roger
79Richm-12

Alexander, Tim
80Ander-6
83Durham-27
84Durham-10

Alexander, Todd
89KS*-54

Alexander, Tommy
85Fresno/Pol-25
87Wichita-3
88Jaxvl/Best-9
88Jaxvl/ProC-982

Alexander, Walter E.
(Walt)
16FleischBrd-3
D328-3
E135-3

Alexander, William H.
(Nin)
No Cards.

Alexis, Juan
91Martins/ClBest-28
91Martins/ProC-3442

Aleys, Maximo
89Everett/Star-1
89Star/IISingl-187
90Clinton/Best-22
90Clinton/ProC-2548
91ClBest/Singl-87
91SanJose/ClBest-13
91SanJose/ProC-1

Alfaro, Flavio
85Durham-18
85T-391OLY

Alfaro, Jesus
80Wichita-14
84CharlO-19
86ElPaso-3
87ElPaso-15
87TexLgAS-30
88MidldA/GS-19
89ElPaso/GS-20
90ElPaso/GS-3
90ElPasoATG/Team-4
90TexLgAS/GS-10

Alfaro, Jose
74Cedar
75Dubuq

Alfonseca, Antonio
93James/ClBest-2

Alfonso, Carlos
75Iowa/TCMA-1
76Indianap-24
82AubAs-18
86Tucson-2MG
92Giant/PGE-1CO
92Mother/Giant-28M

Alfonso, Ossie
84Visalia-6
85OrlanTw-14

Alfonzo, Edgardo
(Edgar)
86QuadC-1
87PalmSp-20
88PalmSp/Cal-96
88QuadC/GS-19
89PalmSp/Cal-44
89PalmSp/ProC-464
91MidldA/OneHour-1
91PalmSp/ProC-2021
92AS/Cal-43
92PalmSp/ClBest-23
92PalmSp/ProC-845
92Pittsfld/ClBest-10
92Pittsfld/ProC-3301
93ClBest/MLG-210
93ClBest/MLG-30
93FExcel/ML-68
93StLucie/ProC-2926
94B-156
94ClBest/Gold-166
94FExcel-232

Alford, Mike
89MissSt-2
90MissSt-2

Alfredson, Tom
86QuadC-2
87PalmSp-19
88MidldA/GS-15
89MidldA/GS-4
90BirmB/Best-5
90BirmB/ProC-1394

Alger, Kevin
92Martins/ClBest-24
92Martins/ProC-3045

Alicano, Pedro
91Peoria/ClBest-2
91Peoria/ProC-1333
91Peoria/Team-4
92WinSalem/ClBest-21
92WinSalem/ProC-1198

Alicea, Edwin
89Greenvl/Best-6
89Greenvl/ProC-1156
89Greenvl/Star-1
90Durham/Team-13
91Miami/ClBest-26
91Miami/ProC-419
92Greenvl/ProC-1163
92Greenvl/SB-226

Alicea, Luis
85Anchora-1
86Erie-1
87ArkTr-16
88D/Rook-52
88F/Up-U116
88Louisvl-7
88Louisvl/CMC-20
88Louisvl/ProC-436
88S/Tr-98T
88Smok/Card-24
88T/Tr-3T
89D-466
89F-443
89Louisvl-8
89Louisvl/CMC-14
89Louisvl/ProC-1263
89Panini/St-175
89RedFoley/St-2
89S-231
89T-261TL
89T-588
89T/St-37
89UD-281
90Louisvl/LBC-6
91AAA/LineD-226
91Louisvl/LineD-226
91Louisvl/ProC-2919
91Louisvl/Team-17
92D-560
92S-607
92StCl-103
93D-416
93F-507
93Pac/Beisbol-28M
93Pac/Beisbol-29
93Pac/Beisbol-30M
93Pac/Spanish-293
93Pol/Card-1
93S-183
93StCl-178
93StCl/1stDay-178
93T-257
93T/Gold-257
93UD-605
94D-534
94F-627
94L-203
94Pac/Cr-585
94Pinn-319
94S-522
94StCl-146
94StCl/1stDay-146
94StCl/Gold-146
94StCl/Team-309
94T-416
94T/Finest-40
94T/FinestRef-40
94T/Gold-416
94UD-239
94UD/CollC-32
94UD/CollC/Gold-32
94UD/CollC/Silv-32
94UD/ElecD-239
94Ultra-562

Alicea, Miguel
80Penin/B-4
80Penin/C-6
85Beloit-24
87CharlO/WBTV-16
88Edmon/CMC-11
88Edmon/ProC-582
89PalmSp/Cal-55

Alimena, Charles
92Clinton/ClBest-19

Alkire, Jeff
91Miami/Bumble-1
92T/Tr-2T
92T/TrGold-2T
93StCl/MurphyS-163
93StCl/MurphyS-174
94ClBest/Gold-157
94FExcel-254

Allaire, Karl
85Osceola/Team-16
86ColumAst-2
87ColAst/ProC-14
88Tucson/CMC-17
88Tucson/JP-1
88Tucson/ProC-167
90AAASingl/ProC-97
90Edmon/CMC-22
90Edmon/ProC-521
90ProC/Singl-499
91AAA/LineD-577
91Toledo/LineD-577
91Toledo/ProC-1937
92Toledo/ProC-1048
92Toledo/SB-576

Allanson, Andy
84BuffB-7
85Water-24
86D/Rook-43
86F/Up-U2
86OhHenry-6
86T/Tr-1T
87BuffB-3
87D-95
87F-241
87Gator-6
87Leaf-102
87T-436
87T/JumboR-1
87T/St-311
87ToysRUs-1
88D-465
88D/Best-5
88F/Up-U21
88Gator-6
88S-586
88T-728
88T/Big-231
89B-83
89D-138
89F-396
89OPC-283
89Panini/St-323
89S-46
89T-283
89T/Big-311
89T/St-207
89UD-217
90F-483
90F/Can-483
90OPC-514
90PublInt/St-551
90S-452
90T-514
90UD-590
91CokeK/Tiger-10
91Leaf-455
92D-42
92Denver/ProC-2642
92F-128
92L-510
92L/BlkGold-510
92OPC-167
92Pol/Brew-1
92S-537
92StCl-238
92T-167
92T/Gold-167
92T/GoldWin-167
92USPlayC/Tiger-2H
92USPlayC/Tiger-7S

Allard, Brian M.
77Ashvl
79Tucson-4
80CharCh-5
80T-673R
81Spokane-10
82T-283
83SLCity-6
84Cram/PCL-171
85IntLgAS-43
85Maine-30
86Watlo-1CO
87Wmsprt-16CO
88EastLAS/ProC-50CO
88Wmsprt/ProC-1311CO
89Kenosha/ProC-1080CO
90AS/Cal-26
90Visalia/Cal-80CO
90Visalia/ProC-2171CO
91Visalia/ClBest-26CO
91Visalia/ProC-1758CO
92Visalia/ClBest-25CO
92Visalia/ProC-1030CO
93Rang/Keeb-48

Allcott, Charles
N172

Allen, Bernard Keith
(Bernie)
61Clover-1
62T-596R
63J-2
63P-2
63T-427
63Twin/Volpe-1
64T-455
65OPC-237
65T-237
66T-327
67CokeCap/Senator-2
67OPC-118
67T-118
68T-548
69MB-5
69MLB/St-100
69OPC-27
69T-27
69T/St-231
70MLB/St-277
70T-577
71MLB/St-529
71OPC-427
71T-427
72MB-6
72T-644
73OPC-293
73T-293
78Twin/Frisz-26
92Yank/WIZ70-3

Allen, Bob
88CapeCod/Sum-157

Allen, Chad
89Burllnd/Star-1
90Watertn/Star-1
91CLAS/ProC-CAR11
91Kinston/ClBest-1
91Kinston/ProC-313
92Canton/SB-101
92Kinston/ProC-2466

Allen, Clint
91MissSt-2
92MissSt-2

Allen, Cyrus Alban
(Jack)
No Cards.

Allen, Dave
85Fresno/Pol-5

Allen, David
88Batavia/ProC-1684
90AubAs/Best-16
90AubAs/ProC-3414
91BurlAs/ClBest-1
91BurlAs/ProC-2792
91ClBest/Singl-222

Allen, Dell
92Martins/ClBest-26
92Martins/ProC-3062

Allen, Edward
83Butte-23
83CharR-10

Allen, Ethan Nathan
(Ethan)
33G-46
34DS-92
35BU-76
35G-1E
35G-3C
35G-5C
35G-6C
92Mega/Ruth-150M
93Conlon-779
94Conlon-1128
R314
R316
V353-46
Allen, Fletcher M.
(Sled)
No Cards.
Allen, Frank Leon
16FleischBrd-4
90Target-9
Allen, George
45Parade*-1
Allen, Greg
78Wisco
Allen, Harold Andrew
(Hank)
67T-569R
68T-426
69MB-6
69T-623
70OPC-14
70T-14
71MLB/St-3
72MB-7
Allen, Harold
88Ashvl/ProC-1060
89Osceola/Star-1
90ColMud/Best-11
90ColMud/ProC-1337
90ColMud/Star-1
90Foil/Best-161
91AAA/LineD-601
91Tucson/LineD-601
91Tucson/ProC-2204
92Jacks/ProC-3991
92Jacks/SB-326
Allen, Hezekiah
No Cards.
Allen, Horace Tanner
No Cards.
Allen, James Bradley
(Jamie)
80LynnS-18
81Spokane-31
82SLCity-2
84Cram/PCL-182
84D-267
84F-604
84Nes/792-744
84T-744
84T/St-350
Allen, James
(Jamie)
82QuadC-17
83QuadC-18
Allen, Jesse Hall
(Pete)
No Cards.
Allen, Jim
75Albuq/Caruso-18
89Johnson/Star-1
Allen, John Marshall
No Cards.
Allen, John Thomas
(Johnny)
32Orbit/num-103
34G-42
35G-8E
35G-9E
37OPC-122
39Wheat-2
90Target-10
92Conlon/Sport-384
93Conlon-722
R312
V300
V354-96
W753
Allen, Kim Bryant
(Kim)
75QuadC
78Cr/PCL-15
80Spokane-19
81F-612
81Spokane-27
89Pac/SenLg-99
89T/SenLg-53
91Pac/SenLg-99
Allen, Larry
86Penin-2
87CharWh-11
Allen, Lee
90LitSun-6
Allen, Lloyd Cecil
71OPC-152R
71T-152R
72OPC-102
72T-102
73OPC-267
73T-267
74OPC-539
74T-539
76SSPC-140
79Iowa/Pol-2
93Rang/Keeb-49
Allen, Matt
91James/ClBest-7
91James/ProC-3547
92Albany/ClBest-5
92Albany/ProC-2308
92James/ClBest-16
92James/ProC-1504
93WPalmB/ClBest-24
93WPalmB/ProC-1342
Allen, Mike
80Buffa-11
80Wichita-13
Allen, Mongo
89KS*-18
Allen, Myron Smith
N172
Allen, Neil
78Tidew
80T-94
81Coke
81D-276
81F-322
81F/St-84
81OPC-322
81T-322
81T/HT
81T/St-198
82D-506
82F-520
82K-20
82OPC-205
82T-205
82T/St-66
83D-98
83F-536
83F/St-22M
83F/St-2M
83K-34
83OPC-268
83OPC/St-265
83T-575
83T/St-265
83T/Tr-1
84D-109
84F-318
84Jacks/Smok-1
84Nes/792-435
84OPC-183
84T-435
84T/St-147
85D-205
85F-219
85OPC-234
85T-731
85T/St-144
86Coke/WS-33
86D-610
86F-98
86F/Up-U3
86T-663
86T/Tr-2T
87Coke/WS-19
87D-507
87F-484
87OPC-113
87RedFoley/St-93
87T-113
87T/St-292
88D-597
88T-384
89ColoSp/CMC-6
89D-196
89F-250
89S-375
89T-61
89UD-567
90AAASingl/ProC-535
90Nashvl/CMC-23
90Nashvl/ProC-223
90ProC/Singl-148
91WIZMets-5
92Yank/WIZ80-3
Allen, Newt
78Laugh/Black-3
86Negro/Frit-104
90Negro/Star-30
94TedW-100
Allen, Paul
89Welland/Pucko-32
Allen, Richard A.
(Richie)
64PhilBull-1
64T-243R
65OldLond-2
65T-460
65T/E-36
65T/trans-38
66Bz-4
66OPC-80
66T-80
66T/RO-3
66T/RO-74
67Bz-4
67CokeCap/AS-1
67CokeCap/NLAS-25
67CokeCap/Phill-1
67T-242LL
67T-244LL
67T-309M
67T-450
67T/Test/SU-18
68Bz-14
68Dexter-3
68T-225
68T/ActionSt-12AM
68T/G-23
68T/Post-15
69Citgo-17
69MB-7
69MLB/St-172
69MLBPA/Pin-33
69NTF
69OPC-6LL
69OPC/DE-1
69T-350
69T-6LL
69T/DE-26
69T/S-53
69T/St-71
69T/decal
69Trans-57
70K-33
70MLB/St-133
70OPC-40
70T-40
70T/SO
71Bz/Test-44
71K-57
71MLB/St-97
71OPC-650
71T-650
71T/S-40
71T/Super-40
71T/tatt-7
71Ticket/Dodg-1
72MB-8
72OPC-240
72T-240
73K-26
73OPC-310
73OPC-62LL
73OPC-63LL
73T-310
73T-62LL
73T-63LL
73T/Comics-2
73T/Lids-2
73T/PinUps-2
74K-33
74OPC-332AS
74OPC-70
74T-332M
74T-70
74T/DE-39
74T/Puzzles-2
74T/St-151
75K-42
75OPC-210MVP
75OPC-307LL
75OPC-400
75SSPC/42-4
75T-210MVP
75T-307LL
75T-400
75T/M-210MVP
75T/M-307LL
75T/M-400
76OPC-455
76SSPC-473
76T-455
81TCMA-415
82KMart-21
89Kodak/WSox-1M
90Target-8
93AP/ASG-155
94TedW-71
PM10/L-1
Allen, Rick
88Alaska/Team-1
89Billings/ProC-2045
90Cedar/Best-8
90Cedar/ProC-2331
91AA/LineD-151
91Chatt/LineD-151
91Chatt/ProC-1964
92Chatt/SB-176
92OrlanSR/ProC-2851
Allen, Robert Earl
No Cards.
Allen, Robert Gilman
(Bob)
N172
Allen, Robert Gray
(Bob)
61T-452
62T-543
63Sugar-33
63T-266
64T-209
66T-538
67OPC-24
67T-24
68OPC-176
68T-176
Allen, Robert
(Bob)
82VeroB-15
84Cram/PCL-156
86ElPaso-2
87MidldA-23
Allen, Roderick B.
(Rod)
79Knoxvl/TCMA-24
82SLCity-3
83SLCity-14
85RochR-10
87BuffB-24
88ColoSp/CMC-19
88ColoSp/ProC-1545
88TripleA/ASCMC-39
89F-397
Allen, Ronald F.
(Ron)
No Cards.
Allen, Ronnie
91Batavia/ClBest-25
91Batavia/ProC-3474
91ClBest/Singl-417
91FrRow/DP-13
92Clearw/ClBest-23
92Clearw/ProC-2046
92StCl/Dome-4
Allen, Scott
88BurlInd/ProC-1784
Allen, Shane
81QuadC-7
Allen, Sterling
76Baton
Allen, Steve
88Butte-26
89Gaston/ProC-1022
89Gaston/Star-1
89Star/IISingl-133
90TexLgAS/GS-36
90Tulsa/ProC-1148
90Tulsa/Team-1
91AA/LineD-526
91SanAn/LineD-526
91SanAn/ProC-2965
92SanAn/ProC-3967
92SanAn/SB-551
Allen, Tracy
90WinHaven/Star-1
91WinHaven/ClBest-1
91WinHaven/ProC-481
Allenson, Gary M.
80T-376
81D-455
81T-128
82Coke/BOS
82D-386
82F-287
82OPC-273
82T-686
83D-30
83F-177
83T-472
84D-335
84F-388
84Nes/792-56
84OPC-56
84T-56
85F-148
85Syrac-3
85T-259
87Oneonta-24
88Oneonta/ProC-2064
89Lynch/Star-23
89Pac/SenLg-41
89TM/SenLg-3
90EliteSenLg-92
90LynchRS/Team-27
91AA/LineD-474MG
91NewBrit/LineD-474MG
91NewBrit/ProC-367
91Pac/SenLg-111
92RedSox/Dunkin-1CO
Allenson, Kelvin
88Oneonta/ProC-2064
Allensworth, Jermaine
93Welland/ProC-3371
94FExcel-250
94FExcel/1stY-6
94UD-541TP
Alley, Leonard Eugene
(Gene)
64T-509R
65OPC-121
65T-121
66EH-14
66T-336
67CokeCap/Pirate-2
67Kahn
67T-283
67T/Test/PP-1
68KDKA-22
68Kahn
68OPC-53
68T-368AS
68T-53
68T/G-25
69MB-8
69MLB/St-181
69Pirate/JITB-1
69T-436
69T/St-81
70MLB/St-97
70T-566
71MLB/St-193
71OPC-416
71T-416
72MB-9
72OPC-286
72T-286
73OPC-635
73T-635
Alleyne, Isaac
87SLCity/Taco-9
88James/ProC-1903
89Rockford/Team-1
90ArkTr/GS-5
Allie, Gair R.
54T-179
55T-59
55T/DH-71
94T/Arc54-179
Allietta, Robert G.
(Bob)
76OPC-623
76T-623
79Tacoma-15
80Tacoma-11

Allinger, Bob
83Miami-21
Allison, Arthur A.
(Art)
No Cards.
Allison, Bubba
86Cram/NWL-151
Allison, Dana
89Medford/Best-28
90Modesto/Cal-153
90Modesto/ProC-2203
91B-238
91S/RookTr-94T
91Tacoma/ProC-2295
91UD/Ext-771
92Huntsvl/ProC-3940
92T/91Debut-2
92Tacoma/SB-526
Allison, Douglas L.
(Doug)
No Cards.
Allison, Jamie
88CalLgAS-21
88Reno/Cal-279
89Kinston/Star-1
90Kinston/Team-13
Allison, Jeff
87Idaho-5
88Miami/Star-1
88SLCity-9
Allison, Jim
83TriCit-12
85BurlR-27
85Utica-1
86DayBe-1
Allison, Mack P.
No Cards.
Allison, Milo Henry
No Cards.
Allison, Tom
90Pittsfld/Pucko-32
91Clmbia/PCPII-5
91Clmbia/PII-7
92Bingham/ProC-521
92Bingham/SB-51
Allison, William R.
(Bob)
59HRDerby-2
59T-116
60Armour-2
60NuCard-66
60T-320
60T/tatt-2
61NuCard-466
61P-91
61T-355
61T/St-176
62Bz
62J-83
62P-83
62P/Can-83
62Salada-22
62Shirriff-22
62T-180
62T/St-73
63J-7
63P-7
63T-75
63Twin/Volpe-2
64T-10LL
64T-290
64T/Coins-19
64Wheat/St-2
65OPC-180
65OldLond-21
65T-180
65T/E-38
65T/trans-1
66T-345
67CokeCap/Twin-2
67OPC-194
67T-194
67T-334M
68Dexter-4
68T-335
69MB-9
69MLB/St-64
69OPC-30
69T-30
69T/St-191
70MLB/St-229
70T-635
72MB-10
78TCMA-26
78Twin/Frisz-1
83MLBPA/Pin-1
89Chatt/II/Team-2
89Pac/Leg-165
89Swell-27
93UD/ATH-3
Allred, Beau
88CLAS/Star-23
88Kinston/Star-1
89BBAmAA/BPro-AA7
89Canton/Best-4
89Canton/ProC-1302
89Canton/Star-1
89EastLgAS/ProC-6
89Star/IISingl-154
90AAASingl/ProC-229
90ColoSp/CMC-9
90ColoSp/ProC-48
90D-691
90F/Up-U88
90OPC-419
90ProC/Singl-461
90S/Tr-70T
90T-419
90T/89Debut-2
91B-80
91F-358
91Indian/McDon-1
91Leaf-316
91S-338RP
91S/100RisSt-56
91S/Rook40-22
91UD/Ext-784
91Ultra-104
92ColoSp/ProC-762
92ColoSp/SB-77
92Sky/AAASingl-34
Almada, Baldomero M.
(Mel)
35BU-147
39PlayBall-43
40Hughes-1
40PlayBall-71
90Target-11
91Conlon/Sport-234
92Conlon/Sport-550
R313
R314
Almante, Tom
86ArkTr-1
Almaraz, Johnny
88Billings/ProC-1825
89Greens/ProC-431
Almeida, Rafael D.
T207
Almon, William F.
(Bill)
74Hawaii
75Hawaii/Caruso-11
77Padre/SchCd-1
77Padre/SchCd-6
77T-490R
78Padre/FamFun-1
78T-392
79K-53
79T-616
80OPC-225
80T-436
81F-332
81T-163
81T/Tr-730
82D-637
82F-335
82F/St-185
82OPC-119
82T-521
82T/St-167
83D-356
83F-228
83OPC-362
83T-362
83T/Tr-2
84D-467
84F-436
84Mother/A's-11
84Nes/792-241
84OPC-241
84T-241
84T/St-334
85D-589
85F-414
85F/Up-U2
85T-273FDP
85T-607
85T/Tr-2T
86D-479
86F-602
86OPC-48
86T-48
86T/St-131
87D-326
87F-601
87OPC-159
87T-447
87T/Tr-1T
88D-487
88Phill/TastyK-2
88T-787
91WIZMets-6
Aloi, Dave
74Cedar
75Dubuq
Aloma, Luis
51B-231
52T-308
54B-134
54T-57
94T/Arc54-57
Alomar, Conde Santos
(Sandy)
65OPC-82R
65T-82R
66T-428
67T-561
68T-541
69JB
69T-283
69T/St-151
70MLB/St-169
70OPC-29
70T-29
71JB
71MLB/St-337
71OPC-745
71T-745
71T/Coins-28
72MB-11
72OPC-253
72T-253
73OPC-123
73T-123
74OPC-347
74T-347
74T/St-141
75OPC-266
75T-266
75T/M-266
76OPC-629
76SSPC-441
76SSPC/MetsY-Y19
76T-629
77T-54
78BK/R-15
78SSPC/270-86
78T-533
79T-144
88Smok/Padres-3CO
89B-258M
89Padre/Mag-9CO
90Padre/MagUno-22CO
91WIZMets-7
92Yank/WIZ70-4
93Rang/Keeb-50
Alomar, Rafael
61Union
Alomar, Roberto
87TexLgAS-8
87Wichita-4
88D-34RR
88D/Best-42
88D/Rook-35
88F/Up-U122
88LasVegas/CMC-20
88LasVegas/ProC-231
88Leaf-34RR
88S/Tr-105T
88Smok/Padres-2
88T/Tr-4T
89B-458
89Bimbo/Discs-12
89Classic-127
89Coke/Padre-1
89D-246
89D/Best-21
89F-299
89F-630M
89F/Superstar-1
89KennerFig-1
89OPC-206
89Padre/Mag-14
89Padre/Mag-9
89Panini/St-191
89RedFoley/St-3
89S-232
89S/HotRook-72
89S/YS/I-28
89Sf-20
89T-206
89T-231TL
89T/Big-102
89T/Gloss60-19
89T/JumboR-1
89T/St-104
89ToysRUs-1
89UD-471
90B-221
90Classic-61
90Coke/Padre-1
90D-111
90D/BestNL-35
90F-149
90F/Can-149
90F/LL-1
90Leaf-75
90OPC-517
90Padre/MagUno-10
90Panini/St-349
90PublInt/St-43
90PublInt/St-607
90S-12
90Sf-93
90T-517
90T/Big-9
90T/Coins-37
90T/Gloss60-27
90T/Mini-77
90T/St-109
90T/TVAS-35
90UD-346
90USPlayC/AS-4D
91B-9
91Cadaco-1
91Classic/200-113
91Classic/I-94
91Classic/II-T81
91Colla/Alomar-Set
91D-12DK
91D-682
91D/SuperDK-12
91F-523
91F/Up-U63
91Leaf-267
91Leaf/Stud-131
91OPC-315
91OPC/Premier-1
91Panini/FrSt-92
91Panini/St-96
91RedFoley/St-3
91S-25
91S-887DT
91S/100SS-100
91S/RookTr-44T
91S/ToroBJ-13
91S/ToroBJ-39AS
91StCl-304
91Sunflower-19
91T-315
91T/Tr-2T
91Tor/Fire-12
91UD-335
91UD-80TC
91UD/Ext-763
91UD/FinalEd-83F
91USPlayC/AS-12H
91Ultra-358
92B-20
92BJ/Fire-1
92Classic/Game200-121
92Classic/I-T4
92Colla/ASG-3
92D-28AS
92D-58
92D/McDon-G1
92DPep/MSA-15
92F-323
92F-698M
92F/Performer-24
92French-12
92Hardee-1
92Kenner/Fig-1
92L-233
92L/BlkGold-233
92MSA/Ben-3
92MooTown-13
92MrTurkey-2
92OPC-225
92OPC/Premier-130
92Panini-26
92Panini-273AS
92Pinn-306SH
92Pinn-45
92Pinn-586M
92Pinn/Team2000-48
92Pinn/TeamP-5
92Post/Can-13
92S-15
92S/100SS-82
92S/Impact-10
92S/Proctor-3
92Seven/Coin-5
92StCl-159
92StCl/Dome-5
92Studio-251
92Studio/Prev-13
92T-225
92T/Gold-225
92T/GoldWin-225
92T/Kids-90
92T/McDonB-4
92TripleP-84
92UD-355
92UD-81M
92UD/ASFF-11
92UD/TWillB-T11
92UD/TmMVPHolo-4
92Ultra-143
92Ultra/AS-2
92Ultra/AwardWin-20
93B-338
93BJ/D/45-2
93BJ/D/McDon-12
93BJ/D/McDon-18A
93BJ/D/McDon-18B
93BJ/D/McDon-28
93BJ/Demp-2
93BJ/Fire-1
93Classic/GameI-2
93Colla/ASG-1
93Colla/DM-1
93Colla/DMArt-1
93Colla/DMProto-1
93D-132M
93D-425
93D/DK-20
93D/Elite-26
93D/EliteDom-10
93D/EliteUp-8
93D/LongBall-LL8
93D/MVP-6
93D/Master-10
93D/Prev-22
93D/Spirit-SG3
93F-330
93F-357
93F/ASAL-2
93F/Atlantic-1
93F/Fruit-1
93F/ProVI-1
93F/TLAL-9
93Flair-287
93Highland-1
93Ho-14
93HumDum/Can-22
93Kenner/Fig-1
93Kraft-2
93L-245
93L/GoldAS-13
93L/UpGoldAS-4
93OPC-4
93OPC/Premier/StarP-3
93OPC/WC-1
93P-22
93Pac/Beisbol-7M
93Pac/Spanish-319
93Pac/SpanishP-7
93Panini-27
93Pinn-30
93Pinn/Cooper-29
93Post/Can-5
93S-14
93S-511AS
93S-542DT
93S/Franchise-14
93S/GoldDT-11
93Select-8

93Select/ChasS-14
93Select/StatL-39
93Select/StatL-51
93StCl-142
93StCl-596MC
93StCl/1stDay-142
93StCl/1stDay-596MC
93StCl/MurphyS-19
93StCl/MurphyS-191
93Studio-4
93T-50
93T/BlkGold-23
93T/Finest-88AS
93T/FinestASJ-88AS
93T/FinestPr-88
93T/FinestRef-88AS
93T/Gold-50
93T/MicroP-50
93T/PreProd-1
93TB/Full-5
93ToysRUs-13
93TripleP-2
93TripleP-200AA
93TripleP/Act-13
93UD-125
93UD-42M
93UD-815TC
93UD-840M
93UD/5thAnn-A3
93UD/Clutch-R1
93UD/Diam-4
93UD/FunPack-10HS
93UD/FunPack-22KS
93UD/FunPack-54GS
93UD/FunPack-55
93UD/FunPackAS-AS4
93UD/Iooss-WI4
93UD/OnDeck-D2
93UD/SP-1AS
93UD/SeasonHL-HI1
93UDFutHero-55
93USPlayC/Ace-2D
93USPlayC/Ace-9H
93Ultra-639
93Ultra/AwardWin-13
94B-609
94Church-11
94D-6
94D/Special-6
94F-324
94F/AS-1
94Flair-115
94Flair/Hot-1
94KingB-20
94L-225
94L/GoldS-1
94L/Pr-1
94L/Slide-5
94OPC-96
94OPC/BJ-6
94OPC/JAS-21
94P-18
94Pac/AllLat-17
94Pac/Cr-632
94Pac/Silv-5
94Panini-134
94Pinn-287
94Pinn/Run-6
94Pinn/Trib-16
94RedFoley-1
94S-43
94S/GoldR-43
94S/GoldS-42
94Sf/2000-177AS
94Sf/2000-31
94StCl-10
94StCl/1stDay-10
94StCl/Gold-10
94StCl/Team-153
94Studio-24
94T-385AS
94T-675
94T/BlkGold-1
94T/Finest-205
94T/FinestRef-205
94T/Gold-385AS
94T/Gold-675
94TripleP-31
94TripleP/Medal-5
94UD-35FT
94UD-455
94UD/CollC-33
94UD/CollC/Gold-33
94UD/CollC/Silv-33
94UD/DColl-E1
94UD/ElecD-35FT
94UD/HoloFX-1
94UD/SP-39
94Ultra-434
94Ultra/AS-3
94Ultra/AwardWin-3
94Ultra/Hit-1
94Ultra/OnBase-1

Alomar, Santos Jr.
(Sandy)
86Beaum-1
87TexLgAS-10
87Wichita-5
88AAA/ProC-20
88LasVegas/CMC-22
88LasVegas/ProC-236
88TripleA/ASCMC-31
89AAA/CMC-31
89AAA/ProC-6
89B-258M
89B-454
89Classic-79
89D-28RR
89D/Rook-21
89F-300
89F-630M
89LasVegas/CMC-11
89LasVegas/ProC-7
89Padre/Mag-2
89Padre/Mag-9
89Panini/St-192
89S-630M
89S/YS/II-1
89Sf-223M
89Star/IISingl-125
89T-648FS
89UD-5
90B-337
90Classic/III-76
90Classic/Up-T3
90D-30
90D/BestAL-97
90D/Learning-40
90D/Rook-1
90F-150
90F/Can-150
90F/Up-U89
90HotRook/St-2
90Kenner/Fig-2
90Leaf-232
90OPC-353
90S-577
90S/McDon-2
90S/Tr-18T
90T-353
90T/Big-265
90T/Tr-2T
90TripleAAS/CMC-31
90UD-655
90UD/Ext-756
90USPlayC/AS-2S
90Windwlk/Discs-1
91B-57
91Bz-20
91Classic/200-194
91Classic/I-39
91Classic/II-T68
91D-13DK
91D-489
91D-51AS
91D-693ROY
91D/SuperDK-13DK
91F-359
91Indian/McDon-2
91JDean-8
91Kenner-2
91KingB/Discs-17
91Leaf-189
91Leaf-528CL
91Leaf/Prev-17
91Leaf/Stud-41
91MajorLg/Pins-18
91MooTown-10
91OPC-165
91OPC/Premier-2
91Panini/FrSt-166
91Panini/FrSt-215
91Panini/St-172
91Panini/Top15-109
91Petro/SU-9
91Post-6
91Post/Can-23
91RedFoley/St-113
91S-400AS
91S-694RF
91S-793
91S-851FRAN
91S-879ROY
91S/100RisSt-1
91S/HotRook-6
91StCl-61
91StCl/Charter*-1
91Sunflower-21
91T-165
91T/CJMini/I-5
91T/JumboR-1
91T/SU-2
91ToysRUs-1
91UD-144
91UD-46
91UD/FinalEd-81F
91USPlayC/AS-11D
91Ultra-105
91Woolwth/HL-6
92B-140
92CJ/DI-10
92Classic/Game200-46
92Classic/II-T50
92Colla/ASG-13
92D-203
92D-29AS
92D/McDon-11
92DPep/MSA-10
92F-103
92F-698M
92French-10
92Hardee-2
92Indian/McDon-1
92L-9
92L/BlkGold-9
92MrTurkey-3
92OPC-420
92OPC/Premier-164
92Panini-271AS
92Panini-44
92Pinn-436
92Pinn-586
92Pinn/Team2000-17
92Post/Can-11
92S-510
92S/100SS-49
92S/Impact-40
92S/Proctor-1
92Seven/Coin-6
92StCl-740
92StCl/Dome-6
92Studio-161
92T-420
92T/Gold-420
92T/GoldWin-420
92T/Kids-71
92TripleP-227
92UD-156
92UD-81M
92UD/ASFF-12
92Ultra-45
93B-93
93Colla/DM-2
93D-39
93F-212
93HumDum/Can-5
93Indian/WUAB-1
93KingB-18
93Kraft-3
93L-83
93OPC-12
93Pac/Beisbol-5M
93Pac/Beisbol-6
93Pac/Beisbol-7
93Pac/Spanish-91
93Pac/SpanishGold-11
93Pac/SpanishP-8
93Panini-47
93Pinn-211
93S-116
93Select-26
93Select/Pr-26
93StCl-400
93StCl/1stDay-400
93StCl/MurphyMP-1AS
93StCl/MurphyS-123
93Studio-13
93T-85
93T/Finest-26
93T/FinestRef-26
93T/Gold-85
93TripleP-251
93UD-255
93UD-45M
93UD/FunPack-106
93UD/SP-118
93Ultra-182
94B-139
94D-65
94F-98
94Finest-251
94L-223
94OPC-201
94Pac/Cr-164
94Panini-53
94Pinn-44
94Pinn/Artist-44
94Pinn/Museum-44
94S-445
94StCl-144
94StCl/1stDay-144
94StCl/Gold-144
94Studio-90
94T-273
94T/Gold-273
94TripleP-111
94UD-415
94UD/CollC-34
94UD/CollC/Gold-34
94UD/CollC/Silv-34
94Ultra-40

Alonso, Julio
77Evansvl/TCMA-2

Alonzo, Ray
83Madis/Frit-6

Alou, Felipe Rojas
59T-102
60L-6
60T-287
61T-565
62AmTract-52A
62AmTract-52B
62AmTract-52C
62J-133
62P-133
62P/Can-133
62Salada-130
62Shirriff-130
62T-133
62T/St-193
63J-107
63P-107
63T-270
64T-65
64T/Coins-11
64T/St-62
65T-383
66Kahn
66OPC-96
66T-96
67CokeCap/Brave-12
67Kahn
67OPC/PI-30
67T-240LL
67T-530
67T/PI-30
68CokeCap/Brave-12
68Dexter-5
68Kahn
68OPC-55
68T-55
69MB-10
69MLB/St-110
69MLBPA/Pin-32
69OPC-2LL
69T-2LL
69T-300
69T/DE-17
69T/S-35
69T/St-2
69T/decal
69Trans-51
70MLB/St-253
70OPC-434
70T-434
71K-7
71MLB/St-505
71OPC-495
71T-495
71T/Coins-8
72MB-12
72OPC-263
72T-263
73OPC-650
73Syrac/Team-1
73T-650
74OPC-485
74T-485
74T/Tr-485T
75SSPC/42-42
78Memphis/Team-1
82D-650
82Wichita-2
83Wichita/Dog-2MG
84Expo/PostC-1CO
84Mother/Giants-19
84Stuart-38CO
84Stuart-6CO
85Indianap-2MG
86WPalmB-1MG
88FSLAS/Star-2CO
88Pac/Leg-58
90FSLAS/Star-23
90WPalmB/Star-29
91WPalmB/ClBest-1MG
91WPalmB/ProC-1244
92Expo/D/Duri-15B
92T/Tr-3TMG
92T/TrGold-3TMG
92Yank/WIZ70-5
93B-701FOIL
93Expo/D/McDon-31MG
93Expo/D/McDon-AU
93T-508M
93T/Gold-508M

Alou, Jesus M. R.
(Jesus)
64T-47R
65T-545
66T-242
66T/RO-3
66T/RO-4
67CokeCap/Giant-18
67T-332
68CokeCap/Giant-18
68Dexter-6
68T-452
69MB-11
69MLB/St-136
69OPC-22
69T-22
69T/St-51
70MLB/St-37
70OPC-248
70T-248
71MLB/St-73
71OPC-337
71T-337
72MB-13
72T-716
73OPC-93
73T-93
74OPC-654
74T-654
75OPC-253
75SSPC/42-42M
75T-253
75T/M-253
76OPC-468
76SSPC-538
76SSPC/MetsY-M6
76T-468
78BK/Ast-22
79T-107
80T-593
81TCMA-406
91WIZMets-8

Alou, Jose
87BurlEx-10
88WPalmB/Star-2
89WPalmB/Star-1

Alou, Mateo Rojas
(Matty)
61T-327
62T-413
63Salada-25
63T-128
64T-204
65T-318
66EH-18
66OPC-94
66T-94
67Bz-47
67CokeCap/Pirate-17
67Kahn
67OPC-10
67OPC/PI-29
67T-10
67T-240LL
67T/PI-29

67T/Test/PP-2
67T/Test/PP-28
68Bz-2
68KDKA-18
68Kahn
68OPC-1LL
68T-1LL
68T-270
68T/G-1
69Kahn
69MB-12
69MLB/St-182
69OPC-2LL
69T-2LL
69T-490
69T/S-56
69T/St-82
69Trans-58
70K-28
70MLB/St-98
70OPC-30
70OPC-460AS
70T-30
70T-460AS
71K-53
71MLB/St-265
71OPC-720
71T-720
71T/Coins-47
72MB-14
72OPC-395
72T-395
73OPC-132
73Syrac/Team-2
73T-132
74OPC-430
74T-430
75SSPC/42-42M
78TCMA-75
88Pac/Leg-37
89WPalmB/Star-27
91Swell/Great-2
92Yank/WIZ70-6
93TWill-74
93UD/ATH-4
Alou, Moises
86Watertn-2
87Watertn-27
88Augusta/ProC-360
89Salem/Star-1
89Star/Wax-93
90A&AASingle/ProC-29
90B-178
90BuffB/Team-1
90F-650M
90F/Can-650M
90Harris/ProC-1204
90Harris/Star-2
90ProC/Singl-790
90S-592
91Classic/I-60
91D-38RR
91Leaf/Stud-191
91OPC-526A
91OPC-526B
91OPC/Premier-3
91S-813
91StCl-31
91T-526A
91T-526B
91T/90Debut-5
91UD-665
92Classic/II-T36
92D/RookPhen-BC1
92F/Up-95
92JDean/Rook-9
92L-426
92L/BlkGold-426
92OPC-401
92Pinn-572
92Pinn/Rook-16
92S/100RisSt-9
92StCl-519
92T/Tr-4T
92T/TrGold-4T
92Ultra-511
93B-452
93B-701FOIL
93Classic/Gamel-3
93Colla/DM-3
93D-510
93Expo/D/McDon-1
93F-70
93F/RookSenII-1
93Flair-78
93HumDum/Can-39
93L-147
93LimeR/Winter-112
93OPC-10
93Pac/Beisbol-26
93Pac/Jugador-19
93Pac/Spanish-180
93Pac/SpanishGold-1
93Panini-232
93Pinn-92
93S-187
93Select-272
93Select/ChasRook-2
93StCl-239
93StCl/1stDay-239
93Studio-11
93T-123
93T/Finest-189
93T/FinestRef-189
93T/Gold-123
93ToysRUs-96
93ToysRUs/MPhoto-1
93TripleP-244
93UD-297
93UD/SP-100
93USPlayC/Rook-11S
93Ultra-61
94B-116
94D-3
94D/DK-23
94D/MVP-8
94D/Special-3
94F-531
94L-252
94OPC-266
94Pac/Cr-372
94Panini-206
94Pinn-7
94Pinn/Artist-7
94Pinn/HobSam-7
94Pinn/Museum-7
94Pinn/RetailSam-7
94S-90
94S/GoldR-90
94Select-159
94Sf/2000-87
94StCl-141
94StCl/1stDay-141
94StCl/Gold-141
94Studio-74
94T-50
94T/Finest-121
94T/Finest/PreProd-121
94T/FinestRef-121
94T/Gold-50
94TripleP-91
94UD-351
94UD/CollC-35
94UD/CollC/Gold-35
94UD/CollC/Silv-35
94UD/SP-82
94Ultra-222
Alperman, Charles A.
(Whitey)
90Target-890
C46-7
E270/2
T204
T206
Alpert, George
81Batavia-25
82Watlo/B-20
82Watlo/Frit-27
Alstead, Jason
91Freder/ClBest-21
91Freder/ProC-2375
92ClBest-106
92Freder/ClBest-9
92Freder/ProC-1816
Alston, Garvin
92Bend/ClBest-5
92FrRow/DP-54
93B-640
93T-661
93T/Gold-661
Alston, Thomas E.
(Tom)
53Mother-24
54Hunter
55B-257
55Hunter
Alston, Walter E.
52Park-66MG
53Exh/Can-61MG
55Gol/Dodg-1MG
56T-8MG
58PacBell-1MG
58T-314M
60BB-18MG
60Morrell
60T-212MG
60Union/Dodg-1MG
61BB-24MG
61T-136MG
61Union/Dodg-1MG
62BB-24MG
62T-217MG
63T-154MG
64T-101MG
65OPC-217MG
65T-217MG
66OPC-116MG
66T-116MG
67T-294MG
68T-472MG
69OPC-24MG
69T-24MG
70OPC-242MG
70T-242MG
71OPC-567MG
71T-567MG
71Ticket/Dodg-2MG
72T-749MG
73OPC-569MG
73T-569MG
74OPC-144MG
74T-144MG
75OPC-361MG
75T-361MG
75T/M-361MG
76SSPC-90MG
76T-46MG
80Pac/Leg-14MG
80Perez/HOF-181
81TCMA-306MG
82Ohio/HOF-15
87Smok/Dodg-1MG
88Smok/Dodg-1MG
89Smok/Dodg-1MG
90Target-12
Alston, Wendell
(Dell)
78Cr/PCL-68
78SSPC/270-4
78T-710R
79T-54
79Tacoma-19
80T-198
80Tacoma-24
81D-322
92Yank/WIZ70-7
Altaffer, Todd
91SoBend/ClBest-12
91SoBend/ProC-2848
92Watlo/ClBest-17
92Watlo/ProC-2132
Altamirano, Porfirio
80OkCty
81OkCty/TCMA-1
83F-153
83Portl-15
83T-432
84Iowa-23
84Nes/792-101
84T-101
Alten, Ernest M.
(Ernie)
No Cards.
Altenberger, Peter
88CapeCod/Sum-48
Altenburg, Jesse H.
No Cards.
Altizer, David Tildon
(Dave)
E254
Altman, George Lee
59T-512
60T-259
61P-195
61T-551
61T/St-1
62J-187
62P-187
62P/Can-187
62Salada-128
62Shirriff-128
62T-240
62T/St-103
62T/bucks
63J-171
63P-171
63Salada-31
63T-357
64Bz-23
64T-95
64T/SU
64T/St-69
65T-528
66OPC-146
66T-146
67CokeCap/Cub-17
67OPC-87
67T-87
91WIZMets-9
Altman, John
77Visalia
Altobelli, Joseph S.
75IntAS/TCMA-16
77T-211MG
78T-256MG
79Pol/Giants-6CO
79T-356MG
80Colum-8
83T/Tr-3
84D-88
84F-643IA
84F/St-125MG
84Nes/792-21MG
84T-21MG
85T-574MG
85T/Gloss22-12MG
88Berg/Cubs-CO
90Cub/Mara-28CO
90T/TVCub-2CO
91Cub/Mara-x
91Cub/Vine-2CO
Alton, George Wilson
No Cards.
Altrock, Nicholas
(Nick)
61F-3
77Galasso-178
87Conlon/2-8
88Conlon/5-1
91Conlon/Sport-226
94Conlon-1119
E210-40
E254
R312/M
WG2-1
Alusik, George J.
62T-261
63T-51
64T-431
Alva, John
86Sumter/ProC-2
87Durham-25
88Greenvl/Best-6
89Greenvl/Best-7
89Greenvl/ProC-1154
89Greenvl/Star-2
90AAASingl/ProC-408
90Greenvl/Star-1
90ProC/Singl-299
90Richm/CMC-23
90Richm/ProC-263
91AAA/LineD-426
91Richm/Bob-19
91Richm/LineD-426
91Richm/ProC-2574
91Richm/Team-13
Alvarado, Arnaldo
75Dubuq
Alvarado, Jose
85Tigres-15
Alvarado, Luis Cesar
70OPC-317R
70T-317R
71OPC-489
71T-489
72T-774
73OPC-627
73T-627
74OPC-462
74T-462
91WIZMets-10
Alvarez, Alex
88CapeCod/Sum-7
Alvarez, Carmelo
82VeroB-16
Alvarez, Chris
86FSLAS-3
86FtLaud-1
87Albany-15
88Colum/CMC-24
88Colum/Pol-13
88Colum/ProC-323
89Colum/ProC-739
90London/ProC-1273
Alvarez, Clemente
88Utica/Pucko-2
89SoBend/GS-30
90Saraso/Star-1
91ClBest/Singl-142
91Saraso/ClBest-12
91Saraso/ProC-1115
92BirmB/ProC-2585
92BirmB/SB-76
92ClBest-29
92Sky/AASingl-36
93B-188
Alvarez, David
89Elmira/Pucko-1
90Elmira/Pucko-2
Alvarez, Emenegilda
91MedHat/ProC-4112
91MedHat/SportP-21
Alvarez, Javier
89Eugene/Best-15
90Eugene/GS-1
Alvarez, Joe
75FtLaud/Sus-14
Alvarez, Jorge
89Salem/Team-5
90BBCity/Star-29CO
90VeroB/Star-1
90VeroB/Star-30CO
91AA/LineD-527
91SanAn/LineD-527
92SanAn/ProC-3979
92SanAn/SB-552
92Sky/AASingl-241
93LimeR/Winter-73
Alvarez, Jose 1
76Dubuq
Alvarez, Jose 2
92Salem/ClBest-12
92Salem/ProC-54
Alvarez, Jose Lino
79Savan-12
81Richm-15
82Richm-1
83Richm-1
84Cram/PCL-51
86Greenvl/Team-2
88F/Up-U70
88Richm/CMC-8
88Richm/ProC-12
89Brave/Dubuq-2
89D-405
89F-585
89Panini/St-31
89T-253
89UD/Ext-734
90D-389
90F-574
90F/Can-574
90OPC-782
90PublInt/St-106
90S-148
90T-782
90UD-634
Alvarez, Mike
81Miami-11
82FtMyr-12
83Omaha-1
84Omaha-19
85FtMyr-27
86FtMyr-2
87AppFx-18
88Savan/ProC-353
91AA/LineD-425M
91Memphis/LineD-425CO
91Memphis/ProC-670CO
92Memphis/ProC-2436CO
92Memphis/SB-450M
Alvarez, Orlando
74Albuq/Team-1
75Albuq/Caruso-1
75IntLgAS/Broder-1
75PCL/AS-1
77SLCity
90Target-891

Alvarez, Oswaldo G.
(Ossie)
59T-504
85Tigres-4
Alvarez, Robbie
81Chatt-3
82Miami-12
Alvarez, Rogelio H.
63T-158R
Alvarez, Tavo
91ClBest/Singl-48
91Sumter/ClBest-1
91Sumter/ProC-2324
92B-165
92ClBest/Up-439
92ProC/Tomorrow-267
92UD/ML-262
92WPalmB/ClBest-3
92WPalmB/ProC-2077
93B-16
93ClBest/MLG-46
93F/Final-88
93FExcel/ML-55
93Ottawa/ProC-2428
93UD-501DD
93Ultra-410
94UD-295UDC
Alvarez, Wilson
88Gaston/ProC-1017
89CharlR/Star-1
89Tulsa/Team-2
90AAASingl/ProC-159
90ProC/Singl-628
90T/89Debut-3
90UD/Ext-765
90Vanco/CMC-1
90Vanco/ProC-481
91AA/LineD-51
91B-354
91BirmB/LineD-51
91BirmB/ProC-1446
91ClBest/Singl-285
91F/UltraUp-U13
91OPC-378
91StCl/Member*-1
91T-378
91UD/FinalEd-42F
92B-69
92Classic/Game200-114
92Classic/I-T5
92D-495HL
92D-630
92F-684RS
92F-74
92L-78
92L/BlkGold-78
92OPC-452
92OPC/Premier-122
92Pinn-192
92ProC/Tomorrow-41
92S-428NH
92S-760
92StCl-761
92T-452
92T/Gold-452
92T/GoldWin-452
92UD-573
92Ultra-32
92WSox-40
93B-387
93D-37
93F-199
93Flair-180
93L-496
93Pac/Spanish-66
93Pinn-441
93Rang/Keeb-51
93S-609
93StCl-181
93StCl/1stDay-181
93StCl/WSox-10
93T-737
93T/Gold-737
93UD-350
93Ultra-170
93WSox-1
94B-54
94D-518
94F-73
94Flair-28
94L-71
94Pac/Cr-118
94Pinn-128
94Pinn/Artist-128
94Pinn/Museum-128
94S-220
94S/GoldR-220
94Select-111
94Sf/2000-97
94StCl-462
94StCl/1stDay-462
94StCl/Gold-462
94StCl/Team-132
94Studio-203
94T-299
94T/Finest-139
94T/FinestRef-139
94T/Gold-299
94TripleP-261
94UD-204
94UD/CollC-36
94UD/CollC/Gold-36
94UD/CollC/Silv-36
94UD/ElecD-204
94UD/SP-188
94Ultra-30
Alvis, Andy
80Batavia-20
Alvis, Dave
86Watlo-2
87Watlo-7
Alvis, Roy Maxwell
(Max)
63Sugar-14
63T-228R
64Kahn
64T-545
64T/Coins-48
64T/S-46
64T/SU
64T/St-7
64T/tatt
65Kahn
65OPC-185
65T-185
65T/E-3
65T/trans-2
66Kahn
66T-415
66T/RO-5
66T/RO-68
67CokeCap/ALAS-34
67CokeCap/AS-24
67CokeCap/Indian-2
67Kahn
67T-520
67T/Test/SU-16
68Bz-9
68Kahn
68T-340
68T/ActionSt-6AM
68T/Post-2
69Kahn
69MB-13
69MLB/St-37
69MLBPA/Pin-1
69OPC-145
69T-145
69T/4in1-5M
69T/St-161
70MLB/St-193
70McDon-6
70OPC-85
70T-85
72MB-15
78TCMA-83
92TX-2
Exh47
Alvord, William C.
(Billy)
N172
Alyea, Brant Jr.
88Gaston/ProC-1007
88SALAS/GS-16
89StLucie/Star-1
90Tulsa/ProC-1165
Alyea, Garrabrant R.
(Brant)
66OPC-11R
66T-11R
69OPC-48
69T-48
70OPC-303
70T-303
71MLB/St-457
71OPC-449
71T-449
72MB-16
72OPC-383
72T-383
Amador, Bruce
82Madis/Frit-30
Amalfitano, John J.
(Joey)
55B-269
55Gol/Giants-1
55T-144
60T-356
61T-87
62J-144
62P-144
62P/Can-144
62Salada-193
62Shirriff-193
62T-456
62T/St-123
63F-36
63T-199
64T-451
65T-402
73OPC-252CO
73T-252CO
74OPC-78CO
74T-78CO
76SSPC-629CO
77Padre/SchCd-2CO
78TCMA-96
81D-522CO
81T-676MG
85Coke/Dodg-1CO
86Coke/Dodg-1CO
89Smok/Ast-15
90Mother/Dodg-28M
90Pol/Dodg-x
91Mother/Dodg-28CO
91Pol/Dodg-x
92Mother/Dodg-28M
92Pol/Dodg-NNO
93Mother/Dodg-28M
93Pol/Dodg-30CO
Aman, Kevan
77Wausau
Amante, Tom
87StPete-10
90SpringDG/Best-4
Amaral, Rich
86Pittsfld-1
87Pittsfld-22
88Pittsfld/ProC-1362
89BirmB/Best-14
89BirmB/ProC-91
90AAASingl/ProC-171
90ProC/Singl-640
90Vanco/CMC-13
90Vanco/ProC-493
91AAA/LineD-51
91Calgary/LineD-51
91Calgary/ProC-520
92B-386
92Calgary/ProC-3737
92D/Rook-3
92Pinn-581
92Sky/AAASingl-291
92StCl-689
92T/91Debut-3
92Ultra-430
93F/Final-263
93Flair-266
93JDean/Rook-1
93L-516
93Mother/Mar-27
93OPC/Premier-114
93Pac/Jugador-1
93Pac/Spanish-617
93S-249
93Select/RookTr-145T
93StCl-264
93StCl/1stDay-264
93StCl/Mar-4
93T-431
93T/Gold-431
93UD-551
93UD/SP-127
93Ultra-265
94B-389
94D-66
94F-278
94L-104
94OPC-149
94Pac/Cr-561
94Panini-120
94Pinn-386
94S-210
94S/GoldR-210
94Select-114
94StCl-44
94StCl/1stDay-44
94StCl/Gold-44
94Studio-98
94T-233
94T/Finest-16
94T/FinestRef-16
94T/Gold-233
94TripleP-121
94UD-211
94UD/CollC-37
94UD/CollC/Gold-37
94UD/CollC/Silv-37
94UD/ElecD-211
94Ultra-116
Amaro, Ruben Jr.
87Salem/ProC-2428
88CalLgAS-32
88PalmSp/Cal-97
88PalmSp/ProC-1434
89QuadC/Best-30
89QuadC/GS-18
90MidldA/GS-4
91AAA/LineD-152
91AAAGame/ProC-12
91B-208
91Classic/III-19
91Edmon/LineD-152
91Edmon/ProC-1526
92B-184
92D-733
92D/Rook-4
92F-52
92L-339
92L/BlkGold-339
92OPC-269
92OPC/Premier-16
92Phill/Med-2
92Pinn-570
92ProC/Tomorrow-30
92S/RookTr-98T
92StCl-870
92T-269
92T/91Debut-4
92T/Gold-269
92T/GoldWin-269
92T/Tr-5T
92T/TrGold-5T
92UD-752
92Ultra-540
93D-488
93F-97
93OPC-18
93Pac/Spanish-229
93Phill/Med-2
93S-341
93ScranWB/Team-2
93StCl-385
93StCl/1stDay-385
93T-43
93T/Gold-43
93USPlayC/Rook-9C
93Ultra-83
94F-581
94Pac/Cr-467
94S-265
94S/GoldR-265
Amaro, Ruben
59T-178
61T-103
62J-194
62P-194
62P/Can-194
62Salada-163
62Shirriff-163
62T-284
62T/St-163
63F-50
63T-455
64PhilBull-2
64T-432
65T-419
66OPC-186
66T-186
67CokeCap/YMet-2
67T-358
68OPC-138
68T-138
69T-598
76OkCty/Team-1
78TCMA-28
83Thorn-26C
89Bristol/Star-29
90Bristol/ProC-3175CO
92Yank/WIZ60-2
Amaya, Ben
86Chatt-1
Ambler, Wayne H.
39PlayBall-117
41G-7
Ambos, Willie
88SLCity-13
89SanBern/Best-9
89SanBern/Cal-66
91SLCity/ProC-3202
91SLCity/SportP-25CO
Ambrose, Mark
87ElPaso-11
88ElPaso/Best-15
89Stockton/Best-10
89Stockton/Cal-159
89Stockton/ProC-377
Ambrosio, Ciro
90StCath/ProC-3467
91Myrtle/ClBest-15
91Myrtle/ProC-2949
Amelung, Edward
(Ed)
81VeroB-1
83Albuq-19
84Cram/PCL-163
85Cram/PCL-158
86Albuq-1
87Edmon-11
88SanDiegoSt-1
89SanDiegoSt-2
90Target-13
Amerson, Archie
78SanJose-21
79Toledo-4
Ames, Doug
86Madis/Pol-1
Ames, Ken
80Ander-10
Ames, Leon Kessling
(Red)
10Domino-1
11Helmar-120
12Sweet/Pin-106
91Conlon/Sport-153
92Conlon/Sport-334
D328-4
D329-5
D350/2-5
E104
E135-4
E254
E270/1
E270/2
E93
E96
M101/4-5
M101/5-5
M116
S74-79
T202
T205
T206
T213/blue
T215/blue
T215/brown
T3-77
W555
WG3-1
Amole, Morris George
(Doc)
No Cards.
Amor, Vincente A.
No Cards.
Amoros, Edmundo I.
(Sandy)
53Exh/Can-43
55Gol/Dodg-2
55T-75
55T/DH-54
56T-42
56T/Pin-49
57T-201
58T-93
60T-531
89Rini/Dodg-2
90Target-14
PM10/Sm-2

Amos, Perry
91Hunting/ClBest-2
91Hunting/ProC-3325
Anaya, Mike
89Star/Wax-22
90Kgsport/Best-15
90Kgsport/Star-1
91Pittsfld/ClBest-22
91Pittsfld/ProC-3414
Ancker, Walter
No Cards.
Anders, Scott
86Peoria-1
Andersen, Larry E.
75OkCty/Team-7
78T-703R
79Tacoma-4
80Port-23
80T-665R
82D-428
82T-52
83D-181
83F-470
83Portl-3
83T-234
84Phill/TastyK-14
85D-570
85F-244
85Phill/TastyK-13
85Phill/TastyK-9
85T-428
86D-355
86F-434
86Phill/TastyK-47
86T-183
87D-640
87F-49
87Mother/Ast-21
87Pol/Ast-1
87T-503
88D-332
88F-438
88Mother/Ast-21
88Pol/Ast-2
88S-133
88T-342
89B-325
89D-359
89F-349
89Lennox/Ast-18
89Mother/Ast-20
89S-523
89T-24
89UD-404
90B-67
90D-359
90F-221
90F/Can-221
90Leaf-386
90Lennox-2
90Mother/Ast-20
90Publlnt/St-86
90S-282
90UD-407
91B-660
91D-665
91F-83
91F/Up-U120
91Leaf-407
91Leaf/Stud-241
91OPC-761
91Padre/MagRal-17
91S-848
91S/RookTr-71T
91StCl-390
91T-761
91UD-41
91UD/Ext-793
92D-687
92F-597
92Mother/Padre-21
92OPC-616
92Padre/Carl-1
92Pinn-399
92Pol/Padre-27
92S-263
92Smok/Padre-1
92StCl-91
92T-616
92T/Gold-616
92T/GoldWin-616
92UD-587
93F-518
93F/Final-108
93L-491
93Pac/Spanish-573
93Phill/Med-3
93S-445
93StCl/Phill-2
94D-71
94F-582
94Pac/Cr-468
94Phill/Med-1
94S-237
94S/GoldR-237
94StCl/Team-223
Andersh, Kevin
86Macon-2
89Augusta/ProC-512
Anderson, Alfred W.
(Alf)
No Cards.
Anderson, Allan
83Wisco/Frit-3
84Visalia-20
85Toledo-1
86D/Rook-3
86Toledo-1
87D-368
87F-533
87Portl-4
87T-336
88F/Up-U41
88Portl/ProC-654
88T-101
89B-149
89Classic/Up/2-178
89D-419
89D/Best-270
89F-102
89F/LL-1
89OPC-20
89Panini/St-381
89S-394
89S/YS/I-34
89Sf-220
89T-672
89T/Mini-60
89UD-85
90B-409
90D-64
90D/BestAL-52
90F-366
90F/Can-366
90Kenner/Fig-3
90Leaf-5
90OPC-71
90Panini/St-117
90Publlnt/St-320
90Publlnt/St-593
90RedFoley/St-1
90S-292
90Sf-59
90T-71
90T/St-296
90UD-219
91B-327
91D-527
91F-603
91Leaf-259
91OPC-223
91S-135
91StCl-188
91T-223
91UD-503
92F-196
92OPC-417
92S-731
92StCl-204
92StCl-767
92T-417
92T/Gold-417
92T/GoldWin-417
92UD-506
92USPlayC/Twin-2C
92USPlayC/Twin-3D
Anderson, Andy Holm
52Park-17
86Negro/Frit-41
Anderson, Andy
88ElPaso/Best-16
88Portl/CMC-1
Anderson, Arnold R.
(Red)
No Cards.
Anderson, Bernie
86Lakeland-2
87Lakeland-10
88GlenF/ProC-928
88London/ProC-1364
Anderson, Blake
93MissSt-2
Anderson, Brady
85Elmira-2
86FSLAS-4
86WinHaven-2
87NewBrit-7
88D/RedSox/Bk-NEW
88D/Rook-14
88S/Tr-70T
88T/Tr-5T
89B-18
89D-519
89F-606
89French-9
89KennerFig-2
89OPC-161
89S-563
89S/YS/I-26
89T-757
89T/JumboR-2
89T/UK-1
89ToysRUs-2
89UD-408
90B-258
90D-638
90F-172
90F/Can-172
90MLBPA/Pins-119
90OPC-598
90Publlnt/St-572
90S-33
90T-598
90UD-290
91B-100
91Crown/Orio-9
91D-668
91F-466
91OPC-97
91S-249
91StCl-410
91T-97A
91T-97B
91UD-349
92F-1
92L-343
92L/BlkGold-343
92OPC-268
92Pinn-452
92S-365
92StCl-303
92Studio-121
92T-268
92T/Gold-268
92T/GoldWin-268
92UD-185
92Ultra-301
93B-409
93Classic/Gamel-4
93Colla/DM-4
93D-89
93D/DK-23
93D/Spirit-SG17
93F-163
93F/Fruit-2
93F/TLAL-7
93Flair-149
93L-177
93MilkBone-19
93OPC-16
93Pac/Spanish-14
93Panini-76
93Pinn-70
93S-140
93Select-56
93Select/StatL-21
93Select/StatL-57
93StCl-507
93StCl/1stDay-507
93StCl/MurphyS-169
93Studio-17
93T-355
93T/BlkGold-24
93T/Finest-71
93T/FinestRef-71
93T/Gold-355
93ToysRUs-52
93TripleP-166
93UD-111
93UD-44M
93UD/FunPack-131
93UD/SP-154
93USPlayC/Ace-11H
93Ultra-138
94B-233
94D-592
94F-1
94L-66
94OPC-3
94Pac/Cr-25
94Panini-17
94Pinn-165
94Pinn/Artist-165
94Pinn/Museum-165
94S-335
94Select-55
94StCl-53
94StCl/1stDay-53
94StCl/Gold-53
94StCl/Team-290
94T-145
94T/Finest-131
94T/FinestRef-131
94T/Gold-145
94TripleP-151
94UD-63
94UD/ElecD-63
94Ultra-301
Anderson, Brian
94B-369
94B-39
94F/MLP-2
94Finest-304
94Flair-19
94L/GRook-17
94Pinn-432
94S-468
94UD-1
94UD/CollC-21
94UD/CollC/Gold-21
94UD/CollC/Silv-21
94UD/ElecD-1
94UD/SP-21
94Ultra-321
Anderson, Chad
90Martins/ProC-3205
91Martins/ClBest-27
91Martins/ProC-3443
92Batavia/ClBest-3
92Batavia/ProC-3254
Anderson, Charles
(Charlie)
90MissSt-3
91MissSt-3
92Johnson/ClBest-7
92Johnson/ProC-3121
92MissSt-3
Anderson, Chris
91Miami/Bumble-2
92Boise/ClBest-15
92Boise/ProC-3634
Anderson, Cliff
92Yakima/ClBest-14
92Yakima/ProC-3455
Anderson, Dave
76Cedar
77Cedar
Anderson, David C.
(Dave)
82Albuq-14
84D-642
84Nes/792-376
84Pol/Dodg-10
84T-376
85Coke/Dodg-2
85D-275
85F-366
85T-654
86Coke/Dodg-2
86F-123
86OPC-29
86Pol/Dodg-10
86T-758
87F-436
87Mother/Dodg-17
87Pol/Dodg-4
87T-73
88D-475
88F-508
88Mother/Dodg-17
88OPC-203
88Panini/St-313
88Pol/Dodg-10
88S-166
88T-456
89D-434
89F-53
89Mother/Dodg-17
89OPC-117
89Pol/Dodg-7
89S-478
89T-117
89UD-89
90D-486
90F/Up-U59
90Mother/Giant-19
90OPC-248
90Publlnt/St-1
90S-238
90T-248
90Target-15
90UD-510
91F-252
91Leaf/Stud-251
91Mother/Giant-19
91OPC-572
91PG&E-18
91S-641
91T-572
91Ultra-314
92Albuq/SB-1
92B-394
92D-759
92F-625
92S-167
92S/RookTr-45T
92UD-290
Anderson, David S.
(Dave)
No Cards.
Anderson, David
92MN-1
Anderson, Doug
91Belling/ClBest-19
91Belling/ProC-3654
Anderson, Dwain C.
72OPC-268R
72T-268R
73OPC-241
73T-241
Anderson, Ed
88SLCity-30M
Anderson, Eddie
90NE-1
Anderson, Edward John
(Goat)
No Cards.
Anderson, Edward
76Dubuq
77Cocoa
Anderson, Eric
82AubAs-6
Anderson, Ferrell J.
90Target-16
Anderson, Fred
16FleischBrd-5
Anderson, Garret
90LitSun/HSPros-19
90LitSun/HSProsG-19
91ClBest/Singl-258
91QuadC/ClBest-22
91QuadC/ProC-2641
92AS/Cal-46
92B-298
92ClBest-209
92MidldA/OneHour-2
92PalmSp/ClBest-12
92PalmSp/ProC-851
92ProC/Tomorrow-34
92UD/ML-292
92UD/POY-PY1
93FExcel/ML-139
93Vanco/ProC-2608
94B-479
94FExcel-23
94FExcel/AS-7
94SigRook-30
94T-84
94T/Gold-84
94Ultra-322
Anderson, George A.J.
No Cards.
Anderson, George Lee
(Sparky)
59T-338
60L-125
60Maple-1
60T-34
61BeeHive-1

70OPC-181MG
70T-181MG
71OPC-688MG
71T-688MG
72OPC-358MG
72T-358MG
73OPC-296MG
73T-296MG
74OPC-326MG
74T-326MG
75OPC-531MG
75T-531MG
75T/M-531MG
76SSPC-22
76T-104MG
77T-287MG
78Pep-1MG
78SSPC/270-129MG
78T-401MG
79T-259MG
81D-370MG
81F-460MG
81T-666MG
81TCMA-300
81Tiger/Detroit-18MG
82D-29MG
83D-533MG
83T-660MG
84Nes/792-259MG
84T-259MG
84Tiger/Wave-1MG
85F-628MG
85F/St-125MG
85Seven-2MG
85T-307MG
85Wendy-1MG
86D/AAS-58MG
86T-411MG
86T/Gloss22-1MG
87T-218MG
88Pac/Leg-46
88Pep/T-11MG
88Pol/T-2MG
88T-14MG
89Mara/Tigers-11MG
89Pol/Tigers-MG
89T-193MG
89T/LJN-132
90CokeK/Tiger-1MG
90OPC-609MG
90T-609MG
91CokeK/Tiger-11MG
91Leaf/Stud-261MG
91OPC-519MG
91Pol/Tiger-1MG
91T-519MG
92OPC-381MG
92T-381MG
92T/Gold-381MG
92T/GoldWin-381MG
93T-506MG
93T/Gold-506MG
93Tiger/Gator-1MG
Anderson, Glen
86Cram/NWL-141
Anderson, Greg
76BurlB
Anderson, Harold
(Hal)
No Cards.
Anderson, Harry W.
57T-404
58T-171
59T-85
60T-285
61T-76
PM10/Sm-3
Anderson, James Lea
(Jim)
78Cr/PCL-93
79T-703R
80T-183
81D-165
81F-598
81Pol/Mariners-4
81T-613
82D-181
82F-503
82T-497
83Rangers-46
84Nes/792-353
84Rangers-14
84T-353
85OKCty-6
87Clinton-5
88Clinton/ProC-703
89Shrev/ProC-1835
93Rang/Keeb-52
Anderson, Jeff
86Penin-3
Anderson, Jesse
81AppFx-1
82AppFx/Frit-10
83Albany-1
Anderson, John 1
84Butte-2
Anderson, John 2
88Martins/Star-1
Anderson, John 3
92MN-20M
Anderson, John C.
62T-266
81TCMA-301
90Target-17
91Crown/Orio-10
Anderson, John Fred
(Fred)
D328-5
E135-5
Anderson, John Joseph
E107
T204
T206
Anderson, Jon
91QuadC/ProC-2629
Anderson, Karl Adam
(Bud)
79Spokane-20
79T-712R
81Chatt-25
82Charl-1
83T-367
83Wheat/Ind-1
84D-590
84F-533
84Maine-8
84Nes/792-497
84T-497
91Pac/SenLg-4
Anderson, Kelly
79Cedar/TCMA-24
Anderson, Kent
86PalmSp-1
88Edmon/CMC-17
88Edmon/ProC-574
89Edmon/CMC-17
89T/Tr-3T
90D-490
90HotRook/St-3
90OPC-16
90PublInt/St-363
90S-412
90S/100Ris-86
90T-16
90T/89Debut-4
90UD-691
91AAA/LineD-153
91B-194
91D-525
91Edmon/LineD-153
91Edmon/ProC-1520
91F-306
91OPC-667
91S-224
91StCl-241
91T-667
92Calgary/ProC-3738
Anderson, Lawrence D.
(Larry)
76OPC-593R
76SSPC-249
76T-593R
77T-487R
80CharlO/Pol-1
80CharlO/W3TV-1
Anderson, Matthew
(Matt)
88OK-9
89Bluefld/Star-26
90ProC/Singl-872
90Wausau/Best-6
90Wausau/ProC-2119
90Wausau/Star-1
91Kane/ClBest-3
91Kane/ProC-2650
91Kane/Team-1
92ClBest-107
92Freder/ClBest-19
92Freder/ProC-1797
92ProC/Tomorrow-11
92UD/ML-89
Anderson, Michael A.
(Mike)
72OPC-14R
72T-14R
73OPC-147
73T-147
74JP
74OPC-619
74T-619
75OPC-118
75T-118
75T/M-118
76OPC-527
76SSPC-469
76T-527T
77T-72
78T-714
79T-102
80BurlB-18
80OkCty
80T-317
81Portl-5
82Vanco-22
84Cram/PCL-46
85Louisvl-29
91Crown/Orio-11
Anderson, Mike
85LitFalls-1
86LitFalls-1
87Columbia-20
87PalmSp-24
88PalmSp/Cal-98
88PalmSp/ProC-1438
89Greens/ProC-428
89Reno/Cal-239
90Cedar/Best-20
90Cedar/ProC-2318
91AA/LineD-152
91Chatt/LineD-152
91Chatt/ProC-1950
91Waverly/Fut-4
92Chatt/ProC-3810
92Chatt/SB-177
Anderson, Norman C.
(Craig)
62T-593R
63T-59
81TCMA-295
91WIZMets-11
Anderson, Ottis
91StCl/Charter*-33
91StCl/Charter*-34
Anderson, Paul
91Spring/ClBest-1
91Spring/ProC-731
92ArkTr/ProC-1120
Anderson, Richard A.
(Rick)
79Jacks-16
81Tidew-26
82Tidew-12
84Tidew-19
85IntLgAS-19
85Tidew-6
86Tidew-1
87F-2
87Omaha-22
87T-594
88Omaha/CMC-1
88Omaha/ProC-1512
89S-441
90Kenosha/Best-28CO
90Kenosha/ProC-2311CO
90Kenosha/Star-26CO
91Kenosha/ClBest-20CO
91Kenosha/ProC-2092CO
91WIZMets-12
92Kenosha/ProC-621CO
Anderson, Richard Lee
(Rick)
76Shrev
77WHave
79Colum-21
80Spokane-20
81Spokane-28
81T-282R
92Yank/WIZ70-8
Anderson, Robert Carl
(Bob)
58T-209
59T-447
60T-412
61T-283
61T/St-2
62T-557
63T-379
Anderson, Roy
85Madis-4
85Madis/Pol-1
86Modesto-1
86Modesto-2
Anderson, Scott
82Madis/Frit-10
85Tulsa-33
88OkCty/CMC-1
89Indianap/CMC-6
89Indianap/ProC-1234
90AAASingl/ProC-563
90Indianap/CMC-7
90Indianap/ProC-280
90ProC/Singl-57
91F-225
91S-734RP
93Edmon/ProC-1129
93Rang/Keeb-53
Anderson, Spike
90WichSt-2
Anderson, Steve 1
83Beloit/Frit-12
Anderson, Steve 2
(Nub)
76Laugh/Clown-14
76Laugh/Clown-25
Anderson, Steve 3
91Oneonta/ProC-4159
92Greens/ClBest-18
92Greens/ProC-784
Anderson, Tim
87Bakers-22
Anderson, Todd
91Pocatel/ProC-3794
91Pocatel/SportP-16
Anderson, Tom 1
78Watlo
Anderson, Tom 2
91AubAS/ClBest-8
92Ashvl/ClBest-4
Anderson, Varney S.
N172
Anderson, Walter Carl
No Cards.
Anderson, William E.
(Bill)
No Cards.
Anderson, William
(Bill)
No Cards.
Anderson, Wingo C.
(Wingo)
No Cards.
Andrade, Herberto
88Peoria/Ko-1
89CharWh/Best-13
89CharWh/ProC-1759
Andre, John Edward
No Cards.
Andres, Ernest Henry
(Ernie)
No Cards.
Andrews, Daniel
90GreatF/SportP-22
91GreatF/SportP-19
Andrews, Elbert D.
No Cards.
Andrews, Fred Jr.
76OkCty/Team-2
78Tidew
Andrews, George E.
N162
N172
N284
N690
WG1-46
Andrews, Hubert Carl
(Hub)
No Cards.
Andrews, Ivy Paul
32Orbit/num-1
32Orbit/un-2
35BU-106
35BU-115M
36Exh/4-15
92Conlon/Sport-420
R300
R305
R313
Andrews, James Pratt
(Jim)
No Cards.
Andrews, Jay III
91BBCity/ClBest-23
91BBCity/ProC-1409
Andrews, Jeff
87PortChar-12
88Tulsa-9CO
89Tulsa/GS-3
89Tulsa/Team-3CO
90Tulsa/ProC-1174CO
90Tulsa/Team-2
91AAA/LineD-303
91OkCty/LineD-303
91OkCty/ProC-194CO
92Jaxvl/SB-375CO
Andrews, John Richard
No Cards.
Andrews, John
88SanDiegoSt-2
89SanDiegoSt-1
Andrews, Michael Jay
(Mike)
67T-314R
67T/Test/RedSox-7
68CokeCap/RedSox-13
68Dexter-7
68T-502
69MB-14
69MLB/St-10
69OPC-52
69T-52
69T/St-131
70MLB/St-157
70OPC-406
70T-406
71OPC-191
71T-191
72MB-17
72OPC-361
72T-361
73OPC-42
73T-42
81TCMA-417
Andrews, Nathan H.
(Nate)
93Conlon-886
Andrews, Robert P.
(Rob)
75IntAS/TCMA-10
76OPC-568
76SSPC-54
76T-568
77T-209
78T-461
79Pol/Giants-21
79T-34
80T-279
Andrews, Shane
90Classic/DP-11
90Classic/III-88
91B-452
91OPC-74
91S-674FDP
91Sumter/ClBest-10
91Sumter/ProC-2339
91T-74
91T/CJMini/II-13
92Albany/ClBest-1
92Albany/ProC-2311
92ClBest-8
92ClBest/BBonusC-3
92ClBest/RBonus-BC3
92UD/ML-290
93B-378
93ClBest/MLG-71
93FExcel/ML-56
93Harris/ProC-273
93SALAS/II-1
93SALAS/IICS-13
94ClBest/Gold-90
94FExcel-222
94UD-2
94UD/ElecD-2
Andrews, Stanley J.
(Stan)
41G-24
90Target-18
Andrews, William W.
(Wally)
N172

Andrezejewski, Joe
89Helena/SP-1
90Beloit/Best-3
90Beloit/Star-1
90Foil/Best-52
90MidwLgAS/GS-2
91Erie/ClBest-15
91Erie/ProC-4059

Andrus, Frederick H.
(Fred)
No Cards.

Andrus, William M.
(Bill)
No Cards.

Andujar, Hector
91Watertn/ClBest-16
91Watertn/ProC-3371

Andujar, Joaquin
77T-67
78BK/Ast-7
78T-158
78T/Zest-1
79OPC-246
79T-471
80K-55
80OPC-324
80T-617
81D-381
81F-63
81F/St-48
81OPC-329
81T-329
81T/Tr-731
82D-607
82F-110
82T-533
83D-316
83D/AAS-27
83F-1
83F/St-15M
83F/St-27M
83OPC-228
83OPC/St-179WS
83T-228
83T-561TL
83T/St-179
84D-181
84F-319
84Nes/792-785
84OPC-371
84T-785
85D-13DK
85D-449
85D/DKsuper-13
85F-220
85F/St-85
85FunFood/Pin-90
85Leaf-13DK
85OPC-231
85Seven-6C
85T-655
85T/Gloss40-12
85T/St-136
85T/Super-38
86D-231
86F-26
86F/LimEd-2
86F/Up-U4
86KAS/Disc-11
86Mother/A's-4
86Mother/Ast-15
86OPC-150
86Sf-101
86Sf-133M
86Sf-185M
86T-150
86T/Mini-58
86T/St-44
86T/Tr-3T
87D-548
87F-385
87F/Hottest-1
87F/Mini-2
87Leaf-162
87OPC-284
87RedFoley/St-11
87Smok/A's-1
87T-775
87T/St-172
88Mother/Ast-26
88Pol/Ast-3
88S-193
88T-47
89S-472
89T/SenLg-93
89UD-79

Andujar, Juan
89Johnson/Star-2
90Foil/Best-13
90Spring/Best-1
91ClBest/Singl-80
91Spring/ClBest-2
91Spring/ProC-746
92StPete/ClBest-6
92StPete/ProC-2032
93Kinston/Team-1

Andujar, Luis
92SoBend/ClBest-4
92SoBend/ProC-168
94FExcel-33

Andux, Orlando
52Laval-107

Angel, Jason
92Billings/ProC-3346
92FrRow/DP-10
93StCl/MurphyS-33

Angelini, Norman S.
(Norm)
73OPC-616R
73T-616R
75Omaha/Team-1

Angelo, Mark
83Erie-12
84Savan-11

Anglero, Jose
87Omaha-2
88BBCity/Star-4
89BBCity/Star-4
90BBCity/Star-1
91Lakeland/ClBest-18
91Lakeland/ProC-271

Angley, Thomas S.
(Tom)
No Cards.

Anglin, Russ
83Ander-25

Angotti, Donald
90Osceola/Star-2
91AubAS/ClBest-12
91AubAS/ProC-4276
92Tucson/ProC-504CO

Angulo, Ken
83Redwd-2
85MidldA-15

Anicich, Mike
82Jacks-14
82Tidew-25
83MidldC-20

Ankenman, Fred N.
(Pat)
90Target-892

Annee, Tim
89Medford/Best-23

Annis, William P.
(Bill)
N172

Ansley, Willie
89Ashvl/ProC-950
89B-332
89SALAS/GS-3
89T-607FDP
90A&AASingle/ProC-57
90ColMud/Best-1
90ColMud/ProC-1356
90ColMud/Star-2
90Foil/Best-3
90ProC/Singl-810
90Star/ISingl-14
91AA/LineD-551
91B-549
91ClBest/Singl-135
91Jacks/LineD-551
91Jacks/ProC-935
92Jacks/ProC-4010

Anson, Adrian C.
(Cap)
50Callahan
50W576-2
60Exh/HOF-2
60F-44
61F-4
63Bz/ATG-39
69Bz/Sm
75F/Pion-1
76Shakey-21
77Shakey-12
80Perez/HOF-17
80SSPC/HOF
89HOF/St-5
90BBWit-66
90HOF/St-9
92Cub/OldStyle-2
E223
N162
N172
N28
N284
N300/unif
WG1-10

Anthony, Andy
86VeroB-1

Anthony, Dane
82Chatt-8
83Watlo/Frit-21

Anthony, Eric
89BBAmAA/BPro-AA11
89ColMud/Best-1
89ColMud/ProC-134
89ColMud/Star-2
89SLAS-3
89Star/Wax-1
89Tucson/JP-1
90B-81
90Classic-70
90ColMud/Star-3
90D-34
90D/BestNL-28
90D/Rook-49
90F-222
90F/Can-222
90HotRook/St-4
90Leaf-82
90Leaf/Prev-7
90Lennox-3
90Mother/Ast-3
90OPC-608
90Panini/St-379
90S-584
90S/100Ris-45
90S/DTRook-B10
90S/YS/I-42
90Sf-179
90T-608
90T/89Debut-5
90T/Big-197
90ToysRUs-2
90UD-28
91AAA/LineD-602
91B-540
91Classic/200-139
91Classic/II-T34
91D-333
91F-498
91Leaf-181
91Leaf/Stud-171
91MajorLg/Pins-44
91OPC-331
91S-146
91S/100RisSt-42
91StCl-229
91T-331
91T/CJMini/II-3
91Tucson/LineD-602
91Tucson/ProC-2223
91UD-533
91Ultra-131
92F-424
92Mother/Ast-7
92Pinn-363
92Pinn/Team2000-28
92S-315
92S/100RisSt-8
92StCl-575
92TripleP-18
93B-152
93Classic/GameI-5
93D-8
93DennyGS-2
93F-45
93Flair-56
93L-218
93Mother/Ast-8
93OPC-2
93Pac/Spanish-474
93Panini-176
93Pinn-84
93Pinn/HRC-34
93S-173
93Select-137
93StCl-141
93StCl/1stDay-141
93StCl/Ast-7
93Studio-3
93T-89
93T/Finest-179
93T/FinestRef-179
93T/Gold-89
93ToysRUs-49
93ToysRUs/MPhoto-2
93TripleP-109
93UD-183
93UD/HRH-HR22
93Ultra-389
94B-445
94D-480
94F-482
94Finest-349
94Flair-98
94L-229
94OPC-61
94Pac/Cr-256
94Panini-188
94Pinn-75
94Pinn/Artist-75
94Pinn/Museum-75
94S-400
94Studio-99
94T-182
94T/Gold-182
94TripleP-122
94UD-361
94UD/CollC-38
94UD/CollC/Gold-38
94UD/CollC/Silv-38
94UD/SP-102
94Ultra-202
94Ultra-415

Anthony, Greg Pepper
91Classic/DP-27
91FrRow/DP-19
92CharRain/ProC-111
92ClBest-51
92OPC-336
92StCl/Dome-7
92T-336DP
92T/Gold-336
92T/GoldWin-336

Anthony, Lee
49B/PCL-1

Anthony, Mark
90LitSun/HSPros-9
90LitSun/HSProsG-9
91Spokane/ClBest-12
91Spokane/ProC-3959
92B-449
92CharRain/ClBest-3
92CharRain/ProC-131
92UD/ML-125

Anthony, Paul
77Salem

Antigua, Felix
89Augusta/ProC-497
89Princet/Star-2
89Star/IISingl-173
90Augusta/ProC-2466
90SALAS/Star-26

Antigua, Jose
93WSox-30CO

Antolick, Jeff
92Oneonta/ClBest-26
93Greens/ClBest-2
93Greens/ProC-876

Antolick, Joseph
(Joe)
No Cards.

Antonelli, John A.
(Johnny)
49Eureka-3
50B-74
51B-243
52T-140
53JC-2
53SpicSpan/3x5-2
53T-106
54B-208
54NYJour
54RM-NL21
54T-119
55Armour-1
55B-124
55Gol/Giants-2
55RM-NL13
56T-138
57T-105
58Hires-50
58Hires/T
58PacBell-2
58SFCallB-1
58T-152
59Armour-2
59T-377
60Bz-35
60T-572AS
60T-80
60T/tatt-3
61P-142
61T-115
61T/St-132
80Marchant-1
84Mother/Giants-13
91T/Arc53-106
92Bz/Quadra-22
94T/Arc54-119
Exh47
PM10/Sm-4
PM10/Sm-5
Rawl

Antonelli, John L.
83Beloit/Frit-6

Antonello, William J.
(Bill)
53T-272
72T/Test-5
90Target-19
91T/Arc53-272

Antonini, Adrian
92LSU/McDag-2
93LSU/McDag-9
94LSU-5

Antoon, Jeff
92Eugene/ClBest-5
92Eugene/ProC-3034
93Rockford/ClBest-2

Antunez, Martin
82Beloit/Frit-23

Anyzeski, Fred
75AppFx

Aparicio, Luis E.
56T-292
56YellBase/Pin-3
57T-7
58T-483AS
58T-85
59T-310
59T-408M
59T-560AS
60Bz-22
60L-1
60T-240
60T-559AS
61Bz-35
61P-19
61T-440
61T-574AS
61T/St-120
62Bz
62Exh
62J-49
62P-49
62P/Can-49
62Salada-71
62Shirriff-71
62T-325
62T-469AS
62T/St-22
63Exh
63J-37
63P-37
63Salada-50
63T-205
63T/SO
64T-540
64T/Coins-127AS
64T/Coins-31
64T/S-39
64Wheat/St-3
65T-410
65T/trans-3
66OPC-90
66T-90
67CokeCap/Orio-2
67OPC-60
67T-60
68CokeCap/Orio-2
68T-310
69Kelly/Pin-1
69MB-15
69MLB/St-28
69MLBPA/Pin-2

69OPC-75
69OPC/DE-2
69T-75
69T/DE-6
69T/S-10
69T/St-152
69T/decal
69Trans-24
70K-22
70MLB/St-181
70OPC-315
70T-315
70T/S-3
70T/SO
70T/Super-3
71Bz
71Bz/Test-8
71K-19
71MD
71MLB/St-313
71MLB/St-554
71OPC-740
71T-740
71T/Coins-16
71T/GM-51
71T/Greatest-51
71T/S-23
71T/Super-23
71T/tatt-6
72MB-18
72OPC-313
72OPC-314IA
72T-313
72T-314A
72T/Cloth-2IA
73OPC-165
73T-165
74OPC-61
74T-61
74T/St-131
77Galasso-42
78TCMA-250
80Perez/HOF-185
81TCMA-358
84TrueVal/WS-2
84West/1-2
86Sf/Dec-37M
87Nestle/DT-15
88Grenada-28
88Pac/Leg-91
89HOF/St-18
89Kodak/WSox-6M
90BBWit-23
90MSA/AGFA-9
90Perez/GreatMom-43
91Crown/Orio-12
93AP/ASG-122
93AP/ASG24K-56G
93TWill-25
Exh47

Apodaca, Robert John
(Bob)
74OPC-608R
74T-608R
75OPC-659
75T-659
75T/M-659
76OPC-16
76SSPC-548
76SSPC/MetsY-M15
76T-16
77T-225
78T-592
79OPC-98
79T-197
80T-633
82Jacks-23
86Columbia-1CO
87Columbia-2CO
89Jacks/GS-21CO
90Jacks/GS-4CO
91AAA/LineD-575M
91Tidew/LineD-575CO
91Tidew/ProC-2527CO
91WIZMets-13
92Tidew/ProC-CO
92Tidew/SB-575M

Apolinario, Oswaldo
90BurlB/Best-6
90BurlB/ProC-2354
90BurlB/Star-1

Aponte, Edwin
80SanJose/JITB-2
81LynnS-15
83Watlo/Frit-2
84BuffB-19

Aponte, Luis Eduardo
81Pawtu-8
83D-109
83F-178
83T-577
84D-371
84F-389
84F/X-2
84Nes/792-187
84T-187
84T/Tr-2
84Wheat/Ind-38
85F-437

Aponte, Newlan
89Wythe/Star-1

Aponte, Ricardo
(Rick)
78DaytB
87AubAs-19
90Ashvl/ClBest-27CO
90Ashvl/ProC-2765CO
91Ashvl/ProC-585CO
92BurlAs/ClBest-27CO
92BurlAs/ProC-564

Appier, Kevin
88BBCity/Star-5
89F/Up-35
89Omaha/CMC-4
89Omaha/ProC-1720
90B-367
90D/Rook-21
90F-100
90F/Can-100
90OPC-167
90S-625
90S/100Ris-13
90T-167
90T/89Debut-6
90UD-102
91B-309
91Bz-21
91D-740
91F-549
91OPC-454
91Panini/Top15-72
91Panini/Top15-95
91Pol/Royal-1
91S-268
91S/100RisSt-73
91StCl-501
91T-454
91T/JumboR-2
91ToysRUs-2
91UD-566
91Ultra-143
92B-640
92D-455
92F-150
92L-31
92L/BlkGold-31
92OPC-281
92Pinn-434
92Pinn/Team2000-5
92Pol/Royal-1
92S-542
92StCl-523
92T-281
92T/Gold-281
92T/GoldWin-281
92TripleP-8
92UD-159
92UD/TmMVPHolo-5
92Ultra-66
93B-41
93Cadaco-1
93D-43
93F-235
93Flair-212
93L-101
93OPC-23
93Pac/Spanish-131
93Panini-101
93Pinn-133
93Pol/Royal-2
93S-154
93Select-102
93Select/Ace-9
93Select/StatL-80
93StCl-374
93StCl/1stDay-374
93StCl/Royal-5
93T-76
93T/Finest-78
93T/FinestRef-78
93T/Gold-76
93T/Hill-8
93TripleP-234
93UD-89
93UD/FunPack-180
93UD/SP-226
93USPlayC/Ace-10S
93Ultra-556
94B-555
94D-47
94D/Special-47
94F-147
94F/LL-6
94Flair-54
94L-70
94OPC-225
94Oscar-2
94Pac/Cr-279
94Panini-71
94Pinn-48
94Pinn/Artist-48
94Pinn/Museum-48
94S-359
94Select-64
94Sf/2000-84
94StCl-340
94StCl/1stDay-340
94StCl/Gold-340
94T-701
94T/Finest-174
94T/FinestRef-174
94T/Gold-701
94TripleP-231
94UD-133
94UD/ElecD-133
94UD/HoloFX-2
94UD/SP-170
94Ultra-61

Applegate, Fred
No Cards.

Applegate, Russ
84Idaho/Team-1
85Madis-5
85Madis/Pol-2
86Modesto-3

Appleton, Edward Sam
(Ed)
90Target-893
D328-6
E135-6

Appleton, Peter W.
(Pete)
33G-83
39PlayBall-137
40PlayBall-128
91Conlon/Sport-76

Appling, Lucas B.
(Luke)
31Exh/4-19
34DS-95
34Exh/4-10
34G-27
35BU-124
35G-1I
35G-2F
35G-6F
35G-7F
36Exh/4-10
36Wheat-3
37Exh/4-10
37OPC-115
38Exh/4-10
39Exh
40Wheat-12
41DP-70
42PlayBall-16
48L-59
49B-175
49Royal-16
50B-37
60F-27
60T-461C
76Rowe-1
76Shakey-95
77Galasso-80
80Pac/Leg-22
80Perez/HOF-95
80SSPC/HOF
83D/HOF-8
84Pol/Atl-55C
88Conlon/AmAS-1
88Pac/Leg-4
89Kodak/WSox-6M
89Swell-30
90Pac/Legend-3
90Swell/Great-18
91Swell/Great-3
92Conlon/Gold-730
92Conlon/Sport-475
93Conlon-730
93TWill-26
94Conlon-1008
Exh47
PR1-1
R303/A
R303/B
R314
R326-7A
R326-7B
R342-7
R346-10
V300
V351B-1
V354-84
V355-113
WG8-1

Aquedo, Vasquez
87FtMyr-16

Aquino, Luis
86Syrac-2
87D-655
87OPC-301
87Syrac-10
87Syrac/TCMA-1
87T-301
88Omaha/CMC-2
88Omaha/ProC-1520
89D-534
89F-275
89T-266
90D-179
90F-101
90F/Can-101
90OPC-707
90PublInt/St-341
90S-432
90T-707
90UD-274
91D-718
91F-550
91OPC-169
91Pol/Royal-2
91StCl-451
91T-169
91UD-504
92D-544
92F-151
92OPC-412
92Pinn-454
92Pol/Royal-2
92S-369
92StCl-365
92T-412
92T/Gold-412
92T/GoldWin-412
92UD-219
93F-615
93F/Final-48
93L-509
93Marlin/Publix-1
93Pac/Spanish-130
93Pol/Royal-3
93T-643
93T/Gold-643
93T/Tr-76T
93UD-711
93Ultra-363
94D-67
94F-458
94Pac/Cr-233
94Pinn-223
94Pinn/Artist-223
94Pinn/Museum-223
94S-255
94S/GoldR-255
94StCl-160
94StCl/1stDay-160
94StCl/Gold-160
94T-76
94T/Gold-76
94UD/CollC-39
94UD/CollC/Gold-39
94UD/CollC/Silv-39
94Ultra-191

Aquino, Pedro
87Spokane-20
88Spokane/ProC-1929

Arace, Pasquale
91Augusta/ClBest-19
91Augusta/ProC-816
92Salem/ClBest-8
92Salem/ProC-74

Aracena, Luinis
92Madis/ClBest-14
92Madis/ProC-1247

Aragon, Angel V. Jr.
(Jack)
No Cards.

Aragon, Angel V. Sr.
No Cards.

Aragon, Joey
86Visalia-2
87Visalia-19
88OrlanTw/Best-11

Aragon, Reno
76Dubuq
77Cocoa

Aragon, Steve
82Wisco/Frit-23
83Visalia/Frit-3
84Visalia-24
85OrlanTw-1
86OrlanTw-1

Arai, Kiyoshi
92Salinas/ClBest-1
92Salinas/ProC-3761

Arango, Fernando
92Oneonta/ClBest-29CO

Arangure, Maurillo
85Tigres-3

Aranzamendi, Alexis
92FrRow/DP-72

Aranzamendi, Jorge
77StPete
79ArkTr-12
80ArkTr-3
81ArkTr-8
82ArkTr-24
83ArkTr-24

Aranzullo, Mike
91SLCity/ProC-3215
91SLCity/SportP-7

Araujo, Andy
86NewBrit-1
87Pawtu-14
87Pawtu/TCMA-1
88Pawtu/CMC-5
88Pawtu/ProC-446
89Pawtu/CMC-8
89Pawtu/Dunkin-23
89Pawtu/ProC-679
93LimeR/Winter-114

Archdeacon, Flash
94Conlon-1307

Archdeacon, Maurice
No Cards.

Archer, Carl
91Pulaski/ClBest-4
91Pulaski/ProC-4010

Archer, James Peter
(Jimmy)
09Buster/Pin-1
10Domino-2
11Helmar-90
12Sweet/Pin-79A
12Sweet/Pin-79B
14CJ-64
15CJ-64
90Target-20
93Conlon-884
BF2-62
D328-7
D329-6
D350/2-6
E135-7
E224
E254
E90/3
E91
M101/4-6
M101/5-6
M116
PM1-1
T202
T204
T205
T222
WG4-1

Archer, James William
(Jim)

61T-552
62J-98
62P-98
62Salada-75
62Shirriff-75
62T-433
62T/St-52
62T/bucks
Archer, Kurt
90Helena/SportP-15
90SDSt-1
91ClBest/Singl-223
91Stockton/ClBest-8
91Stockton/ProC-3023
92Stockton/ClBest-22
92Stockton/ProC-26
Archibald, Dan
88James/ProC-1920
89James/ProC-2142
90Rockford/ProC-2684
90Rockford/Team-1
Archibald, Jaime
86Columbia-2
87Lynch-9
Archie, George Albert
No Cards.
Arcia, Jose R. Orta
68T-258R
69MB-16
69T-473
69T/St-91
70T-587
71MLB/St-217
71OPC-134
71T-134
72MB-19
73OPC-466
73T-466
Ard, Johnny
89AS/Cal-13
89B-153
89Visalia/Cal-96
89Visalia/ProC-1427
90A&AASingle/ProC-39
90B-406
90Foil/Best-60
90OrlanSR/Best-23
90OrlanSR/ProC-1075
90OrlanSR/Star-1
90ProC/Singl-809
91AAA/LineD-385
91B-634
91Phoenix/LineD-385
91Phoenix/ProC-58
92Phoenix/ProC-2814
92Phoenix/SB-376
92ProC/Tomorrow-342
92Sky/AAASingl-173
Ardell, Daniel Miers
(Dan)
No Cards.
Ardizoia, Rinaldo J.
(Rugger)
46Remar-20
Ardner, Joseph
N172
Arduini, Salvatore
52Laval-84
Arellanes, Frank J.
E96
M116
T204
T206
Arena, Rich
89Oneonta/ProC-2120
90Greens/Best-29CO
90Greens/ProC-2681CO
90Greens/Star-26CO
90Tampa/DIMD-28CO
92GulfCY/ProC-3707
Arena, Sam
92FtLaud/Team-1EQMG
Arendas, Dan
87FtLaud-13
88FtLaud/Star-1
Arendas, David
88CapeCod/Sum-100
Arendt, Jim
91Princet/ClBest-29
Arft, Henry Irven
(Hank)
49B-139
51B-173
52B-229
52T-284
53Mother-26
Argo, Billy
88Bakers/Cal-244
89VeroB/Star-1
Arguelles, Fernando
89Salem/Star-2
90SanBern/Best-16
90SanBern/Cal-100
90SanBern/ProC-2636
91AA/LineD-326
91Jaxvl/LineD-326
91Jaxvl/ProC-152
Arias, Alex
88CharWh/Best-9
88SALAS/GS-13
89Peoria/Team-17
90CharlK/Team-5
90T/TVCub-36
91AA/LineD-126
91CharlK/LineD-126
91CharlK/ProC-1693
91ClBest/Singl-10
92F/Up-72
92Iowa/ProC-4055
92Iowa/SB-202
92OPC-551M
92ProC/Tomorrow-202
92Sky/AAASingl-96
92T-551M
92T/Gold-551M
92T/GoldWin-551M
93Classic/GameI-6
93D-254M
93D-4
93D-780
93F/Final-49
93F/MLPI-16
93Flair-45
93L-462
93Marlin/Publix-2
93OPC/Premier-84
93Pac/Spanish-452
93Pinn-483I
93Pinn-612
93S-565
93StCl-741
93StCl/1stDay-741
93StCl/Marlin-4
93T-516
93T/Gold-516
93UD-631
93USPlayC/Marlin-1S
93USPlayC/Marlin-7H
93Ultra-364
94D-97
94F-459
94Pac/Cr-234
94Pinn-390
94S-199
94S/GoldR-199
94Select-137
94StCl-230
94StCl/1stDay-230
94StCl/Gold-230
94StCl/Team-85
94T-104
94T/Gold-104
Arias, Amador
91Cedar/ClBest-16
91Cedar/ProC-2724
91ClBest/Singl-340
91Erie/ClBest-1
91Erie/ProC-4074
92CharWh/ClBest-20
92CharWh/ProC-13
Arias, Francisco
87Pocatel/Bon-26
88Augusta//ProC-2078
Arias, George
94T-369M
94T/Gold-369M
Arias, German
90Martins/ProC-3207
Arias, Jose
90Hamil/Star-2
90Savan/ProC-2058
91Johnson/ClBest-27
Arias, Juan
78Salem
79BuffB/TCMA-11
Arias, Pedro
88BurlInd/ProC-1787
Arias, Rodolfo M.
(Rudy)
59T-537
Arias, Tony
85Madis/Pol-3
86Madis/Pol-2
88Modesto-19
Arigoni, Scott
82ArkTr-1
83Spring/Frit-9
Ariola, Anthony
88SoOreg/ProC-1696
89Madis/Star-2
89Star/Wax-64
90AAASingl/ProC-131
90ProC/Singl-581
90Tacoma/CMC-4
90Tacoma/ProC-84
Arita, Shuzo
91Salinas/ClBest-27CO
91Salinas/ProC-2261CO
Arland, Mark
90CharWh/Best-20
90CharWh/ProC-2250
91CharWh/ClBest-21
91CharWh/ProC-2898
Arlas, Antonio
85Madis-6
Arlett, Russell Loris
(Buzz)
28Exh/PCL-1
31Exh/4-11
WG7-1
Arlich, Donald Louis
(Don)
No Cards.
Arlin, Stephen Ralph
(Steve)
72OPC-78
72T-78
73OPC-294
73T-294
74OPC-406
74T-406
75OPC-159
75T-159
75T/M-159
Arline, James
78Richm
79Richm-23
Armas, Antonio Rafael
(Tony)
77T-492R
78T-298
79T-507
80T-391
81A's/Granny-20
81D-239
81Drake-30
81F-575
81F/St-5
81OPC-151
81Sqt-24
81T-629
81T/SO-6
81T/St-116
82D-365
82Drake-1
82F-85
82F/St-128
82Granny
82K-35
82OPC-60
82PermaGr/CC-17
82T-162LL
82T-60
82T/St-224
82T/St-4LL
83D-71
83F-513
83OPC-353
83OPC/St-108
83OPC/St-191RB
83OPC/St-192RB
83T-1RB
83T-435
83T/St-108
83T/St-191
83T/St-192
83T/Tr-4
84D-294
84F-390
84F/St-21
84Nes/792-105
84OPC-105
84T-105
84T/Gloss40-20
84T/RD-1
84T/St-218
85D-249
85Drake-1
85F-149
85F/St-12
85F/St-28
85FunFood/Pin-24
85Leaf-112
85OPC-394
85T-707AS
85T-785
85T/Gloss40-18
85T/RD-1
85T/St-194
85T/St-209
85T/St-95
85T/Super-10
86D-127
86D-5
86D/DKsuper-5
86F-339
86Leaf-5DK
86OPC-255
86Sf-140M
86Sf-61M
86T-255
86T/St-254
86T/Tatt-11M
86Woolwth-1
87D-498
87F-26
87Mother/A's-21
87OPC-174
87T-535
87T/Board-15
88F-484
88S-487
88Smok/Angels-5
88T-761
89B-51
89D-580
89F-467
89Panini/St-295
89S-182
89T-332
89T/Big-99
89UD-212
90D-525
90F-126
90F/Can-126
90OPC-603
90PublInt/St-364
90S-378
90T-603
90UD-58
Armas, Marcos
89Medford/Best-24
90Madison/Best-4
91AA/LineD-276
91Huntsvl/ClBest-1
91Huntsvl/LineD-276
91HuntsvlProC-1807
91Modesto/ProC-3093
92ClBest-134
92Huntsvl/ProC-3955
92Huntsvl/SB-302
92Sky/AASingl-127
93B-429
93ClBest/MLG-20
93F/Final-253
93L-478
93T/Tr-100T
94D-51
94F-253
94Pac/Cr-444
94Pinn-398
94T-311
94T/Gold-311
Armbrister, Edison R.
(Ed)
72OPC-524R
72T-524R
74OPC-601R
74T-601R
75OPC-622R
75T-622R
75T/M-622R
76OPC-652
76SSPC-42
76T-652
77T-203
78Indianap-8
78SSPC/270-124
78T-556
Armbrust, Orville M.
No Cards.
Armbruster, Charles
No Cards.
Armbruster, Herman
(Harry)
T206
Armer, Rick
77Wausau
Armstrong, Bill
79Memphis/TCMA-3TR
Armstrong, Eldridge Jr.
84Idaho/Team-2
Armstrong, George N.
No Cards.
Armstrong, Howard E.
No Cards.
Armstrong, Jack
88Kahn/Reds-40
88Nashvl/CMC-1
88Nashvl/ProC-484
88Nashvl/Team-1
88S/Tr-78T
88T/Tr-6T
89AAA/CMC-12
89Classic-97
89D-493
89Panini/St-63
89S-462
89S/HotRook-99
89T-317
89UD-257
90Classic/III-74
90D-544
90D/BestNL-142
90F-412
90F/Can-412
90Kahn/Reds-1
90Leaf-374
90OPC-642
90S/YS/II-11
90T-642
90T/Big-314
90TripleAAS/CMC-12
90UD-684
91B-679
91BBBest/Aces-2
91Classic/200-6
91D-439AS
91D-571
91F-55
91Kahn/Reds-40
91Kenner-3
91Leaf-459
91OPC-175
91Panini/FrSt-165
91Panini/St-126
91Pep/Reds-1
91RedFoley/St-114
91S-231
91S/100SS-83
91StCl-510
91T-175
91UD-373
91USPlayC/AS-JK
92B-252
92D-762
92F-398
92Indian/McDon-2
92L-247
92L/BlkGold-247
92OPC-77
92OPC/Premier-192
92S-488
92S/RookTr-58T
92StCl-791
92Studio-162
92T-77
92T/Gold-77
92T/GoldWin-77
92T/Tr-6T
92T/TrGold-6T
92UD-296
92UD-789
92Ultra-344
93D-69
93D-777
93F-417
93F/Final-50

93Flair-46
93L-235
93Marlin/Publix-3
93Pac/Spanish-453
93Pinn-513
93S-655
93StCl-567
93StCl/1stDay-567
93StCl/Marlin-9
93T-434
93T/Gold-434
93T/Tr-80T
93UD-758
93USPlayC/Marlin-11S
93USPlayC/Marlin-2D
93Ultra-365
94D-466
94F-460
94Flair-107
94L-226
94Pac/Cr-235
94Pinn-166
94Pinn/Artist-166
94Pinn/Museum-166
94S-410
94StCl/Team-256
94T-551
94T/Gold-551
94UD-469
94UD/CollC-40
94UD/CollC/Gold-40
94UD/CollC/Silv-40
Armstrong, Jim
91Idaho/ProC-4319
91Idaho/SportP-10
Armstrong, Kevin
85LitFalls-2
86Columbia-3
87Wichita-2
88River/Cal-206
89SanAn/Best-6
Armstrong, Michael D.
(Mike)
80Hawaii-16
81F-503
81Hawaii/TCMA-11
82Omaha-1
82T-731
83F-105
83T-219
84D-217
84F-342
84Nes/792-417
84T-417
84T/Tr-3
85D-602
85F-120
85T-612
86Colum-1
86Colum/Pol-1
87Colum-25
87Colum/Pol-1
92Yank/WIZ80-4
Armstrong, William
83Evansvl-23TR
84Evansvl-20TR
Arnason, Chuck
72Dimanche*-66
Arndt, Harry J.
T206
Arndt, Larry
86Madis/Pol-3
89Tacoma/CMC-22
89Tacoma/ProC-1557
90AAASingl/ProC-144
90ProC/Singl-600
90T/89Debut-7
90Tacoma/CMC-23
90Tacoma/ProC-97
Arner, Michael
90A&AASingle/ProC-80
90Foil/Best-200
90Gaston/Best-19
90Gaston/ProC-2511
90Gaston/Star-1
90ProC/Singl-479
90SALAS/Star-1
90Star/ISingl-96
91CharlR/ClBest-1
91CharlR/ProC-1305
92CharlR/ClBest-24
Arnerich, Ken
82QuadC-18
Arnett, Curt
74Gaston
Arnette, Steve
89TNTech-1
Arney, Jeff
82Wisco/Frit-25
83Visalia/Frit-2
85Water-14
86Water-1
Arnold, Bryan
88Watertn/Pucko-14
Arnold, Chris
72OPC-232R
72T-232R
73OPC-584
73T-584
74OPC-432
74T-432
76SSPC-99
77Phoenix
77T-591
Arnold, Gary
88Geneva/ProC-1636
Arnold, Greg
89Pulaski/ProC-1912
Arnold, Jamie
92ClBest/BBonusC-25
92ClBest/Up-407
92Classic/DP-16
92Classic/DPFoil-BC15
92UD/ML-12
93ClBest/MLG-110
93Macon/ClBest-2
93Macon/ProC-1391
93Pinn-455DP
93S-487DP
93Select-303DP
93StCl/MurphyS-65
93T-559
93T/Gold-559
94ClBest/Gold-113
94FExcel-151
Arnold, Jeff
84Newar-25
Arnold, Ken
91Hunting/ClBest-3
91Hunting/ProC-3339
92Peoria/ClBest-27
92Peoria/Team-2
92ProC/Tomorrow-212
Arnold, Ron
84Albany-2
84Cram/PCL-75
Arnold, Scott
86FSLAS-5
86StPete-2
87ArkTr-13
87TexLgAS-21
88Louisvl-8
88TexLgAS/GS-20
89Louisvl-9
89Louisvl/CMC-2
89Louisvl/ProC-1248
90AAASingl/ProC-508
90Louisvl/CMC-1
90Louisvl/LBC-7
90Louisvl/ProC-394
90ProC/Singl-101
90SpringDG/Best-18
90T/TVCard-38
Arnold, Sheila
88Geneva/ProC-1660
Arnold, Tim
86FSLAS-6
86WPalmB-2
87Jaxvl-2
88Visalia/Cal-149
88Visalia/ProC-97
89OrlanTw/Best-8
89OrlanTw/ProC-1353
Arnold, Tony
84CharlO-26
85CharlO-8
86RochR-1
87French-57
88Albuq/CMC-5
88Albuq/ProC-261
89SanAn/Best-5
90Yakima/Team-19CO
91Crown/Orio-13
91Yakima/ProC-4265CO
92TX-3
92Yakima/ClBest-26CO
Arnovich, Morris
(Morrie)
38Exh/4-6
39PlayBall-46
40PlayBall-97
40Wheat-4
41DP-139
41G-25
41G-25
41PlayBall-57
92Conlon/Sport-500
V351A-1
W711/2
Arnsberg, Brad
84Greens-10
85Albany-1
86Colum-2
86Colum/Pol-2
87Colum-28
87Colum/Pol-2
87Colum/TCMA-1
88F-202
88T-159
89Mother/R-15
89Smok/R-2
90AAASingl/ProC-669
90AlbanyDG/Best-27
90Leaf-495
90OkCty/CMC-7
90OkCty/ProC-423
90ProC/Singl-157
90S/100Ris-72
90T/Tr-3T
91B-279
91D-633
91F-279
91Mother/Rang-25
91OPC-706A
91OPC-706B
91S-510
91StCl-540
91T-706A
91T-706B
91UD-608
91Ultra-346
92ColoSp/ProC-742
92F-298
92Indian/McDon-3
92Iowa/ProC-4045
92StCl-668
92Yank/WIZ80-5
93Pac/Spanish-92
93Rang/Keeb-54
Arnsberg, Tim
86Ashvl-1
87Osceola-26
Arntzen, Brian
90NE-2
92Watertn/ClBest-15
92Watertn/ProC-3237
Arntzen, Orie Edgar
No Cards.
Arocha, Rene
92AAA/ASG/SB-251
92Louisvl/ProC-1879
92Louisvl/SB-251
92Sky/AAASingl-122
92UD/ML-136
93B-276
93D-572RR
93F/Final-123
93FExcel/ML-95
93Flair-119
93L/GRook-15
93OPC/Premier-6
93Pac/Beisbol-29M
93Pac/Spanish-628
93Pinn-599
93Pol/Card-2
93Select/RT/ASRook-9
93Select/RookTr-62T
93StCl-712
93StCl/1stDay-712
93StCl/Card-2
93T-742
93T/Gold-742
93T/Tr-77T
93ToysRUs-78
93UD-3SR
93UD/SP-73
93Ultra-460
93Ultra/AllRook-1
94B-208
94D-60
94F-628
94F/RookSen-1
94Flair-223
94L-228
94OPC-234
94Pac/Cr-586
94Pinn-107
94Pinn/Artist-107
94Pinn/Museum-107
94S-164
94S/GoldR-164
94StCl-306
94StCl/1stDay-306
94StCl/Gold-306
94StCl/Team-315
94T-348
94T/Finest-5
94T/FinestRef-5
94T/Gold-348
94UD-191
94UD/CollC-41
94UD/CollC/Gold-41
94UD/CollC/Silv-41
94UD/ElecD-191
94Ultra-264
Arola, Bruce
88Madis-2
89Boise/ProC-1996
91Salinas/ClBest-22
91Salinas/ProC-2234
92Salinas/ProC-3748
Aronetz, Cam
91GreatF/SportP-22
92Bakers/Cal-2
Arredondo, Joe
90Pittsfld/Pucko-6
91Pittsfld/ClBest-13
91Pittsfld/ProC-3427
Arredondo, Roberto
90CharRain/Best-9
90CharRain/ProC-2045
91MidwLAS/ProC-29
91Waterlo/ClBest-14
91Waterlo/ProC-1261
92ClBest-10
92HighD/ClBest-6
92ProC/Tomorrow-338
Arriete, Nelson
88MissSt-1
89MissSt-3
Arrigo, Gerald W.
(Jerry)
64T-516R
65OPC-39
65T-39
66T-357
67T-488
68Kahn
68T-302
69Kahn
69OPC-213
69T-213
69T/4in1-14M
69T/St-22
70OPC-274
70T-274
72MB-20
78TCMA-64
78TCMA-86
91WIZMets-14
Arrington, Dave
74Wichita-122
Arrington, Sam
82Amari-23
82OrlanTw-23
83Visalia/Frit-4
Arrington, Tom
86BurlEx-1
Arrington, Warren
88Peoria/Ko-2
89Peoria/Team-23
Arroyd, Freddie
86SanJose-1
Arroyo, Carlos R.
79OkCty
80OkCty
81OkCty/TCMA-2
86Clearw-1CO
87Clearw-15CO
88Reading/ProC-888CO
90Batavia/ProC-3084CO
91Batavia/ClBest-18CO
91Batavia/ProC-3501CO
92Reading/ProC-592CO
92Reading/SB-550CO
Arroyo, Felipe
80Ander-11
Arroyo, Fernando
76OPC-614
76T-614
78T-607
81T-408
82D-177
82F-546
82T-18
82T-396TL
91Lakeland/ClBest-17CO
91Lakeland/ProC-283CO
93Edmon/ProC-1153CO
Arroyo, Hector
81CharR-2
Arroyo, Luis Enrique
56T-64
56T/Pin-45
57T-394
61T-142
61T/St-188
62J-12
62P-12
62P/Can-12
62T-455
63T-569
78TCMA-258
92Yank/WIZ60-3
92Yank/WIZAS-1
PM10/L-2
Arroyo, Rudolph Jr.
(Rudy)
No Cards.
Arsenault, Ed
75SanAn
76Wmsprt
Arst, Matt
90WichSt-3
Arteaga, Ivan
93BurlB/ClBest-3
93BurlB/ProC-148
Artiaga, Sal
90AS/Cal-28COM
Arundel, Harry
No Cards.
Arundel, John Thomas
(Tug)
N172
N284
Arvelo, Thomas
92GulfCM/ProC-3486
Arvesen, Scott
89Welland/Pucko-2
90Augusta/ProC-2455
91Augusta/ClBest-2
91Augusta/ProC-795
Arzola, Richard
86StPete-3
Asadoor, Randy
84Tulsa-18
85Cram/PCL-116
86LasVegas-1
87D-574
87F-650M
87LasVegas-7
87Sf-158M
87Sf/TPrev-16M
Asai, Itsuki
90Gate/ProC-3345
90Gate/SportP-2
Asano, Keishi
92Salinas/ClBest-29CO
92Salinas/ProC-3774CO
Asbe, Daryl
86BurlEx-2
Asbell, Frank
40Hughes-2AS
Asbell, James Marion
(Jim)
No Cards.
Asbell, John
81Watlo-5
Asbill, Darin
88MissSt-2
89MissSt-4
Asbjornson, Robert A.
(Asby)
94Conlon-1315
Ascencio, Juan
86Cram/NWL-152

Asche, Scott
91Miami/ClBest-5
91Miami/ProC-399
Aschoff, Jerry
92Belling/ClBest-4
92Belling/ProC-1432
Ash, Kenneth Lowther
(Ken)
92Conlon/Sport-601
Ashburn, Don Richard
(Richie)
49B-214
49Eureka-127
49Lummis
50B-84
51B-186
51BR-A9
51T/BB-3
52B-53
52BR
52Dix
52RM-NL2
52StarCal-89C
52StarCal/L-77A
52T-216
53B/Col-10
53Dix
53NB
53RM-NL3
54B-15
54Dix
54RH
54RM-NL1
54T-45
55B-130
55RFG-22
55RM-NL1
55W605-22
56T-120
56YellBase/Pin-4
57Swift-17
57T-70
58Hires-10
58T-230
59Armour-3
59Bz
59T-300
59T-317M
60Bz-24
60MacGregor-2
60T-305
60T/tatt-4
60T/tatt-87
61P-192
61T-88
61T/St-3
62J-186
62P-186
62P/Can-186
62Salada-171
62Shirriff-171
62T-213
62T/bucks
63J-197
63P-197
63Salada-27
63T-135
63T/SO
77Galasso-14
79TCMA-17
80Marchant-2
80Pac/Leg-94
85West/2-38
88Pac/Leg-8
88Phill/TastyK-39ANN
89B/Ins-1
89Swell-85
90Pac/Legend-70
90Phill/TastyK-29
90Phill/TastyK-35BC
91Swell/Great-4
91T/Arc53-311
91WIZMets-15
92AP/ASG-24
92Bz/Quadra-5
93TWill-70
94T/Arc54-45
Exh47
PM10/Sm-6
R423-1
Rawl
Ashby, Alan Dean
76OPC-209
76SSPC-514
76T-209
77Ho-124
77Ho/Twink-124
77OPC-148
77T-564
77T/CS-1
77T/ClothSt-1
78BJ/PostC-1
78OPC-76
78T-319
79Ho-142
79OPC-14
79T-36
80OPC-105
80T-187
81Coke
81D-259
81F-64
81OPC-146
81T-696
82D-317
82F-212
82OPC-184
82T-433
82T/St-48
83D-144
83F-445
83F/St-11M
83F/St-12M
83F/St-7M
83OPC-84
83OPC/St-241
83T-774
83T/St-241
84D-539
84F-220
84Mother/Ast-3
84Nes/792-217
84OPC-217
84T-217
84T/St-72
85D-283
85F-343
85Mother/Ast-13
85OPC-29
85T-564
86D-405
86F-292
86OPC-331
86Pol/Ast-8
86T-331
87D-332
87D/OD-17
87F-50
87Mother/Ast-11
87Pol/Ast-21
87T-112
88D-163
88D/Best-8
88F-439
88KennerFig-1
88Mother/Ast-11
88OPC-48
88Panini/St-291
88Pol/Ast-4
88RedFoley/St-2
88S-73
88Sf-219
88T-48
88T/St-32
89B-327
89D-88
89F-350
89Mother/Ast-10
89OPC-359
89RedFoley/St-4
89S-366
89T-492
89T/DH-20
89UD-305
90EliteSenLg-63
90MLBPA/Pins-39
Ashby, Andrew
(Andy)
86Cram/NWL-139
87Spartan-13
90A&AASingle/ProC-22
90Foil/Best-46
90ProC/Singl-784
90Reading/Best-7
90Reading/ProC-1211
90Reading/Star-3
91AAA/LineD-478
91B-485
91F/Up-U105
91Phill/Medford-2
91ScranWB/LineD-478
91ScranWB/ProC-2530
91StCl/Member*-2
91UD/FinalEd-64F
92B-286
92Classic/Game200-200
92Classic/I-T6
92D-11RR
92F-521
92L-405
92L/BlkGold-405
92OPC-497
92Phill/Med-3
92Pinn-265
92ProC/Tomorrow-294
92S-396
92S/Rook-18
92StCl-717
92T-497
92T/91Debut-5
92T/Gold-497
92T/GoldWin-497
92TripleP-128
92UD-19SR
92UD/Scout-SR1
92Ultra-541
93D-743
93F-401
93F/Final-21
93Pac/Spanish-420
93Pinn-572
93StCl-700
93StCl/1stDay-700
93StCl/Rockie-18
93T-794
93T/Gold-794
93UD-763
93USPlayC/Rockie-10C
93USPlayC/Rockie-3H
93Ultra-339
94D-70
94F-652
94L-32
94StCl-524
94StCl/1stDay-524
94StCl/Gold-524
94T-648
94T/Gold-648
94Ultra-275
94Finest-255
Ashby, Gary
81Hawaii/TCMA-3
Ashford, Thomas S.
(Tucker)
78Padre/FamFun-2
78T-116
79T-247
80CharCh-16
81Colum-2
82Colum-2
82Colum/Pol-12
83Tidew-26
84Nes/792-492
84T-492
87Jacks/Feder-4
88Jacks/GS-4
91WIZMets-16
92Yank/WIZ80-6
93Rang/Keeb-55
Ashkinazy, Alan
85Greens-2
86Greens-2
Ashley, Billy
90Bakers/Cal-260
91ClBest/Singl-210
91VeroB/ClBest-24
91VeroB/ProC-785
92Albuq/ProC-731
92B-168
92ClBest-243
92D/Rook-5
92SanAn/SB-553
92Sky/AASingl-242
93B-210
93D-56RR
93F/MLPI-9
93L-100
93Pinn-281
93Pinn/Team2001-16
93S-267
93S/Boys-1
93StCl-342
93StCl/1stDay-342
93StCl/Dodg-22
93T-815
93T/Gold-815
93ToysRUs-86
93UD-22SR
94D-420
94F-504
94L-111
94Pinn-324
94Pinn/New-21
94T-53
94T/Gold-53
94TripleP-287
94Ultra-513
Ashley, Duane
91James/ClBest-16
91James/ProC-3534
Ashley, Shon
86Beloit-1
87Beloit-4
88CalLgAS-14
88Stockton/Cal-194
88Stockton/ProC-724
89ElPaso/GS-25
89TexLAS/GS-14
90ElPaso/GS-4
91AA/LineD-176
91ElPaso/LineD-176
91ElPaso/ProC-2758
92Indianap/ProC-1871
92Indianap/SB-176
92ProC/Tomorrow-85
92Sky/AAASingl-84
Ashman, Mike
82Madis/Frit-23
83Albany-11
84Albany-21
85Cram/PCL-136
86Nashua-1
90AlbanyDG/Best-2
Ashmore, Mitch
82CharR-7
82Omaha-13
84Memphis-8
Ashton, Jeff
92Princet/ClBest-3
92Princet/ProC-3092
Ashworth, Kym
94B-157
Ashworth, Mike
88Burllnd/ProC-1793
89SLCity-28
Asmussen, Thomas W.
(Tom)
No Cards.
Asp, Bryan
89Elizab/Star-1
Aspray, Mike
88Peoria/Ko-3
90Visalia/Cal-59
90Visalia/ProC-2151
Aspromonte, Ken
58T-405
59T-424
60T-114
61P-65
61T-176
61T/St-133
62J-19
62P-19
62P/Can-19
62Salada-7A
62Salada-7B
62Shirriff-7
62T-563
63T-464
64T-252
72T-784MG
73OPC-449MG
73T-449MG
74OPC-521MG
74T-521MG
Aspromonte, Robert T.
(Bob)
60T-547
61T-396
62Bz-9
62T-248
62T/St-124
63Exh
63F-37
63J-187
63P-187
63Pep
63T-45
63T/SO
64T-467
64T/Coins-163AS
64T/Coins-84
64T/SU
64T/St-16
65Bz-19
65OPC-175
65T-175
65T/E-61
65T/trans-39
66Bz-24
66T-273M
66T-352
66T/RO-12
66T/RO-6
67Ast/Team-1
67Bz-24
67CokeCap/Astro-2
67T-274
68CokeCap/Astro-2
68Dexter-8
68OPC-95
68T-95
68T/ActionSt-15CM
68T/ActionSt-4CM
69MB-17
69MLB/St-111
69T-542
69T/St-31
70MLB/St-2
70OPC-529
70T-529
71MLB/St-146
71OPC-469
71T-469
72MB-21
72T-659
89Smok/Ast-16
90Target-21
91WIZMets-17
Exh47
Asselstine, Brian H.
77T-479R
78T-372
79T-529
81D-186
81F-256
81Pol/Atl-30
81T-64
82D-184
82F-428
82T-214
83Phoenix/BHN-4
Assenmacher, Paul
84Durham-20
85Durham-1
86D/Rook-28
86F/Up-U5
86Pol/Atl-30
86Sf/Rook-24
86T/Tr-4T
87D-290
87F-511
87Leaf-164
87Sf/TPrev-24M
87Smok/Atl-8
87T-132
87T/St-37
87ToysRUs-2
88F-532
88T-266
89B-265
89Brave/Dubuq-3
89D-357
89F-586
89Panini/St-33
89S-373
89T-454
89UD-566
90Cub/Mara-1
90D-459
90F-25
90F/Can-25
90Leaf-493
90OPC-644
90Publlnt/St-107
90T-644
90T/TVCub-7
90UD-660
91B-431

91Cub/Mara-45
91Cub/Vine-1
91D-144
91F-413
91Leaf-53
91OPC-12
91S-147
91StCl-586
91T-12
91UD-491
92Cub/Mara-45
92D-159
92F-375
92L-117
92L/BlkGold-117
92OPC-753
92Pinn-466
92S-360
92StCl-731
92T-753
92T/Gold-753
92T/GoldWin-753
92UD-590
92USPlayC/Cub-13D
92USPlayC/Cub-7H
92Ultra-172
93Cub/Mara-1
93D-54
93F-17
93Pac/Spanish-375
93StCl-332
93StCl/1stDay-332
93StCl/Cub-13
93T-319
93T/Gold-319
93UD-320
93Ultra-14
94D-57
94F-225
94S-224
94S/GoldR-224
94StCl-133
94StCl/1stDay-133
94StCl/Gold-133
94StCl/Team-195
94T-239
94T/Gold-239

Astacio, Pedro
90VeroB/Star-2
90Yakima/Team-12
91ClBest/Singl-280
91SanAn/ProC-2966
91VeroB/ClBest-1
91VeroB/ProC-762
92Albuq/ProC-710
92Albuq/SB-2
92B-689
92D/Rook-6
92Pinn-551
92Sky/AAASingl-1
93B-238
93Classic/Gamel-7
93D-407RR
93F-57
93F/RookSenII-2
93L-71
93LimeR/Winter-60
93Mother/Dodg-26
93OPC-9
93Pac/Spanish-496
93Pinn-396
93Pol/Dodg-1
93S-231
93Select-325
93Select/ChasRook-13
93StCl-511
93StCl/1stDay-511
93StCl/Dodg-12
93T-93
93T/Gold-93
93ToysRUs-44
93TripleP-29
93UD-367
93USPlayC/Rook-4S
93Ultra-49
94B-294
94D-62
94F-505
94Finest-343
94Flair-177
94L-237
94Pac/Cr-302
94Pinn-454
94Select-82
94StCl-343
94StCl/1stDay-343
94StCl/Gold-343
94T-431
94T/Gold-431
94TripleP-81
94UD-158
94UD/ElecD-158
94Ultra-212

Astacio, Rafael
91Erie/ClBest-2
91Erie/ProC-4075

Astroth, Jon
74Gaston
75Spokane/Caruso-13

Astroth, Joseph Henry
(Joe)
51B-298
52B-170
52T-290
53B/Col-82
53T-103
54B-131
55B-119
55Rodeo
56Rodeo
56T-106
91T/Arc53-103

Atha, Jeff
88James/ProC-1901

Atherton, Charles
No Cards.

Atherton, Keith Rowe
80WHave-16
81WHave-2
82Tacoma-23
83Tacoma-1
84D-497
84F-437
84Mother/A's-26
84Nes/792-529
84T-529
85D-340
85F-415
85Mother/A's-17
85T-166
86F-410
86Mother/A's-17
86T-353
87D-272
87F-534
87T-52
88D-318
88D/Best-270
88F-1
88S-613
88T-451
89D-273
89F-103
89F/Up-24
89S-381
89T-698
89T/Tr-4T
89UD-599
90Publlnt/St-552

Atilano, Luis
75Clinton

Atkins, Francis M.
(Tommy)
E270/2
M116

Atkins, James Curtis
(Jim)
No Cards.

Atkinson, Hubert B.
(Lefty)
No Cards.

Atkinson, William C.
(Bill)
72Dimanche*-1
78OPC-144
78T-43
80OPC-133
80T-415
83AppFx/Frit-19C

Atkisson, Albert W.
(Al)
No Cards.

Attardi, Jay
76AppFx

Attell, Abe
88Pac/8Men-28M
T3/Box-52

Attreau, Richard G.
(Dick)
94Conlon-1289

Atwater, Buck
90Gate/ProC-3353
91Pocatel/ProC-3787

Atwater, Tyrone
90Gate/SportP-3
91Pocatel/SportP-23

Atwell, Gary
75Lafay

Atwell, Maurice D.
(Toby)
52T-356
53B/Col-112
53T-23
54B-123
55B-164
56T-232
57Seattle/Pop-1
91T/Arc53-23
Exh47
V362-34

Atwood, Derek
91Pocatel/ProC-3773
91Pocatel/SportP-13

Atwood, William F.
(Bill)
40PlayBall-240
93Conlon-750

Atz, Jacob Henry
E270/2
T206

Aube, Richard
83CharR-14

Aubel, Mike
92AubAs/ClBest-8
92AubAs/ProC-1365

Aubin, Kevin
91Princet/ClBest-1
91Princet/ProC-3516

Aubin, Yves
52Laval-101

Aubrey, Harvey H.
No Cards.

Auchard, Dan
89Kingspt/Star-1

Aucoin, Derek
90James/Pucko-13
91Sumter/ClBest-2
91Sumter/ProC-2325
92Rockford/ClBest-7
92Rockford/ProC-2106
93WPalmB/ClBest-2
93WPalmB/ProC-1330

Audain, Miguel
87Penin-13

Aude, Rich
90Augusta/ProC-2469
90ProC/Singl-851
91Salem/ClBest-3
91Salem/ProC-957
92Salem/ClBest-3
92Salem/ProC-68
93CaroMud/RBI-3
94B-462
94F/MLP-3
94T-787
94T/Gold-787
94UD/CollC-42
94UD/CollC/Gold-42
94UD/CollC/Silv-42

Audley, Jim
90WichSt-4
91Kane/Team-2
92Freder/ClBest-2
92Freder/ProC-1817

Auerbach, Frederick
(Rick)
72OPC-153
72T-153
73OPC-427
73T-427
74OPC-289
74T-289
75OPC-588
75T-588
75T/M-588
76OPC-622
76SSPC-74
76T-622
78Pep-2
78SSPC/270-126
78T-646
79T-174
80T-354
82T-72
90Target-22

Aufdermauer, Bud
85Anchora-44

August, Don
85T-392OLY
86Tucson-3
87Ashvl-20
87Denver-17
88D-602
88Denver/CMC-8
88Denver/ProC-1259
88F/Up-U37
88S/Tr-104T
88T/Tr-7T
89B-130
89Brewer/YB-38
89D-410
89F-177
89Gard-15
89Panini/St-365
89Pol/Brew-38
89S-419
89S/HotRook-83
89S/YS/II-28
89Sf-131
89T-696
89T/Big-33
89UD-325
90AAASingl/ProC-641
90Classic-124
90D-617
90Denver/CMC-20
90Denver/ProC-616
90OPC-192
90Pol/Brew-38
90ProC/Singl-45
90Publlnt/St-488
90S-144
90T-192
90UD-295
91Brewer/MillB-1
91Pol/Brew-1
92D-140
92London/ProC-623
92S-533
92Ultra-78

August, Sam
88Osceola/Star-2
89ColMud/ProC-140
91AA/LineD-552
91ClBest/Singl-298
91Jacks/LineD-552
91Jacks/ProC-916
92Jacks/SB-327
92Sky/AASingl-139

Augustine, David R.
(Dave)
74OPC-598R
74T-598R
75OPC-616R
75T-616R
75T/M-616R
78Charl
79CharCh-12
81Portl-6
82Portl-18

Augustine, Gerald Lee
(Jerry)
77BurgChef-82
77T-577
78T-133
79T-357
80T-243
81D-445
81F-514
81T-596
82D-332
82F-133
82Pol/Brew-46
82T-46
83F-26
83Pol/Brew-46
83T-424
84F-194
84Nes/792-658
84Pol/Brew-46
84T-658
85RochR-14
92Brew/Carlson-1

Augustine, Rob
92Burllnd/ClBest-15
92Burllnd/ProC-1644

Auker, Eldon Leroy
35BU-120
39PlayBall-4
40PlayBall-139
41PlayBall-45
81Tiger/Detroit-91
88Conlon/3-3
R309/2
R313
W753

Aulds, Leycester D.
No Cards.

Aulenback, Jim
83AlexD-13
84PrWill-14

Ault, Douglas Reagan
(Doug)
75Spokane/Caruso-10
77OPC-202
77T-477R
78BJ/PostC-2
78OPC-202
78T-267
79OPC-205
79Syrac/TCMA-15
79Syrac/Team-17
79T-392
80Syrac/Team-2
81F-424
82Syrac-24
82Syrac/Team-2
83Knoxvl-20
85Syrac-21
86Syrac-3MG
87Syrac-7
87Syrac/TCMA-23
90StCath/ProC-3482MG
91StCath/ClBest-26MG
91StCath/ProC-3411MG
92Myrtle/ClBest-27MG
92Myrtle/ProC-2213MG
92Nabisco-30
93Rang/Keeb-56

Aurila, Brad
92James/ClBest-15
92James/ProC-1506

Aurilia, Rich
94ClBest/Gold-32
94FExcel-130

Ausanio, Joe
88Watertn/Pucko-2
89Salem/Star-3
90A&AASingle/ProC-12
90Harris/ProC-1186
91B-528
91ClBest/Singl-186
92BuffB/BlueS-1
92BuffB/ProC-315
92BuffB/SB-26
92Sky/AAASingl-12

Ausmus, Brad
89Oneonta/ProC-2110
90PrWill/Team-5
91ClBest/Singl-17
91PrWill/ClBest-13
91PrWill/ProC-1429
92ClBest-3
92ColClip/ProC-355
92OPC-58
92ProC/Tomorrow-120
92T-58M
92T/Gold-58
92T/GoldWin-58
93D-773
93Select/RookTr-83T
93StCl-367
93StCl/1stDay-367
93StCl/Rockie-30
94B-504
94D-100
94F-653
94L-239
94Panini-251
94Pinn-391
94S-579
94S/Boys-43
94Select-106
94StCl-412
94StCl/1stDay-412
94StCl/Gold-412

94Studio-129
94T-127
94T/Finest-29
94T/FinestRef-29
94T/Gold-127
94TripleP-161
94UD-232
94UD/CollC-43
94UD/CollC/Gold-43
94UD/CollC/Silv-43
94UD/ElecD-232
94Ultra-276
Aust, Dennis Kay
63Pep/Tul
66OPC-179R
66Pep/Tul
66T-179R
Austelle, Al
86Lipscomb-2ACO
92Lipscomb-2CO
Austerman, Carl
75Sacra/Caruso-16
Austin, Corey
92SoBend/ClBest-8
92SoBend/ProC-188
Austin, Dero
76Laugh/Clown-13
76Laugh/Clown-2
76Laugh/Clown-28
Austin, Frank
52Mother-18
86Negro/Frit-74
Austin, Jacob
92Welland/ClBest-1
Austin, James Parker
(Jim)
86Cram/NWL-178
87CharRain-7
88River/Cal-207
88Wichita-25
89ElPaso/GS-3
90ElPasoATG/Team-22
91AAA/LineD-127
91Brewer/MillB-2
91Denver/LineD-127
91Denver/ProC-114
92ClBest-301
92D/Rook-7
92F/Up-33
92Pol/Brew-2
92S-747
92S/RookTr-107T
92StCl-411
92T/91Debut-6
93D-659
93F/RookSenII-3
93L-12
93OPC-6
93Pac/Spanish-507
93Pol/Brew-1
93S-331
93Select-322
93StCl-587
93StCl/1stDay-587
93T-449
93T/Gold-449
93UD-787
93Ultra-217
94StCl/Team-202
Austin, James Phillip
(Jimmy or Pepper)
10Domino-3
11Helmar-60
12Sweet/Pin-51A
12Sweet/Pin-51B
14CJ-40
15CJ-40
91Conlon/Sport-236
D327
D328-8
D329-7
D350/2-7
E135-8
E220
E224
E254
E286
E94
E97
M101/4-7
M101/5-7
M116
T202
T205
T207
T222
V100
W555
Austin, James Taylor
91James/ClBest-5
91James/ProC-3557
92ProC/Tomorrow-274
92StCl/Dome-8
92WPalmB/ClBest-5
92WPalmB/ProC-2098
93WPalmB/ClBest-3
93WPalmB/ProC-1352
Austin, Pat
87Lakeland-18
88GlenF/ProC-914
89Toledo/CMC-18
89Toledo/ProC-766
90AAASingl/ProC-520
90Hagers/ProC-1418
90Hagers/Star-1
90Louisvl/CMC-23
90Louisvl/ProC-406
90ProC/Singl-123
90S-626
Austin, Paul
89SanDiegoSt/Smok-1
Austin, Rick Gerald
71MLB/St-361
71OPC-41
71T-41
75Sacra/Caruso-14
76OPC-269
76SSPC-248
76T-269
Austin, Rick
82OrlanTw-14
83Toledo-11
Austin, Terry
81QuadC-12
Auten, Jim
83Memphis/TCMA-16
84MidldC-19
Auth, Bob
86QuadC-3
Autry, Albert Jr.
(Al)
75Omaha/Team-2
78Spring/Wiener-15
Autry, Bucky
84LitFalls-18
Autry, Gene
61NuCard-414
92Pol/Angel-2OWN
93Pol/Angel-1OWN
Autry, Martin Gordon
29Exh/4-20
Autry, William Askew
(Chick)
No Cards.
Avent, Stephen
90Bend/Legoe-18
91Spartan/ClBest-13
91Spartan/ProC-898
Averill, Earl D. Jr.
59T-301
60L-110
60T-39
61T-358
62J-80
62P-80
62P/Can-80
62Salada-24A
62Salada-24B
62Shirriff-24
62T-452
63T-139
Averill, Howard Earl
(Earl)
28Exh/PCL-2
29Exh/4-22
31Exh/4-22
32Orbit/num-12
32Orbit/un-3
33DH-3
33Exh/4-11
33G-194
34DS-100
34DS-35
34Exh/4-11
35BU-113
35BU-24
35Exh/4-11
35G-1L
35G-2E
35G-6E
35G-7E
36Exh/4-11
36Wheat
37Exh/4-11
37OPC-103
38Exh/4-11
39Exh
39PlayBall-143
40PlayBall-46
55Salem
60F-71
61F-5
75Shakey-4
76Rowe-5M
76Shakey-147
76Shakey-A
77Galasso-202
77Galasso-79
77Shakey-A
77Shakey/WAS-A
80Marchant-3
80Pac/Leg-4
80Perez/HOF-147
81Conlon-20
82Ohio/HOF-23
86Everett/Pop-1
86Sf/Dec-15M
88Conlon/AmAS-2
89Pac/Leg-203
91Conlon/Sport-31
92Conlon/Sport-597
93Conlon-668
94Conlon-1089
PR1-2
R300
R303/A
R305
R306
R308-160
R310
R311/Gloss
R313
R314
R315-A1
R315-B1
V300
V351B-2
V94-1
W517-51
WG8-2
Aversa, Joe
90Johnson/Star-2
91Spring/ClBest-3
91Spring/ProC-747
92StPete/ClBest-14
Avery, John
92Pulaski/ClBest-2
92Pulaski/ProC-3169
Avery, Larry
81BurlB-29
82BurlR/Frit-2GM
82BurlR/TCMA-27GM
Avery, Steve
89B-268
89BBAmAA/BPro-AA13
89Durham/Star-1
89Durham/Team-1
89Greenvl/Best-28
89Star/Wax-67
89T-784FDP
90AAASingl/ProC-397
90B-9
90Brave/Dubuq/Singl-1
90Classic/Up-T4
90D-39RR
90D/Rook-42
90F/Up-U1
90Leaf-481
90ProC/Singl-277
90Richm/Bob-7
90Richm/CMC-1
90Richm/ProC-252
90Richm/Team-1
90S/Tr-109T
90T/Tr-4T
90UD-65
91B-566
91Brave/Dubuq/Perf-1
91Brave/Dubuq/Stand-1
91Classic/200-138
91Classic/II-T26
91D-187
91F-681
91Leaf-510
91Leaf/Stud-141
91OPC-227
91RedFoley/St-105
91S-80
91S/100RisSt-5
91StCl-48
91T-227
91T/90Debut-6
91T/JumboR-3
91ToysRUs-3
91UD-365
91Ultra-1
92B-180
92Brave/LykePerf-1
92Brave/LykeStand-1
92CJ/DI-4
92Classic/Game200-188
92Classic/I-T7
92Classic/I-xx
92Classic/II-T12
92D-81
92F-349
92F/Smoke-S10
92French-18M
92JDean/18-5
92Kenner/Fig-2
92KingB-11
92L-59
92L/BlkGold-59
92L/GoldPrev-1
92L/Prev-1
92OPC-574
92OPC/Premier-170
92Panini-169
92Pinn-231
92Pinn-585M
92Pinn-612GRIP
92Pinn/Team2000-66
92Pinn/TeamP-2M
92S-241
92S-797HL
92S/100SS-34
92S/Impact-12
92S/Prev-4
92StCl-594MC
92StCl-60
92StCl/Dome-9
92Studio-1
92T-574
92T/Gold-574
92T/GoldWin-574
92T/Kids-36
92T/McDonB-16
92TripleP-85
92UD-41
92UD-475
92UD/ASFF-1
92UD/TmMVPHolo-6
92USPlayC/Brave-10S
92USPlayC/Brave-1D
92Ultra-157
93B-198
93Brave/FLAg-2
93Brave/LykePerf-1
93Brave/LykeStand-1
93Classic/GameI-8
93Colla/DM-5
93D-26
93F-1
93Flair-1
93HumDum/Can-26
93KingB-5
93L-121
93L/Fast-13
93OPC-5
93Pac/Spanish-331
93Pinn-315
93S-169
93Select-109
93StCl-626
93StCl/1stDay-626
93StCl/Brave-10
93Studio-5
93T-615
93T/Finest-160
93T/FinestRef-160
93T/Gold-615
93ToysRUs-95
93TripleP-30
93UD-246
93UD-472M
93UD-816TC
93UD/FunPack-62
93UD/looss-WI5
93UD/SP-55
93UD/SeasonHL-HI2
93Ultra-1
94B-189
94D-41
94D/DK-3
94D/Special-41
94F-350
94F/AS-26
94Finest-359
94L-138
94OPC-196
94Pac/Cr-1
94Pinn-8
94Pinn/Artist-8
94Pinn/HobSam-8
94Pinn/Museum-8
94Pinn/RetailSam-8
94S-166
94S/GoldR-166
94Select-87
94Sf/2000-60
94StCl-254
94StCl/1stDay-254
94StCl/Gold-254
94StCl/Team-32
94Studio-33
94T-137
94T/Gold-137
94TripleP-41
94UD-41FUT
94UD-420
94UD/CollC-44
94UD/CollC/Gold-44
94UD/CollC/Silv-44
94UD/ElecD-41FUT
94UD/SP-47
94Ultra-147
Avila, Roberto G.
(Bobby)
50NumNum
51B-188
52B-167
52NumNum-14
52RM-AL2
52T-257
53B/Col-29
53RM-AL26
54B-68
54DanDee
54RM-AL1
55B-19
55Gol/Ind-1
55RM-AL15
55Salem
56T-132
57Sohio/Ind-1
57T-195
58Hires-33
58T-276
59T-363
60L-59
60T-90
91Crown/Orio-14
Aviles, Brian Keith
84Durham-25
85Greenvl/Team-2
87Greenvl/Best-15
Aviles, Ramon Antonio
78SSPC/270-163
79OkCty
80T-682R
81F-23
81T-644
82F-239
82OkCty-4
82T-152
83Portl-10
86Reading-1CO
87Spartan-11CO
88Maine/CMC-24CO
88Maine/ProC-302CO
89Reading/Best-25CO
89Reading/ProC-671CO
90Reading/Best-6CO
90Reading/ProC-1236CO
90Reading/Star-27CO
91Batavia/ClBest-27MG
91Batavia/ProC-3500MG
92Batavia/ClBest-29M
92Batavia/ProC-3282

Avram, Brian
91Johnson/ClBest-23
91Johnson/ProC-3968
Avrea, James Epherium
(Jim)
No Cards.
Awkard, H.B.
91GulfCR/SportP-29
Ayala, Adan
91CharRain/ClBest-12
91CharRain/ProC-97
92CharRain/ClBest-2
92CharRain/ProC-121
Ayala, Benigno Felix
(Benny)
75OPC-619R
75T-619R
75T/M-619R
75Tidew/Team-1
78Spring/Wiener-8
80T-262
81D-236
81F-185
81T-101
82D-581
82F-157
82T-331
83D-331
83F-52
83T-59
84D-270
84Nes/792-443
84T-443
84T/St-22WS
85Polar/Ind-12
85T-624
85T/Tr-3T
85ThomMc/Discs-1
91Crown/Orio-15
91WIZMets-18
Ayala, Bobby
90Cedar/Best-15
90Cedar/ProC-2314
91AA/LineD-153
91Chatt/LineD-153
91Chatt/ProC-1951
92Chatt/ProC-3811
92Chatt/SB-178
92Sky/AASingl-79
93B-498
93D-30
93F-29
93Pac/Spanish-397
93Reds/Kahn-1
93S/Boys-19
94B-501
94D-75
94F-404
94Finest-409
94L-253
94Pinn-482
94T-673
94T/Gold-673
94UD-506
94Ultra-416
Ayala, Eric
80Ander-20
Ayala, Jason
91Butte/SportP-2
Ayala, Moises
92Bristol/ClBest-15
92Bristol/ProC-1413
Aydelott, Jacob S.
(Jake)
No Cards.
Ayer, Jack
82ArkTr-20
84Louisvl-21
85Louisvl-21
86Louisvl-4
87Louisvl-3
Ayers, Brooks
88MissSt-39M
89MissSt-45M
Ayers, Greg
91Peoria/Team-30M
Ayers, Jason
92MissSt-50M
93MissSt-48M
Ayers, Jim
75Cedar
Ayers, Kevin
86VeroB-2
Ayers, Lenny
91Everett/ClBest-22
Ayers, Scott
86WPalmB-3
87James-19
Ayers, William Oscar
(Bill)
47TipTop
Ayers, Yancy Wyatt
(Doc)
No Cards.
Aylmer, Bobby
90StCath/ProC-3465
91Myrtle/ClBest-1
91Myrtle/ProC-2935
Aylward, Jim
88QuadC/GS-22
88Reno/Cal-280
89QuadC/Best-8
89QuadC/GS-27
90MidldA/GS-14
Aylward, Richard John
(Dick)
No Cards.
Ayoub, Sam
71Richm/Team-2
81Richm-25
82Richm-30
83Richm-7
84Richm-22
85Richm-24
86Richm-1TR
87Richm/Crown-x
87Richm/TCMA-29
88Richm-TR
88Richm/ProC-6
89Richm/CMC-14
89Richm/Ko-TR
89Richm/ProC-820
90ProC/Singl-294TR
90Richm/25Ann-2TR
90Richm/CMC-18TR
90Richm/Team-2TR
Ayrault, Bob
89Reno/Cal-240
90A&AASingle/ProC-23
90EastLAS/ProC-EL31
90Foil/Best-303
90ProC/Singl-800
90Reading/Best-2
90Reading/ProC-1212
90Reading/Star-4
90Star/ISingl-80
91AAA/LineD-479
91ScranWB/LineD-479
91ScranWB/ProC-2531
92D/Rook-8
92Phill/Med-37
92ScranWB/SB-477
92Sky/AAASingl-216
93D-16
93F-484
93Pac/Spanish-574
93Phill/Med-4
93Pinn-229
93S-289
93StCl-4
93StCl/1stDay-4
93StCl/Phill-9
93T-126
93T/Gold-126
94UD/CollC-45
94UD/CollC/Gold-45
94UD/CollC/Silv-45
Ayrault, Joe
91Pulaski/ClBest-1
91Pulaski/ProC-4007
92Macon/ClBest-9
92Macon/ProC-270
93Durham/Team-1
93SALAS/II-2
Ayres, Lenny
90Everett/Best-24
90Everett/ProC-3117
91Everett/ProC-3905
92Clinton/ClBest-8
92Clinton/ProC-3588
Azar, Todd
88Wausau/GS-15
Azcue, Jose Joaquin
(Joe)
62T-417
63T-501
64T-199
64T/Coins-110
65Kahn
65T-514
66T-452
67CokeCap/Indian-9
67T-336
68Bz-4
68T-443
69JB
69MB-18
69MLB/St-38
69OPC-176
69T-176
69T/4in1-21M
69T/St-162
69Trans-1
70MLB/St-170
70OPC-294
70T-294
71MLB/St-338
71OPC-657
71T-657
72MB-22
78TCMA-36
Azocar, Oscar
88Albany/ProC-1347
89Albany/Best-19
89Albany/ProC-332
89Albany/Star-1
90AAASingl/ProC-338
90ColClip/CMC-13
90ColClip/ProC-688
90Colum/Pol-12
90F/Up-111
90ProC/Singl-213
90S/Tr-71T
90T/TVYank-36
91AAA/LineD-276
91B-652
91Classic/I-62
91D-331
91F-655
91LasVegas/LineD-276
91LasVegas/ProC-247
91OPC-659
91Panini/FrSt-329
91Panini/St-270
91S-72
91S/100RisSt-46
91StCl-450
91T-659
91T/90Debut-7
91UD-464
92F-598
92Mother/Padre-12
92OPC-112
92Padre/Carl-2
92Pol/Padre-1
92S-692
92Smok/Padre-2
92StCl-552
92T-112
92T/Gold-112
92T/GoldWin-112
93Panini-263
93StCl-257
93StCl/1stDay-257
Baar, Bryan
89GreatF-19
90Bakers/Cal-256
91AA/LineD-528
91ClBest/Singl-292
91SanAn/LineD-528
91SanAn/ProC-2978
92Albuq/SB-3
92Sky/AAASingl-2
Baase, Michael
92Stockton/ClBest-5
Babb, Charles Amos
(Charlie)
90Target-23
E254
Babbitt, Gene
47Sunbeam
Babbitt, Troy
91Eugene/ClBest-5
91Eugene/ProC-3730
Babcock, Bill
82AppFx/Frit-19
Babcock, Robert E.
(Bob)
77Tucson
78Cr/PCL-106
80CharCh-17
81T-41R
82D-565
82T-567
83SLCity-3
93Rang/Keeb-57
Babcock, Walter Jr.
74Wichita-103
Babe, Loren Rolland
No Cards.
Baber, Larue
90Helena/SportP-13
91Helena/SportP-9
92Beloit/ClBest-21
92Beloit/ProC-417
92ClBest-363
Babich, John Charles
(Johnny)
34DS-82
35BU-167
40PlayBall-191
41DP-127
41PlayBall-40
43Centen-1
44Centen-1
48Signal
48Smith-22
90Target-24
R309/2
Babik, Bill
52Laval-72
Babington, Charles P.
(Charlie)
No Cards.
Babitt, Mack Neal II
(Shooty)
80Ogden-21
80WHave-17
82D-556
82F-86
82T-578
82Tacoma-28
83Memphis/TCMA-1
83Wichita/Dog-3
84Indianap-14
Babki, Blake
91James/ClBest-2
91James/ProC-3558
Baby, Jim
75WPalmB/Sussman-3
Baca, Mark A.
88PalmSp/Cal-99
88PalmSp/ProC-1456
Bacciocu, Jack
49Sommer-19
Bach, Jan
78Clinton
Bach, Rich
78Clinton
80BurlB-16
Bachman, Kent
86WPalmB-4
Backlund, Brett
93B-134
93StCl/MurphyS-61
Backman, Lester John
(Les)
M116
Backman, Walter W.
(Wally)
79Jacks-2
80Tidew-4
81F-336
81Tidew-8
83D-618
83F-537
83T-444
83Tidew-3
84Jacks/Smok-2
85D-319
85F-72
85Leaf-79
85OPC-162
85T-677
85T/Mets/Fan-1
85T/St-106
86D-238
86F-75
86OPC-191
86T-191
86T/Mets/Fan-1
86T/St-97
87D-316
87F-3
87Leaf-59
87OPC-48
87Sf-124
87Sf/TPrev-2M
87T-48
87T/St-100
88D-241
88D/Mets/Bk-241
88F-128
88Kahn/Mets-6
88Leaf-202
88OPC-333
88Panini/St-340
88S-303
88T-333
89B-159
89D-383
89D/Best-186
89D/Tr-10
89F-28
89F/Up-43
89OPC-72
89S-315
89S/Tr-34
89T-508
89T/Big-300
89T/Tr-5T
89UD-188
89UD/Ext-732
90B-177
90D-155
90D/BestNL-130
90F-367
90F/Can-367
90F/Up-U47
90Homer/Pirate-1
90Kenner/Fig-4
90Leaf-341
90OPC-218
90PublInt/St-321
90S-281
90S/Tr-37T
90T-218
90T/Big-233
90T/Tr-5T
90UD-158
91B-490
91D-177
91F-29
91F/UltraUp-U98
91F/Up-U106
91Leaf-482
91OPC-722
91Phill/Medford-3
91RedFoley/St-5
91S-16
91S/RookTr-8T
91StCl-368
91T-722
91T/Tr-3T
91UD-185
91UD/Ext-790
91WIZMets-19
92D-478
92OPC-434
92Phill/Med-4
92S-177
92StCl-4
92T-434
92T/Gold-434
92T/GoldWin-434
92UD-350
Backs, Jason
89Spartan/ProC-1038
89Spartan/Star-1
91AA/LineD-501
91Reading/LineD-501
91Reading/ProC-1362
Backus, Jerry
88Boise/ProC-1618
Bacon, Edgar Suter
(Eddie)
No Cards.
Bacosa, Al
88Idaho/ProC-1848
Bacsik, Michael James
(Mike)
74Gaston
75Spokane/Caruso-18
77T-103
77Tucson
78Cr/PCL-43
80T-453
93Rang/Keeb-58

Baczewski, Fred
54B-60
55B-190
Badacour, Bob
90Martins/ProC-3189
Badcock, Tom
73Wichita-2
75Water
Bader, Arthur Herman
(Art)
No Cards.
Bader, Loren Verne
No Cards.
Badgro, Morris Hiram
(Red)
81Conlon-30
88Conlon/4-2
Badorek, Mike
91Hamil/ClBest-5
91Hamil/ProC-4026
92MidwLAS/Team-1
92Spring/ClBest-9
92Spring/ProC-859
94FExcel-255
Baecht, Edward Joseph
(Ed)
93Conlon-971
Baehr, Dave
82Idaho-1
83Wisco/Frit-25
Baer, Max
33SK*-44
Baerga, Carlos
86CharRain-1
87CharRain-2
88TexLgAS/GS-32
88Wichita-15
89LasVegas/CMC-18
89LasVegas/ProC-9
90B-339
90Classic/III-35
90D/Rook-19
90F/Up-U90
90Leaf-443
90S/Tr-74T
90S/YS/II-32
90T/Big-229
90T/Tr-6T
90UD/Ext-737
91B-69
91Classic/III-22
91D-274
91F-360
91Indian/McDon-3
91Leaf-225
91OPC-147
91Panini/FrSt-218
91Panini/St-180
91S-74
91S/100RisSt-30
91StCl-115
91T-147
91T/90Debut-8
91T/JumboR-4
91ToysRUs-4
91UD-125
91Ultra-106
92B-531
92Classic/II-T48
92D-120
92F-104
92Indian/McDon-4
92L-202
92L/BlkGold-202
92OPC-33
92Panini-47
92Pinn-3
92Pinn/Team2000-56
92S-128
92StCl-143
92StCl/MemberIV*-1
92Studio-163
92T-33
92T/Gold-33
92T/GoldWin-33
92TripleP-235
92UD-231
92Ultra-46
93B-585
93Cadaco-2
93Classic/Gamel-9
93Colla/DM-6
93D-405
93D/DK-13
93D/MVP-16
93D/Spirit-SG15
93Duracel/PPI-15
93F-213
93F-357M
93F/TLAL-6
93Flair-191
93Ho-15
93Indian/WUAB-2
93Kenner/Fig-2
93L-233
93L/Fast-11
93L/GoldAS-4
93OPC-39
93OPC/Premier-51
93Pac/Beisbol-5
93Pac/Beisbol-6M
93Pac/Spanish-93
93Pac/SpanishGold-12
93Pac/SpanishP-9
93Panini-51
93Pinn-6
93Pinn/HRC-39
93Pinn/Slug-29
93Pinn/TP-5M
93Pinn/Team2001-7
93S-9
93S/Franchise-5
93Select-122
93Select/StatL-8
93StCl-593MC
93StCl-61
93StCl/1stDay-593MC
93StCl/1stDay-61
93StCl/MPhoto-1
93StCl/MurphyS-189
93Studio-50
93Studio/Her-9
93T-221
93T-402M
93T/BlkGold-25
93T/Finest-57
93T/FinestRef-57
93T/Gold-221
93T/Gold-402M
93TB/Full-14
93ToysRUs-51
93ToysRUs/MPhoto-3
93TripleP-80
93TripleP/Act-18
93UD-174
93UD-45M
93UD/5thAnn-A8
93UD/Diam-12
93UD/FunPack-105GS
93UD/FunPack-107
93UD/OnDeck-D3
93UD/SP-119
93USPlayC/Ace-4D
93Ultra-183
93Ultra/AS-13
94B-307
94Church-19
94D-14
94D/Special-14
94F-99
94F/AS-2
94F/GoldM-2
94F/ProV-4
94F/TL-5
94Finest-231
94Flair-37
94Flair/Hot-2
94Kraft-1
94L-247
94L/GoldS-9
94L/MVPAL-14
94OPC-106
94OPC/JAS-6
94Pac/Cr-165
94Pac/CrPr-1
94Pac/Silv-16
94Panini-54
94Pinn-2
94Pinn/Artist-2
94Pinn/HobSam-2
94Pinn/Museum-2
94Pinn/Power-12
94Pinn/PowerPr-12
94Pinn/RetailSam-2
94Pinn/Run-15
94Pinn/TeamP-2
94RedFoley-4M
94S-53
94S/Cycle-4
94S/DT-4
94S/GoldR-53
94S/GoldS-38
94Sf/2000-71
94Sf/Mov-11
94StCl-169
94StCl/1stDay-169
94StCl/Gold-169
94Studio-91
94T-450
94T/BlkGold-2
94T/Gold-450
94TripleP-112
94TripleP/Medal-5M
94UD-115
94UD-49FUT
94UD/ElecD-115
94UD/ElecD-49FUT
94UD/SP-96
94Ultra-343
94Ultra/Hit-2
94Ultra/RBIK-6
94Ultra/RisSt-1
Baerns, Scott
89TNTech-3
Baerwald, Rudolph
E254
E270
Baez, Angel
81Buffa-17
Baez, Diogenes
92WinHaven/ClBest-6
92WinHaven/ProC-1790
Baez, Francisco
90AppFox/Box-3
90AppFox/ProC-2087
90Eugene/GS-2
91AppFx/ClBest-1
91AppFx/ProC-1707
92AppFox/ClBest-11
Baez, Igor
89Greens/ProC-408
Baez, Jesse
79LodiD-9
81Wausau-13
83Wausau/Frit-17
Baez, Jose Antonio
75Water
78T-311
Baez, Kevin
88LitFalls/Pucko-2
89Clmbia/Best-12
89Clmbia/GS-6
89SALAS/GS-19
90Jacks/GS-16
91AAA/LineD-551
91T/90Debut-9
91Tidew/LineD-551
91Tidew/ProC-2515
91WIZMets-20
92D/Rook-9
92Sky/AAASingl-247
92StCl-543
92Tidew/ProC-
92Tidew/SB-551
93D-361
93F/Final-98
94D-68
94StCl-247
94StCl/1stDay-247
94StCl/Gold-247
Baez, Pedro
88Madis-3
89Modesto/Cal-267
89Modesto/Chong-8
Bafia, Bob
86WinSalem-2
87WinSalem-8
88Pittsfld/ProC-1363
89CharlK-22
90AAASingl/ProC-630
90Iowa/CMC-11
90Iowa/ProC-323
90ProC/Singl-86
90T/TVCub-37
91AA/LineD-277
91Huntsvl/ClBest-2
91Huntsvl/LineD-277
91HuntsvlProC-1800
Bagby, James C.J. Jr.
(Jim)
39PlayBall-40
40PlayBall-32
42PlayBall-12
61F-92
93Conlon-936
Bagby, James C.J. Sr.
(Jim)
21Exh-3
92Conlon/Sport-487
D327
D328-9
E120
E121
E135-9
E220
V100
W501
W572
W575
WG7-2
Baggott, Dave
89SLCity-4GM
Bagiotti, Aldo
81Redwd-10
Bagley, Eugene T.
(Gene)
No Cards.
Bagnall, Jim
83Butte-16
83CharR-4
Bagshaw, Lance
87SLCity/Taco-7bb
Bagshaw, Ryan
87SLCity/Taco-7bb
Bagwell, Jeff
88CapeCod-4
88CapeCod/Sum-57
90A&AASingle/ProC-26
90EastLAS/ProC-EL40
90Foil/Best-132
90NewBrit/Best-7
90NewBrit/ProC-1324
90NewBrit/Star-1
90ProC/Singl-739
90Star/ISingl-30
91B-183
91Classic/200-90
91Classic/II-T84
91D/Rook-30
91F/UltraUp-U79
91F/Up-U87
91Leaf/GRook-BC14
91Leaf/Stud-172
91Mother/Ast-8
91S/RookTr-96T
91StCl-388
91StCl/Member*-11
91T/Tr-4T
91UD/Ext-702
91UD/Ext-755
92B-200
92CJ/DI-2
92Classic/Game200-187
92Classic/I-T8
92Classic/II-T2
92Colla/Bagwell-Set
92D-358
92D-BC6ROY
92D/BC-BC6ROY
92D/DK-DK11
92D/McDon-24
92F-425
92F/Performer-19
92F/RookSIns-4
92French-1M
92Hardee-3
92JDean/18-3
92L-28
92L/BlkGold-28
92L/GoldPrev-4
92L/Prev-4
92MJB/Bagwell-Set
92MJB/Proto-R1
92MooTown-2
92Mother/Ast-8
92Mother/Bagwell-Set
92OPC-520
92OPC/Premier-107
92P-1
92Panini-152
92Pinn-70
92Pinn/Slug-15
92Pinn/Team2000-10
92S-576
92S-793ROY
92S/100RisSt-35
92S/Impact-2
92StCl-330
92StCl-606MC
92Studio-31
92Studio/Her-12
92Studio/Prev-16
92T-520
92T/91Debut-7
92T/Gold-520
92T/GoldWin-520
92T/Kids-44
92T/McDonB-34
92TripleP-200
92TripleP/Gal-GS7
92UD-276
92UD/ASFF-3
92UD/HRH-HR25
92UD/TWillB-T12
92UD/TmMVPHolo-7
92Ultra-198
92Ultra/AwardWin-3
93B-420
93Classic/Gamel-10
93Colla/DM-7
93D-428
93D/LongBall-LL17
93D/MVP-24
93D/Prev-4
93F-46
93F/Fruit-3
93F/TLNL-9
93Flair-57
93Ho-19
93HumDum/Can-32
93Kenner/Fig-3
93L-125
93L/Fast-17
93L/GoldAS-3M
93Mother/Ast-7
93OPC-29
93Pac/Jugador-20
93Pac/Spanish-117
93Panini-170
93Pinn-10
93Pinn-297I
93Pinn/HRC-28
93Pinn/Slug-14
93Pinn/Team2001-9
93S-89
93S/Franchise-18
93Select-113
93StCl-384
93StCl/1stDay-384
93StCl/Ast-8
93Studio-34
93Studio/Sil-3
93T-227
93T/Finest-11
93T/FinestRef-11
93T/Gold-227
93TB/Full-8
93TWill-156
93TWill-157
93TWill-158
93TWill-159
93ToysRUs-56
93TripleP-43
93TripleP/Act-12
93UD-256
93UD-452IN
93UD-475M
93UD-813TC
93UD/Diam-2
93UD/FunPack-42GS
93UD/FunPack-43
93UD/Iooss-WI2
93UD/SP-28
93Ultra-390
94B-118
94Church-6
94D-365
94D/DK-27
94D/MVP-6
94D/Special-365
94F-483
94F/TL-20
94Kraft-16
94L-221
94L/MVPNL-2
94OPC-212
94OPC/JAS-5
94Oscar-16
94P-29

94Pac/Cr-257
94Pac/Silv-24
94Panini-189
94Pinn-290
94Pinn/Power-16
94Pinn/Run-36
94Pinn/TeamP-1
94RedFoley-2
94S-4
94S/GoldR-4
94S/GoldS-8
94S/HobSam-4
94S/Pr-4
94S/Tomb-1
94Sf/2000-7
94Sf/Shak-3
94StCl-108
94StCl/1stDay-108
94StCl/Gold-108
94Studio-16
94T-40
94T/BlkGold-23
94T/Finest-212
94T/FinestRef-212
94T/Gold-40
94TripleP-21
94TripleP/Medal-4M
94UD-272HFA
94UD-480
94UD/DColl-C1
94UD/ElecD-272HFA
94UD/HoloFX-3
94UD/Mantle-1
94UD/SP-27
94Ultra-203
94Ultra/RisSt-2
Bagwell, William M.
(Bill)
94Conlon-1310
Baham, Leon
82Idaho-16
87SanBern-14
88Tampa/Star-2
Bahns, Ed
79AppFx-4
Bahnsen, Stanley R.
(Stan)
67OPC-93R
67T-93R
68T-214R
69Citgo-9
69T-380
69T/St-201
70T-568
71MD
71MLB/St-482
71OPC-184
71T-184
72T-662
73OPC-20
73T-20
74OPC-254
74T-254
74T/St-152
75OPC-161
75SSPC/18-15
75T-161
75T/M-161
76OPC-534
76SSPC-486
76T-534
77BurgChef-112
77T-383
78OPC-54
78T-97
79OPC-244
79T-468
80OPC-345
80T-653
81D-452
81F-156
81OPC-267
81T-267
81TCMA-369
82D-392
82F-183
82OPC-131
82T-131
83Portl-23
89Pac/SenLg-78
89Swell-39
89T/SenLg-62
89TM/SenLg-4
92Yank/WIZ60-4
92Yank/WIZ70-9
Bahr, Edson Garfield
(Ed)
No Cards.
Bahret, Frank J.
No Cards.
Baich, Dan
57Seattle/Pop-2
Baichley, Grover C.
No Cards.
Baier, Marty
82Clinton/Frit-15
83Clinton/Frit-7
Bailes, Scott
83AlexD-10
85Nashua-1
86D/Rook-25
86F/Up-U6
86OhHenry-43
86Sf/Rook-9
86T/Tr-5T
87D-227
87F-242
87Gator-43
87OPC-134
87T-585
87ToysRUs-3
88D-104
88D/Best-285
88F-600
88Gator-43
88OPC-107
88Panini/St-68
88T-107
88T/St-206
89D-202
89F-398
89S-424
89T-339
89T/St-217
89UD-209
90D-468
90F-484
90F/Can-484
90Leaf-380
90OPC-784
90PublInt/St-553
90RedFoley/St-2
90S-218
90S/Tr-64T
90Smok/Angel-19
90T-784
91B-205
91S-535
91UD-190
92D-357
92F-53
92OPC-95
92S-331
92StCl-167
92T-95
92T/Gold-95
92T/GoldWin-95
93Pac/Spanish-40
Bailey, Abraham L.
(Sweetbreads)
No Cards.
Bailey, Ace
33SK*-29
Bailey, Arthur Eugene
(Gene)
No Cards.
Bailey, Brandon
86Columbia-4
87Columbia-3
88StLucie/Star-1
Bailey, Buddy
80Ander-17
82Durham-23
86Durham-1MG
87Sumter-10
89Greenvl/Best-20
89Greenvl/ProC-1178
89SLAS-23
90Greenvl/ProC-1143MG
90Greenvl/Star-24MG
91CLAS/ProC-CAR21
91LynchRS/ClBest-25
91LynchRS/ProC-1215
92LynchRS/ClBest-26MG
93Pawtu/Ball-1MG
Bailey, Cory
91Elmira/ClBest-16
91Elmira/ProC-3261
92LynchRS/ClBest-5
92LynchRS/ProC-2898
92ProC/Tomorrow-25
93FExcel/ML-129
93Pawtu/Ball-2
93Pawtu/Ballp-2
94F/MLP-4
94Pinn-420
94T-764
94T/Gold-764
Bailey, Darryl
77BurlB
78BurlB
79Holyo-22
Bailey, Greg
83TriCit-21
86Tulsa-18
Bailey, Howard Lee
82Evansvl-1
82Evansvl-1
82T-261R
84D-212
84Evansvl-2
84F-75
84Nes/792-284
84T-284
Bailey, James Hopkins
(Jim)
No Cards.
Bailey, Jay
92MissSt-50M
93MissSt-48M
Bailey, Jim 1
82Idaho-2
Bailey, Jim 2
86Lipscomb-3
Bailey, John Mark
(Mark)
84F/X-3
85D-450
85F-344
85Mother/Ast-17
85OPC-64
85T-64
86D-354
86F-293
86Pol/Ast-14
86T-432
86T/St-30
87D-235
87D-429
87Mother/Ast-15
87Pol/Ast-2
87T-197
88Mother/Ast-15
88Pol/Ast-5
88T/Big-248
89Tidew/CMC-29
89Tidew/ProC-1949
90AAASingl/ProC-39
90Phoenix/CMC-13
90Phoenix/ProC-13
90ProC/Singl-540
91AAA/LineD-377
91Phoenix/LineD-377
91Phoenix/ProC-69
92Phoenix/ProC-2823
92Phoenix/SB-377
Bailey, Lash
89Belling/Legoe-17
90Penin/Star-1
Bailey, Lemuel
(King)
No Cards.
Bailey, Lonas Edgar
(Ed)
53T-206
54T-184
55T-69
55T/DH-30
56Kahn
57Kahn
57Sohio/Reds-1
57Swift-5
57T-128
58Kahn
58T-330
58T-386M
58T-490AS
59Kahn
59T-210
60Kahn
60T-411
61Kahn
61T-418
61T/St-13
62J-137
62P-137
62P/Can-137
62Salada-113A
62Salada-113B
62Shirriff-113
62T-459
62T/St-194
63T-368
64T-437
64Wheat/St-4
65T-559
66T-246
78TCMA-173
78TCMA-37
79TCMA-11
84Mother/Giants-17
91T/Arc53-206
94T/Arc54-184
Exh47
Bailey, Mike
91Eugene/ClBest-25
91Eugene/ProC-3714
Bailey, Otha
92Negro/Retort-1
Bailey, Pat
86Cram/NWL-31
87AppFx-19
Bailey, Robert Jr.
88BBAmer-30
89Welland/Pucko-3
90Salem/Star-1
91Salem/ClBest-4
91Salem/ProC-958
92Salem/ClBest-18
92Salem/ProC-75
Bailey, Robert S.
(Bob)
63IDL-1
63Kahn
63T-228R
64Kahn
64T-91
64T/S-4
65Kahn
65T-412
66EH-7
66Kahn
66T-485
67CokeCap/DodgAngel-2
67OPC-32
67T-32
68T-580
69Fud's-1
69MLB/St-154
69T-399
69T/St-52
70Expo/PostC-6
70Expos/Pins-2
70MLB/St-62
70OPC-293
70T-293
71Expo/ProS-1
71LaPizza-1
71MLB/St-121
71OPC-157
71T-157
71T/Coins-59
72MB-23
72OPC-493KP
72ProStars/PostC-1
72T-493
72T-526
73OPC-505
73T-505
74Expo/West-1
74OPC-97
74T-97
74T/St-51
74Weston-3
75Ho-55
75OPC-365
75T-365
75T/M-365
76OPC-338
76SSPC-333
76T-338
76T/Tr-338T
77T-221
78PapaG/Disc-20
78SSPC/270-173
78T-457
79OPC-282
79T-549
81TCMA-310
86Penin-4MG
87Hawaii-26MG
90Target-25
92Nabisco-11
Bailey, Roger
92Bend/ClBest-2
92Classic/DP-71
92FrRow/DP-96
92UD/ML-23
93B-120
93FExcel/ML-31
93StCl/MurphyS-120
93StCl/Rockie-29
93T-433
93T/Gold-433
Bailey, Roy
90Hamil/Best-2
90Hamil/Star-3
91Savan/ClBest-1
91Savan/ProC-1642
92StPete/ClBest-4
92StPete/ProC-2017
Bailey, Seymour
28LaPresse-4
Bailey, Steven John
(Steve)
No Cards.
Bailey, Troy
88Wythe/ProC-2003
89Wythe/Star-2
Bailey, Vince
79BurlB-18
Bailey, William F.
(Bill)
E254
E90/1
E92
M116
T205
Bailor, Robert M.
(Bob)
76SSPC-386
77OPC-48
77T-474R
78Ho-148
78K-39
78OPC-148
78T-196
78Tastee/Discs-26
79BJ/Bubble-1
79Ho-105
79OPC-259
79T-492
80K-16
80OPC-304
80T-581
81F-409
81OPC-297
81T-297
81T/Tr-732
82D-308
82F-521
82T-79
83D-506
83F-538
83F/St-4M
83F/St-6M
83OPC/St-260
83T-343
83T/St-260
84D-595
84F-580
84F/X-4
84Nes/792-654
84Pol/Dodg-21
84T-654
84T/St-109
84T/Tr-4
85Coke/Dodg-3
85D-397
85F-367
85T-728
86F-124
86T-522
87Dunedin-6
88Syrac/CMC-24
88Syrac/ProC-817
89Syrac/CMC-25
89Syrac/MerchB-25MG
89Syrac/ProC-796
89Syrac/Team-25MG

90AAAGame/ProC-11
90AAASingl/ProC-368MG
90ProC/Singl-674MG
90Syrac/CMC-26MG
90Syrac/MerchB-1MG
90Syrac/ProC-588MG
90Syrac/Team-1MG
90Target-26
91AAA/LineD-524MG
91Crown/Orio-16
91Syrac/LineD-524MG
91Syrac/MerchB-1MG
91Syrac/ProC-2496MG
91WIZMets-21
92BJ/Fire-2CO
92Nabisco-36
93BJ/Fire-2CO
Bain, Herbert Loren
(Loren)
No Cards.
Bain, Paul
77Clinton
78LodiD
79LodiD-3
Baine, David
92Everett/ClBest-24
92Everett/ProC-1676
Baine, John T.
(Tom)
86Erie-2
87Spring/Best-8
88TexLgAS/GS-16
89Louisvl-10
89Louisvl/CMC-20
89Louisvl/ProC-1265
90SpringDG/Best-23
Baines, Harold D.
78Knoxvl
79Iowa/Pol-3
81F-346
81OPC-347
81T-347
82D-568
82F-336
82F/St-184
82OPC-56
82T-684
83D-143
83F-229
83F/St-4M
83F/St-5M
83K-16
83OPC-177
83OPC/St-52
83T-177
83T/St-52
83TrueVal/WSox-3
84D-58
84D/AAS-11
84F-51
84F/St-4
84Nes/792-434
84OPC-197
84T-434
84T/RD-1M
84T/St-242
84TrueVal/WS-3
85Coke/WS-3
85D-58
85D/AAS-58
85Drake-2
85F-507
85F/St-21
85FunFood/Pin-110
85Leaf-231
85OPC-249
85Seven-6G
85T-249
85T-275FDP
85T/Gloss40-34
85T/RD-1M
85T/St-234
85T/Super-51
86Coke/WS-3
86D-13DK
86D-180
86D/AAS-49
86D/DKsuper-13
86Drake-24
86F-198
86F/LimEd-3
86F/Mini-42
86F/Slug-M1
86F/St-1
86GenMills/Book-2M
86Jay's-1
86Leaf-13DK
86OPC-65
86Seven/Coin-C4
86Seven/Coin-E4
86Seven/Coin-S4
86Seven/Coin-W4
86Sf-52M
86Sf-7
86T-755
86T/Mini-8
86T/St-288
86T/Super-9
86T/Tatt-4M
87Classic-42
87Coke/WS-2
87D-429
87D/AAS-25
87D/OD-236
87Drake-22
87F-485
87F-643M
87F/BB-1
87F/GameWin-1
87F/Hottest-2
87F/Mini-3
87F/St-2
87Ho/St-21
87KayBee-1
87Kraft-13
87Leaf-52
87MnM's-8
87OPC-309
87RedFoley/St-119
87Seven-C1
87Sf-153M
87Sf-171
87Sf/TPrev-26M
87Smok/AL-4
87Stuart-17M
87T-772
87T/Board-16
87T/Coins-1
87T/Gloss60-14
87T/St-284
88Coke/WS-1
88D-211
88D/AS-12
88D/Best-11
88F-391
88F/Excit-1
88Grenada-4
88KennerFig-2
88Kodak/WSox-5
88Leaf-157
88OPC-35
88Panini/St-62
88RedFoley/St-3
88S-590
88Sf-33
88T-35
88T/Big-224
88T/Coins-5
88T/RiteAid-16
88T/St-293
88T/UK-1
89B-72
89Cadaco-1
89Coke/WS-5
89D-148
89D/Best-81
89F-491
89F/Excit-1
89F/Superstar-2
89KMart/DT-22
89KennerFig-3
89Kodak/WSox-4M
89OPC-152
89Panini/St-310
89S-128
89S/Tr-62
89Sf-157
89T-585
89T/Big-266
89T/Coins-33
89T/Hills-1
89T/LJN-23
89T/St-304
89T/UK-2
89UD-211
89UD-692TC
90B-501
90Classic-69
90D-402
90D-660AS
90D/BestAL-69
90F-290
90F/ASIns-1
90F/Can-290
90Leaf-126
90Mother/Rang-6
90OPC-345
90Panini/St-167
90Panini/St-200
90PublInt/St-275
90PublInt/St-383
90S-470
90Sf-125
90T-345
90T/Big-157
90T/HillsHM-30
90T/St-158AS
90T/St-245
90UD-353
91B-231
91Cadaco-2
91Classic/200-13
91D-748
91F-2
91F/UltraUp-U45
91Leaf-196
91Leaf/StudPrev-8
91Mother/A's-14
91OPC-166
91RedFoley/St-6
91S-291
91SFExam/A's-1
91StCl-303
91T-166
91UD-562
91USPlayC/AS-9D
92B-171
92Classic/Game200-6
92D-68
92D/DK-DK14
92F-249
92F-707M
92KingB-22
92L-126
92L/BlkGold-126
92Mother/A's-14
92OPC-635
92Pinn-41
92S-137
92StCl-536
92StCl/Dome-10
92Studio-221
92T-635
92T/Gold-635
92T/GoldWin-635
92T/Kids-120
92TripleP-34
92UD-158
92Ultra-109
93B-281
93Cadaco-3
93D-725
93F-659
93F/Final-156
93L-249
93OPC-3
93OPC/Premier-68
93Pac/Spanish-216
93Pinn-111
93Pinn-488HH
93Rang/Keeb-59
93S-585
93Select-257
93Select/RookTr-8T
93StCl-666
93StCl/1stDay-666
93StCl/MurphyS-187
93Studio-190
93T-345
93T/Finest-153
93T/FinestRef-153
93T/Gold-345
93UD-765
93UD-81
93UD/SeasonHL-HI3
93Ultra-492
94B-19
94D-486
94F-2
94Finest-254
94Flair-1
94L-84
94L/CleanUp-12
94OPC-221
94Pac/Cr-26
94Panini-18
94Pinn-408
94S-469
94Select-31
94StCl-16
94StCl/1stDay-16
94StCl/Gold-16
94StCl/Team-278
94Studio-121
94T-420
94T/Gold-420
94TripleP-152
94TripleP/Medal-15M
94UD-188
94UD/ElecD-188
94Ultra-302
Bair, Charles Douglas
(Doug)
78OPC-229
78Pep-3
78SSPC/270-114
78T-353
79Ho-3
79OPC-58
79T-126
80OPC-234
80T-449
81D-73
81F-213
81OPC-73
81T-73
82T-262
83D-372
83F-2
83T-627
83T/Tr-5
84D-369
84F-76
84Nes/792-536
84T-536
84Tiger/Wave-3
85Cain's-1
85D-369
85F-1
85T-744
85Wendy-2
87F-386
87Maine-2
87Phill/TastyK-58
88Syrac/CMC-9
88Syrac/ProC-816
89Syrac/CMC-1
89Syrac/MerchB-1
89Syrac/ProC-807
89Syrac/Team-1
90Homer/Pirate-2
90S-517
Bair, Rich
84Newar-9
Baird, Albert Wells
(Al)
No Cards.
Baird, Allard
89AppFx/ProC-870
Baird, Chris
85Durham-19
Baird, Hal
75Omaha/Team-3
Baird, Howard D.
(Doug)
90Target-894
D328-10
D329-8
E135-10
M101/4-8
Baird, Robert Allen
(Bob)
No Cards.
Bajus, Mark
80Batavia-3
81Batavia-1
81Watlo-6
Bakely, Edward Enoch
(Jersey)
No Cards.
Bakenhaster, David L.
(Dave)
64T-479R
Baker, Albert Jones
(Al)
75Clinton
Baker, Andy
89BurlInd/Star-2
91ColInd/ClBest-8
91ColInd/ProC-1475
92ColRS/ClBest-20
92ColRS/ProC-2378
Baker, Charles A.
(Charlie)
No Cards.
Baker, Charles Joseph
(Chuck)
78Padre/FamFun-3
79Hawaii-16
79T-456
80Hawaii-1
81F-500
82F-561
82T-253
Baker, Charles
(Bock)
No Cards.
Baker, Curt
78Wausau
Baker, Darnell
78Cedar
Baker, David Glen
(Dave)
79Syrac/TCMA-11
79Syrac/Team-5
80Syrac-17
80Syrac/Team-3
81Syrac-11
81Syrac/Team-1
82Syrac-14
82Syrac/Team-3
83Toledo-13
84Toledo-20
Baker, Delmar David
(Del)
54T-133
60T-456C
81Tiger/Detroit-58MG
88Conlon/5-2
94Conlon-1215
94T/Arc54-133
V355-31
Baker, Derek
92GulfCM/ProC-3470
Baker, Derrell
86Indianap-13
87WPalmB-7
88Jaxvl/Best-14
88Jaxvl/ProC-968
89Rockford/Team-28CO
Baker, Douglas
(Doug)
83BirmB-8
84Evansvl-13
84Tiger/Wave-4
85T-269
86Nashvl-1
87Toledo-17
87Toledo/TCMA-20
88Portl/CMC-13
88Portl/ProC-647
89Portl/CMC-14
89Portl/ProC-230
90AAASingl/ProC-252
90BirmDG/Best-4
90F-368
90F/Can-368
90Portl/CMC-18
90Portl/ProC-182
90ProC/Singl-570
90PublInt/St-322
91AAA/LineD-603
91Tucson/LineD-603
91Tucson/ProC-2217
92Durham/ProC-1116
92Pulaski/ClBest-28CO
92Pulaski/ProC-3196CO
Baker, Ernest Gould
(Ernie)
No Cards.
Baker, Ernie
89Johnson/Star-7
89Star/IISingl-162
90Savan/ProC-2059
91StPete/ClBest-1
91StPete/ProC-2265
92StPete/ClBest-23
92StPete/ProC-2018
Baker, Eugene Walter

(Gene)
52Mother-45
55B-7
56T-142
56YellBase/Pin-5
57T-176
58Hires-65
58Kahn
58T-358
59T-238
60T-539
61T-339
79TCMA-48
87Negro/Dixon-32
Exh47
Baker, Floyd Wilson
47TipTop
48L-153
49B-119
50B-146
51B-87
52T-292
53B/BW-49
Baker, Frank Watts
71OPC-213
71T-213
72OPC-409
72T-409
73JP
74OPC-411
74T-411
91Crown/Orio-17
92Yank/WIZ70-10
Baker, Frank
(Home Run)
11Diamond-2
50W576-3
70T-704
71OPC-689
71T-689
76Shakey-78
77Galasso-155
80Perez/HOF-74
92Yank/WIZHOF-1
93Conlon/MasterCol-6
Baker, George F.
No Cards.
Baker, Gerald
86QuadC-4
Baker, Greg
81Shrev-16
Baker, Howard Francis
No Cards.
Baker, Jack Edward
No Cards.
Baker, Jared
92Classic/DP-63
92FrRow/DP-12
92Spokane/ClBest-1
92Spokane/ProC-1284
92UD/ML-22
Baker, Jason
92Elizab/ClBest-20
92Elizab/ProC-3690
Baker, Jay
88Gaston/ProC-999
Baker, Jesse Eugene
No Cards.
Baker, Jesse Ormond
No Cards.
Baker, Jim
80Utica-4
83Syrac-4
84Syrac-29
Baker, John 1
83Ander-7
Baker, John 2
89KS*-23
89KS*-40M
Baker, John Franklin
(Home Run)
10Domino-4
11Helmar-52
12Sweet/Pin-40
14CJ-2
15CJ-2
21Exh-4
40PlayBall-177
50Callahan
60Exh/HOF-3
60F-41
61F-1M
61F-6
61GP-21
75F/Pion-16
80Pac/Leg-41
80SSPC/HOF
89Pac/Leg-146
92Conlon/Sport-565
94Conlon/Col-39
BF2-32
D327
D328-11
D329-9
D350/2-8
E120
E121/80
E122
E135-11
E220
E224
E254
E300
E90/1
E91
E96
L1-120
M101/4-9
M101/5-8
S74-26
S81-95
T201
T202
T205
T206
T208
T213/blue
T215/brown
T227
T3-78
V100
W514-75
W515-15
W573
W575
WG4-2
WG5-2
Baker, Johnny B.
(Dusty)
71OPC-709R
71Richm
71Richm/Team-3
71T-709R
72T-764
73OPC-215
73T-215
73T/Lids-3
74OPC-320
74T-320
74T/St-2
75Ho-117
75OPC-33
75T-33
75T/M-33
76OPC-28
76SSPC-16
76T-28
76T/Tr-28T
77T-146
78Ho-56
78SSPC/270-57
78T-668
79OPC-290
79T-562
80OPC-135
80Pol/Dodg-12
80T-255
81D-179
81F-115
81F/St-62
81PermaGr/CC-27
81Pol/Dodg-12
81Sqt-17
81T-495
81T/HT
81T/SO-71
81T/St-182
82D-336
82F-1
82F/St-4
82K-50
82OPC-375
82Pol/Dodg-12
82T-311TL
82T-375
82T/St-52
83D-462
83F-201
83F/St-2M
83F/St-3M
83F/St-6M
83OPC-220
83OPC/St-245
83Pol/Dodg-12
83Seven-6
83T-220
83T/Gloss40-22
83T/St-245
84D-226
84D/AAS-47
84F-96
84F/X-5
84Nes/792-40
84OPC-40
84Seven-18W
84T-40
84T/St-80
84T/Tr-5
85D-445
85F-602
85F/Up-U3
85Mother/A's-15
85OPC-165
85T-165
85T/Tr-4T
86D-467
86F-411
86Leaf-231
86Mother/A's-3
86OPC-31
86T-645
87F-387
87Smok/Dodg-2
87T-565
88Smok/Dodg-21M
88Smok/Dodg-22
89Smok/Dodg-93
90Mother/Giant-21M
90Pac/Legend-71
90Richm/25Ann-3
90Target-27
91Mother/Giant-27CO
92Giant/PGE-2CO
92Mother/Giant-28M
93Mother/Giant-1MG
93T-514M
93T/Gold-514M
Baker, Ken
89FresnoSt/Smok-1
Baker, Kenny
79WHave-12
82BirmB-10
83Evansvl-17
85Omaha-27
90BirmDG/Best-6
Baker, Kerry
84PrWill-32
85Nashua-2
86Nashua-2
Baker, Kirtley
No Cards.
Baker, Mark
83QuadC-6
85Osceola/Team-3
86ColumAst-3
87ColAst/ProC-13
Baker, Mike
86Elmira-1
87Greens-21
88WinHaven/Star-3
89Lynch/Star-1
Baker, Neal Vernon
No Cards.
Baker, Norman Leslie
(Norm)
No Cards.
Baker, Philip
(Phil)
No Cards.
Baker, Rick
(Ricky)
81Chatt-15
82Chatt-7
83MidldC-25
84MidldC-18
Baker, Sam
90Burllnd/ProC-3001
91Collnd/ClBest-9
91Collnd/ProC-1476
91Watertn/ClBest-1
91Watertn/ProC-3356
92ColRS/ProC-2379
Baker, Scott
90Johnson/Star-3
91Savan/ProC-1643
92StPete/ClBest-10
92StPete/ProC-2019
93StCl/A's-25
Baker, Steven Byrne
(Steve)
80Evansvl/TCMA-12
81Syrac-1
81Syrac/Team-2
83T/Tr-6
84Louisvl-25
85Indianap-6
Baker, Thomas Calvin
(Tom)
90Target-28
93Conlon-739
Baker, Thomas Henry
(Tom)
No Cards.
Baker, Tracy Lee
No Cards.
Baker, William
(Bill)
49Eureka-177
W711/2
Bakkum, Scott
92MN-2
Bakley, Edward
N172
Bako, Paul
94B-158
94T-686
94T/Gold-686
Balabon, Anthony
86FtLaud-2
Balabon, Rick
87PrWill-9
89SanBern/Best-4
89SanBern/Cal-74
90CLAS/CL-45
90Penin/Star-2
91AAA/LineD-52
91Calgary/LineD-52
91Calgary/ProC-508
Balas, Mitchell F.
(Mike)
No Cards.
Balaz, John Lawrence
75SLCity/Caruso-3
76OPC-539
76T-539
Balboni, Stephen C.
(Steve)
80Nashvl
81Colum-11
82Colum-4
82Colum/Pol-35
82T-83R
83Colum-15
83D-73
83OPC-8
83T-8
84F/X-6
84Nes/792-782
84T-782
84T/Tr-6
85D-419
85F-196
85Leaf-95
85OPC-152
85T-486
85T/St-271
86D-222
86Drake-20
86F-1
86Kitty/Disc-17
86Leaf-98
86NatPhoto-45
86OPC-164
86Sf-186M
86T-164
86T/Gloss60-6
86T/Mini-17
86T/St-265
86T/Tatt-21M
87D-102
87D/OD-199
87F-362
87Leaf-262
87OPC-240
87RedFoley/St-85
87T-240
87T/St-263
88D-424
88F-251
88S-273
88S/Tr-46T
88T-638
89D-143
89D/Best-188
89D/Tr-48
89F-538
89F/Up-45
89OPC-336
89S-353
89S/NWest-17
89S/Tr-27
89T-336
89T/St-222
89T/Tr-6T
89UD-111
90B-436
90D-315
90F-436
90F/Can-436
90Leaf-373
90MLBPA/Pins-66
90OPC-716
90Publnt/St-424
90S-327
90S/NWest-25
90T-716
90T/Big-160
90T/TVYank-22
90UD-497
91D-650
91F-656
91OPC-511
91S-159
91StCl-134
91T-511
92OkCty/ProC-1918
92OkCty/SB-302
92Yank/WIZ80-7
93Rang/Keeb-394
Balcena, Robert R.
(Bobby)
52Park-20
Baldrick, Bob
83Wausau/Frit-22
86Chatt-2
Baldschun, Jack
62T-46
62T/St-164
63T-341
64PhilBull-3
64T-520
64T/Coins-69
64T/SU
64T/St-90
65T-555
65T/E-34
66T-272
67OPC-114
67T-114
70OPC-284
70T-284
78TCMA-104
Baldwin, Brian
87Belling/Team-19
88Wausau/GS-21
89SanBern/Best-8
89SanBern/Cal-73
Baldwin, Charles
(Lady)
90Target-895
E223
N172
N403
Scrapp
Baldwin, Clarence G.
(Kid)
N172
Baldwin, Dave
68T-231
69OPC-132
69T-132
69T/4in1-17M
70T-613
71MLB/St-433
71OPC-48
71T-48
81TCMA-309
Baldwin, Frank DeWitt
No Cards.

Baldwin, Henry Clay
No Cards.
Baldwin, James Jr.
92MidwLAS/Team-2
92SoBend/ProC-169
92UD/ML-319
93B-611
93ClBest/MLG-204
93FExcel/ML-149
94B-155
94B-370
94FExcel-34
94FExcel/LL-1
94OPC-210
94StCl/Team-145
94T-766
94T/Gold-766
94UD-3
94UD/ElecD-3
94Ultra-333
Baldwin, Jeff
86Ashvl-2
87Osceola-10
88Osceola/Star-3
89ColMud/Best-13
89ColMud/ProC-135
89ColMud/Star-3
90ColMud/Best-9
90ColMud/ProC-1357
90ColMud/Star-4
90ProC/Singl-753
91AA/LineD-553
91Jacks/LineD-553
91Jacks/ProC-930
91T/90Debut-10
92Jacks/ProC-4011
92Jacks/SB-328
Baldwin, Johnny
83Greens-1
84Nashvl-1
Baldwin, Kirk
89Eugene/Best-3
90AppFox/Box-4
90AppFox/ProC-2088
Baldwin, Marcus E.
(Mark)
E223
N172
Baldwin, O.F.
No Cards.
Baldwin, Reginald C.
(Reggie)
79CharCh-4
80T-678R
80Tidew-13
Baldwin, Rickey Alan
(Rick)
76OPC-372
76SSPC-552
76SSPC/MetsY-M22
76T-372
77T-587
78SanJose-11
91WIZMets-22
Baldwin, Robert H.
(Billy)
76SSPC-370
91WIZMets-23
Baldwin, Tony
88Sumter/ProC-391
89BurlB/ProC-1608
89BurlB/Star-1
90BurlB/Best-19
90BurlB/ProC-2361
90BurlB/Star-2
Balelo, Nesi
87Chatt/Best-19
88Vermont/ProC-949
Balenti, Michael R.
(Mike)
No Cards.
Balentine, Bryant
91Princet/ClBest-24
91Princet/ProC-3504
Bales, Tom
88LitFalls/Pucko-3
Bales, Wesley Owen
(Lee)
67OPC-51R
67T-51R
81TCMA-370
Balfanz, John
88StPete/Star-1
89AS/Cal-37
89Reno/Cal-261
Ball, Arthur
(Art)
No Cards.
Ball, Cornelius
(Neal)
10Domino-5
11Helmar-21
12Sweet/Pin-16
91Conlon/Sport-203
T202
T204
T205
T206
T207
T215/brown
Ball, Harrison
(Harry)
88CapeCod-19
88CapeCod/Sum-27
90Johnson/Star-4
Ball, James Chandler
(Jim)
T204
Ball, Jeff D.
90AubAs/Best-9
90AubAs/ProC-3408
91Osceola/ClBest-16
91Osceola/ProC-690
92Jacks/ProC-4002
92Jacks/SB-329
Ball, Jeff G.
87Hawaii-17
90Boise/ProC-3310
Ball, Jim
77QuadC
Ball, Robert
80Ashvl-10
81Tulsa-26
82Tulsa-21
Balla, Gary
77QuadC
Ballanfant, Lee
55B-295UMP
Ballara, Juan
92Johnson/ClBest-6
92Johnson/ProC-3118
Ballard, Dan
78Green
Ballard, Glenn
(Butch)
77Spartan
80OrlanTw-14
Ballard, Jeff
86Hagers-1
87RochR-25
87RochR/TCMA-1
88D-520
88F-554
88French-34
88RochR/CMC-1
88RochR/ProC-199
88RochR/Team-1
88T-782
89B-7
89D-495
89D/Best-30
89F-607
89French-29
89Panini/St-253
89S-551
89T-69
89T/St-230
89UD-595
90B-244
90Classic-89
90D-51
90D/BestAL-29
90F-173
90F/AwardWin-1
90F/Can-173
90HagersDG/Best-1
90HotRook/St-5
90KMart/SS-27
90Kenner/Fig-5
90Leaf-118
90MLBPA/Pins-110
90OPC-296
90OPC-394AS
90Panini/St-13
90PublInt/St-573
90RedFoley/St-3
90S-349
90S/YS/I-25
90Sf-123
90T-296
90T-394AS
90T/Big-278
90T/DH-2
90T/Gloss60-17
90T/Mini-1
90T/St-232
90T/TVAS-27
90UD-259
91B-98
91Crown/Orio-18
91D-279
91F-467
91Leaf-522
91OPC-546
91S-243
91StCl-283
91T-546
91UD-260
92D-74
92Louisvl/ProC-1880
92Louisvl/SB-252
92OPC-104
92S-129
92StCl-771
92T-104
92T/Gold-104
92T/GoldWin-104
94Pac/Cr-491
Ballard, Matt
89TNTech-2
Ballard, Tim
82CharR-13
Ballenger, Pelham A.
No Cards.
Baller, Jay Scott
(Jay)
82Reading-1
83Charl-1
83Wheat/Ind-2
84BuffB-9
85Iowa-12
86Cub/Unocal-1
86D-613
86F/Up-U7
86Gator-48
87Iowa-5
88Calgary/CMC-5
88Calgary/ProC-792
88T-717
89Indianap/CMC-7
89Indianap/ProC-1231
90Omaha/CMC-1
90ProC/Singl-176
Baller, Jay
92ScranWB/ProC-2439
92ScranWB/SB-478
93D-356
Ballinger, Mark A.
77Jaxvl
Ballou, Bill
89Utica/Pucko-29CO
91Utica/ClBest-22CO
91Utica/ProC-3258CO
Ballou, Win
90Target-896
Balmer, Steve
83QuadC-7
Balsley, Darren
84Idaho/Team-3
86Modesto-4
87Dunedin-9
88Knoxvl/Best-10
89Knoxvl/Best-3
89Knoxvl/ProC-1137
89Knoxvl/Star-5
90StCath/ProC-3484CO
91Myrtle/ClBest-28CO
91Myrtle/ProC-2962CO
92Myrtle/ClBest-29CO
92Myrtle/ProC-2214CO
93Hagers/ClBest-27CO
93Hagers/ProC-1896CO
Balthazar, Doyle
87CharWh-28
87Lakeland-8
88Lakeland/Star-2
89London/ProC-1384
90FSLAS/Star-25
90Lakeland/Star-2
91AA/LineD-376
91London/LineD-376
91London/ProC-1880
92SanBern/ClBest-14
92SanBern/ProC-
Baltz, Nick
76Baton
Bamberger, George I.
50Remar
53Mother-38
59T-529
73OPC-136CO
73T-136C
74OPC-306CO
74T-306C
79T-577MG
80T-659MG
81TCMA-307
83T-246MG
85Gard-1MG
85Pol/Brew-31MG
85T/Tr-5T
86Pol/Brew-31MG
86T-21MG
87T-468MG
90Pac/Legend-11
90Swell/Great-23
91Crown/Orio-19
Bamberger, Harold E.
(Hal)
No Cards.
Ban, Mark
86QuadC-5
92Niagara/ClBest-10
92Niagara/ProC-3314
Banach, Joe
81Clinton-1
Banasiak, Edward
87Elmira/Black-24
87Elmira/Red-24
88WinHaven/Star-4
Bancells, Richard
81RochR-20
83RochR-24
Bancroft, David James
(Dave)
16FleischBrd-6
21Exh-5
25Exh-1
26Exh-4
27Exh-1
28Exh-5
28Yueng-19
29Exh/4-4
61F-7
75Sheraton-13
76Rowe-12M
76Shakey-119
77Galasso-122
80Perez/HOF-119
89HOF/St-20
89Smok/Dodg-2
90Target-29
91Conlon/Sport-17
92Conlon/Sport-598
94Conlon-1065
BF2-82
D327
D328-12
D329-10
D350/2-9
E120
E121/120
E121/80
E126-52
E135-12
E210
E220
M101/4-10
M101/5-9
V100
V61-73
V89-38
W501-64
W502-19
W512-1
W514-40
W515-4
W516-30
W572
W573
W575
WG7-3
Bancroft, Frank C.
T204
Bando, Christopher M.
(Chris)
81Charl-8
81T-451R
82D-551
82T-141R
82Wheat/Ind
83D-33
83F-400
83T-227
83Wheat/Ind-3
84D-224
84F-534
84Nes/792-431
84T-431
84Wheat/Ind-23
85D-520
85F-438
85Leaf-39
85OPC-14
85Polar/Ind-23
85T-14
86D-373
86F-579
86OPC-211
86OhHenry-23
86T-594
87D-501
87D/OD-105
87F-243
87Gator-23
87T-322
88Chatt/Team-1
88D-95
88F-601
88Gator-23
88OPC-51
88Panini/St-71
88S-172
88T-604
88T/St-209
90AS/Cal-29MG
90Stockton/Best-27MG
90Stockton/Cal-200
90Stockton/ProC-2200MG
91Stockton/ClBest-24MG
91Stockton/ProC-3047MG
92ElPaso/ProC-3937
92ElPaso/SB-224MG
Bando, Salvatore L.
(Sal)
67OPC-33R
67T-33R
68A's/JITB-1
68OPC-146
68T-146
69MLB/St-82
69T-371
69T-556M
69T/St-211
70K-51
70MLB/St-254
70OPC-120
70T-120
70T/S-2
70T/SO
70T/Super-2
71MLB/St-506
71OPC-285
71T-285
71T/Coins-132
71T/GM-5
71T/Greatest-5
71T/S-57
71T/Super-57
71T/tatt-1
72K-52
72MB-24
72OPC-348KP
72T-348KP
72T-650
73OPC-155
73T-155
73T/Lids-4
74K-51
74OPC-103
74T-103
74T/St-221
75Ho-4
75Ho/Twink-4
75OPC-380
75SSPC/42-13
75T-380

75T/M-380
76OPC-90
76SSPC-497
76T-90
77BurgChef-87
77Ho-126
77Ho/Twink-126
77OPC-145
77T-498
78Ho-94
78OPC-174
78T-265
78Wiffle/Discs-1
79Ho-119
79OPC-283
79T-550
80OPC-363
80T-715
81D-84
81F-510
81OPC-276
81T-623
82D-592
82F-134
87Mother/A's-4
88Pac/Leg-99
89Swell-63
90Pac/Legend-4
90Swell/Great-7
92AP/ASG-40
93TWill-42
93UD/ATH-5
Bandy, Ken
87QuadC-28
Bane, Craig
90MissSt-4
91MissSt-4
92MissSt-4
93MissSt-3
Bane, Edward Lee
(Ed)
74OPC-592
74T-592
74Tacoma/Caruso-5
75IntLgAS/Broder-2
75PCL/AS-2
75Tacoma/KMMO-13
76SSPC-212
77T-486
Banes, Alan
80Elmira-1
Banes, Dave
82Nashvl-1
Baney, Richard Lee
(Dick)
70OPC-88R
70T-88R
74OPC-608R
74T-608R
Bangert, Greg
81Clinton-10
Bangston, Pat
88Kenosha/ProC-1406
88MidwLAS/GS-34
89OrlanTw/Best-9
89OrlanTw/ProC-1338
90AAASingl/ProC-239
90Portl/CMC-2
90Portl/ProC-169
90ProC/Singl-554
91AA/LineD-476
91OrlanSR/LineD-476
91OrlanSR/ProC-1842
Banister, Jeff
86Watertn-3
87Macon-4
88Harris/ProC-855
89EastLDD/ProC-DD28
89EastLgAS/ProC-23
89Harris/ProC-306
89Harris/Star-2
90Harris/ProC-1195
90Harris/Star-3
91AAA/LineD-26
91BuffB/LineD-26
91BuffB/ProC-544
92T/91Debut-8
Bankhead, Daniel R.
(Dan)
51B-225
52Park-64
79TCMA-159
86Negro/Frit-102
90Target-30
Bankhead, Sam
78Laugh/Black-31
86Negro/Frit-97
Bankhead, Scott
85T-393OLY
86D/Rook-36
86F/Up-U8
86Omaha/ProC-1
86Omaha/TCMA-24
86Sf/Rook-39
87F-363
87F/Up-U1
87Mother/Sea-13
87Sf/TPrev-25M
87T-508
87T/Tr-2T
88D-70
88F-368
88Mother/Sea-13
88OPC-246
88Panini/St-180
88S-238
88S/YS/II-37
88T-738
89B-203
89D-463
89D/Best-219
89F-539
89Mother/Sea-13
89OPC-79
89Panini/St-429
89S-341
89S/YS/I-42
89T-79
89UD-316
90B-466
90D-261
90D/BestAL-40
90F-505
90F/Can-505
90Leaf-127
90Mother/Mar-24
90OPC-213
90Panini/St-147
90PublInt/St-426
90S-555
90Sf-41
90T-213
90T/St-222
90UD-561
91B-254
91CounHrth-11
91D-189
91F-442
91Leaf-345
91OPC-436
91S-817
91StCl-597
91T-436
91UD-294
92D-304
92F/Up-78
92L-485
92L/BlkGold-485
92OPC-155
92OPC/Premier-18
92Pinn-580
92Reds/Kahn-25
92S-594
92S/RookTr-47T
92StCl-375
92StCl-701
92T-155
92T/DQ-6
92T/Gold-155
92T/GoldWin-155
92T/Tr-7T
92T/TrGold-7T
92Ultra-478
93D-690
93F-386
93F/Final-169
93OPC-21
93OPC/Premier-94
93Pac/Spanish-353
93S-584
93Select-265
93Select/RookTr-122T
93StCl-145
93StCl/1stDay-145
93T-361
93T/Gold-361
93UD-329
93UD-760
93Ultra-505
94D-429
94F-25
94Flair-10
94Pac/Cr-48
94S-139
94S/GoldR-139
94T-633
94T/Gold-633
Banko, Joe
89Anchora-1
Bankowski, Chris
81Redwd-27
83Redwd-3
Banks, Brian
94FExcel-77
Banks, Darryl
82QuadC-1
83MidldC-12
84MidldC-8
Banks, Dave
86AubAs-2
Banks, Dean
91Pocatel/ProC-3788
91Pocatel/SportP-10
Banks, Ernest
(Ernie)
54T-94
55B-242
55RFG-26
55T-28
55T/DH-32
55W605-26
56T-15
56T/Pin-5
56YellBase/Pin-6
57T-55
58T-310
58T-482AS
59Armour-4
59Bz
59HRDerby-3
59T-147M
59T-350
59T-469M
59T-559AS
60Armour-3
60Bz-1
60NuCard-20
60T-10
60T-560AS
60T/tatt-5
61Bz-19
61NuCard-420
61P-191
61T-350
61T-43LL
61T-485MVP
61T-575AS
61T/RO
61T/St-4
62Bz
62Exh
62J-188
62P-188
62P/Can-188
62Salada-177A
62Salada-177B
62Shirriff-177
62T-25
62T/St-104
62T/bucks
63Bz-3
63Exh
63J-169
63P-169
63Salada-17
63T-242M
63T-380
63T-3LL
63T/SO
64T-55
64T/Coins-42
64T/SU
64T/St-25
64T/tatt
65OldLond-3
65T-510
65T/E-58
66OPC-110
66T-110
66T/RO
66T/RO-7
67CokeCap/AS-21
67CokeCap/Cub-2
67CokeCap/NLAS-27
67T-215
68T-355
68T/ActionSt-6C
69Kelly/Pin-2
69MB-19
69MLB/St-118
69MLBPA/Pin-34
69OPC-20
69OPC-6LL
69Sunoco/Pin-1
69T-20
69T-6LL
69T/St-11
69Trans-40
70Dunkin-1
70K-40
70MB-3
70MLB/St-13
70T-630
70T/CB
70Trans-3
71K-50
71MD
71MLB/St-25
71MLB/St-555
71OPC-525
71T-525
71T/GM-36
71T/Greatest-36
72MB-25
73OPC-81CO
73T-81C
75OPC-196MVP
75OPC-197MVP
75T-196MVP
75T-197MVP
75T/M-196MVP
75T/M-197MVP
76Laugh/Jub-2
77Galasso-254
77Galasso-29
78TCMA-255
79TCMA-5
80Laugh/3/4/5-27
80Marchant-4
80Pac/Leg-33
80Perez/HOF-158
82CJ-10
84Cub/Uno-2M
84Cub/Uno-3M
84Cub/Uno-4
84Cub/Uno-7M
85CircK-10
85Woolwth-3
86BLChew-9
86Sf/Dec-29
87Nestle/DT-26
88Grenada-64
88Pac/Leg-36
89HOF/St-6
89Kenner/BBGr-2
89T/LJN-65
90BBWit-19
90CollAB-11
90Pac/Legend-5
90Perez/GreatMom-21
90Swell/Great-95
91K/3D-4
91K/SU-2A
91K/SU-2B
91LineD-18
91Swell/Great-5
92Cub/OldStyle-3
92FrRow/Banks-Set
93Nabisco-1
94T/Arc54-94
Exh47
Banks, George Edward
61Clover-2
63T-564
64T-223
65T-348
66T-488
Banks, James
92SoOreg/ClBest-20
92SoOreg/ProC-3404
Banks, Lance
90CharRain/Best-2
90CharRain/ProC-2032
91Waterlo/ClBest-1
91Waterlo/ProC-1248
Banks, William John
(Bill)
No Cards.
Banks, Willie
88Kenosha/ProC-1380
89AS/Cal-4
89Visalia/Cal-101
89Visalia/ProC-1426
90A&AASingle/ProC-40
90B-411
90Classic/III-31
90Foil/Best-11
90OrlanSR/Best-1
90OrlanSR/ProC-1076
90OrlanSR/Star-2
90ProC/Singl-808
90Star/ISingl-45
91AAA/LineD-402
91B-341
91Classic/II-T57
91Leaf/GRook-BC5
91Portl/LineD-402
91Portl/ProC-1559
91UD-74
91Ultra-373MLP
92B-553
92Classic/Game200-160
92D-760
92F-657
92OPC-747
92Pinn-575
92Pinn/RookI-6
92Portl/SB-401
92Portland/ProC-2659
92S/Rook-39
92Sky/AAASingl-182
92StCl-321
92T-747
92T/91Debut-9
92T/Gold-747
92T/GoldWin-747
92UD-14SR
92UD/Scout-SR2
92Ultra-393
93B-76
93D-79
93F-637
93L-351
93Pac/Spanish-518
93Panini-127
93S-235
93Select-314
93StCl-170
93StCl/1stDay-170
93T-226
93T/Gold-226
93ToysRUs-54
93UD-686
93Ultra-579
94D-79
94F-199
94Finest-286
94Flair-134
94L-245
94Pac/Cr-349
94Panini-89
94Pinn-177
94Pinn/Artist-177
94Pinn/Museum-177
94S-185
94S/GoldR-185
94StCl/Team-334
94T-14
94T/Gold-14
94UD-434
94UD/CollC-46
94UD/CollC/Gold-46
94UD/CollC/Silv-46
94Ultra-453
94Ultra-83
Bankston, Wilborn E.
(Bill)
No Cards.
Banning, Doug
86MidldA-1
87Edmon-7
87MidldA-6
90Chatt/GS-4
Banning, James M.
(Jim)
N172
Bannister, Alan
77T-559

78K-38
78SSPC/270-151
78T-213
79T-134
80OPC-317
80T-608
81T-632
82D-159
82F-359
82T-287
82Wheat/Ind
83D-285
83F-401
83OPC-348
83T-348
83Wheat/Ind-4
84D-154
84F-535
84F/X-7
84Mother/Ast-21
84Nes/792-478
84Rangers-2
84T-478
84T/St-257
84T/Tr-7
85F-555
85Rangers-5
85T-76
86D-525
86F-556
86T-784
88Rockford-1
89Jaxvl/Best-2
89Jaxvl/ProC-151
89Pac/SenLg-14
89Rockford-1MG
89T/SenLg-30
89TM/SenLg-5
91AAA/LineD-400M
91Phoenix/LineD-400CO
91Phoenix/ProC-84CO
93Rang/Keeb-60

Bannister, Floyd F.
78BK/Ast-6
78T-39
79OPC-154
79T-306
80OPC-352
80T-699
81D-286
81F-599
81OPC-166
81Pol/Mariners-2
81T-166
81T/St-128
82D-100
82F-504
82T-468
82T/St-234
83D-21DK
83D-50
83F-471
83F/St-1AM
83F/St-1BM
83F/St-7M
83K-41
83OPC-203
83OPC/St-113
83OPC/St-18
83T-545
83T-706LL
83T/St-113
83T/St-18
83T/Tr-7
83TrueVal/WSox-24
84D-366
84F-52
84F/St-84
84Nes/792-280
84OPC-280
84T-280
84T/St-247
84TrueVal/WS-4
85Coke/WS-24
85D-379
85F-508
85OPC-354
85T-274FDP
85T-725
86Coke/WS-19
86D-244
86F-199
86Leaf-118
86OPC-64
86T-64
86T/Mini-9
87Coke/WS-12
87D-211
87F-486
87F/Lim-1
87F/St-3
87OPC-356
87T-737
87T/St-286
88AlaskaAS70/Team-18
88D-383
88D/Best-7
88F-392
88OPC-357
88Panini/St-52
88RedFoley/St-4
88S-622
88S/Tr-63T
88Smok/Royals-8
88T-357
88T/Big-174
88T/Tr-8T
89B-112
89D-262
89F-276
89OPC-194
89RedFoley/St-5
89S-249
89Sf-154
89T-638
89T/St-269
89UD-549
90OPC-116
90Publint/St-342
90T-116
90UD-695
91B-190
91F/Up-U8
91Leaf-439
92Mother/Rang-13
92StCl-743
92Ultra-437
93Rang/Keeb-61

Bannister, Tim
77BurlB
78BurlB

Bannon, James Henry
(Jimmy)
N300/unif

Bannon, Thomas Edward
(Tom)
No Cards.

Banta, John Kay
(Jack)
45Parade*-53
49Eureka-28
50B-224
79TCMA-203
90Target-31

Banton, Scott
89Hamil/Star-1
90Savan/ProC-2079
91Spring/ClBest-4
91Spring/ProC-753

Baptist, Travis
91MedHat/ProC-4089
91MedHat/SportP-10
92Myrtle/ProC-2188
93FExcel/ML-237
93Knoxvl/ProC-1240

Baran, Lorie
92Clinton/ClBest-30M

Baranoski, Jim
89Idaho/ProC-2025

Barba, Doug
84Cedar-4

Barba, Michael
82Holyo-1
83ArkTr-6

Barbara, Daniel
(Dan)
89SanBern/Best-7
89SanBern/Cal-76
90Penin/Star-3
90Star/ISingl-77

Barbara, Don
91MidldA/OneHour-2
91MidwLAS/ProC-24
91QuadC/ClBest-15
91QuadC/ProC-2633
92Edmon/ProC-3543
92Edmon/SB-151
92Sky/AAASingl-73

Barbare, Walter L.
21Exh-6
E120

Barbary, Donald O.
(Red)
No Cards.

Barbe, Jim
(Yogi)
78Ashvl
79Tulsa-17

Barbeau, William J.
(Jap)
E91
T206

Barbee, David Monroe
(Dave)
No Cards.

Barbeln, Joe
92Yakima/ClBest-23
92Yakima/ProC-3438

Barber, Brian
91ClBest/Singl-443
91Classic/DP-18
91FrRow/DP-21
91Johnson/ClBest-18
91Johnson/ProC-3969
92B-29
92ClBest-268
92OPC-594
92Pinn-298DP
92ProC/Tomorrow-324
92S-803
92Spring/ClBest-4
92Spring/ProC-860
92StCl/Dome-11
92StPete/ProC-2020
92T-594
92T/Gold-594
92T/GoldWin-594
92UD/ML-178
93B-136
93FExcel/ML-96
93StCl/Card-29
93Ultra-461
94B-180
94B-364
94ClBest/Gold-13
94FExcel-256
94SigRook-1
94T-788
94T/Gold-788
94Ultra-563

Barber, Charles D.
(Charlie)
No Cards.

Barber, Red
89Rini/Dodg-28M
89Rini/Dodg-29

Barber, Stephen David
(Steve)
60T-514
61P-74
61T-125
61T/St-97
62Salada-11
62Shirriff-11
62T-355
62T-57LL
63Exh
63F-1
63J-64
63P-64
63T-12
64Bz-3
64T-450
64T/Coins-8
64T/SU
64T/St-54
64T/tatt
64Wheat/St-5
65OPC-113
65T-113
66T-477
67OPC-82
67T-82
68T-316
69MB-20
69MLB/St-92
69T-233
69T/St-222
70MLB/St-265
70OPC-224
70T-224
72MB-26
72OPC-333
72T-333
73OPC-36
73T-36
74OPC-631
74T-631
78TCMA-57
91Crown/Orio-20
92Yank/WIZ60-5
Exh47

Barber, Steve Lee
(Steve)
No Cards.

Barber, Tyrus Turner
(Turner)
21Exh-7
E120
E121
E220
V100
W501-60
W573

Barberich, Frank F.
C46-16

Barberie, Bret
88T/Tr-9T
89Star/Wax-32
89T/Big-19
89WPalmB/Star-2
90Jaxvl/Best-3
90Jaxvl/ProC-1379
91AAA/LineD-176
91F/UltraUp-U90
91Indianap/LineD-176
91Indianap/ProC-465
91UD/FinalEd-67F
92B-467
92Classic/I-T9
92D-449
92Expo/D/Duri-1
92F-472
92L-288
92L/BlkGold-288
92L/GoldPrev-6
92L/Prev-6
92OPC-224
92OPC/Premier-36
92Pinn-93
92Pinn/Team2000-50
92ProC/Tomorrow-256
92S-419
92S/100RisSt-14
92StCl-427
92Studio-51
92T-224
92T/91Debut-10
92T/DQ-16
92T/Gold-224
92T/GoldWin-224
92TripleP-134
92UD-363
92Ultra-512
93B-446
93D-12
93D-759
93F-418
93F/Final-51
93Flair-47
93L-256
93Marlin/Publix-4
93Pac/Spanish-454
93Pinn-553
93Pinn/Expan-4
93S-617
93StCl-481
93StCl/1stDay-481
93StCl/Marlin-18
93TripleP-195
93UD-479M
93UD-552
93UD/FunPack-118
93UD/SP-136
93USPlayC/Marlin-11D
93USPlayC/Marlin-6S
93Ultra-366
94B-674
94D-127
94F-461
94L-62
94Panini-179
94Pinn-136
94Pinn/Artist-136
94Pinn/Museum-136
94S-434
94Select-133
94StCl-415
94StCl/1stDay-415
94StCl/Gold-415
94StCl/Team-62
94Studio-106
94T-132
94T/Finest-187
94T/FinestRef-187
94T/Gold-132
94TripleP-131
94UD-151
94UD/CollC-47
94UD/CollC/Gold-47
94UD/CollC/Silv-47
94UD/ElecD-151
94Ultra-192

Barbieri, James P.
(Jim)
67OPC-76
67T-76
90Target-32

Barbosa, Rafael
84Durham-11

Barboza, James
85Clovis-2

Barcelo, Marc
94ClBest/Gold-183
94T-747DP
94T/Gold-747DP

Barclay, Curtis C.
(Curt)
57Seattle/Pop-3
57T-361
58Hires-70
58SFCallB-2
58T-21
59T-307

Barclay, George O.
No Cards.

Barczi, Scott
87Watertn-7
88Augusta/ProC-368
89Salem/Star-4
90Harris/ProC-1196
90Harris/Star-4

Bard, Michael
89KS*-72
91BendB/ClBest-26
91BendB/ProC-3699

Bard, Paul Z.
81VeroB-2
82VeroB-12
84CharlO-21

Barden, Geoff
91Brisbane/Fut-8

Barden, Steve
89Richm/ProC-819

Bardot, Gene
76Wausau

Bare, Raymond Douglas
(Ray)
76OPC-507
76SSPC-613
76T-507
77T-43
78RochR

Barefoot, Mike
89Miami/I/Star-1

Barfield, Jesse Lee
78Dunedin
80Knoxvl/TCMA-13
82OPC-203R
82T-203R
82T/Tr-2T
83D-595
83F-424
83OPC-257
83OPC/St-307
83T-257
83T/St-307
84D-193
84F-147
84Nes/792-488
84OPC-316
84T-488
84T/St-372
84Tor/Fire-4
85D-195
85F-99
85Leaf-209
85OPC-24
85OPC/Post-20

85T-24
85T/St-362
85Tor/Fire-4
86BJ/Ault-3
86D-193
86F-52
86F/Mini-12
86F/St-2
86GenMills/Book-3M
86Leaf-254
86OPC-234
86Seven/Coin-E16
86Sf-76
86T-593
86T/St-192
86T/Tatt-2M
86Tor/Fire-3
87Classic-58
87D-121
87D/AAS-23
87D/OD-34
87F-219
87F-643M
87F/BB-2
87F/Excit-3
87F/LL-1
87F/Mini-4
87F/Slug-2
87F/St-4
87F/WaxBox-C2
87GenMills/Book-1M
87Ho/St-1
87KayBee-2
87Kraft-41
87Leaf-127
87OPC-24
87RedFoley/St-3
87Sf-14
87Sf-153M
87Sf/TPrev-5M
87Stuart-27M
87T-655
87T/Coins-2
87T/Gloss60-35
87T/HL-9
87T/Mini-73
87T/St-184
87Tor/Fire-1
87Woolwth-9
88BJ/5x7-1
88D-442
88D/Best-216
88F-102
88F/RecSet-1
88F/St-70
88Ho/Disc-19
88Leaf-225
88OPC-140
88Panini/St-223
88S-8
88Sf-13
88T-140
88T/Big-92
88T/Gloss60-2
88T/St-192
88T/St/Backs-46
88Tor/Fire-29
89B-257
89Classic-66
89D-425
89D/Best-132
89D/GrandSlam-11
89F-225
89F/Up-46
89OPC-325
89Panini/St-471
89RedFoley/St-6
89S-160
89S/NWest-5
89S/Tr-22
89Sf-9
89T-325
89T/Ames-1
89T/Tr-7T
89Tor/Fire-29
89UD-149
89UD/Ext-702
90B-433
90BJ/HoSt-2M
90BJ/HoSt-2M
90BJ/HoSt-5M
90Classic-99
90D-74
90D/BestAL-109
90F-437
90F/Can-437
90Kenner/Fig-6
90Leaf-201
90MLBPA/Pins-61
90OPC-740
90Pac/Legend-110
90Panini/St-120
90PublInt/St-530
90RedFoley/St-4
90S-222
90S/NWest-5
90Sf-10
90T-740
90T/Big-188
90T/HillsHM-24
90T/St-314
90T/TVYank-29
90UD-476
91B-169
91Classic/200-61
91D-498
91F-657
91Leaf-308
91Leaf/Stud-91
91OPC-85
91Panini/FrSt-330
91S-148
91S-414RIF
91StCl-103
91T-85
91UD-485
91Ultra-228
92B-295
92D-316
92F-221
92OPC-650
92Panini-139
92Pinn-425
92S-565
92StCl-214
92T-650
92T/Gold-650
92T/GoldWin-650
92UD-139
92UD-644DS
92Ultra-99
92Yank/WIZ80-8
93BJ/D/McDon-2
Barfield, John D.
87PortChar-5
88TexLgAS/GS-17
88Tulsa-14
89OkCty/CMC-2
89OkCty/ProC-1518
90AAASingl/ProC-670
90OkCty/CMC-9
90OkCty/ProC-670
90ProC/Singl-159
90T/89Debut-8
91D-688
91F/Up-U58
91Mother/Rang-13
91OPC-428
91S-573
91T-428
91UD-629
92D-168
92OkCty/ProC-1906
92S-683
92StCl-364
92UD-691
93Rang/Keeb-62
Barfoot, Clyde R.
No Cards.
Bargar, Gregory R.
(Greg)
80Memphis-5
83Memphis/TCMA-20
83Wichita/Dog-4
84Indianap-13
84Nes/792-474
84OPC-292
84T-474
85Indianap-13
87Louisvl-4
88Louisvl-9
Bargas, Rob
91WPalmB/ClBest-18
91WPalmB/ProC-1234
Barger, Bob
76Wausau
Barger, Eros Bolivar
(Cy)
10Domino-6
11Helmar-82
12Sweet/Pin-69
14CJ-141
14Piedmont/St-1
15CJ-141
M116
S74-48
T202
T205
T206
T207
T213/blue
Barger, Vince
85Durham-2
Bargerhuff, Brian
89Clinton/Frit-17
86Chatt-3
Bargfeldt, John
79QuadC-19
Barillari, Al
52Laval-50
Bark, Brian
88CapeCod/Sum-114
90Pulaski/Best-1
90Pulaski/ProC-3101
91Durham/ClBest-2
91Durham/ProC-1535
92Greenvl/ProC-1147
92Greenvl/SB-227
92Sky/AASingl-97
93Richm/Bleach-10
93Richm/Pep-3
93Richm/Team-5
Barker, Bob
87Albany-3
Barker, Jeff
78Holyo
Barker, Leonard H.
(Len)
74Gaston
77T-489R
77Tucson
78BK/R-9
78SSPC/270-91
78T-634
79OPC-40
79T-94
80T-227
81D-320
81F-408
81OPC-3
81T-432
81T-6LL
81T/St-5
81T/St-72
82D-137
82D-6DK
82F-360
82F-639M
82F/St-200
82K-37
82OPC-360
82T-166LL
82T-360
82T/St-113
82T/St-12
82T/St-178
82Wheat/Ind
83D-111
83F-402
83F-642
83F/St-13M
83F/St-5M
83K-33
83OPC-120
83OPC/St-57
83T-120
83T/St-57
83Wheat/Ind-5
84D-443
84F-170
84Nes/792-614
84OPC-309
84Pol/Atl-39
84T-614
85D-165
85F-318
85Ho/Braves-2
85Pol/Atl-39
85T-557
86D-409
86F-507
86Indianap-20
86T-24
91Pac/SenLg-153
93Rang/Keeb-63
Barker, Raymond H.
(Ray)
61T-428
65T-546R
66T-323
67T-583
81TCMA-314
91Crown/Orio-21
92Yank/WIZ60-6
Barker, Timothy C.
(Tim)
86Tampa-2
87Beloit-17
88Charl/ProC-1221
Barker, Timothy N..
89GreatF-14
90AS/Cal-8
90Bakers/Cal-255
91AA/LineD-529
91SanAn/LineD-529
91SanAn/ProC-2980
92SanAn/ProC-3980
92SanAn/SB-554
92Sky/AASingl-243
93Ottawa/ProC-2440
Barkett, Andy
93Bz-3
93T/Tr-93T
Barkley, Jeff
83Watlo/Frit-20
84Maine-15
85Maine-1
85Polar/Ind-49
86T-567
Barkley, Red
90Target-33
Barkley, Samuel E.
(Sam)
N172
N284
N284/StL
Barley, Ned
90MedHat/Best-12
Barlick, Al
55B-265UMP
80Perez/HOF-201
90TM/Umpire-71
Barling, Glenn
82Clinton/Frit-6
Barlow, Andy
90James/Pucko-31
Barlow, Clem
91Belling/ClBest-1
91Belling/ProC-3678
Barlow, Mike
76SSPC-298
77SLCity
78Cr/PCL-97
78T-429
80Syrac-13
80Syrac/Team-4
80T-312
81OPC-77
81T-77
82Syrac-1
82Syrac/Team-4
Barlow, Ricky
86GlenF-1
87Toledo-9
87Toledo/TCMA-19
Barlow, Stuart
91Sydney/Fut-16
Barmes, Bruce R.
No Cards.
Barna, Herbert Paul
(Babe)
No Cards.
Barnard, Jeff
81AppFx-2
Barnard, Steve
85PrWill-11
Barnard, Tom
88Watertn/Pucko-32
92Welland/ClBest-30CO
92Welland/ProC-1341CO
Barnes, Brian
88CapeCod/Sum-130
90A&AASingle/ProC-36
90Foil/Best-261
90Jaxvl/Best-14
90Jaxvl/ProC-1365
90ProC/Singl-660
91B-438
91Classic/200-8
91D-415RR
91Leaf/Stud-192
91OPC-211
91OPC/Premier-4
91S-708RP
91S/Rook40-10
91StCl-114
91T-211
91T/90Debut-11
91UD-12
92B-501
92D-117
92Expo/D/Duri-2B
92F-473
92Indianap/SB-177
92OPC-73
92OPC/Premier-52
92S-715
92S/100RisSt-78
92Sky/AASingl-85
92StCl-549
92T-73
92T/Gold-73
92T/GoldWin-73
92UD-361
93D-88
93F-457
93OPC-249
93Pac/Spanish-181
93StCl-500
93StCl/1stDay-500
93T-112
93T/Gold-112
93UD-214
94F-532
94Pac/Cr-373
94S-289
94S/GoldR-289
94T-694
94T/Gold-694
Barnes, Charlie
48Sommer-30M
Barnes, Chris
88CapeCod/Sum-115
Barnes, Colin
91Sydney/Fut-8
Barnes, Craig
75Lafay
Barnes, Donald L.
W753
Barnes, Emile Deering
(Red)
93Conlon-984
Barnes, Everett Duane
(Eppie)
No Cards.
Barnes, Frank
60T-538
92Negro/RetortII-1
Barnes, Harry
92Negro/Retort-2
Barnes, Jeff
91MidldA/OneHour-3
92Modesto/ClBest-12
Barnes, Jesse L.
25Exh-2
90Target-34
92Conlon/Sport-355
E120
V100
V117-1
W514-120
W516-12
W572
W573
W575
Barnes, John Francis
(Honey)
No Cards.
Barnes, John S.
N172
Barnes, Jon
91Classic/DP-47
91FrRow/DP-20
91LitSun/HSPros-10
91LitSun/HSPros-18M
91LitSun/HSProsG-10
91LitSun/HSProsG-18
92CharRain/ClBest-18
92CharRain/ProC-112
92StCl/Dome-12

Barnes, Luther Owen
(Lute)
91WIZMets-24
Barnes, Mike
80Buffa-1
Barnes, Richard
78Knoxvl
79Knoxvl/TCMA-5
80Iowa/Pol-1
82Edmon-19
84D-608
84Maine-6
Barnes, Roscoe C.
(Ross)
No Cards.
Barnes, Samuel Thomas
(Sam)
No Cards.
Barnes, Tom
52Laval-90
Barnes, Virgil
28Exh-17
Barnes, William H.
(Bill)
No Cards.
Barnes, William Henry
(Skeeter)
79Nashvl
80Water-15
81Indianap-29
82Water-13
83Indianap-31
84Wichita/Rock-16
85D-530
85Expo/PostC-1
86Indianap-16
88BuffB/CMC-23
88BuffB/ProC-1487
88Nashvl/Team-2
89AAA/CMC-6
89AAA/ProC-15
89Nashvl/CMC-13
89Nashvl/ProC-1289
89Nashvl/Team-1
90AAASingl/ProC-556
90Nashvl/CMC-13
90Nashvl/ProC-244
90ProC/Singl-138
90TripleAAS/CMC-6
91AAA/LineD-578
91T/Tr-5T
91Toledo/LineD-578
91Toledo/ProC-1942
92D-749
92OPC-221
92Pinn-218
92S-569
92StCl-585
92T-221
92T/Gold-221
92T/GoldWin-221
92UD-470
92USPlayC/Tiger-12C
92USPlayC/Tiger-8C
92Ultra-358
93D-437
93F-603
93Pac/Spanish-441
93Panini-121
93StCl-389
93StCl/1stDay-389
93T-26
93T/Gold-26
93Tiger/Gator-2
94F-124
94Pac/Cr-210
94S-232
94S/GoldR-232
94StCl-50
94StCl/1stDay-50
94StCl/Gold-50
94T-561
94T/Gold-561
Barnett, Larry
88TM/Umpire-7
89TM/Umpire-5
89TM/Umpire-60M
90TM/Umpire-5
Barnett, Mike
90SoBend/Best-26CO
90SoBend/GS-30CO
91Saraso/ClBest-28CO
91Saraso/ProC-1130CO
92Saraso/ClBest-29CO
92Saraso/ProC-225CO
Barney, Edmund J.
(Ed)
No Cards.
Barney, Rex
47HomogBond-1
48B-41
49B-61
49Eureka-29
50B-76
51B-153
90Target-35
D305
Barnhart, Clyde Lee
21Exh-8
E120
E126-2
V61-108
Barnhart, Edgar V.
(Ed)
No Cards.
Barnhart, Leslie Earl
(Les)
No Cards.
Barnhart, Rick
79Wausau-13
Barnhart, Victor Dee
(Vic)
No Cards.
Barnhill, Dave
86Negro/Frit-101
Barnhouse, Scott
83Wausau/Frit-18
Barniak, Jim
90Phill/TastyK-36BC
Barnicle, George B.
No Cards.
Barnicle, Ted
76Cedar
79Knoxvl/TCMA-21
80GlenF/B-11
80GlenF/C-19
Barnie, William H.
(Billy)
90Target-36
N172
Barnowski, Edward A.
(Ed)
66T-442R
67T-507R
91Crown/Orio-22
Barns, Jeff
88PalmSp/Cal-100
88PalmSp/ProC-1451
89MidldA/GS-5
90MidldA/GS-9
90TexLgAS/GS-11
91AA/LineD-427
91MidldA/LineD-427
91MidldA/ProC-438
92Modesto/ProC-3904
93Modesto/ClBest-2
93Modesto/ProC-804
Barnwell, Richard
(Rich)
89Oneonta/ProC-2117
90FtLaud/Star-1
91FtLaud/ClBest-24
91FtLaud/ProC-2438
92Albany/ProC-2236
92Albany/SB-2
Barnwell, Rob
87Watertn-21
Barojas, Salome
83D-67
83F-230
83F/St-27M
83TrueVal/WSox-30
84D-570
84F-53
84TrueVal/WS-5
85D-605
85F-482
85Mother/Mar-19
Baron, Jimmy
93StCl/MurphyS-134
93T-538
93T/Gold-538
Baron, Sean
88BurlInd/ProC-1778
Barone, Richard A.
(Dick)
61Union
Barr, Bob
76Watlo
Barr, Hyder Edward
(Bob)
No Cards.
Barr, James Leland
(Jim)
72OPC-232R
72T-232R
73OPC-387
73T-387
74OPC-233
74T-233
75Ho-13
75Ho/Twink-13
75OPC-107
75T-107
75T/M-107
76OPC-308
76SSPC-92
76T-308
77BurgChef-103
77Ho-83
77Ho/Twink-83
77OPC-119
77T-609
78OPC-19
78T-62
79T-461
80OPC-275
80T-529
81D-412
81F-287
81T-717
83D-398
83F-252
83T-133
84D-79
84F-365
84Nes/792-282
84T-282
88AlaskaAS60/Team-9
Barr, Robert A.
(Bob)
90Target-897
Barr, Robert M.
(Bob)
No Cards.
Barr, Steven Charles
(Steve)
76OPC-595R
76T-595R
93Rang/Keeb-64
Barr, Tim
78Green
80OrlanTw-2
Barragan, Facundo A.
(Cuno)
59DF
62T-66
63T-557
Barragan, Gerry
87Madis-12
88Modesto/Cal-73
Barragan, Jaime
(Jimmy)
88Spartan/ProC-1036
88Spartan/Star-1
89Clearw/Star-1
90Clearw/Star-1
Barranca, German
76Watlo
77Jaxvl
81Indianap-25
83Evansvl-25
84OKCty-24
85Water-17
Barranco, Vince
88BurlInd/ProC-1777
Barreiro, Efrain
90Ashvl/ClBest-1
90AubAs/Best-5
90AubAs/ProC-3413
91Ashvl/ProC-559
Barreiro, Fernando
91Spring/ClBest-5
91Spring/ProC-732
Barrera, Nelson
85BuffB-7
Barrett, Charles H.
(Red)
39Exh
45PlayBall-28
47TipTop
49B-213
49Eureka-4
52Park-14
Barrett, Charles
77LodiD
Barrett, Dick
47Centen-1
Barrett, Francis J.
(Frank)
No Cards.
Barrett, James E.
(Jimmy)
E107
T201
WG2-2
Barrett, Jeff
87Indianap-17
Barrett, John Joseph
(Johnny)
44PlayBall-26
Barrett, Keith
88Belling/Legoe-20
Barrett, Kewpie
47Signal
Barrett, Martin F.
(Marty)
No Cards.
Barrett, Martin Glen
(Marty)
81Pawtu-14
83Pawtu-14
84F/X-8
84Nes/792-683
84T-683
85D-127
85F-150
85Leaf-229
85T-298
85T/St-219
86D-294
86F-340
86Leaf-169
86OPC-314
86T-734
86T/St-250
87Classic-61
87D-523
87D/OD-188
87F-27
87F/AwardWin-1
87F/Lim-2
87F/St-5
87F/WS-6
87Leaf-165
87OPC-39
87Seven-ME2
87Sf-112M
87Sf-182
87Sf/TPrev-9M
87T-39
87T/HL-17
87T/St-18
87Woolwth-17
88D-276
88D/Best-9
88D/RedSox/Bk-276
88F-343
88Leaf-141
88OPC-338
88Panini/St-28
88S-155
88Sf-157
88T-525
88T/Big-54
88T/St-248
89B-28
89D-184
89D/Best-252
89F-78
89KennerFig-4
89OPC-155
89Panini/St-276
89S-63
89Sf-198
89T-155
89T/Big-278
89T/St-257
89UD-173
90B-282
90D-240
90F-266
90F/Can-266
90OPC-355
90Panini/St-15
90Pep/RSox-1
90PublInt/St-446
90S-15
90T-355
90T/Big-44
90T/St-256
90T/TVRSox-21
90UD-133
91B-648
91F-84
91Leaf-474
91OPC-496
91Padre/MagRal-10
91S-228
91T-496
91UD-90
Barrett, Robert S.
(Bob)
90Target-37
Barrett, Tim
86Indianap-34
87Indianap-9
88Indianap/CMC-5
88Indianap/ProC-502
89Indianap/CMC-1
89Indianap/ProC-1229
Barrett, Tom
84Nashvl-2
85Colum-13
85Colum/Pol-1
86Albany/TCMA-5
87Reading-7
88Maine/CMC-16
88Maine/ProC-284
88Phill/TastyK-27
88TripleA/ASCMC-18
89ScranWB/CMC-11
89ScranWB/ProC-725
89T-653
89T/Big-177
90AlbanyDG/Best-15
90S-633
91AAA/LineD-352
91Pawtu/LineD-352
91Pawtu/ProC-44
92Pawtu/ProC-928
92Pawtu/SB-352
Barrett, Tracey S.
(Dick)
No Cards.
Barrett, William J.
(Bill)
93Conlon-977
Barretto, Saul M.
87Gaston/ProC-6
88Gaston/ProC-1022
Barrick, Andy
88Batavia/ProC-1687
Barrilleaux, John
89Oneonta/ProC-2099
Barringer, Reggie
85PrWill-20
86PrWill-1
87Salem-23
Barrios, Eugene
85Greens-24
Barrios, Francisco
77T-222
78SSPC/270-144
78T-552
79Ho-21
79T-386
80OPC-58
80T-107
81F-352
Barrios, Gregg
86WinHaven-3
Barrios, Jose Manuel
76Cedar
80Phoenix/NBank-12
81Phoenix-12
82Phoenix
Barron, Anthony
(Tony)
89Star/Wax-26
89VeroB/Star-2
90Star/ISingl-18
90VeroB/Star-3
91AA/LineD-530
91SanAn/LineD-530
91SanAn/ProC-2986
92Albuq/ProC-732
92SanAn/SB-555

Barron, David Irenus
(Red)
No Cards.
Barros, Ellie
82Danvl/Frit-17
Barrow, Edward G.
50Callahan
50W576-4
60F-23
76Shakey-65
77Galasso-174MG
80Perez/HOF-63
80SSPC/HOF
81Tiger/Detroit-77MG
89HOF/St-94
92Yank/WIZHOF-2
Barrow, Mel
76SanAn/Team-1
79Tucson-22
79Tulsa-21
80Tulsa-11
81Tulsa-6
90TulsaDG/Best-26
Barrows, Roland
(Cuke)
No Cards.
Barrs, Stan
88Savan/ProC-349
Barry, Dan
89GA-12M
90GA-35TR
Barry, Jeff
89Anchora-2
89SanDiegoSt/Smok-2
90James/Pucko-7
90SDSt-2
91ClBest/Singl-365
91WPalmB/ClBest-24
91WPalmB/ProC-1239
92StLucie/ProC-1759
93StLucie/ProC-2931
Barry, John C.
(Shad)
T206
Barry, John Joseph
(Jack)
10Domino-7
11Helmar-53
12Sweet/Pin-41
14CJ-28
14Piedmont/St-2
15CJ-28
16FleischBrd-7
88Conlon/3-4
91Conlon/Sport-139
BF2-1
D303
D304
D327
D328-13
D329-11
D350/2-10
E101
E104
E105
E106
E135-13
E254
E270/1
E300
E90/1
E91
M101/4-11
M101/5-10
M116
S74-27
T201
T202
T205
T206
T207
T208
T216
T222
Barry, John
86Clinton-1
88Fresno/Cal-10
88Fresno/ProC-1227
Barry, Richard D.
(Rich)
No Cards.
Bartell, Mike
75Clinton
Bartell, Richard
(Dick)
29Exh/4-13
31Exh/4-12
32Orbit/num-15
32Orbit/un-4
33DH-4
33Exh/4-6
33G-28
34DS-101
34Exh/4-6
35BU-4
35G-2A
35G-4A
35G-7A
38G-248
38G-272
41DP-56
55B-234
77Galasso-212
88Conlon/4-3
92Conlon/Sport-452
93Conlon-684
94Conlon-1243
PM10/Sm-7
R300
R305
R308-158
R309/2
R310
R314
R337-424
V353-28
V355-37
Bartels, Bill
85Anchora-2
87VeroB-26
88Lynch/Star-1
Barthelson, Robert E.
(Bob)
47Sunbeam
Barthold, John F.
No Cards.
Bartholomew, Lester
No Cards.
Bartholow, Bud
83Reading-1
Bartirome, Anthony J.
(Tony)
52T-332
53T-71
91T/Arc53-71
Bartlett, Bob
75Tidew/Team-2
Bartley, Boyd Owen
90Target-898
Bartley, Greg
84Chatt-29
86Calgary-1
87Chatt/Best-3
Bartley, William J.
(Bill)
E254
Bartling, Irving H.
(Irv)
No Cards.
Bartolomucci, Tony
86AppFx-1
Barton, Harry Lamb
No Cards.
Barton, Jeff
89Spokane/SP-21
90CharRain/Best-3
90CharRain/ProC-2051
Barton, Ken
76Cedar
77Cedar
81Charl-10
Barton, Larry
40Hughes-3
47Signal
Barton, Paul
91StCath/ClBest-18
91StCath/ProC-3386
Barton, Robert Wilbur
(Bob)
66T-511R
67CokeCap/Giant-4
67T-462
68CokeCap/Giant-10
68T-351
69OPC-41
69T-41
70OPC-352
70T-352
71MLB/St-218
71OPC-589
71T-589
72MB-27
72OPC-39
72OPC-40IA
72T-39
72T-40A
73OPC-626
73T-626
Barton, Scott
92Hunting/ClBest-11
92Hunting/ProC-3150
Barton, Shawn
86Reading-2
86SanJose-2
87Maine-6
87Maine/TCMA-1
87Phill/TastyK-x
87SanJose-29
88Jacks/GS-19
89AS/Cal-42
89Reno/Cal-260
89Tidew/CMC-8
89Tidew/ProC-1969
90AAASingl/ProC-265
90ProC/Singl-352
90Reno/Cal-272
90T/TVMets-35
90Tidew/CMC-1
90Tidew/ProC-534
91AA/LineD-327
91Jaxvl/LineD-327
91Jaxvl/ProC-141
92Calgary/SB-53
93Calgary/ProC-1156
93D-53
93Pinn-250
93T-569
93T/Gold-569
Barton, Vincent David
(Vince)
No Cards.
Bartorillo, John
91Brisbane/Fut-1
Bartosch, David R.
(Dave)
No Cards.
Bartson, Charles F.
(Charlie)
No Cards.
Barun, Barton
82Redwd-24
Barwick, Lyall
92Boise/ClBest-9
92Boise/ProC-3641
Basgall, Matt
85Clovis-3
Basgall, Romanus
(Monty)
49Eureka-152
52T-12
73OPC-569CO
73T-569CO
74OPC-144CO
74T-144C
85Coke/Dodg-4CO
86Coke/Dodg-3CO
Bashang, Albert C.
(Al)
No Cards.
Bashore, Walter F.
(Walt)
No Cards.
Basinski, Edward F.
(Eddie)
45PlayBall-29
47TipTop
52Mother-6
53Mother-32
90Target-899
Baskette, James B.
(Jim)
No Cards.
Bass, Barry
83BurlR-1
83BurlR/Frit-9
84Tulsa-22
85Tulsa-26
87ElPaso-27
88ElPaso/Best-17
Bass, Bart
77Cedar
Bass, Ed
85FtMyr-1
Bass, Jerry
78Clinton
79LodiD-16
82BirmB-18
Bass, John E.
No Cards.
Bass, Kevin
77Newar
78BurlB
79Holyo-5
79T-708R
80Holyo-13
81Vanco-24
82Pol/Brew-26
82Vanco-4
84D-450
84F-221
84Nes/792-538
84T-538
85D-136
85F-345
85F/St-52
85Mother/Ast-22
85T-326
86D-548
86D/HL-21
86F-294
86OPC-52
86Pol/Ast-4
86T-458
86T/St-28
87Classic-17
87D-410
87D/AAS-40
87D/OD-14
87Drake-17
87F-51
87F/Hottest-3
87F/Mini-5
87F/Slug-1
87F/St-6
87GenMills/Book-6M
87Leaf-211
87Mother/Ast-9
87OPC-85
87Pol/Ast-22
87Sf-117M
87Sf-175
87Sf/TPrev-8M
87T-85
87T/Gloss60-34
87T/Mini-7
87T/St-34
88D-286
88D/Best-38
88F-440
88F/Excit-2
88F/Mini-77
88F/St-85
88KennerFig-3
88Leaf-137
88Mother/Ast-9
88OPC-175
88Panini/St-298
88Pol/Ast-6
88S-33
88Sf-55
88T-175
88T/Big-77
88T/St-29
89D-325
89F-351
89KennerFig-5
89Lennox/Ast-5
89Mother/Ast-8
89OPC-102
89Panini/St-91
89S-226
89Sf-11
89T-646
89T/Ames-2
89T/Big-187
89T/LJN-63
89T/St-14
89UD-425
90B-240
90D-589
90D/BestNL-36
90D/GSlam-10
90F-223
90F/Can-223
90F/Up-U60
90Leaf-305
90MLBPA/Pins-45
90Mother/Giant-24
90OPC-281
90Panini/St-261
90PublInt/St-87
90S-279
90S/100St-100
90S/Tr-2T
90Sf-198
90T-281
90T/Big-236
90T/St-17
90T/Tr-7T
90UD-302
90UD/Ext-793
91B-625
91D-630
91F-253
91Leaf-365
91Mother/Giant-24
91OPC-752
91PG&E-10
91S-616
91SFExam/Giant-1
91StCl-29
91T-752
91UD-287
91Ultra-315
92D-373
92F-626
92Giant/PGE-3
92L-76
92L/BlkGold-76
92Mother/Giant-24
92OPC-513
92Panini-216
92Pinn-53
92S-139
92S/RookTr-76T
92StCl-6
92Studio-111
92T-513
92T/Gold-513
92T/GoldWin-513
92UD-107
92Ultra-284
93D-745
93F-466
93F/Final-76
93Mother/Ast-16
93S-578
93StCl/Ast-18
93T-672
93T/Gold-672
93UD-679
94F-484
94Pac/Cr-258
94S-128
94S/GoldR-128
94T-362
94T/Gold-362
Bass, Norm
62T-122
63T-461
Bass, Randy William
75Tacoma/KMMO-7
79T-707R
82D-439
82F-566
82T-307
89T/SenLg-50
90EliteSenLg-49
93Rang/Keeb-65
Bass, Regan
86DayBe-2
Bass, William Capers
(Doc)
No Cards.
Basse, Mike
91Helena/SportP-25
92AS/Cal-18
92Stockton/ProC-46
Bassett, Charles E.
(Charley)
N172
N284
WG1-28
Bassett, Matt
84Omaha-29
85Omaha-2

Bassett, Pepper
86Negro/Frit-103
Bassler, John Landis
(Johnny)
21Exh-9
25Exh-89
26Exh-89
27Exh-45
92Conlon/Sport-414
93Conlon-878
E120
E126-55
V100
V117-10
W572
W573
WG7-4
Basso, Michael A.
(Mike)
86Cram/NWL-167
87CharRain-20
88TexLgAS/GS-23
88Wichita-16
89AubAs/ProC-9
89Wichita/Rock-16
89Wichita/Rock/HL-12
90AAASingl/ProC-14
90LasVegas/CMC-11
90LasVegas/ProC-126
90ProC/Singl-514
91AA/LineD-601
91Wichita/LineD-601
91Wichita/ProC-2601
91Wichita/Rock-11
92LasVegas/ProC-2798
Bast, Steven
(Steve)
86Elmira-2
87NewBrit-11
89NewBrit/ProC-608
89Pawtu/Dunkin-30
90AAASingl/ProC-424
90Pawtu/CMC-9
90Pawtu/ProC-452
90ProC/Singl-260
90T/TVRSox-36
Bastable, John M.
76OkCty/Team-3
Bastian, Charles J.
(Charlie)
N172
N284
N690
WG1-47
Bastian, John K.
(Jack)
T206
Bastian, Jose
75WPalmB/Sussman-6
79RochR-17
81Toledo-3
Bastian, Robert
81Redwd-1
83Nashua-1
85Cram/PCL-21
86Edmon-1
Bastien, Aldege
(Bazz)
45Parade*-2
Batch, Emil Henry
C46-48
T205
T206
Batchelder, Joseph E.
(Joe)
No Cards.
Batchelor, Richard
91ClBest/Singl-54
91FSLAS/ProC-FSL11
91FtLaud/ClBest-1
91FtLaud/ProC-2416
92Albany/ProC-2217
92Albany/SB-3
92ProC/Tomorrow-119
92Sky/AASingl-1
94D-649
94Finest-269
94StCl-344
94StCl/1stDay-344
94StCl/Gold-344
94StCl/Team-327
94T-788M
94T/Gold-788M
94Ultra-265
Bateman, John Alvin
63Pep
63T-386R
64T-142
64T/Coins-107
65T-433
66OPC-86
66T-86
67Ast/Team-2
67CokeCap/Astro-9
67T-231
68CokeCap/Astro-9
68Dexter-9
68T-592
69Expos/Pins-1
69Fud's-2
69MB-21
69MLB/St-155
69OPC-138
69T-138
69T/4in1-23M
69T/St-53
70Expo/PostC-14
70Expos/Pins-3
70MLB/St-61
70OPC-417
70T-417
71Expo/ProS-2
71MLB/St-122
71OPC-31
71OPC-628
71T-628
71T/Coins-19
72MB-28
72OPC-5
72T-5
Bates, Billy
86ElPaso-4
87Denver-7
88Denver/CMC-17
88Denver/ProC-1271
89AAA/ProC-41
89Denver/CMC-15
89Denver/ProC-38
90ElPasoATG/Team-1
90Pol/Brew-34
90S-608
90S/100Ris-80
90T/89Debut-9
91AAA/LineD-251
91Nashvl/LineD-251
92Iowa/ProC-4056
92TX-4
Bates, Charles W.
No Cards.
Bates, Delbert O.
No Cards.
Bates, Eric
89Billings/ProC-2061
Bates, Hubert Edgar
(Buddy)
R314/Can
V355-126
Bates, Jason
92AZ/Pol-1
92Bend/ClBest-6
93B-176
93FExcel/ML-32
93T-579M
93T/Gold-579M
94FExcel-183
94T-770
94T/Gold-770
Bates, John William
(Johnny)
10Domino-8
11Helmar-109
12Sweet/Pin-94
E104
E254
E94
M116
S74-97
T202
T204
T205
T206
W555
Bates, Kevin
84Shrev/FB-1
Bates, Raymond
(Ray)
No Cards.
Bates, Richard
(Dick)
No Cards.
Bates, Steve
88Clearw/Star-1
Bates, Tommy
91Watertn/ClBest-17
91Watertn/ProC-3372
92Kinston/ClBest-7
92Kinston/ProC-2480
Batesole, Michael
86Bakers-2
87VeroB-15
88VeroB/Star-1
Bathe, Bill
82WHave-10
83Tacoma-10
84Cram/PCL-80
85Cram/PCL-148
86D/Rook-41
86F/Up-U9
86Mother/A's-23
87D-281
88AAA/ProC-16
88Iowa/CMC-23
88Iowa/ProC-527
88TripleA/ASCMC-1
89Phoenix/CMC-11
89Phoenix/ProC-1495
90B-234
90D-680
90Mother/Giant-22
91OPC-679
91T-679
Bathe, Bob
84Albany-23
85Cram/PCL-143
86Iowa-2
Batina, John
87BYU-11
Batista, Francisco
82Spring/Frit-24
83ArkTr-20
83StPete-20
90SpringDG/Best-5
Batista, Juan
93James/ClBest-3
93James/ProC-3332
Batista, Miguel Jerez
(Decartes)
92WPalmB/ClBest-9
92WPalmB/ProC-2078
93B-564
93Harris/ProC-260
93LimeR/Winter-140
93LimeR/Winter-8
Batista, Miguel
86CharRain-2A
86CharRain-2B
88Bend/Legoe-17
Batista, Rafael
No Cards.
Batiste, Chris
89Bluefld/Star-3
Batiste, Kevin
87Dunedin-19
88Knoxvl/Best-7
89Knoxvl/Best-2
89Knoxvl/ProC-1124
89Knoxvl/Star-7
90Greenvl/Best-18
90Greenvl/ProC-1140
90Greenvl/Star-2
90T/89Debut-10
90UD-115
Batiste, Kim
88Spartan/ProC-1035
88Spartan/Star-2
89Clearw/Star-2
90EastLAS/ProC-EL20
90Foil/Best-227
90ProC/Singl-803
90Reading/Best-15
90Reading/ProC-1225
90Reading/Star-5
90Star/ISingl-81
91AAA/LineD-480
91B-488
91ScranWB/LineD-480
91ScranWB/ProC-2543
92B-44
92Classic/Game200-191
92Classic/I-10
92D-402
92F-522
92L-421
92L/BlkGold-421
92OPC-514
92Phill/Med-5
92Pinn-266
92Pinn/Rook-18
92Pinn/RookI-9
92Pinn/Team2000-69
92ProC/Tomorrow-293
92S-833
92S/Impact-86
92S/Rook-37
92StCl-788
92Studio-71
92T-514
92T/91Debut-11
92T/Gold-514
92T/GoldWin-514
92UD-422
92UD/Scout-SR3
92Ultra-542
93D-148
93F-485
93Pac/Spanish-230
93Phill/Med-5
93Pinn-390
93S-191
93T-679
93T/Gold-679
93UD-516
93Ultra-436
94D-470
94F-583
94Pac/Cr-469
94Phill/Med-2
94Pinn-207
94Pinn/Artist-207
94Pinn/Museum-207
94S-540
94StCl-303
94StCl/1stDay-303
94StCl/Gold-303
94StCl/Team-212
94T-238
94T/Gold-238
94UD/CollC-48
94UD/CollC/Gold-48
94UD/CollC/Silv-48
94Ultra-242
Batiste, Terrance
88NE-10
Batsch, William M.
(Bill)
No Cards.
Battam, Lawrence
(Larry)
No Cards.
Battell, Mark
88Hamil/ProC-1725
89Hamil/Star-2
Batten, George B.
No Cards.
Batten, Mark
80SanJose/JITB-3
81Wausau-8
Battey, Earl Jesse
57T-401
58T-364
59T-114
60L-66
60T-328
61Bz-28
61Clover-3
61P-97
61Peters-22
61T-315
61T-582AS
61T/Dice-1
61T/St-177
62Bz
62J-90
62P-90
62P/Can-90
62Salada-19
62Shirriff-19
62T-371
62T/St-74
62T/bucks
63Exh
63J-8
63P-8
63Salada-44
63T-306M
63T-410
64T-90
64T/Coins-101
64T/Coins-136AS
64T/SU
64T/St-71
64Wheat/St-6
65T-490
65T/E-70
66T-240
66T/RO-55
66T/RO-8
67CokeCap/Twin-3
67OPC-15
67T-15
78TCMA-113
78Twin/Frisz-2
88Pac/Leg-35
94TedW-46
Exh47
Battin, Joseph V.
(Joe)
No Cards.
Battle, Allen
92ClBest-269
92MidwLAS/Team-3
92Spring/ClBest-6
92Spring/ProC-880
93ClBest/MLG-182
Battle, Howard
90MedHat/Best-26
91ClBest/Singl-29
91Myrtle/ClBest-16
91Myrtle/ProC-2950
91SALAS/ProC-SAL36
92B-183
92ClBest-88
92Dunedin/ClBest-5
92Dunedin/ProC-2005
92ProC/Tomorrow-172
92UD/ML-27M
92UD/ML-280
93B-195
93ClBest/MLG-85
93FExcel/ML-238
93Knoxvl/ProC-1256
94ClBest/Gold-108
94FExcel-138
94TedW-118
94TedW/Gardiner-5
Battle, James Milton
(Jim)
No Cards.
Batton, Chris
76Tucson-10
77T-475R
Batts, Matthew Daniel
(Matt)
48L-108
51B-129
52B-216
52T-230
53B/BW-22
53Tiger/Glen-1
54B-183
54T-88
55B-161
76Baton/MG
94T/Arc54-88
Exh47
Bauer, Alice
52Wheat*
Bauer, Dave
89Penin/Star-1
Bauer, Eric
85Spokane/Cram-1
87Wichita-22
88Wichita-33
Bauer, Henry Albert
(Hank)
50B-219
51B-183
51BR-A4
51T/RB-24
52B-65
52BR
52Coke
52T-215
52TipTop
53B/Col-44M
53B/Col-84
53Briggs
53RM-AL2

53SM
54B-129
54DanDee
54NYJour
54RM-AL23
54SM
54T-130
55B-246
55RM-AL22
55SM
55T-166
56T-177
57T-240
58T-9
59T-240
60T-262
61P-90
61T-119M
61T-398
61T/St-156
62T-127M
62T-463
64T-178
65T-323
66T-229
67OPC-1M
67T-1M
67T-534
68A's/JITB-2MG
68T-513
69OPC-124MG
69T-124
69T/4in1-13M
79TCMA-22
89Pac/Leg-144
89Swell-82
91T/Arc53-290
92Yank/WIZAS-2
93UD/ATH-6
94T/Arc54-130
Exh47
PM10/L-3

Bauer, Mark
85Huntsvl/BK-26
85Modesto/Chong-19

Bauer, Marlene
52Wheat*

Bauer, Matt
91Bristol/ClBest-21
91Bristol/ProC-3595
92Lakeland/ClBest-15
92Niagara/ProC-3315

Bauer, Peter
(Pete)
86LitFalls-2
87Lynch-14
88Clmbia/GS-2
89Jacks/GS-23
90Osceola/Star-3
91AA/LineD-554
91Jacks/LineD-554
91Jacks/ProC-917

Bauer, Phil
76Clinton
79AppFx-14

Bauer, Ray
57Seattle/Pop-4

Bauers, Russell
40PlayBall-219
52Park-4

Baugh, Gavin
93T-641M
93T/Gold-641M

Baum, Jeff
88AppFx/ProC-158

Bauman, Brad
81Shrev-10

Baumann, Charles John
(Paddy)
T207

Baumann, David
90GreatF/SportP-13
91VeroB/ClBest-2
91VeroB/ProC-763
91Yakima/ClBest-21

Baumann, Frank
58T-167
59T-161
60T-306
61P-34
61T-46LL
61T-550
62T-161
63T-381
64T-453
65OPC-161
65T-161

Baumer, James Sloan
(Jim)
61T-292

Baumgardner, George
14CJ-131
15CJ-131
T222

Baumgarner, Jeff
92Hagers/ProC-2549

Baumgarten, Ross
79T-704R
80T-138
81D-41
81OPC-328
81T-398
82D-104
82F-337
82OPC-322
82T-563
82T/Tr-3T
83F-302
83T-97

Baumgartner, John E.
No Cards.

Baumgartner, Stan
81Conlon-8
94Conlon-1317

Baumholtz, Frank C.
49B-21
52B-195
52T-225
54B-221
54RH
54T-60
55B-227
55T-172
56T-274
94T/Arc54-60
Exh47
R423-3

Baur, Al
89Martins/Star-1
90Batavia/ProC-3056

Bauta, Ed
61Union
62T-344
63T-336
91WIZMets-25

Bautista, Antonio
77WHave

Bautista, Benny
85Newar-12
87Hagers-6

Bautista, Dan
90Bristol/ProC-3154
91Fayette/ClBest-23
91Fayette/ProC-1182
92Fayette/ClBest-13
92Fayette/ProC-2179
93B-95
93LimeR/Winter-6
94B-97
94D-442
94F/MLP-5
94L/GRook-7
94Pac/Cr-211
94Pinn-234
94Pinn/Artist-234
94Pinn/Museum-234
94Pinn/New-24
94S-559
94S/Boys-51
94Select-186
94StCl-155
94StCl/1stDay-155
94StCl/Gold-155
94T-768
94T/Gold-768
94UD-338
94Finest-435

Bautista, German
86Miami-1

Bautista, Hector
90Wausau/Best-25
90Wausau/ProC-2139
90Wausau/Star-2

Bautista, Jose
85Lynch-9
87Jacks/Feder-3
88D/Rook-41
88F/Up-U1
88French-48
88T/Tr-10T
89B-3
89D-451
89F-608
89French-48
89S-573
89T-469
89T/St-229
89UD-574
90AAASingl/ProC-453
90ProC/Singl-321
90PublInt/St-574
90RochR/CMC-20
90RochR/ProC-696
90Rochester/L&U-28
90UD 8
91Crown/Orio-23
92F-2
92Omaha/ProC-2953
92Omaha/SB-326
93Cub/Mara-2
93F/Final-6
93LimeR/Winter-99
93Pac/Spanish-376
93StCl/Cub-30
94D-458
94F-379
94L-88
94Pac/Cr-94
94Pinn-445
94S-249
94S/GoldR-249
94StCl-421
94StCl/1stDay-421
94StCl/Gold-421
94StCl/Team-340
94T-92
94T/Finest-175
94T/FinestRef-175
94T/Gold-92
94UD-108
94UD/ElecD-108
94Ultra-159

Bautista, Ramon
80Clinton-4
82Clinton/Frit-13
83Clinton/Frit-8
88Watlo/ProC-676
89Kinston/Star-2
90Kinston/Team-16
91AA/LineD-76
91Canton/LineD-76
91Canton/ProC-983

Bavasi, Buzzie
77Padre/SchCd-4GM

Baxes, Jim
59T-547
60T-318
90Target-38

Baxes, Michael
(Mike)
58T-302
59T-381

Baxter, Bob
90James/Pucko-14
91Rockford/ClBest-1
91Rockford/ProC-2037
92WPalmB/ClBest-16
92WPalmB/ProC-2079

Baxter, Jim
88Watlo/ProC-671
89Lakeland/Star-2
91AA/LineD-402
91Memphis/LineD-402
91Memphis/ProC-657

Baxter, John
No Cards.

Baxter, William
C46-80

Bay, Harry Elbert
E107
T206
T213/brown
WG2-3

Bayas, Richard Thomas
(Subby)
87Negro/Dixon-16

Bayer, Chris
86Columbia-5
88StLucie/Star-2

Bayer, Christopher A.
(Burley)
No Cards.

Bayless, Harry Owen
(Dick)
E254
E270/1

Baylor, Don Edward
71OPC-709R
71T-709R
72OPC-474R
72T-474R
73JP
73OPC-384
73T-384
74OPC-187
74T-187
74T/St-121
75OPC-382
75T-382
75T/M-382
76Ho-118
76OPC-125
76SSPC-394
76T-125
77Ho-129
77Ho/Twink-129
77OPC-133
77T-462
78OPC-173
78SSPC/270-208
78T-48
79Ho-63
79OPC-335
79T-635
80BK/PHR-12
80K-56
80OPC-150
80T-203LL
80T-285
80T/S-9
80T/Super-9
81D-413
81F-271
81F/St-122
81K-15
81OPC-309
81T-580
81T/HT
81T/St-51
82D-493
82F-451
82F/St-220
82KMart-35
82OPC-234
82T-415
82T/St-158
83D-493
83Drake-1
83F-77
83F/St-15M
83F/St-19AM
83F/St-19BM
83K-29
83OPC-105
83OPC/St-40
83T-105
83T/Fold-5M
83T/St-40
83T/Tr-8
84D-152
84Drake-1
84F-119
84F/St-45
84Nes/792-335
84Nes/792-486TL
84OPC-335
84T-335
84T-486TL
84T/RD-2
84T/St-320
85D-173
85D/HL-35
85Drake-3
85F-121
85F/St-49
85FunFood/Pin-39
85Leaf-146
85OPC-70
85T-70
85T/RD-2
85T/St-311
86D-347
86F-631M
86F-99
86F/St-3
86F/Up-U10
86OPC-184
86Sf-57M
86T-765
86T/St-300
86T/Tr-6T
86Woolwth-2
87Classic-14
87D-339
87D/OD-186
87F-28
87F/GameWin-2
87F/Hottest-4
87F/Mini-6
87F/St-7
87KayBee-3
87Leaf-232
87OPC-230
87OPC-A
87Seven-E2
87Sf-163
87Sf/TPrev-9M
87Stuart-15M
87T-230
87T-A
87T/Board-17
87T/Gloss60-27
87T/St-252
88D/A's/Bk-NEW
88F-2
88F/St-S1
88F/WS-11
88Mother/A's-8
88OPC-A
88S-250
88S/Tr-55T
88T-545
88T/Big-162
88T/St-10
88T/Tr-11T
88T/WaxBox-A
88Woolwth-1
88Woolwth-29
89F-1
89S-205
89Smok/Angels-13
89T-673
89T/Ames-3
89UD-601
90BBWit-5
90Brewer/MillB-32CO
90Pac/Legend-6
90Pol/Brew-x
91Brewer/MillB-32CO
91Crown/Orio-24
91K/3D-14
91LineD-14
91Pol/Brew-x
91Swell/Great-6
92Yank/WIZ80-9
93T-504M
93T/Gold-504M
93TWill-59
93UD/ATH-7

Bayne, William
E120

Bazydlo, Edward
52Laval-17

BeBop, Spec
76Laugh/Clown-20

Beach, Jackson S.
(Jack)
No Cards.

Beach, Randy
75Tacoma/KMMO-6

Beacom, Chris
89StCath/ProC-2085
90Dunedin/Star-1

Beahan, Scott
83Greens-2

Beal, Sally
78Newar-GM

Beal, Tony
86NewBrit-2

Beall, John Woolf
(Johnny)
No Cards.

Beall, Mike
89AppFx/ProC-864
90BBCity/Star-2

Beall, Robert Brooks
(Bob)
76SSPC-21
79T-222

80Richm-19
81Portl-7
Beall, Walter
94Conlon-1288
Beals, Bryan
88GreatF-19
89Bakers/Cal-197
90Bakers/Cal-257
Beals, Greg
91Pittsfld/ClBest-2
91Pittsfld/ProC-3425
92ColumMet/ClBest-7
92ColumMet/ProC-298
92ColumMet/SAL/II-8
93StLucie/ProC-2923
Beals, Thomas L.
(Tommy)
No Cards.
Beamesderfer, Kurt
87CharlO/WBTV-19
Beamon, Charles Alon.
(Charlie)
59T-192
60HenryH-30
91Crown/Orio-25
Beamon, Charles Alph.
77SanJose-9
78SanJose-12
79Spokane-6
80Spokane-24
80T-672R
81Syrac-12
81Syrac/Team-3
82Syrac-15
82Syrac/Team-5
Beamon, Nick
(Pepper)
79WHave-22M
80WHave-18
Beamon, Trey
92ClBest/Up-431
92Classic/DP-44
93B-302
93StCl/MurphyS-143
94B-518
94ClBest/Gold-10
Beams, Michael
88Ashvl/ProC-1054
88AubAs/ProC-1962
89Ashvl/ProC-968
90Osceola/Star-4
91AA/LineD-451
91NewBrit/LineD-451
91NewBrit/ProC-362
92NewBrit/ProC-444
92NewBrit/SB-476
93Pawtu/Ball-3
Bean, Belve
93Conlon-974
Bean, Billy
87Portl-5
88T-267
88Toledo/CMC-12
88Toledo/ProC-595
89Classic-33
89S/HotRook-19
89Toledo/ProC-772
90AAASingl/ProC-77
90Albuq/CMC-25
90Albuq/ProC-356
90Albuq/Trib-1
90ProC/Singl-427
90Target-39
91AAA/LineD-1
91Albuq/LineD-1
91Albuq/ProC-1152
94F-654
94Pac/Cr-515
Bean, Joseph William
(Joe)
No Cards.
Bean, Kenneth
88Martins/Star-2
89Martins/Star-2
Beanblossom, Brad
88CapeCod/Sum-147
91StPete/ClBest-17
91StPete/ProC-2280
92ArkTr/ProC-1134
92ArkTr/SB-27
Beane, William Lamar
(Billy)
82Jacks-19
84Jacks-17
85IntLgAS-7
85Tidew-14
86D-647
86F/Up-U11
87F-535
87T-114
87Toledo-26
91WIZMets-26
Beard, Cramer T.
(Ted)
51B-308
52T-150
Beard, Dave
80Ogden-15
81T-96R
81Tacoma-24
82F-87
83D-113
83F-514
83F/St-16M
83F/St-9M
83Granny-33
83T-102
84D-218
84F-438
84F/X-9
84Mother/Mar-11
84Nes/792-513
84OPC-149
84T-513
84T/St-336
84T/Tr-8
85F-483
85Maine-2
85T-232
86Richm-2
88Toledo/CMC-1
88Toledo/ProC-586
89Toledo/CMC-10
89Toledo/ProC-777
Beard, Garrett
89Salem/Team-6
90Yakima/Team-1
91Bakers/Cal-23
92Modesto/ClBest-7
92Modesto/ProC-3901
93Modesto/ClBest-3
93Modesto/ProC-805
Beard, Mike
76OPC-53
76T-53
Beard, Oliver Perry
(Ollie)
N172
Beard, Ralph
55B-206
Beard, Ted
81TCMA-302
Bearden, Gene
46Remar-17
49B-57
50NumNum
51B-284
52B-173
52NTea
52T-229
53Exh/Can-3
79TCMA-222
Exh47
Beardman, Larry
84Madis/Pol-24
Beardsley, Chris
89PalmSp/Cal-58
Beare, Gary Ray
78Spokane/Cramer-27
78Spokane/Team-23
78T-516
79OkCty
Bearnarth, Larry
63T-386R
64T-527
65OPC-258
65T-258
66T-464
76Expo/Redp-2CO
78TCMA-61
80Memphis-8
85Expo/PostC-2CO
86Expo/Prov/Pan-14M
86Provigo-14CO
91WIZMets-27
Bearse, Kevin
88CLAS/Star-24
88Kinston/Star-2
89Canton/Best-1
89Canton/ProC-1306
90B-330
90F/Up-U91
90UD/Ext-715
91AAA/LineD-177
91F-361
91Indianap/LineD-177
91Indianap/ProC-453
91T/90Debut-12
Beasley, Andy
90Hamil/Star-4
91Spring/ClBest-6
91Spring/ProC-743
92ClBest-277
92StPete/ClBest-3
92StPete/ProC-2029
Beasley, Bud
46Sunbeam
47Signal
47Sunbeam
Beasley, Chris
86Water-2
87Wmsprt-22
89PalmSp/ProC-488
90AAASingl/ProC-85
90Edmon/CMC-4
90Edmon/ProC-509
90ProC/Singl-501
91Edmon/ProC-1508
92Edmon/ProC-3533
92Edmon/SB-152
92F-54
92Sky/AAASingl-74
92StCl-492
92T/91Debut-12
92UD-614
Beasley, Lewis Paige
(Lew)
77Tucson
93Rang/Keeb-66
Beasley, Tony
89Erie/Star-1
90Freder/Team-4
91CLAS/ProC-CAR5
91Freder/ClBest-16
91Freder/ProC-2370
92Salem/ClBest-25
92Salem/ProC-69
93CaroMud/RBI-4
Beason-Samuels, Cody
92GulfCY/ProC-3795
Beatin, Ebenezer
N172
Beatle, David
(Dave)
No Cards.
Beattie, Burt
87Kenosha-8
Beattie, Jim
77WHave
79BK/Y-7
79Colum-8
79OPC-86
79T-179
80T-334
81D-166
81Spokane-29
81T-443
82D-478
82T-22
83D-176
83F-472
83F/St-9M
83OPC-191
83T-675
83T-711
84D-191
84F-605
84Mother/Mar-12
84Nes/792-288
84OPC-288
84T-288
84T/St-346
85D-313
85F-484
85Leaf-85
85Mother/Mar-15
85OPC-303
85T-505
85T/St-334
86D-196
86F-458
86Mother/Mar-27
86T-729
87T-117
92Yank/WIZ70-11
Beatty, Aloysius D.
(Des)
No Cards.
Beatty, Blaine
87Hagers-12
88Jacks/GS-15
88TexLgAS/GS-18
89Tidew/CMC-9
89Tidew/ProC-1964
90B-130
90F-197
90F/Can-197
90HagersDG/Best-2
90S-632
90T/89Debut-11
90T/TVMets-7
90UD-23
91AAA/LineD-552
91Tidew/LineD-552
91Tidew/ProC-2500
91WIZMets-28
92Indianap/ProC-1852
92Indianap/SB-183
92S-843
92Sky/AAASingl-86
93CaroMud/RBI-12
Beatty, Gary
91Batavia/ClBest-30TR
92Spartan/ClBest-25TR
Beauchamp, James E.
(Jim)
62Kahn/Atl
63Pep/Tul
64T-492R
65T-409R
66OPC-84R
66T-84R
67T-307
69T-613
71MLB/St-266
71OPC-322
71T-322
72T-594
73OPC-137
73T-137
74OPC-424
74T-424
78Charl
79CharCh-2
80Indianap-2MG
81Indianap-2MG
82Syrac-26MG
82Syrac/Team-6
83Syrac-1MG
84Syrac-1MG
85Greenvl/Team-3
86Greenvl/Team-3MG
87Greenvl/Best-1MG
87SLAS-22
88Richm-9MG
88Richm/CMC-23MG
88Richm/ProC-15MG
89AAA/ProC-53MG
89Richm/Bob-1MG
89Richm/CMC-25MG
89Richm/Ko-9MG
89Richm/ProC-822MG
90AAASingl/ProC-419MG
90ProC/Singl-283MG
90Richm/25Ann-4
90Richm/CMC-7MG
90Richm/ProC-274MG
90Richm/Team-3MG
91Brave/Dubuq/Stand-2CO
91WIZMets-29
92Brave/LykeStand-2CO
93Brave/LykeStand-2CO
Beauchamp, Kash
86Knoxvl-1
87Syrac/TCMA-29
88Knoxvl/Best-9
89Richm/Bob-2
89Richm/CMC-23
89Richm/Ko-7
89Richm/ProC-836
90AAASingl/ProC-47
90Phoenix/CMC-17
90Phoenix/ProC-21
90ProC/Singl-544
Beaulac, Joe
90Miami/II/Star-2
Beaumont, Clarence H.
(Ginger)
E107
E254
M116
T206
WG3-2
Beaumont, Matt
93Bz-18
93T/Tr-30T
Beavers, Alan
92Hamil/ClBest-14
92Hamil/ProC-1579
Beavers, Mark
85Anchora-3
86Cram/NWL-55
87Madis-20
88Modesto/Cal-61
89River/Best-2
89River/Cal-23
89River/ProC-1390
Bechtel, George A.
No Cards.
Beck, Brian
90CharRain/Best-4
90CharRain/ProC-2050
91CharRain/ClBest-20
91CharRain/ProC-106
92Augusta/ClBest-21
92Augusta/ProC-249
93Welland/ClBest-2
93Welland/ProC-3347
Beck, Clyde Eugene
29Exh/4-5
Beck, Dion
85Bend/Cram-1
87Reading-8
91Reno/Cal-23
Beck, Ervin Thomas
(Erve)
90Target-900
E107
Beck, Frederick T.
(Fred)
M116
T205
T206
Beck, Rich
66T-234R
81TCMA-476
92Yank/WIZ60-7
Beck, Rod
88Clinton/ProC-695
88MidwLAS/GS-5
89SanJose/Best-2
89SanJose/Cal-209
89SanJose/ProC-459
89SanJose/Star-1
89Star/Wax-82
90Shrev/ProC-1435
90Shrev/Star-2
91AAA/LineD-378
91Phoenix/LineD-378
91Phoenix/ProC-59
92D-461
92F-627
92Giant/PGE-4
92Mother/Giant-14
92OPC/Premier-197
92Pinn-613GRIP
92S-746
92T/91Debut-13
92T/Gold-264
92T/GoldWin-264
92Ultra-586
93B-308
93D-420
93F-150
93Flair-137
93L-232
93Mother/Giant-12
93OPC-11
93Pinn-398
93S-391
93StCl-81
93StCl/1stDay-81
93StCl/Giant-12
93T-604
93T/Gold-604
93UD-73
93UD/SP-109

93Ultra-126
94B-191
94D-604
94F-680
94F/AS-27
94L-224
94OPC-182
94Pac/Cr-538
94Panini-260
94Pinn-118
94Pinn/Artist-118
94Pinn/Museum-118
94S-508
94Sf/2000-129
94StCl-436
94StCl/1stDay-436
94StCl/Gold-436
94StCl/Team-30
94Studio-82
94T-146
94T/Finest-169
94T/Finest/PreProd-169
94T/FinestRef-169
94T/Gold-146
94TripleP-101
94UD-142
94UD-46FUT
94UD/CollC-49
94UD/CollC/Gold-49
94UD/CollC/Silv-49
94UD/ElecD-142
94UD/ElecD-46FUT
94UD/SP-89
94Ultra-285
94Ultra/Fire-7

Beck, Walter
(Boom Boom)
34G-50
40PlayBall-217
90Target-40
93Conlon-734

Beck, Wynn
90Madison/Best-28
90Madison/ProC-2271

Beck, Zinn Bertram
11Helmar-140
D329-12
M101/4-12
S74-42

Beckendorf, Henry W.
(Heinie)
09Buster/Pin-2
M116

Becker, Beals
10Domino-9
11Helmar-121
12Sweet/Pin-107
14CJ-96
14Piedmont/St-3
15CJ-96
16FleischBrd-8
E254
S74-80
T202
T205
T206
T207
T213/brown

Becker, David
92Classic/DP-106

Becker, Gregory
87StPete-23
88MidwLAS/GS-27
88Spring/Best-5
89StPete/Star-2
89Star/Wax-47

Becker, Heinz R.
No Cards.

Becker, Joseph Edward
(Joe)
52Park-1
55Gol/Dodg-3
60T-463CO
60Union/Dodg-23M
79TCMA-187

Becker, July
52Laval-105

Becker, Martin Henry
No Cards.

Becker, Rich
90Elizab/Star-1
91ClBest/Singl-345
91Kenosha/ClBest-25
91Kenosha/ProC-2086
92AS/Cal-37
92B-330
92ClBest-293
92UD/ML-245
92Visalia/ClBest-2
92Visalia/ProC-1025
93B-593
93ClBest/MLG-41
93FExcel/ML-197
93T-658M
93T/Gold-658M
93UD-447TP
94B-216
94B-375
94Flair-72
94L/GRook-16
94Pinn-529
94T-71
94T/Gold-71
94UD-4
94UD/CollC-1
94UD/CollC/Gold-1
94UD/CollC/Silv-1
94UD/ElecD-4
94UD/SP-183
94Ultra-385

Becker, Tim
87FtLaud-1
88Albany/ProC-1341
89Albany/Best-20
89Albany/ProC-315
89Albany/Star-2

Becker, Tom
88LitFalls/Pucko-4

Beckerman, Andy
92Pittsfld/ClBest-5
92Pittsfld/ProC-3286

Beckert, Glenn Alfred
65T-549R
66T-232
67CokeCap/Cub-3
67T-296
68OPC-101
68T-101
69Kelly/Pin-3
69MB-22
69MLB/St-119
69OPC-171
69Sunoco/Pin-2
69T-171
69T/4in1-5M
69T/St-12
70Dunkin-2
70K-43
70MLB/St-14
70OPC-480
70T-480
71K-71
71MD
71MLB/St-26
71OPC-390
71T-390
71T/Coins-143
71T/S-50
71T/Super-50
72K-24
72MB-29
72OPC-45
72OPC-46IA
72OPC-85LL
72T-45
72T-46A
72T-85LL
73OPC-440
73T-440
74McDon
74OPC-241
74T-241
74T/St-11
75Ho-103
75Ho/Twink-103
75OPC-484
75T-484
75T/M-484
81TCMA-367
84Cub/Uno-2M
84Cub/Uno-7M
89Pac/Leg-142
89Swell-116
93UD/ATH-8

Beckett, Robbie
90Classic/DP-25
91B-655
91CharRain/ClBest-1
91CharRain/ProC-87
91ClBest/Singl-162
91S-673FDP
92B-508
92Watlo/ClBest-14
92Watlo/ProC-2133
93B-406
94SigRook-2

Beckley, Jacob Peter
(Jake)
75Sheraton-7
76Shakey-120
80Perez/HOF-120
80SSPC/HOF
E107
N172
T206
WG3-3

Beckman, Bernie
74Albuq/Team-2
83Syrac-2

Beckman, Bill
92Conlon/Sport-623

Beckwith, Joe
78Cr/PCL-36
79Albuq-20
80Albuq-2
80Pol/Dodg-27
80T-679R
81Pol/Dodg-27
81T-231
82Albuq-1
83F-202
83Pol/Dodg-27
84D-337
84F-97
84F/X-10
84Nes/792-454
84T-454
84T/Tr-9
85D-541
85F-197
85T-77
86F-2
86Syrac-4
86T-562
90Target-41

Beckwith, John
74Laugh/Black-6
86Negro/Frit-67
90Negro/Star-22

Becquer, Julio V.
58T-458
59T-93
60L-43
60T-271
61T-329

Bedard, Roger
52Laval-49

Bedell, Howard W.
61T-353
62Salada-217
62Shirriff-217
62T-76

Bedell, Jeff
86FtMyr-3

Bedford, James Elred
(Jim)
No Cards.

Bedrosian, Dave
76Wausau

Bedrosian, Steve
79Savan-14
81Richm-12
82BK/Lids-2
82D-401
82Pol/Atl-32
82T-502R
82T/Tr-4T
83D-173
83F-129
83F/St-5M
83OPC-157
83Pol/Atl-32
83T-157
84D-565
84F-171
84Nes/792-365
84OPC-365
84Pol/Atl-32
84T-365
84T/St-38
85D-628
85F-319
85Ho/Braves-3
85Leaf-51
85OPC-25
85Pol/Atl-32
85Seven-6S
85T-25
85T/St-23
86CIGNA-11
86D-199
86F-508
86F/Up-U12
86OPC-181
86Phill/TastyK-40
86T-648
86T/St-40
86T/Tr-7T
87D-185
87D/HL-9
87F-170
87F/Lim-3
87F/Slug-M1
87F/St-8
87OPC-233
87Phill/TastyK-40
87RedFoley/St-98
87Sf-110
87Sf/TPrev-6M
87Smok/NL-7
87T-736
87T/Mini-27
87T/St-124
88Classic/Blue-222
88D-62
88D/AS-61
88D/Best-16
88F-298
88F-627M
88F/AwardWin-1
88F/Mini-98
88F/SS-1
88F/St-107
88KennerFig-4
88Leaf-82
88MSA/Disc-18
88Nestle-25
88OPC-344
88OPC-B
88Panini/St-351
88Panini/St-440
88Phill/TastyK-3
88S-161
88S-656
88Sf-222M
88Sf-70
88T-407
88T-440
88T/Big-23
88T/Coins-34
88T/Gloss60-28
88T/Mini-64
88T/Revco-11
88T/St-116
88T/St-6
88T/St/Backs-31
88T/UK-2
88T/WaxBox-B
88Woolwth-10
89B-395
89Classic-34
89D-24DK
89D-75
89D/Best-303
89D/DKsuper-24DK
89F-562
89F/BBMVP's-1
89KennerFig-6
89MSA/Disc-15
89Panini/St-145
89Phill/TastyK-1
89S-260
89S/HotStar-29
89S/Tr-49
89Sf-63
89T-20
89T/Big-137
89T/LJN-96
89T/St-112
89T/Tr-8T
89Tetley/Discs-15
89UD-511
90B-226
90Classic-62
90D-295
90D/BestNL-99
90F-50
90F/Can-50
90Kenner/Fig-7
90Leaf-3
90Mother/Giant-6
90OPC-310
90Panini/St-364
90PubIInt/St-232
90S-379
90S/100St-31
90Sf-104
90T-310
90T/Big-275
90T/St-86
90UD-618
91B-317
91D-207
91F-254
91Leaf-505
91Leaf/Stud-82
91OPC-125
91OPC/Premier-5
91RedFoley/St-7
91S-459
91S/RookTr-14T
91StCl-531
91T-125
91T/Tr-6T
91UD-422
91UD/Ext-738
92D-184
92F-197
92OPC-267
92S-17
92T-267
92T/Gold-267
92T/GoldWin-267
92UD-622
92USPlayC/Twin-4H
92USPlayC/Twin-4S
93Brave/LykePerf-2
93Brave/LykeStand-3
93F/Final-1
93StCl-708
93StCl/1stDay-708
93UD-701
93Ultra-301
94D-479
94F-351
94Pac/Cr-2
94S-247
94S/GoldR-247
94StCl-64
94StCl/1stDay-64
94StCl/Gold-64
94StCl/Team-43
94T-617
94T/Gold-617
94Ultra-148

Beebe, Fred
12Sweet/Pin-95
C46-54
E270/2
M116
T204

Beecher, Edward H.
(Ed)
N284

Beecroft, Mike
82BirmB-6

Beeler, Joseph Sam
(Jodie)
No Cards.

Beeler, Pete
87Tampa-27
88Cedar/ProC-1147
88MidwLAS/GS-8
89Cedar/Star-25
89Chatt/Best-11
89Chatt/GS-4
91AA/LineD-154
91Chatt/LineD-154
91Nashvl/ProC-2158
91Waverly/Fut-3
92BuffB/ProC-325
92BuffB/SB-27

Beene, Andy
82ElPaso-14
84Cram/PCL-26

Beene, Fred
70OPC-121R
70T-121R
71MLB/St-219
73OPC-573

73T-573
74OPC-274
74T-274
75OPC-181
75T-181
75T/M-181
76SSPC-504
79OkCty
80Tidew-14
91Crown/Orio-26
92Yank/WIZ70-12
Beene, Steve
76Watlo
77DaytB
Beer, Darrin
89Geneva/ProC-1863
Beerbower, Dan
76QuadC
Beeston, Paul
93BJ/D/McDon-24PR
Befort, Curt
87Clearw-3
Beggs, Joe
Exh47
W711/2
Begley, James L.
(Jim)
No Cards.
Begue, Roger
82Lynch-18
Behel, Steven A. D.
(Steve)
N172/ST
Behenna, Rick
81Durham-15
83Pol/Atl-49
84D-346
85Polar/Ind-32
Behm, Bill
84Tiger/Wave-5
Behney, Mel
72OPC-524R
72T-524R
73OPC-602R
73T-602R
Behnsch, Bobby
87Clearw-7
Behny, Mark
86Erie-3
87Savan-24
88Savan/ProC-339
Behr, George
92Helena/ProC-1719
92MN-3
Behrend, Mike
83Erie-11
84Savan-26
Behrens, Scott
91Idaho/ProC-4320
91Pulaski/ClBest-16
91Pulaski/ProC-3995
92Idaho/ProC-3501
Behrman, Henry
(Hank)
49Eureka-101
50Remar
90Target-42
Beiras, Mike
88Belling/Legoe-26
Beirman, Jim
75FtLaud/Sus-16
Beitey, Dan
75Cedar
Beja, Aaron
91Fayette/ClBest-25
Bejma, Aloysius Frank
(Ollie)
35BU-55
35BU-93
R312/M
Belan, Lance
86PrWill-2
Belanger, Lee
82OrlanTw-2
83Visalia/Frit-1
Belanger, Mark Henry
67T-558R
68CokeCap/Orio-14
68Dexter-10
68OPC-118
68T-118
69T-299
69T/St-121
70MLB/St-145
70T-615
71MLB/St-289
71OPC-99
71T-99
72OPC-224WS
72OPC-456
72Pol/Orio-1
72T-456
73JP
73OPC-253
73T-253
74OPC-329
74T-329
74T/St-122
75OPC-74
75T-74
75T/M-74
76OPC-505
76T-505
77BurgChef-38
77Ho-71
77Ho/Twink-71
77OPC-154
77T-135
78OPC-125
78T-315
79OPC-27
79T-65
80OPC-217
80T-425
81D-472
81F-175
81F/St-39
81T-641
82F-158
82F/St-148
82OPC-42
82Pol/Dodg-8
82T-776
82T/Tr-5T
83D-514
83T-273
90Target-43
91Crown/Orio-27
Belardi, Carroll W.
(Wayne)
55B-36
79TCMA-110
90Target-44
Belbru, Juan
89Savan/ProC-356
90Hamil/Star-5
Belcher, Glenn
87Fayette-27
88Fayette/ProC-1080
89Fayette/ProC-1568
Belcher, Kevin
88Gaston/ProC-1010
89Gaston/ProC-1004
89Gaston/Star-2
89SALAS/GS-30
89Star/IISingl-134
90A&AASingle/ProC-67
90ProC/Singl-744
90TexLgAS/GS-26
90Tulsa/ProC-1166
90Tulsa/Team-3
91AAA/LineD-302
91D-46RR
91F-280
91Leaf/Stud-121
91OkCty/LineD-302
91OkCty/ProC-189
91S-714RP
91S/Rook40-15
91T/90Debut-13
91UD-26
92Tulsa/ProC-2706
92Tulsa/SB-602
93Rang/Keeb-67
Belcher, Tim
84Madis/Pol-9
85Huntsvl/BK-31
85T-281FDP
87Tacoma-21
88D-587
88D/Best-10
88D/Rook-28
88F-509
88Mother/Dodg-23
88Pol/Dodg-49M
88S/Tr-101T
88T/Tr-12T
89B-336
89Bz-1
89Classic-57
89D-203
89D/Best-234
89F-54
89F/Superstar-3
89F/WS-2
89KMart/DT-9
89Mother/Dodg-23
89OPC-177
89Panini/St-21
89Panini/St-95
89Pol/Dodg-25
89S-418
89S/HotRook-94
89S/YS/I-36
89Sf-121
89T-456
89T/Big-145
89T/Gloss60-30
89T/JumboR-3
89T/St-317
89ToysRUs-3
89UD-648
89Woolwth-19
89Woolwth-29
90B-85
90D-79
90D/BestNL-17
90F-389
90F/AwardWin-2
90F/Can-389
90F/LL-2
90F/WaxBox-C2
90Leaf-200
90Mother/Dodg-9
90OPC-173
90Panini/St-281
90Pol/Dodg-49
90PublInt/St-2
90PublInt/St-608
90S-126
90T-173
90T/Big-246
90T/Coins-38
90T/Mini-57
90Target-45
90UD-547
91B-605
91BBBest/Aces-3
91D-70
91F-194
91Leaf-508
91Mother/Dodg-9
91OPC-25
91Pol/Dodg-49
91S-187
91StCl-152
91T-25
91UD-576
91Ultra-159
92B-319
92B-664FOIL
92Classic/II-T78
92D-78
92F-447
92F/Up-79
92L-417
92L/BlkGold-417
92OPC-688
92OPC/Premier-113
92Pinn-384
92Reds/Kahn-31
92S-368
92S/RookTr-65T
92StCl-842
92T-688
92T/Gold-688
92T/GoldWin-688
92T/Tr-8T
92T/TrGold-8T
92UD-668
92UD-761
92USPlayC/Ace-11S
92Ultra-479
93B-118
93D-82
93F-30
93Flair-24
93L-243
93OPC-48
93Pac/Spanish-398
93Pinn-357
93Reds/Kahn-2
93S-423
93Select-191
93Select/RookTr-3T
93StCl-9
93StCl/1stDay-9
93T-382
93T/Gold-382
93TripleP-163
93UD-368
93Ultra-26
94B-677
94D-56
94F-74
94Finest-301
94L-232
94OPC-70
94Pac/Cr-119
94Pinn-491
94S-470
94StCl-255
94StCl/1stDay-255
94StCl/Gold-255
94T-62
94T/Gold-62
94UD-364
94Ultra-353
Belcik, Keith
84LitFalls-2
Belden, Ira Allison
No Cards.
Belen, Lance
85PrWill-14
87Harris-11
88Harris/ProC-844
Belen, Mattie
89Bluefld/Star-4
Belford, John
89Welland/Pucko-35M
Belfour, Ed
91StCl/Charter*-42
91StCl/Charter*-43
Belinda, Stan
87Macon-17
88CLAS/Star-3
88Salem/Star-2
89AAA/CMC-13
89Harris/ProC-305
89Harris/Star-3
90AAASingl/ProC-480
90BuffB/CMC-1
90BuffB/ProC-365
90F/Up-U48
90Leaf-486
90OPC-354
90ProC/Singl-1
90S-634
90T-354
90T/89Debut-12
90TripleAAS/CMC-13
90UD/Ext-759
91D-699
91F-30
91OPC-522
91S-296
91S/100RisSt-8
91StCl-453
91T-522
91UD-161
91Ultra-273
92B-455
92D-501
92F-548
92L-287
92L/BlkGold-287
92OPC-466
92Pinn-370
92Pirate/Nation-1
92S-325
92StCl-75
92T-466
92T/Gold-466
92T/GoldWin-466
92UD-202
92Ultra-550
93B-22
93D-490
93F-110
93Flair-109
93L-339
93Pac/Spanish-242
93Panini-282
93Pinn-142
93Pirate/Nation-1
93S-369
93StCl-268
93StCl/1stDay-268
93T-748
93T/Gold-748
93UD-359
93UD/SP-181
93Ultra-95
94D-77
94F-148
94Flair-55
94S-160
94S/GoldR-160
94StCl-8
94StCl/1stDay-8
94StCl/Gold-8
94T-247
94T/Gold-247
94Ultra-360
Belinskas, Dan
86Cedar/TCMA-1
Belinsky, Bo
62T-592R
63T-33
64T-315
65OPC-225
65T-225
66T-506
67T-447
69T-366
81TCMA-447
89Pac/Leg-130
89Swell-16
Beliveau, Jean
72Dimanche*-67VP
Belk, Chuck
79Wisco-20
Belk, Tim
92Billings/ProC-3360
93FExcel/ML-16
94B-588
94FExcel-172
Bell, Beau
93Conlon-781
Bell, Bobby
86PalmSp-2
86PalmSp/Smok-5
87PalmSp-25
88PalmSp/ProC-1459
Bell, Brent
91Martins/ClBest-14
91Martins/ProC-3457
92Martins/ClBest-18
92Martins/ProC-3063
Bell, Cliff
86Negro/Frit-100
Bell, Curt
92Niagara/ClBest-24
92Niagara/ProC-3326
Bell, David Gus
(Buddy)
73OPC-31
73T-31
74K-10
74OPC-257
74T-257
74T/DE-37
74T/St-161
75Ho-30
75Ho/Twink-30
75OPC-38
75T-38
75T/M-38
76Ho-95
76OPC-358
76OPC-66FS
76SSPC-517
76T-358
76T-66FS
77BurgChef-57
77Ho-69
77Ho/Twink-69
77OPC-86
77Pep-11
77T-590
77T/CS-2
77T/ClothSt-2
78Ho-15
78OPC-234
78PapaG/Disc-34
78Pep-26
78T-280
78Tastee/Discs-1
78Wiffle/Discs-2
79Ho-147

79K-14
79OPC-367
79T-690
80K-53
80OPC-107
80T-190
80T/Super-47
81D-145
81F-625
81F/St-11
81K-64
81MSA/Disc-1
81OPC-66
81T-475
81T/HT
81T/Nat/Super-1
81T/SO-21
81T/St-130
82D-23DK
82D-368
82Drake-2
82F-313
82F/St-172
82F/St-239
82K-33
82OPC-50
82T-50
82T/St-238
83D-215
83D/AAS-40
83F-562
83F-632M
83F/St-19AM
83F/St-19BM
83F/St-23M
83F/St-3M
83K-12
83OPC-330
83OPC/St-119FOIL
83Rangers-25
83T-330
83T-412
83T/Gloss40-9
83T/St-119
84D-56
84D/AAS-12
84F-413
84Nes/792-37TL
84Nes/792-665
84OPC-347
84Rangers-25
84Seven-11W
84T-37TL
84T-665
84T/RD-3
84T/St-351
85D-56
85D/AAS-11
85F-556
85F/LimEd-1
85F/St-7
85FunFood/Pin-76
85GenMills-13
85Leaf-174
85OPC-176
85Rangers-25
85T-131FS
85T-745
85T/RD-3
85T/St-347
85T/Super-53
85ThomMc/Discs-2
86D-447
86F-172
86F/Mini-37
86OPC-285
86Seven/Coin-S10
86Sf-151
86T-285
86T/St-139
86T/Tatt-15M
86TexGold-25
86TrueVal-20
87D-556
87D/OD-196
87F-193
87Kahn-25
87Leaf-169
87OPC-104
87RedFoley/St-38
87Sf-141
87Sf/TPrev-4M
87Stuart-4
87T-545
87T/Board-21
87T/St-143
88D-206
88F-227
88Jiffy-1
88KennerFig-5
88Leaf-192
88Nestle-30
88OPC-130
88Panini/St-279
88RedFoley/St-5
88S-99
88Sf-147
88T-130
88T/St-138
88T/Tr-13T
89B-229
89F-352
89Mother/R-9
89OPC-92
89S-610
89Smok/R-3
89T-461
89T/Big-270
89T/St-18
89UD-112
90AAASingl/ProC-236CO
90ColoSp/ProC-55CO
90Pac/Legend-74
90PublInt/St-404
91Swell/Great-7
93Rang/Keeb-68
93TWill-31

Bell, David Russell
(Gus)
51B-40
51T/RB-17
52T-170
53B/BW-1
53NB
53T-118
54B-124
54RH
54RM-NL19
55B-243
55Kahn
55RFG-16
55RM-NL23
55W605-16
56Kahn
56T-162
57Kahn
57Sohio/Reds-2
57T-180
58Kahn
58T-75
59Kahn
59T-365
60Kahn
60MacGregor-3
60T-235
60T-352M
61Kahn
61P-186
61T-215
61T-25M
61T/St-14
62J-120
62P-120
62P/Can-120
62Salada-158A
62Salada-158B
62Shirriff-158
62T-408
62T/St-153
63T-547
64T-534
76OPC-66FS
76T-66FS
79TCMA-89
82Ohio/HOF-35
85T-131FS
88Pac/Leg-65
91T/Arc53-118
91WIZMets-30
92Bz/Quadra-14
PM10/Sm-8

Bell, David
90Spring/Best-3
91ClBest/Singl-104
91Collnd/ClBest-22
91Collnd/ProC-1489
92Kinston/ClBest-18
92Kinston/ProC-2481
92UD/ML-80
94T-369M
94T/Gold-369M

Bell, Derek
88Myrtle/ProC-1171
88OPC-311
88SALAS/GS-20
89Knoxvl/Best-1
89Knoxvl/ProC-1149
89Knoxvl/Star-1
90AAASingl/ProC-362
90ProC/Singl-340
90S/Tr-81T
90Syrac/CMC-14
90Syrac/MerchB-2
90Syrac/ProC-582
90Syrac/Team-2
91AAA/LineD-501
91AAAGame/ProC-42
91Classic/III-28
91D-32RR
91F-168
91S/100RisSt-32
91S/ToroBJ-20
91Syrac/Kraft-1
91Syrac/LineD-501
91Syrac/MerchB-2
91Syrac/ProC-2491
91T/Tr-7T
91UD/FinalEd-26F
92B-237
92B-559FOIL
92BJ/Fire-3
92Classic/Game200-74
92Classic/I-11
92D-581
92F-324
92L-243
92L/BlkGold-243
92OPC-121
92OPC/Premier-189
92Pinn-250
92Pinn/Rook-7
92Pinn/RookI-18
92ProC/Tomorrow-158
92S-402
92S/100RisSt-64
92S/HotRook-9
92S/Impact-23
92S/Rook-3
92Sky/AAASingl-290
92Sky/AAASingl-292
92StCl-555
92Studio-252
92Syrac/TallT-2
92T-121
92T/91Debut-14
92T/Gold-121
92T/GoldWin-121
92T/McDonB-36
92UD-26SR
92UD/Scout-SR4
92Ultra-448
93BJ/D/45-3
93BJ/D/WS-3M
93BJ/D/WS-7M
93Cadaco-4
93Colla/DM-8
93D-557
93F-331
93F/Final-134
93Flair-131
93L-179
93Mother/Padre-12
93OPC-31
93Pac/Spanish-320
93Panini-32
93Pinn-171
93Pinn/HRC-37
93S-122
93Select-286
93Select/RookTr-132T
93StCl-504
93StCl/1stDay-504
93Studio-18
93T-268
93T/Gold-268
93T/Tr-55T
93ToysRUs-93
93TripleP-255
93UD-158
93UD-696
93UD/SP-163
93USPlayC/Rook-5S
93Ultra-286
93Ultra-469
94B-288
94D-591
94F-655
94Flair-231
94L-113
94OPC-64
94Pac/Cr-517
94Panini-252
94Pinn-22
94Pinn/Artist-22
94Pinn/Museum-22
94Pinn/Power-22
94S-338
94Select-146
94StCl-286
94StCl/1stDay-286
94StCl/Gold-286
94Studio-130
94T-364
94T/Finest-114
94T/FinestRef-114
94T/Gold-364
94TripleP-162
94UD-495
94UD/SP-128
94Ultra-572

Bell, Eric
84Newar-2
87D-39RR
87D/Rook-2
87F/Up-U2
87French-45
87Leaf-39RR
87Sf/Rook-1
87Sf/TPrev-21M
87T/Tr-3T
88Classic/Red-193
88D-125
88F-555
88OPC-383
88Panini/St-4
88RochR/CMC-2
88RochR/ProC-194
88RochR/Team-2
88S-101
88S/YS/II-38
88T-383
88T/St-224
90AAASingl/ProC-454
90HagersDG/Best-3
90RochR/ProC-697
90Rochester/L&U-16
91AA/LineD-77
91Canton/LineD-77
91Canton/ProC-971
91Crown/Orio-28
92ColoSp/ProC-743
92Indian/McDon-5
92L-379
92L/BlkGold-379
93Mother/Ast-25

Bell, Fern Lee
No Cards.

Bell, Frank Gustav
No Cards.

Bell, Gary
59Kahn
59T-327
60Kahn
60T-441
61Kahn
61P-58
61T-274
62Kahn
62Salada-213
62Shirriff-213
62Sugar-2
62T-273
62T/bucks
63Sugar-2
63T-129
64T-234
65T-424
66T-525
67CokeCap/Indian-7
67T-479
68CokeCap/RedSox-3
68Dexter-11
68OPC-43
68T-43
69MB-23
69MLB/St-93
69T-377
69T/St-223
89Pac/Leg-213

Bell, George G.
10Domino-10
11Helmar-83
12Sweet/Pin-70A
12Sweet/Pin-70B
D304
E254
E90/1
M116
S74-49
T20
T204
T205
T3-79

Bell, Greg
86WinSalem-1
87Pittsfld-2

Bell, Herman
(Hi)
34G-52
92Conlon/Sport-632

Bell, James
(Cool Papa)
74Laugh/Black-24
75Sheraton-21
76Shakey-141
80Perez/HOF-141
80SSPC/HOF
83D/HOF-25
86Negro/Frit-3
86Negro/Frit-90
87Leaf/SpecOlym-H12
87Negro/Dixon-24
88Conlon/HardC-1
88Conlon/NegAS-1
88Negro/Duques-14
89Kahn/Coop-1
90Negro/Star-28
90Perez/GreatMom-51
93TWill-97

Bell, Jay
85Visalia-8
86Water-4
87BuffB-4
88D-637
88D/Best-61
88F-602
88Gator-16
88T-637
89AAA/ProC-7
89BuffB/CMC-4
89BuffB/ProC-1679
89D-350
89S-352
89T-144
89UD-489
89VFJuice-3
90B-174
90D-488
90D/BestNL-136
90F-459
90F/Can-459
90Homer/Pirate-4
90Leaf-248
90OPC-523
90OPC-724
90Panini/St-321
90RochR/CMC-13
90RochR/ProC-707
90S-563
90S/YS/II-12
90T-523
90T/89Debut-13
90UD-517
91B-522
91B-96
91Crown/Orio-29
91D-289
91F-31
91F-468
91Leaf-130
91Leaf-262
91Leaf/Stud-221
91Leaf/StudPrev-1
91OPC-293
91OPC/Premier-7
91Panini/FrSt-118
91Panini/St-110
91S-323
91S/100RisSt-59
91StCl-84

91T-293
91UD-183
91UD/FinalEd-59F
91Ultra-274
92B-519
92Classic/I-12
92D-100
92D-479
92D/DK-DK17
92F-3
92F-549
92L-143
92L/BlkGold-143
92OPC-779
92Panini-255
92Pinn-34
92Pirate/Nation-2
92S-180
92S-646
92StCl-507
92Studio-81
92T-52
92T-779
92T/Gold-779
92T/GoldWin-779
92TripleP-184
92UD-115
92Ultra-250
93B-330
93Cadaco-6
93Colla/DM-9
93D-18
93F-111
93Flair-110
93L-116
93OPC-19
93Pac/Spanish-243
93Panini-283
93Pinn-48
93Pirate/Nation-2
93S-32
93Select-81
93StCl-138
93StCl/1stDay-138
93Studio-20
93T-354
93T/Finest-194
93T/FinestRef-194
93T/Gold-354
93TripleP-140
93TripleP-261
93UD-103
93UD-480M
93UD-830TC
93UD/FunPack-149
93UD/SP-182
93Ultra-96
94B-106
94Church-20
94D-21
94D/Special-21
94F-605
94F/AS-28
94F/TL-25
94Finest-411
94Flair-214
94L-12
94OPC-222
94Pac/Cr-492
94Panini-233
94Pinn-151
94Pinn/Artist-151
94Pinn/Museum-151
94Pinn/Run-37
94Pinn/TeamP-4M
94RedFoley-3
94S-32
94S/Cycle-15
94S/GoldR-32
94S/GoldS-12
94S/Tomb-2
94Select-5
94Sf/2000-188AS
94Sf/2000-95
94StCl-18
94StCl/1stDay-18
94StCl/Gold-18
94Studio-144
94T-15
94T/BlkGold-24
94T/Gold-15
94TripleP-181
94TripleP/Medal-8M
94UD-177
94UD-277HFA
94UD/ElecD-177
94UD/ElecD-277HFA
94UD/SP-140
94Ultra-254
94Ultra/AS-14
94Ultra/AwardWin-14

Bell, Jerry
72OPC-162R
72T-162R
73OPC-92
73T-92
74OPC-261
74T-261
74T/St-191
75SanAn

Bell, Jorge Antonio
(George)
82D-54
82F-609
82OPC-254
82Syrac-20
82Syrac/Team-7
82T-254
83Syrac-21
84D-73
84F-148
84Nes/792-278
84OPC-278
84T-278
84Tor/Fire-5
85D-146
85F-100
85F/St-39
85FunFood/Pin-113
85Leaf-248
85OPC-59
85OPC/Post-18
85T-698
85T/St-360
85Tor/Fire-5
86BJ/Ault-4
86D-4
86D-71
86D/DKsuper-4
86F-53
86F/Mini-13
86GenMills/Book-3M
86Leaf-4DK
86OPC-338
86OPC-A
86Seven/Coin-E11
86Sf-102
86T-338
86T-718AS
86T/Gloss60-47
86T/St-187
86T/Super-10
86T/Tatt-3M
86T/WaxBox-A
86Tor/Fire-4
87Classic-56
87D-271
87D/OD-39
87F-220
87F/AS-9
87F/AwardWin-2
87F/GameWin-3
87F/Lim-4
87F/Mini-7
87F/Slug-3
87F/St-9
87GenMills/Book-1M
87Ho/St-3
87Kraft-43
87Leaf-184
87OPC-12
87Sf-51
87Sf-80M
87Sf/TPrev-5M
87Stuart-27
87T-612AS
87T-681
87T/Coins-3
87T/Gloss60-45
87T/Mini-74
87T/St-193
87Tor/Fire-2
88BJ/5x7-2
88Bz-1
88ChefBoy-4
88Classic/Blue-242
88D-656
88D-BC19
88D/AS-6
88D/Best-31
88D/PopUp-6
88Drake-22
88F-103
88F-623M
88F/AS-5
88F/AwardWin-2
88F/BB/AS-1
88F/BB/MVP-1
88F/Excit-3
88F/Hottest-1
88F/LL-1
88F/Mini-59
88F/RecSet-2
88F/SS-2
88F/Slug-1
88F/St-71
88F/TL-1
88FanSam-7
88Grenada-76
88Ho/Disc-22
88KMart-1
88KayBee-1
88KennerFig-6
88Leaf-213CG
88Leaf-214MVP
88Leaf-254
88Nestle-34
88OPC-173
88Panini/St-224
88Panini/St-230M
88RedFoley/St-6
88S-540
88S/WaxBox-6
88Sf-4
88T-390AS
88T-590
88T/Big-15
88T/Coins-1
88T/Gloss22-6
88T/Gloss60-31
88T/Mini-37
88T/Revco-18
88T/RiteAid-26
88T/St-158
88T/St-188
88T/St/Backs-47
88T/UK-3
88Tor/Fire-11
88Woolwth-9
89B-256
89Classic-43
89D-149
89D/Best-272
89F-226
89F/BBAS-2
89F/BBMVP's-2
89F/Heroes-1
89KMart/DT-17
89KennerFig-7
89OPC-50
89Panini/St-472
89RedFoley/St-7
89S-347
89S/HotStar-91
89Sf-25
89T-1RB
89T-50
89T/Ames-4
89T/Big-318
89T/Gloss60-27
89T/LJN-46
89T/Mini-75
89T/St-1
89T/St-193
89T/UK-3
89Tor/Fire-11
89UD-255
89Woolwth-7
90B-515
90BJ/HoSt-1M
90BJ/HoSt-2M
90BJ/HoSt-5M
90Classic-84
90D-206
90D/BestAL-139
90D/Bon/MVP-BC13
90D/Learning-25
90F-628
90F-76
90F/BBMVP-1
90F/Can-628
90F/Can-76
90F/LL-3
90Holsum/Discs-1
90HotPlay/St-1
90Leaf-185
90MCA/Disc-9
90MLBPA/Pins-67
90OPC-170
90Panini/St-180
90PublInt/St-276
90PublInt/St-509
90S-286
90S/100St-27
90S/McDon-20
90Sf-17
90T-170
90T/Ames-22
90T/Big-153
90T/Coins-5
90T/DH-3
90T/Gloss60-24
90T/HillsHM-12
90T/Mini-41
90T/St-192
90T/TVAS-21
90Target-46
90Tetley/Discs-9
90Tor/BJ-11
90UD-127
90UD-95TC
90USPlayC/AS-12C
90Victory-1
90Windwlk/Discs-6
91B-418
91BBBest/HitM-1
91Classic/200-104
91Classic/II-T30
91Cub/Mara-11
91Cub/Vine-3
91Cub/Vine-36MVP
91D-642
91F-169
91F/Up-U77
91Kenner-4
91Leaf-389
91Leaf/Stud-151
91OPC-440
91OPC/Premier-6
91Panini/FrSt-340
91Panini/St-158
91S-195
91S/100SS-40
91S/RookTr-13T
91StCl-504
91T-440
91T/Tr-8T
91UD-532
91UD/Ext-725
91UD/Ext-742
91USPlayC/AS-6S
91Ultra-55
92CJ/DII-6
92Classic/Game200-26
92Classic/II-T86
92D-127
92D/DK-DK7
92D/Up-U12
92F-376
92F/Up-12
92Kenner/Fig-3
92L-462
92L/BlkGold-462
92OPC-320
92OPC/Premier-182
92Panini-188
92Pinn-37
92S-45
92S/100SS-88
92S/RookTr-24T
92StCl-525
92StCl-840
92StCl/Dome-13
92Studio-151
92T-320
92T/Gold-320
92T/GoldWin-320
92T/Kids-3
92T/Tr-9T
92T/TrGold-9T
92TripleP-42
92UD-236
92UD-724
92USPlayC/Cub-1C
92USPlayC/Cub-9D
92Ultra-173
92Ultra-332
92WSox-21
93B-639
93BJ/D/McDon-4
93Cadaco-5
93Classic/GameI-11
93D-95
93D/Spirit-SG6
93F-200
93L-217
93OPC-26
93Pac/Beisbol-3
93Pac/Spanish-67
93Pac/SpanishP-10
93Panini-143
93Pinn-387
93Pinn/Slug-25
93S-387
93Select-100
93StCl-330
93StCl/1stDay-330
93StCl/WSox-22
93Studio-28
93T-790
93T/Finest-175
93T/FinestRef-175
93T/Gold-790
93TripleP-247
93UD-345
93UD/FunPack-198
93UD/HRH-HR12
93Ultra-171
93WSox-2
94F-75
94Panini-44
94S-541
94T-214
94T-390AS
94T/Gold-214
94T/Gold-390AS

Bell, Juan
87Bakers-7
88BBAmer-23
88SanAn/Best-24
88TripleA/ASCMC-44
89B-11
89Classic/Up/2-170
89RochR/CMC-21
89RochR/ProC-1658
89UD-20
89UD/Ext-747
90AAASingl/ProC-464
90ProC/Singl-312
90Rochester/L&U-9
90S-603
90T-724
92F/Up-108
92OPC-52
92RochR/SB-451
92StCl-835
92T/Gold-52
92T/GoldWin-52
93B-48
93D-200
93F-98
93F/Final-222
93L-205
93Pac/Spanish-231
93Phill/Med-6
93Pinn-566
93S-588
93StCl-157
93StCl/1stDay-157
93TripleP-98
93UD-580
93Ultra-84
94F-173
94Pac/Cr-325
94S-282
94S/GoldR-282
94StCl-236
94StCl/1stDay-236
94StCl/Gold-236
94T-651
94T/Gold-651
94Ultra-72

Bell, Kevin Robert
75AppFx
77T-83
78SSPC/270-150
78T-463
79Iowa/Pol-4
79T-662
80OPC-197

80T-379
81D-39
81F-343
81Tacoma-25
82Tacoma-13
Bell, Lenny
88Peoria/Ko-4
89WinSalem/Star-1
Bell, Lester Rowland
(Les)
25Exh-57
26Exh-57
28Yueng-58
92Conlon/Sport-651
E210-58
R309/2
W502-58
Bell, Michael Allen
87Sumter-16
88CLAS/Star-25
88Durham/Star-1
89Greenvl/Best-4
89Greenvl/ProC-1173
89Greenvl/Star-3
89Star/Wax-34
90A&AASingle/ProC-64
90Greenvl/ProC-1134
90Greenvl/Star-3
90Star/ISingl-94
91AAA/LineD-427
91Brave/Dubuq/Stand-3
91F-682
91Richm/Bob-20
91Richm/LineD-427
91Richm/ProC-2575
91Richm/Team-8
91S-375RP
91T/90Debut-14
91UD-644
92F-350
92Greenvl/ProC-1158
92Greenvl/SB-228
92S-249
Bell, Mike
94B-350
94ClBest/Gold-78
94T-201FDP
94T/Gold-201FDP
94UD-542TP
94UD/SP-1PP
Bell, Randy
92Lipscomb-3
Bell, Robert
86Cram/NWL-34
Bell, Ron
77SanJose-20
Bell, Roy Chester
(Beau)
30CEA/Pin-1
37OPC-105
38Exh/4-15
38Wheat-7
39PlayBall-136
40PlayBall-138
V300
Bell, Rudolph Fred
(Rudy)
No Cards.
Bell, Sam
V351A-2
Bell, Stewart
91Parramatta/Fut-15
Bell, Terry
86Chatt-4
86Memphis/GoldT-1
86Memphis/SilverT-1
87Memphis-17
87Memphis/Best-23
88Greenvl/Best-2
88Richm-14
89Greenvl/Best-19
89Greenvl/ProC-1162
89Greenvl/Star-4
Bell, Tito
93LimeR/Winter-58
Bell, Tom
88Fresno/Cal-27
88Fresno/ProC-1248
Bell, William
86Negro/Frit-99
Bella, John
(Zeke)
59T-254

Bellacetin, Juan
85Tigres-27
Bellaman, Mike
86Water-3
87Wmsprt-10
Belle, Joey
(Albert)
88Kinston/Star-3
89Canton/Star-25
89F/Up-25
89S/Tr-106
89Star/IISingl-199
90B-333
90Classic-100
90D-390
90F-485
90F/Can-485
90HotRook/St-6
90Leaf-180
90OPC-283
90S-508
90S/100Ris-9
90S/YS/I-3
90Sf-159
90T-283
90T/89Debut-14
90T/JumboR-2
90T/St-212
90ToysRUs-3
90UD-446
91B-81
91Classic/III-37
91F/Up-U16
91Indian/McDon-4
91Leaf-239
91OPC/Premier-8
91StCl-465
91UD/Ext-764
91Ultra-107
92B-329
92Classic/Game200-140
92Classic/I-13
92D-500
92DennyGS-6
92F-105
92Indian/McDon-6
92Kenner/Fig-4
92L-350
92L/BlkGold-350
92MooTown-1
92OPC-785
92OPC/Premier-100
92Panini-51
92Pinn-31
92Pinn/Team2000-18
92S-31
92S/100SS-39
92StCl-220
92Studio-164
92T-785
92T/Gold-785
92T/GoldWin-785
92T/Kids-73
92TripleP-103
92UD-137
92UD/HRH-HR13
92UD/TWillB-T13
92UD/TmMVPHolo-8
92Ultra-47
93B-445
93Classic/GameI-12
93Colla/DM-10
93D-435
93D/EliteDom-19
93D/LongBall-LL3
93DennyGS-12
93F-590
93F-712RT
93F/Fruit-4
93Flair-192
93Indian/WUAB-3
93L-18
93OPC-66
93Pac/Spanish-94
93Panini-52
93Pinn-93
93Pinn/HRC-5
93Pinn/Slug-11
93S-84
93Select-50
93StCl-102
93StCl/1stDay-102
93Studio-95

93T-635
93T/Finest-16
93T/FinestRef-16
93T/Gold-635
93TripleP-94
93UD-45
93UD-586
93UD-823TC
93UD/FunPack-108
93UD/HRH-HR5
93UD/Iooss-WI12
93UD/OnDeck-D4
93UD/SP-120
93UD/SPPlat-PP1
93USPlayC/Ace-9C
93Ultra-538
93Ultra/HRK-5
94B-411
94D-351
94D/DK-8
94D/Elite-40
94D/MVP-19
94D/Special-351
94F-100
94F/AS-3
94F/LL-2
94F/Lumber-1
94Flair-38
94Flair/Outfield-1
94KingB-9
94L-251
94L/CleanUp-11
94L/MVPAL-1
94L/PBroker-10
94OPC-43
94OPC/JAS-12
94P-27
94Pac/Cr-166
94Pac/Gold-4
94Panini-55
94Panini-7
94Pinn-15
94Pinn/Artist-15
94Pinn/Museum-15
94Pinn/Power-11
94Pinn/Run-8
94RedFoley-4
94S-7
94S/Cycle-20M
94S/GoldR-7
94S/GoldS-46
94S/HobSam-7
94S/Pr-7
94S/Tomb-17
94Sf/2000-10
94StCl-219
94StCl-258
94StCl/1stDay-219
94StCl/1stDay-258
94StCl/Gold-219
94StCl/Gold-258
94Studio-92
94T-480
94T/BlkGold-3
94T/Finest-208
94T/FinestRef-208
94T/Gold-480
94TripleP-113
94TripleP/Bomb-9
94TripleP/Medal-11M
94UD-131
94UD-285HFA
94UD-40FT
94UD/CollC-314TP
94UD/CollC/Gold-314TP
94UD/CollC/Silv-314TP
94UD/CollHR-6
94UD/ElecD-131
94UD/ElecD-40FT
94UD/Mantle-2
94UD/SP-97
94Ultra-41
94Ultra/AS-6
94Ultra/HRK-4
94Ultra/RBIK-1
94Ultra/RisSt-3
Belliard, Rafael
83LynnP-14
87D-538
87D/OD-165
87F-602
87T-541
88F-321
88S-453

88T-221
88T/Big-175
89F-201
89OPC-119
89S-379
89T-723
89T/Big-196
89T/St-133
89UD-90
89VFJuice-6
90D-252
90F-460
90F/Can-460
90Homer/Pirate-3
90OPC-143
90PublInt/St-148
90S-520
90T-143
90UD-208
91B-578
91Brave/Dubuq/Perf-2
91Brave/Dubuq/Stand-4
91F-32
91F/UltraUp-U65
91F/Up-U70
91Leaf-453
91OPC-487
91S/RookTr-76T
91StCl-404
91T-487
91T/Tr-9T
91UD/Ext-706
92B-75
92Brave/LykePerf-2
92Brave/LykeStand-3
92D-107
92F-351
92L-310
92L/BlkGold-310
92OPC-367
92Panini-165
92Pinn-357
92S-116
92StCl-105
92T-367
92T/Gold-367
92T/GoldWin-367
92UD-510
92USPlayC/Brave-12D
92USPlayC/Brave-8S
92Ultra-158
93Brave/LykePerf-3
93Brave/LykeStand-4
93D-398
93F-361
93Pac/Spanish-1
93Pinn-494
93S-478
93Select-267
93StCl-58
93StCl/1stDay-58
93StCl/Brave-20
93T-62
93T/Gold-62
93TripleP-15
93UD-91
93Ultra-2
94F-352
94S-303
94S/GoldR-303
94StCl-426
94StCl/1stDay-426
94StCl/Gold-426
94StCl/Team-59
94T-261
94T/Gold-261
Bellinger, Clay
89Everett/Star-2
90Clinton/Best-1
90Clinton/ProC-2558
90Foil/Best-33
90ProC/Singl-844
91CalLgAS-41
91SanJose/ClBest-4
91SanJose/ProC-15
92Shrev/ProC-3877
92Shrev/SB-576
92Sky/AASingl-253
Bellino, Frank
85Newar-25
86Hagers-2
87Hagers-21
88Fresno/Cal-8
89EastLDD/ProC-DD39

89Reading/Best-18
89Reading/ProC-659
89Reading/Star-2
90Foil/Best-266
90Reading/Best-20
90Reading/ProC-1230
90Reading/Star-6
Bellman, Bill
92Kingspt/ProC-1520
Bellman, John H.
No Cards.
Bello, Duben
88Fayette/ProC-1091
Belloir, Robert E.
(Bob)
77T-312
78T-681
Bellomo, Bill
79Cedar/TCMA-12
Bellomo, Kevin
91Everett/ClBest-28
91Everett/ProC-3926
92ClBest-236
Bellum, Donnie
92Hamil/ClBest-6
92Hamil/ProC-1604
Bellver, Juan
86Miami-2
Belmonte, Nick
91SLCity/ProC-3227MG
91SLCity/SportP-28MG
Belmonte, Pedro
92Kingspt/ClBest-19
92Kingspt/ProC-1521
Belru, Juan
90Hamil/Best-26
Beltran, Alonso
92MedHat/ProC-3201
92MedHat/SportP-7
93StCath/ClBest-3
93StCath/ProC-3966
Beltran, Angel
89Welland/Pucko-4
Beltran, Julio
78DaytB
82Miami-13
Beltran, Rigo
91Hamil/ClBest-6
91Hamil/ProC-4027
92ClBest-367
92Savan/ClBest-17
92Savan/ProC-652
Beltre, Eddy
92Kingspt/ClBest-17
92Kingspt/ProC-1536
Beltre, Esteban
85Utica-12
86WPalmB-5
87Jaxvl-11
88Jaxvl/Best-17
88Jaxvl/ProC-991
89Rockford/Team-2
90AAASingl/ProC-564
90Indianap/CMC-24
90Indianap/ProC-281
90ProC/Singl-74
91AAA/LineD-128
91Denver/LineD-128
91Denver/ProC-127
92B-458
92Classic/II-T84
92D/Rook-10
92F-75
92Pinn-535
92S-766
92S/Rook-24
92StCl-611
92T/91Debut-15
92Ultra-333
93D-595
93LimeR/Winter-106
93StCl-375
93StCl/1stDay-375
93T-13
93T/Gold-13
94StCl/Team-146
Beltre, Sergio
79Jacks-9
81Tidew-10
Belyeu, Randy
91Hunting/ClBest-4
91Hunting/ProC-3336
Bemis, Harry Parker
E101

E105
E107
E254
E90/1
E92
M116
T216
Ben, Elijah
83BurlR-12
83BurlR/Frit-8
Benard, Marvin
92Everett/ClBest-4
92Everett/ProC-1702
Benavides, Al
92ClBest-235
92SanJose/ClBest-25
Benavides, Alfredo
(Freddie)
88Cedar/ProC-1142
89Chatt/Best-12
89Chatt/GS-5
89Nashvl/Team-2
90Chatt/GS-5
91AAA/LineD-252
91B-672
91F/Up-U84
91Kahn/Reds-57
91Nashvl/LineD-252
91Nashvl/ProC-2161
91S/RookTr-98T
91UD/FinalEd-32F
92D-573
92F-399
92Pinn-278
92Reds/Kahn-12
92S-813
92S/100RisSt-53
92StCl-394
92T/91Debut-16
92T/Tr-10T
92T/TrGold-10T
92Ultra-480
93B-472
93D-746
93F-402
93L-244
93Pac/Beisbol-22
93Pac/Spanish-421
93Pinn-548
93Pinn/Expan-6M
93S-627
93StCl-456
93StCl/1stDay-456
93StCl/Rockie-21
93T-356
93T/Gold-356
93T/Tr-7T
93UD-732
93USPlayC/Rockie-13D
93USPlayC/Rockie-4S
93Ultra-340
94D-76
94F-432
94Pac/Cr-187
94Panini-170
94S-229
94S/GoldR-229
94StCl-132
94StCl/1stDay-132
94StCl/Gold-132
94T-553
94T/Gold-553
94Ultra-180
Benbow, Lou Jr.
91StCath/ClBest-3
91StCath/ProC-3401
92StCath/ClBest-12
92StCath/ProC-3391
93Hagers/ClBest-2
93Hagers/ProC-1884
Bench, Johnny Lee
68Kahn
68T-247R
69MB-24
69MLB/St-127
69MLBPA/Pin-35
69OPC-95
69T-430AS
69T-95
69T/St-23
70K-58
70MLB/St-25
70OPC-464AS
70T-464AS
70T-660
70T/PI-11
70T/S-8
70T/Super-8
71Bz
71Bz/Test-29
71MD
71MLB/St-49
71MLB/St-556
71OPC-250
71OPC-64LL
71OPC-66LL
71T-250
71T-64LL
71T-66LL
71T/Coins-149
71T/GM-13
71T/Greatest-13POY
71T/S-32
71T/Super-32
71T/tatt-11
71T/tatt-11a
72Dimanche*-54
72MB-30
72OPC-433
72OPC-434IA
72ProStars/PostC-14
72T-433
72T-434A
73OPC-380
73OPC-62LL
73OPC-63LL
73T-380
73T-62LL
73T-63LL
73T/Comics-3
73T/Lids-5
73T/PinUps-3
74K-28
74OPC-10
74OPC-331AS
74T-10
74T-331M
74T/DE-71
74T/Puzzles-3
74T/St-21
75Ho-83
75K-7
75OPC-208MVP
75OPC-210MVP
75OPC-260
75OPC-308LL
75SSPC/42-29
75SSPC/Puzzle-2
75T-208MVP
75T-210MVP
75T-260
75T-308LL
75T/M-208MVP
75T/M-210MVP
75T/M-260
75T/M-308LL
76Crane-2
76Ho-22
76Ho/Twink-22
76Icee
76K-36
76MSA/Disc
76OPC-195LL
76OPC-300
76SSPC-31
76T-195LL
76T-300
77BurgChef-205
77Ho-6
77Ho/Twink-6
77OPC-100
77Pep-44
77T-411
77T-412
77T-70
77T/ClothSt-3
78Ho-44
78OPC-50
78Pep-4
78SSPC/270-128
78T-700
78Wiffle/Discs-3
79Ho-128
79OPC-101
79T-200
79T/Comics-21
80K-52
80OPC-55
80Perez/HOF-202
80T-100
80T/S-3
80T/Super-3
81Coke
81D-182
81D-62
81F-196
81F/St-37
81K-65
81MSA/Disc-2
81OPC-286
81PermaGr/CC-1
81Sqt-20
81T-201RB
81T-600
81T/HT
81T/Nat/Super-2
81T/SO-64
81T/St-160
82Coke/Reds
82D-400
82D-628M
82Drake-3
82F-57
82F-634M
82F/St-17
82K-30
82KMart-18
82KMart-22
82OPC-18
82OPC-304IA
82PermaGr/CC-1
82T-400
82T-401A
82T/St-35
83D-22DK
83D-500
83D/AAS-14
83F-584
83F/St-19AM
83F/St-19BM
83F/St-9M
83OPC-60
83OPC-61SV
83OPC/St-229
83OPC/St-7
83T-60
83T-61SV
83T/Fold-2M
83T/St-229
84D-660LLB
84D/Champs-51
84F-462
84F-640IA
84F/St-96
84Nes/792-6HL
84T-6HL
84T/Gloss22-22
85CircK-22
87KMart-12
87Nestle/DT-30
88Grenada-1
88Pac/Leg-110
89Kahn/Coop-2
89Kenner/BBGr-3
89T/LJN-53
90BBWit-54
90OPC-664TBC
90Perez/GreatMom-49
90T-664TBC
92UD/Bench-37
92UD/Bench-38
92UD/Bench-39
92UD/Bench-43
92UD/Bench-44
92UD/Bench-AU5AU
93TWill-28
93TWill/Mem-16
93YooHoo-1
Bencomo, Omar
85Kingst-2
87Knoxvl-14
88Knoxvl/Best-17
Bender, Charles A.
(Chief)
10Domino-11
11Diamond-3
11Helmar-54
12Sweet/Pin-42A
12Sweet/Pin-42B
14CJ-19
15CJ-19
40PlayBall-172
50Callahan
50W576-5
60F-7
61F-8
61GP-18
63Bz/ATG-11
69Bz/Sm
75Sheraton-10
76Shakey-66
77Galasso-142
80Pac/Leg-93
80Perez/HOF-64
80SSPC/HOF
86Conlon/1-39
91Conlon/Sport-20
92Conlon/Sport-335
93Conlon-774
BF2-83
D303
D304
D329-13
E101
E102
E103
E104
E105
E106
E107
E224
E286
E90/1
E91
E92
E93
E95
E98
L1-119
M101/4-13
M116
S74-28
S81-94
T201
T202
T204
T205
T206
T207
T208
T213/brown
T214-1
T215/blue
T227
T3-80
W555
WG2-4
WG5-3
WG6-2
Bender, Tony
92MN-21M
Bendorf, Jerry
82VeroB-17
Bene, Bill
88GreatF-1
89B-340
89Bakers/Cal-184
89Salem/Team-7
89T-84FDP
90VeroB/Star-4
91VeroB/ClBest-3
91VeroB/ProC-764
92SanAn/SB-556
92Sky/AASingl-244
Benedetti, Don
75Cedar
Benedict, Arthur M.
(Art)
No Cards.
Benedict, Bruce Edwin
78Richm
79T-715R
80T-675
81D-208
81F-248
81Pol/Atl-20
81T-108
82BK/Lids-1
82D-375
82F-429
82OPC-168
82Pol/Atl-20
82T-424
82T/St-21
82T/StVar-21
83D-299
83F-130
83OPC-204
83OPC/St-151LCS
83OPC/St-152LCS
83OPC/St-154LCS
83OPC/St-217
83Pol/Atl-20
83T-521
83T/St-151
83T/St-152
83T/St-154
83T/St-217
84D-409
84F-172
84Nes/792-255
84OPC-255
84Pol/Atl-20
84T-255
84T/RD-4
84T/St-34
85D-263
85F-320
85Ho/Braves-4
85Leaf-196
85OPC-335
85Pol/Atl-20
85T-335
85T/RD-4
85T/St-31
86D-554
86F-509
86OPC-78
86Pol/Atl-20
86T-78
87D-448
87F-512
87Smok/Atl-11
87Stuart-2
87T-186
88S-423
88T-652
89B-271
89Brave/Dubuq-4
89D-475
89F-587
89OPC-353
89S-502
89T-778
89T/Big-83
89UD-121
90OPC-583
90PublInt/St-108
90T-583
Benedict, Jim
91Butte/SportP-29
Benedict, Tom
91Pac/SenLg-94
Benes, Alan
94B-12
94ClBest/Gold-25
94ClBest/GoldLP-1
94FExcel-257
94SigRook-3
94T-202FDP
94T/Gold-202FDP
94UD-529TP
Benes, Andy
88T/Tr-14T
89AAA/CMC-43
89AubAs/ProC-8
89B-448
89BBAmAA/BPro-AA24
89Star/IISingl-111
89T-437FDP
89T/Big-114
89TexLAS/GS-10
89Wichita/Rock-30
89Wichita/Rock/HL-3
89Wichita/Rock/Up-19
89Wichita/Rock/Up-5
90B-207
90Classic-120
90Coke/Padre-2
90D-41
90D/BestNL-47
90F-151
90F/Can-151
90HotRook/St-7
90Leaf-56
90OPC-193
90Padre/MagUno-9
90Panini/St-382
90S-578
90S/100Ris-69

90S/YS/II-13
90Sf-90
90T-193
90T/89Debut-15
90T/Big-260
90T/JumboR-3
90ToysRUs-4
90TripleAAS/CMC-43
90UD-55
91B-665
91Classic/200-85
91Classic/III-T7
91D-627
91F-524
91Leaf-275
91Leaf/Stud-242
91OPC-307
91Padre/MagRal-18
91Panini/FrSt-99
91Panini/St-92
91S-538
91StCl-51
91T-307
91UD-275
91Ultra-301
92B-249
92B-599FOIL
92Classic/Game200-150
92Classic/I-14
92D-524
92F-599
92F/Smoke-S9
92L-74
92L/BlkGold-74
92L/GoldPrev-29
92Mother/Padre-16
92OPC-682
92Padre/Carl-3
92Pinn-74
92Pinn/Team2000-12
92Pol/Padre-3
92S-133
92S/Impact-88
92Smok/Padre-3
92StCl-423
92Studio-101
92T-682
92T/DQ-13
92T/Gold-682
92T/GoldWin-682
92TripleP-33
92UD-323
92UD/TmMVPHolo-9
92Ultra-274
93B-518
93D-22
93F-519
93Flair-132
93L-192
93Mother/Padre-14
93OPC-17
93Pac/Spanish-255
93Panini-265
93Pinn-42
93S-91
93Select-117
93StCl-581
93StCl/1stDay-581
93Studio-53
93T-568
93T/Finest-19
93T/FinestRef-19
93T/Gold-568
93T/Hill-28
93TripleP-201
93UD-261
93UD/FunPack-137
93UD/SP-164
93Ultra-116
94B-392
94D-332
94D/Special-332
94F-656
94F/AS-29
94Finest-328
94L-143
94OPC-83
94Pac/Cr-516
94Panini-253
94Pinn-51
94Pinn/Artist-51
94Pinn/Museum-51
94RedFoley-5
94S-44
94S/GoldR-44
94Sf/2000-52
94StCl-102
94StCl/1stDay-102
94StCl/Gold-102
94Studio-131
94T-70
94T/Gold-70
94TripleP-163
94UD-388
94UD/SP-129
94Ultra-573

Benes, Joseph Anthony
(Joe)
82Wausau/Frit-7

Benge, Brett
91Bluefld/ClBest-22
91Bluefld/ProC-4119

Benge, Ray
29Exh/4-12
31Exh/4-11
33Exh/4-6
33G-141
34G-24
35BU-11
35BU-99
35G-8A
35G-9A
90Target-47
V354-49
V355-13

Bengough, Bernard O.
(Benny)
29Exh/4-25
33G-1
49Eureka-128
91Conlon/Sport-103
93Conlon-860
94Conlon/Col-32
R315-A2
R315-B2
V353-1

Benhardt, Chris
91Spokane/ClBest-24
91Spokane/ProC-3937
92Watlo/ProC-2134

Beniquez, Juan Jose
74OPC-647
74T-647
75OPC-601
75T-601
75T/M-601
76OPC-496
76SSPC-406
76T-496
77BurgChef-27
77T-81
78SSPC/270-103
78T-238
79BK/Y-22
79T-478
80T-114
81D-518
81F-596
81T-306
81T/Tr-733
82D-587
82F-452
82T-572
83D-640
83F-78
83T-678
84D-207
84F-508
84Nes/792-53
84Smok/Cal-2
84T-53
85D-573
85F-294
85Smok/Cal-14
85T-226
85ThomMc/Discs-3
86D-352
86F-148
86F/St-4
86F/Up-U13
86Leaf-156
86OPC-325
86T-325
86T/St-185
86T/Tr-8T
87D-371
87F-462
87F/Up-U3
87OPC-173
87T-688
87T/Tr-4T
88F-104
88OPC-77
88OPC-C
88T-541
88T/St-12
88T/WaxBox-C
88Tor/Fire-21
89Bimbo/Discs-8
89Pac/SenLg-119
89T/SenLg-131
89TM/SenLg-6
90EliteSenLg-108
91Crown/Orio-30
92Yank/WIZ70-13
93Rang/Keeb-69

Benitez, Armando
92Bluefld/ClBest-21
92Bluefld/ProC-2352
93LimeR/Winter-40
94FExcel-1

Benitez, Christian
89Bluefld/Star-5
90Wausau/Best-22
90Wausau/ProC-2136
90Wausau/Star-3

Benitez, Luis
89CharWh/Best-12
89CharWh/ProC-1749
89Geneva/ProC-1870
90Geneva/ProC-3050
90Geneva/Star-1

Benitez, Manuel
86Bakers-3
87VeroB-12

Benitez, Yamil
92Albany/ClBest-17
92James/ClBest-19
92James/ProC-1511
93BurlB/ClBest-1
93BurlB/ProC-169
93FExcel/ML-57

Benjamin, Alfred S.
(Stan)
No Cards.

Benjamin, Bobby
88NE-11
90NE-3
91Beloit/ClBest-17
91Beloit/ProC-2114
92Stockton/ClBest-3

Benjamin, Jerry
86Negro/Frit-82

Benjamin, Mike
88Shrev/ProC-1283
88TexLgAS/GS-11
89Phoenix/CMC-16
89Phoenix/ProC-1500
90AAASingl/ProC-41
90F-51
90F/Can-51
90Phoenix/CMC-22
90Phoenix/ProC-15
90ProC/Singl-549
90T/89Debut-16
90UD/Ext-750
91Classic/I-6
91D-432RR
91Leaf/Stud-252
91OPC-791
91PG&E-20
91S-345RP
91S/Rook40-25
91SFExam/Giant-2
91StCl-143
91T-791
91UD-651
92Giant/PGE-5
92Phoenix/ProC-2825
92S-649
92S/100RisSt-7
92StCl-314
92UD-268
93D-472
93F-526
93Mother/Giant-19
93OPC-377
93Pac/Spanish-606
93S-603
93StCl-405
93StCl/1stDay-405
93T-384
93T/Gold-384
93Ultra-127
94F-681
94S-273
94S/GoldR-273
94StCl-318
94StCl/1stDay-318
94StCl/Gold-318
94StCl/Team-12
94T-487
94T/Finest-197
94T/FinestRef-197
94T/Gold-487

Benners, Isaac
(Ike)
No Cards.

Bennes, L.D.
91Kingspt/ClBest-25TR

Bennese, Larry
92Pittsfld/ClBest-21TR

Bennett, Albert
88Martins/Star-3
89Batavia/ProC-1920
91Spartan/ClBest-21
91Spartan/ProC-906
92Spartan/ClBest-12
92Spartan/ProC-1273

Bennett, Bob
89FresnoSt/Smok-3
89FresnoSt/Smok-4
91FresnoSt/Smok-1CO
92FrRow/DP-90
92SoOreg/ClBest-2
92SoOreg/ProC-3405

Bennett, Brad
82Spring/Frit-23

Bennett, Brian
89Ashvl/ProC-954

Bennett, Charles W.
(Charlie)
81Tiger/Detroit-2
N172
N28
N284
N526
Scrapp
WG1-19

Bennett, Chris
89WPalmB/Star-3
90Foil/Best-213
90Jaxvl/Best-15
90Jaxvl/ProC-1366
91Indianap/ProC-454

Bennett, Dave
64T-561R
65T-521R

Bennett, Dennis
63T-56
64PhilBull-4
64T-396
65OPC-147
65T-147
66T-491
67CokeCap/RedSox-14
67T-206
67T/Test/RedSox-1
78TCMA-93
91WIZMets-31

Bennett, Doug
90AR-1
91Yakima/ClBest-22
91Yakima/ProC-4237
92StCl/Dome-14
92Yakima/ClBest-1
92Yakima/ProC-3439

Bennett, Erik
88CapeCod/Sum-153
89BendB/Legoe-1
90QuadC/GS-14
92QuadC/ProC-800

Bennett, Gary
90Martins/ProC-3190
91Martins/ClBest-16
91Martins/ProC-3454
92Batavia/ClBest-4
92Batavia/ProC-3267

Bennett, Herschel E.
93Conlon-986

Bennett, James Fred
(Red)
No Cards.

Bennett, Jim
82WHave-20
83Tacoma-14
84Albany-1
87Memphis-25
87Memphis/Best-7
89Wausau/GS-17
90SanBern/Best-4
90SanBern/Cal-91
90SanBern/ProC-2625

Bennett, Joel
92WinHaven/ClBest-15
92WinHaven/ProC-1767
94B-287
94FExcel-18
94FExcel/LL-2

Bennett, Jose
86Cram/NWL-104
87Wausau-11

Bennett, Joseph R.
(Joe)
No Cards.

Bennett, Justin Titus
(Pug)
No Cards.

Bennett, Keith
86Watlo-3
87Erie-13
87Wmsprt-2
88ColoSp/ProC-1535
88Watlo/ProC-684

Bennett, Rick
90OK-19

Bennett, Shayne
94B-587

Bennington, Jeff
91BurlAs/ClBest-23
91BurlAs/ProC-2803

Benoit, Dickens
87Everett-28
89Salinas/Cal-137
89Salinas/ProC-1827

Benoit, Joe
45Parade*-3

Bensching, Bruce
90Spokane/SportP-22
91Waterlo/ClBest-2
91Waterlo/ProC-1249
92Watlo/ClBest-6
92Watlo/ProC-2135

Benson, Coach
80WHave-23bb

Benson, Gene
91Negro/Lewis-27
92Negro/Retort-3
93TWill-99

Benson, Mark
79Cedar/TCMA-3

Benson, Matt
91Helena/SportP-3

Benson, Nate
90Kgsport/Best-18
90Kgsport/Star-2

Benson, Neal
86Lipscomb-4

Benson, Randy
76Baton
80Syrac-18
80Syrac/Team-5

Benson, Steve
80OrlanTw-11
83ColumAst-8

Benson, Tom
89Elizab/Star-2
90Elizab/Star-2

Benson, Vernon A.
(Vern)
53T-205
61Union
73OPC-497CO
73T-497C
74OPC-236CO
74T-236C
78Syrac
79Syrac/TCMA-2
79Syrac/Team-8
80Pol/Giants-8C
91T/Arc53-205

Bentley, Blake
91Princet/ClBest-20
91Princet/ProC-3525

Bentley, Doug
45Parade*-41M

Bentley, John N.
(Jack)
26Exh-41
27Exh-17

93Conlon-919
V89-26
W515-12
WG7-5
Bentley, Max
45Parade*-41M
Benton, Alfred Lee
(Butch)
76Wausau
79Tidew-8
80Tidew-8
82Iowa-1
83Wichita/Dog-5
89Pac/SenLg-24
89T/SenLg-66
91Pac/SenLg-145
91WIZMets-32
Benton, John Alton
50NumNum
52T-374
53Mother-27
81Tiger/Detroit-57
Benton, John C.
(Rube)
L1-113
S81-88
T222
W513-69
WG7-6
Benton, Lawrence
(Larry)
25Exh-3
26Exh-1
29Exh/4-9
33G-45
35G-8L
35G-9L
91Conlon/Sport-182
R310
R315-A3
R315-B3
R316
V353-45
V94-2
Benton, Stanley
(Stan)
No Cards.
Benz, Joseph Louis
15CJ-175
BF2-8
D328-14
D350/2-13
E135-14
E300
M101/5-13
T207
Benza, Brett
82Tulsa-26
83Spring/Frit-10
Benzinger, Todd
86Pawtu-2
87D/Rook-30
87Pawtu-7
87Pawtu/TCMA-13
87Sf/Rook-47
88Classic/Blue-245
88D-297
88D/Best-289
88D/RedSox/Bk-297
88F-344
88F-630M
88Leaf-111
88OPC-96
88S-546
88S/YS/I-31
88T-96
88ToysRUs-1
89B-312
89D-358
89D/Best-174
89D/Tr-47
89F-79
89F/Up-83
89Kahn/Reds-25
89OPC-188
89Panini/St-275
89S-371
89S/Tr-15
89T-493
89T/Tr-9T
89UD-184
89UD/Ext-785
90B-55
90D-257
90D/BestNL-101
90D/GSlam-8
90F-413
90F/Can-413
90Kahn/Reds-2
90Kenner/Fig-8
90Leaf-15
90OPC-712
90Panini/St-250
90PublInt/St-22
90S-65
90Sf-56
90T-712
90T/Big-14
90T/St-138
90UD-186
91D-640
91F-56
91F/UltraUp-U25
91Kahn/Reds-25
91OPC-334
91Panini/FrSt-127
91Pep/Reds-2
91S-90
91StCl-113
91T-334
91UD-280
91UD/FinalEd-41F
91Ultra-87
92B-141
92D-536
92F-152
92L-257
92L/BlkGold-257
92Mother/Dodg-11
92OPC-506
92Panini-94
92Pinn-438
92Pol/Dodg-36
92S-563
92StCl-764
92T-506
92T/Gold-506
92T/GoldWin-506
92T/Tr-11T
92T/TrGold-11T
92UD-518
92Ultra-499
93D-562
93F-58
93F/Final-149
93Mother/Giant-11
93T-620
93T/Gold-620
93UD-790
93Ultra-481
94F-682
94Flair-238
94L-85
94Pac/Cr-539
94Pinn-39
94Pinn/Artist-39
94Pinn/Museum-39
94S-301
94S/GoldR-301
94StCl-61
94StCl/1stDay-61
94StCl/Gold-61
94StCl/Team-29
94T-398
94T/Gold-398
94UD-163
94UD/ElecD-163
94Ultra-586
Berardi, Scott
94LSU-12
Berardino, Dick
79Elmira-21
80Elmira-29
86Pawtu-1CO
87Greens-3
90T/TVRSox-2CO
Berardino, John
(Johnny)
47TipTop
51B-245
52T-253
W753
Berberet, Louis J.
(Lou)
56T-329
57T-315
58T-383
59T-96
60L-24
60MacGregor-4
60T-6
61P-43
Berblinger, Jeff
89KS*-73
94FExcel-258
94FExcel/1stY-3
Bere, Jason
91SoBend/ClBest-13
91SoBend/ProC-2849
92B-358
92ClBest-253
92Saraso/ClBest-6
92Saraso/ProC-198
93B-364FOIL
93B-91
93ClBest/MLG-203
93F/Final-192
93Flair/Wave-1
93L-524
93Select/RookTr-81T
93StCl/WSox-25
93T/Tr-26T
93UD-453IN
93UD/SP-271FOIL
93Ultra-527
93WSox-3
94B-381
94B-567
94D-86
94F-76
94F/RookSen-2
94Flair-29
94L-241
94OPC-206
94OPC/DiamD-13
94Pac/Cr-120
94Pinn-347
94Pinn/New-3
94S-563
94Sf/2000-68
94Sf/Shak-4
94StCl-212
94StCl/1stDay-212
94StCl/Gold-212
94StCl/Team-144
94T-118
94T/Finest-12
94T/FinestRef-12
94T/Gold-118
94TripleP-262
94UD-146
94UD-42FUT
94UD/CollC-50
94UD/CollC/Gold-50
94UD/CollC/Silv-50
94UD/ElecD-146
94UD/ElecD-42FUT
94UD/SP-189
94Ultra-31
94Ultra/Second-1
Berenguer, Juan
78Tidew
79T-721R
79Tacoma-6
80Tidew-3
81T-259R
82D-580
82Evansvl-2
82OPC-107
82OPC/Post-12
82T-437
84D-125
84F-77
84Nes/792-174
84T-174
84Tiger/Wave-6
85Cain's-2
85D-272
85F-2
85T-672
85Wendy-3
86F-221
86Mother/Giants-27
86T-47
86T/Tr-9T
87D-616
87F-265
87F/Up-U4
87T-303
87T/Tr-5T
88D-395
88D/Best-298
88F-3
88Master/Disc-3
88T-526
88T/Big-222
89B-152
89D-81
89D/Best-46
89F-104
89OPC-294
89S-414
89T-294
89T/Big-117
89T/St-291
89UD-232
90B-410
90D-301
90F-369
90F/Can-369
90Leaf-169
90OPC-709
90PublInt/St-323
90S-223
90T-709
90UD-440
91B-572
91Brave/Dubuq/Perf-3
91Brave/Dubuq/Stand-5
91D-340
91F-604
91F/UltraUp-U66
91F/Up-U71
91Leaf-526
91OPC-449
91S-111
91S/RookTr-73T
91StCl-460
91T-449
91UD-411
91WIZMets-33
92Brave/LykePerf-3
92Brave/LykeStand-4
92D-205
92F-352
92OPC-172
92Pinn-515
92S-216
92StCl-44
92T-172
92T/Gold-172
92T/GoldWin-172
92UD-493
92USPlayC/Brave-12H
92USPlayC/Brave-8C
92Ultra-455
Berenyi, Bruce
79Indianap-14
80Indianap-9
81T-606R
82Coke/Reds
82F-58
82T-459
83D-103
83F-585
83OPC-139
83T-139
84D-487
84F-463
84Nes/792-297
84OPC-297
84T-297
84T/Tr-10
85D-625
85F-73
85Indianap-32
85OPC-27
85T-27
85T/Mets/Fan-2
86T-339
87T-582
91WIZMets-34
Berg, Chris
91WA/Via-1
92Kingspt/ProC-1522
Berg, Morris
(Moe)
30CEA/Pin-11
33BU-149
33G-158
39PlayBall-103
40PlayBall-30
88Conlon/5-3
90Target-48
91Conlon/Sport-184
R313
R316
V353-84
Berg, Patty
52Wheat*
Berg, Rich
88Modesto-4
89Madis/Star-3
90Huntsvl/Best-2
91Stockton/ClBest-7
91Stockton/ProC-3024
Berg, Rick
90AAASingl/ProC-423CO
90Richm/Bob-22CO
90Richm/ProC-278CO
90Richm/Team-4
91Richm/Bob-42CO
91Richm/ProC-2584CO
Bergamo, August S.
(Augie)
No Cards.
Berge, Jordan
84Cedar-10
86Vermont-1
Berge, Lou
86LitFalls-3
Bergen, Martin
(Marty)
No Cards.
Bergen, William A.
(Bill)
10Domino-12
12Sweet/Pin-71
90Target-49
E101
E105
E300
E92
M116
S74-50
T201
T202
T205
T206
T216
T3-2
WG3-4
Bergendahl, Wray
83Wausau/Frit-28
85Lynch-7
86Jacks/TCMA-3
Berger Mike P.
92OkCty/ProC-1931CO
Berger, Carl
28Exh/PCL-3
Berger, Charles
(Heinie)
E254
E270/1
M116
T206
Berger, Clarence E.
No Cards.
Berger, John Henne
(Johnny)
No Cards.
Berger, John Henry
(Tun)
No Cards.
Berger, Joseph August
(Joe)
No Cards.
Berger, Ken
77Spartan
Berger, Louis William
(Boze)
35BU-84
Berger, Mike
84PrWill-7
85Nashua-3
86Nashua-3
87Jaxvl-6
88Indianap/CMC-20
88Indianap/ProC-519
89OkCty/CMC-11
89OkCty/ProC-1515
90AAASingl/ProC-680
90OkCty/CMC-10
90OkCty/ProC-434
90ProC/Singl-160
91OkCty/ProC-181
92OkCty/SB-325CO
Berger, Walter Anton
(Wally)
31Exh/4-2

32Orbit/num-51
32Orbit/un-5
33DH-5
33Exh/4-1
33G-98
34DS-108
34DS-25
34Exh/4-1
35BU-1
35BU-172
35Exh/4-1
35Wheat
36Exh/4-1
36G-1
37Exh/4-1
38ONG/Pin-1
39PlayBall-99
40PlayBall-81
77Galasso-220
88Conlon/3-5
88Conlon/NatAS-1
91Conlon/Sport-229
93Conlon-686
94Conlon-1098
R300
R305
R309/2
R310
R313
R326-13A
R326-13B
R328-19
R332-12
R342-13
V351B-3
V355-35
W711/1
Bergeron, Gilles
87James-22
Bergert, Ned
76QuadC
77QuadC
Bergh, John Baptist
No Cards.
Berghammer, Martin A.
(Marty)
No Cards.
Bergman, Alfred Henry
(Al)
No Cards.
Bergman, David Bruce
(Dave)
76SSPC-454
78BK/Ast-21
78T-705R
79CharCh-8
79T-697
81D-139
81F-76
81T-253
81T/Tr-734
82D-146
82T-498
83D-550
83F-253
83Mother/Giants-18
83T-32
84D-624
84F-366
84F/X-11
84Nes/792-522
84T-522
84T/Tr-11
84Tiger/Farmer-1
84Tiger/Wave-7
85Cain's-3
85D-537
85F-3
85OPC-368
85T-368
85Wendy-4
86Cain's-1
86D-471
86F-222
86T-101
87Cain's-4
87Coke/Tigers-9
87D-420
87F-144
87OPC-256
87T-700
88D-373
88F-52
88Pep/T-14
88Pol/T-3
88S-217
88T-289
89D-389
89F-129
89Mara/Tigers-14
89Pol/Tigers-14
89S-469
89T-631
89UD-266
90B-355
90CokeK/Tiger-2
90D-445
90F-600
90F/Can-600
90Leaf-244
90OPC-77
90Panini/St-67
90PublInt/St-468
90S-254
90T-77
90T/St-285
90UD-381
91CokeK/Tiger-14
91D-342
91F-331
91Leaf-92
91OPC-412
91Panini/St-241
91Pol/Tiger-2
91S-562
91StCl-386
91T-412
91UD-599
91Ultra-120
92OPC-354
92S-543
92StCl-171
92T-354
92T/Gold-354
92T/GoldWin-354
92USPlayC/Tiger-3H
92USPlayC/Tiger-9D
92Ultra-56
92Yank/WIZ70-14
Bergman, Sean
91Niagara/ClBest-24
91Niagara/ProC-3624
92Lakeland/ClBest-19
92StCl/Dome-15
93B-531
94B-41
94T-768M
94T/Gold-768M
Bergstrom, John
91MissSt-55M
Beringer, Carroll
73OPC-486CO
73T-486C
74OPC-119CO
74T-119C
78SSPC/270-34CO
Beringhele, Vince
85VeroB-17
Berkelbach, Francis
No Cards.
Berley, John
V355-118
Berlin, Mike
92Bristol/ClBest-1
92Bristol/ProC-1399
Berlin, Randy
89Hamil/Star-12
89Star/IISingl-104
90Spring/Best-4
91Freder/ClBest-17
91Freder/ProC-2371
Berman, Gary
86Cram/NWL-150
87Clearw-18
88Reading/ProC-873
Berman, Robert Leon
(Bob)
No Cards.
Bernabe, Sam
85Iowa-18
Bernal, Vic
77Padre/SchCd-3
79Hawaii-8
Bernard, Curtis Henry
(Curt)
No Cards.
Bernard, Dwight
75Tidew/Team-3
78Tidew
79T-721R
79Tidew-6
81Vanco-4
82Pol/Brew-47
83D-28
83F-27
83Gard-2
83T-244
84Cram/PCL-55
86Macon-4
87Kenosha-16
88Kenosha/ProC-1381
89OrlanTw/Best-4
89OrlanTw/ProC-1342
91WIZMets-35
92Brew/Carlson-2
Bernard, Erik
84Albany-16
85Albany-29
86Alban/TCM-12bb
Bernardo, Rick
87PortChar-18
88CharlR/Star-1
89CharlR/Star-2
89Miami/II/Star-1
Bernardo, Robert
86Wausau-1
Bernazard, Antonio
(Tony)
75WPalmB
75WPalmB/Sussman-29
80OPC-351R
80T-680R
81D-449
81F-168
81OPC-194
81T-413
81T/Tr-735
82D-143
82F-338
82T-206
82T/St-171
82T/StVar-171
83D-482
83F-231
83OPC-369
83OPC/St-49
83T-698
83T/St-49
83T/X-9
83TrueVal/WSox-14
84D-240
84F-606
84F/X-12
84Nes/792-41
84OPC-41
84T-41
84T/St-340
84T/Tr-12
84Wheat/Ind-4
85D-102
85F-439
85OPC-171
85Polar/Ind-4
85T-533
85T/St-252
85ThomMc/Discs-4
86D-520
86F-580
86Leaf-249
86OPC-354
86OhHenry-4
86T-354
86T/St-210
86T/Tatt-14M
87D-377
87D/OD-110
87F-244
87F/GameWin-4
87F/Mini-8
87Gator-4
87OPC-394
87RedFoley/St-105
87Sf-112M
87Sf-60
87Sf/TPrev-3M
87T-607AS
87T-758
87T/Gloss60-43
87T/St-207
88D-344
88F-275
88OPC-122
88S-604
88T-122
91B-143
Bernhard, William H.
E107
T206
T213/brown
Bernhardt, Bill
WG2-5
Bernhardt, Cesar
89SoBend/GS-24
90BirmB/Best-6
90BirmB/ProC-1114
90Foil/Best-80
90ProC/Singl-821
91AAA/LineD-626
91B-360
91Vanco/LineD-626
91Vanco/ProC-1599
92BirmB/SB-77
92OPC-179M
92Sky/AASingl-37
92T-179M
92T/Gold-179M
92T/GoldWin-179M
93LimeR/Winter-51
Bernhardt, Juan Ramon
77T-494R
78SanJose-13
78T-698
79OPC-189
79Spokane-24
79T-366
92Yank/WIZ70-15
Berni, Denny
91LynchRS/ClBest-11
91LynchRS/ProC-1201
92LynchRS/ClBest-8
92LynchRS/ProC-2909
Bernier, Carlos R.
53T-243
54B-171
91T/Arc53-243
Bernstine, Pookie
83Watlo/Frit-16
84BuffB-23
86Iowa-3
87Iowa-16
88Peoria/Ko-5
89Geneva/ProC-1886
89Peoria/Team-29
Bero, Albert
48Sommer-30M
Bero, John George
(Johnny)
No Cards.
Berra, Dale Anthony
78Colum
79T-723R
80T-292
81D-253
81F-369
81OPC-147
81T-147
82D-250
82F-476
82T-588
83D-185
83F-303
83F/St-1M
83F/St-22M
83OPC-271
83OPC/St-279
83T-433
83T/St-279
84D-430
84F-245
84Nes/792-18
84OPC-18
84T-18
84T/St-136
85D-444
85F-461
85F/Up-U4
85OPC-305
85T-132FS
85T-305
85T/St-133
85T/Tr-6T
86D-295
86F-100
86OPC-366
86T-692
87Tucson-8
88RochR/CMC-12
88RochR/Gov-3
88RochR/ProC-193
88RochR/Team-3
92Yank/WIZ80-10
Berra, Lawrence Peter
(Yogi)
47HomogBond-2
47TipTop
48B-6
49B-60
49MP-117
50B-46
50Drake-24
51B-2
51BR-B4
51T/CAS
51T/RB-1
52B-1
52BR
52NTea
52RM-AL3
52StarCal-84BM
52StarCal/L-70C
52T-191
52TipTop
52Wheat*
53B/Col-121
53B/Col-44M
53RM-AL3
53T-104
54B-161
54NYJour
54RM-AL20
54T-50
55Armour-2
55B-168
55RM-AL16
55T-198
56T-110
56T/Pin-27
56YellBase/Pin-7
57T-2
57T-407M
58T-370
59T-180
59YooHoo-1
60Bz-8
60NuCard-28
60T-480
60T/tatt-6
61NuCard-453
61P-1
61T-425
61T-472MVP
61T/RO
61T/St-189
62Exh
62J-7
62P-7
62P/Can-7
62Salada-33
62Shirriff-33
62T-360
62T/St-83
62T/bucks
63Exh
63J-17
63P-17
63Salada-62
63T-340P/CO
64T-21MG
65T-470P/CO
73OPC-257MG
73T-257MG
74OPC-179MG
74T-179MG
75OPC-189M
75OPC-192M
75OPC-193M
75OPC-421MG
75SSPC/18-5MG
75SSPC/42-40MG
75Sheraton-22
75T-189MVP
75T-192MVP
75T-193MVP
75T-421MG
75T/M-189MVP
75T/M-192MVP
75T/M-193MVP
75T/M-421MG
76SSPC/MetsY-M19MG
76Shakey-127

79TCMA-2
80Pac/Leg-67
80Perez/HOF-127
81D-351CO
81TCMA-407M
81TCMA-474M
82D-387CO
83D/HOF-24
83MLBPA/Pin-2
84T/Tr-13MG
85CircK-33
85T-132FS
85T-155MG
85West/2-31
85Woolwth-4
86Sf/Dec-31
87Leaf/SpecOlym-H2
87Nestle/DT-19
88Pac/Leg-53
89B/Ins-2
90BBWit-24
90MSA/AGFA-22
90Pac/Legend-7
90Perez/GreatMom-53
90Swell/Great-105
91CollAB-35
91K/3D-11
91K/SU-3A
91K/SU-3B
91LineD-7
91MDA-11
91Swell/Great-8
91T/Arc53-104
91WIZMets-36
92AP/ASG-1
92AP/ASG24K-1G
92AP/ASGProto-1
92Bz/Quadra-4
92FrRow/Berra-Set
92Perez/Master-26
92Perez/Master-27
92Perez/Master-28
92Perez/Master-29
92Perez/Master-30
92Pinn/MM-25M
92Yank/WIZ60-8
92Yank/WIZAS-3
92Yank/WIZHOF-3
92Ziploc-10
93AP/ASGCoke/Amo-1
93Metallic-3
93TWill-58
93TWill/Locklear-1
93TWill/POG-21
93UD/ATH-9
93YooHoo-2
94Mets/69-30
94T/Arc54-50
94TedW/54-25
D305
Exh47
PM10/L-4
PM10/Sm-10
PM10/Sm-9A
PM10/Sm-9B
R423-5
WG9-1

Berran, Dennis Martin
(Joe)
No Cards.

Berres, Raymond F.
(Ray)
39PlayBall-156
40PlayBall-164
60T-458C
90Target-50

Berringer, John
87Peoria-10
88WinSalem/Star-1

Berrios, Harry
92LSU/McDag-4
93LSU/McDag-10

Berrios, Hector
87Fayette-1
88GlenF/ProC-935
90Lakeland/Star-3
91MidldA/OneHour-4
91PalmSp/ProC-2007
92Albuq/SB-4
92Iowa/ProC-4046

Berroa, Ed
79Elmira-22

Berroa, Geronimo
85Kingst-21
86Ventura-1
87Knoxvl-15
87SLAS-3
88AAA/ProC-36
88D-659
88Syrac/CMC-13
88Syrac/ProC-808
89B-279
89D/Rook-19
89F/Up-72
89S-632
89S/HotRook-30
89S/YS/II-17
89Sf-225M
89T/Big-297
89T/Tr-10T
90AAASingl/ProC-414
90Classic-83
90D-104
90F-575
90F/Can-575
90OPC-617
90ProC/Singl-292
90Richm/Bob-15
90Richm/CMC-16
90Richm/ProC-269
90Richm/Team-5
90S-151
90S/100Ris-36
90T-617
90T/89Debut-17
90UD-531
91ColoSp/ProC-2195
92AAA/ASG/SB-284
92Nashvl/ProC-1843
92Nashvl/SB-284
93D-214
93Edmon/ProC-1147
93F/Final-52
93LimeR/Winter-29
93StCl/Marlin-23
93T/Tr-117T
94Finest-245
94Pinn-387

Berry, Al
91LitSun/HSPros-34CO
91LitSun/HSProsG-34CO

Berry, Allen Kent
(Ken)
65T-368R
66OPC-127
66T-127
67CokeCap/WSox-17
67OPC-67
67T-67
68T-485
69MB-25
69MLB/St-29
69T-494
69T/St-153
70MLB/St-182
70OPC-239
70T-239
71JB
71MLB/St-339
71OPC-466
71T-466
72MB-31
72OPC-379
72T-379
73OPC-445
73T-445
74OPC-163
74T-163
75OPC-432
75T-432
75T/M-432
78TCMA-53
82Oneonta-4MG
87AppFx-24MG
89BirmB/Best-20MG
89BirmB/ProC-89MG
90BirmB/Best-28MG
90BirmB/ProC-1397MG
90BirmDG/Best-3MG

Berry, Charles F.
(Charlie)
31Exh/4-17
33CJ/Pin-1
33Exh/4-10
33Exh/4-9
33G-184
35G-2C
35G-4C
35G-7C
36Exh/4-14
40PlayBall-190
55B-281UMP
92Conlon/Sport-398
94Conlon-1044
R313

Berry, Charles Joseph
(Charlie)
No Cards.

Berry, Claude Elzy
No Cards.

Berry, Cornelius John
(Neil)
49B-180
50B-241
51B-213
52B-219
91Crown/Orio-31

Berry, Joseph H. Jr.
(Joe)
W575

Berry, Joseph H.
(Joe)
No Cards.

Berry, Kevin
90Billings/ProC-3211
91Cedar/ClBest-1
91Cedar/ProC-2709

Berry, Kirk
85Cedar-14
86FSLAS-7
86Macon-3
86Tampa-3
87Vermont-24

Berry, Mark
87Nashvl-1
88Greens/ProC-1575
89Greens/ProC-405
90CharWh/Best-25CO
90CharWh/ProC-2256CO
91Cedar/ClBest-27CO
91Cedar/ProC-2736CO
92Cedar/ClBest-28MG
92Cedar/ProC-1089

Berry, Perry
91Osceola/ClBest-17
91Osceola/ProC-691
92BurlAs/ClBest-20
92BurlAs/ProC-552

Berry, Sean
86Cram/NWL-38
87FtMyr-7
88BBCity/Star-6
89BBCity/Star-5
90A&AASingle/ProC-49
90Foil/Best-86
90Memphis/Best-6
90Memphis/ProC-1016
90Memphis/Star-2
91AAA/LineD-326
91Omaha/LineD-326
91Omaha/ProC-1039
91S-764RP
91T/90Debut-15
91UD-10
92Classic/I-15
92D-651
92F-680
92Omaha/ProC-2966
92Omaha/SB-327
92Pinn-271
92S-678
92Sky/AAASingl-149
92StCl-114
93D-275RR
93F-458
93L-336
93OPC-37
93OPC/Premier-97
93Pac/Spanish-529
93Pinn-212
93S-543
93S/Boys-16
93Select/RookTr-146T
93StCl-184
93StCl/1stDay-184
93T-758
93T/Gold-758
93UD-644
93Ultra-411
94D-461
94F-533
94Finest-342
94Flair-186
94L-42
94Pac/Cr-374
94Panini-207
94Pinn-456
94StCl-67
94StCl/1stDay-67
94StCl/Gold-67
94Studio-75
94T-344
94T/Gold-344
94UD-427
94UD/CollC-51
94UD/CollC/Gold-51
94UD/CollC/Silv-51
94Ultra-223

Berry, Tony
89Gaston/ProC-1009
89Gaston/Star-3

Berryhill, Damon
86Pittsfld-2
87Iowa-15
88Berg/Cubs-9
88D-639
88D/Best-261
88D/Cubs/Bk-639
88D/Rook-31
88F-642R
88F/Up-U75
88Iowa/CMC-12
88Iowa/ProC-537
88S/Tr-82T
88T/Tr-15T
89B-288
89Bz-2
89D-275
89D/Best-116
89F-418
89KMart/DT-8
89KennerFig-8
89Mara/Cubs-9
89OPC-6
89Panini/St-52
89S-336
89S/HotRook-77
89S/YS/I-24
89Sf-216
89T-543
89T/Big-60
89T/Gloss60-39
89T/JumboR-4
89T/St-318
89T/St-51
89ToysRUs-4
89UD-455
90B-33
90D-167
90F-26
90F/Can-26
90Kenner/Fig-9
90MLBPA/Pins-52
90OPC-362
90Panini/St-234
90PeoriaUp/Team-U3
90PublInt/St-190
90S-163
90Sf-164
90T-362
90T/St-49
90T/TVCub-19
90UD-322
91Cub/Mara-9
91Cub/Vine-4
91D-631
91F-414
91Leaf-156
91OPC-188
91S-881
91StCl-28
91T-188
91UD-319
91Ultra-56
92Brave/LykePerf-4
92Brave/LykeStand-5
92D-771
92L-423
92L/BlkGold-423
92OPC-49
92Pinn-390
92StCl-856
92T-49
92T/Gold-49
92T/GoldWin-49
92UD-706
92Ultra-456
93BJ/D/McDon-19M
93Brave/LykePerf-4
93Brave/LykeStand-5
93D-254M
93D-78
93F-362
93L-196
93OPC-32
93Pac/Spanish-332
93Pinn-392
93S-373
93StCl-261
93StCl/1stDay-261
93StCl/Brave-14
93StCl/MurphyS-62
93T-306
93T/Gold-306
93TripleP-113
93UD-606
93UD/SeasonHL-HI4
93Ultra-3
94D-58
94F-353
94Pac/Cr-3
94S-275
94S/GoldR-275
94T-289
94T/Gold-289
94Ultra-149

Bertaina, Frank
65T-396
66T-579R
68OPC-131
68T-131
69MB-26
69T-554
70T-638
71MLB/St-267
71OPC-422
71T-422
72MB-32
81TCMA-446
91Crown/Orio-32

Berte, Harry Thomas
No Cards.

Bertell, Richard G.
(Dick)
61T-441
62T/St-105
63J-176
63P-176
63T-287
64T-424
65OPC-27
65T-27
66T-587

Berthau, Terrell
91Butte/SportP-4

Berthel, Dan
89Erie/Star-2
90CLAS/CL-6
90Freder/Team-19
91Freder/ClBest-22
91Freder/ProC-2376

Berthelot, Eric
94LSU-15

Berti, Don
83DayBe-14

Bertman, Skip
90LSUGreat-1CO
90LSUPol-1CO
91LSU/Pol-3CO
92LSU/McDag-1CO
93LSU/McDag-2CO
94LSU-1CO

Bertoia, Reno Peter
54T-131
55T-94
57T-390
58T-232
59T-84
60T-297
61P-95
61Peter-20
61T-392
61T/St-178
94T/Arc54-131

Bertolani, Jerry
86Penin-5
87DayBe-22
88BirmB/Best-23
88SLAS-8
89BirmB/Best-12

89BirmB/ProC-100
Bertolotti, Fulvio
78StPete
79ArkTr-15
Bertoni, Jeff
80SLCity-9
81SLCity-16
82Spokane-13
83Evansvl-13
Bertotti, Mike
91Utica/ClBest-4
91Utica/ProC-3232
92SoBend/ClBest-11
Bertucio, Charlie
83SanJose-3
Berube, George
(Luc)
87FtLaud-11
87Oneonta-31
88FtLaud/Star-2
Berumen, Andres
91BBCity/ClBest-1
91BBCity/ProC-1388
91ClBest/Singl-65
92AppFox/ClBest-2
93T-627
93T/Gold-627
94B-92
Besana, Fred
91Crown/Orio-33
Bescher, Robert Henry
(Bob)
10Domino-13
11Helmar-110
12Sweet/Pin-96
14CJ-110
15CJ-110
D303
D329-15
D350/2-14
E101
E102
E105
E106
E224
E254
E270/2
E90/1
E92
E94
M101/4-15
M101/5-14
M116
S74-72
T202
T205
T206
T207
T216
T3-81
W555
WG5-4
WG6-3
Besh, Jeff
89GA-1
Bess, Johnny
92Princet/ClBest-10
92Princet/ProC-3089
Bessard, Lloyd
79Elmira-1
Besse, Herman
47Signal
49B/PCL-29
Bessent, Don
56T-184
57T-178
58T-401
59T-71
90Target-51
Best, Bill
81CharR-21
82FtMyr-18
84Memphis-5
Best, Jayson
89Elizab/Star-3
90Foil/Best-225M
90Kenosha/Best-17M
90Kenosha/ProC-2286M
90Kenosha/Star-1M
90MidwLgAS/GS-3
91Visalia/ClBest-1M
91Visalia/ProC-1735M
92ClBest-334
92FtMyr/ProC-2737
92Miracle/ClBest-1
Best, Jim
83AppFx/Frit-6TR
Best, Karl
80LynnS-11
81LynnS-1
82LynnS-2
83SLCity-5
84Cram/PCL-189
85Cram/PCL-76
85F/Up-U5
86D-511
86F-459
86Mother/Mar-19
86Seven/Coin-W16
86Sf-179M
86T-61
87Calgary-10
87D-198
87F-579
87T-439
88Portl/CMC-2
88Portl/ProC-646
88TripleA/ASCMC-43
Beswick, James W.
(Jim)
79Hawaii-10
79T-725R
80Hawaii-8
81Hawaii/TCMA-7
83Nashua-17
Betances, Marcos
88Bristol/ProC-1882
89Fayette/ProC-1574
89Niagara/Pucko-3
90Hamil/Best-3
90Hamil/Star-6
90Savan/ProC-2060
Betcher, Frank Lyle
No Cards.
Betemit, Manuel
77Newar
78BurlB
Bethancourt, Jose
90Elizab/Star-3
Bethea, Scott
90LSUPol-10
91LynchRS/ClBest-14
91LynchRS/ProC-1204
92NewBrit/ProC-438
92NewBrit/SB-477
Bethea, Steve
89Spokane/SP-25
90River/Best-2
90River/Cal-7
90River/ProC-2612
91ClBest/Singl-148
91HighD/ClBest-18
91HighD/ProC-2401
92Wichita/ProC-3660
92Wichita/SB-626
Bethea, William Lamar
(Bill)
60DF
77Fritsch-31
92TX-5
Bethke, James
65T-533R
81TCMA-413
91WIZMets-37
Bethke, Jamie
91GulfCR/SportP-7
Bettencourt, Lawrence
No Cards.
Bettendorf, Dave
88Hagers/Star-2
89Hagers/Best-9
89Hagers/ProC-273
89Hagers/Star-1
89Star/IISingl-132
90Hagers/ProC-1419
90HagersDG/Best-4
Bettendorf, Jeff
83Lynch-4
84Jacks-9
84Mother/A's-25
85Tidew-4
86ColumAst-4
87BirmB/Best-9
87SLAS-21
Betts, Walter
(Huck)
34G-36
E120
V354-83
Betz, Robert
52Park-80
Betzel, Christian
(Bruno)
D328-15
D329-16
D350/2-15
E135-15
M101/4-16
M101/5-15
Beuder, John
87SLCity/Taco-4
88Bakers/Cal-246
Beuder, Mike
83VeroB-1
Beuerlein, Ed
90Ashvl/ProC-2751
91Osceola/ClBest-14
91Osceola/ProC-867
92Ashvl/ClBest-5
Beuerlein, John
86Stockton-1
87Denver-14
Beulac, Joe
89SLCity-24
Beumiller
E254
E270/1
Bevacqua, Kurt A.
72OPC-193
72T-193
74OPC-454
74T-454
74T/Tr-454T
76OPC-427
76OPC-564M
76SSPC-233
76T-427
76T-564M
77T-317
77Tucson
78BK/R-16
78SSPC/270-93
78T-725
79T-44
80T-584
81F-382
81T-118
82F-477
82T-267
82T/Tr-6T
83F-352
83T-674
84D-80
84F-294
84F/St-43
84Mother/Padres-6
84Nes/792-346
84Smok/Padres-1
84T-346
85D-647
85F-26
85Mother/Padres-14
85T-478
85T/St-16WS
86D-528
86F-315
86T-789
93Rang/Keeb-70
Bevan, Harold Joseph
(Hal)
53B/BW-43
55Rodeo
60HenryH-10
60Union-22
61T-456
Bevenour, Keith
89Watertn/Star-2
Bevens, Floyd
(Bill)
45PlayBall-11
47TipTop
48B-22
60NuCard-3
Beverly, Bill
92Negro/Retort-4
Bevil, Brian
92AppFox/ClBest-9
92MidwLAS/Team-4
93B-125
93ClBest/MLG-103
93FExcel/ML-172
94FExcel-64
94SigRook-31
Beville, Henry Monte
(Monte)
No Cards.
Bevington, Terry
78BurlB
79Holyo-2
80Vanco-6
81BurlB-30
82Beloit/Frit-24MG
84ElPaso-12
86Vanco-2MG
87Denver-13
88Vanco/ProC-778
90Coke/WSox-30CO
91Kodak/WSox-x
92WSox-NNO
93WSox-30M
Beyeler, Arnie
87Fayette-19
88Lakeland/Star-3
89London/ProC-1371
90EastLAS/ProC-EL7
90London/ProC-1274
91AAA/LineD-579
91Toledo/LineD-579
91Toledo/ProC-1938
Beyers, Tom
87VeroB-22
89Salem/Team-1MG
90Bakers/Cal-244
91Bakers/Cal-28MG
91CalLgAS-23
92Bakers/Cal-30
Bezdek, Hugo
92Conlon/Sport-396
W514-83
Bhagwat, Tom
80ElPaso-13
Biagini, Greg
87CharlO/WBTV-24
87SLAS-24
88CharlK/Pep-23
89RochR/CMC-25
89RochR/ProC-1660
90AAASingl/ProC-477
90ProC/Singl-326
90RochR/CMC-25MG
90RochR/ProC-720MG
90Rochester/L&U-34MG
91AAA/LineD-474MG
91AAAGame/ProC-39
91RochR/LineD-474MG
91RochR/ProC-1918MG
Bialas, Dave
78Spring/Wiener-7
82Spring/Frit-2MG
83Spring/Frit-22
84ArkTr-14
86FSLAS-8MG
86StPete-4MG
87StPete-18
90ArkTr/GS-1MG
90SpringDG/Best-22MG
91StPete/ClBest-9MG
91StPete/ProC-2292MG
92StPete/ClBest-27MG
92StPete/ProC-2041MG
93Mother/Padre-28M
Biancalana, Roland A.
(Buddy)
82Omaha-14
83Omaha-13
85T-387
86D-605
86F-3
86Kitty/Disc-2
86NatPhoto-1
86Sf-200
86T-99
86T/St-21WS
87D-527
87D/OD-202
87F-364
87Smok/AL-7
87T-554
88Omaha/CMC-20
88Omaha/ProC-1502
88S-383
93UD/ATH-10
Biancamano, John
91Spokane/ClBest-22
91Spokane/ProC-3953
Bianchi, Ben
86Visalia-3
87Portl-16
89OrlanTw/Best-10
89OrlanTw/ProC-1329
Bianchi, Steve
77Ashvl
79Tucson-9
Bianco, Robert
75AppFx
Bianco, Ron
86Sumter/ProC-3
Bianco, Thomas A.
(Tommy)
76SSPC-250
77Evansvl/TCMA-3
78RochR
79RochR-11
Bianco, Toby
75Sacra/Caruso-5
Biasatti, Henry A.
(Hank)
V362-44
Biasucci, Joe
91WinSalem/ClBest-16
91WinSalem/ProC-2833
92Peoria/Team-3
92WinSalem/ClBest-19
94B-346
94FExcel-259
Bibb, Mitch
90Wausau/Star-29TR
91Freder/ClBest-30TR
Bibby, Jim
72OPC-316R
72T-316R
74OPC-11
74T-11
74T/St-231
75OPC-155
75SSPC/18-2
75T-155
75T/M-155
76OPC-324
76T-324
77T-501
78OPC-61
78T-636
79OPC-39
79T-92
80T-229
81Coke
81D-134
81F-370
81F/St-65
81OPC-93
81T-430
81T/SO-105
81T/St-216
81T/St-260
82D-171
82F-478
82F/St-106
82F/St-70
82OPC-170
82T-170
82T/St-86
83T-355
84F-246
84Nes/792-566
84T-566
85Lynch-2CO
86Lynch-2CO
87Lynch-20CO
89Lynch/Star-24CO
89Pac/SenLg-52
89T/SenLg-128
89TM/SenLg-7
90LynchRS/Team-26CO
91LynchRS/ClBest-26CO
91LynchRS/ProC-1216CO
93Rang/Keeb-71
Bibeault, Paul
45Parade*-4
Biberdorf, Cam
88GreatF-24
89Bakers/Cal-190
90FSLAS/Star-1
90VeroB/Star-5
91AA/LineD-531
91SanAn/LineD-531
Bible, Mike
89SLCity-21

Bichette, Dante
86PalmSp-3
88Edmon/CMC-23
88Edmon/ProC-576
89Classic/Up/2-199
89D-634
89D/Rook-29
89F-468
89Panini/St-283
89T-761
89UD-24
90Classic/III-11
90F-127
90F/Can-127
90Leaf-340
90OPC-43
90PublInt/St-365
90S/YS/II-10
90T-43
90UD-688
91B-31
91Brewer/MillB-3
91D-303
91F-307
91F/Up-U29
91Leaf-242
91OPC-564
91Panini/FrSt-186
91Panini/St-139
91Pol/Brew-2
91S-463
91S/RookTr-37T
91StCl-211
91T-564
91T/Tr-10T
91UD-317
91UD/Ext-712
92B-264
92D-347
92F-173
92L-134
92L/BlkGold-134
92OPC-371
92Panini-39
92Pinn-514
92Pol/Brew-3
92S-316
92StCl-7
92Studio-191
92T-371
92T/Gold-371
92T/GoldWin-371
92UD-378
92Ultra-79
93B-92
93Colla/DM-11
93D-45
93D-783
93DennyGS-23
93F-403
93F/Final-22
93Flair-35
93L-258
93MSA/Metz-21
93Pac/Spanish-422
93Pinn-232
93Pinn/Expan-9M
93S-428
93Select-114
93StCl-616
93StCl/1stDay-616
93StCl/Rockie-5
93Studio-24
93T-644
93T/Gold-644
93TripleP-154
93UD-478
93UD-683
93UD/FunPack-174
93UD/SP-217
93USPlayC/Rockie-11H
93USPlayC/Rockie-3D
93Ultra-341
94B-666
94Church-28
94D-418
94F-433
94Flair-151
94L-81
94L/MVPNL-3
94OPC-30
94Pac/Cr-188
94Panini-171
94Pinn-346
94Pinn/Run-41
94S-110
94S/Cycle-9
94S/GoldR-110
94S/GoldS-22
94Select-147
94Sf/2000-22
94StCl-366
94StCl/1stDay-366
94StCl/Gold-366
94StCl/Team-105
94Studio-175
94T-468
94T/Finest-59
94T/Finest/PreProd-59
94T/FinestRef-59
94T/Gold-468
94TripleP-221
94UD-454
94UD/CollC-52
94UD/CollC/Gold-52
94UD/CollC/Silv-52
94UD/SP-164
94Ultra-181

Bickford, Vern
49B-1
50B-57
51B-42
51FB
52B-48
52T-252
53JC-3
53SpicSpan/3x5-3
53T-161
54B-176
79TCMA-114
91Crown/Orio-34
91T/Arc53-161

Bickhardt, Eric
89Butte/SP-5
90Gaston/Best-14
90Gaston/ProC-2512
90Gaston/Star-2
91CharlR/ClBest-2
91CharlR/ProC-1306

Bicknell, Charlie
49Eureka-129

Bicknell, Greg
89StCath/ProC-2090
90Myrtle/ProC-2767
91Myrtle/ClBest-2
91Myrtle/ProC-2936
92Penin/ClBest-20
92Penin/ProC-2924

Bieger, Philip
87Anchora-1
89Anchora-3

Biehl, Rod
91AubAS/ClBest-4
91AubAS/ProC-4267
92BurlAs/ClBest-12
92BurlAs/ProC-536

Bieksha, Steve
87Belling/Team-29
88Wausau/GS-18

Bielanin, Ray
89GreatF-11

Bielaski, Oscar
No Cards.

Bielecki, Mike
82Buffa-16
83LynnP-1
84Cram/PCL-131
85D-28
85F-650M
86F-603
86T/Tr-10T
87D-415
87T-394
87Vanco-1
88AAA/ProC-18
88D-484
88D/Cubs/Bk-NEW
88S-611
88T-436
89D-512
89D/Best-194
89F-419
89Mara/Cubs-36
89T-668
90B-22
90Cub/Mara-2
90D-373
90D-9DK
90D/BestNL-3
90D/SuperDK-9DK
90F-27
90F/Can-27
90Leaf-45
90OPC-114
90Panini/St-242
90PublInt/St-191
90S-484
90T-114
90T/Big-129
90T/Mini-48
90T/St-54
90T/TVCub-8
90UD-359
91B-422
91Cub/Mara-36
91Cub/Vine-5
91D-87
91F-415
91OPC-501
91S-453
91StCl-109
91T-501
91UD-597
91Ultra-57
92Brave/LykePerf-5
92Brave/LykeStand-6
92D-776
92L-505
92L/BlkGold-505
92OPC-26
92Pinn-566
92StCl-656
92T-26
92T/Gold-26
92T/GoldWin-26
92UD-730
92Ultra-457
93F-363
93Indian/WUAB-4
93L-270
93OPC/Premier-112
93S-457
93StCl-721
93StCl/1stDay-721
93T-251
93T/Gold-251
93UD-659
93Ultra-539

Bielenberg, Bruce
85Iowa-33
90Miami/II/Star-30PER

Bienek, Vince
79AppFx-18
80GlenF/B-20
80GlenF/C-11
81GlenF-17

Bierbauer, Louis W.
(Lou)
N172
N690

Biercevicz, Greg
78SanJose-3
79Spokane-21
79T-712R
80Spokane-3
81Spokane-8
81T-282R
82Tidew-17
83Tidew-15
85RochR-30

Bierley, Brad
85Visalia-7
86OrlanTw-2
87OrlanTw-14
88Portl/CMC-16
88Portl/ProC-639
89Portl/CMC-18
89Portl/ProC-231
90AAASingl/ProC-636
90Iowa/CMC-22
90Iowa/ProC-329
90ProC/Singl-97
90T/TVCub-38
91AAA/LineD-201
91Iowa/LineD-201
91Iowa/ProC-1073
92Geneva/ClBest-28CO
92Geneva/ProC-1576

Bierscheid, Gene
87Spartan-3

Bieser, Steve
89Batavia/ProC-1934
90Batavia/ProC-3078
91Spartan/ClBest-22
91Spartan/ProC-907
92Clearw/ClBest-5
92Clearw/ProC-2058

Bigbee, Carson Lee
21Exh-10
25Exh-49
26Exh-49
E120
E121/120
E121/80
V61-54
W501
W573
W575

Bigbee, Lyle Randolph
No Cards.

Bigelow, Elliott A.
94Conlon-1285

Biggers, Allan
89Hamil/Star-3
89Savan/ProC-362

Biggers, Brian
91SLCity/ProC-3210
91SLCity/SportP-8

Biggerstaff, Kent
75Tidew/Team-4
78Holyo
79Vanco-22
80Vanco-12
81Portl-27

Biggio, Craig
88F/Up-U89
88S/Tr-103T
88Tucson/CMC-15
88Tucson/JP-2
88Tucson/ProC-166
89Classic-51
89D-561
89D/Best-176
89F-353
89Lennox/Ast-24
89Mother/Ast-14
89Panini/St-79
89S-237
89S/HotRook-98
89S/YS/II-33
89T-49
89UD-273
90B-78
90Classic-57
90D-306
90D/BestNL-89
90F-224
90F/Can-224
90KMart/SS-8
90Leaf-37
90Lennox-4
90Mother/Ast-5
90OPC-157
90OPC-404AS
90Panini/St-259
90PublInt/St-88
90S-275
90Sf-22
90T-157
90T-404AS
90T/Big-111
90T/Coins-39
90T/Gloss60-54
90T/HeadsUp-6
90T/St-23
90T/TVAS-41
90UD-104
91B-556
91Cadaco-3
91Classic/200-7
91Classic/III-T2
91D-2DK
91D-595
91D/SuperDK-2
91DennyGS-24
91F-499
91JDean-16
91KingB/Discs-13
91Leaf-12
91Leaf/Prev-4
91Leaf/Stud-173
91MooTown-22
91Mother/Ast-5
91OPC-565
91Panini/FrSt-6
91Panini/St-10
91RedFoley/St-8
91S-161
91S-872FRAN
91S/100SS-55
91Seven/3DCoin-1T
91StCl-176
91T-565
91UD-158
91USPlayC/AS-9C
91Ultra-132
92B-484
92CJ/DII-1
92Classic/Game200-2
92D-75
92F-426
92Kenner/Fig-5
92KingB-21
92L-315
92L/BlkGold-315
92Mother/Ast-5
92MrTurkey-4
92OPC-715
92OPC/Premier-135
92Panini-151
92Pinn-140
92S-460
92S-888DT
92S/100SS-52
92S/Impact-22
92Seven/Coin-12
92StCl-200
92StCl/Dome-16
92Studio-32
92T-393AS
92T-715
92T/Gold-393AS
92T/Gold-715
92T/GoldWin-393AS
92T/GoldWin-715
92T/Kids-43
92TripleP-150
92UD-162
92UD-31TC
92Ultra-199
93B-560
93Classic/GameI-13
93Colla/DM-12
93D-84
93D/DK-24
93Duracel/PPI-7
93F-47
93F/Fruit-5
93Flair-58
93L-223
93L/GoldAS-13M
93MilkBone-20
93Mother/Ast-4
93OPC-56
93Pac/Spanish-118
93Panini-171
93Pinn-50
93S-18
93Select-25
93StCl-183
93StCl/1stDay-183
93StCl/Ast-14
93StCl/MurphyS-115
93Studio-86
93T-680
93T/Finest-119
93T/FinestRef-119
93T/Gold-680
93TripleP-100
93UD-114
93UD-475M
93UD/FunPack-44
93UD/SP-29
93Ultra-37
94B-390
94D-12
94D/Special-12
94F-485
94Finest-382
94L-236
94OPC-230
94Pac/Cr-259
94Panini-190
94Pinn-20
94Pinn/Artist-20
94Pinn/Museum-20
94Pinn/Run-33

94S-48
94S/GoldR-48
94StCl-374
94StCl/1stDay-374
94StCl/Gold-374
94Studio-17
94T-305
94T/BlkGold-25
94T/Gold-305
94TripleP-22
94TripleP/Medal-6M
94UD-312
94UD/SP-28
94Ultra-499
Biggs, Doug
88Bristol/ProC-1864
Biggus, Bengie
80BurlB-29
Bigham, Craig
88Spokane/ProC-1931
Bigham, David
89Elizab/Star-4
90Elizab/Star-4
91Kenosha/ClBest-12
91Kenosha/ProC-2066
92Visalia/ClBest-6
92Visalia/ProC-1004
Bigham, Scott
89River/Best-3
89River/Cal-1
89River/ProC-1396
90River/Best-3
90River/Cal-8
90River/ProC-2613
Bigler, Jeff
92Spartan/ClBest-16
92Spartan/ProC-1274
Bignal, George W.
No Cards.
Bigusiak, Mike
76Clinton
86SanJose-3
Biittner, Larry David
72OPC-122
72T-122
73OPC-249
73T-249
75OPC-543
75T-543
75T/M-543
76OPC-238
76SSPC-336
76T-238
77T-64
78SSPC/270-244
78T-346
79OPC-224
79T-433
80OPC-334
80T-639
81D-515
81F-314
81T-718
81T/Tr-736
82Coke/Reds
82D-43
82F-59
82T-159
83D-440
83F-586
83F/St-11M
83F/St-23M
83Rangers-14
83T-527
83T/X-10
84D-342
84F-414
84Nes/792-283
84T-283
93Rang/Keeb-2
Biko, Tom
80OrlanTw-3
82Amari-14
Bilak, Paul
86PalmSp-4TR
86PalmSp/Smok-4
87PalmSp-6
Bilardello, Dann J.
83T/X-11
84D-408
84F-464
84Nes/792-424
84T-424
84T/St-57
85D-243
85T-28
86Expo/Prov/Pan-2
86Provigo-2
86T-253
87F-313
87OPC-217
87T-577
87Vanco-21
88Omaha/CMC-17
88Omaha/ProC-1518
89BuffB/CMC-13
89BuffB/ProC-1677
90AAASingl/ProC-490
90BuffB/CMC-13
90BuffB/ProC-375
90BuffB/Team-2
90OPC-682
90ProC/Singl-13
90T-682
91AAA/LineD-277
91LasVegas/LineD-277
91LasVegas/ProC-237
91S-659
92L-348
92L/BlkGold-348
92Mother/Padre-13
92Padre/Carl-4
92S-719
92Smok/Padre-4
92StCl-254
93Pac/Spanish-256
Bilbert, Roy
91Hagers/LineD-230
Bilello, John
88Boise/ProC-1605
88Fresno/Cal-18
88Fresno/ProC-1224
89Boise/ProC-1997
89Reno/Cal-241
Bilko, Steven Thomas
(Steve)
51B-265
52T-287
53Hunter
54B-206
54Hunter
54T-116
55B-88
55T-93
55T/DH-117
58T-346
59DF
59T-43
60L-106
60T-396
61T-184
62J-74
62P-74
62P/Can-74
62Salada-17A
62Salada-17B
62Shirriff-17
62T-422
62T/St-63
63J-24
63P-24
79TCMA-177
88LitSun/Minor-6
90Target-52
94T/Arc54-116
Exh47
Bill, Bob
79Newar-4
83TriCit-28
86Tulsa-26TR
88Watertn/Pucko-33
Billanueva, Gil
89Reno/Cal-247
Billeci, Craig
91Batavia/ClBest-6
91Batavia/ProC-3488
Billingham, Jack
68T-228R
69OPC-92
69T-92
70T-701
71MLB/St-74
71OPC-162
71T-162
72T-542
73OPC-89
73T-89
74OPC-158
74T-158
74T/St-22
75OPC-235
75T-235
75T/M-235
76OPC-155
76SSPC-23
76T-155
77Pep-53
77T-512
78BK/T-6
78T-47
79T-388
80T-603
85SpokAT/Cram-2
87Osceola-18CO
89Swell-43
90Osceola/Star-28CO
90Target-53
91Osceola/ProC-700CO
92Osceola/ClBest-28CO
92Osceola/ProC-2547CO
93UD/ATH-11
Billings, Haskell
94Conlon-1313
Billings, John A.
(Josh)
No Cards.
Billings, Richard A.
(Dick)
71OPC-729
71T-729
72OPC-148
72T-148
73OPC-94
73T-94
74OPC-466
74T-466
76SSPC-288
93Rang/Keeb-3
Billingsley, Rod
89Spokane/SP-3
90Waterlo/Best-7
90Waterlo/ProC-2380
Billmeyer, Mickey
86Hagers-3
87Miami-11
87PortChar-16
88Miami/Star-2
89CharlR/Star-3
90QuadC/GS-18
91CalLgAS-15
91MidldA/OneHour-5
91PalmSp/ProC-2018
92Edmon/ProC-3541
92Edmon/SB-168
92MidldA/ProC-4030
92MidldA/SB-453
92Sky/AASingl-192
Billoni, Mike
87BuffB-27
89BuffB/CMC-1
Bills, Walter
92MedHat/ProC-3202
92MedHat/SportP-14
Bilyeu, Aaron
90NE-4
Bingham, Dave
89KS*-91CO
Bingham, David
92Idaho/ProC-3524
Bingham, Mark
82Danvl/Frit-5
Binks, George Eugene
45PlayBall-5
V362-21
Biot, Charlie
92Negro/Retort-5
Biras, Stephen A.
(Steve)
No Cards.
Birch, Brent
90AR-2
Birch, Brock
86Cram/NWL-23
86Everett/Pop-2
87Clinton-20
Birchall, A. Judson
(Jud)
No Cards.
Bird, Bill
90Pittsfld/Pucko-29PER
Bird, David
88Alaska/Team-2
89Welland/Pucko-5
90A&AASingle/ProC-75
90Augusta/ProC-2456
91Salem/ClBest-14
91Salem/ProC-944
92CaroMud/ProC-1172
92CaroMud/SB-126
92Sky/AASingl-59
Bird, Doug
74OPC-17
74T-17
75OPC-364
75T-364
75T/M-364
76A&P/KC
76OPC-96
76SSPC-180
76T-96
77BurgChef-68
77OPC-191
77T-556
78SSPC/270-218
78T-183
79BK/P-12
79T-664
80T-421
81F-106
81T-516
81T/Tr-737
82D-504
82F-586
82RedLob
82T-273
83D-48
83F-490
83T-759
83T/X-12
84F-391
84Nes/792-82
84T-82
89Pac/SenLg-90
90EliteSenLg-65
92Yank/WIZ80-11
Bird, Frank Zepherin
No Cards.
Bird, Larry
94TedW-LP1
Bird, Steven
88Kinston/Star-4
Birkbeck, Mike
86Vanco-3
87D-33RR
87D/Rook-19
87F/Up-U5
87Leaf-33
87Pol/Brew-40
87T-229
88D-49
88Pol/Brew-40
88S-369
88T-692
89B-132
89Brewer/YB-40
89D-501
89F-178
89Pol/Brew-40
89S-596
89T-491
90AAASingl/ProC-642
90Denver/CMC-21
90Denver/ProC-617
90Pol/Brew-40
90ProC/Singl-46
90PublInt/St-489
91Canton/ProC-972
92Tidew/ProC-
92Tidew/SB-552
93Richm/Bleach-21
93Richm/Pep-9
93Richm/Team-6
Birkofer, Ralph
35BU-90
90Target-901
Birmingham, Joseph L.
(Dode)
10Domino-14
11Helmar-22
12Sweet/Pin-17
14CJ-106
14Piedmont/St-4
15CJ-106
E254
E270/2
E97
M116
T202
T205
T206
T207
W555
WG5-5
WG6-4
Birrell, Bob
79Elmira-24
83Pawtu-1
Birrer, Werner
(Babe)
56T-84
90Target-54
91Crown/Orio-35
Birriel, Jose
86NewBrit-3
87NewBrit-24
88EastLAS/ProC-19
88NewBrit/ProC-902
89Lynch/Star-2
Birtsas, Tim
82Oneonta-8
85F/Up-U6
86D-462
86F-412
86F/St-5
86Leaf-227
86Mother/A's-25
87Tacoma-23
88F/Up-U82
88Kahn/Reds-48
88Nashvl/CMC-2
88Nashvl/ProC-477
88T-501
89F-152
89Kahn/Reds-48
89S-454
89T-103
89UD-638
90D-493
90F-414
90F/Can-414
90Kahn/Reds-3
90OPC-687
90S-408
90T-687
90UD-137
91OPC-289
91S-648
91T-289
Bisceglia, Dave
81Water-20
Bisceglia, James
86Cram/NWL-90
87QuadC-14
88PalmSp/ProC-1458
89PalmSp/Cal-52
Bischoff, John George
No Cards.
Bish, Brent
90Spokane/SportP-10
91CharRain/ClBest-15
91CharRain/ProC-100
92AS/Cal-36
92HighD/ClBest-3
Bishop, Charles
52Park-98
53T-186
55Rodeo
55T-96
55T/DH-110
91T/Arc53-186
Bishop, Craig
90Bakers/Cal-243
90Yakima/Team-27
Bishop, Frank H.
No Cards.
Bishop, Greg
92MissSt-50M
Bishop, James
83Kinston/Team-1
86Knoxvl-2
87Wmsprt-8
88Cedar/ProC-1165
89Miami/I/Star-2
91Salinas/ClBest-9
91Salinas/ProC-2249
92BirmB/ProC-2587
92BirmB/SB-78
92ClBest-239
Bishop, Max F.
25Exh-105

26Exh-105
29Exh/4-28
33G-61
34DS-6
35G-1G
35G-3E
35G-5E
35G-6E
88Conlon/4-4
91Conlon/Sport-183
94Conlon-1149
R308-187
R315-A4
R315-B4
R316
V353-61

Bishop, Michael D.
(Mike)
77QuadC
80ElPaso-12
81SLCity-14
82Spokane-10
83Tidew-6
87Anchora-2
91WIZMets-38

Bishop, Tim
87Oneonta-28
88PrWill/Star-2

Bishop, William
N172

Bisland, Rivington M.
No Cards.

Bison, Buster T.
92BuffB/BlueS-28

Bispo, Randy
86SanJose-4

Bissant, John L.
92Negro/RetortII-2

Bissonette, Del
28LaPresse-12
29Exh/4-4
31Exh/4-4
90Target-55
R314/Can
R316

Bitker, Joe
86Beaum-2
87LasVegas-1
88LasVegas/CMC-1
88LasVegas/ProC-230
89LasVegas/CMC-1
89LasVegas/ProC-4
90AAAGame/ProC-47
90AAASingl/ProC-132
90ProC/Singl-586
90Tacoma/CMC-9
90Tacoma/ProC-85
91D-624
91F-281
91OkCty/ProC-171
91T/90Debut-16
91UD/Ext-797
92S-743
92S/100RisSt-87
93Rang/Keeb-72

Bitter, Mike
89SanDiegoSt/Smok-3

Bittiger, Jeff
82Jacks-1
83Tidew-13
84Tidew-13
85IntLgAS-20
85Tidew-8
86Portl-1
87Portl-1
88S/Tr-66T
88Vanco/CMC-1
89B-60
89S-512
89T-209
89UD-509
89Vanco/CMC-1
90AAASingl/ProC-56
90Albuq/CMC-2
90Albuq/ProC-335
90Albuq/Trib-2
90ProC/Singl-404
91AAA/LineD-77
91ColoSp/LineD-77
91ColoSp/ProC-2176
92Huntsvl/ProC-3941
92Huntsvl/SB-303

Bittmann, Henry
(Red)
No Cards.

Bivens, William E.
87Spring/Best-10
88Spring/Best-7
89StPete/Star-3
89TexLAS/GS-25

Bivin, Jim
94Conlon-1299

Bjorkman, George A.
80ArkTr-2
82Louisvl-1
83ColumAst-1
84Indianap-20
84Nes/792-116
84T-116
85Indianap-20
85RochR-31

Bjornson, Craig
92Ashvl/ClBest-18
92AubAs/ClBest-22
92AubAs/ProC-1344

Black, Allen
82QuadC-2

Black, Bob
89Richm/CMC-9

Black, Don
R346-28

Black, Harry
(Bud)
80SanJose
80SanJose/JITB-4
81LynnS-2
83D-322
83F-107
83F-644M
83Omaha-2
83T-238
84D-130
84F-343
84Nes/792-26
84T-26
84T/St-283
85D-100
85F-198
85Leaf-202
85OPC-47
85T-412
85T/St-275
86D-374
86F-4
86Kitty/Disc-7
86Leaf-170
86NatPhoto-40
86OPC-319
86T-697
86T/St-261
87D-404
87F-365
87OPC-315
87T-669
88D-301
88F-252
88OPC-301
88S-313
88S/Tr-11T
88SanDiegoSt-3
88SanDiegoSt-4
88Smok/Royals-9
88T-301
88T/Tr-16T
89B-82
89D-556
89OPC-5
89S-404
89SanDiegoSt-3
89SanDiegoSt-4
89T-509
89T/St-209
89UD-466
90D-556
90D/BestAL-118
90F-486
90F/Can-486
90Leaf-451
90OPC-144
90PublInt/St-554
90S-197
90T-144
90T/Big-223
90T/St-213
90UD-498
91B-639
91D-719
91F/UltraUp-U115
91F/Up-U128
91Leaf-312
91Leaf/Stud-260M
91Mother/Giant-7
91OPC-292
91OPC/Premier-9
91PG&E-19
91S/RookTr-46T
91SFExam/Giant-3
91StCl-302
91T-292
91T/Tr-11T
91UD/Ext-799
92B-692
92D-93
92F-628
92Giant/PGE-6
92L-3
92L/BlkGold-3
92Mother/Giant-7
92OPC-774
92Pinn-202
92S-358
92StCl-55
92T-774
92T/Gold-774
92T/GoldWin-774
92UD-697
93B-28
93D-50
93F-151
93L-212
93Mother/Giant-22
93OPC-38
93Pac/Spanish-267
93Pinn-181
93S-131
93Select-221
93StCl-624
93StCl/1stDay-624
93StCl/Giant-24
93T-498
93T/Gold-498
93UD-229
93Ultra-482
94D-64
94F-683
94Pinn-140
94Pinn/Artist-140
94Pinn/Museum-140
94S-176
94S/GoldR-176
94T-89
94T/Gold-89

Black, Joe
52T-321
53RM-NL4
53T-81
54NYJour
54T-98
55Gol/Dodg-4
55T-156
56Kahn
56T-178
56T/Pin-54
79TCMA-160
89Pac/Leg-177
89Swell-69
90Target-56
91Swell/Great-9
91T/Arc53-81
92Bz/Quadra-13
93AP/ASG-143
93TWill-132
93UD/ATH-12
93UD/ATH-154
94T/Arc54-98
PM10/Sm-11
PM10/Sm-12
PM10/Sm-13

Black, John Falconer
(Jack)
No Cards.

Black, John William
(Bill)
No Cards.

Black, Keith
91Hamil/ClBest-23
91Hamil/ProC-4043
92Hamil/ClBest-24
92Hamil/ProC-1596

Black, Robert B.
(Bob)
No Cards.

Black, Stephen
91Melbourne/Fut-18

Blackaby, Ethan Allan
75Phoenix/CircleK-25
76Phoenix/Coke-22GM
77Phoenix
78Cr/PCL-107
79Phoenix
80Phoenix/NBank-27GM
82Phoenix
83Phoenix/BHN-26GM

Blackburn, Earl S.
No Cards.

Blackburn, J.D.
89KS*-6M

Blackburn, Jackie
85FtMyr-24

Blackburn, James Ray
49B-160
51B-287
79TCMA-259

Blackburn, Ron
58T-459
59T-401
60T-209

Blackburne, Russell
(Lena)
91Conlon/Proto-905
93Conlon-905
E90/3
M116
T205
T206
T207

Blackerby, George F.
(George)
No Cards.

Blackmon, Anthony
87SLCity/Taco-22

Blackmon, Tom
80Batavia-7
83Knoxvl-1

Blackmun, Ben
85Bend/Cram-2

Blackshear, Steve
87Reading-18

Blackwell, Barry
85Anchora-4
89Kinston/Star-3

Blackwell, Eric
90GreatF/SportP-14
90Yakima/Team-30
91VeroB/ProC-786
91Yakima/ClBest-8
91Yakima/ProC-4259

Blackwell, Ewell
47HomogBond-3
48B-2
48L-39
49Eureka-77
49Royal-9
50B-63
51B-24
52BR
52RM-NL3
52Royal
52T-344
53T-31
79TCMA-119
80Marchant-5
89Pac/Leg-188
91T/Arc53-31
92Bz/Quadra-18
D305
Exh47
R346-4

Blackwell, Fred
No Cards.

Blackwell, Juan
91FtLaud/ClBest-19
91FtLaud/ProC-2432
92Albany/ProC-2230
92Albany/SB-4

Blackwell, Larry
86Kenosha-2
87OrlanTw-26
88Visalia/Cal-159
88Visalia/ProC-83
89OrlanTw/Best-11
89OrlanTw/ProC-1340

Blackwell, Orlando
83Clinton/Frit-11
84Shrev/FB-2

Blackwell, Teddy
89BurlInd/Star-29TR
90Watertn/Star-26TR
91ColInd/ClBest-30TR
92ColRS/ClBest-29TR

Blackwell, Timothy P.
(Tim)
76SSPC-415
78OPC-223
78T-449
80T-153
81Coke
81D-559
81F-304
81OPC-43
81T-553
81T/HT
82D-99
82Expo/Hygrade-1
82F-587
82Hygrade
82T-374
82T/St-28
82T/Tr-7T
83D-214
83Expo/PostC-1
83OPC-57
83Stuart-26
83T-57
84Cram/PCL-241C
86Fres/Smok-1MG
88Phoenix/CMC-25M
89Pittsfld/Star-24MG
90FSLAS/Star-24
90StLucie/Star-28
91Clmbia/PCPII-7MG
91Clmbia/PII-1MG
91SALAS/ProC-SAL12MG
92ColumMet/ClBest-26MG
92ColumMet/ProC-312
92ColumMet/SAL/II-1

Blackwell, Todd
90Reno/Cal-268

Blackwell, Tom
88Phoenix/ProC-53

Blades, Francis R.
(Ray)
21Exh-11
25Exh-58
26Exh-58
28Exh-30
54T-243CO
91Conlon/Sport-130
92Conlon/Sport-646
94T/Arc54-243

Bladow, Dave
92Eugene/ClBest-6
92Eugene/ProC-3017

Bladt, Richard Alan
74OPC-601R
74Syrac/Team-2
74T-601R
75Syrac/Team-1
76SSPC-444
92Yank/WIZ70-16

Blaeholder, George
32Orbit/num-9
32Orbit/un-6
33G-16
34DS-13
34G-1F
35G-3D
35G-5D
35G-6D
93Conlon-742
R305
R314
V353-12
V353-169

Blaemire, Rae Bertram
No Cards.

Blaine, Tom
88ArkTr/GS-8

Blair, Clarence Vick
(Footsie)
No Cards.

Blair, Dennis
72Dimanche*-2
75OPC-521
75T-521
75T/M-521
76OPC-642

76SSPC-344
76T-642
77OPC-189
77T-593
78T-466
79Hawaii-22
80Hawaii-9
Blair, Dirk
91Pulaski/ClBest-17
91Pulaski/ProC-3996
92Macon/ClBest-2
92Macon/ProC-258
93Durham/Team-2
Blair, Garnett E.
91Negro/Lewis-19
92Negro/RetortII-3
93TWill-98
Blair, Lonnie
91Negro/Lewis-18
Blair, Louis Nathan
(Buddy)
42PlayBall-23
Blair, Paul
65T-473R
66OPC-48
66T-48
67CokeCap/Orio-3
67OPC-153WS
67T-153WS
67T-319
68CokeCap/Orio-3
68Dexter-12
68OPC-135
68T-135
69MB-27
69MLB/St-1
69T-506
70MLB/St-146
70OPC-285
70T-285
71K-35
71MLB/St-290
71OPC-53
71T-53
71T/tatt-6
72MB-33
72Pol/Orio-2
72T-660
73JP
73OPC-528
73T-528
74OPC-92
74T-92
74T/St-123
75Ho-12
75Ho/Twink-12
75OPC-275
75T-275
75T/M-275
76OPC-473
76SSPC-395
76T-473
77BK/Y-21
77BurgChef-39
77T-313
78BK/Y-22
78SSPC/270-20
78T-114
79OPC-304
79T-582
80OPC-149
80T-281
81TCMA-311
84Everett/Cram-19
88CalLgAS-4
88SanJose/Cal-117
88SanJose/ProC-109
89Pac/SenLg-76
89Shrev/ProC-1834
89TM/SenLg-8
90AAASingl/ProC-479CO
90EliteSenLg-77
90ProC/Singl-308CO
90RochR/CMC-7CO
90RochR/ProC-722
90WinSalem/Team-4
91AA/LineD-127
91CharlK/LineD-127
91CharlK/ProC-1694
91Crown/Orio-36
92MCI-8
92Yank/WIZ70-17
92Yank/WIZ80-12
93AP/ASG-158
93MCI-2
93UD/ATH-13
94TedW-8
Blair, Scott
89KS*-24M
Blair, Walter Allan
14CJ-126
14Piedmont/St-5
15CJ-126
T201
T202
T204
Blair, William E.
N172
Blair, Willie
87Dunedin-22
89Syrac/CMC-6
89Syrac/MerchB-2
89Syrac/ProC-805
89Syrac/Team-2
90B-504
90Classic/III-52
90D/Rook-29
90F/Up-126
90Leaf-449
90S/Tr-88T
90T/Tr-8T
90Tor/BJ-27
91AAA/LineD-78
91ColoSp/LineD-78
91ColoSp/ProC-2177
91D-267
91F-170
91OPC-191
91S-57
91S/100RisSt-19
91T-191
91T/90Debut-17
91UD-427
92F-106
92S-730
92StCl-813
92Tucson/ProC-478
92Tucson/SB-NNO
93D-740
93F-404
93F/Final-23
93Flair-36
93Pac/Spanish-423
93T/Tr-96T
93UD-720
93USPlayC/Rockie-10H
93USPlayC/Rockie-8C
93Ultra-342
94D-631
94F-434
94Pac/Cr-189
94S-118
94S/GoldR-118
94StCl-348
94StCl/1stDay-348
94StCl/Gold-348
94StCl/Team-116
94T-439
94T/Gold-439
94Ultra-182
Blais, Jean-Marc
52Laval-111
Blake, Ben
92Watertn/ClBest-8
92Watertn/ProC-3225
Blake, Bob
79Wisco-5
Blake, Ed
52T-144
Blake, Harry Cooper
No Cards.
Blake, John Frederick
(Sherriff)
26Exh-18
92Conlon/Sport-478
Blake, Todd
92Johnson/ClBest-25
92Johnson/ProC-3106
Blake, Toe
45Parade*-49M
Blakely, Dave
85Everett/Cram-1
86Clinton-2
87Visalia-10
Blakely, Lincoln H.
(Link)
R314/Can
Blakeman, Todd
90Elizab/Star-5
91Kenosha/ClBest-3
91Kenosha/ProC-2080
Blakiston, Robert J.
(Bob)
No Cards.
Blanchard, John Edwin
(Johnny)
59T-117
60L-89
60T-283
61P-18
61T-104
61T/St-190
62J-11
62P-11
62P/Can-11
62T-93
63J-21
63P-21
63T-555
64T-118
65T-388
66T-268
81TCMA-474M
89Swell-92
92Yank/WIZ60-9
PM10/L-5
WG10-1
WG9-2
Blanche, Prosper A.
(Al)
35BU-83
Blanchette, Bill
92Boise/ClBest-11
92Boise/ProC-3616
Blanco, Damasco
No Cards.
Blanco, Gil
65T-566R
67T-303
92Yank/WIZ60-10
Blanco, Henry
90Kissim/DIMD-1
91GreatF/SportP-5
92Bakers/Cal-3
92UD/ML-201
Blanco, Oswaldo C.
(Ossie)
No Cards.
Blanco, Pedro
92Elizab/ProC-3684
Blanco, Romauldo
73Cedar
75Dubuq
Bland, Lance
90SanBern/Cal-116TR
Blanding, Fred
(Fritz)
14CJ-109
15CJ-109
T207
Blank, Frank Ignatz
(Coonie)
No Cards.
Blanke, Scott
83Clinton/Frit-26
Blankenship, Bob
89Billings/ProC-2060
90Bend/Legoe-11
Blankenship, Cliff
E90/1
T204
Blankenship, Kevin
84AZ/Pol-1
85Durham-3
86Greenvl/Team-4
87Greenvl/Best-19
88Greenvl/Best-16
88SLAS-28
89AAA/ProC-44
89D-658
89Iowa/CMC-7
89Iowa/ProC-1699
89UD/Ext-762
90AAASingl/ProC-618
90B-24
90F-28
90F/Can-28
90Iowa/CMC-3
90Iowa/ProC-311
90ProC/Singl-78
90S-646
90UD-47
91BuffB/ProC-533
92OkCty/ProC-1907
92OkCty/SB-303
92Sky/AAASingl-139
Blankenship, Lance
86Cram/NWL-69
87Modesto-10
88AAA/ProC-38
88Tacoma/CMC-11
88Tacoma/ProC-630
89D-621
89F-2
89S-641
89S/HotRook-20
89Tacoma/CMC-12
89Tacoma/ProC-1539
89UD-15
90F-1
90F/Can-1
90HotRook/St-8
90Mother/A's-21
90OPC-132
90S-536
90S/100Ris-82
90S/YS/II-36
90T-132
90T/Big-173
90UD-687
91D-701
91F-3
91Mother/A's-21
91OPC-411
91S-303
91StCl-437
91T-411
92D-768
92F-250
92L-410
92L/BlkGold-410
92Mother/A's-21
92OPC-386
92S-279
92StCl-897
92UD-749
92Ultra-418
93B-273
93D-23
93F-290
93L-221
93Mother/A's-22
93OPC-30
93Pac/Spanish-562
93Pinn-338
93StCl-413
93StCl/1stDay-413
93StCl/A's-2
93T-548
93T/Gold-548
93UD-108
93Ultra-253
94D-401
94F-254
94Pac/Cr-445
94StCl-341
94StCl/1stDay-341
94StCl/Gold-341
94T-17
94T/Gold-17
Blankenship, Ted
26Exh-73
27Exh-37
92Conlon/Sport-457
Blanks, Daryl
88Idaho/ProC-1834
89BurlB/ProC-1621
89BurlB/Star-2
90BurlB/Best-23
90BurlB/ProC-2362
90BurlB/Star-3
Blanks, Larvell
73OPC-609R
73T-609R
75OPC-394
75T-394
75T/M-394
76OPC-127
76SSPC-8
76T-127
76T/TR-127T
77Pep-6
77T-441
78OPC-213
78T-61
79T-307
80T-656
89Pac/SenLg-206
89T/SenLg-92
93Rang/Keeb-73
Blanton, Darrell
(Cy)
34DS-57
35BU-88
35G-8K
35G-9K
37Exh/4-7
38Exh/4-7
91Conlon/Sport-134
R312
R313
R314
V351B-4
V355-3
Blanton, Garrett
91Hamil/ClBest-16
91Hamil/ProC-4049
Blaser, Mark
83Greens-16
85Albany-14
86WPalmB-6
Blasingame, Donald L.
(Don)
56T-309
57T-47
58T-199
59Armour-5
59T-491
60T-397
61P-148
61T-294
61T/St-73
62J-117
62P-117
62P/Can-117
62Salada-103
62Shirriff-103
62T-103
63FrBauer-1
63J-126
63Kahn
63P-126
63T-518
64T-327
65OPC-21
65T-21
78TCMA-84
Exh47
Blasingame, Wade
65OPC-44
65T-44
66Kahn
66T-355
67CokeCap/Astro-7
67CokeCap/Brave-14
67OPC-119
67T-119
68T-507
69MB-28
69T-308
71OPC-79
71T-79
72T-581
92Yank/WIZ70-18
Blasingim, Chad
89KS*-1
Blaske, Kevin
92CharlR/ClBest-29TR
Blass, Steve
65OPC-232
65T-232
66EH-28
66T-344
67CokeCap/Pirate-7
67T-562
67T/Test/PP-4
68KDKA-28
68T-499
69Kahn
69OPC-104
69T-104
69T/S-57
69T/St-83
70OPC-396
70T-396
71MLB/St-194
71OPC-143
71T-143

72K-44
72MB-34
72OPC-229WS
72OPC-320
72T-229WS
72T-320
73K-11
73OPC-95
73T-95
74OPC-595
74T-595
93Pirate/Nation-3ANN
93UD/ATH-14
Blasucci, Tony
85PrWill-18
86PrWill-3
87DayBe-5
88BirmB/Best-2
89BirmB/Best-10
89BirmB/ProC-94
90AAASingl/ProC-109
90Calgary/CMC-2
90Calgary/ProC-644
90ProC/Singl-429
Blateric, Steve
73OPC-616R
73T-616R
75SLCity/Caruso-19
92Yank/WIZ70-19
Blatnick, John Louis
(Johnny)
49B-123
Blattner, Robert G.
(Buddy)
40Hughes-4
47TipTop
49Eureka-130
Blauser, Jeff
86Durham-2
87Richm/Crown-2
87Richm/TCMA-11
87Sf/Rook-48
88D-513
88F-533
88Richm-2
88Richm/CMC-22
88Richm/ProC-18
88S-562
88S/YS/II-14
89Brave/Dubuq-5
89D-592
89F-588
89Panini/St-41
89S-589
89T-83
89T/Big-317
89UD-132
90B-15
90Brave/Dubuq/Perf-1
90Brave/Dubuq/Singl-2
90Classic-123
90D-271
90D/BestNL-74
90F-576
90F/Can-576
90Leaf-191
90OPC-251
90Panini/St-217
90PublInt/St-109
90S-178
90T-251
90T/Big-180
90T/St-28
90UD-406
91Brave/Dubuq/Perf-4
91Brave/Dubuq/Stand-6
91D-229
91F-683
91Leaf-115
91OPC-623
91Panini/FrSt-22
91S-52
91StCl-377
91T-623
91UD-382
91Ultra-2
92Brave/LykePerf-6
92Brave/LykeStand-7
92D-228
92F-353
92L-147
92L/BlkGold-147
92OPC-199
92Pinn-477
92S-362
92StCl-168
92T-199
92T/Gold-199
92T/GoldWin-199
92UD-370
92USPlayC/Brave-12C
92USPlayC/Brave-5D
92Ultra-159
93B-142
93Brave/FLAg-3
93Brave/LykePerf-5
93Brave/LykeStand-6
93D-134
93F-364
93Flair-2
93L-86
93OPC-59
93Pac/Spanish-333
93Panini-183
93Pinn-432
93S-142
93StCl-436
93StCl/1stDay-436
93StCl/Brave-5
93Studio/Sil-8
93T-552
93T/Gold-552
93UD-591
93UD/SP-56
93Ultra-302
94B-517
94D-88
94F-354
94F/AS-30
94Flair-124
94L-194
94OPC-214
94Pac/Cr-4
94Panini-143
94Pinn-98
94Pinn/Artist-98
94Pinn/Museum-98
94Pinn/Run-29
94S-54
94S/GoldR-54
94S/GoldS-5
94Select-14
94Sf/2000-111
94StCl-229
94StCl/1stDay-229
94StCl/Gold-229
94StCl/Team-60
94T-318
94T-387M
94T/BlkGold-26
94T/Finest-27
94T/FinestRef-27
94T/Gold-318
94T/Gold-387M
94TripleP-42
94TripleP/Medal-8M
94UD-324
94UD/CollC-53
94UD/CollC/Gold-53
94UD/CollC/Silv-53
94UD/SP-48
94Ultra-150
Blaylock, Gary
59T-539
Blaylock, Marvin E.
(Marv)
55B-292
57T-224
Blaylock, Robert
59T-211
62-Pep/Tul
Blazier, Ron
90Princet/DIMD-2
91Batavia/ClBest-26
91Batavia/ProC-3475
92Spartan/ClBest-10
92Spartan/ProC-1255
93B-244
93FExcel/ML-83
93StCl/Phill-23
Blefary, Curtis LeRoy
(Curt)
65OPC-49R
65T-49R
66Bz-28
66T-460
66T/RO-87
66T/RO-9
67Bz-28
67CokeCap/Orio-13
67OPC-180
67T-180
67T-521M
68CokeCap/Orio-13
68Dexter-13
68T-312
69MB-29
69MLB/St-137
69T-458
69T/S-44
69T/St-122
70MLB/St-242
70OPC-297
70T-297
71MLB/St-483
71OPC-131
71T-131
72MB-35
72T-691
72T-692A
81TCMA-412
91Crown/Orio-37
92Yank/WIZ70-20
Blessitt, Isiah
(Ike)
75Tucson/Caruso-9
77Holyo
89Pac/SenLg-190
89T/SenLg-20
Bleuberg, Jim
91Jaxvl/ProC-142
Blevins, Brad
83QuadC-8
Blevins, Greg
90Butte/SportP-2
91Gaston/ClBest-13
91Gaston/ProC-2690
Bligh, Edwin Forrest
(Ned)
N172
Bliss, Elmer Ward
No Cards.
Bliss, Howard Frank
No Cards.
Bliss, John J.A.
11Helmar-166
E90/1
M116
T206
Bliss, William
(Bill)
91FrRow/DP-45
91Geneva/ClBest-1
91Geneva/ProC-4207
91Peoria/Team-34
92ClBest-218
92Peoria/ClBest-4
92Peoria/Team-4
92StCl/Dome-17
92UD/ML-159
93Peoria/Team-1
Blizzard, Kevin
89GA-2
89GA-28M
Blobaum, Jeff
84Cram/PCL-19
Block, James John
(Bruno)
11Helmar-6
E286
M116
T204
T207
Block, Richard
79Newar-19
Block, Seymour
(Cy)
V362-9
Blocker, Terry
82Jacks-20
84Tidew-20
85IntLgAS-16
85Tidew-19
86Tidew-2
87Tidew-5
87Tidew/TCMA-19
89F-589
89Richm/CMC-17
89Richm/Ko-19
89S-605
89T-76
89UD-399
91WIZMets-39
Blohm, Pete
89Augusta/ProC-516
89SALAS/GS-45
90Dunedin/Star-3
90Knoxvl/Best-3
90Knoxvl/ProC-1246
90Knoxvl/Star-1
91AA/LineD-351
91Knoxvl/LineD-351
91Syrac/MerchB-3
91Syrac/ProC-2475
92Syrac/MerchB-1
92Syrac/ProC-1959
92Syrac/SB-501
93Syrac/ProC-992
Blomberg, Ronald Mark
(Ron)
72OPC-203
72T-203
73OPC-462
73Syrac/Team-3
73T-462
74K-54
74OPC-117
74Syrac/Team-1
74T-117
74T/DE-60
74T/St-211
75OPC-68
75Syrac/Team-1
75Syrac/Team-2
75T-68
75T/M-68
76Ho-38
76Ho/Twink-38
76OPC-354
76SSPC-450
76SSPC/MetsY-Y4
76T-354
77T-543
78Ho-147
78SSPC/270-157
78T-506
79OPC-17
79T-42
88T-663TBC
92Yank/WIZ60-11
92Yank/WIZ70-21
Blomberg, Steve
76Shrev
Blomdahl, Ben
91Niagara/ClBest-19
91Niagara/ProC-3625
92ClBest-99
92Fayette/ClBest-2
92Fayette/ProC-2159
93B-207
93ClBest/MLG-51
Blong, Joseph Myles
(Joe)
No Cards.
Blong, Wesley C.
(Wes)
No Cards.
Blood, Ed
33SK*-9
Bloodworth, James H.
(Jimmy)
40PlayBall-189
49Eureka-78
51B-185
Bloomfield, Clyde S.
62Pep/Tul
63Pep/Tul
64T-532R
Blosser, Greg
89LittleSun-21
90B-278
90CLAS/CL-12
90LynchRS/Team-1
90S-681DC
90T/TVRSox-37
91AA/LineD-452
91B-115
91ClBest/Singl-226
91NewBrit/LineD-452
91NewBrit/ProC-363
91UD-70
92B-251
92ClBest-194
92NewBrit/ProC-445
92NewBrit/SB-478
92Sky/AASingl-203
92UD/ML-260
93B-199
93ClBest/MLG-27
93F/Final-170
93FExcel/ML-130
93Pawtu/Ball-4
93T-798
93T/Gold-798
93Ultra-506
94Finest-402
94Pinn-245
94Pinn/Artist-245
94Pinn/Museum-245
94Select-190
94StCl-172
94StCl/1stDay-172
94StCl/Gold-172
94UD-5
94UD/CollC-2
94UD/CollC/Gold-2
94UD/CollC/Silv-2
94UD/ElecD-5
Blott, Jack Leonard
No Cards.
Blouin, Gary
86Cram/NWL-45
87FtMyr-3
Blount, Bill
85Spokane/Cram-2
86CharRain-3
87LasVegas-16
88River/Cal-230
88River/ProC-1421
Blowers, Michael
86James-1
87WPalmB-13
88Jaxvl/Best-16
88Jaxvl/ProC-975
89Indianap/CMC-14
89Indianap/ProC-1221
90B-441
90Classic/Up-T5
90D-656
90D/Rook-26
90F-438
90F/Can-438
90Leaf-109
90S-624
90S/YS/II-34
90T/89Debut-18
90T/TVYank-23
90T/Tr-9T
90UD/Ext-767
91D-63
91OPC-691
91S-838
91S/100RisSt-17
91T-691
91UD/Ext-730
92Calgary/ProC-3739
92Calgary/SB-54
92Sky/AAASingl-23
92Yank/WIZ80-13
93F/Final-264
93L-457
93Mother/Mar-13
93Pac/Spanish-618
93StCl-144
93StCl/1stDay-144
94D-423
94F-279
94L-218
94Pac/Cr-562
94S-521
94Select-66
94T-717
94T/Finest-183
94T/FinestRef-183
94T/Gold-717
94TripleP-123
94UD-309
94UD/CollC-54
94UD/CollC/Gold-54
94UD/CollC/Silv-54
94Ultra-117
Blue, Bird Wayne
(Bert)
No Cards.
Blue, Luzerne Atwell
(Lu)
26Exh-90
28Exh-57
29Exh/4-30
31Exh/4-20

33Exh/4-10
81Tiger/Detroit-115
90Target-57
94Conlon-1229
E120
E126-54
R316
V61-5
W517-50
W572
W573
Blue, Vida
70OPC-21R
70T-21R
71MLB/St-507
71OPC-544
71T-544
72K-9
72OPC-169
72OPC-170IA
72OPC-92LL
72OPC-94LL
72OPC-96LL
72ProStars/PostC-25
72T-169
72T-170IA
72T-92LL
72T-94LL
72T-96LL
72T/Post-8
73OPC-430
73T-430
74OPC-290
74T-290
74T/St-222
75OPC-209MVP
75OPC-510
75SSPC/42-12
75T-209MVP
75T-510
75T/M-209MVP
75T/M-510
76Crane-3
76Ho-20
76Ho/Twink-20
76K-47
76MSA/Disc
76OPC-140
76OPC-200LL
76SSPC-481
76T-140
76T-200LL
77BurgChef-114
77Ho-52
77Ho/Twink-52
77OPC-75
77T-230
77T/CS-4
77T/ClothSt-4
78OPC-177
78T-680
78Wiffle/Discs-4
79Ho-74
79K-23
79OPC-49
79Pol/Giants-14
79T-110
79T/Comics-33
80BK/PHR-1
80K-42
80OPC-14
80Pol/Giants-14
80T-30
80T/S-59
80T/Super-59
81D-433
81F-432
81F/St-63
81K-23
81OPC-310
81T-310
81T/SO-108
81T/St-239
82D-222
82D-4DK
82F-384
82F/St-61
82FBI/Disc-1
82K-63
82KMart-19
82OPC-267
82OPC-82IA
82T-430
82T-431A
82T-576TL
82T/St-111
82T/Tr-8T
83D-34
83D-648M
83F-106
83F-643M
83F/St-13M
83F/St-16M
83OPC-178
83T-471TL
83T-570
83T/Fold-1M
84Mother/Giants-25
85F/Up-U7
85Mother/Giants-10
86D-509
86F-533
86Leaf-247
86Mother/Giants-10
86Sf-132M
86Sf-142M
86Sf/Dec-63M
86T-770
87D-362
87F-266
87Mother/A's-7
87OPC-260
87RedFoley/St-128
87T-260
89Pac/Leg-198
89Pac/SenLg-215
89T/SenLg-48
89TM/SenLg-9
90EliteSenLg-121
90EliteSenLg-50
90Pac/Legend-8
90Swell/Great-89
91Pac/SenLg-81
91Swell/Great-10
92AP/ASG-44
92UD/Hero-5AU
92UD/Hero-H5
92UD/Hero-H8
93MCI-1
93Metallic-2
93TWill-43
Blueberg, James
86Cram/NWL-120
87Wausau-2
88CalLgAS-30
88SanBern/Best-15
88SanBern/Cal-47
89SanBern/Best-6
90ProC/Singl-795
90Wmsprt/Best-2
90Wmsprt/ProC-1049
90Wmsprt/Star-1
91AA/LineD-328
91Jaxvl/LineD-328
Bluege, Oswald Louis
(Ossie)
25Exh-121
26Exh-121
29Exh/4-31
31Exh/4-32
33G-113
33G-159
34DS-71
35BU-105
36Exh/4-16
61F-93
91Conlon/Sport-295
R313
V353-83
V355-87
Bluege, Otto Adam
94Conlon-1305
Bluestone, Brad
86Erie-4TR
87Sprn/Best-27TR
88Spring/Best-27
90Louisvl/CMC-29TR
90ProC/Singl-680TR
Bluhm, Bill
87Everett-25
88Watlo/ProC-668
89Reno/Cal-262
Bluhm, Brandon
91BurlInd/ProC-3290
92BurlInd/ClBest-6
92BurlInd/ProC-1645
Bluhm, Harvey Fred
(Red)
No Cards.
Blum, Brent
86Albany/TCMA-30
87Albany-22
88PrWill/Star-3
Bluma, Jeff
90WichSt-5
Blumberg, Rob Jr.
89StCath/ProC-2088
90A&AASingle/ProC-89
90Myrtle/ProC-2768
90SALAS/Star-27
91Kane/ClBest-4
91Kane/ProC-2651
92Hagers/SB-252
Blume, David
81Wausau-11
Blundin, Barry
88BurlInd/ProC-1791
Bluthardt, Jay
88Watertn/Pucko-15
Blyleven, Bert
71MLB/St-458
71OPC-26
71T-26
72OPC-515
72T-515
73K-35
73OPC-199
73T-199
74K-46
74OPC-98
74T-98
74T/DE-47
74T/St-201
75Ho-74
75OPC-30
75T-30
75T/M-30
76Ho-116
76K-11
76OPC-204LL
76OPC-235
76SSPC-219
76T-204LL
76T-235
77BurgChef-22
77OPC-101
77T-630
77T/CS-5
77T/ClothSt-5
78Ho-74
78K-53
78OPC-113
78T-131
78Wiffle/Discs-5
79Ho-133
79OPC-155
79T-308
80K-5
80OPC-238
80T-457
81D-135
81F-383
81OPC-294
81T-554
81T/Tr-738
82D-111
82F-361
82F/St-199
82OPC-164
82T-559TL
82T-685
82T/St-173
82Wheat/Ind
83D-589
83OPC-280
83T-280
83T/Fold-1M
83Wheat/Ind-6
84D-129
84D/AAS-45
84D/Champs-42
84F-536
84Nes/792-716LL
84Nes/792-789
84OPC-126
84T-716ATL
84T-789
84T/St-261
84Wheat/Ind-28
85D-224
85D-4DK
85D/DKsuper-4
85F-440
85F/LimEd-2
85F/St-112
85F/St-81
85F/St-92
85FunFood/Pin-106
85Leaf-4DK
85OPC-355
85Polar/Ind-28
85Seven-7G
85T-355
85T/Gloss40-17
85T/St-247
85T/Super-35
86D-649
86D/AAS-52
86D/HL-31
86F-386
86F/Mini-82
86F/Slug-1
86F/St-6
86Leaf-88
86OPC-272
86Quaker-21
86Seven/Coin-C10
86Sf-103
86Sf-142M
86Sf-64M
86T-445
86T/3D-1
86T/Mini-23
86T/St-279
86T/Super-11
86T/Tatt-24M
87D-71
87D/OD-226
87F-536
87F/AwardWin-3
87F/Mini-9
87F/St-10
87F/St-S3
87Leaf-100
87OPC-235
87RedFoley/St-101
87Sf-81
87Sf/TPrev-17M
87T-25
87T/Mini-61
87T/St-278
88D-71
88D/Best-18
88F-4
88F/St-41
88Leaf-52
88Master/Disc-1
88OPC-295
88Panini/St-132
88S-90
88Sf-92
88Smok/Minn-6
88T-295
88T/Big-180
88T/St-20
88T/St-276
88Woolwth-21
89B-41
89D-119
89D/Best-3
89D/Tr-35
89F-105
89F/Up-12
89OPC-204
89S-215
89S/Tr-17
89T-555
89T/LJN-55
89T/St-285
89T/Tr-11T
89UD-225
89UD/Ext-712
90B-285
90Classic-142
90D-331
90D/BestAL-4
90F-128
90F/AwardWin-3
90F/BBMVP-2
90F/Can-128
90KayBee-2
90Leaf-63
90MLBPA/Pins-96
90OPC-130
90Panini/St-28
90PublInt/St-366
90RedFoley/St-5
90S-180
90S/100St-12
90Sf-193
90Smok/Angel-2
90T-130
90T/Big-114
90T/Mini-7
90T/St-165
90UD-527
90Woolwth/HL-7
91BBBest/RecBr-1
91D-453
91F-308
91Leaf/Stud-23
91OPC-615
91OPC/BoxB-A
91S-235
91StCl-175
91T-615
91T/WaxBox-A
91UD-571
91Woolwth/HL-7
92OPC-375
92Pol/Angel-3
92T-375
92T/Gold-375
92T/GoldWin-375
92UD-632
93F-568
93Pac/Spanish-41
93Pinn-296NT
93Pinn-83
93Rang/Keeb-74
93S-577
93Select-252
93T-48
93T/Gold-48
Blyth, Robert
(Bert)
82Iowa-14
Blyzka, Michael
(Mike)
54Esskay
54T-152
91Crown/Orio-38
94T/Arc54-152
Boag, Jack
78StPete
Boak, Chester Robert
(Chet)
No Cards.
Boatman, John
89KS*-2
92Lipscomb-4
93Lipscomb-2
Boatright, Dennis
83Butte-1
Bobb, Jason
92GulfCD/ProC-3557
Bobb, Mark Randall
(Randy)
70OPC-429R
70T-429R
71OPC-83R
71T-83R
Bobel, Jay
87Salem/ProC-2414
Bobo, Elgin
91Boise/ClBest-10
91Boise/ProC-3882
92Boise/ClBest-24
92Boise/ProC-3635
92ClBest/Up-448
92QuadC/ClBest-17
92QuadC/ProC-812
Bobo, Paul
89KS*-3
92Lipscomb-3M
93Lipscomb-3
Boccabella, John D.
64T-192R
66T-482R
67CokeCap/Cub-5
67T-578
68T-542
69MB-30
69T-466
70Expo/PostC-15
70OPC-19
70T-19
71Expo/ProS-3
71LaPizza-2
71MLB/St-123

71OPC-452
71T-452
72Dimanche*-3
72OPC-159
72ProStars/PostC-2
72T-159
73OPC-592
73T-592
74Expo/West-2
74OPC-253
74T-253
74T/St-52
74Weston-12
75OPC-553
75T-553
75T/M-553
78TCMA-291
92Nabisco-35

Bocek, Milton Frank
(Milt)
No Cards.

Bochesa, Greg
86WinHaven-4
87NewBrit-13
88NewBrit/ProC-900

Bochte, Bruce Anton
74SLCity
75OPC-392
75T-392
75T/M-392
76OPC-637
76SSPC-200
76T-637
77T-68
78Ho-81
78PapaG/Disc-29
78T-537
78Tastee/Discs-25
79Ho-123
79OPC-231
79T-443
80K-59
80OPC-80
80T-143
80T/S-55
80T/Super-55
81D-403
81Drake-25
81F-600
81F/St-8
81K-62
81MSA/Disc-3
81OPC-18
81Sqt-31
81T-723
81T/SO-30
81T/St-123
82D-505
82F-505
82F/St-222
82OPC-224
82T-224
82T/St-232
83D-127
83F-473
83F/St-16M
83F/St-4M
83OPC-28
83OPC/St-111
83T-28
83T-711
83T/St-111
84F/X-13
84Mother/A's-6
85D-253
85F-416
85Mother/A's-10
85OPC-391
85T-632
85T/St-331
86D-400
86F-413
86F/Mini-86
86F/St-7
86Leaf-189
86Mother/A's-10
86OPC-378
86T-378
86T/St-170
86T/Tatt-6M
87F-388
87T-496
87T/St-169

Bochtler, Doug
90MidwLgAS/GS-4
90Rockford/ProC-2694
90Rockford/Team-2
91WPalmB/ClBest-2
91WPalmB/ProC-1218
92Harris/ProC-452
92Harris/SB-276
92Sky/AASingl-117
93T-523
93T/Gold-523

Bochy, Bruce Douglas
76Dubuq
77Cocoa
79T-718R
80T-289
81D-20
81F-69
81Tidew-2
82Tidew-6
84Cram/PCL-225
84Nes/792-571
84T-571
85D-505
85Mother/Padres-12
85T-324
86D-551
86T-608
87D-311
87F-411
87T-428
88LasVegas/CMC-21
88LasVegas/ProC-241
88S-469
88T-31
89Pac/SenLg-194
89River/Best-25CO
89River/Cal-29CO
89River/ProC-1405CO
89Spokane/SP-4
90EliteSenLg-51
90River/Best-22MG
90River/Cal-24MG
91HighD/ClBest-29MG
91HighD/ProC-2412MG
91WIZMets-40
92Wichita/ProC-3669MG
92Wichita/SB-649MG
93Mother/Padre-28M

Bock, Doug
88AppFx/ProC-157

Bock, Paul
75AppFx
77Clinton

Bockewitz, Stan
76Wmsprt

Bockhorn, Glen
81Durham-11
85Greenvl/Team-4
86BuffB-1

Bockman, Joseph E.
(Eddie)
49B-195
49Eureka-153

Bockus, Randy
84Shrev/FB-3
86Phoenix-3
87F/Up-U6
87Phoenix-3
88F/Up-U127
88Phoenix/CMC-1
88Phoenix/ProC-55
89B-96
89T-733
89Toledo/CMC-1
89Toledo/ProC-769
91AAA/LineD-155
91Edmon/LineD-155

Boddicker, Mike
80RochR-6
81RochR-1
81T-399R
82RochR-1
84D-123
84F-1
84F-645IA
84F/St-110
84Nes/792-191
84Nes/792-426TL
84Seven-9E
84T-191
84T-426TL
84T/St-13
84T/St-375
85D-291
85Drake-34
85F-170
85F/St-80
85F/St-90
85FunFood/Pin-121
85Leaf-109
85OPC-225
85Seven-6E
85T-225
85T-709AS
85T/3D-26
85T/Gloss40-4
85T/RD-5
85T/St-202
85T/Super-16
85ThomMc/Discs-5
86D-47
86D-8DK
86D/DKsuper-8
86F-269
86F/Mini-57
86Leaf-8DK
86OPC-367
86Seven/Coin-E14
86Sf-104
86T-575
86T/St-233
87D-125
87D/OD-140
87F-463
87F/LL-2
87F/St-11
87French-52
87Leaf-76
87OPC-149
87RedFoley/St-40
87Seven-ME8
87Sf-56
87Sf/TPrev-21M
87T-455
87T/St-227
88AlaskaAS70/Team-23
88D-89
88D/Best-317
88F-556
88F/St-1
88F/Up-U5
88French-52
88KennerFig-7
88OPC-281
88Panini/St-5
88S-67
88Sf-146
88T-725
88T/St-231
89B-21
89Classic-139
89D-612
89D/Best-297
89F-80
89OPC-71
89S-549
89Sf-122
89T-71
89T/Big-296
89T/St-261
89UD-542
90B-267
90D-280
90D/BestAL-3
90F-267
90F/Can-267
90Leaf-19
90OPC-652
90Panini/St-20
90Pep/RSox-2
90PublInt/St-447
90S-31
90T-652
90T/Big-258
90T/St-258
90T/TVRSox-7
90UD-652
91B-296
91Crown/Orio-39
91D-680
91F-85
91Leaf-330
91Leaf/Stud-61
91OPC-303
91OPC/Premier-10
91Panini/Top15-108
91Pol/Royal-3
91S-232
91S/RookTr-45T
91StCl-400
91T-303
91T/Tr-12T
91UD-438
91UD/Ext-719
92B-132
92D-176
92F-153
92L-268
92L/BlkGold-268
92OPC-106
92Pinn-142
92Pol/Royal-3
92S-102
92StCl-39
92T-106
92T/Gold-106
92T/GoldWin-106
92TripleP-12
92UD-213
92Ultra-67
93Cadaco-7
93D-469
93F-616
93Pac/Spanish-132
93Pol/Royal-4
93StCl-192
93StCl/1stDay-192
93T-239
93T/Gold-239
93Ultra-205

Boddie, Eric
89Bakers/Cal-193
90VeroB/Star-6

Boddie, Rodney
(Rod)
88James/ProC-1905
89Rockford/Team-3
90Star/ISingl-6
90WPalmB/Star-1

Bodell, Howard J.
52Laval-81

Bodenhamer, Don
74Gaston

Bodie, Frank Stephan
(Ping)
11Helmar-7
14CJ-79
15CJ-79
28Exh/PCL-4
81Conlon-91
D327
D328-16
E121/80
E122
E135-16
E224
T207
W514-66
W516-3
W575

Bodie, Keith
76Wausau
79Jacks-11
86AubAs-3MG
87Ashvl-4
88FSLAS/Star-3
89Clinton/ProC-898
90SanBern/Best-26MG
90SanBern/Cal-114
90SanBern/ProC-2649
91AAA/LineD-74MG
91Calgary/LineD-74
91Calgary/ProC-530
92Calgary/ProC-3745
92Calgary/SB-74MG
93Calgary/ProC-1181MG

Body, Robert
87Negro/Dixon-9

Boeckel, Norman Doxie
(Tony)
E120
V100
V61-80
W572
W573

Boehler, George
90Target-58

Boehling, John Joseph
14CJ-72
15CJ-72
D328-17
E135-17

Boehlow, Jason
92Hunting/ClBest-3
92Hunting/ProC-3153

Boehmer, Leonard J.
(Len)
69T-519R
81TCMA-355
92Yank/WIZ60-12
92Yank/WIZ70-22

Boehringer, Brian
92ClBest-258
92SoBend/ClBest-1
92SoBend/ProC-171
94ClBest/Gold-193
94FExcel-35

Boelter, Tarry
79Wisco-14

Boemier, Bill
53Mother-63

Boever, Dan
85Cedar-21
88Nashvl/CMC-15
88Nashvl/ProC-476
88Nashvl/Team-3
89Calgary/CMC-12
89Calgary/ProC-535
89Canton/Best-7
89Canton/ProC-1325
89Canton/Star-3
90CedarDG/Best-33

Boever, Joe
83StPete-1
86Louisvl-6
87Louisvl-5
88AAA/ProC-34
88F-534
88Richm-36
88Richm/CMC-9
88Richm/ProC-22
88S-542
88T-627
89Brave/Dubuq-6
89D-168
89T-586
90Brave/Dubuq/Perf-2
90Brave/Dubuq/Singl-3
90D-357
90F-577
90F/Can-577
90Leaf-349
90OPC-410
90Panini/St-220
90PublInt/St-110
90S-81
90SpringDG/Best-14
90T-410
90T/St-34
90UD-408
91B-502
91D-578
91F-387
91Leaf-68
91OPC-159
91Phill/Medford-4
91StCl-462
91T-159
91UD-430
92D-493
92F-523
92L-491
92L/BlkGold-491
92Mother/Ast-13
92OPC-696
92S-647
92StCl-156
92StCl-639
92T-696
92T/Gold-696
92T/GoldWin-696
92T/Tr-12T
92T/TrGold-12T
92UD-402
93D-504
93F-48
93Mother/A's-25
93Pac/Spanish-119
93Pac/Spanish-563
93StCl/A's-15
93T-792
93T/Gold-792
93UD-310
93UD-810

94StCl-458
94StCl/1stDay-458
94StCl/Gold-458
94T-467
94T/Gold-467
Boffek, Scott
91VeroB/ClBest-19
Bogar, Tim
89Jacks/GS-3
90AAASingl/ProC-280
90ProC/Singl-365
90T/TVMets-36
90Tidew/CMC-14
90Tidew/ProC-549
91AA/LineD-626
91Wmsprt/LineD-626
91Wmsprt/ProC-298
92Tidew/ProC-
92Tidew/SB-553
93B-326
93F/Final-99
93L-525
93Mets/Kahn-23
93OPC/Premier-108
93Select/RookTr-54T
93StCl-702
93StCl/1stDay-702
93T/Tr-119T
93UD/SP-145
94D-316
94F-557
94Finest-354
94L-99
94Pac/Cr-395
94S-557
94Select-104
94StCl-170
94StCl/1stDay-170
94StCl/Gold-170
94T-509
94T/Gold-509
94UD-101
94UD/CollC-55
94UD/CollC/Gold-55
94UD/CollC/Silv-55
94UD/ElecD-101
94Ultra-234
Bogart
N172
Bogatyrev, Ilya
89EastLDD/ProC-DD17
93T-633
93T/Gold-633
Bogener, Terrence W.
(Terry)
79Tulsa-15
83D-520
83OKCty-3
84Wichita/Rock-13
93Rang/Keeb-75
Boggess, Dusty
55B-297UMP
Boggetto, Brad
91Yakima/ClBest-20
91Yakima/ProC-4238
Boggs, Tommy
77T-328
78T-518
79Richm-22
79T-384
81D-597
81F-267
81Pol/Atl-40
81T-132
82BK/Lids-3
82D-249
82F-430
82T-61
83D-349
83F-131
83T-649
85OKCty-7
93Rang/Keeb-76
Boggs, Wade Anthony
81Pawtu-15
83D-586
83F-179
83F/St-16M
83F/St-2M
83OPC/St-308
83T-498
83T/St-308
84D-151
84D-26DK
84D/AAS-22
84D/Champs-16
84Drake-2
84F-392
84F-630IA
84F/St-11
84F/St-28
84F/St-52
84MiltBrad-1
84Nes/792-131LL
84Nes/792-30
84Nes/792-786TL
84OPC-30
84Ralston-11
84Seven-10E
84T-131LL
84T-30
84T-786TL
84T/Cereal-11
84T/Gloss40-8
84T/RD-5
84T/St-100
84T/St-216
84T/St/Box-7
84T/Super-7
85D-172
85D/AAS-38
85D/HL-49
85F-151
85F/LimEd-3
85F/St-6
85FunFood/Pin-43
85Leaf-179
85OPC-350
85Seven-7E
85Seven-8C
85T-350
85T/RD-6
85T/St-210
86BK/AP-9
86D-371
86D/AAS-47
86D/AS/WaxBox-PC7
86D/HL-11
86D/HL-13
86Dorman-18
86Drake-27
86F-341
86F-634M
86F-639M
86F/LL-1
86F/LimEd-4
86F/Mini-72
86F/Slug-2
86F/St-8
86F/St-S2
86GenMills/Book-1M
86Jiffy-2
86Leaf-168
86Meadow/Blank-1
86Meadow/Milk-1
86Meadow/Stat-9
86OPC-262
86OPC-B
86Quaker-22
86Seven/Coin-C2
86Seven/Coin-E2
86Seven/Coin-S2
86Seven/Coin-W2
86Sf-180M
86Sf-183M
86Sf-184M
86Sf-3
86Sf-75M
86Sf/Dec-68
86T-510
86T/3D-3
86T/Gloss60-26
86T/Mini-3
86T/St-164
86T/St-247
86T/Super-12
86T/Tatt-22M
86T/WaxBox-B
86TrueVal-30
86Woolwth-3
87BK-1
87Classic-60
87Classic/Up-105
87D-252
87D/AAS-7
87D/HL-14
87D/HL-44
87D/OD-181
87D/PopUp-7
87Drake-16
87F-29
87F-637M
87F/BB-3
87F/Excit-4
87F/GameWin-5
87F/HL-1
87F/LL-3
87F/Mini-10
87F/Slug-4
87F/St-12
87F/St-S2
87F/WS-2M
87GenMills/Book-2M
87Ho/St-19
87Jiffy-20
87KMart-23
87KayBee-4
87Kraft-7
87Leaf-193
87MSA/Discs-13
87MnM's-5
87OPC-150
87Ralston-3
87RedFoley/St-96
87Seven-E5
87Seven-ME6
87Sf-114M
87Sf-197M
87Sf-2
87Sf/TPrev-9M
87Sportflic/DealP-2
87Stuart-15M
87T-150
87T-608AS
87T/Board-31
87T/Coins-4
87T/Gloss22-15
87T/Gloss60-18
87T/HL-10
87T/Mini-41
87T/St-148
87T/St-253
87Woolwth-10
88AP/Test-1
88Bz-2
88ChefBoy-22
88Classic/Blue-214
88Classic/Red-155
88D-153
88D-BC7
88D/AS-31
88D/AS-7
88D/Best-65
88D/PopUp-7
88D/RedSox/Bk-153
88Drake-4
88F-345
88F/AS-8
88F/AwardWin-3
88F/BB/AS-2
88F/BB/MVP-2
88F/Excit-4
88F/Hottest-2
88F/LL-2
88F/Mini-4
88F/RecSet-3
88F/SS-3
88F/Slug-2
88F/St-5
88F/TL-2
88FanSam-8
88Grenada-5
88Jiffy-2
88KMart-2
88KayBee-2
88KennerFig-8
88Leaf-65
88MSA/Disc-1
88Nestle-32
88OPC-200
88Panini/St-228M
88Panini/St-29
88S-2
88S/WaxBox-4
88Sf-50
88Sf/Gamewin-3
88T-200
88T-21TL
88T-388
88T/Big-32
88T/Coins-4
88T/Gloss22-4
88T/Gloss60-51
88T/Mini-1
88T/Revco-16
88T/RiteAid-14
88T/St-157
88T/St-244
88T/St/Backs-40
88T/UK-4
88Woolwth-13
89B-32
89Bz-3
89Cadaco-2
89Classic-102
89Classic-2
89D-68
89D/AS-7
89D/Best-140
89D/PopUp-7
89F-633M
89F-81
89F/BBAS-3
89F/BBMVP's-3
89F/Excit-2
89F/Heroes-2
89F/LL-2
89F/Rec-1
89F/Superstar-4
89F/WaxBox-C2
89Holsum/Discs-2
89KMart/DT-14
89KMart/Lead-1
89KayBee-1
89KennerFig-9
89KingB/Discs-3
89MSA/Disc-7
89Master/Discs-5
89Nissen-2
89OPC-184
89Panini/St-242AS
89Panini/St-245AS
89Panini/St-277
89Panini/St-7
89RedFoley/St-8
89S-175
89S-654HL
89S/HotStar-100
89S/Mast-17
89Sf-100
89Sf-221M
89T-2RB
89T-399AS
89T-600
89T/Big-241
89T/Coins-32
89T/DH-3
89T/Gloss22-4
89T/Gloss60-5
89T/HeadsUp-11
89T/Hills-2
89T/LJN-62
89T/Mini-45
89T/St-147
89T/St-260
89T/St-9
89T/St/Backs-7
89T/UK-4
89Tetley/Discs-7
89UD-389
89UD-687TC
89Woolwth-8
90B-281
90Classic-26
90CollAB-26
90D-68
90D-712AS
90D/BestAL-86
90D/Learning-21
90D/Preview-11
90F-268
90F-632M
90F/AwardWin-4
90F/BB-1
90F/BBMVP-3
90F/Can-268
90F/Can-632
90F/LL-4
90F/LgStand-5
90HotPlay/St-2
90KMart/CBatL-1
90KMart/SS-19
90KayBee-3
90Kenner/Fig-10
90KingB/Discs-9
90Leaf-51
90MCA/Disc-7
90MLBPA/Pins-68
90MSA/Soda-3
90OPC-387AS
90OPC-760
90OPC/BoxB-A
90Panini/St-19
90Panini/St-199M
90Pep/RSox-3
90Post-17
90PublInt/St-277
90PublInt/St-448
90RedFoley/St-6
90S-245
90S-683DT
90S-704
90S/100St-80
90Sf-2
90Starline/LJS-17
90Starline/LJS-22
90Starline/LJS-6
90T-387AS
90T-760
90T/Ames-16
90T/Big-77
90T/Coins-6
90T/DH-4
90T/Gloss22-15
90T/Gloss60-22
90T/HillsHM-19
90T/Mini-3
90T/St-156AS
90T/St-253
90T/St-8HL
90T/TVAS-20
90T/TVRSox-22
90T/WaxBox-A
90Tetley/Discs-7
90UD-555
90USPlayC/AS-11C
90Windwlk/Discs-2
90Woolwth/HL-8
91B-129
91BBBest/HitM-2
91Cadaco-4
91Classic/200-192
91Classic/I-19
91Classic/III-T3
91CollAB-16
91D-178
91D-55AS
91F-86
91KingB/Discs-11
91Leaf-273
91Leaf/Prev-14
91Leaf/Stud-11
91MajorLg/Pins-9
91MooTown-11
91OPC-450
91OPC/Premier-11
91Panini/FrSt-169
91Panini/FrSt-266
91Panini/St-214
91Panini/Top15-30
91RedFoley/St-115
91RedFoley/St-9
91S-12
91S-393AS
91S-889DT
91S/100SS-3
91S/Cooper-B1
91Seven/3DCoin-1NE
91StCl-170
91Sunflower-2
91T-450
91T/CJMini/I-29
91T/SU-3
91UD-546
91UD/FinalEd-84F
91USPlayC/AS-WC
91Ultra-27
92B-70
92CJ/DII-29
92Classic/Game200-70
92Classic/II-T63
92Colla/ASG-7
92D-210
92D-23AS
92D/DK-DK9
92D/Elite-E9
92D/Preview-1
92DPep/MSA-21
92F-32
92F-707M

92F/Performer-9
92F/TmLIns-13
92French-14
92KingB-16
92L-286
92L/BlkGold-286
92OPC-10
92OPC/Premier-1
92P-19
92Panini-274AS
92Panini-87
92Pinn-175
92Pinn-282I
92RedSox/Dunkin-2
92S-434AS
92S-660
92S-885
92S/100SS-30
92S/Proctor-4
92StCl-520
92StCl/Dome-18
92StCl/MPhoto-1
92StCl/MemberI-1
92Studio-131
92Studio/Her-3
92Studio/Prev-14
92T-10
92T-399AS
92T/Gold-10
92T/Gold-399AS
92T/GoldWin-10
92T/GoldWin-399AS
92T/Kids-68
92T/MicroG-10
92TripleP-211
92UD-443
92UD-646DS
92UD/ASFF-13
92UD/TWillB-T1
92UD/TmMVPHolo-10
92USPlayC/Ace-13D
92USPlayC/RedSox-10H
92USPlayC/RedSox-1S
92Ultra-311
92Ultra/AS-4
93B-399
93Cadaco-8
93Colla/ASG-7
93Colla/DM-13
93D-619
93D/Spirit-SG7
93F-554
93F/Final-243
93F/Final/DTrib-DT1
93Flair-245
93L-285
93L/UpGoldAS-5
93MSA/Metz-1
93OPC-196
93OPC/Premier-49
93Pac/Spanish-27
93Pac/Spanish-552
93Panini-152
93Pinn-424
93Pinn-476NT
93Pinn/Cooper-13
93S-592
93Select-48
93Select/RookTr-17T
93StCl-134
93StCl-601
93StCl/1stDay-134
93StCl/1stDay-601
93StCl/MurphyS-15
93StCl/Y-5
93Studio-31
93T-390
93T/Finest-90AS
93T/FinestASJ-90AS
93T/FinestRef-90AS
93T/Gold-390
93T/Tr-47T
93TripleP-143LH
93TripleP-258
93TripleP/Gal-GS3
93UD-556
93UD/Clutch-R2
93UD/FunPack-206
93UD/Iooss-WI20
93UD/OnDeck-D5
93UD/SP-2AS
93UD/Then-TN1
93Ultra-591
94B-305
94D-36
94D/Ann-7
94D/Special-36
94F-226
94F/AS-4
94KingB-5
94L-257
94OPC-193
94Pac/Cr-421
94Pac/Silv-9
94Panini-99
94Pinn-31
94Pinn/Artist-31
94Pinn/Museum-31
94S-101
94S/GoldR-101
94S/GoldS-50
94Select-156
94Sf/2000-102
94StCl-349
94StCl/1stDay-349
94StCl/Gold-349
94StCl/Team-204
94Studio-212
94T-386AS
94T-520
94T-603ST
94T/Finest-173
94T/FinestRef-173
94T/Gold-386AS
94T/Gold-520
94T/Gold-603ST
94T/Prev-390
94TripleP-272
94TripleP/Medal-9M
94UD-112
94UD/ElecD-112
94UD/SP-196
94Ultra-93

Bogues, Muggsy
91Gaston/ClBest-29

Bohanon, Brian
88CharlR/Star-2
90B-489
90D/Rook-13
90F/Up-122
90Mother/Rang-13
90UD/Ext-731
91S/100RisSt-53
91T/90Debut-18
92Classic/Game200-185
92D/Rook-11
92Mother/Rang-18
92OPC-149
92OkCty/ProC-1908
92S-672
92StCl-297
92T-149
92T/Gold-149
92T/GoldWin-149
92Tulsa/ProC-2686
93D-27
93Rang/Keeb-395
93StCl-154
93StCl/1stDay-154
93T-638
93T/Gold-638
93UD-380
94F-302
94StCl-55
94StCl/1stDay-55
94StCl/Gold-55
94StCl/Team-245

Bohlke, Scott
88Durham/Star-2

Bohn, Charles
(Charlie)
No Cards.

Bohn, Matt
88CalLgAS-23

Bohne, Sammy Arthur
21Exh-12
90Target-59
E120
V117-20
V61-67

Bohnenkamp, Dave
89Clinton/ProC-880

Bohnet, Bob
79Wisco-13
82Holyo-14

Bohnet, John
81Chatt-13
82Charl-2
84BuffB-14

Bohringer, Helms
91Bakers/Cal-24

Bohrofen, Brent
89OK-6
90OK-12
91Hamil/ClBest-22
91Hamil/ProC-4050
92Savan/ProC-674

Boisclair, Bruce A.
75Tidew/Team-5
77T-399
78T-277
79OPC-68
79T-148
80T-654
91WIZMets-41

Boitano, Danny
76OkCty/Team-4
79Vanco-9
80T-668R
80Vanco-14
81Tidew-27
91WIZMets-42
93Rang/Keeb-77

Bojan, Tim
92SoOreg/ClBest-19
92SoOreg/ProC-3406

Bojcun, Patrick
(Pat)
91Batavia/ClBest-21
91Batavia/ProC-3476
92Batavia/ClBest-7
92Batavia/ProC-3255

Bokelman, Dick
53T-204
79TCMA-249
91T/Arc53-204

Boken, Robert A.
(Bob)
34G-74

Boker, Mike
91BendB/ClBest-11
91BendB/ProC-3685
92Clinton/ClBest-4
92Clinton/ProC-3589

Bolan, Bob
52Laval-21

Boland, Edward John
(Ed)
No Cards.

Bolar, Wendell
86Cram/NWL-106
87Wausau-9
88Boise/ProC-1607

Bold, Charles Dickens
(Charlie)
No Cards.

Boldt, Sean
92Martins/ClBest-3
92Martins/ProC-3046

Bolek, Ken
76Clinton
78Watlo
83ColumAst-23
86Ashvl-3MG
87Osceola-6
88Watlo/ProC-687
89Kinston/Star-25
90Canton/Best-4MG
90Canton/ProC-1309MG
90Canton/Star-20MG
91AA/LineD-99MG
91Canton/LineD-99
91Canton/ProC-995
92Indian/McDon-30M

Boles, Carl Theodore
63T-428

Boles, John
83AppFx/Frit-25MG
85BuffB-1
86Omaha/ProC-2MG
86Omaha/TCMA-22MG

Boley, John Peter
(Joe)
31Exh/4-27
94Conlon-1141

Bolger, James Cyril
(Jim)
55T-179
57Seattle/Pop-5
57T-289
58T-201
59T-29
61Union

Bolick, Frank C.
88Beloit/GS-4
89Beloit/I/Star-1
89Beloit/II/Star-1
89Star/IISingl-108
90A&AASingle/ProC-152
90AS/Cal-11
90ProC/Singl-713
90Stockton/Best-7
90Stockton/Cal-193
90Stockton/ProC-2192
91AA/LineD-329
91B-534
91ClBest/Singl-381
91Jaxvl/LineD-329
91Jaxvl/ProC-154
92Jacks/ProC-3712
92Jaxvl/SB-351
92OPC-473
92Sky/AASingl-148
92T-473M
92T/Gold-473
92T/GoldWin-473
93B-296
93F/Final-89
93L-231
93OPC/Premier-72
93Pac/Spanish-530
93Pinn-588
93StCl-724
93StCl/1stDay-724
93UD-531
93Ultra-412
94D-63
94Pac/Cr-375

Bolick, Frank
76SanAn/Team-2

Bolin, Bobby
61T-449
62T-329
63T-106
64T-374
65T-341
66OPC-61
66T-61
67CokeCap/Giant-1
67T-252
68CokeCap/Giant-1
68Dexter-14
68OPC-169
68T-169
69OPC-8LL
69T-505
69T-8LL
69T/St-101
70MLB/St-266
70McDon-1
70T-574
71MLB/St-314
71OPC-446
71T-446
72MB-36
72OPC-266
72T-266
73OPC-541
73T-541
74OPC-427
74T-427
78TCMA-109
86BirmB/Team-20CO

Bolin, George
91Melbourne/Fut-10

Boling, John
86AppFx-2
87BirmB/Best-12
88BirmB/Best-18
90Target-60

Bolling, Frank Elmore
55B-204
57T-325
58T-95
59T-280
60T-482
61P-41
61T-335
61T/St-145
62J-146
62P-146
62P/Can-146
62Salada-140
62Shirriff-140
62T-130
62T-211M
62T/St-145
63F-44
63J-149
63P-149
63Salada-18
63T-570
64T-115
65Kahn
65OPC-269
65T-269
66Kahn
78TCMA-9
81Tiger/Detroit-103

Bolling, John Edward
No Cards.

Bolling, Milton J.
(Milt)
53T-280
54B-130
54T-82
55B-48
55T-91
55T/DH-92
56T-315
57T-131
58T-188
91T/Arc53-280
94T/Arc54-82

Bollo, Greg
65T-541R
66T-301
78TCMA-30

Bollweg, Donald R.
(Don)
52T-128
54B-115
55B-54
55Rodeo
PM10/Sm-14

Bolster, Bob
80GlenF/B-29bb
80GlenF/C-23bb

Bolt, James
86SanJose-5

Bolton, Cecil G.
No Cards.

Bolton, Rod
90Utica/Pucko-14
91ClBest/Singl-56
91FSLAS/ProC-FSL27
91Saraso/ClBest-1
91Saraso/ProC-1104
92AAA/ASG/SB-628
92B-240
92ProC/Tomorrow-45
92Sky/AAASingl-279
92UD/ML-117
92Vanco/ProC-2713
92Vanco/SB-628
93B-471
93F/Final-193
93FExcel/ML-150
93L/GRook-12
93Pinn-580
93Select/RookTr-43T
93StCl/WSox-3
93UD-502DD
93Ultra-528
93WSox-4
94B-18
94D-598
94F-77
94Pac/Cr-121
94Pinn-130
94Pinn/Artist-130
94Pinn/Museum-130
94S-553
94StCl-466
94StCl/1stDay-466
94StCl/Gold-466
94StCl/Team-131
94T-766M
94T/Gold-766M

Bolton, Tom
80Elmira-2
87Pawtu-12
87Pawtu/TCMA-27
88F-346
88Pawtu/CMC-9
88Pawtu/ProC-452
88T-442
89AAA/ProC-17
89D-539
89Pawtu/CMC-1

89Pawtu/Dunkin-15
89Pawtu/ProC-680
89S-531
89T-269
89UD-545
90AAASingl/ProC-425
90Pawtu/ProC-453
90T/TVRSox-38
90UD-351
91B-114
91D-609
91F-87
91Leaf-47
91OPC-37
91Pep/RSox-1
91S-781
91StCl-588
91T-37
91UD-86
91Ultra-28
92F-33
92OPC-708
92RedSox/Dunkin-3
92S-99
92S/RookTr-77T
92StCl-561
92T-708
92T/Gold-708
92T/GoldWin-708
92UD-110
92USPlayC/RedSox-2S
92USPlayC/RedSox-7D
93Pac/Spanish-442
93Tiger/Gator-3
93UD-633
94Pac/Cr-212
94UD/CollC-56
94UD/CollC/Gold-56
94UD/CollC/Silv-56

Bolton, William C.
(Cliff)
34DS-47
34G-65
92Conlon/Sport-505
R313
R314
V355-133

Boltz, Brian
90Foil/Best-87
90Greenvl/Best-7
90Greenvl/ProC-1122
90Greenvl/Star-4

Bomback, Mark
77Holyo
79Vanco-7
81F-323
81OPC-264
81T-567
81T/Tr-739
82D-559
82F-610
82OPC-307
82T-707
83Syrac-5
84Syrac-23
89Pac/SenLg-39
91WIZMets-43

Bombard, Marc
86FSLAS-9CO
87Tampa-8
88Cedar/ProC-1144
88MidwLAS/GS-15
89ElPaso/GS-1
90CedarDG/Best-28MG
90EastLAS/ProC-EL29
90Harris/ProC-1208
90Harris/Star-23
91AA/LineD-124MG
91CaroMud/LineD-124
91CaroMud/ProC-1101
92BuffB/BlueS-2
92BuffB/ProC-338
92BuffB/SB-49MG

Bombard, Rich
82AubAs-13
83DayBe-3
86ColumAst-5
87Cedar-26
88Chatt/Best-5
89Chatt/Best-8
89Chatt/GS-2
91Fayette/ClBest-12
92Lakeland/ClBest-28CO
92Lakeland/ProC-2294CO

Bomgardner, Rich
89Clmbia/Best-25
89Clmbia/GS-3

Bonacquista, Jeff
87Anchora-3

Bonaparte, Elijah
77Spartan
80OkCty
81OkCty/TCMA-3
82Toledo-19
83RochR-19

Bonarigo, Nick
43Centen-2

Bonchek, Jeff
88Burllnd/ProC-1779
89Miami/I/Star-3

Boncore, Steve
82VeroB-13
83VeroB-14

Bond, Daven
86AubAs-4
87Ashvl-6
88Osceola/Star-4
89Osceola/Star-2
90ColMud/Best-14
90ColMud/ProC-1338
90ColMud/Star-5
91ColClip/LineD-102
91ColClip/ProC-589
92Jaxvl/SB-352

Bond, David
87Spokane-16
88Charl/ProC-1196
89CharRain/ProC-993

Bond, Doug
88Billings/ProC-1809

Bond, Michael
91Belling/ClBest-11
91Belling/ProC-3670
92Belling/ClBest-21
92Belling/ProC-1449
92Jacks/ProC-3713

Bond, Thomas Henry
(Tommy)
No Cards.

Bond, Walter F.
(Walt)
60T-552
61T-334
62Salada-208
62Shirriff-208
63T-493
64T-339
65OPC-109
65T-109
65T/E-50
65T/trans-4
66T-431
67T-224

Bonds, Barry
86D/Rook-11
86F/Up-U14
86Sf/Rook-13
86T/Tr-11T
87Classic/Up-113
87D-361
87D/OD-163
87F-604
87F/Hottest-5
87Leaf-219
87OPC-320
87Sf/TPrev-18M
87T-320
87T/Gloss60-30
87T/St-131
87ToysRUs-4
88D-326
88D/Best-17
88F-322
88F/SS-4
88KennerFig-9
88KingB/Disc-11
88Leaf-113
88OPC-267
88Panini/St-376
88RedFoley/St-7
88S-265
88S/YS/II-12
88Sf-119
88T-450
88T/Big-89
88T/St-135
88T/UK-5
89B-426
89Classic-117
89D-92
89D/Best-73
89F-202
89F/Heroes-3
89KennerFig-10
89OPC-263
89Panini/St-172
89RedFoley/St-9
89S-127
89S/HotStar-31
89Sf-146
89T-620
89T/Ames-5
89T/Big-5
89T/LJN-95
89T/St-127
89T/St/Backs-46
89T/UK-5
89UD-440
89VFJuice-24
90B-181
90Classic-82
90Classic/III-68
90D-126
90D/BestNL-45
90F-461
90F/Can-461
90Homer/Pirate-5
90Kenner/Fig-11
90Leaf-91
90MLBPA/Pins-37
90OPC-220
90Panini/St-322
90Publnt/St-149
90RedFoley/St-7
90S-4
90S/100St-53
90S/McDon-11
90Sf-143
90Sunflower-9
90T-220
90T/Big-128
90T/Coins-40
90T/DH-5
90T/Mini-70
90T/St-123
90T/St-9HL
90UD-227
90USPlayC/AS-13D
91B-380SLUG
91B-513
91Bz-1
91Cadaco-5
91Classic/200-195
91Classic/I-81
91Classic/II-T78
91CollAB-26
91Colla/Bonds-Set
91D-495
91D-4DK
91D-762MVP
91D/Elite-E1
91D/GSlam-5
91D/Preview-10
91D/SuperDK-4DK
91F-33
91F-710M
91F/ASIns-5
91F/ProVF-1F
91F/UltraG-1
91JDean-4
91Kenner-5
91KingB/Discs-21
91Leaf-261
91Leaf-364CL
91Leaf/Prev-9
91Leaf/Stud-222
91MajorLg/Pins-57
91MooTown-3
91OPC-401AS
91OPC-570
91OPC/Premier-12
91Panini/FrSt-119
91Panini/St-114
91Panini/Top15-105
91Panini/Top15-12
91Panini/Top15-20
91Panini/Top15-33
91Panini/Top15-43
91Pep/SS-7
91Petro/SU-16
91Post-21
91Post/Can-5
91S-330
91S-668AS
91S-868FRAN
91S-876MVP
91S/100SS-26
91Seven/3DCoin-1F
91Seven/3DCoin-2NE
91Seven/3DCoin-2T
91StCl-220
91StCl/Charter*-3
91T-401AS
91T-570
91T/CJMini/I-19
91T/SU-4
91UD-154
91UD-94
91UD/SilSlug-SS5
91Ultra-275
91Ultra-391EP
91Woolwth/HL-1
92B-590FOIL
92B-60
92CJ/DII-14
92Classic/Game200-155
92Classic/I-16
92Classic/I-xx
92Classic/II-T70
92Colla/ASG-22
92D-243
92D/Preview-2
92DPep/MSA-29
92DennyGS-20
92F-550
92F/ASIns-3
92F/Lumber-L8
92F/Performer-23
92French-7M
92JDean/18-2
92Kenner/Fig-6
92L-275
92L/BlkGold-275
92MSA/Ben-18
92OPC-380
92OPC/Premier-157
92P-15
92Panini-258
92Pinn-500
92Pinn/Slug-4
92Pinn/TeamP-8M
92Pirate/Nation-3
92Post/Can-9
92S-555
92S-777AS
92S/100SS-26
92S/Impact-55
92S/Proctor-15
92StCl-604MC
92StCl-620
92StCl/MPhoto-2
92StCl/MemberIII*-1
92Studio-82
92Studio/Prev-15
92T-380
92T-390AS
92T/Gold-380
92T/Gold-390AS
92T/GoldWin-380
92T/GoldWin-390AS
92T/Kids-21
92T/McDonB-12
92T/MicroG-390
92TripleP-116
92UD-134
92UD-711M
92UD-721DS
92UD/ASFF-14
92UD/HRH-HR21
92UD/TWillB-T2
92UD/TmMVPHolo-11
92USPlayC/Ace-10H
92Ultra-251
92Ultra/AS-16
92Ultra/AwardWin-11
93B-140
93B-702FOIL
93Bleach/Bonds-1
93Bleach/Bonds-2
93Bleach/Bonds-3
93Bleach/Pr-1
93Bleach/Pr-2
93Bleach/Pr-3
93ClBest/MLG-1
93Classic/Gamel-14
93Colla/ASG-2
93Colla/DM-14
93Colla/DMArt-2
93D-678
93D/Elite-31
93D/EliteDom-11
93D/EliteUp-13
93D/MVP-25
93D/Master-14
93Duracel/PPI-17
93F-112
93F-350RT
93F/ASNL-7
93F/Atlantic-2
93F/Final-150
93F/Fruit-6
93Flair-138
93Highland-2
93HumDum/Can-49
93JDean/28-10
93Kenner/Fig-4
93KingB-1
93L-269
93L/GoldAS-16M
93MSA/Metz-2
93Metallic-4
93Mother/Giant-4
93OPC-46
93OPC/Premier-1
93OPC/Premier/StarP-14
93P-15
93Pac/Jugador-21
93Pac/Spanish-607
93Panini-165MVP
93Panini-243
93Pinn-484HH
93Pinn-504
93Pinn/Cooper-15
93Pinn/HRC-4
93Pinn/Slug-6
93Pinn/TP-8
93S-482AW
93S-523AS
93S-560
93Select-1
93Select/ChasS-7
93Select/RookTr-23T
93Select/StatL-29
93Select/StatL-40
93Select/StatL-46
93Select/StatL-52
93StCl-51A
93StCl-51B
93StCl-684
93StCl-747MC
93StCl/1stDay-51A
93StCl/1stDay-51B
93StCl/1stDay-684
93StCl/1stDay-747MC
93StCl/Giant-1
93StCl/MPhoto-25
93StCl/MurphyS-161
93StCl/Ultra-1
93StCl/Ultra-10
93StCl/Ultra-1M
93StCl/Ultra-3
93StCl/Ultra-4
93StCl/Ultra-5
93StCl/Ultra-5M
93StCl/Ultra-7
93StCl/Ultra-8
93Studio-12
93Studio/SS-10
93Studio/Sil-2
93T-2
93T-407
93T/BlkGold-1
93T/Finest-103AS
93T/FinestASJ-103AS
93T/FinestRef-103AS
93T/Gold-2
93T/Gold-407
93T/HolPrev-2
93T/Tr-1T
93TB/Full-3
93TripleP/Gal-GS1
93TripleP/LL-L1
93UD-210M
93UD-476M
93UD-486AW
93UD-567
93UD/Clutch-R3
93UD/Diam-11
93UD/FunPack-100

93UD/FunPack-11HS
93UD/FunPack-222CL
93UD/FunPack-99GS
93UD/FunPackAS-AS7M
93UD/HRH-HR6
93UD/SP-10AS
93UD/SPPlat-PP2
93UD/SeasonHL-HI5
93UD/TCr-TC1
93UDFutHero-56
93USPlayC/Ace-10C
93Ultra-483
93Ultra/AS-6
93Ultra/AwardWin-24
93Ultra/AwardWin-7
93Ultra/HRK-6
93Ultra/Perf-1
94B-135
94D-349
94D/AwardWin-1MVP
94D/AwardWin-4
94D/DK-1
94D/DomI-2
94D/DomII-7
94D/Elite-44
94D/LongBall-9
94D/MVP-14
94D/Pr-1
94D/Pr-1SE
94D/Special-349
94D/Spirit-2
94F-684
94F/AS-31
94F/AwardWin-2
94F/LL-8
94F/Lumber-2
94Finest-230
94Flair-239
94Flair/Outfield-2
94KingB-24
94Kraft-17
94L-264
94L/Gamer-8
94L/GoldS-2
94L/MVPNL-4
94L/PBroker-3
94L/Slide-6
94L/Slide-6
94L/StatStand-2
94OPC-200
94OPC/JAS-3
94Oscar-17
94P-11
94Pac/Cr-540
94Pac/Cr-655MVP
94Pac/Gold-11
94Pac/Silv-28
94Panini-12
94Panini-13
94Panini-261
94Pinn-26
94Pinn/Artist-26
94Pinn/Museum-26
94Pinn/Run-23
94Pinn/TeamP-7M
94Pinn/Trib-8
94RedFoley-29
94S-1
94S-632MVP
94S/Cycle-16M
94S/DT-7
94S/GoldR-1
94S/GoldS-1
94S/HobSam-1
94S/Pr-1
94S/Pr-1GR
94S/Tomb-3
94Select/CrCon-5
94Sf/2000-190AS
94Sf/2000-91
94StCl-238
94StCl-259
94StCl-532DL
94StCl/1stDay-238
94StCl/1stDay-259
94StCl/1stDay-532DL
94StCl/Gold-238
94StCl/Gold-259
94StCl/Gold-532DL
94StCl/Pr-238
94StCl/Team-1
94Studio-83
94Studio/Editor-1
94Studio/Her-1
94Studio/S&GStar-2
94T-390M
94T-605ST
94T-700
94T/BlkGold-27
94T/Gold-390M
94T/Gold-605ST
94T/Gold-700
94T/Prev-2
94TripleP-102
94TripleP/Bomb-4
94TripleP/Medal-12
94TripleP/Pr-3
94UD-280HFA
94UD-38FT
94UD-400
94UD/CollC-311TP
94UD/CollC-313M
94UD/CollC/Gold-311TP
94UD/CollC/Gold-313M
94UD/CollC/Silv-311TP
94UD/CollC/Silv-313M
94UD/CollHR-3
94UD/DColl-W1
94UD/ElecD-280HFA
94UD/ElecD-38FT
94UD/HoloFX-4
94UD/Mantle-3
94UD/SP-90
94Ultra-286
94Ultra/AS-16
94Ultra/AwardWin-15
94Ultra/AwardWin-20MVP
94Ultra/HRK-7
94Ultra/Hit-3
94Ultra/OnBase-2
94Ultra/RBIK-7

Bonds, Bobby Jr.
92Classic/DP-84
92Classic/DPFoil-BC17

Bonds, Bobby Lee
69MB-31
69T-630
70MLB/St-121
70OPC-425
70T-425
71MLB/St-241
71OPC-295
71T-295
71T/Coins-13
71Ticket/Giant-1
72MB-37
72T-711
72T-712A
73K-8
73OPC-145
73T-145
73T/Lids-6
74K-39
74Laugh/ASG-73
74OPC-30
74T-30
74T/Puzzles-4
74T/St-101
75Ho-145
75OPC-55
75SSPC/Puzzle-3
75T-55
75T/M-55
76Ho-18
76Ho/Twink-18
76OPC-2RB
76OPC-380
76SSPC-439
76SSPC/MetsY-Y2
76T-2RB
76T-380
76T/Tr-380T
77BurgChef-124
77OPC-173
77T-570
78Ho-42
78OPC-206
78SSPC/270-140
78T-150
78Wiffle/Discs-6
79OPC-142
79T-285
80BK/PHR-23
80OPC-215
80T-410
81D-71
81F-548
81OPC-223
81T-635
81T/Tr-740
82F-588
82OPC-27
82T-580
84Mother/Giants-12
85Polar/Ind
86OhHenry-CO
87Gator-CO
89Pac/SenLg-128
89T/SenLg-40
89TM/SenLg-10
89TM/SenLg-119M
90EliteSenLg-109
90EliteSenLg-122
91MDA-7
91Swell/Great-11
92AP/ASG-62
92UD/ASFF-53
92UD/HeroHL-HI1
92Yank/WIZ70-23
92Yank/WIZAS-4
93B-702FOIL
93L/UpGoldAS-7M
93Mother/Giant-28M
93Rang/Keeb-78
93TWill-51

Bone, George D.
No Cards.

Bone, Pat
82Oneonta-10

Bones, Ricardo
(Ricky)
86Cram/NWL-163
87CharRain-21
88CalLgAS-41
88River/Cal-208
88River/ProC-1426
89AubAs/ProC-16
89Wichita/Rock-10
89Wichita/Rock/HL-2
90TexLgAS/GS-12
90Wichita/Rock-2
91AAA/LineD-278
91B-643
91LasVegas/LineD-278
91LasVegas/ProC-226
92Classic/Game200-60
92Classic/II-T11
92D-545
92F-600
92L-500
92L/BlkGold-500
92OPC-711
92Pol/Brew-4
92S-758
92StCl-109
92Studio-192
92T-711
92T/91Debut-17
92T/Gold-711
92T/GoldWin-711
92T/Tr-13T
92T/TrGold-13T
92UD-623
92UD-762
92Ultra-378
93D-413
93F-247
93L-122
93OPC-33
93Pac/Beisbol-9
93Pac/Spanish-508
93Pinn-393
93Pol/Brew-2
93S-470
93StCl-225
93StCl/1stDay-225
93T-71
93T/Gold-71
93UD-328
93Ultra-568
94D-59
94F-174
94Finest-293
94Flair-63
94L-222
94Pac/Cr-326
94Pinn-123
94Pinn/Artist-123
94Pinn/Museum-123
94Pol/Brew-2
94S-236
94S/GoldR-236
94StCl-398
94StCl/1stDay-398
94StCl/Gold-398
94Studio-42
94T-367
94T/Gold-367
94TripleP-51
94UD/CollC-57
94UD/CollC/Gold-57
94UD/CollC/Silv-57
94UD/SP-56
94Ultra-370

Bonetti, Julio
93Conlon-965

Bongiovanni, Anthony
(Nino)
W711/1

Bonham, Bill
72OPC-29
72T-29
73OPC-328
73T-328
74OPC-528
74T-528
75OPC-85
75T-85
75T/M-85
76OPC-151
76SSPC-303
76T-151
77BurgChef-192
77OPC-95
77T-446
78Pep-5
78SSPC/270-112
78T-276
79K-31
79OPC-182
79T-354
80OPC-26
80T-47
81F-215
81Indianap-13
81T-712
86AubAs-5CO

Bonham, Ernie
(Tiny)
43MP-1
44Yank/St-1
47TipTop
49B-77
49Eureka-154
92Yank/WIZAS-5

Boni, Joel
82Madis/Frit-2

Bonifay, Ken
92Augusta/ClBest-18
92Salem/ProC-70

Bonikowski, Joe
61Clover-4
62T-592R

Bonilla, Bobby
83AlexD-16
86Coke/WS-26
86D/Rook-30
86F/Up-U15
86Sf/Rook-26
86T/Tr-12T
87D-558
87D/OD-167
87F-605
87Sf/TPrev-18M
87T-184
88Classic/Blue-236
88D-238
88D/Best-33
88F-323
88F/BB/AS-3
88F/Hottest-3
88F/Mini-103
88F/Slug-3
88F/St-114
88Grenada-62
88KennerFig-10
88Leaf-188
88OPC-189
88Panini/St-372
88S-116
88S/YS/II-9
88Sf-131
88T-681
88T/Big-25
88T/Coins-37
88T/St-129
89B-422
89Cadaco-3
89D-151
89D-2DK
89D/AS-39
89D/Best-33
89D/DKsuper-2DK
89D/PopUp-39
89F-203
89F-637M
89F/AS-1
89F/BBAS-4
89KennerFig-11
89Nissen-15
89OPC-142
89Panini/St-171
89Panini/St-234AS
89RedFoley/St-10
89S-195
89S/HotStar-42
89Sf-182
89T-388AS
89T-440
89T/Big-159
89T/Coins-5
89T/DH-15
89T/Gloss22-15
89T/Gloss60-24
89T/LJN-127
89T/Mini-30
89T/St-131
89T/St-158
89T/St/Backs-40
89T/UK-6
89UD-578
89VFJuice-25
90B-169
90Classic-143
90Classic/III-73
90D-290
90D/BestNL-70
90D/Bon/MVP-BC16
90F-462
90F/BB-2
90F/BBMVP-4
90F/Can-462
90Homer/Pirate-6
90HotPlay/St-3
90Kenner/Fig-12
90KingB/Discs-8
90Leaf-196
90Leaf/Prev-10
90MCA/Disc-11
90MLBPA/Pins-38
90OPC-273
90Panini/St-325
90PublInt/St-150
90PublInt/St-253
90S-170
90S/100St-37
90Sf-195
90Starline/LJS-31
90Starline/LJS-5
90T-273
90T/Big-208
90T/Coins-41
90T/DH-6
90T/Mini-71
90T/St-129
90T/TVAS-59
90Tetley/Discs-11
90UD-16TC
90UD-366
90USPlayC/AS-11H
91B-381SLUG
91B-525
91Cadaco-6
91Classic/200-144
91Classic/II-T92
91Classic/III-T4
91Classic/III-xx
91D-325
91D/GSlam-2
91DennyGS-17
91F-34
91F-711M
91Kenner-6
91Leaf-357
91Leaf/Stud-223
91OPC-403AS
91OPC-750
91Panini/FrSt-120
91Panini/St-111
91Panini/Top15-18

91Panini/Top15-50
91Pep/SS-15
91Post-14
91RedFoley/St-10
91S-315
91S-402MB
91S-670AS
91S/100SS-42
91StCl-139
91Sunflower-3
91T-403AS
91T-750
91T/CJMini/II-15
91T/SU-5
91UD-152
91UD/FinalEd-99F
91UD/SilSlug-SS15
91USPlayC/AS-JK
91Ultra-276
92B-235
92CJ/DII-18
92Classic/Game200-176
92Classic/II-T47
92D-427AS
92D-610
92D/Up-U20
92F-551
92F-699M
92F/ASIns-4
92F/TmLIns-9
92F/Up-101
92JDean/18-16
92Kenner/Fig-7
92KingB-5
92L-308
92L-463M
92L/BlkGold-308
92L/BlkGold-463M
92MSA/Ben-20
92Mets/Kahn-25
92OPC-160
92OPC/Premier-143
92P-21
92Panini-256
92Pinn-310SH
92Pinn-395
92Pinn/Slug-6
92Rem/Pr-P1
92Rem/Pr-P16M
92Rem/Pr-P17
92Rem/Pr-P18M
92Rem/Pr-P2
92Rem/Pr-P20M
92Rem/Pr-P3
92S-225
92S/100SS-80
92S/RookTr-5T
92StCl-608MC
92StCl-780
92StCl/Dome-19
92Studio-61
92Sunflower-16
92T-160
92T-392AS
92T/Gold-160
92T/Gold-392AS
92T/GoldWin-160
92T/GoldWin-392AS
92T/Kids-22
92T/McDonB-9
92T/Tr-14T
92T/TrGold-14T
92TripleP/Gal-GS1
92UD-225
92UD-755
92UD/ASFF-15
92Ultra-527
93B-158
93Classic/GameI-15
93Colla/DM-15
93D-594
93F-84
93F/Atlantic-3
93Flair-89
93Ho-3
93HumDum/Can-43
93Kraft-16
93L-236
93MSA/Metz-3
93Mets/Kahn-25
93OPC-15
93P-24
93Pac/Jugador-22
93Pac/Spanish-192
93Pac/SpanishGold-2
93Panini-253
93Pinn-43
93Pinn/HRC-41
93Post/Can-12
93S-8
93S/Franchise-21
93Select-11
93StCl-163
93StCl/1stDay-163
93Studio-16
93T-52
93T/Finest-66
93T/FinestRef-66
93T/Gold-52
93T/PreProd-2
93TripleP-173
93TripleP/Act-2
93UD-275
93UD-484M
93UD-826TC
93UD/FunPack-124
93UD/HRH-HR23
93UD/SP-146
93Ultra-422
94B-128
94D-347
94D/DK-13
94D/MVP-9
94D/Special-347
94F-558
94F/AS-32
94F/TL-23
94Finest-234
94Kraft-18
94L-31
94L/Clean-4
94OPC-202
94Oscar-18
94P-10
94Pac/AllLat-6
94Pac/Cr-396
94Pac/Gold-17
94Panini-215
94Pinn-33
94Pinn/Artist-33
94Pinn/Museum-33
94RedFoley-6
94S-378
94S/GoldS-26
94S/Tomb-4
94Sf/2000-49
94StCl-59
94StCl/1stDay-59
94StCl/Gold-59
94Studio-113
94T-730
94T/Gold-730
94TripleP-141
94UD-275HFA
94UD-344
94UD/CollC-58
94UD/CollC/Gold-58
94UD/CollC/Silv-58
94UD/CollHR-4
94UD/ElecD-275HFA
94UD/SP-115
94Ultra-528

Bonilla, George
85Everett/Cram-2A
85Everett/Cram-2B
86Clinton-3
88Shrev/ProC-1289
89Shrev/ProC-1855
90AAASingl/ProC-28
90Phoenix/CMC-4
90Phoenix/ProC-2
90ProC/Singl-531

Bonilla, Juan G.
78Watlo
80Tacoma-19
82D-220
82F-567
82T-464
83D-346
83F-353
83T-563
84D-234
84F-295
84Nes/792-168
84OPC-168
84T-168
84T/St-152
85Colum-26
85IntLgAS-26
86T/Tr-13T
87F-464
87OPC-131
87T-668
88Chatt/Team-2
91Crown/Orio-40
92Yank/WIZ80-14

Bonilla, Miguel
92Welland/ClBest-2
92Welland/ProC-1314

Bonin, Ernest Luther
(Luther)
No Cards

Bonin, Greg
88TM/Umpire-56
89TM/Umpire-54
90TM/Umpire-52

Bonine, Eddie
83Tucson-1
84Cram/PCL-64
85Cram/PCL-70
90Gate/ProC-3363CO
90Gate/SportP-22CO

Bonitto, Arturo
77QuadC

Bonk, Thomas
85Greens-5

Bonneau, Rob
88Wythe/ProC-1976

Bonnell, Robert Barry
(Barry)
78Ho-142
78T-242
79T-496
80OPC-331
80T-632
81D-272
81F-413
81OPC-82
81OPC/Post-19
81T-558
82D-432
82F-611
82OPC-99
82T-99
82T/St-251
82T/StVar-251
83D-430
83F-425
83F/St-27M
83OPC-281
83OPC/St-133
83T-766
83T/St-133
84D-559
84F-149
84F/X-14
84Mother/Mar-2
84Nes/792-302
84OPC-302
84T-302
84T/St-370
84T/Tr-14
85D-191
85F-485
85Leaf-195
85Mother/Mar-10
85OPC-107
85T-423
85T/St-342
86F-460
86Mother/Mar-10
86OPC-119
86T-119
91Pac/SenLg-123
92Nabisco-6

Bonner, Frank J.
No Cards.

Bonner, Jeffry
(Jeff)
89Clinton/ProC-892
90Clinton/Best-5
90Clinton/ProC-2560
91ClBest/Singl-76
91SanJose/ClBest-9
91SanJose/ProC-22

Bonner, Mark
82Danvl/Frit-25
83Redwd-4
85MidldA-5

Bonner, Robert A.
(Bob)
80RochR-1
81RochR-2
82D-610
82T-21R
83F-53
83RochR-14
84RochR-13
91Crown/Orio-41

Bonnici, James
92Belling/ClBest-18
92Belling/ProC-1446
93River/Cal-4

Bonura, Henry John
(Zeke)
34DS-65
35BU-141
35BU-65
35Exh/4-10
35G-8B
35G-9B
36Exh/4-10
36G
37Exh/4-10
37OPC-116
37Wheat
38G-252
38G-276
38Wheat
39PlayBall-144
40PlayBall-131
88Conlon/5-4
91Conlon/Sport-237
93Conlon-738
R312/M
R313
R314
V300
V351A-3
V351B-5
V355-112
WG8-3

Bonura, Tony
86Cram/NWL-93

Booe, Everitt Little
No Cards.

Booker, Eric
90A&AASingle/ProC-168
90SoOreg/Best-10
90SoOreg/ProC-3429
91ClBest/Singl-286
91Modesto/ClBest-16
91Modesto/ProC-3101
92ClBest-34
92Madis/ClBest-11
92Madis/ProC-1248
92Modesto/ClBest-9

Booker, Greg
83LasVegas/BHN-1
84Cram/PCL-218
85F-27
85Mother/Padres-22
85T-262
86LasVegas-2
86T-429
87T/Tr-6T
88Coke/Padres-51
88D-311
88F-577
88S-447
88Smok/Padres-4
88T-727
89S-417
89T-319
89T/Big-194
89UD-641
90AAASingl/ProC-29
90Phoenix/CMC-9
90Phoenix/ProC-3
90ProC/Singl-536
90PublInt/St-44
93Kinston/Team-30CO

Booker, Kevin
92Hunting/ClBest-8
92Hunting/ProC-3160

Booker, Richard Lee
(Buddy)
No Cards.

Booker, Rod
82OrlanTw/A-1
82Toledo-12
83ArkTr-19
84Louisvl-12
86ArkTr-2
86Louisvl-7
87F/Up-U7
87Louisvl-6
88Louisvl-10
88T-483
89Louisvl-11
89Louisvl/CMC-8
89Louisvl/ProC-1264
89T/Big-256
89UD-644
90Phill/TastyK-2
91F-388
91OPC-186
91Phill/Medford-5
91T-186
92Tucson/ProC-493
92Tucson/SB-602

Bool, Albert
(Al)
No Cards.

Boom, Walter
93Conlon-734

Boone, Antonio
91Hamil/ClBest-13
91Hamil/ProC-4028
92Hamil/ClBest-9
92Hamil/ProC-1580

Boone, Bret
88Alaska/Team-3
91AA/LineD-330
91B-261
91Jaxvl/LineD-330
91Jaxvl/ProC-155
92AAA/ASG/SB-55
92B-511
92Calgary/ProC-3740
92Calgary/SB-55
92D/RookPhen-BC2
92F/Up-54
92L/GRook-12
92ProC/Tomorrow-142
92S/RookTr-104T
92Sky/AAASingl-24
92StCl/MemberII-1
92UD-771DD
93B-219
93D-188RR
93F-304
93L-546
93OPC-13
93Pac/Spanish-280
93Pinn-243
93Pinn/RookTP-5M
93Pinn/Team2001-8
93S-335
93S/Proctor-3
93Select-326
93Select/ChasRook-21
93Select/RookTr-58T
93StCl-532
93StCl/1stDay-532
93StCl/Mar-6
93T-808
93T/Gold-808
93ToysRUs-35
93TripleP-133
93UD-65
93UD/SeasonHL-HI6
93Ultra-266
94B-458
94D-413
94F-280
94Finest-386
94Flair-143
94L-233
94OPC-170
94Panini-116
94Pinn-510
94S-568
94Studio-167
94T-659
94T/Gold-659
94UD-448
94UD/CollC-59
94UD/CollC/Gold-59
94UD/CollC/Silv-59
94UD/SP-158
94Ultra-468

Boone, Danny
79SLCity-23
82D-187
82F-568
82T-407
83Tucson-2
84Cram/PCL-36
85Anchora-5

90AAASingl/ProC-455
90ElPasoATG/Team-38
90ProC/Singl-689
90RochR/CMC-27
90RochR/ProC-698
90Rochester/L&U-15
91Crown/Orio-42
91Pac/SenLg-44
91S-715RP

Boone, Isaac Morgan
(Ike)
87Conlon/2-24
88LitSun/Minor-3
90Target-61
R314/Can

Boone, Lute Joseph
(Luke)
D350/2-12
M101/5-12

Boone, Raymond Otis
(Ray)
50NumNum
51B-54
51T/RB-23
52B-214
52NumNum-13
52T-55
53B/Col-79
53T-25
54T-77
55RFG-11
55RM-AL1
55T-65
55T/DH-113
55W605-11
56T-6
56T/Hocus-A7
56T/Hocus-B9
56T/Pin-36
57T-102
58T-185
59T-252
60Lake
60T-281
76OPC-67FS
76T-67FS
79TCMA-179
81Tiger/Detroit-84
83Kaline-15M
85T-133FS
91T/Arc53-25
92Bz/Quadra-6M
93TWill-36
93UD/ATH-15
94T/Arc54-77

Boone, Robert Raymond
(Bob)
73OPC-613R
73T-613R
74JP
74OPC-131
74T-131
74T/St-71
75OPC-351
75T-351
75T/M-351
76OPC-318
76OPC-67FS
76SSPC-471
76T-318
76T-67M
77BurgChef-164
77OPC-68
77T-545
78Ho-29
78OPC-141
78SSPC/270-33
78T-161
79BK/P-2
79Ho-113
79OPC-38
79T-90
80BK/P-2
80OPC-246
80T-470
81Coke
81D-262
81F-4
81F/St-79
81OPC-290
81T-290
81T/HT
81T/St-203
82D-471
82F-240
82OPC-23
82OPC-392IA
82T-615
82T-616A
82T/St-77
82T/StVar-77
82T/Tr-9T
83D-192
83F-79
83F/St-12M
83F/St-5M
83OPC-366
83OPC/St-45
83T-765
83T/St-45
84D-158
84F-509
84F-637
84Nes/792-520
84OPC-174
84Smok/Cal-3
84T-520
84T/St-234
85D-230
85F-295
85OPC-348
85Smok/Cal-3
85T-133FS
85T-348
85T/St-228
86D-17
86D-230
86D/DKsuper-17
86F-149
86Leaf-17DK
86OPC-62
86Smok/Cal-3
86T-62
86T/St-179
87D-233
87D/HL-41
87F-73
87F/AwardWin-4
87Leaf-202
87OPC-166
87T-166
87T/St-180
88AlaskaAS60/Team-10
88D-305
88D/Best-3
88F-485
88Leaf-151
88OPC-158
88OPC-D
88Panini/St-39
88S-63
88Sf-212
88Smok/Angels-9
88T-498
88T/Big-30
88T/St-182
88T/St-5
88T/UK-6
88T/WaxBox-D
89B-119
89Classic/Up/2-187
89D-170
89D/Best-263
89D/Tr-5
89F-469
89F/Up-36
89OPC-243
89Panini/St-287
89S-233
89S/HotStar-81
89S/Tr-74
89Sf-40
89Smok/Angels-17
89T-243
89T-404AS
89T/Big-269
89T/LJN-48
89T/St-175
89T/St/Backs-22
89T/Tr-12T
89UD-119
89UD/Ext-767
90B-373
90D-326
90D/BestAL-50
90F-102
90F/AwardWin-5
90F/Can-102
90Leaf-46
90MLBPA/Pins-107
90OPC-671
90PublInt/St-278
90PublInt/St-343
90S-60
90Sf-40
90T-671
90T/Big-268
90UD-271
91D-356
91F-551
91UD-502
92Tacoma/SB-549MG
94TedW-72

Boone, Ron
75Iowa/TCMA-2

Bootay, Kevin
86Salem-1
86Tulsa-16
88TexLgAS/GS-9
88Tulsa-13
89ScranWB/CMC-24
89ScranWB/ProC-713

Booth, Amos Smith
No Cards.

Booth, David
88Pocatel/ProC-2098
89SanJose/Best-10
89SanJose/Cal-228
89SanJose/ProC-440
89SanJose/Star-2

Booth, Edward H.
(Eddie)
No Cards.

Boothby, John
90Wausau/Star-4
91Brisbane/Fut-12

Boozer, John
63T-29R
64PhilBull-5
64T-16
65OPC-184
65T-184
66T-324
68OPC-173
68T-173
69T-599
89Chatt/II/Team-3

Boras, Scott
77StPete

Borbon, Ernie
82VeroB-2
83Albuq-21
84Cram/PCL-159

Borbon, Pedro Jr.
90A&AASingle/ProC-124
90BurlB/Best-1
90BurlB/ProC-2340
90BurlB/Star-4
90Durham/UpHer-2
90Foil/Best-31
90MidwLgAS/GS-58
91Durham/ClBest-10
91Durham/ProC-1536
92Greenvl/ProC-1148
92Greenvl/SB-229
93B-226
93LimeR/Winter-45
93Richm/Bleach-11
93Richm/Pep-5
93Richm/Team-7
94StCl-233
94StCl/1stDay-233
94StCl/Gold-233
94StCl/Team-42

Borbon, Pedro
70OPC-358
70T-358
71OPC-613
71T-613
73OPC-492
73T-492
74OPC-410
74T-410
74T/St-23
75OPC-157
75T-157
75T/M-157
76OPC-77
76SSPC-24
76T-77
77Pep-54
77T-581
78OPC-199
78Pep-6
78SSPC/270-111
78T-220
79OPC-164
79T-326
80T-627
89Pac/SenLg-49
89T/SenLg-77
89TM/SenLg-11
90EliteSenLg-93

Borcherding, Mark
89Billings/ProC-2066
90Cedar/Best-24
90CharWh/ProC-2232
91Cedar/ClBest-2
91Cedar/ProC-2710
91ClBest/Singl-372
91MidwLAS/ProC-21

Borchers, Rick
79Tacoma-3
80Tacoma-21
81Chatt-18
82Chatt-20

Borchert, Shane
89Clinton/ProC-889
90Madison/Best-27TR
91Madison/ClBest-21
92Reno/Cal-62TR

Bordagaray, Stanley
(Frenchy)
36Exh/4-2
36G-3
39PlayBall-75
90Target-62
R312/M
R314
W711/1

Border, Bob
80ElPaso-10

Border, Mark
82Idaho-3

Borders, Charlie
75Spokane/Caruso-4

Borders, Pat
85Kingst-15
86Knoxvl-3
87Knoxvl-20
88D/Rook-12
88F/Up-U65
88S/Tr-99T
88T/Tr-17T
88Tor/Fire-10
89D-560
89F-227
89OPC-343
89Panini/St-464
89S-325
89S/HotRook-91
89S/YS/I-11
89T-693
89T/St-191
89Tor/Fire-10
89UD-593
90B-521
90Classic/III-39
90D-560
90F-77
90F/Can-77
90Leaf-343
90OPC-191
90Panini/St-175
90PublInt/St-510
90S-288
90Sf-45
90T-191
90T/Big-60
90Tor/BJ-10
90UD-112
91B-14
91D-317
91F-171
91Leaf-23
91OPC-49A
91OPC-49B
91Panini/FrSt-335
91Panini/St-156
91S-425
91S/ToroBJ-11
91StCl-266
91T-49A
91T-49B
91Tor/Fire-10
91UD-147
91Ultra-359
92B-646
92BJ/Fire-4
92D-379
92F-325
92L-324
92L/BlkGold-324
92OPC-563
92Panini-24
92Pinn-421
92S-288
92StCl-77
92StCl/MemberIII*-2
92Studio-253
92T-563
92T/Gold-563
92T/GoldWin-563
92UD-140
92Ultra-144
93B-687
93BJ/D/45-4
93BJ/D/McDon-11
93BJ/D/McDon-25
93BJ/D/McDon-34
93BJ/D/WS-8
93BJ/Demp-21
93BJ/Fire-3
93Colla/DM-16
93D-115
93F-332
93Flair-288
93HumDum/Can-23
93L-157
93OPC-58
93OPC/WC-2
93OPC/WSHero-1
93Pac/Spanish-321
93Panini-25
93Pinn-203
93Post/Can-1
93S-642
93Select-369
93StCl-1
93StCl/1stDay-1
93StCl/MurphyS-136
93Studio-36
93T-322
93T/Finest-133
93T/FinestRef-133
93T/Gold-322
93TripleP-134
93UD-149
93UD/SP-46
93Ultra-287
93Ultra/AwardWin-21
94B-441
94D-54
94F-325
94Finest-266
94L-179
94OPC-178
94OPC/BJ-8
94Pac/Cr-633
94Panini-135
94Pinn-477
94S-343
94Select-74
94StCl-305
94StCl/1stDay-305
94StCl/Gold-305
94StCl/Team-165
94Studio-25
94T-219
94T/Gold-219
94UD-417
94UD/CollC-60
94UD/CollC/Gold-60
94UD/CollC/Silv-60
94Ultra-135

Bordi, Rich
81Tacoma-10
82SLCity-4
82T-531R
83Iowa-1
84SevenUp-42
85D-289
85F-49
85F/Up-U8
85Leaf-166
85T-357
85T/Tr-7T
86D-518
86F-101
86F/Up-U16

86T-94
86T/Tr-14T
87Colum-22
87Colum/Pol-3
87Colum/TCMA-2
87D-213
87F-465
87T-638
88Tacoma/CMC-1
88Tacoma/ProC-627
89Tacoma/CMC-1
89Tacoma/ProC-1544
90AAASingl/ProC-30
90Phoenix/ProC-4
91Crown/Orio-43
92Yank/WIZ80-15
Bordick, Michael
(Mike)
87Modesto-6
88Huntsvl/BK-1
88SLAS-4
89Tacoma/CMC-23
89Tacoma/ProC-1565
90AAASingl/ProC-145
90Tacoma/ProC-98
91AAA/LineD-527
91Classic/II-T58
91S-339RP
91T/90Debut-19
91Tacoma/LineD-527
92B-350
92D-505
92F-251
92L-364
92L/BlkGold-364
92Mother/A's-20
92OPC-317
92OPC/Premier-5
92Pinn-462
92S-681
92StCl-272
92T-317
92T/Gold-317
92T/GoldWin-317
92UD-727
92Ultra-419
93B-401
93Classic/Gamel-16
93D-264M
93D-83
93D/Spirit-SG1
93F-291
93Flair-256
93L-117
93Mother/A's-7
93OPC-57
93Pac/Spanish-217
93Panini-16
93Pinn-85
93S-100
93Select-208
93StCl-80
93StCl/1stDay-80
93StCl/A's-18
93T-639
93T/Gold-639
93ToysRUs-3
93TripleP-45
93TripleP-64M
93UD-189
93UD/SP-37
93Ultra-254
94B-576
94D-81
94F-255
94Flair-89
94L-128
94OPC-264
94Pac/Cr-446
94Panini-107
94Pinn-463
94S-491
94Select-176
94StCl-227
94StCl/1stDay-227
94StCl/Gold-227
94T-188
94T/Finest-81
94T/FinestRef-81
94T/Gold-188
94TripleP-1
94UD-174
94UD/CollC-61
94UD/CollC/Gold-61
94UD/CollC/Silv-61
94UD/ElecD-174
94Ultra-105
Bordley, Bill
79Phoenix
Borg, Gary
86Visalia-4
87OrlanTw-16
88OrlanTw/Best-12
89AS/Cal-34
89Stockton/Best-18
89Stockton/Cal-164
89Stockton/ProC-396
89Stockton/Star-1
Borgatti, Mike
87Hagers-1
88Virgini/Star-2
89Watlo/ProC-1793
89Watlo/Star-1
90Hagers/Best-19
90Hagers/ProC-1402
90Hagers/Star-2
Borges, George
83MidldC-15
84PrWill-33
Borges, Jose
89Butte/SP-9
Borgese, Jeff
88CapeCod/Sum-20
90A&AASingle/ProC-194
90Martins/ProC-3201
Borgmann, Bennie
40Hughes-5
Borgmann, Glenn D.
73OPC-284
73T-284
74OPC-547
74T-547
75OPC-127
75T-127
75T/M-127
76OPC-498
76SSPC-213
76T-498
77T-87
78T-307
78Twin/FriszP-2
79T-431
79Twin/FriszP-2
80T-634
81D-159
81T-716
Borgogno, Mate
88NE-19
89Alaska/Team-17
90ClintUp/Team-U1
90Everett/Best-16
90Everett/ProC-3132
91Clinton/ClBest-11
91Clinton/ProC-839
Borhinger, Helms
90Yakima/Team-4
Boris, Paul
81Colum-7
83T-266
83Toledo-1
84Richm-4
Bork, Frank
65T-592
66OPC-123R
66T-123R
Borkowski, Robert V.
(Bob)
52T-328
53T-7
54T-138
55T-74
55T/DH-63
91T/Arc53-7
94T/Arc54-138
Borland, Scott
83AlexD-4
84PrWill-18
85PrWill-15
Borland, Toby
88Martins/Star-4
89Spartan/ProC-1037
89Spartan/Star-2
90Clearw/Star-2
90Star/ISingl-70
91AA/LineD-502
91ClBest/Singl-336
91Reading/LineD-502
91Reading/ProC-1363
92ScranWB/ProC-2440
92ScranWB/SB-479
92Sky/AAASingl-217
92UD/ML-239
Borland, Tom
60L-26
60T-117
61T-419
89Smok/Ast-6
Borman, Dave
89Utica/Pucko-9
Bormann, Mike
83Durham-16
85Durham-4
Borom, Edward Jones
(Red)
No Cards.
Boros, Stephen
(Steve)
58T-81
59T-331
61T-348
61T/St-146
62J-16
62P-16
62P/Can-16
62Salada-50
62Shirriff-50
62T-62
62T-72M
62T/St-42
63J-47
63P-47
63T-532
65OPC-102
65T-102
78TCMA-88
83Granny-14MG
83T/X-13MG
84Mother/A's-1MG
84Nes/792-531MG
84T-531
86T/Tr-15T
87T-143MG
93Pol/Royal-27CO
Boroski, Stan
83Beloit/Frit-28
86FtMyr-4
87FtMyr-2
Borowicz, Ray
88BurlInd/ProC-1801
Borowski, Joe
91Kane/ClBest-2
91Kane/ProC-2652
91Kane/Team-3
92Freder/ClBest-23
92Freder/ProC-1798
Borowski, Rich
83Idaho-20
84Madis/Pol-23
Borowsky, Erez
83Visalia/Frit-15
84Visalia-3
85OrlanTw-2
Borowy, Henry
(Hank)
39Exh
44Yank/St-2
49B-134
49Eureka-131
49Lummis
50B-177
51B-250
92Yank/WIZAS-6
Borrelli, Dean
88SoOreg/ProC-1705
89Madis/Star-4
90Modesto/Cal-164
90Modesto/Chong-1
90Modesto/ProC-2214
91AA/LineD-278
91Huntsvl/ClBest-3
91Huntsvl/LineD-278
91Huntsvl/Team-2
91HuntsvlProC-1798
92Huntsvl/ProC-3952
92Huntsvl/SB-304
Borriello, Sebby
82Wisco/Frit-13
Borruel, Jeff
78Cedar
Borski, Jeff
91Belling/ClBest-23
91Belling/ProC-3655
91ClBest/Singl-448
92Jacks/ProC-3700
92SanBern/ClBest-7
92SanBern/ProC-
93River/Cal-5
Borton, William Baker
(Babe)
No Cards.
Borucki, Ray
80Penin/B-19
80Penin/C-25
Borzello, Aaire
91Johnson/ClBest-3
Bosarge, Scott
91Belling/ClBest-15
91Belling/ProC-3667
Bosch, Donald John
(Don)
68T-572
69Fud's-3
69T-578
70OPC-527
70T-527
72MB-38
91WIZMets-44
Bosco, Joseph
90Peoria/Team-37ATHR
Bosco, Mike
89Reno/Cal-253
Bosetti, Richard Alan
(Rick)
76OkCty/Team-5
78T-710R
79BJ/Bubble-2
79OPC-279
79T-542
80OPC-146
80T-277
80T/S-51
80T/Super-51
81D-152
81OPC-46
81OPC/Post-18
81T-46
81T/Tr-741
82D-626
82F-88
82T-392
82Tacoma-33
92Nabisco-16
Bosio, Chris
83Beloit/Frit-27
86Vanco-4
87D-478
87D/Rook-20
87F-338
87Pol/Brew-29
87Sf/Rook-2
87T-448
88D-117
88D/Best-295
88F-156
88OPC-137
88Pol/Brew-29
88S-38
88S/YS/I-4
88T-137
89B-134
89Brewer/YB-29
89D-412
89D/Best-109
89F-179
89Pol/Brew-29
89RedFoley/St-11
89S-243
89T-311
89UD-292
90B-389
90Brewer/MillB-1
90Classic/III-42
90D-20DK
90D-57
90D/BestAL-9
90D/SuperDK-20DK
90ElPasoATG/Team-2
90F-316
90F/Can-316
90Kenner/Fig-13
90Leaf-26
90OPC-597
90Panini/St-99
90Pol/Brew-29
90PublInt/St-490
90RedFoley/St-8
90S-283
90Sf-25
90T-597
90T/Big-139
90T/Mini-19
90T/St-205
90UD-293
91B-43
91Brewer/MillB-4
91D-160
91F-576
91Leaf-518
91OPC-217
91Pol/Brew-3
91S-43
91StCl-164
91T-217
91UD-529
92D-471
92L-266
92L/BlkGold-266
92OPC-638
92Panini-42
92Pinn-367
92Pol/Brew-5
92S-37
92StCl-578
92T-638
92T/Gold-638
92T/GoldWin-638
92UD-615
92Ultra-379
93B-191
93D-499
93F-628
93F/Final-265
93Flair-267
93L-255
93MSA/Ben-2
93Mar/DQ-3
93Mother/Mar-20
93OPC-60
93OPC/Premier-3
93Pac/Spanish-619
93Pinn-440
93S-616
93Select/RookTr-108T
93StCl-79
93StCl/1stDay-79
93StCl/Mar-28
93Studio-14
93T-775
93T/Finest-140
93T/FinestRef-140
93T/Gold-775
93T/Tr-28T
93UD-588
93Ultra-614
94B-613
94D-546
94F-281
94F/GoldM-10
94Finest-252
94Flair-99
94L-9
94OPC-134
94Pac/Cr-563
94Pinn-372
94S-264
94S-316
94S/GoldR-264
94S/GoldR-316
94StCl-103
94StCl/1stDay-103
94StCl/Gold-103
94T-60
94T/Gold-60
94TripleP-124
94UD-228
94UD/ElecD-228
94UD/SP-103
94Ultra-417
Boskie, Shawn
87Peoria-8
89CharlK-17
90AAASingl/ProC-619
90Classic/III-43
90Cub/Mara-3
90D/Learning-31
90D/Rook-18
90F/Up-U7
90Iowa/CMC-1
90Iowa/ProC-312
90Leaf-519

90Peoria/Team-20M
90ProC/Singl-76
90S/Tr-94T
90T/TVCub-39
90T/Tr-10T
90UD/Ext-722
91Cub/Mara-47
91Cub/Vine-6
91D-241
91F-416
91Leaf-221
91Leaf/Stud-152
91OPC-254
91S-59
91S/100RisSt-4
91StCl-521
91T-254
91T/90Debut-20
91UD-471
92Cub/Mara-47
92F-377
92L-162
92L/BlkGold-162
92OPC-229
92Pinn-527
92S-713
92StCl-284
92T-229
92T/Gold-229
92T/GoldWin-229
92TripleP-246
92USPlayC/Cub-2D
92USPlayC/Cub-6C
92Ultra-466
93D-500
93F-373
93StCl-583
93StCl/1stDay-583
93T-563
93T/Gold-563
94D-61
94F-380
94Pac/Cr-95
94StCl/Team-353
94T-177
94T/Gold-177

Bosley, Rich
86Beloit-2

Bosley, Thaddis
(Thad)
75QuadC
77SLCity
78SSPC/270-141
78T-619
79T-127
80T-412
81D-162
81F-353
82T-350
83Thorn-20
84Iowa-7
84Nes/792-657
84SevenUp-27
84T-657
85D-388
85SevenUp-27
85T-432
86Cub/Unocal-2
86D-483
86F-361
86Gator-27
86T-512
87D-191
87F-555
87F/Up-U8
87T-58
87T/Tr-7T
88D-348
88F-253
88T-247
89UD-591
90Mother/Rang-16
93Rang/Keeb-79

Bosman, Dick
67T-459R
68T-442
69T-607
70MLB/St-278
70OPC-175
70OPC-68LL
70Pol/SenY-1
70T-175
70T-68LL
70T/S-22
70T/SO
70T/Super-22
71MLB/St-530
71OPC-60
71Pol/SenP-1
71T-60
71T/Coins-70
71T/GM-49
71T/Greatest-49
71T/S-7
71T/Super-7
71T/tatt-1
72MB-39
72OPC-365
72T-365
73OPC-640
73T-640
73T/Lids-7
74OPC-465
74T-465
75Ho-114
75OPC-354
75OPC-7M
75T-354
75T-7M
75T/M-354
75T/M-7M
76OPC-298
76SSPC-483
76T-298
77T-101
86BuffB-2CO
89RochR/CMC-24CO
89RochR/ProC-1641CO
89Swell-124
90AAASingl/ProC-478
90EliteSenLg-3
90ProC/Singl-681CO
90RochR/CMC-26CO
90RochR/ProC-721CO
90Rochester/L&U-35CO
91AAA/LineD-475M
91RochR/LineD-475CO
91RochR/ProC-1919CO
93Rang/Keeb-4

Boss, David
89Hamil/Star-5
90Hamil/Best-8
90Hamil/Star-7

Boss, Elmer Harley
(Harley)
No Cards.

Bostic, Dwain
92ClBest/Up-424
92Classic/DP-34
92GulfCD/ProC-3571

Bostic, Jerry
75Spokane/Caruso-17

Bostic, Randy
89KS*-4ACO

Bostick, Henry L.
No Cards.

Bostock, Lyman Sr.
91Negro/Lewis-4
93TWill-100

Bostock, Lyman W. Jr.
74Tacoma/Caruso-23
76OPC-263
76T-263
77BurgChef-54
77Ho-102
77Ho/Twink-102
77K-16
77OPC-239
77T-531
78Ho-145
78K-46
78SSPC/270-195
78T-655

Boston, D.J. Wooter
91MedHat/ProC-4105
91MedHat/SportP-1
92StCath/ClBest-11
92StCath/ProC-3392
93Hagers/ClBest-3
93Hagers/ProC-1885
94B-347
94ClBest/Gold-21
94FExcel-139
94FExcel/AS-9
94T-448M
94T/Gold-448M
94UD/SP-2PP

Boston, Daryl L.
82AppFx/Frit-24
83GlenF-1
85Coke/WS-8
85D-33RR
85F/Up-U9
85T/Tr-8T
86BuffB-3
86Coke/WS-8
86D-86
86T-139
87Coke/WS-4
87D-137
87F-487
87T-482
88Coke/WS-2
88F-393
88S-582
88T-739
89B-70
89Coke/WS-6
89D-455
89F-492
89Panini/St-011
89S-443
89T-633
89UD-496
90B-317
90D/BestNL-135
90F/Up-U33
90Leaf-514
90OPC-524
90Panini/St-52
90PublInt/St-384
90S-213
90S/Tr-47T
90T-524
90T/Big-54
90T/Tr-11T
90UD-529
91B-476
91D-210
91F-140
91Kahn/Mets-8
91Leaf-202
91Leaf/Stud-201
91OPC-83
91Panini/FrSt-84
91S-618
91StCl-125
91T-83
91UD-159
91Ultra-211
91WIZMets-45
92D-612
92F-495
92Mets/Kahn-6
92OPC-227
92Pinn-343
92S-276
92StCl-328
92T-227
92T/Gold-227
92T/GoldWin-227
92Ultra-227
93B-528
93Colla/DM-17
93D-38
93F-85
93L-281
93Pac/Spanish-193
93Panini-254
93Pinn-545
93S-447
93StCl-3
93StCl-498
93StCl/1stDay-3
93StCl/1stDay-498
93StCl/Rockie-12
93T-399
93T/Gold-399
93T/Tr-126T
93UD-203
93UD-737
93USPlayC/Rockie-6H
93USPlayC/Rockie-9C
93Ultra-343
94F-435
94Pac/Cr-190
94S-396
94T-106
94T/Gold-106
94UD/CollC-62
94UD/CollC/Gold-62
94UD/CollC/Silv-62

Boswell, Dave
67CokeCap/Twin-7
67T-575
68T-322
69T-459
70MLB/St-230
70OPC-325
70OPC-70LL
70T-325
70T-70LL
71MLB/St-459
71OPC-675
71T-675
72MB-40
78Twin/Frisz-3
81TCMA-403
91Crown/Orio-44

Boswell, Kenneth G.
(Ken)
68Dexter-15
69T-402
70OPC-214
70T-214
70Trans/M-22
71MLB/St-147
71OPC-492
71T-492
72MB-41
72OPC-305
72OPC-306IA
72T-305
72T-306A
73OPC-87
73T-87
74OPC-645
74T-645
75OPC-479
75T-479
75T/M-479
76OPC-379
76SSPC-55
76T-379
77T-429
81TCMA-312
91WIZMets-46
94Mets/69-17

Boswell, Mike
88Peoria/Ko-6

Botelho, Derek
83Omaha-3
84Iowa-xx
85Iowa-13
87Omaha-10
88Louisvl-11
90Martins/ProC-3209CO
91CharWh/ClBest-27CO
91CharWh/ProC-2903CO
91Pac/SenLg-38
92CharWh/ProC-24

Botkin, Alan
88CapeCod/Sum-81
89Johnson/Star-3
90Hamil/Star-8
90Spring/Best-5
91Spring/ClBest-7
91Spring/ProC-733
92StPete/ClBest-24
92StPete/ProC-2021

Botkin, Mike
83DayBe-24

Bottalico, Rick
(Ricky)
92ClBest-262
92Spartan/ProC-1256
94B-496
94FExcel-243
94FExcel/LL-3
94OPC-204
94SigRook-32
94UD-6
94UD/ElecD-6
94Ultra-541

Bottarini, John C.
No Cards.

Bottenfield, Brian
92FtLaud/ProC-2629

Bottenfield, Kent
87BurlEx-5
88WPalmB/Star-3
89Jaxvl/Best-9
89Jaxvl/ProC-163
90Jaxvl/Best-16
90Jaxvl/ProC-1367
91AAA/LineD-178
91Indianap/LineD-178
91Indianap/ProC-455
92B-478
92D/Rook-12
92Indianap/ProC-1853
92Indianap/SB-178
92Sky/AAASingl-87
93D-484
93F/Final-90
93F/MLPII-6
93OPC/Premier-64
93Pac/Spanish-531
93Pinn-617
93S-312
93StCl-101
93StCl/1stDay-101
93T-695
93T/Gold-695
93UD-635
93Ultra-62
94D-528
94F-436
94StCl/Team-108
94T-589
94T/Gold-589
94Ultra-183

Bottenfield, Keven
88Boise/ProC-1628

Botting, Ralph
75QuadC
76QuadC
80SLCity-1
80T-663R
81SLCity-2
81T-214R
82Omaha-2

Bottomley, James L.
(Jim)
21Exh-13
25Exh-59
26Exh-59
27Exh-30
29Exh/4-15
31Exh/4-15
33DH-6
33G-44
34DS-59
34Exh/4-4
35BU-115M
35BU-179
35BU-8
35Exh/4-4
35G-1H
35G-1K
35G-3B
35G-3F
35G-4F
35G-5B
35G-6B
40PlayBall-236
60F-45
61F-9
69Bz-7
72F/FFeat-6
72Laugh/GF-13
75Sheraton-12
76Rowe-2
76Shakey-142
77Galasso-67
80Pac/Leg-64
80Perez/HOF-142
90BBWit-83
90HOF/St-26
91Conlon/Sport-22
91Conlon/Sport-302
92Card/McDon/Pac-1
92Conlon/Col-1
92Conlon/Sport-440
92Conlon/Sport-645
93Conlon-909
94Conlon-1004
R300
R308-205
R310
R311/Gloss
R315-A5
R315-B5
R316
V117-19
V353-44
V355-85
V94-3

Bottoms, Derrick
92AubAs/ClBest-19
92AubAs/ProC-1345
Botts, Jacob
91GreatF/SportP-9
Botts, Jake
90Kissim/DIMD-2
Botz, Bob
77Fritsch-41
Bouchard, Emile
(Butch)
45Parade*-5
Bouchard, Pierre
72Dimanche*-68IA
72Dimanche*-69
Bouchee, Edward F.
(Ed)
57T-314
59T-39
60T-347
61T-196
61T/St-5
62J-182
62P-182
62P/Can-182
62Salada-116
62Shirriff-116
62T-497
81TCMA-328
91WIZMets-47
Boucher, Alexander F.
(Al)
No Cards.
Boucher, Denis
88Myrtle/ProC-1168
88SALAS/GS-23
89Dunedin/Star-1
90Dunedin/Star-2
91B-29
91D/Rook-45
91OPC/Premier-13
91Syrac/MerchB-4
91Tor/Fire-35
91UD/Ext-761
92ColoSp/SB-78
92D-604
92S-848
92Sky/AAASingl-35
92StCl-773
92T/91Debut-18
93D-755
93F-405
93OPC-22
93T-541
93T/Gold-541
94Finest-294
94OPC-236
94T-164
94T/Gold-164
Boucher, Medric C.
No Cards.
Boudreau, Jim
84MidldC-4
Boudreau, Louis P.
(Lou)
39Exh
41DP-132
42PlayBall-10MG
43MP-2
47HomogBond-4
48L-106
49B-11
49MP-100
50B-94
50NumNum
51B-62
53B/Col-57MG
55B-89MG
55Rodeo
56Rodeo
60F-16
61F-94
76Rowe-5M
76Shakey-115
77Galasso-19
79TCMA-287
80Marchant/HOF-2
80Pac/Leg-79
80Perez/HOF-115
82Ohio/HOF-16
83D/HOF-12
86Sf/Dec-17
88Pac/Leg-106
89Pac/Leg-166
89Swell-80
90Pac/Legend-9
90Perez/GreatMom-63
90Swell/Great-31
91Swell/Great-12
91T/Arc53-304MG
92AP/ASG-7
92AP/ASG24K-7G
92Bz/Quadra-19MG
93AP/ASGCoke/Amo-7
93TWill-32
93UD/ATH-16
D305
PM10/Sm-15
PM10/Sm-16
R346-22
Boudreau, Tommy
91Belling/ClBest-3
91Belling/ProC-3679
Boudreaux, Corey
93SoEastern-5
Boudreaux, Eric
87Clearw-12
89Reading/Best-19
89Reading/ProC-668
90ProC/Singl-227
90Reading/Best-3
90Reading/ProC-1214
90Reading/Star-7
90ScranWB/CMC-1
Bouie, Tony
92AZ/Pol-2
Bouldin, Carl
63T-496R
64T-518
Bourassa, Jocelyne
72Dimanche*-144
Bourjos, Christopher
(Chris)
77Cedar
79Phoenix
81RochR-21
81T-502R
83Portl-14
Bourne, Kendrick
86Elmira-3
87Elmira/Black-6
87Elmira/Red-6
88WinHaven/Star-5
89Clearw/Star-3
Bournigal, Rafael
89Star/Wax-27
89VeroB/Star-3
90SanAn/GS-5
91VeroB/ClBest-17
91VeroB/ProC-778
92Albuq/ProC-725
92Albuq/SB-5
93D-10
93F/MLPII-7
93Pinn-279
93S-307
93StCl-197
93StCl/1stDay-197
93T-651
93T/Gold-651
93Ultra-50
94Pac/Cr-303
94StCl-500
94StCl/1stDay-500
94StCl/Gold-500
Bourque, Patrick D.
(Pat)
73OPC-605R
73T-605R
74OPC-141
74T-141
75OPC-502
75T-502
75T/M-502
Bourque, Ray
91StCl/Charter*-44
Bouton, Jim
62T-592R
63T-401
64T-219M
64T-470
64T-4LL
64T/Coins-138AS
64T/Coins-4
64T/St-45
64Wheat/St-7
65OPC-137WS
65OPC-30
65T-137WS
65T-30
65T/E-25
65T/trans-5
66T-276
67CokeCap/YMet-7
67T-393
68T-562
78TCMA-77
88Pac/Leg-20
89Swell-66
90LitSun-22
91Swell/Great-123
92Yank/WIZ60-13
92Yank/WIZAS-7
93TWill-60
WG10-2
WG9-3
Bouton, Tony
91Gaston/ClBest-1
91Gaston/ProC-2678
92CharlR/ClBest-11
92CharlR/ProC-2218
Bouvrette, Lionel
45Parade*-6
Bovee, Michael
(Mike)
92AppFox/ClBest-18
92UD/ML-212
93Rockford/ClBest-3
Bowa, Lawrence Robert
(Larry)
70OPC-539R
70T-539R
71MLB/St-169
71OPC-233
71Phill/Arco-1
71T-233
71T/tatt-16
72Dimanche*-55
72OPC-520
72T-520
73OPC-119
73T-119
74JP
74OPC-255
74T-255
74T/DE-70
74T/St-72
75OPC-420
75T-420
75T/M-420
76Crane-4
76Ho-145
76MSA/Disc
76OPC-145
76SSPC-464
76T-145
77BurgChef-170
77Ho-62
77Ho/Twink-62
77OPC-17
77T-310
78Ho-71
78K-26
78OPC-68
78Pep-27
78SSPC/270-49
78T-90
79BK/P-15
79Ho-134
79K-44
79OPC-104
79T-210
80BK/P-7
80K-39
80OPC-330
80T-630
80T/S-34
80T/Super-34
81Coke
81D-142
81F-2
81F-645M
81F/St-20
81F/St-43M
81K-43
81OPC-120
81T-120
81T/HT
81T/St-201
82D-63
82F-241
82F/St-107M
82F/St-56
82OPC-194
82OPC-374IA
82RedLob
82T-515
82T-516A
82T/St-80
82T/Tr-10T
83D-435
83F-491
83F/St-16M
83F/St-17M
83OPC-305
83OPC/St-221
83T-305
83T/Fold-5M
83Thorn-1
84Cub/Uno-7M
84D-239
84F-486
84Nes/792-705LL
84Nes/792-757
84OPC-346
84SevenUp-1
84T-705LL
84T-757
84T/St-46
85D-361
85D/HL-7
85F-50
85FunFood/Pin-126
85OPC-56
85SevenUp-1
85T-484
85T/St-45
86LasVegas-1
87Bohem-10MG
87T/Tr-8T
88Coke/Pad-10MG
88Phill/TastyK-31CO
88T-284MG
89Phill/TastyK-2CO
90Phill/TastyK-34CO
91Phill/Medford-6CO
91WIZMets-48
92Phill/Med-6CO
93Phill/Med-7CO
93TWill-71
94Phill/Med-3CO
Bowcock, Benjamin J.
(Benny)
No Cards.
Bowden, David Timon
(Tim)
No Cards.
Bowden, James
84Butte-3
Bowden, Mark
81Cedar-22
86Reading-3
87Reading-17
88RochR/CMC-4
88RochR/Gov-2
88RochR/ProC-208
88RochR/Team-4
90AAASingl/ProC-620
90Iowa/ProC-313
Bowden, Merritt
89Anchora-4
91Elizab/ProC-4310
Bowden, Steve
85Bend/Cram-3
87Hagers-15
88Fresno/Cal-16
Bowen, Emmons Joseph
(Chick)
No Cards.
Bowen, John
89Erie/Star-3
Bowen, Kenny
88Memphis/Best-5
89Memphis/Best-8
89Memphis/ProC-1207
89Memphis/Star-2
Bowen, Russ
89KS*-13
Bowen, Ryan
87Ashvl-5
88Osceola/Star-5
89ColMud/Best-18
89ColMud/ProC-126
89ColMud/Star-4
90AAASingl/ProC-186
90Foil/Best-245
90ProC/Singl-603
90Tucson/CMC-1
90Tucson/ProC-196
91AAA/LineD-604
91B-539
91Tucson/LineD-604
91Tucson/ProC-2205
91UD/FinalEd-45F
92B-401
92Classic/Game200-117
92Classic/I-17
92D-671
92L-385
92L/BlkGold-385
92OPC-254
92OPC/Premier-28
92Pinn-473
92ProC/Tomorrow-225
92S-762
92StCl-101
92T-254
92T/91Debut-19
92T/Gold-254
92T/GoldWin-254
92Tucson/ProC-479
92UD-354
92Ultra-488
93D-372
93F-419
93F/Final-53
93Marlin/Publix-5
93Pac/Spanish-455
93Pinn-571
93StCl-350
93StCl/1stDay-350
93StCl/Marlin-16
93T/Tr-130T
93UD-780
93USPlayC/Marlin-3S
93USPlayC/Marlin-9D
93Ultra-367
94D-407
94F-462
94L-238
94Pac/Cr-236
94Pinn-117
94Pinn/Artist-117
94Pinn/Museum-117
94S-142
94S/GoldR-142
94Select-59
94StCl-345
94StCl/1stDay-345
94StCl/Gold-345
94StCl/Team-72
94T-494
94T/Finest-30
94T/FinestRef-30
94T/Gold-494
94TripleP-132
94UD-78
94UD/CollC-63
94UD/CollC/Gold-63
94UD/CollC/Silv-63
94UD/ElecD-78
94Ultra-193
Bowen, Samuel Thomas
(Sam)
67CokeCap/Orio-12
78PapaG/Disc-6
81Pawtu-18
81TCMA-313
Bowens, Samuel Edward
(Sam)
64T-201R
65OPC-188
65T-188
66T-412
67T-491
68OPC-82
68T-82
69MB-32
91Crown/Orio-45
Bowens, Steve
83Idaho-1
Bowerman, Frank E.
T204
T206
Bowers, Brent
90MedHat/Best-10
91Myrtle/ClBest-23
91Myrtle/ProC-2957
92Dunedin/ClBest-6

92Dunedin/ProC-2009
93B-407
93Knoxvl/ProC-1261
Bowers, Grover Bill
(Billy)
52Park-6
Bowers, Mickey
80LynnS-15
81LynnS-25
82LynnS-18
83Chatt-12
Bowers, Tom
58SFCallB-3
Bowes, Frank M.
No Cards.
Bowie, Jim Jr.
86Cram/NWL-102
87Wausau-15
88CalLgAS-27
88SanBern/Best-16
88SanBern/Cal-30
89Calgary/CMC-17
89Calgary/ProC-525
90Foil/Best-258
90ProC/Singl-796
90Wmsprt/Best-3
90Wmsprt/ProC-1067
90Wmsprt/Star-2
91AA/LineD-331
91Jaxvl/LineD-331
91Jaxvl/ProC-156
92Calgary/SB-56
92Jacks/ProC-3714
92Sky/AAASingl-25
92Sky/AASingl-291
94FExcel-117
Bowlan, Mark
89Hamil/Star-4
91Spring/ClBest-8
91Spring/ProC-734
Bowles, John
92LitSun/HSPros-13
Bowlin, Allan
80Elmira-3
Bowlin, Lois Weldon
(Hoss)
No Cards.
Bowling, Stephen S.
(Steve)
75Sacra/Caruso-13
79Indianap-20
Bowman, Billy Joe
90Mother/Ast-27CO
93Mother/Ast-28M
Bowman, Don
(General Manager)
88Pulaski/ProC-1771
Bowman, Elmer W.
No Cards.
Bowman, Ernest F.
(Ernie)
62T-231
63T-61
66T-302
81TCMA-352
Bowman, Joseph Emil
(Joe)
39PlayBall-128
40PlayBall-162
94Conlon-1224
Bowman, Michael
89Bristol/Star-1
Bowman, Robert LeRoy
(Bob)
57T-332
58T-415
59T-221
Bowman, Roger
55B-115
57Seattle/Pop-6
Bowman, Scotty
72Dimanche*-70CO
Bowman, William G.
(Bill)
No Cards.
Bowman, William
77StPete
Bowser, James H.
(Red)
No Cards.
Bowsfield, Edward
(Ted)
59T-236
60T-382
61T-216
62T-369
62T/St-64
63T-339
64T-447
Box, Newt
80Cedar-2
Boxberger, Rod
83Nashua-2
Boyan, Michael
88CapeCod/Sum-155
Boyce
N172
Boyce, Bob
82Miami-14
Boyce, Joe
90Erie/Star-1
Boyce, Randy
78Newar
79BurlB-19
Boyce, Tommy
88SLCity-10
89Kenosha/Star-1
89Miami/II/Star-2
89Star/IISingl-141
90Miami/II/Star-3
Boyd, Bob
76QuadC
77QuadC
Boyd, Daryl
86Watertn-4
89WPalmB/Star-4
Boyd, Dennis
(Oil Can)
80Elmira-4
83Pawtu-2
84D-457
84F-393
85D-151
85F-152
85T-116
86D-50
86F-342
86F/St-9
86Leaf-35
86OPC-259
86Sf-152
86T-605
86T/Mini-4
86T/St-249
86T/Tatt-16M
87Classic-85
87D-51
87F-30
87F/BB-4
87F/Excit-5
87Leaf-248
87OPC-285
87RedFoley/St-122
87S/Test-121
87Sf-47
87Sf/TPrev-9M
87Smok/AL-2
87T-285
87T/St-249
88D-462
88D/RedSox/Bk-462
88F-347
88Leaf-252
88Panini/St-20
88S-121
88T-704
89D-476
89F-82
89OPC-326
89Panini/St-269
89S-238
89T-326
89UD-415
90B-102
90D-633
90F/Up-U26
90Leaf-159
90OPC-544
90Publlnt/St-449
90S-137
90S/Tr-24T
90T-544
90T/Tr-12T
90UD-484
90UD/Ext-749
91B-456
91Classic/200-9
91D-194
91F-226
91Leaf-167
91Leaf/Stud-193
91OPC-48
91Panini/FrSt-147
91S-202
91StCl-142
91T-48
91UD-359
91UD/FinalEd-51F
91Ultra-197
92D-447
92OPC-428
92S-531
92StCl-99
92T-428
92T/Gold-428
92T/GoldWin-428
92UD-559
93Rang/Keeb-80
Boyd, Frank John
No Cards.
Boyd, Gary Lee
70OPC-7R
70T-7R
Boyd, Greg
90AR-29M
93T-621M
93T/Gold-621M
Boyd, Jacob Henry
(Jake)
N172
Boyd, Randy
77SanJose-16
Boyd, Robert Richard
(Bob)
53T-257
54B-118
54T-113
57T-26
58Hires-75
58T-279
59T-82
60L-13
60T-207
61T-199
61T/St-157
86Negro/Frit-49
91Crown/Orio-46
91T/Arc53-257
92Negro/Retort-6
94T/Arc54-113
Boyer, Cloyd
51B-228
52T-280
53B/Col-115
53Hunters
53T-60
55B-149
55Rodeo
85Syrac-30
88Pulaski/ProC-1770
90Pulaski/Best-28CO
90Pulaski/ProC-3113CO
91Pulaski/ClBest-20CO
91Pulaski/ProC-4023CO
91T/Arc53-60
92Pulaski/ClBest-29CO
92Pulaski/ProC-3197CO
Boyer, Kenton Lloyd
(Ken)
55Hunter
55T-125
56T-14
56T/Pin-46
57Swift-8
57T-122
58T-350
59Bz
59HRDerby-4
59T-325
59T-557AS
60Armour-4
60Bz-9
60L-12
60T-160M
60T-485
61Bz-14
61P-171
61T-375
61T-43LL
61T-573AS
61T/St-85
62Bz
62J-159
62P-159
62P/Can-159
62Salada-167
62Shirriff-167
62T-370
62T-392AS
62T-52LL
62T/St-183
62T/bucks
63F-60
63J-160
63P-160
63Salada-15
63T-375
63T/SO
64Bz-35
64T-11LL
64T-160
64T/Coins-145AS
64T/Coins-25
64T/S-57
64T/SU
64T/St-61
64T/tatt
64Wheat/St-8
65Bz-35
65OPC-100
65OPC-135WS
65OPC-6LL
65OldLond-4
65T-100
65T-135WS
65T-6LL
65T/E-47
65T/trans-40
66T-385
66T/RO-10
66T/RO-41
67Bz-33
67CokeCap/YMet-28
67Kahn
67OPC-105
67T-105
68T-259
68T/ActionSt-8A
69MB-33
69T-379
74Laugh/ASG-56
75OPC-202MVP
75T-202MVP
75T/M-202MVP
78TCMA-67
79T-192MG
81TCMA-414M
82KMart-6
88Pac/Leg-12
90Target-63
91WIZMets-49
92Card/McDon/Pac-29
93AP/ASG-145
Boyer, Leroy
(Clete)
57T-121
59T-251
60L-46
60T-109
61P-11
61T-19
61T/St-191
62Exh
62J-3
62P-3
62P/Can-3
62Salada-80
62Shirriff-80
62T-163M
62T-490
62T/St-84
63Exh
63J-14
63Kahn
63P-14
63T-361
64T-69
65T-475
66OPC-9
66T-9
67CokeCap/Brave-13
67T-328
68Bz-1
68CokeCap/Brave-13
68Dexter-16
68Kahn
68T-550
69T-489
69T/St-3
70OPC-206
70T-206
71MLB/St-4
71OPC-374
71T-374
72MB-42
78Green
81TCMA-477
87Colum-3
88Pac/Leg-13
89Pac/SenLg-149
89Swell-94
89T/SenLg-4
89TM/SenLg-12
90AAASingl/ProC-343M
90ColClip/CMC-24CO
90ColClip/ProC-693CO
90Colum/Pol-2CO
90EliteSenLg-34
90Pac/Legend-10
90ProC/Singl-224M
90Swell/Great-102
91AAA/LineD-125M
91ColClip/LineD-125CO
91Pac/SenLg-43MG
91Pac/SenLg-54M
91Swell/Great-109
92Yank/WIZ60-14
Exh47
PM10/L-6
WG10-3
WG9-4
Boyer, Mickey
84Idaho/Team-4
Boykin, Deral
89KS*-20
Boykin, Tyrone
91Boise/ClBest-5
91Boise/ProC-3893
92QuadC/ClBest-23
92QuadC/ProC-821
Boylan, Brad
84Cram/PCL-193TR
86Toledo-2TR
87Portl-24
88Portl/ProC-648
Boyland, Dorian Scott
78Colum
79Portl-7
80Port-2
80T-683R
81Portl-8
82Phoenix
Boyle, Edward J.
(Eddie)
No Cards.
Boyle, Gary
76QuadC
Boyle, Henry J.
N172
N284
WG1-29
Boyle, John Anthony
(Jack)
No Cards.
Boyle, John Bellew
(Jack)
No Cards.
Boyle, Ralph Francis
(Buzz)
90Target-64
R310
Boyles, John
85Cedar-1
86Vermont-2
89Wausau/GS-6
Boyne, Bryan
76Cedar
Boyzuick, Mike
91GreatF/SportP-12
92Bakers/Cal-4
92VeroB/ProC-2881
Boze, Marshall
91Helena/SportP-5
92Beloit/ClBest-6
92Beloit/ProC-395
93B-675
94B-37
94ClBest/Gold-174
94FExcel-78

Braase, John
88GreatF-14
90Bakers/Cal-241
Brabender, Gene
66T-579R
67OPC-22
67T-22
68OPC-163
68T-163
69T-393
70McDon-3
70OPC-289
70T-289
71MLB/St-340
71OPC-666
71T-666
91Crown/Orio-47
Brabinski, Marek
90Idaho/ProC-3268
Bracho, Jose
52Park-24
Brack, Gilbert Herman
(Gib)
39PlayBall-127
Bradbury, Miah
88Alaska/Team-4
90Miami/I/Star-1
91ClBest/Singl-110
91Miami/ClBest-16
91Miami/ProC-410
92Penin/ClBest-3
92Penin/ProC-2935
93FExcel/ML-220
93Harris/ProC-271
Braddy, Leonard
84Visalia-9
Brader, Tim
88Bristol/ProC-1865
89Fayette/ProC-1583
Bradford, Charles W.
(Buddy)
68OPC-142R
68T-142R
69MB-34
69OPC-97
69T-97
70MLB/St-183
70OPC-299
70T-299
71MLB/St-362
71OPC-552
71T-552
72MB-43
74OPC-357
74T-357
75OPC-504
75T-504
75T/M-504
76OPC-451
76SSPC-281
76T-451
Bradford, Henry V.
(Vic)
No Cards.
Bradford, Larry
78Richm
79Richm-17
80T-675R
81D-584
81F-265
81Pol/Atl-34
81T-542
82D-553
82F-431
82T-271
83Portl-24
85Greenvl/Team-5
Bradford, Mark
88Batavia/ProC-1672
Bradford, Troy
88CapeCod/Sum-103
90AZ/Pol-1
90Geneva/ProC-3030
90Geneva/Star-2
91CLAS/ProC-CAR39
91WinSalem/ClBest-1
91WinSalem/ProC-2820
92CharlK/ProC-2764
92Peoria/ClBest-24
Bradford, Vincent
90Bristol/ProC-3169
90Bristol/Star-2
90LitSun/HSPros-16
90LitSun/HSProsG-16
91Bristol/ClBest-15
91Bristol/ProC-3617
Bradish, Mike
90Utica/Pucko-29
92Salinas/ClBest-23
Bradley, Bert
80WHave-10
81WHave-3
82WHave-2
83Tacoma-2
84Cram/PCL-92
85Colum-2
85Colum/Pol-2
87Madis-1
88Madis-4
90Madison/Best-26CO
90Madison/ProC-2284CO
90MidwLgAS/GS-26M
91AA/LineD-300CO
91Huntsvl/ClBest-17CO
91Huntsvl/LineD-300CO
91Huntsvl/Team-24CO
91HuntsvlProC-1812CO
92Huntsvl/ProC-3965CO
92Huntsvl/SB-325CO
Bradley, Byron
92Geneva/ProC-1565
Bradley, David
91Welland/ClBest-23
Bradley, Eric
90Myrtle/ProC-2769
Bradley, George W.
90HOF/St-1
N172
Bradley, Hugh F.
M116
T207
Bradley, J. Nichols
(Nick)
No Cards.
Bradley, John Thomas
(Jack)
No Cards.
Bradley, Kenny
92Kingspt/ClBest-2
92Kingspt/ProC-1537
Bradley, Len
80GlenF/C-2
81GlenF-23
82Edmon-17
Bradley, London
92Geneva/ClBest-25
93Peoria/Team-2
Bradley, M.
N172
Bradley, Mark
77LodiD
82Albuq-19
83Pol/Dodg-22
84F-581
84Nes/792-316
84T-316
90Target-65
91WIZMets-50
Bradley, Mike
90Spokane/SportP-18
91CharRain/ClBest-2
91CharRain/ProC-88
Bradley, Otis
79Clinton/TCMA-7
Bradley, Paul
85Modesto/Chong-2
Bradley, Philip Poole
(Phil)
83SLCity-11
84F/X-15
84Mother/Mar-24
84T/Tr-15
85D-631
85F-486
85Leaf-50
85Mother/Mar-21
85OPC-69
85T-449
86D-191
86D-22DK
86D/AAS-41
86D/DKsuper-22
86F-461
86F/LimEd-5
86F/Mini-96
86F/St-10
86GenMills/Book-2M
86Leaf-22DK
86Mother/Mar-8
86OPC-305
86Seven/Coin-W11
86Sf-77
86T-305
86T/Gloss60-54
86T/St-217
86T/Super-13
86T/Tatt-14M
87D-270
87D/OD-122
87F-580
87F/LL-4
87F/Mini-11
87F/St-13
87GenMills/Book-3M
87Ho/St-29
87Leaf-200
87Mother/Sea-6
87OPC-170
87Sf-89
87Sf/TPrev-25M
87Stuart-25M
87T-525
87T/Mini-70
87T/St-221
88D-243
88D/Best-47
88F-369
88F/Up-U107
88OPC-55
88Panini/St-191
88Phill/TastyK-4
88S-66
88S/Tr-34T
88Sf-93
88T-55
88T/Mini-33
88T/St-218
88T/Tr-18T
89B-17
89D-369
89D/Best-198
89D/Tr-41
89F-563
89F/Up-1
89French-16
89KennerFig-12
89OPC-308
89Panini/St-154
89S-79
89S/Tr-44
89T-608
89T/Ames-6
89T/St-113
89T/Tr-13T
89UD-229
89UD/Ext-749
90B-261
90D-259
90F-174
90F/Can-174
90KMart/CBatL-20
90Leaf-138
90OPC-163
90Panini/St-4
90PublInt/St-575
90S-24
90S/100St-36
90S/Tr-44T
90Sf-95
90T-163
90T/Big-202
90T/Mini-2
90T/St-241
90UD-194
91Crown/Orio-48
91D-646
91F-114
91OPC-717
91S-560
91T-717
91UD-641
92Edmon/ProC-3550
Bradley, Rick
75Phoenix/Caruso-7
77Phoenix
78Cr/PCL-75
79Phoenix
Bradley, Scott W.
83Nashvl-1
84Colum-11
84Colum/Pol-2
85D-37RR
86BuffB-4
86D-396
86T-481
87D-440
87F-580
87F/BB-5
87Mother/Sea-14
87Sf/TPrev-25M
87T-376
87T/St-217
88D-147
88D/Best-24
88F-370
88Leaf-75
88Mother/Sea-14
88OPC-199
88Panini/St-183
88RedFoley/St-8
88S-151
88T-762
88T/St-222
89B-209
89D-261
89F-540
89Mother/Sea-14
89OPC-279
89Panini/St-432
89S-324
89T-279
89T/St-225
89UD-226
90B-483
90D-581
90F-506
90F/Can-506
90Leaf-404
90Mother/Mar-25
90OPC-593
90PublInt/St-427
90S-228
90T-593
90T/Big-181
90T/St-229
90UD-383
91B-239
91CounHrth-5
91D-287
91F-443
91Leaf-99
91OPC-38
91S-113
91StCl-252
91T-38
91UD-130
91Ultra-332
92D-713
92F-273
92OPC-608
92S-304
92StCl-146
92T-608
92T/Gold-608
92T/GoldWin-608
92UD-390
92Yank/WIZ80-16
Bradley, Tom
71OPC-588
71T-588
72OPC-248
72T-248
73OPC-336
73T-336
74OPC-455
74T-455
74T/St-102
75OPC-179
75Phoenix/CircleK-9
75T-179
75T/M-179
76OPC-644
76T-644
76Tucson-35
Bradley, Wayne
75Cedar
Bradley, William J.
(Bill)
E107
E90/1
E97
T206
T213/blue
W555
WG2-6
Bradshaw, Craig
92Idaho/ProC-3502
Bradshaw, Dallas C.
No Cards.
Bradshaw, George T.
No Cards.
Bradshaw, Joe
90Target-903
Bradshaw, Kevin
87Lakeland-7
88GlenF/ProC-934
89Toledo/CMC-19
89Toledo/ProC-783
91Bristol/ClBest-30CO
92Toledo/ProC-1058CO
92Toledo/SB-600CO
Bradshaw, Terry
90Hamil/Best-23
91ClBest/Singl-269
91SALAS/ProC-SAL41
91Savan/ClBest-23
91Savan/ProC-1664
92ProC/Tomorrow-320
94B-648
94FExcel-260
Brady, Brian
86MidldA-2
87MidldA-5
88Edmon/CMC-16
88Edmon/ProC-572
90AAASingl/ProC-42
90Phoenix/CMC-12
90Phoenix/ProC-16
90ProC/Singl-539
90T/89Debut-19
Brady, Clifford F.
(Cliff)
No Cards.
Brady, Dave
83Redwd-6
Brady, Doug
91Utica/ClBest-2
91Utica/ProC-3244
92ClBest-377
92Saraso/ClBest-25
92Saraso/ProC-211
92SoBend/ClBest-9
Brady, James J.
56T-126
Brady, Jim
77Salem
Brady, Lawrence
86Watertn-5
Brady, Mike
89Myrtle/ProC-1476
90StLucie/Star-1
91StLucie/ProC-702
91VeroB/ClBest-4
91VeroB/ProC-765
92StCl/MemberIII*-8
92VeroB/ClBest-21
Brady, Pat
89Salinas/Cal-138
89Salinas/ProC-1815
90SanJose/Best-4
90SanJose/Cal-31
90SanJose/ProC-2023
90SanJose/Star-1
90SanJose/Star-26M
91Clearw/ClBest-15
91Clearw/ProC-1626
91FSLAS/ProC-FSL6
92Clearw/ClBest-22
92Clearw/ProC-2068
Brady, Robert Jay
(Bob)
No Cards.
Brady, Stephen A.
(Steve)
E223
N172/ST
Bragan, Jimmy
89Chatt/II/Team-4MG
Bragan, Peter
89Jaxvl/Best-23
Bragan, Robert R.
(Bobby)
47TipTop
53Mother-4
59DF
60T-463CO
60Union/Dodg-23M
63T-73MG

64T-506MG
65T-346MG
66T-476MG
81TCMA-410MG
90Target-66
Bragg, Darren
92ClBest-213
92Penin/ClBest-23
92Penin/ProC-2945
93FExcel/ML-221
Braggs, Glenn
86Sf/Rook-21
86Vanco-5
87D-337
87D/OD-52
87F-339
87Pol/Brew-26
87Sf/TPrev-19M
87T-622
88D-240
88D/Best-15
88F-157
88OPC-263
88Panini/St-127
88Pol/Brew-26
88S-59
88S/YS/II-2
88T-263
88T-639TL
88T/St-197
89B-145
89Brewer/YB-26
89Classic/Up/2-169
89D-103
89D/Best-277
89F-180
89Gard-12
89KennerFig-13
89OPC-271
89Panini/St-375
89Pol/Brew-26
89S-147
89Sf-29
89T-718
89T/Big-204
89T/St-196
89UD-504
90B-403
90D-264
90ElPasoATG/Team-3
90F-317
90F/Can-317
90F/Up-U11
90Kahn/Reds-4
90Leaf-466
90OPC-88
90Panini/St-97
90Pol/Brew-26
90PublInt/St-491
90S-105
90S/Tr-56T
90T-88
90T/Big-10
90T/St-206
90T/Tr-13T
90UD-456
90UD/Ext-714
91B-669
91D-253
91F-57
91Kahn/Reds-15
91Leaf-362
91OPC-444
91Pep/Reds-3
91S-18
91StCl-187
91T-444
91UD-631
91Ultra-88
92D-363
92F-400
92OPC-197
92Panini-268
92Pinn-502
92Reds/Kahn-15
92S-393
92StCl-13
92T-197
92T/Gold-197
92T/GoldWin-197
92TripleP-61
92UD-341
92Ultra-185
Brahms, Russ
82QuadC-3
Brain, David Leonard
(Dave)
T206
Brainerd, Frederick
(Fred)
No Cards.
Brake, Greg
85Madis/Pol-4
Brakebill, Mark
89Belling/Legoe-21
90Penin/Star-4
91Penin/ClBesf-18
91Penin/ProC-383
92QuadC/ClBest-24
92QuadC/ProC-815
Brakeley, Bill
89Helena/SP-9
90Helena/SportP-27
91Beloit/ClBest-1
91Beloit/ProC-2094
Braley, Jeffrey
(Jeff)
89Bristol/Star-2
90A&AASingle/ProC-85
90Fayette/ProC-2397
90SALAS/Star-2
91FSLAS/ProC-FSL19
91Lakeland/ClBest-1
91Lakeland/ProC-257
92London/ProC-624
92London/SB-401
92Sky/AASingl-170
Brame, Ervin Beckham
(Erv)
93Conlon-959
Bramhall, Arthur W.
(Art)
No Cards.
Branca, Ralph
47HomogBond-5
47TipTop
49B-194
49Eureka-30
50B-59
51B-56
51FB
51T/BB-20
52B-96
52T-274
52TipTop
53B/BW-52
53Exh/Can-8
79TCMA-32
89Rini/Dodg-7
89Smok/Dodg-51
90Pac/Legend-13
90Swell/Great-133
90Target-67
91B-410M
91Swell/Great-14
91T/Arc53-293
92AP/ASG-41
92Bz/Quadra-7
93TWill-8
D305
Exh47
R423-4
Brancato, Albert
(Al)
41DP-48
41PlayBall-43
45PlayBall-22
Branch, Roy
80Spokane-7
89Pac/SenLg-210
91Pac/SenLg-57
Branconier, Paul
89Salem/Team-8
90Ashvl/ClBest-2
90Yakima/Team-31
91Ashvl/ProC-560
Brand, Ronald George
(Ron)
64T-326
65OPC-212
65T-212
66T-394
67CokeCap/Astro-10
68CokeCap/Astro-10
68Dexter-17
68T-317
69Expos/Pins-2
69T-549
70Expo/PostC-16
70MLB/St-63
70OPC-221
70T-221
71Expo/ProS-4
71MLB/St-124
71OPC-304
71T-304
72MB-44
72T-773
78TCMA-41
Brandon, Darrell
66T-456R
67CokeCap/RedSox-5
67OPC-117
67T-117
67T/Test/RedSox-2
68CokeCap/RedSox-5
68Dexter-18
68OPC-26
68T-26
69MB-35
69T-301
72OPC-283
72T-283
73OPC-326
73T-326
89Pac/SenLg-44
Brandow, Derek
91OKSt-1
92OKSt-1
92StCath/ClBest-24
92StCath/ProC-3377
93Hagers/ClBest-4
93Hagers/ProC-1870
Brandt, Ed
(Dutch/Lefty)
33DH-7
33G-50
34Exh/4-1
34T-5
35BU-107
35BU-2
35Exh/4-1
35G-1J
35G-2E
35G-3A
35G-4A
35G-4E
35G-5A
35G-7E
36Exh/4-2
90Target-68
91Conlon/Sport-298
R306
R328-28
V353-50
V354-62
Brandt, John George
(Jackie)
59T-297
60T-53
61P-76
61T-515
61T/RO-27
61T/St-98
62J-31
62P-31
62P/Can-31
62Salada-53A
62Salada-53B
62Shirriff-53
62T-165
62T/St-3
62T/bucks
63J-58
63P-58
63T-65
64T-399
65OPC-33
65T-33
66T-383
67OPC-142
67T-142
78TCMA-33
91Crown/Orio-49
Exh47
Brandt, Randy
77Salem
Branham, Luther H.
92Negro/RetortII-5
Brannan, Otis Owen
No Cards.
Brannon, Cliff
89Hamil/Star-6
90Savan/ProC-2080
91AA/LineD-27
91ArkTr/LineD-27
91ArkTr/ProC-1298
92ArkTr/ProC-1141
92ArkTr/SB-28
92Sky/AASingl-12
Brannon, Paul
92SanBern/ClBest-25
92SanBern/ProC-
Branom, Edgar Dudley
(Dudley)
No Cards.
Bransfield, William
(Kitty)
12Sweet/Pin-124
94Conlon-1193UMP
E104
E254
E270/1
E90/1
E97
M116
T204
T205
T206
T3-82
W555
Branson, Jeff
88T/Tr-19T
89Cedar/Best-1
89Cedar/ProC-928
89Cedar/Star-1
89T/Big-69
90B-52
90CedarDG/Best-20
90Chatt/GS-6
91AA/LineD-155
91Chatt/LineD-155
91Chatt/ProC-1965
92B-512
92D/Rook-13
92Nashvl/ProC-1836
92Pinn-533
92StCl-716
93D-138
93F-31
93L-481
93Pac/Spanish-399
93Reds/Kahn-3
93S-308
93StCl-188
93StCl/1stDay-188
93T-784
93T/Gold-784
93UD-642
93USPlayC/Rook-6H
93Ultra-27
94D-642
94F-405
94Pac/Cr-141
94S-225
94S/GoldR-225
94StCl-20
94StCl/1stDay-20
94StCl/Gold-20
94T-368
94T/Finest-189
94T/FinestRef-189
94T/Gold-368
94UD/CollC-64
94UD/CollC/Gold-64
94UD/CollC/Silv-64
Brant, Marshall Lee
78Tidew
79Tidew-13
80Colum-20
81Colum-13
82Colum-6
82Colum/Pol-33
83Colum-16
92Yank/WIZ80-17
Brantley, Cliff
88Clearw/Star-2
89Reading/Best-11
89Reading/ProC-662
90Clearw/Star-3
90Reading/Star-8
91AA/LineD-503
91Reading/LineD-503
91Reading/ProC-1364
92B-120
92D-722
92F-662
92L-434
92L/BlkGold-434
92OPC-544
92Phill/Med-7
92Pinn-557
92ProC/Tomorrow-299
92S-854
92StCl-583
92T-544
92T/91Debut-20
92T/Gold-544
92T/GoldWin-544
92Ultra-543
93D-250
93F-486
93ScranWB/Team-3
93StCl-253
93StCl/1stDay-253
93T-773
93T/Gold-773
Brantley, Jeff
86Shrev-1
87Phoenix-28
87Shrev-13
88Phoenix/CMC-5
88Phoenix/ProC-78
89D/Rook-41
89F/Up-127
89Mother/Giants-17
89S/Tr-101
89T/Tr-14T
90D-466
90F-52
90F/Can-52
90HotRook/St-9
90Leaf-357
90Mother/Giant-25
90OPC-703
90S-371
90S/100Ris-22
90S/YS/I-24
90T-703
90UD-358
90USPlayC/AS-3H
91B-620
91Classic/200-143
91Classic/II-T47
91D-319
91F-255
91Leaf-136
91MissSt-5
91Mother/Giant-25
91OPC-17
91PG&E-7
91Panini/FrSt-75
91Panini/St-70
91S-160
91SFExam/Giant-4
91StCl-567
91T-17
91UD-424
91Ultra-316
92D-295
92F-629
92Giant/PGE-7
92L-56
92L/BlkGold-56
92Mother/Giant-25
92OPC-491
92Pinn-470
92S-157
92StCl-294
92Studio-112
92T-491
92T/Gold-491
92T/GoldWin-491
92UD-581
92Ultra-285
93D-100
93F-152
93L-102
93Mother/Giant-17
93OPC-65
93Pac/Spanish-608
93Pinn-512
93S-153
93StCl-260
93StCl/1stDay-260
93StCl/Giant-14

93T-631
93T/Gold-631
93TripleP-213
93UD-581
93Ultra-128
94D-94
94F-685
94Pac/Cr-541
94Pinn-198
94Pinn/Artist-198
94Pinn/Museum-198
94T-116
94T/Gold-116

Brantley, Mickey
84Chatt-26
85Cram/PCL-88
86Calgary-2
86F-651R
86Sf/Rook-45
87D-656
87D/Rook-27
87F-582
87Mother/Sea-15
87Sf/TPrev-25M
87T-347
88D-610
88D/Best-80
88F-371
88F/Excit-5
88F/Mini-51
88Leaf-258
88Mother/Sea-15
88Panini/St-192
88S-213
88S/YS/II-15
88T-687
89Chatt/II/Team-5
89D-212
89F-541
89KennerFig-14
89Mother/Sea-7
89OPC-369
89Panini/St-439
89S-89
89Sf-6
89T-568
89T/Big-38
89T/St-219
89UD-550
90Calgary/CMC-15
90ProC/Singl-442
90PublInt/St-428
91AAA/LineD-129
91Denver/LineD-129
91Denver/ProC-133
92Tucson/SB-603

Brashear, Robert N.
(Kitty)
No Cards.

Brashear, Roy Parks
T206

Brassil, Tom
85Beaum-14
86Beaum-3
87Wichita-19
88LasVegas/CMC-23
88LasVegas/ProC-238
89Spokane/SP-13

Bratcher, Joseph W.
(Joe)
No Cards.

Bratchi, Frederick O.
(Fred)
No Cards.

Brathwaite, Alonso
52Laval-58

Bratlien, Erik
88Batavia/ProC-1673
89Batavia/ProC-1941
89Reading/Star-3

Braun, Bart
81Redwd-29

Braun, John Paul
65OPC-82R
65T-82R

Braun, Randy
83DayBe-17
86Calgary-3
87Calgary-15
88Jaxvl/Best-21
88Jaxvl/ProC-976
88SLAS-20
89Indianap/CMC-16
89Indianap/ProC-1213
90AAASingl/ProC-566
90Indianap/CMC-19
90Indianap/ProC-283
90ProC/Singl-69

Braun, Stephen R.
(Steve)
72OPC-244
72T-244
73OPC-16
73T-16
74OPC-321
74T-321
74T/St-202
75K-41
75OPC-273
75T-273
75T/M-273
76Ho-96
76OPC-183
76SSPC-221
76T-183
77Ho-134
77Ho/Twink-134
77OPC-123
77T-606
77T/CS-6
77T/ClothSt-6
78T-422
79T-502
80T-9
81F-427
82D-418
82F-111
82T-316
83F-3
83T-734
84F-320
84F/St-42
84Nes/792-227
84T-227
85F-221
85F/St-51
85T-152
86D-534
86F-27
86KAS/Disc-4
86Louisvl-5
86T-631
88Louisvl-4
90T/TVCard-2CO
92WinHaven/ClBest-29

Braunecker, Darek
91James/ClBest-24
91James/ProC-3535

Brauning, Jeff
90SanJose/Best-5
90SanJose/Cal-34
90SanJose/ProC-2015
90SanJose/Star-2

Bravo, Angel Alfonso
(Angel)
70OPC-283
70T-283
71MLB/St-50
71OPC-538
71T-538

Bravo, Dino
72Dimanche*-114

Bravo, Luis
79Wisco-17
83Albany-17

Braxton, Garland
91Conlon/Sport-248

Braxton, Glenn
86AppFx-3
87Penin-16
89Utica/Pucko-2

Bray, Clarence W.
(Buster)
No Cards.

Bray, Scott
89SLCity-23

Brazeau, Jay
90Columbia/GS-29AMG

Brazell, Don
78Wausau

Brazill, Frank Leo
(Frank)
V100

Brazle, Alpha
47TipTop
49B-126
49Eureka-178
50B-126
51B-157
52B-134
52T-228
53B/Col-140
53Hunter
54B-142
54Hunter
55B-230

Breadon, Sam
W754

Bream, Scott
90CharRain/ProC-2049
91CharRain/ClBest-16
91CharRain/ProC-101
91ClBest/Singl-184
91Spokane/ClBest-23
91Spokane/ProC-3954
92Watlo/ClBest-3
92Watlo/ProC-2148

Bream, Sidney Eugene
(Sid)
82VeroB-18
83Albuq-15
84Cram/PCL-149
85D-470
85T-253
86D-566
86F-604
86T-589
87D-79
87D/OD-168
87F-606
87F/Excit-6
87F/Mini-12
87F/Slug-5
87F/St-14
87Leaf-239
87OPC-35
87Sf/TPrev-18M
87T-35
87T/St-126
88D-188
88D/Best-45
88F-324
88F/Excit-6
88F/St-113
88KennerFig-11
88OPC-304
88Panini/St-370
88S-260
88Sf-98
88T-478
88T/Big-205
88T/St-130
89B-419
89D-252
89D/Best-89
89F-204
89OPC-126
89S-48
89T-126
89T/Big-106
89T/Mini-31
89T/St-125
89UD-556
89VFJuice-5
90B-175
90D-329
90D/BestNL-33
90F-463
90F/Can-463
90Homer/Pirate-7
90OPC-622
90PublInt/St-151
90S-423
90T-622
90Target-69
90UD-250
91B-585
91Brave/Dubuq/Perf-5
91Brave/Dubuq/Stand-7
91D-644
91F-35
91F/Up-U72
91Leaf-379
91Leaf/Stud-142
91OPC-354
91Panini/FrSt-115
91Panini/St-119
91S-304
91S/RookTr-12T
91StCl-427
91T-354
91T/Tr-13T
91UD-109
91UD/Ext-710
92B-356
92Brave/LykePerf-7
92Brave/LykeStand-8
92D-202
92DennyGS-7
92F-354
92L-242
92L/BlkGold-242
92OPC-770
92Panini-162
92Pinn-446
92S-131
92StCl-478
92Studio-2
92T-770
92T/Gold-770
92T/GoldWin-770
92TripleP-258
92UD-495
92USPlayC/Brave-4H
92USPlayC/Brave-7S
92Ultra-160
93B-689
93Brave/FLAg-4
93Brave/LykePerf-6
93Brave/LykeStand-7
93D-526
93F-2
93L-178
93OPC-84
93Pac/Spanish-2
93Panini-181
93Pinn-204
93S-396
93Select-382
93StCl-151
93StCl/1stDay-151
93StCl/Brave-15
93Studio-38
93T-224
93T/Gold-224
93UD-104
93Ultra-4
94D-118
94F-355
94Pac/Cr-5
94StCl-79
94StCl/1stDay-79
94StCl/Gold-79
94T-528
94T/Gold-528

Breard, Stan
45Parade*-54

Breaux, Greg
88Martins/Star-5

Breazeale, James Leo
(Jim)
71Richm/Team-4
73OPC-33
73T-33
79AppFx-17
83Miami-25

Brecheen, Harry
47HomogBond-6
48L-158
49B-158
49Eureka-179
50B-90
51B-86
51FB
51T/BB-28
52B-176
52T-263
53Exh/Can-14
54Esskay
54T-203CO
55Esskay
55T-113CO
55T/DH-74CO
56T-229CO
60L-132CO
60T-455C
79TCMA-166
92Card/McDon/Pac-48
94T/Arc54-203
D305
Exh47
R423-8

Brecht, Mike
83Phoenix/BHN-17

Brechtel, Johnny
93SoEastern-3ACO

Breckinridge
N172/PCL

Brede, Brent
90Elizab/Star-6
91Elizab/ProC-4311
91Kenosha/ClBest-7
91Kenosha/ProC-2087
92ClBest-147
92Kenosha/ProC-615
94ClBest/Gold-65

Bree, Charlie
89Pac/SenLg-217M

Breeden, Daniel R.
(Danny)
69T-536R
70OPC-36R
70T-36R
71MLB/St-27

Breeden, Harold Noel
(Hal)
72T-684
73OPC-173
73T-173
74OPC-297
74T-297
75OPC-341
75T-341
75T/M-341
76SSPC-329

Breeden, Joe
89Memphis/Best-25
89Memphis/ProC-1193
90AppFox/Box-5
90AppFox/ProC-2111MG
91AppFx/ClBest-26
91AppFx/ProC-1731

Breeden, Scott
82Iowa-26
83Iowa-27
85Cedar-32
86TexGold-CO
88Kahn/Reds-CO
93StCath/ClBest-27CO

Breeding, Marvin E.
(Marv)
60T-525
61P-77
61T-321
61T/St-99
62J-28
62P-28
62P/Can-28
62Salada-65A
62Salada-65B
62Shirriff-65
62T-6
63T-149
90Target-70
91Crown/Orio-50

Breedlove, Larry R.
87Spring/Best-21

Breen, Dick
C46-88

Breining, Fred
78Colum
79BuffB/TCMA-13
82D-186
82F-385
82T-144
83D-503
83F-254
83F/St-2M
83Mother/Giants-7
83T-747
84D-387
84Expo/PostC-2
84F-367
84F/X-16
84Nes/792-428
84Stuart-35
84T-428
84T/Tr-16
85F-392
85Indianap-10
85OPC-36
85T-36
86Nashvl-2

Breitenbucher, Karl
87Pocatel/Bon-21
89Clinton/ProC-888

Breitenstein, Ted
T206
T213/brown

Bremer, Bernard
85Albany-28
Bremer, Herbert F.
(Herb)
No Cards.
Bremigan, Nick
88TM/Umpire-19
89TM/Umpire-15
90TM/Umpire-63
Brenegan, Olaf Selmer
(Sam)
No Cards.
Brenly, Robert Earl
(Bob)
77Cedar
80Phoenix/NBank-4
81Phoenix-4
82D-574
82T-171R
83D-377
83F-255
83Mother/Giants-6
83T-494
84D-616
84F-368
84Nes/792-378
84T-378
84T/St-174
85D-187
85D-26
85D/DKsuper-26
85F-603
85Leaf-26DK
85Mother/Giants-7
85OPC-215
85T-215
85T/Gloss40-3
85T/St-158
86D-323
86F-534
86Leaf-194
86Mother/Giants-5
86OPC-307
86T-625
86T/St-92
86T/Tatt-3M
87D-485
87D/OD-95
87F-267
87Mother/SFG-4
87OPC-125
87Sf/TPrev-10M
87T-125
87T/St-87
88D-189
88F-77
88Mother/Giants-4
88OPC-69
88Panini/St-419
88S-134
88T-703
88T/Big-143
88T/St-92
89B-249
89D-453
89OPC-52
89S-395
89T-52
89Tor/Fire-9
89UD-479
92Giant/PGE-8CO
92Mother/Giant-28M
93Mother/Giant-28M
Brennaman, Marty
93Reds/Kahn-4ANN
Brennan, Addison
14CJ-115
15CJ-115
Brennan, James A.
(Jim)
N172
Brennan, James D.
32Orbit/num-92
35BU-178
Brennan, Thomas M.
(Tom)
75OkCty/Team-5
77Watlo
79Tacoma-5
80Tacoma-12
81Charl-1
81T-451R
82T-141R
82Wheat/Ind
83F-403
83T-524
84D-102
84F-537
84Nes/792-662
84T-662
84TrueVal/WS-6
85Coke/Dodg-5
90Target-71
Brennan, Tom
80Wausau-1
81Wausau-5
83GlenF-12
Brennan, William
(Bill)
85VeroB-15
87Albuq/Pol-5
88Albuq/CMC-6
88Albuq/ProC-250
88TripleA/ASCMC-41
89Albuq/CMC-1
89Albuq/ProC-65
89D-589
89S-622
89S/HotRook-9
89UD-16
90AAASingl/ProC-187
90ProC/Singl-610
90Target-72
90Tucson/CMC-8
90Tucson/ProC-197
92Toledo/ProC-1032
92Toledo/SB-577
94T/Gold-395
Brenneman, Jim
77Fritsch-21
81TCMA-409
92Yank/WIZ60-15
Brennen, James
87DayBe-9
Brenner, Jack
52Laval-11
Brenzel, William R.
(Bill)
94Conlon-1302
Bresnahan, Dave
86Watlo-4
87Wmsprt-14
Bresnahan, Roger P.
10Domino-15
11Helmar-167
12Sweet/Pin-145A
12Sweet/Pin-145B
14CJ-17
15CJ-17
48Exh/HOF
50Callahan
50W576-6
60Exh/HOF-4
60F-8
61F-10
75F/Pion-7
76Shakey-29
77Galasso-179MG
80Marchant/HOF-3
80Pac/Leg-102
80Perez/HOF-29
80SSPC/HOF
81Conlon-74
89HOF/St-55
92Conlon/Sport-459
93Conlon-871
D303
D350/2-16
E103
E106
E254
E270/2
E90/1
E91
E98
L1-129
M101/5-16
M116
S74-117
S81-104
T201
T202
T204
T205
T206
T207
T213/blue
T214-2
T215/blue
T216
T222
T3-4
WG3-5
WG5-6
WG6-5
Bressler, Raymond B.
(Rube)
25Exh-25
26Exh-25
27Exh-13
90Target-73
91Conlon/Sport-173
94Conlon-1280
W514-28
Bressoud, Edward F.
(Ed)
58SFCallB-4
58T-263
59T-19
60T-253
61P-152
61T-203
61T/St-74
62Salada-182A
62Salada-182B
62Shirriff-182
62T-504
63J-78
63P-78
63T-188
64T-352
65T-525
66T-516
67CokeCap/YMet-29
67OPC-121
67T-121
78TCMA-164
78TCMA-39
91WIZMets-51
PM10/Sm-17
Breton, John F.
(Jim)
No Cards.
Brett, George Howard
75OPC-228
75T-228
75T/M-228
76A&P/KC
76Ho-114
76OPC-19
76SSPC-167
76T-19
77BurgChef-71
77Ho-36
77Ho/Twink-36
77K-6
77OPC-170
77OPC-1LL
77OPC-261RB
77Pep-32
77T-1LL
77T-231M
77T-580RB
77T-631M
77T/CS-7
77T/ClothSt-7
78Ho-27
78OPC-215
78PapaG/Disc-36
78Pep-28
78SSPC/270-217
78T-100
78Tastee/Discs-9
78Wiffle/Discs-7
79Ho-68
79K-50
79OPC-167
79T-330
79T/Comics-9
80BK/PHR-13
80K-9
80OPC-235
80T-450
80T/S-14
80T/Super-14TP
81Coke
81D-100
81D-491MVP
81Drake-5
81F-28
81F-655
81F/St-116
81K-8
81MSA/Disc-4
81OPC-113
81PermaGr/AS-10
81PermaGr/CC-3
81Pol/Royals-2
81Sqt-1
81T-1LL
81T-700
81T/Nat/Super-3
81T/SO-1
81T/St-243
81T/St-82
81T/St-9
82D-15DK
82D-34
82Drake-4
82F-405
82F/St-202
82K-3
82KMart-38
82OPC-200
82OPC-201IA
82OPC-261AS
82PermaGr/AS-9
82PermaGr/CC-19
82Sqt-3
82T-200
82T-201A
82T-549AS
82T-96TL
82T/St-133
82T/St-190
83D-338
83D/AAS-42
83F-108
83F/St-1M
83F/St-25AM
83F/St-25BM
83K-4
83OPC-3
83OPC-388AS
83OPC/St-76
83PermaGr/AS-1
83PermaGr/CC-19
83Pol/Royals-2
83T-388AS
83T-600
83T/Fold-3M
83T/Gloss40-31
84D-53
84D/AAS-55
84D/Champs-15
84Drake-3
84F-344
84F-638IA
84F/St-36
84MiltBrad-2
84Nes/792-399AS
84Nes/792-500
84Nes/792-710LL
84Nestle/DT-3
84OPC-212
84OPC-223AS
84Ralston-13
84Seven-5C
84Seven-5E
84Seven-5W
84T-399AS
84T-500
84T-710LL
84T/Cereal-13
84T/Gloss22-4
84T/Gloss40-12
84T/RD-6
84T/St-198
84T/St-275
84T/Super-13
85D-53
85D/AAS-26
85D/HL-11
85D/HL-25
85Drake-4
85F-199
85F/LimEd-4
85FunFood/Pin-6
85GenMills-14
85Leaf-176
85OPC-100
85Seven-2C
85Seven-2E
85Seven-2G
85T-100
85T-703AS
85T/3D-4
85T/Gloss22-15
85T/RD-7
85T/St-188
85T/St-268
85T/Super-46
86BK/AP-20
86D-53
86D/AAS-12
86D/HL-3
86D/PopUp-12
86Dorman-1
86Drake-14
86F-5
86F-634M
86F/AS-3
86F/LL-2
86F/LimEd-6
86F/Mini-1
86F/Slug-3
86F/St-11
86F/WaxBox-C2
86GenMills/Book-2M
86Jiffy-4
86Kitty/Disc-20
86Leaf-42
86Meadow/Blank-2
86Meadow/Milk-2
86Meadow/Stat-1
86NatPhoto-5
86OPC-300
86OPC-C
86Quaker-23
86Seven/Coin-C2M
86Seven/Coin-E2M
86Seven/Coin-S2M
86Seven/Coin-W2M
86Sf-1
86Sf-180M
86Sf-186M
86Sf-52M
86Sf-63M
86Sf/Dec-64
86T-300
86T-714AS
86T/3D-5
86T/Gloss22-4
86T/Gloss60-18
86T/Mini-18
86T/St-157
86T/St-16ALCS
86T/St-23
86T/St-256
86T/St-3
86T/Super-14
86T/Tatt-6M
86T/WaxBox-C
86TrueVal-17
86Woolwth-4
87Classic-47
87D-15DK
87D-54
87D/AAS-27
87D/DKsuper-15
87D/OD-206
87Drake-14
87F-366
87F/GameWin-6
87F/Hottest-6
87F/LL-5
87F/Lim-5
87F/Mini-13
87F/RecSet-1
87F/Slug-6
87F/St-15
87F/WaxBox-C3
87GenMills/Book-3M
87Ho/St-24
87Jiffy-5
87KMart-24
87KayBee-5
87Kraft-21
87Leaf-15DK
87Leaf-96
87MnM's-14
87OPC-126
87RedFoley/St-111
87Sf-114M
87Sf-197M
87Sf-5
87Sf/TPrev-13M
87Sportflic/DealP-4
87Stuart-20M

87T-400
87T/Board-13
87T/Coins-5
87T/Gloss60-31
87T/Mini-57
87T/St-254
88Classic/Blue-248
88D-102
88D/Best-39
88F-254
88F/BB/AS-4
88F/Hottest-4
88F/St-30
88FanSam-2
88Grenada-55
88KMart-3
88KennerFig-12
88KingB/Disc-7
88Leaf-93
88OPC-312
88Panini/St-104
88S-11
88Sf-150
88Smok/Royals-20
88T-700
88T/Big-157
88T/Gloss60-53
88T/St-259
88T/St/Backs-41
88T/UK-7
89B-121
89Cadaco-4
89Classic-47
89D-204
89D/AS-11
89D/Best-7
89D/MVP-BC7
89F-277
89F/BBMVP's-4
89F/Superstar-5
89F/WaxBox-C3
89KMart/Lead-5
89KayBee-2
89KennerFig-15
89MSA/SS-9
89Master/Discs-9
89OPC-200
89OPC/BoxB-A
89Panini/St-355
89RedFoley/St-12
89S-75
89S/HotStar-4
89S/Mast-11
89Sf-64
89T-200
89T/Big-46
89T/Coins-34
89T/Crunch-9
89T/Gloss60-14
89T/Hills-3
89T/LJN-42
89T/Mini-54
89T/St-270
89T/St/Backs-1
89T/UK-7
89T/WaxBox-A
89Tastee/Discs-1
89UD-215
89UD-689TC
90B-382
90Classic/Up-T6
90CollAB-21
90D-144
90D/BestAL-35
90D/Learning-1DK
90F-103
90F-621MVP
90F/BBMVP-5
90F/Can-103
90F/Can-621
90HOF/St-93
90KMart/CBatL-5
90KayBee-4
90Leaf-178
90MLBPA/Pins-101
90MSA/Soda-1
90OPC-60
90OPC/BoxB-B
90Panini/St-91
90Post-4
90PublInt/St-344
90RedFoley/St-9
90S-140
90S/100St-76
90S/McDon-19
90Sf-214
90T-60
90T/Ames-2
90T/HillsHM-10
90T/St-265
90T/WaxBox-B
90UD-124
90Woolwth/HL-9
91B-300
91BBBest/HitM-3
91Bz-10
91Classic/200-137
91Classic/I-46
91Classic/II-T70
91CollAB-28
91D-201
91D-396MVP
91D-BC19
91D/BC-BC19
91D/Elite-E2
91F-552
91JDean-12
91Leaf-264CL
91Leaf-335
91Leaf/Stud-62
91MajorLg/Pins-21
91MooTown-19
91OPC-2RB
91OPC-540
91OPC/BoxB-B
91OPC/Premier-14
91Panini/FrSt-276
91Panini/St-224
91Panini/Top15-5
91Petro/SU-13
91Pol/Royal-4
91Post-26
91Post/Can-29
91RedFoley/St-11
91S-120
91S-769HL
91S-853FRAN
91S/100SS-85
91S/Cooper-B5
91Seven/3DCoin-1MW
91Seven/3DCoin-1NW
91Seven/3DCoin-2F
91StCl-159
91StCl/Charter*-2
91Sunflower-4
91T-2RB
91T-540
91T/CJMini/I-15
91T/SU-6
91T/WaxBox-B
91UD-525
91Ultra-144
91Woolwth/HL-8
92B-500
92CJ/DII-30
92Classic/Game200-81
92Classic/II-T79
92D-143
92D/McDon-3
92F-154
92JDean/Living-1
92L-255
92L/BlkGold-255
92L/GoldPrev-19
92L/Prev-19
92MooTown-21
92MrTurkey-5
92OPC-620
92OPC/Premier-114
92P-11
92Panini-102
92Pinn-282M
92Pinn-60
92Pinn/RookI-3M
92Pol/Royal-4
92S-650
92S/100SS-21
92Seven/Coin-25
92StCl-150
92StCl-609MC
92StCl/MemberI-2
92StCl/MemberII-2
92Studio-181
92T-620
92T/Gold-620
92T/GoldWin-620
92T/Kids-105
92T/McDonB-6
92TripleP-115
92UD-444
92UD/ASFF-16
92UD/TmMVPHolo-12
92Ultra-68
93B-265
93Classic/GameI-17
93Colla/DM-18
93D/EliteDom-16
93D/MVP-3
93D/Prev-16
93Duracel/PPII-5
93F-236
93F/Final/DTrib-DT2
93F/Fruit-7
93F/GoldMI-1
93Flair-213
93Highland-3
93HumDum/Can-9
93JDean/28-15
93KingB-9
93Kraft-4
93L-146
93L/Heading-7
93OPC-50
93P-25
93Pac/Jugador-2
93Pac/Spanish-133
93Panini-110
93Pinn-131
93Pinn-294NT
93Pinn/Cooper-2
93Pinn/Trib-1
93Pinn/Trib-2
93Pinn/Trib-3
93Pinn/Trib-4
93Pinn/Trib-5
93Pol/Royal-5
93S-517HL
93S-57
93Select-78
93StCl-424
93StCl/1stDay-424
93StCl/I/Ins-2
93StCl/MPhoto-13
93StCl/Royal-1
93Studio-25
93Studio/Her-1
93T-397
93T/Finest-63
93T/FinestRef-63
93T/Gold-397
93T/MicroP-397
93TripleP-214
93TripleP-64
93UD-54M
93UD-56
93UD-SP5
93UD/Diam-24
93UD/FunPack-181
93UD/Iooss-WI22
93UD/OnDeck-D6
93UD/SP-227
93UD/SeasonHL-HI7
93UD/Then-TN2
93Ultra-206
94D-107
94D/Ann-3
94F-149
94F/GoldM-6
94StCl-5
94StCl/1stDay-5
94StCl/Gold-5
94T-180
94T/Gold-180
94T/Prev-397
94UD/CollC-65
94UD/CollC/Gold-65
94UD/CollC/Silv-65

Brett, Kenneth Alvin
(Ken)
69T-476R
71MLB/St-315
71OPC-89
71T-89
72MB-45
72OPC-517
72T-517
73OPC-444
73T-444
74OPC-237
74T-237
75K-52
75OPC-250
75T-250
75T/M-250
76OPC-401
76SSPC-569
76T-401
76T/Tr-401T
77Ho-65
77Ho/Twink-65
77OPC-21
77T-157
77T-631M
78SSPC/270-192
78T-682
79T-557
80Pol/Dodg-34
80T-521
81T-47
82D-364
82F-406
82T-397
85Utica-24
90Swell/Great-52
90Target-74
92Yank/WIZ70-24
93UD/ATH-17

Breuer, Marvin
44Yank/St-3

Brevell, Ron
(Bubba)
86Kinston-2
88Miami/Star-3

Brewer, Anthony Bruce
(Tony)
83Albuq-20
84Cram/PCL-161
85Cram/PCL-152
85D-31RR
90Target-76

Brewer, Billy
90James/Pucko-15
92WPalmB/ClBest-20
92WPalmB/ProC-2080
93B-561
93F/Final-215
93OPC/Premier-99
93Pac/Spanish-485
93Pinn-606
93Select/RookTr-143T
93Ultra-557
94D-137
94F-150
94Pac/Cr-280
94S-564
94StCl-490
94StCl/1stDay-490
94StCl/Gold-490
94T-123
94T/Gold-123

Brewer, Chet
78Laugh/Black-23
87Negro/Dixon-29

Brewer, Jim
61T-317
61T/St-6
62T-191
63T-309
64T-553
65T-416
66OPC-158
66T-158
67CokeCap/DodgAngel-7
67OPC-31
67T-31
68T-298
69MB-36
69T-241
70T-571
71MLB/St-98
71OPC-549
71T-549
71Ticket/Dodg-3
72MB-46
72OPC-151
72T-151
73OPC-126
73T-126
74K-14
74OPC-189
74T-189
75OPC-163
75T-163
75T/M-163
76OPC-459
76T-459
78TCMA-243
87Smok/Dodg-3
88Smok/Dodg-14
89Smok/Dodg-79
90Target-75

Brewer, John H.
48Sommer-2
49B/PCL-8
49Sommer-2

Brewer, Mark
91SLCity/ProC-3228CO
91SLCity/SportP-26CO

Brewer, Marvin
40PlayBall-183

Brewer, Matt
91ClBest/Singl-420
91Everett/ClBest-21
91Everett/ProC-3927
92ProC/Tomorrow-359
92SanJose/ClBest-1

Brewer, Mike
84Omaha-9
85Maine-26
86Omaha/ProC-3
86Omaha/TCMA-13

Brewer, Omar
88CharlR/Star-3

Brewer, Rodney
88Spring/Best-19
89ArkTr/GS-3
90AAASingl/ProC-521
90Louisvl/CMC-12
90Louisvl/LBC-8
90Louisvl/ProC-407
90ProC/Singl-112
90T/TVCard-39
91AAA/LineD-227
91Classic/I-92
91Louisvl/LineD-227
91Louisvl/ProC-2925
91Louisvl/Team-14
91T/90Debut-21
92AAA/ASG/SB-253
92Louisvl/ProC-1897
92Louisvl/SB-253
92S-864
92Sky/AAASingl-123
93F/MLPI-17
93Pac/Spanish-629
93Pol/Card-3
93StCl-527
93StCl/1stDay-527
93StCl/Card-7
93T-566
93T/Gold-566
93UD-381
94D-400
94F-629
94S-297
94S/GoldR-297
94StCl/Team-326

Brewer, Sherwood
(Woody)
92Negro/RetortII-6

Brewer, Tom
55B-178
55T-83
55T/DH-128
56T-34
57T-112
58T-220
59T-346M
59T-55
60T-439
61P-50
61T-434
61T/St-108
62Salada-4
62Shirriff-4
Exh47

Brewington, Jamie
92Everett/ClBest-18
92Everett/ProC-1677
93ClBest/MLG-159

Brewington, Michael
(Mike)
89Welland/Pucko-6
90Augusta/ProC-2476
90ProC/Singl-725
91Salem/ClBest-10
91Salem/ProC-964

Brewster, Charles L.
(Charlie)
No Cards.

Brewster, Rich
76QuadC
77QuadC
80ElPaso-20
Brian, Braden
87James-17
Brickell, Fritz D.
(Fritzie)
61BeeHive-2
61T-333
81TCMA-294
Brickell, George F.
(Fred)
33G-38
35G-1E
35G-3C
35G-5C
35G-6C
93Conlon-808
V353-38
Brickey, Josh
90Kgsport/Star-30BB
Brickhouse, Jack
89Pac/Leg-209
Brickler, Tim
93MissSt-4
Brickley, Geroge V.
No Cards.
Brideweser, James E.
(Jim)
53B/Col-136
55B-151
57T-382
91Crown/Orio-51
Bridge, Eric
89FresnoSt/Smok-5
Bridge, Mark
85Clovis-5
Bridges, Everett L.
(Rocky)
52T-239
53B/BW-32
54B-156
55B-136
56T-324
57Sohio/Reds-3
57T-294
58T-274
59T-318
60L-31
60T-22
61T-508
62J-75
62P-75
62P/Can-75
75Phoenix/CircleK-1
76Phoenix/Coke-23MG
77Phoenix
78Cr/PCL-50
79Phoenix
80Phoenix/NBank-25MG
81Phoenix-25
82Phoenix
84Everett/Cram-28MG
86PrWill-4MG
87Vanco-8
88BuffB/CMC-25
88BuffB/Polar-1
88BuffB/ProC-1478
89Salem/Star-25
90Target-77
90Welland/Pucko-33CO
V362-1
Bridges, Jason
88Oneonta/ProC-2045
89PrWill/Star-1
90PrWill/Team-6
Bridges, Jim
85BurlR-28
Bridges, Marshall
58Union
78TCMA-48
92Yank/WIZ60-16
WG9-5
Bridges, Thomas
33G-199
34DS-5
34G-44
35BU-81
35BU-9
35G-1D
35G-2D
35G-6D
35G-7D
35Wheat
37OPC-133
37Wheat
38Exh/4-12
38Wheat
39PlayBall-104
41PlayBall-65
61F-95
81Tiger/Detroit-56
88Conlon/AmAS-3
91Conlon/Sport-180
93Conlon-723
R308-177
R313
R313A-1
R314
V300
V354-87
V355-33
V94-4
Bridges-Clements, Tony
88BBCity/Star-9
89Memphis/Best-7
89Memphis/ProC-1202
89Memphis/Star-3
91Memphis/ProC-659
92BBCity/ProC-3850
92ClBest-237
92Memphis/ProC-2430
92Memphis/SB-427
92Sky/AASingl-179
Bridwell, Albert H.
(Al)
10Domino-16
11Helmar-77
12Sweet/Pin-108
14CJ-42
14Piedmont/St-6
15CJ-42
91Conlon/Sport-170
D303
E101
E104
E105
E106
E254
E90/1
E91
E92
E98
M116
S74-81
T201
T202
T204
T205
T206
T213/blue
T215/brown
T216
T3-83
Brief, Anthony V.
(Bunny)
94Conlon-1290
Brier, Coe
83Wisco/Frit-1
Briggs, Daniel Lee
(Dan)
75SLCity/Caruso-5
77T-592
79T-77
80T-352
82OPC-102
82T-102
82T/Tr-11T
84Colum-5
84Colum/Pol-3
85Colum-14
85Colum/Pol-3
85IntLgAS-33
Briggs, David
88Spokane/ProC-1938
89CharRain/ProC-994
Briggs, Grant
No Cards.
Briggs, John Edward
64PhilBull-6
64T-482R
65OPC-163
65T-163
66T-359
67CokeCap/Phill-3
67Pol/Phill-2
67T-268
68T-284
69MB-37
69MLB/St-173
69OPC-73
69T-73
69T/St-72
70MLB/St-85
70T-564
71MLB/St-170
71OPC-297
71T-297
72MB-47
72OPC-197
72T-197
73OPC-71
73T-71
74OPC-218
74T-218
74T/St-192
75K-16
75OPC-123
75T-123
75T/M-123
76OPC-373
76T-373
81TCMA-424
Briggs, John T.
57Seattle/Pop-7
59T-177
60T-376
Briggs, Ken
91Salinas/ClBest-1
91Salinas/ProC-2246
Briggs, Kenny
83Wausau/Frit-29
Briggs, Stoney
91MedHat/ProC-4113
92Myrtle/ClBest-16
92Myrtle/ProC-2209
Briggs, Walter O.
81Tiger/Detroit-50WN
Briggs, William
91MedHat/SportP-20
Bright, Brian
91Elmira/ClBest-1
91Elmira/ProC-3281
92WinHaven/ClBest-23
92WinHaven/ProC-1791
94ClBest/Gold-64
Bright, Don
74Gaston
75Anderson/TCMA-1
76SanAn/Team-3
78Cr/PCL-86
Bright, Harry James
59T-523
60T-277
61T-447
62T-551
63J-95
63P-95
63T-304
64T-259
65T-584
76Tucson-23MG
78TCMA-214
85Durham-14
92Yank/WIZ60-17
WG9-6
Bright, Tom
77AppFx
Briles, Nelson
(Nellie)
65T-431R
66T-243
67T-404
68OPC-153WS
68T-153WS
68T-540
69MB-38
69MLB/St-208
69OPC-60
69T-60
69T/St-111
70MLB/St-134
70OPC-435
70T-435
71MLB/St-195
71OPC-257
71T-257
72MB-48
72OPC-227WS
72T-605
73OPC-303
73T-303
74OPC-123
74T-123
74T/St-81
74T/Tr-123T
75OPC-495
75T-495
75T/M-495
76OPC-569
76SSPC-159
76T-569
77T-174
78T-717
79T-262
81TCMA-308
89Swell-79
91Crown/Orio-52
93Rang/Keeb-81
93UD/ATH-18
Briley, Greg
86Cram/NWL-107
87Chatt/Best-17
88Calgary/CMC-13
88Calgary/ProC-799
88S/Tr-74T
89F/Up-57
89S/HotRook-54
89T-781
89T/Big-247
89UD/Ext-770
90B-482
90Bz-17
90Classic-54
90D-463
90F-507
90F/Can-507
90Leaf-391
90Mother/Mar-14
90OPC-288
90Panini/St-148
90S-303
90S/100Ris-60
90S/YS/I-12
90Sf-43
90T-288
90T/Big-35
90T/Gloss60-19
90T/JumboR-4
90T/St-226
90T/St-320FS
90ToysRUs-5
90UD-455
91B-256
91CounHrth-4
91D-352
91F-444
91Leaf-194
91OPC-133
91S-494
91StCl-130
91T-133
91UD-479
92D-487
92F-274
92L-65
92L/BlkGold-65
92Mother/Mar-15
92OPC-502
92Panini-61
92S-387
92StCl-228
92T-502
92T/Gold-502
92T/GoldWin-502
92UD-369
92Ultra-120
93D-695
93F-670
93F/Final-54
93Marlin/Publix-6
93Pac/Spanish-281
93StCl-440
93StCl/1stDay-440
93T-14
93T/Gold-14
93T/Tr-35T
93UD-634
93USPlayC/Marlin-8S
93Ultra-368
Briley, Paxton
92Boise/ClBest-25
92Boise/ProC-3617
93StCl/MurphyS-158
Brilinski, Tyler
86Modesto-5
88Tacoma/CMC-12
88Tacoma/ProC-617
89Tacoma/CMC-13
89Tacoma/ProC-1561
Brill, Clinton
83Ander-26
Brill, Tim
78Watlo
79Savan-6
Brill, Todd
88Oneonta/ProC-2042
Brimhall, Bradley
90Madison/ProC-2260
90SoOreg/Best-22
90SoOreg/ProC-3439
91Madison/ClBest-5
91Madison/ProC-2122
92Kane/Team-2
Brimsek, Frank
45Parade*-7
Bringhurst, Stewart
78Wausau
Brink, Brad
87Clearw-23
88Maine/CMC-5
88Maine/ProC-289
88Phill/TastyK-27
89ScranWB/ProC-721
92D/Rook-14
92Phill/Med-38
92Reading/SB-527
92ScranWB/SB-484
92Sky/AASingl-227
93S-224
93ScranWB/Team-4
93T-818
93T/Gold-818
Brink, Craig
88Oneonta/ProC-2051
Brink, Mike
85Clovis-6
Brinker, William H.
(Bill)
No Cards.
Brinkman, Charles E.
(Chuck)
71OPC-13R
71T-13R
72T-786
73OPC-404
73T-404
74OPC-641
74T-641
Brinkman, Edwin A.
(Ed)
63T-479
64T-46
64T/Coins-108
64T/S-27
65T-417
66T-251
67CokeCap/Senator-3
67T-311
68OPC-49
68T-49
69MB-39
69MLB/St-101
69OPC-153
69T-153
69T/4in1-16M
69T/St-232
70MLB/St-279
70Pol/SenY-2
70T-711
71MLB/St-385
71OPC-389
71T-389
71T/Coins-46
72MB-49
72T-535
73OPC-5
73T-5
74OPC-138
74T-138
74T/St-171
75OPC-439
75T-439
75T/M-439
76SSPC-447
76SSPC/MetsY-Y3
81Tiger/Detroit-70

82BirmB-24MG
92Yank/WIZ70-25
93Rang/Keeb-82
Brinkman, Greg
84Butte-8
88Vermont/ProC-957
89OrlanTw/Best-30
89Visalia/ProC-1428
Brinkman, Joe
88TM/Umpire-15
89TM/Umpire-13
90TM/Umpire-13
Brinkopf, Leon C.
77Fritsch-18
Brinson, Hugh
86Ventura-2
87Dunedin-5
88Knoxvl/Best-24
Briody, Charles F.
(Fatty)
No Cards.
Brisbin, Steve
75QuadC
Brisco, Jamie
83Erie-9
84Savan-13
86Stockton-2
87ElPaso-10
88ElPaso/Best-4
Briscoe, John
90Modesto/Cal-150
90Modesto/Chong-2
90Modesto/ProC-2204
91AA/LineD-279
91Huntsvl/LineD-279
91S/RookTr-108T
92D/Rook-15
92Sky/AAASingl-235
92StCl-681
92T/91Debut-21
92Tacoma/ProC-2495
92Tacoma/SB-539
Briskey, Dick
45Centen-2
Brison, Sam
76Laugh/Clown-11
76Laugh/Clown-29
76Laugh/Clown-37
76Laugh/Clown-4
Brissie, Lou
48L-31
49B-41
49Royal-8
50B-48
50Drake-4
51B-155
51T/BB-31
52B-79
52NTea
52NumNum-1
52Royal
52T-270
52TipTop
Exh47
Bristol, Dave
67OPC-21MG
67T-21
68OPC-148MG
68T-148MG
69T-234MG
70McDon-5MG
70T-556MG
71OPC-637MG
71T-637MG
72Dimanche*-5CO
72T-602MG
73OPC-377CO
73T-377C
74OPC-531CO
74T-531C
76T-631MG
77T-442MG
79Pol/SFG-1MG
80Pol/SFG-1MG
80T-499MG
81D-436MG
81T-686MG
84Phill/TastyK-9CO
85Phill/TastyK-3CO
85Phill/TastyK-8CO
88Phill/TastyK-29CO
Bristow, George
No Cards.
Bristow, Richie
90Kgsport/Best-21
90Kgsport/Star-3
91Clmbia/PCPII-2
91Clmbia/PII-12
Brito, Adan
84Idaho/Team-5
Brito, Bernardo
81Batavia-20
81Watlo-31
83Watlo/Frit-17
86Water-5
87Wmsprt-23
88OrlanTw/Best-28
88SLAS-13
89Portl/CMC-21
89Portl/ProC-212
90AAASingl/ProC-260
90Portl/CMC-23
90Portl/ProC-190
90ProC/Singl-575
91AAA/LineD-403
91Portl/LineD-403
91Portl/ProC-1575
92Portl/SB-402
92Portland/ProC-2677
92Sky/AAASingl-183
93LimeR/Winter-79
93Pinn-274
93S-306
94F-200
94Pac/Cr-350
Brito, Frank
88Bend/Legoe-6
Brito, Gino
72Dimanche*-114M
Brito, Jorge
88Modesto-17
88Modesto/Cal-68
89Modesto/Cal-282
90Foil/Best-180
90Huntsvl/Best-13
91AAA/LineD-528
91Huntsvl/Team-3
91Tacoma/LineD-528
91Tacoma/ProC-2309
92Huntsvl/ProC-3953
92Tacoma/SB-527
Brito, Jose Oscar
80Water-12
81Indianap-11
81Louisvl-14
82Louisvl-3
83Louisvl/Riley-14
85CharlO-26
85RochR-15
Brito, Luis
89Martins/Star-3
90Princet/DIMD-3
91Martins/ClBest-13
91Martins/ProC-3458
92Clearw/ProC-2061
92Spartan/ClBest-17
92Spartan/ProC-1267
Brito, Mario
87James-20
88MidwLAS/GS-45
88Rockford-3
89Rockford-2
90Jaxvl/Best-17
90Jaxvl/ProC-1368
90ProC/Singl-660
91AAA/LineD-627
91Vanco/LineD-627
91Vanco/ProC-1586
92Harris/ProC-453
92Harris/SB-277
93Harris/ProC-261
93LimeR/Winter-9
Brito, Tilson
93Dunedin/ClBest-2
93Dunedin/ProC-1801
Britt, Bob
88Spartan/ProC-1046
Britt, Doug
78Charl
81Buffa-3
82DayBe-10
Britt, Ken
92Hamil/ClBest-16
92Hamil/ProC-1581
Britt, Patrick
87Modesto-21
Britt, Stephan
92Lipscomb-23M
92Lipscomb-5
Brittain, August S.
(Gus)
No Cards.
Brittain, Grant
90A&AASingle/ProC-198
90Idaho/ProC-3251
91Macon/ClBest-17
91Macon/ProC-870
92Durham/ClBest-10
92Durham/Team-9
Britton, James Allan
64T-94R
68OPC-76R
68T-76R
69OPC-154
69T-154
69T/4in1-3M
70T-646
71OPC-699
71T-699
72MB-50
Britton, Jimmy W.
72OPC-351R
72T-351R
Britton, Stephen G.
(Gil)
No Cards.
Brizzolara, Tony
79Richm-25
80OPC-86
80Richm-7
80T-156
81Richm-2
82Richm-2
83Richm-2
84Richm-9
85IntLgAS-11
85Richm-1
86BuffB-5
90Richm/25Ann-5
Broaca, Johnny
35BU-192
92Conlon/Sport-517
94Conlon-995
Broadfoot, Scott
87Erie-15
88StPete/Star-2
89Spring/Best-6
Broas, Rick
77Newar
Broberg, Pete
72OPC-64
72T-64
73K-41
73OPC-162
73T-162
74OPC-425
74T-425
75OPC-542
75T-542
75T/M-542
76A&P/Milw
76Ho-74
76OPC-39
76SSPC-245
76T-39
77Ho-145
77Ho/Twink-145
77OPC-55
77T-409
78T-722
79OPC-301
79T-578
89T/SenLg-87
93Rang/Keeb-5
Brocail, Doug
87CharRain-23
88Charl/ProC-1211
89AubAs/ProC-13
89Wichita/Rock-28
90Wichita/Rock-3
91AA/LineD-602
91Wichita/LineD-602
91Wichita/ProC-2590
91Wichita/Rock-1
92D/Rook-16
92LasVegas/ProC-2789
92LasVegas/SB-226
92Sky/AAASingl-110
93D-418
93F/Final-135
93T-821
93T/Gold-821
94D-615
94F-657
94L-165
94Pac/Cr-518
94T-579
94T/Gold-579
94TripleP-164
Brock, Chris
92Idaho/ProC-3503
93Macon/ClBest-3
93Macon/ProC-1392
94FExcel-152
Brock, Don
88Pocatel/ProC-2073
89SanJose/Best-6
89SanJose/Cal-210
89SanJose/ProC-442
89SanJose/Star-3
90SanJose/Best-18
90SanJose/Cal-50
90SanJose/ProC-2004
90SanJose/Star-3
Brock, Gregory Allen
(Greg)
82Albuq-15
83D-579
83F-203
83Pol/Dodg-17
83Seven-12
83T/X-14
84D-296
84F-98
84Nes/792-555
84OPC-242
84Pol/Dodg-9
84T-555
84T/St-376YS
85Coke/Dodg-6
85F-368
85OPC-242
85T-753
86Coke/Dodg-4
86D-296
86F-125
86OPC-368
86Pol/Dodg-9
86T-368
86T/St-67
87D/OD-50
87F-437
87F/Up-U9
87OPC-26
87Pol/Brew-9
87T-26
87T/St-68
87T/Tr-9T
88D-337
88D/Best-71
88F-158
88Leaf-148
88OPC-212
88Panini/St-121
88Pol/Brew-9
88S-234
88Sf-184
88T-212
88T/Big-217
89B-143
89Brewer/YB-9
89D-57
89D/Best-239
89F-181
89Gard-11
89OPC-163
89Panini/St-371
89Pol/Brew-9
89S-307
89T-517
89T/Big-100
89T/St-201
89UD-543
90B-395
90Brewer/MillB-2
90D-293
90D/BestAL-142
90F-318
90F/Can-318
90Leaf-454
90OPC-139
90Panini/St-104
90PublInt/St-492
90S-485
90T-139
90T/Big-47
90T/St-208
90Target-78
90UD-514
91B-41
91D-572
91F-577
91OPC-663
91Panini/FrSt-204
91Pol/Brew-4
91RedFoley/St-12
91S-522
91StCl-269
91T-663
91UD-289
91Ultra-172
Brock, John Roy
No Cards.
Brock, Louis Clark
(Lou)
62T-387
63T-472
64T-29
64T/Coins-97
65T-540
66OPC-125
66T-125
67OPC-63M
67T-285
67T-63M
68Bz-15
68OPC-151WS
68T-151WS
68T-372AS
68T-520
69Kelly/Pin-4
69MB-40
69MLB/St-209
69MLBPA/Pin-36
69NTF
69OPC-165WS
69OPC-85
69T-165WS
69T-428AS
69T-85
69T/4in1-4M
69T/St-112
69Trans-31
70K-44
70MB-2
70MLB/St-135
70OPC-330
70T-330
70T/PI-4
70T/S-11
70T/Super-11
71K-17
71MD
71MLB/St-268
71OPC-625
71T-625
71T/Coins-87
71T/GM-27
71T/Greatest-27
71T/S-25
71T/Super-25
72K-48
72MB-51
72OPC-200
72T-200
73K-40
73OPC-320
73OPC-64LL
73T-320
73T-64LL
73T/Lids-8
74Greyhound-2
74Greyhound-6M
74OPC-204LL
74OPC-60
74T-204LL
74T-60
74T/DE-20
74T/St-111
75Ho-23
75Ho/Twink-23
75K-39
75OPC-2RB
75OPC-309LL
75OPC-540
75T-2RB
75T-309LL

75T-540
75T/M-2M
75T/M-309LL
75T/M-540
76Crane-5
76Ho-7
76Ho/Twink-7
76K-40
76Laugh/Jub-14
76MSA/Disc
76OPC-10
76OPC-197LL
76SSPC-275
76SSPC-590M
76T-10
76T-197LL
77BurgChef-15
77Galasso-269
77Ho-32
77Ho/Twink-32
77OPC-51
77T-355
77T/CS-8
77T/ClothSt-8
78K-7
78OPC-204
78OPC-236RB
78T-170
78T-1RB
78Tastee/Discs-6
78Wiffle/Discs-8
79OPC-350
79T-415HL
79T-665
80Marchant-6
80Perez/HOF-190
80T-1M
81TCMA-341
85West/2-28
85Woolwth-5
86Sf/Dec-59
87KMart-13
89Kahn/Coop-3
89T-662TBC
89T/LJN-101
90HOF/St-86
90Pac/Legend-12
90Perez/GreatMom-66
90Swell/Great-71
91CollAB-11
91K/3D-10
91K/SU-4A
91K/SU-4B
91LineD-24
91Swell/Great-13
91UD-636A
91UD-636B
92AP/ASG-2
92AP/ASG24K-2G
92Card/McDon/Pac-30
92UD/ASFF-48
92UD/Hero-6AU
92UD/Hero-H6
92UD/Hero-H8M
92UD/HeroHL-HI2
93AP/ASGCoke/Amo-2
93FrRow/Brock-Set
93Metallic-5
93TWill-86
93TWill/Locklear-2
93YooHoo-3

Brock, Norman
86FSLAS-10
86Osceola-1
87ColAst/ProC-24
88ColAst/Best-27
89Cedar/Best-18
89Cedar/ProC-938
89Cedar/Star-2

Brock, Russell
91SoOreg/ClBest-10
91SoOreg/ProC-3832
92ProC/Tomorrow-136
92Reno/Cal-46
92StCl/Dome-20
93Modesto/ClBest-4
93Modesto/ProC-790
94FExcel-118

Brock, Tarrik
91Bristol/ClBest-6
91ClBest/Singl-407
91FrRow/DP-52
91LitSun/HSPros-8
91LitSun/HSProsG-8
92B-345
92Fayette/ClBest-6
92Fayette/ProC-2180
92StCl/Dome-21
92UD/ML-189

Brocker, John
(Gene)
49Sommer-26

Brockett, Lew
11Helmar-39
C46-55
E254
E270/1

Brocki, Mike
87SanBern-16
88SanBern/Best-26
88SanBern/Cal-40
89Wmsprt/ProC-629
91Pac/SenLg-92

Brockil, Dave
86Cram/NWL-162

Brocklander, Fred
88TM/Umpire-38
89TM/Umpire-36
90TM/Umpire-34

Brockway, Kevin
86Cram/NWL-188

Broda, Turk
45Parade*-8

Broderick, Matthew T.
(Matt)
No Cards.

Broderick, Stan
83QuadC-24

Brodie, Walter Scott
(Steve)
No Cards.

Brodowski, Dick
52T-404
53T-69
54T-221
55T-171
56T-157
59Kahn
59T-371
91T/Arc53-69
94T/Arc54-221

Broersma, Eric
82OrlanTw/A-13
82OrlanTw/B-3
83OrlanTw-19
83Toledo-26
84Toledo-17
85Toledo-2
86Toledo-3
87Tacoma-11

Broglio, Ernie
59T-296
60L-41
60T-16
61Bz-16
61P-179
61T-420
61T-451M
61T-45LL
61T-47LL
61T-49LL
62J-164
62P-164
62P/Can-164
62Salada-132
62Shirriff-132
62T-507
63J-165
63P-165
63T-313
64T-59
64T/Coins-95
64T/SU
64T/St-77
65T-565
66T-423
78TCMA-18

Brogna, Dennis
81Watlo-3
83MidldC-6
84MidldC-13
92Myrtle/ClBest-30TR
93Hagers/ClBest-28TR

Brogna, Rico
88Bristol/ProC-1885
89B-102
89Lakeland/Star-3
90A&AASingle/ProC-30
90B-351
90EastLAS/ProC-EL4
90London/ProC-1275
91AAA/LineD-580
91B-134
91Classic/200-197
91Classic/II-T12
91Leaf/GRook-BC11
91S-741RP
91Toledo/LineD-580
91Toledo/ProC-1939
91UD-73
92B-256
92D/Rook-17
92F/Up-19
92OPC-126M
92ProC/Tomorrow-63
92Sky/AAASingl-258
92T-126M
92T/Gold-126M
92T/GoldWin-126M
92Toledo/ProC-1049
92Toledo/SB-578
92UD-74TP
93D-41
93F/MLPI-15
93Pinn-240
93S-114
93S/Boys-17
93StCl-530
93StCl/1stDay-530
93T-598
93T/Gold-598
93UD-386

Brohamer, John A.
(Jack)
73OPC-181
73T-181
74OPC-586
74T-586
75OPC-552
75T-552
75T/M-552
76OPC-618
76SSPC-518
76T-618
76T/Tr-618T
77BurgChef-78
77T-293
78PapaG/Disc-3
78SSPC/270-166
78T-416
79OPC-25
79T-63
80T-349
81F-393
81T-462

Brohm, Jeff
90Burlind/ProC-3019
91Watertn/ClBest-24
91Watertn/ProC-3379

Bromby, Scott
88Rockford-2
89Rockford-3
89Rockford/Team-4

Bronkey, Jeff
87OrlanTw-21
88Visalia/Cal-166
88Visalia/ProC-95
89OrlanTw/Best-12
89OrlanTw/ProC-1337
91AAA/LineD-305
91OkCty/LineD-305
91OkCty/ProC-172
92Tulsa/ProC-2687
92Tulsa/SB-603
93F/Final-277
93Rang/Keeb-396
94Flair-64
94Pac/Cr-609
94Pol/Brew-3
94T/Gold-396

Bronkie, Herman C.
No Cards.

Bronson, Aaron
93Lipscomb-25M

Brookens, Andy
91Eugene/ClBest-3
91Eugene/ProC-3731

Brookens, Thomas D.
(Tom)
77Evansvl/TCMA-4
80T-416
81D-6
81F-473
81T-251
82D-202
82F-263
82OPC-11
82T-753
83D-454
83F-327
83F/St-3M
83T-119
84D-578
84F-78
84Nes/792-14
84T-14
84Tiger/Wave-8
85Cain's-4
85D-593
85F-4
85T-512
85Wendy-5
86Cain's-2
86D-537
86F-223
86OPC-286
86T-643
87Cain's-1
87Coke/Tigers-17
87D-296
87F-145
87OPC-232
87T-713
88D-107
88F-53
88Panini/St-93
88Pep/T-16
88Pol/T-4
88S-233
88T-474
89D-508
89D/Tr-53
89F-130
89KennerFig-16
89OPC-342
89Panini/St-340
89S-269
89S/NWest-21
89S/Tr-73
89T-342
89T/St-278
89UD-106
90F-439
90F/Can-439
90S-297
90UD-138
91D-658
91F-362
91OPC-268
91S-106
91T-268
91UD-102
92Yank/WIZ80-18

Brookens, Tim
75Anderson/TCMA-2

Brooks, Billy
87Bakers-6
88Bakers/Cal-250

Brooks, Bob
89AS/Cal-54UMP
90AS/Cal-33UMP
91CalLgAS-28UMP

Brooks, Brian Todd
87CharRain-1
88River/Cal-216
88River/ProC-1410
89Wichita/Rock-25
89Wichita/Rock/Up-12

Brooks, Craig
81Bristol-1

Brooks, Damon
86AubAs-6
87AubAs-5

Brooks, Desi
86Lynch-3
87Lynch-6

Brooks, Eric
89Myrtle/ProC-1460
91Dunedin/ClBest-12
91Dunedin/ProC-208
92Dunedin/ClBest-4
92Dunedin/ProC-2002
93Dunedin/ClBest-3
93Dunedin/ProC-1798

Brooks, Hubert
(Hubie)
79Jacks-3
80Tidew-15
81T-259R
81T/Tr-742
82D-476
82F-522
82F/St-81
82K-10
82OPC-266
82T-246TL
82T-494
82T/St-68
83D-49
83F-539
83F/St-7M
83OPC-134
83OPC/St-261
83T-134
83T/St-261
84D-607
84F-582
84Jacks/Smok-3
84Nes/792-368
84OPC-368
84T-368
84T/St-103
85D-197
85Expo/PostC-3
85F-74
85F/Up-U10
85Leaf-214
85OPC-222
85OPC/Post-5
85T-222
85T/St-104
85T/Tr-9T
86D-55
86D/HL-15
86Expo/Prov/Pan-1
86Expo/Prov/Post-3
86F-244
86F/LimEd-7
86F/Mini-52
86F/St-12
86GenMills/Book-6M
86Leaf-44
86OPC-308
86Provigo-1
86Sf-187
86T-555
86T/St-77
86T/Super-15
86T/Tatt-13M
87D-17DK
87D-88
87D/AAS-48
87D/DKsuper-17
87D/OD-91
87F-314
87F/GameWin-7
87F/LL-6
87F/Mini-14
87F/St-16
87GenMills/Book-4M
87Ho/St-4
87KayBee-6
87Kraft-42
87Leaf-142
87Leaf-17DK
87OPC-3
87RedFoley/St-91
87Sf-18
87Sf-197M
87Sf-79M
87Sf/TPrev-20M
87Stuart-8M
87T-650
87T/Coins-27
87T/Gloss60-46
87T/St-76
88D-468
88D/AS-45
88D/Best-12
88F-179
88Grenada-17
88Ho/Disc-5
88Leaf-257
88OPC-50
88Panini/St-328
88S-305
88Sf-187
88T-50
88T/Big-81
88T/St-81

88T/St/Backs-10
88T/UK-8
89B-367
89D-220
89D/Best-292
89F-371
89F/BBMVP's-5
89OPC-221
89Panini/St-123
89RedFoley/St-13
89S-53
89Sf-96
89T-485
89T/Big-301
89T/LJN-40
89T/Mini-21
89T/St-72
89T/UK-8
89UD-122
90B-100
90Classic-129
90Classic/III-75
90D-130
90D/BestNL-115
90F-341
90F/Can-341
90F/Up-U19
90Leaf-16
90Mother/Dodg-10
90OPC-745
90Pol/Dodg-21
90Publlnt/St-169
90S-299
90S/Tr-34T
90T-745
90T/Big-262
90T/St-77
90T/Tr-14T
90UD-197
90UD/Ext-791
91B-461
91BBBest/HitM-4
91Classic/200-77
91D-349
91F-195
91F/UltraUp-U94
91F/Up-U100
91Kahn/Mets-7
91Leaf-295
91OPC-115
91OPC/Premier-15
91Panini/FrSt-59
91Panini/St-56
91RedFoley/St-13
91S-196
91S/RookTr-5T
91StCl-325
91T-115
91T/Tr-14T
91UD-217
91UD/Ext-787
91WIZMets-52
92B-97
92D-64
92F-496
92L-378
92L/BlkGold-378
92OPC-457
92OPC/Premier-198
92Panini-226
92Pinn-449
92Pol/Angel-4
92S-107
92S/RookTr-69T
92StCl-754
92Studio-142
92T-457
92T/Gold-457
92T/GoldWin-457
92T/Tr-15T
92T/TrGold-15T
92UD-114
92UD-709
92Ultra-322
93Cadaco-9
93D-563
93StCl/Royal-26
93UD-680
94D-166
94F-151
94S-125
94S/GoldR-125

Brooks, Jerry
88GreatF-11
89AS/Cal-18
89Bakers/Cal-203
90SanAn/GS-6
91AAA/LineD-2
91AAAGame/ProC-1
91Albuq/LineD-2
91Albuq/ProC-1153
92Albuq/ProC-733
92Albuq/SB-6

Brooks, John
25Exh-19

Brooks, Jonathan J.
(Mandy)
No Cards.

Brooks, Kevin
88Virgini/Star-3

Brooks, Michael
75OkCty/Team-22
75SanAn
76Baton
82Redwd-1

Brooks, Monte
87Spokane-12
88Charl/ProC-1204
89River/Best-27
89River/Cal-10
89River/ProC-1417
90CharRain/ProC-2048

Brooks, Ramy Jr.
90Eugene/GS-3
91Eugene/ClBest-7
91Eugene/ProC-3728
92Eugene/ClBest-7
92Eugene/ProC-3032
93Rockford/ClBest-4

Brooks, Robert
(Bobby)
70OPC-381R
70T-381R
71OPC-633R
71T-633R

Brooks, Rodney
88Hamil/ProC-1740

Brooks, Trey
83MidldC-16
84Iowa-14
85Iowa-3
86Iowa-4

Broome, Kim
89Welland/Pucko-7

Brophy, E.J.
92Martins/ClBest-25
92Martins/ProC-3057

Brosious, Frank
82BurlR/Frit-8
82BurlR/TCMA-14

Brosius, Scott
88Madis-5
88MidwLAS/GS-50
89Huntsvl/Best-12
90Foil/Best-74
90Huntsvl/Best-15
91AAA/LineD-529
91Tacoma/LineD-529
91Tacoma/ProC-2310
92B-527
92Classic/I-19
92Classic/II-T5
92D-591
92F-671
92Mother/A's-27
92Pinn-274
92S-846
92T/91Debut-22
92Tacoma/ProC-2508
92UD-312
92Ultra-420
93D-419
93Pac/Spanish-218
93StCl-62
93StCl/1stDay-62
93StCl/A's-27
93T-796
93T/Gold-796
93UD-681
93Ultra-603
94D-630
94F-256
94Finest-396
94L-208
94StCl-164
94StCl/1stDay-164
94StCl/Gold-164
94T-74
94T/Gold-74
94UD-306

Broskie, Sigmund T.
(Siggy)
No Cards.

Brosnan, Jason
89GreatF-10
90AS/Cal-17
90Bakers/Cal-234
91AA/LineD-532
91SanAn/LineD-532
92Albuq/SB-7
92VeroB/ProC-2866

Brosnan, Jim
55B-229
57T-155
58T-342
59T-194
60L-124
60T-449
61T-513
61T/RO-25
61T/St-15
62J-125
62Kahn
62P-125
62T-2
63T-116
90LitSun-10

Brosnan, Timothy
N172

Bross, Terry
88LitFalls/Pucko-15
89StLucie/Star-2
90B-129
90D-502
90Jacks/GS-7
90T/TVMets-37
90TexLgAS/GS-32
91D-34RR
91Tidew/ProC-2501
92F-653
92LasVegas/SB-227
92S-763
92S/Rook-21
92Sky/AAASingl-111
92T/91Debut-23
92UD-531

Brothers, John
91Princet/ClBest-25
91Princet/ProC-3505

Brottem, Anton C.
(Tony)
No Cards.

Broughton, Cecil C.
(Cal)
N172

Brouhard, Mark Steven
82D-154
82F-135
82Pol/Brew-29
82T-517
83D-532
83F-28
83Gard-3
83T-167
84D-211
84F-195
84Gard-2
84Nes/792-528
84Pol/Brew-29
84T-528
85D-149
85F-576
85Gard-2
85Pol/Brew-29
85T-653
86OPC-21
86T-473
92Brew/Carlson-3

Brousseau, Fernand
52Laval-95

Brouthers, Arthur H.
(Art)
No Cards.

Brouthers, Dennis J.
(Dan)
50Callahan
50W576-7
75F/Pion-6
76Shakey-30
80Perez/HOF-30
80SSPC/HOF
81Tiger/Detroit-80
89HOF/St-7
89Smok/Dodg-3
90BBWit-102
90Target-79
N162
N172
N284
N300/unif
Scrapp
WG1-20

Brovia, Joseph John
(Joe)
48Sommer-11
52Mother-51
53Mother-18
77Fritsch-3

Brow, Dennis
88PrWill/Star-4
89PrWill/Star-2

Brow, Scott
90StCath/ProC-3458
91Dunedin/ClBest-1
91Dunedin/ProC-197
92Dunedin/ClBest-3
92Dunedin/ProC-1990
93B-435
93F/Final-286
93Knoxvl/ProC-1241
94Pac/Cr-634
94StCl/Team-169
94Ultra-435

Brow, Steve
87FtLaud-28

Browder, Bubba
88Wythe/ProC-1987

Brower, Bob
83BurlR-13
83BurlR/Frit-11
83Tulsa-13
85OKCty-21
86OKCty-1
87D-651
87D/Rook-49
87F/Up-U10
87Mother/Rang-18
87Sf/Rook-3
87Smok/R-26
87T/Tr-10T
88D-346
88F-461
88Mother/R-18
88OPC-252
88RedFoley/St-9
88S-236
88Smok/R-16
88T-252
88ToysRUs-2
89B-182
89D-411
89F-514
89S-344
89T-754
89UD-439
90Publlnt/St-531
90T/TVYank-37
92OkCty/ProC-1925
92OkCty/SB-305
92Yank/WIZ80-19
93Rang/Keeb-83

Brower, Jim
92MN-21M

Brower, Louis Lester
(Lou)
No Cards.

Brown, Adam
88Bakers/Cal-242
88CalLgAS-48
89SanAn/Best-10
90AAASingl/ProC-68
90Albuq/CMC-14
90Albuq/ProC-347
90Albuq/Trib-3
90ProC/Singl-416
90SanAn/GS-7
91FSLAS/ProC-FSL36
91VeroB/ClBest-14
91VeroB/ProC-775
92SanAn/ProC-3977
92SanAn/SB-557

Brown, Alvin
91Elizab/ProC-4302
91Kenosha/ClBest-1
91Kenosha/ProC-2077

Brown, Anthony
90Welland/Pucko-10
91Augusta/ClBest-23
91Augusta/ProC-817
91ClBest/Singl-246

Brown, Bob
94Conlon-1281
V94-5

Brown, Brant
92Classic/DP-58
92FrRow/DP-83
92Peoria/Team-5
93B-284
93StCl/MurphyS-194
94B-494
94FExcel-163
94SigRook-33

Brown, Bryan
92WinHaven/ClBest-18
92WinHaven/ProC-1792

Brown, Carmon
86Lipscomb-5

Brown, Chad
92MedHat/ProC-3203
92MedHat/SportP-2
93StCath/ClBest-4
93StCath/ProC-3967

Brown, Charles E.
(Buster)
E90/1
M116

Brown, Charlie
92GulfCY/ProC-3780

Brown, Clinton
35BU-189
35BU-82
91Conlon/Sport-132

Brown, Craig
83AlexD-19
84PrWill-26
85Nashua-4
86Nashua-4
87Harris-8

Brown, Curt S.
84Colum-15
84Colum/Pol-1
85Colum-3
85Colum/Pol-4
86Indianap-25
87Indianap-13
88CharlK/Pep-24
88RochR/Gov-4
92Yank/WIZ80-21

Brown, Curtis Jr.
(Curt)
81Holyo-11

Brown, Dan
89SanDiegoSt/Smok-4
91Martins/ClBest-26
91Martins/ProC-3444
92Clearw/ProC-2047
92ProC/Tomorrow-304

Brown, Dana
88CapeCod/Sum-95
89Batavia/ProC-1932
90Spartan/Best-19
90Spartan/ProC-2502
90Spartan/Star-2
91AA/LineD-504
91Reading/LineD-504
91Reading/ProC-1380

Brown, Danny
90AR-3

Brown, Daren
89StCath/ProC-2073
90Myrtle/ProC-2770
91Dunedin/ClBest-2
91Dunedin/ProC-198
92Knoxvl/ProC-2981
92Knoxvl/SB-376
93Knoxvl/ProC-1242

Brown, Darrell Wayne
80Evansvl/TCMA-11
84F-556
84Nes/792-193
84T-193
84T/St-311
85D-558
85F-270
85RochR-11
85T-767
85T/St-306

Brown, Dave 1

78Laugh/Black-27
90Negro/Star-12
Brown, Dave 2
89Erie/Star-4
Brown, Delos Hight
No Cards.
Brown, Dickie
90BurlInd/ProC-3002
91ColInd/ClBest-10
91ColInd/ProC-1477
92ColRS/ClBest-2
92ColRS/ProC-2380
92Kinston/ClBest-5
93Kinston/Team-2
Brown, Don
87Cedar-22
88Greens/ProC-1572
89Cedar/Star-26
89Chatt/Best-22
89Chatt/GS-6
Brown, Drummond Nic.
No Cards.
Brown, Duane
90Ashvl/ClBest-3
91Ashvl/ProC-561
92Ashvl/ClBest-10
Brown, Edward P.
(Ed)
No Cards.
Brown, Edward William
(Eddie)
28Exh-1
90Target-80
E126-44
E126-50
W575
Brown, Edwin Randolph
(Randy)
No Cards.
Brown, Elmer
90Target-81
Brown, Eric
74Cedar
82Idaho-4
Brown, Fred Herbert
No Cards.
Brown, George
WG3-6
Brown, Gerry
72Dimanche*-129M
Brown, Greg 1
78Wausau
Brown, Greg 2
91Batavia/ClBest-24
91Batavia/ProC-3477
92Spartan/ProC-1257
Brown, Hector Harold
(Skinny)
53T-184
54T-172
55B-221
55T-148
57T-194
58Hires-18
58T-394
59T-487
60T-89
61T-218
61T-46LL
62T-488
63T-289
64T-56
91CharRain/ProC-89
91Crown/Orio-54
91T/Arc53-184
92Yank/WIZ60-18
94T/Arc54-172
Brown, Isaac
(Ike)
70OPC-152
70T-152
71MLB/St-387
71OPC-669
71T-669
72OPC-284
72T-284
72T/Cloth-3
73OPC-633
73T-633
74OPC-409
74T-409
Brown, J.B.
83GlenF-2

Brown, Jackie G.
71MLB/St-531
71OPC-591
71T-591
72Dimanche*-6
74OPC-89
74T-89
75OPC-316
75T-316
75T/M-316
76OPC-301
76T-301
77OPC-36
77T-147
78Cr/PCL-23
78OPC-126
78T-699
86Hawaii-1CO
87Vanco-2CO
88BuffB/ProC-1479CO
89BuffB/CMC-25CO
89BuffB/ProC-1683CO
90AAASingl/ProC-505CO
90BuffB/ProC-390CO
90BuffB/Team-3CO
91AAA/LineD-50CO
91BuffB/LineD-50CO
91BuffB/ProC-557CO
92WSox-NNO
93Rang/Keeb-84
93WSox-30M
Brown, James D.
(Don)
No Cards.
Brown, James Kevin
(Kevin)
87D-627
88BBAmer-25
88Tulsa-15
89D-613
89D/Best-256
89D/Rook-44
89F-641M
89F/Up-63
89Mother/R-18
89S/Tr-89
89Smok/R-4
89T/Tr-15T
89UD/Ext-752
90B-488
90Classic/III-41
90D-343
90D/BestAL-13
90F-291
90Leaf-47
90Mother/Rang-21
90OPC-136
90Panini/St-168
90PublInt/St-405
90S-210
90S/100Ris-28
90S/YS/I-29
90Sf-73
90T-136
90T/Big-261
90T/JumboR-5
90T/St-248
90ToysRUs-6
90TulsaDG/Best-32
90UD-123
91B-274
91D-314
91F-282
91Leaf-250
91Mother/Rang-21
91OPC-584
91Panini/St-208
91S-846
91StCl-56
91T-584
91T/90Debut-22
91UD-472
91Ultra-347
92B-191
92D-55
92F-299
92L-326
92L/BlkGold-326
92Mother/Rang-21
92OPC-297
92Pinn-405
92S-709
92S/Proctor-9

92StCl-123
92T-297
92T/Gold-297
92T/GoldWin-297
92TripleP-226
92UD-578
92Ultra-438
93B-685
93D-377
93F-317
93Flair-277
93Kenner/Fig-5
93L-202
93OPC-20
93Pac/Spanish-306
93Panini-156LL
93Panini-79
93Pinn-356
93Rang/Keeb-397
93S-146
93Select-204
93Select/Ace-7
93Select/StatL-62
93Select/StatL-85M
93StCl-396
93StCl/1stDay-396
93StCl/MurphyS-176
93StCl/Rang-20
93Studio-21
93T-785
93T/Finest-134
93T/FinestRef-134
93T/Gold-785
93T/Hill-14
93TripleP-252
93UD-76
93UD/FunPack-154
93UD/SP-190
93Ultra-276
94B-325
94D-22
94D/Special-22
94F-303
94Finest-257
94L-231
94OPC-205
94Pac/Cr-610
94Pinn-71
94Pinn/Artist-71
94Pinn/Museum-71
94RedFoley-8M
94S-99
94S/GoldR-99
94Sf/2000-132
94StCl-382
94StCl/1stDay-382
94StCl/Gold-382
94StCl/Team-260
94Studio-151
94T-345
94T/Gold-345
94TripleP-191
94TripleP/Medal-13M
94UD-487
94Ultra-126
Brown, James Murray
(John)
67OPC-72R
67T-72R
Brown, James Roberson
(Jimmy)
39PlayBall-132
40PlayBall-112
41DP-146
41PlayBall-12
W754
Brown, Jarvis
87Kenosha-14
88Kenosha/ProC-1390
88MidwLAS/GS-33
89Visalia/Cal-106
89Visalia/ProC-1437
90OrlanSR/Best-9
90OrlanSR/ProC-1095
90OrlanSR/Star-3
91AAA/LineD-404
91Portl/LineD-404
91Portl/ProC-1576
92D-770
92F-669
92Pinn-544
92ProC/Tomorrow-92
92S-870
92S/Rook-27

92StCl-515
92T/91Debut-24
92Ultra-394
94F-658
94Pac/Cr-519
94S-281
94S/GoldR-281
94StCl/Team-36
Brown, Jeff
85Anchora-6
85FtMyr-14
87SanAn-12
87VeroB-16
88Bakers/Cal-234
88CalLgAS-46
91CharRain/ClBest-3
92Bristol/ClBest-2
92Bristol/ProC-1400
92Watlo/ClBest-8
92Watlo/ProC-2136
94ClBest/Gold-140
Brown, Jerald Ray
(Jake)
75Lafay
Brown, Jim
76QuadC
76Wausau
Brown, Jimmy
90Kissim/DIMD-3
91Niagara/ClBest-2
91Niagara/ProC-3639
Brown, John C.
(Chris)
80Clinton-16
84Cram/PCL-23
85F/Up-U11
85Mother/Giants-18
85T/Tr-10T
86D-553
86F-535
86F/LimEd-8
86F/Mini-108
86F/St-13
86KayBee-2
86Leaf-215
86Mother/Giants-18
86OPC-383
86Seven/Coin-W13
86Sf-78
86T-383
86T/Gloss60-10
86T/St-311
86T/St-85
86T/Tatt-18M
87Classic-65
87D-11DK
87D-80
87D/AAS-44
87D/DKsuper-11
87D/OD-100
87F-268
87F/LL-7
87F/Mini-15
87F/RecSet-2
87F/Up-U11
87Leaf-11DK
87Leaf-236
87Mother/SFG-5
87OPC-180
87Sf-115M
87Sf-13
87Sf/TPrev-10M
87T-180
87T/St-86
88Coke/Padres-35
88D-483
88D/Best-77
88F-578
88KennerFig-13
88Leaf-221
88OPC-112
88Panini/St-408
88S-363
88Smok/Padres-5
88T-568
88T/Big-130
88T/St-111
89B-106
89D-183
89D/Tr-9
89F-301
89S-369
89T-481
89T/St-103

89UD-193
89UD/Ext-784
90PublInt/St-469
Brown, John Lindsay
(Lindsay)
90Target-82
Brown, Keith
87Cedar-10
88Chatt/Best-3
88Nashvl/Team-4
89Chatt/II/Team-6
89D-115
89F-154
89Nashvl/CMC-2
89Nashvl/ProC-1296
89Nashvl/Team-3
90AAASingl/ProC-536
90CedarDG/Best-32
90Nashvl/CMC-9
90Nashvl/ProC-224
90ProC/Singl-134
91AAA/LineD-253
91F-58
91Nashvl/LineD-253
91Nashvl/ProC-2149
92Nashvl/SB-279
93T/Gold-823
Brown, Ken
88PrWill/Star-5
Brown, Kevin D.
86Lynch-4
87Sumter-7
87Wichita-21
88StLucie/Star-3
88Wichita-32
89Jacks/GS-26
89Tidew/ProC-1962
90AAASingl/ProC-266
90B-127
90F/Can-291
90ProC/Singl-353
90StLucie/Star-2
90T/TVMets-38
90Tidew/CMC-2
90Tidew/ProC-535
91B-49
91Brewer/MillB-5
91D-674
91Leaf-475
91Pol/Brew-5
91WIZMets-53
92Calgary/ProC-3726
92Calgary/SB-52
92F-174
Brown, Knock-out
T3/Box-66
Brown, Kurt
86AppFx-4
87Penin-26
88Tampa/Star-3
89Saraso/Star-1
90BirmB/Best-2
90BirmB/ProC-1111
90Foil/Best-189
91AAA/LineD-628
91Vanco/LineD-628
91Vanco/ProC-1596
Brown, Larry Lesley
64T-301
65T-468
66OPC-16
66T-16
67CokeCap/Indian-3
67OPC-145
67T-145
68Kahn
68T-197
69MB-42
69MLB/St-39
69T-503
69T/St-163
70MLB/St-194
70OPC-391
70T-391
71MLB/St-363
71OPC-539
71T-539
72MB-53
72OPC-279
72T-279
73JP
81TCMA-416
83LasVegas/BHN-3
84Cram/PCL-238

91Crown/Orio-55
93Rang/Keeb-85
94TedW-102
Brown, Larry
78Laugh/Black-2
86Negro/Frit-26
Brown, Leon
75Phoenix/Caruso-1
75Phoenix/CircleK-21
91WIZMets-54
Brown, Lewis J.
(Lew)
No Cards.
Brown, Lloyd
90Target-83
91Conlon/Sport-181
Brown, Mace
40PlayBall-220
41DP-36
90Target-84
R303/A
R312
V351B-6
Brown, Mark
81Miami-4
83RochR-2
85Toledo-3
86T-451
86Toledo-4
89Erie/Star-28
91Crown/Orio-56
Brown, Marty
86Cedar/TCMA-14
87Vermont-5
88AAA/ProC-26
88Nashvl/CMC-18
88Nashvl/ProC-481
88Nashvl/Team-5
89F-645M
89Nashvl/CMC-14
89Nashvl/ProC-1292
89Nashvl/Team-4
89S/HotRook-70
90CedarDG/Best-29
90D/Rook-39
90Rochester/L&U-17
91AAA/LineD-79
91ColoSp/LineD-79
91ColoSp/ProC-2188
91Crown/Orio-57
Brown, Matt
90Elizab/Star-7
91ClBest/Singl-93
91Visalia/ClBest-12
91Visalia/ProC-1743
92Visalia/ClBest-16
92Visalia/ProC-1017
Brown, Michael C.
(Mike)
81Holyo-8
82Spokane-19
84Cram/PCL-117
84D-42
84F/X-17
84Nes/792-643
84T-643
85D-207
85F-296
85Smok/Cal-4
85T-258
86D-642
86F-605
86F/Mini-117
86Leaf-256
86T-114
87D-168
87F-607
87Richm/Crown-42
87Richm/TCMA-27
87T-341
88Toledo/CMC-24
88Toledo/ProC-611
89Edmon/CMC-18
89Edmon/ProC-558
Brown, Michael G.
(Mike)
83T/X-15
84D-517
84F-394
84Nes/792-472
84T-472
86Pawtu-3
87Calgary-7
87D-563
87F-583
87T-271
88ColoSp/CMC-2
88ColoSp/ProC-1526
90PrWill/Team-1
91FtLaud/ClBest-29CO
91FtLaud/ProC-2444
92ColClip/Pol-2M
92ColClip/SB-125CO
93ColClip/Pol-24M
Brown, Mike 1
(Michael)
90Welland/Pucko-2
91Augusta/ClBest-24
91Augusta/ProC-809
91ClBest/Singl-88
92Augusta/ProC-243
94FExcel-251
Brown, Mike 2
91GreatF/SportP-3
92Yakima/ProC-3452
Brown, Mike 3
86Osceola-2
87Osceola-3
89Kinston/Star-26
90Reno/Cal-286MG
91ColInd/ProC-1504MG
92ColRS/ClBest-27MG
92ColRS/ProC-2407
Brown, Mordecai
10Domino-17
11Diamond-4
11Helmar-91
12Sweet/Pin-80A
12Sweet/Pin-80B
14CJ-32
14Piedmont/St-7
15CJ-32
50Callahan
50W576-8
60Exh/HOF-5
60F-9
61F-11
63Bz/ATG-13
69Bz/Sm
75F/Pion-23
76Motor-5
76Shakey-57
80Pac/Leg-71
80Perez/HOF-56
80SSPC/HOF
89HOF/St-60
90BBWit-89
92Conlon/Sport-555
92Cub/OldStyle-4
93Conlon-883
93CrackJack-18
BF2-63
D329-17
D350/2-23
E103
E270/2
E300
E90/1
E90/3
E91
E93
E96
E98
M101/4-17
M101/5-23
M116
S74-58
T201
T202
T204
T205
T206
T213/blue
T215/blue
T222
T3-1
W555
WG1-1
WG3-7
Brown, Ollie Lee
66T-524R
67CokeCap/Giant-2
67OPC-83
67T-83
68CokeCap/Giant-2
68T-223
69MLB/St-190
69OPC-149
69T-149
69T/4in1-8M
69T/S-63
69T/St-92
70K-55
70MLB/St-109
70OPC-130
70T-130
70T/PI-18
70T/S-36
70T/Super-36
71MLB/St-220
71OPC-505
71T-505
71T/Coins-133
72MB-54
72T-551
72T-552A
73OPC-526
73T-526
74OPC-625
74T-625
75OPC-596
75T-596
75T/M-596
76OPC-223
76SSPC-466
76T-223
77T-84
81TCMA-368
Brown, Oscar Lee
71MLB/St-5
71OPC-52R
71T-52R
72OPC-516
72T-516
73OPC-312
73T-312
Brown, Paul D.
62T-181
63T-478
64T-319
Brown, Paul
87Elmira/Black-34
87Hawaii-28
88Lynch/Star-2
90LynchRS/Team-15
91WinHaven/ClBest-2
91WinHaven/ProC-482
Brown, Randy
76Wausau
Brown, Randy J.
90Elmira/Pucko-3
91ClBest/Singl-131
91WinHaven/ClBest-15
91WinHaven/ProC-495
92WinHaven/ClBest-3
92WinHaven/ProC-1783
Brown, Reggie
89Helena/SP-3
Brown, Renard
87Stockton-9
Brown, Richard Ernest
(Dick)
58T-456
59T-61
60T-256
61T-192
62J-21
62P-21
62P/Can-21
62Salada-37
62Shirriff-37
62T-438
63J-52
63P-52
63T-112
78TCMA-95
91Crown/Orio-53
Brown, Rick
86LitFalls-4
87Columbia-12
88StLucie/Star-4
Brown, Rob
89SanDiegoSt/Smok-5
90CharlR/Star-2
91AA/LineD-576
91Tulsa/LineD-576
91Tulsa/ProC-2765
91Tulsa/Team-2
92Tulsa/ProC-2688
92Tulsa/SB-604
Brown, Robert M.
34G-81
Brown, Robert W.
(Bobby)
47TipTop
49B-19
50B-101
51B-110
51BR-B6
52B-105
52BR
91Swell/Great-15
93TWill-61
R346-9
Brown, Rogers Lee
(Bobby)
79Colum-27
80T-670R
81D-469
81F-95
81OPC-107
81T-418
82D-552
82F-30
82T-791
82T/Tr-12T
83LasVegas/BHN-2
83T-287
84D-478
84F-296
84Mother/Padres-14
84Nes/792-261
84Smok/Padres-2
84T-261
84T/St-157
85D-383
85F-28
85Mother/Padres-23
85OPC-92
85T-583
85Utica-17
86T-182
92Yank/WIZ70-26
92Yank/WIZ80-20
93UD/ATH-19
Brown, Ron
91MissSt-6
92MissSt-5
93MissSt-5
Brown, Ronnie
89Wythe/Star-3
Brown, Samuel W.
(Sam)
No Cards.
Brown, Scott
80Indianap-17
81Indianap-19
82F-60
82T-351R
83Omaha-4
Brown, Sid
89Panini/St-169
Brown, Stacy
89Burllnd/Star-3
Brown, Steven E.
80ElPaso-16
81SLCity-3
82Spokane-1
85Indianap-24
Brown, Tab
89Pulaski/ProC-1899
90Foil/Best-62
90ProC/Singl-828
90Sumter/Best-2
90Sumter/ProC-2425
Brown, Terry M.
87Beloit-15
89Kenosha/ProC-1068
89Kenosha/Star-2
Brown, Terry
89KS*-49
Brown, Thomas D.
76Baton
78SanJose-16
79Tacoma-2
80Syrac-8
81Syrac-2
Brown, Thomas Michael
(Tom)
49B-178
49Eureka-31
52B-236
52T-281
53B/Col-42
90Target-85
Brown, Thomas T.
(Tom)
N172
N284
N526
Brown, Thomas William
(Tom)
64T-311
Brown, Tibor
92FrRow/DP-62
Brown, Timothy
88StCath/ProC-2007
89Myrtle/ProC-1464
90Dunedin/Star-4
91Dunedin/ClBest-3
91Dunedin/ProC-199
92ClBest-158
92Knoxvl/ProC-2982
92Knoxvl/SB-377
93Syrac/ProC-993
Brown, Todd
86Stockton-3
87ElPaso-17
88Denver/CMC-19
88Denver/ProC-1278
Brown, Tom
80Syrac/Team-6
81Syrac/Team-4
89Hagers/Best-11
89Hagers/ProC-283
89Pac/SenLg-139
90Hagers/Best-5CO
90Hagers/ProC-1432CO
90Hagers/Star-27CO
Brown, Tony
86Reading-4
87Reading-2
88EastLAS/ProC-31
88Reading/ProC-867
89Tidew/CMC-27
89Tidew/ProC-1974
90Foil/Best-298
90Huntsvl/Best-20
92MidldA/OneHour-3
92MidldA/ProC-4036
92MidldA/SB-455
Brown, Walter G.
(Jumbo)
28LaPresse-19
33G-192
39PlayBall-124
40PlayBall-154
92Conlon/Sport-454
Brown, Willard
E223
N172
N338/2
Brown, Willard Jessie
90Negro/Star-7
94TedW-101
Brown, William James
(Gates)
64T-471
65OPC-19
65T-19
66T-362
67OPC-134
67T-134
68CokeCap/Tiger-7
68T-583
69MB-41
69T-256
70OPC-98
70T-98
71MLB/St-386
71OPC-503
71T-503
72MB-52
72OPC-187
72T-187
73OPC-508
73T-508
74OPC-389
74T-389
75OPC-371
75T-371
75T/M-371
76SSPC-371
81Tiger/Detroit-106
84Tiger/Wave-9CO
86Tiger/Sport-18
88Domino-1
89Pac/SenLg-199

89TM/SenLg-13
Brown, William Verna
(Bill)
No Cards.
Brown, Willie
92Erie/ClBest-1
92Erie/ProC-1635
93StCl/MurphyS-54
93T-497M
93T/Gold-497M
Brown, Winston 1
61T-391
Brown, Winston 2
89Spring/Best-8
Browne, Byron Ellis
66OPC-139R
66T-139R
67CokeCap/Cub-18
67T-439
68T-296
70OPC-388
70T-388
71MLB/St-171
71OPC-659
71T-659
Browne, Byron
92Beloit/ClBest-4
92Beloit/ProC-396
Browne, Earl James
No Cards.
Browne, George Edward
E90/3
E91
T206
T3-84
Browne, Jerry
86Tulsa-9A
87Classic/Up-146
87D-41RR
87D/OD-170
87D/Rook-29
87F-647M
87F/Up-U12
87Leaf-41RR
87Mother/Rang-22
87Sf/Rook-4
87Smok/R-31
87T/Tr-11T
88D-408
88F-462
88Leaf-236
88Mother/R-22
88OPC-139
88Panini/St-201
88S-278
88S/YS/II-13
88Smok/R-15
88T-139
88T/Big-163
88T/JumboR-21
88ToysRUs-3
89B-85
89D-529
89D/Best-280
89D/Tr-44
89F/Up-26
89T-532
89T/Big-236
89T/Tr-16T
89UD-314
90B-332
90Classic-53
90D-138
90F-487
90F/Can-487
90Leaf-48
90OPC-442
90Panini/St-54
90PublInt/St-555
90S-52
90Sf-111
90T-442
90T/Big-256
90T/Coins-7
90T/St-210
90TulsaDG/Best-27
90UD-426
91B-71
91D-162
91F-363
91Indian/McDon-5
91Leaf-43
91OPC-76
91Panini/FrSt-217
91S-481
91StCl-25
91T-76
91UD-116
91Ultra-108
92F-107
92F/Up-47
92OPC-219
92Pinn-208
92S-496
92StCl-251
92T-219
92T/Gold-219
92T/GoldWin-219
92T/Tr-16T
92T/TrGold-16T
92TripleP-130M
92UD-340
92Ultra-48
93D-447
93F-292
93L-150
93Mother/A's-13
93OPC-234
93Pac/Spanish-219
93Panini-18
93Pinn-391
93Rang/Keeb-86
93S-382
93StCl-509
93StCl/1stDay-509
93StCl/A's-4
93StCl/MurphyS-167
93T-383
93T/Gold-383
93UD-129
93Ultra-255
94F-257
94Pinn-489
94S-349
94StCl/Team-68
94T-624
94T/Gold-624
Browne, Prentice A.
(Pidge)
77Fritsch-50
89Smok/Ast-20
Brownholtz, Joe
92CharlR/ProC-2219
92Gaston/ClBest-8
Browning, Jim
33SK*-41
Browning, Louis R.
(Pete)
90Target-86
N172
Browning, Mike
82Nashvl-2
83Nashvl-2
84Cram/PCL-114
86Miami-3
87Miami-15
88Miami/Star-4
89ColMud/Best-17
89ColMud/ProC-122
89ColMud/Star-5
90ColMud/Best-20
90ColMud/ProC-1339
90ColMud/Star-6
Browning, Tom
83Tampa-5
84Wichita/Rock-5
85D-634
85D/HL-43
85F/Up-U12
85T/Tr-11T
86D-384
86Drake-37
86F-173
86F/Mini-38
86F/Slug-4
86F/St-14
86F/WaxBox-C6
86KayBee-3
86Leaf-179
86Seven/Coin-S15
86Sf-185M
86Sf-79
86T-652
86T/Gloss60-49
86T/Mini-40
86T/St-141
86T/St-313
86T/Super-16
86T/Tatt-10M
86TexGold-32
87Classic-78
87D-63
87D/OD-194
87F-194
87Kahn-32
87Leaf-138
87OPC-65
87Sf/TPrev-4M
87T-65
87T/St-137
88D-63
88D/Best-335
88F-228
88Kahn/Reds-32
88S-132
88T-577
88T/Big-96
89B-306
89Classic-126
89D-71
89D/Best-62
89F-153
89F-629M
89Kahn/Reds-32
89OPC-234
89Panini/St-4
89Panini/St-65
89S-554
89S-658HL
89S/HotStar-61
89Sf-180
89Sf-222M
89T-234
89T/Big-14
89T/Gloss60-46
89T/Mini-6
89T/St-141
89T/St-7
89T/St/Backs-61
89UD-617
89Woolwth-9
90B-43
90Classic/Up-T7
90D-308
90D/BestNL-27
90D/Learning-54
90F-415
90F/Can-415
90Kahn/Reds-5
90Leaf-110
90MLBPA/Pins-20
90OPC-418
90Panini/St-247
90PublInt/St-23
90S-165
90S/100St-33
90Sf-91
90T-418
90T/Big-48
90T/St-135
90UD-189
91B-684
91Classic/200-10
91D-528
91F-59
91Kahn/Reds-32
91Kenner-7
91Leaf-88
91Leaf/Stud-161
91OPC-151
91Pep/Reds-4
91S-229
91S/100SS-32
91StCl-235
91T-151
91UD-633
91USPlayC/AS-5S
91Ultra-89
92B-161
92D-136
92F-401
92L-46
92L/BlkGold-46
92OPC-339
92Pinn-101
92Reds/Kahn-32
92S-642
92StCl-624
92StCl/Dome-22
92T-339
92T/Gold-339
92T/GoldWin-339
92UD-461
92Ultra-186
93D-190
93F-387
93L-359
93OPC-74
93Pac/Spanish-79
93Pinn-405
93Reds/Kahn-5
93S-404
93Select-249
93T-733
93T/Gold-733
93TripleP-91
93UD-270
93Ultra-325
94F-406
94Finest-337
94Flair-144
94Pac/Cr-142
94Panini-161
94Pinn-335
94S-168
94S/GoldR-168
94StCl-433
94StCl/1stDay-433
94StCl/Gold-433
94T-619
94T/Gold-619
94Ultra-469
Broyles, Jason
90Kissim/DIMD-4
91Yakima/ClBest-19
91Yakima/ProC-4239
Brubaker, Bruce
65T-493R
67T-276
90Target-904
Brubaker, John
89Oneonta/ProC-2128
90FtLaud/Star-2
Brubaker, Wilbur L.
(Bill)
34G-4
36G
39PlayBall-130
40PlayBall-166
94Conlon-1133
R314
Brucato, Bob
89CharRain/ProC-973
Bruce, Andy
91Johnson/ClBest-5
91Johnson/ProC-3981
92ProC/Tomorrow-325
92StPete/ProC-2033
Bruce, Bob
60T-118
61T-83
62T-419
63Pep
63T-24
64T-282
65OPC-240
65T-240
66OPC-64
66T-64
66T/RO-11
66T/RO-8
67CokeCap/Brave-11
67T-417
89Smok/Ast-1
Bruce, Louis
(Lou)
No Cards.
Bruck, Tom
90BurlB/Best-5
90BurlB/ProC-2341
90BurlB/Star-5
Brucker, Earle F. Jr.
No Cards.
Brueggemann, Jeff
80Toledo-18
83Visalia/Frit-14GM
Brueggemann, Steve
85LitFalls-3
Bruehl, Darin
89AubAs/ProC-2179
Bruett, Joseph T.
(J.T.)
88CapeCod/Sum-168
89Kenosha/ProC-1074
89Kenosha/Star-3
90A&AASingle/ProC-154
90AS/Cal-13
90Portl/CMC-24
90ProC/Singl-576
90Visalia/Cal-74
90Visalia/ProC-2165
91AAA/LineD-405
91Portl/LineD-405
91Portl/ProC-1577
92B-112
92D/Rook-18
92Portl/SB-403
92Portland/ProC-2678
92Sky/AAASingl-184
93F/MLPII-8
93Pac/Spanish-519
93Pinn-241
93S-275
93StCl-397
93StCl/1stDay-397
93T-309
93T/Gold-309
93Ultra-229
Bruggy, Frank Leo
No Cards.
Brugo, Dale
91LynchRS/ClBest-1
Bruhert, Mike
78Tidew
79T-172
79Tucson-3
82Colum-7
82Colum/Pol-25
91WIZMets-55
Brumfield, Harvey
87Clearw-9
88Reading/ProC-881
89Reading/Best-20
89Reading/ProC-667
89Reading/Star-4
Brumfield, Jacob
87FtMyr-33
88Memphis/Best-6
89Memphis/Best-3
89Memphis/ProC-1188
89Memphis/Star-4
90BBCity/Star-3
90FSLAS/Star-26
90Star/ISingl-43
91AAA/LineD-327
91Omaha/LineD-327
91Omaha/ProC-1045
92D/Rook-19
92L-499
92L/BlkGold-499
92Nashvl/ProC-1844
92OPC-591M
92Pinn-553
92T-591M
92T/Gold-591M
92T/GoldWin-591M
92Ultra-481
93Pac/Spanish-80
93Reds/Kahn-6
93S-292
94D-473
94F-407
94Pac/Cr-143
94StCl-166
94StCl/1stDay-166
94StCl/Gold-166
94T-69
94T/Gold-69
Brumley, Duff
90Johnson/Star-5
91Hamil/ClBest-10
91Hamil/ProC-4029
92Hamil/ClBest-8
92Hamil/ProC-1582
94B-73
94FExcel-261
94FExcel/LL-5
94T-316M
94T/Gold-316M
94Ultra-427
Brumley, Mike
86Iowa-5
87Iowa-13
88AAA/ProC-21
88D-609
88LasVegas/CMC-19
88LasVegas/ProC-235
88TripleA/ASCMC-35
89D-302
89D/Rook-39

89F-302
89F/Up-30
89Mara/Tigers-12
89T/Big-324
90D-533
90Mother/Mar-26
90OPC-471
90S/100Ris-88
90T-471
90UD-312
91AAA/LineD-353
91F-445
91Pawtu/LineD-353
91Pawtu/ProC-45
91S-624
92OPC-407
92Pawtu/ProC-929
92Pawtu/SB-353
92S-363
92TX-6
Brumley, Tony Mike
(Mike)
60DF
64T-167R
65T-523
66OPC-29
66T-29
Brummer, Glenn Edward
82Louisvl-2
82T-561R
83D-418
83F-4
83T-311
84D-138
84F-321
84Nes/792-152
84T-152
85D-290
85Rangers-7
86F-557
86Hawaii-2
86T-616
93Rang/Keeb-87
Brummer, Jeff
90Yakima/Team-7
Brummett, Greg
88Alaska/Team-5
89Everett/Star-26
90Clinton/Best-7
90Clinton/ProC-2546
91Clinton/ClBest-23
92SanJose/ClBest-16
93F/Final-151
93StCl/Giant-28
Brunansky, Thomas A.
(Tom)
80ElPaso-17
81SLCity-21
82Spokane-20
82T-653R
82T/Tr-13T
83D-555
83F-607
83F/St-13M
83F/St-8M
83OPC-232
83OPC/St-309
83OPC/St-90
83T-232
83T/St-309
83T/St-90
83Twin/Team-17
83Twin/Team-33M
84D-242
84F-557
84Nes/792-447
84OPC-98
84T-447
84T/RD-7
84T/St-304
85D-364
85F-271
85FunFood/Pin-130
85GenMills-15
85Leaf-36
85OPC-122
85Seven/Minn-7
85T-122
85T/Gloss40-39
85T/RD-8
85T/St-299
85T/Super-57
85Twin/Seven-7
85Twin/Team-19
86D-192
86D-24DK
86D/AAS-44
86D/DKsuper-24
86F-387
86F/LimEd-9
86F/Mini-83
86F/St-15
86KayBee-4
86Leaf-24DK
86OPC-392
86Seven/Coin-C15
86Sf-80
86T-565
86T/St-276
86T/Tatt-18M
87D-194
87D/OD-222
87F-537
87F/Hottest-7
87F/St-17
87Leaf-244
87OPC-261
87RedFoley/St-75
87Sf-134
87Sf/TPrev-17M
87Stuart-22M
87T-776
87T/St-280
88D-245
88D/Best-19
88F-5
88F/Slug-4
88F/St-42
88F/Up-U117
88KennerFig-14
88Master/Disc-12
88OPC-375
88Panini/St-142
88S-194
88S/Tr-5T
88Sf-194
88Smok/Card-25
88T-375
88T/Big-211
88T/St-15
88T/St-275
88T/Tr-20T
89B-444
89Classic/Up/2-186
89D-112
89D/Best-187
89F-444
89F/Heroes-4
89KennerFig-17
89OPC-60
89Panini/St-187
89RedFoley/St-14
89S-184
89Sf-161
89Smok/Cards-1
89T-261TL
89T-60
89T/Big-54
89T/Hills-4
89T/LJN-152
89T/St-41
89T/UK-9
89UD-272
90B-202
90Classic-119
90D-399
90D/BestAL-130
90ElPasoATG/Team-34
90F-242
90F/Can-242
90F/Up-U70
90Leaf-447
90MLBPA/Pins-31
90OPC-409
90Panini/St-344
90PublInt/St-211
90S-72
90S/Tr-49T
90T-409
90T/Big-94
90T/St-45
90T/TVCard-31
90T/Tr-15T
90UD-257
90UD/Ext-708
91B-125
91Classic/200-11
91D-513
91F-88
91Leaf-164
91OPC-675
91Panini/FrSt-270
91Pep/RSox-2
91RedFoley/St-14
91S-245
91StCl-297
91T-675
91UD-163
91Ultra-29
92D-490
92F-34
92OPC-296
92Panini-89
92Pinn-314
92RedSox/Dunkin-4
92S-46
92StCl-464
92T-296
92T/Gold-296
92T/GoldWin-296
92UD-543
92USPlayC/RedSox-11D
92USPlayC/RedSox-6S
92Ultra-12
93D-693
93F-555
93F/Final-223
93L-226
93OPC-217
93OPC/Premier-34
93Pac/Spanish-28
93Pinn-534
93Pol/Brew-3
93S-612
93Select-210
93Select/RookTr-134T
93StCl-625
93StCl/1stDay-625
93T-532
93T/Gold-532
93TripleP-217
93UD-806
93UD/HRH-HR26
93Ultra-569
94Pol/Brew-4
94S-423
Brundage, Dave
87Clearw-20
88Vermont/ProC-951
89Wmsprt/ProC-642
89Wmsprt/Star-1
90Wmsprt/Star-3
91AAA/LineD-53
91Calgary/LineD-53
91Calgary/ProC-525
92Calgary/ProC-3742
92Calgary/SB-57
92Sky/AAASingl-26
93Calgary/ProC-1182CO
Brune, Jim
88Billings/ProC-1804
88Cedar/ProC-1154
Brunelle, Rodney
85Bend/Cram-4
87CharWh-7
88Clearw/Star-3
Brunenkant, Barry
84OKCty-15
85Tulsa-14
86Maine-1
87BuffB-5
Brunet, George
58T-139
63T-538
64T-322
65OPC-242
65T-242
66T-393
67CokeCap/DodgAngel-31
67OPC-122
67T-122
68T-347
69MB-43
69MLB/St-19
69MLBPA/Pin-3
69T-645
69T/St-141
70MLB/St-267
70OPC-328
70T-328
71MLB/St-269
71OPC-73
71T-73
72MB-55
91Crown/Orio-58
Bruneteau, Eddie
45Parade*-9
Bruneteau, Modere
45Parade*-10
Brunner, Tom
79Elmira-26
Bruno, Joe
80Penin/B-15
80Penin/C-21
87Cedar-12
88Chatt/Best-17
88SLAS-37
89Chatt/Best-21
89Chatt/GS-7
89SLAS-18
90Chatt/GS-7
Bruno, Julio
90CharRain/Best-5
90CharRain/ProC-2046
90Spokane/SportP-20
91ClBest/Singl-367
91Waterlo/ClBest-15
91Waterlo/ProC-1262
92ClBest-23
92HighD/ClBest-25
93B-546
94B-420
Bruno, Paul
91ClBest/Singl-343
91Kenosha/ClBest-23
91Kenosha/ProC-2078
Bruno, Thomas
77OPC-32
78Spring/Wiener-16
79T-724R
Brunsberg, Arlo A.
77Fritsch-24
Brunson, Bill
92Princet/ProC-3077
Brunson, Eddie
78Newar
80Holyo-7
Brunson, Matt
94B-28
94Pinn-433
94S-532
94UD-296UDC
94UD-547TP
94UD/CollC-27
94UD/CollC/Gold-27
94UD/CollC/Silv-27
Brunson, Will
92Princet/ClBest-14
Brunswick, Mark
85LitFalls-13
86Columbia-6
87Lynch-25
Brunswick, Tom
77Spartan
Brush, Robert
(Bob)
No Cards.
Bruske, James
87Kinston-17
88Wmsprt/ProC-1323
89Kinston/Star-4
90Canton/Best-18
90Canton/ProC-1285
90Canton/Star-1
90Star/ISingl-12
91AA/LineD-78
91Canton/LineD-78
91Canton/ProC-973
92Jacks/ProC-3992
94FExcel-197
Brusky, Brad
86Cedar/TCMA-2
87Vermont-1
88Cedar/ProC-1156
89Wmsprt/ProC-644
89Wmsprt/Star-2
Brusstar, Warren
78SSPC/270-54
78T-297
79BK/P-9
79T-653
80T-52
81OkCty/TCMA-4
81T-426
82F-242
82T-647
83Thorn-41
84D-442
84F-487
84Nes/792-304
84SevenUp-41
84T-304
85D-533
85F-51
85SevenUp-41
85T-189
86D-555
86F-362
86T-564
87SanJose-21
Brust, Dave
90Durham/Team-20
91Durham/ClBest-8
91Durham/ProC-1550
Brust, Jerry
76QuadC
Brutcher, Lenny
90Foil/Best-28
90MidwLgAS/GS-5
90SoBend/Best-1
90SoBend/GS-1
91Saraso/ClBest-2
91Saraso/ProC-1105
91UD-75
Bruton, William Haron
(Bill)
53JC-22
53SpicSpan/3x5-4
53SpicSpan/7x10-2
53T-214
54B-224
54JC-38
54SpicSpan/PostC-3
54T-109
55B-11
55Gol/Braves-3
55JC-38
55RFG-15
55SpicSpan/DC-3
55W605-15
56T-185
56YellBase/Pin-8
57SpicSpan/4x5-3
57T-48
58T-355
59T-165
60Lake
60SpicSpan-3
60T-37
61P-109
61T-251
61T/St-39
62J-18
62P-18
62P/Can-18
62Salada-92
62Shirriff-92
62T-335
62T/St-43
63J-49
63P-49
63T-437
64Det/Lids-2
64T-98
81Tiger/Detroit-101
91T/Arc53-214
92Bz/Quadra-12
94T/Arc54-109
Exh47
PM10/Sm-18
Bruyette, Edward T.
(Ed)
No Cards.
Bryan, Frank
85Clovis-7
87SanJose-9
88Fresno/Cal-17
88Fresno/ProC-1222
89PalmSp/Cal-47
89PalmSp/ProC-487
Bryan, William Ronald
(Billy)
63T-236
65OPC-51
65T-51
66T-332
67T-601
68T-498
78TCMA-47
92Yank/WIZ60-19

Bryand, Renay
88Spokane/ProC-1941
89CharRain/ProC-996
90River/Best-4
90River/Cal-13
90River/ProC-2597
91HighD/ClBest-1
91HighD/ProC-2384
91Wichita/ProC-2591
92Wichita/ProC-3651
92Wichita/SB-627
Bryans, Jason
91Eugene/ClBest-27
91Eugene/ProC-3715
Bryant, Allen
92Negro/Retort-7
Bryant, Bobby
79Jacks-19
79Tidew-21
Bryant, Chris
87Idaho-12
Bryant, Clay
74OPC-521CO
74T-521CO
Bryant, Craig
92ClBest-246
92SanBern/ClBest-13
92SanBern/ProC-
Bryant, Derek Roszell
77SanJose-4
80Ogden-4
80T-671R
81Tacoma-9
Bryant, Donald Ray
(Don)
67CokeCap/Cub-9
69T-499R
70OPC-473
70T-473
74OPC-403CO
74T-403C
77T-597C
Bryant, Erick
87Belling/Team-2
88Belling/Legoe-25
89Wausau/GS-25
Bryant, Erwin
81Bristol-16
Bryant, Franklin S.
81VeroB-3
Bryant, George
No Cards.
Bryant, James
86Chatt-5
87Chatt/Best-7
Bryant, John
82CharR-5
83CharR-15
86Cedar/TCMA-23
87Vermont-15
Bryant, Keith
89Belling/Legoe-3
Bryant, Mike
80Elmira-25
Bryant, Neil
82Amari-15
83MidldC-5
Bryant, Patrick
91ClBest/Singl-57
91Collnd/ClBest-29
91Collnd/ProC-1496
92ClBest-85
92ColRS/ClBest-3
92ColRS/ProC-2402
92Watertn/ClBest-18
92Watertn/ProC-3245
Bryant, Phil
87Gaston/ProC-7
88CharlR/Star-4
89Tulsa/GS-6
89Tulsa/Team-4
90ProC/Singl-740
90Tulsa/ProC-1149
Bryant, Ralph
82VeroB-21
83VeroB-22
85Cram/PCL-161
86Albuq-2
87Albuq/Pol-25
87D-587
87F-649M
87F/Up-U13
87Pol/Dodg-24
87Sf/TPrev-14M
87T/Tr-12T
88F-510
90Target-87
Bryant, Ron
70OPC-433
70T-433
71MLB/St-242
71OPC-621
71T-621
72OPC-185
72OPC-186IA
72T-185
72T-186IA
73OPC-298
73T-298
74OPC-104
74OPC-205LL
74T-104
74T-205LL
74T/DE-21
74T/St-103
75OPC-265
75T-265
75T/M-265
Bryant, Scott
90A&AASingle/ProC-129
90B-59
90Cedar/Best-1
90Cedar/ProC-2336
90CedarDG/Best-30
90Foil/Best-64
90ProC/Singl-877
90S-667DC
91AA/LineD-156
91Chatt/LineD-156
91Chatt/ProC-1970
91ClBest/Singl-69
91UD/FinalEd-5F
92Iowa/ProC-4059
92Iowa/SB-203
92Sky/AAASingl-97
Bryant, Shawn
90BurlInd/ProC-3003
91Kinston/ClBest-2
91Kinston/ProC-314
92ClBest-153
92Kinston/ClBest-1
92Kinston/ProC-2467
Bryden, Thomas R.
(T.R.)
82Danvl/Frit-4
83Redwd-7
85MidldA-11
87Edmon-21
87T-387
88Portl/CMC-3
88Portl/ProC-663
Brye, Stephen Robert
(Steve)
71OPC-391R
71T-391R
72OPC-28R
72T-28
73OPC-353
73T-353
74OPC-232
74T-232
75OPC-151
75T-151
75T/M-151
76OPC-519
76SSPC-215
76T-519
77T-424
78T-673
79Hawaii-12
79T-28
Bryeans, Chris
82CharR-10
83CharR-5
Brynan, Charles
N172
Brzezinski, George
88Geneva/ProC-1657
Bubalo, Mike
90Bend/Legoe-8MG
91Everett/ProC-3934
Bubrewicz, Tim
91Elmira/ProC-3262
Bubser, Harold Fred
(Hal)
No Cards.
Buccheri, James
88SoOreg/ProC-1692
89Madis/Star-5
89Star/Wax-65
90Modesto/Cal-162
90Modesto/Chong-3
90Modesto/ProC-2217
91AA/LineD-280
91Huntsvl/ClBest-5
91Huntsvl/LineD-280
91Huntsvl/Team-4
91HuntsvlProC-1801
92Huntsvl/SB-305
92Sky/AASingl-128
Bucci, Mike
76SanAn/Team-4
78Cr/PCL-115
79Tucson-5
80Tacoma-13
81Charl-11
82Wausau/Frit-12CO
83Chatt-9
85BurlR-10
86Salem-2MG
87BuffB-26MG
88BurlInd/ProC-1786
Buccola, Vic
47Signal
48Smith-16
Bucha, John George
(Johnny)
52T-19
53Tiger/Glen-2
54B-215
Buchanan, Bob
81Cedar-23
82Water-7
83Indianap-28
87Tidew-26
87Tidew/TCMA-27
88Omaha/CMC-3
88Omaha/ProC-1514
89Omaha/CMC-1
89Omaha/ProC-1724
91AAA/LineD-328
91Omaha/LineD-328
91Omaha/ProC-1027
92Nashvl/SB-277
92Sky/AAASingl-131
Buchanan, Donald
52Laval-12
Buchanan, Reggie
81Buffa-25
Buchanan, Rob
88Eugene/Best-13
89AppFx/ProC-868
89Eugene/Best-21
Buchanan, Shawn
88NE-1
90NE-5
91Utica/ClBest-5
91Utica/ProC-3252
92Saraso/ClBest-17
92Saraso/ProC-218
Buchek, Gerald Peter
(Jerry)
61Union
62Kahn/Atl
62T-439
64T-314
65T-397
66T-454
67T-574
68T-277
69MB-44
91WIZMets-56
Bucher, James Quinter
(Jim)
90Target-88
R313
Buchheister, Don
(Bucky)
73Cedar
74Cedar
75Cedar
76Cedar
77Cedar
78Cedar
79Cedar/TCMA-29
80Cedar-21
81Cedar-20
82Cedar-27
83Cedar-26
84Cedar-19
85Cedar-28
86Cedar/TCMA-27
88Cedar/ProC-1136
89Cedar/Best-24
89Cedar/ProC-931
90CedarDG/Best-34GM
Buckels, Gary
87Salem/ProC-2413
88MidwLAS/GS-25
88QuadC/GS-28
89MidldA/GS-6
90AAASingl/ProC-85
90Edmon/CMC-3
90Edmon/ProC-510
90ProC/Singl-480
91AAA/LineD-156
91Edmon/LineD-156
91Edmon/ProC-1509
Buckenberger, Albert
N172
Buckeye, Garland
93Conlon-981
Buckholz, Steven
88Watertn/Pucko-3
90Salem/Star-2
91Salem/ProC-945
92CaroMud/ProC-1173
92CaroMud/SB-127
Buckle, Larry
80Cedar-5
82Water-2
Buckley, Brian
81Redwd-2
82Holyo-2
84PrWill-10
Buckley, Joe
89Spokane/SP-7
Buckley, Kevin John
82BurlR/Frit-3
82BurlR/TCMA-15
83BurlR-2
83BurlR/Frit-20
83Tulsa-16
84OKCty-16
84Tulsa-27
85Maine-15
86Maine-2
87LasVegas-8
90TulsaDG/Best-14
93Rang/Keeb-88
Buckley, Mike
81QuadC-6
Buckley, Richard D.
(Dick)
N172
Buckley, Terrell
93Macon/ClBest-4
93Macon/ProC-1405
Buckley, Travis
90A&AASingle/ProC-78
90Gaston/Best-4
90Gaston/ProC-2513
90Gaston/Star-3
91CharlR/ClBest-3
91CharlR/ProC-1307
92Harris/ProC-454
92Harris/SB-278
92Sky/AASingl-118
93T-732
93T/Gold-732
Buckley, Troy
88CapeCod/Sum-170
90AS/Cal-15
90ProC/Singl-863
90Visalia/Cal-75
90Visalia/ProC-2157
91ClBest/Singl-203
91Visalia/ClBest-13
91Visalia/ProC-1744
92FtMyr/ProC-2748
92Miracle/ClBest-19
93ClBest/MLG-64
Buckmier, Jim
83AlexD-29
84PrWill-2
Buckner, Jim
79Tidew-10
79Toledo-14
80Buffa-5
81Omaha-20
Buckner, Rex
89MissSt-5
90MissSt-5
91MissSt-7
92MissSt-6
93MissSt-6
Buckner, William J.
(Bill)
70OPC-286R
70T-286R
71MLB/St-99
71OPC-529R
71T-529R
72OPC-114
72T-114
73OPC-368
73T-368
74OPC-505
74T-505
74T/St-41
75Ho-97
75K-32
75OPC-244
75T-244
75T/M-244
76OPC-253
76SSPC-91
76T-253
77BurgChef-195
77Ho-54
77Ho/Twink-54
77T-27
78Ho-46
78OPC-127
78SSPC/270-264
78T-473
78Wiffle/Discs-10
79Ho-27
79OPC-177
79T-346
80OPC-75
80T-135
81Coke
81D-482
81Drake-13
81F-292
81F/St-29
81MSA/Disc-5
81OPC-202
81Sqt-6
81T-1LL
81T-625
81T/HT
81T/SO-55
81T/St-153
81T/St-17
82D-403
82Drake-5
82F-589
82F/St-96
82K-2
82OPC-124
82RedLob
82T-456TL
82T-760
82T/St-29
82T/StVar-29
83D-14DK
83D-99
83D/AAS-7
83Drake-2
83F-492
83F/St-3M
83F/St-6M
83K-59
83OPC-250
83OPC/St-223
83PermaGr/CC-1
83T-250
83T/Gloss40-24
83T/St-223
83Thorn-22
84D-117
84D/AAS-28
84D/Champs-18
84Drake-4
84F-488
84F/X-18
84Nes/792-545
84OPC-96
84T-545
84T/RD-8
84T/St-42
84T/Super-14
84T/Tr-17
85D-416
85F-153

85FunFood/Pin-100
85Leaf-254
85OPC-65
85SpokAT/Cram-3
85T-65
85T/RD-9
85T/St-214
85ThomMc/Discs-6
86D-151
86Drake-17
86F-343
86F/St-16
86Leaf-77
86OPC-239
86Sf-135M
86Sf-81
86T-443
86T/St-252
86T/Super-17
86T/Tatt-14M
86Woolwth-5
87D-462
87D/OD-183
87F-31
87F/LimWaxBox-C2
87Leaf-241
87OPC-306
87Sf-70
87T-764
87T/Board-14
87T/St-250
88D-456
88F-486
88OPC-147
88S-591
88S/Tr-36T
88T-147
89F-278
89OPC/BoxB-B
89S-214
89T/WaxBox-B
89UD-639
90D-474
90Pep/RSox-4
90PublInt/St-345
90S-396
90T/TVRSox-23
90Target-89
90UD-252
93TWill-20
93UD/ATH-20
Buckthorpe, David
91Waverly/Fut-8
Bucz, Bruce
88Visalia/Cal-171
90Visalia/Cal-81GM
Bucz, Joseph
90Visalia/Cal-83PER
Budaska, Mark David
79Ogden/TCMA-18
80Ogden-7
81Tacoma-13
82T-531R
Budde, Chip
89KS*-7
Buddie, Mike
92Classic/DP-77
92FrRow/DP-13
92Oneonta/ClBest-2
93Greens/ClBest-3
93Greens/ProC-877
Buddin, Donald Thomas
(Don)
58T-297
59T-32
60T-520
61P-53
61T-99
62J-59
62P-59
62P/Can-59
62Salada-68A
62Salada-68B
62Shirriff-68
62T-332
89Smok/Ast-19
Buddy, Lorenzo
92Albany/ProC-2321
Budke, Todd
85Visalia-17
86OrlanTw-3
Budner, Scott
90SoOreg/Best-30CO
90SoOreg/ProC-3450CO
91Madison/ClBest-13CO
91Madison/ProC-2147CO
92Reno/Cal-60CO
Budnick, Michael
47TipTop
Budrewicz, Timothy
91Elmira/ClBest-17
92WinSalem/ClBest-25
92WinSalem/ProC-1199
Buechele, Steve
82Tulsa-27
83Tulsa-22
84OKCty-13
85OKCty-17
86D-544
86F-558
86Rangers-22
86T-397
87D-180
87D/OD-179
87F-121
87Mother/Rang-7
87OPC-176
87Smok/R-11
87T-176
87T/St-242
88D-224
88D/Best-312
88F-463
88Mother/R-7
88OPC-2
88Panini/St-204
88S-306
88Smok/R-12
88T-537
88T/Big-104
88T/St-235
89B-232
89D-174
89D/Best-223
89F-515
89KennerFig-18
89Mother/R-8
89OPC-83
89Panini/St-453
89S-368
89Smok/R-5
89T-729TL
89T-732
89T/Big-156
89T/St-250
89UD-418
90B-493
90D-107
90F-292
90F/Can-292
90Leaf-179
90Mother/Rang-14
90OPC-279
90Panini/St-169
90PublInt/St-406
90S-221
90T-279
90T/Big-63
90T/St-251
90TulsaDG/Best-15
90UD-685
91B-268
91D-357
91F-283
91Mother/Rang-5
91OPC-464
91Panini/FrSt-254
91Panini/St-209
91S-257
91S/RookTr-77T
91StCl-337
91T-464
91UD-650
92B-335
92Classic/Game200-66
92D-699
92F-552
92L-91
92L/BlkGold-91
92OPC-622
92Panini-254
92Pinn-430
92Pirate/Nation-4
92S-695
92S/RookTr-21T
92StCl-405
92Studio-83
92T-622
92T/Gold-622
92T/GoldWin-622
92TripleP-50
92UD-488
92Ultra-252
93B-608
93Cub/Mara-3
93D-104
93F-18
93Flair-13
93L-106
93OPC-8
93Pac/Spanish-53
93Panini-206
93Pinn-176
93Rang/Keeb-89
93S-97
93Select-129
93StCl-494
93StCl/1stDay-494
93StCl/Cub-7
93Studio-8
93T-74
93T/Gold-74
93TripleP-79
93UD-159
93UD/SP-82
93Ultra-15
94B-522
94D-555
94F-381
94Flair-135
94L-180
94OPC-78
94Pac/Cr-96
94Pinn-200
94Pinn/Artist-200
94Pinn/Museum-200
94S-346
94Select-166
94StCl-204
94StCl/1stDay-204
94StCl/Gold-204
94StCl/Team-333
94Studio-58
94T-666
94T/Finest-51
94T/FinestRef-51
94T/Gold-666
94TripleP-71
94UD-136
94UD/CollC-66
94UD/CollC/Gold-66
94UD/CollC/Silv-66
94UD/ElecD-136
94Ultra-160
Buelow, Frederick W.
(Fritz)
E107
Bues, Arthur F.
(Art)
No Cards.
Buettemeyer, Kim
80Wichita-3
Buffamoyer, John
75BurlB
77Holyo
78Spokane/Cramer-20
78Spokane/Team-18CO
80CharlO/Pol-2
80CharlO/W3TV-2
Buffinton, Charles G.
(Charlie)
E223
N172
N690
Buffolino, Rocco
87Pocatel/Bon-24
88Fresno/Cal-24
88Fresno/ProC-1231
Buford, Bobby
76Clinton
Buford, Damon
91ClBest/Singl-198
91Freder/ClBest-23
91Freder/ProC-2377
92B-224
92ClBest-120
92Hagers/ProC-2567
92Hagers/SB-253
92Sky/AASingl-105
92UD/ML-221
92UD/ML-51DS
93B-141
93F/Final-157
93FExcel/ML-122
93L-492
93Select/RookTr-149T
93StCl-742
93StCl/1stDay-742
93T-576M
93T/Gold-576M
93T/Tr-63T
93UD-691
94D-605
94Pac/Cr-27
94Pinn-423
94S-582
94S/Boys-55
94StCl/Team-283
94T-61
94T/Gold-61
94Ultra-303
Buford, Don Jr.
88Hagers/Star-3
89EastLDD/ProC-DD38
89Hagers/Best-15
89Hagers/ProC-277
89Hagers/Star-2
90Hagers/ProC-1420
90Hagers/Star-3
91Freder/ProC-2382DIR
Buford, Donald Alvin
(Don)
64T-368R
65OPC-81
65T-81
66T-465
67CokeCap/WSox-6
67OPC-143M
67T-143M
67T-232
68Dexter-19
68OPC-194
68T-194
69MB-45
69MLB/St-2
69T-478
69T/St-123
70MLB/St-147
70OPC-305WS
70OPC-428
70T-428
71MLB/St-291
71OPC-29
71OPC-328WS
71T-29
71T-328WS
72MB-56
72OPC-370
72Pol/Orio-3
72T-370
73OPC-183
73T-183
74Greyhound-5M
81TCMA-299
86Indianap-29
88French-2CO
90Smok/SoCal-1
91Crown/Orio-59
92Hagers/ProC-2570MG
92Hagers/SB-274MG
93UD/ATH-21
Buggs, Michael J.
82AppFx/Frit-26
Buggs, Ron
(Doc)
77Newar
78Newar
79BurlB-9
Buhe, Tim
89Kingspt/Star-2
90Pittsfld/Pucko-9
Buheller, Tim
86Elmira-4
87WinHaven-1
88Lynch/Star-3
89Lynch/Star-3
Buher, Brad
89KS*-5
92Lipscomb-6
93Lipscomb-4
Buhl, Bob
53JC-4
53SpicSpan/3x5-5
53SpicSpan/7x10-3
54JC-10
54SpicSpan/PostC-4
54T-210
55B-43
55Gol/Braves-4
55JC-10
55SpicSpan/DC-4
56T-244
57SpicSpan/4x5-4
57T-127
58T-176
59T-347
60Lake
60SpicSpan-4
60T-230M
60T-374
61P-103
61T-145
61T/St-40
62J-154
62P-154
62P/Can-154
62Salada-117
62Shirriff-117
62T-458
63T-175
64T-96
65OPC-264
65T-264
66OPC-185
66T-185
67OPC-68
67T-68
89Swell-21
94T/Arc54-210
Buhner, Jay
87Colum-19
87Colum/Pol-4
87Colum/TCMA-19
88Classic/Blue-244
88Colum/CMC-23
88Colum/Pol-18
88Colum/ProC-329
88D-545
88D/Rook-11
88D/Y/Bk-545
88S/Tr-95T
88Sf-223
88T/Tr-21T
89B-219
89Bz-4
89Calgary/CMC-13
89Calgary/ProC-544
89D-581
89D/Best-136
89F-542
89KMart/DT-5
89OPC-223
89Panini/St-440
89S-530
89S/YS/I-6
89Sf-89
89T-223
89T/Big-20
89T/Coins-35
89T/Gloss60-9
89T/JumboR-5
89T/St-319
89T/UK-10
89ToysRUs-5
89UD-220
90B-477
90D-448
90F-508
90F/Can-508
90Leaf-114
90Mother/Mar-7
90OPC-554
90S-521
90T-554
90UD-534
91B-247
91CounHrth-13
91D-509
91D/GSlam-6
91F-446
91F/UltraUp-U49
91Leaf-62
91OPC-154
91Panini/FrSt-234
91Panini/St-190
91S-125
91StCl-153
91T-154
91UD-128
92B-248

92Classic/I-20
92D-61
92DennyGS-23
92F-275
92L-128
92L/BlkGold-128
92Mother/Mar-6
92OPC-327
92Panini-59
92Pinn-27
92Pinn-305SH
92S-64
92StCl-213
92Studio-231
92T-327
92T/Gold-327
92T/GoldWin-327
92UD-441
92UD/HRH-HR18
92Ultra-121
92Yank/WIZ80-22
93B-23
93D-111
93F-305
93Flair-268
93L-271
93Mother/Mar-6
93OPC-40
93Pac/Jugador-3
93Pac/Spanish-282
93Panini-65
93Pinn-68
93Pinn/HRC-36
93S-172
93Select-202
93StCl-310
93StCl/1stDay-310
93StCl/Mar-23
93Studio-52
93T-718
93T/Finest-124
93T/FinestRef-124
93T/Gold-718
93TripleP-231
93UD-224
93UD-55M
93UD/FunPack-112
93UD/SP-128
93Ultra-267
94B-557
94D-369
94D/Special-369
94F-282
94L-131
94OPC-268
94Pac/Cr-564
94Panini-117
94Pinn-343
94Pinn/Run-17
94RedFoley-7
94S-353
94Select-79
94Sf/2000-18
94StCl-299
94StCl/1stDay-299
94StCl/Gold-299
94Studio-100
94T-472
94T/Finest-122
94T/FinestRef-122
94T/Gold-472
94TripleP-125
94UD-61
94UD/ElecD-61
94UD/SP-104
94Ultra-118

Buice, DeWayne
78Cedar
81WHave-4
82Tacoma-1
83Tacoma-3
86MidldA-3
87D/Rook-6
87F/Up-U14
87Sf/Rook-26
87T/Tr-13T
88D-58
88F-487
88OPC-396
88S-376
88Smok/Angels-7
88T-649
88T/JumboR-4
88T/Mini-4
88T/St-180
88ToysRUs-4
88UD/Sample-1
89S-153
89Syrac/CMC-8
89Syrac/MerchB-3
89Syrac/ProC-811
89Syrac/Team-3
89T-147
89UD-147

Buitimea, Martin
85Tigres-5

Buker, Cy
77Fritsch-7

Buker, Henry L.
(Harry)
No Cards.

Buksa, Ken
88Watertn/Pucko-16

Bulkeley, Morgan G.
50Callahan
50W576-9
76Shakey-9
80Perez/HOF-6
80SSPC/HOF

Bullard, George D.
No Cards.

Bullard, Jason
91Welland/ClBest-28
91Welland/ProC-3563
92CaroMud/ProC-1174
92CaroMud/SB-128

Bullard, Larry
(Rocky)
78Dunedin

Bullas, Simeon E.
(Sam)
No Cards.

Bullett, Scott
90Welland/Pucko-11
91Augusta/ClBest-25
91Augusta/ProC-818
91ClBest/Singl-245
91SALAS/ProC-SAL3
92B-321
92CaroMud/ProC-1191
92CaroMud/SB-129
92ClBest-42
92ClBest/BBonusC-4
92ClBest/RBonus-BC4
92ProC/Tomorrow-312
92Sky/AASingl-60
92StCl-288
92T/91Debut-25
92Ultra-551
93B-402
93L-497
94D-431
94Pac/Cr-493
94T-584
94T/Gold-584

Bulling, Terry C.
(Bud)
78OrlanTw
78T-432
79Spokane-23
80Spokane-10
82D-612
82T-98
83D-226
83F-630
83SLCity-15
83T-519

Bullinger, Jim
86Geneva-1
87WinSalem-10
88Pittsfld/ProC-1367
89CharlK-6
90WinSalem/Team-17
91AA/LineD-128
91CharlK/LineD-128
91CharlK/ProC-1681
91ClBest/Singl-176
92D/Rook-20
92F/Up-73
92Iowa/SB-204
92S/RookTr-101T
92Sky/AAASingl-98
92StCl-714
92StCl/MemberII-3
92T/Tr-17T
92T/TrGold-17T
93D-556
93F-374
93L-31
93S-339
93Select-285
93StCl-118
93StCl/1stDay-118
93StCl/Cub-26
93T-101
93T/Gold-101
93ToysRUs-6
93UD-379
94StCl/Team-360

Bullinger, Kirk
92Hamil/ClBest-2
92Hamil/ProC-1583
94FExcel-262

Bullinger, Matt
81Chatt-6
82Jacks-2

Bullock, Craig
91CharRain/ClBest-17
91CharRain/ProC-102
92ColumMet/ClBest-18
92ColumMet/ProC-301
92ColumMet/SAL/II-25

Bullock, Eric
82DayBe-12
83ColumAst-9
85Cram/PCL-52
87Tucson-19
88Portl/CMC-17
88Portl/ProC-640
89F-106
89Phill/TastyK-38
90AAASingl/ProC-568
90Indianap/CMC-17
90Indianap/ProC-285
90ProC/Singl-67
91B-457
91Leaf-470
92D-683
92F-474
92Indianap/ProC-1872
92S-661
92StCl-659

Bullock, Josh
90NE-6
93James/ClBest-4
93James/ProC-3318

Bullock, Renaldo
92Belling/ClBest-26
92Belling/ProC-1455

Bullock, Wynn
75T/Photo-104

Bulls, Dave
86Portl-2

Bumbry, Alonza B.
(Al)
73JP
73OPC-614R
73T-614R
74OPC-137
74T-137
75OPC-358
75T-358
75T/M-358
76OPC-307
76SSPC-396
76T-307
77BurgChef-37
77Ho-90
77Ho/Twink-90
77OPC-192
77T-626
78T-188
79T-517
80OPC-36
80T-65
81D-355
81F-172
81F/St-30
81OPC-34
81T-425
81T/SO-29
81T/St-35
82D-153
82F-159
82F/St-147
82OPC-265
82T-265
83D-383
83F-54
83F/St-14M
83F/St-26M
83OPC-272
83T-655
83T/Fold-5M
84D-210
84F-2
84Nes/792-319
84T-319
85D-350
85F-171
85F/Up-U13
85Mother/Padres-25
85T-726
85T/St-205
85T/Tr-12T
86F-316
86T-583
87Elmira/Black-29
87Elmira/Red-29
89Pac/SenLg-47
89T/SenLg-27
89TM/SenLg-14
90EliteSenLg-94
90Swell/Great-29
90T/TVRSox-3CO
91Crown/Orio-60
92RedSox/Dunkin-5CO
93TWill-82
93UD/ATH-22

Bumgarner, Jeff
86Kenosha-3
87ColAst/ProC-25
87OrlanTw-1
88Portl/CMC-4
88Portl/ProC-659
89Jacks/GS-10
90Freder/Team-27
91AA/LineD-226
91Hagers/LineD-226
91Hagers/ProC-2447
92Hagers/SB-254

Bumstead, Mark
78StPete

Bunce, Joshua
(Josh)
No Cards.

Bunch, Melvin Jr.
93Rockford/ClBest-5
94ClBest/Gold-195
94FExcel-65

Bundy, Lorenzo
83AlexD-31
84Cram/PCL-127
89Indianap/CMC-17
89Indianap/ProC-1223
90Jaxvl/Best-27CO
90Jaxvl/ProC-1389CO
91Sumter/ClBest-26MG
91Sumter/ProC-2351
92Albany/ClBest-27MG
92Albany/ProC-2321MG
93BurlB/ClBest-26MG
93BurlB/ProC-173MG

Bunker, Wally
64T-201R
65OPC-9LL
65T-290
65T-9LL
66T-499
67CokeCap/Orio-15
67T-585
68CokeCap/Orio-15
68T-489
69MLB/St-56
69OPC-137
69T-137
69T/4in1-2M
69T/St-182
70K-70
70MLB/St-218
70OPC-266
70T-266
70T/CB
71MLB/St-410
71OPC-528
71T-528
72MB-57
81TCMA-408
91Crown/Orio-61

Bunning, Jim
57T-338
58T-115
59T-149
60L-144
60T-502
61P-39
61T-46LL
61T-490
61T-50LL
61T/St-147
62J-26
62P-26
62P/Can-26
62Salada-13
62Shirriff-13
62T-460
62T-57LL
62T-59LL
62T/St-44
62T/bucks
63J-53
63P-53
63Salada-33
63T-10LL
63T-218M
63T-365
63T-8LL
63T/SO
64PhilBull-7
64T-265
64T-6LL
64T/Coins-93
64T/S-10
64Wheat/St-9
65Bz-21
65OPC-20
65OldLond-5
65T-20
65T/E-17
65T/trans-6
66Bz-31
66T-435
66T/RO-12
66T/RO-78
67Bz-31
67CokeCap/AS-15
67CokeCap/NLAS-20
67CokeCap/Phill-16
67Pol/Phill-1
67T-238LL
67T-560
68Bz-7
68KDKA-14
68OPC-11LL
68OPC-7LL
68OPC-9LL
68T-11LL
68T-215
68T-7LL
68T-9LL
68T/ActionSt-8AM
69Citgo-20
69MB-46
69MLB/St-183
69OPC-175
69T-175
69T/4in1-8M
69T/St-84
70MLB/St-86
70OPC-403
70T-403
71MLB/St-172
71OPC-574
71Phill/Arco-2
71T-574
71T/Coins-3
71T/GM-43
71T/Greatest-43
72MB-58
74Laugh/ASG-61
76Laugh/Jub-10
76OkCty/Team-6
81TCMA-454
81Tiger/Detroit-97
83Kaline-15M
83Kaline-24M
86Tiger/Sport-13
88Pac/Leg-92
89Swell-7
90Pac/Legend-76
90Target-90
PM10/L-7

Buonantony, Rich
82QuadC-4
86Louisvl-8
87Louisvl-7
88Louisvl-12
88Louisvl/CMC-7
88Louisvl/ProC-445
90Reading/Star-9

91Reno/Cal-19
Burba, Dave
88SanBern/Best-17
88SanBern/Cal-49
89Wmsprt/ProC-630
90AAASingl/ProC-110
90Calgary/CMC-6
90Calgary/ProC-645
90ProC/Singl-433
91AAA/LineD-54
91B-263
91Calgary/LineD-54
91Calgary/ProC-509
91D/Rook-12
91F-447
91S-742RP
91T/90Debut-23
92B-190
92Classic/I-21
92D-566
92Giant/PGE-9
92L-471
92L/BlkGold-471
92Mother/Giant-26
92OPC-728
92OPC/Premier-160
92Pinn-529
92S-611
92S/RookTr-51T
92StCl-348
92StCl-718
92T-728
92T/Gold-728
92T/GoldWin-728
92T/Tr-18T
92T/TrGold-18T
92Ultra-587
93D-128
93F-527
93Mother/Giant-18
93Pac/Spanish-609
93StCl-245
93StCl/1stDay-245
93UD-809
93Ultra-484
94D-124
94F-686
94Pac/Cr-542
94S-219
94S/GoldR-219
94StCl/Team-8
94T-433
94T/Gold-433
94UD/CollC-67
94UD/CollC/Gold-67
94UD/CollC/Silv-67
94Ultra-287
Burbach, Bill
69T-658R
70OPC-167
70T-167
71MLB/St-484
71OPC-683
71T-683
92Yank/WIZ60-20
92Yank/WIZ70-27
Burbank, Dennis
88CapeCod-6
88CapeCod/Sum-151
91OKSt-2
91Oneonta/ProC-4145
92FtLaud/ProC-2602
92FtLaud/Team-2
Burbrink, Nelson E.
(Nels)
56T-27
Burch, Albert William
(Al)
E254
E270/2
M116
T206
Burch, Ernest W.
N172
N28
Burcham, Timothy
(Tim)
86QuadC-6
87PalmSp-21
88MidldA/GS-6
89Edmon/CMC-5
89Edmon/ProC-553
89MidldA/GS-7
90AAASingl/ProC-87
90Edmon/CMC-4
90Edmon/ProC-511
90ProC/Singl-481
91AAA/LineD-157
91Edmon/LineD-157
91Edmon/ProC-1510
Burchart, Larry
69T-597R
70OPC-412
70T-412
Burchell, Fred
C46-14
T204
T206
Burchett, Kerry D.
81ArkTr-10
Burckel, Brad
91MissSt-8
Burda, Edward Robert
(Bob)
61Union
62Kahn/Atl
69T-392
70OPC-357
70T-357
71OPC-541
71T-541
72T-734
Burden, John
80Wausau-2
81Chatt-2
83Chatt-20
86Chatt-6CO
Burdette, Freddie
64T-408R
Burdette, Lew
52B-244
53B/BW-51
53JC-5
53SpicSpan/3x5-6
53SpicSpan/7x10-4
54B-192
54JC-33
54RM-NL24
54SpicSpan/PostC-5
55B-70
55Gol/Braves-5
55JC-33
55SpicSpan/DC-5
56T-219
57SpicSpan/4x5-5
57T-208
58T-10
58T-289M
59T-440
60Lake
60NuCard-35
60SpicSpan-5
60T-230M
60T-70
60T/tatt-7
61NuCard-408
61NuCard-435
61P-102
61T-320
61T-47LL
62Exh
62J-153
62P-153
62P/Can-153
62Salada-166
62Shirriff-166
62T-380
62T/St-146
62T/bucks
63Exh
63J-155
63P-155
63T-429
64T-523
65OPC-64
65T-64
66T-299
67CokeCap/DodgAngel-22
67T-265
73OPC-237CO
73T-237CO
78TCMA-276
88Pac/Leg-68
91LineD-15
91Swell/Great-16
91T/Arc53-310
92Bz/Quadra-13M
93AP/ASG-142
93Metallic-6
93TWill-46
93UD/ATH-23
Exh47
Burdette, Ricky
77Spartan
80Ashvl-24
Burdick, Kevin
87Watertn-11
88Salem/Star-3
89EastLDD/ProC-DD22
89Harris/ProC-297
89Harris/Star-4
89Star/Wax-19
90AAASingl/ProC-493
90BuffB/CMC-16
90BuffB/ProC-378
90BuffB/Team-4
90ProC/Singl-16
91AAA/LineD-80
91ColoSp/LineD-80
91ColoSp/ProC-2189
Burdick, Stacey
87Miami-3
89Freder/Star-1
90EastLAS/ProC-EL43
90Foil/Best-255
90Hagers/Best-17
90Hagers/ProC-1403
90Hagers/Star-4
91AA/LineD-227
91Hagers/LineD-227
91Hagers/ProC-2448
Burdick, William B.
N172
Burdock, John Joseph
(Jack)
90Target-91
N172
N284
Burdy, B.J.
(Mascot)
91Tor/Fire-x
Bure, Pavel
91StCl/Member*-38
Burg, Joseph Peter
(Pete)
No Cards.
Burgen, Chris
88OK-24
Burgess, Bob
89Welland/Pucko-34GM
90Welland/Pucko-34GM
Burgess, Forrest H.
(Smoky)
49Eureka-52
51B-317
52B-112
52T-357
53B/Col-28
53T-10
54B-31
55B-209
55RFG-12
55W605-12
56Kahn
56T-192
57Kahn
57Sohio/Reds-4
57T-228
58Kahn
58T-49
59Kahn
59T-432
60Kahn
60T-393
61Kahn
61P-138
61T-461
61T/St-61
62J-176
62Kahn
62P-176
62P/Can-176
62Salada-114
62Shirriff-114
62T-389
62T/St-173
63F-55
63IDL-2
63J-144
63Kahn
63P-144
63T-18M
63T-425
64T-37
65OPC-198
65T-198
66T-354
67T-506
72Laugh/GF-28
77Galasso-6
78Green
78TCMA-1
88Pulaski/ProC-1750
89Pac/Leg-201
89Swell-32
90Pac/Legend-77
91T/Arc53-10
92Bz/Quadra-9
93AP/ASG-141
Burgess, Gus
80Elmira-26
83Pawtu-20
84Pawtu-9
85Pawtu-1
Burgess, Kurt
92Macon/ClBest-23
92Macon/ProC-259
93Durham/Team-3
Burgess, Thomas R.
54Hunter
79Richm-15MG
80CharCh-1MG
81Tulsa-20MG
82Tulsa-22MG
83OKCty-2MG
84OKCty-3MG
86Lakeland-3MG
87GlenF-3MG
90TulsaDG/Best-28MG
Burgmeier, Tom
69T-558
70OPC-108
70T-108
71MLB/St-411
71OPC-431
71T-431
72OPC-246
72T-246
73OPC-306
73T-306
75OPC-478
75T-478
75T/M-478
76OPC-87
76SSPC-206
76T-87
77T-398
78PapaG/Disc-16
78T-678
79OPC-272
79T-524
80T-128
81Coke
81D-97
81F-228
81OPC-320
81T-228
81T/HT
82Coke/BOS
82D-361
82F-288
82T-455
83D-235
83F-180
83F/St-4M
83Granny-39
83OPC-213
83T-213
83T/Fold-4M
83T/X-16
84D-522
84F-439
84Mother/A's-18
84Nes/792-33
84OPC-33
84T-33
85D-400
85F-417
93Rockford/ClBest-29CO
Burgo, Dale
88WinHaven/Star-6
89Lynch/Star-4
91LynchRS/ProC-1190
Burgo, William Ross
(Bill)
No Cards.
Burgos, Enrique
87Knoxvl-17
88Syrac/ProC-815
89Dunedin/Star-2
Burgos, John
87Gaston/ProC-27
89Savan/ProC-351
90ArkTr/GS-6
91AA/LineD-505
91Reading/LineD-505
91Reading/ProC-1365
Burgos, Paco
87SanJose-17
88CharlR/Star-5
89CharlR/Star-4
90Tulsa/ProC-1160
90Tulsa/Team-4
91AAA/LineD-306
91OkCty/LineD-306
91OkCty/ProC-183
91Tulsa/Team-3
92AppFox/ClBest-12
92Memphis/ProC-2424
92Memphis/SB-428
92Sky/AASingl-180
Burguillos, Carlos
91Niagara/ClBest-17
91Niagara/ProC-3644
92ClBest-101
92Fayette/ProC-2181
Burich, William Max
(Bill)
No Cards.
Burk, Mack Edwin
57T-91
58T-278
Burkam, Robert
(Bob)
No Cards.
Burke, Alan
92Batavia/ClBest-10
92Batavia/ProC-3270
94ClBest/Gold-163
94FExcel-244
Burke, Curtis
83DayBe-25
85Osceola/Team-22
Burke, Daniel L.
(Dan)
No Cards.
Burke, Don
86James-2
87WPalmB-12
87WPalmB-24
Burke, Edward D.
(Eddie)
33SK*-33
Burke, Edward
N566-177
Burke, Frank A.
No Cards.
Burke, Glenn L.
75Water
78SSPC/270-76
78T-562
79OPC-78
79T-163
90Target-92
Burke, James Timothy
(Jimmy)
T206
W514-89
Burke, John Patrick
No Cards.
Burke, John
92Bend/ClBest-1
92ClBest/BBonusC-29
92ClBest/Up-412
92Classic/DP-79
92UD/ML-17
93B-388
93ClBest/MLG-205
93FExcel/ML-33
93StCl-513
93StCl/1stDay-513
93UD-444TP
94B-226
94B-356
94ClBest/Gold-27
94FExcel-184
94SigRook-4
94SigRook/Hot-1
94T-770M

94T/Gold-770M
94TedW-119
94Ultra-477
Burke, Kevin
85Newar-24
87Hagers-20
Burke, Leo Patrick
63T-249
64T-557
65OPC-202
65T-202
91Crown/Orio-62
Burke, Leslie K.
(Les)
No Cards.
Burke, Matt
90OK-3
Burke, Michael E.
(Mike)
86Bakers-4
87VeroB-25
Burke, Patrick Edward
(Pat)
No Cards.
Burke, Robert J.
(Bobby)
33G-71
35G-2C
35G-4C
35G-7C
92Conlon/Sport-362
94Conlon-1183
V354-25
Burke, Steve
77Jaxvl
78T-709R
79Spokane-22
Burke, Tim
82Buffa-15
83Colum-7
83Nashvl-3
84Indianap-23
85Expo/PostC-4
85F/Up-U14
86D-421
86Expo/Prov/Pan-17
86F-245
86Leaf-198
86OPC-258
86Provigo-17
86Seven/Coin-E15
86T-258
87D-222
87F-315
87Leaf-205
87OPC-132
87Sf/TPrev-20M
87T-624
87T/St-78
88D-98
88D/Best-34
88F-180
88F/Mini-87
88F/St-95
88Ho/Disc-2
88Leaf-84
88OPC-14
88S-187
88T-529
89B-360
89D-274
89D/Best-180
89F-372
89OPC-48
89Panini/St-113
89RedFoley/St-15
89S-228
89Sf-73
89T-48
89T/St-69
89UD-456
90B-103
90D-334
90D/BestNL-42
90F-342
90F/BB-3
90F/Can-342
90Leaf-28
90OPC-195
90Panini/St-294
90PublInt/St-170
90RedFoley/St-10
90S-127
90S/100St-34
90Sf-199
90T-195
90T/Big-187
90T/Mini-61
90T/St-72
90T/TVAS-60
90UD-515
91D-125
91F-227
91F/UltraUp-U95
91Leaf-124
91OPC-715
91Panini/FrSt-148
91RedFoley/St-15
91S-181
91StCl-514
91T-715
91UD-215
91UD/FinalEd-70F
91Ultra-198
92D-366
92F-497
92L-44
92L/BlkGold-44
92Mets/Kahn-44
92OPC-322
92Pinn-471
92S-651
92StCl-392
92Studio-62
92T-322
92T/Gold-322
92T/GoldWin-322
92TripleP-14
92UD-433
92Ultra-228
93F-647
93T-249
93T/Gold-249
Burke, Todd
87Visalia-18
Burke, Tom
77Charl
Burke, William I.
E254
T206
Burkett, Jesse Cail
50Callahan
50W576-10
76Shakey-39
80Perez/HOF-39
80SSPC/HOF
81Conlon-75
89HOF/St-33
E254
E286
T204
W575
Burkett, John
85Fresno/Pol-22
86Shrev-2
87Shrev-14
87TexLgAS-33
88F-651
88Phoenix/CMC-2
88Phoenix/ProC-76
89Phoenix/CMC-1
89Phoenix/ProC-1483
90AAASingl/ProC-31
90Classic/III-T6
90D/BestNL-12
90D/Rook-51
90F/Up-U61
90Leaf-384
90Mother/Giant-26
90Phoenix/ProC-5
90S/Tr-73T
90T/Tr-16T
90UD/Ext-735
91B-637
91Classic/200-86
91D-638
91F-256
91Leaf-56
91Leaf/Stud-253
91Mother/Giant-26
91OPC-447
91PG&E-3
91Panini/FrSt-74
91Panini/St-78
91S-70
91S/100RisSt-7
91SFExam/Giant-5
91Seven/3DCoin-1NC
91StCl-119
91T-447
91T/JumboR-5
91UD-577
91Ultra-317
92D-257
92F-630
92Giant/PGE-10
92L-179
92L/BlkGold-179
92Mother/Giant-5
92OPC-762
92Pinn-292SIDE
92Pinn-578
92S-522
92StCl-136
92Studio-113
92T-762
92T/Gold-762
92T/GoldWin-762
92UD-148
92Ultra-286
93B-520
93Colla/DM-19
93D-156
93F-153
93Flair-139
93L-342
93Mother/Giant-7
93OPC-89
93Pac/Spanish-268
93Pinn-375
93S-174
93StCl-412
93StCl/1stDay-412
93StCl/Giant-10
93Studio-44
93T-66
93T/Finest-44
93T/FinestRef-44
93T/Gold-66
93UD-160
93UD/SP-110
93Ultra-129
94B-463
94D-13
94D/Special-13
94F-687
94F/AS-33
94Finest-295
94Flair-240
94L-73
94OPC-19
94Pac/Cr-543
94Pac/Silv-19
94Panini-262
94Pinn-24
94Pinn/Artist-24
94Pinn/Museum-24
94S-5
94S/GoldR-5
94S/GoldS-21
94S/HobSam-5
94S/HobSam-5G
94S/Pr-5
94Sf/2000-29
94StCl-88
94StCl/1stDay-88
94StCl/Gold-88
94StCl/Team-28
94T-213
94T/Gold-213
94TripleP-103
94UD-403
94UD/CollC-306M
94UD/CollC-68
94UD/CollC/Gold-306M
94UD/CollC/Gold-68
94UD/CollC/Silv-306M
94UD/CollC/Silv-68
94UD/SP-91
94Ultra-587
Burkhart, Ken
47TipTop
Burks, Ellis
86NewBrit-4
87D/Rook-5
87F/Up-U15
87Pawtu-23
87Pawtu/TCMA-22
87Sf/Rook-5
87T/Tr-14T
88Classic/Blue-229
88D-174
88D/Best-121
88D/RedSox/Bk-174
88F-348
88F-630M
88F/Slug-5
88F/St-6
88KennerFig-15
88Leaf-174
88MSA/Disc-2
88OPC-269
88Panini/St-31
88RedFoley/St-10
88S-472
88S/YS/I-37
88Sf-144
88T-269
88T/Big-80
88T/Gloss60-50
88T/JumboR-2
88T/St-250
88T/St-310
88ToysRUs-5
89B-36
89Classic/Up/2-152
89Classic/Up/2-175M
89D-303
89D/Best-9
89D/GrandSlam-12
89F-83
89KennerFig-19
89Nissen-3
89OPC-311
89Panini/St-278
89S-9
89S/HotStar-43
89S/Mast-25
89Sf-191
89T-785
89T/Ames-7
89T/Big-259
89T/HeadsUp-12
89T/St-254
89UD-434
90B-280
90Classic/Up-T8
90D-228
90D-23DK
90D/BestAL-30
90D/SuperDK-23DK
90F-269
90F/Can-269
90Kenner/Fig-14
90Leaf-261
90OPC-155
90Panini/St-21
90Pep/RSox-5
90PublInt/St-450
90PublInt/St-594
90RedFoley/St-11
90S-340
90S/100St-16
90Sf-80
90T-155
90T/Big-107
90T/Coins-8
90T/DH-7
90T/St-259
90T/TVRSox-28
90UD-343
90USPlayC/AS-7C
91B-109
91B-373SLUG
91Classic/200-12
91D-235
91DennyGS-1
91F-89
91Leaf-121
91Leaf/Stud-12
91MajorLg/Pins-11
91OPC-70
91Panini/FrSt-269
91Panini/St-212
91Panini/Top15-114
91Pep/RSox-3
91S-8
91S/100SS-48
91StCl-108
91StCl/Charter*-4
91T-70
91T/CJMini/II-8
91UD-436
91UD/SilSlug-SS10
91Ultra-30
92B-570
92Classic/Game200-71
92D-234
92F-35
92L-314
92L/BlkGold-314
92OPC-416
92Panini-90
92Pinn-26
92RedSox/Dunkin-6
92S-270
92S/100SS-83
92S/Impact-78
92StCl-399
92T-416
92T/Gold-416
92T/GoldWin-416
92T/Kids-70
92UD-525
92UD-94TC
92USPlayC/RedSox-13D
92USPlayC/RedSox-9S
92Ultra-13
93B-231
93D-33
93F-176
93F/Final-194
93Flair-181
93L-252
93OPC/Premier-93
93Pac/Spanish-29
93Pac/Spanish-386
93Panini-95
93Pinn-46
93S-78
93Select-68
93Select/RookTr-10T
93StCl-187
93StCl-607
93StCl/1stDay-187
93StCl/1stDay-607
93StCl/WSox-27
93Studio-33
93T-351
93T/Gold-351
93T/Tr-104T
93UD-265
93UD-526
93Ultra-529
93WSox-5
94B-414
94D-145
94F-78
94Finest-275
94Flair-152
94L-242
94OPC-90
94Pac/Cr-122
94Panini-45
94Pinn-496
94S-431
94StCl/Team-115
94Studio-176
94T-538
94T/Gold-538
94TripleP-222
94UD-483
94UD/SP-165
94Ultra-478
Burks, Robert E.
N172
Burks, Will
86Lipscomb-6
Burleson, Richard P.
(Rick)
75OPC-302
75T-302
75T/M-302
76Ho-44
76Ho/Twink-44
76OPC-29
76SSPC-410
76T-29
77BurgChef-28
77Ho-68
77Ho/Twink-68
77OPC-237
77T-585
78OPC-37
78PapaG/Disc-7
78SSPC/270-175
78T-245
79OPC-57
79T-125
80OPC-339

80T-645
81D-454
81F-225
81F/St-33
81K-49
81OPC-172
81Sqt-13
81T-455
81T/HT
81T/SO-37
81T/St-52
81T/Tr-743
82D-342
82F-453
82F/St-219
82K-44
82OPC-55
82T-55
82T/St-134
82T/St-157
83D-318
83F-80
83OPC-315
83T-315
84F-510
84Nes/792-735
84OPC-376
84Smok/Cal-4
84T-735
84T/St-238
86Smok/Cal-15
86T/Tr-16T
87D/OD-134
87F-74
87OPC-152
87T-579
91Crown/Orio-63
91Mother/A's-28CO
92RedSox/Dunkin-7CO

Burley, Rick
93Rockford/ClBest-6

Burley, Tony
82Cedar-16
83Tampa-1

Burley, Travis
90MedHat/Best-4

Burlingame, Ben
91Geneva/ClBest-2
91Geneva/ProC-4208
92WinSalem/ClBest-24
92WinSalem/ProC-1200
93Peoria/Team-3

Burlingame, Dennis
88SALAS/GS-28
88Sumter/ProC-393
89Durham/Star-2
89Durham/Team-2
91Durham/ClBest-7
91Durham/ProC-1537
92Greenvl/ProC-1149
92Greenvl/SB-230
92Sky/AASingl-98
92UD/ML-299
93Richm/Pep-19

Burlingame, Greg
87Hawaii-22
89SanBern/Best-5
89SanBern/Cal-70

Burn
T222

Burnau, Ben
89Wausau/GS-10

Burnett, Hercules H.
No Cards.

Burnett, John H.
(Johnny)
91Conlon/Sport-82
92Conlon/Sport-543
R314/Can

Burnett, John P.
No Cards.

Burnett, Lance
88Pocatel/ProC-2083

Burnett, Ora
46Remar-9
47Remar-5
47Signal
47Smith-17
49B/PCL-36

Burnett, Roger
91Oneonta/ProC-4160
92PrWill/ClBest-12
92PrWill/ProC-154

Burnette, Wallace
57T-13
58T-69

Burney, Wayne
74Albuq/Team-3
75Albuq/Caruso-10

Burnham, George W.
N172

Burnitz, Jeromy
88CapeCod/Sum-145
90Classic/DP-17
90Pittsfld/Pucko-31
91AA/LineD-627
91B-474
91ClBest/Gold-5
91ClBest/Singl-68
91Classic/I-4
91S-380FDP
91Wmsprt/LineD-627
91Wmsprt/ProC-304
92B-189
92OPC-591
92ProC/Tomorrow-280
92Sky/AAASingl-248
92T-591M
92T/Gold-591
92T/GoldWin-591
92Tidew/ProC-
92Tidew/SB-554
92UD-65TP
92UD/ML-130
93B-622
93D-787RR
93F/Final-100
93FExcel/ML-69
93Flair/Wave-2
93L-503
93Select/RookTr-85T
93T-658
93T/Gold-658
93T/Tr-110T
93UD/SP-147
93Ultra-423
94B-512
94D-575
94F-559
94Flair-195
94L-230
94OPC-110
94Pac/Cr-397
94Panini-216
94Pinn-395
94Pinn/New-23
94S-570
94StCl-201
94StCl/1stDay-201
94StCl/Gold-201
94T-122
94T/Finest-15
94T/FinestRef-15
94T/Gold-122
94TripleP-142
94UD-190
94UD/CollC-69
94UD/CollC/Gold-69
94UD/CollC/Silv-69
94UD/ElecD-190
94Ultra-235

Burnos, Jim
83Wisco/Frit-20

Burns, Bill
(Sleepy)
88Pac/8Men-17M
88Pac/8Men-18

Burns, Britt
79Knoxvl/TCMA-6
81Coke
81D-279
81F-342
81OPC-218
81T-412
81T/HT
81T/St-63
82D-230
82F-339
82F/St-189
82T-44
83D-193
83D-23DK
83F-232
83F/St-17M
83K-43
83OPC/St-48
83T-541
83T/St-48
83TrueVal/WSox-40
84D-424
84F-54
84Nes/792-125
84OPC-125
84T-125
84TrueVal/WS-7
85Coke/WS-40
85D-257
85F-509
85OPC-338
85T-338
86D-58
86F-200
86F/St-17
86OPC-174
86Sf-105
86T-679
86T/Mini-10
86T/St-292
90T/TVYank-38

Burns, Dan
83ElPaso-1

Burns, Daren
88Wythe/ProC-1985

Burns, Edward James
(Ed)
11Helmar-111
16FleischBrd-9
D327
D328-18
D329-18
D350/2-17
E135-18
E270/2
M101/4-18
M101/5-17

Burns, George Henry
21Exh-14
26Exh-81
27Exh-41
94Conlon-1153
94Conlon-1272IA
D327
D328-19
D329-19
E120
E121/80
E135-19
E210-9
E220
M101/4-19
V100
W502-9
W514-24
W516-10
W572
W573
W575

Burns, George Joseph
16FleischBrd-10
21Exh-15
28Yueng-9
32Orbit/num-64
32Orbit/un-7
91Conlon/Sport-158
91Conlon/Sport-201
91Conlon/Sport-309
D327
D328-20
D329-20
D350/2-18
E120
E121/80
E122
E135-20
E220
M101/4-20
M101/5-18
V100
W515-54
W572
W573
W575

Burns, George
21Exh-16
21Exh-17
75Shakey-7
80Laugh/FFeat-35
BF2-73
V61-1
V61-70
WG7-7

Burns, Gregory
85Madis-7

Burns, Ian
91Daikyo/Fut-11

Burns, J.J.
92CharRain/ClBest-5

Burns, James M.
(Jim)
N172

Burns, James
83StPete-16

Burns, Jerry
92CharRain/ProC-113

Burns, John Irving
(Jack)
33G-198
34DS-75
34Exh/4-15
35BU-18
35BU-191
35Exh/4-15
35G-8C
35G-9C
91Conlon/Sport-131
R305
R326-1A
R326-1B
R342-1

Burns, John Joseph
No Cards.

Burns, Jonathan
89KS*-1M

Burns, Joseph Francis
(Joe)
No Cards.

Burns, Joseph James
(Joe)
No Cards.

Burns, Kerry
83TriCit-4

Burns, Michael
91BurlAs/ClBest-24
91BurlAs/ProC-2804
92Osceola/ClBest-5
92Osceola/ProC-2532

Burns, Patrick
(Pat)
No Cards.

Burns, Richard Simon
(Dick)
No Cards.

Burns, Thomas E.
(Tom)
80Batavia-8
81Batavia-2
81Watlo-7
83Wausau/Frit-4
85Lynch-11
86Tidew-3

Burns, Thomas P.
(Oyster)
90Target-905
E223
N172
N284
WG1-11

Burns, Todd
85Madis-8
85Madis/Pol-5
86SLAS-18
88F/Up-U52
88S/Tr-106T
88Tacoma/CMC-2
88Tacoma/ProC-632
89Classic/Up/2-171
89D-564
89F-3
89Mother/A's-24
89Panini/St-411
89S-465
89S/HotRook-100
89S/YS/II-4
89Sf-87
89T-174
89T/Big-10
89UD/Ext-718
90D-446
90F-2
90F/Can-2
90Leaf-458
90Mother/A's-20
90OPC-369
90PublInt/St-299
90S-64
90T-369
90UD-689
91B-221
91D-479
91F-4
91Mother/A's-20
91OPC-608
91S-41
91StCl-207
91T-608
91UD-405
91Ultra-243
92OkCty/SB-306
92S-341
92Sky/AAASingl-140
93D-641
93F-318
93Pac/Spanish-307
93Rang/Keeb-398
93StCl-210
93StCl/1stDay-210
93StCl/Rang-27
93T-279
93T/Gold-279
93UD-749

Burns, Tom
87Jacks/Feder-21

Burns, William T.
T206
T3-85

Burnside, Pete
58T-211
59T-354
60T-261
61P-46
61T-507
62T-207
63T-19
91Crown/Orio-64

Burnside, Sheldon
80Indianap-3
81F-220

Burr, Alexander T.
(Alex)
No Cards.

Burr, Chris
93ClBest/MLG-113

Burrell, Frank Andrew
(Buster)
90Target-93

Burrell, Kevin
85Lynch-14
86Shrev-3
87Phoenix-8
88Memphis/Best-11
88SLAS-2
89Omaha/CMC-10
89Omaha/ProC-1733
90AAASingl/ProC-603
90Omaha/ProC-68
91AAA/LineD-329
91Omaha/LineD-329
91Omaha/ProC-1037

Burrell, Scott
92UD/ML-71

Burress, Davey
76Clinton

Burright, Larry
62T-348
63T-174
81TCMA-464
90Target-94
91WIZMets-57

Burris, Paul Robert
54JC-29

Burris, Pierre
91Billing/SportP-2
91Billings/ProC-3765

Burris, Ray
74OPC-161
74T-161
75OPC-566
75T-566
75T/M-566
76Ho-60
76Ho/Twink-60
76OPC-51
76T-51
77BurgChef-194
77Ho-67
77Ho/Twink-67
77OPC-197
77T-190

78SSPC/270-261
78T-371
78Wiffle/Discs-9
79OPC-43
79T-98
80T-364
81D-524
81F-328
81OPC-323
81T-654
81T/Tr-744
82D-414
82Expo/Hygrade-2
82F-184
82Hygrade
82OPC-227
82T-227
82Zeller-20
83D-36
83F-277
83OPC-12
83Stuart-16
83T-474
84D-331
84F-270
84F/X-19
84Mother/A's-22
84Nes/792-552
84OPC-319
84T-552
84T/Tr-18
85D-218
85F-418
85F/Up-U15
85Leaf-116
85OPC-238
85Pol/Brew-48
85T-758
85T/St-328
85T/Tr-13T
86D-107
86F-482
86T-106
89Helena/SP-26
89T/SenLg-108
90Brewer/MillB-32CO
90EliteSenLg-18
90Pol/Brew-x
91Brewer/MillB-32CO
91Pol/Brew-x
91WIZMets-58
92Mother/Rang-28M
92Yank/WIZ70-28
93Rang/Keeb-90

Burritt, Mike
92BurlInd/ClBest-8
92BurlInd/ProC-1646

Burrough, Butch
92Elizab/ClBest-7
92Elizab/ProC-3691

Burroughs, Darren
82OkCty-23
83Reading-2
84Cram/PCL-235
86BuffB-6
88Calgary/CMC-1
88Calgary/ProC-780

Burroughs, Eric
90Billings/ProC-3233

Burroughs, Jeffrey A.
(Jeff)
72OPC-191
72T-191
73OPC-489
73T-489
74K-16
74OPC-223
74T-223
74T/DE-48
74T/St-232
75Ho-94
75K-8
75OPC-212MVP
75OPC-308LL
75OPC-470
75SSPC/42-27
75SSPC/Puzzle-4
75T-212MVP
75T-308LL
75T-470
75T/M-212MVP
75T/M-308LL
75T/M-470
76Crane-6
76Ho-111
76MSA/Disc
76OPC-360
76SSPC-269
76T-360
77BurgChef-214
77OPC-209
77Pep-58
77T-55
78Ho-61
78K-15
78OPC-134
78Pep-29
78T-130
78Tastee/Discs-4
78Wiffle/Discs-11
79Ho-20
79K-12
79OPC-124
79T-245
80OPC-283
80T-545
81D-66
81F-245
81Pol/Mariners-1
81T-20
81T/Tr-745
82D-379
82F-506
82F/St-220
82KMart-25
82OPC-309
82T-440
82T/St-231
82T/StVar-231
82T/Tr-14T
83D-323
83F-515
83F/St-16M
83F/St-9M
84D-156
84D/Champs-7
84F-440
84Mother/A's-17
84Nes/792-354
84OPC-354
84T-354
84T/St-329
85D-542
85F/Up-U16
85OPC-91
85T-272FDP
85T-91
85T/Tr-14T
85Tor/Fire-6
86F-54
86OPC-168
86T-168
92MCI-9
93Rang/Keeb-6
93UD/ATH-24
94TedW-86

Burroughs, Kenny
89Utica/Pucko-3
90Yakima/Team-8

Burrows, Terry
90Butte/SportP-5
91ClBest/Singl-265
91Gaston/ClBest-2
91Gaston/ProC-2679
92CharlR/ClBest-25
92ClBest-65
93B-573

Burrus, Daryl
87Belling/Team-25

Burrus, Maurice L.
(Dick)
25Exh-4
26Exh-3
94Conlon-1238

Burt, Frank J.
No Cards.

Burt, Jon
93MissSt-48M

Burton, Bob
89Wausau/GS-4
90Columbia/GS-27TR
90SALAS/Star-48TR
91Clmbia/PII-4
92StLucie/ClBest-29TR

Burton, Chris
89Idaho/ProC-2022
90Idaho/ProC-3259
91ClBest/Singl-163
91Miami/ClBest-27
91Miami/ProC-420

Burton, Darren
91AppFx/ClBest-22
91AppFx/ProC-1727
91MidwLAS/ProC-1
92B-424
92BBCity/ClBest-23
92BBCity/ProC-3856
92ClBest-20
92UD/ML-303
93B-181
93ClBest/MLG-81
94B-639

Burton, Ellis N.
59T-231
60T-446
61BeeHive-3
63T-262
64T-269

Burton, Essex
92SoBend/ClBest-20
92SoBend/ProC-182
93FExcel/ML-151

Burton, Jim
76OPC-471
76SSPC-418
76T-471
78SSPC/270-168

Burton, Ken
76Cedar

Burton, Michael
89FresnoSt/Smok-6
90A&AASingle/ProC-99
90Foil/Best-268
90Gaston/ProC-2526
90Gaston/Star-4
90SALAS/Star-3
91AA/LineD-577
91Tulsa/LineD-577
91Tulsa/ProC-2777
91Tulsa/Team-4
92CharlR/ClBest-2
92CharlR/ProC-2229

Burton, Steve
91GulfCR/SportP-23
92Gaston/ClBest-21
92Gaston/ProC-2258

Burton, Terry
89TNTech-4

Burtschy, Ed
55B-120
55Rodeo

Burtt, Dennis
81Bristol-21
83Pawtu-3
84Pawtu-5
85IntLgAS-39
85Toledo-4
87Albuq/Pol-6
88Albuq/CMC-7
88Albuq/ProC-276
89Albuq/CMC-2
89Albuq/ProC-68
90AAASingl/ProC-372
90ProC/Singl-380
90Toledo/CMC-3
90Toledo/ProC-142
91Kissim/ProC-4205CO
92FtMyr/ProC-2762
92Miracle/ClBest-27CO

Burwell, Bill
60T-467C

Burwell, Phil
83Erie-17

Busby, James F.
(Jim)
51B-302
52B-68
52BR
52StarCal-87DM
52StarCal/L-73F
52T-309
53B/Col-15
53Briggs
53NB
54B-8
54RM-AL2
55B-166
55RFG-8
55RM-AL2
55Salem
55W605-8
56T-330
57Sohio/Ind-2
57T-309
58Hires-68
58Hires/T
58T-28
59T-185
60L-11
60T-232
62Salada-30
62Shirriff-30
73OPC-237CO
73T-237CO
74OPC-634CO
74T-634CO
77T-597CO
79TCMA-66
91Crown/Orio-65

Busby, Mike
91LitSun/HSPros-14
91LitSun/HSProsG-14
92Savan/ProC-653
94ClBest/Gold-158
94FExcel-263

Busby, Paul Miller
No Cards.

Busby, Steve
73OPC-608R
73T-608R
74OPC-365
74T-365
74T/St-181
75Ho-124
75K-24
75OPC-120
75OPC-7M
75SSPC/42-39
75T-120
75T-7M
75T/M-120
75T/M-7M
76A&P/KC
76Ho-71
76K-33
76Laugh/Jub-15
76OPC-260
76SSPC-183
76T-260
78T-336
80T-474
81F-33
90Smok/SoCal-2

Busby, Wayne
89SoBend/GS-23
90Saraso/Star-2
91AA/LineD-52
91BirmB/LineD-52
91BirmB/ProC-1458
92BirmB/ProC-2588
92BirmB/SB-79
92Sky/AASingl-38

Busch, Edgar John
(Ed)
44PlayBall-16

Busch, Gussie
81TCMA-362M

Busch, Mike
90GreatF/SportP-3
91Bakers/Cal-25
92ClBest-346
92SanAn/SB-558
94B-650
94FExcel-210
94FExcel/LL-4

Buschorn, Don
65T-577R

Bush, Chuck
91Helena/SportP-26
92Stockton/ClBest-2
92Stockton/ProC-27

Bush, Craig
92Elmira/ClBest-5
92Elmira/ProC-1374

Bush, George W.
80Perez/HOF-F
92Mega/Ruth-149M
92Mega/Ruth-150M

Bush, Guy T.
30CEA/Pin-12
32Orbit/num-16
32Orbit/un-8
33G-67
35BU-158
35Exh/4-7
35G-1E
35G-3C
35G-4C
35G-5C
36Exh/4-7
88Conlon/NatAS-2
91Conlon/Sport-196
R305
R306
R308-189
R316
V353-67

Bush, Homer
92CharRain/ClBest-16
92CharRain/ProC-124
92ClBest-52
94B-8
94FExcel-277

Bush, Kalani
89Geneva/ProC-1872

Bush, Leslie Ambrose
(Joe)
15CJ-166
21Exh-18
92Conlon/Sport-345
93CrackJack-24
94Conlon-1279
D328-21
D329-21
D350/2-19
E120
E121/120
E121/80
E126-3
E135-21
E220
M101/4-21
M101/5-19
V61-4
V89-5
W501-34
W515-27
W572
W575
WG7-8

Bush, Owen Joseph
(Donie)
09Buster/Pin-3
11Diamond-5
11Helmar-27
14CJ-122
15CJ-122
21Exh-19
81Tiger/Detroit-38MG
86Indianap-2
94Conlon-1234
BF2-24
D303
D327
D328-22
D329-22
D350/2-20
E106
E135-22
E224
E254
E270/2
E286
E90/1
F61-96
M101/4-22
M101/5-20
M116
T206
T216
T222
W514-30
W575

Bush, Ricky
92Martins/ClBest-10
92Martins/ProC-3058

Bush, Robert Randall
(Randy)
80Toledo-8
82OrlanTw/A-2
82Toledo-20
83T/X-17
83Twin/Team-18
84D-513
84F-558
84Nes/792-429
84OPC-84
84T-429
84T/St-314
85D-633

85F-272
85T-692
85Twin/Team-20
86F-388
86OPC-214
86T-214
87D-441
87F-538
87T-364
88D-272
88F-6
88F/WS-2
88Master/Disc-7
88Panini/St-450IA
88S-292
88Smok/Minn-9
88T-73
89B-164
89D-537
89D/Best-214
89F-107
89OPC-288
89Panini/St-391
89S-212
89T-577
89T/Big-282
89UD-158
90B-416
90D-199
90F-370
90F/Can-370
90Leaf-83
90OPC-747
90Panini/St-109
90PublInt/St-324
90S-278
90T-747
90T/Big-92
90T/St-294
90UD-493
91D-382
91F-605
91F/UltraUp-U34
91Leaf-26
91OPC-124
91S-574
91T-124
92D-728
92F-198
92L-467
92L/BlkGold-467
92OPC-476
92S-377
92StCl-84
92T-476
92T/Gold-476
92T/GoldWin-476
92USPlayC/Twin-12D
92USPlayC/Twin-8S
93D-781
93F-638
93StCl-645
93StCl/1stDay-645

Bush, Todd
91Miami/Bumble-3

Busha, Rodney
90Butte/SportP-1

Bushell, James
91Adelaide/Fut-6

Bushelman, John
(Jack)
T207

Bushing, Chris
89Penin/Star-2
90A&AASingle/ProC-111
90Rockford/ProC-2695
90Rockford/Team-3
91WPalmB/ClBest-3
91WPalmB/ProC-1219
92Reading/ProC-566
92Reading/SB-528

Bushong, Albert John
(Doc)
90Target-95
N172
N172/BC
N284
N370
Scrapps

Busick, Warren
86DayBe-3

Buskey, Joseph Henry
(Joe)
No Cards.

Buskey, Michael T.
(Tom)
74Syrac/Team-3
75OPC-403
75T-403
75T/M-403
76OPC-178
76OkCty/Team-7
76SSPC-505
76T-178
77T-236
79BJ/Bubble-3
79Syrac/Team-29
80OPC-265
80T-506
81D-270
92Yank/WIZ70-29

Buss, Scott
86Chatt-7
87Kinston-5

Bussa, Todd
92Fayette/ClBest-11
92Fayette/ProC-2160

Busse, Raymond Edward
(Ray)
72OPC-101R
72T-101R
73OPC-607R
73T-607R
75Iowa/TCMA-3

Bustabad, Juan
83Pawtu-15
84Pawtu-25
85Pawtu-2
87SanAn-9
88SanAn/Best-12
89Albuq/CMC-20
89Albuq/ProC-78
90Yakima/Team-5

Bustamante, Eddie
89FresnoSt/Smok-7

Bustamante, Rafael
90CharWh/Best-14
90CharWh/ProC-2245
90Foil/Best-201
91CharWh/ClBest-15
91CharWh/ProC-2892

Bustillos, Albert
89Star/Wax-28
89VeroB/Star-4
91Bakers/Cal-26
92Albuq/ProC-711
92SanAn/SB-559

Buszka, John
77Watlo
78Watlo

Butcher, Arthur
89Beloit/II/Star-2
90Beloit/Best-20
90Beloit/Star-2
92Salinas/ClBest-17

Butcher, Henry Joseph
(Hank)
T207

Butcher, Jason
92GreatF/SportP-22

Butcher, John
78Ashvl
79Tulsa-16
80CharCh-13
81F-635
81T-41R
82T-418
83D-37
83F-563
83Rangers-29
83T-534
84D-220
84F-415
84F/X-20
84Nes/792-299
84T-299
84T/Tr-19
85D-314
85F-273
85Leaf-71
85OPC-356
85Seven/Minn-5
85T-741
85T/St-305
85Twin/Seven-5
85Twin/Team-22
86D-120
86F-389
86T-638
87F-245
87T-107
93Rang/Keeb-91

Butcher, Matthew
84Visalia-17

Butcher, A. Maxwell
(Max)
40PlayBall-222
90Target-96
93Conlon-756
94Conlon-1073

Butcher, Mike
86Cram/NWL-40
87AppFx-10
88BBCity/Star-7
89MidldA/GS-8
90MidldA/GS-15
91AA/LineD-428
91MidldA/LineD-428
91MidldA/OneHour-6
91MidldA/ProC-427
92Edmon/ProC-3534
92Edmon/SB-153
92F/Up-7
92Sky/AAASingl-75
93D-665
93F-569
93Pac/Spanish-364
93Pinn-262
93S-277
93StCl-407
93StCl/1stDay-407
93T-104
93T/Gold-104
94D-52
94F-48
94Pac/Cr-71
94StCl-78
94StCl/1stDay-78
94StCl/Gold-78
94T-236
94T/Gold-236
94Ultra-20

Butcher, Ryan
90GA-1

Butera, Brian
80Elmira-35

Butera, Salvatore P.
(Sal)
79Toledo-8
81D-530
81F-570
81T-243
82D-532
82F-548
82T-676
83T-67
84Indianap-5
85Expo/PostC-5
85Indianap-15
86OPC-261
86T-407
86TexGold-22
87F-195
87T-358
88S-361
88Syrac/CMC-16
88Syrac/ProC-826
88T-772
89Pac/SenLg-209
89Syrac/CMC-11
89Syrac/MerchB-4
89Syrac/ProC-802
89Syrac/Team-4
89T/SenLg-42
89TM/SenLg-15
89Tor/Fire-26
90Osceola/Star-27MG
91Osceola/ClBest-26
91Osceola/ProC-700
92Osceola/ClBest-26MG
92Osceola/ProC-2545MG

Buther, Brad
89KS*-17M

Butka, Edward Luke
(Ed)
No Cards.

Butler, Arthur Edward
(Art)
D329-23
D350/2-21
E90/1
M101/4-23
M101/5-21
T201

Butler, Brett Morgan
80Ander-26
81Richm-8
82BK/Lids-4
82D-275
82Pol/Atl-22
82T-502R
83D-636
83F-132
83Pol/Atl-22
83T-364
84D-141
84F-173
84F/X-21
84Nes/792-77
84T-77
84T/Tr-20
84Wheat/Ind-2
85D-216
85D/AAS-23
85F-441
85F/St-56
85Leaf-186
85OPC-241
85Polar/Ind-2
85T-637
85T/St-246
86D-102
86D-12DK
86D/DKsuper-12
86F-581
86F/Mini-114
86F/St-18
86Leaf-12DK
86OPC-149
86OhHenry-2
86Seven/Coin-C14
86Sf-26
86T-149
86T/Gloss60-52
86T/Mini-12
86T/St-206
86T/Super-18
86T/Tatt-9M
87Classic-36
87D-219
87D/OD-113
87F-246
87F/Hottest-8
87Gator-2
87Leaf-183
87OPC-197
87RedFoley/St-79
87Sf-69
87Sf/TPrev-3M
87T-723
88D-279
88D/Best-23
88F-603
88F/Up-U128
88Mother/Giants-14
88OPC-202
88Panini/St-78
88S-122
88S/Tr-3T
88Sf-153
88T-479
88T/Big-166
88T/St-212
88T/Tr-22T
89B-480
89Classic-38
89D-217
89D/Best-274
89F-324
89KennerFig-20
89Mother/Giants-5
89OPC-241
89Panini/St-220
89S-216
89Sf-31
89T-241
89T/Big-62
89T/Coins-6
89T/LJN-128
89T/Mini-39
89T/St-85
89T/UK-11
89UD-218
90B-237
90D-249
90D/BestNL-139
90F-53
90F/Can-53
90Leaf-251
90MLBPA/Pins-27
90Mother/Giant-7
90OPC-571
90Panini/St-365
90PublInt/St-64
90RedFoley/St-12
90Richm/25Ann-6
90S-236
90S/100St-47
90Sf-136
90T-571
90T/Big-259
90T/Mini-83
90T/St-87
90UD-119
91B-597
91Classic/200-4
91D-143
91F-257
91F/UltraUp-U85
91F/Up-U91
91Leaf-411
91Leaf/Stud-181
91Mother/Dodg-6
91OPC-325
91OPC/BoxB-C
91OPC/Premier-16
91Panini/FrSt-72
91Panini/St-75
91Panini/Top15-25
91Panini/Top15-44
91Panini/Top15-51
91Pol/Dodg-22
91S-455
91S/RookTr-23T
91StCl-389
91T-325
91T/Tr-15T
91T/WaxBox-C
91UD-270
91UD/Ext-732
91USPlayC/AS-8S
92B-597
92CJ/DI-9
92Classic/Game200-32
92D-369
92D/DK-DK18
92F-448
92F-702M
92Hardee-4
92L-186
92L/BlkGold-186
92Mother/Dodg-2
92OPC-655
92OPC/Premier-145
92Panini-197
92Pinn-133
92Pinn-619TECH
92Pinn/TeamP-9M
92Pol/Dodg-22
92Post/Can-8
92S-465
92S-778AS
92StCl-292
92StCl/Dome-23
92Studio-41
92Studio/Prev-19
92Sunflower-21
92T-655
92T/GPro-655
92T/Gold-655
92T/GoldWin-655
92T/Kids-49
92T/Pr-325
92TripleP-243LH
92TripleP-59
92UD-307
92Ultra-209
93B-422
93Colla/DM-20
93D-86
93F-59
93F/Fruit-8
93Flair-68
93Ho-20
93KingB-16
93L-230
93MilkBone-17
93Mother/Dodg-3
93OPC-36

93Pac/Spanish-143
93Panini-218
93Pinn-487HH
93Pinn-91
93Pol/Dodg-2
93S-20
93S/Franchise-19
93Select-115
93Select/StatL-54
93StCl-216
93StCl/1stDay-216
93StCl/Dodg-14
93Studio-9
93T-65
93T/Finest-6
93T/FinestRef-6
93T/Gold-65
93TripleP-136
93UD-259
93UD/FunPack-210ASA
93UD/FunPack-87
93UD/SP-91
93Ultra-51
94B-382
94B-622
94D-543
94F-506
94F-711
94Finest-367
94L-187
94OPC-215
94Pac/Cr-304
94Panini-197
94Pinn-369
94Pinn/Run-43
94S-46
94S/Cycle-1
94S/Cycle-14M
94S/GoldR-46
94S/GoldS-28
94StCl-121
94StCl/1stDay-121
94StCl/Gold-121
94Studio-66
94T-172
94T/Gold-172
94TripleP-82
94UD-183
94UD/CollC-70
94UD/CollC/Gold-70
94UD/CollC/Silv-70
94UD/ElecD-183
94UD/SP-75
94Ultra-213

Butler, Cecil
62T-239
63T-201

Butler, Chris
89Kingspt/Star-3
89Star/IISingl-181

Butler, Frank Dean
No Cards.

Butler, Frank E.
No Cards.

Butler, Jason
91Pulaski/ClBest-21
91Pulaski/ProC-3997
92Macon/ClBest-15
92Macon/ProC-260
93Macon/ClBest-5
93Macon/ProC-1393

Butler, John Albert
90Target-906

Butler, John S.
(Johnny)
C46-46
T206

Butler, John Stephen
(Johnny)
26Exh-9
27Exh-5
90Target-97

Butler, John
90Peoria/Team-3GM

Butler, Mark
83SanJose-11

Butler, Mick
86PalmSp-5
86PalmSp/Smok-17

Butler, Mike
92Boise/ClBest-20
92Boise/ProC-3618

Butler, Rich
92Myrtle/ClBest-12
92Myrtle/ProC-2210
93Dunedin/ClBest-4
93Dunedin/ProC-1807
94ClBest/Gold-54
94FExcel-140

Butler, Richard H.
(Dick)
No Cards.

Butler, Robert
91StCath/ClBest-8
91StCath/ProC-3406
92B-603FOIL
92ClBest-89
92Dunedin/ClBest-7
92Dunedin/ProC-2010
92ProC/Tomorrow-174
92UD/ML-315
93B-547
93ClBest/Fisher-3
93ClBest/MLG-86
93FExcel/ML-239
93Syrac/ProC-1009
93T/Tr-15T
94D-558
94Finest-313
94L-17
94OPC-232
94Pac/Cr-635
94Pinn-397
94StCl/Team-178
94T-361
94T/Gold-361
94UD-176
94UD/CollC-71
94UD/CollC/Gold-71
94UD/CollC/Silv-71
94UD/ElecD-176

Butler, Todd
88BurlInd/ProC-1782
88OK-17

Butler, W. J.
(Bill)
69T-619R
70MLB/St-219
70OPC-377
70T-377
71MLB/St-412
71OPC-681
71T-681
72MB-59
75OPC-549
75T-549
75T/M-549
76OPC-619
76SSPC-207
76T-619
78Cr/PCL-1
78SSPC/270-61

Butler, Willis E.
(Kid)
No Cards.

Butterfield, Brian J.
82Nashvl-3
87Oneonta-14
89Oneonta/ProC-2098
90Greens/Best-27MG
90Greens/ProC-2679
90Greens/Star-26
92FtLaud/ClBest-23MG
92FtLaud/Team-3

Butterfield, Chris
89Pittsfld/Star-1
89Star/IISingl-157
90StLucie/Star-3
91StLucie/ClBest-10
91StLucie/ProC-715
92Bingham/ProC-522
92Bingham/SB-52
92Sky/AASingl-22

Butters, Dave
85PrWill-28

Butters, Tom
63T-299R
64T-74R
65OPC-246
65T-246

Butterworth, Gary
91MissSt-9

Button, Dick
51BR-B17

Butts, David
87Sumter-29
88Durham/Star-3
89Durham/Star-3
89Durham/Team-3

Butts, Randy
86Erie-5
87StPete-24
88Hamil/ProC-1735

Butts, Tom
82Iowa-29

Butts, Tommy
78Laugh/Black-11

Buxowatz, Jack
52Laval-92

Buxton, Ralph
(Buck)
46Remar-21
47Remar-6
47Signal
47Smith-11
48Signal
48Smith-11
49Remar

Buzard, Brian
90WichSt-6
91Watertn/ClBest-2
91Watertn/ProC-3357
92ColRS/ClBest-25

Buzas, Joseph John
(Joe)
47Centen-2

Buzhardt, John
59T-118
60T-549
61T-3
61T/St-49
62J-200
62P-200
62P/Can-200
62Salada-129A
62Salada-129B
62Shirriff-129
62T-555
63T-35
64T-323
65T-458
66T-245
67CokeCap/WSox-7
67OPC-178
67T-178
68T-403
81TCMA-361
91Crown/Orio-66

Buzzard, Buddy
87Kenosha-7

Buzzard, Dale
89James/ProC-2130

Byam, George
V362-47

Byerly, Eldred
(Bud)
52T-161
58T-72
60T-371

Byerly, Jim
92SoOreg/ClBest-18
92SoOreg/ProC-3407

Byerly, Rodney
(Rod)
89Augusta/ProC-518
89Welland/Pucko-8
90BurlB/Best-26
90BurlB/ProC-2342
90BurlB/Star-6
90Durham/UpHer-5

Byers, James W.
(Bill)
No Cards.

Byers, John William
C46-74
E254

Byers, Randell
86Beaum-4
87LasVegas-14
88D-605
88F-653R
88LasVegas/CMC-13
88LasVegas/ProC-224
89LasVegas/CMC-12
89LasVegas/ProC-6
89Louisvl-12
89Louisvl/CMC-23
89Louisvl/ProC-1245

Byington, John
88CapeCod/Sum-21
89Beloit/II/Star-3
90Beloit/Best-15
90Beloit/Star-3
90Foil/Best-254
90MidwLgAS/GS-6
91AA/LineD-177
91ClBest/Singl-356
91ElPaso/LineD-177
91ElPaso/ProC-2752
92ClBest-336
92ElPaso/ProC-3926
92ElPaso/SB-201
92Sky/AASingl-90
92UD/ML-86
93FExcel/ML-181

Byrd, Anthony
92Kenosha/ProC-616
94FExcel-91

Byrd, Bill
86Negro/Frit-52

Byrd, Felan
76Clinton

Byrd, Harry
53B/Col-38
53T-131
54B-49
54NYJour
55B-159
55Esskay
58T-154
79TCMA-172
91Crown/Orio-67
91T/Arc53-131

Byrd, Jeff
75Anderson/TCMA-3
76SanAn/Team-5
78OPC-211
78Syrac
78T-667

Byrd, Jim
89Star/Wax-10
89WinHaven/Star-2
90CLAS/CL-13
90LynchRS/Team-5
91LynchRS/ClBest-15
91LynchRS/ProC-1205
92Pawtu/ProC-930
92WinHaven/ClBest-9
93F/Final-171
93Pawtu/Ball-5

Byrd, Leland
77Visalia

Byrd, Paul
90LSUPol-4
91LSU/Pol-14
92B-349
92Canton/ProC-682
92Canton/SB-102
92ClBest-37
92Sky/AASingl-47
92UD/ML-242
93B-233
93FExcel/ML-158

Byrd, Samuel D.
(Sammy)
32Orbit/num-96
33G-157
35BU-56
35G-2F
35G-4F
35G-7F
91Conlon/Sport-281
R313
R314
V353-86

Byrne, Clayton
92Kane/ClBest-25
92Kane/ProC-103
92Kane/Team-3
94ClBest/Gold-4

Byrne, Robert M.
(Bobby)
10Domino-18
11Helmar-154
12Sweet/Pin-133
16FleischBrd-11
D322
D328-23
D329-24
D350/2-22
E135-23
E224
E270/2
E300
E94
M101/4-24
M101/5-22
M116
S74-106
T201
T202
T205
T206
T207
T213/blue
T213/brown
T215/blue
T215/brown
T222

Byrne, T.J.
81Holyo-4

Byrne, Thomas Joseph
(Tommy)
44Yank/St-4
51B-73
51BR-D4
51T/BB-35
52B-61
52T-241
53T-123
55B-300
56T-215
57T-108
79TCMA-198
91T/Arc53-123
92Yank/WIZAS-8

Byrnes, Chris
87Oneonta-20

Byrnes, James Joseph
(Jim)
No Cards.

Byrnes, Milton John
(Milt)
No Cards.

Byron, Bill
73F/Wild-20
93Conlon-731UMP

Byron, Tim
82Oneonta-11
85Albany-2

Bystrom, Marty
77Spartan
79OkCty
80OkCty
81T-526R
82D-93
82T-416R
83D-93
83F-154
83T-199
84D-259
84F-24
84Nes/792-511
84Phill/TastyK-15
84T-511
85F-122
85T-284
86D-591
86F-102
86T-723
87FtLaud-2
88Maine/CMC-1
88Maine/ProC-292

Ca, Adam
87SLCity/Taco-19
92Yank/WIZ80-23

Caballero, Ed
88Peoria/Ko-7
89WinSalem/Star-2
90WinSalem/Team-18
91WinSalem/ClBest-2
91WinSalem/ProC-2821

Caballero, Jose
82Miami-8

Caballero, Ralph J.
(Putsy)
49Eureka-132
91Jesuit-4

Cabana, Gerry
52Laval-37

Cabassa, Carlos
80Penin/B-3
80Penin/C-3

Cabell, Billy
83Clinton/Frit-4

Cabell, Enos Milton
73OPC-605R
73T-605R
75OPC-247
75T-247

75T/M-247
76OPC-404
76SSPC-61
76T-404
77BurgChef-2
77Ho-94
77Ho/Twink-94
77T-567
78BK/Ast-14
78Ho-9
78OPC-44
78T-132
79Ho-70
79OPC-269
79T-515
80BK/PHR-24
80OPC-201
80T-385
81D-138
81F-58
81F/St-36
81OPC-45
81T-45
81T/Tr-746
82D-272
82F-386
82F/St-64
82OPC-311
82T-627
82T/St-105
82T/StVar-105
82T/Tr-15T
83D-202
83F-328
83F/St-15M
83OPC-225
83T-225
84D-456
84F-79
84F/X-22
84Mother/Ast-11
84Nes/792-482
84T-482
84T/St-273
84T/Tr-21
85D-110
85F-346
85Leaf-161
85Mother/Ast-10
85T-786
85T/St-61
86Coke/Dodg-5
86D-418
86F-126
86Pol/Dodg-23
86T-197
87F-438
87T-509
90Target-98
91Crown/Orio-68
94TedW-35
Cabella, Jim
89BurlInd/Star-27
Cabello, Bobby
86Cram/NWL-83
Cabral, Irene
91Erie/ClBest-3
91Erie/ProC-4080
Cabral, Joaquin
91Hunting/ClBest-5
91Hunting/ProC-3340
Cabrera, Alfredo A.
(Al)
No Cards.
Cabrera, Antonio
(Tony)
84Idaho/Team-6
85Modesto/Chong-3
86Madis/Pol-4
Cabrera, Basilio
87Fayette-5
88Lakeland/Star-4
89Lakeland/Star-4
90London/ProC-1278
91AA/LineD-377
91London/LineD-377
91London/ProC-1888
92London/ProC-643
92London/SB-402
Cabrera, Carlos
80Utica-3
93Dunedin/ProC-1802
Cabrera, Francisco
86Ventura-3
87Myrtle-28
88BBAmer-20
88Dunedin/Star-1
88SLAS-22
89AAA/CMC-16
89AAA/ProC-16
89F/Up-68
89Syrac/CMC-20
89Syrac/MerchB-5
89Syrac/ProC-791
89Syrac/Team-5
90AAASingl/ProC-409
90Brave/Dubuq/Perf-3
90Brave/Dubuq/Singl-4
90D-646
90F/Up-U2
90OPC-254
90ProC/Singl-289
90Richm/CMC-13
90Richm/ProC-264
90Richm/Team-6
90S/Tr-67T
90T-254
90T/89Debut-20
90TripleAAS/CMC-16
90UD-64
91Brave/Dubuq/Perf-6
91Brave/Dubuq/Stand-8
91D-341
91F-684
91OPC-693
91S-63
91S/100RisSt-33
91T-693
91UD-439
91Ultra-3
92Brave/LykePerf-8
92Brave/LykeStand-9
92D-482
92F-355
92Richm/Bleach-21
92Richm/Comix-1
92Richm/ProC-379
92S-581
92StCl-797
93Brave/LykePerf-7
93Brave/LykeStand-8
93D-184
93F-365
93LimeR/Winter-46
93OPC-383
93Pac/Spanish-3
93Pac/SpanishP-1
93S-472
93StCl/Brave-8
93StCl/MurphyS-172
93T-769
93T/Gold-769
93UD-611
93UD/SeasonHL-HI8
93Ultra-303
94F-356
94Pac/Cr-6
94S-222
94S/GoldR-222
Cabrera, Fremio
86Wausau-2
Cabrera, Jolbert
91Sumter/ProC-2340
92Albany/ClBest-7
92Albany/ProC-2312
93BurlB/ClBest-4
93BurlB/ProC-164
Cabrera, Jose
92BurlInd/ClBest-9
92BurlInd/ProC-1647
93ClBest/MLG-107
Cabrera, Juan
91Beloit/ClBest-13
91Beloit/ProC-2107
91SoOreg/ProC-3852
Cabrera, Miguel
91AubAS/ProC-4284
92Ashvl/ClBest-17
Cabrera, Nasusel
88Madis-6
Cabrera, Victor
86CharRain-4
Cacciatore, Frank
88AubAs/ProC-1967
89Tucson/JP-2
89Tucson/ProC-202
90Ashvl/ClBest-26MG
90Ashvl/ProC-2764
91Ashvl/ProC-584
92Osceola/ClBest-29CO
92Osceola/ProC-2546CO
Cacciatore, Paul
76Wausau
77Wausau
79Jacks-10
Cacek, Craig Thomas
78Charl
79Portl-18
80Port-3
81Portl-9
82Spokane-14
Caceres, Edgar
86WPalmB-7
87Jaxvl-9
89Saraso/Star-2
90BirmB/Best-7
90BirmB/ProC-1395
90Foil/Best-206
92ElPaso/ProC-3927
92ElPaso/SB-202
93FExcel/ML-182
Caci, Bob
86Beloit-3
Cacini, Ron
91AubAS/ProC-4279
92Ashvl/ClBest-13
Cadahia, Aurelio
(Chino)
80OrlanTw-13
81Toledo-11
82OrlanTw/A-3
82OrlanTw/B-15
83OrlanTw-10
86DayBe-4MG
87Gaston/ProC-3
Cadahia, Ben
81CharR-15
82FtMyr-4
86Tulsa-12
Cadahia, Chino
91GulfCR/SportP-30MG
Cadaret, Greg
85Huntsvl/BK-34
88D-528
88D/A's/Bk-528
88Modesto-35
88Mother/A's-26
88T-328
89D-479
89F-4
89Mother/A's-20
89S-340
89S/Tr-69
89T-552
90D-545
90F-440
90F/Can-440
90OPC-659
90PublInt/St-300
90S/NWest-19
90T-659
90T/TVYank-7
90UD-549
91B-157
91D-236
91F-658
91Leaf-415
91OPC-187
91S-188
91StCl-536
91T-187
91UD-343
91Ultra-229
92B-231
92D-628
92F-222
92L-24
92L/BlkGold-24
92OPC-18
92Pinn-402
92S-454
92StCl-176
92T-18
92T/Gold-18
92T/GoldWin-18
92UD-412
92Ultra-404
92Yank/WIZ80-24
93D-610
93F/Final-14
93Pac/Spanish-204
93Reds/Kahn-7
93T-478
93T/Gold-478
94StCl/Team-166
94T-303
94T/Gold-303
Cadian, Larry
89Portl/CMC-7
Cadore, Leon
21Exh-20
61T-403M
72F/FFeat-19M
72Laugh/GF-37M
90HOF/St-22
90Target-99
E120
E220
V100
V61-97
W572
Cady, Charles B.
(Charlie)
No Cards.
Cady, Forrest LeRoy
(Hick)
BF2-2
D328-24
D329-25
E135-24
M101/4-25
T205
Cafego, Thomas
(Tom)
No Cards.
Caffie, Joseph C.
(Joe)
58T-182
Caffrey, Bob
85T-394OLY
87WPalmB-10
88Jaxvl/Best-25
88Jaxvl/ProC-979
88SLAS-19
Caffyn, Benjamin T.
(Ben)
No Cards.
Cage, Wayne Levell
76Wmsprt
78T-706R
79OPC-70
79T-150
79Tacoma-26
80T-208
80Tacoma-4
Cahill, John F.P.
(Patsy)
N172
N284
Cahill, Mark
80Wausau-3
81LynnS-3
83Chatt-21
Cahill, Thomas H.
(Tom)
No Cards.
Cain, Aaron
81Hawaii-9
82Hawaii-9
Cain, Bob
50B-236
51B-197
52B-19
52T-349
53B/Col-56
53T-266
54B-195
54T-61
91T/Arc53-266
94T/Arc54-61
Cain, Cal
86Cedar/TCMA-19
87Cedar-18
Cain, Jerald
83VeroB-23
Cain, John
88Rockford-4
89Rockford-4TR
90Rockford/Team-4TR
Cain, Les
69T-324R
71K-29
71MLB/St-388
71OPC-101
71T-101
72T-783
Cain, Merritt
(Sugar)
93Conlon-952
Cain, Tim
91BendB/ClBest-2
91BendB/ProC-3686
Caines, Arturo
(Art)
89Bristol/Star-3
90Fayette/ProC-2419
Cairncross, Cameron
91Brisbane/Fut-11
91CharRain/ClBest-4
91CharRain/ProC-90
92Watlo/ClBest-12
92Watlo/ProC-2137
93B-658
94B-644
Cairo, Miguel
92GulfCD/ProC-3572
Cairo, Sergio
89Bluefld/Star-6
90Wausau/Best-14
90Wausau/ProC-2142
90Wausau/Star-5
91CLAS/ProC-CAR6
91Freder/ClBest-24
91Freder/ProC-2378
92Hagers/ProC-2568
92Hagers/SB-255
93LimeR/Winter-53
Caithamer, George T.
No Cards.
Cajide, Al
78DaytB
Cakora, Matthew
(Matt)
88CharWh/Best-17
89CharWh/Best-22
89CharWh/ProC-1770
89CharlK-20
90Miami/I/Star-2
Cala, Craig A.
88CapeCod/Sum-92
90SanJose/Best-6
90SanJose/Cal-35
90SanJose/ProC-2022
90SanJose/Star-4
Calcagno, Dan
91Everett/ProC-3916
92Clinton/ProC-3600
92SanJose/ClBest-11
Calcaterra, Jeff
92GulfCY/ProC-3781
Calder, Joe
92Augusta/ClBest-23
92Augusta/ProC-244
92UD/ML-101
Calderon, Ivan
81Wausau-26
82Wausau/Frit-10
83Chatt-27
84Cram/PCL-173
85F/Up-U17
85Mother/Mar-26
86D-435
86F-462
86Leaf-204
86Mother/Mar-15
86OPC-382
86Seven/Coin-W13M
86T-382
87Coke/WS-14
87D/OD-230
87F-488
87F/Slug-7
87T/Tr-15T
88Coke/WS-3
88D-182
88D-25DK
88D-BC5
88D/Best-25
88D/DKsuper-25DK
88F-394
88F/BB/MVP-4
88F/LL-3
88F/Mini-14
88F/St-14
88Kodak/WSox-4
88Leaf-175
88Leaf-25DK
88OPC-184
88Panini/St-63

88S-607
88S/YS/II-22
88Sf-166
88T-184
88T/Big-63
88T/Coins-6
88T/Mini-7
88T/St-285
88T/UK-9
89B-68
89Coke/WS-7
89D-371
89D/Best-193
89F-493
89KennerFig-21
89OPC-101
89RedFoley/St-16
89S-331
89T-656
89T/Big-289
89T/St-297
89UD-650
90B-316
90Coke/WSox-1
90D-294
90D/BestAL-141
90F-529
90F/Can-529
90Leaf-89
90OPC-569
90Panini/St-47
90PublInt/St-385
90RedFoley/St-13
90S-94
90Sf-167
90T-569
90T/Big-80
90T/Coins-9
90T/Mini-11
90T/St-299
90UD-503
91B-440
91Classic/III-T5
91D-203
91Expo/PostC-1
91F-115
91F/Up-U97
91Leaf-338
91Leaf/Stud-194
91OPC-93
91OPC/Premier-17
91Panini/FrSt-318
91Panini/St-258
91S-254
91S/RookTr-6T
91StCl-383
91T-93
91T/Tr-16T
91UD-285
91UD/Ext-786
91UD/FinalEd-96F
91USPlayC/AS-13C
91Ultra-199
92B-179
92CJ/DII-9
92D-431
92D-48
92Expo/D/Duri-4
92F-475
92Kenner/Fig-8
92L-283
92L/BlkGold-283
92OPC-775
92Panini-208
92Panini-287AS
92Pinn-58
92S-83
92S/100SS-61
92Seven/Coin-4
92StCl-73
92StCl/Dome-24
92Studio-52
92T-775
92T/Gold-775
92T/GoldWin-775
92T/Kids-7
92TripleP-196
92UD-226
92UD/HRH-HR24
92UD/TmMVPHolo-13
92Ultra-513
93B-663
93D-196
93F-71
93F/Final-172
93L-242
93OPC-88
93OPC/Premier-105
93Pac/Spanish-354
93Panini-98
93Pinn-150
93S-95
93Select-125
93Select/RookTr-118T
93StCl-119
93StCl-647
93StCl/1stDay-119
93StCl/1stDay-647
93T-540
93T/Finest-55
93T/FinestRef-55
93T/Gold-540
93UD-751
93Ultra-507
94Pinn-192
94Pinn/Artist-192
94Pinn/Museum-192

Calderon, Jose
81Buffa-16
84Cram/PCL-207
85Maine-3
87ArkTr-4
87Louisvl-8

Calderone, Jeff
90BurlB/Best-10
90BurlB/ProC-2343
90BurlB/Star-7

Calderone, Samuel F.
(Sammy)
53T-260
54JC-42
54T-68
79TCMA-236
91T/Arc53-260
94T/Arc54-68

Caldwell, Bruce
90Target-100

Caldwell, Earl W.
47TipTop

Caldwell, Earl
V351A-4

Caldwell, Ralph M.
(Mike)
73OPC-182
73T-182
74OPC-344
74T-344
75OPC-347
75T-347
75T/M-347
76OPC-157
76SSPC-93
76T-157
77T-452
78T-212
79Ho-14
79OPC-356
79T-651
80OPC-269
80T-515
81D-86
81F-512
81OPC-85
81T-85
81T/St-97
82D-330
82F-136
82OPC-378
82Pol/Brew-48
82T-378
83D-154
83F-29
83F/St-5M
83Gard-4
83OPC-142
83OPC/St-184WS
83OPC/St-185WS
83Pol/Brew-48
83T-142
83T/St-184
83T/St-185
84D-237
84F-196
84Gard-3
84Nes/792-605
84OPC-326
84Pol/Brew-48
84T-605
85D-490
85F-577
85T-419
85T/St-289
92Brew/Carlson-4
92Helena/ProC-1733CO

Caldwell, Raymond B.
(Ray)
14CJ-129
15CJ-129
16FleischBrd-12
93Conlon-705
D329-27
D350/2-25
M101/4-27
M101/5-25

Caldwell, Rich
84Newar-17
85CharlO-19

Calhoon, Greg
92Stockton/ClBest-25TR

Calhoun, Brad
77AppFx

Calhoun, Gary
90Helena/SportP-29MG
91Niagara/ClBest-29MG
91Niagara/ProC-3650MG

Calhoun, Jeff
83ColumAst-13
85F/Up-U18
85Mother/Ast-24
86D-426
86F-295
86Pol/Ast-19
86T-534
87D-578
87F-52
87Maine-14
87Maine/TCMA-2
87T-282
87T/Tr-16T
88D-509
88F-299
88Phill/TastyK-5
88T-38
89UD-33

Calhoun, John Charles
No Cards.

Calhoun, Ray
89GreatF-30
90VeroB/Star-7
91FSLAS/ProC-FSL37
91VeroB/ClBest-5
91VeroB/ProC-766
92SanAn/ProC-3968
92SanAn/SB-560

Calhoun, William D.
(Bill)
No Cards.

Calini, Ron
91AubAS/ClBest-11

Calise, Michael S.
(Mike)
80ArkTr-6
81Louisvl-21
82Louisvl-4
83Louisvl/Riley-21
84RochR-5
85Cram/PCL-63

Call, Keith
82Madis/Frit-26
83Madis/Frit-14
84Nashvl-3

Callaghan, Martin F.
(Marty)
E120
V61-66
W573

Callahan, Ben
82Nashvl-4
83Colum-14
83Nashvl-4

Callahan, Brian
88AZ/Pol-1

Callahan, Edward J.
(Ed)
No Cards.

Callahan, Harry
75T/Photo-18

Callahan, James J.
(Nixey)
10Domino-19
11Helmar-8
12Sweet/Pin-8
14CJ-111
16FleischBrd-13
D329-26
D350/2-24
E107
E224
E270/2
E300
M101/4-26
M101/5-24
T207
WG5-7
WG6-6

Callahan, Leo
90Target-107A

Callahan, Mike
83DayBe-4

Callahan, Patrick B.
79WHave-6
81Colum-4
82Nashvl-5

Callahan, Patrick H.
(Pat)
No Cards.

Callahan, Steve
89Everett/Star-3
89Star/IISingl-196
90Clinton/Best-2
90Clinton/ProC-2545
91SanJose/ClBest-14
91SanJose/ProC-2
92Modesto/ClBest-13
92Modesto/ProC-3891

Callahan, Wesley L.
(Wes)
No Cards.

Callari, Ray
91ClBest/Singl-316
91Rockford/ClBest-17
91Rockford/ProC-2052

Callas, Pete
87CharWh-6
88Clearw/Star-4

Callaway, Frank B.
E120

Calley, Robert
85Visalia-10
86Visalia-5

Callihan, John
92Yakima/ClBest-20
92Yakima/ProC-3456

Callis, Al
75Clinton

Callison, John W.
(Johnny)
59T-119
60L-118
60T-17
61T-468
61T/St-50
62Bz
62P/Can-118
62Salada-204
62Shirriff-204
62T-17
62T/St-165
63Bz-15
63Exh
63F-51
63J-179
63P-179
63Salada-26
63T-434
63T/SO
64Bz-15
64PhilBull-8
64T-135
64T/Coins-50
64T/S-36
64T/SU
64T/St-80
64T/tatt
65Bz-15
65OPC-4LL
65T-310
65T-4LL
65T/E-32
65T/trans-41
66Bz-12
66OPC-52M
66T-230
66T-52M
66T/RO
66T/RO-13
67Bz-12
67CokeCap/Phill-4
67OPC-85
67OPC/PI-14
67Pol/Phill-3
67T-309M
67T-85
67T/PI-14
68T-415
68T/ActionSt-15C
68T/ActionSt-4C
69MB-47
69MLB/St-174
69MLBPA/Pin-37
69OPC-133
69T-133
69T/4in1-6M
69T/St-73
70MLB/St-15
70OPC-375
70T-375
71MLB/St-28
71OPC-12
71T-12
72MB-60
72OPC-364
72T-364
72T/Cloth-4
73OPC-535
73Syrac/Team-4
73T-535
74Laugh/ASG-64
78TCMA-29
92Yank/WIZ70-30
93AP/ASG-146
93UD/ATH-25
Exh47
PM10/L-8

Callistro, Robby
91Pocatel/ProC-3774
91Pocatel/SportP-2

Calloway, Rick
89KS*-44

Calmus, Dick
64T-231
68T-427
90Target-101

Calufetti, Larry
76Wausau

Calui, Mark
92Belling/ProC-1447

Calvert, Art
87PrWill-8
88FtLaud/Star-3
89StPete/Star-4
89Star/Wax-48

Calvert, Chris
85Visalia-12
87Visalia-13
88Clearw/Star-5
88Reading/ProC-886
89EastLDD/ProC-DD34
89Reading/Best-21
89Reading/ProC-664
89Reading/Star-5

Calvert, Mark
80Phoenix/NBank-9
81Phoenix-9
83Phoenix/BHN-2
84Cram/PCL-2
85Maine-4

Calvert, Steve
92MN-4

Calvey, Jack
46Sunbeam

Calvi, Mark
92Belling/ClBest-19

Calvo, Jacinto
(Jack)
No Cards.

Calzado, Francis
84Everett/Cram-23

Calzado, Johnny
89Johnson/Star-4
90Savan/ProC-2081
91ClBest/Singl-79
91Spring/ClBest-9
91Spring/ProC-754

Calzado, Lorenzo
89Savan/ProC-360

Camacho, Adulfo
85Tigres-18

Camacho, Ernie
81T-96R

84Wheat/Ind-13
85D-129
85F-442
85Polar/Ind-13
85T-739
85T/St-253
86F-582
86OhHenry-13
86T-509
87D-350
87F-247
87Gator-13
87OPC-353
87T-353
87T/St-209
88Mother/Ast-16
88Tucson/ProC-189
89Phoenix/CMC-6
89Phoenix/ProC-1494
90B-229
90Louisvl/LBC-9
90Mother/Giant-27
90T/TVCard-51
91Pac/SenLg-132

Camacho, Joe
93Rang/Keeb-40CO

Camara, Gerry
89KS*-75

Camarena, Miguel
90Hunting/ProC-3272
91Hunting/ClBest-6
91Hunting/ProC-3326

Cambria, Fred
71OPC-27R
71T-27R
72OPC-392R
72T-392R
92Spokane/ClBest-28CO
92Spokane/ProC-1311CO

Camelli, Henry R.
(Hank)
47TipTop

Camelo, Pete
86Jaxvl/TCMA-6
87Jaxvl-4

Cameron, John S.
No Cards.

Cameron, Paul
84CharlO-5
85CharlO-30
87CharlO/WBTV-xx

Cameron, Stanton
89Pittsfld/Star-2
90Clmbia/PCPII-4
90Columbia/GS-25
91StLucie/ClBest-4
91StLucie/ProC-722
92Freder/ClBest-8
92Freder/ProC-1818
93ClBest/MLG-62
93FExcel/ML-123
94FExcel-2
94T-79M
94T/Gold-79M

Camilli, Adolf Louis
(Dolph)
34G-91
35BU-150
36Exh/4-6
36G-5
37Exh/4-6
38Exh/4-2
38Wheat-16
39Exh
39PlayBall-86
40PlayBall-68
40Wheat-11
41DP-20
41PlayBall-51
43Playball-31
61F-97
89Smok/Dodg-42
90Target-102
PM10/Sm-19
R302
R312
R313
R314
WG8-4

Camilli, Douglass J.
(Doug)
61Union
62T-594R
63T-196
64T-249
65OPC-77
65T-77
66T-593
67T-551
73OPC-131CO
73T-131C
85Greens-1MG
86Greens-3MG
87WinHaven-24
90Target-103
90WinHaven/Star-27CO

Camilli, Kevin
86Greens-4
88Fayette/ProC-1099

Camilli, Louis Steven
(Lou)
71MLB/St-364
71OPC-612R
71T-612R

Caminiti, Ken
85Osceola/Team-17
86ColumAst-6
87SLAS-10
87Sf/Rook-37
88Classic/Blue-228
88D-308
88F-441
88OPC-64
88S-164
88S/YS/I-29
88Sf-124
88T-64
88T/St-33
88ToysRUs-6
88Tucson/CMC-11
88Tucson/JP-3
88Tucson/ProC-182
89D-542
89D/Best-262
89Lennox/Ast-21
89Mother/Ast-25
89T-369
89T/Big-210
89UD-141
90B-73
90D-424
90D/BestNL-126
90F-225
90F/Can-225
90Leaf-253
90Lennox-5
90MLBPA/Pins-42
90Mother/Ast-6
90OPC-531
90Panini/St-260
90PublInt/St-89
90S-76
90Sf-209
90T-531
90T/Big-170
90T/St-20
90T/TVAS-37
90UD-122
91B-543
91D-221
91F-500
91Leaf-502
91Leaf/Stud-174
91Mother/Ast-6
91OPC-174
91Panini/FrSt-9
91Panini/St-17
91S-186
91S-415RIF
91StCl-520
91T-174
91UD-180
91Ultra-133
92B-538
92D-66
92DennyGS-2
92F-427
92L-140
92L/BlkGold-140
92Mother/Ast-6
92OPC-740
92Panini-154
92Pinn-43
92S-69
92StCl-142
92Studio-33
92T-740
92T/Gold-740
92T/GoldWin-740
92T/Kids-45
92TripleP-78
92UD-279
92Ultra-200
93B-504
93Colla/DM-21
93D-140
93F-432
93Flair-59
93Kraft-17
93L-261
93MilkBone-6
93Mother/Ast-9
93OPC-81
93Panini-173
93Pinn-59
93S-40
93Select-47
93StCl-464
93StCl/1stDay-464
93StCl/Ast-4
93Studio-143
93T-448
93T/Finest-131
93T/FinestRef-131
93T/Gold-448
93TripleP-149
93TripleP-61AA
93UD-305
93UD/FunPack-45
93UD/SP-30
93Ultra-38
94B-230
94D-53
94F-486
94L-244
94Pac/Cr-260
94Panini-191
94Pinn-193
94Pinn/Artist-193
94Pinn/Museum-193
94S-342
94StCl-322
94StCl/1stDay-322
94StCl/Gold-322
94Studio-18
94T-646
94T/Finest-191
94T/FinestRef-191
94T/Gold-646
94TripleP-23
94UD-409
94UD/CollC-72
94UD/CollC/Gold-72
94UD/CollC/Silv-72
94UD/SP-29
94Ultra-500

Camnitz, Samuel H.
(Howard)
10Domino-20
11Helmar-155
12Sweet/Pin-134A
12Sweet/Pin-134B
14CJ-16
14Piedmont/St-8
15CJ-16
D322
E224
E254
E270/1
E90/1
E97
L1-124
M116
S74-107
S81-99
T202
T205
T206
T207
T213/blue
T214-3
T215/blue
T215/brown
T3-7

Camp, Howard Lee
(Howie)
No Cards.

Camp, Llewellan R.
No Cards.

Camp, Rick
77T-475R
78T-349
79Richm-21
79T-105
81D-197
81F-246
81OPC-87
81Pol/Atl-37
81T-87
81T/St-150
82BK/Lids-5
82D-223
82F-432
82OPC-138
82Pol/Atl-37
82T-637
83D-149
83F-133
83F/St-5M
83Pol/Atl-37
83T-207
84D-165
84F-174
84Nes/792-597
84OPC-136
84Pol/Atl-37
84T-597
85D-409
85F-321
85Ho/Braves-5
85Leaf-130
85OPC-167
85Pol/Atl-37
85T-491
86D-385
86F-510
86T-319

Camp, Scott
86Osceola-3

Campa, Eric
90Madison/Best-5

Campagno, Steve
82Oneonta-9

Campanella, Roy
49B-84
49Eureka-32
50B-75
50Drake-6
51B-31
52B-44
52BR
52StarCal-91B
52StarCal/L-79C
52T-314
52TipTop
52Wheat*
53B/Col-46
53Exh/Can-20
53RM-NL5
53SM
53T-27
54B-90
54NYJour
54RM-NL13
54Wilson
55B-22
55Gol/Dodg-5
56T-101
57T-210
57T-400M
58BB
59T-550
60NuCard-29
61NuCard-429
61T-480MVP
75OPC-189MVP
75OPC-191MVP
75OPC-193MVP
75T-189MVP
75T-191MVP
75T-193MVP
75T/M-189MVP
75T/M-191MVP
75T/M-193MVP
76Shakey-111
77Galasso-251
77Galasso-5
79TCMA-43
79TCMA-8
80Marchant/HOF-4
80Pac/Leg-90
80Perez/HOF-111
80SSPC/HOF
83D/HOF-39
83MLBPA/Pin-20
84West/1-22
86Sf/Dec-33
87Leaf/SpecOlym-H3
88Pac/Leg-47
89HOF/St-54
89Rini/Dodg-9
89Smok/Dodg-4
90BBWit-30
90Perez/GreatMom-7
90Target-104
91T/Arc53-27
92Bz/Quadra-20
92FrRow/ATGHolo-2
93TWill-133
93TWill-141
93TWill-9
93TWill/Mem-1
93TWill/POG-21M
93TWill/POG-22
Exh47
PM10/Sm-20A
PM10/Sm-20B
PM10/Sm-21
R423-12

Campaneris, Blanco D.
(Bert)
65OPC-266
65T-266
66Bz-44
66OPC-175
66T-175
66T/RO-108
66T/RO-14
67Bz-44
67OPC/PI-2
67T-515
67T/PI-2
68A's/JITB-3
68OPC-109
68T-109
68T/ActionSt-5A
69MB-48
69MLB/St-83
69T-423AS
69T-495
69T-556M
69T/S-29
69T/St-212
70K-39
70MLB/St-255
70OPC-205
70T-205
70T/PI-23
71Bz
71Bz/Test-31
71MLB/St-508
71OPC-440
71T-440
71T/Coins-64
71T/GM-6
71T/Greatest-6
71T/S-31
71T/Super-31
71T/tatt-7
72MB-61
72OPC-75
72T-75
73OPC-209WS
73OPC-295
73OPC-64LL
73T-209WS
73T-295
73T-64LL
74Greyhound-5M
74K-4
74OPC-155
74OPC-335AS
74OPC-474WS
74OPC-478WS
74T-155
74T-335AS
74T-474WS
74T-478WS
74T/DE-46
74T/St-223
75Ho-28
75Ho/Twink-28
75OPC-170
75SSPC/42-14
75T-170
75T/M-170
76Ho-61
76OPC-580
76SSPC-492
76T-580

77BurgChef-19
77Ho-149
77Ho/Twink-149
77K-2
77OPC-74
77T-373
78BK/R-14
78SSPC/270-101
78T-260
78T/Zest-2
78Wiffle/Discs-12
79OPC-326
79T-620
80OPC-264
80T-505
81D-50
81F-280
81T-410
82D-593
82F-454
82T-772
83Colum-17
83T/Tr-18
84F-120
84Nes/792-139
84Nes/792-711LL
84Nes/792-714LL
84T-139
84T-711LL
84T-714LL
87Mother/A's-1
89Pac/Leg-157
89Pac/SenLg-63
89T/SenLg-32
89TM/SenLg-16
90EliteSenLg-78
90HOF/St-67
90Pac/Legend-15
90Swell/Great-121
91K/Leyenda-1
91Swell/Great-110
92AP/ASG-42
92MCI-4
92Yank/WIZ80-25
93Rang/Keeb-92
93TWill-44
93UD/ATH-26

Campanis, Alexander
(Al)
90Target-105

Campanis, James A.
(Jim)
67OPC-12R
67T-12R
68T-281
69T-396
70T-671
71MLB/St-196
74OPC-513
74T-513
90Target-106

Campanis, Jim Jr.
88T/Tr-23T
89SanBern/Best-1
89SanBern/Cal-85
90Penin/Star-5
91AA/LineD-332
91Jaxvl/LineD-332
91Jaxvl/ProC-153
92B-144
92ClBest-328
92D-647
92Jacks/ProC-3709
92Jaxvl/SB-353
92OPC-58M
92ProC/Tomorrow-143
92Sky/AASingl-149
92T-58M
92T/Gold-58M
92T/GoldWin-58M
92UD/ML-223

Campas, Mike
89Hamil/Star-7
89Star/IISingl-105
90Spring/Best-6
91StPete/ClBest-18
91StPete/ProC-2281

Campau, Charles C.
(Count)
N172

Campbell, Arthur V.
(Vin)
15CJ-168
D322
M116

Campbell, Bill
74OPC-26
74T-26
75OPC-226
75T-226
75T/M-226
76OPC-288
76SSPC-208
76T-288
77OPC-12
77OPC-8LL
77T-166
77T-8LL
78Ho-107
78OPC-87
78OPC-8LL
78PapaG/Disc-22
78SSPC/270-169
78T-208LL
78T-545
79OPC-195
79T-375
80T-15
81F-240
81OPC-256
81T-396
82D-487
82F-289
82RedLob
82T-619
82T/Tr-16T
83D-504
83F-493
83F/St-20M
83T-436
83T/Fold-4M
83Thorn-39
84D-555
84F-489
84F/X-23
84Nes/792-787
84Phill/TastyK-16
84T-787
84T/Tr-22
85D-163
85F-245
85F/Up-U19
85OPC-209
85Phill/TastyK-9
85T-209
85T/Tr-15T
86D-571
86F-28
86F/Up-U17
86T-112
86T/Tr-17T
87F-146
87OPC-362
87T-674
89Pac/Leg-191
89Pac/SenLg-34
89T/SenLg-106
89TM/SenLg-17
90EliteSenLg-95
91Pac/SenLg-125
92Denver/ProC-2656
92Denver/SB-150M

Campbell, Bruce D.
35BU-152
41PlayBall-37
92Conlon/Sport-539
93Conlon-881
94Conlon-1228
R305
R313

Campbell, Clarence
(Soup)
40PlayBall-200
41DP-131

Campbell, D.C
90Durham/Team-8

Campbell, Darrin
89Saraso/Star-3
90Saraso/Star-3
91AA/LineD-53
91BirmB/LineD-53
91BirmB/ProC-1456

Campbell, David Alan
(Dave)
78T-402
79T-9

Campbell, David W.
(Dave)
69T-324R
70MLB/St-110
70T-639
71MLB/St-221
71OPC-46
71T-46
72OPC-384
72T-384
73OPC-488
73T-488
74OPC-556
74T-556
78Padre/FamFun-4ANN
84Smok/Padres-3ANN

Campbell, Donovan
88Idaho/ProC-1845
89BurlB/ProC-1620
89BurlB/Star-3
92StPete/ClBest-7

Campbell, Greg
82BurlR/Frit-26TR
83BurlR-28
83BurlR/Frit-25TR
84Tulsa-TR
85OKCty-14
86OKCty-2TR

Campbell, James A.
81Tiger/Detroit-130GM
83Kaline-22GM
83Kaline-44GM
83Kaline-54GM

Campbell, James R.
(Jim)
63Pep
63T-373
64T-303

Campbell, Jim
88Memphis/Best-10
89F-646M
89Memphis/Best-17
89Memphis/ProC-1194
89Memphis/Star-5
89Smok/Ast-13
90A&AASingle/ProC-15
90Foil/Best-311
90Memphis/Best-22
90Memphis/ProC-1002
90Memphis/Star-3
91Spokane/ClBest-3
91Spokane/ProC-3938
91T/90Debut-24
92ClBest-267
92Omaha/ProC-2954

Campbell, Joseph Earl
(Joe)
No Cards.

Campbell, Keiver
91StCath/ClBest-2
91StCath/ProC-3407
92StCath/ClBest-14
92StCath/ProC-3397

Campbell, Kevin
87VeroB-17
88VeroB/Star-2
89Bakers/Cal-182
90SanAn/GS-8
90TexLgAS/GS-16
91AAA/LineD-530
91AAAGame/ProC-45
91Tacoma/LineD-530
91Tacoma/ProC-2296
92D/Rook-21
92F/Up-48
92S-855
92Sky/AAASingl-236
92StCl-647
92T/91Debut-26
92T/Tr-19T
92T/TrGold-19T
92Tacoma/SB-528
93D-155
93F-660
93StCl-235
93StCl/1stDay-235
93T-236
93T/Gold-236

Campbell, Marc T.
(Hutch)
No Cards.

Campbell, Mark
82DayBe-17

Campbell, Mike
86Cedar/TCMA-4
87Calgary-14
87Tampa-21
88D-30
88D/Best-163
88D/Rook-2
88F-372
88Leaf-30RR
88Mother/Sea-18
88T-246
89D-497
89F-543
89Mother/Sea-18
89S-568
89S/HotRook-86
89S/YS/II-30
89T-143
89UD-337
90AAASingl/ProC-160
90ProC/Singl-634
90Vanco/CMC-7
90Vanco/ProC-482
91Tulsa/Team-5
92OkCty/ProC-1909
92OkCty/SB-307
93Rang/Keeb-93

Campbell, Paul M.
No Cards.

Campbell, Ronald T.
(Ron)
67CokeCap/Cub-6
67T-497

Campbell, Samuel
(Sam)
No Cards.

Campbell, Scott
90OK-8
91James/ClBest-8
91James/ProC-3550
92WPalmB/ClBest-10
92WPalmB/ProC-2093

Campbell, Steve
82Idaho-23

Campbell, William G.
(Gilly)
32Orbit/num-34
32Orbit/un-9
35BU-164
35G-8D
35G-9D
90Target-107B

Campbell, William J.
E270/1
T206
T213/blue
T213/brown

Campeau, Jean Claude
45Parade*-11

Camper, Cardell
78T-711R
91Pac/SenLg-96

Campillo, Robert
92James/ClBest-8
92James/ProC-1505

Campisi, Sal
70T-716R
71OPC-568
71T-568

Campos, Francisco J.
(Frank)
52T-307
53T-51
91T/Arc53-51

Campos, Frank
88CharWh/Best-24
89CharWh/Best-23
89CharWh/ProC-1767
90SoBend/GS-23
90Utica/Pucko-15
91SoBend/ClBest-14
91SoBend/ProC-2850
92BirmB/ProC-2574
92Saraso/ClBest-18
92UD/ML-180

Campos, Jesus
93James/ClBest-5
93James/ProC-3337

Campos, Tony
52Laval-103

Campusano, Genaro
90Welland/Pucko-3
91Augusta/ClBest-29
91Augusta/ProC-810
91ClBest/Singl-161
92Salem/ClBest-9

Campusano, Silvestre
(Sil)
86Knoxvl-4
87Syrac-1
87Syrac/TCMA-18
88D/Rook-42
88F/Up-U66
88S/Tr-93T
88T/Tr-24T
88Tor/Fire-6
89Classic-137
89D-584
89OPC-191
89S-473
89Syrac/CMC-21
89Syrac/MerchB-6
89Syrac/ProC-808
89Syrac/Team-6
89T-191
89Tor/Fire-6
89UD-45
90Classic/III-66
90Phill/TastyK-3
91F-389
91OPC-618
91Phill/Medford-7
91S-847
91ScranWB/ProC-2549
91StCl-484
91T-618
91UD-469
93LimeR/Winter-81

Campusano, Teo
89AubAs/ProC-2162

Canady, Chuckie
82BurlR/Frit-16
82BurlR/TCMA-16
83Tulsa-14
84OKCty-17
85OKCty-29
90TulsaDG/Best-2

Canale, George
87Stockton-18
88ElPaso/Best-5
89Denver/CMC-19
89Denver/ProC-35
90AAASingl/ProC-655
90B-392
90D-699
90Denver/CMC-17
90Denver/ProC-630
90ElPasoATG/Team-28
90F-641R
90F/Can-641
90OPC-344
90ProC/Singl-42
90S-656
90T-344
90T/89Debut-21
90UD-59
91AAA/LineD-130
91Denver/LineD-130
91Denver/ProC-128
91F-578
91S/100RisSt-27

Canan, Dick
86Peoria-2
87Peoria-5
89WinSalem/Star-3
90CharlK/Team-3
91AA/LineD-129
91CharlK/LineD-129
91CharlK/ProC-1695

Canate, William
90Watertn/Star-2
91Kinston/ClBest-23
91Kinston/ProC-335
92ClBest-86
92ColRS/ClBest-4
92ColRS/ProC-2403
93ClBest/MLG-11
93F/Final-287
93FExcel/ML-159
93Pac/Spanish-650
93SALAS/II-3
93SALAS/IICS-15
94StCl/Team-163
94T-124
94T/Gold-124

Canavan, James Edward
(Jimmy)
90Target-108
N172

Cancel, Danny
91Peoria/ProC-1353
Cancel, Victor
88Wythe/ProC-1980
89Wythe/Star-4
90Geneva/ProC-3034
90Geneva/Star-3
90Peoria/Team-15
91Peoria/ClBest-18
91Peoria/Team-23
Candaele, Casey
85Indianap-25
86Indianap-33
87Classic/Up-128
87D-549
87D/Rook-33
87F/Up-U16
87Sf-158M
87Sf/Rook-6
87Sf/TPrev-20M
87T/Tr-17T
88D-179
88D/Best-68
88F-181
88Ho/Disc-12
88Leaf-199
88OPC-87
88Panini/St-329
88RedFoley/St-11
88S-97
88S/YS/I-34
88Sf-140
88T-431
88T/Gloss60-60
88T/JumboR-11
88T/St-305
88T/St-77
88ToysRUs-7
89Tucson/CMC-16
89Tucson/JP-3
89Tucson/ProC-197
89UD-58
90Lennox-6
90Mother/Ast-25
90T/Tr-17T
91B-559
91D-324
91F-501
91Leaf-114
91Mother/Ast-25
91OPC-602
91Panini/FrSt-8
91S-577
91StCl-434
91T-602
91UD-511
91Ultra-134
92D-150
92F-428
92Mother/Ast-25
92OPC-161
92Panini-153
92S-147
92StCl-178
92T-161
92T/Gold-161
92T/GoldWin-161
92UD-387
92Ultra-489
93D-536
93F-49
93L-15
93Mother/Ast-24
93OPC-105
93Pac/Spanish-120
93Panini-177
93StCl-70
93StCl/1stDay-70
93StCl/Ast-28
93T-584
93T/Gold-584
93UD-294
94S-285
94S/GoldR-285
Candelari, Rick
88Belling/Legoe-1
89Wausau/GS-21
Candelaria, Al
83Ander-9
85Fresno/Pol-20
Candelaria, Ben
93MedHat/ProC-3748
93MedHat/SportP-13
Candelaria, John
76Crane-7
76Ho-92
76MSA/Disc
76OPC-317
76SSPC-563
76T-317
77BurgChef-188
77Ho-80
77Ho/Twink-80
77K-7
77OPC-59
77Pep-63
77T-510
78Ho-104
78K-18
78OPC-221
78OPC-7LL
78T-190
78T-207LL
79Ho-86
79K-34
79OPC-29
79T-70
80OPC-332
80T-635
81Coke
81D-374
81F-375
81OPC-265
81T-265
82D-297
82F-479
82OPC-3
82T-425
83D-549
83F-304
83F/St-6M
83OPC-127
83OPC/St-282
83T-291TL
83T-755
83T/St-282
84D-357
84F-247
84F/St-57
84Nes/792-330
84OPC-330
84T-330
84T/St-127
85D-430
85F-462
85F/St-98
85FunFood/Pin-50
85Leaf-157
85OPC-50
85T-50
85T/St-123
86D-499
86F-150
86OPC-140
86Sf-129M
86Smok/Cal-16
86T-140
86T/Tatt-5M
87D-551
87F-75
87F/AwardWin-5
87F/LimWaxBox-C3
87Leaf-242
87OPC-313
87Sf-148
87Sf/TPrev-11M
87Smok/AL-3
87Smok/Cal-1
87T-630
88D-608
88D/Best-20
88D/Y/Bk-NEW
88F/Up-U46
88S-293
88S/Tr-40T
88T-546
88T/Tr-25T
89B-171
89D-192
89F-251
89OPC-285
89Panini/St-397
89S-246
89S/NWest-8
89Sf-202
89T-285
89T/St-306
89UD-248
90KayBee-5
90Leaf-492
90OPC-485
90PublInt/St-532
90S/Tr-54T
90T-485
90T/Tr-18T
90UD/Ext-720
91F/Up-U92
91Leaf-324
91Mother/Dodg-22
91OPC-777
91Pol/Dodg-54
91S-791
91S/RookTr-32T
91StCl-538
91T-777
91T/Tr-17T
91UD/FinalEd-40F
91WIZMets-59
92D-125
92F-449
92Mother/Dodg-12
92OPC-363
92Pol/Dodg-54
92S-350
92StCl-164
92T-363
92T/Gold-363
92T/GoldWin-363
92UD-482
92Ultra-500
92Yank/WIZ80-26
93F-443
93Pac/Spanish-584
93Pirate/Nation-4
93S-448
93T-682
93T/Gold-682
93UD-690
Candelaria, Jorge
88Oneonta/ProC-2055
89Boise/ProC-1998
89Reno/Cal-242
Candini, Mario
49Remar
51B-255
Candiotti, Tom
81ElPaso-22
84Cram/PCL-32
84D-393
84F-197
84Nes/792-262
84T-262
86F/Up-U18
86OhHenry-49
86T/Tr-18T
87D-342
87D/OD-104
87F-248
87F/Mini-16
87F/St-18
87Gator-49
87Leaf-81
87OPC-296
87Sf/TPrev-3M
87T-463
87T/Mini-50
87T/St-211
88D-377
88D/Best-112
88F-604
88Gator-49
88OPC-123
88Panini/St-69
88S-595
88Sf-37
88T-123
88T/Big-93
89B-80
89D-256
89D/Best-117
89F-399
89Panini/St-317
89RedFoley/St-17
89S-239
89T-599
89T/Big-267
89T/St-211
89UD-470
90B-324
90D-256
90D/BestAL-89
90ElPasoATG/Team-32
90F-488
90F/Can-488
90Leaf-55
90OPC-743
90Panini/St-57
90PublInt/St-556
90S-269
90Sf-126
90T-743
90T/Coins-10
90T/St-216
90UD-388
91B-62
91Classic/200-54
91D-115
91F-364
91F/UltraUp-U59
91F/Up-U64
91Indian/McDon-6
91Leaf-79
91Leaf/Stud-132
91OPC-624
91Panini/FrSt-223
91Panini/St-174
91RedFoley/St-16
91S-488
91S/100SS-36
91S/RookTr-31T
91S/ToroBJ-28
91StCl-405
91T-624
91T/Tr-18T
91UD-218
91UD/FinalEd-49F
91Ultra-109
92B-606
92D-459
92F-326
92F/Up-89
92L-409
92L/BlkGold-409
92Mother/Dodg-3
92OPC-38
92OPC/Premier-142
92Pinn-459
92Pinn-610GRIP
92Pol/Dodg-49
92S-575
92S/RookTr-68T
92StCl-113
92StCl-875
92Studio-42
92T-38
92T/Gold-38
92T/GoldWin-38
92T/Tr-20T
92T/TrGold-20T
92UD-447
92UD-760
92USPlayC/Ace-9S
92Ultra-501
93B-322
93D-142
93F-60
93L-487
93Mother/Dodg-11
93OPC-63
93Pac/Spanish-497
93Pinn-147
93Pol/Dodg-3
93S-175
93Select-143
93StCl-325
93StCl/1stDay-325
93StCl/Dodg-19
93T-365
93T/Finest-132
93T/FinestRef-132
93T/Gold-365
93T/Hill-22
93UD-98
93Ultra-52
94B-126
94D-521
94F-507
94L-72
94Pac/Cr-305
94Panini-198
94Pinn-115
94Pinn/Artist-115
94Pinn/Museum-115
94S-203
94S/GoldR-203
94StCl-32
94StCl/1stDay-32
94StCl/Gold-32
94T-211
94T/Finest-107
94T/FinestRef-107
94T/Gold-211
94UD-260
94UD/ElecD-260
94Ultra-514
Caneira, John
75QuadC
77SLCity
78Cr/PCL-55
Canepa, Vincent
52Laval-52
Canestro, Art
88Oneonta/ProC-2060
89Oneonta/ProC-2104
90PrWill/Team-7
91FtLaud/ClBest-2
91FtLaud/ProC-2417
Cangelosi, John
83AppFx/Frit-13
86Coke/WS-44
86D/HL-51
86D/Rook-51
86F/Up-U19
86Sf/Rook-31
86T/Tr-19T
87D-162
87F-489
87Leaf-251
87OPC-201
87Seven-C3
87Sf-157M
87Sf/TPrev-26M
87T-201
87T/JumboR-2
87T/Mini-49
87T/St-293
87T/Tr-18T
88D-435
88F-325
88OPC-328
88Panini/St-377
88S-418
88T-506
89S-601
89T-592
89UD-67
89VFJuice-44
90D-565
90Homer/Pirate-8
90OPC-29
90S-367
90T-29
90UD-370
91AAA/LineD-629
91Vanco/LineD-629
91Vanco/ProC-1605
92B-442
92Mother/Rang-27
92Ultra-439
93Rang/Keeb-94
Cangemi, Jamie
87Beloit-7
89Beloit/II/Star-4
89Stockton/Best-6
89Stockton/Cal-150
89Stockton/ProC-389
89Stockton/Star-13
90Stockton/Best-21
90Stockton/Cal-182
90Stockton/ProC-2182
91Stockton/ClBest-1
91Stockton/ProC-3025
Caniglia, Pete
52Laval-45
Canino, Carlos
88Geneva/ProC-1655
Canizaro, Jay
92OKSt-2
Cannaday, Aaron
92Welland/ClBest-3
92Welland/ProC-1325
93Welland/ClBest-3
93Welland/ProC-3359
Cannell, Virgin Wirt
(Rip)
No Cards.
Cannizzaro, Chris Jr.
86Pawtu-4

87Pawtu-27
87Pawtu/TCMA-2
88Pawtu/CMC-15
88Pawtu/ProC-451
89Pawtu/CMC-11
89Pawtu/Dunkin-7
89Pawtu/ProC-686
Cannizzaro, Chris
61T-118
62T-26
65OPC-61
65T-61
66T-497
69OPC-131
69T-131
69T/4in1-24M
70OPC-329
70T-329
71MLB/St-222
71OPC-426
71T-426
71T/Coins-109
71T/tatt-6
72T-759
75OPC-355
75T-355
75T/M-355
81Redwd-28MG
82Redwd-25MG
90Target-109
91WIZMets-60
Cannon, Joseph Jerome
(J.J.)
75Dubuq
78Charl
79Syrac/TCMA-7
79Syrac/Team-23
80OPC-118
80T-221
81Syrac-17
81Syrac/Team-5
82Knoxvl-18
83Kinston/Team-2
86Knoxvl-5
87Knoxvl-26
89Knoxvl/Best-25
89Knoxvl/ProC-1129
89Knoxvl/Star-24
90Knoxvl/Best-10CO
90Knoxvl/ProC-1260CO
90Knoxvl/Star-25CO
91MedHat/ProC-4117MG
91MedHat/SportP-26MG
92StCath/ClBest-27MG
92StCath/ProC-3401MG
93StCath/ClBest-25MG
93StCath/ProC-3989MG
Cannon, Robby
91Boise/ProC-3894
Cannon, Scott
86Kinston-3
Cannon, Stan
79Wisco-16
Cannon, Tim
83Miami-22
Cano, Jose
83Ander-8
84Durham-22
87Osceola-27
88Tucson/CMC-7
88Tucson/JP-4
88Tucson/ProC-171
89ColMud/Best-25
90B-68
90ColMud/Best-25
90ColMud/ProC-1340
90Lennox-7
90T/89Debut-22
90UD-43
93LimeR/Winter-116
Canseco, Jose
83Madis/Frit-13
85Huntsvl/BK-44
86D-39RR
86D/HL-55
86D/Rook-22
86F-649R
86F/LL-3
86F/Mini-87
86F/Slug-5
86F/St-19
86F/Up-U20
86Mother/A's-9
86SLAS-14
86Sf-178R
86Sf/Rook-11
86T/Tr-20T
87Classic-46
87Classic/Up-125
87D-6DK
87D-97
87D-PC12
87D/AAS-21
87D/DKsuper-6
87D/HL-40M
87D/OD-24
87D/WaxBox-PC12
87Drake-4
87F-389
87F-625M
87F-628M
87F-633M
87F/AwardWin-6
87F/BB-6
87F/Excit-7
87F/GameWin-8
87F/HL-2
87F/Hottest-9
87F/LL-8
87F/Lim-6
87F/Mini-17
87F/RecSet-3
87F/Slug-8
87F/St-131M
87F/St-19
87GenMills/Book-3M
87Ho/St-28
87KayBee-7
87Kraft-35
87Leaf-151
87Leaf-6DK
87MSA/Discs-17
87MnM's-10
87Mother/A's-26
87Mother/A's-27M
87OPC-247
87RedFoley/St-63
87Sf-80M
87Sf-90
87Sf/TPrev-23M
87Smok/A's-2
87Smok/AL-1
87Stuart-24M
87T-620
87T/Coins-6
87T/Gloss60-59
87T/HL-12
87T/JumboR-3
87T/Mini-68
87T/St-164
87T/St-304
87ToysRUs-5
87Woolwth-12
88Bz-3
88Classic/Red-165
88Classic/Red-197M
88D-302
88D/A's/Bk-302
88D/Best-22
88F-276
88F-624M
88F/AwardWin-4
88F/BB/AS-5
88F/BB/MVP-3
88F/Excit-7
88F/Hottest-5
88F/LL-4
88F/Mini-45
88F/RecSet-4
88F/SS-5
88F/Slug-6
88F/St-54
88F/TL-3
88KMart-4
88KayBee-3
88KennerFig-16
88Leaf-138
88Mother/A's-7
88Nestle-37
88OPC-370
88Panini/St-173
88S-45
88S/YS/I-30
88Sf-201
88T-370
88T/Big-13
88T/Coins-7
88T/Gloss60-55
88T/Mini-30
88T/St-173
88T/St/Backs-48
88T/UK-10
89B-201
89Bz-5
89CMC/Canseco-Set
89Cadaco-5
89Classic-103
89Classic-3
89D-643HL
89D-91
89D/AS-2
89D/AS-30
89D/Best-57
89D/GrandSlam-1
89D/MVP-BC5
89D/PopUp-2
89F-5
89F-628M
89F-634M
89F/AS-2
89F/BBAS-5
89F/BBMVP's-6
89F/Excit-3
89F/Heroes-5
89F/LL-3
89F/Superstar-6
89F/WS-3
89F/WaxBox-C4
89Holsum/Discs-5
89KMart/DT-18
89KayBee-3
89KennerFig-22
89KingB/Discs-17
89MSA/Disc-18
89MSA/SS-12
89Master/Discs-10
89Modesto/Chong-34
89Mother/A's-7
89Mother/Canseco-1
89Mother/Canseco-2
89Mother/Canseco-3
89Mother/Canseco-4
89Mother/ROY's-1
89Mother/ROY's-4M
89Nissen-5
89OPC-389
89Panini/St-238AS
89Panini/St-246
89Panini/St-422
89Panini/St-477
89Panini/St-480
89Panini/St-8
89RedFoley/St-18
89S-1
89S-582M
89S-655HL
89S/HotStar-1
89S/Mast-40
89Sf-1
89Sf-221M
89T-401AS
89T-500
89T/Ames-8
89T/Big-190
89T/Coins-29
89T/Crunch-1
89T/DH-5
89T/Gloss22-6
89T/Gloss60-12
89T/HeadsUp-18
89T/Hills-5
89T/LJN-74
89T/Mini-68
89T/St-11
89T/St-148
89T/St-171
89T/St/Backs-13
89T/UK-12
89Tacoma/ProC-1536
89Tetley/Discs-18
89UD-371
89UD-659MVP
89UD-670TC
89Woolwth-1
89Woolwth-23
90B-460
90BBWit-11
90Classic-22
90Classic/III-32
90CollAB-25
90Colla/Canseco-Set
90D-125
90D/BestAL-81
90D/Learning-6
90F-3
90F-629MVP
90F/AwardWin-6
90F/BB-4
90F/BBMVP-6
90F/Can-3
90F/Can-629
90F/LL-5
90F/LgStand-4
90F/WS-10M
90F/WS-5
90HOF/St-95
90HotPlay/St-4
90KMart/SS-21
90Kenner/Fig-15
90Leaf-108
90MCA/Disc-4
90MLBPA/Pins-78
90MSA/Soda-15
90Mother/A's-6
90Mother/Canseco-1
90Mother/Canseco-2
90Mother/Canseco-3
90Mother/Canseco-4
90OPC-250
90Panini/St-142
90Pep/Canseco-Set
90Post-16
90PublInt/St-279
90PublInt/St-301
90RedFoley/St-14
90S-375
90S/100St-5
90Sf-23
90T-250
90T/Ames-29
90T/Big-270
90T/DH-8
90T/Gloss60-31
90T/HeadsUp-18
90T/HillsHM-7
90T/St-177
90T/TVAS-11
90Tetley/Discs-4
90UD-66
90USPlayC/AS-WC
90Windwlk/Discs-8
90WonderBrd-14
91B-227
91B-372SLUG
91BBBest/RecBr-2
91Cadaco-7
91Classic/200-135
91Classic/II-T19
91Classic/III-T6
91CollAB-13
91D-50AS
91D-536
91D/Elite-E3
91D/GSlam-4
91D/Preview-11
91F-5
91F/ASIns-8
91F/ProV-6
91F/WS-3
91JDean-19
91Kenner-8
91Leaf-182
91Leaf/Stud-101
91MajorLg/Pins-38
91MooTown-1
91Mother/A's-6
91OPC-390AS
91OPC-700
91OPC/Premier-18
91Panini/FrSt-173
91Panini/FrSt-198
91Panini/St-149
91Panini/Top15-15
91Panini/Top15-24
91Panini/Top15-39
91Pep/SS-17
91Post-4
91RedFoley/St-116
91RedFoley/St-17
91S-1
91S-398AS
91S-441DT
91S-690MB
91S/100SS-1
91SFExam/A's-2
91Seven/3DCoin-2NC
91Seven/3DCoin-2NW
91Seven/3DCoin-2SC
91Seven/3DCoin-3T
91Seven/3DCoin-6A
91StCl-155
91StCl/Member*-29M
91T-390AS
91T-700
91T/CJMini/I-10
91T/SU-7
91UD-155
91UD/SilSlug-SS4
91Ultra-244
92B-600
92CJ/DI-25
92Classic/Game200-110
92Classic/I-22
92Classic/II-NNO
92Classic/II-T3
92Colla/ASG-21
92D-548
92D/McDon-13
92DPep/MSA-24
92DennyGS-22
92F-252
92F-688LL
92F/ASIns-24
92F/Lumber-L5
92F/Performer-13
92F/TmLIns-19
92F/Up-59
92French-4
92Kenner/Fig-9
92L-267
92L/BlkGold-267
92L/GoldPrev-23
92L/Prev-23
92MSA/Ben-12
92Mother/A's-6
92OPC-100
92OPC/Premier-24
92P-25
92Panini-144M
92Panini-19
92Pinn-130
92Pinn/Slug-3
92Post/Can-16
92Rem/Pr-P19
92Rem/Pr-P4
92Rem/Pr-P5
92Rem/Pr-P6
92S-500
92S/100SS-67
92S/Impact-52
92S/Proctor-8
92S/RookTr-9T
92Seven/Coin-21
92StCl-370
92StCl-597MC
92StCl/MPhoto-3
92Studio-222
92Studio/Her-4
92Sunflower-18
92T-100
92T-401AS
92T/Gold-100
92T/Gold-401AS
92T/GoldWin-100
92T/GoldWin-401AS
92T/Kids-115
92T/McDonB-22
92T/MicroG-100
92TripleP-214
92UD-333
92UD-640CL
92UD-649DS
92UD/ASFF-17
92UD/HRH-HR1
92UD/TWillB-T3
92UD/TmMVPHolo-14
92USPlayC/Ace-13H
92USPlayC/Ace-1C
92Ultra-110
93B-545
93Cadaco-10
93Classic/Gamel-18
93Colla/DM-22
93D-159
93D/LongBall-LL6
93D/Master-7
93D/Prev-21
93D/Spirit-SG5M
93Duracel/PPII-19
93F-319

93F/Fruit-9
93Flair-278
93Ho-10
93Kenner/Fig-6
93L-241
93L/GoldAS-9
93MSA/Metz-22
93OPC-47
93OPC/Premier-81
93Pac/Beisbol-14M
93Pac/Beisbol-15M
93Pac/Beisbol-27M
93Pac/Spanish-308
93Pac/SpanishGold-13
93Pac/SpanishP-11
93Panini-85
93Pinn-49
93Pinn/HRC-10
93Pinn/Slug-24
93Rang/Keeb-399
93S-13
93Select-364
93StCl-499
93StCl/1stDay-499
93StCl/MPhoto-14
93StCl/Rang-28
93Studio-47
93Studio/SS-2
93T-500
93T/Finest-99AS
93T/FinestASJ-99AS
93T/FinestRef-99AS
93T/Gold-500
93TripleP-243
93UD-365
93UD-52M
93UD/Clutch-R4
93UD/FunPack-12HS
93UD/FunPack-155
93UD/OnDeck-D7
93UD/SP-191
93UD/TCr-TC2
93Ultra-627
94B-600
94D-372
94D/Doml-7
94D/Special-372
94F-304
94Finest-222
94L-249
94L/MVPAL-2
94OPC-169
94Pac/AllLat-15
94Pac/Cr-611
94Panini-125
94Pinn-306
94RedFoley-8
94S-61
94S/GoldR-61
94Sf/2000-141
94StCl-171
94StCl/1stDay-171
94StCl/Gold-171
94StCl/Team-250
94Studio-152
94T-80
94T/Gold-80
94TripleP-192
94UD-140
94UD/ElecD-140
94UD/HoloFX-5
94UD/Mantle-4
94UD/SP-146
94Ultra-428
Canseco, Ozzie
83Greens-3
87Madis-6
88Madis-7
88MidwLAS/GS-51
89Huntsvl/Best-28
89UD/Ext-756
90F/Up-117
90Foil/Best-162
90Huntsvl/Best-21
90Leaf-516
91MajorLg/Pins-41
91OPC-162
91S-346RP
91T-162
91T/90Debut-25
91UD-146
92Louisvl/ProC-1898
92Louisvl/SB-254
92Sky/AAASingl-124
93B-164
93D-336
93Pac/Beisbol-27
93Pac/Spanish-630
93Pinn-272
93Pol/Card-4
93S-241
93S/Boys-25
93StCl-634
93StCl/1stDay-634
93StCl/Card-14
Canton, Michael
92Elmira/ClBest-4
92Elmira/ProC-1387
Cantrell, Dave
89Salinas/Cal-129
89Salinas/ProC-1826
Cantrell, Derrick
92Classic/DP-111
Cantrell, Guy
90Target-110
Cantrelle, Lee
91OKSt-3
Cantres, Jorge
90Yakima/Team-35
Cantu, Mike
91Hamil/ClBest-19
91Hamil/ProC-4044
92StPete/ProC-2034
94ClBest/Gold-169
Cantwell, Ben
33G-139
35BU-96
35G-8L
35G-9L
90Target-111
91Conlon/Sport-211
R308-168
R332-25
V354-14
WG8-5
Cantwell, Rob
88Spokane/ProC-1924
89Watlo/ProC-1780
89Watlo/Star-2
Cantz, Bartholomew L.
(Bart)
N172
Capel, Mike
84MidldC-10
86Pittsfld-3
87Iowa-4
88D/Rook-46
88Iowa/CMC-1
88Iowa/ProC-547
89F-643R
89Iowa/CMC-1
89Iowa/ProC-1706
89T-767
90AAASingl/ProC-643
90Denver/CMC-5
90Denver/ProC-618
90ProC/Singl-30
91AAA/LineD-605
91Tucson/LineD-605
91Tucson/ProC-2206
92F-429
92S-687
92TX-7
92Tucson/ProC-480
92Tucson/SB-604
Capellan, Carlos
88Kenosha/ProC-1396
89AS/Cal-6
89Visalia/Cal-112
89Visalia/ProC-1441
90AS/Cal-9
90Visalia/Cal-71
90Visalia/ProC-2159
91AA/LineD-477
91OrlanSR/LineD-477
91OrlanSR/ProC-1854
93LimeR/Winter-132
Capello, Pete
87AppFx-4
88Virgini/Star-4
89AppFx/ProC-865
Capilla, Doug
78OPC-11
78SSPC/270-127
78T-477
80T-628
81D-587
81F-309
81T-136
82T-537
82Wichita-3
89Pac/SenLg-172
Caple, Kyle
92Kenosha/ProC-607
Caplinger, Roger
91Helena/SportP-28TR
Capowski, Jim
78Ashvl
79Tulsa-4
Cappadona, Pete
86NewBrit-5
Cappuzzello, George
77Evansvl/TCMA-5
78Indianap-15
79Indianap-16
81Evansvl-2
82F-264
82T-137
82Tucson-20
83T-422
84Colum-7
84Colum/Pol-4
Capra, Lee
(Buzz)
72OPC-141R
72T-141R
75OPC-105
75OPC-311LL
75T-105
75T-311LL
75T/M-105
75T/M-311LL
76Ho-85
76OPC-153
76SSPC-1
76T-153
77T-432
78T-578
83Ander-6
86AppFx-5CO
87BurlEx-21
88Spartan/ProC-1047
88Spartan/Star-23
88Spartan/Star-7
90Spartan/Best-26CO
90Spartan/ProC-2508CO
90Spartan/Star-27CO
91Spartan/ClBest-29CO
91Spartan/ProC-914CO
91WIZMets-61
92Spartan/ClBest-24CO
92Spartan/ProC-1281CO
Capra, Nick Lee
79Tulsa-20
80Tulsa-8
83OKCty-4
84OKCty-11
85OKCty-25
86BuffB-7
87OKCty-23
88Omaha/CMC-12
88Omaha/ProC-1499
89F-279
89Omaha/CMC-19
89Omaha/ProC-1742
90AAASingl/ProC-689
90OkCty/CMC-16
90OkCty/ProC-443
90ProC/Singl-166
91AAA/LineD-307
91OkCty/LineD-307
91OkCty/ProC-190
92Nashvl/ProC-1845
92Nashvl/SB-280
93Edmon/ProC-1148
93Rang/Keeb-95
Capri, Patrick N.
(Pat)
No Cards.
Capriati, Jeff
91Pac/SenLg-76
Capron, Ralph Earl
No Cards.
Caraballo, Felix
88Madis-8
88Modesto-5
90Reno/Cal-281
Caraballo, Gary
90AppFox/Box-6
90AppFox/ProC-2100
91AppFx/ClBest-15
91AppFx/ProC-1721
91ClBest/Singl-211
91MidwLAS/ProC-2
92B-54
92BBCity/ClBest-19
92UD/ML-289
Caraballo, Ramon
85Phill/TastyK-41
86Phill/TastyK-x
87Clearw-11
88Clearw/Star-6
90A&AASingle/ProC-131
90BurlB/Best-4
90BurlB/ProC-2360
90BurlB/Star-8
90Foil/Best-260
90MidwLgAS/GS-27
91B-584
91ClBest/Singl-376
91Durham/ClBest-24
91Durham/ProC-1551
92D/RookPhen-BC13
92Greenvl/SB-231
92ProC/Tomorrow-187
92Richm/Bleach-11
92Sky/AASingl-99
92UD/ML-210
93Richm/Bleach-2
93Richm/Pep-11
93Richm/Pep-12
93Richm/Team-8
93StCl/Brave-30
93T-451
93T/Gold-451
94Pac/Cr-7
94Pinn-260
94Pinn/Artist-260
94Pinn/Museum-260
94StCl/Team-44
Caraballo, Wilmer
85Lynch-21
86Lynch-5
87BirmB/Best-6
Carabba, Robbie
92Albany/ClBest-10
92Albany/ProC-2313
Carabello, Nelson
89Welland/Pucko-9
Caray, Harry
88Peoria/Ko-8
Carballo, Gary
92ClBest-176
Carballo, Jay
90Eugene/GS-4
Carballo, Lee
88SLCity-28
88Virgini/Star-5
Carbine, John C.
No Cards.
Carbo, Bernardo
(Bernie)
70OPC-36R
70T-36R
71MLB/St-51
71OPC-478
71T-478
72OPC-463
72T-463
73OPC-171
73T-171
74OPC-621
74T-621
75OPC-379
75T-379
75T/M-379
76OPC-278
76SSPC-411
76T-278
77T-159
78SSPC/270-185
78T-524
79T-38
80T-266
89Pac/SenLg-45
89T/SenLg-13
89TM/SenLg-18
90EliteSenLg-96
94TedW-2
94TedW/54-33
Carbonneau, Guy
91StCl/Member*-39
Carbonnet, Mark
92ColRS/ProC-2395
Carcia, Carlos
91AAA/LineD-29
Carcione, Thomas
(Tom)
88SoOreg/ProC-1699
89Madis/Star-6
89Modesto/Chong-19
90Modesto/Cal-167
90Modesto/Chong-4
90Modesto/ProC-2215
91AA/LineD-281
91Huntsvl/ClBest-6
91Huntsvl/LineD-281
91HuntsvlProC-1799
92Huntsvl/SB-306
92Modesto/ClBest-24
92Modesto/ProC-3902
Cardenal, Jose
65T-374R
66T-505
66T/RO-15
66T/RO-80
67CokeCap/DodgAngel-29
67OPC-193
67T-193
68OPC-102
68T-102
69MB-49
69MLB/St-40
69T-325
69T/S-15
69T/St-164
69Trans-5
70MLB/St-136
70T-675
71K-26
71MLB/St-270
71OPC-435
71T-435
72MB-62
72OPC-12
72T-12
72T-757TR
73OPC-393
73T-393
74Greyhound-6M
74OPC-185
74T-185
74T/DE-55
74T/St-12
75Ho-65
75Ho/Twink-65
75K-29
75OPC-15
75T-15
75T/M-15
76Crane-8
76Ho-37
76Ho/Twink-37
76MSA/Disc
76OPC-430
76T-430
77BurgChef-197
77Ho-85
77Ho/Twink-85
77OPC-127
77T-610
77T/CS-9
77T/ClothSt-9
78T-210
79BK/P-18
79T-317
80T-512
81T-473
89Pac/Leg-149
89Swell-61
91WIZMets-62
93Reds/Kahn-8CO
Cardenas, Daniel
90Yakima/Team-10
91Bakers/Cal-22
Cardenas, Epi
92Watertn/ClBest-14
92Watertn/ProC-3240
Cardenas, Leonardo L.
(Leo)
60T-119
61T-244
61T/St-16
62Kahn
62T-381
63FrBauer-2
63J-127
63Kahn
63P-127

63T-203
64Kahn
64T-72
65Kahn
65T-437
66Kahn
66T-370
67CokeCap/Reds-2
67Kahn
67OPC/PI-10
67T-325
67T/PI-10
68Kahn
68OPC-23
68T-23
68T-480M
69MB-50
69T-265
70MLB/St-231
70OPC-245
70T-245
71MLB/St-460
71OPC-405
71T-405
71T/Coins-148
71T/tatt-8
72K-30
72MB-63
72T-561
72T-562A
73OPC-522
73T-522
75OPC-518
75T-518
75T/M-518
76OPC-587
76SSPC-261
76T-587
78TCMA-69
78Twin/Frisz-27
83Wisco/Frit-15
93Rang/Keeb-96

Cardieri, Ron
82Miami-9

Cardinal, Conrad
(Randy)
63T-562R

Cardona, Isbel
91MedHat/ProC-4090
91MedHat/SportP-11

Cardona, James
91Welland/ClBest-6
91Welland/ProC-3585

Cardona, Jose
90Butte/SportP-9
91Gaston/ClBest-3
91Gaston/ProC-2680

Cardoz, Don
78RochR

Cardwell, Buddy
77Wausau

Cardwell, Don
57T-374
58T-372
59T-314
60T-384
61NuCard-410
61P-194
61T-393M
61T-564
62T-495
62T/St-106
62T/bucks
63IDL-3
63Sugar-A
63T-575
64T-417
65T-502
66EH-43
66T-235
67CokeCap/YMet-23
67T-555
68T-437
69MB-51
69OPC-193
69T-193
69T/4in1-2M
70OPC-83
70T-83
72MB-64
78TCMA-89
90Swell/Great-72
91WIZMets-63
94Mets/69-26

Cardwood, Alfredo
85OrlanTw-15
86Visalia-6
87WPalmB-4

Carew, Jeff
91GulfCR/SportP-17

Carew, Rodney Cline
(Rod)
67T-569R
68Bz-13
68Dexter-20
68OPC-80
68T-363AS
68T-80
68T/ActionSt-7C
68T/G-29
69MB-52
69MLB/St-65
69MLBPA/Pin-4
69OPC/DE-3
69T-419AS
69T-510
69T/DE-12
69T/St-192
70K-47
70MB-4
70MLB/St-232
70OPC-290
70OPC-453AS
70OPC-62LL
70T-290
70T-453AS
70T-62LL
70T/PI-16
71MLB/St-461
71OPC-210
71T-210
71T/Coins-24
71T/tatt-15
72MB-65
72T-695
72T-696IA
73K-51
73OPC-330
73OPC-61LL
73T-330
73T-61LL
73T/Lids-9
74Greyhound-3
74Greyhound-5M
74K-30
74OPC-201LL
74OPC-333AS
74OPC-50
74T-201LL
74T-333AS
74T-50
74T/DE-32
74T/DE-36
74T/St-203
75Ho-56
75K-33
75OPC-306LL
75OPC-600
75SSPC/42-32
75SSPC/Puzzle-5
75T-306LL
75T-600
75T/M-306LL
75T/M-600
76Crane-9
76Ho-33
76Ho/Twink-33
76K-48
76MSA/Disc
76OPC-192LL
76OPC-400
76SSPC-214
76T-192LL
76T-400
77BurgChef-51
77Ho-9
77Ho/Twink-9
77K-53
77OPC-143
77Pep-2
77T-120
77T/CS-10
77T/ClothSt-10
78Ho-140
78K-29
78OPC-1LL
78OPC-230
78PapaG/Disc-35
78Pep-30
78T-201LL
78T-580
78Tastee/Discs-8
78Twin/FriszP-3
78Wiffle/Discs-13
79Ho-38
79K-13
79OPC-151
79T-1LL
79T-300
79T/Comics-11
80BK/PHR-14
80K-60
80OPC-353
80T-700
80T/S-12
80T/Super-12TP
81D-169
81D-49
81Drake-2
81F-268
81F/St-40
81K-26
81MSA/Disc-6
81OPC-100
81PermaGr/AS-11
81PermaGr/CC-22
81Sqt-9
81T-100
81T/HT
81T/Nat/Super-4
81T/SO-18
81T/St-49
82D-216
82Drake-6
82F-455
82F/St-217
82FBI/Disc-2
82K-51
82KMart-31
82OPC-187
82OPC-363IA
82OPC-36AS
82PermaGr/CC-21
82T-276TL
82T-500
82T-501IA
82T-547AS
82T/St-131
82T/St-160
83D-8DK
83D-90
83D/AAS-38
83Drake-3
83F-81
83F/St-12M
83F/St-7M
83K-1
83OPC-200
83OPC-201SV
83OPC-386AS
83OPC/St-39
83PermaGr/AS-2
83PermaGr/CC-20
83Seven-1
83T-200
83T-201SV
83T-386AS
83T-651TL
83T/Fold-3M
83T/Fold-5M
83T/Gloss40-29
83T/St-39
84D-352
84D/Champs-21
84Drake-5
84F-511
84F/St-103
84F/St-12
84F/St-54
84MiltBrad-3
84Nes/792-276TL
84Nes/792-600
84Nes/792-710LL
84Nes/792-711LL
84OPC-26
84Ralston-17
84Seven-8W
84Smok/Cal-5
84T-276TL
84T-600
84T-710LL
84T-711LL
84T/Cereal-17
84T/Gloss22-2
84T/Gloss40-26
84T/RD-9
84T/St-227
84T/St/Box-11
85D-85
85D/HL-31
85F-297
85F/LimEd-5
85FunFood/Pin-35
85Leaf-132
85OPC-300
85Seven-6W
85Smok/Cal-5
85T-300
85T/Gloss22-13
85T/RD-5M
85T/St-184
85T/St-223
85ThomMc/Discs-7
86D-280
86F-151
86F-629M
86F/HOF-4
86F/LL-4
86F/St-20
86OPC-371
86Seven/Coin-W10
86Sf-106
86Sf-146M
86Sf-180M
86Sf-182M
86Sf-69M
86Sf-74M
86T-400
86T/Gloss60-16
86T/St-176
86T/St-4
86Woolwth-6
87KMart-14
87Nestle/DT-12
88Grenada-48
89Smok/Angels-10
89T/LJN-97
90MSA/AGFA-7
90Pac/Legend-17
90Swell/Great-4
91B-1
91B-2
91B-3
91B-4
91B-5
91K/Leyenda-2
91Perez/HOF-207
91Swell/Great-103
91T/Ruth-8
92K/CornAS-4
92K/FrAS-1
92Pinn-584
93AP/ASG-128
93AP/ASG24K-62G
93Metallic-7
93Mother/Angel-28M
93Pol/Angel-4CO
93YooHoo-4
94TedW-47

Carey, Andrew Arthur
(Andy)
53T-188
54NYJour
54T-105
55T-20
55T/DH-36
56T-12
57T-290
58T-333
59T-45
60T-196
61T-518
61T/St-158
62J-52
62P-52
62P/Can-52
62Salada-86A
62Salada-86B
62Shirriff-86
62T-418
79TCMA-243
90Target-112
91T/Arc53-188
92Yank/WIZ60-21
94T/Arc54-105
PM10/L-9

Carey, Brooks M.
80CharlO/Pol-3
80CharlO/W3TV-3
81RochR-3
82Indianap-9

Carey, Frank
90Clinton/Best-4
90Clinton/ProC-2555
90Foil/Best-67
90MidwLgAS/GS-28
91AA/LineD-301
91Shrev/LineD-301
91Shrev/ProC-1826

Carey, George C.
(Scoops)
E107
T206

Carey, Jeff
82WHave-3

Carey, Max George
11Helmar-156
14CJ-73
15CJ-73
21Exh-21
25Exh-50
26Exh-50
28Exh-6
28Yueng-32
40PlayBall-178
61F-12
72Laugh/GF-9
76Rowe-11M
76Shakey-85
77Galasso-103
77Galasso-214CO
80Laugh/FFeat-12
80Perez/HOF-85
80SSPC/HOF
89HOF/St-38
89Smok/Dodg-5
90BBWit-88
90Perez/GreatMom-50
90Target-113
91Conlon/Sport-24
93Conlon-797
94Conlon-1232
BF2-90
D327
D329-28
D350/2-26
E120
E121/120
E121/80
E122
E126-32
E126-32
E210-32
E220
M101/4-28
M101/5-26
T206
T207
T213/brown
V100
V61-71
V89-28
W501-86
W502-32
W514-22
W573
W575

Carey, P.J.
88Belling/Legoe-28MG
89Belling/Legoe-30MG
91Billing/SportP-28MG
91Billings/ProC-3770MG
92CharWh/ClBest-23MG
92CharWh/ProC-23
93SALAS/II-4MG

Carey, Paul
90Miami/I/Star-3
91AA/LineD-228
91ClBest/Singl-190
91Hagers/LineD-228
91Hagers/ProC-2466
92ClBest-392
92Freder/ClBest-1
92RochR/ProC-1949
93F/Final-158
94D-465
94Pac/Cr-28
94Pinn-403
94StCl/Team-275

94T-4
94T/Gold-4
Carey, Pete
86FtMyr-5
87Tampa-2
Carey, Roger J.
No Cards.
Carey, Thomas Francis
(Tom)
35BU-89
39PlayBall-62
40PlayBall-39
93Conlon-698
Carey, Todd
92Elmira/ClBest-9
92Elmira/ProC-1388
Cargo, Robert J.
(Chick)
No Cards.
Caridad, Rolando
90Utica/Pucko-16
91SoBend/ClBest-15
91SoBend/ProC-2851
92Saraso/ClBest-11
92Saraso/ProC-199
Caridad, Ron
90LitSun/HSPros-11
90LitSun/HSProsG-11
91Elizab/ProC-4293
92Elizab/ClBest-21
92Elizab/ProC-3672
Cariel, Rafael
76Shrev
Carisch, Frederick B.
(Fred)
No Cards.
Carisen, Robert
91Madison/ClBest-25
Carista, Mike
85Elmira-3
86WinHaven-5
87Greens-5
88EastLAS/ProC-20
88NewBrit/ProC-909
89NewBrit/ProC-605
90NewBrit/Best-12
90NewBrit/ProC-1311
90NewBrit/Star-2
Carl, Frederick E.
(Fred)
No Cards.
Carl, Jeff
83Memphis/TCMA-5
Carleton, James
(Tex)
34G-48
35G-1A
35G-2A
35G-6A
35G-7A
90Target-114
92Conlon/Sport-378
R310
V354-90
Carley, David
86AZ/Pol-1
87Beloit-19
Carlin, James Arthur
(Jim)
No Cards.
Carlin, Mike
89Spartan/ProC-1035
89Spartan/Star-3
Carlisle, Matthew
86Negro/Frit-85
Carlisle, Walter G.
No Cards.
Carlo
C46-85
Carlos, Cisco
68T-287R
69OPC-54
69T-54
70OPC-487
70T-487
72MB-66
Carlsen, Robert
91Madison/ProC-2137
92CharWh/ProC-14
Carlson, Bill
87Clinton-11
87Pocatel/Bon-13
88Clinton/ProC-700
89SanJose/Best-9
89SanJose/Cal-229
89SanJose/ProC-439
89SanJose/Star-4
90Salinas/Cal-131
90Salinas/ProC-2730
91Salinas/ClBest-30
91Salinas/ProC-2250
Carlson, Bob
91Elizab/ProC-4294
92ProC/Tomorrow-103
Carlson, Dan
90Everett/Best-3
90Everett/ProC-3119
91Clinton/ClBest-1
91Clinton/ProC-826
92ClBest-183
92Shrev/ProC-3864
92Shrev/SB-577
92Sky/AASingl-254
93FExcel/ML-113
93StCl/Giant-26
94B-331
Carlson, Hal
94Conlon-1116
R316
V100
W513-75
Carlson, Lynn
90Welland/Pucko-19
91Augusta/ClBest-3
91Augusta/ProC-796
Carlson, Tom
76Clinton
Carlstrom, Albin O.
(Swede)
No Cards.
Carlton, Andy
90StCath/ProC-3476
91Myrtle/ClBest-17
91Myrtle/ProC-2951
Carlton, Scott
91Spartan/ClBest-1
91Spartan/ProC-886
Carlton, Steve
65T-477R
67OPC-146
67T-146
68T-408
69T-255
70MLB/St-137
70OPC-220
70OPC-67LL
70T-220
70T-67LL
71MLB/St-271
71OPC-55
71T-55
71T/Coins-115
72Dimanche*-56
72MB-67
72OPC-420
72OPC-93LL
72T-420
72T-751TR
72T-93LL
73K-7
73OPC-300
73OPC-65LL
73OPC-66LL
73OPC-67LL
73T-300
73T-65LL
73T-66LL
73T-67LL
73T/Comics-4
73T/Lids-10
73T/PinUps-4
74JP
74OPC-95
74T-95
74T/DE-5
74T/St-73
75Ho-63
75OPC-185
75OPC-312LL
75T-185
75T-312LL
75T/M-185
75T/M-312LL
76Crane-10
76MSA/Disc
76OPC-355
76SSPC-459
76T-355
77BurgChef-171
77Ho-117
77Ho/Twink-117
77K-57
77OPC-93
77T-110
77T/CS-11
77T/ClothSt-11
78Ho-49
78K-1
78OPC-170
78OPC-5LL
78SSPC/270-29
78T-205LL
78T-540
78Wiffle/Discs-14
79BK/P-4
79Ho-71
79K-18
79OPC-9
79T-25
80BK/P-15
80BK/PHR-2
80K-14
80OPC-113
80Perez/HOF-217
80T-210
81Coke
81D-33
81D-481CY
81F-6
81F-660M
81F/St-85
81K-50
81MSA/Disc-7
81OPC-203
81PermaGr/CC-16
81T-202HL
81T-5LL
81T-630
81T-6LL
81T/HT
81T/SO-104
81T/St-206
81T/St-25
81T/St-261
81T/St-28
81T/St-29
82D-42
82Drake-7
82F-243
82F-632M
82F-641M
82F/St-240M
82F/St-241M
82F/St-54
82FBI/Disc-3
82K-27
82OPC-122IA
82OPC-68
82PermaGr/CC-10
82T-1M
82T-480
82T-481IA
82T-636TL
82T/St-129
82T/St-75
83D-16DK
83D-219
83D/AAS-24
83F-155
83F/St-16M
83F/St-24M
83K-45
83OPC-384AS
83OPC-70
83OPC-71SV
83OPC/St-176
83OPC/St-203
83OPC/St-204
83OPC/St-267FOIL
83PermaGr/CC-2
83T-229TL
83T-406AS
83T-70
83T-705LL
83T-706LL
83T-71SV
83T/Fold-1M
83T/Gloss40-36
83T/LeadS-5
83T/St-203
83T/St-204
83T/St-267
84D-111
84D/AAS-24
84D/Champs-38
84F-25
84F-642IA
84F/St-101
84F/St-78
84MiltBrad-4
84Nes/792-136LL
84Nes/792-1HL
84Nes/792-395AS
84Nes/792-4HL
84Nes/792-706LL
84Nes/792-707LL
84Nes/792-708LL
84Nes/792-780
84Nestle/DT-21
84OPC-214
84OPC-395AS
84Phill/TastyK-17
84Phill/TastyK-5HOF
84Ralston-16
84Seven-12E
84T-136LL
84T-1HL
84T-395AS
84T-4HL
84T-706LL
84T-707LL
84T-708LL
84T-780
84T/Cereal-16
84T/Gloss40-27
84T/RD-10
84T/St-1
84T/St-119
84T/St-15
84T/St-184
84T/St-2
84T/Super-16
85CIGNA-12
85D-305
85D/AAS-55
85Drake-35
85F-246
85F/LimEd-6
85FunFood/Pin-30
85Leaf-113
85OPC-360
85Phill/TastyK-14
85Phill/TastyK-9M
85Seven-2S
85Seven-3E
85T-360
85T/3D-25
85T/RD-10
85T/St-112
85T/Super-24
85ThomMc/Discs-25
85Woolwth-6
86BK/AP-6
86D-183
86D/HL-35
86F-435
86F/HOF-2
86F/Mini-91
86F/Slug-M2
86F/St-21
86Keller-1
86Leaf-117
86Meadow/Milk-3
86OPC-120
86Phill/TastyK-32
86Seven/Coin-C8
86Seven/Coin-E8
86Seven/Coin-S8
86Seven/Coin-W8
86Sf-27
86Sf-70M
86Sf/Dec-54
86T-120
86T-246M
86T/St-116
86T/Tatt-3M
87D-617
87F-490
87F-635M
87F/Excit-8
87F/Up-U17
87KMart-15
87OPC-271
87OPC-B
87Sf-200
87T-718
87T-B
87T/HL-1
87T/Tr-19T
87Woolwth-1
88F-7
89Swell-95
89T/LJN-37
90BBWit-43
90HOF/St-78
90MSA/AGFA-15
90Pac/Legend-16
90Phill/TastyK-30
90Swell/Great-110
91K/3D-8
91K/SU-5A
91K/SU-5B
91LineD-9
91MDA-1
91Swell/Great-17
93TWill-72
Carlucci, Dave
86Bakers-5
Carlucci, Rich
81Water-1
82Indianap-19
83Indianap-16
84RochR-2
86Syrac-6
Carlucci, Tony
83TriCit-14
Carlyle, Hiram Cleo
(Cleo)
No Cards.
Carlyle, Kenny
92Fayette/ProC-2161
92FrRow/DP-6
93B-151
93ClBest/MLG-207
93StCl/MurphyS-116
Carlyle, Roy Edward
No Cards.
Carman, Don
80Penin/B-11
80Penin/C-5
82OkCty-24
83Reading-3
84Cram/PCL-204
84Phill/TastyK-41
85F/Up-U20
85Phill/TastyK-15
85Phill/TastyK-9M
85T/Tr-16T
86CIGNA-2
86D-427
86F-436
86F/St-22
86Leaf-200
86Phill/TastyK-42
86T-532
87D-432
87F-171
87Leaf-174
87OPC-355
87Phill/TastyK-42
87Sf-108
87Sf/TPrev-6M
87T-355
87T/St-122
88D-385
88D/Best-72
88F-300
88Phill/TastyK-6
88S-401
88T-415
89B-392
89D-396
89F-564
89OPC-154
89Panini/St-146
89Phill/TastyK-3
89S-222
89T-154
89T/St-121
89UD-409
90D-604
90F-552
90F/Can-552
90OPC-731
90Phill/TastyK-4
90PublInt/St-233
90T-731
90UD-420
91D-377
91F-390

91Kahn/Reds-36
91OPC-282
91S-237
91T-282
91UD-288
92OkCty/ProC-1910
92Tulsa/ProC-2689
92Tulsa/SB-616
93Rang/Keeb-97
Carman, George W.
No Cards.
Carmel, Leon James
(Duke)
60T-120
61Union
63T-544R
64T-44
64T/Coins-81
65OPC-261
65T-261
91WIZMets-64
92Yank/WIZ60-22
WG10-4
Carmichael, Al
85Lynch-15
86Lynch-6
87Jacks/Feder-12
Carmody, Kevin
89Beloit/I/Star-2
89Beloit/II/Star-5
90Stockton/Best-20
90Stockton/Cal-181
90Stockton/ProC-2181
Carmona, Greg
89StPete/Star-5
90ArkTr/GS-7
90T/TVCard-40
91AA/LineD-28
91ArkTr/LineD-28
91ArkTr/ProC-1291
91B-392
91Louisvl/ProC-2920
91Louisvl/Team-21
92Louisvl/ProC-1892
92Louisvl/SB-255
93LimeR/Winter-74
Carmona, William
89Martins/Star-4
90Martins/ProC-3181
91Pocatel/ProC-3795
91Pocatel/SportP-27
92Martins/ClBest-21
92Martins/ProC-3068
Carnegie, Olie
28LaPresse-26
Carnelius, Brian
92London/SB-403
Carnera, Primo
33SK*-43
47HomogBond-7BOX
D305
Carnes, Scott
77QuadC
80ElPaso-3
81SLCity-17
82Spokane-15
Carnett, Edwin E.
(Eddie)
43Centen-3
Carnevale, Anthony
89Anchora-5
Carney, John Joseph
(Jack)
N172
Carney, Patrick J.
(Pat)
No Cards.
Carney, Ron
78Ashvl
79Tulsa-18
80Ashvl-14
81Tulsa-10
Carney, William John
(Bill)
No Cards.
Caro, Joe
91Boise/ProC-3900CO
Caro, Jorge
91Bristol/ClBest-2
91Bristol/ProC-3611
Caroland, Kevin
89TNTech-6
Carosielli, Marc
88Wythe/ProC-1999
Carothers, Ron
91Waverly/Fut-12
Carpenter, Bubba
90AR-4
92Albany/ProC-2237
92Albany/SB-5
Carpenter, Cris
87PanAm/USAB-19
87PanAm/USAR-19
88D/Rook-50
88Louisvl-13
88Louisvl/CMC-8
88Louisvl/ProC-428
89Classic/Up/2-185
89D-39RR
89D/Rook-40
89F/Up-117
89Louisvl-13
89S/Tr-81
89S/YS/II-37
89T-282
89T/Big-307
89UD-8
90AAASingl/ProC-509
90D-634
90F-243
90F/Can-243
90HotRook/St-10
90Louisvl/CMC-3
90Louisvl/LBC-10
90Louisvl/ProC-395
90OPC-443
90ProC/Singl-103
90PublInt/St-212
90S/100Ris-74
90T-443
90T/TVCard-7
90TeamUSA/87-19
90UD-523
91F-628
91F/UltraUp-U105
91Leaf-507
91OPC-518
91StCl-499
91T-518
92D-79
92F-575
92OPC-147
92Pol/Card-2
92S-160
92StCl-429
92T-147
92T/Gold-147
92T/GoldWin-147
92UD-686
92Ultra-563
93D-734
93F-420
93F/Final-55
93Pac/Spanish-456
93Pinn-562
93Rang/Keeb-400
93S-633
93StCl-706
93StCl/1stDay-706
93StCl/Marlin-11
93T-629
93T/Gold-629
93UD-726
93USPlayC/Marlin-13D
93USPlayC/Marlin-3C
93Ultra-369
94L-261
94SigRook-5
94StCl-239
94StCl/1stDay-239
94StCl/Gold-239
94StCl/Team-259
94T-317
94T/Gold-317
94UD/CollC-73
94UD/CollC/Gold-73
94UD/CollC/Silv-73
Carpenter, Doug
84Greens-9
85Albany-20
86FtLaud-3
87Miami-7
89Reno/Cal-254
90Lakeland/Star-27CO
91Lakeland/ClBest-10CO
91Lakeland/ProC-284CO
Carpenter, Glenn
83DayBe-18
86Tucson-4
87Tucson-2
88Tucson/CMC-12
88Tucson/JP-5
88Tucson/ProC-173
Carpenter, Jay
90AR-5
Carpenter, John
45Centen-3
Carpenter, Kevin
90Johnson/Star-6
Carpenter, Matt
91MissSt-10
92MissSt-7
93MissSt-7
Carpenter, Paul
44Centen-2
47Centen-3
Carpenter, Rob
90Kgsport/Best-10
90Kgsport/Star-4
91Clmbia/PII-26
Carpenter, Warren W.
(Hick)
N172
Carpentier, Edouard
72Dimanche*-115
Carpentier, Georges
52LaPatrie-2
52Laval-54
Carpentier, Rob
91Clmbia/PCPII-1
92StLucie/ClBest-12
92StLucie/ProC-1737
93StLucie/ProC-2912
Carper, Mark
88CapeCod/Sum-172
91Freder/ClBest-1
91Freder/ProC-2355
92Albany/ProC-2218
92Hagers/SB-256
Carpin, Frank
66OPC-71
66T-71
Carpine, Bill
91Clinton/ClBest-16TR
92Clinton/ClBest-29TR
Carpio, Jorge
82QuadC-5
84MidldC-6
Carr, Bobby
92GulfCM/ProC-3471
Carr, Charles Carbitt
(Charlie)
E107
E254
E270/1
E270/2
T206
Carr, Chuck
87Belling/Team-9
88MidwLAS/GS-56
88Wausau/GS-8
89Jacks/GS-2
89TexLAS/GS-28
90F/Up-U34
90Jacks/GS-24
91F-141
91T/90Debut-26
91Tidew/ProC-2521
91UD-514
91WIZMets-65
92ArkTr/SB-29
92Louisvl/ProC-1899
92S-857
92Sky/AASingl-13
93B-474
93D-124
93D-762
93F-421
93F/Final-56
93Flair-48
93L-541
93Marlin/Publix-7
93Pac/Spanish-457
93Pinn-618
93S-545
93Select/RookTr-37T
93StCl-564
93StCl/1stDay-564
93StCl/Marlin-25
93T-722
93T/Gold-722
93UD-590
93UD/SP-137
93USPlayC/Marlin-12D
93USPlayC/Marlin-6H
93Ultra-370
94B-66
94D-509
94F-463
94F/LL-10
94F/RookSen-4
94L-408
94OPC-220
94Pac/Cr-237
94Panini-180
94Pinn-195
94Pinn/Artist-195
94Pinn/Museum-195
94S-512
94S/Boys-31
94Select-11
94StCl-29
94StCl/1stDay-29
94StCl/Gold-29
94StCl/Team-84
94Studio-107
94T-653
94T/Finest-8
94T/FinestRef-8
94T/Gold-653
94TripleP-133
94UD-202
94UD/ElecD-202
94UD/SP-108
94Ultra-194
94Ultra/LL-8
94Ultra/Second-6
Carr, Ernie
88GreatF-4
89Bakers/Cal-200
90SanAn/GS-9
Carr, Lewis Smith
(Lew)
No Cards.
Carr, Terence
86Cram/NWL-95
87QuadC-1
88QuadC/GS-9
89Reno/Cal-255
90PalmSp/Cal-203
90PalmSp/ProC-2589
Carrano, Rick
86Miami-4TR
Carranza, Javier
83StPete-2
Carrara, Giovanni
91StCath/ClBest-13
91StCath/ProC-3387
92Dunedin/ClBest-17
92Myrtle/ClBest-25
92ProC/Tomorrow-175
93Dunedin/ClBest-5
93Dunedin/ProC-1787
93SALAS/II-5
Carrasco, Carlos
88Bakers/Cal-251
89Reno/Cal-243
90Salinas/Cal-127
90Salinas/ProC-2718
91Salinas/ClBest-23
91Salinas/ProC-2235
Carrasco, Claudio
86Watlo-5
87Watlo-26
88Wmsprt/ProC-1320
89QuadC/Best-23
89QuadC/GS-29
89Reno/Cal-259
Carrasco, Ernie
83Erie-22
84Savan-15
86ArkTr-3
Carrasco, Hector
89Kgsport/Star-4
90Kgsport/Best-16
90Kgsport/Star-5
91Pittsfld/ClBest-21
91Pittsfld/ProC-3415
92Ashvl/ClBest-24
93B-262
94B-130
94Finest-316
94Flair-145
94L/GRook-20
94UD-511DD
94Ultra-470
Carrasco, Norman
82Danvl/Frit-28
83Redwd-5
85Cram/PCL-22
86Edmon-2
87Edmon-19
88MidldA/GS-25
89Toledo/CMC-20
89Toledo/ProC-768
Carrasquel, Alex
93Conlon-956
Carrasquel, Alfonso
(Chico)
51B-60
51FB
51T/BB-26
52B-41
52BR
52Dix-53
52StarCal-87B
52StarCal/L-73D
52T-251
53B/Col-54
53Exh/Can-4
54B-54
54RM-AL19
55B-173
55RFG-4
55RM-AL23
55Salem
55W605-4
56T-230
57Sohio/Ind-3
57T-67
58Hires-11
58T-55
59T-264
79TCMA-74
91Crown/Orio-69
Exh47
PM10/Sm-22
R423-9
Carrasquel, Emilio
82BirmB-22
Carrasquillo, Angel
88Bend/Legoe-1
Carraway, Rod
82Watlo/B-14
82Watlo/Frit-9
Carreno, Amalio
87PrWill-19
88Albany/ProC-1329
89Reading/Star-6
90Foil/Best-140
90Reading/Best-5
90Reading/ProC-1213
90Reading/Star-11
91AAA/LineD-481
91ScranWB/LineD-481
91ScranWB/ProC-2532
92S-867
92T/91Debut-27
Carreon, Camilo G.
(Cam)
60L-88
60T-121
61T-509
62T-178
62T/St-23
63T-308
64T-421
65T-578
66T-513
91Crown/Orio-70
Carreon, Mark
83Lynch-14
84Jacks-20
85Tidew-25
86Tidew-4
87Tidew-21
87Tidew/TCMA-20
88AAA/ProC-39
88F-129
88Tidew/CANDL-14
88Tidew/CMC-22
88Tidew/ProC-1588
88TripleA/ASCMC-23
89B-389
89Classic-84
89D/Rook-18
89F-29
89Kahn/Mets-32
89S/HotRook-16

89S/Tr-108
89Tidew/CMC-24
89Tidew/Candl-14
90Classic-112
90D-454
90F-198
90F/Can-198
90HotRook/St-11
90Kahn/Mets-45
90Leaf-488
90OPC-434
90S-363
90S/100Ris-67
90S/YS/I-17
90T-434
90T/JumboR-6
90T/TVMets-30
90ToysRUs-7
90UD-135
91D-731
91F-142
91Kahn/Mets-45
91OPC-764
91S-165
91StCl-196
91T-764
91WIZMets-66
92B-111
92D-465
92F-498
92L-259
92L/BlkGold-259
92OPC-111
92OPC/Premier-88
92Pinn-441
92S-19
92S/RookTr-37T
92StCl-678
92T-111
92T/Gold-111
92T/GoldWin-111
92T/Tr-21T
92T/TrGold-21T
92UD-398
92UD-739
92Ultra-359
93D-71
93F-604
93F/Final-152
93Mother/Giant-15
93Pac/Spanish-104
93Pinn-136
93S-366
93StCl-680
93StCl/1stDay-680
93StCl/Giant-23
93T-567
93T/Gold-567
93UD-570
94F-688
94S-132
94S/GoldR-132
94StCl/Team-13
94T-327
94T/Gold-327
94Ultra-288

Carrick, William
E107

Carrier, Brent
89TNTech-35M
89TNTech-5

Carrigan, William F.
(Bill)
10Domino-21
11Diamond-6
11Helmar-1
12Sweet/Pin-1A
12Sweet/Pin-1B
14CJ-27
14Piedmont/St-9
15CJ-27
16FleischBrd-14
93Conlon-828
94Conlon-1056
E95
E97
M116
S74-1
T202
T204
T205
T206
T207
T3-86
WG6-7

Carriger, Rick
87Hagers-18
88Jaxvl/Best-1
88Jaxvl/ProC-988
89Jaxvl/Best-19
89Jaxvl/ProC-168

Carrillo, Joe
92Johnson/ClBest-24
92Johnson/ProC-3107

Carrillo, Matias
85Tigres-25
86Nashua-5
87Salem-10
88ElPaso/Best-12
89Denver/CMC-22
89Denver/ProC-49
91AAA/LineD-131
91Denver/LineD-131
91Denver/ProC-134
92T/91Debut-28
94Pac/Cr-238
94StCl-235
94StCl/1stDay-235
94StCl/Gold-235
94Ultra-490

Carrillo, Paul
85Clovis-8

Carrion, German
92CharRain/ClBest-15
92CharRain/ProC-125

Carrion, Jesus
86Osceola-4

Carrion, Leonel
80Memphis-12
83Memphis/TCMA-15
84Indianap-3C
86Jaxvl/TCMA-9C

Carrithers, Don
71MLB/St-243
72Dimanche*-7
72OPC-76
72T-76
73OPC-651
73T-651
74OPC-361
74T-361
75OPC-438
75T-438
75T/M-438
76Expo/Redp-3
76OPC-312
76SSPC-348
76T-312
77OPC-18
77T-579
78Cr/PCL-80
78T-113
79Phoenix

Carroll, Bob
75Anderson/TCMA-4
77Visalia

Carroll, Carson
83OrlanTw-25
83Wisco/Frit-7
84Visalia-15
86Albany/TCMA-3
87Albany-14

Carroll, Chris
86FtLaud-4
87FtLaud-5

Carroll, Clay
65T-461R
66T-307
67T-219
68Dexter-21
68T-412
69Kahn
69OPC-26
69T-26
70OPC-133
70T-133
71MLB/St-52
71OPC-394
71T-394
72MB-68
72OPC-311
72OPC-312IA
72T-311
72T-312A
73OPC-195
73OPC-68LL
73T-195
73T-68LL
74OPC-111
74T-111
75OPC-345
75T-345
75T/M-345
76K-6
76OPC-211
76SSPC-25
76T-211
76T/Tr-211T
77T-497
78T-615
79Vanco-14

Carroll, Don
88GreatF-12
89Salem/Team-9
90Kissim/DIMD-5
91Bakers/Cal-27
91Yakima/ClBest-18
91Yakima/ProC-4240

Carroll, Dorsey Lee
(Dixie)
No Cards.

Carroll, Ed
78Holyo
79Holyo-4
80Holyo-19

Carroll, Edward
(Chick)
No Cards.

Carroll, Frederick H.
(Fred)
N172
N284

Carroll, James
86Cram/NWL-71
87Madis-21
88Madis-9
88Modesto-6
89Clearw/Star-4

Carroll, Joe
78Ashvl

Carroll, John E.
(Scrappy)
N172

Carroll, Kevin
90Clmbia/PCPII-2
90Columbia/GS-23
91StLucie/ClBest-12
91StLucie/ProC-713
92LynchRS/ClBest-17
92LynchRS/ProC-2910

Carroll, Owen
33DH-8
33G-72
90Target-115
92Conlon/Sport-496
R310
R316
V354-46
V94-6

Carroll, Patrick
(Pat)
No Cards.

Carroll, Ralph A.
(Doc)
No Cards.

Carroll, Samuel C.
(Cliff)
N172
N284
WG1-55

Carroll, Shadow
C46-39

Carroll, Steve
83Iowa-24
85Iowa-30

Carroll, Thomas E.
(Tommy)
55T-158
56T-139
57T-164
59T-513

Carroll, Thomas M.
75OPC-507
75T-507
75T/M-507
76Indianap-12
76OPC-561
76T-561

Carruth, Jim
76Baton

Carsey, Wilfred
(Kid)
90Target-908

Carsley, Jeff
78Dunedin

Carson, Henry
83StPete-3
86StPete-5

Carson, Paul
89Martins/Star-5

Carson, Ted
84Savan-23

Carson, Walter Lloyd
(Kit)
R313

Carstensen, Chris
77Newar
78BurlB

Carswell, Frank W.
53Tiger/Glen-3

Cartaya, Joel
86Salem-3
87PortChar-21
88Tulsa-16
89CharlR/Star-5

Carte, Nick
72Dimanche*-116

Cartelli, John
(Doc)
85Modesto/Chong-28TR
86Modesto-6TR
87Modesto-22

Carter, Andy
88SALAS/GS-27
88Spartan/Star-3
89Clearw/Star-5
90Clearw/Star-4
91AA/LineD-506
91Reading/LineD-506
91Reading/ProC-1366
92Clearw/ProC-2048
92Reading/SB-529
92Sky/AASingl-228

Carter, Bart
89MissSt-5

Carter, Bruce
86Clearw-2
86Cram/NWL-189

Carter, Bubba
92MissSt-8

Carter, Conrad P.
W514-45

Carter, Dale
92StCl/MemberIV*-9

Carter, David
90Gate/ProC-3361
90Gate/SportP-4
91Erie/ClBest-14
91Erie/ProC-4060

Carter, Dell
85Elmira-4

Carter, Dennis
87ArkTr-1
88StPete/Star-3
89ArkTr/GS-4
90AAASingl/ProC-528
90Louisvl/CMC-10
90Louisvl/ProC-414
90ProC/Singl-110

Carter, Dick
60T-466C

Carter, Don
83Memphis/TCMA-7
84BuffB-21

Carter, Dwight
75Clinton

Carter, Ed
90StPete/Star-1

Carter, Eddie
87Erie-7
88Savan/ProC-354
89Savan/ProC-358

Carter, Fred
87FtLaud-29
88Reno/Cal-290
89PalmSp/Cal-45
89PalmSp/ProC-479

Carter, Gary Edmund
75IntAS/TCMA-21
75OPC-620R
75T-620R
75T/M-620R
76Expo/Redp-4
76Ho-62
76K-34
76OPC-441
76SSPC-334
76T-441
77BurgChef-154
77Expo/PostC-1
77Ho-41
77Ho/Twink-41
77OPC-45
77T-295
78Ho-146
78OPC-135
78T-120
79Ho-24
79OPC-270
79T-520
80OPC-37
80T-70
80T/S-52
80T/Super-52
81D-90
81Drake-23
81F-142
81F/St-73
81OPC-6
81OPC/Post-8
81PermaGr/AS-1
81PermaGr/CC-32
81T-660
81T/SO-66
81T/St-184
81T/St-259
82D-114
82D-2DK
82Drake-7
82Expo/Hygrade-3
82F-185
82F-635M
82F-638M
82F/St-39
82FBI/Disc-4
82Hygrade
82K-24
82OPC-244
82OPC-344AS
82OPC/Post-16
82PermaGr/AS-10
82PermaGr/CC-4
82Sqt-19
82T-344AS
82T-730
82T/St-128
82T/St-61
82T/StVar-61
82Zeller-1
82Zeller-13
82Zeller-16
82Zeller-19
82Zeller-6
83D-340
83D/AAS-58
83Drake-4
83Expo/PostC-2
83F-278
83F-637M
83F-638M
83F/St-12M
83F/St-19AM
83F/St-19BM
83K-55
83OPC-314AS
83OPC-370
83OPC/St-178
83OPC/St-255
83PermaGr/AS-10
83PermaGr/CC-3
83Stuart-8
83T-370
83T-404AS
83T/Gloss40-20
83T/St-178
83T/St-255
83T/St/Box-2
84D-55
84D/Champs-58
84Drake-6
84Expo/PostC-3
84F-271
84MiltBrad-5
84Nes/792-393AS
84Nes/792-450
84OPC-366
84OPC-393AS
84Ralston-28
84Seven-15C
84Stuart-15

84Stuart-36AS
84T-393AS
84T-450
84T/Cereal-28
84T/Gloss22-20
84T/Gloss40-9
84T/RD-11
84T/St-183FOIL
84T/St-90
84T/Super-18
85D-55
85D/AAS-57
85D/HL-21M
85D/HL-47
85Drake-5
85F-393
85F-631IA
85F-632M
85F/St-16
85F/St-26
85F/St-35
85F/Up-U21
85FunFood/Pin-3
85GenMills-1DP
85Leaf-241
85OPC-230
85Pol/MetYank-M2
85Seven-9C
85T-230
85T-719AS
85T/3D-5
85T/Gloss22-9
85T/Gloss40-36
85T/Mets/Fan-3
85T/RD-11
85T/St-180
85T/St-192
85T/St-83
85T/Super-13
85T/Tr-17T
86D-68
86Dorman-3
86Drake-1
86F-76
86F/AS-4
86F/LL-5
86F/LimEd-10
86F/Mini-17
86F/Slug-M3
86F/St-23
86F/WaxBox-C7
86GenMills/Book-4M
86Jiffy-19
86Leaf-63
86OPC-170
86Quaker-4
86Seven/Coin-E16M
86Sf-126M
86Sf-137M
86Sf-28
86Sf/Dec-72M
86T-170
86T-708AS
86T/3D-2
86T/Gloss60-23
86T/Mets/Fan-2
86T/Mini-50
86T/St-96
86T/Super-19
86T/Tatt-20M
86TrueVal-16
86Woolwth-7
87BK-2
87Classic-5
87D-69
87D/AAS-19
87D/OD-130
87D/PopUp-19
87Drake-20
87F-4
87F-629M
87F-634M
87F/AS-2
87F/AwardWin-7
87F/BB-7
87F/Excit-9
87F/GameWin-9
87F/Mini-18
87F/St-20
87F/WS-4
87GenMills/Book-5M
87Ho/St-12
87KMart-25
87KayBee-8
87Leaf-109
87MSA/Discs-8
87MnM's-12
87OPC-20
87Ralston-9
87RedFoley/St-110
87Seven-E1
87Seven-ME1
87Sf-151M
87Sf-50
87Sf/TPrev-2M
87Stuart-1M
87T-20
87T-602AS
87T/Board-11
87T/Coins-28
87T/Gloss22-9
87T/Gloss60-11
87T/HL-25
87T/Mets/Fan-1
87T/Mini-20
87T/St-101
87T/St-14LCS
87T/St-158
87T/St-22WS
87Woolwth-25
88ChefBoy-10
88D-199
88D/AS-41
88D/Best-14
88D/Mets/Bk-199
88D/PopUp-19
88Drake-10
88F-130
88F-636M
88F/St-S2
88Grenada-37
88Jiffy-3
88Kahn/Mets-8
88KennerFig-17
88Leaf-156
88Nestle-26
88OPC-157
88Panini/St-232M
88Panini/St-338
88S-325
88S/WxBx-10
88Sf-28
88Sf/Gamewin-14
88T-530
88T/Big-37
88T/Gloss22-20
88T/Gloss60-7
88T/Mets/Fan-8
88T/St-105
88T/St-152
88T/St/Backs-22
88T/UK-11
89B-379
89Cadaco-6
89Classic-64
89D-53
89D/AS-41
89D/Best-182
89D/PopUp-41
89F-30
89F/Superstar-7
89Kahn/Mets-8
89KayBee-4
89KennerFig-23
89OPC-324
89Panini/St-136
89Panini/St-228AS
89RedFoley/St-19
89S-240
89Sf-155
89T-393AS
89T-3RB
89T-680
89T/Big-325
89T/DHTest-4
89T/Gloss22-20
89T/Gloss60-17
89T/LJN-138
89T/Mets/Fan-8
89T/St-160
89T/St-2
89T/St-94
89T/St/Backs-55
89UD-390
89Woolwth-10
90B-236
90BBWit-32
90D-147
90D/BestNL-48
90D/Learning-5
90F-199
90F/Can-199
90F/Up-U62
90KayBee-6
90Leaf-134
90MLBPA/Pins-17
90Mother/Giant-3
90OPC-790
90PublInt/St-128
90S-416
90S/Tr-35T
90T-790
90T/Tr-19T
90UD-168
90UD/Ext-774
91B-598
91BBBest/RecBr-3
91D-151
91D-BC8
91D/BC-BC8
91F-258
91F/UltraUp-U86
91F/Up-U93
91Leaf-457
91Leaf/Stud-182
91Mother/Dodg-16
91OPC-310
91OPC/Premier-19
91Pol/Dodg-12
91S-215
91S/RookTr-26T
91StCl-424
91T-310
91T/Tr-19T
91UD-176
91UD/Ext-758
91WIZMets-67
92B-385
92D-36
92D/Up-U19
92DPep/MSA-12
92Expo/D/Duri-5
92F-450
92L-442
92L/BlkGold-442
92OPC-387TRI
92OPC-389TRI
92OPC-399TRI
92OPC-402TRI
92OPC-45
92OPC/Premier-29
92Pinn-321
92S-489
92S/RookTr-59T
92StCl-845
92StCl/MemberI-3
92Studio-53
92T-45
92T/Gold-45
92T/GoldWin-45
92T/Tr-22T
92T/TrGold-22T
92TripleP-26M
92TripleP/Prev-5
92UD-267
92UD-767
92Ultra-514
93D-122M
93Expo/D/McDon-12
93Select-55
93T-205
93T/Gold-205
93T/PreProd-3
93UD-219
94TedW-135
94TedW-50

Carter, Glenn
88Bend/Legoe-21
89QuadC/Best-1
89QuadC/GS-8
90MidldA/GS-18
91AA/LineD-429
91ClBest/Singl-305
91MidldA/LineD-429
91MidldA/ProC-428

Carter, Herbert
82Wisco/Frit-10

Carter, Jeffrey A.
87James-27
88Rockford-5
89Rockford-5
89WPalmB/Star-5
90A&AASingle/ProC-38
90AAASingl/ProC-43
90Foil/Best-316
90Jaxvl/Best-18
90Jaxvl/ProC-1369
90Phoenix/CMC-18
90Phoenix/ProC-17
90ProC/Singl-545
91AAA/LineD-379
91AAA/LineD-630
91B-348
91Phoenix/LineD-379
91Phoenix/ProC-71
91Vanco/LineD-630
91Vanco/ProC-1587
92Pinn-280
92S-770
92Sky/AAASingl-237
92StCl-381
92T/91Debut-29
92Vanco/ProC-2714
92Vanco/SB-630

Carter, Jeffrey D.
85Everett/II/Cram-1
86Clinton-4
88Shrev/ProC-1291
89Shrev/ProC-1846
89TexLAS/GS-29
92Tacoma/ProC-2509
92Tacoma/SB-529

Carter, Joe
83Iowa-20
83Thorn-33
84D-41RR
84Iowa-25
84Wheat/Ind-30
85D-616
85F-443
85Polar/Ind-30
85T-694
86D-224
86D/HL-42
86F-583
86OPC-377
86OhHenry-30
86T-377
86T/St-213
86T/Tatt-15M
87Classic/Up-127
87D-156
87D/OD-109
87F-249
87F/AwardWin-8
87F/BB-8
87F/LL-9
87F/Lim-7
87F/Mini-19
87F/St-21
87Gator-30
87KayBee-9
87Kraft-15
87Leaf-133
87MnM's-16
87OPC-220
87RedFoley/St-27
87Sf-176
87Sf/TPrev-3M
87Smok/AL-5
87Stuart-18
87T-220
87T/Coins-7
87T/Gloss60-16
87T/Mini-51
87T/St-208
88D-254
88D-BC9
88D/Best-56
88F-605
88F/Mini-18
88F/SS-6
88F/Slug-7
88F/St-18
88Gator-30
88Grenada-56
88KayBee-4
88KennerFig-18
88Leaf-184
88Nestle-36
88OPC-75
88OPC-I
88Panini/St-72
88S-80
88Sf-5
88T-75
88T/Big-71
88T/Coins-8
88T/Gloss60-44
88T/RiteAid-17
88T/St-213
88T/St/Backs-49
88T/UK-12
88T/WaxBox-I
89B-91
89Cadaco-7
89Classic-11
89D-83
89D/Best-56
89D/MVP-BC3
89F-400
89F/Excit-4
89F/Heroes-6
89KennerFig-24
89KingB/Discs-8
89OPC-164
89Panini/St-327
89RedFoley/St-20
89S-213
89S/HotStar-55
89S/Mast-34
89Sf-104
89T-420
89T/Ames-9
89T/Big-155
89T/Coins-36
89T/Gloss60-3
89T/Hills-6
89T/LJN-87
89T/St-216
89T/St/Backs-14
89T/UK-13
89UD-190
90B-220
90Classic-138
90Classic/Up-T9
90Coke/Padre-3
90D-114
90D/BestNL-72
90F-489
90F/Can-489
90F/Up-U55
90HotPlay/St-5
90Kenner/Fig-16
90Leaf-379
90Leaf/Prev-2
90OPC-580
90Padre/MagUno-27
90Panini/St-65
90Post-30
90PublInt/St-280
90PublInt/St-557
90RedFoley/St-15
90S-319
90S/100St-59
90S/Tr-19T
90Sf-120
90T-580
90T/Ames-27
90T/Big-245
90T/Coins-42
90T/DH-9
90T/Gloss60-33
90T/HillsHM-28
90T/Mini-13
90T/St-209
90T/TVAS-43
90T/Tr-20T
90UD-375
90UD-53TC
90UD/Ext-754
90WichSt-7
91B-11
91Classic/200-91
91Classic/I-21
91Classic/II-T98
91Colla/Carter-Set
91D-298
91D-409MVP
91D/GSlam-1
91F-525
91F/Up-U65
91Leaf-353
91Leaf/Stud-133
91OPC-120
91OPC/Premier-20
91Panini/FrSt-95
91Panini/St-90
91Panini/Top15-19
91S-9

91S/100SS-81
91S/RookTr-11T
91S/ToroBJ-1
91S/ToroBJ-37AS
91StCl-513
91T-120
91T/Tr-20T
91Tor/Fire-29
91UD-226
91UD/Ext-765
91USPlayC/AS-4H
91Ultra-360
92B-573
92B-667FOIL
92BJ/Fire-5
92CJ/DII-21
92Classic/Game200-11
92Colla/ASG-12
92D-677HL
92D-693
92D/DK-DK3
92D/Elite-E10
92D/McDon-G2
92DPep/MSA-25
92DennyGS-26
92F-327
92F-685RS
92F-703M
92F/ASIns-21
92F/TmLIns-14
92French-16
92KingB-24
92L-375
92L/BlkGold-375
92L/GoldPrev-26
92L/Prev-26
92MSA/Ben-2
92OPC-790
92OPC/Premier-194
92P-12
92Panini-29
92Pinn-148
92S-435AS
92S-90
92S/100SS-35
92StCl-10
92StCl/Dome-25
92Studio-254
92Sunflower-12
92T-402AS
92T-790
92T/Gold-402AS
92T/Gold-790
92T/GoldWin-402AS
92T/GoldWin-790
92T/Kids-89
92T/McDonB-29
92TripleP-108
92UD-224
92UD/HRH-HR6
92USPlayC/Ace-6H
92USPlayC/Ace-9C
92Ultra-145
93B-575
93BJ/D/45-5
93BJ/D/McDon-22
93BJ/D/McDon-32
93BJ/D/WS-2
93BJ/Demp-6
93BJ/Fire-4
93Classic/Gamel-19
93Colla/ASG-19
93Colla/DM-23
93D-615
93DennyGS-4
93F-333
93F-713RT
93F/ASAL-8
93F/Fruit-10
93Flair-289
93HumDum/Can-20
93KingB-13
93L-228
93L/GoldAS-8
93L/UpGoldAS-9
93MSA/Metz-4
93OPC-83
93OPC/Premier/StarP-13
93OPC/WC-3
93Pac/Spanish-322
93Panini-31
93Pinn-427
93Pinn/Cooper-21
93Pinn/HRC-7
93Pinn/Slug-4
93Pinn/TP-10M
93Post/Can-4
93S-506AS
93S-575
93Select-96
93Select/ChasS-20
93Select/StatL-32
93StCl-279
93StCl-749MC
93StCl/1stDay-279
93StCl/1stDay-749MC
93StCl/MurphyS-74
93Studio-87
93Studio/SS-5
93T-350
93T-407M
93T/BlkGold-26
93T/Finest-94AS
93T/FinestASJ-94AS
93T/FinestRef-94AS
93T/Gold-350
93T/Gold-407M
93TripleP-123
93TripleP/Act-30
93UD-223
93UD-41M
93UD-42
93UD/Clutch-R5
93UD/FunPack-56
93UD/HRH-HR7
93UD/SP-3AS
93UD/SPPlat-PP3
93USPlayC/Ace-8C
93Ultra-288
93Ultra/HRK-7
94B-1
94D-366
94D/Ann-1
94D/Doml-5
94D/Special-366
94F-326
94F/AS-5
94Flair-116
94Flair/Outfield-3
94L-193
94L/CleanUp-8
94L/MVPAL-3
94L/PBroker-9
94L/StatStand-7
94OPC-145
94OPC/BJ-4
94OPC/JAS-23
94Pac/Cr-636
94Pac/CrPr-2
94Pac/Gold-6
94Panini-136
94Pinn-345
94RedFoley-30
94S-625WS
94S-73
94S/GoldR-73
94S/GoldS-31
94Select-12
94Sf/2000-12
94Sf/2000-183AS
94Sf/Mov-10
94StCl-300
94StCl-527DL
94StCl/1stDay-300
94StCl/1stDay-527DL
94StCl/Gold-300
94StCl/Gold-527DL
94StCl/Team-151
94Studio-26
94Studio/Her-3
94Studio/S&GStar-5
94T-645
94T/BlkGold-4
94T/Finest-207
94T/FinestRef-207
94T/Gold-645
94TripleP-32
94TripleP/Nick-4
94UD-91
94UD/ElecD-91
94UD/Mantle-5
94UD/SP-40
94Ultra-136
94Ultra/Career-1
94Ultra/HRK-6
94Ultra/RBIK-3
Carter, John Howard
(Howard)
No Cards.
Carter, John
92Welland/ClBest-4
92Welland/ProC-1315
94B-663
Carter, Larry G.
89Salinas/Cal-126
89Salinas/ProC-1816
91Shrev/LineD-302
91Shrev/ProC-1814
Carter, Larry L.
89Beloit/II/Star-6
90Beloit/Best-4
90Beloit/Star-4
91AA/LineD-302
91Beloit/ClBest-2
91Beloit/ProC-2095
91MidwLAS/ProC-32
92Phoenix/ProC-2815
92Phoenix/SB-378
92ProC/Tomorrow-347
92Sky/AAASingl-174
92Sky/AASingl-294
92Stockton/ClBest-1
93B-168
93D-76
93S-300
93S/Boys-18
Carter, Marlin
86Negro/Frit-50
92Negro/Retort-8
93TWill-101
Carter, Michael
90Helena/SportP-24
91Beloit/ClBest-22
91Beloit/ProC-2108
91ClBest/Singl-214
91MidwLAS/ProC-33
92B-243
92ElPaso/ProC-3933
92Stockton/ProC-47
92UD/ML-270
Carter, Otis Leonard
(Jackie)
No Cards.
Carter, Richard
87Lakeland-13
88Lakeland/Star-6
89SanBern/Best-3
89SanBern/Cal-68
Carter, Richie
86PalmSp-6
86PalmSp/Smok-14
Carter, Ron
86Madis/Pol-5
87SanBern-8
Carter, Steve
87Watertn-10
88Augusta/ProC-385
89BuffB/ProC-1665
89D/Rook-8
90AAAGame/ProC-17
90AAASingl/ProC-500
90B-179
90BuffB/CMC-22
90BuffB/ProC-385
90BuffB/Team-5
90OPC-482
90ProC/Singl-22
90T-482
90T/89Debut-23
90UD-368
91AAA/LineD-202
91D-418RR
91Iowa/LineD-202
91Iowa/ProC-1074
91Lakeland/ClBest-8
91Ultra-374MLP
92Sky/AAASingl-259
92Toledo/ProC-1053
92Toledo/SB-579
Carter, Tim
90Helena/SportP-1
91Beloit/ClBest-14
91Beloit/ProC-2109
92Stockton/ClBest-6
92Stockton/ProC-38
Carter, Tom
92FtLaud/ClBest-9
92FtLaud/ProC-2603
92FtLaud/Team-4
Cartwright, Alan
84ElPaso-19
86ElPaso-5
87Denver-19
88ElPaso/Best-13
Cartwright, Alexander J.
50Call
50W576-11
76Shakey-15
80Perez/HOF-15
80SSPC/HOF
89HOF/St-90
90BBWit-96
Cartwright, Edward C.
(Ed)
N172
N300/SC
Cartwright, Mark
83Visalia/Frit-16
Carty, Jorge
77Charl
Carty, Ricardo Adolfo Jacobo
(Rico)
64T-476R
65Kahn
65OPC-2LL
65T-2LL
65T-305
65T/trans-7
66OPC-153
66T-153
67CokeCap/Brave-17
67Kahn
67OPC-35
67T-240LL
67T-35
68CokeCap/Brave-17
68Dexter-22
68T-455
69MLB/St-112
69T-590
70MLB/St-3
70OPC-145
70T-145
71Bz
71Bz/Test-28
71MD
71MLB/St-557
71MLB/St-6
71OPC-270
71OPC-62LL
71T-270
71T-62LL
71T/Coins-113
71T/GM-3
71T/Greatest-3
71T/S-29
71T/Super-29
71T/tatt-11
72T-740
73OPC-435
73T-435
75OPC-655
75T-655
75T/M-655
76OPC-156
76SSPC-519
76T-156
77OPC-114
77Pep-9
77T-465
78BJ/PostC-3
78T-305
79BJ/Bubble-4
79OPC-291
79T-565
80OPC-25
80T-46
91K/Leyenda-3
91Swell/Great-18
92AP/ASG-74
93Rang/Keeb-98
93UD/ATH-27
94TedW-41
Caruso, Joe
92LynchRS/ClBest-20
92LynchRS/ProC-2899
92StCl/Dome-26
92UD/ML-111
93FExcel/ML-131
93Pawtu/Ball-6
Caruthers, Robert Lee
(Bob)
90Target-116
N162
N172
N172/BC
N28
N284
N370
Scrapps
Carvajal, Jovina
90Oneonta/ProC-3375
91FSLAS/ProC-FSL12
91FtLaud/ClBest-25
91FtLaud/ProC-2439
92ClBest-110
92FtLaud/ClBest-2
92FtLaud/ProC-2624
92FtLaud/Team-5
Carver, Billy Paul
87AubAs-6
88Ashvl/ProC-1049
88SALAS/GS-4
89ColMud/Best-23
89Osceola/Star-3
Carveth, Joe
45Parade*-12
Cary, Chuck
82BirmB-9
83BirmB-14
86F/Up-U21
86Nashvl-3
87D-461
87F-147
87Richm/Bob-1
87Richm/Crown-47
87Richm/TCMA-1
87T-171
89Colum/CMC-7
89Colum/Pol-1
89Colum/ProC-745
89S/NWest-27
89T/Tr-17T
89UD-396
90Classic-125
90D-429
90Leaf-50
90OPC-691
90Panini/St-123
90S-393
90S/NWest-15
90T-691
90T/St-315
90T/TVYank-8
90UD-528
91B-176
91D-179
91F-659
91Leaf-66
91OPC-359
91Panini/FrSt-331
91S-566
91StCl-40
91T-359
91UD-409
92Yank/WIZ80-27
93WSox-6
Cary, Jeff
80LynnS-12
81Wausau-15
82Madis/Frit-31
Casado, Cancio
89Martins/Star-6
Casagrande,Tom
55T-167
Casale, Jerry
59T-456
60MacGregor-5
60T-38
61T-195
61T/St-169
Casano, Andy
88Watlo/ProC-666
89Kinston/Star-5
Casanova, Ortiz P.
(Paul)
67CokeCap/ALAS-35
67CokeCap/AS-9
67CokeCap/Senator-9
67OPC-115
67T-115
68Bz-1
68T-560
68T/ActionSt-14C
68T/ActionSt-3C
69MB-53
69MLB/St-102
69NTF
69T-486

69T/St-233
70MLB/St-280
70OPC-84
70Pol/SenY-3
70T-84
71MLB/St-532
71OPC-139
71Pol/SenP-2
71T-139
71T/Coins-146
72MB-69
72T-591
73OPC-452
73T-452
74OPC-272
74T-272
75OPC-633
75T-633
75T/M-633
76Laugh/Clown-24
89Pac/SenLg-58

Casanova, Raul
92ColumMet/ClBest-19
92ColumMet/ProC-200
92Kingspt/ClBest-10
92Kingspt/ProC-1533

Casarotti, Rich
88BurlB/ProC-21
88MidwLAS/GS-17
89Durham/Star-4
89Durham/Team-4
89Star/Wax-68
90Greenvl/Best-10
90Greenvl/ProC-1135
90Greenvl/Star-5
91AA/LineD-201
91Greenvl/ClBest-14
91Greenvl/LineD-201
91Greenvl/ProC-3008
91Richm/Bob-28
92CharlK/ProC-2776

Casavant, Denys
45Parade*-13

Cascarella, Joe
35BU-162
W711/1

Case, George W.
39PlayBall-138
40PlayBall-15
41DP-76
41DP-88
41G-16
41PlayBall-69
42Playball-20
Exh47
R303/A
R303/B
V351B-7

Case, Michael
92Bend/ClBest-8
93T-661M
93T/Gold-661M

Casey, Dan
N172
N284
N690
WG1-48

Casey, Dennis Patrick
No Cards.

Casey, Hugh
39PlayBall-151
40PlayBall-148
47TipTop
49B-179
49Eureka-155
80Laugh/FFeat-27
90Target-118
Exh47

Casey, James Peter
(Doc)
90Target-117
E107
T206

Casey, Jas.
WG3-8

Casey, Joie
87SLCity/Taco-x
88SLCity-30M

Casey, Joseph Felix
(Joe)
14CJ-87
15CJ-87
E101
E92

Casey, Keith
90Gate/ProC-3338
90Gate/SportP-5

Casey, Kim
87SLCity/Taco-x

Casey, Orrin Robinson
(Bob)
No Cards.

Casey, Pat
83Beaum-16
84Beaum-16
85Cram/PCL-86
86Calgary-4
87Portl-7

Casey, Timothy
(Tim)
86Stockton-4
87ElPaso-13
89Huntsvl/Best-14
90AAASingl/ProC-151
90ProC/Singl-589
90Tacoma/CMC-12
90Tacoma/ProC-104

Cash, Bill
86Negro/Frit-57
91Negro/Lewis-2
92Negro/Retort-9

Cash, David
(Dave)
69Pirate/JITB-2
70OPC-141R
70T-141R
71MLB/St-197
71OPC-582
71T-582
72OPC-125
72T-125
73OPC-397
73T-397
74JP
74OPC-198
74T-198
75Ho-93
75K-48
75OPC-22
75SSPC/Puzzle-6
75T-22
75T/M-22
76Crane-11
76Ho-40
76Ho/Twink-40
76K-16
76MSA/Disc
76OPC-295
76SSPC-465
76T-295
77BurgChef-162
77Ho-133
77Ho/Twink-133
77OPC-180
77Pep-66
77T-649
77T/CS-12
77T/ClothSt-12
78Ho-23
78OPC-18
78T-495
78Tastee/Discs-17
78Wiffle/Discs-15
79OPC-207
79T-395
80OPC-3
80T-14
81D-121
81F-492
81T-707
88Batavia/ProC-1663
89Pac/SenLg-192
89ScranWB/CMC-6
89T/SenLg-64
89TM/SenLg-19
90Batavia/ProC-3084MG
91Pac/SenLg-58
91Pac/SenLg-80
93Expo/D/McDon-13
93ScranWB/Team-5CO
93UD/ATH-28

Cash, Earl
85Osceola/Team-4
86Osceola-5
87ColAst/ProC-19

Cash, Johnny
86Durham-3

Cash, Mike
75Cedar
78Cr/PCL-94

Cash, Norman Dalton
(Norm)
59T-509
60T-488
61P-40
61T-95
61T/St-148
62Bz
62Exh
62J-14
62P-14
62P/Can-14
62Salada-72
62Shirriff-72
62T-250
62T-466AS
62T-51LL
62T-90LL
62T/St-45
62T/bucks
63Exh
63J-46
63P-46
63T-445
63T-4LL
64Bz-20
64Det/Lids-3
64T-331M
64T-425
64T/Coins-79
64T/SU
64T/St-49
64T/tatt
65OPC-153
65T-153
66T-218LL
66T-315
67CokeCap/Tiger-2
67T-216M
67T-540
68CokeCap/Tiger-2
68T-256
69MB-54
69MLB/St-46
69OPC-80
69T-80
69T/St-171
70MLB/St-205
70T-611
71MLB/St-389
71OPC-599
71T-599
72MB-70
72OPC-150
72OPC-90LL
72T-150
72T-90LL
73OPC-485
73T-485
74OPC-367
74T-367
74T/St-172
75SSPC/42-38
78TCMA-49
81Tiger/Detroit-73
83Kaline-19M
83Kaline-22M
83Kaline-24M
83MLBPA/Pin-3
85CircK-25
86Tiger/Sport-14
88Domino-2
93AP/ASG-147
94TedW-29
94TedW/54-29
Exh47

Cash, Ronald Forrest
(Ron)
74OPC-600R
74T-600R

Cash, Timothy
88VeroB/Star-3

Cash, Todd
86Clinton-5

Cashion, Jay Carl
14CJ-62
E270/1

Casian, Larry
88OrlanTw/Best-20
88SLAS-29
89Portl/ProC-223
90AAASingl/ProC-240
90Portl/CMC-3
90Portl/ProC-170
90ProC/Singl-555
91B-325
91Leaf-481
91OPC-374
91T-374
91T/90Debut-27
92AAA/ASG/SB-404
92F-199
92Portl/SB-404
92Portland/ProC-2660
92S/100RisSt-94
92Sky/AAASingl-185
93D-343
93F/Final-233
93L-498
94D-109
94F-201
94StCl-479
94StCl/1stDay-479
94StCl/Gold-479
94T-543
94T/Gold-543
94Ultra-84

Casillas, Adam
88Greens/ProC-1562
89Cedar/Best-14
89Cedar/ProC-922
89Cedar/Star-3
89Star/IISingl-198
90CedarDG/Best-18
91AAA/LineD-254
91Nashvl/LineD-254
91Nashvl/ProC-2168
92Memphis/SB-430
92Omaha/ProC-2973
92Sky/AASingl-181

Caskin, Edward James
(Ed)
No Cards.

Casper, Tim
91Everett/ClBest-13
91Everett/ProC-3920

Cassady, Harry D.
No Cards.

Cassel, Grahame
91Parramatta/Fut-9

Cassels, Chris
88Beloit/GS-23
89Stockton/Best-19
89Stockton/Cal-163
89Stockton/ProC-392
89Stockton/Star-14
90AS/Cal-41
90Stockton/Best-14
90Stockton/Cal-199
90Stockton/ProC-2199
91AA/LineD-251
91Harris/LineD-251
91Harris/ProC-640

Cassidy, David
(Dave)
89Hamil/Star-9
91StPete/ProC-2266
92ArkTr/ProC-1121

Cassidy, Howard
(Hop)
79Colum-25
90Tampa/DIMD-28CO
92ColClip/Pol-2M
92ColClip/SB-125M
93ColClip/Pol-24M

Cassidy, John P.
No Cards.

Cassidy, Joseph P.
(Joe)
No Cards.

Cassidy, Mike
91StPete/ClBest-2

Cassidy, Peter F.
(Pete)
90Target-909
T206

Cassillas, Adam
90Chatt/GS-8

Cassinelli, David
90AR-32M

Cassini, Jack Dempsey
No Cards.

Castaigne, Arcilio
80Ander-2

Castain, Maurice
83Idaho-26
84Madis/Pol-22

Castaldo, Gregg
92Kane/Team-4

Castaldo, Joe
91Hamil/ClBest-1
91Hamil/ProC-4030

Castaldo, Vince
90Helena/SportP-16
91ClBest/Singl-264
91Stockton/ClBest-19
91Stockton/ProC-3036
92ElPaso/ProC-3934
92ElPaso/SB-203
93Ottawa/ProC-2441

Castaneda, Nick
82AlexD-13
83AlexD-5
84PrWill-31
85Tigres-23
89Omaha/CMC-13
89Omaha/ProC-1722
91AAA/LineD-228
91Louisvl/LineD-228
91Louisvl/ProC-2921

Castaneda, Robbie
91BendB/ProC-3687

Casteel, Brent
86WinSalem-3

Castellano, Miguel
90Butte/SportP-3
91Gaston/ClBest-16
91Gaston/ProC-2693
92CharlR/ClBest-14

Castellano, Pedro
89Star/IISingl-163
89Wythe/Star-5
90MidwLgAS/GS-29
90Peoria/Team-8
90Peoria/Team-9M
91CLAS/ProC-CAR40
91ClBest/Singl-173
91WinSalem/ClBest-17
91WinSalem/ProC-2834
92B-271
92B-649
92D/Rook-22
92Iowa/ProC-4057
92Iowa/SB-205
92ProC/Tomorrow-204
92Sky/AAASingl-99
92UD/ML-133
93B-232
93D-761
93F/Final-24
93FExcel/ML-7
93T/Tr-69T
94D-449
94Pac/Cr-191
94Pinn-229
94Pinn/Artist-229
94Pinn/Museum-229
94StCl/Team-97

Castellanos, Miquel
92CharlR/ProC-2230

Castello, Brian
89Salinas/Cal-149TR

Caster, George
W753

Castiglione, Peter P.
(Pete)
49Eureka-156
50B-201
51B-17
52B-47
52T-260
54B-174

Castilla, Vinicio
(Vinny)
90Foil/Best-278
90ProC/Singl-727
90SALAS/Star-28
90Sumter/Best-28
90Sumter/ProC-2439
91AA/LineD-202
91Greenvl/ClBest-15
91Greenvl/LineD-202
91Greenvl/ProC-3009
91Richm/Bob-29
92F-666
92ProC/Tomorrow-183
92Richm/Bleach-2

92Richm/Comix-2
92Richm/ProC-382
92Richm/SB-427
92S-860
92Sky/AAASingl-195
92T/91Debut-30
93B-556
93D-102
93D-770
93F-406
93F/Final-25
93JDean/Rook-2
93L-495
93OPC/Premier-65
93Pac/Jugador-23
93Pac/Spanish-424
93StCl-547
93StCl/1stDay-547
93StCl/Rockie-23
93Studio-212
93T/Tr-33T
93UD-560
93USPlayC/Rockie-13C
93USPlayC/Rockie-4H
93Ultra-344
94D-549
94F-437
94L-214
94Pac/Cr-192
94Panini-172
94Pinn-191
94Pinn/Artist-191
94Pinn/Museum-191
94S-305
94S/GoldR-305
94StCl-244
94StCl/1stDay-244
94StCl/Gold-244
94StCl/Team-92
94T-163
94T/Gold-163
94UD/CollC-74
94UD/CollC/Gold-74
94UD/CollC/Silv-74

Castillo, Ace
75QuadC

Castillo, Alberto
89Kingspt/Star-5
90Clmbia/PCPII-2
90Columbia/GS-19
90Pittsfld/Pucko-23
91Clmbia/PCPII-7
91Clmbia/PII-10
92StLucie/ClBest-15
92StLucie/ProC-1748
93StLucie/ProC-2924
94B-23

Castillo, Anthony
(Tony)
79Hawaii-24
80Hawaii-21

Castillo, Antonio Jose
(Tony)
85Iowa-1
85Kingst-3
87Dunedin-12
88Dunedin/Star-2
89B-244
89D/Rook-12
90Brave/Dubuq/Perf-4
90D-592
90OPC-620
90T-620
90UD-551
91AAA/LineD-428
91F-685
91OPC-353
91Richm/Bob-7
91Richm/LineD-428
91Richm/ProC-2560
91Richm/Team-6
91S-582
91T-353
91UD-458
92D-739
92F-499
92S-682
92Toledo/ProC-1033
92Toledo/SB-580
93F/Final-288
94D-601
94F-327
94Pac/Cr-637
94S-177
94S/GoldR-177
94StCl-470
94StCl/1stDay-470
94StCl/Gold-470
94StCl/Team-167

Castillo, Axel
88BurlInd/ProC-1781

Castillo, Ben
(Benny)
88Bristol/ProC-1892
89Fayette/ProC-1580
91SLCity/ProC-3222
91SLCity/SportP-16

Castillo, Benigno
92CharlR/ClBest-3
92CharlR/ProC-2236

Castillo, Bobby
79Albuq-22
79T-641
80Pol/Dodg-37
81D-298
81F-137
81Pol/Dodg-37
81T-146
82D-236
82F-2
82T-48
82T/Tr-17T
83F-608
83F/St-3M
83F/St-9M
83T-327
83T-771TL
83Twin/Team-23
84D-436
84F-559
84Nes/792-491
84OPC-329
84T-491
85Coke/Dodg-7
85F-274
85F/Up-U22
85T-588
85T/Tr-18T
86F-127
86T-252
90Target-119

Castillo, Braulio
89AS/Cal-9
89Bakers/Cal-202
90SanAn/GS-10
91AA/LineD-533
91ClBest/Singl-307
91Classic/II-T85
91SanAn/LineD-533
91SanAn/ProC-2987
92B-104
92D-753
92OPC-353
92ProC/Tomorrow-245
92S-824
92S/Rook-32
92ScranWB/ProC-2458
92ScranWB/SB-480
92Sky/AAASingl-218
92StCl-124
92T-353
92T/91Debut-31
92T/Gold-353
92T/GoldWin-353
92UD-21SR
93D-386
93F-407
93LimeR/Winter-80
93S-629
93Select-340
93USPlayC/Rockie-5C
93USPlayC/Rockie-8S

Castillo, Carlos
91Yakima/ClBest-23
91Yakima/ProC-4241
92Bakers/Cal-5
92Visalia/ProC-1005

Castillo, Esteban M.
(Manny)
78Spring/Wiener-9
81Omaha-15
81T-66R
83D-253
83F-474
83T-258
84F-607
84Nes/792-562
84Syrac-24
84T-562

Castillo, Felipe
87Gaston/ProC-1
88Gaston/ProC-1008
89CharlR/Star-6
89Tulsa/GS-7
89Tulsa/Team-5
90ProC/Singl-741
90Tulsa/ProC-1150
90Tulsa/Team-5

Castillo, Frank
89WinSalem/Star-4
90CharlK/Team-20
91AAA/LineD-203
91D/Rook-20
91Iowa/LineD-203
91UD/FinalEd-27F
92Cub/Mara-49
92D-492
92F-378
92L-290
92L/BlkGold-290
92OPC-196
92OPC/Premier-159
92Pinn-504
92S-399
92S/100RisSt-61
92StCl-65
92T-196
92T/91Debut-32
92T/Gold-196
92T/GoldWin-196
92UD-526
92USPlayC/Cub-10D
92USPlayC/Cub-2S
92Ultra-467
93Cub/Mara-4
93D-400
93F-375
93L-141
93Pac/Beisbol-17M
93Pac/Spanish-54
93Pinn-208
93S-462
93StCl-346
93StCl/1stDay-346
93StCl/Cub-21
93T-533
93T/Gold-533
93UD-408
93Ultra-16
94D-91
94F-382
94L-217
94Pac/Cr-97
94StCl-337
94StCl/1stDay-337
94StCl/Gold-337
94StCl/Team-341
94T-399
94T/Gold-399
94UD-464

Castillo, Jeff
88GreatF-8

Castillo, Juan
80BurlB-22
80Utica-13
81BurlB-20
83ElPaso-10
84ElPaso-16
85Cram/PCL-205
86F/Up-U22
86Pol/Brew-3
87D-249
87F/Up-U18
87Pol/Brew-3
87T/Tr-20T
88D-363
88F-159
88OPC-362
88Pol/Brew-3
88S-429
88T-362
88T/Big-117
89D-530
89T-538
89T/Big-9
89UD-522
90AAASingl/ProC-222
90ColoSp/ProC-41
90Pittsfld/Pucko-20
91AAA/LineD-132
91Clmbia/PCPII-3
91Clmbia/PII-14
91Denver/LineD-132
91Denver/ProC-129
91SALAS/ProC-SAL13
92StLucie/ClBest-13
92StLucie/ProC-1738
93B-538

Castillo, Luis T.
82Wausau/Frit-16
87Stockton-17
88ElPaso/Best-8

Castillo, M. Carmelo
(Carmen)
81Chatt-16
82Charl-19
83F-404
84Wheat/Ind-8
85D-590
85F-444
85OPC-184
85Polar/Ind-8
85T-184
85T/St-255
86D-460
86F-584
86OhHenry-8
86T/Tr-21T
87D-588
87F-250
87Gator-8
87T-513
88D-403
88F-606
88Gator-8
88S-581
88T-341
89D-374
89F-401
89S-497
89S/Tr-23
89T-637
89T/Big-91
89T/Tr-18T
89UD-487
90D-554
90F-371
90F/Can-371
90OPC-427
90S-123
90T-427
90UD-281
91F-606
91OPC-266
91S-608
91T-266
93LimeR/Winter-93

Castillo, Martin H.
(Marty)
80Evansvl-19
81Evans
82Evansvl-11
82F-265
82T-261R
83Evansvl-11
84D-247
84Nes/792-303
84T-303
84Tiger/Wave-10
85Cain's-5
85D-394
85F-5
85T-461
85Wendy-6
86T-788
89Pac/SenLg-88
89T/SenLg-10
90EliteSenLg-66
91Pac/SenLg-2

Castillo, Roberto
90QuadC/GS-8

Castillo, Tomas
80Utica-12

Castillo, Tony
81Hawaii/TCMA-6

Castino, John A.
77Orlan
78OrlanTw
79Twin/FriszP-3
80OPC-76
80T-137
81D-488
81Drake-29
81F-554
81F/St-112
81OPC-304
81Sqt-29
81T-304
81T/SO-33
81T/St-99
82D-256
82F-549
82F/St-230
82K-29
82OPC-73
82T-396TL
82T-644
82T/St-209
83D-303
83F-609
83OPC-93
83OPC/St-89
83T-93
83T/St-89
83Twin/Team-1
84D-120
84D-4
84D/AAS-7
84F-560
84Nes/792-237
84OPC-237
84T-237
84T/St-307
85OPC-298
85T-452

Castle, Donald Hardy
(Don)
77WHave
93Rang/Keeb-99

Castle, John Francis
No Cards.

Castleberry, Kevin
88CapeCod/Sum-111
88OK-8
89OK-7
90Durham/Team-6
91Miami/ClBest-18
91Miami/ProC-412
92BirmB/ProC-2589
92Saraso/ClBest-8

Castleman, Clydell
36G
R314
V355-36

Castleman, Foster E.
55Gol/Giants-3
56T-271
57T-237
58T-416
79TCMA-225
91Crown/Orio-71

Castner, Rodger
87Watertn-2
88Watertn/Pucko-4

Castor, John
91OKSt-4

Castro, Antionio
85Tigres-24

Castro, Bill
76OPC-293
76T-293
77T-528
78T-448
79T-133
80T-303
81D-578
81F-517
81T-271
82Tacoma-4
83F-109
92Pol/Brew-30M
92Yank/WIZ80-28

Castro, Earnest
89Wausau/GS-3

Castro, Edgar
82Miami-15

Castro, Fidel
88LitSun/Minor-11

Castro, Frank
85Beaum-15
86Beaum-5

Castro, Genaro
86LitFalls-5

Castro, Guillermo
82DayBe-1
83DayBe-5

Castro, Jose
81OkCty/TCMA-24
82Edmon-2
85BuffB-8

86Syrac-7
87Syrac-18
87Syrac/TCMA-12
88Omaha/CMC-24
88Omaha/ProC-1509
89Omaha/CMC-14
89Omaha/ProC-1731
90AAASingl/ProC-570
90Indianap/CMC-23
90Indianap/ProC-287
90James/Pucko-29CO
90ProC/Singl-73
91Rockford/ClBest-13CO
91Rockford/ProC-2063CO
92Erie/ProC-1643
Castro, Juan
91GreatF/SportP-26
92Bakers/Cal-6
Castro, Liliano
87Fayette-21
88Fayette/ProC-1101
Castro, Louis M.
No Cards.
Castro, Nelson
90Kissim/DIMD-6
91GreatF/SportP-4
92Bakers/Cal-7
Castro, Pablo
88StCath/ProC-2012
Castro, Tony
91Eugene/ClBest-1
91Eugene/ProC-3737
Cataline, Dan
81QuadC-16
83VeroB-24
Cater, Danny Anderson
64PhilBull-9
64T-482R
65OPC-253
65T-253
66T-398
67CokeCap/A's-17
67OPC-157
67T-157
68A's/JITB-4
68T-535
69MB-55
69MLB/St-84
69OPC-1LL
69OPC-44
69T-1LL
69T-44
69T-556M
69T/St-213
69Trans-12
70MLB/St-243
70OPC-437
70T-437
71K-30
71MD
71MLB/St-485
71OPC-358
71T-358
71T/Coins-14
72MB-71
72T-676
73OPC-317
73T-317
74OPC-543
74T-543
75OPC-645
75T-645
75T/M-645
92Yank/WIZ70-31
Cater, Michael
92Stockton/ClBest-19
Cates, Eli Eldo
No Cards.
Cates, Tim
83Memphis/TCMA-11
85Indianap-8
Cathcart, Gary
86FtLaud-5
87Albany-9
88Albany/ProC-1335
Cather, Theodore P.
(Ted)
15CJ-145
Catlett, David
94B-665
Cato, Keefe
81Water-2
82Water-3
83Water-1
84Wichita/Rock-14
85Cram/PCL-118
85T-367
86Omaha/ProC-4
Cato, Wayne
76Cedar
79Cedar/TCMA-15
80Clinton-26MG
Caton, James Howard
(Buster)
No Cards.
Catterson, Thomas H.
(Tom)
90Target-910
Caudill, Bill
76ArkTr
78SSPC/270-262
80T-103
81D-586
81F-306
81OPC-346
81T-574
81T/St-152
82D-426
82F-590
82T-303
82T/Tr-18T
83D-302
83F-475
83F/St-8M
83F/St-9M
83Nalley-5
83OPC-78
83OPC/St-118
83T-78
83T/St-118
84D-118
84F-608
84F/St-76
84F/X-24
84Mother/A's-12
84Nes/792-769
84OPC-299
84T-769
84T/St-345
84T/Tr-23
85D-96
85F-419
85F/St-100
85F/Up-U23
85Leaf-154
85OPC-275
85OPC/Post-23
85T-685
85T/St-322
85T/Tr-19T
85Tor/Fire-7
86BJ/Ault-5
86D-317
86F-55
86GenMills/Book-3M
86OPC-207
86T-435
86Tor/Fire-5
87F-221
87Mother/A's-24
87OPC-156
87T-733
Caughey, Wayne
79Toledo-11
80Albuq-18
81Albuq/TCMA-14
82Portl-12
Cauley, Chris
88Tampa/Star-4
89Saraso/Star-4
Caulfield, John J.
No Cards.
Caulfield, Tom
83Erie-23
Causey, Cecil
(Red)
E120
E121/80
E122
W501-65
Causey, James Wayne
(Wayne)
62Salada-100
62Shirriff-100
62T-496
63T-539
64T-75
64T/Coins-102
64T/Coins-161AAS
64T/Coins-161BAS
64T/S-45
64T/SU
64T/St-87
64T/tatt
65T-425
65T/E-21
65T/trans-8
66T-366
67CokeCap/WSox-8
67T-286
68T-522
69OPC-33
69T-33
78TCMA-8
91Crown/Orio-72
Cavalier, Kevin
87James-26
88WPalmB/Star-4
Cavalli, Brian
90OK-2
92OKSt-3
Cavallo, Pablo
77Newar
78Newar
Cavanagh, Michael
92Everett/ClBest-21
92Everett/ProC-1692
Cavanaugh, John J.
No Cards.
Cavarretta, Phil
35BU-101
39Exh
41DP-104
43Playball-35
47TipTop
48L-168
49B-6
49Eureka-53
50B-195
51B-138
52B-126
52StarCal-92A
52StarCal/L-80F
52T-295
52TipTop
53B/Col-30MG
54T-55MG
55B-282MG
74Laugh/ASG-44
76SSPC-617CO
84Cub/Uno-3M
89Pac/Leg-131
91T/Arc53-295MG
92Cub/OldStyle-5
94T/Arc54-55
PM10/Sm-23
PR1-3
R312/M
R314
R423-13
V355-54
WG8-6
Cavazzoni, Ken
91Princet/ClBest-5
91Princet/ProC-3519
Caveney, James C.
(Ike or Jimmy)
21Exh-22
E120
V61-116
W573
Cavers, Mike
89Freder/Star-2
90Hagers/Best-25
90Hagers/ProC-1404
90Hagers/Star-5
Cayson, Tony
87Belling/Team-20
88Belling/Legoe-3
89Belling/Legoe-25
Cebuhar, John
88Hamil/ProC-1721
89Hamil/Star-8
Ceccarelli, Art
55Rodeo
58T-191
59T-226
60T-156
91Crown/Orio-73
Cecchetti, George
81Chatt-14
82Chatt-14
83BuffB-22
84BuffB-2
85Water-20
86Maine-3
Cecchini, Jim
86Jaxvl/TCMA-3
Cecena, Jose
86Reading-5
88D/Rook-6
88F/Up-U62
88Mother/R-12
88T/Tr-26T
89F-516
89S/HotRook-35
89T-683
89UD-560
93CaroMud/RBI-15
93Rang/Keeb-100
Ceci, Sam
74Tacoma/Caruso-15
Cecil, Rex
47Centen-4
49Remar
Cecil, Timothy
90CharWh/Best-12
90CharWh/ProC-2233
90ProC/Singl-708
91CharWh/ClBest-1
91CharWh/ProC-2878
91ClBest/Singl-262
Cedarburg, John
91MissSt-54M
Cedeno, Andujar
89Ashvl/ProC-952
90A&AASingle/ProC-58
90B-77
90ColMud/Best-3
90ColMud/ProC-1351
90ColMud/Star-7
90Foil/Best-72
90ProC/Singl-811
91AAA/LineD-606
91B-563
91Classic/200-200
91Classic/I-43
91F-502
91Leaf/GRook-BC20
91Leaf/StudPrev-12
91MajorLg/Pins-45
91OPC-646
91S-753RP
91S/Rook40-40
91StCl-476
91T-646
91T/90Debut-28
91Tucson/LineD-606
91Tucson/ProC-2218
91UD-23SR
91Ultra-135
92B-9
92Classic/I-23
92D-549
92F-430
92L-341
92L/BlkGold-341
92Mother/Ast-9
92OPC-288
92OPC/Premier-156
92Panini-155
92Pinn-84
92Pinn/Team2000-33
92ProC/Tomorrow-224
92S-599
92S/100RisSt-65
92StCl-310
92StCl/MemberII-4
92Studio-34
92T-288
92T/Gold-288
92T/GoldWin-288
92TripleP-68
92Tucson/ProC-494
92UD-257
92Ultra-201
93B-672
93D-456
93F-433
93Flair-60
93L-108
93LimeR/Winter-136
93Mother/Ast-10
93OPC-129
93Pac/Beisbol-24M
93Pac/Jugador-24
93Pac/Spanish-121
93Panini-172
93Pinn-32
93S-127
93StCl-207
93StCl/1stDay-207
93StCl/Ast-20
93T-553
93T/Gold-553
93UD-562
93UD/SP-31
93Ultra-391
94B-558
94D-519
94F-487
94Flair-168
94L-260
94OPC-10
94Pac/Cr-261
94Panini-192
94Pinn-292
94S-104
94S/GoldR-104
94StCl-138
94StCl/1stDay-138
94StCl/Gold-138
94Studio-19
94T-11
94T/Finest-97
94T/FinestRef-97
94T/Gold-11
94TripleP-24
94UD-354
94UD/CollC-75
94UD/CollC/Gold-75
94UD/CollC/Silv-75
94Ultra-204
Cedeno, Blas
91Bristol/ClBest-19
91Bristol/ProC-3596
92Bristol/ClBest-3
92Bristol/ProC-1401
Cedeno, Cesar
71OPC-237
71T-237
71T/S-15
71T/Super-15
72OPC-65
72T-65
73K-13
73OPC-290
73T-290
74OPC-200
74OPC-337AS
74T-200
74T-337AS
74T/St-31
75Ho-17
75Ho/Twink-17
75OPC-590
75SSPC/42-26
75SSPC/Puzzle-7
75T-590
75T/M-590
76Crane-12
76Ho-47
76Ho/Twink-47
76MSA/Disc
76OPC-460
76SSPC-63
76T-460
77BurgChef-7
77Ho-58
77Ho/Twink-58
77OPC-131
77T-90
77T/ClothSt-13
77T/S-13
78BK/Ast-18
78Ho-50
78OPC-226
78T-650
78Wiffle/Discs-16
79Ho-91
79OPC-294
79T-570
80BK/PHR-25
80K-36
80OPC-193
80T-370
80T/S-56
80T/Super-56
81Coke
81D-263

81Drake-20
81F-59
81F/St-35
81K-14
81MSA/Disc-8
81OPC-190
81PermaGr/CC-25
81T-190
81T/HT
81T/SO-77
81T/St-167
81T/St-258
82Coke/Reds
82D-118
82F-213
82F/St-41
82OPC-48
82T-640
82T/St-47
82T/Tr-19T
83D-43
83F-587
83F/St-15M
83F/St-9M
83OPC-238
83OPC/St-231
83T-351TL
83T-475
83T/Fold-5M
83T/St-231
84D-306
84F-465
84Nes/792-705LL
84Nes/792-725
84OPC-191
84T-705LL
84T-725
84T/St-54
85D-447
85F-531
85FunFood/Pin-42
85Leaf-87
85OPC-54
85T-54
85T/St-55
85ThomMc/Discs-26
86Coke/Dodg-6
86D-648
86F-29
86Mother/Ast-11
86OPC-224
86T-224
89Pac/SenLg-62
89T/SenLg-69
89TM/SenLg-118M
89TM/SenLg-20
90EliteSenLg-79
90Swell/Great-41
90Target-120
91K/Leyenda-4
91LineD-36
91Pac/SenLg-40
91Pac/SenLg-53
91Swell/Great-104
92AP/ASG-29
93TWill-41
93UD/ATH-29

Cedeno, Domingo
89Myrtle/ProC-1456
90Dunedin/Star-5
90Visalia/Cal-68
90Visalia/ProC-2166
91AA/LineD-352
91Knoxvl/LineD-352
91Knoxvl/ProC-1773
92Knoxvl/ProC-2995
92Knoxvl/SB-378
93F/Final-289
93L-486
93LimeR/Winter-133
93Syrac/ProC-1002
94D-455
94StCl/Team-164
94T-776
94T/Gold-776
94Ultra-436

Cedeno, Ramon
88Ashvl/ProC-1053
89Osceola/Star-4

Cedeno, Roger
92GreatF/SportP-19
93B-534
93StCl/Dodg-24
93UD/SP-272FOIL
94B-238
94FExcel-211

Cedeno, Vinicio
86MidldA-4
87MidldA-8
88MidldA/GS-4
89MidldA/GS-9

Cederblad, Brett
91Daikyo/Fut-6

Centala, Scott
88CapeCod/Sum-123
89Eugene/Best-7
90Foil/Best-29
90Memphis/Best-14
90Memphis/ProC-1001
90Memphis/Star-4
90ProC/Singl-748
90Star/ISingl-83

Centeno, Henry
92Ashvl/ClBest-3

Centeno, Jose
75Clinton

Cento, Tony
86AppFx-6
87Penin-28

Cepeda, Octavio
86Macon-5
87Salem-5

Cepeda, Orlando M.
58SFCallB-5
58T-343
59Bz
59T-390
59T-553AS
60Bz-10
60L-128
60T-450
60T/tatt-8
61P-144
61T-435
61T/St-75
62Bz
62Exh
62J-136
62P-136
62P/Can-136
62Salada-175
62Shirriff-175
62T-390AS
62T-40
62T-401M
62T-54LL
62T/St-195
62T/bucks
63Bz-22
63Exh
63F-64
63J-101
63P-101
63Salada-13
63T-3LL
63T-520
63T/SO
64T-306M
64T-390
64T-9LL
64T/Coins-142AS
64T/Coins-63
64T/S-55
64T/SU
64T/St-50
64T/tatt
64Wheat/St-10
65OPC-4LL
65OldLond-6
65T-360
65T-4LL
65T/E-45
65T/trans-9
66OPC-132
66T-132
67OPC-20
67OPC/PI-9
67T-20
67T/PI-9
67T/Test/SU-13
68Bz-6
68OPC-3LL
68T-200
68T-278
68T-362AS
68T-3LL
68T/ActionSt-14AM
68T/ActionSt-1AM
68T/ActionSt-9B
68T/G-32
68T/Post-12
69MB-56
69MLB/St-113
69MLBPA/Pin-38
69T-385
69T/St-113
70MLB/St-4
70T-555
70T/CB
71Bz
71Bz/Test-33
71MD
71MLB/St-7
71OPC-605
71T-605
71T/Coins-61
71T/GM-26
71T/Greatest-26
71T/tatt-3
72MB-72
72OPC-195
72T-195
73OPC-545
73T-545
74K-24
74OPC-83
74T-83
74T/St-132
75OPC-205MVP
75T-205MVP
75T/M-205MVP
78TCMA-50
80GlenF/B-26CO
80GlenF/C-25CO
82KMart-12
83Kaline-51M
83MLBPA/Pin-21
84Mother/Giants-11
85CircK-24
86Sf/Dec-48M
88Pac/Leg-94
89Swell-8
90Pac/Legend-65
90Swell/Great-28
91K/Leyenda-5
91Swell/Great-105
92AP/ASG-66
92Card/McDon/Pac-26
92Kodak-1
93TWill-87
Exh47
PM10/Sm-24
PM10/Sm-25

Cepicky, Scott
90Foil/Best-173
90MidwLgAS/GS-7
90SoBend/Best-2
90SoBend/GS-2
91ClBest/Singl-86
91FSLAS/ProC-FSL28
91Saraso/ClBest-15
91Saraso/ProC-1118
92B-297
92B-614FOIL
92BirmB/ProC-2590
92BirmB/SB-80
92ClBest-30
92ProC/Tomorrow-44
92Sky/AASingl-39
92UD/ML-304
93FExcel/ML-152

Cerame, Mike
89Pulaski/ProC-1903
90Pulaski/Best-29
91Pulaski/ClBest-30TR

Ceravolo, Steve
93SoEastern-6

Cerdan, Marcel
47HomogBond-8BOX
D305

Cerefin, Mike
85Osceola/Team-5

Cerio, Steve
92Spring/ClBest-25
92Spring/ProC-871

Cermak, Edward Hugo
(Ed)
No Cards.

Cerny, Chris
88Bakers/Cal-252
89Boise/ProC-1999

Cerny, Mark
89Billings/ProC-2054
90Erie/Star-2

Cerny, Marty
87PortChar-7
88Gaston/ProC-1016
89Miami/I/Star-4
89Miami/II/Star-3

Cerny, Scott
86Cram/NWL-86
87QuadC-24
88CalLgAS-33
88PalmSp/Cal-101
88PalmSp/ProC-1440
89MidldA/GS-10
90MidldA/GS-8

Cerone, Richard Aldo
(Rick)
76SSPC-516
77OPC-76
77T-476R
78OPC-129
78T-469
79BJ/Bubble-5
79OPC-72
79T-152
80OPC-311
80T-591
81D-346
81F-83
81F/St-88
81OPC-335
81T-335
81T/HT
81T/SO-28
81T/St-109
81T/St-248
82D-199
82F-31
82F/St-118
82F/St-238M
82OPC-45
82T-45
82T/St-218
83D-577
83F-376
83F/St-13M
83F/St-8M
83OPC-254
83RoyRog/Disc-1
83T-254
84D-492
84F-121
84Nes/792-617
84OPC-228
84T-617
85D-274
85F-123
85F/Up-U24
85Ho/Braves-6
85OPC-337
85Pol/Atl-5
85T-429
85T/Tr-20T
86D-310
86F-511
86F/Up-U23
86OPC-203
86Pol/Brew-11
86T-747
86T/Tr-22T
87F-340
87T-129
87T/Tr-21T
88D-351
88D/Best-332
88D/RedSox/Bk-NEW
88F-203
88F/Up-U6
88Panini/St-151
88S-486
88S/Tr-21T
88T-561
88T/Tr-27T
89D-398
89D/Best-308
89F-84
89OPC-96
89S-396
89T-96
89T/Big-119
89UD-152
90B-435
90D-305
90F-270
90F/Can-270
90OPC-303
90PublInt/St-451
90S-139
90S/NWest-28
90S/Tr-63T
90T-303
90T/St-1HL
90T/TVYank-20
90T/Tr-21T
90UD-405
91B-468
91F-660
91F/UltraUp-U96
91F/Up-U101
91Kahn/Mets-13
91Leaf-493
91OPC-237
91S-580
91S/RookTr-41T
91StCl-511
91T-237
91T/Tr-21T
92D-335
92L-523
92L/BlkGold-523
92OPC-643
92OPC/Premier-90
92Panini-221
92StCl-705
92T-643
92T/Gold-643
92T/GoldWin-643
92Yank/WIZ80-29

Cerqueira, Jeff
88CapeCod/Sum-83

Cerrud, Roberto
80Utica-14

Cerutti, John
83Knoxvl-3
84Syrac-31
85Syrac-27
86D/Rook-20
86F/Up-U24
86Sf/Rook-36
86Syrac-8
86T/Tr-23T
87D-442
87F-222
87Leaf-210
87OPC-282
87Sf/TPrev-5M
87T-557
87Tor/Fire-3
87ToysRUs-6
88D-321
88F-105
88Leaf-152
88OPC-191
88S-98
88T-191
88Tor/Fire-55
89B-247
89D-467
89F-228
89OPC-347
89S-304
89T-347
89Tor/Fire-55
89UD-129
90B-507
90D-645
90F-78
90F/Can-78
90Leaf-27
90OPC-211
90Panini/St-177
90PublInt/St-511
90S-429
90Sf-86
90T-211
90T/St-195
90Tor/BJ-55
90UD-485
91B-139
91CokeK/Tiger-55
91D-467
91F-172
91F/Up-U22
91Leaf-270
91OPC-687A
91OPC-687B

91S-786
91S/RookTr-40T
91StCl-445
91T-687A
91T-687B
91UD-585
92D-709
92F-129
92OPC-487
92Pawtu/ProC-915
92Pawtu/SB-354
92S-179
92StCl-71
92T-487
92T/Gold-487
92T/GoldWin-487
92UD-487
92USPlayC/Tiger-10H
92USPlayC/Tiger-2D

Cerv, Robert Henry
(Bob)
53T-210
55B-306
56T-288
57T-269
58T-329
59Armour-6
59Bz
59HRDerby-5
59T-100
60Bz-15
60T-415
61P-13
61T-563
61T/St-170
62T-169
79TCMA-162
91T/Arc53-210
92Yank/WIZ60-23
Exh47

Cervantes, Manny
92ClBest-151
92SanBern/ClBest-16
92SanBern/ProC-
93ClBest/MLG-142
93River/Cal-30CO

Cervantes, Raymond
92Erie/ClBest-22
92Erie/ProC-1629

Cesari, Jeff
89Geneva/ProC-1868

Cesarlo, Jim
83TriCit-23

Cespedes, Teodoro
89Everett/Star-4

Cey, Ronald Charles
(Ron)
72T-761R
73OPC-615R
73T-615R
74OPC-315
74T-315
74T/St-42
75Ho-61
75Ho/Twink-61
75OPC-390
75T-390
75T/M-390
76Crane-13
76Ho-63
76MSA/Disc
76OPC-370
76SSPC-75
76T-370
77BurgChef-153
77Ho-89
77Ho/Twink-89
77K-18
77OPC-199
77T-50
77T/CS-14
77T/ClothSt-14
78Ho-93
78K-24
78OPC-130
78SSPC/270-62
78T-630
78Wiffle/Discs-17
79Ho-28
79OPC-94
79T-190
80K-19
80OPC-267
80Pol/Dodg-10
80T-510
81D-296
81F-126
81F/St-3
81OPC-260
81Pol/Dodg-10
81T-260
81T/HT
81T/SO-73
81T/St-177
82D-210
82F-3
82F/St-3
82K-46
82OPC-216
82OPC-367IA
82Pol/Dodg-10
82T-410
82T-411IA
82T/St-51
83D-84
83D/AAS-21
83F-204
83F/St-11M
83F/St-15M
83OPC-15
83OPC/St-244
83T-15
83T/Fold-2M
83T/St-244
83T/Tr-19
83Thorn-11
84Cub/Uno-7M
84D-361
84Drake-7
84F-490
84Nes/792-357
84OPC-357
84SevenUp-11
84T-357
84T/RD-12
84T/St-41
85D-320
85Drake-6
85F-52
85F/St-19
85FunFood/Pin-89
85Leaf-84
85OPC-366
85SevenUp-11
85T-768
85T/St-42
86Cub/Unocal-3
86D-198
86F-363
86Gator-11
86OPC-194
86Sf-130M
86T-669
87F-556
87OPC-322
87OPC-C
87Smok/Dodg-4
87T-767
87T-C
87T/Tr-22T
88Smok/Dodg-15M
88Smok/Dodg-21M
88Smok/Dodg-27
89Smok/Dodg-82
90Target-121
93AP/ASG-163
93TWill-10

Chacon, Elio R.
60T-543
62T-256
66Pep/Tul
91WIZMets-68

Chacon, Troy
88CapeCod/Sum-183

Chadbourne, Chester
No Cards.

Chadwick, Henry
50Call
50W576-12
76Shakey-16
80Perez/HOF-16
80SSPC/HOF
90LitSun-2

Chadwick, Ray
86Edmon-3
87D-505
88BirmB/Best-4
90AAASingl/ProC-593
90Omaha/CMC-2
90Omaha/ProC-58
90ProC/Singl-177

Chadwick, Robert
86NewBrit-6TR
87NewBrit-9TR
88NewBrit/ProC-893

Chafin, John
88Utica/Pucko-14
91Elmira/ClBest-23
91Elmira/ProC-3263

Chagnon, Leon
R314/Can

Chajin, David
91Johnson/ProC-3970

Chakales, Bob
52NumNum-9
52T-120
55B-148
57T-261
60Maple-2
61BeeHive-4
91Crown/Orio-74

Chalk, David Lee
(Dave)
74OPC-597R
74T-597R
75Ho-46
75Ho/Twink-46
75OPC-64
75T-64
75T/M-64
76Ho-59
76Ho/Twink-59
76OPC-52
76SSPC-194
76T-52
77BurgChef-119
77T-315
78SSPC/270-198
78T-178
79OPC-362
79T-682
80OPC-137
80T-261
81D-101
81F-35
82D-590
82F-407
82T-462
93Rang/Keeb-101

Chalmers, George
D329-29
D350/2-27
M101/4-29
M101/5-27
T207
T222

Chamberlain, Bill
78Wausau

Chamberlain, Craig
80T-417
81Omaha-4
81T-274
82Phoenix
83Phoenix/BHN-23
88CharlK/Pep-12

Chamberlain, Elton
N172

Chamberlain, Joseph
No Cards.

Chamberlain, Matt
93LSU/McDag-11
93Welland/ProC-3348

Chamberlain, Tom
78StPete
79ArkTr-19

Chamberlain, Wesley
(Wes)
87Watertn-12
88Augusta/ProC-359
89BBAmAA/BPro-AA1
89EastLgAS/ProC-5
89Harris/ProC-296
89Harris/Star-5
89Star/IISingl-171
90AAASingl/ProC-501
90BuffB/CMC-23
90BuffB/ProC-386
90BuffB/Team-6
90ProC/Singl-23
91B-505
91Classic/200-92
91Classic/I-80
91Classic/III-T8
91D-423RR
91D/Rook-3
91F-391
91Leaf-178
91Leaf/Stud-211
91OPC-603
91Phill/Medford-8
91S-713RP
91S/Rook40-14
91ScranWB/ProC-2550
91StCl-317
91T-603A
91T-603B
91T/90Debut-29
91UD-626
91Ultra-258
92B-412
92CJ/DI-18
92Classic/Game200-63
92Classic/II-T55
92D-384
92F-524
92F/RookSIns-16
92JDean/18-17
92L-453
92L/BlkGold-453
92OPC-14
92Phill/Med-8
92Pinn-36
92ProC/Tomorrow-295
92S-384
92S/100RisSt-25
92S/Impact-11
92ScranWB/ProC-2459
92StCl-396
92Studio-72
92T-14
92T/Gold-14
92T/GoldWin-14
92UD-347
92Ultra-239
93B-456
93D-304
93F-99
93L-338
93OPC-45
93Pac/Spanish-232
93Panini-275
93Phill/Med-8
93Pinn-328
93S-168
93Select-217
93StCl-34
93StCl/1stDay-34
93StCl/Phill-13
93Studio-19
93T-154
93T/Gold-154
93UD-267
93Ultra-85
94D-101
94F-584
94L-243
94OPC-27
94Pac/Cr-470
94Phill/Med-4
94Pinn-201
94Pinn/Artist-201
94Pinn/Museum-201
94S-438
94Select-67
94StCl-432
94StCl/1stDay-432
94StCl/Gold-432
94StCl/Team-238
94T-419
94T/Finest-123
94T/FinestRef-123
94T/Gold-419
94UD-148
94UD/CollC-76
94UD/CollC/Gold-76
94UD/CollC/Silv-76
94UD/ElecD-148
94Ultra-542

Chamberlin, Buck
79Toledo-13
80Toledo-14
81Toledo-2
82Toledo-24

Chambers, Albert E.
(Al)
81LynnS-20
82SLCity-5
83D-649
83SLCity-21
84Cram/PCL-188
85Cram/PCL-80
85D-389
85T-277FDP
87ColAst/ProC-1

Chambers, Carl
87Watlo-17

Chambers, Cliff
47Signal
49Eureka-157
50B-202
51B-131
51FB
51T/RB-25
52B-14
52RM-NL4
52StarCal-93C
52StarCal/L-81C
52T-68
53Hunter
54B-126

Chambers, Jeff
89Elizab/Star-31

Chambers, Mark
91Pulaski/ClBest-11
91Pulaski/ProC-4017
92Pulaski/ClBest-5
92Pulaski/ProC-3189
93Macon/ClBest-6
93Macon/ProC-1412

Chambers, Travis
86Clearw-3
87Maine-19
87Maine/TCMA-3
88Maine/CMC-2
88Maine/ProC-283
89Jaxvl/Best-10
89Jaxvl/ProC-162
90AAASingl/ProC-565
90Indianap/CMC-4
90Indianap/ProC-282
90ProC/Singl-54

Chambliss, Carroll C.
(Chris)
72OPC-142
72T-142
73OPC-11
73T-11
74OPC-384
74T-384
74T/DE-15
74T/St-162
75OPC-585
75T-585
75T/M-585
76Ho-58
76Ho/Twink-58
76OPC-65
76SSPC-434
76SSPC/MetsY-Y14
76T-65
77BK/Y-12
77BurgChef-173
77Ho-98
77Ho/Twink-98
77K-52
77OPC-49
77T-220
78BK/Y-12
78K-13
78OPC-145
78SSPC/270-7
78T-485
78Wiffle/Discs-18
79BK/Y-12
79K-37
79OPC-171
79T-335
80OPC-328
80T-625
81D-219
81F-252
81F/St-81
81OPC-155
81Pol/Atl-10
81T-155
81T/St-147
82BK/Lids-6
82D-47
82F-433
82F/St-70

82K-52
82OPC-320
82OPC-321IA
82Pol/Atl-10
82T-320
82T-321IA
82T/St-17
82T/StVar-17
83D-123
83F-134
83F/St-10M
83F/St-5M
83OPC-11
83OPC/St-212
83Pol/Atl-10
83T-792
83T/St-212
84D-537
84D/AAS-29
84F-175
84Nes/792-50
84OPC-50
84Pol/Atl-10
84T-50
84T/RD-13
84T/St-28
85D-287
85F-322
85FunFood/Pin-123
85Ho/Braves-7
85Leaf-168
85OPC-187
85Pol/Atl-10
85T-518
85T/St-29
86D-618
86F-512
86Pol/Atl-10
86T-293
87F-513
87OPC-204
87T-777
89London/ProC-1378MG
91AA/LineD-224MG
91Greenvl/ClBest-25MG
91Greenvl/LineD-224MG
91Greenvl/ProC-3018MG
92AP/ASG-55
92Richm/Bleach-5MG
92Richm/Comix-3MG
92Richm/ProC-391MG
92Richm/SB-449MG
92Yank/WIZ70-32
92Yank/WIZ80-30
92Yank/WIZAS-9

Champ, Jeff
89Penin/Star-3

Champagne, Andre
89OK-8
90OK-4

Champagne, Boo
86Cram/NWL-44
87FtMyr-8

Champion, Billy
70OPC-149
70T-149
71MLB/St-173
71OPC-323
71T-323
72T-599
73OPC-74
73T-74
74OPC-391
74T-391
75Ho-118
75OPC-256
75T-256
75T/M-256
76OPC-501
76T-501

Champion, Brian
88BurlB/ProC-10
89Durham/Star-5
89Durham/Team-5
89Star/Wax-69
90CLAS/CL-31
90Durham/Team-3
90Greenvl/Best-3
91AA/LineD-203
91ClBest/Singl-177
91Greenvl/ClBest-16
91Greenvl/LineD-203
91Greenvl/ProC-3010

Champion, Keith
88Savan/ProC-337
89Savan/ProC-344
90Spring/Best-26MG
92Watlo/ClBest-26MG
92Watlo/ProC-2156MG

Champion, Kirk
89SoBend/GS-5
90SoBend/Best-27CO
90SoBend/GS-28CO
91SoBend/ClBest-26CO
91SoBend/ProC-2874CO
92Saraso/ClBest-28CO
92Saraso/ProC-226CO

Champion, Randall
83StPete-14
87ArkTr-8

Champion, Robert M.
(Mike)
77Padre/SchCd-5
77Padre/SchCd-6
77T-494R
78Padre/FamFun-5
78T-683
79Tacoma-14
80Tacoma-16

Champlin, Kelly
91FresnoSt/Smok-2

Chance, Dean
62T-194
63Exh
63J-32
63P-32
63T-355
63T-6LL
64T-32
64T/Coins-67
64T/S-16
65Bz-5
65OPC-11LL
65OPC-140
65OPC-7LL
65OPC-9LL
65OldLond-22
65T-11LL
65T-140
65T-7LL
65T-9LL
65T/E-66
65T/trans-10
65T/trans-42
66Bz-25
66T-340
66T/RO-16
66T/RO-83
67Bz-25
67CokeCap/Twin-14
67T-380
67T/Test/SU-12
68Bz-10
68Dexter-23
68OPC-10LL
68OPC-12LL
68T-10LL
68T-12LL
68T-255
68T/ActionSt-13AM
68T/ActionSt-4AM
68T/G-16
68T/Post-1
69MB-57
69MLB/St-66
69MLBPA/Pin-5
69T-620
69T/S-21
69T/St-193
70K-67
70MLB/St-195
70T-625
71MLB/St-148
71OPC-36
71T-36
72MB-73
78Twin/Frisz-4
80Marchant-7
82Ohio/HOF-4
89Smok/Angels-2
89Swell-89
91WIZMets-69
94TedW-14
Exh47

Chance, Frank Leroy
10Domino-22
11Diamond-7
11Helmar-92
12Sweet/Pin-81A
12Sweet/Pin-81BLL
14CJ-99
14Piedmont/St-10
40PlayBall-234
48Exh/HOF
50Callahan
50W576-13
60Exh/HOF-6
60F-50
61F-98
63Bz/ATG-25
69Bz/Sm
73F/Wild-2
76Motor-11
76Shakey-40
77Galasso-161
80Marchant/HOF-5
80Pac/Leg-84
80Perez/HOF-40
80SSPC/HOF
81Conlon-12
84Cub/Uno-7
84Cub/Uno-8MG
90Perez/GreatMom-40M
92Cub/OldStyle-6
92Yank/WIZHOF-4
93Conlon-819
93UD/ATH-148M
93UD/ATH-30
93UD/T202-9M
94Conlon-1166
D304
D350/2-28
E101
E103
E105
E107
E224
E254
E270/1
E270/2
E286
E90/1
E90/3
E91
E92
E93
E94
E95
E98
M101/5-28
M116
PM1-2
S74-59
T201
T202
T204
T205
T206
T207
T213/blue
T213/brown
T215/blue
T215/brown
T216
T222
T3-47
W555
WG3-9
WG4-3
WG5-8
WG6-8

Chance, Robert
(Bob)
64T-146R
65Bz-18
65OPC-224
65T-224
66T-564
67T-349
69T-523
78TCMA-82

Chance, Tony
86Macon-6
86PrWill-5
87Salem-25
88Harris/ProC-854
89UD-3SR
90AAASingl/ProC-470
90ProC/Singl-319
90RochR/CMC-19
90RochR/ProC-713
90Rochester/L&U-19
91AAA/LineD-451
91RochR/LineD-451
91RochR/ProC-1913
92Iowa/ProC-4060
92Iowa/SB-206

Chandler, A.B.
(Happy)
49Eureka-1
50Callahan
50W576-14
80Perez/HOF-178
80SSPC/HOF
89HOF/St-97

Chandler, Bob
90Padre/MagUno-16ANN
91Padre/Coke-1ANN

Chandler, Chris
92StCath/ClBest-21
92StCath/ProC-3393

Chandler, Ed
52Mother-63
90Target-122

Chandler, George
85Clovis-9ACO

Chandler, Ken
81Wisco-13

Chandler, Spud
40PlayBall-181
43Playball-1
44Yank/St-5
89Pac/Leg-136
92Yank/WIZAS-10
93Conlon-763
94Conlon-1068
Exh47

Chaney, Darrel Lee
69T-624R
70OPC-3
70T-3
71MLB/St-53
71OPC-632
71T-632
72OPC-136
72T-136
73OPC-507
73T-507
74OPC-559
74T-559
75OPC-581
75T-581
75T/M-581
76OPC-259
76SSPC-33
76T-259
76T/Tr-259T
77BurgChef-216
77Ho-57
77Ho/Twink-57
77OPC-134
77T-384
78T-443
79OPC-91
79T-184

Chaney, Keith
91Pulaski/ClBest-5
91Pulaski/ProC-4011

Chaney, Norma
89Welland/Pucko-35M

Channell, Lester C.
(Les)
No Cards.

Chant, Charles J.
(Charlie)
75IntLgAS/Broder-3
75PCL/AS-3
75Tucson-7
75Tucson/Caruso-8
75Tucson/Team-2

Chanye, Bruce
83MidldC-10

Chapin, Darrin
88FtLaud/Star-4
89Albany/ProC-340
89Albany/Star-3
89Colum/CMC-30
90A&AASingle/ProC-19
90AAASingl/ProC-318
90Albany/ProC-1029
90Albany/Star-1
90ColClip/CMC-20
90ColClip/ProC-668
90ProC/Singl-220
90Star/ISingl-51
91AAA/LineD-103
91ColClip/LineD-103
91ColClip/ProC-590
92D-745
92ScranWB/ProC-2441
92ScranWB/SB-481
92Sky/AAASingl-219
92T/91Debut-33

Chaplin, Bert Edgar
(Ed)
No Cards.

Chaplin, Tiny
94Conlon-1308

Chapman, Calvin Louis
No Cards.

Chapman, Dan
(AGM)
88Stockton/Cal-205
88Stockton/ProC-751
89Stockton/Best-28
89Stockton/Cal-174
89Stockton/ProC-398
89Stockton/Star-23

Chapman, Dave
79Ashvl/TCMA-7

Chapman, Glenn J.
90Target-911

Chapman, Harry E.
No Cards.

Chapman, John Curtis
(Jack)
No Cards.

Chapman, Kelvin Keith
77Wausau
79Tidew-18
80Tidew-18
81Syrac-13
81Syrac/Team-6
82Tidew-2
83Tidew-7
84Tidew-27
85D-626
85F-75
85T-751
86T-492
91WIZMets-70

Chapman, Ken
92Yakima/ClBest-12
92Yakima/ProC-3457

Chapman, Mark
88Beloit/GS-10
88MidwLAS/GS-59
89ElPaso/GS-4
90ElPaso/GS-6
91AA/LineD-178
91ElPaso/LineD-178
91ElPaso/ProC-2739
92Harris/ProC-455
92Harris/SB-279

Chapman, Nathan
79Colum-22
82Nashvl-6

Chapman, Raymond J.
(Ray)
BF2-21
D327
D328-26
D329-30
D350/2-29
E135-26
M101/4-30
M101/5-29

Chapman, Ron
85Albany-15

Chapman, Samuel Blake
(Sam)
40PlayBall-194
41DP-125
41PlayBall-44
48L-26
49B-112
50B-104
51B-9
51T/BB-52
52Mother-33
52NTea

Chapman, William B.
(Ben)
32Orbit/num-99
33G-191
34DS-38
34G-9
35BU-188

35BU-62
37OPC-130
41DP-74
52T-391MG
77Galasso-197
88Conlon/3-6
88Conlon/AmAS-4
90Target-123
92Yank/WIZAS-11
93Conlon-688
94Conlon-1081
R303/A
R303/B
R310
R313
R332-40
V300
V351B-8
V354-5I
V355-90

Chappas, Harold Perry
(Harry)
79Iowa/Pol-5
80T-347

Chappell, Laverne A.
(Larry)
No Cards.

Chappelle, William
T206
T213/blue

Charboneau, Joseph
(Joe)
81D-82
81Drake-21
81F-397
81K-54
81OPC-13
81Sqt-32
81T-13
81T/SO-12
81T/St-66
82D-363
82F-362
82F/St-192
82OPC-211
82T-630
82Wheat/Ind
83BuffB-23
84PrWill-15
88Chatt/Team-3
93MCI-6
93UD/ATH-31

Charbonnet, Mark
89BurlInd/Star-4
90Reno/Cal-269
90Watertn/Star-3
91ColInd/ClBest-7
91ColInd/ProC-1497
92ColRS/ClBest-13
93Kinston/Team-3

Charland, Colin
86Cram/NWL-76
87PalmSp-9
88CalLgAS-31
88PalmSp/Cal-85
88PalmSp/ProC-1447
89Edmon/CMC-6
89Edmon/ProC-565
90F-640M
90F/Can-640M
92Canton/ProC-683
92Canton/SB-110
92Sky/AASingl-48

Charles, Edwin
(Ed)
52Laval-19
62T-595R
63J-89
63P-89
63T-67
64T-475
64T/Coins-117
64T/SU
64T/St-1
65OPC-35
65T-35
66T-422
66T/RO-106
66T/RO-17
67CokeCap/A's-3
67CokeCap/ALAS-25
67CokeCap/AS-35
67OPC-182
67T-182
68T-563
69MB-58
69MLB/St-164
69T-245
69T/St-62
78TCMA-25
90Swell/Great-123
91WIZMets-71
94Mets/69-18

Charles, Ezzard
51BR-A13

Charles, Frank
91Everett/ClBest-11
91Everett/ProC-3917
92ProC/Tomorrow-357

Charles, Raymond
(Chappy)
M116
T206
T213/brown

Charleston, Oscar
74Laugh/Black-34
76Laugh/Clown-30
76Shakey-152
80Perez/HOF-152
86Negro/Frit-24
86Negro/Frit-4
86Negro/Frit-8
88Conlon/NegAS-2
88Negro/Duques-7
90Negro/Star-36
93TWill-102

Charlton, Norm
86Vermont-3
87Nashvl-2
88Nashvl/CMC-3
88Nashvl/ProC-488
88Nashvl/Team-6
88TripleA/ASCMC-12
89D-544
89F-155
89Kahn/Reds-37
89S-646
89S/YS/II-15
89T-737
89UD/Ext-783
90D-426
90F-416
90F/Can-416
90Kahn/Reds-6
90Leaf-334
90OPC-289
90PublInt/St-24
90S-248
90T-289
90UD-566
91B-690
91D-384
91F-60
91Kahn/Reds-37
91Leaf-414
91OPC-309
91Pep/Reds-5
91S-530
91StCl-305
91T-309
91UD-394
91Ultra-90
92D-102
92F-402
92L-120
92L/BlkGold-120
92OPC-649
92Pinn-216
92Reds/Kahn-37
92S-267
92StCl-530
92Studio-21
92T-649
92T/Gold-649
92T/GoldWin-649
92TripleP-163
92UD-677
92Ultra-482
93B-655
93D-238
93F-32
93F/Final-266
93Flair-269
93L-287
93Mother/Mar-10
93OPC-98
93OPC/Premier-50
93Pac/Spanish-620
93Pinn-439
93S-375
93Select-207
93Select/RookTr-96T
93StCl-659
93StCl/1stDay-659
93StCl/Mar-13
93StCl/MurphyS-144
93T-57
93T/Finest-178
93T/FinestRef-178
93T/Gold-57
93T/Tr-123T
93UD-663
93UD/SP-129
93Ultra-615
94D-96
94F-283
94Pac/Cr-565
94Pinn-216
94Pinn/Artist-216
94Pinn/Museum-216
94S-549

Charno, Joe
88Ashvl/ProC-1055
89Ashvl/ProC-962

Charpia, Reed
89Helena/SP-16

Charry, Stephen
83Madis/Frit-2TD

Chartak, Michael G.
(Mike)
No Cards.

Charton, Frank
(Pete)
64T-459R
66T-329

Chase, Dave
80Ander-12

Chase, Harold Homer
(Hal)
10Domino-23
11Diamond-8
11Helmar-40
12Sweet/Pin-32A
12Sweet/Pin-32B
14Piedmont/St-11
75F/Pion-22
75Shakey-13
77Galasso-146
88Conlon/4-5
91Conlon/Sport-160
D303
D304
E101
E102
E103
E106
E254
E270/2
E300
E90/1
E92
E93
E98
M116
S74-20
T201
T202
T205
T206
T213/blue
T213/brown
T216
T3-6
W514-114
W555
WG5-9
WG6-9

Chase, Ken
39PlayBall-59
40PlayBall-19

Chase, Scott
89Oneonta/ProC-2107

Chasey, Mark
88Utica/Pucko-4
89SoBend/GS-21
90Saraso/Star-4
91AA/LineD-54
91BirmB/LineD-54
91BirmB/ProC-1459

Chasin, David
91Johnson/ClBest-22

Chasteen, Steve
83Idaho-2

Chatham, Charles L.
(Buster)
94Conlon-1287

Chatterton, Christopher
92Bluefld/ClBest-14
92Bluefld/ProC-2353

Chatterton, James M.
(Jim)
No Cards.

Chauncey, Keathel
75Anderson/TCMA-5
76SanAn/Team-6
77Tucson
78Cr/PCL-58
79Tucson-19
80WHave-21
81Toledo-19

Chavarria, Oswaldo Q.
(Ossie)
67CokeCap/A's-6
67T-344

Chaves, Rafael
86CharRain-5
92HighD/ClBest-23
93ClBest/MLG-56

Chavez, Anthony
92Boise/ClBest-19
92Boise/ProC-3619

Chavez, Carlos
92Bluefld/ClBest-22
92Bluefld/ProC-2354

Chavez, Devin
91Hunting/ClBest-7
91Hunting/ProC-3341

Chavez, Eric
92Bluefld/ProC-2364
94ClBest/Gold-5
94FExcel-3

Chavez, Harold P.
WG7-9

Chavez, Joe
86Beaum-6TR
88Wichita-TR
89Wichita/Rock-TR

Chavez, Pedro
83BirmB-21
86Nashvl-4
87GlenF-21
88Toledo/CMC-17
88Toledo/ProC-601

Chavez, Rafael
88CalLgAS-42
88River/Cal-209
88River/ProC-1429
89AubAs/ProC-25
89Wichita/Rock-14
90Wichita/Rock-4
91AA/LineD-603
91Wichita/LineD-603
91Wichita/ProC-2592
91Wichita/Rock-2

Chavez, Raul
91BurlAs/ClBest-13
91BurlAs/ProC-2807
92Ashvl/ClBest-8

Chavez, Samuel
(Sam)
88Cedar/ProC-1160
89SoBend/GS-9
90Huntsvl/Best-3

Chech, Charles
E90/1
T204

Checo, Pedro
89Bristol/Star-4

Cheek, Carey
86PrWill-6

Cheek, Harry G.
(Harry)
No Cards.

Cheek, Jeff
93StCath/ClBest-5
93StCath/ProC-3968

Cheek, Patrick
90Princet/DIMD-4
91Batavia/ClBest-7
91Batavia/ProC-3489

Cheetham, Sean
90A&AASingle/ProC-185
90Hunting/ProC-3273
90LitSun/HSPros-5
90LitSun/HSProsG-5
91B-414
91ClBest/Singl-231
91WinSalem/ClBest-3
91WinSalem/ProC-2822
92ClBest-315
92WinSalem/ClBest-6
92WinSalem/ProC-1201

Cheeves, Virgil
(Chief)
E120
E126-23
V61-84

Chelette, Mark
80SanJose/JITB-5
81Wausau-23

Chelini, Dan
83Butte-2

Chelini, Italo
35BU-114

Chenevey, Jim
88Madis-10
88MidwLAS/GS-53

Cheney, Larry
14CJ-89
15CJ-89
16FleischBrd-15
90Target-124
D328-27
D329-31
D350/2-30
E135-27
M101/4-31
M101/5-30
WG4-4

Cheney, Tom
57T-359
61T-494
63Exh
63F-27
63J-99
63P-99
78TCMA-85
Exh47
WG9-27

Cherry, Gus
85Omaha-6

Cherry, Joe
76Laugh/Clown-15
76Laugh/Clown-32

Cherry, Lamar
90LitSun/HSPros-3
90LitSun/HSProsG-3
91Martins/ClBest-12
91Martins/ProC-3459
92Batavia/ClBest-5
92Batavia/ProC-3271
92Spartan/ClBest-15
92Spartan/ProC-1275

Cherry, Michael
85VeroB-23
86VeroB-3

Cherry, Paul
83Spring/Frit-3
86ArkTr-4
87Louisvl-9
88Toledo/CMC-9
88Toledo/ProC-591

Chervinko, Paul
90Target-912

Chesbro, Jack
48Exh/HOF
50Callahan
50W576-15
61F-13
61T-407M
63Bz/ATG-3
69Bz/Sm
72F/FFeat-39
72Laugh/GF-12
76Shakey-41
79T-416M
80Perez/HOF-41
80SSPC/HOF
85Woolwth-7
92Yank/WIZHOF-5
E107
T206
WG2-7

Cheshire, Donnie
78StPete

Chesnes, Bob
49B-13
50B-70

Cheso, Reno
49Sommer-11
53Mother-33
Chestnut, Troy
87Knoxvl-7
Chevalier, Bonel
89Belling/Legoe-23
90Bend/Legoe-7
Chevez, Tony
78RochR
79RochR-19
91Crown/Orio-75
Chevolek, Tom
80ElPaso-5
Chewning, David
93MissSt-48M
Chiamparino, Scott
88Huntsvl/BK-2
88Modesto-8
88Modesto/Cal-64
90AAAGame/ProC-49
90AAASingl/ProC-133
90ProC/Singl-580
90S/Tr-108T
90Tacoma/CMC-3
90Tacoma/ProC-86
91B-282
91Classic/200-183
91Classic/I-84
91D-42RR
91D/Preview-3
91Leaf-401
91Leaf/Stud-122
91MajorLg/Pins-37
91Mother/Rang-14
91OPC-676
91S-352A
91S-352B
91S/100RisSt-14
91S/Rook40-29
91StCl-384
91T-676
91T/90Debut-30
91UD-8SR
91Ultra-375MLP
92Mother/Rang-14
92OPC-277
92S-688
92StCl-896
92T-277
92T/Gold-277
92T/GoldWin-277
93D-738
93F-422
93Rang/Keeb-102
93S-386
93StCl/Marlin-7
93T-64
93T-711
93T/Gold-64
93T/Gold-711
93TripleP-63
Chick, Bruce
91CLAS/ProC-CAR22
91ClBest/Singl-13
91LynchRS/ClBest-20
91LynchRS/ProC-1210
92NewBrit/ProC-446
92NewBrit/SB-480
92Sky/AASingl-204
Chicken, San Diego
82D-531
83D-645
84D-651
84Smok/Padres-4
Chiffer, Floyd
81Hawaii
81Hawaii/TCMA-18
83D-44
83F-354
83T-298
85Toledo-32
87Richm/Bob-2
87Richm/Crown-28
87Richm/TCMA-2
Chikida, Honen
89Salinas/ProC-1812
Childers, Bob
88Alaska/Team-6
Childers, Chabon
92OKSt-4
Childers, Jeffrey
85Beaum-1
88Modesto-7
88Wichita-30
Childress, Billy
92Hunting/ProC-3137
Childress, Chip
83Durham-1
84Durham-13
85Durham-20
86Greenvl/Team-5
Childress, Rocky
85Cram/PCL-31
85Phill/TastyK-45
86Phill/TastyK-50
87Tucson-10
88D-554
88F-442
88T-643
88Tucson/CMC-8
88Tucson/JP-6
88Tucson/ProC-181
89Tucson/CMC-1
89Tucson/JP-4
89Tucson/ProC-194
90AAASingl/ProC-267
90ProC/Singl-354
90Tidew/CMC-3
90Tidew/ProC-536
Childress, Willie J.
87Greenvl/Best-11
Childs, Clarence A.
(Cupid)
N172
Childs, Mike
79Ashvl/TCMA-20
Childs, Peter Pierre
(Pete)
No Cards.
Chiles, Barry
90Pulaski/Best-2
90Pulaski/ProC-3100
91Macon/ClBest-1
91Macon/ProC-855
92Durham/ClBest-20
92Durham/ProC-1092
92Durham/Team-34
93Durham/Team-4
Chiles, Pearce Nuget
No Cards.
Chiles, Richard F.
(Rich)
72OPC-56
72T-56
73OPC-617
73T-617
78T-193
78Twin/FriszP-4
79T-498
79Tacoma-20
91WIZMets-72
92CaroMud/ProC-1196
92CaroMud/SB-150CO
Chimelis, Joel
88SoOreg/ProC-1703
89Modesto/Cal-279
89Modesto/Chong-22
90Modesto/Chong-5
90Reno/Cal-267
91AA/LineD-282
91Huntsvl/ClBest-7
91Huntsvl/LineD-282
91Huntsvl/Team-5
91HuntsvlProC-1802
92ClBest/Up-446
92Shrev/ProC-3878
92Shrev/SB-578
93B-464
93FExcel/ML-114
Ching, Maurice
(Mo)
83Greens-17
84Greens-22
86Albany/TCMA-18
Chiozza, Louis Peo
(Lou)
34DS-80
38ONG/Pin-2
39PlayBall-58
40PlayBall-157
41G-3
41G-3
94Conlon-1074
Chipman, Robert
(Bob)
44Playball-33
47TipTop
49B-184
49Eureka-54
50B-192
52B-228
52T-388
90Target-125
Chipple, Walter John
(Walt)
No Cards.
Chireno, Manny
87Beloit-24
Chism, Thomas R.
(Tom)
78RochR
79RochR-18
81RochR-4
82RochR-21
83RochR-23
91Crown/Orio-76
Chisum, Dave
91BurlInd/ProC-3306
92Watertn/ClBest-16
92Watertn/ProC-3246
Chiti, Dom
79Savan-1
85CharlO-13C
86RochR-2C
87RochR-15C
87RochR/TCMA-25C
88RochR/Gov-28
88RochR/ProC-212
88RochR/Team-5
92Indian/McDon-30M
Chiti, Harry Dominick
53B/Col-7
55B-304
56T-179
58T-119
59T-79
60T-339
61T-269
61T/St-149
62T-253
91WIZMets-73
Chitren, Stephen
(Steve)
87Anchora-4
89Medford/Best-20
90Foil/Best-279
90Huntsvl/Best-4
91B-214
91D-431RR
91Leaf-486
91Mother/A's-27
91S-760RP
91T/90Debut-31
91UD/Ext-753
91Ultra-376MLP
92B-506
92D-385
92F-253
92F/RookSIns-14
92L-32
92L/BlkGold-32
92OPC-379
92Pinn-236
92S-202
92Sky/AAASingl-238
92StCl-518
92T-379
92T/Gold-379
92T/GoldWin-379
92Tacoma/ProC-2496
92Tacoma/SB-530
92UD-471
Chittum, Nelson
60T-296
Chiyomaru, Akihiko
90Gate/ProC-3339
90Gate/SportP-6
Chlan, Greg
75Omaha/Team-4
Chlupsa, Bob
71OPC-594R
71T-594R
Chmil, Steve
83Durham-2
Choate, Don
61Union
Choate, Mark
90MedHat/Best-6
91Myrtle/ClBest-18
91Myrtle/ProC-2952
92StCath/ClBest-13
92StCath/ProC-3394
Cholowsky, Dan
91Classic/DP-35
91FrRow/DP-5
92ClBest-370
92Savan/ClBest-18
92Savan/ProC-667
92StCl/Dome-27
93B-488
93ClBest/MLG-95
93SALAS/II-6
93SALAS/IICS-8
Chouinard, Bobby
92Kane/ClBest-20
92Kane/ProC-82
92Kane/Team-5
92MidwLAS/Team-5
93Modesto/ClBest-5
93Modesto/ProC-791
Chouinard, Felix G.
No Cards.
Chozen, Harry Kenneth
No Cards.
Chris, Mike
80Evansvl-5
80T-666R
81Evansvl-3
82Phoenix
85Cram/PCL-149
Chrisley, Barbra O.
(Neil)
57T-320
58T-303
59T-189
60L-117
60T-273
62T-308
Chrisman, Jim
91AppFx/ClBest-2
91AppFx/ProC-1708
92BBCity/ClBest-10
92BBCity/ProC-3837
Christ, Michael
87Chatt/Best-11
88Calgary/CMC-6
Christenbury, Lloyd
V100
Christensen, Bruce R.
75Phoenix/Caruso-10
75Phoenix/CircleK-15
76Phoenix/Coke-2
Christensen, Jim
82Toledo-13
83Tacoma-30A
Christensen, John L.
84Tidew-4
86D-360
86Pawtu-5
86Pawtu-6
86T-287
87Mother/Sea-27
87T/Tr-23T
88Calgary/CMC-17
88Calgary/ProC-794
88S-419
88T-413
89F-108
89Portl/CMC-19
89Portl/ProC-214
91WIZMets-74
Christensen, Walter
(Cuckoo)
No Cards.
Christenson, Gary
81Omaha-5
Christenson, Kim
83AppFx/Frit-4
84PrWill-25
85Nashua-5
Christenson, Larry
74OPC-587
74T-587
75OPC-551
75T-551
75T/M-551
76OPC-634
76SSPC-460
76T-634
77OPC-194
77T-59
78OPC-17
78SSPC/270-47
78T-247
79BK/P-5
79OPC-260
79T-493
80BK/P-16
80OPC-89
80T-161
81F-8
81T-346
82D-219
82F-244
82T-544
83D-345
83F-156
83F/St-13M
83OPC-286
83T-668
84Nes/792-252
84T-252
Christian, Eddie
92FrRow/DP-46
93T-683M
93T/Gold-683M
Christian, Rick
86Erie-6
87Erie-1
88Hamil/ProC-1724
89StPete/Star-6
90ArkTr/GS-8
91AA/LineD-29
91ArkTr/LineD-29
91ArkTr/ProC-1299
92Louisvl/SB-256
Christian, Robert
69OPC-173R
69T-173R
69T/4in1-21
70OPC-51
70T-51
Christiansen, Clay
82Nashvl-7
83Colum-9
84Colum-12
84Colum/Pol-5
85Colum-4
85Colum/Pol-5
85D-396
85T-211
86Albany/TCMA-28
86Colum-3
86Colum/Pol-3
88Tucson/ProC-179
92Yank/WIZ80-31
Christiansen, Jason
92Augusta/ClBest-7
92Salem/ClBest-11
92Salem/ProC-55
Christiansen, Jeff
89Anchora-6
Christianson, Alex
79Wausau-19
Christman, Mark J.
44Playball-2
49B-121
Christman, Scott
94B-211
94ClBest/Gold-153
94ClBest/GoldLP-2
94Pinn-266
94Pinn/Artist-266
94Pinn/Museum-266
Christmas, Maurice
93ClBest/MLG-148
Christmas, Scott
94S-548
Christmas, Stephen R.
(Steve)
80Water-3
81Water-12
82Indianap-22
83Tucson-12
85BuffB-4
86Gator-18
86Iowa-6
Christofferson, Bob
83Tacoma-25B
Christopher, Fred
86Cram/NWL-143
87Spartan-27
88Clearw/Star-7
89Clearw/Star-6
89Reading/Star-7
90Reading/ProC-1215
Christopher, Joe
61T-82

63T-217
64T-546
65Bz-20
65T-495
65T/E-52
65T/trans-43
66T-343
78TCMA-7
91WIZMets-75
WG10-25
Christopher, Lloyd
43Centen-4
44Centen-3
47Signal
47TipTop
48Signal
48Smith
49Remar
50Remar
Christopher, Mike
86FtLaud-6
87FtLaud-8
88Albany/ProC-1337
89Albany/Best-22
89Albany/ProC-321
89Albany/Star-4
90AAASingl/ProC-57
90Albuq/CMC-1
90Albuq/ProC-336
90Albuq/Trib-4
90ProC/Singl-403
91AAA/LineD-3
91Albuq/LineD-3
91Albuq/ProC-1134
92B-374
92ColoSp/ProC-744
92ColoSp/SB-80
92D/Rook-23
92F-654
92Sky/AAASingl-36
92StCl-612
92T/91Debut-34
93Indian/WUAB-5
93OPC/Premier-11
93Pac/Spanish-408
93StCl-308
93StCl/1stDay-308
93T-786
93T/Gold-786
Christopher, Terry
92Beloit/ClBest-3
92Beloit/ProC-397
Christopher, Tyron
92GulfCY/ProC-3782
Christopherson, Eric
89Anchora-7
89SanDiegoSt/Smok-6
90A&AASingle/ProC-170
90Classic/DP-19
90Classic/III-87
90Everett/Best-13
90Everett/ProC-3129
90SDSt-3
91B-635
91ClBest/Singl-320
91Clinton/ClBest-14
91Clinton/ProC-836
91MidwLAS/ProC-3
91S-672FDP
92B-38
92ClBest-254
92ProC/Tomorrow-354
92Shrev/ProC-3874
92Shrev/SB-579
92Sky/AASingl-255
92UD/ML-128
93FExcel/ML-115
Christopherson, Gary
91BurlAs/ClBest-14
91BurlAs/ProC-2808
92Osceola/ClBest-8
92Osceola/ProC-2535
Christy, Al
83Peoria/Frit-19
Christy, Claude
53Mother-47
Chue, Jose
79Cedar/TCMA-18
80Clinton-3
81Clinton-7
Chumas, Steve
83Idaho-18
Chun, Bo
92VeroB/ProC-2894CO
Church, Dan
80Ander-1
Church, Donald
86Cram/NWL-138
Church, Emory
(Bubba)
51B-149
52B-40
52T-323
53B/Col-138
53T-47
55B-273
91T/Arc53-47
Exh47
Church, Hiram Lincoln
(Hi)
No Cards.
Churchill, James
82AlexD-16
Churchill, Norman
77Watlo
79QuadC-27
Churchill, Tim
88Martins/Star-6
89Batavia/ProC-1919
89Spartan/ProC-1053
89Spartan/Star-4
90Spartan/Best-14
90Spartan/ProC-2496
90Spartan/Star-3
Churn, Chuck
59DF
60DF-13
90Target-126
Churry, John
No Cards.
Chylak, Nestar
55B-283UMP
Ciaffone, Lawrence T.
(Larry)
No Cards.
Ciaglo, Paul
88CapeCod/Sum-6
89James/ProC-2135
90WPalmB/Star-2
Ciampa, Mike
80Elmira-27
Cianfrocco, Archie
87James-2
88Rockford-6
89Jaxvl/Best-11
89Jaxvl/ProC-160
89Rockford-6
90Jaxvl/Best-4
90Jaxvl/ProC-1380
91AA/LineD-252
91Harris/LineD-252
91Harris/ProC-634
92B-450
92D/Rook-24
92L-493
92L/BlkGold-493
92Pinn-510
92S/RookTr-99T
92StCl-802
92T/Tr-23T
92T/TrGold-23T
92UD-772DD
92UD/Scout-SR5
92Ultra-515
92Ultra/AllRook-4
93D-246
93F-72
93OPC-112
93Pac/Spanish-182
93Pinn-349
93S-340
93StCl-388
93StCl/1stDay-388
93T-151
93T/Gold-151
93UD-736
93UD/SP-165
93Ultra-63
94B-672
94D-493
94F-659
94Flair-232
94L-79
94Pinn-331
94Select-138
94StCl-221
94StCl/1stDay-221
94StCl/Gold-221
94T-704
94T/Finest-144
94T/FinestRef-144
94T/Gold-704
94TripleP-165
94UD-75
94UD/CollC-77
94UD/CollC/Gold-77
94UD/CollC/Silv-77
94UD/ElecD-75
94Ultra-574
Ciardi, Mark
86Vanco-6
87Pol/Brew-34
88Denver/CMC-9
88Denver/ProC-1272
88T-417
Cias, Darryl
80WHave-14
81WHave-5
82Tacoma-11
83Tacoma-9
84Nes/792-159
84T-159
86SanJose-6
Ciccarella, Joe
89Alaska/Team-4
92ClBest-185
92UD/ML-99
92WinHaven/ClBest-2
92WinHaven/ProC-1768
93B-551
93Pawtu/Ball-7
Cicero, Joseph F.
No Cards.
Cicione, Mike
84Everett/Cram-3
Cicotte, Al
57T-398
58T-382
59T-57
60Maple-3
60T-473
61T-241
62T-126
89Smok/Ast-2
Cicotte, Eddie
10Domino-24
11Helmar-2
12Sweet/Pin-2
14CJ-94
15CJ-94
77Galasso-175
87Conlon/2-29
88Pac/8Men-104
88Pac/8Men-14
88Pac/8Men-19
88Pac/8Men-22M
88Pac/8Men-38
88Pac/8Men-58
88Pac/8Men-59
88Pac/8Men-6
94Conlon-1034
94Conlon-1041M
D327
D328-28
D329-31
E135-28
E270/1
E286
E94
E95
M101/4-31
M116
S74-2
T201
T202
T204
T205
T206
T207
W514-81
W516-21
Cicotte, Greg
80BurlB-17
Ciczczon, Steve
89ColoSp/CMC-25
Cienscyzk, Frank
90Mother/A's-28EQMG
93Mother/A's-28M
Ciesla, Theodore
90James/Pucko-1
91Rockford/ClBest-18
91Rockford/ProC-2053
Cieslak, Mark
85Cedar-2
Cieslak, Thaddeus W.
(Ted)
No Cards.
Cifarelli, Gerard
89CharRain/ProC-980
Cihocki, Albert J.
(Al)
V362-4
Cihocki, Edward J.
(Ed)
No Cards.
Cijntje, Sherwin
85Newar-13
86Hagers-4
87CharlO/WBTV-2
88CharlK/Pep-25
88RochR/CMC-20
88RochR/ProC-198
88RochR/Team-6
89Hagers/Best-7
89Hagers/Star-3
89RochR/CMC-15
89RochR/ProC-1632
Cimino, Pete
66T-563R
67OPC-34
67T-34
68OPC-143
68T-143
Cimo, Matt
87CharlO/WBTV-15
88RochR/CMC-11
88RochR/Gov-5
88RochR/ProC-203
88RochR/Team-7
89ScranWB/CMC-14
89ScranWB/ProC-730
Cimoli, Gino Nicholas
52Park-70
57T-319
58BB
58Hires-63
58T-286
59T-418
60Kahn
60L-142
60T-58
61Kahn
61P-136
61T-165
62J-150
62P-150
62P/Can-150
62Salada-148
62Shirriff-148
62T-402
63J-88
63P-88
63T-321
64T-26
65T-569
89Smok/Dodg-62
90Target-127
91Crown/Orio-77
V362-22
Cimorelli, Frank
89Johnson/Star-5
90Spring/Best-23
91Spring/ClBest-10
91Spring/ProC-735
92MidwLAS/Team-6
92Spring/ClBest-23
92Spring/ProC-861
94B-223
Cina, Randy
88Lynch/Star-4
Cindrich, Jeff
92GulfCY/ProC-3783
93Greens/ClBest-4
93Greens/ProC-878
Cinnella, Doug
87Hagers-29
88FSLAS/Star-4
88WPalmB/Star-5
89WPalmB/Star-6
90Jacks/GS-15
91AAA/LineD-553
91Tidew/LineD-553
91Tidew/ProC-2502
Ciocca, Eric
91Spokane/ClBest-1
91Spokane/ProC-3939
92CharRain/ProC-114
Cipolloni, Joe
86Phill/TastyK-x
86Portl-3
87Maine-18
87Maine/TCMA-8
87Phill/TastyK-23
Cipot, Ed
76Wausau
78Tidew
79Tidew-14
80Tidew-7
81Toledo-20
Cipres, Mark
83TriCit-6
Ciprian, Francis
88Modesto-18
88Modesto/Cal-78
Cipriani, Frank D.
62T-333
Cirbo, Dennis
78StPete
Cirillo, Jeff
91Helena/SportP-12
92Beloit/ClBest-25
92Beloit/ProC-409
92MidwLAS/Team-7
93FExcel/ML-183
94FExcel-79
Cisar, George Joseph
90Target-913
Cisarik, Brian
88Spokane/ProC-1940
89AubAs/ProC-5
89Wichita/Rock-32
90Wichita/Rock-5
91AA/LineD-604
91Wichita/LineD-604
91Wichita/ProC-2609
91Wichita/Rock-19
Cisco, Galen
61Union
62T-301
63T-93
64T-202
64TS-47
65T-364
67T-596
69OPC-211
69T-211
73OPC-593CO
73T-593CO
74T-166CO
83Expo/PostC-3CO
83Stuart-13CO
84Expo/PostC-4CO
84Stuart-4CO
88Syrac/CMC-25CO
88Syrac/ProC-818CO
89Syrac/MerchB-25M
89Syrac/ProC-799CO
89Syrac/Team-25CO
90Tor/BJ-42CO
91Tor/Fire-42CO
91WIZMets-76
92BJ/Fire-6CO
93BJ/Fire-5CO
Cisco, Jeff
86CharRain-6
Cissell, Chalmer W.
(Bill)
28Exh-37
29Exh/4-19
30CEA/Pin-13
31Exh/4-19
32Orbit/num-23
32Orbit/un-10
33CJ/Pin-2
33G-26
34Exh/4-9
35BU-13
35G-1G
35G-3E
35G-5E
35G-6E
92Conlon/Sport-411
R305
R315-C1
R315-D1
R316
V353-26
W517-5

Ciszczon, Steve
80Tacoma-26
83Charl-21TR
85Maine-31
86Maine-4TR
88ColoSp/ProC-1539
89ColoSp/ProC-250
Ciszkowski, Jeff
84LitFalls-16
86Lynch-7
87Lynch-13
88StLucie/Star-5
89Stockton/Best-11
89Stockton/Cal-154
89Stockton/ProC-399
89Stockton/Star-17
Citarella, Ralph A.
81ArkTr-18
81Louisvl-16
82Louisvl-5
83Louisvl/Riley-16
84Louisvl-16
85Cram/PCL-44
85D-504
85Phill/TastyK-46
86Louisvl-9
86Tacoma-2
87Hawaii-6
Citari, Joe
86Omaha/ProC-5
86Omaha/TCMA-14
87Omaha-9
88Omaha/CMC-21
88Omaha/ProC-1519
89Reading/Star-8
Citronnelli, Ed
87SLCity/Taco-13
Clabaugh, John W.
(Moose)
90Target-128
Clack, Marvin
82AlexD-12
83AlexD-7
Clack, Robert S.
(Bobby)
No Cards.
Claire, David M.
(Danny)
No Cards.
Claire, Mark S.
92Pulaski/ClBest-6
92Pulaski/ProC-3182
Claire, Randy S.
85Expo/PostC-21
87Expo/PostC-7
87Sf/TPrev-20M
90AAASingl/ProC-193
90ProC/Singl-607
91AAA/LineD-443
91Richm/Bob-16
91Richm/Team-10
92Richm/Bleach-14
92Richm/Comix-19
92Richm/ProC-377
92Richm/SB-443
92Sky/AAASingl-204
Clancey, William E.
(Bill)
E254
T206
Clancy, Albert H.
No Cards.
Clancy, Jim
75Anderson/TCMA-6
76SanAn/Team-7
78BJ/PostC-4
78OPC-103DP
78T-496
79BJ/Bubble-6
79OPC-61
79T-131
80OPC-132
80T-249
81F-412
81OPC-19
81OPC/Post-21
81T-19
81T/St-143
82D-227
82F-612
82OPC-28
82T-665
83D-101
83F-426
83F/St-14M
83F/St-7M
83OPC-345
83OPC/St-132
83T-345
83T/St-132
84D-119
84D-19DK
84D/AAS-49
84F-150
84Nes/792-575
84OPC-337
84T-575
84T/St-367
84Tor/Fire-6
85D-439
85F-101
85OPC-188
85T-746
85Tor/Fire-8
86BJ/Ault-6
86D-268
86F-56
86Leaf-141
86OPC-213
86T-412
86T-96M
86Tor/Fire-6
87D-639
87D/HL-11
87F-223
87Leaf-90
87OPC-122
87Sf-189
87T-122
87T/St-189
87Tor/Fire-5
88BJ/5x7-3
88D-74
88D/Best-48
88F-106
88Ho/Disc-13
88Leaf-73
88OPC-54
88S-530
88Sf-215
88T-54
88T/Big-258
88T/St-184
88Tor/Fire-18
89B-324
89D-267
89D/Best-206
89D/Tr-32
89F-229
89F/Up-88
89Lennox/Ast-7
89Mother/Ast-15
89OPC-219
89S-538
89S/Tr-42
89T-219
89T/Tr-19T
89UD-282
90BJ/HoSt-4M
90D-69
90F-226
90F/Can-226
90Lennox-8
90Mother/Ast-23
90OPC-648
90PublInt/St-90
90S-424
90T-648
90UD-203
91B-554
91Brave/Dubuq/Stand-9
91Mother/Ast-23
91UD-682
92D-639
92OPC-279
92S-627
92T-279
92T/Gold-279
92T/GoldWin-279
92USPlayC/Brave-2S
92USPlayC/Brave-6D
Clancy, John William
(Bud)
28LaPresse-21
29Exh/4-19
33G-32
90Target-129
94Conlon-1131
R315-D2
V353-32
Clanton, Ucal
(Uke)
No Cards.
Clapham, Mark
78OrlanTw
Clapp, Aaron Bronson
No Cards.
Clapp, John Edgar
No Cards.
Clapp, Steve
89TNTech-7
Clarey, Douglas W.
(Doug)
77Holyo
Clark, Al
88TM/Umpire-24
89TM/Umpire-22
90TM/Umpire-21
Clark, Alfred A.
(Allie)
49B-150
50B-233
50NumNum
51B-29
52B-130
52T-278
53B/Col-155
Clark, Alfred Robert
(Fred)
No Cards.
Clark, Bailey Earl
(Earl)
33G-57
40Wheat-4
V354-41
Clark, Bob
84Nes/792-626
86OPC-352
90Target-130
Clark, Brian
92MissSt-9
93MissSt-8
Clark, Bryan
77Salem
78Charl
80Spokane-8
82D-596
82F-507
82SLCity-6
82T-632
83D-603
83F-476
83T-789
84D-562
84F-609
84F/X-26
84Nes/792-22
84T-22
84T/Tr-25
84Tor/Fire-7
85Maine-5
85OPC-217
85Polar/Ind-43
85T-489
85T/Tr-21T
86BuffB-8
89AAA/CMC-41
89AAA/ProC-39
89Tacoma/CMC-7
89Tacoma/ProC-1563
90TripleAAS/CMC-41
Clark, Casey
77Salem
78Charl
Clark, Chris
81Holyo-9
82Holyo-19
84Cram/PCL-108
85Cram/PCL-18
Clark, Dan
84Butte-4
Clark, Daniel Curran
(Danny)
21Exh-23
Clark, Dave
85Water-15
86Maine-5
87BuffB-6
87D-623
87F-644M
87Gator-12
87Sf-118M
88D-473
88Gator-25
88Rockford-7
88S-633
88T-49
89D-585
89F-402
89Rockford-7
89T-574
89UD-517
90Cub/Mara-4
90D-492
90F-490
90F/Can-490
90OPC-339
90PublInt/St-558
90S-141
90T-339
90T/TVCub-29
90UD-449
91D-616
91F-417
91OPC-241
91S-542
91T-241
91UD-314
92BuffB/BlueS-3
92BuffB/ProC-332
92BuffB/SB-28
92S-657
93Pirate/Nation-5
94F-606
94Pac/Cr-494
94S-267
94S/GoldR-267
94StCl-498
94StCl/1stDay-498
94StCl/Gold-498
94UD/CollC-78
94UD/CollC/Gold-78
94UD/CollC/Silv-78
Clark, Dera
88BBCity/Star-8
89Memphis/Best-18
89Memphis/ProC-1199
89Memphis/Star-6
89Star/Wax-40
90AAASingl/ProC-594
90Omaha/CMC-3
90Omaha/ProC-59
90ProC/Singl-178
92Omaha/ProC-2955
Clark, Doug
90AR-26ACO
Clark, Garry
87Clearw-13
87Spartan-7
88Clearw/Star-8
90Reno/Cal-284
Clark, Geoff
89Salem/Team-4TR
91Yakima/ClBest-30TR
Clark, Glen Ester
No Cards.
Clark, Harry
(Pep)
No Cards.
Clark, Isaiah
86Beloit-4
87Stockton-11
88Modesto-20
89River/Best-29
89River/Cal-9
89River/ProC-1404
90Foil/Best-196
90ProC/Singl-720
90SanBern/Best-7
90SanBern/Cal-103
90SanBern/ProC-2638
Clark, Jack Anthony
75Lafay
76Phoenix/Coke-3
77T-488R
78T-384
79Ho-116
79K-40
79OPC-268
79Pol/Giants-22
79T-512
79T/Comics-32
80K-57
80OPC-93
80Pol/Giants-22
80T-167
80T/S-54
80T/Super-54
81D-315
81Drake-15
81F-433
81F/St-52
81MSA/Disc-9
81OPC-30
81Sqt-18
81T-30
81T/SO-70
81T/St-234
82D-46
82Drake-8
82F-387
82F/St-65
82T-460
82T/St-106
83D-222
83D/AAS-29
83Drake-5
83F-256
83F/St-11M
83F/St-1M
83K-48
83Mother/Giants-2
83OPC-210
83OPC/St-162
83OPC/St-300FOIL
83T-210
83T/Gloss40-32
83T/St-162
83T/St-300
84D-65
84D-7DK
84D/AAS-31
84F-369
84Mother/Giants-7
84Nes/792-690
84OPC-381
84T-690
84T/RD-14
84T/St-167
85D-65
85D/AAS-30
85F-604
85F/Up-U25
85FunFood/Pin-19
85Leaf-207
85OPC-208
85T-740
85T/RD-12
85T/St-160
85T/Tr-22T
86D-168
86D/AAS-23
86F-30
86F/LL-6
86F/Mini-6
86F/St-24
86GenMills/Book-4M
86KAS/Disc-9
86Leaf-96
86OPC-350
86Quaker-5
86Schnucks-1
86Seven/Coin-S13
86Sf-107
86T-350
86T/Gloss60-4
86T/Mini-59
86T/St-50
86T/Tatt-19M
87Classic/Up-148
87D-111
87D/OD-67
87F-289
87F/LimWaxBox-C4
87F/Slug-9
87OPC-331
87Sf/TPrev-12M
87Smok/Cards-13
87Stuart-11M
87T-520
87T/Board-25
87T/St-52
88Classic/Blue-205
88D-15DK
88D-183
88D/AS-33
88D/Best-49
88D/DKsuper-15DK
88D/PopUp-11

88D/Y/Bk-NEW
88F-26
88F/AS-11
88F/BB/AS-6
88F/Excit-8
88F/Mini-39
88F/RecSet-5
88F/SS-7
88F/Up-U47
88Jiffy-4
88KMart-5
88KayBee-5
88KennerFig-19
88Leaf-15DK
88Leaf-181
88Nestle-17
88OPC-100
88Panini/St-232M
88Panini/St-388
88RedFoley/St-12
88S-100
88S-650
88S/Tr-1T
88S/WxBx-11
88Sf-18
88Sf/Gamewin-25
88T-100
88T-397
88T/Big-262
88T/Coins-9
88T/Gloss22-13
88T/Gloss60-41
88T/Mini-69
88T/Revco-4
88T/RiteAid-10
88T/St-150
88T/St-46
88T/St/Backs-1
88T/Tr-28T
88T/UK-13
89B-456
89Classic/Up/2-158
89Coke/Padre-2
89D-311
89D/Best-98
89D/Tr-2
89F-252
89F/Up-123
89KayBee-5
89OPC-3
89Padre/Mag-6
89RedFoley/St-21
89S-25
89S/HotStar-27
89S/Tr-3
89Sf-26
89T-410
89T/Big-240
89T/Coins-7
89T/Crunch-14
89T/Gloss60-56
89T/LJN-94
89T/Mini-65
89T/St-308
89T/Tr-20T
89T/UK-14
89UD-346
89UD/Ext-773
90B-214
90Coke/Padre-4
90D-128
90D/BestNL-109
90D/GSlam-11
90F-152
90F/AwardWin-8
90F/Can-152
90Leaf-287
90MLBPA/Pins-56
90OPC-90
90Padre/MagUno-18
90Panini/St-348
90PublInt/St-45
90RedFoley/St-16
90S-20
90Sf-28
90T-90
90T/Ames-12
90T/Big-39
90T/HillsHM-18
90T/Mini-78
90T/St-104
90T/TVAS-44
90UD-342
91B-122
91Classic/200-154
91Classic/II-T99
91D-618
91F-526
91F/UltraUp-U5
91F/Up-U4
91Leaf-201
91Leaf/Stud-13
91OPC-650
91OPC/Premier-21
91Panini/FrSt-91
91Panini/St-98
91Pep/RSox-4
91RedFoley/St-18
91S-523
91S/RookTr-4T
91StCl-500
91T-650
91T/Tr-22T
91UD-331
91UD/Ext-735
92B-233
92D-169
92DennyGS-5
92F-36
92L-366
92L/BlkGold-366
92OPC-207
92Pinn-85
92RedSox/Dunkin-8
92S-318
92StCl-186
92T-207
92T/Gold-207
92T/GoldWin-207
92UD-521
92UD/HRH-HR14
92USPlayC/RedSox-11H
92USPlayC/RedSox-9C
92Ultra-14
92Yank/WIZ80-32
93D-63
93F-556
93OPC-240
93Pinn-221
93Select-188
93StCl-20
93StCl/1stDay-20
93T-781
93T/Gold-781
93Ultra-148

Clark, James Edward
(Jim)
No Cards.

Clark, James Francis
(Jim)
E96

Clark, James
(Jim)
No Cards.

Clark, Jeff
89Pulaski/ProC-1910
90BurlB/Best-16
90BurlB/ProC-2363
90BurlB/Star-9
91Durham/ClBest-20
91Durham/ProC-1558

Clark, Jerald
85Spokane/Cram-3
87Wichita-24
88LasVegas/CMC-12
88LasVegas/ProC-229
89AAA/CMC-37
89AAA/ProC-49
89B-462
89D-599
89F-642M
89LasVegas/CMC-13
89LasVegas/ProC-10
89S-644
89Sf-179
89UD-30
90Classic/Up-10
90D-593
90D/Rook-48
90Leaf-510
90PublInt/St-46
90S-660
90S/YS/II-41
90TripleAAS/CMC-37
90UD-624
91B-658
91D-74
91F/UltraUp-U110
91F/Up-U121
91Leaf-265
91OPC-513
91Padre/MagRal-15
91Padre/MagRal-7
91S-242
91StCl-468
91T-513
91UD-624
92B-323
92D-144
92F-601
92L-55
92L/BlkGold-55
92Mother/Padre-9
92OPC-749
92Padre/Carl-5
92Pinn-48
92Pol/Padre-4
92S-257
92Smok/Padre-5
92StCl-149
92Studio-102
92T-749
92T/Gold-749
92T/GoldWin-749
92UD-292
92Ultra-275
93B-612
93D-74
93D-790
93F-137
93F/Final-26
93Flair-37
93L-290
93OPC-44
93OPC/Premier-91
93Pac/Spanish-425
93Pinn-234
93Pinn/Expan-7M
93S-405
93StCl-671
93StCl/1stDay-671
93StCl/Rockie-13
93Studio-41
93T-194
93T-565
93T/Gold-194
93T/Gold-565
93TripleP-126
93UD-140
93UD-797
93UD/FunPack-175
93UD/SP-218
93USPlayC/Rockie-12H
93USPlayC/Rockie-7C
93Ultra-345
94D-136
94F-438
94Pac/Cr-193
94Panini-173
94Pinn-103
94Pinn/Artist-103
94Pinn/Museum-103
94S-362
94StCl-98
94StCl/1stDay-98
94StCl/Gold-98
94T-77
94T/Gold-77
94UD/CollC-79
94UD/CollC/Gold-79
94UD/CollC/Silv-79
94Ultra-184

Clark, John Carroll
(Cap)
No Cards.

Clark, Joshua B.
(Pepper)
T206

Clark, Leroy
76Dubuq

Clark, Mark
87Sumter-11
88Hamil/ProC-1736
89Savan/ProC-370
90StPete/Star-2
90T/TVCard-41
91Louisvl/Team-2
92B-109
92D/Rook-25
92F/Up-118
92Louisvl/SB-257
92Sky/AAASingl-125
92T/91Debut-35
92UD-702
92UD-773DD
92Ultra-564
93D-152
93F-508
93Indian/WUAB-6
93L-172
93S-320
93Select-301
93StCl-60
93StCl/1stDay-60
93T-339
93T/Gold-339
93UD-629
94D-656
94F-101
94Flair-39
94Pac/Cr-167
94StCl-207
94StCl/1stDay-207
94StCl/Gold-207
94T-696
94T/Gold-696

Clark, Melvin Earl
(Mel)
53B/Col-67
54B-175
55B-41

Clark, Mike J.
53Hunter
53T-193
91T/Arc53-193

Clark, Owen F.
(Spider)
No Cards.

Clark, Phil
87Fayette-23
88FSLAS/Star-31
88Lakeland/Star-7
89London/ProC-1383
90AAASingl/ProC-382
90ProC/Singl-400
90Toledo/CMC-23
90Toledo/ProC-152
91AAA/LineD-581
91F-332
91S-756RP
91S/Rook40-7
91Toledo/LineD-581
91Toledo/ProC-1934
92T/Tr-24T
92T/TrGold-24T
92Toledo/SB-581
93D-391
93F/Final-136
93Mother/Padre-21
93Pinn-287
93Select-335
93T-802
93T/Gold-802
93Ultra-470
94D-130
94F-660
94Pac/Cr-520
94Panini-254
94Pinn-167
94Pinn/Artist-167
94Pinn/Museum-167
94S-241
94S/GoldR-241
94Select-153
94StCl-399
94StCl/1stDay-399
94StCl/Gold-399
94T-408
94T/Gold-408
94Ultra-277

Clark, Philip J.
58T-423
59T-454

Clark, Randy
79QuadC-14

Clark, Rickey
70T-586
71OPC-697
71T-697
72OPC-462
72T-462
73OPC-636
73T-636

Clark, Rob
83Tulsa-4
84OKCty-2
85Tulsa-27
86OKCty-3
90TulsaDG/Best-33

Clark, Robert Cale
(Bobby)
76QuadC
79SLCity-12
80SLCity-23
80T-663R
81D-572
81T-288
82D-318
82F-456
82T-74
83D-444
83F-82
83T-184
84D-524
84F-512
84F/X-25
84Gard-4
84Nes/792-626
84Pol/Brew-25
84T-626
84T/Tr-24
85Cram/PCL-204
85D-481
85F-578
85Gard-3
85T-553
86Edmon-4
86T-452
87Tacoma-4

Clark, Robert H.
(Bob)
N172

Clark, Rodney
85Utica-13

Clark, Ronald Bruce
(Ron)
67OPC-137R
67T-137R
68T-589R
69T-561
70OPC-531
70T-531
71MLB/St-509
75IntAS/TCMA-13
76OkCty/Team-8
82OkCty-6MG
83Kinston/Team-3MG
86Clearw-4MG
90Coke/WSox-30CO
92Indian/McDon-30M

Clark, Roy 1
79Tulsa-24M

Clark, Roy 2
80LynnS-20
81Spokane-6
82SLCity-7

Clark, Royal
No Cards.

Clark, Russell
76Wausau
79Jacks-20
79Tidew-22

Clark, Skip
81Miami-12

Clark, Stephen C.
80Perez/HOF-B

Clark, Terry
83ArkTr-3
84Louisvl-24
86MidldA-5
87Edmon-22
88Edmon/CMC-1
88Edmon/ProC-569
89AAA/ProC-27
89D-607
89F-470
89OPC-129
89S-566
89S/HotRook-89
89T-129
89UD-234
90AAASingl/ProC-188
90ProC/Singl-605
90Tucson/CMC-3
90Tucson/ProC-198
91AAA/LineD-607
91Tucson/LineD-607
91Tucson/ProC-2207
92ColoSp/ProC-745
92ColoSp/SB-81

Clark, Tim
90Beloit/Star-5
90LSUPol-14
91Stockton/ClBest-23
91Stockton/ProC-3042
93B-699FOIL
94B-343
94B-562
94ClBest/Gold-94
94FExcel-189
94T-79M
94T/Gold-79M
Clark, Tom
90LitSun-18
Clark, Tony
86DayBe-5
90A&AASingle/ProC-189
90Bristol/ProC-3173
90Bristol/Star-3
91Niagara/ClBest-13
91Niagara/ProC-3645
92Niagara/ClBest-1
92Niagara/ProC-3336
92UD/ML-182
94B-209
Clark, Will
86D/HL-1
86D/Rook-32
86F/Slug-6
86F/Up-U25
86Mother/Giants-7
86Sf/Rook-6
86T/Tr-24T
87BK-3
87D-66
87D/OD-96
87F-269
87F/Excit-10
87F/Lim-8
87F/Slug-M2
87F/St-22
87Leaf-144
87Mother/SFG-2
87OPC-361
87RedFoley/St-50
87Sf-195M
87Sf-95
87Sf/TPrev-10M
87T-420
87T/St-88
87ToysRUs-7
88Classic/Blue-225
88D-204
88D-21DK
88D-BC24
88D/Best-79
88D/DKsuper-21DK
88Drake-27
88F-78
88F/AwardWin-5
88F/BB/AS-7
88F/BB/MVP-5
88F/Excit-9
88F/Hottest-6
88F/LL-5
88F/Mini-116
88F/RecSet-6
88F/SS-8
88F/Slug-8
88F/St-126
88F/TL-4
88FanSam-12
88Jiffy-5
88KMart-6
88KennerFig-20
88Leaf-170
88Leaf-21DK
88MSA/Disc-10
88Mother/Giants-2
88Mother/WClark-1
88Mother/WClark-2
88Mother/WClark-3
88Mother/WClark-4
88Nestle-14
88OPC-350
88Panini/St-420
88Panini/St-421TL
88S-78
88S/YS/I-25
88Sf-9
88Sf/Gamewin-4
88T-261TL
88T-350
88T/Big-9
88T/Coins-38
88T/RiteAid-12
88T/St-87
88T/UK-14
89B-476
89Cadaco-8
89Classic-150
89Classic-18
89Classic/Up/2-180
89D-249
89D/AS-33
89D/Best-23
89D/MVP-BC22
89D/PopUp-33
89F-325
89F-631M
89F-632M
89F/AS-3
89F/BBAS-6
89F/BBMVP's-7
89F/Excit-5
89F/Heroes-7
89F/LL-4
89F/Superstar-8
89F/WaxBox-C6
89KMart/DT-23
89KayBee-6
89KennerFig-25
89KingB/Discs-22
89MSA/Disc-4
89Mother/Giants-2
89Mother/WClark-1
89Mother/WClark-2
89Mother/WClark-3
89Mother/WClark-4
89OPC-321
89Panini/St-212
89Panini/St-232AS
89RedFoley/St-22
89S-450
89S/HotStar-85
89S/Mast-10
89Sf-170
89T-660
89T/Big-146
89T/Coins-8
89T/Crunch-19
89T/DH-13
89T/Gloss22-13
89T/Gloss60-11
89T/HeadsUp-2
89T/Hills-7
89T/LJN-22
89T/Mini-40
89T/St-159
89T/St-88
89T/St/Backs-34
89T/UK-15
89Tetley/Discs-4
89UD-155
89UD-678TC
90B-231
90B/Ins-1
90Classic-150
90Classic-6
90Classic-87
90Classic/III-T7
90Classic/Up-11
90CollAB-4
90Colla/Clark-Set
90D-230
90D-707AS
90D/BestNL-24
90D/GSlam-6
90D/Learning-23
90D/Preview-4
90F-54
90F-630MVP
90F-637M
90F/ASIns-2
90F/AwardWin-7
90F/BB-5
90F/BBMVP-7
90F/Can-54
90F/Can-630
90F/Can-637
90F/LL-6
90F/WS-10M
90F/WS-4
90Holsum/Discs-11
90HotPlay/St-6
90KMart/SS-1
90Kenner/Fig-17
90Kenner/Fig-18
90Leaf-172
90Leaf-444CL
90MCA/Disc-1
90MLBPA/Pins-28
90MSA/Soda-18
90Mother/Clark-1
90Mother/Clark-2
90Mother/Clark-3
90Mother/Clark-4
90Mother/Giant-2
90OPC-100
90OPC-397AS
90Panini/St-207M
90Panini/St-363
90Post-7
90PublInt/St-254
90PublInt/St-65
90RedFoley/St-17
90S-300
90S-684DT
90S-699M
90S/100St-30
90S/McDon-1
90Sf-5
90Sunflower-17
90T-100
90T-397AS
90T/Ames-31
90T/Big-224
90T/Coins-43
90T/DH-10
90T/Gloss22-2
90T/Gloss60-52
90T/HeadsUp-2
90T/HillsHM-2
90T/Mini-84
90T/St-147AS
90T/St-85
90T/TVAS-34
90UD-50M
90UD-556
90USPlayC/AS-12D
90WonderBrd-19
90Woolwth/HL-24
91B-616
91BBBest/HitM-5
91Cadaco-8
91Classic/200-48
91Classic/II-T94
91Classic/III-T9
91Classic/III-xx
91D-441AS
91D-86
91DennyGS-3
91F-259
91F/ProV-2
91F/UltraG-2
91JDean-1
91Jesuit-8
91Kenner-9
91KingB/Discs-15
91Leaf-238
91Leaf/Prev-12
91Leaf/Stud-254
91MajorLg/Pins-63
91MissSt-11
91Mother/Giant-2
91OPC-500
91OPC/Premier-22
91PG&E-14
91Panini/FrSt-158
91Panini/FrSt-67
91Panini/St-79
91Petro/SU-20
91Post-3
91Post/Can-9
91RedFoley/St-117
91RedFoley/St-19
91S-664AS
91S-7
91S-871FRAN
91S-886DT
91S/100SS-4
91S/Cooper-B6
91SFExam/Giant-6
91Seven/3DCoin-3NC
91StCl-5
91T-500
91T/CJMini/I-35
91T/SU-8
91UD-445
91UD/FinalEd-92F
91USPlayC/AS-WC
91Ultra-318
92B-260
92B-673FOIL
92CJ/DI-14
92Classic/Game200-136
92Classic/I-24
92Classic/II-T37
92Colla/ASG-2
92D-214
92D-428AS
92D/DK-DK2
92D/Elite-E11
92D/McDon-18
92D/Preview-3
92DPep/MSA-14
92DennyGS-24
92F-631
92F-699M
92F/ASIns-13
92F/Performer-22
92F/TmLIns-8
92French-11M
92Giant/PGE-11
92Giant/PGE-12AS
92Highland-24T
92JDean/18-7
92Kenner/Fig-10
92L-241
92L/BlkGold-241
92L/GoldPrev-12
92L/Prev-12
92MSA/Ben-17
92MooTown-8
92Mother/Giant-2
92MrTurkey-6
92OPC-330
92OPC/Premier-146
92P-14
92Panini-212
92Panini-281AS
92Pinn-122
92Pinn/Slug-12
92Pinn/TeamP-4M
92Post/Can-3
92S-3
92S-773AS
92S-883DT
92S/100SS-24
92S/Impact-51
92Seven/Coin-20
92StCl-460
92StCl-598MC
92StCl/Dome-28
92StCl/MPhoto-4
92Studio-114
92Studio/Her-8
92Studio/Prev-11
92Sunflower-8
92T-330
92T-386AS
92T/DQ-2
92T/Gold-330
92T/Gold-386AS
92T/GoldWin-330
92T/GoldWin-386AS
92T/Kids-58
92T/McDonB-18
92TripleP-155
92UD-175
92UD-718DS
92UD/ASFF-18
92UD/TWillB-T4
92UD/TmMVPHolo-15
92USPlayC/Ace-11H
92Ultra-287
92Ultra/AS-11
92Ultra/AwardWin-14
93B-252
93Colla/DM-24
93Colla/DMProto-2
93D-446
93D/Elite-S3AU
93D/MVP-13
93D/Master-9
93D/Prev-11
93D/Spirit-SG8
93DennyGS-11
93Duracel/PPI-22
93F-154
93F/Atlantic-4
93F/Fruit-11
93F/TLNL-1
93Flair-140
93Flair/Pr-1
93Ho-17
93Kenner/Fig-7
93Kraft-18
93L-247
93L/GoldAS-11M
93MSA/Metz-23
93MilkBone-7
93Mother/Giant-2
93OPC-113
93OPC/Premier/StarP-12
93P-2
93Pac/Spanish-269
93Panini-236
93Pinn-16
93Pinn/Cooper-16
93Pinn/HRC-38
93Pinn/Slug-20
93S-22
93S/Franchise-26
93Select-3
93Select/StatL-17M
93StCl-562
93StCl/1stDay-562
93StCl/Giant-9
93StCl/II/Ins-1
93StCl/MPhoto-15
93StCl/MurphyS-139
93Studio-48
93T-10
93T/BlkGold-2
93T/Finest-108AS
93T/FinestASJ-108AS
93T/FinestRef-108AS
93T/Gold-10
93TripleP-107
93TripleP/Act-11
93TripleP/Nick-4
93UD-315M
93UD-476
93UD-576
93UD/Clutch-R6
93UD/FunPack-101
93UD/FunPack-13HS
93UD/FunPackAS-AS3M
93UD/Iooss-WI11
93UD/OnDeck-D8
93UD/SP-111
93UD/SPPlat-PP4
93UD/TCr-TC3
93Ultra-130
93Ultra/AS-2
94B-485
94D-38
94D/Special-38
94F-689
94F/TL-28
94Finest-238
94Flair-108
94Flair/Hot-3
94L-404
94L/Gamer-10
94L/MVPAL-4
94OPC-187
94P-22
94Pac/Cr-544
94Panini-263
94Pinn-513
94RedFoley-9
94S-10
94S/GoldR-10
94Sf/2000-146
94StCl-203
94StCl/1stDay-203
94StCl/Gold-203
94StCl/Team-258
94Studio-153
94T-240
94T/Gold-240
94TripleP-193
94UD-350
94UD/SP-147
94Ultra-429
Clark, William Otis
(Willie)
No Cards.
Clark, William Watson
(Lefty)
32Orbit/num-8
32Orbit/un-11
33DH-9
33G-17
35G-1G
35G-3E
35G-4E

35G-5E
90Target-131
R305
R337-407
V353-17
V355-86
Clark, William Winf.
(Bill)
No Cards.
Clarke, Arthur F.
(Archie)
No Cards.
Clarke, Fred C.
10Domino-25
11Helmar-112
11Helmar-157
12Sweet/Pin-135A
12Sweet/Pin-135B
14CJ-70
14Piedmont/St-12
15CJ-70
48Exh/HOF
50Callahan
50W576-16
63Bz/ATG-26
73F/Wild-21
75Sheraton-11
76Shakey-31
77Galasso-164
80Perez/HOF-31
80SSPC/HOF
86Conlon/1-53
93CrackJack-13MG
D322
E107
E254
E270/1
E270/2
E300
E90/1
E90/2
E91
E93
E96
E98
M116
S74-108
T201
T205
T206
T3-8
W555
WG3-10
WG5-10
WG6-10
Clarke, Harry Corson
No Cards.
Clarke, Horace M.
66T-547
67CokeCap/YMet-6
67OPC-169
67T-169
68T-263
69MB-59
69MLB/St-73
69OPC-87
69T-87
69T/St-202
70MLB/St-244
70T-623
71MLB/St-486
71OPC-715
71T-715
72MB-74
72OPC-387
72T-387
73OPC-198
73Syrac/Team-5
73T-198
74OPC-529
74T-529
92Yank/WIZ60-24
92Yank/WIZ70-33
Clarke, Jay Austin
(Nig)
E254
E270/1
E270/2
M116
T202
T206
Clarke, Jeff
91AppFx/ClBest-16
91AppFx/ProC-1722
92AppFox/ClBest-13
Clarke, Joshua B.
(Josh)
No Cards.
Clarke, Richard Grey
(Dick)
No Cards.
Clarke, Stan
83Knoxvl-2
84Syrac-19
84Tor/Fire-8
85Syrac-4
86Syrac-5
87Calgary-18
88T-556
88Toledo/CMC-2
88Toledo/ProC-607
89Omaha/CMC-2
89Omaha/ProC-1737
90AAASingl/ProC-510
90Louisvl/CMC-4
90Louisvl/LBC-11
90Louisvl/ProC-396
90ProC/Singl-104
90T/TVCard-42
91AAA/LineD-229
91Louisvl/LineD-229
Clarke, Sumpter Mills
No Cards.
Clarke, Thomas A.
(Tommy)
16FleischBrd-16
D328-29
D329-33
D350/2-32
E135-29
M101/4-33
M101/5-32
M116
T207
Clarke, Tim
82QuadC-6
Clarke, William H.
N172
Clarke, William Jones
(Boileryard)
E107
E270/2
Clarke, William S.
(Stu)
No Cards.
Clarkin, Mike
86WinHaven-6
87NewBrit-1
88NewBrit/ProC-891
Clarkson, Buster
86Negro/Frit-44
Clarkson, David
91Waverly/Fut-14
Clarkson, James B.
(Buzz)
No Cards.
Clarkson, John Gibson
75F/Pion-26
76Shakey-91
80Perez/HOF-91
80SSPC/HOF
E223
N172
N28
N284
N300/unif
N403
WG1-2
Clary, Ellis
60T-470C
88Chatt/Team-5
Clary, Marty
85Richm-2
86D-36RR
87Richm/Bob-3
87Richm/Crown-34
87Richm/TCMA-3
88F-535
88Richm-32
88Richm/CMC-10
88Richm/ProC-11
89Brave/Dubuq-8
89Richm/CMC-1
89Richm/Ko-32
89Richm/ProC-826
90Brave/Dubuq/Perf-5
90D-381
90F-578
90F/Can-578
90OPC-304
90T-304
90UD/Ext-779
91AAA/LineD-230
91F-686
91Louisvl/LineD-230
91Louisvl/ProC-2906
91OPC-582
91T-582
91UD-478
Classet, Gowell
28LaPresse-16
Clatterbuck, Don
79Newar-9
Claudio, Patricio
92Burllnd/ClBest-21
92Burllnd/ProC-1668
93LimeR/Winter-91
Claus, Marc
92Kenosha/ProC-609
Claus, Todd
91Boise/ClBest-1
91Boise/ProC-3885
92ClBest-226
92QuadC/ClBest-2
92QuadC/ProC-816
Clawson, Chris
86Ashvl-4
Clawson, Ken
87PortChar-1
Clay, Billy
79Newar-17
Clay, Dain Elmer
No Cards.
Clay, Danny
83Wisco/Frit-16
85OrlanTw-16
86Toledo-5
87Portl-11
88F/Up-U108
88Maine/ProC-297
89ScranWB/ProC-706
90AAASingl/ProC-567
90Indianap/CMC-2
90Indianap/ProC-284
90ProC/Singl-52
90T/TVCub-40
Clay, Dave
82Durham-14
83Durham-17
85Richm-3
86ElPaso-6
87Denver-1
Clay, Frederick C.
(Bill)
No Cards.
Clay, Jeff
81Cedar-21
82Cedar-26
86Salem-4TR
Clay, Ken
78SSPC/270-16
78T-89
79OPC-225
79T-434
80T-159
81F-633
81Pol/Mariners-8
81T-305
81T/Tr-747
82F-508
82T-649
89Pac/SenLg-72
92Yank/WIZ70-34
93Rang/Keeb-103
Clayton, Craig
91Belling/ClBest-13
91Belling/ProC-3671
92ClBest-114
92SanBern/ClBest-21
92SanBern/ProC-
93River/Cal-6
94B-74
Clayton, Kenny
82Beloit/Frit-14
82Idaho-22
Clayton, Royal
88CLAS/Star-4
88PrWill/Star-6
89Albany/Best-6
89Albany/ProC-318
89Albany/Star-5
89Star/Wax-96
90Albany/Best-23
90Albany/ProC-1030
90Albany/Star-2
90AlbanyDG/Best-10
90EastLAS/ProC-EL13
90Foil/Best-287
90ProC/Singl-785
90Star/ISingl-50
91AAA/LineD-104
91ColClip/LineD-104
91ColClip/ProC-591
92ColClip/Pol-3
92ColClip/ProC-343
92ColClip/SB-101
92Sky/AAASingl-44
93ColClip/Pol-1
Clayton, Royce
89B-472
89Clinton/ProC-895
90A&AASingle/ProC-156
90AS/Cal-49
90Foil/Best-114
90ProC/Singl-855
90SanJose/Best-7
90SanJose/Cal-36
90SanJose/ProC-2018
90SanJose/Star-5
91B-641
91ClBest/Gold-12
91ClBest/Singl-251
91Classic/III-10
91Shrev/LineD-303
91Shrev/ProC-1827
91UD-61TP
91UD/FinalEd-4F
92B-212
92CJ/DII-10
92ClBest/BBonusC-200
92Classic/Game200-179
92Classic/I-25
92Classic/II-T35
92D-397RR
92F-632
92Giant/PGE-13
92L-272
92L/BlkGold-272
92Mother/Giant-4
92OPC-786
92OPC/Premier-39
92Pinn-268
92Pinn/Rook-26
92Pinn/RookI-15
92Pinn/Team2000-34
92ProC/Tomorrow-343
92S-841
92S/HotRook-2
92S/Impact-24
92S/Rook-12
92StCl-630
92Studio-115
92T-786
92T/91Debut-36
92T/Gold-786
92T/GoldWin-786
92T/McDonB-38
92TripleP-123
92UD-2SR
92UD/ASFF-5
92UD/Scout-SR6
92Ultra-288
93B-548
93Classic/GameI-20
93D-208
93F-155
93Flair-141
93L-176
93Mother/Giant-6
93OPC-138
93Pac/Spanish-270
93Panini-238
93Pinn-321
93Pinn/Team2001-11
93S-157
93Select-400
93StCl-39
93StCl/1stDay-39
93StCl/Giant-4
93Studio-94
93T-542
93T/Gold-542
93ToysRUs-16
93TripleP-39
93UD-151
93UD/SP-112
93USPlayC/Rook-10S
93Ultra-131
94B-519
94D-153
94F-690
94Flair-241
94L-381
94OPC-164
94Pac/Cr-545
94Panini-264
94Pinn-111
94Pinn/Artist-111
94Pinn/Museum-111
94S-448
94Sf/2000-86
94StCl-39
94StCl/1stDay-39
94StCl/Gold-39
94StCl/Team-2
94Studio-84
94T-267
94T/Finest-28
94T/FinestRef-28
94T/Gold-267
94TripleP-104
94UD-221
94UD/CollC-80
94UD/CollC/Gold-80
94UD/CollC/Silv-80
94UD/ElecD-221
94UD/SP-92
94Ultra-289
Clear, Mark
76QuadC
77QuadC
80T-638
81D-291
81T-12
81T/Tr-748
82Coke/BOS
82D-452
82F-290
82OPC-169
82T-421
82T/St-154
83D-361
83F-181
83F-629M
83F/St-12M
83F/St-7M
83OPC-162
83OPC/St-36
83T-162
83T/St-36
84D-611
84F-395
84Nes/792-577
84OPC-148
84T-577
85D-538
85F-154
85Leaf-32
85T-207
86D-493
86F-344
86F/Up-U26
86Pol/Brew-25
86T-349
86T/Tr-25T
87D-355
87F-341
87F/BB-9
87F/St-23
87OPC-244
87Pol/Brew-25
87T-640
87T/St-195
88D-372
88F-160
88Pol/Brew-25
88S-446
88T-742
89D-528
89F-182
89S-430
89T-63
90ElPasoATG/Team-37
Cleary, Tony
79Elmira-16
86Pawtu-7TR
87Pawtu-15
88Pawtu/CMC-14
88Pawtu/ProC-467
89Pawtu/Dunkin-TR

89Pawtu/ProC-683
Clelland, Rick
92Albany/ClBest-14
92Albany/ProC-2297
92ClBest-378
93BurlB/ClBest-5
93BurlB/ProC-149
Clem, Brad
92Erie/ClBest-23
92Erie/ProC-1636
Clem, Brian
85Clovis-10
Clem, John
86Wausau-3
Clemans, Sherri
90Miami/II/Star-30
Clemens, Chester S.
(Chet)
No Cards.
Clemens, Clement L.
(Clem)
No Cards.
Clemens, Douglas H.
(Doug)
67CokeCap/Phill-5
67T-489
Clemens, Roger
84F/X-27
84Pawtu-22
85D-273
85F-155
85F/St-123
85Leaf-99
85T-181
86D-172
86D/HL-17
86D/HL-18
86D/HL-26
86D/HL-5
86D/HL-6
86F-345
86F/Mini-73
86F/Slug-7
86OPC-98
86T-661
87BK-4
87Classic-84
87Classic/Up-114
87D-276
87D-2DK
87D/AAS-8
87D/AS/Wax-PC14
87D/DKsuper-2
87D/PopUp-8
87Drake-31
87F-32
87F-634M
87F-640M
87F/AS-11
87F/AwardWin-9
87F/BB-10
87F/Excit-11
87F/GameWin-10
87F/Hottest-10
87F/LL-10
87F/Lim-9
87F/Mini-20
87F/RecSet-4
87F/Slug-10
87F/St-24
87F/WS-3
87GenMills/Book-2M
87Jiffy-12
87KayBee-10
87Kraft-45
87Leaf-190
87Leaf-2DK
87MSA/Discs-2
87MnM's-7
87OPC-340
87Ralston-10
87RedFoley/St-70
87Seven-E8
87Seven-ME10
87Sf-10
87Sf-111M
87Sf-159M
87Sf-196M
87Sf/TPrev-9M
87Sportflic/DealP-1
87Stuart-15
87T-1RB
87T-340
87T-614AS
87T/Coins-8
87T/Gloss22-21
87T/Gloss60-5
87T/HL-7
87T/Mini-42
87T/St-154
87T/St-2
87T/St-244
87T/St-3
87Woolwth-7
88Bz-4
88ChefBoy-23
88Classic/Blue-217
88Classic/Red-158
88D-51
88D/Best-57
88D/RedSox/Bk-51
88Drake-30
88F-349
88F/AS-4
88F/AwardWin-6
88F/BB/AS-8
88F/BB/MVP-6
88F/Excit-10
88F/Hottest-7
88F/LL-6
88F/Mini-5
88F/RecSet-7
88F/SS-9
88F/Slug-9
88F/St-7
88F/TL-5
88Grenada-47
88Jiffy-6
88KMart-7
88KennerFig-21
88KingB/Disc-20
88Leaf-56
88MSA/Disc-9
88Nestle-1
88OPC-70
88Panini/St-21
88RedFoley/St-13
88S-110
88S/YS/II-23
88Sf-207
88Sf/Gamewin-20
88T-394
88T-70
88T/Big-118
88T/Coins-2
88T/Gloss60-13
88T/Mini-2
88T/Revco-28
88T/St-251
88T/St/Backs-58
88T/UK-15
88Woolwth-11
89B-26
89Cadaco-9
89Classic-119
89D-280
89D/AS-14
89D/Best-65
89F-85
89F/BBAS-7
89F/BBMVP's-8
89F/Excit-6
89F/Heroes-8
89F/LL-5
89F/Rec-2
89F/Superstar-9
89Holsum/Discs-16
89KMart/DT-20
89KayBee-7
89KennerFig-26
89MSA/Disc-8
89MSA/SS-7
89Nissen-16
89OPC-121
89Panini/St-249
89Panini/St-270
89RedFoley/St-23
89S-350
89S/HotStar-90
89S/Mast-20
89Sf-3
89T-405AS
89T-450
89T/Big-42
89T/Coins-37
89T/Crunch-18
89T/DH-9
89T/Gloss60-23
89T/Hills-8
89T/LJN-66
89T/Mini-46
89T/St-259
89T/St/Backs-25
89T/UK-16
89Tetley/Discs-8
89UD-195
90B-268
90Classic-51
90CollAB-19
90D-184
90D/BestAL-58
90F-271
90F-627MVP
90F/BBMVP-8
90F/Can-271
90F/Can-627
90F/WaxBox-C3
90HotPlay/St-7
90Kenner/Fig-19
90Leaf-12
90MLBPA/Pins-69
90MSA/Soda-8
90OPC-245
90Panini/St-24
90Pep/RSox-6
90Post-2
90PublInt/St-281
90PublInt/St-452
90RedFoley/St-18
90S-310
90S/100St-79
90S/McDon-18
90Sf-149
90Sunflower-18
90T-245
90T/Big-22
90T/DH-11
90T/Mini-4
90T/St-255
90T/TVAS-25
90T/TVRSox-8
90UD-323
90UD-57TC
90USPlayC/AS-1S
90Windwlk/Discs-3
90WonderBrd-2
91B-118
91BBBest/Aces-4
91Cadaco-9
91Classic/200-149
91Classic/I-18
91Classic/II-T65
91Classic/II-T97
91CollAB-1
91D-395MVP
91D-81
91D-9DK
91D/SuperDK-9DK
91F-90
91F/ASIns-10
91F/ProV-9
91JDean-18
91Leaf-174CL
91Leaf-488
91Leaf/Stud-14
91Leaf/StudPrev-2
91MSA/Holsum-13
91MajorLg/Pins-8
91OPC-530
91OPC/Premier-23
91Panini/FrSt-271
91Panini/St-215
91Panini/Top15-63
91Panini/Top15-69
91Panini/Top15-80
91Panini/Top15-94
91Pep/RSox-5
91Pep/SS-6
91Petro/SU-3
91Post-12
91Post/Can-18
91RedFoley/St-20
91S-399AS
91S-655
91S-684KM
91S-850FRAN
91S/100SS-50
91Seven/3DCoin-3F
91Seven/3DCoin-3NE
91Seven/3DCoin-4T
91StCl-309
91StCl/Member*-12
91T-530
91T/CJMini/I-22
91T/SU-9
91UD-655
91USPlayC/AS-10H
91Ultra-31
92B-691
92CJ/DI-17
92Classic/Game200-189
92Classic/I-26
92Classic/I-xx
92Classic/II-T61
92Colla/ASG-19
92D-244
92D-BC3CY
92D/BC-BC3CY
92D/McDon-10
92DPep/MSA-1
92F-37
92F/ClemIns-Set
92F/Clemens-1
92F/Performer-6
92F/Smoke-S4
92French-2
92Hardee-5
92Highland-181
92JDean/18-10
92Kenner/Fig-11
92KingB-9
92L-19
92L/BlkGold-19
92MooTown-4
92MrTurkey-7
92OPC-150
92OPC/Premier-105
92P-16
92Panini-146
92Panini-92
92Pinn-95
92Pinn/RookI-4M
92Pinn/TeamP-1
92Post/Can-10
92RedSox/Dunkin-9
92S-21
92S-790CY
92S/100SS-74
92S/Impact-57
92Seven/Coin-3
92StCl-593MC
92StCl-80
92StCl/Dome-29
92StCl/MemberI-9
92Studio-132
92T-150
92T-405AS
92T/Gold-150
92T/Gold-405AS
92T/GoldWin-150
92T/GoldWin-405AS
92T/Kids-67
92T/McDonB-10
92TX-8
92TripleP-216
92UD-545
92UD-641DS
92UD/ASFF-19
92UD/TmMVPHolo-16
92USPlayC/Ace-10S
92USPlayC/Ace-JK
92USPlayC/RedSox-10C
92USPlayC/RedSox-1H
92Ultra-15
92Ultra/AwardWin-6
93B-635
93Cadaco-11
93Classic/GameI-21
93Colla/DM-25
93D-119
93D/DK-3
93D/MVP-15
93D/Prev-13
93Duracel/PPI-1
93F-177
93F-348LL
93F-717SS
93F/Atlantic-5
93F/Fruit-12
93F/TLAL-4
93Flair-160
93Ho-27
93HumDum/Can-3
93JDean/28-7
93Kenner/Fig-8
93KingB-21
93Kraft-5
93L-279
93L/GoldAS-20
93L/Heading-6
93MSA/Ben-12
93MSA/Metz-5
93OPC-259
93OPC/Premier/StarP-18
93P-4
93Pac/Jugador-4
93Pac/Spanish-30
93Panini-90
93Pinn-25
93Pinn/Cooper-18
93Post/Can-3
93S-7
93S/Franchise-2
93Select-14
93Select/Ace-1
93Select/ChasS-21
93Select/StatL-62M
93Select/StatL-75
93Select/StatL-79
93Select/StatL-87
93StCl-220
93StCl-748MC
93StCl/1stDay-220
93StCl/1stDay-748MC
93StCl/MurphyS-97
93Studio-22
93Studio/Her-3
93T-4
93T-409M
93T/BlkGold-27
93T/Finest-104AS
93T/FinestASJ-104AS
93T/FinestRef-104AS
93T/Gold-4
93T/Gold-409M
93T/Hill-3
93TB/Full-15
93TripleP-118
93TripleP/Act-14
93TripleP/Nick-2
93UD-135
93UD-48M
93UD-630M
93UD/Clutch-R7
93UD/Diam-21
93UD/FunPack-14HS
93UD/FunPack-161GS
93UD/FunPack-162
93UD/FunPack-23KS
93UD/FunPack-29HERO
93UD/OnDeck-D9
93UD/SP-199
93UDFutHero-57
93USPlayC/Ace-11S
93Ultra-508
93Ultra/Strike-1
94B-475
94Church-13
94D-356
94D/Special-356
94F-26
94F/Smoke-1
94L-255
94OPC-67
94OPC/JAS-18
94Oscar-3
94Pac/Cr-49
94Panini-26
94Pinn-25
94Pinn/Artist-25
94Pinn/Museum-25
94RedFoley-31
94S-25
94S/GoldR-25
94Select-61
94Select/CrCon-2
94Sf/2000-15
94StCl-534QS
94StCl/1stDay-534QS
94StCl/Gold-534QS
94Studio-159
94T-720
94T/Finest-217
94T/FinestRef-217
94T/Gold-720
94TripleP-201
94UD-450
94UD/DColl-E2
94UD/HoloFX-6
94UD/SP-152

94Ultra-11
Clemens, Troy
90Spring/Best-7
91Reno/Cal-17
92SanJose/ClBest-13
Clement, Wallace Oaks
(Wally)
90Target-914
E90/1
Clemente, Joe
93MissSt-9
Clemente, Roberto W.
55T-164
56T-33
57Kahn
57T-76
58Kahn
58T-52
59Kahn
59T-478
59T-543M
60Bz-7
60Kahn
60T-326
61Kahn
61P-132
61T-388
61T-41LL
62Bz-11
62Exh
62J-173
62Kahn
62P-173
62P/Can-173
62Salada-150
62Shirriff-150
62Sugar-B
62T-10
62T-52LL
62T/St-174
62T/bucks
63Bz-14
63Exh
63F-56
63IDL-4
63J-143
63Kahn
63P-143
63Salada-23
63T-18M
63T-540
63T/SO
64Bz-14
64Kahn
64T-440
64T-7LL
64T/Coins-150AS
64T/Coins-55
64T/S-11
64T/SU
64T/St-27
64Wheat/St-11
65Bz-14
65MacGregor-1
65OPC-160
65OPC-2LL
65T-160
65T-2LL
65T/E-19
65T/trans-44
66Bz-26
66EH-21
66Kahn
66T-215LL
66T-300
66T/RO-18
66T/RO-47
67Bz-26
67CokeCap/Pirate-18
67OPC/PI-11
67T-242LL
67T-361CL
67T-400
67T/PI-11
67T/Test/PP-27
67T/Test/PP-6
67T/Test/SU-7
68Bz-12
68Dexter-24
68KDKA-21
68OPC-150
68OPC-1LL
68OPC-3LL
68T-150
68T-1LL
68T-374AS
68T-3LL
68T-480M
68T/3D
68T/ActionSt-12B
68T/ActionSt-9C
68T/G-6
68T/Post-6
69MB-60
69MLB/St-184
69MLBPA/Pin-39
69OPC-50
69OPC/DE-4
69T-50
69T/DE-27
69T/S-58
69T/St-85
69T/decal
69Trans-56
70K-27
70MB-5
70MLB/St-99
70OPC-350
70OPC-61LL
70T-350
70T-61LL
70T/PI-21
70T/S-12
70T/Super-12
70Trans-5
71Bz
71Bz/Test-38
71K-5
71MLB/St-198
71MLB/St-558
71OPC-630
71T-630
71T/Coins-71
71T/S-37
71T/Super-37
72Dimanche*-57
72K-49
72MB-75
72OPC-226WS
72OPC-309
72OPC-310IA
72ProStars/PostC-15
72T-226WS
72T-309
72T-310A
72T/Cloth-6
73OPC-50
73T-50
74Laugh/ASG-62
75OPC-204MVP
75T-204MVP
75T/M-204MVP
76Shakey-135
77Galasso-252
77Galasso-41
78TCMA-13
79TCMA-23
80Laugh/FFeat-21
80Pac/Leg-50
80Perez/HOF-135
82KMart-10
83D/HOF-17
83MLBPA/Pin-22
84West/1-3
86CharRain-7
86Sf/Dec-43
87D-612PUZ
87D/AS/WaxBox-PUZ
87D/DKsuper-28
87D/WaxBox-PUZ
87KMart-2
87Leaf-163
87Nestle/DT-27
87T-313TBC
88Grenada-73
89HOF/St-46
89Kenner/BBGr-4
89Pac/Leg-135
89Swell-125
89T/LJN-149
89USPS-1
90CollAB-35
90MSA/AGFA-8
90Perez/GreatMom-32
90Swell/Great-20
91Cadaco-10
91Homer/Classic-7
91K/Leyenda-6
91LineD-39
91Swell/Great-132
93AP/ASG-119
93AP/ASG24K-53G
93Cadaco-12
93CityP/Clemente-Set
93TWill/Clemente-Set
93TWill/Mem-11
94T/Arc54-251
Exh47
PM10/Sm-26
Clements, Dave
83Spring/Frit-2
84ArkTr-2
85Louisvl-14
86ArkTr-5
Clements, Edward
(Ed)
89Pac/SenLg-54
Clements, John T.
(Jack)
N172
N284
N690
WG1-49
Clements, Pat
85F/Up-U26
85Smok/Cal-22
85T/Tr-23T
86D-600
86F-606
86OPC-283
86T-754
87D-390
87F-608
87T-16
88Colum/CMC-1
88Colum/Pol-1
88Colum/ProC-318
88D-52
88F-204
88S-389
88T-484
89B-452
89LasVegas/ProC-15
89T-159
90F-153
90F/Can-153
90OPC-548
90T-548
91LasVegas/ProC-227
92B-533
92F-602
92Mother/Padre-23
92S-714
92Smok/Padre-6
92Yank/WIZ80-33
Clements, Tony
91AA/LineD-403
91Memphis/LineD-403
Clements, Wes
83Tucson-14
84Cram/PCL-53
85Beloit-14
87GlenF-5
89Pac/SenLg-176
Clemo, Scott
86James-3
87Indianap-28
88WPalmB/Star-6
Clemons, Lance
72OPC-372R
72T-372R
Clemons, Mark
85Kingst-1
86OrlanTw-4
87OrlanTw-10
88Jaxvl/Best-8
88Jaxvl/ProC-977
Clemons, Robert
E270/2
Clemons, Verne James
E120
V100
W573
Clemons, Verne
V61-85
Clendenon, Donn Alvin
62T-86
63IDL-5
63Kahn
63T-477
64Kahn
64T-163
64T/Coins-15
64T/SU
64T/St-76
65Kahn
65T-325
65T/E-9
66EH-17
66OPC-99M
66T-375
66T-99M
67CokeCap/Pirate-3
67T-266M
67T-535
67T/Test/PP-30
67T/Test/PP-7
68KDKA-17
68T-344
69MB-61
69OPC-208
69T-208
69T/4in1-3
69T/St-54
69T/decal
70MLB/St-74
70OPC-280
70OPC-306WS
70T-280
70T-306WS
70Trans/M-24
71MLB/St-149
71OPC-115
71T-115
71T/Coins-151
71T/S-4
71T/Super-4
71T/tatt-6
72MB-76
72T-671
78TCMA-237
90Swell/Great-82
91WIZMets-77
94Mets/69-10
Cleveland, Elmer E.
N172
Cleveland, Reggie
70T-716R
71OPC-216R
71T-216R
72OPC-375
72T-375
73OPC-104
73T-104
74OPC-175
74T-175
74T/St-112
74T/Tr-175T
75OPC-32
75T-32
75T/M-32
76OPC-419
76T-419
77OPC-111
77T-613
78BK/R-10
78SSPC/270-165
78T-105
79OPC-103
79T-209
80T-394
81D-206
81F-523
81T-576
82D-456
82F-137
82T-737
91Pac/SenLg-61
91Pac/SenLg-79
92StCath/ClBest-28CO
93Rang/Keeb-104
93StCath/ClBest-28CO
Clevenger, Tex
58T-31
59T-298
60T-392
61T-291
63T-457
92Yank/WIZ60-25
Cleverly, Gary
75SanAn
Cliburn, Stanley Gene
(Stan)
75QuadC
76QuadC
78Cr/PCL-74
82Portl-10
83LynnP-11
84Cram/PCL-132
85Cram/PCL-242
86Edmon-5M
86Edmon-6
87Richm/Crown-29
87Richm/TCMA-28
88BuffB/CMC-24
88BuffB/ProC-1480
88Watertn/Pucko-31
89Augusta/ProC-514
89Pac/SenLg-150
89SALAS/GS-1
89T/SenLg-54
90Salem/Star-25MG
91Pac/SenLg-30
91Pac/SenLg-51M
91Salem/ClBest-25MG
91Salem/ProC-968MG
92Gaston/ClBest-26CO
92Gaston/ProC-2269
Cliburn, Stewart
77Salem
79BuffB/TCMA-2
80Port-13
81Buffa-9
83Nashua-3
84Cram/PCL-113
85Cram/PCL-19
85F/Up-U27
86D-301
86Edmon-5M
86Edmon-7
86F-152
86Seven/Coin-W16M
86Sf-177M
86T-179
87D-530
88Smok/Angels-19
89D-462
89Edmon/CMC-7
89Edmon/ProC-566
89F-471
89S-445
89T-649
89UD-483
91Pac/SenLg-29
91Pac/SenLg-51M
91PalmSp/ProC-2034CO
92AS/Cal-51
92PalmSp/ClBest-30CO
92PalmSp/ProC-856CO
Clifford, James
92Belling/ClBest-22
92Belling/ProC-1450
Clifford, Jeff
90SoOreg/Best-13
90SoOreg/ProC-3440
Clift, Harland Benton
36Exh/4-15
37Exh/4-15
37OPC-104
38Exh/4-15
38Wheat
41DP-148
41G-2
41PlayBall-66
43Playball-15
94Conlon-1124
V300
W753
Clifton, Herman Earl
(Flea)
R314
V351A-5
V355-32
Cline, John
(Monk)
N172
Cline, Steve
75Cedar
81Clinton-3
82Clinton/Frit-3CO
84Shrev/FB-4CO
88Shrev/ProC-1286
89Shrev/ProC-1837
90Clinton/Best-10CO
91Clinton/ClBest-27CO
91Clinton/ProC-853CO
92Shrev/ProC-3888CO
92Shrev/SB-600M
Cline, Tyrone A.
(Ty)

61T-421
62Kahn
62Sugar-8
62T-362
62T/St-32
63J-74
63P-74
63T-414
64T-171
65OPC-63
65T-63
66T-306
67CokeCap/Brave-2
67T-591
68T-469
69MB-62
69MLB/St-156
69T-442
70MLB/St-64
70OPC-164
70T-164
71MLB/St-54
71OPC-199NLCS
71OPC-201NLCS
71OPC-319
71T-199NLCS
71T-201NLCS
71T-319
72MB-77
78TCMA-149
78TCMA-191
Clines, Eugene
(Gene)
71OPC-27R
71T-27R
72OPC-152
72T-152
73OPC-333
73T-333
74OPC-172
74T-172
75OPC-575
75T-575
75T/M-575
76OPC-417
76SSPC-543
76SSPC/MetsY-M17
76T-417
77T-237
78SSPC/270-253
78T-639
79T-171
89Pac/SenLg-146
89TM/SenLg-21
90Mother/Mar-27M
91WIZMets-78
92Mother/Mar-27M
93Rang/Keeb-105
Clingman, William F.
(Billy)
No Cards.
Clinkscales, Sherard
92ClBest/Up-414
92Classic/DP-22
92Eugene/ClBest-1
92Eugene/ProC-3018
92FrRow/DP-3
93ClBest/MLG-184
93Rockford/ClBest-7
93StCl/MurphyS-6
93T-706
93T/Gold-706
94ClBest/Gold-146
Clinton, Bill
93TripleP-32
Clinton, James L.
(Jim)
No Cards.
Clinton, James
(Jim)
89Butte/SP-11
90Gaston/Best-24
90Gaston/ProC-2527
90Gaston/Star-5
91CharlR/ProC-1320
92CharlR/ClBest-15
92CharlR/ProC-2231
Clinton, Luciean L.
(Lu)
60T-533
61Union
62T-457
63F-6
63J-82
63P-82
63T-96
64T-526
65OPC-229
65T-229
67T-426
92Yank/WIZ60-26
Cloherty, John
76Dubuq
78DaytB
Cloninger, Darin
85Albany-3
Cloninger, Greg
88Sumter/ProC-406
89BurlB/ProC-1601
89BurlB/Star-4
Cloninger, Todd
86Geneva-2
87WinSalem-3
Cloninger, Tom
87Oneonta-33
Cloninger, Tony
62T-63
63J-157
63P-157
63T-367
64T-575
65Kahn
65T-520
66Bz-27
66Kahn
66OPC-10
66T-10
66T-223LL
66T/RO-116
66T/RO-19
67Bz-27
67CokeCap/Brave-5
67Kahn
67T-396M
67T-490
68CokeCap/Brave-5
68Dexter-25
68OPC-93
68T-93
69Kahn
69MLB/St-128
69T-492
70MLB/St-26
70T-705
71MLB/St-55
71OPC-218
71T-218
72T-779
78TCMA-20
88Albany/ProC-1353
90HOF/St-70
91Pac/SenLg-31
Clontz, Brad
92Pulaski/ClBest-13
92Pulaski/ProC-3170
93Durham/Team-5
94B-641
Close, Casey
88Colum/CMC-21
88Colum/Pol-19
88Colum/ProC-325
90AAASingl/ProC-126
90Calgary/CMC-19
90Calgary/ProC-661
90ProC/Singl-446
Clossen, Bill
86Durham-4
87PrWill-15
Closter, Alan
66T-549R
69OPC-114R
69T-114R
69T/4in1-24
72OPC-124R
72T-124R
73OPC-634
73Syrac/Team-6
73T-634
92Yank/WIZ70-35
Cloud, David
89KS*-25M
Clough, Edgar George
(Ed)
No Cards.
Clougherty, Pat
93Bz-8
93T/Tr-34T
Club, Lachine
28LaPresse-2
Cluck, Bob
74Cedar
75Dubuq
76Dubuq
81Tucson-5
84Cram/PCL-239MG
85Cram/PCL-110MG
90Mother/Ast-27CO
91Mother/Ast-28CO
92Mother/Ast-27M
93Mother/Ast-28M
Cluff, Paul
87BYU-14
89Boise/ProC-2006
Clutterbuck, Bryan
82Beloit/Frit-20
83ElPaso-15
84ElPaso-5
85Cram/PCL-222
86Vanco-7
87D-397
87Denver-23
87F-342
87T-562
89Pol/Brew-48
89T/Tr-21T
90OPC-264
90T-264
90UD-239
Clyburn, Danny
92ClBest/Up-422
92Classic/DP-32
92FrRow/DP-18
93B-542
93ClBest/MLG-194
93StCl/MurphyS-12
94B-406
Clyde, David
74OPC-133
74T-133
74T/St-233
75OPC-12
75T-12
75T/M-12
76Laugh/Jub-19
77Tucson
79T-399
80T-697
93Rang/Keeb-106
Clymer, Otis Edgar
E254
E270/2
T204
Clymer, William J.
T206
Coachman, Pete
86PalmSp-7
86PalmSp/Smok-22
87Edmon-13
88Edmon/CMC-13
88Edmon/ProC-578
89Edmon/CMC-12
89Edmon/ProC-563
90AAASingl/ProC-98
90Edmon/CMC-20
90Edmon/ProC-522
90ProC/Singl-497
91AAA/LineD-531
91S-344RP
91T/90Debut-32
91Tacoma/LineD-531
91Tacoma/ProC-2311
Coakley, Andrew
T204
Coan, Gilbert F.
(Gil)
49B-90
50B-54
51B-18
52B-51
52RM-AL4
52T-291
53B/Col-34
53T-133
54B-40
54Esskay
55B-78
55Esskay
88Chatt/Team-6
91Crown/Orio-78
91T/Arc53-133
R302-114
Coates, Jim
59T-525
60L-35
60T-51
61P-17
61T-531
62T-553
63T-237
67T-401
78TCMA-217
78TCMA-267
92Yank/WIZ60-27
92Yank/WIZAS-12
Coates, Thomas
91Idaho/ProC-4339
91Idaho/SportP-6
92Pulaski/ClBest-7
92Pulaski/ProC-3190
93Durham/Team-6
Coatney, Rick
81Durham-16
82Durham-15
Cobb, Joseph S.
No Cards.
Cobb, Mark
88Spartan/Star-4
89Clearw/Star-7
89Star/Wax-11
Cobb, Marvin
88OK-16
89BendB/Legoe-2
89OK-9
90PalmSp/Cal-219
90PalmSp/ProC-2570
91AA/LineD-430
91MidldA/LineD-430
91MidldA/OneHour-7
91MidldA/ProC-429
92MidldA/ProC-4019
92MidldA/SB-456
92Sky/AASingl-193
Cobb, Mickey
75Omaha/Team-5
Cobb, Tyrus Raymond
(Ty)
09Buster/Pin-4
10Domino-26
11Diamond-9
11Helmar-28
12Sweet/Pin-22A
12Sweet/Pin-22B
14CJ-30
14Piedmont/St-13
15CJ-30
16FleischBrd-17
21Exh-24
24Sherlock-2
25Exh-90
26Exh-91
27Exh-53
28Yueng-27
33SK*-1
48Exh/HOF-2
50Callahan
50W576-17
60Exh/HOF-7
60F-42
60NuCard-43
61F-14
61F-1M
61GP-25
61NuCard-443
63Bz/ATG-35
69Bz-1
69Bz-7
69Bz-8
72F/FFeat-15
72K/ATG-15
72Laugh/GF-35
73F/Wild-35M
73OPC-471LL
73OPC-475LL
73T-471LL
73T-475LL
75F/Pion-14
75McCallum-Set
76Motor-3
76OPC-346AS
76Rowe-7M
76Shakey-1
76T-346AS
77Galasso-100
77Galasso-136
77Shakey-19
79T-411M
79T-414M
80Laugh/3/4/5-4
80Laugh/FFeat-28
80Marchant/HOF-6
80Pac/Leg-31
80Perez/HOF-1
80SSPC/HOF
81Conlon-1
81Tiger/Detroit-17
83D-653Pz
83D/HOF-1
84D/Champs-26
84West/1-8
85Woolwth-8
86Conlon/1-2
86Conlon/1-24
86Conlon/1-41
86Conlon/1-6
86Tiger/Sport-1
87Conlon/2-5
87Nestle/DT-7
88Conlon/4-6
88Conlon/HardC-2
88Grenada-40
89HOF/St-37
89Pac/Leg-117
89Swell-2
89T/LJN-85
90BBWit-56
90HOF/St-19
90Perez/GreatMom-12
90Swell/Great-15
91Cadaco-11
91Conlon/Proto-13
91Conlon/Proto-250
91Conlon/Proto-500
91Conlon/Sport-250
91Homer/Classic-4
91LineD-48
91Swell/Great-127
92Conlon/Col-10
92Conlon/Gold-1000G
92Conlon/Sport-425
92Conlon/Sport-525
92Mega/Ruth-125M
92Mega/Ruth-160M
92S-878
92Whitehall-1
92Whitehall/Proto-1
93AP/ASG-88
93AP/ASG24K-22G
93Cadaco-13
93Conlon-796
93Conlon-838
93Conlon/MasterBW-7
93CrackJack-1
93Spectrum/HOFI-2
93TWill-125
93UD/ATH-145M
93UD/ATH-146M
93UD/ATH-160
93UD/ATH-32
93UD/T202-2M
93UD/T202-6M
93UD/T202-7M
93UD/T202-8M
94Conlon-1000
94Conlon-1011
94TedW-30
94TedW/Lock-11
B18
BF2-25
D303
D304
D327
D328-30
D329-38
E101
E102
E103
E105
E106
E120
E121/120
E121/80
E126-17
E135-30
E210-27
E220
E224
E254
E270/1

E270/2
E300
E90/1
E92
E93
E94
E95
E98
L1-127
M101/4-38
M116
PM1-3
R328-14
R423-14
S74-13
S81-102
T201
T202
T205
T206
T213/blue
T213/brown
T214-4
T215/blue
T215/brown
T216
T227
T3-9
V100
V117-22
V61-30
V89-46
W501-8
W502-27
W512-3
W514-43
W515-10
W516-6
W555
W572
W573
WG4-5
WG5-11
WG6-11

Coble, David Lamar
(Dave)
No Cards.

Coble, Drew
88TM/Umpire-45
89TM/Umpire-43
90TM/Umpire-41

Coble, Tony
90Helena/SportP-4

Cobleigh, Mike
89Modesto/Chong-5

Cocanower, Jaime
81Vanco-1
82Vanco-20
84F/X-28
84Pol/Brew-47
84T/Tr-26
85Cram/PCL-210
85D-455
85F-579
85Gard-4
85Pol/Brew-47
85T-576
85T/St-288
86D-393
86F-483
86Pol/Brew-47
86T-277
86T/Tr-24T
87Albuq/Pol-7
87T-423
87T/JumboR-4

Coccia, Dan
88Martins/Star-7

Cochran, Arnold
81Batavia-12
81Watlo-20

Cochran, Dave
84Jacks-21

Cochran, George L.
No Cards.

Cochran, Greg
79Colum-17
80Colum-21
81Colum-12
82Colum-8
82Colum/Pol-27

Cochran, Jamie
91Johnson/ClBest-17
91Johnson/ProC-3971
92Hamil/ClBest-5
92Hamil/ProC-1584
92ProC/Tomorrow-327
93FExcel/ML-97
94FExcel-264
94FExcel/LL-6

Cochrane, Dave
86BirmB/Team-11
87Hawaii-13
87Seven-C5
87Sf-158M
87Sf/TPrev-26M
88Calgary/CMC-14
88Calgary/ProC-785
89Calgary/CMC-14
89Calgary/ProC-542
90Calgary/CMC-11
90OPC-491
90ProC/Singl-438
90T-491
91AAA/LineD-55
91Calgary/LineD-55
91Calgary/ProC-518
92D-539
92L-398
92L/BlkGold-398
92Mother/Mar-14
92S-461
92S/100RisSt-70
92StCl-69
92Ultra-431
93D-481
93F-671
93T-288
93T/Gold-288

Cochrane, Gordon S.
(Mickey)
28Exh-53
29Exh/4-27
31Exh/4-28
32Orbit/num-28
32Orbit/un-12
33DH-10
33DL-6
33Exh/4-14
33G-76
34DS-4
34Exh/4-12
34Exh/4-14
34G-2
35BU-25
35Exh/4-12
35G-1D
35G-1J
35G-2D
35G-3A
35G-5A
35G-6A
35G-6D
35G-7D
35Wheat
36Exh/4-12
36G
36Wheat
37Exh/4-12
40PlayBall-180
48Exh/HOF
49Leaf/Prem-2
50Callahan
50W576-18B
51T/CMAS
60F-24
60NuCard-19
61F-15
61GP-12
61NuCard-419
63Bz/ATG-34
69Bz/Sm
72K/ATG-4
76OPC-348AS
76Rowe-13M
76Shakey-50
76T-348AS
77Galasso-238
77Galasso-61
77Shakey-8
80Marchant/HOF-7
80Pac/Leg-38
80Perez/HOF-50
80SSPC/HOF
81Tiger/Detroit-3
85West/2-29
86Conlon/1-7
86Sf/Dec-13
86Tiger/Sport-5
87Nestle/DT-8
88Conlon/3-7
88Conlon/AmAS-5
89HOF/St-56
89Pac/Leg-151
90Swell/Great-3
91Conlon/Sport-266
91Conlon/Sport-51
91LineD-49
91Swell/Great-142
92Conlon/Sport-432
92Conlon/Sport-551
93AP/ASG-98
93AP/ASG24K-32G
93Conlon-866
93Conlon/MasterBW-5
94Conlon-1087
94Conlon-1146
94TedW-65
R305
R306
R308-155
R308-186
R309/2
R310
R311/Gloss
R312
R313A-2
R314
R328-12
R332-32
V353-69
V354-59
V355-45
V94-7
W517-37
W517-54

Cock, J.R.
91BendB/ClBest-1
91BendB/ProC-3688

Cockman, James
(Jim)
No Cards.

Cockrell, Alan
86Shrev-4
87Phoenix-15
88Phoenix/CMC-19
88Phoenix/ProC-68
89Portl/CMC-20
89Portl/ProC-224
90AAAGame/ProC-50
90AAASingl/ProC-230
90ColoSp/CMC-23
90ColoSp/ProC-49
90ProC/Singl-475
91AAA/LineD-56
91Calgary/LineD-56
91Calgary/ProC-526
92ColoSp/ProC-753
92ColoSp/SB-82
92OPC-591M
92T-591M
92T/Gold-591M
92T/GoldWin-591M

Codinach, Antonio
84Visalia-19

Codiroli, Chris
82WHave-4
83T/Tr-20
84D-345
84F-441
84Mother/A's-10
84Nes/792-61
84OPC-61
84T-61
84T/St-330
85D-462
85F-420
85Mother/A's-9
85T-552
85T/St-327
86D-278
86F-414
86Leaf-151
86Mother/A's-15
86OPC-388
86T-433
86T/St-173
86T/Tatt-9M
87D-226
87F-390
87T-217
89T-6

Cody
N172

Cody, Ron
92Belling/ClBest-8

Cody, William
92Belling/ProC-1433

Coentopp, Kevin
86Cram/NWL-175

Cofer, Brian
90Watertn/Star-4
91Collnd/ClBest-11
91Collnd/ProC-1478
92Kinston/ClBest-3
92Kinston/ProC-2468

Coffey, John Francis
(Jack)
No Cards.

Coffey, Mike
85Cedar-3
86Elmira-5
87WinHaven-11

Coffey, Paul
91StCl/Charter*-45
91StCl/Member*-40

Coffey, Stephen
90Geneva/ProC-3047
90Geneva/Star-4
91Peoria/ProC-1346

Coffman, George David
39PlayBall-147
40PlayBall-55
41G-32

Coffman, Jim
82Amari-12

Coffman, Kevin
85Durham-5
86Durham-5
87Greenvl/Best-20
87SLAS-19
88D/Rook-49
88F-536
88T/Tr-29T
89B-282
89OPC-44
89T-488
91AA/LineD-555
91Jacks/LineD-555
91Jacks/ProC-918
92Greenvl/SB-232
92Richm/ProC-370
93Calgary/ProC-1157

Coffman, Samuel R.
(Dick)
33G-101
35BU-92
35G-1F
35G-3D
35G-5D
35G-6D
39PlayBall-24
40PlayBall-140
91Conlon/Sport-321
V354-23

Coggins, Franklin
68OPC-96R
68T-96R

Coggins, Richard A.
(Rich)
73JP
73OPC-611R
73T-611R
74OPC-353
74T-353
75OPC-167
75T-167
75T/M-167
76OPC-572
76SSPC-446
76T-572
91Crown/Orio-79
92Yank/WIZ70-36

Coghen, Al
77Wausau
78Wausau

Coghill, Dave
80Ander-7

Cogswell, Edward
(Ed)
No Cards.

Cohea, Dave
77Clinton
82Albuq-25
83Albuq-24

Cohen, Albert
(Alta)
90Target-132

Cohen, Andrew Howard
(Andy)
33G-52
60T-466C
V353-52

Cohen, Jim
92Negro/Kraft-13
92Negro/Retort-10

Cohen, John
88MissSt-3
89MissSt-7
90MissSt-6
91ClBest/Singl-78
91Visalia/ClBest-20
91Visalia/ProC-1752

Cohen, Tony
87Macon-23
88Augusta/ProC-380

Cohick, Emmitt
91QuadC/ClBest-23
91QuadC/ProC-2642
92PalmSp/ClBest-21
92PalmSp/ProC-852

Cohoon, Don
86Wausau-4
88CharWh/Best-18
89WinSalem/Star-5

Coin, Mike
85Beloit-5

Coker, Jimmie Goodwin
60T-438
61T-144
63T-456
64T-211
65OPC-192
65T-192
66T-292
67OPC-158
67T-158

Coker, Kerry
92Lipscomb-7
93Lipscomb-5

Coker, Kyle
92Lipscomb-23M
92Lipscomb-8

Coker, Larry
88Fayette/ProC-1084

Colarusso, Sam
88CapeCod/Sum-105
89Anchora-8

Colavito, Rocco D.
(Rocky)
55Salem
57Sohio/Ind-4
57Swift
57T-212
58T-368
59Bz
59HRDerby-6
59Kahn
59T-166M
59T-420
59T-462HL
60Armour-5
60Bz-30
60NuCard-68
60T-260M
60T-400
60T/tatt-88
60T/tatt-9
61Bz-17
61NuCard-468
61P-36
61T-330
61T-44LL
62Exh
62P-19
62P/Can-19
62Salada-28
62Shirriff-28
62T-20
62T-314IA
62T-472AS
62T/St-46
62T/bucks
63Bz-33
63Exh
63J-50
63P-50
63Salada-58

63T-240
63T-4LL
63T/SO
64Bz-33
64T-320
64T/Coins-46
64T/S-9
64T/SU
64T/St-65
64T/tatt
65Bz-33
65OldLond-23
65T-380
65T/E-46
65T/trans-45
66Bz-15
66OPC-150
66T-150
66T-220LL
66T/RO-20
66T/RO-72
67Bz-15
67CokeCap/Indian-4
67OPC-109M
67T-109M
67T-580
68OPC-99
68T-99
73OPC-449CO
73T-449CO
79TCMA-216
81Tiger/Detroit-99
82Ohio/HOF-36
83Kaline-19M
85CircK-27
89Swell-126
90Pac/Legend-18
90Swell/Great-119
90Target-133
91Swell/Great-116
92AP/ASG-65
92Yank/WIZ60-28
93Metallic-8
93TWill-33
94TedW-146
Exh47
Colavito, Steve
88Watlo/ProC-679
Colbern, Michael M.
(Mike)
79Iowa/Pol-6
79T-704R
80Iowa/Pol-2A
80Iowa/Pol-2B
80T-664R
81T-522
82Richm-22
88Indianap/ProC-499M
Colbert, Craig
88Clinton/ProC-707
89Shrev/ProC-1844
89TexLAS/GS-30
90AAASingl/ProC-44
90Phoenix/CMC-16
90Phoenix/ProC-18
90ProC/Singl-543
91AAA/LineD-380
91Phoenix/LineD-380
91Phoenix/ProC-70
92D/Rook-26
92Phoenix/ProC-2826
92StCl-891
92Ultra-588
93F-528
93Mother/Giant-21
93Pac/Spanish-610
93S-255
93Select-338
93StCl/Giant-27
93T-91
93T/Gold-91
Colbert, Nathan
(Nate)
66T-596R
69MB-63
69T-408
70MLB/St-111
70OPC-11
70T-11
70T/SO
71K-72
71MLB/St-223
71OPC-235
71T-235
71T/Coins-77
71T/GM-28
71T/Greatest-28
71T/S-22
71T/Super-22
71T/tatt-1
72K-41
72MB-78
72T-571
72T-572IA
73K-33
73OPC-340
73T-340
73T/Comics-5
73T/Lids-11
73T/PinUps-5
74K-19
74McDon
74OPC-125
74T-125
74T/DE-34
74T/St-91
75Ho-76
75OPC-599
75T-599
75T/M-599
76Laugh/Jub-16
76OPC-495
76SSPC-330
76T-495
77T-433HL
87Wichita-6
88Wichita-17
89Padre/Mag-12
89River/Best-24
89River/Cal-27CO
89River/ProC-1391CO
90HOF/St-80
90River/Best-19CO
90River/Cal-26CO
90River/ProC-2622CO
94TedW-85
Colbert, Rick
81Bristol-10
85Cram/PCL-59
87Louisvl-10
88ArkTr/GS-1
89Spring/Best-27
90Savan/ProC-2084MG
91Hamil/ClBest-29
91Hamil/ProC-4056
92Spring/ClBest-27MG
92Spring/ProC-885MG
Colbert, Vince
71MLB/St-365
71OPC-231R
71T-231R
72OPC-84
72T-84
Colborn, Jim
71MLB/St-29
71OPC-38
71T-38
72OPC-386
72T-386
73OPC-408
73T-408
74OPC-75
74T-75
74T/DE-49
74T/St-193
75OPC-305
75T-305
75T/M-305
76A&P/Milw
76OPC-521
76SSPC-226
76T-521
77T-331
78OPC-116
78SSPC/270-238
78T-129
79OPC-137
79T-276
85Iowa-29CO
86Iowa-7CO
Colbrunn, Greg
88MidwLAS/GS-42
88Rockford-8
89Rockford-8
89WPalmB/Star-7
90A&AASingle/ProC-53
90Foil/Best-5
90Jaxvl/Best-1
90Jaxvl/ProC-1377
91B-449
91D-425RR
91OPC-91
91StCl-215
91T-91
91UD-15SR
92D-557
92F/Up-96
92Indianap/ProC-1864
93Classic/Gamel-22
93D-328
93F/Final-91
93F/MLPII-3
93Flair-79
93L-55
93OPC-137
93Panini-225
93Pinn-538
93S-271
93Select-295
93StCl-522
93StCl/1stDay-522
93T-464
93T/Gold-464
93ToysRUs-74
93UD-342
93USPlayC/Rook-3H
93Ultra-64
94D-93
94F-534
94Pinn-474
94T-134
94T/Gold-134
Cole, Albert G.
E120
V100
W573
Cole, Alex
86FSLAS-11
86StPete-6
87ArkTr-20
88Louisvl-14
88Louisvl/CMC-11
88Louisvl/ProC-438
89AAA/CMC-14
89Louisvl-14
89Louisvl/CMC-21
89Louisvl/ProC-1266
89StPete/Star-7
90AAASingl/ProC-21
90F-244
90F/Can-244
90LasVegas/CMC-16
90LasVegas/ProC-133
90ProC/Singl-519
90TripleAAS/CMC-14
90UD/Ext-751
91B-64
91Classic/I-36
91D-383
91F-365
91Indian/McDon-7
91Leaf-108
91OPC-421
91OPC/Premier-24
91Panini/FrSt-222
91Panini/Top15-48
91S-555
91S/100RisSt-13
91StCl-392
91T-421
91T/90Debut-33
91T/JumboR-6
91ToysRUs-5
91UD-654
91Ultra-110
92B-173
92D-220
92F-108
92Indian/McDon-7
92L-307
92L/BlkGold-307
92OPC-170
92Panini-50
92Pinn-66
92S-463
92StCl-437
92Studio-165
92T-170
92T/Gold-170
92T/GoldWin-170
92TripleP-49
92UD-197
92Ultra-345
93B-36
93Cadaco-14
93D-70
93D-786
93F-408
93F/Final-27
93Flair-38
93L-312
93Pac/Spanish-426
93Pinn-556
93Pinn/Expan-8M
93S-400
93StCl-458
93StCl/1stDay-458
93StCl/Rockie-6
93Studio-106
93T-591
93T/Finest-12
93T/FinestRef-12
93T/Gold-591
93UD-538
93UD/SP-219
93USPlayC/Rockie-12C
93USPlayC/Rockie-7H
93Ultra-346
94F-439
94Finest-292
94Pac/Cr-194
94Pinn-467
94S-336
94Ultra-386
Cole, Bert
V61-28
Cole, Butch
91AppFx/ClBest-23
91AppFx/ProC-1728
92BBCity/ClBest-15
92BBCity/ProC-3857
Cole, Chris
89BurlInd/Star-5
Cole, David
52B-132
53B/BW-38
53JC-6
Cole, Howard
90Reno/Cal-283
Cole, Joey
79QuadC-13
Cole, Leonard
(King)
11Helmar-93
E286
E300
E90/3
T201
T207
Cole, Mark
88OK-10
89OK-10
90Lakeland/Star-4
92Stockton/ClBest-20
92Stockton/ProC-39
Cole, Marvin
88Wythe/ProC-1982
90PeoriaUp/Team-U5
91WinSalem/ClBest-18
91WinSalem/ProC-2835
Cole, Michael
81Wisco-15
Cole, Richard Roy
(Dick)
52Mother-35
53SpicSpan/3x5-7
54B-27
54T-84
55B-28
57T-234
58Union
94T/Arc54-84
Cole, Robert
(Popeye)
88Sumter/ProC-392
89BurlB/ProC-1627
89BurlB/Star-5
90CLAS/CL-30
90Durham/Team-12
91AA/LineD-204
91Greenvl/ClBest-20
91Greenvl/LineD-204
91Greenvl/ProC-3014
Cole, Rodger
85Cram/PCL-45
85Phill/TastyK-42
86Indianap-17
Cole, Stewart
(Stu)
89Memphis/Best-9
89Memphis/ProC-1184
89Memphis/Star-7
89Star/Wax-41
90Memphis/Best-4
90Memphis/ProC-1014
90Memphis/Star-5
90Star/ISingl-84
91AAA/LineD-330
91Omaha/LineD-330
91Omaha/ProC-1040
92Omaha/ProC-2967
92Omaha/SB-328
92Sky/AAASingl-150
92StCl-553
92T/91Debut-37
Cole, Tim
78Green
79Savan-20
82Richm-3
83Durham-18
Cole, Victor
89Memphis/Best-19
89Memphis/ProC-1185
89Memphis/Star-8
90Memphis/Best-20
90Memphis/ProC-1006
90Memphis/Star-6
90ProC/Singl-830
91AAA/LineD-331
91Omaha/LineD-331
91Omaha/ProC-1028
92B-239
92BuffB/ProC-316
92BuffB/SB-29
92D/Rook-27
92F/Up-113
92Sky/AAASingl-13
93D-120
93T-453
93T/Gold-453
Cole, Willis Russell
No Cards.
Cole, Winston
76Baton
77Salem
Coleman, Billy
91Oneonta/ProC-4146
92Greens/ClBest-14
92Greens/ProC-770
93Greens/ClBest-5
93Greens/ProC-879
Coleman, Clarence
(Choo Choo)
61T-502
63Exh
63T-27
64T-251
66T-561
81TCMA-298
89Tidew/Candl-5
91WIZMets-79
Exh47
Coleman, Curtis H.
(Curt)
No Cards.
Coleman, Dale
90SanAn/GS-11
91SanAn/ProC-2967
91VeroB/ClBest-6
91VeroB/ProC-767
Coleman, David Lee
(Dave)
79Toledo-17
80Colum-19
81Colum-18
Coleman, DeWayne
86Visalia-7
87WinSalem-25
88CharWh/Best-19
Coleman, Ed
93Conlon-921
Coleman, Elliot
92Negro/Retort-11
Coleman, Gerald F.
(Jerry)
49B-225
50B-47
50Drake-26
51B-49
51BR-A6

51T/RB-18
52B-73
52BR
52StarCal-84CM
52StarCal/L-70E
52T-237
54B-81
55B-99
55RFG-25
55W605-25
56T-316
57T-192
78Padre/FamFun-6
79TCMA-36
84Smok/Padres-5
90Padre/MagUno-8ANN
91Padre/Coke-2ANN
91Swell/Great-19
92Yank/WIZAS-13
93UD/ATH-33
Exh47
PM10/L-10
PM10/Sm-27
R423-10

Coleman, Glenn
91Bluefld/ClBest-14
91Bluefld/ProC-4139

Coleman, Gordon C.
(Gordy)
60HenryH-5
60T-257
60Union-19
61Kahn
61T-194
62J-116
62Kahn
62P-116
62P/Can-116
62Salada-110
62Shirriff-110
62T-508
62T/St-113
63FrBauer-3
63J-125
63Kahn
63P-125
63T-90
64T-577
65Kahn
65T-289
66T-494
67CokeCap/Reds-3
67OPC-61
67T-61
Exh47

Coleman, Guy
52Laval-46

Coleman, Hampton
52LaPatrie-3

Coleman, J. Dale
89VeroB/Star-5

Coleman, Jeff
85Clovis-11

Coleman, Joe H.
66T-333R
67OPC-167R
67T-167R
68T-573
69MB-64
69MLB/St-103
69T-246
69T/St-234
70MLB/St-281
70OPC-127
70T-127
71MLB/St-390
71OPC-403
71T-403
72K-18
72MB-79
72OPC-96LL
72T-640
72T-96LL
73K-48
73OPC-120
73T-120
74K-3
74OPC-240
74T-240
74T/DE-53
74T/St-173
75OPC-42
75T-42
75T/M-42
76OPC-456
76OPC-68FS
76SSPC-358
76T-456
76T-68FS
77T-219
78T-554
79OPC-166
79Portl-11
79T-329
80Spokane-5
80T-542
81Spokane-19
81Tiger/Detroit-126
83Peor/Frit-29MG
89Pac/SenLg-109

Coleman, Joe P.
50B-141
51B-120
53T-279
54Esskay
54NYJour
54T-156
55B-3
55Esskay
55RFG-20
55RM-AL17
55T-162
55W605-20
76OPC-68FS
76T-68FS
91Crown/Orio-80
91T/Arc53-279
94T/Arc54-156

Coleman, John Francis
E223
N172
N284
WG1-56

Coleman, Ken
89Utica/Pucko-4
92Saraso/ClBest-2
92Saraso/ProC-212

Coleman, Matthew
89Bristol/Star-5

Coleman, Parke Edward
(Ed)
34G-28
35G-8J
35G-9J
V354-76

Coleman, Paul
89Johnson/Star-6
89LittleSun-10
90B-199
90OPC-654FDP
90ProC/Singl-842
90S-662DC
90Savan/ProC-2082
90T-654
90T/TVCard-43
91B-385
91Spring/ProC-755

Coleman, Raymond L.
(Ray)
50B-250
51B-136
52B-201
52Hawth/Pin-1
52T-211

Coleman, Rickey
85Beaum-2

Coleman, Rico
89Spokane/SP-24
90CharRain/Best-6
90CharRain/ProC-2053

Coleman, Ronnie
91Burlind/ProC-3314
92Burlind/ClBest-26
92Burlind/ProC-1669

Coleman, Scott
91Martins/ClBest-25
91Martins/ProC-3445
92Martins/ClBest-13
92Martins/ProC-3047

Coleman, Solomon
(Hampton)
52Park-65
53Exh/Can-52

Coleman, Ty
80BurlB-14

Coleman, Vince
84Louisvl-20
85D/HL-29M
85D/HL-54
85F/Up-U28
85Louisvl-5
85T/Tr-24T
86D-181
86D-651M
86F-31
86F-636M
86F-637IA
86F/LL-7
86F/LimEd-11
86F/Mini-7
86F/Slug-M4
86F/St-25
86KAS/Disc-1
86KayBee-5
86Leaf-115
86Leaf-225M
86OPC-370
86OPC-D
86Quaker-3
86Schnucks-2
86Seven/Coin-S9
86Sf-136M
86Sf-176M
86Sf-24
86T-201RB
86T-370
86T-D
86T/Gloss60-21
86T/Mini-60
86T/St-306
86T/St-47
86T/St-5
86T/Super-8
86T/Tatt-16M
86T/WaxBox-D
87Classic-30
87D-263
87D/HL-36
87D/OD-60
87F-290
87F/LL-11
87F/Lim-10
87F/Mini-21
87F/Slug-M3
87F/St-25
87KayBee-11
87Kraft-18
87Leaf-194
87OPC-119
87RedFoley/St-8
87Sf-152M
87Sf-199M
87Sf-65
87Sf/TPrev-12M
87Smok/Cards-24
87Stuart-11M
87T-590
87T/Coins-29
87T/Gloss60-38
87T/Mini-32
87T/St-50
88Bz-5
88Classic/Blue-223
88D-293
88D/Best-44
88F-27
88F-634M
88F/BB/MVP-7
88F/Excit-11
88F/LL-7
88F/Mini-106
88F/St-117
88F/WS-6
88Jiffy-7
88KMart-8
88KennerFig-22
88Leaf-128
88MSA/Disc-11
88OPC-260
88Panini/St-394
88S-652HL
88S-68
88S/YS/II-24
88Sf-221
88Sf-67
88Smok/Card-19
88T-1RB
88T-260
88T/Big-5
88T/Mini-70
88T/Revco-3
88T/St-4
88T/St-47
88T/UK-16
88Woolwth-2
89B-443
89Bz-6
89Cadaco-10
89D-181
89D-19DK
89D/AS-38
89D/Best-19
89D/DKsuper-19DK
89D/PopUp-38
89F-445
89F/BBAS-8
89F/Excit-7
89F/LL-6
89KennerFig-27
89OPC-90
89Panini/St-188
89Panini/St-229AS
89S-155
89S/HotStar-86
89S/Mast-35
89Sf-113
89Smok/Cards-2
89T-90
89T/Big-124
89T/Gloss22-17
89T/LJN-59
89T/Mini-34
89T/St-154
89T/St-43
89UD-253
90B-198
90BBWit-45
90Bz-8
90Classic-105
90D-279
90D/BestNL-138
90F-245
90F/AwardWin-9
90F/Can-245
90HOF/St-100
90Holsum/Discs-15
90KayBee-7
90Kenner/Fig-20
90Leaf-90
90MLBPA/Pins-35
90OPC-660
90OPC-6RB
90Panini/St-216
90Panini/St-336
90Panini/St-383
90PublInt/St-213
90PublInt/St-609
90RedFoley/St-19
90S-260
90S/100St-73
90Sf-142
90Smok/Card-1
90SpringDG/Best-31
90T-660
90T-6RB
90T/Big-184
90T/DH-12
90T/Mini-73
90T/St-39
90T/St-4HL
90T/TVCard-32
90UD-223
90UD-68TC
90Woolwth/HL-10
91B-471
91BBBest/RecBr-4
91Bz-12
91Cadaco-12
91Classic/200-93
91Classic/I-91
91D-487
91F-629
91F/Up-U102
91Kahn/Mets-1
91Kenner-10
91Leaf-427
91Leaf/Stud-202
91OPC-160
91OPC/Premier-25
91Panini/FrSt-35
91Panini/St-35
91Panini/Top15-41
91Post-5
91RedFoley/St-21
91S-450
91S/RookTr-57T
91StCl-498
91T-160
91T/Tr-23T
91UD-461
91UD/Ext-768
91Ultra-212
92B-613
92Card/McDon/Pac-42
92Classic/Game200-52
92D-218
92F-500
92L-42
92L/BlkGold-42
92Mets/Kahn-1
92OPC-500
92Panini-227
92Pinn-39
92S-95
92S/100SS-79
92StCl-40
92Studio-63
92T-500
92T/Gold-500
92T/GoldWin-500
92TripleP-208
92UD-131
92Ultra-229
93B-186
93D-618
93F-467
93Flair-90
93L-57
93Mets/Kahn-11
93Pac/Spanish-194
93Panini-252
93Pinn-69
93S-650
93Select-175
93StCl-195
93StCl/1stDay-195
93Studio-56
93T-765
93T/Gold-765
93TripleP-14
93UD-748
93UD/SP-148
93Ultra-424
94B-499
94Finest-326
94Flair-56
94L-240
94UD-376
94Ultra-361

Coleman, W. Rip
57T-354
59T-51
60Maple-4
60T-179
61BeeHive-5
91Crown/Orio-81
D301

Coles, Cadwallader R.
(Cad)
T206

Coles, Charles Edward
(Chuck)
59T-120

Coles, Darnell
81Wausau-19
83Chatt-1
84Cram/PCL-190
84D-630
84Mother/Mar-26
85Cram/PCL-96
85D-118
85T-108
86D-557
86F/Up-U27
86T-337
86T/Tr-26T
87Cain's-2
87Coke/Tigers-14
87D-230
87D/OD-215
87F-148
87OPC-388
87Seven-DT1
87Sf/TPrev-15M
87T-411
87T/St-271
88D-572
88D/Best-185
88OPC-46
88S-554

88T-46
88T/Big-255
89B-217
89D-566
89F-544
89Mother/Sea-23
89S-83
89T-738
89T/Big-133
89UD-339
90B-480
90D-212
90F-509
90F/Can-509
90Mother/Mar-22
90OPC-232
90Panini/St-145
90PublInt/St-429
90S-62
90T-232
90T/St-227
90UD-311
91AAA/LineD-381
91F-333
91OPC-506
91Phoenix/LineD-381
91Phoenix/ProC-79
91S-629
91T-506
92B-382
92Nashvl/SB-281
92Reds/Kahn-26
93BJ/Demp-16
93BJ/Fire-6
93F-388
93F/Final-290
93Pac/Spanish-651
93S-416
93Select/RookTr-105T
93UD-721
94F-328
94S-537
94StCl/Team-162
94Ultra-137

Colescott, Rob
85LitFalls-15
86LitFalls-6
87Columbia-27
88SALAS/GS-24
88Savan/ProC-335
89Spring/Best-5

Coletta, Chris
75IntAS/TCMA-12
75IntAS/TCMA-27

Coletti, John
91Billing/SportP-13

Coletti, Mike
91Billings/ProC-3745

Colgan, William H.
(Bill)
No Cards.

Coliver, William J.
(Bill)
No Cards.

Colletti, Manny
82Omaha-15
82OrlanTw/A-4

Colley, Jay
88RochR/ProC-220

Collier, Anthony
89GreatF-22
90Star/ISingl-20
90VeroB/Star-8
91Bakers/Cal-20
91CalLgAS-17
92ClBest-204
92VeroB/ClBest-11
92VeroB/ProC-2888

Collier, Dan
92Elmira/ClBest-2
92Elmira/ProC-1394

Collier, Ervin
92Kingspt/ClBest-20
92Kingspt/ProC-1523

Collier, Lou
93Welland/ClBest-4
93Welland/ProC-3362

Collins, Allen
86WPalmB-8
87WPalmB-15
88WPalmB/Star-7
90Canton/Best-25
90Canton/ProC-1286
90Canton/Star-2

Collins, Charles
(Chub)
No Cards.

Collins, Chris
86QuadC-7
87MidldA-4
88MidldA/GS-7

Collins, Cyril Wilson
No Cards.

Collins, Daniel T.
(Dan)
No Cards.

Collins, David S.
(Dave)
75SLCity/Caruso-2
76OPC-363
76SSPC-191
76T-363
77OPC-248
77T-431
78Pep-7
78SSPC/270-135
78T-254
79T-622
80T-73
81Coke
81D-185
81F-201
81OPC-175
81T-175
81T/HT
81T/SO-84
81T/St-162
82D-169
82F-61
82F/St-14
82OPC-349
82T-595
82T/St-33
82T/StVar-33
82T/Tr-20T
83D-234
83F-377
83F/St-9M
83Madis/Frit-3DB
83OPC-359
83T-359
83T/Tr-21
84D-650
84F-151
84Nes/792-733
84OPC-38
84T-733
84Tor/Fire-9
85D-241
85F-102
85F/St-55
85F/Up-U29
85Leaf-172
85Mother/A's-14
85OPC-164
85T-463
85T/St-363
85T/Tr-25T
86Cain's-3
86D-218
86F-415
86F/Up-U28
86OPC-271
86T-271
86T/St-172
86T/Tr-27T
87D-215
87F-149
87Sf/TPrev-20M
87T-148
88Kahn/Reds-22
88S-371
89Kodak/WSox-2M
89S-267
89TM/SenLg-22
89UD-351
90BJ/HoSt-5M
90Smok/Card-2
90T/TVCard-33
92Yank/WIZ80-34

Collins, Don
80Tacoma-5
82Spring/Frit-18

Collins, Edw.T. Jr.
(Eddie)
No Cards.

Collins, Edw.T. Sr.
(Eddie)
10Domino-27
11Diamond-10
11Helmar-55
12Sweet/Pin-43A
12Sweet/Pin-43B
14CJ-7
14Piedmont/St-14
15CJ-7
21Exh-25
25Exh-73
26Exh-74
27Exh-54
33G-42
48Exh/HOF
50Callahan
50W576-19
51T/CM
60Exh/HOF-8
60F-20
61F-16
61GP-28
63Bz/ATG-41
69Bz/Sm
72F/FFeat-18
72K/ATG-10
72Laugh/GF-43
75F/Pion-20
76Rowe-13M
76Shakey-17
77Galasso-111
77Galasso-182
77Shakey-16
80Laugh/FFeat-32
80Pac/Leg-26
80Perez/HOF-18
80SSPC/HOF
81Conlon-39
87Conlon/2-27
88Conlon/5-5
88Pac/8Men-8
88Pac/8Men-99
90BBWit-76
90Perez/GreatMom-45
91Conlon/Sport-21
91Conlon/Sport-312
92Conlon/Sport-582
93AP/ASG-89
93AP/ASG24K-23G
93CrackJack-17
94Conlon-1040
94Conlon-1142
94TedW-19
BF2-9
D303
D304
D327
D328-31
D329-34
E101
E102
E103
E104
E105
E106
E120
E121/120
E121/80
E122
E126-16
E135-31
E210-47
E221
E254
E90/1
E92
E93
E98
L1-125
M101/4-34
M116
R328-1
S74-29
S81-100
T202
T204
T205
T206
T207
T208
T213/blue
T215/blue
T215/brown
T216
V117-4
V353-42
V61-29
V89-35
W501-38
W514-25
W515-58
W517-52
W555
W572
W573
W575
WG4-6

Collins, Frankie
80GlenF/C-29M

Collins, George H.
(Hub)
N172

Collins, Harry W.
(Rip)
W575

Collins, Hugh
No Cards.

Collins, James A.
(Rip)
35BU-146
35BU-78
35G-51
88Conlon/NatAS-3
92Card/McDon/Pac-2
92Conlon/Sport-656
94Conlon-1237
94Conlon-1261
R312
R312/M
R313
V355-18
WG8-7

Collins, James Joseph
(Jimmy)
35Wheat
50Callahan
50W576-20
51T/CMAS
60Exh/HOF-9
60F-25
61F-99
63Bz/ATG-23
69Bz/Sm
76Shakey-32
80Perez/HOF-32
80SSPC/HOF
89HOF/St-23
E104
E107
E220
E91
E95
R310
T204
T205
T206
T3-87
W555
WG2-8

Collins, John Edgar
(Zip)
No Cards.

Collins, John Francis
(Shano)
11Helmar-9
21Exh-26
88Pac/8Men-98
93Conlon-745
94Conlon-1042M
BF2-10
D327
D328-32
D329-35
D350/2-34
E120
E135-32
M101/4-35
M101/5-34
V100
W572

Collins, Joseph E.
(Joe)
52B-181
52BR
52T-202
53T-9
54NYJour
54T-83
55T-63
55T/DH-65
56T-21
56T/Pin-28
57T-295
79TCMA-21
91T/Arc53-9
94T/Arc54-83
PM10/L-11

Collins, Kevin M.
65T-581R
69OPC-127
69T-127
69T/4in1-13M
70T-707
71OPC-553
71T-553
91WIZMets-80

Collins, Mike
92Billings/ProC-3361

Collins, Orth Stein
No Cards.

Collins, Patrick T.
26Exh-97
28Exh-49
29Exh/4-1
91Conlon/Sport-118
E126-35
V61-35

Collins, Phil
32Orbit/num-22
32Orbit/un-13
33G-21
35Exh/4-6
93Conlon-785
R305
V353-21

Collins, Ray
15CJ-169
16FleischBrd-18
M116

Collins, Robert J.
(Bob)
No Cards.

Collins, Ron
88Eugene/Best-18
89Eugene/Best-20

Collins, Scott
81Batavia-19

Collins, Sean
89Eugene/Best-24
90BBCity/Star-4

Collins, Sherman
89VeroB/Star-6

Collins, Stacey
91Rockford/ClBest-3
91Rockford/ProC-2038

Collins, Terry
75Albuq/Caruso-8
78Cr/PCL-41
80Albuq-19
82VeroB-26
84Cram/PCL-167
85Cram/PCL-156MG
86Albuq-3MG
87Albuq/Pol-1MG
88AAA/ProC-47
88Albuq/CMC-25
88Albuq/ProC-270
89BuffB/CMC-24
89BuffB/ProC-1668
90AAAGame/ProC-36MG
90AAASingl/ProC-504MG
90BuffB/CMC-3MG
90BuffB/ProC-389MG
90BuffB/Team-7MG
90ProC/Singl-3MG
91AAA/LineD-49MG
91BuffB/LineD-49MG
91BuffB/ProC-556MG
92Pirate/Nation-5CO
93Pirate/Nation-6CO

Collins, Tharon L.
(Pat)
E120
W573

Collins, Tim
85Bend/Cram-5

Collins, Tony
86Geneva-3
86Peoria-3

Collins, William J.
(Bill)
N172

Collins, William S.
(Bill)
90Target-915
C46-34
Collum, Jack
54B-204
55B-189
57T-268
90Target-134
V362-30
Colman, Frank Lloyd
52Park-9
Colmenares, Carlos
92MedHat/ProC-3212
92MedHat/SportP-18
93MedHat/ProC-3742
93MedHat/SportP-1
Colombino, Carlo
86Ashvl-5
87Osceola-4
88ColAst/Best-19
88SLAS-10
89Tucson/CMC-21
89Tucson/JP-5
89Tucson/ProC-206
91AAA/LineD-608
91Tucson/LineD-608
91Tucson/ProC-2219
92Canton/ProC-695
92Canton/SB-103
Colombino, Chris
90Osceola/Star-5
Colon, Angel
92Welland/ClBest-6
92Welland/ProC-1328
Colon, Charlie
88NE-2
90NE-7
Colon, Cris
87PortChar-22
88Gaston/ProC-1005
89Gaston/ProC-1014
89Gaston/Star-4
90CharlR/Star-3
90SALAS/Star-4
91CharlR/ClBest-17
91CharlR/ProC-1321
91ClBest/Singl-183
92B-405
92Sky/AASingl-266
92Tulsa/ProC-2700
92Tulsa/SB-605
93D-353
93Rang/Keeb-107
93S-314
93T-809
93T/Gold-809
93UD-14SR
Colon, David
88Sumter/ProC-411
90ProC/Singl-702
90Waterlo/Best-2
90Waterlo/ProC-2389
91PalmSp/ProC-2027
92PalmSp/ClBest-24
92PalmSp/ProC-853
Colon, Dennis
92BurlAs/ClBest-19
92BurlAs/ProC-553
Colon, Felix
90WinHaven/Star-2
91Elmira/ClBest-2
91Elmira/ProC-3275
92WinHaven/ProC-1784
94FExcel-19
Colon, Hector
91Johnson/ClBest-14
91Johnson/ProC-3988
92Johnson/ClBest-22
92Johnson/ProC-3129
Colon, Jose
91Burllnd/ProC-3291
Colon, Roque
92Hunting/ClBest-7
92Hunting/ProC-3161
Colon, Tony
89Geneva/ProC-1875
Colpaert, Dick
73OPC-608R
73T-608R
Colpitt, Mike
87Spartan-28
Colson, Brent
92Yakima/ProC-3440
Colson, Bruce
88Cedar/ProC-1145
Colson, Loyd
71OPC-111R
71T-111R
92Yank/WIZ70-37
Colston, Frank
87Miami-16
87SLCity/Taco-18
88Wausau/GS-24
Colton, Lawrence
68T-348R
69T-454R
Coluccio, Robert P.
(Bob)
74OPC-124
74T-124
74T/St-194
75OPC-456
75T-456
75T/M-456
76OPC-333
76SSPC-150
76T-333
78Charl
Colvard, Benny
(Ben)
88Billings/ProC-1830
89Cedar/Best-19
89Cedar/ProC-916
89Cedar/Star-4
89Star/IISingl-197
90Chatt/GS-9
91Chatt/ProC-1971
92Chatt/ProC-3829
92Chatt/SB-179
92ClBest-69
Colvin, Jeff
92Lipscomb-9
Colzie, Rick
80Batavia-22
81Watlo-2
Combe, Geoff
79Indianap-19
80Indianap-7
81Indianap-3
81T-606R
82Edmon-23
82F-62
82T-351R
Combs, Bobby
75AppFx
77AppFx
Combs, Earle Bryan
26Exh-98
28Yueng-21
29Exh/4-25
31Exh/4-25
32Orbit/num-111
33G-103
40PlayBall-124
44Yank/St-6
54T-183
61F-17
76Rowe-2M
76Shakey-116
77Galasso-109
80Pac/Leg-105
80Perez/HOF-116
80SSPC/HOF
91Conlon/Sport-105
91Conlon/Sport-262
92Conlon/Sport-466
92Conlon/Sport-583
92Yank/WIZHOF-6
93Conlon-732
94T/Arc54-183
R314
R316
R328-5
R332-28
V354-21
W502-21
W513-86
W517-1
Combs, Mark
87SanBern-9
88Fresno/Cal-2
Combs, Merrill R.
48Signal
48Smith-23
52T-18
93Rang/Keeb-108CO
Combs, Pat
87PanAm/USAB-5
87PanAm/USAR-5
88T/Tr-30T
89B-398
89BBAmAA/BPro-AA10
89Clearw/Star-8
89Reading/ProC-676
89Reading/Star-9
89Star/Wax-12
89T/Big-227
90B-148
90Classic/Up-12
90D-44
90D/BestNL-49
90D/Rook-3
90F-553
90F/Can-553
90Leaf-78
90OPC-384
90Phill/TastyK-5
90S-623RP
90S/DTRook-B2
90S/YS/II-4
90T-384
90T/89Debut-24
90T/Big-136
90TeamUSA/87-5
90UD/Ext-763
91B-498
91Classic/200-94
91Classic/II-T41
91D-60
91F-392
91Leaf-32
91OPC-571
91Phill/Medford-9
91S-440
91S/100RisSt-72
91StCl-36
91T-571
91T/JumboR-7
91ToysRUs-6
91UD-537
91Ultra-259
92D-76
92F-525
92OPC-456
92Phill/Med-39
92S-106
92ScranWB/ProC-2442
92ScranWB/SB-482
92StCl-443
92T-456
92T/Gold-456
92T/GoldWin-456
92TripleP-170
92UD-442
93ScranWB/Team-6
Comeau, Drew
88CapeCod/Sum-124
Comer, H. Wayne
69T-346
70MLB/St-268
70McDon-2
70OPC-323
70T-323
88Domino-3
Comer, Steve
79T-463
80T-144
81T-592
82D-341
82F-314
82F/St-177
82T-16
82T/St-242
83D-163
83F-564
83T-353
84Wheat/Ind-31
85T-788
86Maine-6C
88OrlanTw/Best-7
93Rang/Keeb-109
Comforti, Dave
81Holyo-5M
Comimbre, Francisco
(Pancho)
87Negro/Dixon-38
Comiskey, Charles A.
(Charlie)
14CJ-23
15CJ-23
50Callahan
50W576-21
61F-18
76Shakey-22
80Perez/HOF-20
80SSPC/HOF
87Conlon/2-26
88Pac/8Men-24
88Pac/8Men-80
BF2-11
D329-36
D350/2-35
M101/4-36
M101/5-35
N172
N172/BC
N28
N284
N370
Scrapps
Command, James Dalton
(Jim)
No Cards.
Como, George
82Holyo-25
83Nashua-26
85Nashua-28
Comoletti, Glenn
78StPete
Comorosky, Adam A.
31Exh/4-13
33G-77
34G-85
35BU-44
35G-1H
35G-1K
35G-3B
35G-3F
35G-4F
35G-5B
35G-5F
35G-6B
91Conlon/Sport-73
V353-70
Compos, Rafael
89Ashvl/ProC-949
Compres, Fidel
87Watlo-1
90CharlR/Star-4
91AAA/LineD-231
91ArkTr/ProC-1276
91Louisvl/LineD-231
92ArkTr/ProC-1122
92ArkTr/SB-30
92ClBest-331
92Sky/AASingl-14
93LimeR/Winter-7
Compton, Anna S.
(Pete)
No Cards.
Compton, Clint 1
73Wichita-3
Compton, Clint 2
92CharRain/ClBest-17
Compton, Kenny
86Fres/Smok-27bb
Compton, Michael Lynn
(Mike)
71MLB/St-174
71OPC-77
71T-77
77Spartan
80Water-10
Comstock, Brad
87Everett-27
88Fresno/Cal-25
88Fresno/ProC-1226
Comstock, Keith
77QuadC
80WHave-19
81WHave-6
82Tacoma-39
82WHave-5
83BirmB-22
84Toledo-16
88F-579
88LasVegas/CMC-2
88LasVegas/ProC-246
88S-438
88T-778
89LasVegas/CMC-2
89LasVegas/ProC-14
90B-467
90BirmDG/Best-5
90F-510
90F/Can-510
90Leaf-522
90Mother/Mar-23
91CounHrth-20
91D-246
91OPC-337
91S-502
91StCl-556
91T-337A
91T-337B
Conatser, Clinton A.
(Clint)
49Eureka-5
Concepcion, Carlos
84CharlO-6
Concepcion, David E.
(Dave)
71MLB/St-56
71OPC-14
71T-14
72OPC-267
72T-267
72T/Cloth-7
73OPC-554
73T-554
74OPC-435
74T-435
74T/St-24
75Ho-47
75OPC-17
75T-17
75T/M-17
76Ho-128
76Icee
76OPC-48
76SSPC-34
76T-48
77BurgChef-200
77Ho-95
77Ho/Twink-95
77OPC-258
77Pepsi-47
77T-560
78Ho-108
78OPC-220
78Pep-8
78SSPC/270-133
78T-180
78Wiffle/Discs-19
79Ho-85
79OPC-234
79T-450
80OPC-117
80T-220
81Coke
81D-181
81F-197
81F/St-101
81K-28
81OPC-83
81PermaGr/AS-2
81T-375
81T/HT
81T/SO-95
81T/St-161
82Coke/Reds
82D-421
82F-63
82F-630M
82F/St-109M
82K-22
82OPC-221IA
82OPC-340AS
82OPC-86
82PermaGr/AS-11
82Sqt-15
82T-340
82T-660
82T-661A
82T/St-124
82T/St-37
82T/StVar-37
83D-148
83D/AAS-47
83F-588
83F-631M
83F/St-21M
83F/St-4M
83K-57
83OPC-102
83OPC-32AS
83OPC/St-227

83T-400
83T-720
83T/Fold-5M
83T/Gloss40-34
83T/St-227
84D-121
84D-2
84F-466
84MiltBrad-6
84Nes/792-55
84OPC-55
84Ralston-20
84T-55
84T/Cereal-20
84T/RD-15
84T/St-56
85D-203
85D/HL-8
85F-532
85FunFood/Pin-23
85Leaf-131
85OPC-21
85T-515
85T/RD-13
85T/St-48
86D-243
86F-174
86GenMills/Book-5M
86OPC-195
86Sf-131M
86Sf-153
86T-195
86T-366M
86T/St-137
86T/Tatt-22M
86TexGold-13
87F-196
87Kahn-13
87OPC-193
87RedFoley/St-12
87T-731
88D-329
88F-229
88Kahn/Reds-13
88OPC-336
88Panini/St-275
88S-210
88Sf-218
88T-422
88T/Big-144
89F-156
89S-166
89UD-196
91MDA-6

Concepcion, Onix
81Omaha-16
83D-516
83F-110
83T-52
84D-95
84F-345
84Nes/792-247
84T-247
85D-155
85F-200
85T-697
85ThomMc/Discs-8
86D-252
86F-6
86Kitty/Disc-5
86OPC-163
86T-596

Concepcion, Yamil
91Princet/ClBest-19
91Princet/ProC-3520
92Princet/ClBest-6
92Princet/ProC-3078

Conde, Ramon Luis
60DF-14
61Union

Cone, David
82CharR-19
84Memphis-25
85Omaha-25
86Omaha/ProC-6
86Omaha/TCMA-16
87D-502
87D/Rook-35
87Sf/Rook-39
87T/Tr-24T
88D-653
88D/Best-40
88D/Mets/Bk-653
88F-131
88Kahn/Mets-44
88S-49
88T-181
88ToysRUs-8
89B-375
89Cadaco-11
89Classic-100
89Classic-125
89D-388
89D-9DK
89D/AS-44
89D/Best-96
89D/DKsuper-9DK
89F-31
89F-636M
89F/BBAS-9
89F/Excit-8
89F/Heroes-9
89F/LL-7
89F/WaxBox-C7
89Holsum/Discs-19
89Kahn/Mets-44
89KennerFig-28
89MSA/Disc-2
89Nissen-19
89OPC-384
89Panini/St-129
89RedFoley/St-24
89S-221
89S/HotStar-2
89S/YS/I-9
89Sf-51
89T-710
89T/DHTest-6
89T/Gloss60-6
89T/Hills-9
89T/Mets/Fan-44
89T/Mini-24
89T/St-96
89T/St/Backs-58
89T/UK-17
89Tetley/Discs-2
89UD-584
90B-125
90D-265
90D/BestNL-43
90F-200
90F/Can-200
90F/LL-7
90Kahn/Mets-44
90Leaf-40
90MLBPA/Pins-11
90Mets/Fan-44
90OPC-30
90Panini/St-301
90PublInt/St-129
90S-430
90Sf-201
90T-30
90T/Big-11
90T/Mini-65
90T/St-93
90T/TVMets-8
90UD-224
91B-460
91D-154
91F-143
91Kahn/Mets-17
91Leaf-253
91OPC-680
91Panini/St-80
91Panini/Top15-73
91S-409KM
91S-549
91StCl-367
91StCl/Member*-13
91T-680
91UD-366
91Ultra-213
91WIZMets-81
92B-238
92Classic/Game200-143
92Classic/I-27
92Classic/II-T45
92D-97
92F-501
92F-687RS
92F/Smoke-S3
92F/Up-63
92L-92
92L/BlkGold-92
92Mets/Kahn-17
92OPC-195
92OPC/Premier-175
92Pinn-450
92Pinn-590M
92Pinn-611GRIP
92S-680
92S-795HL
92S/100SS-16
92S/Impact-90
92S/RookTr-27T
92StCl-17
92T-195
92T/Gold-195
92T/GoldWin-195
92T/Kids-16
92TripleP-35
92TripleP-64
92UD-364
92UD/TmMVPHolo-17
92Ultra-230
92Ultra/AS-19
93B-97
93BJ/D/45-15
93Classic/GameI-23
93D-712
93F-691
93F/Final-216
93Flair-214
93Kenner/Fig-9
93L-250
93OPC-107
93OPC/Premier-92
93OPC/WC-4
93Pac/Spanish-486
93Pinn-489HH
93Pinn-544
93Pol/Royal-6
93S-654
93Select-361
93Select/RookTr-18T
93Select/StatL-77
93StCl-703
93StCl/1stDay-703
93StCl/MurphyS-154
93StCl/Royal-17
93T-720
93T/Finest-115AS
93T/FinestASJ-115AS
93T/FinestRef-115AS
93T/Gold-720
93T/Tr-125T
93UD-335
93UD-534
93UD/FunPack-179GS
93UD/FunPack-182
93UD/SP-228
93Ultra-558
94B-593
94D-194
94F-152
94F/Smoke-2
94L-274
94OPC-260
94Pac/Cr-281
94Pinn-325
94RedFoley-19M
94S-405
94Select-76
94Sf/2000-39
94StCl-292
94StCl/1stDay-292
94StCl/Gold-292
94Studio-182
94T-510
94T/Finest-52
94T/Finest/PreProd-52
94T/FinestRef-52
94T/Gold-510
94TripleP-232
94UD-413
94UD/CollC-81
94UD/CollC/Gold-81
94UD/CollC/Silv-81
94UD/SP-171
94Ultra-362

Confreda, Gene
83Beaum-23
87Ashvl-3
88Ashvl/ProC-1076
90Osceola/Star-30TR

Congalton, William M.
(Bunk)
E254
E270/2
T206

Conger, Jeff
92Augusta/ClBest-24
92Augusta/ProC-250
92ClBest-16

Conigliaro, Anthony
(Tony)
64T-287R
65OPC-55
65T-55
65T/trans-11
66Bz-6
66T-218LL
66T-380
66T/RO-113
66T/RO-21
67Bz-6
67T-280
67T/Test/RSox-3
67T/Test/RSox-30
68Bz-4
68OPC-140
68T-140
68T/ActionSt-8C
69T-330
70OPC-340
70T-340
71Bz/Test-45
71JB
71MLB/St-342
71OPC-105
71OPC-63LL
71T-105
71T-63LL
71T/Coins-142
71T/tatt-10
78TCMA-206
94TedW-137
PM10/Sm-28
PM10/Sm-29

Conigliaro, William
(Billy)
69T-628R
70OPC-317R
70T-317R
71MLB/St-316
71OPC-114
71T-114
72MB-80
72OPC-481
72T-481
74OPC-545
74T-545

Conine, Jeff
88BBCity/Star-10
89BBCity/Star-6
90A&AASingle/ProC-48
90Foil/Best-156
90Memphis/Best-8
90Memphis/ProC-1017
90Memphis/Star-7
90ProC/Singl-743
90Star/ISingl-85
91AAA/LineD-332
91B-184
91Classic/200-96
91Classic/I-47
91D-427RR
91F-553
91Leaf/Stud-63
91OPC/Premier-26
91Omaha/LineD-332
91Omaha/ProC-1041
91S-722RP
91S/HotRook-5
91S/Rook40-19
91StCl-578
91T/90Debut-34
91UD-27RS
91Ultra-145
92AAA/ASG/SB-329
92D/RookPhen-BC3
92Omaha/ProC-2968
92Omaha/SB-329
92S/100RisSt-21
92Sky/AAASingl-151
92StCl-683
93B-670
93Cadaco-15
93D-101
93D-765
93F-423
93F/Final-57
93Flair-49
93JDean/Rook-3
93L-288
93Marlin/Publix-8
93OPC/Premier-119
93Pac/Spanish-458
93Pinn-479I
93Pinn-601
93Pinn/Expan-7
93S-402
93Select-321
93Select/ChasRook-12
93Select/RT/ASRook-1
93StCl-340
93StCl/1stDay-340
93StCl/Marlin-13
93Studio-54
93T-789
93T/Finest-54
93T/FinestRef-54
93T/Gold-789
93TripleP-93
93UD-479M
93UD-754
93UD/FunPack-119
93UD/SP-138
93USPlayC/Marlin-11H
93USPlayC/Marlin-5S
93USPlayC/Marlin-9C
93Ultra-371
93Ultra/AllRook-2
94B-383
94B-394
94D-156
94F-464
94F/RookSen-5
94Flair-161
94L-41
94OPC-238
94OPC/DiamD-12
94Oscar-19
94Pac/Cr-239
94Pac/Silv-23
94Panini-181
94Pinn-30
94Pinn/Artist-30
94Pinn/Museum-30
94S-484
94S/GoldS-30
94Select-26
94Sf/2000-62
94StCl-406
94StCl/1stDay-406
94StCl/Gold-406
94StCl/Team-90
94Studio-108
94T-466
94T/Finest-4
94T/FinestRef-4
94T/Gold-466
94TripleP-134
94UD-162
94UD/CollC-82
94UD/CollC/Gold-82
94UD/CollC/Silv-82
94UD/ElecD-162
94UD/SP-109
94Ultra-491
94Ultra/Second-7

Conklin, Chip
82Wausau/Frit-28
83Wausau/Frit-11
85Huntsvl/BK-17

Conkright, Dan
88BirmB/Best-21

Conlan, John Bertrand
(Jocko)
55B-303UMP
75Sheraton-3
76Shakey-143
77Galasso-87
80Pac/Leg-59
80Perez/HOF-143
80SSPC/HOF
88TM/Umpire-63
89HOF/St-98
94Conlon-1196UMP

Conley, Bob
78Watlo

Conley, D. Eugene
(Gene)
53T-215
54JC-22
54SpicSpan/PostC-6
54T-59

55Gol/Braves-6
55JC-22
55SpicSpan/DC-6
55T-81
55T/DH-34
56T-17
56T/Pin-17
57SpicSpan/4x5-6
57T-28
58T-431
59T-492
60Armour-6
60T-293
61P-124
61T-193
61T/St-119
62T-187
63T-216
64T-571
90Pac/Legend-79
91T/Arc53-215
94T/Arc54-59

Conley, Greg
88Spokane/ProC-1922
89CharRain/ProC-974
90Waterlo/Best-22
90Waterlo/ProC-2381
91HighD/ClBest-15
91HighD/ProC-2398

Conley, Matt
91Sumter/ClBest-3
91Sumter/ProC-2326
92Albany/ClBest-18
92Albany/ProC-2298

Conley, Robert Burns
(Bob)
59T-121

Conley, Virgil
83Tampa-2
84Cedar-8
85Cedar-4
86Penin-6
87Penin-27
88Jacks/GS-11

Conlon, Angel
92Welland/ClBest-6

Conlon, Arthur Joseph
(Art)
No Cards.

Conlon, Charles M.
86Conlon/1-59
91Conlon/Sport-327
94Conlon-1266

Conn, Albert Thomas
(Bert)
No Cards.

Conn, Gary
75BurlB
76BurlB
77Holyo

Connally, Fritzie Lee
81QuadC-5
83Iowa-13
84Cram/PCL-224
85F/Up-U30
91Crown/Orio-82

Connally, George
(Sarge)
33G-27
91Conlon/Sport-247
R337-406
V353-27

Connally, Mervin T.
(Bud)
No Cards.

Connatser, Broadus M.
(Bruce)
No Cards.

Connaughton, Frank H.
No Cards.

Connell, Eugene J.
(Gene)
No Cards.

Connell, Joseph B.
(Joe)
No Cards.

Connell, Lino
92Boise/ClBest-14
92Boise/ProC-3636

Connell, Monty
89GA-3

Connell, Peter J.
(Pete)
N172

Connelly, Bill
53T-126
79TCMA-60
91T/Arc53-126

Connelly, Daron
86Cram/NWL-196
87Clinton-24
88SanJose/Cal-130
88SanJose/ProC-135

Connelly, David
86Cram/NWL-197

Connelly, Thomas M.
(Tom)
No Cards.

Conner, Greg
88SanJose/Cal-118
88SanJose/ProC-129
89Shrev/ProC-1839

Conner, Jeff
81Holyo-12
82Holyo-3
83Nashua-4
84Evansvl-18
86Nashvl-5

Conner, John
90AppFox/Box-7
90AppFox/ProC-2089
91BBCity/ClBest-2
91BBCity/ProC-1389
91ClBest/Singl-71

Connolly, Chris
91Eugene/ClBest-29
91Eugene/ProC-3716
93Rockford/ClBest-8

Connolly, Craig
90SoOreg/Best-20
90SoOreg/ProC-3441
91Madison/ClBest-6
91Madison/ProC-2123
92Reno/Cal-37
93Modesto/ClBest-6
93Modesto/ProC-792

Connolly, Edward J.
(Ed)
65T-543

Connolly, John M.
(Red)
No Cards.

Connolly, Joseph A.
(Joe)
15CJ-155
D329-37
D350/2-36
M101/4-37
M101/5-36

Connolly, Joseph G.
(Joe)
No Cards.

Connolly, Matt
91Erie/ClBest-16
91Erie/ProC-4061
92Visalia/ClBest-4
92Visalia/ProC-1006
93WPalmB/ProC-1331

Connolly, Steve
87Pocatel/Bon-4
88Clinton/ProC-696
88MidwLAS/GS-6
89Shrev/ProC-1830
90Shrev/ProC-1437
90Shrev/Star-3

Connolly, Thomas F.
(Blackie)
No Cards.

Connolly, Thomas H.
50Callahan
50W576-22
76Shakey-67
77Galasso-149UMP
80Perez/HOF-65
80SSPC/HOF
89TM/Umpire-63
92Conlon/Sport-469
94Conlon-1186UMP

Connor, James Matthew
(Jim)
No Cards.

Connor, Joseph F.
(Joe)
No Cards.

Connor, Joseph
(Joe)
No Cards.

Connor, Mark
90T/TVYank-2CO

Connor, Roger
76Shakey-153
80Perez/HOF-153
80SSPC/HOF
89HOF/St-9
E223
N167
N167-1
N172
N284
N690
WG1-37

Connors, Billy
67T-272R
83Thorn-26CO
90T/TVYank-3CO
91Cub/Mara-x
91WIZMets-82CO
92Cub/Mara-NNO
93Cub/Mara-5CO

Connors, Jeremiah
(Jerry)
No Cards.

Connors, Joseph P.
(Joe)
No Cards.

Connors, Kevin Joseph
(Chuck)
52Mother-4
77Fritsch-2
80Pac/Leg-28
88Pac/Leg-71
89Rini/Dodg-21
90Target-135
V362-2

Connors, Mervyn James
(Merv)
No Cards.

Conquest, Tom
82Idaho-5
83Madis/Frit-12

Conroy, Bernard P.
(Ben)
No Cards.

Conroy, Brian
90CLAS/CL-9
90LynchRS/Team-16
91AA/LineD-453
91NewBrit/LineD-453
91NewBrit/ProC-344
92NewBrit/ProC-425
92Pawtu/SB-355
92Sky/AAASingl-160
93B-579
93Pawtu/Ball-8

Conroy, Mike
88Stockton/ProC-752
89Stockton/Best-31M
89Stockton/ProC-402M
89Stockton/Star-28M

Conroy, Tim
80WHave-22
81WHave-7
84D-340
84F-442
84Mother/A's-24
84Nes/792-156TL
84Nes/792-189
84T-156TL
84T-189
85D-156
85F-421
85Mother/A's-16
85T-503
86F/Up-U29
86Schnucks-3
86T/Tr-28T
87F-291
87T-338
88Louisvl-15
88Louisvl/CMC-5
88S-384
88T-658
89Harris/ProC-288
89Harris/Star-6

Conroy, William E.
(Wid)
11Helmar-67
46Sunbeam
E254
E91
M116
T204
T206
T215/brown

Conroy, William F.
(Pep)
No Cards.

Conroy, William G.
(Bill)
No Cards.

Consolo, William A.
(Billy)
54T-195
55T-207
57T-399
58T-148
59T-112
60T-508
61P-100
61Peters-26
61T-504
84Tiger/Wave-11CO
88Pep/T-CO
89Mara/Tigers-CO
90CokeK/Tiger-28CO
91CokeK/Tiger-x
94T/Arc54-195

Constable, Jimmy
59T-451
63T-411

Constant, Andres
89Freder/Star-3
90Freder/Team-25
91Freder/ClBest-2
91Freder/ProC-2356

Constantino, Kraig
92Spokane/ClBest-16
92Spokane/ProC-1298

Consuegra, Sandy
51B-96
52B-143
53B/Col-89
54B-166
55B-116
55RM-AL25
56T-265
79TCMA-170
91Crown/Orio-83

Conte, Michael
(Mike)
89Medford/Best-1
90Madison/ProC-2276
90Modesto/Chong-6
91Huntsvl/ClBest-4
91Huntsvl/Team-6
91HuntsvlProC-1808
92Huntsvl/ProC-3959
92Huntsvl/SB-307

Conti, Guy
86Watertn-6CO
88Bakers/Cal-263CO
89AS/Cal-24CO
89Bakers/Cal-207CO
90GreatF/SportP-29CO
92GreatF/SportP-30CO

Conti, Joe
88CapeCod/Sum-15

Contreras, Frank
82Miami-21

Contreras, Henry
81BurlB-15

Contreras, Joaquin
85LitFalls-22
86Columbia-7
87Jacks/Feder-15
87TexLgAS-16
88Jacks/GS-20
88Tidew/CANDL-15
88Tidew/CMC-17
89Tidew/CMC-16
89Tidew/ProC-1960
90AAASingl/ProC-476
90RochR/ProC-719
90Rochester/L&U-25
91AAA/LineD-452
91RochR/LineD-452

Contreras, Nardi
75Tidew/Team-6
80Iowa/Pol-3
82Edmon-14CO
85BuffB-2CO
87Richm/Crown-43CO
87Richm/TCMA-22CO
88Jaxvl/Best-23CO
88Jaxvl/ProC-969CO
88SLAS-40CO
89Jaxvl/Best-26CO
89Jaxvl/ProC-173CO
90Jaxvl/Best-26CO
90Jaxvl/ProC-1392CO
91AAA/LineD-200M
91Indianap/LineD-200CO
91Indianap/ProC-478CO

Converse, Jim
90LitSun/HSPros-22
90LitSun/HSProsG-22
91Penin/ClBest-2
92Jacks/ProC-3701
92Jaxvl/SB-354
92Sky/AASingl-150
92UD/ML-259
93B-543
93Calgary/ProC-1158
93F/Final-267
93FExcel/ML-222
93StCl-683
93StCl/1stDay-683
93T/Tr-40T
93Ultra-616
94Pac/Cr-566

Converse, Mike
86Cedar/TCMA-3
87Tampa-3

Conway, Jack Clements
No Cards.

Conway, Jack
92TX-9

Conway, James P.
N172

Conway, John
52Park-96

Conway, Owen S.
No Cards.

Conway, Peter J.
(Pete)
N172
Scrapps

Conway, Richard D.
(Rip)
N172

Conway, William
(Bill)
No Cards.

Conwell, Edward J.
(Ed)
No Cards.

Conyers, Herbert L.
(Herb)
No Cards.

Coogan, Dale Roger
50B-244
52T-87

Coogan, Daniel George
(Dan)
No Cards.

Cook, Andy
88Oneonta/ProC-2041
89PrWill/Star-3
90Albany/Best-2
90Albany/ProC-1031
90Albany/Star-3
90ProC/Singl-731
91AA/LineD-1
91Albany/LineD-1
91Albany/ProC-999
92ColClip/ProC-342
93B-124
93ColClip/Pol-2
93F/Final-244
94Pinn-257
94Pinn/Artist-257
94Pinn/Museum-257

Cook, Brian
90AR-6

Cook, Dennis
86Fresno/Smok-16
87Shrev-4
88Phoenix/CMC-3
88Phoenix/ProC-80
89D-646
89D/Best-327
89F-652R
89F/Up-104
89Panini/St-207
89Phill/TastyK-39
89Phoenix/CMC-3
89Phoenix/ProC-1482
89UD/Ext-779

90Classic-80
90D-193
90D/BestNL-93
90F-554
90F/Can-554
90HotRook/St-12
90Leaf-342
90OPC-633
90Panini/St-320
90Phill/TastyK-6
90S-545
90S/100Ris-75
90T-633
90UD-71
91AAA/LineD-4
91Albuq/LineD-4
91D-657
91F-196
91Leaf-257
91OPC-467
91Pol/Dodg-25
91StCl-411
91T-467
91UD-612
92B-497
92F-451
92Indian/McDon-8
92L-503
92L/BlkGold-503
92Pinn-493
92StCl-887
92TX-10
92Ultra-346
93D-625
93F-214
93Indian/WUAB-7
93L-193
93Pac/Spanish-409
93StCl-153
93StCl/1stDay-153
93T-141
93T/Gold-141
93UD-202

Cook, Doug
81CharR-12
83CharR-16
84Memphis-12
91Idaho/ProC-4321

Cook, Glen
82BurlR/Frit-23
82BurlR/TCMA-17
83BurlR-3
83BurlR/Frit-12
83Tulsa-2
84OKCty-22
85OKCty-8
86OKCty-4
86T-502
87OKCty-14
93Rang/Keeb-110

Cook, James Fitchie
(Jim)
No Cards.

Cook, James
86Kenosha-4

Cook, Jeff
86PrWill-7
87Harris-10
88EastLAS/ProC-13
88Harris/ProC-835
89Harris/ProC-304
89Harris/Star-7
90AAASingl/ProC-502
90BuffB/CMC-24
90BuffB/ProC-387
90ProC/Singl-24

Cook, Kenny
92GulfCD/ProC-3558

Cook, Kerry
83SanJose-13
86WPalmB-9

Cook, Kyle
93MissSt-10

Cook, Larry
86PalmSp-8
86PalmSp/Smok-11

Cook, Luther Almus
(Doc)
D350/2-37
M101/5-37

Cook, Mike
86MidldA-6
88Edmon/CMC-2
88Edmon/ProC-567
89F-472
90AAAGame/ProC-21
90AAASingl/ProC-241
90Portl/CMC-4
90Portl/ProC-171
90ProC/Singl-556
91AAA/LineD-57
91Calgary/LineD-57
92Louisvl/ProC-1881
92Louisvl/SB-258
94StCl/Team-289

Cook, Mitch
83QuadC-9
86ColumAst-7
87ColAst/ProC-9

Cook, Paul
N172

Cook, Raymond C.
(Cliff)
61T-399
62T-41
63T-566
81TCMA-296
91WIZMets-83

Cook, Ron W.
71MLB/St-75
71OPC-583
71T-583
72OPC-339
72T-339
72T/Cloth-8

Cook, Ron
88Fayette/ProC-1096
89Lakeland/Star-5
90Lakeland/Star-5
90Star/ISingl-33
91AA/LineD-378
91London/LineD-378

Cook, Stan
89Boise/ProC-1982
90Erie/Star-3

Cook, Tim
79Holyo-12
81ElPaso-20
82Vanco-12
83LasVegas/BHN-4
84Beaum-12

Cooke, Allan Lindsey
(Dusty)
35BU-148
92Conlon/Sport-418
W711/1

Cooke, Frederick B.
(Fred)
No Cards.

Cooke, Mitch
82QuadC-7

Cooke, Scott
89MissSt-8

Cooke, Steve
90Welland/Pucko-20
91Augusta/ClBest-4
91Augusta/ProC-797
92B-274
92BuffB/BlueS-4
92CaroMud/SB-130
92ClBest-43
92D/Rook-28
92Sky/AASingl-61
93B-514
93D-150
93F/MLPII-16
93Flair-111
93L-240
93OPC/Premier-19
93Pac/Spanish-585
93Pinn-260
93Pirate/Nation-7
93S-296
93Select/RookTr-69T
93StCl-726
93StCl/1stDay-726
93T-716
93T/Gold-716
93UD-599
93UD/SP-183
93Ultra-449
94B-434
94D-72
94F-607
94F/RookSen-6
94Flair-215
94L-169
94OPC-85
94Pac/Cr-495
94Panini-234
94Pinn-93
94Pinn/Artist-93
94Pinn/Museum-93
94S-186
94S/GoldR-186
94Select-130
94StCl-47
94StCl/1stDay-47
94StCl/Gold-47
94T-72
94T/Finest-19
94T/FinestRef-19
94T/Gold-72
94TripleP-182
94UD-132
94UD/CollC-83
94UD/CollC/Gold-83
94UD/CollC/Silv-83
94UD/ElecD-132
94Ultra-255

Cookson, Brent
91SoOreg/ClBest-11
91SoOreg/ProC-3860
92Clinton/ClBest-5

Coolbaugh, Mike
90MedHat/Best-1
91StCath/ClBest-7
91StCath/ProC-3402
92StCath/ClBest-3
92StCath/ProC-3395
93Hagers/ClBest-5
93Hagers/ProC-1886

Coolbaugh, Scott
88TexLgAS/GS-12
88Tulsa-18
89AAA/CMC-5
89AAA/ProC-26
89OkCty/CMC-21
89OkCty/ProC-1512
90B-494
90Classic/III-24
90D-43
90D/Rook-32
90F-293
90F/Can-293
90F/SoarSt-5
90HotRook/St-13
90Leaf-363
90S-612
90S/100Ris-79
90Sf-180
90T/89Debut-25
90T/Tr-22T
90TripleAAS/CMC-5
90TulsaDG/Best-1
90UD-42
91AAA/LineD-280
91B-649
91F/Up-U122
91LasVegas/LineD-280
91LasVegas/ProC-241
91Leaf-397
91OPC-277
91S/100RisSt-36
91StCl-493
91T-277
91T/Tr-24T
91UD-451
91UD/FinalEd-37F
92LasVegas/SB-228
92S-205
92Sky/AAASingl-112
92TX-11
93Rang/Keeb-111

Cooley, Chad
94LSU-11

Cooley, Dick Gordon
(Duff)
E107

Cooley, Fred
89Medford/Best-9
90A&AASingle/ProC-126
90Madison/Best-6
90Madison/ProC-2275
90MidwLgAS/GS-8
91AA/LineD-283
91ClBest/Singl-228
91Huntsvl/ClBest-8
91Huntsvl/LineD-283
91HuntsvlProC-1803
91Modesto/ProC-3094
92OrlanSR/SB-502

Cooley, Jack
91Pac/SenLg-90

Coombs, Cecil L.
(Cecil)
No Cards.

Coombs, Daniel
65T-553R
66T-414
67T-464
68T-547
69T-389
71OPC-126
71T-126
71T/Coins-49

Coombs, Glenn
91Welland/ClBest-25
91Welland/ProC-3564
92Augusta/ProC-229

Coombs, John W.
(Jack)
16FleischBrd-19
86Conlon/1-40
90Target-136
D350/2-38
E224
E270/2
E286
E98
M101/5-38
M116
T201
T204

Coombs, Mike
90Helena/SportP-28CO

Coomer, Ronald
(Ron)
88CalLgAS-9
88Modesto-21
88Modesto/Cal-72
90Huntsvl/Best-16
91AA/LineD-55
91BirmB/LineD-55
91BirmB/ProC-1460
92Sky/AAASingl-280
92Vanco/ProC-2727
92Vanco/SB-631
94FExcel-36

Coonan, Bill
86Cram/NWL-58

Cooney, Ed
88CapeCod/Sum-14

Cooney, James E.
26Exh-19

Cooney, James Edward
(Jimmy)
N172

Cooney, John Walter
(Johnny)
39PlayBall-85
40PlayBall-60
41DP-41
41PlayBall-50
54JC-28CO
55Gol/Braves-7CO
55JC-28CO
60T-458C
90Target-137
91Conlon/Sport-94

Cooney, Phillip
(Phil)
No Cards.

Cooney, Terry
88TM/Umpire-21
89TM/Umpire-19
90TM/Umpire-18

Cooney, William A.
(Bill)
No Cards.

Coons, Wilbur K.
(William)
No Cards.

Cooper, Alfred
(Army)
87Negro/Dixon-11

Cooper, Arley Wilbur
16FleischBrd-20
E120
E121/120
E220
W501-80
W514-42
W516-19
W572
W573

Cooper, Bill
86Lakeland-4
87GlenF-8
88GlenF/ProC-933

Cooper, Cecil C.
72OPC-79R
72T-79R
74OPC-523
74T-523
75OPC-489
75T-489
75T/M-489
76OPC-78
76SSPC-404
76T-78
77OPC-102
77T-235
78Ho-119
78K-41
78OPC-71
78T-154
79Ho-36
79OPC-163
79T-325
80OPC-52
80T-95
80T/S-33
80T/Super-33
81D-83
81Drake-16
81F-639
81F/St-16
81K-32
81MSA/Disc-10
81OPC-356
81PermaGr/CC-15
81Sqt-30
81T-3LL
81T-555
81T/Nat/Super-5
81T/SO-2
81T/St-10
81T/St-13
81T/St-241
81T/St-93
82D-258
82Drake-9
82F-138
82F/St-140
82K-60
82OPC-167
82PermaGr/AS-2
82PermaGr/CC-18
82Pol/Brew-15
82Sqt-1
82T-675
82T-703TL
82T/St-199
83D-106
83D/AAS-19
83Drake-6
83F-30
83F/St-11M
83F/St-11M
83Gard-5
83K-28
83OPC-190
83OPC/St-173
83OPC/St-181WS
83OPC/St-80
83PermaGr/CC-21
83Pol/Brew-15
83T-190
83T/Fold-3M
83T/Gloss40-15
83T/St-173
83T/St-181
83T/St-80
84D-351
84D/Champs-24
84Drake-8
84F-198
84F/St-31
84Gard-5
84MiltBrad-7
84Nes/792-133LL
84Nes/792-420
84Nes/792-710LL
84OPC-43
84Pol/Brew-15
84Ralston-27
84Seven-8C
84T-133LL

84T-420
84T-710LL
84T/Cereal-27
84T/Gloss40-34
84T/RD-15M
84T/St-200A
84T/St-291
85D-170
85F-580
85FunFood/Pin-48
85Gard-5
85Leaf-246
85OPC-290
85Pol/Brew-15
85T-290
85T/RD-13M
85T/St-287
85ThomMc/Discs-9
86D-170
86D-7DK
86D/AAS-54
86D/AS/WaxBox-PC9
86D/DKsuper-7
86F-484
86F/LimEd-12
86F/Mini-100
86F/St-26
86Jay's-2
86Leaf-7DK
86OPC-385
86Pol/Brew-15
86Seven/Coin-C15M
86Sf-140M
86Sf-180M
86Sf-29
86T-385
86T/St-196
86T/Super-20
86T/Tatt-6M
86Woolwth-8
87D-363
87F-343
87F/AwardWin-10
87F/Mini-22
87Leaf-230
87OPC-10
87OPC-D
87Pol/Brew-15
87RedFoley/St-48
87Sf-169
87Stuart-21M
87T-10
87T-D
87T/Board-6
87T/HL-2
87T/St-198
87Woolwth-2
88F-161
88S-169
88T-769
89Pac/SenLg-42
89TM/SenLg-23
92Brew/Carlson-5
93AP/ASG-164
93TWill-49
93UD/ATH-34

Cooper, Chris
87BYU-5

Cooper, Claude W.
No Cards.

Cooper, Craig
86Cram/NWL-168
88Wichita-24
89Wichita/Rock-34
89Wichita/Rock/Up-8
90ElPaso/GS-7
92Canton/SB-104

Cooper, Darren
90Martins/ProC-3200

Cooper, Dave
84AZ/Pol-2
87Lakeland-23
88Toledo/CMC-8
88Toledo/ProC-608
89London/ProC-1362

Cooper, David
94T-761DP
94T/Gold-761DP

Cooper, Don
79WHave-3
82F-550
82T-409
82Toledo-1
83Syrac-6
84Colum-17
84Colum/Pol-6
85Colum-5
85Colum/Pol-6
86Syrac-9
90Saraso/Star-27CO
91Pac/SenLg-22
91Saraso/ClBest-16CO
91Saraso/ProC-1131CO
92BirmB/ProC-2600
92BirmB/SB-100CO
92Yank/WIZ80-35

Cooper, Gary N.
74Gaston
79Savan-2
81Durham-6

Cooper, Gary
86AubAs-7
87Osceola-21
88ColAst/Best-21
89Tucson/CMC-22
89Tucson/JP-6
89Tucson/ProC-184
90AAASingl/ProC-203
90Hamil/Best-19
90Hamil/Star-9
90ProC/Singl-612
90Tucson/CMC-10
90Tucson/ProC-213
91AAA/LineD-609
91AAAGame/ProC-51
91Tucson/LineD-609
91Tucson/ProC-2224
92AAA/ASG/SB-605
92D-774
92Mega/Ruth-134M
92Pinn/RookI-3
92S-840
92S/Impact-25
92S/Rook-28
92Sky/AAASingl-270
92T/91Debut-38
92Tucson/ProC-495
92Tucson/SB-605
93FExcel/ML-40

Cooper, Jamie
87Everett-9
88Clinton/ProC-715
88MidwLAS/GS-4
89SanJose/Best-3
89SanJose/Cal-230
89SanJose/ProC-458
89SanJose/Star-5
89Star/Wax-83
90Shrev/ProC-1457
90Shrev/Star-4
91Shrev/ProC-1833
92Phoenix/SB-380
92Sky/AAASingl-179

Cooper, Jeff
91SLCity/ProC-3217

Cooper, Kent
84Everett/Cram-7

Cooper, Mark
85Kingst-12

Cooper, Morton
(Mort)
39PlayBall-131
40PlayBall-113
43Playball-25
91Conlon/Sport-301
92Card/McDon/Pac-19
92Conlon/Sport-624
Exh47
PM10/Sm-30
R302
W754

Cooper, Neal
76Dubuq

Cooper, Orge
(Pat)
No Cards.

Cooper, Paul
78DaytB

Cooper, Scott
86Elmira-6
87Greens-10
88CLAS/Star-5
88Lynch/Star-5
89BBAmAA/BPro-AA9
89NewBrit/ProC-609
89NewBrit/Star-3
89Star/IISingl-126
90AAASingl/ProC-439
90B-277
90Classic/Up-13
90Pawtu/CMC-14
90Pawtu/ProC-467
90ProC/Singl-265
90S-651RPs
90T/TVRSox-39
91AAA/LineD-354
91AAAGame/ProC-29
91D-496
91F-91
91Pawtu/LineD-354
91Pawtu/ProC-46
91T/90Debut-35
91UD-22
92B-129
92Classic/Game200-142
92Classic/I-28
92D-570
92L-182
92L/BlkGold-182
92OPC-488
92Pinn-252
92Pinn/Rook-2
92ProC/Tomorrow-16
92S-876
92S/100RisSt-88
92S/HotRook-5
92S/Impact-26
92S/Rook-13
92StCl-377
92T-488
92T/Gold-488
92T/GoldWin-488
92TripleP-180
92UD-541
92Ultra-312
93B-467
93D-135
93F-178
93Flair-161
93L-175
93OPC-385
93OPC/Premier-13
93Pac/Spanish-355
93Panini-93
93Pinn-330
93S-198
93Select-302
93StCl-368
93StCl/1stDay-368
93Studio-45
93T-655
93T/Finest-7
93T/FinestRef-7
93T/Gold-655
93ToysRUs-29
93TripleP-25
93UD-57
93UD/SP-200
93USPlayC/Rook-11D
93Ultra-149
94B-203
94D-417
94F-27
94F/AS-6
94Flair-11
94L-75
94OPC-4
94Pac/Cr-50
94Panini-27
94Pinn-72
94Pinn/Artist-72
94Pinn/Museum-72
94S-388
94Select-39
94StCl-396
94StCl/1stDay-396
94StCl/Gold-396
94Studio-160
94T-235
94T/Finest-168
94T/Finest/PreProd-168
94T/FinestRef-168
94T/Gold-235
94TripleP-202
94UD-502
94UD/CollC-84
94UD/CollC/Gold-84
94UD/CollC/Silv-84
94UD/SP-153
94Ultra-313

Cooper, Tim
90Tampa/DIMD-1
91Greens/ProC-3064
92Greens/ClBest-21
92Greens/ProC-785
94ClBest/Gold-148

Cooper, Virgil
88Utica/Pucko-15
89SoBend/GS-10

Cooper, Wilbur
21Exh-27
77Galasso-166
V61-57

Cooper, William W.
(Walker)
43Playball-24
48B-9
49B-117
49Eureka-79
50B-111
51B-135
52B-208
52T-294
53B/BW-30
53Exh/Can-58
53JC-14
53SpicSpan/3x5-8
54DanDee
56T-273
57T-380
60T-462C
79TCMA-69
92Card/McDon/Pac-14
92Conlon/Sport-633
Exh47
R302
R423-11
W754

Cope, Gary
91Kissim/ProC-4175
92GreatF/SportP-5

Copeland, Mark
90AubAs/Best-24TR

Coplon, Mitch
82DayBe-2

Copp, Bill
86Watertn-7
87Salem-19
88Harris/ProC-853

Coppell, Shannon
89Clinton/ProC-902

Coppenbarger, Frank
77QuadC

Copper, Jeff
91SLCity/SportP-22

Coppeta, Greg
90Niagara/Pucko-16
91Fayette/ClBest-1
91Fayette/ProC-1161
92Lakeland/ClBest-12

Coppock, Mark
90AR-30M

Cora, Joey
85Spokane/Cram-4
86Beaum-7
87Bohem-4
87D/OD-147
88AAA/ProC-22
88F-580
88LasVegas/CMC-18
88LasVegas/ProC-234
88S-420
88T-91
89AAA/CMC-33
89LasVegas/CMC-14
89LasVegas/ProC-23
90B-211
90D-538
90F-154
90F/Can-154
90Leaf-366
90S/YS/II-14
90TripleAAS/CMC-33
90UD-601
91F-527
91F/Up-U11
91Kodak/WSox-21
91Leaf-375
91S-253
91UD-291
92D-108
92F-76
92OPC-302
92Panini-126
92S-326
92StCl-535
92T-302
92T/Gold-302
92T/GoldWin-302
92UD-359
92Ultra-334
92WSox-28
93D-697
93F-580
93Flair-182
93L-461
93Pac/Spanish-68
93S-454
93StCl-54
93StCl/1stDay-54
93StCl/WSox-6
93T-122
93T/Gold-122
93UD-742
93Ultra-172
93WSox-7
94D-447
94F-79
94L-175
94Pac/Cr-123
94Panini-46
94Pinn-318
94S-485
94S/Cycle-12
94Select-132
94StCl-100
94StCl/1stDay-100
94StCl/Gold-100
94StCl/Team-143
94T-478
94T/Finest-146
94T/FinestRef-146
94T/Gold-478
94UD-371
94UD/CollC-85
94UD/CollC/Gold-85
94UD/CollC/Silv-85
94Ultra-32

Cora, Manny
92CharRain/ClBest-1
92CharRain/ProC-126
92ClBest-53
92UD/ML-203
93SALAS/II-7
93SALAS/IICS-12

Corbell, Charlie
85Fresno/Pol-17
86Shrev-5
87Phoenix-6
88Tacoma/CMC-3
88Tacoma/ProC-636

Corbell, Eric
91Kingspt/ClBest-17
91Kingspt/ProC-3804

Corbett
N284

Corbett, Doug
79Indianap-12
81D-546
81F-555
81F/St-227
81OPC-162
81T-162
81T/St-106
82D-53
82F-551
82OPC-157
82T-560
82T/St-210
82T/Tr-21T
83F-83
83T-27
84Cram/PCL-111
85D-474
85F-298
85Smok/Cal-18
85T-682
86Smok/Cal-8
86T-234
87D-333
87F-76
87T-359
89Pac/SenLg-193
89T/SenLg-114
89TM/SenLg-24
90EliteSenLg-52
91Crown/Orio-84

Corbett, Eugene Louis
(Gene)
46Sunbeam

Corbett, Ray
81Cedar-8
82Water-11
83Indianap-15
85RochR-1
90CedarDG/Best-25
Corbett, Sherman
86MidldA-7
87Edmon-18
88F/Up-U11
89D-407
89Edmon/CMC-8
89Edmon/ProC-547
89F-473
89T-99
89ToysRUs-6
89UD-464
90AAASingl/ProC-88
90Edmon/CMC-5
90Edmon/ProC-512
90ProC/Singl-482
91AA/LineD-431
91MidldA/LineD-431
91MidldA/OneHour-8
91MidldA/ProC-430
92London/ProC-625
Corbin, A. Ray
72OPC-66
72T-66
73OPC-411
73T-411
74OPC-296
74T-296
74T/St-204
75OPC-78
75T-78
75T/M-78
76OPC-474
76SSPC-209
76T-474
78Twin/Frisz-28
Corbin, Archie
89Clmbia/Best-5
89Clmbia/GS-7
90StLucie/Star-4
91AA/LineD-404
91ClBest/Singl-293
91Memphis/LineD-404
91Memphis/ProC-646
92ClBest-180
92D-400RR
92Memphis/ProC-2410
92Memphis/SB-431
92ProC/Tomorrow-75
92Sky/AASingl-182
92StCl-473
92T/91Debut-39
93ClBest/MLG-125
93Harris/ProC-262
Corbin, Ted
92Classic/DP-97
92FrRow/DP-8
92FtMyr/ProC-2751
92Miracle/ClBest-2
Corbitt, Claude E.
47Royal/Mont-1
Corbitt, Cord
91Spokane/ClBest-19
91Spokane/ProC-3940
Corcino, Luis
86BurlEx-3
87FtMyr-22
88Virgini/Star-6
Corcoran, Arthur A.
(Art)
No Cards.
Corcoran, John A.
No Cards.
Corcoran, John H.
No Cards.
Corcoran, Lawrence J.
(Larry)
N167-2
N172
Corcoran, Lori
83GlenF-23
Corcoran, Michael J.
(Mickey)
C46-49
Corcoran, Thomas W.
(Tommy)
90Target-138
E107
E270/2
N300/unif
WG3-11
Corcoran, Timothy M.
(Tim)
77Evansvl/TCMA-6
78BK/T-20
78T-515
79T-272
81D-367
81Evansvl-18
81F-479
81T-448
82OkCty-3
83Portl-11
84Phill/TastyK-34
85CIGNA-6
85D-381
85F-247
85Phill/TastyK-12M
85Phill/TastyK-34
85T-302
86D-381
86F-437
86T-664
86Tidew-5
87Maine/TCMA-24
88Reading/ProC-887
91WIZMets-84
Cordani, Richard
88CapeCod/Sum-8
90LSUPol-6
91LSU/Pol-8
Cordeiro, Richard
52Laval-6
Corder, Daniel
74Wichita-108
Cordero, Wil
(Wilfredo)
89WPalmB/Star-8
90Foil/Best-128
90Jaxvl/Best-5
90Jaxvl/ProC-1381
90ProC/Singl-682
91AAA/LineD-179
91B-436
91Classic/II-T2
91Indianap/LineD-179
91Indianap/ProC-466
91Leaf/GRook-BC3
91UD-60TP
92B-194
92D-2RR
92D/RookPhen-BC20
92F/Up-97
92Indianap/ProC-1865
92Indianap/SB-179
92OPC-551
92ProC/Tomorrow-254
92S/RookTr-110T
92Sky/AAASingl-88
92T-551M
92T/Gold-551
92T/GoldWin-551
92TripleP-179
92UD-16SR
93B-508
93D-432
93F-73
93Flair-80
93HumDum/Can-36
93L-37
93L/GRook-2
93OPC-161
93OPC/Premier-29
93Pac/Beisbol-25
93Pac/Beisbol-26M
93Pac/Spanish-532
93Panini-227
93Pinn-280
93Pinn/RookTP-7
93Pinn/Team2001-1
93S-334
93S/Proctor-1
93Select-336
93Select/ChasRook-18
93Select/RookTr-150T
93StCl-361
93StCl/1stDay-361
93Studio-93
93T-256
93T/Finest-123
93T/FinestRef-123
93T/Gold-256
93ToysRUs-90
93TripleP-27
93UD-60
93UD/Diam-32
93UD/FunPack-1SOT
93UD/SP-101
93USPlayC/Rook-3S
93Ultra-65
94B-153
94D-545
94Flair-187
94L-103
94OPC-252
94OPC/DiamD-10
94Pac/Cr-376
94Panini-208
94Pinn-89
94Pinn/Artist-89
94Pinn/Museum-89
94Pinn/New-7
94S-412
94Select-81
94Sf/2000-36
94StCl-393
94StCl/1stDay-393
94StCl/Gold-393
94Studio-76
94T-21
94T/Finest-20
94T/FinestRef-20
94T/Gold-21
94TripleP-92
94UD-97
94UD/ElecD-97
94Ultra-224
Cordner, Steve
83QuadC-19
Cordoba, Wilfrido
82AlexD-9
83LynnP-2
84PrWill-13
Cordova, Antonio
82QuadC-21
84MidldC-2
Cordova, Luis
92Erie/ClBest-25
92Erie/ProC-1637
Cordova, Marty
89Elizab/Star-5
92AS/Cal-32
92UD/ML-115
92UD/POY-PY24
92Visalia/ClBest-14
92Visalia/ProC-1026
93B-345FOIL
93ClBest/MLG-42
93FExcel/ML-198
94B-544
94F/MLP-6
94FExcel-92
Cordova, Rocky
78Clinton
79LodiD-7
Corey, Frederick H.
(Fred)
No Cards.
Corey, Mark M.
79RochR-15
79T-701R
80RochR-5
80T-661R
81F-193
81T-399R
82Evansvl-23
86Jaxvl/TCMA-20
87Indianap-30
89Pac/SenLg-195
91Crown/Orio-85
Corgan, Charles H.
(Chuck)
90Target-916
Corhan, Roy George
No Cards.
Corkhill, John S.
(Pop)
90Target-139
N172
Corkins, Mike
70T-573R
71MLB/St-224
71OPC-179
71T-179
72T-608
73OPC-461
73T-461
74OPC-546
74T-546
Cormack, Terry
83Durham-3
84Durham-6
85Durham-21
Corman, Dave
85Beaum-20
90HagersDG/Best-5
Cormier, Rheal
89StPete/Star-8
90ArkTr/GS-9
90Louisvl/LBC-12
91B-396
91Louisvl/ProC-2907
91Louisvl/Team-5
92B-473
92D-712
92F/Up-119
92L-469
92L/BlkGold-469
92OPC-346
92ProC/Tomorrow-315
92S-851
92StCl-506
92T-346
92T/91Debut-40
92T/Gold-346
92T/GoldWin-346
92UD-574
93B-80
93D-228
93F-124
93L-209
93MSA/Ben-20
93OPC-34
93Pac/Spanish-631
93Pinn-360
93Pol/Card-5
93S-371
93StCl-15
93StCl/1stDay-15
93StCl/Card-18
93T-149
93T/Gold-149
93ToysRUs-21
93UD-79
93Ultra-462
94D-622
94F-630
94Finest-248
94Flair-224
94L-110
94Pac/Cr-587
94StCl-437
94StCl/1stDay-437
94StCl/Gold-437
94StCl/Team-303
94T-594
94T/Gold-594
94UD-422
Cormier, Russ
89Medford/Best-21
90Modesto/Chong-7
91AA/LineD-284
91Huntsvl/ClBest-9
91Huntsvl/LineD-284
91HuntsvlProC-1788
Cornejo, Mardie
78Tidew
91WIZMets-85
Cornelius, Brian
89Niagara/Pucko-4
90Fayette/ProC-2420
91ClBest/Singl-15
91FSLAS/ProC-FSL20
91Lakeland/ClBest-23
91Lakeland/ProC-277
92London/ProC-644
92Sky/AASingl-171
Cornelius, Reid
89Rockford/Team-5
90WPalmB/Star-3
91B-458
91ClBest/Singl-52
91FSLAS/ProC-FSL42
91WPalmB/ClBest-4
91WPalmB/ProC-1220
92ClBest-124
92Harris/SB-280
92ProC/Tomorrow-264
92Sky/AASingl-119
93Harris/ProC-263
94FExcel-223
Cornelius, Willie
78Laugh/Black-17
Cornell, Daren
90Beloit/Best-16
Cornell, David
92Eugene/ProC-3041
Cornell, Jeff
83Phoenix/BHN-7
84Cram/PCL-12
85Cram/PCL-200
85T-514
86Iowa-8
Cornett, Brad
92StCath/ClBest-22
92StCath/ProC-3378
93Hagers/ClBest-6
93Hagers/ProC-1871
94ClBest/Gold-88
94FExcel-141
Cornish, Tim
92Martins/ClBest-14
92Martins/ProC-3069
Cornutt, Terry
75Lafay
76Phoenix/Coke-4
78Cr/PCL-71
79Phoenix
Corona, John
90Spring/Best-22
91StPete/ClBest-3
91StPete/ProC-2267
Corrado, Gary
77Wausau
Corrales, Patrick
(Pat)
65OPC-107R
65T-107R
66OPC-137
66T-137
67OPC-78
67T-78
69T-382
70OPC-507
70T-507
71MLB/St-57
71OPC-293
71T-293
72T-705
72T-706IA
73OPC-542
73T-542
74OPC-498
74T-498
79T-499MG
81F-623MG
83D-626MG
83T-637MG
84Nes/792-141MG
84T-141MG
84Wheat/Ind-18MG
85Polar/Ind-18MG
85T-119MG
86OhHenry-7MG
86T-699MG
87Gator-7MG
87Gator-MG
87T-268MG
88Chatt/Team-4
88Toledo/CMC-25
88Toledo/ProC-590
90Brave/Dubuq/Singl-5CO
91Brave/Dubuq/Stand-
10CO
92Brave/Lyke/Stand-10CO
93Brave/Lyke/Stand-9CO
93Rang/Keeb-112MG
Correa, Amilcar
89Wythe/Star-6
90Geneva/ProC-3051
90Geneva/Star-5
91Peoria/ClBest-3
91Peoria/ProC-1334
91Peoria/Team-5
92WinSalem/ClBest-16
92WinSalem/ProC-1202
Correa, Edwin
83AppFx/Frit-17
86D/Rook-4
86F/Up-U30
86Rangers-18
86Sf/Rook-2
87Classic/Up-143
87D-57

87F-122
87Leaf-145
87Mother/Rang-19
87OPC-334
87Smok/R-22
87T-334
88D-57
88F-464
88Panini/St-196
88S-523
88Smok/R-18
88T-227
89RedFoley/St-25
89UD-598
90VeroB/Star-9
93Rang/Keeb-113

Correa, Jorge
92AubAs/ClBest-26
92AubAs/ProC-1346

Correa, Jose
92Elizab/ClBest-16
92Elizab/ProC-3673

Correa, Miguel
92Idaho/ProC-3525
93Macon/ClBest-7
93Macon/ProC-1413

Correa, Ramser
89Helena/SP-15
90Beloit/Best-1
90Foil/Best-24
92Stockton/ProC-28

Correia, Rod
88SoOreg/ProC-1702
89Modesto/Cal-277
89Modesto/Chong-23
90Modesto/Cal-163
90Modesto/Chong-8
90Modesto/ProC-2218
91Huntsvl/Team-7
91Tacoma/ProC-2312
92MidldA/OneHour-4
92MidldA/ProC-4032
92MidldA/SB-457
93F/Final-179
93FExcel/ML-140
93Select/RookTr-142T
93StCl/Angel-10
93Vanco/ProC-2603
94F-49
94Pac/Cr-72
94S-594
94StCl-352
94StCl/1stDay-352
94StCl/Gold-352
94T-532
94T/Gold-532
94Ultra-21

Correll, Victor C.
(Vic)
75OPC-177
75T-177
75T/M-177
76OPC-608
76SSPC-14
76T-608
77T-364
78Indianap-19
78T-527
79T-281
80T-419
81T-628

Correnti, Chris
91BurlAs/ClBest-28TR
92BurlAs/ClBest-29TR

Corridan, Phillip
No Cards.

Corriden, John M. Jr.
90Target-140
R346-17

Corriden, John M. Sr.
(Red)
No Cards.

Corridon, Frank
C46-17
E90/1
M116
T205

Corrigan, Larry
75Water

Corry, DeLynn
92Hamil/ClBest-29
92Hamil/ProC-1585

Corsaro, Robby
89Batavia/ProC-1945

Corsi, James
(Jim)
83Greens-4
85Greens-16
86NewBrit-7
87Modesto-25
88Tacoma/CMC-7
88Tacoma/ProC-625
89F-649R
89S/HotRook-36
89T-292
89Tacoma/CMC-2
89Tacoma/ProC-1560
90D-422
90F-4
90F/Can-4
90OPC-623
90S-553
90T-623
90UD-521
91F/UltraUp-U80
91Mother/Ast-21
92D-467
92F-431
92S-524
92Tacoma/SB-531
93D-741
93F-424
93F/Final-58
93T-753
93T/Gold-753
93USPlayC/Marlin-10H
93USPlayC/Marlin-8D

Cort, Barry
75BurlB
78Spokane/Cramer-18
78Spokane/Team-16
79Holyo-26
80Holyo-4

Cortazzo, John F.
(Shine)
No Cards.

Cortes, Hernan
89Penin/Star-4
90FtLaud/Star-3
90Star/ISingl-39
91AA/LineD-628
91Wmsprt/LineD-628
91Wmsprt/ProC-299

Cortez, Argenis
(Conde)
87DayBe-12
91AA/LineD-56
91BirmB/LineD-56
91BirmB/ProC-1447

Cortez, Dave
87Wichita-18

Corwin, Elmer
(Al)
52B-121
53B/Col-126
53B/Col-149
54B-137
55B-122
55Gol/Giants-4
79TCMA-232

Cosby, Darin
88OK-15
89OK-11

Cosby, Rob
84Everett/Cram-13A

Coscarart, Joseph M.
(Joe)
No Cards.

Coscarart, Peter J.
(Pete)
36G
39PlayBall-141
40PlayBall-63
45Playball-33
49B/PCL-21
89Smok/Dodg-46
90Target-141
R314

Cosenza, Vincent
52Laval-40

Cosey, Donald Ray
(Ray)
79Ogden/TCMA-16
80Ogden-2

Cosgrove, Mike
75Iowa/TCMA-4
75OPC-96
75T-96
75T/M-96
76Ho-96
76OPC-122
76T-122
77T-589

Cosio, Raymundo
78Cedar
79Cedar/TCMA-27

Cosman, James H.
66Pep/Tul
67T-384R
70OPC-429R
70T-429R

Cosman, Jim
89Martins/Star-7

Coss, Mike
91Bluefld/ClBest-10
91Bluefld/ProC-4133
92Freder/ProC-1810

Costa, Tim
92Martins/ProC-3048

Costa, Tony
92Martins/ClBest-6

Costas, Bob
89Chatt/II/Team-7ANN

Costell, Arnie
75Dubuq

Costello, Bob
83Wisco/Frit-14

Costello, Brian
89Salinas/ProC-1828
90Clinton/Best-12
92SanJose/ClBest-29TR

Costello, Chris
92GulfCD/ProC-3559

Costello, Daniel F.
(Dan)
D350/2-39
M101/5-39

Costello, Fred
88Ashvl/ProC-1063
89ColMud/Best-16
89ColMud/ProC-129
89ColMud/Star-6
90ColMud/Best-16
90ColMud/ProC-1341
90ColMud/Star-8
90Foil/Best-218
91Osceola/ClBest-1
91Osceola/ProC-673
92Jacks/ProC-3993
92Osceola/ClBest-11

Costello, John
83Erie-18
84Savan-4
85Spring-5
86StPete-7
87ArkTr-25
88F/Up-U118
88Louisvl-16
88Louisvl/CMC-1
88Louisvl/ProC-440
88S/Tr-107T
89Classic-142
89D-518
89F-446
89Panini/St-176
89S-534
89S/HotRook-75
89Smok/Cards-3
89T-184
89UD-625
90D-555
90F-246
90F/Can-246
90OPC-36
90Publlnt/St-214
90S-347
90SpringDG/Best-10
90T-36
90T/TVCard-8
90UD-486
91AAA/LineD-281
91LasVegas/LineD-281
91LasVegas/ProC-228
92S-614

Costello, Mike
86Beaum-8
87Wichita-15
88Wichita-26
89Denver/CMC-5
89Denver/ProC-45
89ElPaso/GS-5

Costello, Tim
77Visalia

Costic, Tim
91FresnoSt/Smok-3
92Elizab/ClBest-5
92Elizab/ProC-3692

Costner, Kevin
89Durham/Star-29

Costo, Tim
90Classic/DP-8
91AA/LineD-79
91B-79
91Canton/LineD-79
91Canton/ProC-984
91ClBest/Singl-389
91ClBest/Singl-438
91Classic/200-58
91Classic/I-38
91Leaf/GRook-BC18
91OPC-103
91PreRookPrev/LineD-79
91S-680FDP
91T-103FDP
91UD-62TP
92B-489
92Chatt/ProC-3824
92Chatt/SB-180
92ClBest-70
92D/Rook-29
92ProC/Tomorrow-51
92Sky/AASingl-80
93B-314
93D-270
93F/MLPI-3
93L-529
93Pinn-582
93S-265
93StCl-390
93StCl/1stDay-390
93T-577
93T/Gold-577
93ToysRUs-25
93UD-11SR
93Ultra-326
94B-416
94D-561
94F-408
94L-53
94Pac/Cr-144
94S-552
94S/Boys-48
94StCl-119
94StCl/1stDay-119
94StCl/Gold-119
94T-513
94T/Gold-513
94UD-168
94UD/CollC-86
94UD/CollC/Gold-86
94UD/CollC/Silv-86
94UD/ElecD-168

Cota, Chris
87DayBe-20
89BendB/Legoe-3

Cota, Francisco
83Miami-4
85Tigres-11

Cota, Tim
87Visalia-4

Cote, Brice
80Elmira-5

Cote, Gerard
45Parade*-64

Cote, Henry Joseph
No Cards.

Cote, Warren Peter
(Pete)
No Cards.

Cotes, Eugenio
77Salem
79Portl-10
79T-723R

Cotner, Andrew
91Kingspt/ClBest-28
91Kingspt/ProC-3805
92Kingspt/ClBest-22
92Kingspt/ProC-1524
93StLucie/ProC-2913

Cotter, Edward C.
(Ed)
No Cards.

Cotter, Harvey L.
No Cards.

Cotter, Richard R.
(Dick)
No Cards.

Cotter, Thomas B.
(Tom)
No Cards.

Cottier, Charles K.
(Chuck)
60L-138
60Lake
60SpicSpan-6
60T-417
61P-113
61T-13
62J-66
62P-66
62P/Can-66
62Salada-20
62Shirriff-20
62T-27
62T/St-93
62T/bucks
63F-28
63J-98
63P-98
63T-219
64T-397
69T-252
77QuadC
78TCMA-189
85Mother/Mar-1MG
85T-656MG
86T-141MG
88Berg/Cubs-CO
90Cub/Mara-28CO
90T/TVCub-3CO
91Cub/Mara-x
91Cub/Vine-7CO
92Cub/Mara-NNO
93Cub/Mara-6CO

Cotto, Hector
88Miami/Star-5

Cotto, Henry
81QuadC-15
83Iowa-21
84SevenUp-28
85D-411
85F-53
85F/Up-U31
85T-267
87Colum/Pro-39
87Colum/TCMA-20
87T-174
88D/Best-51
88F-205
88F/Up-U58
88Mother/Sea-6
88OPC-172
88S-368
88S/Tr-48T
88T-766
88T/Big-125
88T/Tr-31T
89D-109
89F-545
89Mother/Sea-6
89OPC-207
89Panini/St-441
89S-209
89T-468
89T/Big-160
89T/St-218
89UD-134
90B-476
90D-644
90F-511
90F/Can-511
90Mother/Mar-9
90OPC-31
90Publlnt/St-430
90S-161
90T-31
90T/Big-156
90UD-207
91B-244
91CounHrth-18
91D-343
91F-448
91Leaf-113
91OPC-634
91Panini/FrSt-232
91S-282
91StCl-525

91T-634
91UD-110
91Ultra-333
92D-356
92F-276
92L-472
92L/BlkGold-472
92Mother/Mar-9
92OPC-311
92Pinn-342
92S-390
92StCl-14
92T-311
92T/Gold-311
92T/GoldWin-311
92UD-616
92Ultra-432
92Yank/WIZ80-36
93D-705
93F-672
93Marlin/Publix-9
93Mother/Mar-5
93Pac/Spanish-283
93Panini-64
93Pinn-323
93StCl-565
93StCl/1stDay-565
93T-206
93T/Gold-206
93T/Tr-121T
93UD-411
94D-184
94F-465
94Pac/Cr-240
94S-161
94S/GoldR-161
94T-522
94T/Gold-522

Cotton, John
89BurlInd/Star-6
90Watertn/Star-5
91CollInd/ClBest-23
91CollInd/ProC-1490
92Kinston/ClBest-16
92Kinston/ProC-2482
92UD/ML-321
93Kinston/Team-4

Cottrell, Steve
84Everett/Cram-8

Couch, Johnny
94Conlon-1297

Couch, Richard
77Ashvl

Couchee, Mike
82Amari-16
85CharlO-31
85Cram/PCL-123
86Tulsa-4CO
88QuadC/GS-2
88SanDiegoSt-5
89SanDiegoSt-5

Coughlin
N172

Coughlin, Kevin
90Utica/Pucko-1
91SoBend/ClBest-9
91SoBend/ProC-2868
92Saraso/ClBest-19
94ClBest/Gold-154

Coughlin, Red
85Syrac-24
86Syrac-10TR
87Syrac/TCMA-33
88Syrac/ProC-819

Coughlin, William P.
(Bill)
E107

Coughlon, Kevin
82Madis/Frit-7
84Madis/Pol-21
85Modesto/Chong-12

Coughtry, James M.
(Marlan)
61Union
62T-595R

Coulon, Johnny
T3/Box-54

Coulson, Robert
T207

Coulson, Steven
77WHave

Coulter, Chris
91BurlInd/ProC-3292

Coulter, Darrell
88Spartan/ProC-1029
88Spartan/Star-5
89Spartan/ProC-1042
89Spartan/Star-5

Coulter, Roy
75AppFx
76AppFx

Coulter, Thomas Lee
(Tom)
No Cards.

Coumbe, Fred
(Fritz)
D328-33
E135-33

Counsell, Craig
92Bend/ClBest-9

Counts, Rick
78Dunedin

Cournoyer, Yvan
72Dimanche*-71IA
72Dimanche*-72

Courtney, Clinton D.
(Clint)
53B/Col-70
53NB
53T-127
54B-69
54Dix
55B-34
56T-159
57T-51
58T-92
59T-483
60T-344
61T-342
79TCMA-169
91Crown/Orio-86
91T/Arc53-127

Courtney, Ernest E.
(Ernie)
E254

Courtney, Harry
E120

Courtright, John
91Billing/SportP-15
91Billings/ProC-3746
92CharWh/ClBest-14
92CharWh/ProC-1
93SALAS/II-8
94B-570

Cousineau, Edward T.
(Dee)
No Cards.

Cousins, Derryl
88TM/Umpire-40
89TM/Umpire-38
90TM/Umpire-36

Cousy, Bob
51BR-A11
60P*

Couture, Mike
90Helena/SportP-11
91Stockton/ClBest-15
91Stockton/ProC-3043
92Beloit/ClBest-10
92Beloit/ProC-418
92MidwLAS/Team-8

Coveleski, Harry
81Tiger/Detroit-39
94Conlon-1172
BF2-26
D327
D328-34
D329-39
D350/2-40
E135-34
M101/4-39
M101/5-40
M116
T206

Coveleski, Stan
21Exh-28
25Exh-122
26Exh-122
28Yueng-57
61F-100
76Shakey-113
77Galasso-118
80Perez/HOF-112
80SSPC/HOF
82Ohio/HOF-24
92Conlon/Sport-462
92Yank/WIZHOF-7
93Conlon-707
94Conlon-1172M
E120
E121/120
E210-57
E220
E254
E93
T3-88
V100
W501-21
W502-57
W555
W572
W575

Coveney, Jim
89Ashvl/ProC-961

Coveney, John P.
(John)
No Cards.

Coveney, Patrick
84AZ/Pol-3
86Clearw-5
87DayBe-13

Covington, Clarence
(Sam)
No Cards.

Covington, John W.
(Wes)
57SpicSpan/4x5-7
57T-283
58T-140
59T-290
59T-565AS
60Lake
60T-158
61P-108
61T-296
61T/St-41
62Salada-105
62Shirriff-105
62T-157
63J-182
63P-182
63T-529
64PhilBull-10
64T-208
65T-583
66OPC-52M
66T-484
66T-52M
78TCMA-132
90Target-142

Covington, William
(Tex)
T207

Cowan, Billy Roland
64T-192R
65OPC-186
65T-186
69T-643
71MLB/St-341
71OPC-614
71T-614
72OPC-19
72T-19
78TCMA-282
91WIZMets-86
92Yank/WIZ60-29

Cowan, Ed
77DaytB

Cowan, Johnnie
92Negro/Retort-12

Cowens, Alfred Edward
(Al)
75OPC-437
75T-437
75T/M-437
76A&P/KC
76Ho-28
76Ho/Twink-28
76OPC-648
76SSPC-175
76T-648
77T-262
78Ho-67
78K-5
78OPC-143
78SSPC/270-240
78T-46
79OPC-258
79T-490
80OPC-174
80T-330
81Coke
81D-369
81F-471
81OPC-123
81T-123
82D-207
82F-266
82OPC-103
82T-575
82T/St-182
82T/Tr-22T
83D-554
83F-477
83F/St-17M
83Nalley-2
83OPC-193
83OPC/St-115
83T-763
83T/St-115
84D-511
84F-610
84Mother/Mar-19
84Nes/792-622
84T-622
84T/St-344
85D-196
85F-487
85Leaf-239
85Mother/Mar-6
85OPC-224
85T-224
85T/St-333
85ThomMc/Discs-10
86D-389
86F-463
86Leaf-184
86Mother/Mar-6
86OPC-92
86T-92
89Pac/SenLg-145
89TM/SenLg-25

Cowger, Tracy
79Ashvl/TCMA-2
80Tulsa-18
81Tulsa-2
82Tulsa-12
83OKCty-5
83Tulsa-17

Cowley, Bill
45Parade*-14

Cowley, Joe
78Green
79Savan-15
82Pol/Atl-38
83Richm-3
83T-288
84Colum-13
84Colum/Pol-7
85D-613
85F-124
85Leaf-58
85T-769
85T/St-318
86BuffB-9
86Coke/WS-40
86D-608
86D/HL-44
86F-103
86F/Up-U31
86T-427
86T/Tr-29T
87D-552
87F-491
87F/LL-12
87Leaf-240
87Phill/TastyK-39A
87Sf-196M
87Sf/TPrev-26M
87T-27
87T/St-290
92Yank/WIZ80-37

Cox, Boyce
89Bristol/Star-31
90Bristol/Star-30PRES

Cox, Carl 1
47Signal

Cox, Carl 2
86VeroB-4

Cox, Carter
87BYU-16

Cox, Dalene
81ArkTr-23M

Cox, Danny
82Spring/Frit-12
83StPete-4
84D-449
85D-571
85F-222
85T-499
86D-382
86F-32
86KAS/Disc-5
86Leaf-177
86OPC-294
86Schnucks-4
86Sf-108
86T-294
86T/Mini-61
86T/St-48
87D-553
87F-292
87F/Excit-12
87Leaf-160
87OPC-202
87Sf/TPrev-12M
87Smok/Cards-6
87T-621
87T/Mini-33
88D-60
88D/Best-75
88F-28
88Leaf-72
88Louisvl-17
88OPC-59
88Panini/St-383
88S-415
88Sf-84
88Smok/Card-2
88T-59
88T/Big-111
88Woolwth-27
89D-348
89F-447
89OPC-158
89S-613
89T-562
89UD-535
90Louisvl/LBC-13
90OPC-184
90PublInt/St-215
90Smok/Card-3
90SpringDG/Best-9
90T-184
90T/TVCard-9
91Leaf-350
91Phill/Medford-10
91T/Tr-25T
92BuffB/BlueS-5
92D-614
92F-526
92OPC-791
92Phill/Med-9
92S-568
92StCl-351
92T-791
92T/Gold-791
92T/GoldWin-791
93BJ/Demp-3
93BJ/Fire-7
93D-466
93F-499
93F/Final-291
94D-114
94F-329
94L-87
94S-242
94S/GoldR-242
94StCl/Team-152
94T-582
94T/Gold-582

Cox, Darren
87Idaho-21

Cox, Darron
88CapeCod/Sum-97
88OK-12
89Billings/ProC-2067
89OK-12
90CharWh/Best-1
90CharWh/ProC-2243
90Foil/Best-20
90ProC/Singl-840
90SALAS/Star-5
91Cedar/ClBest-13
91Cedar/ProC-2720
92Chatt/ProC-3822

92Chatt/SB-181
Cox, Doug
87Bakers-13
88VeroB/Star-4
Cox, Elmer Joseph
(Dick)
90Target-917
E120
E126-5
W573
Cox, Frank Bernhardt
No Cards.
Cox, J. Casey
66T-549R
67CokeCap/Senator-7
67T-414
68OPC-66
68T-66
69T-383
70OPC-281
70T-281
71MLB/St-533
71OPC-82
71T-82
72MB-81
72OPC-231
72T-231
73OPC-419
73T-419
92Yank/WIZ70-38
93Rang/Keeb-7
Cox, James Charles
(Jim)
72Dimanche*-8
74OPC-600R
74T-600R
76SSPC-325
Cox, Jeffrey Linden
(Jeff)
79Ogden/TCMA-12
80Ogden-19
81D-230
81T-133
81Tacoma-19
82Evansvl-14
83Omaha-14
86Vermont-4
87Vanco-3
87Watertn-30
88Augusta/ProC-382
88Chatt/Team-7
89Memphis/Best-24
89Memphis/ProC-1195
90Memphis/Best-26MG
90Memphis/ProC-1025MG
90Memphis/Star-26MG
91AA/LineD-424MG
91Memphis/LineD-424
91Memphis/ProC-669MG
92Omaha/ProC-2977MG
92Omaha/SB-349MG
Cox, Jim
85Elmira-5
Cox, Larry Eugene
76SSPC-596
77T-379
78SSPC/270-258
78T-541
79T-489
80OPC-63
80T-116
81D-285
81F-604
81T-249
81T/Tr-749
83QuadC-2
85Iowa-28
86Iowa-9MG
87Iowa-22MG
88Berg/Cubs-CO
93Rang/Keeb-114
Cox, Robbie
76Baton
Cox, Robert Joe
(Bobby)
69MB-65
69T-237
75Syrac/Team-2MG
75Syrac/Team-3
78T-93MG
79T-302MG
80T-192MG
81D-426MG
81F-247MG
81Pol/Atl-6MG
81T-675MG
83OPC-34MG
83T-606MG
84Nes/792-202MG
84OPC-202MG
84T-202MG
84Tor/Fire-10MG
85OPC-135MG
85T-411
85Tor/Fire-9MG
86OPC-359MG
86T-471MG
90Brave/Dubuq/Singl-6MG
90T/Tr-23TMG
91Brave/Dubuq/Perf-7MG
91Brave/Dubuq/Stand-11MG
91OPC-759MG
91T-759MG
92Brave/LykePerf-9MG
92Brave/LykeStand-11MG
92OPC-489MG
92T-489MG
92T/Gold-489MG
92T/GoldWin-489MG
92Yank/WIZ60-30
93BJ/D/McDon-15MG
93Brave/LykePerf-8MG
93Brave/LykeStand-10MG
93T-501M
93T/Gold-501M
Cox, Stan
86Lipscomb-7
Cox, Steven
92Classic/DP-85
92FrRow/DP-98
93B-653
Cox, Ted
91Peoria/Team-30M
Cox, Terry
71OPC-559R
71T-559R
Cox, William Richard
(Billy)
47TipTop
49B-73
49Eureka-33
50B-194
51B-224
51T/BB-48
52B-152
52Dix
52T-232
53B/BW-60
53NB
54B-26
54NYJour
54RH
54RM-NL2
55B-56
55Esskay
79TCMA-83
90Target-143
91Crown/Orio-87
PM10/Sm-31
PM10/Sm-32
Cox, William Ted
(Ted)
78T-706R
79T-79
80T-252
81D-283
81F-602
81Spokane-16
Coyle, Joseph
(Rocky)
87Knoxvl-6
87Syrac/TCMA-27
Coyne, Toots
No Cards.
Cozzi, Dante
52Laval-73
Cozzolino, Paul
82VeroB-3
Crabbe, Bruce
86Pittsfld-4
87Iowa-12
88Iowa/CMC-13
88Iowa/ProC-550
89Iowa/CMC-14
89Iowa/ProC-1714
90AAASingl/ProC-410
90ProC/Singl-290
90Richm/Bob-5
90Richm/CMC-14
90Richm/ProC-265
90Richm/Team-7
91AAA/LineD-429
91Richm/Bob-2
91Richm/LineD-429
91Richm/ProC-2576
91Richm/Team-21
92Syrac/MerchB-2
92Syrac/ProC-1973
92Syrac/SB-502
Crable, George
90Target-918
Crabtree, Chris
91Yakima/ClBest-24
91Yakima/ProC-4242
Crabtree, Estel C.
82Ohio/HOF-45
V355-134
W754
Crabtree, Tim
92ClBest/Up-432
92Classic/DP-45
92FrRow/DP-9
92StCath/ClBest-23
92StCath/ProC-3379
93ClBest/MLG-208
93FExcel/ML-240
93Knoxvl/ProC-1243
93StCl/MurphyS-29
93T-742M
93T/Gold-742M
Craddock, Walt
59T-281
Cradle, Rickey
92MedHat/ProC-3218
92MedHat/SportP-15
93Hagers/ClBest-7
93Hagers/ProC-1890
Craft, Harry Francis
39PlayBall-65
40PlayBall-79
55Rodeo
62T-12MG
63T-491MG
64T-298MG
78TCMA-244MG
89Smok/Ast-27
W711/1
W711/2
Craft, Mark
90SoOreg/Best-16
90SoOreg/ProC-3442
Craig, Dale
89Wythe/Star-7
90WinSalem/Team-8
91Geneva/ClBest-3
91Geneva/ProC-4220
Craig, Dean
78Clinton
79Wausau-18
82Nashvl-8
Craig, Morris
90Hunting/ProC-3287
91Geneva/ClBest-4
91Peoria/ProC-1347
92Peoria/ClBest-23
Craig, Pete
65T-466R
66OPC-11R
66T-11R
67T-459R
Craig, Rodney Paul
79Spokane-5
80T-672R
81Charl-19
81D-288
81F-597
81T-282R
82Wheat/Ind
83Charl-15
83D-515
84Maine-19
Craig, Roger
56T-63
57T-173
58T-194
60BB-15
60L-8
60Morrell
60T-62
60Union/Dodg-2
61BB-38
61T-543
61Union/Dodg-2
62Salada-189
62Shirriff-189
62T-183
62T/St-154
62T/bucks
63Exh
63F-47
63J-200
63P-200
63T-197
64T-295
65T-411
66T-543
74OPC-31CO
74T-31CO
76SSPC-628CO
77Padre/SchCd-7CO
78Padre/FamFun-7MG
78TCMA-201
79T-479MG
80Marchant-8
81TCMA-482M
84Tiger/Wave-16CO
86Mother/SFG-1MG
86T-111MG
87Mother/SFG-1MG
87T-193MG
88Mother/Giants-1MG
88T-654MG
89Mother/Giants-1MG
89Pac/Leg-145
89Rini/Dodg-15
89T-744MG
89T/LJN-79MG
90KMart/SS-33MG
90Mother/Giant-1MG
90OPC-351MG
90T-351MG
90T/TVAS-66MGM
90Target-144
91Mother/Giant-1MG
91OPC-579MG
91PG&E-6MG
91T-579MG
91WIZMets-87
92Giant/PGE-14MG
92Mother/Giant-1MG
92OPC-109MG
92T-109MG
92T/Gold-109MG
92T/GoldWin-109MG
Exh47
Craig, Tom
82Syrac-25
83Syrac-3
84Syrac-3
Crain, Gregg
91Cedar/ClBest-29TR
Crall, Jim
75Anderson/TCMA-7
Cram, Jerry
71OPC-247R
71T-247R
75Tidew/Team-7
76SSPC-559
81Omaha-2
82Omaha-26
83Omaha-25
84Omaha-13
91WIZMets-88
Cramer, Bill
90Rockford/ProC-2698
90Rockford/Team-5
91WPalmB/ClBest-15
91WPalmB/ProC-1231
Cramer, George
35Exh/4-14
Cramer, Michael J.
(Mike)
75Phoenix/CircleK-26
Cramer, Rob
86Visalia-8
Cramer, Roger Maxwell
(Doc)
34G-25
35BU-53
35G-8J
35G-9J
39PlayBall-101
40PlayBall-29
43Playball-12
77Galasso-71
81Tiger/Detroit-24
89Pac/Leg-181
92Conlon/Sport-451
93Conlon-903
94Conlon-1154
R314
V354-74
V94-8
Cramer, William B.
(Dick)
No Cards.
Crandall, Bob
80Elmira-33
Crandall, Delmar W.
(Del)
50B-56
51B-20
52T-162
53JC-15
53SpicSpan/3x5-9
53SpicSpan/7x10-5
53T-197
54B-32
54JC-1
54RM-NL3
54SpicSpan/PostC-7
54T-12
55Armour-3
55B-217
55Gol/Braves-8
55JC-1
55RM-NL2
55SpicSpan/DC-7
56T-175
57SpicSpan/4x5-7
57T-133
58T-351M
58T-390
59Armour-7
59Bz
59T-425
59T-567AS
60Armour-7
60Bz-36
60Lake
60MacGregor-6
60SpicSpan-7A
60SpicSpan-7B
60T-170
60T-568AS
61P-110
61T-390
61T-583AS
61T/Dice-2
61T/St-42
62T-351M
62T-443
62T/St-147
63J-153
63P-153
63Salada-11
63T-460
64T-169
65OPC-68
65T-68
66T-339
73OPC-646MG
73T-646MG
74T-99MG
75OPC-384MG
75T-384MG
75T/M-384MG
78Cr/PCL-30MG
78TCMA-144
79TCMA-68
80Albuq-23MG
81Albuq/TCMA-25MG
82Albuq-24MG
83Albuq-23MG
84D-632MG
84Mother/Mar-1MG
84Nes/792-721MG
84T-721MG
88Pac/Leg-98
89Swell-132
91T/Arc53-197
92Bz/Quadra-4M
94T/Arc54-12
Exh47
PM10/L-12
WG9-28

Crandall, Ducky
75Lafay
Crandall, James Otis
(Doc)
10Domino-28
11Helmar-122
12Sweet/Pin-109
14CJ-67
15CJ-67
D304
E104
E254
M116
S74-82
T202
T204
T205
T206
T207
T213/blue
T215/blue
T215/brown
Crane, Edward N.
(Cannonball)
N172
Crane, Gordy
75Sacra/Caruso-18
Crane, Rich
89FresnoSt/Smok-8
89GreatF-3
90Bakers/Cal-235
Crane, Samuel Byren
(Sam)
E120
Crane, Samuel N.
(Sam)
90Target-919
N172
N284
Scrapps
Cranford, John
92Welland/ClBest-5
92Welland/ProC-1329
Cranston, William
T206
Cravath, Clifford C.
(Gavvy)
14CJ-82
15CJ-82
91Conlon/Sport-277
93Conlon-803
BF2-84
D327
D328-35
D329-40
D350/2-41
E135-35
E254
E270/1
M101/4-40
M101/5-41
T206
W514-11
Craven, Britt
91QuadC/ClBest-2
91QuadC/ProC-2619
Craver, William H.
(Bill)
No Cards.
Crawford, Carlos
91BurlInd/ProC-3293
92ColRS/ClBest-6
92ColRS/ProC-2381
93Kinston/Team-5
Crawford, Clifford R.
(Pat)
No Cards.
Crawford, Forrest
No Cards.
Crawford, George
No Cards.
Crawford, Glenn M.
47Remar-25
Crawford, Jack
82Danvl/Frit-8
83Peoria/Frit-15
Crawford, Jerry
88TM/Umpire-28
89TM/Umpire-26
90TM/Umpire-25
Crawford, Jim
74OPC-279
74T-279
76OPC-428
76SSPC-47
76T-428
76T/Tr-428T
77T-69
89Gaston/ProC-1015
Crawford, Joe
91Kingspt/ClBest-16
91Kingspt/ProC-3806
92ColumMet/SAL/II-39
92ProC/Tomorrow-290
92StLucie/ClBest-5
92StLucie/ProC-1739
93StLucie/ProC-2914
Crawford, Kenneth D.
(Ken)
No Cards.
Crawford, Pat
94Conlon-1293
Crawford, Rufus
55B-121
Crawford, Samuel Earl
(Sam)
11Helmar-29
14CJ-14
15CJ-14
72F/FFeat-27
75Shakey-9
76Shakey-82
77Galasso-140
77Galasso-267
80Pac/Leg-55
80Perez/HOF-82
80SSPC/HOF
81Conlon-98
81Tiger/Detroit-121
87Conlon/2-30
89HOF/St-50
90BBWit-78
94Conlon-1221
BF2-27
D303
D304
D327
D328-36
E101
E102
E103
E104
E106
E135-36
E90/1
E92
E94
E95
M116
T201
T206
T213/blue
T215/brown
T216
T3-5
W514-95
W555
WG2-9
WG5-12
WG6-12
Crawford, Shag
89Pac/Leg-199UMP
Crawford, Steve
82Coke/BOS
82D-564
82F-291
82T-157
83Pawtu-4
83T-419
84Pawtu-14
85D-395
85F-156
85T-661
86D-416
86F-346
86Leaf-193
86T-91
87D-399
87F-33
87T-589
88F-350
88S-289
88T-299
90Leaf-494
91F-554
91OPC-718
91Pol/Royal-5
91S-287
91T-718
92S-349
Crawford, Willie M.
65T-453R
68T-417
69T-327
70K-26
70OPC-34
70T-34
71MLB/St-100
71OPC-519
71T-519
71Ticket/Dodg-4
72T-669
73OPC-639
73T-639
74OPC-480
74T-480
74T/St-43
75OPC-186
75T-186
75T/M-186
76OPC-76
76SSPC-84
76T-76
77BurgChef-107
77T-642
78T-507
78TCMA-157
85SpokAT/Cram-4
90Target-146
Creager, Mack
66Pep/Tul
Creamer, George W.
No Cards.
Creamer, Robert
90LitSun-14
Credeur, Todd
85Anchora-7
86Ashvl-6
87Osceola-28
88Osceola/Star-6
89ColMud/Best-26
89Osceola/Star-5
90ColMud/Best-17
90ColMud/ProC-1342
90ColMud/Star-9
Cree, William F.
(Birdie)
10Domino-29
11Helmar-41
12Sweet/Pin-33
E224
M116
T206
T213/blue
T213/brown
T214-5
T215/blue
T215/brown
Creech, Ed
90Gate/SportP-24MG
91James/ClBest-28MG
91James/ProC-3561MG
Creed, Bennett
90Miami/II/Star-30PER
Creeden, Patrick F.
(Pat)
No Cards.
Creedon, Cornelius C.
(Connie)
No Cards.
Creegan, Martin
(Marty)
No Cards.
Creek, Doug
91Hamil/ProC-4031
94B-3
Creekmore, Niles
87SLCity/Taco-17
Creel, Keith
82Omaha-3
83D-574
83Omaha-5
84F-346
84Omaha-15
85Maine-6
86Maine-7
87OKCty-7
93Rang/Keeb-115
Creely, August L.
(Gus)
No Cards.
Cregan, Peter James
(Pete)
No Cards.
Creger, Bernard Odell
(Bernie)
47TipTop
Crema, Pat
92MedHat/ProC-3204
92MedHat/SportP-4
Crenshaw, Ken
89Princet/Star-28
Crespi, Frank A.
(Creepy)
41DP-145
W754
Crespo, Felipe
91MedHat/ProC-4106
91MedHat/SportP-22
92B-77
92Myrtle/ClBest-19
92Myrtle/ProC-2202
93Dunedin/ClBest-6
93Dunedin/ProC-1803
94ClBest/Gold-55
Crespo, Michael
91Butte/SportP-7
91Gaston/ClBest-14
91Gaston/ProC-2691
92Gaston/ClBest-3
92Gaston/ProC-2255
Cresse, Mark
85Coke/Dodg-8CO
86Coke/Dodg-7CO
90Mother/Dodg-28M
90Pol/Dodg-x
91Mother/Dodg-28CO
91Pol/Dodg-x
92Mother/Dodg-28M
92Pol/Dodg-NNO
93Mother/Dodg-28M
93Pol/Dodg-30M
Crew, Ken
86Memphis/GoldT-2
86Memphis/SilverT-2
87Memphis-20
87Memphis/Best-8
88ColAst/Best-6
Crews, Larry
82Clinton/Frit-19
84Shrev/FB-5
85Cram/PCL-178
Crews, Tim
81BurlB-10
83ElPaso-17
84ElPaso-10
86ElPaso-7
87Albuq/Pol-8
88Albuq/CMC-8
88Albuq/ProC-264
88D-464
88D/Rook-20
88F-511
88Pol/Dodg-52M
88S-641RP
88Sf-224
88T-57
89D-486
89Mother/Dodg-24
89Panini/St-96
89Pol/Dodg-27
89S-505
89T-22
89UD-611
90D-550
90ElPasoATG/Team-29
90F-390
90F/Can-390
90Mother/Dodg-26
90OPC-551
90Pol/Dodg-52
90S-164
90T-551
90Target-147
90UD-670
91D-294
91F-197
91F/UltraUp-U87
91Leaf-141
91Mother/Dodg-26
91OPC-737
91Pol/Dodg-52
91S-302
91StCl-375
91T-737
91UD-596
92D-437
92F-452
92Mother/Dodg-13
92OPC-642
92Pol/Dodg-52
92S-238
92StCl-349
92T-642
92T/Gold-642
92T/GoldWin-642
92UD-687
92Ultra-502
93F-444
93Pinn-554
Cribb, Buddy
89Alaska/Team-19
Crider, Jerry
69T-491R
71OPC-113
71T-113
Criger, Louis
E107
E90/1
M116
T205
T206
T3-89
WG2-10
Crim, Chuck
83Beloit/Frit-22
84ElPaso-6
85Cram/PCL-220
86Vanco-8
87D/Rook-18
87F/Up-U19
87Pol/Brew-32
87T/Tr-25T
88D-355
88F-162
88Pol/Brew-32
88S-402
88T-286
89B-136
89Brewer/YB-32
89D-617
89D/Best-127
89F-183
89OPC-99
89Pol/Brew-32
89S-272
89T-466
89UD-501
90Brewer/MillB-3
90D-221
90ElPasoATG/Team-7
90F-319
90F/Can-319
90Leaf-58
90OPC-768
90Panini/St-103
90Pol/Brew-32
90PublInt/St-493
90S-108
90T-768
90UD-511
91B-51
91Brewer/MillB-6
91D-684
91F-579
91Leaf-28
91OPC-644
91Pol/Brew-6
91S-99
91StCl-112
91T-644
91UD-391
91Ultra-173
92D-103
92F-175
92L-312
92L/BlkGold-312
92OPC-169
92S-22
92S/RookTr-53T
92StCl-823
92T-169
92T/Gold-169
92T/GoldWin-169
92UD-496
93D-649
93F-570
93Mother/Angel-20

93Pac/Spanish-365
93S-455
93StCl-327
93StCl/1stDay-327
93StCl/Angel-2
93T-499
93T/Gold-499
Crimian, Jack
53Hunter
56T-319
57T-297
Criminger, John
92Beloit/ProC-398
Crimmins, John
92Elmira/ClBest-8
92Elmira/ProC-1384
Cripe, David Gordon
(Dave)
83DayBe-1
85Osceola/Team-1
86ColumAst-8MG
Criscione, Dave G.
75Spokane/Caruso-12
78RochR
91Crown/Orio-88
Criscola, Anthony P.
(Tony)
47Centen-5
Crisham, Patrick L.
(Pat)
No Cards.
Crisler, Joel
77QuadC
79SLCity-15
80ElPaso-11
Crisler, Thomas
81Redwd-3
Crisp, Joseph Shelby
(Joe)
No Cards.
Criss, Dode
E254
M116
T206
Criss, Matt
90WichSt-8
Crist, Chester Arthur
(Ches)
No Cards.
Crist, Clark
81LynnS-28
81Wausau-21
82LynnS-10
84Chatt-7
91AubAS/ClBest-24CO
91AubAS/ProC-4291CO
92AubAs/ClBest-28
92AubAs/ProC-1372
Crist, Jack
71Richm/Team-5
Cristelli, Pat
77SLCity
78Cr/PCL-5
Criswell, Brian
85Madis-9
85Madis/Pol-6
86Madis/Pol-6
88Huntsvl/BK-3
Criswell, Tim
86Durham-6
87Durham-7
Critz, Hugh Melville
(Hughie)
25Exh-26
26Exh-26
28Exh-13
29Exh/4-7
31Exh/4-9
33Exh/4-5
33G-238
33G-3
34G-17
35Exh/4-5
35G-2A
35G-4A
35G-7A
61F-101
87Conlon/2-10
88Conlon/5-6
91Conlon/Sport-290
R316
R332-46
V353-3
V354-72
W517-25
WG7-10
Crnich, Jeff
88Belling/Legoe-30BB CL
89Belling/Legoe-36BB
Croak, David
90Martins/ProC-3188
Crockett, Claude
77StPete
Crockett, David S.
(Davey)
No Cards.
Crockett, Rusty
88Peoria/Ko-9
89WinSalem/Star-6
90CharlK/Team-21
90T/TVCub-41
91AA/LineD-130
91CharlK/LineD-130
91CharlK/ProC-1696
92ChalK/SB-151
92CharlK/ProC-2777
Croft, Arthur F.
(Art)
No Cards.
Croft, Henry T.
No Cards.
Croft, Paul
78Wisco
90HagersDG/Best-6
Croghan, Andrew
89Alaska/Team-10
91Oneonta/ProC-4147
92Greens/ClBest-5
92Greens/ProC-771
Croghan, John
N172
Crolius, Fred J.
No Cards.
Cromartie, Warren L.
78OPC-117
78T-468
79OPC-32
79T-76
80OPC-102
80T-180
81D-332
81F-142
81F/St-92
81OPC-345
81OPC/Post-5
81T-345
81T/SO-78
81T/St-188
82D-340
82Expo/Hygrade-4
82F-186
82F/St-33
82FBI/Disc-5
82Hygrade
82OPC-61
82OPC-94TL
82OPC/Post-13
82T-526TL
82T-695
82T/St-60
82Zeller-18
82Zeller-7
83D-466
83F-279
83F/St-3M
83F/St-7M
83OPC-351
83Stuart-18
83T-495
84F-272
84Nes/792-287
84OPC-287
84T-287
91B-315
91F/Up-U25
91Leaf-458
91Leaf/Stud-64
92S-637
93Expo/D/McDon-14
Crombie, Kevin
92Niagara/ClBest-19
92Niagara/ProC-3316
Cromer, Brandon
92ClBest/Up-416
92Classic/DP-25
92FrRow/DP-36
92UD/ML-18
93ClBest/MLG-173
93StCath/ClBest-6
93StCath/ProC-3979
93StCl/MurphyS-190
Cromer, Burke
92Idaho/ProC-3504
Cromer, David T.
92SoOreg/ClBest-7
92SoOreg/ProC-3431
Cromer, Tripp
89Hamil/Star-10
90StPete/Star-3
91StPete/ClBest-19
91StPete/ProC-2282
92ArkTr/ProC-1135
92ArkTr/SB-31
92Sky/AASingl-15
93B-52
94D-419
94F/MLP-7
94Pac/Cr-588
94Pinn-425
94StCl/Team-328
94T-139
94T/Gold-139
94UD-113
94UD/ElecD-113
Crompton, Edward
(Ned)
No Cards.
Crompton, Herbert B.
(Herb)
52Laval-80
Cromwell, Brian
89KS*-6
Cromwell, Nate
88Myrtle/ProC-1174
89Dunedin/Star-3
90Knoxvl/Best-27
90Knoxvl/ProC-1238
90Knoxvl/Star-2
90ProC/Singl-816
91AA/LineD-353
91ClBest/Singl-91
91Knoxvl/LineD-353
91Knoxvl/ProC-1760
92Knoxvl/ProC-2983
92Knoxvl/SB-379
93Knoxvl/ProC-1244
Cron, Chris
86Durham-7
87QuadC-23
88CalLgAS-34
88PalmSp/Cal-102
88PalmSp/ProC-1441
89MidldA/GS-11
89TexLAS/GS-2
90AAASingl/ProC-99
90Edmon/CMC-21
90Edmon/ProC-523
90ProC/Singl-498
91AAA/LineD-158
91Edmon/LineD-158
91Edmon/ProC-1521
92Classic/I-29
92D-698
92F-656
92S-847
92Sky/AAASingl-281
92T/91Debut-41
92Vanco/ProC-2728
92Vanco/SB-632
93F-581
Crone, Bill
81LynnS-16
82LynnS-11
83SLCity-18
84Cram/PCL-172
85Cram/PCL-93
86Calgary-5
87Tucson-4
Crone, Ray
85Newar-18
Crone, Raymond H.
54JC-20
54SpicSpan/PostC-8
54T-206
55Gol/Braves-9
55JC-12
55T-149
56T-76
57SpicSpan/4x5-8
57T-68
58SFCallB-6
58T-272
94T/Arc54-206
Cronin, Chuck
47Sunbeam
Cronin, Daniel
(Dan)
No Cards.
Cronin, James John
94Conlon-1158
Cronin, Jeff
91Durham/ClBest-5
91Durham/ProC-1538
Cronin, John J.
90Target-148
Cronin, Joseph Edward
(Joe)
31Exh/4-31
33DH-11
33G-109
33G-63
34Exh/4-16
35BU-183
35BU-32
35Exh/4-9
35G-1G
35G-3E
35G-5E
35G-6E
36Exh/4-9
37Exh/4-9
37OPC-124
38Exh/4-9
38ONG/Pin-3
40PlayBall-134
40Wheat-7
41DP-59
41DP-82
41PlayBall-15
61GP-14
75Shakey-6
76Rowe-16M
76Shakey-80
77Galasso-198
77Galasso-65
80Pac/Leg-39
80Perez/HOF-80
80SSPC/HOF
81Conlon-65
83D/HOF-20
86Conlon/1-9
86Sf/Dec-7
88Conlon/AmAS-6
89HOF/St-19
89Pac/Leg-167
91Conlon/Sport-314
91Conlon/Sport-50
92Conlon/Sport-600
93Conlon-676
93Conlon-843
94Conlon-1085
R300
R302
R303/A
R303/B
R306
R308-176
R310
R311/Gloss
R312/M
R313
R314
R328-7
R332-37
V300
V351B-9
V353-63
V355-63
V94-9
WG8-8
Cronin, William P.
(Bill)
No Cards.
Cronk, Doug
89Gaston/ProC-1013
89Gaston/Star-5
89SALAS/GS-29
89Star/IISingl-135
90CharlR/Star-5
Cronkright, Dan
86Penin-7
Cronkright, Dave
87DayBe-24
Crooks, John Charles
N172
Crooks, Thomas A.
(Tom)
No Cards.
Crosby, Edward C.
(Ed)
71OPC-672
71T-672
73OPC-599
73T-599
76OPC-457
76SSPC-520
76T-457
78SanJose-5
79Spokane-1
Crosby, Ken
76OPC-593R
76SSPC-602
76T-593R
Crosby, Mike
92ColRS/ClBest-9
92ColRS/ProC-2393
93B-177
93Kinston/Team-6
Crosby, Pat
86LitFalls-7
Crosby, Todd
87Spartan-15
88Clearw/Star-9
89StPete/Star-9
89Star/Wax-49
90AAASingl/ProC-522
90Louisvl/CMC-24
90Louisvl/LBC-14
90Louisvl/ProC-408
90ProC/Singl-124
90T/TVCard-44
91AAA/LineD-232
91Louisvl/LineD-232
91Louisvl/ProC-2922
91Louisvl/Team-18
92Shrev/ProC-3879
92Shrev/SB-580
Crosetti, Frank P.
(Frankie)
33G-217
34DS-86
35BU-182
36G-9
38ONG/Pin-4
41DP-113
43Playball-2
44Yank/St-7
47TipTop
52B-252CO
52T-384CO
60T-465C
68Bz-13
81TCMA-481M
88Conlon/3-8
90Pac/Legend-19
90Swell/Great-48
91Swell/Great-20
92AP/ASG-45
92Yank/WIZAS-14
93UD/ATH-35
R303/A
R311/Leath
R313
R314
R346-24
R423-17
V351A-6
V351B-10
V355-91
WG8-9
Crosnoe, Cory
91Pulaski/ClBest-6
91Pulaski/ProC-4012
92Macon/ClBest-11
92Macon/ProC-272
Cross, Amos C.
No Cards.
Cross, Bob
79Newar-16
Cross, Clarence
No Cards.
Cross, Frank Atwell
No Cards.
Cross, Jesse
89Myrtle/ProC-1473
90Dunedin/Star-6
90FSLAS/Star-27
90Star/ISingl-63

91AA/LineD-354
91Knoxvl/LineD-354
91Knoxvl/ProC-1761
92Knoxvl/ProC-2984
92Syrac/SB-503
93Syrac/ProC-994
94FExcel-142
Cross, Joffre
(Jeff)
47TipTop
Cross, LaFayette N.
(Lave)
90Target-149
E107
N172
N300/unif
WG2-11
Cross, Leach
T3/Box-69
Cross, Mike
92Freder/ClBest-4
Cross, Montford M.
(Monte)
E107
T206
WG2-12
Crossin, Frank P.
No Cards.
Crossley, William
N172
Crotty, Joseph P.
(Joe)
N172
N172/ST
Crouch, Bill
41G-27
90Target-150
W754
Crouch, Jack Albert
No Cards.
Crouch, Matt
86BurlEx-4
88Memphis/Best-8
89Omaha/CMC-5
89Omaha/ProC-1717
Crouch, Zach
85Greens-9
87NewBrit-2
88Pawtu/CMC-6
88Pawtu/ProC-457
89NewBrit/ProC-612
89NewBrit/Star-4
90T/TVRSox-40
Croucher, Frank D.
No Cards.
Crough, Bill
41G-27
Crouse, Buck
28LaPresse-25
Crouse, Clyde E.
(Buck)
92Conlon/Sport-509
Crouwel, Michael
92Martins/ClBest-2
92Martins/ProC-3059
Crow, Donald Leroy
(Don)
80Albuq-27
81Albuq/TCMA-13
82Albuq-12
90Target-151
Crow, Roger
(Gabby)
79QuadC-4
81QuadC-32
82QuadC-12
83QuadC-1
Crowder, Alvin
(General)
33G-122
33G-95
34DS-93
34Exh/4-16
34G-15
35BU-161
35G-1H
35G-3F
35G-5F
35G-6F
61F-102
77Galasso-187
88Conlon/AmAS-7
91Conlon/Sport-257
93Conlon-682
94Conlon-1277
R308-185
R310
R312/M
V353-71
V354-65
V94-10
Crowe, George Daniel
52T-360
53JC-18
53SpicSpan/3x5-10
53T-3
55JC-39
56T-254
57Kahn
57T-73
58Kahn
58T-12
59T-337
60T-419
61T-52
91T/Arc53-3
Crowe, Ron
88NE-3
89Everett/Star-5
89Star/IISingl-195
90Clinton/Best-21
90Clinton/ProC-2557
90Foil/Best-170
91SanJose/ClBest-5
91SanJose/ProC-16
92Shrev/ProC-3875
92Shrev/SB-581
Crowell, William
N172
Crowley, Brian
89Butte/SP-8
Crowley, Edgar Jewel
(Ed)
No Cards.
Crowley, Jim
91Elmira/ClBest-3
91Elmira/ProC-3276
92LynchRS/ClBest-18
92LynchRS/ProC-2912
Crowley, John A.
No Cards.
Crowley, Ray
78Memphis/Team-2
79Memphis/TCMA-16
80Memphis-11
Crowley, Terrence M.
(Terry)
70OPC-121R
70T-121R
71MLB/St-292
71OPC-453
71T-453
72T-628
73JP
73OPC-302
73T-302
74OPC-648
74T-648
74T/Tr-648T
75OPC-447
75T-447
75T/M-447
76OPC-491
76SSPC-35
76T-491
79T-91
80T-188
81D-507
81F-190
81OPC-342
81T-543
82D-383
82F-160
82T-232
83D-457
83F-55
83T-372
83T/Tr-22
84Nes/792-732
84OPC-246
84T-732
87French-10CO
88French-10CO
91Crown/Orio-89
Crowley, Terry Jr.
88Salem/Star-4
89Salem/Star-5
90Harris/ProC-1198
90Harris/Star-5
90ProC/Singl-762
91AA/LineD-104
91CaroMud/LineD-104
91CaroMud/ProC-1091
92Canton/ProC-696
Crowley, William M.
N284
Crownover, Derek
86Lipscomb-8
Cruise, Walton Edwin
(Walt)
21Exh-29
E120
E220
V100
Crum, George
83BurlR-14
83BurlR/Frit-4
85Tulsa-4
86Water-6
Crumling, Eugene Leon
(Gene)
No Cards.
Crump, Arthur Elliott
(Buddy)
No Cards.
Crump, Jamie
90Pulaski/Best-15
90Pulaski/ProC-3095
Crutcher, Dave
79Tulsa-19
80Tulsa-2
81Tulsa-15
Crutchfield, Jim
(Jimmie)
78Laugh/Black-35
86Negro/Frit-29
91Negro/Lewis-8
92Negro/Kraft-6
92Negro/Retort-13
Cruthers, Charles P.
(Press)
No Cards.
Cruz, Andres
90Memphis/Best-23
90Memphis/ProC-1003
90Memphis/Star-8
91AA/LineD-405
91Memphis/LineD-405
91Memphis/ProC-647
Cruz, Arcadio
77Charl
Cruz, Cirilio Dilan
(Tommy)
78Cr/PCL-105
79Colum-13
Cruz, Daniel
90Bristol/ProC-3162
90Bristol/Star-4
Cruz, Fausto
91Modesto/ProC-3095
92AS/Cal-9
92Reno/Cal-38
92UD/ML-157
93LimeR/Winter-141
93LimeR/Winter-18
93Modesto/ClBest-7
93Modesto/ProC-806
94B-436
94FExcel-119
94Ultra-406
Cruz, Georgie
83Memphis/TCMA-2
Cruz, Hector Dilan
(Heity)
76OPC-598R
76T-598R
77T-624
78SSPC/270-248
78T-257
79Pol/Giants-9
79T-436
80T-516
81F-206
81T-52
81T/Tr-750
82D-57
82F-214
82OPC-364
82T-663
91Pac/SenLg-60
Cruz, Henry Acosta
74Albuq/Team-4
76OPC-590R
76SSPC-85
76T-590R
78SSPC/270-152
78T-316
80Iowa/Pol-4
90Target-152
Cruz, Ismael
89Martins/Star-8
90Batavia/ProC-3071
Cruz, Ivan
90FSLAS/Star-28
90Lakeland/Star-6
90Star/ISingl-34
91AA/LineD-379
91B-153
91ClBest/Singl-18
91London/LineD-379
91London/ProC-1882
92B-170
92ClBest-171
92London/ProC-638
92London/SB-404
92Sky/AASingl-172
92UD/ML-241
92UD/POY-PY23
93B-319
93FExcel/ML-170
93T-423M
93T/Gold-423M
Cruz, J.J.
91Erie/ClBest-4
91Erie/ProC-4071
92Batavia/ClBest-6
92Batavia/ProC-3268
Cruz, Javier
85Tigres-26
Cruz, Jesus
79Cedar/TCMA-2
Cruz, Jose Dilan
72OPC-107
72T-107
73OPC-292
73T-292
74OPC-464
74T-464
74T/St-113
75OPC-514
75T-514
75T/M-514
76OPC-321
76SSPC-62
76T-321
77BurgChef-9
77Ho-75
77Ho/Twink-75
77K-50
77OPC-147
77T-42
78BK/Ast-17
78Ho-72
78K-16
78OPC-131
78T-625
79Ho-58
79OPC-143
79T-289
80OPC-367
80T-722
81Coke
81D-383
81F-60
81F/St-78
81OPC-105
81T-105
81T/HT
81T/SO-83
81T/St-169
82D-244
82Drake-10
82F-214
82F/St-50
82OPC-325
82T-325
82T/St-44
83D-41
83F-446
83F/St-15M
83F/St-16M
83OPC-327
83OPC/St-242
83T-585
83T/Fold-5M
83T/St-242
84D-182
84F-222
84F/St-24
84F/St-8
84Mother/Ast-8
84Nes/792-422
84Nes/792-66TL
84OPC-189
84Seven-19W
84T-422
84T-66TL
84T/RD-16
84T/St-65
84T/St/Box-13
85D-20DK
85D-304
85D/DKsuper-20
85Drake-7
85F-347
85FunFood/Pin-129
85Leaf-20DK
85Mother/Ast-4
85OPC-95
85Seven-10C
85T-95
85T/Gloss40-20
85T/RD-14
85T/St-59
85T/Super-34
85ThomMc/Discs-27
86D-60
86D/AAS-19
86F-296
86F/LL-8
86F/LimEd-13
86F/Mini-62
86F/St-27
86Leaf-49
86Mother/Ast-20
86OPC-96
86Pol/Ast-12
86Seven/Coin-S13M
86Sf-30
86T-186M
86T-640
86T/St-26
86T/Tatt-11M
87D-85
87D/OD-13
87F-53
87F/BB-11
87F/St-26
87F/St-S4
87Leaf-116
87Mother/Ast-3
87OPC-343
87Pol/Ast-3
87RedFoley/St-95
87Sf-152M
87Sf-42
87Sf/TPrev-8M
87T-670
87T/St-29
88D/Y/Bk-NEW
88F-443
88Grenada-10
88Panini/St-299
88S-28
88T-278
89Pac/SenLg-188
89T/SenLg-78
89TM/SenLg-26
90EliteSenLg-53
90Kissim/DIMD-7
91Pac/SenLg-36
92Yank/WIZ80-38
Cruz, Juan-1
83Madis/Frit-21
85MidldA-23
Cruz, Juan-2
92CharRain/ClBest-11
92Spokane/ClBest-25
92Spokane/ProC-1305
Cruz, Julio Luis
75QuadC
78T-687
79Ho-111
79OPC-305
79T-583
80BK/PHR-26
80OPC-16
80T-32
81D-163
81F-601

81OPC-121
81Pol/Mariners-6
81T-397
81T/St-126
82D-250
82F-509
82F/St-225
82OPC-130
82T-130
82T/St-114
82T/St-235
83D-379
83F-478
83OPC-113
83OPC/St-112
83T-414
83T/Fold-5M
83T/St-112
83T/Tr-23
84D-379
84F-55
84F/St-95
84Nes/792-257
84OPC-257
84T-257
84T/St-248
84TrueVal/WS-9
85Coke/WS-12
85D-452
85F-510
85OPC-71
85T-749
85T/St-239
86Coke/WS-12
86D-257
86F-201
86OPC-14
86T-14
87F-492
87OPC-53
87T-790
89Stockton/Cal-179CO
90Swell/Great-88
91LineD-32
91Swell/Great-21
Cruz, Luis
83Wisco/Frit-19
86Pittsfld-5
87WinSalem-9
88CLAS/Star-26
88WinSalem/Star-2
89CharlK-8
89Iowa/CMC-15
89Iowa/ProC-1692
89Niagara/Pucko-5A
Cruz, Nandi
90Saraso/Star-5
91Dunedin/ClBest-16
91Dunedin/ProC-213
Cruz, Pablo
77Salem
78Salem
Cruz, Rafael
86DayBe-6
87Gaston/ProC-13
Cruz, Ruben
91BurlAs/ClBest-19
91BurlAs/ProC-2813
92Osceola/ClBest-22
92Osceola/ProC-2541
Cruz, Todd Ruben
80T-492
81Coke
81F-341
81T-571
83D-505
83F-479
83Nalley-4
83OPC-132
83T-132
84D-148
84F-3
84Nes/792-773
84T-773
85F-172
85T-366
87SanBern-20
91Crown/Orio-90
91Pac/SenLg-147
91Salinas/ClBest-5
91Salinas/ProC-2251
Cruz, Tommy
75IntLgAS/Broder-4
75PCL/AS-4
75Spokane/Caruso-8
92Penin/ClBest-28CO
92Penin/ProC-2949CO
Cruz, Victor
78Syrac
79T-714R
80OPC-54
80T-99
81D-321
81F-407
81OPC-252
81T-252
81T/Tr-751
82F-480
82T-263
83OKCty-6
84OKCty-20
88Pocatel/ProC-2089
93Rang/Keeb-116
Csefalvay, John
83ColumAst-3
84Nashvl-4
Cubanich, Creighton
91SoOreg/ClBest-23
Cubbage, Michael Lee
(Mike)
75OPC-617R
75Spokane/Caruso-14
75T-617R
75T/M-617R
76OPC-615
76T-615
77BurgChef-50
77T-149
78T-219
78Twin/FriszP-5
79OPC-187
79T-362
79Twin/FriszP-4
80OPC-262
80T-503
81D-492
81F-566
81T-657
81T/Tr-752
82F-523
82T-43
82Tidew-26
85Lynch-1
86Jacks/TCMA-24
87Tidew-12
87Tidew/TCMA-23
88AAA/ProC-54
88Tidew/CANDL-3MG
88Tidew/CMC-24MG
88Tidew/ProC-1586MG
89Tidew/CMC-21MG
90Kahn/Mets-4CO
90T/TVMets-2CO
91Kahn/Mets-4CO
91WIZMets-89
92Mets/Kahn-4CO
93Rang/Keeb-117
Cuccinello, Alfred E.
(Al)
94Conlon-1171M
Cuccinello, Anthony
(Tony)
33G-99
34DS-55
35BU-79
35Exh/4-2
38Exh/4-1
39Exh
39PlayBall-61
40PlayBall-61
49Eureka-80
55Gol/Ind-3
55Salem
60T-458C
77Galasso-223
89Pac/Leg-170
89Smok/Dodg-37
90Target-153
94Conlon-1171
R314
Cucjen, Romy
85Fresno/Pol-13
87Shrev-9
88Shrev/ProC-1293
89Louisvl-15
89Louisvl/CMC-15
89Louisvl/ProC-1257
90AAASingl/ProC-572
90Indianap/CMC-22
90Indianap/ProC-289
90ProC/Singl-72
Cudjo, Lavell
89Greens/ProC-406
89SALAS/GS-34
90Cedar/Best-9
90Cedar/ProC-2332
Cudworth, James A.
(Jim)
N172
Cuellar, Bobby
76SanAn/Team-8
77Tucson
78Cr/PCL-111
79Tacoma-7
80T-665R
80Tacoma-6
81Charl-2
84Cram/PCL-192
85Cram/PCL-84
86Wausau-5MG
87Wausau-1MG
88SanBern/Best-27
88SanBern/Cal-54
89Wmsprt/ProC-627
89Wmsprt/Star-3
90Wmsprt/Best-26CO
90Wmsprt/ProC-1073CO
90Wmsprt/Star-26CO
91AA/LineD-350M
91Jaxvl/LineD-350CO
91Jaxvl/ProC-167CO
93Rang/Keeb-118
Cuellar, Mike Jr.
80Knoxvl/TCMA-12
Cuellar, Mike
59T-518
60T-398
65T-337
66T-566
67Ast/Team-3
67CokeCap/Astro-14
67OPC-97
67T-234LL
67T-97
68CokeCap/Astro-14
68Dexter-26
68T-274
68T/ActionSt-8CM
69MB-66
69T-453
69T-532M
70MLB/St-148
70OPC-199ALCS
70OPC-68LL
70OPC-70LL
70T-199ALCS
70T-590
70T-68LL
70T-70LL
70T/CB
71K-49
71MLB/St-293
71OPC-170
71OPC-69LL
71T-170
71T-69LL
71T/Coins-150
71T/tatt-16
72K-27
72MB-82
72OPC-70
72Pol/Orio-4
72T-70
73JP
73K-47
73OPC-470
73T-470
74OPC-560
74T-560
75Ho-42
75OPC-410
75SSPC/42-24
75T-410
75T/M-410
76Ho-121
76OPC-285
76SSPC-375
76T-285
77T-162
86Mother/Ast-5
89Pac/SenLg-46
89TM/SenLg-27
91Crown/Orio-91
91K/Leyenda-7
Cuen, Eleno
73Cedar
75Dubuq
81Portl-26
82Buffa-14
Cuervo, Ed
78Wausau
83ColumAst-2
Cuesta, Jamie
88BurlB/ProC-17
89Durham/Star-6
89Durham/Team-6
Cueto, Manuel Melo
No Cards.
Cuevas, Angelo
86Lynch-8
88Jacks/GS-21
88TexLgAS/GS-10
89Jacks/GS-14
Cuevas, Johnny
86Sumter/ProC-4
87Durham-8
88Sumter/ProC-397
89BurlB/ProC-1597
89BurlB/Star-6
90Durham/Team-16
91AA/LineD-205
91Greenvl/ClBest-11
91Greenvl/LineD-205
91Greenvl/ProC-3005
92Durham/ClBest-2
92Durham/ProC-1103
92Durham/Team-28
Cuevas, Rafael
78Newar
Cuff, John J.
No Cards.
Culberson, Calvain
88Pulaski/ProC-1760
89Sumter/ProC-1101
92Cedar/ClBest-24
92Cedar/ProC-1061
Culberson, Charles
85Fresno/Pol-3
86Fresno/Smok-25
87FtMyr-15
88Memphis/Best-17
91Utica/ClBest-24CO
91Utica/ProC-3259CO
Culberson, Delbert Leon
47TipTop-1
Culberson, Don
92SoBend/ClBest-2
92SoBend/ProC-172
Culkar, Steve
88Virgini/Star-7
89Hagers/Best-8
89Hagers/ProC-276
89Hagers/Star-4
90Hagers/Best-16
90Hagers/ProC-1405
90Hagers/Star-6
91Hagers/ProC-2449
Cullen, John
(Jack)
63T-54R
66OPC-31
66T-31
92Yank/WIZ60-31
Cullen, Mike
85Kingst-4
Cullen, Tim
67OPC-167R
67T-167R
68T-209
69T-586
70K-30
70OPC-49
70T-49
71MLB/St-534
71OPC-566
71Pol/SenP-3
71T-566
72OPC-461
72T-461
Cullenbine, Roy
45Playball-3
81Tiger/Detroit-43
90Target-154
93Conlon-849
W753
Culler, Dick
45Playball-38
47TipTop
Cullers, Steve
85BurlR-5
Cullop, Glen
92Princet/ClBest-27
92Princet/ProC-2685
Cullop, Henry Nick
29Exh/4-3
31Exh/4-7
82Ohio/HOF-3
82Ohio/HOF-3
87Conlon/2-11
88Conlon/4-7
90Target-156
W514-59
Culmer, Will
80Penin/B-8
80Penin/C-19
82OkCty-25
83Charl-16
83Wheat/Ind-7
84Maine-14
Culp, Ray
60L-75
63T-29R
64PhilBull-11
64T-412
64T/Coins-35
64T/SU
64T/St-96
64T/tatt
64Wheat/St-12
65T-505
66OPC-4
66T-4
67CokeCap/Cub-7
67OPC-168
67T-168
68CokeCap/RedSox-7
68T-272
69MB-67
69MLB/St-11
69T-391
69T/S-6
69T/St-132
70K-35
70MLB/St-158
70OPC-144
70T-144
71MD
71MLB/St-317
71OPC-660
71T-660
71T/tatt-13
72MB-83
72OPC-2
72T-2
78TCMA-197
Culpepper, Kevin
92Kingspt/ClBest-25TR
Culver, George
65OPC-166R
65T-166R
67T-499R
68T-319
69Kahn
69T-635
70OPC-92
70T-92
71MLB/St-76
71OPC-291
71T-291
72MB-84
72T-732
73OPC-242
73T-242
74OPC-632
74T-632
83Portl-12
84Cram/PCL-215
86Reading-6MG
87Reading-1MG
88Maine/CMC-23
88Maine/ProC-300
89ScranWB/ProC-724
90Reading/Best-25CO
90Reading/ProC-1235CO
90Reading/Star-28CO
90Target-155
93ScranWB/Team-7MG
Culver, Lanell C.

83Tampa-3
84Cedar-16
Cumberbatch, Abdiel
90Tampa/DIMD-2
92Oneonta/ClBest-4
93Greens/ClBest-6
93Greens/ProC-897
Cumberland, John
69OPC-114R
69T-114R
69T/4in1-24M
71MLB/St-244
71OPC-108
71T-108
72OPC-403
72T-403
83Lynch-13
85Tidew-26CO
86Tidew-6CO
87Tidew-18CO
87Tidew/TCMA-24CO
88Tidew/CANDL-2PC
88Tidew/CMC-25CO
88Tidew/ProC-1579CO
90AAASingl/ProC-292CO
90ProC/Singl-685CO
90Tidew/CMC-28CO
90Tidew/ProC-561CO
91AA/LineD-625M
91Wichita/LineD-625CO
91Wichita/ProC-2615CO
91Wichita/Rock-25CO
92Yank/WIZ60-32
92Yank/WIZ70-39
Cummings, Audelle
89GreatF-8
Cummings, Bob
79Cedar/TCMA-32
80Clinton-24
84Shrev/FB-6
85Cram/PCL-197
Cummings, Brian
88Batavia/ProC-1689
88BurlB/ProC-12
89Batavia/ProC-1943
89BurlB/ProC-1618
89BurlB/Star-7
90Durham/Team-19
Cummings, Dick
84Iowa-21
85Iowa-25
92Geneva/ClBest-29TR
Cummings, John
89Anchora-9
91SanBern/ClBest-1
91SanBern/ProC-1977
92Penin/ClBest-17
92Penin/ProC-2925
92UD/ML-179
93B-135
93ClBest/MLG-33
93F/Final-268
93FExcel/ML-223
93L-303
93Mother/Mar-26
93OPC/Premier-69
93Pac/Spanish-621
93Pinn-595
93StCl/Mar-21
93T/Tr-129T
93UD-503DD
93Ultra-617
94D-126
94T-443
94T/Gold-443
Cummings, Midre
91ClBest/Singl-318
91Kenosha/ClBest-24
91Kenosha/ProC-2088
92ClBest-240
92ClBest/BBonusC-13
92ClBest/RBonus-BC13
92ProC/Tomorrow-98
92Salem/ClBest-1
92Salem/ProC-76
92UD/ML-277
92UD/ML-41M
92UD/ML/TPHolo-TP1
92UD/POY-PY18
93B-357FOIL
93B-598
93CaroMud/RBI-22
93ClBest/Fisher-12
93ClBest/MLG-76
93FExcel/ML-90
93T-616M
93T/Gold-616M
93UD-440TP
94B-363
94B-630
94D-608
94F/MLP-8
94L/GRook-4
94Pac/Cr-496
94T-787M
94T/Gold-787M
94TripleP-292
94UD-7
94UD/CollC-3
94UD/CollC/Gold-3
94UD/CollC/Silv-3
94UD/ElecD-7
Cummings, Steve
87Dunedin-2
88Knoxvl/Best-20
88SLAS-27
89Syrac/CMC-7
89Syrac/MerchB-7
89Syrac/ProC-803
89Syrac/Team-7
90D-698
90OPC-374
90ProC/Singl-329
90S/Tr-78T
90Syrac/CMC-3
90Syrac/MerchB-3
90Syrac/Team-3
90T-374
90T/89Debut-26
91AAA/LineD-81
91ColoSp/LineD-81
91ColoSp/ProC-2178
92Sky/AAASingl-260
92Toledo/ProC-1034
92Toledo/SB-582
Cummings, William
(Candy)
50Callahan
50W576-23
76Shakey-23
80Perez/HOF-19
80SSPC/HOF
89HOF/St-64
90BBWit-60
Cunha, Steve
91SLCity/ProC-3223
91SLCity/SportP-11
Cunningham, Bill 1
86WPalmB-10
87Jaxvl-17
Cunningham, Bill 2
V61-112
Cunningham, Chip
85PrWill-5
Cunningham, Dave
88Ashvl/ProC-1075
89Watlo/ProC-1795
89Watlo/Star-3
Cunningham, Earl
89LittleSun-2
89Wythe/Star-8
90B-34
90OPC-134FDP
90Peoria/Team-1
90Peoria/Team-2
90Peoria/Team-9M
90PeoriaCol/Team-1
90PeoriaCol/Team-2
90PeoriaCol/Team-3
90PeoriaCol/Team-4
90S-670DC
90T-134FDP
90T/TVCub-42
91B-420
91ClBest/Singl-435
91Peoria/ClBest-8
91Peoria/ProC-1354
91Peoria/Team-24
92B-81
92ClBest-316
92Peoria/ClBest-1
92Peoria/Team-6
92ProC/Tomorrow-208
92WinSalem/ClBest-2
93Peoria/Team-4
Cunningham, Ellsworth
N172
Cunningham, Everett
88Butte-27
89Gaston/ProC-1000
89Gaston/Star-6
89SALAS/GS-43
90CharlR/Star-6
90FSLAS/Star-29
90Star/ISingl-23
90Tulsa/Team-6
91AA/LineD-578
91Tulsa/LineD-578
91Tulsa/ProC-2766
91Tulsa/Team-6
Cunningham, Glen
51BR-D16
Cunningham, Joseph Jr.
87StPete-8
88StPete/Star-4
89Hamil/Star-28
90Johnson/Star-29CO
91Johnson/ClBest-30CO
91Johnson/ProC-4172CO
Cunningham, Joseph R.
(Joe)
55T-37
55T/DH-38
57T-304
58T-168
59T-285
60Bz-27
60T-40
60T-562AS
60T/tatt-10
61P-172
61T-520
62J-195
62P-162
62P/Can-162
62Salada-173A
62Salada-173B
62Shirriff-173
62T-162
63Exh
63J-35
63P-35
63T-100
64T-340
65T-496
65T/E-63
66T-531
79TCMA-105
92Card/McDon/Pac-33
Exh47
Cunningham, Kenn
90Bristol/ProC-3174MG
90Bristol/Star-27MG
Cunningham, O'Brian
91LitSun/HSPros-13
91LitSun/HSProsG-13
Cunningham, Randall
91StCl/Charter*-35
Cunningham, Scott
91OKSt-5
92OKSt-6
Cunningham, Sean
87BurlEx-25
88Rockford-9
89Jaxvl/Best-22
89Jaxvl/ProC-158
89Rockford-9TR
90WPalmB/Star-31
91WPalmB/ClBest-30TR
Cunningham, Shawn
88Bend/Legoe-3
88Bend/Legoe-33
Cunningham, Troy
89Spokane/SP-17
90CharRain/Best-7
90CharRain/ProC-2034
Cunningham, Wm. A.
E120
W515-1
W573
W575
Cunningham, Wm. J.
E102
E220
T207
Cupit, Wayne
92AubAs/ClBest-23
92AubAs/ProC-1347
Cupples, Michael
84Idaho/Team-7
85Madis-10
85Madis/Pol-7
86Madis/Pol-7
87Madis-16
Curbelo, Jorge
82Miami-10
Curley, Tim
89Princet/Star-3
Curnal, Jim
78Cr/PCL-96
Curnow, Robert
88Spokane/ProC-1939
89Watlo/ProC-1777
89Watlo/Star-4
90CharRain/Best-8
90CharRain/ProC-2042
Curran, Bud
79Cedar/TCMA-14
88Cedar/ProC-1161
Curran, Dave
80Holyo-22
Curran, Mike
75WPalmB/Sussman-15
Curran, Shawn
91Classic/DP-48
91FrRow/DP-27
91LitSun/HSPros-25
91LitSun/HSProsG-25
92StCl/Dome-30
Currence, Delaney
(Lafayette)
76SSPC-251
Current, Matt
88Martins/Star-8
89Martins/Star-9
89Star/IISingl-143
90Spartan/Best-13
90Spartan/ProC-2494
90Spartan/Star-4
91Clearw/ClBest-13
91Clearw/ProC-1624
Currie, Brian
89Boise/ProC-2000
90Erie/Star-4
Currier, Bryan
92Eugene/ClBest-8
92Eugene/ProC-3019
93Rockford/ClBest-9
Currier, Lenny
86Albuq-4TR
87Albuq/Pol-4TR
88Albuq/ProC-272TR
Currin, Wes
88Sumter/ProC-395
89Durham/Star-7
89Durham/Team-7
89Star/Wax-70
Curron, Bud
85Cedar-30
Curry, Clinton
83TriCit-25
Curry, Dell
91Gaston/ClBest-27
Curry, Floyd
45Parade*-15
Curry, G. Tony
60T-541
61P-120
61T-262
61T/St-51
81TCMA-452
Curry, Stephen T.
(Steve)
86NewBrit-8
87Pawtu-3
87Pawtu/TCMA-3
88AAA/ProC-31
88Pawtu/CMC-7
88Pawtu/ProC-468
88S/Tr-81T
89F-86
89Panini/St-267
89Pawtu/CMC-2
89Pawtu/Dunkin-35
89Pawtu/ProC-691
89S/HotRook-53
89T-471
90Pawtu/ProC-454
90T/TVRSox-41
92Memphis/ProC-2411
92Memphis/SB-432
Curry, Steve
81Richm-17
86Greenvl/Team-6
86Richm-3
89BurlB/ProC-1613
90AAASingl/ProC-426
90Idaho/ProC-3262MG
91Idaho/ProC-4344MG
91Richm/Bob-43CO
92BurlAs/ClBest-26MG
92BurlAs/ProC-563
Curtis, Chad
91AAA/LineD-159
91AAAGame/ProC-13
91Edmon/LineD-159
91Edmon/ProC-1522
92B-627
92Classic/II-T96
92D/Rook-30
92D/Up-U5RR
92F/Up-8
92L/GRook-1
92Pinn-523
92Pinn/Rook-29
92Pinn/RookI-17
92Pinn/Team2000-40
92Pol/Angel-5
92ProC/Tomorrow-29
92S/RookTr-87T
92Studio-143
92T/Tr-25T
92T/TrGold-25T
92UD-774DD
92Ultra-323
92Ultra/AllRook-6
93B-313
93Colla/DM-26
93D-93
93F-571
93F/RookSenII-4
93Flair-170
93L-227
93Mother/Angel-12
93OPC-28
93OPC/Premier-2
93Pac/Spanish-42
93Panini-10
93Pinn-411
93Pol/Angel-7
93S-354
93Select-290
93Select/ChasRook-9
93StCl-543
93StCl/1stDay-543
93StCl/Angel-23
93Studio-2
93T-699
93T/Finest-146
93T/FinestRef-146
93T/Gold-699
93ToysRUs-2
93TripleP-70
93TripleP/Act-26
93UD-235
93UD/SP-19
93USPlayC/Ace-2H
93USPlayC/Rook-13S
93Ultra-159
94B-179
94D-11
94D/Special-11
94F-50
94Finest-358
94L-19
94OPC-98
94Pac/Cr-73
94Panini-35
94Pinn-282
94S-95
94S/GoldR-95
94S/GoldS-56
94Sf/2000-119
94StCl-295
94StCl/1stDay-295
94StCl/Gold-295
94Studio-8
94T-56
94T/Gold-56
94TripleP-11
94UD-82
94UD/CollC-87
94UD/CollC/Gold-87
94UD/CollC/Silv-87
94UD/ElecD-82
94UD/SP-22
94Ultra-323

Curtis, Chris
91Butte/SportP-10
92ClBest-327
92Gaston/ClBest-19
92Gaston/ProC-2243
92StCl/Dome-31
Curtis, Clinton
(Cliff)
90Target-920
M116
Curtis, Craig
90Ashvl/ProC-2753
91Osceola/ClBest-22
91Osceola/ProC-696
92BurlAs/ClBest-18
92BurlAs/ProC-554
Curtis, Harry
C46-90
Curtis, Irvin
N172
Curtis, Jack P.
61T-533
62T-372
Curtis, John D.
72T-724R
73OPC-143
73T-143
74OPC-373
74T-373
74T/Tr-373T
75OPC-381
75T-381
75T/M-381
76OPC-239
76T-239
77T-324
78T-486
79Pol/Giants-40
79T-649
80T-12
81F-491
81OPC-158
81T-531
81T/St-231
82F-569
82T-219
83D-170
83F-84
83T-777
84F-513
84Nes/792-158
84Smok/Cal-6
84T-158
89Princet/Star-4
90Welland/Pucko-12
Curtis, Mike
86Geneva-4
87WinSalem-27
88Harris/ProC-843
90Canton/Best-26
90Canton/ProC-1287
90Canton/Star-3
90EastLAS/ProC-EL38
90Foil/Best-119
90ProC/Singl-733
91AA/LineD-80
91Canton/LineD-80
91Canton/ProC-974
Curtis, Randy
91Pittsfld/ClBest-6
91Pittsfld/ProC-3434
92ClBest-80
92ColumMet/ClBest-24
92ColumMet/ProC-307
92ColumMet/SAL/II-13
92ColumMet/SAL/II-31
93StLucie/ProC-2932
94B-345
94ClBest/Gold-167
94FExcel-233
Curtwright, Guy
Exh47
Cusack, Rocky
87Lakeland-12
88CharlK/Pep-13
Cusak, John
88Pac/8Men-12
Cusey, Lee
92Madis/ClBest-13
92Madis/ProC-1226
Cushing, Steve
81Batavia-4
81Watlo-32
82Watlo/B-1
82Watlo/Frit-15
Cushman, Ed
N172
N172/ST
N284
N690
Cusick, Anthony
N172
Cusick, Jack
52B-192
Cutler, Brad
75Tacoma/KMMO-16
Cutshall, Bill
86Jaxvl/TCMA-24
87Nashvl-3
88OrlanTw/Best-27
Cutshaw, George
16FleischBrd-21
21Exh-30
90Target-157
D327
D328-37
E100
E120
E135-37
E220
E99
V100
W573
Cutty, Fran
81CharR-11
82FtMyr-15
Cuyler, Hazen
(KiKi)
25Exh-51
26Exh-51
27Exh-25
29Exh/4-6
30CEA/Pin-2
31Exh/4-6
32Orbit/num-6
32Orbit/un-14
33CJ/Pin-3
33DL-8
33G-23
34DS-31
34G-90
35G-1F
35G-3D
35G-4D
35G-5D
36G
36G-10
38Wheat
60F-75
61F-19
73F/Wild-14
76Rowe-9M
76Shakey-109
77Galasso-72
80Pac/Leg-92
80Perez/HOF-108
80SSPC/HOF
89Smok/Dodg-6
90Target-158
91Conlon/Sport-12
92Conlon/Sport-587
92Cub/OldStyle-7
92Mega/Ruth-158M
93Conlon-741
94Conlon-1096
R305
R308-152
R312
R312/M
R314
R332-29
R332-3
V353-23
V355-55
W517-19
WG8-10
Cuyler, Milt
87Fayette-8
88FSLAS/Star-32
88Lakeland/Star-8
89Toledo/CMC-21
89Toledo/ProC-787
90AAASingl/ProC-390
90B-358
90ProC/Singl-398
90S-583
90S/100Ris-84
90Toledo/CMC-21
90Toledo/ProC-160
91B-141
91Classic/200-191
91Classic/I-42
91CokeK/Tiger-22
91D-40RR
91D/Rook-6
91F-334
91F/UltraUp-U22
91Leaf-251
91Leaf/Stud-51
91OPC-684
91OPC/Premier-27
91StCl-470
91T-684
91T/90Debut-36
91UD-556
92B-196
92Classic/Game200-87
92D-232
92F-130
92F/RookSIns-7
92L-75
92L/BlkGold-75
92OPC-522
92Panini-110
92Pinn-174
92Pinn/Team2000-44
92S-26
92S/100RisSt-1
92S/Impact-4
92StCl-5
92Studio-171
92T-522
92T/Gold-522
92T/GoldWin-522
92TripleP-100
92UD-536
92USPlayC/Tiger-11D
92USPlayC/Tiger-6S
92Ultra-57
93D-173
93F-224
93L-38
93Pac/Spanish-105
93Pinn-193
93S-82
93Select-166
93StCl-156
93StCl/1stDay-156
93T-429
93T/Gold-429
93Tiger/Gator-4
93TripleP-44
93UD-162
93Ultra-194
94D-475
94F-125
94Pinn-359
Cvejdlik, Kent
76Watlo
Cyburt, Phil
78Salem
Cypret, Greg
81Tucson-1
82Tucson-6
83Tucson-15
84Cram/PCL-54
Czajkowski, Jim
87Sumter-19
88Durham/Star-4
89Durham/Star-8
89Durham/Team-8
90Harris/ProC-1187
90Harris/Star-6
91AA/LineD-179
91ElPaso/LineD-179
91ElPaso/ProC-2740
92ElPaso/ProC-3913
92ElPaso/SB-204
Czarkowski, Mark
92Jacks/ProC-3702
93Calgary/ProC-1159
Czarnik, Chris
89BurlB/ProC-1617
89BurlB/Star-8
89Star/IISingl-110
90Durham/Team-9
D'Acquisto, John F.
(John)
74OPC-608R
74T-608R
75OPC-372
75T-372
75T/M-372
76OPC-628
76SSPC-94
76T-628
77Padre/SchCd-8
77T-19
78Padre/FamFun-8
79T-506
80T-339
81F-163
81OPC-204
81T-427
82Richm-4
82T-58
83F-516
89Pac/SenLg-121
89T/SenLg-31
D'Alessandro, Sal
85Durham-22
86Greenvl/Team-7
87Richm/Bob-4
87Richm/Crown-10
88Greenvl/Best-3
D'Alexander, Greg
90AR-10
90Miami/I/Star-4
91Miami/ClBest-19
91Miami/ProC-413
D'Amato, Brian
92CharRain/ClBest-8
92CharRain/ProC-115
D'Amico, Jeff
94B-205
94B-374
94ClBest/Gold-2
94ClBest/GoldLP-3
94Pol/Brew-5DP
94SigRook-6
94T-759DP
94T/Gold-759DP
D'Amore, Louis
81Clinton-14
D'Andrea, Michael
(Mike)
92Pulaski/ClBest-25
92Pulaski/ProC-3171
93FExcel/ML-1
93Macon/ClBest-8
93Macon/ProC-1394
D'Boever, William
86James-4
D'Onofrio, Gary
83DayBe-20
D'Vincenzo, Mark
86LitFalls-8
D'laCruz, Marcelino
92Spokane/ClBest-26
DaSilva, Fernando
93BurlB/ClBest-6
93BurlB/ProC-150
93ClBest/MLG-112
93James/ClBest-6
93James/ProC-3319
DaVanon, Frank G.
(Jerry)
69T-637R
71OPC-32
71T-32
75Iowa/TCMA-5
76OPC-551
76T-551
77T-283
91Crown/Orio-95
Daal, Omar
92Albuq/ProC-712
92SanAn/SB-561
93B-42
93F/Final-81
93Mother/Dodg-15
94F-508
94Pac/Cr-306
94T-29
94T/Gold-29
94Ultra-214
Dabney, Fred
88Utica/Pucko-16
89SoBend/GS-11
90Saraso/Star-6
91Saraso/ClBest-3
91Saraso/ProC-1106
92BirmB/ProC-2575
92BirmB/SB-81
Dabney, Ty
85Everett/Cram-3
86Fresno/Smok-19
87Shrev-3
87TexLgAS-32
88Phoenix/CMC-22
88Phoenix/ProC-72
Daboll, Dennis
65T-561R
Dacko, Mark
82Evansvl-3
83Evansvl-1
84Evansvl-6
Dacosta, Bill
87Oneonta-11
88PrWill/Star-7
Dacus, Barry
86PalmSp-9
86PalmSp/Smok-19
87MidldA-28
88Edmon/CMC-10
88Edmon/ProC-568
Dade, Lonnie Paul
(Paul)
78K-14
78OPC-86
78T-662
79OPC-3
79T-13
80OPC-134
80T-254
81T-496
Dafforn, Mike
88Martins/Star-9
89Martins/Star-10
Dagres, Angelo George
(Angie)
91Crown/Orio-92
Dahle, Dave
52Mother-15
Dahlen, William F.
(Bill)
10Domino-30
11Helmar-84
12Sweet/Pin-72
14Piedmont/St-15
90Target-159
E107
E254
E286
E98
M116
N300/SC
S74-51
T202
T205
T206
T3-11
WG3-12
WG5-13
Dahlgren, Ellsworth
(Babe)
39PlayBall-81
40PlayBall-3
41PlayBall-49
90Target-160
Dahse, David
84Newar-4
Dailey, Steve
91OKSt-6
92OKSt-7
Dailey, William G.
63T-391
63Twin/Volpe-3
64T-156
Daily, Cornelius F.
(Con)
90Target-922
N172
N284
Daily, Edward M.
(Ed)
E223
N172
N284
N690/2
Dakin, Brian
90Everett/Best-17
90Everett/ProC-3133
Dal Canton, John B.
(Bruce)
69T-468R
70OPC-52

70T-52
71MLB/St-413
71OPC-168
71T-168
72T-717
73OPC-487
73T-487
74OPC-308
74T-308
75OPC-472
75T-472
75T/M-472
76OPC-486
76T-486
77T-114
79Knoxvl/TCMA-18
82Durham-22
85IntLgAS-23
85Richm-23CO
86Richm-4CO
89Brave/Dubuq-7CO
91AAA/LineD-450M
91Richm/Bob-40CO
91Richm/LineD-450CO
91Richm/ProC-2585CO
92Richm/Bleach-23M
92Richm/Comix-4CO
92Richm/ProC-392CO
92Richm/SB-450CO
93Richm/Team-2CO

Dale, Emmett Eugene
(Gene)
D329-42
D350/2-43
M101/4-42
M101/5-43

Dale, Phil
86Tampa-4
87Cedar-2
88Chatt/Best-18
89Greens/ProC-427
90CedarDG/Best-22
91Idaho/ProC-4345CO
91Waverly/Fut-NNO

Dalena, Pete
83Nashvl-5
84Colum-18
84Colum/Pol-8
84Nashvl-5
85Colum-15
85Colum/Pol-7
86Colum-4
86Colum/Pol-4
87Colum-11
87Colum/Pol-5
87Colum/TCMA-12
88Colum/CMC-16
88Colum/Pol-14
88Colum/ProC-321
89AAA/ProC-36
89ColoSp/CMC-12
89ColoSp/ProC-235
90AAASingl/ProC-172
90ProC/Singl-641
90T/89Debut-27
90Vanco/CMC-14
90Vanco/ProC-494
91AA/LineD-275M
91Harris/ProC-617CO
93BurlB/ClBest-27CO

Dalesandro, Mark
90A&AASingle/ProC-166
90Boise/ProC-3324
91ClBest/Singl-259
91MidwLAS/ProC-25
91QuadC/ClBest-16
91QuadC/ProC-2634
92AS/Cal-38
92PalmSp/ClBest-20
92PalmSp/ProC-846

Daley, Jud
90Target-923

Daley, Leavitt Leo
(Buddy)
55Salem
58T-222
59T-263
60Armour-8
60Bz-2
60T-8
60T/tatt-11
61Bz-4
61P-83
61T-422
61T-48LL
61T/St-159
61T/St-201
62Salada-203
62Shirriff-203
62T-376
63T-38
64T-164
65OPC-262
65T-262
78TCMA-257
92Yank/WIZ60-33
Exh47

Daley, Peter Harvey
(Pete)
55T-206
57T-388
58T-73
59T-276
60T-108
61T-158
62T/St-94

Daley, William
(Bill)
N172

Dalkowski, Steve
63T-496R

Dallas, Gershon
90Ashvl/ProC-2759
91Osceola/ClBest-23
91Osceola/ProC-697
92ColRS/ClBest-14
92ColRS/ProC-2404

Dallessandro, Dom
41DP-101
44Playball-32
49B/PCL-9

Dalrymple, Abner F.
(Abner)
N172
WG1-57

Dalrymple, Clayton E.
(Clay)
60L-143
60T-523
61T-299
61T/St-52
62J-197
62P-197
62P/Can-197
62Salada-141
62Shirriff-141
62T-434
62T/St-166
63F-52
63J-184
63P-184
63T-192
64PhilBull-12
64T-191
65T-372
66T-202
67CokeCap/Phill-9
67OPC-53
67Pol/Phill-4
67T-53
68T-567
69MB-68
69OPC-151
69T-151
69T/4in1-12M
69T/St-74
70OPC-319
70T-319
71MLB/St-294
71OPC-617
71T-617
78TCMA-203
91Crown/Orio-93
PM10/L-13

Dalson, Kevin
89Wythe/Star-9

Dalton, Harry
82Pol/Brew-GM

Dalton, Jack
90Target-161

Dalton, Mike
86Pawtu-8
87Pawtu-16
87Pawtu/TCMA-4
88NewBrit/ProC-896
89NewBrit/ProC-607
89Pawtu/Dunkin-27
90AAASingl/ProC-427
90Pawtu/CMC-24
90Pawtu/ProC-455
90ProC/Singl-275
90T/TVRSox-42
91AAA/LineD-582
91Toledo/LineD-582
91Toledo/ProC-1923
92BuffB/BlueS-6
92BuffB/ProC-317
92BuffB/SB-30
92F-131
92S/100RisSt-95
92T/91Debut-42

Dalton, Rich
78OrlanTw

Daly, Bob
92GulfCM/ProC-3487

Daly, James J.
(Sun)
N172

Daly, Mark
81Tidew-25

Daly, Thomas Peter
(Tom)
28LaPresse-6
90Target-162
E107
N172
N300/SC

Dalzachio, Paul
91Butte/SportP-6

Damian, Leonard
(Len)
86Peoria-4
87Pittsfld-13
88Iowa/CMC-2
88Iowa/ProC-544
89Iowa/CMC-2
89Iowa/ProC-1705
90T/TVCub-43

Damon, John
83Memphis/TCMA-4

Damon, Johnny
92ClBest/Up-417
92UD/ML-19
93ClBest/MLG-201
93Rockford/ClBest-1
93UD/SP-273FOIL
94B-373
94FExcel-66
94FExcel/AS-6
94UD-546TP

Dana, Derek
91Everett/ClBest-12
91Everett/ProC-3918
92Clinton/ClBest-14
92Clinton/ProC-3601

Danapilis, Eric
94FExcel-52

Dancer, Faye
94TedW-93

Dancy, Bill
80Penin/B-27MG
80Penin/C-12MG
83Reading-23
85Cram/PCL-35MG
87Maine/TCMA-23
89ScranWB/CMC-25
89ScranWB/ProC-1208
90AAAGame/ProC-27
90ProC/Singl-244MG
90ScranWB/CMC-18MG
91AAA/LineD-499MG
91ScranWB/LineD-499MG
91ScranWB/ProC-2555MG
92Clearw/ProC-2073

Dando, Patrick
90A&AASingle/ProC-191
90Pulaski/Best-16
90Pulaski/ProC-3096
91Durham/ClBest-18
91Durham/ProC-1552
92BBCity/ClBest-3
92BBCity/ProC-3851

Dandos, Mike
85Everett/II/Cram-2

Dandridge, Ray
(Hooks)
74Laugh/Black-26
80Perez/HOF-197
86Negro/Frit-7
87D/HL-18
88Negro/Duques-17
89HOF/St-26
90Negro/Star-14
90Perez/GreatMom-34
91Negro/Lewis-5
92FrRow/Dandridge-Set
92Negro/Lee-4
93TWill-103

Danek, Bill
86Peoria-5
87WinSalem-5

Danforth, David C.
(Dave)
21Exh-31
93Conlon-719
E120
E121/120
T207
V61-26
W501-101
W572
W573

Danforth, Perry
77Spoka

Daniel, Chuck
88MissSt-4
89MissSt-9
90MissSt-7
91MissSt-12
92Geneva/ClBest-23
92Geneva/ProC-1551
92MissSt-10

Daniel, Clay
85Cedar-5
86Vermont-5
88Harris/ProC-860
90Miami/I/Star-5

Daniel, Dian
81ArkTr-23M

Daniel, Jake
90Target-924

Daniel, Jim
86CharRain-8TR
86Memphis/GoldT-3
86Memphis/SilverT-3
87CharlO/WBTV-11
88CharlK/Pep-16
88River/Cal-231
88River/ProC-1412
89River/Best-28
89River/ProC-1407
90River/Best-21TR

Daniel, Keith
90Kissim/DIMD-8

Daniel, Lee
90MedHat/Best-21

Daniel, Michael
91James/ProC-3548
91OKSt-7
92ClBest-302
92ProC/Tomorrow-273
92WPalmB/ClBest-23
92WPalmB/ProC-2090
93WPalmB/ClBest-4
93WPalmB/ProC-1343

Daniel, Scott
91James/ClBest-29PER

Daniel, Steve
85BurlR-25

Daniels, B.A.
94Conlon-1268IA

Daniels, Bennie
58T-392
59T-122
60L-7
60T-91
61T-368
62Salada-42
62Shirriff-42
62T-378
62T/St-95
62T/bucks
63T-497
64T-587
65OPC-129
65T-129
78TCMA-145

Daniels, Bernard E.
(Bert)
E270/1
E286
T207

Daniels, Dave
79AppFx-11
82VeroB-4

Daniels, Gary
90Erie/Star-5

Daniels, Greg
87Miami-19

Daniels, Harold Jack
(Jack)
53B/Col-83

Daniels, Jerry
87Erie-23
88StPete/Star-5

Daniels, Jim
89River/Cal-28TR

Daniels, Kal
83Cedar-22
83Cedar/Frit-17
86D-27RR
86F-646M
86Sf/Rook-43
86TexGold-28
87Classic/Up-130
87D-142
87D/OD-192
87F-197
87F/LL-13
87Kahn-28
87Sf/TPrev-4M
87T-466
87ToysRUs-8
88Classic/Red-161
88D-14DK
88D-289
88D/Best-6
88D/DKsuper-14DK
88F-230
88F/AwardWin-7
88F/Mini-72
88F/St-82
88Kahn/Reds-28
88KennerFig-23
88Leaf-14DK
88Leaf-150
88OPC-53
88Panini/St-281
88RedFoley/St-14
88S-86
88S/YS/I-39
88Sf-112
88T-622
88T/Big-48
88T/St-139
89B-314
89Classic-74
89D-198
89D/Best-118
89D/MVP-BC18
89F-157
89F/LL-8
89F/Superstar-10
89Kahn/Reds-28
89KennerFig-29
89OPC-45
89Panini/St-75
89RedFoley/St-26
89S-7
89S/Tr-48
89Sf-52
89T-45
89T/Ames-10
89T/Big-323
89T/LJN-59
89T/Mini-7
89T/St-144
89UD-160
90B-99
90CedarDG/Best-2
90Classic/III-64
90D-432
90D/BestNL-127
90F/Up-U20
90Leaf-313
90Mother/Dodg-3
90OPC-585
90Panini/St-280
90Pol/Dodg-28
90PublInt/St-25
90PublInt/St-610
90S-490
90T-585
90T/Big-238
90Target-925
90UD-603
91B-600
91Classic/200-14

91D-336
91D/GSlam-3
91F-198
91Leaf-112
91MooTown-7
91Mother/Dodg-3
91OPC-245
91Panini/FrSt-60
91Panini/St-58
91Pol/Dodg-28
91RedFoley/St-22
91S-20
91S/100SS-53
91StCl-116
91Sunflower-5
91T-245
91UD-166
91Ultra-160
92B-487
92Classic/Game200-125
92D-343
92DennyGS-14
92F-453
92Mother/Dodg-14
92OPC-767
92Panini-198
92Pinn-374
92Pol/Dodg-28
92S-110
92S/RookTr-70T
92StCl-514
92T-767
92T/Gold-767
92T/GoldWin-767
92T/Kids-51
92UD-284
92Ultra-210
93Panini-207
93Select-181
93T-128
93T/Gold-128
Daniels, Lance
89Bristol/Star-6
Daniels, Lawrence L.
(Law)
N172
Daniels, Lee
91MedHat/ProC-4114
91MedHat/SportP-14
92StCath/ClBest-9
92StCath/ProC-3380
94B-197
Daniels, Steve
80Cedar-24
Dann, Tom
79Newar-1
Danner, Deon
91Welland/ClBest-18
91Welland/ProC-3565
92Augusta/ClBest-8
92Augusta/ProC-230
Danning, Harry
(Harry)
39PlayBall-18
40PlayBall-93
41DP-25
41DP-91
41PlayBall-7
41Wheat-20
R302
V351A-7
V355-22
Danrel, Mike
91James/ClBest-6
Danson, Roger
76BurlB
Dantonio, Fats
90Target-921
91Jesuit-1
Dantzler, Shawn
86Clearw-6
87Clearw-10
88Clearw/Star-10
Dapper, Cliff
90Target-163
Darby, Mike
86Wausau-6
Darcy, Patrick L.
(Pat)
75OPC-615R
75T-615R
75T/M-615R
76OPC-538
76SSPC-26
76T-538
Dare, Brian
90Idaho/ProC-3241
Darensbourg, Vic
94B-234
94FExcel-190
Dark, Alvin Ralph
(Alvin)
48L-51
49B-67
49Eureka-6
49Royal-18
50B-64
50Drake-20
51B-14
52B-34
52BR
52Royal
52StarCal-90CM
52StarCal/L-78B
52T-351
53B/Col-19
53T-109
54B-41
54NYJour
54RH
55B-2
55Gol/Giants-5
56T-148
57T-98
58T-125
59T-502
60T-472
61T-220MG
62T-322MG
63T-258MG
64T-529MG
66T-433MG
67T-389MG
68T-237MG
69OPC-91MG
69T-91MG
70OPC-524MG
70T-524MG
71OPC-397MG
71T-397MG
75OPC-561MG
75T-561MG
75T/M-561MG
76SSPC-488MG
78T-467MG
79TCMA-25
80Pac/Leg-80
87Mother/A's-13
88Pac/Leg-28
89Swell-77
90Pac/Legend-69
91LineD-23
91Swell/Great-22
91T/Arc53-109
92Bz/Quadra-15
93TWill-52
93UD/ATH-36
Exh47
PM10/Sm-33
R302-116
R423-20
Dark, David
92Geneva/ClBest-22
92Geneva/ProC-1552
Darkis, Willie
83Reading-18
84Cram/PCL-211
86GlenF-2
Darley, Ned
91MedHat/ProC-4091
91MedHat/SportP-19
92StCath/ClBest-8
92StCath/ProC-3381
93Hagers/ClBest-8
93Hagers/ProC-1872
Darling, Dell Conrad
(Dell)
N172
N184
Darling, Gary
89TM/Umpire-58
90TM/Umpire-56
Darling, Ronald M.
(Ron)
81Tulsa-18
82Tidew-13
83Tidew-1
84D-30RR
84F/X-29
84T/Mets/Fan-2
84T/Tr-27
85D-434
85F-76
85F/St-117
85Leaf-256
85OPC-138
85T-415
85T/St-105
86D-563
86D/AAS-37
86F-77
86F/Mini-18
86F/St-28
86KayBee-6
86Leaf-221
86OPC-225
86Seven/Coin-E14M
86Sf-109
86T-225
86T/Mets/Fan-3
86T/St-98
86T/Tatt-10M
87BK-6
87D-192
87Drake-28
87F-5
87F/Hottest-11
87F/LimWaxBox-C1
87F/Mini-23
87F/St-27
87F/WS-5
87Kraft-28
87Leaf-85
87MSA/Discs-3
87OPC-75
87Sf-53
87Sf/TPrev-2M
87T-75
87T/HL-26
87T/Mets/Fan-2
87T/Mini-21
87T/St-105
87Woolwth-26
88D-6DK
88D-76
88D/Best-41
88D/DKsuper-6DK
88D/Mets/Bk-76
88F-132
88F/Slug-C1
88F/St-100
88Kahn/Mets-12
88Leaf-6DK
88Leaf-78
88OPC-38
88Panini/St-335
88S-141
88Sf-73
88T-685
88T/Big-85
88T/St-98
89B-372
89D-171
89D/Best-41
89F-32
89Kahn/Mets-12
89OPC-105
89Panini/St-130
89S-180
89S/HotStar-71
89Sf-32
89T-105
89T/Big-166
89T/DHTest-7
89T/LJN-15
89T/St-100
89UD-159
90D-289
90D/Learning-29
90F-201
90F/Can-201
90Kahn/Mets-15
90Kenner/Fig-21
90Leaf-304
90MLBPA/Pins-14
90OPC-330
90Panini/St-295
90PublInt/St-130
90S-446
90T-330
90T/Big-113
90T/St-98
90T/TVMets-9
90TulsaDG/Best-18
90UD-241
91B-483
91D-472
91F-144
91Kahn/Mets-15
91Leaf-378
91OPC-735
91S-456
91StCl-60
91T-735
91UD-198
91UD/FinalEd-69F
91Ultra-214
91WIZMets-90
92B-30
92D-723
92F-254
92L-447
92L/BlkGold-447
92Mother/A's-24
92OPC-259
92Pinn-378
92S-710
92StCl-685
92T-259
92T/Gold-259
92T/GoldWin-259
92UD-669
92Ultra-111
93B-189
93D-700
93F-661
93L-182
93Mother/A's-12
93OPC-82
93Pac/Spanish-220
93Panini-22
93Pinn-199
93S-619
93Select-10
93StCl-305
93StCl/1stDay-305
93StCl/A's-14
93T-182
93T/Gold-182
93UD-168
93Ultra-256
94D-452
94F-258
94Finest-243
94Flair-90
94L-57
94Pac/Cr-447
94Pinn-90
94Pinn/Artist-90
94Pinn/Museum-90
94S-159
94S/GoldR-159
94StCl-428
94StCl/1stDay-428
94StCl/Gold-428
94T-549
94T/Gold-549
94UD-498
94UD/CollC-88
94UD/CollC/Gold-88
94UD/CollC/Silv-88
94Ultra-106
Darnbrough, William
N172
Darnell, Robert Jack
(Bob)
55B-39
79TCMA-257
90Target-164
Darnell, Steve
76Wausau
Darr, Michael Edward
(Mike)
78Syrac
Darretta, Dave
85BurlR-9
Darrow, Darrell
75SLCity/Caruso-9
79SLCity-17
Darrow, George Oliver
(George)
34G-87
Darwin, Arthur B.
(Bobby)
69T-641R
73OPC-228
73T-228
74OPC-527
74T-527
74T/St-205
75Ho-98
75OPC-346
75T-346
75T/M-346
76Ho-31
76Ho/Twink-31
76OPC-63
76SSPC-247
76T-63
77T-617
90Lennox-9
90Target-165
Darwin, Danny Wayne
78Cr/PCL-81
79T-713R
80T-498
81D-147
81F-632
81OPC-22
81T-22
81T/St-136
82D-231
82F-315
82T-298
82T/St-237
83D-289
83F-565
83F/St-12M
83F/St-14M
83OPC/St-121
83Rangers-44
83T-609
83T/St-121
84D-544
84F-416
84Nes/792-377
84Rangers-44
84T-377
84T/St-359
85D-98
85F-557
85F/Up-U32
85OPC-227
85Pol/Brew-18
85T-227
85T/St-352
85T/Tr-26T
86D-149
86F-485
86Leaf-75
86OPC-206
86Pol/Brew-18
86T-519
86T/St-205
87D-508
87F-54
87Mother/Ast-14
87OPC-157
87Pol/Ast-4
87T-157
88D-358
88F-444
88Mother/Ast-14
88Pol/Ast-7
88S-184
88T-461
89D-390
89F-354
89Lennox/Ast-13
89Mother/Ast-13
89S-553
89T-719
89UD-97
90B-66
90D-561
90D/BestNL-53
90F-227
90F/Can-227
90Leaf-346
90Mother/Ast-15
90OPC-64
90PublInt/St-91
90S-402
90Sf-83
90T-64
90T/St-14
90UD-305
91B-111
91Classic/200-170
91Classic/I-44

91D-165
91D-401MVP
91F-503
91F/Up-U5
91Leaf-405
91OPC-666
91OPC/Premier-28
91Panini/FrSt-15
91Panini/St-18
91Panini/Top15-65
91Pep/RSox-6
91S-51
91S/RookTr-24T
91StCl-394
91T-666
91T/Tr-26T
91UD-586
91UD/Ext-705
92D-87
92F-38
92OPC-324
92RedSox/Dunkin-10
92S-138
92StCl-539
92T-324
92T/Gold-324
92T/GoldWin-324
92UD-678
92USPlayC/RedSox-2C
92USPlayC/RedSox-5H
93D-647
93F-179
93L-455
93Pac/Spanish-356
93Rang/Keeb-119
93StCl-484
93StCl/1stDay-484
93T-214
93T/Gold-214
93UD-220
93Ultra-150
94D-469
94F-28
94Flair-12
94L-114
94Pac/Cr-51
94Pinn-303
94S-192
94S/GoldR-192
94Select-110
94StCl-251
94StCl/1stDay-251
94StCl/Gold-251
94T-292
94T/Finest-58
94T/FinestRef-58
94T/Gold-292
94UD-123
94UD/CollC-89
94UD/CollC/Gold-89
94UD/CollC/Silv-89
94UD/ElecD-123
94Ultra-12

Darwin, Jeff
89Belling/Legoe-4
90Penin/Star-6
91ClBest/Singl-51
91SanBern/ClBest-2
91SanBern/ProC-1978
92Penin/ClBest-16
92Penin/ProC-2926
93B-627

Dascenzo, Doug
86WinSalem-4
87Pittsfld-23
88Iowa/CMC-19
88Iowa/ProC-528
89D-491
89F-420
89Iowa/CMC-20
89Iowa/ProC-1702
89Panini/St-47
89S-621
89S/HotRook-4
89Sf-42
89T-149
89UD-10SR
90Cub/Mara-5
90OPC-762
90S/YS/II-40
90T-762
90T/TVCub-30
90UD-211
91Cub/Mara-29
91Cub/Vine-8
91D-749
91F-418
91Leaf-483
91OPC-437
91S-209
91T-437
92B-287
92Cub/Mara-29
92D-38
92L-51
92L/BlkGold-51
92OPC-509
92Pinn-160
92S-319
92StCl-252
92Studio-11
92T-509
92T/Gold-509
92T/GoldWin-509
92UD-239
92USPlayC/Cub-12C
92USPlayC/Cub-4H
93B-193
93D-212
93F-376
93Pac/Spanish-55
93Panini-210
93Pinn-555
93Rang/Keeb-401
93S-446
93StCl-664
93StCl/1stDay-664
93StCl/Rang-15
93T-211
93T/Gold-211
93UD-64
93UD-739
94Pac/Cr-612

Dascoli, Frank
55B-291UMP

Dashefsky, Howard
87Hawaii-30M

Daspit, James
(Jim)
90GreatF/SportP-5
91Bakers/Cal-21
92VeroB/ClBest-18
92VeroB/ProC-2867

Dasso, Francis J.
(Frank)
47Signal

Dattola, Kevin
90SoOreg/Best-4
91ClBest/Singl-115
91Huntsvl/Team-8
91Modesto/ClBest-25
91Modesto/ProC-3102
92Huntsvl/ProC-3960
92Huntsvl/SB-308

Datz, Jeff
82AubAs-11
83DayBe-15
86ColumAst-9
87ColAst/ProC-2
88Tucson/CMC-9
88Tucson/JP-7
88Tucson/ProC-187
89Toledo/CMC-11
89Toledo/ProC-761
90AAASingl/ProC-328
90ColClip/CMC-19
90ColClip/ProC-678
90ProC/Singl-507
90T/89Debut-28

Daub, Dan
90Target-926

Daubach, Brian
91Kingspt/ClBest-6
91Kingspt/ProC-3818
92Pittsfld/ClBest-15
92Pittsfld/ProC-3302

Daubert, Jacob E.
(Jake)
11Helmar-85
14CJ-143
14Piedmont/St-16
15CJ-143
16FleischBrd-22
21Exh-32
75F/Pion-24
87Conlon/2-12
88Pac/8Men-95
90Target-166
91Conlon/Sport-307
93Conlon-805
94Conlon-1019
BF2-57
D327
D328-38
D329-43
D350/2-44
E120
E121/80
E122
E135-38
E220
E254
E270/1
M101/4-43
M101/5-44
S74-52
T201
T202
T205
T207
V100
V61-99
V89-48
W501-52
W514-68
W572
W575
WG5-14
WG6-13
WG7-11

Dauer, Richard F.
(Rich)
77T-477R
78T-237
79T-666
80OPC-56
80T-102
81D-232
81F-182
81OPC-314
81T-314
81T/St-36
82D-256
82F-161
82OPC-8
82T-8
82T/St-147
83D-477
83F-57
83F/St-14M
83F/St-6M
83OPC-192
83OPC/St-27
83T-579
83T/St-27
84D-350
84F-4
84Nes/792-723
84OPC-374
84T-723
84T/St-214
85D-106
85F-173
85OPC-58
85T-494
85T/St-203
86F-270
86OPC-251
86T-251
87SanBer-7
89ColoSp/CMC-24
89ColoSp/ProC-242
89SanBer/Best-28M
90Smok/SoCal-3
91Crown/Orio-94
91Indian/McDon-30M
91Pac/SenLg-105
92Kane/Team-6CO

Daugherty, Jack
86Jaxvl/TCMA-25
87Indianap-10
88Indianap/CMC-21
88Indianap/ProC-521
89OkCty/CMC-13
89OkCty/ProC-1525
90B-503
90D-461
90F-294
90F/Can-294
90Leaf-521
90Mother/Rang-11
90OPC-52
90S-564
90S/100Ris-61
90T-52
90UD-614
91B-277
91D-576
91F-284
91Leaf-17
91Mother/Rang-11
91OPC-622
91S-309
91StCl-276
91T-622
91UD-284
92D-569
92F-300
92Mother/Rang-11
92OPC-344
92S-622
92StCl-634
92T-344
92T/Gold-344
92T/GoldWin-344
93F-682
93Rang/Keeb-120
94S-146
94S/GoldR-146

Daugherty, Jim
90Ashvl/ClBest-4
91Ashvl/ProC-562
91SALAS/ProC-SAL1
92ProC/Tomorrow-235

Daugherty, Pat
90James/Pucko-27MG

Daughterty, Mike
83SanJose-19

Daughtry, Dorian
87Belling/Team-4
88Belling/Legoe-2
89SanBern/Best-2
89SanBern/Cal-88

Daulton, Darren
83Reading-11
84Cram/PCL-198
85Cram/PCL-42
85F/Up-U33
85Phill/TastyK-10M
85Phill/TastyK-24
86CIGNA-7
86D-477
86F-438
86Phill/TastyK-10
86T-264
87D-262
87F-172
87Maine/TCMA-21
87OPC-57
87Phill/TastyK-10
87T-636
88D-309
88Phill/TastyK-7
88S-473
88T-468
89D-549
89D/Best-128
89Phill/TastyK-4
89S-413
89T-187
89UD-448
90B-158
90D-194
90D/BestNL-20
90F-555
90F/Can-555
90Leaf-369
90OPC-542
90Phill/TastyK-7
90PublInt/St-234
90S-389
90T-542
90UD-418
91B-507
91Classic/200-81
91D-316
91F-393
91Leaf-192
91Leaf/Stud-212
91OPC-89
91Panini/FrSt-102
91Panini/St-109
91Phill/Medford-11
91S-246
91StCl-4
91T-89
91UD-408
91Ultra-260
92B-440
92D-198
92F-527
92L-335
92L/BlkGold-335
92OPC-244
92Panini-241
92Phill/Med-10
92Pinn-241
92S-506
92StCl-529
92Studio-73
92Studio/Her-13
92T-244
92T/Gold-244
92T/GoldWin-244
92TripleP-143
92UD-429
92Ultra-240
93B-160
93Classic/Gamel-24
93Colla/ASG-6
93Colla/DM-27
93D-92
93D/DK-17
93D/Elite-29
93D/EliteUp-11
93D/MVP-11
93D/Prev-8
93F-100
93F-352RT
93F-705LL
93F-715M
93F/ASNL-9
93F/Atlantic-6
93F/Fruit-13
93Flair-97
93Flair/Pr-2
93JDean/28-5
93KingB-10
93Kraft-19
93L-95
93L/GoldAS-1M
93L/UpGoldAS-2M
93OPC-71
93OPC/Premier-12
93P-18
93Pac/Spanish-233
93Panini-269
93Phill/Med-9
93Pinn-99
93Pinn/HRC-9
93Pinn/TP-3
93Post/Can-10
93S-10
93S-526AS
93S/Franchise-22
93Select-13
93Select/ChasS-5
93Select/StatL-34
93StCl-313
93StCl/1stDay-313
93StCl/MurphyS-91
93StCl/Phill-1
93Studio-51
93Studio/SS-7
93T-180
93T-408
93T/BlkGold-3
93T/Finest-171
93T/FinestRef-171
93T/Gold-180
93T/Gold-408
93TB/Full-13
93TripleP-229LH
93TripleP-7
93TripleP/Act-5
93TripleP/LL-L5
93UD-137
93UD-485M
93UD-498AW
93UD-829TC
93UD/FunPack-142GS
93UD/FunPack-143
93UD/FunPackAS-AS2M
93UD/HRH-HR8
93UD/Iooss-WI17
93UD/SP-11AS
93UD/SPPlat-PP5
93USPlayC/Ace-3C
93Ultra-86
93Ultra/AS-1

93Ultra/HRK-9
94B-140
94B-384
94D-333
94D/Pr-2
94D/Special-333
94F-585
94F/AS-34
94F/ProV-1
94Flair-204
94KingB-4
94L-170
94L/MVPNL-5
94L/Pr-2
94L/Slide-3
94OPC-123
94P-9
94Pac/Cr-471
94Pac/Silv-31
94Panini-224
94Phill/Med-5
94Pinn-91
94Pinn/Artist-91
94Pinn/Museum-91
94Pinn/Run-31
94S-34
94S/GoldR-34
94S/GoldS-4
94Select-9
94Sf/2000-128
94StCl-450
94StCl/1stDay-450
94StCl/Gold-450
94StCl/Team-237
94Studio-136
94T-380
94T-608ST
94T/BlkGold-28
94T/Finest-220
94T/FinestRef-220
94T/Gold-380
94T/Gold-608ST
94TripleP-171
94TripleP/Medal-2
94UD-65
94UD/ElecD-65
94UD/SP-134
94Ultra-243
94Ultra/PhillFinest-1
94Ultra/PhillFinest-2
94Ultra/PhillFinest-3
94Ultra/PhillFinest-4
94Ultra/PhillFinest-5
94Ultra/Pr-243
94Ultra/Pr-243
94Ultra/RBIK-12

Daunic, Willie
93MedHat/ProC-3743
93MedHat/SportP-7

Dauphin, Philip J.
90Geneva/ProC-3036
90Geneva/Star-6
91MidwLAS/ProC-7
91Peoria/ClBest-25
91Peoria/ProC-1355
91Peoria/Team-25
92B-169
92ChalK/SB-152
92CharlK/ProC-2782
92ClBest-60
92ProC/Tomorrow-209
92Sky/AASingl-70
92UD/ML-305
93StCl/Cub-25

Dauss, George August
(Hooks)
21Exh-33
25Exh-91
26Exh-92
27Exh-46
81Tiger/Detroit-74
88Conlon/5-7
94Conlon-1070
D327
D328-39
E120
E121/120
E121/80
E122
E135-39
V100
V117-11
V61-18
W501-110
W573
W575

Davalillo, Victor J.
(Vic)
63Sugar-24
63T-324R
64Kahn
64T-435
64T/Coins-86
64T/St-100
64T/tatt
65Kahn
65OPC-128
65OldLond-24
65T-128
66Kahn
66T-216LL
66T-325
66T/RO-22
66T/RO-70
67CokeCap/Indian-17
67OPC-69
67T-69
68T-397
69MB-70
69MLB/St-20
69T-275
69T/S-9
69T/St-142
70MLB/St-138
70OPC-256
70T-256
71MLB/St-199
71OPC-4
71T-4
72MB-86
72T-785
73OPC-163
73T-163
74OPC-444
74T-444
78SSPC/270-66
78T-539
79T-228
81F-132
90Target-167
WG10-26

Davenport, Adell
87Anchora-5
89Clinton/ProC-882
90AS/Cal-47
90Foil/Best-58
90ProC/Singl-715
90SanJose/Best-8
90SanJose/Cal-39
90SanJose/ProC-2019
90SanJose/Star-6
91CalLgAS-29
91SanJose/ClBest-6
91SanJose/ProC-17
92ClBest/Up-435
92Shrev/ProC-3880
92Shrev/SB-582
92Sky/AASingl-256
93B-408
93ClBest/MLG-211
93FExcel/ML-116
93StCl/Giant-17
93T-494M
93T/Gold-494M

Davenport, Arthur D.
(Dave)
D327

Davenport, Gary
86Fresno/Smok-2CO

Davenport, James H.
(Jim)
58SFCallB-7
58T-413
59Bz
59T-198
60T-154
61P-149
61T-55
61T/Dice-3
61T/St-76
62J-134
62P-134
62P/Can-134
62Salada-169
62Shirriff-169
62T-9
62T/St-196
63F-65
63J-104
63P-104
63Salada-19
63T-388
64T-82
64T/St-63
65OPC-213
65T-213
66OPC-176
66T-176
67CokeCap/Giant-3
67T-441
68CokeCap/Giant-3
68Dexter-27
68T-525
69MB-69
69OPC-102
69T-102
69T/St-102
70MLB/St-122
70OPC-378
70T-378
72MB-85
76SSPC-626
78TCMA-131
79Pol/SFG-12
79TCMA-288
80Pol/SFG-12
84Mother/SFG-6
85Mother/SFG-1MG
85T/Tr-27T
86Phill/TastyK-2CO
87Phill/TastyK-x
89Pac/Leg-118
91CokeK/Tiger-x
91Hamil/ClBest-24
91Hamil/ProC-4051
PM10/Sm-34

Davenport, Neal
86Cedar/TCMA-26
87Tampa-23TR

Daves, Eddie
78Spring/Wiener-11

Davey, Michael Gerard
(Mike)
79Spokane-14
80Port-19

Daviault, Ray
91WIZMets-91

David, Andre
82OrlanTw/A-5
82OrlanTw/B-16
83Toledo-19
84Toledo-11
85T-43
85Toledo-20
85Twin/Team-16
86Toledo-7
87D-519
87Tidew-24
87Tidew/TCMA-12
88Tidew/CANDL-7
88Tidew/CMC-18
88Tidew/ProC-1596
89ElPaso/GS-26
92Kingspt/ClBest-23MG
92Kingspt/ProC-1547MG

David, Brian
83Wausau/Frit-6
86Chatt-8
87Chatt/Best-23

David, Gerald
92Elmira/ClBest-15

David, Greg
87Dunedin-20
88Myrtle/ProC-1176
89Myrtle/ProC-1454
90Wichita/Rock-6
91AA/LineD-605
91Kingspt/ClBest-24MG
91Kingspt/ProC-3829MG
91Wichita/LineD-605
91Wichita/ProC-2603
91Wichita/Rock-13
92Memphis/ProC-2421
92Memphis/SB-433

Davidsmeier, Dan
82ElPaso-5
84Cram/PCL-29
85Cram/PCL-201
86Vanco-9
87Denver-22

Davidson, Bob
88TM/Umpire-44
89TM/Umpire-42
90TM/Umpire-40

Davidson, Bobby
86Albany/TCMA-31
87PrWill-3
88Albany/ProC-1334
89Albany/Best-3
89Albany/ProC-327
89Albany/Star-6
89Star/Wax-97
90AAASingl/ProC-319
90ColClip/CMC-26
90ColClip/ProC-669
90Colum/Pol-10
90ProC/Singl-226
90T/89Debut-29
90T/TVYank-39
91AAA/LineD-233
91Louisvl/LineD-233
91Louisvl/ProC-2908
92Yank/WIZ80-39

Davidson, Grady
91Watertn/ClBest-3
91Watertn/ProC-3358

Davidson, Jackie
86Pittsfld-6
87Iowa-3
88Pittsfld/ProC-1375
89CharlK-19

Davidson, John
91Kissim/ProC-4176

Davidson, Mark
85OrlanTw-3
86Toledo-6
87D/OD-225
87D/Rook-22
87F/Up-U20
88D-519
88F-8
88S-570
88T-19
89F-109
89Portl/CMC-22
89Portl/ProC-227
89S-107
89T-451
89T/Big-320
89UD-577
90Lennox-10
90Mother/Ast-11
90OPC-267
90T-267
91D-540
91F-504
91Leaf-143
91Mother/Ast-11
91OPC-678
91StCl-584
91T-678
91Ultra-136
92ColoSp/ProC-763
92ColoSp/SB-83
92F-432
92S-289

Davidson, Mike
88Bristol/ProC-1871
89Fayette/ProC-1593

Davidson, Randy
78Indianap-24
79Indianap-13
81Cedar-19
82Cedar-25

Davidson, Scott
93MissSt-11

Davidson, Thomas E.
(Ted)
65OPC-243R
65T-243R
66OPC-89
66T-89
67T-519
68OPC-48
68T-48

Davidson, William J.
M116
T206

Davie, Gerald Lee
(Jerry)
59T-256
60T-301

Davies, Bob
52Wheat*

Davies, Dan
85Miami-1

Davila, J.D.
(Jose)
91Spokane/ClBest-18
91Spokane/ProC-3941
92Watlo/ClBest-10
92Watlo/ProC-2138

Davila, Vic
83Butte-17

Davin, D.
N172

Davino, Mike
89Utica/Pucko-5
90Saraso/Star-7
91AA/LineD-57
91BirmB/LineD-57
91BirmB/ProC-1448

Davins, Jim
86Macon-7
87Kenosha-1
88Portl/CMC-10
88Portl/ProC-660
89Portl/CMC-1
89Portl/ProC-211
90AAASingl/ProC-569
90Indianap/CMC-11
90Indianap/ProC-286
90ProC/Singl-61
91AAA/LineD-133
91Denver/LineD-133
91Denver/ProC-115

Davis, Allen
(Bo)
89Bluefld/Star-7
90Wausau/Best-26
90Wausau/ProC-2140
90Wausau/Star-6
91Kane/ClBest-21
91Kane/ProC-2668

Davis, Alvin
83Chatt-8
84F/X-30
84Mother/Mar-23
84T/Tr-28
85D-18DKs86D-
85D-69
85D/AAS-16
85D/DKsuper-18
85Drake-8
85F-488
85F/LimEd-7
85F/St-15
85FunFood/Pin-37
85GenMills-16
85Leaf-18DK
85Mother/Mar-2
85OPC-145
85Seven-7W
85T-145
85T/Gloss40-8
85T/RD-15
85T/St-332
85T/St-368YS
85T/Super-6
86D-69
86F-464
86F/LL-9
86F/Mini-97
86F/Slug-8
86F/St-29
86KayBee-7
86Leaf-65
86Mother/Mar-2
86OPC-309
86Sf-31
86Sf-74M
86T-440
86T/St-218
86T/Tatt-12M
86TrueVal-21
87D-75
87D/OD-115
87F-584
87F/Excit-13
87F/Mini-24
87F/RecSet-5
87F/St-28
87Kraft-37
87Leaf-118
87Mother/Sea-2
87OPC-235
87RedFoley/St-71
87Sf-21
87Sf/TPrev-25M

87Stuart-25M
87T-235
87T/Coins-9
87T/St-220
88D-193
88D-BC25
88D/Best-107
88F-373
88F/RecSet-8
88F/SS-10
88F/St-59
88Grenada-78
88KayBee-6
88KennerFig-24
88KingB/Disc-17
88Leaf-196
88Mother/Sea-2
88OPC-349
88Panini/St-185
88S-83
88Sf-52
88T-785
88T/Big-64
88T/Coins-10
88T/RiteAid-24
88T/St-219
88T/UK-17
89B-215
89Chatt/II/Team-8
89Classic-81
89D-345
89D/Best-24
89D/MVP-BC25
89F-546
89KennerFig-30
89Mother/Sea-2
89OPC-57
89Panini/St-435
89RedFoley/St-27
89S-51
89S/HotStar-78
89Sf-33
89T-687
89T/Big-218
89T/Coins-38
89T/LJN-70
89T/Mini-72
89T/St-227
89T/UK-18
89UD-105
89UD-680TC
90B-479
90Classic-136
90D-109
90D/BestAL-26
90D/Bon/MVP-BC9
90F-512
90F/Can-512
90HotPlay/St-8
90Leaf-35
90MLBPA/Pins-116
90Mother/Mar-2
90OPC-373
90Panini/St-149
90PublInt/St-431
90S-205
90S/100St-26
90Sf-112
90T-373
90T/Ames-26
90T/Big-315
90T/Coins-11
90T/DH-13
90T/HillsHM-26
90T/Mini-33
90T/St-220
90UD-364
91B-258
91CounHrth-14
91D-482
91DennyGS-19
91F-449
91Leaf-429
91Leaf/Stud-111
91OPC-515
91Panini/St-185
91S-482
91Seven/3DCoin-3NW
91StCl-82
91T-515
91UD-457
91Ultra-334
92B-341
92D-124
92F-277
92L-168
92L/BlkGold-168
92OPC-130
92OPC/Premier-183
92Pinn-467
92Pol/Angel-6
92S-76
92StCl-617
92StCl-90
92T-130
92T/Gold-130
92T/GoldWin-130
92UD-386
92Ultra-324

Davis, Anthony
91Pac/SenLg-95

Davis, Arthur W.
(Bill)
65T-546R
66OPC-44R
66T-44R
67T-253R
68T-432R
69T-304R

Davis, Bill
82Idaho-17

Davis, Brad
85FtMyr-3

Davis, Braz
88CharWh/Best-20
89Peoria/Team-2P

Davis, Brent
92MN-5

Davis, Bret
85Anchora-8
86Wausau-7
88James/ProC-1897
89Rockford/Team-6
90WPalmB/Star-4

Davis, Brian
88Tampa/Star-5
89Utica/Pucko-6
90Clmbia/PCPII-5
90Columbia/GS-12
90SALAS/Star-29
91StLucie/ProC-723

Davis, Bryshear B.
(Brock)
63T-553R
71OPC-576R
71T-576R
72OPC-161
72T-161
73OPC-366
73T-366

Davis, Charles T.
(Chili)
78Cedar
82T-171R
82T/Tr-23T
83D-348
83F-257
83F/St-4M
83Mother/Giants-3
83OPC-115
83OPC/St-319
83T-115
83T/St-319
84D-114
84F-370
84Nes/792-494
84OPC-367
84T-494
84T/St-171
85D-480
85Drake-9
85F-605
85F/St-10
85FunFood/Pin-38
85Leaf-66
85Mother/Giants-2
85OPC-245
85T-245
85T/St-162
85T/Super-40
86D-65
86D-6DK
86D/DKsuper-6
86F-536
86F/Mini-109
86Leaf-6DK
86Mother/Giants-2
86Sf-82
87D-268
87D/AAS-38
87D/OD-97
87F-270
87F/BB-12
87F/Mini-25
87F/St-29
87Kraft-46
87Leaf-208
87Mother/SFG-3
87OPC-162
87RedFoley/St-76
87Sf-45
87Sf/TPrev-10M
87Stuart-13M
87T-672
87T/St-95
88D-313
88F-79
88F/Up-U12
88OPC-15
88S-605
88S/Tr-28T
88Sf-172
88Smok/Angels-10
88T-15
88T/Big-235
88T/Tr-32T
89B-50
89Classic-80
89D-449
89D/Best-115
89F-474
89F/LL-9
89KennerFig-31
89OPC-103
89Panini/St-296
89RedFoley/St-28
89S-54
89Sf-129
89T-525
89T/Big-294
89T/LJN-44
89T/St-177
89UD-126
90B-301
90D-136
90D/Bon/MVP-BC20
90E-129
90F/Can-129
90Leaf-288
90OPC-765
90Panini/St-39
90PublInt/St-367
90S-326
90Sf-21
90Smok/Angel-3
90T-765
90T/Big-280
90T/Coins-12
90T/St-173
90UD-38
91B-331
91Classic/III-12
91D-580
91F-309
91F/UltraUp-U35
91F/Up-U36
91Leaf-374
91OPC-355
91Panini/St-134
91S-803
91S/RookTr-70T
91StCl-329
91T-355
91T/Tr-27T
91UD-339
91UD/Ext-722
92B-195
92Classic/Game200-92
92D-115
92F-200
92Hardee-6
92L-395
92L/BlkGold-395
92OPC-118
92Pinn-46
92S-94
92StCl-18
92StCl/Dome-32
92T-118
92T/Gold-118
92T/GoldWin-118
92T/Kids-113
92TripleP-27
92UD-126
92UD/HRH-HR12
92USPlayC/Ace-2C
92USPlayC/Twin-13D
92USPlayC/Twin-9S
92Ultra-89
93B-553
93D-679
93DennyGS-1
93F-262
93F/Final-180
93Flair-171
93L-254
93Mother/Angel-6
93OPC-52
93OPC/Premier-24
93Pac/Spanish-366
93Panini-131
93Pinn-536
93Pol/Angel-6
93S-583
93Select-238
93Select/RookTr-124T
93StCl-222
93StCl-611
93StCl/1stDay-222
93StCl/1stDay-611
93StCl/Angel-3
93Studio-32
93T-455
93T/Gold-455
93UD-239
93UD-794
93UD/FunPack-38
93UD/SP-20
93Ultra-518
94B-451
94D-82
94F-51
94L-258
94OPC-143
94Pac/Cr-74
94Pinn-458
94S-345
94StCl-173
94StCl/1stDay-173
94StCl/Gold-173
94Studio-9
94T-265
94T/Finest-112
94T/FinestRef-112
94T/Gold-265
94TripleP-12
94UD-74
94UD/ElecD-74
94UD/SP-23
94Ultra-324

Davis, Chris 1
78StPete
79ArkTr-17

Davis, Chris 2
90Elmira/Pucko-15
91Elmira/ClBest-18
91Elmira/ProC-3264
92ProC/Tomorrow-24
92WinHaven/ClBest-1

Davis, Chuck
86NewBrit-9
87Pawtu-24
87Pawtu/TCMA-5

Davis, Clint
92Savan/ClBest-7
92Savan/ProC-654
94B-564
94ClBest/Gold-170
94FExcel-265
94Ultra-564

Davis, Corbin
90MissSt-8
91MissSt-13

Davis, Courtney
90ClintUp/Team-U2
90Everett/Best-22
90Everett/ProC-3138
91Clinton/ProC-845

Davis, Curtis Benton
(Curt)
35BU-97
36Exh/4-6
36Wheat
90Target-168
91Conlon/Sport-282
R314

Davis, Darwin
91Kingspt/ClBest-3
91Kingspt/ProC-3819

Davis, Douglas
(Doug)
82BurlR/Frit-22
82BurlR/TCMA-18
85MidldA-14
86MidldA-8
87MidldA-10
88Edmon/CMC-18
88Edmon/ProC-559
89Belling/Legoe-18
89Edmon/CMC-15
89Edmon/ProC-551
90AAASingl/ProC-95
90Edmon/CMC-18
90Edmon/ProC-519
90ProC/Singl-495
91AAA/LineD-160
91Edmon/LineD-160
91Edmon/ProC-1518
92B-490
92D/Rook-31
92OkCty/ProC-1916
92OkCty/SB-308
92StCl-692
93Rang/Keeb-121

Davis, Eddie
94T-237M
94T/Gold-237M

Davis, Eric Keith
(Eric)
82Cedar-20
83Water-15
84Borden-44
84Wichita/Rock-15
85D-325
85F-533
85T-627
86D-164
86D/HL-30
86F-175
86Seven/Coin-S9M
86T-28
86TexGold-44
87Classic-21
87Classic/Up-102
87Classic/Up-150M
87D-22DK
87D-265
87D/DKsuper-22
87D/HL-3
87D/HL-8
87D/OD-197
87F-198
87F/AwardWin-11
87F/Excit-14
87F/GameWin-11
87F/Hottest-12
87F/Mini-26
87F/Slug-11
87F/St-132M
87F/St-30
87GenMills/Book-6M
87Ho/St-9
87Kahn-44
87Kraft-10
87Leaf-179
87Leaf-22DK
87MSA/Discs-7
87OPC-228
87Sf-155M
87Sf-199M
87Sf-22
87Sf/TPrev-4M
87Stuart-4M
87T-412
87T/Coins-30
87T/Gloss60-44
87T/Mini-4
87T/St-136
88Bz-6
88ChefBoy-2
88Classic/Blue-201M
88Classic/Blue-213
88Classic/Red-154
88D-369
88D-BC2
88D/AS-38
88D/Best-62
88D/PopUp-16
88Drake-24

88F-231
88F-637M
88F/AS-7
88F/AwardWin-8
88F/BB/AS-9
88F/BB/MVP-8
88F/Excit-12
88F/Hottest-8
88F/LL-8
88F/Mini-73
88F/RecSet-9
88F/SS-11
88F/Slug-10
88F/St-83
88F/St-S6M
88F/TL-6
88FanSam-14
88Grenada-32
88Kahn/Reds-44
88KayBee-7
88KennerFig-25
88KingB/Disc-22
88Leaf-149
88MSA/Disc-12
88Nestle-3
88OPC-150
88OPC-J
88Panini/St-235M
88Panini/St-282
88RedFoley/St-15
88S-10
88S-649M
88S/WaxBox-15
88S/YS/II-10
88Sf-10
88Sf/Gamewin-5
88T-150
88T/Big-20
88T/Coins-39
88T/Gloss22-17
88T/Gloss60-16
88T/Mini-46
88T/RiteAid-3
88T/St-141
88T/St-146
88T/St/Backs-14
88T/UK-18
88T/WaxBox-J
89B-316
89Cadaco-12
89Classic-109
89Classic-9
89D-80
89D/Best-6
89F-158
89F-639M
89F/BBMVP's-9
89F/Excit-9
89F/Heroes-10
89F/LL-10
89F/Superstar-11
89Holsum/Discs-7
89Kahn/Reds-44
89KayBee-8
89KennerFig-32
89MSA/Disc-11
89Nissen-7
89OPC-330
89Panini/St-76
89RedFoley/St-29
89S-109
89S/HotStar-58
89S/Mast-18
89Sf-69
89T-111TL
89T-330
89T/Ames-11
89T/Big-273
89T/Coins-9
89T/Crunch-13
89T/Gloss60-2
89T/HeadsUp-21
89T/LJN-38
89T/Mini-8
89T/St-138
89T/St/Backs-47
89T/UK-19
89Tetley/Discs-11
89UD-410
89UD-688TC
90B-58
90CedarDG/Best-1
90Classic-11
90CollAB-28
90D-233
90D-695AS
90D/BestNL-1
90D/Bon/MVP-BC23
90F-417
90F/AwardWin-10
90F/BB-6
90F/BBMVP-9
90F/Can-417
90F/LL-8
90F/WaxBox-C4
90HotPlay/St-9
90Kahn/Reds-7
90Kenner/Fig-22
90Leaf-189
90MLBPA/Pins-22
90OPC-260
90OPC-402AS
90Panini/St-209
90Panini/St-246
90Post-24
90PublInt/St-255
90PublInt/St-26
90RedFoley/St-20
90S-185
90S/100St-95
90Sf-97
90Starline/LJS-3
90Starline/LJS-38
90Sunflower-21
90T-260
90T-402AS
90T/Ames-28
90T/Big-72
90T/Coins-44
90T/DH-14
90T/Gloss22-7
90T/Gloss60-25
90T/HillsHM-1
90T/Mini-53
90T/St-134
90T/St-149AS
90T/TVAS-38
90UD-116
91B-686
91Cadaco-13
91Classic/200-136
91Classic/I-34
91Classic/III-13
91D-84
91DennyGS-4
91F-61
91F/ProV-10
91F/WS-1
91Kahn/Reds-44
91Kenner-11
91Leaf-37
91Leaf/Stud-162
91Leaf/StudPrev-11
91MSA/Holsum-2
91MajorLg/Pins-70
91OPC-550
91OPC/Premier-29
91Panini/FrSt-131
91Panini/St-124
91Pep/Reds-6
91Petro/SU-6
91S-137
91S-403MB
91S-669AS
91S-696RF
91S-863FRAN
91S/100SS-9
91Seven/3DCoin-6SC
91StCl-37
91StCl/Charter*-5
91T-550
91T/CJMini/I-16
91T/SU-10
91UD-355
91Ultra-91
91Woolwth/HL-25
92B-671
92CJ/DII-8
92Classic/Game200-161
92Classic/II-T25
92D-503
92F-403
92F/Up-90
92Kenner/Fig-12
92L-430
92L/BlkGold-430
92Mother/Dodg-4
92OPC-610
92OPC/Premier-129
92Panini-267
92Pinn-323
92Pinn-602SH
92Pinn/RookI-1M
92Pol/Dodg-33
92S-44
92S/100SS-44
92S/RookTr-62T
92StCl-660
92Studio-43
92T-610
92T/Gold-610
92T/GoldWin-610
92T/Kids-38
92T/Tr-26T
92T/TrGold-26T
92UD-125
92UD-756
92UD/ASFF-20
92Ultra-503
93B-450
93Colla/DM-28
93D-482
93F-445
93L-267
93Mother/Dodg-7
93OPC-87
93Pac/Spanish-144
93Panini-221
93Pinn-429
93Pol/Dodg-4
93S-570
93Select-91
93Select/RookTr-92T
93StCl-381
93StCl/1stDay-381
93StCl/Dodg-20
93T-745
93T/Finest-126
93T/FinestRef-126
93T/Gold-745
93TripleP-112
93UD-477
93UD-595
93UD/SP-92
93Ultra-53
94B-293
94D-618
94F-126
94Flair-46
94L-256
94OPC-226
94Pac/Cr-213
94Panini-62
94Pinn-388
94S-504
94Sf/2000-124
94StCl-209
94StCl/1stDay-209
94StCl/Gold-209
94Studio-189
94T-488
94T/Finest-80
94T/FinestRef-80
94T/Gold-488
94TripleP-241
94UD-261
94UD/ElecD-261
94Ultra-354

Davis, Frank
(Dixie)
E120
E121/120
V100
V61-36
W501-3
W514-48
W573
W575

Davis, Freddie Jr.
87Salem/ProC-2439
89Lynch/Star-5
90CLAS/CL-10
90LynchRS/Team-17
90WinHaven/Star-3
91AA/LineD-454
91ClBest/Singl-123
91NewBrit/LineD-454
91NewBrit/ProC-345

Davis, Geff
86BurlEx-5
87WPalmB-27

Davis, George 1
(Storm)
83D-619
83F-56
83OPC/St-310
83T-268
83T/St-310
84D-585
84F-5
84Nes/792-140
84OPC-140
84T-140
85D-454
85F-174
85FunFood/Pin-120
85Leaf-81
85OPC-73
85T-599
86D-169
86F-271
86Leaf-99
86OPC-179
86T-469
86T/St-231
87Bohem-34
87D-273
87F-466
87F/Up-U22
87OPC-349
87T-349
87T/St-230
87T/Tr-26T
88D-595
88D/A's/Bk-595
88D/Best-282
88F-278
88Mother/A's-19
88T-248
89B-192
89D-210
89F-6
89Mother/A's-18
89Panini/St-413
89S-248
89T-701
89T/Big-121
89UD-153
90B-368
90Classic/Up-15
90D-479
90F-5
90F/Can-5
90F/Up-102
90Leaf-362
90OPC-606
90PublInt/St-302
90S-266
90S/Tr-21T
90T-606
90T/Mini-26
90T/Tr-25T
90UD-292
90UD/Ext-712
91B-293
91Classic/200-16
91Crown/Orio-97
91D-185
91F-556
91F/UltraUp-U26
91Leaf-161
91Leaf/Stud-65
91OPC-22
91Pol/Royal-7
91S-511
91StCl-67
91T-22
91UD-639
92D-529
92F-155
92L-465
92L/BlkGold-465
92OPC-556
92Pinn-312
92S-264
92S/RookTr-34T
92StCl-728
92T-556
92T/Gold-556
92T/GoldWin-556
92UD-499
93D-769
93F-541
93L-259
93Mother/A's-18
93Pac/Spanish-564
93S-449
93StCl-174
93StCl/1stDay-174
93StCl/A's-6
93UD-746
93Ultra-604
94Pac/Cr-214
94T-682
94T/Gold-682

Davis, George 2
76Clinton

Davis, George 3
94Conlon-1235

Davis, George Allen
(George)
D350/2-45
M101/5-45

Davis, George Stacey
(George)
11Helmar-23
E107
E254
E90/1
N142
T206
V355-17

Davis, George Willis
(Kiddo)
33G-236
92Conlon/Sport-502
W711/1

Davis, Gerald Edward
(Jerry)
82Amari-5
83LasVegas/BHN-5
84Cram/PCL-222
85D-162
85F/Up-U34
85Mother/Padres-26
85T/Tr-28T
86D-429
86F-317
86T-323
87Toledo-30
87Toledo/TCMA-24

Davis, Gerald
92Elmira/ProC-1395

Davis, Gerrod
90Kgsport/Best-3
92StLucie/ClBest-19

Davis, Gerry
88TM/Umpire-52
89TM/Umpire-50
90TM/Umpire-48

Davis, Glenn Earle
(Glenn)
82DayBe-20
83ColumAst-11
84Cram/PCL-62
85Cram/PCL-65
85F-652R
86D-380
86F-297
86F/Mini-63
86Leaf-175
86OPC-389
86Pol/Ast-22
86Sf-188
86T-389
86T/Gloss60-59
86T/St-29
86T/St-314
86T/Tatt-18M
87Classic-28
87Classic/Up-107
87D-61
87D/AAS-42
87D/OD-16
87F-55
87F-636M
87F/GameWin-12
87F/LL-14
87F/Lim-11
87F/Mini-27
87F/St-31
87F/St-S5
87KayBee-12
87Kraft-36
87Leaf-115
87Mother/Ast-10
87OPC-56
87Pol/Ast-23

87RedFoley/St-43
87Sf-17
87Sf-195M
87Sf/TPrev-8M
87Stuart-5M
87T-560
87T/Coins-31
87T/Gloss60-4
87T/Mini-8
87T/St-26
88Classic/Red-182
88D-184
88D/Best-64
88F-445
88F/Mini-78
88F/SS-12
88F/Slug-11
88F/St-86
88KennerFig-26
88Leaf-186
88Mother/Ast-10
88OPC-159
88Panini/St-292
88Pol/Ast-8
88S-460
88Sf-102
88T-430
88T/Big-192
88T/St-35
88T/UK-19
89B-331
89Cadaco-13
89Classic-17
89Classic/Up/2-168
89D-236
89D-25DK
89D/Best-8
89D/DKsuper-25DK
89F-355
89F/BBMVP's-10
89F/Excit-10
89F/Heroes-11
89F/LL-11
89KennerFig-33
89Lennox/Ast-26
89Mother/Ast-9
89OPC-378
89Panini/St-88
89RedFoley/St-30
89S-164
89S/HotStar-46
89Sf-137
89T-579TL
89T-765
89T/Big-89
89T/Coins-10
89T/Gloss60-32
89T/Hills-10
89T/LJN-67
89T/St-21
89T/St/Backs-35
89T/UK-20
89UD-443
90B-80
90Classic-71
90D-118
90D/BestNL-65
90D/Bon/MVP-BC21
90D/Learning-22
90F-228
90F/BB-7
90F/BBMVP-10
90F/Can-228
90F/LL-9
90F/WaxBox-C5
90HotPlay/St-10
90KMart/SS-16
90Leaf-30
90Lennox-11
90MLBPA/Pins-41
90Mother/Ast-2
90OPC-50
90Panini/St-258
90Publint/St-92
90RedFoley/St-21
90S-272
90S/100St-52
90Sf-19
90Starline/LJS-15
90Starline/LJS-30
90T-50
90T/Big-122
90T/Coins-45
90T/DH-15
90T/Gloss60-3
90T/HillsHM-22
90T/Mini-55
90T/St-13
90T/TVAS-45
90UD-245
91B-83
91Cadaco-14
91Classic/200-169
91Classic/II-T6
91Crown/Orio-496
91D-474
91F-505
91F/Up-U1
91Kenner-12
91Leaf-398
91Leaf/Stud-1
91OPC-350
91OPC/Premier-30
91Panini/FrSt-7
91Panini/St-19
91Post/Can-14
91RedFoley/St-23
91S-405MB
91S-830
91S/RookTr-7T
91Seven/3DCoin-1A
91Seven/3DCoin-4F
91Seven/3DCoin-5T
91StCl-391
91Sunflower-6
91T-350
91T/Tr-28T
91UD-535
91UD-81TC
91UD/Ext-757
91Ultra-14
92B-428
92Classic/Game200-174
92D-597
92F-4
92L-316
92L/BlkGold-316
92OPC-190
92Pinn-138
92S-615
92StCl-808
92Studio-122
92T-190
92T/Gold-190
92T/GoldWin-190
92T/Kids-65
92TripleP-60
92UD-565
92Ultra-1
93B-1
93D-163
93F-164
93L-45
93OPC-69
93Pac/Spanish-15
93Pinn-217
93S-383
93Select-378
93StCl-326
93StCl/1stDay-326
93T-485
93T/Finest-41
93T/FinestRef-41
93T/Gold-485
93TripleP-73
93UD-353
93UD-827TC
93Ultra-139

Davis, Glenn
52Wheat*

Davis, Grant
93MissSt-12

Davis, Greg
90Kissim/DIMD-9
91GreatF/SportP-15

Davis, Harry H.
(Harry)
11Diamond-11
91Conlon/Sport-269
E101
E103
E104
E105
E107
E254
E270/1
E286
E90/1
E91
E92
E94
E96
E97
E98
M116
T206
T207
T208
T213/blue
T215/blue
T215/brown
T216
T222
W555
WG2-13

Davis, Harry
84Everett/Cram-5
86Fresno/Smok-26
88Shrev/ProC-1299
89Wmsprt/ProC-641
89Wmsprt/Star-4

Davis, Herman Thomas
(Tommy)
59DF
60T-509
60Union/Dodg-3
61BB-12
61Morrell
61P-165
61T-168
61T/St-25
61Union/Dodg-3
62BB-12
62J-105
62P-105
62P/Can-105
62Salada-154A
62Salada-154B
62Shirriff-154
62T-358
63Bz-36
63F-40
63J-117
63P-117
63T-1LL
63T-310
63T/SO
64Bz-36
64T-180
64T-7LL
64T/Coins-153AS
64T/Coins-57
64T/S-43
64T/SU
64T/St-64
64Wheat/St-13
65Bz-36
65T-370
65T/E-49
65T/trans-46
66OPC-75
66T-75
67Bz-37
67CokeCap/YMet-30
67Kahn
67T-370
68Bz-10
68T-265
68T/G-10
69MB-72
69MLB/St-94
69OPC-135
69T-135
69T/4in1-4
69T/DE-15
69T/S-32
69T/St-224
69T/decal
70MB-6
70MLB/St-38
70T-559
71OPC-151
71T-151
71T/Coins-93
72MB-87
72OPC-41
72OPC-42IA
72T-41
72T-42IA
73JP
74K-43
74OPC-396
74T-396
74T/St-124
75OPC-564
75SSPC/42-7
75T-564
75T/M-564
76OPC-149
76SSPC-398
76T-149
77T-362
78TCMA-87
82D-648CO
87Smok/Dodg-5
88Bakers/Cal-265
88Pac/Leg-83
88Smok/Dodg-8
89Smok/Dodg-70
90Target-171
91Crown/Orio-98
91WIZMets-92
93TWill-11
93TWill/Mem-7
93TWill/POG-25
93UD/ATH-37

Davis, I.M.
25Exh-77

Davis, Jacke S.
(Jacke)
62T-521
63T-117

Davis, James Bennett
(Jim)
52Mother-2
53Mother-46
55T-68
55T/DH-28
56T-102
57T-273

Davis, James J.
(Jumbo)
N172

Davis, Jay
90Kgsport/Star-6
91Clmbia/PCPII-1
91Clmbia/PII-24
91SALAS/ProC-SAL14
92StLucie/ProC-1760
93FExcel/ML-70

Davis, Jerry
90Johnson/Star-7

Davis, Jody Richard
(Jody)
79Jacks-7
82D-225
82F-592
82RedLob
82T-508
83D-183
83F-494
83OPC/St-226
83T-542
83T/St-226
83Thorn-7
84Cub/Uno-6M
84D-433
84F-491
84Jacks/Smok-4
84Nes/792-73
84OPC-73
84SevenUp-7
84T-73
84T/St-43
85D-76
85D/AAS-54
85F-54
85FunFood/Pin-51
85Leaf-180
85OPC-384
85SevenUp-7
85T-384
85T/St-37
86Cub/Unocal-4
86D-289
86F-364
86F/St-30
86Gator-7
86Jay's-3
86OPC-176
86T-767
86T/St-58
86T/Tatt-13M
87Berg/Cubs-7
87D-269
87D/AAS-50
87D/OD-72
87F-557
87F/BB-13
87F/LL-15
87Kraft-6
87Leaf-48
87OPC-270
87RedFoley/St-68
87Seven-C2
87Seven-ME3
87Sf-170
87Sf/TPrev-22M
87Smok/NL-3
87Stuart-3M
87T-270
87T/St-64
88Berg/Cubs-7
88D-119
88D/Cubs/Bk-119
88F-414
88KennerFig-27
88Leaf-69
88OPC-376
88Panini/St-258
88S-551
88Sf-60
88T-615
88T/St-60
88T/St/Backs-23
89B-270
89Brave/Dubuq-9
89D-650
89D/Best-58
89F-421
89OPC-115
89RedFoley/St-31
89S-173
89S/Tr-64
89Sf-187
89T-115
89T/Big-3
89T/Tr-22T
89UD-148
89UD/Ext-795
90F-579
90F/Can-579
90OPC-453
90Publint/St-111
90S-328
90T-453
90T/Big-26
90UD-429

Davis, Joe
89Anchora-10

Davis, Joel
86Coke/WS-52
86D-623
86F-202
86T/Tr-30T
87Coke/WS-26
87D-124
87T-299
88T-511
88Vanco/CMC-2
88Vanco/ProC-763
89ColoSp/CMC-7
89ColoSp/ProC-237

Davis, John Humphrey
(John or Red)
52Mother-27
61Union
75OkCty/Team-23
76Wmsprt

Davis, John Kirk
83CharR-17
86Memphis/GoldT-4
86Memphis/SilverT-4
87Omaha-19
88CapeCod/Sum-56
88Coke/WS-5
88D-594
88D/Rook-48
88F-255
88F/Up-U15
88S-636
88Sf-224
88T-672
89S-608
89T-162
89UD-548
89Vanco/CMC-9
89Vanco/ProC-582
91AAA/LineD-430
91Richm/Bob-6

91Richm/LineD-430
91Richm/Team-22
Davis, John
91Peoria/Team-28CO
Davis, Johnny
86Negro/Frit-95
Davis, Kelvin
88Eugene/Best-17
Davis, Kenny
87Visalia-15
88Visalia/Cal-145
88Visalia/ProC-81
Davis, Kevin
83Peoria/Frit-3
83Redwd-8
85MidldA-18
87Salem-30F
88EastLAS/ProC-14
88Harris/ProC-837
89BirmB/Best-6
89BirmB/ProC-98
91AA/LineD-432
91MidldA/LineD-432
91MidldA/OneHour-9
91MidldA/ProC-439
92Salinas/ProC-3762
Davis, Larry
75Tucson/Team-22
81Tacoma-1
82Tacoma-20
83Tacoma-22
90Mother/A's-28TR
Davis, Lavonne
(Pepper)
93TWill-118
Davis, Lefty
90Target-1102
Davis, Lorenzo
(Piper)
53Mother-54
86Negro/Frit-12
86Negro/Frit-47
87Negro/Dixon-37
92Negro/Retort-15
Davis, Mark William
(Mark)
81OkCty/TCMA-6
82OkCty-12
82T-231R
83Phoenix/BHN-20
84D-201
84F-371
84Nes/792-343
84T-343
85D-553
85F-606
85Mother/Giants-20
85T-541
86D-265
86F-537
86Mother/Giants-20
86T-138
86T/St-91
87D-313
87F-271
87F/Up-U21
87Mother/SFG-14
87T-21
88Coke/Padres-48
88D-64
88D/Best-98
88F-581
88S-391
88Smok/Padres-6
88T-482
89B-447
89Coke/Padre-3
89D-65
89D/AS-46
89D/Best-133
89F-303
89F-635M
89F/BBAS-10
89F/Up-18
89KennerFig-34
89OPC-59
89Padre/Mag-13
89RedFoley/St-32
89S-490
89S/HotStar-62
89Sf-74
89T-59
89T/St-110
89T/St/Backs-64
89UD-268
90B-369
90B/Ins-2
90Bz-3
90Classic/Up-14
90Classic/Up-NNO
90D-302
90D/BestAL-8
90F-155
90F-631M
90F/ASIns-3
90F/Can-155
90F/Can-631
90F/Up-101
90Holsum/Discs-6
90HotPlay/St-11
90KMart/SS-14
90Leaf-468
90OPC-205
90OPC-407AS
90Panini/St-215
90Panini/St-352
90PublInt/St-47
90RedFoley/St-22
90S-259
90S/100St-51
90S/Tr-26T
90Sf-62
90T-205
90T-407AS
90T/Big-312
90T/Coins-34
90T/DH-16
90T/Gloss60-58
90T/Mini-79
90T/St-102
90T/TVAS-12
90T/Tr-24T
90UD-431
90UD/Ext-710
90Woolwth/HL-4CY
91B-306
91BBBest/RecBr-5
91Classic/200-15
91D-560
91F-555
91Leaf-16
91OPC-116
91Pol/Royal-6
91RedFoley/St-24
91S-136
91StCl-136
91T-116
91UD-589
92D-54
92L-163
92L/BlkGold-163
92OPC-766
92Pinn-359
92Pol/Royal-5
92S-718
92StCl-212
92T-766
92T/91Debut-43
92T/Gold-766
92T/GoldWin-766
92TripleP-247
92UD-607
92Ultra-369
93D-52
93Pinn-425
93StCl-371
93StCl/1stDay-371
93Ultra-437
94D-657
94F-661
94Pac/Cr-521
94StCl-497
94StCl/1stDay-497
94StCl/Gold-497
Davis, Mark
84LitFalls-22
86Kenosha-5
87Penin-1
87Savan-12
88BirmB/Best-14
88Sumter/ProC-396
89BurlB/ProC-1599
89BurlB/Star-9
89Vanco/CMC-22
89Vanco/ProC-585
90MidldA/GS-10
91AAA/LineD-161
91Edmon/LineD-161
91Edmon/ProC-1527
Davis, Marty
91GulfCR/SportP-18
Davis, Matt
91Clinton/ClBest-12
91Clinton/ProC-840
92AS/Cal-14
92SanJose/ClBest-23
Davis, Michael Dwayne
(Mike)
81D-470
81F-586
81T-364
81Tacoma-11
82T-671
82Tacoma-34
83Granny-16
83T/Tr-24
84D-298
84F-443
84Mother/A's-5
84Nes/792-558
84T-558
84T/St-338
85D-223
85D/HL-3
85F-422
85Mother/A's-7
85T-778
86D-14DK
86D-96
86D/DKsuper-14
86F-416
86F/LimEd-14
86F/Mini-88
86F/St-31
86Leaf-14DK
86Mother/A's-7
86OPC-165
86Sf-83
86T-165
86T/St-166
87D-133
87D/OD-21
87F-391
87F/Lim-12
87F/Mini-28
87F/St-32
87Smok/A's-3
87T-83
87T/St-168
88D-281
88D/Best-36
88F-277
88Mother/Dodg-12
88OPC-217
88Panini/St-174
88Pol/Dodg-37
88RedFoley/St-16
88S-211
88S/Tr-53T
88Sf-206
88T-448
88T/Big-154
88T/St-171
88T/Tr-33T
89B-352
89D-316
89F-55
89Mother/Dodg-12
89OPC-277
89Panini/St-193
89Panini/St-24
89Pol/Dodg-11
89S-376
89T-277
89T/Ames-12
89T/Big-225
89UD-146
89Woolwth-32
90D-552
90F-391
90OPC-697
90PublInt/St-3
90S-437
90T-697
90Target-169
90UD-258
91Indianap/LineD-180
91Indianap/ProC-472
Davis, Michael
82Tidew-3
83Pawtu-16
84Pawtu-26
84Pawtu-7
85Tidew-23
86T/Tatt-4M
86Tidew-7
87Sf/TPrev-23M
89BurlInd/Star-7
89Kingspt/Star-6
90F/Can-391
90Watertn/Star-6
91AAA/LineD-180
Davis, Nick
90Clmbia/PCPII-6
90Columbia/GS-5
Davis, Nicky
90Ashvl/ClBest-12
90Pittsfld/Pucko-11
91Ashvl/ProC-573
91ClBest/Singl-49
Davis, Odie Ernest
(Odie)
79Tucson-18
80CharCh-15
81Charl-16
93Rang/Keeb-122
Davis, Ray
(Peaches)
39PlayBall-123
W711/1
Davis, Richard Earl
(Dick)
77Spoka
79T-474
80T-553
81D-528
81F-527
81T-183
81T/Tr-753
82D-147
82F-245
82T-352
82T/Tr-24T
83D-647
83F-305
83Portl-16
83T-667
Davis, Rick
89Spokane/SP-11
90Foil/Best-78
90River/Best-5
90River/Cal-14
90River/ProC-2598
91AA/LineD-606
91Wichita/LineD-606
91Wichita/ProC-2593
91Wichita/Rock-3
92LasVegas/ProC-2790
92LasVegas/SB-229
92Sky/AAASingl-113
Davis, Robert Edward
(Bob)
61T-246
Davis, Robert John
75Hawaii/Caruso-3
75IntLgAS/Broder-5
75PCL/AS-5
76OPC-472
76T-472
77Padre/SchCd-9
77T-78
78Padre/FamFun-9
78T-713
80OPC-185
80T-351
81D-30
81F-428
81OPC-221
81SLCity-26
81T-221
Davis, Robert
86FtMyr-6
89Bristol/Star-7
Davis, Ronald E.
(Ron)
67CokeCap/Astro-3
67T-298
68CokeCap/Astro-3
68Dexter-28
68OPC-21
68T-21
69MB-71
69MLB/St-185
69T-553
70MLB/St-100
Davis, Ronald Gene
(Ron)
79Colum-14
80OPC-101
80T-179
81D-467
81F-86
81OPC-16
81T-16
82D-451
82F-32
82F/St-117
82F/St-242M
82OPC-283
82T-2M
82T-635
82T/Tr-25T
83D-228
83F-610
83F/St-14M
83F/St-5M
83OPC-380
83OPC/St-94
83T-380
83T/St-94
83Twin/Team-25
84D-269
84F-561
84F/St-75
84Nes/792-519
84OPC-101
84T-519
84T/RD-17
84T/St-309
85D-120
85F-275
85F/St-103
85FunFood/Pin-112
85OPC-78
85Seven/Minn-8
85T-430
85T/RD-16
85T/St-297
85Twin/Seven-8
85Twin/Team-29
86D-364
86F-390
86OPC-265
86T-265
86T/St-281
86T/Tatt-18M
87Berg/Cubs-39
87D-438
87F-558
87OPC-383
87T-383
89Phoenix/ProC-1505
90Colum/Pol-9
90Target-170
91Pac/SenLg-115
92Yank/WIZ70-40
92Yank/WIZ80-40
92Yank/WIZAS-15
93B-342FOIL
Davis, Russell
89FtLaud/Star-2
89Oneonta/ProC-2109
90CLAS/CL-18
90PrWill/Team-8
90Saraso/Star-29TR
91AA/LineD-2
91Albany/LineD-2
91Albany/ProC-1014
91ClBest/Singl-182
92Albany/ProC-2231
92Albany/SB-6
92ClBest-115
92Sky/AASingl-2
92UD/ML-132
93ColClip/Pol-13
93F/Final-245
93FExcel/ML-205
93Flair/Wave-3
93UD/SP-274FOIL
93Ultra-592
94B-109
94F-227
94FExcel-100
94FExcel/AS-4
94L/GRook-8
94SigRook-34
94SigRook/Hot-2
94StCl/Team-194

94T-772
94T/Gold-772
Davis, Sammy
78Watlo
Davis, Saul
92Negro/Retort-14
Davis, Scott
90Eugene/GS-5
Davis, Stan
77Newar
78Newar
79BurlB-21
81ElPaso-6
82Vanco-9
83ElPaso-6
84ElPaso-14
Davis, Steven K.
80Syrac/Team-7
81Syrac/Team-7
86BJ/Ault-7
86Tor/Fire-7
87Syrac-21
87Syrac/TCMA-2
88Syrac/CMC-1
88Syrac/ProC-814
89ColoSp/CMC-1
89ColoSp/ProC-249
90AAASingl/ProC-58
90Albuq/CMC-4
90Albuq/ProC-337
90Albuq/Trib-6
90Jacks/GS-28
90OPC-428
90ProC/Singl-406
90S-187
90T-428
91AA/LineD-629
91Geneva/ClBest-5
91Geneva/ProC-4209
Davis, Steven Michael 1
(Steve)
81Syrac-14
Davis, Steven Michael 2
87Tampa-19
88Cedar/ProC-1150
91Wmsprt/LineD-629
91Wmsprt/ProC-305
Davis, Ted
78Ashvl
79Wausau-20
80Tulsa-4
81Tulsa-8
82Jacks-3
83BirmB-18
Davis, Thomas Oscar
(Tod)
47Signal
Davis, Tim
90Elmira/Pucko-4
92T/Tr-27T
92T/TrGold-27T
93StCl/MurphyS-103
94B-257
94ClBest/Gold-12
94FExcel-125
94Flair-100
94T-167
94T/Gold-167
94UD-512DD
94Ultra-418
Davis, Trench
82Portl-19
84Cram/PCL-139
85Cram/PCL-238
86Hawaii-3
87Richm/Bob-5
87Richm/Crown-32
87Richm/TCMA-17
Davis, Virgil L.
(Spud)
33G-210
39PlayBall-37
40PlayBall-163
88Conlon/NatAS-4
91Conlon -269
93Conlon-863
94Conlon-1072
R314
V355-12
W711/1
WG8-11
Davis, Wallace M.
(Butch)
84D-277
85Omaha-12
85T-49
87Vanco-17
88CharlK/Pep-3
89AAA/CMC-21
89RochR/CMC-22
89RochR/ProC-1652
90AAASingl/ProC-78
90Albuq/CMC-22
90Albuq/ProC-357
90Albuq/Trib-5
90ProC/Singl-424
90TripleAAS/CMC-21
91AAA/LineD-5
91Albuq/LineD-5
91Albuq/ProC-1154
91Crown/Orio-96
92AAA/ASG/SB-503
92Sky/AAASingl-224
92Syrac/MerchB-3
92Syrac/ProC-1980
92Syrac/SB-504
93Rang/Keeb-402
93StCl/Rang-8
94Pac/Cr-613
Davis, Wayne
87Myrtle-20
88Dunedin/Star-3
Davis, Willie Henry
(Willie)
60DF-8
61BB-3
61T-506
61Union/Dodg-4
62BB-3
62J-106
62P-106
62P/Can-106
62Salada-161
62Shirriff-161
62T-108
63J-119
63P-119
63Salada-21
63T-229
64T-68
65OldLond-7
65T-435
66T-535
66T/RO-17
66T/RO-23
67CokeCap/DodgAngel-17
67OPC-160
67T-160
68T-208
68T/3D
69MB-73
69MLB/St-145
69MLBPA/Pin-40
69OPC-65
69T-65
69T/S-45
69T/St-41
69Trans-45
70MLB/St-49
70OPC-390
70T-390
70T/PI-3
70T/S-39
70T/Super-39
70Trans-2
71K-16
71MD
71MLB/St-101
71OPC-585
71T-585
71Ticket/Dodg-5
72Dimanche*-58
72Dimanche*-9
72K-3
72MB-88
72OPC-390
72T-390
72T/Cloth-9
73K-43
73OPC-35
73T-35
73T/Comics-6
73T/Lids-12
73T/PinUps-6
74K-45
74OPC-165
74T-165
74T/DE-42
74T/St-44
74T/Tr-165T
75OPC-10
75SSPC/18-11
75T-10
75T/M-10
76OPC-265
76SSPC-279
76T-265
77T-603
78TCMA-24
87Smok/Dodg-6
88Smok/Dodg-12
89Smok/Dodg-77
90Target-172
92Pinn-591M
93Rang/Keeb-123
Davison, Julio
(Coco)
91StCath/ClBest-25CO
91StCath/ProC-3412CO
Davison, Michael Lynn
(Mike)
71MLB/St-245
71OPC-276R
71T-276R
Davison, Nathan
91Adelaide/Fut-5
Davison, Scott
89James/ProC-2145
90Rockford/ProC-2699
90Rockford/Team-6
91WPalmB/ClBest-19
91WPalmB/ProC-1235
Davisson, Jay
83Reading-4
84Cram/PCL-213
85Cram/PCL-41
Dawley, Bill
79Nashvl
80Indianap-25
81Indianap-28
82Indianap-7
84D-328
84F-223
84F/St-108
84Mother/Ast-22
84Nes/792-248
84OPC-248
84T-248
84T/St-71
85D-354
85F-348
85Mother/Ast-16
85OPC-363
85T-634
86F-298
86F/Up-U32
86Mother/Ast-25
86T-376
87D-628
87F-493
87F/Up-U23
87Smok/Cards-9
87T-54
88D-331
88F-29
88S-328
88T-509
89Tacoma/CMC-5
89Tacoma/ProC-1555
Dawson, Andre Nolan
(Andre)
77Expo/PostC-2
77Expo/PostC-3
77T-473R
78OPC-180
78T-72
79OPC-179
79T-348
80OPC-124
80T-235
81D-212
81F-145
81F/St-123
81OPC-125
81OPC/Post-6
81PermaGr/AS-3
81T-125
81T/SO-90
81T/St-187
82D-88
82Expo/Hygrade-5
82F-187
82F/St-35
82FBI/Disc-6
82Hygrade
82OPC-341AS
82OPC-379
82OPC/Post-18
82PermaGr/AS-12
82Sqt-17
82T-341AS
82T-540
82T/St-125
82T/St-57
82T/StVar-57
82Zeller-10
82Zeller-14
82Zeller-4
83D-518
83D/AAS-9
83F-280
83F/St-12M
83F/St-5M
83OPC-173AS
83OPC-303
83OPC/St-164
83OPC/St-252
83PermaGr/AS-11
83PermaGr/CC-4
83Stuart-4
83T-402
83T-680
83T/St-164
83T/St-252
84D-97
84D/AAS-18
84Drake-9
84Expo/PostC-5
84F-273
84F/St-18
84F/St-25
84F/St-33
84MiltBrad-8
84Nes/792-200
84Nes/792-392AS
84Nestle/DT-16
84OPC-200
84OPC-392AS
84Ralston-6
84Seven-1C
84Seven-1E
84Seven-1W
84Stuart-11
84Stuart-36AS
84Stuart-37M
84T-200
84T-392AS
84T/Cereal-6
84T/Gloss22-18
84T/Gloss40-35
84T/RD-6M
84T/St-181
84T/St-92
84T/Super-20
85D-421
85D/HL-41
85F-394
85F/LimEd-8
85FunFood/Pin-22
85GenMills-2
85Leaf-133
85OPC-133
85OPC/Post-9
85Seven-7S
85T-420
85T/RD-7M
85T/St-86
86D-25DK
86D-87
86D/DKsuper-25
86Expo/Prov/Pan-9
86Expo/Prov/Post-9
86F-246
86F/Mini-53
86F/St-32
86GenMills/Book-6M
86Leaf-25DK
86OPC-256
86Provigo-9
86Seven/Coin-E13
86Sf-110
86Sf-66M
86T-576TL
86T-760
86T/St-74
86T/Tatt-20M
86TrueVal-29
87Berg/Cubs-8
87Classic/Up-124
87D-458
87D/HL-28
87D/HL-31
87D/OD-70
87F-316
87F/Hottest-13
87F/Slug-12
87F/St-33
87F/Up-U24
87Leaf-212
87OPC-345
87RedFoley/St-13
87Sf-139
87Stuart-3M
87T-345
87T/Board-10
87T/St-77
87T/Tr-27T
88AP/Test-2
88Berg/Cubs-8
88ChefBoy-18
88Classic/Blue-216
88Classic/Red-157
88D-269
88D-9DK
88D-BC10
88D/AS-36
88D/Best-225
88D/Cubs/Bk-269
88D/DKsuper-9DK
88D/PopUp-14
88Drake-16
88F-415
88F/AS-6
88F/AwardWin-9
88F/BB/AS-10
88F/BB/MVP-9
88F/Excit-13
88F/Hottest-9
88F/LL-9
88F/Mini-67
88F/RecSet-10
88F/SS-13
88F/Slug-12
88F/St-79
88F/TL-7
88FanSam-15
88Grenada-41
88Jiffy-8
88KMart-9
88KayBee-8
88KennerFig-28
88KingB/Disc-14
88Leaf-126
88Leaf-9DK
88Nestle-9
88OPC-247
88Panini/St-236M
88Panini/St-265
88RedFoley/St-17
88S-4
88S/WaxBox-16
88Sf-3
88T-401AS
88T-500
88T/Big-153
88T/Coins-33
88T/Gloss22-18
88T/Gloss60-1
88T/Mini-43
88T/Revco-2
88T/RiteAid-2
88T/St-148
88T/St-56
88T/St/Backs-13
88T/UK-20
88Woolwth-8
89B-298
89Cadaco-14
89Classic-37
89D-167
89D/AS-36
89D/Best-4
89D/MVP-BC8
89D/PopUp-36
89F-422
89F/BBAS-11
89F/BBMVP's-11
89F/Excit-11
89F/Heroes-12
89F/LL-12

89F/Superstar-12
89KayBee-9
89KennerFig-35
89MSA/Disc-14
89MSA/SS-2
89Mara/Cubs-8
89OPC-10
89Panini/St-230AS
89Panini/St-59
89RedFoley/St-33
89S-2
89S/HotStar-80
89S/Mast-28
89Sf-95
89T-10
89T-391AS
89T-4RB
89T/Ames-13
89T/Big-120
89T/Coins-11
89T/Crunch-10
89T/DH-17
89T/Gloss22-18
89T/Hills-11
89T/LJN-148
89T/Mini-3
89T/St-156
89T/St-5
89T/St-54
89T/St/Backs-48
89T/UK-21
89Tetley/Discs-14
89UD-205
89Woolwth-11
90B-39
90Classic-85
90Cub/Mara-6
90D-223
90D/BestNL-97
90D/Learning-52
90F-29
90F/Can-29
90HOF/St-96
90KayBee-8
90Kenner/Fig-23
90Leaf-177
90MLBPA/Pins-54
90MSA/Soda-24
90OPC-140
90OPC/BoxB-C
90Panini/St-240
90PublInt/St-192
90PublInt/St-256
90RedFoley/St-23
90S-265
90S/100St-74
90S/McDon-10
90Sf-108
90T-140
90T/Ames-9
90T/Big-91
90T/DH-17
90T/Gloss60-41
90T/HillsHM-15
90T/St-47
90T/TVCub-31
90T/WaxBox-C
90UD-357
90UD-73TC
90USPlayC/AS-9H
90Woolwth/HL-11
91B-429
91Cadaco-15
91Classic/200-26
91Classic/III-14
91Cub/Mara-8
91Cub/Vine-36MVP
91Cub/Vine-9
91D-129
91D-435AS
91D/Elite-E4
91DennyGS-14
91F-419A
91F-419B
91F-713M
91Kenner-13
91Leaf-400
91Leaf/Stud-153
91MajorLg/Pins-67
91OPC-640
91OPC/BoxB-D
91OPC/Premier-31
91Panini/FrSt-49
91Panini/St-41
91Pep/SS-2
91Post/Can-7
91RedFoley/St-118
91RedFoley/St-25
91S-445
91S/100SS-87
91Seven/3DCoin-2MW
91StCl-310
91Sunflower-14
91T-640
91T/CJMini/II-7
91T/SU-11
91T/WaxBox-D
91UD-454
91UD/Ext-725
91UD/FinalEd-98FAS
91USPlayC/AS-11C
91Ultra-58
91Woolwth/HL-9
92B-625
92Classic/Game200-27
92Classic/II-T24
92Cub/Mara-8
92D-119
92D-422AS
92D/Preview-4
92F-379
92F/TmLIns-20
92Hardee-7
92L-183
92L/BlkGold-183
92MooTown-15
92OPC-460
92OPC/Premier-45
92Panini-186
92Panini-285AS
92Pinn-115
92S-75
92S/100SS-48
92StCl-810
92StCl/Dome-33
92Studio-12
92Studio/Her-9
92T-460
92T/Gold-460
92T/GoldWin-460
92T/Kids-2
92T/McDonB-31
92T/MicroG-460
92TripleP-113AA
92TripleP-174
92UD-124
92UD/HRH-HR9
92USPlayC/Ace-3H
92USPlayC/Ace-6C
92USPlayC/Cub-1H
92USPlayC/Cub-9C
92Ultra-468
93B-495
93Cadaco-16
93Colla/DM-29
93D-632
93Duracel/PPI-3
93Expo/D/McDon-2
93F-377
93F/Final-173
93F/Final/DTrib-DT3
93F/Fruit-14
93Flair-162
93L-310
93OPC-35
93OPC/Premier-18
93Pac/Spanish-56
93Panini-97
93Pinn-497
93Pinn/Cooper-11
93Pinn/HRC-16
93Pinn/Slug-26
93S-552
93Select-9
93Select/RookTr-11T
93StCl-203
93StCl-655
93StCl/1stDay-203
93StCl/1stDay-655
93Studio-104
93T-265
93T/BlkGold-4
93T/Finest-84AS
93T/FinestASJ-84AS
93T/FinestRef-84AS
93T/Gold-265
93T/PreProd-4
93T/Tr-92T
93TripleP/Gal-GS2
93UD-308
93UD-777
93UD-832TC
93UD/FunPack-163
93UD/SP-201
93Ultra-509
94B-531
94D-448
94F-29
94Flair-13
94L-142
94OPC-138
94Pac/Cr-52
94Panini-28
94Pinn-320
94S-471
94Select-93
94Sf/2000-79
94StCl-371
94StCl/1stDay-371
94StCl/Gold-371
94Studio-161
94T-595
94T/Finest-50
94T/FinestRef-50
94T/Gold-595
94TripleP-203
94UD-96
94UD/ElecD-96
94UD/SP-154
94Ultra-13

Dawson, David
89Bakers/Cal-180

Dawson, Dwayne
92AubAs/ClBest-20
92AubAs/ProC-1348

Dawson, Gary
83Madis/Frit-24

Dawson, Joe
94Conlon-1311

Dawson, Larry
88AppFx/ProC-164

Day, Charles F.
(Boots)
70Expos/Pins-4
70T-654R
71Expo/ProS-5
71MLB/St-125
71OPC-42
71T-42
72OPC-254
72ProStars/PostC-3
72T-254
73OPC-307
73T-307
74Expo/West-3
74OPC-589
74T-589
74Weston-8
77Evansvl/TCMA-7

Day, Clyde Henry
(Pea Ridge)
90Target-173

Day, Dexter
83Water-16
84Cedar-13

Day, George
91AppFx/ClBest-17
91AppFx/ProC-1723

Day, Kevin
89Ashvl/ProC-943

Day, Leon
78Laugh/Black-5
90Negro/Star-13
91Negro/Lewis-6
92Negro/Kraft-1
92Negro/Retort-16
94TedW-103

Day, Mike
86WPalmB-11

Day, Ned
52Wheat*

Day, Paul
88Augusta/ProC-388

Day, Randy
86Phill/TastyK-x
86Portl-4
87Syrac/TCMA-31

Day, Steve 1
94FExcel-287

Day, Steve 2
77Newar

Day, Tim
91Adelaide/Fut-4

Dayett, Brian Kelly
(Brian)
79WHave-4
82Nashvl-9
83Colum-26
84Colum-4
84Colum/Pol-9
84D-45RR
85D-152
85F-125
85F/Up-U35
85Iowa-8
85SevenUp-24
85T-534
85T/Tr-29T
86T-284
87Berg/Cubs-24
87D/OD-73
87F/Up-U25
87T-369
88D-416
88F-416
88OPC-136
88S-205
88T-136
92Yank/WIZ80-41

Dayle, Snookie
94TedW-94

Dayley, Kenneth Grant
(Ken)
81Richm-19
82BK/Lids-7
82D-501
82Richm-25
83D-375
83F-135
83Richm-4
83T-314
84D-199
84F-176
84Nes/792-104
84T-104
84T/Tr-29
86D-303
86F-33
86KAS/Disc-2
86OPC-202
86Schnucks-5
86T-607
87D-357
87F-293
87T-59
88D-357
88D/Best-299
88F-30
88S-517
88Smok/Card-3
88T-234
89B-428
89D-299
89D/Best-268
89F-448
89OPC-396
89Smok/Cards-4
89T-409
89UD-114
90B-191
90D-281
90D/BestNL-22
90F-247
90F/Can-247
90Leaf-275
90OPC-561
90PublInt/St-216
90Richm/25Ann-7
90S-556
90Smok/Card-4
90T-561
90T/St-36
90T/TVCard-10
90UD-280
91B-27
91D-735
91F-630
91Leaf/Stud-134
91OPC-41
91OPC/Premier-32
91S-607
91S/ToroBJ-27
91StCl-552
91T-41
91Tor/Fire-46
91UD-628
91UD/Ext-781
92BJ/Fire-7
92OPC-717
92S-685
92StCl-137
92T-717
92T/Gold-717
92T/GoldWin-717
93BJ/D/45-30
93BJ/Fire-8

DeAngelis, Steve
86Reading-7
87Maine-13
88Phill/TastyK-27
88Reading/ProC-877
89QuadC/Best-29
89QuadC/GS-26
90MidldA/GS-3

DeArmas, Roly
87Clearw-19
88Martins/Star-10
90Martins/ProC-3209MG
91Martins/ClBest-29MG
92Martins/ClBest-30MG
92Martins/ProC-3075MG

DeBattista, Dan
77Salem

DeBerry, Joe
91Billing/SportP-14
91Billings/ProC-3759
91FrRow/DP-30
92Cedar/ClBest-14
92Cedar/ProC-1076
92ClBest-46
92StCl/Dome-34
92UD/ML-126

DeBerry, John Herman
(Hank)
25Exh-9
29Exh/4-4
90Target-175
E120
E126-30
R316
V61-101
W572
W573

DeBold, Rusty
85Miami-2

DeBord, Bob
83CharR-18

DeBottis, Marc
88Syrac/ProC-828

DeBrand, Genaro
90Niagara/Pucko-12

DeBriyn, Norm
90AR-28CO

DeBusschere, David A.
(Dave)
63T-54R
64T-247
65T-297
78TCMA-246

DeButch, Mike
86Beaum-9
87TexLgAS-1
87Wichita-1
88Wichita-10
89Jacks/GS-19
89Tidew/ProC-1959
90ProC/Singl-366
90T/TVMets-39
90Tidew/CMC-15
90Tidew/ProC-550
92London/ProC-639

DeChavez, Oscar
83Idaho-3
85Modesto/Chong-5

DeCillis, Dean
90AAASingl/ProC-384
92Toledo/ProC-1050

DeCinces, Douglas V.
(Doug)
75OPC-617R
75T-617R
75T/M-617R
76OPC-438
76SSPC-387
76T-438
77BurgChef-44
77Ho-15
77Ho/Twink-15

77OPC-228
77T-216
78Ho-10
78OPC-192
78T-9
79Ho-54
79OPC-217
79T-421
80OPC-322
80T-615
81D-352
81F-173
81F/St-90
81OPC-188
81T-188
82D-279
82F-162
82F/St-142
82OPC-174
82T-564
82T/St-142
82T/Tr-26T
83D-216
83F-85
83F/St-20M
83F/St-4M
83OPC-341
83OPC/St-155LCS
83OPC/St-171
83OPC/St-46
83PermaGr/CC-22
83Seven-7
83T-341
83T/St-155
83T/St-171
83T/St-46
84D-230
84D/AAS-6
84F-514
84Nes/792-790
84OPC-82
84Smok/Cal-7
84T-790
84T/St-229
85D-179
85D-2DK
85D/AAS-51
85D/DKsuper-2
85F-299
85FunFood/Pin-73
85Leaf-2DK
85OPC-111
85Smok/Cal-6
85T-111
85T/St-222
86D-57
86D/HL-39
86D/WaxBox-PC6
86F-153
86OPC-257
86Sf-173
86Smok/Cal-6
86T-257
86T/St-178
86T/Tatt-12M
87D-356
87D/OD-1
87F-77
87F/Hottest-14
87F/Mini-29
87F/St-34
87OPC-22
87Seven-W1
87Sf-106
87Sf/TPrev-11M
87Smok/Cal-17
87Stuart-16M
87T-22
87T/Gloss60-52
87T/St-182
88F-31
88OPC-141
88S-239
88Sf-185
88T-446
89Smok/Angels-16
91Crown/Orio-99
91LineD-19
91Swell/Great-23
93UD/ATH-39
94TedW-15

DeCordova, David
87StPete-14

DeCosta, Bob
83Visalia/Frit-8

DeDario, Joe
90Niagara/Pucko-31HOST

DeFillippis, Art
75Spokane/Caruso-20
76OPC-595R
76T-595R

DeFord, Logan
92MissSt-11

DeFrancesco, Anthony
85Greens-25
86WinHaven-7
87NewBrit-15
88Chatt/Best-7
88Nashvl/Team-7
89Chatt/Best-3
89Chatt/GS-8
90AAASingl/ProC-547
90Chatt/GS-10
90Nashvl/ProC-235
91AAA/LineD-255
91Nashvl/LineD-255
91Nashvl/ProC-2159
92Reno/Cal-39
92SoOreg/ClBest-30CO

DeFreites, Arturo S.
(Art)
76Indianap-4
77Indianap-20
78Indianap-22
80T-677R
91Pac/SenLg-77

DeGrasse, Tim
91Hamil/ClBest-2
91Hamil/ProC-4032
92Hamil/ClBest-15
92Hamil/ProC-1586

DeHart, Greg
78Newar
79BurlB-20
80BurlB-6
83SanJose-25

DeHart, Rick 1
87Birm/Best-28TR

DeHart, Rick 2
92Albany/ClBest-15
92Albany/ProC-2299

DeJardin, Bob
(Bobby)
88Oneonta/ProC-2044
89PrWill/Star-4
90Albany/Best-14
90Albany/ProC-1039
90Foil/Best-212
91AA/LineD-3
91Albany/LineD-3
91Albany/ProC-1015
92ColClip/Pol-16
92ColClip/ProC-358
92ColClip/SB-102
92OPC-179
92Sky/AAASingl-45
92T-179M
92T/Gold-179
92T/GoldWin-179

DeJardin, Brad
88Alaska/Team-8
91Kinston/ProC-336
91Sydney/Fut-13

DeJean, Mike
92Oneonta/ClBest-18
93Greens/ClBest-7
93Greens/ProC-880

DeJesus, Ivan
74Albuq/Team-5
76SSPC-76
78OPC-158
78SSPC/270-256
78T-152
79Ho-88
79OPC-209
79T-398
80OPC-349
80T-691
81Coke
81D-483
81F-297
81OPC-54
81T-54
81T/HT
81T/SO-94
81T/St-156
82D-14DK
82D-48
82F-593
82F/St-95
82OPC-313
82T-484
82T/St-32
82T/Tr-27T
83D-399
83F-157
83F/St-12M
83F/St-16M
83OPC-233
83OPC/St-271
83T-587
83T/St-271
84D-427
84F-26
84Nes/792-279
84OPC-279
84Phill/TastyK-29
84T-279
84T/St-121
85D-204
85F-248
85Phill/TastyK-11
85T-791
85T/Tr-30T
85ThomMc/Discs-28
86D-449
86F-34
86T-178
89Toledo/ProC-774
89UD-355
90EliteSenLg-4
90Kissim/DIMD-29MG
90Target-178
91Kissim/ProC-4205MG
92SanBern/ClBest-27MG
92SanBern/ProC-MG
92Yank/WIZ80-42

DeJesus, Jorge
78Newar
80BurlB-21

DeJesus, Jose
85FtMyr-12
85Tigres-19
86FtMyr-7
87Memphis-5
87Memphis/Best-9
88BBAmer-14
88Memphis/Best-18
89D-558
89F-280
89Omaha/CMC-6
89Omaha/ProC-1735
89UD/Ext-769
90AAASingl/ProC-294
90F-104
90F/Can-104
90F/Up-U42
90Leaf-415
90OPC-596
90S-587RP
90S/100Ris-95
90ScranWB/ProC-592
90Sf-131
90T-596
90UD-255
91D-596
91F-394
91Leaf-200
91OPC-232
91Phill/Medford-12
91S-623
91S/100RisSt-16
91StCl-104
91T-232
91UD-486
91Ultra-261
92D-300
92F-528
92OPC-471
92Pinn-172
92S-380
92T-471
92T/Gold-471
92T/GoldWin-471
92UD-631

DeJesus, Malvin
92Niagara/ClBest-4
92Niagara/ProC-3329

DeJohn, Mark Stephen
(Mark)
75Tidew/Team-8
80Evansvl-2
81Evansvl-13
83Evansvl-24
87Savan-26
88Spring/Best-26
89Johnson/Star-24MG
90Johnson/Star-28MG
91AAA/LineD-249MG
91Louisvl/LineD-249MG
91Louisvl/ProC-2932MG
91Louisvl/Team-30
92London/ProC-648MG

DeJohn, Mark
92London/SB-424MG

DeJonghe, Emile
V351A-9

DeKneef, Mike
91ClBest/Singl-171
91WinHaven/ClBest-17
91WinHaven/ProC-496
92NewBrit/ProC-440

DeKraai, Brad
81BurlB-21
82Beloit/Frit-22

DeLaCruz, Carlos
87DayBe-6
88Utica/Pucko-17
89SoBend/GS-12
90BirmB/Best-14
90BirmB/ProC-1102
93LimeR/Winter-32

DeLaCruz, Francisco
87Spokane-15

DeLaCruz, Gerry
77Clinton

DeLaCruz, Hector
87Dunedin-16
88Knoxvl/Best-8
89Syrac/CMC-18
89Syrac/MerchB-8
89Syrac/ProC-816
89Syrac/Team-8
90AAASingl/ProC-363
90ProC/Singl-346
90Syrac/CMC-20
90Syrac/MerchB-4
90Syrac/ProC-583
90Syrac/Team-4

DeLaCruz, Lorenzo
93MedHat/ProC-3749
93MedHat/SportP-20

DeLaCruz, Marcelino
92CharRain/ClBest-9
92Spokane/ProC-1299

DeLaHoya, Javier
89LittleSun-13
90VeroB/Star-10
90Yakima/Team-2
91Bakers/Cal-18
92VeroB/ClBest-22
92VeroB/ProC-2868
94B-178

DeLaHoz, Miguel A.
(Mike)
61T-191
62T-123
63Sugar-8
63T-561
64T-216
65OPC-182
65T-182
66T-346
67T-372

DeLaMata, Fred
87Miami-21

DeLaNuez, Rex
89Elizab/Star-24
90Foil/Best-118
90Kenosha/Best-2
90Kenosha/ProC-2305
90Kenosha/Star-8
91ClBest/Singl-147
91Visalia/ClBest-21
91Visalia/ProC-1753
92ClBest-199
92OrlanSR/ProC-2857
92OrlanSR/SB-503
92Sky/AASingl-216

DeLaRosa, Benny
77Charl
81Buffa-6

DeLaRosa, Cesar
87Spartan-24
88QuadC/GS-23
89PalmSp/Cal-43
89PalmSp/ProC-475

DeLaRosa, Domingo
87Pocatel/Bon-11
89Clinton/ProC-905

DeLaRosa, Francisco
89Freder/Star-4
90A&AASingle/ProC-3
90Hagers/Best-23
90Hagers/ProC-1406
90Hagers/Star-7
90ProC/Singl-764
90Rochester/L&U-29
91AAA/LineD-453
91RochR/LineD-453
91RochR/ProC-1895
92ColClip/Pol-4
92ColClip/Pol-4
92ColClip/ProC-344
92ColClip/SB-103
92StCl-61
92T/91Debut-44
93ColClip/Pol-3
93LimeR/Winter-39

DeLaRosa, Jesus
75Iowa/TCMA-10
80Knoxvl/TCMA-20
89Pac/SenLg-57

DeLaRosa, Juan
88Myrtle/ProC-1175
89Myrtle/ProC-1458
90Dunedin/Star-7
91AA/LineD-355
91Knoxvl/LineD-355
91Knoxvl/ProC-1779
92ClBest/Up-436
92Knoxvl/ProC-3002
92Knoxvl/SB-380
92UD/ML-73
93B-519
93ClBest/MLG-92
93FExcel/ML-241
93LimeR/Winter-28
93Syrac/ProC-1010

DeLaRosa, Maximo
92BurlInd/ClBest-30CL
92BurlInd/ProC-1670

DeLaRosa, Nelson
82AlexD-25
83AlexD-23
85Nashua-6

DeLancey, William P.
(Bill)
34DS-81
35Wheat
92Conlon/Sport-625
V355-15

DeLao, Mike
85Durham-17
88Fayette/ProC-1105
89London/ProC-1367
90EastLAS/ProC-EL48TR
91Fayette/ClBest-30TR

DeLeeuw, Karel
76Watlo

DeLeon, Felix
63Pep/Tul

DeLeon, Gerbacio
90Madison/Best-14

DeLeon, Huascar
90BBCity/Star-5
91BBCity/ClBest-13
92BBCity/ClBest-11

DeLeon, Jesus
87FtMyr-11
88AppFx/ProC-155
88MidwLAS/GS-39
89RedFoley/St-35

DeLeon, John
81Miami-7

DeLeon, Jose
81Buffa-4
82Portl-1
84D-628
84F-248
84Nes/792-581
84T-581
85D-308
85F-463
85OPC-385
85T-385
86D-235
86F-607

86OPC-75
86T-75
86T/Tatt-3M
87Coke/WS-16
87D-457
87F-494
87T-421
88D-59
88F-395
88F/St-15
88F/Up-U119
88OPC-23
88S-508
88S/Tr-7T
88Smok/Card-4
88T-634
88T/Big-194
88T/Tr-34T
89B-431
89D-437
89F-449
89OPC-107
89Panini/St-177
89S-115
89Smok/Cards-5
89T-107
89T/Mini-35
89UD-293
90B-186
90D-536
90D/BestNL-59
90F-248
90F/AwardWin-11
90F/Can-248
90Leaf-485
90OPC-257
90Panini/St-334
90PublInt/St-217
90RedFoley/St-25
90S-309
90Sf-76
90Smok/Card-6
90T-257
90T/Big-31
90T/Mini-74
90T/St-38
90T/TVCard-11
90UD-697
91B-400
91D-128
91F-631
91Leaf-190
91OPC-711
91Pol/Card-48
91S-221
91StCl-455
91T-711
91UD-220
91Ultra-288
92B-265
92D-246
92F-576
92L-227
92L/BlkGold-227
92OPC-85
92Panini-178
92Pinn-341
92Pol/Card-3
92S-81
92StCl-67
92T-85
92T/Gold-85
92T/GoldWin-85
92T/Kids-30
92UD-458
92USPlayC/Ace-7S
92Ultra-565
93D-464
93F-487
93Pac/Spanish-575
93Phill/Med-10
93StCl/Phill-25
93Ultra-438
94StCl/Team-130

DeLeon, Julio
87PortChar-20

DeLeon, Luis Antonio
(Luis)
80ArkTr-7
80Tacoma-27
81Chatt-4
82Charl-14
82D-588
82T-561R
83Charl-9
83D-296
83F-355
83F/St-4M
83OPC-323
83T-323
84D-162
84F-297
84Mother/Padres-17
84Nes/792-38
84Smok/Padres-6
84T-38
85D-406
85F-29
85Mother/Padres-11
85T-689
85ThomMc/Discs-29
86F-318
86T-286
87RochR-16
87RochR/TCMA-2
88Tucson/CMC-10
88Tucson/JP-8
88Tucson/ProC-174
89Calgary/CMC-1
91Crown/Orio-100

DeLeon, Paulo
73Cedar
74Cedar
75Dubuq

DeLeon, Pedro
86Ashvl-7
88Osceola/Star-8
89PrWill/Star-5
89Star/Wax-88

DeLeon, Pichy
84Maine-11

DeLeon, Rafael
86FtMyr-8

DeLeon, Roberto 1
89Sumter/ProC-1113
90BurlB/Best-11
90BurlB/ProC-2351
90BurlB/Star-10
90Foil/Best-166

DeLeon, Roberto 2
92Spokane/ClBest-12
92Spokane/ProC-1300

DeLeon, Yobanne
92AppFox/ClBest-16
92BBCity/ProC-3848

DeLima, Rafael
86Kenosha-8
87Kenosha-6
88BBAmer-15
88OrlanTw/Best-22
88SLAS-11
89Portl/CMC-23
89Portl/ProC-222
90Portl/CMC-22
90Portl/ProC-191
90ProC/Singl-574
91AA/LineD-478
91OrlanSR/LineD-478
91OrlanSR/ProC-1861
92OrlanSR/SB-504

DeLoach, Bobby
87Savan-1
89Savan/ProC-346
90FSLAS/Star-2
90StPete/Star-4
90Star/ISingl-62
91AA/LineD-356
91Knoxvl/LineD-356
91Knoxvl/ProC-1780

DeLoach, Lee
89GreatF-16

DeLosSantos, Alberto
89Princet/Star-5
91ClBest/Singl-152
91Salem/ClBest-5
91Salem/ProC-959
92CaroMud/ProC-1192
92CaroMud/SB-131
92Sky/AASingl-62
93CaroMud/RBI-24
93LimeR/Winter-138

DeLosSantos, German
75Cedar
76Cedar

DeLosSantos, Luis
85FtMyr-28
86Memphis/GoldT-5
86Memphis/SilverT-5
86SLAS-9
87Omaha-25
88AAA/ProC-30
88Omaha/CMC-22
88Omaha/ProC-1506
88TripleA/ASCMC-2
89AAA/CMC-2
89D-562
89D/Rook-33
89F-646M
89F/Up-37
89Omaha/ProC-1729
89Panini/St-347
89S-648
89S/HotRook-52
89UD-12
90AAASingl/ProC-605
90Classic-9
90F-105
90F/Can-105
90HotRook/St-14
90OPC-452
90Omaha/CMC-11
90Omaha/ProC-70
90ProC/Singl-186
90S-659
90S/100Ris-100
90S/DTRook-B4
90T-452
90TripleAAS/CMC-2
91B-152
93Edmon/ProC-1142
93LimeR/Winter-19

DeLosSantos, Mariano
92Augusta/ClBest-14
92Augusta/ProC-231
93LimeR/Winter-10

DeLosSantos, Pedro
89Ashvl/ProC-951

DeLosSantos, Ramon
75Iowa/TCMA-11
84Cram/PCL-76
92Batavia/ClBest-8
92Batavia/ProC-3276

DeLosSantos, Reynoldo
91Martins/ClBest-5
91Martins/ProC-3466

DeLuca, Kurt
85LitFalls-16
86Columbia-8

DeLucia, Richard
(Rich)
86Cram/NWL-121
88SanBern/Best-8
88SanBern/Cal-50
89Wmsprt/ProC-649
89Wmsprt/Star-5
90A&AASingle/ProC-134
90Foil/Best-228
90SanBern/Best-2
90SanBern/Cal-88
90SanBern/ProC-2626
90Star/ISingl-48
90Wmsprt/Star-4
91B-242
91CounHrth-27
91D-426RR
91D/Rook-2
91F/UltraUp-U50
91F/Up-U52
91Leaf-222
91S-728RP
91S/Rook40-37
91T/90Debut-38
91T/Tr-31T
91UD/Ext-727
92B-665
92D-118
92F-278
92F/RookSIns-11
92L-155
92L/BlkGold-155
92OPC-686
92OPC/Premier-171
92Pinn-388
92S-135
92S/100RisSt-54
92S/Impact-6
92StCl-511
92T-686
92T/Gold-686
92T/GoldWin-686
92UD-637
92Ultra-122
93D-185
93F-673
93Mother/Mar-18
93Pac/Spanish-284
93StCl-402
93StCl/1stDay-402
93T-152
93T/Gold-152
94Pac/Cr-567

DeMaestri, Joseph P.
(Joe)
52T-286
54B-147
55B-176
55Rodeo
56Rodeo
56T-161
57T-44
58T-62
59T-64
60L-139
60T-358
61T-116
92Yank/WIZ60-34

DeMars, William L.
(Billy)
50B-252
51B-43
52Park-8
73OPC-486CO
73T-486CO
74OPC-119CO
74T-119CO
78SSPC/270-45CO
82Zeller-9
83Expo/PostC-4CO
83Stuart-11CO
84Expo/PostC-6CO
84Stuart-3CO
86TexGold-CO

DeMeo, Bob M.
79OkCty
81OkCty/TCMA-21

DeMerit, John Stephen
(John)
61T-501
62Salada-192
62Shirriff-192
62T-4
78TCMA-129
91WIZMets-93

DeMerit, Thomas
88VeroB/Star-5

DeMerritt, Martin
75BurlB
76Dubuq
83Clinton/Frit-25
85Fresno/Pol-2CO
86Shrev-6
87Shrev-24
88Phoenix/CMC-25M
88Phoenix/ProC-67
89Phoenix/CMC-7
89Phoenix/ProC-1486
92Erie/ProC-1643

DeMola, Donald John
(Don)
72Dimanche*-10
75OPC-391
75T-391
75T/M-391
76OPC-571
76T-571

DeMontreville, Eugene
90Target-180
E107

DeMoss, Bingo
74Laugh/Black-4
86Negro/Frit-66
90Negro/Star-6

DeMoss, Dave
92Geneva/ClBest-21
92Geneva/ProC-1571

DeMuth, Dana
88TM/Umpire-53
89TM/Umpire-51
90TM/Umpire-49

DeMuth, Don
89Spartan/ProC-1056

DePalo, Jim
79TCMA-82

DePastino, Rich
87Myrtle-22
88Dunedin/Star-5
89Myrtle/ProC-1628
90Dunedin/Star-8

DePew, Daren
88Boise/ProC-1627

DePrimo, John
85Greens-28

DeRicco, John
90Geneva/ProC-3043
90Geneva/Star-8

DeRosa, Tom
77Newar
78BurlB

DeRosa, Tony
75FtLaud/Sus-9
80Syrac/Team-8TR
81Syrac-24TR

DeSa, Joseph
(Joe)
79ArkTr-10
81Louisvl-7
82Louisvl-6
83Louisvl/Riley-7
85Coke/WS-20
86BuffB-10
86D-546
86T-313

DeSalvo, Steve
85FtMyr-22

DeSantis, Dominic
91Martins/ClBest-24
91Martins/ProC-3446
92Spartan/ProC-1258

DeSanto, Tom
79Elmira-27

DeSapio, Jim
88AubAs/ProC-1968
89AubAs/ProC-2172

DeShields, Delino
88MidwLAS/GS-44
88OPC-88DP
88Rockford-10
89BBAmAA/BPro-AA15
89Jaxvl/Best-15
89Jaxvl/ProC-152
89Rockford-10
89SLAS-5
90B-119
90Classic-55
90Classic/III-95
90D-42RR
90D/BestNL-116
90D/Learning-47
90D/Rook-6
90F-653R
90F/Can-653
90F/Up-U27
90Leaf-193
90OPC-224
90S-645RP
90S/YS/II-3
90T-224
90T/Big-231
90UD/Ext-702M
90UD/Ext-746
91B-445
91Bz-14
91Cadaco-16
91Classic/200-134
91Classic/I-61
91Classic/II-T71
91D-11DK
91D-555
91D-BC16
91D/BC-BC16
91D/SuperDK-11DK
91F-228
91Kenner-14
91Leaf-139
91Leaf/Stud-195
91MajorLg/Pins-78
91OPC-432
91OPC/Premier-34
91Panini/FrSt-140
91Panini/St-69
91Post/Can-1
91RedFoley/St-27
91S-545
91S/100RisSt-55
91StCl-194
91StCl/Charter*-6
91T-432
91T/90Debut-39
91T/CJMini/II-35
91T/JumboR-8

91ToysRUs-7
91UD-364
91Ultra-200
92B-47
92Classic/Game200-38
92Classic/II-T34
92D-277
92Expo/D/Duri-6
92F-476
92Hardee-8
92L-138
92L/BlkGold-138
92OPC-515
92OPC/Premier-163
92Panini-203
92Pinn-24
92Pinn/Team2000-22
92S-16
92StCl-505
92Studio-54
92T-515
92T/Gold-515
92T/GoldWin-515
92T/Kids-9
92TripleP-209
92UD-167
92UD-36TC
92UD/ASFF-4
92Ultra-220
93B-424
93Classic/GameI-25
93Colla/DM-30
93D-564
93Duracel/PPII-22
93Expo/D/McDon-3
93F-74
93F/ASNL-2
93F/Fruit-15
93Flair-81
93HumDum/Can-35
93Kraft-21
93L-268
93L/GoldAS-5M
93OPC-183
93OPC/Premier-7
93Pac/Spanish-183
93Panini-226
93Pinn-121
93Pinn-302I
93Pinn/TP-5
93Pinn/Team2001-12
93S-145
93Select-43
93Select/StatL-59
93StCl-78
93StCl/1stDay-78
93StCl/MPhoto-2
93Studio-150
93T-368
93T/BlkGold-5
93T/Finest-168
93T/FinestRef-168
93T/Gold-368
93ToysRUs-61
93TripleP-102
93UD-142
93UD-454IN
93UD-481M
93UD/FunPack-94
93UD/Iooss-WI10
93UD/SP-102
93USPlayC/Ace-7H
93Ultra-66
94B-454
94D-350
94D/Special-350
94F-535
94Finest-270
94Kraft-19
94L-277
94OPC-59
94Pac/Cr-377
94Panini-209
94Pinn-147
94Pinn/Artist-147
94Pinn/Museum-147
94S-38
94S/GoldR-38
94Studio-67
94T-109
94T/Gold-109
94TripleP-83
94UD-465
94UD/CollC-92
94UD/CollC/Gold-92
94UD/CollC/Silv-92
94UD/SP-76
94Ultra-515

DeSilva, John
87BYU-6
89Niagara/Pucko-6
90FSLAS/Star-30
90Lakeland/Star-8
91B-148
91London/LineD-381
91London/ProC-1869
92B-229
92Sky/AAASingl-269
92Toledo/ProC-1035
92UD/ML-137

DeSimone, Jerry
81Hawaii-7
82Hawaii-7
83LasVegas/BHN-6
84Cram/PCL-223

DeSonnaville, Erik
89AS/Cal-53UMP

DeVincenzo, Rich 1
83AppFx/Frit-7

DeVincenzo, Rich 2
86BirmB/Team-27

DeViveiros, Bernie
94Conlon-1282

DeVoe, Dan
92Kinston/ClBest-29TR
93Kinston/Team-29TR

DeVormer, Albert E.
(Al)
E120
E121/120
W501-105
W513-80
W572
W573
W575

DeWillis, Jeff
88S-583

DeWitt, William O.
63FrBauer-4
W753

DeWolf, Rob
85Beloit-7
86Stockton-6
87ElPaso-6
88ElPaso/Best-14
89Wichita/Rock-9
89Wichita/Rock/Up-15

DeWright, Wayne
78Dunedin

DeYoung, Rob
87BurlEx-28
88WPalmB/Star-8
89WPalmB/Star-9

Deabenderfer, Blaine
87Madis-22

Deak, Brian
87Sumter-26
88BurlB/ProC-27
88MidwLAS/GS-16
89Durham/Star-9
89Durham/Team-9
89Star/Wax-71
90Durham/Team-4
91AA/LineD-206
91Greenvl/ClBest-12
91Greenvl/LineD-206
91Greenvl/ProC-3006
92Richm/Bleach-13
92Richm/Comix-5
92Richm/ProC-380
92Richm/SB-428
93Calgary/ProC-1168
93StCl/Mar-5

Deak, Darrel
88Alaska/Team-7
89Alaska/Team-12
91Johnson/ClBest-6
91Johnson/ProC-3982
92Spring/ClBest-18
93StCl/Card-11
94B-620

Deal, Charles Albert
(Charlie)
21Exh-34
D327
D328-40
D329-44
D350/2-46
E121/80
E122
E135-40
E220
M101/4-44
M101/5-46
V100
W514-18
W575

Deal, Ellis Fergason
(Cot)
54Hunter
54T-192
60T-459C
78Colum
79OkCty
81OkCty/TCMA-22
82OkCty-5
94T/Arc54-192

Deal, Jamon
92Belling/ClBest-7
92Belling/ProC-1434

Deal, Lindsay
90Target-927

Dealey, Patrick E.
(Pat)
N172

Dean, Alfred Lovill
(Chubby)
40PlayBall-193

Dean, Bob
73Cedar
75Dubuq

Dean, Chris
92LitSun/HSPros-10

Dean, Jay Hanna
(Dizzy)
32Orbit/num-14
32Orbit/un-15
33CJ/Pin-4
33G-223
34G-6
34Ward's/Pin-1
35BU-64
35Exh/4-8
35G-1A
35G-2A
35G-6A
35G-7A
35Wheat
36Exh/4-8
37Exh/4-8
38Exh/4-3
38ONG/Pin-5
38Wheat-1
39Exh
50Callahan
50W576-24
60NuCard-14M
61GP-8
61NuCard-476M
74Laugh/ASG-36
76Rowe-3
76Shakey-63
77Galasso-52
80Laugh/FFeat-5
80Marchant/HOF-8
80Pac/Leg-12
80Perez/HOF-66
80SSPC/HOF
81Conlon-21
83D/HOF-29
86Conlon/1-10
86Sf/Dec-14M
88Conlon/4-8
88Conlon/NatAS-5
88Grenada-27
90BBWit-71
90Perez/GreatMom-18
90Swell/Great-6
91Conlon/Proto-34
91Conlon/Sport-3
91Homer/Classic-8
91LineD-50
91Swell/Great-138
91T/Arc53-326M
92Card/McDon/Pac-15
92Conlon/Col-19
92Conlon/Sport-428
92Conlon/Sport-635
93AP/ASG-106
93AP/ASG24K-40G
93Conlon-928
93Spectrum/HOFI-5
93UD/ATH-38
94Conlon-1109
94Conlon-1170
94Conlon/Pr-1170
94TedW-82
PM10/Sm-35
PR1-4
R300
R305
R308-202
R310
R311/Gloss
R313A-3
R332-31
R332-35
R423-21
RiceStix
V351A-8
V354-55
V355-19
V94-11

Dean, Jeff
83Miami-11

Dean, Jimmy
92Negro/RetortII-7

Dean, John
77Salem

Dean, Kevin
87WPalmB-9
88Jaxvl/Best-13
88Jaxvl/ProC-984
89Indianap/CMC-21
89Indianap/ProC-1225
90AAASingl/ProC-204
90Greenvl/Star-6
90ProC/Singl-625
90Tucson/CMC-23
90Tucson/ProC-214
91AA/LineD-556
91Jacks/LineD-556
91Jacks/ProC-936
92Jacks/SB-330

Dean, Paul Dee
(Daffy)
35BU-143
35Exh/4-8
35Wheat
36Exh/4-8
39PlayBall-19
40PlayBall-156
60NuCard-14M
61NuCard-476M
81Conlon-22
88Conlon/3-9
92Conlon/Sport-363
92Conlon/Sport-631
94Conlon-1170M
94Conlon/Pr-1170M
R313A-4
RiceStix

Dean, Roger
85Utica-9

Dean, Steve
90OK-10

Dean, Tommy Douglas
(Tommy)
69T-641R
70OPC-234
70T-234
71MLB/St-225
71OPC-364
71T-364
90Target-174

Dearse, Ed
46Remar-14

Dease, Don'l
90Idaho/ProC-3247

Deasley, Thomas H.
(Pat)
E223
N172
N403

Debee, Rich
90Omaha/CMC-23CO

Debrand, Rafael
93StCath/ClBest-7
93StCath/ProC-3985

Debus, John Eric
81VeroB-4
84Cram/PCL-164
86Albuq-5
87Albuq/Pol-15
88Albuq/CMC-15
88Albuq/ProC-269
89Albuq/CMC-12
89Albuq/ProC-76
90SanAn/GS-3CO
91VeroB/ProC-792CO
92GreatF/SportP-29MG

Debutch, Mike
90AAASingl/ProC-281
92London/SB-405

Decatur, A.R.
(Art)
25Exh-10
27Exh-21
90Target-176

Decillis, Dean
88Lakeland/Star-9
89London/ProC-1372
90ProC/Singl-397
90Toledo/CMC-20
90Toledo/ProC-154
91AA/LineD-380
91London/LineD-380
91London/ProC-1883
92Toledo/SB-583

Deck, Todd
85Clovis-12

Decker, Dee Martin
(Marty)
82OkCty-22
83Portl-18
84Cram/PCL-226
85Cram/PCL-107

Decker, Edward
N172

Decker, George Henry
(Joe)
71MLB/St-30
71OPC-98
71T-98
72T-612
73OPC-311
73T-311
74OPC-469
74T-469
74T/St-206
75Ho-96
75OPC-102
75T-102
75T/M-102
76OPC-636
76SSPC-210
76T-636
78SanJose-6
78Twin/Frisz-29
79Spokane-12
82SLCity-25
83SLCity-10
89T/SenLg-112
90Niagara/Pucko-29CO
91Pac/SenLg-101

Decker, Steve
89SanJose/Best-11
89SanJose/Cal-227
89SanJose/ProC-446
89SanJose/Star-6
89Star/Wax-84
90A&AASingle/ProC-72
90Shrev/ProC-1445
90Shrev/Star-5
90TexLgAS/GS-24
91B-622
91Classic/200-198
91Classic/I-7
91Classic/II-T100
91Classic/II-T64
91D-428RR
91F-260
91Leaf-441
91Leaf/Stud-260M
91Leaf/StudPrev-16
91Mother/Giant-3
91OPC/Premier-33
91PG&E-13
91S-710RP
91S/ASFan-2
91S/HotRook-8
91S/Rook40-12
91SFExam/Giant-7
91Seven/3DCoin-4NC
91StCl-569
91T/90Debut-37
91T/Tr-29T
91UD-25SR
91Ultra-319
92AAA/ASG/SB-381

92D-389
92F-633
92OPC-593
92Panini-211
92Phoenix/ProC-2824
92Phoenix/SB-381
92Pinn-63
92S-317
92S/100RisSt-56
92Sky/AAASingl-175
92StCl-417
92T-593
92T/Gold-593
92T/GoldWin-593
92UD-173
92Ultra-289
93D-260
93D-768
93F-425
93Pac/Spanish-459
93Pinn-233
93S-653
93StCl-692
93StCl/1stDay-692
93StCl/Marlin-15
93T-544
93T/Gold-544
93UD-744
93USPlayC/Marlin-4S
93USPlayC/Marlin-8C
93Ultra-372
Dede, Artie
90Target-928
Dedeaux, Raoul
(Rod)
85T-389OLY
90Smok/SoCal-4CO
90Target-177
Dedmon, Jeffrey L.
(Jeff)
81Durham-17
82Durham-16
84T/Tr-30
85D-554
85F-323
85Richm-4
85T-602
86D-443
86F-513
86Pol/Atl-49
86T-129
87D-314
87F-514
87Smok/Atl-7
87T-373
88D-325
88F-537
88Gator-50
88S-498
88T-469
89Indianap/ProC-1214
Dedos, Felix
87WinHaven-2
89WinHaven/Star-3
Dedrick, James
91Kane/ClBest-5
91Kane/ProC-2653
91Kane/Team-4
92Freder/ClBest-15
Dedrick, Tim
92Freder/ProC-1799
Dee, Mike
92MN-20M
Deer, Robert George
(Rob)
79Cedar/TCMA-28
80Clinton-20
84Cram/PCL-4
85F-648R
85Mother/Giants-25
86F-538
86F/Up-U33
86Pol/Brew-45
86T-249
86T/Tr-31T
87Classic-43
87Classic/Up-141
87D-274
87D/OD-57
87F-344
87F/BB-14
87F/Excit-15
87F/Mini-30
87OPC-188
87Pol/Brew-45
87Sf-172
87Sf/TPrev-19M
87T-547
87T/Coins-10
87T/Gloss60-22
87T/Mini-59
87T/St-194
88D-274
88D/Best-109
88F-163
88F/St-36
88KennerFig-29
88OPC-33
88Panini/St-128
88Pol/Brew-45
88RedFoley/St-18
88S-95
88Sf-183
88T-33
88T/Big-151
88T/St-198
89B-146
89Brewer/YB-45
89Classic-39
89D-173
89D/Best-71
89F-184
89Gard-4
89KennerFig-36
89OPC-364
89Panini/St-376
89Pol/Brew-45
89RedFoley/St-34
89S-72
89Sf-111
89T-364
89T-759TL
89T/Big-78
89T/St-202
89UD-442
90B-401
90Brewer/MillB-4
90D-55
90F-320
90F/Can-320
90Leaf-322
90MLBPA/Pins-80
90OPC-615
90Panini/St-102
90Pol/Brew-45
90PublInt/St-494
90RedFoley/St-24
90S-390
90Sf-137
90T-615
90T/Big-74
90T/St-204
90UD-176
91B-132
91CokeK/Tiger-44
91D-729
91F-580
91F/Up-U23
91Leaf-237
91Leaf/Stud-52
91OPC-192
91Panini/FrSt-209
91RedFoley/St-26
91S-248
91S/RookTr-47T
91StCl-539
91T-192
91T/Tr-30T
91UD-272
91UD/Ext-726
92B-363
92D-532
92F-132
92L-193
92L/BlkGold-193
92OPC-441
92Panini-109
92Pinn-348
92S-56
92StCl-92
92Studio-172
92T-441
92T/Gold-441
92T/GoldWin-441
92UD-294
92USPlayC/Tiger-11C
92USPlayC/Tiger-5S
92Ultra-58
93B-332
93D-231
93D/LongBall-LL1
93D/Spirit-SG10M
93F-225
93L-246
93Pac/Spanish-106
93Panini-119
93Pinn-167
93Pinn/HRC-15
93S-636
93Select-186
93Select/RookTr-2T
93StCl-357
93StCl/1stDay-357
93Studio-26
93T-243
93T/Gold-243
93Tiger/Gator-5
93TripleP-137
93UD-217
93UD/SP-235
93USPlayC/Ace-5C
93Ultra-195
94D-74
94F-30
94S-475
94StCl-139
94StCl/1stDay-139
94StCl/Gold-139
94T-531
94T/Gold-531
94UD/CollC-90
94UD/CollC/Gold-90
94UD/CollC/Silv-90
Dees, Charles Henry
(Charlie)
64T-159
Degifico, Vincent
(Vince)
87Elmira/Black-16
87Elmira/Red-16
89Star/IISingl-119
89WinHaven/Star-4
90NewBrit/Best-16
90NewBrit/ProC-1325
90NewBrit/Star-3
Deguero, Jerry
86Modesto-7
Dehart, Rick
92Albany/ClBest-15
92Albany/ProC-2299
Dehdashtion, Derek
92Rockford/ClBest-14
92Rockford/ProC-2118
Deidel, Jim
92Yank/WIZ70-41
Deiley, Lou
87Ashvl-23
88Osceola/Star-7
Deisel, Pat
90Target-929
Deitz, Tim
86Cedar/TCMA-5
88Chatt/Best-15
89Greenvl/Best-12
89Greenvl/ProC-1175
89Greenvl/Star-5
Dejak, Tom
78Dunedin
80Knoxvl/TCMA-16
Dejarld, John
90GreatF/SportP-24
Dejulio, Frank
80Cedar-15
Dekneef, Mike
92NewBrit/SB-481
DelGreco, Robert G.
(Bobby)
52T-353
53T-48
57T-94
60T-486
61T-154
61T/St-53
62Salada-16
62Shirriff-16
62T-548
63J-91
63P-91
63T-282
78TCMA-259
91T/Arc53-48
DelOrbe, Chico
75Lafay
DelPozo, Roberto
90SanBern/Best-10
90SanBern/Cal-104
90SanBern/ProC-2643
91Penin/ClBest-23
91Penin/ProC-388
DelRosario, Manny
83Miami-18
DelRosario, Maximo
83Ander-16
85Durham-6
86Durham-8
87Greenvl/Best-18
88Greenvl/Best-17
89Greenvl/Best-11
89Greenvl/ProC-1161
89Greenvl/Star-6
90Greenvl/ProC-1123
90Greenvl/Star-7
DelRosario, Sergio
83Miami-6
DelVecchio, Jim
77Clinton
DelVecchio, Nick
92Oneonta/ClBest-19
DelaCruz, Anthony
89BurlInd/Star-8
89Star/IISingl-177
Delafield, Glenn
92GulfCY/ProC-3701
Delahanty, Edward J.
(Ed)
50Callahan
50W576-25
72F/FFeat-38
72Laugh/GF-10
75F/Pion-10
76Shakey-33
80Perez/HOF-33
80SSPC/HOF
89HOF/St-31
90BBWit-70
N142
N172
N300/SC
Delahanty, Frank G.
(Frank)
14CJ-81
15CJ-81
T206
Delahanty, James C.
(Jim)
10Domino-31
11Helmar-30
12Sweet/Pin-23
E104
E107
E254
E300
E91
E93
E96
M116
S74-14
T202
T205
T206
T207
W555
Delahanty, Joseph
C46-67
Delancer, Julio
86Kenosha-7
Delaney, Sean
93Rockford/ClBest-10
Delany, Dennis
79ArkTr-16
81ArkTr-4
Delarwelle, Chris
90Foil/Best-229
91Visalia/ClBest-14
91Visalia/ProC-1746
92OrlanSR/ProC-2852
92ProC/Tomorrow-96
Delas, Mickey
88Bristol/ProC-1883
89Fayette/ProC-1590
Delbianco, Ronnie
52Laval-29
Delgado, Alex
90WinHaven/Star-4
91LynchRS/ClBest-16
91LynchRS/ProC-1206
92WinHaven/ProC-1779
Delgado, Carlos
89StCath/ProC-2077
90A&AASingle/ProC-184
90StCath/ProC-3454
91ClBest/Singl-63
91Myrtle/ClBest-12
91Myrtle/ProC-2946
91SALAS/ProC-SAL37
92B-127
92ClBest-90
92ClBest/BBonusC-6
92ClBest/RBonus-BC6
92Dunedin/ClBest-20
92Dunedin/ProC-2003
92ProC/Tomorrow-170
92Syrac/MerchB-4
92UD/ML-264
92UD/ML-53DS
92UD/POY-PY4
93B-379
93B-693FOIL
93ClBest/Fisher-4
93ClBest/MLG-87
93ClBest/MLGPrev-5
93ClBest/Pr-2
93FExcel/ML-242
93FExcel/MLAS-6
93Knoxvl/ProC-1252
93StCl-520
93StCl/1stDay-520
93T-701M
93T/Gold-701M
93UD-425TP
93UD/SP-275FOIL
94B-341
94B-637
94D-568
94F/MLP-9
94Finest-423
94Flair-117
94Flair/Wave-2
94L/GRook-10
94OPC-100
94OPC/HotPros-5
94Pinn-413
94Pinn/New-18
94Pinn/RookTPinn-1
94S-614
94S/Boys-45
94Select-193
94Select/RookSurg-4
94StCl/Team-168
94Studio-27
94TripleP-296
94UD-8
94UD/CollC-4
94UD/CollC/Gold-4
94UD/CollC/Silv-4
94UD/ElecD-8
94UD/HoloFX-7
94UD/Mantle-6
94UD/SP-41
94Ultra-437
94Ultra/AllRook-2
Delgado, Eugenio
92Kane/Team-7
Delgado, Howard
94T-686M
94T/Gold-686M
Delgado, Juan
83DayBe-19
86ColumAst-10
87Osceola-22
Delgado, Luis Felipe
(Luis)
78SanJose-14
Delgado, Pablo
89Geneva/ProC-1879
90Hunting/ProC-3296
Delgado, Richard
91Elmira/ClBest-19
91Elmira/ProC-3265
91WinHaven/ClBest-29
Delgado, Roberto
92Clinton/ClBest-7
93LimeR/Winter-130
Delgado, Tim
90Geneva/ProC-3045
90Miami/II/Star-4
91Peoria/ClBest-4
91Peoria/ProC-1335

91Peoria/Team-6
92WinSalem/ClBest-14
92WinSalem/ProC-1203
Delgatti, Scott
75FtLaud/Sus-27
Delima, Rafael
90AAASingl/ProC-261
Delker, Edward
V94-12
Delkus, Pete
88Kenosha/ProC-1398
88MidwLAS/GS-35
89OrlanTw/Best-13
89OrlanTw/ProC-1331
90AAASingl/ProC-242
90Portl/CMC-5
90Portl/ProC-172
90ProC/Singl-557
91OrlanSR/ProC-1843
Dell, Tim
88Batavia/ProC-1674
89Spartan/ProC-1052
89Spartan/Star-6
89Star/Wax-54
90Clearw/Star-5
91Stockton/ProC-3026
92ElPaso/ProC-3914
92ElPaso/SB-205
Dell, William George
(Wheezer)
16FleischBrd-23
D328-41
WG7-12
Deller, Bob
90Oneonta/ProC-3388
91Greens/ProC-3071
92FtLaud/ProC-2625
Deller, Tom
87Anchora-6
89Welland/Pucko-10
90Salem/Star-3
DelliCarri, Joseph
(Joe)
88CapeCod/Sum-16
89Pittsfld/Star-3
90Jacks/GS-9
90StLucie/Star-5
91AA/LineD-630
91Wmsprt/LineD-630
91Wmsprt/ProC-300
92Bingham/ProC-523
92Bingham/SB-53
Delmas, Bert
90Target-930
Delmonte, John
82Lynch-4
Delock, Ivan Martin
(Ike)
52B-250
52T-329
55B-276
56T-284
57T-63
58T-328
59T-437
60T-336
61T-268
61T/St-110
62T-201
63T-136
91Crown/Orio-101
Delpiano, Marc
89BurlInd/Star-9
90Watertn/Star-7
Delsing, James Henry
(Jim)
47Signal
51B-279
52B-157
52T-271
53B/BW-44
53T-239
53Tiger/Glen-4
54B-55
54RM-AL24
54T-111
55B-274
55T-192
56T-338
59T-386
91T/Arc53-239
94T/Arc54-111
Delucchi, Ron
86PrWill-8
Delvecchio, Nick
93Greens/ClBest-8
93Greens/ProC-890
94ClBest/Gold-82
94FExcel-101
Delyon, Gene
77Holyo
Delzer, Ed
85MidldA-22
86Kinston-4
Demaree, Albert W.
(Al)
14CJ-92
15CJ-92
37Wheat
94Conlon-1216
D329-45
D350/2-47
M101/4-45
M101/5-47
PM1-4
Demaree, Joseph F.
(Frank)
33G-224
35BU-166
38G-244
38G-268
38ONG/Pin-6
39PlayBall-34
40PlayBall-90
41PlayBall-58
91Conlon/Sport-212
WG8-12
Dembowski, Steve
79Newar-7
Demers, Tony
45Parade*-16
Demerson, Tim
90Tampa/DIMD-3
92FtLaud/ClBest-21
92FtLaud/Team-6
92Greens/ProC-791
Demery, Lawrence C.
(Larry)
75OPC-433
75T-433
75T/M-433
76OPC-563
76SSPC-564
76T-563
77T-607
78T-138
Demeter, Donald Lee
(Don)
58T-244
59T-324
60BB-14
60T-234
60Union/Dodg-4
61BB-16
61T-23
62J-195
62P-195
62P/Can-195
62Salada-170
62Shirriff-170
62T-146
62T/St-167
62T/bucks
63F-53
63J-180
63P-180
63T-268
64Det/Lids-4
64T-58
64T/Coins-116
65T-429
66OPC-98
66T-98
67CokeCap/RedSox-3
67T-572
67T/Test/RSox-4
78TCMA-198
79TCMA-237
90Target-179
Demeter, Stephen
(Steve)
60Maple-5
61BeeHive-6
77Salem
79BuffB/TCMA-7
80Buffa-16
87Salem-29
Demeter, Todd
85Spring-6
Demetral, Chris
91Yakima/ClBest-7
91Yakima/ProC-4252
92Bakers/Cal-8
94ClBest/Gold-184
94FExcel-212
Demetre, Doug
90Oneonta/ProC-3383
Demmitt, Charles R.
(Ray)
C46-11
D303
E106
E254
E270/1
E90/1
M116
T206
T213/blue
T214-6
T216
T222
Demoran, Joe
43Centen-5
44Centen-4
45Centen-4
Dempsay, Adam
87Lakeland-24
88GlenF/ProC-932
Dempsey, Cornelius F.
(Con)
48Sommer-3
49Sommer-4
52T-44
Dempsey, Jack
33SK*-17
Dempsey, John Rikard
(Rick)
72T-778R
74OPC-569
74Syrac/Team-4
74T-569
75OPC-451
75Syrac/Team-3
75Syrac/Team-4
75T-451
75T/M-451
76OPC-272
76SSPC-438
76SSPC/MetsY-Y12
76T-272
77T-189
78T-367
79Ho-73
79OPC-312
79T-593
80OPC-51
80T-91
81D-113
81F-177
81OPC-132
81T-615
81T/St-38
82D-77
82F-163
82F/St-146
82OPC-262
82T-489
83D-329
83F-58
83OPC-138
83OPC/St-30
83T-138
83T/St-30
84D-413
84F-6
84F-644
84F/St-115
84Nes/792-272
84OPC-272
84Seven-21E
84T-272
84T/RD-5M
84T/St-213
84T/St-23WS
85D-332
85F-175
85OPC-94
85T-521
85T/RD-6M
85T/St-199
86D-106
86F-272
86OPC-358
86Sf-147M
86T-358
86T-726M
86T/St-232
86T/Tatt-5M
87D-294
87F-467
87F/Up-U26
87Gator-24
87OPC-28
87RedFoley/St-92
87T-28
87T/St-225
87T/Tr-28T
88Mother/Dodg-15
88S-262
88S/Tr-32T
89B-343
89D-432
89Mother/Dodg-15
89Pol/Dodg-10
89S-556
89T-606
89T/Big-108
89UD/Ext-713
90D-557
90D/Learning-15
90F-392
90F/Can-392
90Mother/Dodg-16
90OPC-736
90Pol/Dodg-17
90PublInt/St-4
90S-414
90T-736
90Target-181
91Brewer/MillB-7
91Crown/Orio-102
91Leaf-484
91OPC-427
91Pol/Brew-7
91S-816
91StCl-553
91T-427
92Yank/WIZ70-42
93Orio/SUI-1
Dempsey, John
90Johnson/Star-8
91Johnson/ClBest-2
91Johnson/ProC-3979
91Spring/ClBest-12
91Spring/ProC-744
92Savan/ClBest-13
Dempsey, Mark S.
(Mark)
81Shrev-11
82Phoenix
83Phoenix/BHN-21
Dempsey, Mike
76BurlB
77BurlB
78Holyo
Dempsey, Pat
77Modesto
79Ogden/TCMA-20
80Ogden-22
81T-96R
81Tacoma-7
82Tacoma-26
84Nashvl-6
85Maine-14
86Toledo-8
87Portl-2
Dempsey, Pete
82Syrac/Team-8
Dempster, Kurt
88Billings/ProC-1828
89Billings/ProC-2053
89Greens/ProC-426
Demus, Joe
90Elmira/Pucko-13
91WinHaven/ClBest-11
91WinHaven/ProC-491
92NewBrit/ProC-436
92NewBrit/SB-482
92WinHaven/ProC-1780
Denbo, Gary
84Cedar-26
85Cedar-16
86Vermont-6
87Tampa-1
88Cedar/ProC-1143
89Greens/ProC-404
90CLAS/CL-19
90PrWill/Team-2
91AAA/LineD-125M
91ColClip/LineD-125CO
92GulfCY/ProC-3706
93Greens/ProC-904CO
Denby, Darryl
83Lynch-6
84Jacks-19
86Greenvl/Team-8
Denehy, William F.
(Bill)
67T-581R
68T-526
91WIZMets-94
Denevi, Mike
77Jaxvl
Denkenberger, Ralph
88Watertn/Pucko-17
Denkinger, Don
88TM/Umpire-8
89TM/Umpire-6
90TM/Umpire-6
Denman, Brian John
(Brian)
81Bristol-7
83Pawtu-5
84Pawtu-24
86Nashvl-6
Denman, John
80CharlO/Pol-4
80CharlO/W3TV-4
Dennis, Donald Ray
(Don)
63Pep/Tul
66OPC-142
66T-142
67T-259
Dennis, Ed
(Eddie)
78Dunedin
80Knoxvl/TCMA-14
82Knoxvl-16
83Knoxvl-16
86Knoxvl-6
88StCath/ProC-2014
91Pac/SenLg-71
Dennis, Michael
91Sydney/Fut-7
Dennison, Brian
90AR-30M
91Helena/SportP-15
92Beloit/ClBest-12
92Beloit/ProC-399
Dennison, Jim
90Elmira/Pucko-16
90WinHaven/Star-5
91LynchRS/ClBest-2
91LynchRS/ProC-1191
92LynchRS/ClBest-24
92LynchRS/ProC-2900
Dennison, Scott
91James/ClBest-10
91James/ProC-3551
92Rockford/ClBest-2
92Rockford/ProC-2121
Denny, Jeremiah D.
(Jerry)
N172
N284
WG1-30
Denny, John Allen
(John)
75OPC-621R
75T-621R
75T/M-621R
76OPC-339
76SSPC-295
76T-339
77BurgChef-14
77Ho-42
77Ho/Twink-42
77OPC-109
77OPC-7LL
77T-541
77T-7LL
78Ho-129
78T-609
79Ho-1
79T-59
80OPC-242
80T-464

81T-122
82D-572
82F-363
82F/St-194
82T-773
82Wheat/Ind
83D-237
83F-158
83T-211
84D-407
84F-27
84F/St-56
84Nes/792-135LL
84Nes/792-17
84Nes/792-637TL
84Phill/TastyK-18
84Seven-19E
84T-135LL
84T-17
84T-637TL
84T/RD-18
84T/St-122
84T/St-177
84T/St-19WS
84T/Super-4
85CIGNA-13
85D-111
85F-249
85FunFood/Pin-49
85Leaf-228
85OPC-325
85Phill/TastyK-16
85Phill/TastyK-9M
85T-325
85T/RD-17
85T/St-119
86D-204
86F-439
86F/Up-U34
86OPC-268
86Sf-132M
86Sf-134M
86Sf-64M
86T-556
86T/Tr-32T
86TexGold-40
87D-329
87F-199
87OPC-139
87T-644
90Swell/Great-116

Denson, Andrew
(Drew)
86Durham-9
87Greenvl/Best-7
88Greenvl/Best-9
88SLAS-17
89Richm/Bob-4
89Richm/CMC-18
89Richm/Ko-39
89Richm/ProC-847
90AAASingl/ProC-411
90ProC/Singl-287
90Richm/CMC-11
90Richm/ProC-266
90Richm/Team-8
90T/89Debut-30
92Vanco/ProC-2729
92Vanco/SB-637
94Pinn-241
94Pinn/Artist-241
94Pinn/Museum-241

Dent, Eddie
90Target-182

Dent, Russell Earl
(Bucky)
74OPC-582
74T-582
75OPC-299
75SSPC/Puzzle-8
75T-299
75T/M-299
76Ho-119
76OPC-154
76SSPC-143
76T-154
77BK/Y-14
77BurgChef-81
77Ho-91
77Ho/Twink-91
77OPC-122
77T-29
78BK/Y-15
78K-2
78OPC-164
78SSPC/270-24
78T-335
79BK/Y-14
79Ho-131
79OPC-254
79T-485
80OPC-33
80T-60
81D-465
81F-80
81F/St-110
81K-7
81MSA/Disc-11
81OPC-164
81PermaGr/AS-12
81T-650
81T/HT
81T/St-110
82D-209
82F-33
82F-629M
82OPC-240
82OPC-241IA
82OPC-298AS
82T-240
82T-241A
82T-550AS
83F-566
83OPC-279
83OPC/St-122
83Rangers-7
83T-565
83T/St-122
84D-300
84F-417
84Nes/792-331
84OPC-331
84T-331
84T/St-362
87Colum-1MG
87Colum/Pol-6MG
87Colum/TCMA-23MG
88Colum/CMC-25MG
88Colum/Pol-24MG
88Colum/Pol-25MG
88Colum/ProC-306MG
89AAA/ProC-21MG
89Colum/CMC-25MG
89Colum/Pol-25MG
89Colum/ProC-757MG
89Swell-72
90OPC-519MG
90T-519MG
90T/TVYank-1MG
92Yank/WIZ70-43
92Yank/WIZ80-43
92Yank/WIZAS-16
93Rang/Keeb-124
93UD/ATH-40

Dente, Samuel Joseph
(Sam)
50B-107
51B-133
52Hawth/Pin-2
52T-304
53B/Col-137
55Gol/Ind-4
55Salem

Derdivannis, Kent
93Pirate/Nation-8ANN

Deriso, Phil
81Batavia-8

Derksen, Rob
85Beloit-25
86Stockton-5CO
87Stockton-2
88CalLgAS-18
88Stockton/Cal-201
88Stockton/ProC-721
89Stockton/Best-30
89Stockton/Cal-177CO
89Stockton/ProC-385
89Stockton/Star-25
90Beloit/Best-26MG
90Beloit/Star-25MG
91Beloit/ClBest-27
91Beloit/ProC-2119
92ElPaso/ProC-3938
92ElPaso/SB-225CO

Dernier, Robert E.
(Bob)
80Reading
81OkCty/TCMA-5
82T-231R
82T/Tr-28T
83D-189
83F-159
83OPC-43
83OPC/St-320
83T-43
83T/St-320
84Cub/Uno-2
84D-541
84F-28
84F/X-31
84Nes/792-358
84OPC-358
84SevenUp-20
84T-358
84T/Tr-31
85D-510
85F-55
85FunFood/Pin-127
85Leaf-57
85OPC-334
85SevenUp-20
85T-589
85T/St-38
86Cub/Unocal-5
86D-266
86F-365
86Gator-20
86Jay's-4
86Leaf-139
86OPC-188
86T-188
86T/St-63
87Berg/Cubs-20
87D-146
87D/OD-68
87F-559
87OPC-138
87T-715
88D-392
88F-417
88OPC-183
88Phill/TastyK-8
88S-451
88S/Tr-45T
88T-642
89D-430
89F-565
89Panini/St-155
89Phill/TastyK-5
89S-357
89T-418
89T/Big-265
89UD-340
90OPC-204
90PublInt/St-235
90T-204
93MCI-12

Derr, Jason
90GreatF/SportP-15

Derrick, Claud Lester
(Claud)
T207

Derringer, Paul
34G-84
35BU-190
35Exh/4-4
36Exh/4-4
36G
37Exh/4-4
38Exh/4-4
39Exh
39PlayBall-15
40PlayBall-74
41DP-7
41PlayBall-4
45Playball-23
60F-43
61F-20
77Galasso-74
80Pac/Leg-113
82Ohio/HOF-55
86Sf/Dec-14M
91Conlon/Sport-213
PR1-5
R303/A
R310
R311/Leath
R313
R314
R326-9A
R326-9B
R342-9
V351A-10
V351B-11
V355-66
W711/1
W711/2
WG8-13

Derrington, Charles
39PlayBall-116
40PlayBall-28
53Mother-60

Derrington, Chas. J.
(Jim)
58T-129

Derryberry, Tim
82RochR-9

Dersin, Eric
86Albany/TCMA-14

Dertli, Chuck
87WinSalem-21

DesJardins, Brad
89Watertn/Star-29

Desantis, Dominic
92Spartan/ClBest-9

Desautels, Eugene A.
(Gene)
39PlayBall-116
40PlayBall-28

Desert, Harry
52Park-92

Deshaies, Jim
85Colum-23
85Colum/Pol-8
85IntLgAS-34
86D/HL-45
86D/Rook-34
86F/Up-U35
86Pol/Ast-24
86Sf/Rook-15
87Classic/Up-137
87D-184
87F-56
87F/Mini-31
87Leaf-255
87Mother/Ast-23
87Pol/Ast-19
87Sf-156M
87Sf/TPrev-8M
87T-167
87T-2RB
87T/Gloss60-20
87T/St-1
87ToysRUs-9
88D-85
88D/Best-94
88F-446
88Leaf-96
88Mother/Ast-23
88OPC-24
88Panini/St-287
88Pol/Ast-9
88S-354
88Sf-190
88T-24
88T/St-27
89B-320
89D-241
89D/Best-120
89F-356
89Lennox/Ast-11
89Mother/Ast-22
89OPC-341
89S-546
89T-341
89T/Big-29
89UD-76
90B-70
90D-187
90D-7DK
90D/BestNL-4
90D/SuperDK-7
90F-229
90F/Can-229
90Leaf-168
90Lennox-12
90Mother/Ast-12
90OPC-225
90Panini/St-267
90PublInt/St-93
90RedFoley/St-26
90S-154
90Sf-32
90T-225
90T/Big-212
90T/St-21
90UD-221
91B-541
91D-652
91F-506
91Leaf-49
91Leaf/Stud-175
91Mother/Ast-9
91OPC-782
91Panini/St-11
91S-193
91StCl-262
91T-782
91UD-208
91Ultra-137
92D-515
92LasVegas/ProC-2791
92OPC-415
92Pol/Padre-5
92S-364
92T-415
92T/Gold-415
92T/GoldWin-415
92UD-297
92Yank/WIZ80-44
93F-520
93F/Final-234
93Flair-234
93L-522
93UD-648
93Ultra-580
94Pinn-301
94T/Finest-190
94T/FinestRef-190
94UD/CollC-91
94UD/CollC/Gold-91
94UD/CollC/Silv-91

Deshong, James B.
(Jimmie)
34G-96
35G-8E
35G-9E
39PlayBall-10

Desilva, John
91AA/LineD-381
92Toledo/SB-598

Desjarlais, Keith
81AppFx-3
82Edmon-7
83GlenF-13

Dessau, Frank Rolland
(Rube)
90Target-931
C46-61
M116
T206

Dessellier, Chris
93ClBest/MLG-144

Dest, Blanch
80WHave-18M

Dest, Vanna
80WHave-18M

Destrade, Orestes
82Oneonta-1
85Albany-16
86Colum-5
86Colum/Pol-5
87Colum-12
87Colum/Pol-7
87Colum/TCMA-13
88BuffB/CMC-20
88BuffB/ProC-1486
88S/Tr-110T
89BuffB/ProC-1687
89T-27
90AlbanyDG/Best-21
92Yank/WIZ80-45
93B-418
93Colla/DM-31
93F/Final-59
93Flair-50
93L-304
93Marlin/Publix-10
93OPC/Premier-32
93Pac/Jugador-25
93Pac/Spanish-460
93Pinn-526
93Pinn/Expan-3
93StCl-554
93StCl/1stDay-554
93StCl/Marlin-29
93Studio-97
93T/Finest-144
93T/FinestRef-144
93T/Tr-11T

93UD-479M
93UD-524
93UD/SP-139
93USPlayC/Marlin-10D
93USPlayC/Marlin-11C
93USPlayC/Marlin-7S
93Ultra-373
94B-506
94D-212
94F-466
94Finest-272
94Flair-162
94L-191
94OPC-23
94Pac/Cr-241
94Pac/Silv-22
94Panini-182
94Pinn-373
94S-372
94Select-150
94StCl-387
94StCl/1stDay-387
94StCl/Gold-387
94StCl/Team-70
94T-710
94T/Gold-710
94TripleP-135
94UD-304
94Ultra-195

Detherage, Robert W.
(Bob)
75Water
81Omaha-21

Dettmer, John
91T/Tr-32T
92Gaston/ProC-2244
92StCl/Dome-35
92T/DQ-19
94B-129
94FExcel-131
94FExcel/LL-7

Dettola, Kevin
92Sky/AASingl-129

Dettore, Thomas A.
(Tom)
74Wichita-106
75OPC-469
75T-469
75T/M-469
76OPC-126
76T-126
89Princet/Star-27
91Salem/ProC-969CO

Deutsch, John
89GreatF-17
90AS/Cal-3
90Bakers/Cal-249
91VeroB/ClBest-18
91VeroB/ProC-779
92SanAn/ProC-3981
92SanAn/SB-562
92Sky/AASingl-245

Deutsch, Melvin
92TX-12

Deutsch, Mike
89Freder/Star-5
90Freder/Team-5

Devares, Cesar
89Bluefld/Star-8
90Foil/Best-133
90Wausau/Best-17
90Wausau/ProC-2130
90Wausau/Star-7
91CLAS/ProC-CAR7
91Freder/ClBest-12
91Freder/ProC-2366
92Hagers/ProC-2559
92Hagers/SB-257
92Sky/AASingl-106
93LimeR/Winter-48

Devens, Charlie
94Conlon-1284

Devereaux, Mike
87SanAn-10
87TexLgAS-28
88AAA/ProC-1
88Albuq/CMC-18
88Albuq/ProC-252
88D-546
88F-512
88Mother/Dodg-27
88S-637
88TripleA/ASCMC-36
89Classic/Up/2-181
89D-603
89D/Best-326
89D/Rook-51
89D/Tr-30
89F-56
89F/Up-2
89French-12
89S/HotRook-11
89S/YS/II-22
89T/Tr-23T
89UD-68
90B-260
90D-282
90F-175
90F/Can-175
90Leaf-223
90OPC-127
90Panini/St-12
90PublInt/St-576
90S-232
90S/100Ris-90
90Sf-114
90T-127
90T/Big-178
90T/JumboR-7
90Target-183
90ToysRUs-8
90UD-681
91B-93
91Crown/Orio-103
91D-444
91F-469A
91F-469B
91Leaf-138
91OPC-758
91Panini/FrSt-245
91Panini/St-196
91S-258
91StCl-555
91T-758
91UD-308
91Ultra-15
92B-688
92D-354
92F-5
92L-79
92L/BlkGold-79
92OPC-492
92Panini-70
92Pinn-165
92S-36
92StCl-199
92Studio-123
92T-492
92T/Gold-492
92T/GoldWin-492
92UD-209
92Ultra-2
93B-605
93D-455
93F-165
93Flair-150
93L-67
93OPC-93
93Pac/Spanish-16
93Panini-75
93Pinn-400
93S-170
93Select-170
93Select/StatL-20
93StCl-56
93StCl/1stDay-56
93Studio-55
93T-741
93T/BlkGold-28
93T/Finest-74
93T/FinestRef-74
93T/Gold-741
93ToysRUs-8
93TripleP-34
93UD-167
93UD/FunPack-132
93UD/HRH-HR14
93UD/SP-155
93Ultra-493
94B-403
94D-69
94F-3
94L-154
94OPC-203
94Pac/Cr-29
94Panini-19
94Pinn-13
94Pinn/Artist-13
94Pinn/Museum-13
94S-386
94Select-131
94StCl-424
94StCl/1stDay-424
94StCl/Gold-424
94StCl/Team-299
94Studio-122
94T-534
94T/Finest-117
94T/FinestRef-117
94T/Gold-534
94TripleP-153
94UD-356
94Ultra-304

Devereaux, Todd
88AZ/Pol-2
90FtLaud/Star-4

Devich, John
83Butte-24

Deville, Dan
89Spokane/SP-10
90River/Best-6
90River/Cal-15
90River/ProC-2599
91HighD/ClBest-2
91HighD/ProC-2385

Devine, Kevin
86VeroB-5
87VeroB-23

Devine, Paul Adrian
(Adrian)
74OPC-614
74T-614
77T-339
78T-92
79T-257
80T-528
81T-464
93Rang/Keeb-125

Devito, Fred
80WHave-13

Devlin, Arthur M.
(Art)
10Domino-32
11Helmar-123
12Sweet/Pin-110
93UD/T202-1
E101
E103
E254
E91
E92
E94
E95
M116
S74-83
T202
T204
T205
T206
T207
T3-10
W555

Devlin, Bob
84Greens-21
86WPalmB-12
87Jaxvl-18

Devlin, James H.
(Tim)
N172
N690

Devlin, Paul
88Lynch/Star-6
89Lynch/Star-6

Devlin, Steven
91Brisbane/Fut-4

Devoe, Dan
91Kinston/ClBest-29TR

Devore, Joshua
(Josh)
10Domino-33
11Helmar-124
12Sweet/Pin-111
14CJ-47
15CJ-47
BF2-85
D329-46
E270/2
E300
E94
E97
M101/4-46
M116
S74-84
T202
T205
T206
T207
T213/blue
T215/blue
T215/brown
W555

Devore, Ted
91CharRain/ClBest-5
91CharRain/ProC-91
92HighD/ClBest-14

Dewechter, Pat
85Greens-14

Deweerdt, Dan
88Rockford-11
89Rockford-11

Deweese, Brent
92MissSt-13
93MissSt-13

Dewey, Mark
87Everett-32
88Clinton/ProC-711
89AS/Cal-43
89SanJose/Best-7
89SanJose/Cal-211
89SanJose/ProC-448
89SanJose/Star-7
89Star/Wax-85
90A&AASingle/ProC-65
90Shrev/ProC-1436
90Shrev/Star-6
91AAA/LineD-382
91Phoenix/LineD-382
91Phoenix/ProC-60
91S-371RP
91T/90Debut-40
91Tidew/ProC-2503
92StCl-817
92Tidew/ProC-
92Tidew/SB-564
93F-468
94D-102
94Finest-298
94Flair-216
94L-82
94Pac/Cr-497
94T-101
94T/Gold-101

Dewey, Todd Alan
86Durham-10
87Greenvl/Best-10
88Richm/CMC-11
88Richm/ProC-4
89Durham/Star-10
89Durham/Team-10
90Durham/Team-25

Dews, Robert
(Bobby)
66Pep/Tul
82Durham-25MG
85Pol/Atl-53C

DiBartolomeo, Steve
90CLAS/CL-52
90WinSalem/Team-16
91AA/LineD-131
91CharlK/LineD-131
91CharlK/ProC-1682

DiCeglio, Tom
85Visalia-11
86Kenosha-6

DiFelice, Mike
91Hamil/ClBest-15
91Hamil/ProC-4041
92Hamil/ProC-1593

DiGiacomo, Kevin
92Watertn/ClBest-25
92Watertn/ProC-3241

DiGioia, John
85Spring-7
86PalmSp-10
86PalmSp/Smok-7

DiGiovanna, Charlie
55Gol/Dodg-6bb

DiGrandi, Vince
90NE-8

DiHigo, Martin
74Laugh/Black-29
80Perez/HOF-159
86Negro/Frit-19
88Conlon/NegAS-3
88Negro/Duques-10
89HOF/St-63
90Negro/Star-23

DiLauro, Jack Edward
(Jack)
70OPC-382
70T-382
71MLB/St-78
71OPC-677
71T-677
91WIZMets-95
94Mets/69-21

DiMaggio, Dominic P.
(Dom)
41DP-108
41PlayBall-63
47HomogBond-9
47TipTop
48L-75
49B-64
49Royal-4
50B-3
50Drake-33
51BR-A8
51T/RB-20
52BR
52NTea
52RM-AL5
52Royal
52StarCal-85B
52StarCal/L-71F
52T-22
53Exh/Can-23
53RM-AL22
53T-149
91T/Arc53-149
D305
Exh47
PM10/Sm-37
PM10/Sm-38
R423-24

DiMaggio, Joseph Paul
(Joe)
37Exh/4-13
37OPC-118
37Wheat
38Exh/4-13
38G-250
38G-274
38ONG/Pin-7
38Wheat
39Exh
39PlayBall-26
40PlayBall-1
40Wheat
41DP-63
41PlayBall-7
41Wheat
42Playball-2
47HomogBond-10
48L-1
48Swell-15
50Callahan
50W576-27
51BR-B5
52BR
53Exh/Can-28
60NuCard-38
60NuCard-7
61GP-9
61NuCard-438
61NuCard-467
68A's/JITB-5CO
72Laugh/GF-1
73Syrac/Team-7
74Laugh/ASG-39
74Syrac/Team-5
75Shakey-1
76Laugh/Jub-25
76Rowe-4
76Shakey-74
77Galasso-1
77Galasso-235
77Shakey-24
79TCMA-1
80Marchant/HOF-10
80Pac/Leg-5
80Perez/HOF-75
80SSPC/HOF
83MLBPA/Pin-4
84West/1-5
85Sportflic/Proto-1
86Sf/Dec-20
88Pac/Leg-100
89HOF/St-39
89Kenner/BBGr-5

90BBWit-49
90HOF/St-39
92S/DiMag-1
92S/DiMag-2
92S/DiMag-3
92S/DiMag-4
92S/DiMag-5
92S/DiMag-x
92S/Factory-B12
92S/Factory-B13
92S/Factory-B14
92Yank/WIZAS-18
92Yank/WIZHOF-9
93Pinn/DiMag-11
93Pinn/DiMag-Set
93Pinn/DiMagAU-Set
D305
PM10/Sm-39
PM10/Sm-40
PM10/Sm-41A
PM10/Sm-41B
PM10/Sm-42
PM10/Sm-43
PR1-7
R302
R303/A
R303/B
R311/Leath
R312
R314
R314/M
R326-4A
R326-4B
R342-4
R346-16
R423-25
V300
V351A-11
V351B-13
V355-51

DiMaggio, Vincent P.
(Vince)
38Exh/4-1
41PlayBall-61
42Playball-38
47Signal
V351A-12

DiMarco, Steven
91Erie/ClBest-5
91Erie/ProC-4077
91Kane/ClBest-15
91Kane/ProC-2662

DiMare, Gino
91Miami/Bumble-4

DiMascio, Dan
87GlenF-22
88EastLAS/ProC-6
88GlenF/ProC-931
89Toledo/CMC-17
89Toledo/ProC-788

DiMichele, Frank
86QuadC-8
87PalmSp-27
88Edmon/ProC-565
88MidldA/GS-8
89MidldA/GS-12
90MidldA/GS-22

DiPietro, Fred
76Clinton

DiPino, Frank M.
78BurlB
80Holyo-12
81Vanco-17
82T-333R
82Vanco-16
83T/Tr-25
84D-502
84F-224
84F/St-72
84Mother/Ast-17
84Nes/792-172
84T-172
84T/St-74
85D-232
85F-349
85Mother/Ast-11
85OPC-376
85T-532
85T/St-66
86D-304
86F-299
86Pol/Ast-25
86T-26
87Berg/Cubs-33
87D-416
87F-560
87OPC-297
87T-662
88Berg/Cubs-33
88D-570
88D/Best-205
88D/Cubs/Bk-570
88F-418
88S-413
88T-211
89B-434
89D-393
89F-423
89F/Up-118
89S-146
89Smok/Cards-6
89T-439
89T/Tr-24T
89UD-61
90B-187
90D-518
90F-249
90F/Can-249
90Leaf-103
90OPC-788
90PublInt/St-218
90S-462
90Smok/Card-5
90T-788
90T/TVCard-12
90UD-202
91D-360
91F-632
91OPC-112
91Pol/Card-35
91S-553
91StCl-439
91T-112
91UD-350
92StCl-886

DiPino, Paul
90Idaho/ProC-3254

DiPoto, Jerry
89Watertn/Star-3
90CLAS/CL-36
90Kinston/Team-1
91AA/LineD-81
91Canton/LineD-81
91Canton/ProC-975
92B-92
92ColoSp/ProC-746
92ColoSp/SB-84
92Sky/AAASingl-39
93F/Final-199
94F-102
94S-278
94S/GoldR-278
94StCl-380
94StCl/1stDay-380
94StCl/Gold-380
94T-767
94T/Gold-767

DiSalvo, Pio
77Evansvl/TCMA-8TR
84Tiger/Wave-12

DiSarcina, Gary
88Bend/Legoe-33M
88Bend/Legoe-7
89BBAmAA/BPro-AA30
89MidldA/GS-13
89TexLAS/GS-4
90AAASingl/ProC-100
90B-290
90Edmon/CMC-19
90Edmon/ProC-524
90ProC/Singl-496
90S/Tr-68T
90T/89Debut-31
90UD/Ext-761
91AAA/LineD-162
91Edmon/LineD-162
91Edmon/ProC-1523
91S-768RP
91S/100RisSt-26
92B-159
92Classic/II-T8
92D-497
92D/Rook-32
92F-664
92L-48
92L/BlkGold-48
92L/GRook-21
92L/GoldPrev-30
92Pinn-52
92Pinn/Rook-8
92Pinn/Team2000-38
92Pol/Angel-7
92S/Rook-25
92StCl-458
92Studio-144
92T/Tr-28T
92T/TrGold-28T
92TripleP-251
92UD-726
92UD/Scout-SR7
92Ultra-24
92Ultra/AllRook-3
93B-145
93Colla/DM-32
93D-121
93F-188
93F/RookSenII-5
93Flair-172
93L-260
93Mother/Angel-2
93OPC-80
93Pac/Spanish-43
93Panini-6
93Pinn-337
93Pol/Angel-17
93S-374
93Select-281
93StCl-196
93StCl/1stDay-196
93StCl/Angel-27
93Studio-85
93T-157
93T/Gold-157
93TripleP-58
93UD-230
93UD/SP-21
93USPlayC/Rook-13H
93Ultra-160
94B-507
94D-478
94F-52
94Flair-20
94L-173
94Pac/Cr-75
94Panini-36
94Pinn-97
94Pinn/Artist-97
94Pinn/Museum-97
94S-377
94StCl-213
94StCl/1stDay-213
94StCl/Gold-213
94Studio-10
94T-351
94T/Finest-171
94T/FinestRef-171
94T/Gold-351
94TripleP-13
94UD-165
94UD/CollC-94
94UD/CollC/Gold-94
94UD/CollC/Silv-94
94UD/ElecD-165
94Ultra-325

DiSarcina, Glenn
91Utica/ClBest-16
91Utica/ProC-3245
92ClBest-259
92SoBend/ClBest-15
92SoBend/ProC-183
94B-99

Diagostino, Gary
89GA-4

Dial, Bryan
85BurlR-20
86Salem-5

Dials, Lou
86Negro/Frit-14
86Negro/Frit-20
92Negro/Retort-17

Diaz, Alberto
89Kingspt/Star-7
90Clmbia/PCPII-2
90Columbia/GS-14
91StLucie/ClBest-9
91StLucie/ProC-716

Diaz, Alex
88Clmbia/GS-14
89StLucie/Star-3
90AAASingl/ProC-286
90ProC/Singl-374
90T/TVMets-40
90Tidew/CMC-23
90Tidew/ProC-555
91AAA/LineD-181
91Indianap/LineD-181
91Indianap/ProC-473
92Denver/ProC-2645
92Denver/SB-126
93Pac/Spanish-509
93Pol/Brew-4
94Flair-65
94L-250
94Pac/Cr-327
94Pinn-416
94T-519
94T/Gold-519

Diaz, Andres
90Kissim/DIMD-10

Diaz, Angel
89Helena/SP-2

Diaz, Armando
52Laval-76

Diaz, Baudilio Jose
(Bo)
78T-708R
79T-61
80T-483
81D-517
81F-404
81T-362
82D-263
82F-364
82F-639M
82F/St-197
82OPC-258
82T-258
82T/St-176
82T/StVar-176
82T/Tr-29T
83D-147
83F-160
83F-637M
83F/St-6M
83F/St-6M
83OPC-175
83OPC/St-273
83T-175
83T-229TL
83T/St-273
84D-137
84F-29
84F/St-118
84Nes/792-535
84OPC-131
84Phill/TastyK-25
84T-535
84T/St-120
85F-250
85OPC-219
85Phill/TastyK-10
85Phill/TastyK-25
85T-737
86D-530
86F-176
86Leaf-258
86OPC-253
86T-639
86TexGold-6
87D-246
87D/HL-21
87D/OD-190
87F-200
87F/Mini-32
87Kahn-6
87OPC-41
87T-41
87T/St-142
88D-186
88D/AS-47
88D/Best-110
88F-232
88Kahn/Reds-6
88Leaf-191
88OPC-265
88Panini/St-273
88S-206
88Sf-117
88T-265
88T/St-143
89B-307
89D-242
89D/Best-293
89F-159
89Kahn/Reds-6
89KennerFig-37
89OPC-201
89Panini/St-71
89RedFoley/St-36
89S-187
89T-422
89T/St-135
89UD-169
90D-139
90PublInt/St-27
90S-434
90UD-664

Diaz, Carlos Antonio
(Carlos)
80Spokane-4
81Richm-13
82Richm-5
83D-562
83F-540
84D-600
84F-583
84F/X-32
84Nes/792-524
84Pol/Dodg-27
84T-524
84T/Tr-32
85Coke/Dodg-9
85F-369
85T-159
86Coke/Dodg-9
86D-348
86F-128
86Pol/Dodg-27
86T-343
90Target-184
91WIZMets-96

Diaz, Carlos Francisco
87Dunedin-1
88Knoxvl/Best-12
89Knoxvl/Best-4
89Knoxvl/ProC-1125
89Knoxvl/Star-2
90ProC/Singl-336
90Syrac/CMC-10
90Syrac/MerchB-5
90Syrac/Team-5
91AAA/LineD-134
91Bristol/ClBest-18
91Bristol/ProC-3612
91Denver/LineD-134
91Denver/ProC-124
91T/90Debut-41
92Memphis/ProC-2422
92Memphis/SB-434
92Omaha/ProC-2963

Diaz, Cesar
91Kingspt/ClBest-27
91Kingspt/ProC-3815
92ColumMet/SAL/II-11
92Pittsfld/ClBest-11
92Pittsfld/ProC-3298
93FExcel/ML-71

Diaz, Derek
85Beloit-23
86ElPaso-8
87ElPaso-16

Diaz, Ed
92SanBern/ClBest-20
92SanBern/ProC-
94ClBest/Gold-101
94ClBest/Gold-79

Diaz, Eddie
83Watlo/Frit-4

Diaz, Edgar
(Kiki)
83Beloit/Frit-23
86Vanco-10
87Pol/Brew-2
88Denver/CMC-18
88Denver/ProC-1256
89Denver/CMC-12
89Denver/ProC-47
90Brewer/MillB-5
90ElPasoATG/Team-16
90F/Up-105
90Leaf-335
90Pol/Brew-2
90T/Tr-26T
91Belling/ClBest-5
91Belling/ProC-3672
91D-197
91F-581
91OPC-164
91S-576
91T-164

91UD-286
Diaz, Einar
92BurlInd/ClBest-28
92BurlInd/ProC-1662
Diaz, Enrique
80Wausau-15
81Wausau-16
Diaz, German
90Geneva/ProC-3039
90Geneva/Star-9
91Peoria/ClBest-16
91Peoria/ProC-1348
91Peoria/Team-16
92ClBest-219
92Geneva/ClBest-20
92Geneva/ProC-1566
92Peoria/ClBest-10
Diaz, Johnny
87Elmira/Black-22
87Elmira/Red-22
88WinHaven/Star-7
89Elmira/Pucko-2
Diaz, Jorge
83Madis/Frit-8
Diaz, Jose
87Myrtle-3
88Dunedin/Star-4
88FSLAS/Star-33
89Knoxvl/Best-5
89Knoxvl/Star-3
Diaz, Kiki
92Chatt/SB-182
92Nashvl/SB-288
Diaz, Mario
80Wausau-14
81LynnS-17
82LynnS-12
84Chatt-25
86Calgary-6
87Calgary-11
88Calgary/ProC-804
88F-649R
88F/Up-U59
88Mother/Sea-21
89F-547
89Mother/Sea-21
89Panini/St-427
89T-309
89UD-318
90AAASingl/ProC-120
90Calgary/ProC-655
90OPC-781
90PublInt/St-432
90T-781
91Leaf-363
91Mother/Rang-24
91WIZMets-97
92Calgary/SB-58
92D-149
92F-301
92OkCty/ProC-1919
93L-470
93Rang/Keeb-126
94D-73
94F-305
94Pac/Cr-614
94S-169
94S/GoldR-169
94StCl/Team-71
Diaz, Mike
83Iowa-11
85Cram/PCL-50
85Phill/TastyK-41
86Sf/Rook-50
87D-267
87F-609
87Sf/TPrev-18M
87T-469
88D-267
88F-326
88OPC-239
88Panini/St-378
88S-143
88T-567
89D-655
89F-494
89S-603
89T-142
89UD-606
Diaz, Rafael
90James/Pucko-16
91Rockford/ClBest-4
91Rockford/ProC-2039
92WPalmB/ClBest-14
92WPalmB/ProC-2081
93Harris/ProC-264
Diaz, Remigio
90Stockton/Best-6
90Stockton/Cal-192
90Stockton/ProC-2191
91Stockton/ClBest-13
91Stockton/ProC-3037
Diaz, Rich
83Watlo/Frit-25
Diaz, Roberto
78Newar
79BurlB-16
Diaz, Sandy
89Elizab/Star-6
90Elizab/Star-8
90Kenosha/Best-18
90Kenosha/ProC-2287
90Kenosha/Star-2
91Elizab/ProC-4295
92Kenosha/ProC-595
92ProC/Tomorrow-104
Diaz, Steve
89Beloit/II/Star-7
90Stockton/Best-3
90Stockton/Cal-188
90Stockton/ProC-2187
91Beloit/ClBest-11
91Beloit/ProC-2105
Diaz, Tony
84Butte-9
88Miami/Star-6
89StLucie/Star-4
Diaz, Victor
87Myrtle-23
89BirmB/Best-4
89BirmB/ProC-101
Diaz, William
86Wausau-8
88SanBern/Best-9
88SanBern/Cal-37
89Wmsprt/ProC-640
89Wmsprt/Star-6
Dibble, Rob
85Cedar-6
86Vermont-7
87Nashvl-4
88F/Up-U83
88Nashvl/CMC-4
88Nashvl/ProC-493
88Nashvl/Team-8
88S/Tr-86T
89B-305
89Classic-76
89D-426
89D/Best-334
89F-160
89Kahn/Reds-49
89S-618
89T-264
89UD-375
90B-42
90CedarDG/Best-16
90Classic-43
90D-189
90D/BestNL-76
90F-418
90F/Can-418
90Kahn/Reds-8
90Kenner/Fig-24
90Leaf-57
90OPC-46
90Panini/St-249
90PublInt/St-28
90S-277
90S/YS/II-15
90T-46
90UD-586
90USPlayC/AS-WC
91B-667
91Classic/200-168
91Classic/I-23
91Classic/III-15
91D-321
91F-62
91Kahn/Reds-49
91Leaf-282
91Leaf/Stud-163
91OPC-662
91Panini/St-128
91Pep/Reds-7
91RedFoley/St-4
91S-17
91S-407KM
91StCl-131
91T-662
91UD-635
91USPlayC/AS-10S
91Ultra-92
91Woolwth/HL-23M
92B-242
92Classic/Game200-75
92Classic/II-T76
92D-139
92F-404
92Kenner/Fig-13
92L-69
92L/BlkGold-69
92OPC-757
92OPC/Premier-53
92Pinn-180
92Pinn/TeamP-11M
92Reds/Kahn-49
92S-455
92S-891DT
92S/100SS-41
92S/Impact-71
92StCl-584
92StCl/Dome-36
92Studio-22
92Studio/Prev-12
92T-757
92T/GPro-757
92T/Gold-757
92T/GoldWin-757
92T/Kids-40
92T/Pr-131
92TripleP-257
92UD-142
92UD-30TC
92UD/ASFF-21
92Ultra-187
93B-526
93Classic/GameI-26
93D-322
93F-389
93F/Fruit-16
93Flair-25
93L-280
93L/GoldAS-10M
93MilkBone-16
93OPC-122
93Pac/Spanish-81
93Panini-297
93Pinn-101
93Pinn/TP-B11
93Reds/Kahn-9
93S-651
93Select-65
93StCl-369
93StCl/1stDay-369
93T-470
93T/Finest-180
93T/FinestRef-180
93T/Gold-470
93TripleP-52
93UD-473M
93UD-675
93UD/FunPack-168
93UD/SP-208
93Ultra-327
94D-451
94F-409
94L-166
94OPC-224
94Pac/Cr-145
94Pinn-41
94Pinn/Artist-41
94Pinn/Museum-41
94S-114
94S/GoldR-114
94Sf/2000-14
94StCl-202
94StCl/1stDay-202
94StCl/Gold-202
94T-183
94T/Finest-88
94T/FinestRef-88
94T/Gold-183
94TripleP-211
94UD-308
94UD/CollC-93
94UD/CollC/Gold-93
94UD/CollC/Silv-93
94Ultra-471
Dick, Bill
76BurlB
77BurlB
77Holyo
78BurlB
78Holyo
Dick, Ed
79TCMA-81
Dick, Ralph
88SanBern/Best-14
88SanBern/Cal-53
89SanBern/Best-11
89SanBern/Cal-90MG
Dicken, Rongie
92Johnson/ClBest-5
92Johnson/ProC-3122
Dickens, John
92Eugene/ClBest-9
92Eugene/ProC-3020
93Rockford/ClBest-11
Dickerman, Leo
90Target-932
Dickerson, Bob
(Bobby)
87Oneonta-27
88FtLaud/Star-5
89Albany/Best-16
89Albany/ProC-319
89Albany/Star-7
90Albany/Best-15
90Albany/ProC-1040
90Albany/Star-4
91AA/LineD-229
91Hagers/LineD-229
91Hagers/ProC-2461
92RochR/ProC-1944
92RochR/SB-452
Dickerson, Jim
86Pittsfld-7
Dickerson, Robert
92Niagara/ClBest-9
92Niagara/ProC-3337
Dickey, Chad
85Clovis-13
Dickey, George W.
47TipTop
Dickey, William M.
(Bill)
31Exh/4-25
33Exh/4-13
33G-19
34DS-103
34DS-11
34Exh/4-13
35BU-117
35BU-30
35Exh/4-13
35G-2D
35G-4D
35G-7D
37OPC-119
38Exh/4-13
39Exh
39PlayBall-30
40PlayBall-7
41DP-66
41PlayBall-70
42Playball-3
44Yank/St-8
48Swell-6
50Callahan
50W576-26
51B-290CO
52T-400CO
60NuCard-34
60T-465C
61GP-27
61NuCard-434
63Bz/ATG-40
76Rowe-4M
76Shakey-71
77Galasso-188
77Galasso-68
77Shakey-9
80Marchant/HOF-9
80Pac/Leg-44
80Perez/HOF-71
80SSPC/HOF
83D/HOF-26
86Sf/Dec-13
88Conlon/AmAS-8
90Perez/GreatMom-37
92Conlon/Sport-474
92Yank/WIZAS-17
92Yank/WIZHOF-8
93Conlon-755
93Conlon-869
94Conlon-1086
94Conlon/Col-36
PM10/Sm-36
PR1-6
R300
R302
R303/A
R303/B
R308-161
R310
R312
R314
R328-4
R332-11
R423-22
V300
V351B-12
V353-19
V355-34
V94-13
WG8-14
Dickman, Dave
89Pulaski/ProC-1888
89Sumter/ProC-1100
Dickman, Geo. Emerson
39PlayBall-17
40PlayBall-37
41G-6
94Conlon-1167
Dickman, Mark
85Kingst-5
86Ventura-4
Dickshot, Johnny
45Playball-16
94Conlon-1286
Dickson, James Edward
(Jim)
64T-524R
65T-286R
66T-201
Dickson, Ken
87AubAs-21
88Ashvl/ProC-1050
Dickson, Lance
90A&AASingle/ProC-173
90AZ/Pol-2
90CharlK/Team-1
90Classic/DP-23
90Classic/III-85
90Geneva/ProC-3029
90Geneva/Star-10
90PeoriaUp/Team-U1
91AAA/LineD-204
91B-411
91Classic/II-T55
91D-424RR
91Iowa/LineD-204
91Iowa/ProC-1053
91Leaf/Stud-154
91OPC-114
91OPC/Premier-35
91S-385FDP
91S/Rook40-24
91StCl-44
91T-114
91T/90Debut-42
91UD-9SR
91UD/FinalEd-3F
92B-316
92CJ/DI-7
92D-421
92Iowa/SB-207
92Pinn-272
92ProC/Tomorrow-199
92S/100RisSt-96
92S/Impact-85
92Sky/AAASingl-100
92StCl-836
92TripleP-97
92UD/ML-74
93StCl/Cub-15
94StCl/Team-352
Dickson, Murry Monroe
(Murry)
49B-8
49Eureka-158
50B-34
51B-167
51T/BB-16
52B-59
52RM-NL5
52T-266
52TipTop
53RM-NL22

54B-111
55B-236
56T-211
57T-71
58T-349
59T-23
Exh47
R423-23

Dickson, Walter R.
(Walt)
T205

Didier, Robert Daniel
(Bob)
69T-611R
70MLB/St-5
70OPC-232
70T-232
71MLB/St-8
71OPC-432
71T-432
73OPC-574
73T-574
74OPC-482
74T-482
75Iowa/TCMA-6
80Vanco-11
81WHave-1
82WHave-26
83Tacoma-18
87Tucson-24
88Tucson/CMC-24
88Tucson/JP-9
88Tucson/ProC-190
90Mother/Mar-27M

Didrickson, Babe
33SK*-45

Diehl, Charles
52Wheat*

Diehl, Greg
75FtLaud/Sus-8

Diemido, Chet
87Penin-3
91Saraso/ProC-1132CO

Dierderger, George
78Wisco
79Wisco-4

Diering, Charles E.
(Chuck)
47TipTop
49Eureka-180
50B-179
51B-158
52B-198
52NTea
52T-265
54Esskay
55Esskay
55T-105
55T/DH-2
56T-19
56T/Pin-1
57Seattle/Pop-8
79TCMA-51
91Crown/Orio-104

Dierker, Lawrence E.
(Larry)
65T-409R
66T-228
67Ast/Team-4
67CokeCap/Astro-15
67T-498
68CokeCap/Astro-15
68T-565
69MLB/St-138
69T-411
69T/St-32
70MLB/St-39
70OPC-15
70T-15
70T/PI-15
70T/S-6
70T/Super-6
71Bz
71Bz/Test-24
71K-48
71MLB/St-77
71OPC-540
71T-540
71T/Coins-141
71T/GM-32
71T/Greatest-32
71T/S-30
71T/Super-30
71T/tatt-6
72MB-89
72OPC-155
72T-155
73K-53
73OPC-375
73T-375
73T/Lids-13
74OPC-660
74T-660
75OPC-49
75T-49
75T/M-49
76Ho-25
76Ho/Twink-25
76OPC-75
76T-75
77T-350
78T-195
86Mother/Ast-8
89Swell-78
93UD/ATH-41

Dietrich, William J.
(Bill)
41G-9
44Playball-19
91Conlon/Sport-133
92Conlon/Sport-366
R313

Dietrick, Patrick J.
(Pat)
85Madis-12
85Madis/Pol-9
86Madis/Pol-8
88Huntsvl/BK-4
89Tacoma/CMC-24
89Tacoma/ProC-1553
90AAASingl/ProC-152
90ProC/Singl-590
90Tacoma/CMC-13
90Tacoma/ProC-105

Dietz, Don
87Vermont-11

Dietz, Jim
89SanDiegoSt/Smok-7CO

Dietz, Richard Allen
(Dick)
62Kahn/Atl
67T-341R
68OPC-104
68T-104
69T-293
69T/St-103
70MLB/St-123
70OPC-135
70T-135
71K-42
71MD
71MLB/St-246
71OPC-545
71T-545
71T/Coins-33
71T/tatt-4
71Ticket/Giant-2
72MB-90
72OPC-295
72OPC-296IA
72T-295
72T-296IA
73OPC-442
73T-442
84Mother/Giants-21
90SanJose/Best-28CO
90SanJose/ProC-2027
90SanJose/Star-28
90Target-185
91SanJose/ClBest-25
91SanJose/ProC-28
92Shrev/ProC-3889CO
92Shrev/SB-600CO

Diez, Scott
87Miami-14
88FSLAS/Star-5
88Miami/Star-7
90Durham/UpHer-3

Difelice, Mike
92Hamil/ClBest-23

Diggle, Ron
75Tidew/Team-9
77Spoka
78Spokane/Cramer-3
78Spokane/Team-3
79RochR-14

Diggs, Tony
89Helena/SP-8
90Helena/SportP-9
91Beloit/ClBest-18
91Beloit/ProC-2115
92ElPaso/ProC-3935
92ElPaso/SB-206
92Sky/AASingl-91

Digirolama, Dave
83Butte-3

Digrace, Jack
52Laval-87

Dilks, Darren
84Indianap-27

Dill, Walter
(Chip)
84AZ/Pol-4

Dillard, David Donald
(Don)
57Seattle/Pop-9
59T-123
60Maple-6
60T-122
61T-172
63T-298

Dillard, Gordon
87Hagers-25
88CharlK/Pep-20
88RochR/Gov-6
89ScranWB/CMC-7
89ScranWB/ProC-714
90AAASingl/ProC-481
90BuffB/CMC-2
90BuffB/ProC-366
90ProC/Singl-2
91Crown/Orio-105

Dillard, Harrison
51BR-D18

Dillard, Jay
75Lafay

Dillard, Mike
87Elmira/Red-32

Dillard, Ron
81Miami-1
82Tulsa-18
83BurlR-15
83BurlR/Frit-14

Dillard, Stephen B.
75IntAS/TCMA-22
77T-142
78BK/T-16
78T-597
79T-217
80T-452
81D-502
81F-298
81T-78
82D-174
82Edmon-4
82F-594
82T-324
89Pac/SenLg-140
90EliteSenLg-35
91AubAS/ClBest-26MG
91AubAS/ProC-4289
92AubAs/ClBest-27
92AubAs/ProC-1370

Dillhoefer, William
(Pickles)
W514-71

Dillinger, John
92FrRow/DP-51
93ClBest/MLG-198

Dillinger, Robert B.
(Bob)
48L-144
49B-143
50B-105
51B-63
53Mother-61
Exh47
R346-14

Dillingham, J.J.
89KS*-13M

Dillman, William H.
(Bill)
67T-558R
68T-466
69OPC-141
69T-141
69T/4in1-9M
70OPC-386
70T-386
91Crown/Orio-106

Dillmore, Phillip
87Kinston-6

Dillon, Frank Edward
(Pop)
90Target-186
E107

Dillon, James
(Jim)
90SoOreg/Best-11
90SoOreg/ProC-3443
91Madison/ClBest-7
91Madison/ProC-2124
91MidwLAS/ProC-40
92Modesto/ClBest-21
92Modesto/ProC-3892

Dillon, Stephen E.
(Steve)
64T-556R
91WIZMets-98

Dilone, Miguel Angel
(Miguel)
78T-705R
79Ho-118
79OPC-256
79T-487
80T-541
81D-441
81F-391
81F/St-86
81OPC-141
81T-141
81T/St-67
82D-515
82F-365
82F/St-196
82OPC-77
82T-77
82Wheat/Ind
83D-85
83F-405
83T-303
83Wheat/Ind-8
84Expo/PostC-7
84Stuart-25
85D-453
85F-395
85Leaf-135
85OPC-178
85T-178
93LimeR/Winter-94

Dilorenzo, Joe
52Laval-30

Dimartino, John
52Laval-43

Dimas, Rodolfo
85Tigres-7

Dimeda, Jose
91Macon/ClBest-21

Dimmel, Michael Wayne
(Mike)
75Water
78RochR
80ArkTr-8
91Crown/Orio-107

Dimuro, Ray
91CalLgAS-53

Dineen, Kerry Michael
(Kerry)
76SSPC-452
79OkCty
92Yank/WIZ70-44

Dinger, David
86Lipscomb-9

Dinkelmeyer, John
75Clinton

Dinneen, William H.
(Bill)
92Conlon/Sport-374
94Conlon-1200UMP
E107
T204
T206
WG2-14

Diorio, Ronald M.
(Ron)
74OPC-599R
74T-599R

Disher, Dan
87Wausau-4
88SanBern/Best-10
88SanBern/Cal-31

Disher, David
86Cram/NWL-122

Dishington, Nate
94ClBest/Gold-104

Dishman, Glenn
94FExcel-278

Dismuke, Jamie
91Cedar/ClBest-17
91Cedar/ProC-2725
91ClBest/Singl-368
92CharWh/ClBest-16
92CharWh/ProC-15
92ClBest-57
93ClBest/MLG-185
93FExcel/ML-17
94FExcel-173

Dismukes, William
(Dizzy)
87Negro/Dixon-15M
92Negro/RetortII-48M

Distaso, Alec John
(Alec)
69T-602R

Distefano, Benny
83LynnP-19
84Cram/PCL-144
85Cram/PCL-231
85D-166
85T-162
86D-78
86Hawaii-4
87D-514
87T-651
88AAA/ProC-4
88BuffB/CMC-11
88BuffB/Polar-6
88BuffB/ProC-1489
89BuffB/CMC-11
89BuffB/ProC-1682
89F-205
89T/Tr-25T
89VFJuice-30
90F-464
90F/Can-464
90PublInt/St-152
91AAA/LineD-454
91RochR/LineD-454
91RochR/ProC-1907
92B-414
92Mother/Ast-14
92Tucson/SB-606

Ditmar, Arthur J.
(Art)
55B-90
55Rodeo
56Rodeo
56T-258
57T-132
58T-354
59T-374
60L-78
60MacGregor-7
60T-430
61P-16
61T-46LL
61T-48LL
61T-510
61T/St-192
62J-100
62P-100
62P/Can-100
62Salada-202
62Shirriff-202
62T-246
79TCMA-220
92Yank/WIZ60-35

Dittmar, Carl
28Exh/PCL-5

Dittmer, John D.
(Jack)
53JC-19
53SpicSpan/3x5-11
53SpicSpan/7x10-6
53T-212
54B-48
54JC-6
54SpicSpan/PostC-9
54T-53
55B-212
55Gol/Braves-10
55JC-6
55SpicSpan/DC-8
57T-282
91T/Arc53-212
94T/Arc54-53

Ditton, Julian
76Clinton

Divison, Julio
75Lafay
Dixon, Andrew
86Cram/NWL-11
86Everett/Pop-3
88Shrev/ProC-1287
Dixon, Bryan
88StCath/ProC-2030
Dixon, Colin
90WinHaven/Star-6
91AA/LineD-455
91NewBrit/LineD-455
91NewBrit/ProC-356
92NewBrit/ProC-439
92NewBrit/SB-483
92Sky/AASingl-205
Dixon, Dan
79Ashvl/TCMA-23
79Tulsa-7
Dixon, Dee
87Clinton-15
89Shrev/ProC-1836
90ElPaso/GS-8
90TexLgAS/GS-9
Dixon, Dickie
91Kenosha/ClBest-13
91Kenosha/ProC-2067
92Visalia/ClBest-3
92Visalia/ProC-1007
Dixon, Eddie
86WPalmB-13
87WPalmB-21
88Jaxvl/Best-6
88Jaxvl/ProC-967
89Jaxvl/Best-5
89Jaxvl/ProC-159
90AAASingl/ProC-571
90Indianap/CMC-10
90Indianap/ProC-288
90ProC/Singl-60
91AAA/LineD-182
91Indianap/LineD-182
91Indianap/ProC-456
92BuffB/ProC-318
92BuffB/SB-31
Dixon, Hal
55B-309UMP
Dixon, John Craig
(Sonny)
53Briggs
55B-211
55Rodeo
Dixon, John
88Chatt/Team-8
Dixon, Ken
84CharlO-17
85D-270
85F/Up-U36
85T/Tr-31T
86D-148
86F-273
86T-198
87D-171
87F-468
87French-39
87T-528
88D-48
88F-557
88S-411
88T-676
91Crown/Orio-108
Dixon, King
89KS*-37
Dixon, Mason
90ColMud/Star-28
Dixon, Mike
81Watlo-8
Dixon, Rap
74Laugh/Black-2
86Negro/Frit-78
Dixon, Roger
90Elizab/Star-9
Dixon, Ronn
82Wausau/Frit-14
83Wausau/Frit-7
Dixon, Steve
89Johnson/Star-8
90Savan/ProC-2061
91StPete/ClBest-4
91StPete/ProC-2268
92ArkTr/ProC-1123
92ArkTr/SB-32
92ClBest-13
93B-192
94StCl/Team-314
94T-168
94T/Gold-168
Dixon, Thomas Earl
(Tom)
75Dubuq
79OPC-186
79T-361
80T-513
80Tidew-12
81Tidew-14
82Syrac-2
82Syrac/Team-9
83Wichita/Dog-6
Dixon, Troy
83BirmB-23
Djakonow, Paul
75Shrev/TCMA-1
76Shrev
79BuffB/TCMA-21
80Buffa-10
82Evansvl-15
Doak, William L.
(Bill)
21Exh-35
21Exh-36
59T-124
60T-123
61Peters-24
61T-108
62T-267
90Target-187
D327
D328-42
D329-47
D350/2-48
Dobbek, Daniel J.
E120
E121/120
E121/80
E122
E135-42
E220
M101/4-47
M101/5-48
V100
V61-65
W501-78
W514-51
W572
W573
W575
Dobbins, Joe
43Centen-6
44Centen-5
45Centen-5
Dobbs, Gary
78Wisco
79Wisco-15
Dobbs, John
90Target-188
Doberenz, Mark
82Idaho-32
83Idaho-33
Dobernic, Andrew J.
(Jess)
49B-200
49Eureka-81
Dobie, Reggie
85Lynch-5
86Jacks/TCMA-2
87Tidew-3
87Tidew/TCMA-1
88Tidew/ProC-1590
89Calgary/CMC-5
89Calgary/ProC-528
Dobrolsky, Bill
92Beloit/ClBest-19
92Beloit/ProC-407
92Helena/ProC-1717
Dobson, Charles T.
(Chuck)
66T-588R
67CokeCap/A's-14
67T-438
68A's/JITB-6
68OPC-62
68T-62
69MB-74
69T-397
70MLB/St-256
70OPC-331
70T-331
71K-32
71MLB/St-510
71OPC-238
71T-238
72MB-91
72OPC-523
72T-523
75OPC-635
75T-635
75T/M-635
77SLCity
Dobson, Joseph Gordon
(Joe)
47TipTop-3
49B-7
50B-44
51B-36
52Hawth/Pin-3
52T-254
53B/Col-88
53RM-AL15
53T-5
91T/Arc53-5
Exh47
Dobson, Patrick E.
(Pat)
67T-526R
68OPC-22
68T-22
69T-231
70MLB/St-112
70OPC-421
70T-421
71MLB/St-295
71OPC-547
71T-547
72MB-92
72OPC-140
72T-140
73OPC-34
73T-34
74OPC-463
74Syrac/Team-6
74T-463
75OPC-44
75Syrac/Team-4
75Syrac/Team-5
75T-44
75T/M-44
76OPC-296
76SSPC-431
76SSPC/MetsY-Y16
76T-296
76T/Tr-296T
77Pep-8
77T-618
78T-575
83Pol/Brew-45C
88Domino-4
88Smok/Padres-7CO
89Pac/SenLg-219M
89Pac/SenLg-87
89T/SenLg-96
89TM/SenLg-28
90EliteSenLg-64
90Padre/MagUno-22CO
91Crown/Orio-109
91Pac/SenLg-9
92Brew/Carlson-NNO
92Yank/WIZ70-45
Doby, Lawrence Eugene
(Larry)
48L-138
49B-233
50B-39
50NumNum
51B-151
51T/CAS
52B-115
52BR
52NumNum-18
52RM-AL6
52StarCal-88B
52StarCal/L-74A
52T-243
53B/Col-40
53Exh/Can-11
54B-84
54DanDee
54T-70
55Armour-4
55Gol/Ind-5
55RM-AL18
55Salem
56T-250
56YellBase/Pin-9
57T-85
58Hires-17
58T-424
59T-166M
59T-455
72Dimanche*-11CO
73OPC-377CO
73T-377C
74OPC-531CO
74T-531C
76Expo/Redp-5CO
78SSPC/270-153CO
79TCMA-27
82CJ-1
88Pac/Leg-102
89Swell-115
90Pac/Legend-20
90Swell/Great-43
91Swell/Great-24
91T/Arc53-333
92AP/ASG-27
93TWill-134
93UD/ATH-153
93UD/ATH-42
94T/Arc54-70
Exh47
PM10/Sm-44
PM10/Sm-45
PM10/Sm-46
R302-124
R423-18
Dockins, George
90Target-189
Dodd, Bill
88Cedar/ProC-1138
88MidwLAS/GS-11
89Chatt/Best-14
89Chatt/GS-9
90Chatt/GS-11
91AA/LineD-157
91Chatt/LineD-157
91Chatt/ProC-1952
Dodd, Daniel
88StCath/ProC-2018
89Myrtle/ProC-1471
Dodd, Lance
82AlexD-8
Dodd, Mike
75Cedar
Dodd, Rob
90AR-7
91Boise/ClBest-26
91Boise/ProC-3869
Dodd, Scott
91Billing/SportP-11
91Billings/ProC-3747
92Cedar/ProC-1062
Dodd, Tim
83Tampa-7
84Cedar-11
Dodd, Tom
86SLAS-12
87CharlO/WBTV-8
87SLAS-6
88Omaha/CMC-19
88Omaha/ProC-1505
89Omaha/CMC-11
89Omaha/ProC-1727
90AAASingl/ProC-127
90Calgary/CMC-16
90Calgary/ProC-662
90ProC/Singl-443
91Crown/Orio-110
Dodd, Tommie
82Nashvl-10
Dodge, Tom
91QuadC/ClBest-12
91QuadC/ProC-2630
92PalmSp/ClBest-19
92PalmSp/ProC-842
Dodig, Jeff
87Idaho-25
88Durham/Star-5
Dodson, Bo
89Helena/SP-17
89LittleSun-11
90A&AASingle/ProC-150
90AS/Cal-38
90Stockton/Best-26
90Stockton/Cal-190
90Stockton/ProC-2189
91B-38
91CalLgAS-55
91ClBest/Singl-358
91Stockton/ClBest-20
91Stockton/ProC-3038
92ElPaso/ProC-3928
92ElPaso/SB-207
92ProC/Tomorrow-87
92Sky/AASingl-92
92UD/ML-311
94FExcel-80
Dodson, Pat
84Pawtu-19
85Pawtu-3
86Pawtu-9
87Classic-8
87D-44RR
87Leaf-44RR
87Pawt/TCMA-24
87Seven-E11
87Sf-118M
87Sf/TPrev-9M
87T-449FS
88Pawtu/CMC-16
88Pawtu/ProC-466
88S-352
90AAASingl/ProC-683
90OkCty/ProC-437
91Pol/Royal-25CO
Doerr, Robert P.
(Bobby)
38G-258
38G-282
39PlayBall-7
40PlayBall-38
41DP-106
41PlayBall-64
47HomogBond-11
47TipTop-4
48L-83
49B-23
50B-43
50Drake-13
51T/BB-37
52BR
53Exh/Can-24
74Laugh/ASG-43
75Shakey-14
79BJ/Bubble-7CO
80Perez/HOF-194
83MLBPA/Pin-5
86D/HL-32
88Pac/Leg-73
89HOF/St-11
89Pac/Leg-150
89Swell-110
89T/Gloss22-11
90Pac/Legend-21
90Perez/GreatMom-36
90Swell/Great-96
91Swell/Great-25
92AP/ASG-8
92AP/ASG24K-8G
92Conlon/Sport-467
93AP/ASGCoke/Amo-8
93Conlon-913
94TedW-3
D305
Exh47
R314
Rawl
Doerr, Tim
76Clinton
Does, Raymond
89Welland/Pucko-11
Doescher, Edward
C46-50
Doffek, Scott
90Yakima/Team-15
91VeroB/ProC-780
92SanAn/ProC-3982
92SanAn/SB-563
Doggett, George
85Lynch-26
Doggett, Jerry
60Union/Dodg-22M
61Union/Dodg-24M
71Ticket/Dodg-20ANN
Doherty, John Harold
75OPC-524
75SLCity/Caruso-6
75T-524
75T/M-524
Doherty, John Michael
(John)

89Niagara/Pucko-7
90Lakeland/Star-7
91AA/LineD-382
91London/LineD-382
91London/ProC-1870
92B-518
92Classic/II-T99
92D/Rook-33
92F/Up-20
92L/GRook-24
92Pinn-513
92Pinn/Rook-4
92S/RookTr-81T
92Ultra-360
93D-277
93F-226
93Flair-200
93L-534
93Pinn-407
93S-353
93Select-298
93T-713
93T/Gold-713
93Tiger/Gator-6
93UD-757
93USPlayC/Rook-7D
93Ultra-196
94D-78
94F-127
94Finest-277
94Flair-47
94L-371
94Pac/Cr-215
94Pinn-96
94Pinn/Artist-96
94Pinn/Museum-96
94S-531
94StCl-184
94StCl/1stDay-184
94StCl/Gold-184
94T-371
94T/Gold-371
94TripleP-242
94UD-247
94UD/ElecD-247
94Ultra-51
Dohne, Heriberto
88Modesto/Cal-76
Doiron, Serge
91Geneva/ClBest-6
91Geneva/ProC-4221
Dolan, Cozy
81Conlon-41
90Target-190
V117-9
Dolan, John
88Elmira-7
89Lynch/Star-7
Dolan, Thomas J.
(Tom)
N172
Dolejsi, Brad
91OKSt-8
Dolf, Mike
76Wmsprt
Doll, Chris
88Belling/Legoe-24
88Wausau/GS-4
Dolson, Andrew
91MedHat/ProC-4092
91MedHat/SportP-17
92MedHat/ProC-3205
92MedHat/SportP-8
93Hagers/ProC-1873
Doman, Roger
92StCath/ClBest-7
92StCath/ProC-3382
93Hagers/ClBest-9
93Hagers/ProC-1874
Dombrowski, Robert
89Billings/ProC-2055
90Cedar/ProC-2328
Domecq, Ray
90Martins/ProC-3192
91Spartan/ClBest-2
91Spartan/ProC-887
Domingo, Tyrone
92LitSun/HSPros-28
Dominguez, Frank
85Miami-3
89Reno/Cal-256
90PalmSp/Cal-209
90PalmSp/ProC-2580
91PalmSp/ProC-2019
Dominguez, Jose
86OrlanTw-5
88Shrev/ProC-1281
88TexLgAS/GS-19
89Shrev/ProC-1854
Dominguez, Ken
90Oneonta/ProC-3390CO
92PrWill/ClBest-28CO
92PrWill/ProC-165CO
93Greens/ClBest-28CO
Dominico, Ron
84LitFalls-26
85LitFalls-4
Dominquez, Jose
85Visalia-22
Donaghue, Ray
77StPete
Donahue, Chuck
86Tampa-5
Donahue, James A.
(Jim)
No Cards.
Donahue, Matt
92Erie/ClBest-27
92Erie/ProC-1611
Donahue, Patrick W.
(Pat)
E107
E91
M116
T204
T205
T206
Donahue, Tim
90Reno/Cal-270
91Collnd/ClBest-24
91Collnd/ProC-1491
92Kinston/ClBest-11
92Kinston/ProC-2483
Donald, Richard Atley
(Atley)
40PlayBall-121
41PlayBall-38
44Yank/St-9
Donald, Tremayne
90Johnson/Star-9
92StPete/ClBest-19
92StPete/ProC-2038
Donaldson, James
91Sydney/Fut-20
Donaldson, John David
(John)
68T-244
69MB-75
69MLB/St-85
69OPC-217
69T-217
70MLB/St-269
70OPC-418
70T-418
72MB-93
Donaldson, John
78Laugh/Black-28
86Negro/Frit-77
90Negro/Star-8
94TedW-104
Donatelli, Andy
85Utica-18
Donatelli, Augie
55B-313UMP
Donati, John
92StCl/Dome-37
Donlin, Michael J.
(Mike)
11Helmar-158
75F/Pion-25
92Conlon/Sport-450
94Conlon-1051
E107
E90/1
E91
T204
T206
T207
T213/blue
T215/blue
T215/brown
WG3-13
Donnelly, Edward
(Ed)
T207
Donnelly, James B.
(Jim)
N172
N284
WG1-64
Donnelly, Rich
74Gaston
77Tucson
78Cr/PCL-8
79Tucson-8
89VFJuice-39CO
90Homer/Pirate-9CO
92Pirate/Nation-6CO
93Pirate/Nation-9CO
93Rang/Keeb-127CO
Donnelly, Sylvester
(Blix)
49B-145
49Eureka-133
50B-176
51B-208
Donnels, Chris
88Clmbia/GS-26
88StLucie/Star-6
89StLucie/Star-5
89Star/IISingl-116
90Jacks/GS-12
90T/TVMets-41
91AAA/LineD-554
91AAAGame/ProC-47
91B-465
91Classic/III-16
91Leaf-447
91S/RookTr-104T
91Tidew/LineD-554
91Tidew/ProC-2516
91UD/FinalEd-61F
92D-619
92OPC-376
92Pinn-168
92ProC/Tomorrow-275
92S-212
92S/100RisSt-79
92S/Rook-29
92Sky/AAASingl-249
92StCl-353
92T-376
92T/91Debut-45
92T/Gold-376
92T/GoldWin-376
92Tidew/ProC-
92Tidew/SB-555
92UD-44
93D-747
93F-426
93Mother/Ast-22
93Pac/Spanish-475
93StCl/Ast-23
93T-238
93T/Gold-238
94F-488
94Pac/Cr-262
94S-172
94S/GoldR-172
94StCl-334
94StCl/1stDay-334
94StCl/Gold-334
94T-153
94T/Gold-153
Donofrio, Larry
80Ashvl-22
81AppFx-13
Donohoe, Kelly
89KS*-1
89KS*-39M
Donohue, J.A.
E91
Donohue, Jack
N172
N172/ST
Donohue, James A.
(Jim)
N172
N284
N690
Donohue, James T.
(Jim)
60T-124
61T-151
62T-498
Donohue, John F.
(Jiggs)
No Cards.
Donohue, Peter J.
(Pete)
25Exh-27
26Exh-27
91Conlon/Sport-322
E120
R316
V61-77
W517-26
W572
Donohue, Steve
79WHave-19
82Colum-24M
Donohue, Thomas J.
(Tom)
77SLCity
78Cr/PCL-52
80T-454
81D-51
81F-281
81T-621
Donovan, Bret
88CapeCod/Sum-165
92ClBest-322
92Elmira/ClBest-3
92Elmira/ProC-1375
92WinHaven/ClBest-22
Donovan, Gary
77BurlB
Donovan, Jack
81Tucson-25
Donovan, Michael B.
(Mike)
80BurlB-3
Donovan, Patrick J.
(Patsy)
09Buster/Pin-5
11Helmar-31
12Sweet/Pin-24
90Target-191
E107
M116
WG2-15
Donovan, Richard E.
(Dick)
55T-146
56T-18
56T/Pin-32
57T-181
58T-290
59T-5
60L-72
60T-199
61Bz-10
61T-414
61T/St-202
62J-73
62Kahn
62P-73
62P/Can-73
62Sugar-3
62T-15
62T-55LL
62T/St-33
63Bz-10
63F-11
63J-75
63P-75
63Salada-34
63Sugar-3
63T-370
63T-8LL
63T/SO
64Kahn
79TCMA-34
Exh47
Donovan, William E.
(Wild Bill)
16FleischBrd-24
81Tiger/Detroit-29
87Conlon/2-13
90Target-192
D303
D327
D328-43
D329-48
D350/2-49
E101
E102
E103
E104
E105
E106
E121/80
E122
E254
E300
E90/1
E92
E93
E96
M116
T201
T204
T206
T213/blue
T213/brown
T216
T3-12
V100
W555
W575
Dooin, Charles S.
(Red)
10Domino-34
11Diamond-12
11Helmar-141
12Sweet/Pin-125A
12Sweet/Pin-125B
14CJ-38
15CJ-38
BF2-74
D303
D329-49
D350/2-50
E101
E103
E104
E105
E106
E224
E270/2
E300
E90/1
E92
E93
E96
E98
L1-126
M101/4-49
M101/5-50
M116
S74-98
S81-101
T201
T202
T205
T206
T207
T215/blue
T215/brown
T216
T3-14
W555
WG3-14
WG5-15
WG6-14
Doolan, Blake
92Batavia/ClBest-25
92Batavia/ProC-3256
Doolan, Michael J.
(Mickey)
10Domino-35
11Helmar-142
12Sweet/Pin-126A
12Sweet/Pin-126B
14CJ-120
15CJ-120
90Target-193
D303
D329-50
D350/2-51
E101
E104
E105
E106
E224
E254
E270/1
E92
E94
E97
M101/4-50
M101/5-51
M116
S74-99
T202
T205
T206
T213/blue
T213/brown

T214-7
T215/blue
T215/brown
T216
T3-90
W555
WG3-15
Dooley
N172/PCL
Dooley, Marvin
89Princet/Star-6
Doolittle, James
33SK*-28
Dooner, Glenn
82Toledo-2
Doornenweerd, Dave
91FrRow/DP-36
92Augusta/ProC-232
92B-146
92StCl/Dome-38
92UD/ML-169
Dophied, Tracy
82AubAs-12
Dopson, John
86Indianap-12
88D/Rook-43
88F/Up-U99
88S/Tr-88T
89B-24
89Classic/Up/2-161
89D-392
89D/Best-177
89D/Tr-7
89F-373
89F/Up-8
89OPC-251
89S-466
89S/Tr-40
89T-251
89T/Tr-26T
89UD-57
90D-162
90F-272
90F/Can-272
90Leaf-130
90OPC-733
90Panini/St-18
90Pep/RSox-7
90S-331
90S/YS/I-26
90T-733
90T/St-260
90T/TVRSox-9
90UD-671
91D-193
91F-92
91OPC-94
91S-772
91T-94
91UD-88
92OPC-400
92Pawtu/SB-360
92StCl-287
93F-557
93Pac/Spanish-31
93StCl-41
93StCl/1stDay-41
93T-187
93T/Gold-187
93UD-409
93Ultra-151
94D-104
94F-31
94Pac/Cr-53
94S-113
94S/GoldR-113
94T-321
94T/Gold-321
Doran, Bill
82Tucson-7
83T/Tr-26
84D-580
84F-225
84Mother/Ast-4
84Nes/792-198
84OPC-198
84T-198
84T/St-377
85D-84
85F-350
85Mother/Ast-8
85OPC-299
85T-684
85T/St-68
86D-10DK
86D-110
86D/DKsuper-10
86F-300
86Leaf-10DK
86OPC-57
86Pol/Ast-5
86Seven/Coin-S14
86T-57
86T/St-25
86T/Tatt-19M
87D-286
87D/OD-11
87F-57
87GenMills/Book-6M
87Leaf-197
87Mother/Ast-4
87OPC-243
87Pol/Ast-5
87RedFoley/St-69
87Sf-116M
87Sf-162
87Sf/TPrev-8M
87T-472
87T/Mini-9
87T/St-31
88D-235
88D/Best-120
88F-447
88F/LL-10
88F/St-87
88Leaf-183
88Mother/Ast-4
88Nestle-19
88OPC-166
88Panini/St-295
88Pol/Ast-10
88S-52
88Sf-48
88T-745
88T/Big-51
88T/St-34
89B-329
89D-306
89D/Best-38
89F-357
89KennerFig-38
89Lennox/Ast-8
89Mother/Ast-4
89OPC-226
89Panini/St-89
89RedFoley/St-37
89S-21
89Sf-57
89T-226
89T/Big-168
89T/St-16
89T/UK-22
89UD-101
90B-76
90D-236
90D/BestNL-102
90F-230
90F/Can-230
90Leaf-161
90Lennox-13
90MLBPA/Pins-44
90Mother/Ast-7
90OPC-368
90Panini/St-268
90Publlnt/St-257
90Publlnt/St-94
90S-182
90S/100St-8
90T-368
90T/Big-159
90T/St-15
90UD-198
91B-682
91D-756
91F-63
91Kahn/Reds-19
91Leaf-197
91OPC-577
91Pep/Reds-8
91S-775
91StCl-148
91T-577
91UD-398
91Ultra-93
92B-234
92D-293
92F-405
92L-231
92L/BlkGold-231
92OPC-136
92Panini-263
92Pinn-47
92Reds/Kahn-19
92S-77
92StCl-38
92T-136
92T/Gold-136
92T/GoldWin-136
92UD-280
92Ultra-188
93D-370
93F-390
93Pac/Spanish-82
93Pol/Brew-5
93T-608
93T/Gold-608
93UD-107
93Ultra-28
Doran, John F.
(John)
N172
Doran, Mark
86PalmSp-11
87MidldA-21
88Edmon/CMC-24
88Edmon/ProC-570
89MidldA/GS-14
Dorante, Luis
87Elmira/Black-14
87Elmira/Red-14
88Elmira-12
89Elmira/Pucko-3
90LynchRS/Team-11
91WinHaven/ClBest-12
91WinHaven/ProC-492
Dorgan, Charles
77Clinton
Dorgan, Michael C.
(Mike)
N167-3
N172
N284
N403
N690
Dorish, Harry
51B-266
52T-303
53T-145
54B-86
54T-110
55B-248
56T-167
79BuffB/TCMA-12
80Port-14C
91Crown/Orio-111
91T/Arc53-145
94T/Arc54-110
Dorlarque, Aaron
92Eugene/ClBest-10
92Eugene/ProC-3021
93Rockford/ClBest-12
Dorn, Chris
89Pittsfld/Star-4
90Clmbia/PCPII-5
90Columbia/GS-20
91StLucie/ClBest-22
91StLucie/ProC-703
92Bingham/ProC-508
92Bingham/SB-54
Dorner, Augustus
(Gus)
T204
T206
Dorsett, Brian
85Huntsvl/BK-22
85Madis-11
85Madis/Pol-8
86Tacoma-3
87Tacoma-22
88F-607
89Colum/CMC-14
89Colum/Pol-2
89Colum/ProC-759
90AAAGame/ProC-14
90AAASingl/ProC-329
90ColClip/ProC-679
90Colum/Pol-18
90T/TVYank-40
91AAA/LineD-279
91LasVegas/LineD-279
91LasVegas/ProC-238
92BuffB/BlueS-7
92BuffB/ProC-326
92BuffB/SB-32
92Yank/WIZ80-46
94Pac/Cr-146
94T-688
94T/Gold-688
Dorsett, Cal
94Conlon-1295
Dorsey, James Edward
(Jim)
75QuadC
79SLCity-14
80SLCity-16
81Pawtu-9
81T-214R
83Pawtu-6
84Pawtu-6
Dorsey, Lee
90Utica/Pucko-30
Doscher, Jack
90Target-194
Doss, Dennis
77Watlo
Doss, Greg
88Savan/ProC-357
Doss, Jason
88Wythe/ProC-1998
89CharWh/Best-20
89CharWh/ProC-1765
90Peoria/Team-19
91Peoria/ClBest-5
91Peoria/ProC-1336
91Peoria/Team-7
92WinSalem/ClBest-9
92WinSalem/ProC-1204
Doss, Larry
87James-9
Doss, Rick
79Cedar/TCMA-10
Dostal, Bruce
88Bakers/Cal-247
89VeroB/Star-7
90FSLAS/Star-3
90VeroB/Star-11
91AA/LineD-507
91Reading/LineD-507
91Reading/ProC-1381
92Reading/ProC-586
92ScranWB/SB-483
92Sky/AAASingl-220
93ScranWB/Team-8
Doster, Zach
87Fayette-7
88Fayette/ProC-1090
89Miami/I/Star-5
Dotel, Angel
92Bakers/Cal-9
Dotel, Mariano
91Myrtle/ClBest-19
91Myrtle/ProC-2953
92Dunedin/ClBest-12
92Dunedin/ProC-2006
93Hagers/ClBest-10
93Hagers/ProC-1887
Dotelson, Angel
91Kissim/ProC-4200
Dotolo, C.L.
92Clinton/ClBest-25
92Clinton/ProC-3603
Dotson, J.
(Gene)
79ArkTr-8
81Louisvl-15
83Louisvl/Riley-15
Dotson, Larry
81Watlo-25
Dotson, Richard E.
(Rich)
78Knoxvl
79Knoxvl/TCMA-8
81Coke
81D-280
81F-356
81OPC-138
81T-138
81T/HT
81T/St-62
82D-356
82F-340
82F/St-186
82OPC-257
82T-461
82T/St-166
82T/StVar-166
83D-319
83F-233
83OPC-46
83T-46
83TrueVal/WSox-34
84D-180
84F-56
84F/St-62
84Nes/792-216TL
84Nes/792-759
84OPC-24
84T-216TL
84T-759
84T/St-241
84TrueVal/WS-10
85Coke/WS-34
85D-302
85D-3DK
85D/DKsuper-3
85F-511
85Leaf-3DK
85OPC-364
85T-364
85T/St-233
86Coke/WS-34
86D-160
86F-203
86Jay's-5
86OPC-233
86Sf-133M
86T-156M
86T-612
87Coke/WS-20
87D-383
87D/OD-238
87F-495
87F/Mini-33
87OPC-211
87T-720
88D-124
88D/Best-52
88D/Y/Bk-NEW
88F-396
88F/Up-U48
88OPC-209
88Panini/St-53
88S-480
88S/Tr-60T
88T-209
88T/St-291
88T/Tr-35T
89D-277
89F-253
89OPC-357
89Panini/St-398
89S-278
89S/NWest-23
89S/Tr-80
89Sf-194
89T-511
89T/DHTest-22
89T/St-316
89UD-80
90OPC-169
90Publlnt/St-533
90S-19
90T-169
92Yank/WIZ80-47
Dotter, Gary Richard
(Gary)
65T-421R
Dotterer, Henry John
(Dutch)
58T-396
59T-288
60T-21
61T-332
61T/RO-24
Doty, Derrin
91WA/Via-2
Doty, Sean
89Billings/ProC-2052
90Billings/ProC-3212
91CharWh/ClBest-2
91CharWh/ProC-2879
92Cedar/ClBest-25
92Cedar/ProC-1063
Dotzler, Mike
86DayBe-7
87Salem-12
88OrlanTw/Best-21
89Visalia/Cal-105
89Visalia/ProC-1438

Doubleday, Abner
80Perez/HOF-A
90BBWit-108
Doucet, Eric
89Boise/ProC-1983
Doucette, Darren
92Hamil/ClBest-22
92Hamil/ProC-1598
Dougherty, James
88CapeCod/Sum-55
92ClBest-351
92Osceola/ClBest-17
92Osceola/ProC-2521
93ClBest/MLG-65
93FExcel/ML-41
94FExcel-198
Dougherty, Mark
83Erie-7
86ArkTr-6
87Louisvl-11
88Louisvl-18
88Louisvl/CMC-23
88Louisvl/ProC-444
Dougherty, Pat
86BurlEx-6
Dougherty, Patrick H.
(Patsy)
10Domino-36
11Helmar-10
12Sweet/Pin-9
E101
E102
E105
E107
E254
E90/1
E90/3
E92
E94
M116
T201
T205
T206
T215/blue
T215/brown
T216
WG2-16
Doughty, Jamie
85Tulsa-9
86Tulsa-11
Douglas, Charles 1
(Whammy)
58T-306
59T-431
Douglas, Charles 2
88Boise/ProC-1624
Douglas, Dave
87Harris-16
Douglas, John 1
90Target-933
Douglas, John 2
88OK-7
89OK-13
Douglas, Maurice
89KS*-32
Douglas, Murray
93SoEastern-7
Douglas, Phillip B.
(Phil)
90Target-195
E120
E121/120
W501-74
W514-5
W575
Douglas, Preston
88Utica/Pucko-27
Douglas, Steve
82OrlanTw/A-6
82OrlanTw/B-17
Douglas, William B.
(Klondike)
E107
Douma, Todd
90Pittsfld/Pucko-13
91FSLAS/ProC-FSL30
91StLucie/ClBest-24
91StLucie/ProC-704
92Bingham/ProC-509
92Bingham/SB-55
92ProC/Tomorrow-286
92Sky/AASingl-23
93FExcel/ML-72

Dour, Brian
88CapeCod/Sum-64
89Everett/Star-6
90Foil/Best-253
90SanJose/Best-21
90SanJose/Cal-42
90SanJose/ProC-2009
90SanJose/Star-7
91SanJose/ClBest-15
91SanJose/ProC-3
Douris, John D.
91Welland/ClBest-21
91Welland/ProC-3566
Douthit, Taylor Lee
(Taylor)
29Exh/4-16
31Exh/4-16
33Exh/4-4
33G-40
91Conlon/Sport-264
94Conlon-1214
R316
V353-40
Dovalis, Alex
79Wisco-6
Dovey, Troy
89Ashvl/ProC-956
90Ashvl/ProC-2739
90Osceola/Star-6
91BurlAs/ClBest-2
91BurlAs/ProC-2793
92Osceola/ProC-2522
Dowd, Snooks
90Target-196
Dowell, Ken
83Reading-13
84Cram/PCL-210
85Cram/PCL-46
86Portl-5
87F/Up-U27
87Maine-16
87Maine/TCMA-10
88Tidew/CANDL-8
88Tidew/CMC-14
88Tidew/ProC-1595
89Tidew/CMC-11
89Tidew/ProC-1963
90AAASingl/ProC-412
90ProC/Singl-298
90Richm/CMC-22
90Richm/ProC-267
90Richm/Team-9
Dowies, Butch
82Danvl/Frit-10
Dowless, Mike
81Water-3
82Indianap-16
83Indianap-23
84Cedar-24
Dowling, David B.
(Dave)
65OPC-116R
65T-116R
66T-482R
67T-272R
88AlaskaAS60/Team-12
Down, Rick
90Albany/ProC-1180MG
90Albany/Star-24
91AAA/LineD-124MG
91ColClip/LineD-124
91ColClip/ProC-614
92ColClip/Pol-1M
92ColClip/ProC-367
92ColClip/SB-124MG
Downey, Alexander C.
(Red)
90Target-934
Downey, Charles
90AR-8
Downey, Thomas E.
(Tom)
10Domino-37
11Helmar-143
12Sweet/Pin-97A
12Sweet/Pin-97B
14CJ-107
15CJ-107
E254
M116
S74-73
T201
T205

T206
T207
T213/blue
T214-8
T3-91
Downing, Alphonso E.
(Al)
62T-219
64T-219M
64T-86
64T/Coins-109
65MacGregor-2
65OPC-11LL
65T-11LL
65T-598
66T-384
67CokeCap/YMet-14
67T-308
68Bz-12
68OPC-105
68T-105
68T/ActionSt-5AM
69MB-76
69T-292
70T-584
71MLB/St-102
71OPC-182
71T-182
72MB-94
72OPC-460
72OPC-93LL
72T-460
72T-93LL
73OPC-324
73T-324
74OPC-620
74T-620
75OPC-498
75T-498
75T/M-498
76OPC-605
76SSPC-66
76T-605
81TCMA-450
90Target-197
92Yank/WIZ60-36
92Yank/WIZAS-19
WG10-5
WG9-7
Downing, Brian Jay
(Brian)
74OPC-601R
74T-601R
75OPC-422
75T-422
75T/M-422
76OPC-23
76SSPC-141
76T-23
77Ho-138
77Ho/Twink-138
77OPC-246
77T-344
78T-519
79T-71
80OPC-315
80T-602
80T/S-49
80T/Super-49
81D-410
81F-282
81OPC-263
81T-263
81T/St-50
82D-115
82F-457
82F/St-215
82OPC-158
82T-158
83D-367
83F-86
83F/St-22M
83F/St-2M
83OPC-298
83T-442
84D-423
84F-515
84Nes/792-574
84OPC-135
84Smok/Cal-8
84T-574
84T/St-236
85D-158
85F-300

85Leaf-223
85OPC-374
85Smok/Cal-7
85T-374
85T/St-224
86D-108
86F-154
86Leaf-39
86OPC-205
86Sf-154
86Smok/Cal-7
86T-772
86T/St-183
86T/Tatt-14M
87D-86
87D/HL-5
87D/OD-9
87F-78
87F/BB-15
87F/Excit-16
87F/Mini-34
87F/St-35
87OPC-88
87Sf-161
87Sf/TPrev-11M
87Smok/Cal-19
87T-782
87T/St-178
88D-258
88D/Best-27
88F-488
88F/Mini-10
88F/St-11
88KennerFig-30
88Leaf-203
88OPC-331
88Panini/St-46
88RedFoley/St-19
88S-44
88Sf-181
88Smok/Angels-18
88T-331
88T/Big-78
88T/Mini-5
88T/Revco-23
88T/St-181
89B-53
89D-254
89D/Best-321
89F-475
89OPC-17
89Panini/St-288
89S-76
89Sf-117
89Smok/Angels-12
89T-17
89T/St-178
89UD-485
90B-294
90D-10DK
90D-352
90D/SuperDK-10DK
90F-130
90F/Can-130
90OPC-635
90Panini/St-27
90PublInt/St-368
90S-26
90S/100St-46
90Sf-77
90Smok/Angel-4
90T-635
90T/St-169
90UD-146
91F-310
91F/UltraUp-U54
91Leaf-269
91Mother/Rang-17
91OPC-255
91S-104
91S/RookTr-30T
91StCl-348
91T-255
91T/Tr-33T
91UD-231A
91UD-231B
91UD/Ext-770
92D-167
92F-302
92L-440
92L/BlkGold-440
92Mother/Rang-17
92OPC-173
92Pinn-368

92S-579
92StCl-494
92T-173
92T/Gold-173
92T/GoldWin-173
92UD-483
92Ultra-440
93Panini-88
93Rang/Keeb-128
Downs, Dorley
84PrWill-12
85Nashua-7
86Macon-8
Downs, Jerome Willis
(Red)
90Target-198
T201
T206
Downs, John
91Eugene/ClBest-22
91Eugene/ProC-3717
Downs, Kelly
82OkCty-21
83Portl-9
84Cram/PCL-201
85Cram/PCL-189
86Phoenix-4
87D-573
87F-272
87Mother/SFG-17
87Sf/TPrev-10M
87T-438
88Classic/Red-194
88D-145
88D/Best-106
88F-80
88Mother/Giants-17
88OPC-187
88Panini/St-415
88S-27
88S/YS/I-19
88Sf-203
88T-629
88T/JumboR-19
88ToysRUs-9
89B-465
89D-367
89D/Best-247
89F-326
89Mother/Giants-4
89OPC-361
89Panini/St-209
89S-124
89Sf-39
89T-361
89T/Big-112
89T/St-81
89UD-476
90D-177
90F-55
90F/Can-55
90Mother/Giant-4
90OPC-17
90PublInt/St-66
90S-534
90T-17
90UD-699
91B-633
91D-738
91F-261
91F/UltraUp-U116
91Mother/Giant-4
91OPC-733
91PG&E-4
91S-654
91StCl-193
91T-733
91UD-441
92B-343
92D-303
92F-634
92Giant/PGE-15
92Mother/Giant-21
92OPC-573
92Pinn-492
92S-191
92StCl-517
92T-573
92T/Gold-573
92T/GoldWin-573
92UD-583
92Ultra-290
93F-662
93Mother/A's-20

93Pac/Spanish-565
93UD-636
94F-259
Downs, Kirk
80BurlB-24
Downs, Ron
88Augusta/ProC-378
88SALAS/GS-5
89Salem/Star-6
Doxtator, Melvil
52Laval-74
Doyel, Dan
89Savan/ProC-347
90ArkTr/GS-3TR
91StPete/ClBest-30TR
92StPete/ClBest-29TR
Doyle
N172/PCL
Doyle, Blake
78RochR
79RochR-4
80Indianap-20
Doyle, Brian Reed
(Brian)
78Cr/PCL-14
79T-710R
80Colum-13
80T-582
81F-104
81T-159
81T/Tr-754
82Syrac-16
82Syrac/Team-10
92Yank/WIZ70-46
92Yank/WIZ80-48
Doyle, Carl
90Target-935
Doyle, Ian
91BurlInd/ProC-3294
92ColRS/ClBest-18
92ColRS/ProC-2382
93ClBest/MLG-15
93Kinston/Team-7
93SALAS/II-9
94FExcel-42
Doyle, James
M116
Doyle, Jeffrey D.
(Jeff)
81ArkTr-7
81Louisvl-11
82Louisvl-7
83Louisvl/Riley-11
Doyle, John Joseph
(Jack)
90Target-199
E107
N566-178
Doyle, Judd Bruce
(Slow Joe)
T206
Doyle, Lawrence J.
(Larry)
10Domino-38
11Diamond-13
11Helmar-125
12Sweet/Pin-112A
12Sweet/Pin-112B
14CJ-4
14Piedmont/St-19
15CJ-4
16FleischBrd-25
77Galasso-157
91Conlon/Sport-317
BF2-75
D303
D328-44
D329-51
D350/2-52
E101
E102
E103
E104
E105
E106
E135-44
E224
E254
E270/2
E286
E91
E92
E95
M101/4-51
M101/5-52
M116
S74-85
T201
T202
T205
T206
T207
T213/blue
T215/blue
T215/brown
T216
T3-13
W514-81
W516-13
WG4-7
Doyle, Paul S.
(Paul)
70OPC-277
70T-277
72T-629
Doyle, Rich
82Watlo/B-2
82Watlo/Frit-23
83BuffB-3
84BuffB-11
85Water-6
86Beaum-10
88SanBern/Best-24
88SanBern/Cal-52
89Calgary/CMC-7
89Calgary/ProC-541
89EastLDD/ProC-DD32
Doyle, Robert Dennis
(Denny)
70OPC-539R
70T-539R
71MLB/St-175
71OPC-352
71T-352
72T-768
73OPC-424
73T-424
74OPC-552
74T-552
75OPC-187
75SSPC/18-17
75T-187
75T/M-187
76Ho-107
76OPC-381
76SSPC-407
76T-381
77Ashvl
77T-336
78OPC-111
78T-642
Doyle, Tim
91SoOreg/ClBest-4
91SoOreg/ProC-3833
Doyle, Tom
86Columbia-9TR
87Columbia-23
88Jacks/GS-7
88Martins/Star-11
90Waterlo/Best-26
90Waterlo/ProC-2383
91CharRain/ClBest-18
91CharRain/ProC-103
92James/ClBest-3
92MN-6
93BurlB/ClBest-7
93BurlB/ProC-165
Doyle, William Carl
R313
Dozier, D.J.
90FSLAS/Star-4
90S/Tr-97T
90StLucie/Star-6
90Star/ISingl-9
91AA/LineD-631
91B-478
91ClBest/Singl-387
91Classic/200-89
91Classic/II-T4
91UD-3SR
91Wmsprt/LineD-631
91Wmsprt/ProC-306
92B-219
92D-20RR
92OPC-591M
92ProC/Tomorrow-282
92Sky/AAASingl-250
92T-591M
92T/Gold-591M
92T/GoldWin-591M
92Tidew/ProC-
92Tidew/SB-556
93D-90
Dozier, Tom
82Spring/Frit-15
83StPete-5
84Albany-11
85Cram/PCL-145
85Huntsvl/BK-15
86Tacoma-4
87Tacoma-1
88Greenvl/Best-18
90SpringDG/Best-8
Drabek, Doug
85Albany-4
86Colum-6
86Colum/Pol-6
86D/Rook-31
86F/Up-U36
87D-251
87D/HL-32
87F-96
87T-283
87T/Tr-29T
88D-79
88D/Best-73
88F-327
88Leaf-88
88OPC-143
88RedFoley/St-20
88S-51
88T-591
88T/Big-124
88T/St-134
89B-416
89D-211
89D/Best-17
89F-206
89KennerFig-39
89OPC-37
89Panini/St-161
89S-117
89S/HotStar-87
89S/YS/I-21
89Sf-27
89T-478
89UD-597
89VFJuice-15
90AlbanyDG/Best-22
90B-164
90D-92
90D/BestNL-9
90F-465
90F/Can-465
90Homer/Pirate-10
90Leaf-296
90OPC-197
90Panini/St-332
90PublInt/St-153
90RedFoley/St-27
90S-505
90T-197
90T/Big-185
90T/St-130
90UD-422
91B-515
91BBBest/Aces-5
91Bz-4
91Classic/200-167
91Classic/I-82
91Classic/II-T79
91CollAB-29
91D-269
91D-411MVP
91D-750CY
91D/Elite-E5
91D/Preview-2
91F-36
91F/UltraG-3
91Kenner-15
91Leaf-516
91Leaf/Stud-224
91Leaf/StudPrev-15
91MSA/Holsum-7
91MajorLg/Pins-59
91OPC-405AS
91OPC-685
91Panini/FrSt-122
91Panini/St-116
91Panini/Top15-57
91Panini/Top15-92
91RedFoley/St-28
91S-472
91S-661AS
91S-878CY
91S/100SS-6
91StCl-202
91StCl/Charter*-7
91T-405
91T-685
91T/CJMini/I-12
91UD-278
91Ultra-277
91Woolwth/HL-3
92B-465
92CJ/DI-34
92Classic/Game200-67
92Classic/II-T68
92D-209
92F-553
92L-11
92L/BlkGold-11
92OPC-440
92OPC/Premier-32
92Panini-259
92Pinn-96
92Pirate/Nation-7
92S-115
92S/100SS-53
92StCl-170
92Studio-84
92T-440
92T/Gold-440
92T/GoldWin-440
92T/Kids-24
92TripleP-106
92UD-221
92UD-39TC
92UD/TmMVPHolo-18
92Ultra-253
92Yank/WIZ80-49
93B-208
93D-622
93Duracel/PPI-12
93F-500
93F/Final-77
93F/Fruit-17
93Flair-61
93JDean/28-19
93KingB-23
93Kraft-20
93L-293
93L/GoldAS-20M
93MSA/Ben-7
93MSA/Metz-6
93Mother/Ast-5
93OPC-72
93OPC/Premier-73
93Pac/Spanish-476
93Pinn-423
93Pinn-485HH
93S-580
93Select-153
93Select/Ace-16
93Select/RookTr-97T
93Select/StatL-65M
93StCl-167
93StCl-672
93StCl/1stDay-167
93StCl/1stDay-672
93StCl/Ast-1
93Studio-194
93T-190
93T/Finest-127
93T/FinestRef-127
93T/Gold-190
93T/Hill-26
93T/Tr-94T
93TripleP-232
93UD-475
93UD-664
93UD/FunPack-46
93UD/SP-32
93Ultra-392
94B-174
94D-632
94F-489
94Finest-345
94L-271
94OPC-248
94Pac/Cr-263
94Panini-193
94Pinn-104
94Pinn/Artist-104
94Pinn/Museum-104
94RedFoley-2M
94S-426
94Sf/2000-17
94StCl-408
94StCl/1stDay-408
94StCl/Gold-408
94Studio-20
94T-220
94T/Gold-220
94TripleP-25
94UD-452
94UD/CollC-95
94UD/CollC/Gold-95
94UD/CollC/Silv-95
94UD/SP-30
94Ultra-501
Drabinski, Marek
91Macon/ClBest-14
91Macon/ProC-867
Drabowsky, Myron W.
(Moe)
57T-84
58T-135
59T-407
60L-68
60T-349
61T-364
62T-331
64T-42
64T/St-82
64T/tatt-36
65T-439
66T-291
67CokeCap/Orio-16
67OPC-125
67OPC-151WS
67T-125
67T-151WS
68CokeCap/Orio-16
68Dexter-29
68T-242
69MB-77
69MLB/St-57
69T-508
69T/St-183
70MLB/St-220
70T-653
71MLB/St-272
71OPC-685
71T-685
72MB-95
72T-627
78TCMA-121
87Birm/Best-3CO
88BirmB/Best-7CO
89Pac/Leg-215
89Swell-103
89Vanco/CMC-25CO
89Vanco/ProC-581CO
90AAASingl/ProC-184CO
90ProC/Singl-175CO
90Vanco/CMC-26CO
90Vanco/ProC-506CO
91AAA/LineD-650M
91Crown/Orio-112
91Vanco/LineD-650CO
91Vanco/ProC-1610CO
92Hagers/ProC-2572CO
92Hagers/SB-275CO
93UD/ATH-43
Drago, Richard A.
(Dick)
69T-662R
70OPC-37
70T-37
71MLB/St-414
71OPC-752
71T-752
72K-40
72OPC-205
72T-205
73OPC-392
73T-392
74OPC-113
74T-113
75OPC-333
75T-333
75T/M-333
76OPC-142
76SSPC-422
76T-142
77T-426
78PapaG/Disc-11
78SSPC/270-171
78T-567

79OPC-2
79T-12
80T-271
81D-336
81F-239
81OPC-332
81T-647
81T/Tr-755
82F-510
82T-742
89T/SenLg-17
89TM/SenLg-29
91Crown/Orio-113
Drahman, Brian
87Beloit-10
88Stockton/Cal-186
88Stockton/ProC-734
89ElPaso/GS-6
90BirmB/Best-15
90BirmB/ProC-1103
91B-363
91Kodak/WSox-50
91S/RookTr-81T
92F-77
92OPC-231
92S-734
92S/100RisSt-55
92StCl-744
92T-231
92T/91Debut-46
92T/Gold-231
92T/GoldWin-231
92Vanco/SB-633
93D-672
94StCl/Team-82
Drake, Delos Daniel
(Delos)
T207
Drake, H.P.
78LodiD
Drake, Kevin
74Cedar
75Dubuq
Drake, Sam
88CapeCod/Sum-131
89Helena/SP-22
90Beloit/Best-6
90Beloit/Star-6
91Stockton/ClBest-9
91Stockton/ProC-3027
Drake, Samuel H.
(Sammy)
62T-162
91WIZMets-99
Drake, Solomon L.
(Solly)
57T-159
59T-406
90Target-200
Drake, Tex
85Kingst-26
86Kinston-5bb
89Richm/ProC-819
Drake, Tom
90Target-201
Drake, William
(Plunk)
78Laugh/Black-8
86Negro/Frit-69
87Negro/Dixon-10
Dramer, Tommy
90Kinston/Team-2
Draper, Mike
88Oneonta/ProC-2059
89PrWill/Star-6
90FtLaud/Star-5
91AA/LineD-4
91Albany/LineD-4
91Albany/ProC-1000
92AAA/ASG/SB-104
92ColClip/Pol-5
92ColClip/ProC-345
92ColClip/SB-104
92D/Rook-34
92Sky/AAASingl-46
93B-482
93F/Final-101
93FExcel/ML-206
93Mets/Kahn-47
93Pac/Spanish-540
93StCl-732
93StCl/1stDay-732
93Ultra-425
94Pac/Cr-398

Dravecky, David F.
(Dave)
79BuffB
79BuffB/TCMA-1
80Buffa-4
81Hawaii-20
82Hawaii-20
83F-356
83T-384
84D-551
84D-8DK
84F-298
84Mother/Padres-11
84Nes/792-290
84Nes/792-366TL
84OPC-290
84Smok/Padres-7
84T-290
84T-366TL
84T/St-155
85D-112
85F-30
85Mother/Padres-8
85OPC-32
85T-530
85T/St-154
86D-162
86F-319
86Leaf-92
86OPC-276
86T-735
87Bohem-43
87D-187
87F-412
87F/Up-U28
87OPC-62
87T-470
87T/St-107
88D-485
88D/Best-135
88F-81
88F/BB/MVP-10
88F/St-127
88Mother/Giants-9
88S-564
88T-68
89F-327
89Mother/Giants-9
89T-601
89UD-39
90OPC-124
90Pac/Legend-80
90Panini/St-360
90Panini/St-386
90S-550
90T-124
90UD-679
93TWill-53
93UD/ATH-44
Drawdy, Duke
77WHave
Drayton, Kenny
89KS*-29
Drees, Tom
86Penin-8
87DayBe-4
88BirmB/Best-3
88SLAS-34
89AAA/ProC-29
89Vanco/CMC-10
89Vanco/ProC-588
90AAAGame/ProC-38
90AAASingl/ProC-161
90BirmDG/Best-7
90F-644R
90F/Can-644
90ProC/Singl-630
90UD-3SR
90Vanco/CMC-3
90Vanco/ProC-483
91AAA/LineD-631
91Vanco/LineD-631
91Vanco/ProC-1588
92OkCty/SB-309
92Sky/AAASingl-141
92T/91Debut-47
Dreifort, Darren
91T/Tr-34TUSA
92StCl/Dome-39
92T/Tr-29T
92T/TrGold-29T
93StCl/MurphyS-13
94Pinn-540

94UD-513DD
94UD/SP-3PP
Dreifort, Todd
90WichSt-9
92James/ClBest-7
92James/ProC-1512
Dreisbach, Bill
91Princet/ClBest-12
91Princet/ProC-3517
92Billings/ProC-3357
Drell, Tom
88CapeCod-1
88CapeCod/Sum-18
89Anchora-11
90Niagara/Pucko-17
91Lakeland/ClBest-2
91Lakeland/ProC-258
92Lakeland/ClBest-21
Dressen, Charles W.
(Chuck)
25Exh-28
26Exh-28
40PlayBall-72
49Remar
50Remar
51B-259MG
52B-188MG
52T-377MG
53B/Col-124MG
53RM-NL1MG
53T-50MG
60Lake
60SpicSpan-8MG
60T-213MG
61T-137MG
64Det/Lids-5MG
64T-443MG
65T-538MG
66OPC-187MG
66T-187MG
79TCMA-56MG
83Kaline-29M
87Conlon/2-31
88Conlon/4-9
89Smok/Dodg-59
90Target-202
91T/Arc53-50MG
92Conlon/Sport-400
93Conlon-832
94Conlon-1120
R312
R316
R346-8
Dressendorfer, Kirk
88CapeCod/Sum-134
90A&AASingle/ProC-163
90SoOreg/Best-3
90SoOreg/ProC-3425
91B-235
91Classic/200-159
91Classic/I-77
91Classic/II-T20
91D/Rook-24
91F/Up-U50
91Leaf/GRook-BC13
91Mother/A's-19
91OPC/Premier-36
91S/RookTr-97T
91T/Tr-35T
91UD/Ext-756
92B-91
92Classic/Game200-7
92D-594
92OPC-716
92Pinn-270
92S-728
92S/100RisSt-37
92StCl-806
92T-716
92T/91Debut-48
92T/Gold-716
92T/GoldWin-716
92TX-13
92TripleP-177
Dressler, Robert Alan
(Rob)
75IntLgAS/Broder-6
75Lafay
75PCL/AS-6
75Phoenix-11
75Phoenix/Caruso-14
75Phoenix/CircleK-11
76OPC-599R
76Phoenix/Coke-5

76T-599R
77Phoenix
77T-11
78Cram/PCL-57
79Spokane-19
80T-366
81D-405
81OPC-163
81T-508
Drew, Bob
74Wichita-126MG
75Lafay
82Madis/Frit-34MVP
Drew, Cameron
86Ashvl-8
87ColAst/ProC-7
87SLAS-7
88TripleA/ASCMC-37
88Tucson/CMC-14
88Tucson/JP-10
88Tucson/ProC-188
89B-334
89Classic-135
89D-30RR
89F-640R
89S-643RP
89S/HotRook-3
89Sf-225R
Drews, Karl August
(Karl)
49B-188
52T-352
53B/Col-113
53T-59
54B-191
91T/Arc53-59
Drews, Matt
94B-53
94Pinn-265
94Pinn/Artist-265
94Pinn/Museum-265
94S-506
94SigRook-7
94UD/CollC-30
94UD/CollC/Gold-30
94UD/CollC/Silv-30
Dreyer, Darren
92Geneva/ClBest-19
92Geneva/ProC-1553
Dreyer, Steve
91Gaston/ClBest-4
91Gaston/ProC-2681
91SALAS/ProC-SAL22
92CharlR/ClBest-23
92CharlR/ProC-2220
92UD/ML-129
93Rang/Keeb-403
94F/MLP-10
94StCl/Team-244
94T-193
94T/Gold-193
94UD-9
94UD/CollC-5
94UD/CollC/Gold-5
94UD/CollC/Silv-5
94UD/ElecD-9
94Ultra-430
Dreyfuss, Barney
D322
Drezek, Karl
88AppFx/ProC-148
88Eugene/Best-21
Driessen, Daniel
(Dan)
74OPC-341
74T-341
74T/St-25
75OPC-133
75T-133
75T/M-133
76OPC-514
76SSPC-36
76T-514
77BurgChef-199
77OPC-31
77Pep-45
77T-23
78Ho-64
78OPC-84
78Pep-9
78SSPC/270-123
78T-246
79K-26
79OPC-247

79T-475
80OPC-173
80T-325
81Coke
81D-301
81F-205
81F/St-22
81OPC-14
81T-655
81T/HT
81T/St-164
82Coke/Reds
82D-248
82F-630M
82F-64
82OPC-373
82T-785
83D-274
83F-589
83F/St-13M
83F/St-3M
83OPC-165
83OPC/St-228
83T-165
83T/St-228
84D-243
84F-467
84Nes/792-585
84OPC-44
84T-585
84T/St-55
85D-619
85Expo/PostC-6
85F-396
85Leaf-255
85OPC-285
85OPC/Post-2
85T-285
85T/St-92
86D-641
86F-539
86Leaf-255
86Mother/Giants-14
86T-65
86T/St-89
86T/Tatt-14M
87Louisvl-12
88F/WS-7M
89Pac/SenLg-102
89Pac/SenLg-105IA
89T/SenLg-46
89TM/SenLg-30
90EliteSenLg-67
91Pac/SenLg-1
Driggers, Lee
90Augusta/ProC-2480MG
91Welland/ProC-3591MG
Drill, Lewis L.
(Lew)
E107
Drilling, Robert
49Sommer-20
Drinkwater, Sean
92Spokane/ClBest-15
92Spokane/ProC-1301
94FExcel-279
Driscoll, James B.
(Jim)
71OPC-317R
71T-317R
85Water-19
86Water-7CO
93Rang/Keeb-8
Driscoll, Jim
T3/Box-51
Driscoll, Mary Ellen
85Fresno/Pol-31
Driver, Ron
77Newar
78Holyo
79Holyo-11
Drizmala, Tom
83CharR-19
Drohan, Bill
88Eugene/Best-5
89AppFx/ProC-854
90BBCity/Star-6
Droll, Jeff
92Helena/ProC-1708
Dromerhauser, Rob
85Newar-17
Dropo, Walter
(Walt)
50B-246

51T/CAS
52B-169
52T-235
53B/Col-45
53RM-AL4
53T-121
53Tiger/Glen-5
54B-7
54T-18
55B-285
56T-238
57T-257
58T-338
59T-158
60T-79
61T-489
79TCMA-116
80Laugh/FFeat-36
89Swell-108
90Pac/Legend-22
90Swell/Great-57
91Crown/Orio-114
91Swell/Great-111
91T/Arc53-121
92Bz/Quadra-20M
94T/Arc54-18
Exh47
R423-19

Droschak, Dave
83Spring/Frit-5

Drott, Richard Fred
(Dick)
58T-80
59T-15
60L-76
60T-27
61T-231
79TCMA-64

Drucke, Louis
10Domino-39
11Helmar-126
12Sweet/Pin-113

Drummond, Tim
86PrWill-9
87Vanco-13
88Tidew/CANDL-18
88Tidew/CMC-4
88Tidew/ProC-1593
89Tidew/CMC-1
89Tidew/ProC-1952
90D-510
90D/Rook-50
90F/Up-107
90OPC-713
90S/Tr-103T
90T-713
91AAA/LineD-406
91D-694
91F-607
91OPC-46
91Portl/LineD-406
91Portl/ProC-1560
91S-76
91S/100RisSt-95
91T-46
91UD-698
92Hagers/ProC-2550

Drummonds, Lamar
63Pep/Tul

Drumright, Keith A.
78Charl
79CharCh-1
81Tacoma-17
82D-616
82F-89
82T-673
82Tacoma-29

Drury, Scott
88Batavia/ProC-1668

Dryden, Ken
72Dimanche*-73

Dryer, Steve
90Butte/SportP-10

Drysdale, Donald S.
(Don)
57T-18
58BB
58Hires-55
58T-25
59Bz
59Morrell
59T-262M
59T-387
60Armour-9
60Morrell
60P*
60T-475
60T-570AS
60T/tatt-12
60Union/Dodg-5
61Bz-26
61Morrell
61P-160
61T-260
61T-45LL
61T-49LL
61T/Dice-4
61T/St-26
61Union/Dodg-5
62BB-53
62J-110
62P-110
62P/Can-110
62T-340
62T-398AS
62T-60LL
62T/St-133
62T/bucks
63Bz-17
63Exh
63F-41
63J-123
63P-123
63Salada-1
63T-360
63T-412M
63T-5LL
63T-7LL
63T-9LL
63T/SO
64T-120
64T-5LL
64T/Coins-34
64T/SU
64T/St-79
65OPC-12LL
65OPC-260
65OPC-8LL
65T-12LL
65T-260
65T-8LL
65T/E-15
65T/trans-47
66Bz-42
66T-223LL
66T-430
66T/RO-16
66T/RO-24
67Bz-42
67OPC-55
67OPC/PI-16
67T-55
67T/PI-16
67T/Test/SU-11
68Bz-15
68Bz-6
68OPC-145
68T-145
68T/ActionSt-11B
68T/ActionSt-13CM
68T/ActionSt-2CM
68T/Post-7
69MLBPA/Pin-41
69T-400
69T/S-46
69T/St-42
69T/decal
72Laugh/GF-38
77Galasso-246
78TCMA-3
80Perez/HOF-186
82KMart-42
83MLBPA/Pin-23
84West/1-9
87Smok/Dodg-7
88Grenada-45
88Smok/Dodg-11
89AS/Cal-28
89Kenner/BBGr-6
89Rini/Dodg-8
89Smok/Dodg-7
89T/LJN-153
90HOF/St-73
90Pac/Legend-29
90Swell/Great-62
90T/Gloss22-11CAPT
90Target-203
91CollAB-10
91LineD-1
91Swell/Great-26
93AP/ASG-121
93AP/ASG24K-55G
93Nabisco-2
93TWill-12
93TWill/Mem-6
Exh47

Drzayich, Emil
80Cedar-4
81Cedar-10

DuBeau, Jack
78Watlo

DuBois, Brian
86Hagers-5
87Hagers-4
88CLAS/Star-6
88Virgini/Star-8
89Hagers/Best-13
89Hagers/ProC-274
89Hagers/Star-5
90B-349
90Classic/Up-17
90CokeK/Tiger-3
90D-38RR
90D/Rook-4
90F-601
90F/Can-601
90HagersDG/Best-7
90Leaf-266
90OPC-413
90S-657RP
90T-413
90T/89Debut-32
90T/Big-272
90UD-78
91S/100RisSt-85

DuBose, Brian
90Bristol/ProC-3163
90Bristol/Star-5
91Niagara/ClBest-10
91Niagara/ProC-3640
92ClBest-103
92Fayette/ClBest-5
92Fayette/ProC-2174
94TedW-120

DuPlessis, Dave
92Salinas/ClBest-21
92Salinas/ProC-3763

DuRussel, Scott
91Niagara/ProC-3626
92Niagara/ClBest-18
92Niagara/ProC-3317

DuVall, Brad
88Hamil/ProC-1722
89B-430
89Spring/Best-4
90StPete/Star-5
90T/TVCard-45

Duant, Rich
86LitFalls-9

Duarte, Luis
80Batavia-16
81Watlo

Dube, Greg
85Osceola/Team-6
87Wmsprt-19

Dubee, Rich
76Watlo
77DaytB
84Memphis-2
85Omaha-11
86Memphis/GoldT-6CO
86Memphis/SilverT-6CO
87Memphis-11
87Memphis/Best-3CO
88Omaha/CMC-23
88Omaha/ProC-1494
89Omaha/ProC-1739
90AAASingl/ProC-617CO
90Omaha/ProC-82CO
90ProC/Singl-198M
91Rockford/ClBest-16CO
91Rockford/ProC-2064CO
92Indianap/ProC-1876CO
92Indianap/SB-200M
93WPalmB/ClBest-27CO
93WPalmB/ProC-1358CO

Dubiel, Walter John
(Monk)
47Centen-6
49Eureka-55
51B-283
52T-164

Dubuc, Jean J.
(Jean)
15CJ-156
BF2-28
D329-52
D350/2-53
M101/4-52
M101/5-52
T206
T213/blue
T213/brown
T215/blue

Ducey, Rob
86Ventura-5
87D/HL-39
87Syrac-16
87Syrac/TCMA-19
87Tor/Fire-6
88F-107
88OPC-106
88S-629
88Syrac/CMC-14
88Syrac/ProC-825
88T-438
88Tor/Fire-40
89OPC-203
89Panini/St-459
89S/HotRook-7
89T-203
89T/Big-280
89Tor/Fire-40
89UD/Ext-721
90AAASingl/ProC-364
90OPC-619
90ProC/Singl-347
90PublInt/St-512
90S/YS/I-34
90Syrac/CMC-21
90Syrac/MerchB-6
90Syrac/ProC-584
90Syrac/Team-6
90T-619
90UD-464
91AAA/LineD-502
91AAAGame/ProC-43
91D-705
91OPC-101
91S-821
91S/ToroBJ-22
91StCl-374
91Syrac/LineD-502
91Syrac/MerchB-5
91Syrac/ProC-2492
91T-101
91Tor/Fire-20
92BJ/Fire-8
92D-466
92F-328
92OPC-739
92ProC/Tomorrow-163
92S-609
92StCl-422
92T-739
92T/Gold-739
92T/GoldWin-739
93BJ/D/45-40
93D-489
93OPC-55
93Rang/Keeb-404
93StCl-69
93StCl/1stDay-69
93T-293
93T/Gold-293
94StCl/Team-257
94T-618
94T/Gold-618

Duchin, David
90LynchRS/Team-25TR
91LynchRS/ClBest-27TR
92LynchRS/ClBest-27TR

Duckett, Mahlon
86Negro/Frit-40
91Negro/Lewis-11
92Negro/Retort-18
93TWill-104

Duckhorn, Steve
79Cedar/TCMA-1

Duckworth, James R.
(Jim)
78TCMA-151
78TCMA-23

Dudek, Steve
91Johnson/ClBest-9
91Johnson/ProC-3983
92Johnson/ClBest-4
92Johnson/ProC-3123

Dudley, Clise
90Target-204

Duenas, Vernon
88CharWh/Best-11

Duensing, Larry
80Hawaii-3
81Hawaii-25
81Hawaii/TCMA-20
82Hawaii-25
84Cram/PCL-244TR

Dues, Hal Joseph
(Hal)
75WPalmB/Sussman-10
79OPC-373
79T-699
81OPC-71
81T-71

Duey, Kody
86James-5

Duey, Kyle
90MedHat/Best-5
91Myrtle/ClBest-3
91Myrtle/ProC-2937
92Dunedin/ClBest-22
92Dunedin/ProC-1991
93Knoxvl/ProC-1255

Duezabou, Mel
47Remar-20
47Signal
47Smith-23
48Signal
48Smith-14
49Remar
50Remar

Dufault, Monte
92Kenosha/ProC-610

Duff, Dave
82Jacks-12

Duff, Scott
90Billings/ProC-3213
91CharWh/ClBest-3
91CharWh/ProC-2880
92Cedar/ClBest-23
92Cedar/ProC-1064

Duffalo, Jim
62T-578
63T-567
64T-573
65OPC-159
65T-159
78TCMA-204
78TCMA-249
81Shrev-13

Duffee, Charles E.
(Charlie)
N172

Duffie, John
77Fritsch-29
90Target-936

Duffy, Allen
86GlenF-3

Duffy, Darrin
86Cram/NWL-72
88Modesto-22
89WinSalem/Star-7
90CharlK/Team-4
90T/TVCub-44
91Peoria/Team-33
92ChalK/SB-153
92Iowa/ProC-4058

Duffy, Frank Thomas
(Frank)
71OPC-164R
71T-164R
72T-607
73OPC-376
73T-376
74OPC-81
74T-81
74T/St-163
75OPC-448
75T-448
75T/M-448
76Ho-115
76OPC-232
76SSPC-521
76T-232
77BurgChef-63
77OPC-253
77Pep-18
77T-542

78PapaG/Disc-17
78SSPC/270-184
78T-511
79OPC-47
79T-106
Duffy, Hugh
12Sweet/Pin-10A
12Sweet/Pin-10B
48Exh/HOF
50Callahan
50W576-28
63Bz/ATG-33
69Bz-4
76Shakey-34
77Galasso-147
80Perez/HOF-34
80SSPC/HOF
81Conlon-18
87Conlon/2-33
90BBWit-67
90HOF/St-8
92Conlon/Sport-532
94Conlon-1014
E90/1
M116
N172
N300/unif
S74-5
T205
T206
V100
WG3-16
Duffy, John
87GlenF-23
88Toledo/CMC-10
88Toledo/ProC-596
89Memphis/Best-2
89Memphis/ProC-1181
89Memphis/Star-9
Duffy, Tom
83VeroB-2
Dugan, Joseph Anthony
(Joe)
21Exh-37
21Exh-38
21Exh-39
28Yueng-3
29Exh/4-1
61F-103
88Conlon/5-8
91Conlon/Sport-112
94Conlon-1059
E120
E210-3
E220
V100
W502-3
W513-66
W515-30
W573
WG7-13
Dugan, Ken
86Lipscomb-10CO
89KS*-7CO
92Lipscomb-10CO
93Lipscomb-6CO
Dugan, Kurt
89KS*-8
92Lipscomb-11
93Lipscomb-7
Dugan, Mike
86Lipscomb-11
Dugas, Augustin J.
(Gus)
R314/Can
Dugas, Shanie
81Watlo-21
82Chatt-13
83BuffB-15
84Maine-23
85Maine-17
87Albuq/Pol-18
88Albuq/CMC-22
88Albuq/ProC-266
89Albuq/CMC-13
89Albuq/ProC-85
Dugdale, Daniel E.
(Dan)
N172
Dugey, Oscar Joseph
(Oscar)
15CJ-60
D329-53
D350/2-54
M101/4-53
M101/5-54
Duggan, Tom
83Wausau/Frit-21
86Salem-6
Dugger, Keith
91Spokane/ClBest-30
Dugger, Lonnie
81Holyo-13
82Holyo-4
Dugrahm
N172
Duke, Andy
89Billings/ProC-2056
Duke, Doug
87BurlEx-7
88Jaxvl/Best-22
89Jaxvl/Best-6
89Jaxvl/ProC-167
Duke, Ed
86ColumAst-11TR
Duke, Jerome
86James-6
Duke, Kyle
90Penin/Star-7
91BendB/ClBest-4
91BendB/ProC-3689
92SanBern/ClBest-4
92SanBern/ProC-
Duke, Martin F.
N172
Duke, Marvin
V355-116
Duke, Richard
87Idaho-6
Dukes, Jan Noble
(Jan)
70OPC-154R
70T-154R
93Rang/Keeb-9
Dukes, Kevin
82LynnS-3
83Chatt-19
Dukes, Thomas Earl
(Tom)
68OPC-128R
68T-128R
69T-223
71OPC-106
71T-106
91Crown/Orio-115
Dukes, Willie Jr.
90Elmira/Pucko-9
90WinHaven/Star-7
91WinHaven/ClBest-13
91WinHaven/ProC-493
Duliba, Robert John
(Bob)
60L-77
60T-401
62Kahn/Atl
62T-149
63T-97
64T-441
66OPC-53
66T-53
67T-599
Dulin, Tim
86Miami-5
87Hagers-10
88CharlK/Pep-5
88SLAS-9
89RochR/CMC-20
89RochR/ProC-1646
90AAASingl/ProC-465
90ProC/Singl-316
90RochR/CMC-16
90RochR/ProC-708
90Rochester/L&U-5
Dull, Darrell
83Idaho-19
Dull, Mike
87BurlEx-9
88WPalmB/Star-9
89Jaxvl/Best-7
89Jaxvl/ProC-164
Dulom, Kirk
90FtLaud/Star-6
Dumas, Don
87Savan-21
Dumont, Serge
72Dimanche*-117
Dumouchelle, Pat
81Miami-8
84CharlO-13
90HagersDG/Best-8
Dumoulin, Dan
77Indianap-13
78Indianap-7
79Indianap-26
Dunbar, Matt
88CapeCod/Sum-65
90Oneonta/ProC-3382
91Greens/ProC-3050
92PrWill/ClBest-9
92PrWill/ProC-139
Dunbar, Thomas Jerome
(Tommy)
82Tulsa-10
83OKCty-7
84D-28RR
84OKCty-18
84Rangers-13
85D-159
85F/Up-U37
85Rangers-13
85T-102
86D-221
86OKCty-5
86T-559
87Vanco-6
88Greenvl/Best-21
89Greenvl/Best-26
89Greenvl/ProC-1179
89Greenvl/Star-7
90Memphis/Best-11
90Memphis/ProC-1023
90Memphis/Star-9
90TulsaDG/Best-24
91AAA/LineD-333
91Omaha/LineD-333
91Omaha/ProC-1046
93Rang/Keeb-129
Duncan, Andres
91ClBest/Singl-322
91Clinton/ClBest-13
91Clinton/ProC-841
92SanJose/ClBest-10
92UD/ML-215
Duncan, C.
(Duke)
78Newar
79Holyo-27
Duncan, Chip
87Watertn-6
88Salem/Star-5
89Salem/Star-7
90Salem/Star-4
91AA/LineD-105
91CaroMud/LineD-105
91CaroMud/ProC-1079
91Parramatta/Fut-18
92Memphis/ProC-2412
Duncan, David Edwin
(Dave)
64T-528R
68T-261
69OPC-68
69T-68
69T/St-214
70T-678
71MLB/St-511
71OPC-178
71T-178
72OPC-17
72T-17
73OPC-337
73T-337
74OPC-284
74T-284
74T/St-164
75OPC-238
75OPC-626
75T-238
75T/M-238
76OPC-49
76SSPC-383
76T-49
77T-338
87Mother/A's-8CO
90Mother/A's-27M
91Crown/Orio-116
91Mother/A's-28CO
92Mother/A's-28M
93Mother/A's-27M
Duncan, Doug
76SanAn/Team-9
77Visalia
Duncan, Frank Jr.
(Dunk)
86Negro/Frit-118
87Negro/Dixon-45
92Negro/RetortII-8
Duncan, Jeff
92Madis/ClBest-3
92Madis/ProC-1240
Duncan, John
83Wausau/Frit-26
Duncan, Lindy
81Tulsa-25
Duncan, Louis Baird
(Pat)
21Exh-40
88Pac/8Men-94
94Conlon-1026
E120
V100
V61-109
W572
WG7-14
Duncan, Mariano
83VeroB-16
85Coke/Dodg-10
85F/Up-U38
85T/Tr-32T
86Coke/Dodg-8
86D-128
86F-129
86F/LL-10
86F/Mini-27
86F/St-33
86KayBee-8
86Leaf-50
86OPC-296
86Pol/Dodg-25
86Seven/Coin-W13M
86T-602
87D-253
87D/OD-84
87F-439
87Mother/Dodg-7
87OPC-199
87Pol/Dodg-12
87Seven-W2
87Sf/TPrev-14M
87T-199
87T/Mini-13
87T/St-74
88Albuq/CMC-23
88Albuq/ProC-255
88D-155
88F-513
88OPC-181
88Pol/Dodg-25
88S-321
88T-481
89Mother/Dodg-26
89Pol/Dodg-15
90D-684
90D/BestNL-113
90F/Up-U12
90Kahn/Reds-9
90Leaf-202
90OPC-234
90S-506
90T-234
90T/Big-243
90Target-205
90UD-430
91B-675
91D-309
91F-64
91Kahn/Reds-7
91Leaf-494
91Leaf/Stud-164
91OPC-13
91Panini/FrSt-128
91Panini/St-123
91Pep/Reds-9
91S-479
91StCl-251
91T-13
91UD-112
91Ultra-94
92D-540
92F-406
92F/Up-109
92L-311
92L/BlkGold-311
92OPC-589
92Phill/Med-11
92Pinn-377
92S-352
92S/RookTr-54T
92StCl-614
92Studio-74
92T-589
92T/Gold-589
92T/GoldWin-589
92T/Tr-30T
92T/TrGold-30T
92UD-659
92UD-792
92Ultra-544
93D-382
93F-101
93Flair-98
93L-187
93OPC-95
93Pac/Spanish-234
93Panini-272
93Phill/Med-11
93Pinn-218
93S-201
93Select-151
93Select/StatL-17
93StCl-276
93StCl/1stDay-276
93StCl/Phill-21
93T-371
93T/Gold-371
93UD-201
93UD/SP-172
93Ultra-87
94B-196
94D-614
94F-586
94Finest-352
94L-11
94Pac/AllLat-8
94Pac/Cr-472
94Panini-225
94Phill/Med-6
94Pinn-479
94S-490
94StCl-54
94StCl/1stDay-54
94StCl/Gold-54
94StCl/Team-217
94Studio-137
94T-663
94T/Gold-663
94TripleP-172
94UD-181
94UD/ElecD-181
94Ultra-543
Duncan, Michael
86Modesto-8
87Modesto-4
Duncan, Rick
78OrlanTw
Duncan, Taylor M.
79T-658
89Pac/SenLg-70
Duncan, Tim
80Elmira-20
Dunckel, Bill
92Boise/ClBest-23
92Boise/ProC-3642
Duncun, John
86Chatt-9
Dundik, Alexander
89EastLDD/ProC-DD10
Dunegan, James W. Jr.
(Jim)
71OPC-121R
71T-121R
Dunlap, Frederick C.
(Fred)
N162
N172
N284
Scrapps
WG1-58
Dunlap, Joe
86Cedar/TCMA-15
87Vermont-10
89Calgary/CMC-18
89Calgary/ProC-529
89EastLDD/ProC-DD30
Dunlap, Paul
V355-125
Dunlap, Travis
90Pulaski/Best-3
90Pulaski/ProC-3099

91Idaho/SportP-11
92Macon/ClBest-10
92Macon/ProC-261
Dunleavy, John E.
WG3-17
Dunlop, Harry
73OPC-593CO
73T-593CO
74T-166CO
83LasVegas/BHN-7
84Smok/SDP-8CO
91Helena/SportP-30MG
92Helena/ProC-1732MG
Dunn
N172
Dunn, Brian
89SanDiegoSt/Smok-8
90Pittsfld/Pucko-12
91Clmbia/PCPII-7
91Clmbia/PII-19
Dunn, Bubba
91BBCity/ClBest-3
91BBCity/ProC-1390
Dunn, Geoff
91Waverly/Fut-1
Dunn, Greg
82Spring/Frit-13
83Spring/Frit-14
85Spring-8
86Louisvl-10
Dunn, James William
(Jim)
81Shrev-3
Dunn, John Joseph
(Jack)
90Target-206
C46-19
E107
E254
T205
T206
Dunn, Joseph Edward
(Joe)
T205
T206
T213/brown
Dunn, Mike
82Clinton/Frit-14
Dunn, Nathan
92GreatF/SportP-3
Dunn, Ronald Ray
(Ron)
74Wichita-119
76SSPC-322
Dunn, Steve R.
89Elizab/Star-7
89Kenosha/ProC-1073
89Kenosha/Star-4
90Foil/Best-12
90Kenosha/Best-1
90Kenosha/ProC-2299
90Kenosha/Star-3
90PalmSp/Cal-220
90PalmSp/ProC-2571
91ClBest/Singl-241
91Visalia/ClBest-15
91Visalia/ProC-1747
Dunn, Steve
88QuadC/GS-10
89Star/IISingl-147
90MidwLgAS/GS-9
90Star/ISingl-55
92UD/ML-216
92Visalia/ClBest-19
92Visalia/ProC-1019
93B-17
93FExcel/ML-199
94F/MLP-11
94FExcel-93
94Ultra-387
Dunn, Todd
93Bz-19
93T/Tr-67T
94B-657
94UD-528TP
Dunne, Mike
85T-395OLY
86Louisvl-11
87D/Rook-38
87F/Up-U29
87Sf/Rook-40
87T/Tr-30T
87Vanco-15
88Classic/Blue-237
88D-390
88D/Best-89
88F-328
88F/AwardWin-10
88F/BB/MVP-11
88F/Mini-104
88F/RecSet-11
88F/St-115
88KennerFig-31
88Leaf-235
88OPC-224
88Panini/St-367
88S-432
88S/YS/I-26
88Sf-171
88T-619
88T/Big-236
88T/Coins-40
88T/Gloss60-19
88T/JumboR-16
88T/Mini-68
88T/RiteAid-9
88T/St-132
88T/St-307
88T/UK-21
88ToysRUs-10
89B-412
89D-269
89F-207
89OPC-165
89Panini/St-162
89S-285
89T-165
89T/St-130
89UD-518
89VFJuice-41
90Leaf-418
90OPC-522
90Padre/MagUno-19
90T-522
91OPC-238
91T-238
92Vanco/ProC-2715
92Vanco/SB-634
Dunnegan, Steve
82DayBe-11
Dunner, Mike
82Clinton/Frit-14
Dunning, Stephen John
(Steve)
71OPC-294
71T-294
72T-658
73OPC-53
73T-53
76Expo/Redp-6
78T-647
93Rang/Keeb-130
Dunnum, Rick
88AubAs/ProC-1969
89Ashvl/ProC-964
90Osceola/Star-7
91AA/LineD-508
91Reading/LineD-508
91Reading/ProC-1367
Dunster, Don
86Osceola-6
87Osceola-19
88ColAst/Best-2
Dunston, Shawon
83QuadC-20
84MidldC-22
85D-39RR
85F-649R
85T-280FDP
86Cub/Unocal-6
86D-311
86F-366
86F/Mini-77
86F/St-34
86Gator-12
86Jay's-6
86KayBee-9
86Leaf-181
86Seven/Coin-C13
86Sf-155
86T-72
86T/Tatt-2M
87Berg/Cubs-12
87D-119
87D/OD-76
87F-561
87F/GameWin-13
87F/Mini-35
87F/RecSet-6
87F/St-36
87Leaf-128
87OPC-346
87RedFoley/St-94
87Seven-C4
87Sf-79M
87Sf-98
87Sf/TPrev-22M
87T-346
87T/St-59
88Berg/Cubs-12
88D-146
88D/Best-37
88D/Cubs/Bk-146
88F-419
88KennerFig-32
88Leaf-70
88OPC-277
88Panini/St-264
88S-529
88S/YS/II-18
88Sf-163
88T-695
88T/Big-225
88T/St-65
88T/St/Backs-11
89B-294
89Cadaco-15
89D-137
89D/AS-43
89D/Best-93
89F-424
89KMart/DT-26
89KennerFig-40
89Mara/Cubs-12
89OPC-140
89Panini/St-58
89RedFoley/St-38
89S-235
89Sf-190
89T-140
89T/Big-233
89T/St-49
89T/St/Backs-43
89UD-107
90B-38
90Cub/Mara-7
90D-49
90D/BestNL-112
90F-30
90F/Can-30
90Leaf-229
90MLBPA/Pins-46
90OPC-415
90Panini/St-236
90PublInt/St-193
90S-169
90T-415
90T/Big-62
90T/DH-18
90T/Gloss60-45
90T/St-53
90T/TVCub-22
90UD-231
90USPlayC/AS-10D
91B-424
91Cadaco-17
91Classic/200-27
91Cub/Mara-12
91Cub/Vine-10
91D-686
91F-420
91Kenner-16
91Leaf-25
91Leaf/Stud-155
91OPC-765
91OPC/Premier-37
91Panini/FrSt-46
91Panini/St-47
91RedFoley/St-29
91S-201
91S-413RIF
91S/100SS-45
91StCl-3
91T-765
91T/CJMini/II-23
91UD-111
91Ultra-59
92Classic/Game200-28
92Cub/Mara-12
92D-613
92F-380
92L-249
92L/BlkGold-249
92OPC-370
92OPC/Premier-125
92Panini-185
92Pinn-244
92S-634
92S/Impact-70
92StCl-540
92T-370
92T/GPro-370
92T/Gold-370
92T/GoldWin-370
92T/Kids-5
92T/Pr-3
92TripleP-160
92UD-122
92UD-35TC
92UD-714DS
92USPlayC/Cub-13C
92USPlayC/Cub-7S
92Ultra-174
93Cadaco-17
93D-268
93F-19
93MSA/Metz-24
93OPC-62
93Pac/Spanish-57
93Panini-205
93Pinn-89
93S-26
93Select-121
93StCl-393
93StCl/1stDay-393
93StCl/Cub-9
93T-595
93T/Gold-595
93TripleP-40
93UD-101
93Ultra-17
94D-490
94Finest-368
94Flair-136
94L-316
94Panini-152
94Pinn-523
94Select-136
94StCl/Team-354
94Studio-59
94UD-477
94Ultra-454
Dunton, Kevin
86WPalmB-14
Dupont, Margaret
51BR-D13
Dupree, Michael D.
(Mike)
77T-491R
79Hawaii-19
Dupuy, Jerry
93MissSt-14
Duquette, Bryan
83ElPaso-5
84ElPaso-11
85Cram/PCL-212
86Vanco-11
Duquette, Chuck
88Fayette/ProC-1089
Duran, Daniel James
(Dan)
74Gaston
76SanAn/Team-10
80CharCh-12
93Rang/Keeb-131
Duran, Dave
(Pitcher)
81Holyo-14
82Holyo-5
Duran, Felipe
91BurlInd/ProC-3307
92ColRS/ClBest-24
92ColRS/ProC-2396
Duran, Ignacio
90Savan/ProC-2072
91ClBest/Singl-283
91Spring/ClBest-13
91Spring/ProC-748
92Savan/ProC-668
Duran, Rick
79Holyo-14
Duran, Roberto
92GulfCD/ProC-3560
Durant, Mike
91Classic/DP-42
91FrRow/DP-17
92AS/Cal-47
92ClBest-294
92StCl/Dome-40
92UD/ML-288
92Visalia/ClBest-21
92Visalia/ProC-1018
93ClBest/MLG-43
93FExcel/ML-200
Durant, Richard
87Columbia-25
88Clmbia/GS-3
89Stockton/Best-7
89Stockton/Cal-155
89Stockton/ProC-388
89Stockton/Star-19
Duren, Rinold George
(Ryne)
58T-296
59T-485
60L-22
60T-204
60T/tatt-13
61P-14
61T-356
62J-81
62P-81
62P/Can-81
62Salada-46A
62Salada-46B
62Shirriff-46
62T-388
63T-17
64T-173
65T-339
79TCMA-135
89Pac/Leg-141
91Crown/Orio-117
92Yank/WIZ60-37
92Yank/WIZAS-20
Durham, Donald Gary
(Don)
73OPC-548
73T-548
93Rang/Keeb-132
Durham, Edward Fant
(Bull)
34G-79
90Target-207
Durham, Joseph Vann
(Joe)
58T-96
90Hagers/Best-6CO
90Hagers/ProC-1433CO
90Hagers/Star-28CO
91AA/LineD-250CO
91Crown/Orio-118
91Hagers/LineD-250CO
91Hagers/ProC-2472CO
92Hagers/ProC-2571CO
92Hagers/SB-275M
Durham, Leon
81Coke
81D-427
81F-540
81OPC-321
81T-321
81T/HT
81T/Tr-756
82D-151
82F-595
82F/St-94
82OPC-206
82RedLob
82T-607
82T/St-25
82T/StVar-25
83D-477
83D/AAS-55
83F-495
83F/St-13M
83F/St-14M
83K-27
83OPC-125
83OPC/St-219FOIL
83T-125
83T-51TL
83T/St-219
83Thorn-10
84Cub/Uno-7M
84D-5DK
84D-67
84F-492
84Nes/792-565
84OPC-209

84SevenUp-10
84T-565
84T/RD-19
84T/St-40
85D-189
85D/AAS-46
85F-56
85FunFood/Pin-107
85Leaf-238
85OPC-330
85Seven-8G
85SevenUp-10
85T-330
85T/Gloss40-11
85T/RD-18
85T/St-36
86Cub/Unocal-7
86D-320
86F-367
86F/LL-11
86F/Mini-78
86F/St-35
86Gator-10
86Leaf-190
86OPC-58
86Sf-111
86T-460
86T/St-60
86T/Tatt-4M
87Berg/Cubs-10
87D-242
87D/OD-74
87F-562
87F/Hottest-15
87Leaf-125
87OPC-290
87RedFoley/St-120
87Seven-C6
87Sf-185
87Sf/TPrev-22M
87Stuart-3
87T-290
87T/Board-26
87T/St-57
88D-191
88D/Cubs/Bk-191
88F-420
88Kahn/Reds-10
88KennerFig-33
88OPC-65
88Panini/St-259
88S-378
88T-65
88T/Big-42
88T/St-63
89Louisvl-16
89Louisvl/CMC-16
89Louisvl/ProC-1260
89UD-354
Durham, Louis
E97
T206
W555
Durham, Ray
91Utica/ClBest-6
91Utica/ProC-3246
92Saraso/ProC-219
94FExcel-37
94Ultra-334
Durham, Shane
87Anchora-7
Durkin, Chris
91AubAS/ClBest-19
91AubAS/ProC-4285
91ClBest/Singl-410
91FrRow/DP-8
92Ashvl/ClBest-21
92ClBest-15
92StCl/Dome-41
92UD/ML-177
Durkin, Martin
(Marty)
88CapeCod/Sum-128
89Watertn/Star-4
90Miami/I/Star-6
90Miami/II/Star-5
91WPalmB/ClBest-25
91WPalmB/ProC-1240
92WinHaven/ProC-1785
Durnan, Bill
51BR-A17
Durney, Bill
88PalmSp/Cal-115
88PalmSp/ProC-1462
89BendB/Legoe-29TR
Durning, Dick
90Target-937
Durocher, Francois
86Osceola-7
Durocher, Leo Ernest
(Leo)
29Exh/4-26
31Exh/4-7
33G-147
34G-7
35BU-156
38Exh/4-2
39PlayBall-6
41DP-142
49Eureka-102
50B-220MG
51B-233MG
52B-146MG
52RM-NL1
52T-315MG
53B/Col-55MG
55Gol/Giants-6
67T-481MG
68T-321MG
69OPC-147MG
69T-147
69T/4in1-12M
70OPC-291MG
70T-291MG
71OPC-609MG
71T-609MG
72T-576MG
73OPC-624MG
73T-624MG
79TCMA-201MG
80Pac/Leg-40
80Perez/HOF-218
84Cub/Uno-8M
86Conlon/1-11
88Conlon/3-10
88Pac/Leg-27
89Rini/Dodg-28M
89Rini/Dodg-30
89Smok/Dodg-39
90Target-208
91T/Arc53-309MG
92Bz/Quadra-5M
R310
R346-2
V353-74
V354-69
V355-25
Durrett, Red
45Parade*-55
90Target-938
Durrman, Jim
81WHave-8
83Albany-9
Durso, Joe
93StCath/ClBest-8
93StCath/ProC-3977
Durst, Cedric
91Conlon/Sport-108
Duryea, James Whitney
(Jesse)
N172
Dusak, Ervin Frank
(Erv)
47TipTop
51B-310
52T-183
79TCMA-122
Dusan, Gene
75OkCty/Team-21
77Watlo
79Tacoma-24
80Tacoma-23
82Jacks-22
84Wichita/Rock-22
86Cedr/TCM-25MG
90Bend/Legoe-2CO
Dusan, John
92Bend/ClBest-28BB
Dussault, Normand
45Parade*-17
Dustal, Robert Andrew
(Bob)
63T-299R
Duty, Darrell
89Anchora-12
Duval, Michael
(Mickey)
79Indianap-27
82Madis/Frit-34GM
Dwight, Edward Joseph
(Pee Wee)
87Negro/Dixon-4
Dworak, John
52Laval-61
Dwyer, James Edward
(Jim)
75OPC-429
75T-429
75T/M-429
76Expo/Redp-7
76OPC-94
76SSPC-341
76T-94
78T-644
79T-236
80T-577
81D-577
81F-235
81OPC-184
81T-184
81T/Tr-757
82D-64
82F-164
82T-359
83D-583
83F-59
83T-718
84D-454
84F-7
84F/St-117
84Nes/792-473
84T-473
85F-176
85T-56
86D-413
86F-274
86OPC-339
86T-653
87D-418
87F-469
87French-9
87T-246
88D-459
88F-558
88French-9
88S-229
88T-521
89D/Best-311
90D-484
90PublInt/St-325
91AAA/LineD-425M
91Crown/Orio-119
91Pac/SenLg-118
91Portl/LineD-425CO
91Portl/ProC-1582CO
91WIZMets-100
92Kenosha/ProC-620MG
Dwyer, John Francis
(Frank)
N172
Dybzinski, Jerome M.
(Jerry)
78Watlo
79Tacoma-13
81D-438
81F-399
81OPC-198
81T-198
82D-647
82F-366
82T-512
82Wheat/Ind
83D-576
83F-406
83T-289
83T/Tr-27
84D-160
84F-57
84Nes/792-619
84T-619
84TrueVal/WS-11
85Cram/PCL-250
85F-512
85T-52
86Calgary-7
Dyce, George
89Nashvl/Team-27VP
Dyck, James Robert
(Jim)
53B/C-111
53NB
53T-177
54B-85
56T-303
57Seattle/Pop-10
91Crown/Orio-120
91T/Arc53-177
Dye, Jermaine
94B-433
Dye, Mark
82Idaho-18
Dye, Scott
80Water-8
81Tidew-15
82Jacks-4
83Tidew-14
Dye, Steve
89Modesto/Cal-269
89Modesto/Chong-9
Dyer, Don Robert
(Duffy)
69T-624R
70T-692
71MLB/St-150
71OPC-136
71T-136
72Dimanche*-12
72OPC-127
72T-127
73OPC-493
73T-493
74OPC-536
74T-536
75OPC-538
75T-538
75T/M-538
76OPC-88
76SSPC-581
76T-88
77BurgChef-185
77T-318
78T-637
79T-286
80OPC-232
80T-446
81D-7
81T-196
83Thorn-26CO
86ElPaso-9MG
87ElPaso-14MG
88Denver/CMC-25
88Denver/ProC-1264
90Brewer/MillB-32CO
90ElPasoATG/Team-20
90Pol/Brew-x
91Brewer/MillB-32
91Pol/Brew-x
91WIZMets-101
92Pol/Brew-30M
94Mets/69-22
Dyer, Eddie
49Eureka-181
92Conlon/Sport-618
Dyer, Hal
87CharWh-14
93MedHat/ProC-3753CO
93MedHat/SportP-24CO
Dyer, John
78Green
Dyer, Linton
88AppFx/ProC-143
89AppFx/ProC-867
90BBCity/Star-7
Dyer, Mike
87Kenosha-11
88OrlanTw/Best-9
89Portl/CMC-8
89Portl/ProC-228
90AAASingl/ProC-243
90D-642
90F-372
90F/Can-372
90OPC-576
90Portl/CMC-6
90Portl/ProC-173
90ProC/Singl-558
90S-571
90T-576
90T/89Debut-33
90UD-374
Dyes, Andy
78Syrac
79Hawaii-5
80Hawaii-24
Dygert, James Henry
(Jimmy)
12Sweet/Pin-44
C46-45
E104
E90/1
E97
M116
S74-30
T201
T205
T206
T208
T3-92
W555
Dyke, Bill
89Knoxvl/ProC-1120
Dykes, James Joseph
(Jimmy)
21Exh-41
25Exh-106
26Exh-107
29Exh/4-28
31Exh/4-27
32Orbit/num-11
32Orbit/un-16
33DH-12
33DL-18
33G-6
34DS-42
34Ward's/Pin-2
35BU-159
35BU-29
35Exh/4-10
35G-1I
35G-2F
35G-6F
35G-7F
36Exh/4-10
36G
37Exh/4-10
40PlayBall-187
47Signal
51B-226MG
52B-98MG
53B/Col-31MG
54Esskay
60T-214MG
61Kahn
61T-222MG
77Galasso-120
77Galasso-201
78TCMA-224
87Conlon/2-37
88Conlon/4-10
91Conlon/Sport-92
91T/Arc53-281MG
93Conlon-678
93Conlon-848
94Conlon-1150
E120
E210-51
E220
R300
R305
R308-167
R311/Gloss
R314
R316
R337-410
V100
V353-6
V355-1
W517-22
W572
Dykstra, Kevin
90AS/Cal-32UMP
Dykstra, Len
83Lynch-15
84Jacks-18
85Tidew-20
86D-482
86F-78
86OPC-53
86T-53
87Classic-2
87D-611
87F-6
87F/Lim-13
87Leaf-88
87OPC-295
87Seven-E4
87Seven-ME5
87Sf-58
87Sf/TPrev-2M
87T-295

87T/HL-23
87T/Mets/Fan-3
87T/St-13
87T/St-21WS
87T/St-98
87Woolwth-23
88D-364
88D/Best-264
88D/Mets/Bk-364
88F-133
88Kahn/Mets-4
88KennerFig-34
88Leaf-135
88OPC-299
88Panini/St-345
88S-370
88S/YS/II-19
88Sf-106
88T-655
88T/Big-203
88T/Mini-59
89Classic-36
89D-353
89D/Best-159
89F-33
89F/Up-105
89KennerFig-41
89OPC-349
89Panini/St-138
89Phill/TastyK-40
89S-84
89S/Tr-28
89Sf-123
89T-435
89T/Big-41
89T/DHTest-12
89T/St-90
89T/Tr-27T
89UD-369
90B-152
90Classic/Up-18
90D-313
90D/BestNL-118
90F-556
90F/Can-556
90Kenner/Fig-25
90Leaf-262
90MLBPA/Pins-5
90OPC-515
90Panini/St-313
90Phill/TastyK-8
90PublInt/St-131
90RedFoley/St-28
90S-427
90S/McDon-14
90Sf-156
90T-515
90T/Big-300
90T/St-118
90UD-472
90USPlayC/AS-9D
91B-501
91BBBest/HitM-6
91Classic/200-133
91Classic/I-78
91CollAB-8
91D-410MVP
91D-434AS
91D-523
91D-744M
91D-7DK
91D/SuperDK-7DK
91F-395
91Kenner-17
91Leaf-163
91Leaf/Prev-8
91Leaf/Stud-213
91MajorLg/Pins-60
91MooTown-18
91OPC-345
91Panini/FrSt-108
91Panini/FrSt-163
91Panini/St-103
91Panini/Top15-26
91Panini/Top15-4
91Pep/SS-16
91Phill/Medford-13
91Post-8
91Post/Can-6
91RedFoley/St-119
91RedFoley/St-30
91S-250
91S-867FRAN
91S/100SS-11
91Seven/3DCoin-4NE
91StCl-150
91Sunflower-9
91T-345
91T/CJMini/I-21
91T/SU-12
91UD-267
91UD-97TC
91Ultra-262
91WIZMets-102
92B-635
92CJ/DII-13
92Classic/Game200-152
92Classic/I-30
92Classic/II-T51
92D-57
92D/McDon-8
92F-529
92F/TmLIns-10
92L-504
92L/BlkGold-504
92OPC-200
92OPC/Premier-184
92Panini-247
92Phill/Med-12
92Pinn-12
92S-560
92S/100SS-86
92S/Impact-74
92Seven/Coin-8
92StCl-470
92Studio-75
92T-200
92T/Gold-200
92T/GoldWin-200
92T/Kids-17
92TripleP-94
92UD-246
92Ultra-241
93B-300
93Cadaco-18
93Colla/DM-33
93D-544
93F-488
93Flair-99
93HumDum/Can-44
93L-59
93OPC-119
93Pac/Spanish-235
93Panini-274
93Phill/Med-12
93Pinn-45
93Pinn-477I
93S-30
93Select-59
93StCl-477
93StCl/1stDay-477
93StCl/Phill-15
93Studio-101
93T-740
93T/Finest-177
93T/FinestRef-177
93T/Gold-740
93TripleP-185
93UD-485M
93UD-69
93UD/FunPack-144
93UD/SP-173
93Ultra-439
94B-440
94Church-8
94D-373
94D/DomII-9
94D/MVP-10
94D/Special-373
94D/Spirit-10
94F-587
94F/LL-9
94F/TL-24
94Finest-237
94Flair-205
94Flair/Outfield-4
94KingB-15
94Kraft-20
94L-97
94L/Gamer-2
94L/GoldS-5
94OPC-168
94Oscar-20
94P-20
94Pac/Cr-473
94Pac/Silv-33
94Panini-226
94Phill/Med-7
94Pinn-34
94Pinn/Artist-34
94Pinn/Museum-34
94Pinn/Run-24
94Pinn/TeamP-6
94Pinn/Trib-6
94S-60
94S-624WS
94S/Cycle-8
94S/GoldR-60
94S/GoldS-17
94Select-89
94Select/CrCon-10
94SelectSam-CC1
94Sf/2000-1
94Sf/2000-191AS
94Sf/2000Sam-1
94Sf/Mov-12
94StCl-165
94StCl/1stDay-165
94StCl/Gold-165
94StCl/Team-211
94Studio-138
94T-388M
94T-635
94T/BlkGold-29
94T/Gold-388M
94T/Gold-635
94TripleP-173
94TripleP/Medal-12M
94TripleP/Pr-8
94UD-172
94UD/DColl-E3
94UD/ElecD-172
94UD/SP-135
94Ultra-544
94Ultra/AS-17
94Ultra/LL-7
94Ultra/OnBase-3

Dyson, Theodore Timothy
(Ted or Tim)
88PalmSp/Cal-103
88PalmSp/ProC-1453

Dzafic, Bernie
88Elmira-5
89WinHaven/Star-5
92WinHaven/ProC-1769

Dziadkowiec, Andy
87Myrtle-27
89Dunedin/Star-4
90AAASingl/ProC-353
90Knoxvl/Best-17
90Knoxvl/Star-3
90ProC/Singl-351
90Syrac/CMC-25
90Syrac/ProC-573
91Miami/ClBest-17
91Miami/ProC-411
92Bingham/ProC-519
92Bingham/SB-56

Eaddy, Don
77Fritsch-54

Eaddy, Keith
92Bluefld/ClBest-13
92Bluefld/ProC-2370

Eagar, Brad
87Anchora-8
87BYU-18
89Medford/Best-7

Eagar, Steve
86Lakeland-5

Eagelston, Chris
86Hagers-6

Eagen, Charles
E254
M116

Eagle, Johnny
(War)
72Dimanche*-118

Eakes, Steven
82Redwd-2
83Redwd-9

Ealy, Thomas
(Tom)
85Everett/Cram-4
86Clinton-6
86Cram/NWL-200
87Clinton-12
88Clinton/ProC-718
89SanJose/Best-14
89SanJose/Cal-231
89SanJose/ProC-434
89SanJose/Star-8
90Shrev/ProC-1454
90Shrev/Star-7
91AA/LineD-304
91Shrev/LineD-304
91Shrev/ProC-1834
92Lakeland/ClBest-23
92Lakeland/ProC-2290

Ealy, Tracey
90Johnson/Star-10
91Savan/ClBest-24
91Savan/ProC-1665
92Eugene/ClBest-11
92Eugene/ProC-3042

Eaman, Bob
89London/ProC-1359

Earl, Scottie
83BirmB-17
84Evansvl-14
85D-491
86Nashvl-7
87Toledo-1
87Toledo/TCMA-10
88Nashvl/CMC-19
88Nashvl/ProC-471
88Nashvl/Team-9
90BirmDG/Best-8

Earle, William
(Billy)
90Target-209
N172

Earley, Arnold Carl
(Arnie)
67T-388
78TCMA-209

Earley, Bill
83Iowa-2
84Iowa-2
85OKCty-30
86Louisvl-12
87Louisvl-13
88Wythe/ProC-1989
89CharWh/Best-24
89CharWh/ProC-1754
90WinSalem/Team-28
91WinSalem/ClBest-21
91WinSalem/ProC-2846CO
92ChalK/SB-175CO
92CharlK/ProC-2787

Earls, Peter
82Tucson-28M

Early, Jacob Willard
(Jake)
48L-61
49B-106
93Conlon-749

Earnshaw, George L.
(George)
32Orbit/num-38
32Orbit/un-17
33DH-13
34Exh/4-10
34G-41
35G-1I
35G-2F
35G-6F
35G-7F
40PlayBall-233
90Target-210
91Conlon/Sport-88
94Conlon-1137
R305
R306
R308-169
R310
R312/M
R328-29
R332-13
V354-93
W517-8

Easler, Michael A.
(Mike)
75Iowa/TCMA-7
76Tulsa
78Colum
78T-710R
80T-194
81Coke
81D-256
81F-372
81F/St-74
81OPC-92
81T-92
81T/SO-81
81T/St-212
82D-221
82F-481
82K-49
82OPC-235
82T-235
82T/St-84
83D-221
83F-306
83F/St-11M
83F/St-3M
83OPC-385
83T-385
84D-444
84F-249
84F/X-33
84Nes/792-589
84OPC-353
84T-589
84T/St-137
84T/Tr-33
85D-213
85F-157
85F/St-46
85Leaf-206
85OPC-349
85T-686
85T/St-213
86D-395
86F-347
86F/Up-U37
86T-477
86T/St-255
86T/Tatt-21M
86T/Tr-33T
87D-277
87D/OD-155
87F-97
87F/AS-7
87Leaf-192
87OPC-135
87Phill/TastyK-34
87Sf-92
87T-135
87T/St-295
88F-206
88OPC-9
88S-220
88T-741
89T/SenLg-80
90EliteSenLg-19
90Miami/I/Star-28MG
90Miami/II/Star-26MG
92Pol/Brew-30CO
92Yank/WIZ80-50

Easley, Damion
89BendB/Legoe-16
90MidwLgAS/GS-31
90QuadC/GS-24
91AA/LineD-433
91ClBest/Singl-121
91MidldA/LineD-433
91MidldA/OneHour-10
91MidldA/ProC-440
92B-672
92Edmon/ProC-3544
92Edmon/SB-154
92F/Up-9
92Sky/AAASingl-76
93B-257
93D-457RR
93F-189
93Flair-173
93L-286
93Mother/Angel-26
93OPC-104
93Pac/Spanish-367
93Panini-7
93Pinn-227
93Pol/Angel-13
93S-222
93Select-328
93StCl-6
93StCl/1stDay-6
93StCl/Angel-21
93Studio-142
93T-184
93T/Gold-184
93ToysRUs-43
93TripleP-103
93UD-377
93UD/SP-22
93Ultra-161
94B-563
94D-112

94F-53
94Finest-332
94L-86
94OPC-9
94Pac/Cr-76
94Panini-37
94Pinn-340
94S-17
94S/GoldR-17
94StCl-124
94StCl/1stDay-124
94StCl/Gold-124
94Studio-11
94T-418
94T/Gold-418
94TripleP-14
94UD-66
94UD/ElecD-66
94Ultra-326
Easley, Logan
83Greens-5
85Albany-5
86Albany/TCMA-17
88BuffB/CMC-1
88BuffB/ProC-1490
90AAASingl/ProC-644
90AlbanyDG/Best-5
90Denver/ProC-619
Easley, Mike
90Reno/Cal-266
91CLAS/ProC-CAR12
91Kinston/ClBest-15
91Kinston/ProC-327
92Shrev/ProC-3881
92Shrev/SB-583
Eason, Greg
80Ashvl-26
Eason, Mal
90Target-939
92Conlon/Sport-375
Eason, Tommy
91Batavia/ClBest-3
91Batavia/ProC-3485
92ClBest-263
92Spartan/ProC-1265
93ClBest/MLG-135
93FExcel/ML-84
Easter, Dick
84Iowa-4
Easter, Luscious Luke
(Luke)
50NumNum
51B-258
51T/RB-26
52B-95
52NumNum-12
52T-24
53B/Col-104
53Exh/Can-2
53T-2
54B-116
54DanDee
54T-23
79TCMA-80
86Negro/Frit-83
88LitSun/Minor-5
91T/Arc53-2
92Bz/Quadra-6M
94T/Arc54-23
D301
Exh47
PM10/Sm-47
Easterly, James M.
(Jamie)
75OPC-618R
75T-618R
75T/M-618R
76OPC-511
76T-511
78T-264
79Richm-11
79T-684
82D-623
82F-139
82Pol/Brew-28
82T-122
83D-280
83F-31
83Pol/Brew-28
83T-528
83T/Tr-28
84F-538
84Nes/792-367
84T-367
84T/St-258
85F-445
85Polar/Ind-36
85T-764
86D-582
86F-585
86OhHenry-36
86T-31
87Gator-11
89Pac/SenLg-189
89TM/SenLg-31
90EliteSenLg-54
Easterly, Theodore H.
(Ted)
14CJ-117
15CJ-117
T206
T207
Eastman, Doug
88Cedar/ProC-1153
89Cedar/Best-20
89Cedar/ProC-923
89Cedar/Star-5
Eastwick, Rawlins J.
(Rawley)
75OPC-621R
75T-621R
75T/M-621R
76Icee
76OPC-469
76T-469
77OPC-140
77OPC-8LL
77Pep-55
77T-45
77T-8LL
78BK/Y-11
78T-405
79T-271
80T-692
82F-596
82T-117
92Yank/WIZ70-47
Eatinger, Michael
90Foil/Best-222
90MidwLgAS/GS-10
90SoBend/Best-18
90SoBend/GS-3
92Saraso/ClBest-9
92Saraso/ProC-213
Eaton, Craig
76Watlo
77DaytB
80SLCity-3
81SLCity-4
82Spokane-2
83Evansvl-2
84Indianap-8
Eaton, Dann
91Spring/ClBest-14
91Spring/ProC-736
Eaton, Tommy
80CharlO/Pol-5
80CharlO/W3TV-5
81RochR-5
Eave, Gary
87Durham-19
88Richm-31
88Richm/CMC-5
88Richm/ProC-26
89Richm/Bob-5
89Richm/CMC-2
89Richm/Ko-31
89Richm/ProC-828
90B-471
90D-713
90S-621
91AA/LineD-333
91Jaxvl/LineD-333
91Jaxvl/ProC-143
Ebanks, Weddison
90Eugene/GS-6
Ebbetts, Charlie
90Target-940
Ebel, Brian
89Hagers/Best-16
89Hagers/ProC-284
Ebel, Dino
89VeroB/Star-8
90VeroB/Star-12
91Adelaide/Fut-7
91Bakers/Cal-19
91SanAn/ProC-2981
92Bakers/Cal-31
Eberle, Greg
89Peoria/Team-27MG
Eberle, Mike
88CLAS/Star-7
88Hagers/Star-4
89Hagers/Best-12
89Hagers/ProC-270
89Hagers/Star-6
90Foil/Best-199
90Hagers/Best-4
90Hagers/ProC-1415
90Hagers/Star-8
91AAA/LineD-455
91RochR/LineD-455
91RochR/ProC-1905
Eberly, Ryan
90Tampa/DIMD-4
Ebersberger, Randy
82Clinton/Frit-24
Ebert, Scott
88Pocatel/ProC-2080
89Everett/Star-7
90ClintUp/Team-U3
90Everett/ProC-3118
Ebright, Chris
88CapeCod/Sum-33
88OK-3
89Geneva/ProC-1876
89OK-14
90Peoria/Team-16
91CLAS/ProC-CAR41
91WinSalem/ClBest-23
91WinSalem/ProC-3840
92ChalK/SB-154
92CharlK/ProC-2778
92Sky/AASingl-71
Ebright, Hiram C.
(Hi)
N172
Eccles, John
85Anchora-9
87OrlanTw-4
88CalLgAS-38
88Visalia/Cal-150
88Visalia/ProC-84
89OrlanTw/ProC-1351
90OrlanSR/Best-2
90OrlanSR/ProC-1086
90OrlanSR/Star-4
Eccleston, Tom
86Wausau-9
Echemendia, Idaiberto
(Bert)
88James/ProC-1906
89Star/Wax-33
89WPalmB/Star-10
Echevarria, Angel
92Bend/ClBest-10
94B-610
Echevarria, Francisco
84Everett/Cram-17
Echevarria, Robert
87Elmira/Black-7
87Elmira/Red-7
Echeverria, Phil
90AZ/Pol-3
92AZ/Pol-3
Echols, Tony
76Wausau
Echols, Tracy
89MissSt-10
90MissSt-9
Eckard, Paul
91Everett/ClBest-29TR
Eckersley, Dennis Lee
(Dennis)
76Ho-137
76K-19
76OPC-202LL
76OPC-98
76SSPC-506
76T-202LL
76T-98
77BurgChef-58
77Ho-106
77Ho/Twink-106
77OPC-15
77Pep-13
77T-525
78Ho-78
78OPC-138
78PapaG/Disc-5
78SSPC/270-178
78T-122
78Wiffle/Discs-20
79Ho-145
79K-9
79OPC-16
79T-40
80OPC-169
80T-320
81Coke
81D-96
81F-226
81F/St-34
81OPC-109
81T-620
81T/HT
81T/St-48
82Coke/BOS
82D-30
82F-292
82F/St-165
82OPC-287
82PermaGr/AS-1
82T-490
83D-487
83F-182
83F-629M
83F/St-13M
83F/St-5M
83OPC-270
83OPC/St-34
83T-270
83T/St-34
84D-639
84F-396
84F/X-34
84Nes/792-745
84OPC-218
84SevenUp-43
84T-745
84T/St-224
84T/Tr-34
85D-442
85F-57
85OPC-163
85SevenUp-43
85T-163
86Cub/Unocal-8
86D-239
86F-368
86Gator-43
86Leaf-113
86OPC-199
86Sf-129M
86T-538
86T/St-62
86T/Tatt-2M
87D-365
87F-563
87F/Up-U30
87OPC-381
87Seven-C8
87Sf/TPrev-22M
87T-459
87T/St-63
87T/Tr-31T
88D-349
88D/A's/Bk-349
88D/Best-43
88F-279
88F/Slug-13
88Mother/A's-10
88OPC-72
88S-104
88T-72
88T/St-170
89B-190
89Cadaco-16
89Classic-90
89D-67
89D/AS-16
89D/Best-134
89F-7
89F/AS-4
89F/BBAS-12
89F/Heroes-13
89KennerFig-42
89Mother/A's-10
89OPC-370
89Panini/St-12
89Panini/St-414
89RedFoley/St-39
89S-276
89S/HotStar-16
89Sf-101
89Sf-222M
89T-370
89T/DH-11
89T/Gloss60-16
89T/Hills-12
89T/LJN-20
89T/Mini-69
89T/St-167
89T/St/Backs-31
89T/UK-23
89UD-289
89UD-664MVP
89Woolwth-20
90B-451
90D-210
90D/BestAL-12
90F-6
90F/Can-6
90F/LL-11
90KMart/SS-29
90KayBee-9
90Kenner/Fig-26
90Leaf-29
90Leaf/Prev-3
90MLBPA/Pins-75
90Mother/A's-7
90OPC-670
90Panini/St-137
90PublInt/St-282
90PublInt/St-303
90RedFoley/St-29
90S-315
90Sf-170
90T-670
90T/Big-50
90T/DH-19
90T/Gloss60-53
90T/HeadsUp-4
90T/Mini-27
90T/St-182
90T/TVAS-13
90UD-513
90USPlayC/AS-8C
91B-237
91BBBest/Aces-6
91Classic/200-126
91Classic/II-T18
91D-270
91F-6
91Leaf-285
91Leaf/Stud-102
91Mother/A's-7
91OPC-250
91OPC/Premier-38
91Panini/FrSt-200
91Panini/St-148
91Panini/Top15-86
91RedFoley/St-31
91S-485
91S/100SS-73
91SFExam/A's-3
91Seven/3DCoin-5NC
91StCl-332
91T-250
91UD-172
91USPlayC/AS-10D
91Ultra-245
92B-431
92CJ/DI-1
92Classic/Game200-8
92Colla/ASG-17
92D-147
92D/Preview-5
92DPep/MSA-7
92F-255
92L-100
92L/BlkGold-100
92Mother/A's-7
92OPC-738
92OPC/Premier-188
92Panini-22
92Pinn-25
92Pinn/TeamP-11
92S-190
92S/100SS-56
92StCl-190
92StCl/Dome-42
92StCl/MemberII-5
92StCl/MemberIII*-4
92Studio-223
92T-738
92T/Gold-738
92T/GoldWin-738
92T/Kids-119

92TripleP-195
92UD-331
92UD/TmMVPHolo-19
92Ultra-421
93B-485
93Classic/Gamel-27
93Colla/DM-34
93Colla/DMProto-3
93D-215
93D-396M
93D/Elite-25
93D/EliteUp-7
93D/Prev-19
93D/Spirit-SG4
93Duracel/PPII-23
93F-293
93F-717M
93F/Atlantic-7
93F/Fruit-18
93F/GoldMII-1
93F/ProVI-2
93Flair-257
93Ho-11
93Kraft-6
93L-72
93L/GoldAS-10
93MSA/Ben-1
93MSA/Metz-25
93Mother/A's-4
93OPC-106
93OPC/Premier/StarP-22
93Pac/Spanish-221
93Panini-13
93Panini-157LL
93Panini-161CY
93Panini-162MVP
93Pinn-100
93Pinn-474NT
93Pinn/Cooper-6
93S-21
93S-481AW
93S-483AW
93S-509AS
93S-513HL
93S-540DT
93S/Franchise-11
93S/GoldDT-9
93Select-38
93Select/ChasS-24
93Select/StatL-67
93StCl-291MC
93StCl-461
93StCl/1stDay-291MC
93StCl/1stDay-461
93StCl/A's-1
93StCl/MurphyS-179
93Studio-1
93T-155
93T-411M
93T/BlkGold-29
93T/Finest-100AS
93T/FinestASJ-100AS
93T/FinestRef-100AS
93T/Gold-155
93T/Gold-411M
93T/Hill-1
93T/MicroP-155
93TripleP-9
93TripleP/LL-L1M
93TripleP/LL-L2M
93UD-271
93UD-487AW
93UD-489AW
93UD-814TC
93UD/Clutch-R8
93UD/FunPack-49
93UD/OnDeck-D10
93UD/SP-38
93UD/Then-TN10
93Ultra-257
93Ultra/AwardWin-23
93Ultra/Eck-Set
93Ultra/EckComm-1
94B-520
94D-16
94D/Special-16
94F-260
94Flair-91
94KingB-8
94Kraft-2
94L-234
94OPC-144
94Pac/Cr-448
94Panini-108
94Pinn-32
94Pinn/Artist-32
94Pinn/Museum-32
94RedFoley-18M
94S-109
94S/GoldR-109
94Sf/2000-50
94StCl-125
94StCl/1stDay-125
94StCl/Gold-125
94StCl/Pr-125
94StCl/PreProd-125
94Studio-1
94T-465
94T/Finest-206
94T/FinestRef-206
94T/Gold-465
94TripleP-2
94UD-365
94Ultra-407
94Ultra/Fire-5

Eckhardt, Ox
90Target-211

Eckhardt, Tom
89Idaho/ProC-2030

Economy, Scott
88Billings/ProC-1814
89Cedar/Best-9
89Cedar/ProC-921
89Cedar/Star-6
90Cedar/ProC-2317

Eddings, Jay
88CharWh/Best-12
89CharWh/Best-21
89CharWh/ProC-1766
89Peoria/Team-6
90Peoria/Team-21

Eddins, Glenn Jr.
79Elmira-6
81Bristol-18

Eddy, Chris
92Classic/DP-57
92Eugene/ClBest-12
92Eugene/ProC-3022
92FrRow/DP-56
93B-477
93StCl/MurphyS-82
93StCl/Royal-27
94FExcel-67

Eddy, Donald Eugene
(Don)
72OPC-413R
72T-413R

Eddy, Jim
90Rockford/ProC-2691
90Rockford/Team-7
91WPalmB/ClBest-5
91WPalmB/ProC-1221

Eddy, Martin
88BurlInd/ProC-1775

Eddy, Steven Allen
(Steve)
76QuadC
80SLCity-17

Edelen, Benny Joe
(Joe)
77StPete
80ArkTr-1
82F-65
83Indianap-8

Eden, Edward Michael
(Mike)
75Phoenix/Caruso-11
75Phoenix/CircleK-16
76Phoenix/Coke-6
78SSPC/270-136
79RochR-9
80RochR-12

Edenfield, Ken
90Boise/ProC-3308
91ClBest/Singl-260
91QuadC/ClBest-3
91QuadC/ProC-2620
92MidldA/OneHour-5
92MidldA/ProC-4020
92PalmSp/ClBest-13

Edens, Tom
83Butte-4
86Jacks/TCMA-4
87Tidew-9
87Tidew/TCMA-2
88Tidew/CANDL-19
88Tidew/CMC-5
88Tidew/ProC-1581
89Tidew/CMC-2
89Tidew/ProC-1956
90AAASingl/ProC-645
90Brewer/MillB-6
90Denver/CMC-4
90Denver/ProC-620
90ProC/Singl-29
91AAA/LineD-407
91AAAGame/ProC-35
91D-590
91F-582
91OPC-118
91Portl/LineD-407
91Portl/ProC-1561
91S-78
91S/100RisSt-2
91T-118
91UD-616
91WIZMets-103
92F/Up-39
92S-720
92StCl-662
93D-729
93F-434
93F/Final-78
93Mother/Ast-27
93S-450
94D-456
94Flair-169
94Pac/Cr-264
94T-427
94T/Gold-427

Edge, Alvin
76BurlB
78BurlB

Edge, Claude Lee Jr.
(Butch)
76BurlB
78Syrac
79Syrac/TCMA-9
79Syrac/Team-19
80OPC-329R
80Richm-3
80T-674R
81Richm-11
82Portl-2

Edge, Greg
86Clearw-7
87Reading-4
88EastLAS/ProC-32
88Reading/ProC-880
89ElPaso/GS-21
89Reading/Best-16
89Reading/ProC-666
90ElPaso/GS-9
91AA/LineD-106
91CaroMud/LineD-106
91CaroMud/ProC-1092
92CaroMud/SB-132

Edge, Tim
90Welland/Pucko-16
91Salem/ClBest-1
91Salem/ProC-955
92Salem/ClBest-19
92Salem/ProC-66
93CaroMud/RBI-1

Edgerton, Bill
No Cards.

Ediger, Lance
78Newar

Edler, David Delmar
(Dave)
80Spokane-15
81F-610
81Pol/Mariners-7
82Omaha-16
82T-711
83T-622

Edmonds, Bobby Joe
89Reading/Best-17
89Reading/ProC-673
89Reading/Star-10

Edmonds, Jim
88Bend/Legoe-10
89QuadC/Best-27
89QuadC/GS-6
90AS/Cal-6
91PalmSp/ProC-2028
92ClBest-343
92MidldA/OneHour-6
92MidldA/ProC-4037
92MidldA/SB-458
92Sky/AASingl-194
93F/Final-181
93FExcel/ML-141
93Flair/Wave-4
93T-799
93T/Gold-799
93Ultra-519
93Vanco/ProC-2609
94B-423
94F-54
94Flair-21
94Pinn-394
94Select-198
94T-404
94T/Gold-404
94Ultra-327

Edmonds, Stan
82Wausau/Frit-4

Edmondson, Brian
91Bristol/ClBest-26
91Bristol/ProC-3597
92Fayette/ClBest-3
92Fayette/ProC-2162
92StCl/Dome-43
93B-291
94B-265
94FExcel-53

Edmondson, Gavin
92GulfCD/ProC-3568

Edmondson, Paul M.
(Paul)
70OPC-414
70T-414

Eduardo, Hector
77StPete
78StPete
79ArkTr-19

Edwards, Allen
82Madis/Frit-17
83Albany-2

Edwards, Bobby
88SLCity-11

Edwards, Charles B.
(Bruce)
47HomogBond-12
47TipTop
48B-43
49B-206
49Eureka-34
50B-165
51B-116
51T/BB-42
52B-88
52NTea
52T-224
89Smok/Dodg-52
90Target-212
D305
Exh47
R346-26

Edwards, Chuck
89Johnson/Star-9

Edwards, David L.
(Dave)
79Twin/FriszP-5
80T-657
81D-595
81F-568
81T-386
81T/Tr-758
82D-247
82T-151
83D-565
83F-357
83T-94
87Pocatel/Bon-17
88Pocatel/ProC-2084
90Everett/Best-28

Edwards, Glenn
85Water-5

Edwards, Henry Albert
(Hank)
43Playball-7
48L-72
49B-136
49Eureka-56
50B-169
52B-141
52T-176
53T-90
90Target-213
91T/Arc53-90

Edwards, Howard R.
(Doc)
62T-594R
63T-296
64T-174
65OPC-239
65T-239
79RochR-10
80RochR-13
81RochR-22
81TCMA-426
82Charl-23
83Charl-22
84Maine-10
85IntLgAS-24
85Maine-29
86OhHenry-CO
87Gator-CO
88Gator-32MG
88T-374MG
89T-534MG
90Kahn/Mets-32CO
90T/TVMets-3CO
91Kahn/Mets-32CO
92BuffB/BlueS-8CO
92BuffB/ProC-339
92BuffB/SB-50CO
92Yank/WIZ60-38

Edwards, Jeff
86Ashvl-9
86AubAs-8
87Albuq/Pol-9
87Ashvl-25
87SanBern-3
88ColAst/Best-16
89Canton/ProC-1316
89Canton/Star-4
89EastLDD/ProC-DD41
90ColoSp/CMC-6
90ProC/Singl-458
92GulfCM/ProC-3499

Edwards, Jerome
90Princet/DIMD-5
91Batavia/ClBest-12
91Batavia/ProC-3495
92Spartan/ClBest-2
92Spartan/ProC-1276

Edwards, Jim
93Conlon-985

Edwards, John Alban
(Johnny)
62Kahn
62Salada-191
62Shirriff-191
62T-236WS
62T-302
62T/St-114
63FrBauer-5
63J-132
63Kahn
63P-132
63T-178
64Kahn
64T-507
64Wheat/St-14
65Kahn
65MacGregor-3
65T-418
66Kahn
66T-507
67CokeCap/Reds-10
67Kahn
67T-202
68T-558
69MLB/St-139
69OPC-186
69T-186
69T/4in1-22M
69T/St-33
70MLB/St-40
70OPC-339
70T-339
71MLB/St-79
71OPC-44
71T-44
72MB-96
72OPC-416
72T-416
73OPC-519
73T-519
74OPC-635
74T-635

Edwards, Jovon
86Bakers-6
88StLucie/Star-7

Edwards, Larry
77BurlB
78BurlB

79BurlB-1
80Ander-5
81GlenF-24
Edwards, Marshall L.
78Holyo
79Vanco-4
80Vanco-19
82F-140
82T-333R
83D-406
83F-32
83Gard-6
83Pol/Brew-16
83T-582
84Cram/PCL-47
84D-490
84Nes/792-167
84T-167
92Brew/Carlson-6
Edwards, Mel
91Spokane/ProC-3955
Edwards, Michael L.
(Mike)
75Shrev/TCMA-2
76Shrev
79T-201M
79T-613
80OPC-158
80T-301
81D-497
Edwards, Mike
91Butte/SportP-9
92ClBest-310
92Gaston/ClBest-12
92Gaston/ProC-2259
Edwards, Otis
91Watertn/ClBest-25
91Watertn/ProC-3380
Edwards, Ryan
90Billings/ProC-3223
91Cedar/ClBest-3
91Cedar/ProC-2711
92Cedar/ClBest-27
92Cedar/ProC-1065
Edwards, Samuel
90Princet/DIMD-6
91Martins/ClBest-23
91Martins/ProC-3447
92Martins/ClBest-23
92Martins/ProC-3049
Edwards, Todd
86Miami-6
90Helena/SportP-19
91Beloit/ClBest-19
91Beloit/ProC-2116
91SLCity/ProC-3224
91SLCity/SportP-4
92Geneva/ClBest-18
92Geneva/ProC-1554
Edwards, Wayne
86Penin-9
87DayBe-15
88BirmB/Best-1
89BBAmAA/BPro-AA22
89BirmB/Best-21
89BirmB/ProC-110
89SLAS-16
90B-309
90BirmDG/Best-9
90Coke/WSox-2
90Coke/WSox-28
90D/Rook-17
90F-652M
90F/Can-652M
90F/Up-U83
90Leaf-352
90S/Tr-85T
90T/89Debut-34
90T/Tr-27T
90UD/Ext-762
91B-364
91D-327
91F-116
91Kodak/WSox-45
91Leaf-454
91OPC-751
91S-66
91S/100RisSt-10
91StCl-129
91T-751
91UD-697
92OPC-404
92StCl-674
92Syrac/MerchB-5
92Syrac/ProC-1960
92Syrac/SB-505
Eenhoorn, Robert
90A&AASingle/ProC-182
90Oneonta/ProC-3384
91B-172
91PrWill/ClBest-16
91PrWill/ProC-1432
91UD/FinalEd-16F
92B-278
92ClBest-229
92FtLaud/ClBest-4
92FtLaud/ProC-2617
92FtLaud/Team-7
92ProC/Tomorrow-121
92UD/ML-326
93B-567
93StCl/Y-25
94B-277
94FExcel-102
94UD-514DD
Effrig, Mark
83ElPaso-7
84ElPaso-1
Egan, Jack
94Conlon-1185UMP
Egan, Richard Joseph
(Joe)
14Piedmont/St-20
16FleischBrd-26
T202
T205
T206
Egan, Richard Wallis
(Dick)
63T-169R
64T-572R
66T-536
67T-539
81TCMA-434
89Smok/R-6CO
90OkCty/CMC-22CO
90OkCty/ProC-449CO
90ProC/Singl-172CO
90Target-214
91Butte/SportP-30
93Rang/Keeb-133CO
Egan, Thomas Patrick
(Tom)
65T-486R
66T-263
67OPC-147
67T-147
69T-407
70MLB/St-171
70OPC-4
70T-4
71OPC-537
71T-537
72MB-97
72OPC-207
72T-207
73OPC-648
73T-648
75OPC-88
75T-88
75T/M-88
77Wausau-MG
Eggert, David
92James/ClBest-25
92James/ProC-1492
93BurlB/ClBest-8
93BurlB/ProC-151
Eggertsen, Todd
86PalmSp-12
86PalmSp/Smok-16
87PalmSp-29
88MidldA/GS-9
Eggleston, Darren
88CharWh/Best-10
Eggleston, Scott
91Spokane/ClBest-17
91Spokane/ProC-3942
92Spokane/ClBest-20
92Spokane/ProC-1285
Eggleston, Skip
88Geneva/ProC-1639
Egins, Paul C. III
88BurlB/ProC-30TR
89BurlB/ProC-1625
Egloff, Bruce
87Watlo-15
89Watertn/Star-5
90A&AASingle/ProC-11
90Canton/Best-20
90Canton/ProC-1288
90Foil/Best-251
91B-78
91Indian/McDon-8
92ColoSp/ProC-747
92S-751
92StCl-503
92T/91Debut-49
Ehardt, Rube
90Target-941
Ehler, Dan
94T-751DP
94T/Gold-751DP
Ehmann, Kurt
92Classic/DP-83
92Everett/ClBest-23
93StCl/MurphyS-70
94ClBest/Gold-150
94FExcel-288
Ehmig, Greg
88SLCity-14
Ehmke, Howard J.
(Howard)
21Exh-42
21Exh-43
25Exh-65
28Exh-54
61F-21
88Conlon/5-9
92Conlon/Sport-357
93Conlon-759
94Conlon-1135
E120
R316
V100
W573
WG7-15
Ehret, Philip S.
(Red)
N172
Ehrhard, Jim
88FtLaud/Star-6
Ehrhard, Rod
87Oneonta-23
88Oneonta/ProC-2072
89PrWill/Star-7
90FtLaud/Star-7
Eichelberger, Juan T.
79Hawaii-21
80Hawaii-4
81T-478
81T/St-97
82D-442
82F-570
82T-366TL
82T-614
82T/StVar-97
83D-422
83F-358
83OPC-168
83T-168
83T/Tr-29
84D-398
84F-539
84Nes/792-226
84T-226
86Richm-5
87Richm/Bob-6
87Richm/Crown-15
87Richm/TCMA-4
88Richm/CMC-6
88Richm/ProC-10
89Pac/SenLg-175
89T/SenLg-123
89TM/SenLg-32
90EliteSenLg-20
91Pac/SenLg-119
Eicher, Mike
92Spring/ClBest-17
92Spring/ProC-881
Eichhorn, Dave
86Albuq-6
87SanAn-20
88SanAn/Best-13
89Albuq/CMC-6
89Albuq/ProC-61
Eichhorn, Mark A.
82Syrac-3
82Syrac/Team-11
83Syrac-7
84Syrac-18
86D/Rook-13
86F/Up-U38
86Sf/Rook-38
86T/Tr-34T
86Tor/Fire-8
87D-321
87F-224
87F/GameWin-14
87F/Hottest-16
87F/Mini-36
87F/St-37
87Leaf-173CG
87Leaf-229
87OPC-371
87Sf-194M
87Sf/TPrev-5M
87T-371
87T/Gloss60-49
87T/JumboR-5
87T/St-187
87Tor/Fire-7
87ToysRUs-10
88BJ/5x7-4
88D-121
88F-108
88F/Mini-60
88Ho/Disc-18
88Leaf-74
88OPC-116
88Panini/St-212
88S-198
88Sf-210
88T-749
88T/Big-208
88T/Revco-30
88Tor/Fire-38
89AAA/CMC-26
89Brave/Dubuq-10
89F-230
89OPC-274
89Richm/ProC-825
89S-152
89T-274
89T/Big-188
90F-580
90F/Can-580
90F/Up-U77
90Leaf-472
90OPC-513
90T-513
90T/Tr-28T
90TripleAAS/CMC-26
91D-318
91F-311
91OPC-129
91S-504
91Smok/Angel-16
91T-129
91UD-519
92D-181
92F-55
92L-97
92L/BlkGold-97
92OPC-435
92Pinn-353
92S-221
92StCl-857
92T-435
92T/Gold-435
92T/GoldWin-435
92UD-287
93BJ/D/45-16
93BJ/Demp-15
93BJ/Fire-9
93F/Final-292
93StCl-617
93StCl/1stDay-617
94D-144
94F-330
94Pac/Cr-638
94Pinn-511
94S-266
94S/GoldR-266
94StCl/Team-282
Eierman, John
91Elmira/ClBest-4
91Elmira/ProC-3282
92LynchRS/ClBest-2
92LynchRS/ProC-2918
Eiffert, Michael
92Bend/ClBest-11
Eiland, Dave
87Oneonta-17
88Albany/ProC-1336
88EastLAS/ProC-1
89Colum/CMC-8
89Colum/Pol-3
89Colum/ProC-750
89D-481
89T-8
90AAASingl/ProC-320
90AlbanyDG/Best-26
90ColClip/CMC-2
90ColClip/ProC-670
90Colum/Pol-13
90ProC/Singl-202
90S-652
90T/TVYank-41
91D-354
91F-661
91Leaf-184
91OPC-611
91S-826
91StCl-477
91T-611
92F-223
92L-488
92L/BlkGold-488
92Mother/Padre-10
92OPC-406
92Pol/Padre-6
92S-679
92Smok/Padre-7
92StCl-133
92StCl-879
92StCl/MemberI-4
92Ultra-575
92Yank/WIZ80-51
93Mother/Padre-7
93UD-709
Eilers, David Louis
(Dave)
66T-534R
78TCMA-245
91WIZMets-104
Einstein, Charles
90LitSun-11
Eischen, Joe
(Joey)
89Butte/SP-13
90Gaston/Best-6
90Gaston/ProC-2514
90Gaston/Star-6
91CharlR/ClBest-4
91CharlR/ProC-1308
92ClBest-303
92WPalmB/ClBest-18
92WPalmB/ProC-2082
93B-240
93Harris/ProC-265
94B-528
94ClBest/Gold-137
94FExcel-224
94FExcel/LL-8
94SigRook-35
94UD-10
94UD/ElecD-10
94Ultra-522
Eisenreich, Charlie
87AppFx-15
Eisenreich, James M.
(Jim)
81Wisco-21
83T-197
83Twin/Team-2
83Twin/Team-31M
87Memphis-27
87Memphis/Best-21
88D-343
88OPC-348
88S-456
88Smok/Royals-26
88T-348
89D/Best-306
89F/Up-38
89S-594
89T/Tr-28T
89UD-44
90B-374
90D-238
90D/BestAL-120
90F-106
90F/Can-106
90Leaf-278
90OPC-246
90Panini/St-80
90PublInt/St-346
90S-179
90Sf-166
90T-246

90T/Big-234
90T/St-271
90UD-294
91B-304
91D-448
91F-557
91OPC-707
91Panini/FrSt-280
91Panini/St-229
91Pol/Royal-8
91S-154
91StCl-373
91T-707
91UD-658
91Ultra-146
92D-297
92F-156
92L-295
92L/BlkGold-295
92OPC-469
92Pinn-468
92Pol/Royal-6
92S-158
92StCl-409
92T-469
92T/Gold-469
92T/GoldWin-469
92TripleP-140
92UD-539
92Ultra-69
93D-722
93F-617
93F/Final-109
93Flair-100
93L-507
93Pac/Spanish-576
93Panini-104
93Phill/Med-13
93S-551
93Select-241
93StCl-224
93StCl/1stDay-224
93StCl/Phill-7
93T-22
93T/Gold-22
93UD-800
93Ultra-440
94D-548
94F-588
94Flair-206
94L-176
94Pac/Cr-474
94Panini-227
94Phill/Med-8
94Pinn-149
94Pinn/Artist-149
94Pinn/Museum-149
94StCl-27
94StCl/1stDay-27
94StCl/Gold-27
94StCl/Team-224
94T-504
94T/Gold-504
94UD-157
94UD/ElecD-157
94Ultra-545

Eisenstat, Harry
40PlayBall-204
90Target-215

Eissens, Simon
91Perth/Fut-1

Eiterman, Tom
90AS/Cal-39
90Reno/Cal-263
91CLAS/ProC-CAR13
91Kinston/ClBest-25
91Kinston/ProC-337
92Canton/ProC-700
92Canton/SB-105

Eklund, Troy
89Butte/SP-16
90Gaston/Best-12
90Gaston/ProC-2532
90Gaston/Star-7

Ekman, Rich
91Pocatel/ProC-3775
91Pocatel/SportP-9

Elam, Scott
82Knoxvl-2
83Kinston/Team-4

Elam, Todd
88Batavia/ProC-1682
89Spartan/ProC-1028
89Spartan/Star-7
90Clearw/Star-6

Elberfeld, Norman A.
(Kid)
12Sweet/Pin-57A
12Sweet/Pin-57B
89Chatt/II/Team-9
90Target-216
92Conlon/Sport-557
E107
E254
M116
S74-38
T201
T202
T204
T205
T206
T213/blue
T214-9
T215/blue
T215/brown
T3-15
WG2-17

Elder, Isaac
89James/ProC-2147
90Rockford/ProC-2706

Elders, Mike
76Clinton

Eldred, Calvin
(Cal)
89Beloit/II/Star-8
90A&AASingle/ProC-138
90B-387
90ElPaso/GS-10
90Foil/Best-61
90ProC/Singl-866
90S-669DC
90Stockton/Best-1
90Stockton/Cal-174
90Stockton/ProC-2178
91AAA/LineD-135
91B-56
91Denver/LineD-135
91Denver/ProC-116
92B-299
92Classic/Game200-126
92Classic/I-31
92D-718
92Denver/ProC-2631
92Denver/SB-127
92F-679
92L-2
92L/BlkGold-2
92OPC-433
92Pinn-249
92Pinn/Team2000-36
92ProC/Tomorrow-81
92S-834
92S/HotRook-1
92S/Impact-89
92S/Rook-33
92Sky/AAASingl-61
92StCl-327
92T-433
92T/91Debut-50
92T/Gold-433
92T/GoldWin-433
92TripleP-213
92UD-477
92Ultra-380
93B-127
93Classic/Gamel-28
93D-131
93F-248
93F/RookSenl-2
93Flair-223
93HumDum/Can-10
93L-34
93L/Fast-16
93OPC-85
93OPC/Premier-4
93Pinn-2
93Pinn/Team2001-2
93Pol/Brew-6
93S-368
93Select-296
93Select/Ace-21
93Select/ChasRook-15
93StCl-475
93StCl/1stDay-475
93Studio-6
93T-590
93T/Finest-147
93T/FinestRef-147
93T/Gold-590
93ToysRUs-80
93TripleP-18
93UD-375
93UD/FunPack-70
93UD/SP-64
93USPlayC/Rook-13C
93Ultra-218
94B-393
94D-89
94F-175
94Finest-288
94Flair-66
94L-267
94OPC-179
94Pac/Cr-328
94Pinn-19
94Pinn/Artist-19
94Pinn/Museum-19
94Pol/Brew-6
94RedFoley-28M
94S-449
94Sf/2000-107
94StCl-329
94StCl/1stDay-329
94StCl/Gold-329
94T-45
94T/Gold-45
94TripleP-52
94UD-431
94UD/SP-57
94Ultra-73

Eldredge, Ted
88Belling/Legoe-23
88SanBern/Best-11
88SanBern/Cal-41
89Wausau/GS-9

Eldridge, Brian
89Anchora-13
90AZ/Pol-4

Eldridge, Rodney
90Hamil/Best-20
90Hamil/Star-10
91ClBest/Singl-180
91Savan/ClBest-16
91Savan/ProC-1657
92StPete/ClBest-15

Elenes, Larry
74Cedar

Elerman, John
92ClBest-388

Elguezabal, Jose
78SanJose-7

Elia, Lee Constantine
(Lee)
66T-529R
67T-406
68T-561
69T-312
75IntAS/TCMA-26
75IntAS/TCMA-8
79OkCty
81TCMA-428
82RedLob
83D-614MG
83T-456MG
83Thorn-26MG
84Cram/PCL-200MG
85Phill/TastyK-4CO
85Phill/TastyK-8CO
86Phill/TastyK-4CO
87Phill/TastyK-x
87T/Tr-32T
88Chatt/Team-9
88Phill/TastyK-32CO
88Phill/TastyK-9A
88Phill/TastyK-9B
88T-254MG
90Clearw/Star-26MG
91Clearw/ClBest-18MG
91Clearw/ProC-1638MG
92ScranWB/ProC-2462MG
92ScranWB/SB-499MG
93Mother/Mar-28M

Elick, Jason
90Visalia/Cal-84BB

Elkin, Rick
80Batavia-15
81Batavia-11

Elkins, Mark
89TNTech-8

Ellam, Roy
T206
T213/brown

Eller, Horace Owen
(Hod)
88Pac/8Men-93
92Conlon/Sport-352
94Conlon-1027
W514-38

Ellerbe, Francis R.
(Frank)
E120
V100
V61-51
W573

Elli, Rocky
88Clmbia/GS-4
90Jacks/GS-22
91AAA/LineD-482
91ScranWB/LineD-482
91ScranWB/ProC-2533
92Clearw/ProC-2049

Ellingsen, H. Bruce
75OPC-288
75OkCty/Team-6
75T-288
75T/M-288

Elliot, Corey
84Visalia-7

Elliot, Greg
92AubAs/ClBest-2
92AubAs/ProC-1359

Elliot, Lawrence L.
(Larry)
63T-407R
64T-536R
67OPC-23
67T-23
91WIZMets-105

Elliot, Paul
91Parramatta/Fut-2CO

Elliot, Rowdy
90Target-942

Elliot, Terry
88StPete/Star-6
89StPete/Star-10

Elliott, Clay
79Savan-11

Elliott, Donnie
88Martins/Star-12
89Batavia/ProC-1925
90Spartan/Best-16
90Spartan/ProC-2482
90Spartan/Star-5
91Spartan/ClBest-3
91Spartan/ProC-888
92ClBest-369
92Greenvl/ProC-1150
93B-58
93Richm/Bleach-18
93Richm/Pep-8
93Richm/Team-9
94B-255

Elliott, Glenn
43Centen-7
44Centen-6
45Centen-6
49Eureka-8

Elliott, Greg
93ClBest/MLG-155

Elliott, Harry Lewis
(Harry)
55Hunters
55T-137

Elliott, James Thomas
(Jumbo)
33G-132
90Target-217
V354-6
W513-64

Elliott, Jim
90Spokane/SportP-11

Elliott, John
86Ashvl-10
87Osceola-17
88ColAst/Best-13

Elliott, Mark
78Clinton
79Clinton/TCMA-1

Elliott, Randy Lee
(Randy)
75Hawaii/Caruso-4
78T-719R

Elliott, Robert I.
(Bob)
39Exh
42Playball-37
47HomogBond-13
48B-1
48L-65
49B-58
49Eureka-7
50B-20
50Drake-35
51B-66
51T/BB-32
52BR
52T-14
53Exh/Can-26
60T-215MG
D305
R346-38
R423-28

Ellis, Bruce
87BYU-20

Ellis, Bull
91Utica/ProC-3233

Ellis, Dock Phillip
(Dock)
69Pirate/JITB-3
69T-286
70T-551
71MLB/St-200
71OPC-2
71T-2
71T/Coins-99
72OPC-179
72OPC-180IA
72T-179
72T-180IA
73OPC-575
73T-575
74OPC-145
74T-145
74T/St-82
75OPC-385
75T-385
75T/M-385
76OPC-528
76T-528
76T/Tr-528T
77K-4
77OPC-146
77T-71
78BK/R-6
78SSPC/270-96
78T-209
79T-691
80OPC-64
80T-117
89Pac/SenLg-15
89T/SenLg-116
89TM/SenLg-33
90EliteSenLg-5
91WIZMets-106
92Yank/WIZ70-48
93Rang/Keeb-134
94TedW-76

Ellis, Doug
87Macon-15

Ellis, George W.
(Rube)
E254
E270/1
E286
E90/1
M116
T207

Ellis, Jim
77Fritsch-28
91MissSt-14
92MissSt-12

Ellis, John Charles
(John)
70OPC-516R
70T-516R
71MLB/St-487
71OPC-263
71T-263
72OPC-47
72OPC-48IA
72T-47
72T-48IA
73OPC-656
74OPC-128
74T-128
74T/St-165
75Ho-54
75OPC-605
75T-605

75T/M-605
76Ho-27
76Ho/Twink-27
76OPC-383
76SSPC-515
76T-383
76T/Tr-383T
77T-36
78BK/R-3
78SSPC/270-100
78T-438
79T-539
80T-283
81D-26
81T-339
82D-642
82F-316
82T-177
92Yank/WIZ60-39
92Yank/WIZ70-49
93Rang/Keeb-135
T73-656

Ellis, Paul
90Hamil/Best-13
90Hamil/Star-11
91ClBest/Singl-81
91FSLAS/ProC-FSL34
91StPete/ClBest-15
91StPete/ProC-2278
92ClBest-278
92StPete/ClBest-5
92StPete/ProC-2030
93B-336
93ClBest/MLG-97

Ellis, Robert Walter
(Rob)
75Sacra/Caruso-11
76SSPC-240
77Spoka
79Tacoma-23
80Port-5
89Anchora-14ACO
91Everett/ProC-3933MG

Ellis, Robert
91Utica/ClBest-7
92SoBend/ClBest-3
94B-183
94FExcel-38

Ellis, Rufus
86FSLAS-12
86FtMyr-9
87FtMyr-18
88CharlR/Star-6

Ellis, Samuel Joseph
(Sammy)
63T-29R
64T-33R
65Kahn
65T-507
66Kahn
66T-250
66T/RO
66T/RO-25
67Kahn
67OPC-176
67T-176
68T-453
69OPC-32
69T-32
78TCMA-293
80Colum-14
81Colum-26
82Colum-24M
90Coke/WSox-30CO
91Kodak/WSox-x
92Cub/Mara-NNO
93Mother/Mar-28M

Ellis, Terry
88MissSt-5

Ellis, Tim
88Geneva/ProC-1643
90Kinston/Team-26
90Watertn/Star-8

Ellison, Darold
80Batavia-18

Ellison, Jeff
76Dubuq
77Cocoa

Ellison, Paul
88Spartan/Star-6
89Spartan/ProC-1041
89Spartan/Star-8

Ellsworth, Ben
90Johnson/Star-11
91Hamil/ClBest-25
91Hamil/ProC-4045
92Savan/ClBest-5
92Savan/ProC-669

Ellsworth, Richard C.
(Dick)
60T-125
61T-427
61T/St-7
62T-264
62T/St-107
63T-399
64Bz-28
64T-1LL
64T-220
64T/Coins-56
64T/S-17
64T/SU
64T/St-5
64T/tatt
65OPC-165
65T-165
65T/E-67
66T-447
66T/RO-26
67CokeCap/Phill-7
67Pol/Phill-5
67T-359
68CokeCap/RedSox-14
68Dexter-30
68T-406
69MB-78
69MLB/St-12
69T-605
70MLB/St-196
70OPC-59
70T-59
71MLB/St-435
71OPC-309
71T-309
72MB-98

Ellsworth, Steve
86NewBrit-10
87Pawtu-17
87Pawtu/TCMA-6
88D/RedSox/Bk-NEW
88D/Rook-54
88S/Tr-83T
89Pawtu/CMC-7
89Pawtu/Dunkin-28
89Pawtu/ProC-704
89T-299

Elpin, Ralph
81Watlo-33
82Watlo/B-3
82Watlo/Frit-12

Elrod, Greg
85Clovis-14

Elsbecker, Andy
92Hunting/ClBest-16
92Hunting/ProC-3138

Elsea, Dottie
89Kingspt/Star-30
90Kgsport/Star-29GM

Elster, Kevin
84LitFalls-19
85Lynch-19
86Jacks/TCMA-13
87D-635
87F-7
87Tidew-32
87Tidew/TCMA-13
88Classic/Red-190
88D-37RR
88D/Best-70
88D/Mets/Bk-37
88D/Rook-34
88F/Up-U104
88Kahn/Mets-21
88Leaf-37RR
88S-624
88S/YS/II-40
88Sf/Gamewin-24
88T-8FS
88T/Mets/Fan-21
89B-383
89Classic-75
89D-289
89D/Best-97
89F-34
89Kahn/Mets-21
89KennerFig-43
89Panini/St-127
89S-130
89Sf-71
89T-356
89T/Big-16
89T/JumboR-6
89Tidew/Candl-15
89ToysRUs-7
89UD-269
90B-137
90D-152
90D/BestNL-31
90F-202
90F/Can-202
90Kahn/Mets-21
90Leaf-8
90MLBPA/Pins-12
90Mets/Fan-21
90OPC-734
90Panini/St-296
90Publlnt/St-132
90S-443
90Sf-118
90T-734
90T/Big-143
90T/St-2HL
90T/St-97
90T/TVMets-23
90UD-187
91B-469
91D-304
91F-145
91Kahn/Mets-21
91Leaf-305
91OPC-134
91Panini/FrSt-82
91RedFoley/St-32
91S-633
91StCl-149
91T-134
91UD-101
91Ultra-215
91WIZMets-107
92D-307
92F-502
92Mets/Kahn-15
92OPC-251
92Panini-225
92Pinn-89
92S-103
92StCl-201
92T-251
92T/Gold-251
92T/GoldWin-251
92TripleP-66
92UD-385
92Ultra-231
93F-469
93Pac/Spanish-195

Elston, Carey
89Burllnd/Star-10

Elston, Curt
C46-23

Elston, Donald Ray
(Don)
57T-376
58T-363
59T-520
60T-233
61P-200
61T-169
61T/St-8
62J-190
62P-190
62P/Can-190
62Salada-101
62Shirriff-101
62T-446
63T-515
64T-111
65T-436
78TCMA-143
84Cub/Uno-9
90Target-218

Elston, Guy
82Nashvl-11
83Colum-13
84Maine-13

Elvira, Narciso
88Stockton/Cal-183
88Stockton/ProC-748
89Stockton/Star-6
91AAA/LineD-136
91B-47
91Denver/LineD-136
91Denver/ProC-117
91T/90Debut-43
91UD-13
92OkCty/ProC-1911
92OkCty/SB-323

Elway, John
82Oneonta-13

Elwert
E270/2

Ely, Bones
90Target-943

Embree, Alan
90Burllnd/ProC-3004
91Collnd/ClBest-12
91Collnd/ProC-1479
92B-387
92Kinston/ClBest-17
92Kinston/ProC-2469
93B-389
93D-333
93F/MLPI-5
93Pinn-593
93S/Boys-20
93StCl-379
93StCl/1stDay-379
93T-742M
93T/Gold-742M
93ToysRUs-59
93UD-12SR

Embree, Charles W.
(Red)
52Mother-22

Embry, Todd
90Waterlo/Best-4
90Waterlo/ProC-2370

Embser, Rich
85Spring-2
86ArkTr-7

Emerick, Chris
90Gate/ProC-3357
90Gate/SportP-7

Emerson, Scott
92Bluefld/ClBest-15
92Bluefld/ProC-2355

Emery, Calvin Wayne
(Cal)
81Charl-24
89Vanco/CMC-21
89Vanco/ProC-572

Emm, Art
90Clmbia/PCPII-1
90Columbia/GS-17

Emmerke, R.
N172

Emoto, Kouichi
90Salinas/Cal-121
90Salinas/ProC-2715

Empting, Mike
83Clinton/Frit-15

Emslie, Bob
94Conlon-1203UMP

Encarcion, Miguel
76BurlB

Encarnacion, Angelo
91Welland/ClBest-10
91Welland/ProC-3574
92Augusta/ProC-241

Encarnacion, Juan
90Ashvl/ProC-2760

Encarnacion, Luis
86Water-8
87Wmsprt-5
88Memphis/Best-12
89Memphis/Best-20
89Memphis/ProC-1187
89Memphis/Star-10
89SLAS-22
90AAASingl/ProC-595
90Omaha/CMC-4
90Omaha/ProC-60
90ProC/Singl-179
91AAA/LineD-334
91Omaha/LineD-334
91Omaha/ProC-1029
91T/90Debut-44
93LimeR/Winter-1

Endebrock, Kurt
91SoOreg/ClBest-25
91SoOreg/ProC-3853
92SoOreg/ClBest-27
92SoOreg/ProC-3432

Ender, Scott
81Cedar-24

Engel, Bob
88TM/Umpire-5
89TM/Umpire-3
90TM/Umpire-3

Engel, Joe
88Chatt/Team-10

Engel, Steve
86D-510
86Iowa-10
88ArkTr/GS-3

Engelkin, Gary
88Jaxvl/Best-28
88Jaxvl/ProC-990
89James/ProC-2149

Engelmeyer, Bob
77DaytB

Engeln, William
55B-301UMP

England, Dave
82ArkTr-23
83ArkTr-25
92Helena/ProC-1709

Engle, Arthur Clyde
(Hack)
10Domino-40
11Helmar-3
12Sweet/Pin-3A
12Sweet/Pin-3B
14Piedmont/St-21
D303
E106
E254
E90/1
M116
T205
T206
T207
T213/brown
T216

Engle, Eleanor
91T/Arc53-332

Engle, Ralph David
(Dave)
79Toledo-7
80Toledo-15
81T-328R
82D-102
82F-552
82T-738
83D-646
83T-294
83Twin/Team-14
83Twin/Team-32M
84D-598
84F-562
84Nes/792-463
84T-463
84T/St-313
85D-72
85F-276
85Leaf-173
85OPC-199
85T-667
85T/St-298
85Twin/Team-15
86D-438
86F-391
86F/Up-U39
86T-43
88OPC-196
88S-617
88T-196
89Pol/Brew-25
90AAASingl/ProC-681
90OkCty/ProC-435
91AAA/LineD-625CO
91Tucson/LineD-625CO
91Tucson/ProC-2229CO
92Tucson/ProC-505CO
92Tucson/SB-625M

Engle, Rick
79Memphis/TCMA-14

Engle, Scott
84AZ/Pol-5

Engle, Tom
89Kingspt/Star-8
89LittleSun-3
90Kgsport/Best-22
90Kgsport/Star-7
91Clmbia/PCPII-5
91Clmbia/PII-31M
91Clmbia/PII-5
92ColumMet/SAL/II-29
94B-70

Englehart, Bill
84Greens-26

Englehart, Scott
92Erie/ClBest-12
92Erie/ProC-1612
English, Elwood G.
(Woody)
28Exh-9
29Exh/4-6
30CEA/Pin-3
31Exh/4-6
32Orbit/num-32A
32Orbit/num-32B
32Orbit/un-18
33Exh/4-3
33G-135
34Exh/4-3
34G-4
35G-1F
35G-3D
35G-4D
35G-5D
37Exh/4-2
77Galasso-210
90Target-944
93Conlon-689
94Conlon-1240
R305
R308-156
R308-193
R316
R332-18
V354-11
V354-50
WG8-15
English, Gil
90Target-219
English, Maddy
94TedW-95
Englishby, Steve
73Cedar
78DaytB
Englund, Tim
86Knoxvl-7
87Knoxvl-8
Engram, Duane
86Penin-10
Engram, Graylyn
87DayBe-21
Ennen, Chuck
85Clovis-15
Ennis, Alan
84Newar-8
Ennis, Delmar
(Del)
47HomogBond-14
48L-49
49Eureka-134
49Lummis
50B-31
50Drake-21
51B-4
51BR-A10
51T/BB-4
52B-76
52BR
52NTea
52T-223
53B/Col-103
53Exh/Can-60
53RM-N17
54B-127
54Wilson
55B-17
56T-220
57T-260
58T-60
59T-255
79TCMA-18
89Pac/Leg-121
89Swell-19
93UD/ATH-45
94TedW-73
D305
Exh47
PM10/Sm-48
R302
Enno, Clayton
89Salem/Team-10
Enos, Dave
82Reading-13
Enos, Eric
88Batavia/ProC-1671
Enright, George A.
(George)
82QuadC-26
84MidldC-15
Enriquez, Graciano
91Beloit/ClBest-20
91Beloit/ProC-2117
92Beloit/ClBest-17
92Beloit/ProC-419
Enriquez, Martin
82Wausau/Frit-15
83Wausau/Frit-5
Ens, Jewel
92Conlon/Sport-499
Enyart, Terry Gene
(Terry)
79Ogden/TCMA-1
80Ogden-8
Enzmann, Johnny
90Target-220
Epley, Daren
89Kinston/Star-6
90Canton/Best-5
90Canton/ProC-1296
90Canton/Star-4
91AA/LineD-82
91Canton/LineD-82
91Canton/ProC-985
92ColoSp/SB-85
92Sky/AAASingl-37
Eppard, Jim
84Albany-24
85Modesto/Chong-13
86Tacoma-5
87Edmon-1
88Edmon/CMC-21
88Edmon/ProC-558
88F-645
88F/Up-U13
89Edmon/CMC-14
89Edmon/ProC-548
89F-476
89S-607
89T-42
89UD-614
90AAASingl/ProC-356
90ProC/Singl-339
90Syrac/CMC-13
90Syrac/MerchB-7
90Syrac/ProC-576
90Syrac/Team-7
92Indianap/ProC-1873
92Indianap/SB-180
Epperly, Al
90Target-221
Epperson, Chad
92GulfCM/ProC-3483
Epple, Tom
82Spring/Frit-8
83StPete-6
Epps, Riley
86Salem-7
Epps, Scott
90AR-9
Epstein, Michael P.
(Mike)
67T-204R
68T-358
69MB-79
69MLB/St-104
69T-461
69T-539M
69T/St-235
69Trans-25
70K-24
70MLB/St-282
70OPC-235
70Pol/SenY-4
70T-235
70T/CB
71K-34
71MLB/St-535
71OPC-655
71T-655
71T/Coins-126
72MB-99
72T-715
73OPC-38
73T-38
73T/Lids-14
74OPC-650
74T-650
74T/St-142
78TCMA-261
91Crown/Orio-121
93Rang/Keeb-136
Erardi, Joseph G.
(Joe)
77Holyo
Erautt, Edward L.S.
(Eddie)
49Eureka-82
52Mother-43
52T-171
53T-226
57Seattle/Pop-11
91T/Arc53-226
Erautt, Joseph M.
(Joe)
No Cards.
Erb, Gerry
77Newar
Erb, Mike
87Salem/ProC-2435
88PalmSp/Cal-86
88PalmSp/ProC-1443
89QuadC/Best-10
89QuadC/GS-14
90AAASingl/ProC-89
90Edmon/CMC-6
90Edmon/ProC-513
90ProC/Singl-483
91AAA/LineD-154
91Edmon/LineD-154
91Edmon/ProC-1511
92Jaxvl/SB-369
Erdahl, Jay Michael
82Wausau/Frit-21
Erdman, Brad
90Geneva/ProC-3033
90Geneva/Star-11
90Peoria/Team-4
91MidwLAS/ProC-8
91Peoria/ClBest-10
91Peoria/ProC-1344
91Peoria/Team-14
92ClBest-317
92WinSalem/ClBest-11
92WinSalem/ProC-1210
Erhard, Barney
91Belling/ClBest-9
91Belling/ProC-3673
92Belling/ClBest-23
92Belling/ProC-1451
Erhardt, Herb
88Oneonta/ProC-2046
89FtLaud/Star-3
90PrWill/Team-9
91CharWh/ClBest-16
91CharWh/ProC-2893
Ericks, John
89B-433
89SALAS/GS-36
89Savan/ProC-371
90ArkTr/GS-10
90B-190
90StPete/Star-6
90T/TVCard-46
91AA/LineD-30
91ArkTr/LineD-30
91ArkTr/ProC-1277
91B-393
91ClBest/Singl-287
91UD-57TP
92ArkTr/ProC-1124
92ArkTr/SB-33
92B-48
92ClBest-332
92Sky/AASingl-16
Erickson, Don
89Beloit/I/Star-3
Erickson, Eric G.
82Clinton/Frit-22
86Fresn/Smok-14
87Lynch-7
Erickson, Greg
92FtLaud/Team-8
Erickson, Harold J.
(Hal)
53Tiger/Glen-6
Erickson, Henry Nels
(Hank)
R314/Can
Erickson, Roger F.
78Twin/FriszP-6
79Ho-94
79OPC-34
79T-81
79Twin/FriszP-6
80T-256
81D-549
81F-561
81OPC-80
81T-434
81T/St-105
82D-303
82F-553
82T-153
82T/St-211
82T/StVar-211
82T/Tr-30T
83F-378
83T-539
87SanJose-23
89Louisvl-17
89Louisvl/CMC-3
89Louisvl/ProC-1242
90Spring/Best-27CO
91Pac/SenLg-98
91Spring/ClBest-29CO
91Spring/ProC-760CO
92Yank/WIZ80-52
Erickson, Scott
90A&AASingle/ProC-41
90Butte/SportP-13
90Foil/Best-106
90OrlanSR/Best-16
90OrlanSR/ProC-1077
90OrlanSR/Star-5
90T/Tr-29T
91B-335
91Classic/200-160
91Classic/II-T16
91Classic/III-17
91Classic/III-xx
91D-767
91F-608
91F/UltraUp-U36
91Gaston/ClBest-5
91Gaston/ProC-2682
91Leaf-527
91Leaf/Stud-83
91OPC-234
91S-812
91StCl-560
91T-234
91T/90Debut-45
91UD-522
92B-53
92CJ/DII-33
92Classic/Game200-93
92D-463
92D/DK-DK21
92F-201
92F-693LL
92F/ASIns-10
92F/Smoke-S6
92French-5
92Kenner/Fig-14
92KingB-23
92L-166
92L/BlkGold-166
92L/GoldPrev-21
92L/Prev-21
92OPC-605
92P-18
92Pinn-106
92Pinn/Team2000-60
92Rem/Pr-P10
92Rem/Pr-P11
92Rem/Pr-P12
92S-438AS
92S-60
92S-889DT
92S/100SS-2
92S/Impact-13
92StCl-110
92Studio-202
92Sunflower-23
92T-605
92T/Gold-605
92T/GoldWin-605
92T/Kids-110
92TripleP-3
92UD-146
92UD-89TC
92UD/TmMVPHolo-20
92USPlayC/Twin-10H
92USPlayC/Twin-1S
92Ultra-90
93B-425
93Classic/GameI-29
93D-211
93F-263
93L-142
93OPC-77
93Pac/Spanish-169
93Panini-123
93Pinn-163
93S-206
93Select-253
93StCl-443
93StCl/1stDay-443
93T-90
93T/Finest-142
93T/FinestRef-142
93T/Gold-90
93TripleP-33
93UD-397
93UD/FunPack-192
93UD/SP-245
93Ultra-230
94D-437
94F-202
94Flair-73
94L-227
94Pac/Cr-351
94Pinn-361
94S-461
94Select-171
94T-365
94T/Finest-166
94T/Finest/PreProd-166
94T/FinestRef-166
94T/Gold-365
94TripleP-252
94UD-503
94UD/CollC-96
94UD/CollC/Gold-96
94UD/CollC/Silv-96
94UD/SP-184
94Ultra-85
Erickson, Steve
87Oneonta-8
88FtLaud/Star-7
89FtLaud/Star-4
Erickson, Tim
87Wausau-28
Ericson, E.G.
V100
Ericson, Mark
88Kenosha/ProC-1394
Ericson, Mike
89Anchora-15
90Miami/I/Star-7
91Miami/ClBest-6
91Miami/ProC-400
92Visalia/ClBest-8
92Visalia/ProC-1008
Erikson, Greg
92FtLaud/ProC-2618
Ermer, Calvin C.
(Cal)
68T-206MG
70McDon-2
74Tacoma/Caruso-4MG
75Tacoma/KMMO-10MG
79Toledo-3
80Toledo-3
81Toledo-1
82Toledo-23
83Toledo-23
84Toledo-6
85Toledo-26
88Chatt/Team-12
Ermis, Chris
91MedHat/ProC-4093
91MedHat/SportP-5
Erskine, Carl Daniel
(Carl)
51B-260
52B-70
52T-250
53B/Col-12
53Briggs
54B-10
54NYJour
54RH
54RM-NL4
54SM
54Wilson
55B-170
55Gol/Dodg-8
55RM-NL14
55SM
56T-233
57T-252

58T-258
59T-217
60NuCard-69
61NuCard-469
79TCMA-146
88Pac/Leg-75
89Rini/Dodg-23
89Rini/Dodg-25
89Smok/Dodg-60
89Swell-44
90Pac/Legend-14
90Swell/Great-36
90Target-222
91Swell/Great-27
91T/Arc53-308
92AP/ASG-54
92Bz/Quadra-11
93TWill-13
93UD/ATH-46
PM10/Sm-49

Ervin, Chris
91Beloit/ClBest-21

Erwin, Ross Emil
(Tex)
10Domino-41
11Helmar-86
12Sweet/Pin-73
90Target-223
M116
T207

Erwin, Scott
88CapeCod/Sum-78
89Medford/Best-5
90Modesto/Cal-149
90Modesto/Chong-9
90Modesto/ProC-2205
91Modesto/ProC-3079
92ClBest-135
92Huntsvl/ProC-3942
92Huntsvl/SB-309
92Sky/AASingl-130
92UD/ML-92

Erwin, Terry
75BurlB

Esasky, Nicholas A.
(Nick)
80Water-21
81Indianap-15
82Indianap-4
83Indianap-5
84D-602
84F-468
84Nes/792-192
84OPC-192
84T-192
84T/St-378YS
85D-121
85F-534
85Indianap-35
85OPC-253
85T-779
85T/St-51
86D-286
86F-177
86Leaf-162
86OPC-201
86T-677
86TexGold-12
87D-166
87F-201
87Kahn-12
87OPC-13
87T-13
88D-413
88D/Best-118
88F-233
88Kahn/Reds-12
88Leaf-240
88OPC-364
88Panini/St-274
88S-163
88T-364
88T/Big-167
88T/St-137
89B-31
89D-189
89D/Best-284
89D/Tr-18
89F-161
89F/Up-9
89OPC-262
89Panini/St-72
89S-64
89S/Tr-37
89T-554
89T/Big-316
89T/St-134
89T/Tr-29T
89UD-299
89UD/Ext-757
90B-20
90Brave/Dubuq/Perf-6
90Brave/Dubuq/Singl-7
90D-303
90D/BestNL-13
90F-273
90F/Can-273
90F/LL-10
90F/Up-U3
90Kenner/Fig-27
90Leaf-164
90OPC-206
90Panini/St-26
90PublInt/St-453
90S-91
90S/Tr-3T
90Sf-72
90T-206
90T/Big-251
90T/Mini-5
90T/St-263
90T/Tr-30T
90UD-463
90UD/Ext-758
91Brave/Dubuq/Perf-8
91Brave/Dubuq/Stand-12
91F-687
91Leaf/Stud-143
91OPC-418
91T-418
92Brave/LykePerf-10
92OPC-405
92StCl-497

Escalera, Carlos
86Beloit-5
86Cram/NWL-30
87AppFx-6
88BBCity/Star-11
88FSLAS/Star-34
89Memphis/Best-10
89Memphis/ProC-1182
89Memphis/Star-11

Escalera, Nino
77Fritsch-10

Escalera, Ruben
87Stockton-14
88CalLgAS-17
88Stockton/Cal-200
88Stockton/ProC-735
89ElPaso/GS-27
90AAASingl/ProC-662
90Denver/CMC-24
90Denver/ProC-637
90ElPaso/GS-11
90ProC/Singl-49
91AA/LineD-180
91ElPaso/LineD-180
91ElPaso/ProC-2759
92Nashvl/SB-283

Escarrega, Ernesto
(Acosta)
83D-291
83F-234

Eschen, Jim
77Evansvl/TCMA-9
89Kingspt/Star-26
90Pittsfld/Pucko-25MG
91AA/LineD-650CO
91Wmsprt/LineD-650CO
91Wmsprt/ProC-310CO

Escobar, Angel
85Fresno/Pol-4
86Shrev-7
87Phoenix-7
88Phoenix/CMC-14
88Phoenix/ProC-63
89Huntsvl/Best-25

Escobar, John
88Martins/Star-13
89Batavia/ProC-1940
90Spartan/Best-15
90Spartan/ProC-2497
90Spartan/Star-6
91Clearw/ClBest-16
91Clearw/ProC-1627
92Reading/SB-530

Escobar, Jose
80Utica-15
83Kinston/Team-5
87Syrac-17
87Syrac/TCMA-13
88Knoxvl/Best-13
89Syrac/MerchB-9
89Syrac/Team-9
90AAASingl/ProC-357
90ProC/Singl-341
90Syrac/CMC-15
90Syrac/MerchB-8
90Syrac/ProC-577
90Syrac/Team-8
91B-74
91Indian/McDon-9
92Reading/ProC-580
92T/91Debut-51

Escobar, Oscar
86Ventura-6
87Myrtle-2
88Salem/Star-6

Escobar, Rodney
90WichSt-10

Escribano, Eddie
83Madis/Frit-17

Eshelman, Vaughn
91Bluefld/ClBest-7
91Bluefld/ProC-4120
91Kane/Team-5
92B-318
92StCl/Dome-44
94B-431

Eskew, Dan
88SoOreg/ProC-1711
89Modesto/Chong-10
90Foil/Best-51
90Huntsvl/Best-5
91AAA/LineD-532
91Huntsvl/Team-9
91Tacoma/LineD-532
91Tacoma/ProC-2297

Eskins, Mark
88Idaho/ProC-1856

Esmond, James J.
(Jimmy)
E270/2

Espinal, Bill
(Willie)
89Johnson/Star-11
90A&AASingle/ProC-76
90Savan/ProC-2062
91Spring/ClBest-15
91Spring/ProC-737

Espinal, Josue
88SoOreg/ProC-1700

Espinal, Mendy
87Cedar-9

Espinal, Sergio
86Geneva-5
87Peoria-4
88Peoria/Ko-10

Espino, Francisco
88Geneva/ProC-1648
89Geneva/ProC-1860
89Peoria/Team-3

Espino, Juan
79WHave-24
80Colum-28
81Colum-15
82Colum-23
82Colum/Pol-29
83Colum-3
84D-92
84Maine-17
85Colum-11
85Colum/Pol-9
85IntLgAS-32
86Colum-7
86Colum/Pol-7
87Colum-8
87Colum/Pol-8
87Colum/TCMA-10
87T-239
88Richm-29
88Richm/CMC-20
88Richm/ProC-7
92Yank/WIZ80-53

Espinosa, Anulfo A.
(Nino)
75Tidew/Team-10
77T-376
78T-197
79BK/P-11
79OPC-292
79T-566
80BK/P-17
80OPC-233
80T-447
81F-20
81T-405
89Tidew/Candl-7
91WIZMets-108

Espinosa, Philip
87Anchora-9

Espinosa, Ramon
92Welland/ClBest-7
92Welland/ProC-1336

Espinosa, Santiago
86Cram/NWL-98
86QuadC-9
87QuadC-4

Espinoza, Alvaro
82Wisco/Frit-7
83Visalia/Frit-23
84Toledo-3
85Toledo-15
85Twin/Team-1
86Toledo-9
87Portl-14
87T-529
88Colum/CMC-15
88Colum/Pol-15
88Colum/ProC-320
89D/Best-161
89F/Up-47
89S/NWest-3
89T/Tr-30T
90B-431
90D-245
90D/BestAL-123
90F-441
90F/Can-441
90Leaf-240
90OPC-791
90Panini/St-121
90S-101
90S/NWest-4
90T-791
90T/Big-8
90T/St-311
90T/TVYank-24
90UD-163
91B-163
91D-226
91F-662
91Leaf-198
91OPC-28
91Panini/FrSt-327
91Panini/St-269
91S-127
91StCl-242
91T-28
91UD-204
91Ultra-230
92ColoSp/ProC-757
92ColoSp/SB-86
92D-474
92F-224
92OPC-243
92Panini-138
92S-41
92StCl-527
92T-243
92T/Gold-243
92T/GoldWin-243
92UD-119
92Ultra-100
92Yank/WIZ80-54
93F/Final-200
93Indian/WUAB-8
93Pac/Beisbol-6M
93Pac/Spanish-410
94F-103
94Pac/Cr-168
94S-141
94S/GoldR-141
94StCl-461
94StCl/1stDay-461
94StCl/Gold-461
94T-726
94T/Gold-726

Espinoza, Andres
85LitFalls-17
86QuadC-10
87PalmSp-31

Espinoza, Carlos
90Gate/ProC-3343

Espinoza, Jose
92GulfCM/ProC-3488

Espinsosa, Santiago
87Salem/ProC-2429

Esposito, Nick
83TriCit-9

Esposito, Samuel
(Sammy)
57T-301
58T-425
59T-438
60T-31
61T-323
62T-586
63T-181

Espy, Cecil Edward
(Cecil)
81AppFx-14
82VeroB-22
86Hawaii-5
87OKCty-16
88D/Rook-9
88F-465
88Mother/R-13
88S/Tr-73T
88T/Tr-36T
89B-236
89Bz-7
89Classic-143
89D-292
89D/Best-335
89F-517
89KMart/DT-6
89Mother/R-12
89Panini/St-443
89S-401
89S/YS/II-10
89Smok/R-7
89T-221
89T/Big-36
89T/Gloss60-59
89T/JumboR-7
89T/St-240
89T/St-320
89ToysRUs-8
89UD-92
90B-502
90D-260
90F-295
90F/Can-295
90Mother/Rang-25
90OPC-496
90PublInt/St-407
90S-69
90T-496
90T/Big-37
90T/Mini-36
90T/St-249
90Target-224
90UD-371
91AAA/LineD-27
91BuffB/LineD-27
91BuffB/ProC-551
92D-678
92Pirate/Nation-8
92S-673
92StCl-95
92Ultra-552
93Rang/Keeb-137

Espy, Duane
75Sacra/Caruso-7
77Spoka
78Spokane/Cramer-1
78Spokane/Team-1
79BurlB-17
80BurlB-10
84Shrev/FB-7MG
86Phoenix-5CO
87Phoenix-22
88SanJose/Cal-141
88SanJose/ProC-125
89AS/Cal-49MG
89SanJose/Best-28
89SanJose/Cal-235
89SanJose/ProC-453
90AAASingl/ProC-53MG
90Phoenix/CMC-24
90Phoenix/ProC-27
90ProC/Singl-551MG
91AAA/LineD-399MG
91Phoenix/LineD-399
91Phoenix/ProC-83

Esquer, David
(Dave)
89QuadC/Best-7

89QuadC/GS-25
90PalmSp/Cal-204
90PalmSp/ProC-2583
Esquer, Mercedes
83Knoxvl-4
Essegian, Charles A.
(Chuck)
58T-460
59T-278
60BB-11
60T-166
60Union/Dodg-6
61T-384
62J-45
62P-45
62P/Can-45
62T-379
63J-71
63P-71
63T-103
90Target-225
91Crown/Orio-122
Esser, Mark Gerald
(Mark)
80GlenF/B-14
80GlenF/C-5
Essian, James Sarkis
(Jim)
76SSPC-142
77T-529
78T-98
79OPC-239
79T-458
80OPC-179
80T-341
81Coke
81D-503
81F-593
81T-178
81T/Tr-759
82D-369
82F-341
82T-269
82T/Tr-31T
83D-478
83OPC/St-117
83T-646
83T/St-117
83T/Tr-30
83Wheat/Ind-10
84D-629
84F-540
84F/X-35
84Mother/A's-19
84Nes/792-737
84T-737
84T/Tr-35
85F-423
85T-472
86WinSalem-7MG
87Pittsfld-4MG
88EastLAS/ProC-47MG
88Pittsfld/ProC-1360MG
89CharlK-3MG
90AAASingl/ProC-640MG
90Iowa/CMC-24MG
90Iowa/ProC-333MG
90ProC/Singl-99MG
91AAA/LineD-224
91Cub/Mara-41MG
91Iowa/LineD-224MG
91Iowa/ProC-1076MG
91T/Tr-36T
Estalella, Roberto M.
(Bobby)
W753
Esteban, Felipe
87VeroB-21
88VeroB/Star-6
Estelle, Richard H.
(Dick)
65OPC-282R
65T-282R
66T-373R
Estep, Chad
89KS*-9
92Lipscomb-11M
93Lipscomb-8
Estep, Chris
87Anchora-10
88Watertn/Pucko-18
89Augusta/ProC-499
90CLAS/CL-25
90Salem/Star-5
91AA/LineD-107
91CaroMud/LineD-107
91CaroMud/ProC-1097
92CaroMud/SB-133
92Cedar/ProC-1082
92Chatt/ProC-3830
Estep, Richie
89KS*-19M
Estepa, Ramon
80SanJose/JITB-6
81LynnS-21
82LynnS-14
83Chatt-5
84Chatt-3
Estepan, Rafael
80Clinton-18
Esterbrook, Thomas J.
(Dude)
90Target-226
E223
N167
N167-4
N172
N284
N690
WG1-31
Esterday, Henry
N172
Estes, Frank
(Doc)
78OrlanTw
80OrlanTw-9
81Toledo-21
85IntLgAS-8
85Richm-18
86Richm-6
87Syrac-22
87Syrac/TCMA-22
Estes, Joel
84AZ/Pol-6
86AZ/Pol-2
86AubAs-9
87Osceola-20
89ColMud/ProC-128
89ColMud/Star-7
90Foil/Best-97
90SanJose/Best-17
90SanJose/Cal-45
90SanJose/ProC-2007
90SanJose/Star-8
Estes, Marc
86Miami-7
Estes, Mark
89GA-5
90GA-2
Estes, Shawn
91Belling/ClBest-29
91Belling/ProC-3656
91ClBest/Singl-429
91Classic/DP-8
91LitSun/HSPros-11
91LitSun/HSProsG-11
92B-151
92Belling/ClBest-1
92Belling/ProC-1435
92OPC-624
92ProC/Tomorrow-146
92StCl/Dome-45
92T-624DP
92T/Gold-624
92T/GoldWin-624
92UD/ML-164
93B-275
93ClBest/MLG-191
93FExcel/ML-224
93StCl/Mar-30
94B-473
Estevez, Carlos
92FtMyr/ProC-2752
92Miracle/ClBest-13
Estevez, Juan
88Bristol/ProC-1866
Estrada, Charles L.
(Chuck)
60T-126
61Bz-13
61P-73
61T-395
61T-48LL
61T/St-100
62J-36
62P-36
62P/Can-36
62Salada-212
62Shirriff-212
62T-560
62T/St-4
62T/bucks
63T-465
64T-263
65T-378
67T-537
73OPC-549CO
73T-549C
78Padre/FamFun-10CO
82Charl-24
85Cram/PCL-129
86Tacoma-6CO
87Tacoma-12CO
88Tacoma/ProC-623CO
89Tacoma/CMC-9CO
89Tacoma/ProC-1564CO
90AAASingl/ProC-158CO
90Tacoma/ProC-111CO
91Crown/Orio-123
91WIZMets-109
93Rang/Keeb-138CO
Estrada, Eduardo
86NewBrit-11
87NewBrit-25
88EastLAS/ProC-21
88NewBrit/ProC-903
89NewBrit/Star-1
89Pawtu/CMC-23
89Pawtu/ProC-698
Estrada, Francisco
91WIZMets-110
Estrada, Jay
87Spokane-5
88Charl/ProC-1213
89River/Best-4
89River/Cal-21
89River/ProC-1409
90River/Best-7
90River/Cal-16
90River/ProC-2600
91HighD/ClBest-3
91HighD/ProC-2386
Estrada, Josue
94ClBest/Gold-71
94T-741DP
94T/Gold-741DP
Estrada, Luis
79AppFx-16
81GlenF-1
Estrada, Manuel
(Manny)
78SanJose-22
79Spokane-25
80LynnS-13
81Spokane-2
82SLCity-15
83SLCity-25
84Butte-1
Estrada, Peter
(Pete)
88Elmira-8
89WinHaven/Star-6
90LynchRS/Team-18
91AA/LineD-456
91NewBrit/LineD-456
91NewBrit/ProC-346
92LynchRS/ClBest-3
92LynchRS/ProC-2901
Etchandy, Curt
76AppFx
Etchebarren, Andy
66OPC-27R
66T-27R
67CokeCap/Orio-9
67T-457
68CokeCap/Orio-9
68Dexter-31
68T-204
69MB-80
69MLB/St-3
69T-634
70MLB/St-159
70OPC-213
70T-213
71MLB/St-296
71OPC-501
71T-501
72MB-100
72OPC-26
72T-26
73JP
73OPC-618
73T-618
74OPC-488
74T-488
75OPC-583
75T-583
75T/M-583
76OPC-129
76T-129
77T-454
78T-313
86Pol/Brew-8C
90Brewer/MillB-32CO
90Pol/Brew-x
91Brewer/MillB-32
91Crown/Orio-124
91Pol/Brew-x
94TedW-9
Etchebarren, Ray
84Beaum-24
Etheredge, Jeff
89Batavia/ProC-1917
Etheridge, Bobby L.
(Bobby)
68OPC-126
68T-126
69T-604
70OPC-107
70T-107
Etheridge, Haden
90AR-12
Etheridge, Roger
92Princet/ClBest-9
92Princet/ProC-3079
Ethifier, Edouard
72Dimanche*-119
Etler, Todd
92Classic/DP-54
92FrRow/DP-63
92LitSun/HSPros-7
92Princet/ClBest-1
92Princet/ProC-3080
93StCl/MurphyS-68
Etten, Nicholas R.
(Nick)
41DP-123
44Yank/St-10
48Signal
48Smith-4
Ettles, Mark
89Niagara/Pucko-8
90Lakeland/Star-9
91Lakeland/ClBest-3
91Lakeland/ProC-259
92Wichita/ProC-3652
92Wichita/SB-628
93F/Final-137
Etzweiler, Dan
88Myrtle/ProC-1177
Eubanks, Craig
91CharRain/ClBest-6
91CharRain/ProC-92
Eubanks, Larry
77Cocoa
Eufemia, Frank
83Visalia/Frit-11
85Toledo-6
86D-513
86F-392
86T-236
86Toledo-10
Eusebio, Tony
88Osceola/Star-9
89ColMud/Best-15
89ColMud/ProC-125
89ColMud/Star-8
90ColMud/Best-5
90ColMud/ProC-1350
90ColMud/Star-10
90Foil/Best-112
90Star/ISingl-15
91AA/LineD-557
91Jacks/LineD-557
91Jacks/ProC-928
92ClBest-338
92Jacks/SB-331
92S-858
92Sky/AASingl-140
92StCl-546
92T/91Debut-52
93FExcel/ML-42
93LimeR/Winter-16
93StCl/Ast-29
94FExcel-199
94Pinn-537
94Select-192
94Ultra-502
Evangelista, George
91GulfCR/SportP-19
92ClBest-84
92FtMyr/ProC-2753
92Miracle/ClBest-3
Evans, Alfred Hubert
(Al)
48L-22
49B-132
50B-144
51B-38
52T-152
Evans, Barry Steven
(Barry)
81F-499
81OPC-72
81T-72
82D-271
82F-571
82T-541
83Colum-19
85Maine-18
86Maine-8
92Yank/WIZ80-55
Evans, Bart
92Eugene/ClBest-13
92Eugene/ProC-3023
93Rockford/ClBest-13
Evans, Brian
89CharlR/Star-7
90A&AASingle/ProC-81
90Gaston/Best-13
90Gaston/ProC-2515
90Gaston/Star-8
Evans, Darrell
70T-621R
72OPC-171
72OPC-172IA
72T-171
72T-172IA
73OPC-374
73T-374
74OPC-140
74T-140
74T/DE-2
74T/St-3
75Ho-3
75Ho/Twink-3
75OPC-475
75T-475
75T/M-475
76Ho-24
76Ho/Twink-24
76OPC-81
76SSPC-9
76T-81
77T-571
78T-215
79Ho-64
79OPC-215
79Pol/Giants-41
79T-410
80OPC-81
80Pol/Giants-41
80T-145
81D-192
81F-436
81OPC-69
81T-648
81T/St-235
82D-398
82F-388
82OPC-17
82T-17
82T/St-112
83D-251
83F-258
83Mother/Giants-9
83OPC-329
83OPC/St-305
83T-448
83T/Fold-2M
83T/St-305
84D-431
84F-372
84F/St-3
84F/X-36
84Mother/Giants-27
84Nes/792-325
84OPC-325
84T-325
84T/Gloss40-11

84T/St-163
84T/Tr-36
84Tiger/Farmer-2
84Tiger/Wave-13
85Cain's-6
85D-227
85D/HL-51
85F-6
85FunFood/Pin-117
85Leaf-215
85OPC-319
85Seven-3D
85T-792
85Wendy-7
86Cain's-4
86D-369
86F-224
86F/St-36
86OPC-103
86Quaker-24
86Seven/Coin-C15M
86Sf-183M
86Sf-189
86T-515
86T/3D-7
86T/Gloss60-60
86T/Mini-13
86T/St-165
86T/St-269
86T/Super-21
86T/Tatt-4M
86Woolwth-9
87Cain's-6
87Coke/Tigers-13
87D-398
87D/OD-210
87F-150
87F/LL-16
87OPC-265
87Seven-DT2
87Sf-132
87Sf/TPrev-15M
87T-265
87T/St-264
88D-250
88D/Best-35
88F-54
88KayBee-9
88KingB/Disc-12
88Leaf-173
88OPC-390
88OPC/WaxBox-E
88Panini/St-441
88Panini/St-89
88Pep/T-41
88Pol/T-5
88S-75
88Sf-188
88T-630
88T/Big-82
88T/Mini-10
88T/St-265
88T/St-8
88T/WaxBox-E
88Woolwth-3
89B-275
89D-533
89OPC/BoxB-C
89S-171
89S/Tr-65
89T/Tr-31T
89T/WaxBox-C
89UD-394
90F-581
90F/Can-581
90KayBee-10
90OPC-55
90OPC/BoxB-D
90PublInt/St-112
90Richm/25Ann-8
90S-302
90T-55
90T/St-31
90T/WaxBox-D
90UD-143
92SanAn/ProC-3989CO
93TWill-37

Evans, Dave
90ProC/Singl-839
90SanBern/Best-5
90SanBern/Cal-97
90SanBern/ProC-2627
91AA/LineD-334
91Jaxvl/LineD-334
91Jaxvl/ProC-144

Evans, Duane
82Lynch-13

Evans, Dwight Michael
(Dwight)
73OPC-614R
73T-614R
74OPC-351
74T-351
75Ho-18
75Ho/Twink-18
75K-38
75OPC-255
75T-255
75T/M-255
76Ho-87
76OPC-575
76SSPC-408
76T-575
77BurgChef-30
77Ho-21
77Ho/Twink-21
77OPC-259
77T-25
78Ho-54
78PapaG/Disc-24
78SSPC/270-181
78T-695
79Ho-33
79K-41
79OPC-73
79T-155
80OPC-210
80T-405
81Coke
81F-232
81OPC-275
81T-275
81T/HT
82Coke/BOS
82D-109
82Drake-11
82Drake-45
82F-293
82F-642M
82F/St-167
82OPC-355
82T-162LL
82T-355
82T/St-135
82T/St-153
82T/St-4LL
83D-452
83D-7DK
83D/AAS-2
83Drake-7
83F-183
83F/St-12M
83F/St-6M
83OPC-135
83OPC/St-38
83T-135
84D-395
84F-397
84Nes/792-720
84OPC-244
84T-720
84T/RD-13M
84T/St-219
85D-294
85D/AAS-15
85Drake-10
85F-158
85F/St-40
85FunFood/Pin-62
85Leaf-150
85OPC-271
85Seven-8E
85T-580
85T/RD-19
85T/St-212
85T/Super-33
86D-249
86Drake-2
86F-348
86F/Mini-74
86Leaf-127
86OPC-60
86Seven/Coin-E13M
86Sf-32
86T-396M
86T-60
86T/Mini-5
86T/St-251
86T/Super-22
86T/Tatt-13M
86Woolwth-10
87D-129
87D/HL-33
87D/OD-184
87F-34
87F/LL-17
87F/Mini-37
87F/St-38
87F/WS-9M
87Leaf-57
87OPC-368
87Sf-128
87Sf/TPrev-9M
87T-3RB
87T-645
87T/Board-7
87T/HL-21
87T/St-20WS
87T/St-251
87T/St-4
87Woolwth-21
88D-16DK
88D-216
88D/AS-23
88D/Best-84
88D/DKsuper-16DK
88D/RedSox/Bk-216
88Drake-9
88F-351
88F/AwardWin-11
88F/BB/MVP-12
88F/LL-11
88F/Mini-6
88F/St-8
88F/WaxBox-C2
88KayBee-10
88KennerFig-35
88Leaf-16DK
88Leaf-171
88OPC-221
88Panini/St-25
88RedFoley/St-21
88S-65
88Sf-137
88T-470
88T/Big-6
88T/Coins-11
88T/Coins-42
88T/Gloss60-21
88T/Mini-3
88T/Revco-24
88T/St-245
88T/St/Backs-50
88T/UK-22
89B-35
89Classic-44
89D-240
89D/Best-121
89F-87
89F/Excit-12
89KayBee-10
89OPC-205
89Panini/St-279
89RedFoley/St-40
89S-193
89S/HotStar-8
89Sf-204
89T-205
89T/Big-193
89T/Gloss60-36
89T/LJN-107
89T/Mini-47
89T/St-252
89T/St/Backs-15
89T/UK-24
89UD-366
90B-279
90Classic-77
90D-122
90D/BestAL-102
90D/GSlam-5
90F-274
90F/Can-274
90KayBee-11
90Leaf-235
90OPC-375
90Panini/St-17
90Pep/RSox-8
90PublInt/St-454
90S-3
90S/100St-54
90Sf-217
90T-375
90T/Ames-4
90T/Big-1
90T/HillsHM-23
90T/St-257
90T/TVAS-28
90T/TVRSox-29
90UD-113
90Woolwth/HL-12
91B-103
91Crown/Orio-497
91D-122
91F-93
91F/UltraUp-U1
91F/Up-U2
91Leaf-266
91Leaf/Stud-2
91OPC-155A
91OPC-155B
91OPC/BoxB-E
91OPC/Premier-39
91Panini/St-213
91S-225
91S/100SS-99
91S/RookTr-62T
91Seven/3DCoin-2A
91StCl-351
91T-155A
91T-155B
91T/Tr-37T
91T/WaxBox-E
91UD-549
91UD/Ext-776
91Woolwth/HL-10
92D-502
92F-6
92OPC-705
92Panini-69
92S-150
92StCl-463
92T-705
92T/Gold-705
92T/GoldWin-705
92TripleP-67
92UD-248
92Ultra-3

Evans, Felix
92Negro/Retort-19

Evans, Frank 1
91Negro/Lewis-23

Evans, Frank 2
85Louisvl-3

Evans, Freeman
75Anderson/TCMA-8
76Clinton

Evans, Gary
82Beloit/Frit-17

Evans, Glenn
92Elizab/ClBest-19
92Elizab/ProC-3693

Evans, Godfrey
75WPalmB/Sussman-12
78Memphis/Team-3
79Memphis/TCMA-24

Evans, Jamie
91AubAS/ClBest-7
91AubAS/ProC-4268
92Ashvl/ClBest-12

Evans, Jim 1
77Clinton

Evans, Jim 2
88TM/Umpire-13
89TM/Umpire-11
90TM/Umpire-11

Evans, Joe
93Conlon-949

Evans, John
79BurlB-15
80BurlB-25
81ElPaso-21
82Tacoma-16

Evans, Louis Richard
10Domino-42
11Helmar-168
12Sweet/Pin-146
14CJ-128
15CJ-128
E254
M116
S74-118
T202
T205
T206
T207
T213/blue

Evans, Matt
92Bristol/ClBest-18
92Bristol/ProC-1417

Evans, Michael
91SoOreg/ClBest-18
91SoOreg/ProC-3834

Evans, Mike
82Wausau/Frit-22
84Chatt-1
87Erie-17
88Hamil/ProC-1734
89Hamil/Star-29
90Spring/Best-28TR
91Spring/ClBest-30TR
92Spring/ClBest-29TR

Evans, Park
90MissSt-10
91MissSt-15
92MissSt-14

Evans, Phil
89SLCity-25

Evans, Randy
80GlenF/B-4
80GlenF/C-15
81GlenF-2

Evans, Richard (Dr.)
82Iowa-32

Evans, Rick
(Bubba)
76AppFx
77Charl
78Salem
79BuffB/TCMA-9
80Buffa-8
89GA-6

Evans, Rob
87Tidew-29

Evans, Roy
90Target-945

Evans, Russell Edison
(Red)
39PlayBall-159
90Target-227

Evans, Scott
87Miami-4
88Hagers/Star-5

Evans, Sean
92Augusta/ClBest-10
92Salem/ProC-56

Evans, Stanley
92Martins/ClBest-29
92Martins/ProC-3070
94ClBest/Gold-35

Evans, Tim
92Osceola/ProC-2536

Evans, Tom
92Classic/DP-108
92LitSun/HSPros-24
92MedHat/SportP-24
93Hagers/ClBest-11
93Hagers/ProC-1888
93StCl/MurphyS-79

Evans, Tony
83Tampa-4

Evans, Tory
89SanBern/Cal-65

Evans, Van
85PrWill-25
86Kinston-6

Evans, William L.
(Billy)
21Exh-44UMP
61F-22
76Shakey-136
77Galasso-134
80Perez/HOF-136
80SSPC/HOF
89HOF/St-100
92Conlon/Sport-472
94Conlon-1210UMP

Evaschuk, Brad
88StCath/ProC-2010

Eveline, William
(Billy)
86AppFx-7
87DayBe-18
88Tampa/Star-6
89QuadC/Best-26
89QuadC/GS-30

Everett, Carl
90Classic/DP-10
90LitSun/HSPros-13
90LitSun/HSProsG-13

90Tampa/DIMD-5
91B-156
91Greens/ProC-3072
91OPC-113DP
91S-386DP
91SALAS/ProC-SAL25
91T-113DP
92B-258
92FtLaud/ProC-2626
92FtLaud/Team-9
92ProC/Tomorrow-124
92UD/ML-155
92UD/ML-56DS
93B-94
93FExcel/ML-207
93StCl/Marlin-30
93T/Tr-74T
93UD/SP-276FOIL
94B-318
94D-241
94Pinn-252
94Pinn/Artist-252
94Pinn/Museum-252
94S-601
94Sf/2000-168
94StCl/Team-73
94T-781
94T/Gold-781
94UD-11
94UD/CollC-6
94UD/CollC/Gold-6
94UD/CollC/Silv-6
94UD/ElecD-11
94UD/SP-110

Everett, Smokey
81Wisco-3
82OrlanTw-4

Everingham, Matt
91Sydney/Fut-3

Evers, Bill
83Greens-28
86Clinton-7CO
87Clinton-17
88Clinton/ProC-712
89Shrev/ProC-1838
90Shrev/ProC-1458MG
90Shrev/Star-25MG
90TexLgAS/GS-37MG
91AA/LineD-324MG
91Shrev/LineD-324MG
91Shrev/ProC-1838MG
92Phoenix/ProC-2837MG
92Phoenix/SB-399MG
93Greens/ClBest-27MG
93Greens/ProC-903MG

Evers, John Joseph
(Johnny)
10Domino-43
11Diamond-14
11Helmar-94
12Sweet/Pin-82
14CJ-118
15CJ-118
16FleischBrd-27
40PlayBall-174
48Exh/HOF
50Callahan
50W576-29
60Exh/HOF-10
60F-57
61F-23
63Bz/ATG-21
69Bz/Sm
72F/FFeat-7
75F/Pion-17
76Shakey-42
77Galasso-159
80Marchant/HOF-11
80Perez/HOF-42
80SSPC/HOF
81Conlon-13
84Cub/Uno-7M
90Perez/GreatMom-40M
91Conlon/Sport-15
92Cub/OldStyle-8
93Conlon-818
93Conlon-892
93CrackJack-11
93UD/ATH-147M
93UD/ATH-148
93UD/ATH-47
94Conlon-1165
BF2-50
D303
D304
D327
D328-45
D329-54
D350/2-55
E101
E102
E105
E106
E121/80
E122
E135-45
E254
E270/1
E90/3
E91
E92
E93
E94
E95
E98
L1-134
M101/4-54
M101/5-55
M116
PM1-5
S74-60
S81-109
T201
T202
T204
T205
T206
T213/blue
T213/brown
T215/blue
T216
V100
W555
W575
WG5-16
WG6-15

Evers, Troy
87FtLaud-4
88Albany/ProC-1340
90Wmsprt/Best-4
90Wmsprt/ProC-1050
90Wmsprt/Star-5

Evers, Walter Arthur
(Hoot)
47TipTop
48L-78
49B-42
50B-41
51B-23
51FB
51T/CAS
52B-111
52StarCal-86B
52StarCal/L-71H
52StarCal/L-72C
52T-222
53B/Col-25
54B-18
55Esskay
79TCMA-264
81Tiger/Detroit-44
91Crown/Orio-125
91T/Arc53-291
Exh47
R302-123

Eversgerd, Bryan
89Johnson/Star-10
91Savan/ClBest-3
91Savan/ProC-1644
92ProC/Tomorrow-321
92StPete/ClBest-12
92StPete/ProC-2022
94B-244

Everson, Gregory
(Greg)
88FSLAS/Star-35
88Lakeland/Star-10
89London/ProC-1380
90Memphis/Best-15
90Memphis/ProC-1005
90Memphis/Star-10
91AAA/LineD-335
91Omaha/LineD-335
91Omaha/ProC-1030

Ewart, Ron
86WinSalem-8

Ewell, Doc
90Mother/Ast-28TR
92Mother/Ast-28M

Ewell, Mark
75WPalmB/Sussman-5

Ewing, Bill
76QuadC
79SLCity-13

Ewing, George L.
(Long Bob)
E103
M116
S74-100
T204
T205
T206
WG3-18

Ewing, Jim
84Everett/Cram-10B

Ewing, John
(Long John)
N172

Ewing, Justin
90MissSt-11
93MissSt-15

Ewing, Samuel James
(Sam)
77OPC-221
78BJ/PostC-5
78OPC-112
78Syrac
78T-344
79OPC-271
79T-521
81AppFx-28

Ewing, William
(Buck)
50Callahan
50W576-30
75F/Pion-3
76Shakey-24
80Perez/HOF-21
80SSPC/HOF
89HOF/St-57
90BBWit-68
E223
N172
N284
N29
N300/unif
N338/2
N403
N43
WG1-38

Eyre, Scott
93B-277
94ClBest/Gold-29
94FExcel-132

Ezell, Glenn
86Ventura-7MG
87Knoxvl-23
88Omaha/CMC-25
88Omaha/ProC-1503
91Pol/Royal-26CO
92Pol/Royal-27CO
93Pol/Royal-27M
93Rang/Keeb-139CO

Faatz, Jay
N172

Fabbro, Arthur
52Park-55
53Exh/Can-45

Faber, Dick
52Mother-28

Faber, Urban
(Red)
21Exh-45
28Yueng-4
30CEA/Pin-14
33G-79
40PlayBall-230
61F-24
75Sheraton-20
76Rowe-1M
76Shakey-96
77Galasso-121
80Perez/HOF-96
80SSPC/HOF
88Pac/8Men-96
89HOF/St-61
91Conlon/Proto-710
91Conlon/Sport-41
92Conlon/Sport-483
93Conlon-710
94Conlon-1251
94Conlon/Col-26
BF2-12
D327
D328-46
D329-55
D350/2-56
E120
E121/120
E121/80
E126-6
E135-46
E210-4
E220
M101/4-55
M101/5-56
R316
V100
V353-54
V61-14
W501-48
W502-4
W514-69
W515-60
W572
W573
W575

Fabregas, Jorge
91Classic/DP-30
91Miami/Bumble-5
92B-8
92ClBest-359
92PalmSp/ClBest-18
92PalmSp/ProC-843
92StCl/Dome-46
92UD/ML-329
93B-5
93ClBest/MLG-31
93StCl/Angel-8
94B-171
94FExcel-24
94UD-515DD

Fabri, Isidro
86Negro/Frit-73

Fabrique, Bunny
90Target-228

Fabrizio, Kurt
80CharlO/Pol-6
80CharlO/W3TV-6

Faccio, John
89Beloit/I/Star-4
89Star/Wax-4

Faccio, Luis
85Bend/Cram-6
88PrWill/Star-8
89Spring/Best-7
90Savan/ProC-2063
91StPete/ClBest-6
91StPete/ProC-2269

Face, Elroy
53T-246
54T-87
56T-13
57Kahn
57T-166
58Hires-59
58Kahn
58T-74
59Kahn
59T-339
59T-425M
60Kahn
60L-16
60T-115M
60T-20
60T/tatt-14
60T/tatt-89
61Kahn
61P-133
61T-250M
61T-370
61T/St-62
62J-177
62P-177
62P/Can-177
62Salada-174
62Shirriff-174
62T-210
62T-423M
62T/St-175
63F-57
63IDL-6
63J-147
63P-147
63T-409
64T-539
65T-347
66EH-26
66T-461
67CokeCap/Pirate-14
67OPC-49
67T-49
67T/Test/PP-8
68KDKA-26
68T-198
69OPC-207
69T-207
69T/4in1-16M
72Laugh/GF-26
78TCMA-5
89Pac/Leg-178
89Swell-51
90HOF/St-58
91Swell/Great-28
91T/Arc53-246
92AP/ASG-26
92Bz/Quadra-19M
93UD/ATH-48
94T/Arc54-87
94TedW-77

Faedo, Len
80OrlanTw-10
81Charl-12
82T-766R
83F-611
83T-671
83Twin/Team-8
84Evansvl-10
84F-563
84Nes/792-84
84T-84
84T/St-310

Fagan, Pete
87StPete-26
91Savan/ClBest-4TR
92Savan/ClBest-25TR

Fagan, William
N172

Fagnano, Phil
88Spartan/ProC-1032

Fagnant, Ray
90WinHaven/Star-8
91AA/LineD-457
91NewBrit/LineD-457
91NewBrit/ProC-354

Faherty, Sean
83AlexD-18
84PrWill-3

Fahey, Bill
72OPC-334R
72T-334R
73OPC-186
73T-186
74OPC-558
74T-558
75OPC-644
75T-644
75T/M-644
76OPC-436
76SSPC-259
76T-436
77T-511
78Cr/PCL-67
78SSPC/270-97
78T-388
80OPC-23
80T-44
81D-361
81F-490
81T-653
81T/Tr-760
82T-286
83D-281
83T-196
85Tulsa-28CO
89T-351TL
90Mother/Giant-21M
91Mother/Giant-27CO
93Rang/Keeb-10

Fahr, Gerald
52Park-23

Fahrow, Bryant
75QuadC

Fain, Ferris
48B-21
49B-9
49Royal-24
50B-13
51T/RB-3
52B-154

52BR
52Dix-53
52NTea
52RM-AL7
52Royal
52StarCal-89B
52StarCal/L-76B
52T-21
52TipTop
53T-24
54B-214
54RH
54RM-AL22
54T-27
54Wilson
55T-11
55T/DH-116
91T/Arc53-24
92Bz/Quadra-3
94T/Arc54-27
Exh47
Faino, Jeffrey
92Classic/DP-109
92Elmira/ProC-1376
Fairchild, Glenn
86Watlo-6
87Watlo-25
88Kinston/Star-5
Fairey, Jim
68T-228R
69MLB/St-157
69OPC-117
69T-117
69T/4in1-22M
71Expo/ProS-6
71MLB/St-126
71OPC-474
71T-474
72Dimanche*-13
72ProStars/PostC-4
72T-653
73OPC-429
73T-429
74Tacoma/Caruso-24
75Hawaii/Caruso-7
81TCMA-334
85SpokAT/Cram-5
90Target-229
Fairfax, Kenny
93Welland/ClBest-5
93Welland/ProC-3349
Fairley, Craig
90NE-9
Fairly, Pat
92Geneva/ClBest-17
92Geneva/ProC-1567
Fairly, Ron
59T-125
60DF-21
60T-321
61T-492
61Union/Dodg-7
62BB-6
62T-375
62T/St-134
63T-105
64T-490
64T/Coins-54
65OPC-196
65OldLond-8
65T-196
65T/E-2
66Bz-20
66T-330
66T/RO-18
66T/RO-27
67Bz-20
67CokeCap/DodgAngel-3
67OPC-94
67T-94
68T-510
68T/3D
69Expos/Pins-3
69MB-81
69MLB/St-146
69MLBPA/Pin-42
69OPC-122
69T-122
69T/4in1-5
69T/St-43
70Expos/Pins-5
70MLB/St-65
70T-690
70T/PI-10
71Expo/ProS-7
71LaPizza-3
71MLB/St-127
71OPC-315
71T-315
71T/Coins-83
72Dimanche*-14
72MB-101
72OPC-405
72T-405
73OPC-125
73T-125
74K-27
74OPC-146
74T-146
74T/St-53
75OPC-270
75T-270
75T/M-270
76OPC-375
76SSPC-276
76T-375
77T-127
78OPC-40
78SSPC/270-205
78T-85
79T-580
81TCMA-324
90Smok/SoCal-5
90Target-230
92Nabisco-19
Fairman, Andy
91Helena/SportP-16
92Beloit/ClBest-20
92Beloit/ProC-410
Fajardo, Hector
91Augusta/ClBest-5
91Augusta/ProC-798
91SALAS/ProC-SAL4
92B-22
92Classic/I-32
92D-419RR
92Pinn-573
92Pinn/RookI-2
92ProC/Tomorrow-311
92S-842
92S/Rook-23
92T/91Debut-53
93Pac/Spanish-309
93Rang/Keeb-140
93StCl-430
93StCl/1stDay-430
Falco, Chris
91FresnoSt/Smok-4
91James/ClBest-9
91James/ProC-3552
92Rockford/ClBest-23
92Rockford/ProC-2122
Falcone, Dave
84CharlO-16
85RochR-4
87CharlO/WBTV-36
87SLAS-1
90HagersDG/Best-9
Falcone, Pete
76OPC-524
76T-524
76T/Tr-524T
77BurgChef-12
77Ho-24
77Ho/Twink-24
77OPC-177
77T-205
78T-669
79OPC-36
79T-87
80T-401
81D-395
81F-327
81OPC-117
81T-117
82D-380
82F-524
82T-326
83D-182
83F-541
83Pol/Atl-33
83T-764
83T/Tr-31
84D-385
84F-177
84Nes/792-521
84OPC-51
84Pol/Atl-33
84T-521
85T-618
89Pac/SenLg-208
89T/SenLg-56
90EliteSenLg-55
91Pac/SenLg-110
91WIZMets-111
Falk, Bibb A.
21Exh-46
25Exh-74
26Exh-75
28Exh-38
29Exh/4-22
31Exh/4-22
39Yueng
61F-104
92Conlon/Sport-518
E120
E121/120
E210-39
V100
V61-15
W501-41
W502-39
W572
W573
W575
Falkenburg, Frederick
(Cy)
14CJ-20
15CJ-20
M116
T201
Falkner, Richard
88BurlInd/ProC-1773
89Kinston/Star-7
89Star/Wax-75
90Kinston/Team-18
Fallon, George
90Target-231
Fallon, Robert
81GlenF-3
85BuffB-17
85F/Up-U39
Falls, Bobby
86ColumAst-12
Falteisek, Steven
92James/ClBest-4
92James/ProC-1493
Falzone, Jim
87Miami-2
Fancher, Terry
89MissSt-11
Fancher, Tim
89MissSt-12
Fandozzi, Mike
52Laval-15
Faneyte, Rikkert
(Ricky)
91Clinton/ClBest-22
92SanJose/ClBest-7
92UD/ML-116
94B-51
94T-790
94T/Gold-790
94UD/CollC-97
94UD/CollC/Gold-97
94UD/CollC/Silv-97
Fanio, Jeff
92Elmira/ClBest-21
Fann, Brian
93Lipscomb-22M
Fannin, Cliff
47TipTop
48L-123
49B-120
50B-106
51B-244
51T/BB-36
52T-285
53T-203
91T/Arc53-203
Fanning, Jim
82D-492MG
82Expo/Hygrade-6MG
82Hygrade
85OPC-267MG
85T-759MG
Fanning, Steve
88Hamil/ProC-1739
89Savan/ProC-363
90ArkTr/GS-11
91AA/LineD-31
91ArkTr/LineD-31
91ArkTr/ProC-1292
92ArkTr/ProC-1136
92ArkTr/SB-34
Fanok, Harry
62Kahn/Atl
63T-54R
64T-262R
Fanovich, Frank
49Eureka-83
52Park-84
54Esskay
Fansler, Stan
85Nashua-8
86Hawaii-7
87Vanco-7
88BuffB/CMC-2
88BuffB/ProC-1469
91AA/LineD-102
91CaroMud/LineD-102
91CaroMud/ProC-1080
92CaroMud/ProC-1175
92CaroMud/SB-134
92Sky/AASingl-63
Fanucchi, Paul
90NE-10
Fanzone, Carmen
73OPC-139
73T-139
74OPC-484
74T-484
75OPC-363
75T-363
75T/M-363
Faria, Joe
47Smith-25
Faries, Paul
87Spokane-17
88CalLgAS-43
88River/Cal-217
88River/ProC-1422
89AubAs/ProC-18
89TexLAS/GS-7
89Wichita/Rock-22
89Wichita/Rock/HL-17
89Wichita/Rock/Up-3
90AAAGame/ProC-8
90AAASingl/ProC-16
90LasVegas/CMC-14
90LasVegas/ProC-128
90ProC/Singl-517
91B-664
91D/Rook-16
91F-528
91Leaf/Stud-243
91MajorLg/Pins-55
91Padre/Coke-3
91Padre/MagRal-20
91S-711RP
91StCl-557
91T/90Debut-46
91UD/Ext-751
91Ultra-302
92AAA/ASG/SB-230
92F-603
92LasVegas/ProC-2799
92LasVegas/SB-230
92OPC-162
92Pinn-332
92S-509
92S/100RisSt-22
92StCl-513
92T-162
92T/Gold-162
92T/GoldWin-162
92UD-310
Fariss, Monty
88Butte-22
88Tulsa-3
89B-233
89T-177FDP
89Tulsa/GS-8
89Tulsa/Team-6
90B-500
90ProC/Singl-799
90Tulsa/ProC-1161
90Tulsa/Team-7
91AAA/LineD-308
91AAAGame/ProC-25
91B-285
91Classic/III-18
91D-455
91OkCty/LineD-308
91OkCty/ProC-184
92Classic/Game200-107
92D/Rook-35
92F-668
92L-354
92L/BlkGold-354
92Mother/Rang-24
92OPC-138
92OkCty/ProC-1926
92Pinn-560
92Pinn/Rook-14
92Pinn/Team2000-74
92ProC/Tomorrow-152
92S-772
92S/Rook-30
92StCl-803
92T-138
92T/91Debut-54
92T/Gold-138
92T/GoldWin-138
92UD-462
92Ultra-441
93D-245
93D-753
93F-427
93L-320
93Pac/Spanish-461
93Rang/Keeb-141
93S-432
93StCl-535
93StCl/1stDay-535
93StCl/Marlin-19
93T-575
93T/Gold-575
93T/Tr-111T
93UD-717
93USPlayC/Marlin-3H
93USPlayC/Rook-7H
93Ultra-374
Farkas, Ron
78Spring/Wiener-2
82Indianap-24
Farley, Bob
61Union
62T-426
Farley, Brian
83Erie-10
87Spring/Best-20
Farlow, Kevin
90Spokane/SportP-23
91Waterlo/ClBest-16
91Waterlo/ProC-1263
92Watlo/ClBest-1
92Watlo/ProC-2149
Farmar, Damon
83QuadC-25
85Modesto/Chong-20
87MidldA-14
Farmer, Al
86Salem-8
Farmer, Billy
70OPC-444R
70T-444R
Farmer, Bryan Pierce
87Greenvl/Best-16
88Greenvl/Best-13
89Richm/Bob-6
89Richm/CMC-8
89Richm/Ko-12
89Richm/ProC-834
Farmer, Ed
72OPC-116
72T-116
73OPC-272
73T-272
74OPC-506
74T-506
78Spokane/Cramer-22
78Spokane/Team-20
80T-702
81Coke
81D-40
81F-339
81F/St-114
81OPC-36
81T-36
81T/HT
81T/SO-54
81T/St-64
82D-482
82F-342
82OPC-328
82T-328
82T/Tr-32T
83D-471
83F-161

83T-459
83T/Fold-4M
84Cram/PCL-247
86Hawaii-8
91Crown/Orio-126
93Rang/Keeb-142
Farmer, Gordon
88AubAs/ProC-1970
89Ashvl/ProC-953
91Osceola/ClBest-2
91Osceola/ProC-674
Farmer, Howard
87James-24
88MidwLAS/GS-46
88Rockford-12
89BBAmAA/BPro-AA20
89Jaxvl/Best-12
89Jaxvl/ProC-155
89Rockford-12
90AAASingl/ProC-573
90B-107
90Indianap/CMC-3
90Indianap/ProC-290
90ProC/Singl-53
90S/Tr-91T
90UD/Ext-753
91D-734
91MajorLg/Pins-79
91OPC/Premier-40
91S-718RP
91S/100RisSt-20
91T/90Debut-47
91UD-362
92D-779
92Indianap/ProC-1854
92Indianap/SB-181
92StCl-367
Farmer, Ken
86LitFalls-10
Farmer, Kevin
87Spokane-14
88River/Cal-218
88River/ProC-1408
89River/Best-5
89River/Cal-7
89River/ProC-1412
Farmer, Michael
90Martins/ProC-3182
91SALAS/ProC-SAL43
91Spartan/ClBest-23
91Spartan/ProC-908
92ClBest-75
92Clearw/ClBest-8
92Clearw/ProC-2069
93B-624
Farmer, Randy
91Kingspt/ClBest-13
91Kingspt/ProC-3820
92ColumMet/ClBest-14
92ColumMet/ProC-302
92ColumMet/SAL/II-31M
92ColumMet/SAL/II-6
Farmer, Reggie
87Spokane-11
88Charl/ProC-1216
89Watlo/ProC-1796
89Watlo/Star-5
90River/Best-8
90River/Cal-9
90River/ProC-2618
91HighD/ClBest-24
91HighD/ProC-2407
Farmer, William
N172
Farner, Matt
94ClBest/Gold-68
94T-203FDP
94T/Gold-203FDP
Farnsworth, Mark
82CharR-23
83CharR-26
85FtMyr-21
86FtMyr-10TR
87FtMyr-31
90BBCity/Star-31TR
Farnsworth, Ross
90Kissim/DIMD-11
91GreatF/SportP-11
92Bakers/Cal-10
Faron, Robert J.
87Spring/Best-11
88ArkTr/GS-9
90SpringDG/Best-21

Farr, Jim
79Ashvl/TCMA-6
80Tulsa-7
83OKCty-22
84Cram/PCL-9
93Rang/Keeb-143
Farr, Michael
86Watlo-7
87Kinston-15
88Wmsprt/ProC-1307
Farr, Steve
78Charl
80Buffa-7
81Buffa-18
82Buffa-13
84Maine-4
84Wheat/Ind-27
85D-653
85F-446
85T-664
86D-588
86NatPhoto-26
86T/Tr-35T
87D-301
87F-367
87OPC-216
87T-473
87T/St-255
88D-378
88F-256
88S-466
88Smok/Royals-10
88T-222
89B-114
89D-356
89D/Best-151
89F-281
89OPC-356
89Panini/St-349
89S-183
89T-507
89T/St-272
89Tastee/Discs-12
89UD-308
90B-366
90D-356
90F-107
90F/Can-107
90OPC-149
90PublInt/St-347
90RedFoley/St-30
90S-356
90T-149
90T/St-270
90UD-680
91B-168
91D-365
91F-558
91Leaf-348
91Leaf/Stud-92
91OPC-301
91S-172
91S/RookTr-21T
91StCl-419
91T-301
91T/Tr-38T
91UD-660
91UD/Ext-717
92B-622
92D-735
92F-225
92L-20
92L/BlkGold-20
92OPC-46
92Pinn-206
92S-47
92StCl-793
92T-46
92T/Gold-46
92T/GoldWin-46
92UD-48
92Ultra-405
93B-539
93D-21
93F-276
93L-504
93OPC-27
93Pac/Spanish-553
93Pinn-196
93S-162
93Select-172
93StCl-176
93StCl/1stDay-176

93StCl/Y-7
93T-717
93T/Gold-717
93UD-410
93UD/SP-263
93Ultra-593
94D-531
94F-228
94Finest-348
94L-270
94S-535
94T-641
94T/Gold-641
94UD-467
Farrar, Sid
N172
N284
N690
WG1-50
Farrar, Terry
91Bluefld/ClBest-4
91Bluefld/ProC-4121
91Kane/Team-6
92Freder/ClBest-18
92Freder/ProC-1800
94B-78
Farrell, Charles A.
(Duke)
90Target-233
E107
N172
Farrell, Dick
(Turk)
58Hires-43
58T-76
59T-175
60T-103
61P-115
61T-522
61T/St-54
61Union/Dodg-6
62Salada-184
62Shirriff-184
62T-304
62T/St-125
62T/bucks
63Bz-8
63Exh
63F-38
63J-192
63P-192
63Pep
63Salada-2
63T-277
63T-9LL
63T/SO
64Bz-8
64T-560
64T/Coins-91
64T/S-22
64T/SU
64T/St-98
65OPC-80
65OldLond-9
65T-80
66T-377
66T/RO-28
67OPC-190
67T-190
68CokeCap/Astro-16
68T-217
69MB-82
69T-531
78TCMA-202
78TCMA-256
86Mother/Ast-1
89Smok/Ast-8
90Target-232
Exh47
Farrell, Edward S.
(Doc)
26Exh-33
29Exh/4-1
33G-148
91Conlon/Sport-324
V353-73
Farrell, John A.
N172
N284
Farrell, John
85Water-21
86Water-9
87BuffB-15
88CapeCod/Sum-76

88Classic/Blue-239
88D-42RR
88D/Best-117
88F-608
88Gator-52
88Leaf-42RR
88S-620
88S/YS/I-33
88Sf-132
88T-533
88T/Big-213
89B-74
89D-320
89D/Best-285
89F-403
89OPC-227
89Panini/St-318
89S-266
89Sf-37
89T-227
89T/Big-135
89T/St-214
89UD-468
90D-232
90D/BestAL-19
90F-491
90F/Can-491
90Leaf-22
90OPC-32
90Panini/St-53
90PublInt/St-559
90S-103
90T-32
90T/Big-237
90T/St-217
90UD-570
91B-82
91Classic/DP-20
91D-106
91F-366
91FrRow/DPPr-1
91Indian/McDon-12
91Leaf/Stud-42
91OPC-664
91S-50
91StCl-185
91T-664
91UD-692
91Ultra-111
92StCl-693
93Mother/Angel-21
93StCl/Angel-20
93UD-689
94Pac/Cr-77
Farrell, Jon
91ClBest/Singl-422
91FrRow/DP-12
91Welland/ClBest-1
91Welland/ProC-3575
92Augusta/ClBest-1
92Augusta/ProC-251
92B-393
92ClBest-17
92OPC-9
92Pinn-299DP
92ProC/Tomorrow-313
92S-804FDP
92StCl/Dome-47
92T-9DP
92T/Gold-9
92T/GoldWin-9
92UD-69TP
92UD/ML-108
93FExcel/ML-91
Farrell, Mike 1
76AppFx
Farrell, Mike 2
92AS/Cal-15
92ElPaso/ProC-3915
92GulfCM/ProC-3489
92Stockton/ClBest-21
92Stockton/ProC-29
93B-211
93FExcel/ML-184
Farrish, Keoki
90GreatF/SportP-8
91Yakima/ClBest-9
91Yakima/ProC-4260
92VeroB/ClBest-2
92VeroB/ProC-2890
Farrow, Doug
82Idaho-6
Farsaci, Dave
91Eugene/ClBest-17

91Eugene/ProC-3718
Farson, George
78Holyo
79Holyo-8
80Penin/C-11C
Farwell, Fred
87Bakers-20
Fascher, Stan
86Ashvl-11
87Osceola-11
Fassero, Jeff
85Spring-9
86FSLAS-13
86StPete-8
87ArkTr-6
88ArkTr/GS-5
89Louisvl-18
89Louisvl/CMC-4
89Louisvl/ProC-1246
90Canton/Best-19
90Canton/ProC-1289
90Canton/Star-5
91AAA/LineD-183
91D/Rook-28
91Expo/PostC-2
91Indianap/LineD-183
91Indianap/ProC-457
91T/Tr-39T
92D-717
92Expo/D/Duri-7
92F-477
92F/RookSIns-5
92OPC-423
92OPC/Premier-119
92S-738
92StCl-469
92T-423
92T/91Debut-55
92T/Gold-423
92T/GoldWin-423
92UD-685
92Ultra-516
93D-642
93F-459
93Flair-82
93L-91
93OPC-192
93Pac/Spanish-533
93T-178
93T/Gold-178
93UD-609
94D-123
94F-536
94Finest-250
94L-181
94Pac/Cr-378
94S-261
94S/GoldR-261
94Select-124
94StCl-379
94StCl/1stDay-379
94StCl/Gold-379
94T-554
94T/Gold-554
94TripleP-93
94UD-192
94UD/CollC-98
94UD/CollC/Gold-98
94UD/CollC/Silv-98
94UD/ElecD-192
94Ultra-225
Fast, Darcy
72OPC-457R
72T-457R
Faszholz, John
55Hunter
Fator, Laverne
33SK*-13
Faul, Bill
63T-558R
64T-236
66T-322
Faulk, James
(Jim)
88Rockford-13
89Rockford-13
90FSLAS/Star-5
90Star/ISingl-7
90WPalmB/Star-5
Faulk, Kelly
80Penin/B-6
80Penin/C-13
82Reading-2
85Colum-6

85Colum/Pol-10
86Colum-8
86Colum/Pol-8
87Indianap-24
Faulkner, Craig
88Hagers/Star-6
89Hagers/Best-14
89Hagers/ProC-266
89Hagers/Star-7
90Hagers/Best-10
90Hagers/ProC-1421
90Hagers/Star-9
90LSUGreat-6
90ProC/Singl-742
91AA/LineD-181
91ElPaso/LineD-181
91ElPaso/ProC-2750
92ElPaso/ProC-3924
92ElPaso/SB-208
92Sky/AASingl-93
Faulkner, Jim
90Target-234
Faurot, Scott
90Yakima/Team-21TR
Faust, Nancy
84TrueVal/WS-12ORG
85Coke/WS-ORG
86Coke/WS-ORG
87Coke/WS-28ORG
88Coke/WS-6ORG
89Coke/WS-29ORG
Fava, Andres
85Anchora-10
Faw, Brian
90Tampa/DIMD-6
91Greens/ProC-3051
92FtLaud/ClBest-19
92FtLaud/ProC-2604
92FtLaud/Team-10
Fax, Steve
87Sf/TPrev-14M
Fayne, Jeff
89Johnson/Star-13
90Hamil/Star-12
91Spring/ClBest-16
91Spring/ProC-756
Fazekas, Robert
88CapeCod/Sum-160
90Niagara/Pucko-18
91Fayette/ClBest-9
91Fayette/ProC-1162
Fazio, Ernie
63Pep
78TCMA-215
Fazzini, Frank
86Beloit-6
Fears, Tom
52Wheat*
Feder, Mike
76Wausau
Federici, Rick
78Charl
80Buffa-3
Federico, Gustavo
89Helena/SP-14
Federico, Joe
87Anchora-11
88Hamil/ProC-1738
88NE-20
89StPete/Star-11
90Foil/Best-93
90Spring/Best-8
91StPete/ClBest-20
91StPete/ProC-2283
Federoff, Al
53Mother-62
Fedor, Chris
84Greens-11
Fedor, Fritz
82Beloit/Frit-9
83Beloit/Frit-24
86BurlEx-7
87Kinston-10
Feeley, James
82Madis/Frit-20
Feeley, Peter
91Niagara/ClBest-16
91Niagara/ProC-3646
92Niagara/ClBest-5
92Niagara/ProC-3330
Feinburg, Ken
77Cedar
78Cedar

Feist, Ken
91Everett/ClBest-9
91Everett/ProC-3928
92Clinton/ClBest-6
92Clinton/ProC-3608
Felda, Brian
75Cedar
Felden, Keith
88Utica/Pucko-18
89Miami/I/Star-6
Felder, Kenny
92Classic/DP-9
92Classic/DPFoil-BC9
92Helena/ProC-1726
93B-563
93FExcel/ML-185
93StCl/MurphyS-99
93T-723
93T/Gold-723
94B-421
Felder, Mike
83ElPaso-9
84ElPaso-23
85Cram/PCL-211
86D-634
86Pol/Brew-16
87D-295
87Pol/Brew-16
87T-352
88D-397
88F-164
88Pol/Brew-16
88S-388
88T-718
89Pol/Brew-16
89T-263
89UD-252
90Brewer/MillB-7
90D-609
90ElPasoATG/Team-12
90F-321
90F/Can-321
90Leaf-480
90OPC-159
90Pol/Brew-16
90PublInt/St-495
90S-268
90T-159
90UD-178
91D-535
91F-583
91F/UltraUp-U117
91F/Up-U129
91Leaf-445
91Mother/Giant-15
91OPC-44
91PG&E-28
91S-97
91StCl-307
91T-44
91UD-395
92B-93
92D-182
92F-635
92Giant/PGE-16
92Mother/Giant-15
92OPC-697
92Pinn-311
92S-251
92StCl-194
92T-697
92T/Gold-697
92T/GoldWin-697
92UD-288
92Ultra-291
93B-247
93F-529
93F/Final-269
93L-248
93Mother/Mar-9
93Pac/Spanish-622
93Pinn-148
93S-621
93Select/RookTr-106T
93StCl-675
93StCl/1stDay-675
93StCl/Mar-29
93T-466
93T/Gold-466
93UD-186
93UD-714
93Ultra-618
94D-155

94F-284
94L-348
94Pac/Cr-568
94Pinn-352
94S-411
94T-569
94T/Gold-569
Felice, Jason
83Tampa-8
86Jacks/TCMA-20
87Tidew-7
Feliciano, Felix
80Utica-5
Felitz, Bill
89Johnson/Star-12
Felix, Albert
92CharlR/ClBest-9
Felix, Antonio
89Augusta/ProC-510
90Salem/Star-6
Felix, Gus
90Target-946
Felix, Junior
87Myrtle-21
88Knoxvl/Best-2
88SLAS-24
89D/Best-199
89D/Rook-55
89F/Up-69
89S/Tr-83
89Syrac/CMC-19
89Syrac/MerchB-10
89Syrac/ProC-810
89Syrac/Team-10
89T/Tr-32T
89UD/Ext-743
90B-522
90BJ/HoSt-5M
90BJ/HoSt-6M
90Classic-50
90D-70
90D/BestAL-70
90F-79
90F/Can-79
90F/SoarSt-9
90HotRook/St-15
90Leaf-422
90OPC-347
90Panini/St-377
90S-258
90S/100Ris-18
90S/YS/I-9
90Sf-186
90T-347
90T/89Debut-35
90T/Big-210
90T/JumboR-8
90T/St-188
90Tor/BJ-47
90ToysRUs-9
90UD-106
91B-201
91Classic/200-190
91Classic/II-T48
91D-323
91F-173
91Leaf-435
91OPC-543
91OPC/Premier-41
91Panini/FrSt-342
91S-203
91S/RookTr-20T
91Smok/Angel-2
91StCl-457
91T-543
91T/Tr-40T
91UD-563
91UD/Ext-711
92B-404
92D-217
92L-118
92L/BlkGold-118
92OPC-189
92Panini-9
92Pinn-220
92Pol/Angel-8
92S-519
92StCl-141
92T-189
92T/Gold-189
92T/GoldWin-189
92TripleP-168
92UD-303
92Ultra-325

93B-122
93Classic/Gamel-30
93D-197
93D-771
93F-190
93F/Final-60
93L-333
93OPC-128
93Pac/Spanish-462
93Pinn-515
93Pinn/Expan-9
93S-425
93Select-28
93StCl-457
93StCl/1stDay-457
93StCl/Marlin-8
93Studio-181
93T-77
93T/Finest-173
93T/FinestRef-173
93T/Gold-77
93UD-157
93UD-771
93USPlayC/Marlin-12S
93USPlayC/Marlin-6C
93USPlayC/Marlin-9H
93Ultra-375
94Flair-48
Felix, Lauro
93Modesto/ClBest-8
93Modesto/ProC-807
Felix, Nathanael
90Tampa/DIMD-7
Felix, Nick
88Belling/Legoe-22
89Wausau/GS-16
90SanBern/Cal-92
91CharlR/ClBest-5
91CharlR/ProC-1309
Felix, Paul
83Wisco/Frit-6
85OrlanTw-4
86GlenF-4
87GlenF-19
88Toledo/CMC-20
88Toledo/ProC-600
Feliz, Adolfo
81Water-13
82Cedar-15
83Tampa-9
83Water-11
Feliz, Janiero
90Welland/Pucko-5
Feller, Robert
(Bob)
37Exh/4-11
37OPC-120
38Dix
38Exh/4-11
38G-264
38G-288
38ONG/Pin-8
38Wheat
39Exh
40Wheat
41DP-78
47HomogBond-15
48B-5
48L-93
48Swell-19
49B-27
50B-6
50NumNum
51B-30
51T/RB-22
51Wheat
52B-43
52BR
52NumNum-5
52RM-AL8
52StarCal-88BM
52StarCal/L-74E
52T-88
52Wheat*
53B/Col-114
53Exh/Can-17
53T-54
54B-132
54DanDee
54Wilson
55B-134
55Gol/Ind-6
55Salem
56Carling-1

56T-200
60F-26
60NuCard-60
61F-25
61NuCard-460
72Laugh/GF-44
75Sheraton-1
76Rowe-5
76Shakey-87
77Galasso-12
79TCMA-28
80Pac/Leg-53
80Perez/HOF-87
80SSPC/HOF
81Watlo-34
82CJ-2
82Ohio/HOF-5
83D/HOF-36
83MLBPA/Pin-6
84West/1-10
86Sf/Dec-16
87Nestle/DT-20
88Grenada-75
88Pac/Leg-101
89HOF/St-62
89Pac/Leg-156
89Swell-75
90BBWit-13
90CollAB-36
90Pac/Legend-85
90Swell/Great-60
91Conlon/Sport-35
91Homer/Classic-6
91LineD-43
91Swell/Great-145
91T/Arc53-54
92Bz/Quadra-7M
92Conlon/Col-23
92Conlon/Sport-370
92MCI-14
93AP/ASG-110
93AP/ASG24K-44G
93Conlon-933
93MCI-5
93Pinn/DiMag-11M
93YooHoo-5
94TedW-25
94TedW/Lock-12
D305
PM10/Sm-50
PM10/Sm-51
PR1-8
R302-103
R303/A
R303/B
R326-8A
R326-8B
R342-8
R346-43
R423-31
V300
V351B-14
Fellows, Mark
82Madis/Frit-14
83Albany-3
Felsch, Oscar
(Happy)
88Pac/8Men-10
88Pac/8Men-109
88Pac/8Men-41
88Pac/8Men-55M
88Pac/8Men-76
94Conlon-1042M
D327
D328-47
D329-56
D350/2-57
E135-47
M101/4-56
M101/5-57
W514-3
Felske, John
73OPC-332
73OPC-45
73T-332
73T-45
77Spoka
78Spokane/Cramer-26
78Spokane/Team-22
79Vanco-20
82Reading-22
83Portl-13
84Phill/TastyK-10CO
85Phill/TastyK-2MG

85Phill/TastyK-8MG
85T/Tr-33T
86Phill/TastyK-7MG
86T-621MG
87Phill/TastyK-7MG
87T-443MG

Felt, Jim
82AlexD-24
83AlexD-22
84PrWill-5

Felt, Rich
82VeroB-5
83VeroB-3

Felton, Fred
88Batavia/ProC-1686

Felton, Terry
79Toledo-9
80Toledo-7
81Toledo-4
83D-354
83F-612
83T-181
83Toledo-2

Felton, Todd
88Spartan/ProC-1043

Fendrick, Dave
74Gaston

Fenn, Harry
57Seattle/Pop-12

Fennell, Mike
82Oneonta-14
83Greens-18
85Albany-26

Fennelly, Francis
N172

Feno, Quinn
92Elmira/ClBest-11
92Elmira/ProC-1396

Fenwick, Bob
72T-679R
73OPC-567
73T-567

Feola, Lawrence
(Larry)
75Clinton
87SanJose-22

Ferguson, Alex
90Target-235
93Conlon-793
E126-40

Ferguson, Bruce
78Wausau

Ferguson, Charles
N172
N284
N690

Ferguson, Fergy
83Tampa-10

Ferguson, George
10Domino-44
12Sweet/Pin-66
E254
E270/1
E286
M116
T204
T205
T206

Ferguson, Greg
88SoOreg/ProC-1708

Ferguson, James
(Jim)
82Oneonta-15
87SLCity/Taco-6
88Savan/ProC-348
89Savan/ProC-354
90Savan/ProC-2075
91James/ClBest-23
91James/ProC-3536
92Albany/ClBest-2
92James/ClBest-10
92James/ProC-1494

Ferguson, Joe
72T-616
73OPC-621
73T-621
74OPC-86
74T-86
74T/DE-67
74T/St-45
75OPC-115
75T-115
75T/M-115
76OPC-329
76SSPC-81
76T-329
77BurgChef-8
77OPC-107
77T-573
78BK/Ast-2
78Ho-109
78T-226
79T-671
80OPC-29
80Pol/Dodg-13
80T-51
81D-177
81F-124
81Pol/Dodg-13
81T-711
82T-514
83D-604
83F-87
83T-416
87Smok/R-24CO
90Mother/Dodg-28M
90Pol/Dodg-x
90Target-236
91Mother/Dodg-28CO
91Pol/Dodg-x
92Mother/Dodg-28M
92Pol/Dodg-NNO
93Mother/Dodg-28M
93Pol/Dodg-30M
93Rang/Keeb-144

Ferguson, Mark
83Albany-4
84Greens-19
85Albany-6

Ferguson, Mike
82Cedar-8

Ferguson, Shane
92GulfCY/ProC-3784

Ferlenda, Greg
86Salem-9
86Tulsa-15
88Kinston/Star-6
89Canton/Best-14
89Canton/Star-5
89Kinston/Star-8
90CLAS/CL-35
90Kinston/Team-19
92Watertn/ClBest-27
92Watertn/ProC-3251CO

Ferm, Ed
88Bristol/ProC-1886
90Lakeland/Star-10
91ClBest/Singl-289
91Lakeland/ClBest-4
91Lakeland/ProC-260

Fermaint, Mike
91Penin/ClBest-19
91Penin/ProC-384

Fermin, Carlos
90Bristol/ProC-3149
90Bristol/Star-6
91ClBest/Singl-374
91Fayette/ClBest-18
91Fayette/ProC-1177
92Niagara/ClBest-17
92Niagara/ProC-3331
93LimeR/Winter-108

Fermin, Felix
84PrWill-16
85Nashua-9
86Hawaii-9
87Harris-6
88BuffB/CMC-21
88BuffB/ProC-1465
88D-144
88F-643R
88T-547
88TripleA/ASCMC-5
89D-565
89D/Best-229
89D/Tr-33
89F-208
89F/Up-27
89S-620
89S/Tr-78
89T-303
89T/Tr-33T
89UD-88
90B-334
90D-191
90F-492
90F/Can-492
90OPC-722
90Panini/St-60
90Publint/St-560
90S-256
90S/YS/I-6
90T-722
90UD-409
91D-537
91F-367
91Indian/McDon-10
91Leaf-137
91OPC-193
91Panini/FrSt-219
91S-139
91StCl-238
91T-193
91UD-104
91Ultra-112
92D-242
92F-109
92Indian/McDon-9
92OPC-632
92Panini-48
92Pinn-152
92S-148
92StCl-102
92T-632
92T/Gold-632
92T/GoldWin-632
92UD-160
92Ultra-49
93D-597
93F-591
93Indian/WUAB-9
93L-215
93LimeR/Winter-107
93OPC-90
93Pac/Beisbol-6M
93Pac/Spanish-95
93Panini-50
93Pinn-331
93Select-256
93StCl-139
93StCl/1stDay-139
93T-462
93T/Gold-462
93UD-615
93Ultra-184
94D-573
94F-104
94Finest-271
94Flair-101
94Pac/Cr-169
94Panini-56
94Pinn-102
94Pinn/Artist-102
94Pinn/Museum-102
94S-107
94S/GoldR-107
94StCl-81
94StCl/1stDay-81
94StCl/Gold-81
94T-36
94T/Gold-36
94UD-389
94Ultra-42

Fermin, Miguel
93LimeR/Winter-97

Fermin, Pompilio
76Clinton

Fermin, Ramon
92Madis/ClBest-2
92Madis/ProC-1227
93Modesto/ClBest-9
93Modesto/ProC-793

Fernandes, Eddie
47Sunbeam

Fernandez, Alex
90Classic/DP-4
90Classic/III-99
90F/Up-U84
90Foil/Best-250
90Foil/Best-321
91B-351
91Bz-5
91Classic/200-184
91Classic/II-T7
91D-59
91F-117
91F/UltraUp-U14
91Kodak/WSox-32
91Kodak/WSox-x
91Leaf-296
91Leaf/Stud-31
91OPC-278
91OPC/Premier-42
91S-382FDP
91S/100RisSt-66
91Seven/3DCoin-5F
91Seven/3DCoin-9MW
91StCl-147
91T-278
91T/90Debut-48
91T/CJMini/II-36
91UD-645
91Woolwth/HL-11
92B-201
92Classic/Game200-95
92D-191
92F-78
92L-85
92L/BlkGold-85
92OPC-755
92Pinn-30
92S-82
92StCl-467
92Studio-152
92T-755
92T/Gold-755
92T/GoldWin-755
92TripleP-74
92UD-551
92Ultra-335
92WSox-32
93D-139
93F-201
93Flair-183
93L-41
93OPC-53
93Pac/Spanish-69
93Pac/SpanishP-12
93Pinn-383
93S-412
93StCl-552
93StCl/1stDay-552
93StCl/WSox-23
93T-41
93T/Finest-27
93T/FinestRef-27
93T/Gold-41
93UD-362
93UD/SP-253
93Ultra-173
93WSox-8
94B-239
94D-582
94F-80
94Flair-30
94L-268
94OPC-6
94Pac/AllLat-19
94Pac/Cr-124
94Pinn-289
94S-153
94S/GoldR-153
94Sf/2000-3
94StCl/Team-142
94Studio-204
94T-599
94T/Finest-26
94T/Finest/PreProd-26
94T/FinestRef-26
94T/Gold-599
94TripleP-263
94UD-231
94UD-43FUT
94UD/CollC-99
94UD/CollC/Gold-99
94UD/CollC/Silv-99
94UD/ElecD-231
94UD/ElecD-43FUT
94UD/SP-190
94Ultra-33

Fernandez, Chris
87Tampa-22

Fernandez, Dan
89SanJose/Best-8
89SanJose/Cal-232
89SanJose/ProC-441
89SanJose/Star-9
90SanJose/Best-12
90SanJose/Cal-40
90SanJose/ProC-2012
90SanJose/Star-9
91SanJose/ClBest-1
91SanJose/ProC-12
92Shrev/ProC-3876
92Shrev/SB-584

Fernandez, Frank
66T-584R
68T-214R
69T-557
70OPC-82
70T-82
71MLB/St-512
71OPC-468
71T-468
72MB-102
92Yank/WIZ60-40

Fernandez, Froilan
(Nanny)
47TipTop
49Royal-23

Fernandez, Humberto
(Chico)
55B-270
57T-305
58Hires-16
58Hires/T
58T-348
59T-452
60T-314
61T-112
61T/St-150
62J-17
62P-17
62P/Can-17
62Salada-3
62Shirriff-3
62T-173
63T-278
79TCMA-274
88Cedar/ProC-1141
90Target-237
91Crown/Orio-127
91WIZMets-113

Fernandez, James
88StPete/Star-7

Fernandez, Jose 1
89Hamil/Star-11
89StPete/Star-12
90ArkTr/GS-12
90StPete/Star-7
91AA/LineD-32
91AA/LineD-33
91ArkTr/LineD-32
91ArkTr/LineD-33
91ArkTr/ProC-1288
91ArkTr/ProC-1293
91Louisvl/ProC-2926
91Louisvl/Team-15
92ArkTr/ProC-1132
92Louisvl/SB-260
92Louisvl/SB-261
92Sky/AAASingl-126

Fernandez, Jose 2
91Hunting/ClBest-8
91Hunting/ProC-3346

Fernandez, Jose Maria
86Negro/Frit-72

Fernandez, Julio
89Clinton/ProC-900
91Belling/ClBest-17
91Belling/ProC-3680
92SanBern/ClBest-19

Fernandez, Mike
91Elizab/ProC-4305
92Kenosha/ProC-611

Fernandez, Reynaldo
88Oneonta/ProC-2053
88PrWill/Star-9

Fernandez, Rolando
90Hunting/ProC-3297
91Peoria/ClBest-19
91Peoria/ProC-1356
91Peoria/Team-26
92WinSalem/ClBest-12
92WinSalem/ProC-1218

Fernandez, Rudy
92Negro/Retort-20

Fernandez, Sid
82VeroB-6
84D-44RR
84Tidew-2
85D-563
85F-77
85OPC-390
85T-649
85Tidew-3
86D-625
86F-79

86KayBee-10
86Leaf-242
86T-104
86T/Mini-51
87Classic-74
87D-323
87D/AAS-26
87D/HL-4
87F-629M
87F-8
87F/BB-16
87F/Slug-13
87Leaf-93
87OPC-337
87Sf-63
87Sf/TPrev-2M
87T-570
87T/Mini-22
87T/St-97
88D-118
88D/AS-58
88D/Mets/Bk-118
88F-134
88F/BB/MVP-13
88F/St-101
88Kahn/Mets-50
88Leaf-63
88OPC-30
88Panini/St-336
88RedFoley/St-22
88S-615
88Sf-177
88T-30
88T/Mets/Fan-50
88T/St-103
88T/St/Backs-28
89B-377
89D-471
89F-35
89Kahn/Mets-50
89OPC-34
89S-268
89T-790
89T/Big-276
89T/Mini-25
89UD-168
90B-131
90D-572
90D/BestNL-105
90F-203
90F/Can-203
90KMart/SS-11
90Kahn/Mets-50
90Leaf-66
90Mets/Fan-50
90OPC-480
90Panini/St-299
90PublInt/St-133
90S-18
90Sf-113
90T-480
90T/Big-155
90T/Coins-46
90T/DH-20
90T/Mini-66
90T/St-92
90T/TVAS-61
90T/TVMets-10
90Target-238
90UD-261
91B-462
91D-97
91F-146
91Kahn/Mets-50
91OPC-230
91S-180
91StCl-225
91T-230
91UD-242
91Ultra-216
91WIZMets-112
92B-296
92D-719
92F-503
92L-519
92L/BlkGold-519
92Mets/Kahn-50
92OPC-382
92Pinn-509
92S-675
92StCl-655
92T-382
92T/Gold-382
92T/GoldWin-382
92UD-671
92Ultra-528
93B-214
93D-566
93F-86
93L-2
93Mets/Kahn-50
93OPC-42
93Pac/Spanish-196
93Panini-248
93Pinn-500
93S-556
93Select-243
93StCl-351
93StCl/1stDay-351
93T-188
93T/Finest-5
93T/FinestRef-5
93T/Gold-188
93T/Hill-24
93UD-361
93USPlayC/Ace-3S
93Ultra-72
94B-571
94D-396
94F-560
94Finest-379
94L-246
94OPC-63
94Pac/Cr-399
94Pinn-483
94S-182
94S/GoldR-182
94StCl/Team-273
94T-615
94T/Gold-615
94UD-433
94Ultra-305

Fernandez, Tony
82Syrac-17
82Syrac/Team-12
83Syrac-16
84D-32
84F-152
84Syrac-9
84Tor/Fire-11
85D-390
85F-103
85Leaf-91
85OPC-48
85OPC/Post-16
85T-48
85Tor/Fire-10
86BJ/Ault-8
86D-119
86F-57
86F/Mini-14
86F/St-37
86GenMills/Book-3M
86KayBee-11
86Leaf-45
86OPC-241
86Sf-112
86T-241
86T/St-194
86T/Tatt-15M
86Tor/Fire-9
87Classic-57
87D-72
87D/AAS-35
87D/OD-35
87F-225
87F/AS-3
87F/AwardWin-12
87F/Mini-38
87F/RecSet-7
87F/St-39
87GenMills/Book-1M
87Leaf-106
87OPC-329
87RedFoley/St-29
87Sf-113M
87Sf-187
87Sf/TPrev-5M
87Stuart-27M
87T-485
87T/Mini-75
87T/St-191
87Tor/Fire-8
88BJ/5x7-5
88Bz-7
88D-12DK
88D-319
88D/AS-25
88D/Best-87
88D/DKsuper-12DK
88F-109
88F-635M
88F/BB/MVP-14
88F/Hottest-10
88F/Mini-61
88F/SS-C3
88F/St-72
88Ho/Disc-21
88Leaf-12DK
88Leaf-133
88OPC-290
88Panini/St-222
88S-20
88S-651M
88S/YS/II-6
88Sf-26
88T-290
88T/Big-187
88T/Coins-12
88T/Gloss60-15
88T/St-193
88T/St/Backs-43
88T/UK-23
88Tor/Fire-1
89B-254
89Classic-115
89D-206
89D/Best-48
89F-231
89F/Superstar-13
89OPC-170
89Panini/St-470
89RedFoley/St-41
89S-57
89S/HotStar-53
89Sf-93
89T-170
89T/Big-157
89T/Coins-39
89T/Gloss60-52
89T/LJN-92
89T/Mini-76
89T/St-189
89T/St/Backs-10
89T/UK-25
89Tor/Fire-1
89UD-139
90B-524
90BJ/HoSt-5M
90BJ/HoSt-5M
90D-149
90D/BestAL-113
90F-634M
90F-80
90F/AwardWin-12
90F/BB-9
90F/BBMVP-11
90F/Can-634
90F/Can-80
90KMart/CBatL-16
90Leaf-53
90OPC-685
90Panini/St-176
90PublInt/St-283
90PublInt/St-513
90RedFoley/St-31
90S-89
90Sf-6
90T-685
90T/Big-165
90T/DH-21
90T/Mini-42
90T/St-11HL
90T/St-194
90Tor/BJ-1
90UD-130
91B-642
91Cadaco-19
91Classic/200-161
91Classic/II-T45
91D-524
91F-174
91F/UltraUp-U111
91F/Up-U123
91Leaf-315
91Leaf/Stud-244
91OPC-320
91OPC/Premier-43
91Panini/FrSt-339
91Panini/St-152
91RedFoley/St-33
91S-432
91S/RookTr-66T
91StCl-515
91T-320
91T/Tr-41T
91UD-126
91UD/Ext-754
92B-293
92Colla/ASG-24
92D-362
92F-604
92L-187
92L/BlkGold-187
92Mother/Padre-8
92OPC-60
92Padre/Carl-6
92Panini-235
92Pinn-137
92Pol/Padre-7
92S-645
92Smok/Padre-8
92StCl-203
92Studio-103
92T-60
92T/Gold-60
92T/GoldWin-60
92T/Kids-57
92TripleP-102AA
92TripleP-165
92UD-272
92Ultra-276
93B-18
93Classic/Gamel-31
93D-674
93F-470
93F/Final-293
93L-273
93Mets/Kahn-1
93OPC-70
93OPC/Premier-20
93Pac/Spanish-541
93Pac/SpanishGold-3
93Panini-249
93Pinn-533
93S-572
93Select-93
93Select/RookTr-19T
93StCl-644
93StCl/1stDay-644
93StCl/MurphyS-32
93Studio-98
93T-465
93T/Finest-36
93T/FinestRef-36
93T/Gold-465
93T/Tr-9T
93UD-672
93UD/FunPack-125
93UD/SP-47
93Ultra-426
94D-172
94F-331
94L-266
94OPC/BJ-9
94Pac/Cr-639
94Panini-137
94Pinn-427
94S-62
94S/Cycle-13
94S/GoldR-62
94StCl-214
94StCl/1stDay-214
94StCl/Gold-214
94T-702
94T/Gold-702
94TripleP/Medal-7
94UD-437

Ferran, Alex
89Watertn/Star-6
90Reno/Cal-265

Ferran, George
86Shrev-8
87Phoenix-4

Ferrand, Ray
93SoEastern-8

Ferrante, Joe
82DayBe-3

Ferrara, Al
64T-337R
65T-331R
66T-487
67CokeCap/DodgAngel-18
67T-557
68OPC-34
68T-34
69MLB/St-191
69NTF
69T-452
69T/DE-30
69T/St-93
70MLB/St-113
70OPC-345
70T-345
70T/CB
71MLB/St-226
71OPC-214
71T-214
71T/Coins-25
72MB-103
81TCMA-330
90Target-239

Ferrarese, Don
55T-185
56T-266
57T-146
58T-469
59T-247
60T-477
61T-558
62T-547
91Crown/Orio-128

Ferraro, Carl
86CharRain-9

Ferraro, Mike
68T-539R
69OPC-83
69T-83
72T-613
75FtLaud/Sus-2
77WHave
78Cr/PCL-119MG
81TCMA-436
83T/Tr-32MG
83Wheat/Ind-11MG
90T/TVYank-4CO
92Yank/WIZ60-41

Ferraro, Vincent
84Visalia-5

Ferre, Jean
(Andre The Giant)
72Dimanche*-120

Ferrebee, Anthony
87Idaho-2

Ferreira, Arturo J.
(Jose)
84Idaho/Team-8
85Madis-13
85Madis/Pol-10

Ferreira, Tony
82FtMyr-11
84Omaha-3
85Omaha-10
86Tidew-8
87Calgary-20
88Albany/ProC-1339
90AAASingl/ProC-596
90Omaha/CMC-8
90Omaha/ProC-61
90ProC/Singl-183
92WinHaven/ClBest-7
92WinHaven/ProC-1786

Ferreiras, Sal
86PrWill-10

Ferrell, Frank
75Cedar

Ferrell, Rick
31Exh/4-30
33Exh/4-15
33G-197
34DS-48
34Exh/4-9
35BU-10
35BU-126
35Exh/4-9
35G-8G
35G-9G
36Exh/4-9
36G
37Exh/4-9
37OPC-132
38Exh/4-16
39PlayBall-39
40PlayBall-21
44Playball-20
61F-105
77Galasso-199
80Perez/HOF-187
81Conlon-49
90Pac/Legend-23

90Perez/GreatMom-70
90Swell/Great-86
91Swell/Great-29
92Conlon/Sport-471
93Conlon-674
93Conlon-861
93TWill-2
93UD/ATH-49
94Conlon-1169M
94Conlon-994
R310
R312/M
R314
V300
V94-14
W753
WG8-17
Ferrell, Wes
31Exh/4-21
33CJ/Pin-5
33DH-14
33Exh/4-11
33G-218
34DS-94
34Exh/4-11
35BU-12
35BU-174
35G-8G
35G-9G
37OPC-138
38Exh/4-16
61F-26
77Galasso-189
81Conlon-50
88Conlon/3-11
90HOF/St-30
90Target-240
91Conlon/Sport-198
92Conlon/Sport-361
92Conlon/Sport-446
94Conlon-1169
R300
R306
R308-162
R311/Leath
R314
R332-21
V300
V355-40
Ferrer, Sergio
74Tacoma/Caruso-17
76OkCty/Team-9
78Tidew
79T-397
80T-619
80Tidew-5
81Indianap-31
89Pac/SenLg-2
90EliteSenLg-110
91WIZMets-114
Ferretti, Sam
88Watlo/ProC-680
89Canton/ProC-1307
89Kinston/Star-9
90Canton/Best-7
90Canton/ProC-1297
90Canton/Star-6
90Foil/Best-309
91AA/LineD-83
91Canton/LineD-83
91Canton/ProC-986
92Hagers/ProC-2561
92Hagers/SB-258
Ferreyra, Raul
77Indianap-19
78Indianap-21
78SSPC/270-130
Ferrick, Tom
39Exh
51B-182
60T-461C
Ferris, Albert
(Hobe)
E107
E254
E270/1
E270/2
T204
T206
WG2-18
Ferris, Bob
76QuadC
78Cr/PCL-60
79SLCity-10
80SLCity-24
81SLCity-5
Ferris, David
(Boo)
47TipTop
49B-211
Ferro, Bob
83Wisco/Frit-11
Ferroni, Frank
81Miami-14
Ferry, John
11Helmar-159
T207
Ferry, Mike
90A&AASingle/ProC-195
90Billings/ProC-3214
91Cedar/ClBest-4
91Cedar/ProC-2712
92Cedar/ClBest-7
92Cedar/ProC-1066
92MidwLAS/Team-9
94B-486
94FExcel-174
Ferson, Alexander
N172
Ferst, Larry
78Clinton
79Clinton/TCMA-28
Fessenden, Wallace
N172
Fette, Lou
38Wheat
90Target-241
PR1-9
Fetters, Michael
86Cram/NWL-97
87PalmSp-26
88MidldA/GS-10
89Edmon/CMC-9
90AAASingl/ProC-90
90B-286
90D-35
90Edmon/CMC-7
90Edmon/ProC-514
90F-131
90F/Can-131
90OPC-14
90ProC/Singl-484
90T-14
90T/89Debut-36
90UD/Ext-742
91AAA/LineD-163
91D-565
91Edmon/LineD-163
91Edmon/ProC-1512
91F-312
91OPC-477
91S-497
91S/100RisSt-74
91StCl-228
91T-477
91UD-696
92D-491
92F-56
92L-460
92L/BlkGold-460
92OPC-602
92Pol/Brew-6
92S-606
92S/100RisSt-38
92StCl-696
92T-602
92T/Gold-602
92T/GoldWin-602
93D-573
93F-249
93OPC-109
93Pac/Spanish-510
93Pol/Brew-7
93S-420
93Select-174
93StCl-633
93StCl/1stDay-633
93T-527
93T/Gold-527
93UD-193
94D-603
94F-176
94Pol/Brew-7
94S-200
94S/GoldR-200
94T-159
94T/Gold-159
Fetty, Pat
92Beloit/ClBest-23
92Beloit/ProC-400
Fetzer, John E.
81Tiger/Detroit-81OWN
83Kaline-39OWN
83Kaline-44OWN
Fewster, Wilson
(Chick)
25Exh-81
26Exh-12
27Exh-6
28LaPresse-5
90Target-242
E121/120
E220
V89-29
W501-120
W575
Fiacco, Charlie
90Geneva/ProC-3035
90Geneva/Star-12
Fiala, Mike
86Bakers-7
Fiala, Neil
78StPete
79ArkTr-13
82Indianap-29
Fiala, Walter
52LaPatrie-4
52Park-67
53Exh/Can-48
Fichman, Mal
79Newar-6
88Boise/ProC-1632
90Erie/Star-29MG
91Reno/Cal-29MG
Fichter, Bob
75T/Photo-128
Fick, Barry
85Cedar-7
Fick, Chuck
82WHave-11
90EliteSenLg-111
91Pac/SenLg-93
Ficklin, Winston
81Watlo-29
82Watlo/B-15
82Watlo/Frit-19
83Watlo/Frit-18
85Water-4
86Water-10
87Wmsprt-3
88Portl/CMC-18
88Portl/ProC-652
89Iowa/CMC-21
89Iowa/ProC-1711
Fidler, Andy
89Kingspt/Star-9
90Pittsfld/Pucko-19
91Clmbia/PCPII-1
Fidrych, Mark
77BurgChef-92
77Ho-46
77Ho/Twink-46
77K-26
77OPC-115
77OPC-7LL
77Pep-30
77T-265
77T-7LL
77T/CS-15
77T/ClothSt-15
77Tiger/BK-1
78BK/T-4
78OPC-235
78PapaG/Disc-32
78T-45
78Tastee/Discs-22
78Wiffle/Discs-21
79Ho-77
79OPC-329
79T-625
80Evansvl-6
80OPC-231
80T-445
81D-8
81Evansvl-4
81F-462
81OPC-150
81T-150
81Tiger/Detroit-6
83Pawtu-7
88Pac/Leg-62
90Swell/Great-122
92AP/ASG-25
93UD/ATH-50
94TedW-31
Fiedler, Dick
57Seattle/Pop-13
Fiedler, Mark
86LitFalls-11
Fiegel, Todd
91Kingspt/ClBest-15
91Kingspt/ProC-3807
92ColumMet/ClBest-11
92ColumMet/ProC-288
92ColumMet/SAL/II-18
92ColumMet/SAL/II-30
92ProC/Tomorrow-291
93StLucie/ProC-2915
Field, Greg
79Portl-3
83Richm-5
84Toledo-18
Field, James
E254
Fielder, Cecil
1994 Donruss MVP'S-20
86BJ/Ault-9
86D-512
86F-653R
86OPC-386
86T-386
86Tor/Fire-10
87F/Up-U31
87OPC-178
87T-178
87Tor/Fire-9
88D-565
88F-110
88OPC-21
88S-399
88T-618
88Tor/Fire-23
89D-442
89F-232
89OPC-224
89S-120
89T-541
89UD-364
90B-357
90Classic/III-94
90CokeK/Tiger-4
90D/BestAL-133
90D/Learning-26
90F/Up-U95
90Leaf-165
90S/McDon-16
90S/Tr-9T
90T/Big-313
90T/Tr-31T
90UD/Ext-786
90USPlayC/AS-13S
90Windwlk/Discs-4
91B-136
91B-367SLUG
91Bz-8
91Cadaco-18
91Classic/200-127
91Classic/I-41
91Classic/II-T69
91CokeK/Tiger-45
91CollAB-14
91D-397MVP
91D-3DK
91D-451
91D-BC5
91D/BC-BC5
91D/Elite-E6
91D/GSlam-7
91D/SuperDK-3
91DennyGS-2
91F-335
91F-709M
91F/ASIns-4
91JDean-21
91Kenner-18
91KingB/Discs-14
91Leaf-106
91Leaf/Prev-18
91Leaf/Stud-53
91MSA/Holsum-17
91MajorLg/Pins-32
91MooTown-24
91OPC-386AS
91OPC-720
91OPC/Premier-44
91Panini/FrSt-288
91Panini/St-232
91Panini/Top15-13
91Panini/Top15-21
91Panini/Top15-37
91Panini/Top15-54
91Pep/SS-10
91Petro/SU-11
91Pol/Tiger-3
91Post-23
91Post/Can-19
91RedFoley/St-34
91S-168
91S-395AS
91S-693MB
91S-770HL
91S/100SS-88
91Seven/3DCoin-3MW
91Seven/3DCoin-6F
91StCl-186
91StCl/Charter*-8
91StCl/Member*-29
91Sunflower-8
91T-386AS
91T-720
91T/CJMini/I-31
91T/SU-13
91UD-244
91UD-83TC
91UD/FinalEd-82F
91UD/SilSlug-SS12
91USPlayC/AS-12D
91Ultra-121
91Ultra-392EP
92B-90
92CJ/DI-22
92Classic/Game200-129
92Classic/I-33
92Classic/II-T73
92D-206
92D-27AS
92D/McDon-20
92DPep/MSA-13
92DennyGS-13
92F-133
92F-692LL
92F-705M
92F/Lumber-L1
92F/Performer-7
92F/TmLIns-6
92F/Up-H4
92JDean/18-15
92Kenner/Fig-15
92KingB-17
92L-153
92L/BlkGold-153
92L/GoldPrev-18
92L/Prev-18
92MSA/Ben-1
92MooTown-10
92MrTurkey-8
92OPC-425
92OPC/Premier-70
92P-13
92Panini-105
92Panini-144
92Panini-272AS
92Pinn-4
92Pinn/Slug-1
92Post/Can-12
92S-431AS
92S-50
92S/100SS-66
92S/Impact-60
92Seven/Coin-19
92StCl-250
92StCl-599MC
92StCl/Dome-48
92StCl/MPhoto-5
92Studio-173
92T-397AS
92T-425
92T/Gold-397AS
92T/Gold-425
92T/GoldWin-397AS
92T/GoldWin-425
92T/Kids-76
92T/McDonB-1
92T/MicroG-397
92TripleP-29
92UD-255
92UD-647DS
92UD-96TC

92UD/ASFF-22
92UD/HRH-HR2
92UD/TWillB-T5
92UD/TmMVPHolo-21
92USPlayC/Ace-13C
92USPlayC/Ace-1H
92USPlayC/Tiger-10C
92USPlayC/Tiger-1H
92Ultra-59
93B-475
93Classic/Gamel-32
93Colla/DM-35
93D-541
93D/DK-15
93D/Elite-34
93D/EliteUp-16
93D/LongBall-LL13
93D/MVP-17
93D/Prev-15
93D/Spirit-SG10
93DennyGS-25
93Duracel/PPI-23
93F-227
93F-345LL
93F-711RT
93F-714SS
93F/ASAL-5
93F/Atlantic-8
93F/Fruit-19
93F/ProVII-3
93Flair-201
93Ho-16
93HumDum/Can-8
93JDean/28-12
93KingB-11
93Kraft-7
93L-283
93L/GoldAS-3
93MSA/Metz-7
93OPC-51
93OPC/Premier-96
93P-10
93Pac/Spanish-107
93Panini-114
93Pinn-26
93Pinn/Cooper-28
93Pinn/HRC-3
93Pinn/Slug-3
93S-31
93S/Franchise-6
93Select-20
93Select/ChasS-13
93Select/StatL-27
93Select/StatL-31
93StCl-503
93StCl/1stDay-503
93Studio-37
93T-80
93T/BlkGold-30
93T/Finest-111AS
93T/FinestASJ-111AS
93T/FinestRef-111AS
93T/Gold-80
93Tiger/Gator-7
93TripleP-5
93TripleP/Act-15
93TripleP/LL-L5M
93UD-46
93UD-499AW
93UD-564
93UD/Clutch-R9
93UD/FunPack-185GS
93UD/FunPack-186
93UD/HRH-HR3
93UD/looss-WI23
93UD/OnDeck-D11
93UD/SP-236
93UD/SPPlat-PP6
93USPlayC/Ace-12C
93Ultra-548
93Ultra/HRK-3
94B-69
94D-27
94D/DK-22
94D/Doml-1
94D/LongBall-1
94D/Special-27
94F-128
94F/AS-7
94F/TL-6
94Flair-49
94Kraft-3
94L-50
94L/Clean-5
94L/MVPAL-5
94L/PBroker-7
94OPC-126
94OPC/JAS-20
94Oscar-4
94P-17
94Pac/Cr-216
94Pac/Silv-18
94Panini-63
94Pinn-10
94Pinn/Artist-10
94Pinn/HobSam-10
94Pinn/Museum-10
94Pinn/RetailSam-10
94RedFoley-10
94S-393
94S/GoldS-40
94S/Tomb-18
94Sf/2000-78
94Sf/Mov-3
94StCl-25
94StCl-535QS
94StCl/1stDay-25
94StCl/1stDay-535QS
94StCl/Gold-25
94StCl/Gold-535QS
94Studio-190
94T-190
94T/BlkGold-5
94T/Finest-219
94T/FinestRef-219
94T/Gold-190
94TripleP-243
94TripleP/Bomb-2
94TripleP/Nick-1
94UD-220
94UD-286HFA
94UD/CollC-100
94UD/CollC/Gold-100
94UD/CollC/Silv-100
94UD/CollHR-5
94UD/DColl-E4
94UD/ElecD-220
94UD/HoloFX-8
94UD/Mantle-7
94UD/SP-176
94Ultra-52
94Ultra/RBIK-5

Fields, Bruce
82BirmB-11
83SanJose-14
86Nashvl-8
87D-47RR
87Leaf-47RR
87Toledo-14
87Toledo/TCMA-9
88Mother/Sea-16
89AAA/CMC-36
89Calgary/CMC-19
89Calgary/ProC-534
89S/HotRook-43
89T-556
89UD-238
90AAASingl/ProC-153
90BirmDG/Best-10
90ProC/Singl-591
90Tacoma/CMC-14
90Tacoma/ProC-106
90TripleAAS/CMC-36
91Richm/Bob-24
91Richm/ProC-2580
91Richm/Team-5
92London/ProC-649CO
92London/SB-425CO

Fields, John James
N172

Fields, Wilmer
(Red)
52Park-21
91Negro/Lewis-17
92Negro/RetortII-9

Fiene, Lou
T206

Fiepke, Scott
86Nashua-6

Fier, Mike
90Gate/ProC-3350
90Gate/SportP-9

Fierro, John
80Penin/B-24TR
80Penin/C-10TR
86Peoria-6

Fife, Dan
74OPC-421
74T-421
74Tacoma/Caruso-6

Figga, Michael
90Tampa/DIMD-8
91PrWill/ClBest-14
91PrWill/ProC-1430
92FtLaud/ClBest-10
92FtLaud/ProC-2614
92FtLaud/Team-11

Figueroa, Alexis
89Watlo/ProC-1774
89Watlo/Star-6

Figueroa, Bienvenido
(Bien)
86Erie-7
87Spring/Best-22
88ArkTr/GS-6
89Louisvl-19
89Louisvl/CMC-17
89Louisvl/ProC-1262
90AAASingl/ProC-523
90Louisvl/CMC-17
90Louisvl/LBC-15
90Louisvl/ProC-409
90ProC/Singl-117
90T/TVCard-47
91AAA/LineD-234
91Louisvl/LineD-234
91Louisvl/ProC-2923
91Louisvl/Team-20
92D/Rook-36
92Louisvl/ProC-1893
92Louisvl/SB-262
93LimeR/Winter-5
93Pinn-263
93S-281
93StCl-304
93StCl/1stDay-304
93T-690
93T/Gold-690

Figueroa, Danny
93T-704M
93T/Gold-704M

Figueroa, Ed
75OPC-476
75T-476
75T/M-476
76OPC-27
76SSPC-190
76T-27
76T/Tr-27T
77BK/Y-5
77K-42
77OPC-164
77T-195
78BK/Y-5
78SSPC/270-9
78T-365
78T/Zest-3
79BK/Y-11
79OPC-13
79T-35
80OPC-288
80T-555
81F-624
81T-245
81Tacoma-32
82Tacoma-10
89Pac/SenLg-75
89T/SenLg-43
89TM/SenLg-34
90EliteSenLg-80
91K/Leyenda-8
92Yank/WIZ70-50
92Yank/WIZ80-56
93Rang/Keeb-145

Figueroa, Fernando
87PrWill-22
88FtLaud/Star-8
89Miami/II/Star-4
90Wmsprt/Best-5
90Wmsprt/ProC-1051
90Wmsprt/Star-6
91AA/LineD-335
91Jaxvl/LineD-335
91Jaxvl/ProC-145
92Jacks/ProC-3703
92Jaxvl/SB-355

Figueroa, Jesus
75FtLaud/Sus-22
77WHave
80Wichita-9
81D-556
81T-533
87Pocatel/Bon-25

Figueroa, Matt
90AZ/Pol-5
91James/ClBest-22
91James/ProC-3537

Figueroa, Ray
88Geneva/ProC-1637

Figueroa, Rich
80Clinton-23
81Clinton-28

Figueroa, Vic
86Modesto-9

Filer, Thomas
79WHave-11
81Colum-24
82Iowa-15
83Iowa-3
83T-508
84Iowa-28
85Syrac-6
86D-439
86F-58
86Leaf-211
86OPC-312
86T-312
86Tor/Fire-11
88Denver/CMC-10
88Denver/ProC-1257
88T/Tr-37T
89F-185
89T-419
90B-385
90Brewer/MillB-8
90D-687
90F-322
90F/Can-322
90Pol/Brew-28
92Tidew/ProC-

Filippi, James
86AppFx-8
87SanBern-10

Filkins, Les
81Evansvl-19
82Evansvl-19

Fillingim, Dana
21Exh-47
E120

Fillmore, Joe
86Negro/Frit-59
92Negro/Retort-21

Filosa, Brian
92SoBend/ClBest-14
92SoBend/ProC-184

Filotei, Bobby
90Billings/ProC-3227
91Cedar/ProC-2726

Filson, Matt
92Yakima/ClBest-22
92Yakima/ProC-3461

Filson, Pete
82Colum-9
82Colum/Pol-30
82Toledo-26
83Twin/Team-16
84D-194
84F-564
84Nes/792-568
84T-568
85D-607
85F-277
85T-97
85Twin/Team-18
86BuffB-11
86D-436
86F-393
86T-122
87Colum-29
87Colum/Pol-9
87Colum/TCMA-3
90AAAGame/ProC-23
90AAASingl/ProC-597
90Omaha/CMC-9
90Omaha/ProC-62
90ProC/Singl-184
91BBCity/ClBest-30CO
91BBCity/ProC-1414CO
92BBCity/ClBest-26CO
92BBCity/ProC-3862
92Yank/WIZ80-57

Filter, Rusty
89SanDiegoSt/Smok-9
90SDSt-4
90StCath/ProC-3468

Fimple, Jack
81Watlo-18
82VeroB-14
83Albuq-11
84Cram/PCL-146
84D-372
84F-99
84Nes/792-263
84Pol/Dodg-31
84T-263
85Cram/PCL-163
86Albuq-7
87Edmon-23
90Target-243

Finch, Joel
79T-702R
80T-662R
81Pawtu-1

Finch, Steve
77Ashvl
79Tulsa-6
81Spokane-11
82SLCity-8
84Cram/PCL-106
85MidldA-13
86Edmon-8

Fincher, Matt
89GA-7ACO
90GA-3

Findlay, Bill
88Gaston/ProC-997

Fine, Tom
89Penin/Star-5
90Visalia/Cal-61
90Visalia/ProC-2147

Fine, Tommy
48Sommer-4

Fingers, Bob
87Modesto-18

Fingers, Rollie
69T-597R
70OPC-502
70T-502
71MLB/St-513
71OPC-384
71T-384
72OPC-241
72T-241
73OPC-84
73T-84
74OPC-212
74T-212
75Ho-52
75Ho/Twink-52
75K-55
75OPC-21
75OPC-463WS
75SSPC/Puzzle-9
75T-21
75T-463WS
75T/M-21
75T/M-463WS
76Ho-104
76OPC-405
76SSPC-480
76T-405
77BurgChef-133
77Ho-137
77Ho/Twink-137
77K-51
77OPC-52
77Padre/SchCd-10
77T-523
78Ho-144
78OPC-201
78OPC-8LL
78Padre/FamFun-11
78T-140
78T-208LL
78Wiffle/Discs-22
79OPC-203
79T-390
79T-8LL
80BK/PHR-3
80OPC-343
80Perez/HOF-212
80T-651
81D-2
81F-485
81F/St-47
81OPC-229
81T-229
81T-8LL

81T/St-31M
81T/Tr-761
82D-28
82F-141
82F-644M
82F/St-132
82K-7
82KMart-40
82OPC-176
82OPC-44
82PermaGr/CC-16
82Pol/Brew-34
82Sqt-11
82T-168LL
82T-585
82T-586IA
82T/St-16
82T/St-198
83D-2DK
83D-78
83D/AAS-33
83F-33
83F/St-18M
83F/St-8M
83Gard-7
83K-2
83OPC-35
83OPC-36SV
83OPC/St-79
83PermaGr/CC-23
83Pol/Brew-34
83T-35
83T-36SV
83T/Fold-4M
83T/St-79
83T/St/Box-6
84D-LLA
84D/Champs-45
84F-199
84Gard-6
84Nes/792-495
84Nes/792-717LL
84Nes/792-718LL
84OPC-283
84Pol/Brew-34
84T-495
84T-717LL
84T-718LL
85D-292
85D/AAS-36
85D/HL-2
85F-581
85FunFood/Pin-10
85Gard-6
85Leaf-190
85OPC-182
85Pol/Brew-34
85T-750
85T/St-285
85Woolwth-10
86D-229
86F-486
86OPC-185
86Seven/Coin-C11
86Sf-130M
86Sf-146M
86Sf-150M
86Sf-65M
86T-185
86T/St-198
87Mother/A's-10
88Pac/Leg-103
89Pac/SenLg-161
89Padre/Mag-8
89T/SenLg-65
89TM/SenLg-35
90BBWit-51
90EliteSenLg-123
90EliteSenLg-21
90MSA/AGFA-18
91K/3D-7
91Pac/SenLg-126
91Swell/Great-30
92Brew/Carlson-7
92UD/ASFF-45
92UD/Hero-7AU
92UD/Hero-H7
92UD/Hero-H8M
92UD/HeroHL-HI3
92Ziploc-3
93AP/ASG-130
93AP/ASG24K-64G
94TedW-66

Finigan, Jim
55Armour-5
55RFG-17
55Rodeo
55T-14
55T/DH-50
55W605-17
56Rodeo
56T-22
56T/Pin-12
57T-248
58T-136
59T-47
79TCMA-128
91Crown/Orio-129

Finigan, Kevin
87BurlEx-13
88James/ProC-1915

Fink, Eric
84PrWill-11

Finken, Steve
88GreatF-15
89AS/Cal-22
89Bakers/Cal-205
90SanAn/GS-12
91AA/LineD-534
91SanAn/LineD-534
91SanAn/ProC-2982
92Shrev/SB-592
92Sky/AASingl-257

Finlayson, Mike
75WPalmB/Sussman-23
79Memphis/TCMA-12

Finley, Bob
44Playball-45
45Centen-7

Finley, Brian
83Beloit/Frit-18
86ElPaso-10
88Chatt/Best-13
90Chatt/GS-12

Finley, Chris
93SoEastern-9

Finley, Chuck
86QuadC-11
87D-407
87F-79
87Smok/Cal-6
87T-446
88D-530
88D/Best-283
88F-489
88Smok/Angels-15
88T-99
88T/Big-254
89B-37
89D-226
89D/Best-333
89F-477
89S-503
89T-708
89T/Big-76
89UD-632
90B-289
90D-344
90D/BestAL-103
90F-132
90F/Can-132
90KMart/SS-28
90Leaf-162
90OPC-147
90Panini/St-32
90PublInt/St-369
90S-380
90S/100St-24
90Sf-172
90Smok/Angel-5
90T-147
90T/Big-319
90T/Coins-13
90T/DH-22
90T/Mini-8
90T/St-171
90T/TVAS-14
90UD-667
90USPlayC/AS-9S
90Windwlk/Discs-5
91B-196
91BBBest/Aces-7
91Classic/I-95
91Classic/III-20
91D-26DK
91D-692
91D/SuperDK-26
91F-313
91Leaf-45
91Leaf/Prev-15
91Leaf/Stud-24
91OPC-395AS
91OPC-505
91Panini/FrSt-187
91Panini/St-135
91Panini/Top15-70
91RedFoley/St-35
91S-100
91S/100SS-90
91Smok/Angel-9
91StCl-81
91Sunflower-7
91T-395AS
91T-505
91T/CJMini/II-12
91UD-31
91UD-437
91Ultra-44
92B-32
92Classic/Game200-1
92D-255
92F-57
92Kenner/Fig-16
92L-450
92L/BlkGold-450
92OPC-247
92OPC/Premier-155
92Pinn-42
92Pol/Angel-9
92S-585
92S/100SS-6
92StCl-315
92Studio-145
92T-247
92T/Gold-247
92T/GoldWin-247
92T/Kids-94
92TripleP-91
92UD-244
92Ultra-25
93B-385
93D-225
93F-191
93Flair-174
93HumDum/Can-4
93L-292
93Mother/Angel-3
93OPC-153
93Pac/Spanish-44
93Pinn-201
93Pol/Angel-19
93S-158
93Select-198
93StCl-301
93StCl/1stDay-301
93StCl/Angel-16
93T-605
93T/Finest-72
93T/FinestRef-72
93T/Gold-605
93TripleP-169
93UD-53M
93UD-77
93UD/FunPack-39
93UD/SP-23
93Ultra-162
94B-67
94D-363
94D/Special-363
94F-55
94Flair-22
94L-394
94OPC-158
94Pac/Cr-78
94Pinn-38
94Pinn/Artist-38
94Pinn/Museum-38
94S-151
94S/GoldR-151
94Sf/2000-21
94StCl-211
94StCl/1stDay-211
94StCl/Gold-211
94T-381
94T/Finest-143
94T/FinestRef-143
94T/Gold-381
94TripleP-15
94UD-314
94Ultra-328

Finley, David
88Modesto-23
88Modesto/Cal-70

Finley, Steve
88AAA/ProC-29
88Hagers/Star-7
88RochR/Gov-7
88TripleA/ASCMC-21
89B-15
89D/Rook-47
89F/Up-3
89French-10
89RochR/ProC-1639
89S/Tr-95
89UD/Ext-742
90D-215
90F-176
90F/Can-176
90HagersDG/Best-10
90Leaf-329
90OPC-349
90S-339
90S/100Ris-58
90S/YS/I-11
90T-349
90T/89Debut-37
90UD-602
91B-561
91Crown/Orio-130
91D-355
91F-470
91F/UltraUp-U81
91F/Up-U88
91Leaf-231
91Leaf/Stud-176
91Mother/Ast-2
91OPC-212
91Panini/FrSt-244
91S-266
91StCl-376
91T-212
91T/Tr-42T
91UD-330
91UD/Ext-794
92B-574
92D-197
92F-433
92L-66
92L/BlkGold-66
92Mother/Ast-2
92OPC-86
92Panini-157
92Pinn-19
92S-176
92StCl-29
92Studio-35
92T-86
92T/Gold-86
92T/GoldWin-86
92T/Kids-46
92TripleP-26
92TripleP-43
92TripleP/Prev-5M
92UD-368
92Ultra-202
93B-96
93Classic/Gamel-33
93D-192
93F-50
93Flair-62
93L-325
93Mother/Ast-2
93OPC-154
93Pac/Spanish-122
93Panini-174
93Pinn-172
93S-65
93Select-88
93Select/StatL-23
93Select/StatL-60M
93StCl-556
93StCl/1stDay-556
93StCl/Ast-10
93T-148
93T/Finest-9
93T/FinestRef-9
93T/Gold-148
93TripleP-203
93UD-231
93UD/FunPack-47
93UD/SP-33
93USPlayC/Ace-5H
93Ultra-39
94B-502
94D-402
94F-490
94L-383
94OPC-129
94Pac/Cr-265
94Panini-194
94Pinn-351
94S-364
94S/Cycle-12M
94Sf/2000-135
94StCl-308
94StCl/1stDay-308
94StCl/Gold-308
94Studio-21
94T-580
94T/Finest-31
94T/Finest/PreProd-31
94T/FinestRef-31
94T/Gold-580
94TripleP-26
94UD-346
94Ultra-503

Finn, John
89Beloit/II/Star-9
90Stockton/Best-11
90Stockton/Cal-196
90Stockton/ProC-2196
91CalLgAS-30
91Stockton/ClBest-18
91Stockton/ProC-3044
92ClBest-96
92ElPaso/ProC-3929
92ElPaso/SB-209
92UD/ML-141

Finn, Neal
(Mickey)
28Exh/PCL-7
33DH-15
90Target-244

Finney, Lou
40PlayBall-197
41PlayBall-30
92Conlon/Sport-512
R314
V355-64

Finney, Mark
91BendB/ClBest-5
91BendB/ProC-3690

Finnvold, Gar
90Elmira/Pucko-17
91ClBest/Singl-192
91LynchRS/ClBest-3
91LynchRS/ProC-1192
92ClBest-195
92NewBrit/ProC-426
92NewBrit/SB-484
92Sky/AASingl-206
93Pawtu/Ball-9
94B-231

Finzer, Kory
91AubAS/ClBest-27DIR

Fiore, Mike Jr.
85Miami-4
87PanAm/USAB-6
87PanAm/USAR-6
88T/Tr-38T
89Spring/Best-1
89T/Big-8
90StPete/Star-8
90TeamUSA/87-6
91AA/LineD-34
91ArkTr/LineD-34
91ArkTr/ProC-1294

Fiore, Mike
69T-376R
70T-709
71MLB/St-318
71OPC-287
71T-287
72MB-104
72OPC-199
72T-199
78Colum
91Crown/Orio-131

Fiore, Tom
86Kenosha-9TR

Fiore, Tony
92Martins/ClBest-22
92Martins/ProC-3050

Fiorillo, Nicholas
80Water-1
82Water-10
83Tampa-27

Fireovid, Steve
81Hawaii-13
81Hawaii/TCMA-12
82Hawaii-13
83LasVegas/BHN-8
84Cram/PCL-214
85BuffB-18
86Calgary-8
87F-653M
87Sf/TPrev-25M
87Syrac-6
87Syrac/TCMA-30
87T-357
88Omaha/CMC-4
88Omaha/ProC-1513
89Omaha/CMC-3
89Omaha/ProC-1718
90AAASingl/ProC-575
90Indianap/CMC-1
90Indianap/ProC-292
90ProC/Singl-51
91AAA/LineD-28
91BuffB/LineD-28
91BuffB/ProC-534
92B-334
92OkCty/ProC-1912
93Rang/Keeb-146
Firova, Dan
80Spokane-22
86Calgary-9
89UD-32
Firsich, Steve
91Bluefld/ClBest-20
91Bluefld/ProC-4122
92Kane/ClBest-24
92Kane/ProC-83
92Kane/Team-8
Fischback, Bruce
86Kinston-7TR
Fischer
N172
Fischer, Brad
82Madis/Frit-19MG
83Madis/Frit-31MG
84Madis/Pol-1MG
85Huntsv/BK-25MG
88Tacoma/ProC-622MG
89Tacoma/CMC-25MG
89Tacoma/ProC-1551MG
90AAASingl/ProC-157MG
90Tacoma/ProC-110MG
Fischer, Carl
43Centen-8
44Centen-7
45Centen-8
92Conlon/Sport-409
Fischer, Dan
81Omaha-7
82Omaha-4
Fischer, Hank
63T-554
64T-218
65T-585
66T-381
67CokeCap/RedSox-15
67T-342
67T/Test/RSox-5
Fischer, Jeff
86FSLAS-14
86WPalmB-15
87Indianap-15
88Indianap/CMC-6
88Indianap/ProC-503
89Albuq/CMC-3
89Albuq/ProC-86
90AAASingl/ProC-59
90Albuq/CMC-3
90Albuq/ProC-338
90Albuq/Trib-7
90ProC/Singl-405
90S-654
90Target-948
93BurlB/ClBest-28CO
93BurlB/ProC-174CO
Fischer, Todd
82Idaho-7
83Madis/Frit-4
84Albany-12
86Edmon-9
Fischer, Tom
89B-20
89Lynch/Star-8
90NewBrit/Best-2
90NewBrit/ProC-1312
90NewBrit/Star-4
90ProC/Singl-806
91AA/LineD-458
91ClBest/Singl-306
91Crown/Orio-134
91NewBrit/LineD-458
91NewBrit/ProC-347
92Pawtu/ProC-916
92Pawtu/SB-356
Fischer, William C.
58T-56
59T-230
60T-76
61T-553
63T-301
64T-409
72Laugh/GF-47
90HOF/St-64
90T/TVRSox-4CO
90Target-947
D328-48
D329-57
D350/2-58
E135-48
M101/4-57
M101/5-58
W514-27
Fischetti, Art
75Water
Fischlin, Mike
78Charl
79CharCh-6
79T-718R
80Tucson-17
81Charl-13
82Wheat/Ind
83D-489
83F-407
83T-182
83Wheat/Ind-12
84F-541
84Nes/792-689
84T-689
84Wheat/Ind-22
85D-495
85F-447
85Polar/Ind-22
85T-41
86F/Up-U40
86T-283
87F-98
87Richm/Bob-7
87Richm/Crown-18
87Richm/TCMA-12
87T-434
88Greenvl/Best-23
88Richm-4
89Myrtle/ProC-1465
90Myrtle/ProC-2792MG
90SALAS/Star-47CO
92Yank/WIZ80-58
Fishel, John
86FSLAS-15
86Osceola-8
87ColAst/ProC-12
88F/Up-U88
88Tucson/CMC-19
88Tucson/JP-11
88Tucson/ProC-178
89Colum/CMC-18
89Colum/Pol-4
89Colum/ProC-735
89D-443
89F-358
89Panini/St-80
89S/HotRook-42
90AAASingl/ProC-339
90ColClip/CMC-14
90ColClip/ProC-689
90Colum/Pol-6
90ProC/Singl-214
90T/TVYank-42
Fisher, Brian K.
82Durham-17
84Richm-20
85Colum-7
85Colum/Pol-11
85F/Up-U40
86D-492
86F-104
86KayBee-12
86Seven/Coin-E15M
86Sf-177M
86T-584
86T/Gloss60-30
86T/St-312
86T/Tatt-2M
87D-340
87F-99
87F/Up-U32
87OPC-316
87Sf/TPrev-18M
87T-316
87T/Tr-33T
88D-415
88D/Best-101
88F-329
88Leaf-244
88OPC-193
88Panini/St-368
88S-130
88T-193
88T/Big-159
89B-415
89D-126
89F-209
89OPC-303
89RedFoley/St-42
89S-24
89T-423
89UD-69
89VFJuice-54
90AAASingl/ProC-189
90OPC-666
90ProC/Singl-626
90PublInt/St-154
90S-547
90T-666
90Tucson/CMC-24
90Tucson/ProC-199
90UD-97
91AAA/LineD-137
91Denver/LineD-137
91Denver/ProC-118
92Nashvl/ProC-1826
92Nashvl/SB-278
92Yank/WIZ80-59
93F-674
Fisher, Brian
77Newar
Fisher, Chauncey
90Target-949
Fisher, David
92Martins/ClBest-20
92Martins/ProC-3064
Fisher, Eddie
60T-23
61T-366
63T-223
63T-6LL
64T-66
65T-328
66Bz-47
66OPC-85
66T-222LL
66T-85
66T/RO-22
66T/RO-29
67CokeCap/Orio-14
67T-434
68T-418
69T-315
69T/St-143
70OPC-156
70T-156
71MLB/St-343
71OPC-631
71T-631
72T-689
73OPC-439
73T-439
91Crown/Orio-132
Fisher, Frederick
(Fritz)
64T-312R
66T-209R
Fisher, Glen
79Cedar/TCMA-13
81Shrev-6
82Redwd-20
Fisher, Jack H.
60T-399M
60T-46
61T-463
62T-203
63T-474
64T-422
65OPC-93
65T-93
66T-316
66T/RO-30
66T/RO-6
67CokeCap/YMet-32
67Kahn
67T-533
68T-444
69T-318
70T-684
81TCMA-478
89Clmbia/Best-23
89Clmbia/GS-2
90Clmbia/PCPII-6
90Columbia/GS-2CO
91Crown/Orio-133
91WIZMets-115
Fisher, Kyle
89Augusta/ProC-521
Fisher, Ray
11Helmar-42
14CJ-102
15CJ-102
16FleischBrd-28
88Pac/8Men-92
93Conlon-702
D328-49
D329-58
D350/2-59
E135-49
M101/4-58
M101/5-59
T205
T207
Fisher, Robert
90Target-245
C46-43
Fisher, Tom
77Fritsch-37
Fisk, Carlton
72OPC-79R
72T-79R
73K-27
73OPC-193
73T-193
73T/Lids-15
74K-5
74OPC-105
74OPC-331AS
74T-105
74T-331AS
74T/DE-64
74T/St-133
75Ho-143
75OPC-80
75T-80
75T/M-80
76Crane-14
76Ho-64
76MSA/Disc
76OPC-365
76SSPC-403
76T-365
77BurgChef-33
77Ho-104
77Ho/Twink-104
77OPC-137
77Pep-22
77T-640
78OPC-210
78PapaG/Disc-25
78SSPC/270-180
78T-270
78Wiffle/Discs-23
79Ho-106
79OPC-360
79T-680
80K-41
80OPC-20
80T-40
81D-335
81Drake-32
81F-224
81F/St-58
81MSA/Disc-12
81OPC-116
81PermaGr/AS-13
81T-480
81T/HT
81T/St-46
81T/Tr-762
82D-20DK
82D-495
82Drake-12
82F-343
82F-632M
82F/St-183
82K-25
82OPC-110
82OPC-111IA
82OPC-58AS
82PermaGr/AS-3
82Sqt-8
82T-110
82T-111IA
82T-554AS
82T/St-138
82T/St-170
83D-104
83D/AAS-43
83F-235
83F-638M
83F/St-11M
83F/St-13M
83F/St-23M
83K-56
83OPC-20
83OPC-393AS
83OPC/St-177
83OPC/St-54
83T-20
83T-393
83T/Gloss40-17
83T/St-177
83T/St-54
83TrueVal/WSox-72
84D-302
84D/Champs-52
84F-58
84F/St-39
84MiltBrad-9
84Nes/792-216TL
84Nes/792-560
84OPC-127
84Ralston-33
84Seven-12C
84T-216TL
84T-560
84T/Cereal-33
84T/Gloss40-40
84T/RD-9M
84T/St-243
84T/Super-15
84TrueVal/WS-13
85Coke/WS-72
85D-208
85F-513
85FunFood/Pin-72
85GenMills-17
85Leaf-155
85OPC-49
85T-1RB
85T-770
85T/RD-5M
85T/St-243
86Coke/WS-72
86D-366
86D/AAS-17
86D/PopUp-17
86F-204
86F-643M
86F/LL-12
86F/LimEd-15
86F/Mini-43
86F/St-38
86F/WaxBox-C8
86GenMills/Book-2M
86Jay's-7
86Leaf-163
86Meadow/Blank-3
86Meadow/Stat-13
86OPC-290
86OPC-E
86Seven/Coin-C12
86Sf-125
86Sf-67M
86Sf/Dec-62M
86T-290
86T-719AS
86T/Gloss22-9
86T/Gloss60-28
86T/Mini-11
86T/St-162
86T/St-286
86T/Super-23
86T/Tatt-23M
86T/WaxBox-E

87Classic-41
87Coke/WS-27
87D-247
87D/OD-232
87F-496
87F/RecSet-8
87GenMills/Book-3M
87Leaf-199
87OPC-164
87RedFoley/St-41
87Seven-C7
87Sf-140
87Sf/TPrev-26M
87Stuart-17M
87T-756
87T/St-288
88Coke/WS-8
88D-260
88D/Best-67
88F-397
88F/AwardWin-12
88KennerFig-36
88KingB/Disc-18
88Kodak/WSox-2
88Leaf-208
88Nestle-38
88OPC-385
88Panini/St-55
88RedFoley/St-23
88S-592
88Sf-43
88T-385
88T/Big-197
88T/Mini-8
88T/St-290
89B-62
89Cadaco-17
89Coke/WS-8
89D-101
89D-7DK
89D/Best-11
89D/DKsuper-7DK
89F-495
89KayBee-11
89Kodak/WSox-3M
89OPC-46
89Panini/St-304
89RedFoley/St-43
89S-449
89S/HotStar-39
89S/Mast-9
89Sf-219
89T-695
89T/Big-24
89T/Coins-40
89T/DH-8
89T/LJN-134
89T/St-299
89T/St/Backs-23
89T/UK-26
89UD-609
90B-314
90Classic-116
90Coke/WSox-29
90Coke/WSox-3
90D-58
90D/BestAL-5
90D/Bon/MVP-BC19
90D/Learning-49
90F-530
90F/AwardWin-13
90F/Can-530
90HotPlay/St-12
90KayBee-12
90Kodak/WSox-1
90Leaf-10
90Leaf-174CL
90MSA/Soda-21
90OPC-392AS
90OPC-420
90Panini/St-44
90PublInt/St-284
90PublInt/St-386
90RedFoley/St-32
90S-290
90S/100St-70
90S/McDon-4
90Sf-204
90T-392AS
90T-420
90T/Big-176
90T/DH-23
90T/Gloss60-46
90T/HillsHM-29
90T/St-303
90T/TVAS-8
90UD-367
90Woolwth/HL-13
91B-345
91BBBest/RecBr-6
91Cadaco-20
91Classic/200-51
91Classic/III-21
91D-108
91D-BC6
91D/BC-BC6
91F-118
91KingB/Discs-22
91Kodak/WSox-72
91Kodak/WSox-x
91Leaf-384
91Leaf/Prev-16
91Leaf/Stud-32
91MajorLg/Pins-14
91OPC-170
91OPC-393AS
91OPC-3RB
91OPC/BoxB-F
91OPC/Premier-45
91Panini/FrSt-311
91Panini/St-255
91Petro/SU-7
91RedFoley/St-36
91S-265
91S-421HL
91S/100SS-41
91Seven/3DCoin-4MW
91StCl-180
91StCl/Charter*-9
91StCl/Member*-14
91T-170
91T-393AS
91T-3RB
91T/CJMini/II-2
91T/SU-14
91T/WaxBox-F
91UD-29TC
91UD-643
91UD-677M
91USPlayC/AS-2D
91Ultra-72
91Woolwth/HL-12
92B-585
92Classic/Game200-96
92D-543
92DPep/MSA-11
92F-79
92F/TmLIns-4
92JDean/Living-2
92L-303
92L/BlkGold-303
92MrTurkey-9
92OPC-630
92OPC/Premier-86
92Panini-124
92Pinn-361
92S-72
92S/100SS-72
92S/Factory-B8
92StCl-480
92StCl/Dome-49
92Studio/Her-2
92T-630
92T/Gold-630
92T/GoldWin-630
92T/McDonB-15
92TripleP-149
92UD-571
92Ultra-33
92WSox-72
93B-175
93Cadaco-19
93D-519
93F-582
93F/Final/DTrib-DT4
93L-284
93MSA/Metz-26
93OPC-78
93Pac/Spanish-70
93Panini-135
93Pinn-421
93Pinn-475NT
93Pinn/Cooper-4
93S-579
93Select-76
93StCl-221
93StCl/1stDay-221
93StCl/WSox-16
93T-230
93T/Finest-125
93T/FinestRef-125
93T/Gold-230
93T/HolPrev-230
93UD-272
93Ultra-530

Fister, Corby
90Idaho/ProC-3256

Fittipaldi, Emerson
72Dimanche*-140

Fitzer, Doug
91ClBest/Singl-362
91SanBern/ClBest-3
91SanBern/ProC-1979
92Penin/ClBest-11
92Penin/ProC-2927

Fitzgerald, Dave
89Beloit/I/Star-5
89Beloit/II/Star-10
90AS/Cal-54
90Stockton/Best-17
90Stockton/Cal-178
90Stockton/ProC-2177
91Helena/SportP-18
91Stockton/ClBest-11
92ElPaso/SB-210

Fitzgerald, Ed
47Signal
47Sunbeam
49B-109
49Eureka-159
50B-178
52B-180
52T-236
53Briggs
54B-168
55B-208
56T-198
57T-367
58T-236
59T-33
60T-423

Fitzgerald, Kevin
86Cram/NWL-1
86Everett/Pop-4

Fitzgerald, Matthew
E254
E270/1

Fitzgerald, Mike P.
85Spring-11
87ArkTr-21
87TexLgAS-26
88Louisvl-19
88Louisvl/CMC-18
88Louisvl/ProC-427
89Louisvl-20
89Louisvl/CMC-18
89Louisvl/ProC-1259
90ArkTr/GS-13
90SpringDG/Best-34

Fitzgerald, Mike R.
82Tidew-4
83Tidew-2
84D-482
84F/X-37
84T/Tr-37
85D-238
85Expo/PostC-7
85F-78
85F/Up-U41
85OPC-104
85OPC/Post-1
85T-104
85T/St-108
85T/St-372YS
85T/Tr-34T
86D-97
86Expo/Prov/Pan-26
86Expo/Prov/Post-7
86F-247
86GenMills/Book-6M
86Leaf-32
86OPC-313
86Provigo-26
86T-503
87D-345
87F-317
87GenMills/Book-4M
87Leaf-222
87OPC-212
87Sf/TPrev-20M
87Smok/NL-14
87T-212
88D-159
88F-182
88Ho/Disc-6
88Leaf-81
88OPC-386
88Panini/St-322
88S-318
88T-674
88T/St-78
89D-456
89F-374
89OPC-23
89S-511
89T-23
89UD-133
90D-392
90F-343
90F/Can-343
90OPC-484
90PublInt/St-171
90S-361
90T-484
90T/Big-84
90UD-558
91B-453
91D-82
91F-229
91Leaf/Stud-196
91OPC-317
91Panini/FrSt-138
91S-198
91StCl-128
91T-317
91UD-516
91Ultra-201
91WIZMets-116
92B-186
92F-478
92L-371
92L/BlkGold-371
92OPC-761
92S-667
92StCl-844
92T-761
92T/Gold-761
92T/GoldWin-761
92T/Tr-31T
92T/TrGold-31T
92UD-210
93D-757
93Pac/Spanish-45

Fitzgerald, Richard
52Laval-100

Fitzmaurice, Shaun
71Richm/Team-6
91WIZMets-117

Fitzmorris, Al
70OPC-241R
70T-241R
71OPC-564
71T-564
72OPC-349
72T-349
72T/Cloth-10
73OPC-643
73T-643
74OPC-191
74T-191
75OPC-24
75T-24
75T/M-24
76A&P/KC
76Ho-8
76Ho/Twink-8
76OPC-144
76SSPC-160
76T-144
77T-449
78T-227
79Hawaii-17
79T-638

Fitzpatrick, Dan
84Newar-7
86Beloit-7
87Stockton-6
88CalLgAS-11
88Stockton/Cal-187
88Stockton/ProC-745
89Stockton/Best-12
89Stockton/Cal-151
89Stockton/ProC-395

Fitzpatrick, David
91Kissim/ProC-4177
92GreatF/SportP-16

Fitzpatrick, Edward
C46-70
T201

Fitzpatrick, Gary
83LynnP-27

Fitzpatrick, John
54T-213CO
94T/Arc54-213CO

Fitzpatrick, Mike
89EastLDD/ProC-48UMP

Fitzpatrick, Robert
(Rob)
90James/Pucko-2
91ClBest/Singl-254
91Rockford/ClBest-14
91Rockford/ProC-2049
92WPalmB/ClBest-4
92WPalmB/ProC-2091
93Harris/ProC-272
94B-256

Fitzsimmons, Fred
(Freddie)
31Exh/4-10
33Exh/4-5
33G-130
33G-235
35BU-72
35G-8A
35G-9A
39PlayBall-110
40PlayBall-65
41DP-143
52B-234
60T-462C
77Galasso-75
90Target-246
91Conlon/Sport-260
94Conlon-1117
R315-A6
R315-B6
R316
V354-20
V355-14
WG8-16

Fitzsimmons, Tom
90Target-950

Fix, Greg
86Cram/NWL-91
87QuadC-17

Flachsbarth, Lance
89KS*-5

Flack, Max
25Exh-60
D329-59
D350/2-60
E120
E121/120
M101/4-59
M101/5-60
V100
W501-117
W573

Flagg, Paul
92GulfCD/ProC-3578

Flagstead, Ira
21Exh-48
25Exh-66
26Exh-65
27Exh-33
28Exh-33
87Conlon/2-34
91Conlon/Sport-291
E120
E121/120
E210-21
W501-7
W514-1
W573

Flaherty, John Timothy
88Elmira-13
89WinHaven/Star-7
90AAASingl/ProC-436
90Pawtu/CMC-11
90Pawtu/ProC-464
90ProC/Singl-262
90T/TVRSox-43
91AA/LineD-459
91NewBrit/LineD-459
91NewBrit/ProC-355
92D/Rook-37
92L-439
92L/BlkGold-439
92T/Tr-32T

92T/TrGold-32T
92Ultra-313
93D-561
93Pac/Spanish-32
93Pawtu/Ball-10
93S-278
94D-596
94Pinn-443
94S-313
94S/GoldR-313
94T-197
94T/Gold-197

Flaherty, John
55B-272UMP

Flaherty, Patrick
E254

Flammang, Chris
80SanJose/JITB-7
81Spokane-1

Flanagan, Dan
90ClintUp/Team-U4
90Everett/Best-4
90Everett/ProC-3120
91Clinton/ClBest-2
91Clinton/ProC-827
92AS/Cal-7
92SanJose/ClBest-12

Flanagan, James
T206

Flanagan, Mike
76OPC-589R
76T-589R
77T-106
78Ho-134
78OPC-231
78T-341
79K-48
79OPC-76
79T-160
80K-3
80OPC-335
80T-205LL
80T-640
81D-234
81F-171
81F/St-56
81K-60
81OPC-10
81T-10
82D-329
82F-165
82F/St-145
82OPC-153
82T-520
82T/St-148
82T/StVar-148
83D-105
83F-60
83F/St-17M
83F/St-2M
83OPC-172
83OPC/St-25
83T-445
83T/St-25
84D-169
84F-8
84F/St-63
84Nes/792-295
84OPC-295
84T-295
84T/St-12LCS
84T/St-210
85D-88
85F-177
85Leaf-175
85OPC-46
85T-780
85T/St-207
86D-576
86F-275
86Sf-57M
86T-365
87D-459
87F-470
87French-46
87OPC-112
87T-748
88D-636
88D/Best-272
88F/Up-U67
88OPC-164
88S-427
88T-623
88Tor/Fire-46
89B-241
89D-324
89D/Best-316
89F-233
89OPC-139
89RedFoley/St-44
89S-475
89T-139
89T/Big-243
89T/LJN-103
89T/St-190
89Tor/Fire-46
89UD-385
90D-324
90F-81
90F/Can-81
90OPC-78
90PublInt/St-514
90S-67
90T-78
90UD-483
91Crown/Orio-135
91Leaf-479
91S/RookTr-2T
91StCl/Member*-10M
92D-196
92F-7
92OPC-218
92Pinn-475
92S-333
92S-427NH
92StCl-30
92T-218
92T/Gold-218
92T/GoldWin-218
92UD-380
93StCl-123
93StCl/1stDay-123
93T-381
93T/Gold-381

Flanigan, Thomas
N172

Flannelly, Tim
91Oneonta/ProC-4161
92Greens/ClBest-3
92Greens/ProC-786
92ProC/Tomorrow-128
92StCl/Dome-50

Flannery, John
76QuadC
79Knoxvl/TCMA-10
82BirmB-15

Flannery, Kevin
81AppFx-4
82AppFx/Frit-21
83Toledo-3

Flannery, Tim
80Hawaii-19
80T-685R
81F-493
81Hawaii/TCMA-1
81T-579
82D-61
82F-572
82T-249
83D-472
83F-359
83F/St-8M
83T-38
84D-202
84F-299
84Mother/Padres-12
84Nes/792-674
84Smok/Padres-9
84T-674
85D-551
85F-31
85Mother/Padres-20
85T-182
86D-383
86F-320
86OPC-387
86T-413
86T/St-112
87Bohem-11
87D-287
87F-413
87OPC-52
87T-763
87T/St-114
88Coke/Padres-11
88D-328
88F-582
88OPC-262
88Panini/St-404
88S-483
88Smok/Padres-8
88T-513
88T/St-108
89B-457
89Coke/Padre-4
89D-364
89Padre/Mag-15
89S-513
89T-379
89T/Big-174
89UD-603
90PublInt/St-48

Flater, John
E254

Flath, Daniel
90Saraso/Star-30BB

Fleeman, Brad
89KS*-6

Fleet, Joe
91Watertn/ClBest-4
91Watertn/ProC-3359
93Kinston/Team-8

Fleet, Kenyatta
92ColRS/ClBest-26
92ColRS/ProC-2383

Fleischer, Herb
52Laval-47

Fleita, Oneri
89Freder/Star-6
90Wausau/ProC-2145CO
90Wausau/Star-28CO
91Kane/ClBest-28CO
91Kane/ProC-2675CO
91Kane/Team-26M
92Freder/ClBest-28CO
92Freder/ProC-1823

Fleming, Bill
91Pac/SenLg-84

Fleming, Carlton
92Classic/DP-98
92Oneonta/ClBest-5

Fleming, Dave
90Foil/Best-57
91AA/LineD-336
91B-249
91ClBest/Singl-284
91Jaxvl/LineD-336
91Jaxvl/ProC-146
92B-624
92Classic/Game200-163
92Classic/I-34
92D-404RR
92D/RookPhen-BC4
92F/Up-55
92JDean/Rook-6
92L-494
92L/BlkGold-494
92Mother/Mar-17
92OPC-192
92Pinn-275
92Pinn/Rook-13
92Pinn/RookI-14
92ProC/Tomorrow-141
92S/RookTr-85T
92StCl-814
92T-192
92T/91Debut-56
92T/Gold-192
92T/GoldWin-192
92UD-4SR
92UD/Scout-SR8
93B-487
93Classic/GameI-34
93D-243
93F-306
93F/ASAL-11
93F/RookSenI-5
93Mother/Mar-2
93OPC-67
93P-1
93Pac/Spanish-285
93Panini-57
93Pinn-5
93Pinn/Team2001-23
93S-356
93Select-271
93Select/Ace-23
93Select/ChasRook-20
93Select/ChasS-22
93StCl-358
93StCl/1stDay-358
93StCl/Mar-8
93T-410M
93T-45
93T/Finest-196
93T/FinestRef-196
93T/Gold-410M
93T/Gold-45
93T/Hill-13
93T/PreProd-5
93ToysRUs-77
93TripleP-99
93UD-141
93UD/FunPack-113
93UD/SP-130
93USPlayC/Rook-1D
93Ultra-268
94B-117
94D-183
94F-285
94Flair-102
94L-149
94OPC-183
94Pac/Cr-569
94Pinn-158
94Pinn/Artist-158
94Pinn/Museum-158
94S-135
94S/GoldR-135
94Select-173
94StCl-409
94StCl/1stDay-409
94StCl/Gold-409
94T-415
94T/Finest-172
94T/FinestRef-172
94T/Gold-415
94TripleP-126
94UD-246
94UD/CollC-101
94UD/CollC/Gold-101
94UD/CollC/Silv-101
94UD/ElecD-246
94Ultra-119

Fleming, Hap
91MissSt-16
92MissSt-15
93MissSt-16

Fleming, Jack
77DaytB
80Tucson-7

Fleming, Jim
88OK-4CO
89OK-3ACO
91James/ClBest-28CO
91James/ProC-3561CO
92James/ClBest-27CO
92James/ProC-1517CO

Fleming, Keith
87Stockton-20
88Stockton/Cal-185
88Stockton/ProC-725
89ElPaso/GS-7
90Beloit/Best-25
90Beloit/Star-7

Fleming, Les
49Eureka-160

Fleming, Paul
82Wisco/Frit-8

Fleming, Ricky
86Everett/Pop-5

Flener, Huck
90StCath/ProC-3470
91Myrtle/ClBest-4
91Myrtle/ProC-2938
92Dunedin/ClBest-24
92Dunedin/ProC-1992
92ProC/Tomorrow-173
93Knoxvl/ProC-1246
94Pac/Cr-640
94StCl/Team-177
94T-39
94T/Gold-39

Flesher, Jay
89GA-8

Fleshman, Richard
75FtLaud/Sus-10
77WHave

Fletcher, Arthur
11Helmar-127
21Exh-49
40PlayBall-125
44Yank/St-11CO
61F-106
77Galasso-183CO
87Conlon/2-32
88Conlon/4-11
91Conlon/Sport-117
92Conlon/Sport-490
D304
D327
D328-50
D329-60
D350/2-61
E120
E135-50
E220
M101/4-60
M101/5-61
M116
S74-86
T202
T205
T206
T207
T213/brown
T222
V61-107
W514-14
W516-14
W573
WG4-8

Fletcher, Bob
89GreatF-27
89Saraso/Star-5
90VeroB/Star-13

Fletcher, Darrin
88SanAn/Best-15
89Albuq/CMC-18
89Albuq/ProC-58
90AAAGame/ProC-44
90AAASingl/ProC-69
90Albuq/CMC-15
90Albuq/ProC-348
90Albuq/Trib-8
90ProC/Singl-417
90S-622RP
90T/89Debut-38
90Target-951
91AAA/LineD-483
91B-496
91Classic/II-T5
91D-47RR
91F/Up-U107
91OPC-9
91Phill/Medford-14
91ScranWB/LineD-483
91ScranWB/ProC-2541
91T-9
91UD-428
91Ultra-377MLP
92B-609
92D-319
92Expo/D/Duri-8
92F-530
92Indianap/ProC-1861
92L-264
92L/BlkGold-264
92OPC-159
92OPC/Premier-41
92S-193
92S/RookTr-64T
92T-159
92T/Gold-159
92T/GoldWin-159
92T/Tr-33T
92T/TrGold-33T
92UD-108
92Ultra-517
93B-620
93Cadaco-20
93D-378
93F-460
93L-165
93OPC-64
93Pac/Spanish-184
93Panini-224
93S-216
93StCl-272
93StCl/1stDay-272
93T-665
93T/Gold-665
93UD-614
93UD/SP-103
93Ultra-67
94B-612
94D-152
94F-537
94Flair-188
94L-118

94Pac/Cr-379
94Pinn-205
94Pinn/Artist-205
94Pinn/Museum-205
94S-436
94Select-168
94StCl-42
94StCl/1stDay-42
94StCl/Gold-42
94T-412
94T/Finest-137
94T/FinestRef-137
94T/Gold-412
94TripleP-94
94UD-459
94UD/CollC-102
94UD/CollC/Gold-102
94UD/CollC/Silv-102
94Ultra-226
Fletcher, David
90MedHat/Best-17
Fletcher, Dennis
90A&AASingle/ProC-77
90Savan/ProC-2064
91Spring/ClBest-17
91Spring/ProC-738
92StPete/ClBest-2
92StPete/ProC-2023
Fletcher, Don
76Clinton
91Pac/SenLg-103
Fletcher, Edward Paul
(Paul)
88Martins/Star-14
89Batavia/ProC-1921
90Spartan/Best-2
90Spartan/ProC-2483
90Spartan/Star-7
91ClBest/Singl-111
91Clearw/ClBest-2
91Clearw/ProC-1613
92Reading/ProC-567
92Reading/SB-535
93B-272
93ScranWB/Team-9
Fletcher, Elburt
39PlayBall-69
40PlayBall-103
41DP-150
41G-26
41PlayBall-62
43Playball-32
47TipTop
49Eureka-9
R314
Fletcher, Mitch
80Tulsa-26
Fletcher, Paul
92Eugene/ClBest-14
92Eugene/ProC-3024
Fletcher, Rob
90WPalmB/Star-6
91Modesto/ClBest-4
91Modesto/ProC-3096
Fletcher, Scott
82D-554
82Iowa-2
83TrueVal/WSox-1
84D-452
84F-59
84Nes/792-364
84T-364
84T/St-250
84TrueVal/WS-14
85Coke/WS-1
85D-330
85F-514
85T-78
85T/St-240
86D-282
86D/HL-28
86F-205
86F/Up-U41
86OPC-187
86Rangers-1
86T-187
86T/Tr-36T
87Classic/Up-118
87D-304
87D/OD-171
87F-123
87F/AwardWin-13
87Leaf-226
87Mother/Rang-6
87Sf-113M
87Sf-136
87Sf/TPrev-1M
87Smok/R-13
87T-462
87T/St-237
88D-11DK
88D-180
88D/Best-32
88D/DKsuper-11DK
88F-466
88F/Mini-54
88F/St-63
88Leaf-11DK
88Leaf-155
88Mother/R-6
88OPC-345
88Panini/St-206
88RedFoley/St-24
88S-251
88Sf-77
88Smok/R-10
88T-345
88T/Big-19
88T/St-241
89B-230
89Cadaco-18
89D-142
89D/Best-167
89F-518
89F/Superstar-14
89KennerFig-44
89Mother/R-13
89OPC-295
89Panini/St-454
89S-78
89S/Tr-47
89Sf-185
89Smok/R-8
89T-295
89T/Big-205
89T/St-246
89UD-420
90B-319
90Coke/WSox-4
90D-455
90D/BestAL-88
90F-531
90F/Can-531
90Kodak/WSox-5
90Leaf-141
90OPC-565
90Panini/St-43
90PublInt/St-408
90S-58
90Sf-220
90T-565
90T/Big-207
90T/St-307
90UD-310
91B-359
91D-276
91F-119
91Kodak/WSox-7
91Leaf-306
91Leaf/Stud-33
91OPC-785
91Panini/FrSt-313
91S-36
91StCl-30
91T-785
91UD-321
91Ultra-73
92B-7
92F-80
92F/Up-34
92L-234
92L/BlkGold-234
92OPC-648
92Pol/Brew-7
92S-203
92StCl-116
92StCl-792
92Studio-193
92T-648
92T/Gold-648
92T/GoldWin-648
92T/Tr-34T
92T/TrGold-34T
92UD-186
92Ultra-381
93B-383
93D-631
93F-629
93F/Final-174
93Flair-163
93L-344
93OPC-133
93OPC/Premier-48
93Pac/Spanish-357
93Pinn-495
93Rang/Keeb-147
93S-632
93Select-140
93Select/RookTr-98T
93StCl-112
93StCl-623
93StCl/1stDay-112
93StCl/1stDay-623
93T-97
93T/Gold-97
93UD-523
93Ultra-510
94B-503
94D-134
94F-32
94L-422
94Pac/Cr-54
94Panini-29
94Pinn-146
94Pinn/Artist-146
94Pinn/Museum-146
94S-367
94StCl-198
94StCl/1stDay-198
94StCl/Gold-198
94T-169
94T/Finest-181
94T/FinestRef-181
94T/Gold-169
94UD/CollC-103
94UD/CollC/Gold-103
94UD/CollC/Silv-103
94Ultra-14
Fletcher, Van
(Guy)
46Sunbeam
47Signal
47Sunbeam
Flick, Elmer
76Shakey-92
80Perez/HOF-92
80SSPC/HOF
89HOF/St-53
E107
E254
E270/1
M116
T206
WG2-19
Flinn, Geoff
89Butte/SP-15
Flinn, John
79T-701R
81T-659R
81Vanco-21
82RochR-2
83RochR-3
85CharlO-24
87CharlO/WBTV-25
91Crown/Orio-136
Flinn, Mike
82Madis/Frit-4
Flint, Frank S.
E223
N172
N284
WG1-12
Floethe, Chris
72OPC-268R
72T-268R
Flood, Curt
58T-464
59T-353
60L-141
60T-275
61P-178
61T-438
61T/St-86
62J-166
62P-166
62P/Can-166
62Salada-139
62Shirriff-139
62T-590
63J-162
63P-162
63T-505
64T-103
64T/Coins-65
64T/St-28
64T/tatt
65T-415
66OPC-60
66T-60
66T/RO-31
67OPC-63M
67T-245
67T-63M
68Bz-11
68OPC-180
68T-180
68T/3D
69Kelly/Pin-5
69MB-83
69MLB/St-210
69MLBPA/Pin-43
69OPC/DE-5
69T-426AS
69T-540
69T/DE-28
69T/S-59
69T/St-114
70K-48
70MLB/St-87
70OPC-360
70T-360
71MLB/St-536
71OPC-535
71T-535
71T/S-41
71T/Super-41
72MB-105
78TCMA-240
89Pac/SenLg-220COM
89TM/SenLg-1COM
90EliteSenLg-1COM
92AP/ASG-72
92Card/McDon/Pac-32
93TWill-88
93UD/ATH-51
Flood, Thomas J.
N172
Flood, Tim
90Target-247
Flora, Kevin
87Salem/ProC-2433
88QuadC/GS-5
89QuadC/Best-6
89QuadC/GS-11
90MidldA/GS-24
91AA/LineD-434
91ClBest/Singl-19
91MidldA/LineD-434
91MidldA/OneHour-11
91MidldA/ProC-441
92B-283
92Edmon/ProC-3545
92Edmon/SB-156
92ProC/Tomorrow-33
92Sky/AAASingl-77
92T/91Debut-57
92UD/ML-96
93T-521
93T/Gold-521
Florence, Donald
88WinHaven/Star-8
89WinHaven/Star-8
90NewBrit/Best-10
90NewBrit/ProC-1313
90NewBrit/Star-5
91AA/LineD-460
91NewBrit/LineD-460
91NewBrit/ProC-348
92NewBrit/ProC-427
92NewBrit/SB-485
93Pawtu/Ball-11
Florence, Paul
V355-177
Flores, Adalberto
76BurlB
77BurlB
77Newar
Flores, Alex
87Greens-18
Flores, Gil
77SLCity
78Cr/PCL-40
78SSPC/270-209
78T-268
80T-478
80Tidew-6
81Tidew-11
82Tidew-7
83Tidew-22
84Tidew-7
91WIZMets-118
Flores, Jesse
80Knoxvl/TCMA-8
87Salem/ProC-2442CO
Flores, Joe
92Kingspt/ClBest-21
92Kingspt/ProC-1538
92Pittsfld/ProC-3303
Flores, Jose
85Greens-23
86Greens-5
90Ashvl/ClBest-13
90AubAs/Best-6
90AubAs/ProC-3411
91Ashvl/ProC-574
92Ashvl/ClBest-2
Flores, Juan
90Helena/SportP-3
91Stockton/ClBest-22
91Stockton/ProC-3034
Flores, Miguel
90BurlInd/ProC-3013
91CLAS/ProC-CAR14
91Kinston/ClBest-16
91Kinston/ProC-328
92Canton/ProC-697
92Canton/SB-106
92ProC/Tomorrow-55
92Sky/AASingl-49
92UD/ML-140
Flores, Norberto
(Bert)
85VeroB-12
86Bakers-8
Flores, Willi
82Wisco/Frit-21
Florez, Tim
91Everett/ClBest-10
91Everett/ProC-3921
92Clinton/ClBest-22
Florie, Bryce
89CharRain/ProC-983
90Foil/Best-130
90Waterlo/Best-3
90Waterlo/ProC-2371
91Waterlo/ClBest-3
91Waterlo/ProC-1250
92HighD/ClBest-20
94B-316
94FExcel-280
Flower, George
86WPalmB-16
Flowers, Bennett
55B-254
Flowers, D'Arcy
(Jake)
29Exh/4-3
31Exh/4-3
33G-151
90Target-248
V353-81
Flowers, Doug
91Kane/ClBest-29
Flowers, Kim
85Everett/Cram-5A
85Everett/Cram-5B
87Clinton-16
88Fresno/Cal-11
88Fresno/ProC-1223
Flowers, Larry
90GA-4
Flowers, Perry
86Clinton-8
Flowers, Wes
90Target-952
Flowers, Willie
78Newar
Floyd, Chris
88Myrtle/ProC-1173
Floyd, Cliff
91Classic/DP-11
91FrRow/DP-49
91LitSun/HSPros-19
91LitSun/HSProsG-19
92Albany/ClBest-22
92Albany/ProC-2314
92B-678
92ClBest-380
92ClBest/BBonusC-19
92ClBest/RBonus-BC19

92OPC-186
92Pinn-296DP
92S-801
92StCl/Dome-51
92T-186
92T/Gold-186
92T/GoldWin-186
92UD/ML-267
92UD/ML-63DS
92UD/ML/TPHolo-TP2
92UD/POY-PY10
93B-128
93B-354FOIL
93ClBest/Fisher-17
93ClBest/MLG-72
93F/Final-92
93FExcel/ML-58
93Flair/Wave-5
93Harris/ProC-274
93T-576M
93T/Gold-576M
93UD-431TP
93UD/SP-277FOIL
93Ultra-413
94B-200
94B-340
94D-651
94F-538
94F/RookSen-7
94Finest-427
94Flair-189
94L/GRook-18
94OPC-223
94OPC/HotPros-1
94Pac/Cr-380
94Pinn-392
94Pinn/New-10
94Pinn/Power-19
94Pinn/RookTPinn-7M
94S-587
94S/Boys-60
94Select-185
94Select/RookSurg-1
94SelectSam-RS1
94Sf/2000-173
94Sf/2000-NNO
94SigRook/Floyd-Set
94SigRook/Pr-1
94StCl-127
94StCl/1stDay-127
94StCl/Gold-127
94Studio-77
94T-259
94T/Gold-259
94TedW-154
94TedW-155
94TedW-156
94TedW-157
94TripleP-289
94UD-12
94UD/CollC-7
94UD/CollC/Gold-7
94UD/CollC/Silv-7
94UD/DColl-E5
94UD/ElecD-12
94UD/HoloFX-9
94UD/Mantle-8
94UD/SP-83
94Ultra-227
94Ultra/AllRook-3
94Ultra/RisSt-4

Floyd, D.J.
90Erie/Star-6

Floyd, Robert
(Bobby)
69T-597R
70OPC-101
70T-101
71MLB/St-415
71OPC-646
71T-646
72OPC-273
72T-273
72T/Cloth-11
74OPC-41
74T-41
75Omaha/Team-6
80LynnS-4MG
81LynnS-24MG
82SLCity-24MG
83SLCity-24MG
84Cram/PCL-191
85Cram/PCL-78MG
86Lynch-9MG
91Crown/Orio-137

Floyd, Stan
77Charl

Floyd, Tony
88SoOreg/ProC-1707

Flynn, Bob
75AppFx
76AppFx

Flynn, David
88CapeCod/Sum-13

Flynn, Errol
88Pulaski/ProC-1758

Flynn, John A.
(Jocko)
N172

Flynn, John Anthony
12Sweet/Pin-136
D322
M116
S74-109
T205

Flynn, R. Doug
76OPC-518
76SSPC-37
76T-518
77T-186
78T-453
79Ho-81
79OPC-116
79T-229
80OPC-32
80T-58
81Coke
81D-394
81F-330
81OPC-311
81T-634
81T/HT
81T/SO-93
81T/St-192
82D-427
82F-525
82F/St-87
82OPC-302
82T-302
82T/St-70
82T/Tr-33T
83D-240
83F-282
83OPC-169
83Stuart-7
83T-169
84D-254
84Expo/PostC-8
84F-274
84Nes/792-749
84OPC-262
84Stuart-29
84T-749
84T/St-97
85D-463
85F-397
85Leaf-257
85OPC-112
85T-554
85T/St-93
86Cain's-5
86T-436
91WIZMets-119
92MCI-3
93Rang/Keeb-148

Fobbs, Larry
78LodiD
81Albuq/TCMA-15
82Albuq-16

Fodge, Gene
58T-449

Fogarty, James
N172
N284
N29
N43
N690
WG1-51

Fogg, Kevin
76Baton

Foggie, Cornell
89Watertn/Star-7

Fogler, Seth
90Miami/II/Star-29TR
90Miami/II/Star-30PER

Fohl, Lee
V100
V117-5

Foiles, Hank
52Park-85
53T-252
55Gol/Ind-7
57T-104
58Hires-71
58Kahn
58T-4
59T-294
60T-77
61T-277
62T-112
63T-326
64T-554
91Crown/Orio-138
91T/Arc53-252

Foit, Jim
83Tulsa-20

Fojas, Francisco
79Cedar/TCMA-9

Foldman, Harry
(Hal)
49Sommer-29

Foley, Bill
77Newar
78BurlB
79Holyo-3
82ElPaso-6

Foley, Jack
83Tampa-11

Foley, Jim
88Modesto-9
89Madis/Star-8
90Clinton/ProC-2549

Foley, Joe
87Anchora-12

Foley, Keith
86WPalmB-17
88Vermont/ProC-948

Foley, Mark
87Penin-4

Foley, Martin
87Spartan-17
88Spartan/ProC-1038
88Spartan/Star-7
89Reading/Best-15
89Reading/ProC-672
89Reading/Star-11
90Reading/Best-16
90Reading/ProC-1226
90Reading/Star-12

Foley, Marvis
77AppFx
78Knoxvl
81D-399
81T-646
83D-652
83T-409
84Rangers-30
85D-500
85T-621
86BirmB/Team-23CO
89Vanco/CMC-23
89Vanco/ProC-573
90AAAGame/ProC-39
90AAASingl/ProC-183
90ProC/Singl-632MG
90Vanco/CMC-5MG
90Vanco/ProC-505MG
91AAA/LineD-649MG
91Pac/SenLg-23
91Vanco/LineD-649MG
91Vanco/ProC-1609MG
92ChalK/SB-174MG
92CharlK/ProC-2786
93Rang/Keeb-149

Foley, Rick
79SLCity-18
80SLCity-15
81Holyo-15
82Spokane-3

Foley, Thomas
(Tom)
80Water-19
81Indianap-7
82Indianap-20
84D-81
84Nes/792-632
84T-632
85D-569
85F-535
85T-107
86D-549
86F-440
86Phill/TastyK-11
86T-466
87D-504
87F-318
87OPC-78
87T-78
88D-303
88F-183
88Ho/Disc-3
88Leaf-143
88OPC-251
88S-159
88T-251
89D-342
89D/Best-314
89F-375
89OPC-159
89Panini/St-121
89S-405
89T-529
89T/Big-261
89UD-441
90B-120
90D-274
90F-344
90F/Can-344
90Leaf-292
90OPC-341
90Panini/St-292
90PublInt/St-172
90S-32
90T-341
90T/Big-58
90UD-489
91D-180
91F-230
91Leaf/StudPrev-13
91OPC-773
91S-526
91T-773
91UD-381
92D-538
92L-372
92L/BlkGold-372
92OPC-666
92S-486
92StCl-19
92T-666
92T/Gold-666
92T/GoldWin-666
92TripleP-2
92UD-492
92Ultra-221
93D-727
93MilkBone-13
93Pac/Spanish-586
93Pirate/Nation-10
94D-132
94F-608
94L-335
94StCl-142
94StCl/1stDay-142
94StCl/Gold-142

Folga, Mike
85PrWill-12
87Peoria-26

Foli, Tim
71OPC-83R
71T-83R
72Dimanche*-15
72ProStars/PostC-5
72T-707
72T-708IA
73OPC-19
73T-19
73T/Lids-16
74Expo/West-4
74OPC-217
74T-217
74T/DE-19
74T/St-54
74Weston-19
75Ho-9
75Ho/Twink-9
75OPC-149
75T-149
75T/M-149
76Expo/Redp-8
76OPC-397
76SSPC-328
76T-397
77BurgChef-156
77OPC-162
77T-76
78OPC-169
78T-167
79OPC-213
79T-403
80OPC-131
80T-246
81Coke
81D-13
81F-379
81OPC-38
81T-501
82D-376
82F-482
82F/St-75
82OPC-97
82T-618
82T/St-88
82T/Tr-34T
83D-342
83F-88
83OPC-319
83T-738
84D-474
84F-516
84F/X-38
84Nes/792-342
84OPC-342
84T-342
84T/Tr-38
85F-126
85T-271FDP
85T-456
87Smok/R-29CO
91WIZMets-120
92Pol/Brew-30M
92Yank/WIZ80-60
93Rang/Keeb-150

Folkers, Rich
71OPC-648R
71T-648R
73OPC-649
73T-649
74OPC-417
74T-417
75OPC-98
75T-98
75T/M-98
76OPC-611
76SSPC-114
76T-611
77Spoka
77T-372
91WIZMets-121

Followell, Vern
81Evansvl-14
82Evansvl-18
85Cram/PCL-57

Fondy, Dee
52B-231
52T-359
53B/BW-5
54B-173
54RH
55B-224
56T-112
57Seattle/Pop-14
57T-42
58Kahn
58T-157
79TCMA-47

Fong, Steve
87SLCity/Taco-21TR

Fonseca, Angel
82Wausau/Frit-25

Fonseca, Dave
80Clinton-13

Fonseca, Lew
29Exh/4-21
31Exh/4-22
32Orbit/num-20
32Orbit/un-19
33DH-16
33G-43
34DS-7
61F-27
82Ohio/HOF-61
91Conlon/Sport-283
R305
R308-184
R310
R316
V353-43
V94-15

W517-48
WG7-16
Fontenot, Ray
82Nashvl-12
83Colum-5
84D-370
84F-122
84Nes/792-19
84T-19
85D-248
85F-127
85F/Up-U42
85SevenUp-31
85T-507
85T/Tr-35T
86Cub/Unocal-9
86D-361
86F-369
86Gator-31
86T-308
87T-124
87Tucson-12
92Yank/WIZ80-61
Fontes, Brad
88Butte-24
89Kenosha/ProC-1062
89Kenosha/Star-5
Fonville, Chad
92ClBest/Up-449
92Everett/ClBest-28
92Everett/ProC-1695
93ClBest/MLG-160
94ClBest/Gold-41
94FExcel-289
Fonville, Charlie
84Butte-10
Foor, Jim
72OPC-257R
72T-257R
Foote, Barry
72Dimanche*-16
72Dimanche*-17
74OPC-603R
74T-603R
75Ho-39
75OPC-229
75T-229
75T/M-229
76Expo/Redp-9
76OPC-42
76T-42
77BurgChef-157
77OPC-207
77T-612
78SSPC/270-40
78T-513
79T-161
80OPC-208
80T-398
81D-558
81F-313
81OPC-305
81T-492
81T/St-154
81T/Tr-763
82D-83
82F-34
82T-706
83T-697
85Albany-23
86Colum-9MG
87Myrtle-7
89Knoxvl/Best-28
89Knoxvl/ProC-1128
89SLAS-24
90Coke/WSox-30CO
91Kodak/WSox-x
92Mets/Kahn-26CO
92Yank/WIZ80-62
Forbes, Andre
78Green
Forbes, P.J.
90Boise/ProC-3320
90WichSt-11
91PalmSp/ProC-2022
92ClBest-376
92QuadC/ClBest-18
92QuadC/ProC-817
94FExcel-25
Forbes, Willie
88Charl/ProC-1193
Ford, Allen
91MedHat/ProC-4094
Ford, Calvin
89Wythe/Star-15
90Hunting/ProC-3298
Ford, Curt
83Spring/Frit-6
84ArkTr-16
85Louisvl-13
86F-648R
86Louisvl-13
87D-454
87F-294
87Smok/Cards-21
87T-399
88D-417
88F-32
88Panini/St-395
88S-288
88Smok/Card-20
88T-612
88T/St-23
88Woolwth-28
89B-408
89F-450
89Phill/TastyK-6
89T-132
89UD-309
90D-694
90F-557
90F/Can-557
90OPC-39
90Phill/TastyK-9
90S-183
90SpringDG/Best-30
90T-39
90UD-490
91AAA/LineD-583
91Toledo/LineD-583
91Toledo/ProC-1943
92Louisvl/ProC-1900
Ford, Dale
88TM/Umpire-23
89TM/Umpire-21
89TM/Umpire-60M
90TM/Umpire-20
Ford, Darnell
(Dan)
76OPC-313
76SSPC-216
76T-313
77BurgChef-48
77Ho-121
77Ho/Twink-121
77OPC-104
77T-555
77T/CS-16
77T/ClothSt-16
78Ho-18
78OPC-34
78T-275
78Twin/FriszP-7
79OPC-201
79T-385
80OPC-7
80T-20
81D-54
81F-273
81OPC-303
81T-422
82D-468
82F-458
82F/St-216
82OPC-134
82T-134
82T/St-163
82T/Tr-35T
83D-509
83F-61
83OPC-357
83T-683
84D-367
84F-9
84Nes/792-530
84OPC-349
84T-530
84T/St-212
85D-489
85F-178
85T-252
86T-753
91Crown/Orio-139
Ford, Dave
79RochR-20
80T-661R
81D-552
81F-192
81T-706
82D-597
82F-166
82T-174
83RochR-4
84Cram/PCL-94
91Crown/Orio-140
Ford, Doug
47Centen-7
Ford, Edward C.
(Whitey)
51B-1
51BR-D5
53B/Col-153
53T-207
54B-177
54NYJour
54RM-AL16
54T-37
55Armour-6
55B-59
55RM-AL3
56T-240
57T-25
58T-320
59Armour-8
59T-430
59YooHoo-2
60Armour-10
60T-35
60T/tatt-15
61P-6
61T-160
61T-586AS
61T/St-193
62Bz
62Exh
62J-9
62P-9
62P/Can-9
62Salada-8
62Shirriff-8
62T-310
62T-315IA
62T-475AS
62T-57LL
62T-59LL
62T/St-85
62T/bucks
63Exh
63J-19
63P-19
63T-446
63T-6LL
64T-380
64T-4LL
64T/Coins-139AS
64T/S-7
64Wheat/St-15
65T-330
66OPC-160
66T-160
66T/RO-32
66T/RO-60
67OPC-5
67T-5
74Syrac/Team-30
75SSPC/42-33CO
75Syrac/Team-5CO
75Syrac/Team-6
76Shakey-144
77Galasso-25
78TCMA-21
80Perez/HOF-144
80SSPC/HOF
81TCMA-450M
82CJ-3
83Kaline-16M
83MLBPA/Pin-7
85Woolwth-11
86Sf/Dec-44
87Nestle/DT-21
89B/Ins-3
89HOF/St-70
89Kahn/Coop-4
89Pac/Leg-210
89Swell-50
89T/LJN-121
90MSA/AGFA-16
90Perez/GreatMom-5
90Swell/Great-8
91MDA-10
91T/Arc53-207
92Bz/Quadra-12M
92FrRow/Ford-Set
92Pinn/MM-25
92Yank/WIZ60-42
92Yank/WIZAS-21
92Yank/WIZHOF-10
93AP/ASG-116
93AP/ASG24K-50G
93TWill-62
93UD/ATH-140M
93UD/ATH-152M
93UD/ATH-158M
93UD/ATH-52
93YooHoo-6
94T/Arc54-37
Exh47
PM10/L-14
PM10/Sm-52
WG10-6
WG9-8
Ford, Horace E.
(Hod)
29Exh/4-8
31Exh/4-8
33G-24
90Target-249
93Conlon-923
E120
E126-57
R316
V353-24
V61-111
W573
Ford, Ken
82AlexD-23
83LynnP-20
85Nashua-10
86Nashua-7
Ford, Ondra
86Cram/NWL-33
89AppFx/ProC-859
Ford, Randy
82Knoxvl-3
Ford, Rick
76BurlB
77BurlB
77Holyo
78Clinton
Ford, Russ
10Domino-45
11Helmar-43
12Sweet/Pin-34A
12Sweet/Pin-34B
14CJ-83
14Piedmont/St-22
15CJ-83
E270/2
E286
E98
L1-115
M116
S74-21
S81-90
T201
T202
T205
T206
T213/blue
T214-10
T215/blue
T215/brown
Ford, Rusty
86Beaum-11
87LasVegas-9
88Wichita-41
Ford, Scott
86Lipscomb-12
Ford, Steve
90Yakima/Team-20VP/GM
Ford, Stewart
90Pulaski/Best-4
90Pulaski/ProC-3098
91Pulaski/ClBest-18
91Pulaski/ProC-3998
92Idaho/ProC-3505
Ford, Ted
71OPC-612R
71T-612R
72OPC-24
72T-24
73OPC-299
73T-299
74OPC-617
74T-617
93Rang/Keeb-11
Fordyce, Brook
89Kingspt/Star-10
89Star/IISingl-191
90Clmbia/PCPII-4
90Columbia/GS-22
90SALAS/Star-30
91ClBest/Gold-10
91ClBest/Singl-220
91Clmbia/PCPII-7
91FSLAS/ProC-FSL31
91StLucie/ClBest-11
91StLucie/ProC-714
91UD-64
92B-56
92Bingham/ProC-520
92Bingham/SB-57
92ClBest-25
92ProC/Tomorrow-285
92Sky/AASingl-24
92UD/ML-287
93B-333
93FExcel/ML-73
93T-701M
93T/Gold-701M
94B-540
94SigRook-36
94T-785
94T/Gold-785
Fore, Chuck L.
78Syrac
79Syrac/TCMA-14
80Knoxvl/TCMA-1
81Syrac-3
81Syrac/Team-8
83Richm-6
Foreman, Dave
87Anchora-40STAT
Foreman, Francis
N172
Foreman, Toby
91Belling/ClBest-21
91Belling/ProC-3657
Forer, Daniel Lynn
81VeroB-5
Forgeur, Freddy
79QuadC-21
Forgione, Chris
85Visalia-9
86Visalia-9
87Kenosha-22
88OrlanTw/Best-16
Fornasiere, Bob
92MN-20
Forney, Jeff
87Tampa-25
88Cedar/ProC-1151
88MidwLAS/GS-10
90Chatt/GS-13
Forney, Rick
92Kane/ClBest-22
92Kane/ProC-84
92Kane/Team-9
92MidwLAS/Team-10
94B-327
94FExcel-4
Fornieles, Mike
54T-154
55B-266
57T-116
58T-361
59T-473
60T-54
61T-113
62T-512
62T/St-12
63T-28
79TCMA-132
91Crown/Orio-141
94T/Arc54-154
Forrest, Chris
87StPete-15
89Boise/ProC-2001
Forrest, Joel
87Macon-3
88Augusta/ProC-381
88Watertn/Pucko-5
Forrester, Gary
89Salem/Team-11
90Bakers/Cal-251
91QuadC/ProC-2635
Forrester, Tom
86BirmB/Team-15

87Hawaii-7
88BirmB/Best-12
89Vanco/CMC-20
89Vanco/ProC-597
90BirmDG/Best-11
90SoBend/Best-19
90SoBend/GS-4
Forry, Dewey
75Water
Forsch, Ken
71OPC-102R
71T-102R
72OPC-394
72T-394
73OPC-589
73T-589
74OPC-91
74T-91
75OPC-357
75T-357
75T/M-357
76OPC-357
76SSPC-48
76T-357
77BurgChef-4
77OPC-78
77T-21
77T-632M
78BK/Ast-8
78T-181
79Ho-51
79OPC-276
79T-534
80OPC-337
80T-642
81D-141
81F-52
81OPC-269
81T-269
81T/Tr-764
82D-393
82F-459
82F/St-221
82OPC-385
82T-276TL
82T-385
82T/St-159
83D-164
83F-89
83F/St-17M
83F/St-4M
83OPC-346
83T-625
84D-280
84F-517
84Nes/792-765
84OPC-193
84Smok/Cal-9
84T-765
84T/St-237
85F-301
85OPC-141
85Smok/Cal-8
85T-442
86F-155
86Mother/Ast-14
90Swell/Great-37
Forsch, Robert
75OPC-51
75T-51
75T/M-51
76OPC-426
76SSPC-294
76T-426
77T-381
77T-632M
78Ho-3
78K-50
78T-58
79K-38
79OPC-117
79T-230
80OPC-279
80T-535
81Coke
81D-69
81F-537
81OPC-140
81T-140
82D-91
82F-112
82F/St-22
82OPC-34
82T-186TL
82T-775
82T/St-90
83D-64
83F-5
83F/St-16M
83F/St-4M
83OPC-197
83OPC/St-289
83T-415
83T/St-289
84D-168
84F-322
84F-639M
84Nes/792-5HL
84Nes/792-75
84OPC-75
84T-5HL
84T-75
84T/St-288A
85F-223
85OPC-137
85T-631
86D-353
86F-35
86KAS/Disc-6
86Schnucks-6
86Sf-129M
86T-322
86T-66M
87D-540
87F-295
87F/AwardWin-14
87F/St-40
87Leaf-161
87OPC-257
87Sf-191
87Sf/TPrev-12M
87Smok/Cards-7
87T-257
87T/St-47
88D-111
88F-33
88Panini/St-384
88S-264
88Sf-199
88Smok/Card-5
88T-586
89D-118
89Lennox/Ast-23
89Mother/Ast-11
89S-525
89T-163
90F-231
90F/Can-231
90PublInt/St-95
90S-219
92Card/McDon/Pac-51
Forster, Guillermo
73Cedar
74Cedar
Forster, Terry
72T-539
73OPC-129
73T-129
74OPC-310
74T-310
74T/St-153
75Ho-14
75OPC-137
75OPC-313LL
75T-137
75T-313LL
75T/M-137
75T/M-313LL
76Ho-14
76Ho/Twink-14
76OPC-437
76SSPC-157
76T-437
77T-271
78SSPC/270-68
78T-347
79OPC-7
79T-23
80T-605
81Pol/Dodg-51
81T-104
82D-362
82F-4
82Pol/Dodg-51
82T-444
83D-453
83F-205
83Pol/Atl-51
83T-583
83T/Fold-4M
83T/Tr-33
84F-178
84Nes/792-791
84OPC-109
84Pol/Atl-51
84T-791
85F-324
85Ho/Braves-8
85OPC-248
85Pol/Atl-51
85T-248
86D-432
86F-514
86F/Up-U42
86Leaf-202
86Smok/Cal-23
86T-363
86T/Tr-37T
87F-80
87T-652
90Target-250
Forster, Tom
N172
N284
Fortaleza, Ray
84Greens-2
Fortenberry, Jim
86Clearw-8
86FSLAS-16
87Reading-21
Fortinberry, Bill
80Port-12
Fortugno, Tim
86Cram/NWL-115
88Reading/ProC-876
89Reno/Cal-244
89Stockton/Star-7
90Beloit/Best-7
90Beloit/Star-8
91AA/LineD-182
91ElPaso/LineD-182
91ElPaso/ProC-2741
92D/Rook-38
92Edmon/ProC-3535
92Edmon/SB-157
92Sky/AAASingl-78
93D-299
93F-572
93Ottawa/ProC-2429
93S-262
93StCl-231
93StCl/1stDay-231
93T-320
93T/Gold-320
93Ultra-163
Fortuna, Mike
89Salem/Star-8
89Welland/Pucko-12
Fortune, Steve
79Elmira-9
Fosnow, Gerald
65T-529
Foss, Larry
91WIZMets-122
Fossa, Dick
88CalLgAS-24
Fossas, Tony
80Ashvl-7
81Tulsa-16
83Tulsa-3
84OKCty-12
85OKCty-10
86Edmon-10
87Edmon-20
88OkCty/CMC-9
88OkCty/ProC-34
89Denver/CMC-3
89Denver/ProC-55
90D-457
90F-323
90F/Can-323
90OPC-34
90Pol/Brew-36
90S-567
90T-34
91Leaf-276
91OPC-747
91S-634
91T-747
92D-645
92OPC-249
92RedSox/Dunkin-11
92S-389
92StCl-144
92T-249
92T/Gold-249
92T/GoldWin-249
92UD-503
92USPlayC/RedSox-4D
92USPlayC/RedSox-8H
93D-195
93F-180
93Pac/Spanish-358
93Rang/Keeb-151
93StCl-247
93StCl/1stDay-247
94Pac/Cr-55
94StCl-26
94StCl/1stDay-26
94StCl/Gold-26
94T-378
94T/Gold-378
Fosse, Ray
69T-244R
70OPC-184
70T-184
71K-39
71MD
71MLB/St-366
71OPC-125
71T-125
71T/Coins-42
71T/S-51
71T/Super-51
71T/tatt-16
72OPC-470
72T-470
72T/Post-4
73K-18
73OPC-226
73T-226
73T/Lids-17
74OPC-420
74T-420
75OPC-486
75T-486
75T/M-486
76OPC-554
76SSPC-500
76T-554
76T/Tr-554T
77BurgChef-62
77Ho-122
77Ho/Twink-122
77OPC-39
77Pep-17
77T-267
78Ho-57
78T-415
79T-51
80T-327
Foster, Alan
69T-266R
70OPC-369
70T-369
71MLB/St-367
71OPC-207
71T-207
72OPC-521
72T-521
73OPC-543
73T-543
74OPC-442
74T-442
75OPC-296
75T-296
75T/M-296
76OPC-266
76SSPC-115
76T-266
77T-108
81TCMA-465
85SpokAT/Cram-6
90Target-251
Foster, Andrew
(Rube)
74Laugh/Black-35
80Perez/HOF-174
86Negro/Frit-18
87Negro/Dixon-25
88Conlon/NegAS-4
88Negro/Duques-1
90Negro/Star-16
91Conlon/Sport-138
94TedW-105
Foster, Bob
79LodiD-17
Foster, Bryan
88Beloit/GS-12
89Stockton/Best-21
89Stockton/Cal-171
89Stockton/ProC-393
89Stockton/Star-20
Foster, Bud
46Remar-15
47Remar-9
47Signal
48Signal
49Remar
Foster, Clifton
92SoOreg/ClBest-24
92SoOreg/ProC-3408
Foster, Doug
78Clinton
Foster, Edward C.
BF2-44
D327
D328-51
D329-61
D350/2-62
E121/120
E121/80
E122
E135-51
E270/2
M101/4-61
M101/5-62
M116
T201
W575
Foster, Edward Lee
M116
T206
Foster, Elmer
N172/ST
N338/2
N690
WG1-39
Foster, George
71OPC-276R
71T-276R
72OPC-256
72T-256
73OPC-202
73OPC-399
73T-399
74OPC-646
74T-646
75OPC-87
75T-87
75T/M-87
76Ho-106
76Icee
76OPC-179
76SSPC-44
76T-179
77BurgChef-201
77Ho-40
77Ho/Twink-40
77K-1
77OPC-120
77OPC-3LL
77Pepsi-48
77T-347
77T-3LL
78Ho-2
78K-10
78OPC-2LL
78OPC-3LL
78OPC-70
78Pep-10
78SSPC/270-113
78T-202LL
78T-203LL
78T-500
78Wiffle/Discs-24
79Ho-107
79K-32
79OPC-316
79T-2LL
79T-3LL
79T-600
80BK/PHR-15
80K-50
80OPC-209
80T-400
80T/S-24
80T/Super-24

81Coke
81D-65
81Drake-18
81F-202
81F-216
81F/St-41
81K-1
81OPC-200
81PermaGr/AS-4
81PermaGr/CC-9
81Sqt-2
81T-200
81T/HT
81T/SO-65
81T/St-159
82D-274
82Drake-13
82F-630M
82F-66
82F/St-12
82K-56
82KMart-32
82OPC-177IA
82OPC-336
82OPC-342AS
82Sqt-18
82T-342AS
82T-700
82T-701IA
82T/St-126
82T/St-40
82T/Tr-36T
83D-427
83D-6DK
83Drake-8
83F-542
83F/St-2M
83F/St-8M
83K-22
83OPC-80
83OPC/St-263
83T-80
83T/Fold-2M
83T/St-263
84D-312
84D/Champs-2
84F-584
84Nes/792-350
84OPC-350
84T-350
84T/Mets/Fan-3
84T/RD-20
84T/St-105
85D-603
85F-79
85FunFood/Pin-46
85Leaf-42
85OPC-170
85Pol/MetYank-M1
85T-170
85T/Mets/Fan-4
85T/RD-20
85T/St-99
86D-116
86F-80
86GenMills/Book-4M
86OPC-69
86Sf-126M
86Sf-131M
86Sf-139M
86Sf-68M
86T-680
86T/St-100
86Woolwth-11
89Pac/Leg-173
89Pac/SenLg-114
89T/SenLg-1
89TM/SenLg-119
89TM/SenLg-36
90EliteSenLg-112
90EliteSenLg-124
90Pac/Legend-72
90Swell/Great-97
91LineD-37
91MDA-8
91Swell/Great-112
91WIZMets-123
92AP/ASG-61
93Metallic-9
93TWill-29
93TWill/Mem-17
93TWill/POG-25M
93UD/ATH-53

Foster, Jim
94FExcel-5
94FExcel/1stY-1

Foster, John
82Wisco/Frit-19

Foster, Ken
81Wisco-16
82OrlanTw/B-18
83OrlanTw-11
86SanJose-7

Foster, Kevin
89Rockford/Team-7
90WPalmB/Star-7
91Sumter/ClBest-4
91Sumter/ProC-2327
92WPalmB/ProC-2083
94StCl/Team-236
94T-786
94T/Gold-786

Foster, Lamar
89Martins/Star-11
90Martins/ProC-3179
91Batavia/ClBest-8
91Batavia/ProC-3490

Foster, Leo
74OPC-607R
74T-607R
75OPC-418
75T-418
75T/M-418
75Tidew/Team-11
77T-458
78T-229
91WIZMets-124

Foster, Lindsay
87Myrtle-15
88Dunedin/Star-6
89Canton/Best-15
89Canton/ProC-1304
89Canton/Star-6
90Kinston/Team-14
91AA/LineD-58
91BirmB/LineD-58
91BirmB/ProC-1461
92BirmB/ProC-2591
92BirmB/SB-82

Foster, Paul
87Fayette-16
88Lakeland/Star-11

Foster, Randy
87Oneonta-21
88PrWill/Star-10

Foster, Roy
71MLB/St-368
71OPC-107
71T-107
72OPC-329
72T-329
72T/Cloth-12
89Tidew/Candl-2

Foster, Russ
91Pac/SenLg-75

Foster, Stephen
(Steve)
88Billings/ProC-1818
89Cedar/Best-2
89Cedar/ProC-936
89Cedar/Star-7
89Star/IISingl-194
90Chatt/GS-14
91AA/LineD-158
91Chatt/LineD-158
91Chatt/ProC-1953
92Classic/I-35
92D-420RR
92F/Up-80
92Nashvl/ProC-1827
92OPC-528
92ProC/Tomorrow-216
92StCl-826
92T-528
92T/91Debut-58
92T/Gold-528
92T/GoldWin-528
93D-666
93F-33
93S-284
93T-193
93T/Gold-193
93Ultra-328
94Pac/Cr-147

Foster, Willie
74Laugh/Black-5
90Negro/Star-24

Fothergill, Robert
(Bob)
28Exh-45
81Tiger/Detroit-85
91Conlon/Sport-72

Foucault, Steve
74OPC-294
74T-294
75OPC-283
75T-283
75T/M-283
76OPC-303
76SSPC-252
76T-303
77T-459
78BK/T-10
78T-68
92Beloit/ClBest-29CO
92Beloit/ProC-423
93Rang/Keeb-152

Foulk, Leon
52Park-15

Fournier, Bruce
80Ogden-16
80WHave-5
81WHave-10

Fournier, Jacques F.
21Exh-50
21Exh-51
25Exh-11
26Exh-10
90Target-252
92Conlon/Sport-541
D327
D328-52
D329-62
D350/2-63
E120
E135-52
M101/4-62
M101/5-63
T207
V100
W573

Foussianes, George
83BirmB-11
85Tulsa-6
90BirmDG/Best-12

Foutz, Dave
90Target-253
N172/BC
N284
N300/unif
N370
N566-181
Scrapps

Fowble, Greg
87AZ/Pol-2
88AZ/Pol-3

Fowler, Dick
49B-171
50B-214
52B-190
52T-210
Exh47

Fowler, Don
81Tacoma-14
82Tacoma-2
84Colum-6
84Colum/Pol-10
84Nashvl-7
89Watlo/ProC-1792
89Watlo/Star-7

Fowler, Dwayne
91Pulaski/ClBest-19
91Pulaski/ProC-3999

Fowler, Eddie
89Wythe/Star-10

Fowler, J. Art
55T-3
55T/DH-80
56Kahn
56T-47
56T/Pin-55
57T-233
59T-508
62T-128
63T-454
64T-349
73OPC-323CO
73T-323C
74OPC-379CO
74T-379C
90Target-254
93Rang/Keeb-153CO
94TedW-106

Fowler, John
89Bluefld/Star-9
90Wausau/Best-21
90Wausau/ProC-2134
90Wausau/Star-8

Fowler, Mike
88Durham/Star-6
89Durham/Star-11
89Durham/Team-11

Fowler, Yale
89GreatF-13
90Yakima/Team-32

Fowlkes, Alan Kim
81Shrev-7
83D-46
83F-259
83T-543
84Cram/PCL-16
86Edmon-11
88Reno/Cal-268

Fowlkes, David
77Watlo

Fox, Andy
89LittleSun-8
90Foil/Best-263
90Greens/Best-16
90Greens/ProC-2668
90Greens/Star-1
90ProC/Singl-825
90SALAS/Star-6
90T/TVYank-43
91CLAS/ProC-CAR30
91ClBest/Singl-132
91PrWill/ClBest-17
91PrWill/ProC-1433
92PrWill/ClBest-2
92PrWill/ProC-155

Fox, Blane
87Lakeland-22
88FSLAS/Star-36
88Lakeland/Star-12
89ColMud/Best-14
89ColMud/ProC-143
89ColMud/Star-9
91AA/LineD-461
91NewBrit/LineD-461
91NewBrit/ProC-364

Fox, Chad
92Classic/DP-100
92Princet/ClBest-13
92Princet/ProC-3081
93FExcel/ML-18

Fox, Charlie
71OPC-517MG
71T-517MG
71Ticket/Giant-3MG
72OPC-129MG
72T-129MG
73OPC-252MG
73T-252MG
74OPC-78MG
74T-78MG

Fox, Dan
89Kenosha/ProC-1085
90Kenosha/Best-29TR
90Kenosha/Star-27TR
91Kenosha/ClBest-21TR

Fox, Eric
85Anchora-11
87Chatt/Best-16
88Vermont/ProC-945
89Huntsvl/Best-9
90AAASingl/ProC-154
90ProC/Singl-592
90Tacoma/CMC-15
90Tacoma/ProC-107
91AAA/LineD-533
91Tacoma/LineD-533
91Tacoma/ProC-2317
92D/Rook-39
92Huntsvl/ProC-3961
92S/RookTr-88T
92Tacoma/SB-532
93D-287
93F-663
93Pac/Spanish-566
93Pinn-567
93S-352
93Select-313
93StCl-131
93StCl/1stDay-131
93T-46
93T/Gold-46
93UD-781
93USPlayC/Rook-2C
93Ultra-605

Fox, Ervin
(Pete)
34G-70
35BU-195
35G-8F
35G-9F
38G-242
38G-266
39PlayBall-80
40PlayBall-43
81Tiger/Detroit-110
91Conlon/Sport-197
R309/2
R312/M
R313
R314
V355-30
WG8-18

Fox, Howard
(Howie)
45Playball-41
49Eureka-84
50B-80
51B-180
52B-125
52T-209
53B/Col-158
53T-22
54Esskay
54T-246
91Crown/Orio-142
91T/Arc53-22
94T/Arc54-246

Fox, Jacob Nelson
(Nellie)
51B-232
52B-21
52BR
52Dix-53
52Hawth/Pin-4
52RM-AL9
52StarCal-87CM
52StarCal/L-73G
53B/Col-18
53NB
53RM-AL5
54B-6
54RH
54RM-AL3
54Wilson
55B-33
55RM-AL4
56T-118
56YellBase/Pin-11
57Swift-7
57T-38
58T-400
58T-479AS
59Armour-9
59Bz
59T-30
59T-408M
59T-556AS
60Armour-11
60Bz-25
60NuCard-72
60T-100
60T-429M
60T-555AS
60T/tatt-16
61NuCard-472
61P-20
61T-30
61T-477MVP
61T-570AS
62Exh
62J-47
62P-47
62P/Can-47
62Salada-12
62Shirriff-12
62T-73
62T/St-24
62T/bucks
63Exh
63J-36
63P-36
63T-525
64T-205

64T-81M
64T/S-13
64Wheat/St-16
65T-485P/CO
74Laugh/ASG-58
75OPC-197MVP
75T-197MVP
75T/M-197MVP
76Laugh/Jub-24
79TCMA-15
80Laugh/FFeat-7
80Pac/Leg-68
83Kaline-20
83MLBPA/Pin-8
86Sf/Dec-37M
87Nestle/DT-13
88Grenada-25
88Pac/Leg-57
89Kodak/WSox-2M
91T/Arc53-331
92Bz/Quadra-17
92Ziploc-9
93AP/ASG-139
93Rang/Keeb-41CO
94TedW-20
Exh47
PM10/Sm-53

Fox, Kenneth
86James-7

Fox, Mike
87StPete-11
89ArkTr/GS-5

Fox, Nickie
94TedW-96

Fox, Terry
61T-459
62T-196
63T-44
64T-387
65T-576
66T-472
67OPC-181
67T-181

Foxen, Bill
M116
S74-61
T202
T205

Foxover, David
91Daikyo/Fut-4

Foxx, James Emory
(Jimmie)
29Exh/4-27
31Exh/4-28
32Orbit/num-18
32Orbit/un-20
33DH-17
33DL-21
33Exh/4-14
33G-154
33G-29
34DS-64
34Exh/4-14
34G-1
34Ward's/Pin-3
35BU-144
35BU-28
35Exh/4-14
35G-1B
35G-2B
35G-6B
35G-7B
35Wheat
36Exh/4-9
36Wheat
37Exh/4-9
37OPC-106
38Dix
38Exh/4-9
38G-249
38G-273
38ONG/Pin-9
38Wheat
39Exh
39Wheat-5
40PlayBall-133
40Wheat-3
41DP-60
41PlayBall-13
41Wheat-14
50Callahan
50W576-31
60F-53
61F-28
61GP-22
72F/FFeat-16
72Laugh/GF-19
73F/Wild-41
74Laugh/ASG-35
76Rowe-6
76Shakey-59
77Galasso-184
77Galasso-57
77Shakey-13
80Laugh/3/4/5-21
80Laugh/FFeat-23
80Marchant/HOF-12
80Pac/Leg-16
80Perez/HOF-59
80SSPC/HOF
81Conlon-80
83D/HOF-13
85CircK-7
86BLChew-7
86Conlon/1-12
86Sf/Dec-2
87Nestle/DT-11
88Conlon/5-10
88Conlon/AmAS-9
90BBWit-61
90Swell/Great-101
91Conlon/Sport-2
91Conlon/Sport-303
91LineD-44
91Swell/Great-143
92Conlon/Col-16
92Conlon/Sport-526
92Conlon/Sport-560
93AP/ASG-100
93AP/ASG24K-34G
93Conlon-917
93TWill-123
93UD/ATH-54
94Conlon-1083
94Conlon-1152
94TedW/500-5
PR1-10
R300
R302-153
R303/A
R303/B
R305
R306
R308-153
R310
R311/
R311/Gloss
R312/M
R314
R315-A7
R315-B7
R316
R326-12A
R326-12B
R328-23
R337
R342-12
V300
V351B-15
V353-29
V353-85
V354-58
V355-47
V94-16
W517-21
WG8-19

Foy, Joe
66T-456R
67CokeCap/RedSox-6
67T-331
67T/Test/RSox-6
68CokeCap/RedSox-6
68Dexter-32
68T-387
69MB-84
69MLB/St-58
69OPC-93
69T-93
69T/DE-22
69T/S-22
69T/St-184
69T/decal
70MLB/St-75
70OPC-138
70T-138
71MLB/St-537
71OPC-706
71Pol/SenP-4
71T-706
72MB-106
81TCMA-321
91WIZMets-125

Foytack, Paul
53Tiger/Glen-7
57T-77
58T-282
59T-233
60T-364
61P-62
61T-171
62T-349
63T-327
64T-149
81TCMA-323

Frailing, Ken
74OPC-605R
74T-605R
75OPC-436
75T-436
75T/M-436
76SSPC-305
78Knoxvl

Fralick, Bob
90Miami/I/Star-28CO
90Miami/II/Star-27CO
91Miami/ClBest-30CO
91Miami/ProC-424

Frame, Michael
(Mike)
89GreatF-2
90Bakers/Cal-236

France, Todd
86Stockton-7TR
87Stockton-5

Franceschi, Sean
90Eugene/GS-7

Franchi, Kevin
86Macon-9
87Salem-1

Franchuk, Orv
90Boise/ProC-3332CO
91Boise/ProC-3901CO

Francis, Earl
61T-54
62T-252
63IDL-7
63T-303
64T-117
78TCMA-226

Francis, Harry
81Redwd-13
82Holyo-20
83Nashua-12

Francis, Scott
91Pulaski/ClBest-22
91Pulaski/ProC-4000
92Macon/ProC-262

Francis, Todd
83Wausau/Frit-14

Francis, Tommy
83Miami-23

Francisco, Rene
89Geneva/ProC-1862
90Peoria/Team-17

Francisco, Vicente
91SoOreg/ClBest-22
91SoOreg/ProC-3854
92Madis/ClBest-25
92Madis/ProC-1241

Franco, John
82Albuq-2
84F/X-39
84Wichita/Rock-19
85D-164
85F-536
85F/St-120
85T-417
86D-487
86F-178
86F/St-39
86KayBee-13
86Leaf-240
86OPC-54
86Sf-156
86T-54
86T/St-142
86T/Tatt-7M
86TexGold-31
87Classic-100
87D-289
87D/AAS-22
87F-202
87F-631M
87F/BB-17
87F/LL-18
87F/Lim-14
87F/Slug-14
87F/St-41
87Kahn-31
87Leaf-178
87OPC-305
87RedFoley/St-116
87Sf-192
87Sf/TPrev-4M
87T-305
87T/Mini-5
87T/St-138
88D-123
88D/AS-53
88D/Best-54
88F-234
88F-627M
88F/Mini-74
88F/RecSet-12
88F/St-84
88Kahn/Reds-31
88KennerFig-37
88Leaf-79
88Nestle-8
88OPC-341
88Panini/St-271
88S-535
88Sf-195
88T-730
88T/Big-232
88T/Coins-41
88T/Mini-47
88T/St-142
88T/St/Backs-32
88T/UK-24
89B-301
89Cadaco-19
89D-233
89D/Best-166
89F-162
89F/Heroes-14
89F/LL-13
89Kahn/Reds-31
89KennerFig-45
89OPC-290
89Panini/St-66
89RedFoley/St-45
89S-575
89S/HotStar-97
89Sf-176
89T-290
89T/Coins-12
89T/DH-23
89T/LJN-28
89T/Mini-9
89T/St-136
89T/St-4
89T/St/Backs-65
89T/UK-27
89UD-407
89Woolwth-12
90B-128
90Classic-86
90Classic/Up-19
90D-124
90D-14DK
90D/BestNL-92
90D/SuperDK-14DK
90F-419
90F/Can-419
90F/Up-U35
90F/WaxBox-C7
90HotPlay/St-13
90Kahn/Mets-31
90Leaf-356
90OPC-120
90Panini/St-244
90PublInt/St-258
90PublInt/St-29
90RedFoley/St-33
90S-273
90S/100St-49
90S/McDon-7
90S/Tr-15T
90Sf-138
90T-120
90T/Big-264
90T/HeadsUp-11
90T/Mini-54
90T/St-144
90T/TVMets-11
90T/Tr-32T
90UD-139
90UD/Ext-709
90USPlayC/AS-7H
91B-475
91Classic/200-125
91Classic/I-65
91D-322
91F-147
91F-712M
91Kahn/Mets-31
91Kenner-19
91Leaf-437
91Leaf/Stud-203
91OPC-407AS
91OPC-510
91Panini/St-87
91Panini/Top15-81
91S-14
91S/100SS-29
91StCl-22
91T-407AS
91T-510
91UD-290
91Ultra-217
91WIZMets-126
92B-546
92D-186
92F-504
92L-174
92L/BlkGold-174
92Mets/Kahn-31
92OPC-690
92OPC/Premier-73
92Pinn-64
92Pinn/TeamP-12M
92S-605
92S/100SS-57
92S/Impact-61
92StCl-565
92Studio-64
92T-690
92T/Gold-690
92T/GoldWin-690
92T/Kids-13
92TripleP-182
92TripleP-64M
92UD-514
92Ultra-529
93B-298
93D-146
93F-471
93L-112
93Mets/Kahn-31
93OPC-68
93Pac/Spanish-197
93Pinn-216
93Pinn-310HH
93S-139
93Select-167
93Select/ChasS-11
93StCl-316
93StCl/1stDay-316
93Studio-70
93T-25
93T/Finest-191
93T/FinestRef-191
93T/Gold-25
93TripleP-90
93UD-321
93Ultra-73
94B-184
94D-98
94F-561
94Flair-196
94L-144
94OPC-256
94Pac/Cr-400
94Pinn-368
94S-122
94S/GoldR-122
94StCl-339
94StCl/1stDay-339
94StCl/Gold-339
94T-481
94T/Finest-170
94T/FinestRef-170
94T/Gold-481
94UD-323

Franco, Julio
80Penin/B-21
80Penin/C-17
82OkCty-11
83D-525

83T/Tr-34
83Wheat/Ind-13
84D-216
84F-542
84F/St-111
84Nes/792-48
84OPC-48
84T-48
84T/RD-13M
84T/St-379
84Wheat/Ind-14
85D-94
85F-448
85Leaf-213
85OPC-237
85Polar/Ind-14
85T-237
85T/RD-19M
85T/St-245
86D-216
86F-586
86F/LL-13
86F/LimEd-16
86F/Mini-115
86F/Slug-9
86F/St-40
86KayBee-14
86Leaf-93
86OPC-391
86OhHenry-14
86Sf-33
86T-391
86T/St-211
86T/Tatt-1M
87D-131
87D/OD-111
87F-251
87F/LL-19
87F/Lim-15
87F/Mini-39
87F/St-42
87Gator-14
87Leaf-131
87OPC-160
87RedFoley/St-1
87Sf-84
87Sf/TPrev-3M
87Stuart-18M
87T-160
87T/St-210
88Classic/Red-187
88D-10DK
88D-156
88D/Best-168
88D/DKsuper-10DK
88F-609
88F/AwardWin-13
88F/BB/AS-11
88F/BB/MVP-15
88F/Excit-14
88F/Hottest-11
88F/LL-12
88F/Mini-19
88F/RecSet-13
88F/St-19
88F/TL-8
88FanSam-10
88Gator-14
88Grenada-66
88KennerFig-38
88Leaf-10DK
88Leaf-71
88OPC-49
88Panini/St-77
88RedFoley/St-25
88S-60
88S/YS/II-7
88Sf-58
88T-683
88T/Big-135
88T/St-207
89B-228
89Cadaco-20
89D-310
89D/Best-32
89D/Tr-31
89F-404
89F/AS-5
89F/Up-64
89KMart/Lead-14
89Master/Discs-11
89Mother/R-3
89OPC-55
89Panini/St-325
89S-11
89S/HotStar-36
89S/Mast-29
89S/Tr-35
89Sf-149
89Smok/R-9
89T-398AS
89T-55
89T/Big-288
89T/DH-2
89T/St-208
89T/St/Backs-4
89T/Tr-34T
89UD-186
89UD/Ext-793
90B-497
90Classic-67
90D-142
90D-701AS
90D/BestAL-112
90D/Bon/MVP-BC14
90D/Learning-17
90F-296
90F/BB-8
90F/Can-296
90KMart/CBatL-11
90KMart/SS-18
90Leaf-205
90Mother/Rang-10
90OPC-386AS
90OPC-550
90Panini/St-163
90Panini/St-201
90PublInt/St-285
90PublInt/St-409
90RedFoley/St-34
90S-160
90S/100St-84
90S/McDon-3
90Sf-158
90T-386AS
90T-550
90T/Ames-21
90T/Big-205
90T/DH-24
90T/Gloss22-14
90T/Gloss60-35
90T/Mini-37
90T/St-159AS
90T/St-243
90T/TVAS-2
90UD-103
90UD-82TC
90USPlayC/AS-JK
90Windwlk/Discs-6
91B-265
91B-368SLUG
91Cadaco-21
91D-192
91F-285
91Leaf-228
91Leaf/Stud-123
91Mother/Rang-10
91OPC-387AS
91OPC-775
91Panini/FrSt-253
91Panini/St-210
91S-392AS
91S-493
91S/100SS-84
91Seven/3DCoin-6T
91StCl-173
91StCl/Member*-15
91T-387AS
91T-775
91UD-227
91UD/SilSlug-SS1
91USPlayC/AS-6H
91Ultra-348
92B-206
92CJ/DII-27
92Classic/Game200-157
92Classic/I-36
92D-741
92D/DK-DK4
92F-303
92F-690LL
92F/ASIns-18
92French-3
92L-119
92L/BlkGold-119
92MSA/Ben-9
92Mother/Rang-10
92OPC-490
92OPC/Premier-15
92Panini-145
92Panini-76
92Pinn-150
92Pinn/RookI-5M
92S-108
92S-432AS
92S/100SS-38
92StCl-440
92StCl/Dome-52
92Studio-241
92T-398AS
92T-490
92T/Gold-398AS
92T/Gold-490
92T/GoldWin-398AS
92T/GoldWin-490
92T/Kids-129
92T/McDonB-27
92TripleP-83
92UD-241
92USPlayC/Ace-1D
92Ultra-131
93B-657
93D-451
93F-320
93Flair-279
93L-27
93OPC-73
93Pac/Beisbol-13M
93Pac/Beisbol-14
93Pac/Beisbol-3M
93Pac/Spanish-310
93Pac/SpanishP-13
93Panini-82
93Pinn-104
93Rang/Keeb-405
93S-394
93Select-58
93StCl-651
93StCl/1stDay-651
93StCl/Rang-25
93Studio-103
93T-670
93T/Finest-161
93T/FinestRef-161
93T/Gold-670
93TripleP-148
93UD-656
93UD/SP-192
93Ultra-277
94B-399
94D-481
94F-306
94Finest-278
94L-364
94OPC-142
94Pac/Cr-615
94Panini-126
94Pinn-520
94S-413
94StCl/Team-147
94Studio-205
94T-260
94T/Gold-260
94UD-57
94UD/ElecD-57
94UD/SP-191
94Ultra-335

Franco, Matthew
(Matt)
89CharWh/Best-11
89CharWh/ProC-1748
89SALAS/GS-14
90Peoria/Team-11
91ClBest/Singl-134
91WinSalem/ClBest-19
91WinSalem/ProC-2836
92ChalK/SB-155
92CharlK/ProC-2779
94FExcel-164

Francois, Manny
85VeroB-5
87VeroB-11
88SanAn/Best-14
89SanAn/Best-2
90Canton/Best-8
90Canton/ProC-1298

Francona, John
(Tito)
57T-184
58T-316
59T-268
60Kahn
60T-260M
60T-30
60T/tatt-17
61Kahn
61P-64
61T-503
61T/St-134
62Exh
62J-40
62Kahn
62P-40
62P/Can-40
62Salada-15
62Shirriff-15
62Sugar-9
62T-97
62T/St-34
63Exh
63F-12
63J-67
63P-67
63Sugar-9
63T-248
63T-392M
64T-583
65OPC-256
65T-256
66OPC-163
66T-163
67T-443
68CokeCap/Brave-2
68T-527
69MB-85
69T-398
69T/St-4
70MLB/St-257
70T-663
72MB-107
78TCMA-205
78TCMA-231
85T-134FS
89Pac/Leg-133
89Swell-76
91Crown/Orio-143
Exh47
WG9-29

Francona, Terry
80Memphis-13
82D-627
82Expo/Hygrade-7
82F-188
82Hygrade
82OPC-118R
82OPC/Post-19
82T-118R
82Zeller-11
82Zeller-5
83D-592
83F-281
83OPC-267
83OPC/St-321
83Stuart-14
83T-267
83T/St-321
84D-463
84Expo/PostC-9
84F-275
84Nes/792-496
84OPC-89
84Stuart-18
84T-496
85D-132
85F-398
85Leaf-245
85OPC-258
85T-134FS
85T-578
85T/St-88
86D-401
86F-248
86F/Up-U43
86Gator-16
86Iowa-11
86Leaf-191
86OPC-374
86T-374
86T/St-80
86T/Tr-38T
87D/OD-193
87F-564
87Kahn-10
87OPC-294
87T-785
87T/Tr-34T
88ColoSp/CMC-20
88ColoSp/ProC-1541
88S-297
88T-686
89Pol/Brew-30
89S-597
89T-31
89T/Tr-35T
89UD-536
90Louisvl/LBC-16
90OPC-214
90Pol/Brew-30
90S-216
90T-214
90T/TVCard-48
90UD-180
92SoBend/ClBest-24MG
92SoBend/ProC-193MG

Franek, Ken
88CalLgAS-49

Franjul, Miguel
78Clinton
79LodiD-15

Frankhouse, Fred
33G-131
34DS-62
35BU-75
35G-2E
35G-4E
35G-7E
39PlayBall-70
90Target-255
92Conlon/Sport-498
93Conlon-725
94Conlon-1110
V354-19

Franklin, Elliott
76BurlB

Franklin, Glen
80Memphis-10
82Water-17
83Indianap-24

Franklin, Jay
89Butte/SP-17
90Gaston/Best-11
90Gaston/ProC-2516
90Gaston/Star-9
92Gaston/ProC-2245

Franklin, Jeff
78Wausau

Franklin, Micah
90Kgsport/Best-7
90Kgsport/Star-8
91Pittsfld/ClBest-12
91Pittsfld/ProC-3428
92Billings/ProC-3367
93FExcel/ML-19

Franklin, Tony
76Indianap-23
79RochR-7
90Saraso/Star-26MG
91AA/LineD-74MG
91BirmB/LineD-74MG
91BirmB/ProC-1469MG
92BirmB/ProC-2598
92BirmB/SB-99MG

Franko, Kris
94FExcel-290

Franko, Phil
82Wisco/Frit-18
83Visalia/Frit-5

Franks, Herman
45Parade*-56
52T-385
65OPC-32MG
65T-32MG
66T-537MG
67OPC-116MG
67T-116MG
68T-267MG
77T-518MG
78SSPC/270-268MG
78T-234MG
79T-551MG
90Target-256
Rawl

Frascatore, John
91Hamil/ClBest-3
91Hamil/ProC-4033
92Savan/ClBest-8
92Savan/ProC-655

Fraser, Chick
WG3-19

Fraser, Gretchen
52Wheat*
Fraser, Ron
85Miami-5CO
91Miami/Bumble-6CO
92T/DQ-33CO
92T/Tr-35TCO USA
92T/TrGold-35TCO USA
Fraser, Will
(Willie)
86PalmSp-13
86PalmSp/Smok-9
87D-40RR
87D/Rook-9
87F-646R
87F/Up-U33
87Leaf-40RR
87Sf/Rook-27
87Smok/Cal-7
87T/Tr-35T
88D-135
88F-490
88OPC-363
88S-394
88Smok/Angels-14
88T-363
88T/Big-183
89D-567
89F-478
89S-157
89T-679
89T/Big-272
89UD-613
90D-587
90F-133
90F/Can-133
90OPC-477
90PublInt/St-370
90S-358
90Smok/Angel-6
90T-477
90UD-85
91B-6
91D-379
91F-314
91OPC-784
91OPC/Premier-46
91S-96
91StCl-496
91T-784
91UD-699
92D-755
92Edmon/ProC-3536
92Edmon/SB-158
92S-721
92StCl-33
Frash, Roger
82Lynch-12
Frasier, Brad
89KS*-10
Frasier, Vic
93Conlon-982
Frassa, Bob
88Bristol/ProC-1867
Fraticelli, Carl
90Visalia/Cal-66
90Visalia/ProC-2160
Frattare, Lanny
93Pirate/Nation-11ANN
Frauenhoffer, Mike
90GreatF/SportP-21
Frazier, Brad
92Erie/ClBest-3
92Erie/ProC-1613
Frazier, Fred
74Syrac/Team-7
75IntAS/TCMA-15
75IntAS/TCMA-20
77SLCity
78Knoxvl
79Iowa/Pol-7
80Iowa/Pol-5
Frazier, George
76BurlB
77Holyo
79T-724R
80T-684R
81D-310
82D-584
82F-35
82T-349
83D-535
83F-379
83T-123
84D-591
84F-123
84F/X-40
84Nes/792-539
84OPC-139
84SevenUp-39
84T-539
84T/Tr-39
85D-167
85F-58
85OPC-19
85SevenUp-39
85T-19
86Cub/Unocal-10
86D-411
86F-370
86Gator-39
86T-431
87D-564
87F-539
87T-207
88D-443
88F-9
88S-332
88T-709
92Yank/WIZ80-63
Frazier, Joseph F.
(Joe)
55Hunter
55T-89
55T/DH-83
56T-141
60DF-22
75Tidew/Team-12
76SSPC-610MG
76T-531MG
77T-259MG
82Louisvl-8
91Crown/Orio-144
Frazier, Keith
45Centen-9
Frazier, Ken
81Clinton-18
Frazier, Lou
87Ashvl-7
88Osceola/Star-10
89ColMud/Best-12
89ColMud/ProC-145
89ColMud/Star-10
90London/ProC-1276
91AA/LineD-383
91London/LineD-383
91London/ProC-1889
92London/ProC-645
92London/SB-406
92Sky/AASingl-173
93F/Final-93
93FExcel/ML-171
93L-515
93Select/RookTr-49T
94D-524
94F-539
94Pac/Cr-381
94S-577
94StCl-517
94StCl/1stDay-517
94StCl/Gold-517
94T-192
94T/Gold-192
Frazier, Ron
88CapeCod/Sum-90
90Oneonta/ProC-3376
91Greens/ProC-3052
92PrWill/ClBest-21
92PrWill/ProC-140
94B-541
94FExcel-103
Frazier, Shawn
86Sumter/ProC-5
Frazier, Terance
89FresnoSt/Smok-9
92SoOreg/ClBest-8
92SoOreg/ProC-3423
93Modesto/ClBest-10
93Modesto/ProC-811
Freck
E254
Frederick, Charlie
84CharlO-3
85CharlO-29
87CharlO/WBTV-xx
Frederick, Chuck
90Eugene/GS-8
Frederick, Jim
89GA-9
Frederick, John
34G-47
85Woolwth-12
88Conlon/NatAS-6
90HOF/St-34
90Target-257
R315-A8
R315-B8
V354-85
Frederiksen, Kelly
90Gate/ProC-3359
90Gate/SportP-10
Fredlund, Jay
79Elmira-2
81Bristol-15
Fredrickson, Scott
90Spokane/SportP-16
91Waterlo/ClBest-4
91Waterlo/ProC-1251
92Sky/AASingl-278
92Wichita/ProC-3653
92Wichita/SB-629
93F/Final-28
93T-489
93T/Gold-489
Fredymond, Juan
85Durham-23
86Durham-11
87Durham-21
88Sumter/ProC-409
Freeberger, George
92Bluefld/ClBest-20
92Bluefld/ProC-2362
Freeburg, Larry
82Cedar-11
Freeburg, Ryan
92Bend/ClBest-4
93StCl/MurphyS-46
93T-616M
93T/Gold-616M
Freed, Daniel
(Dan)
88James/ProC-1899
89Rockford/Team-8
90FSLAS/Star-6
90Star/ISingl-8
90WPalmB/Star-8
91AA/LineD-253
91Harris/LineD-253
91Harris/ProC-619
92London/ProC-626
92London/SB-407
Freed, Roger
70OPC-477R
70T-477R
71MLB/St-176
71OPC-362R
71Phill/Arco-3
71T-362R
72OPC-69
72T-69
78T-504
79T-111
80T-418
91Crown/Orio-145
Freehan, Bill
63T-466R
64Det/Lids-6
64T-407
64T/Coins-87
64T/S-30
64T/St-68
64T/tatt
65T-390
65T/E-41
65T/trans-12
66OPC-145
66T-145
66T/RO-33
66T/RO-63
67CokeCap/Tiger-9
67OPC-48
67T-48
68Bz-2
68CokeCap/Tiger-9
68Dexter-33
68Kahn
68T-375AS
68T-470
68T/ActionSt-11AM
68T/G-11
69Kahn
69MB-86
69MLB/St-47
69MLBPA/Pin-6
69NTF
69OPC/DE-6
69T-390
69T-431AS
69T/DE-10
69T/S-18
69T/St-172
70K-57
70MB-7
70MLB/St-206
70OPC-335
70OPC-465AS
70T-335
70T-465AS
70T/CB
70T/S-7
70T/Super-7
71Bz
71Bz/Test-37
71K-31
71MD
71MLB/St-391
71OPC-575
71T-575
71T/Coins-38
71T/GM-22
71T/Greatest-22
71T/S-12
71T/Super-12
71T/tatt-12
72MB-108
72OPC-120
72T-120
73OPC-460
73T-460
73T/Comics-7
73T/Lids-18
73T/PinUps-7
74OPC-162
74T-162
74T/St-174
75Ho-120
75OPC-397
75T-397
75T/M-397
76Ho-6
76Ho/Twink-6
76OPC-540
76T-540
77BurgChef-94
77T-22
78TCMA-285
81Tiger/Detroit-72
83Kaline-33M
86Sf/Dec-49M
86Tiger/Sport-17
88Domino-5
88Pac/Leg-93
89Swell-106
93AP/ASG-150
WG10-27
Freehling, Rick
92Erie/ClBest-21
92Erie/ProC-1638
Freeland, Dean
85Beloit-15
86Clinton-9
87Shrev-5
88Shrev/ProC-1285
89Shrev/ProC-1852
90ElPaso/GS-12
91AA/LineD-558
91Jacks/LineD-558
91Tucson/ProC-2208
Freeman, Clem Jr.
82Water-6
83Tampa-12
Freeman, Herschel
(Hersh)
55B-290
56Kahn
56T-242
57Kahn
57Sohio/Reds-5
57T-32
58T-27
79TCMA-120
Freeman, James J.
(Buck)
T204
T206
WG2-20
Freeman, Jimmy
73OPC-610R
73T-610R
Freeman, John
N172
Freeman, Julius
N172
Freeman, LaVell
86ElPaso-11
87ElPaso-1
87TexLgAS-25
88AAA/ProC-12
88Denver/CMC-20
88Denver/ProC-1277
88TripleA/ASCMC-10
89Denver/CMC-14
89Denver/ProC-48
89UD/Ext-788
90AAASingl/ProC-391
90ElPasoATG/Team-31
90ProC/Singl-394
90T/89Debut-39
90Toledo/CMC-17
90Toledo/ProC-161
Freeman, Mark
59T-532
79TCMA-265
Freeman, Marty
86GlenF-5
Freeman, Marvin
86Reading-8
87D-576
87F-651R
87Maine-12
87Maine/TCMA-4
87Phill/TastyK-48
87Sf/Rook-4
87Sf/TPrev-6M
88Maine/CMC-4
88Maine/ProC-279
89D-631
89F-566
89S/HotRook-34
89ScranWB/CMC-1
89T-634
90AAASingl/ProC-295
90OPC-103
90ProC/Singl-228
90PublInt/St-236
90ScranWB/CMC-2
90ScranWB/ProC-593
90T-103
91Brave/Dubuq/Perf-9
91Brave/Dubuq/Stand-13
91D-619
91F/Up-U73
92Brave/LykePerf-11
92Brave/LykeStand-12
92D-603
92F-356
92L-110
92L/BlkGold-110
92OPC-68
92S-307
92StCl-264
92T-68
92T/Gold-68
92T/GoldWin-68
92UD-491
92USPlayC/Brave-2D
92USPlayC/Brave-5C
92Ultra-458
93Brave/LykePerf-9
93Brave/LykeStand-11
93D-662
93F-366
93L-11
93Pac/Spanish-4
93StCl-309
93StCl/1stDay-309
93StCl/Brave-24
93T-583
93T/Gold-583
93UD-519
93Ultra-304
94F-357
94Finest-327
94StCl/Team-106
94T-374
94T/Gold-374
94Ultra-479

Freeman, Pete
87Watertn-9
88Augusta/ProC-367
90Martins/ProC-3193
Freeman, Rick
89Elizab/Star-8
Freeman, Scott
90Yakima/Team-28
91ClBest/Singl-357
91VeroB/ClBest-7
91VeroB/ProC-768
92Bakers/Cal-11
Freer, Mike
91Osceola/ClBest-27TR
92Osceola/ClBest-27TR
Freese, Gene
55T-205
56T-46
58T-293
59T-472
60L-140
60MacGregor-8
60T-435
60T/tatt-18
61Kahn
61P-30
61T-175
61T/St-17
62J-118
62Kahn
62P-118
62P/Can-118
62Salada-137
62Shirriff-137
62T-205
62T/St-115
63F-33
63Kahn
63T-133
64T-266
65T-492
66T-319
81TCMA-304
Freese, George
55B-84
Fregin, Doug
82Toledo-27
Fregosi, Jim Jr.
85Spring-3
86StPete-9
87ArkTr-11
88ArkTr/GS-16MG
89WPalmB/Star-11
91BendB/ClBest-12CO
91BendB/ProC-3711CO
Fregosi, Jim
62T-209
63T-167
64Bz-22
64T-97
64T/Coins-128AS
64T/Coins-98
64T/S-18
64T/SU
64T/St-60
64T/tatt
65Bz-22
65OPC-210
65OldLond-25
65T-210
65T/E-39
65T/trans-13
66Bz-19
66OPC-5
66T-5
66T/RO-34
66T/RO-84
67Bz-19
67CokeCap/ALAS-24
67CokeCap/AS-8
67CokeCap/DodgAngel-30
67T-385
67T/Test/SU-9
68Dexter-34
68OPC-170
68T-170
68T-367AS
68T/ActionSt-9AM
68T/G-33
68T/Post-4
69Bz-28
69Citgo-7
69JB
69MB-87
69MLB/St-21
69MLBPA/Pin-7
69NTF
69T-365
69T/DE-5
69T/S-7
69T/St-144
69T/decal
69Trans-14
70K-36
70MB-8
70MLB/St-172
70T-570
70T/S-30
70T/Super-30
70Trans-14
71Bz
71Bz/Test-25
71JB
71K-64
71MD
71MLB/St-344
71OPC-360
71T-360
71T/Coins-136
71T/GM-16
71T/Greatest-16
71T/tatt-3
71T/tatt-3a
72MB-109
72OPC-115
72OPC-346KP
72T-115
72T-346KP
72T-755TR
72T/Cloth-13KP
73OPC-525
73T-525
74T-196
74T/St-234
75OPC-339
75T-339
75T/M-339
76OPC-635
76SSPC-262
76T-635
78T-323
78TCMA-170
79T-424MG
81F-274MG
81Louisvl-1MG
81T-663MG
83Louisvl/Riley-1MG
84Louisvl-1MG
85Louisvl-1MG
86Louisvl-1MG
86T/Tr-39T
87Coke/WS-10MG
87T-318MG
88Coke/WS-7MG
88T-714MG
89Smok/Angels-3
89T-414MG
91MDA-15
91T/Tr-43TMG
91WIZMets-127
92OPC-669MG
92Phill/Med-13MG
92T-669MG
92T/Gold-669MG
92T/GoldWin-669MG
93Phill/Med-14MG
93Rang/Keeb-154
93T-510M
93T/Gold-510M
93TWill-18
93UD/ATH-55
94Phill/Med-9MG
Fregoso, Dan
92Bluefld/ClBest-4
92Bluefld/ProC-2356
Freigau, Howard
21Exh-52
25Exh-20
26Exh-20
90Target-953
Freiling, Howard
88VeroB/Star-7
89Jacks/GS-18
90Jacks/GS-11
91Clmbia/PII-3CO
92Pittsfld/ClBest-20CO
92Pittsfld/ProC-3311CO
Freisleben, Dave
74OPC-599R
74T-599R
75OPC-37
75T-37
75T/M-37
76OPC-217
76SSPC-116
76T-217
77Padre/SchCd-11
77T-407
78Padre/FamFun-12
78T-594
79BJ/Bubble-8
79T-168
80OPC-199
80T-382
89Butte/SP-30
Freitag, Dusty
92Rockford/ClBest-26
92Rockford/ProC-2119
Freitas, Antonio
40Hughes-6
46Sunbeam
47Signal
47Sunbeam
49B/PCL-11
R314
Freitas, Mike
90Pittsfld/Pucko-24
91Clmbia/PCPII-2
91Clmbia/PII-23
92StLucie/ClBest-7
92StLucie/ProC-1740
93ClBest/MLG-170
French, Charlie
C46-25
French, Kevin
90NE-11
French, Larry
34G-29
35BU-132
41DP-1
42Playball-30
88Conlon/NatAS-7
90Target-258
92Conlon/Sport-416
V354-79
WG8-20
French, Ray
28Exh/PCL-31
WG7-17
French, Richard J.
66T-333R
69OPC-199
69T-199
69T-199
69T/4in1-6
70T-617
71MLB/St-538
71OPC-399
71Richm/Team-7
71T-399
71T-399
French, Ron
90Johnson/Star-12
91Hamil/ClBest-27
91Hamil/ProC-4052
92Hamil/ClBest-7
92Hamil/ProC-1605
French, Steve
84Butte-11
French, Walter
92Conlon/Sport-397
94Conlon-1143
Frew, Mike
85Beloit-16
86Stockton-8
87Stockton-15
Frey, Benjamin R.
92Conlon/Sport-381
Frey, Eric
77Newar
Frey, Jim
73OPC-136CO
73T-136CO
74OPC-306CO
74T-306CO
81D-464MG
81T-667MG
84Cub/Uno-10
84Cub/Uno-12M
84Cub/Uno-8M
84Nes/792-51MG
84SevenUp-MG
84T-51MG
85SevenUp-MG
85T-241MG
86T-231MG
Frey, Linus R.
(Lonny)
34G-89
35G-1G
35G-3E
35G-4E
35G-5E
39PlayBall-161
40PlayBall-76
41DP-5
42Playball-36
90Target-259
93Conlon-812
R310
R312
R314
W711/1
W711/2
Frey, Steve
85Albany-7
87Albany-23
87FtLaud-3
88Tidew/CANDL-20
88Tidew/CMC-6
88Tidew/ProC-1602
89Indianap/CMC-3
89Indianap/ProC-1218
90F-649R
90F/Can-649M
90F/Up-U28
90OPC-91
90T-91
90T/89Debut-40
91B-451
91D-292
91F-231
91Leaf-153
91OPC-462
91Panini/FrSt-154
91S-436
91T-462
91UD-397
91Ultra-202
92D-660
92F-479
92L-418
92L/BlkGold-418
92OPC-174
92StCl-572
92T-174
92T/Gold-174
92T/GoldWin-174
92Ultra-222
93D-533
93F-573
93L-488
93Mother/Angel-22
93Pac/Spanish-368
93StCl/Angel-12
93T-728
93T/Gold-728
93UD-750
94D-142
94F-56
94Pinn-185
94Pinn/Artist-185
94Pinn/Museum-185
94S-250
94S/GoldR-250
94StCl/Team-26
94T-503
94T/Gold-503
94Ultra-22
Frias, Israel
89Bluefld/Star-10
Frias, Jesus M.
(Pepe)
72Dimanche*-18
73OPC-607R
73T-607R
74OPC-468
74T-468
75OPC-496
75T-496
75T/M-496
76Expo/Redp-10
76OPC-544
76SSPC-231
76T-544
77OPC-225
77T-199
78OPC-171
78T-654
79OPC-146
79T-294
80OPC-48
80T-87
81F-134
81Pol/Dodg-36
89Pac/SenLg-106
90Bend/Legoe-25
90Target-260
91Clinton/ClBest-18
92SanJose/ClBest-21
93Rang/Keeb-155
Frias, Joe
91Spokane/ClBest-27
91Spokane/ProC-3956
Friberg, A. Bernhardt
(Barney)
26Exh-42
29Exh/4-11
31Exh/4-12
33G-105
91Conlon/Sport-297
V354-10
Fricano, Marion
53T-199
54B-3
54T-124
55B-316
55Rodeo
91T/Arc53-199
94T/Arc54-124
Frick, Ford
49Eureka-2
59T-1COM
60F-74
61F-29
76Shakey-117COMM
80Perez/HOF-117
80SSPC/HOF
Frick, James
T205
Frick, Tod
91SoOreg/ProC-3848
Fricke, Dave
90Kgsport/Best-28
90Kgsport/Star-28TR
92ColumMet/ClBest-29TR
92ColumMet/SAL/II-32
Friday, Paul
89KS*-27
Fridley, Jim
52T-399
53T-187
54Esskay
72T/Test-6
91Crown/Orio-146
91T/Arc53-187
Fridman, Jason
91Elmira/ClBest-5
Friedel, Chuck
84LitFalls-5
Friederich, Mike
85Osceola/Team-7
86ColumAst-13
Friedland, Michael
90James/Pucko-12
91Rockford/ClBest-19
91Rockford/ProC-2054
Friedman, Jason
90Elmira/Pucko-5
90WinHaven/Star-9
91Elmira/ProC-3277
92LynchRS/ClBest-6
92LynchRS/ProC-2913
93FExcel/ML-132
Friel, Bill
E107
E270/2
Friend, Bob
52B-191
52T-233
53B/Col-16
54B-43
54DanDee
55B-57
56T-221
56YellBase/Pin-10
57Kahn
57T-150

58Hires-24
58Hires/T
58Kahn
58T-315
58T-334M
58T-492AS
59Kahn
59T-428M
59T-460
59T-569AS
60Kahn
60L-53
60T-437
61Kahn
61P-125
61T-270
61T-45LL
61T-585AS
61T/St-63
62J-178
62Kahn
62P-178
62P/Can-178
62Salada-157
62Shirriff-157
62T-520
62T/St-176
62T/bucks
63IDL-8
63J-145
63Kahn
63P-145
63T-450
64Bz-6
64Kahn
64T-1LL
64T-20
64T/Coins-77
64T/S-28
64T/SU
64T/St-66
64T/tatt
64Wheat/St-17
65Kahn
65OldLond-10
65T-392
66T-519
78TCMA-160
88Pac/Leg-78
89Swell-86
91T/Arc53-298
91WIZMets-128
92Bz/Quadra-22M
92Yank/WIZ60-43
Exh47

Friend, Owen
50B-189
51B-101
52T-160
53Tiger/Glen-8
54B-212
55B-256
57Seattle/Pop-15

Frierson, John
83Miami-19

Frierson, Mike
80Wausau-19

Friesen, Rob
87Fayette-26

Frill, John E.
E270/2
M116
T206

Frink, Keith
88Wausau/GS-7

Frisch, Frank
(Frankie)
21Exh-53
25Exh-33
26Exh-34
28Exh-31
28Yueng-50
29Exh/4-15
31Exh/4-15
33CJ/Pin-6
33DH-18
33Exh/4-8
33G-49
34DS-17
34Exh/4-8
34G-13
34Ward's/Pin-4
35BU-173
35BU-33
35Exh/4-8
35G-1A
35G-2A
35G-6A
35G-7A
35Wheat
36Exh/4-8
40PlayBall-167
45Playball-34MG
48Exh/HOF
50B-229MG
50Callahan
50W576-32
51B-282MG
61F-30
61GP-19
76Motor-7
76Rowe-3M
76Shakey-51
77Galasso-207
77Galasso-53
80Pac/Leg-46
80Perez/HOF-51
80SSPC/HOF
81Conlon-23
85Woolwth-13
86Conlon/1-14M
88Conlon/5-11
88Conlon/NatAS-8
89HOF/St-13
89Pac/Leg-113
90Perez/GreatMom-57
91Conlon/Proto-664
91Conlon/Sport-11
91Conlon/Sport-305
92Card/McDon/Pac-7
92Conlon/ASP-664G
92Conlon/Sport-634
93Conlon-664
93Conlon-835
94Conlon-1091MG
94Conlon-1233
E120
E121/120
E121/80
E210-50
E220
R300
R306
R310
R311/Gloss
R313
R313A-5
R314
R315-A9
R315-B9
R316
R328-30
R332-4
R337-419
R423-32
V100
V353-49
V354-64
V355-107
V61-62
V89-24
W501-104
W501-62
W502-50
W512-8
W515-14
W517-16
W572
W573
W575
WG8-21

Frisella, Dan
(Danny)
68OPC-191
68T-191
69T-343
71MLB/St-151
71OPC-104
71T-104
72OPC-293
72OPC-294IA
72T-293
72T-294A
72T/Cloth-14IA
73OPC-432
73T-432
74OPC-71
74T-71
75OPC-343
75T-343
75T/M-343
76OPC-32
76SSPC-117
76T-32
77T-278
81TCMA-470
89Tidew/Candl-1
91WIZMets-129

Fritch, John
89KS*-12

Fritsch, Ted Sr.
77Fritsch-8

Fritz, Charles
T206
T213 brown

Fritz, Greg
91Utica/ClBest-19
91Utica/ProC-3234
92Salinas/ClBest-2

Fritz, John
88Bend/Legoe-20
88PalmSp/Cal-87
88PalmSp/ProC-1445
90PalmSp/Cal-221
90PalmSp/ProC-2572
91Melbourne/Fut-7
91Miami/ClBest-7
91Miami/ProC-401
92QuadC/ClBest-10
92QuadC/ProC-801
93FExcel/ML-142
94FExcel-26

Frobel, Doug
78Charl
81Buffa-22
82Portl-20
84D-38
84Nes/792-264
84T-264
85F-464
85T-587
85T/St-128
86Tidew-9
87BuffB-7
89BirmB/Best-7
89BirmB/ProC-105

Frock, Sam
C46-13
M116

Froemming, Bruce
88TM/Umpire-11
89TM/Umpire-9
90TM/Umpire-9

Frohwirth, Todd
86Clearw-9
87Phill/TastyK-52
87Reading-19
88D/Rook-3
88F-301
88Maine/CMC-10
88Maine/ProC-296
88Phill/TastyK-10
88T-378
89D-587
89F-567
89Phill/TastyK-7
89S-647
89S/HotRook-14
89T-542
90AAASingl/ProC-296
90D-631
90OPC-69
90ProC/Singl-250
90ScranWB/CMC-24
90ScranWB/ProC-594
90T-69
90UD-443
91AAA/LineD-456
91RochR/LineD-456
91RochR/ProC-1896
92D-317
92F/Up-1
92OPC-158
92Pinn-411
92ProC/Tomorrow-3
92S-534
92StCl-358
92T-158
92T/Gold-158
92T/GoldWin-158
92T/Pr-18
92UD-318
92Ultra-302
93D-513
93F-166
93Pac/Spanish-342
93StCl-445
93StCl/1stDay-445
93T-415
93T/Gold-415
93UD-191
93Ultra-494
94D-389
94F-4
94Pac/Cr-30
94S-226
94S/GoldR-226
94StCl-248
94StCl/1stDay-248
94StCl/Gold-248
94T-242
94T/Gold-242

Frolin, Darrel
75Anderson/TCMA-9

Fromme, Art
10Domino-46
11Helmar-113
12Sweet/Pin-98
14Piedmont/St-23
D303
E106
E254
E270/2
E90/1
M116
S74-74
T202
T204
T205
T206
T207
T213/blue
T214-11
T215/blue
T215/brown
T216
T3-93

Fronio, Jason
91Watertn/ClBest-5
91Watertn/ProC-3360
92Watertn/ClBest-3
92Watertn/ProC-3226
93Kinston/Team-9
94FExcel-43

Frost, C. David
78Cr/PCL-83
79T-703R
80T-423
81D-52
81F-275
81SLCity-6
81T-286
82D-290
82F-460
82T-24
82T/Tr-37T
83F-111
83T-656

Frost, Jerald
87Sumter-1
88BurlB/ProC-8
89Durham/Star-12
89Durham/Team-12

Fruge, Chris
90Utica/Pucko-17

Fruge, Jeff
82QuadC-8
83QuadC-10

Fry, Brian
89Billings/ProC-2051
90Billings/ProC-3215

Fry, Jerry
75WPalmB/Sussman-13
79T-720R

Fry, W.J.
N172

Frye, Dan
92Princet/ClBest-23
92Princet/ProC-3093
93B-698FOIL
93ClBest/MLG-212
93FExcel/ML-20

Frye, Jeff
88Butte-14
89Gaston/ProC-1023
89Gaston/Star-7
89SALAS/GS-27
89Star/IISingl-137
90CharlR/Star-7
91AA/LineD-579
91Tulsa/LineD-579
91Tulsa/ProC-2778
91Tulsa/Team-7
92D/Rook-40
92F/Up-60
92OkCty/ProC-1920
92OkCty/SB-310
92Sky/AAASingl-142
93D-724
93F-321
93Pinn-496
93Rang/Keeb-406
93S-274
93StCl-133
93StCl/1stDay-133
93T-197
93T/Gold-197
93UD-371
93USPlayC/Rook-7C
93Ultra-278
94StCl/Team-261

Frye, Paul
86James-8
87WPalmB-3
88Rockford-14
89Rockford-14

Fryer, Paul
82Reading-14

Fryhoff, John
83TriCit-10

Fryman, Travis
88Fayette/ProC-1094
89BBAmAA/BPro-AA2
89EastLgAS/ProC-4
89London/ProC-1366
90AAAGame/ProC-30
90AAASingl/ProC-385
90B-360
90F/Up-U96
90ProC/Singl-395
90T/Tr-33T
90Toledo/CMC-18
90Toledo/ProC-155
91B-145
91Classic/200-124
91Classic/I-40
91CokeK/Tiger-24
91D-768
91F-336
91Leaf-149
91Leaf/Stud-54
91MajorLg/Pins-34
91OPC-128
91Pol/Tiger-4
91RedFoley/St-106
91S-570
91S/100RisSt-68
91Seven/3DCoin-5MW
91StCl-355
91T-128
91T/90Debut-49
91T/JumboR-9
91ToysRUs-8
91UD-225
91Ultra-122
92B-37
92CJ/DI-11
92Classic/Game200-88
92D-349
92F-134
92L-304
92L/BlkGold-304
92OPC-750
92Panini-107
92Pinn-110
92Pinn/Team2000-4
92S-65
92S/Impact-47
92StCl-59
92Studio-174
92T-750
92T/Gold-750
92T/GoldWin-750
92T/Kids-78
92TripleP-86
92UD-466
92UD-643DS
92USPlayC/Tiger-12D
92USPlayC/Tiger-6C
92Ultra-60

93B-67
93Classic/Gamel-35
93D-127
93F-228
93F/Fruit-20
93Flair-202
93Kenner/Fig-10
93L-16
93L/Fast-19
93OPC-76
93OPC/Premier-102
93Pac/Spanish-108
93Panini-117
93Pinn-79
93Pinn/HRC-48
93Pinn/Slug-30
93Pinn/Team2001-10
93S-11
93Select-44
93StCl-298MC
93StCl-448
93StCl/1stDay-298MC
93StCl/1stDay-448
93StCl/MPhoto-16
93StCl/MurphyS-168
93Studio-108
93Studio/Sil-5
93T-392
93T-404M
93T/BlkGold-31
93T/Finest-135
93T/FinestRef-135
93T/Gold-392
93T/Gold-404M
93Tiger/Gator-8
93ToysRUs-87
93TripleP-59
93UD-364
93UD-455IN
93UD-836TC
93UD/Diam-25
93UD/FunPack-187
93UD/SP-237
93Ultra-197
94B-621
94Church-15
94D-378
94D/Special-378
94F-129
94F/AS-8
94Finest-228
94KingB-10
94L-405
94OPC-209
94Pac/Cr-217
94Panini-64
94Pinn-183
94Pinn/Artist-183
94Pinn/Museum-183
94Pinn/Power-14
94Pinn/Run-9
94S-11
94S/GoldR-11
94S/GoldS-48
94Sf/2000-16
94Sf/2000-178AS
94StCl-309
94StCl/1stDay-309
94StCl/Gold-309
94Studio-191
94T-285
94T/BlkGold-6
94T/Gold-285
94TripleP-244
94TripleP/Medal-9M
94UD-345
94UD-37FT
94UD-51FUT
94UD/ElecD-37FT
94UD/ElecD-51FUT
94UD/HoloFX-10
94UD/SP-177
94Ultra-53
94Ultra/RisSt-5
Fryman, Troy
91Utica/ClBest-27
91Utica/ProC-3247
92SoBend/ClBest-21
92SoBend/ProC-185
94ClBest/Gold-155
Fryman, Woodie
66EH-22
66T-498R
67CokeCap/Pirate-15
67T-221
67T/Test/PP-9
68OPC-112
68T-112
69MB-88
69MLB/St-175
69OPC-51
69T-51
69T/St-75
70MLB/St-88
70T-677
71MLB/St-177
71OPC-414
71T-414
72MB-110
72OPC-357
72T-357
72T/Cloth-15
73OPC-146
73T-146
74OPC-555
74T-555
75OPC-166
75T-166
75T/M-166
76Expo/Redp-11
76OPC-467
76SSPC-345
76T-467
77OPC-126
77T-28
78SSPC/270-249
78T-585
79OPC-135
79T-269
80OPC-316
80T-607
81D-331
81F-159
81OPC-170
81OPC/Post-10
81T-394
82D-68
82Expo/Hygrade-8
82F-189
82Hygrade
82OPC-181
82T-788
82Zeller-12
83D-162
83Expo/PostC-5
83F-283
83F/St-4M
83OPC-137
83Stuart-2
83T-137
93Expo/D/McDon-22
Fucci, Dom
80GlenF/B-19
80GlenF/C-14
80GlenF/C-20M
81GlenF-11
82Edmon-18
Fuchs, Charlie
90Target-261
Fuduric, Tony
94FExcel-54
94T-757DP
94T/Gold-757DP
Fuentes, Miguel
70OPC-88R
70T-88R
Fuentes, Mike
83Wichita/Dog-7
84D-40RR
84Expo/PostC-10
84Indianap-12
84Stuart-32
85Indianap-7
87Memphis-1
87Memphis/Best-25
Fuentes, Roberto
85Elmira-6
86WinHaven-8
Fuentes, Tito
66T-511R
67OPC-177
67T-177
68CokeCap/Giant-4
70OPC-42
70T-42
71MLB/St-247
71OPC-378
71T-378
71Ticket/Giant-4
72OPC-427
72OPC-428IA
72T-427
72T-428IA
73OPC-236
73T-236
74OPC-305
74T-305
74T/St-104
75Ho-108
75OPC-425
75T-425
75T/M-425
76Crane-15
76MSA/Disc
76OPC-8
76SSPC-124
76T-8
77T-63
78T-385
Fuhrman, Alfred
(Ollie)
E120
W573
Fujimoto, Kenji
89Visalia/Cal-116
89Visalia/ProC-1432
Fulcar, Manuel
93LimeR/Winter-101
Fulgencio, Elvin
85Cedar-22
Fulgham, John
77StPete
80T-152
81D-70
81Louisvl-20
81T-523
82Louisvl-9
83Louisvl/Riley-20
Fuller, Charles F.
(Nig)
90Target-954
Fuller, Harry
88AubAs/ProC-1956
89Ashvl/ProC-957
Fuller, James H.
(Jim)
74OPC-606R
74T-606R
75OPC-594
75T-594
75T/M-594
78Colum
91Crown/Orio-147
Fuller, Jon
90CharWh/ProC-2244
91Cedar/ClBest-14
91Cedar/ProC-2721
92Cedar/ClBest-12
92Cedar/ProC-1074
92MidwLAS/Team-11
Fuller, Mark
92Pittsfld/ClBest-14
92Pittsfld/ProC-3287
93StLucie/ProC-2916
Fuller, Paul
88Utica/Pucko-5
89Saraso/Star-6
89Star/Wax-58
Fuller, Scott
88Utica/Pucko-19
Fuller, Tom
80Ander-4
Fuller, Vern
68OPC-71
68T-71
69T-291
70MLB/St-197
70T-558
72MB-111
Fuller, Wayne
88Batavia/ProC-1669
Fuller, William B.
N172
N566-179
Fullerton, Darren
91Sydney/Fut-9
Fullerton, Hugh
88Pac/8Men-29
88Pac/8Men-35M
88Pac/8Men-42M
88Pac/8Men-64
Fullis, Charles
(Chick)
33DH-19
35BU-74
88Conlon/NatAS-9
92Conlon/Sport-514
R308-166
V94-17
Fullmer, Brad
94B-76
94UD-532TP
94UD/SP-4PP
Fully, Edward
90Kgsport/Best-11
90Kgsport/Star-9
91Clmbia/PCPII-3
91Clmbia/PII-11
91SALAS/ProC-SAL15
92StLucie/ClBest-20
92StLucie/ProC-1761
93StLucie/ProC-2933
Fulmer, Chris
N172
N284
Fulmer, Mike
84Madis/Pol-20
85Modesto/Chong-10
86Stockton-9
Fulton, Bill
84Greens-12
86Albany/TCMA-26
87Colum-31
87Colum/Pol-10
87Colum/TCMA-4
88Colum/CMC-4
88Colum/Pol-2
88Colum/ProC-312
89Colum/CMC-1
89Colum/Pol-5
89Colum/ProC-746
92Yank/WIZ80-64
Fulton, Ed
88Spring/Best-24
89StPete/Star-13
90ArkTr/GS-14
90Louisvl/LBC-17
90T/TVCard-49
91AAA/LineD-235
91Louisvl/LineD-235
91Louisvl/ProC-2916
91Louisvl/Team-28
92Louisvl/ProC-1889
Fulton, Greg
87Chatt/Best-18
88Vermont/ProC-942
89Calgary/ProC-524
89Wmsprt/ProC-648
90AAASingl/ProC-121
90Calgary/CMC-9
90Calgary/ProC-656
90ProC/Singl-436
91AA/LineD-254
91Harris/LineD-254
91Harris/ProC-631
92Harris/SB-281
92Indianap/ProC-1866
93Harris/ProC-283CO
Fults, Nathan
90Idaho/ProC-3260
Fultz, Aaron
93ClBest/MLG-169
94FExcel-291
Fultz, Bill
82Lynch-20
83Lynch-5
84Jacks-7
Fultz, David
E107
Fultz, Vince
92Albany/ClBest-16
92Rockford/ProC-2107
Funderburk, Mark
78Wisco
80OrlanTw-19
82OrlanTw-7
83Omaha-15
85OrlanTw-5
86D-630
86F-652M
86Sf-178M
86Toledo-11
87OrlanTw-25
88OrlanTw/Best-5
89OrlanTw/Best-3
89OrlanTw/ProC-1344
90OrlanSR/Best-29CO
90OrlanSR/ProC-1099CO
90OrlanSR/Star-25CO
91AA/LineD-500CO
91OrlanSR/LineD-500CO
91OrlanSR/ProC-1866CO
92OrlanSR/ProC-2863CO
92OrlanSR/SB-526CO
Funk, Art
R314/Can
Funk, Brian
83Water-2
84Cedar-6
Funk, E.
31Exh/4-24
Funk, Frank
60Maple-7
61T-362
62Sugar-4
62T-587
63T-476
64T-289
80Penin/B-26C
86Omaha/ProC-7CO
86Omaha/TCMA-23CO
87Omaha-1
91Cedar/ClBest-26MG
91Cedar/ProC-2735MG
92Nashvl/ProC-1849CO
92Nashvl/SB-300CO
Funk, Tom
86ColumAst-14
87Tucson-25
88ColAst/Best-18
Fuqua, David
75Lafay
Furcal, Lorenzo
89Madis/Star-9
89Medford/Best-17
Furcal, Manuel
90SanBern/Best-11
90SanBern/Cal-98
90SanBern/ProC-2628
91Penin/ClBest-4
91Penin/ProC-370
Furch, John
89Utica/Pucko-7
Furillo, Carl
47HomogBond-16
48Swell-20
49B-70
49Eureka-35
50B-58
50Drake-18
51B-81
52B-24
52Coke
52TipTop
53B/Col-78
54B-122
54NYJour
55B-169
55Gol/Dodg-9
56T-190
57T-400M
57T-45
58T-417
59Morrell
59T-206
60BB-8
60Morrell
60NuCard-32
60T-408
61NuCard-432
72T/Test-5
77Galasso-11
79TCMA-43
89Rini/Dodg-14
89Smok/Dodg-58
90Target-262
91T/Arc53-305
92Bz/Quadra-2
D305
Exh47
PM10/Sm-54
PM10/Sm-55
PM10/Sm-56
PM10/Sm-57
Furman, Jon
83BirmB-20
Furmanik, Dan
89Clmbia/Best-6

89Clmbia/GS-8
90StLucie/Star-7
91SLCity/ProC-3203
91SLCity/SportP-2
Furtado, Tim
93River/Cal-7
Furtak, Mark
87Hawaii-16
Fusco, Thomas
90Hamil/Best-5
90Hamil/Star-13
91Savan/ProC-1645
92Savan/ClBest-20
92Savan/ProC-656
Fuson, Grady
82Idaho-31
83Idaho-31
89Medford/Best-18
90SoOreg/Best-30MG
90SoOreg/ProC-3449MG
91SoOreg/ProC-3866MG
Fuson, Robin
78Watlo
82Chatt-18
83BuffB-1
84BuffB-24
85Pawtu-13
Fussell, Denny
92Princet/ClBest-15
92Princet/ProC-3082
Fusselman, Les
52T-378
53Hunter
53T-218
91T/Arc53-218
Futrell, Mark
90Welland/Pucko-21
91Augusta/ClBest-6
91Augusta/ProC-799
Fye, Chris
89Clinton/ProC-885
90Foil/Best-159
90SanJose/Best-16
90SanJose/Cal-43
90SanJose/ProC-2002
90SanJose/ProC-2172M
90SanJose/Star-10
Fyhrie, Mike
92BBCity/ClBest-21
92BBCity/ProC-3838
Fynan, Kevin
88Clearw/Star-11
89Clearw/Star-9
90Clearw/Star-7
Fyock, Wade
90LitSun/HSPros-23
90LitSun/HSProsG-23
91AppFx/ClBest-3
91AppFx/ProC-1709
91ClBest/Singl-249
Fzelykovskyi, Andrei
89EastLDD/ProC-DD13#
Gabbani, Mike
90Hunting/ProC-3284
91Sydney/Fut-18
91WinSalem/ClBest-13
91WinSalem/ProC-2831
92WinSalem/ClBest-20
92WinSalem/ProC-1211
Gabbard, John
45Parade*-57
Gabella, Jim
90Watertn/Star-24MG
91AAA/LineD-100M
91ColoSp/LineD-100CO
91ColoSp/ProC-2202CO
92Canton/ProC-707
92Canton/SB-125M
Gabler, Frank
35BU-91
92Conlon/Sport-606
Gabler, John
60L-62
92Yank/WIZ60-44
Gables, Kenneth
48Sommers-5
49Sommers-3
Gabriele, Dan
85Elmira-7
86Greens-6
87WinHaven-10
88NewBrit/ProC-898
89EastLgAS/ProC-13
89NewBrit/ProC-604
89NewBrit/Star-6
Gabriele, Mike
90Sumter/Best-3
90Sumter/ProC-2426
Gabrielson, Len
63T-253R
64T-198
65OPC-14
65T-14
66T-395
67CokeCap/DodgAngel-19
67T-469
68T-357
69MB-89
69MLB/St-147
69T-615
69T/St-44
70MLB/St-50
70OPC-204
70T-204
90Target-263
PM10/Sm-58
Gabrielson, Leonard
43Centen-9
Gaddie, Mike
90Johnson/Star-30TR
92Johnson/ClBest-28
Gaddy, Robert
89Batavia/ProC-1928
90A&AASingle/ProC-95
90SALAS/Star-7
90Spartan/Best-3
90Spartan/ProC-2484
90Spartan/Star-8
91Clearw/ClBest-3
91Clearw/ProC-1614
92Clearw/ClBest-4
92Clearw/ProC-2050
Gaeckle, Chris
86Greens-7
87Greens-25
Gaedel, Eddie
60NuCard-26
61NuCard-426
73F/Wild-4
77Fritsch-1
Gaeta, Chris
85Newar-19
Gaeta, Frank
52Laval-25
Gaetti, Gary
80Wisco
82OrlanTw/A-7
83D-53
83F-613
83OPC/St-87
83T-431
83T/St-87
83Twin/Team-33M
83Twin/Team-5
84D-314
84F-565
84Nes/792-157
84OPC-157
84T-157
84T/RD-20M
84T/St-306
85D-242
85F-278
85FunFood/Pin-131
85Leaf-145
85OPC-304
85Seven/Minn-9
85T-304
85T/RD-20M
85T/St-302
85Twin/Seven-9
85Twin/Team-5
86D-314
86F-394
86OPC-97
86T-97
86T/St-283
87Classic-54
87D-122
87D/OD-219
87F-540
87F/GameWin-15
87F/Mini-40
87F/RecSet-9
87F/St-43
87Leaf-245
87OPC-179
87Sf-114M
87Sf-64
87Sf/TPrev-17M
87T-710
87T/Gloss60-3
87T/Mini-62
87T/St-279
88Classic/Blue-233
88D-194
88D-19DK
88D/Best-46
88D/DKsuper-19DK
88F-10
88F/Hottest-12
88F/LL-13
88F/Mini-34
88F/St-43
88Grenada-24
88KayBee-11
88KennerFig-39
88Leaf-19DK
88Leaf-200
88Master/Disc-9
88Nestle-4
88OPC-257
88Panini/St-140
88Panini/St-445
88RedFoley/St-26
88S-62
88Sf-154
88Smok/Minn-2
88T-578
88T/Big-127
88T/Coins-13
88T/RiteAid-31
88T/St-17
88T/St-277
88T/UK-25
88Woolwth-18
88Woolwth-22
89B-158
89Cadaco-21
89Classic-41
89D-64
89D/AS-13
89D/Best-102
89F-110
89F/Heroes-15
89KennerFig-46
89Master/Discs-3
89OPC-220
89Panini/St-389
89RedFoley/St-46
89S-8
89S/HotStar-21
89S/Mast-16
89Sf-48
89T-220
89T/Big-264
89T/Gloss60-33
89T/LJN-35
89T/Mini-61
89T/St-289
89T/St/Backs-8
89UD-203
90B-417
90D-151
90D/BestAL-10
90F-373
90F/BB-10
90F/Can-373
90HotPlay/St-14
90Kenner/Fig-28
90Leaf-97
90Leaf/Prev-11
90MLBPA/Pins-100
90OPC-630
90Panini/St-106
90PublInt/St-286
90PublInt/St-326
90S-145
90S/100St-22
90Sf-51
90T-630
90T/Big-254
90T/Coins-14
90T/DH-25
90T/Gloss60-28
90T/St-288
90UD-454
91B-207
91Cadaco-22
91Classic/200-49
91D-547
91F-609
91F/UltraUp-U8
91F/Up-U9
91Leaf-303
91Leaf/Stud-25
91OPC-430
91OPC/Premier-47
91Panini/FrSt-302
91Panini/St-250
91S-325
91S/RookTr-39T
91Smok/Angel-13
91StCl-353
91T-430
91T/Tr-44T
91UD-233
91UD-34TC
91UD/Ext-731
92B-564
92D-96
92F-58
92L-107
92L/BlkGold-107
92OPC-70
92Panini-7
92Pinn-81
92Pol/Angel-10
92S-39
92StCl-436
92T-70
92T/Gold-70
92T/GoldWin-70
92TripleP-223
92UD-321
92Ultra-26
93Cadaco-21
93D-517
93D/Spirit-SG15M
93F-574
93L-514
93Mother/Angel-5
93Pac/Spanish-46
93Panini-4
93Pinn-112
93S-644
93Select-262
93Select/RookTr-95T
93StCl-512
93StCl/1stDay-512
93T-139
93T/Gold-139
93UD-370
93UD/HRH-HR28
93Ultra-520
94D-502
94F-153
94Finest-394
94L-427
94S-300
94S/GoldR-300
94StCl-485
94StCl/1stDay-485
94StCl/Gold-485
94Studio-183
94T-403
94T/Gold-403
94UD-466
94Ultra-363
Gaff, Brent
78Wausau
79Wausau-1
81Tidew-17
82Tidew-20
83D-553
83Tidew-16
84Tidew-8
85F-80
85T-546
86T-18
91WIZMets-130
Gaffke, Fabian
94Conlon-1306
Gaffney, Bill
80SanJose/JITB-8
Gaffney, John H.
90Target-955
N172
Gagliano, Manny
91OKSt-9
92OKSt-8
92Spokane/ClBest-17
92Spokane/ProC-1302
Gagliano, Phil
61Union
62Kahn/Atl
64T-568R
65T-503
66T-418
67T-304
68T-479
69T-609
70OPC-143
70T-143
71OPC-302
71T-302
72MB-112
72OPC-472
72T-472
73OPC-69
73T-69
74OPC-622
74T-622
Gagliano, Ralph
65T-501R
Gagliardi, Joe
88CalLgAS-25
89AS/Cal-56PRES
90AS/Cal-27PRES
91CalLgAS-26
Gagne, Greg
82OrlanTw-8
83Toledo-14
84D-39RR
85F/Up-U43
85T/Tr-36T
85Twin/Team-21
86D-558
86F-395
86T-162
87D-395
87D/OD-223
87F-541
87Sf/TPrev-17M
87T-558
87T/St-283
88D-441
88D/Best-74
88F-11
88Master/Disc-11
88OPC-343
88Panini/St-141
88S-214
88Smok/Minn-8
88T-343
88T/Big-58
88Woolwth-32WS7
89B-161
89D-318
89D/Best-158
89F-111
89OPC-19
89Panini/St-390
89S-159
89T-19
89T-429TL
89T/Big-186
89T/St-288
89UD-166
90B-414
90D-237
90D/BestAL-135
90F-374
90F/Can-374
90Leaf-302
90MLBPA/Pins-99
90OPC-448
90Panini/St-115
90PublInt/St-327
90S-102
90T-448
90T/Big-78
90T/St-295
90UD-217
91B-338
91D-284
91F-610
91Leaf-426
91Leaf/Stud-84
91OPC-216
91Panini/FrSt-303
91Panini/St-245
91RedFoley/St-37
91S-211
91StCl-277
91T-216
91UD-415
91Ultra-186
92B-660
92D-204

92F-202
92L-146
92L/BlkGold-146
92OPC-663
92Panini-118
92Pinn-262
92S-182
92S/Factory-B1M
92StCl-376
92StCl/Dome-53
92Studio-203
92T-663
92T/Gold-663
92T/GoldWin-663
92TripleP-230
92UD-168
92USPlayC/Twin-11S
92USPlayC/Twin-7H
92Ultra-395
93B-449
93Cadaco-22
93D-633
93D/Spirit-SG13
93F-264
93F/Final-217
93L-282
93OPC-101
93OPC/Premier-117
93Pac/Spanish-487
93Panini-105
93Pinn-510
93Pol/Royal-7
93S-555
93Select-178
93Select/RookTr-28T
93StCl-631
93StCl/1stDay-631
93StCl/Royal-16
93Studio-39
93T-715
93T/Gold-715
93UD-708
93Ultra-559
94B-283
94D-595
94F-154
94Finest-276
94Flair-57
94L-122
94OPC-141
94Pac/Cr-282
94Panini-72
94Pinn-354
94S-91
94S/GoldR-91
94StCl-159
94StCl/1stDay-159
94StCl/Gold-159
94Studio-184
94T-151
94T/Gold-151
94TripleP-233
94UD-79
94UD/ElecD-79
94Ultra-62

Gagnon, Johnny
45Parade*-18

Gahbrielson, Rick
86Bakers-9CO

Gaiko, Rob
92OKSt-9

Gainer, Chris
89KS*-11
93Lipscomb-9

Gainer, Delos C.
BF2-3
D328-53
D329-63
D350/2-64
E135-53
M101/4-63
M101/5-64
T207
V89-3

Gainer, Jay
90Spokane/SportP-12
91CalLgAS-7
91ClBest/Singl-230
91HighD/ClBest-19
91HighD/ProC-2402
92ClBest-312
92ProC/Tomorrow-336
92Sky/AASingl-279
92Wichita/ProC-3661
92Wichita/SB-630
93B-444
93F/Final-29
93FExcel/ML-109
93T/Tr-10T

Gainer, Keith
79Newar-18

Gaines, A. Joe
62T-414
63T-319
64T-364
65T-595
66OPC-122
66T-122
91Crown/Orio-148

Gaines, Jerry
77Ashvl

Gainey, Bob
72Dimanche*-74

Gainey, Ty
82DayBe-13
83ColumAst-10
85Cram/PCL-69
86D-31RR
86Tucson-5
87D-533
87Sf-118M
87Sf/TPrev-8M
87Tucson-23
88D-578
88F-448
89ColoSp/CMC-22
89ColoSp/ProC-258
90AAASingl/ProC-231
90ColoSp/CMC-11
90ColoSp/ProC-50
90ProC/Singl-463

Gainous, Trey
88AppFx/ProC-151

Gaither, Horace
90Saraso/Star-8
91SoBend/ClBest-2
91SoBend/ProC-2862

Gajkowski, Steve
90BurlInd/ProC-3005
91CollInd/ClBest-13
91CollInd/ProC-1480
91Watertn/ClBest-6
91Watertn/ProC-3361

Gakeler, Dan
85Greens-20
86Greens-8
87NewBrit-19
88NewBrit/ProC-904
89Jaxvl/Best-24
89Jaxvl/ProC-157
90AAASingl/ProC-577
90Indianap/CMC-6
90Indianap/ProC-294
90ProC/Singl-56
90WPalmB/Star-9
91AAA/LineD-584
91B-144
91Toledo/LineD-584
91Toledo/ProC-1924
92F-135
92OPC-621
92S-831
92StCl-276
92T-621
92T/91Debut-59
92T/Gold-621
92T/GoldWin-621
92USPlayC/Tiger-2C
92USPlayC/Tiger-5H

Galan, Augie
35BU-135
36Exh/4-3
37Exh/4-3
38Exh/4-3
41DP-102
44Playball-42
48B-39
49B-230
49Eureka-103
50Remar
53Mother-7
54T-233
89Smok/Dodg-48
90Target-264
94T/Arc54-233
Exh47
R312/M
R314
V355-106
WG8-22

Galante, Joe
79BuffB/TCMA-4

Galante, Matt
75BurlB
76BurlB
77Holyo
83Tucson-23
84Cram/PCL-50
90Mother/Ast-27CO
91Mother/Ast-28CO
92Mother/Ast-27M
93Mother/Ast-28M

Galarraga, Andres
85Indianap-3
86D-33
86D/Rook-7
86Expo/Prov/Pan-10
86F-647R
86F/Up-U44
86Leaf-27RR
86Provigo-10
86Sf/Rook-27
86T/Tr-40T
87Classic-71
87D-303
87D/OD-90
87F-319
87F/BB-18
87F/Mini-41
87GenMills/Book-4M
87Leaf-221
87OPC-272
87Sf/TPrev-20M
87T-272
87T/St-84
88D-282
88D/Best-90
88F-184
88F/LL-14
88F/Mini-88
88F/Slug-14
88F/St-96
88F/TL-9
88F/WaxBox-C3
88Ho/Disc-8
88Leaf-121
88OPC-25
88Panini/St-323
88S-19
88S/YS/II-8
88Sf-182
88T-25
88T/Big-55
88T/Gloss60-58
88T/Mini-56
88T/St-79
88T/St/Backs-2
89B-365
89Cadaco-22
89Classic-46
89D-130
89D-14DK
89D/AS-45
89D/Best-12
89D/DKsuper-14DK
89D/MVP-BC16
89F-376
89F-638M
89F/BBAS-13
89F/BBMVP's-12
89F/Excit-13
89F/Heroes-16
89F/LL-14
89F/Rec-3
89F/Superstar-15
89F/WaxBox-C8
89KayBee-12
89OPC-93
89Panini/St-119
89Panini/St-224
89RedFoley/St-47
89S-144
89S/HotStar-74
89S/Mast-33
89Sf-139
89T-386AS
89T-590
89T/Big-173
89T/Coins-13
89T/Gloss60-44
89T/Hills-13
89T/LJN-159
89T/Mini-22
89T/St-76
89T/St/Backs-36
89T/UK-28
89UD-115
89UD-677TC
90B-113
90Classic-115
90D-97
90D/BestNL-67
90F-345
90F/Can-345
90Holsum/Discs-4
90HotPlay/St-15
90Kenner/Fig-29
90Leaf-450
90OPC-720
90Panini/St-284
90PublInt/St-173
90PublInt/St-611
90RedFoley/St-35
90S-25
90S/100St-14
90Sf-148
90T-720
90T/Big-108
90T/HillsHM-31
90T/St-75
90T/TVAS-62
90UD-356
91B-446
91Classic/200-75
91D-68
91D/GSlam-9
91F-232
91Leaf-110
91Leaf/Stud-197
91OPC-610
91OPC/Premier-48
91Panini/FrSt-139
91Panini/Top15-100
91Post/Can-3
91S-443
91StCl-69
91T-610
91UD-456
91Ultra-203
92B-320
92D-355
92F-480
92L-449
92L/BlkGold-449
92MrTurkey-10
92OPC-240
92OPC/Premier-191
92Panini-202
92Pinn-381
92Pol/Card-4
92S-35
92S/RookTr-60T
92StCl-652
92T-240
92T/Gold-240
92T/GoldWin-240
92T/Tr-36T
92T/TrGold-36T
92UD-474
92UD-758
93B-204
93Colla/DM-36
93D-764
93Expo/D/McDon-4
93F-409
93F/Final-30
93Flair-39
93Flair/Pr-3
93L-322
93MSA/Metz-27
93OPC/Premier-58
93Pac/Beisbol-22M
93Pac/Jugador-26
93Pac/Spanish-427
93Pinn-434
93Pinn/Expan-3M
93S-649
93Select/RookTr-102T
93StCl-454
93StCl/1stDay-454
93StCl/Rockie-11
93Studio-163
93Studio/SS-9
93T-173
93T/Finest-130
93T/FinestRef-130
93T/Gold-173
93T/Tr-31T
93TB/Full-20
93UD-478M
93UD-593
93UD/FunPack-173GS
93UD/FunPack-176
93UD/SP-220
93USPlayC/Rockie-1D
93USPlayC/Rockie-2S
93Ultra-347
94B-526
94D-346
94D/DK-7
94D/Elite-48
94D/LongBall-3
94D/MVP-4
94D/Special-346
94F-440
94F/AS-35
94F/LL-7
94F/TL-18
94KingB-16
94Kraft-21
94L-156
94L/Clean-2
94L/GoldS-7
94L/MVPNL-6
94OPC-69
94Oscar-21
94P-23
94Pac/AllLat-3
94Pac/Cr-195
94Pac/Silv-20
94Panini-11
94Panini-174
94Pinn-446
94Pinn/Run-30
94RedFoley-12M
94S-8
94S/GoldR-8
94S/GoldS-11
94S/HobSam-8
94S/Pr-8
94S/Tomb-5
94Select-63
94Sf/2000-55
94Sf/Mov-6
94StCl-454
94StCl/1stDay-454
94StCl/Gold-454
94StCl/Team-91
94Studio-177
94Studio/Editor-4
94T-525
94T/BlkGold-30
94T/Finest-35
94T/Finest/PreProd-35
94T/FinestRef-35
94T/Gold-525
94TripleP-223
94UD-270HFA
94UD-315
94UD/CollC-312TP
94UD/CollC/Gold-312TP
94UD/CollC/Silv-312TP
94UD/DColl-W2
94UD/ElecD-270HFA
94UD/HoloFX-11
94UD/SP-166
94Ultra-480
94Ultra/Hit-4
94Ultra/LL-6
94Ultra/OnBase-4

Galasso, Bob
78Spokane/Cramer-21
78Spokane/Team-19
80T-711R
80Vanco-20
81Spokane-9
82T-598
84Richm-16
89Pac/SenLg-200
89T/SenLg-100
90EliteSenLg-56
91Pac/SenLg-114

Galatzer, Milt
R313

Galbato, Chan
86James-9

Galbraith, Moe
89TNTech-9

Galbreath, John W.
82Ohio/HOF-56

Gale, Bill
91StPete/ProC-2287
Gale, Rich
76Watlo
77Jaxvl
78SSPC/270-235
79OPC-149
79T-298
80T-433
81D-462
81F-40
81OPC-363
81Pol/Royals-3
81T-544
82D-138
82F-408
82OPC-67
82T-67
82T/Tr-38T
83D-172
83F-260
83OPC-243
83T-719
83T/Tr-35
84D-140
84F-469
84F/X-41
84Nes/792-142
84Pawtu-23
84T-142
84T/Tr-40
85T-606
89EastLDD/ProC-DD43CO
89NewBrit/ProC-602
89NewBrit/Star-24
89Pac/SenLg-95
90NewBrit/Best-26CO
90NewBrit/ProC-1335CO
90NewBrit/Star-26CO
91AAA/LineD-375
91Pac/SenLg-19
91Pawtu/LineD-375CO
91Pawtu/ProC-55CO
92RedSox/Dunkin-12CO
Galehouse, Dennis
40PlayBall-198
42Playball-9
47TipTop
61F-107
W753
Galinas, Marck
79BuffB/TCMA-10
Galindez, Luis
89Watlo/ProC-1789
89Watlo/Star-8
90Foil/Best-171
90MidwLgAS/GS-32
90Waterlo/Best-5
90Waterlo/ProC-2372
91ClBest/Singl-179
91HighD/ClBest-4
91HighD/ProC-2387
92ClBest-129
92HighD/ClBest-16
Galindez, Vilato
90Foil/Best-172
Galindo, Luis
88Lakeland/Star-5
89Lakeland/Star-6
90London/ProC-1277
91AA/LineD-384
91London/LineD-384
91London/ProC-1884
Gallagher
N690
Gallagher, Alan
71OPC-224
71T-224
72T-693
72T-694IA
78Green
81Durham-14
82Chatt-23
83BuffB-24
Gallagher, Allen
92BurlInd/ClBest-17
92BurlInd/ProC-1648
Gallagher, Bob
74OPC-21
74T-21
75OPC-406
75T-406
75T/M-406
76Phoenix/Coke-7
76SSPC-608
91WIZMets-131
Gallagher, Dave
80Batavia-25
81Watlo-26
82Chatt-17
82Watlo/Frit-11
83BuffB-19
84Maine-7
85IntLgAS-35
85Maine-27
86Maine-9CO
87Calgary-22
88D/Rook-7
88F/Up-U16
88S/Tr-89T
88Vanco/CMC-24
88Vanco/ProC-771
89B-71
89Bz-8
89Chatt/II/Team-10
89Coke/WS-9
89D-384
89D/Best-67
89F-496
89KMart/DT-7
89Panini/St-299
89S-455
89S/HotRook-96
89S/YS/I-4
89Sf-88
89T-156
89T/Big-310
89T/Gloss60-49
89T/JumboR-8
89T/St-295
89T/St-321
89ToysRUs-9
89UD-164
90Classic-49
90Coke/WSox-5
90D-219
90F-532
90F/Can-532
90OPC-612
90Panini/St-46
90Publint/St-387
90S-115
90S/100St-56
90Sf-105
90T-612
90T/St-305
90UD-328
91Crown/Orio-498
91F-471
91F/UltraUp-U9
91OPC-349
91StCl-563
91T-349
91UD-508
92D-377
92F-59
92L-224
92L/BlkGold-224
92Mets/Kahn-8
92OPC-552
92OPC/Premier-128
92S-239
92S/RookTr-55T
92StCl-841
92T-552
92T/Gold-552
92T/GoldWin-552
92T/Tr-37T
92T/TrGold-37T
92UD-289
92Ultra-530
93D-170
93F-472
93L-479
93Mets/Kahn-8
93StCl-476
93StCl/1stDay-476
93T-471
93T/Gold-471
93Ultra-74
94D-626
94F-562
94Pac/Cr-401
94S-235
94S/GoldR-235
94StCl/Team-37
94T-274
94T/Gold-274
Gallagher, Doug
77Fritsch-52
Gallagher, Joe
90Target-265
Gallagher, Sean
85Clovis-16
Gallaher, Kevin
92BurlAs/ProC-537
94B-202
94FExcel-200
Gallardo, Luis
87QuadC-31
87Salem/ProC-2436
90Oneonta/ProC-3366
91Greens/ProC-3065
92FtLaud/ClBest-11
92FtLaud/ProC-2619
92FtLaud/Team-12
Galle, Mike
89GreatF-28
90Yakima/Team-26
91Bakers/Cal-16
Gallego, Mike
82Tacoma-30
82WHave-12
84Cram/PCL-81
85Mother/A's-24
86D-156
86T-304
86Tacoma-7
88D-379
88D/A's/Bk-379
88Modesto-33
88Mother/A's-22
88S-428
88T-702
88T/Big-103
89D-422
89F-8
89Mother/A's-23
89S-537
89T-102
89UD-583
90B-459
90D-361
90F-7
90F/Can-7
90Leaf-121
90Mother/A's-25
90OPC-293
90Publint/St-304
90S-323
90T-293
90T/Big-73
90UD-230
91B-219
91D-158
91F-7
91Leaf-78
91Mother/A's-25
91OPC-686
91S-476
91SFExam/A's-4
91StCl-151
91T-686
91UD-151
91Ultra-246
92B-273
92D-314
92F-256
92L-236
92L/BlkGold-236
92OPC-76
92OPC/Premier-131
92Panini-16
92Pinn-387
92S-43
92S/RookTr-30T
92StCl-106
92StCl-627
92Studio-211
92T-76
92T/Gold-76
92T/GoldWin-76
92T/Tr-38T
92T/TrGold-38T
92UD-193
92UD-750
92Ultra-112
92Ultra-406
93Cadaco-23
93D-81
93F-648
93L-96
93Pinn-388
93Select-220
93StCl-126
93StCl/1stDay-126
93StCl/Y-11
93T-287
93T/Gold-287
93TripleP-226
93UD-600
93Ultra-240
94D-495
94F-229
94Flair-80
94L-136
94Pac/Cr-422
94Panini-100
94Pinn-451
94S-244
94S/GoldR-244
94Select-53
94StCl-388
94StCl/1stDay-388
94StCl/Gold-388
94StCl/Team-183
94T-432
94T/Finest-75
94T/FinestRef-75
94T/Gold-432
94TripleP-273
94UD-412
94UD/CollC-104
94UD/CollC/Gold-104
94UD/CollC/Silv-104
94Ultra-398
Gallegos, Matt
83Nashvl-6
Gallia, Melvin
(Bert)
D328-54
E135-54
W514-76
Galligani, Marcel
92FrRow/DP-67
92SoOreg/ClBest-3
92SoOreg/ProC-3424
Galliher, Marve
75Hawaii/Caruso-9
Gallivan, Phil
90Target-266
Gallo, Ben
81Clinton-6
90Reno/Cal-287CO
Gallo, Raymond
81BurlB-6
83ElPaso-14
Galloway, Clarence E.
(Chick)
21Exh-54
61F-108
93Conlon-967
E120
E126-15
E210-58
V100
W572
W573
Galloway, Gill
89Billings/ProC-2065
Galloway, Ike
88Batavia/ProC-1680
Galloway, Joseph
26Exh-106
Galloway, Troy
85Visalia-24
86OrlanTw-6
87Visalia-9
Galvan, Mike
88Utica/Pucko-20
89Utica/Pucko-8
90Saraso/Star-9
90Star/ISingl-58
91Saraso/ClBest-4
91Saraso/ProC-1107
Galvez, Balvino
86Albuq-8
89Colum/CMC-10
89Colum/Pol-6
89Colum/ProC-748
90AAASingl/ProC-579
90Indianap/ProC-296
90Target-267
92SanAn/ProC-3969
92SanAn/SB-564
93LimeR/Winter-61
Galvez, Roberto
78Dunedin
Galvin, James
(Pud)
75F/Pion-11
76Motor-8
76Shakey-102
80Perez/HOF-102
80SSPC/HOF
89HOF/St-80
N172
WG1-59
Gamba, Tom J.
87Watlo-8
88Watlo/ProC-673
Gambee, Brad
86Cram/NWL-4
86Everett/Pop-6
87Everett-29
Gambeski, Mike
83Spring/Frit-23
Gamble, Billy
88Wythe/ProC-2000
Gamble, Freddie
89Bristol/Star-8
92Erie/ClBest-4
92Erie/ProC-1630
Gamble, John
74OPC-597R
74T-597R
Gamble, Lee
40PlayBall-208
W711/1
Gamble, Oscar
70T-654R
71MLB/St-178
71OPC-23
71T-23
72OPC-423
72T-423
73OPC-372
73T-372
74OPC-152
74T-152
74T/St-166
75Ho-147
75OPC-213
75T-213
75T/M-213
76OPC-74
76SSPC-526
76T-74
76T/Tr-74T
77T-505
78Ho-100
78Padre/FamFun-13
78T-390
79OPC-132
79T-263
80T-698
81D-229
81F-98
81OPC-139
81T-139
82D-360
82F-36
82OPC-229
82T-472
83D-461
83F-380
83OPC-19
83T-19
84F-124
84Nes/792-512
84OPC-13
84T-512
85Coke/WS-0
85F/Up-U44
85OPC-93
85T-724
85T/Tr-37T
89Pac/SenLg-116
89TM/SenLg-37
92Yank/WIZ70-51
92Yank/WIZ80-65
93Rang/Keeb-156
Gamble, Robert
N172
Gamboa, Tom
90AAASingl/ProC-394MG
90ProC/Singl-691MG
90Toledo/CMC-22MG
90Toledo/ProC-164MG

Gambrell, Glen
91Melbourne/Fut-19
Gambs, Chris
92ClBest-320
92Clinton/ClBest-13
92Clinton/ProC-3590
92StCl/Dome-54
93B-280
Gamby, Steve
75Clinton
Gamez, Bobby
90Boise/ProC-3317
91QuadC/ClBest-4
91QuadC/ProC-2621
92PalmSp/ClBest-8
92PalmSp/ProC-830
Gamez, Francisco
91Beloit/ClBest-3
91Beloit/ProC-2096
92ClBest-283
92Stockton/ClBest-16
92Stockton/ProC-30
93B-267
Gammage, Mark
82BurlR/Frit-17
82BurlR/TCMA-19
Gammill, Jimmy
88MissSt-6
89MissSt-13
90MissSt-12
91MissSt-17
Ganch, Tim
78Charl
Gandarillas, Gus
92Classic/DP-118
92Elizab/ProC-3674
93StCl/MurphyS-138
93T-786M
93T/Gold-786M
94FExcel-94
Gandil, Charles
(Chick)
14CJ-39
15CJ-39
88Pac/8Men-106
88Pac/8Men-22M
88Pac/8Men-25
88Pac/8Men-46
88Pac/8Men-48M
88Pac/8Men-9
94Conlon-1031
BF2-22
C46-65
D328-55
D329-64
E135-55
E90/3
M101/4-64
T206
T213/blue
W514-31
Gandolph, David
91GulfCR/SportP-4
92Gaston/ClBest-16
92Gaston/ProC-2246
Gandy, Chris
79Clinton/TCMA-13
Ganley, Robert
E91
T204
T206
Ganote, Joe
90StCath/ProC-3461
91Myrtle/ClBest-5
91Myrtle/ProC-2939
91SALAS/ProC-SAL38
92Dunedin/ProC-1993
93Knoxvl/ProC-1247
Gant, Ronald Edwin
(Ronnie)
86Durham-12
87Greenvl/Best-13
87SLAS-13
88D-654
88D/Best-2
88D/Rook-47
88F-538
88Richm/CMC-12
88Richm/ProC-3
88S-647
88T/Big-249
88T/Tr-39T
89B-274
89Brave/Dubuq-11
89Bz-9
89Classic-35
89D-50
89F-590
89KMart/DT-2
89KennerFig-47
89OPC-196
89Panini/St-42
89S-372
89S/HotRook-87
89S/YS/I-16
89Sf-28
89T-296
89T/Big-43
89T/Gloss60-10
89T/JumboR-9
89T/St-322
89T/St-34
89T/UK-29
89ToysRUs-10
89UD-378
90Brave/Dubuq/Perf-7
90Brave/Dubuq/Singl-8
90D-475
90D/BestNL-111
90F-582
90F/Can-582
90Leaf-376
90OPC-567
90PublInt/St-113
90PublInt/St-612
90T-567
90T/Big-66
90UD-232
91B-583
91Brave/Dubuq/Perf-10
91Brave/Dubuq/Stand-14
91Classic/200-123
91Classic/I-5
91Classic/III-23
91Classic/III-24
91D-10DK
91D-507
91D/SuperDK-10
91F-688
91Leaf-129
91Leaf/Stud-144
91MajorLg/Pins-47
91OPC-725
91OPC/Premier-49
91Panini/FrSt-23
91Panini/St-27
91Panini/Top15-36
91Panini/Top15-52
91RedFoley/St-38
91S-448
91S/100SS-14
91StCl-454
91T-725
91T/CJMini/II-19
91UD-361
91UD-82TC
91Ultra-4
92B-534
92Brave/LykePerf-12
92Brave/LykeStand-13
92Classic/Game200-15
92Classic/II-T19
92D-284
92F-357
92F/Lumber-L9
92Hardee-9
92L-15
92L/BlkGold-15
92OPC-25
92OPC/Premier-4
92Panini-167
92Pinn-128
92Pinn/Slug-8
92S-25
92S/100SS-76
92S/Impact-65
92StCl-730
92StCl/Dome-55
92Studio-3
92T-25
92T-391AS
92T/Gold-25
92T/Gold-391AS
92T/GoldWin-25
92T/GoldWin-391AS
92T/Kids-32
92T/McDonB-14
92TripleP-126
92UD-345
92UD/HRH-HR7
92USPlayC/Ace-4H
92USPlayC/Ace-8C
92USPlayC/Brave-13H
92USPlayC/Brave-9C
92Ultra-161
93B-382
93Brave/LykePerf-10
93Brave/LykeStand-12
93Colla/DM-37
93D-210
93D/EliteDom-4
93F-3
93Flair-3
93L-225
93OPC-108
93Pac/Spanish-5
93Panini-185
93Pinn-445
93Pinn/HRC-20
93S-220
93Select-133
93StCl-28
93StCl/1stDay-28
93StCl/Brave-6
93StCl/MurphyS-98
93Studio-88
93T-393
93T/Finest-68
93T/FinestRef-68
93T/Gold-393
93TripleP-199
93UD-264
93UD/SP-57
93UD/SPPlat-PP7
93Ultra-5
94D-34
94D/DomI-8
94D/Special-34
94F-358
94F-706M
94F/Lumber-3
94Pac/Cr-8
94Pac/Gold-15
94Panini-144
94S-332
94S/GoldS-14
94Sf/2000-90
94StCl-123
94StCl-260
94StCl/1stDay-123
94StCl/1stDay-260
94StCl/Gold-123
94StCl/Gold-260
94StCl/Pr-123
94StCl/Team-41
94T-166
94T/BlkGold-31
94T/Finest-165
94T/FinestRef-165
94T/Gold-166
94TripleP-43
94TripleP/Bomb-7
94Ultra/HRK-11
94Ultra/RBIK-9
Gantner, Jim
77Spoka
77T-494R
79T-154
80T-374
81D-204
81F-522
81F/St-133
81OPC-122
81T-482
82D-406
82F-142
82OPC-207
82Pol/Brew-17
82T-613
83D-232
83F-34
83F/St-17M
83Gard-8
83OPC-88
83Pol/Brew-17
83T-88
84D-115
84F-200
84Gard-7
84Nes/792-298
84OPC-298
84Pol/Brew-17
84T-298
84T/St-298
85D-229
85D/AAS-2
85F-582
85Gard-7
85Leaf-217
85OPC-216
85Pol/Brew-17
85T-781
85T/St-295
86D-115
86F-487
86Jay's-8
86Leaf-43
86OPC-51
86Pol/Brew-17
86T-582
86T/St-202
86T/Tatt-9M
87D-172
87D/OD-53
87F-345
87OPC-108
87Pol/Brew-17
87Smok/AL-15
87T-108
87T/St-197
88D-214
88D/Best-53
88F-165
88Leaf-161
88OPC-337
88Panini/St-124
88Pol/Brew-17
88S-197
88Sf-130
88T-337
88T/St-195
89B-141
89Brewer/YB-17
89D-264
89D/Best-295
89F-186
89Gard-3
89OPC-134
89Panini/St-372
89Pol/Brew-17
89S-313
89T-671
89T/Big-184
89T/St-203
89UD-274
90B-400
90Brewer/MillB-9
90D-291
90F-324
90F/Can-324
90MLBPA/Pins-81
90OPC-417
90Panini/St-94
90Pol/Brew-17
90PublInt/St-496
90S-382
90T-417
90T/Big-124
90T/St-207
90UD-218
91B-48
91Brewer/MillB-8
91D-703
91F-584
91Leaf-145
91OPC-23
91Pol/Brew-8
91S-532
91StCl-183
91T-23
91UD-618
91Ultra-174
92B-301
92Brew/Carlson-8
92D-574
92F-176
92OPC-248
92Panini-37
92Pinn-71
92Pol/Brew-8
92S-246
92StCl-502
92T-248
92T/Gold-248
92T/GoldWin-248
92UD-360
92Ultra-382
93F-630
93Pac/Spanish-156
93Pinn-207
Ganzel, Charles
N172
N300/unif
N526
Scrapp
Ganzel, John Henry
C46-26
T206
Garagiola, Joe
47TipTop
49Eureka-182
51B-122
52B-27
52T-227
53B/Col-21
54B-141
79TCMA-262
80Pac/Leg-76
90Pac/Legend-24
90Swell/Great-14
91Swell/Great-31
91T/Arc53-314
92AP/ASG-43
92Bz/Quadra-21
93TWill-89
Garagozzo, Keith
91Oneonta/ProC-4148
92ClBest-290
92Greens/ClBest-2
92Greens/ProC-772
94B-656
94Flair-74
94Ultra-388
Garbark, Bob
93Conlon-946
Garbark, Mike
44Playball-8
Garber, Gene
74OPC-431
74T-431
75OPC-444
75T-444
75T/M-444
76OPC-14
76SSPC-458
76T-14
77T-286
78SSPC/270-38
78T-177
79OPC-331
79T-629
80OPC-263
80T-504
81D-77
81F-249
81OPC-307
81Pol/Atl-26
81T-307
81T/SO-42
81T/St-137
82BK/Lids-8
82D-123
82F-434
82F/St-234
82Pol/Atl-26
82T-32
82T/St-245
83D-223
83F-136
83F/St-14M
83F/St-9M
83OPC-255
83OPC-256SV
83OPC/St-213
83Pol/Atl-26
83T-255
83T-256IA
83T/Fold-4M
83T/St-213
84D-287
84F-179
84Nes/792-466
84Nes/792-709LL
84OPC-167
84Pol/Atl-26
84T-466
84T-709LL
84T/St-35
85F-325

85Ho/Braves-9
85Pol/Atl-26
85T-129
86F-515
86Pol/Atl-26
86T-776
87D-414
87F-515
87F/Excit-17
87F/RecSet-10
87F/St-44
87Leaf-172
87Sf/TPrev-24M
87Smok/Atl-9
87T-351
87T/St-40
88D-618
88D/Best-63
88F-257
88OPC-289
88S-565
88Sf-88
88Smok/Royals-11
88T-597

Garber, Jeff
88Eugene/Best-16
89AppFx/ProC-863
90BBCity/Star-8
91AA/LineD-406
91Memphis/LineD-406
91Memphis/ProC-660
92Memphis/ProC-2425
92Memphis/SB-435

Garbey, Barbaro
81BirmB
82BirmB-2
83Evansvl-18
84F/X-42
84T/Tr-41
84Tiger/Farmer-3
84Tiger/Wave-14
85Cain's-7
85D-456
85F-7
85F/St-121
85Leaf-121
85OPC-243
85T-243
85T/St-263
85Wendy-8
86D-349
86F-225
86OPC-88
86T-609
88OkCty/CMC-16
88OkCty/ProC-45
90BirmDG/Best-13
93Rang/Keeb-157

Garbould, Bob
44Centen-8

Garces, Jesus
90Princet/DIMD-7
91Batavia/ClBest-9
91Batavia/ProC-3491
92Spartan/ClBest-5
92Spartan/ProC-1268

Garces, Maduro
89Hagers/Best-6

Garces, Richard
(Rich)
89Kenosha/ProC-1076
89Kenosha/Star-6
89Star/Wax-51
90A&AASingle/ProC-140
90AS/Cal-18
90Visalia/Cal-62
90Visalia/ProC-2148
91AAA/LineD-408
91B-324
91Classic/I-59
91D-420RR
91OPC-594
91Portl/LineD-408
91Portl/ProC-1562
91StCl-370
91T-594
91T/90Debut-50
91UD/Ext-741
91Ultra-378MLP
92D-516
92OrlanSR/ProC-2840
92OrlanSR/SB-505
92Sky/AASingl-217

Garces, Robinson
87Lakeland-21
88Fayette/ProC-1087
89Hagers/ProC-281
89Hagers/Star-8
90ElPaso/GS-13

Garcia, Adrian
92Pulaski/ClBest-11
92Pulaski/ProC-3180
93Macon/ClBest-9
93Macon/ProC-1402

Garcia, Alfonso
(Kiko)
77T-474R
78T-287
79T-543
80T-37
81D-514
81F-191
81OPC-192
81T-688
81T/Tr-765
82D-476
82F-215
82T-377
83D-569
83F-447
83Portl-25
83T-198
83T/Tr-36
84D-545
84F-30
84Nes/792-458
84Phill/TastyK-30
84T-458
85Phill/TastyK-29
85T-763
91Crown/Orio-150

Garcia, Amadeo
89Elizab/Star-26

Garcia, Anastacio
90MedHat/Best-13
91Dunedin/ClBest-13
91Dunedin/ProC-209
92Myrtle/ClBest-5
92Myrtle/ProC-2199
93Knoxvl/ProC-1253

Garcia, Anthony
89Salem/Team-3TR
90Bakers/Cal-245TR

Garcia, Apolinar
89Madis/Star-10
90Modesto/Chong-10
90Modesto/ProC-2206
91AAA/LineD-534
91Huntsvl/Team-10
91Tacoma/LineD-534
91Tacoma/ProC-2298
92FtMyr/ProC-2738
92Miracle/ClBest-5
93LimeR/Winter-98

Garcia, Butch
90CharlK/Team-10

Garcia, Carlos
88Augusta/ProC-365
89Salem/Star-9
90A&AASingle/ProC-28
90EastLAS/ProC-EL25
90Harris/ProC-1199
90Harris/Star-7
90ProC/Singl-761
91B-531
91BuffB/LineD-29
91BuffB/ProC-546
91F-37
91T/90Debut-51
91Ultra-278
92AAA/ASG/SB-33
92B-576
92BuffB/BlueS-9
92BuffB/ProC-327
92BuffB/SB-33
92Classic/I-37
92D-14RR
92Pinn-264
92ProC/Tomorrow-305
92S-821
92Sky/AAASingl-14
92UD-665
93B-626
93D-598
93F-501
93Flair-112
93L-277
93OPC/Premier-111
93Pac/Spanish-244
93Pinn-558
93Pirate/Nation-12
93S-246
93S/Boys-14
93Select-403
93Select/RookTr-40T
93StCl-545
93StCl/1stDay-545
93Studio-49
93T-27
93T/Finest-4
93T/FinestRef-4
93T/Gold-27
93ToysRUs-70
93TripleP-65
93UD-334
93UD/SP-184
93Ultra-450
94B-218
94D-161
94F-609
94L-248
94OPC-112
94OPC/DiamD-18
94Pac/Cr-498
94Panini-235
94Pinn-108
94Pinn/Artist-108
94Pinn/Museum-108
94S-520
94Select-119
94StCl-206
94StCl/1stDay-206
94StCl/Gold-206
94Studio-145
94T-309
94T/Finest-57
94T/FinestRef-57
94T/Gold-309
94TripleP-183
94UD-198
94UD/CollC-105
94UD/CollC/Gold-105
94UD/CollC/Silv-105
94UD/ElecD-198
94UD/SP-141
94Ultra-555

Garcia, Cheo
89Kenosha/ProC-1083
89Kenosha/Star-7
91AA/LineD-480
91OrlanSR/LineD-480
91OrlanSR/ProC-1855
92OrlanSR/ProC-2853
92OrlanSR/SB-501
92ProC/Tomorrow-94
93Pawtu/Ball-12

Garcia, Cornelio
(Chidez)
86AppFx-9
88FSLAS/Star-37
88Tampa/Star-7
89BirmB/Best-9
89BirmB/ProC-102
90BirmB/Best-9
90BirmB/ProC-1117

Garcia, Damaso
76FtLaud
77WHave
78Cr/PCL-49
79Colum-4
81D-269
81F-415
81OPC-233
81OPC/Post-14
81T-488
82D-479
82F-613
82OPC-293
82OPC/Post-2
82T-596
83D-54
83D/AAS-17
83F-427
83F/St-11M
83F/St-9M
83OPC-202TL
83OPC-222
83OPC/St-134
83PermaGr/CC-24
83T-202TL
83T-222
83T/St-134
84D-241
84F-153
84Nes/792-124
84OPC-124
84T-124
84T/RD-14M
84T/St-364
84Tor/Fire-12
85D-315
85D/AAS-6
85F-104
85Leaf-65
85OPC-353
85OPC/Post-15
85T-645
85T-702AS
85T/RD-12M
85T/St-357
85Tor/Fire-11
86BJ/Ault-10
86D-241
86D/AAS-40
86F-59
86F/LimEd-17
86F/Mini-15
86F/St-41
86GenMills/Book-3M
86Leaf-116
86OPC-45
86Sf-34
86T-45
86T-713
86T/St-190
86T/Tatt-24M
86Tor/Fire-12
87D-614
87F-226
87Leaf-92
87OPC-395
87Sf-183
87Smok/Atl-22
87T-395
87T/St-188
88D-414
88T-241
89T/Big-275
90BJ/HoSt-1M
90F-346
90F/Can-346
90OPC-432
90T-432
90UD-649
92Nabisco-20
92Yank/WIZ70-52

Garcia, Danny
76Watlo
91Spokane/ClBest-28CO
91Spokane/ProC-3966CO
92Wichita/ProC-3670CO
92Wichita/SB-650M

Garcia, Dave
73OPC-12CO
73T-12C
78SSPC/270-193MG
78T-656MG
81D-442MG
81T-665MG
82BK/Indians-1MG
82BK/Indians-2MG
82D-337MG
82Wheat/Ind
83Pol/Brew-C
83T-546MG

Garcia, Eduardo
92GulfCD/ProC-3579

Garcia, Edward M.
(Mike)
50B-147
50NumNum
51B-150
51T/RB-40
52B-7
52NumNum-7
52T-272
53B/Col-43
53T-75
54B-100
54DanDee
55B-128
55Gol/Ind-8
55Salem
56Carling-2
56T-210
57Sohio/Ind-5
57T-300
58T-196
59T-516
60T-532
91T/Arc53-75
94TedW-26

Garcia, Fermin
91Princet/ClBest-27
91Princet/ProC-3506
92Billings/ProC-3347
92CharWh/ClBest-4
92CharWh/ProC-2

Garcia, Francisco
90AppFox/Box-8
90AppFox/ProC-2107

Garcia, Frank
80Ashvl-23
80Tulsa-12
83StPete-17

Garcia, Freddy
93MedHat/ProC-3744
93MedHat/SportP-14

Garcia, Guillermo
91Kingspt/ClBest-14
91Kingspt/ProC-3821
92Pittsfld/ClBest-6
92Pittsfld/ProC-3299

Garcia, Jaime
92SoBend/ClBest-26CO
92SoBend/ProC-194CO

Garcia, Joe
75SanAn

Garcia, Jose Luis
90AS/Cal-4
90ProC/Singl-714
90Visalia/Cal-78
90Visalia/ProC-2161
93LimeR/Winter-55

Garcia, Julio
89Princet/Star-26
91Augusta/ClBest-1CO
91Augusta/ProC-823CO
92Augusta/ClBest-26
92Welland/ClBest-29CO
92Welland/ProC-1342CO
93Welland/ClBest-30CO

Garcia, Leo
81AppFx-15
82AppFx/Frit-3
83Water-17
84Wichita/Rock-4
87Nashvl-5
89Toledo/CMC-16
89Toledo/ProC-767
90AAASingl/ProC-557
90Nashvl/CMC-15
90Nashvl/ProC-245
90ProC/Singl-140
91AAA/LineD-256
91Nashvl/LineD-256
91Nashvl/ProC-2169
92Omaha/ProC-2974
92Omaha/SB-330

Garcia, Leonard
77SLCity
78Cr/PCL-88
79SLCity-23
80SLCity-19
81SLCity-1
86Edmon-12TR

Garcia, Librado
89Beloit/I/Star-6
89Beloit/II/Star-11
90Miami/I/Star-8

Garcia, Longo
87PanAm/USAB-14
87PanAm/USAR-14
89Miami/I/Star-7
89Miami/II/Star-5
90TeamUSA/87-14

Garcia, Luis
90LSUPol-13
92Kenosha/ProC-596

Garcia, Manny
89Butte/SP-19
91Kane/ClBest-16
91Kane/ProC-2663
91Kane/Team-7

Garcia, Marcelino
92Spokane/ClBest-11
92Spokane/ProC-1296

Garcia, Marcos
90Penin/Star-8
91CalLgAS-22
91SanBern/ClBest-4
91SanBern/ProC-1980
92Jaxvl/SB-356
Garcia, Mario
90Princet/DIMD-8
91Hunting/ClBest-9
91Hunting/ProC-3327
92Hunting/ProC-3139
Garcia, Michael
89Bristol/Star-9
90A&AASingle/ProC-84
90Fayette/ProC-2398
90SALAS/Star-8
91Lakeland/ClBest-5
91Lakeland/ProC-261
92London/ProC-627
92London/SB-408
Garcia, Miguel
75BurlB
76Clinton
80Ander-22
81Durham-2
82Durham-1
86PalmSp-14
86PalmSp/Smok-8
87MidldA-1
89BuffB/CMC-7
89BuffB/ProC-1686
89D-622
89F-647R
90Harris/ProC-1188
90Harris/Star-8
90UD-538
93LimeR/Winter-92
Garcia, Nelson Jose
75OkCty/Team-19
80ArkTr-17
Garcia, Omar
90Kgsport/Best-13
90Kgsport/Star-10
91Clmbia/PCPII-6
91Clmbia/PII-30M
91Clmbia/PII-9
92ClBest-337
92ColumMet/ClBest-21
92ColumMet/ProC-303
92ColumMet/SAL/II-7
93ClBest/MLG-157
93SALAS/II-11
93StLucie/ProC-2927
94FExcel-234
Garcia, Oscar
89StCath/ProC-2075
Garcia, Pedro
73OPC-609R
73T-609R
74OPC-142
74T-142
74T/St-195
75OPC-147
75T-147
75T/M-147
76OPC-187
76SSPC-234
76T-187
77OPC-166
77T-453
77Watlo
Garcia, Ralph
73OPC-602R
73T-602R
Garcia, Ramon
90Saraso/Star-10
91AA/LineD-59
91BirmB/LineD-59
91BirmB/ProC-1449
91D/Rook-13
92Classic/Game200-97
92D-658
92D/Rook-41
92OPC-176
92ProC/Tomorrow-42
92S-745
92Sky/AAASingl-282
92StCl-866
92T-176
92T/91Debut-60
92T/Gold-176
92T/GoldWin-176
92Vanco/ProC-2716
92Vanco/SB-635
Garcia, Raphael
90MedHat/Best-25
91Myrtle/ClBest-6
91Myrtle/ProC-2940
92Dunedin/ClBest-14
92Myrtle/ProC-2189
Garcia, Ray
85Utica-19
Garcia, Reggie
88Martins/Star-15
89Spartan/ProC-1039
89Spartan/Star-9
Garcia, Rene
86Bakers-10
87VeroB-27
Garcia, Rich
88TM/Umpire-22
89TM/Umpire-20
90TM/Umpire-19
Garcia, Santiago
88Vanco/CMC-13
88Vanco/ProC-764
Garcia, Steve
83Beaum-12
84Beaum-18
85Cram/PCL-115
86LasVegas-3
87LasVegas-20
88Albuq/CMC-24
88Albuq/ProC-249
Garcia, Victor
(Butch)
87Columbia-16
87Peoria-2
87Peoria/PW-1
88CLAS/Star-27
88PrWill/Star-11
88WinSalem/Star-3
89CharlK-7
89FtLaud/Star-5
89Greens/ProC-407
89Iowa/CMC-11
89Iowa/ProC-1693
90A&AASingle/ProC-122
90Cedar/Best-16
90Cedar/ProC-2315
90FtLaud/Star-8
90MidwLgAS/GS-33
91AA/LineD-159
91AA/LineD-5
91Albany/LineD-5
91Albany/ProC-1001
91Chatt/LineD-159
91Chatt/ProC-1954
92Canton/ProC-684
92Canton/SB-107
93LimeR/Winter-102
Garcia, Vinicio U.
(Chico)
54Esskay
91Crown/Orio-149
Garcia-Luna, Frank
92Welland/ClBest-8
92Welland/ProC-1316
Garciaparra, Nomar
92T/Tr-39T
92T/TrGold-39T
93StCl/MurphyS-93
Garczyk, Ed
(Eddie)
89SLCity-9
90Miami/II/Star-6
Gardella, Danny
45Playball-36
Gardella, Mike
88CapeCod/Sum-69
89Oneonta/ProC-2103
90CLAS/CL-15
90PrWill/Team-10
91AA/LineD-6
91Albany/LineD-6
91Albany/ProC-1002
91ClBest/Singl-46
92Albany/SB-7
92B-52
92Canton/ProC-685
92ClBest-4
Gardenhire, Ron
81Tidew-5
82D-649
82T-623R
82T/Tr-39T
83D-175
83F-543
83T-469
83Tidew-20
85D-360
85F-81
85T-144
86T-274
86Tidew-10
87Portl-25
88Kenosha/ProC-1402
88MidwLAS/GS-36
89OrlanTw/Best-5
89OrlanTw/ProC-1355
90OrlanSR/Best-28MG
90OrlanSR/ProC-1098MG
90OrlanSR/Star-24MG
91WIZMets-132
92TX-14
Gardey, Rudy
88Idaho/ProC-1855
90Salinas/Cal-123
Gardiner, Mike
88Wausau/GS-25
89Wausau/GS-28
90A&AASingle/ProC-16
90EastLAS/ProC-EL17
90Star/ISingl-49
90Wmsprt/Best-6
90Wmsprt/ProC-1052
90Wmsprt/Star-7
91AAA/LineD-355
91Classic/III-25
91D-417RR
91D/Rook-46
91Pawtu/LineD-355
91Pawtu/ProC-31
91S-721RP
91T/90Debut-52
91UD-14RP
92D-290
92L-482
92L/BlkGold-482
92OPC-694
92Pinn-505
92ProC/Tomorrow-17
92RedSox/Dunkin-13
92S-694
92StCl-732
92T-694
92T/Gold-694
92T/GoldWin-694
92UD-588
93D-515
93F-558
93F/Final-94
93T-241
93T/Gold-241
93UD-640
93Ultra-414
94StCl-474
94StCl/1stDay-474
94StCl/Gold-474
Gardner, Art
73Cedar
75Iowa/TCMA-8
78Cr/PCL-2
86Tulsa-5CO
87Gaston/ProC-24
Gardner, Billy F.
52Park-88
55B-249
55Gol/Giants-7
55T-27
55T/DH-61
57T-17
58Hires-37
58T-105
59T-89
60T-106
61Clover-5
61P-96
61Peters-14
61T-123
61T/St-179
62Salada-211
62Shirriff-211
62T-163M
62T-338
63T-408
79Memphis/TCMA-21MG
82D-591MG
83T-11MG
83Twin/Team-27MG
83Twin/Team-34M
84Nes/792-771MG
84T-771MG
85T-213MG
85Twin/Team-31MG
87T/Tr-36T
91Crown/Orio-151
92Yank/WIZ60-45
Gardner, Billy Jr.
88Eugene/Best-19
90Pittsfld/Pucko-27CO
91Pittsfld/ClBest-27CO
91Pittsfld/ProC-3439CO
92StLucie/ClBest-27CO
92StLucie/ProC-1764
Gardner, Chris
90Ashvl/ProC-2741
91Jacks/ProC-919
92B-457
92D-413RR
92L-8
92L/BlkGold-8
92Pinn-599
92ProC/Tomorrow-227
92Sky/AAASingl-271
92T/91Debut-61
92Tucson/ProC-481
92Tucson/SB-607
Gardner, Chuck
77Clinton
Gardner, Damon
90MissSt-13
91MissSt-18
Gardner, Earl M.
11Helmar-44
M116
T201
T205
T207
Gardner, Floyd
(Jelly)
74Laugh/Black-7
Gardner, Franklin W.
N172
Gardner, Glen
88Pulaski/ProC-1756
89SALAS/GS-42
89Sumter/ProC-1097
90BurlB/Best-3
90BurlB/ProC-2355
90BurlB/Star-11
90Foil/Best-217
Gardner, Harry R.
16FleischBrd-29
Gardner, Jeff
86Lynch-10
87Jacks/Feder-9
87TexLgAS-7
88Jacks/GS-10
89Tidew/CMC-20
89Tidew/ProC-1966
90AAASingl/ProC-282
90ProC/Singl-367
90T/TVMets-42
90Tidew/CMC-16
90Tidew/ProC-551
91AAA/LineD-555
91AAAGame/ProC-48
91Tidew/LineD-555
91Tidew/ProC-2517
92F-675
92LasVegas/ProC-2800
92LasVegas/SB-231
92ProC/Tomorrow-279
92S-869
92Sky/AAASingl-114
92T/91Debut-62
93D-470
93F/Final-138
93L-238
93Mother/Padre-22
93Select/RookTr-140T
93T-663
93T/Gold-663
93UD-639
94D-406
94F-662
94Pac/Cr-522
94Panini-255
94Pinn-296
94S-478
94StCl-58
94StCl/1stDay-58
94StCl/Gold-58
94T-544
94T/Finest-196
94T/FinestRef-196
94T/Gold-544
94UD/CollC-106
94UD/CollC/Gold-106
94UD/CollC/Silv-106
94Ultra-278
Gardner, Jimmie
T3/Box-62
Gardner, John
86Geneva-6
86Peoria-7
87CharWh-20
88CharWh/Best-15
89CharWh/Best-19
89CharWh/ProC-1769
90WinSalem/Team-6
91AA/LineD-132
91CharlK/LineD-132
91CharlK/ProC-1683
92Iowa/ProC-4047
92Iowa/SB-208
92Sky/AAASingl-101
Gardner, Mark
86Jaxvl/TCMA-15
87Indianap-19
88Jaxvl/Best-7
88Jaxvl/ProC-987
89AAA/CMC-10
89AAA/ProC-10
89Indianap/CMC-8
89Indianap/ProC-1224
90B-106
90Classic/III-T4
90D-40RR
90D/Rook-20
90F-646R
90F/Can-646M
90F/Up-U29
90Foil/Best-262
90HotRook/St-16
90Leaf-371
90OPC-284
90S-639
90S/100Ris-66
90T-284
90T/89Debut-41
90ToysRUs-10
90TripleAAS/CMC-10
90UD/Ext-743
91D-443
91Expo/PostC-3
91F-233
91OPC-757
91Panini/St-67
91Panini/Top15-91
91S-518
91S/100RisSt-71
91StCl-592
91T-757
91UD-663
92B-562
92D-238
92Expo/D/Duri-9
92F-481
92L-512
92L/BlkGold-512
92OPC-119
92Pinn-215
92S-586
92S-785HL
92StCl-42
92T-119
92T/Gold-119
92T/GoldWin-119
92UD-557
93B-421
93D-64
93F-75
93F/Final-218
93L-313
93OPC/Premier-21
93Pol/Royal-8
93S-390
93Select-185
93StCl-159
93StCl-663
93StCl/1stDay-159
93StCl/1stDay-663
93StCl/Royal-24
93T-314
93T/Gold-314
93UD-348
93UD-641

93Ultra-560
94StCl/Team-83
Gardner, Myron
86Watlo-8
88SLCity-20
Gardner, Rob
66T-534R
67T-217
68T-219
710PC-734
71T-734
720PC-22
72T-22
730PC-222
73T-222
91WIZMets-133
92Yank/WIZ70-53
Gardner, Scott
82DayBe-4
83Miami-3
90Hunting/ProC-3274
91Hunting/ClBest-10
91Hunting/ProC-3328
92Geneva/ClBest-16
92Geneva/ProC-1555
93Peoria/Team-5
Gardner, Vassie
81Charl-20
82Knoxvl-19
Gardner, Wes
83Lynch-23
84Tidew-3
85IntLgAS-21
85Tidew-9
88D-634
88D/RedSox/Bk-634
88F-352
88T-189
89B-23
89D-541
89F-88
89S-412
89T-526
90B-266
90D-541
90F-275
90F/Can-275
90Leaf-407
900PC-38
90Pep/RSox-9
90PublInt/St-455
90S-348
90T-38
90T/TVRSox-10
91B-653
91F-94
910PC-629
91S-592
91T-629
91UD-214
91WIZMets-134
Gardner, William L.
(Larry)
21Exh-55
91Conlon/Sport-147
D327
D328-56
D329-65
D350/2-65
E120
E121/120
E121/80
E135-56
E220
E254
M101/4-65
M101/5-65
M116
V100
W501-24
W575
Gardner, Willie
90Hunting/ProC-3299
91Geneva/ClBest-7
91Geneva/ProC-4229
91Peoria/ClBest-20
91Peoria/ProC-1357
92ClBest-220
92Peoria/ClBest-14
92Peoria/Team-7
Garham, John
91AubAS/ClBest-29GM
Garia, Mike
92Bz/Quadra-14M

Garibaldi, Art
40Hughes-7
Garibaldi, Bob
70T-681
710PC-701
71T-701
Garibaldo, Chris
89AppFx/ProC-862
90BBCity/Star-9
Gariglio, Robert
81Chatt-1
Garland, Chaon
90SoOreg/Best-14
90SoOreg/ProC-3428
91Modesto/ClBest-5
91Modesto/ProC-3080
92Modesto/ClBest-11
92Modesto/ProC-3893
Garland, Tim
(Nookie)
90Greens/Best-21
90Greens/ProC-2673
90Greens/Star-2
91FtLaud/ClBest-26
91FtLaud/ProC-2440
92ClBest-222
92PrWill/ClBest-15
92PrWill/ProC-160
Garland, Wayne
740PC-596R
74T-596R
760PC-414
76SSPC-376
76T-414
77BurgChef-59
77Ho-144
77Ho/Twink-144
77K-21
770PC-138
77Pep-14
77T-33
77T/CS-17
77T/ClothSt-17
78Ho-137
780PC-15
78T-174
78Wiffle/Discs-25
79T-636
80T-361
81D-440
81F-394
810PC-272
81T-511
82D-489
82F-367
82T-446
87Nashvl-6CO
88Nashvl/CMC-24CO
88Nashvl/ProC-494CO
88Nashvl/Team-25CO
89Pac/SenLg-100
89TM/SenLg-38
90EliteSenLg-68
91Crown/Orio-152
Garlick, Gene
85Clovis-17
Garman, Mike
710PC-512R
71T-512R
720PC-79R
72T-79R
730PC-616R
73T-616R
750PC-584
75T-584
75T/M-584
760PC-34
76SSPC-293
76T-34
77T-302
78SSPC/270-70
78T-417
790PC-88
79Portl-15
79T-181
90Target-268
Garman, Pat
88Gaston/ProC-1014
89CharlR/Star-8
90AAASingl/ProC-684
900kCty/CMC-12
900kCty/ProC-438
90ProC/Singl-162

91AA/LineD-580
91Tulsa/LineD-580
91Tulsa/ProC-2779
Garms, Debs
39PlayBall-72
40PlayBall-161
41DP-149
41G-29
41PlayBall-11
91Conlon/Sport-296
Garner, Darrin
86DayBe-8
87Gaston/ProC-22
88CharlR/Star-7
88FSLAS/Star-38
89Tulsa/GS-9
89Tulsa/Team-7
90Tulsa/ProC-1162
90Tulsa/Team-8
91AAA/LineD-309
910kCty/LineD-309
910kCty/ProC-185
Garner, Kevin
88River/Cal-220
88River/ProC-1431
89AubAs/ProC-17
89Wichita/Rock-33OF
91AA/LineD-60
91BirmB/LineD-60
91BirmB/ProC-1462
91Brisbane/Fut-19
92BirmB/ProC-2592
92Chatt/ProC-3825
Garner, Mike
87VeroB-13
88Reno/Cal-277
Garner, Phil
750PC-623R
75T-623R
75T/M-623R
760PC-57
76SSPC-495
76T-57
77BurgChef-109
77Ho-11
77Ho/Twink-11
770PC-34
77T-261
78Ho-52
780PC-203
78T-53
79Ho-75
790PC-200
79T-383
800PC-65
80T-118
81Coke
81D-372
81F-364
81F/St-71
81K-44
810PC-99
81T-573
81T/SO-102
81T/St-209
81T/St-253
82D-544
82F-216
82Sqt-13
82T-683
83D-270
83F-448
83F/St-13M
83F/St-8M
830PC-128
830PC/St-170
830PC/St-237
83T-478
83T/St-170
83T/St-237
84D-354
84F-226
84Mother/Ast-5
84Nes/792-752
840PC-119
84T-752
84T/RD-11M
84T/St-63
85D-161
85F-351
85Mother/Ast-3
850PC-206
85T-206
85T/RD-11M

85T/St-64
86D-527
86F-301
86F/Mini-64
860PC-83
86Pol/Ast-9
86T-83
86T/St-32
86T/Tatt-24M
87D-358
87D/OD-12
87F-58
87Mother/A's-16
87Mother/Ast-6
870PC-304
87Pol/Ast-24
87T-304
87T/St-30
88Mother/Giants-25
88S-431
88T-174
90Mother/Ast-27CO
90Target-269
91Mother/Ast-28CO
91Swell/Great-113
920PC-291MG
92Pol/Brew-9MG
92T-291MG
92T/Gold-291MG
92T/GoldWin-291MG
93Pol/Brew-8MG
93T-508MG
93T/Gold-508MG
93UD/ATH-56
94Pol/Brew-8MG
94TedW-78
Garnett, Brad
82AlexD-11
Garr, Ralph
700PC-172R
70T-172R
71MLB/St-9
710PC-494R
71T-494R
72K-21
720PC-260
720PC-85LL
72T-260
72T-85LL
73K-37
730PC-15
73T-15
740PC-570
74T-570
74T/St-4
75Ho-87
75K-35
750PC-306LL
750PC-550
75T-306LL
75T-550
75T/M-306LL
75T/M-550
760PC-410
76SSPC-17
76T-410
76T/Tr-410T
77BurgChef-80
77Ho-108
77Ho/Twink-108
77K-13
770PC-77
77Pep-26
77T-133
77T/ClothSt-18
78K-37
780PC-195
78PapaG/Disc-37
78SSPC/270-155
78T-628
78Tastee/Discs-21
78Wiffle/Discs-26
790PC-156
79T-309
800PC-142
80T-272
90Pac/Legend-25
90Richm/25Ann-9
90Swell/Great-46
92Idaho/ProC-3526
93UD/ATH-57
94TedW-42
Garrelts, Scott
80Clinton-10

81Shrev-20
83Phoenix/BHN-3
84Cram/PCL-5
84D-646
85Mother/Giants-23
85T/Tr-38T
86D-309
86D/AAS-35
86F-540
86F/LL-14
86F/Mini-110
86F/St-42
86Leaf-180
86Mother/Giants-19
860PC-395
86Sf-157
86T-395
86T/St-86
86T/Tatt-16M
87D-116
87F-273
87F/Hottest-17
87F/Mini-42
87F/St-45
87Leaf-75
87Mother/SFG-11
870PC-37
87RedFoley/St-24
87Sf-68
87Sf/TPrev-10M
87T-475
87T/St-89
88D-80
88D/Best-162
88F-82
88Mother/Giants-11
880PC-97
88Panini/St-416
88S-533
88Sf-44
88T-97
88T/Big-240
88T/St-90
89B-467
89D-295
89D/Best-218
89F-328
89Mother/Giants-11
890PC-214
89RedFoley/St-48
89S-258
89T-703
89UD-50
90B-228
90D-217
90D/BestNL-110
90F-56
90F/AwardWin-14
90F/BB-11
90F/Can-56
90Leaf-41
90Mother/Giant-16
900PC-602
90Panini/St-367
90PublInt/St-67
90S-246
90Sf-39
90T-602
90T/Big-51
90T/Mini-85
90T/St-82
90UD-478
91B-626
91D-311
91F-262
91Leaf-5
91Leaf/Stud-255
91Mother/Giant-16
910PC-361
91PG&E-29
91S-541
91SFExam/Giant-8
91StCl-182
91T-361
91UD-443
91Ultra-320
92F-636
92Giant/PGE-17
920PC-558
92S-117
92StCl-832
92T-558
92T/Gold-558
92T/GoldWin-558

Garret, Neil
93T-579
93T/Gold-579
Garrett, Bobby
81WHave-9
Garrett, Clifton
90Boise/ProC-3330
91ClBest/Singl-248
91MidwLAS/ProC-26
91QuadC/ClBest-24
91QuadC/ProC-2643
92B-51
92ClBest-210
92PalmSp/ClBest-25
92PalmSp/ProC-854
92UD/ML-314
93ClBest/MLG-131
Garrett, Eric
83Idaho-15
84Madis/Pol-19
85Modesto/Chong-6
Garrett, Greg
70T-642R
71MLB/St-58
71OPC-377
71T-377
Garrett, H. Adrian
(Pat)
66T-553R
71OPC-576R
71T-576R
74OPC-656
74T-656
76OPC-562
76T-562
82AppFx/Frit-31MG
83GlenF-22
87Omaha-16
91Pol/Royal-25CO
92Pol/Royal-27M
93Edmon/ProC-1154CO
Garrett, Lee
80Water-9
81Water-23
82Indianap-31TR
83Indianap-32TR
Garrett, Lynn
81WHave-11
82WHave-21
83Tacoma-15
Garrett, R. Wayne
70T-628
71MLB/St-152
71OPC-228
71T-228
72Dimanche*-19
72OPC-518
72T-518
73OPC-562
73T-562
74OPC-510
74T-510
74T/St-61
75OPC-111
75T-111
75T/M-111
76Expo/Redp-12
76OPC-222
76SSPC-539
76SSPC/MetsY-M5
76T-222
77OPC-117
77T-417
78OPC-198
78T-679
79T-319
89Pac/SenLg-156
89TM/SenLg-39
91WIZMets-135
94Mets/69-23
Garrett, Steve
80Elmira-6
Garrick, Darren
86SanJose-8
Garrido, Gil
61Union
64T-452R
69T-331R
70OPC-48
70T-48
71MLB/St-10
71OPC-173
71T-173
72T-758
88BurlB/ProC-26CO
89Sumter/ProC-1094CO
90BurlB/ProC-2366CO
90BurlB/Star-28CO
91Durham/ProC-1677CO
Garrigan, Pat
92SanBern/ClBest-3
92SanBern/ProC-
Garriott, Cece
47Signal
Garrison, Ford
44Playball-14
Garrison, Jim
87Watertn-18
88Augusta/ProC-369
Garrison, Marv
77LodiD
78LodiD
Garrison, Venoy
75Clinton
Garrison, Webster
85Kingst-16
87Dunedin-15
88SLAS-23
89Knoxvl/Best-6
89Knoxvl/ProC-1131
89Knoxvl/Star-4
90AAASingl/ProC-358
90ProC/Singl-342
90Syrac/CMC-16
90Syrac/MerchB-9
90Syrac/ProC-578
90Syrac/Team-9
91AAA/LineD-535
91Tacoma/LineD-535
91Tacoma/ProC-2313
92Huntsvl/ProC-3956
92Tacoma/SB-533
Garrity, Pat
90LSUPol-3
91LSU/Pol-4
Garrow, David
92Kenosha/ProC-612
Garside, Russ
90CharRain/Best-1
90CharRain/ProC-2038
90Foil/Best-35
90Spokane/SportP-7
Gartner, Mike
91StCl/Member*-41
91StCl/Member*-42
92StCl/MemberIV*-5
Garver, Ned
49B-15
50B-51
51B-172
51FB
51T/BB-18
52B-29
52BR
52StarCal-89A
52StarCal-89AM
52StarCal/L-75A
52T-212
52TipTop
53B/Col-47
53T-112
53Tiger/Glen-9
54B-39
54T-44
55B-188
56T-189
57T-285
58T-292
59T-245
60T-471
61T-331
61T/St-171
89Pac/Leg-183
91T/Arc53-112
94T/Arc54-44
PM10/Sm-59
Garvey, Brian
75AppFx
Garvey, Don
91Welland/ClBest-4
91Welland/ProC-3577
92Augusta/ProC-245
Garvey, Steve
71MLB/St-103
71OPC-341
71T-341
71Ticket/Dodg-6
72T-686
73OPC-213
73T-213
74OPC-575
74T-575
75Ho-49
75Ho/Twink-49
75K-17
75OPC-140
75OPC-212M
75OPC-460NLCS
75SSPC/Puzzle-10
75T-140
75T-212MVP
75T-460NLCS
75T/M-140
75T/M-212MVP
75T/M-460NLCS
76Crane-16
76Ho-19
76Ho/Twink-19
76K-54
76MSA/Disc
76OPC-150
76SSPC-77
76T-150
77BurgChef-150
77Ho-35
77Ho/Twink-35
77K-14
77OPC-255
77Pep-61
77T-400
77T/CS-19
77T/ClothSt-19
78OPC-190
78Pep-31
78SSPC/270-71
78T-350
78Tastee/Discs-3
78Wiffle/Discs-27
79Ho-8
79OPC-21
79T-50
79T/Comics-24
80K-31
80OPC-152
80Pol/Dodg-6
80T-290
80T/S-13
80T/Super-13TP
81D-176
81D-56
81Drake-11
81F-110
81F-606HL
81F/St-1
81K-10
81MSA/Disc-13
81OPC-251
81PermaGr/CC-12
81Pol/Dodg-6
81Sqt-4
81T-530
81T/HT
81T/Nat/Super-6
81T/SO-56
81T/St-176
81T/St-252
82D-3DK
82D-84
82Drake-14
82F-5
82F/St-9
82FBI/Disc-7
82HB/LS
82K-47
82KMart-26
82OPC-179
82OPC-180IA
82P/Tips-1
82P/Tips-12
82PermaGr/CC-11
82Pol/Dodg-6
82T-179
82T-180IA
82T/St-54
83D-488
83F-206
83F/St-14M
83F/St-5M
83OPC-198
83OPC/St-243
83T-610
83T/Fold-3M
83T/St-243
83T/Tr-37
84D-63
84D/AAS-38
84D/Champs-56
84Drake-10
84F-300
84F-628IA
84MiltBrad-10
84Mother/Padres-7
84Nes/792-380
84Nestle/DT-12
84OPC-380
84Ralston-18
84Seven-7W
84Smok/Padres-10
84T-380
84T/Cereal-18
84T/RD-21
84T/St-156
84T/Super-22
85D-307
85Drake-11
85F-32
85F-631IA
85F/LimEd-9
85FunFood/Pin-9
85GenMills-3
85Leaf-94
85Mother/Padres-6
85OPC-177
85Seven-8W
85SpokAT/Cram-7
85T-2RB
85T-450
85T/Gloss22-2
85T/RD-21
85T/St-1
85T/St-13
85T/St-14
85T/St-149
85T/St-176
85T/St-2
85T/Super-26
86BK/AP-18
86D-63
86D/AAS-3
86D/PopUp-3
86F-321
86F-640M
86F/LL-15
86F/Mini-67
86F/St-43
86F/St-S3
86Jiffy-18
86Leaf-56
86Meadow/Blank-4
86Meadow/Stat-15
86OPC-4
86Quaker-6
86Seven/Coin-W14
86Sf-137M
86Sf-35
86Sf-51M
86Sf/Dec-61
86T-660
86T/Gloss22-13
86T/Gloss60-38
86T/St-104
86T/St-148
86T/Super-24
86T/Tatt-5M
86TrueVal-2
87BK-5
87Bohem-6
87Classic-27
87D-81
87D/OD-143
87F-414
87F/Excit-18
87F/GameWin-16
87F/Lim-16
87F/Mini-43
87F/St-46
87Kraft-20
87Leaf-114
87MnM's-20
87OPC-100
87Ralston-2
87RedFoley/St-61
87Sf-40
87Sf/TPrev-16M
87Smok/Dodg-8
87Smok/NL-10
87Stuart-12M
87T-100
87T/Board-18
87T/Coins-32
87T/St-115
88S-225
88Smok/Dodg-15M
88Smok/Dodg-17
88Smok/Dodg-21M
89Padre/Mag-20
89Smok/Dodg-83
90BBWit-26
90Pac/Legend-27
90Swell/Great-103
90Target-270
91LineD-8
91Swell/Great-32
92AP/ASG-64
92MCI-2
93TWill-14
93YooHoo-7
Garvin, Ned
90Target-271
Garvin, Theodore
(Jerry)
78BJ/PostC-6
78OPC-49
78T-419
79OPC-145
79Syrac/Team-25
79T-293
80OPC-320
80T-611
81D-150
81F-429
81OPC-124
81T-124
82D-430
82F-614
82OPC-264
82T-768
83D-227
83F-428
83T-358
92Nabisco-14
Garvin, Virgil
E107
Garza, Alejandro
93CaroMud/RBI-7
Garza, Armando
90NE-12
Garza, Lonnie
83Redwd-10
Garza, Mark
85Clovis-18
Garza, Roberto
92BurlInd/ClBest-16
92BurlInd/ProC-1649
Garza, Willie
88Watlo/ProC-670
Gasgue, Ed
57Seattle/Pop-16
Gash, Darius
90Spokane/SportP-24
91Waterlo/ClBest-20
91Waterlo/ProC-1267
92ClBest-2
92HighD/ClBest-27
Gaspar, Harry
10Domino-47
11Helmar-114
12Sweet/Pin-99
E254
M116
T201
T202
T205
T206
Gaspar, Rod
70OPC-371
70T-371
71MLB/St-227
71OPC-383
71T-383
75Hawaii/Caruso-6
91WIZMets-136
94Mets/69-25
Gass, Jeff
83Erie-16
Gassaway, Charles
46Remar-7
47Remar-4
47Signal

47Smith-8
48Signal
48Smith-10
49B/PCL-10
49Remar
50Remar
Gasser, Steve
86Kenosha-10
87OrlanTw-11
87SLAS-18
88OrlanTw/Best-23
89Pittsfld/Star-5
Gast, Joe
89Penin/Star-6
Gast, John
91Princet/ClBest-4
91Princet/ProC-3521
Gastall, Tommy
91Crown/Orio-153
Gastelum, Macario
87Bakers-3
89Bakers/Cal-185
Gastfield, Ed
N172
Gaston, Alex
81Conlon-69
E121/120
W501-11
W575
Gaston, Clarence
(Cito)
69MB-90
69T-304R
70T-604
71Bz
71Bz/Test-12
71K-41
71MLB/St-228
71OPC-25
71T-25
71T/Coins-1
71T/Super-52
71T/tatt-4
72MB-113
72OPC-431
72OPC-432IA
72T-431
72T-432IA
73OPC-159
73T-159
74OPC-364SD
74T-364
75OPC-427
75T-427
75T/M-427
76OPC-558
76SSPC-18
76T-558
77T-192
78T-716
79T-208
84Tor/Fire-13CO
85Tor/Fire-12CO
86Tor/Fire-13CO
87Tor/Fire-10CO
88Tor/Fire-43CO
89T/Tr-36T
89Tor/Fire-43MG
90OPC-201MG
90T-201MG
90T/TVAS-33MG
90Tor/BJ-43MG
91OPC-81MG
91S/ToroBJ-36MG
91T-81MG
91Tor/Fire-43MG
92BJ/Fire-9MG
92OPC-699MG
92T-699MG
92T/Gold-699MG
92T/GoldWin-699MG
93BJ/D/45-28MG
93BJ/D/McDon-15M
93BJ/D/McDon-24M
93BJ/Demp-13MG
93BJ/Fire-10MG
93OPC/WC-18MG
93T-514MG
93T/Gold-514MG
Gaston, John
83Greens-6
Gaston, Milt
33G-65
81Conlon-70
V353-65
Gaston, Russell
90Savan/ProC-2065
91Johnson/ClBest-19
91Savan/ClBest-5
91Savan/ProC-1646
Gaston, Welcome
90Target-956
Gastreich, Henry
N172
Gastright, Hank
90Target-272
Gate, Bill
91StPete/ClBest-24
Gateman, Wareham
88CapeCod-25
Gates, Brent
91ClBest/Singl-414
91Classic/DP-22
91FrRow/DP-22
91SoOreg/ClBest-24
91SoOreg/ProC-3855
92AS/Cal-1
92ClBest-187
92D/Rook-42
92L/GRook-2
92Modesto/ClBest-15
92Modesto/ProC-3905
92OPC-216
92ProC/Tomorrow-133
92S-805DP
92StCl/Dome-56
92T-216DP
92T/Gold-216
92T/GoldWin-216
92UD/ML-145
93B-457
93ClBest/Fisher-9
93ClBest/MLG-74
93F/Final-254
93FExcel/ML-216
93FExcel/MLAS-8
93Flair-258
93JDean/Rook-4
93L-536
93Mother/A's-17
93Select/RT/ASRook-2
93Select/RookTr-61T
93StCl/A's-19
93T-451M
93T/Gold-451M
93T/Tr-91T
93UD-500M
93UD-504DD
93UD/FunPack-2SOT
93UD/SP-39
94B-304
94D-111
94F-261
94L-161
94OPC-231
94OPC/DiamD-15
94Pac/Cr-449
94Pinn-299
94S-187
94S/GoldR-187
94StCl-65
94StCl/1stDay-65
94StCl/Gold-65
94Studio-2
94T-586
94T/Finest-7
94T/FinestRef-7
94T/Gold-586
94TripleP-3
94UD-110
94UD/CollC-107
94UD/CollC/Gold-107
94UD/CollC/Silv-107
94UD/ElecD-110
94UD/SP-33
94Ultra-107
94Ultra/Second-2
Gates, Bryan
87Anchora-34BB
Gates, Eddie
81Evansvl-20
82Evansvl-20
Gates, Joe
77Jaxvl
78Knoxvl
80Iowa/Pol-6
Gates, Mathew
91Brisbane/Fut-6
Gates, Michael
80Memphis-9
82Wichita-4
83D-114
83OPC-195
83T-657
83Wichita/Dog-8
84Indianap-29
Gates, Todd
91Butte/SportP-13
Gatewood, Aubrey
64T-127R
65T-422
66OPC-42
66T-42
Gatewood, Henry
85VeroB-11
86Visalia-10
87OrlanTw-5
88WinSalem/Star-4
Gatins, Frank
90Target-957
Gatlin, Mike
82Oneonta-16
Gaton, Frank
75BurlB
76BurlB
Gattis, Jim
89Miami/II/Star-6
Gaudet, Jim
77Jaxvl
79T-707R
80Evansvl-3
81Omaha-13
82Syrac-11
91Jesuit-7
Gaudreault, Armand
45Parade*-19
Gaughan, Hank
82Chatt-25
Gault, Raymond
77Watlo
Gaunt
C46-69
Gausepohl, Dan
81Hawaii-8
82Hawaii-8
Gauthier, Fernand
45Parade*-20
45Parade*-21
Gautreau, Doc
92Conlon/Sport-545
Gautreau, Walter
28LaPresse-9
Gautreaux, Sid
90Target-273
Gavaghan, Sean
92Kenosha/ProC-597
Gavan, John
E120
W573
Gavin, Dave
88Madis-11
89Modesto/Chong-28
89Watlo/ProC-1776
89Watlo/Star-9
Gavin, Tom
90Elizab/Star-10
91Visalia/ClBest-22
91Visalia/ProC-1754
Gavlick, Daryle
92Hunting/ClBest-26
92Hunting/ProC-3140
93Peoria/Team-7
Gay, Jeff
86Cram/NWL-78
87QuadC-26
89PalmSp/Cal-34
89PalmSp/ProC-466
90QuadC/GS-16
91AA/LineD-61
91BirmB/LineD-61
91BirmB/ProC-1457
Gay, Scott
87FtLaud-17
88FtLaud/Star-9
89Salinas/ProC-1823
Gay, Steve
86Lynch-11
Gaylor, Bobby
86James-10
87BurlEx-18
88WPalmB/Star-10
Gaynor, John
91Parramatta/Fut-10
Gaynor, Richard Kent
83Reading-5
84Cram/PCL-212
87BirmB/Best-11
88BirmB/Best-17
Gazella, Mike
91Conlon/Sport-121
Gazzilli, Dan
85Utica-26
Gebhard, Bob
72OPC-28R
72T-28R
75IntAS/TCMA-29
Geddes, Jim
73OPC-561
73T-561
Gedeon, Elmer Joe
16FleischBrd-30
D327
D328-57
D329-66
D350/2-66
E135-57
M101/4-66
M101/5-66
W514-39
Gedman, Rich
81Pawtu-24
82Coke/BOS
82D-512
82F-294
82T-59
83D-156
83F-184
83T-602
84D-579
84F-398
84Nes/792-498
84OPC-296
84T-498
84T/St-222
85D-457
85F-159
85OPC-18
85T-529
85T/St-217
86D-273
86D/AAS-56
86F-349
86F-643M
86F/LimEd-18
86F/Mini-75
86F/St-44
86Leaf-145
86OPC-375
86Sf-84
86T-375
86T/St-248
86T/Tatt-17M
87Classic-49
87D-153
87D/AAS-39
87F-35
87F/RecSet-11
87F/WS-9M
87Leaf-254
87OPC-137
87Sf-149
87Sf-154M
87T-740
87T/St-247
88D-129
88D/Best-140
88D/RedSox/Bk-129
88F-353
88OPC-245
88Panini/St-24
88S-241
88T-245
88T/Big-152
88T/St-252
89B-27
89D-162
89F-89
89OPC-178
89S-345
89T-652
89T/Big-72
89T/St-253
89UD-368
90D-346
90F-276
90F/Can-276
90Leaf-478
90MLBPA/Pins-72
90OPC-123
90Pep/RSox-10
90Publint/St-456
90S-173
90T-123
90T/TVRSox-18
90UD-402
91Leaf-418
91Pol/Card-29
91UD-588
92D-553
92F-577
92Pol/Card-5
92S-689
92StCl-58
92Ultra-566
Gee, Steve
82Tucson-28M
Geeve, David
92CharlR/ClBest-18
92CharlR/ProC-2221
94FExcel-133
Gegan, Fred
87VeroB-9
Gehrig, Henry Louis
(Lou)
25Exh-97
26Exh-99
27Exh-49
28Exh-50
28Yueng-26
29Exh/4-26
31Exh/4-26
33CJ/Pin-7
33DL-7
33G-160
33G-92
34Exh/4-13
34G-37
34G-61
35Exh/4-13
35Wheat
36Exh/4-13
36Wheat
37Exh/4-13
38Exh/4-13
38ONG/Pin-11
39Exh
48Exh/HOF
48Swell-14
49Leaf/Prem-3
50Callahan
50W576-33
51T/CM
60Exh/HOF-11
60F-28
60NuCard-24
61F-31
61GP-16
61NuCard-424
61T-405M
63Bz/ATG-15
69Bz-5
69Bz/Sm
72F/FFeat-5
72K/ATG-13
72Laugh/GF-8
73OPC-472LL
73Syrac/Team-8
73T-472LL
74Syrac/Team-8
76Laugh/Jub-28
76OPC-341AS
76Rowe-4M
76Shakey-18
76T-341M
77Galasso-236
77Galasso-46
77Galasso-M
77Shakey-10
80Laugh/3/4/5-29
80Laugh/FFeat-10
80Marchant-9
80Pac/Leg-13
80Perez/HOF-22
80SSPC/HOF
81Conlon-5
85CircK-14
85D-635PUZ
85D/HOF-3

85D/WaxBox-PUZ
85Leaf-635PUZ
85West/2-25
85Woolwth-14
86Conlon/1-1
86Conlon/1-17
86Conlon/1-52
86Conlon/1-57
86Sf/Dec-10
87Conlon/2-1
87Nestle/DT-1
88Conlon/5-12
88Conlon/AmAS-10
88Conlon/HardC-3
88Grenada-30
89HOF/St-1
89Kenner/BBGr-7
89Pac/Leg-174
89Swell-25
89T/LJN-81
89USPS-2
90BBWit-73
90CollAB-34
90HOF/St-38
90Perez/GreatMom-4
90Swell/Great-25
91Cadaco-23
91Conlon/Proto-111
91Conlon/Sport-111
91Conlon/Sport-310
91Homer/Classic-9
91Swell/Great-125
92Conlon/Col-3
92Conlon/Col-8
92Conlon/Sport-529
92Mega/Ruth-122M
92Mega/Ruth-128M
92Mega/RuthProto-154M
92Pinn-286M
92S-881
92Whitehall-2
92Whitehall/Proto-2
92Yank/WIZAS-22
92Yank/WIZHOF-11
93AP/ASG-97
93AP/ASG24K-31G
93Cadaco-24
93Conlon-673
93Spectrum/HOFII-1
93TWill-122
93TWill-63
93TWill/POG-23
93TWill/POG-24
93UD/ATH-131M
93UD/ATH-133
93UD/ATH-58
94Conlon-1082
94Conlon-1249
94Conlon/Col-31
94TedW-147
94TedW/Lock-13
PM10/Sm-60
PR1-11
R310
R315-A10
R315-B10
R316
R328-26
R332-20
R346-29
R423-35
V353-55
V354-92
V355-96
W502-26
W517-35

Gehringer, Charles
(Charlie)
26Exh-95
27Exh-47
29Exh/4-23
31Exh/4-23
33DH-20
33DL-5
33Exh/4-12
33G-222
34DS-77
34Exh/4-12
34G-23
34Ward's/Pin-5
35BU-130
35BU-42
35Exh/4-12
35G-1D
35G-2D
35G-6D
35G-7D
36Exh/4-12
36Wheat
37Dix
37Exh/4-12
37OPC-112
37Wheat-4
38Exh/4-12
38G-241
38G-265
38ONG/Pin-10
38Wheat
39Exh
39PlayBall-50
40PlayBall-41
41DP-54
41PlayBall-19
50Callahan
50W576-34
60F-58
61F-32
61GP-10
76Rowe-7M
76Shakey-56
77Galasso-200
80Perez/HOF-57
80SSPC/HOF
81Conlon-78
81Tiger/Detroit-14
83D/HOF-28
83Kaline-33M
83Kaline-39M
84West/1-16
86Conlon/1-43
86Sf/Dec-12
86Tiger/Sport-4
88Conlon/5-13
88Conlon/AmAS-11
90Pac/Legend-81
90Perez/GreatMom-31
90Perez/Master-1
90Perez/Master-2
90Perez/Master-3
90Perez/Master-4
90Perez/Master-5
92Conlon/Gold-667
92Conlon/Sport-461
92Conlon/Sport-553
93Conlon-667
94Conlon-1076
94Conlon-1122
94Conlon/Col-34
R300
R303/A
R308-183
R310
R311/Leath
R313
R314
R316
V300
V351A-13
V351B-16
V354-57
V355-42
V94-18
WG8-23

Geiger, Burt
82Albuq-3
83Albuq-2

Geiger, Gary Jr.
87Everett-24
88Fresno/Cal-23
88Fresno/ProC-1229

Geiger, Gary Merle
58T-462
59T-521
60T-184
61T-33
61T/St-111
62J-60
62P-60
62P/Can-60
62Salada-38A
62Salada-38B
62Shirriff-38
62T-117
62T/St-13
63J-81
63P-81
63T-513
64T-93
65T-452
66T-286
67CokeCap/Brave-1
67T-566
69T-278
77Evans/TCMA-10CO

Geis, Jason
92SoOreg/ClBest-13
92SoOreg/ProC-3433

Geisel, Harry
94Conlon-1205UMP

Geisel, J. Dave
79T-716R
80T-676R
82D-633
82Syrac-4
82Syrac/Team-13
84Cram/PCL-175
84D-645
84F-154
84Nes/792-256
84OPC-256
84T-256
85Mother/Mar-22
86OKCty-6

Geishert, Vern
70T-683R

Geiske, Mark
90River/Cal-10

Geisler, Phil
91Martins/ClBest-11
91Martins/ProC-3460
92Clearw/ClBest-18
92Clearw/ProC-2062
94B-336
94FExcel-245
94Ultra-546

Geiss, Emil
N172

Geist, Pete
86FSLAS-17
86VeroB-6
87VeroB-6
88Dunedin/Star-7

Geivett, Billy
86PalmSp-15
86PalmSp/Smok-23
87MidldA-3

Gelatt, Dave
85LitFalls-18
86Columbia-10
87Lynch-18
88StLucie/Star-8

Gelb, Jac
89Wythe/Star-11
90Peoria/Team-22

Gelbert, Charles M.
(Charlie)
29Exh/4-16
31Exh/4-16
33Exh/4-8
39PlayBall-93
40PlayBall-18
91Conlon/Sport-70
R306
R313
R314
V355-49

Gelfarb, Steve
81WHave-12
82WHave-13

Gelinas, Marc
78Salem

Gellinger, Mike
87DayBe-25
89Utica/Pucko-30CO
90BirmB/Best-24CO
90BirmB/ProC-1400CO
91Utica/ClBest-23MG
91Utica/ProC-3257MG

Gelnar, John
65OPC-143R
65T-143R
67T-472R
70McDon-4
70OPC-393
70T-393
71MLB/St-436
71OPC-604
71T-604

Genao, Huascar
92BurlInd/ClBest-23
92BurlInd/ProC-1663

Gendron, Bob
84Shrev/FB-8

Gendron, Jonnie
92Classic/DP-104

Genewich, Joseph
(Joe)
21Exh-56
25Exh-5
26Exh-5
27Exh-2
92Conlon/Sport-573

Genins, C. Frank
N172

Genovese, George
91LitSun/HSPros-35SC
91LitSun/HSProsG-35SC

Gentile, Gene
78Charl
81Bristol-4
83Pawtu-21
84Albany-3
86Kinston-8
87Harris-21
88Harris/ProC-856

Gentile, Jim
60T-448
61NuCard-401
61P-68
61T-559
61T/St-101
62Bz
62Exh
62J-27
62P-27
62P/Can-27
62Salada-1
62Shirriff-1
62T-290
62T-53LL
62T/St-5
62T/bucks
63Bz-11
63Exh
63J-57
63P-57
63T-260
63T-4LL
63T/SO
64Bz-11
64T-196
64T/S-15
64T/SU
64T/St-75
65T-365
66OPC-45
66T-45
78TCMA-4
85Woolwth-15
90Target-274
91Crown/Orio-154
Exh47
WG10-28

Gentile, Randy
89Elizab/Star-9
90Kenosha/Best-3
90Kenosha/ProC-2300
90Kenosha/Star-4

Gentile, Scott
92Classic/DP-74
92FrRow/DP-43
92James/ClBest-17
92James/ProC-1495
93ClBest/MLG-122
93StCl/MurphyS-52
93WPalmB/ClBest-5
93WPalmB/ProC-1332

Gentle, Mike
83VeroB-4

Gentleman, J.P.
(Jean)
88Hamil/ProC-1743
88Savan/ProC-356

Gentry, Andry
90GA-5

Gentry, Gary
69OPC-31R
69T-31R
70OPC-153
70T-153
70Trans/M-23
71MLB/St-153
71OPC-725
71T-725
72OPC-105
72T-105
73OPC-288
73T-288
74OPC-415
74T-415
75OPC-393
75T-393
75T/M-393
91WIZMets-137
94Mets/69-16

Genzale, Henry
90Mother/Mar-28EQMG

George, Andre
88Pocatel/ProC-2075

George, Chris
89AS/Cal-38
89MissSt-14
89Stockton/Best-2
89Stockton/Cal-153
89Stockton/ProC-391
89Stockton/Star-8
90ElPaso/GS-14
90ElPasoATG/Team-21
90MissSt-14
90TexLgAS/GS-17
91AAA/LineD-138
91B-35
91Classic/II-T50
91Denver/LineD-138
91Denver/ProC-119
91MissSt-19
91Pittsfld/ClBest-23
91Pittsfld/ProC-3416
92B-213
92Classic/Game200-20
92D-746
92Denver/ProC-2632
92Denver/SB-128
92Pittsfld/ClBest-16
92Pittsfld/ProC-3288
92S-835
92S/Rook-9
92Sky/AAASingl-62
92StCl-354
92StLucie/ClBest-25
92T/91Debut-63
92UD-9SR
93T-744
93T/Gold-744

George, Curtis
92Watertn/ClBest-22
92Watertn/ProC-3242

George, Don
33SK*-40

George, Frankie
75SLCity/Caruso-7
77SLCity

George, Greek
90Target-275

George, Leo
82QuadC-14

George, Nattie
84Greens-7

George, Phil
83Butte-5
85FtMyr-11
86FtMyr-11
86Memphis/GoldT-7
86Memphis/SilverT-7
87Memphis-2
87Memphis/Best-11

George, Steve
83Greens-7
84Greens-18
86Albany/TCMA-29
88T-18

George, Thomas
(Lefty)
T207

George, Will
80CharlO/Pol-7
80CharlO/W3TV-7
82Miami-1
83Miami-1
87Hagers-3
89Kinston/Star-27
90Canton/Best-2CO
90Canton/ProC-1363CO
91Canton/ProC-996CO

George, William
N172
N338/2

Georger, Joe
80LynnS-17
81LynnS-4
82LynnS-4
86Wausau-10CO
87Belling/Team-12CO
89QuadC/Best-3CO
89QuadC/GS-3CO
90QuadC/GS-2CO
91QuadC/ClBest-28CO
91QuadC/ProC-2646CO
92QuadC/ClBest-29CO
92QuadC/ProC-827CO
Gerace, Joanne
88Utica/Pucko-29
89Utica/Pucko-32GM
Geraghty, Ben
90Target-276
Gerald, Dwayne
91LitSun/HSPros-23
91LitSun/HSProsG-23
92StCl/Dome-57
Gerald, Edward
(Ed)
89LittleSun-19
91AppFx/ClBest-24
91AppFx/ProC-1729
92AppFox/ClBest-25
Gerard, Alfonzo
52Laval-88
Gerber, Craig
82Redwd-3
83Nashua-13
84Cram/PCL-109
86D-545
86Edmon-13
86F-156
86T-222
88Edmon/ProC-583
88MidldA/GS-24
Gerber, Walter
(Wally)
21Exh-57
25Exh-113
26Exh-117
92Conlon/Sport-501
E120
E220
V61-49
W573
Geren, Bob
83Spring/Frit-13
84ArkTr-11
87Albany-5
88AAA/ProC-9
88Colum/CMC-11
88Colum/Pol-12
88Colum/ProC-303
88TripleA/ASCMC-16
89Colum/CMC-11
89Colum/Pol-7
89Colum/ProC-758
89D/Rook-11
89F/Up-48
89S/HotRook-66
89S/NWest-25
89S/Tr-93
89T/Tr-37T
90AlbanyDG/Best-4
90B-438
90Bz-20
90Classic-25
90D-395
90F-442
90F/Can-442
90Leaf-182
90OPC-536
90Panini/St-128
90S-464
90S/100Ris-50
90S/NWest-9
90Sf-205
90SpringDG/Best-28
90T-536
90T/Big-209
90T/Gloss60-40
90T/JumboR-9
90T/St-316
90T/St-321FS
90T/TVYank-21
90ToysRUs-11
90UD-608
91D-114
91F-663
91OPC-716
91Panini/FrSt-323
91Panini/St-265
91S-435
91StCl-171
91T-716
91UD-202
91Ultra-231
92F-226
92OPC-341
92Pawtu/ProC-925
92S-170
92T-341
92T/Gold-341
92T/GoldWin-341
92Yank/WIZ80-66
93Mother/Padre-13
Gergen, Bob
83BurlR-16
83BurlR/Frit-13
84Tulsa-26
85Tulsa-25
86Tulsa-14
Gerhardt, Allen
83Beaum-22
87Gaston/ProC-10
Gerhardt, Bill
83Miami-7
Gerhardt, Joe
N167-5
Gerhardt, John
N172
N284
N338/2
Gerhardt, Rusty
84OKCty-5
85OKCty-24
86OKCty-7CO
89CharlR/Star-27CO
Gerhart, Bert
91GulfCR/SportP-21
92Gaston/ClBest-4
Gerhart, Ken
84CharlO-22
85CharlO-1
86RochR-3
87D-30RR
87D/OD-141
87D/Rook-24
87F/Up-U34
87French-38
87Leaf-30
87Sf/Rook-7
87Sf/TPrev-21M
87T/Tr-37T
88D-213
88F-559
88French-38
88OPC-271
88Panini/St-14
88RedFoley/St-27
88S-58
88T-271
88ToysRUs-11
89F-609
89OPC-192
89Phoenix/CMC-20
89Phoenix/ProC-1499
89S-506
89T-598
89UD-426
90HagersDG/Best-11
91Crown/Orio-155
Gering, Scott
79Elmira-13
Gerlach, Jim
81QuadC-27
83MidldC-21
German, Rene
83QuadC-11
Germann, Mark
86Cedar/TCMA-16
87Vermont-20
88Chatt/Best-10
89Nashvl/CMC-15
89Nashvl/ProC-1275
Germer, Glen
81Durham-18
Gernert, Dick
52StarCal/L-71G
52T-343
53B/BW-11
54B-146
57T-202
58T-38
59T-13
59T-519M
60T-86
61T-284
61T/St-151
62T-536
62T/bucks
89Smok/Ast-18
93Rang/Keeb-158CO
Geronimo, Cesar
71OPC-447
71T-447
72T-719
73OPC-156
73T-156
74OPC-181
74T-181
74T/St-26
75Ho-121
75K-50
75OPC-41
75T-41
75T/M-41
76Ho-150
76Icee
76OPC-24
76SSPC-45
76T-24
77BurgChef-202
77Ho-76
77Ho/Twink-76
77K-40
77OPC-160
77Pep-49
77T-535
78OPC-32
78Pep-11
78SSPC/270-115
78T-354
79OPC-111
79T-220
80OPC-247
80T-475
81D-305
81T-390
81T/Tr-766
82D-322
82F-409
82T-693
83D-448
83F-112
83T-194
84D-252
84Nes/792-544
84T-544
Gershberg, Howie
88Bend/Legoe-28CO
89BendB/Legoe-27CO
90Boise/ProC-3333CO
91Boise/ProC-3902CO
92Boise/ProC-3647
Gerstein, Ron
91Sumter/ClBest-5
91Sumter/ProC-2328
92Rockford/ClBest-8
92Rockford/ProC-2108
Gertz, Mike
82Watlo/B-16
82Watlo/Frit-14
83Watlo/Frit-22
Gessler, Harry
(Doc)
14CJ-59
15CJ-59
M116
Gettel, Allen
50Remar
51B-304
52Mother-3
Getter, Kerry
75Anderson/TCMA-10
76Clinton
Gettler, Chris
88Bakers/Cal-253
Gettman, Jake
C46-40
Getz, Gustave
(Gus)
90Target-277
D328-58
D329-67
D350/2-67
E135-58
E254
E270/2
M101/4-67
M101/5-67
Getzein, Charles
N172
N284
N29
N43
Scrapps
WG1-21
Gewecke, Steve
90Spring/Best-21
Geyer, Jacob
(Rube)
T213/blue
T214-12
Gharriey, Joe
W514-109
Gharrity, Edward P.
(Patsy)
E120
E121/120
V100
V61-50
W501-12
W572
W573
W575
WG7-18
Ghelfi, Andrew
(Tony)
84Phill/TastyK-19
85Cram/PCL-40
85Phill/TastyK-17
86Watlo-9
87Kinston-16
88Wmsprt/ProC-1308
88Wmsprt/ProC-1314
89LasVegas/CMC-5
89LasVegas/ProC-1
Gholston, Rico
92Welland/ClBest-9
92Welland/ProC-1330
Ghostlaw, Derek
91Helena/SportP-2
Giallombardo, Bob
59DF
59T-321
60DF-9
61Union
90Target-278
Giamatti, A.Bartlett
89Wichita/Rc/HL-16
90D-716
90OPC-396
90S/DTRook-B1
90T-396
90TM/Umpire-65
Giambi, Jason
91T/Tr-45T
92Classic/DP-42
92FrRow/DP-40
92StCl/Dome-58
92T/DQ-31
92T/Tr-40T
92T/TrGold-40T
92UD/ML-20
93Modesto/ClBest-11
93Modesto/ProC-808
93StCl/MurphyS-156
93StCl/MurphyS-200
94ClBest/Gold-125
94FExcel-120
94T-369M
94T/Gold-369M
94TedW-123
94UD-525TP
Giannelli, Ray
89Myrtle/ProC-1469
89SALAS/GS-35
90Dunedin/Star-9
90Star/ISingl-64
91AA/LineD-357
91ClBest/Singl-26
91Knoxvl/LineD-357
91Knoxvl/ProC-1774
91S/ToroBJ-33
92Sky/AAASingl-225
92Syrac/MerchB-6
92Syrac/ProC-1974
92Syrac/SB-506
92T/91Debut-64
93Syrac/ProC-1003
Giannotta, Go
80Evansvl-13
Giansanti, Ralph
83Ander-21
Gianukakis, John
86Cram/NWL-146
Giard, Joe
91Conlon/Sport-119
Giard, Ken
92Idaho/ProC-3506
93Macon/ClBest-10
93Macon/ProC-1395
Giaudrone, Charlie
90WichSt-12
Gibbon, Joe
60T-512
61T-523
62Kahn
62T-448
63IDL-9
63Kahn
63T-101
64T-307
65OPC-54
65T-54
66T-457
67T-541
68OPC-32
68T-32
69OPC-158
69T-158
69T/4in1-2M
70OPC-517
70T-517
72OPC-382
72T-382
78TCMA-219
Gibbons, Bill
89Clinton/ProC-907
Gibbons, John
82Beloit/Frit-8
85D-116
85IntLgAS-15
85Tidew-15
86ElPaso-12
86Tidew-11
87Chatt/Best-22
87D-626
87Tidew-6
87Tidew/TCMA-10
88Albuq/CMC-20
88Albuq/ProC-260
88Vermont/ProC-950
89OkCty/CMC-12
89OkCty/ProC-1531
90AAASingl/ProC-304
90ProC/Singl-236
90ScranWB/CMC-10
90ScranWB/ProC-602
91WIZMets-138
Gibbons, Michael
88SLCity-15
89Rockford/Team-9
Gibbs, Jake
62T-281
64T-281R
65OPC-226R
65T-226R
66OPC-117
66T-117
67CokeCap/YMet-3
67T-375
68OPC-89
68T-89
69MB-91
69MLB/St-74
69T-401
69T/St-203
70MLB/St-245
70T-594
71MLB/St-488
71OPC-382
71T-382
72MB-114
92Yank/WIZ60-46
92Yank/WIZ70-54
WG10-7
WG9-9
Gibbs, James
(Jim)
88Spring/Best-9
89Medford/Best-4
90Bend/Legoe-30

90Madison/Best-15
Gibbs, Paul
92Watertn/ClBest-2
92Watertn/ProC-3227
Gibert, Pat
89Huntsvl/Best-21
Giberti, Dave
91Butte/SportP-8
92FtMyr/ProC-2739
92Miracle/ClBest-15
94ClBest/Gold-33
Gibralter, Steve
91CharWh/ClBest-22
91CharWh/ProC-2899
91SALAS/ProC-SAL7
92Cedar/ClBest-17
92Cedar/ProC-1083
92ClBest-47
92MidwLAS/Team-12
92UD/ML-284
92UD/ML-69DS
92UD/POY-PY21
93B-694FOIL
93ClBest/Fisher-2
93ClBest/MLG-214
93FExcel/ML-21
Gibree, Bob
86Wausau-11
Gibson, Dave
80Knoxvl/TCMA-19
Gibson, Frank
25Exh-6
Gibson, George
10Domino-48
11Helmar-160
12Sweet/Pin-137
92Conlon/Sport-516
93Conlon-825
D303
D322
D329-68
D350/2-68
E101
E103
E105
E106
E121/120
E254
E270/1
E270/2
E90/1
E90/2
E91
E92
E93
E96
M101/4-68
M101/5-68
M116
S74-110
T201
T202
T205
T206
T216
T3-94
V100
W501-88
W514-63
W555
Gibson, Hoot
81Durham-19
Gibson, J. Russ
67T-547R
68T-297
69MB-92
69OPC-89
69T-89
69T/St-133
70OPC-237
70T-237
71MLB/St-248
71OPC-738
71T-738
72MB-115
72T-643
Gibson, Joel
65T-368R
78TCMA-208
Gibson, Josh Jr.
91Negro/Lewis-24
Gibson, Josh Sr.
74Laugh/Black-8
76Shakey-128
80Perez/HOF-128
80SSPC/HOF
83D/HOF-4
86Negro/Frit-23
86Negro/Frit-30
86Negro/Frit-31
86Negro/Frit-4
86Negro/Frit-9
87Negro/Dixon-6
88Conlon/NegAS-5
88Negro/Duques-12
90Negro/Star-2
91Negro/Lewis-24
92Negro/Kraft-17
92Negro/Lee-3
93TWill-105
94TedW/Lock-14
Gibson, Kirk
81Coke
81F-481
81OPC-315
81T-315
81T/St-78
81Tiger/Detroit-20
82D-407
82Drake-15
82F-267
82F/St-161
82K-40
82OPC-105
82PermaGr/CC-24
82Sqt-6
82T-105
82T/St-184
83D-459
83F-329
83OPC-321
83OPC/St-67
83T-430
83T/St-67
84D-593
84F-80
84Nes/792-65
84OPC-65
84T-65
84T/St-272
84Tiger/Farmer-4
84Tiger/Wave-15
85Cain's-8
85D-471
85Drake-12
85F-8
85F/St-22
85FunFood/Pin-21
85Leaf-103
85OPC-372
85Seven-13D
85Seven-8S
85T-565
85T/RD-22
85T/St-11ALCS
85T/St-19WS
85T/St-267
85T/Super-27
85Wendy-9
86BK/AP-13
86Cain's-6
86D-125
86D-1DK
86D/DKsuper-1
86D/WaxBox-PC4
86Drake-28
86F-226
86F/LimEd-19
86F/Mini-47
86F/Slug-10
86F/St-45
86GenMills/Book-1M
86Leaf-1DK
86OPC-295
86Seven/Coin-C16
86Sf-21
86T-295
86T/Gloss60-29
86T/St-266
86T/Super-25
86T/Tatt-22M
86TrueVal-8
87Cain's-9
87Classic-9
87Coke/Tigers-1
87D-50
87F-151
87F/GameWin-17
87F/Lim-17
87F/Mini-44
87F/St-47
87GenMills/Book-2M
87Kraft-19
87Leaf-104
87OPC-386
87RedFoley/St-10
87Seven-DT3
87Sf-48
87Sf/TPrev-15M
87Stuart-19
87T-765
87T/Board-29
87T/Coins-11
87T/Mini-53
87T/St-273
87Toledo-28
88D-275
88D/Best-66
88F-55
88F/Mini-82
88F/St-24
88F/Up-U93
88Leaf-136
88Mother/Dodg-8
88OPC-201
88Panini/St-95
88Pol/Dodg-23
88S-525
88S/Tr-10T
88Sf-111
88T-605
88T/Big-191
88T/St-267
88T/Tr-40T
88T/UK-26
89B-351
89Bz-10
89Cadaco-23
89Classic-120
89D-132
89D-15DK
89D/Best-10
89D/DKsuper-15DK
89F-57
89F/BBAS-14
89F/BBMVP's-13
89F/Excit-14
89F/Heroes-17
89F/LL-15
89F/Rec-4
89F/Superstar-16
89F/WS-5
89F/WaxBox-C10
89Holsum/Discs-20
89KayBee-13
89KennerFig-48
89KingB/Discs-1
89Mother/Dodg-8
89OPC-340
89OPC-382
89Panini/St-107
89Panini/St-16
89Panini/St-17
89Panini/St-479
89Pol/Dodg-14
89RedFoley/St-49
89S-210
89S-582M
89S/HotStar-30
89Sf-65
89T-340
89T-396AS
89T/Ames-14
89T/Big-299
89T/Coins-1
89T/Crunch-2
89T/DH-24
89T/Gloss60-55
89T/Hills-14
89T/LJN-102
89T/Mini-17
89T/St-66
89T/St/Backs-49
89T/UK-30
89UD-633
89UD-662MVP
89UD-676TC
89Woolwth-2
89Woolwth-24
90B-97
90Classic/Up-20
90D-368
90D/BestNL-41
90F-393
90F/Can-393
90Kenner/Fig-30
90KingB/Discs-5
90Leaf-173
90MLBPA/Pins-6
90Mother/Dodg-13
90OPC-150
90Panini/St-271
90Pol/Dodg-23
90Publlnt/St-259
90Publlnt/St-5
90S-487
90T-150
90T/Ames-20
90T/Big-326
90T/HillsHM-25
90T/St-60
90Target-279
90UD-264
91B-302
91Cadaco-24
91Classic/200-57
91D-445
91F-199
91F/UltraUp-U27
91F/Up-U26
91Leaf-249
91Leaf/Stud-66
91OPC-490
91OPC/Premier-50
91Pol/Royal-9
91S-800
91S/RookTr-18T
91StCl-344
91T-490
91T/Tr-46T
91UD-634
91UD/Ext-737
92D-39
92F-157
92OPC-720
92Panini-100
92Pinn-481
92Pol/Royal-7
92S-520
92StCl-495
92StCl-784
92T-720
92T/Gold-720
92T/GoldWin-720
92UD-180
93Cadaco-25
93F/Final-209
93Flair-203
93L-314
93MSA/Metz-28
93Pac/Jugador-5
93Pac/Spanish-443
93StCl-673
93StCl/1stDay-673
93Studio-165
93T/Tr-8T
93Tiger/Gator-9
93UD-766
93Ultra-549
94D-108
94F-130
94Flair-50
94L-342
94Pac/Cr-218
94Pinn-453
94S-421
94T-228
94T/Gold-228
94Ultra-355
Gibson, Leighton
N172
N690
Gibson, Monty
91Pocatel/ProC-3776
91Pocatel/SportP-18
Gibson, Paul
80Cedar-18
82BirmB-23
83OrlanTw-20
86GlenF-6
86Nashvl-9
87Toledo-10
87Toledo/TCMA-17
88D/Rook-19
88F/Up-U26
88Pep/T-48
89B-99
89Bz-11
89Classic-140
89D-445
89F-131
89KMart/DT-10
89Mara/Tigers-48
89Panini/St-331
89S-595
89T-583
89T/Big-230
89T/Gloss60-20
89T/JumboR-10
89T/St-323
89ToysRUs-11
89UD-47
90BirmDG/Best-14
90CokeK/Tiger-5
90D-657
90F-602
90F/Can-602
90Leaf-298
90OPC-11
90Publlnt/St-470
90S-261
90T-11
90UD-496
91CokeK/Tiger-48
91D-353
91F-337
91F/UltraUp-U23
91Leaf-55
91OPC-431
91Pol/Tiger-5
91S-152
91T-431
91UD-579
92D-375
92F-136
92L-461
92L/BlkGold-461
92Mets/Kahn-45
92OPC-143
92OPC/Premier-174
92S-261
92StCl-223
92StCl-694
92T-143
92T/Gold-143
92T/GoldWin-143
92UD-489
92USPlayC/Tiger-7H
92USPlayC/Tiger-8S
92Ultra-531
93F-473
93StCl-29
93StCl/1stDay-29
94F-230
94StCl/Team-185
Gibson, Robert L.
(Bob L.)
79BurlB-14
82ElPaso-21
83Pol/Brew-40
84Cram/PCL-40
84D-246
84F-201
84Nes/792-349
84T-349
85D-393
85Pol/Brew-40
85T/Tr-39T
86D-271
86F-488
86T-499
86Vanco-12
87Tidew-33
87Tidew/TCMA-3
88RochR/CMC-5
88RochR/ProC-196
88RochR/Team-8
91WIZMets-139
Gibson, Robert
(Bob)
59T-514
60T-73
61T-211
62T-530
63F-61
63J-166
63P-166
63Salada-3
63T-415
63T-5LL

63T-9LL
64T-460
64T/Coins-59
64T/S-41
65Bz-23
65OPC-12LL
65OPC-138WS
65T-12LL
65T-138WS
65T-320
65T/E-69
65T/trans-14
66Bz-21
66T-225LL
66T-320
66T/RO-35
66T/RO-39
67Bz-21
67T-210
67T-236LL
68Bz-9
68OPC-100
68OPC-154WS
68T-100
68T-154WS
68T-378AS
68T/ActionSt-10CM
69Kelly/Pin-6
69MLB/St-211
69MLBPA/Pin-44
69NTF
69OPC-107CL
69OPC-10LL
69OPC-12LL
69OPC-162WS
69OPC-168WS
69OPC-200
69OPC-8LL
69OPC/DE-7
69T-107
69T-10LL
69T-12LL
69T-162WS
69T-168WS
69T-200
69T-432AS
69T-8LL
69T/4in1-14M
69T/4in1-18M
69T/4in1-7
69T/DE-29
69T/S-60
69T/St-115
69T/decal
69Trans-33
70K-71
70MLB/St-139
70OPC-530
70OPC-67LL
70OPC-71LL
70T-530
70T-67LL
70T-71LL
70T/CB
70T/S-33
70T/Super-33
70Trans-5
71Bz
71Bz/Test-41
71K-51
71MD
71MLB/St-273
71MLB/St-559
71OPC-450
71OPC-70LL
71OPC-72LL
71T-450
71T-70LL
71T-72LL
71T/Coins-63
71T/GM-24
71T/Greatest-24
71T/S-48
71T/Super-48
71T/tatt-15
71T/tatt-15a
72Dimanche*-59
72K-26
72OPC-130
72T-130
73K-14
73OPC-190
73T-190
73T/Lids-19
74K-1
74OPC-350
74T-350
74T/DE-3
74T/Puzzles-5
74T/St-114
75Ho-119
75OPC-150
75OPC-206M
75OPC-3RB
75T-150
75T-206MVP
75T-3RB
75T/M-150
75T/M-206MVP
75T/M-3RB
78TCMA-60
80Perez/HOF-175
82KMart-14
82Pol/Atl-45CO
83Pol/Atl-45CO
84Pol/Atl-45CO
86Sf/Dec-42
87KMart-3
87Nestle/DT-31
88T-664TBC
89Kahn/Coop-5
89Kenner/BBGr-8
89T/LJN-23
90BBWit-31
90HOF/St-74
90Pac/Legend-28
90Swell/Great-120
91CollAB-23
91K/3D-5
91K/SU-6A
91K/SU-6B
91LineD-3
91Swell/Great-33
92AP/ASG-3
92AP/ASG24K-3G
92AP/ASGProto-2
92Card/McDon/Pac-46
92UD/ASFF-52
92UD/HeroHL-HI4
92Ziploc-2
93AP/ASGCoke/Amo-3
93Metallic-10
93TWill-142
93TWill-90

Gibson, Sam
93Conlon-962

Gibson, Scott
82AppFx/Frit-22
84Visalia-22

Gibson, Steve
78Newar
79BurlB-13
80BurlB-1
81BurlB-11

Gibson, Thomas
91Niagara/ClBest-4

Giddens, Ron
84Cedar-20
86Macon-10

Giddings, Wayne
83Idaho-4
84Madis/Pol-18
85Huntsvl/BK-42

Gideon
BF2-33

Gideon, Brett
86PrWill-11
87Harris-18
88BuffB/CMC-3
88BuffB/ProC-1492
88F-330
89Indianap/CMC-5
89Indianap/ProC-1230
90B-105
92Canton/ProC-686

Gideon, Jim
77T-478R
82Tulsa-9
89Pac/SenLg-81
89T/SenLg-26
92TX-15
93Rang/Keeb-159

Gideon, Ron
86Lynch-12
87Lynch-8
88Jacks/GS-1
89StLucie/Star-7
90Jacks/GS-23
91StLucie/ClBest-27CO
91StLucie/ProC-728CO
92Bingham/ProC-533
92Bingham/SB-75M

Giebell, Floyd
81Tiger/Detroit-88

Giegling, Matt
91Cedar/ClBest-15
91Cedar/ProC-2722
92Cedar/ClBest-6
92Cedar/ProC-1075

Giel, Paul
55B-125
55Gol/Giants-9
58SFCallB-8
58T-308
59T-9
60T-526
61Clover-6
61Peters-19
61T-374

Gienger, Craig
92SoOreg/ClBest-14
92SoOreg/ProC-3409

Gierhan, Sam
78Newar
79BurlB-5

Gies, Chris
90Butte/SportP-22
91ClBest/Singl-191
91Gaston/ClBest-6
91Gaston/ProC-2683
92CharlR/ClBest-10
92ClBest-66

Giesdal, Brent
82Oneonta-3

Giesecke, Bob
79Clinton/TCMA-21

Giesecke, Rob
(Doc)
82VeroB-27
83VeroB-27
85VeroB-24
86VeroB-7TR
87VeroB-18
90SanAn/GS-4TR
90TexLgAS/GS-19TR

Gieseke, Mark
89Watlo/Star-30
90River/ProC-2614
91CalLgAS-20
91HighD/ClBest-20
91HighD/ProC-2403
92Wichita/ProC-3662

Giesen, Dan
87Reading-6
88Reading/ProC-874

Gietzen, Peter
92Greens/ClBest-16
92Greens/ProC-773

Gifford, Frank
60P*

Giggie, Bob
60Lake

Gigon, Norm
67T-576R

Gil, Benji
91Classic/DP-15
91FrRow/DP-50B
91LitSun/HSPros-27
91LitSun/HSPros-27
91LitSun/HSProsG-27
92B-339
92ClBest-309
92Gaston/ClBest-1
92Gaston/ProC-2260
92OPC-534
92Pinn-302DP
92S-808
92StCl/Dome-59
92T-534DP
92T/Gold-534
92T/GoldWin-534
92UD/ML-174
93B-629
93ClBest/MLG-50
93F/Final-278
93FExcel/ML-234
93L/GRook-18
93OPC/Premier-27
93Pac/Beisbol-16M
93Pac/Spanish-639
93Pinn-597
93Rang/Keeb-407
93SALAS/II-12
93SALAS/IICS-5
93Select/RookTr-42T
93StCl-697
93StCl/1stDay-697
93StCl/Rang-9
93T-529M
93T/Gold-529M
93T/Tr-60T
93UD-441TP
93UD/FunPack-3SOT
93UD/SP-193
93Ultra-628
94B-185
94B-379
94D-103
94Pac/Cr-616
94Pinn-194
94Pinn/Artist-194
94Pinn/Museum-194
94S-606
94StCl/Team-246
94T-231
94T/Gold-231
94UD-135
94UD/CollC-108
94UD/CollC/Gold-108
94UD/CollC/Silv-108
94UD/ElecD-135

Gil, Carlos
83MidldC-7

Gil, Danny
90Boise/ProC-3336
91PalmSp/ProC-2020

Gil, Jose
82Wisco/Frit-15

Gil, T. Gus
67T-253R
69T-651
75Hawaii/Caruso-1
82Danvl/Frit-2MG

Gilbert, Andrew
(Andy)
73OPC-252CO
73T-252CO
74OPC-78CO
74T-78CO

Gilbert, Angelo
80Batavia-1
82Idaho-8

Gilbert, Brent
90Tampa/DIMD-9
91PrWill/ClBest-1
91PrWill/ProC-1417

Gilbert, Charles M.
(Charlie)
90Target-280
91Jesuit-2

Gilbert, Dennis
80ElPaso-2
81Holyo-10
82Holyo-21
83Redwd-11

Gilbert, Donald
92Kane/ClBest-4
92Kane/ProC-97
92Kane/Team-10

Gilbert, Drew E.
(Buddy)
60HenryH-16
60T-359
60Union-6

Gilbert, Greg
84Everett/Cram-6A
85Fresno/Pol-10
86Fresno/Smok-7
87Anchora-13
87Idaho-15
88Sumter/ProC-405

Gilbert, Harold
(Tookie)
50B-235
52Mother-31
52T-61
91Jesuit-5

Gilbert, Jeff
83SanJose-21
84CharlO-18
85CharlO-20

Gilbert, Lawrence W.
(Larry)
16FleischBrd-31

Gilbert, Mark
79QuadC-12
80Water-14
81Water-19
82Water-18
83Indianap-22
84Wichita/Rock-12
85BuffB-13

Gilbert, Pat
86Cram/NWL-59
87Madis-7
88Modesto-26
88Modesto/Cal-79

Gilbert, Pete
90Target-958

Gilbert, Robbie
86Cram/NWL-62

Gilbert, Roy
89Freder/Star-7
90Freder/Team-14
91AA/LineD-230
91Freder/ProC-2379

Gilbert, Shawn
88MidwLAS/GS-32
88Visalia/Cal-151
88Visalia/ProC-91
89Visalia/Cal-104
89Visalia/ProC-1439
90Foil/Best-88
90OrlanSR/Best-4
90OrlanSR/ProC-1089
90OrlanSR/Star-6
90ProC/Singl-750
91AA/LineD-481
91OrlanSR/LineD-481
91OrlanSR/ProC-1856
92Portl/SB-406
92Portland/ProC-2672
92Sky/AAASingl-186
93StCl/WSox-30

Gilbert, Walter John
(Wally)
90Target-959
92Conlon/Sport-404

Gilbert, William O.
(Billy)
E107
T206

Gilbreath, Rod
74OPC-93
74T-93
75OPC-431
75T-431
75T/M-431
76OPC-306
76SSPC-10
76T-306
77T-126
78T-217
79OPC-296
79T-572
80Port-22
87Idaho-9

Gilchrist, John
88Eugene/Best-24
89Eugene/Best-22
90AppFox/Box-9
90AppFox/ProC-2108
91BBCity/ClBest-24
91BBCity/ProC-1410

Gilcrease, Doug
84Memphis-19
85FtMyr-17
86Memphis/GoldT-8
86Memphis/SilverT-8

Gilday, William
(Bill)
52Laval-75

Gile, Don
61T-236
62T-244

Gile, Mark
83TriCit-16
85Tulsa-10

Giles, Brian Jeffrey
81Tidew-4
82Tidew-8
83F-544
83OPC/St-322
83T-548
83T/St-322
84D-563
84F-585
84Jacks/Smok-5
84Nes/792-676
84OPC-324

84T-676
84T/St-111
84Tidew-24
85Pol/Brew-26
87Hawaii-8
88Calgary/CMC-15
88Calgary/ProC-784
89ColoSp/CMC-13
89ColoSp/ProC-253
91WIZMets-140
Giles, Brian Stephen
90Watertn/Star-9
91CLAS/ProC-CAR15
91ClBest/Singl-16
91Kinston/ClBest-26
91Kinston/ProC-338
92Canton/ProC-701
92Canton/SB-108
92ClBest-38
92ProC/Tomorrow-56
92Sky/AASingl-50
Giles, George
86Negro/Frit-51
91Negro/Lewis-1
92Negro/Retort-22
Giles, Troy
87QuadC-2
87Salem/ProC-2415
88QuadC/GS-15
89PalmSp/Cal-32
89PalmSp/ProC-473
Giles, Warren
56T-2PRES
57T-100M
58T-300M
59T-200PRES
60F-73
61F-33
80Perez/HOF-167
80SSPC/HOF
82Ohio/HOF-17
89HOF/St-92
Gilhooley, Frank
16FleischBrd-32
D328-59
E135-59
Gilkey, Otis Bernard
(Bernard)
87Spring/Best-25
88Spring/Best-13
89ArkTr/GS-6
90AAAGame/ProC-19
90AAASingl/ProC-529
90Leaf-353
90Louisvl/CMC-9
90Louisvl/LBC-18
90Louisvl/LBC-2MVP
90Louisvl/ProC-415
90ProC/Singl-109
90S/Tr-106T
90T/TVCard-50
91B-408
91Classic/200-165
91Classic/I-93
91D-30RR
91F-633
91Leaf-286
91Leaf/Stud-231
91Louisvl/Team-23
91OPC-126
91OPC/Premier-51
91Pol/Card-23
91S-709RP
91S/Rook40-11
91StCl-402
91T-126
91T/90Debut-53
91UD-16
92B-403
92D-376
92F-578
92L-502
92L/BlkGold-502
92OPC-746
92Pinn-88
92Pol/Card-6
92S-544
92S/100RisSt-24
92StCl-234
92T-746
92T/Gold-746
92T/GoldWin-746
92UD-552
92Ultra-567
93B-684
93D-284
93F-125
93Flair-120
93L-99
93OPC-61
93Pac/Spanish-294
93Panini-197
93Pinn-304HH
93Pinn-88
93Pol/Card-6
93S-81
93Select-173
93StCl-230
93StCl/1stDay-230
93StCl/Card-3
93Studio-7
93T-203
93T/Gold-203
93ToysRUs-81
93TripleP-208
93UD-394
93UD-482M
93UD/SP-74
93Ultra-106
94B-592
94D-90
94F-631
94L-152
94Pac/Cr-589
94Panini-242
94Pinn-79
94Pinn/Artist-79
94Pinn/Museum-79
94Pinn/Run-42
94S-420
94Select-20
94Sf/2000-140
94StCl-231
94StCl/1stDay-231
94StCl/Gold-231
94StCl/Team-316
94Studio-50
94T-377
94T/Finest-111
94T/FinestRef-111
94T/Gold-377
94TripleP-61
94UD-406
94UD/CollC-109
94UD/CollC/Gold-109
94UD/CollC/Silv-109
94UD/SP-62
94Ultra-565
Gilks, Robert
N172
Gill, Carlos
84Iowa-20
Gill, Chris
89Billings/ProC-2046F
90CharWh/Best-15
90CharWh/ProC-2246
90Foil/Best-141
91CharWh/ClBest-17
91CharWh/ProC-2894
Gill, John
45Centen-10
WG8-24
Gill, Shawn
82Idaho-14
83Madis/Frit-11
84Madis/Pol-17
Gill, Sheldon
75FtLaud/Sus-20
Gill, Steve
90AZ/Pol-6
91Waterlo/ClBest-21
91Waterlo/ProC-1268
92HighD/ClBest-2
Gill, Turner
87Wmsprt-25
88Wmsprt/ProC-1312
Gillaspie, Mark
83Beaum-15
84Beaum-5
85IowaC-22
88Memphis/Best-13
Gilleaudeau, Joseph (Mrs.)
94Conlon-1112M
94Conlon-1112M
Gilleaudeau, Joseph
94Conlon-1112M
94Conlon-1112M
Gillen, Kevin
76Watlo
77Jaxvl
Gillenwater, Carden
90Target-960
V362-32
Gilles, Bob
83VeroB-15
Gilles, Mark
87Kinston-3
88Kinston/Star-7
89Canton/Best-13
89Canton/ProC-1323
89Canton/Star-7
Gilles, Tom
87AppFx-16
88Kenosha/ProC-1387
89Knoxvl/Best-7
89Knoxvl/ProC-1143
90AAASingl/ProC-344
90ProC/Singl-330
90Syrac/CMC-4
90Syrac/MerchB-10
90Syrac/ProC-564
90Syrac/Team-10
91Reno/Cal-16
91T/90Debut-54
Gilles, Wayne
87AZ/Pol-3
Gillespie, Don
89Wythe/Star-12
Gillespie, John
E120
Gillespie, Mark
84Idaho/Team-9
Gillespie, Patrick
N172
N284
N690
Gillespie, Paul
47Smith-20
Gillespie, Pete
N167-6
Gillespie, Robert
52Mother-21
Gillette, Mike
90Fayette/ProC-2409
91Lakeland/ClBest-15
91Lakeland/ProC-269
92London/ProC-636
92London/SB-409
Gilliam, Bo
86Lipscomb-13
92FtLaud/ClBest-18
92FtLaud/ProC-2627
92FtLaud/Team-13
Gilliam, Darryl
86Bakers-11
86Cram/NWL-199
Gilliam, Ed
78BurlB
Gilliam, James
(Junior)
52LaPatrie-5
52Park-68
53T-258
54B-74
54NYJour
54RH
54RM-NL14
54T-35
55Armour-7
55B-98
55Gol/Dodg-10
55T-5
55T/DH-129
56T-280
57Swift-10
57T-115
58BB
58PacBell-3
58T-215
59Morrell
59T-306
60BB-4
60L-18
60MacGregor-9
60T-255
60T/tatt-19
60Union/Dodg-7
61BB-19
61P-158
61T-238
61Union/Dodg-8
62BB-19
62J-112
62P-112
62P/Can-112
62Salada-201
62Shirriff-201
62T-486
63J-114
63P-114
63T-80
64T-310
64Wheat/St-18
73OPC-569CO
73T-569CO
74OPC-144CO
74T-144CO
78TCMA-45
79TCMA-290
86Negro/Frit-76
88Pac/Leg-44
90Target-281
91T/Arc53-258
92Bz/Quadra-8
93TWill-135
93TWill-149
93TWill/Mem-2
94T/Arc54-35
PM10/L-15
PM10/Sm-61
PM10/Sm-62
Gilliam, Keith
83Kinston/Team-6
85Syrac-7
86Knoxvl-8
87Knoxvl-13
Gilliam, Melvin
80Ashvl-4
Gilliam, Sean
90Greens/Best-22
90Greens/ProC-2674
90Greens/Star-3
90ProC/Singl-705
91Greens/ProC-3073
Gilliford, Paul
77Fritsch-40
91Crown/Orio-156
Gilligan, Andrew
N172
N284
Gilligan, Jim
87SLCity/Taco-11MG
Gilligan, John
90MedHat/Best-19
91SLCity/ProC-3204
91SLCity/SportP-12
Gilligan, Larry
91Johnson/ClBest-7
91Johnson/ProC-3984
92Hamil/ClBest-18
92Hamil/ProC-1599
Gillis, Jack
91Oneonta/ProC-4168MG
92Oneonta/ClBest-27MG
Gillis, Louis
92Negro/Retort-23
Gillis, Tim
90BurlB/Best-13
90BurlB/ProC-2356
90BurlB/Star-12
90Foil/Best-134
91CLAS/ProC-CAR1
91Durham/ClBest-17
91Durham/ProC-1553
92Durham/ClBest-11
92Durham/ProC-1107
92Durham/Team-18
Gills, Amy
85Anchora-35TR
87Anchora-14TR
Gills, Jack
87Oneonta-32
Gillum, K.C.
(Kenneth)
89Billings/ProC-2042
90A&AASingle/ProC-196
90Billings/ProC-3237
90CharWh/ProC-2251
91Cedar/ClBest-25
91Cedar/ProC-2731
91ClBest/Singl-369
92CharWh/ClBest-15
92CharWh/ProC-19
92ClBest-58
93SALAS/II-13
93SALAS/IICS-17
Gilmartin, Dan
78Newar
79BurlB-10
82Beloit/Frit-18
Gilmore, Bill
87AppFx-2
Gilmore, Bob
79Richm-9M
Gilmore, Frank T.
N172
Gilmore, Joel
91Martins/ProC-3448
92ClBest-264
92Clearw/ProC-2051
Gilmore, Lenny
88BurlInd/ProC-1774
Gilmore, Matt
90BurlInd/ProC-3014
Gilmore, Quincy Jordan
87Negro/Dixon-23
Gilmore, Terry
87Spokane-19
88TexLgAS/GS-29
88Wichita-20
89LasVegas/CMC-4
89LasVegas/ProC-16
90AAAGame/ProC-18
90AAASingl/ProC-1
90LasVegas/CMC-4
90LasVegas/ProC-113
90ProC/Singl-506
91AAA/LineD-282
91LasVegas/LineD-282
91LasVegas/ProC-229
Gilmore, Tony R.
90AR-13
90AubAs/ProC-3397
91BurlAs/ClBest-25
91BurlAs/ProC-2805
91MidwLAS/ProC-15
92Osceola/ClBest-2
92Osceola/ProC-2533
Gilmore, Tony
80Utica-16
Gilson, Bob
89London/ProC-1358
Gilson, Hal
66Pep/Tul
68OPC-162R
68T-162R
69OPC-156R
69T-156R
69T/4in1-2
Gimenez, Issac
75Clinton
Gimenez, Ray
75Clinton
Ging, Adam
85Spokane/Cram-5
87Columbia-8
88StLucie/Star-9
Gingrich, Gary
75WPalmB/Sussman-2
76BurlB
77BurlB
Gingrich, Jeff
79Memphis/TCMA-18
Ginsberg, Myron
(Joe)
52T-192
53B/Col-6
53Tiger/Glen-10
54B-52
57T-236
58T-67
59T-66
60T-304
61T-79
79TCMA-52
91Crown/Orio-157
91WIZMets-141
Gioia, Joe
86Cram/NWL-194
Gionfriddo, Al
48Swell-9
90Target-282
V362-24
Giordano, Marc
89Princet/Star-7
90Miami/I/Star-9
90Miami/II/Star-7
91Miami/ClBest-20

91Miami/ProC-414
Giordano, Mike
83OrlanTw-21
Giovanola, Ed
90Idaho/ProC-3267
91Durham/ClBest-14
91Durham/ProC-1554
92Greenvl/ProC-1159
92Greenvl/SB-233
Gipner, Marcus
92GulfCY/ProC-3793
92StCl/Dome-60
Girardi, Joe
87WinSalem-17
88BBAmer-8
88EastLAS/ProC-25
88Pittsfld/ProC-1359
89D/Rook-23
89F-644R
89Mara/Cubs-7
89S/Tr-84
89UD/Ext-776
90Cub/Mara-8
90D-404
90D/BestNL-87
90F-31
90F/Can-31
90Leaf-289
90OPC-12
90S-535
90S/100Ris-33
90S/YS/II-29
90T-12
90T/89Debut-42
90T/TVCub-20
90UD-304
91B-415
91Cub/Mara-7
91Cub/Vine-11
91D-184
91F-421
91Leaf-258
91Leaf/Stud-156
91OPC-214
91Panini/FrSt-42
91Panini/St-49
91S-585
91StCl-247
91T-214
91UD-113
91Ultra-60
92B-636
92Cub/Mara-7
92D-175
92L-72
92L/BlkGold-72
92OPC-529
92Pinn-498
92S-701
92StCl-132
92Studio-13
92T-529
92T/Gold-529
92T/GoldWin-529
92TripleP-151
92UD-351
92Ultra-469
93B-668
93D-736
93F-410
93F/Final-31
93Flair-40
93L-332
93MilkBone-18
93Pac/Spanish-428
93Pinn-236
93Pinn/Expan-2M
93S-419
93Select-53
93StCl-620
93StCl/1stDay-620
93StCl/Rockie-10
93Studio-188
93T-425
93T/Gold-425
93TripleP-237
93UD-571
93UD/SP-221
93USPlayC/Rockie-13S
93USPlayC/Rockie-4D
93Ultra-348
94B-30
94D-165
94F-441
94Flair-153
94L-3
94Pac/Cr-196
94Pinn-74
94Pinn/Artist-74
94Pinn/Museum-74
94S-76
94S/GoldR-76
94Select-70
94StCl-323
94StCl/1stDay-323
94StCl/Gold-323
94StCl/Team-107
94Studio-178
94T-372
94T/Finest-72
94T/FinestRef-72
94T/Gold-372
94TripleP-224
94UD-76
94UD/ElecD-76
94Ultra-185
Giron, Ysidro
86FtLaud-7
87PrWill-17
Gisselman, Bob
82Wausau/Frit-31EQMG
Githens, John
86Watlo-10
87Watlo-13
88Kinston/Star-8
89Hagers/Best-2
89Hagers/ProC-262
89Hagers/Star-9
Giuliani, Tony
90Target-283
Giusti, Dave
62T-509
63T-189
64T-354
65T-524
66T-258
67Ast/Team-5
67CokeCap/Astro-1
67T-318
68CokeCap/Astro-1
68Dexter-36
68OPC-182
68T-182
69MB-93
69OPC-98
69Pirate/JITB-4
69T-98
69T/St-95
70OPC-372
70T-372
71MLB/St-202
71OPC-562
71T-562
72MB-116
72OPC-190
72T-190
73OPC-465
73T-465
74OPC-82
74T-82
74T/St-83
75OPC-53
75T-53
75T/M-53
76OPC-352
76SSPC-565
76T-352
77T-154
89Smok/Ast-3
89Swell-58
Giustino, Gerard
89SLCity-26
Givens, Brian
85LitFalls-5
86Columbia-11A
86Columbia-11B
87Lynch-28
88Jacks/GS-14
89Jacks/GS-27
90AAASingl/ProC-268
90ProC/Singl-355
90Tidew/CMC-4
90Tidew/ProC-537
Givens, James
91Bristol/ClBest-1
91Bristol/ProC-3613
92ClBest-165
92Lakeland/ClBest-22
92Lakeland/ProC-2285
93ClBest/MLG-162
Givler, Doug
87Chatt/Best-9
88ColAst/Best-7
89ColMud/Best-11
89ColMud/ProC-124
89ColMud/Star-11
Gjesdal, Brent
86Beaum-12
Glabman, Barry
76Dubuq
Gladd, Jim
52Mother-53
53Mother-29
Gladden, Dan
(Danny)
81Shrev-9
82Phoenix
83Phoenix/BHN-8
84Cram/PCL-17
85D-567
85F-607
85F/St-118
85Leaf-30
85Mother/Giants-3
85T-386
85T/St-166
85T/St-374YS
86D-187
86F-541
86Mother/Giants-3
86OPC-336
86T-678
86T/St-90
87D-189
87D/OD-224
87F-274
87F/Up-U36
87OPC-46
87T-46
87T/St-93
87T/Tr-38T
88D-491
88D/Best-130
88F-12
88F/WS-1
88OPC-206
88Panini/St-143
88S-324
88Smok/Minn-10
88T-502
88T/St-19
88T/St-281
88Woolwth-20
89B-163
89D-391
89D/Best-298
89F-112
89KennerFig-49
89OPC-387
89Panini/St-392
89RedFoley/St-50
89S-62
89T-426
89T/St-286
89UD-400
90B-420
90Classic-148
90D-182
90D-22DK
90D/BestAL-108
90D/SuperDK-22DK
90F-375
90F/Can-375
90Leaf-254
90OPC-298
90Panini/St-111
90PublInt/St-328
90S-61
90Sf-190
90T-298
90T/Big-147
90T/St-292
90UD-238
91B-318
91D-228
91F-611
91Leaf-76
91Leaf/Stud-85
91OPC-778
91Panini/FrSt-304
91S-163
91StCl-54
91T-778
91UD-659
91Ultra-187
92D-585
92F-203
92F/Up-21
92L-239
92L/BlkGold-239
92OPC-177
92OPC/Premier-11
92Panini-121
92Pinn-318
92S-28
92S/RookTr-28T
92StCl-801
92StCl/Dome-61
92T-177
92T/Gold-177
92T/GoldWin-177
92T/Tr-41T
92T/TrGold-41T
92UD-332
92UD-737
92USPlayC/Twin-12C
92USPlayC/Twin-8D
92Ultra-361
93D-467
93F-605
93L-60
93OPC-100
93Pac/Spanish-109
93Panini-118
93Pinn-333
93S-207
93Select-244
93StCl-191
93StCl/1stDay-191
93T-626
93T/Gold-626
93Tiger/Gator-10
93UD-251
93Ultra-198
94D-138
94F-131
94Pac/Cr-219
94S-215
94S/GoldR-215
94T-342
94T/Gold-342
Gladden, Jeff
81CharR-17
82FtMyr-13
83Clinton/Frit-28
Gladding, Fred
64T-312R
65OPC-37
65T-37
66T-337
67CokeCap/Astro-5
67CokeCap/Tiger-7
67OPC-192
67T-192
68T-423
69OPC-58
69T-58
70MLB/St-41
70OPC-208
70T-208
71MLB/St-80
71OPC-381
71T-381
72MB-117
72OPC-507
72T-507
73OPC-17
73T-17
78TCMA-158
79Tacoma-25
86Ashvl-12CO
87ColAst/ProC-3
88ColAst/Best-20
89ColMud/Best-10
89ColMud/ProC-139
90Kinston/Team-27CO
91Kinston/ClBest-17CO
91Kinston/ProC-341CO
92ColRS/ProC-2408CO
Glade, Fred
WG2-21
Gladu, Jean-Paul
45Parade*-22
Gladu, Mike
88Wythe/ProC-1993
Gladu, Roland
45Parade*-58
Glanville, Doug
91ClBest/Singl-402
91Classic/DP-9
91Geneva/ClBest-24
91Geneva/ProC-4230
92Classic/DP-92FB
92ProC/Tomorrow-210
92UD/ML-173
92WinSalem/ClBest-1
92WinSalem/ProC-1219
93ClBest/MLG-39
93FExcel/ML-8
94B-177
Glanz, Scott
83Peoria/Frit-4
Glaser, Gordy
81Charl-3
82Charl-3
83BuffB-4
Glaser, Kris
91Eugene/ClBest-28
91Eugene/ProC-3719
Glasker, Stephen
86Salem-10
87PortChar-15
89CharlR/Star-9
Glass, Bobby
77Jaxvl
Glass, Steve
87Idaho-22
88BurlB/ProC-9
89BurlB/ProC-1607
89BurlB/Star-10
90Sumter/Best-29CO
90Sumter/ProC-2452CO
Glass, Tim
78Watlo
81Chatt-11
82Chatt-6
83BuffB-11
84BuffB-3
85Water-18
Glasscock, John
(Jack)
75F/Pion-21
86Indianap-5
N162
N172
N284
N300
WG1-32
Glasscock, Larry
83Memphis/TCMA-18
Glaviano, Thomas
(Tommy)
49Eureka-183
51B-301
51T/RB-47
52T-56
53T-140
91T/Arc53-140
Glavine, Tom
86Greenvl/Team-9
86SLAS-23
87Richm/Bob-8
87Richm/Crown-14
87Richm/TCMA-5
87Sf/TPrev-24M
88D-644
88F-539
88S-638
88T-779
88T/St-44
89B-267
89Brave/Dubuq-12
89Classic/Up/2-159
89D-381
89D/Best-2
89F-591
89Panini/St-34
89S-442
89S/YS/II-23
89T-157
89UD-360
90B-2
90Brave/Dubuq/Perf-8
90Brave/Dubuq/Singl-9
90Classic-36
90D-145
90D/BestNL-2
90D/Learning-53

90F-583
90F/Can-583
90Leaf-13
90OPC-506
90Panini/St-219
90RedFoley/St-36
90S-481
90Sf-34
90T-506
90T/Big-99
90T/St-26
90UD-571
91B-576
91Brave/Dubuq/Perf-11
91Brave/Dubuq/Stand-15
91Classic/200-17
91Classic/III-26
91D-132
91F-689
91Leaf-172
91Leaf/Stud-145
91OPC-82
91RedFoley/St-39
91S-206
91StCl-558
91StCl/Member*-16
91T-82
91UD-480
91UD/FinalEd-90FAS
91USPlayC/AS-1S
91Ultra-5
92B-699
92Brave/LykePerf-13
92Brave/LykeStand-14
92CJ/DII-2
92Classic/Game200-124
92Classic/I-38
92Classic/II-T17
92D-426AS
92D-629
92D-BC4CY
92D/BC-BC4CY
92DPep/MSA-5
92F-358
92F-694LL
92F/ASIns-6
92F/Performer-20
92F/Smoke-S7
92F/TmLIns-11
92French-2M
92Hardee-10
92Kenner/Fig-17
92L-279
92L/BlkGold-279
92MooTown-22
92OPC-305
92OPC/Premier-49
92Panini-288AS
92Pinn-594SIDE
92Pinn-75
92S-450
92S-791CY
92S-890DT
92S/100SS-15
92S/Impact-49
92S/Proctor-18
92StCl-395
92StCl/Dome-62
92Studio-4
92Sunflower-19
92T-305
92T-395AS
92T/Gold-305
92T/Gold-395AS
92T/GoldWin-305
92T/GoldWin-395AS
92T/Kids-34
92TripleP-7
92UD-342
92UD-713DS
92USPlayC/Ace-12S
92USPlayC/Ace-JK
92USPlayC/Brave-10H
92USPlayC/Brave-1S
92Ultra-162
92Ultra/AS-20
92Ultra/AwardWin-7
93B-410
93Brave/FLAg-5
93Brave/LykePerf-11
93Brave/LykeStand-13
93Cadaco-26
93Classic/GameI-36
93Colla/ASG-14
93Colla/DM-38
93D-554
93D/DK-19
93D/EliteDom-18
93D/Prev-1
93Duracel/PPI-21
93F-4
93F/ASNL-11
93F/Atlantic-9
93F/Fruit-21
93F/Glavine-Set
93F/ProVII-2
93Flair-4
93Ho-22
93JDean/28-14
93Kenner/Fig-11
93KingB-19
93Kraft-22
93L-295
93L/GoldAS-18M
93MSA/Ben-6
93MilkBone-2
93OPC-132
93OPC/Premier/StarP-21
93P-21
93Pac/Spanish-6
93Panini-159LL
93Panini-179
93Pinn-90
93Pinn/TP-2
93S-15
93S-539DT
93S/GoldDT-8
93Select-7
93Select/Ace-2
93Select/ChasS-10
93Select/StatL-88
93StCl-296MC
93StCl-650
93StCl/1stDay-296MC
93StCl/1stDay-650
93StCl/Brave-1
93StCl/MurphyMP-2AS
93StCl/MurphyS-106
93Studio-145
93T-280
93T-410
93T/BlkGold-6
93T/Finest-87AS
93T/FinestASJ-87AS
93T/FinestRef-87AS
93T/Gold-280
93T/Gold-410
93T/Hill-18
93TB/Full-19
93TripleP-117
93TripleP-209LH
93UD-472M
93UD-75
93UD/FunPack-61GS
93UD/FunPack-63
93UD/SP-58
93USPlayC/Ace-2S
93Ultra-6
94B-21
94D-364
94D/Special-364
94F-359
94F/AS-36
94F/LL-11
94Finest-267
94Flair-125
94Kraft-22
94L-235
94OPC-250
94P-16
94Pac/Cr-9
94Panini-14
94Panini-145
94Pinn-284
94RedFoley-16M
94S-30
94S/DT-2
94S/GoldR-30
94S/GoldS-16
94Sf/2000-80
94StCl-538QS
94StCl/1stDay-538QS
94StCl/Gold-538QS
94StCl/Team-56
94Studio-34
94T-393M
94T-475
94T/BlkGold-32
94T/Gold-393M
94T/Gold-475
94TripleP-44
94UD-144
94UD/CollC-306M
94UD/CollC/Gold-306M
94UD/CollC/Silv-306M
94UD/ElecD-144
94UD/SP-49
94Ultra-151
94Ultra/AS-19
94Ultra/LL-9

Glaze, Gettys
92Elmira/ClBest-20
92Elmira/ProC-1377
93B-311

Glazner, Charles
(Whitey)
E120
E121/120
E220
W501-87
W572
W573
W575

Gleason, Harry
E107

Gleason, Jackie
92Pinn-590

Gleason, Roy
77Fritsch-44
90Target-961

Gleason, William G.
N172
N172/BC
N284
N370
Scrapps

Gleason, William J.
(Kid)
88Conlon/5-14
88Pac/8Men-102
88Pac/8Men-23
88Pac/8Men-73
94Conlon-1038MG
E107
E223
N172

Gleason, William P.
D327
D328-60
E121/120
E121/80
E122
E135-60
V100
W501-39
W514-112
W575

Gleaton, Jerry Don
80T-673R
80Tulsa-1
81T-41R
82T-371
83SLCity-2
84Cram/PCL-186
85BuffB-19
85T-216
86BuffB-12
86T-447
88D-547
88F-258
88Omaha/CMC-5
88Omaha/ProC-1497
88S-343
88Smok/Royals-7
88T-116
89D-444
89F-282
89S-423
89T-724
90CokeK/Tiger-6
90TulsaDG/Best-17
91CokeK/Tiger-19
91D-661
91F-338
91Leaf-135
91OPC-597
91Pol/Tiger-6
91S-316
91StCl-574
91T-597
92D-607
92OPC-272
92S-375
92T-272
92T/Gold-272
92T/GoldWin-272
92TX-16
92UD-601
92USPlayC/Tiger-12S
92USPlayC/Tiger-6H
93Edmon/ProC-1130
93Rang/Keeb-160
93StCl/Marlin-14

Gleckel, Scott
82OrlanTw/A-14

Gledhill, Chance
91Boise/ClBest-4
91Boise/ProC-3870
92QuadC/ClBest-14
92QuadC/ProC-802

Gleeson, Jim
94Conlon-1291

Gleissner, James
82FtMyr-17

Glenn, Edward C.
N172

Glenn, Joe
35BU-87
92Conlon/Sport-510

Glenn, John
62Kahn/Atl

Glenn, Leon Jr.
90Beloit/Best-17
90Beloit/Star-9
90Foil/Best-271
91Beloit/ClBest-24
91Beloit/ProC-2110
91BendB/ClBest-25
91BendB/ProC-3700
91ClBest/Singl-215
92ClBest-284
92Stockton/ClBest-12
92Stockton/ProC-40

Glenn, Simon
80Elmira-28

Glenn, Stanley
92Negro/Retort-24

Glick, Tom
90James/Pucko-31

Glinatsis, George
92AS/Cal-28
92ClBest-394
92SanBern/ClBest-15
92SanBern/ProC-
93ClBest/MLG-143

Glinatsis, Mike
76Cedar
82Miami-2

Gline, Steve
90Clinton/ProC-2566CO

Glinton, James
91CharlR/ClBest-16

Glisson, Robert
86Erie-8
87Spring/Best-18
88Spring/Best-1

Globig, Dave
76BurlB

Glossop, Alban
(Al)
47Signal
49B/PCL-17
90Target-284

Glover, Jeff
86Cram/NWL-68
87Madis-17
88Modesto-10
88Modesto/Cal-60

Glover, Reggie
88Reno/Cal-271

Glover, Terence
88SLCity-23

Glynn, Dennis
86Jacks/TCMA-14

Glynn, Ed
77Evansvl/TCMA-11
77T-487R
79T-343
80T-509
81Charl-4
81T-93
82Charl-4
83Charl-19
83D-537
83F-408
83T-614
83Wheat/Ind-14
84Maine-22
86Tidew-12
87Tidew-15
87Tidew/TCMA-4
89Pac/SenLg-129
91Pac/SenLg-82
91WIZMets-142

Glynn, Gene
83Wichita/Dog-9
84Indianap-22
85Utica-25
86WPalmB-18CO
87James-16
88Rockford-15
89Jaxvl/Best-27
89Jaxvl/ProC-174
89Rockford-15CO
90Spokane/SportP-26MG
90Waterlo/Best-23CO
90Waterlo/ProC-2395CO
91Spokane/ClBest-29MG
91Spokane/ProC-3965MG
92Bend/ClBest-24MG

Glynn, William V.
(Bill)
52Mother-56
53T-171
54T-178
55T-39
55T/DH-59
91T/Arc53-171
94T/Arc54-178
V362-42

Gmitter, Joe
91Helena/SportP-10

Gnacinski, Paul
84Pawtu-8
86Greenvl/Team-10

Gobbo, Michael
85Beloit-8
86Stockton-10
87ElPaso-26

Gobel, Donnie
91Augusta/ClBest-7
91Augusta/ProC-800

Gochnaur, John
90Target-285
E107

Godfrey, Tyson
90Hunting/ProC-3275
91ClBest/Singl-432
91Peoria/ClBest-12
91Peoria/ProC-1337
91Peoria/Team-8
92Peoria/ClBest-17
92Peoria/Team-8

Godin, Steve
91Kane/ClBest-22
91Kane/ProC-2669
91Kane/Team-8
92Freder/ClBest-13
92Freder/ProC-1819

Godwin, Glenn
83Madis/Frit-25

Goedde, Mike
85Cedar-8
89Billings/ProC-2049

Goedhart, Darrell
89Martins/Star-12
90Spartan/Best-4
90Spartan/ProC-2485
90Spartan/Star-9
91Clearw/ClBest-4
91Clearw/ProC-1615
92Clearw/ClBest-3
92Reading/ProC-568

Goergen, Todd
89Batavia/ProC-1927
90Spartan/Best-5
90Spartan/ProC-2486
90Spartan/Star-10
91Spartan/ClBest-4
91Spartan/ProC-889
92Clearw/ProC-2052

Goettsch, Jeff
87Salem/ProC-2441

Goetz, Barry
91CharlR/ClBest-6
91CharlR/ProC-1310
92CharlR/ClBest-20
92CharlR/ProC-2222

Goetz, Jack
75Dubuq

Goetz, Lawrence
55B-311UMP
Goff, Jerry L.
86Cram/NWL-110
87Wausau-17
88SanBern/Best-12
88SanBern/Cal-33
89Wmsprt/ProC-631
89Wmsprt/Star-7
90AAASingl/ProC-574
90B-112
90Indianap/CMC-13
90Indianap/ProC-291
90Leaf-476
90ProC/Singl-63
91AAA/LineD-184
91D-499
91Indianap/LineD-184
91Indianap/ProC-467
91Panini/FrSt-153
91S-834
91T/90Debut-55
92Indianap/ProC-1867
92Indianap/SB-182
92Sky/AAASingl-89
94T-463
94T/Gold-463
Goff, Mike
86Greens-9
87Belling/Team-18
88MidwLAS/GS-57
88Wausau/GS-27
89AS/Cal-14
89SanBern/Best-24
89SanBern/Cal-72
90Wmsprt/Best-7
90Wmsprt/ProC-1053
90Wmsprt/Star-8
92Jaxvl/SB-375M
Goff, Tim
86Cram/NWL-32
87FtMyr-17
Goff, Wally
79Wausau-8
80Penin/B-7
80Penin/C-14
Gogas, Keith
91Melbourne/Fut-3
Goggin, Chuck
74OPC-457
74T-457
Gogolewski, Bill
71MLB/St-539
71OPC-559R
71T-559R
72OPC-424
72T-424
73OPC-27
73T-27
74OPC-242
74T-242
93Rang/Keeb-12
Gogolewski, Doug
(Gogo)
87Oneonta-10
88FtLaud/Star-10
89FtLaud/Star-6
90Albany/ProC-1032
90Albany/Star-5
90ProC/Singl-730
92FtLaud/ClBest-3
92FtLaud/ProC-2605
92FtLaud/Team-14
Goguen, Phil
88NE-21
Gohl, Lefty
52Park-78
Gohmann, Ken
86Lakeland-6
87Lakeland-26
88GlenF/ProC-930
89Saraso/Star-7
Gohr, Greg
90B-347
90Lakeland/Star-11
90S-679DC
91AA/LineD-385
91B-142
91London/LineD-385
91London/ProC-1871
91Toledo/ProC-1925
92B-453
92Fayette/ClBest-27TR
92ProC/Tomorrow-65
92Sky/AAASingl-261
92Toledo/ProC-1036
92Toledo/SB-584
92UD/ML-195
93B-671
93D-605RR
93F/Final-210
93L/GRook-6
93OPC/Premier-17
93Pinn-615
93StCl-685
93StCl/1stDay-685
93UD-685
93Ultra-550
94D-167
94F-132
94T-711
94T/Gold-711
Goins, Scott
87Everett-3
89SanJose/Best-27
89SanJose/Cal-233
89SanJose/ProC-438
89SanJose/Star-10
Goins, Tim
92Watlo/ClBest-15
92Watlo/ProC-2143
Gokey, Steve
87Modesto-8
88Modesto-30
89Modesto/Cal-289CO
89Modesto/Chong-6
Gold, Bret
81Miami-20
Gold, Mark
87Wausau-23
Goldberg, Marc
90StLucie/Star-31
91StLucie/ClBest-29DIR
92WPalmB/ClBest-27
Golden, Brian
89Hamil/Star-16
90Erie/Star-7
Golden, Ike
81AppFx-16
Golden, Jim
61T-298
62T-568
63T-297
89Smok/Ast-4
90Target-286
Goldetsky, Larry
78Memphis/Team-4
79Memphis/TCMA-6
80Memphis-7
83Memphis/TCMA-6CO
Goldgrabe, Curt
85Fresno/Pol-30AGM
Goldman, J.
31Exh/4-21
Goldsberry, Gordon
52T-46
53T-200
91T/Arc53-200
Goldsby, Walt
N172
Goldstein, David R.
80WHave-20
Goldstein, Ike
87Visalia-12
Goldthorn, Burk
82AlexD-15
83LynnP-12
85PrWill-30
86Hawaii-10
Goldy, Purnal
63T-516
Golenbock, Peter
90LitSun-21
Goliat, Mike
50B-205
51B-77
51BR-B10
61Union
Gollehon, Chris
88Bristol/ProC-1875
89Spokane/SP-20
Golmont, Van
90Erie/Star-8
Goltz, Dave
73OPC-148
73T-148
74OPC-636
74T-636
75OPC-419
75T-419
75T/M-419
76OPC-136
76SSPC-218
76T-136
77BurgChef-47
77Ho-48
77Ho/Twink-48
77OPC-73
77T-321
78Ho-96
78K-35
78OPC-142
78OPC-5LL
78T-205LL
78T-249
78Twin/FriszP-8
79Ho-16
79OPC-10
79T-27
79Twin/FriszP-7
80OPC-108
80Pol/Dodg-38
80T-193
81F-127
81OPC-289
81Pol/Dodg-38
81T-548
82D-604
82F-6
82Pol/Dodg-38
82T-674
83F-90
83T-468
90Target-287
Gomes, Wayne
94B-608
94ClBest/Gold-36
94ClBest/GoldLP-4
94Pinn-434
94S-494
94SigRook-8
94T-742DP
94T/Gold-742DP
94UD-540TP
94UD/CollC-22
94UD/CollC/Gold-22
94UD/CollC/Silv-22
94Ultra-547
Gomez, Art
81Clinton-8
Gomez, Chris
92Classic/DP-62
92FrRow/DP-34
93B-39
93Select/RookTr-80T
93StCl/MurphyS-133
94B-321
94D-628
94F-133
94OPC/DiamD-5
94Pac/Cr-220
94Pinn-414
94S-309
94S/GoldR-309
94Select-194
94StCl-73
94StCl/1stDay-73
94StCl/Gold-73
94T-626
94T/Gold-626
94UD-93
94UD/CollC-110
94UD/CollC/Gold-110
94UD/CollC/Silv-110
94UD/ElecD-93
94Ultra-54
Gomez, Dana
87WinHaven-30
Gomez, Fabio
88BurlInd/ProC-1788
89Star/IISingl-180
89Watertn/Star-8
90Kinston/Team-7
91CollInd/ClBest-27
91Kinston/ProC-329
92AS/Cal-2
92Reno/Cal-40
Gomez, Henry
88CharWh/Best-14
90Peoria/Team-23
91AA/LineD-133
91CharlK/LineD-133
91CharlK/ProC-1684
Gomez, Jorge
80Ashvl-3
82BurlR/Frit-12
82BurlR/TCMA-20
83Tulsa-1
84Tulsa-4
Gomez, Jose Luis 1
(Sanchez)
77T-13
78BJ/PostC-7
78OPC-121
78T-573
79BJ/Bubble-9
79OPC-128
79T-254
80OPC-95
80T-169
81D-88
81F-253
81Pol/Atl-9
81T-477
82T-372
89Pac/SenLg-17
89T/SenLg-16
91Pac/SenLg-143
Gomez, Jose Luis 2
(Rodriguez)
R313
Gomez, Jose
83Miami-14
Gomez, Juan A.
75Tucson-9
75Tucson/Caruso-12
75Tucson/Team-3
76Tucson-33
Gomez, Leo
87Hagers-5
89EastLgAS/ProC-3
89Hagers/Best-1
89Hagers/ProC-280
89Hagers/Star-10
90AAAGame/ProC-10
90AAASingl/ProC-466
90B-262
90HagersDG/Best-12
90ProC/Singl-311
90RochR/CMC-10
90RochR/ProC-709
90Rochester/L&U-6
91B-88
91Classic/200-164
91Classic/I-12
91Classic/III-31
91Crown/Orio-158
91D-35RR
91F-472
91Leaf-35
91Leaf/Prev-13
91Leaf/Stud-3
91OPC/Premier-52
91S-725RP
91S/Rook40-20
91Seven/3DCoin-3A
91T/90Debut-56
91T/Tr-47T
91UD-6
91Ultra-16
92B-344
92Classic/Game200-58
92Classic/II-T58
92D-199
92F-8
92L-87
92L/BlkGold-87
92OPC-84
92OPC/Premier-161
92Panini-67
92Pinn-356
92Pinn/Team2000-52
92S-240
92S/100RisSt-66
92S/Impact-16
92StCl-664
92T-84
92T/Gold-84
92T/GoldWin-84
92TripleP-131
92UD-161
92Ultra-4
93B-381
93D-31
93F-167
93L-155
93OPC-117
93Pac/Spanish-17
93Panini-74
93Pinn-351
93S-104
93Select-66
93StCl-536
93StCl/1stDay-536
93Studio-99
93T-164
93T/Gold-164
93UD-132
93Ultra-140
94D-576
94Pac/Cr-31
94Pinn-180
94Pinn/Artist-180
94Pinn/Museum-180
94S-55
94S/GoldR-55
94T-506
94T/Gold-506
Gomez, Marcos
82Beloit/Frit-10
Gomez, Miguel
78Dunedin
Gomez, Mike
92Batavia/ClBest-18
92Batavia/ProC-3272
Gomez, Orlando
82Tulsa-23
83BurlR-26
83BurlR/Frit-27MG
84Tulsa-23MG
85Tulsa-23MG
86Water-11MG
87BuffB-25
88Gaston/ProC-1009MG
89Gaston/ProC-1017MG
89SALAS/GS-2
90Gaston/Best-25MG
90Gaston/ProC-2536MG
90Gaston/Star-26MG
90SALAS/Star-24CO
91Mother/Rang-28CO
92Mother/Rang-28M
93Rang/Keeb-161CO
Gomez, Pat
87Peoria-13
87Peoria/PW-2
88CharWh/Best-13
89WinSalem/Star-8
90Foil/Best-49
90Greenvl/Best-4
91AA/LineD-207
91Greenvl/ClBest-1
91Greenvl/LineD-207
91Greenvl/ProC-2995
91Huntsvl/ClBest-26
91Richm/Bob-34
92Richm/Bleach-15
92Richm/Comix-6
92Richm/ProC-371
92Richm/SB-429
92Sky/AAASingl-196
93B-82
93D-266
93F/Final-139
93Pac/Spanish-595
93Pinn-610
93S-310
93Ultra-471
94F-663
94Pac/Cr-523
Gomez, Pedro
(Preston)
60DF-10
61Union
69OPC-74MG
69T-74MG
70OPC-513MG
70T-513MG
71OPC-737MG
71T-737MG
72T-637MG
73OPC-624CO
73T-624CO
74OPC-31MG
74T-31MG
75OPC-487MG
75SSPC/18-6MG
75T-487MG
75T/M-487MG

Gomez, Pierre
90Miami/II/Star-8
Gomez, Randy
84Cram/PCL-20
85Cram/PCL-179
86Phoenix-6
87Hawaii-24
Gomez, Ruben
54NYJour
54T-220
55Gol/Giants-10
55T-71
55T/DH-89
56T-9
56T/Pin-39P
57T-58
58SFCallB-9
58T-335
59T-535
60T-82
61T-377
67T-427
79TCMA-98
94T/Arc54-220
PM10/L-16
PM10/Sm-64
Gomez, Rudy
91Geneva/ClBest-8
91Geneva/ProC-4223
92WinSalem/ClBest-18
92WinSalem/ProC-1213
Gomez, Steve
86OrlanTw-7
87OrlanTw-13
Gomez, Vernon
(Lefty)
32Orbit/num-120
33CJ/Pin-8
33DL-14
33G-216
34Exh/4-13
35BU-23
35BU-86
35Exh/4-13
36Exh/4-13
36G
36Wheat-1
37Exh/4-13
38Exh/4-13
38ONG/Pin-12
39Exh
39PlayBall-48
39Wheat-3
40PlayBall-6
41DP-61
41PlayBall-72
60F-54
61F-34
72Laugh/GF-18
75Shakey-3
76Rowe-4M
76Shakey-129
77Galasso-185
77Galasso-265
77Galasso-76
80Marchant/HOF-13
80Pac/Leg-117
80Perez/HOF-129
80SSPC/HOF
81Conlon-44
86Conlon/1-45
86Sf/Dec-9
87Conlon/2-2
88Conlon/5-15
88Conlon/AmAS-12
89HOF/St-76
90Perez/GreatMom-44
90Swell/Great-84
91Conlon/Proto-662
91Conlon/Sport-67
91Homer/Classic-3
91Swell/Great-129
92Conlon/ASP-662G
92Conlon/Sport-536
92Yank/WIZAS-23
92Yank/WIZHOF-12
93AP/ASG-105
93AP/ASG24K-39G
93Conlon-662
94Conlon-1063
94Conlon-1088
PM10/Sm-63
PR1-12
R303/A
R303/B
R308-151
R309/2
R310
R312/M
R313
R314
R328-31
V351B-17
V355-56
V94-19
Gonder, Jesse
63FrBauer-6
63T-29R
64T-457
64T/Coins-43
64T/SU
64T/St-30
65T-423
66EH-20
66T-528
67CokeCap/Pirate-10
67T-301
67T/Test/PP-10
69T-617
78TCMA-122
78TCMA-238
91WIZMets-143
92Yank/WIZ60-47
Goninger, Gerry
89Cedar/ProC-930
Gonring, Doug
87Ashvl-8
Gonsalves, Dennis
83Madis/Frit-7
84Madis/Pol-16
Gonzales, Benjamin
(Ben)
89AubAs/ProC-2171
90Ashvl/ProC-2740
91BurlAs/ClBest-3
91BurlAs/ProC-2794
92ClBest/Up-437
92Osceola/ClBest-16
92Osceola/ProC-2523
Gonzales, Dan
77Evansvl/TCMA-12
80Evansvl-20
Gonzales, Eddie
87SanJose-25
Gonzales, John
90Ashvl/ClBest-21
91Ashvl/ProC-579
Gonzales, Jose
80CharlO/Pol-8
80CharlO/W3TV-8
Gonzales, Larry
87Hawaii-7
87PanAm/USAB-10
87PanAm/USAR-10
89QuadC/Best-21
89QuadC/GS-28
89Salem/Team-12
90QuadC/GS-17
90TeamUSA/87-10
91AA/LineD-435
91Melbourne/Fut-4
91MidldA/LineD-435
91MidldA/OneHour-12
91MidldA/ProC-436
92Edmon/ProC-3542
92Edmon/SB-159
92Sky/AAASingl-79
93Vanco/ProC-2601
Gonzales, Rene C.
83Memphis/TCMA-3
84Indianap-25
85Indianap-11
86Indianap-10
88D-582
88F-560
88French-88
88T-98
88T/Big-209
89D-377
89French-88
89OPC-213
89S-585
89T-213
89T/Big-87
89T/St-234
90D-401
90OPC-787
90S-118
90T-787
91B-25
91Crown/Orio-159
91F-473
91Leaf-490
91OPC-377
91OPC/Premier-53
91S-638
91S/ToroBJ-14
91StCl-406
91T-377
91Tor/Fire-88
92D-274
92OPC-681
92Pol/Angel-11
92S-582
92S/RookTr-75T
92StCl-704
92T-681
92T/Gold-681
92T/GoldWin-681
92T/Tr-42T
92T/TrGold-42T
92UD-729
93D-785
93F/Final-182
93L-345
93Mother/Angel-14
93OPC-184
93Pac/Spanish-47
93Panini-11
93Pinn-55
93Pol/Angel-11
93S-604
93Select-379
93StCl-121
93StCl/1stDay-121
93StCl/Angel-15
93T-266
93T/Gold-266
93UD-188
93Ultra-164
94D-640
94F-57
94Pinn-364
94S-455
94T-141
94T/Gold-141
Gonzales, Todd
87Watlo-11
88Kinston/Star-9
89Canton/Best-16
89Canton/ProC-1320
89Canton/Star-8
Gonzales, Tommy
76Phoenix/Coke-24M
80Phoenix/NBank-26SVR
Gonzalez, Alex
92B-596
92Myrtle/ClBest-11
92Myrtle/ProC-2203
92UD/ML-317
92UD/ML-60DS
93B-374FOIL
93B-603
93ClBest/MLG-128
93FExcel/ML-243
93Knoxvl/ProC-1257
93UD-456IN
93UD/SP-278FOIL
94B-380
94B-469
94FExcel-143
94FExcel/AS-5
94Finest-433
94OPC-258
94OPC/HotPros-8
94Pinn-505
94Select-178
94T-67
94T/Gold-67
94TedW-121
94UD-13
94UD/CollC-8
94UD/CollC/Gold-8
94UD/CollC/Silv-8
94UD/ElecD-13
94UD/SP-42
Gonzalez, Angel
86WinHaven-9
87NewBrit-4
88NewBrit/ProC-910
88Pawtu/CMC-17
88Pawtu/ProC-462
89Pawtu/CMC-22
89Pawtu/Dunkin-12
89Pawtu/ProC-684
90AAASingl/ProC-440
90Pawtu/CMC-15
90Pawtu/ProC-468
90ProC/Singl-266
90T/TVRSox-44
91AAA/LineD-257
91Nashvl/LineD-257
91Nashvl/ProC-2162
Gonzalez, Arturo
73Cedar
74Cedar
85Cram/PCL-33
86Phill/TastyK-x
86Portl-6
Gonzalez, Carlos
86FtMyr-12
87AppFx-14
88BBCity/Star-12
89BBCity/Star-7
Gonzalez, Cecilio
90Johnson/Star-13
91Johnson/ClBest-26
91Johnson/ProC-3972
Gonzalez, Chris
85Clovis-19
Gonzalez, Cliff
85LitFalls-23
86LitFalls-12
87Columbia-4
89Saraso/Star-8
90Saraso/Star-11
91CalLgAS-46
91Reno/Cal-12
92Salinas/ClBest-20
92Salinas/ProC-3767
Gonzalez, David
91AA/LineD-407
91Memphis/LineD-407
91Memphis/ProC-661
Gonzalez, Denio
(Denny)
82Portl-13
84Cram/PCL-130
85Cram/PCL-229
85D-600
86D-410
86F-608
86T-746
88BuffB/CMC-15
88BuffB/ProC-1473
89ColoSp/CMC-14
89ColoSp/ProC-248
90AAASingl/ProC-283
90ProC/Singl-368
90T/TVMets-43
90Tidew/CMC-17
90Tidew/ProC-552
91AAA/LineD-258
91Nashvl/LineD-258
91Nashvl/ProC-2163
93LimeR/DomPr-P2
93LimeR/Winter-137
93LimeR/Winter-P2
Gonzalez, Eddie
90WPalmB/Star-10
Gonzalez, Felipe
86Fresno/Smok-5
87Clinton-7
Gonzalez, Ferdi
83Greens-14
84Greens-6
86Albany/TCMA-6
86FtLaud-8
87Albany-20
90Miami/I/Star-28CO
90Miami/II/Star-28CO
91Miami/ClBest-1MG
91Miami/ProC-423MG
92Erie/ClBest-30MG
92Erie/ProC-1640
Gonzalez, Frank
90Fayette/ProC-2399
91Lakeland/ClBest-6
91Lakeland/ProC-262
92ClBest-172
92London/ProC-628
92London/SB-410
92Sky/AASingl-174
Gonzalez, Fred
(Freddy)
90VeroB/Star-14
91AA/LineD-535
91SanAn/LineD-535
92SanAn/SB-565
92VeroB/ProC-2889
93LimeR/Winter-75
Gonzalez, German
87Kenosha-26
88BBAmer-18
88OrlanTw/Best-17
88SLAS-30
89D-590
89D/Rook-24
89F-113
89Panini/St-379
89S/HotRook-49
89T-746
90F-376
90F/Can-376
90HotRook/St-17
90OPC-266
90S-133
90S/100Ris-81
90T-266
90UD-352
91Kissim/ProC-4193
92GreatF/SportP-26
Gonzalez, Gilberto
80Elmira-32
Gonzalez, Henry
84Newar-18
85Newar-10
Gonzalez, Jamie
91ClBest/Singl-449
Gonzalez, Javier
88Clmbia/GS-12
90Jacks/GS-13
91AA/LineD-632
91Wmsprt/LineD-632
91Wmsprt/ProC-296
92Tidew/ProC-
92Tidew/SB-560
Gonzalez, Jesus
91Burllnd/ProC-3295
Gonzalez, Jim
92BurlAs/ClBest-22
92BurlAs/ProC-549
Gonzalez, Jimmy
91Classic/DP-36
91FrRow/DP-32
92OPC-564
92StCl/Dome-63
92T-564DP
92T/Gold-564
92T/GoldWin-564
93B-292
Gonzalez, John
84Idaho/Team-10
Gonzalez, Jose Fern.
(Fernando)
74OPC-649
74T-649
74T/Tr-649T
78Colum
78Padre/FamFun-14
78T-433
79T-531
80SLCity-25
80T-171
81SLCity-18
82AlexD-7
83LynnP-3
92Yank/WIZ70-55
Gonzalez, Jose Rafael
86Albuq-9
87Albuq/Pol-26
87D-525
87F-649M
87Pol/Dodg-25
87Sf/TPrev-14M
88Albuq/CMC-19
88Albuq/ProC-258
88D-341
88S-364
89Albuq/CMC-17
89Albuq/ProC-80
89D/Best-260
89S/HotRook-29
89UD-626
90Classic-96
90D-314
90F-394
90F/Can-394
90Mother/Dodg-11

90OPC-98
90Pol/Dodg-38
90S-368
90S/YS/I-16
90T-98
90Target-288
90UD-666
91D-543
91Mother/Dodg-11
91OPC-279
91Pol/Dodg-38
91S-614
91StCl-208
91T-279A
91T-279B
92Edmon/SB-160
92S-733
92StCl-774
93LimeR/Winter-83
Gonzalez, Jose
82ArkTr-13
83Louisvl/Riley-13
Gonzalez, Juan A.
87Gaston/ProC-4
88CharlR/Star-8
89BBAmAA/BPro-AA26
89TexLAS/GS-34
89Tulsa/GS-10
89Tulsa/Team-8
90AAAGame/ProC-12
90AAASingl/ProC-690
90B-492
90Classic/Up-21
90D-33
90F-297
90F/Can-297
90OPC-331
90OkCty/CMC-17
90OkCty/ProC-444
90ProC/Singl-167
90S-637
90T-331
90T/89Debut-43
90TulsaDG/Best-25
90UD-72
91B-180
91Classic/200-122
91Classic/I-70
91Classic/II-T74
91D-371
91F-286
91F/UltraUp-U55
91Leaf-119
91Leaf/Stud-124
91MajorLg/Pins-36
91Mother/Rang-4
91OPC-224
91OPC/Premier-54
91RedFoley/St-107
91S-805
91S/100RisSt-41
91S/HotRook-9
91Seven/3DCoin-7T
91StCl-237
91T-224
91Tulsa/Team-30
91UD-646
92B-84
92Classic/Game200-158
92D-393
92F-304
92JDean/18-14
92Kenner/Fig-18
92L-62
92L/BlkGold-62
92Mother/Rang-4
92OPC-27
92Panini-81
92Pinn-127
92Pinn/Team2000-26
92S-11
92S/100SS-69
92S/Impact-27
92StCl-240
92Studio-242
92T-27
92T/Gold-27
92T/GoldWin-27
92T/Kids-131
92TripleP-112
92UD-243
92UD/ASFF-9
92UD/HRH-HR19
92UD/TWillB-T14
92USPlayC/Ace-2H
92Ultra-132
93B-305
93Classic/Gamel-37
93Colla/ASG-15
93Colla/DM-40
93Colla/DMProto-4
93D-555
93D/DK-7
93D/Elite-36
93D/EliteDom-20
93D/EliteDom-20AU
93D/EliteUp-18
93D/LongBall-LL14
93D/MVP-21
93D/Master-11
93D/Spirit-SG5
93DennyGS-20
93F-322
93F-709RT
93F/ASAL-6
93F/Atlantic-10
93F/Fruit-22
93F/GoldMII-3M
93F/TLAL-8
93Flair-280
93JDean/28-8
93Kenner/Fig-12
93L-170
93L/Fast-5
93OPC-97
93OPC/Premier/StarP-7
93P-23
93Pac/Beisbol-12
93Pac/Beisbol-13
93Pac/Beisbol-15
93Pac/Jugador-6
93Pac/Spanish-311
93Pac/SpanishGold-14
93Pac/SpanishP-14
93Panini-86
93Pinn-191
93Pinn/Cooper-25
93Pinn/HRC-1
93Pinn/Slug-1
93Pinn/TP-8M
93Pinn/Team2001-13
93Rang/Keeb-408
93S-51
93S/Franchise-13
93Select-40
93Select/StatL-25
93StCl-297MC
93StCl-540
93StCl/1stDay-297MC
93StCl/1stDay-540
93StCl/Rang-21
93Studio-160
93Studio/Her-2
93Studio/Sil-4
93T-34
93T/BlkGold-32
93T/Finest-116AS
93T/FinestASJ-116AS
93T/FinestRef-116AS
93T/Gold-34
93TB/Full-4
93TWill-151
93TWill-152
93TWill-153
93TWill-154
93TWill-AU151
93TWill-AU152
93TWill-AU153
93TWill-AU154
93TWill/Pr-160
93ToysRUs-85
93TripleP-221
93TripleP/Act-22
93TripleP/LL-L4M
93UD-497AW
93UD-52
93UD-755
93UD-831TC
93UD/5thAnn-A6
93UD/Clutch-R10
93UD/Diam-20
93UD/FunPack-153GS
93UD/FunPack-156
93UD/FunPack-15HS
93UD/FunPack-223CL
93UD/FunPackAS-AS7
93UD/HRH-HR1
93UD/OnDeck-D12
93UD/SP-194
93UD/SPPlat-PP8
93UDFutHero-58
93USPlayC/Ace-1C
93Ultra-279
93Ultra/AS-16
93Ultra/HRK-1
93Ultra/Perf-2
94B-45
94D-49
94D/AwardWin-9
94D/Doml-6
94D/Elite-42
94D/LongBall-10
94D/MVP-27
94D/Special-49
94D/Spirit-5
94F-307
94F-710M
94F/AS-9
94F/Lumber4
94F/ProV-6
94F/TL-13
94Flair-109
94Flair/Outfield-5
94Kraft-4
94L-418
94L/CleanUp-7
94L/Gamer-3
94L/GoldS-13
94L/MVPAL-6
94L/PBroker-4
94L/Slide-7
94L/Slide-7
94L/StatStand-3
94OPC-28
94OPC/JAS-4
94Oscar-5
94P-3
94Pac/AllLat-14
94Pac/Cr-617
94Pac/CrPr-3
94Pac/Gold-1
94Pac/Silv-2
94Panini-127
94Panini-6
94Pinn-350
94Pinn/Power-24
94Pinn/Run-7
94Pinn/TeamP-7
94Pinn/Trib-15
94RedFoley-32
94S-27
94S/Cycle-16
94S/GoldR-27
94S/GoldS-33
94S/Tomb-19
94Select/CrCon-6
94Sf/2000-182AS
94Sf/2000-35
94StCl-261
94StCl/1stDay-261
94StCl/Gold-261
94StCl/Team-241
94Studio-154
94Studio/Editor-5
94Studio/S&GStar-9
94T-389AS
94T-685
94T/BlkGold-7
94T/Finest-211
94T/FinestRef-211
94T/Gold-389AS
94T/Gold-685
94T/Prev-34
94TripleP-194
94TripleP/Bomb-3
94TripleP/Pr-1
94UD-155
94UD-293HFA
94UD-52FUT
94UD/CollC-313TP
94UD/CollC/Gold-313TP
94UD/CollC/Silv-313TP
94UD/CollHR-1
94UD/DColl-W3
94UD/ElecD-155
94UD/ElecD-52FUT
94UD/HoloFX-12
94UD/Mantle-9
94UD/SP-148
94Ultra-127
94Ultra/AS-7
94Ultra/HRK-1
94Ultra/Hit-5
94Ultra/RBIK-4
Gonzalez, Juan
76Clinton
Gonzalez, Julian
83Peoria/Frit-23
85MidldA-25
87SanJose-24
Gonzalez, Julio C.
78BK/Ast-13
78T-389
79T-268
80T-696
81F-73
82D-645
82T-503
83Evansvl-14
83T-74
Gonzalez, Luis E.
88AubAs/ProC-1973
89Osceola/Star-6
89Star/Wax-15
90A&AASingle/ProC-59
90ColMud/Best-4
90ColMud/ProC-1352
90ColMud/Star-11
90Foil/Best-95
90ProC/Singl-760
90Star/ISingl-16
91B-550
91Classic/II-T91
91D-690
91D/Rook-17
91F-507
91F/UltraUp-U82
91Leaf/GRook-BC2
91Mother/Ast-13
91S/RookTr-99T
91StCl-576
91T/90Debut-57
91T/Tr-48T
91UD-567
91UD/Ext-702
92B-145
92Classic/Game200-3
92D-270
92F-434
92L-160
92L/BlkGold-160
92OPC-12
92OPC/Premier-103
92Panini-158
92Pinn-163
92Pinn/Team2000-68
92S-210
92S/100RisSt-6
92StCl-227
92T-12
92T/Gold-12
92T/GoldWin-12
92TripleP-210
92UD-372
92Ultra-203
93B-40
93Colla/DM-39
93D-404
93F-51
93Flair-63
93L-90
93Mother/Ast-15
93OPC-178
93Pac/Beisbol-24
93Pac/Spanish-123
93Panini-175
93Pinn-312
93S-151
93Select-205
93StCl-302
93StCl/1stDay-302
93StCl/Ast-26
93Studio-171
93T-362
93T/Finest-195
93T/FinestRef-195
93T/Gold-362
93UD-572
93UD/SP-34
93Ultra-40
94B-62
94D-83
94F-491
94Finest-290
94Flair-170
94L-292
94OPC-263
94Pac/AllLat-4
94Pac/Cr-266
94Pinn-323
94S-474
94StCl-35
94StCl/1stDay-35
94StCl/Gold-35
94Studio-22
94T-484
94T/Gold-484
94TripleP-27
94UD-396
94UD/CollC-111
94UD/CollC/Gold-111
94UD/CollC/Silv-111
94Ultra-205
Gonzalez, Luis
78Ashvl
79Ashvl/TCMA-1
80Tulsa-14
Gonzalez, Marcos
82Miami-3
87Fayette-20
Gonzalez, Melvin
91Elmira/ClBest-21
91Elmira/ProC-3266
Gonzalez, Miguel
21Exh-58
28Yueng-34
40PlayBall-115
86Conlon/1-14M
92Conlon/Sport-655
D328-61
E121/80
E135-61
E210-34
W502-34
W575
W754
Gonzalez, Mike 1
(Pitcher)
75Shrev/TCMA-3
76Shrev
Gonzalez, Mike 2
89Burllnd/Star-11
90Watertn/Star-10
Gonzalez, Orlando
75OkCty/Team-13
77T-477R
79OkCty
80BurlB-7
80OkCty
81F-585
83Tampa-13
87Nashvl-7
88Miami/Star-8
89Pac/SenLg-82
89T/SenLg-83
91Pac/SenLg-35
Gonzalez, Otto
82BurlR/Frit-27
82BurlR/TCMA-21
83BurlR-17
83BurlR/Frit-17
85Tulsa-35
86DayBe-9
86FSLAS-18
88OkCty/CMC-12
88OkCty/ProC-47
89MidldA/GS-15
Gonzalez, Paul
91ClBest/Singl-82
91HighD/ClBest-21
91HighD/ProC-2404
92Sky/AASingl-280
92Wichita/ProC-3663
92Wichita/SB-632
Gonzalez, Pedro 1
63T-537R
64T-581R
65OPC-97
65T-97
66Kahn
66T-266
67CokeCap/Indian-6
67T-424
92Yank/WIZ60-48
WG10-8
WG9-10
Gonzalez, Pedro 2
(Pete)
90VeroB/Star-15
91VeroB/ClBest-15

91VeroB/ProC-776
92Fayette/ClBest-20
92Lakeland/ProC-2281
92Toledo/ProC-1045
Gonzalez, Raul
92AppFox/ClBest-19
Gonzalez, Rich
91StPete/ClBest-25
91StPete/ProC-2288
Gonzalez, Ruben
87Belling/Team-23
88Wausau/GS-6
89AS/Cal-12
89SanBern/Best-23
89SanBern/Cal-82
90Foil/Best-198
90ProC/Singl-797
90Wmsprt/Best-8
90Wmsprt/ProC-1062
91AA/LineD-337
91ClBest/Singl-28
91Jaxvl/LineD-337
91Jaxvl/ProC-157
Gonzalez, Tommy
75Phoenix-5
79Phoenix
81Phoenix-26
82Phoenix
83Phoenix/BHN-28
Gonzalez, Tony
60T-518
61T-93
61T/St-55
62T-534
62T/St-168
63Exh
63J-181
63P-181
63T-32
64PhilBull-13
64T-379
64T/Coins-58
64T/S-14
64T/SU
64T/St-58S6
65OPC-72
65T-72
66T-478
67CokeCap/Phill-17
67Pol/Phill-6
67T-548
68Bz-8
68OPC-1LL
68T-1LL
68T-245
68T/ActionSt-7CM
68T/G-20
69MB-94
69MLB/St-192
69T-501
69T/St-94
69T/decal
70MLB/St-6
70OPC-105
70T-105
71MLB/St-345
71OPC-256
71T-256
72MB-118
75Phoenix/Caruso-19
75Phoenix/CircleK-5
77Spartan/C
82Danvl/Frit-13CO
Exh47
Gonzalez, Wallace
90Pulaski/Best-13
90Pulaski/ProC-3093
91Macon/ClBest-15
91Macon/ProC-868
Gooch, John B.
(Johnny)
31Exh/4-8
90Target-289
91Conlon/Sport-244
E120
E126-1
Gooch, Ron
79Tucson-7
79Tulsa-11
80Tulsa-17
81Tulsa-28
Good, Wilbur
D329-69
D350/2-69
M101/4-69
M101/5-69
T205
T206
Goodale, Jeff
89Niagara/Pucko-9
90Lakeland/Star-12
91Lakeland/ClBest-24
91Lakeland/ProC-278
Goodale, Wes
75Anderson/TCMA-11
Goodchild, Chris
80Clinton-6
Goode, William
14Piedmont/St-24
Gooden, Dwight
(Doc)
83Lynch-10
84F/X-43
84T/Tr-42
85D-190
85D/AAS-47
85D/HL-32
85D/HL-33
85D/HL-48
85D/WaxBox-PC1
85Drake-36
85F-634IA
85F-82
85F/St-113
85F/St-87
85F/St-95
85FunFood/Pin-27
85Leaf-234
85OPC-41
85Pol/MetYank-M3
85Seven-9E
85T-3RB
85T-620
85T/3D-19
85T/Gloss40-38
85T/Mets/Fan-5
85T/RD-19M
85T/St-107
85T/St-280
85T/St-3
85T/St-371M
85T/St-4
85T/Super-7
85Woolwth-16
86BK/AP-17
86D-26DK
86D-75
86D/AAS-28
86D/DKsuper-26
86D/HL-8
86Dorman-5
86Drake-35
86F-626M
86F-638M
86F-641M
86F-81
86F/AS-10
86F/LL-16
86F/LimEd-20
86F/Mini-19A
86F/Mini-19B
86F/Slug-11
86F/St-132CL
86F/St-46
86GenMills/Book-4M
86Jiffy-20
86KayBee-16
86Leaf-26DK
86Meadow/Blank-5
86Meadow/Milk-4
86Meadow/Stat-3
86OPC-250
86OPC-F
86Quaker-2
86Seven/Coin-C1
86Seven/Coin-E1
86Seven/Coin-S1
86Seven/Coin-W1
86Sf-100
86Sf-136M
86Sf-143M
86Sf-176M
86Sf-184M
86Sf-185M
86Sf/Dec-75
86Sf/Rook-47M
86T-202RB
86T-250
86T-709AS
86T/3D-4
86T/Gloss60-41
86T/Mets/Fan-4
86T/Mini-52
86T/St-6
86T/St-94
86T/Super-4
86T/Tatt-20M
86T/WaxBox-F
87Classic-72
87D-199
87D/AAS-18
87D/PopUp-18
87Drake-26
87F-629M
87F-9
87F/AwardWin-15
87F/BB-19
87F/Excit-19
87F/GameWin-18
87F/HL-3
87F/Hottest-18
87F/LL-20
87F/Lim-18
87F/Mini-45
87F/RecSet-12
87F/Slug-15
87F/St-48
87F/WS-7
87F/WaxBox-C4
87GenMills/Book-5M
87Jiffy-9
87KMart-26
87KayBee-13
87Leaf-84
87OPC-130
87RedFoley/St-6
87Seven-E7
87Seven-ME9
87Sf-100
87Sf-120M
87Sf-159M
87Sf/TPrev-2M
87Sportflic/DealP-4
87T-130
87T-603AS
87T/Coins-33
87T/Gloss22-10
87T/Gloss60-51
87T/Mini-23
87T/St-163
87T/St-5
87T/St-6
87T/St-96
87Tidew-31
87Tidew/TCMA-30
88AP/Test-3
88Bz-8
88Classic/Red-171
88D-69
88D/Best-96
88D/Mets/Bk-69
88Drake-28
88F-135
88F/AwardWin-14
88F/BB/AS-12
88F/BB/MVP-16
88F/Excit-15
88F/Head-5
88F/Hottest-13
88F/LL-15
88F/Mini-92
88F/RecSet-14
88F/SS-14
88F/Slug-15
88F/St-102
88F/TL-10
88Grenada-20
88KMart-10
88Kahn/Mets-16
88KennerFig-40
88Leaf-48
88MSA/Disc-19
88Nestle-21
88OPC-287
88Panini/St-337
88S-350
88S/YS/II-3
88Sf-200
88Sf/Gamewin-9
88T-405ASs
88T-480
88T/Big-11
88T/Gloss60-54
88T/Mets/Fan-16
88T/Mini-60
88T/St-101
88T/St/Backs-25
88T/UK-27
89B-376
89Classic-107
89Classic-7
89Classic/Up/2-189
89D-270
89D/AS-40
89D/Best-14
89D/PopUp-40
89F-36
89F-635M
89F/BBAS-15
89F/BBMVP's-14
89F/Excit-15
89F/Heroes-18
89F/LL-16
89F/Superstar-17
89KMart/DT-31
89Kahn/Mets-16
89KayBee-14
89KennerFig-50
89MSA/Disc-6
89OPC-30
89Panini/St-131
89Panini/St-227AS
89RedFoley/St-51
89S-200
89S/HotStar-15
89S/Mast-26
89Sf-140
89T-30
89T-661TBC84
89T/Big-304
89T/Coins-14
89T/Crunch-17
89T/DHTest-5
89T/Gloss22-21
89T/Gloss60-37
89T/HeadsUp-3
89T/LJN-86
89T/Mets/Fan-16
89T/Mini-26
89T/St-162
89T/St-99
89T/St/Backs-59
89T/UK-31
89Tetley/Discs-6
89UD-565
90B-126
90B/Ins-3
90BBWit-35
90Classic-58
90CollAB-2
90D-171
90D/BestNL-7
90D/Learning-10
90F-204
90F/BBMVP-12
90F/Can-204
90HOF/St-98
90HotPlay/St-16
90KMart/SS-10
90Kahn/Mets-16
90Kenner/Fig-31
90Leaf-139
90MCA/Disc-10
90MLBPA/Pins-9
90MSA/Soda-6
90Mets/Fan-16
90OPC-510
90OPC/BoxB-E
90Panini/St-297
90Post-29
90PublInt/St-134
90PublInt/St-260
90RedFoley/St-37
90S-313
90S/100St-99
90Sf-145
90T-510
90T/Big-174
90T/DH-26
90T/Gloss60-23
90T/HeadsUp-3
90T/St-96
90T/TVAS-58
90T/TVMets-12
90T/WaxBox-E
90Tetley/Discs-10
90UD-114
90UD-62TC
91B-472
91BBBest/Aces-8
91Classic/200-121
91Classic/I-99
91Classic/II-T39
91CollAB-17
91Colla/Gooden-Set
91D-266
91D/Preview-8
91F-148
91F/ProV-7
91JDean-25
91Kahn/Mets-16
91Kenner-20
91KingB/Discs-8
91Leaf-165
91Leaf/Prev-7
91Leaf/Stud-204
91Leaf/StudPrev-14
91MajorLg/Pins-74
91OPC-330
91OPC/Premier-55
91Panini/FrSt-86
91Panini/St-89
91Panini/Top15-60
91Panini/Top15-74
91Pep/SS-1
91Petro/SU-12
91RedFoley/St-40
91S-540
91S-685KM
91S-866FRAN
91S/100SS-65
91Seven/3DCoin-5NE
91Seven/3DCoin-8F
91StCl-100
91Sunflower-10
91T-330
91T/CJMini/I-28
91T/SU-15
91UD-224
91Ultra-218
91WIZMets-144
92B-480
92CJ/DI-23
92Classic/Game200-53
92Classic/II-T43
92D-446
92D/DK-DK15
92D/Elite-E12
92DPep/MSA-2
92F-505
92F/Smoke-S8
92L-112
92L/BlkGold-112
92Mets/Kahn-16
92MooTown-18
92MrTurkey-11
92OPC-725
92OPC/Premier-47
92P-5
92Pinn-111
92Pinn/Rookl-6M
92S-10
92S/100SS-25
92S/Impact-54
92Seven/Coin-1
92StCl-455
92StCl-602MC
92StCl/MPhoto-6
92StCl/MemberI-10M
92Studio-65
92Studio/Prev-7
92T-725
92T/Gold-725
92T/GoldWin-725
92T/Kids-11
92T/McDonB-32
92T/MicroG-725
92TripleP-167
92UD-135
92UD-84M
92UD/ASFF-23
92Ultra-232
93B-242
93Colla/DM-41
93D-462
93Duracel/PPI-13
93F-474
93F/Fruit-23
93Flair-91
93KingB-14

93L-203
93MSA/Metz-8
93Mets/Kahn-16
93OPC-92
93Pac/Spanish-198
93Panini-245
93Pinn-96
93Pinn/Cooper-19
93S-53
93Select-57
93Select/Ace-8
93StCl-514
93StCl/1stDay-514
93StCl/II/Ins-2
93StCl/MPhoto-17
93Studio-155
93T-640
93T/Finest-113AS
93T/FinestASJ-113AS
93T/FinestRef-113AS
93T/Gold-640
93TripleP-146
93TripleP/Nick-6
93UD-665
93UD/Diam-15
93UD/FunPack-123GS
93UD/FunPack-126
93UD/SP-149
93Ultra-427
94B-400
94Church-2
94D-17
94D/Special-17
94F-563
94Flair-197
94L-10
94OPC-24
94Pac/Cr-402
94Panini-217
94Pinn-62
94Pinn/Artist-62
94Pinn/Museum-62
94RedFoley-6M
94S-22
94S/GoldR-22
94Select-54
94Sf/2000-94
94StCl-220
94StCl/1stDay-220
94StCl/Gold-220
94Studio-114
94T-150
94T/Finest-82
94T/Finest/PreProd-82
94T/FinestRef-82
94T/Gold-150
94TripleP-143
94UD-205
94UD/DColl-E6
94UD/ElecD-205
94UD/SP-116
94Ultra-236

Gooden, Maury
85LitFalls-24

Goodenough, Randy
86Cram/NWL-39
87FtMyr-23

Goodfellow, Michael
N172

Goodin, Craig
83CharR-6

Goodin, Rick
(Rich)
83CharR-20
86Memphis/GoldT-9
86Memphis/SilverT-9

Goodlow, Sebastian
89Salem/Team-13

Goodman, Billy
48L-30
49B-39
50B-99
51B-237
51BR-C2
51FB
51T/RB-46
52B-81
52StarCal-85CM
52StarCal/L-71E
52T-23
53B/Col-148
53Exh/Can-63
54B-82
55B-126
56T-245
57T-303
58T-225
59T-103
60T-69
61T-247
77Galasso-21
79TCMA-96
80Ashvl-1
91Crown/Orio-160
91T/Arc53-334
Exh47
PM10/Sm-65

Goodman, Douglas
92Johnson/ClBest-3
92Johnson/ProC-3108

Goodman, Ival
35BU-127
35G-8D
35G-9D
38Exh/4-4
41DP-115
93Conlon-854
R303/A
R303/B
V351B-18
W711/1
W711/2

Goodrich, Jon
93T-704
93T/Gold-704

Goodson, J. Ed
73OPC-197
73T-197
74K-18
74OPC-494
74T-494
74T/St-105
75OPC-322
75T-322
75T/M-322
76OPC-386
76SSPC-588
76T-386
77T-584
78SSPC/270-65
78T-586
90Target-290

Goodson, Kirk
91Hunting/ClBest-11
91Hunting/ProC-3329

Goodwin, Curtis
92Kane/ClBest-5
92Kane/ProC-104
92Kane/Team-11
94B-487
94FExcel-6

Goodwin, Danny
77SLCity
78SSPC/270-204
79Ogden/TCMA-15
79T-322
80T-362
81D-474
81T-527
82D-305
82F-554
82T-123
82Tacoma-14
83Tacoma-25A
84Cram/PCL-91
85Cram/PCL-134

Goodwin, David
88Geneva/ProC-1641
89CharWh/Best-18
89CharWh/ProC-1768

Goodwin, Mike
86PrWill-12

Goodwin, Tom
89FresnoSt/Smok-10
89FresnoSt/Smok-11
89GreatF-1
90B-96
90Bakers/Cal-261
90S-668DC
90SanAn/GS-13
91AAA/LineD-6
91Albuq/LineD-6
91Albuq/ProC-1155
91B-608
91Classic/III-32
91UD/FinalEd-9F
92Albuq/ProC-734
92Albuq/SB-8
92Classic/I-39
92D/Rook-43
92F-652
92ProC/Tomorrow-243
92S-830
92S/Rook-34
92Sky/AAASingl-3
92StCl-322
92T/91Debut-65
92UD-20SR
93D-640
93F-446
93Pac/Spanish-498
93Pol/Dodg-5
93Select-349
93StCl-446
93StCl/1stDay-446
93T-228
93T/Gold-228
93Ultra-398

Goossen, Greg
67T-287R
68T-386
70McDon-5
70OPC-271
70T-271
91WIZMets-145

Gorbould, Bob
45Centen-11

Gorbous, Glen
56T-174

Gordon, Anthony
89Belling/Legoe-5
90Penin/Star-9
92BBCity/ClBest-16
92Saraso/ClBest-24

Gordon, David
89KS*-34

Gordon, Don
83BirmB-2
85Syrac-13
86BJ/Ault-11
86Tor/Fire-14
87RochR/TCMA-29
87Syrac-5
87Syrac/TCMA-26
87Syrac/TCMA-4
88ColoSp/CMC-3
88ColoSp/ProC-1538
88S/Tr-92T
88T-144
89ColoSp/CMC-2
89ColoSp/ProC-260
89F-405
89S-547
90AAASingl/ProC-646
90Denver/CMC-18
90Denver/ProC-621
90ProC/Singl-43
91AA/LineD-183
91ElPaso/LineD-183
91ElPaso/ProC-2742

Gordon, Harold
(Beebop)
92Negro/RetortII-10

Gordon, Joe
39Exh
41DP-67
41DP-83
41Wheat-21
42Playball-1
44Yank/St-12
47HomogBond-17
48L-117
49B-210
49Royal-13
50B-129
50NumNum
52Mother-19
59Kahn
60T-216MG
61T-224MG
61T/RO-30
69T-484MG
86Sf/Dec-24M
92Yank/WIZAS-24
93AP/ASG-133
D305
R303/A
R303/B
R423-36
V351B-19

Gordon, Keith
90Billings/ProC-3228
91CharWh/ClBest-23
92Cedar/ClBest-1
92Cedar/ProC-1084
92UD/ML-204
93B-174

Gordon, Kevin
85PrWill-21
86Nashua-8

Gordon, Mike W.
78SSPC/270-251

Gordon, Mike
92GulfCY/ProC-3785

Gordon, Sid
43Playball-45
47HomogBond-18
47TipTop
48B-27
48L-131
49B-101
49Eureka-104
50B-109
50Drake-16
51B-19
51T/RB-2
52B-60
52Dix
52NTea
52RM-NL6
52T-267
52TipTop
53B/Col-5
53Dix
53JC-23
53NB
53SpicSpan/3x5-12
53T-117
54B-11
54DanDee
54Dix
55B-163
55RFG-24
55W605-24
79TCMA-67
91T/Arc53-117
D305

Gordon, Tom
(Tommy)
87FtMyr-25
88AppFx/ProC-149
88MidwLAS/GS-40
89B-115
89Classic/Up/2-182
89D-45RR
89D/Best-287
89D/Rook-4
89F-284
89S-634RP
89S/HotRook-68
89S/Mast-7
89S/YS/II-2
89T/Tr-38T
89UD/Ext-736
90B-365
90Bz-21
90Classic-4
90D-297
90F-108
90F/AwardWin-15
90F/Can-108
90F/SoarSt-7
90HotRook/St-18
90Leaf-14
90OPC-752
90Panini/St-89
90PublInt/St-348
90S-472
90S/100Ris-1
90Sf-30
90T-752
90T/Big-252
90T/Coins-15
90T/Gloss60-30
90T/HeadsUp-21
90T/JumboR-10
90T/Mini-15
90T/St-268
90T/St-322FS
90ToysRUs-12
90UD-365
91B-311
91D-242
91F-559
91Leaf-132
91OPC-248
91Panini/FrSt-284
91Panini/St-231
91Pol/Royal-10
91S-197
91StCl-254
91T-248
91UD-431
91Ultra-147
92B-477
92Classic/Game200-82
92D-250
92F-158
92L-68
92L/BlkGold-68
92OPC-431
92Pinn-238
92Pinn/Team2000-58
92Pol/Royal-8
92S-130
92S/Impact-69
92StCl-388
92Studio-182
92T-431
92T/Gold-431
92T/GoldWin-431
92UD-476
92Ultra-370
93D-497
93F-237
93Flair-215
93L-211
93OPC-75
93Pac/Spanish-134
93Pinn-105
93Pol/Royal-9
93S-184
93StCl-523
93StCl/1stDay-523
93StCl/Royal-3
93T-611
93T/Gold-611
93UD-221
93Ultra-207
94D-450
94F-155
94Finest-397
94L-389
94Pac/Cr-283
94Panini-73
94Pinn-317
94S-234
94S/GoldR-234
94Select-118
94T-66
94T/Gold-66
94TripleP-234
94UD-474
94UD/CollC-112
94UD/CollC/Gold-112
94UD/CollC/Silv-112
94Ultra-364

Gordon, Tony
92Saraso/ProC-200

Gore, Arthur
55B-289UMP

Gore, Brad
91OKSt-10
92OKSt-10

Gore, Bryan
90CharlR/Star-8
91AA/LineD-581
91Tulsa/LineD-581
91Tulsa/ProC-2767
91Tulsa/Team-8
92Tulsa/ProC-2690
92Tulsa/SB-606

Gore, George
90HOF/St-6
N172
N284
N338/2
WG1-40

Gore, Kevin
89Geneva/ProC-1865

Gore, Ricky
89Idaho/ProC-2017

Gorecki, Rick
91GreatF/SportP-24
91LitSun/HSPros-20
91LitSun/HSProsG-20
92Bakers/Cal-12
92UD/ML-109
93B-266
94B-482

94FExcel-213
Gorham, Bobby
92Everett/ClBest-25
92Everett/ProC-1678
Gorin, Charles
54JC-15
55Gol/Braves-11
55JC-15
92TX-17
Gorinski, Bob
75Tacoma/KMMO-9
78T-386
79Tidew-24
Gorman, Bill
82Omaha-24
83Omaha-23
84Omaha-14
85Omaha-1
Gorman, Dave
89Utica/Pucko-9
90Utica/Pucko-18
Gorman, Dirk
90Kissim/DIMD-12
Gorman, Mike
86GlenF-7
Gorman, Paul
91Daikyo/Fut-14
Gorman, Thomas A.
(Tom)
53B/BW-61
54B-17
55Rodeo
56T-246
57T-87
58T-235
59T-449
Gorman, Thomas P.
(Tom)
80Memphis-4
82Wichita-5
83Tidew-11
84Nes/792-774
84T-774
84Tidew-14
85F-83
85T-53
86F-82
86Portl-7
86T-414
91WIZMets-146
Gorman, Tom
55B-293UMP
Gorsica, John
47TipTop
Gorski, Gary
86Cram/NWL-82
88Modesto-11
88Modesto/Cal-62
89Modesto/Chong-12
Gorton, Chris
89Hamil/Star-15
90Foil/Best-181
90Spring/Best-20
91StPete/ClBest-7
91StPete/ProC-2270
Goryl, John
58T-384
59T-77
61Clover-7
62T-558
63T-314
64T-194
78OrlanTw
78Twin/Frisz-30
79Twin/FriszP-8CO
81D-527MG
81T-669MG
82BK/Indians-3CO
82BK/Indians-4CO
82Wheat/Ind
83Wheat/Ind-15CO
85Polar/Ind-xx
86OhHenry-CO
87Gator-CO
88Gator-45CO
Goselin, Scott
88Pulaski/ProC-1751
89Sumter/ProC-1107
Gosger, Jim
63T-553R
66OPC-114
66T-114
67CokeCap/A's-18
67OPC-17
67T-17
68T-343
69MB-95
69T-482
70Expos/Pins-6
70T-651
71Expo/ProS-8
71LaPizza-4
71MLB/St-128
71OPC-284
71T-284
72MB-119
91WIZMets-147
Goshay, Henry Lee
88VeroB/Star-8
89Dunedin/Star-5
Goshgarian, Dee Marge
91Salinas/ClBest-28
Goslin, Leon
(Goose)
25Exh-123
26Exh-123
27Exh-61
28Exh-61
29Exh/4-31
31Exh/4-29
33CJ/Pin-9
33DH-21
33Exh/4-15
33G-110
33G-168
34Exh/4-12
35BU-85
35Exh/4-12
35G-1H
35G-3F
35G-5F
35G-6F
36Exh/4-12
37Exh/4-12
37OPC-111
40PlayBall-232
48Swell-13
61F-35
76Rowe-7M
76Shakey-110
77Galasso-60
80Pac/Leg-104
80Perez/HOF-109
80SSPC/HOF
81Tiger/Detroit-124
87Conlon/2-38
91Conlon/Proto-520
91Conlon/Sport-62
92Conlon/Sport-437
93Conlon-907
E120
E210-49
R300
R308-173
R309/2
R312/M
R313
R313A-6
R314
R315-A11
R315-B11
R316
R332-27
V300
V355-43
V61-8
W502-49
W517-47
W573
Gosnell, Mark
93SoEastern-4ACO
Goss, Howie
62T-598R
63T-364
Gossage, Rich
(Goose)
73OPC-174
73T-174
74OPC-542
74T-542
75OPC-554
75T-554
75T/M-554
76Ho-77
76OPC-180
76OPC-205LL
76SSPC-156
76T-180
76T-205LL
77Ho-128
77Ho/Twink-128
77T-319
78BK/Y-10
78K-8
78T-70
79BK/Y-10
79Ho-48
79OPC-114
79T-225
79T-8LL
80OPC-77
80T-140
81D-347
81F-89
81F/St-118
81K-41
81MSA/Disc-1[illegible]
81OPC-48
81T-460
81T/HT
81T/Nat/Super-7
81T/St-113
81T/St-251
81T/St-8
82D-283
82F-37
82F/St-116
82FBI/Disc-8
82K-32
82OPC-117IA
82OPC-286AS
82OPC-396
82T-557AS
82T-770
82T-771IA
82T/St-140
82T/St-217
83D-157
83F-381
83F/St-15M
83F/St-6M
83K-10
83OPC-240
83OPC-241SV
83OPC/St-100
83RoyRog/Disc-2
83T-240
83T-241SV
83T/Fold-4M
83T/Gloss40-11
83T/St-100
84D-396
84F-125
84F/X-44
84Mother/Padres-2
84Nes/792-670
84Nes/792-718LL
84OPC-121
84Seven-22E
84T-670
84T-718LL
84T/RD-8M
84T/St-316
84T/Tr-43
85D-185
85D/AAS-14
85F-33
85F/LimEd-10
85F/St-108
85FunFood/Pin-05
85Leaf-204
85Mother/Padres-5
85OPC-90
85Seven-9W
85T-90
85T/3D-27
85T/Gloss40-19
85T/RD-22M
85T/St-147
85T/Super-49
85ThomMc/Discs-30
86D-185
86D-2DK
86D/AAS-31
86D/DKsuper-2
86F-322
86F/Mini-68
86F/Slug-12
86Leaf-2DK
86Meadow/Stat-20
86OPC-104
86Seven/Coin-C7
86Seven/Coin-E7
86Seven/Coin-S7
86Seven/Coin-W7
86Sf-190
86Sf-55M
86T-530
86T/3D-6
86T/Gloss60-56
86T/St-107
86T/Super-26
86T/Tatt-1M
87Bohem-54
87Classic-96
87D-483
87F-415
87F/LL-21
87OPC-380
87RedFoley/St-9
87T-380
87T/St-109
88Berg/Cubs-54
88D-434
88D/Best-26
88D/Cubs/Bk-NEW
88F-583
88F/Up-U76
88OPC-170
88S-331
88S/Tr-14T
88T-170
88T/Tr-41T
89D-158
89F-425
89Mother/Giants-27
89OPC-162
89OPC/BoxB-D
89S-223
89T-415
89T/LJN-75
89T/WaxBox-D
89UD-452
90D-678
90Publint/St-68
91B-271
91Classic/III-98
91F/Up-U59
91Leaf-236
91Leaf/Stud-125
91Mother/Rang-16
92D-555
92F-305
92L-474
92L/BlkGold-474
92Mother/A's-12
92OPC-215
92S-538
92StCl-719
92T-215
92T/Gold-215
92T/GoldWin-215
92Yank/WIZ70-56
92Yank/WIZ80-67
92Yank/WIZAS-25
93F/Final-255
93Flair-259
93Mother/A's-16
93Pac/Spanish-567
93Rang/Keeb-162
93StCl-17
93StCl/1stDay-17
93Ultra-606
94F-262
94Pac/Cr-450
94S-260
94S/GoldR-260
94StCl-191
94StCl/1stDay-191
94StCl/Gold-191
Gosse, John
80WHave-19
Gosselin, Pat
93Welland/ProC-3363
Gotay, Julio
62T-489
63IDL-10
63J-161
63P-161
63T-122
65T-552
67CokeCap/Astro-4
68Dexter-35
68OPC-41
68T-41
69MB-96
Gotay, Ruben
83ArkTr-2
Gott, James
(Jim)
81ArkTr-17
83D-353
83OPC-62
83T-506
84D-268
84F-155
84Nes/792-9
84OPC-9
84T-9
84Tor/Fire-14
85D-632
85F-105
85F/Up-U45
85Leaf-136
85Mother/Giants-21
85OPC-311
85T-311
85T/Tr-40T
86D-358
86F-542
86Mother/Giants-21
86OPC-106
86T-463
87F/Up-U35
87Mother/SFG-19
87T/Tr-39T
88D-606
88D/Best-213
88F/Up-U112
88Leaf-253
88S-320
88T-127
89B-411
89D-362
89F-210
89F/Excit-16
89F/Superstar-18
89OPC-172
89Panini/St-163
89S-257
89S/HotStar-98
89Sf-83
89T-752
89T/Mini-41
89UD-539
89VFJuice-35
90D-605
90F-466
90F/Can-466
90Mother/Dodg-24
90OPC-292
90Pol/Dodg-35
90Publnt/St-155
90S-515
90T-292
90UD-89
90UD/Ext-701
91D-601
91F-200
91Leaf-229
91Mother/Dodg-24
91OPC-606
91Pol/Dodg-35
91S-621
91T-606
91UD-690
92D-601
92F-454
92Mother/Dodg-15
92OPC-517
92Pinn-228
92Pinn-596SIDE
92Pol/Dodg-35
92S-172
92StCl-483
92T-517
92T/Gold-517
92T/GoldWin-517
92Ultra-504
93D-670
93F-447
93Flair-69
93L-511
93Mother/Dodg-17
93Pac/Spanish-499
93Pinn-435
93Pol/Dodg-6
93S-422
93StCl-487

93StCl/1stDay-487
93StCl/Dodg-7
93T-418
93T/Gold-418
93UD-666
94D-92
94F-509
94L-205
94Pac/Cr-307
94Pinn-307
94S-402
94T-87
94T/Finest-49
94T/FinestRef-49
94T/Gold-87
94UD-336
94UD/CollC-113
94UD/CollC/Gold-113
94UD/CollC/Silv-113
94Ultra-215

Goucher, Steve
89SanDiegoSt/Smok-10
91BendB/ClBest-6
91BendB/ProC-3691

Goughan, Bob
88RochR/Gov-32

Gould, Bob
85Madis-14
85Madis/Pol-11
86Madis/Pol-9
87Modesto-11

Gould, Frank
90Everett/Best-5
90Everett/ProC-3121

Goulding, Rich
77Clinton
78LodiD

Gouldrup, Gary
85Elmira-8

Goulet, Michel
91StCl/Member*-43

Gousha, Sean
92Erie/ClBest-18
92Erie/ProC-1626

Governor, Tony
28Exh/PCL-8

Gowdy, Hank
11Helmar-78
14CJ-138
15CJ-138
16FleischBrd-33
21Exh-59
21Exh-60
40PlayBall-82
72F/FFeat-33
81Conlon-26
87Conlon/2-39
88Conlon/3-12
91Conlon/Sport-209
BF2-51
D327
D328-62
D329-70
D350/2-70
E120
E121/120
E121/80
E122
E135-62
E220
M101/4-70
M101/5-70
R313
T207
V100
W501-90
W514-67
W516-23
W572
W573
W575
W711/1
W711/2

Gowell, Larry
73Syrac/Team-9
92Yank/WIZ70-57

Gozzo, Mauro
(Goose)
84LitFalls-21
86Lynch-13
87Memphis-3
87Memphis/Best-20
88Memphis/Best-16
89Knoxvl/Best-8
89Knoxvl/ProC-1145
89Knoxvl/Star-6
89Star/IISingl-121
90AAASingl/ProC-345
90D-655
90F-82
90F/Can-82
90OPC-274
90ProC/Singl-328
90S-610
90S/100Ris-48
90Sf-168
90Syrac/CMC-2
90Syrac/MerchB-11
90Syrac/ProC-565
90Syrac/Team-11
90T-274
90T/89Debut-44
91AAA/LineD-82
91ColoSp/LineD-82
91ColoSp/ProC-2179
91MajorLg/Pins-19
91S-843
92Portl/SB-407
92Portland/ProC-2661

Grabarkewitz, Bill
70OPC-446
70T-446
71K-56
71MD
71MLB/St-104
71OPC-85
71T-85
71T/Coins-21
71T/tatt-5
71Ticket/Dodg-7
72T-578
73OPC-301
73T-301
74OPC-214
74T-214
74T/St-74
75OPC-233
75T-233
75T/M-233
75Tucson-8
75Tucson/Caruso-1
75Tucson/Team-4
87Smok/Dodg-9
89Smok/Dodg-76
90Target-291

Graber, Red
61Union

Grable, Rob
91Niagara/ClBest-14
91Niagara/ProC-3641
92Fayette/ClBest-18
92ProC/Tomorrow-69

Grabowski, Al F.
No Cards.

Grabowski, Joe
R310

Grabowski, Johnny
28LaPresse-20
91Conlon/Sport-124

Grabowski, Mike
75WPalmB/Sussman-19

Grabowski, Reggie J.
No Cards.

Grace, Earl
93Conlon-938

Grace, Joe
52Mother-5
V355-103
W753

Grace, Mark
86Peoria-8
87Pittsfld-10
88Berg/Cubs-17
88D-40RR
88D/Best-4
88D/Cubs/Bk-40
88D/Rook-1
88F-641R
88F/Mini-68
88F/Up-U77
88IowaC/CMC-14
88IowaC/ProC-539
88Leaf-40RR
88Peoria/Ko-11
88Peoria/Ko-34M
88S/Tr-80T
88T/Tr-42T
89B-291
89Bz-12
89Classic-13
89Classic/Up/2-155
89D-17DK
89D-255
89D/DKsuper-17DK
89F-426
89F/BBMVP's-15
89F/Excit-17
89F/LL-17
89F/Superstar-19
89Holsum/Discs-12
89KMart/DT-1
89KennerFig-51
89Mara/Cubs-17
89Nissen-12
89OPC-297
89Panini/St-55
89S-362
89S/HotRook-78
89S/Mast-22
89S/YS/I-3
89Sf-15
89T-465
89T/Big-189
89T/Coins-15
89T/Gloss60-29
89T/HeadsUp-15
89T/JumboR-11
89T/St-324
89T/St-50
89ToysRUs-12
89UD-140
90B-29
90Classic-8
90CollAB-31
90Cub/Mara-9
90D-577
90D/BestNL-51
90F-32
90F/BB-12
90F/Can-32
90F/LL-12
90F/LgStand-6
90HotPlay/St-17
90Kenner/Fig-32
90Kenner/Fig-33
90Leaf-137
90MLBPA/Pins-51
90OPC-240
90Panini/St-241
90Post-19
90PublInt/St-194
90PublInt/St-613
90RedFoley/St-38
90S-150
90S/100St-60
90Sf-15
90Starline/LJS-16
90Starline/LJS-2
90Starline/LJS-40
90T-240
90T/Big-19
90T/DH-27
90T/Gloss60-12
90T/Mini-49
90T/St-56
90T/TVAS-63
90T/TVCub-23
90UD-128
91B-433
91Cadaco-25
91Classic/200-105
91Classic/I-27
91CollAB-20
91Cub/Mara-17
91Cub/Vine-12
91D-199
91F-422
91Kenner-21
91Leaf-170
91Leaf/Stud-157
91MajorLg/Pins-66
91OPC-520
91Panini/FrSt-43
91Panini/St-48
91Post-22
91S-175
91S/100SS-91
91Seven/3DCoin-6MW
91StCl-290
91T-520
91T/CJMini/I-24
91T/SU-16
91UD-134
91UD-99TC
91Ultra-61
92B-580
92CJ/DII-5
92Classic/Game200-29
92Cub/Mara-17
92D-281
92F-381
92L-26
92L/BlkGold-26
92OPC-140
92Panini-182
92Pinn-136
92S-445
92S/100SS-20
92StCl-174
92Studio-14
92T-140
92T/Gold-140
92T/GoldWin-140
92T/Kids-4
92TripleP-114
92UD-143
92USPlayC/Cub-13S
92USPlayC/Cub-8H
92Ultra-175
93B-440
93Cadaco-27
93Colla/DM-42
93Cub/Mara-7
93D-532
93F-20
93F/Fruit-24
93Flair-14
93HumDum/Can-28
93L-198
93L/GoldAS-12M
93L/UpGoldAS-10M
93MSA/Metz-29
93OPC-86
93Pac/Jugador-27
93Pac/Spanish-58
93Panini-203
93Pinn-34
93S-50
93Select-73
93Select/StatL-12
93StCl-419
93StCl/1stDay-419
93StCl/Cub-8
93StCl/MPhoto-18
93Studio-42
93Studio/Her-5
93Studio/SS-8
93T-630
93T/Finest-73
93T/FinestRef-73
93T/Gold-630
93TripleP-11LH
93TripleP-211
93UD-483M
93UD-573
93UD/FunPack-81
93UD/looss-WI8
93UD/SP-83
93Ultra-18
93Ultra/AwardWin-3
94B-410
94D-358
94D/MVP-2
94D/Special-358
94F-383
94F/AS-37
94Finest-390
94Kraft-23
94L-43
94L/Gamer-6
94OPC-146
94P-14
94Pac/Cr-98
94Pac/Silv-25
94Panini-153
94Pinn-336
94Pinn/Run-34
94RedFoley-11
94S-42
94S/GoldR-42
94S/GoldS-3
94S/Tomb-6
94Sf/2000-120
94StCl-403
94StCl/1stDay-403
94StCl/Gold-403
94StCl/Team-339
94Studio-60
94T-360
94T/BlkGold-33
94T/Gold-360
94TripleP-72
94TripleP/Medal-4
94UD-440
94UD/CollC-114
94UD/CollC/Gold-114
94UD/CollC/Silv-114
94UD/SP-69
94Ultra-455
94Ultra/AwardWin-11
94Ultra/OnBase-5

Grace, Michael
87Anchora-15
89SLCity-14
90Rockford/ProC-2702
90Rockford/Team-9
91Batavia/ClBest-22
91Batavia/ProC-3478
91ClBest/Singl-431
91WinSalem/ClBest-20
91WinSalem/ProC-2837
92ChalK/SB-156
92CharlK/ProC-2780
92Sky/AASingl-72
92UD/ML-217

Grace, Mike
77Indianap-12
78Indianap-16
79Indianap-18
80Indianap-4
83ColumAst-4

Grace, Robert Earl
34DS-69
34G-58
35BU-69
R314

Grace, Willie
92Negro/Retort-25

Grachen, Tim
83QuadC-12

Grady, Pat
80Batavia-26

Graff, Milt
57T-369
58T-192
59T-182

Graff, Stephen
86Erie-9

Graffanino, Anthony
(Tony)
91Idaho/ProC-4335
91Idaho/SportP-5
92ClBest-372
92Macon/ClBest-1
92Macon/ProC-273
92ProC/Tomorrow-195
93Durham/Team-7
94B-601
94FExcel-153

Graham, Bert
M116

Graham, Bill
77Fritsch-46
91WIZMets-148

Graham, Brian
83Madis/Frit-28
84Albany-6
85Huntsvl/BK-14
87Kinston-11
88EastLAS/ProC-51
88Wmsprt/ProC-1313
89Watertn/Star-11
90CLAS/CL-32MG
90Kinston/Team-28MG
91CLAS/ProC-CAR16MG
91Kinston/ClBest-28MG
91Kinston/ProC-340MG
92Canton/ProC-706
92Canton/SB-124MG

Graham, Bruce
85Everett/II/Cram-3TR
86Everett/Pop-7
87Everett-33TR
89Phoenix/ProC-1488TR

Graham, Dan
79Toledo-6
80T-669R
81D-233
81F-189
81OPC-161

81T-161
82D-455
82F-167
82RochR-10
82T-37
91Crown/Orio-161
Graham, Derrick
91Billing/SportP-9
91Billings/ProC-3766
92Billings/ProC-3362
Graham, Everett
82Clinton/Frit-10
86Phoenix-7
87Shrev-1
88Phoenix/CMC-20
88Phoenix/ProC-60
89MidldA/GS-16
Graham, George
(Peaches)
11Helmar-95
C46-63
E270/2
E90/1
M116
S74-43
S74-62
T201
T202
T204
T205
T206
T207
T3-95
Graham, Gordie
91Bluefld/ClBest-2
91Bluefld/ProC-4134
Graham, Greg
91WinHaven/ClBest-18
91WinHaven/ProC-497
92NewBrit/ProC-441
92NewBrit/SB-486
93StLucie/ProC-2928
Graham, Jack
50B-145
90Target-292
Graham, Jeffrey L.
87Spring/Best-9
Graham, Jeremy
92Lipscomb-21M
93Lipscomb-10
Graham, John
(Johnny)
88AubAs/ProC-1971
89AubAs/ProC-2177
90AubAs/Best-20MG
Graham, Lee
81Pawtu-19
83Pawtu-22
84Pawtu-2
85Richm-19
86Richm-7
Graham, Lew
84LitFalls-23
Graham, Lindsey
74Gaston
Graham, Nancy
92WPalmB/ClBest-28
Graham, Otto
52Wheat*
Graham, Randy
83Greens-8
84Nashvl 8
85Albany-8
86Colum-10
86Colum/Pol-9
87Colum-23
87Colum/Pol-11
87Colum/TCMA-5
Graham, Richard
92Belling/ClBest-5
92Belling/ProC-1436
Graham, Steve
88Hamil/ProC-1745
89Hamil/Star-13
90StPete/Star-9
Graham, Tim
90Elmira/Pucko-1
91Elmira/ClBest-6
91Elmira/ProC-3283
92LynchRS/ClBest-12
92LynchRS/ProC-2919
Graham, Wayne
91WIZMets-149
92TX-18
Graham, William
T206
Grahe, Joe
90MidldA/GS-12
91AAA/LineD-164
91Classic/200-50
91Classic/III-27
91D-737
91Edmon/LineD-164
91Edmon/ProC-1513
91OPC-426
91S-367RP
91T-426
91T/90Debut-58
91UD-657
92Classic/Game200-68
92D-445
92L-137
92L/BlkGold-137
92OPC-496
92OPC/Premier-158
92Pinn-371
92S-674
92S/100RisSt-97
92StCl-579
92T-496
92T/Gold-496
92T/GoldWin-496
92UD-542
93B-201
93D-401
93F-192
93L-372
93Mother/Angel-27
93OPC-199
93Pac/Spanish-369
93Pinn-412
93S-188
93Select-374
93StCl-262
93StCl/1stDay-262
93StCl/Angel-18
93T-129
93T/Gold-129
93TripleP-256
93UD-290
93Ultra-165
94D-454
94F-58
94L-69
94Pac/Cr-79
94S-202
94S/GoldR-202
94T-691
94T/Finest-193
94T/FinestRef-193
94T/Gold-691
94TripleP-16
94UD-401
94Ultra-329
Grahek, Larry
81CharR-22
Grahovac, Mike
89Everett/Star-8
90ClintUp/Team-U5
91Clinton/ProC-837
Grain, Gregg
90Chatt/GS-3TR
Grajeda, Billy
92AZ/Pol-4
Gralewski, Bob
88CapeCod-5
88CapeCod/Sum-154
Grammas, Alex
54Hunter
54T-151
55B-186
55Hunter
55T-21
55T/DH-107
56T-37
57Sohio/Reds-6
57T-222
58T-254
59T-6
60T-168
61P-177
61T-64
61T/St-87
62J-168
62P-168
62P/Can-168
62Salada-197
62Shirriff-197
62T-223
63T-416
73OPC-296CO
73T-296CO
74OPC-326CO
74T-326CO
76SSPC-620
76T-606MG
77T-51MG
84Tiger/Wave-17CO
88Pep/T-CO
89Mara/Tigers-CO
90CokeK/Tiger-28CO
91CokeK/Tiger-xCO
94T/Arc54-151
Granco, Julio
86Cram/NWL-79
Grandas, Bob
79Ogden/TCMA-25
80Ogden-11
81Tacoma-27
82Tacoma-35
83Evansvl-19
Grandquist, Ken
82IowaC-27
83IowaC-29
84IowaC-5
85IowaC-26
Grandy, Jack
92Watlo/ClBest-29MG
Graney, Jack
92Conlon/Sport-481
94Conlon-1247
D327
D328-63
D329-71
D350/2-71
E120
E121/120
E121/80
E135-63
E220
M101/4-71
M101/5-71
T207
W501-112
W573
W575
Grange, Red
33SK*-4
Granger, George
R314/Can
Granger, Jeff
91T/Tr-49T
92StCl/Dome-64
92T/DQ-18
92T/Tr-43T
92T/TrGold-43T
93StCl/MurphyS-22
94B-527
94F/MLP-12
94OPC-51
94Pinn-269
94Pinn/Artist-269
94Pinn/HobSam-269
94Pinn/HobSam-NNO
94Pinn/Museum-269
94Pinn/RetailSam-269
94Pinn/RetailSam-NNO
94S-574
94S/Boys-59
94T-204FDP
94T/Gold-204FDP
94UD-14
94UD/CollC-23
94UD/CollC/Gold-23
94UD/CollC/Silv-23
94UD/ElecD-14
94UD/SP-172
Granger, Lee
82Miami-19
83SanJose-4
84RochR-7
85CharlO-2
Granger, Wayne
69T-551
70MLB/St-27
70OPC-73
70T-73
71MLB/St-59
71OPC-379
71T-379
72T-545
73OPC-523
73T-523
74OPC-644
74T-644
76Expo/Redp-13
76OPC-516
76T-516
89Pac/SenLg-202
92Yank/WIZ70-58
Grant, Bob
77Wausau
Grant, Brian
93MedHat/ProC-3730
93MedHat/SportP-5
Grant, Charles
52Park-10
Grant, Charlie
74Laugh/Black-23
86Negro/Frit-70
Grant, Ed
10Domino-49
11Helmar-115
12Sweet/Pin-100
E104
E270/2
E90/1
E94
M116
S74-75
T201
T202
T205
Grant, Frank
74Laugh/Black-17
Grant, George
93Conlon-957
Grant, Jim
(Mudcat)
58T-394
59Kahn
59T-186
60Kahn
60L-25
60T-14
61Kahn
61P-60
61T-18
61T/St-135
62Kahn
62Salada-26
62Shirriff-26
62T-307
63Sugar-23
63T-227
64Kahn
64T-133
64T/Coins-99
64T/St-37S4
64Wheat/St-19
65T-432
66Bz-37
66OPC-40
66T-224LL
66T-40
66T/RO-3
66T/RO-36
67CokeCap/Twin-15
67T-545
68T-398
69Fud's-4
69MLB/St-158
69T-306
69T/St-55
71MLB/St-201
71OPC-509
71T-509
72MB-120
72OPC-111
72T-111
78TCMA-200
78Twin/Frisz-5
85Durham-15C
89Pac/Leg-186
89Swell-84
90Target-293
91Swell/Great-34
93MCI-3
93TWill-34
Grant, Ken
86QuadC-12
87PalmSp-7
88QuadC/GS-21
88Visalia/Cal-152
88Visalia/ProC-86
Grant, Larry
90Elmira/Pucko-6
91WinHaven/ClBest-19
91WinHaven/ProC-498
Grant, Mark
82Clinton/Frit-23
84Cram/PCL-3
85Cram/PCL-199
85D-601
86Phoenix-8
87D-644
87Mother/SFG-26
87Sf/TPrev-10M
88Coke/Padres-55PAN
88D-511
88D/Best-133
88F-584
88Smok/Padres-9
88T-752
89Coke/Padre-5
89F-304
89S-349
89S/YS/I-12
89T-178
89T/Big-154
89UD-622
90Brave/Dubuq/Singl-10
90Coke/Padre-5
90D-441
90F-156
90F/Can-156
90OPC-537
90Padre/MagUno-20
90PublInt/St-49
90S-466
90T-537
90UD-412
91Brave/Dubuq/Perf-12
91Brave/Dubuq/Stand-16
91D-361
91F-690
91OPC-287
91S-824
91T-287
91UD-301
92Calgary/ProC-3727
92OPC-392
93F-675
93Mother/Ast-26
Grant, Tom
82IowaC-3
83IowaC-22
84IowaC-30
85IowaC-9
Grantham, George
25Exh-52
26Exh-52
31Exh/4-14
33CJ/Pin-10
33Exh/4-4
33G-66
91Conlon/Sport-292
R316
V353-66
W513-76
Grapenthien, Dan
92StCl/Dome-65
Grapenthin, Dick
83Wichita/Dog-10
84Indianap-16
86LasVegas-4
87Louisvl-14
88AAA/ProC-24
88Louisvl-20
88Louisvl/CMC-2
88Louisvl/ProC-426
89Colum/CMC-23
89Colum/Pol-9
89Colum/ProC-747
Graser, Rick
80SanJose/JITB-9
80Wausau-18
Grass, Darren
92MN-22M
93Bz-13
93T/Tr-101T
Grasso, Newton M.
(Mickey)
49B/PCL-6
51B-205
52B-174
52T-90
53B/Col-77

53Briggs
53T-148
54B-184
91T/Arc53-148
Grate, Don
88Chatt/Team-13
Grater, Mark
87Savan-11
88Spring/Best-2
89StPete/Star-14
90AAASingl/ProC-511
90ArkTr/GS-15
90Louisvl/CMC-21
90Louisvl/ProC-397
90ProC/Singl-121
91AAA/LineD-236
91Louisvl/LineD-236
91Louisvl/ProC-2909
91Louisvl/Team-7
92Louisvl/ProC-1882
92Louisvl/SB-263
92T/91Debut-66
Graupmann, Tim
83Wisco/Frit-9
84Visalia-16
Gravelle, Leo
45Parade*-23
Graven, Tim
79Savan-7
Graves, Chris
87QuadC-22
88QuadC/GS-27
89PalmSp/Cal-40
89PalmSp/ProC-483
Graves, Danny
93Bz-9
93T/Tr-97T
Graves, Frank M.
N172
Graves, Joe
83Lynch-20
84Jacks-8
86Jaxvl/TCMA-11
Graves, John
89Butte/SP-21
90A&AASingle/ProC-82
90Gaston/Best-23
90Gaston/ProC-2517
90Gaston/Star-10
90SALAS/Star-9
Graves, Jon
92Yakima/ClBest-2
92Yakima/ProC-3441
Graves, Kenley
85Bend/Cram-7
Graves, Kenny
90StLucie/Star-8
90T/TVMets-44
Graves, Randy
90Kissim/DIMD-13
91GreatF/SportP-16
Gray, Dan
90GreatF/SportP-2
91Yakima/ClBest-10
91Yakima/ProC-4250
92VeroB/ClBest-20
92Yakima/ClBest-4
92Yakima/ProC-3453
Gray, Dave
64T-572R
Gray, David
88Lynch/Star-7
89Lynch/Star-9
Gray, Dennis Jr.
89Alaska/Team-16
91StCath/ClBest-16
91StCath/ProC-3388
92Myrtle/ClBest-7
92Myrtle/ProC-2190
92StCl/Dome-66
93Dunedin/ClBest-7
93Dunedin/ProC-1788
Gray, Dick
58T-146
59T-244
60T-24
90Target-294
Gray, Elliott
89Martins/Star-13
90Batavia/ProC-3057
91ClBest/Singl-141
91Clearw/ClBest-1
91Clearw/ProC-1616
92Clearw/ClBest-12
92Clearw/ProC-2053
92ProC/Tomorrow-301
Gray, Gary
75Anderson/TCMA-12
76SanAn/Team-11
77Tucson
78Cr/PCL-38
79Tucson-1
80Tacoma-17
81F-402
81T/Tr-767
82F-511
82OPC-78
82SLCity-9
82T-523
82T/St-233
83D-637
83F-480
83T-313
93Rang/Keeb-163
Gray, Jeff
86Vermont-8
87Nashvl-8
88Nashvl/CMC-5
88Nashvl/ProC-478
88Nashvl/Team-10
89Nashvl/CMC-3
89Nashvl/ProC-1288
89Nashvl/Team-5
90AAASingl/ProC-428
90Pawtu/CMC-25
90Pawtu/ProC-456
90ProC/Singl-276
91D-721
91F-95
91Leaf-356
91OPC-731
91Pep/RSox-7
91S-586
91StCl-271
91T-731
91UD-685
92D-122
92S-187
92StCl-222
92USPlayC/RedSox-12H
92USPlayC/RedSox-8C
Gray, John L.
55Rodeo
55T-101
55T/DH-48
Gray, Lorenzo
77AppFx
80GlenF/B-22
80GlenF/C-20M
80GlenF/C-26
82Edmon-10
84Maine-12
84Nes/792-163
84T-163
86SanJose-9
Gray, Pete
77Fritsch-6
77Galasso-229
88LitSun/Minor-2
Gray, Samuel
25Exh-107
29Exh/4-29
31Exh/4-30
33Exh/4-15
91Conlon/Sport-75
Gray, Scott
86AubAs-10
Gray, Stanley
43Centen-10
44Centen-9
Gray, Steve
89Clinton/ProC-899
89Salinas/ProC-1802
Gray, Ted
49B-10
50B-210
51B-178
52B-199
52T-86
53B/Col-72
53T-52
53Tiger/Glen-11
54B-71
55B-86
81Tiger/Detroit-131
91Crown/Orio-162
91T/Arc53-52
Gray, Terry
77StPete
Gray, William
(Dolly)
11Helmar-68
12Sweet/Pin-58
E90/1
T202
T205
T206
Graybill, Dave
87Jaxvl-15
89PalmSp/Cal-59
Grayner, Paul
82Nashvl-13
83Nashvl-7TR
Grayson, Mike
89Beloit/I/Star-7
Grayston, Joe
85BurlR-1
Grayum, Richie
88MissSt-7
89Geneva/ProC-1871
89MissSt-15
90CharlK/Team-23
91WinSalem/ClBest-24
91WinSalem/ProC-2841
92ChalK/SB-157
92CharlK/ProC-2783
Graziano, Andy
92Gaston/ClBest-27TR
Grba, Eli
60T-183
61T-121
62T-96
63T-231
64T-464
65T-203
82Vanco-23
88Vanco/ProC-769
89Reno/Cal-265MG
90Princet/DIMD-28MG
91Martins/ProC-3471CO
92Yank/WIZ60-49
Greason, Bill
92Negro/RetortII-11
Grebe, Brett
90Pulaski/Best-5
90Pulaski/ProC-3103
Grebeck, Brian
90Boise/ProC-3321
90SDSt-5
91QuadC/ClBest-17
91QuadC/ProC-2636
92PalmSp/ClBest-11
92PalmSp/ProC-847
93B-33
93FExcel/ML-143
Grebeck, Craig
87Penin-10
88BirmB/Best-24
89BirmB/Best-17
89BirmB/ProC-111
90B-318
90BirmDG/Best-15
90Coke/WSox-28
90Coke/WSox-6
90D/Rook-9
90F/Up-U85
90S/Tr-105T
90UD/Ext-721
91D-378
91F-120
91F/UltraUp-U15
91Kodak/WSox-14
91OPC-446
91S-69
91S/100RisSt-35
91StCl-559
91T-446
91T/90Debut-59
92D-546
92F-81
92L-344
92L/BlkGold-344
92OPC-273
92Pinn-334
92S-561
92StCl-145
92T-273
92T/Gold-273
92T/GoldWin-273
92UD-603
92Ultra-34
92WSox-14
93D-199
93F-202
93Pac/Spanish-71
93Pinn-362
93S-126
93Select-389
93StCl-136
93StCl/1stDay-136
93StCl/WSox-14
93T-259
93T/Gold-259
93UD-738
93Ultra-531
93WSox-9
94F-81
94Pac/Cr-126
94StCl-225
94StCl/1stDay-225
94StCl/Gold-225
94StCl/Team-133
94T-176
94T/Gold-176
94Ultra-336
Greco, George
80Elmira-7
Greely, Jim
93LSU/McDag-3
Green, Bob
86FtLaud-9
87FtLaud-6
88Albany/ProC-1331
89Albany/Best-10
89Colum/CMC-20
89Colum/Pol-8
89Colum/ProC-734
Green, Charlie
87Watertn-29
Green, Christopher
82AlexD-6
85Cram/PCL-240
86Edmon-14
87RochR/TCMA-22
Green, Daryl
86Cram/NWL-88
87QuadC-10
88QuadC/GS-13
89Modesto/Cal-271
89Modesto/Chong-11
90Huntsvl/Best-6
91StPete/ClBest-8
91StPete/ProC-2271
Green, David A.
80Holyo-14
82Louisvl-10
83D-166
83F-6
83OPC/St-323
83T-578
83T/St-323
84D-425
84D-625
84F-323
84Nes/792-362
84OPC-362
84T-362
84T/St-149
85D-303
85F-224
85F/Up-U46
85Leaf-191
85Mother/Giants-17
85OPC-87
85T-87
85T/St-145
85T/Tr-41T
86D-114
86F-543
86OPC-122
86T-727
87Louisvl-15
88F-34
88Louisvl-21
88Louisvl/CMC-14
88Louisvl/ProC-421
91AA/LineD-582
91Tulsa/LineD-582
91Tulsa/ProC-2784
91Tulsa/Team-9
Green, Donald
(Don)
89Hamil/Star-18
90Savan/ProC-2066
Green, Edward
(Danny)
E107
Green, Elijah
(Pumpsie)
60T-317
61T-454
62Salada-187
62Shirriff-187
62T-153
63T-292
64T-442
81TCMA-297
91WIZMets-151
Green, Fred
60T-272
61T-181
Green, G. Dallas
60L-52
60T-366
61T-359
62Salada-219
62Shirriff-219
62T-111
63T-91
64T-464
65OPC-203
65T-203
78TCMA-187
80BK/P-1MG
81D-415MG
81T-682MG
84Cub/Uno-12M
89S/NWest-31MG
89T-104MG
91WIZMets-150
93T/Tr-36TMG
Green, Gary
85Beaum-18
85T-396OLY
86LasVegas-5
87LasVegas-22
88LasVegas/CMC-17
88LasVegas/ProC-232
89UD/Ext-722
90AAASingl/ProC-685
90OkCty/CMC-13
90OkCty/ProC-439
90ProC/Singl-163
91OPC-184
91StCl-323
91T-184
92Nashvl/ProC-1837
93Rang/Keeb-164
Green, Gene
58T-366
59T-37
60L-82
60T-269
61T-206
62J-72
62P-72
62P/Can-72
62Salada-70
62Shirriff-70
62T-78
63Sugar-10
63T-506
91Crown/Orio-163
Green, Harvey
90Target-962
Green, Jason
94B-545
Green, Jeff
83BuffB-8
Green, Joe
87Negro/Dixon-8
Green, Joey
90OK-5
Green, John
86Geneva-7
86Peoria-9
87Peoria-3
87Peoria/PW-3
89FtLaud/Star-7
Green, Larry
76Dubuq
Green, Lenny
58T-471
59T-209
60T-99
61Clover-8H
61Peters-15

61T-4
62J-87
62P-87
62P/Can-87
62Salada-69A
62Salada-69B
62Shirriff-69
62T-84
62T/St-75
62T/bucks
63J-6
63P-6
63T-198
63Twin/Volpe-4
64T-386
65T-588
66T-502
91Crown/Orio-164
Green, Nat
85Bend/Cram-8
Green, Otis
86Syrac-11
87Syrac-15
87Syrac/TCMA-14
88Syrac/CMC-19
88Syrac/ProC-831
89Syrac/CMC-12
89Syrac/MerchB-11
89Syrac/ProC-793
89Syrac/Team-11
90AAASingl/ProC-576
90Indianap/CMC-18
90Indianap/ProC-293
90ProC/Singl-68
91Stockton/ClBest-2
91Stockton/ProC-3028
92Denver/ProC-2633
92Denver/SB-129
92ProC/Tomorrow-88
92Sky/AAASingl-63
93Vanco/ProC-2589
Green, Randy
80Ogden-5
Green, Richard
(Dick)
64T-466R
65OPC-168
65T-168
66T-545
67CokeCap/A's-8
67OPC-54
67T-54
68A's/JITB-7
68T-303
69MB-97
69T-515
69T/St-215
70MLB/St-258
70OPC-311
70T-311
71MLB/St-514
71OPC-258
71T-258
72MB-121
72T-780
73OPC-456
73T-456
74OPC-392
74T-392
75OPC-91
75T-91
75T/M-91
Green, Rick
92Salinas/ProC-3749
Green, Shawn
92ClBest-348
92Dunedin/ClBest-8
92Dunedin/ProC-2011
92OPC-276
92StCl/Dome-67
92T-276
92T/Gold-276
92T/GoldWin-276
92UD-55TP
92UD/ML-225
93B-27
93Knoxvl/ProC-1262
94B-253
94D-607
94StCl-66
94StCl/1stDay-66
94StCl/Gold-66
94StCl/Team-159
94T-237M
94T/Gold-237M
94UD-15
94UD-297UDC
94UD/CollC-9
94UD/CollC/Gold-9
94UD/CollC/Silv-9
94UD/ElecD-15
Green, Stephen W.
88Bakers/Cal-248
89VeroB/Star-9
90London/ProC-1279
Green, Steve R.
77Visalia
78Holyo
80OrlanTw/B-4
82OrlanTw/A-15
Green, Terry
86Osceola-9
87Osceola-25
88ColAst/Best-22
Green, Tom
(Tom)
90Welland/Pucko-13
91Augusta/ClBest-20
91Augusta/ProC-819
92BuffB/BlueS-10
92CaroMud/ProC-1193
92ClBest-241
92Salem/ClBest-17
93CaroMud/RBI-14
Green, Trent
92FrRow/Green-6M
92Lipscomb-12
Green, Tyler
89Wichita-1
90WichSt-13
91Batavia/ClBest-20
91Batavia/ProC-3479
91ClBest/Gold-19
91ClBest/Singl-416
91Classic/DP-7
91Classic/DPPr-1
91FrRow/DP-34
92ClBest-230
92D/RookPhen-BC5
92FrRow/Green-1
92FrRow/Green-2
92FrRow/Green-3
92FrRow/Green-4
92FrRow/Green-5
92FrRow/Green-6
92FrRow/Green-7
92FrRow/Green-Set
92OPC-764
92Pinn-303DP
92ProC/Tomorrow-303
92Reading/ProC-569
92Reading/SB-531
92S-810DP
92Sky/AASingl-229
92StCl/Dome-68
92T-764DP
92T/Gold-764
92T/GoldWin-764
92UD-68TP
92UD/ML-167
92UD/ML-40M
92UD/ML-68DS
93B-400
93ClBest/MLG-36
93FExcel/ML-85
93Phill/Med-15
93Pinn-581
93ScranWB/Team-10
93T/Tr-37T
93UD-505DD
94B-362
94B-422
94D-433
94Finest-256
94Phill/Med-10
94Pinn-503
94StCl/Team-239
94T-294
94T/Gold-294
94UD-72
94UD/ElecD-72
Greenberg, Hank
34DS-54
34G-62
35BU-57
35G-8F
35G-9F
36G
36Wheat
37OPC-107
38Exh/4-12
38G-253
38G-277
38ONG/Pin-13
38Wheat
39Exh
39PlayBall-56
39Wheat-7
40PlayBall-40
41DP-52
41DP-85
41PlayBall-18
41Wheat-16
55Gol/Ind-9
60NuCard-42
61GP-4
61NuCard-442
63Bz-19
76Rowe-7
76Shakey-81
77Galasso-82
80Marchant/HOF-14
80Pac/Leg-30
80Perez/HOF-81
80SSPC/HOF
81Conlon-79
81Tiger/Detroit-133
83D/HOF-16
83Kaline-39M
85T/Gloss22-22
85West/2-33
86Sf/Dec-4
86Tiger/Sport-6
89Pac/Leg-195
91Conlon/Sport-14
92Conlon/Sport-430
92Conlon/Sport-590
93AP/ASG-107
93AP/ASG24K-41G
93Conlon-733
94Conlon-1005
94TedW-32
PR1-13
R302
R303-B
R303/A
R309/2
R311/Gloss
R312
R313
R314
R346-35
R423-38
V300
V351B-20
V355-41
Greenberg, Steve
76Dubuq
Greene, Altar
(Al)
80Evansvl-8
80T-666R
Greene, Bart
92Bristol/ClBest-23
92Bristol/ProC-1424
Greene, Carl
57Seattle/Pop-17
Greene, Charlie
92CharRain/ClBest-12
92CharRain/ProC-122
Greene, Ed
86Beloit-8
Greene, Grant
76Laugh/Clown-8
Greene, Henry
77DaytB
Greene, Ira Thomas
(Tommy)
86Sumter/ProC-7
87Greenvl/Best-23
88Richm-33
88Richm/CMC-1
88Richm/ProC-2
89AAA/ProC-54
89Richm/Bob-7
89Richm/CMC-3
89Richm/Ko-33
89Richm/ProC-831
90AAASingl/ProC-398
90B-1
90Classic/Up-22
90D-576
90F-584
90F/Can-584
90ProC/Singl-296
90Richm/Bob-9
90Richm/CMC-20
90Richm/ProC-253
90Richm/Team-10
90S-640
90S/YS/II-24
90Sf-224
90T/89Debut-45
90UD-49
91Classic/200-66
91D-635
91F/UltraUp-U99
91F/Up-U108
91Leaf-524
91OPC-486
91Phill/Medford-15
91S-808
91StCl-549
91StCl/Member*-3
91T-486
91UD/FinalEd-62F
92B-227
92Classic/Game200-64
92D-109
92D-94HL
92F-531
92L-292
92L/BlkGold-292
92OPC-83
92Phill/Med-14
92Pinn-155
92Pinn/Team2000-53
92S-336
92S-426NH
92StCl-27
92T-83
92T/Gold-83
92T/GoldWin-83
92UD-567
92Ultra-242
93D-568
93F-489
93Flair-101
93L-132
93OPC-144
93Phill/Med-16
93Pinn-313
93S-464
93StCl-559
93StCl/1stDay-559
93StCl/Phill-27
93T-291
93T/Finest-149
93T/FinestRef-149
93T/Gold-291
93UD-549
93UD/SP-174
93Ultra-441
94B-580
94D-482
94F-589
94L-133
94OPC-137
94Pac/Cr-475
94Phill/Med-11
94Pinn-78
94Pinn/Artist-78
94Pinn/Museum-78
94RedFoley-13M
94S-380
94Select-155
94StCl/Team-222
94T-570
94T/Finest-152
94T/FinestRef-152
94T/Gold-570
94TripleP-174
94UD-203
94UD/CollC-115
94UD/CollC/Gold-115
94UD/CollC/Silv-115
94UD/ElecD-203
94Ultra-244
Greene, James
(Joe)
78Laugh/Black-13
Greene, Jeff
86Sumter/ProC-6
87Durham-22
87Penin-20
88BurlB/ProC-14
88Tampa/Star-8
Greene, Keith
86Cram/NWL-137
87Spartan-8
Greene, Nelson
90Target-963
Greene, Rick
92B-563FOIL
92Classic/DP-12
92LSU/McDag-5
92T/Tr-44T
92T/TrGold-44T
92UD/ML-9
93B-263
93StCl/MurphyS-188
93T-233
93T/Gold-233
93UD-446TP
94B-425
94ClBest/Gold-110
94FExcel-55
94FExcel-55
94SigRook-9
94Ultra-356
Greene, Steve
77BurlB
Greene, Todd
91T/Tr-50T
92StCl/Dome-69
92T/DQ-20
94FExcel-27
94FExcel/1stY-7
Greene, Willie
90A&AASingle/ProC-96
90Augusta/ProC-2470
90B-173
90ProC/Singl-849
90S-682DC
91B-448
91ClBest/Singl-350
91WPalmB/ClBest-20
91WPalmB/ProC-1236
92B-429
92Cedar/ClBest-20
92Chatt/ProC-3826
92ClBest-48
92F/Up-81
92ProC/Tomorrow-263
93B-349FOIL
93B-638
93D-143RR
93F-34
93L-456
93Pinn-285
93S-250
93S/Boys-12
93S/Proctor-8
93Select-348
93StCl-704
93StCl/1stDay-704
93T-764
93T/Finest-148
93T/FinestRef-148
93T/Gold-764
93ToysRUs-46
93ToysRUs/MPhoto-4
93UD-4SR
94B-430
94D-539
94F-410
94L-326
94Pinn-522
94S/Boys-34
94Select-102
94T-428
94T/Gold-428
94TripleP-212
94UD-230
94UD/CollC-116
94UD/CollC/Gold-116
94UD/CollC/Silv-116
94UD/ElecD-230
94Ultra-170
Greenfield, Kent
90Target-295
92Conlon/Sport-617
Greengrass, Jim
53T-209
54B-28
54T-22
55B-49
56T-275
56YellBase/Pin-12
58Union

91T/Arc53-209
94T/Arc54-22
Exh47
Greenhalgh, Ted
46Sunbeam
Greenlee, Gus
88Negro/Duques-5OWN
Greenlee, Robert
87SanBern-19
Greenwell, Mike
85IntLgAS-44
85Pawtu-4
86Pawtu-10
86Sf-178R
87D-585
87D/Rook-4
87F/Up-U37
87Sf/Rook-8
87Sf/TPrev-9M
87T-259
88Classic/Blue-227
88D-339
88D/Best-177
88D/RedSox/Bk-339
88F-354
88F-630M
88F/Excit-16
88F/Hottest-14
88F/Mini-7
88F/St-9
88Leaf-153
88OPC-274
88Panini/St-32
88S-175
88S/YS/I-24
88Sf-118
88T-493
88T/Big-233
88T/Coins-14
88T/Gloss60-20
88T/JumboR-3
88T/St-249
88T/St-312
88ToysRUs-12
89B-34
89Cadaco-24
89Classic-149
89D-186
89D-1DK
89D/AS-15
89D/Best-28
89D/DKsuper-1DK
89D/GrandSlam-5
89D/MVP-BC13
89F-90
89F/AS-6
89F/BBAS-16
89F/BBMVP's-16
89F/Excit-18
89F/Heroes-19
89F/LL-18
89F/Superstar-20
89F/WaxBox-C11
89KayBee-15
89KennerFig-52
89Nissen-6
89OPC-374
89Panini/St-280
89S-659HL
89S-66
89S/HotStar-70
89S/Mast-36
89Sf-143
89Sf-221M
89T-402AS
89T-630
89T/Big-211
89T/Coins-41
89T/DH-6
89T/Gloss60-31
89T/HeadsUp-22
89T/Hills-15
89T/LJN-147
89T/Mini-48
89T/St-255
89T/St/Backs-16
89T/UK-32
89UD-432
90B-274
90Classic-47
90D-66
90D/BestAL-115
90D/Bon/MVP-BC17
90D/Learning-32
90F-277
90F-632M
90F/BB-13
90F/BBMVP-13
90F/Can-277
90F/Can-632M
90F/LL-13
90F/WaxBox-C8
90Kenner/Fig-34
90Leaf-143
90MCA/Disc-18
90MLBPA/Pins-71
90OPC-70
90Panini/St-16
90Pep/RSox-11
90PublInt/St-287
90PublInt/St-457
90RedFoley/St-39
90S-345
90S/100St-67
90Sf-50
90T-70
90T/Big-61
90T/DH-28
90T/St-254
90T/TVAS-22
90T/TVRSox-30
90Tetley/Discs-18
90UD-354
91B-116
91Classic/200-18
91Classic/III-29
91D-553
91D/GSlam-14
91F-96
91F/ProV-8
91Leaf-19
91Leaf/Stud-15
91OPC-792
91Panini/FrSt-268
91Panini/Top15-32
91Pep/RSox-8
91S-130
91S/100SS-82
91StCl-253
91T-792
91T/CJMini/II-34
91UD-165
91UD-43TC
91Ultra-32
92B-615
92Classic/Game200-72
92D-523
92F-39
92L-89
92L/BlkGold-89
92OPC-113
92Panini-91
92Pinn-131
92RedSox/Dunkin-14
92S-545
92S/100SS-10
92StCl-446
92T-113
92T/Gold-113
92T/GoldWin-113
92T/Kids-69
92TripleP-252
92UD-275
92USPlayC/RedSox-10D
92USPlayC/RedSox-1C
92Ultra-16
93B-607
93Colla/DM-43
93D-223
93F-559
93Flair-164
93L-197
93OPC-285
93Pac/Spanish-33
93Panini-96
93Pinn-102
93S-385
93Select-228
93StCl-86
93StCl/1stDay-86
93Studio-161
93T-323
93T/Finest-197
93T/FinestRef-197
93T/Gold-323
93TripleP-46
93UD-154
93UD/FunPack-164
93UD/SP-202
93Ultra-152
94B-259
94D-163
94F-33
94Finest-322
94L-182
94OPC-49
94Pac/Cr-56
94Panini-30
94Pinn-285
94S-83
94S/GoldR-83
94S/Tomb-20
94Select-10
94Sf/2000-110
94StCl-386
94StCl/1stDay-386
94StCl/Gold-386
94Studio-162
94T-502
94T/Gold-502
94TripleP-204
94UD-187
94UD/ElecD-187
94UD/SP-155
94Ultra-314
Greenwell, Richard
89LittleSun-12
Greenwood, Bob
55B-42
Greenwood, John
88Pulaski/ProC-1753
Greenwood, Mike
87Pocatel/Bon-9
Greenwood, William
N172
Greer, Brian K.
80T-685R
82Amari-2
Greer, Edward C.
N172
N403
Greer, Ken
88Oneonta/ProC-2047
89PrWill/Star-8
90FtLaud/Star-9
91FtLaud/ClBest-4
91FtLaud/ProC-2418
92Albany/ProC-2219
93ColClip/Pol-4
Greer, Randy
80Penin/B-14
80Penin/C-20
Greer, Rusty
90Butte/SportP-4
90TexLgAS/GS-3
91CharlR/ClBest-21
91CharlR/ProC-1325
91ClBest/Singl-172
91FSLAS/ProC-FSL4
92ProC/Tomorrow-156
92Sky/AASingl-267
92Tulsa/ProC-2701
92Tulsa/SB-607
Gregg, Eric
88TM/Umpire-34
89TM/Umpire-32
90TM/Umpire-31
Gregg, Hal
47TipTop
49Eureka-161
52T-318
90Target-296
Gregg, Sylvanus
16FleischBrd-34
Gregg, Tommy
86Nashua-9
87Harris-19
88BuffB/CMC-12
88BuffB/ProC-1474
88D-203
88F/Up-U113
88S/Tr-69T
89Brave/Dubuq-13
89Classic/Up/2-192
89D-121
89D/Best-170
89F-592
89Panini/St-32
89T/Tr-39T
89UD/Ext-751
90Brave/Dubuq/Perf-9
90Brave/Dubuq/Singl-11
90D-239
90F-585
90F/Can-585
90Leaf-86
90OPC-223
90Panini/St-224
90PublInt/St-114
90S-78
90S/YS/I-39
90T-223
90UD-121
91Brave/Dubuq/Perf-13
91Brave/Dubuq/Stand-17
91D-244
91F-691
91Leaf-144
91OPC-742
91Panini/FrSt-19
91S-606
91StCl-571
91T-742
91Ultra-6
92Brave/LykePerf-14
92Brave/LykeStand-15
92D-485
92OPC-53
92S-623
92StCl-244
92T-53
92T/Gold-53
92T/GoldWin-53
Gregg, Vean
14CJ-29
15CJ-29
T207
W514-33
WG5-17
WG6-16
Gregory, Brad
90Miami/I/Star-10
Gregory, Bull
72Dimanche*-121
Gregory, Grover
(Lee)
62Kahn/Atl
Gregory, John
83VeroB-17
Gregory, Paul
47Signal
Gregory, Scott
78Dunedin
Gregson, Glenn
(Goose)
83MidldC-3
84MidldC-14
87WinSalem-12
88GreatF-27
89GreatF-33
90Bakers/Cal-246
91Bakers/Cal-29CO
91CalLgAS-24
92Bakers/Cal-31M
Greif, Bill
72OPC-101R
72T-101R
73OPC-583
73T-583
74McDon
74OPC-102
74T-102
74T/St-92
75OPC-168
75T-168
75T/M-168
76OPC-184
76T-184
77OPC-243
77T-112
Greiner, Dan
W514-80
Grejtak, Bryan
90OK-1
91Bluefld/ClBest-13
91Bluefld/ProC-4130
Greminger, Edward
T206
T213/brown
Grennan, Steve
91Pocatel/ProC-3777
91Pocatel/SportP-19
92Kingspt/ClBest-7
92Kingspt/ProC-1525
Gresham, Kris
91Bluefld/ClBest-1
91Bluefld/ProC-4131
92Kane/ClBest-9
92Kane/ProC-93
92Kane/Team-12
Gress, Loren
90Idaho/ProC-3270
91Idaho/ProC-4336
91Macon/ProC-871
Gretzky, Wayne
91StCl/Charter*-46
91StCl/Charter*-47
91StCl/Member*-44
Grewal, Ranbir
90James/Pucko-17
91MidwLAS/ProC-45
91Rockford/ClBest-5
91Rockford/ProC-2040
92ClBest-304
92WPalmB/ClBest-12
92WPalmB/ProC-2084
Grich, Bob
71OPC-193
71T-193
72OPC-338
72T-338
73JP
73K-39
73OPC-418
73T-418
74OPC-109
74T-109
74T/DE-8
74T/St-125
75Ho-72
75K-4
75OPC-225
75T-225
75T/M-225
76Ho-13
76Ho/Twink-13
76OPC-335
76SSPC-388
76T-335
77BurgChef-126
77Ho-131
77Ho/Twink-131
77K-39
77OPC-28
77Pepsi-25
77T-521
78Ho-62
78OPC-133
78SSPC/270-194
78T-18
79Ho-112
79OPC-248
79T-447
80OPC-326
80T-621
81D-289
81F-269
81F/St-50
81OPC-182
81T-182
81T/HT
81T/St-53
82D-90
82F-461
82F/St-218
82K-38
82OPC-284
82PermaGr/AS-5
82T-162LL
82T-284
82T/St-162
82T/St-4LL
83D-468
83F-91
83K-60
83OPC-381
83OPC-387AS
83OPC/St-43
83Seven-11
83T-387
83T-790
83T/St-43
84D-179
84F-518
84Nes/792-315
84OPC-315
84Smok/Cal-10
84T-315
84T/RD-20M
84T/St-228

85D-280
85F-302
85Leaf-88
85OPC-155
85Smok/Cal-12
85T-465
85T/RD-20M
85T/St-230
86D-207
86F-157
86OPC-155
86Smok/Cal-12
86T-155
86T-486M
86T/St-181
86T/Tatt-23M
86Woolwth-12
87D-456
87F-81
87OPC-4
87RedFoley/St-30
87Sf-184
87T-677
89Smok/Angels-11
90Pac/Legend-31
90Swell/Great-58
91Crown/Orio-165
92AP/ASG-71
93Orio/SUII-1
93TWill-19
93UD/ATH-59

Grief

E270/2

Grier, Antron

87Erie-12
88Hamil/ProC-1723
88Savan/ProC-355
89Spring/Best-3
90StPete/Star-10

Grier, Dave

80BurlB-5
82ElPaso-17

Grier, Mark

79Newar-14

Griesser, Grant

90AppFox/Box-10
90AppFox/ProC-2097

Grieve, Tom

71MLB/St-540
71OPC-167
71T-167
72T-609
73OPC-579
73T-579
74OPC-268
74T-268
75Ho-38
75OPC-234
75T-234
75T/M-234
76Ho-130
76OPC-106
76SSPC-270
76T-106
77BurgChef-25
77Ho-93
77Ho/Twink-93
77T-403
78T-337
79OPC-138
79T-277
79Tucson-14
91WIZMets-152
93Rang/Keeb-13

Grieve, William

55B-275UMP

Griffen, Leonard

91Cedar/ClBest-5
91Cedar/ProC-2713
92Cedar/ClBest-3
92Cedar/ProC-1067

Griffey, Craig

92Belling/ClBest-25
92Belling/ProC-1456
92LimeR/GriffeyHolo-3
92UD-51CL
92UD-85M
93River/Cal-27

Griffey, Ken Jr.

87Belling/Team-15
88CalLgAS-26
88SanBern/Best-1
88SanBern/Cal-34
89B-220
89B-259FS
89Classic-131
89Classic/Up/2-193
89D-33RR
89D/Best-192
89D/Rook-3
89F-548
89Mother/Griffey-1
89Mother/Griffey-2
89Mother/Griffey-3
89Mother/Griffey-4
89Mother/Sea-3
89S/Mast-30
89S/Tr-100
89S/YS/II-18
89T/HeadsUp-5
89T/Tr-41T
89UD-1
90B-481
90Bz-18
90Classic-20
90Classic/III-T1
90CollAB-3
90D-365
90D-4DK
90D/BestAL-1
90D/Learning-8
90D/SuperDK-4DK
90F-513
90F/AwardWin-16
90F/BB-14
90F/BBMVP-14
90F/Can-513
90F/LL-14
90F/SoarSt-6
90F/WaxBox-C10
90HotRook/St-19
90Kenner/Fig-35
90Kenner/Fig-36
90KingB/Discs-16
90Leaf-245
90Leaf/Prev-4
90MCA/Disc-8
90MLBPA/Pins-117
90MSA/Soda-17
90Mother/Mar-3
90OPC-336
90Panini/St-155
90Post-23
90PublInt/St-433
90PublInt/St-595
90RedFoley/St-40
90S-560
90S/100Ris-3
90Sf-7
90Sunflower-2
90T-336
90T/89Debut-46
90T/Big-250
90T/Coins-16
90T/DH-29
90T/Gloss60-20
90T/HeadsUp-5
90T/JumboR-11
90T/St-225
90T/St-323FS
90Tetley/Discs-8
90ToysRUs-13
90UD-156
90UD-24TC
90USPlayC/AS-11S
90Windwlk/Discs-7
90WonderBrd-18
91Arena*-2
91B-255
91BBBest/HitM-7
91Bleach/Pr-1
91Bleach/Griffey-1
91Bleach/Griffey-2
91Bleach/Griffey-3
91Cadaco-26
91Classic/200-120
91Classic/I-3
91Classic/II-T1
91Classic/III-30
91CollAB-4
91Colla/Griffey-Set
91CounHrth-15
91CounHrth-28M
91D-392MVP
91D-49AS
91D-77
91D/Preview-4
91F-450A
91F-450B
91F-710M
91F/ASIns-7
91F/UltraG-4
91FrRow/Griffey-Set
91Griffey-1
91Griffey-2
91Griffey-3
91Griffey-4M
91JDean-2
91Kenner-22
91Kenner-23
91KingB/Discs-6
91Leaf-372
91Leaf/Stud-112
91MSA/Holsum-9
91MajorLg/Pins-4
91MooTown-4
91Mother/Griffey-1
91Mother/Griffey-3M
91Mother/Griffey-4M
91OPC-392AS
91OPC-790
91OPC/Premier-56
91Panini/FrSt-172
91Panini/FrSt-233
91Panini/St-189
91Panini/Top15-116
91Pep/Griffey-Set
91Petro/SU-23
91Post-11
91Post/Can-26
91RedFoley/St-120
91RedFoley/St-41
91S-2
91S-396AS
91S-697RF
91S-841M
91S-858FRAN
91S-892DT
91S/100SS-5
91S/Cooper-B3
91Seven/3DCoin-3SC
91Seven/3DCoin-4A
91Seven/3DCoin-4NW
91Seven/3DCoin-5NW
91Seven/3DCoin-6NC
91Seven/3DCoin-6NE
91Seven/3DCoin-7F
91Seven/3DCoin-7MW
91Seven/3DCoin-8T
91StCl-270
91StCl/Charter*-10
91Sunflower-11
91T-392AS
91T-790
91T/CJMini/I-36
91T/SU-17
91UD-555
91UD/FinalEd-79FCL
91UD/FinalEd-87FAS
91USPlayC/AS-1D
91Ultra-336
92AlGrif/GoldMom-1
92AlGrif/GoldMom-10
92AlGrif/GoldMom-2
92AlGrif/GoldMom-3
92AlGrif/GoldMom-4
92AlGrif/GoldMom-5
92AlGrif/GoldMom-6
92AlGrif/GoldMom-7
92AlGrif/GoldMom-8
92AlGrif/GoldMom-9
92AlGrif/McDon-1
92AlGrif/McDon-2
92AlGrif/McDon-3
92Arena/KidGriff-1
92Arena/KidGriff-2
92Arena/KidGriff-3
92Arena/KidGriff-4
92Arena/KidGriff-5
92B-100
92CJ/DI-12
92ClBest-200
92ClBest/BBonusC-12
92ClBest/RBonus-BC12
92Classic/Game200-186
92Classic/I-40
92Classic/II-T44
92Colla/ASG-11
92D-165
92D-24AS
92D/Elite-E13
92D/McDon-22
92D/Preview-7
92DPep/MSA-26
92F-279
92F-709PV
92F/ASIns-23
92F/Performer-4
92F/TmLIns-15
92F/Up-H1
92FrRow/Griffey-NNO
92FrRow/GriffeyClub-Set
92FrRow/GriffeyGold-Set
92FrRow/GriffeyHolo-Set
92French-15
92Highland-50
92JDean/18-11
92Kenner/Fig-19
92Kenner/Fig-20
92KingB-8
92L-392
92L/BlkGold-392
92L/GoldPrev-24
92L/Prev-24
92LimeR/GriffeyHolo-2
92MSA/Ben-10
92MTV-3
92MooTown-7
92Mother/Mar-2
92MrTurkey-12
92OPC-50
92OPC/Premier-167
92P-20
92Panini-277AS
92Panini-60
92Pinn-283I
92Pinn-549
92Pinn/Slug-7
92Pinn/Team2000-47
92Pinn/TeamP-9
92S-1
92S-436AS
92S/100SS-1
92S/Impact-28
92S/Prev-1
92S/Proctor-7
92Seven/Coin-26
92StCl-400
92StCl-603MC
92StCl/Dome-70
92StCl/MPhoto-7
92StCl/MemberII-6
92Studio-232
92Sunflower-14
92T-50
92T/Gold-50
92T/GoldWin-50
92T/Kids-122
92T/McDonB-8
92T/MicroG-50
92TripleP-152
92TripleP/Gal-GS8
92TripleP/Prev-1
92UD-424
92UD-650DS
92UD-85M
92UD/ASFF-24
92UD/TWillB-T15
92UD/TmMVPHolo-22
92USPlayC/Ace-11D
92Ultra-123
92Ultra/AS-6
92Ultra/AwardWin-22
93AlGrif/24Taco-1
93AlGrif/24Taco-2
93AlGrif/24Taco-3
93AlGrif/24Taco-4
93AlGrif/24Taco-5
93AlGrif/24Taco-6
93AlGrif/TripleP-1
93B-375
93B-703FOIL
93Cadaco-28
93Classic/GameI-38
93Colla/ASG-3
93Colla/DM-44
93Colla/DMArt-3
93Colla/DMProto-5
93D-553
93D/DK-1
93D/EliteDom-7
93D/LongBall-LL9
93D/MVP-20
93D/Master-8
93D/Prev-20
93Duracel/PPII-15
93F-307
93F/ASAL-7
93F/Atlantic-11
93F/Fruit-25
93F/TLAL-10
93Flair-270
93Ho-25
93HumDum/Can-15
93JDean/28-11
93Kenner/Fig-13
93KingB-2
93Kraft-8
93L-319
93L/GoldAS-7
93L/UpGoldAS-8
93MSA/Metz-9
93Mar/DQ-4
93Mother/Mar-4
93OPC-91
93OPC/Premier/StarP-9
93P-7
93Pac/Jugador-7
93Pac/Spanish-286
93Panini-63
93Pinn-110
93Pinn/Cooper-22
93Pinn/HRC-13
93Pinn/Slug-28
93Post/Can-9
93S-1
93S-504AS
93S-536DT
93S/Franchise-12
93S/GoldDT-5
93Select-2
93Select/ChasS-19
93Select/StatL-15
93StCl-591MC
93StCl-707
93StCl/1stDay-591MC
93StCl/1stDay-707
93StCl/II/Ins-4M
93StCl/MPhoto-26
93StCl/Mar-1
93StCl/MurphyMP-3AS
93StCl/MurphyS-56
93Studio-96
93Studio/SS-1
93T-179
93T-405M
93T/BlkGold-33
93T/Finest-110AS
93T/FinestASJ-110AS
93T/FinestRef-110AS
93T/Gold-179
93T/Gold-405M
93T/HolPrev-179
93T/MicroP-179
93T/PreProd-6
93TB/Full-2
93ToysRUs-1
93ToysRUs/MPhoto-5
93TripleP-1
93TripleP/Act-24
93TripleP/Nick-5
93UD-355
93UD-525M
93UD-55M
93UD/5thAnn-A1
93UD/Clutch-R11
93UD/Diam-13
93UD/FunPack-111GS
93UD/FunPack-114
93UD/FunPack-16HS
93UD/FunPack-224CL
93UD/FunPack-24KS
93UD/FunPack-30HERO
93UD/FunPackAS-AS8
93UD/HRH-HR9
93UD/Iooss-WI13
93UD/OnDeck-D13
93UD/SP-4AS
93UD/SPPlat-PP9
93UD/SeasonHL-HI9
93UD/TCr-TC4
93UDFutHero-59
93USPlayC/Ace-4C
93Ultra-619
93Ultra/AS-17
93Ultra/AwardWin-16
93Ultra/Perf-3
94B-5
94D-4
94D/DK-14

94D/DomI-9
94D/DomII-6
94D/Elite-45
94D/LongBall-5
94D/MVP-26
94D/Pr-7
94D/Special-4
94D/Spirit-3
94DQ/Griffey-Set
94F-286
94F/AS-10
94F/GoldM-4
94F/Lumber-5
94F/TL-12
94Finest-232
94Flair-103
94Flair/Outfield-6
94KingB-6
94Kraft-5
94L-368
94L/Gamer-1
94L/GoldS-4
94L/MVPAL-7
94L/PBroker-5
94L/Pr-3
94L/Slide-9
94L/StatStand-6
94OPC-22
94OPC/JAS-8
94Oscar-6
94P-15
94Pac/Cr-570
94Pac/CrPr-4
94Pac/Gold-2
94Pac/Silv-8
94Panini-118
94Pinn-100
94Pinn/Artist-100
94Pinn/Museum-100
94Pinn/Power-23
94Pinn/Run-3
94Pinn/TeamP-6M
94Pinn/Trib-17
94RedFoley-33
94S-3
94S-628HL
94S/Cycle-17
94S/GoldR-3
94S/GoldS-32
94S/HobSam-3
94S/Pr-3
94S/Pr-3GR
94S/Tomb-21
94Select-1
94Select/CrCon-9
94Sf/2000-143
94Sf/2000-181AS
94StCl-262
94StCl-529DL
94StCl-85
94StCl/1stDay-262
94StCl/1stDay-529DL
94StCl/1stDay-85
94StCl/Gold-262
94StCl/Gold-529DL
94StCl/Gold-85
94Studio-101
94Studio/Editor-3
94Studio/S&GStar-4
94T-388AS
94T-400
94T-606ST
94T/BlkGold-8
94T/Gold-388AS
94T/Gold-400
94T/Gold-606ST
94TripleP-127
94TripleP/Bomb-8
94TripleP/Medal-11
94TripleP/Pr-4
94UD-224
94UD-292HFA
94UD-53FUT
94UD/CollC-117
94UD/CollC/Gold-117
94UD/CollC/Silv-117
94UD/CollCPr-50
94UD/CollHR-2
94UD/DColl-W4
94UD/ElecD-224
94UD/ElecD-53FUT
94UD/GriffeyJ-Set
94UD/HoloFX-13
94UD/Mantle-10
94UD/Pr-224
94UD/SP-105
94Ultra-120
94Ultra/AS-8
94Ultra/AwardWin-6
94Ultra/HRK-2
94Ultra/OnBase-6

Griffey, Ken Sr.
74OPC-598R
74T-598R
75OPC-284
75T-284
75T/M-284
76Crane-17
76Icee
76K-44
76MSA/Disc
76OPC-128
76SSPC-40
76T-128
77BurgChef-206
77Ho-59
77Ho/Twink-59
77K-49
77OPC-11
77Pep-50
77T-320
78K-4
78OPC-140
78Pep-12
78SSPC/270-118
78T-80
79Ho-45
79K-39
79OPC-216
79T-420
80OPC-285
80T-550
81Coke
81D-184
81F-199
81F/St-60
81OPC-280
81T-280
81T/HT
81T/SO-91
81T/St-163
82D-634
82F-67
82F/St-16
82OPC-171IA
82OPC-330
82T-620
82T-621SA
82T-756TL
82T/St-38
82T/St-38
82T/Tr-40T
83D-486
83F-382
83F/St-2M
83F/St-7M
83OPC-330
83OPC/St-98
83RoyRog/Disc-3
83T-110
83T/Fold-3M
83T/St-98
84D-613
84D/AAS-21
84D/Champs-25
84F-126
84Nes/792-770
84OPC-306
84T-770
84T/St-317
85D-347
85F-128
85Leaf-193
85OPC-380
85T-380
86D-126
86F-105
86Leaf-48
86OPC-40
86T-40
86T/Tr-41T
87D-513
87D/OD-42
87F-516
87F/Mini-46
87F/St-49
87OPC-114
87Sf/TPrev-24M
87Smok/Atl-19
87Stuart-2M
87T-711
88D-202
88D/Best-141
88F-540
88KennerFig-41
88Leaf-165
88OPC-255
88Panini/St-248
88RedFoley/St-28
88S-390
88Sf-178
88T-443
88T/Big-110
88T/St-38
89B-259FS
89F/Up-84
89Kahn/Reds-30
89S-609
89T/Tr-40T
90B-60
90D-469
90F-420
90F/Can-420
90Kahn/Reds-10
90KayBee-13
90OPC-581
90PublInt/St-30
90S-338
90T-581
90T/Big-100
90UD-682
91B-246
91Classic/200-141
91Classic/II-T21
91CounHrth-19
91CounHrth-28M
91D-452
91Griffey-4M
91Kenner-24
91Leaf-503
91Leaf/Stud-113
91MSA/Holsum-11
91MajorLg/Pins-5
91Mother/Griffey-2
91Mother/Griffey-3M
91Mother/Griffey-4M
91OPC-465
91S-835
91S-841M
91Seven/3DCoin-4NW
91StCl-342
91StCl/Charter*-10M
91T-465
91UD-572
91Ultra-335
92AlGrif/GoldMom-10M
92AlGrif/GoldMom-5M
92LimeR/GriffeyHolo-1
92OPC-250
92T-250
92T/Gold-250
92T/GoldWin-250
92UD-335
92UD-85M
92Yank/WIZ80-69
93B-703FOIL
93Mother/Mar-28M

Griffin, Alan
75Tucson-21
75Tucson/Caruso-18
75Tucson/Team-5
76Tucson-34
78SanJose-9

Griffin, Alfredo
79BJ/Bubble-10
79T-705R
80OPC-290
80T-558
81D-149
81F-430
81OPC-277
81OPC/Post-15
81T-277
81T/St-140
82D-101
82F-615
82F/St-236
82OPC-148
82T-677
82T/St-252
83D-180
83F-429
83OPC-294
83OPC/St-129
83T-488
83T/St-129
84D-605
84F-156
84Nes/792-76
84OPC-76
84T-76
84T/St-369
84Tor/Fire-15
85D-73
85F-106
85F/Up-U47
85Leaf-230
85Mother/A's-5
85OPC-361
85T-361
85T/St-366
85T/Tr-42T
86D-101
86F-417
86Leaf-34
86Mother/A's-5
86OPC-121
86Sf-136M
86T-566
86T/St-168
86T/Tatt-16M
87D-256
87D/OD-28
87F-392
87Leaf-198
87OPC-111
87Sf-164
87Sf/TPrev-23M
87Smok/A's-4
87Stuart-24
87T-111
87T/St-166
88D-226
88D/Best-92
88F-280
88F/Up-U94
88Mother/Dodg-7
88OPC-42
88Panini/St-172
88Pol/Dodg-7
88S-88
88S/Tr-37T
88Sf-156
88T-726
88T/Big-247
88T/St-169
88T/Tr-43T
89B-345
89D-79
89D/Best-178
89F-58
89Mother/Dodg-7
89OPC-62
89Pol/Dodg-5
89S-167
89T-62
89T/St-59
89UD-631
90B-95
90D-195
90D/BestNL-103
90F-395
90F/Can-395
90Leaf-95
90Mother/Dodg-8
90OPC-643
90Panini/St-270
90Pol/Dodg-7
90PublInt/St-6
90S-156
90T-643
90T/Big-18
90T/St-58
90Target-297
90UD-338
91B-592
91D-488
91F-201
91Leaf-344
91Mother/Dodg-8
91OPC-226
91OPC/BoxB-G
91Panini/FrSt-58
91Pol/Dodg-7
91S-442
91StCl-524
91T-226
91T/WaxBox-G
91UD-119
91Ultra-161
92BJ/Fire-10
92D-692
92F-455
92OPC-418
92Panini-195
92S-254
92T-418
92T/Gold-418
92T/GoldWin-418
92UD-282
93BJ/D/45-6
93BJ/Demp-12
93BJ/Fire-11
93F-692
93StCl-561
93StCl/1stDay-561
94F-332
94Pac/Cr-641

Griffin, Barry
88Boise/ProC-1614

Griffin, Bob
88MissSt-8

Griffin, Dave
83Ander-20
84Durham-8
85Durham-24
86Greenvl/Team-11
87Richm/Bob-9
87Richm/Crown-24
87Richm/TCMA-13
88Richm-34
88Richm/CMC-19
88Richm/ProC-20
88TripleA/ASCMC-17
89Colum/CMC-27
89Toledo/CMC-12
89Toledo/ProC-785

Griffin, Doug
71OPC-176R
71T-176R
72T-703
72T-704IA
73OPC-96
73T-96
74OPC-219
74T-219
75OPC-454
75T-454
75T/M-454
76OPC-654
76SSPC-412
76T-654
77T-191
89Pac/SenLg-53

Griffin, Frankie
83Reading-6

Griffin, Greg
83Knoxvl-17

Griffin, Ivy M.
V100

Griffin, Mark
89Star/Wax-29
89VeroB/Star-10
90VeroB/Star-16
91ClBest/Singl-236
91FSLAS/ProC-FSL38
91VeroB/ClBest-27
91VeroB/ProC-787
93WPalmB/ClBest-6
93WPalmB/ProC-1353

Griffin, Michael
N172
N300/unif

Griffin, Mike
77Ashvl
79WHave-17
81Colum-10
81F-107
81T-483
82D-553
82T-146
83OKCty-8
84OKCty-7
85Omaha-13
86Omaha/ProC-8
86Omaha/TCMA-15
87French-42
87RochR-9
87RochR/TCMA-3
88D-494

88F-561
88RochR/CMC-7
88RochR/Gov-8
88RochR/ProC-210
88RochR/Team-9
89Nashvl/CMC-4
89Nashvl/ProC-1274
89Nashvl/Team-6
90CharWh/Best-27CO
90CharWh/ProC-2258CO
90Target-298
91AA/LineD-175CO
91Chatt/LineD-175CO
91Chatt/ProC-1975CO
92Chatt/ProC-3834
92Chatt/SB-200M
92Yank/WIZ70-59
92Yank/WIZ80-68

Griffin, Nuje
91Crown/Orio-166

Griffin, Rick
90Mother/Mar-28TR

Griffin, Steve
91FresnoSt/Smok-5
92SoOreg/ClBest-15
92SoOreg/ProC-3410

Griffin, Terry
88LitFalls/Pucko-16
89StLucie/Star-8

Griffin, Tim
90GreatF/SportP-25
91VeroB/ClBest-20
91VeroB/ProC-781
91Yakima/ClBest-11
91Yakima/ProC-4253
92VeroB/ClBest-6

Griffin, Tom
69T-614R
70T-578
71MLB/St-81
71OPC-471
71T-471
72MB-122
73OPC-468
73T-468
74OPC-256
74T-256
75OPC-188
75T-188
75T/M-188
76OPC-454
76T-454
77Padre/SchCd-12
77T-39
78T-318
79Pol/Giants-43
79T-291
80Pol/Giants-43
80T-649
81D-75
81F-456
81T-538
82D-474
82F-389
82T-777

Griffin, Ty
87PanAm/USAB-2
87PanAm/USAR-2
88T/Tr-44T
89B-289
89CharlK-14
89Peoria/Team-1
89T-713FDP
89T/Big-170
90B-37
90CharlK/Team-14
90T/TVCub-45
90TeamUSA/87-2
91AA/LineD-134
91CharlK/LineD-134
91CharlK/ProC-1700
92Chatt/ProC-3827
92Chatt/SB-183
92Sky/AASingl-81

Griffith, Calvin
78Twin/Frisz-6PRES

Griffith, Clark C.
10Domino-50
11Helmar-69
12Sweet/Pin-101A
12Sweet/Pin-101B
14Piedmont/St-25
48Exh/HOF
50Callahan
50W576-35
60Exh/HOF-12
60F-15
61F-36
63Bz/ATG-37
76Shakey-43
77Galasso-150
80Pac/Leg-37
80Perez/HOF-43
80SSPC/HOF
92Conlon/Sport-464
92Yank/WIZHOF-13
93Conlon-840
D329-72
E220
E93
M101/4-72
M116
N172
S74-76
T202
T204
T205
T206
T213/blue
T214-13MG
T215/blue
T215/brown
T3-77
W514-41
W555
WG2-22
WG5-18
WG6-17

Griffith, Jeff
87Watertn-22
88Augusta/ProC-363

Griffith, Kerry
86Erie-10

Griffith, Lynn
89KS*-12
93Lipscomb-23M

Griffith, Robert D.
(Derrell)
65OPC-112
65T-112
66T-573
67T-502
90Target-299

Griffith, Thomas H.
(Tommy)
15CJ-167
16FleischBrd-35
90Target-300
D327
D328-64
D329-73
D350/2-72
E120
E121/120
E121/80
E122
E135-64
M101/4-73
M101/5-72
V100
V61-58
W501-106
W515-35
W572
W575

Griffith, Tommy
89Boise/ProC-1984
91Salinas/ClBest-6
91Salinas/ProC-2255

Griffiths, Brian
89Ashvl/ProC-955
90Osceola/Star-8
91Osceola/ClBest-3
91Osceola/ProC-675
92ClBest-324
92Jacks/ProC-3994
92Jacks/SB-332
92Sky/AASingl-141
93T-483
93T/Gold-483

Grifol, Pedro
91Elizab/ProC-4303
92ClBest-12
92FtMyr/ProC-2749
92Miracle/ClBest-6
92ProC/Tomorrow-101
93B-185

Griggs, Acie
(Skeet)
92Negro/RetortII-12

Griggs, Hal
58T-455
59T-434
60L-34
60T-244

Griggs, Wiley
92Negro/Retort-26

Grigsby, Benji
92Classic/DP-15
92Classic/DPFoil-BC14
92UD/ML-11
93Modesto/ClBest-1
93Modesto/ProC-794
93Pinn-463DP
93S-495DP
93Select-354DP
93StCl/MurphyS-151
93T-518
93T/Gold-518

Grijak, Kevin
91Idaho/ProC-4337
91Idaho/SportP-17
92ProC/Tomorrow-197
92Pulaski/ClBest-17
92Pulaski/ProC-3191
93Macon/ClBest-11
93Macon/ProC-1406

Grilione, Dave
86Cram/NWL-94
87QuadC-29

Grilk, Jim
40Hughes-8

Grilli, Guido
66T-558R

Grilli, Steve
76OPC-591R
76T-591R
77T-506
78Syrac
79Syrac/TCMA-17
79Syrac/Team-21
80Syrac/Team-9
81Syrac-4

Grilone, Dave
88BurlB/ProC-18

Grim, Bob
55B-167
55RM-AL5
55T-80
55T/DH-58
56T-52
57T-36
58T-224
59T-423
60L-10
60T-78
62T-564
92Yank/WIZAS-26
94T/Arc54-252

Grim, John
90Target-964

Grimes, Bob
88CharWh/Best-27
89Peoria/Team-32TR
90CharlK/Team-24TR

Grimes, Burleigh A.
21Exh-61
25Exh-12
26Exh-11
27Exh-7
28Yueng-1
32Orbit/num-26
32Orbit/un-21
33G-64
35G-1F
35G-3D
35G-4D
35G-5D
60F-59
61F-37
75Sheraton-6
76Rowe-11M
76Shakey-97
77Galasso-97
80Pac/Leg-51
80Perez/HOF-97
80SSPC/HOF
83D/HOF-21
89Smok/Dodg-8
90Target-301
91Conlon/Sport-25
92Card/McDon/Pac-20
92Conlon/Sport-433
92Yank/WIZHOF-14
93Conlon-706
94Conlon-997
E120
E210-1
R305
R308-191
R315-A12
R315-B12
R316
V100
V353-64
V61-89
V89-31
W502-1
W513-72
W515-16
W572

Grimes, David
(Dave)
89Spring/Best-2
90StPete/Star-11
91AA/LineD-35
91ArkTr/LineD-35
91ArkTr/ProC-1278

Grimes, John
84Everett/Cram-25
85Fresno/Pol-14
86Shrev-9
87Shrev-22

Grimes, Lee
87WinSalem-14
88CharWh/Best-6

Grimes, Michael
(Mike)
88CapeCod/Sum-122
89Medford/Best-6
91Madison/ClBest-4
92ClBest-36
92Modesto/ClBest-20
92Modesto/ProC-3894

Grimes, Oscar Ray
21Exh-62
44Yank/St-13
E120
V61-105
W572
W573

Grimes, Steve
76Cedar
78Holyo

Grimm, Charlie
21Exh-63
25Exh-21
26Exh-21
27Exh-10
29Exh/4-6
30CEA/Pin-4
31Exh/4-6
32Orbit/num-37
32Orbit/un-22
33CJ/Pin-11
33Exh/4-3
33G-51
34Exh/4-3
34G-3
34Ward's/Pin-6
35Exh/4-3
40PlayBall-228
53B/Col-69MG
53JC-1MG
54JC-40MG
55B-298MG
55Gol/Braves-12MG
55JC-40MG
60T-217MG
77Galasso-115
80Pac/Leg-75
84Cub/Uno-8M
87Conlon/2-40
88Conlon/4-12
91Conlon/Sport-95
91T/Arc53-321MG
92Cub/OldStyle-9
93Conlon-821
E120
E121/120
E126-19
E220
R300
R305
R332-15
R337-423
V100
V353-51
V354-61
V355-89
V89-43
W501-82
W575
WG8-25

Grimm, John
92Bristol/ClBest-12
92Bristol/ProC-1402

Grimshaw, Myron
(Moose)
E254
T206

Grimsley, Jason
85Bend/Cram-9
88Clearw/Star-12
89BBAmAA/BPro-AA4
89EastLgAS/ProC-16
89Reading/Best-10
89Reading/ProC-670
89Reading/Star-12
90AAASingl/ProC-297
90B-151
90F-653R
90F/Can-653M
90OPC-493
90Phill/TastyK-10
90ProC/Singl-229
90S-649RP
90ScranWB/CMC-3
90ScranWB/ProC-595
90T-493
90T/89Debut-47
90UD-27SR
91D-653
91F-396
91Leaf-288
91OPC-173
91Phill/Medford-16
91S-818
91StCl-294
91T-173
92D-599
92F-532
92S-711
92StCl-418
92Tucson/ProC-482
92Tucson/SB-608
92UD-406

Grimsley, Ross
72OPC-99
72T-99
73OPC-357
73T-357
74OPC-59
74T-59
74T/Tr-59T
75K-2
75OPC-458
75T-458
75T/M-458
76OPC-257
76SSPC-377
76T-257
77BurgChef-40
77Fritsch-4
77OPC-47
77T-572
78T-691
79Ho-5
79K-3
79OPC-4
79T-15
79T/Comics-26
80K-1
80OPC-195
80T-375
81F-406
81T-170
84Chatt-8
86Calgary-10C
87Calgary-5CO
89BurlB/ProC-1614
89Pac/SenLg-117
89TM/SenLg-40
90EliteSenLg-81
90Penin/Star-26CO
91AAA/LineD-75CO
91Calgary/LineD-75CO
91Calgary/ProC-531CO

91Crown/Orio-167
92Calgary/ProC-3746CO
92Calgary/SB-75CO
93Calgary/ProC-1183CO
Griner, Craig
90GA-6
Griner, Dan
90Target-965
Grisham, Wes
90LSUPol-2
90Welland/Pucko-15
Grissom, Antonio
90Martins/ProC-3195
91Batavia/ClBest-13
91Batavia/ProC-3496
91Spartan/ClBest-24
91Spartan/ProC-909
92Albany/ClBest-26
92Albany/ProC-2316
93BurlB/ClBest-9
93BurlB/ProC-170
93FExcel/ML-59
Grissom, Lee
38Wheat
39PlayBall-2
90Target-302
W711/1
Grissom, Marquis
88James/ProC-1910
89BBAmAA/BPro-AA14
89Jaxvl/Best-1
89Jaxvl/ProC-175
90B-115
90Classic-65
90D-36RR
90D/BestNL-128
90D/Rook-45
90F-347
90F/Can-347
90HotRook/St-20
90Leaf-107
90OPC-714
90S-591RP
90S/100Ris-99
90S/DTRook-B9
90S/YS/II-6
90Sf-134
90T-714
90T/89Debut-48
90T/Big-138
90UD-9SR
90UD/Ext-702M
91B-435
91Classic/200-119
91Classic/II-T38
91D-307
91Expo/PostC-4
91F-234
91Leaf-22
91Leaf/Stud-198
91OPC-283
91Panini/FrSt-151
91S-234
91S/100RisSt-38
91StCl-8
91T-283
91T/JumboR-10
91ToysRUs-9
91UD-477
91Ultra-204
92B-14
92CJ/DI-21
92Classic/Game200-39
92D-137
92DennyGS-1
92Expo/D/Duri-10
92F-482
92L-273
92L/BlkGold-273
92OPC-647
92OPC/Premier-176
92Panini-207
92Pinn-129
92Pinn/Team2000-11
92S-66
92S/Impact-63
92StCl-120
92Studio-55
92T-647
92T/Gold-647
92T/GoldWin-647
92T/Kids-8
92TripleP-47
92UD-455
92UD-719DS
92Ultra-518
93B-268
93Classic/GameI-39
93Colla/DM-45
93D-300
93DennyGS-10
93Expo/D/McDon-5
93F-461
93F-706LL
93F/Fruit-26
93F/TLNL-7
93Flair-83
93HumDum/Can-37
93Kenner/Fig-14
93L-129
93L/Fast-20
93L/UpGoldAS-8M
93OPC-209
93Pac/Spanish-185
93Panini-230
93Pinn-346
93Pinn/Team2001-17
93S-28
93Select-99
93Select/StatL-18
93Select/StatL-58
93StCl-529
93StCl-598MC
93StCl/1stDay-529
93StCl/1stDay-598MC
93Studio-178
93T-15
93T/BlkGold-7
93T/Finest-40
93T/FinestRef-40
93T/Gold-15
93ToysRUs-30
93ToysRUs/MPhoto-6
93TripleP-159
93UD-356
93UD-481
93UD/Diam-10
93UD/FunPack-216FOLD
93UD/FunPack-93GS
93UD/FunPack-95
93UD/FunPackAS-AS8M
93UD/SP-12AS
93USPlayC/Ace-1H
93Ultra-415
94B-284
94Church-24
94D-37
94D/Special-37
94F-540
94F/AS-38
94F/TL-22
94Finest-229
94Flair-190
94L-174
94OPC-18
94OPC/JAS-11
94Oscar-22
94Pac/Cr-382
94Panini-210
94Pinn-358
94Pinn/Run-38
94RedFoley-27M
94S-352
94S/GoldS-25
94S/Tomb-7
94Sf/2000-48
94Studio-78
94T-590
94T/BlkGold-34
94T/Gold-590
94TripleP-95
94UD-390
94UD-39FT
94UD/ElecD-39FT
94UD/SP-84
94Ultra-228
94Ultra/AwardWin-16
94Ultra/RisSt-6
Grissom, Marv
54NYJour
55B-123
55Gol/Giants-11
55RM-NL25
56T-301
57T-216
58Hires-64
58SFCallB-10
58T-399
59T-243
Grissom, Scott
89KS*-13
Groat, Dick
52T-369
53T-154
54T-43
55T-26
55T/DH-100
56T-24
56T/Hocus-A1
56T/Hocus-B3
56T/Pin-42SS
57Kahn
57T-12
58Hires-21
58Kahn
58T-45
59Kahn
59T-160
60Kahn
60T-258
60T/tatt-20
61Bz-8
61Kahn
61NuCard-413
61P-129
61T-1
61T-41LL
61T-486MVP
61T/Dice-5
61T/St-64
62Exh
62J-172
62Kahn
62P-172
62P/Can-172
62Salada-138
62Shirriff-138
62Sugar-A
62T-270
62T/St-177
62T/bucks
63Exh
63J-139
63Kahn
63P-139
63Salada-16
63T-130
64Bz-2
64T-40
64T-7LL
64T/Coins-147AS
64T/Coins-5
64T/S-19
64T/SU
64T/St-81S9
64T/tatt
64Wheat/St-20
65OPC-275
65OldLond-11
65T-275
65T/trans-15
66OPC-103
66T-103
67CokeCap/Phill-6
67Pol/Phill-7
67T-205
75OPC-198MVP
75T-198MVP
75T/M-198MVP
78TCMA-150
81TCMA-414M
85West/2-40
88Pac/Leg-108
89Swell-91
90Pac/Legend-26
90Swell/Great-49
91Swell/Great-35
91T/Arc53-154
92AP/ASG-28
92Bz/Quadra-15M
92Card/McDon/Pac-28
94T/Arc54-43
Exh47
WG10-29
WG9-30
Grob, Connie
59DF
Groch, Dick
89EastLDD/ProC-DD47CO
Grodzicki, Johnny
81TCMA-362M
Groennert, John
87SLCity/Taco-8
88Billings/ProC-1815
Groh, Don
83Peoria/Frit-5
85Cram/PCL-4
Groh, Heinie
15CJ-159
16FleischBrd-36
21Exh-64
21Exh-65
25Exh-34
77Galasso-139
81Conlon-90
88Pac/8Men-81
91Conlon/Sport-163
94Conlon-1270IA
D327
D328-65
D329-74
D350/2-73
E120
E121/120
E121/80
E135-65
E220
M101/4-74
M101/5-73
V61-88
V89-23
W501-67
W514-46
W515-52
W516-2
W572
W573
W575
WG7-19
Grohs, Michael
91Spokane/ClBest-4
91Spokane/ProC-3943
92CharRain/ProC-117
Gromek, Steve
49B-198
50B-131
50NumNum
51B-115
52B-203
52NumNum-8
52T-258
53B/BW-63
54B-199
55B-203
56T-310
56YellBase/Pin-13
57T-258
79TCMA-133
Exh47
Groninger, Gerry
88Billings/ProC-1803
89Cedar/Best-23
89Cedar/Star-23
90Billings/ProC-3238MG
91Fayette/ClBest-14MG
91Fayette/ProC-1186MG
92Fayette/ClBest-24MG
92Fayette/ProC-2184
Groom, Bob
10Domino-51
11Helmar-70
12Sweet/Pin-59
14CJ-46
14Piedmont/St-26
15CJ-46
92Conlon/Sport-350
D328-66
E135-66
E270/2
E90/1
E91
T202
T205
T206
T213/blue
T214-14
T215
T3-96
Groom, Buddy
88Tampa/Star-9
89BirmB/Best-24
89BirmB/ProC-109
89SLAS-17
90BirmB/Best-16
90BirmB/ProC-1104
91AA/LineD-386
91London/LineD-386
91London/ProC-1872
92D/Rook-44
92F/Up-22
92Toledo/ProC-1037
92Toledo/SB-585
93D-569
93T-353
93T/Gold-353
93Tiger/Gator-11
94D-637
Groot, Franz
92GreatF/SportP-14
Groppuso, Mike
91Classic/DP-39
91FrRow/DP-39
92Osceola/ClBest-13
92Osceola/ProC-2537
92Pinn-543
Gross, Bob
87Gaston/ProC-5
Gross, Deryk
89Kenosha/ProC-1064
89Kenosha/Star-8
90Kenosha/Best-4
90Kenosha/ProC-2306
90Kenosha/Star-5
Gross, Don
57Kahn
57Sohio/Reds-7
57T-341
58T-172
59T-228
60T-284
Gross, George
78DaytB
80Tucson-10
81Tucson-22
Gross, Greg
75Ho-101
75K-5
75OPC-334
75T-334
75T/M-334
76Ho-90
76K-56
76OPC-171
76SSPC-64
76T-171
77T-614
78SSPC/270-257
78T-397
79BK/P-22
79OPC-302
79T-579
80BK/P-12
80OPC-364
80T-718
81D-598
81F-18
81T-459
82D-371
82F-246
82T-53
83D-441
83F-162
83T-279
84D-285
84F-31
84Nes/792-613
84Phill/TastyK-35
84T-613
85CIGNA-5
85D-407
85F-251
85F/St-53
85OPC-117
85Phill/TastyK-12M
85Phill/TastyK-35
85T-117
86CIGNA-5
86D-163
86F-441
86OPC-302
86Phill/TastyK-21
86T-302
87D-385
87F-173
87OPC-338
87Phill/TastyK-21
87RedFoley/St-20
87T-702

88D-412
88F-302
88Phill/TastyK-11
88S-386
88T-518
89F-568
89Lennox/Ast-2
89Mother/Ast-12
89OPC/BoxB-E
89S-125
89T-438
89T/WaxBox-E
89UD-534
91Padre/MagRal-12CO
Gross, John
90AppFox/Box-11
91BBCity/ClBest-4
91BBCity/ProC-1391
91ClBest/Singl-35
92BBCity/ClBest-9
92BBCity/ProC-3839
Gross, Kevin
83Portl-5
84D-381
84F-32
84Nes/792-332
84Phill/TastyK-20
84T-332
85CIGNA-14
85D-477
85F-252
85Phill/TastyK-18
85Phill/TastyK-9M
85T-584
86CIGNA-8
86D-529
86F-442
86Phill/TastyK-46
86T-764
86T/St-119
87D-236
87F-174
87OPC-163
87Phill/TastyK-46
87Sf/TPrev-6M
87T-163
88D-113
88D/Best-103
88F-303
88OPC-20
88Phill/TastyK-12
88S-468
88T-20
88T/St-118
89B-355
89D-194
89D/AS-48
89D/Best-202
89D/MVP-BC12
89D/Tr-3
89F-569
89F/Up-96
89OPC-215
89Panini/St-147
89S-227
89S/Tr-39
89Sf-213
89T-215
89T/St-116
89T/Tr-42T
89UD-31
89UD/Ext-719
90B-109
90D-248
90D/BestNL-18
90F-348
90F/Can-348
90Leaf-61
90OPC-465
90PublInt/St-174
90S-251
90T-465
90T/Big-3
90T/St-76
90UD-468
91B-611
91D-569
91F-235
91F/Up-U94
91Leaf-279
91Mother/Dodg-17
91OPC-674A
91OPC-674B
91Pol/Dodg-45
91S-22
91S/RookTr-51T
91T-674A
91T-674B
91UD-380
91UD/Ext-713
92D-279
92F-456
92L-33
92L/BlkGold-33
92Mother/Dodg-16
92OPC-334
92Pinn-344
92Pol/Dodg-46
92S-34
92StCl-72
92StCl/MemberII-7
92T-334
92T/Gold-334
92T/GoldWin-334
92UD-515
93D-458
93D/Spirit-SG19
93F-448
93L-181
93Mother/Dodg-19
93OPC-111
93Pac/Spanish-145
93Pinn-177
93Pol/Dodg-7
93S-519HL
93StCl-473
93StCl/1stDay-473
93StCl/Dodg-5
93T-714
93T/Gold-714
93UD-198
93Ultra-399
94D-587
94F-510
94L-153
94Pac/Cr-308
94S-530
94Select-157
94StCl-281
94StCl/1stDay-281
94StCl/Gold-281
94T-516
94T/Gold-516
94UD-166
94UD/ElecD-166
94Ultra-516
Gross, Kip
87Lynch-5
88FSLAS/Star-6
88StLucie/Star-10
89Jacks/GS-22
91AAA/LineD-259
91Nashvl/LineD-259
91Nashvl/ProC-2150
91T/90Debut-60
92F-407
92OPC-372
92Pol/Dodg-57
92S-740
92S/100RisSt-92
92StCl-247
92T-372
92T/Gold-372
92T/GoldWin-372
93D-194
93Pol/Dodg-8
93StCl-7
93StCl/1stDay-7
Gross, Wayne
76Tucson-25
77T-479R
78Ho-141
78OPC-106
78T-139
79T-528
80OPC-189
80T-363
81A's/Granny-10
81D-237
81F-587
81OPC-86
81T-86
81T/St-118
82D-139
82F-90
82F/St-124
82Granny-2
82OPC-303
82T-692
83D-591
83F-517
83Granny-10
83T-233
84D-375
84F-444
84F/X-45
84Nes/792-741
84OPC-263
84T-741
84T/St-333
84T/Tr-44
85D-228
85F-179
85OPC-233
85T-416
86D-535
86F-276
86OPC-173
86T-173
87Mother/A's-17
91Crown/Orio-168
Grossman, Bob
75OkCty/Team-1
75SanAn
76Wmsprt
Grossman, Dave
82Edmon-24
86IowaC-12TR
88IowaC/ProC-531
89IowaC/ProC-1703
Grossman, Jim
87Kinston-8
Grote, Bob
79Jacks-8
Grote, Gerald
(Jerry)
64T-226R
65T-504
66T-328
67CokeCap/YMet-34
67T-413
68T-582
69MB-98
69MLB/St-165
69OPC-55
69T-55
69T/St-63
70MLB/St-76
70OPC-183
70T-183
70Trans-22
71MLB/St-154
71OPC-278
71T-278
71T/GM-54
71T/Greatest-54
72MB-123
72T-655
73OPC-113
73T-113
74OPC-311
74T-311
74T/St-62
75OPC-158
75T-158
75T/M-158
76Ho-78
76OPC-143
76T-143
78SSPC/270-60
78T-464
79T-279
81TCMA-438
89Pac/SenLg-120IA
89Pac/SenLg-125
89T/SenLg-34
89TM/SenLg-41
90Target-303
91LineD-17
91Swell/Great-36
91WIZMets-153
93UD/ATH-60
94Mets/69-8
Grotewald, Jeff
87Spartan-21
88Clearw/Star-13
89Clearw/Star-10
90Reading/Best-17
90Reading/ProC-1227
90Reading/Star-10
91AAA/LineD-484
91ScranWB/LineD-484
91ScranWB/ProC-2544
92D/Rook-45
92F/Up-110
92Phill/Med-40
92Ultra-545
93F-490
93S-305
93StCl-63
93StCl/1stDay-63
93T-72
93T/Gold-72
Groth, Bill
52StarCal-86C
52StarCal/L-72F
Groth, Ernest
50Remar
Groth, John
(Johnny)
50B-243
51B-249
51T/BB-11
52B-67
52NTea
52RM-AL10
52T-25
52TipTop
53T-36
54B-165
54Wilson
55B-117
56T-279
56YellBase/Pin-14
57T-360
58T-262
59T-164
60L-133
60T-171
79TCMA-38
81Tiger/Detroit-33
91T/Arc53-36
Exh47
Grott, Matthew
90A&AASingle/ProC-115
90Madison/ProC-2261
90MidwLgAS/GS-54
90Modesto/Chong-11
91AA/LineD-285
91Huntsvl/ClBest-11
91Huntsvl/LineD-285
91Huntsvl/Team-11
91HuntsvlProC-1789
92Chatt/ProC-3812
92Chatt/SB-184
Grout, Ron
79Wisco-7
Grove, George M.
WG7-20
Grove, LeRoy Orval
43Playball-11
48L-66
Exh47
Grove, Robert M.
(Lefty)
29Exh/4-27
31Exh/4-28
32Orbit/un-23
33CJ/Pin-12
33DL-23
33Exh/4-14
33G-220
34DS-1
34Exh/4-14
34Exh/4-9
34G-19
35BU-153
35BU-31
35Exh/4-9
35Wheat
36Exh/4-9
36Wheat
37Exh/4-9
37OPC-137
37Wheat-9
38Exh/4-9
38Wheat
39Exh
41DP-105
48Exh/HOF
50Callahan
50W576-36
60F-60
61F-38
61GP-17
72K/ATG-7
72Laugh/GF-16
76OPC-350AS
76Rowe-13M
76Shakey-52
76T-350AS
77Galasso-195
77Galasso-55
77Shakey-7
80Laugh/3/4/5-19
80Laugh/FFeat-8
80Pac/Leg-27
80Perez/HOF-52
80SSPC/HOF
81Conlon-38
82Ohio/HOF-25
86Conlon/1-47
86Sf/Dec-3
88Conlon/4-13
88Conlon/AmAS-13
88Grenada-69
89HOF/St-74
89Pac/Leg-185
89Swell-15
90BBWit-94
90HOF/St-31
90Swell/Great-70
91Conlon/Sport-23
91Conlon/Sport-255
91Swell/Great-139
92Conlon/Col-2
92Conlon/Sport-431
92Conlon/Sport-533
93AP/ASG-99
93AP/ASG24K-33G
93Conlon-669
93Conlon-930
94Conlon-1140
94Conlon-999
94Conlon/Pr-1140
94TedW-67
PR1-14
R300
R305
R306
R308-182
R310
R312/M
R313
R315-A13
R315-B13
R316
R328-27
R332-49
R337-408
R423-39
V300
V354-54
V355-88
V94-20
W517-39
Grove, Scott
88Pulaski/ProC-1752
89Sumter/ProC-1114
90BurlB/Best-18
90BurlB/ProC-2344
90BurlB/Star-13
92Dunedin/ClBest-13
92Dunedin/ProC-1994
93Dunedin/ClBest-8
93Dunedin/ProC-1789
93Knoxvl/ProC-1248
Groves, Jeff
86Greenvl/Team-12
Groves, Larry
86Indianap-27
Grovom, Carl
86AubAs-11
87CharWh-15
88Osceola/Star-11
91Jacks/ProC-920
Grow, Lorin
76Indianap-14
Grubb, Cary
87Salem/ProC-2437
88Reno/Cal-281
Grubb, Christopher
93James/ClBest-7
93James/ProC-3333
Grubb, John
(Johnny)
74McDon
74OPC-32SD
74T-32
74T/St-93

75Ho-109
75K-43
75OPC-298
75SSPC/Puzzle-11
75T-298
75T/M-298
76OPC-422
76SSPC-130
76T-422
77OPC-165
77Pep-10
77T-286
78T-608
79OPC-99
79T-198
80OPC-165
80T-313
81D-148
81F-631
81T-545
82D-467
82F-317
82OPC-193
82T-496
83D-341
83F-567
83F/St-14M
83F/St-5M
83OPC/St-123
83T-724
83T/St-123
83T/Tr-38
84D-90
84F-81
84Nes/792-42
84T-42
84Tiger/Farmer-5
84Tiger/Wave-18
85Cain's-9
85D-578
85F-9
85T-643
85Wendy-10
86Cain's-7
86D-615
86F-227
86T-243
87Cain's-12
87Coke/Tigers-18
87D-476
87F-152
87T-384
87T/St-265
88Richm-27
88S-199
88T-128
89Pac/SenLg-191
89Richm/Bob-8CO
89Richm/CMC-24CO
89Richm/Ko-CO
89Richm/ProC-821CO
89TM/SenLg-42
90AAASingl/ProC-420CO
90EliteSenLg-57
90ProC/Singl-278M
90Richm/CMC-2CO
90Richm/ProC-275CO
90Richm/Team-11CO
91Richm/Bob-41CO
91Richm/ProC-2586CO
93Rang/Keeb-165

Grubb, Sean
89Hamil/Star-17

Grube, Frank
32Orbit/num-5
32Orbit/un-24
34G-64
35G-8C
35G-9C
92Conlon/Sport-399
94Conlon-1162
R305
W753

Gruber, Henry
N172

Gruber, Kelly
80Batavia-21
81Watlo-22
82Chatt-16
83BuffB-16
84Syrac-27
84Tor/Fire-16
85F-645R
85IntLgAS-37
85Syrac-22
85Tor/Fire-13
86BJ/Ault-12
86D/Rook-16
86Tor/Fire-15
87D-444
87F-227
87GenMills/Book-1M
87OPC-191
87T-458
87Tor/Fire-11
88D-244
88D/Best-255
88F-111
88OPC-113
88Panini/St-221
88S-422
88T-113
88T/Big-134
88Tor/Fire-17
89B-251
89D-113
89D/Best-31
89F-234
89OPC-29
89Panini/St-469
89S-194
89S/YS/II-12
89Sf-163
89T-201TL
89T-29
89T/Big-95
89T/St-187
89Tor/Fire-17
89UD-575
90B-519
90BJ/HoSt-1M
90BJ/HoSt-5M
90Classic/III-70
90D-113
90D-12DK
90D/BestAL-84
90D/Learning-30
90D/SuperDK-12DK
90F-83
90F/Can-83
90Leaf-106
90OPC-505
90Panini/St-171
90PublInt/St-515
90RedFoley/St-41
90S-425
90S/McDon-9
90Sf-57
90T-505
90T/Big-17
90T/St-193
90Tor/BJ-17
90UD-111
90USPlayC/AS-5S
90Windwlk/Discs-5
91B-18
91B-369SLUG
91Cadaco-27
91Classic/200-19
91D-149
91DennyGS-6
91F-175
91Kenner-25
91Leaf-9
91Leaf/Stud-135
91MSA/Holsum-15
91OPC-370
91OPC-388AS
91OPC/Premier-57
91Panini/FrSt-338
91Panini/St-161
91Panini/Top15-112
91Panini/Top15-22
91Petro/SU-26
91Post/Can-15
91RedFoley/St-42
91S-595
91S/100SS-64
91S/ToroBJ-15
91StCl-331
91Sunflower-12
91T-370
91T-388AS
91T/CJMini/II-4
91Tor/Fire-17
91UD-374
91UD-44TC
91UD/SilSlug-SS7
91Ultra-361
92B-510
92BJ/Fire-11
92CJ/DI-5
92Classic/Game200-122
92Classic/II-T20
92D-65
92D/McDon-G3
92D/Preview-8
92DPep/MSA-20
92F-329
92Hardee-11
92L-27
92L/BlkGold-27
92MSA/Ben-5
92OPC-298
92OPC/Premier-116
92Panini-27
92Pinn-134
92Post/Can-14
92S-495
92S/100SS-64
92StCl-570
92StCl/Dome-71
92Studio-255
92T-298
92T/Gold-298
92T/GoldWin-298
92T/Kids-92
92TripleP-242
92UD-324
92Ultra-146
93BJ/D/45-7
93BJ/D/McDon-17
93BJ/D/McDon-18AM
93BJ/D/McDon-18BM
93BJ/D/McDon-19
93BJ/D/McDon-5
93D-453
93F-334
93L-532
93Mother/Angel-13
93OPC-156
93OPC/WC-5
93Pac/Spanish-323
93Panini-5
93Pinn-198
93Pol/Angel-5
93S-156
93Select-200
93StCl/MurphyS-31
93T-628
93T/Gold-628
93UD-406
93UD-807

Grudzielanek, Mark
91James/ClBest-4
91James/ProC-3553
92Rockford/ClBest-20
92Rockford/ProC-2123
93WPalmB/ClBest-7
93WPalmB/ProC-1346

Grudzinski, Gary
85PrWill-19

Grundler, Frank
75Shrev/TCMA-4
76Shrev

Grundt, Ken
91Everett/ClBest-18
91Everett/ProC-3906
92Clinton/ClBest-23
92Clinton/ProC-3591
92MidwLAS/Team-13
92ProC/Tomorrow-358
93FExcel/ML-117

Grunhard, Dan
(Danny)
85Anchora-12
86QuadC-13
87PalmSp-8
88MidldA/GS-16
89MidldA/GS-17
90AAASingl/ProC-104
90Edmon/CMC-16
90Edmon/ProC-528
90ProC/Singl-493
91AAA/LineD-165
91Edmon/LineD-165
91Edmon/ProC-1528
92Tacoma/ProC-2514
92Tacoma/SB-534

Grunsky, Gary
76Baton

Grunwald, Al
60T-427

Grygiel, Joe
91Spokane/ClBest-16
91Spokane/ProC-3944

Gryskevich, Larry
89Hamil/Star-14
90Savan/ProC-2073

Grzelaczyk, Kenneth
92Spokane/ClBest-2
92Spokane/ProC-1286

Grzenda, Joe
69OPC-121
69T-121
69T/4in1-20M
70T-691
71MLB/St-541
71OPC-518
71T-518
72OPC-13
72T-13
91WIZMets-154

Grzybeck, Ben
77DaytB

Gsellman, Bob
87CharWh-8

Guanchez, Harry
90Eugene/GS-9
91AppFx/ClBest-18
91AppFx/ProC-1724

Guante, Cecilio
81Portl-10
82Portl-3
83D-423
84D-78
84F-250
84Nes/792-122
84T-122
85D-357
85F-465
85T-457
86D-142
86F-609
86T-668
86T/Tatt-8M
87D-238
87F-610
87F/Up-U38
87OPC-219
87T-219
87T/St-127
87T/Tr-40T
88D/Best-276
88D/Y/Bk-NEW
88T-84
89D-260
89F-519
89Mother/R-23
89S-439
89Smok/R-10
89T-766
89UD-576
90D-403
90F-298
90F/Can-298
90Leaf-365
90OPC-532
90PublInt/St-410
90S-438
90T-532
92Yank/WIZ80-70
93LimeR/Winter-117
93Rang/Keeb-166

Guarache, Jose
88StCath/ProC-2011

Guardado, Eddie
91Elizab/ProC-4296
92Kenosha/ProC-598
92ProC/Tomorrow-102
93F/Final-235
94D-139
94F-203
94T-677
94T/Gold-677
94Ultra-86

Guarnera, Rick
75Spokane/Caruso-5

Gubanich, Creighton
91SoOreg/ProC-3850
92ClBest-177
92Madis/ClBest-1
92Madis/ProC-1238

Gubicza, Mark
84F/X-46
84T/Tr-45
85D-344
85F-201
85OPC-127
85T-127
86D-583
86F-8
86Kitty/Disc-19
86Leaf-226
86NatPhoto-23
86T-644
87D-466
87F-368
87F/Excit-20
87F/Mini-47
87Leaf-238
87OPC-326
87Sf/TPrev-13M
87T-326
88D-54
88D/Best-95
88F-259
88F/RecSet-15
88OPC-378
88S-516
88Smok/Royals-12
88T-507
88T/Big-199
88T/St-262
89B-117
89Cadaco-25
89Classic-138
89D-179
89D/AS-18
89D/Best-119
89F-283
89F/BBAS-17
89F/Excit-19
89KennerFig-53
89OPC-379
89Panini/St-350
89S-291
89S/HotStar-69
89S/YS/II-14
89Sf-102
89T-430
89T/Big-26
89T/Mini-55
89T/St-271
89T/St/Backs-26
89T/UK-33
89Tastee/Discs-9
89UD-202
90B-363
90D-204
90D/BestAL-77
90F-109
90F-633M
90F/BB-15
90F/Can-109
90F/Can-633
90F/LL-15
90Leaf-145
90MLBPA/Pins-105
90OPC-20
90Panini/St-82
90PublInt/St-349
90S-121
90T-20
90T/Big-201
90T/St-272
90UD-676
91Classic/200-20
91D-145
91F-560
91Leaf/Stud-67
91OPC-265
91Panini/St-228
91Pol/Royal-11
91S-212
91StCl-240
91T-265
91UD-541
91Ultra-148
92B-215
92Classic/Game200-83
92D-282
92F-159
92L-332
92L/BlkGold-332
92OPC-741
92Pinn-102
92Pol/Royal-9

92S-459
92StCl-542
92Studio-183
92T-741
92T/Gold-741
92T/GoldWin-741
92TripleP-233
92UD-459
92Ultra-70
93D-703
93F-618
93OPC-99
93Pac/Spanish-135
93Pinn-81
93Pol/Royal-10
93S-581
93Select-227
93StCl-555
93StCl/1stDay-555
93StCl/Royal-11
93T-674
93T/Gold-674
93TripleP-168
93UD-85
93Ultra-208
94F-156
94StCl-197
94StCl/1stDay-197
94StCl/Gold-197
94T-357
94T/Gold-357

Gueldner, Jeff
89KS*-42

Guenther, Bob
87Myrtle-26

Guercio, Maurice
86FSLAS-19
86FtLaud-10
87Albany-6

Guerra, Esmili
92Peoria/ClBest-16
93Peoria/Team-6

Guerra, Fermin
(Mike)
49B-155
50B-157
51B-202

Guerra, Pete
91BurlInd/ProC-3303

Guerra, Rich
75SanAn
76Wmsprt

Guerrero, Alex
75QuadC

Guerrero, Epifano
(Sandy)
86Ventura-8
87Stockton-4
88CalLgAS-15
88Stockton/Cal-196
88Stockton/ProC-727
89ElPaso/GS-22
91Denver/LineD-139
91Denver/ProC-130

Guerrero, Inocencio
(Ino)
83Durham-4
85Greenvl/Team-6
86Greenvl/Team-13
87Greenvl/Best-17
87Richm/Bob-10
88Greenvl/Best-4
89Durham/Star-28
89Durham/Team-26CO

Guerrero, Juan
87Pocatel/Bon-27
88Clinton/ProC-701
89SanJose/Best-21
89SanJose/Cal-219
89SanJose/ProC-451
89SanJose/Star-11
89Star/Wax-86
90Shrev/ProC-1450
90Shrev/Star-8
91AA/LineD-305
91Shrev/LineD-305
91Shrev/ProC-1828
92D/Rook-46
92F/Up-85
92L-428
92L/BlkGold-428
92Mother/Ast-15
92Pinn-552
92ProC/Tomorrow-348
92StCl-775
92Ultra-490
93D-240
93F-435
93LimeR/Winter-72
93S-259
93StCl-16
93StCl/1stDay-16
93T-414
93T/Gold-414
93Ultra-41

Guerrero, Mario
73OPC-607R
73T-607R
74OPC-192
74T-192
75OPC-152
75T-152
75T/M-152
76OPC-499
76SSPC-285
76T-499
77T-628
78T-339
79Ho-78
79K-43
79OPC-131
79T-261
80T-49
81F-591
81T-547
89Pac/SenLg-36
89TM/SenLg-43

Guerrero, Mike
88Beloit/GS-15
89Beloit/I/Star-8
90Stockton/Best-8
90Stockton/ProC-2193
91ElPaso/ProC-2754
92ClBest-97
92ElPaso/ProC-3930
92ElPaso/SB-211
93LimeR/Winter-20

Guerrero, Patrick
88StCath/ProC-2038

Guerrero, Pedro
78Cr/PCL-11
79Albuq-16
79T-719R
80Pol/Dodg-28
81Pol/Dodg-28
81T-651
82D-136
82F-7
82F/St-6
82OPC-247
82Pol/Dodg-28
82T-247
82T/St-260
82T/St-55
83D-110
83Drake-9
83F-207
83F/St-27M
83K-20
83OPC-116
83OPC/St-248
83PermaGr/CC-5
83Pol/Dodg-28
83Seven-4
83T-425
83T-681
83T/Fold-3M
83T/St-248
84D-174
84D-24DK
84D/AAS-17
84Drake-11
84F-100
84F/St-19
84F/St-34
84MiltBrad-11
84Nes/792-306TL
84Nes/792-90
84OPC-90
84Pol/Dodg-28
84Ralston-30
84Seven-14W
84T-306TL
84T-90
84T/Cereal-30
84T/Gloss40-25
84T/RD-7M
84T/St-75
84T/Super-24
85Coke/Dodg-11
85D-174
85D/AAS-34
85D/HL-19
85Drake-13
85F-370
85FunFood/Pin-26
85Leaf-211
85OPC-34
85Seven-10W
85T-575
85T/RD-8M
85T/St-70
85T/Super-44
85ThomMc/Discs-31
86Coke/Dodg-10
86D-174
86Drake-6
86F-130
86F/AS-8
86F/LimEd-21
86F/Mini-28
86F/Slug-13
86F/St-47
86GenMills/Book-5M
86Leaf-105
86Meadow/Blank-6
86Meadow/Stat-18
86OPC-145
86OPC/WaxBox-G
86Pol/Dodg-28
86Seven/Coin-C4M
86Seven/Coin-E4M
86Seven/Coin-S4M
86Seven/Coin-W4M
86Sf-14
86Sf-148M
86Sf-181M
86Sf/Dec-74M
86T-145
86T-706AS
86T/3D-8
86T/Gloss60-25
86T/Mini-44
86T/St-65
86T/Super-27
86T/Tatt-23M
86T/WaxBox-G
86TrueVal-1
87BK-7
87Classic-39
87D-53
87F-440
87F/Slug-16
87GenMills/Book-6M
87Jiffy-10
87KayBee-14
87Leaf-237
87Mother/Dodg-2
87OPC-360
87Pol/Dodg-14
87RedFoley/St-83
87Seven-W4
87Sf-27
87Sf/TPrev-14M
87Smok/Dodg-10
87Stuart-6M
87T-360
87T/Board-27
87T/St-69
88D-278
88D-BC16
88D/AS-48
88D/Best-122
88Drake-26
88F-514
88F-623M
88F/AwardWin-15
88F/Mini-83
88F/Slug-16
88F/St-91
88FanSam-20
88KMart-11
88KayBee-12
88KennerFig-42
88Leaf-101
88Mother/Dodg-2
88Nestle-24
88OPC-111
88Panini/St-314
88Pol/Dodg-28
88RedFoley/St-29
88S-9
88Sf-97
88Smok/Dodg-28
88T-409TL
88T-550
88T/Big-171
88T/Coins-43
88T/Gloss60-24
88T/Mini-52
88T/RiteAid-5
88T/St-75
88T/St/Backs-15
88T/UK-28
89B-440
89Cadaco-26
89Classic-60
89D-418
89D/Best-75
89F-451
89KMart/DT-33
89KMart/Lead-6
89KayBee-16
89KennerFig-54
89KingB/Discs-20
89OPC-68
89Panini/St-183
89RedFoley/St-52
89S-564
89S/HotStar-44
89Smok/Cards-7
89Smok/Dodg-94
89T-780
89T/Ames-15
89T/Big-285
89T/Coins-16
89T/LJN-74
89T/St-40
89T/UK-34
89UD-306
90B-201
90Classic-146
90D-63
90D-674AS
90D/BestNL-95
90D/Bon/MVP-BC6
90F-250
90F/BB-16
90F/BBMVP-15
90F/Can-250
90F/LL-16
90F/WaxBox-C11
90HOF/St-85
90HotPlay/St-18
90KMart/CBatL-6
90KMart/SS-15
90Kenner/Fig-37
90Leaf-44
90MLBPA/Pins-32
90OPC-610
90Panini/St-211
90Panini/St-335
90Post-22
90PublInt/St-219
90RedFoley/St-42
90S-13
90S/100St-61
90Sf-66
90Smok/Card-7
90Sunflower-10
90T-610
90T/Big-13
90T/Coins-47
90T/DH-30
90T/Gloss60-32
90T/HillsHM-6
90T/Mini-75
90T/St-151AS
90T/St-35
90T/Stbk-3
90T/TVAS-50
90T/TVCard-25
90Target-304
90UD-244
91B-403
91BBBest/HitM-8
91Classic/200-21
91D-25DK
91D-558
91D/SuperDK-25DK
91DennyGS-22
91F-634
91Leaf-204
91Leaf/Stud-232
91Louisvl/Team-16
91OPC-20
91OPC/Premier-58
91Panini/FrSt-31
91Panini/St-37
91Pol/Card-28
91RedFoley/St-43
91S-140
91StCl-314
91T-20
91T/CJMini/I-8
91UD-327
91UD-98TC
91Ultra-289
92B-377
92Classic/Game200-80
92D-158
92F-579
92L-18
92L/BlkGold-18
92OPC-470
92Panini-172
92Pinn-392
92Pol/Card-7
92S-376
92StCl-320
92Studio-91
92T-470
92T/Gold-470
92T/GoldWin-470
92T/Kids-26
92TripleP-9
92UD-357
92Ultra-263
93D-600
93F-509

Guerrero, Rafael
92GulfCM/ProC-3493

Guerrero, Ramces
88Idaho/ProC-1844
89Idaho/ProC-2010

Guerrero, Sandy
90ElPaso/GS-15
91AAA/LineD-139
92Denver/ProC-2646
92ElPaso/SB-212
93LimeR/Winter-119

Guerrero, Tony
81Wisco-4
83OrlanTw-22
85Visalia-21

Guetterman, Lee
84Chatt-16
86F/Up-U45
87D-322
87F-585
87T-307
88D-270
88D/Y/Bk-NEW
88F-374
88OPC-382
88S-323
88Sf-45
88T-656
89D/Best-108
89S/NWest-24
89T/Tr-43T
90D-127
90F-443
90F/Can-443
90Leaf-333
90OPC-286
90Panini/St-118
90PublInt/St-534
90S-294
90S/NWest-17
90T-286
90T/TVYank-9
90UD-318
91D-124
91F-664
91Leaf-52
91OPC-62
91S-34
91StCl-361
91T-62
91UD-481
91Ultra-232
92D-507
92F-227
92L-320
92L/BlkGold-320
92OPC-578
92S-244
92S/RookTr-74T
92StCl-346

92T-578
92T/Gold-578
92T/GoldWin-578
92UD-610
92Yank/WIZ80-71
93D-542
93F-475
93StCl-214
93StCl/1stDay-214
93T-134
93T/Gold-134
94F-632
94Pac/Cr-590
94StCl-216
94StCl/1stDay-216
94StCl/Gold-216
Guggiana, Todd
90Butte/SportP-30
91B-697
91CharlR/ClBest-18
91CharlR/ProC-1322
91ClBest/Singl-204
Guidi, Jim
91SLCity/ProC-3205
91SLCity/SportP-24
Guidry, Ron
76OPC-599R
76T-599R
77BK/Y-11
77T-656
78BK/Y-4
78Ho-25
78PapaG/Disc-28
78SSPC/270-17
78T-135
79BK/Y-4
79Ho-89
79K-11
79OPC-264
79T-202RB
79T-500
79T-5LL
79T-7LL
79T/Comics-13
80BK/PHR-4
80K-4
80OPC-157
80T-207LL
80T-300
80T/S-7
80T/Super-7
81D-227
81F-88
81F/St-76
81K-45
81OPC-250
81T-250
81T/St-112
82D-548
82D-558M
82F-38
82F/St-120
82K-26
82OPC-10IA
82OPC-9
82Sqt-9
82T-10IA
82T-9
83D-17DK
83D-31
83D/AAS-15
83F-383
83F/St-13M
83F/St-5M
83OPC-104
83OPC/St-102
83RoyRog/Disc-4
83T-440
83T/St-102
84D-173
84D/AAS-51
84F-127
84MiltBrad-12
84Nes/792-110
84Nes/792-406AS
84Nes/792-486TL
84Nes/792-717LL
84Nestle/DT-10
84OPC-110
84OPC-204AS
84Ralston-31
84Seven-16E
84T-110
84T-406AS
84T-486TL
84T-717LL
84T/Cereal-31
84T/Gloss40-14
84T/RD-11M
84T/St-194
84T/St-318
84T/Super-17
85D-214
85F-129
85FunFood/Pin-96
85Leaf-237
85OPC-388
85Pol/MetYank-Y3
85T-790
85T/RD-11M
85T/St-313
85ThomMc/Discs-11
86D-103
86Drake-32
86F-106
86F/Mini-22
86F/Slug-14
86F/St-48
86Leaf-36
86OPC-109
86OPC/WaxBox-H
86Seven/Coin-C6
86Seven/Coin-E6
86Seven/Coin-S6
86Seven/Coin-W6
86Sf-149M
86Sf-18
86Sf-185M
86Sf-57M
86Sf/Dec-71
86T-610
86T-721
86T/3D-9
86T/Gloss60-12
86T/Mini-26
86T/St-302
86T/Super-28
86T/Tatt-14M
86T/WaxBox-H
87Classic-68
87D-93
87F-100
87F/AwardWin-16
87Leaf-101
87OPC-375
87RedFoley/St-54
87Sf-83
87T-375
87T/St-301
88D-175
88D/Y/Bk-175
88F-207
88F/St-S3
88Leaf-180
88OPC-127
88S-310
88T-535
88T/Big-50
88T/St-296
88T/St/Backs-61
89S-342
89S/NWest-28
89T-255
89T/LJN-111
89UD-307
90HOF/St-97
92Yank/WIZ70-60
92Yank/WIZ80-72
92Yank/WIZAS-27
Guiheen
T206
Guilfoyle, Mike
90Bristol/ProC-3166
90Bristol/Star-7
91Fayette/ClBest-2
91Fayette/ProC-1163
92Lakeland/ClBest-13
92Lakeland/ProC-2272
Guillen, Ozzie
83Beaum-2
84Cram/PCL-236
85Coke/WS-13
85D/HL-55
85F/Up-U48
85T/Tr-43T
86Coke/WS-13
86D-208
86F-206
86F/LL-17
86F/Mini-44
86F/St-49
86F/WaxBox-C3
86GenMills/Book-2M
86Jay's-9
86KayBee-16
86Leaf-140
86OPC-254
86Quaker-20
86Seven/Coin-C13M
86Sf-176M
86Sf-22
86T-254
86T/Gloss60-58
86T/St-294
86T/St-309
86T/Super-7
86T/Tatt-5M
87Coke/WS-7
87D-87
87D/OD-235
87F-497
87F/AwardWin-17
87F/Mini-48
87F/RecSet-13
87F/St-50
87Kraft-11
87Leaf-117
87OPC-89
87RedFoley/St-67
87Seven-C9
87Sf-186
87Sf/TPrev-26M
87Stuart-17
87T-89
87T/St-287
88Coke/WS-9
88D-137
88D/Best-81
88F-398
88F/Mini-15
88F/RecSet-16
88F/St-16
88KennerFig-43
88Kodak/WSox-1
88Leaf-59
88Nestle-7
88OPC-296
88Panini/St-61
88S-603
88S/YS/I-21
88Sf-83
88T-585
88T/Big-27
88T/St-284
89B-64
89Classic/Up/2-175M
89Coke/WS-10
89D-176
89D/Best-137
89D/MVP-BC23
89F-497
89F/BBAS-18
89KennerFig-55
89KingB/Discs-6
89Kodak/WSox-6M
89OPC-195
89Panini/St-309
89RedFoley/St-53
89S-433
89S/HotStar-51
89Sf-85
89T-195
89T/Big-148
89T/LJN-104
89T/St-303
89T/UK-35
89UD-175
90B-315
90Classic-92
90Coke/WSox-29
90Coke/WSox-7
90D-135
90D-15DK
90D/BestAL-74
90D/Learning-13
90D/SuperDK-15DK
90F-533
90F/Can-533
90Kodak/WSox-3
90Leaf-128
90OPC-365
90Panini/St-41
90PublInt/St-388
90S-6
90S/McDon-21
90Sf-48
90T-365
90T/Big-215
90T/St-298
90T/TVAS-3
90UD-267
90UD-79TC
90USPlayC/AS-6C
90Windwlk/Discs-9
91B-356
91BBBest/HitM-9
91Classic/200-53
91D-577
91F-121
91Kenner-26
91Kodak/WSox-13
91Kodak/WSox-xM
91Leaf-331
91MooTown-12
91OPC-620
91Panini/FrSt-315
91Panini/St-261
91Panini/Top15-113
91RedFoley/St-44
91S-11
91S-394AS
91S/100SS-15
91Seven/3DCoin-8MW
91StCl-70
91T-620
91UD-325
91USPlayC/AS-2H
91Ultra-74
92B-565
92Classic/Game200-98
92D-229
92F-706M
92F-82
92Hardee-12
92L-149
92L/BlkGold-149
92OPC-210
92Panini-128
92Pinn-79
92S-92
92S/100SS-13
92S/Impact-84
92StCl-20
92StCl/Dome-72
92T-210
92T/Gold-210
92T/GoldWin-210
92T/Kids-100
92UD-436
92Ultra-35
92WSox-13
93B-287
93D-255
93F-203
93Flair-184
93L-85
93OPC-102
93Pac/Beisbol-4
93Pac/Spanish-72
93Pac/SpanishP-15
93Panini-138
93Pinn-166
93S-94
93Select-128
93StCl-517
93StCl/1stDay-517
93StCl/WSox-12
93Studio-167
93T-474
93T/Finest-128
93T/FinestRef-128
93T/Gold-474
93TripleP-115
93UD-139
93UD/SP-254
93Ultra-532
93WSox-10
94B-511
94D-359
94D/Special-359
94F-82
94Finest-393
94Flair-31
94L-107
94OPC-115
94Pac/Cr-125
94Panini-47
94Pinn-428
94S-93
94S/GoldR-93
94Select-25
94Sf/2000-33
94StCl-389
94StCl/1stDay-389
94StCl/Gold-389
94StCl/Team-141
94Studio-206
94T-5
94T/Gold-5
94TripleP-264
94UD-156
94UD/ElecD-156
94Ultra-337
Guillot, Don
87PanAm/USAB-9
87PanAm/USAR-9
90TeamUSA/87-9
Guin, Greg
82ArkTr-14
83ArkTr-17
84ArkTr-10
Guindon, Bob
65T-509R
Guinn, Brian
85Modesto/Chong-7
86SLAS-8
87Pittsfld-11
88IowaC/CMC-15
88IowaC/ProC-526
89IowaC/CMC-16
89IowaC/ProC-1709
90AAASingl/ProC-631
90Iowa/CMC-12
90Iowa/ProC-324
90ProC/Singl-87
90T/TVCub-46
91AAA/LineD-206
91Iowa/LineD-206
91Iowa/ProC-1066
92Vanco/SB-629
Guinn, Drannon E.
(Skip)
69T-614R
70OPC-316
70T-316
71MLB/St-82
71OPC-741
71T-741
Guinn, Wayne
80Cedar-26
Guintini, Ben
48Sommer-14
Guise, Witt
W711/2
Guisto, Lou
D328-67
E135-67
Gulan, Mike
92ClBest/Up-426
92Classic/DP-38
92FrRow/DP-11
92Hamil/ClBest-26
92Hamil/ProC-1597
93B-656
93FExcel/ML-98
93StCl/MurphyS-90
94FExcel-266
Gulbit, German
89EastLDD/ProC-DD3
Gulden, Brad
77LodiD
78Cr/PCL-46
79Colum-1
80Colum-6
80T-670R
81Spokane-30
83Colum-4
85D-365
85F-537
85OPC-251
85T-251
86Mother/Giants-25
90Target-305
92Yank/WIZ70-61
92Yank/WIZ80-73
Gull, Sterling
80SLCity-20
Gulledge, Hugh
90Madison/Best-16
91Madison/ClBest-8

91Madison/ProC-2125
92Reno/Cal-41
Gullett, Don
71MLB/St-60
71OPC-124
71T-124
72OPC-157
72T-157
73OPC-595
73T-595
74OPC-385
74T-385
74T/St-27
75Ho-107
75OPC-65
75T-65
75T/M-65
76Crane-18
76Ho-45
76Ho/Twink-45
76Icee
76K-3
76MSA/Disc
76OPC-390
76SSPC-27
76T-390
77BK/Y-6
77BurgChef-172
77Ho-143
77Ho/Twink-143
77OPC-250
77Pepsi-35
77T-15
78BK/Y-8
78OPC-30
78SSPC/270-18
78T-225
78Wiffle/Discs-28
79OPC-64
79T-140
80T-435
90Chatt/GS-2CO
91AAA/LineD-275M
91Nashvl/LineD-275CO
91Nashvl/ProC-2173CO
92Yank/WIZ70-62
92Yank/WIZ80-74
93Reds/Kahn-8M
Gulley, Napolean
92Negro/RetortII-13
Gullickson, Bill
81D-91
81F-150
81OPC-41
81T-203RB
81T-578
82D-162
82Expo/Hygrade-9
82F-190
82FBI/Disc-9
82Hygrade
82OPC-172
82OPC-94TC
82OPC/Post-21
82T-172
82T-526TL
82Zeller-15
83D-288
83Expo/PostC-6
83F-284
83F/St-6M
83OPC-31
83Stuart-15
83T-31
84D-401
84Expo/PostC-11
84F-276
84Nes/792-318
84OPC-318
84Stuart-16
84T-318
84T/St-96
85D-97
85F-399
85Leaf-236
85OPC-143
85T-687
85T/St-91
86D-331
86D/HL-40
86F-249
86F/Up-U46
86OPC-229
86T-229
86T/St-78
86T/Tr-42T
86TexGold-34
87D-369
87F-203
87F/AwardWin-18
87F/Mini-49
87F/RecSet-14
87F/St-51
87Kahn-34
87Sf/TPrev-4M
87Smok/NL-4
87T-489
87T/St-140
88D-586
88F-208
88OPC-329
88S-585
88T-711
90B-65
90Lennox-14
90Mother/Ast-13
90T/Tr-34T
90UD/Ext-799
91B-133
91CokeK/Tiger-36
91F-508
91Leaf-402
91Leaf/Stud-55
91S-177
91S/RookTr-56T
91UD-590
92B-558
92D-131
92F-137
92L-61
92L/BlkGold-61
92OPC-508
92Panini-112
92Pinn-87
92S-242
92StCl-119
92Sunflower-2
92T-508
92T/Gold-508
92T/GoldWin-508
92TripleP-161
92UD-317
92UD/TmMVPHolo-23
92USPlayC/Tiger-10S
92USPlayC/Tiger-1D
92Ultra-362
92Yank/WIZ80-75
93D-523
93F-606
93L-103
93OPC-124
93Pac/Spanish-110
93Panini-112
93Pinn-352
93S-643
93Select-85
93StCl-574
93StCl/1stDay-574
93T-325
93T/Gold-325
93T/Hill-7
93Tiger/Gator-12
93UD-398
94D-195
94F-134
94Finest-398
94L-147
94Panini-65
94S-198
94S/GoldR-198
94StCl-370
94StCl/1stDay-370
94StCl/Gold-370
94T-654
94T/Gold-654
94TripleP-245
94UD-458
94UD/CollC-118
94UD/CollC/Gold-118
94UD/CollC/Silv-118
Gulliver, Glenn
77Evansvl/TCMA-13
80Evansvl-21
81Evansvl-15
82RochR-12
83D-131
83F-62
83RochR-15
83T-293
84RochR-11
85Richm-13
86Hagers-7
86RochR-4
87Hagers-11
91Crown/Orio-169
91Pac/SenLg-155
Gully, Scott
91Oneonta/ProC-4149
92Greens/ClBest-13
92Greens/ProC-774
Gumbert, Addison
90Target-306
N172
Gumbert, Harry
39PlayBall-54
40PlayBall-86
41DP-27
41DP-92
41PlayBall-26
49B-192
50B-171
W754
Gumbert, Rich
83Greens-9
Gumbs, Lincoln Jr.
90AubAs/Best-17
90AubAs/ProC-3409
Gump, Chris
92AZ/Pol-5
Gumpert, Dave
82BirmB-5
83Evansvl-3
84Evansvl-8
84Nes/792-371
84T-371
85IowaC-14
86IowaC-13
87F-565
87T-487
90BirmDG/Best-16
Gumpert, Randy
49B-87
50B-184
51B-59
52B-106
52T-247
Gumpf, John
90Elizab/Star-11
91Kenosha/ClBest-9
91Kenosha/ProC-2089
92FtMyr/ProC-2756
92Miracle/ClBest-22
Gundelfinger, Matt
81Redwd-14
83Spring/Frit-18
Gunderson, Eric
87Everett-13
88CalLgAS-5
88SanJose/Cal-131
88SanJose/ProC-114
89Shrev/ProC-1833
90B-225
90Phoenix/CMC-7
90ProC/Singl-534
90S/Tr-99T
90UD/Ext-752
91B-628
91D-416RR
91S-744RP
91S/100RisSt-57
91T/90Debut-61
91UD-315
92Classic/Game200-41
92F-637
92Jaxvl/SB-357
92StCl-397
93Calgary/ProC-1160
Gunderson, Greg
89Batavia/ProC-1938
90Spartan/Best-6
90Spartan/ProC-2487
90Spartan/Star-11
Gunn, Clay
86Cram/NWL-126
87Wausau-10
88SanBern/Best-18
88SanBern/Cal-32
Gunn, Jeffrey
90Princet/DIMD-9
Gunnarson, Bob
86Chatt-10
87Chatt/Best-13
Gunning, Thomas
N172
N690
Gunson, Joseph
N172
Gunter, Chet
76Shrev
Gunter, Reid
87Pocatel/Bon-8
Gura, Larry
71OPC-203
71T-203
73OPC-501
73T-501
74OPC-616
74T-616
74T/Tr-616T
75OPC-557
75T-557
75T/M-557
76OPC-319
76SSPC/MetsY-Y7
76T-319
77T-193
78SSPC/270-237
78T-441
79T-19
80OPC-154
80T-295
81Coke
81D-461
81F-38
81F/St-102
81K-59
81OPC-130
81T-130
81T/SO-51
81T/St-88
82D-338
82F-410
82F/St-205
82OPC-147
82T-790
82T-96TL
82T/St-195
83D-160
83F-113
83F/St-8M
83K-42
83OPC-340
83OPC-395AS
83OPC/St-77
83T-340
83T-395AS
83T/St-77
84D-100
84F-347
84Nes/792-625
84Nes/792-96TL
84OPC-264
84T-625
84T-96TL
84T/St-285
85D-217
85F-202
85T-595
85T/St-278
92Yank/WIZ70-63
Gurchiek, Chris
88AppFx/ProC-156
88Boise/ProC-1609
Gurtcheff, Jeff
86Watertn-8
Gust, Chris
88Madis-12
Gustafson, Cliff
92TX-19
93TX-1CO
Gustafson, Edward (Ed)
89Everett/Star-9
90A&AASingle/ProC-118
90Clinton/Best-6
90Clinton/ProC-2550
90Foil/Best-85
91Visalia/ClBest-2
91Visalia/ProC-1736
92OrlanSR/ProC-2841
92OrlanSR/SB-506
Gustave, Michael
78Wisco
Gustavson, Dan
92Hunting/ClBest-13
92Hunting/ProC-3141
Gustavson, Duane
82FtMyr-10
83CharR-25
85FtMyr-26
86FtMyr-13MG
87Memphis-21
87Memphis/Best-2C
88OrlanTw/Best-3
Gustine, Frank
43Playball-33
47TipTop
48L-88
49B-99
49Eureka-57
Exh47
Guthrie, Mark
88Visalia/Cal-167
89OrlanTw/Best-14
89OrlanTw/ProC-1335
89SLAS-19
90AAASingl/ProC-244
90D-622
90LSUGreat-9
90OPC-317
90Portl/ProC-174
90T-317
90T/89Debut-49
90UD-436
91D-64
91F-612
91Leaf-171
91OPC-698
91S-778
91StCl-219
91T-698
91UD-505
92D-691
92L-263
92L/BlkGold-263
92OPC-548
92Pinn-511
92S-164
92StCl-456
92T-548
92T/Gold-548
92T/GoldWin-548
92UD-604
92USPlayC/Twin-5S
92USPlayC/Twin-6D
92Ultra-396
93D-714
93F-265
93L-251
93Pac/Spanish-170
93Pinn-361
93StCl-550
93StCl/1stDay-550
93T-777
93T/Gold-777
93UD-399
93Ultra-581
94D-530
94F-204
94Pac/Cr-352
Gutierrez, Anthony
90Ashvl/ProC-2742
90ProC/Singl-677
91BurlAs/ClBest-4
91BurlAs/ProC-2795
92Osceola/ClBest-18
92Osceola/ProC-2524
Gutierrez, Cesar
69OPC-16R
69T-16R
70OPC-269
70T-269
71MLB/St-392
71OPC-154
71T-154
72T-743
Gutierrez, Dimas
85PrWill-8
86Nashua-10
87Harris-22
88EastLAS/ProC-15
88Harris/ProC-841
89Miami/I/Star-8
Gutierrez, Felipe
85VeroB-7
Gutierrez, Israel
78Ashvl
79Wausau-7

Gutierrez, Jim
89Belling/Legoe-6
90Penin/Star-10
91SanBern/ClBest-5
91SanBern/ProC-1981
93River/Cal-8
Gutierrez, Joaquin
(Jackie)
79Elmira-7
84F/X-47
84T/Tr-46
85D-335
85F-160
85T-89
85T/St-216
85T/St-373YS
86D-335
86F-350
86F/Up-U47
86OPC-73
86T-633
87D-601
87F-471
87T-276
88Phill/TastyK-33
89Pawtu/CMC-19
89Pawtu/Dunkin-21
89Pawtu/ProC-694
89UD-430
90Miami/I/Star-11
90Miami/II/Star-9
91Crown/Orio-170
Gutierrez, Julian
78StPete
80ArkTr-16
82ArkTr-15
Gutierrez, Rafael
90Eugene/GS-10
92VeroB/ClBest-23
92Yakima/ClBest-21
92Yakima/ProC-3442
Gutierrez, Ricky
89Freder/Star-8
90CLAS/CL-4
90Freder/Team-18
91AA/LineD-231
91ClBest/Singl-55
91Hagers/LineD-231
91Hagers/ProC-2462
92B-103
92RochR/ProC-1945
92RochR/SB-453
92Sky/AAASingl-206
93B-462
93F/Final-140
93L-493
93Mother/Padre-10
93Pac/Spanish-596
93Pinn-577
93Select/RookTr-63T
93StCl-676
93StCl/1stDay-676
93T/Tr-21T
93UD-660
93UD/SP-166
94B-560
94D-159
94F-664
94Flair-233
94L-196
94OPC-47
94Pac/Cr-524
94Pinn-138
94Pinn/Artist-138
94Pinn/Museum-138
94S-271
94S/GoldR-271
94Select-175
94StCl-75
94StCl/1stDay-75
94StCl/Gold-75
94T-42
94T/Finest-53
94T/FinestRef-53
94T/Gold-42
94TripleP-166
94UD-104
94UD/CollC-119
94UD/CollC/Gold-119
94UD/CollC/Silv-119
94UD/ElecD-104
94Ultra-279
Gutierrez, Robert
(Bob)
84Newar-21
85Newar-15
Gutierrez, Willie
79Knoxvl/TCMA-13
Gutteridge, Don
44Playball-1
60T-458C
70OPC-123MG
70T-123MG
92Conlon/Sport-636
Guy, Mark
91Melbourne/Fut-9
Guyton, Duffy
92Johnson/ClBest-23
92Johnson/ProC-3109
Guzik, Rob
(Robbi)
89Kingspt/Star-11
90Pittsfld/Pucko-5
91Clmbia/PCPII-2
91Clmbia/PII-22
92ColumMet/ClBest-13
92ColumMet/ProC-289
92ColumMet/SAL/II-15
92ColumMet/SAL/II-30M
93StLucie/ProC-2917
Guzman, Doinini
89Medford/Best-10
Guzman, Hector
83VeroB-18
Guzman, Johnny
90A&AASingle/ProC-144
90Modesto/Chong-12
90Modesto/ProC-2207
90ProC/Singl-665
91AAA/LineD-536
91Tacoma/LineD-536
91Tacoma/ProC-2299
92ClBest-136
92D/Rook-47
92Huntsvl/ProC-3943
92Huntsvl/SB-310
92Sky/AASingl-131
92StCl-498
92T/91Debut-67
93LimeR/Winter-100
93Pinn-261
93S-270
93StCl-284
93StCl/1stDay-284
93StCl/A's-23
Guzman, Jose Alberto
83BurlR-4
83BurlR/Frit-7
84Tulsa-29
85OKCty-11
86D-30RR
86D/Rook-24
86F-559
86Rangers-23
86T/Tr-43T
87D-101
87F-124
87Leaf-50
87Mother/Rang-23
87Smok/R-3
87T-363
88D-136
88D/Best-88
88F-467
88Leaf-55
88Mother/R-23
88OPC-98
88S-322
88Smok/R-20
88T-563
89Bimbo/Discs-11
89D-284
89F-520
89Mother/R-25
89OPC-209
89Panini/St-445
89S-143
89S/YS/II-11
89Smok/R-11
89T-462
89T/St-241
89UD-73
90OPC-308
90PublInt/St-411
90T-308
90UD-617
91F/Up-U60
92D-271
92F-306
92S-502
92T-188
92UD-204
Guzman, Jose Antonio
89Bristol/Star-10
90Fayette/ProC-2400
Guzman, Jose
92B-668
92L-222
92L/BlkGold-222
92Mother/Rang-19
92OPC-188
92Pinn-98
92StCl-153
92Studio-243
92T/Gold-188
92T/GoldWin-188
92TripleP-215
92Ultra-442
93B-412
93Cub/Mara-8
93D-687
93F-323
93F/Final-7
93L-266
93OPC-121
93OPC/Premier-23
93Pac/Beisbol-17
93Pac/Spanish-377
93Pinn-505
93Rang/Keeb-167
93S-256
93Select/RookTr-107T
93StCl-648
93StCl/1stDay-648
93StCl/Cub-19
93Studio-91
93T-253
93T/Finest-145
93T/FinestRef-145
93T/Gold-253
93TripleP-142M
93UD-323
93UD-515
93UD/SP-84
93Ultra-313
94B-578
94D-507
94F-384
94Flair-137
94L-186
94OPC-180
94Pac/Cr-99
94Pinn-55
94Pinn/Artist-55
94Pinn/Museum-55
94S-178
94S/GoldR-178
94Select-90
94StCl/Team-342
94T-35
94T/Finest-93
94T/Finest/PreProd-93
94T/FinestRef-93
94T/Gold-35
94TripleP-73
94UD-196
94UD/ElecD-196
94Ultra-456
Guzman, Juan
(Correa)
86VeroB-8
87Bakers-5
88Knoxvl/Best-18
89Syrac/CMC-9
89Syrac/MerchB-12
89Syrac/ProC-797
89Syrac/Team-12
90Foil/Best-79
90Knoxvl/Best-8
90Knoxvl/ProC-1242
90ProC/Singl-814
91AAA/LineD-504
91F/UltraUp-U60
91S/ToroBJ-25
91Syrac/LineD-504
91Syrac/MerchB-6
91Syrac/ProC-2476
92B-294
92BJ/Fire-12
92Classic/Game200-12
92Classic/II-T18
92D-534
92F-330
92F/RookSIns-13
92L-35
92L/BlkGold-35
92OPC-662
92OPC/Premier-168
92Pinn-183
92Pinn/Team2000-27A
92Pinn/Team2000-27B
92ProC/Tomorrow-161
92S-424
92S/100RisSt-27
92S/Impact-3
92StCl-402
92Studio-256
92Syrac/TallT-3
92T-662
92T/91Debut-68
92T/Gold-662
92T/GoldWin-662
92UD-625
92UD/TmMVPHolo-24
92Ultra-449
93B-55
93BJ/D/45-17
93BJ/Demp-1
93BJ/Fire-12
93Classic/Gamel-40
93Colla/DM-46
93D-189
93F-693
93F/Fruit-27
93Flair-290
93HumDum/Can-25
93Kenner/Fig-15
93L-3
93L/Fast-9
93MSA/Ben-14
93OPC-187
93OPC/Premier-36
93OPC/WC-6
93Pac/Spanish-324
93Pac/SpanishGold-15
93Panini-33
93Pinn-364
93Post/Can-2
93S-372
93Select-180
93Select/Ace-11
93StCl-244
93StCl/1stDay-244
93StCl/MurphyS-2
93StCl/MurphyS-63
93Studio-144
93T-75
93T/Finest-56
93T/FinestRef-56
93T/Gold-75
93T/Hill-15
93ToysRUs-73
93TripleP-28
93TripleP/Act-28
93UD-266
93UD/FunPack-57
93UD/SP-48
93USPlayC/Ace-5S
93Ultra-640
93Ultra/Strike-2
94B-553
94D-404
94F-333
94F/Smoke-3
94L-262
94OPC-177
94Pac/Cr-642
94Panini-138
94Pinn-172
94Pinn/Artist-172
94Pinn/Museum-172
94S-375
94Sf/2000-116
94StCl-149
94StCl/1stDay-149
94StCl/Gold-149
94StCl/Team-170
94T-181
94T/Finest-132
94T/FinestRef-132
94T/Gold-181
94TripleP-33
94UD-430
94UD/CollC-120
94UD/CollC/Gold-120
94UD/CollC/Silv-120
94UD/SP-43
94Ultra-438
Guzman, Luis
79Knoxvl/TCMA-3
80Utica-17
Guzman, Pedro
(Pete)
90CharRain/Best-10
90CharRain/ProC-2037
Guzman, Ramon
92SoBend/ClBest-19
Guzman, Ruben
83Water-18
86GlenF-8
87GlenF-1
Guzman, Santiago
70T-716R
72OPC-316R
72T-316R
Gwinn, Tony
87PrWill-27
Gwosdz, Doug
81Hawaii
81Hawaii/TCMA-5
82T-731R
84D-383
84Mother/Padres-16
84Nes/792-753
84Smok/Padres-11
84T-753
85Mother/Giants-22
86Jacks/TCMA-11
87Calgary-23
88Nashvl/CMC-16
88Nashvl/ProC-480
88Nashvl/Team-11
89Nashvl/CMC-11
89Nashvl/ProC-1277
89Nashvl/Team-7
Gwynn, Anthony
(Tony)
82Hawaii-10
83D-598
83F-360
83OPC-143
83T-482
84D-324
84F-301
84Mother/Padres-9
84Nes/792-251
84Smok/Padres-12
84T-251
84T/St-160
85D-25DK
85D-63
85D/AAS-19
85D/DKsuper-25
85Drake-14
85F-34
85F/LimEd-11
85F/St-8
85FunFood/Pin-28
85Leaf-25DK
85Mother/Padres-2
85OPC-383
85Seven-11W
85T-660
85T-717AS
85T/3D-13
85T/Gloss22-6
85T/Gloss40-29
85T/RD-3M
85T/St-146
85T/St-170
85T/St-174
85T/Super-5
85ThomMc/Discs-32
86D-112
86D/AAS-1
86D/PopUp-1
86F-323
86F/LimEd-22
86F/Mini-69
86F/Slug-15
86F/St-50
86KayBee-17
86Leaf-41
86OPC-10
86Quaker-7
86Seven/Coin-W10M
86Sf-13
86Sf-135M
86Sf-181M

86T-10
86T/Gloss22-17
86T/Gloss60-57
86T/Mini-65
86T/St-105
86T/St-146
86T/Super-29
86T/Tatt-24M
86Woolwth-13
87Bohem-19
87Classic-26
87D-64
87D/AAS-16
87D/HL-12
87D/OD-146
87D/PopUp-16
87Drake-11
87F-416
87F/AwardWin-19
87F/BB-19
87F/Lim-19
87F/Mini-50
87F/Slug-17
87F/St-52
87GenMills/Book-6M
87Ho/St-16
87KayBee-15
87Kraft-44
87Leaf-235
87MSA/Discs-16
87MnM's-23
87OPC-198
87RedFoley/St-113
87Sf-117M
87Sf-197M
87Sf-31
87Sf/TPrev-16
87Sportflic/DealP-3
87Stuart-12M
87T-530
87T-599AS
87T/Coins-34
87T/Gloss22-6
87T/Gloss60-2
87T/HL-16
87T/Mini-35
87T/St-106
87T/St-155
87Woolwth-16
88Bz-9
88ChefBoy-6
88Classic/Blue-220
88Coke/Padres-19
88D-164
88D/AS-51
88D/Best-154
88D/MVP-BC6
88Drake-14
88F-585
88F-631M
88F-634M
88F/AwardWin-16
88F/BB/AS-13
88F/BB/MVP-17
88F/Excit-17
88F/Hottest-15
88F/LL-16
88F/Mini-112
88F/RecSet-17
88F/Slug-17
88F/St-123
88F/TL-11
88FanSam-18
88Grenada-26
88KMart-12
88KayBee-13
88KennerFig-44
88KingB/Disc-5
88Leaf-90
88Nestle-40
88OPC-F
88OPC/WaxBox-360
88Panini/St-410
88Panini/St-437
88S-385
88SanDiegoSt-7M
88SanDiegoSt-8
88Sf-16
88Smok/Padres-10
88T-360
88T-402AS
88T-699M
88T/Big-161
88T/Coins-36
88T/Gloss60-38
88T/Mini-74
88T/Revco-1
88T/RiteAid-11
88T/St-115
88T/St/Backs-16
88T/UK-29
88T/WaxBox-F
88Woolwth-12
89B-461
89Bz-13
89Cadaco-27
89Classic-30
89Coke/Padre-6
89D-128
89D-6DK
89D/Best-42
89D/DKsuper-6DK
89D/MVP-BC20
89F-305
89F/BBAS-19
89F/BBMVP's-17
89F/Excit-20
89F/Heroes-20
89F/LL-19
89F/Superstar-21
89F/WaxBox-C12
89Holsum/Discs-6
89KMart/DT-29
89KMart/Lead-2
89KayBee-17
89KennerFig-56
89KingB/Discs-21
89OPC-51
89Padre/Mag-3
89Panini/St-203
89Panini/St-222
89RedFoley/St-54
89S-90
89S/HotStar-40
89S/Mast-37
89SanDiegoSt-6M
89SanDiegoSt-8
89Sf-160
89T-570
89T-699M
89T/Big-58
89T/Coins-4
89T/Crunch-5
89T/Gloss60-58
89T/HeadsUp-1
89T/Hills-16
89T/LJN-82
89T/Mini-38
89T/St-109
89T/St/Backs-50
89T/UK-36
89UD-384
89UD-683TC
90B-217
90BBWit-2
90Bz-6
90Classic-17
90Classic-87
90Coke/Padre-6
90CollAB-17
90D-705AS
90D-86
90D/BestNL-11
90D/Bon/MVP-BC4
90D/Learning-48
90D/Preview-6
90F-157
90F/BBMVP-16
90F/Can-157
90F/LL-17
90F/WaxBox-C12
90Holsum/Discs-18
90HotPlay/St-19
90KMart/CBatL-2
90KMart/SS-5
90KayBee-14
90KingB/Discs-3
90Leaf-154
90MLBPA/Pins-55
90MSA/Soda-14
90OPC-403AS
90OPC-730
90Padre/MagUno-1
90Padre/MagUno-15
90Panini/St-207M
90Panini/St-351
90Post-5
90PublInt/St-261
90PublInt/St-50
90RedFoley/St-43
90S-255
90S-685DT
90S/100St-3
90Sf-98
90Starline/LJS-29
90Starline/LJS-4
90Sunflower-11
90T-403AS
90T-730
90T/Big-93
90T/Coins-36
90T/DH-31
90T/Gloss22-8
90T/Gloss60-56
90T/HeadsUp-1
90T/Mini-80
90T/St-101
90T/St-146AS
90T/TVAS-39
90UD-344
90USPlayC/AS-11D
90WonderBrd-12
91B-647
91BBBest/HitM-10
91Cadaco-28
91Classic/200-156
91Classic/II-T93
91Classic/III-33
91CollAB-19
91D-243
91F-529
91Leaf-290
91Leaf/Prev-11
91Leaf/Stud-245
91MSA/Holsum-5
91MajorLg/Pins-54
91MooTown-6
91OPC-180
91OPC/Premier-59
91Padre/MagRal-22
91Panini/FrSt-97
91Panini/St-99
91Panini/Top15-104
91Petro/SU-24
91Post-10
91S-500
91S/100SS-94
91Seven/3DCoin-4SC
91StCl-308
91T-180
91T/CJMini/I-26
91T/SU-18
91UD-255
91UD/FinalEd-97FAS
91USPlayC/AS-1C
91Ultra-303
92B-50
92CJ/DI-16
92Classic/Game200-61
92Classic/II-T52
92Colla/ASG-18
92Colla/Gwynn-Set
92D-425AS
92D-441
92D/Elite-E14
92F-605
92F/ASIns-2
92F/Performer-10
92F/TmLIns-7
92French-16M
92JDean/18-13
92Kenner/Fig-21
92KingB-10
92L-206
92L/BlkGold-206
92MSA/Ben-15
92Mother/Padre-7
92MrTurkey-13
92OPC-270
92OPC/Premier-106
92P-26
92Padre/Carl-7
92Panini-236
92Panini-286AS
92Pinn-400
92Pinn-591
92Pol/Padre-8
92S-625
92S-779AS
92S-886DT
92S/100SS-81
92S/Proctor-16
92Seven/Coin-23
92Smok/Padre-9
92StCl-825
92StCl/Dome-73
92Studio-104
92Studio/Prev-22
92T-270
92T/Gold-270
92T/GoldWin-270
92T/Kids-53
92T/MicroG-270
92TripleP-219
92UD-274
92UD-717DS
92UD-83TC
92UD/ASFF-25
92UD/TWillB-T6
92USPlayC/Ace-3D
92Ultra-277
92Ultra/AwardWin-12
92Ultra/Gwynn-Set
93B-630
93Cadaco-29
93Classic/GameI-41
93Colla/ASG-18
93Colla/DM-47
93D-126
93Duracel/PPI-14
93F-138
93F/Fruit-28
93Flair-133
93HumDum/Can-47
93Kraft-23
93L-28
93L/GoldAS-9M
93L/Heading-2
93MSA/Metz-10
93Mother/Padre-3
93OPC-94
93P-8
93Pac/Jugador-28
93Pac/Spanish-257
93Panini-262
93Pinn-289NT
93Pinn-98
93Pinn/Cooper-20
93S-24
93S-525AS
93Select-5
93Select/ChasS-8
93StCl-538
93StCl/1stDay-538
93StCl/MurphyMP-4AS
93StCl/MurphyS-3
93Studio-100
93T-5
93T/BlkGold-8
93T/Finest-77
93T/FinestRef-77
93T/Gold-5
93TB/Full-7
93TripleP-51
93UD-165
93UD-474M
93UD/Diam-17
93UD/FunPack-138
93UD/FunPack-211ASA
93UD/FunPackAS-AS9M
93UD/OnDeck-D14
93UD/SP-167
93UD/Then-TN11
93USPlayC/Ace-6D
93Ultra-472
94B-120
94D-10
94D/Ann-10
94D/DK-11
94D/DomII-1
94D/Elite-38
94D/MVP-13
94D/Special-10
94F-665
94F-711M
94F/AS-39
94F/ProV-9
94F/TL-27
94Kraft-24
94L-254
94L/StatStand-9
94OPC-109
94Oscar-23
94P-13
94Pac/Cr-525
94Pac/Silv-35
94Panini-256
94Pinn-4
94Pinn/Artist-4
94Pinn/Museum-4
94Pinn/Run-35
94RedFoley-5M
94S-12
94S/GoldR-12
94S/GoldS-23
94S/Tomb-8
94Select-77
94Sf/2000-25
94Sf/Mov-5
94StCl-151
94StCl-537QS
94StCl/1stDay-151
94StCl/1stDay-537QS
94StCl/Gold-151
94StCl/Gold-537QS
94Studio-132
94Studio/S&GStar-1
94T-620
94T/Finest-201
94T/FinestRef-201
94T/Gold-620
94TripleP-167
94UD-219
94UD-279HFA
94UD/CollC-122
94UD/CollC/Gold-122
94UD/CollC/Silv-122
94UD/DColl-W5
94UD/ElecD-219
94UD/ElecD-279HFA
94UD/HoloFX-14
94UD/SP-130
94Ultra-280
94Ultra/Hit-6

Gwynn, Chris

87Albuq/Pol-27
88AAA/ProC-2
88Albuq/CMC-12
88Albuq/ProC-259
88F-647R
88S-640RP
88SanDiegoSt-6
88SanDiegoSt-7M
89Albuq/CMC-15
89Albuq/ProC-64
89F-59
89S/HotRook-21
89SanDiegoSt-6
89SanDiegoSt-7
89UD-607
90Classic-111
90Leaf-411
90Mother/Dodg-14
90OPC-456
90Pol/Dodg-15
90S/YS/II-39
90T-456
90Target-307
90UD-526
91D-598
91F-202
91Mother/Dodg-14
91OPC-99
91Pol/Dodg-15
91S-178
91StCl-480
91T-99
91UD-560
92D-648
92F-457
92L-518
92L/BlkGold-518
92OPC-604
92OPC/Premier-9
92Pol/Royal-10
92S-449
92S/RookTr-56T
92StCl-815
92T-604
92T/Gold-604
92T/GoldWin-604
92UD-689
92Ultra-371
93D-657
93L-453
93Pol/Royal-11
93StCl/Royal-9
93T-472
93T/Gold-472
93UD-632

94D-223
94F-157
94L-209
94Pac/Cr-284
94Pinn-297
94S-381
94T-731
94T/Gold-731
94UD/CollC-121
94UD/CollC/Gold-121
94UD/CollC/Silv-121
94Ultra-63
Gyarmati, Jeff
83Beloit/Frit-4
89Boise/ProC-1985
Gyselman, Dick
43Centen-11
44Centen-10
Haag, Mike
93James/ClBest-28TR
Haar, Rich
93James/ClBest-8
93James/ProC-3334
Haas, Berthold
(Bert)
49Eureka-105
90Target-308
Exh47
Haas, Bill
63T-544R
64T-398R
Haas, Bryan
(Moose)
75BurlB
78T-649
79T-448
80T-181
81D-85
81F-516
81OPC-327
81T-327
81T/St-98
82D-206
82F-143
82F/St-139
82OPC-12
82Pol/Brew-30
82T-12
83D-204
83F-35
83Gard-9
83OPC-317
83Pol/Brew-30
83T-503
84D-368
84F-202
84F/St-61
84Gard-8
84Nes/792-271
84Nes/792-726TL
84OPC-271
84Pol/Brew-30
84T-271
84T-726TL
84T/RD-22
84T/St-292
85D-473
85F-583
85Gard-8
85OPC-151
85Pol/Brew-30
85T-151
85T/RD-23
85T/St-293
86D-237
86F-489
86F/Up-U48
86Mother/A's-16
86OPC-9
86T-759
86T/St-201
86T/Tatt-2M
86T/Tr-44T
87D-528
87F-393
87Leaf-54
87OPC-369
87Smok/A's-5
87T-413
88S-177
88T-606
92Brew/Carlson-9
Haas, Dave
87Anchora-16
89Lakeland/Star-7
90London/ProC-1263
91AAA/LineD-585
91B-151
91Toledo/LineD-585
91Toledo/ProC-1926
92OPC-665
92S-825
92Sky/AAASingl-262
92StCl-362
92T-665
92T/91Debut-69
92T/Gold-665
92T/GoldWin-665
92Toledo/ProC-1038
92Toledo/SB-586
92USPlayC/Tiger-4C
92USPlayC/Tiger-4D
93D-335
93S-215
93T-536
93T/Gold-536
93Tiger/Gator-13
93USPlayC/Rook-8S
93Ultra-551
94Pac/Cr-221
Haas, G. Edwin
(Eddie)
59T-126
79Savan-16
81Richm-21
82Richm-27
83Richm-23
84Richm-27
85Ho/Braves-1MG
85Pol/Atl-22MG
85T/Tr-44T
Haas, George W.
(Mule)
29Exh/4-27
31Exh/4-28
32Orbit/num-19
32Orbit/un-25
33G-219
35BU-170
35G-8B
35G-9B
40PlayBall-184
61F-109
81Conlon-60
91Conlon/Sport-323
94Conlon-1138
PR1-15
R305
R310
R312/M
R314
R315-A14
R315-B14
V355-68
V94-21
W517-32
WG8-26
Haas, Jeff
92Eugene/ClBest-3
92Eugene/ProC-3025
93Rockford/ClBest-14
93StCl/MurphyS-119
Haas, Randy
75Clinton
Haase, Dean
91Utica/ClBest-11
91Utica/ProC-3242
92Saraso/ClBest-10
92SoBend/ProC-179
Haber, Dave
90Eugene/GS-11
Haberle, Dave
83Cedar-18
83Cedar/Frit-11
84Cedar-28
91Eugene/ClBest-2
91Eugene/ProC-3732
Habyan, John
85CharlO-21
86D-45RR
86RochR-5
87Classic-95
87D-494
87French-54
87RochR-24
87RochR/TCMA-4
88D-354
88F-562
88RochR/CMC-6
88RochR/Gov-9
88RochR/ProC-215
88RochR/Team-10
88S-353
88T-153
90AAASingl/ProC-321
90ColClip/CMC-3
90ColClip/ProC-671
90Colum/Pol-16
90ProC/Singl-203
90T/TVYank-44
91B-167
91Crown/Orio-171
91F/UltraUp-U40
91F/Up-U42
91Leaf-480
91StCl-590
92D-32
92F-228
92L-189
92L/BlkGold-189
92OPC-698
92Pinn-433
92S-451
92StCl-576
92T-698
92T/Gold-698
92T/GoldWin-698
92TripleP-228
93D-107
93F-277
93L-162
93Pac/Spanish-205
93Pinn-409
93S-459
93StCl-383
93StCl/1stDay-383
93StCl/Y-20
93T-86
93T/Gold-86
93UD-719
93Ultra-241
94D-562
94F-158
94Pac/Cr-285
94S-294
94S/GoldR-294
94StCl/Team-325
94T-614
94T/Gold-614
Hack, Stan
34DS-107
34DS-34
35BU-137
40Wheat-12
41DP-2
41DP-97
41Wheat-21
42Playball-40
47TipTop
52Mother-60
53Mother-49
54Wilson
55T-6MG
55T/DH-24MG
61F-110
75Shakey-18
77Galasso-78
80Pac/Leg-83
91Conlon/Sport-126
92Cub/OldStyle-10
R302
R312/M
R313
V355-105
WG8-27
Hacker, Rich
90T/TVCard-3CO
91Tor/Fire-7
92BJ/Fire-13CO
93BJ/Fire-13CO
Hacker, Warren
51B-318
52Dix
52StarCal/L-80G
52T-324
53B/Col-144
53Dix
53NB
53RM-NL23
54B-125
55B-8
56T-282
57Kahn
57Sohio/Reds-8
57T-370
58T-251
Hackett, John
86Erie-11
Hackett, Tom
52LaPatrie-6
52Laval-108
Hacopian, Derek
92Classic/DP-96
92Watertn/ClBest-24
92Watertn/ProC-3252CO
94ClBest/Gold-44
94FExcel-44
Haddan, Russell
91Sydney/Fut-17
Haddix, Harvey
53Hunter
53T-273
54Hunter
54T-9
55Armour-8
55Hunter
55T-43
55T/DH-42
56T-77
56T/Hocus-A6
56T/Hocus-B8
56T/Pin-47P
57T-265
58Kahn
58T-118
59T-184
60Kahn
60NuCard-9
60T-340
61Kahn
61NuCard-478
61P-134
61T-100
61T-410HL
61T/RO-33
62J-180
62Kahn
62P-180
62P/Can-180
62T-67
63IDL-11
63Kahn
63T-239
64T-439
65OPC-67
65T-67
76Laugh/Jub-31
76SSPC-623CO
77Galasso-241
79TCMA-39
82D-651CO
82Ohio/HOF-46
88Pac/Leg-11
89Swell-13
90HOF/St-57
90Swell/Great-73
91Crown/Orio-172
91T/Arc53-273
92AP/ASG-63
92Bz/Quadra-19M
93TWill-75
93UD/ATH-61
94T/Arc54-9
Haddock, Darren
91BendB/ClBest-7
91BendB/ProC-3692
Haddock, George
N172
N300/unif
Haden, Paris
90Hagers/Best-11
Hadley, Irving
(Bump)
32Orbit/num-24
32Orbit/un-26
33G-140
34Exh/4-15
35G-1C
35G-275
35G-2C
35G-6C
35G-7C
38G-251
38ONG/Pin-14
61F-111
92Conlon/Sport-508
R305
R316
V354-15
Hadley, Kent
59T-127
60L-135
60T-102
61Union
92Yank/WIZ60-50
Haeberle, Kevin
89Idaho/ProC-2037
90Sumter/Best-27
90Sumter/ProC-2427
Haefner, Mickey
44Playball-22
49B-144
50B-183
Haeger, Greg
90Bristol/ProC-3159
90Bristol/Star-8
91Fayette/ClBest-3
91Fayette/ProC-1164
92Fayette/ClBest-9
92Fayette/ProC-2163
Hafey, Charles J.
(Chick)
29Exh/4-16
31Exh/4-16
32Orbit/un-27
33DL-19
33Exh/4-4
34DS-18
34Exh/4-4
34G-34
35BU-16
35Exh/4-4
61F-39
76Rowe-8
76Shakey-121
77Galasso-217
80Pac/Leg-116
80Perez/HOF-121
80SSPC/HOF
87Conlon/2-14
88Conlon/NatAS-10
89HOF/St-34
91Conlon -259
91Conlon/Sport-33
92Card/McDon/Pac-11
92Conlon/Sport-657
93Conlon-677
93Conlon-889
R300
R305
R308-207
R310
R316
R328-8
R332-5
V354-78
V355-94
V94-22
W517-29
Hafey, Daniel A.
(Bud)
35BU-163
Hafey, Tom
46Remar-12
47Remar-11
47Signal
47Smith-18
48Smith-12
Hafey, Will
47Remar-16
47Smith-19
48Signal
48Smith-3
Haffley, Jay
90WichSt-15
Haffner, Les
90QuadC/GS-11
Hagan, Kevin
81Louisvl-6
83Louisvl/Riley-6
84Louisvl-11
84Nes/792-337
85Louisvl-7
88Tucson/CMC-5
88Tucson/JP-12
88Tucson/ProC-180
Hageman, Kurt
T207
Hagemann, Tim
80Clinton-9

Hagen, Kevin
81ArkTr-16
82ArkTr-2
84T-337
86Maine-10
87Portl-13
87Tucson-17
Hagen, Walter
33SK*-8
Hagermann, Ken
79Elmira-3
Haggas, Josh
92GulfCM/ProC-3490
Haggerty, Roger
86Elmira-7
87WinHaven-26
88WinHaven/Star-9
Haggins, Ray
92Negro/RetortII-14
Hagman, Keith
81Durham-9
82Durham-2
Hague, Joe
69T-559R
70OPC-362
70T-362
71MLB/St-274
71OPC-96
71T-96
71T/Coins-139
72T-546
73OPC-447
73T-447
81TCMA-427
Hagy, Gary
91Boise/ClBest-19
91Boise/ProC-3886
92MidwLAS/Team-14
92QuadC/ClBest-22
92QuadC/ProC-818
Hahn, Brent
90Salinas/Cal-134
90Salinas/ProC-2725
Hahn, Don
71Expo/ProS-9
71MLB/St-129
71OPC-94
71T-94
72OPC-269
72T-269
74OPC-291
74T-291
75OPC-182
75T-182
75T/M-182
77Phoenix
91WIZMets-155
Hahn, Ed
E254
E90/3
M116
T206
Hahn, Eric
87Savan-5
Hahn, Frank
(Noodles)
82Ohio/HOF-47
E107
Hahn, Willie
N172
Hailey, Fred
(Freddie)
87Oneonta-15
88FtLaud/Star-11
89FtLaud/Star-8
90Albany/Best-20
90Albany/ProC-1044
90Albany/Star-6
Hailey, Roger
88Pulaski/ProC-1766
89Pulaski/ProC-1907
90A&AASingle/ProC-93
90Foil/Best-160
90ProC/Singl-728
90SALAS/Star-31
90Sumter/Best-4
90Sumter/ProC-2428
91Durham/ProC-1539
92Durham/ProC-1093
92Durham/Team-32
Hain, Bill
60HenryH-6
60Union-7
Haines, Allan
(Abner)
80GlenF/B-27TR
80GlenF/C-22TR
Haines, Dennis
77SanJose-11
79Ogden/TCMA-8
Haines, Jesse
21Exh-66
32Orbit/un-28
33G-73
40PlayBall-227
61F-40
76Rowe-3M
76Shakey-118
77Galasso-125
80Perez/HOF-118
80SSPC/HOF
82Ohio/HOF-6
89Pac/Leg-208
91Conlon/Sport-43
92Card/McDon/Pac-17
92Conlon/Sport-358
92Conlon/Sport-647
93Conlon-768
E120
E121/120
E210-30
R305
R316
V100
V354-44
V355-93
V61-103
W501-76
W513
W573
W575
Haines, Michael
86James-11
Hainline, Jeff
88Butte-25
Hairston, Jerry
74OPC-96
74T-96
75OPC-327
75T-327
75T/M-327
76OPC-391
76SSPC-153
76T-391
83D-616
83F-236
83T-487
83TrueVal/WSox-17
84D-86
84F-60
84Nes/792-177
84T-177
84TrueVal/WS-15
85Coke/WS-17
85D-135
85F-515
85T-596
86Coke/WS-17
86D-424
86F-207
86T-778
87Coke/WS-11
87D-285
87F-498
87OPC-299
87T-685
88D-285
88T-281
Hairston, John
90SoBend/Best-3
90SoBend/GS-5
91SoBend/ClBest-8
91SoBend/ProC-2863
Hairston, Rodd
91BurlInd/ProC-3308
Hairston, Sam Sr.
86BirmB/Team-26CO
87BirmB/Best-2CO
87Negro/Dixon-1
89BirmB/Best-29CO
89BirmB/ProC-112CO
90BirmB/Best-26CO
90BirmB/ProC-1398CO
91AA/LineD-75M
91BirmB/LineD-75CO
91BirmB/ProC-1470CO
92BirmB/SB-100M
Hajeck, David
90A&AASingle/ProC-102
90Ashvl/ProC-2754
90ProC/Singl-675
90SALAS/Star-10
91Osceola/ClBest-18
91Osceola/ProC-692
92Jacks/ProC-4003
Halama, Scott
87Erie-22
88Hamil/ProC-1720
89Johnson/Star-14
Halberg, Eric
83Clinton/Frit-2
Halcovich, Frank
87AZ/Pol-4
88AZ/Pol-4
Hale, A. Odell
(Odell)
36Wheat-8
37OPC-128
38Exh/4-11
81Conlon-55
92Conlon/Sport-415
R313
R314
V300
Hale, Bob
56T-231
57T-406
59T-507
60T-309
61T-532
79TCMA-129
91Crown/Orio-173
92Yank/WIZ60-51
Hale, Chip
84AZ/Pol-7
86AZ/Pol-3
87AZ/Pol-5
88OrlanTw/Best-18
89Portl/CMC-24
89Portl/ProC-208
90AAASingl/ProC-253
90D-690
90OPC-704
90Portl/CMC-19
90Portl/ProC-183
90ProC/Singl-571
90S-588RP
90S/100Ris-98
90Sf-223
90T-704
90T/89Debut-50
90UD-475
91AAA/LineD-409
91Portl/LineD-409
91Portl/ProC-1570
91S/100RisSt-39
92Portl/SB-408
92Portland/ProC-2673
93F/Final-236
93Select/RookTr-74T
94D-168
94F-205
94L-115
94Pac/Cr-353
94S-609
94Select-162
94StCl-501
94StCl/1stDay-501
94StCl/Gold-501
94T-583
94T/Gold-583
Hale, Dan
86Greens-10
87Greens-20
Hale, DeMarlo
86NewBrit-12
88Huntsvl/BK-5
88Madis-13
92NewBrit/SB-500CO
Hale, Diane
81ArkTr-23M
Hale, John
75Albuq/Caruso-5
76OPC-228
76T-228
77T-523
78T-584
79OPC-23
79T-56
80Indianap-6
81RochR-6
90Target-309
Hale, Samuel
(Sammy)
25Exh-108
29Exh/4-28
81Conlon-56
91Conlon/Sport-293
94Conlon-1155
W517-44
Hale, Shane
91Freder/ClBest-3
91Freder/ProC-2357
Haley, Bart
86Elmira-8
87WinHaven-6
88Lynch/Star-8
89Lynch/Star-10
Haley, Bill
78Green
Haley, Mark
85Anchora-13CO
91SoBend/ClBest-23CO
91SoBend/ProC-2875CO
92SoBend/ClBest-25CO
92SoBend/ProC-195CO
Haley, Ryan
91Niagara/ClBest-5
91Niagara/ProC-3635
Haley, Sam
83Wausau/Frit-23
86WPalmB-19
Halicki, Ed
75OPC-467
75T-467
75T/M-467
76OPC-423
76T-423
77T-343
78Ho-12
78T-107
79OPC-354
79Pol/Giants-28
79T-672
80OPC-115
80Pol/Giants-28
80T-217
81D-53
81T-69
89Pac/SenLg-74
Halicki, Kevin
82Redwd-4
Hall, Albert
82Richm-19
83Richm-18
85F-326
85Ho/Braves-10
85Pol/Atl-2
85T-676
86Richm-8
87F/Up-U39
87Smok/Atl-25
87T/Tr-41T
88D-290
88D/Best-253
88F-541
88OPC-213
88Panini/St-249
88S-148
88T-213
88T/St-39
89F-593
89KennerFig-57
89OPC-153
89S-74
89T-433
89T/Big-104
89T/St-30
89UD-93
Hall, Andy
86Cram/NWL-198
86Macon-11
88CLAS/Star-8
88Salem/Star-7
89BuffB/CMC-10
89BuffB/ProC-1672
89Harris/Star-8
90MidldA/GS-21
Hall, Billy
90WichSt-16
92AS/Cal-39
92HighD/ClBest-7
92UD/ML-285
93B-306
93ClBest/MLG-57
94FExcel-281
94UD-175
94UD/ElecD-175
Hall, Bob
49Eureka-10
90Target-1103
Hall, Carl
90WichSt-17
Hall, Charles Louis
E90/1
M116
T207
Hall, Chris
89Bristol/Star-11
90Bristol/ProC-3155
90Bristol/Star-9
Hall, Darren
87Myrtle-4
88Dunedin/Star-8
89Dunedin/Star-6
90Knoxvl/Best-21
90Knoxvl/ProC-1244
90Knoxvl/Star-4
91AA/LineD-358
91Knoxvl/LineD-358
91Knoxvl/ProC-1762
92ProC/Tomorrow-165
92Syrac/MerchB-7
92Syrac/ProC-1961
92Syrac/SB-507
93Syrac/ProC-995
94B-85
Hall, Dave 1
63MilSau-1
Hall, Dave 2
81Cedar-26
82Cedar-19
83Tampa-14
Hall, Dean
78Newar
Hall, Drew
86Pittsfld-8
87D-594
87Iowa-2
88D/Cubs/Bk-NEW
88T-262
89B-221
89D-522
89F-643R
89OkCty/ProC-1517
89Smok/R-12
89T-593
89UD-324
90F-299
90F/Can-299
90Leaf-423
90OPC-463
90S-516
90T-463
90UD-631
91F-236
91OPC-77
91S-581
91T-77
93Rang/Keeb-168
93ScranWB/Team-11
Hall, Grady
(Gardner C.)
87BirmB/Best-14
88Vanco/CMC-8
88Vanco/ProC-761
89BirmB/Best-11
89BirmB/ProC-108
89F-650R
90AAASingl/ProC-162
90ProC/Singl-633
90Vanco/CMC-6
90Vanco/ProC-484
91AAA/LineD-632
91Vanco/LineD-632
91Vanco/ProC-1589
92Albuq/ProC-713
Hall, Greg
85Spokane/Cram-6
87CharRain-5
88River/Cal-219
88River/ProC-1415
89River/Best-26
89River/Cal-6
89River/ProC-1397
89Spokane/SP-8
Hall, Irv
44Playball-15

Hall, Jeff
80Elmira-11
Hall, Jimmie
64T-73
64T/Coins-16
64T/St-3
65T-580
66OPC-190
66T-190
66T/RO-37
66T/RO-51
67CokeCap/DodgAngel-23
67T-432
68OPC-121
68T-121
69MB-99
69OPC-61
69T-61
70T-649
78Twin/Frisz-7
92Yank/WIZ60-52
Hall, Joe
88Hamil/ProC-1747
89StPete/Star-15
90ArkTr/GS-16
90TexLgAS/GS-30
91AAA/LineD-633
91Vanco/LineD-633
91Vanco/ProC-1600
92Vanco/ProC-2730
92Vanco/SB-636
94B-651
94Flair-32
94Ultra-338
Hall, Johnny
90Target-968
Hall, Kevin
88Pocatel/ProC-2093
89Everett/Star-10
Hall, Lamar
88Idaho/ProC-1840
89Sumter/ProC-1106
Hall, Marty
86Madis/Pol-10
87Ashvl-10
Hall, Matthew
86Chatt-11
87Chatt/Best-21
Hall, Mel
82Iowa-4
83D-126
83T/Tr-39
83Thorn-27
84D-411
84F-493
84F/St-106
84Nes/792-508
84OPC-4
84T-508
84T/St-380YS
84T/Tr-47
84Wheat/Ind-34
85D-338
85F-449
85OPC-263
85Polar/Ind-27
85T-263
85T/St-254
86D-276
86F-587
86OPC-138
86OhHenry-27
86T-647
87D-473
87F-252
87F/Excit-21
87F/St-53
87Gator-27
87OPC-51
87Sf-180
87Sf/TPrev-3M
87T-51
87T/St-206
88D-342
88D/Best-173
88F-610
88Gator-27
88KennerFig-45
88Leaf-109
88OPC-318
88Panini/St-79
88S-441
88Sf-189
88T-318
88T/Big-114
88T/St-205
89D-73
89D/Tr-36
89F-406
89F/Up-49
89KennerFig-58
89OPC-173
89Panini/St-328
89RedFoley/St-55
89S-17
89S/NWest-20
89S/Tr-54
89Sf-144
89T-173
89T/Big-13
89T/Tr-44T
89UD-538
89UD/Ext-729
90B-437
90D-598
90D/BestAL-66
90F-444
90F/Can-444
90Leaf-227
90MLBPA/Pins-92
90OPC-436
90Panini/St-122
90PubliInt/St-535
90S-383
90S/NWest-7
90T-436
90T/Big-123
90T/St-313
90T/TVYank-30
90UD-458
91B-179
91Classic/III-34
91D-442
91F-665
91Leaf-283
91OPC-738
91S-166
91StCl-333
91T-738
91UD-392
91Ultra-233
92B-425
92Classic/II-T83
92D-248
92F-229
92L-88
92L/BlkGold-88
92OPC-223
92Panini-141
92Pinn-144
92S-154
92StCl-9
92T-223
92T/Gold-223
92T/GoldWin-223
92T/Kids-87
92UD-291
92Ultra-101
92Yank/WIZ80-76
93F-278
93Select-89
93T-114
93T/Gold-114
93UD-291
Hall, Richard W.
55T-126
55T/DH-57
56T-331
57T-308
60T-308
61T-197
61T/St-160
62T-189
63T-526
67T-508
68OPC-17
68T-17
70OPC-182
70T-182
71MLB/St-297
71OPC-417
71T-417
91Crown/Orio-174
Hall, Robert L.
55B-113
Hall, Robert P.
T206
Hall, Rocky
78Newar
79BurlB-6
79Holyo-24
Hall, Roy
85Greens-15
Hall, Tim
91Spokane/ClBest-26
91Spokane/ProC-3950
92CharRain/ProC-123
Hall, Todd
87Penin-24
88Tampa/Star-10
89Saraso/Star-9
90BirmB/Best-17
90BirmB/ProC-1105
90ProC/Singl-747
Hall, Tom E.
69T-658R
70OPC-169
70T-169
71MLB/St-462
71OPC-313
71T-313
72MB-124
72OPC-417
72T-417
73OPC-8
73T-8
74OPC-248
74T-248
75OPC-108
75T-108
75T/M-108
76OPC-621
76SSPC-556
76SSPC/MetsY-M3
76T-621
78Twin/Frisz-31
91WIZMets-156
Hall, William B.
(Bill)
90Target-967
Hall, William
(Bill)
59T-49
Halla, John
E254
E270/1
Hallahan, Bill
31Exh/4-16
32Orbit/num-72
32Orbit/un-29
33Exh/4-8
33G-200
34DS-23
34Exh/4-8
34G-82
35BU-121
35BU-40
77Galasso-211
87Conlon/2-15
91Conlon/Sport-214
92Card/McDon/Pac-18
92Conlon/Sport-639
93Conlon-685
R305
R313
R313A-7
R314
V355-70
WG8-28
Halland, Jon
91Belling/ClBest-4
91Belling/ProC-3674
91Penin/ProC-385
Hallas, Bob
83Madis/Frit-16
84Albany-13
Hallberg, Lance
78Wisco
80OrlanTw-8
82OrlanTw/A-11
Halle, Andrew
88BurlInd/ProC-1797
Haller, Jim 1
75Albuq/Caruso-19
Haller, Jim 2
90A&AASingle/ProC-87
90Greens/Best-7
90Greens/ProC-2653
90Greens/Star-4
91ClBest/Singl-144
91PrWill/ClBest-29
91PrWill/ProC-1418
92FtLaud/ProC-2606
92FtLaud/Team-15
Haller, Tom
62T-356
63J-108
63P-108
63T-85
64T-485
65T-465
65T/trans-16
66T-308
67OPC-65
67T-65
68CokeCap/Giant-9
68OPC-185
68T-185
69MB-100
69MLB/St-148
69OPC/DE-10
69T-310
69T/DE-23
69T/S-47
69T/St-45
69T/decal
70K-25
70MB-9
70MLB/St-51
70T-685
71MLB/St-105
71OPC-639
71T-639
72MB-125
72OPC-175
72OPC-176IA
72T-175
72T-176IA
73OPC-454
73T-454
79Pol/Giants-5
84Mother/Giants-5
86BirmB/Team-25MG
87Smok/Dodg-11
89Smok/Dodg-74
90Target-310
Hallgren, Robert
76Dubuq
77Cocoa
78Ashvl
Hallgren, Tim
80SanJose/JITB-11
86Salem-11C
Halliday, Doc
90Idaho/ProC-3264
Halliday, Troy
91Parramatta/Fut-6
Hallinan, Ed
T207
Hallion, Tom
88TM/Umpire-57
89TM/Umpire-55
90TM/Umpire-53
Hallman, William W.
(Bill)
90Target-311
E107
N172
N300/SC
T206
Halls, Gary
77BurlB
Hallstrom, Charles
N172
Hally
E254
Halter, Shane
91Eugene/ClBest-4
91Eugene/ProC-3733
92AppFox/ClBest-8
92MidwLAS/Team-15
92StCl/Dome-74
93FExcel/ML-173
94B-31
Ham, Michael
(Mike)
87Everett-17
88Clinton/ProC-709
89Phoenix/ProC-1478
89SanJose/Best-26
89SanJose/Cal-220
89SanJose/ProC-461
89SanJose/Star-12
90Shrev/ProC-1447
90Shrev/Star-9
Hambright, Roger
72OPC-124R
72T-124R
74Syrac/Team-9
92Yank/WIZ70-64
Hamel, Todd
85Clovis-20
Hamelin, Bob
88Eugene/Best-1
89BBAmAA/BPro-AA17
89Memphis/Best-1
89Memphis/ProC-1201
89Memphis/Star-12
89SLAS-9
89Star/Wax-42
90AAASingl/ProC-606
90B-379
90Omaha/CMC-24
90Omaha/ProC-71
90ProC/Singl-199
90UD-45
91AAA/LineD-336
91B-310
91Omaha/LineD-336
91Omaha/ProC-1042
92F-672
93B-617
94B-143
94D-435
94Flair-58
94L-363
94L/GRook-11
94Pinn-404
94Pinn/RookTPinn-2
94S-622
94S/Boys-44
94Select-191
94Select/RookSurg-2
94Sf/2000-152
94StCl-294
94StCl/1stDay-294
94StCl/Gold-294
94T-769
94T/Finest-110
94T/FinestRef-110
94T/Gold-769
94UD-249
94UD/ElecD-249
94Ultra-64
Hamilton, Bill
52Laval-55
Hamilton, Billy
61F-112
76Shakey-86
80Perez/HOF-86
80SSPC/HOF
89HOF/St-43
BF2-40
N172
N300/SC
Hamilton, Bob
85VeroB-1
87SanAn-18
Hamilton, Carl
86Pittsfld-9
87Iowa-1
88Peoria/Ko-13
90MidldA/GS-17
91AA/LineD-108
91CaroMud/LineD-108
91CaroMud/ProC-1081
Hamilton, Charlie
91Kissim/ProC-4205TR
Hamilton, Darryl
85Anchora-14
87Stockton-8
88Denver/CMC-24
88Denver/ProC-1274
88F/Up-U38
88S/Tr-72T
89Denver/CMC-13
89Denver/ProC-39
89F-187
89S/HotRook-44
89T-88
89UD-301
90B-397
90Brewer/MillB-10
90F-325
90F/Can-325
90Pol/Brew-24
90T/Tr-35T
91Brewer/MillB-9

91D-517
91F-585
91F/UltraUp-U30
91OPC-781
91Pol/Brew-9
91S-107
91StCl-234
91T-781
91UD-42
92B-74
92D-593
92F-177
92L-12
92L/BlkGold-12
92OPC-278
92Pinn-151
92Pol/Brew-10
92S-497
92StCl-253
92T-278
92T/Gold-278
92T/GoldWin-278
92TripleP-250
92UD-460
92Ultra-383
93B-239
93Colla/DM-48
93D-527
93F-250
93Flair-224
93L-199
93OPC-158
93Pac/Spanish-157
93Panini-41
93Pinn-144
93Pol/Brew-9
93S-118
93Select-168
93StCl-303
93StCl/1stDay-303
93Studio-40
93T-556
93T/Finest-45
93T/FinestRef-45
93T/Gold-556
93UD-192
93UD/SP-65
93Ultra-219
94B-289
94D-398
94F-177
94Flair-67
94L-281
94OPC-58
94Pac/Cr-329
94Panini-80
94Pinn-94
94Pinn/Artist-94
94Pinn/Museum-94
94Pol/Brew-9
94S-395
94Sf/2000-57
94StCl-188
94StCl/1stDay-188
94StCl/Gold-188
94Studio-43
94T-435
94T/Finest-142
94T/FinestRef-142
94T/Gold-435
94TripleP-53
94UD-326
94Ultra-74

Hamilton, Dave
73OPC-214
73T-214
74OPC-633
74T-633
75OPC-428
75T-428
75T/M-428
76OPC-237
76T-237
77OPC-224
77T-367
78T-288
79T-147
80T-86
81Tacoma-8

Hamilton, Earl
15CJ-171
92Conlon/Sport-339
D328-68
D329-75
D350/2-74
E120
E135-68
M101/4-75
M101/5-74
T207
T222
V61-68
W573

Hamilton, Jack
62T-593R
63T-132
65T-288
66T-262
67CokeCap/YMet-35
67OPC-2
67T-2
68OPC-193
68T-193
69T-629
91WIZMets-157

Hamilton, Jamie
80ElPaso-23

Hamilton, Jeff
86Albuq-10
87Albuq/Pol-19
87D-464
87Pol/Dodg-16
87T-266
88D-525
88F-515
88Mother/Dodg-19
88Panini/St-312
88Pol/Dodg-33
88T-62
89D-550
89D/Best-290
89F-60
89Mother/Dodg-19
89Pol/Dodg-3
89S-570
89T-736
89UD-615
90B-94
90D-321
90F-396
90F/Can-396
90Leaf-306
90Mother/Dodg-23
90OPC-426
90Pol/Dodg-3
90PublInt/St-7
90S-132
90S/YS/II-17
90T-426
90T/Big-98
90T/St-67
90Target-312
90UD-296
91Leaf-509
91Mother/Dodg-23
91OPC-552
91Pol/Dodg-3
91StCl-550
91T-552
91UD/Ext-779
92Albuq/ProC-726
92Albuq/SB-10
92OPC-151
92Pol/Dodg-3
92S-684
92Sky/AAASingl-4
92StCl-339
92T-151
92T/Gold-151
92T/GoldWin-151

Hamilton, Joe
92FrRow/DP-35
93StCl/MurphyS-49

Hamilton, Joey
88MissSt-9
89MissSt-16
90MissSt-15
91MissSt-20
92AS/Cal-42
92CharRain/ClBest-21
92ClBest-54
92Classic/DP-90FB
92UD-67TP
92UD/ML-39M
92UD/ML-76
94B-525
94SigRook-10
94UD/SP-5PP
94Ultra-575

Hamilton, Kenny
90GreatF/SportP-19
91Yakima/ClBest-17
91Yakima/ProC-4243
92VeroB/ClBest-5
92VeroB/ProC-2869

Hamilton, Mike
88Butte-1

Hamilton, Robert
80Water-13

Hamilton, Scott W.
86Erie-12
87Spring/Best-17
88StPete/Star-8
90Stockton/Best-19
90Stockton/Cal-180
90Stockton/ProC-2180

Hamilton, Steve
63T-171
64T-206
65T-309
66T-503
67CokeCap/YMet-15
67T-567
68T-496
69MB-101
69MLB/St-75
69OPC-69
69T-69
70MLB/St-246
70OPC-349
70T-349
71OPC-627
71T-627
72MB-126
72T-766
92Yank/WIZ60-53
92Yank/WIZ70-65
WG10-9
WG9-11

Hamilton, Z.B.
89Princet/Star-8

Hamlin, Jonas
91StPete/ClBest-21
91StPete/ProC-2284
92Savan/ClBest-12
92Savan/ProC-670

Hamlin, Ken
60T-542
61P-89
61T-263
62Salada-34A
62Salada-34B
62Shirriff-34
62T-296
66OPC-69
66T-69

Hamlin, Luke
39PlayBall-13
40PlayBall-70
41PlayBall-53
90Target-313

Hamm, Pete
71OPC-74R
71T-74R
72OPC-501
72T-501

Hamm, Stacy
91Pocatel/ProC-3796
91Pocatel/SportP-26
92CharRain/ClBest-4
92CharRain/ProC-132
92Spokane/ClBest-23
92Spokane/ProC-1306

Hamm, Tim
81Hawaii-18
82Hawaii-18

Hammagren, Tucker
(Roy)
88CapeCod/Sum-166
90Billings/ProC-3225
91CharWh/ClBest-12
91CharWh/ProC-2889
92CharWh/ClBest-7
92CharWh/ProC-10
93ClBest/MLG-186
93SALAS/II-14

Hammaker, Atlee
81Omaha-6
82T-471R
83D-298
83F-261
83F/St-15M
83F/St-20M
83Mother/Giants-13
83OPC/St-324
83T-342
83T/St-324
84D-236
84F-373
84F/St-65
84Mother/Giants-9
84Nes/792-137LL
84Nes/792-576TL
84Nes/792-85
84OPC-85
84Seven-15W
84T-137TL
84T-576TL
84T-85
84T/Gloss40-7
84T/RD-4M
84T/St-165
84T/St-175
85D-509
85F-608
85Mother/Giants-6
85OPC-351
85T-674
85T/RD-4M
85T/St-165
86D-445
86F-544
86Leaf-220
86Mother/Giants-6
86T-223
87F/Up-U40
87OPC-358
87Phoenix-24
87T-781
88D-450
88F-83
88Mother/Giants-19
88S-528
88T-157
88T/Big-259
89D-414
89F-329
89Mother/Giants-19
89OPC-2
89S-422
89T-572
89T/Big-21
89UD-544
90D-532
90F-57
90F/Can-57
90Mother/Giant-13
90OPC-447
90PublInt/St-69
90S-231
90T-447
90UD-620
91D-707
91F-530
91Leaf/Stud-246
91OPC-34
91StCl-347
91T-34
92S-233

Hamman, Ed
76Laugh/Clown-1
76Laugh/Clown-12
76Laugh/Clown-23
76Laugh/Clown-32
76Laugh/Clown-40

Hammell, Al
92GulfCM/ProC-3484

Hammer, James
(Pete)
77Wausau
79Jacks-12

Hammerschmidt, Andy
92MN-22M

Hammett, Ann
81ArkTr-23M

Hammon, Randy
78Cr/PCL-85
79Phoenix

Hammond, Allan
92Savan/ClBest-19
92Savan/ProC-657

Hammond, Arthur S.
81VeroB-6

Hammond, Chris
87Tampa-15
88BBAmer-17
88Chatt/Best-2
88SLAS-36
89Nashvl/ProC-1279
89Nashvl/Team-8
90AAAGame/ProC-51
90AAASingl/ProC-537
90F-421
90F/Can-421
90Nashvl/CMC-5
90Nashvl/ProC-225
90ProC/Singl-130
90S-629RP
90UD-52
91B-680
91D-759
91D/Rook-19
91F-65
91F/UltraUp-U76
91Kahn/Reds-45
91Leaf-373
91Leaf/Stud-165
91OPC-258
91OPC/Premier-60
91StCl-575
91T-258
91T/90Debut-62
91UD/Ext-748
92B-328
92D-172
92F-408
92L-178
92L/BlkGold-178
92OPC-744
92Pinn-335
92Reds/Kahn-45
92S-513
92S/100RisSt-89
92StCl-751
92T-744
92T/Gold-744
92T/GoldWin-744
92UD-105
92Ultra-189
93D-346
93F-35
93F/Final-61
93Flair-51
93L-475
93Marlin/Publix-11
93Pinn-449
93S-195
93Select/RookTr-104T
93StCl-209
93StCl/1stDay-209
93T-437
93T/Gold-437
93T/Tr-86T
93UD-216
93UD-661
93UD/SP-140
93USPlayC/Marlin-12C
93USPlayC/Marlin-4H
93Ultra-29
93Ultra-376
94B-150
94D-315
94F-467
94Flair-163
94L-284
94Pac/Cr-242
94Pinn-59
94Pinn/Artist-59
94Pinn/Museum-59
94S-124
94S/GoldR-124
94StCl-367
94StCl/1stDay-367
94StCl/Gold-367
94StCl/Team-64
94Studio-109
94T-189
94T/Finest-200
94T/FinestRef-200
94T/Gold-189
94TripleP-136
94UD-209
94UD/ElecD-209
94UD/SP-111
94Ultra-492

Hammond, David
90Princet/DIMD-10

Hammond, Greg
91CharWh/ClBest-13
91CharWh/ProC-2890

92CharWh/ClBest-17
92CharWh/ProC-11
Hammond, Steve
78Green
80Richm-6
81Richm-16
83F-114
83Omaha-18
84Omaha-10
86Iowa-14
Hammonds, Jeffrey
91T/Tr-51T
92B-617FOIL
92Classic/DP-4
92Classic/DPFoil-BC4
92Classic/DPPr-1
92Classic/DPPr-1
92Classic/DPPrev-BB4
92StCl/Dome-75
92T/DQ-21
92T/Tr-45T
92T/TrGold-45T
92UD/ML-3
93ClBest/MLG-166
93F/Final-159
93Flair/Wave-6
93L/UpGRook-2
93Select/RT/ASRook-6
93Select/RookTr-82T
93StCl/MurphyS-73
93UD/SP-156
94D-629
94F-5
94F/RookSen-8
94Flair-2
94L-403
94Pac/Cr-32
94Pinn-417
94Pinn/New-4
94Pinn/RookTPinn-7
94S-560
94Select-180
94Select/RookSurg-5
94Sf/2000-150
94Studio-123
94TripleP-284
94UD-210
94UD/CollC-123
94UD/CollC/Gold-123
94UD/CollC/Silv-123
94UD/ElecD-210
94UD/HoloFX-15
94UD/SP-121
94Ultra-1
94Ultra/AllRook-4
94Ultra/Second-3
Hammonds, Reggie
86Nashua-11
Hamner, Granny
49Eureka-135
49Lummis
50B-204
51B-148
51BR-B7
51T/BB-29
52B-35
52NTea
52RM-NL7
52T-221
52TipTop
53B/Col-60
53RM-NL18
53T-146
54B-47
54T-24
55B-112
55RFG-18
55RM-NL15
55W605-18
56T-197
57T-335
58Hires-20
58T-268
59T-436
79TCMA-309
91T/Arc53-146
94T/Arc54-24
PM10/Sm-66
Rawl
Hamner, Ralph
49B-212
Hampton, Anthony
86Osceola-10
Hampton, Isaac
(Ike)
75SLCity/Caruso-11
76SSPC-601
78SSPC/270-196
78T-503
91WIZMets-158
Hampton, Mark
90AubAs/Best-14
90AubAs/ProC-3401
92Gaston/ClBest-5
92Gaston/ProC-2247
Hampton, Mike
90LitSun/HSPros-20
90LitSun/HSProsG-20
91SanBern/ClBest-6
91SanBern/ProC-1982
92AS/Cal-40
92B-638
92ProC/Tomorrow-145
92SanBern/ClBest-17
92SanBern/ProC-
92UD/ML-252
93B-459
93F/Final-270
93FExcel/ML-225
93Mother/Mar-24
93OPC/Premier-80
93StCl-731
93StCl/1stDay-731
93StCl/Mar-22
93T/Tr-58T
93UD-783
93Ultra-620
94Finest-407
94Pinn-415
94StCl-237
94StCl/1stDay-237
94StCl/Gold-237
Hampton, Ray
82Evansvl-21
Hampton, Scott
89TNTech-10
Hampton, Tony
85Osceola/Team-23
Hamric, Odbert
(Bert)
55T-199
58T-336
91Crown/Orio-175
Hamric, Rusty
80Penin/B-18
80Penin/C-24
82OkCty-10
84Cram/PCL-216
Hamrick, Ray
47Remar-17
47Smith-6
48Signal
48Smith-7
49Remar
50Remar
Hamrick, Stephen
78SanJose-15
Hamza, Tony
86Geneva-8
86Peoria-10
Hance, Bill
83TriCit-13
84Tulsa-28
Hancock, Andy
80Ashvl-5
Hancock, Brian
92UD/ML-188
Hancock, Chris
89Clinton/ProC-890
89Everett/Star-11
90A&AASingle/ProC-119
90Clinton/Best-8
90Clinton/ProC-2543
90Foil/Best-113
90MidwLgAS/GS-34
92SanJose/ClBest-19
93StCl/Giant-16
Hancock, Garry
79T-702R
81F-229
82Coke/BOS
82D-608
82F-295
82T-322
84F-445
84Mother/A's-16
84Nes/792-197
84T-197
Hancock, Jeff
89Watertn/Star-9
Hancock, Lee
88Belling/Legoe-14
89SanBern/Best-16
89SanBern/Cal-71
90Foil/Best-32
90Wmsprt/Best-1
90Wmsprt/ProC-1054
90Wmsprt/Star-9
91AA/LineD-109
91CaroMud/LineD-109
91CaroMud/ProC-1082
92CaroMud/ProC-1176
92CaroMud/SB-135
93CaroMud/RBI-19
Hancock, Michael
92Stockton/ClBest-14
92Stockton/ProC-31
Hancock, Ryan
94B-619
94T-760DP
94T/Gold-760DP
94UD-523TP
Hand, James
82Tucson-23
Hand, Rich
71MLB/St-369
71OPC-24
71T-24
71T/tatt-8
72OPC-317
72T-317
73OPC-398
73T-398
74OPC-571
74T-571
93Rang/Keeb-14
Handford, Charles
C46-21
Handler, Marve
80Elmira-34
Handley, Gene
40Hughes-9
49B/PCL-34
52Mother-7
53Mother-21
Handley, Jim
76AppFx
Handley, Lee E.
40PlayBall-221
41DP-33
49B/PCL-28
93Conlon-744
Hands, William Alfred
(Bill)
66T-392R
67OPC-16
67T-16
68T-279
69MLB/St-120
69OPC-115
69T-115
69T/4in1-10M
69T/St-13
70MLB/St-16
70OPC-405
70T-405
71MLB/St-31
71OPC-670
71T-670
72MB-127
72OPC-335
72T-335
73OPC-555
73T-555
74OPC-271
74T-271
75OPC-412
75T-412
75T/M-412
76OPC-509
76SSPC-253
76T-509
78Twin/Frisz-32
93Rang/Keeb-169
Hanebrink, Harry
58T-454
59T-322
Hanel, Marcus
90Welland/Pucko-17
91Augusta/ClBest-13
91Augusta/ProC-807
92ClBest-242
92Salem/ClBest-14
92Salem/ProC-67
Haney, Chris
90James/Pucko-18
91AA/LineD-255
91B-443
91ClBest/Singl-23
91D/Rook-44
91Harris/LineD-255
91Harris/ProC-620
91UD/FinalEd-23F
92Classic/Game200-133
92Classic/I-41
92D-291
92Expo/D/Duri-2A
92F-483
92OPC-626
92OPC/Premier-186
92Pinn-521
92ProC/Tomorrow-258
92S-873
92S/100RisSt-15
92StCl-449
92T-626
92T/91Debut-70
92T/Gold-626
92T/GoldWin-626
92UD-662
92Ultra-519
93D-279
93F/Final-219
93L-538
93Pinn-194
93Pol/Royal-12
93T-581
93T/Gold-581
94D-251
94F-159
94Pac/Cr-286
94S-279
94S/GoldR-279
94StCl-154
94StCl/1stDay-154
94StCl/Gold-154
94T-9
94T/Gold-9
94Ultra-65
Haney, Fred G.
26Exh-66
27Exh-34
29Exh/4-16
47Signal
52Mother-13
54T-75MG
57SpicSpan/4x5-9MG
58T-475AS
59T-551AS
87Conlon/2-16
91T/Arc53-316MG
93Conlon-856
94T/Arc54-75
Haney, Joe
86Beloit-9
Haney, Todd
87Belling/Team-11
88Wausau/GS-14
89SanBern/Best-25
89SanBern/Cal-81
89Wmsprt/Star-8
90AAAGame/ProC-43
90AAASingl/ProC-122
90Calgary/CMC-18
90Calgary/ProC-657
90ProC/Singl-445
91AAA/LineD-185
91Indianap/LineD-185
91Indianap/ProC-468
92ProC/Tomorrow-257
93D-342
93Ottawa/ProC-2442
Haney, Wallace Larry
(Larry)
67CokeCap/Orio-17
67T-507R
68CokeCap/Orio-17
68OPC-42
68T-42
69OPC-209
69T-209
69T/4in1-7M
70T-648
73OPC-563
73T-563
75OPC-626
75T-626
75T/M-626
76OPC-446
76SSPC-502
76T-446
77T-12
78T-391
78TCMA-228
83Pol/Brew-12CO
86Pol/Brew-12CO
90Brewer/MillB-32CO
90Pol/Brew-x
91Brewer/MillB-32CO
91Crown/Orio-176
91Pol/Brew-x
92Brew/Carlson-NNO
Hanford, Charles
E254
E270/2
T205
Hanggie, Dan
84Chatt-4
85OrlanTw-6
Hanifin, Pat
90Target-970
Hanisch, Ron
89Beloit/II/Star-12
90Ashvl/ClBest-29TR
90Stockton/Best-23
90Stockton/Cal-202
Hanker, Fred
88Madis-14
Hankins, Jay
77Fritsch-25
Hankins, Mike
90Oneonta/ProC-3385
91CLAS/ProC-CAR31
91ClBest/Singl-143
91PrWill/ClBest-5
91PrWill/ProC-1434
92FtLaud/ProC-2620
92PrWill/ClBest-4
Hankinson, Frank
E223
N172
N172/ST
N284
N690/2
Hanks, Chris
89Elmira/Pucko-4
89WinHaven/Star-9
90LynchRS/Team-12
Hanley, John
79Knoxvl/TCMA-15
81AppFx-17
Hanlin, Rich
89Belling/Legoe-26
Hanlon, Edward J.
(Ned)
75F/Pion-9
90Target-314
E107
N172
N284
Scrapps
WG1-22
WG3-20
Hanlon, Lawrence
(Larry)
92CharlR/ClBest-12
92CharlR/ProC-2232
92StCl/Dome-76
Hanna, Dave
83Idaho-5
Hanna, Jim
89KS*-76
Hanna, Preston
79T-296
80T-489
81D-523
81F-264
81Pol/Atl-49
81T-594
82BK/Lids-9
82F-435
82Pol/Atl-49
83T-127
Hannah, Joe
61BeeHive-7
Hannah, Mike
75OkCty/Team-18
75SanAn

76Wmsprt
Hannah, Truck
28Exh/PCL-9
Hannahs, Gerald
(Gerry)
79Albuq-9
80Albuq-25
81Toledo-5
90Target-315
Hannahs, Mitch
88CapeCod/Sum-45
89Beloit/II/Star-13
90ElPaso/GS-16
91AA/LineD-184
91ElPaso/LineD-184
91ElPaso/ProC-2755
Hannan, Jim
63T-121
64T-261
65T-394
66T-479
67CokeCap/Senator-14
67T-291
69OPC-106
69T-106
69T/St-236
70T-697
71OPC-229
71T-229
72MB-128
Hanneman, Blair
92Everett/ClBest-5
Hannifan, John J.
T206
Hannon, John
76BurlB
77Holyo
Hannon, Phil
87WinSalem-6
88Peoria/Ko-12
89WinSalem/Star-9
90CharlK/Team-2
90T/TVCub-47
91Geneva/ClBest-29CO
91Geneva/ProC-4235CO
92Hunting/ClBest-28MG
Hanrahan, William
N172
Hansel, Damon
87Macon-18
Hansell, Greg
90WinHaven/Star-10
91Bakers/Cal-17
91CalLgAS-14
92Albuq/ProC-714
92B-314
92ClBest-344
92SanAn/SB-566
92Sky/AASingl-246
92UD/ML-150
93B-478
Hanselman, Carl
88Pocatel/ProC-2099
89Clinton/ProC-903
89Everett/Star-12
90Clinton/Best-14
90Clinton/ProC-2540
91CalLgAS-45
91SanJose/ClBest-16
91SanJose/ProC-4
92SanJose/ClBest-18
93B-84
Hansen, Andy
49Eureka-106
52T-74
53B/BW-64
Hansen, Bob
75IntLgAS/Broder-7
75OPC-508
75PCL/AS-7
75Sacra/Caruso-1
75T-508
75T/M-508
Hansen, Darel
83Idaho-6
84Madis/Pol-15
85Madis-15
85Madis/Pol-12
86Modesto-10
Hansen, Dave
87Bakers-21
88FSLAS/Star-7
88VeroB/Star-9
89SanAn/Best-17
90AAAGame/ProC-45
90AAASingl/ProC-71
90Albuq/CMC-17
90Albuq/ProC-350
90Albuq/Trib-9
90B-93
90F-642R
90F/Can-642M
90F/Up-U21
90ProC/Singl-419
91AAA/LineD-7
91Albuq/LineD-7
91Albuq/ProC-1145
91Classic/200-155
91Classic/II-T35
91D-45RR
91F-203
91T/90Debut-63
91UD-4
92Classic/Game200-103
92Classic/II-T23
92D-506
92L-389
92L/BlkGold-389
92Mother/Dodg-17
92Pol/Dodg-15
92ProC/Tomorrow-238
92S-754
92StCl-36
92Ultra-505
93D-244
93F-449
93Mother/Dodg-24
93Pac/Spanish-146
93Pinn-209
93Pol/Dodg-9
93Rem/Karros-5M
93StCl-263
93StCl/1stDay-263
93T-469
93T/Gold-469
93UD-537
94D-616
94F-511
94Pac/Cr-309
94Panini-199
94S-259
94S/GoldR-259
94T-697
94T/Gold-697
Hansen, Elston
92B-548FOIL
92ClBest-148
92FtLaud/ClBest-13
92FtLaud/Team-16
92Greens/ProC-787
93Greens/ClBest-9
93Greens/ProC-891
Hansen, Guy
83Butte-31
89Memphis/Best-26CO
89Memphis/ProC-1192CO
90Memphis/Best-25CO
90Memphis/ProC-1026CO
90Memphis/Star-26CO
91AAA/LineD-350M
91Omaha/LineD-350CO
91Omaha/ProC-1050CO
92Pol/Royal-27M
93Pol/Royal-27M
Hansen, Jon
82ElPaso-11
Hansen, Mike
87Lakeland-16
88FSLAS/Star-39
88Lakeland/Star-13
89London/ProC-1376
Hansen, Ray
86Greens-11
87Greens-17
Hansen, Roger
81CharR-6
82CharR-2
84Memphis-18
86Omaha/ProC-9
86Omaha/TCMA-5
87Chatt/Best-14
88Calgary/CMC-21
88Calgary/ProC-790
89Calgary/CMC-15
89Calgary/ProC-530
92Mother/Mar-27M
Hansen, Ron Jr.
83TriCit-17
Hansen, Ron
59T-444
60T-127
61P-72
61T-240
61T/St-102
62J-30
62P-30
62P/Can-30
62Salada-89
62Shirriff-89
62T-245
62T/St-6
63F-2
63J-60
63P-60
63T-88
64T-384
64T/Coins-41
65MacGregor-4
65OPC-146
65T-146
66T-261
67CokeCap/WSox-10
67OPC-9
67T-9
68T-411
69MB-102
69T-566
70MLB/St-184
70OPC-217
70T-217
71MLB/St-489
71OPC-419
71T-419
72MB-129
72T-763
78TCMA-142
83Pol/Brew-18C
85Expo/PostC-8CO
86Expo/Prov/Pan-28M
86Provigo-28CO
91Crown/Orio-177
92Brew/Carlson-NNO
92Yank/WIZ70-66
Hansen, Roy
(Snipe)
93Conlon-953
Hansen, Terrel
87James-10
89Rockford/Team-10
90A&AASingle/ProC-54
90Foil/Best-169
90Jaxvl/Best-9
90Jaxvl/ProC-1384
90ProC/Singl-690
91AAA/LineD-556
91Tidew/LineD-556
91Tidew/ProC-2522
92Sky/AAASingl-251
92StCl-878
92Tidew/ProC-
92Tidew/SB-557
93Ottawa/ProC-2445
Hansen, Todd
86Macon-12
88Charl/ProC-1206
89River/Best-6
89River/Cal-22
89River/ProC-1413
90Wichita/Rock-7
Hanson, Craig
91Spokane/ClBest-15
91Spokane/ProC-3945
92CharRain/ProC-118
Hanson, Erik
87Chatt/Best-10
88Calgary/ProC-786
89B-206
89Chatt/II/Team-11
89Classic-145
89D-32RR
89D/Best-320
89D/Rook-49
89F-549
89Mother/Sea-16
89T/Tr-45T
89UD/Ext-766
90B-469
90Classic/III-78
90D-345
90D/BestAL-68
90F-514
90F/Can-514
90Leaf-430
90Mother/Mar-8
90OPC-118
90PublInt/St-434
90S-530
90S/100Ris-85
90S/YS/II-18
90T-118
90T/Big-289
90UD-235
91B-260
91Classic/200-147
91Classic/II-T22
91CounHrth-24
91D-550
91F-451
91Leaf-142
91Leaf/Stud-114
91OPC-655
91Panini/FrSt-235
91Panini/St-186
91Panini/Top15-79
91S-486
91S-688KM
91Seven/3DCoin-6NW
91StCl-9
91T-655
91UD-551
91Ultra-337
92B-583
92D-138
92F-280
92L-23
92L/BlkGold-23
92Mother/Mar-7
92OPC-71
92Pinn-188
92S-8
92StCl-37
92Studio-233
92T-71
92T/Gold-71
92T/GoldWin-71
92T/Kids-124
92TripleP-20
92UD-572
92Ultra-124
93D-317
93F-308
93Flair-271
93L-354
93Mother/Mar-12
93OPC-115
93Pac/Spanish-287
93Pinn-152
93S-136
93StCl-423
93StCl/1stDay-423
93StCl/Mar-17
93T-342
93T/Finest-150
93T/FinestRef-150
93T/Gold-342
93UD-338
93UD/SP-131
93Ultra-621
94D-211
94F-287
94Finest-395
94L-426
94OPC-243
94Pinn-472
94S-387
94T-529
94T/Gold-529
94UD-508
94UD/CollC-124
94UD/CollC/Gold-124
94UD/CollC/Silv-124
94Ultra-472
Hanyuda, Tad
88SanJose/Cal-119
88SanJose/ProC-128
Hara, Hidefumi
92Salinas/ClBest-18
92Salinas/ProC-3768
Haraguchi, Ted
87SanJose-10
Hard, Shelby
90Everett/Best-23
Hardamon, Derrick
86Geneva-9
Harden, Curry
88CapeCod/Sum-67
Harden, Jon
88MissSt-10
89MissSt-17
90MissSt-16
91MissSt-21
92MissSt-16
Harden, Nat
92MissSt-17
93MissSt-17
Harden, Ty
85BurlR-21
86DayBe-10
Harder, Mel
32Orbit/num-29
32Orbit/un-30
34G-66
35BU-134
35Exh/4-11
35G-8I
35G-9I
36Exh/4-11
41DP-134
55Gol/Ind-10CO
55Salem
60T-460C
62Sugar-15
63Sugar-15
77Galasso-81
82Ohio/HOF-37
88Conlon/AmAS-14
89Pac/Leg-205
89Swell-41
94Conlon-1079
R305
R311/Gloss
R311/Leath
R312
R313
R314
WG8-29
Hardge, Michael
92Rockford/ClBest-6
92Rockford/ProC-2124
93WPalmB/ClBest-8
93WPalmB/ProC-1347
Hardgrave, Eric
86Beaum-13
87ElPaso-7
88GlenF/ProC-915
Hardgrove, Tom
88CapeCod/Sum-132
89Martins/Star-14
89Star/IISingl-144
90Foil/Best-38
90Spartan/Best-1
90Spartan/ProC-2498
90Spartan/Star-12
Hardin, Jim
68T-222
69MB-103
69T-532M
69T-610
69T/St-124
70T-656
71MLB/St-298
71OPC-491
71T-491
72MB-130
72OPC-287
72T-287
73OPC-124
73T-124
91Crown/Orio-178
92Yank/WIZ70-67
Harding, Greg
88StCath/ProC-2029
89Myrtle/ProC-1468
Harding, Warren G.
92Mega/Ruth-141M
Hardtke, Jason
91ClBest/Singl-7
91CollInd/ClBest-25
91CollInd/ProC-1492
92MidwLAS/Team-16
92ProC/Tomorrow-59
92UD/ML-98
92Watlo/ClBest-21
92Watlo/ProC-2150
94ClBest/Gold-141
94FExcel-282
Hardtke, Martin

94T-527
94T/Gold-527
Hardwick, Anthony
86Bakers-12
Hardwick, Bill
94ClBest/Gold-175
Hardwick, Joe
92Boise/ClBest-3
92Boise/ProC-3643
Hardwick, Willie
82Amari-19
83Beaum-18
84ArkTr-15
Hardy, Alex
C46-78
Hardy, Carlton
91Martins/ClBest-10
91Martins/ProC-3461
Hardy, Carroll
58T-446
59T-168
60T-341
61T-257
62Salada-220
62Shirriff-220
62T-101
63Pep
63T-468
Hardy, Howard L.
(Larry)
75Hawaii/Caruso-15
75OPC-112
75T-112
75T/M-112
76SSPC-120
78Charl
79CharCh-15
80Knoxvl/TCMA-18
80Utica-1
82Knoxvl-21
84Syrac-2
86Knoxvl-9MG
87Phoenix-11
90AAASingl/ProC-55CO
90Phoenix/CMC-26CO
90Phoenix/ProC-29CO
90ProC/Singl-688CO
91AAA/LineD-400M
91Phoenix/LineD-400CO
91Phoenix/ProC-85CO
92TX-20
Hardy, Jack
86BirmB/Team-16
87BirmB/Best-18
87Hawaii-3
88Vanco/CMC-10
88Vanco/ProC-755
89Vanco/CMC-5
89Vanco/ProC-586
90AAASingl/ProC-671
90OkCty/CMC-1
90OkCty/ProC-425
90ProC/Singl-151
90T/89Debut-51
Hardy, Mark
86James-12
Hare, Shawn
89Lakeland/Star-8
89Star/IISingl-156
90AAASingl/ProC-392
90ProC/Singl-391
90Toledo/CMC-14
90Toledo/ProC-162
91AAA/LineD-586
91Toledo/LineD-586
91Toledo/ProC-1944
92D/Rook-48
92F/Up-23
92Pinn-598
92S-828RP
92Sky/AAASingl-263
92StCl-465
92T/91Debut-71
92Toledo/SB-587
92Ultra-363
93D-305
93T-491
93T/Gold-491
Harer, Wayne
80Colum-4
81Colum-19
82Colum-3
82Colum/Pol-22

Harford, Bill
90Peoria/Team-34VP
Hargan, Steve
66T-508
67Kahn
67T-233LL
67T-440
68Kahn
68OPC-35
68T-35
68T/ActionSt-7AM
68T/G-15
69T-348
70OPC-136
70T-136
71MLB/St-370
71OPC-375
71T-375
71T/Coins-110
72MB-131
72T-615
75OPC-362
75T-362
75T/M-362
76K-1
76OPC-463
76SSPC-254
76T-463
77OPC-247
77T-37
93Rang/Keeb-170
Hargesheimer, Al
80Phoenix/NBank-13
81F-457
81Phoenix-13
81T-502R
82Phoenix
83Iowa-4
84Omaha-4
85Omaha-26
86Omaha/TCMA-20
87Omaha-13
88Omaha/CMC-6
88Omaha/ProC-1517
Hargis, Dan
89Rockford/Team-11
90James/Pucko-34
91Rockford/ProC-2050
Hargis, Gary
76Shrev
78Colum
79Portl-13
80Port-15
81Buffa-15
Hargis, Steve
91Rockford/ClBest-29
Hargrave, Eugene F.
(Bubbles)
28Exh-14
28Yueng-33
81Conlon-96
94Conlon-1179
E120
V61-60
W501-33
W572
W573
WG7-21
Hargrave, William M.
(Pinky)
26Exh-113
27Exh-57
33G-172
81Conlon-97
91Conlon/Sport-245
94Conlon-1179M
Hargraves, Charles R.
28Exh-7
29Exh/4-14
90Target-316
Hargrove, Dudley M.
(Mike)
75Ho-106
75OPC-106
75T-106
75T/M-106
76Ho-88
76K-51
76OPC-485
76SSPC-263
76T-485
77BurgChef-24
77Ho-18

77Ho/Twink-18
77K-30
77OPC-35
77Pep-5
77T-275
77T/CS-20
77T/ClothSt-20
78BK/R-11
78Ho-41
78K-56
78OPC-176
78SSPC/270-82
78T-172
79Ho-148
79OPC-311
79T-591
80OPC-162
80T-308
81D-78
81F-387
81K-66
81MSA/Disc-15
81OPC-74
81T-74
81T/SO-32
81T/St-68
82D-389
82Drake-16
82F-368
82F/St-198
82OPC-310
82T-310
82T-559TL
82T/St-180
82Wheat/Ind
83D-450
83F-409
83F/St-10M
83F/St-14M
83OPC-37
83OPC/St-56
83T-660
83T/St-56
83Wheat/Ind-16
84D-495
84F-543
84Nes/792-546TL
84Nes/792-764
84OPC-79
84Seven-10C
84T-546TL
84T-764
84T/St-260
84Wheat/Ind-21
85D-398
85F-450
85FunFood/Pin-101
85GenMills-18
85OPC-252
85Polar/Ind-21
85T-425
85T/St-248
85ThomMc/Discs-12
86D-590
86F-588
86Leaf-228
86T-136
88EastLAS/ProC-52
88Wmsprt/ProC-1306
89ColoSp/CMC-10
89ColoSp/ProC-246
91Indian/McDon-30M
91T/Tr-52TMG
92Indian/McDon-10MG
92OPC-609MG
92T-609MG
92T/Gold-609MG
92T/GoldWin-609MG
93Indian/WUAB-10MG
93Rang/Keeb-171
93T-505MG
93T/Gold-505MG
Harigen, Charlie
81Tacoma-29M
Harikkala, Tim
92Belling/ClBest-9
92Belling/ProC-1437
Harker, Paul
92Penin/ClBest-30TR
Harkey, Mike
88BBAmer-2
88EastLAS/ProC-26
88Peoria/Ko-35M
88Pittsfld/ProC-1377

88TripleA/ASCMC-15
89B-286
89D-43RR
89F-427
89Iowa/CMC-5
89Iowa/ProC-1704
89Panini/St-48
89S-624RP
89S/HotRook-48
89S/YS/II-31
89Sf-132
89T-742FS
89UD-14SR
90B-28
90Classic/III-47
90Cub/Mara-10
90D-522
90D/Rook-22
90F-33
90F/Can-33
90Leaf-309
90Peoria/Team-20M
90T/TVCub-9
90T/Tr-36T
90UD-107
91B-417
91Classic/200-22
91Cub/Mara-22
91Cub/Vine-13
91D-447
91F-423
91Leaf-90
91OPC-376
91Panini/FrSt-51
91Panini/St-46
91S-322
91S/100RisSt-63
91StCl-197
91T-376
91T/JumboR-11
91ToysRUs-10
91UD-475
91Ultra-62
92D-241
92F-382
92OPC-98
92Pinn-197
92S-67
92StCl-501
92T-98
92T/Gold-98
92T/GoldWin-98
92UD-218
92USPlayC/Cub-3S
92USPlayC/Cub-7D
93Cub/Mara-9
93D-450
93F-378
93L-533
93OPC-110
93Pinn-395
93S-111
93Select-397
93StCl-656
93StCl/1stDay-656
93StCl/Cub-14
93T-657
93T/Gold-657
93UD-610
93Ultra-314
94D-121
94F-385
94Finest-259
94Flair-154
94L-276
94Pac/Cr-100
94Pinn-171
94Pinn/Artist-171
94Pinn/Museum-171
94S-96
94S/GoldR-96
94StCl-41
94StCl/1stDay-41
94StCl/Gold-41
94StCl/Team-95
94T-272
94T/Gold-272
94UD-372
94Ultra-161
Harkins, John
N172
Harkness, Don
77Cocoa
78DaytB

Harkness, Thomas W.
(Tim)
61Union
62T-404
63T-436
64T-57
90Target-317
91WIZMets-159
Harkrider, Tim
93TX-2
94B-201
Harlan, Dan
88BBCity/Star-13
Harley, Al
90Ashvl/ClBest-14
91Ashvl/ProC-575
91ClBest/Singl-101
92BurlAs/ClBest-23
92BurlAs/ProC-555
Harley, Richard
E107
Harlow, Larry
76SSPC-397
78T-543
79T-314
80T-68
81F-289
81T-121
82F-462
82T-257
83LasVegas/BHN-9
89T/SenLg-103
91Crown/Orio-179
91Pac/SenLg-20
Harmes, Kris
90MedHat/Best-20
91Dunedin/ClBest-29
91Dunedin/ProC-210
91StCath/ClBest-4
91StCath/ProC-3397
92Dunedin/ClBest-9
92StCath/ClBest-16
92StCath/ProC-3388
93Hagers/ClBest-12
93Hagers/ProC-1881
94ClBest/Gold-89
Harmon, Charles
(Chuck)
54T-182
55T-82
55T/DH-55
56T-308
57T-299
58T-48
94T/Arc54-182
Harmon, Glen
45Parade*-24
Harmon, Kevin
86Sumter/ProC-8TR
87Sumter-12
Harmon, Mark
89SanBern/Best-28M
Harmon, Robert
10Domino-52
11Helmar-169
12Sweet/Pin-147
16FleischBrd-37
D329-76
E286
E300
M101/4-76
M116
T202
T205
T207
Harmon, Terry
69T-624R
70OPC-486
70T-486
71MLB/St-179
71OPC-682
71Phill/Arco-4
71T-682
72OPC-377
72T-377
72T/Cloth-16
73OPC-166
73T-166
74OPC-642
74T-642
75OPC-399
75T-399
75T/M-399

76OPC-247
76T-247
77T-388
78SSPC/270-37
78T-118
Harmon, Tommy
83MidldC-2
92TX-21
Harmon, Wayne
83Cedar-28
83Cedar/Frit-6TR
Harms, Tom
88Hagers/Star-8
89Freder/Star-9
Harnisch, Pete
88BBAmer-11
88CharlK/Pep-18
88RochR/Gov-10
88SLAS-32
89B-4
89D-44RR
89French-42
89RochR/ProC-1649
89S/Tr-110
89UD/Ext-744
90B-247
90Classic-44
90D-596
90D/BestAL-101
90F-177
90F/Can-177
90Leaf-39
90OPC-324
90S-355
90S/100Ris-76
90S/YS/II-19
90T-324
90T/JumboR-12
90ToysRUs-14
90UD-623
91B-555
91Crown/Orio-180
91D-181
91F-474
91F/UltraUp-U83
91F/Up-U89
91Leaf-245
91Leaf/Stud-177
91Mother/Ast-3
91OPC-179
91RedFoley/St-45
91S-492
91S/RookTr-36T
91StCl-343
91StCl/Member*-17
91T-179
91T/Tr-53T
91UD-302
91UD/Ext-772
91USPlayC/AS-3S
92B-514
92Classic/Game200-4
92Classic/II-T9
92D-235
92F-435
92L-77
92L/BlkGold-77
92Mother/Ast-3
92OPC-765
92Panini-159
92Pinn-196
92Pinn/Team2000-67
92S-224
92S/100SS-12
92StCl-391
92StCl/Dome-77
92Studio-36
92T-765
92T/Gold-765
92T/GoldWin-765
92TripleP-175
92UD-635
92UD/TmMVPHolo-25
92USPlayC/Ace-8S
92Ultra-204
93B-448
93D-272
93F-52
93Flair-64
93L-51
93Mother/Ast-3
93OPC-185
93Pac/Spanish-124
93Panini-168
93Pinn-113
93S-395
93Select-219
93StCl-110
93StCl/1stDay-110
93StCl/Ast-19
93T-195
93T/Finest-62
93T/FinestRef-62
93T/Gold-195
93T/Hill-21
93TripleP-241
93UD-97
93UD/SP-35
93Ultra-42
94B-286
94D-113
94F-492
94F/Smoke-4
94Flair-171
94L-398
94OPC-73
94Pac/Cr-267
94Pinn-45
94Pinn/Artist-45
94Pinn/Museum-45
94S-78
94S/GoldR-78
94Sf/2000-113
94StCl-190
94StCl/1stDay-190
94StCl/Gold-190
94T-456
94T/Finest-120
94T/FinestRef-120
94T/Gold-456
94TripleP-28
94UD-379
94Ultra-504
Harnisch, Ron
92Ashvl/ClBest-30CL
Haro, Sam
84PrWill-22
85Nashua-11
86Hawaii-11
87Vanco-10
Harper, Brian
80ElPaso-9
81SLCity-15
84D-142
84Nes/792-144
84T-144
85D-566
85F-466
85T-332
86D-547
86F-36
86KAS/Disc-8
86Nashvl-10
86T-656
88F/Up-U42
88Martins/Star-16
88Portl/CMC-11
88Portl/ProC-651
89B-155
89D-641
89F-114
89S-408
89T-472
89UD-379
90D-355
90D/BestAL-37
90ElPasoATG/Team-35
90F-377
90F/Can-377
90Leaf-479
90OPC-47
90Panini/St-116
90PublInt/St-329
90S-189
90Sf-121
90T-47
90T/St-290
90UD-391
91B-333
91Classic/III-35
91D-22DK
91D-398MVP
91D-582
91D/SuperDK-22DK
91F-613
91Leaf-54
91Leaf/Stud-86
91OPC-554
91Panini/FrSt-299
91Panini/St-242
91S-312
91S/100SS-46
91StCl-589
91T-554
91UD-212
91Ultra-188
92B-149
92D-83
92F-204
92L-131
92L/BlkGold-131
92OPC-217
92Panini-114
92Pinn-73
92S-215
92S/Factory-B4M
92StCl-296
92Studio-204
92T-217
92T/Gold-217
92T/GoldWin-217
92TripleP-76
92UD-527
92USPlayC/Twin-10S
92USPlayC/Twin-1D
92Ultra-91
93B-537
93Colla/ASG-21
93D-547
93F-266
93F/ASAL-10
93Flair-235
93L-186
93OPC-125
93Pac/Spanish-520
93Panini-124
93Pinn-54
93S-72
93Select-154
93StCl-95
93StCl/1stDay-95
93Studio-27
93T-389
93T-408M
93T/BlkGold-34
93T/Finest-51
93T/FinestRef-51
93T/Gold-389
93T/Gold-408M
93TripleP-250
93TripleP-68M
93UD-110
93UD/SP-246
93Ultra-582
94B-645
94D-196
94D/DK-6
94F-206
94Finest-247
94L-290
94OPC-102
94Pac/Cr-354
94Panini-90
94Pinn-494
94Pol/Brew-10
94S-37
94S/GoldR-37
94S/GoldS-55
94Studio-44
94T-706
94T/Gold-706
94TripleP/Medal-1M
94UD-441
94UD/SP-58
94Ultra-371
Harper, Charles W.
E107
Harper, David
77Tucson
78Cr/PCL-28
Harper, Devallon
83Kinston/Team-7
Harper, George W.
21Exh-68
25Exh-41
26Exh-43
27Exh-18
29Exh/4-2
91Conlon/Sport-246
E121/120
W501-107
W513-85
Harper, Greg
88Idaho/ProC-1847
88Sumter/ProC-401
89Sumter/ProC-1117
90BurlB/Best-22
90BurlB/Star-14
Harper, Harry C.
90Target-318
D327
D328-69
E135-69
W575
Harper, Jon
77Cedar
Harper, Marshal
76AppFx
77AppFx
Harper, Milt
86Water-12
87Kinston-22
88Wmsprt/ProC-1327
90Reno/Cal-275
Harper, Terry Joe
(Terry)
79Richm-14
80Richm-17
81Pol/Atl-19
81T-192R
82BK/Lids-10
82Richm-24
82T-507
83D-607
83F-137
83Pol/Atl-19
83T-339
84F-180
84Nes/792-624
84Pol/Atl-19
84T-624
85F-327
85Pol/Atl-19
85T/Tr-45T
86D-627
86F-516
86Leaf-246
86OPC-247
86Pol/Atl-19
86T-247
86T/St-41
87D/OD-217
87F-517
87F/Excit-22
87T-49
87T/Tr-42T
88F-331
90Greenvl/ProC-1145CO
90Greenvl/Star-24CO
91AA/LineD-225M
91Greenvl/ClBest-27CO
91Greenvl/LineD-225CO
91Greenvl/ProC-3019CO
Harper, Terry
82Redwd-22
83Redwd-12
Harper, Tommy
63FrBauer-7
63T-158R
64Kahn
64T-330
64T/Coins-40
64T/St-43
65Kahn
65OPC-47
65T-47
66Kahn
66T-214
67CokeCap/Reds-4
67Kahn
67T-392
68T-590
69MB-104
69MLB/St-95
69OPC-42
69Sunoco/Pin-10
69T-42
69T/St-225
70K-74
70MLB/St-270
70McDon-5
70OPC-370
70T-370
70T/CB
70T/S-9
70T/Super-9
71Bz
71Bz/Test-30
71K-47
71MD
71MLB/St-437
71OPC-260
71T-260
71T/Coins-140
71T/GM-42
71T/Greatest-42
71T/S-63
71T/Super-63
71T/tatt-2
72MB-132
72OPC-455
72T-455
73OPC-620
73T-620
74Greyhound-5M
74OPC-204LL
74OPC-325
74T-204LL
74T-325
74T/St-134
75OPC-537
75T-537
75T/M-537
76OPC-274
76T-274
77T-414
81TCMA-399
91Crown/Orio-181
Harrah, Doug
92Salem/ClBest-6
92Salem/ProC-57
93CaroMud/RBI-10
Harrah, Toby
71Pol/SenP-5
72OPC-104
72T-104
73OPC-216
73T-216
74OPC-511
74T-511
74T/St-235
75Ho-14
75Ho/Twink-14
75OPC-131
75T-131
75T/M-131
76Ho-48
76Ho/Twink-48
76OPC-412
76SSPC-264
76T-412
77BurgChef-26
77Ho-37
77Ho/Twink-37
77OPC-208
77T-301
78BK/R-13
78Ho-123
78OPC-74
78SSPC/270-89
78T-44
79Ho-150
79OPC-119
79T-234
80OPC-333
80T-636
81D-318
81F-389
81OPC-67
81T-721
81T/SO-46
81T/St-65
82D-72
82F-369
82F/St-193
82OPC-16
82T-532
82T/St-177
82Wheat/Ind
83D-13DK
83D-337
83D/AAS-39
83F-410
83F-635M
83F/St-16M
83F/St-1M
83K-44
83OPC-356
83OPC/St-58

83PermaGr/CC-25
83T-141TL
83T-480
83T/Gloss40-13
83T/St-58
83Wheat/Ind-17
84D-251
84F-544
84F/X-48
84Nes/792-348
84OPC-348
84T-348
84T/RD-23
84T/St-251
84T/Tr-48
85F-130
85F/Up-U49
85Rang-11
85T-94
85T/Tr-46T
86D-159
86F-560
86Leaf-86
86OPC-72
86Rang-11
86T-535
86T/Mini-32
86T/St-238
86T/Tatt-19M
87D-408
87F-125
87OKCty-12
87T-152
88AAA/ProC-51
88OkCty/CMC-25
88OkCty/ProC-46
89Pac/SenLg-162
89Smok/R-13
89T/SenLg-58
89TM/SenLg-44
90EliteSenLg-22
90Mother/Rang-27M
91LineD-10
91Mother/Rang-28CO
91Swell/Great-37
92Mother/Rang-28M
92Yank/WIZ80-77
93Rang/Keeb-15
93Rang/Keeb-172
93UD/ATH-62

Harrel, Donny
90Eugene/GS-12
91AppFx/ClBest-12
91AppFx/ProC-1718

Harrell, Bill
58T-443
59T-433
61T-354
63MilSau-2

Harrell, Greg
87PortChar-13
88Tulsa-27TR
89Tulsa/GS-4
89Tulsa/Team-9TR
90TexLgAS/GS-38TR
90Tulsa/Team-9TR
91Tulsa/Team-10

Harrell, John
70OPC-401R
70T-401R

Harrell, Matt
93James/ClBest-9
93James/ProC-3329

Harrell, Ray
93Conlon-960

Harrelson, Bill
69T-224R

Harrelson, Derrel M.
(Bud)
67T-306
68OPC-132
68T-132
69MB-105
69MLB/St-166
69MLBPA/Pin-45
69T-456
69T/St-64
70K-68
70MLB/St-77
70T-634
70Trans/M-25
71K-66
71MD
71MLB/St-155
71OPC-355
71T-355
71T/Coins-67
71T/GM-55
71T/Greatest-55SS
71T/tatt-13
72MB-133
72OPC-496KP
72OPC-53
72OPC-54IA
72T-496KP
72T-53
72T-54IA
72T/Post-22
73OPC-223
73T-223
73T/Lids-20
74OPC-380
74T-380
74T/St-63
75Ho-45
75OPC-395
75SSPC/42-16
75T-395
75T/M-395
76Ho-52
76Ho/Twink-52
76OPC-337
76SSPC-545
76T-337
77BurgChef-144
77OPC-172
77T-44
78T-403
79T-118
80OPC-294
80T-566
81T-694
81TCMA-425
84LitFalls-13
88Kahn/Mets-3CO
89Kahn/Mets-3CO
90Kahn/Mets-3CO
90Swell/Great-111
90T/TVMets-4MG
90T/Tr-37TMG
91Kahn/Mets-3MG
91OPC-261MG
91Swell/Great-38
91T-261MG
91WIZMets-160
92AP/ASG-58
93Rang/Keeb-173
93TWill-56
93UD/ATH-63
94Mets/69-6

Harrelson, Ken
64T-419
65T-479
66OPC-55
66T-55
66T/RO-107
66T/RO-38
67CokeCap/Senator-17
67OPC-188
67T-188
68T-566
68T/ActionSt-10CM
69MB-106
69MLB/St-13
69MLBPA/Pin-8
69OPC-3LL
69OPC-5LL
69OPC/DE-8
69T-240
69T-3LL
69T-417AS
69T-5LL
69T/DE-3
69T/S-4
69T/St-134
70K-68
70MLB/St-198
70OPC-545
70T-545
70T/PI-6
71Bz/Test-15
71MLB/St-371
71OPC-510
71T-510
71T/Coins-134
72MB-134
78TCMA-247
86Coke/WS-xx
88Pac/Leg-14

Harridge, Will
56T-1PRES
57T-100M
58T-300M
76Shakey-130PRES
80Perez/HOF-130
80SSPC/HOF

Harriger, Dennis
89Pittsfld/Star-6
90StLucie/Star-9
91StLucie/ClBest-21
92StLucie/ClBest-8
92StLucie/ProC-1741

Harring, Ken Jr.
89Idaho/ProC-2014
90Durham/Team-5

Harrington, Jody
89Elizab/Star-10
90Kenosha/Best-19
90Kenosha/ProC-2288
90Kenosha/Star-6

Harrington, John
86Miami-8
87Miami-20

Harris, Adoldo
90Tampa/DIMD-10

Harris, Alonzo
(Candy)
67T-564R
68OPC-128R
68T-128R

Harris, Anthony S.
(Spence)
E120
E220

Harris, B. Gail
56T-91
57T-281
58T-309
59T-378
60T-152
79TCMA-275

Harris, Carry
83Knoxvl-10

Harris, Craig
80WHave-11

Harris, Dannie
90Foil/Best-126
90Huntsvl/Best-7

Harris, David Stanley
25Exh-7
33G-9
R337-412
V353-9

Harris, Donald
89Butte/SP-4
90B-499
90OPC-314FDP
90ProC/Singl-793
90S-661DC
90T-314FDP
90Tulsa/ProC-1167
90Tulsa/Team-10
91AA/LineD-583
91B-269
91ClBest/Singl-12
91Tulsa/LineD-583
91Tulsa/ProC-2785
91Tulsa/Team-11
92B-332
92ClBest-287
92D-652
92F-660
92OPC-554
92Pinn-597
92Pinn/Rookl-16
92ProC/Tomorrow-155
92Sky/AASingl-268
92StCl-691
92T-554
92T/91Debut-72
92T/Gold-554
92T/GoldWin-554
92Tulsa/SB-608
92UD-11SR
92Ultra-443
93D-291
93Rang/Keeb-174
93S-254
93S/Boys-21
93Select-341
93StCl-318
93StCl/1stDay-318
93StCl/Rang-7
93T-731
93T/Gold-731
94D-133
94StCl/Team-249

Harris, Doug
90Eugene/GS-13
91AppFx/ClBest-4
91AppFx/ProC-1710
92BBCity/ProC-3840

Harris, Doyle
81Louisvl-29
83Louisvl/Riley-29
84Louisvl-7

Harris, Elander Victor
(Vic)
87Negro/Dixon-2
94TedW-107

Harris, Eric
92Kingspt/ClBest-8
92Kingspt/ProC-1534

Harris, Frank
77Evansvl/TCMA-14
80Ogden-12
82Madis/Frit-18CO
89Clmbia/Best-26
89Medford/Best-3

Harris, G.G.
93Welland/ClBest-6
93Welland/ProC-3364

Harris, Gary
90AR-14

Harris, Gene
86James-13
87WPalmB-26
88Jaxvl/Best-5
88Jaxvl/ProC-980
89D/Best-325
89F/Up-58
89T/Tr-46T
90D-247
90F-515
90F/Can-515
90Leaf-378
90Mother/Mar-15
90OPC-738
90S-548
90S/100Ris-54
90T-738
90T/89Debut-52
90UD-565
91D-651
91F-452
91OPC-203
91S-627
91T-203
92OPC-390
92Smok/Padre-10
92StCl-425
93D-494
93F/Final-141
93Flair-134
93L-517
93Mother/Padre-18
93Pac/Spanish-597
93T/Tr-64T
93UD-657
93UD/SP-168
94D-468
94F-666
94Finest-340
94L-407
94Pac/Cr-526
94Pinn-363
94S-138
94S/GoldR-138
94Select-125
94StCl-325
94StCl/1stDay-325
94StCl/Gold-325
94T-514
94T/Gold-514
94TripleP-168
94UD-307
94UD/CollC-125
94UD/CollC/Gold-125
94UD/CollC/Silv-125
94Ultra-576

Harris, Glenn
84Savan-18

Harris, Greg A.
79Jacks-21
80Tidew-11
81Tidew-23
82Coke/Reds
82Indianap-13
82T-783
82T/Tr-41T
83D-295
83F-590
83Indianap-6
83T-296
84Expo/PostC-12
84Stuart-22
85F-35
85Rang-27
85T-242
85T/Tr-47T
86D-465
86F-561
86OPC-128
86Rang-27
86T-586
86T/St-245
87D-382
87F-126
87F/St-54
87Leaf-82
87Mother/Rang-11
87OPC-44
87Sf-126
87Sf/TPrev-1M
87Smok/R-2
87T-44
87T/St-238
88AlaskaAS70/Team-15
88D-427
88F-468
88F/Up-U109
88Phill/TastyK-34
88S-179
88T-369
89D-548
89F-570
89Phill/TastyK-8
89S-476
89T-627
90D-582
90F/Up-U71
90Leaf-499
90OPC-529
90PublInt/St-237
90T-529
90T/TVRSox-11
91D-306
91F-97
91Leaf-83
91OPC-123
91Pep/RSox-9
91S-109
91StCl-324
91T-123
91UD-509
91WIZMets-161
92D-113
92L-154
92L/BlkGold-154
92OPC-468
92RedSox/Dunkin-15
92S-156
92StCl-49
92Studio-133
92T-468
92T/Gold-468
92T/GoldWin-468
92UD-658
92USPlayC/RedSox-13H
92USPlayC/RedSox-5C
93D-663
93F-560
93Flair-165
93L-131
93Pac/Spanish-359
93Rang/Keeb-175
93S-640
93StCl-315
93StCl/1stDay-315
93UD-414
93Ultra-511
94D-512
94F-34
94Pinn-476
94S-272
94S/GoldR-272
94StCl-407
94StCl/1stDay-407
94StCl/Gold-407
94T-18

94T-738
94T/Gold-18
94T/Gold-738
94Ultra-15
Harris, Greg W.
85Spokane/Cram-7
86Cram/NWL-161
87TexLgAS-23
87Wichita-11
88AAA/ProC-23
88LasVegas/CMC-3
88LasVegas/ProC-227
88Wichita-19
89D-34
89D/Rook-46
89F-306
89Padre/Mag-18
89S/Tr-87
89T-194
89UD/Ext-724
89Wichita/Rock-19
90Classic/III-13
90Coke/Padre-7
90D-65
90F-158
90F/Can-158
90Leaf-452
90OPC-572
90Padre/MagUno-24
90Panini/St-353
90S-257
90S/100Ris-24
90S/YS/I-18
90T-572
90T/JumboR-13
90UD-622
91B-657
91D-131
91F-531
91Leaf-422
91OPC-749
91Padre/MagRal-13
91S-251
91StCl-205
91T-749
91UD-489
91Ultra-304
91Ultra-33
92B-269
92D-49
92F-606
92L-10
92L/BlkGold-10
92Mother/Padre-2
92OPC-636
92Padre/Carl-8
92Pinn-169
92Pol/Padre-9
92S-378
92Smok/Padre-11
92StCl-275
92Studio-105
92T-636
92T/Gold-636
92T/GoldWin-636
92TripleP-157
92UD-306
92Ultra-278
93D-154
93F-139
93L-82
93Mother/Padre-5
93Pac/Spanish-258
93S-599
93StCl-312
93StCl/1stDay-312
93T-436
93T-78
93T/Gold-436
93T/Gold-78
93UD-724
93Ultra-117
94D-193
94F-442
94L-416
94Pinn-470
94S-374
94StCl/Team-99
94UD-194
94UD/CollC-126
94UD/CollC/Gold-126
94UD/CollC/Silv-126
94UD/ElecD-194
94Ultra-481

Harris, Greg
94Finest-303
94Finest-372
Harris, Gregg S.
86CharRain-10
87CharRain-3
Harris, James William
(Billy)
69T-569
70OPC-512
70T-512
Harris, James
89Kingspt/Star-12
89Star/IISingl-172
90Clmbia/PCPII-5
90Columbia/GS-7
90SALAS/Star-32
90Star/ISingl-99
91StLucie/ClBest-8
91StLucie/ProC-717
92StLucie/ClBest-6
92StLucie/ProC-1751
Harris, Joe
28Yueng-51
90Target-319
94Conlon-1241
E120
W502-51
W513-81
W572
Harris, John 1
77QuadC
79SLCity-16
80SLCity-12
81T-214R
82D-444
82F-463
82Spokane-16
82T-313
83Indianap-29
84Evansvl-15
Harris, John 2
92GulfCM/ProC-3472
Harris, Keith
89Utica/Pucko-10
Harris, Larry
81Wisco-5
Harris, Lenny
84Cedar-25
86Vermont-9
87Nashvl-9
88Nashvl/CMC-12
88Nashvl/ProC-489
88Nashvl/Team-12
89F-645R
89Kahn/Reds-7
89UD/Ext-781
90CedarDG/Best-3
90D-434
90F-397
90F/Can-397
90Leaf-437
90Mother/Dodg-18
90OPC-277
90Pol/Dodg-29
90PublInt/St-31
90S-23
90S/100Ris-83
90S/YS/I-37
90T-277
90Target-320
90UD-423
91B-607
91D-224
91F-204
91Mother/Dodg-18
91OPC-453
91Panini/FrSt-57
91Panini/St-51
91Pol/Dodg-29
91S-144
91StCl-65
91T-453
91UD-239
91Ultra-162
92D-226
92F-458
92L-213
92L/BlkGold-213
92Mother/Dodg-5
92OPC-92
92Panini-194
92Pinn-57

92Pol/Dodg-29
92S-291
92StCl-121
92T-92
92T/Gold-92
92T/GoldWin-92
92UD-191
92Ultra-211
93D-590
93F-61
93L-127
93Mother/Dodg-13
93Pac/Spanish-147
93Panini-220
93Pinn-119
93Pol/Dodg-10
93S-546
93Select-384
93StCl-98
93StCl/1stDay-98
93StCl/Dodg-13
93T-177
93T/Gold-177
93UD-184
93Ultra-54
94S-152
94S/GoldR-152
Harris, Luman
43Playball-21
60T-455CO
65OPC-274MG
65T-274MG
66OPC-147MG
66T-147MG
68T-439MG
69OPC-196MG
69T-196MG
69T/4in1-6M
70OPC-86MG
70T-86MG
71OPC-346MG
71T-346MG
72OPC-484MG
72T-484MG
Harris, Mark 1
(Infielder)
79WHave-26
Harris, Mark 2
90LitSun-19
Harris, Maurice
(Mickey)
47TipTop
48L-27
49B-151
50B-160
51B-311
52B-135
52T-207
Harris, Michael
92Stockton/ProC-48
Harris, Mike
82Spring/Frit-19
83ArkTr-13
84ArkTr-26
86BirmB/Team-10
Harris, Moon
81Conlon-66
Harris, Pep
91BurlInd/ProC-3296
91LitSun/HSPros-18M
91LitSun/HSPros-26
91LitSun/HSProsG-18M
91LitSun/HSProsG-26
92ColRS/ClBest-15
92ColRS/ProC-2384
Harris, Rafael
80Utica-6
Harris, Ray
88SoOreg/ProC-1713
Harris, Reggie
87Elmira/Cain-1
87Elmira/Red-30
88Lynch/Star-9
89WinHaven/Star-10
90B-446
91Classic/I-71
91D-704
91OPC-177
91S-643RP
91S/100RisSt-49
91T-177
91T/90Debut-64
91Tacoma/ProC-2300
91UD-672

92D-781
92S/100RisSt-48
92Sky/AAASingl-239
92StCl-158
92Tacoma/ProC-2497
92Tacoma/SB-535
Harris, Robbie
85Clovis-21
Harris, Robert A.
W753
Harris, Robert
87Watertn-3
88Augusta/ProC-386
90Harris/ProC-1205
90Harris/Star-9
92BirmB/ProC-2594
92BirmB/SB-83
Harris, Rusty
87AubAs-2
88Osceola/Star-12
89Osceola/Star-7
90ColMud/Best-7
90ColMud/ProC-1353
90ColMud/Star-12
91AA/LineD-559
91Jacks/LineD-559
91Jacks/ProC-931
92Jacks/ProC-4004
92Jacks/SB-333
Harris, Sam
21Exh-69
Harris, Sheriff
81Conlon-67
Harris, Stanley
(Bucky)
25Exh-124
26Exh-124
28Exh-62
28Yueng-41
34DS-91
36G
40PlayBall-129
51B-275MG
52B-158MG
53B/BW-46
76Rowe-10M
76Shakey-148
77Galasso-132
80Perez/HOF-148
80SSPC/HOF
81Conlon-68
81Tiger/Detroit-105MG
86Conlon/1-25
91Conlon/Sport-61
91T/Arc53-313MG
92Conlon/Sport-593
92Yank/WIZHOF-15
93Conlon-845MG
E120
E210-41
E220
R310
R312/M
R313
R314
V100
V117-21
V355-130
V94-23
W502-14
W517-9
W572
Harris, Steve
85Bend/Cram-10
Harris, Tony
91Adelaide/Fut-3
Harris, Tracy
80SanJose/JITB-10
81LynnS-5
82SLCity-10
83Chatt-17
Harris, Twayne
83Idaho-21
85Modesto/Chong-4
86Modesto-11
Harris, Vic
73OPC-594
73T-594
74OPC-157
74T-157
74T/St-13
75OPC-658
75T-658
75T/M-658

76SSPC-321
77Phoenix
78T-436
79T-338
79Vanco-2
80Vanco-21
84Louisvl-18
93Rang/Keeb-16
Harris, Vince
88Utica/Pucko-6
89CharRain/ProC-976
90AS/Cal-5
90Foil/Best-315
90ProC/Singl-718
90River/Best-9
90River/Cal-12
90River/ProC-2619
91AA/LineD-607
91Wichita/LineD-607
91Wichita/ProC-2610
91Wichita/Rock-20
92Sky/AASingl-281
92Wichita/ProC-3666
92Wichita/SB-633
Harris, Walt
88Hagers/Star-9
89RochR/CMC-19
89RochR/ProC-1651
90Hagers/Star-10
Harris, Walter
(Buddy)
71OPC-404R
71T-404R
Harris, William 1
(Bill)
60DF-18
60T-128
90Target-971
Harris, William 2
V100
Harris, Wilmer
92Negro/RetortII-15
Harrison, Brett
87StPete-7
88ArkTr/GS-13
88TexLgAS/GS-13
Harrison, Brian Lee
86Cram/NWL-164
87CharRain-8
88River/Cal-210
88River/ProC-1428
89River/Best-7
89River/Cal-17
89River/ProC-1410
90A&AASingle/ProC-133
90Foil/Best-27
90River/Best-10
90River/Cal-17
90River/ProC-2601
Harrison, Charles
(Chuck)
66T-244R
67OPC-8
67T-8
68CokeCap/Astro-6
69OPC-116
69T-116
69T/4in1-10M
Harrison, Craig
89SanDiegoSt/Smok-11
Harrison, Doug
78Clinton
80Albuq-9
Harrison, Keith
86Cram/NWL-173
86Elmira-9
87CharRain-22
88Charl/ProC-1207
Harrison, Mack
79Ogden/TCMA-7
Harrison, Mathew
(Matt)
86FSLAS-20
86FtLaud-11
87Albany-13
88Colum/CMC-5
88Colum/Pol-3
88Colum/ProC-317
90AlbanyDG/Best-8
Harrison, Mike
91Billing/SportP-21
91Billings/ProC-3756
92CharWh/ClBest-8
92CharWh/ProC-12

92StCl/Dome-78
Harrison, Pat
89Alaska/Team-7
Harrison, Phil
86Geneva-10
87Peoria-23
88CLAS/Star-28
88WinSalem/Star-5
89CharlK-21
90T/TVCub-48
Harrison, R.J.
80LynnS-19
81LynnS-6
82Wausau/Frit-17MG
83Wausau/Frit-30MG
86Chatt-12MG
Harrison, Robert 1
77StPete
Harrison, Robert 2
89Johnson/Star-26TR
90Hamil/Star-28TR
Harrison, Robert Lee
(Bob)
79TCMA-76
91Crown/Orio-182
Harrison, Ron
82Madis/Frit-21
83Albany-18
87Beloit-16
87Denver-8
Harrison, Roric E.
72OPC-474R
72T-474R
73OPC-229
73T-229
74OPC-298
74T-298
74T/St-5
75OPC-287
75T-287
75T/M-287
76OPC-547
76SSPC-507
76T-547
77Evansvl/TCMA-15
78T-536
91Crown/Orio-183
Harrison, Scott
92James/ClBest-20
92James/ProC-1496
93James/ClBest-10
93James/ProC-3320
Harrison, Wayne
85Durham-25
86Durham-13
Harriss, Bryan
(Slim)
28Exh-34
E126-46
V61-38
Harriss, William
(Slim)
21Exh-70
E120
W573
Harrist, Earl
50Remar
52T-402
53T-65
91T/Arc53-65
Harry, Whitney
82BurlR/Frit-24
82BurlR/TCMA-22
83BurlR-18
83BurlR/Frit-15
84Tulsa-20
Harryman, Jeff
77Newar
78BurlB
Harsh, Nick
82FtMyr-7
Harshman, Jack
54T-173
55RM-AL6
55T-104
55T/DH-66
56T-29
56T/Pin-33
57T-152
58T-217
59T-475
60T-112
79TCMA-33
91Crown/Orio-184
94T/Arc54-173
Hart, Bob
94Conlon-1195UMP
Hart, Brian
89Burllnd/Star-12
Hart, Chris
85Miami-6
90SoOreg/Best-18
90SoOreg/ProC-3431
91Modesto/ProC-3103
91SoOreg/ProC-3861
92Modesto/ClBest-5
Hart, Darrin
89Watlo/Star-10
89Watlo/Star-29
Hart, James Henry
T206
T213/brown
Hart, James M.
79Tucson-17
80CharCh-10
81RochR-7
83Colum-24
88CLAS/Star-2
89Reading/ProC-658
90FtLaud/Star-23MG
91CLAS/ProC-CAR32MG
91PrWill/ClBest-24
91PrWill/ProC-1442MG
Hart, Jeff
89CharRain/ProC-987
89Watlo/ProC-1781
90ProC/Singl-703
90Waterlo/Best-6
90Waterlo/ProC-2373
Hart, Jim Ray
64T-452R
65OPC-4LL
65T-395
65T-4LL
65T/E-4
66T-295
66T/RO-28
66T/RO-39
67CokeCap/Giant-6
67T-220
68CokeCap/Giant-6
68Dexter-37
68OPC-73
68T-73
69MB-107
69MLB/St-199
69MLBPA/Pin-46
69T-555
69T/St-104
70MLB/St-124
70OPC-176
70T-176
71MLB/St-249
71OPC-461
71T-461
72MB-135
72T-733
73OPC-538
73T-538
74OPC-159
74T-159
78TCMA-269
84Mother/Giants-20
92Yank/WIZ70-68
PM10/Sm-67
Hart, John
85CharlO-14
86RochR-6MG
87RochR-3
87RochR/TCMA-24
88French-47CO
90OPC-141MG
90T-141MG
Hart, Kim
82Iowa-31
83Iowa-28
Hart, Michael Lawrence
(Mike)
80LynnS-7
81Spokane-7
82SLCity-11
83Toledo-20
85IntLgAS-30
85Toledo-21
86RochR-7
87RochR-10
87RochR/TCMA-18
88T-69
91Crown/Orio-185
92PrWill/ClBest-26MG
92PrWill/ProC-164MG
93Rang/Keeb-176
Hart, Shelby
90Everett/ProC-3139
91Clinton/ClBest-17
91Clinton/ProC-846
92Everett/ClBest-11
92Everett/ProC-1696
Hart, William F.
90Target-321
N172
N284
N526
T206
T213/brown
Hart, William W.
46Remar-6
47Smith-15
90Target-972
Hartas, Peter
91Daikyo/Fut-13
Hartenstein, Chuck
68OPC-13
68T-13
69T-596
70OPC-216
70T-216
75IntLgAS/Broder-8
75PCL/AS-8
77OPC-157
77T-416
80Hawaii-11
81Hawaii-24
81Hawaii/TCMA-22
82Hawaii-24
84Cram/PCL-134CO
86Penin-11CO
92TX-22
Harter, Andy
88Ashvl/ProC-1052
Hartgraves, Dean
87AubAs-24
88Ashvl/ProC-1072
89Ashvl/ProC-960
90ColMud/Best-6
90ColMud/ProC-1343
90ColMud/Star-13
91AA/LineD-560
91Jacks/LineD-560
91Jacks/ProC-921
92Jacks/ProC-3995
92Tucson/SB-609
Hartje, Chris
90Target-973
Hartley, Grover
11Helmar-128
92Conlon/Sport-520
D328-70
E135-70
T207
W753
Hartley, Michael
(Mike)
83StPete-7
85Spring-13
87Bakers-1
88Albuq/CMC-9
88Albuq/ProC-263
89Albuq/CMC-4
89Albuq/ProC-67
90B-87
90Classic/III-63
90D/Rook-34
90F-651R
90F/Can-651M
90F/Up-U22
90Pol/Dodg-46
90S-641
90SpringDG/Best-15
90T/89Debut-53
90Target-974
91D-545
91F-205
91Mother/Dodg-19
91OPC-199
91Pol/Dodg-46
91S-252
91S/100RisSt-67
91T-199
91UD-686
92D-726
92OPC-484
92Phill/Med-41
92S-670
92ScranWB/SB-485
92T-484
92T/Gold-484
92T/GoldWin-484
92UD-613
93D-596
93F-102
93OPC/Premier-67
93StCl-124
93StCl/1stDay-124
93T-208
93T/Gold-208
94D-225
94F-207
Hartley, Todd
86Cram/NWL-63
Hartley, Tom
86AppFx-10
Hartman, Albert
82BurlR/Frit-5
82BurlR/TCMA-23
Hartman, Ed
87Watertn-16
88Augusta/ProC-366
89Salem/Star-10
89Star/Wax-94
Hartman, Harry
W711/1ANN
W711/2ANN
Hartman, J.C.
61T/St-161
63Pep
63T-442
Hartman, Jeff
86VeroB-9
88VeroB/Star-10
Hartman, Kelly
92Belling/ClBest-10
92Belling/ProC-1438
Hartman, Ralph
(Doc)
81Redwd-26
82Redwd-27
Hartman, Robert
59T-128
60T-129
Hartman, Trey
86Lipscomb-14
Hartmann, Brian
92MN-7
Hartmann, Reid
89Kingspt/Star-13
90Clmbia/PCPII-4
90Columbia/GS-8
Hartnett, Charles
(Gabby)
21Exh-67
25Exh-22
26Exh-22
27Exh-11
28Exh-10
28Yueng-5
29Exh/4-5
30CEA/Pin-5
31Exh/4-5
32Orbit/un-31
33CJ/Pin-13
33G-202
35BU-136
35Exh/4-3
36Exh/4-3
36Wheat
37Dix
37Exh/4-3
38Dix
38Exh/4-3
38ONG/Pin-15
39Exh
50Callahan
50W576-37
60F-29
61F-41
61GP-11
76Rowe-9M
76Shakey-75
77Galasso-206
77Galasso-62
80Pac/Leg-72
80Perez/HOF-76
80SSPC/HOF
81Conlon-89
84Cub/Uno-3M
84Cub/Uno-6
86Sf/Dec-13
87Conlon/2-17
91Conlon/Sport-313
91Conlon/Sport-59
92Conlon/Gold-880
92Conlon/Sport-586
92Cub/OldStyle-11
93Conlon-675
93Conlon-880
94Conlon-1052
94Conlon-1103
94TedW-16
E120
E210-5
PM10/Sm-68
PR1-16
R305
R306
R308-200
R311/Leath
R312/M
R314
R332-38
V355-57
W502-5
WG8-30
Hartnett, Dave
86Cram/NWL-101
87Wausau-22
Harts, Greg
91WIZMets-162
Hartsel, Tully
(Topsy)
10Domino-53
12Sweet/Pin-45
E101
E106
E107
E254
E90/1
E92
E97
S74-31
T205
T206
T208
T213/brown
T215/blue
T215/brown
T216
W555
Hartsfield, Bob
75Cedar
76Clinton
82AubAs-2MG
92Jacks/ProC-3724MG
92Jaxvl/SB-374MG
Hartsfield, Roy
51B-277
52B-28
52T-264
73OPC-237CO
73T-237CO
75IntLgAS/Broder-9
75PCL/AS-9
77OPC-238MG
77T-113MG
78BJ/PostC-8MG
78OPC-218MG
78T-444MG
79BJ/Bubble-11MG
79OPC-262MG
79T-282MG
79TCMA-123
83Indianap-3MG
Hartshorn, Kyle
85Lynch-12
86Jacks/TCMA-5
87Jacks/Feder-19
88Jacks/GS-6
Hartsock, Brian
82Danvl/Frit-24
83Peoria/Frit-24
86MidldA-9
87SanBern-13
89Reno/Cal-249
Hartsock, Jeff
88GreatF-21
89AS/Cal-15
89Bakers/Cal-183
90SanAn/GS-14
91AAA/LineD-8
91Albuq/LineD-8

91Albuq/ProC-1135
92Iowa/ProC-4048
92Iowa/SB-209
92Sky/AAASingl-102
93B-648
93D-160
Hartung, Andrew
90A&AASingle/ProC-180
90Geneva/ProC-3044
90Geneva/Star-13
91ClBest/Singl-433
91Peoria/ClBest-28
91Peoria/ProC-1349
91Peoria/Team-17
92ClBest/Up-430
92WinSalem/ClBest-13
92WinSalem/ProC-1214
93FExcel/ML-9
Hartung, Clinton
47TipTop
48B-37
49B-154
49Eureka-107
50B-118
50Drake-2
51B-234
52BR
52T-141
R346-47
Hartwig, Dan
77Cedar
Hartwig, Rob
90Batavia/ProC-3079
91Spartan/ClBest-25
91Spartan/ProC-910
Hartzell, Paul
75QuadC
77BurgChef-118
77T-179
78SSPC/270-191
78T-529
79OPC-212
79T-402
79Twin/FriszP-9
80OPC-366
80T-721
84ElPaso-20
91Crown/Orio-186
Hartzell, Roy A.
16FleischBrd-38
92Conlon/Sport-544
D303
D329-77
D350/2-76
E126
E254
E270/1
E90/1
E91
M101/4-77
M101/5-76
M116
T201
T204
T216
Hartzog, Cullen
90PrWill/Team-11
90T/TVYank-45
91AA/LineD-7
91Albany/LineD-7
91Albany/ProC-1003
Harvell, Rod
89GreatF-26
Harvey, Bob
91Negro/Lewis-3
92Negro/RetortII-16
Harvey, Bryan
86PalmSp-16
86PalmSp/Smok-12
87MidldA-25
88D/Rook-53
88Edmon/CMC-5
88F/Up-U14
88S/Tr-87T
88Smok/Angels-21
88T/Tr-45T
89B-40
89D-525
89D/Best-317
89F-479
89F/BBMVP's-18
89F/Heroes-21
89OPC-287
89Panini/St-284
89S-185
89S/HotRook-92
89S/YS/I-30
89Sf-130
89T-632
89T/St-180
89ToysRUs-13
89UD-594
90D-372
90F-134
90F/Can-134
90Leaf-116
90OPC-272
90RedFoley/St-44
90S-8
90Sf-31
90Smok/Angel-7
90T-272
90T/St-175
90UD-686
91B-211
91D-206
91F-315
91Leaf-213
91OPC-153
91S-108
91Smok/Angel-17
91StCl-98
91T-153
91UD-592
91USPlayC/AS-7D
91Ultra-45
92B-172
92Classic/Game200-57
92Classic/I-42
92D-211
92DPep/MSA-9
92F-61
92F-696LL
92French-6
92L-309
92L/BlkGold-309
92OPC-568
92Pinn-145
92S-322
92StCl-410
92StCl/Dome-79
92Studio-146
92T-407AS
92T-568
92T/Gold-407AS
92T/Gold-568
92T/GoldWin-407AS
92T/GoldWin-568
92TripleP-37
92UD-434
92UD/ASFF-26
92Ultra-27
93B-234
93D-728
93F-193
93F/Final-62
93Flair-52
93Flair/Pr-4
93L-361
93Marlin/Publix-12
93OPC-14
93OPC/Premier-90
93Pac/Spanish-463
93Pinn-235
93S-558
93S/Franchise-27
93Select-126
93StCl-604
93StCl/1stDay-604
93StCl/Marlin-2
93T-439
93T/Finest-3
93T/FinestRef-3
93T/Gold-439
93TripleP-225
93UD-684
93UD/FunPack-120
93UD/SP-141
93USPlayC/Marlin-10C
93USPlayC/Marlin-3D
93Ultra-377
94B-10
94D-374
94D/MVP-5
94D/Special-374
94F-468
94F/AS-40
94Flair-164
94L-140
94OPC-239
94Pac/Cr-243
94Panini-183
94Pinn-344
94RedFoley-24M
94S-66
94S/GoldR-66
94S/Tomb-9
94Select-103
94Sf/2000-47
94StCl-452
94StCl/1stDay-452
94StCl/Gold-452
94StCl/Team-61
94Studio-110
94T-20
94T/Finest-164
94T/FinestRef-164
94T/Gold-20
94TripleP-137
94UD-405
94UD/CollC-127
94UD/CollC/Gold-127
94UD/CollC/Silv-127
94UD/SP-112
94Ultra-493
94Ultra/Fire-8
Harvey, Craig
77Watlo
Harvey, Don
88Pac/8Men-16
Harvey, Greg
88Eugene/Best-3
89AppFx/ProC-853
90BBCity/Star-10
90FSLAS/Star-31
91BBCity/ClBest-5
91BBCity/ProC-1392
92Memphis/ProC-2413
Harvey, Harold
(Doug)
84Smok/SDP-13UMP
88TM/Umpire-1
89TM/Umpire-1
90TM/Umpire-1
Harvey, Ken
87SanAn-23
Harvey, Randy
82BirmB-12
85Modesto/Chong-11
86QuadC-14
Harvey, Raymond
91CollInd/ClBest-1
91CollInd/ProC-1498
92Kinston/ClBest-12
92Kinston/ProC-2484
93Kinston/Team-10
Harvey, Robert
90SanBern/Cal-BB
Harvey, Steve
82Reading-20
Harvey, Terry
93Bz-1
93T/Tr-41T
Harvey, Wayne
91Parramatta/Fut-17
Harvick, Brad
87Erie-19
88Savan/ProC-345
89Savan/ProC-365
Harwell, David
88Kinston/Star-10
Harwell, Ernie
81Tiger/Detroit-62ANN
83Kaline-26ANN
88Domino-6ANN
89Pac/Leg-172ANN
Harwell, Jim
61Union
Haryd, Mark
87BurlEx-20
Haselman, Bill
88CharlR/Star-9
89TexLAS/GS-33
89Tulsa/GS-11
89Tulsa/Team-10
90A&AASingle/ProC-68
90ProC/Singl-745
90TexLgAS/GS-25
90Tulsa/ProC-1158
90Tulsa/Team-11
91AAA/LineD-310
91D-679
91F-287
91OkCty/LineD-310
91OkCty/ProC-182
91S-377RP
91T/90Debut-65
92Calgary/ProC-3734
92StCl-574
93B-79
93F/Final-271
93Pac/Spanish-623
93Rang/Keeb-177
93StCl/Mar-7
93Ultra-622
94D-654
94F-288
94L-58
94Pac/Cr-571
94S-189
94S/GoldR-189
94StCl-114
94StCl/1stDay-114
94StCl/Gold-114
94T-138
94T/Gold-138
Hasler, Curt
89Saraso/Star-10
91AAA/LineD-634
91Vanco/LineD-634
91Vanco/ProC-1590
Haslerig, Bill
78Green
79Savan-4
Hasley, Mike
75Dubuq
76Dubuq
Haslin, Mickey
35BU-104
Haslock, Chris
88Spokane/ProC-1945
89CharRain/ProC-981
90River/Best-11
90River/Cal-18
90River/ProC-2602
91HighD/ClBest-5
91HighD/ProC-2388
Hassamaer, William L.
N172
Hassan, Theodore
92Pulaski/ClBest-1
92Pulaski/ProC-3172
Hassel, Bob
84Idaho/Team-11
Hassel, Jay
92Hunting/ClBest-25
92Hunting/ProC-3142
93FExcel/ML-10
93Peoria/Team-8
Hassett, John
(Buddy)
39Exh
39PlayBall-57
40PlayBall-62
41DP-121
90Target-322
93Conlon-752
94Conlon-1067
R303/A
V351B-21
Hassey, Ron
79Tacoma-1
80T-222
81D-80
81F-405
81OPC-187
81T-564
81T/St-71
82D-463
82F-370
82OPC-54
82T-54
82Wheat/Ind
83D-159
83F-411
83F-642M
83OPC/St-62
83T-689
83T/St-62
83Wheat/Ind-18
84D-460
84F-545
84F/X-49
84Nes/792-308
84OPC-308
84SevenUp-15
84T-308
84T/St-262
84T/Tr-49
85F/Up-U50
85T-742
85T/Tr-48T
86D-370
86F-107
86OPC-157
86T-157
86T/Tatt-13M
87Coke/WS-15
87D-532
87F-499
87OPC-61
87Sf/TPrev-26M
87T-667
87T/St-285
88D-580
88D/A's/Bk-NEW
88D/Best-302
88F-399
88Mother/A's-16
88S/Tr-33T
88T-458
88T/Tr-46T
89B-194
89D-361
89F-9
89Mother/A's-15
89OPC-272
89S-334
89T-272
89T/Big-171
89T/St-173
89UD-564
90B-464
90D-450
90F-8
90F/Can-8
90Leaf-326
90Mother/A's-12
90OPC-527
90PublInt/St-305
90S-168
90T-527
90T/Big-4
90UD-195
91D-476
91F-8
91F/Up-U98
91Leaf-359
91OPC-327
91OPC/Premier-61
91S-806
91S/RookTr-43T
91StCl-490
91T-327
91UD-401
92S-273
92Yank/WIZ80-78
Hassinger, Brad
90Princet/DIMD-11
91ClBest/Singl-140
91Spartan/ClBest-5
91Spartan/ProC-890
92Spartan/ProC-1259
Hassler, Andy
75OPC-261
75T-261
75T/M-261
76OPC-207
76SSPC-186
76T-207
77T-602
78SSPC/270-225
78T-73
79T-696
80T-353
81D-581
81F-290
81T-454
81T/St-55
82D-519
82F-464
82T-94
83D-290
83F-92
83T-573
84ArkTr-25
84D-255
84F-519
84Nes/792-719
84T-719

85Louisvl-6
91WIZMets-163
Hasson, Gene
V351A-14
Hasty, Robert
E120
V100
Hatcher, Billy
83MidldC-13
84Iowa-24
85D-41RR
85F-649R
85Iowa-10
85SevenUp-22
86D-433
86F-371
86F/Up-U49
86Pol/Ast-23
86T-46
86T/Tr-45T
87D-481
87D/OD-18
87F-59
87F/RecSet-15
87Mother/Ast-26
87Pol/Ast-6
87T-578
88D-23DK
88D-261
88D/Best-150
88D/DKsuper-23DK
88F-449
88KennerFig-46
88Leaf-110
88Leaf-23DK
88Mother/Ast-6
88OPC-306
88Panini/St-300
88Pol/Ast-11
88RedFoley/St-30
88S-505
88Sf-63
88T-306
88T/Big-3
88T/Mini-49
88T/St-28
88T/UK-30
89D-187
89D/Best-150
89F-359
89KennerFig-59
89Lennox/Ast-1
89Mother/Ast-5
89OPC-252
89Panini/St-92
89S-61
89Sf-174
89T-252
89T/Big-118
89T/St-19
89UD-344
90D-616
90D/BestNL-125
90F-467
90F/Can-467
90F/Up-U13
90Homer/Pirate-11
90Kahn/Reds-11
90Leaf-241
90OPC-119
90PublInt/St-96
90S-562
90S/Tr-42T
90T-119
90T/Big-222
90T/Tr-38T
90UD-598
90UD/Ext-778
91B-670
91D-196
91D-763WS
91F-66
91F/WS-2
91Kahn/Reds-22
91Leaf-205
91Leaf/Stud-166
91OPC-604
91Panini/FrSt-132
91Pep/Reds-10
91RedFoley/St-46
91S-469
91StCl-371
91StCl/Charter*-11
91T-604
91UD-114
91Ultra-95
91Woolwth/HL-27
92D-537
92F-409
92OPC-432
92Pinn-460
92S-447
92S/RookTr-72T
92StCl-363
92T-432
92T/Gold-432
92T/GoldWin-432
92TripleP-222
92UD-699
92Ultra-190
93D-754
93F-561
93Flair-166
93L-109
93Pac/Spanish-83
93S-657
93Select-225
93Studio-186
93T-725
93T/Gold-725
93TripleP-157
93UD-618
93Ultra-512
94D-434
94F-35
94Flair-14
94L-34
94Pac/Cr-57
94Panini-31
94Pinn-362
94S-443
94Select-96
94T-26
94T/Gold-26
94TripleP-205
94UD-461
94UD/CollC-128
94UD/CollC/Gold-128
94UD/CollC/Silv-128
94Ultra-16
Hatcher, Chris
90AubAs/ProC-3395
91BurlAs/ClBest-20
91BurlAs/ProC-2814
91ClBest/Singl-312
91MidwLAS/ProC-16
92Osceola/ClBest-6
92Osceola/ProC-2542
92ProC/Tomorrow-230
93ClBest/MLG-167
93FExcel/ML-43
Hatcher, Hal
81CharR-5
82FtMyr-2
84Memphis-20
Hatcher, Johnny
83Durham-5
84Durham-5
85Durham-26
87Greenvl/Best-25
Hatcher, Ken
52Laval-39
Hatcher, Mickey
79Albuq-11
80Pol/Dodg-44
80T-679R
81D-526
81F-135
81Pol/Dodg-44A
81T-289
81T/Tr-768
82D-480
82F-467
82OPC-291
82T-467
82T/St-212
83D-615
83F-614
83T-121
83Twin/Team-6
84D-147
84F-566
84Nes/792-746
84T-746
85D-194
85F-279
85Leaf-224
85Seven/Minn-3
85T-18
85T/St-304
85Twin/Seven-3
85Twin/Team-6
86D-269
86F-396
86Leaf-143
86OPC-356
86T-356
86T-786M
87D-491
87F-542
87F/Up-U41
87Mother/Dodg-25
87OPC-341
87T-504
87T/St-276
87T/Tr-43T
88D-299
88F-516
88Leaf-122
88Mother/Dodg-25
88OPC-339
88Pol/Dodg-9
88S-298
88T-607
88T/St-71
89B-347
89D-346
89F/WS-1
89Mother/Dodg-25
89OPC-254
89OPC-390
89Panini/St-105
89Panini/St-23
89Pol/Dodg-6
89S-332
89T-483
89T/Big-63
89UD/Ext-709
89Woolwth-31
90D-439
90F-398
90F/Can-398
90Leaf-332
90Mother/Dodg-6
90OPC-226
90Pol/Dodg-8
90PublInt/St-8
90S-359
90T-226
90Target-323
90UD-283
91F-206
91OPC-152
91S-153
91T-152
91UD-666
92Albuq/ProC-738
92Albuq/SB-25M
93Rang/Keeb-436CO
Hatcher, Rick
82Durham-18
Hatchett, Frank
89KS*-26
Hatfield, Fred
52B-153
52T-354
53B/Col-125
53T-163
53Tiger/Glen-12
54B-119
55B-187
56T-318
57T-278
58T-339
59DF
80Richm-5MG
86Miami-9MG
91T/Arc53-163
Hatfield, Gilbert
(Gil)
90Target-975
N172
N338/2
Hatfield, Rob
86Macon-13
87Salem-4
Hathaway, Hilly
90A&AASingle/ProC-157
90Boise/ProC-3311
92MidldA/OneHour-7
92PalmSp/ProC-831
93B-61
93D-329
93F/Final-183
93Select/RookTr-55T
93T/Tr-87T
93Vanco/ProC-2590
94D-170
94F-59
94Pinn-127
94Pinn/Artist-127
94Pinn/Museum-127
94S-612
94StCl-385
94StCl/1stDay-385
94StCl/Gold-385
94T-596
94T/Gold-596
94UD/CollC-129
94UD/CollC/Gold-129
94UD/CollC/Silv-129
Hathaway, Ray
45Parade*-59
Hathaway, Shawn
88Spring/Best-6
89StPete/Star-16
89Star/Wax-50
Hattabaugh, Matt
91Utica/ClBest-10
91Utica/ProC-3243
Hattaway, Wayne
85OrlanTw-23
88OrlanTw/Best-26
89OrlanTw/Best-27
89OrlanTw/ProC-1336
90OrlanSR/Best-26
90OrlanSR/Star-28MG
Hatteberg, Scott
91ClBest/Singl-442
91Classic/DP-38
91FrRow/DP-15
92B-83
92ClBest-196
92NewBrit/ProC-437
92NewBrit/SB-487
92OPC-734
92Pinn-569
92Sky/AASingl-207
92StCl/Dome-80
92T-734
92T/Gold-734
92T/GoldWin-734
92UD/ML-238
93B-87
93ClBest/MLG-28
94SigRook-37
94T-764M
94T/Gold-764M
Hatten, Joe
47HomogBond-19
47TipTop
49B-116
49Eureka-36
50B-166
51B-190
52B-144
52T-194
90Target-324
D305
Hatton, Grady
49B-62
49Eureka-85
50B-26
51B-47
51T/RB-34
52T-6
53T-45
54T-208
55T-131
55T/DH-72
56T-26
56T/Pin-23
66T-504MG
67Ast/Team-6MG
67T-347MG
68T-392MG
73OPC-624CO
73T-624C
74OPC-31CO
74T-31C
91Crown/Orio-187
91T/Arc53-45
92TX-23
94T/Arc54-208
Exh47
PM10/Sm-69
Haugen, Troy
89Helena/SP-7
90Beloit/Best-24
90Beloit/Star-10
91Stockton/ClBest-12
91Stockton/ProC-3039
Haughey, Chris
90Target-976
Haughney, Trevor
91GulfCR/SportP-14
Haught, Gary
92SoOreg/ClBest-17
92SoOreg/ProC-3411
Haugstad, Phil
52T-198
90Target-325
Haurado, Yanko
87PrWill-2
Hause, Brendan
92LitSun/HSPros-8
Hauser, Arnold
10Domino-54
11Helmar-170
12Sweet/Pin-148
14Piedmont/St-27
S74-119
T201
T202
T205
Hauser, Jeff
88Rockford-16
89Rockford-16
Hauser, Joe
26Exh-108
28Exh-55
28LaPresse-15
61F-113
88LitSun/Minor-10
92Conlon/Sport-548
94Conlon-1071
E120
V61-53
W572
Hausladen, Bob
83BurlR-19
83BurlR/Frit-1
Hausman, Thomas
(Tom)
74Sacra
76OPC-452
76T-452
77Spoka
77T-99
78Tidew
79OPC-339
79T-643
80T-151
81D-396
81F-333
81T-359
82D-301
82F-526
82T-524
83T-417
91WIZMets-164
Hausmann, Clem
V362-13
Hausmann, George
44Playball-36
49Eureka-109
Hausmann, Jeff
88NE-4
Hausterman, David
86DayBe-11TR
Hauswirth, Trentor
93Rockford/ClBest-15
Havens, Brad
82D-382
82OrlanTw/A-16
82T-92
83D-480
83F-615
83T-751
83Twin/Team-19
84Nes/792-509
84T-509
84Toledo-8
85IntLgAS-40
85RochR-16
86D-599
87F-472
87RochR-17
87RochR/TCMA-5

87T-398
87T/Tr-44T
88F-517
88Mother/Dodg-22
88Pol/Dodg-41
88T-698
89F-407
89T-204
90Target-326
91Crown/Orio-188
Havens, Tom
92Madis/ClBest-8
92Madis/ProC-1242
Havens, Will
92Pulaski/ClBest-15
92Pulaski/ProC-3173
Hawarny, Dave
82BirmB-16
83BirmB-6
Hawblitzel, Ryan
90Hunting/ProC-3276
91CLAS/ProC-CAR42
91WinSalem/ClBest-4
91WinSalem/ProC-2823
92B-138
92ChalK/SB-158
92CharlK/ProC-2765
92ClBest-61
92D/Rook-49
92ProC/Tomorrow-205
92Sky/AASingl-73
92UD-59TP
92UD/ML-298
92UD/ML-31M
93B-64
93ClBest/MLG-91
93F/Final-32
93FExcel/ML-11
93T-648
93T/Gold-648
93Ultra-349
Hawes, Roy Lee
55B-268
88Chatt/Team-14
Hawkins, Andy
81Hawaii-14
82Hawaii-14
84F-302
84Mother/Padres-18
84Nes/792-778
84T-778
85D-528
85D/HL-14
85D/HL-15
85F-36
85Mother/Padres-13
85T-299
86D-284
86F-324
86F/Mini-70
86F/St-51
86Leaf-158
86OPC-5
86Seven/Coin-W12
86Sf-191
86T-478
86T/St-108
86T/Tatt-12M
87Bohem-40
87D-264
87F-417
87Sf/TPrev-16M
87T-183
88F-586
88S-347
88Smok/Padres-11
88T-9
88T/Big-257
89B-166
89D-583
89D/Best-52
89D/Tr-52
89F-307
89F/Up-50
89Panini/St-194
89S-118
89S/NWest-19
89S/Tr-14
89Sf-84
89T-533
89T/St-111
89T/Tr-47T
89UD-495
89UD/Ext-708
90Classic-135
90D-159
90F-445
90F/Can-445
90Leaf-281
90OPC-335
90Panini/St-130
90PublInt/St-536
90S/NWest-18
90T-335
90T/Big-36
90T/St-317
90T/TVYank-10
90UD-339
91D-611
91D-BC12A
91D-BC12B
91D/BC-BC12A
91D/BC-BC12B
91F-666
91F/WaxBox-6
91OPC-635
91Panini/FrSt-357
91Panini/St-6
91S-47
91S-704NH
91StCl-487
91StCl/Charter*-12
91T-635
91UD-333
91Ultra-234
92Calgary/SB-59
92Yank/WIZ80-79
Hawkins, Cedric
86LitFalls-13
Hawkins, Chris
87AubAs-11
Hawkins, Craig
91Elizab/ProC-4306
92Elizab/ClBest-14
92Elizab/ProC-3694
Hawkins, Hersey
88Peoria/Ko-14
Hawkins, Joe
90Pittsfld/Pucko-28TR
91StLucie/ClBest-30TR
Hawkins, John
84Nashvl-9
85Albany-32
86FSLAS-21
86FtLaud-12
91SoBend/ClBest-28
Hawkins, Kraig
92Oneonta/ClBest-25
93Greens/ClBest-10
93Greens/ProC-898
94FExcel-104
Hawkins, LaTroy
94FExcel-95
94FExcel/LL-9
94UD-248TP
94Ultra-389
Hawkins, Todd
87Everett-18
88Fresno/Cal-9
88Fresno/ProC-1242
Hawkins, Ty
91SoBend/ProC-2869
Hawkins, Walter
87Idaho-11
Hawkins, Wynn
60T-536
61T-34
63T-334
Hawks, Larry
90Spokane/SportP-5
91BendB/ClBest-24
91BendB/ProC-3696
91Waterlo/ClBest-28
91Waterlo/ProC-1258
Hawks, Nelson
25Exh-42
W575
Hawley, Billy
83Cedar/Frit-10
86Vermont-10
87Tampa-26
Haws, Scott
92Martins/ClBest-16
92Martins/ProC-3060
Haydel, Hal
71OPC-692R
71T-692R
72OPC-28R
72T-28R
Hayden, Alan
86Columbia-12
87Jacks/Feder-22
87Lynch-11
88Jacks/GS-25
89Chatt/Best-25
89Chatt/GS-23
89Jacks/GS-30
89Nashvl/Team-9
90Chatt/GS-15
Hayden, David
91Batavia/ClBest-10
91Batavia/ProC-3492
92Spartan/ClBest-18
92Spartan/ProC-1269
Hayden, John F.
T206
Hayden, Paris
89Freder/Star-10
90Freder/Team-13
90Hagers/ProC-1427
90Hagers/Star-11
91FSLAS/ProC-FSL22
91Miami/ClBest-28
91Miami/ProC-421
Hayden, Richard
84Butte-12
Hayes, Ben
82Indianap-21
83F-591
84F-470
84Nes/792-448
84T-448
85Louisvl-25
Hayes, Bill
80Wichita-5
82Iowa-5
83Iowa-12
84Iowa-15
85Iowa-2
86Omaha/ProC-10
86Omaha/TCMA-1
87Iowa-14
88Geneva/ProC-1654
90Geneva/ProC-3053MG
90Geneva/Star-26MG
91Peoria/ClBest-22MG
91Peoria/ProC-1359MG
91Peoria/Team-1MG
92WinSalem/ClBest-26
92WinSalem/ProC-1223MG
Hayes, Brian
78LodiD
79LodiD-19
Hayes, Charlie
85Fresno/Pol-11
86Shrev-11
87Shrev-17
87TexLgAS-27
88Phoenix/CMC-15
88Phoenix/ProC-57
89F-330
89F/Up-106
89Phill/TastyK-41
89Phoenix/CMC-13
89Phoenix/ProC-1487
89S-628
89S/HotRook-39
89UD/Ext-707
90Classic-98
90D-548
90D/BestNL-106
90F-558
90F/Can-558
90HotRook/St-21
90Leaf-131
90OPC-577
90Phill/TastyK-11
90S-507
90S/100Ris-12
90S/YS/I-38
90Sf-36
90T-577
90T/Big-69
90UD-437
91B-508
91D-278
91F-397
91Leaf-214
91Leaf/Stud-214
91OPC-312
91Panini/FrSt-105
91Panini/St-102
91Phill/Medford-17
91S-238
91S/100SS-19
91StCl-163
91T-312
91UD-269
91Ultra-263
92B-147
92D-547
92F-533
92F/Up-42
92L-220
92L/BlkGold-220
92OPC-754
92OPC/Premier-6
92Panini-244
92Pinn-497
92S-301
92S/RookTr-16T
92StCl-711
92Studio-212
92T-754
92T/Gold-754
92T/GoldWin-754
92T/Tr-46T
92T/TrGold-46T
92UD-208
92UD-768
92Ultra-243
92Ultra-407
93B-500
93Cadaco-30
93Colla/DM-49
93D-181
93D-776
93Duracel/PPII-4
93F-279
93F/Final-33
93Flair-41
93JDean/28-26
93L-360
93OPC-54
93OPC/Premier-66
93Pac/Spanish-429
93Pinn-447
93Pinn/Expan-5M
93Pinn/HRC-19
93S-411
93Select-194
93StCl-743
93StCl/1stDay-743
93StCl/Rockie-3
93Studio-136
93T-142
93T-759
93T/Finest-60
93T/FinestRef-60
93T/Gold-142
93T/Gold-759
93TripleP-257
93UD-647
93UD/FunPack-177
93UD/SP-222
93USPlayC/Rockie-1H
93USPlayC/Rockie-2C
93Ultra-350
94B-254
94D-46
94D/Special-46
94F-443
94L-134
94OPC-171
94Pac/Cr-197
94Pac/Silv-21
94Panini-175
94Pinn-14
94Pinn/Artist-14
94Pinn/Museum-14
94Pinn/Run-40
94RedFoley-12
94S-50
94S/Cycle-7
94S/GoldR-50
94Select-42
94Sf/2000-82
94StCl-249
94StCl/1stDay-249
94StCl/Gold-249
94StCl/Team-114
94Studio-179
94T-655
94T/Finest-32
94T/FinestRef-32
94T/Gold-655
94TripleP-225
94UD-167
94UD/CollC-130
94UD/CollC/Gold-130
94UD/CollC/Silv-130
94UD/ElecD-167
94UD/SP-167
94Ultra-482
Hayes, Chris
87Modesto-13
Hayes, Damon
47Remar-21
47Smith-21
48Smith-13
Hayes, Dan
84Newar-13
Hayes, Emanuel
92MedHat/ProC-3213
92MedHat/SportP-5
93StCath/ClBest-9
93StCath/ProC-3980
Hayes, Frank
(Blimp)
39PlayBall-108
40PlayBall-24
41DP-47
41G-13
41PlayBall-41
47TipTop
92Conlon/Sport-380
93Conlon-864
Hayes, Jim
(Jimmy)
88Bristol/ProC-1874
90Tampa/DIMD-11
Hayes, Minter
(Jackie)
29Exh/4-32
34G-63
35BU-111M
35G-8B
35G-9B
37OPC-102
81Conlon-36
91Conlon/Sport-71
V300
Hayes, Randy
84AZ/Pol-8
Hayes, Robbie
91MissSt-22
92MissSt-18
93MissSt-18
Hayes, Terry
82Wausau/Frit-29
Hayes, Todd
87SanBern-22
88SanBern/Best-25
88SanBern/Cal-51
Hayes, Tom
81Durham-7
84Richm-6
85Greenvl/Team-7
Hayes, Von
80Watlo
81Charl-15
82D-237
82F-371
82T-141R
82T/Tr-42T
82Wheat/Ind
83D-324
83F-412
83OPC-325
83OPC/St-311
83T-325
83T/St-311
83T/Tr-40
84D-477
84F-33
84Nes/792-587
84OPC-259
84Phill/TastyK-36
84T-587
84T/St-124
85CIGNA-2
85D-326
85D/HL-16
85F-253
85Leaf-93
85OPC-68
85Phill/TastyK-12M
85Phill/TastyK-36
85T-68

85T/St-115
86CIGNA-3
86D-305
86F-443
86F/Mini-92
86F/St-52
86Keller-2
86Leaf-176
86OPC-146
86Phill/TastyK-9
86T-420
86T/St-120
86T/Tatt-10M
87BK-8
87Champion-1
87Classic-63
87D-113
87D-12DK
87D/DKsuper-12
87D/OD-152
87Drake-3
87F-175
87F/Excit-23
87F/GameWin-19
87F/Mini-51
87F/St-55
87Kraft-24
87Leaf-12Dk
87Leaf-130
87OPC-389
87Phill/TastyK-9
87RedFoley/St-72
87Sf-193
87Sf/TPrev-6
87T-666
87T/Coins-35
87T/Mini-28
87T/St-121
88D-207
88D/Best-128
88Drake-17
88F-304
88F/Excit-18
88F/Mini-99
88F/St-108
88KennerFig-47
88Leaf-197
88OPC-215
88Panini/St-356
88Phill/TastyK-13
88S-515
88Sf-62
88T-215
88T/Big-139
88T/St-117
89B-406
89D-160
89D/Best-47
89F-571
89KennerFig-60
89KingB/Discs-18
89OPC-385
89Panini/St-151
89Phill/TastyK-9
89RedFoley/St-56
89S-38
89Sf-181
89T-385
89T/Big-302
89T/St-115
89UD-246
90B-160
90Classic-113
90D-278
90D/BestNL-140
90D/Bon/MVP-BC25
90D/Learning-18
90F-559
90F/AwardWin-17
90F/BB-17
90F/Can-559
90Kenner/Fig-38
90KingB/sDiscs-7
90Leaf-52
90MLBPA/Pins-2
90OPC-710
90Panini/St-319
90Phill/TastyK-12
90Post-27
90PublInt/St-238
90RedFoley/St-45
90S-36
90S/100St-62
90Sf-147
90Sunflower-12
90T-710
90T/Coins-48
90T/DH-32
90T/Mini-69
90T/St-114
90T/TVAS-54
90UD-453
90UD-7TC
91B-487
91Classic/200-25
91D-222
91F-398
91Leaf-280
91OPC-15
91Panini/FrSt-107
91Panini/St-105
91Phill/Medford-18
91RedFoley/St-47
91S-426
91StCl-127
91T-15
91T/CJMini/II-5
91UD-368
91Ultra-264
91Ultra-398CL
92B-197
92D-580
92F-534
92L-177
92L/BlkGold-177
92OPC-135
92OPC/Premier-127
92Panini-248
92Pinn-326
92Pol/Angel-12
92S-207
92StCl-880
92Studio-147
92T-135
92T/Gold-135
92T/GoldWin-135
92T/Kids-19
92T/Tr-47T
92T/TrGold-47T
92UD-427
92UD-707
92Ultra-326

Hayford, Don
79Elmira-10

Hayman, David
93MissSt-19

Haynes, Heath
91James/ClBest-25
91James/ProC-3538
92MidwLAS/Team-17
92ProC/Tomorrow-272
92Rockford/ClBest-21
92Rockford/ProC-2109
93ClBest/MLG-37
93Harris/ProC-266
94FExcel-225

Haynes, Jimmy
91LitSun/HSPros-6
91LitSun/HSProsG-6
92Kane/ClBest-18
92Kane/ProC-85
92Kane/Team-13
92UD/ML-168
93B-493
94B-543
94FExcel-7

Haynes, Joe
49B-191
51B-240
52B-103
52T-145
54T-223
94T/Arc54-223

Haynes, Marvin
87Vermont-26

Haynes, Rick
75Dubuq

Hays, Darrin
89Butte/SP-23
90CharlR/Star-9

Hays, David
89EastLDD/ProC-50EQ

Hays, Rob
90Spokane/SportP-9
91Waterlo/ClBest-5
91Waterlo/ProC-1252

Hayward, Brent
92GulfCM/ProC-3473

Hayward, Jeff
86Tampa-6

Hayward, Ray
83Beaum-19
84Cram/PCL-219
85Cram/PCL-104
86LasVegas-6
87D-632
87LasVegas-12
88F/Up-U63
88Mother/R-16
88OkCty/CMC-7
88OkCty/ProC-49
88S/Tr-67T
88T/Tr-47T
89D-521
89F-521
89S-514
90AAASingl/ProC-672
90OkCty/ProC-426
93Rang/Keeb-178

Haywood, Albert
(Buster)
78Laugh/Black-20
86Negro/Frit-42
87Negro/Dixon-36
92Negro/Kraft-8
92Negro/Retort-27

Hayworth, Ray
34DS-90
35BU-165
39PlayBall-140
40PlayBall-155
90Target-327
R300
R314
V355-50
WG8-31

Hazelette, Moe
83Kinston/Team-8

Hazewood, Drungo L.
80CharlO/Pol-9
80CharlO/W3TV-9
81RochR-8
83RochR-20
91Crown/Orio-189

Hazle, Robert S.
(Hurricane)
58T-83

Hazlett, Steve
91Elizab/ProC-4307
92Kenosha/ProC-617
92MidwLAS/Team-18
94ClBest/Gold-66

Head, Ed
90Target-328

Headley, Kent
88Virgini/Star-9

Heakins, Craig
86Watertn-9
87Macon-19

Healey, John
N172
N284

Healy, Bob
77QuadC

Healy, Fran
72T-663
73OPC-361
73T-361
74OPC-238
74T-238
74T/St-182
75OPC-120
75OPC-251
75T-251
75T/M-251
76OPC-394
76SSPC-184
76T-394
77BK/Y-3
77T-148
78SSPC/270-19
78T-582
92Yank/WIZ70-69

Heap, James
52Laval-79

Heaps, Chris
92GulfCY/ProC-3796

Heard, Jehosie
54Esskay
54T-226
91Crown/Orio-190
91Negro/Lewis-15
92Negro/RetortII-17
94T/Arc54-226

Hearn, Ed
83Lynch-22
84Jacks-xx
85IntLgAS-10
85Tidew-21
86D/Rook-54
86Tidew-13
87D-446
87D/OD-201
87F-10
87T-433
87ToysRUs-11
88S-569
88T-56
89AAA/ProC-4
89D-297
89Omaha/CMC-12
89Omaha/ProC-1732
89T-348
89UD-42
91WIZMets-165

Hearn, Jim
49B-190
49Eureka-184
50B-208
51B-61
52B-49
52BR
52RM-NL8
52T-337
52TipTop
53B/Col-76
53NB
53T-38
54NYJour
55B-220
55Gol/Giants-12
56T-202
57T-348
58T-298
59T-63
79TCMA-97
91T/Arc53-38
R423-44

Hearn, Sean
92MedHat/ProC-3219
92MedHat/SportP-3
93StCath/ClBest-10
93StCath/ProC-3986

Hearn, Tommy
86Miami-10

Hearne, Hugh
90Target-977

Hearne, John
91Perth/Fut-14

Hearron, Jeff
86Tor/Fire-16
87D-490
87Knoxvl-21
87OPC-274
87Syrac/TCMA-3
87T-274
87Tor/Fire-13
89LasVegas/CMC-17
89LasVegas/ProC-11
90AAASingl/ProC-627
90Iowa/CMC-23
90Iowa/ProC-320
90ProC/Singl-98
90T/TVCub-49

Heath, Al
82AppFx/Frit-28
83AppFx/Frit-29
84Madis/Pol-8
85Modesto/Chong-8
86Kinston-9
87PalmSp-2

Heath, Dave
83Peoria/Frit-6
85MidldA-6
86MidldA-10
87Edmon-3

Heath, Jason
92OKSt-11

Heath, John Jeffrey
(Jeff)
39Exh
45Playball-15
47TipTop
49B-169
49Eureka-11
79TCMA-97
93Conlon-939
R303/A
R303/B
V351B-22

Heath, Kelly
81Omaha-17
83Omaha-16
84Colum-2
84Colum/Pol-11
85Colum-16
85Colum/Pol-12
85IntLgAS-31
86Richm-9
87Richm/Bob-11
87Richm/Crown-1
87Richm/TCMA-18
88Syrac/CMC-20
88Syrac/ProC-811
89Syrac/CMC-17
89Syrac/MerchB-13
89Syrac/ProC-800
89Syrac/Team-13
90AAASingl/ProC-307
90ProC/Singl-239
90ScranWB/CMC-13
90ScranWB/ProC-605
92Reading/ProC-593CO
92Reading/SB-550M

Heath, Lee
89Pulaski/ProC-1911
90Sumter/Best-5
90Sumter/ProC-2445
91Macon/ClBest-23
91Macon/ProC-876
92Durham/ClBest-7
92Durham/ProC-1112
92Durham/Team-33
92UD/ML-88
93B-114

Heath, Mickey
28Exh/PCL-10

Heath, Mike
75FtLaud/Sus-19
76FtLaud
77WHave
79T-710R
80T-687
81A's/Granny-2
81D-120
81F-583
81T-437
82D-413
82F-91
82Granny-3
82OPC-318
82T-318
83D-517
83F-518
83Granny-2
83OPC/St-104
83T-23
83T/St-104
84D-223
84F-446
84Mother/A's-9
84Nes/792-567
84T-567
84T/St-337
85D-298
85F-422
85F-424
85Mother/A's-4
85OPC-396
85T-662
85T/St-326
86D-253
86F-418
86F/Up-U50
86OPC-148
86Schnucks-7
86T-148
86T/St-174
86T/Tr-46T
87Cain's-3
87Coke/Tigers-8
87D-496
87D/OD-214
87F/Up-U42
87T-492
88D-338
88D/Best-69
88F-56
88Pep/T-8

88RedFoley/St-31
88S-156
88T-237
89D-271
89D/Best-147
89F-132
89Mara/Tigers-8
89S-131
89T-609TL
89T-743
89UD-654
90B-352
90Classic/III-40
90CokeK/Tiger-7
90D-209
90D/BestAL-90
90F-603
90F/Can-603
90Leaf-60
90MLBPA/Pins-91
90OPC-366
90Panini/St-66
90PublInt/St-471
90S-172
90T-366
90T/Big-166
90T/St-280
90UD-306
91B-589
91Brave/Dubuq/Perf-14
91Brave/Dubuq/Stand-18
91D-230
91F-339
91Leaf-320
91OPC-16
91Panini/FrSt-287
91Panini/St-237
91S-112
91S/RookTr-69T
91StCl-393
91T-16
91UD-318
91UD/Ext-701
92OPC-512
92S-344
92StCl-128
92T-512
92T/GPro-512
92T/Gold-512
92T/GoldWin-512
92T/Pr-16
92Tacoma/ProC-2506
92UD-304
92USPlayC/Brave-4D
92USPlayC/Brave-5S
92Yank/WIZ70-70

Heath, Thomas
52Mother-46
53Mother-43
R314/Can

Heath, William
(Bill)
66T-539R
67Ast/Team-7
67OPC-172
67T-172
68CokeCap/Astro-7
70OPC-541
70T-541

Heathcock, Jeff
83ColumAst-14
84Cram/PCL-65
86D-182
86F-302
86Tucson-6
87Tucson-18
88F-450
88Mother/Ast-18
88Pol/Ast-12
89Tucson/CMC-7
89Tucson/JP-7
89Tucson/ProC-196
90AAASingl/ProC-91
90Edmon/CMC-9
90Edmon/ProC-515
90ProC/Singl-486

Heathcote, Clifton E.
21Exh-71
26Exh-23
27Exh-12
33G-115
94Conlon-1058
E120
E210-35
V354-9

Heathcott, Mike
91Utica/CIBest-8
91Utica/ProC-3235

Heaton, Neal
82Charl-5
83Wheat/Ind-19
84D-373
84F-546
84F/St-113
84Wheat/Ind-44
85D-373
85F-451
85Polar/Ind-44
86D-338
86F-589
86Leaf-203
86OhHenry-44
87D-615
87F-543
87F/Up-U43
87T/Tr-45T
88D-134
88D/Best-124
88F-185
88F/Mini-89
88Ho/Disc-10
88OPC-354
88Panini/St-319
88RedFoley/St-32
88S-430
88Sf-81
88T-765
88T/Big-33
88T/St-80
88T/St/Backs-29
89D-224
89F-377
89F/Up-113
89OPC-197
89S-253
89T-197
89UD-99
89VFJuice-26
90D-658
90F-468
90F/Can-468
90Homer/Pirate-12
90Leaf-460
90OPC-539
90PublInt/St-156
90T-539
90T/Big-255
90UD-86
90USPlayC/AS-7D
91BBBest/Aces-9
91D-475
91F-38
91OPC-451
91Panini/FrSt-123
91Panini/St-115
91S-233
91StCl-53
91T-451
91UD-36
91Ultra-279
92D-522
92F-554
92OPC-89
92S-723
92StCl-357
92StCl-877
92T-89
92T/Gold-89
92T/GoldWin-89
92UD-417
93Pac/Spanish-554

Heaverlo, Dave
76OPC-213
76SSPC-95
76T-213
77Phoenix
77T-97
78T-338
79T-432
80T-177
81D-407
81F-594
81Tacoma-26
82Tacoma-3
83Tacoma-21

Hebb, Michael
91Kane/CIBest-6
91Kane/ProC-2654
91Kane/Team-9

Heberling, Keith
94FExcel-105
94SigRook-38

Hebert, Roger
52Laval-65

Heble, Kurt
91StCath/CIBest-11
91StCath/ProC-3403
92Myrtle/CIBest-26
92Myrtle/ProC-2191
93Dunedin/CIBest-9
93Dunedin/ProC-1790
94FExcel-144

Hebner, Rich
69OPC-82R
69T-82R
70MLB/St-101
70OPC-264
70T-264
71MLB/St-203
71OPC-212
71T-212
72MB-136
72T-630
73OPC-2
73T-2
74/DE-35
74OPC-450
74T-450
74T/St-84
75Ho-57
75K-57
75OPC-492
75T-492
75T/M-492
76OPC-376
76SSPC-579
76T-376
77OPC-168
77T-167
78OPC-194
78SSPC/270-35
78T-26
79OPC-293
79T-567
80OPC-175
80T-331
81Coke
81D-125
81F-474
81OPC-217
81T-217
82D-328
82F-268
82OPC-96
82T-603
83F-307
83T-778
84F-251
84F/X-50
84Nes/792-433
84SevenUp-18
84T-433
84T/Tr-50
85D-564
85F-59
85SevenUp-18
85T-124
86T-19
88Myrtle/ProC-1188
88SALAS/GS-1MG
90T/TVRSox-5CO
91WIZMets-166

Hebrard, Mike
82Amari-24

Hechinger, Mike
90Target-978

Hecht, Steve
87PanAm/USAB-7
87PanAm/USAR-7
89AS/Cal-35
89SanJose/Best-24
89SanJose/Cal-221
89SanJose/ProC-457
89SanJose/Star-13
90Shrev/ProC-1451
90Shrev/Star-10
90TeamUSA/87-7
91AAA/LineD-186
91Indianap/LineD-186
91Indianap/ProC-474
92Harris/ProC-470
92Harris/SB-282

Heckel, Wally
90StCath/ProC-3477

Hecker, Doug
92Classic/DP-64
92FrRow/DP-24
93B-411
93CIBest/MLG-151
93StCl/MurphyS-64

Hecker, Guy
90HOF/St-3
N172

Heckman, Andy
92Everett/CIBest-29
92Everett/ProC-1680

Heckman, Tom
82Madis/Frit-8

Hedfelt, Pancho
85Utica-10

Hedge, Pat
89Erie/Star-5
91Freder/CIBest-25
91Freder/ProC-2380

Hedgearner, Pat
90Freder/Team-28

Hedley, Darren
90Martins/ProC-3183

Hedlund, Mike
65T-546R
69T-591
70OPC-187
70T-187
71OPC-662
71T-662
72MB-137
72OPC-81
72T-81
73OPC-591
73T-591

Hedrick, Craig
78Cedar
79Cedar/TCMA-23

Heep, Danny
80Tucson-1
81F-72
81T-82R
82F-217
82T-441
83D-443
83F-449
83T-538
83T/Tr-41
84D-434
84F-586
84Nes/792-29
84T-29
85D-556
85F-84
85OPC-339
85T-339
86D-556
86F-83
86T-619
87D-649
87F-11
87T-241
88Mother/Dodg-20
88Pol/Dodg-12
88S-417
88T-753
89D-368
89F-61
89S-343
89S/Tr-57
89T-198
90B-276
90D-358
90F-278
90F/Can-278
90OPC-573
90S-113
90T-573
90T/Big-90
90T/TVRSox-24
90Target-329
91AAA/LineD-635
91Brave/Dubuq/Perf-15
91S-827
91Vanco/LineD-635
91Vanco/ProC-1601
91WIZMets-167

Heffernan, Bert
87PanAm/USAB-18
87PanAm/USAR-18
89Beloit/I/Star-9
89Beloit/II/Star-14
89Star/IISingl-109
90ElPaso/GS-17
90TeamUSA/87-18
90TexLgAS/GS-5
91AAA/LineD-9
91Albuq/LineD-9
91Albuq/ProC-1143
92Calgary/SB-60
92D/Rook-50
93Calgary/ProC-1169

Heffernan, Jerry
45Parade*-25

Heffner, Don
39PlayBall-44
40PlayBall-51
41DP-147
41G-11
60T-462C
66T-269MG
92Conlon/Sport-521
W753

Heffner, Robert
64T-79
65OPC-199
65T-199
66T-432

Heflin, Bailey
92Lipscomb-13
93Lipscomb-11

Hegan, J. Mike
67T-553R
68T-402
69Sunoco/Pin-11
69T-577
70MLB/St-271
70McDon-3
70OPC-111
70T-111
70T/SO
71MLB/St-438
71OPC-415
71T-415
71T/Coins-116
72T-632
73OPC-382
73T-382
74OPC-517
74Syrac/Team-10
74T-517
75OPC-99
75T-99
75T/M-99
76A&P/Milw
76Laugh/Jub-21
76OPC-377
76OPC-69FS
76SSPC-235
76T-377
76T-69FS
77T-507
92Yank/WIZ60-54
92Yank/WIZ70-71

Hegan, Jim
48L-28
50B-7
50NumNum
51B-79
51T/RB-12
52B-187
52NumNum-2
52RM-AL11
52StarCal-88AM
52StarCal/L-74D
52T-17
53B/Col-102
53T-80
54DanDee
54RH
54T-29
55Gol/Ind-11
55RFG-5
55RM-AL7
55Salem
55T-7
55T/DH-67
55W605-5
56Carling-3
56T-48
56T/Pin-8C
57Sohio/Ind-6
57T-136
58T-345

59T-372
73OPC-116CO
73T-116CO
76OPC-69FS
76T-69FS
79TCMA-139
81TCMA-481M
83Kaline-15M
91T/Arc53-80
93UD/ATH-64
94T/Arc54-29
Exh47
PM10/Sm-70
Hegan, Steve
90MissSt-17
91MissSt-23
92MissSt-19
93MissSt-20
Hegman, Bob
81CharR-10
84Memphis-13
85Omaha-30
86Omaha/ProC-11
86Omaha/TCMA-8
Hehl, Jake
90Target-979
Heidelberg, Khary
91LitSun/HSPros-15
91LitSun/HSProsG-15
Heidemann, Jack
71MLB/St-372
71OPC-87
71T-87
72OPC-374
72T-374
73OPC-644
73T-644
75OPC-649
75T-649
75T/M-649
76SSPC-544
77T-553
78Spokane/Cramer-9
78Spokane/Team-9
79Spokane-15
91WIZMets-168
Heiden, Shawn
89Bluefld/Star-11
90Foil/Best-110
90Wausau/Best-13
90Wausau/ProC-2126
90Wausau/Star-9
Heidenreich, Curt
82Cedar-3
83Water-3
84Wichita/Rock-9
Heiderscheit, Pat
89James/ProC-2143
93James/ClBest-27CO
93James/ProC-3343CO
Heidrick, John
E107
Heifferon, Mike
86Albany/TCMA-11
87PrWill-14
88Albany/ProC-1354
89AAA/ProC-3
89Colum/Pol-24M
90AAASingl/ProC-343M
90ColClip/CMC-24CO
90ColClip/ProC-693CO
90ProC/Singl-224M
92ColClip/Pol-2M
Height, Ron
88LitFalls/Pucko-5
Heilgeist, Jim
90Gate/ProC-3346
90Gate/SportP-11
Heilmann, Harry E.
21Exh-72
25Exh-92
26Exh-93
27Exh-48
29Exh/4-24
31Exh/4-7
50Callahan
50W576-38
60F-65
61F-42
63Bz/ATG-2
76Shakey-61
77Galasso-95
80Laugh/3/4/5-28
80Perez/HOF-61
80SSPC/HOF
81Conlon-76
81Tiger/Detroit-4
86Conlon/1-42
86Tiger/Sport-3
90Perez/GreatMom-47
91Conlon/Sport-52
93Conlon-915
D327
D328-71
E120
E121/120
E122
E135-71
E210-22
E220
R423-46
V100
V61-27
V89-22
W501-6
W502-22
W515-18
W517-14
W573
W575
Heimach, Fred
90Target-330
92Conlon/Sport-480
Heimer, Todd
79Tacoma-8
80Tacoma-18
81Chatt-10
Heimueller, Gorman
81WHave-20
82Tacoma-5
83Tacoma-4
84Cram/PCL-95
84D-131
85OrlanTw-25
86Toledo-12
87Visalia-24
88Visalia/Cal-174
88Visalia/ProC-105
89Visalia/Cal-119CO
89Visalia/ProC-1420
90OrlanSR/Best-24CO
90OrlanSR/ProC-1100CO
90OrlanSR/Star-26CO
91AAA/LineD-425M
91Portl/LineD-425CO
91Portl/ProC-1583CO
92Portl/SB-425M
92Portland/ProC-2683CO
Heinen, Joe
75Cedar
Heinkel, Don
83BirmB-9
84Evansvl-19
86Nashvl-11
87Toledo-7
87Toledo/TCMA-2
88F/Up-U27
88S/Tr-79T
89B-427
89F-133
89Louisvl-21
89S-168
89T-499
90BirmDG/Best-17
90WichSt-14
Heinle, Dana
87Kenosha-15
88Visalia/Cal-168
88Visalia/ProC-82
89VeroB/Star-11
Heins, Jim
89Niagara/Pucko-10
Heintzelman, Ken
49B-108
49Eureka-136
50B-85
51B-147
51BR-C10
52B-148
52T-362
53T-136
79TCMA-78
91T/Arc53-136
R423-42
Heintzelman, Tom
74OPC-607R
74T-607R
75Phoenix-17
75Phoenix/Caruso-13
75Phoenix/CircleK-17
76Phoenix/Coke-8
79Phoenix
Heise, Benjamin
75OkCty/Team-12
Heise, Larry Wayne
84Newar-19
87Greenvl/Best-22
Heise, Robert
70OPC-478
70T-478
71MLB/St-250
71OPC-691
71T-691
72OPC-402
72T-402
73OPC-547
73T-547
74OPC-51
74T-51
74T/Tr-51T
75OPC-441
75T-441
75T/M-441
91WIZMets-169
Heisler, Laurence
92Batavia/ClBest-16
92Batavia/ProC-3257
Heist, Al
58Union
61T-302
62Salada-195
62Shirriff-195
62T-373
62T/St-126
89Smok/Ast-24
Heitmuller, William
(Heinie)
E90/1
M116
Held, Matt
83Idaho-16
Held, Mel
91Crown/Orio-191
Held, Woodie
58T-202
59Kahn
59T-226
60Kahn
60L-2
60T-178
61Bz-33
61Kahn
61NuCard-405
61T-60
61T/St-136
62Bz
62J-44
62Kahn
62P-44
62P/Can-44
62Salada-5
62Shirriff-5
62Sugar-12
62T-215
62T/St-35
62T/bucks
63J-69
63P-69
63Sugar-12
63T-435
64Kahn
64T-105
64T/Coins-29
64T/SU
64T/St-29S3
64T/tatt
65T-336
66OPC-136
66T-136
67T-251
68T-289
69MB-108
69T-636
78TCMA-284
79TCMA-174
91Crown/Orio-192
Helfand, Eric
88NE-5
89Alaska/Team-3
90A&AASingle/ProC-167
90SoOreg/Best-2
90SoOreg/ProC-3426
91ClBest/Singl-128
91Modesto/ClBest-21
92AS/Cal-3
92ClBest-188
92Modesto/ClBest-3
92Modesto/ProC-3903
93FExcel/ML-217
94T-363
94T/Gold-363
Heller, John
83Lynch-17
Heller, Mark
86Albuq-11
Helling, Rick
91T/Tr-54T
92B-641FOIL
92Classic/DP-17
92FrRow/DP-81
92StCl/Dome-81
92T/Tr-48T
92T/TrGold-48T
92UD/ML-13
93B-165
93Pinn-459DP
93S-491DP
93Select-358DP
93StCl/MurphyS-96
94B-297
94ClBest/Gold-181
94FExcel-134
94Finest-434
94Flair-110
94Pinn-525
94SigRook/Bonus-3
94UD-516DD
94UD/SP-149
94Ultra-431
Hellman, Anthony
N172
Hellman, Jeff
87FtLaud-25
Helm, J. Ross
T206
Helm, Wayne
89BendB/Legoe-4
90Boise/ProC-3315
Helmick, Tony
89GreatF-6
90Bakers/Cal-238
Helmquist, Doug
84BuffB-25
Helms, Mike
90Everett/Best-18
90Everett/ProC-3134
Helms, Tommy
65OPC-243R
65T-243R
66T-311R
67CokeCap/Reds-5
67Kahn
67T-505
68T-405
69MB-109
69MLB/St-129
69MLBPA/Pin-47
69OPC-70
69OPC/DE-9
69T-418AS
69T-70
69T/DE-20
69T/S-40
69T/St-24
69T/decal
70MLB/St-28
70OPC-159
70T-159
71MLB/St-61
71OPC-272
71T-272
72MB-138
72OPC-204
72T-204
73OPC-495
73T-495
74OPC-67
74T-67
74T/St-32
75OPC-119
75T-119
75T/M-119
76OPC-583
76SSPC-56
76T-583
76T/Tr-583T
77T-402
78T-618
86TexGold-CO
88Kahn/Reds-CO
90CharlK/Team-19MG
90OPC-110MG
90T-110MG
91Utica/ClBest-17
91Utica/ProC-3248
92Salinas/ClBest-12
93Rang/Keeb-179
Helsel, Ronald
93Dunedin/ProC-1808
Helsom, Bob
83StPete-21
84ArkTr-7
Helton, Keith
87Belling/Team-6
88CalLgAS-29
88SanBern/Best-19
88SanBern/Cal-44
89Star/IISingl-123
89Wmsprt/ProC-645
89Wmsprt/Star-9
90AAASingl/ProC-111
90Calgary/CMC-21
90Calgary/ProC-646
90ProC/Singl-448
91AAA/LineD-58
91Calgary/LineD-58
91Calgary/ProC-510
92Jacks/ProC-3996
Helton, Todd
93Bz-11
93T/Tr-19T
Heman, Russell
59T-283
60Maple-8
Heming, Tom
92Eugene/ClBest-15
92Eugene/ProC-3026
Hemm, Warren
78Memphis/Team-5
79Memphis/TCMA-23
Hemmerich, Mike
89Pittsfld/Star-7
Hemmerly, John
89Erie/Star-6
89SanDiegoSt/Smok-12
Hemond, Scott
87Madis-3
88Huntsvl/BK-6
89Huntsvl/Best-1
90AAASingl/ProC-146
90B-453
90F-646R
90F/Can-646
90ProC/Singl-593
90S-598RP
90T/89Debut-54
90Tacoma/CMC-16
90Tacoma/ProC-99
90UD/Ext-727
91B-232
91S/100RisSt-22
91Tacoma/ProC-2314
92D-637
92Mother/A's-26
92S-617
92StCl-62
92Ultra-422
93D-623
93Mother/A's-19
93StCl/A's-21
93Ultra-607
94D-141
94F-263
94Pac/Cr-451
94StCl-12
94StCl/1stDay-12
94StCl/Gold-12
94T-226
94T/Gold-226
Hempen, Hal
88Savan/ProC-342
Hempfield, Keith
83CharR-7
Hemphill, Charles
12Sweet/Pin-35
E107
E97
S74-22
T204
T205

T206
W555
Hemsley, Ralston (Rollie)
34Exh/4-15
35BU-71
35Exh/4-15
35G-8C
35G-9C
36Exh/4-15
36G
36Wheat
37Exh/4-15
40PlayBall-205
41DP-133
41PlayBall-34
44Yank/St-14
47Centen-8
54T-143CO
91Conlon/Sport-299
92Yank/WIZAS-28
94T/Arc54-143
PR1-17
R312/M
R314
WG8-32
Hemus, Solly
52B-212
52T-196
53B/Col-85
53Hunter
53T-231
54B-94
54Hunter
54T-117
55B-107
55Hunter
57T-231
58T-207
59T-527
60T-218MG
61T-139MG
79TCMA-93
81TCMA-362MG
91T/Arc53-231
94T/Arc54-117
Hence, Sam
90BurlInd/ProC-3020
91BurlInd/ProC-3315
92ColRS/ClBest-7
92ColRS/ProC-2405
92Watertn/ProC-3247
Henderson, Bill
88Fayette/ProC-1102
89Lakeland/Star-9
Henderson, Brad
86FSLAS-22TR
86StPete-10TR
87ArkTr-24TR
88ArkTr/GS-2TR
Henderson, Carl
90MissSt-18
91MissSt-24
92MissSt-20
93MissSt-21
Henderson, Chris
92Bend/ClBest-12
Henderson, Craig
82Wisco/Frit-26
83Visalia/Frit-20
85OrlanTw-26
Henderson, Daryl
91GulfCR/SportP-22
92Gaston/ClBest-10
92Gaston/ProC-2248
92UD/ML-243
93B-25
Henderson, Dave
80Spokane-16
82T-711R
83F-481
83T-732
84D-557
84F-611
84Mother/Mar-3
84Nes/792-154
84OPC-154
84T-154
84T/St-343
85F-489
85Mother/Mar-4
85OPC-344
85T-344
85T/St-338
86D-318
86F-465
86Leaf-187
86Mother/Mar-4
86OPC-221
86T-221
86T-546M
86T/St-222
87D-622
87D/OD-189
87F-36
87F/Hottest-19
87F/WS-10M
87Leaf-103
87Sf/TPrev-9M
87T-452
87T/HL-22
87T/St-23WS
87Woolwth-22
88D/A's/Bk-NEW
88F-84
88F/Up-U53
88Mother/A's-14
88S-228
88S/Tr-49T
88T-628
88T/Big-131
88T/Tr-48T
89AubAs/ProC-2185
89B-200
89D-20DK
89D-450
89D/Best-190
89D/DKsuper-20DK
89F-10
89Mother/A's-13
89OPC-327
89Panini/St-423
89S-533
89Sf-127
89T-527
89T/Big-326
89T/St-164
89T/St/Backs-17
89UD-174
90B-458
90D-243
90D/BestAL-39
90F-9
90F/Can-9
90Kenner/Fig-39
90Mother/A's-18
90OPC-68
90Osceola/Star-9
90Panini/St-133
90PublInt/St-306
90S-325
90T-68
90T/Big-309
90T/St-184
90UD-206
90Woolwth/HL-29
91B-226
91BurlAs/ClBest-15
91BurlAs/ProC-2809
91Classic/III-36
91D-326
91F-9
91Leaf-232
91Leaf/Stud-103
91Mother/A's-18
91OPC-144
91Panini/FrSt-197
91Panini/St-150
91S-644
91SFExam/A's-5
91StCl-284
91T-144
91UD-108
91UD/FinalEd-88FAS
91USPlayC/AS-13H
91Ultra-247
92B-488
92Classic/Game200-9
92D-21AS
92D-311
92F-257
92Hardee-13
92Kenner/Fig-22
92L-232
92L/BlkGold-232
92Mother/A's-18
92OPC-335
92Panini-20
92Panini-276AS
92Pinn-16
92Pinn/Rookl-8M
92S-5
92S/100SS-92
92StCl-218
92StCl/Dome-82
92Studio-224
92T-335
92T/Gold-335
92T/GoldWin-335
92T/Kids-116
92TripleP-130
92TripleP-166
92UD-172
92Ultra-113
93D-373
93F-664
93L-139
93Mother/A's-9
93OPC-155
93Pac/Spanish-568
93Panini-20
93Pinn-170
93S-134
93StCl-349
93StCl/1stDay-349
93StCl/A's-11
93Studio-30
93T-473
93T/Gold-473
93TripleP-119
93UD-607
93Ultra-608
94D-513
94F-264
94Finest-260
94Flair-59
94Pac/Cr-452
94Panini-109
94Pinn-508
94S-463
94StCl-253
94StCl/1stDay-253
94StCl/Gold-253
94T-708
94T/Gold-708
94UD-507
94Ultra-365
Henderson, David
92SanBern/ProC-
Henderson, Derek
89Pittsfld/Star-8
91StLucie/ClBest-7
91StLucie/ProC-718
92Knoxvl/ProC-2996
92Knoxvl/SB-381
93Knoxvl/ProC-1258
Henderson, Frank
88AppFx/ProC-154
88Eugene/Best-23
89AppFx/ProC-857
Henderson, Harry IV
89Billings/ProC-2059
Henderson, James H. (Hardie)
N172
N184
Henderson, Jeff
91Kingspt/ClBest-1
91Kingspt/ProC-3808
Henderson, Jim
92James/ClBest-2
Henderson, Joe
81Clinton-22
82Beloit/Frit-2
83ElPaso-3
84MidldC-1
Henderson, John
77QuadC
Henderson, Joseph Lee
76Indianap-5
77Indianap-3
77T-487R
Henderson, Kenneth J.
91Everett/ClBest-19
91Everett/ProC-3929
92Everett/ClBest-6
92Everett/ProC-1681
Henderson, Kenneth Jos.
65T-497R
66OPC-39
66T-39
67T-383
68T-309
70OPC-298
70T-298
71MLB/St-251
71OPC-155
71T-155
71T/Coins-97
71T/tatt-2
71Ticket/Giant-5
72OPC-443
72OPC-444IA
72T-443
72T-444IA
73OPC-101
73T-101
74OPC-394
74T-394
74T/St-154
75Ho-136
75Ho/Twink-136
75OPC-59
75T-59
75T/M-59
76OPC-464
76SSPC-147
76T-464
76T/Tr-464T
77T-242
78Ho-126
78Pep-13
78T-212
79T-73
80T-523
91WIZMets-170
93Rang/Keeb-180
Henderson, Lee
89GA-10
90CharRain/Best-11
90CharRain/ProC-2041
90GA-33M
90GA-7
91Waterlo/ClBest-12
91Waterlo/ProC-1259
92HighD/ClBest-26
Henderson, Matt
79Wisco-8
Henderson, Mike
78Holyo
79Holyo-17
80Vanco-17
Henderson, Pedro
90BurlInd/ProC-3021
91ColInd/ProC-1499
91Watertn/ClBest-26
91Watertn/ProC-3381
Henderson, Ramon
86Reading-9
87Reading-15
88Maine/CMC-19
88Maine/ProC-295
89Reading/Best-13
89Reading/ProC-653
89Reading/Star-13
90Princet/DIMD-29CO
91Clearw/ClBest-5CO
91Clearw/ProC-1639CO
92Clearw/ClBest-24CO
92Clearw/ProC-2074
Henderson, Rats
86Negro/Frit-34
Henderson, Rickey
77Modesto
79Ogden/TCMA-9
80T-482
81A's/Granny-35
81D-119
81F-351HL
81F-574
81F/St-54
81K-33
81OPC-261
81PermaGr/CC-19
81Sqt-28
81T-261
81T-4LL
81T/SO-39
81T/St-115
81T/St-15
82D-113
82F-643HL
82F-92
82F/St-123
82Granny-4
82K-4
82OPC-268
82PermaGr/AS-6
82PermaGr/CC-23
82T-156TL
82T-164LL
82T-610
82T/St-221
82T/St-8
82T/StVar-221
83D-11DK
83D-35
83D/AAS-22
83F-519
83F-639HL
83F-646IA
83F/St-1AM
83F/St-1BM
83F/St-25AM
83F/St-25BM
83F/St-7M
83Granny-35
83K-8
83OPC-180
83OPC-391AS
83OPC/St-103FOIL
83OPC/St-159
83OPC/St-197RB
83OPC/St-198RB
83OPC/St-199RB
83OPC/St-200RB
83OPC/St-201RB
83OPC/St-202RB
83OPC/St-21
83PermaGr/CC-26
83T-180
83T-2M
83T-391AS
83T-531TL
83T-704LL
83T/Fold-5M
83T/Gloss40-33
83T/St-103
83T/St-159
83T/St-197
83T/St-198
83T/St-199
83T/St-200
83T/St-201
83T/St-202
83T/St-21
83T/St/Box-8
84D-54
84D/AAS-9
84F-447
84F/St-53
84F/St-92
84MiltBrad-13
84Mother/A's-2
84Nes/792-134LL
84Nes/792-156TL
84Nes/792-230
84Nes/792-2HL
84OPC-230
84Ralston-15
84Seven-21W
84T-134LL
84T-156TL
84T-230
84T-2LL
84T/Cereal-15
84T/Gloss40-6
84T/RD-24
84T/St-202
84T/St-3
84T/St-327
84T/St-4
84T/Super-19
85D-176
85D/HL-17
85D/HL-42
85F-425
85F-629IA
85F/St-54
85F/Up-U51
85FunFood/Pin-17
85Leaf-208
85OPC-115
85Seven-12W
85T-115
85T-706AS
85T/3D-10
85T/RD-24
85T/St-283
85T/St-321

85T/Super-14
85T/Tr-49T
85Woolwth-17
86D-51
86D/AAS-10
86D/PopUp-10
86Dorman-7
86Drake-5
86F-108
86F/AS-7
86F/LimEd-23
86F/Mini-23
86F/St-53
86GenMills/Book-1M
86Leaf-37
86OPC-243
86Quaker-25
86Seven/Coin-E12
86Sf-184M
86Sf-6
86Sf/Dec-69
86T-500
86T-716AS
86T/3D-11
86T/Gloss22-7
86T/Gloss60-5
86T/Mini-27
86T/St-155
86T/St-297
86T/Super-30
86T/Tatt-24M
87BK-9
87Classic-12
87D-228
87D/AAS-6
87D/OD-248
87D/PopUp-6
87Drake-12
87F-101
87F/Excit-24
87F/HL-4
87F/Hottest-20
87F/Mini-52
87F/Slug-18
87F/St-56
87GenMills/Book-2M
87Jiffy-14
87KMart-27
87KayBee-16
87Kraft-31
87Leaf-191
87MSA/Discs-18
87Mother/A's-20
87OPC-7
87OPC/WaxBox-E
87RedFoley/St-80
87Seven-E3
87Sf-157M
87Sf-159M
87Sf-198M
87Sf-4
87Sf/TPrev-7M
87Sportflic/DealP-4
87Stuart-23M
87T-311TBC
87T-735
87T/Board-8
87T/Coins-12
87T/Gloss22-18
87T/Gloss60-21
87T/HL-3
87T/Mini-64
87T/St-147
87T/St-296
87T/WaxBox-E
87Woolwth-3
88ChefBoy-20
88Classic/Blue-234
88D-277
88D/AS-4
88D/Best-76
88D/PopUp-4
88D/Y/Bk-277
88Drake-7
88F-209
88F/Hottest-16
88F/Mini-40
88F/SS-C2
88F/Slug-C2
88F/St-S4
88KMart-13
88KennerFig-48
88Leaf-145
88OPC-60
88OPC/WaxBox-M
88Panini/St-158
88Panini/St-231M
88Panini/St-434
88S-13
88S/WaxBox-7
88Sf-11
88Sf/Gamewin-8
88T-60
88T/Big-165
88T/Gloss22-7
88T/Gloss60-25
88T/Mini-26
88T/St-155
88T/St-297
88T/St/Backs-51
88T/UK-31
88T/WaxBox-M
89B-181
89Bz-14
89Cadaco-28
89Classic-50
89D-245
89D/AS-4
89D/Best-78
89D/PopUp-4
89F-254
89F/BBAS-20
89F/Excit-21
89F/Superstar-22
89F/Up-54
89KMart/Lead-15
89KayBee-18
89KennerFig-61
89Modesto/Chong-33
89OPC-282
89OPC/BoxB-F
89Panini/St-239AS
89Panini/St-408
89S-657HL
89S-70
89S/HotStar-45
89S/Tr-50
89Sf-145
89T-380
89T/Ames-16
89T/Big-271
89T/DHTest-16
89T/Gloss22-7
89T/Gloss60-35
89T/LJN-54
89T/Mini-66
89T/St-145
89T/St-312
89T/St/Backs-18
89T/Tr-48T
89T/UK-37
89T/WaxBox-F
89UD-210
90B-457
90BBWit-37
90Bz-9
90Classic-37
90Classic/III-27
90CollAB-8
90D-304
90D/BestAL-124
90D/Learning-7
90F-10
90F/AwardWin-18
90F/BBMVP-17
90F/Can-10
90F/LL-18
90F/WS-11
90HOF/St-87
90Holsum/Discs-8
90HotPlay/St-20
90KMart/CBatL-21
90KMart/SS-23
90KayBee-15
90Kenner/Fig-40
90KingB/Discs-19
90Leaf-160
90Leaf-84CL
90MSA/Soda-5
90Mother/A's-4
90OPC-450
90OPC-7RB
90OPC/BoxB-F
90Panini/St-138
90Post-25
90PublInt/St-288
90PublInt/St-537
90S-360
90S-686DT
90S-698M
90S/100St-90
90S/McDon-5
90Sf-208
90Sunflower-13
90T-450
90T-7RB
90T/Ames-13
90T/Big-292
90T/Coins-17
90T/DH-33
90T/Gloss60-37
90T/Mini-28
90T/St-181
90T/St-7HL
90T/TVAS-10
90T/WaxBox-F
90UD-334
90USPlayC/AS-13C
90Windwlk/Discs-8
90Woolwth/HL-14
90Woolwth/HL-23
90Woolwth/HL-31
91B-213
91B-371SLUG
91B-692
91BBBest/RecBr-7
91Bz-2
91Cadaco-29
91Classic/200-189
91Classic/I-72
91Classic/II-T75
91CollAB-25
91D-387MVP
91D-53AS
91D-648
91D-761MVP
91D/Elite-E7
91F-10
91F/ASIns-6
91F/ProVF-2F
91F/UltraG-5
91F/WS-4
91JDean-17
91Kenner-27
91KingB/Discs-5
91Leaf-101
91Leaf/GRook-BC26
91Leaf/Prev-23
91Leaf/Stud-104
91MSA/Holsum-12
91MajorLg/Pins-40
91Mother/A's-4
91OPC-391AS
91OPC-670
91OPC/BoxB-H
91OPC/Premier-62
91Panini/FrSt-171
91Panini/FrSt-196
91Panini/St-146
91Panini/Top15-38
91Panini/Top15-45
91Panini/Top15-53
91Panini/Top15-6
91Pep/Henderson-Set
91Pepsi/Discs-1
91Pepsi/Discs-2
91Pepsi/Discs-3
91Pepsi/Discs-4
91Petro/SU-21
91Post-27
91Post/Can-24
91RedFoley/St-121
91RedFoley/St-48
91S-10
91S-397AS
91S-857FRAN
91S-875MVP
91S-890DT
91S/100SS-10
91S/Cooper-B4
91SFExam/A's-6
91Seven/3DCoin-5A
91Seven/3DCoin-7NC
91Seven/3DCoin-7NE
91Seven/3DCoin-7NW
91SilverSt-1
91StCl-120
91StCl/Charter*-13
91StCl/Charter*-14
91StCl/Member*-18
91StCl/Member*-4
91T-391AS
91T-670
91T/CJMini/I-18
91T/SU-19
91T/WaxBox-H
91UD-444
91UD-636
91UD/Ext-SP2M
91UD/FinalEd-86FAS
91UD/SilSlug-SS3
91USPlayC/AS-11H
91Ultra-248
91Ultra-393EP
91Woolwth/HL-2
91Woolwth/HL-26
92B-166
92CJ/DII-19
92Classic/Game200-118
92Classic/I-43
92D-193
92D-215HL
92D-30AS
92D/Elite-L1
92DPep/MSA-28
92F-258
92F-681RS
92F/Performer-17
92French-17
92Kenner/Fig-23
92L-116
92L/BlkGold-116
92MooTown-19
92Mother/A's-4
92MrTurkey-14
92OPC-2RB
92OPC-560
92OPC/Premier-147
92Panini-21
92Panini-278AS
92Pinn-283M
92Pinn-401
92Pinn-614TECH
92Pinn/RookI-7M
92Post/Can-18
92S-430HL
92S-441DT
92S-480
92S/100SS-100
92StCl-750
92StCl/Dome-83
92StCl/MPhoto-8
92T-2RB
92T-560
92T/Gold-2RB
92T/Gold-560
92T/GoldWin-2RB
92T/GoldWin-560
92T/Kids-118
92T/McDonB-3
92T/MicroG-2
92TripleP-63
92UD-155
92UD-640CL
92UD-648DS
92UD-782
92UD-90TC
92UD/ASFF-27
92UD/TWillB-T7
92Ultra-114
92Yank/WIZ80-80
92Yank/WIZAS-29
93B-625
93Cadaco-31
93Classic/Gamel-42
93Colla/DM-50
93D-315
93DennyGS-3
93F-294
93F/Fruit-29
93Flair-260
93Ho-23
93HumDum/Can-14
93L-291
93L/GoldAS-16
93MSA/Metz-30
93Mother/A's-6
93OPC-130
93Pac/Spanish-222
93Panini-19
93Pinn-29
93Pinn-308HH
93Pinn/Cooper-7
93Pinn/HRC-21
93S-71
93Select-106
93Select/RookTr-1T
93StCl-558
93StCl/1stDay-558
93StCl/A's-8
93StCl/MPhoto-19
93Studio-84
93T-750
93T/Finest-86AS
93T/FinestASJ-86AS
93T/FinestRef-86AS
93T/Gold-750
93TripleP-219
93UD-136
93UD/Clutch-R12
93UD/Diam-29
93UD/FunPack-212ASA
93UD/FunPack-50
93UD/SP-40
93UD/SeasonHL-HI10
93UD/Then-TN3
93USPlayC/Ace-8H
93Ultra-258
94B-80
94D-19
94D-290M
94D/Ann-4
94D/Special-19
94F-334
94Finest-223
94L-259
94OPC-37
94OPC/BJ-1
94Pac/Cr-643
94Panini-139
94Pinn-450
94Pinn/Run-10
94S-35
94S/GoldR-35
94S/GoldS-34
94Sf/Mov-8
94StCl-107
94StCl/1stDay-107
94StCl/Gold-107
94Studio-3
94T-248
94T/Gold-248
94TripleP-4
94UD-60
94UD/CollC-131
94UD/CollC/Gold-131
94UD/CollC/Silv-131
94UD/DColl-W6
94UD/ElecD-60
94UD/SP-34
94Ultra-408

Henderson, Robbie
79Cedar/TCMA-6

Henderson, Rodney
92Classic/DP-76
92James/ClBest-1
92James/ProC-1497
93OPC/Premier/TDP-3
93StCl/MurphyS-178
93WPalmB/ClBest-9
93WPalmB/ProC-1333
94B-584
94ClBest/Gold-189
94FExcel-226
94Flair-191
94SigRook-39
94UD-517DD
94Ultra-523

Henderson, Ryan
92GreatF/SportP-17
94FExcel-214

Henderson, Steve
77Indianap-14
78OPC-53
78T-134
79OPC-232
79T-445
80OPC-156
80T-299
81Coke
81D-157
81F-321
81K-25
81OPC-44
81T-619
81T/SO-79
81T/St-193
81T/Tr-769
82D-183
82F-597

82F/St-98
82FBI/Disc-10
82OPC-89
82RedLob
82T-89
82T/St-30
83D-252
83F-496
83T-335
83T/Tr-42
84D-389
84F-612
84Mother/Mar-21
84Nes/792-501
84OPC-274
84T-501
84T/RD-25
84T/St-341
85D-145
85F-490
85F/Up-U52
85Mother/A's-26
85OPC-38
85T-640
85T/RD-25
85T/Tr-50T
86D-375
86F-419
86Mother/A's-20
86T-748
87Tacoma-13
88Mother/Ast-12
88Pol/Ast-13
88S-547
88T-527
89AAA/CMC-9
89AAA/ProC-22
89BuffB/CMC-14
89BuffB/ProC-1676
89Pac/SenLg-5
89T/SenLg-9
89TM/SenLg-45
90AAASingl/ProC-506CO
90BuffB/ProC-391CO
90BuffB/Team-8CO
90EliteSenLg-17
90TripleAAS/CMC-9
91Pac/SenLg-144
91WIZMets-171
Henderson, Ted
81Tacoma-29M
Henderson, Tim
89MissSt-18
90MissSt-19
Henderson, Todd
92Hamil/ClBest-27
92Hamil/ProC-1606
Henderson, Valentine
89Welland/Pucko-13
Henderson, Wendell
82QuadC-15
Hendley, Brett
90Modesto/Chong-13
91Madison/ClBest-15
91Madison/ProC-2134
91MidwLAS/ProC-41
92Modesto/ClBest-16
92Modesto/ProC-3906
Hendley, C. Bob
61T-372
62T-361
63T-62
64T-189
64T/Coins-94
65T-444
66OPC-82
66T-82
67CokeCap/Cub-4
67T-256
68T-345
69OPC-144
69T-144
69T/4in1-24M
91WIZMets-172
Hendrick, George
72OPC-406
72T-406
73OPC-13
73OPC-201ALCS
73T-13
73T-201ALCS
74OPC-303
74T-303
74T/St-167
75Ho-140
75K-46
75OPC-109
75T-109
75T/M-109
76OPC-570
76SSPC-527
76T-570
77BurgChef-129
77Ho-123
77Ho/Twink-123
77OPC-218
77Padre/SchCd-13
77Pep-40
77T-330
78Ho-82
78OPC-178
78T-30
79Ho-66
79OPC-82
79T-175
80OPC-184
80T-350
81Coke
81D-430
81Drake-22
81F-542
81K-35
81OPC-230
81T-230
81T/SO-85
81T/St-22
81T/St-220
81T/St-256
82D-40
82D-9DK
82Drake-17
82F-113
82F/St-25
82OPC-295
82Sqt-16
82T-420
82T/St-91
83D-404
83Drake-10
83F-7
83F/St-14M
83K-25
83OPC-148
83OPC/St-153LCS
83OPC/St-285
83PermaGr/CC-6
83T-650
83T/St-153
83T/St-285
84D-475
84D/AAS-32
84Drake-12
84F-324
84F/St-9
84Nes/792-386AS
84Nes/792-540
84OPC-163
84OPC-386AS
84T-386AS
84T-540
84T/Gloss40-23
84T/RD-2M
84T/St-139
84T/St-185
84T/St/Box-11
85D-181
85F-225
85F/St-27
85F/Up-U53
85FunFood/Pin-52
85Leaf-259
85OPC-60
85T-60
85T/RD-2M
85T/St-134
85T/Tr-51T
86F-158
86OPC-190
86Smok/Cal-14
86T-190
87D/OD-3
87F-82
87OPC-248
87Smok/Cal-22
87T-725
88D-479
88S-308
88Smok/Angels-24
88T-304
89Pac/SenLg-61
89T/SenLg-12
89TM/SenLg-46
90EliteSenLg-82
92Card/McDon/Pac-45
Hendrick, Harvey
29Exh/4-3
34DS-41
90Target-331
92Conlon/Sport-522
R315-C2
R316
W513-63
Hendrick, Pete
86ElPaso-14
Hendricks, Elrod
(Ellie)
69MB-110
69T-277
70OPC-528
70T-528
71MLB/St-299
71OPC-219
71T-219
72MB-139
72OPC-508
72T-508
75OPC-609
75T-609
75T/M-609
76OPC-371
76SSPC-384
76T-371
87French-44CO
88French-44CO
89French-44CO
89Swell-64
91Crown/Orio-193
92Yank/WIZ70-72
Hendricks, Kacy
92GulfCD/ProC-3561
Hendricks, Steve
87Spokane-22
88River/Cal-221
88River/ProC-1409
89AubAs/ProC-7
89Watlo/ProC-1772
89Watlo/Star-11
90AS/Cal-7
90River/Best-12
90River/Cal-11
90River/ProC-2615
91AA/LineD-462
91NewBrit/LineD-462
91NewBrit/ProC-357
Hendrickson, Craig
77QuadC
Hendrickson, Dan
89Everett/Star-13
Hendriksen, Claude
16FleischBrd-39
Hendrix, Claude
14CJ-76
15CJ-76
92Conlon/Sport-343
BF2-64
D328-72
D329-78
D350/2-77
E135-72
E220
M101/4-78
M101/5-77
W514-9
WG4-9
Hendrix, James
87CharWh-2
88Virgini/Star-10
Hendry, Ted
88TM/Umpire-35
89TM/Umpire-33
90TM/Umpire-32
Henerson, Rob
78Cedar
Hengel, Dave
86Calgary-11
87Calgary-9
88Calgary/CMC-18
88Calgary/ProC-1550
88D-629
88F-375
89Chatt/II/Team-12
89ColoSp/CMC-18
89ColoSp/ProC-243
89T-531
92Phoenix/SB-382
Hengle, Emory
N172
Henika, Ron
84Cedar-27
86Vermont-11
87Nashvl-10
90CedarDG/Best-17
Henion, Scott
87Columbia-17
88Salem/Star-8
89WPalmB/Star-12
Henke, Rick
83Watlo/Frit-26TR
86Water-13TR
87Wmsprt-15
Henke, Tom
82Tulsa-1
83OKCty-9
84D-134
84OKCty-10
85D-403
85IntLgAS-41
85Syrac-8
85Tor/Fire-14
86BJ/Ault-13
86D-437
86F-60
86F/St-54
86Leaf-206
86OPC-333
86T-333
86T/St-189
86Tor/Fire-17
87D-197
87F-228
87F/Excit-25
87F/Slug-19
87F/St-57
87GenMills/Book-1M
87Leaf-73
87OPC-277
87Sf/TPrev-5M
87Smok/AL-14
87T-510
87T/Mini-76
87T/St-185
87Tor/Fire-12
88BJ/5x7-6
88D-490
88D/AS-28
88D/Best-104
88F-112
88F/AS-2
88F/AwardWin-18
88F/Excit-19
88F/LL-17
88F/Mini-62
88F/St-73
88F/TL-12
88Ho/Disc-23
88OPC-220
88Panini/St-213
88RedFoley/St-33
88S-57
88Sf-65
88T-220
88T-396
88T/Big-41
88T/Gloss60-35
88T/Mini-38
88T/Revco-31
88T/St-186
88T/St/Backs-64
88T/UK-32
88Tor/Fire-50
89B-246
89D-385
89D/Best-301
89F-235
89F/Excit-22
89OPC-75
89Panini/St-461
89S-318
89S/HotStar-63
89Sf-126
89T-75
89T/LJN-143
89T/St-195
89Tor/Fire-50
89UD-264
90B-506
90BJ/HoSt-3M
90BJ/HoSt-4M
90D-349
90D/BestAL-14
90F-84
90F/Can-84
90Holsum/Discs-3
90Leaf-158
90OPC-695
90PublInt/St-516
90S-157
90Sf-42
90T-695
90T/Big-101
90T/St-196
90Tor/BJ-50
90Tulsa/Team-28
90TulsaDG/Best-19
90UD-282
91B-16
91D-205
91F-176
91Leaf-517
91OPC-110
91OPC/Premier-63
91Panini/FrSt-345
91S-579
91S/ToroBJ-2
91StCl-24
91T-110
91Tor/Fire-50
91UD-149
91Ultra-362
92BJ/Fire-14
92D-141
92D/McDon-G5
92DPep/MSA-3
92F-331
92L-159
92L/BlkGold-159
92OPC-451
92Pinn-417
92S-385
92S-439AS
92S/100SS-31
92StCl-819
92Syrac/TallT-4
92T-451
92T/Gold-451
92T/GoldWin-451
92T/Kids-93
92UD-395
92Ultra-450
93B-461
93BJ/D/45-18
93BJ/D/McDon-7
93D-723
93F-335
93F/Final-279
93Flair-281
93KingB-15
93L-278
93MSA/Ben-16
93OPC-202
93OPC/Premier-77
93OPC/WC-7
93Pac/Spanish-640
93Pinn-546
93Rang/Keeb-409
93S-602
93Select-211
93Select/RookTr-15T
93StCl-637
93StCl/1stDay-637
93StCl/Rang-17
93T-376
93T/Finest-164
93T/FinestRef-164
93T/Gold-376
93T/Tr-14T
93UD-557
93UD/SP-195
93Ultra-629
94B-269
94D-162
94F-308
94Flair-111
94L-434
94OPC-242
94Pac/Cr-618
94Panini-128
94Pinn-42
94Pinn/Artist-42
94Pinn/Museum-42

94S-542
94Sf/2000-104
94StCl-19
94StCl/1stDay-19
94StCl/Gold-19
94StCl/Team-270
94T-644
94T/Finest-64
94T/FinestRef-64
94T/Gold-644
94TripleP-195
94UD-367
94Ultra-128
94Ultra/Fire-3
Henkel, Rob
91Elmira/ClBest-20
91Elmira/ProC-3267
92ProC/Tomorrow-26
92WinHaven/ProC-1770
Henkemeyer, Dick
82Wisco/Frit-17
Henley, Bobby
93James/ClBest-11
93James/ProC-3330
Henley, Dan
85Anchora-15
88Bakers/Cal-235
89SanAn/Best-12
90AAASingl/ProC-72
90Albuq/CMC-18
90Albuq/ProC-351
90Albuq/Trib-10
90ProC/Singl-420
91AAA/LineD-636
91Vanco/LineD-636
91Vanco/ProC-1602
Henley, Mike
83AppFx/Frit-11
Henley, Weldon
90Target-332
E107
E254
Henline, Noah
C46-64
Henline, Walter
(Butch)
25Exh-43
26Exh-44
27Exh-8
87Conlon/2-18
90Target-333
92Conlon/Sport-581
E120
E126-31
E220
V100
V61-59
W572
Henneman, Blair
92Everett/ProC-1679
Henneman, Mike
86Nashvl-12
87D/Rook-32
87F/Up-U44
87Sf/Rook-29
87T/Tr-46T
87Toledo-16
87Toledo/TCMA-13
88Classic/Blue-241
88D-420
88D/Best-91
88F-57
88F/St-25
88OPC-3
88Pep/T-39
88S-520
88S/YS/I-15
88Sf-129
88T-582
88T/Big-256
88T/Gloss60-10
88T/JumboR-7
88ToysRUs-13
89B-98
89Classic-94
89D-327
89D/Best-237
89F-134
89F/Excit-23
89KennerFig-62
89Mara/Tigers-39
89OPC-365
89Panini/St-333
89Pol/Tigers-39
89S-293
89S/HotStar-59
89Sf-56
89T-365
89T/Big-252
89T/St-273
89UD-373
90B-345
90BirmDG/Best-18
90CokeK/Tiger-8
90D-296
90D/BestAL-105
90F-604
90F/Can-604
90Leaf-2
90OPC-177
90Panini/St-69
90PublInt/St-472
90S-184
90Sf-144
90T-177
90T/Big-41
90T/St-282
90Tiger/Milk-Set
90UD-537
91CokeK/Tiger-39
91D-76
91F-340
91Leaf-18
91OPC-641
91Panini/St-236
91RedFoley/St-49
91S-142
91S/100SS-51
91StCl-287
91T-641
91UD-386
91Ultra-123
92B-441
92D-253
92F-138
92L-325
92L/BlkGold-325
92OPC-293
92Pinn-164
92S-217
92StCl-34
92Studio-175
92T-293
92T/Gold-293
92T/GoldWin-293
92UD-339
92USPlayC/Tiger-13S
92USPlayC/Tiger-8D
92Ultra-364
93B-559
93D-259
93F-229
93Flair-204
93L-81
93OPC-149
93Pinn-385
93S-166
93Select-138
93StCl-480
93StCl/1stDay-480
93T-756
93T/Gold-756
93Tiger/Gator-14
93UD-403
93UD/SP-238
93Ultra-199
94B-181
94D-496
94F-135
94L-183
94OPC-52
94Pinn-154
94Pinn/Artist-154
94Pinn/Museum-154
94RedFoley-10M
94S-117
94S/GoldR-117
94StCl-401
94StCl/1stDay-401
94StCl/Gold-401
94T-438
94T/Finest-34
94T/FinestRef-34
94T/Gold-438
94TripleP-246
94UD-321
94UD/CollC-132
94UD/CollC/Gold-132
94UD/CollC/Silv-132
94UD/SP-178
94Ultra-55
Hennessey, Scott
91BBCity/ClBest-25
91BBCity/ProC-1411
Hennessy, Brendan
83BurlR-20
83BurlR/Frit-18
83TriCit-24
Hennessy, Mike
82Cedar-9
86Sumter/ProC-9
Hennigan, Phil
71MLB/St-373
71OPC-211
71T-211
72T-748
73OPC-107
73T-107
91WIZMets-173
Henning, Rich
85Fresno/Pol-24
90Bristol/ProC-3176CO
90Bristol/Star-28CO
Henninger, Rai
88Idaho/ProC-1852
Henninger, Rich
74OPC-602R
74T-602R
75OkCty/Team-4
93Rang/Keeb-181
Hennis, Randall
(Randy)
87AubAs-10
88FSLAS/Star-8
88Osceola/Star-13
89ColMud/Best-9
89ColMud/ProC-137
89ColMud/Star-12
90ProC/Singl-608
90Tucson/CMC-6
90Tucson/ProC-200
91AAA/LineD-611
91Classic/I-45
91S-752RP
91T/90Debut-66
91Tucson/LineD-611
91Tucson/ProC-2209
Hennisaire, Randy
90AAASingl/ProC-190
Henrich, Bobby
58T-131
Henrich, Tom
39PlayBall-52
40PlayBall-4
41DP-111
41PlayBall-39
47TipTop
48B-19
48L-55
49B-69
49Royal-12
50B-10
50Drake-23
51B-291
51BR-B3
53Exh/Can-27
79TCMA-35
82Ohio/HOF-38
92Conlon/Gold-770
92Yank/WIZAS-30
93Conlon-770
94Conlon-1061
Exh47
PM10/Sm-71
PM10/Sm-72
R302
R303/A
R346-42
R423-47
V351A-15
V351B-23
Henrichs, Shawn
91Everett/ClBest-16
91Everett/ProC-3907
Henriksen, Olaf
16FleischBrd-40
D328-73
D329-79
D350/2-78
E135-73
M101/4-79
M101/5-78
T207
Henrikson, Dan
90Bend/Legoe-12
91Clinton/ClBest-3
91Clinton/ProC-828
Henriquez, Oscar
94B-418
Henry Allen, Newton
(Colt)
87Negro/Dixon-41
Henry, Antoine
92Johnson/ClBest-12
92Johnson/ProC-3130
Henry, Bill F.
68T-384R
92Yank/WIZ60-55
Henry, Bill R.
55B-264
59T-46
60Kahn
60T-524
61T-66
62Kahn
62T-562
63FrBauer-8
63T-378
64T-49
65T-456
66OPC-115
66T-115
67T-579
68T-239
Henry, Butch
88Cedar/ProC-1159
88MidwLAS/GS-12
89Chatt/Best-9
89Chatt/GS-11
90CedarDG/Best-23
90Chatt/GS-16
91AAA/LineD-612
91Tucson/LineD-612
91Tucson/ProC-2210
92B-502
92D/Rook-51
92F/Up-86
92L-435
92L/BlkGold-435
92Mother/Ast-18
92Pinn-567
92StCl-742
92Studio-37
92T/Tr-49T
92T/TrGold-49T
92UD-796
92UD/Scout-SR9
93D-348
93D-767
93F-411
93OPC-200
93OPC/Premier-30
93Pac/Spanish-430
93Pinn-511
93S-569
93StCl-311
93StCl/1stDay-311
93StCl/Rockie-24
93T-281
93T-719
93T/Gold-281
93T/Gold-719
93UD-770
93USPlayC/Rockie-11C
93USPlayC/Rockie-5S
93USPlayC/Rook-2S
93Ultra-351
94F-541
Henry, Carlos
88Ashvl/ProC-1074
89Ashvl/ProC-965
Henry, Chris
80Wausau-17
Henry, Dan
77Clinton
77LodiD
Henry, Doug
86Beloit-10
87Beloit-12
88Stockton/Cal-177
88Stockton/ProC-747
89ElPaso/GS-8
90Stockton/Cal-184
91AAA/LineD-140
91AAAGame/ProC-9
91Denver/LineD-140
91Denver/ProC-120
92Classic/Game200-78
92D-663
92L-80
92L/BlkGold-80
92OPC-776
92Pol/Brew-11
92ProC/Tomorrow-82
92S-421
92S/Impact-17
92StCl-615
92T-776
92T/91Debut-73
92T/Gold-776
92T/GoldWin-776
92UD-43
92Ultra-384
93D-471
93F-251
93L-530
93OPC-181
93Pac/Spanish-158
93Pinn-415
93Pol/Brew-10
93S-177
93Select-399
93StCl-521
93StCl/1stDay-521
93T-343
93T/Gold-343
93UD-395
93Ultra-220
94D-119
94F-178
94Finest-404
94L-393
94Pac/Cr-330
94Pinn-283
94Pol/Brew-11
94S-119
94S/GoldR-119
94T-16
94T/Gold-16
94Ultra-75
Henry, Dutch
90Target-334
93Conlon-783
Henry, Dwayne
82BurlR/Frit-4
82BurlR/TCMA-24
83Tulsa-11
84Tulsa-36
85Tulsa-29
86D-603
86F-562
86Sf-179R
87D-637
87OKCty-18
88OkCty/CMC-2
88OkCty/ProC-33
88T-178
89Richm/Bob-9
89Richm/CMC-4
89Richm/Ko-38
89Richm/ProC-844
89T-496
89UD-51
90Brave/Dubuq/Perf-10
90Brave/Dubuq/Singl-12
91F-692
91Leaf-329
91Mother/Ast-24
91OPC-567
91T-567
92D-114
92F-436
92L-433
92L/BlkGold-433
92OPC-668
92Reds/Kahn-48
92S-204
92StCl-892
92T-668
92T/Gold-668
92T/GoldWin-668
92UD-430
92Ultra-483
93D-478
93F-391
93F/Final-272
93Mother/Mar-8
93Rang/Keeb-182
93S-474
93StCl-577

93StCl/1stDay-577
93T-29
93T/Gold-29
94Pac/Cr-572
Henry, Harold
91Utica/ClBest-18
91Utica/ProC-3253
92SoBend/ClBest-16
92SoBend/ProC-189
Henry, Jim
(Sugar)
45Parade*-26
Henry, Jimmy
90Bristol/ProC-3171
90Bristol/Star-10
91Niagara/ClBest-25
91Niagara/ProC-3627
92Lakeland/ClBest-17
92London/ProC-629
Henry, John M.
N172
Henry, John Park
D327
D328-74
D329-80
D350/2-79
E135-74
M101/4-80
M101/5-79
T222
Henry, Jon
90Elizab/Star-12
91Visalia/ClBest-3
91Visalia/ProC-1737
92OrlanSR/ProC-2842
92OrlanSR/SB-507
Henry, Kevin
88Idaho/ProC-1846
Henry, Mark
86Penin-12
87DayBe-10
Henry, Michael
87Savan-10
88Spring/Best-4
Henry, Paul
88NE-6
Henry, Ron
77Fritsch-48
Henry, Santiago
92StCath/ClBest-10
92StCath/ProC-3396
93Hagers/ClBest-13
93Hagers/ProC-1889
Henry, Scott
90Madison/Best-7
90SoOreg/Best-29
91Madison/ClBest-17
91Madison/ProC-2135
92Reno/Cal-42
Henry, Tim
82BurlR/Frit-14
82BurlR/TCMA-1
82Tulsa-6
83Tulsa-10
Henshaw, Roy
90Target-335
Hensich, Phil
R314/Can
V355-123
Hensley, Chuck
82WHave-6
83Tacoma-5
84Cram/PCL-86
86Phoenix-9
87Richm/Bob-12
87Richm/Crown-37
87Richm/TCMA-6
88Albuq/CMC-10
88Albuq/ProC-273
89Calgary/CMC-2
89Calgary/ProC-531
90Wmsprt/Best-9
90Wmsprt/ProC-1055
90Wmsprt/Star-10
Hensley, Mike
88OK-2
89Savan/ProC-364
90Foil/Best-235
90Spring/Best-19
91StPete/ProC-2272
Henson, Hunter
89KS*-14
93Lipscomb-25M
Henson, Joey
92Lipscomb-14
93Lipscomb-12
Henson, Mickey
91ClBest/Singl-22
91Gaston/ClBest-7
91Gaston/ProC-2684
Hentgen, Pat
87Myrtle-10
88Dunedin/Star-9
89Dunedin/Star-7
90A&AASingle/ProC-45
90Foil/Best-295
90Knoxvl/Best-4
90Knoxvl/ProC-1240
90Knoxvl/Star-5
91AAA/LineD-505
91B-23
91Syrac/Kraft-2
91Syrac/LineD-505
91Syrac/MerchB-7
91Syrac/ProC-2477
92B-696
92Classic/II-T16
92D-704
92F/Up-64
92Pinn-563
92S/RookTr-96T
92Syrac/MerchB-8
92Syrac/ProC-1962
92T/91Debut-74
93BJ/D/45-33
93BJ/Demp-19
93BJ/Fire-14
93D-247
93F-694
93Flair-291
93L-540
93OPC-245
93S-343
93Select-309
93StCl-26
93StCl/1stDay-26
93T-752
93T/Gold-752
93UD-693
93UD/SP-49
93Ultra-641
94B-323
94D-200
94F-335
94F/AS-11
94Finest-400
94Flair-118
94L-185
94Pac/Cr-644
94Pinn-316
94S-509
94Select-48
94Sf/2000-133
94StCl-242
94StCl/1stDay-242
94StCl/Gold-242
94StCl/Team-158
94Studio-28
94T-304
94T/Gold-304
94TripleP-34
94UD-126
94UD/CollC-133
94UD/CollC/Gold-133
94UD/CollC/Silv-133
94UD/ElecD-126
94Ultra-138
Hepler, William
66T-574R
67OPC-144
67T-144
91WIZMets-174
Herbel, Ron
61Union
63T-208R
64T-47R
65OPC-84
65T-84
66T-331
67CokeCap/Giant-10
67OPC-156
67T-156
68T-333
69T-251
70OPC-526
70T-526
71MLB/St-11
71OPC-387
71T-387
72MB-140
72OPC-469
72T-469
91WIZMets-175
Herberholz, Craig
81BurlB-7
Herbert, Ray
53Tiger/Glen-13
54T-190
55Rodeo
55T-138
55T/DH-106
58T-379
59T-154
60T-252
60T/tatt-21
61P-87
61T-498
61T/St-162
62Salada-6
62Shirriff-6
62T-8
62T/St-25
63Bz-29
63Exh
63F-9
63J-45
63P-45
63Salada-42
63T-560
63T-8LL
63T/SO
64T-215
65T-399
66OPC-121
66T-121
94T/Arc54-190
Exh47
Heredia, Geysi
86Osceola-11
Heredia, Gilbert
(Gil)
86AZ/Pol-4
87AZ/Pol-6
87Everett-2
88CalLgAS-2
88SanJose/Cal-132
88SanJose/ProC-130
90AAASingl/ProC-32
90Phoenix/CMC-3
90Phoenix/ProC-6
90ProC/Singl-530
91AAA/LineD-383
91Phoenix/LineD-383
91Phoenix/ProC-61
92D-737
92F-665
92Giant/PGE-18
92S-771
92Sky/AAASingl-294
92StCl-895
92T/91Debut-75
93Ottawa/ProC-2430
94Pac/Cr-383
Heredia, Hector
87Albuq/Pol-10
88Albuq/CMC-11
88Albuq/ProC-274
89Albuq/CMC-5
89Albuq/ProC-66
Heredia, Julian
91Boise/ClBest-29
91Boise/ProC-3871
91ClBest/Singl-444
92ClBest-227
92ProC/Tomorrow-40
92QuadC/ClBest-1
92QuadC/ProC-803
93LimeR/Winter-41
Heredia, Ubaldo
77LodiD
78LodiD
87Indianap-11
Heredia, Wilson
91GulfCR/SportP-6
92Gaston/ClBest-7
92Gaston/ProC-2249
93LimeR/Winter-124
Herges, Matt
92Yakima/ClBest-15
92Yakima/ProC-3443
Herman, Billy
28Yueng-22
32Orbit/num-67
32Orbit/un-33
33G-227
35BU-138
36Exh/4-3
36Wheat
37Exh/4-3
37Wheat-10
38Exh/4-3
38Wheat
40Wheat-10
41DP-3
50Remar
52T-394CO
54T-86CO
55Gol/Dodg-11CO
55T-19CO
55T/DH-53CO
60T-456CO
65OPC-251MG
65T-251MG
66OPC-37MG
66T-37MG
76Rowe-9M
76Shakey-149
77Galasso-84
78Padre/FamFun-15CO
80Pac/Leg-23
80Perez/HOF-149
80SSPC/HOF
89Kahn/Coop-6
89Smok/Dodg-9
90Pac/Legend-30
90Perez/GreatMom-41
90Swell/Great-59
90Target-337
91Swell/Great-39
92AP/ASG-9
92AP/ASG24K-9G
92Conlon/Sport-421
92Conlon/Sport-473
92Cub/OldStyle-12
93Conlon-787
93TWill-21
94Conlon-1092
94T/Arc54-86
R303/A
R303/B
R305
R312/M
V351B-24
V355-16
WG8-33
Herman, Floyd C.
(Babe)
29Exh/4-4
31Exh/4-4
32Orbit/un-32
33G-5
35G-8K
35G-9K
36Exh/4-4
61F-114
88Conlon/5-16
90Target-336
91Conlon/Sport-169
R305
R306
R308-195
R312/M
R314
R315-A15
R315-B15
R316
R337-418
V353-5
W513-84
Herman, Greg
77AppFx
Herman, Ty
80Elmira-8
Hermann, Jeff
86GlenF-9
87GlenF-18
88Wichita-27
Hermann, LeRoy
R314/Can
Hermanski, Gene
47TipTop
48L-102
49B-20
49Eureka-37
50B-113
51B-55
51T/RB-11
52B-136
52T-16
52TipTop
53T-179
54T-228
79TCMA-165
89Rini/Dodg-36
90Target-338
91T/Arc53-179
94T/Arc54-228
Exh47
Hermanson, Dustin
93Bz-7
93T/Tr-22T
Hermanson, Mike
92Spokane/ClBest-9
92Spokane/ProC-1287
Hermoso, Angel
70OPC-147
70T-147
Hernaiz, Jesus R.
76OkCty/Team-10
83Colum-12
84Idaho/Team-12
88SoOreg/ProC-1718
91Kingspt/ClBest-26CO
91Kingspt/ProC-3830CO
92Kingspt/ClBest-24CO
92Kingspt/ProC-1549CO
Hernaiz, Juan
92GulfCD/ProC-3580
Hernandez, Arned
90AppFox/Box-12
90AppFox/ProC-2110
Hernandez, Carlos
85BurlR-19
87Bakers-25
88Bakers/Cal-243
89SanAn/Best-13
89TexLAS/GS-17
90AAASingl/ProC-70
90Albuq/CMC-16
90Albuq/ProC-349
90Albuq/Trib-11
90D/Rook-37
90ProC/Singl-418
91AAA/LineD-10
91AAAGame/ProC-2
91Albuq/LineD-10
91Albuq/ProC-1144
91D-711
91F-207
91Madison/ClBest-24
91Madison/ProC-2138
91T/90Debut-67
92B-5
92Classic/I-44
92D-778
92F/Up-91
92L-54
92L/BlkGold-54
92Mother/Dodg-18
92Pinn-456
92Pinn/Rook-30
92Pol/Dodg-41
92ProC/Tomorrow-239
92S/RookTr-91T
92T/Tr-50T
92T/TrGold-50T
92UD-797
92Ultra-506
93D-406
93F-62
93L-442
93Mother/Dodg-18
93Pac/Spanish-148
93Pinn-146
93Pol/Dodg-11
93S-348
93Select-317
93StCl-149
93StCl/1stDay-149
93StCl/Dodg-4
93T-589
93T/Gold-589
93UD-148
93Ultra-400
94D-122
94F-512
94Pac/Cr-310

94S-174
94S/GoldR-174
94StCl-145
94StCl/1stDay-145
94StCl/Gold-145
94T-353
94T/Gold-353

Hernandez, Cesar
86BurlEx-8
87WPalmB-14
88Rockford-17
89Rockford-17
90Jaxvl/Best-10
90Jaxvl/ProC-1385
91AA/LineD-256
91Harris/LineD-256
91Harris/ProC-641
92Chatt/SB-185
92D/Rook-52
92OPC-618
92Sky/AASingl-82
92T-618R
92T/Gold-618
92T/GoldWin-618
93D-558
93F-392
93LimeR/Winter-54
93Pac/Spanish-400
93Pinn-591
93S-302
93T-301
93T/Gold-301
94Pac/Cr-148

Hernandez, Chuck
86PalmS-17C
86PalmS/Smk-3C
87MidldA-18
88Edmon/ProC-563
89Edmon/CMC-24
89Edmon/ProC-562
90AAASingl/ProC-108
90Edmon/CMC-8CO
90Edmon/ProC-532CO
90ProC/Singl-485CO
93Mother/Angel-28M

Hernandez, Daniel
90LitSun/HSPros-8
90LitSun/HSProsG-8

Hernandez, Enrique
(Kiki)
89Oneonta/ProC-2100
90PrWill/Team-12
91Greens/ProC-3062
91SALAS/ProC-SAL26
92Albany/ProC-2228
92Albany/SB-23
92B-637FOIL
92ClBest-102
92FtLaud/Team-17
92ProC/Tomorrow-125
92Sky/AASingl-3
92UD/ML-158
93ClBest/MLG-101
93ColClip/Pol-11

Hernandez, Enzo
71MLB/St-229
71OPC-529R
71T-529R
72OPC-7
72T-7
73OPC-438
73T-438
74McDon
74OPC-572
74T-572
75OPC-84
75T-84
75T/M-84
76OPC-289
76SSPC-125
76T-289
77BurgChef-135
77Padre/SchCd-14
77T-522
78Cr/PCL-84
90Target-339

Hernandez, Fernando
91BurlInd/ProC-3297
92ColRS/ClBest-16
92ColRS/ProC-2385
93Kinston/Team-11
93LimeR/Winter-103

Hernandez, Henry
90StPete/Star-12

Hernandez, Jackie
67CokeCap/DodgAngel-20
68T-352
69T-258
69T/St-185
70MLB/St-221
70T-686
71MLB/St-204
71OPC-144
71T-144
72MB-141
72OPC-502
72T-502
73OPC-363
73T-363
74OPC-566
74T-566

Hernandez, Javier
90Ashvl/ClBest-5
91Ashvl/ProC-563
92Osceola/ProC-2525

Hernandez, Jeremy
87Erie-26
88Spring/Best-3
89StPete/Star-17
90TexLgAS/GS-13
90Wichita/Rock-8
91AAA/LineD-283
91LasVegas/LineD-283
91LasVegas/ProC-230
92B-73
92D-756
92F/Up-122
92LasVegas/ProC-2792
92Mother/Padre-18
92OPC-211
92Smok/Padre-12
92StCl-734
92T-211
92T/91Debut-76
92T/Gold-211
92T/GoldWin-211
92UD-42
92Ultra-576
93D-180
93F-140
93L-502
93Pac/Spanish-598
93StCl-392
93StCl/1stDay-392
93T-388
93T/Gold-388
93UD-811
93Ultra-473
93Ultra-649M
94D-95
94F-105
94S-204
94S/GoldR-204
94StCl-420
94StCl/1stDay-420
94StCl/Gold-420
94T-537
94T/Gold-537

Hernandez, Jose
89Gaston/ProC-1018
89Gaston/Star-8
90CharlR/Star-10
91AA/LineD-584
91ClBest/Singl-94
91Tulsa/LineD-584
91Tulsa/ProC-2780
91Tulsa/Team-12
92Canton/ProC-698
92Canton/SB-109
92D-530
92F-307
92OPC-237
92S-866
92Sky/AASingl-51
92T-237
92T/91Debut-77
92T/Gold-237
92T/GoldWin-237
93Rang/Keeb-183
94Ultra-457

Hernandez, Keith
75OPC-623R
75T-623R
75T/M-623R
76OPC-542
76SSPC-590M
76T-542
77BurgChef-11
77Ho-115
77Ho/Twink-115
77OPC-150
77T-95
78Ho-22
78OPC-109
78T-143
79Ho-108
79OPC-371
79T-695
80BK/PHR-16
80K-43
80OPC-170
80T-201LL
80T-321
80T/S-26
80T/Super-26
81Coke
81D-67
81F-545
81K-31
81MSA/Disc-16
81OPC-195
81PermaGr/CC-8
81T-420
81T/SO-67
81T/St-18
81T/St-219
82D-278
82F-114
82F/St-23
82FBI/Disc-11
82K-23
82KMart-36
82OPC-210
82PermaGr/CC-8
82T-186TL
82T-210
82T/St-92
83D-152
83D-20DK
83D/AAS-20
83F-8
83F/St-20M
83F/St-3M
83K-49
83OPC-262
83OPC/St-188WS
83OPC/St-290
83PermaGr/CC-7
83T-700
83T/Fold-3M
83T/Gloss40-4
83T/St-188
83T/St-290
83T/Tr-43
84D-238
84D/AAS-23
84D/Champs-46
84Drake-13
84F-587
84F/St-49
84Nes/792-120
84OPC-120
84Ralston-32
84Seven-24E
84T-120
84T/Cereal-32
84T/Mets/Fan-4
84T/RD-5M
84T/St-107
84T/St/Box-6
84T/Super-26
85D-68
85D/AAS-41
85D/HL-21M
85D/HL-27
85Drake-15
85F-85
85F/LimEd-12
85F/St-25
85FunFood/Pin-104
85Leaf-62
85OPC-80
85Pol/MetYank-M5
85Seven-10E
85T-712AS
85T-80
85T/3D-11
85T/Gloss40-13
85T/Mets/Fan-6
85T/RD-6M
85T/St-98
85T/Super-36
85ThomMc/Discs-33
86D-190
86Dorman-9
86Drake-10
86F-84
86F/Mini-20
86F/St-55
86Leaf-124
86OPC-252
86Seven/Coin-C3
86Seven/Coin-C9
86Seven/Coin-E3
86Seven/Coin-S3
86Seven/Coin-W3
86Sf-127M
86Sf-15
86Sf-181M
86Sf-62M
86T-203HL
86T-520
86T-701AS
86T/3D-10
86T/Gloss60-7
86T/Mets/Fan-5
86T/Mini-53
86T/St-99
86T/Super-31
86T/Tatt-1M
86Woolwth-14
87BK-10
87Classic-4
87D-76
87D/AAS-11
87D/OD-124
87D/PopUp-11
87Drake-10
87F-12
87F-629M
87F-637M
87F/HL-5
87F/Hottest-21
87F/Lim-20
87F/Mini-53
87F/St-58
87F/WS-2M
87F/WaxBox-C6
87GenMills/Book-5M
87Jiffy-4
87KayBee-17
87Leaf-233
87MSA/Discs-4
87OPC-350
87RedFoley/St-32
87Seven-E10
87Seven-ME13
87Sf-133
87Sf-195M
87Sf/TPrev-2M
87Sportflic/DealP-3
87Stuart-1M
87T-350
87T-595AS
87T/Board-12
87T/Coins-36
87T/Gloss22-2
87T/Gloss60-26
87T/HL-31
87T/Mini-24
87T/St-102
87T/St-157
87Woolwth-31
88ChefBoy-12
88D-316
88D/AS-49
88D/Best-152
88D/Mets/Bk-316
88Drake-5
88F-136
88F-639M
88F/Hottest-17
88F/LL-18
88F/Mini-93
88F/St-103
88Jiffy-9
88KMart-14
88Kahn/Mets-17
88KennerFig-49
88Leaf-117
88Nestle-42
88OPC-68
88Panini/St-339
88S-400
88Sf-31
88Sf/Gamewin-11
88T-610
88T/Big-59
88T/Gloss60-32
88T/Mets/Fan-17
88T/St-97
88T/St/Backs-3
88T/UK-33
89B-385
89Classic-59
89D-117
89D/Best-208
89D/GrandSlam-8
89F-37
89KMart/Lead-8
89Kahn/Mets-17
89KennerFig-63
89OPC-63
89OPC/BoxB-G
89Panini/St-137
89RedFoley/St-57
89S-41
89S/HotStar-23
89Sf-60
89T-291TL
89T-480
89T/Big-185
89T/DHTest-8
89T/LJN-26
89T/St-93
89T/WaxBox-G
89UD-612
90B-342
90BBWit-20
90Classic/III-36
90D-388
90D/BestAL-33
90F-205
90F/Can-205
90KMart/CBatL-10
90KayBee-16
90Leaf-470
90MLBPA/Pins-10
90OPC-230
90PublInt/St-135
90PublInt/St-262
90S-193
90S/100St-29
90S/Tr-57T
90Sf-106
90T-230
90T/Ames-8
90T/Big-301
90T/Tr-39T
90UD-222
90UD/Ext-777
91F-368
91S-89
91WIZMets-177
92Card/McDon/Pac-24
93AP/ASG-148

Hernandez, Krandall
91Hunting/ClBest-12
91Hunting/ProC-3337

Hernandez, Leonardo Jesus
(Leo)
78Clinton
79Clinton/TCMA-16
83T/Tr-44
84Nes/792-71
84RochR-15
84T-71
85RochR-5
86Colum-11
86Colum/Pol-10
91Crown/Orio-194
92Yank/WIZ80-81

Hernandez, Luis
90Bristol/ProC-3153
90Bristol/Star-11
91Bristol/ClBest-5
91Bristol/ProC-3614
92Bristol/ProC-1418

Hernandez, Manny
82DayBe-5
83DayBe-6
84Cram/PCL-59
85Cram/PCL-56
86Tucson-7
87Tucson-7
88D-481
88Tucson/CMC-1
88Tucson/JP-13

88Tucson/ProC-169
89Portl/CMC-2
89Portl/ProC-221
90AAASingl/ProC-269
90ProC/Singl-356
90T/TVMets-45
90Tidew/CMC-5
90Tidew/ProC-538
91AAA/LineD-557
91Tidew/LineD-557
91Tidew/ProC-2504
91WIZMets-176

Hernandez, Marino
88Pocatel/ProC-2085
89Clinton/ProC-884
90Clinton/Best-16

Hernandez, Martin
86Nashua-12
87Salem-11

Hernandez, Nick
78Newar
79BurlB-8

Hernandez, Pedro Julio
(Pete)
78DaytB
81Syrac-15
82Syrac-21
85Cram/PCL-71

Hernandez, Pedro
80Knoxvl/TCMA-17
81Syrac/Team-9
82Syrac/Team-14

Hernandez, Rafael
91Kingspt/ClBest-11
91Kingspt/ProC-3822
92Pittsfld/ClBest-8
92Pittsfld/ProC-3304

Hernandez, Ramon 1
(Pitcher)
67T-576R
68T-382
73OPC-117
73T-117
74OPC-222
74T-222
75OPC-224
75T-224
75T/M-224
76OPC-647
76SSPC-567
76T-647
77T-468

Hernandez, Ramon 2
91Billing/SportP-17
91Billings/ProC-3760
92Princet/ClBest-22
92Princet/ProC-3094

Hernandez, Roberto M.
87QuadC-8
88QuadC/GS-20
89MidldA/GS-18
90BirmB/Best-18
90BirmB/ProC-1106
90Foil/Best-216
90ProC/Singl-820
91AAA/LineD-637
91B-343
91Vanco/LineD-637
91Vanco/ProC-1591
92B-133
92Classic/Game200-115
92Classic/I-45
92D-19RR
92F-677
92F/Up-13
92OPC-667
92Pinn-253
92Pinn/Rook-9
92S-874
92Sky/AAASingl-284
92StCl-356
92T-667
92T/91Debut-78
92T/Gold-667
92T/GoldWin-667
92UD-7SR
92Ultra-336
92Vanco/SB-640
92WSox-39
93D-403
93F-583
93F/RookSenl-4
93Flair-185
93L-346
93OPC-126
93Pac/Spanish-387
93Pinn-129
93S-376
93Select-311
93StCl-21
93StCl/1stDay-21
93StCl/WSox-8
93T-70
93T/Gold-70
93ToysRUs-88
93UD-352
93USPlayC/Rook-9D
93Ultra-533
93WSox-11
94B-138
94D-116
94F-83
94Finest-376
94L-167
94OPC-94
94Pac/Cr-127
94Panini-48
94Pinn-164
94Pinn/Artist-164
94Pinn/Museum-164
94S-457
94StCl-182
94StCl/1stDay-182
94StCl/Gold-182
94StCl/Team-129
94T-572
94T/Gold-572
94TripleP-265
94UD-468
94UD/CollC-134
94UD/CollC/Gold-134
94UD/CollC/Silv-134
94Ultra-34
94Ultra/Fire-4

Hernandez, Roberto
(Bobby)
86Cram/NWL-100
86LitFalls-14
87Columbia-15
87Kenosha-2
88StLucie/Star-11

Hernandez, Rudolph Albert
(Rudy)
61T-229

Hernandez, Rudy J.
89StLucie/Star-9
90Jacks/GS-21
90TexLgAS/GS-21
91AA/LineD-633
91Wmsprt/LineD-633
91Wmsprt/ProC-301

Hernandez, Toby
80Utica-18
83Syrac-14
84Syrac-15
85Toledo-13

Hernandez, Tom
91Gaston/ClBest-15
91Gaston/ProC-2692

Hernandez, Willie
(Guillermo)
76OkCty/Team-11
78SSPC/270-255
78T-99
79T-614
80T-472
81D-589
81F-310
81T-238
82RedLob
82T-23
83D-174
83F-497
83T-568
83T/Tr-45
84D-163
84F-34
84F/X-51
84Nes/792-199
84OPC-199
84T-199
84T/Tr-51
84Tiger/Farmer-6
84Tiger/Wave-19
85Cain's-10
85D-212
85Drake-37
85F-10
85F/St-101
85FunFood/Pin-79
85Leaf-235
85OPC-333
85Seven-10D
85Seven-1G
85Seven-7C
85T-333
85T/RD-18M
85T/St-257
85T/Super-2
85Wendy-11
86Cain's-8
86D-227
86D/AAS-43
86D/WaxBox-PC5
86F-228
86F/LL-18
86F/St-56
86Leaf-102
86OPC-341
86Sf-65M
86Sf-85
86T-670
86T/St-275
86T/Tatt-8M
87Cain's-13
87Coke/Tigers-15
87D-522
87D/AAS-43
87F-153
87F/Excit-26
87F/GameWin-20
87F/Mini-54
87F/St-59
87OPC-339
87Seven-DT4
87Sf-105
87Sf/TPrev-15M
87T-515
87T/Mini-54
87T/St-272
87Toledo-27
88D-398
88D/Best-125
88F-58
88KennerFig-50
88Panini/St-84
88Pep/T-21
88S-507
88T-713
88T/Big-206
89Bimbo/Discs-9
89D-62
89F-135
89Mara/Tigers-21
89OPC-43
89Pol/Tigers-21
89S-275
89T-43
89UD-279
90D-610
90F-605
90F/Can-605
90PublInt/St-473
90RedFoley/St-46
90S-267
90UD-518

Hernandez, Xavier
88Myrtle/ProC-1178
88SALAS/GS-21
89Knoxvl/Best-9
89Knoxvl/ProC-1144
89Syrac/MerchB-14
89Syrac/Team-14
90D-682
90D/Rook-33
90Leaf-517
90Lennox-15
90T/89Debut-55
90UD-26
91B-545
91D-708
91F-509
91Leaf-462
91Mother/Ast-26
91OPC-194
91S-564
91StCl-74
91T-194
92D-782
92F-437
92Mother/Ast-26
92OPC-640
92StCl-736
92T-640
92T/Gold-640
92T/GoldWin-640
92Ultra-205
93D-636
93F-53
93L-543
93Mother/Ast-23
93OPC-233
93Pac/Spanish-477
93Pinn-453
93S-417
93StCl-271
93StCl/1stDay-271
93StCl/Ast-24
93T-252
93T/Gold-252
93UD-319
93Ultra-43
94D-143
94F-493
94Finest-373
94Flair-81
94L-273
94Pac/Cr-268
94Pinn-471
94StCl/Team-201
94T-512
94T/Gold-512
94UD-342
94Ultra-206
94Ultra-399

Herndon, Larry
75Phoenix-20
75Phoenix/Caruso-9
75Phoenix/CircleK-20
76Phoenix/Coke-9
77BurgChef-104
77Ho-47
77Ho/Twink-47
77OPC-169
77T-397
78T-512
79OPC-328
79Pol/Giants-31
79T-624
80Pol/Giants-31
80T-257
81D-196
81F-451
81OPC-108
81T-409
81T/St-236
82D-172
82F-390
82OPC-182
82T-182
82T/St-109
82T/StVar-109
82T/Tr-43T
83D-585
83D/AAS-5
83F-330
83F/St-11M
83F/St-20M
83OPC-13
83OPC/St-68
83T-13
83T-261TL
83T/St-68
84D-349
84F-82
84Nes/792-333
84OPC-333
84T-334
84T/St-264
84Tiger/Farmer-7
84Tiger/Wave-20
85Cain's-11
85D-150
85F-11
85Leaf-249
85OPC-9
85Seven-4D
85T-591
85T/St-266
85Wendy-12
86Cain's-9
86D-593
86F-229
86Leaf-230
86OPC-61
86T-688
86T/St-271
87Cain's-11
87Coke/Tigers-2
87D/OD-211
87F-154
87Seven-DT5
87T-298
88D-353
88F-59
88OPC-146
88Pep/T-31
88Pol/T-6
88RedFoley/St-34
88S-138
88T-743
88T/Big-56
89S-279
89UD-49
93Tiger/Gator-28M

Herold, Bob
92Omaha/ProC-2978CO
92Omaha/SB-350CO

Heron, Chico
57Seattle/Pop-18

Herr, Edward
N172

Herr, Thomas
(Tommy)
77StPete
80T-684R
81Coke
81D-68
81F-550
81T-266
82D-530
82F-115
82F/St-30
82T-27
83D-217
83F-9
83F/St-16M
83OPC-97
83OPC/St-286
83T-489
83T/St-286
84D-596
84F-325
84Nes/792-649
84OPC-117
84T-649
84T/St-142
85D-425
85D/AAS-43
85F-226
85OPC-113
85T-113
85T/St-142
86D-83
86D/AAS-2
86D/PopUp-2
86Drake-21
86F-37
86F/AS-2
86F/Mini-8
86F/St-57
86KAS/Disc-15
86Leaf-79
86OPC-94
86Schnucks-8
86Seven/Coin-S14M
86Sf-113
86T-550
86T-702AS
86T/Gloss22-14
86T/Gloss60-32
86T/Mini-62
86T/St-147
86T/St-49
86T/Super-32
86T/Tatt-22M
87D-140
87D/OD-61
87F-296
87F/LL-22
87Leaf-121
87OPC-181
87RedFoley/St-60
87Sf/TPrev-12M
87Smok/Cards-20
87T-721
87T/St-49
88D-208
88D/Best-326
88F-35

88F/Hottest-18
88F/Up-U43
88F/WS-10
88F/WS-7M
88KennerFig-51
88Leaf-201
88OPC-310
88Panini/St-389
88Panini/St-391
88S-84
88S/Tr-8T
88Sf-141
88T-310
88T/Big-31
88T/St-50
88T/St/Backs-4
88T/Tr-49T
89B-403
89Classic/Up/2-166
89D-301
89D/Best-72
89D/Tr-4
89F-115
89F/Up-107
89Phill/TastyK-10
89S-191
89S/Tr-9T
89T-709
89T/Big-283
89T/Tr-49T
89UD-558
89UD/Ext-720
90B-159
90D-21DK
90D-75
90D/BestNL-32
90D/Learning-16
90D/SuperDK-21DK
90F-560
90F/BBMVP-18
90F/Can-560
90Kenner/Fig-41
90Leaf-184
90MLBPA/Pins-1
90OPC-297
90Panini/St-309
90Phill/TastyK-13
90PublInt/St-239
90RedFoley/St-47
90S-171
90S/100St-77
90Sf-63
90T-297
90T/Big-206
90T/Coins-49
90T/St-122
90UD-488
91B-480
91D-610
91F-149
91Kahn/Mets-28
91Leaf-48
91Leaf/Stud-205
91OPC-64
91S-820
91StCl-532
91T-64
91UD-416
91Ultra-219
91WIZMets-178
92Card/McDon/Pac-37

Herrera, Edgar
89GA-11
90GA-34M
90GA-8
93B-241

Herrera, Ezequiel
90Foil/Best-41
90Spring/Best-9
91StPete/ClBest-26
91StPete/ProC-2289
92StPete/ClBest-22
92StPete/ProC-2039

Herrera, Hector
87AubAs-20

Herrera, Jose C.
69T-378

Herrera, Jose
91MedHat/ProC-4115
91MedHat/SportP-9
92MedHat/ProC-3220
92MedHat/SportP-9
93Hagers/ClBest-1
93Hagers/ProC-1891
94B-604
94FExcel-145
94TedW-122

Herrera, Juan
(Poncho)
58T-433
59T-129
60L-5
60T-130
61Bz-27
61P-121
61T-569AS
61T/RO-36
61T/St-56
62J-192
62P-192
62Salada-122
62Shirriff-122

Herrera, Pascuel
92MedHat/SportP-12

Herrera, Paul
87BYU-14M

Herrera, Ramon
26Exh-67
86Negro/Frit-84

Herrera, Raul
93ClBest/MLG-102

Herrholtz, John
91Utica/ClBest-3
91Utica/ProC-3236
92SoBend/ProC-173

Herrick, Neal
81Miami-16

Herring, Art
90Target-340

Herring, Paul
80Water-5
81Indianap-27
82Water-16

Herring, Vince
90SanJose/Best-20
90SanJose/Cal-48
90SanJose/ProC-2010
90SanJose/Star-11
91SanJose/ClBest-17
91SanJose/ProC-5
92SanJose/ClBest-22

Herrmann, Ed
69T-439R
70OPC-368
70T-368
71OPC-169
71T-169
72OPC-452
72T-452
73OPC-73
73T-73
74OPC-438
74T-438
74T/St-155
75Ho-86
75OPC-219
75T-219
75T/M-219
76OPC-406
76SSPC-440
76SSPC/MetsY-Y8
76T-406
77T-143
78BK/Ast-3
78T-677
79OPC-194
79T-374
92Yank/WIZ70-73

Herrmann, Gary
92Batavia/ClBest-13
92Batavia/ProC-3258

Herrmann, Leroy
93Conlon-973

Herrmann, Tim
89Niagara/Pucko-11
90Fayette/ProC-2401

Herrnstein, John
63T-553R
64PhilBull-14
64T-243R
65T-534
66T-304
78TCMA-124

Herron, Tony
84Pawtu-11A
84Pawtu-11B
85Pawtu-16

Herrscher, Rick
91WIZMets-179

Herry, David
92LSU/McDag-15

Hersh, Dave
77BurlB

Hersh, Earl
60Maple-9
61BeeHive-8

Hershberger, N. Mike
62T-341
63T-254
64T-465
65OPC-89
65T-89
66T-236
67CokeCap/A's-11
67T-323
68OPC-18
68T-18
69MB-111
69MLB/St-86
69T-655
70MLB/St-272
70McDon-3
70T-596
71OPC-149
71T-149
72MB-142
78TCMA-287

Hershberger, Willard
39PlayBall-119
40PlayBall-77
W711/1
W711/2

Hershiser, Gordon
88VeroB/Star-11
89SanAn/Best-7

Hershiser, Orel
82Albuq-4
83Albuq-3
84Pol/Dodg-55
85Coke/Dodg-12
85D-581
85F-371
85F/St-96
85FunFood/Pin-83
85Leaf-38
85OPC-273
85T-493
85T/St-74
86Coke/Dodg-11
86D-18
86D-226
86D/DKsuper-18
86Drake-31
86F-131
86F/LimEd-24
86F/Slug-16
86F/St-58
86Leaf-18DK
86OPC-159
86Pol/Dodg-55
86Seven/Coin-W12M
86Sf-9
86T-159
86T/3D-12
86T/Gloss60-24
86T/Mini-45
86T/St-73
86T/Super-33
86T/Tatt-20M
87Classic-92
87D-106
87D/HL-13
87D/OD-79
87F-441
87F/RecSet-16
87Leaf-246
87Mother/Dodg-6
87OPC-385
87Pol/Dodg-28
87RedFoley/St-5
87Seven-W6
87Sf-43
87Sf/TPrev-14M
87Smok/Dodg-12
87T-385
87T/Mini-14
88D-94
88D/AS-56
88D/Best-148
88F-518
88F-632M
88F/AwardWin-17
88F/BB/AS-14
88F/Excit-20
88F/Hottest-19
88F/LL-19
88F/Mini-84
88F/RecSet-18
88F/SS-15
88F/Slug-18
88F/St-92
88F/TL-13
88Leaf-62
88Mother/Dodg-6
88OPC-40
88Panini/St-303
88Pol/Dodg-55
88S-470
88Sf-160
88T-40
88T/Big-91
88T/Mini-53
88T/Revco-12
88T/St-68
88T/UK-34
89B-341
89Bz-15
89Cadaco-29
89Classic-1
89Classic-105
89Classic/Up/2-173
89D-197
89D-648HL
89D/AS-50
89D/Best-225
89D/MVP-BC4
89F-62
89F/AS-7
89F/BBAS-21
89F/BBMVP's-19
89F/Excit-24
89F/Heroes-22
89F/LL-20
89F/Superstar-23
89F/WS-11
89F/WS-6
89F/WaxBox-C14
89Holsum/Discs-18
89KayBee-19
89KennerFig-64
89KingB/Discs-12
89MSA/Disc-10
89MSA/SS-5
89Mother/Dodg-6
89Nissen-18
89OPC-380
89OPC-41
89Panini/St-13LCS
89Panini/St-18
89Panini/St-19
89Panini/St-225
89Panini/St-25
89Panini/St-474
89Panini/St-9
89Panini/St-97
89Pol/Dodg-29
89RedFoley/St-58
89S-370
89S-582M
89S-653HL
89S/HotStar-35
89S/Mast-21
89Sf-222M
89Sf-36
89Smok/Dodg-100
89Socko-Set
89T-394AS
89T-550
89T-5RB
89T-669TL
89T/Big-1
89T/Coins-2
89T/Crunch-3
89T/DH-21
89T/Gloss60-48
89T/Hills-17
89T/LJN-162
89T/Mini-18
89T/St-12
89T/St-65
89T/St/Backs-60
89T/UK-38
89Tetley/Discs-10
89UD-130
89UD-661CY
89UD-665M
89UD-667M
89Woolwth-21
89Woolwth-25
89Woolwth-33
89Woolwth-4
90B-84
90BBWit-1
90Classic-81
90CollAB-6
90D-197
90D/BestNL-54
90D/Bon/MVP-BC5
90F-399
90F/BB-18
90F/BBMVP-19
90F/Can-399
90F/WaxBox-C14
90HOF/St-99
90Holsum/Discs-12
90HotPlay/St-21
90Kenner/Fig-42
90Leaf-280
90MLBPA/Pins-8
90MSA/Soda-9
90Mother/Dodg-12
90OPC-780
90Panini/St-275
90Pol/Dodg-55
90Post-8
90PublInt/St-263
90PublInt/St-9
90RedFoley/St-48
90S-50
90S/100St-94
90Sf-197
90T-780
90T/Big-82
90T/DH-34
90T/Mini-58
90T/St-63
90T/TVAS-46
90Target-341
90UD-10TC
90UD-256
90WonderBrd-4
91B-595
91Cadaco-30
91Classic/200-23
91Classic/III-38
91D-280
91F-208
91F/UltraUp-U88
91Leaf-243
91Leaf/Stud-183
91Mother/Dodg-12
91OPC-690
91OPC/Premier-64
91Petro/SU-22
91Pol/Dodg-55
91S-550
91SanAn/ProC-2968
91Seven/3DCoin-5SC
91StCl-244
91T-690
91T/CJMini/II-17
91UD-524
92B-517
92Classic/Game200-33
92D-247
92F-459
92L-81
92L/BlkGold-81
92Mother/Dodg-6
92OPC-175
92OPC/Premier-162
92Panini-199
92Pinn-21
92Pinn-592SIDE
92Pol/Dodg-55
92S-653
92StCl-431
92Studio-44
92T-175
92T/Gold-175
92T/GoldWin-175
92T/Kids-52
92TripleP-212
92UD-261
92Ultra-507
93B-394
93Cadaco-32
93Colla/DM-51

93D-274
93D/DK-14
93Duracel/PPI-4
93F-63
93Flair-70
93Kraft-24
93L-53
93Mother/Dodg-10
93OPC-136
93Pac/Spanish-149
93Pinn-319
93Pol/Dodg-12
93S-90
93Select-49
93StCl-544
93StCl/1stDay-544
93StCl/Dodg-23
93T-255
93T/Finest-184
93T/FinestRef-184
93T/Gold-255
93TripleP-121
93UD-169
93UD/FunPack-88
93UD/SP-93
93Ultra-55
94B-566
94D-151
94F-513
94Flair-178
94L-16
94OPC-133
94Pac/Cr-311
94Panini-200
94Pinn-58
94Pinn/Artist-58
94Pinn/Museum-58
94RedFoley-20M
94S-102
94S/GoldR-102
94Select-134
94Sf/2000-125
94StCl-400
94StCl/1stDay-400
94StCl/Gold-400
94Studio-68
94T-460
94T/Finest-98
94T/FinestRef-98
94T/Gold-460
94TripleP-84
94UD-355
94UD/CollC-135
94UD/CollC/Gold-135
94UD/CollC/Silv-135
94UD/SP-77
94Ultra-517

Hershmann, William
87StPete-21
88Savan/ProC-340
89Savan/ProC-366

Hertel, Rick
78Dunedin

Hertz, Steve
64T-544R

Hertzler, Paul
85Indianap-18
86Jacks/TCMA-15

Herz, Steve
80Toledo-13
81Toledo-12
82Spokane-11
82Vanco-11
84Cram/PCL-142
85Cram/PCL-244

Herzig, Lynn
(Spike)
77Holyo
78Holyo

Herzog, Charles
(Buck)
11Helmar-129
12Sweet/Pin-114
12Sweet/Pin-67
14CJ-85
15CJ-85
16FleischBrd-41
40PlayBall-229
75F/Pion-27
92Conlon/Sport-489
BF2-71
D304
D327
D328-75
D329-81
D350/2-80
E135-75
E96
M101/4-81
M101/5-80
M116
S74-44
T201
T205
T206
T207
T213/blue
T215/blue
T3-45
W514-104

Herzog, Hans
84Savan-8
86StPete-11
87StPete-16

Herzog, Whitey
57T-29
58T-438
59T-392
60L-71
60T-92
61P-88
61T-106
61T/St-163
62T-513
63T-302
73OPC-549MG
73T-549MG
75SSPC/18-13CO
76SSPC-185
76T-236MG
77T-371MG
78SSPC/270-224MG
78T-299MG
79T-451MG
81T-684MG
82D-190MG
83D-530MG
83T-186MG
84Nes/792-561MG
84T-561MG
84T/Gloss22-12MG
85T-683MG
86T-441MG
87D/AAS-20MG
87D/PopUp-20MG
87Smok/Cards-25MG
87T-243MG
87T/Gloss22-1MG
88Smok/Card-1MG
88T-744MG
89D/AS-42MG
89D/PopUp-42MG
89Smok/Cards-8MG
89T-654MG
89T/Gloss22-12MG
90OPC-261MG
90Smok/Card-8MG
90T-261MG
90T/TVCard-1MG
91Crown/Orio-195
92Card/McDon/Pac-47MG
93Rang/Keeb-184MG
Exh47

Hesketh, Joe
83Memphis/TCMA-19
84Indianap-6
85D-157
85Expo/PostC-9
85F-652R
85T/Tr-52T
86D-341
86Expo/Prov/Pan-21
86Expo/Prov/Post-6
86F-250
86Leaf-150
86OPC-42
86Provigo-21
86Seven/Coin-S15M
86Sf-177M
86T-472
86T/Gloss60-19
87D-134
87Expo/PostC-1
87F-320
87Leaf-62
87OPC-189
87T-189
88D-504
88Indianap/ProC-512
88OPC-371
88T-371
89D-460
89F-378
89OPC-74
89S-498
89T-614
89UD-60
90Brave/Dubuq/Perf-11
90D-511
90F-349
90F/Can-349
90Leaf-507
90OPC-24
90PublInt/St-175
90S-483
90T-24
90T/Tr-40T
90UD-512
91OPC-269
91T-269
92D-611
92F-40
92L-22
92L/BlkGold-22
92OPC-521
92Pinn-415
92RedSox/Dunkin-16
92S-359
92StCl-636
92T-521
92T/Gold-521
92T/GoldWin-521
92UD-570
92USPlayC/RedSox-1D
92USPlayC/RedSox-8S
92Ultra-17
93F-562
93Pac/Spanish-360
93Pinn-448
93S-467
93StCl-107
93StCl/1stDay-107
93T-162
93T/Gold-162
93UD-620
94StCl-455
94StCl/1stDay-455
94StCl/Gold-455

Heslet, Harry
V362-27

Hess, Mark
91Daikyo/Fut-3

Hester, Marshall
80CharlO/W3TV-10

Hester, Steve
88Greens/ProC-1570
89Cedar/Best-29
89Cedar/ProC-919
89Cedar/Star-27
89Cedar/Star-8
90Cedar/Best-26
90Cedar/ProC-2323

Hetki, John
53T-235
54T-161
55T/DH-62
91T/Arc53-235
94T/Arc54-161

Hetrick, Kent
87SLCity/Taco-3
88Beloit/GS-13
89Stockton/Best-9
89Stockton/Cal-161
89Stockton/ProC-376
89Stockton/Star-10

Hetzel, Eric
85Greens-18
87WinHaven-22
88Pawtu/CMC-8
88Pawtu/ProC-449
89D-660
89Pawtu/CMC-3
89Pawtu/Dunkin-31
89Pawtu/ProC-703
90D-539
90F-279
90F/Can-279
90LSUGreat-5
90OPC-629
90S-543
90S/100Ris-23
90T-629
90T/89Debut-56
90T/TVRSox-45
90UD-673
91AAA/LineD-356
91Pawtu/LineD-356
91Pawtu/ProC-32

Heuer, Mark
87SanAn-24

Heusser, Ed
93Conlon-970

Heving, John A.
(Johnnie)
81Conlon-48
92Conlon/Sport-455
94Conlon-1176

Heving, Joseph W.
(Joe)
29Exh/4-17
35BU-43
39PlayBall-20
40PlayBall-35
41DP-136
81Conlon-47
94Conlon-1176M

Hewatt, B.
88Pocatel/ProC-2090

Hewes, Pat
87Savan-9
88StPete/Star-9
89Penin/Star-7

Heydeman, Greg
74Albuq/Team-6

Heydler, John (Mrs.)
94Conlon-1112M
94Conlon-1112M

Heydler, John
94Conlon-1112M
94Conlon-1112M

Hiatt, Jack
65T-497R
66T-373R
67CokeCap/Giant-5
67T-368
68Dexter-38
68T-419
69MB-112
69OPC-204
69T-204
69T/4in1-11M
70OPC-13
70T-13
71MLB/St-83
71OPC-371
71T-371
72MB-143
72T-633
73OPC-402
73T-402
74Wichita-117CO
80Wichita-8
82Holyo-23
83ColumAst-22
88Pocatel/ProC-2101

Hiatt, Phil
90Eugene/GS-14
91BBCity/ClBest-17
91BBCity/ProC-1403
91ClBest/Singl-151
91FSLAS/ProC-FSL1
92B-529
92ClBest-181
92Memphis/ProC-2426
92Memphis/SB-436
92ProC/Tomorrow-76
92Sky/AASingl-183
92UD/ML-176
92UD/ML-45M
92UD/POY-PY22
93B-69
93ClBest/MLG-25
93D-393
93F/Final-220
93FExcel/ML-174
93FExcel/MLAS-9
93Flair-216
93L/GRook-14
93Pac/Spanish-488
93Pinn-611
93Select/RookTr-66T
93StCl-695
93StCl/1stDay-695
93StCl/Royal-6
93Studio-107
93T/Tr-29T
93UD-457IN
93UD-645
93UD/Diam-33
93UD/FunPack-4SOT
93UD/SP-229
93Ultra-561
93Ultra/AllRook-3
94D-279
94F-160
94L-90
94Pac/Cr-287
94Pinn-327
94S-515
94T-94
94T/Finest-56
94T/FinestRef-56
94T/Gold-94
94UD/CollC-136
94UD/CollC/Gold-136
94UD/CollC/Silv-136
94Ultra-66

Hibbard, Greg
86Cram/NWL-43
87AppFx-27
87FtMyr-6
88Vanco/CMC-11
88Vanco/ProC-770
89Vanco/CMC-3
89Vanco/ProC-584
90B-303
90Coke/WSox-8
90D-384
90F-534
90F/Can-534
90Leaf-523
90OPC-769
90S-369
90S/100Ris-77
90S/YS/II-20
90T-769
90T/89Debut-57
90T/JumboR-14
90UD-543
91D-159
91F-122
91Kodak/WSox-27
91Leaf-438
91Leaf/Stud-34
91OPC-256
91Panini/FrSt-319
91Panini/St-254
91S-128
91T-256
91UD-679
91Ultra-75
92B-325
92D-178
92F-83
92L-169
92L/BlkGold-169
92OPC-477
92Pinn-364
92S-266
92StCl-586
92Studio-153
92T-477
92T/Gold-477
92T/GoldWin-477
92TripleP-261
92UD-420
92Ultra-36
92WSox-27
93B-88
93Cub/Mara-10
93D-271
93F-379
93F/Final-8
93Flair-15
93L-298
93Pac/Spanish-378
93Pinn-527
93S-622
93Select-216
93Select/RookTr-103T
93StCl-606
93StCl/1stDay-606
93StCl/Cub-3
93T-313
93T/Gold-313
93UD-539
93Ultra-315
94D-542
94F-386
94Finest-389

94Flair-104
94L-402
94Pac/Cr-101
94Pinn-480
94S-432
94T-148
94T/Gold-148
94UD-472
94Ultra-162
Hibbett, Wendell
78Charl
Hibbs, Al
85Utica-11
86Cram/NWL-132
Hibbs, Jim
73Wichita-4
77Fritsch-39
Hibbs, Loren
84Everett/Cram-15
90WichSt-40
Hibner, Dave
78Ashvl
79Ashvl/TCMA-25
80Ashvl-8
Hice, Bob
84CharlO-1
85CharlO-27
87CharlO/WBTV-xx
Hickerson, Bryan
87Clinton-28
89SanJose/Best-15
89SanJose/Cal-212
89SanJose/ProC-443
89SanJose/Star-14
90Shrev/ProC-1438
90Shrev/Star-11
91AA/LineD-306
91Shrev/LineD-306
91Shrev/ProC-1815
92Classic/Game200-135
92D-783
92F-638
92Giant/PGE-19
92L-280
92L/BlkGold-280
92Mother/Giant-16
92OPC-8
92OPC/Premier-65
92ProC/Tomorrow-349
92S-750
92StCl-686
92T-8
92T/91Debut-79
92T/Gold-8
92T/GoldWin-8
92UD-667
92Ultra-589
93D-496
93F-530
93L-501
93Mother/Giant-26
93OPC-162
93Pac/Spanish-271
93StCl-217
93StCl/1stDay-217
93StCl/Giant-29
93T-147
93T/Gold-147
93UD-778
93Ultra-485
94D-181
94F-691
94Flair-242
94Pac/Cr-546
94StCl/Team-11
94T-429
94T/Gold-429
94Ultra-588
Hickey, Bob
75SanAn
Hickey, James Joseph
85BuffB-20
86BirmB/Team-18
87BirmB/Best-16
89ColMud/Best-19
91BurlAs/ClBest-26CO
91BurlAs/ProC-2818CO
92Ashvl/ClBest-28
Hickey, Kevin
79AppFx-6
80GlenF/B-10
80GlenF/C-7
82D-631
82F-344
82OPC-362
82T-778
83D-445
83F-237
83T-278
83TrueVal/WSox-45
84D-135
84F-61
84Nes/792-459
84T-459
86Portl-8
87Hawaii-18
88RochR/Gov-11
89F/Up-4
89French-23
90D-583
90F-178
90F/Can-178
90OPC-546
90PublInt/St-577
90S-214
90T-546
90UD-299
91AA/LineD-237
91Crown/Orio-196
91F-475
91Hagers/LineD-237
91Hagers/ProC-2450
Hickey, Michael
90OK-6
92Belling/ClBest-28
92Belling/ProC-1452
92Classic/DP-123
92FrRow/DP-5
Hickman, Braxton
93TX-3
Hickman, Charles
E107
T201
T213/brown
WG2-23
Hickman, Dave J.
90Target-342
Hickman, Gordon J.
T206
Hickman, Jess
77Fritsch-36
Hickman, Jim
61Union
62T-598R
63T-107
64T-514
64T/Coins-92
65OPC-114
65T-114
66T-402
67T-346
69MB-113
69OPC-63
69Sunoco/Pin-3
69T-63
70T-612
71K-11
71MD
71MLB/St-32
71OPC-175
71T-175
71T/Coins-27
72T-534
73OPC-565
73T-565
90Target-343
91WIZMets-180
Hickox, Tom
88CapeCod/Sum-86
91Helena/SportP-21
Hicks, Aman
89Erie/Star-7
90Wausau/Best-24
90Wausau/ProC-2138
90Wausau/Star-10
91Kane/ClBest-23
91Kane/ProC-2670
91Kane/Team-10
Hicks, Charlie
92Everett/ClBest-27
92Everett/ProC-1682
Hicks, Clay
77AppFx
Hicks, Ed
76Wausau
89Pac/SenLg-130
Hicks, Jim
67T-532
69T-559R
70OPC-173
70T-173
Hicks, Joseph A.
79QuadC-11CO
83Iowa-14CO
84Iowa-9CO
86Iowa-15CO
87PrWill-26CO
89Pac/SenLg-69
89T/SenLg-105
Hicks, Mike
77Ashvl
Hicks, Rob
86Portl-9
87Reading-26
88ElPaso/Best-27
Hicks, Robert
82Spring/Frit-7
Hicks, William J.
(Joe)
60L-74
61T-386
62T-428
91WIZMets-181
Hidalgo, Richard
94B-586
Hierholzer, David
90Eugene/GS-15
91AppFx/ClBest-5
91AppFx/ProC-1711
Higbe, Kirby
39Exh
41DP-24
41PlayBall-52
47TipTop
48L-129
49B-215
49Eureka-108
50B-200
89Smok/Dodg-50
90Target-344
93Conlon-764
94Conlon-1213
Exh47
Higginbotham, Robin
91Niagara/ClBest-15
91Niagara/ProC-3647
92Niagara/ProC-3338
Higgins, Bill
90Martins/ProC-3184
Higgins, Bob
90Target-980
T207
Higgins, Dennis
66T-529R
67OPC-52
67T-52
68T-509
69T-441
69T/St-237
70OPC-257
70T-257
71MLB/St-374
71OPC-479
71T-479
72MB-144
72OPC-278
72T-278
Higgins, Frank
36Exh/4-14
V351B-25
V94-24
WG8-34
Higgins, Kevin
89Spokane/SP-19
90Foil/Best-102
90River/Best-13
90River/Cal-6
90River/ProC-2610
91AAA/LineD-284
91LasVegas/LineD-284
91LasVegas/ProC-239
92LasVegas/ProC-2801
92LasVegas/SB-232
93B-574
93F/Final-142
93L-441
93Select/RookTr-136T
94D-387
94F-667
94Pac/Cr-527
94Pinn-215
94Pinn/Artist-215
94Pinn/Museum-215
94S-642
94StCl-83
94StCl/1stDay-83
94StCl/Gold-83
94T-279
94T/Gold-279
Higgins, Mark Douglas
86Watlo-11
87Wmsprt-9
88ColoSp/CMC-13
88ColoSp/ProC-1544
89ColoSp/CMC-15
89ColoSp/ProC-255
90Denver/CMC-16
90Denver/ProC-631
90T/89Debut-58
Higgins, Mark
80BurlB-23
81BurlB-23
90AAASingl/ProC-656
90ProC/Singl-41
Higgins, Mike
(Pinky)
34G-78
35BU-171
35G-1B
35G-2B
35G-6B
35G-7B
36B
40PlayBall-199
41DP-55
41PlayBall-35
43Playball-13
55T-150MG
61T-221MG
62T-559MG
72F/FFeat-30
72Laugh/GF-11
81Tiger/Detroit-89
88Conlon/AmAS-15
90HOF/St-37
94Conlon-1115
PM10/Sm-73
R303/A
R303/B
R313
R314
W501-26
Higgins, Ted
86FSLAS-23
86FtLaud-13
87Albany-8
Higginson, Bob
92Niagara/ClBest-14
92Niagara/ProC-3339
94FExcel-56
Higgs, Darrel
87OrlanTw-24
High, Andrew
(Andy)
21Exh-73
26Exh-2
27Exh-3
33G-182
88Conlon/3-13
90Target-345
92Conlon/Sport-648
94Conlon-1174
R316
High, Brent
89KS*-15
93Lipscomb-17M
High, Hugh
16FleischBrd-42
94Conlon-1174M
D328-76
D329-82
D350/2-81
E135-76
M101/4-82
M101/5-81
Hightower, Barry
86Columbia-13
87Columbia-1
88Spokane/ProC-1942
Hightower, Mark
90GA-9
Hightower, Vee
93Peoria/Team-9
Higson, Chuck
86Cram/NWL-185
86Everett/Pop-8
88Fresno/Cal-22
88Fresno/ProC-1225
Higuchi, Alan
87Hawaii-29
Higuera, Ted
(Teddy)
84ElPaso-15
85F/Up-U54
85Pol/Brew-49
85T/Tr-53T
86D-351
86F-490
86F/St-59
86Jay's-10
86Leaf-157
86Pol/Brew-49
86Sf-114
86T-347
87Classic/Up-147
87D-16DK
87D-49
87D/AAS-57
87D/DKsuper-16
87D/OD-56
87F-346
87F/Excit-27
87F/GameWin-21
87F/Hottest-22
87F/LL-23
87F/Lim-21
87F/Mini-55
87F/Slug-20
87F/St-60
87Leaf-16DK
87Leaf-95
87OPC-250
87Pol/Brew-49
87RedFoley/St-74
87Sf-74
87Sf-111M
87Sf/TPrev-19M
87T-250
87T-615AS
87T/Gloss22-22
87T/Mini-60
87T/St-199
88D-90
88D/Best-127
88F-166
88F/AS-3
88F/AwardWin-19
88F/BB/AS-15
88F/BB/MVP-18
88F/Excit-21
88F/Hottest-20
88F/LL-20
88F/Mini-30
88F/RecSet-19
88F/SS-16
88F/Slug-19
88F/St-37
88F/TL-15
88Grenada-60
88KennerFig-52
88Leaf-53
88OPC-110
88Panini/St-116
88Pol/Brew-49
88S-280
88Sf-20
88T-110
88T/Big-87
88T/Mini-18
88T/St-196
88T/UK-35
89B-129
89Brewer/YB-49
89Classic-136
89D-175
89D/Best-183
89ElPaso/GS-16
89F-188
89F/BBMVP's-20
89F/Heroes-23
89F/Superstar-24
89Gard-7
89KennerFig-65
89OPC-292
89Panini/St-366
89Pol/Brew-49
89RedFoley/St-59
89S-132
89S/HotStar-49
89Sf-47

89T-595
89T/Mini-57
89T/St-198
89T/St/Backs-28
89T/UK-39
89UD-424
90B-384
90Brewer/MillB-11
90Classic/III-T9
90D-339
90D/BestAL-92
90ElPasoATG/Team-6
90F-326
90F/Can-326
90Leaf-506
90MLBPA/Pins-83
90OPC-15
90Panini/St-96
90Pol/Brew-49
90PublInt/St-289
90PublInt/St-497
90S-305
90Sf-44
90T-15
90T/Big-322
90T/St-201
90UD-627
91B-54
91BBBest/Aces-10
91Brewer/MillB-10
91Classic/200-24
91D-629
91F-586
91Leaf/StudPrev-6
91OPC-475
91Pol/Brew-10
91S-260
91StCl-46
91T-475
91UD-341
91Ultra-175
92B-223
92D-294
92F-178
92OPC-265
92Pinn-439
92Pol/Brew-12
92S-126
92StCl-208
92T-265
92T/Gold-265
92T/GoldWin-265
92UD-138
92Ultra-80
93Pac/Spanish-511
93Pac/SpanishP-16
93Pol/Brew-11
94Panini-81
94Pol/Brew-12
94S-348
94StCl-273
94StCl/1stDay-273
94StCl/Gold-273
Hilbert, Adam
88Pocatel/ProC-2081
Hildebrand, George
21Exh-74
90Target-346
93Conlon-708
94Conlon-1208UMP
Hildebrand, Oral
34G-38
35BU-123
35G-1L
35G-2E
35G-6E
35G-7E
36G
37Exh/4-15
40PlayBall-123
77Galasso-186
91Conlon/Sport-278
R308-163
R313
R314
Hildebrand, Tom
86Penin-13
Hildreth, Brad 1
89Erie/Star-8
90Freder/Team-30
90Wausau/Star-11
Hildreth, Brad 2
88MissSt-11
89MissSt-19
Hilgenberg, Scot
86Cedar/TCMA-17
87Tampa-24
Hilgendorf, Tom
63Pep/Tul
70OPC-482
70T-482
74OPC-13
74T-13
75OPC-377
75T-377
75T/M-377
76OPC-168
76T-168
Hiljus, Erik
92Kingspt/ClBest-13
92Kingspt/ProC-1526
Hill, A.J.
77AppFx
80GlenF/B-21
80GlenF/C-20M
80GlenF/C-30
81AppFx-18
83MidldC-26
84Chatt-20
Hill, Brad
85BurlR-4
86Salem-12
Hill, Carmen
93Conlon-987
Hill, Chris
88LitFalls/Pucko-17
89Clmbia/Best-13
89Clmbia/GS-9
89SALAS/GS-15
90StLucie/Star-10
91AA/LineD-634
91Wmsprt/LineD-634
91Wmsprt/ProC-286
92Osceola/ClBest-3
92Osceola/ProC-2526
93ClBest/MLG-66
93FExcel/ML-44
Hill, Darryl
78Dunedin
Hill, Don
(Clay)
83Chatt-15
84Chatt-27
85Cram/PCL-100
86Calgary-12
88Miami/Star-9
Hill, Donnie
82WHave-14
83Tacoma-11
84D-96
84F-448
84Mother/A's-13
84Nes/792-265
84T-265
85D-375
85F-426
85Mother/A's-12
85T/Tr-54T
86D-340
86F-420
86Leaf-148
86Mother/A's-12
86OPC-310
86T-484
87Coke/WS-9
87D-405
87D/OD-237
87F-394
87T-339
87T/Tr-47T
88Coke/WS-10
88D-87
88F-400
88OPC-132
88S-572
88T-132
88T/Big-137
88T/St-286
89S-583
89T-512
89Tacoma/CMC-18
89Tacoma/ProC-1562
89UD-527
91D-376
91F-316
91Leaf-177
91OPC-36
91Smok/Angel-12
91T-36
91UD-211
91Ultra-46
92F-60
92L-498
92L/BlkGold-498
92OPC-731
92S-183
92StCl-702
92T-731
92T/Gold-731
92T/GoldWin-731
92UD-413
Hill, Elmore
(Moe)
78Wisco
Hill, Eric
90Batavia/ProC-3058
91Spartan/ClBest-6
91Spartan/ProC-891
92Clearw/ClBest-2
92Reading/ProC-570
Hill, Fred
89Wythe/Star-13
Hill, Garry
70OPC-172R
70T-172R
Hill, Glenallen
85Kingst-19
86Knoxvl-10
86SLAS-16
87D-561
87Sf/TPrev-5M
87Syrac-23
87Syrac/TCMA-20
88Syrac/CMC-15
88Syrac/ProC-812
89AAA/CMC-22
89AAA/ProC-31
89Syrac/CMC-15
89Syrac/MerchB-15
89Syrac/ProC-804
89Syrac/Team-15
90B-514
90Classic-88
90D-627
90D/Rook-24
90F/Up-127
90Leaf-317
90OPC-194
90S-601RP
90S/YS/II-33
90T-194
90T/89Debut-59
90Tor/BJ-24
90TripleAAS/CMC-22
90UD/Ext-776
91B-24
91D-380
91F-177
91F/UltraUp-U19
91F/Up-U17
91Leaf-311
91Leaf/Stud-43
91OPC-509
91Panini/FrSt-347
91S-514
91S/100RisSt-60
91StCl-425
91T-509
91T/JumboR-12
91T/Tr-55T
91Tor/Fire-24
91ToysRUs-11
91UD-276
91UD/FinalEd-52F
91Ultra-363
92B-659
92CJ/DII-23
92D-643
92F-110
92Indian/McDon-11
92L-70
92L/BlkGold-70
92OPC-364
92Pinn-420
92S-448
92StCl-413
92Studio-166
92T-364
92T/Gold-364
92T/GoldWin-364
92TripleP-181
92UD-558
92Ultra-347
93B-65
93D-201
93F-592
93Indian/WUAB-11
93L-128
93OPC-114
93Pac/Spanish-411
93Pinn-123
93S-398
93StCl-576
93StCl/1stDay-576
93T-666
93T/Gold-666
93TripleP-212
93UD-584
93Ultra-540
94D-150
94F-387
94Flair-138
94L-18
94StCl/Team-351
94T-63
94T/Gold-63
94UD-149
94UD/CollC-137
94UD/CollC/Gold-137
94UD/CollC/Silv-137
94UD/ElecD-149
94Ultra-458
Hill, H.A.
79Knoxvl/TCMA-22
Hill, Herman
70OPC-267R
70T-267R
Hill, Jim
47Centen-9
92Negro/Retort-28
Hill, Ken
87ArkTr-19
89D-536
89D/Best-304
89D/Rook-31
89F-652R
89F/Up-119
89Louisvl-22
89Louisvl/ProC-1268
89S/Tr-98
89Smok/Cards-9
89T/Tr-50T
90AAAGame/ProC-53
90D-397
90F-251
90F/Can-251
90Louisvl/LBC-19
90OPC-233
90S-233
90S/100Ris-34
90S/YS/I-32
90T-233
90T/JumboR-15
90T/TVCard-13
90ToysRUs-15
90UD-336
91B-390
91D-670
91F-635
91F/UltraUp-U106
91Leaf-376
91Louisvl/Team-4
91OPC-591
91Pol/Card-43
91S-567
91StCl-435
91T-591
91UD-647
92B-507
92Classic/Game200-168
92D-31
92Expo/D/Duri-11
92F-580
92F/Up-98
92L-468
92L/BlkGold-468
92OPC-664
92OPC/Premier-89
92Pinn-486
92S-104
92S/RookTr-61T
92StCl-138
92StCl-735
92Studio-56
92T-664
92T/Gold-664
92T/GoldWin-664
92T/Tr-51T
92T/TrGold-51T
92UD-628
92UD-790
92Ultra-520
93B-324
93D-220
93Expo/D/McDon-9
93F-76
93Flair-84
93HumDum/Can-38
93L-201
93OPC-239
93Pac/Spanish-186
93Panini-223
93Pinn-66
93S-48
93Select-169
93Select/Ace-14
93Select/StatL-89
93StCl-227
93StCl/1stDay-227
93T-495
93T/Finest-35
93T/FinestRef-35
93T/Gold-495
93TripleP-174
93UD-138
93UD/FunPack-96
93UD/SP-104
93Ultra-68
94B-444
94D-180
94F-542
94Flair-192
94L-282
94OPC-140
94Panini-211
94Pinn-355
94S-64
94S/GoldR-64
94StCl-445
94StCl/1stDay-445
94StCl/Gold-445
94Studio-79
94T-315
94T/Finest-25
94T/FinestRef-25
94T/Gold-315
94TripleP-96
94UD-173
94UD/CollC-138
94UD/CollC/Gold-138
94UD/CollC/Silv-138
94UD/ElecD-173
94Ultra-229
Hill, Lew
87Oneonta-1
89Oneonta/ProC-2111
90Greens/Best-23
90Greens/ProC-2675
91Greens/ProC-3074
92ClBest/Up-438
92Greens/ClBest-20
92Greens/ProC-792
93ClBest/MLG-116
93FExcel/ML-208
93SALAS/II-15
93SALAS/IICS-3
Hill, Marc
75OPC-620R
75T-620R
75T/M-620R
76OPC-577
76SSPC-100
76T-577
77T-57
78T-359
79Pol/Giants-2
79T-11
80OPC-125
80Pol/Giants-2
80T-236
81T-486
81T/Tr-770
82T-748
83D-230
83T-124
83TrueVal/WSox-7
84D-330
84F-62
84Nes/792-698

84T-698
84TrueVal/WS-16
85Coke/WS-7
85D-160
85F-516
85T-312
86Coke/WS-7
86T-552
92Penin/ClBest-27MG
92Penin/ProC-2948MG
93ClBest/MLG-132
Hill, Milton
88Cedar/ProC-1163
89Chatt/Best-6
89Chatt/GS-10
90AAASingl/ProC-538
90Nashvl/CMC-1
90Nashvl/ProC-226
90ProC/Singl-126
91AAA/LineD-261
91Nashvl/LineD-261
91Nashvl/ProC-2151
92D-659
92Nashvl/ProC-1828
92Nashvl/SB-282
92S-820
92StCl-733
92T/91Debut-80
93D-502
93F-36
93T-642
93T/Gold-642
94StCl/Team-33
Hill, Nate
85Spokane/Cram-8
Hill, Orsino
83Cedar-23
83Cedar/Frit-23
88Jaxvl/Best-12
88Jaxvl/ProC-965
89CharlK-24
90AAAGame/ProC-41
90AAASingl/ProC-177
90ProC/Singl-644
90Vanco/CMC-17
90Vanco/ProC-499
91AAA/LineD-638
91Vanco/LineD-638
91Vanco/ProC-1606
92Tacoma/ProC-2515
92Tacoma/SB-536
Hill, Perry W.
86DayBe-12C
90Gaston/Star-28INS
91Gaston/ProC-2705INS
93Rang/Keeb-437CO
Hill, Pete
74Laugh/Black-10
Hill, Quency
76OkCty/Team-12
78Knoxvl
82QuadC-27
Hill, Roger
88Watlo/ProC-685
Hill, Ron
80Elmira-9
Hill, Sandy
78Salem
Hill, Stephen F.
(Steve)
85Anchora-16
86StPete-12
87Peoria-7
87Peoria/PW-4
87Spring/Best-12
88StPete/Star-10
88WinSalem/Star-6
89ArkTr/GS-7
89SanBern/Best-15
89SanBern/Cal-84
Hill, Tony
86Elmira-10
87Greens-14
Hill, Tripp
90MissSt-20
91MissSt-25
92MissSt-21
93MissSt-22
Hill, Tyrone
91Classic/DP-12
91Helena/SportP-8
91LitSun/HSPros-3
91LitSun/HSProsG-3
92Beloit/ClBest-1
92Beloit/ProC-401
92ClBest-364
92MidwLAS/Team-19
92OPC-444
92Pinn-301DP
92S-807DP
92StCl/Dome-84
92T-444DP
92T/Gold-444
92T/GoldWin-444
92UD/ML-135
92UD/ML-29M
93B-368FOIL
93B-619
93FExcel/ML-186
93UD-427TP
94F/MLP-13
94SigRook-40
94Ultra-372
Hill, William C.
(Still Bill)
90Target-981
Hillegas, Shawn
87Albuq/Pol-11
87Sf/Rook-30
88Albuq/CMC-1
88Albuq/ProC-265
88D-35RR
88F-519
88Leaf-35RR
88Pol/Dodg-57M
88S-612
88T-455
89B-58
89Coke/WS-11
89D-503
89F-498
89Panini/St-301
89S-488
89S/YS/II-29
89T-247
89UD-478
90AAASingl/ProC-163
90D-619
90F-535
90F/Can-535
90OPC-93
90ProC/Singl-635
90Publint/St-389
90S-329
90T-93
90Target-982
90UD-541
90Vanco/CMC-8
90Vanco/ProC-485
91D-589
91F/Up-U18
91Indian/McDon-13
91Leaf-513
91S/RookTr-65T
92ColClip/ProC-346
92D-72
92F-111
92OPC-523
92S-93
92StCl-76
92T-523
92T/Gold-523
92T/GoldWin-523
93Mother/A's-26
93Pac/Spanish-569
93StCl/A's-20
94Pac/Cr-453
Hillemann, Charles
(Charlie)
87Spokane-9
88Charl/ProC-1197
89AubAs/ProC-4
89TexLAS/GS-9
89Wichita/Rock-18
89Wichita/Rock/Up-6
90AAASingl/ProC-22
90LasVegas/CMC-18
90LasVegas/ProC-134
90ProC/Singl-521
90Wichita/Rock-9
91AA/LineD-608
91ClBest/Singl-50
91Wichita/LineD-608
91Wichita/ProC-2611
Hiller, Chuck
61T-538
62Salada-106
62Shirriff-106
62T-188
63J-102
63P-102
63T-185
64T-313
65T-531
66OPC-154
66T-154
67CokeCap/YMet-19
67T-198
68T-461
73OPC-549CO
73T-549CO
91WIZMets-182
93Rang/Keeb-185CO
Hiller, Dutch
45Parade*-21M
45Parade*-27
Hiller, Frank
52B-114
52T-156
R346-37
Hiller, John
66T-209R
68T-307
69MB-114
69T-642
70OPC-12
70T-12
71MLB/St-393
71OPC-629
71T-629
72MB-146
73OPC-448
73T-448
74/DE-17
74OPC-208LL
74OPC-24
74T-208LL
74T-24
74T/St-175
75K-19
75OPC-415
75T-415
75T/M-415
76OPC-37
76SSPC-353
76T-37
77BurgChef-95
77Ho-28
77Ho/Twink-28
77OPC-257
77T-595
78BK/T-9
78T-258
79OPC-71
79T-151
80OPC-229
80T-614
81Tiger/Detroit-12
83Kaline-52M
86GlenF-10CO
86Tiger/Sport-22
87Toledo-25
88Domino-7
Hillerman, Charlie
91Wichita/Rock-21
Hillman, Dave
57T-351
58T-41
59T-319
60T-68
61T-326
62T-282
91WIZMets-183
Hillman, Eric
88Clmbia/GS-5
89Clmbia/Best-11
89Clmbia/GS-10
91AAA/LineD-558
91Tidew/LineD-558
91Tidew/ProC-2505
92B-326
92F/Up-102
92Sky/AAASingl-252
92StCl-847
92Tidew/ProC-
92Tidew/SB-558
93F-87
93S-280
93Select-350
93T-751
93T/Gold-751
94D-514
94F-564
94Pac/Cr-403
94StCl-480
94StCl/1stDay-480
94StCl/Gold-480
94T-453
94T/Gold-453
94UD/CollC-139
94UD/CollC/Gold-139
94UD/CollC/Silv-139
Hillman, Joe
88SoOreg/ProC-1716
89Modesto/Cal-275
89Modesto/Chong-29
Hillman, Stewart
90Clinton/Best-18
90Clinton/ProC-2542
Hillman, Trey
86Watlo-12
87Kinston-19
90AAASingl/ProC-343M
90ColClip/CMC-24CO
90ColClip/ProC-693CO
90Oneonta/ProC-3389MG
91Greens/ProC-3075MG
91SALAS/ProC-SAL27MG
92Greens/ClBest-26MG
92Greens/ProC-796
Hillman, Troy
90ProC/Singl-224M
Hilpert, Adam
89Clinton/ProC-883
Hilton, Howard
86StPete-13
87Spring/Best-13
88ArkTr/GS-12
89Louisvl-23
89Louisvl/CMC-6
89Louisvl/ProC-1251
90AAASingl/ProC-512
90B-189
90Louisvl/CMC-6
90Louisvl/LBC-20
90Louisvl/ProC-398
90ProC/Singl-106
90T/TVCard-14
91T/90Debut-68
Hilton, John David
73T-615R
74OPC-148
74T-148
75OPC-509
75T-509
75T/M-509
77OPC-139
77T-163
81Portl-11
84Visalia-10
89Pac/SenLg-216
89SnJos/Cal-238C
90EliteSenLg-113
91Pac/SenLg-124
91Pac/SenLg-133
92Idaho/ProC-3531MG
Hilton, Stan
85Modesto/Chong-22
88Wmsprt/ProC-1316
89Burllnd/Star-28CO
89ColoSp/ProC-244
90Burllnd/ProC-3027
91Burllnd/ProC-3321CO
Hina, Fred
88Clmbia/GS-18
90Jacks/GS-6TR
Hinch, A.J.
93Bz-14
93T/Tr-12T
Hinchman, Harry
E254
E270/1
T201
T206
Hinchman, William
(Bill)
91Conlon/Sport-155
94Conlon-1113
E97
T206
W555
Hinde, Michael
88CapeCod/Sum-62
89Elizab/Star-11
Hindman, Randy
86Cedar/TCMA-18
Hinds, Kevin
81Cedar-11
Hinds, Robert
92Oneonta/ClBest-14
93Greens/ClBest-11
93Greens/ProC-892
Hinds, Sam
77Spoka
78Spokane/Cramer-19
78Spokane/Team-17
78T-303
79Holyo-29
79Vanco-19
Hine, Frank
85Clovis-22
Hines, Ben
86Coke/Dodg-12CO
87Albuq/Pol-2CO
90Mother/Dodg-28M
90Pol/Dodg-x
91Mother/Dodg-28CO
91Pol/Dodg-x
92Mother/Dodg-28M
92Pol/Dodg-NNO
93Mother/Dodg-28M
93Pol/Dodg-30M
Hines, Henry
(Hunkey)
90Target-347
N172
Hines, Keith
90MedHat/Best-14
91StCath/ClBest-12
91StCath/ProC-3408
92StCath/ClBest-2
93Hagers/ClBest-14
93Hagers/ProC-1892
Hines, Maurice
90Martins/ProC-3187
Hines, Paul
N172
N284
WG1-33
Hines, Richard
90Tampa/DIMD-12
91Greens/ProC-3053
91SALAS/ProC-SAL28
92PrWill/ClBest-6
92PrWill/ProC-141
Hines, Tim
89Pittsfld/Star-9
89StLucie/Star-10
89Star/IISingl-158
90Salem/Star-7
91AA/LineD-110
91CaroMud/LineD-110
91CaroMud/ProC-1089
93WPalmB/ProC-1344
Hingle, Larry
92Boise/ClBest-30CL
92Boise/ProC-3620
92FrRow/DP-73
Hinkel, John
78Wausau
Hinkle, Brad
89KS*-57
Hinkle, Mike
87Erie-28
88Savan/ProC-331
89ArkTr/GS-8
90AAASingl/ProC-513
90Louisvl/CMC-5
90Louisvl/LBC-21
90Louisvl/ProC-399
90ProC/Singl-105
90T/TVCard-52
91Louisvl/Team-10
92Louisvl/ProC-1883
92Louisvl/SB-264
Hinnrichs, Dave
84Everett/Cram-16
86Fresn/Smok-13
Hinrichs, Phil
80Phoenix/NBank-17
81Phoenix-17
83Phoenix/BHN-11
Hinshaw, George
82Amari-1
83LasVegas/BHN-10
84Cram/PCL-234
85Cram/PCL-113
87Albuq/Pol-28
88Albuq/CMC-13

88Albuq/ProC-268
88TripleA/ASCMC-40
90AAASingl/ProC-48
90Phoenix/CMC-15
90Phoenix/ProC-22
90ProC/Singl-542

Hinsley, Jerry
64T-576R
65T-449R
91WIZMets-184

Hinson, Bo
82AubAs-10

Hinson, Dean
91Welland/ClBest-9II
91Welland/ProC-3576

Hinson, Gary
82BirmB-14

Hinton, Chuck
62T-347
62T/St-96
63Bz-25
63Exh
63J-93
63P-93
63T-2LL
63T-330
63T/SO
64Bz-25
64T-52
64T/Coins-162AS
64T/Coins-38
64T/S-20
64T/SU
64T/St-47
65Bz-3
65Kahn
65OPC-235
65OldLond-26
65T-235
65T/E-60
65T/trans-48
66T-391
67CokeCap/Indian-18
67OPC-189
67T-189
68T-531
69MB-115
69MLB/St-22
69T-644
70MLB/St-199
70OPC-27
70T-27
71MLB/St-375
71OPC-429
71T-429
72MB-147
78TCMA-252
78TCMA-265
89Swell-93
Exh47

Hinton, Rich
72T-724R
73OPC-321
73T-321
76Indianap-20
76OPC-607
76SSPC-158
76T-607
92Yank/WIZ70-74
93Rang/Keeb-17

Hinton, Steve
91Eugene/ClBest-9
91Eugene/ProC-3734
92AppFox/ClBest-23
92MidwLAS/Team-20

Hinzo, Thomas
86AZ/Pol-5
87Kinston-21
88ColoSp/CMC-14
88ColoSp/ProC-1527
88D-526
88F-611
88OPC-294
88Panini/St-73
88S-567
88T-576
89ColoSp/CMC-16
89ColoSp/ProC-256
89UD-34

Hipp, Mike
93SoEastern-10

Hippauf, Herb A.
66T-518R
87Idaho-18CO
88Idaho/ProC-1860CO

Hiraldo, Jerry
92GulfCM/ProC-3494

Hird, Jeff
86AZ/Pol-6

Hirose, Sam
87SanJose-1
88SanJose/Cal-142
88SanJose/ProC-123

Hirsch, Chris
91Sumter/ClBest-13
91Sumter/ProC-2336

Hirsch, Jeff
86Peoria-11
87WinSalem-23
88Iowa/CMC-6
88Iowa/ProC-532
89CharlK-18
90Peoria/Team-20M

Hirschbeck, John
88TM/Umpire-50
89TM/Umpire-48
90TM/Umpire-46

Hirschbeck, Mark
89TM/Umpire-59
89Umpires-59
90TM/Umpire-57

Hirtensteiner, Rick
87PanAm/USAB-17
87PanAm/USAR-17
88CapeCod/Sum-25
89BendB/Legoe-20
90QuadC/GS-27
90TeamUSA/87-17
91SLCity/ProC-3225
91SLCity/SportP-6
92B-658
92Harris/ProC-471
92Harris/SB-283
93Ottawa/ProC-2445

Hiser, Gene
72OPC-61R
72T-61R
74OPC-452
74T-452
74Wichita-120
76SSPC-314

Hisey, Jason
88Alaska/Team-9
90AZ/Pol-7
91Hamil/ClBest-11
91Hamil/ProC-4034
92Savan/ClBest-16
92Savan/ProC-658
94ClBest/Gold-171

Hisey, Steve
88SanBern/Best-20
88SanBern/Cal-39

Hisle, Larry
68T-579R
69OPC-206R
69T-206R
69T/4in1-22M
70K-45
70MLB/St-89
70OPC-288
70T-288
71MLB/St-180
71OPC-616
71Phill/Arco-5
71T-616
72MB-148
72OPC-398
72T-398
73OPC-622
73T-622
74OPC-366
74T-366
75Ho-128
75OPC-526
75T-526
75T/M-526
76Ho-73
76OPC-59
76SSPC-220
76T-59
77BurgChef-49
77OPC-33
77T-375
78Ho-13
78OPC-3LL
78PapaG/Disc-38
78T-203LL
78T-520
78Tastee/Discs-24
78Wiffle/Discs-29
79Ho-95
79OPC-87
79T-180
79T/Comics-10
80K-22
80OPC-222
80T-430
81D-87
81F-509
81F/St-94
81OPC-215
81T-215
82D-358
82F-144
82Pol/Brew-9
82T-93
83T-773
92BJ/Fire-15CO
93BJ/Fire-15CO

Hiss, William
75SanAn
77Watlo

Hitchcock, Billy
51B-191
52B-89
52T-182
53T-17
53Tiger/Glen-14
60T-461C
62T-121MG
63T-213MG
67T-199MG
91T/Arc53-17

Hitchcock, Sterling
90A&AASingle/ProC-88
90Greens/Best-2
90Greens/ProC-2654
90Greens/Star-5
90ProC/Singl-822
90T/TVYank-46
91ClBest/Singl-385
91PrWill/ClBest-2
91PrWill/ProC-1419
92Albany/ProC-2220
92Albany/SB-8
92Sky/AASingl-4
93B-606
93ColClip/Pol-5
93D-345
93F/MLPI-2
93Pinn-579
93Pinn/RookTP-2M
93Pinn/Team2001-30
93S-311
93S/Boys-22
93Select/RookTr-53T
93StCl/Y-17
93T-530
93T/Gold-530
93UD-16SR
94B-333
94D-638
94Pinn-213
94Pinn/Artist-213
94Pinn/Museum-213
94S-565
94Sf/2000-157
94StCl/Team-203
94T-103
94T/Gold-103
94UD-138
94UD/ElecD-138

Hitchcox, Wally
92Lipscomb-19M
93Lipscomb-24M

Hithe, Victor
87Ashvl-19
88Osceola/Star-14
89EastLgAS/ProC-21
89Hagers/Best-5
89Hagers/ProC-272
89Hagers/Star-11
90AAASingl/ProC-471
90Foil/Best-135
90Hagers/Best-14
90Hagers/ProC-1426
90ProC/Singl-323
90RochR/CMC-22
90RochR/ProC-714
90Rochester/L&U-24

Hitt, Daniel
(Danny)
89Savan/ProC-369
90StPete/Star-13

Hitta, Chief Powa
78Richm

Hitting, Scott
90Batavia/ProC-3084CO

Hittle, Floyd
(Red)
48Smith-21
53Mother-42

Hivizda, Jim
88Butte-2

Hixon, Alan
86Miami-11

Hiyama, Yasuhiro
87SLCity/Taco-20

Hmielewski, Chris
92Albany/ClBest-8
92Albany/ProC-2317
93BurlB/ClBest-10
93BurlB/ProC-166

Hoag, Myril
34G-95
39PlayBall-109
40PlayBall-52
91Conlon/Sport-233
93Conlon-894
R312/M
R313
R314

Hoak, Don
52LaPatrie-7
52Park-57
53Exh/Can-33
53T-176
54T-211
55B-21
55Gol/Dodg-13
55T-40
55T/DH-26
56T-335
57Kahn
57Sohio/Reds-9
57T-274
58Kahn
58T-160
59Kahn
59T-25
60Kahn
60T-373
61Kahn
61P-130
61T-230
61T/St-65
62Exh
62J-171
62Kahn
62P-171
62P/Can-171
62Salada-107
62Shirriff-107
62Sugar-C
62T-95
62T/St-178
62T/bucks
63Exh
63J-140
63P-140
63T-305
64T-254
79TCMA-273
81TCMA-388
90Target-348
91T/Arc53-176
94T/Arc54-211
Exh47

Hoban, John
81Watlo-9
82Beloit/Frit-7

Hobaugh, Brian
83Wisco/Frit-17
84Visalia-12

Hobaugh, Ed
60T-131
61T-129
62T-79
63T-423

Hobbie, Glen
58T-467
59T-334
60Bz-32
60L-20
60T-182
60T/tatt-22
61P-197
61T-264
61T-393M
62Salada-145
62Shirriff-145
62T-585
62T/St-108
63F-31
63T-212
64T-578

Hobbs, Jack
82OrlanTw/A-17
82OrlanTw/B-5
83OrlanTw-16

Hobbs, Jon
88Fresno/Cal-4
88Fresno/ProC-1237

Hobbs, Rodney
80LynnS-3
81LynnS-22
82WHave-22
84Albany-4
86Nashvl-13

Hoblitzell, Richard C.
(Doc)
10Domino-55
11Helmar-116
12Sweet/Pin-102
14CJ-55
15CJ-55
16FleischBrd-43
91Conlon/Sport-148
D328-77
D329-83
D350/2-82
E135-77
E270/2
M101/4-83
M101/5-82
M116
PM1-6
S74-77
T202
T204
T206
T213/blue
T215/blue
T215/brown
T3-97
WG5-19
WG6-18

Hobson, Butch
77T-89
78Ho-1
78OPC-187
78PapaG/Disc-4
78SSPC/270-172
78T-155
79Ho-129
79OPC-136
79T-270
80OPC-216
80T-420
81D-542
81F-227
81OPC-7
81T-595
81T/HT
81T/St-54
81T/Tr-771
82D-577
82F-465
82F/St-213
82OPC-357
82T-357
82T/St-164
83Colum-21
83T-652
84Colum-16
84Colum/Pol-12
85Colum-17
85Colum/Pol-13
87Columbia-10
88Clmbia/GS-1
89NewBrit/ProC-617
89NewBrit/Star-23
89Pac/SenLg-32
89T/SenLg-49
89TM/SenLg-47
90EastLAS/ProC-EL11MG
90NewBrit/Best-23MG
90NewBrit/ProC-1334
90NewBrit/Star-25MG
91AAA/LineD-374MG

91Pawtu/LineD-374MG
91Pawtu/ProC-54MG
92RedSox/Dunkin-17MG
92T/Tr-52T
92T/TrGold-52T
92Yank/WIZ80-82
93T-502MG
93T/Gold-502MG

Hobson, Todd
90AR-15
91AubAS/ClBest-18
91AubAS/ProC-4286
92Ashvl/ClBest-6

Hockenberry, Charlie
75SLCity/Caruso-13

Hockenbury, Bill
52Park-81

Hockett, Oris
44Playball-12
90Target-349

Hocking, David
89Everett/Star-14

Hocking, Denny
91Kenosha/ClBest-4
91Kenosha/ProC-2081
91MidwLAS/ProC-37
92ClBest-295
92Visalia/ClBest-20
92Visalia/ProC-1020
93B-73
93FExcel/ML-201
94F/MLP-14
94Pinn-421
94StCl-9
94StCl/1stDay-9
94StCl/Gold-9
94T-771
94T/Gold-771
94UD-114
94UD/ElecD-114

Hocutt, Mike
86Indianap-22
87Jacks/Feder-10
88Louisvl-22

Hodapp, Urban J.
(Johnny)
33DH-22
88Conlon/AmAS-16
92Conlon/Sport-538
93Conlon-810
R316

Hodde, Rodney
82BurlR/Frit-11
82BurlR/TCMA-2

Hoderlein, Mel
53Briggs
54B-120

Hodge, Clarence
E120
E121/120
W501-42
W573

Hodge, Eddie
80OrlanTw-5
82OrlanTw-24
83Toledo-4
84F/X-52
85F-280
85T-639
85Toledo-8

Hodge, Gomer
81Watlo-1
82Watlo/B-26MG
82Watlo/Frit-2MG
83Watlo/Frit-28MG
86Beloit-11MG
87Beloit-18MG
88Beloit/GS-1MG
89Jaxvl/Best-20
90AAASingl/ProC-591CO
90Indianap/ProC-308CO
91AAA/LineD-200M
91Indianap/LineD-200CO
91Indianap/ProC-479CO
92Indianap/ProC-1877CO
92Indianap/SB-200CO
93Harris/ProC-285CO

Hodge, Kevin
88BuffB/ProC-1482

Hodge, Nick
92Indianap/ProC-NNO

Hodge, Pat
83Durham-6
84Durham-4

Hodge, Roy
92Bluefld/ClBest-12
92Bluefld/ProC-2371
92Kane/ClBest-3
92Kane/ProC-105

Hodge, Tim
88StCath/ProC-2016
89Myrtle/ProC-1457
90Dunedin/Star-10
91Dunedin/ClBest-20
91Dunedin/ProC-218
92Dunedin/ClBest-15
92Dunedin/ProC-2012
93Knoxvl/ProC-1263

Hodges, Darren
90A&AASingle/ProC-177
90Oneonta/ProC-3377
91CLAS/ProC-CAR33
91PrWill/ClBest-3
91PrWill/ProC-1420
92Albany/ProC-2221
92Albany/SB-9
92Sky/AASingl-5

Hodges, Gil
47HomogBond-20
49B-100
49Eureka-38
50B-112
50Drake-11
51B-7
51FB
51T/RB-31
52B-80
52BR
52Coke
52StarCal-91A
52StarCal/L-79A
52T-36
52TipTop
53B/Col-92
53Briggs
53Exh/Can-13
53SM
54B-138
54DanDee
54NYJour
54RM-NL22
54SM
54T-102
54Wilson
55B-158
55Gol/Dodg-12
55RM-NL3
55SM
55T-187
56T-145
56T/Pin-50
56YellBase/Pin-15
57T-400M
57T-80
58BB
58PacBell-4
58T-162
59HRDerby-7
59Morrell
59T-270
60Bz-23
60Morrell
60NuCard-41
60T-295
60Union/Dodg-8
61BB-14
61NuCard-441
61P-168
61T-460
61Union/Dodg-9
62Bz
62J-101
62P-101
62P/Can-101
62Salada-146A
62Salada-146B
62Shirriff-146
62T-85
62T/St-155
62T/bucks
63J-193
63P-193
63T-245
63T-68M
64T-547MG
65OPC-99MG
65T-99MG
66T-386MG
67T-228MG
68OPC-27MG
68T-27MG
69T-564MG
70OPC-394MG
70T-394MG
71OPC-183MG
71T-183MG
72OPC-465MG
72T-465MG
77Galasso-15
77Galasso-233
79TCMA-43
79TCMA-71
80Marchant-10
80Pac/Leg-63
81TCMA-315MG
81TCMA-407MG
81TCMA-423MG
81TCMA-482
85CircK-29
85West/2-30
86Sf/Dec-38M
88Pac/Leg-87
89B/Ins-4
89Rini/Dodg-31
89Smok/Dodg-54
89Swell-33
89T-664TBC
90Swell/Great-132
90Target-350
91Swell/Great-131
91T/Arc53-296
91WIZMets-185
92Bz/Quadra-16
93AP/ASG-137
93TWill/Mem-3
93UD/ATH-65
94Mets/69-29
94T/Arc54-102
94TedW-11
94TedW-148
D305
Exh47
PM10/Sm-74A
PM10/Sm-74B
PM10/Sm-75
PM10/Sm-76

Hodges, Ronald W.
(Ron)
74OPC-448
74T-448
75Cedar
75OPC-134
75T-134
75T/M-134
75Tidew/Team-13
76Cedar
77T-329
78T-653
79T-46
80T-172
81T-537
82F-527
82T-234
83D-476
83F-445
83T-713
84D-603
84F-588
84Nes/792-418
84T-418
85T-363
91WIZMets-186

Hodges, Steve
90Idaho/ProC-3242

Hodgin, Elmer Ralph
47TipTop
49B/PCL-3

Hodgson, Gordon
79QuadC-18

Hodgson, Paul
80Knoxvl/TCMA-5
82Knoxvl-13
83Knoxvl-18

Hodkinson, Chris
91Parramatta/Fut-7

Hodo, Doug
86Cram/NWL-134

Hoeft, Billy
52T-370
53B/BW-18
53T-165
53Tiger/Glen-15
54B-167
54Dix
56T-152
57T-60
58T-13
59T-343
60L-90
60T-369
61T-256
62T-134
63T-346
64T-551
65T-471
66T-409
79TCMA-37
81Tiger/Detroit-32
91Crown/Orio-197
91T/Arc53-165

Hoeksema, Dave
83Memphis/TCMA-9
85Indianap-23

Hoeme, Steve
88Eugene/Best-2
89AppFx/ProC-852
90BBCity/Star-11
92Watlo/ClBest-9
92Wichita/ProC-3654

Hoenstine, Dave
80Cedar-3
81Cedar-12

Hoerner, Joe
64T-544R
66T-544R
67OPC-41
67T-41
68T-227
69T-522
70MLB/St-90
70OPC-511
70T-511
71MLB/St-181
71OPC-166
71Phill/Arco-6
71T-166
72OPC-482
72T-482
73OPC-653
73T-653
74OPC-493
74T-493
75OPC-629
75T-629
75T/M-629
77T-256
93Rang/Keeb-186

Hoerner, Troy
90Kenosha/Best-5
90Kenosha/ProC-2307
90Kenosha/Star-7

Hofer, John
89AppFx/ProC-878

Hoff, Chester
(Red)
T207

Hoff, Jim
83Tampa-28
88Billings/ProC-1827

Hoffinger, Glenn
86Cram/NWL-61

Hoffman, Danny
14CJ-9
15CJ-9
E300
E90/3
E91
E95
M116
T205
T206
T213/brown
W575

Hoffman, Dennis
88Martins/Star-17

Hoffman, Frank J.
N172

Hoffman, Fred
28Exh-35
92Conlon/Sport-575
W753

Hoffman, Glenn
81D-95
81F-237
81OPC-349
81T-349
81T/HT
82Coke/BOS
82D-460
82F-296
82F/St-168
82T-189
83D-282
83F-185
83OPC-108
83T-108
84D-606
84F-399
84Nes/792-523
84OPC-141
84T-523
84T/St-223
85T-633
86D-457
86F-351
86OPC-38
86T-38
87Pawtu-63
87T-374
88Pawtu/CMC-13
88Pawtu/ProC-465
88T-202
90AAASingl/ProC-73
90Albuq/CMC-26CO
90Albuq/ProC-352
90Albuq/Trib-12
90D-407
90ProC/Singl-653CO
90Target-351
91Bakers/Cal-30CO
92VeroB/ClBest-29MG
92VeroB/ProC-2893MG

Hoffman, Guy
79Iowa/Pol-8
80Iowa/Pol-7
80T-664R
82Edmon-6
86F/Up-U51
86Gator-50
86Iowa-16
87F-566
87F/Up-U45
87Kahn-30
87T/Tr-48T
88D-452
88F-235
88S-609
88T-496
93Rang/Keeb-187

Hoffman, Harry C.
T206

Hoffman, Hunter
89Wausau/GS-18
90Fayette/ProC-2410

Hoffman, Jeff
88Oneonta/ProC-2057
90Foil/Best-230
90Greens/Best-3
90Greens/ProC-2655
90Greens/Star-6
90ProC/Singl-704
90SALAS/Star-11
90Star/ISingl-92
91PrWill/ClBest-4
91PrWill/ProC-1421
92Albany/ProC-2222
92Albany/SB-10
92Sky/AASingl-6

Hoffman, John
87Belling/Team-7
88Wausau/GS-9
89SanBern/Cal-77

Hoffman, John Edward
77Fritsch-33

Hoffman, Rich
89StPete/Star-18
90ArkTr/GS-17

Hoffman, Rob
90Kissim/DIMD-14

Hoffman, Trevor
88AZ/Pol-5
89Billings/ProC-2068
90CharWh/Best-16
90CharWh/ProC-2247
91Cedar/ClBest-6
91Cedar/ProC-2714
92B-11
92Chatt/SB-186
92Nashvl/ProC-1829

92ProC/Tomorrow-219
92Sky/AASingl-83
92UD/ML-105
93B-390
93F/Final-143
93Flair-135
93Flair/Wave-7
93L-531
93OPC/Premier-113
93Pac/Spanish-464
93Pinn-602
93StCl-451
93StCl/1stDay-451
93StCl/Marlin-20
93T-572
93T/Gold-572
93UD-773
93UD/SP-169
93USPlayC/Marlin-12H
93USPlayC/Marlin-7D
93Ultra-378
94D-187
94F-668
94Finest-417
94Flair-234
94L-421
94Pac/Cr-528
94Panini-257
94Pinn-272
94StCl-312
94StCl/1stDay-312
94StCl/Gold-312
94Studio-133
94T-222
94T/Gold-222
94UD-153
94UD/ElecD-153
94UD/SP-131
94Ultra-577
Hoffmann, Greg
85Iowa-24
Hoffner, Jamie
89Pittsfld/Star-27
91StLucie/ClBest-6
91StLucie/ProC-719
92Bingham/ProC-524
92Bingham/SB-58
Hoffner, William
N172
Hofman, Arthur
(Solly)
10Domino-56
11Helmar-96
12Sweet/Pin-52
E254
M116
T201
T206
T213/blue
T215/blue
T215/brown
T3-98
Hofman, Rich
92LitSun/HSPros-29
Hofman, Robert G.
(Bobby)
49B-223
50Remar
52T-371
53T-182
54NYJour
54T-99
55Gol/Giants-13
55T-17
55T/DH-96
56T-28
56T/Pin-40
78TCMA-59
91T/Arc53-182
94T/Arc54-99
Hogan, Ben
51BR-A16
52Wheat*
Hogan, David
91Brisbane/Fut-16
Hogan, J. Francis
(Shanty)
28Exh-18
29Exh/4-10
31Exh/4-9
33DH-23
33G-30
34DS-20
34Exh/4-1
34G-20
35Exh/4-1
35G-2E
35G-4E
35G-7E
87Conlon/2-42
91Conlon/Sport-294
R310
R316
V353-30
V354-66
Hogan, Mike
82AubAs-8
83DayBe-8
86Modesto-12
88Phoenix/CMC-6
88Phoenix/ProC-73
Hogan, Rob
91Waverly/Fut-6
Hogan, Robert
N172
Hogan, Shorty
V94-25
Hogan, William
(Happy)
E270/2
T207
Hoganson, Dale
72Dimanche*-75
Hogdin, Ralph
44Playball-17
Hogg, David
82Edmon-16
Hogsett, Elon
(Chief)
28LaPresse-11
93Conlon-969
Hogue, Bobby
49Eureka-12
52T-9
Hogue, Cal
53T-238
54T-134
91T/Arc53-238
94T/Arc54-134
Hohlmeyer, Alice
(Lefty)
93TWill-116
Hohn, Bill
90TM/Umpire-60
Hohn, Eric
86Erie-13
Hohno, Takayuki
92Salinas/ClBest-26CO
Hoiles, Chris
87GlenF-2
88Toledo/CMC-19
88Toledo/ProC-597
89RochR/ProC-1640
90AAASingl/ProC-461
90B-259
90F/Up-U65
90Leaf-513
90ProC/Singl-313
90RochR/CMC-14
90RochR/ProC-704
90Rochester/L&U-4
90S/Tr-96T
90T/89Debut-60
91B-99
91Classic/I-13
91Crown/Orio-198
91D-358
91F-476
91Leaf-131
91Leaf/Stud-4
91OPC-42
91OPC/Premier-65
91S-334RP
91S/100RisSt-34
91StCl-489
91StCl/Member*-10M
91T-42
91UD-306
91Ultra-17
92B-472
92D-156
92F-9
92L-211
92L/BlkGold-211
92L/GoldPrev-31
92OPC-125
92Panini-64
92Pinn-83
92S-641
92StCl-161
92Studio-124
92T-125
92T/Gold-125
92T/GoldWin-125
92TripleP-256
92UD-183
92UD/TWillB-T16
92Ultra-5
93B-549
93D-323
93F-168
93Flair-151
93L-133
93OPC-142
93Pac/Spanish-18
93Panini-70
93Pinn-186
93S-54
93Select-144
93StCl-345
93StCl/1stDay-345
93Studio-156
93T-524
93T/Gold-524
93TripleP-205
93UD-402
93UD/SP-157
93Ultra-495
94B-131
94D-99
94F-6
94Flair-3
94KingB-11
94L-195
94OPC-167
94Pac/Cr-33
94Panini-20
94Pinn-112
94Pinn/Artist-112
94Pinn/Museum-112
94Pinn/Power-2
94Pinn/Run-18
94S-357
94Select-15
94Sf/2000-114
94Sf/2000-180AS
94StCl-451
94StCl/1stDay-451
94StCl/Gold-451
94StCl/Team-288
94T-295
94T/BlkGold-9
94T/Finest-141
94T/Finest/PreProd-141
94T/FinestRef-141
94T/Gold-295
94TripleP-154
94TripleP/Medal-1
94UD-77
94UD/CollC-140
94UD/CollC/Gold-140
94UD/CollC/Silv-140
94UD/ElecD-77
94UD/SP-122
94Ultra-2
94Ultra/AS-1
Hokanson, Mark
91Kingspt/ClBest-21
91Kingspt/ProC-3809
92Pittsfld/ProC-3289
Hoke, Leon
81Miami-17
83SanJose-23
Hokuf, Ken
91Modesto/ClBest-6
91Modesto/ProC-3081
92Modesto/ClBest-22
92Modesto/ProC-3895
Holbert, Aaron
90Classic/DP-18
90Johnson/Star-14
90LitSun/HSPros-4
90LitSun/HSProsG-4
91B-399
91S-676FDP
92Savan/ClBest-21
92Savan/ProC-671
92UD/ML-172
93B-304
93SALAS/II-16
93SALAS/IICS-2
93StCl/Card-30
94B-68
94FExcel-267
Holbert, Ray
89Watlo/ProC-1791
89Watlo/Star-12
90Foil/Best-9
90Waterlo/Best-1
90Waterlo/ProC-2384
91HighD/ClBest-22
91HighD/ProC-2405
92Sky/AASingl-282
92UD/ML-103
92Wichita/ProC-3664
92Wichita/SB-634
93B-194
94B-532
94FExcel-283
94UD-518DD
Holbert, William
N172
N172/ST
Holcomb, Scott
87Modesto-24
88Huntsvl/BK-7
89Huntsvl/Best-16
92Albany/SB-11
Holcomb, Shawn
92FrRow/DP-65
Holcomb, Ted
86Bakers-13
87Bakers-18
88Durham/Star-7
Holcombe, Ken
49B/PCL-19
51B-267
52T-95
Holden, Gary
81Batavia-21
Holder, Brooks
46Remar
47Remar-3
47Signal
47Smith-4
48Signal
48Smith-2
49Sommer
Holdridge, Dave
88QuadC/GS-11
89Clearw/Star-11
90Foil/Best-17
90ProC/Singl-802
90Reading/Best-1
90Reading/ProC-1216
90Reading/Star-13
91AA/LineD-510
91ClBest/Singl-155
91Reading/LineD-510
91Reading/ProC-1368
92PalmSp/ClBest-9
92PalmSp/ProC-832
Holdsworth, Fred
74OPC-596R
74T-596R
75OPC-323
75T-323
75T/M-323
77T-466
80Vanco-18
81Tacoma-21
91Crown/Orio-199
Holifield, Rick
(Rickey)
89StCath/ProC-2096
90Myrtle/ProC-2787
91Myrtle/ClBest-24
91Myrtle/ProC-2958
92Myrtle/ClBest-13
92Myrtle/ProC-2211
93Dunedin/ClBest-10
93Dunedin/ProC-1809
Holke, Walter
21Exh-75
21Exh-76
25Exh-44
91Conlon/Sport-207
92Conlon/Sport-491
D327
D328-78
E120
E121/120
E121/80
E122
E135-78
V100
W501-91
W575
Hollacher, Charlie
V61-110
Holladay, Kolin
89KS*-16ACO
92Lipscomb-15CO
93Lipscomb-23M
Holland, Al
77Shrev
78Colum
79Portl-1
80Pol/Giants-19
81F-445
81T-213
82D-377
82F-391
82T-406
83D-146
83F-262
83F/St-11M
83F/St-21M
83OPC/St-306
83T-58
83T/St-306
83T/Tr-46
84D-204
84F-35
84F/St-68
84Nes/792-138LL
84Nes/792-564
84Nestle/DT-22
84OPC-206
84Phill/TastyK-21
84T-138LL
84T-564
84T/St-125
84T/St-289
84T/Super-10
85D-427
85F-254
85F-637IA
85F/St-107
85F/Up-U55
85FunFood/Pin-87
85Leaf-151
85OPC-185
85Phill/TastyK-19
85Phill/TastyK-9M
85T-185
85T/St-113
85T/Tr-55T
86Colum-12
86Colum/Pol-11
86D-573
86F-159
86OPC-369
86T-369
87Colum-26
87Colum/Pol-12
87Colum/TCMA-6
89Pac/SenLg-113
89Pac/SenLg-26
90EliteSenLg-114
91Pac/SenLg-139
92Yank/WIZ80-83
Holland, Bill
78Laugh/Black-21
Holland, Donny
82Wausau/Frit-20
Holland, Jay
92Bend/ClBest-13
Holland, John
81Buffa-2
82Buffa-12
Holland, Michael
90Erie/Star-9
Holland, Mike
74Cedar
Holland, Monty
80Batavia-9
Holland, Randy
86Knoxvl-11TR
87Knoxvl-22
88AAA/ProC-53
88Syrac/CMC-2
88Syrac/ProC-829
89Syrac/CMC-13
89Syrac/MerchB-25M
89Syrac/ProC-795
89Syrac/Team-25TR
90Syrac/MerchB-12
90Syrac/Team-12
91Syrac/MerchB-8TR

Holland, Sid
91Gaston/ClBest-23
91Gaston/ProC-2700
92CharlR/ClBest-16
92CharlR/ProC-2237
Holland, Smith
89KS*-14
Holland, Tim
89Watlo/ProC-1779
89Watlo/Star-13
90CLAS/CL-5
90Freder/Team-15
91AA/LineD-232
91Hagers/LineD-232
91Hagers/ProC-2463
91Perth/Fut-8
92Hagers/ProC-2562
92Hagers/SB-259
Hollandsworth, Todd
91FrRow/DP-46
92Bakers/Cal-1
92StCl/Dome-85
92UD/ML-160
92UD/POY-PY9
93B-98
93StCl/Dodg-28
94B-359
94B-426
94FExcel-215
94SigRook-41
94SigRook/Hot-3
94UD-531TP
94UD/SP-6PP
Holle, Gary
77Holyo
78Holyo
93Rang/Keeb-188
Holleday, Juan
92AubAs/ClBest-25
92AubAs/ProC-1349
Hollenback, Dave
88Modesto-3TR
88Modesto/Cal-83TR
89Modesto/Cal-290TR
89Modesto/Chong-3TR
90Modesto/Cal-173TR
90Modesto/Chong-14
91Modesto/ClBest-19TR
92AS/Cal-23
92Modesto/ClBest-27TR
Holley, Bobby
88Eugene/Best-22
90BBCity/Star-12
91CLAS/ProC-CAR28
91Penin/ClBest-21
91Penin/ProC-386
92Jacks/ProC-3715
92Jaxvl/SB-359
92Sky/AASingl-151
Holley, Ed
34G-55
R310
V94-26
Holley, Kenny
88Wythe/ProC-1994
Holliday, Brian
92BurlAs/ClBest-15
92BurlAs/ProC-538
92StCl/Dome-86
Holliday, James
N172
Holliday, Tom
91OKSt-11ACO
92OKSt-5M
Hollifield, David
76QuadC
77QuadC
Hollinger, Adrian
92Spokane/ClBest-19
92Spokane/ProC-1288
Hollingsworth, Al
90Target-352
W711/1
Hollingsworth, Scot
91MissSt-26
Hollins, Damon
92LitSun/HSPros-25
93B-170
93ClBest/MLG-149
93StCl/MurphyS-185
94B-161
94FExcel-154
Hollins, Dave
87Spokane-8
88CalLgAS-44
88River/Cal-222
88River/ProC-1418
89AubAs/ProC-12
89Wichita/Rock-7
89Wichita/Rock/HL-11
90B-161
90Classic/III-14
90D/Rook-47
90F/Up-U43
90Phill/TastyK-14
90S/Tr-75T
90S/YS/II-35
90T/Tr-41T
90UD/Ext-785
91F-399
91OPC-264
91Phill/Medford-19
91S-61
91S/100RisSt-96
91ScranWB/ProC-2545
91T-264
91T/90Debut-69
91UD-518
92B-6
92D-685
92F-535
92L-278
92L/BlkGold-278
92OPC-383
92Phill/Med-15
92Pinn-67
92Pinn/Team2000-16
92ProC/Tomorrow-296
92S-553
92StCl-246
92T-383
92T/Gold-383
92T/GoldWin-383
92UD-586
92Ultra-244
93B-216
93Colla/DM-52
93D-68
93DennyGS-18
93F-353RT
93F-491
93Flair-102
93L-239
93OPC-169
93Pac/Spanish-236
93Panini-273
93Phill/Med-17
93Pinn-127
93Pinn/HRC-11
93Pinn/Slug-8
93S-99
93Select-187
93Select/StatL-41
93StCl-339
93StCl/1stDay-339
93StCl/Phill-11
93Studio-158
93T-17
93T/Finest-23
93T/FinestRef-23
93T/Gold-17
93ToysRUs-18
93TripleP-38
93UD-153
93UD-458IN
93UD-485M
93UD/Diam-18
93UD/FunPack-145
93UD/HRH-HR10
93UD/SP-175
93UD/SPPlat-PP10
93USPlayC/Ace-2C
93Ultra-88
93Ultra/HRK-10
94B-524
94D-29
94D/Special-29
94F-590
94F/AS-41
94Flair-207
94L-54
94L/Clean-3
94OPC-186
94Pac/Cr-476
94Panini-228
94Phill/Med-12
94Pinn-121
94Pinn/Artist-121
94Pinn/Museum-121
94S-354
94Select-28
94Sf/2000-145
94StCl-96
94StCl/1stDay-96
94StCl/Gold-96
94StCl/Team-225
94Studio-139
94T-476
94T/Finest-47
94T/Finest/PreProd-47
94T/FinestRef-47
94T/Gold-476
94TripleP-175
94TripleP/Medal-10M
94UD-432
94UD/CollC-141
94UD/CollC/Gold-141
94UD/CollC/Silv-141
94UD/SP-136
94Ultra-245
Hollins, Jessie
89Wythe/Star-16
90A&AASingle/ProC-175
90Geneva/ProC-3041
90Geneva/Star-14
91B-423
91ClBest/Singl-36
91WinSalem/ClBest-5
91WinSalem/ProC-2824
92ChalK/SB-159
92CharlK/ProC-2766
92Sky/AASingl-74
93B-348FOIL
93B-580
93D-368
93StCl/Cub-27
93T-487
93T/Gold-487
93UD-18SR
94B-278
Hollins, Paul
86Chatt-13
Hollins, Steve
90Princet/DIMD-12
Hollinshed, Joe
86Erie-14
Hollis, Jack 1
52Mother-62
Hollis, Jack 2
78Dunedin
Hollis, Jack 3
90CharWh/Best-21
90CharWh/ProC-2252
Hollmig, Stan
49Eureka-137
Hollocher, Charles J.
21Exh-77
93Conlon-799
E120
E121/120
E121/80
E122
E220
V100
W501-57
W514-53
W515-59
W572
W573
W575
Holloman, Bobo
77Fritsch-11
90BBWit-69
90HOF/St-47
91T/Arc53-306
Holloway, Crush
78Laugh/Black-24
86Negro/Frit-22
Holloway, Ken
29Exh/4-22
93Conlon-700
Holloway, Rick
81WHave-13
Hollowell, Chuck
80Batavia-12
Holly, Chuck**
88MissSt-12
89MissSt-20
90MissSt-21
91MissSt-27
Holly, Jeff
78OrlanTw
79T-371
79Twin/FriszP-10
Holm, Dave
75Clinton
Holm, Mike
85Newar-8
Holm, Roscoe
33G-173
Holm, Wattie
93Conlon-691
Holman, Brad
90Eugene/GS-16
91Penin/ClBest-5
91Penin/ProC-371
92Jacks/ProC-3704
92Penin/ClBest-24
93Calgary/ProC-1161
94D-462
94F-289
94L-35
94Pac/Cr-573
94StCl-76
94StCl/1stDay-76
94StCl/Gold-76
94T-631
94T/Gold-631
Holman, Brian
86Jaxvl/TCMA-23
86SLAS-21
87Jaxvl-24
88F/Up-U100
88Indianap/CMC-9
88Indianap/ProC-504
89B-357
89D-511
89F-379
89T/Tr-51T
89UD-356
90Classic-66
90D-143
90F-516
90F/Can-516
90Leaf-273
90Mother/Mar-20
90OPC-616
90Panini/St-146
90PublInt/St-176
90S-387
90S/YS/I-7
90T-616
90T/Big-282
90UD-362
91B-240
91CounHrth-21
91D-539
91F-453
91Leaf-11
91Leaf/Stud-115
91OPC-458
91S-285
91StCl-106
91T-458
91UD-252
91Ultra-338
92D-43
92F-281
92Mother/Mar-26
92OPC-239
92Pinn-520
92S-228
92StCl-295
92T-239
92T/Gold-239
92T/GoldWin-239
92UD-595
93D-385
93StCl/Mar-15
93UD-799
Holman, Craig
91Batavia/ClBest-28
91Batavia/ProC-3480
92Spartan/ClBest-1
92Spartan/ProC-1260
Holman, Dale
82Albuq-20
84Syrac-28
85Syrac-5
86Syrac-12
87Richm/Bob-13
87Richm/Crown-25
87Richm/TCMA-23
Holman, Ed
76SanAn/Team-12
Holman, Gary
69T-361
Holman, Nat
33SK*-3
Holman, R. Scott
77Wausau
79Tidew-17
82Tidew-18
83D-224
84F-589
84Nes/792-13
84T-13
84Tidew-1
85Iowa-15
91WIZMets-187
Holman, Shawn
84PrWill-4
85PrWill-16
86Nashua-13
87Harris-1
88EastLAS/ProC-7
88GlenF/ProC-929
89Toledo/CMC-5
89Toledo/ProC-781
90AAASingl/ProC-373
90F-606
90F/Can-606
90ProC/Singl-381
90S-620RP
90T/89Debut-61
90Toledo/CMC-4
90Toledo/ProC-143
93Richm/Bleach-14
93Richm/Pep-23
93Richm/Team-10
Holman, Steve
78Cedar
Holmberg, Dennis
75BurlB
76BurlB
77Newar
78Dunedin
85Syrac-28
87Dunedin-7C
90Dunedin/Star-26MG
90FSLAS/Star-48
91Dunedin/ClBest-25MG
91Dunedin/ProC-223MG
92Dunedin/ClBest-26MG
92Dunedin/ProC-2013MG
93Dunedin/ClBest-26MG
93Dunedin/ProC-1811MG
Holmberg, Kenny
92Dunedin/ClBest-30
93Dunedin/ClBest-29BB
Holmes, Bill
89Princet/Star-9
90Augusta/ProC-2471
Holmes, Bob
C46-79
Holmes, Carl
86Cram/NWL-158
Holmes, Chris
88Reno/Cal-282
Holmes, Darren
86VeroB-10
87VeroB-5
89SanAn/Best-4
90AAASingl/ProC-60
90Albuq/CMC-6
90Albuq/ProC-339
90Albuq/Trib-13
90ProC/Singl-408
91AAA/LineD-141
91Brewer/MillB-11
91D-669
91Denver/LineD-141
91Leaf-387
91T/90Debut-70
92D-504
92Denver/SB-130
92F-179
92OPC-454
92S-753
92S/100RisSt-39
92StCl-155
92T-454
92T/Gold-454
92T/GoldWin-454
93D-149
93D-779

93F-412
93F/Final-34
93L-383
93OPC/Premier-104
93Pac/Spanish-431
93Pinn-521
93S-600
93StCl-506
93StCl/1stDay-506
93StCl/Rockie-17
93T-681
93T/Gold-681
93TripleP-22
93UD-668
93USPlayC/Rockie-6D
93USPlayC/Rockie-9S
93Ultra-352
94B-310
94D-222
94F-444
94Finest-307
94L-119
94Pac/Cr-198
94Pinn-375
94S-207
94S/GoldR-207
94StCl/Team-117
94T-562
94T/Gold-562
94TripleP-226
94UD-128
94UD/ElecD-128
94Ultra-483
Holmes, Ducky
C46-60
Holmes, Stan
83Visalia/Frit-10
85Toledo-22
86OrlanTw-8
87MidldA-17
88Edmon/CMC-14
88Edmon/ProC-571
89Edmon/CMC-11
89Edmon/ProC-555
Holmes, Tim
88Watertn/Pucko-6
Holmes, Tommy
39Exh
42Playball-43
45Playball-39
47HomogBond-21
48L-133
49B-72
49Eureka-13
50B-110
51T/RB-52
52T-289
53Exh/Can-18
90Target-353
D305
Holmes, William
WG2-24
Holmquist, Doug
83Nashvl-8MG
85Colum-25
Holsman, Richard
(Rich)
87Spokane-6
88River/Cal-211
88River/ProC-1427
89AubAs/ProC-20
89TexLAS/GS-12
89Wichita/Rock-17
89Wichita/Rock/Up-20
90Wichita/Rock-10
91AA/LineD-257
91Harris/LineD-257
91Harris/ProC-621
Holt, Chris
92AubAs/ClBest-1
92AubAs/ProC-1350
92Classic/DP-50
92FrRow/DP-33
93B-264
93StCl/MurphyS-75
94FExcel-201
Holt, Darren
90Visalia/Cal-86PER
Holt, Dave
79Elmira-14
86FSLAS-24MG
86WinHaven-10
87NewBrit-18
90WinHaven/Star-26MG
91Elmira/ClBest-27MG
91Elmira/ProC-3287MG
92Elmira/ClBest-24MG
Holt, Gene
44Centen-11
Holt, Goldie
49Eureka-162
Holt, Jim
71MLB/St-463
71OPC-7
71T-7
72T-588
73OPC-259
73T-259
74OPC-122
74T-122
74T/St-207
75OPC-607
75T-607
75T/M-607
76OPC-603
76SSPC-498
76T-603
76Tucson-37
77T-349
78Twin/Frisz-33
Holt, Mike
78Clinton
Holt, Norman
87Hawaii-20
Holt, Red
28LaPresse-7
Holt, Roger
79Colum-18
80Colum-7
92Yank/WIZ80-84
Holter, Brian
92BurlInd/ClBest-27
92BurlInd/ProC-1650
Holtgrave, Vern
77Fritsch-30
Holton, Brian
81Albuq/TCMA-10
82Albuq-5
83Albuq-4
84Cram/PCL-168
85Cram/PCL-164
86Albuq-12
87D-598
87D/Rook-54
87Mother/Dodg-26
87Pol/Dodg-27
87T/Tr-49T
88D-402
88Mother/Dodg-26
88Pol/Dodg-51
88RedFoley/St-35
88S-208
88T-338
89B-2
89D-439
89D/Tr-20
89F-63
89F/Up-5
89French-37
89S-507
89S/Tr-59
89T-368
89T/Tr-52T
89UD-72
90D-635
90F-179
90F/Can-179
90Leaf-487
90OPC-179
90PublInt/St-578
90Rochester/L&U-32
90S-177
90T-179
90Target-354
90UD-175
91Crown/Orio-200
92Albuq/ProC-715
Holton, Mark
80Utica-19
Holtz, Ed
76AppFx-GM
80Knoxvl/TCMA-28
84Chatt-6GM
88Sumter/ProC-420GM
89Sumter/ProC-1088GM
Holtz, Fred
75AppFx
76AppFx
Holtz, Gerald
87CharlO/WBTV-17
88CharlK/Pep-19
88RochR/Gov-12
89Reading/Star-14
Holtzclaw, Shawn
90A&AASingle/ProC-100
90Myrtle/ProC-2788
90SALAS/Star-33
91Dunedin/ClBest-21
91Dunedin/ProC-219
Holtzman, Ken
67CokeCap/Cub-14
67OPC-185
67T-185
68Bz-4
68OPC-60
68T-380AS
68T-60
69MB-116
69T-288
70MLB/St-18
70OPC-505
70T-505
71MD
71MLB/St-33
71OPC-410
71T-410
72MB-149
72T-670
73OPC-60
73T-60
74K-31
74OPC-180
74T-180
74T/St-224
75Ho-16
75Ho/Twink-16
75OPC-145
75T-145
75T/M-145
76OPC-115
76SSPC-482
76T-115
77BK/Y-8
77T-625
78SSPC/270-6
78T-387
79T-522
80T-298
87Mother/A's-11
89Pac/Leg-138
89Swell-129
91Crown/Orio-201
91LineD-21
91Swell/Great-40
92AP/ASG-57
92Yank/WIZ70-75
93TWill-45
93UD/ATH-66
Holub, Edward
88Boise/ProC-1612
Holub, Sean
92Helena/ProC-1720
Holum, Brett
90Ashvl/ProC-2755
Holway, John
90LitSun-20
Holyfield, Vince
85Bend/Cram-11
87Spartan-20
88Reading/ProC-883
89Reading/Best-14
89Reading/ProC-661
89Reading/Star-15
90EastLAS/ProC-EL23
90Reading/Best-21
90Reading/ProC-1231
90Reading/Star-14
Holzemer, Mark
88Bend/Legoe-22
89QuadC/Best-9
89QuadC/GS-21
90MidldA/GS-16
92MidldA/ProC-4021
92PalmSp/ClBest-27
93B-117
93Vanco/ProC-2591
94D-583
94T-765
94T/Gold-765
Homstedt, Vic
78Watlo
Honeycutt, Rick
79T-612
80T-307
81D-46
81OPC-33
81T-33
81T/Tr-772
82D-494
82F-318
82T-751
83D-415
83F-568
83Rang-40
83T-557
84D-494
84F-101
84F/St-66
84Nes/792-137LL
84Nes/792-222
84Nes/792-37TL
84OPC-222
84Pol/Dodg-40
84T-137LL
84T-222
84T-37TL
84T/St-176
84T/St-84
85Coke/Dodg-13
85D-215
85F-372
85Leaf-156
85OPC-174
85T-174
85T/St-78
86Coke/Dodg-13
86D-372
86F-132
86Pol/Dodg-40
86T-439
87Classic-93
87D-402
87F-442
87F/Excit-28
87Mother/Dodg-16
87OPC-167
87Pol/Dodg-20
87T-753
87T/St-71
88D-590
88D/A's/Bk-590
88D/Best-211
88F-281
88Mother/A's-23
88S-87
88T-641
89B-187
89D-328
89D/Best-313
89F-11
89Mother/A's-25
89S-416
89T-328
89UD-278
89Woolwth-28
90B-450
90D-386
90F-11
90F/Can-11
90Leaf-372
90Mother/A's-13
90OPC-582
90PublInt/St-307
90S-317
90T-582
90T/Big-42
90Target-355
90UD-151
91D-373
91F-11
91Leaf-210
91Leaf/Stud-105
91Mother/A's-13
91OPC-67
91S-539
91SFExam/A's-7
91StCl-415
91T-67
91UD-379
91Ultra-249
92D-269
92F-259
92Mother/A's-13
92OPC-202
92S-456
92StCl-581
92T-202
92T/Gold-202
92T/GoldWin-202
92UD-684
93F-665
93Mother/A's-8
93Pac/Spanish-223
93Rang/Keeb-189
93StCl/A's-13
94D-169
94F-265
94Pac/Cr-454
94S-208
94S/GoldR-208
94StCl/Team-242
Honeywell, Brent
90Augusta/ProC-2457
Honochick, Jim
55B-267UMP
Hood, Dennis
86Sumter/ProC-10
87Durham-27
88Greenvl/Best-5
89Greenvl/Best-1
89Greenvl/ProC-1169
89Greenvl/Star-8
90AAASingl/ProC-415
90ProC/Singl-291
90Richm/Bob-18
90Richm/CMC-15
90Richm/ProC-270
90Richm/Team-12
91AAA/LineD-59
91Calgary/LineD-59
91Calgary/ProC-527
Hood, Don
74OPC-436
74T-436
75OPC-516
75T-516
75T/M-516
76OPC-132
76SSPC-508
76T-132
77T-296
78T-398
79T-667
80T-89
81Omaha-8
82Omaha-5
83D-390
83F-115
83T-443
84F-348
84Nes/792-743
84T-743
89Pac/SenLg-108
91Crown/Orio-202
92Yank/WIZ70-76
Hood, Mike
80Wausau-16
Hood, Randall
91Helena/SportP-23
91Stockton/ClBest-16
91Stockton/ProC-3045
92Saraso/ClBest-16
92Saraso/ProC-220
Hood, Scott
82Durham-3
83Durham-7
84Durham-17
Hood, Wally
28Exh/PCL-11
90Target-983
Hoog, James
88CapeCod/Sum-178
Hoog, Michael
90Idaho/ProC-3244
Hook, Chris
90CharWh/Best-2
90CharWh/ProC-2234
91CharWh/ClBest-4
91CharWh/ProC-2881
92Cedar/ClBest-10
92Cedar/ProC-1068
94FExcel-175
Hook, Ed
90HagersDG/Best-13
Hook, Jay
60Kahn
60T-187
61Kahn

61T-162
62T-94
62T/St-156
63T-469
64T-361
91WIZMets-188
Hook, Mike
88Ashvl/ProC-1073
89FtLaud/Star-9
90MidwLgAS/GS-35
90QuadC/GS-6
91Freder/ClBest-4
91Freder/ProC-2358
92Hagers/SB-260
Hooker, W.E.
(Buck)
T206
Hooks, Alex
R314
Hooks, Maurice
89KS*-25
Hooper, Ed
W516-27
Hooper, Harry
12Sweet/Pin-4
14CJ-35
15CJ-35
25Exh-75
40PlayBall-226
76Shakey-122
77Galasso-172
80Perez/HOF-122
80SSPC/HOF
81Conlon-15
87Conlon/2-35
89HOF/St-52
91Conlon/Sport-135
92Conlon/Sport-470
93Conlon-802
93CrackJack-14
BF2-4
D327
D328-79
D329-84
D350/2-83
E120
E121/120
E121/80
E135-79
E220
E224
E254
E270/1
E91
M101/4-84
M101/5-83
M116
T207
V100
V61-13
W501-47
W514-64
W572
W573
W575
Hooper, Jeff
87Belling/Team-1
88Wausau/GS-16
89Wmsprt/ProC-639
89Wmsprt/Star-10
90Wmsprt/Best-10
90Wmsprt/ProC-1060
90Wmsprt/Star-11
Hooper, Mike
90Helena/SportP-2
91Beloit/ClBest-25
91Beloit/ProC-2097
92Salinas/ProC-3750
92Saraso/ClBest-26
Hooper, Robert
(Bob)
51B-33
52B-10
52T-340
53T-84
54B-4
55B-271
55Salem
91T/Arc53-84
Hooper, Troy
92Salinas/ProC-3751
Hooten, Leon
75IntLgAS/Broder-10
75PCL/AS-10
75Tucson-10
75Tucson/Caruso-17
75Tucson/Team-6
76Tucson-16
77OPC-67
77T-478R
Hooton, Burt
72OPC-61R
72T-61R
73OPC-367
73T-367
74OPC-378
74T-378
74T/St-14
75Ho-11
75Ho/Twink-11
75OPC-176
75T-176
75T/M-176
76OPC-280
76SSPC-67
76T-280
77T-284
78K-42
78SSPC/270-55
78T-41
79Ho-49
79OPC-370
79T-694
80OPC-96
80Pol/Dodg-46
80T-170
81D-541
81F-113
81F/St-61
81OPC-53
81Pol/Dodg-46
81T-565
81T/HT
81T/St-180
82D-32
82F-8
82F/St-5
82K-15
82OPC-315
82Pol/Dodg-46
82T-311TL
82T-315
82T/St-53
82T/StVar-53
83D-32
83F-208
83F/St-11M
83F/St-3M
83OPC-82
83Pol/Dodg-46
83T-775
84D-459
84F-102
84Nes/792-15
84OPC-15
84Pol/Dodg-46
84T-15
85D-104
85F-373
85F/Up-U56
85OPC-201
85Rang-46
85T-201
85T/Tr-56T
86D-300
86F-563
86OPC-36
86T-454
86T/St-242
86T/Tatt-18M
87Smok/Dodg-13
88Smok/Dodg-19
89Pac/Leg-219
89Salem/Team-2CO
89Smok/Dodg-95
90SanAn/GS-2CO
90Target-356
91SanAn/ProC-2992CO
92TX-24
93Rang/Keeb-190
Hoover, Charles
N172
Hoover, John
85CharlO-22
85T-397OLY
87CharlO/WBTV-20
88Jaxvl/Best-4
88Jaxvl/ProC-989
89Tulsa/Team-11
90AAASingl/ProC-673
90OkCty/CMC-3
90OkCty/ProC-427
90ProC/Singl-153
91T/90Debut-71
93Rang/Keeb-191
Hoover, William
N172
Hope, John
89LittleSun-18
91Welland/ClBest-26
91Welland/ProC-3567
92Salem/ClBest-15
92Salem/ProC-58
93CaroMud/RBI-11
94F/MLP-15
94T-491
94T/Gold-491
Hopke, Fred
60L-91
Hopkins, Dave
83BurlR-5
83BurlR/Frit-23
Hopkins, Don
75SSPC/18-12
76Tucson-11
77SanJose-13
Hopkins, Gail
70OPC-483
70T-483
71MLB/St-416
71OPC-269
71T-269
72T-728
73OPC-441
73T-441
74OPC-652
74T-652
90Target-357
Hopkins, Gordon
(Hoppy)
92Negro/RetortII-18
Hopkins, Randy
75Shrev/TCMA-5
76Shrev
78Colum
Hopkins, Rick
86WinSalem-9
87Pittsfld-20
Hopp, Dean
91Martins/ClBest-17
91Martins/ProC-3455
92Batavia/ClBest-24
92Batavia/ProC-3269
Hopp, John
(Johnny)
44Playball-24
48L-139
49B-207
49Eureka-163
50B-122
51B-146
52T-214
54T-193
89Pac/Leg-139
90Target-358
94T/Arc54-193
Exh47
W754
Hoppe, Denny
91ClBest/Singl-341
91Kenosha/ClBest-10
91Kenosha/ProC-2068
92FtMyr/ProC-2740
92Miracle/ClBest-21
Hoppe, Willie
33SK*-36
Hoppel, Monty
90MidldA/GS-NNO
Hopper, Brad
88Eugene/Best-9
90BBCity/Star-13
91BBCity/ClBest-6
91BBCity/ProC-1393
Hopper, Clay
52Mother-55MG
53Mother-51MG
Hopper, Jim
47Centen-10
Hopper, Lefty
90Target-984
Horan, Dave
89Salinas/Cal-128
89Salinas/ProC-1800
Horincewich, Thomas
92Elizab/ClBest-6
92Elizab/ProC-3685
Horlen, Joel
62T-479
63T-332
64T-584
65OPC-7LL
65T-480
65T-7LL
66T-560
66T/RO-40
66T/RO-5
67CokeCap/WSox-14
67OPC-107
67T-107
67T-233LL
68Bz-11
68Kahn
68OPC-125
68OPC-8LL
68T-125
68T-377AS
68T-8LL
68T/ActionSt-14A
68T/ActionSt-1A
68T/ActionSt-8B
69Kahn
69Kelly/Pin-7
69MB-117
69MLB/St-30
69MLBPA/Pin-9
69T-328
69T/S-12
69T/St-154
70K-23
70MLB/St-185
70OPC-35
70T-35
70T/PI-1
70T/S-20
70T/Super-20
71OPC-345
71T-345
71T/Coins-120
72MB-150
72T-685
81TCMA-318
88Clmbia/GS-28CO
89Pac/Leg-217
90StLucie/Star-29
91AA/LineD-638CO
91Wmsprt/LineD-638CO
91Wmsprt/ProC-311CO
92Omaha/ProC-2979CO
92Omaha/SB-350M
Horn, Herman
(Doc)
92Negro/RetortII-19
Horn, Jeff
92Elizab/ClBest-10
92Elizab/ProC-3682
Horn, Larry
75WPalmB/Sussman-25
Horn, Sam
86NewBrit-13
87Pawtu-2
87Pawtu/TCMA-14
87Sf/Rook-38
88Classic/Blue-204
88D-498
88D/RedSox/Bk-498
88F-355
88F/Mini-8
88Leaf-237
88OPC-377
88S-201
88S/YS/I-3
88Sf-114
88T-377
88T/Big-252
88T/St-246
88ToysRUs-14
90Classic/III-28
90PublInt/St-458
90Rochester/L&U-11
90T/Big-307
90T/Tr-42T
90UD/Ext-796
91Crown/Orio-203
91D-733
91F-477
91Leaf-332
91Leaf/Stud-5
91OPC-598
91S-605
91StCl-316
91T-598
91UD-530
92B-177
92D-278
92F-10
92L-219
92L/BlkGold-219
92OPC-422
92Pinn-221
92S-290
92StCl-269
92Studio-125
92T-422
92T/Gold-422
92T/GoldWin-422
92UD-338
92Ultra-6
93D-617
93F-542
93Pinn-128
93T-109
93T/Gold-109
94Pinn-170
94Pinn/Artist-170
94Pinn/Museum-170
94S-543
94StCl/Team-187
Horn, Terry
91Classic/DP-46
91FrRow/DP-24
91LitSun/HSPros-24
91LitSun/HSProsG-24
92StCl/Dome-87
Horn, Tim
89TNTech-11
Horn, Walt
82WHave-29TR
86Tacoma-8TR
89Tacoma/ProC-1543TR
Hornacek, Jay
86Bakers-14
87VeroB-20
88Bakers/Cal-245
89SoBend/GS-29
90Saraso/Star-12
Horne, Geoff
91MedHat/SportP-25TR
Horne, Jeffrey
82AlexD-5
84Greens-5
Horne, Tyrone
90Gate/ProC-3348
90Gate/SportP-12
91Sumter/ClBest-23
91Sumter/ProC-2348
92MidwLAS/Team-21
92Rockford/ClBest-24
92Rockford/ProC-2127
93FExcel/ML-60
93WPalmB/ClBest-10
93WPalmB/ProC-1354
Horner, Bob
79Ho-98
79T-586
79T/Comics-18
80OPC-59
80T-108
80T/S-27
80T/Super-27
81D-99
81Drake-17
81F-244
81F/St-99
81K-61
81MSA/Disc-17
81OPC-355
81PermaGr/CC-6
81Pol/Atl-5
81T-355
81T/SO-61
81T/St-145
81T/St-20
82BK/Lids-11
82D-173
82Drake-18
82F-436
82F/St-69
82K-13
82OPC-145
82Pol/Atl-5

93Pinn/Team2001-21
93S-303
93Select-346
93StCl-333
93StCl/1stDay-333
93StCl/Giant-15
93T-653
93T/Gold-653
93TripleP-54
93UD-15SR
93Ultra-132
94D-655
94Sf/2000-155
94StCl/Team-7
94T-547
94T/Gold-547

Hoskins, Dave
54T-81
55Salem
55T-133
55T/DH-7
86Negro/Frit-81
94T/Arc54-81

Hoskinson, Keith
86Lakeland-7

Hosley, Tim
72OPC-257R
72T-257R
76OPC-482
76SSPC-313
76T-482
77SanJose-10
78T-261
79Ogden/TCMA-2
80Ogden-1
82Tacoma-12
89Pac/SenLg-93

Hostetler, Brian
92Helena/ProC-1718
93FExcel/ML-187

Hostetler, Dave
79Memphis
79Memphis/TCMA-9
83D-89
83F-569
83OPC-339
83OPC/St-312
83Rang-12
83T-584
83T/St-312
84D-159
84F-418
84Nes/792-62
84OPC-62
84T-62
85Indianap-17
85Iowa-23
93Rang/Keeb-193

Hostetler, Jeff
91FrRow/DP-37
91James/ClBest-20
91James/ProC-3539
92StCl/Dome-88
93BurlB/ClBest-11
93BurlB/ProC-152

Hostetler, Mike
92Durham/ClBest-17
92Durham/ProC-1094
92Durham/Team-24
92UD/ML-206
93B-30
93ClBest/MLG-89
93Richm/Bleach-7
93Richm/Team-11
94FExcel-155

Hostetler, Tom
87Everett-16
88Clinton/ProC-697
88MidwLAS/GS-7
89SanJose/Best-19
89SanJose/Cal-213
89SanJose/ProC-444
89SanJose/Star-15
90A&AASingle/ProC-66
90Shrev/ProC-1439
90Shrev/Star-12
91AA/LineD-308
91Shrev/LineD-308
91Shrev/ProC-1816

Hotaling, Pete
E223
N172

Hotchkiss, John
83Tacoma-12
84Cram/PCL-93
86MidldA-11
87MidldA-11

Hotchkiss, Thomas
90MedHat/Best-23
92Dunedin/ClBest-23
92Dunedin/ProC-1995
93Dunedin/ClBest-11
93Dunedin/ProC-1791

Hotz, Todd
90Utica/Pucko-19

Houck, Byron Simon
T222

Houck, Jeff
90AR-16

Hough, Charlie
72OPC-198R
72T-198R
73OPC-610R
73T-610R
74OPC-408
74T-408
75OPC-71
75T-71
75T/M-71
76OPC-174
76SSPC-68
76T-174
77K-47
77T-298
78SSPC/270-81
78T-22
79OPC-266
79T-508
80Pol/Dodg-49
80T-644
81T-371
82D-447
82F-319
82T-718
83D-69
83F-570
83F/St-11M
83OPC-343
83OPC/St-125
83Rang-49
83T-412TL
83T-479
83T/St-125
83T/St-312
84D-638
84F-419
84Nes/792-118
84OPC-118
84Rang-49
84T-118
84T/St-356
85D-422
85F-558
85FunFood/Pin-114
85Leaf-108
85OPC-276
85Rang-49
85SpokAT/Cram-8
85T-571
85T/St-345
86D-342
86F-564
86F/St-61
86Leaf-152
86OPC-275
86Rang-49
86T-275
86T-666M
86T/Mini-33
86T/St-241
86T/Tatt-9M
87D-470
87D-7DK
87D/AAS-49
87D/DKsuper-7
87D/OD-178
87F-127
87F-641M
87F/BB-21
87F/Mini-56
87F/St-62
87Leaf-7DK
87Mother/Rang-3
87OPC-70
87RedFoley/St-26
87Sf/TPrev-1M
87Smok/AL-12
87Smok/R-1
87T-70
87T/St-240
88D-99
88D/Best-256
88F-469
88F/AwardWin-20
88F/BB/AS-16
88F/BB/MVP-19
88F/Mini-55
88F/St-64
88Grenada-42
88KennerFig-53
88Leaf-89
88Mother/R-3
88OPC-121
88Panini/St-197
88S-140
88Sf-87
88Smok/R-13
88T-680
88T/Big-47
88T/Coins-15
88T/Mini-36
88T/Revco-32
88T/St-236
88T/UK-36
89B-224
89D-165
89F-522
89Mother/R-4
89OPC-345
89Panini/St-446
89RedFoley/St-60
89S-295
89Sf-92
89Smok/R-14
89T-345
89T/LJN-146
89T/St-245
89T/UK-40
89UD-437
90D-411
90F-300
90F/Can-300
90KayBee-17
90Leaf-390
90Mother/Rang-5
90OPC-735
90PublInt/St-412
90S-202
90T-735
90T/Big-242
90Target-359
90UD-314
91B-355
91D-146
91F-288
91F/Up-U12
91Kodak/WSox-49
91Leaf-472
91Leaf/Stud-35
91OPC-495
91S-141
91StCl-579
91T-495
91T/Tr-56T
91UD-313
91UD/Ext-792
92B-153
92D-69
92F-84
92L-39
92L/BlkGold-39
92OPC-191
92Pinn-422
92S-302
92StCl-894
92T-191
92T/Gold-191
92T/GoldWin-191
92UD-418
92Ultra-37
92WSox-49
93B-530
93F-584
93F/Final-63
93L-384
93Marlin/Publix-13
93OPC-41
93Pac/Spanish-465
93Pinn-523
93Pinn/Expan-1
93Rang/Keeb-194
93S-223
93Select/RookTr-117T
93StCl-610
93StCl/1stDay-610
93StCl/III/Ins-2
93StCl/Marlin-6
93Studio-205
93T-520
93T/Finest-169
93T/FinestRef-169
93T/Gold-520
93UD-207
93UD-518
93USPlayC/Marlin-8H
93USPlayC/Marlin-9S
93Ultra-379
94B-618
94D-269
94F-469
94L-188
94OPC-62
94Pac/Cr-244
94Pinn-288
94S-452
94StCl-245
94StCl/1stDay-245
94StCl/Gold-245
94StCl/Team-69
94T-625
94T/Finest-180
94T/FinestRef-180
94T/Gold-625
94UD-449
94Ultra-494

Hough, Stan
79Jacks-22
79Tidew-16
83DayBe-2
85Cram/PCL-62
86Osceola-12C
88Tulsa-11CO
89OkCty/CMC-24CO
89OkCty/ProC-1521CO
90OkCty/CMC-23CO
90OkCty/ProC-450CO
90ProC/Singl-173CO
91AAA/LineD-325CO
91OkCty/LineD-325CO
91OkCty/ProC-195CO

Houk, Ralph
52T-200
60T-465C
61T-133MG
62T-88MG
63T-382MG
67T-468MG
68OPC-47MG
68T-47MG
69T-447MG
70OPC-273MG
70T-273MG
71OPC-146MG
71T-146MG
72T-533MG
73OPC-116MG
73Syrac/Team-10MG
73T-116MG
74OPC-578MG
74T-578MG
75OPC-18MG
75T-18MG
75T/M-18MG
76SSPC-352MG
76T-361MG
77T-621MG
78BK/T-1MG
78T-684MG
81T-662MG
81TCMA-455MG
81TCMA-481MG
82D-282MG
83T-786MG
84Nes/792-381MG
84T-381MG
85T-11MG
89Swell-42
90Swell/Great-131
91LineD-25
91Swell/Great-42
91T/Arc53-282

Houk, Tom
91ClBest/Singl-351
91Kenosha/ClBest-26
91Kenosha/ProC-2082
92Visalia/ClBest-12
92Visalia/ProC-1021

Houle, Rejean
72Dimanche*-76

Houp, Scott
85Osceola/Team-24

House, Brian
86WinSalem-10
87Pittsfld-7
88EastLAS/ProC-27
88Pittsfld/ProC-1361
89Iowa/CMC-17
89Iowa/ProC-1700
90AAASingl/ProC-686
90OkCty/CMC-14
90OkCty/ProC-440
90ProC/Singl-164

House, Gary
77Newar

House, H. Frank
52T-146
54T-163
55T-87
55T/DH-14
56T-32
56T/Pin-37
57T-223
58T-318
59T-313
60T-372
79TCMA-214
94T/Arc54-163

House, Howard
92B-581FOIL

House, Mike
89Elizab/Star-12
89Star/IISingl-149
90Visalia/Cal-73
90Visalia/ProC-2167

House, Mitch
91Welland/ClBest-7
91Welland/ProC-3578
93Welland/ClBest-1
93Welland/ProC-3365

House, Pat
77Fritsch-22

House, Thomas R.
69T-331R
72OPC-351R
72T-351R
74OPC-164
74T-164
75OPC-525
75T-525
75T/M-525
76OPC-231
76SSPC-2
76T-231
76T/Tr-231T
77T-358
78T-643
79T-31
82Amari-25C
83LasVegas/BHN-11
84Cram/PCL-232C
87Smok/R-20CO
88AlaskaAS60/Team-8
89Smok/R-15CO
90Mother/Rang-27M
90Richm/25Ann-10
91Mother/Rang-28CO
92Mother/Rang-28M
93Rang/Keeb-195

House, Trini
92Beloit/ClBest-14
92Beloit/ProC-420

Householder, Brian
87CharlO/WBTV-21
88CharlK/Pep-1
88SLAS-33

Householder, Ed
90Target-986

Householder, Paul
79Nashvl
80Indianap-15
81D-303
81F-217
81Indianap-4
81T-606R
82Coke/Reds
82D-314
82F-68
82T-351R
83D-566
83F-592

83T-34
84F-471
84Nes/792-214
84T-214
84T/St-61
85Pol/Brew-7
86D-414
86F-491
86Pol/Brew-7
86T-554
Houser, Ben
T207
Houser, Brett
78StPete
Houser, Chris
87Erie-24
88Hamil/ProC-1719
Housey, Joe
81QuadC-20
84MidldC-7
86Geneva-12
87Peoria-11
89WinSalem/Star-20
90Geneva/ProC-3054CO
91Geneva/ClBest-28CO
Housie, Wayne
87Lakeland-1
88GlenF/ProC-913
89London/ProC-1382
90Salinas/ProC-2731
91AA/LineD-463
91NewBrit/LineD-463
91NewBrit/ProC-365
92OPC-639
92Pawtu/ProC-935
92Pawtu/SB-357
92S-836
92Sky/AAASingl-161
92StCl-352
92T-639
92T/91Debut-82
92T/Gold-639
92T/GoldWin-639
92UD-664
92Ultra-314
Houston, Barry
82Wisco/Frit-16
Houston, K.R.
(Ken)
81Evansvl-21TR
82Evansvl-24TR
83Wausau/Frit-1TR
86Osceola-13TR
87Osceola-24TR
Houston, Kevin
78DaytB
82Buffa-10
Houston, Maceo
91Hunting/ClBest-13
91Hunting/ProC-3347
91LitSun/HSPros-29
91LitSun/HSProsG-29
92Hunting/ClBest-9
92Hunting/ProC-3162
Houston, Mel
86WPalmB-20
87WPalmB-19
88Indianap/CMC-23
88Indianap/ProC-507
89Jaxvl/Best-3
89Jaxvl/ProC-170
90AAASingl/ProC-578
90Indianap/CMC-20
90Indianap/ProC-295
90ProC/Singl-70
91AAA/LineD-196
91Indianap/LineD-196
91Indianap/ProC-469
Houston, Pete
88Reno/Cal-289
Houston, Tyler
89Idaho/ProC-2021
89LittleSun-5
90A&AASingle/ProC-104
90B-14
90Foil/Best-16
90Foil/Best-324
90OPC-564FDP
90ProC/Singl-827
90S-677DC
90Sumter/Best-1
90Sumter/ProC-2436
90T-564FDP
91B-581
91ClBest/Singl-267
91Macon/ClBest-16
91Macon/ProC-869
91SALAS/ProC-SAL32
92ClBest-91
92Durham/ClBest-16
92Durham/ProC-1104
92Durham/Team-19
92UD/ML-151
94StCl/Team-45
Houtteman, Art
50B-42
51B-45
52T-238
53B/Col-4
53Tiger/Glen-16
54B-20
54DanDee
55B-144
55Gol/Ind-12
55Salem
56Carling-4
56T-281
57T-385
79TCMA-242
81Tiger/Detroit-46
91Crown/Orio-204
Hovey, James
92Bend/ClBest-14
Hovley, Steve
70MLB/St-273
70McDon-2
70OPC-514
70T-514
71MLB/St-515
71OPC-109
71T-109
72T-683
73OPC-282
73T-282
Howard, Brent
89AS/Cal-52UMP
90AS/Cal-35UMP
Howard, Bruce
64T-107R
65OPC-41R
65T-41R
66T-281
67OPC-159
67T-159
68T-293
69T-226
91Crown/Orio-205
Howard, Christian
(Chris)
87PrWill-11
88CLAS/Star-9
88PrWill/Star-12
89FtLaud/Star-10
89Star/Wax-78
90Albany/ProC-1033
91AA/LineD-62
91BirmB/LineD-62
91BirmB/ProC-1450
Howard, Christopher Hugh
89Wausau/GS-27
90Foil/Best-239
90Wmsprt/Best-11
90Wmsprt/ProC-1061
90Wmsprt/Star-12
91AAA/LineD-60
91Calgary/LineD-60
91Calgary/ProC-519
92B-309
92Calgary/ProC-3735
92Calgary/SB-61
92Sky/AAASingl-283
92T/91Debut-83
92Vanco/ProC-2717
92Vanco/SB-638
93Calgary/ProC-1170
Howard, David
(Dave)
87FtMyr-32
88AppFx/ProC-145
89BBCity/Star-9
89Princet/Star-10
90Memphis/Best-5
90Memphis/ProC-1015
90Memphis/Star-11
91B-295
91F/Up-U27
91Leaf-325
91S/RookTr-83T
92B-307
92D-567
92F-160
92L-4
92L/BlkGold-4
92OPC-641
92Pinn-86
92Pol/Royal-11
92S-704
92S/100RisSt-2
92StCl-245
92T-641
92T/91Debut-84
92T/Gold-641
92T/GoldWin-641
92TripleP-201
92UD-216
92Ultra-71
93F-619
93Pac/Spanish-136
93S-645
93T-519
93T/Gold-519
94Pac/Cr-288
94S-206
94S/GoldR-206
Howard, Dennis
80Utica-20
82Knoxvl-4
83Syrac-8
84Syrac-4
85Syrac-9
86Syrac-13
Howard, Doug
74Tacoma/Caruso-18
77OPC-112
88SLCity-19
Howard, Elston
55B-68
56T-208
57T-82
58T-275
59T-395
60T-65
61P-2
61T-495
61T/St-194
62J-8
62P-8
62P/Can-8
62Salada-95
62Shirriff-95
62T-400
62T-473AS
62T-51LL
62T/St-86
62T/bucks
63J-18
63Kahn
63P-18
63Salada-45
63T-306M
63T-60
64Bz-29
64T-100
64T/Coins-135AS
64T/Coins-23
64T/S-21
64T/SU
64T/St-72
64Wheat/St-21
65Bz-29
65OPC-1LL
65T-1LL
65T-450
65T/trans
66T-405
67CokeCap/ALAS-29
67CokeCap/AS-25
67CokeCap/YMet-9
67OPC-25
67T-25
68CokeCap/RedSox-18
68OPC-167
68T-167
73OPC-116CO
73T-116CO
74Syrac/Team-11
75OPC-201MVP
75Syrac/Team-6CO
75Syrac/Team-7
75T-201MVP
75T/M-201MVP
76SSPC-619CO
78TCMA-236
79TCMA-271
82KMart-3
86Sf/Dec-49M
88Pac/Leg-19
92Yank/WIZ60-56
92Yank/WIZAS-31
94T/Arc54-253
94TedW-59
94TedW/54-26
Exh47
PM10/L-17
PM10/Sm-77
WG10-10
WG9-12
Howard, Ernest E.
T206
Howard, Frank
60DF-17
60T-132
60Union/Dodg-9
61Morrell
61T-280
61T/RO-34
61T/St-27
61Union/Dodg-10
62BB-25
62Bz
62T-175
62T/St-135
62T/bucks
63Exh
63T-123
64T-371
64T/Coins-61
64T/S-24
64T/SU
64T/St-83
64T/tatt
65OPC-40
65T-40
65T/trans-49
66Bz-3
66T-515
66T/RO-33
66T/RO-42
67Bz-3
67CokeCap/ALAS-20
67CokeCap/Senator-6
67OPC/PI-7
67T-255
67T/PI-7
67T/Test/SU-15
68Bz-7
68OPC-6LL
68T-320
68T-6LL
68T/ActionSt-11C
68T/G-21
68T/Post-3
69Citgo-10
69MB-120
69MLB/St-105
69MLBPA/Pin-12
69OPC-170
69OPC-3LL
69OPC-5LL
69OPC/DE-12
69T-170
69T-3LL
69T-5LL
69T/4in1-20M
69T/DE-16
69T/S-30
69T/St-238
69T/decal
69Trans-29
70K-6
70MB-10
70MLB/St-283
70OPC-66LL
70Pol/SenY-5
70T-550
70T-66LL
70T/PI-22
70T/S-16
70T/Super-16
70Trans-12
71Bz
71Bz/Test-20
71K-14
71MD
71MLB/St-542
71MLB/St-561
71OPC-620
71OPC-63LL
71OPC-65LL
71Pol/SenP-6
71T-620
71T-63LL
71T-65LL
71T/Coins-22
71T/GM-48
71T/Greatest-48
71T/S-17
71T/Super-17
71T/tatt-8
71T/tatt-8a
72MB-153
72OPC-350
72T-350
72T/Cloth-17
73OPC-560
73T-560
78TCMA-220
81T-685MG
81TCMA-474M
83MLBPA/Pin-9
83T/Tr-47MG
84Nes/792-621MG
84T-621MG
85CircK-23
85Woolwth-19
86Pol/Brew-33C
87Mother/Mar-28CO
88Mother/Mar-27CO
88Pac/Leg-17
88Smok/Dodg-3
90HOF/St-75
90Target-360
93Rang/Keeb-18
94TedW-88
Exh47
Howard, Fred
77AppFx
78Knoxvl
80T-72
Howard, George Elmer
(Del)
E254
T204
T206
T215/brown
WG3-21
Howard, Ivan Chester
D328-81
D329-85
D350/2-84
E135-81
M101/4-85
M101/5-84
Howard, Jamie
94ClBest/Gold-47
Howard, Jim
86Knoxvl-12
87Albany-12
Howard, Larry
71OPC-102R
71T-102R
Howard, Mathew
(Matt)
88CapeCod/Sum-120
89GreatF-23
90AS/Cal-14
90Bakers/Cal-253
91FSLAS/ProC-FSL39
91VeroB/ClBest-21
91VeroB/ProC-782
92ClBest-244
92ProC/Tomorrow-246
92SanAn/ProC-3983
92SanAn/SB-567
92Sky/AASingl-247
Howard, Michael Frederick
(Mike)
79Jacks-14
81Tidew-12
82Tidew-5
83Tidew-18
84Cram/PCL-135
91WIZMets-189
Howard, Michael Stephen
(Mike)
81Pawtu-2
Howard, Mike
75QuadC
Howard, Ron
88Bristol/ProC-1870

89Fayette/ProC-1592
90Fayette/ProC-2413
91Lakeland/ClBest-19
91Lakeland/ProC-272
92Lakeland/ClBest-6
92Lakeland/ProC-2286

Howard, Steve
83Idaho-27
85Modesto/Chong-16
86Modesto-13
88Huntsvl/BK-8
88SLAS-3
89Tacoma/CMC-21
89Tacoma/ProC-1552
90AAASingl/ProC-155
90ProC/Singl-594
90T/Tr-43T
90Tacoma/CMC-17
90Tacoma/ProC-108
91S-364RP
91T/90Debut-72
91UD-277
92Richm/SB-426

Howard, Thomas
86Cram/NWL-171
87TexLgAS-18
87Wichita-13
88LasVegas/CMC-11
88LasVegas/ProC-239
89LasVegas/CMC-15
89LasVegas/ProC-8
89UD/Ext-726
90AAASingl/ProC-23
90B-212
90F/Up-U56
90LasVegas/ProC-135
91B-644
91D-746
91F-532
91LasVegas/ProC-248
91Padre/MagRal-3
91S-335RP
91S/100RisSt-9
91StCl-403
91T/90Debut-73
91UD/FinalEd-39F
91Ultra-305
92D-266
92F-607
92F/Up-15
92Indian/McDon-12
92L-456
92L-84
92L/BlkGold-456
92L/BlkGold-84
92OPC-539
92S-293
92StCl-401
92T-539
92T/Gold-539
92T/GoldWin-539
92UD-416
92Ultra-279
92Ultra-348
93D-257
93F-215
93Indian/WUAB-12
93OPC-139
93Pinn-399
93S-426
93StCl-515
93StCl/1stDay-515
93T-113
93T/Gold-113
93UD-299
93Ultra-185
94D-164
94F-411
94S-501
94StCl-496
94StCl/1stDay-496
94StCl/Gold-496
94T-246
94T/Gold-246
94Ultra-473

Howard, Tim
89Pittsfld/Star-10
90Clmbia/PCPII-6
90Columbia/GS-11
90SALAS/Star-34
91B-538
91ClBest/Singl-232
91StLucie/ClBest-23
91StLucie/ProC-720
92Bingham/ProC-527
92Bingham/SB-59
92Sky/AASingl-25
92UD/ML-218

Howard, Wilbur
74OPC-606R
74T-606R
75OPC-563
75T-563
75T/M-563
76OPC-97
76SSPC-65
76T-97
77T-248
78BK/Ast-20
78T-534
79CharCh-17
79T-642

Howarth, Jim
73OPC-459
74OPC-404
74T-404
?3T-459

Howe, Art
76SSPC-585
78BK/Ast-16
78T-13
79OPC-165
79T-327
80OPC-287
80T-554
81Coke
81D-258
81F-51
81OPC-129
81T-129
81T/HT
81T/SO-99
81T/St-170
82D-92
82F-218
82K-34
82OPC-248
82T-453
82T-66TL
82T/St-43
82T/Tr-48T
83D-396
83F-450
83F/St-10M
83F/St-9M
83OPC-372
83OPC/St-236
83T-639
83T/St-236
84F-227
84F/X-54
84Nes/792-679
84T-679
84T/Tr-53
85F-228
85T-204
87Smok/R-25CO
89Lennox/Ast-25CO
89Mother/Ast-1MG
89T/Tr-53MG
90Lennox-16MG
90Mother/Ast-1MG
90OPC-579MG
90T-579MG
91Mother/Ast-1MG
91OPC-51MG
91T-51MG
92Mother/Ast-1MG
92OPC-729MG
92T-729
92T/Gold-729MG
92T/GoldWin-729MG
93Mother/Ast-1MG
93Rang/Keeb-196CO
93T-506M
93T/Gold-506M

Howe, Gordie
83Kaline-13M

Howe, Greg
83Visalia/Frit-21
85Toledo-23

Howe, Steve
81D-511
81F-136
81OPC-159
81Pol/Dodg-57
81T-693
81T/HT
82D-158
82F-9
82OPC-14
82Pol/Dodg-57
82T-14
83D-630
83F-209
83F/St-15M
83F/St-2M
83OPC-170
83Pol/Dodg-57
83T-170
84F-103
84Nes/792-425
84OPC-196
84T-425
85Coke/Dodg-14
86SanJose-10
87Smok/Dodg-14
88D-593
88S-543
89London/ProC-1357
89Smok/Dodg-98
90Salinas/Cal-117
90Target-361
91AAA/LineD-105
91ColClip/LineD-105
91ColClip/ProC-592
91F/Up-U43
91Leaf-440
91Leaf/Stud-93
91StCl-401
91UD/FinalEd-31F
92D-106
92F-230
92OPC-318
92Pinn-507
92S-275
92StCl-827
92T-318
92T/Gold-318
92T/GoldWin-318
92UD-630
92Ultra-408
93D-763
93Pac/Spanish-555
93Pinn-559
93Rang/Keeb-197
93StCl-738
93StCl/1stDay-738
93UD-707
93Ultra-594
94F-231
94StCl/Team-193
94T-637
94T/Gold-637

Howe, Tom
91MissSt-28
92MissSt-22

Howell, David
(Dave)
89Oneonta/ProC-2113
90PrWill/Team-13
91FtLaud/ClBest-20
91FtLaud/ProC-2433
92ArkTr/ProC-1137
92StPete/ClBest-11

Howell, Harry
90Target-363
E107
E90
E92
M116
T204
T206
T213/brown
WG2-25

Howell, Homer
(Dixie)
48Sommer-19
49Eureka-86
51B-252
52B-222
52T-135
53T-255
90Target-362
91T/Arc53-255

Howell, Jack
85Cram/PCL-24
86D-524
86Edmon-15
86OPC-127
86T-127
87D-305
87F-83
87OPC-2
87Smok/Cal-16
87T-422
88D-333
88D/Best-59
88F-491
88OPC-114
88Panini/St-44
88S-124
88Smok/Angels-3
88T-631
88T/Big-121
88T/St-175
89B-48
89D-288
89D/Best-307
89F-480
89KennerFig-66
89OPC-216
89Panini/St-293
89RedFoley/St-61
89S-261
89T-216
89T/Big-228
89T/St-181
89UD-138
90B-296
90D-254
90D/BestAL-45
90F-135
90F/Can-135
90Leaf-327
90OPC-547
90PublInt/St-371
90S-206
90Smok/Angel-8
90T-547
90T/Big-34
90UD-19
91D-247
91OPC-57
91Panini/FrSt-182
91S-842
91Smok/Angel-11
91StCl-198
91T-57
91UD-213
91Ultra-47
92D-646
92OPC-769
92Panini-234
92S-706
92T-769
92T/Gold-769
92T/GoldWin-769
92UD-419

Howell, Jay
79Indianap-24
80Indianap-11
82Iowa-16
82T-51R
83D-587
84F-128
84Nes/792-239
84T-239
85D-103
85D/HL-18
85F-131
85F/Up-U57
85Leaf-244
85Mother/A's-18
85T-559
85T/Tr-57T
86D-223
86D/AAS-57
86F-421
86F/Mini-89
86F/St-62
86Leaf-100
86Mother/A's-18
86OPC-115
86Seven/Coin-W15
86Sf-192
86T-115
86T/St-175
86T/Super-34
86T/Tatt-11M
87D-503
87F-395
87F/St-63
87Mother/A's-25
87OPC-391
87RedFoley/St-89
87Smok/A's-6
87T-391
88D-55
88D/AS-11
88F-282
88F/Up-U95
88Mother/Dodg-16
88OPC-91
88Pol/Dodg-50
88S-522
88S/Tr-35T
88Sf-86
88T-690
88T/St-166
88T/Tr-52T
89B-335
89D-610
89D/Best-36
89F-64
89Mother/Dodg-16
89OPC-212
89Panini/St-22
89Panini/St-98
89Pol/Dodg-26
89S-378
89Smok/Dodg-89
89T-425
89T/Big-79
89T/St-61
89UD-610
89Woolwth-30
90B-83
90D-203
90D/BestNL-66
90F-400
90F/Can-400
90KMart/SS-13
90Leaf-42
90Mother/Dodg-15
90OPC-40
90Panini/St-274
90Pol/Dodg-50
90PublInt/St-11
90RedFoley/St-49
90S-227
90Sf-78
90T-40
90T/Mini-59
90T/St-65
90T/TVAS-47
90Target-364
90UD-508
91B-603
91D-486
91F-209
91Leaf-98
91Mother/Dodg-15
91OPC-770
91Pol/Dodg-50
91S-29
91StCl-278
91T-770
91UD-558
91Ultra-163
92B-408
92D-395
92F-460
92Mother/Dodg-19
92OPC-205
92Pinn-444
92Pol/Dodg-50
92S-119
92StCl-457
92T-205
92T/Gold-205
92T/GoldWin-205
92UD-511
92Yank/WIZ80-85
93Brave/LykePerf-12
93Brave/LykeStand-15
93D-538
93F-450
93F/Final-2
93OPC-160
93Pac/Spanish-150
93StCl/Brave-19
93T-311
93T/Gold-311
93UD-731
94F-360
94L-322
94StCl/Team-262
94T-592
94T/Gold-592

Howell, Ken
84Cram/PCL-165
85Coke/Dodg-15
85D-592
85F-374
85T/Tr-58T
86Coke/Dodg-14
86D-275
86F-133
86OPC-349
86Pol/Dodg-43
86T-654
86T/St-69
87D-229
87F-443
87Mother/Dodg-19
87OPC-187
87Phill/TastyK-37
87Pol/Dodg-22
87T-477
88D-130
88F-520
88Mother/Dodg-24
88OPC-149
88Pol/Dodg-43
88S-406
88T-149
89B-394
89D/Best-184
89F/Up-108
89Phill/TastyK-11
89T-93
89T/Tr-54T
90B-147
90D-430
90D/BestNL-44
90F-561
90F/Can-561
90Leaf-316
90OPC-756
90Panini/St-314
90Phill/TastyK-15
90PublInt/St-240
90T-756
90T/Big-269
90T/St-116
90Target-365
90UD-559
91D-204
91F-400
91OPC-209
91Panini/FrSt-110
91Panini/St-108
91Phill/Medford-20
91S-458
91StCl-71
91T-209
91UD-488
91Ultra-265
Howell, Millard
(Dixie)
56T-149
57T-221
58T-421
Howell, Pat
89Pittsfld/Star-11
89Star/IISingl-159
90Clmbia/PCPII-3
90Columbia/GS-9
90SALAS/Star-35
91ClBest/Singl-217
91FSLAS/ProC-FSL32
91StLucie/ClBest-25
91StLucie/ProC-724
92D/Rook-55
92F/Up-103
92ProC/Tomorrow-284
92Sky/AAASingl-253
92Tidew/ProC-
92Tidew/SB-559
93D-116
93T-215
93T/Gold-215
93UD-161
Howell, Peter
92Kane/ClBest-28TR
92Kane/Team-14TR
Howell, Roy Lee
74Spoka
76OPC-279
76SSPC-265
76T-279
77T-608
78BJ/PostC-9
78Ho-84
78OPC-31
78T-394
79BJ/Bubble-12
79Ho-137
79K-54
79OPC-45
79T-101
80OPC-254
80T-488
81D-392
81F-417
81OPC-40
81T-581
81T/Tr-773
82D-204
82F-145
82Pol/Brew-13
82T-68
83D-358
83F-36
83Pol/Brew-13
83T-218
84F-203
84Gard-9
84Nes/792-687
84Pol/Brew-13
84T-687
85D-577
85T-372
89Pac/SenLg-12
89T/SenLg-88
89TM/SenLg-48
90EliteSenLg-6
92Brew/Carlson-10
93Rang/Keeb-198
Howerton, Bill
50B-239
51B-229
52B-119
52T-167
53Mother-16
Howerton, Rick
77Watlo
Howerton, Troy
84Newar-3
Howes, Jeff
84LitFalls-12
87Hawaii-25
Howes, John
87BurlEx-22
88WPalmB/Star-11
Howes, William
N172
Howey, Todd
87Clearw-26
88Clearw/Star-14
Howie, Mark
85Madis-16
85Madis/Pol-13
86Madis/Pol-11
88EastLAS/ProC-39
88Wmsprt/ProC-1322
89MidldA/GS-19
90LSUGreat-2
90MidldA/GS-7
91AA/LineD-436
91MidldA/LineD-436
91MidldA/OneHour-13
91MidldA/ProC-442
92Nashvl/ProC-1838
92Nashvl/SB-285
92ProC/Tomorrow-31
92Sky/AASingl-132
92Sky/AASingl-292
Howitt, Dann
86Cram/NWL-67
87Modesto-20
88Modesto-27
88Modesto/Cal-67
89Huntsvl/Best-7
90AAASingl/ProC-147
90F-644R
90F/Can-644M
90ProC/Singl-597
90T/89Debut-62
90Tacoma/CMC-20
90Tacoma/ProC-100
90UD/Ext-747
91AAA/LineD-538
91B-229
91Tacoma/LineD-538
91Tacoma/ProC-2315
91UD-442
92B-521
92D-751
92S-861
92S/100RisSt-68
92Sky/AAASingl-240
92Tacoma/SB-537
93Calgary/ProC-1177
93D-349
Howley, Dan
33G-175
Howser, Dick
61T-416
62Bz-10
62J-94
62P-94
62P/Can-94
62Salada-31
62Shirriff-31
62T-13
62T/St-53
62T/bucks
63F-15
63T-124
64T-478
65Kahn
65OPC-92
65T-92
66T-567
67T-411
68T-467
69MB-121
73OPC-116CO
73T-116C
78TCMA-233
81F-84MG
83D-590MG
83T-96MG
84Nes/792-471MG
84T-471MG
85T-334MG
86NatPhoto-10MG
86T-199MG
87D/AAS-10MG
87D/PopUp-10MG
87T-18MG
87T/Gloss22-12MG
90OPC-661TBC
90T-661TBC
92Yank/WIZ60-57
Howze, Ben
89Rockford/Team-12
90Rockford/Team-10
91Rockford/ClBest-6
91Rockford/ProC-2041
Hoy, Pete
89Elmira/Pucko-5
90WinHaven/Star-11
91AA/LineD-464
91NewBrit/LineD-464
91NewBrit/ProC-349
92B-292
92Classic/II-T92
92D/Rook-56
92L-515
92L/BlkGold-515
92Pawtu/ProC-917
92Pinn-526
92Ultra-315
93S-230
Hoy, William
(Dummy)
73F/Wild-8
N172
WG1-65
Hoyer, Brad
88Spokane/ProC-1937
89Watlo/ProC-1794
89Watlo/Star-14
90Waterlo/Best-8
90Waterlo/ProC-2374
91LynchRS/ClBest-4
91LynchRS/ProC-1193
Hoyt, Dave
82Wisco/Frit-5
83Spring/Frit-16
Hoyt, LaMarr
(Dewey)
78AppFx
79Iowa/Pol-9
80Iowa/Pol-8
81D-160
81T-164
82D-117
82F-345
82F/St-190
82T-428
83D-632
83F-238
83F/St-15M
83F/St-7M
83OPC-226
83OPC/St-16
83OPC/St-53
83T-591TL
83T-618
83T-705LL
83T/LeadS-4
83T/St-16
83T/St-53
83TrueVal/WSox-31
84D-488
84F-63
84Nes/792-135LL
84Nes/792-405AS
84Nes/792-97
84Nestle/DT-9
84OPC-177AS
84OPC-97
84Seven-23C
84T-135LL
84T-405AS
84T-97
84T/Gloss40-32
84T/RD-26
84T/St-11LCS
84T/St-178
84T/St-192
84T/St-240
84T/Super-3
84TrueVal/WS-17
85D-86
85D/HL-23
85F-517
85F/Up-U58
85FunFood/Pin-91
85Leaf-37
85Mother/Padres-17
85OPC-312
85T-520
85T/RD-26
85T/Tr-59T
86D-139
86D/AAS-9
86D/PopUp-9
86F-325
86F/LimEd-25
86F/St-63
86Leaf-61
86OPC-380
86Sf-193
86Sf-57M
86T-380
86T/Gloss22-21
86T/St-113
86T/St-154
86T/Tatt-14M
87D-434
87F-418
87T-275
Hoyt, Waite
28Yueng-30
29Exh/4-25
31Exh/4-24
33G-60
35G-1E
35G-3C
35G-4C
35G-5C
40PlayBall-118
60F-69
61F-44
76Shakey-114
77Galasso-117
80Perez/HOF-113
80SSPC/HOF
82Ohio/HOF-7
86Conlon/1-26
89HOF/St-71
89Smok/Dodg-10
90Target-366
91Conlon/Sport-115
92Conlon/Sport-468
92Yank/WIZHOF-16
93Conlon-757
E120
E220
R310
R313
R314
R316
V100
V117-7
V353-60
V355-39
V61-44
V89-32
V94-27
W501-32
W502-30
W513-62
W515-8
W572
W573
W575
Hrabar, Shaun
91Kane/ClBest-1
91Kane/ProC-2671
91Kane/Team-11
91Perth/Fut-3
Hrabcsak, Edward
52Park-87
Hrabosky, Al
71OPC-594R
71T-594R
73OPC-153
73T-153
74OPC-108
74T-108
75OPC-122
75T-122
75T/M-122
76Crane-20
76Ho-50
76Ho/Twink-50
76K-23
76MSA/Disc
76OPC-205LL
76OPC-315
76SSPC-291
76T-205LL
76T-315
77BurgChef-10
77Pep-37
77T-495
78SSPC/270-228
78T-230
78Wiffle/Discs-30
79Ho-25
79OPC-19
79T-45
80OPC-306
80T-585
81D-550
81F-262
81OPC-354
81Pol/Atl-39
81T-636
82BK/Lids-12
82D-97
82F-438
82OPC-393
82Pol/Atl-39
82T-393
83D-475
89Pac/Leg-115
89Pac/SenLg-179
89T/SenLg-15
89TM/SenLg-49
91Swell/Great-43
92Card/McDon/Pac-55
Hrbek, Kent
80Wisco
82D-557
82T-766R
82T/Tr-44T
83D-179
83D-19DK
83D/AAS-49
83F-616
83F-633M
83F/St-11M
83F/St-18M
83K-53
83OPC-251
83OPC/St-313
83OPC/St-88FOIL
83T-690
83T-771TL
83T/Gloss40-35
83T/St-313
83T/St-88

83Twin/Team-31M
83Twin/Team-33M
83Twin/Team-9
84D-70
84D/AAS-37
84F-567
84Nes/792-11TL
84Nes/792-345
84OPC-345
84Seven-11C
84T-11TL
84T-345
84T/RD-17M
84T/St-305
85D-70
85D/AAS-40
85Drake-16
85F-281
85F/LimEd-13
85FunFood/Pin-111
85Leaf-200
85OPC-308
85Seven-11C
85Seven/Minn-4
85T-510
85T/RD-16M
85T/St-296
85T/Super-41
85ThomMc/Discs-13
85Twin/Seven-4
85Twin/Team-10
86D-70
86D/HL-19
86Dorman-6
86F-397
86F/LL-20
86F/Mini-84
86F/Slug-17
86F/St-64
86GenMills/Book-2M
86Leaf-67
86OPC-63
86Sf-36
86T-430
86T/St-277
86T/Tatt-17M
86TrueVal-24
87Classic-53
87D-73
87D/OD-228
87F-544
87F/Excit-29
87F/Lim-22
87F/Mini-57
87F/St-64
87Kraft-25
87Leaf-99
87OPC-161
87RedFoley/St-49
87Sf-15
87Sf/TPrev-17M
87Stuart-22M
87T-679
87T/Board-28
87T/Coins-13
87T/Gloss60-25
87T/St-281
88Classic/Red-192
88D-320
88D/Best-102
88F-13
88F/BB/AS-17
88F/LL-21
88F/Mini-35
88F/SS-17
88F/St-44
88F/TL-14
88F/WS-9
88Jiffy-10
88KennerFig-54
88Leaf-139
88Master/Disc-10
88OPC-45
88Panini/St-136
88S-43
88Sf-95
88Smok/Minn-3
88T-45
88T/Big-84
88T/Gloss60-8
88T/Mini-22
88T/St-24
88T/St-274
88T/UK-37
88Woolwth-30WS6
89B-157
89Cadaco-30
89Classic-55
89D-199
89D/Best-18
89F-116
89KMart/Lead-16
89KennerFig-67
89OPC-265
89Panini/St-387
89RedFoley/St-62
89S-382
89S/HotStar-14
89Sf-188
89T-265
89T/Big-209
89T/Coins-42
89T/Gloss60-7
89T/LJN-112
89T/St-287
89T/UK-41
89UD-213
90B-418
90Classic/Up-23
90D-81
90D/BestAL-65
90D/Learning-36
90F-378
90F/BBMVP-20
90F/Can-378
90KMart/CBatL-22
90Kenner/Fig-43
90Leaf-228
90MLBPA/Pins-97
90MSA/Soda-20
90OPC-125
90Panini/St-112
90PublInt/St-290
90PublInt/St-330
90RedFoley/St-50
90S-381
90Sf-203
90T-125
90T/Ames-19
90T/Big-27
90T/Coins-18
90T/HillsHM-11
90T/St-287
90UD-452
91B-321
91Classic/200-118
91Classic/II-T15
91D-95
91DennyGS-7
91F-614
91Leaf-313
91Leaf/Stud-87
91OPC-710
91Panini/FrSt-300
91Panini/St-251
91RedFoley/St-50
91S-292
91S/100SS-78
91StCl-248
91Sunflower-13
91T-710
91T/CJMini/II-24
91UD-167
91Ultra-189
92B-445
92CJ/DI-29
92Classic/Game200-94
92D-326
92DennyGS-19
92F-205
92L-362
92L/BlkGold-362
92OPC-347
92OPC/Premier-46
92Panini-115
92Pinn-68
92S-530
92S/100SS-98
92StCl-235
92StCl/Dome-89
92Studio-205
92T-347
92T/Gold-347
92T/GoldWin-347
92T/Kids-111
92TripleP-135
92UD-334
92USPlayC/Twin-13C
92USPlayC/Twin-9D
92Ultra-92
93B-677
93Colla/DM-53
93D-283
93D/LongBall-LL7
93F-267
93Flair-236
93L-76
93MSA/Metz-31
93OPC-150
93Pac/Spanish-171
93Panini-125
93Pinn-27
93Pinn-307HH
93Pinn/HRC-45
93S-98
93Select-80
93StCl-525
93StCl/1stDay-525
93Studio-35
93T-9
93T/Finest-117
93T/FinestRef-117
93T/Gold-9
93TripleP-128
93UD-50
93UD-74
93UD/SP-247
93Ultra-231
94D-443
94F-208
94Finest-261
94Flair-75
94L-269
94OPC-261
94Pac/Cr-355
94Panini-91
94Pinn-206
94Pinn/Artist-206
94Pinn/Museum-206
94S-65
94S/GoldR-65
94Sf/2000-100
94StCl-224
94StCl/1stDay-224
94StCl/Gold-224
94Studio-196
94T-490
94T/Gold-490
94TripleP-253
94UD-98
94UD/ElecD-98
94Ultra-87

Hreha, Dan
90AR-17

Hriniak, Walt
69T-611R
70OPC-392
70T-392
90Coke/WSox-30CO
91Kodak/WSox-x
92WSox-NNO
93WSox-30M

Hrovat, Dale
76Watlo
77Holyo
78Spokane/Cramer-4
78Spokane/Team-4

Hrusovsky, John
91Princet/ClBest-8
91Princet/ProC-3507
92CharWh/ClBest-3
92CharWh/ProC-3
92ProC/Tomorrow-221
93ClBest/MLG-187
93SALAS/II-17
94FExcel-176

Hrynko, Larry
81Watlo-4
82Charl-6
83Charl-3

Hubacek, Doug
57Seattle/Pop-19

Hubbard, Cal
55B-315UMP
76Shakey-154
80Perez/HOF-154
80SSPC/HOF
89HOF/St-99
90BBWit-75

Hubbard, Don
78Watlo

Hubbard, Glenn
78Richm
79T-715R
80Richm-15
81D-459
81F-260
81OPC-247
81Pol/Atl-17
81T-247
81T/St-149
82BK/Lids-13
82D-436
82F-437
82Pol/Atl-17
82T-482
82T/St-23
83D-184
83F-139
83OPC-322
83OPC/St-215
83Pol/Atl-17
83T-624
83T/St-215
84D-432
84F-182
84Nes/792-25
84OPC-25
84Pol/Atl-17
84T-25
84T/St-29
85D-199
85F-329
85Ho/Braves-12
85Leaf-242
85OPC-195
85Pol/Atl-17
85T-195
85T/St-33
86D-141
86F-518
86Leaf-71
86OPC-112
86Pol/Atl-17
86T-539
86T/St-36
86T/Tatt-4M
87D-634
87D/OD-48
87F-519
87OPC-68
87Sf/TPrev-24M
87Smok/Atl-21
87T-745
88D-22DK
88D-314
88D/A's/Bk-NEW
88D/DKsuper-22DK
88F-542
88Leaf-22DK
88Mother/A's-18
88OPC-325
88Panini/St-243
88RedFoley/St-36
88S-111
88S/Tr-58T
88T-325
88T/Big-200
88T/Tr-53T
89B-199
89D-568
89F-12
89Mother/A's-19
89S-34
89T-237
89T/Big-232
89UD-395
90Richm/25Ann-11
91Macon/ClBest-10CO
91Macon/ProC-882CO
92Macon/ClBest-27CO
92Macon/ProC-285CO
93Richm/Team-3CO

Hubbard, Jeff
89CharlR/Star-28CO
90CharlR/Star-30CO
91AA/LineD-600M
91Tulsa/LineD-600CO
91Tulsa/ProC-2790CO
91Tulsa/Team-13CO

Hubbard, Joe
90Elizab/Star-26TR

Hubbard, Mark
91Oneonta/ProC-4165
92ClBest-306
92Greens/ClBest-24
92Greens/ProC-793
92StCl/Dome-90

Hubbard, Mike
92Geneva/ClBest-15
92Geneva/ProC-1563
94B-606
94ClBest/Gold-50

Hubbard, Trent
86AubAs-12
87Ashvl-2
88Osceola/Star-15
89ColMud/ProC-132
89ColMud/Star-13
91AA/LineD-561
91Jacks/LineD-561
91Jacks/ProC-932
92Tucson/ProC-496
92Tucson/SB-610
93FExcel/ML-45

Hubbard, Ty III
83Tampa-15

Hubbell, Carl
33G-230
33G-234
33SK*-42
34DS-39
34Exh/4-5
34G-12
35BU-5
35Exh/4-5
35Wheat
36Exh/4-5
36Wheat
37Dix
37Exh/4-5
37Wheat-6
38Dix
38Exh/4-5
38ONG/Pin-16
38Wheat
39Exh
39PlayBall-53
40PlayBall-87
41DP-140
41G-20
41G-20
41PlayBall-6
42Playball-34
48Exh/HOF
48Swell-8
50Callahan
50W576-40
60F-4
60NuCard-11
61F-45
61GP-6
61NuCard-479
72Laugh/GF-36
74Laugh/ASG-34
75Sheraton-2
76Rowe-12M
76Shakey-53
77Galasso-208
77Galasso-240
77Galasso-88
80Pac/Leg-89
80Perez/HOF-53
80SSPC/HOF
83D/HOF-33
84D/Champs-55
85West/2-32
86Conlon/1-15
86Sf/Dec-6
87Nestle/DT-10
88Conlon/3-15
88Conlon/NatAS-11
89HOF/St-75
90BBWit-95
90HOF/St-32
90Perez/GreatMom-35
91Conlon/Sport-10
91Conlon/Sport-253
92Conlon/Col-12
92Conlon/Gold-665
92Conlon/Sport-360
92Conlon/Sport-552
93AP/ASG-103
93AP/ASG24K-37G
93Conlon-665
93UD/ATH-136M
93UD/ATH-69
94Conlon-1105

94Conlon/Pr-1105
PM10/Sm-78A
PM10/Sm-78B
R302
R314
R315-A17
R315-B17
R332-22
V354-71
WG8-35
Hubbell, Wilbert
21Exh-79
25Exh-45
90Target-987
E120
E220
V61-96
W572
Hubbs, Ken
62T-461
63Bz-27
63Exh
63J-174
63P-174
63T-15
63T/SO
64T-550
84Cub/Uno-2M
92Cub/OldStyle-14
Exh47
Huber, Clarence
26Exh-45
Huber, Jeff
91CharRain/ClBest-7
91CharRain/ProC-93
92CharRain/ClBest-10
92CharRain/ProC-119
Huble, Ian
91Waverly/Fut-5
Huckaby, Ken
91GreatF/SportP-17
92ClBest-353
92VeroB/ClBest-27
92VeroB/ProC-2878
94FExcel-216
Hudak, Joe
88MissSt-37M
90MissSt-41M
91MissSt-29CO
Hudek, John
89Saraso/Star-11
89Star/Wax-59
90BirmB/Best-19
90BirmB/ProC-1107
90Foil/Best-296
90ProC/Singl-771
91AA/LineD-63
91BirmB/LineD-63
91BirmB/ProC-1451
92BirmB/SB-84
92Sky/AASingl-40
92Vanco/ProC-2718
92Vanco/SB-641
94B-34
94UD/SP-31
Hudgens, Dave
83Tacoma-16
84Cram/PCL-74
Hudik, Matt
90StCath/ProC-3452
Hudler, Rex
82Nashvl-14
84Colum-8
84Colum/Pol-13
85Colum-18
85Colum/Pol-14
85D-469
86RochR-8
87RochR/TCMA-28
88F/Up-U101
88Indianap/CMC-10
88Indianap/ProC-513
89B-364
89D-452
89F-380
89OPC-346
89S-470
89T-346
89T/Big-248
89UD-405
90D-366
90Leaf-439
90OPC-647
90Publint/St-177
90S-287
90Smok/Card-10
90T-647
90UD-411
91B-409
91Crown/Orio-206
91D-599
91F/Up-U116
91Leaf-212
91Leaf/Stud-233
91OPC-228
91Panini/FrSt-37
91Pol/Card-10
91S-589
91StCl-280
91T-228
91UD-482
92D-438
92F-581
92L-25
92L/BlkGold-25
92OPC-47
92Pinn-315
92Pinn-589M
92Pol/Card-8
92S-184
92StCl-851
92Studio-92
92T-47
92T/Gold-47
92T/GoldWin-47
92TripleP-207
92TripleP-41AA
92UD-670
92Ultra-568
92Yank/WIZ80-86
93D-96
93F-510
93StCl-113
93StCl/1stDay-113
Hudlin, Willis
33G-96
34DS-79
35BU-103
35BU-48
35G-1K
35G-3B
35G-5B
35G-6B
R313
R316
V353-72
Hudson, Charles
83Portl-19
84D-448
84F-36
84Nes/792-432
84Phill/TastyK-22
84T-432
84T/St-17
85CIGNA-16
85D-355
85F-255
85OPC-379
85Phill/TastyK-20
85Phill/TastyK-9M
85T-379
85T/St-120
86CIGNA-13
86D-622
86F-444
86Leaf-239
86Phill/TastyK-49
86T-792
86T/Tatt-13M
87D-630
87F-176
87F/Up-U46
87T-191
87T/Tr-50T
88D-374
88D/Y/Bk-374
88F-210
88T-636
88T/Big-212
89D-514
89D/Tr-50
89Mara/Tigers-27
89OPC-236
89S-415
89T-236
89T/Big-88
89UD-586
90Publint/St-474
90UD-520
92Yank/WIZ80-87
93Rang/Keeb-199
Hudson, Charlie
75SLCity/Caruso-18
Hudson, David
(Hap)
86Louisvl-3TR
87Louisvl-29
88Louisvl-51
88Louisvl/ProC-434
89AAA/ProC-12
89Louisvl-38
89Louisvl/CMC-5
89Louisvl/ProC-1253
Hudson, Deryk
90Rockford/ProC-2701
90Rockford/Team-11
Hudson, Jack
76Watlo
Hudson, Jesse James
70OPC-348R
70T-348R
91WIZMets-190
Hudson, Jim
89BBCity/Star-10
Hudson, Joe
92Elmira/ClBest-18
92Elmira/ProC-1378
Hudson, John
39PlayBall-154
40PlayBall-147
90Target-367
Hudson, Kevin
89Billings/ProC-2039
91Billing/SportP-26TR
Hudson, Lance
86Miami-12
88Lakeland/Star-14
90Miami/II/Star-10
Hudson, Nathaniel
N172
N172/BC
N370
Scrapps
Hudson, Rex
74Albuq/Team-7
75Albuq/Caruso-13
Hudson, Robert
81Wausau-3
83Chatt-14
Hudson, Sid
41PlayBall-46
48L-84
50B-17
51B-169
51T/RB-44
52B-123
52T-60
53B/BW-29
53T-251
54B-194
54T-93
55B-318
91T/Arc53-251
93Rang/Keeb-42CO
94T/Arc54-93
Hudson, Stan
75Albuq/Caruso-14
Hudson, Teressa
81ArkTr-23M
Hudson, Tony
80Tulsa-3
81Tulsa-21
82BurlR/Frit-21
82BurlR/TCMA-3
85Tulsa-20
86Knoxvl-13
87Syrac-12
Huebner, John
88GreatF-18
89Bakers/Cal-196
Huenneke, Derek
86AZ/Pol-7
Huey, John
83Madis/Frit-26
84MidldC-5
Huff, Brad
88Wythe/ProC-1979
89Wythe/Star-14
90Geneva/ProC-3032
90Geneva/Star-15
91WinSalem/ClBest-14
Huff, Matt
87SLCity/Taco-23
88Miami/Star-10
Huff, Mike
86VeroB-11
87SanAn-16
88SanAn/Best-19
88TexLgAS/GS-33
89AAA/CMC-38
89AAA/ProC-48
89Albuq/CMC-24
89Albuq/ProC-79
90AAAGame/ProC-46
90AAASingl/ProC-79
90Albuq/CMC-24
90Albuq/ProC-358
90Albuq/Trib-14
90Classic/Up-24
90F-649
90F/Can-649
90ProC/Singl-426
90S-597
90T/89Debut-63
90TripleAAS/CMC-38
91B-73
91F-210
91Indian/McDon-14
91Leaf/GRook-BC22
91S/RookTr-52T
92D-579
92F-85
92L-342
92L/BlkGold-342
92OPC-532
92OPC/Premier-21
92Pinn-485
92S-664
92StCl-329
92T-532
92T/Gold-532
92T/GoldWin-532
92Ultra-337
92WSox-12
93D-788
93Pac/Spanish-388
93StCl/WSox-24
93WSox-12
94StCl/Team-140
Huffman, Kris
88Savan/ProC-351
89Spring/Best-9
Huffman, Phil
79BJ/Bubble-13
80OPC-79
80Syrac-9
80Syrac/Team-10
80T-142
81OPC-2
81Syrac-5
81Syrac/Team-10
81T-506
82Omaha-6
85RochR-17
86RochR-9
87RochR-1
87RochR/TCMA-6
91Crown/Orio-207
Huffman, Rod
91Clinton/ClBest-5
91Clinton/ProC-829
91MidwLAS/ProC-4
92ProC/Tomorrow-355
92SanJose/ClBest-20
Huffman, Ryan
94LSU-10
Hufford, Scott
87Spartan-26
88Lakeland/Star-15
Huffstickler, Danny
79Elmira-4
Hufft, Fuzzy
28Exh/PCL-12
Huggins, Miller
10Domino-57
11Diamond-15
11Helmar-171
12Sweet/Pin-149A
12Sweet/Pin-149B
14CJ-75
14Piedmont/St-28
15CJ-75
61F-46
76Shakey-98
77Galasso-128
80Perez/HOF-98
80SSPC/HOF
81Conlon-3
82Ohio/HOF-39
86Conlon/1-16
91Conlon/Sport-101
91Conlon/Sport-271
92Card/McDon/Pac-5
92Conlon/Sport-649
92Mega/Ruth-124M
92Yank/WIZHOF-17
93Conlon-830
93CrackJack-22
BF2-93
D329-86
D350/2-85
E121/120
E121/80
E270/2
E300
M101/4-86
M101/5-85
M116
S74-120
T201
T202
T204
T205
T206
T207
T213/blue
T213/brown
T215/blue
T215/brown
T222
V100
V89-10MG
W514-34
W515-36
W575
WG3-22
WG5-20
WG6-19
Hughes, Bobby
92Classic/DP-35
93B-507
94FExcel-81
Hughes, Butch
82Reading-3
83Phoenix/BHN-18
86Modesto-14
87Modesto-9
Hughes, Danan
92Helena/ProC-1727
93FExcel/ML-188
Hughes, Gregory
80Water-22
81Tulsa-23
Hughes, James Michael
(Jim)
74Tacoma/Caruso-7
76Ho/Twink-53
76OPC-11
76SSPC-211
76T-11
77T-304
78Cr/PCL-62
78T-395
90Target-368
Hughes, James Robert
(Jim)
52Park-56
53T-216
54NYJour
54T-169
55B-156
55Gol/Dodg-14
55T-51
55T/DH-20
79TCMA-268
90Target-369
91T/Arc53-216
94T/Arc54-169
Hughes, John
83Clinton/Frit-16
Hughes, Keith
85Albany-35
86Albany/TCMA-7
87Colum-21
87Colum/Pol-13
87Colum/TCMA-21
88D-643
88F-305

88RochR/CMC-15
88RochR/Gov-13
88RochR/ProC-213
88RochR/Team-11
88S-635
88T-781
89AAA/ProC-23
89RochR/CMC-13
89RochR/ProC-1659
90AAAGame/ProC-6
90AAASingl/ProC-287
90AlbanyDG/Best-32
90ProC/Singl-375
90T/TVMets-46
90Tidew/CMC-24
90Tidew/ProC-556
91AAA/LineD-106
91ColClip/LineD-106
91ColClip/ProC-601
91Crown/Orio-208
91WIZMets-191
92Portl/SB-409
92Portland/ProC-2674
92Yank/WIZ80-88

Hughes, Kiley
93SoEastern-11

Hughes, Leo
(Doc)
48Sommer-29
49Sommer-23

Hughes, Michael
(Mickey)
90Target-370

Hughes, Mickey J.
N172

Hughes, Richard
(Dick)
62Kahn/Atl
62Pep/Tul
67T-384R
68T-253
69OPC-39
69T-39

Hughes, Roy
47Royal/Mont-2
92Conlon/Sport-566
94Conlon-1069

Hughes, Sammy T.
78Laugh/Black-15
86Negro/Frit-111
90Negro/Star-35

Hughes, Steve
80Cedar-8

Hughes, Terry W.
73OPC-603R
73T-603R
74OPC-604R
74T-604R
75OPC-612
75T-612
75T/M-612

Hughes, Thomas
(Tom)
11Helmar-71
91Conlon/Sport-161
C46-66
E254
E91
M116

Hughes, Tim
75Cedar

Hughes, Troy
90Pulaski/Best-20
90Pulaski/ProC-3088
91Macon/ClBest-24
91Macon/ProC-877
92ClBest-92
92Durham/ClBest-15
92Durham/ProC-1113
92Durham/Team-27
92ProC/Tomorrow-191

Hughs, Eric
89Alaska/Team-18

Hughson, Cecil
(Tex)
42Playball-5
47TipTop
49B-199
92TX-25
Exh47

Hugo, Sean
92OKSt-12

Huisman, Rick
90ClintUp/Team-U6
91CalLgAS-31
91ClBest/Singl-32
91SanJose/ClBest-27
91SanJose/ProC-6
92B-217
92ClBest-255
92ProC/Tomorrow-350
92Shrev/ProC-3865
92Shrev/SB-585
92Sky/AASingl-258
92UD/ML-186
93FExcel/ML-118

Huismann, Mark
81CharR-18
82FtMyr-16
84D-339
85D-583
85F-203
85Omaha-15
85T-644
86NatPhoto-38
87F-586
87Mother/Sea-16
87T-187
88AAA/ProC-42
88Toledo/CMC-11
88Toledo/ProC-588
88TripleA/ASCMC-26
89RochR/CMC-10
89RochR/ProC-1650
90AAASingl/ProC-482
90BuffB/CMC-4
90BuffB/ProC-367
90BuffB/Team-9
90ProC/Singl-4
91AAA/LineD-30
91BuffB/LineD-30
91BuffB/ProC-535
91Crown/Orio-209
92Omaha/ProC-2956
92Omaha/SB-331

Hulett, Tim
81GlenF-12
84TrueVal/WS-18
85Coke/WS-32
85D-645
85F/Up-U59
85T/Tr-60T
86Coke/WS-32
86D-404
86F-208
86OPC-87
86T-724
86T/St-295
87Coke/WS-18
87D-260
87D/OD-231
87F-500
87OPC-286
87T-566
87T/St-289
88Indianap/CMC-17
88Indianap/ProC-522
88T-158
89RochR/CMC-16
89RochR/ProC-1653
90F/Up-U66
91Crown/Orio-210
91D-706
91F-478
91OPC-468
91S-632
91StCl-517
91T-468
92F-11
92OPC-396
92S-391
92StCl-104
93D-661
93F-543
93OPC-167
93Pac/Spanish-343
93StCl-14
93StCl/1stDay-14
93T-327
93T/Gold-327
94D-129
94F-7
94Pac/Cr-34
94S-165
94S/GoldR-165
94StCl-430
94StCl/1stDay-430
94StCl/Gold-430
94StCl/Team-298
94T-32
94T/Gold-32

Hull, Brett
91StCl/Charter*-48
91StCl/Charter*-49
91StCl/Member*-45

Hull, Jeff
85FtMyr-8
86FtMyr-14
88EastLAS/ProC-35
88Vermont/ProC-961
89Calgary/CMC-8
89Calgary/ProC-526
90OrlanSR/Best-8
90OrlanSR/ProC-1085

Hulme, Pat
90Utica/Pucko-20

Hulse, David
90Butte/SportP-8
91CharlR/ClBest-22
91CharlR/ProC-1326
91ClBest/Singl-197
92Sky/AASingl-269
92Tulsa/ProC-2707
92Tulsa/SB-609
93B-601
93D-706
93F-683
93Flair-282
93L-355
93OPC-146
93OPC/Premier-40
93Pac/Spanish-641
93Pinn-269
93Pinn/RookTP-10M
93Rang/Keeb-410
93S-293
93S/Boys-26
93Select/RT/ASRook-7
93Select/RookTr-35T
93StCl-705
93StCl/1stDay-705
93StCl/Rang-4
93T-118
93T/Gold-118
93ToysRUs-75
93UD-374
93Ultra-630
94D-560
94F-309
94Flair-112
94L-278
94Pac/Cr-620
94Pinn-162
94Pinn/Artist-162
94Pinn/Museum-162
94S-523
94S/Cycle-14
94StCl-449
94StCl/1stDay-449
94StCl/Gold-449
94StCl/Team-251
94Studio-155
94T-498
94T/Finest-148
94T/FinestRef-148
94T/Gold-498
94TripleP-196
94UD-377
94UD/CollC-142
94UD/CollC/Gold-142
94UD/CollC/Silv-142
94Ultra-129

Hulse, Jeff
88Eugene/Best-14
89AppFx/ProC-866
90Clearw/Star-8

Hulstrom, Bruce
87Penin-14

Hulswitt, Rudy
E254
E270/1
E270/2
M116
T206

Humber, Frank
89GreatF-21
90Bakers/Cal-239

Hume, Thomas
(Tom)
76Indianap-9
77Indianap-5
78Pep-14
78SSPC/270-120
78T-701R
79T-301
80T-149
81F-211
81OPC-292
81T-419
81T-8LL
81T/HT
81T/St-166
81T/St-31M
82Coke/Reds
82D-229
82F-69
82OPC-79
82T-763
83D-229
83F-593
83F/St-18M
83F/St-24M
83F/St-8M
83OPC-86
83T-86
84D-550
84F-472
84Nes/792-607
84OPC-186
84T-607
84T/St-59
85D-408
85F-538
85OPC-223
85T-223
86D-365
86F-179
86F/Up-U52
86Phill/TastyK-41
86T-573
86T/Tr-47T
87F-177
87OPC-251
87Phill/TastyK-41
87T-719
88F-236
88S-494

Hummel, Dean
86Shrev-10

Hummel, John E.
10Domino-58
11Helmar-87
12Sweet/Pin-74
14CJ-50
14Piedmont/St-29
15CJ-50
90Target-371
E254
E270/2
E300
M116
S74-53
T202
T204
T205
T206
T213/blue
T215/blue
T215/brown

Hummel, Mark
89KS*-59

Humphrey, Al
90Target-988

Humphrey, Daryl
83Greens-10

Humphrey, Sly
83Idaho-28

Humphrey, Terry
72Dimanche*-20
72OPC-489R
72T-489R
73OPC-106
73T-106
76OPC-552
76SSPC-373
76T-552
77T-369
78SSPC/270-210
78T-71
79T-503

Humphrey, Trevor
92Classic/DP-59

Humphreys, Mike
87SLCity/Taco-16
88Spokane/ProC-1926
89AS/Cal-10
89River/Best-8
89River/Cal-5
89River/ProC-1400
90TexLgAS/GS-7
90Wichita/Rock-11
91AAA/LineD-107
91B-162
91ColClip/LineD-107
91ColClip/ProC-608
91UD/FinalEd-35F
92ColClip/Pol-21
92ColClip/ProC-363
92ColClip/SB-105
92D-769
92F-231
92Pinn-277
92S-815
92S/Rook-26
92Sky/AAASingl-47
92StCl-319
92T/91Debut-85
92UD 432
93ColClip/Pol-21
93F/Final-246
93StCl/Y-10
93Ultra-595

Humphreys, Robert W.
(Bob)
65OPC-154
65T-154
66T-342
67CokeCap/Senator-1
67T-478
68T-268
69OPC-84
69T-84
70OPC-538
70T-538
71MLB/St-439
71OPC-236
71T-236
72MB-154
80Knoxvl/TCMA-25
81Syrac-23MG
81Syrac/Team-11
83Syrac-26MG

Humphries, Joe
87Myrtle-25
88SanAn/Best-20

Humphries, John
93Conlon-951

Humphry, Brandt
80ElPaso-1
81Holyo-22

Humphry, Trevor
92Martins/ProC-3051
93StCl/MurphyS-87
93StCl/Phill-16

Hund, John
75QuadC

Hundelt, Bill
89KS*-8

Hundhammer, Paul
84Pawtu-10A
84Pawtu-10B
85Pawtu-5

Hundley, Randy
66T-392R
67CokeCap/Cub-10
67OPC-106
67T-106
68OPC-136
68T-136
69MB-122
69MLB/St-121
69Sunoco/Pin-4
69T-347
69T/St-14
70Dunkin-3
70K-31
70MLB/St-17
70OPC-265
70T-265
71Bz
71Bz/Test-46
71MD
71MLB/St-34
71OPC-592
71T-592
71T/Coins-51
71T/tatt-3
72MB-155
72OPC-258
72T-258

73OPC-21
73T-21
74OPC-319
74T-319
74T/St-15
74T/Tr-319T
76OPC-351
76SSPC-121
76T-351
77T-502
78Twin/Frisz-34
84Cub/Uno-2M
84Cub/Uno-6M
89Pac/Leg-207
92Cub/OldStyle-15

Hundley, Todd
88LitFalls/Pucko-6
89Clmbia/Best-1
89Clmbia/GS-11
89SALAS/GS-17
90B-142
90Classic/III-100
90F/Up-U36
90Jacks/GS-1
90S/Tr-76T
90T/TVMets-47
90T/Tr-44T
90UD/Ext-726
91AAA/LineD-559
91AAAGame/ProC-49
91B-467
91D-641
91F-150
91MajorLg/Pins-75
91OPC-457
91OPC/Premier-66
91RedFoley/St-108
91S-340RP
91S/100RisSt-79
91S/Rook40-23
91StCl-349
91T-457
91T/90Debut-74
91Tidew/LineD-559
91Tidew/ProC-2513
91UD-440
91Ultra-220
91WIZMets-192
92B-101
92Classic/Game200-54
92D-568
92F-506
92L/GRook-7
92Mets/Kahn-9
92OPC-673
92Pinn-571
92Pinn/Rook-17
92Pinn/RookI-10
92Pinn/Team2000-78
92ProC/Tomorrow-277
92S-602
92S/100RisSt-80
92S/HotRook-6
92S/Impact-31
92S/Rook-6
92StCl-290
92Studio-66
92T-673
92T/Gold-673
92T/GoldWin-673
92T/McDonB-42
92TripleP-104
92UD-260
92UD/Scout-SR10
92Ultra-233
93B-398
93D-66
93F-88
93Flair-92
93L-75
93Mets/Kahn-9
93OPC-116
93Pac/Spanish-542
93Panini-246
93Pinn-126
93S-167
93Select-293
93Select/ChasRook-19
93StCl-72
93StCl/1stDay-72
93Studio-206
93T-380
93T/Gold-380
93ToysRUs-12
93TripleP-218
93UD-293
93UD/SP-150
93Ultra-75
94B-456
94D-128
94F-565
94Finest-319
94Flair-198
94L-323
94Pac/Cr-404
94Panini-218
94Pinn-155
94Pinn/Artist-155
94Pinn/Museum-155
94S-458
94Select-73
94StCl-82
94StCl/1stDay-82
94StCl/Gold-82
94Studio-115
94T-8
94T/Gold-8
94TripleP-144
94UD-242
94UD/CollC-143
94UD/CollC/Gold-143
94UD/CollC/Silv-143
94UD/ElecD-242
94UD/SP-117
94Ultra-237

Hunger, Chris
81Wausau-9
83Chatt-3

Hungler
N172

Hungling, Bernard
(Bernie)
90Target-989
E120

Hunington, Neal
91James/ClBest-29PER

Hunnefield, William
26Exh-76
27Exh-38
30CEA/Pin-15
31Exh/4-21
93Conlon-696

Hunsacker, Frank
77StPete
80ArkTr-15

Hunsinger, Alan
82Spring/Frit-17
83ArkTr-18
90SpringDG/Best-7

Hunt, Ben
75Clinton

Hunt, Chris
92Boise/ProC-3630

Hunt, Ken L.
60L-33
60T-522
61T-156
61T/St-172
62J-79
62P-79
62P/Can-79
62Salada-76A
62Salada-76B
62Shirriff-76
62T-68
62T/St-65
62T/bucks
63T-207
64Bz-26
64T-294
64T/Coins-89
65Bz-26
92Yank/WIZ60-58

Hunt, Ken R.
61T-556
62J-129
62Kahn
62P-129
62P/Can-129
62T-364

Hunt, Randy
82Spring/Frit-20
83ArkTr-11
85Louisvl-11
86Indianap-6
86T-218
87D-625
88Memphis/Best-15
90SpringDG/Best-33

Hunt, Riegal
92Welland/ClBest-10
92Welland/ProC-1337
93Welland/ClBest-7
93Welland/ProC-3372

Hunt, Ronald K.
(Ron)
63T-558R
64T-235
64T/Coins-164AS
64T/S-6
64T/SU
64T/St-93
65OldLond-12
65T-285
65T/E-35
65T/trans-50
66T-360
67CokeCap/DodgAngel-6
67CokeCap/Giant-9
67OPC/PI-31
67T-525
67T/PI-31
68Dexter-39
68OPC-15
68T-15
69MB-123
69MLB/St-200
69T-664
69T/St-105
70Expos/Pins-7
70MLB/St-125
70OPC-276
70T-276
71Expo/ProS-10
71MLB/St-130
71OPC-161
71T-578
72Dimanche*-21
72MB-156
72OPC-110
72ProStars/PostC-6
72T-110
73OPC-149
73T-149
74Expo/West-5
74K-25
74OPC-275
74T-275
74T/St-55
74Weston-33
75OPC-610
75T-610
75T/M-610
78TCMA-212
81TCMA-357
90Pac/Legend-84
90Target-372
91WIZMets-193
92Nabisco-5
93UD/ATH-70

Hunt, Ronald
81Redwd-15
82Holyo-15
82Redwd-21

Hunt, Shannon
90Bend/Legoe-28

Hunt, Tom
80LynnS-16
81Wausau-28
82Wausau/Frit-30TR
83Chatt-23
84Chatt-10
86Chatt-14TR
87Chatt/Best-26TR

Hunt, Will
93LSU/McDag-6

Hunter, Bert
86Ashvl-14
86AubAs-13
87Ashvl-16
88Osceola/Star-16
89ColMud/ProC-148
89ColMud/Star-14
90ColMud/Best-8
90ColMud/ProC-1358
90ColMud/Star-14
91AA/LineD-562
91Jacks/LineD-562
91Jacks/ProC-937
92Bingham/ProC-528
92Bingham/SB-60

Hunter, Bob
(Bobby)
88Oneonta/ProC-2056
91Augusta/ClBest-8
92CaroMud/ProC-1177
92Salem/ClBest-13
92Salem/ProC-59
93CaroMud/RBI-19

Hunter, Brian L.
90Ashvl/ProC-2761
90ProC/Singl-295
90ProC/Singl-848
91Osceola/ClBest-24
91Osceola/ProC-698
92ClBest-206
92Osceola/ClBest-9
92Osceola/ProC-2543
92UD/ML-324
93B-12
94B-670
94FExcel-202
94FExcel-8
94FExcel/AS-8
94Select-91
94TedW/Gardiner-7
94UD-16
94UD/ElecD-16

Hunter, Brian R.
88BurlB/ProC-25
88MidwLAS/GS-18
89Greenvl/Best-2
89Greenvl/ProC-1158
89Greenvl/Star-9
89Star/Wax-35
90AAASingl/ProC-416
90Richm/CMC-19
90Richm/ProC-271
90Richm/Team-13
91AAA/LineD-431
91Brave/Dubuq/Stand-19
91Classic/III-39
91D/Rook-9
91F/UltraUp-U67
91Richm/Bob-25
91Richm/LineD-431
91Richm/ProC-2581
91Richm/Team-18
91UD/FinalEd-54F
92B-662
92Brave/LykePerf-15
92Brave/LykeStand-17
92Classic/Game200-16
92D-163
92F-359
92L-374
92L/BlkGold-374
92OPC-611
92OPC/Premier-78
92Pinn-412
92Pinn/Team2000-29
92ProC/Tomorrow-177
92S-417
92S/100RisSt-3
92S/Impact-9
92StCl-432
92T-611
92T/91Debut-86
92T/Gold-611
92T/GoldWin-611
92UD-366
92USPlayC/Brave-11D
92USPlayC/Brave-6H
92Ultra-163
93Brave/LykePerf-13
93Brave/LykeStand-16
93D-290
93F-5
93OPC-157
93Pac/Spanish-7
93Pinn-414
93S-549
93Select-189
93StCl-491
93StCl/1stDay-491
93StCl/Ast-21
93StCl/Brave-23
93T-102
93T/Gold-102
93UD-582
93Ultra-305
94Finest-336
94L-275
94Pinn-502
94UD/SP-7PP
94Ultra-505

Hunter, George
90Target-990
E254
M116
T206
T213/brown

Hunter, Gordon
(Billy)
53T-166
54B-5
54T-48
55B-69
57T-207
58T-98
59T-11
73OPC-136CO
73T-136CO
74OPC-306CO
74T-306CO
78BK/R-1MG
78SSPC/270-104MG
78T-548CO
79TCMA-118
91Crown/Orio-211
91T/Arc53-166
93Rang/Keeb-200MG
94T/Arc54-48

Hunter, Greg
91ClBest/Singl-178
91SanBern/ClBest-15
91SanBern/ProC-1992
92Penin/ClBest-19
92Penin/ProC-2938

Hunter, Herb H.
16FleischBrd-44

Hunter, James McGregor
86BurlEx-9
86Sf/Dec-63M
87Stockton-19
88ElPaso/Best-28
89ElPaso/GS-9
91Brewer/MillB-12
92Denver/ProC-2634
92Denver/SB-148
92ElPaso/SB-214
92S-741
92Sky/AASingl-94
92T/91Debut-87

Hunter, Jeff
80Elmira-21

Hunter, Jim
(Catfish)
65T-526R
66OPC-36
66T-36
67CokeCap/A's-15
67T-369
67T/Test/SU-23
68A's/JITB-8
68Bz-2
68T-385
68T/ActionSt-10AM
68T/Post-5
69MB-124
69MLB/St-87
69T-235
69T/St-216
70MLB/St-259
70T-565
71Bz
71Bz/Test-48
71MD
71MLB/St-516
71OPC-45
71T-45
71T/Coins-80
71T/tatt-9
72K-22
72MB-157
72OPC-330
72T-330
73K-20
73OPC-235
73OPC-344KP
73T-235
73T-344KP
73T/Lids-21
74K-44
74OPC-196
74OPC-339AS
74T-339AS
74T-7

74T/DE-6
74T/St-225
75Ho-148
75K-44
75OPC-230
75OPC-310LL
75OPC-311LL
75SSPC/Sam-2
75T-230
75T-310LL
75T-311LL
75T/M-230
75T/M-310LL
75T/M-311LL
76Crane-21
76Ho-141
76K-5
76Laugh/Jub-7
76MSA/Disc
76OPC-100
76OPC-200LL
76OPC-202LL
76SSPC-425
76SSPC/MetsY-Y1
76T-100
76T-200LL
76T-202LL
77BK/Y-4
77BurgChef-178
77Ho-79
77Ho/Twink-79
77OPC-10
77T-280
77T/CS-21
77T/ClothSt-21
78BK/Y-7
78OPC-69
78SSPC/270-23
78T-460
78Wiffle/Discs-31
79BK/Y-6
79OPC-352
79T-670
80Perez/HOF-198
83MLBPA/Pin-10
87D/HL-19
87Mother/A's-6
88Pac/Leg-16
88T/Gloss22-11
89HOF/St-82
89Pac/Leg-193
89Swell-10
90Pac/Legend-68
90Perez/GreatMom-62
92Pinn-587
92Yank/WIZ70-77
92Yank/WIZAS-32
92Yank/WIZHOF-18
93AP/ASG-126
93AP/ASG24K-60G
93MCI-8
93Nabisco-3
94TedW-68

Hunter, Marion
81Redwd-16

Hunter, Marty
90Bend/Legoe-5CO

Hunter, Torii
94B-104
94ClBest/Gold-80
94ClBest/GoldLP-5
94Pinn-267
94Pinn/Artist-267
94Pinn/Museum-267
94S-640

Hunter, Traver
92OKSt-13

Hunter, Willard
90Target-373
91WIZMets-194

Huntz, Steve
69OPC-136R
69T-136R
69T/4in1-25M
70OPC-282
70T-282
71MLB/St-252
71OPC-486
71T-486
72OPC-73
72T-73
75Hawaii/Caruso-2
75IntLgAS/Broder-11
75PCL/AS-11
76SSPC-126

Hunziker, Kent
76Clinton
77AppFx

Huppert, David B.
(Dave)
80CharlO/Pol-10
80CharlO/W3TV-10
81RochR-9
83RochR-11
84Cram/PCL-37
86ElPaso-13
88CalLgAS-19
88Stockton/Cal-202MG
88Stockton/ProC-740
89Stockton/Best-29MG
89Stockton/Cal-176MG
89Stockton/ProC-386MG
89Stockton/Star-22MG
90ElPaso/GS-1MG
90TexLgAS/GS-18MG
91AA/LineD-199MG
91Crown/Orio-212MG
91ElPaso/LineD-199MG
91ElPaso/ProC-2762MG
92WSox-NNO

Hurd, Thomas
55T-116
55T/DH-120
56T-256

Hurdle, Clinton
(Clint)
76Watlo
78SSPC/270-229
78T-705R
79T-547
80OPC-273
80T-525
81D-224
81F-45
81OPC-98
81Pol/Royals-4
81T-98
81T/St-85
82Coke/Reds
82D-516
82F-411
82T-297
83Tidew-4
84Tidew-28
86D-434
86Schnucks-10
86T-438
87F-298
87OPC-317
87T-317
87Tidew-1
87Tidew/TCMA-22
89Pac/SenLg-111
89StLucie/Star-6
89T/SenLg-98
89TM/SenLg-50
89Tidew/Candl-12
90EliteSenLg-115
90Jacks/GS-5MG
91AA/LineD-649MG
91WIZMets-195
91Wmsprt/LineD-649MG
91Wmsprt/ProC-309MG
92Tidew/ProC-MG
92Tidew/SB-574MG

Hurdle, Mike
80Utica-29

Hurlbert, Gordon
90EastLAS/ProC-EL47TR
90NewBrit/Best-15TR
90NewBrit/Star-27TR

Hurlbutt, Robert
90Ashvl/ClBest-18
90AubAs/Best-7
90AubAs/ProC-3416
91Ashvl/ProC-570

Hurley, Battling
T3/Box-71

Hurley, Edwin
55B-260UMP

Hurley, Mike
89OK-15

Hurley, Pat
90Target-991

Hurni, Rick
88SLCity-12

Hursey, Darren
87Fayette-13
88Lakeland/Star-16
89London/ProC-1370
90Lakeland/Star-13
91AA/LineD-387
91London/LineD-387
91London/ProC-1873

Hurst, Bill
91Johnson/ProC-3973

Hurst, Bruce
81Pawtu-3
81T-689R
82F-297
82T-381R
83D-134
83F-186
83T-82
84D-213
84F-400
84Nes/792-213
84OPC-213
84T-213
84T/St-226
85D-493
85F-161
85Leaf-73
85OPC-134
85T-451
85T/St-211
86D-517
86D/HL-47
86F-352
86OPC-193
86T-581
86T/Mini-6
87Classic-83
87D-174
87F-37
87F/BB-22
87F/St-65
87F/WS-1
87Leaf-253
87OPC-31
87Sf-38
87Sf/TPrev-9M
87T-705
87T/HL-19
87T/HL-28
87T/Mini-43
87T/St-19WS
87Woolwth-19
87Woolwth-28
88D-252
88D/AS-14
88D/Best-233
88D/RedSox/Bk-252
88F-356
88F/BB/AS-18
88F/St-10
88Leaf-179
88OPC-125
88Panini/St-22
88RedFoley/St-37
88S-380
88Sf-197
88T-125
88T/St-253
88T/St/Backs-62
89B-451
89Classic/Up/2-194
89Coke/Padre-7
89D-423
89D/Best-77
89D/Tr-45
89F-91
89F/Up-124
89Padre/Mag-21
89Panini/St-271
89S-325
89S/HotStar-79
89S/Tr-19
89Sf-175
89T-675
89T/Gloss60-28
89T/LJN-115
89T/Mini-49
89T/St/Backs-29
89T/Tr-55T
89T/UK-42
89UD-387
89UD/Ext-792
90B-208
90Classic-102
90Coke/Padre-8
90D-183
90D/BestNL-84
90F-159
90F/BB-19
90F/Can-159
90Leaf-23
90MLBPA/Pins-57
90OPC-315
90Padre/MagUno-23
90Panini/St-357
90PubInt/St-51
90S-270
90S/100St-18
90Sf-47
90T-315
90T/Big-324
90T/Mini-81
90T/St-108
90T/TVAS-48
90UD-433
91B-661
91Classic/200-84
91D-83
91F-533
91Leaf-469
91MajorLg/Pins-56
91OPC-65
91Padre/MagRal-19
91Padre/MagRal-5
91Panini/Top15-90
91S-145
91StCl-475
91T-65
91UD-602
91Ultra-306
92B-187
92D-123
92F-608
92L-216
92L/BlkGold-216
92Mother/Padre-20
92OPC-595
92Padre/Carl-9
92Panini-238
92Pinn-40
92Pol/Padre-10
92S-111
92Smok/Padre-13
92StCl-312
92T-595
92T/Gold-595
92T/GoldWin-595
92TripleP-57
92UD-437
92Ultra-280
93D-576
93F-521
93L-341
93Mother/Padre-9
93OPC-118
93Panini-256
93Pinn-327
93S-133
93Select-141
93Select/Ace-19
93StCl-347
93StCl/1stDay-347
93T-111
93T/Gold-111
93UD-304
93Ultra-474
94Pinn-504
94StCl/Team-243

Hurst, Charles
(Charlie)
89Martins/Star-15
90Batavia/ProC-3059
91Spartan/ClBest-7
91Spartan/ProC-892
92Spartan/ClBest-13
92Spartan/ProC-1261

Hurst, Frank O.
(Don)
29Exh/4-11
31Exh/4-12
33Exh/4-6
34Exh/4-6
34G-33
92Conlon/Sport-519
R316
V354-80

Hurst, Harry
45Parade*-66

Hurst, James
92CharlR/ClBest-7
92CharlR/ProC-2223
94B-483
94B-625
94Select-199

Hurst, Jody
88CapeCod/Sum-110
88MissSt-13
89MissSt-21
89Niagara/Pucko-12
90Lakeland/Star-14
90Star/ISingl-35
92Toledo/ProC-1054
92Toledo/SB-588

Hurst, Jonathan
88CharlR/Star-10
89CharlR/Star-10
90Foil/Best-105
90Gaston/Best-9
90Gaston/ProC-2518
90Gaston/Star-11
90SALAS/Star-12
91ClBest/Singl-199
91FSLAS/ProC-FSL23
91Miami/ClBoct-8
91Miami/ProC-402
92B-388
92D/Rook-57
92Indianap/SB-184
92Sky/AAASingl-90
93Ottawa/ProC-2431
93Pinn-242
93S-299
93StCl-306
93StCl/1stDay-306
93T-727
93T/Gold-727
94Ultra-529

Hurt, Mike
89Reading/Best-26

Hurta, Robert 1
(Bob)
88Spartan/ProC-1026
88Spartan/Star-8

Hurta, Robert 2
(Bob)
90AubAs/Best-2
90AubAs/ProC-3399
91BurlAs/ClBest-5
91BurlAs/ProC-2796
92Jacks/ProC-3997
92Jacks/SB-334
92Tucson/ProC-483

Hurtado, Edwin
93StCath/ClBest-11
93StCath/ProC-3969

Hurtado, Jose
85Bend/Cram-12

Husband, Perry
85Visalia-3

Huseby, Ken
87Tampa-4
88Greens/ProC-1564
89Augusta/ProC-503

Huskey, Butch
90Kgsport/Star-11
91Clmbia/PCPII-5
91Clmbia/PII-29
91Clmbia/PII-30M
91SALAS/ProC-SAL16
92B-539
92ClBest-273
92ColumMet/SAL/II-42FB
92StLucie/ClBest-1
92StLucie/ProC-1752
92UD/ML-269
92UD/ML-37M
93B-46
93ClBest/MLG-70
93D-506RR
93FExcel/ML-74
93UD-436TP
94B-100
94D-426
94F/MLP-16
94L/GRook-3
94Pac/Cr-405
94Pinn-235
94Pinn/Artist-235
94Pinn/Museum-235
94Pinn/New-12
94Pinn/RookTPinn-4M
94S-605
94S/Boys-52
94Sf/2000-149

94T-179
94T/Gold-179
94TripleP-297
94UD-17
94UD/CollC-10
94UD/CollC/Gold-10
94UD/CollC/Silv-10
94UD/ElecD-17
Huslig, James
88OK-1
89OK-16
90ClintUp/Team-U7
90Everett/Best-6
90Everett/ProC-3122
90OK-14
Huson, Jeff
86BurlEx-10
87WPalmB-23
88Jaxvl/Best-18
88Jaxvl/ProC-966
88SLAS-18
89AAA/CMC-4
89AAA/ProC-11
89Indianap/CMC-18
89Indianap/ProC-1233
89S/HotRook-69
90D-693
90D/BestAL-83
90D/Rook-11
90F-350
90F/Can-350
90F/Up-123
90Leaf-285
90Mother/Rang-23
90OPC-72
90S-615
90S/100Ris-14
90S/DTRook-B7
90S/Tr-41T
90S/YS/I-41
90Sf-176
90T-72
90T/Tr-45T
90TripleAAS/CMC-4
90UD-434
90UD/Ext-788
91B-273
91Bz-16
91D-305
91F-289
91Leaf-134
91Mother/Rang-23
91OPC-756
91Panini/FrSt-255
91Panini/St-206
91S-263
91S/100RisSt-18
91StCl-160
91T-756
91T/JumboR-13
91ToysRUs-12
91UD-195
91Ultra-349
92D-456
92F-308
92L-251
92L/BlkGold-251
92Mother/Rang-23
92OPC-314
92Panini-78
92S-466
92StCl-341
92T-314
92T/Gold-314
92T/GoldWin-314
92UD-196
92Ultra-133
93D-583
93F-324
93L-137
93Pac/Spanish-312
93Panini-83
93Rang/Keeb-411
93StCl-281
93StCl/1stDay-281
93StCl/Rang-12
93T-143
93T/Gold-143
93UD-289
93Ultra-280
94D-432
94Pac/Cr-619
94StCl/Team-253
Hust, Gary
90LitSun/HSPros-15
90LitSun/HSProsG-15
91SoOreg/ClBest-16
91SoOreg/ProC-3862
92Madis/ClBest-9
92Madis/ProC-1249
92ProC/Tomorrow-134
Huston, Pat
91Geneva/ClBest-9
91Geneva/ProC-4224
Hutcheon, Mike
88MissSt-37M
89MissSt-44M
Hutcheson, Dave
93Peoria/Team-10
Hutcheson, Joe
90Target-992
Hutcheson, Todd
83Miami-28TR
84Beaum-23TR
85Beaum-23TR
86LasVegas-7TR
87LasVegas-13TR
88LasVegas/ProC-226TR
89LasVegas/ProC-28TR
90LasVegas/CMC-25TR
90ProC/Singl-683TR
Hutchings, John R.
W711/2
Hutchingson, Chris
86Osceola-14
Hutchins, Jason
92Bend/ClBest-15
93B-584
93FExcel/ML-34
93T-537
93T/Gold-537
Hutchins, Lance
88SanJose/Cal-144
88SanJose/ProC-124
Hutchinson, Don
88CapeCod/Sum-68
Hutchinson, Fred
47TipTop
48L-163
49B-196
50B-151
51B-141
52B-3
52StarCal-86CM
52StarCal/L-72E
52T-126
53B/Col-132
53NB
53T-72
60T-219MG
61T-135MG
62T-172MG
63FrBauer-9MG
63T-422MG
64T-207MG
75Shakey-11
79TCMA-138
80Pac/Leg-25
81Tiger/Detroit-48MG
82Ohio/HOF-40
91T/Arc53-72
Exh47
R303/A
V351A-16
V351B-26
Hutchinson, Ira
39PlayBall-142
90Target-374
W754
Hutchinson, Ray
(Harpo)
76Dubuq
Hutchinson, Sean
89Pulaski/ProC-1909
Hutchinson, William
N172
Huth, Ken
84Savan-7
Hutson, Jason
90Myrtle/ProC-2771
Hutson, Roy
90Target-993
Hutson, Scott
89StCath/ProC-2074
Hutto, Jim
75IntAS/TCMA-11
75IntAS/TCMA-17
76SSPC-385
84Newar-23
84RochR-4
91Crown/Orio-213
Hutto, Paul
90Gate/ProC-3351
90Gate/SportP-13
Hutton, Mark
89Oneonta/ProC-2118
90Greens/Best-4
90Greens/ProC-2656
90Greens/Star-7
91FSLAS/ProC-FSL13
91FtLaud/ClBest-5
91FtLaud/ProC-2419
92Albany/ProC-2223
92Albany/SB-12
92B-598
92ClBest-5
92ClBest/BBonusC-2
92ClBest/RBonus-BC2
92D/Rook-58
92L/GRook-6
92Sky/AASingl-7
92UD/ML-147
93B-651
93ClBest/MLG-2
93ColClip/Pol-8
93D-671RR
93FExcel/ML-209
93StCl/Y-24
93T-806
93T/Gold-806
94B-437
94D-87
94Pac/Cr-423
94Pinn-412
94Pinn/RookTPinn-9
94S-608
94S/Boys-32
94Sf/2000-166
94StCl-279
94StCl/1stDay-279
94StCl/Gold-279
94StCl/Team-182
94T-269
94T/Gold-269
94UD-18
94UD/CollC-11
94UD/CollC/Gold-11
94UD/CollC/Silv-11
94UD/ElecD-18
Hutton, Tom
67T-428R
69T-266R
72Dimanche*-22
72T-741R
73OPC-271
73T-271
74OPC-443
74T-443
75OPC-477
75T-477
75T/M-477
76OPC-91
76SSPC-472
76T-91
77T-264
78Ho-103
78T-568
79OPC-355
79T-673
80OPC-219
80T-427
81D-93
81F-164
81OPC-374
81T-374
85SpokAT/Cram-9
90Swell/Great-87
90Target-375
Huyke, Woody
78Charl
Huyler, Mike
88Watertn/Pucko-19
89Augusta/ProC-509
90CLAS/CL-22
90Salem/Star-8
91AA/LineD-111
91CaroMud/LineD-111
91CaroMud/ProC-1093
91ClBest/Singl-300
92Beloit/ClBest-26
92Beloit/ProC-411
Hvizda, James
(Jim)
89Gaston/ProC-1019
89Gaston/Star-9
89SALAS/GS-25
89Star/IISingl-140
90CharlR/Star-11
90Tulsa/Team-12
91Beloit/ClBest-28
91Beloit/ProC-2098
Hyatt, Robert Ham
D322
E104
E286
E90/2
M116
T207
Hyde, Bubba
91Negro/Lewis-29
Hyde, Cowan
92Negro/Retort-29
93TWill-106
Hyde, Dick
57T-403
58T-156
59T-498
60T-193
91Crown/Orio-214
Hyde, Matt
91QuadC/ClBest-5CO
91QuadC/ProC-2647CO
92QuadC/ClBest-28CO
92QuadC/ProC-828CO
Hyde, Mickey
89Batavia/ProC-1931
90Bend/Legoe-4
91Clearw/ClBest-21
91Clearw/ProC-1632
92Clearw/ClBest-6
92Reading/ProC-587
Hyde, Rich
91Everett/ProC-3908
92Clinton/ClBest-2
Hyde, Scott
75T/Photo-123
Hydes, Kyle
75Phoenix/Caruso-20
Hyers, Tim
90MedHat/Best-3
91Myrtle/ClBest-20
91Myrtle/ProC-2954
92Dunedin/ClBest-10
92Dunedin/ProC-2007
93Knoxvl/ProC-1259
94B-148
94ClBest/Gold-109
94Pinn-530
94Ultra-578
Hyman, Don
81QuadC-2
83MidldC-17
84MidldC-3
Hyman, Pat
89Clmbia/Best-24
Hymel, Gary
90LSUPol-7
91LSU/Pol-12M
91LSU/Pol-7
92Albany/ClBest-24
92Albany/ProC-2309
92ClBest-9
93BurlB/ClBest-12
93BurlB/ProC-160
93Ottawa/ProC-2438
Hypes, Kyle
75Lafay
76Phoenix/Coke-10
77Phoenix
78Cr/PCL-22
79Phoenix
Hyson, Cole
89AubAs/ProC-2170
90Osceola/Star-10
91Osceola/ClBest-4
91Osceola/ProC-676
92Watlo/ClBest-25
Hyzdu, Adam
90A&AASingle/ProC-169
90Classic/DP-15
90Classic/III-90
90Everett/Best-1
90Everett/ProC-3140
91B-617
91ClBest/Singl-321
91Clinton/ClBest-20
91Clinton/ProC-847
91S-388FDP
92AS/Cal-5
92SanJose/ClBest-8
92UD/ML-244
Iacona, Andy
87SLCity/Taco-7BB
Iadarola, George
80WHave-18
Iannini, Steve
87Modesto-15
Iasparro, Donnie
86Visalia-11
Iavarone, Greg
87Peoria-9
90Tulsa/ProC-1159
90Tulsa/Team-13
91AA/LineD-585
91Tulsa/LineD-585
91Tulsa/ProC-2775
91Tulsa/Team-14
Ibarguen, Ricky
89Bristol/Star-12
Ibarguen, Steve
82Jacks-5
Ibarra, Carlos
82Edmon-1
Ibarra, Luis
85Tigres-28
Ice, Lee
89KS*-89
Ickes, Mike
87WinHaven-25
Iglesias, Luis
87Spartan-18
88Clearw/Star-15
Iglesias, Michael
91Kissim/ProC-4178
Ignasiak, Mike
89AS/Cal-39
89Stockton/Best-3
89Stockton/Cal-157
89Stockton/ProC-400
89Stockton/Star-5
90ElPaso/GS-18
90Stockton/Best-16
90Stockton/Cal-177
90Stockton/ProC-2176
91AAA/LineD-142
91Denver/LineD-142
91Denver/ProC-121
92B-15
92Denver/ProC-2635
92Denver/SB-131
92S-837RP
92Sky/AAASingl-64
92T/91Debut-88
93F/Final-224
94F-179
94Pol/Brew-13
94StCl-489
94StCl/1stDay-489
94StCl/Gold-489
94T-564
94T/Gold-564
94Ultra-76
Ikesue, Kazutaka
91Salinas/ClBest-21
91Salinas/ProC-2236
Ikeue, Kouichi
87SLCity/Taco-15
Ilsley, Blaise
86Ashvl-15
87ColAst/ProC-8
88ColAst/Best-17
89Osceola/Star-8
91AAA/LineD-613
91Tucson/LineD-613
91Tucson/ProC-2211
92Louisvl/ProC-1884
92Louisvl/SB-265
94B-188
94Ultra-459
Imes, Rodney
(Rod)
87Oneonta-25
88FtLaud/Star-12
89Albany/Best-21
89Albany/ProC-314
89Albany/Star-8
89BBAmAA/BPro-AA8
89EastLgAS/ProC-10

90AAASingl/ProC-539
90AlbanyDG/Best-16
90Nashvl/CMC-7
90Nashvl/ProC-227
90ProC/Singl-132
91AAA/LineD-262
91Nashvl/LineD-262
91Nashvl/ProC-2152
92Chatt/ProC-3813
92Chatt/SB-187
Impagliazzo, Joe
86Albany/TCMA-27
Imperial, Jason
92Beloit/ProC-412
Inabata, Nelson
87Hawaii-2
Inagaki, Shuji
87Miami-13
88Miami/Star-12
Incaviglia, Pete
86D/Rook-23
86F/Up-U53
86Rang-29
86Sf/Rook-3
86T/Tr-48T
87Classic-16
87Classic/Up-131
87D-224
87D/OD-175
87F-128
87F-625M
87F/Hottest-24
87F/LL-25
87F/Mini-58
87F/Slug-21
87F/St-66
87Kraft-39
87Leaf-185
87Mother/Rang-2
87OPC-384
87RedFoley/St-130
87Sf-37
87Sf/TPrev-1
87Smok/R-15
87Stuart-26M
87T-550
87T/Coins-14
87T/Gloss60-29
87T/JumboR-6
87T/St-236
87T/St-308
87ToysRUs-12
88Classic/Red-177
88D-304
88D/Best-55
88F-470
88F/Mini-56
88F/SS-C1
88F/Slug-20
88F/St-65
88Grenada-33
88KennerFig-55
88Leaf-147
88Mother/R-2
88Nestle-20
88OPC-280
88Panini/St-207
88S-485
88S/YS/I-32
88Sf-169
88Smok/R-4
88T-280
88T/Big-73
88T/St-239
89B-238
89D-3DK
89D-56
89D/Best-144
89D/DKsuper-3DK
89F-523
89F/LL-21
89KennerFig-68
89KingB/Discs-24
89Mother/R-10
89OPC-42
89Panini/St-455
89RedFoley/St-63
89S-201
89Sf-112
89Smok/R-16
89T-706
89T/Big-127
89T/LJN-16
89T/St-249
89UD-484
90B-491
90D-48
90F-301
90F/Can-301
90Leaf-231
90Mother/Rang-4
90OPC-430
90Panini/St-157
90PublInt/St-413
90S-93
90T-430
90T/Big-81
90T/St-247
90UD-333
91B-131
91CokeK/Tiger-29
91D-464
91F-290
91Leaf-366
91OPC-172
91OPC/Premier-67
91Panini/FrSt-258
91RedFoley/St-51
91S-278
91S/RookTr-3T
91StCl-78
91T-172
91T/Tr-57T
91UD-453
91UD/Ext-747
92B-43
92F-139
92L-458
92L/BlkGold-458
92Mother/Ast-4
92OPC-679
92OPC/Premier-126
92Pinn-325
92S-306
92S/RookTr-17T
92StCl-874
92T-679
92T/Gold-679
92T/GoldWin-679
92T/Tr-54T
92T/TrGold-54T
92UD-271
92UD-759
92USPlayC/Tiger-13C
92USPlayC/Tiger-5C
92Ultra-491
93D-480
93F-436
93F/Final-110
93Flair-103
93L-276
93OPC-242
93OPC/Premier-95
93Pac/Spanish-577
93Phill/Med-18
93Pinn-492
93Rang/Keeb-201
93S-568
93Select/RookTr-114T
93StCl-47
93StCl-636
93StCl/1stDay-47
93StCl/1stDay-636
93StCl/Phill-22
93T-7
93T/Gold-7
93T/PreProd-7
93T/Tr-73T
93UD-522
93UD/SP-176
93Ultra-442
94B-84
94D-594
94F-591
94L-265
94Pac/Cr-477
94Phill/Med-13
94Pinn-468
94S-416
94StCl/Team-215
94Studio-140
94T-323
94T/Finest-140
94T/FinestRef-140
94T/Gold-323
94UD-491
94UD/CollC-144
94UD/CollC/Gold-144
94UD/CollC/Silv-144
94Ultra-246
Incavigua, Tony
81Buffa-20
Indriago, Juan
92AppFox/ClBest-24
Infante, Alexis
85Syrac-14
86Syrac-14
87Syrac-8
87Syrac/TCMA-15
88Syrac/CMC-21
88Syrac/ProC-813
89D/Rook-30
90B-17
90Brave/Dubuq/Perf-12
90Brave/Dubuq/Singl-14
90PublInt/St-517
Infante, Kennedy
(Ken)
86StPete-14
87ArkTr-5
88ArkTr/GS-11
89Cedar/Best-15
89Cedar/Star-28
90Clearw/Star-9
Infante, Tom
89Hamil/Star-19
90Spring/Best-17
Ingalls, Rick
88Bend/Legoe-29CO
89BendB/Legoe-28CO
Ingle, Mike
86Kinston-10
Ingle, Randy
83Ander-4
84Durham-29
85Greenvl/Team-8
86Greenvl/Team-14
87Greenvl/Best-4
89Greenvl/Best-21
89Greenvl/ProC-1177
90Greenvl/ProC-1146CO
90Greenvl/Star-24CO
90Pulaski/Best-26MG
90Pulaski/ProC-3114MG
91AA/LineD-225M
91Greenvl/ClBest-28CO
91Pulaski/ClBest-14MG
91Pulaski/ProC-4022MG
92Greenvl/SB-250CO
92Pulaski/ClBest-27MG
92Pulaski/ProC-3195MG
93Macon/ClBest-27MG
93Macon/ProC-1417MG
Ingram, Gerald
(Garey)
88Eugene/Best-26
90GreatF/SportP-18
91Bakers/Cal-14
91CalLgAS-12
92SanAn/ProC-3986
Ingram, Jeff
89Utica/Pucko-11
90SoBend/Best-5
90SoBend/GS-6
Ingram, John
90Batavia/ProC-3061
91Martins/ClBest-22
91Martins/ProC-3449
Ingram, Linty
89Fayette/ProC-1572
90Fayette/ProC-2402
92HighD/ClBest-10
92LasVegas/SB-242
Ingram, Riccardo
89Lakeland/Star-10
90London/ProC-1280
91AA/LineD-388
91London/LineD-388
91London/ProC-1890
92B-164
92Sky/AAASingl-264
92Toledo/ProC-1055
92Toledo/SB-589
92UD/ML-213
Ingram, Todd
91SoOreg/ClBest-9
91SoOreg/ProC-3835
92Reno/Cal-43
93Modesto/ClBest-12
93Modesto/ProC-795
Inks, Bert
90Target-994
Inman, Bert
90OK-16
91Oneonta/ProC-4150
92Greens/ClBest-17
92Greens/ProC-775
92Oneonta/ClBest-11
93Greens/ClBest-12
93Greens/ProC-881
Inman, Wade
88OK-21
89OK-17
Innis, Brian
83VeroB-5
Innis, Jeff
84Jacks-6
85Lynch-4
86Jacks/TCMA-6
87Tidew-8
87Tidew/TCMA-5
88D/Mets/Bk-NEW
88F/Up-U105
88T/Tr-54T
88Tidew/CANDL-21
88Tidew/CMC-3
88Tidew/ProC-1582
89Tidew/CMC-3
89Tidew/ProC-1950
90AAASingl/ProC-270
90D-408
90F-206
90F/Can-206
90Kahn/Mets-40
90OPC-557
90ProC/Singl-357
90T-557
90T/TVMets-13
90Tidew/CMC-6
90Tidew/ProC-539
90UD-562
91F/UltraUp-U97
91F/Up-U103
91Kahn/Mets-40
91OPC-443
91StCl-547
91T-443
91WIZMets-196
92D-587
92F-507
92Mets/Kahn-40
92OPC-139
92S-327
92StCl-863
92T-139
92T/Gold-139
92T/GoldWin-139
92TripleP-64M
92UD-298
92Ultra-234
93D-330
93F-476
93Mets/Kahn-40
93OPC-141
93Pac/Spanish-543
93Pinn-557
93S-409
93StCl-433
93StCl/1stDay-433
93T-297
93T/Gold-297
93UD-119
93Ultra-428
94F-566
94Pac/Cr-406
94S-291
94S/GoldR-291
94T-37
94T/Gold-37
Intorcia, Trent
87Wausau-21
88Miami/Star-13
Iorg, Dane
76OkCty/Team-13
80T-139
81D-311
81F-543
81T-334
82D-166
82F-116
82F/St-24
82T-86
83D-469
83F-10
83F/St-17M
83OPC/St-189WS
83OPC/St-190WS
83T-788
83T/Fold-3M
83T/St-189
83T/St-190
84D-571
84F-326
84F/X-55
84Nes/792-416
84T-416
84T/Tr-54
85D-252
85F-204
85T-671
86F-9
86F/Up-U54
86Kitty/Disc-9
86Sf-186M
86T-269
86T/St-18WS
86T/Tr-49T
87OPC-151
87T-690
Iorg, Garth
75FtLaud
75FtLaud/Sus-26
78T-704R
79Syrac/TCMA-12
79Syrac/Team-9
80Syrac-1
80Syrac/Team-11
81F-423
81OPC-78
81OPC/Post-16
81T-444
82D-353
82F-616
82OPC-83
82T-518
83D-306
83F-430
83F/St-2M
83F/St-7M
83OPC-326
83T-326
84D-561
84F-157
84Nes/792-39
84OPC-39
84T-39
84Tor/Fire-17
85D-363
85F-107
85OPC-168
85T-168
85Tor/Fire-15
86BJ/Ault-14
86D-640
86F-61
86Leaf-252
86OPC-277
86T-694
86Tor/Fire-18
87D-394
87F-229
87OPC-59
87T-751
87Tor/Fire-14
88D-444
88F-113
88OPC-273
88Panini/St-220
88S-204
88T-273
89Pac/SenLg-152
89T/SenLg-86
89TM/SenLg-51
90EliteSenLg-36
91Myrtle/ClBest-27MG
91Myrtle/ProC-2961MG
91Pac/SenLg-41
92Knoxvl/ProC-3006MG
92Knoxvl/SB-399MG
92Nabisco-28
93Knoxvl/ProC-1265MG
Ippolito, Rob
92AZ/Pol-6
Ireland, Billy
83Miami-13
Ireland, Rich
92Classic/DP-72
92FrRow/DP-61
93ClBest/MLG-190

93StCl/MurphyS-192
93T-767
93T/Gold-767
Ireland, Tim
77Jaxvl
81Omaha-18
81T-66R
89Pac/SenLg-104
89Salinas/Cal-146MG
89Salinas/ProC-1822MG
89T/SenLg-67
89TM/SenLg-52
90AAASingl/ProC-54CO
90EliteSenLg-69
90Phoenix/CMC-25CO
90Phoenix/ProC-28CO
90ProC/Singl-552CO
92Stockton/ClBest-23MG
92Stockton/ProC-51MG
Irish, Jeffrey
90Dunedin/Star-12
90StCath/ProC-3475
Irons, Alex
92Lipscomb-24M
93Lipscomb-13
Irvin, Kyle
88Eugene/Best-7
Irvin, Monte
51B-198
51T/RB-50
52B-162
52BR
52Dix
52RM-NL9
52StarCal-90AM
52StarCal/L-78F
52T-26
53B/Col-51
53Briggs
53Dix
53Exh/Can-6
53NB
53SM
53T-62
54DanDee
54Dix
54NYJour
54RM-NL5
54SM
54T-3
55Gol/Giants-14
55SM
55T-100
55T/DH-3
56T-194
76Shakey-137
77Galasso-26
79TCMA-168
80Perez/HOF-137
80SSPC/HOF
83D/HOF-15
86Negro/Frit-6
86Negro/Frit-89
88Negro/Duques-20
88Pac/Leg-79
89HOF/St-32
90Negro/Star-9
90Pac/Legend-32
90Perez/GreatMom-27
90Swell/Great-85
91LineD-42
91Negro/Lewis-20
91Swell/Great-44
91T/Arc53-62
92AP/ASG-10
92AP/ASG24K-10G
92Bz/Quadra-10
92FrRow/Irvin-Set
92Negro/Kraft-4
92Negro/Lee-1
92Negro/Retort-30
93AP/ASGCoke/Amo-10
93TWill-136
93TWill-146
93TWill-54
93UD/ATH-154M
93UD/ATH-163M
93UD/ATH-71
94T/Arc54-3
94TedW/54-21
Exh47
PM10/Sm-79
PM10/Sm-80
PM10/Sm-81
Irvine, Daryl
85Greens-17
86WinHaven-11
87NewBrit-14
88NewBrit/ProC-890
89EastLgAS/ProC-12
89NewBrit/ProC-611
89NewBrit/Star-7
89Star/IISingl-127
90AAASingl/ProC-429
90Pawtu/CMC-5
90Pawtu/ProC-457
90ProC/Singl-256
90T/TVRSox-46
91AAAGame/ProC-30
91F-98
91OPC-189
91Pawtu/ProC-33
91S-333RP
91StCl-122
91T-189
91T/90Debut-75
91Ultra-34
92F-41
92Pawtu/ProC-918
92Pawtu/SB-358
92S-726
92Sky/AAASingl-162
Irvine, Ed
81ElPaso-1
82Vanco-8
84Cram/PCL-44
Irwin, Arthur
N172
N284
N690
WG1-52
WG1-66
Irwin, Charles
90Target-376
E90/1
Irwin, Dennis
78Cr/PCL-9
Irwin, John
N172
Irwin, Michael
90AubAs/Best-13
90AubAs/ProC-3412
Irwin, Tom
92Batavia/ClBest-27
92Batavia/ProC-3259
Isa, Kelsey
87Penin-21
Isaac, Joe Keith
78Wisco
Isaac, Luis
76Wmsprt
81Batavia-28
88Gator-7CO
91Indian/McDon-30M
92ColoSp/ProC-767
92ColoSp/SB-100CO
Isaacson, Christopher
88Kinston/Star-11
Isakson, Herb
92MN-20M
Isales, Orlando
79OkCty
80OkCty
81OkCty/TCMA-8
82Indianap-10
83Indianap-18
Isbell, Frank
WG2-26
Isbell, William
E107
E90/1
T206
Ishibashi, Keith
87Hawaii-9
Ishmael, Michael
(Mike)
87BurlEx-19
87James-3
Isom, Jeff
93Welland/ClBest-8
93Welland/ProC-3350
Isringhausen, Jason
92GulfCM/ProC-3474
94B-326
94FExcel-235
Issac, Richard
86AppFx-11
Ithier, Pete
76Wmsprt
78SanJose-10
Iverson, Tom
89Greens/ProC-430
90CharWh/Best-28TR
91Princet/ClBest-30TR
92Cedar/ClBest-30TR
Ivie, Lonnie
81Miami-15
Ivie, Mike
72OPC-457R
72T-457R
73OPC-613R
73T-613R
76Ho-103
76OPC-134
76SSPC-127
76T-134
77BurgChef-134
77OPC-241
77Padre/SchCd-15
77T-325
78T-445
79Pol/Giants-15
79T-538
80OPC-34
80Pol/Giants-15
80T-62
81D-312
81F-435
81OPC-236
81T-236
81T/Tr-744
82D-396
82T-734
82T/Tr-45T
83D-485
83F-331
83OPC-117
83T-613
Ivie, Ryan
92Watlo/ClBest-7
92Watlo/ProC-2139
Ivie, Tom
91CharRain/ClBest-27
Ivory, James
(Sap)
92Negro/RetortII-20
Iwema, Todd
91Helena/SportP-17
Jabalera, Francisco
83ColumAst-12
Jablonowski, Pete
33G-83
V354-34
Jablonski, Ray
53Hunter
53T-189
54Hunter
54T-26
54Wilson
55RM-NL21
55T-56
55T/DH-51
56Kahn
56T-86
57Kahn
57T-218
58Hires-35
58SFCallB-11
58T-362
59T-342
61Union-H1
91T/Arc53-189
94T/Arc54-26
Jacas, Andre
86Madis/Pol-12
88StLucie/Star-12
Jacas, David
(Dave)
87Kenosha-12
88Kenosha/ProC-1389
89AS/Cal-8
89Visalia/Cal-109
89Visalia/ProC-1447
90AAASingl/ProC-262
90Portl/CMC-20
90Portl/ProC-192
90ProC/Singl-572
91AA/LineD-186
91ElPaso/LineD-186
91ElPaso/ProC-2760
92Huntsvl/ProC-3962
92Huntsvl/SB-311
92Sky/AASingl-132
Jaccar, Mike
77Ashvl
Jacinto, Larry
91GreatF/SportP-8
Jacklitsch, Fred
90Target-377
C46-62
D303
E101
E104
E105
E106
E107
E92
M116
T205
T206
T216
Jackman, Bill
86Negro/Frit-68
Jackowski, Bill
55B-284UMP
Jackson, Alvin
62T-464
63Bz-19
63F-48
63T-111
63T/SO
64T-494
64T/Coins-17
64T/SU
64T/St-85
64T/tatt
65T-381
65T/trans-17
66T-206
67OPC-195
67T-195
68T-503
69MB-125
69T-649
70OPC-443
70T-443
83Tidew-24CO
84Tidew-22CO
88LitFalls/Pucko-27
89French-31
91WIZMets-197
Jackson, Bo
86D/HL-43
86D/Rook-38
86Memphis/GoldT-10
86Memphis/SilverT-10
86SLAS-13
86Sf/Rook-40
86T/Tr-50T
87Classic-15
87Classic/Up-109
87D-35RR
87D/OD-205
87D/Rook-14
87F-369
87F/Slug-M4
87F/St-132M
87Leaf-35RR
87Sf-190
87Sf/TPrev-13
87T-170
87ToysRUs-13
88Classic/Blue-208
88D-220
88D/Best-119
88F-260
88Leaf-187
88OPC-8
88Panini/St-110
88RedFoley/St-38
88S-180
88Sf-148
88Smok/Royals-5
88T-750
88T/Big-49
88T/St-258
89B-126
89Classic-122
89Classic/Up/2-157
89D-208
89D/Best-169
89F-285
89KennerFig-69
89KingB/Discs-11
89OPC-84
89Panini/St-358
89RedFoley/St-64
89S-330
89S/Mast-1
89S/YS/I-5
89Sf-70
89T-540
89T-789TL
89T/Ames-17
89T/Big-238
89T/HeadsUp-8
89T/St-265
89T/UK-43
89Tastee/Discs-6
89UD-221
90B-378
90B/Ins-4
90Classic-2
90Classic-59
90Classic/Up-25
90CollAB-1
90D-1DK
90D-61
90D-650AS
90D/BestAL-63
90D/Bon/MVP-BC1
90D/GSlam-12
90D/Learning-38
90D/Preview-1
90D/SuperDK-1DK
90F-110
90F-635M
90F/AwardWin-19
90F/BB-20
90F/BBMVP-21
90F/Can-110
90F/Can-635M
90F/LL-19
90F/WaxBox-C15
90HotPlay/St-22
90Kenner/Fig-44
90KingB/Discs-17
90Leaf-125
90MCA/Disc-5
90MLBPA/Pins-104
90MSA/Soda-7
90OPC-300
90Panini/St-198M
90Panini/St-384
90Panini/St-84
90Post-14
90PublInt/St-350
90PublInt/St-596
90RedFoley/St-51
90S-280
90S-566AS
90S-687DT
90S-697M
90S/100St-40
90S/YS/I-1
90Sf-200
90Sunflower-4
90T-300
90T/Big-6
90T/Coins-19
90T/DH-35
90T/Gloss22-17
90T/Gloss60-44
90T/HeadsUp-8
90T/Mini-16
90T/St-155AS
90T/St-264
90T/TVAS-5
90Tetley/Discs-5
90UD-105
90UD-32TC
90UD-75HL
90WonderBrd-1
91Cadaco-32
91Classic/200-186
91Classic/I-48
91D-632
91D-BC10
91D/BC-BC10
91F-561
91F/ProV-5
91F/UltraG-6
91Kenner-28
91Kenner-29
91Kodak/WSox-8
91Leaf/Prev-19
91MajorLg/Pins-20
91OPC-600

91Panini/FrSt-281
91Panini/St-226
91Pol/Royal-12
91S-412RIF
91S-420HL
91S-5
91S-692MB
91S-773HL
91S/100SS-2
91S/RookTr-1T
91StCl-224
91T-600
91T/CJMini/I-25
91T/SU-20
91T/Tr-58T
91UD-545
91UD/Ext-744
91Ultra-149
92Classic/Game200-108
92D-470
92F-701M
92F-86
92Kenner/Fig-24
92Kenner/Fig-25
92OPC-290
92S-361
92S/Impact-53
92StCl-654
92StCl/MemberIV*-2
92T-290
92T/Gold-290
92T/GoldWin-290
92T/Kids-103
92T/McDonB-33
92TripleP-164
92UD-555
93B-415
93Cadaco-33
93Colla/DM-54
93F/Final-195
93Flair-186
93L-316
93OPC-151
93Pac/Jugador-8
93Pac/Spanish-389
93Pinn-524
93Pinn/HRC-43
93StCl-495
93StCl/1stDay-495
93StCl/WSox-2
93Studio-110
93T-400
93T/Finest-91AS
93T/FinestASJ-91AS
93T/FinestRef-91AS
93T/Gold-400
93UD-775
93UD/FunPack-199
93UD/FunPack-31HERO
93UD/OnDeck-D15
93UD/SP-255
93Ultra-534
93WSox-13
94B-535
94D-173
94D/LongBall-4
94F-84
94F/GoldM-5
94Finest-241
94Flair-23
94L-307
94OPC-116
94Pac/Cr-128
94Panini-49
94Pinn-509
94Pinn/Trib-4
94S-513
94S/GoldS-35
94StCl-167
94StCl/1stDay-167
94StCl/Gold-167
94Studio-12
94T-500
94T/Gold-500
94UD-117
94UD/DColl-W7
94UD/ElecD-117
94UD/HoloFX-16
94UD/SP-24
94Ultra-330

Jackson, Bubba
88Tulsa-17

Jackson, Chief
92ColClip/Pol-25

Jackson, Chuck
85Cram/PCL-67
86Tucson-8
87D/Rook-55
87F/Up-U47
88Mother/Ast-25
88Pol/Ast-14
88S-222
88T-94
89S-584
89Tucson/CMC-20
89Tucson/JP-8
89Tucson/ProC-205
89UD-323
91AAA/LineD-61
91Calgary/LineD-61
91Calgary/ProC-521
92OkCty/ProC-1921
92OkCty/SB-311
92Sky/AAASingl-143
93Edmon/ProC-1143

Jackson, Damian
92Burllnd/ClBest-3
92Burllnd/ProC-1664

Jackson, Danny
82CharR-6
83Omaha-6
84D-461
85D-374
85F-205
86D-95
86F-10
86Kitty/Disc-16
86Leaf-30
86NatPhoto-25
86Sf-186M
87D-157
87D/OD-203
87F-370
87T/Tr-51T
88D-132
88D/Best-166
88F-261
88F/Slug-21
88F/Up-U84
88Kahn/Reds-20
88OPC-324
88S-398
88S/Tr-2T
88T-324
88T/Tr-55T
89B-304
89Cadaco-31
89Classic-123
89D-124
89D/AS-52
89D/Best-54
89F-163
89F-636M
89F/BBAS-22
89F/BBMVP's-21
89F/Excit-25
89F/Heroes-24
89F/LL-22
89F/WaxBox-C15
89Kahn/Reds-20
89KennerFig-70
89KingB/Discs-23
89OPC-319
89Panini/St-225
89Panini/St-67
89Richm/Ko-CO
89S-555
89S/HotStar-75
89S/YS/II-41
89Sf-80
89T-395AS
89T-730
89T/DH-22
89T/Gloss60-57
89T/Hills-18
89T/LJN-99
89T/Mini-10
89T/St-143
89T/St/Backs-62
89UD-640
90B-44
90D-80
90F-422
90F/Can-422
90Kahn/Reds-13
90Leaf-279
90OPC-445
90Panini/St-255
90PublInt/St-264
90PublInt/St-32
90S-289
90Sf-89
90T-445
90T/St-142
90UD-120
91B-412
91Classic/200-69
91Cub/Mara-32
91Cub/Vine-14
91D-678
91D-96
91F-67
91F/UltraUp-U70
91F/Up-U78
91Leaf-268
91OPC-92
91OPC/Premier-68
91S-601
91S/RookTr-17T
91StCl-433
91T-92
91T/Tr-59T
91UD-414
91UD/Ext-723
92B-142
92Classic/Game200-86
92Cub/Mara-32
92D-91
92F-383
92L-381
92L/BlkGold-381
92OPC-619
92Pinn-457
92S-120
92StCl-406
92T-619
92T/Gold-619
92T/GoldWin-619
92UD-104
92USPlayC/Cub-10H
92USPlayC/Cub-5C
92Ultra-176
93D-202
93F-492
93F/Final-111
93Flair-104
93L-308
93Pac/Spanish-578
93Phill/Med-19
93Pinn-514
93S-421
93Select-371
93Select/RookTr-94T
93StCl/Phill-5
93UD-753
93Ultra-443
94D-131
94F-592
94Finest-320
94Flair-208
94L-83
94OPC-240
94Pac/Cr-478
94Phill/Med-14
94Pinn-144
94Pinn/Artist-144
94Pinn/Museum-144
94S-209
94S/GoldR-209
94StCl-296
94StCl/1stDay-296
94StCl/Gold-296
94StCl/Team-235
94Studio-141
94T-199
94T/Gold-199
94TripleP-176
94UD-453
94UD/CollC-145
94UD/CollC/Gold-145
94UD/CollC/Silv-145
94UD/SP-137
94Ultra-247

Jackson, Darrell
78OrlanTw
79T-246
79Toledo-18
80T-386
81D-547
81F-567
81OPC-89
81T-89
82D-179
82F-555
82T-193

Jackson, Darrin
82QuadC-22
84MidldC-16
86Pittsfld-10
87Iowa-25
88Berg/Cubs-30
88D/Cubs/Bk-NEW
88D/Rook-45
88F-641R
88F/Up-U78
88S/Tr-109T
88T/Tr-56T
89F-428
89S-360
89T-286
89T/JumboR-12
89ToysRUs-14
89UD-214
90D-641
90F-160
90F/Can-160
90OPC-624
90Padre/MagUno-6
90PublInt/St-195
90S-541
90T-624
90UD-414
91F/UltraUp-U112
91F/Up-U124
91Leaf-346
91OPC-373
91Padre/MagRal-6
91S-169
91T-373
92B-456
92D-292
92F-609
92L-129
92L/BlkGold-129
92Mother/Padre-15
92OPC-88
92Padre/Carl-10
92Panini-237
92Pinn-207
92Pol/Padre-11
92S-521
92Smok/Padre-14
92StCl-226
92T-88
92T/Gold-88
92T/GoldWin-88
92TripleP-189
92UD-328
93BJ/D/McDon-33
93BJ/Demp-22
93BJ/Fire-16
93D-230
93F-141
93F/Final-102
93L-140
93OPC-143
93Pac/Spanish-259
93Panini-264
93Pinn-125
93S-155
93Select-199
93Select/RookTr-133T
93StCl-19
93StCl/1stDay-19
93T-761
93T/Gold-761
93TripleP-138
93UD-258
93UD-673
93Ultra-118
93Ultra-642
94F-567
94Finest-262
94Flair-33
94L-300
94Pinn-531
94StCl-157
94StCl/1stDay-157
94StCl/Gold-157
94StCl/Team-150
94T-576
94T/Gold-576
94UD-411
94Ultra-339

Jackson, Doug
78DaytB

Jackson, Gayron
86AubAs-14

Jackson, Grant
66T-591R
67T-402R
68T-512
69OPC-174
69T-174
69T/4in1-21M
70MLB/St-91
70OPC-6
70T-6
71Bz
71MLB/St-300
71OPC-392
71T-392
72MB-158
72OPC-212
72T-212
73JP
73OPC-396
73T-396
74OPC-68
74T-68
74T/St-126
75OPC-303
75T-303
75T/M-303
76OPC-233
76SSPC-378
76T-233
77T-49
78T-661
79T-117
80OPC-218
80T-426
81D-15
81F-378
81OPC-232
81T-519
82D-518
82F-191
82OPC-104
82T-779
82T/Tr-46T
88EastLAS/ProC-48
89CharlK-2
89Chatt/II/Team-13
89Pac/SenLg-66
89TM/SenLg-53
91AAA/LineD-225
91Crown/Orio-215
91Iowa/LineD-225CO
91Iowa/ProC-1077CO
92Yank/WIZ70-78

Jackson, Greg
86Cram/NWL-85
87QuadC-30
87Salem/ProC-2420

Jackson, James B.
T206

Jackson, James
84Idaho/Team-13

Jackson, Jason
87BYU-8
88NewBrit/ProC-912
90Canton/Star-7

Jackson, Jeff
89Martins/Star-16
90B-157
90Batavia/ProC-3080
90OPC-74DP
90S-678DC
90T-74DP
91B-491
91ClBest/Singl-125
91Spartan/ClBest-26
91Spartan/ProC-911
92B-72
92Clearw/ClBest-1
92Clearw/ProC-2070
92UD/ML-301
93ClBest/MLG-99
93StCl/Phill-24

Jackson, Jelly
86Negro/Frit-96

Jackson, Joe 1
(Shoeless)
14CJ-103
15CJ-103
40PlayBall-225
77Galasso-154
77Galasso-259
77Shakey-21

80Laugh/3/4/5-13
80Laugh/FFeat-24
80Pac/Leg-107
82Ohio/HOF-48
88Pac/8Men-110
88Pac/8Men-13
88Pac/8Men-31
88Pac/8Men-32
88Pac/8Men-36
88Pac/8Men-37
88Pac/8Men-55M
88Pac/8Men-62
88Pac/8Men-69
88Pac/8Men-77
89Pac/Leg-220
91Conlon/Proto-14
91Conlon/Proto-400
92Conlon/13Nat-400
92Conlon/Col-21
92Conlon/Sport-444
93AP/ASG-131
93CrackJack-2
94Conlon-1030
94Conlon-1042M
94Conlon/Pr-1030
D327
D328-82
D329-87
D350/2-86
E135-82
E224
E90/1
M101/4-87
M101/5-86
W514-15

Jackson, Joe 2
76Clinton

Jackson, John
90Everett/Best-25
90Everett/ProC-3141
91ClBest/Singl-255
91SanJose/ClBest-26
91SanJose/ProC-23
91SanJose/ProC-26M
92ClBest-186
92MidldA/OneHour-8
92MidldA/SB-459
92UD/ML-205

Jackson, Kenneth
(Ken)
85Phill/TastyK-44
86Reading-10
87Maine-7
87Maine/TCMA-11
87Phill/TastyK-51
88Maine/CMC-17
88Maine/ProC-287
89ScranWB/CMC-17
89ScranWB/ProC-729

Jackson, Kenny 1
86Cram/NWL-37
87AppFx-28
88BBCity/Star-14
89Beloit/II/Star-15
90Stockton/Best-12
90Stockton/Cal-197
90Stockton/ProC-2197
91AA/LineD-187
91ElPaso/LineD-187
91ElPaso/ProC-2761
92Denver/ProC-2653
92Denver/SB-132

Jackson, Kenny 2
92LSU/McDag-13
93LSU/McDag-7

Jackson, LaVerne
85Greens-26
86WinHaven-12
87WinHaven-8
89EastLDD/ProC-DD31
89NewBrit/ProC-615
89NewBrit/Star-2
90Canton/ProC-1303

Jackson, Larry
81Cedar-1

Jackson, Lawrence C.
(Larry)
55Hunters-1
56T-119
57T-196
58T-97
59T-399
60L-15
60T-492
61P-174
61T-535
61T-75M
61T/St-88
62J-165
62P-165
62P/Can-165
62T-306M
62T-83
62T/St-184
62T/bucks
63T-95
64T-444
64T/Coins-114
64T/St-13
64T/tatt
64Wheat/St-22
65Bz-2
65OPC-10LL
65T-10LL
65T-420
66T-595
67CokeCap/Phill-14
67T-229
68OPC-81
68T-81
69MB-126
78TCMA-222
78TCMA-286
84Cub/Uno-2M

Jackson, Lee
90Canton/Best-13

Jackson, Lloyd
85Everett/II/Cram-5
86Clinton-11

Jackson, Lonnie
91Kissim/ProC-4201

Jackson, Lou
59T-130
61BeeHive-9
64T-511
78TCMA-115
91Crown/Orio-216

Jackson, Mark
86Cedar/TCMA-20
87Tampa-18

Jackson, Martinez
92Negro/Kraft-18

Jackson, Miccal
91Savan/ClBest-17
91Savan/ProC-1658

Jackson, Michael
86Reading-11
87D/Rook-36
87F/Up-U48
87Phill/TastyK-33
87Sf/Rook-33
88D-139
88F-306
88F/Up-U60
88Mother/Sea-19
88RedFoley/St-39
88S-144
88S/Tr-62T
88T-651
89B-207
89D-652
89F-550
89F/BBMVP's-22
89Mother/Sea-19
89OPC-169
89S-398
89S/YS/I-14
89T-169
89UD-142
90F-517
90F/Can-517
90Leaf-351
90Mother/Mar-19
90OPC-761
90PublInt/St-435
90S-546
90T-761
90UD-494
91CounHrth-23
91D-676
91F-454
91F/UltraUp-U51
91Leaf-452
91OPC-534
91S-91
91T-534
91UD-496
92B-513
92D-584
92F-282
92F/Up-128
92Giant/PGE-20
92L-481
92L/BlkGold-481
92Mother/Giant-12
92OPC-411
92Pinn-437
92S-194
92S/RookTr-40T
92StCl-653
92Studio-116
92T-411
92T/Gold-411
92T/GoldWin-411
92UD-593
92UD-738
92Ultra-590
93D-314
93F-156
93Flair-142
93L-84
93Mother/Giant-20
93Pac/Spanish-611
93StCl-373
93StCl/1stDay-373
93StCl/Giant-18
93T-283
93T/Gold-283
93UD-170
93Ultra-133
94D-525
94F-692
94Finest-311
94Flair-243
94L-301
94Pac/Cr-547
94S-243
94S/GoldR-243
94StCl/Team-25
94T-58
94T/Gold-58
94UD-311
94Ultra-290

Jackson, Mikki
83Madis/Frit-20
88OK-19M

Jackson, Ransom
(Randy)
52B-175
52StarCal-92B
52StarCal/L-80C
52T-322
53B/BW-12
54B-189
55B-87
56T-223
57T-190
58T-301
59T-394
90Target-378
92TX-26

Jackson, Ray
91Everett/ClBest-7
91Everett/ProC-3930
92ClBest-78
92Clinton/ClBest-9
92Clinton/ProC-3609

Jackson, Reggie
83Lynch-1
84Jacks-5

Jackson, Reginald M.
(Reggie)
68A's/JITB-9
69MB-127
69T-260
69T/S-28
69T/decal
70K-32
70MB-11
70MLB/St-260
70OPC-140
70OPC-459AS
70OPC-64LL
70OPC-66LL
70T-140
70T-459AS
70T-64LL
70T-66LL
70T/CB
70T/S-28
70T/Super-28
70Trans-11
71Bz/Test-18
71MLB/St-517
71MLB/St-562
71OPC-20
71T-20
71T/Coins-108
71T/GM-47
71T/Greatest-47
71T/S-38
71T/Super-38
71T/tatt-3
72K-20
72MB-159
72OPC-435
72OPC-436IA
72OPC-90LL
72ProStars/PostC-26
72T-435
72T-436IA
72T-90LL
73K-22
73OPC-255
73T-255
73T/Comics-8
73T/Lids-22
73T/PinUps-8
74K-20
74Laugh/ASG-71
74OPC-130
74OPC-202LL
74OPC-203LL
74OPC-338AS
74OPC-470ALCS
74OPC-477WS
74T-130
74T-202LL
74T-203LL
74T-338AS
74T-470ALCS
74T-477WS
74T/DE-61
74T/Puzzles-6
74T/St-226
75Ho-88
75K-54
75OPC-211M
75OPC-300
75OPC-461WS
75SSPC/42-11
75SSPC/Puzzle-12
75T-211MVP
75T-300
75T-461WS
75T/M-211MVP
75T/M-300
75T/M-461WS
76Crane-22
76Ho-146
76K-8
76MSA/Disc
76OPC-194LL
76OPC-500
76SSPC-494
76T-194LL
76T-500
77BK/Y-17
77BurgChef-176
77Ho-3
77Ho/Twink-3
77OPC-200
77Pep-34
77T-10
77T/CS-22
77T/ClothSt-22
78BK/Y-21
78Ho-47
78OPC-110
78OPC-242RB
78PapaG/Disc-26
78Pep-32
78SSPC/270-26
78T-200
78T-413WS
78T-7RB
78Wiffle/Discs-32
79BK/Y-21
79K-46
79OPC-374
79T-700
79T/Comics-12
80BK/PHR-17
80K-26
80OPC-314
80Perez/HOF-216
80T-600
80T/S-6
80T/Super-6TP
81D-228
81D-348
81D-468
81Drake-10
81F-650HL
81F-79
81F/St-115
81F/St-CLI
81K-3
81MSA/Disc-18
81OPC-370
81PermaGr/AS-14
81PermaGr/CC-7
81Sqt-5
81T-2LL
81T-400
81T/HT
81T/Nat/Super-8
81T/SO-3
81T/St-107
81T/St-11M
81T/St-245
82D-535
82D-575M
82Drake-19
82F-39
82F-646M
82F/St-110M
82F/St-112
82K-14
82KMart-23
82OPC-300
82OPC-301IA
82OPC-377AS
82PermaGr/AS-7
82PermaGr/CC-20
82Sqt-5
82T-300
82T-301IA
82T-551AS
82T/St-216
82T/StVar-216
82T/Tr-47T
83D-115
83D-3DK
83D/AAS-3
83Drake-12
83F-640M
83F-645M
83F-93
83F/St-27M
83F/St-3M
83K-3
83OPC-219SV
83OPC-390AS
83OPC-56
83OPC/St-163
83OPC/St-17
83OPC/St-41FOIL
83OPC/St-5
83PermaGr/CC-27
83Seven-5
83T-390AS
83T-500
83T-501SV
83T-702LL
83T/Fold-2M
83T/Gloss40-39
83T/LeadS-2
83T/St-163
83T/St-17M
83T/St-41
83T/St-5
83T/St/Box-4
84D-57
84D/AAS-36
84D/Champs-9
84Drake-15
84F-520
84MiltBrad-14
84Nes/792-100
84Nes/792-711LL
84Nes/792-712LL
84Nes/792-713LL
84OPC-100
84Ralston-19
84Seven-12W
84Smok/Cal-11
84T-100
84T-711LL
84T-712LL

84T-713LL
84T/Cereal-19
84T/RD-27
84T/St-102B
84T/St-231
84T/Super-21
85CircK-13
85D-57
85D/AAS-39
85Drake-17
85F-303
85F-639IA
85F/LimEd-14
85FunFood/Pin-16
85GenMills-19
85Leaf-170
85OPC-200
85Seven-12C
85Seven-13W
85Smok/Cal-2
85T-200
85T/3D-14
85T/Gloss22-19
85T/Gloss40-15
85T/RD-27
85T/St-187
85T/St-220
85T/Super-29
86BK/AP-12
86D-377
86D/HL-10
86Dorman-11
86Drake-3
86F-160
86F/HOF-6
86F/LimEd-26
86F/Mini-32
86F/Slug-18
86F/St-65
86GenMills/Book-2M
86Jiffy-8
86Leaf-173
86Meadow/Blank-7
86Meadow/Stat-6
86OPC-394
86OPC/WaxBox-I
86Quaker-26
86Seven/Coin-W9
86Sf-145M
86Sf-147M
86Sf-37
86Sf-59M
86Sf-61M
86Sf-71M
86Sf/Dec-53
86Smok/Cal-2
86T-700
86T/3D-13
86T/Gloss60-2
86T/St-177
86T/Super-35
86T/Tatt-17M
86T/WaxBox-I
86TrueVal-13
86Woolwth-15
87Classic-24
87D-210
87D/OD-22
87F-84
87F/Up-U49
87GenMills/Book-3M
87KMart-16
87Leaf-201
87Mother/A's-27M
87Mother/A's-5
87OPC-300
87RedFoley/St-108
87Sf-44
87Sf/TPrev-23M
87Smok/A's-7
87T-300
87T-312TBC
87T/Coins-15
87T/Gloss60-54
87T/HL-4
87T/Tr-52T
87Woolwth-4
88F-283
88Grenada-3
88Panini/St-175
88S-500
88S-501
88S-502
88S-503
88S-504
88Sf-120
89Kenner/BBGr-9
89Pac/Leg-111
89Smok/Angels-15
89T/LJN-33
90BBWit-42
90HOF/St-88
90UD/Jackson-Set
91BBBest/RecBr-8
91Crown/Orio-217
91Mother/A's-28CO
92UD/ASFF-46
92UD/HeroHL-HI5
92Yank/WIZ70-79
92Yank/WIZ80-89
92Yank/WIZAS-33
93UD/5thAnn-A9
93UD/ATH-135M
93UD/ATH-165
93UD/ATH-72
93UD/ATHPrev-2
93UD/ATHPrev-3M
93UD/ATHPrev-4
93UD/Clark-Set
93UD/FunPack-28HERO
93UD/Then-TN16
94TedW/500-2

Jackson, Robert
85Everett/II/Cram-6

Jackson, Roland
(Sonny)
65OPC-16R
65T-16R
66T-244R
67Ast/Team-8
67T-415
68CokeCap/Astro-8
68CokeCap/Brave-14
68Dexter-40
68OPC-187
68T-187
69MB-128
69OPC-53
69T-53
69T/St-5
70OPC-413
70T-413
71MLB/St-12
71OPC-587
71T-587
72MB-160
72OPC-318
72T-318
73OPC-403
73T-403
74Greyhound-6M
74OPC-591
74T-591
75Hawaii/Caruso-10
79Savan-8CO
80Ander-8CO
83Pol/Atl-36
84Durham-30CO
85Richm-25CO
87Greenvl/Best-3CO
89Richm/Bob-10CO
89Richm/CMC-24CO
89Richm/ProC-832
90AAASingl/ProC-422CO
90ProC/Singl-278M
90Richm/CMC-2CO
90Richm/ProC-277CO
90Richm/Team-14CO
91AAA/LineD-450M
91Richm/Bob-39CO
91Richm/LineD-450CO
91Richm/ProC-2587CO
92Richm/Bleach-23
92Richm/Comix-7
92Richm/ProC-393CO
92Richm/SB-450M

Jackson, Ron H.
55Armour-9
55T-66
55T/DH-49
56T-186
58T-26
59T-73
60L-29
60T-426

Jackson, Ron
85Louisvl-30
86Bakers-15
87Gaston/ProC-20

Jackson, Ronnie D.
75IntLgAS/Broder-12
75PCL/AS-12
75SLCity
75SLCity/Caruso-4
77BurgChef-120
77T-153
78SSPC/270-213
78T-718
79K-59
79OPC-173
79T-339
79Twin/FriszP-11
80OPC-5
80T-18
81D-489
81F-557
81OPC-271
81T-631
81T/St-103
82D-602
82F-269
82OPC-359
82Spokane-21
82T-488
82T/Tr-48T
83D-639
83F-94
83T-262
84D-133
84F-521
84Nes/792-548
84Smok/Cal-12
84T-548
88Vanco/ProC-768
89BirmB/Best-26
89BirmB/ProC-113
89Pac/SenLg-92
89T/SenLg-117
89TM/SenLg-54
90EliteSenLg-70
90Saraso/Star-28CO
91Crown/Orio-218
91Pac/SenLg-5

Jackson, Roy Lee
78Tidew
79Tidew-1
80Tidew-19
81D-36
81T-223
81T/Tr-775
82D-541
82OPC-71
82OPC/Post-7
82T-71
83D-479
83F-431
83OPC-194
83T-427
84D-195
84F-158
84Nes/792-339
84OPC-339
84T-339
84Tor/Fire-18
85D-606
85F-108
85Leaf-106
85OPC-37
85T-516
85T/St-364
86F-326
86T-634
87F-545
87T-138
91WIZMets-198

Jackson, Travis C.
(Stonewall)
25Exh-35
29Exh/4-10
31Exh/4-9
33CJ/Pin-14
33G-102
34DS-63
35BU-180
35G-1K
35G-3B
35G-4B
35G-5B
35Wheat
40PlayBall-158
61F-115
80Pac/Leg-87
80Perez/HOF-179
91Conlon/Sport-42
94Conlon-1101
R315-A18
R315-B18
V354-24
V89-36
W517-12
WG4-10
WG5-21
WG6-20

Jackson, Vince
91Kissim/ProC-4202
91LitSun/HSPros-9
91LitSun/HSProsG-9
92GreatF/SportP-2

Jackson, William
52Laval-34

Jacob, Mark
83SanJose-12

Jacobo, Ed
85VeroB-10
86VeroB-12

Jacobs, Anthony R.
55T-183

Jacobs, Elmer
WG7-22

Jacobs, Forrest
(Spook)
52Park-54
53Exh/Can-46
54T-129
55Rodeo
55T-61
55T/DH-47
56T-151
56T/Hocus-A17
88Chatt/Team-15
94T/Arc54-129
PM10/Sm-82

Jacobs, Frank
91ClBest/Singl-398
91Pittsfld/ClBest-4
91Pittsfld/ProC-3429
92ClBest-274
92StLucie/ClBest-24
92StLucie/ProC-1753

Jacobs, Jake
89Eugene/Best-4
90AppFox/Box-13
90AppFox/ProC-2090
91BBCity/ClBest-7
91BBCity/ProC-1394

Jacobs, Ron
77Holyo
78Holyo
79Vanco-3

Jacobsen, Nels
87BurlEx-3
88FSLAS/Star-9
88WPalmB/Star-12

Jacobsen, Robert
85VeroB-16
86VeroB-13

Jacobson, Albert
WG2-27

Jacobson, Jeff
82AubAs-3
85CharlO-3

Jacobson, Kevin
82Redwd-23

Jacobson, Merwin
90Target-379

Jacobson, William
(Baby Doll)
21Exh-80
25Exh-114
26Exh-114
87Conlon/2-43
88Conlon/4-14
93Conlon-740M
D327
E120
E121/120
E121/80
E122
E126-45
E220
V100
V117-18
W514-61
W572
W573
W575

Jacobucci, Steve
89Pittsfld/Star-26TR
90StLucie/Star-30
91Elmira/ClBest-30

Jacoby, Brook
80Ander-27
82Richm-13
83Richm-13
84D-542
84F/X-56
84T/Tr-55
84Wheat/Ind-26
85D-154
85F-452
85OPC-327
85Polar/Ind-26
85T-327
85T/St-251
85T/St-370YS
86D-154
86F-590
86F/Mini-116
86Leaf-82
86OPC-116
86OhHenry-26
86T-116
86T/St-207
86T/Tatt-5M
87Classic-40
87D-104
87D-8DK
87D/AAS-37
87D/DKsuper-8
87D/OD-112
87F-253
87Gator-26
87Ho/St-22
87Leaf-134
87Leaf-8DK
87OPC-98
87RedFoley/St-53
87Sf-109
87Sf/TPrev-3M
87T-405
87T/St-212
88D-131
88D/Best-229
88F-612
88F/Excit-22
88F/St-20
88Gator-26
88Leaf-51
88OPC-248
88Panini/St-76
88S-39
88Sf-72
88T-555
88T/Big-17
88T/St-211
88T/UK-38
89B-86
89D-114
89D/Best-61
89F-408
89KennerFig-71
89OPC-1
89Panini/St-326
89RedFoley/St-65
89S-19
89Sf-192
89T-141TL
89T-739
89T/Big-195
89T/St-212
89UD-198
90B-341
90D-83
90D/BestAL-75
90F-493
90F/Can-493
90Leaf-74
90OPC-208
90Panini/St-58
90PublInt/St-561
90Richm/25Ann-12
90S-56
90Sf-155
90T-208
90T/Big-276
90T/St-219
90UD-459
90USPlayC/AS-5C
91B-59
91D-176

91DennyGS-9
91F-369
91F/UltraUp-U46
91Indian/McDon-11
91Leaf-421
91Leaf/Stud-44
91OPC-47
91Panini/FrSt-216
91Panini/St-178
91S-162
91S/100SS-92
91StCl-286
91T-47
91UD-137
91UD/FinalEd-78F
91Ultra-113
92Classic/I-46
92D-670
92F-260
92Indian/McDon-13
92OPC-606
92Pinn-376
92S-577
92StCl-828
92T-606
92T/Gold-606
92T/GoldWin-606
92UD-528
92Ultra-349
93D-493
93F-593
93S-567
93T-303
93T/Gold-303
93UD-200
Jacoby, Don
91BurlInd/ProC-3322CO
Jacome, Jason
91Kingspt/ClBest-23
91Kingspt/ProC-3810
92ColumMet/ClBest-10
92ColumMet/SAL/II-28
92ColumMet/SAL/II-30M
92ProC/Tomorrow-292
92StLucie/ProC-1742
93StLucie/ProC-2918
94B-210
Jacques, Eric
89Wythe/Star-17
90Peoria/Team-24
91WinSalem/ClBest-6
91WinSalem/ProC-2825
Jaeckel, Paul
65T-386R
Jaffee, Irving
33SK*-34
Jagnow, Jim
85BurlR-17
Jaha, John
86Cram/NWL-195
87Beloit-3
88Stockton/Cal-193
88Stockton/ProC-743
89AS/Cal-45
89Stockton/Best-16
89Stockton/Cal-165
89Stockton/ProC-380
89Stockton/Star-3
91AA/LineD-188
91ClBest/Singl-291
91Daikyo/Fut-18
91ElPaso/LineD-188
91ElPaso/ProC-2756
92B-399
92B-542FOIL
92D-398RR
92Denver/ProC-2647
92Denver/SB-133
92F/Up-35
92OPC-126M
92ProC/Tomorrow-84
92Sky/AAASingl-65
92Sky/AASingl-290
92T-126M
92T/Gold-126M
92T/GoldWin-126M
93B-183
93D-207
93F-252
93Flair-225
93L-350
93OPC-190
93Pac/Spanish-159
93Pinn-228
93Pol/Brew-12
93S-236
93Select-308
93StCl-701
93StCl/1stDay-701
93Studio-89
93T-181
93T/Finest-152
93T/FinestRef-152
93T/Gold-181
93ToysRUs-91
93UD-177
93UD/SP-66
93Ultra-221
94B-65
94D-569
94F-180
94Flair-68
94L-317
94OPC-131
94Pac/Cr-331
94Panini-82
94Pinn-312
94Pol/Brew-14
94S-173
94S/GoldR-173
94Sf/2000-40
94StCl-105
94StCl/1stDay-105
94StCl/Gold-105
94Studio-45
94T-283
94T/Finest-106
94T/FinestRef-106
94T/Gold-283
94TripleP-54
94UD-476
94UD/CollC-146
94UD/CollC/Gold-146
94UD/CollC/Silv-146
94Ultra-77
Jaime, Angel
92GreatF/SportP-23
Jaime, Ismael
85Tigres-16
Jaime, Jorge
89LittleSun-17
Jaime, Juan
90Myrtle/ProC-2780
91Myrtle/ClBest-13
91Myrtle/ProC-2947
Jakubowski, John
81Batavia-30
Jakubowski, Stan
77Ashvl
79Tucson-6
Jakucki, Sigmund
(Jack)
47Centen-11
47Signal
James, Arthur
(Artie)
77Evansvl/TCMA-16
79RochR-6
James, Bevan
91Sydney/Fut-5
James, Bob
82Expo/Hygrade-10
82Hygrade
83Expo/PostC-7
83Wichita/Dog-11
84D-87
84Expo/PostC-13
84F-277
84Nes/792-579
84OPC-336
84Stuart-10
84T-579
85Coke/WS-43
85D-279
85F-400
85F/Up-U60
85OPC-114
85T-114
85T/Tr-61T
86Coke/WS-43
86D-379
86F-209
86F/St-66
86OPC-284
86Seven/Coin-C11M
86Sf-158
86T-467
86T/St-290
86T/Super-36
86T/Tatt-3M
87Coke/WS-24
87D-493
87F-501
87F/St-67
87OPC-342
87RedFoley/St-15
87Sf/TPrev-26M
87T-342
88D-507
88F-401
88OPC-232
88Panini/St-54
88T-232
88T/St-289
James, Calvin
85Miami-7
86Osceola-15
87Osceola-7
88ColAst/Best-26
James, Charles
(Charlie)
60T-517
61T-561
62T-412
63J-163
63P-163
63T-83
64T-357
65OPC-141
65T-141
78TCMA-292
James, Chris
85Cram/PCL-29
85Phill/TastyK-43
86F/Up-U55
86Phill/TastyK-26
86Portl-10
87D-42RR
87F/Up-U50
87Leaf-42RR
87Phill/TastyK-18
87T/Tr-53T
88D-453
88D/Best-159
88F-307
88OPC-1
88Panini/St-362
88Phill/TastyK-14
88S-409
88S/YS/I-14
88T-572
88T/St-122
89B-404
89Coke/Padre-8
89D-312
89D/Best-266
89F-572
89KennerFig-72
89OPC-298
89Padre/Mag-23
89Panini/St-156
89Phill/TastyK-12
89RedFoley/St-66
89S-202
89S/Tr-46
89T-298
89T/St-119
89T/Tr-56T
89UD-513
90B-340
90D-323
90D/GSlam-3
90F-161
90F/Can-161
90F/Up-U92
90Leaf-319
90OPC-178
90Panini/St-350
90PublInt/St-241
90S-498
90S/Tr-60T
90T-178
90T/St-105
90T/Tr-46T
90UD-435
90UD/Ext-798
91B-67
91D-227
91F-370
91Indian/McDon-15
91Leaf-175
91Leaf/Stud-45
91OPC-494
91Panini/St-181
91S-491
91StCl-422
91T-494
91UD-140
91Ultra-114
92D-82
92F-112
92Giant/PGE-21
92L-497
92L/BlkGold-497
92Mother/Giant-27
92OPC-709
92OPC/Premier-20
92S-262
92StCl-23
92StCl-747
92T-709
92T/Gold-709
92T/GoldWin-709
92UD-560
93D-604
93F-531
93F/Final-79
93Mother/Ast-21
93Pac/Spanish-272
93Pinn-120
93Rang/Keeb-412
93StCl/Ast-5
93T-38
93T/Gold-38
94Finest-385
94L-358
94UD-398
94Ultra-432
James, Cleo
72OPC-117
72T-117
74Wichita-113
90Target-380
James, Darin
84Everett/Cram-6B
85Everett/II/Cram-7
James, Dewey
82Beloit/Frit-11
83Beloit/Frit-3
James, Dion
82ElPaso-2
84D-31RR
84F/X-57
84Pol/Brew-14
85D-211
85F-584
85Gard-9
85Leaf-162
85Pol/Brew-14
85T-228
86D-89
86T-76
86Vanco-13
87Classic/Up-144
87D/OD-44
87F/Up-U51
87Sf/TPrev-24M
87Smok/Atl-24
87T/Tr-54T
88D-190
88D/Best-29
88F-543
88F/Mini-64
88F/St-76
88OPC-82
88Panini/St-250
88S-395
88S/YS/I-7
88Sf-36
88T-408
88T/Big-220
88T/Coins-44
88T/Mini-40
88T/St-42
88T/UK-39
89B-277
89D-340
89D/Best-253
89F-594
89KennerFig-73
89Panini/St-44
89S-163
89S/Tr-51T
89T-678
89T/Big-223
89T/St-24
89UD-587
90B-331
90D-428
90ElPasoATG/Team-14
90F-494
90F/Can-494
90OPC-319
90Panini/St-64
90PublInt/St-115
90S-514
90T-319
90T/Big-132
90UD-591
91D-348
91F-371
91OPC-117
91S-131
91T-117
91UD-399
92B-494
92L-365
92L/BlkGold-365
92StCl-884
92Ultra-409
93D-735
93F-649
93Pac/Spanish-556
93StCl-266
93StCl/1stDay-266
94D-446
94F-232
94Pac/Cr-424
94S-175
94S/GoldR-175
James, Duane
85Tulsa-29
86Salem-13
James, Howard
90Cedar/Best-27GM
James, Jeff
69T-477
70OPC-302
70T-302
James, Joey
89Watertn/Star-10
90A&AASingle/ProC-127
90Clinton/Best-20
90Clinton/ProC-2554
90Foil/Best-127
90MidwLgAS/GS-36
91CalLgAS-33
91ClBest/Singl-378
91SanJose/ClBest-29
91SanJose/ProC-18
James, John
60T-499
61T-457
92Yank/WIZ60-59
James, Keith
87Pocatel/Bon-22
James, Mike
88GreatF-23
89Bakers/Cal-186
90SanAn/GS-15
90TexLgAS/GS-14
91AA/LineD-536
91SanAn/LineD-536
91SanAn/ProC-2969
92Albuq/SB-11
92SanAn/ProC-3970
93B-674
93StCl/Dodg-26
James, Paul
86DayBe-13
James, Richard
83StPete-22
James, Robert Byrne
33G-208
James, Skip
75Phoenix-14
75Phoenix/Caruso-5
75Phoenix/CircleK-14
76Phoenix/Coke-11
77Phoenix
79Vanco-1
James, Sonny
84Savan-1
James, Todd
88Bend/Legoe-23
89PalmSp/Cal-56
91AA/LineD-437
91MidldA/LineD-437
91MidldA/ProC-431
92Edmon/SB-161

92MidldA/OneHour-9
92MidldA/ProC-4022
92Sky/AAASingl-80
James, Troy
86Columbia-14
87Lynch-23
88Visalia/Cal-164
88Visalia/ProC-88
James, William
15CJ-153
88Conlon/5-17
94Conlon-1035
94Conlon-1041M
BF2-52
D328-84
D329-88
D350/2-87
E135-84
M101/4-88
M101/5-87
Jameyson, Rick
92Watertn/ClBest-29
Jamieson, Charles
21Exh-81
25Exh-82
28Exh-41
33G-171
93Conlon-692
D328-85
E120
E126-21
E135-85
R316
V100
W572
Jamison, Alonzo
89KS*-47
Jamison, Bob
87Nashvl-25M
89Nashvl/Team-26ANN
Jamison, David
85Clovis-23
Janeski, Gerry
71MLB/St-543
71OPC-673
71T-673
93Rang/Keeb-19
Janiak, Joseph
52Laval-8
Janicki, Pete
92Classic/DP-119
93B-641
93Pinn-468DP
93S-500DP
93UD-422TP
Janikowski, Randy
88Boise/ProC-1619
Janney, Barry
77Spartan
Janowicz, Vic
53T-222
54B-203
54T-16
55B-114
72T/Test-8
91T/Arc53-222
94T/Arc54-16
Jansen, Larry
47HomogBond-22
48B-23
48L-56
49B-202
49Eureka-110
50B-66
51B-162
51FB
51T/RB-21
52B-90
52BR
52RM-NL10
52StarCal-90B
52StarCal/L-78D
52T-5
52TipTop
53B/BW-40
54B-169
54NYJour
54T-200
57Seattle/Pop-20
73OPC-81CO
73T-81C
79TCMA-255
93UD/ATH-73
94T/Arc54-200
D305
R346-6
Jantzen, A.C.
N172
Janus, Ed
82Madis/Frit-33MG
83Madis/Frit-1GM
Janvrin, Harold
15CJ-149
16FleischBrd-45
90Target-381
91Conlon/Sport-144
D327
D328-83
D329-89
D350/2-88
E135-83
M101/4-89
M101/5-88
Janzen, Marty
92GulfCY/ProC-3786
Jaques, Eric
89Star/IISingl-164
92ChalK/SB-160
92CharlK/ProC-2767
Jaqutte, Brian
92Beloit/ClBest-30TR
Jaramillo, Rudy
76SanAn/Team-13
90Mother/Ast-27CO
91Mother/Ast-28CO
92Mother/Ast-27CO
93Mother/Ast-28M
Jarlett, Al
46Sunbeam
Jarolimek, Jonathan
92Geneva/ClBest-14
92Geneva/ProC-1556
Jarquin, Gersan
(Skeeter)
78RochR
79Holyo-13
Jarrell, Joe
86Memphis/GoldT-11
86Memphis/SilverT-11
87CharlO/WBTV-13
88CharlK/Pep-9
Jarrett, Mark
82Madis/Frit-12
Jarvis, John
90Greens/Best-14
90Greens/ProC-2666
90Greens/Star-8
91PrWill/ClBest-15
91PrWill/ProC-1431
Jarvis, Kevin
91Princet/ClBest-23
91Princet/ProC-3508
92CharWh/ClBest-12
92CharWh/ProC-4
94B-48
Jarvis, LeRoy
47TipTop
49Sommer-9
90Target-382
Jarvis, Matt
92Kane/ClBest-6
92Kane/ProC-86
92Kane/Team-15
94B-599
94ClBest/Gold-6
Jarvis, Ray
70OPC-361
70T-361
71OPC-526
71T-526
Jarvis, Robert Pat
(Pat)
67OPC-57
67T-57
68CokeCap/Brave-4
68Dexter-41
68OPC-134
68T-134
69MB-129
69MLB/St-114
69T-282
69T/St-6
70MLB/St-7
70OPC-438
70T-438
71MLB/St-13
71OPC-623
71T-623
71T/Coins-85
72MB-161
72T-675
73OPC-192
73T-192
78TCMA-264
Jaster, Larry
66Pep/Tul
67T-356
68OPC-117
68T-117
69T-496
69T/St-56
70OPC-124
70T-124
71MLB/St-14
71Richm/Team-8
72MB-162
86Durham-14CO
87Sumter-21
88Sumter/ProC-415
89Durham/Star 27
90Durham/Team-28CO
91Durham/ClBest-16CO
91Durham/ProC-1678CO
92Macon/ClBest-28CO
92Macon/ProC-286CO
93Macon/ClBest-29CO
93Macon/ProC-1418CO
Jaster, Scott
86Columbia-15
87Lynch-21
88Clmbia/GS-25
88StLucie/Star-13
89StLucie/Star-11
90Salinas/ProC-2732
91AA/LineD-64
91BirmB/LineD-64
91BirmB/ProC-1465
92BirmB/ProC-2595
92BirmB/SB-85
92Sky/AASingl-41
Jaszczak, Steve
93MissSt-23
Jata, Paul
72OPC-257R
72T-257R
Jauss, Dave
90WPalmB/Star-30
91WPalmB/ClBest-27
91WPalmB/ProC-1245CO
92WPalmB/ClBest-26MG
92WPalmB/ProC-2103MG
Javery, Al
43Playball-39
Javier, Ignacio Alfredo
73Cedar
75Iowa/TCMA-9
80Wichita-10
Javier, M. Julian
60T-133
61T-148
61T/St-89
62T-118
62T/St-185
63J-159
63P-159
63T-226
64T-446
64Wheat/St-23
65T-447
66T-436
67T-226
68Bz-5
68OPC-25
68T-25
69MB-130
69MLB/St-212
69T-497
69T/St-116
70MLB/St-140
70OPC-415
70T-415
71MLB/St-275
71OPC-185
71T-185
71T/Coins-39
72MB-163
72T-745
78TCMA-288
81TCMA-414M
92Card/McDon/Pac-27
Javier, Stan
83Greens-24
84Nashvl-10
85Huntsvl/BK-20
86D-584
86F/Up-U56
86Tacoma-9
87D-590
87F/Up-U52
87T-263
88D/A's/Bk-NEW
88D/Best-155
88Mother/A's-15
88S-367
89D-185
89F-13
89Mother/A's-21
89OPC-248
89S-322
89T-622
89T/Big-277
89UD-581
90D-568
90F-12
90F/Can-12
90F/Up-U23
90Leaf-445
90Mother/A's-23
90OPC-102
90PublInt/St-308
90S-394
90S/Tr-52T
90S/YS/II-21
90T-102
90T/Tr-47T
90UD-209
91B-599
91D-239
91F-211
91Leaf-155
91Mother/Dodg-27
91OPC-61
91Panini/FrSt-61
91Pol/Dodg-5
91S-281
91StCl-39
91T-61
91UD-688
92D-322
92F-461
92Mother/Dodg-20
92OPC-581
92Pol/Dodg-5
92S-583
92StCl-187
92T-581
92T/Gold-581
92T/GoldWin-581
92Ultra-212
92Yank/WIZ80-90
93D-280
93F-493
93Mother/Angel-23
93Pac/Beisbol-2M
93Pac/Spanish-237
93Panini-276
93T-712
93T/Gold-712
93UD-249
93UD-730
94F-60
94Finest-403
94Flair-92
94L-325
94Pac/Cr-80
94Pinn-313
94S-252
94S/GoldR-252
94Select-115
94T-446
94T/Gold-446
94UD-384
94Ultra-409
Javier, Vicente
88Billings/ProC-1824
89Greens/ProC-422
90Cedar/Best-4
90Cedar/ProC-2327
91Cedar/ClBest-18
91Cedar/ProC-2727
Jay, Joe
54JC-47
54T-141
55Gol/Braves-13
55JC-47
55T-134
58T-472
59T-273
60L-23
60Lake
60SpicSpan-9
60T-266
61Kahn
61T-233
61T/St-43
62Bz-13
62J-124
62Kahn
62P-124
62P/Can-124
62Salada-126
62Shirriff-126
62T-232WS
62T-263M
62T-440
62T-58LL
62T/St-116
62T/bucks
63Exh
63FrBauer-10
63J-133
63Kahn
63P-133
63T-225
63T-7LL
64Kahn
64T-346
65Kahn
65OPC-174
65T-174
66T-406
78TCMA-216
90BBWit-81
94T/Arc54-141
Exh47
Jean, Domingo
91MidwLAS/ProC-10
91SoBend/ClBest-16
91SoBend/ProC-2852
92B-130
92FtLaud/ProC-2607
92FtLaud/Team-18
92UD/ML-307
93B-159
93Flair/Wave-8
93StCl/Y-30
94B-90
94D-117
94F-233
94Pac/Cr-425
94Pinn-238
94Pinn/Artist-238
94Pinn/Museum-238
94S-256
94S/GoldR-256
94T-212
94T/Gold-212
94UD/CollC-147
94UD/CollC/Gold-147
94UD/CollC/Silv-147
94Ultra-506
Jeannette, Joe
T3/Box-68
Jeansonne, Kevin
77Watlo
Jeffcoat, George
90Target-383
Jeffcoat, Hal
49Eureka-58
51B-211
52B-104
52T-341
53B/BW-37
53T-29
54B-205
55B-223
56T-289
57Kahn
57Sohio/Reds-10
57T-93
58Kahn
58T-294
59T-81
91T/Arc53-29
Jeffcoat, Mike
81Watlo-10
82Watlo-4
83Charl-2
84D-43RR
84F/X-58

84T/Tr-56
84Wheat/Ind-46
85D-251
85F-453
85T-303
86F-545
86Phoenix-10
86T-571
87OKCty-10
89F-524
89OkCty/CMC-4
89OkCty/ProC-1520
90D-521
90F-302
90F/Can-302
90Leaf-416
90Mother/Rang-19
90OPC-778
90S-158
90T-778
91B-278
91F-291
91Leaf-386
91Mother/Rang-19
91OPC-244
91S-174
91StCl-216
91T-244
92D-351
92F-309
92OPC-464
92OkCty/SB-312
92S-174
92StCl-265
92T-464
92T/Gold-464
92T/GoldWin-464
92UD-597
92Ultra-134
93Rang/Keeb-202

Jefferies, Gregg

86Columbia-16
87Jacks/Feder-24
87TexLgAS-11
88AAA/ProC-40
88Classic/Blue-243
88D-657
88D/Mets/Bk-657
88F-137
88F/Mini-94
88Leaf-259
88S-645
88Tidew/CANDL-9
88Tidew/CMC-15
88Tidew/ProC-1600
88TripleA/ASCMC-27
89B-381
89Bz-16
89Classic-6
89Classic/Up/2-154
89D-35RR
89D/Best-152
89D/Rook-2
89F-38
89F/Excit-26
89F/LL-23
89F/Superstar-25
89Holsum/Discs-11
89KMart/DT-11
89Kahn/Mets-9
89KennerFig-74
89Nissen-11
89OPC-233FS
89Panini/St-128
89S-600
89S/HotRook-1
89S/Mast-39
89S/YS/I-1
89Sf-223R
89Sf-90
89T-233FS
89T/Big-253
89T/DHTest-2
89T/HeadsUp-10
89T/JumboR-13
89T/LJN-19
89T/Mets/Fan-9
89T/UK-44
89ToysRUs-15
89UD-9RS
89Woolwth-22
90B-140
90Bz-14
90Classic/Up-T1
90D-270
90D/BestNL-117
90F-207
90F/Can-207
90HotRook/St-22
90Kahn/Mets-9
90Kenner/Fig-45
90Leaf-171
90MLBPA/Pins-18
90Mets/Fan-9
90OPC-457
90Panini/St-298
90PublInt/St-136
90PublInt/St-614
90S-468
90S/100Ris-10
90Sf-14
90Starline/LJS-12
90Starline/LJS-32
90T-457
90T/Big-57
90T/DH-36
90T/Gloss60-60
90T/JumboR-16
90T/St-324FS
90T/TVMets-24
90ToysRUs-16
90UD-166
91B-481
91BBBest/HitM-11
91Classic/200-117
91Classic/II-T40
91D-79
91F-151
91Kahn/Mets-9
91Kenner-30
91Leaf-465
91Leaf/Stud-206
91MajorLg/Pins-77
91OPC-30
91Panini/FrSt-80
91Panini/St-83
91Post-9
91S-660
91S/100SS-80
91Seven/3DCoin-8NE
91StCl-257
91T-30
91UD-156
91UD-95TC
91Ultra-221
91Ultra-397CL
91WIZMets-199
92B-13
92Classic/Game200-171
92D-372
92F-508
92F/Up-26
92L-215
92L/BlkGold-215
92OPC-707
92OPC/Premier-95
92Panini-223
92Pinn-330
92Pinn/Team2000-45
92Pol/Royal-12
92S-192
92S/RookTr-39T
92StCl-737
92Studio-184
92T-707
92T/Gold-707
92T/GoldWin-707
92T/Kids-14
92T/Tr-55T
92T/TrGold-55T
92UD-133
92UD-725
92Ultra-372
93B-544
93Colla/DM-55
93D-307
93F-238
93F/Final-124
93Flair-121
93L-265
93OPC-123
93OPC/Premier-98
93Pac/Spanish-137
93Panini-106
93Pinn-24
93Pinn-480I
93Pol/Card-7
93S-17
93S/Franchise-7
93Select-152
93Select/RookTr-12T
93StCl-628
93StCl/1stDay-628
93StCl/Card-12
93Studio-90
93T-105
93T/Finest-83
93T/FinestRef-83
93T/Gold-105
93T/Tr-122T
93TripleP-130
93UD-176
93UD-545
93UD-54M
93UD-818TC
93UD/FunPack-75
93UD/SP-75
93Ultra-209
93Ultra-463
94B-536
94D-9
94D/DK-21
94D/MVP-12
94D/Special-9
94F-633
94F/TL-26
94L-56
94L/MVPNL-7
94OPC-77
94Oscar-24
94P-28
94Pac/Cr-591
94Pac/Silv-27
94Panini-243
94Pinn-204
94Pinn/Artist-204
94Pinn/Museum-204
94Pinn/Run-27
94S-29
94S/Cycle-5
94S/GoldR-29
94S/GoldS-9
94S/Tomb-10
94Sf/2000-74
94Sf/Mov-1
94StCl-109
94StCl-531DL
94StCl/1stDay-109
94StCl/1stDay-531DL
94StCl/Gold-109
94StCl/Gold-531DL
94StCl/Team-317
94Studio-51
94Studio/Her-7
94T-660
94T/BlkGold-35
94T/Finest-92
94T/Finest/PreProd-92
94T/FinestRef-92
94T/Gold-660
94TripleP-62
94TripleP/Nick-8
94UD-265
94UD/CollC-148
94UD/CollC/Gold-148
94UD/CollC/Silv-148
94UD/ElecD-265
94UD/SP-63
94Ultra-266
94Ultra/OnBase-7

Jeffers, Steve

87Erie-6
88Spring/Best-20

Jefferson, George

86Negro/Frit-105

Jefferson, Jesse

73OPC-604R
73T-604R
74OPC-509
74T-509
75OPC-539
75T-539
75T/M-539
76OPC-47
76T-47
77OPC-184
77T-326
78BJ/PostC-10
78BK/R-8
78OPC-22
78T-144
79BJ/Bubble-14
79OPC-112
79T-221
80OPC-244
80T-467
81F-419
82F-466
82F/St-173
82RedLob
82T-682
82T/Tr-49T
91Crown/Orio-219
92Nabisco-32

Jefferson, Jim

86FSLAS-25
86Tampa-7
87Vermont-2
88Chatt/Best-19
88Nashvl/Team-13

Jefferson, Reggie

87Cedar-14
88Cedar/ProC-1146
89Chatt/Best-1
89Chatt/GS-12
90AAASingl/ProC-550
90B-51
90CedarDG/Best-9
90Nashvl/CMC-22
90Nashvl/ProC-238
90ProC/Singl-147
91AAA/LineD-263
91B-678
91Classic/I-35
91D/Rook-55
91Leaf-514
91Nashvl/LineD-263
91Nashvl/ProC-2164
91T/Tr-60T
91UD/Ext-746
91UD/FinalEd-73F
91Ultra-379MLP
92B-25
92Classic/Game200-47
92D-12RR
92F-113
92Indian/McDon-14
92L-86
92L/BlkGold-86
92OPC-93
92Pinn-476
92Pinn/Team2000-79
92ProC/Tomorrow-213
92S-409
92S/HotRook-10
92StCl-335
92T-93
92T/91Debut-89
92T/Gold-93
92T/GoldWin-93
92TripleP-24
92UD-656
92Ultra-50
93B-557
93D-303
93F-594
93Indian/WUAB-13
93L-302
93OPC-163
93Pac/Spanish-412
93Panini-48
93Pinn-550
93S-433
93Select-330
93StCl-425
93StCl/1stDay-425
93Studio-152
93T-496
93T/Finest-139
93T/FinestRef-139
93T/Gold-496
93ToysRUs-83
93UD-544
93UD/SP-121
93USPlayC/Rook-2D
93Ultra-541
94D-653
94F-106
94Finest-333
94Flair-105
94L-298
94Pac/Cr-170
94Pinn-161
94Pinn/Artist-161
94Pinn/Museum-161
94S-391
94T-121
94T/Gold-121
94UD-478
94UD/CollC-149
94UD/CollC/Gold-149
94UD/CollC/Silv-149

Jefferson, Stan

86Tidew-14
87Bohem-22
87D-642
87D/Rook-43
87F/Up-U53
87Sf/Rook-9
87T/Tr-55T
88Coke/Padres-22
88D-187
88F-587
88OPC-223
88Panini/St-411
88S-114
88S/YS/I-11
88Smok/Padres-12
88T-223
88T/Big-86
88T/St-109
89B-180
89Colum/CMC-28
89S-519
89T-689
89T/Big-165
91AAA/LineD-84
91ColoSp/LineD-84
91Crown/Orio-220
91WIZMets-200
92Yank/WIZ80-91

Jefferson, Thomas
(T.J.)

87Negro/Dixon-28

Jeffery, Scott 1

88Greens/ProC-1553
89Cedar/Best-3
89Cedar/ProC-913
89Cedar/Star-9
90Cedar/Best-25
91Chatt/ProC-1955

Jeffrey, Scott 2

93MedHat/ProC-3734
93MedHat/SportP-17

Jeffries, James 1

T3/Box-55

Jeffries, James 2

82BurlR/Frit-25
82BurlR/TCMA-4

Jefts, Chris

86Penin-14
87DayBe-16

Jelic, Chris

86FtMyr-15
87Lynch-4
88Jacks/GS-8
89Jacks/GS-5
90AAASingl/ProC-284
90ProC/Singl-369
90T/TVMets-48
90Tidew/CMC-18
90Tidew/ProC-553
91AAA/LineD-285
91Classic/I-66
91LasVegas/LineD-285
91LasVegas/ProC-249
91T/90Debut-76
91WIZMets-201
92LasVegas/ProC-2802
92Wichita/SB-636

Jelinek, Joey

91Martins/ClBest-9
91Martins/ProC-3462
92Martins/ClBest-8
92Martins/ProC-3065

Jelks, Greg

86Portl-11
87Maine-9
87Maine/TCMA-12
87Phill/TastyK-45
88F-648
88Maine/CMC-18
88Maine/ProC-298
89Louisvl-24
89Louisvl/CMC-19
89Louisvl/ProC-1258

Jelks, Pat

85Greens-22
86NewBrit-14
88River/Cal-228

88River/ProC-1411
88Wichita-28
Jeltz, Steve
82Reading-15
83Portl-6
84Cram/PCL-205
85CIGNA-10
85D-44RR
85F-653R
85Phill/TastyK-11M
85Phill/TastyK-30
85T/Tr-62T
86CIGNA-9
86Phill/TastyK-30
86T-453
87Champion-2
87D-359
87D/OD-157
87F-178
87Phill/TastyK-30
87T-294
88D-576
88F-308
88OPC-126
88Panini/St-361
88Phill/TastyK-15
88S-435
88T-126
89D-431
89D/Best-271
89F-573
89Phill/TastyK-13
89S-355
89T-707
89T/Big-52
89T/St-114
89UD-219
90D-133
90F-562
90F/Can-562
90OPC-607
90PublInt/St-242
90RedFoley/St-52
90S-421
90S/Tr-59T
90T-607
90T/St-113
90UD-495
91AAA/LineD-457
91OPC-507
91RochR/LineD-457
91RochR/ProC-1908
91S-272
91T-507
Jemison, Greg
77Ashvl
79WHave-15
83BurlR-27CO
83BurlR/Frit-26CO
84Tulsa-14CO
Jendra, Rick
80Cedar-11
Jenkins, Anthony
91Savan/ClBest-25
91Savan/ProC-1666
Jenkins, Bernie
88AubAs/ProC-1959
89Osceola/Star-9
90ColMud/Best-10
90ColMud/ProC-1359
90ColMud/Star-15
90Foil/Best-66
91AA/LineD-563
91Jacks/LineD-563
91Jacks/ProC-938
92Cedar/ProC-1085
Jenkins, Bob
57Seattle/Pop-21
Jenkins, Brett
92WPalmB/ClBest-21
92WPalmB/ProC-2094
Jenkins, Buddy Jr.
91James/ClBest-21
91James/ProC-3540
Jenkins, Dee
91Princet/ClBest-14
91Princet/ProC-3522
92Billings/ProC-3363
93FExcel/ML-22
Jenkins, Fats
74Laugh/Black-28
86Negro/Frit-113
Jenkins, Fergie
66T-254R
67CokeCap/Cub-1
67T-333
68Bz-10
68Kahn
68OPC-11LL
68OPC-9LL
68T-11LL
68T-410
68T-9LL
68T/ActionSt-11CM
69MB-131
69MLB/St-122
69OPC-10LL
69OPC-12LL
69Sunoco/Pin-5
69T-10LL
69T-12LL
69T-640
69T/S-37
69T/St-15
69T/decal
70MLB/St-19
70OPC-240
70OPC-69LL
70OPC-71LL
70T-240
70T-69LL
70T-71LL
71Bz/Test-13
71MD
71MLB/St-35
71MLB/St-563
71OPC-280
71OPC-70LL
71OPC-72LL
71T-280
71T-70LL
71T-72LL
71T/Coins-7
71T/S-42
71T/Super-42
71T/tatt-10
71T/tatt-10a
72Dimanche*-60
72K-8
72MB-164
72OPC-410
72OPC-93LL
72OPC-95LL
72ProStars/PostC-16
72T-410
72T-93LL
72T-95LL
72T/Post-10
73K-28
73OPC-180
73T-180
73T/Lids-23
74Laugh/ASG-67
74OPC-87
74T-87
74T/DE-59
74T/St-236
75Ho-116
75K-22
75OPC-310LL
75OPC-60
75T-310LL
75T-60
75T/M-310LL
75T/M-60
76Ho-138
76OPC-250
76SSPC-255
76T-250
76T/Tr-250T
77BurgChef-31
77K-3
77OPC-187
77T-430
78BK/R-8
78SSPC/270-84
78T-420
79T-544
80K-47
80OPC-203
80T-390
81D-146
81F-622
81F/St-84
81T-158
82D-643
82F-320
82OPC-137
82T-624
82T/Tr-49T
83D-300
83F-498
83F/St-14M
83F/St-15M
83OPC-230
83OPC-231SV
83OPC/St-224
83T-230
83T-231SV
83T-51TL
83T/Fold-1M
83T/St-224
83Thorn-31
84Cub/Uno-5
84D-189
84D/Champs-33
84F-494
84Nes/792-456TL
84Nes/792-483
84Nes/792-706LL
84OPC-343
84Seven-20C
84T-456TL
84T-483
84T-706LL
84T/St-48
85West/2-46
88OkCty/CMC-6
88OkCty/ProC-50
88Pac/Leg-43
89Chatt/II/Team-14
89OkCty/CMC-25
89OkCty/ProC-1513
89Pac/SenLg-29
89T/SenLg-119
89TM/SenLg-55
90EliteSenLg-125
90EliteSenLg-97
91Cub/Vine-15CO
91Pac/SenLg-108
91Perez/HOF-208
91Swell/Great-45
91UD/HOF-H3
91UD/HOF-x
92AP/ASG-4
92AP/ASG24K-4G
92Cub/OldStyle-16
92MCI-13
92MCI-15
93Rang/Keeb-203
93TWill-22
93UD/ATH-159M
93UD/ATH-74
Jenkins, Garrett
89Elmira/Pucko-6
90FSLAS/Star-32
90WinHaven/Star-12
91ClBest/Singl-72
91WinHaven/ClBest-22
91WinHaven/ProC-501
Jenkins, Jack
70OPC-286R
70T-286R
90Target-384
Jenkins, Jerry
77Newar
78BurlB
82ElPaso-13
Jenkins, Jonathan
(Jon)
90Utica/Pucko-21
91ClBest/Singl-219
91SoBend/ClBest-17
91SoBend/ProC-2853
92SoBend/ClBest-12
Jenkins, Mack
88Greens/ProC-1566
90Billings/ProC-3239CO
91Billing/SportP-27CO
91Billings/ProC-3771CO
91Cedar/ClBest-28CO
91Cedar/ProC-2737CO
92Cedar/ClBest-29CO
Jenkins, Norm
90Peoria/Team-3DIR
91Peoria/Team-30M
Jennings, Doug
86PalmSp-18
86PalmSp/Smok-26
87MidldA-16
87TexLgAS-4
88D/A's/Bk-NEW
88D/Rook-13
88F/Slug-22
88F/Up-U54
88Mother/A's-24
89D-505
89F-14
89S-459
89T-166
89Tacoma/CMC-19
89Tacoma/ProC-1541
89UD-585
90AAASingl/ProC-148
90ProC/Singl-595
90Tacoma/CMC-18
90Tacoma/ProC-101
91AAA/LineD-539
91F-12
91S-819
91Tacoma/LineD-539
92RochR/ProC-1950
92RochR/SB-454
93Cub/Mara-11
94Pac/Cr-102
Jennings, Hugh
09Buster/Pin-6
10Domino-59
11Diamond-16MG
11Helmar-32
12Sweet/Pin-25A
12Sweet/Pin-25B
14CJ-77
15CJ-77
16FleischBrd-46
40PlayBall-223
48Exh/HOF
50Callahan
50W576-41
60F-67
61F-47
72Laugh/GF-23
76Shakey-35
77Galasso-176MG
80Perez/HOF-35
80SSPC/HOF
81Conlon-2
81Tiger/Detroit-34MG
86Tiger/Sport-2
89HOF/St-16
89Smok/Dodg-11
90Target-385
91Conlon/Proto-450
91Conlon/Sport-16
92Conlon/Sport-556
93Conlon-847
93Conlon/MasterCol-9MG
93UD/T202-2
93UD/T202-5M
94Conlon/Col-25
D303
D327
D328-86
D329-90
D350/2-89
E101
E103
E104
E105
E106
E121/80
E135-86
E254
E270/2
E90/1
E92
E93
E94
E96
E98
L1-128
M101/4-90
M101/5-89
M116
S81-103
T201
T202
T205
T206
T213/blue
T215/blue
T215/brown
T216
T222
T3-18
W514-206
W515-34
W555
W575
WG4-11
WG5-22
WG6-21
Jennings, Lance
91AppFx/ClBest-13
91AppFx/ProC-1719
92B-633
92BBCity/ClBest-5
92ClBest-21
92Memphis/ProC-2423
92UD/ML-107
93FExcel/ML-175
Jennings, Robin
92Geneva/ClBest-13
92Geneva/ProC-1572
93Peoria/Team-11
Jennings, William
52Park-5
Jenny, Shane
88Kenosha/ProC-1401
Jensen, Dave
85Lynch-8
Jensen, Forrest
(Woody)
R313
R314
Jensen, Jackie
49Remar
51B-254
52B-161
52Dix-53
52T-122
53B/Col-24
53Briggs
53Dix
53NB
53RM-AL6
53T-265
54B-2
54Dix
54T-80
55Armour-10
55RM-AL19
55T-200
56T-115
56T/Pin-24OF
57Swift-15
57T-220
58Hires-56
58T-130
58T-489AS
59Armour-10
59Bz
59HRDerby-8
59T-400
60Bz-21
60T/tatt-23
60T/tatt-90
61T-173M
61T-476MVP
61T-540
61T/St-112
62J-62
62P-62
62P/Can-62
62Salada-73
62Shirriff-73
75OPC-196MVP
75T-196MVP
75T/M-196MVP
77Galasso-18
79TCMA-229
80Marchant-11
91T/Arc53-265
92Bz/Quadra-11M
94T/Arc54-80
Exh47
PM10/Sm-83
PM10/Sm-84
PM10/Sm-85
Jensen, John 1
(Swede)
49B/PCL-13
Jensen, John 2
89WinSalem/Star-10
90WinSalem/Team-15
91CLAS/ProC-CAR43
91WinSalem/ClBest-25
91WinSalem/ProC-2842
92ChalK/SB-161
92CharlK/ProC-2784

92ProC/Tomorrow-206
Jensen, Marcus
90A&AASingle/ProC-171
90Everett/Best-14
90Everett/ProC-3130
92Clinton/ClBest-24
92Clinton/ProC-3602
94FExcel-292
Jenson, Jeff
91SoOreg/ProC-3836
Jernigan, Pete
63MilSau-3
63T-253R
Jersild, Aaron
92StCath/ClBest-26
92StCath/ProC-3383
93Hagers/ClBest-15
93Hagers/ProC-1875
Jesperson, Bob
91Billing/SportP-24
91Billings/ProC-3767
92CharWh/ProC-20
Jessop, Kim
91Brisbane/Fut-15
Jessup, Steve
88Utica/Pucko-28
Jestadt, Garry
70OPC-109R
70T-109R
71OPC-576R
71T-576R
72OPC-143
72T-143
77Phoenix
Jester, Billy
86Clearw-10
Jeter, Derek
92ClBest/BBonusC-22
92ClBest/Up-402
92Classic/DP-6
92Classic/DPFoil-BC6
92FrRow/DP-55
92GulfCY/ProC-3797
92LitSun/HSPros-2
92UD/ML-5
93B-511
93ClBest/MLG-115
93ClBest/Pr-1
93FExcel/ML-210
93Greens/ClBest-1
93Greens/ProC-893
93Pinn-457DP
93S-489DP
93Select-360DP
93StCl/MurphyS-117
93T-98
93T/Gold-98
93UD-449TP
93UD/SP-279FOIL
94B-376
94B-633
94ClBest/GAce-3
94ClBest/Gold-83
94FExcel-106
94FExcel/LL-10
94SigRook-11
94SigRook/Hot-4
94T-158M
94T/Gold-158M
94TedW-124
94TedW/Gardiner-3
94UD-550TP
Jeter, John
70OPC-141R
70T-141R
71MLB/St-205
71OPC-47
71T-47
72OPC-288
72T-288
73OPC-423
73T-423
74OPC-615
74T-615
Jeter, Shawn
87Dunedin-21
88Dunedin/Star-12
89Knoxvl/Best-10
89Knoxvl/ProC-1130
89Knoxvl/Star-8
90Knoxvl/Best-6
90Knoxvl/ProC-1257
90Knoxvl/Star-6
91AAA/LineD-506
91Syrac/LineD-506
91Syrac/MerchB-9
91Syrac/ProC-2493
92D/Rook-59
92F/Up-14
92Vanco/SB-639
93Pinn-265
93StCl-453
93StCl/1stDay-453
93T-800
93T/Gold-800
Jethroe, Sam
50B-248
51B-242
51BR-D10
51T/BB-12
52B-84
52T-27
53B/Col-3
53Exh/Can-10
79TCMA-44
86Negro/Frit-38
89Pac/Leg-206
89Swell-62
92Negro/Kraft-10
92Negro/Retort-31
93TWill-137
Jevne, Frederick
N172
Jewell, Jim
43Centen-12
Jewell, Mike
91Watertn/ClBest-7
91Watertn/ProC-3362
92Watertn/ClBest-6
92Watertn/ProC-3228
Jewett, Earl
89Pulaski/ProC-1897
90Sumter/Best-7
90Sumter/ProC-2429
91Macon/ClBest-2
91Macon/ProC-856
Jewett, Trent
89Salem/Star-11
90Harris/ProC-1197
90Harris/Star-10
91AA/LineD-125M
91CaroMud/LineD-125CO
92Welland/ClBest-28MG
92Welland/ProC-1340MG
Jewtraw, C.
33SK*-11
Jimaki, Jim
88CapeCod/Sum-84
Jimenez, Alex
88Clmbia/GS-15
89Clmbia/Best-29
89Clmbia/GS-12
90Jacks/GS-3
91AAA/LineD-560
91Tidew/LineD-560
91Tidew/ProC-2518
Jimenez, Alfonso
(Houston)
83Toledo-15
84Nes/792-411
84T-411
85D-269
85F-282
85T-562
85Toledo-16
87Vanco-12
Jimenez, Cesar
86Durham-15
87Durham-1
88Durham/Star-8
88F/Up-U72
Jimenez, Felix
(Elvio)
65OPC-226R
65T-226R
69T-567R
92Yank/WIZ60-62
Jimenez, German
88F/Up-U72
89Greenvl/Best-23
89Greenvl/ProC-1153
89Greenvl/Star-10
89T-569
89UD-113
Jimenez, Juan
86BurlEx-11C
Jimenez, Manuel 1
62T-598R
63J-87
63P-87
63T-195
64T-574
66T-458
67T-586
68T-538
69MB-132
Jimenez, Manuel 2
75QuadC
Jimenez, Manuel 3
91Pulaski/ClBest-7
91Pulaski/ProC-4013
92Macon/ClBest-8
92Macon/ProC-274
92ProC/Tomorrow-194
93Durham/Team-8
Jimenez, Miguel
91SoOreg/ClBest-14
91SoOreg/ProC-3837
92Madis/ClBest-7
92Madis/ProC-1228
93B-133
93LimeR/Winter-86
94B-108
94F/MLP-17
94L/GRook-13
94StCl-356
94StCl/1stDay-356
94StCl/Gold-356
94T-773M
94T/Gold-773M
94UD-19
94UD/CollC-12
94UD/CollC/Gold-12
94UD/CollC/Silv-12
94UD/ElecD-19
94Ultra-108
Jimenez, Oscar
94B-583
Jimenez, Ramon
90Foil/Best-40
90Greens/Best-17
90Greens/ProC-2669
90Greens/Star-9
90ProC/Singl-697
90SALAS/Star-13
90Star/ISingl-93
91PrWill/ClBest-18
91PrWill/ProC-1435
92PrWill/ClBest-11
92PrWill/ProC-156
Jimenez, Ray
83Peoria/Frit-1
Jimenez, Roberto
90Burllnd/ProC-3011
Jimenez, Steve
93SoEastern-12
Jimenez, Vincent
91Idaho/SportP-21
Jiminez, Alex
86LitFalls-15
87Columbia-28
Jiminez, Luis
78Charl
Jiminez, Vincent
90Pulaski/Best-14
90Pulaski/ProC-3092
Jirschele, Mike
78Ashvl
79Wausau-21
80Ashvl-28
80Tulsa-15
81Tulsa-29
82Tulsa-19
83OKCty-10
84OKCty-9
85OKCty-4
89Omaha/CMC-17
90AppFox/Box-14CO
90AppFox/ProC-2112CO
90TulsaDG/Best-20
91AppFx/ClBest-27CO
91AppFx/ProC-1732CO
93Rockford/ClBest-28MG
Job, Ryan
85Osceola/Team-18
86ColumAst-15
Jobes, Tracy
88MissSt-14
89MissSt-22
90MissSt-22
Jockish, Mike
88StCath/ProC-2031
89StCath/ProC-2078
90Erie/Star-10
Jodo, Daijiro
88SanJose/Cal-120
Joe, Tokio
72Dimanche*-130
Johdo, Joe
88SanJose/ProC-136
John, Oliver
E270/2
John, Tommy
64T-146R
65OPC-208
65T-208
66T-486
67CokeCap/WSox-15
67T-609
68OPC-72
68T-72
69MB-133
69MLB/St-31
69NTF
69T-465
69T/St-155
69Trans-22
70MLB/St-186
70OPC-180
70T-180
71K-74
71MD
71OPC-520
71T-520
71T/Coins-56
72MB-165
72OPC-264
72T-264
73OPC-258
73T-258
74OPC-451
74T-451
75OPC-47
75T-47
75T/M-47
76OPC-416
76SSPC-69
76T-416
77T-128
78Ho-7
78K-36
78SSPC/270-75
78T-375
79BK/Y-9
79OPC-129
79T-255
80OPC-348
80T-690
80T/Super-23
81D-107
81F-81
81F/St-121
81K-52
81OPC-96
81T-550
81T/HT
81T/SO-52
81T/St-114
81T/St-250
81T/St-2M
82D-409
82D-558M
82F-40
82F/St-115
82OPC-75
82T-486TL
82T-75
82T/St-214
83D-570
83F-95
83F/St-7M
83F/St-8M
83OPC-144SV
83OPC-196
83Seven-9
83T-735
83T-736A
83T/Fold-1M
84D-301
84D/Champs-36
84F-522
84Nes/792-415
84Nes/792-715LL
84OPC-284
84Smok/Cal-13
84T-415
84T-715LL
84T/RD-28
84T/St-232
85D-423
85F-304
85FunFood/Pin-92
85OPC-179
85Smok/Cal-23
85T-179
85T/St-229
86F-422
86F/Up-U57
86T-240
87F-102
87OPC-236
87Smok/Dodg-15
87T-236
88D-17DK
88D-401
88D/Best-220
88D/DKsuper-17DK
88D/Y/Bk-401
88F-211
88Leaf-17DK
88Leaf-230
88Panini/St-148
88S-240
88Sf-122
88T-611
89Classic-40
89F-255
89S-477
89Smok/Dodg-91
89T-359
89T/LJN-64
89T/St-310
89UD-230
90Target-386
92Yank/WIZ70-80
92Yank/WIZ80-92
92Yank/WIZAS-34
93AP/ASG-157
93UD/ATH-75
94TedW-12
Johnigan, Steve 1
87Watlo-4
Johnigan, Steve 2
92MissSt-23
93MissSt-24CO
Johns, Douglas
90SoOreg/Best-5
91Madison/ClBest-9
91Madison/ProC-2126
92Reno/Cal-44
Johns, Keith
92FrRow/DP-52
92Hamil/ClBest-12
92Hamil/ProC-1600
93ClBest/MLG-118
93FExcel/ML-99
Johns, Ronald M.
86FSLAS-26
86StPete-15
87Spring/Best-6
88Harris/ProC-849
Johnson, Abner
78Wisco
81CharR-19
Johnson, Alex
64PhilBull-15
65T-352
66OPC-104
66Pep/Tul
66T-104
67OPC-108
67T-108
68T-441
69Kahn
69T-280
69T/St-25
70MLB/St-173
70OPC-115
70T-115
71JB
71K-54
71MD
71MLB/St-346
71MLB/St-564
71OPC-590
71OPC-61LL
71T-590
71T-61LL
71T/Coins-84
71T/GM-17

71T/Greatest-17
71T/S-8
71T/Super-8
71T/tatt-15
72MB-166
72OPC-215
72T-215
73OPC-425
73T-425
74OPC-107
74T-107
74T/St-237
75OPC-534
75T-534
75T/M-534
76SSPC/MetsY-Y17
77T-637
92Yank/WIZ70-81
93Rang/Keeb-204
Johnson, Andre
91Pulaski/ClBest-12
91Pulaski/ProC-4018
92Idaho/ProC-3527
Johnson, Angela
89GA-12MG
90GA-35M
Johnson, Anthony 1
79Memphis/TCMA-10
80Memphis-3
83D-629
83Syrac-22
84Syrac-7
Johnson, Anthony 2
89SanDiegoSt/Smok-13
90Pulaski/Best-21
90Pulaski/ProC-3086
Johnson, Arthur
91Niagara/ClBest-3
92Bristol/ProC-1419
Johnson, Avery
89BurlInd/Star-13
Johnson, Ban
50Callahan
50W576-42
61F-48
63Bz/ATG-16
69Bz-Sm
76Shakey-10PRES
77Galasso-170PRES
80Perez/HOF-7
80SSPC/HOF
88Pac/8Men-78
89HOF/St-96
WG1-4
WG2-28
Johnson, Barry
90AZ/Pol-8
Johnson, Benjamin F.
(Ben)
60T-528
Johnson, Ben
88Alaska/Team-10
90Welland/Pucko-6
Johnson, Bert
82CharR-9
Johnson, Bill
83Reading-7
84Iowa-29
85Iowa-16
Johnson, Billy
87Louisvl-30
89Spokane/SP-12
90CharRain/Best-12
90CharRain/ProC-2040
91CharRain/ClBest-8
91CharRain/ProC-94
92Watlo/ClBest-5
Johnson, Bob
79Wausau-12
Johnson, Bobby E.
78Ashvl
80Tulsa-21
82T-418R
83D-494
83Rang-8
83T/Tr-48
84D-500
84F-420
84Nes/792-608
84T-608
93Rang/Keeb-205
Johnson, Brian David
90CLAS/CL-40
90Foil/Best-214
90Greens/Best-13
90Greens/ProC-2665
90Greens/Star-10
90Kinston/Team-6
90SALAS/Star-14
90T/TVYank-47
91ClBest/Singl-9
91FSLAS/ProC-FSL14
91FtLaud/ClBest-16
91FtLaud/ProC-2429
92Wichita/ProC-3659
92Wichita/SB-637
94FExcel-284
94T-789
94T/Gold-789
94Ultra-579
Johnson, Brian Lloyd
(B.J.)
88BurlInd/ProC-1798
89Kinston/Star-10
91AAA/LineD-85
91ColoSp/LineD-85
91ColoSp/ProC-2186
92ColoSp/ProC-754
Johnson, C. Barth
(Bart)
70T-669R
71OPC-156
71T-156
72OPC-126
72T-126
73OPC-506
73T-506
74OPC-147
74T-147
75OPC-446
75T-446
75T/M-446
76OPC-513
76T-513
77BurgChef-77
77T-177
Johnson, Carl
88VeroB/Star-12
89Kenosha/ProC-1065
89Kenosha/Star-9
90BurlInd/ProC-3006
91Kinston/ClBest-3
91Kinston/ProC-315
92Kinston/ClBest-13
Johnson, Charles 1
81GlenF-4
Johnson, Charles 2
(Chuck)
87Savan-2
88Spring/Best-12
89StPete/Star-19
Johnson, Charles Edward
91Miami/Bumble-7
91T/Tr-61T
92B-661
92StCl/Dome-91
92T/DQ-27
92T/Tr-56T
92T/TrGold-56T
93StCl/MurphyS-76
93UD-435TP
94ClBest/Gold-105
94FExcel-191
94FExcel/AS-1
94SigRook/Bonus-2
94TedW-125
94TedW/Gardiner-4
94UD-536TP
94UD/SP-113
Johnson, Chet
45Centen-12
Johnson, Ching
33SK*-30
Johnson, Chip
91OKSt-12
Johnson, Chris
88Beloit/GS-25
89Beloit/I/Star-10
89Beloit/II/Star-16
90A&AASingle/ProC-137
90AS/Cal-56
90ProC/Singl-712
90Stockton/Best-15
90Stockton/Cal-176
90Stockton/ProC-2174
91AA/LineD-189
91B-45
91ClBest/Singl-282
91ElPaso/LineD-189
91ElPaso/ProC-2743
91UD-56
92Harris/ProC-456
92Harris/SB-284
92Sky/AASingl-120
93Harris/ProC-267
Johnson, Chuck
86AZ/Pol-8
Johnson, Cliff
75OPC-143
75T-143
75T/M-143
76OPC-249
76SSPC-51
76T-249
77T-514
78BK/Y-3
78SSPC/270-2
78T-309
79BK/Y-3
79OPC 50
79T-114
80OPC-321
80T-612
81D-484
81F-303
81OPC-17
81T-17
81T/Tr-776
82F-93
82Granny-5
82OPC-333
82T-422
82T/St-226
82T/StVar-226
83D-601
83F-520
83T-762
83T/Tr-49
84D-512
84F-159
84Nes/792-221
84OPC-221
84T-221
84T/St-366
84Tor/Fire-19
85D-512
85F-109
85F/Up-U61
85Leaf-115
85OPC-7
85Rang-44
85T-4RB
85T-568
85T/St-367
85T/Tr-63T
85Woolwth-20
86BJ/Ault-15
86D-639
86F-62
86Leaf-250
86OPC-348
86T-348
86Tor/Fire-19
87D-645
87F-230
87OPC-118
87T-663
90EliteSenLg-83
92Nabisco-2
92Yank/WIZ70-82
93Rang/Keeb-206
93UD/ATH-76
Johnson, Clifford
(Connie)
56T-326
57T-43
58T-266
59T-21
87Negro/Dixon-43
91Crown/Orio-222
92Negro/Retort-32
Johnson, Clinton
81Bristol-20
Johnson, Curtis
88StCath/ProC-2022
89Myrtle/ProC-1470
Johnson, Dana
87Dunedin-8
Johnson, Dante
88Billings/ProC-1812
89Greens/ProC-417
Johnson, Darrell
54Esskay
57T-306
58T-61
59T-533
60T-263
62T-16
74OPC-403MG
74T-403MG
75OPC-172MG
75T-172MG
75T/M-172MG
76SSPC-417MG
76T-118MG
77T-597MG
78T-79MG
79T-659MG
83T-37MG
91Crown/Orio-223
93Rang/Keeb-207MG
Johnson, Darron
90Eugene/GS-17
Johnson, David Allen
(Davey)
65T-473R
66T-579R
67CokeCap/Orio-8
67T-363
68CokeCap/Orio-8
68Dexter-42
68T-273
69MB-135
69MLB/St-4
69OPC-203
69T-203
69T/4in1-11M
69T/St-125
70MLB/St-150
70OPC-45
70T-45
71MD
71MLB/St-301
71OPC-595
71T-595
71T/Coins-2
71T/tatt-4
72K-43
72MB-168
72OPC-224WS
72Pol/Orio-5
72T-224WS
72T-680
73OPC-550
73T-550
74K-50
74OPC-45
74T-45
74T/St-6
75OPC-57
75T-57
75T/M-57
78T-317
78Twin/FriszP-9
83Tidew-23
84Jacks/Smk-6MG
84T/Mets/Fan-1MG
84T/Tr-57MG
85Pol/MetYank-M2MG
85T-492MG
86T-501MG
87T-543MG
88D/AS-42MG
88D/PopUp-20MG
88Kahn/Mets-5MG
88T-164MG
88T/Gloss22-12MG
89Kahn/Mets-5MG
89T-684MG
90Kahn/Mets-5MG
90OPC-291MG
90Pac/Legend-33
90Swell/Great-61
90T-291MG
90T/TVMets-1MG
91Crown/Orio-224
91LineD-34
91MDA-13
91Swell/Great-46
92AP/ASG-75
92OPC-657
92T/Gold-657
92T/GoldWin-657
93Reds/Kahn-10MG
93T/Tr-36TM
93TWill-83
93UD/ATH-77
Johnson, David C.
77T-478R
78T-627
91Crown/Orio-225
Johnson, David M.
77SanJose-24
78StPete
79ArkTr-21
80ArkTr-14
Johnson, David Wayne
(Dave)
84PrWill-30
85Nashua-12
86Hawaii-12
86QuadC-15
87Vanco-9
88BuffB/CMC-4
88BuffB/Polar-2
88BuffB/ProC-1476
89RochR/CMC-11
89RochR/ProC-1656
90D-702
90F/Up-U67
90Leaf-434
90OPC-416
90S-528
90S/100Ris-43
90T-416
90UD-425
91Crown/Orio-226
91D-126
91F-479
91Leaf-248
91OPC-163
91Panini/St-199
91StCl-117
91T-163
91UD-299
91Ultra-18
92Edmon/SB-162
92F-12
92S-604
92T-657
Johnson, David
83AlexD-20
87PalmSp-3
Johnson, Dean
85LitFalls-25
Johnson, Deron Andre
88Watertn/Pucko-20
89Welland/Pucko-14
90Augusta/ProC-2472
Johnson, Deron Jr.
86Cram/NWL-105
87Wausau-18
Johnson, Deron Roger
59T-131
60T-134
61T-68
62T-82
64T-449
65Kahn
65MacGregor-5
65OPC-75
65T-75
66Kahn
66T-219LL
66T-440
66T/RO-43
67CokeCap/Reds-6
67Kahn
67OPC-135
67T-135
68CokeCap/Brave-15
68Kahn
68T-323
69MB-136
69T-297
70OPC-125
70T-125
70T/CB
71MLB/St-182
71OPC-490
71Phill/Arco-7
71T-490
71T/Coins-79
71T/S-58
71T/Super-58
72MB-169
72OPC-167
72OPC-168IA
72T-167
72T-168A

73OPC-590
73T-590
74OPC-312
74T-312
74T/St-227
75SSPC/18-18
76OPC-529
76T-529
78Cr/PCL-10
78TCMA-213
84Phill/TastyK-11CO
85Mother/Mar-27CO
86Mother/Mar-28CO
88Albany/ProC-1351CO
90Swell/Great-34
92Yank/WIZ60-60
Johnson, Dodd
86Sumter/ProC-11
87Durham-28
88Durham/Star-9
89Penin/Star-8
91Reno/Cal-22
91Sydney/Fut-14
Johnson, Dominick
87Pocatel/Bon-15
89Clinton/ProC-904
90SanJose/Best-25
90SanJose/Cal-47
90SanJose/ProC-2011
90SanJose/Star-13
91Reno/Cal-6
92PalmSp/ProC-833
Johnson, Don
47TipTop
52T-190
53B/BW-55
54T-146
55B-101
55Esskay
55T-165
91Crown/Orio-227
94T/Arc54-146
Johnson, Drew
92Kane/ClBest-2
92Kane/ProC-98
92Kane/Team-16
Johnson, Earl
47TipTop
49B-231
50B-188
51B-321
52Mother-14
Johnson, Earnie
90SoBend/GS-7
91Saraso/ClBest-5
91Saraso/ProC-1108
92BirmB/ProC-2576
Johnson, Erik
87Pocatel/Bon-29
88Clinton/ProC-708
88MidwLAS/GS-3
89Shrev/ProC-1845
90AAASingl/ProC-45
90Phoenix/ProC-19
90Shrev/Star-13
91AA/LineD-309
91Shrev/LineD-309
91Shrev/ProC-1829
92Phoenix/ProC-2827
92Phoenix/SB-384
Johnson, Ernest R.
21Exh-82
E120
E220
V100
W573
Johnson, Ernest T.
53JC-7
53SpicSpan/3x5-13
54B-144
54JC-32
54SpicSpan/PostC-10
55B-157
55Gol/Braves-14
55JC-32
55SpicSpan/DC-9
56T-294
57SpicSpan/4x5-10
57T-333
58T-78
59T-279
60T-228
91Crown/Orio-228
Johnson, Frank
69T-227
71MLB/St-253
71OPC-128
71T-128
75Phoenix-23
75Phoenix/CircleK-23
Johnson, Gary
89KS*-17
89KS*-18
92Lipscomb-16
93Lipscomb-14
Johnson, George
78Laugh/Black-25
Johnson, Greg 1
77QuadC
79Savan-10
Johnson, Greg 2
87AubAs-18
88Ashvl/ProC-1051
89Ashvl/ProC-959
90A&AASingle/ProC-42
90OrlanSR/Best-15
90OrlanSR/ProC-1078
90OrlanSR/Star-7
91AA/LineD-482
91ClBest/Singl-105
91OrlanSR/LineD-482
91OrlanSR/ProC-1844
92Kenosha/ProC-613
92Portl/SB-410
92Portland/ProC-2662
92Sky/AAASingl-187
Johnson, Hank
33G-14
92Conlon/Sport-382
R314/Can
R337-409
V353-14
Johnson, Herman
92SoOreg/ClBest-23
92SoOreg/ProC-3418
Johnson, Home Run
74Laugh/Black-22
86Negro/Frit-109
Johnson, Howard
81BirmB
83D-328
83F-332
84Tiger/Farmer-8
84Tiger/Wave-21
85D-247
85F-12
85F/Up-U62
85OPC-192
85T-192
85T/St-262
85T/Tr-64T
86D-312
86F-85
86OPC-304
86T-751
86T/Mets/Fan-6
86T/St-101
87D-646
87D/HL-43
87D/OD-132
87F-13
87OPC-267
87T-267
88D-569
88D/Best-97
88D/Mets/Bk-569
88F-138
88F/Mini-95
88F/RecSet-20
88F/St-104
88Kahn/Mets-20
88KayBee-14
88KennerFig-56
88Leaf-238
88OPC-85
88OPC/Waxbox-K
88Panini/St-343
88Panini/St-439
88RedFoley/St-40
88S-69
88Sf-138
88Sf/Gamewin-17
88T-85
88T/Big-129
88T/Gloss60-52
88T/Mets/Fan-20
88T/Mini-61
88T/St-99
88T/WaxBox-K
89D-235
89D/Best-126
89F-39
89Kahn/Mets-20
89OPC-383
89S-136
89T-383
89T/Ames-18
89T/Big-208
89T/DHTest-10
89T/Gloss60-22
89T/St-91
89T/St/Backs-41
89UD-582
90B-133
90BirmDG/Best-2
90Classic-144
90D-18DK
90D-654AS
90D-99
90D/BestNL-19
90D/Bon/MVP-BC2
90D/Preview-8
90D/SuperDK-18DK
90F-208
90F-639M
90F/ASIns-4
90F/AwardWin-20
90F/BB-21
90F/BBMVP-22
90F/Can-208
90F/Can-639
90F/WaxBox-C16
90Holsum/Discs-10
90KMart/SS-3
90Kahn/Mets-20
90Kenner/Fig-46
90Leaf-272
90MCA/Disc-2
90MLBPA/Pins-16
90Mets/Fan-20
90OPC-399AS
90OPC-680
90Panini/St-210
90Panini/St-306
90Panini/St-385
90PublInt/St-137
90PublInt/St-265
90S-124
90S/100St-83
90Sf-109
90Sunflower-3
90T-399AS
90T-680
90T/Big-216
90T/Coins-50
90T/DH-37
90T/Gloss22-4
90T/Gloss60-43
90T/HillsHM-33
90T/Mini-67
90T/St-150AS
90T/St-90
90T/TVAS-53
90T/TVMets-25
90Tetley/Discs-2
90UD-263
90WonderBrd-17
91B-464
91BBBest/RecBr-9
91Cadaco-33
91Classic/200-76
91Classic/III-40
91D-454
91DennyGS-11
91F-152
91Kahn/Mets-20
91Kenner-31
91Leaf-34
91Leaf/Stud-207
91OPC-470
91Panini/FrSt-81
91Panini/St-86
91RedFoley/St-52
91S-185
91S/100SS-86
91StCl-86
91StCl/Member*-19
91T-470
91T/CJMini/II-33
91UD-124
91USPlayC/AS-4C
91Ultra-222
91WIZMets-203
92B-10
92CJ/DII-17
92Classic/Game200-145
92Classic/I-47
92Classic/II-T41
92D-341
92D/Elite-E15
92D/McDon-25
92DPep/MSA-23
92DennyGS-16
92F-509
92F-689LL
92F/TmLIns-2
92French-4M
92Kenner/Fig-26
92KingB-6
92L-132
92L/BlkGold-132
92L/GoldPrev-7
92L/Prev-7
92MSA/Ben-16
92Mets/Kahn-20
92OPC-590
92OPC/Premier-42
92P-28
92Panini-147
92Panini-224
92Pinn-15
92S-550
92S-776AS
92S/100SS-68
92StCl-430
92StCl-610MC
92StCl/Dome-92
92Studio-67
92Sunflower-6
92T-388AS
92T-590
92T/Gold-388AS
92T/Gold-590
92T/GoldWin-388AS
92T/GoldWin-590
92T/Kids-12
92T/McDonB-23
92TripleP-236
92UD-256
92UD-37TC
92UD-720DS
92UD/ASFF-28
92UD/HRH-HR3
92UD/TmMVPHolo-26
92USPlayC/Ace-12C
92USPlayC/Ace-12H
92Ultra-235
93B-130
93Cadaco-34
93Colla/DM-56
93D-434
93F-89
93Flair-93
93L-39
93MSA/Metz-11
93Mets/Kahn-20
93OPC-166
93Pac/Spanish-199
93Panini-251
93Pinn-389
93Pinn/HRC-44
93Pinn/Slug-18
93S-62
93Select-101
93StCl-404
93StCl/1stDay-404
93Studio-128
93T-106
93T/Finest-143
93T/FinestRef-143
93T/Gold-106
93TripleP-86
93UD-484M
93UD-676
93UD/FunPack-127
93UD/looss-WI14
93UD/SP-151
93UD/Then-TN12
93Ultra-76
94B-142
94D-487
94F-568
94Finest-374
94L-432
94OPC-31
94Pac/Cr-407
94Panini-219
94Pinn-518
94S-414
94StCl/Team-109
94T-302
94T/Gold-302
94TripleP-227
94UD-462
94Ultra-484
Johnson, J.J.
91Classic/DP-33
91FrRow/DP-48
91Yakima/ClBest-6
92Pinn-577
94B-7
Johnson, Jack 1
T3/Box-76
Johnson, Jack 2
89Anchora-16
90AZ/Pol-9
92Bakers/Cal-13
Johnson, James H.
21Exh-83
Johnson, James
81Clinton-19
Johnson, Jason
94B-498
Johnson, Jay
87Sumter-30
Johnson, Jeff
88Oneonta/ProC-2069
89PrWill/Star-9
90FtLaud/Star-10
91AAA/LineD-108
91B-159
91ColClip/LineD-108
91ColClip/ProC-593
91D/Rook-47
91F/Up-U44
91S/RookTr-110T
91T/Tr-62T
92B-362
92ColClip/Pol-11
92D-275
92OPC-449
92Pinn-464
92Pinn/Team2000-23
92ProC/Tomorrow-109
92S-523
92S/100RisSt-40
92StCl-471
92T-449
92T/91Debut-90
92T/Gold-449
92T/GoldWin-449
92TripleP-93
92UD-626
92Ultra-410
93F-650
Johnson, Jerry
81ArkTr-11
81Hawaii-5
82Hawaii-5
83ArkTr-9
83LasVegas/BHN-12
84Beaum-19
85RochR-18
Johnson, Jerry Michael
69T-253
70OPC-162
70T-162
71MLB/St-254
71OPC-412
71T-412
72OPC-35
72OPC-36IA
72T-35
72T-36A
73OPC-248
73T-248
75Hawaii/Caruso-18
75IntLgAS/Broder-13
75OPC-218
75PCL/AS-13
75T-218
75T/M-218
76OPC-658
76T-658
78OPC-184
78T-169
81TCMA-440
84Louisvl-26
Johnson, Jim 1
(Jimmy)

80Tucson-9
81Tucson-12
82Tucson-24MG
85Cram/PCL-53MG
Johnson, Jim 2
88GreatF-26
Johnson, Jody
89GA-13
Johnson, Joe
84Richm-21
85Greenvl/Team-9
85IntLgAS-17
86D-624
86F-519
86Pol/Atl-38
86Syrac-15
87D-650
87F-231
87Leaf-91
87T/Tr-56T
87Tor/Fire-15
88Edmon/CMC-7
88Edmon/ProC-560
88OPC-347
88T-347
90AAASingl/ProC-430
90Pawtu/CMC-7
90Pawtu/ProC-458
90ProC/Singl-258
90T/TVRSox-47
Johnson, Joel
91Eugene/ClBest-26
91Eugene/ProC-3720
92ClRS/ProC-2386
92Ultra-72
Johnson, John Henry
75Cedar
76Cedar
79Ho-39
79K-6
79OPC-361
79T-681
80OPC-97
80T-173
81T-216
82D-550
82F-321
82T-527
84D-91
84F-401
84Nes/792-419
84T-419
85Cram/PCL-246
85F-162
85T-734
86Vanco-14
87F-347
87Pol/Brew-38
87T-377
93Rang/Keeb-208
Johnson, John Ralph
N172
Johnson, John
86BirmB/Team-9
87FtLaud-23
Johnson, Josh
86Negro/Frit-13
86Negro/Frit-63
91Negro/Lewis-26
92Negro/Retort-33
Johnson, Judd
89Sumter/ProC-1102
90Foil/Best-193
90Greenvl/Best-13
90Greenvl/Star-8
91AA/LineD-208
91Greenvl/ClBest-2
91Greenvl/LineD-208
91Greenvl/ProC-2996
92Greenvl/ProC-1151
92Greenvl/SB-234
93Richm/Bleach-22
93Richm/Pep-24
93Richm/Team-12
Johnson, Karl
89Elizab/Star-13
Johnson, Keith
92FrRow/DP-21
92Yakima/ClBest-6
92Yakima/ProC-3458
93StCl/MurphyS-110
Johnson, Kenneth Travis
(Ken)
60T-135
61BeeHive-10
61T-24
62T-278
63Pepsi
63T-352
64T-158
64T/S-2
64T/SU
64T/St-70
64T/tatt
65OldLond-13
65T-359
66T-466
66T/RO-96
67CokeCap/Brave-10
67Kahn
67OPC-101
67T-101
68CokeCap/Brave-10
68Dexter-43
68T-342
69T-238
78TCMA-232
89Smok/Ast-5
92Yank/WIZ60-61
D301
Johnson, Kenneth Wandersee
(Hook)
49Eureka-185
51B-293
Johnson, Kent
79Clinton/TCMA-14
Johnson, Kevin 1
80Clinton-12
Johnson, Kevin 2
91Spokane/ClBest-20
91Spokane/ProC-3951
Johnson, Lamar
76OPC-596R
76T-596R
77BurgChef-76
77T-443
78Ho-59
78SSPC/270-137
78T-693
79Ho-43
79OPC-192
79T-372
80T-242
81Coke
81D-38
81F-350
81OPC-366
81T-589
81T/HT
81T/SO-26
81T/St-58
82D-269
82F-346
82T-13
82T/Tr-50T
83D-142
83F-571
83T-453
90EliteSenLg-7
91AAA/LineD-150M
91Denver/LineD-150CO
91Denver/ProC-138CO
92Denver/ProC-2657
92Denver/SB-150CO
93Rang/Keeb-209
Johnson, Lance
83F/St-15M
86ArkTr-8
87Louisvl-16
88Coke/WS-12
88D-31RR
88F-37
88Leaf-31RR
88T/Big-251
89AAA/ProC-30
89D-606
89F-499
89Panini/St-312
89RedFoley/St-67
89S/HotRook-33
89T-122
89Vanco/CMC-18
89Vanco/ProC-576
90Coke/WSox-9
90D-573
90F-536
90F/Can-536
90Leaf-259
90OPC-587
90S-570
90S/YS/II-38
90T-587
90T/Big-274
90UD-90
91B-349
91D-259
91F-123
91Kodak/WSox-1
91Leaf-403
91OPC-243
91Panini/FrSt-317
91Panini/St-253
91S-157
91StCl-199
91T-243
91UD-248
91Ultra-76
92B-208
92D-267
92F-87
92L-237
92L/BlkGold-237
92OPC-736
92Panini-130
92Pinn-373
92S-146
92StCl-444
92StCl/MPhoto-9
92Studio-154
92T-736
92T/Gold-736
92T/GoldWin-736
92TripleP-239
92UD-188
92Ultra-38
92WSox-1
93D-301
93F-204
93Flair-187
93L-373
93OPC-176
93Pac/Spanish-390
93Panini-141
93Pinn-137
93S-109
93Select-266
93Select/StatL-19
93StCl-359
93StCl/1stDay-359
93StCl/WSox-15
93Studio-192
93T-94
93T/Finest-64
93T/FinestRef-64
93T/Gold-94
93UD-280
93UD/SP-256
93Ultra-174
93WSox-14
94B-623
94D-552
94F-85
94L-13
94OPC-262
94Pac/Cr-129
94Pinn-86
94Pinn/Artist-86
94Pinn/Museum-86
94S-69
94S/Cycle-11
94S/GoldR-69
94Select-13
94Sf/2000-123
94StCl-194
94StCl/1stDay-194
94StCl/Gold-194
94StCl/Team-134
94T-452
94T/Finest-54
94T/FinestRef-54
94T/Gold-452
94TripleP-266
94UD-118
94UD/CollC-150
94UD/CollC/Gold-150
94UD/CollC/Silv-150
94UD/ElecD-118
94Ultra-35
Johnson, Larry D.
80RochR-20
81Evansvl-12
Johnson, Lee
90Durham/UpHer-1
90Greenvl/ProC-1124
90Greenvl/Star-9
91Osceola/ClBest-5
91Osceola/ProC-677
Johnson, Lindsey
86Kinston-11
89Miami/I/Star-9
89Miami/II/Star-7
Johnson, Lloyd
34G-86
Johnson, Lou
60T-476
61BeeHive-11
63T-238
66OPC-13
66T-13
67CokeCap/DodgAngel-8
67T-410
68OPC-184
68T-184
69JB
69MB-137
69T-367
90Target-387
Johnson, Luther
88Martins/Star-18
89AubAs/ProC-2176
90Ashvl/ProC-2762
91Osceola/ClBest-25
91Osceola/ProC-699
Johnson, Marcel
88NE-22
90Kgsport/Best-23
90Kgsport/Star-12
92Pulaski/ClBest-9
92Pulaski/ProC-3184
Johnson, Mark 1
86Lipscomb-15
88CapeCod-2
88CapeCod/Sum-1
91Augusta/ClBest-15
91Augusta/ProC-811
92CaroMud/ProC-1187
92CaroMud/SB-136
92MidwLAS/Team-22
92ProC/Tomorrow-79
93CaroMud/RBI-17
93ClBest/MLG-104
Johnson, Mark 2
90AR-18
91Eugene/ClBest-11
91Eugene/ProC-3738
92AppFox/ClBest-10
Johnson, Mark 3
88TM/Umpire-51
89TM/Umpire-49
90TM/Umpire-47
Johnson, Matt
92MedHat/ProC-3214
92MedHat/SportP-1
93Dunedin/ClBest-12
93Dunedin/ProC-1804
Johnson, Mike
79AppFx-10
82Wausau/Frit-18
84Chatt-14
Johnson, Mitch
80Elmira-18
85Pawtu-19
86Pawtu-11
87Pawtu-8
87Pawtu/TCMA-7
88Pawtu/CMC-3
88Pawtu/ProC-455
89Tucson/CMC-2
89Tucson/JP-9
89Tucson/ProC-187
Johnson, North
91Kinston/ClBest-30
Johnson, Otis
T201
Johnson, Owen
66T-356R
Johnson, Paul
89Pittsfld/Star-12
89Star/IISingl-160
90StLucie/Star-11
Johnson, Perry
83Idaho-7
Johnson, Randall David
(Randy)
86WPalmB-21
87Jaxvl-23
87SLAS-16
88Indianap/CMC-1
88Indianap/ProC-510
88TripleA/ASCMC-13
89Classic-95
89D-42RR
89D/Best-80
89D/Rook-43
89F-381
89F/Up-59
89OPC-186
89Panini/St-111
89S-645RP
89S/HotRook-63
89S/Tr-77T
89S/YS/II-32
89Sf-224R
89T-647
89T/Big-287
89T/Tr-57T
89UD-25
89Woolwth-13
90B-468
90Classic/III-22
90D-379
90D/BestAL-111
90F-518
90F/Can-518
90HotRook/St-23
90Leaf-483
90Mother/Mar-13
90OPC-431
90Panini/St-154
90S-415
90S/100Ris-52
90Sf-64
90T-431
90T/St-230
90UD-563
90USPlayC/AS-3S
91B-253
91Brisbane/Fut-17
91Classic/200-35
91CounHrth-26
91D-134
91D-BC2
91D/BC-BC2
91F-455
91F/WaxBox-2
91Leaf-319
91Leaf/Stud-116
91MajorLg/Pins-6
91OPC-225
91Panini/FrSt-353
91Panini/St-188
91Panini/St-2
91RedFoley/St-53
91S-290
91S-700NH
91Seven/3DCoin-9NW
91StCl-409
91StCl/Charter*-15
91T-225
91UD-376
91Ultra-339
92B-178
92D-207
92D/DK-DK22
92F-283
92F/Smoke-S11
92L-302
92L/BlkGold-302
92Mother/Mar-13
92OPC-525
92OPC/Premier-173
92Panini-62
92Pinn-379
92Pinn-595SIDE
92S-584
92StCl-720
92Studio-234
92Sunflower-15
92T-525
92T/Gold-525
92T/GoldWin-525
92T/Kids-126
92TripleP-71
92UD-164
92UD/TmMVPHolo-27
92Ultra-125
93B-431
93Cadaco-35
93D-581

93F-676
93Flair-272
93L-380
93Mar/DQ-1
93Mother/Mar-15
93OPC-140
93Pac/Spanish-288
93Panini-60
93Pinn-41
93S-384
93Select-118
93Select/StatL-73
93StCl-501
93StCl/1stDay-501
93StCl/Mar-16
93Studio-153
93T-460
93T/Finest-154
93T/FinestRef-154
93T/Gold-460
93T/Hill-16
93TripleP-167
93UD-336
93UD-824TC
93UD/FunPack-115
93UD/SP-132
93Ultra-269
93Ultra/Strike-3
94B-285
94D-352
94D/Special-352
94F-290
94F/AS-12
94F/Smoke-5
94L-164
94OPC-81
94Pac/Cr-574
94Pac/Silv-7
94Panini-119
94Panini-9
94Pinn-278
94Pinn/Trib-9
94RedFoley-7M
94S-33
94S/GoldR-33
94S/GoldS-43
94Select-19
94Select/CrCon-3
94SelectSam-19
94Sf/2000-30
94StCl-438
94StCl/1stDay-438
94StCl/Gold-438
94Studio-102
94T-290
94T/BlkGold-10
94T/Finest-213
94T/FinestRef-213
94T/Gold-290
94TripleP-128
94TripleP/Medal-13M
94UD-31FT
94UD-330
94UD/CollC-307TP
94UD/CollC/Gold-307TP
94UD/CollC/Silv-307TP
94UD/ElecD-31FT
94UD/SP-106
94Ultra-419
94Ultra/LL-5
94Ultra/Strike-1

Johnson, Randall Glenn
81Richm-22
82BK/Lids-14
82Pol/Atl-6
83Pol/Atl-6
83T-596
84D-321
84F-183
84Nes/792-289
84Pol/Atl-6
84T-289
85D-531
85F-330
85Richm-14
85T-458
86Phoenix-11
89Everett/Star-16
90Clinton/Best-15
90Clinton/ProC-2561

Johnson, Randall Stuart
(Randy)
80GlenF/B-18
80GlenF/C-4
81GlenF-18
82T/Tr-51T
83D-305
83F-617
83T-354
83Toledo-21
85BuffB-14
89Pac/SenLg-181
90EliteSenLg-23

Johnson, Reginald
92GreatF/SportP-11

Johnson, Rich
86Ashvl-16
87ColAst/ProC-23
88ColAst/Best-14

Johnson, Robert Dale
70T-702R
71OPC-365
71OPC-71LL
71T-365
71T-71LL
72MB-167
72OPC-27
72T-27
73OPC-657
73T-657
74OPC-269
74T-269
74T/Tr-269T
91WIZMets-202

Johnson, Robert Lee
(Indian Bob)
34G-68
35BU-20
35Exh/4-14
35G-8J
35G-9J
36Exh/4-14
37Exh/4-14
37OPC-123
38Exh/4-14
38Wheat-6
39Exh
39PlayBall-97
40PlayBall-25
41DP-49
41PlayBall-22
42Playball-22
44Playball-10
47Centen-12
47Signal
75Sheraton-17
77Shakey-C
77Shakey/WAS-C
81Conlon-33
91Conlon/Sport-96
92Conlon/Sport-547
93Conlon-776
94Conlon-1173
R314
V100
V351B-27

Johnson, Robert Wallace
62T-519
62T/St-97
63J-96
63P-96
63T-504
64T-304
65T-363
66OPC-148
66T-148
67OPC-38
67T-38
68T-338
69MB-134
69T-261
70T-693
78TCMA-79
91Crown/Orio-221
91WIZMets-204

Johnson, Rocky
88NE-12

Johnson, Roger
86Kinston-12

Johnson, Rondin
(Ron)
81Omaha-19
82Omaha-17
84Indianap-24
84Omaha-25
85Omaha-21
86Omaha/ProC-12
86Omaha/TCMA-2
87FtMyr-34
87Omaha-11
88Omaha/CMC-10
88Omaha/ProC-1515
90BBCity/Star-30CO
91BBCity/ClBest-29CO
91BBCity/ProC-1415CO
91Daikyo/Fut-5
92BBCity/ClBest-24MG
92BBCity/ProC-3860

Johnson, Roy Cleveland
32Orbit/un-35
33G-8
34Exh/4-9
35BU-63
38Exh/4-1
44Centen-12
81Conlon-32
88Conlon/AmAS-17
91Conlon/Sport-199
93Conlon-777
94Conlon-1173M
R305
R316
R337
V353-8

Johnson, Roy Edward
82Wichita-6
82Wichita-7M
83D-492
83Wichita/Dog-12
83Wichita/Dog-24
84Expo/PostC-14
84Indianap-7
85Indianap-5
87Tacoma-15
88Tacoma/CMC-15
88Tacoma/ProC-621

Johnson, Russ
92LSU/McDag-14
93Bz-12
93LSU/McDag-13
93T/Tr-115T
94LSU-3

Johnson, Scott
81Miami-21
87Watlo-9
88Kinston/Star-12
89SoBend/GS-6
90SoBend/Best-25TR
90SoBend/GS-8TR
92Saraso/ClBest-30TR

Johnson, Sean
88SLCity-30M

Johnson, Silas
33DH-24
35BU-54
47TipTop
R332-34

Johnson, Stan
61Union

Johnson, Steve 1
83Beaum-3
84Beaum-20
86Watlo-13

Johnson, Steve 2
92Savan/ClBest-9
92Savan/ProC-659

Johnson, Sylvester
39PlayBall-28
40PlayBall-99
43Centen-13
44Centen-13
45Centen-13
92Conlon/Sport-654
93Conlon-901
E120
V117-13
V61-24
W572
W573

Johnson, Terence
(T.J.)
84LitFalls-14
85LitFalls-19

Johnson, Terry
83BurlR-6
83BurlR/Frit-10
83Tulsa-24
84Tulsa-34
85Tulsa-30

Johnson, Tim
74OPC-554
74T-554
75OPC-556
75T-556
75T/M-556
76A&P/Milw
76OPC-613
76T-613
77T-406
78BJ/PostC-11
78T-542
79OPC-89
79T-182
80OPC-155
80T-297
88GreatF/Team-25MG
89AS/Cal-23MG
89Bak/Cal-206MG
90AAASingl/ProC-590MG
90Indianap/CMC-25MG
90Indianap/ProC-307MG
90ProC/Singl-75MG

Johnson, Todd
91FresnoSt/Smok-6
91T/Tr-63T
92StCl/Dome-93
92T/DQ-24

Johnson, Tom R.
75OPC-618R
75T-618R
75T/M-618R
75Tacoma/KMMO-11
76OPC-448
76T-448
77BurgChef-46
77T-202
78K-9
78T-54
78Twin/FriszP-10
79OPC-77
79T-162
80GlenF/B-3
80GlenF/C-28
81QuadC-13

Johnson, Tom
83MidldC-23
86BurlEx-12
87FtMyr-19
88Virgini/Star-11
89BBCity/Star-11

Johnson, Tony
84Idaho/Team-14

Johnson, Tookie
90LSUPol-16
91LSU/Pol-5

Johnson, Wallace
(Wally)
82F-192
82Wichita-8
83F-285
85Indianap-21
86Indianap-19
87F-321
87OPC-234
87T-588
88F-186
88OPC-228
88S-433
88T-228
89D-484
89F-382
89OPC-138
89Panini/St-120
89S-196
89T-138
89UD-124
90D-570
90F-351
90F/Can-351
90Leaf-344
90OPC-318
90PublInt/St-178
90S-479
90T-318
90T/Big-46

Johnson, Walter P.
10Domino-60
11Helmar-72
12Sweet/Pin-60A
12Sweet/Pin-60B
14CJ-57
15CJ-57
21Exh-84
24Sherlock-4
25Exh-125
26Exh-125
27Exh-62
40PlayBall-120
48Exh/HOF
48Swell-4
49Leaf/Prem-4
50Callahan
50W576-43
51T/CM
60Exh/HOF-13
60F-6
60NuCard-40
61F-49
61GP-29
61NuCard-440
61T-409HL
63Bz/ATG-12
69Bz-6
69Bz-Sm
72F/FFeat-8
72K/ATG-1
72Laugh/GF-2
73OPC-476LL
73OPC-478LL
73T-476LL
73T-478LL
75Sheraton-15
76OPC-349AS
76Rowe-10M
76Shakey-3
76T-349AS
77Galasso-105
77Galasso-144
77Galasso-234
77Shakey-4
79T-417LL
79T-418LL
80Laugh/3/4/5-3
80Laugh/FFeat-25
80Pac/Leg-45
80Perez/HOF-2
80SSPC/HOF
81Conlon-37
83D/HOF-2
84D/Champs-37
85Woolwth-21
86Conlon/1-4
87Conlon/2-6
87Nestle/DT-9
89Pac/Leg-192
89Swell-3
90BBWit-62
90HOF/St-28
90Perez/GreatMom-8
90Swell/Great-75
91Conlon/Sport-258
91Conlon/Sport-9
91LineD-45
91Swell/Great-130
92Conlon/Col-7
92Conlon/Gold-934
92Conlon/Gold-934G
92Conlon/Sport-353
92Conlon/Sport-564
92Mega/Ruth-126M
93AP/ASG-90
93AP/ASG24K-24G
93Conlon-758
93Conlon-804
93Conlon-934
93Conlon/MasterBW-3
93Conlon/MasterCol-3M
93Conlon/Proto-934
93CrackJack-5
93UD/ATH-138M
93UD/ATH-142M
93UD/ATH-143M
93UD/ATH-78
93UD/T202-4M
94Conlon-1255
94Conlon/Col-30
94TedW-89
94TedW/Lock-15
BF2-45
D327
D328-87
D329-91
D350/2-90
E120
E121/120
E121/80
E122
E126-28
E135-87
E210-45

E224
E300
E91
L1-135
M101/4-91
M101/5-90
M116
PM1-7
PM10/Sm-86
R310
R423-54
S74-39
S81-110
T201
T202
T204
T205
T206
T207
T213/blue
T214-15
T215/blue
T215/brown
T222
T3-99
V100
V117-30
V61-47
V89-47
W501-17
W514-94
W515-38
W516-8
W573
W575
WG5-23
WG6-22
WG7-23

Johnson, Wayne
82Watlo/B-5
82Watlo/Frit-25
83BuffB-2
85Water-10
91Martins/ClBest-4
91Martins/ProC-3467
92Batavia/ClBest-9
92Batavia/ProC-3277

Johnson, Wes
88MissSt-15

Johnson, William Julius
(Judy)
74Laugh/Black-36
76Shakey-150
78Laugh/Black-29
80Perez/HOF-150
86Negro/Frit-4
86Negro/Frit-5
88Conlon/NegAS-6
88Negro/Duques-9
90Negro/Star-18
90Perez/GreatMom-46
93TWill-107

Johnson, William Russell
44Yank/St-15
48B-33
48L-14
49B-129
50B-102
51B-74
51BR-A5
51T/BB-21
52B-122
52T-83
53Hunter
53T-21
79TCMA-230
91T/Arc53-21
Exh47
R346-1

Johnson, Willy
88Sumter/ProC-417
89Sumter/ProC-1092
90Sumter/Best-26TR
93Macon/ClBest-30TR

Johnston, Chris
83Knoxvl-11

Johnston, Craig
88Martins/Star-19
89Kingspt/Star-14
91Sydney/Fut-11

Johnston, Dan
88Geneva/ProC-1644
90Greens/Best-5
90Greens/ProC-2657
90Greens/Star-11
91PrWill/ClBest-6
91PrWill/ProC-1422
92FtLaud/ClBest-8
92FtLaud/ProC-2608
92FtLaud/Team-19

Johnston, Fred Ivy
90Target-388

Johnston, Greg
78Cr/PCL-47
79Phoenix
79T-726R
80T-686R
81T-328R
91Parramatta/Fut-12

Johnston, James H.
25Exh-13
90Target-389
D327
D328-88
E120
E121/80
E122
E135-88
E220
V100
W515-41
W572
W575

Johnston, Jody
82Jacks-6
82Lynch-22

Johnston, Joel
88Eugene/Best-11
89BBCity/Star-12
90Memphis/Best-17
90Memphis/ProC-1010
91AAA/LineD-337
91B-297
91Omaha/LineD-337
91Omaha/ProC-1031
92B-199
92D/Rook-60
92F-673
92OPC-328
92Pinn-259
92Pinn/Rook-10
92Pol/Royal-13
92ProC/Tomorrow-73
92S-764
92S/Rook-15
92StCl-345
92T-328
92T/91Debut-91
92T/Gold-328
92T/GoldWin-328
93D-791
93Select/RookTr-137T
94D-246
94F-610
94S-308
94S/GoldR-308
94T-557
94T/Gold-557
94TripleP-184

Johnston, John
16FleischBrd-47

Johnston, Len
92Bluefld/ClBest-24CO

Johnston, Mark
79WHave-1
82ElPaso-10
83Beloit/Frit-10

Johnston, Richard
E223
N172
N284
N526

Johnston, Ryan
88Savan/ProC-352

Johnston, Sean
94ClBest/Gold-156

Johnston, Stan
86Bakers-16TR
87Bakers-14TR
88Bakers/Cal-264
89Albuq/ProC-74

Johnston, Tom
93Welland/ClBest-9
93Welland/ProC-3366

Johnston, Wheeler
(Doc)
15CJ-150
E120
W573

Johnstone, Jay
67CokeCap/DodgAngel-34
67T-213
68T-389
69JB
69MB-138
69OPC-59
69T-59
70MLB/St-174
70OPC-485
70T-485
70T/CB
71OPC-292
71T-292
72MB-170
72OPC-233
72T-233
75OPC-242
75T-242
75T/M-242
76OPC-114
76SSPC-463
76T-114
77BurgChef-166
77K-35
77OPC-226
77Pep-71
77T-415
78SSPC/270-43
78T-675
79BK/Y-5
79OPC-287
79T-558
80OPC-15
80Pol/Dodg-21
80T-31
81D-300
81F-128
81OPC-372
81Pol/Dodg-21
81T-372
82D-262
82F-10
82Pol/Dodg-21
82RedLob
82T-774
82T/Tr-52T
83D-561
83F-499
83OPC-152
83OPC/St-220
83T-152
83T/St-220
83Thorn-21
84D-540
84F-495
84Nes/792-249
84SevenUp-21
84T-249
84T/St-50
85Coke/Dodg-16
86T-496
90Target-390
92Yank/WIZ70-83

Johnstone, John
89Pittsfld/Star-13
89Star/IISingl-169
90FSLAS/Star-7
90StLucie/Star-12
91AA/LineD-635
91ClBest/Singl-64
91Wmsprt/LineD-635
91Wmsprt/ProC-287
92Bingham/ProC-510
92Bingham/SB-61
92Sky/AASingl-26
92UD/ML-310
93D-784
93Edmon/ProC-1131
93StCl-734
93StCl/1stDay-734
93T-454
93T/Gold-454

Joiner, Dave
88Clmbia/GS-16
89Clmbia/Best-8
89Clmbia/GS-13

Joiner, Roy
(Pop)
40PlayBall-211

Jok, Stan
52Park-93
54T-196
55B-251
94T/Arc54-196

Jolley, Mike
91Savan/ClBest-6
91Savan/ProC-1647
92Savan/ClBest-2
92Savan/ProC-660

Jolley, Smead
28Exh/PCL-13
30CEA/Pin-16
31Exh/4-20
32Orbit/num-25
32Orbit/un-36
87Conlon/2-23
88LitSun/Minor-8
93Conlon-858
R305
R315-C3
R315-D3
V355-98

Jolly, Dave
53JC-8
53SpicSpan/3x5-14
54JC-17
54SpicSpan/PostC-11
54T-188
55B-71
55Gol/Braves-15
55JC-16
55SpicSpan/DC-10
55T-35
55T/DH-95
57T-389
58T-183
94T/Arc54-188

Jonas, John
90Salinas/Cal-144GM

Jonas, Pete
43Centen-14
47Centen-13
47Signal

Jonathan, Don Leo
72Dimanche*-122

Jones, Al
82AppFx/Frit-7
83AppFx/Frit-20
85D-404
85T-437
86BuffB-13
86T-227
87Denver-26

Jones, Alan
72Dimanche*-141

Jones, Allen
60Maple-10

Jones, Barry
85PrWill-3
86Hawaii-13
86Sumter/ProC-12
87D-602
87Durham-2
87F-611
87T-494
88F/Up-U114
88Greenvl/Best-8
88SLAS-14
88T-168
89Coke/WS-12
89D-647
89F-500
89Richm/Bob-11
89Richm/CMC-20
89Richm/Ko-18
89Richm/ProC-846
89S-333
89T-539
89T/SenLg-3
89UD-457
90AAASingl/ProC-417
90Coke/WSox-10
90Leaf-431
90OPC-243
90ProC/Singl-288
90PublInt/St-390
90Richm/Bob-11
90Richm/CMC-12
90Richm/ProC-272
90Richm/Team-15
90S-152
90T-243
91AAA/LineD-86
91B-439
91ColoSp/LineD-86
91ColoSp/ProC-2196
91D-534
91F-124
91F/UltraUp-U91
91Leaf-406
91OPC-33
91OPC/Premier-69
91Panini/St-259
91S-115
91S/RookTr-75T
91StCl-551
91T-33
91T/Tr-64T
91UD-39
91UD/Ext-789
92D-155
92F-484
92L-484
92L/BlkGold-484
92OPC-361
92Phill/Med-16
92S-297
92StCl-671
92T-361
92T/Gold-361
92T/GoldWin-361
92UD-681
92Ultra-546
93Richm/Bleach-17
93Richm/Team-13

Jones, Ben
92Classic/DP-102
92FrRow/DP-66

Jones, Bill
86StPete-16

Jones, Bobby 1
(Ducky)
28Exh/PCL-14

Jones, Bobby 2
89BendB/Legoe-21
90QuadC/GS-30
91AA/LineD-438
91MidldA/LineD-438
91MidldA/OneHour-14
91MidldA/ProC-445
92MidldA/OneHour-10
92MidldA/SB-460

Jones, Bobby 3
(Golfer)
33SK*-38

Jones, Bobby 4
92Helena/ProC-1710

Jones, Brian
85PrWill-31
86PrWill-13
87Harris-17

Jones, Bryan
76Watlo

Jones, Butter
92Everett/ClBest-13
92Everett/ProC-1703

Jones, Calvin
87Chatt/Best-6
88Vermont/ProC-962
89SanBern/Cal-64
89Wmsprt/Star-11
90SanBern/Best-3
90SanBern/Cal-96
90SanBern/ProC-2629
91AAA/LineD-62
91Calgary/LineD-62
91Calgary/ProC-511
92D-690
92L-71
92L/BlkGold-71
92Mother/Mar-21
92ProC/Tomorrow-139
92S-868
92StCl-127
92T/91Debut-92
92UD-731
92Ultra-433
93D-749
93F-413
93StCl-578
93StCl/1stDay-578
93T-664
93T/Gold-664

Jones, Carl
87Sumter-14

Jones, Charles
E107
T204

Jones, Charlie
83VeroB-6

Jones, Chipper
90Classic/DP-1
90Classic/DP-NNO
90Classic/III-92
90Classic/III-NO
91B-569
91ClBest/Singl-268
91Macon/ClBest-19
91Macon/ProC-872
91OPC-333FDP
91S-671FDP
91SALAS/ProC-SAL33
91T-333FDP
91UD-55TP
92B-28
92ClBest-93
92ClBest/BBonusC-7
92ClBest/RBonus-BC7
92Durham/ClBest-1
92Durham/ProC-1108
92Durham/Team-10
92OPC-551M
92ProC/Tomorrow-190
92StCl/1stDP-1
92T-551M
92T/Gold-551M
92T/GoldWin-551M
92UD/ML-165
92UD/ML-66DS
92UD/ML/TPHolo-TP3
92UD/POY-PY5
93B-347FOIL
93B-86
93ClBest/Fisher-5
93ClBest/MLG-172
93D-721RR
93FExcel/ML-2
93FExcel/MLAS-2
93L/GRook-19
93Richm/Bleach-13
93Richm/Pep-6
93Richm/Team-14
93StCl-638
93StCl/1stDay-638
93StCl/Brave-9
93T-529M
93T/Gold-529M
93UD-24SR
93UD-459IN
93UD/5thAnn-A11
93UD/OnDeck-D16
93UD/SP-280FOIL
94B-353
94B-489
94D-453
94F/MLP-18
94L-46
94OPC-57
94Pac/Cr-10
94Pinn-236
94Pinn/Artist-236
94Pinn/Museum-236
94Pinn/New-20
94Pinn/RookTPinn-5M
94S-572
94S/Boys-58
94Sf/2000-160
94StCl/Team-50
94T-777
94T/Gold-777
94TripleP-281
94UD-185
94UD/CollC-152
94UD/CollC/Gold-152
94UD/CollC/Silv-152
94UD/ElecD-185
94Ultra-152

Jones, Chris C.
86Cedar/TCMA-21
86Phoenix-12
87Dunedin-17
87Phoenix-1
87Vermont-22
88Chatt/Best-6
88Idaho/ProC-1843
88Knoxvl/Best-16
88SanDiegoSt-9
89Knoxvl/Best-11
89Knoxvl/ProC-1134
89Knoxvl/Star-9
89Nashvl/CMC-20
89Nashvl/ProC-1290
89SanDiegoSt-9
90AAASingl/ProC-558
90Knoxvl/Best-20
90Knoxvl/ProC-1243
90Knoxvl/Star-7
90Nashvl/CMC-16
90Nashvl/ProC-246
90ProC/Singl-141
91AAA/LineD-11
91Albuq/LineD-11
91Albuq/ProC-1136
91B-676
91D/Rook-50
91S/RookTr-92T
91T/Tr-65T
92D-464
92F-410
92L-444
92L/BlkGold-444
92Mother/Ast-22
92OPC-332
92S-811
92S/100RisSt-69
92StCl-698
92T-332
92T/91Debut-93
92T/Gold-332
92T/GoldWin-332
93F/Final-35
93Flair-42
93StCl/Rockie-19
93T/Tr-102T
94D-510
94F-445
94Pac/Cr-199
94Panini-176
94S-148
94S/GoldR-148
94T-496
94T/Gold-496

Jones, Chris L.
88CapeCod/Sum-164

Jones, Chris
78Wausau
82Tucson-2
83Tucson-19
84Cram/PCL-52
85Cram/PCL-51

Jones, Clarence W.
68T-506
86Sumter/ProC-13
87Sumter-6
88Richm/CMC-25
88Richm/ProC-17
89Brave/Dubuq-14CO
90Brave/Dubuq/Singl-15CO
91Brave/Dubuq/Stand-20CO
92Brave/Lyke/Stand-18CO
93Brave/Lyke/Stand-17CO

Jones, Cleon Joseph
65T-308R
66OPC-67R
66T-67R
67CokeCap/AS-31
67CokeCap/NLAS-35
67CokeCap/YMet-24
67Kahn
67OPC-165
67OPC/PI-13
67T-165
67T/PI-13
68T-254
69MB-139
69MLB/St-167
69T-512
69T/S-50
69T/St-65
70K-3
70MLB/St-78
70OPC-61LL
70T-575
70T-61LL
70T/CB
70Trans-1
70Trans/M-24
71MLB/St-156
71OPC-527
71T-527
71T/Coins-103
71T/tatt-1
72MB-171
72OPC-31
72OPC-32IA
72T-31
72T-32IA
73OPC-540
73T-540
74OPC-245
74OPC-476WS
74T-245
74T-476WS
74T/St-64
75Ho-123
75K-21
75OPC-43
75T-43
75T/M-43
76SSPC/MetsY-M11
81TCMA-322
91WIZMets-207
94Mets/69-14

Jones, Cliff
92Pittsfld/ClBest-17
92Pittsfld/ProC-3290

Jones, Clinton
(Casey)
92Negro/Kraft-2
92Negro/Retort-34

Jones, Craig
84Richm-13

Jones, D.J.
87Durham-23

Jones, Dan 1
83Miami-15

Jones, Dan 2
91ClBest/Singl-423
91Welland/ClBest-29
91Welland/ProC-3568
92Salem/ClBest-21
92Salem/ProC-60
92StCl/Dome-95
93CaroMud/RBI-9

Jones, Darryl
78Cr/PCL-24
79Colum-28
80T-670R
92Yank/WIZ70-84

Jones, David Jefferson
(Davy)
11Helmar-33
81Tiger/Detroit-19
93Conlon-753
E103
E104
E107
E254
E270/1
E93
M116
S74-15
T202
T205
T3-100
W555

Jones, David
85Durham-7
86Sumter/ProC-14

Jones, Dax
91ClBest/Singl-421
91Everett/ClBest-8
91Everett/ProC-3931
92ClBest-79
92Clinton/ClBest-1
92Clinton/ProC-3610

Jones, DeWayne
88SoOreg/ProC-1698

Jones, Dennis
87Myrtle-13
88BBAmer-19
88Knoxvl/Best-19
89Knoxvl/Best-12
89Knoxvl/ProC-1136
89Knoxvl/Star-10
90Knoxvl/Best-24
90Knoxvl/Star-8

Jones, Donny
77QuadC
80ElPaso-18

Jones, Doug
78Newar
79BurlB-12
81ElPaso-11
82Pol/Brew-45
82Vanco-13
84Cram/PCL-39
84ElPaso-7
85Water-12
86Maine-11
87Gator-46
88D-588
88D/Best-325
88F-613
88Gator-11
88S-594
88T-293
89B-78
89Classic-89
89D-438
89D/AS-20
89D/Best-173
89F-409
89F/BBAS-23
89F/BBMVP's-23
89KennerFig-75
89OPC-312
89Panini/St-319
89Panini/St-5
89S-387
89S-656HL
89S/HotStar-41
89Sf-38
89T-690
89T-6RB
89T/LJN-152
89T/Mini-51
89T/St-215
89T/St-3
89T/St/Backs-32
89UD-540
89Woolwth-14
90B-328
90Classic-114
90D-320
90D/BestAL-61
90ElPasoATG/Team-15
90F-495
90F/BB-22
90F/Can-495
90F/LL-20
90GA-10
90Leaf-153
90OPC-75
90Panini/St-63
90PublInt/St-562
90S-130
90Sf-96
90T-75
90T/Big-316
90T/St-215
90UD-632
90USPlayC/AS-7S
91B-77
91Classic/200-55
91D-232
91F-372
91Indian/McDon-16
91Leaf-57
91Leaf/Stud-46
91OPC-745
91Panini/FrSt-224
91Panini/St-173
91Panini/Top15-87
91RedFoley/St-54
91S-45
91S-884DT
91S/100SS-54
91StCl-145
91T-745
91UD-216
91Ultra-115
92D-674
92F-114
92F/Up-87
92L-253
92L/BlkGold-253
92Mother/Ast-16
92OPC-461
92OPC/Premier-51
92Pinn-499
92S-53
92S/RookTr-38T
92StCl-616
92Studio-38
92T-461
92T/Gold-461
92T/GoldWin-461
92T/Tr-57T
92T/TrGold-57T
92UD-798
93B-532
93D-296
93F-54
93Flair-65
93L-161
93Mother/Ast-14
93OPC-267
93Pac/Spanish-478
93Pinn-443
93S-197
93Select-67
93StCl-411
93StCl/1stDay-411
93StCl/Ast-15
93StCl/MurphyS-53
93Studio-115
93T-171
93T/Finest-69
93T/FinestRef-69
93T/Gold-171
93TripleP-175
93UD-171
93Ultra-44
94D-533
94F-494
94Finest-380
94Flair-209
94L-377
94Panini-195
94Phill/Med-15
94Pinn-222
94Pinn/Artist-222
94Pinn/Museum-222
94S-544
94StCl/Team-216
94T-334
94T/Gold-334
94UD-374
94Ultra-207
94Ultra-548

Jones, Earl
(Lefty)
48Signal
49Remar

Jones, Elijah
C46-52

Jones, Eric
81Batavia-22

Jones, Eugene
89Greens/ProC-416
90CharWh/Best-22
90CharWh/ProC-2253
90Foil/Best-207
90ProC/Singl-695
91Cedar/ClBest-22
91Cedar/ProC-2732
92CharWh/ProC-21

Jones, Fielder
87Conlon/2-44
90HOF/St-20
90Target-391
BF2-41
D328-89
D329-92
D350/2-91
E135-89
M101/4-92
M101/5-91
T206
W514-50
WG2-29

Jones, Gareth Howell
(Gary)
71OPC-559R
71T-559R
92Yank/WIZ70-85

Jones, Gary 1
91Madison/ClBest-22MG
91Madison/ProC-2146MG
92Reno/Cal-59MG

Jones, Gary 2
83QuadC-21
86Fresno/Smok-4
87Tacoma-5
88SanJose/Cal-121
88SanJose/ProC-112
88Tacoma/CMC-23
88Tacoma/ProC-612
89Huntsvl/Best-17

Jones, Geary
86Columbia-17
87Lynch-17
88Jacks/GS-3
88StLucie/Star-14
92Kingspt/ClBest-26CO
92Kingspt/ProC-1548CO

Jones, George

85Everett/Cram-6A
85Everett/Cram-6B
Jones, Glenn
82Clinton/Frit-21
91Adelaide/Fut-1
Jones, Gordon 1
55Hunter
55T-78
55T/DH-6
57Seattle/Pop-22
59T-458
60L-73
60T-98
61T-442
91Crown/Orio-229
Jones, Gordon 2
82Redwd-5
Jones, Grover
(Deacon)
63T-253R
Jones, Gus
86Cram/NWL-47
87FtMyr-14
Jones, Hank
77LodiD
78LodiD
79LodiD-20
Jones, Harold
62T-49
Jones, J. Dalton
64T-459R
65OPC-178
65T-178
66T-317
67CokeCap/RedSox-8
67OPC-139
67T-139
67T/Test/RSox-8
68CokeCap/RedSox-8
68Dexter-44
68OPC-106
68T-106
69MB-140
69T-457
70T-682
71MLB/St-395
71OPC-367
71T-367
72MB-172
72OPC-83
72T-83
73OPC-512
73T-512
89Pac/SenLg-55
93Rang/Keeb-20
Jones, James C.
(Jimmy)
84Beaum-1
85Beaum-8
86Cram/NWL-25
86Everett/Pop-9
86LasVegas-8
87D-557
87F-650R
87F/Up-U54
87LasVegas-17
87Sf/Rook-35
87Sf/TPrev-16M
88Coke/Padres-45PAN
88D-141
88D/Best-189
88F-588
88S-246
88Smok/Padres-13
88T-63
89B-169
89Colum/CMC-9
89Colum/Pol-10
89Colum/ProC-752
89D-247
89D/Best-217
89Denver/CMC-17
89F-308
89S-294
89S/NWest-26
89T-748
89T/Tr-58T
89UD-286
90AAASingl/ProC-322
90ColClip/CMC-23
90ColClip/ProC-672
90Colum/Pol-19
90OPC-359
90ProC/Singl-223
90S/NWest-21
90T-359
90T/TVYank-48
91B-553
91F-667
91Leaf-371
91Mother/Ast-12
91S-583
92D-272
92F-438
92Mother/Ast-12
92OPC-184
92S-33
92StCl-53
92T-184
92T/Gold-184
92T/GoldWin-184
92UD-392
92Yank/WIZ80-93
93D-324
93F-437
93OPC-293
93Pac/Spanish-125
93S-463
93T-477
93T/Gold-477
93UD-698
Jones, James
88CapeCod-3
88CapeCod/Sum-70
89BendB/Legoe-5
Jones, Jeffrey A.
79Ogden/TCMA-23
81T-687
82D-213
82F-94
82F/St-130
82T-139
82Tacoma-24
83D-651
83T-259
83Tacoma-28
84Cram/PCL-82
84Nes/792-464
84T-464
85T-319
Jones, Jeffrey R.
80Cedar-19
81Cedar-16
82Cedar-24
84D-262
84MidldC-20
87GlenF-4
88GlenF/ProC-936
89Fayette/ProC-1570
90AAASingl/ProC-395CO
90CedarDG/Best-19
90ProC/Singl-399CO
90Toledo/CMC-26CO
90Toledo/ProC-165CO
91AA/LineD-400M
91London/LineD-400CO
91London/ProC-1893CO
91Pac/SenLg-32
92London/ProC-650CO
Jones, Jim
84Madis/Pol-14
85Modesto/Chong-15
86Modesto-15
87Pocatel/Bon-7
87SLAS-12
88Huntsvl/BK-9
88Tacoma/CMC-21
88Tacoma/ProC-618
89AS/Cal-30
89Denver/ProC-40
89SanJose/Best-23
89SanJose/Cal-222
89SanJose/ProC-460
89SanJose/Star-16
90SanJose/Best-11
90SanJose/Cal-38
90SanJose/ProC-2016
90SanJose/Star-14
91Reno/Cal-5
Jones, Joe
77Spartan
Jones, Keith Tyrone
(Kiki)
89GreatF-18
90AS/Cal-20
90B-86
90Bakers/Cal-230
90S-676DC
91ClBest/Singl-212
91Johnson/ClBest-16
91Johnson/ProC-3989
91UD-59TP
91VeroB/ClBest-8
91VeroB/ProC-769
92ClBest-292
92VeroB/ClBest-1
Jones, Keith 1
82BurlR/Frit-10
82BurlR/TCMA-5
84Tulsa-6
Jones, Keith 2
92Spring/ClBest-10
92Spring/ProC-882
Jones, Ken
78Wausau
81Water-4
82Water-4
83Water-4
87Madis-14
Jones, Kevin
85Osceola/Team-28BB
89Everett/Star-17
90Billings/ProC-3229
90CharWh/Best-17
Jones, Kirk 1
80Batavia-6
Jones, Kirk 2
85Osceola/Team-29BB
Jones, Lance
88CapeCod/Sum-133
Jones, Larry K.
80RochR-7
81RochR-19
82Iowa-17
82WHave-17
83Iowa-5
Jones, Lee
83Redwd-13
Jones, Lynn
78Indianap-20
80T-123
81T-337
82D-542
82F-270
82T-64
83F-333
83T-483
84Nes/792-731
84T-731
84T/Tr-58
85T-513
86D-466
86F-11
86NatPhoto-35
86T-671
91Pol/Royal-26CO
92Pol/Royal-27M
Jones, Mack
62T-186
63T-137
65OPC-241
65T-241
66Kahn
66T-446
67CokeCap/Brave-18
67T-435
68CokeCap/Brave-18
68Kahn
68T-353
69Fud's-5
69MLB/St-159
69T-625
69T/St-57
70Expo/PostC-10
70Expos/Pins-8
70MLB/St-66
70OPC-38
70T-38
70T/SO
71Expo/ProS-11
71MLB/St-131
71OPC-142
71T-142
71T/Coins-135
72MB-173
76Laugh/Jub-20
92Nabisco-27
93Expo/D/McDon-15
Jones, Mark
88Visalia/Cal-173
Jones, Marty
90AubAs/Best-15
90AubAs/ProC-3403
Jones, Matt
92Welland/ClBest-11
92Welland/ProC-1331
Jones, Michael C.
(Mike)
81Omaha-9
81T-66R
82Clinton/Frit-7
82F-412
82T-471R
84Omaha-20
84Shrev/FB-9
85D-640
85Fresno/Pol-6
85T-244
86D-419
86F-12
86Richm-10
86Shrev-12
86T-514
86Ventura-9
87Dunedin-4
Jones, Mike 1
74Cedar
Jones, Mike 2
88Bristol/ProC-1889
88Knoxvl/Best-4
88Nashvl/CMC-6
88Nashvl/ProC-485
88Nashvl/Team-14
89Lakeland/Star-11
89RochR/CMC-1
89RochR/ProC-1657
89Star/Wax-31
90RochR/CMC-4
Jones, Mike 3
90ProC/Singl-305
90WichSt-18
91Billing/SportP-18
91Billings/ProC-3761
92Cedar/ClBest-16
92Cedar/ProC-1077
Jones, Motorboat
92CharWh/ClBest-10
Jones, Neil
91Melbourne/Fut-2
Jones, Norm
89Denver/ProC-56
Jones, Odell
78Colum
78T-407
80Port-17
80T-342
81Portl-13
82Portl-4
83Rang-21
83T/Tr-50
84D-256
84F-421
84Nes/792-734
84OPC-382
84Rang-21
84T-734
85D-525
85F-560
85RochR-19
85T-29
86RochR-10
87D-582
87Syrac/TCMA-5
88Pol/Brew-28
89F-189
89Pac/SenLg-171
89S-579
89TM/SenLg-56
89UD-608
91Crown/Orio-231
91Pac/SenLg-27
93Rang/Keeb-211
Jones, Oscar
90Target-392
Jones, Paul
92Bluefld/ClBest-18
92Bluefld/ProC-2365
Jones, Percy
92Conlon/Sport-456
E120
E126-18
R316
Jones, Randy
74McDon
74OPC-173SD
74T-173
74T/St-94
75OPC-248
75T-248
75T/M-248
76Crane-23
76Ho-143
76K-4
76MSA/Disc
76OPC-199LL
76OPC-201LL
76OPC-310
76SSPC-118
76T-199LL
76T-201LL
76T-310
77BurgChef-132
77Ho-26
77Ho/Twink-26
77K-17
77OPC-113
77OPC-5LL
77Padre/SchCd-16
77Padre/SchCd-17
77T-550
77T 6LL
77T/ClothSt-23
78Ho-121
78OPC-101
78Padre/FamFun-16
78T-56
78Wiffle/Discs-33
79Ho-99
79OPC-95
79T-194
80OPC-160
80T-305
80T/Super-48
81Coke
81D-122
81F-487
81OPC-148
81T-458
81T/Tr-777
82F-528
82OPC-274
82T-626
83F-546
83F/St-5M
83OPC-29
83T-29
88Grenada-36
89Padre/Mag-16
91WIZMets-205
94TedW-84
Jones, Rex
83ColumAst-24
84Cram/PCL-56
85Cram/PCL-74TR
86Tucson-9TR
88Tucson/ProC-192
Jones, Rick
88Portl/CMC-14
88Portl/ProC-656
89Spartan/ProC-1032
90Spartan/Best-27CO
90Spartan/ProC-2509CO
90Spartan/Star-27CO
91Crown/Orio-230
Jones, Ricky
83RochR-16
85CharlO-23
85RochR-6
86RochR-11
87CharlO/WBTV-7
Jones, Robert Joseph
(Bobby)
91Classic/DP-32
91FrRow/DP-11
91FresnoSt/Smok-7
92B-389
92Bingham/ProC-511
92Bingham/SB-62
92ClBest-341
92Pinn-548
92Sky/AASingl-27
92StCl/Dome-94
92UD/ML-294
92UD/POY-PY14
93B-355FOIL
93B-650
93ClBest/MLG-61
93FExcel/ML-75
93FExcel/MLAS-5
93T-817

93T/Gold-817
93UD-19SR
93Ultra-429
94B-652
94D-501
94F-569
94Flair-199
94L-304
94OPC-108
94OPC/DiamD-6
94Pinn-380
94Pinn/New-14
94Select-167
94Sf/2000-148
94Studio-116
94T-539
94T/Finest-109
94T/FinestRef-109
94T/Gold-539
94TripleP-145
94UD-119
94UD/CollC-151
94UD/CollC/Gold-151
94UD/CollC/Silv-151
94UD/ElecD-119
94UD/SP-118
94Ultra-530

Jones, Robert O.
(Bobby)
75IntLgAS/Broder-14
75PCL/AS-14
75Spokane/Caruso-9
77T-16
78Cr/PCL-79
83OKCty-11
83Rang-6
84Nes/792-451
84Rang-6
84T-451
85D-134
85F-559
85Rang-6
85T-648
86OKCty-8
86T-142]
89CharlR/Star-26MG
89Pac/SenLg-98
90CharlR/Star-29MG
90EliteSenLg-71
90FSLAS/Star-50
91AA/LineD-599MG
91Pac/SenLg-59
91Tulsa/LineD-599MG
91Tulsa/ProC-2788MG
91Tulsa/Team-15
92Tulsa/ProC-2709MG
92Tulsa/SB-624MG
93Rang/Keeb-210

Jones, Robert T.
(Bobby)
87Beloit-8
88CalLgAS-13
88Stockton/Cal-190
88Stockton/ProC-732
89AS/Cal-32
89Stockton/Best-24
89Stockton/Cal-166
89Stockton/ProC-383
89Stockton/Star-15

Jones, Robert Walter
E120
V100

Jones, Ron
85Bend/Cram-13
86Clearw-11
86FSLAS-27
87Maine-23
87Maine/TCMA-17
88Maine/CMC-14
88Maine/ProC-280
88Phill/TastyK-27
89B-407
89Classic-96
89D-40RR
89D/Rook-42
89F-574
89Panini/St-143
89Phill/TastyK-14
89S-639RP
89S/HotRook-25
89S/YS/II-3
89Sf-178
89Sf-225M
89T-349
89ToysRUs-16
89UD-11
90AAASingl/ProC-312
90D-487
90F-563
90F/Can-563
90OPC-129
90Phill/TastyK-16
90ProC/Singl-245
90PublInt/St-243
90S-364
90S/100Ris-31
90ScranWB/CMC-19
90ScranWB/ProC-610
90T-129
90UD-94
91S-653
92D-738
92S-342
93Richm/Bleach-9
93Richm/Pep-14
93Richm/Team-15

Jones, Ronnie
81BurlB-25

Jones, Ross
82Albuq-17
83Albuq-16
84Tidew-18
85BurlR-26
85Tidew-22
85Utica-2
86Chatt-15
86DayBe-14
87Gaston/ProC-17
88F-262
88S-598
88T-169
88WPalmB/Star-13
89WPalmB/Star-13
91WIZMets-208

Jones, Ruppert
75Omaha/Team-7
77T-488R
78OPC-20
78T-141
79OPC-218
79T-422
80OPC-43
80T-78
81D-349
81F-101
81OPC-225
81T-225
81T/HT
81T/Tr-778
82D-346
82F-573
82F/St-102
82OPC-217
82T-511
82T/St-99
83D-373
83F-361
83F/St-1M
83OPC-287
83OPC/St-295
83T-695
83T/Gloss40-38
83T/St-295
84D-261
84F-303
84F/X-U59
84Nes/792-327
84OPC-327
84T-327
84T/St-158
84T/Tr-59
84Tiger/Wave-22
85D-612
85F-13
85F/Up-U63
85Smok/Cal-19
85T-126
85T/Tr-65T
86D-423
86F-161
86OPC-186
86Smok/Cal-19
86T-464
86T/St-184
87D-428
87F-85
87Sf/TPrev-11M
87Smok/Cal-21
87T-53
88F-492
88Panini/St-47
88S-333
92Yank/WIZ80-94

Jones, Ryan
93MedHat/ProC-3745
94FExcel-146

Jones, Sam P.
21Exh-85
28Exh-63
28Yueng
29Exh/4-32
33G-81
91Conlon/Sport-140
91Conlon/Sport-174
92Conlon/Sport-356
94Conlon-1003
E120
R316
V100
V354-31
V61-43
V89-17
W502-38
W514-8
W515-43
W573

Jones, Sam
75BurlB
76BurlB
77DaytB

Jones, Samuel
(Sad Sam)
52NumNum-19
52T-382
53T-6
56T-259
57T-287
58T-287
59T-75
60L-14
60T-410
60T/tatt-24
61P-143
61T-49LL
61T-555
61T/RO-31
62J-138
62P-138
62P/Can-138
62Salada-162
62Shirriff-162
62T-92
62T/St-127
77Galasso-129
84Mother/Giants-15
86Negro/Frit-80
91Crown/Orio-232
91T/Arc53-6
93Conlon-801

Jones, Scott
83Cedar-2
83Cedar/Frit-18

Jones, Sean
91Perth/Fut-9

Jones, Shannon
89Geneva/ProC-1881
90CLAS/CL-46
90WinSalem/Team-12
91AA/LineD-135
91CharlK/LineD-135
91CharlK/ProC-1685

Jones, Sheldon
(Available)
47HomogBond-23
48B-34
49B-68
49Eureka-111
50B-83
50Drake-7
51B-199
52B-215
52BR
52NTea
52T-130
D305

Jones, Sherman
61T-161
91WIZMets-206

Jones, Slim
86Negro/Frit-79

Jones, Stacy
89Freder/Star-11
90Freder/Team-12
91AA/LineD-233
91Hagers/LineD-233
91Hagers/ProC-2451
92F-701M
92Freder/ClBest-25
92Freder/ProC-1801
92ProC/Tomorrow-7
92S-832RP
92T/91Debut-94

Jones, Steve H.
69OPC-49R
69T-49R

Jones, Steve
91Johnson/ClBest-25
91Johnson/ProC-3974
92Hamil/ClBest-10
92Hamil/ProC-1587
92ProC/Tomorrow-328

Jones, Terry R.
76OkCty/Team-14

Jones, Terry
87FtMyr-21

Jones, Thomas F.
(Rick)
77T-118
79Portl-23
82RochR-13

Jones, Thomas
09Buster/Pin-7
12Sweet/Pin-26
E254
E270/1
M116
T205
T206

Jones, Tim
92Bristol/ClBest-13
92Bristol/ProC-1403

Jones, Timothy Byron
75Shrev/TCMA-6
77Clinton
78Clinton
78T-703R

Jones, Todd
90Osceola/Star-12
91ClBest/Singl-333
91Osceola/ClBest-6
91Osceola/ProC-678
92B-202
92Jacks/ProC-3998
92Jacks/SB-335
92Sky/AASingl-142
92UD/ML-219
93B-352FOIL
93B-392
93FExcel/ML-46
93StCl/Ast-25
93UD-423TP
94B-22
94D-171
94F-495
94Finest-265
94Flair-172
94L-415
94Pac/Cr-269
94S-246
94S/GoldR-246
94StCl-226
94StCl/1stDay-226
94StCl/Gold-226
94T-97
94T/Gold-97
94UD/CollC-153
94UD/CollC/Gold-153
94UD/CollC/Silv-153
94Ultra-507

Jones, Tommy
80Clinton-27
80Phoenix/NBank-16CO
81Phoenix-16
83Butte-30
86Memphis/GoldT-12MG
86Memphis/SilverT-12MG
87Albany-19
88Albany/ProC-1352
89Wausau/GS-2
90AAASingl/ProC-129
90Batavia/ProC-3060
90Calgary/CMC-23MG
90Calgary/ProC-664MG
90ProC/Singl-450MG
91SanBern/ClBest-27MG
91SanBern/ProC-2003MG

Jones, Tracy
83Tampa-26
86D/Rook-2
86F/Up-U58
86TexGold-29
87D-413
87F-651M
87F/Up-U55
87Kahn-29
87Sf/TPrev-4M
87T-146
88Classic/Red-185
88D-310
88D/Best-174
88F-237
88Kahn/Reds-29
88Leaf-107
88OPC-101
88Panini/St-283
88S-326
88S/YS/I-38
88Sf-38
88T-553
89B-479
89D-574
89F-383
89F/Up-31
89Mother/Giants-14
89OPC-373
89Panini/St-124
89S-510
89S/Tr-43
89T-373
89UD-96
89UD/Ext-798
90CokeK/Tiger-9
90D-636
90F-607
90F/Can-607
90OPC-767
90PublInt/St-70
90S-291
90T-767
90UD-309
91CounHrth-16
91D-594
91F/Up-U53
91OPC-87
91S-87
91StCl-446
91T-87
92D-519
92F-284
92OPC-271
92S-206
92T-271
92T/Gold-271
92T/GoldWin-271

Jones, Vernal
(Nippy)
49Eureka-186
50B-238
52T-213
58Union
R302-111
R423-51

Jones, Victor
91CollInd/ClBest-2
91CollInd/ProC-1500

Jones, William Timothy
(Tim)
87ArkTr-14
87Louisvl-17
88Louisvl-23
88Louisvl/CMC-13
88Louisvl/ProC-433
89B-439
89D-555
89D/Rook-28
89F-453
89S-649
89S/HotRook-28
89Smok/Cards-10
89UD-348
90D-686
90OPC-533
90S-579
90S/100Ris-62
90Smok/Card-11
90T-533
90T/TVCard-26
90UD-501
91D-66
91F/Up-U117

91Louisvl/Team-19
91OPC-262
91StCl-121
91T-262
92StCl-206
92Ultra-569
93D-624
93StCl-280
93StCl/1stDay-280
94Pac/Cr-592
Jones, Willie
49B-92
49Eureka-138
49Lummis
50B-67
51B-112
51BR-B8
51FB
51T/BB-43
52B-20
52RM-NI 11
52T-47
52TipTop
53B/Col-133
53T-88
54B-143
54T-41
55B-172
56T-127
57T-174
58Hires-60
58T-181
59T-208
60L-98
60T-289
61T-497
79TCMA-29
91T/Arc53-88
94T/Arc54-41
PM10/Sm-87
Jongewaard, Steve
87Erie-8
Jonnard, Clarence
35G-1E
35G-3C
35G-5C
35G-6C
Jonson, Greg
81CharR-1
82FtMyr-6
Joost, Edwin
(Eddie)
39PlayBall-67
40PlayBall-151
41DP-117
47HomogBond-24
48B-15
48L-62
49B-55
50B-103
51B-119
51FB
51T/BB-15
52B-26
52RM-AL12
52T-45
52TipTop
53B/Col-105
53RM-AL7
54B-35
55B-263
61F-116
D305
R302-115
R423-50
W711/1
W711/2
Jordan
N172
Jordan, Adolph
(Dutch)
90Target-995
E254
E270/1
T206
T213/brown
Jordan, Adonis
89KS*-55
Jordan, Adrian
90Bristol/ProC-3152
90Bristol/Star-12
Jordan, Baxter
(Buck)
34DS-49
34G-31
38Wheat
R314
V354-75
Jordan, Brian
90ArkTr/GS-18
91AAA/LineD-238
91Louisvl/LineD-238
91Louisvl/ProC-2927
91Louisvl/Team-24
91Louisvl/Team-32
92B-464
92D/RookPhen-BC14
92D/Up-U3RR
92JDean/Rook-3
92L-337
92L/BlkGold-337
92Pinn-555
92Pinn/Team2000-39
92S/RookTr-83T
92Studio-93
92T/Tr 58T
92T/TrGold-58T
92UD-3SR
92UD-702M
92UD/Scout-SR11
93D-442
93F-511
93L-229
93OPC-134
93Pac/Spanish-632
93Pinn-540
93Pol/Card-8
93S-217
93Select-280
93StCl-435
93StCl/1stDay-435
93StCl/Card-25
93T-754
93T/Gold-754
93ToysRUs-97
93TripleP-62
93UD-596
93USPlayC/Rook-6D
93Ultra-107
94B-676
94D-586
94F-634
94Finest-360
94Flair-225
94L-272
94Panini-244
94Pinn-124
94Pinn/Artist-124
94Pinn/Museum-124
94S-201
94S/GoldR-201
94Select-62
94Sf/2000-105
94StCl-63
94StCl/1stDay-63
94StCl/Gold-63
94StCl/Team-308
94T-632
94T/Gold-632
94TripleP-63
94UD-223
94UD/CollC-154
94UD/CollC/Gold-154
94UD/CollC/Silv-154
94UD/ElecD-223
94Ultra-267
Jordan, Harry K.
75Phoenix-24
75Phoenix/CircleK-24
76Phoenix/Coke-24TR
77Phoenix
78Cr/PCL-117
79Phoenix
80Phoenix/NBank-2TR
81Phoenix-2
82Phoenix
Jordan, Jim 1
78BurlB
Jordan, Jim 2
R310
V94-28
Jordan, Joe 1
85Everett/II/Cram-8
Jordan, Joe 2
89OK-4ACO
Jordan, Kevin
90A&AASingle/ProC-181
90NE-13
90Oneonta/ProC-3386
91ClBest/Singl-96
91FSLAS/ProC-FSL15
91FtLaud/ClBest-21
91FtLaud/ProC-2434
92ClBest-223
92PrWill/ClBest-22
92PrWill/ProC-157
93ClBest/MLG-35
93FExcel/ML-211
94B-224
94FExcel-107
Jordan, Michael
91UD-SP1
94TedW/Gardiner-1
94UD/DColl-C2
94UD/HoloFX-17
94UD/SP-8PP
Jordan, Milton
53Tiger/Glen-17
Jordan, Ricardo
91Myrtle/ClBest-7
91Myrtle/ProC-2941
92Dunedin/ClBest-11
92Dunedin/ProC-1996
Jordan, Ricky
86Phill/TastyK-x
86Reading-12
87Reading-16
88F/Up-U110
88Maine/CMC-11
88Maine/ProC-286
88Phill/TastyK-35
88S/Tr-68T
88TripleA/ASCMC-28
89B-401
89Bz-17
89Classic-129
89D-624
89D/Best-103
89F-575
89F/BBAS-24
89F/Excit-27
89F/Heroes-25
89Panini/St-144
89Phill/TastyK-15
89S-548
89S/HotRook-88
89S/YS/I-15
89Sf-44
89T-358
89T/Big-246
89T/Coins-17
89T/HeadsUp-4
89T/JumboR-14
89T/UK-45
89ToysRUs-17
89UD-35
90B-156
90Classic-32
90D-76
90D/BestNL-8
90F-564
90F/Can-564
90F/LL-21
90F/SoarSt-11
90HotPlay/St-23
90Kenner/Fig-47
90Leaf-236
90MLBPA/Pins-3
90OPC-216
90Panini/St-315
90Phill/TastyK-17
90PublInt/St-244
90PublInt/St-615
90S-16
90Sf-153
90T-216
90T/Big-172
90T/DH-38
90T/St-112
90UD-576
91B-494
91D-466
91DennyGS-13
91F-401
91F/UltraUp-U100
91Leaf/Stud-215
91OPC-712
91Panini/FrSt-103
91Phill/Medford-21
91RedFoley/St-55
91S-15
91StCl-192
91T-712
91UD-160
92D-458
92F-536
92OPC-103
92Phill/Med-42
92Pinn-530
92S-476
92StCl-188
92T-103
92T/Gold-103
92T/GoldWin-103
92UD-106
92Ultra-245
93Cadaco-36
93D-514
93F-103
93L-169
93Pac/Spanish-579
93Phill/Med-20
93Pinn-187
93S-141
93StCl-229
93StCl/1stDay-229
93T-585
93T/Gold-585
93UD-561
93Ultra-89
94D-394
94F-593
94Finest-297
94Phill/Med-16
94S-116
94S/GoldR-116
94Select-95
94StCl/Team-228
94T-86
94T/Gold-86
94Ultra-248
Jordan, Rocky
75SLCity/Caruso-10
Jordan, Scott
86Watlo-14
87Kinston-12
88EastLAS/ProC-40
88Wmsprt/ProC-1326
89D-609
Jordan, Steve
81BurlB-16
Jordan, Tim 1
77Newar
78Newar
Jordan, Tim 2
90Johnson/Star-15
91Savan/ClBest-26
91Savan/ProC-1667
92Hamil/ClBest-20
92Hamil/ProC-1607
Jordan, Tim Joseph
90Target-393
C46-87
E103
E254
E90/1
M116
T206
T213/blue
T3-20
Jordan, Tony
80Wausau-4
Jorgens, Arndt
34G-72
39PlayBall-42
40PlayBall-2
91Conlon/Sport-78
Jorgensen, Mike
70OPC-348R
70T-348R
71OPC-596
71T-596
72Dimanche*-23
72Dimanche*-65M
72OPC-16
72ProStars/PostC-7
72T-16
73OPC-281
73T-281
74Expo/West-6
74OPC-549
74T-549
74T/St-56
74Weston-16
75Ho-105
75OPC-286
75T-286
75T/M-286
76Expo/Redp-14
76Ho-144
76OPC-117
76SSPC-327
76T-117
77OPC-9
77T-368
78SSPC/270-107
78T-406
79T-22
80T-213
81D-274
81F-324
81T-698
82D-224
82F-529
82T-566
83F-547
83T-107
83T/Tr-51
84Nes/792-313
84Pol/Atl-11
84T-313
84T/Tr-60
85F-229
85T-783
86T-422
87Louisvl-1MG
88Louisvl-1MG
88Louisvl/CMC-25
88Louisvl/ProC-441MG
89Louisvl-6MG
89Louisvl/CMC-25MG
89Louisvl/ProC-1256MGs
91WIZMets-209
93Rang/Keeb-212
Jorgensen, Terry
88OrlanTw/Best-15
89OrlanTw/Best-15
89OrlanTw/ProC-1352
89SLAS-12
90AAASingl/ProC-254
90Portl/CMC-17
90Portl/ProC-184
90ProC/Singl-569
90S-655
90T/89Debut-64
91AAA/LineD-410
91Portl/LineD-410
91Portl/ProC-1571
92Portl/SB-411
92Portland/ProC-2675
92Sky/AAASingl-188
93D-151
93F-268
93OPC/Premier-106
93Pac/Spanish-521
93Pinn-594
93S-458
93Select/RookTr-144T
93T-805
93T/Gold-805
93UD-697
93Ultra-232
94D-563
94F-209
94Pac/Cr-356
94Ultra-88
Jorgenson, John
(Spider)
45Parade*-60
47TipTop
49Eureka-39
53Mother-55
90Target-394
Jorn, David A.
78StPete
80ArkTr-25
81ArkTr-12
90Greens/Best-30CO
90Greens/ProC-2680CO
90Greens/Star-26CO
91AA/LineD-25M
91Albany/LineD-25CO
91Albany/ProC-1024CO
92Albany/ProC-2349
92Albany/SB-25
Jose, Domingo Felix
84Idaho/Team-15
85Madis-17
85Madis/Pol-14
86Modesto-16

88Tacoma/CMC-24
88Tacoma/ProC-614
89D-38RR
89F-15
89Mother/A's-22
89S-629RP
89S/HotRook-22
89Tacoma/CMC-14
89Tacoma/ProC-1542
89UD-22SR
90B-455
90Classic/III-33
90D-564
90D/Rook-5
90F-13
90F/Can-13
90HotRook/St-24
90Leaf-385
90Mother/A's-17
90OPC-238
90S-321
90S/YS/I-19
90T-238
90UD-228
91B-401
91Bz-17
91Classic/200-64
91Classic/III-41
91D-656
91F-636
91F/UltraUp-U107
91Leaf-392
91OPC-368
91Pol/Card-34
91S-784
91S/100RisSt-90
91StCl-366
91T-368
91T/GlossRk-14
91T/JumboR-14
91ToysRUs-13
91UD-387
91USPlayC/AS-9S
92B-176
92Classic/II-T53
92D-233
92D/DK-DK13
92DennyGS-4
92F-582
92F/ASIns-1
92Kenner/Fig-27
92L-63
92L/BlkGold-63
92L/GoldPrev-10
92L/Prev-10
92MooTown-9
92OPC-105
92Panini-176
92Pinn-159
92Pol/Card-9
92S-40
92S/100SS-99
92StCl-407
92StCl/Dome-96
92Studio-94
92T-105
92T/Gold-105
92T/GoldWin-105
92T/Kids-29
92TripleP-75
92UD-264
92Ultra-264
93B-393
93Classic/GameI-43
93D-574
93D/LongBall-LL12
93F-126
93F/ASNL-5
93Flair-217
93L-349
93L/Fast-12
93LimeR/Winter-82
93OPC-182
93OPC/Premier-128
93Pac/Beisbol-8M
93Pac/Spanish-295
93Pac/SpanishGold-4
93Panini-198
93Pinn-36
93Pol/Royal-13
93S-110
93Select-131
93Select/RookTr-110T
93StCl-653
93StCl/1stDay-653
93StCl/Royal-21
93T-67
93T/Finest-81
93T/FinestRef-81
93T/Gold-67
93T/Tr-66T
93TripleP-114
93UD-156
93UD-542
93UD-835TC
93UD/FunPack-183
93UD/SP-230
93Ultra-562
94B-667
94D-529
94F-161
94Finest-306
94L-168
94OPC-191
94Pac/Cr-289
94Panini-74
94Pinn-77
94Pinn/Artist-77
94Pinn/Museum-77
94S-433
94Select-37
94StCl-298
94StCl/1stDay-298
94StCl/Gold-298
94Studio-185
94T-672
94T/Gold-672
94TripleP-235
94UD-226
94UD/ElecD-226
94UD/SP-173
94Ultra-67

Jose, Elio
88CharWh/Best-23

Jose, Manny
85Greens-4
86WinHaven-13
87WinHaven-17
88NewBrit/ProC-897
89London/ProC-1385
91AAA/LineD-265
91Nashvl/LineD-265
91Nashvl/ProC-2170
93LimeR/Winter-123

Joseph, Ricardo
68T-434
69T-329
70OPC-186
70T-186
72MB-174

Joseph, Sam
86QuadC-16TR

Joseph, Walter Lee
(Newt)
87Negro/Dixon-31

Josephina, Michael
92Macon/ClBest-16
92Macon/ProC-279

Josephson, Duane
67T-373R
68T-329
69MB-141
69MLB/St-32
69T-222
69T/St-156
70MLB/St-187
70OPC-263
70T-263
71OPC-56
71T-56
71T/Coins-92
72MB-175
72T-543

Josephson, Paul
83Albany-5
84Durham-21

Joshua, Von
71OPC-57
71T-57
73OPC-544
73T-544
74OPC-551
74T-551
75OPC-547
75T-547
75T/M-547
76A&P/Milw
76K-39
76OPC-82
76SSPC-109
76T-82
77BurgChef-85
77T-651
78T-108
80T-209
85SpokAT/Cram-10
88Albuq/ProC-254
89Albuq/ProC-73
90AAASingl/ProC-84CO
90Albuq/CMC-28CO
90Albuq/ProC-362CO
90Albuq/Trib-15CO
90ProC/Singl-658M
90Target-395
91AAA/LineD-25M
91Albuq/LineD-25CO
91Albuq/ProC-1158CO
92Albuq/ProC-739
92Albuq/SB-25CO

Joslin, Chris
83BurlR-7
83BurlR/Frit-16

Joslin, Spanky
92Mega/Ruth-160M

Joslyn, John
88Virgini/Star-12

Joss, Adrian
(Addie)
61F-117
77Galasso-168
80Pac/Leg-114
80Perez/HOF-164
80SSPC/HOF
91Conlon/Sport-272
94Conlon-1016
E107
E254
E90/1
E93
M116
T205
T206
T3-19
W555
WG2-30

Joyce, Dick
77Fritsch-27

Joyce, James
91Pocatel/ProC-3784

Joyce, Jim
90TM/Umpire-59

Joyce, Kevin
78Clinton
79Clinton/TCMA-24

Joyce, Michael
63T-66
64T-477

Joyce, Richard
91Pocatel/SportP-4

Joyce, Robert Emmett
48Sommer-6

Joyce, Tom
76AppFx

Joyce, William
(Bill)
90Target-396
N300/unif

Joyner, Wally
85Cram/PCL-2
86D/HL-23
86D/Rook-1
86F/Slug-19
86F/Up-U59
86Sf/Rook-7
86Smok/Cal-22
86T/Tr-51T
87BK-11
87Classic-6
87Classic/Up-108
87D-135
87D-1DK
87D/AAS-1
87D/DKsuper-1
87D/HL-35
87D/OD-7
87D/PopUp-1
87Drake-2
87F-628M
87F-86
87F/BB-23
87F/Excit-30
87F/GameWin-22
87F/Hottest-25
87F/LL-26
87F/Lim-23
87F/Mini-59
87F/RecSet-17
87F/Slug-22
87F/St-68
87F/WaxBox-C7
87GenMills/Book-3M
87Ho/St-20
87KayBee-18
87Kraft-9
87Leaf-1DK
87Leaf-252
87MSA/Discs-10
87MnM's-1
87OPC-80
87RedFoley/St-82
87Seven-W3
87Sf-26
87Sf-75M
87Sf/TPrev-11M
87Smok/Cal-12
87Sportflic/DealP-2
87Stuart-16M
87T-80
87T/Coins-16
87T/Gloss22-13
87T/Gloss60-39
87T/JumboR-7
87T/Mini-45
87T/St-150
87T/St-174
87T/St-313
87ToysRUs-14
88Bz-10
88Classic/Blue-206
88D-110
88D-BC13
88D/Best-115
88F-493
88F-622M
88F/AwardWin-21
88F/BB/AS-19
88F/BB/MVP-20
88F/Excit-23
88F/Hottest-21
88F/LL-22
88F/Mini-11
88F/RecSet-21
88F/SS-18
88F/St-12
88F/TL-16
88F/WaxBox-C4
88FanSam-4
88Grenada-8
88Jiffy-11
88KayBee-15
88KennerFig-57
88KingB/Disc-9
88Leaf-50
88Nestle-44
88OPC-168
88Panini/St-40
88RedFoley/St-41
88S-7
88S/YS/I-27
88Sf-75
88Smok/Angels-17
88T-420
88T/Big-52
88T/Coins-16
88T/Gloss60-48
88T/Mini-6
88T/RiteAid-15
88T/St-179
88T/St/Backs-34
88T/UK-40
88UD/Sample-700
89B-47
89Classic-29
89D-52
89D/Best-139
89D/MVP-BC21
89F-481
89F/Excit-28
89F/Superstar-26
89F/WaxBox-C16
89Holsum/Discs-1
89KennerFig-76
89Master/Discs-7
89Nissen-1
89OPC-270
89Panini/St-291
89RedFoley/St-68
89S-65
89S/HotStar-73
89Sf-2
89Smok/Angels-18
89T-270
89T/Big-201
89T/LJN-30
89T/St-183
89T/UK-46
89UD-573
89UD-668TC
90B-299
90Classic/Up-42
90D-94
90D/BestAL-31
90F-136
90F/Can-136
90HotPlay/St-24
90Leaf-24
90MLBPA/Pins-93
90OPC-525
90Panini/St-31
90PublInt/St-372
90S-120
90S/100St-81
90Sf-49
90Smok/Angel-9
90Sunflower-19
90T-525
90T/Ames-30
90T/Big-168
90T/St-166
90UD-693
91B-195
91Classic/III-42
91D-677
91DennyGS-23
91F-317
91Leaf-31
91Leaf/Stud-26
91OPC-195
91Panini/FrSt-180
91Panini/St-141
91RedFoley/St-56
91S-470
91S-873FRAN
91S/100SS-57
91Seven/3DCoin-7SC
91Smok/Angel-6
91StCl-2
91T-195
91UD-575
91Ultra-48
92B-435
92Classic/Game200-164
92D-333
92D/Up-U14
92F-62
92F/Up-27
92L-438
92L/BlkGold-438
92OPC-629
92OPC/Premier-61
92P-4
92Panini-5
92Pinn-284I
92Pinn-537
92Pol/Royal-14
92S-535
92S/100SS-29
92S/RookTr-13T
92StCl-122
92StCl-710
92Studio-185
92Studio/Prev-10
92T-629
92T/Gold-629
92T/GoldWin-629
92T/Kids-95
92T/Tr-59T
92T/TrGold-59T
92TripleP/Gal-GS2
92UD-343
92UD-744
92UD/ASFF-29
92Ultra-373
93B-645
93Classic/GameI-44
93Colla/DM-57
93D-129
93D/DK-8
93DennyGS-24
93F-239

94Pinn/TeamP-8M
94Pinn/Trib-5
94S-422
94S/Cycle-19
94S/GoldS-24
94S/Tomb-11
94Sf/2000-192AS
94Sf/2000-6
94StCl-263
94StCl-530DL
94StCl-94
94StCl/1stDay-263
94StCl/1stDay-530DL
94StCl/1stDay-94
94StCl/Gold-263
94StCl/Gold-530DL
94StCl/Gold-94
94StCl/Team-49
94Studio-35
94T-389M
94T-630
94T/BlkGold-36
94T/Gold-389M
94T/Gold-630
94TripleP-45
94TripleP/Bomb-5
94UD-267HFA
94UD-375
94UD/CollC-156
94UD/CollC/Gold-156
94UD/CollC/Silv-156
94UD/CollHR-7
94UD/DColl-E7
94UD/ElecD-267HFA
94UD/HoloFX-18
94UD/Mantle-11
94UD/SP-50
94Ultra-442
94Ultra/AS-18
94Ultra/HRK-8
94Ultra/RBIK-8

Justis, Walter
C46-42

Jutze, Alfred Henry
(Skip)
73OPC-613R
73T-613R
74OPC-328
74T-328
76OPC-489
76SSPC-52
76T-489
78T-532

Kaage, George
77Clinton
78LodiD

Kaaihue, Kala
87Hawaii-20

Kaat, Jim
60T-136
61Clover-9
61Peters-7
61T-63
61T/St-180
62T-21
63F-22
63J-10
63P-10
63Salada-40
63T-10LL
63T-165
64T-567
65OPC-62
65T-62
66T-224LL
66T-445
67Bz-18
67CokeCap/Twin-16
67T-235LL
67T-237LL
67T-300
68Dexter-45
68OPC-67CL
68T-450
68T-67CL
69MB-142
69MLB/St-67
69T-290
69T/St-194
70MLB/St-233
70OPC-75
70T-75
71MLB/St-464
71OPC-245
71T-245
71T/GM-7
71T/Greatest-7
72MB-176
72T-709
72T-710IA
73OPC-530
73T-530
74OPC-440
74T-440
75Ho/Twink-110
75OPC-243
75SSPC/Puzzle-13
75T-243
75T/M-243
76Crane-24
76Ho-110
76K-25
76MSA/Disc
76OPC-80
76SSPC-136
76T-80
76T/Tr-80T
77BurgChef-169
77T-638
78T-715
79T-136
80T-250
81D-536
81F-536
81T-563
82D-217
82F-117
82F/St-240M
82T-367
83D-343
83F-11
83OPC-211
83OPC-383SV
83OPC/St-135RB
83OPC/St-136RB
83T-672
83T-673SV
83T/Fold-1M
83T/St-135
83T/St-136
88Chatt/Team-16
88Pac/Leg-88
89Swell-88
92Yank/WIZ70-86
92Yank/WIZ80-95
93AP/ASG-149
94TedW-48

Kable, David
81ArkTr-9
81Louisvl-28
82Louisvl-12
83Louisvl/Riley-28
84Louisvl-29
85Louisvl-9
86ArkTr-9

Kaczmarski, Randy
82Amari-21
83Beaum-4

Kaelin, Kris
91Pocatel/ProC-3789
91Pocatel/SportP-20

Kagawa, Ross
87Hawaii-11

Kahanamoku, Duke
33SK*-20

Kahmann, Jim
86WPalmB-22TR
87Jaxvl-28
88Jaxvl/ProC-974
89OrlanTw/Best-6
89OrlanTw/ProC-1349

Kahn, Roger
90LitSun-13

Kahoe, Michael
E107
T204

Kain, Marty
82Amari-20
84Cram/PCL-100
85Cram/PCL-11

Kainer, Don W.
79Tucson-11
93Rang/Keeb-213

Kainer, Ronald
76Watlo

Kairis, Bob
88BurlInd/ProC-1794

Kaiser, Bart
86Clearw-12
87Clearw-25

Kaiser, C. Don
56T-124
57T-134

Kaiser, Jeff
85Mother/A's-25
86Tacoma-10
87BuffB-16
88ColoSp/CMC-4
88ColoSp/ProC-1531
88Gator-47
89ColoSp/CMC-3
89F-410
89Salinas/Cal-142
89Salinas/ProC-1805
90ColoSp/CMC-10
90ProC/Singl-462
90T/Tr-49T
91AAA/LineD-143
91Denver/LineD-143
91Denver/ProC-122
91OPC-576
91T-576
92AAA/ASG/SB-590
92StCl-526
92Toledo/ProC-1039
92Toledo/SB-590

Kaiser, Keith
88Greens/ProC-1573
89Chatt/Best-2
89Chatt/GS-13
90Chatt/GS-17
91AA/LineD-565
91Jacks/LineD-565
91Jacks/ProC-923

Kaiser, Ken
88TM/Umpire-31
89TM/Umpire-29
90TM/Umpire-28

Kaiser, Nick
91Eugene/ClBest-6
91Eugene/ProC-3735

Kaiserling, George
15CJ-157

Kajima, Ken
89Salinas/Cal-148CO

Kalas, Harry
88Phill/TastyK-39ANN
90Phill/TastyK-35BC

Kaler
T207

Kalin, Frank
53Mother-44

Kaline, Al
54T-201
55B-23
55T-4
55T/DH-45
56T-20
56T/Pin-38OF
56YellBase/Pin-16
57T-125
58T-304M
58T-70
59HRDerby-9
59T-360
59T-463HL
59T-562AS
60Armour-12
60Bz-18
60NuCard-65
60P*
60T-50
60T-561AS
60T/tatt-25
61Bz-20
61NuCard-465
61P-35
61T-429
61T-580AS
61T/Dice-6
61T/St-152A
61T/St-152B
62Bz-12
62Exh
62J-20
62P-20
62P/Can-20
62Salada-67
62Shirriff-67
62T-150
62T-470AS
62T-51LL
62T/St-47
62T/bucks
63Bz-34
63Exh
63J-51
63P-51
63Salada-63
63T-25
63T/SO
64Bz-34
64Det/Lids-7
64T-12LL
64T-250
64T-331M
64T-8LL
64T/Coins-100
64T/Coins-129AS
64T/S-12
64T/SU
64T/St-95
64T/tatt
64Wheat/St-24
65Bz-34
65OPC-130
65OldLond-27
65T-130
65T/E-13
65T/trans-51
66Bz-46
66T-410
66T/RO-44
66T/RO-66
67Bz-46
67CokeCap/ALAS-19
67CokeCap/AS-22
67CokeCap/Tiger-17
67OPC-30
67OPC/PI-21
67T-216M
67T-239LL
67T-30
67T/PI-21
67T/Test/SU-10
68Bz-1
68CokeCap/Tiger-17
68OPC-2LL
68T-240
68T-2LL
68T/ActionSt-16CM
68T/ActionSt-1CM
68T/ActionSt-6B
68T/G-13
68T/Post-9
69Kelly/Pin-8
69MB-143
69MLB/St-49
69MLBPA/Pin-13
69NTF
69OPC-166WS
69T-166WS
69T-410
69T/4in1-24M
69T/St-174
69Trans-6
70K-52
70MLB/St-208
70T-640
70T/SO
70Trans-14
71Bz/Test-14
71K-44
71MLB/St-396
71MLB/St-565
71OPC-180
71T-180
71T/Coins-62
71T/GM-19
71T/Greatest-19
71T/S-54
71T/Super-54
71T/tatt-5
71T/tatt-5a
72MB-177
72ProStars/PostC-27
72T-600
73K-52
73OPC-280
73T-280
73T/Lids-24
74Laugh/ASG-57
74OPC-215
74T-215
74T/St-177
75OPC-4RB
75SSPC/42-34
75T-4HL
75T/M-4HL
78TCMA-40
79TCMA-184
80Pac/Leg-65
80Perez/HOF-170
80SSPC/HOF
81Tiger/Detroit-100
81Tiger/Detroit-132
82CJ-4
83D/HOF-18
83Kaline-Set
83MLBPA/Pin-11
84West/1-12
85CircK-21
86Sf/Dec-51M
86Tiger/Sport-12
87Leaf/SpecOlym-H10
88Domino-9
88Grenada-12
88Pac/Leg-104
89Swell-40
89T/LJN-93
90HOF/St-52
90MSA/AGFA-5
90Perez/GreatMom-2
91MDA-18
91Swell/Great-53
92AP/ASG-6
92AP/ASG24K-6G
93AP/ASGCoke/Amo-6
93TWill-38
93YooHoo-8
94T/Arc54-201
94TedW/54-30
Exh47
Rawl
WG10-30
WG9-31

Kaline, Louise
83Kaline-32M
83Kaline-7M

Kaline, Mark
83Kaline-28M
83Kaline-32M

Kaline, Michael
83Kaline-28M
83Kaline-32M

Kaline, Naomi
83Kaline-65M

Kaline, Nicholas
83Kaline-65M

Kallevig, Dane
90Watertn/Star-11

Kallevig, Greg
86Peoria-12
87WinSalem-2
88MidwLAS/GS-28
88Peoria/Ko-18
89CharlK-16
90AAASingl/ProC-621
90Iowa/CMC-4
90Iowa/ProC-314
90ProC/Singl-79
90T/TVCub-50

Kallio, Rudy
28Exh/PCL-15

Kamanaka, Masaaki
89VeroB/Star-12

Kamei, Kat
87SanJose-8

Kamenshek, Dotty
93TWill-117

Kamerschen, Robbie
90Martins/ProC-3199

Kamieniecki, Scott
87PrWill-6
88FtLaud/Star-13
89Albany/Best-25
89Albany/ProC-316
89EastLgAS/ProC-15
90Albany/Best-5
90Albany/ProC-1034
90Albany/Star-7
90Foil/Best-63
90T/TVYank-49
91AAA/LineD-109
91ColClip/LineD-109
91ColClip/ProC-594
91D/Rook-51
91F/Up-U45
91StCl-568
91T/Tr-66T

91UD/FinalEd-33F
92D-195
92F-232
92FtLaud/ClBest-14
92OPC-102
92OPC/Premier-110
92ProC/Tomorrow-110
92S-415
92S/100RisSt-23
92StCl-649
92T-102
92T/91Debut-96
92T/Gold-102
92T/GoldWin-102
92UD-46
93D-681
93F-651
93L-520
93Pac/Spanish-557
93Pinn-570
93S-377
93StCl-410
93StCl/1stDay-410
93StCl/Y-19
93T-749
93T/Gold-749
94D-553
94F-234
94Pinn-309
94S-350
94StCl-101
94StCl/1stDay-101
94StCl/Gold-101
94StCl/Team-186
94T-489
94T/Finest-60
94T/FinestRef-60
94T/Gold-489
94Ultra-94

Kamm, Willie
21Exh-87
25Exh-76
26Exh-77
27Exh-39
28Yueng-40
29Exh/4-19
30CEA/Pin-17
31Exh/4-19
32Orbit/num-10
32Orbit/un-38
33G-75
34Exh/4-11
34G-14
35BU-39
35Exh/4-11
35G-1J
35G-1L
35G-2E
35G-3A
35G-5A
35G-6A
35G-6E
35G-7E
91Conlon/Sport-166
93Conlon-899
R305
R308-164
R316
V353-68
V354-60
V89-7
W502-40
W515-42
W517-13

Kammeyer, Bob
78Cr/PCL-34
79Colum-23
80Colum-10
92Yank/WIZ70-87

Kammeyer, Tim
82Redwd-6
83Redwd-15

Kampouris, Alex
35G-8D
35G-9D
36Exh/4-4
41DP-13
90Target-398
R314
W711/1

Kampsen, Doug
85Cedar-9

Kane, Frank
90Target-997

Kane, Joey
88Alaska/Team-11
89Alaska/Team-13

Kane, John
M116

Kane, Kevin
81Bristol-3
85Pawtu-18

Kane, Thomas
91AA/LineD-465
91NewBrit/LineD-465
91NewBrit/ProC-350

Kane, Tom
86Greens-12
87Greens-1

Kanehl, Rod
62T-597R
63F-49
63J-199
63P-19
63T-371
64T 582
90Swell/Great-44
91WIZMets-210

Kaney, Joe
47Centen-14

Kannenberg, Scott
86QuadC-17
87QuadC-9
88PalmSp/Cal-88
88PalmSp/ProC-1444

Kanter, John
85Madis-18
85Madis/Pol-15
86Modesto-17

Kantlehner, Erving
16FleischBrd-48

Kantor, Brad
91Watertn/ClBest-18
91Watertn/ProC-3373
92Watertn/ClBest-20
92Watertn/ProC-3243

Kanwisher, Billy
91OKSt-13
92OKSt-14

Kanwisher, Gary
85Beloit-20
86Stockton-11
87Stockton-25

Kapano, Corey
89BendB/Legoe-17
90QuadC/GS-19
91CalLgAS-16
91PalmSp/ProC-2023
92MidldA/OneHour-11
92MidldA/SB-461
92Sky/AASingl-195
92WinSalem/ProC-1220

Kappell, Henry
N172

Kappesser, Bob
89Helena/SP-19
90AS/Cal-48
90Stockton/Best-4
90Stockton/Cal-189
90Stockton/ProC-2188
91Visalia/ClBest-25
91Visalia/ProC-1745
92ElPaso/ProC-3925
92ElPaso/SB-215

Karakas, Michael
45Parade*-28

Karasinski, Dave
88BurlB/ProC-16
89BurlB/ProC-1611
89BurlB/Star-11
90Durham/Team-26
91Salinas/ClBest-20
91Salinas/ProC-2237

Karcher, Carl
92Pol/Angel-13
93Pol/Angel-2

Karcher, Kevin
86Cram/NWL-41

Karcher, Rick
90Idaho/ProC-3255
91Macon/ClBest-20
91Macon/ProC-873
92Durham/ClBest-3
92Durham/ProC-1109
92Durham/Team-22

Karchner, Matt
89Eugene/Best-6
90AppFox/Box-15
90AppFox/ProC-2091
91BBCity/ClBest-8
91BBCity/ProC-1395
92Memphis/ProC-2414
92Memphis/SB-437
93ClBest/MLG-126

Karczewski, Ray
88SLCity-7
89SLCity-7SS

Karger, Edwin
10Domino-61
12Sweet/Pin-5
E90/1
E91
E96
M116
T204
T205
T206

Karkovice, Ron
83AppFx/Frit-22
86SLAS-5
87Coke/WS-3
87D-334
87D/OD-234
87F-645R
87Seven-C11
87Sf/TPrev-26M
87T-491
88S-374
88T-86
88Vanco/CMC-15
88Vanco/ProC-773
89Coke/WS-13
89T-308
89UD-183
90BirmDG/Best-19
90Coke/WSox-11
90D-413
90Leaf-307
90OPC-717
90PublInt/St-391
90S-22
90T-717
90UD-69
91D-220
91D/GSlam-12
91F-125
91F/UltraUp-U16
91Kodak/WSox-20
91Leaf-515
91OPC-568
91S-833
91StCl-102
91T-568
91UD-209
92D-374
92F-88
92L-105
92L/BlkGold-105
92OPC-153
92Pinn-413
92S-532
92StCl-257
92T-153
92T/Gold-153
92T/GoldWin-153
92UD-169
92Ultra-39
92WSox-20
93D-331
93F-205
93L-63
93OPC-198
93Pac/Spanish-391
93Panini-142
93Pinn-195
93S-152
93Select-381
93StCl-427
93StCl/1stDay-427
93StCl/WSox-17
93T-286
93T/Gold-286
93TripleP-216
93UD-199
93UD/SP-257
93Ultra-175
93WSox-15
94B-71
94D-416
94F-86
94L-184
94OPC-71
94Pac/Cr-130
94Pinn-116
94Pinn/Artist-116
94Pinn/Museum-116
94S-403
94Select-33
94StCl-57
94StCl/1stDay-57
94StCl/Gold-57
94StCl/Team-123
94T-684
94T/Finest-71
94T/FinestRef-71
94T/Gold-684
94UD-121
94UD/CollC-157
94UD/CollC/Gold-157
94UD/CollC/Silv-157
94UD/ElecD-121
94Ultra-36

Karl, Andy
45Playball-44

Karl, Scott
92Helena/ProC-1711
93FExcel/ML-189
94B-477
94FExcel-82

Karli, Todd
90Reno/Cal-291ANN

Karlin, Pat
89KS*-60

Karmeris, Joe
85VeroB-14

Karp, Ryan
92Oneonta/ClBest-7
93Greens/ClBest-13
93Greens/ProC-882
94B-552
94ClBest/Gold-84
94FExcel-108
94FExcel/LL-11

Karpuk, Greg
86Watlo-15
87Wmsprt-26

Karr, Benjamin
E120
E126-20
W573

Karr, Jeff
84LitFalls-7

Karrmann, Jason
92MN-8

Karros, Eric
88GreatF-2
89AS/Cal-2
89Bakers/Cal-201
90SanAn/GS-16
90TexLgAS/GS-1
91AAA/LineD-12
91Albuq/LineD-12
91Albuq/ProC-1164
91B-604
91Classic/200-171
91Classic/II-T36
91UD-24
91Ultra-380MLP
92B-288
92Classic/Game200-34
92Classic/II-T21
92D-16RR
92D/RookPhen-BC6
92F-462
92JDean/Rook-4
92L-293
92L/BlkGold-293
92Mother/Dodg-21
92OPC-194
92OPC/Premier-63
92Pinn-256
92Pinn/Rook-24
92Pinn/Team2000-76
92Pol/Dodg-23
92ProC/Tomorrow-240
92S-827
92S/Rook-31
92StCl-236
92StCl/MemberIII*-3
92Studio-45
92T-194
92T/91Debut-97
92T/Gold-194
92T/GoldWin-194
92T/McDonB-43
92UD-534
92UD/Scout-SR12
92Ultra-508
92Ultra/AllRook-1
93B-14
93Classic/GameI-46
93Colla/DM-59
93D-430
93D/DK-30ROY
93D/MVP-8
93D/Prev-5
93F-64
93F/Fruit-31
93F/RookSenI-6
93F/TLNL-4
93Flair-71
93HumDum/Can-34
93JDean/28-24
93Kenner/Fig-16
93L-234
93L/Fast-7
93Mother/Dodg-2
93OPC-208
93OPC/Premier/StarP-8
93P-6
93Pac/Spanish-151
93Panini-166ROY
93Panini-214
93Pinn-14
93Pinn/Team2001-26
93Pol/Dodg-13
93Rem/Karros-1
93Rem/Karros-2
93Rem/Karros-3
93Rem/Karros-4
93Rem/Karros-5
93S-486AW
93S-63
93Select-278
93Select/ChasRook-5
93StCl-292MC
93StCl-528
93StCl/1stDay-292MC
93StCl/1stDay-528
93StCl/Dodg-8
93Studio-92
93Studio/Her-10
93T-11
93T/BlkGold-9
93T/Finest-32
93T/FinestRef-32
93T/Gold-11
93T/HolPrev-11
93ToysRUs-63
93TripleP-4
93TripleP/Act-7
93TripleP/LL-L3
93UD-385
93UD-490AW
93UD/5thAnn-A10
93UD/FunPack-86GS
93UD/FunPack-89
93UD/HRH-HR19
93UD/Iooss-WI9
93UD/OnDeck-D17
93UD/SP-94
93USPlayC/Rook-1S
93USPlayC/Rook-JK
93Ultra-56
93Ultra/AwardWin-20
93Ultra/Perf-4
94B-14
94D-338
94D/Special-338
94F-514
94F-713M
94Finest-356
94L-171
94OPC-163
94Pac/Cr-312
94Panini-201
94Pinn-87
94Pinn/Artist-87
94Pinn/Museum-87
94Pinn/Power-18
94S-26
94S/GoldR-26
94Select-44
94Sf/2000-5
94StCl-240
94StCl/1stDay-240
94StCl/Gold-240
94Studio-69
94T-115
94T/Gold-115

94TripleP-85
94UD-208
94UD/CollC-158
94UD/CollC/Gold-158
94UD/CollC/Silv-158
94UD/ElecD-208
94UD/SP-78
94Ultra-518
Karsay, Steve
90A&AASingle/ProC-179
90StCath/ProC-3472
91B-12
91ClBest/Singl-119
91Classic/200-88
91Classic/II-T60
91Myrtle/ClBest-8
91Myrtle/ProC-2942
91S-675FDP
91S/ToroBJ-31
91UD-54TP
92B-158
92ClBest-193
92Dunedin/ClBest-1
92Dunedin/ProC-1997
92ProC/Tomorrow-171
92UD/ML-154
93B-83
93FExcel/ML-244
93Knoxvl/ProC-1249
94B-220
94B-377
94D-197
94F/MLP-19
94Finest-438
94Flair-93
94Flair/Wave-3
94L/GRook-9
94OPC-11
94Pinn-247
94Pinn/Artist-247
94Pinn/Museum-247
94S-558
94S/Boys-50
94Select-179
94Select/RookSurg-8
94Sf/2000-163
94T-131
94T/Gold-131
94TripleP-291
94UD-20
94UD/CollC-13
94UD/CollC/Gold-13
94UD/CollC/Silv-13
94UD/ElecD-20
94UD/HoloFX-19
94UD/SP-35
94Ultra-109
Kaseda, Yuki
89Salinas/Cal-130
89Salinas/ProC-1808
Kasko, Eddie
57T-363
58T-8
59T-232
60Kahn
60L-9
60T-61
61Kahn
61P-185
61T-534
61T/St-18
62J-119
62Kahn
62P-119
62P/Can-119
62Salada-147
62Shirriff-147
62T-193
62T/St-117
63FrBauer-11
63J-128
63Kahn
63P-128
63T-498
70OPC-489MG
70T-489MG
71OPC-578MG
71T-31MG
72OPC-218MG
72T-218MG
73OPC-131MG
73T-131MG
78TCMA-249
Kasper, Kevin
89Everett/Star-18
90Clinton/Best-17
90Clinton/ProC-2556
91SanJose/ClBest-7
91SanJose/ProC-19
92Shrev/ProC-3882
92Shrev/SB-586
Kaspryzak, Dennis
77Jaxvl
Kastelic, Bruce
82Lynch-5
Kasunick, Joe
83Butte-29
Katalinas, Ed
81Tiger/Detroit-127
Kating, Jim
87Bakers-11
88SanAn/Best-9
89Huntsvl/Best-6
90Huntsvl/Best-17
Kato, Hideki
92Salinas/ClBest-10
92Salinas/ProC-3764
Kats, Bill
43Centen-15
45Centen-14
Katt, Ray
54B-121
54NYJour
55B-183
55Gol/Giants-15
57T-331
58Hires-57
58T-284
60T-468C
61Union
62Sugar-17
79TCMA-235
Katzaroff, Robert
(Rob)
88CapeCod/Sum-163
90James/Pucko-8
91AA/LineD-258
91ClBest/Singl-20
91Harris/LineD-258
91Harris/ProC-642
92Bingham/ProC-529
92Bingham/SB-63
92ClBest-26
92ProC/Tomorrow-262
92Sky/AASingl-28
Kaub, Keith
88James/ProC-1911
89Miami/I/Star-21
89Rockford/Team-13
90Rockford/ProC-2704
Kauff, Benjamin
(Bennie)
15CJ-160
16FleischBrd-49
92Conlon/Sport-484
94Conlon-1269IA
BF2-76
D327
D328-92
D329-94
D350/2-92
E135-92
M101/4-94
M101/5-92
PM1-9
W514-100
W516-16
Kaufman, Al
T3/Box-73
Kaufman, Curt
82Colum-5
82Colum/Pol-24
83Colum-11
84Smok/Cal-14
85Cram/PCL-20
85D-524
85F-305
85T-61
92Yank/WIZ80-96
Kaufman, Ron
82QuadC-9
Kaufmann, Anthony
(Tony)
21Exh-88
47TipTop
93Conlon-927
Kaull, Kurt
83Erie-25
84Savan-5
Kausnicka, Jay
90Visalia/Cal-72
Kautz, Scott
88Harris/ProC-862
Kautzer, Bill
75AppFx
76AppFx
Kavanagh, Mike
75Shrev/TCMA-7
Kavanaugh, Tim
83Erie-19
Kawabata, Yasuhiro
89VeroB/Star-13
Kawakami, Mark
87Hawaii-13
Kawano, Rye
91Salinas/ClBest-11
91Salinas/ProC-2256
Kay, Belinda
90ColMud/Star-29
Kaye, Jeff
86Clearw-13
87Clearw-8
87Phill/TastyK-x
88Reading/ProC-872
Kayser, Tom
77Holyo
79Holyo-30
80Holyo-10
81Holyo-3
Kazak, Edward
(Eddie)
49Eureka-187
50B-36
51B-85
52T-165
53T-194
79TCMA-250
91T/Arc53-194
Kazanski, Ted
54T-78
55T-46
55T/DH-5
57T-27
58T-36
59T-99
94T/Arc54-78
Kazmierczak, William
(Bill)
87Peoria-28
88WinSalem/Star-7
90CharlK/Team-13
Kea, Rusty
89GA-14
90GA-12
Keagle, Greg
94T-753DP
94T/Gold-753DP
Kealey, Steve
69T-224R
71OPC-43
71T-43
72OPC-146
72T-146
73OPC-581
73T-581
Keane, Johnny
60T-468C
62T-198MG
63T-166MG
64T-413MG
65OPC-131MG
65T-131MG
66T-296MG
81TCMA-371MG
Kearney, Robert
(Bob)
78Cedar
81Tacoma-5
82Tacoma-27
83D-539
83T/Tr-52T
84D-462
84F-449
84F/X-U60
84Mother/Mar-4
84Nes/792-326
84T-326
84T/St-381YS
84T/Tr-61T
85D-362
85F-491
85Mother/Mar-13
85OPC-386
85T-679
85T/St-335
86D-74
86F-466
86Mother/Mar-23
86OPC-13
86T-13
87D-445
87F-587
87Mother/Sea-12
87OPC-73
87T-498
92TX-27
Kearns, John
83Wisco/Frit-10
Kearse, Edward
47Remar-7
47Smith-14
Keas
N172
Keathley, Don
91Modesto/ProC-3090
Keathley, Robin
83TriCit-8
85BurlR-22
Keating, Dave
89Niagara/Pucko-5B
90Bristol/Star-13
Keating, Dennis
79AppFx-2
Keating, Mike
90Savan/ProC-2074
Keating, Ray H.
14CJ-95
15CJ-95
16FleischBrd-50
28Exh/PCL-32
T222
Keatley, Greg
81Omaha-14
82Omaha-11
Kebedgy, Nik
45Parade*-67
Keckler, Mike
85FtMyr-23
Keedy, Pat
81Holyo-16
82Holyo-16
84Cram/PCL-118
85Cram/PCL-1
86Edmon-16
87Hawaii-27
88T-486
88Tucson/CMC-22
88Tucson/JP-14
88Tucson/ProC-175
Keefe, Dave
93Conlon-885
Keefe, George
N172
Keefe, Jim
(Jamie)
92FrRow/DP-42
93ClBest/MLG-199
Keefe, Kevin
78Cr/PCL-104
79Albuq-8
80Albuq-17
81Albuq/TCMA-11
Keefe, Timothy
(Tim)
76Shakey-99
80Perez/HOF-99
80SSPC/HOF
90HOF/St-4
E223
N162
N167-7
N172
N28
N284
N403
WG1-41
Keefer, Paul
89Welland/Pucko-15
Keegan, Ed
61T-248
62T-249
Keegan, Robert
(Bob)
53T-196
54T-100
55T-10
55T/DH-52
56T-54
57T-99
58T-200
59T-86
60T-291
77T-436M
91T/Arc53-196
94T/Arc54-100
Keehn, Mike
83TriCit-18
Keeler, Jay
(Devo)
83Watlo/Frit-9
Keeler, Willie
40PlayBall-237
48Exh/HOF
50Callahan
50W576-44
63Bz/ATG-31
69Bz/Sm
72F/FFeat-40
72Laugh/GF-31
76Shakey-19
80Pac/Leg-99
80Perez/HOF-23
80SSPC/HOF
89HOF/St-51
89Smok/Dodg-12
90BBWit-74
90Perez/GreatMom-25
90Target-399
92Yank/WIZHOF-19
94Conlon-1018
E107
E254
E270/2
E90/1
E97
T204
T206
T3-101
W555
WG2-31
Keeley, Robert
54JC-35
54T-176
55JC-35
94T/Arc54-176
Keeline, Jason
91Pulaski/ClBest-8
91Pulaski/ProC-4014
92Macon/ClBest-19
92Macon/ProC-275
93Macon/ClBest-12
93Macon/ProC-1407
Keen, Vic
93Conlon-976
Keenan, Brad
92Billings/ProC-3364
Keenan, James
N172
V100
Keenan, Kerry
77Ashvl
79Wausau-4
80Ashvl-15
Keenan, Kevin
80Elmira-10
Keene, Andre
92Clinton/ClBest-10
92Clinton/ProC-3604
92MidwLAS/Team-23
92UD/ML-123
93FExcel/ML-119
Keener, Jeff
81Louisvl-10
82ArkTr-4
83Louisvl/Riley-10
84Louisvl-22
85Louisvl-8
Keenum, Larry
76Baton
Keeter, Lonnie
90Wichita/Rock-26CO
91HighD/ProC-2413CO
Keeton, Garry
83AppFx/Frit-26
Keeton, Rickey
(Buster)
79Vanco-10
82D-618
82F-146
82T-268

82Tucson-13
83Tucson-3
84Omaha-6
85Omaha-28
91Augusta/ClBest-27CO
91Augusta/ProC-824CO
92Salem/ClBest-27CO
92Salem/ProC-80CO
Kehn, Chet
90Target-998
Keighley, Steve
91Rockford/ClBest-15
91Rockford/ProC-2051
92WPalmB/ClBest-6
92WPalmB/ProC-2092
Keim, Chris
89Billings/ProC-2062
90Billings/ProC-3216
Keister, Tripp
92Pittsfld/ClBest-3
92Pittsfld/ProC-3306
Keitges, Jeff
89Wausau/GS-24
90SanBern/Best-6
90SanBern/Cal-110
90SanBern/ProC-2639
91SanBern/ClBest-16
91SanBern/ProC-1993
Keith, James
92Classic/DP-69
Kekich, Mike
65T-561R
69T-262
70OPC-536
70T-536
71MLB/St-490
71OPC-703
71T-703
72OPC-138
72T-138
73OPC-371
73Syrac/Team-11
73T-371
74OPC-199
74T-199
76OPC-582
76T-582
78SanJose-24
89Pac/SenLg-73
89TM/SenLg-57
90EliteSenLg-84
90Target-400
92Yank/WIZ60-64
92Yank/WIZ70-88
93Rang/Keeb-214
Kelbe, Frank
89Watertn/Star-27
Keliher, Paul
91Pulaski/ClBest-2
Keliipuleole, Carl
88Kinston/Star-13
89Canton/Best-18
89Canton/ProC-1300
89Canton/Star-9
90Canton/Best-21
90Canton/ProC-1290
90Canton/Star-8
90Foil/Best-137
90ProC/Singl-835
91Harris/ProC-622
Keling, Korey
88OK-14
89OK-18
90OK-23
91Boise/ClBest-25
91Boise/ProC-3872
92AS/Cal-31
92PalmSp/ClBest-10
92PalmSp/ProC-834
92ProC/Tomorrow-37
Kelipuleole, Carl
87BYU-4
Kell, Everett
(Skeeter)
52B-242
Kell, George
47TipTop
48L-120
49B-26
49Royal-3
50B-8
51B-46
51FB
51T/CAS
52B-75
52BR
52RM-AL13
52Royal
52StarCal-86A
52StarCal/L-72A
52T-246
52TipTop
53B/Col-61
53RM-AL8
53T-138
54B-50
54RH
54RM-AL4
55B-213
56T-195
57T-230
58T-40
77Galasso-9
79TCMA-86
80Marchant-13
80Pac/Leg-118
80Perez/HOF-182
81Tiger/Detroit-10
83Kaline-26ANN
83Kaline-30M
83Kaline-39M
83Kaline-57M
83Kaline-58M
86Sf/Dec-24M
86Tiger/Sport-10
88Pac/Leg-69
89HOF/St-24
90Pac/Legend-86
90Perez/GreatMom-59
91Crown/Orio-233
91Swell/Great-47
91T/Arc53-138
92AP/ASG-11
92AP/ASG24K-11G
92Bz/Quadra-11M
93AP/ASGCoke/Amo-11
93TWill-39
93UD/ATH-79
Exh47
R423-57
Kelleher, Frank
47Signal
49B/PCL-27
53Mother-37
Kelleher, Hal
93Conlon-968
Kelleher, John
90Target-401
E120
V61-87
Kelleher, Mick
76SSPC-605
77T-657
78SSPC/270-269
78T-564
79T-53
80T-323
81D-513
81T-429
81T/Tr-779
82D-601
82T-184
82T/Tr-53T
83T-79
Kellelmark, Joe
87VeroB-19
Keller, Carlton
(Buzz)
77ArkTr
Keller, Charlie
39Exh
39PlayBall-88
40PlayBall-9
41DP-64
41DP-84
41PlayBall-21
44Yank/St-16
47HomogBond-25
47TipTop
49B-209
50B-211
51B-177
80Marchant-12
89Pac/Leg-194
90Swell/Great-22
91Swell/Great-48
92Yank/WIZAS-36
93TWill-64
D305
Exh47
R346-48
Keller, Clyde
87PanAm/USAB-21
87PanAm/USAR-21
90Foil/Best-82
90MidwLgAS/GS-37
90Spring/Best-18
90TeamUSA/87-21
91MidwLAS/ProC-14
91Spring/ClBest-18
91Spring/ProC-739
92ProC/Tomorrow-318
92StLucie/ClBest-11
Keller, David
(Dave)
86Tampa-8C
88Billings/ProC-1802
89Billings/ProC-2048
90Burllnd/ProC-3026
91AA/LineD-100CO
91Burllnd/ProC-3320MG
91Canton/LineD-100CO
91Canton/ProC-997CO
92Kinston/ClBest-26CO
92Kinston/ProC-2491MG
93Kinston/Team-12MG
Keller, Edward
94Conlon-1113M
Keller, Jerry
79Richm-19
80Richm-12
81Richm-3
82Richm-10
83Portl-7
84Syrac-10
85Syrac-18
90Richm/25Ann-13
Keller, Phil
74Albuq/Team-8
Keller, Ron
77Fritsch-51
Keller, Steve
89Spartan/ProC-1055
89Spartan/Star-10
Kellert, Frank
55Gol/Dodg-15
56T-291
90Target-402
91Crown/Orio-234
Kelley, Anthony
86ColumAst-16
86SLAS-22
87Tucson-21
88Tucson/CMC-2
88Tucson/JP-15
88Tucson/ProC-186
89Tucson/CMC-3
89Tucson/JP-10
89Tucson/ProC-186
90FSLAS/Star-9
90Miami/I/Star-13
90Miami/II/Star-11
90Rochester/L&U-30
90Star/ISingl-73
Kelley, Dean Alan
87Oneonta-29
88CLAS/Star-10
88PrWill/Star-13
89FtLaud/Star-11
90Wichita/Rock-12
91AAA/LineD-286
91LasVegas/LineD-286
91LasVegas/ProC-242
Kelley, Erskine
92Welland/ClBest-12
92Welland/ProC-1338
93Welland/ClBest-10
93Welland/ProC-3373
Kelley, Harry
37Exh/4-14
37OPC-121
38Exh/4-14
93Conlon-721
V300
Kelley, Jack
C46-15
Kelley, Joe
76Shakey-123
80Perez/HOF-123
80SSPC/HOF
89HOF/St-35
89Smok/Dodg-13
90Target-403
C46-27
E107
T206
WG3-23
Kelley, M.
W516-26
Kelley, Rich
91Niagara/ClBest-18
91Niagara/ProC-3628
92Fayette/ProC-2164
Kelley, Richard
64T-476R
66OPC-84R
66T-84R
67CokeCap/Brave-16
67OPC-138
67T-138
68CokeCap/Brave-16
68T-203
69MLB/St-193
69T-359
70MLB/St-114
70OPC-474
70T-474
72MB-178
72OPC-412
72T-412
Kelley, Steve
75QuadC
Kelley, Thomas
64T-552R
66OPC-44R
66T-44R
67T-214
71OPC-463
71T-463
72OPC-97
72T-97
Kelliher, Paul
91Idaho/ProC-4332
91Pulaski/ProC-4008
Kellman, Howard
88Indianap/ProC-525M
89Indianap/ProC-1216
Kellner, Alex
49B-222
50B-14
51B-57
51FB
52B-226
52T-201
53B/Col-107
53Exh/Can-64
54B-51
55B-53
55Rodeo
56T-176
57T-280
58T-3
59T-101
79TCMA-55
80Marchant-14
Exh47
Kellner, Frank
90Osceola/Star-13
91Osceola/ClBest-19
91Osceola/ProC-693
92Jacks/ProC-4005
92Jacks/SB-336
Kellogg, Geoff
90Helena/SportP-17
91Beloit/ClBest-4
91Beloit/ProC-2099
92HighD/ClBest-18
Kellogg, Jeff
89EastLDD/ProC-48UMP
Kelly, Bill 1
47Signal
Kelly, Bill 2
80Indianap-23
81Indianap-22
82Omaha-7
Kelly, Brian
75Clinton
Kelly, Bryan
83Evansvl-4
86Nashvl-14
87Toledo-29
Kelly, Charles H.
N172
Kelly, Dale Patrick
(Pat)
75QuadC
78Syrac
79Syrac/Team-6
79T-714R
80OPC-329R
80Syrac-15
80Syrac/Team-12
80T-674R
83GlenF-11
86CharRain-11MG
88Wichita-40MG
89Pac/SenLg-134
89TexLAS/GS-1MG
89Wichita/Rock-6MG
89Wichita/Rock/Up-2MG
90AAASingl/ProC-25MG
90LasVegas/CMC-22MG
90LasVegas/ProC-136MG
90ProC/Singl-525MG
91Pac/SenLg-56
91Rockford/ClBest-27MG
91Rockford/ProC-2062MG
92Indianap/ProC-1875MG
92Indianap/SB-199MG
Kelly, Eliqio
78Newar
Kelly, George L.
21Exh-89
28Yueng-20
29Exh/4-7
40PlayBall-141
49Remar
50Remar
76Rowe-8M
76Shakey-138
77Galasso-119
80Pac/Leg-62
80Perez/HOF-138
80SSPC/HOF
87Conlon/2-45
89HOF/St-8
89Smok/Dodg-14
90Target-404
91Conlon/Sport-60
92Conlon/Sport-561
93Conlon-908
E120
E121/120
E121/80
E122
E126-60
E210-20
E220
V100
V61-119
V89-15
W501-72
W502-20
W515-32
W517-11
W572
W575
Kelly, Hal
79Tulsa-22
Kelly, Harold Patrick
(Pat)
69T-619R
70MLB/St-222
70OPC-57
70T-57
71OPC-413
71T-413
72MB-179
72OPC-326
72T-326
73OPC-261
73T-261
74K-47
74OPC-46
74T-46
74T/St-156
75OPC-82
75T-82
75T/M-82
76OPC-212
76SSPC-152
76T-212
77T-469
78T-616
79T-188
80T-543
81D-600
82F-372
82T-417
91Crown/Orio-235

Kelly, Jim
88Knoxvl/Best-5
89Dunedin/Star-9
90StLucie/Star-13
Kelly, John O.
N172
Kelly, John
90Johnson/Star-16
91ClBest/Singl-166
91SALAS/ProC-SAL42
91Savan/ClBest-7
91Savan/ProC-1648
92ClBest-279
92ProC/Tomorrow-319
92StPete/ClBest-20
92StPete/ProC-2024
93FExcel/ML-100
94FExcel-268
Kelly, Joseph
(Joe)
88CapeCod/Sum-173
90Yakima/Team-17
Kelly, Kevin
89BurlB/ProC-1623
89BurlB/Star-12
90BurlB/Best-21
90BurlB/ProC-2345
90BurlB/Star-15
Kelly, Leonard
87BurlEx-1
Kelly, Michael Joseph
(King)
50Callahan
50W576-45
75F/Pion-8
76Shakey-36
80Perez/HOF-36
80SSPC/HOF
90Perez/GreatMom-61
E223
N162
N172
N172
N28
N284
N403
N526
N690/2
WG1-5
Kelly, Michael Raymond
91ClBest/Gold-16
91ClBest/Singl-399
91Classic/DP-2
91Classic/DPPr-2
91Durham/ClBest-6
91Durham/ProC-DUR1
91DurhamUp/ProC-1
92ClBest-116
92ClBest/BBonusC-9
92ClBest/RBonus-BC9
92Classic/DP-87FB
92Classic/DPFoil-BC19FB
92Greenvl/ProC-1164
92Greenvl/SB-235
92ProC/Tomorrow-185
92Sky/AASingl-100
92UD-794
92UD/CollHolo-CP2
92UD/ML-275
92UD/ML-28M
92UD/ML/TPHolo-TP4
93ClBest/Fisher-6
93ClBest/GLP-1
93ClBest/GPr-1
93ClBest/MLG-18
93ClBest/MLGPr-1
93ClBest/MLGPrev-4
93FExcel/ML-3
93Richm/Bleach-8
93Richm/Pep-16
93UD-756
94B-261
94ClBest/Gold-144
94F/MLP-20
94FExcel-156
94Finest-329
94Flair-127
94Pinn-534
94SigRook-12
94SigRook/Hot-5
94UD-519DD
94Ultra-443
Kelly, Mike
87Elmira/Black-15
87Elmira/Red-15
88CapeCod/Sum-10
88WinHaven/Star-10
89Alaska/Team-6
89Lynch/Star-11
90EastLAS/ProC-EL39
90Foil/Best-191
90NewBrit/Best-11
90NewBrit/ProC-1330
90NewBrit/Star-6
Kelly, Pat F.
88Oneonta/ProC-2043
89PrWill/Star-10
89Star/Wax-89
90A&AASingle/ProC-32
90Albany/Best-16
90Albany/ProC-1041
90Albany/Star-8
90EastLAS/ProC-EL21
90ProC/Singl-787
91AAA/LineD-110
91Albany/ClBest-1
91B-155
91Classic/III-44
91ColClip/LineD-110
91ColClip/ProC-602
91D/Rook-1
91F/UltraUp-U41
91F/Up-U46
91Leaf/GRook-BC17
91S/RookTr-107T
91StCl-381
91T/Tr-67T
91UD-76
91Ultra-381MLP
92B-535
92Classic/I-48
92D-370
92F-233
92L-104
92L/BlkGold-104
92OPC-612
92OPC/Premier-71
92Panini-137
92Pinn-54
92Pinn/Team2000-7
92ProC/Tomorrow-108
92S-185
92S/100RisSt-5
92StCl-89
92Studio-213
92T-612
92T/91Debut-98
92T/Gold-612
92T/GoldWin-612
92TripleP-193
92TripleP-46
92UD-435
92Ultra-102
93B-187
93D-503
93F-280
93Flair-246
93L-447
93OPC-24
93Pac/Spanish-206
93Panini-150
93Pinn-134
93S-370
93Select-255
93StCl-155
93StCl/1stDay-155
93StCl/Y-16
93Studio-111
93T-196
93T/Gold-196
93UD-215
93Ultra-242
94B-549
94D-483
94F-235
94L-51
94OPC-156
94Pac/Cr-426
94Panini-101
94Pinn-197
94Pinn/Artist-197
94Pinn/Museum-197
94S-397
94Select-142
94StCl-52
94StCl/1stDay-52
94StCl/Gold-52
94StCl/Team-196
94Studio-213
94T-88
94T/Finest-63
94T/FinestRef-63
94T/Gold-88
94TripleP-274
94UD-264
94UD/ElecD-264
94Ultra-95
Kelly, Patrick Anthony
90Sumter/Best-8MG
90Sumter/ProC-2440MG
91Durham/ProC-1555MG
92Greenvl/ProC-1160
92Greenvl/SB-236
93Durham/Team-9
Kelly, Rafael
75QuadC
76QuadC
Kelly, Rich
92Fayette/ClBest-14
93ClBest/MLG-52
93SALAS/II-18
Kelly, Robert Edward
52T-348
Kelly, Roberto
83Greens-19
84Greens-4
86Albany/TCMA-2
87Colum-18
87Colum/Pol-14
87Colum/TCMA-22
88D-635
88D/Rook-16
88D/Y/Bk-635
88F-212
88S-634RP
88T/Tr-57T
89B-183
89Classic/Up/2-167
89D-433
89D/Best-273
89F-256
89Panini/St-395
89S-487
89S/HotRook-90
89S/NWest-18
89S/YS/II-25
89T-691
89T/Big-152
89ToysRUs-18
89UD-590
90AlbanyDG/Best-3
90B-444
90Classic/Up-27
90D-192
90D/BestAL-94
90F-446
90F/Can-446
90Kenner/Fig-48
90Leaf-17
90OPC-109
90Panini/St-119
90PublInt/St-538
90PublInt/St-597
90S-100
90S/100St-57
90S/NWest-6
90Sf-184
90T-109
90T/Big-247
90T/St-312
90T/TVYank-31
90UD-193
91B-166
91Classic/200-28
91D-400MVP
91D-538
91F-668
91Kenner-33
91Leaf-38
91Leaf/Stud-94
91OPC-11
91Panini/FrSt-328
91Panini/St-268
91Panini/Top15-31
91Panini/Top15-47
91RedFoley/St-57
91S-119
91S/100SS-96
91Seven/3DCoin-9NE
91StCl-319
91T-11
91T/CJMini/II-16
91UD-372
91Ultra-235
92B-12
92Classic/Game200-51
92Classic/II-T81
92D-73
92D/McDon-4
92F-234
92L-156
92L/BlkGold-156
92OPC-266
92OPC/Premier-83
92Panini-140
92Pinn-114
92S-324
92S/100SS-96
92S/Impact-80
92StCl-393
92Studio-214
92T-266
92T/Gold-266
92T/GoldWin-266
92T/Kids-88
92TripleP-72
92UD-577
92Ultra-103
92Ultra/AS-7
92Yank/WIZ80-97
93B-610
93Classic/Gamel-47
93Colla/DM-60
93D-313
93D/DK-12
93F-393
93F/Final-15
93Flair-26
93Kenner/Fig-17
93L-289
93OPC-79
93OPC/Premier-109
93Pac/Jugador-29
93Pac/Spanish-401
93Panini-295
93Pinn-520
93Reds/Kahn-11
93S-438
93Select-64
93Select/RookTr-20T
93StCl-632
93StCl/1stDay-632
93StCl/MurphyS-162
93Studio-23
93T-60
93T/Finest-120
93T/FinestRef-120
93T/Gold-60
93T/Tr-105T
93UD-47
93UD-473M
93UD-655
93UD/FunPack-169
93UD/SP-209
93Ultra-329
94B-626
94D-344
94D/Special-344
94F-412
94L-40
94OPC-139
94Pac/Cr-149
94Panini-162
94Pinn-286
94S-334
94StCl-372
94StCl/1stDay-372
94StCl/Gold-372
94Studio-36
94T-457
94T/Finest-163
94T/Finest/PreProd-163
94T/FinestRef-163
94T/Gold-457
94TripleP-213
94UD-387
94UD/SP-51
94Ultra-171
Kelly, Tim
86Bakers-17CO
87PalmSp-18
88MidldA/GS-3
Kelly, Tom
74Tacoma/Caruso-25
75Tacoma/KMMO-19
82OrlanTw/A-12MG
82OrlanTw/B-13MG
83Twin/Team-26CO
83Twin/Team-34M
85Twin/Team-30CO
87T-618MG
88T-194MG
89D/AS-10MG
89D/PopUp-10MG
89T-14MG
89T/Gloss22-1MG
90OPC-429MG
90T-429MG
91OPC-201MG
91T-201MG
92OPC-459MG
92T-459MG
92T/Gold-459MG
92T/GoldWin-459MG
93T-509MG
93T/Gold-509MG
Kelly, Van
71Richm/Team-9
Kelly, William J.
D304
E254
E270/2
E97
T207
T213/blue
T215/blue
Kelso, Bill
65OPC-194R
65T-194R
67T-367R
68T-511
92AubAs/ClBest-29
92AubAs/ProC-1371
Kelso, Jeff
88Bend/Legoe-9
89BendB/Legoe-22
90PalmSp/Cal-214
90PalmSp/ProC-2590
Keltner, Ken
39Exh
41DP-79
42Playball-11
47HomogBond-26
48L-45
49B-125
50B-186
75Sheraton-19
89Pac/Leg-143
89Swell-87
94Conlon-M
D305
Exh47
R303/A
R303/B
R311/Gloss
V351B-28
Kemmerer, Russ
55B-222
55T-18
55T/DH-4
58T-137
59T-191
60T-362
61T-56
61T/St-121
62T-576
63T-338
Kemmler, Rudolph
N172
N172/BC
N370
Scrapps
Kemnitz, Brent
85Anchora-17CO
87Anchora-17CO
90WichSt-41
Kemp, Bill
90GA-13
Kemp, Hugh
84Cedar-7
87Nashvl-11
88AAA/ProC-27
88Nashvl/CMC-7
88Nashvl/ProC-479
88Nashvl/Team-15
89Nashvl/CMC-5
89Nashvl/ProC-1294
89Nashvl/Team-10
90AAASingl/ProC-483
90BuffB/CMC-5

90BuffB/ProC-368
90BuffB/Team-10
90ProC/Singl-5
Kemp, Joe
88SanBern/Best-21
88SanBern/Cal-35
89Modesto/Cal-280
Kemp, Rick
75Spokane/Caruso-15
Kemp, Rod
79LodiD-1
Kemp, Steve
77T-492R
78BK/T-18
78Ho-55
78OPC-167
78T-21
79Ho-15
79OPC-97
79T-196
80K-33
80OPC-166
80T-315
80T/S-29
80T/Super-29
81Coke
81D-249
81Drake-27
81F-459
81F/St-7
81MSA/Disc-19
81OPC-152
81Sqt-27SP
81T-593
81T/SO-11
81T/St-74
81Tiger/Detroit-86
82D-594
82F-271
82F/St-160
82K-39
82OPC-296
82T-666TL
82T-670
82T/St-185
82T/Tr-54T
83D-269
83Drake-13
83F-239
83F/St-10M
83F/St-14M
83OPC-260
83OPC/St-50
83RoyRog/Disc-5
83T-260
83T/St-50
83T/Tr-53
84D-469
84Drake-16
84F-129
84Nes/792-440
84OPC-301
84T-440
84T/RD-12M
85D-225
85F-132
85F/Up-U64
85FunFoodPin-58
85Leaf-100
85OPC-120
85T-120
85T/RD-15M
85T/Tr-66T
86D-200
86F-610
86LasVegas-9
86T-387
87OKCty-11
88AlaskaAS70/Team-19
88Mother/R-8
89Pac/SenLg-10
89T/SenLg-52
89TM/SenLg-58
90EliteSenLg-8
90Smok/SoCal-6
92Yank/WIZ80-98
93Rang/Keeb-215
Kemper, Robbie
89Clinton/ProC-896
90Erie/Star-11
Kempfer, Jason
91Idaho/SportP-24
92Pulaski/ClBest-16
92Pulaski/ProC-3174
Kenaga, Jeff
82Evansvl-22
83Evansvl-20
84CharlO-8
Kendall, Fred
72T-532
73OPC-221
73T-221
74McDon
74OPC-53SD
74T-53
74T/St-95
75OPC-332
75T-332
75T/M-332
76OPC-639
76SSPC-122
76T-639
77OPC-213
77T-576
78PapaG/Disc-13
78SSPC/270-182
78T-426
79T-83
80T-598
Kendall, Jason
92ClBest/BBonusC-26
92ClBest/Up-408
92Classic/DP-18
92FrRow/DP-89
92LitSun/HSPros-11
92UD/ML-14
93B-162
93ClBest/MLG-195
93Pinn-458DP
93S-490DP
93Select-359DP
93StCl/MurphyS-148
93T-334
93T/Gold-334
94B-246
94ClBest/Gold-19
94FExcel-252
94SigRook-13
94T-686
94T/Gold-686
Kendall, Jeremy
92Martins/ClBest-15
92Martins/ProC-3071
Kendall, Phil
91Billing/SportP-25
91Billings/ProC-3748
Kendrena, Ken
92Erie/ClBest-15
92Erie/ProC-1614
93T-726M
93T/Gold-726M
Kendrick, Patrick
92Hunting/ClBest-22
92Hunting/ProC-3143
Kendrick, Pete
83Madis/Frit-23
84Albany-14
85Modesto/Chong-14
87ElPaso-4
88Denver/ProC-1269
Kenins, John N.
N172
Kennedy, Bo
87Penin-23
89Saraso/Star-12
90BirmB/Best-20
90BirmB/ProC-1108
90ProC/Singl-770
91AA/LineD-65
91BirmB/LineD-65
91BirmB/ProC-1452
92BirmB/ProC-2577
92BirmB/SB-86
92Sky/AASingl-42
92Vanco/ProC-2719
Kennedy, Dan
89WinSalem/Star-11
89Wythe/Star-18
Kennedy, Darryl
92Gaston/ClBest-11
Kennedy, Dave
89Elmira/Pucko-23
Kennedy, James
91GulfCR/SportP-12
Kennedy, Joel
93MissSt-48M
Kennedy, John E.
64T-203
65OPC-119
65T-119
66T-407
67CokeCap/DodgAngel-11
67OPC-111
67T-111
69T-631
70McDon-2
70OPC-53
70T-53
71MLB/St-319
71OPC-498
71T-498
72T-674
73OPC-437
73T-437
86Alban/TCM-24C
90Target-407
92Yank/WIZ60-65
Kennedy, Junior
76Indianap-13
77Phoenix
78Pep-15
78SSPC/270-134
79T-501
80T-377
81D-424
81F-203
81T-447
82D-188
82F-70
82RedLob
82T-723
82T/Tr-55T
83D-529
83F-500
83T-204
Kennedy, Kevin
78RochR
79RochR-3
80RochR-11
81RochR-10
87Bakers-15
88SanAn/Best-23
88TexLgAS/GS-22
89Albuq/ProC-72
90AAAGame/ProC-32MG
90AAASingl/ProC-82MG
90Albuq/CMC-27MG
90Albuq/ProC-361MG
90Albuq/Trib-16MG
90ProC/Singl-667MG
91AAA/LineD-24MG
91Albuq/LineD-24MG
91Albuq/ProC-1157MG
93Rang/Keeb-393MG
93T-513MG
93T/Gold-513MG
Kennedy, Kyle
92MissSt-24
93MissSt-25
Kennedy, Lloyd Vernon
37Exh/4-10
37OPC-135
38G-256
38G-280
92Conlon/Sport-365
V300
WG8-37
Kennedy, Mike
90Modesto/Chong-16
91SoOreg/ClBest-21
91SoOreg/ProC-3849
Kennedy, Monte
47TipTop
49B-237
49Eureka-112
50B-175
51B-163
52B-213
52BR
52T-124
Kennedy, Robert D.
47TipTop
51B-296
51T/RB-29
52NumNum-16
52T-77
53T-33
54Esskay
54T-155
55Esskay
55T-48
55T/DH-87
56T-38
56T/Pin-34
57T-149
64T-486CO
65T-457CO
68OPC-183MG
68T-183
85T-135FS
90Target-405
91Crown/Orio-236
91T/Arc53-33
94T/Arc54-155
Kennedy, Scott
93MedHat/ProC-3731
93MedHat/SportP-6
Kennedy, Shawn
91Butte/SportP-12
Kennedy, Terry
78ArkTr
79T-724R
80T-569
81D-428
81F-541
81OPC-353
81T-353
81T/Tr-780
82D-121
82Drake-20
82F-574
82F/St-105
82OPC-65
82T-65
82T/St-100
83D-220
83D-26DK
83D/AAS-11
83F-362
83F/St-1AM
83F/St-1BM
83OPC-274
83OPC/St-293FOIL
83T-274
83T-742TL
83T/Gloss40-6
83T/St-293
84D-112
84D/AAS-8
84F-304
84Mother/Pad-5
84Nes/792-366TL
84Nes/792-455
84OPC-166
84Seven-17W
84Smok/Pad-14
84T-366TL
84T-455
84T/RD-28M
84T/St-154
85D-429
85F-37
85FunFoodPin-47
85Leaf-33
85Mother/Pad-10
85OPC-194
85T-135FS
85T-635
85T/RD-28
85T/St-148
86D-356
86D/AAS-7
86D/PopUp-7
86F-327
86GenMills/Book-5M
86OPC-230
86T-230
86T-306M
86T/Gloss22-20
86T/St-111
86T/St-152
87D-205
87D/OD-142
87F-419
87F/Up-U56
87French-15
87OPC-303
87Sf/TPrev-21M
87T-540
87T/St-108
87T/Tr-57T
88D-150
88D/AS-9
88D/Best-30
88D/PopUp-9
88F-563
88French-15
88KennerFig-58
88Leaf-99
88OPC-180
88Panini/St-227M
88Panini/St-7
88S-123
88S/WaxBox-1
88Sf-94
88T-180
88T/Gloss22-9
88T/St-161
88T/St-225
88T/St/Backs-55
89B-470
89D-141
89F-610
89F/Up-128
89Mother/Giants-8
89OPC-309
89Panini/St-256
89S-123
89S/Tr-30T
89T-705
89T/Big-180
89T/St-235
89T/Tr-59T
89UD-469
90B-241
90D-602
90D/BestNL-132
90F-58
90F/Can-58
90Leaf-67
90Mother/Giant-12
90OPC-372
90PublInt/St-71
90S-7
90T-372
90T/Big-16
90UD-397
91B-631
91Crown/Orio-237
91D-94
91F-263
91Leaf-216
91Mother/Giant-12
91OPC-66
91PG&E-5
91Panini/FrSt-66
91S-548
91StCl-91
91T-66
91UD-404
91Ultra-321
91Ultra-399CL
92OPC-253
92S-503
92T-253
92T/Gold-253
92T/GoldWin-253
92UD-192
Kennedy, Theodore A.
N172
Kennedy, Vern
94Conlon-1123
Kennedy, William G.
(Bill)
49B-105
52T-102
53T-94
60HenryH-25
91T/Arc53-94
Kennedy, William V.
(Brickyard)
90Target-406
Kennedy, William
N284
N300/unif
Kennelley, Steve
87Columbia-11
Kennemur, Paul
76Baton
Kenner, Jeff
86ArkTr-10
Kenney, Jerry
69T-519R
70OPC-219
70T-219
71MLB/St-491
71OPC-572
71T-572
72MB-180
72OPC-158

72T-158
73OPC-514
73T-514
75Syrac/Team-7
75Syrac/Team-8
92Yank/WIZ60-66
92Yank/WIZ70-89
Kenny, Brian
91Geneva/ClBest-10
91Geneva/ProC-4210
92MidwLAS/Team-24
92Peoria/ClBest-7
92Peoria/Team-31M
92Peoria/Team-9
Kenny, Terry
75Cedar
Kent, Bernard
85Beloit-12
Kent, Dave
89Oneonta/ProC-2119
Kent, Jeff
88CapeCod/Sum-169
89StCath/ProC-2091
90Dunedin/Star-13
90FSLAS/Star-33
90Star/ISingl-65
91AA/LineD-360
91ClBest/Singl-108
91Knoxvl/LineD-360
91Knoxvl/ProC-1775
92D/Rook-61
92F/Up-104
92L-445
92L/BlkGold-445
92Pinn-522
92S/RookTr-84T
93B-426
93BJ/D/45-41
93D-302
93F-90
93L-185
93Mets/Kahn-12
93OPC-213
93Pinn-155
93S-189
93Select-318
93StCl-269
93StCl/1stDay-269
93T-703
93T/Gold-703
93ToysRUs-84
93UD-401
93USPlayC/Rook-7S
93Ultra-77
94B-296
94B-385
94D-185
94F-570
94Flair-200
94L-112
94OPC-166
94Pac/Cr-408
94Panini-220
94Pinn-122
94Pinn/Artist-122
94Pinn/Museum-122
94S-516
94Select-85
94StCl-362
94StCl/1stDay-362
94StCl/Gold-362
94Studio-117
94T-424
94T/Finest-33
94T/FinestRef-33
94T/Gold-424
94TripleP-146
94UD-178
94UD/CollC-159
94UD/CollC/Gold-159
94UD/CollC/Silv-159
94UD/ElecD-178
94UD/HoloFX-20
94UD/SP-119
94Ultra-238
Kent, John
(Bo)
86Cram/NWL-73
87Modesto-1
88Huntsvl/BK-10
Kent, Lewis
87Kinston-7
88Kinston/Star-14
Kent, Matt
86Stockton-12
Kent, Maury
90Target-999
Kent, Troy
88Martins/Star-20
89Spartan/ProC-1033
89Spartan/Star-11
91SanBern/ClBest-7
91SanBern/ProC-1983
92Jacks/ProC-3705
92Jaxvl/SB-360
92Sky/AASingl-152
93Calgary/ProC-1162
Kent, Wes
81AppFx-26
82AppFx/Frit-13
83GlenF-3
Kenworthy, Dick
68OPC-63
68T-63
81TCMA-332
Kenworthy, William
(Duke)
WG7-24
Kenyon, J.J.
N172
Kenyon, Robert
81VeroB-7
82VeroB-7
Keon, Kevin
90Niagara/Pucko-19
Keough, Joseph
69T-603
70T-589
71MLB/St-417
71OPC-451
71T-451
72OPC-133
72T-133
Keough, Matt
78T-709R
79Ho-59
79OPC-284
79T-554
80OPC-74
80T-134
81A's/Granny-27
81D-358
81F-588
81OPC-301
81T-301
82D-71
82F-95
82F/St-129
82Granny-6
82OPC-87
82T-87
82T/St-225
83D-239
83F-521
83Granny-27
83OPC/St-109
83T-413
83T/St-109
83T/Tr-54
84D-627
84F-130
84Nes/792-203
84OPC-203
84T-203
85Louisvl-16
87Mother/A's-18
88Chatt/Team-17
90Swell/Great-127
92Yank/WIZ80-99
Keough, R. Marty
58T-371
59T-303
60T-71
61T-146
62J-69
62P-69
62P/Can-69
62Salada-79
62Shirriff-79
62T-258
63FrBauer-12
63J-135
63P-135
63T-21
64T-166
65OPC-263
65T-263
66T-334
Kepshire, Kurt
81Cedar-2
82Cedar-5
83ArkTr-4
84Louisvl-17
85D-382
85F-230
85T-474
86D-504
86F-39
86KAS/Disc-13
86Louisvl-14
86Schnucks-11
86T-256
88Indianap/CMC-2
88Indianap/ProC-506
89Portl/CMC-3
89Portl/ProC-215
Kerdoon, Randy
87SLCity/Taco-21ANN
Kerfeld, Charlie
85Cram/PCL-73
86D/Rook-6
86F-303
86Pol/Ast-10
86Sf/Rook-23
86T/Tr-52T
87D-209
87F-60
87F/Excit-31
87Leaf-195
87Mother/Ast-12
87OPC-145
87Sf-146
87Sf/TPrev-8M
87T-145
87T/St-28
87ToysRUs-15
88ColAst/Best-1
88OPC-392
88S-479
88T-608
89Tucson/CMC-8
89Tucson/JP-11
89Tucson/ProC-188
90Brave/Dubuq/Perf-14
Kerfut, George
90FSLAS/Star-10
90Miami/I/Star-14
90Miami/II/Star-12
90Star/ISingl-74
91Miami/ClBest-15
91Miami/ProC-403
Keriazakos, Const.
(Gus)
55B-14
Kerkes, Kevin
89Wausau/GS-22
Kerley, Collin
92Geneva/ClBest-12
92Geneva/ProC-1557
93Peoria/Team-12
Kermode, Al
92James/ClBest-11
92James/ProC-1498
Kern, James
(Jim)
75OPC-621R
75OkCty/Team-8
75T-621R
75T/M-621R
76SSPC-509
77Pep-7
77T-41
78OPC-165
78T-253
79OPC-297
79T-573
80OPC-192
80T-369
81D-27
81F-618
81F/St-18
81OPC-197
81T-197
82Coke/Reds
82D-89
82F-322
82OPC-59
82T-463
82T/Tr-56T
83D-355
83F-240
83T-772
83T/Fold-4M
83TrueVal/WSox-67
86OhHenry-46
93Rang/Keeb-216
Kern, Lloyd D.
77WHave
79WHave-28
79WHave-29M
80LynnS-22
81LynnS-26
Kernek, George B.
66Pep/Tul
66T-544R
Kernick, Craig
91Waverly/Fut-7
Kerns, Mickey
92Boise/ClBest-13
92Boise/ProC-3637
Kerns, Russ
V362-38
Kerr, Jason
91Yakima/ClBest-16
91Yakima/ProC-4244
92ProC/Tomorrow-250
92VeroB/ClBest-9
92VeroB/ProC-2870
Kerr, John Francis
33G-214
49Remar
Kerr, John J.
(Buddy)
45Playball-37
47HomogBond-27
48B-20
49B-186
49Eureka-113
50B-55
50Drake-15
51B-171
79TCMA-113
D305
R302-102
Kerr, John L.
28Exh/PCL-16
29Exh/4-19
Kerr, Paul S.
80Perez/HOF-C
Kerr, Richard
(Dickie)
21Exh-90
88Pac/8Men-47
88Pac/8Men-56
88Pac/8Men-97
94Conlon-1037
94Conlon-1041M
E121/120
E121/80
E122
E220
W501-37
W514-23
W575
Kerr, Zackary
(Zach)
89Erie/Star-10
90CLAS/CL-1
90Freder/Team-10
91Freder/ClBest-5
Kerrigan, Joe
75WPalmB/Sussman-9
76Expo/Redp-15
77OPC-171
77T-341
78OPC-108
78T-549
79RochR-2
79T-37
81Indianap-24
82OkCty-13
83Expo/PostC-8CO
84Expo/PostC-15CO
84Stuart-33
86Expo/Prov/Pan-14CO
86Provigo-14CO
87Jaxvl-26
88Indianap/ProC-499M
90AAASingl/ProC-592CO
90Indianap/ProC-309CO
91AA/LineD-275M
91Crown/Orio-238
91Harris/LineD-275CO
91Harris/ProC-618CO
Kerrigan, Rob
87James-21
88James/ProC-1898
88Rockford-18
89Rockford-18
89Rockford/Team-14
90WPalmB/Star-11
Kershaw, Scott
86AppFx-12
Keshock, Christopher
87CharWh-22
Kesler, Mike
87QuadC-13
Kesselmark, Joe
88SanAn/Best-11
89SanAn/Best-9
90Canton/Best-10
90Canton/ProC-1304
Kesses, Steve
76Wausau
Kessinger, Don
66OPC-24
66T-24
67T-419
68OPC-159
68T-159
69Kelly/Pin-9
69MB-144
69MLB/St-123
69MLBPA/Pin-48
69Sunoco/Pin-6
69T-225
69T-422AS
69T/S-18
69T/St-16
70Dunkin-4
70MLB/St-20
70OPC-456AS
70OPC-80
70T-456AS
70T-80
71K-9
71MD
71MLB/St-36
71OPC-455
71T-455
71T/Coins-119
71T/tatt-15
72MB-181
72OPC-145
72T-145
73OPC-285
73T-285
74OPC-38
74T-38
74T/DE-52
74T/St-16
75Ho-77
75Ho/Twink-77
75OPC-315
75T-315
75T/M-315
76Crane-25
76Ho-134
76MSA/Disc
76OPC-574
76SSPC-315
76T-574
77T-229
78SSPC/270-154
78T-672
79T-404MG
79T-467
84Cub/Uno-2M
84Cub/Uno-7M
89Swell-112
90Pac/Legend-34
90Swell/Great-69
91Swell/Great-115
92AP/ASG-76
93UD/ATH-80
94TedW-17
Kessinger, Keith
89Bluefld/Star-12
90Wausau/Best-18
90Wausau/ProC-2131
90Wausau/Star-12
91Freder/ClBest-29
92Cedar/ClBest-8
92Cedar/ProC-1078
94Pinn-251
94Pinn/Artist-251
94Pinn/Museum-251
94Pinn/RookTPinn-3M
94S-621
94S/Boys-42

92StCl-837
92Studio-39
92T-134
92T/91Debut-100
92T/Gold-134
92T/GoldWin-134
92UD-374
92Ultra-206
93D-668
93F-438
93Flair-66
93L-143
93Mother/Ast-19
93Pac/Spanish-479
93Pinn-430
93S-430
93StCl-518
93StCl/1stDay-518
93StCl/Ast-17
93T-308
93T/Gold-308
93UD-314
93UD/SP-36
93Ultra-393
94B-614
94D-32
94D/Special-32
94F-496
94F/AS-43
94F/GoldM-10M
94Finest-244
94Flair-173
94L-314
94OPC-176
94Pac/Cr-270
94Panini-196
94Pinn-321
94S-231
94S-630HL
94S/GoldR-231
94Sf/2000-72
94StCl-327
94StCl/1stDay-327
94StCl/Gold-327
94Studio-23
94T-703
94T/Gold-703
94TripleP-29
94UD-435
94UD/CollC-162
94UD/CollC/Gold-162
94UD/CollC/Silv-162
94Ultra-208

Kiley, Craig
84LitFalls-15

Kilgo, Rusty
89James/ProC-2156
90A&AASingle/ProC-110
90MidwLgAS/GS-11
90Rockford/ProC-2685
90Rockford/Team-12
91FSLAS/ProC-FSL43
91WPalmB/ClBest-6
91WPalmB/ProC-1222
92Cedar/ClBest-15
92Cedar/ProC-1069
92Chatt/ProC-3814
92Rockford/ClBest-4

Kilgus, Paul
86Tulsa-20
87OKCty-1
88D-469
88D/Best-111
88F-471
88Mother/R-19
88S-536
88T-427
89B-285
89D-283
89D/Best-149
89D/Tr-42
89F-525
89F/Up-76
89Mara/Cubs-39
89OPC-276
89S-271
89T-276
89T/Tr-60T
89UD-335
89UD/Ext-797
90AAASingl/ProC-346
90B-508
90D-276
90F-34
90F/Can-34
90OPC-86
90ProC/Singl-335
90PublInt/St-196
90S-196
90Syrac/CMC-9
90Syrac/MerchB-13
90Syrac/ProC-566
90Syrac/Team-13
90T-86
90Tor/BJ-39
90UD-155
91Crown/Orio-499
92Louisvl/ProC-1885
92Louisvl/SB-266
92S-268
92StCl-722
93F/Final-125
93Rang/Keeb-217
94Pac/Cr-593
94StCl/Team-324
94T-737
94T/Gold-737

Kilkenny, Mike
69T-544
70MLB/St-209
70OPC-424
70T-424
71MLB/St-397
71OPC-86
71T-86
72OPC-337
72T-337
73OPC-551
73T-551

Killebrew, Cameron
79Wausau-22

Killebrew, Harmon
55T-124
55T/DH-111
56T-164
58T-288
59HRDerby-10
59T-515
60Bz-20
60NuCard-49
60P*
60T-210
60T/tatt-26
60T/tatt-91
61Clover-10
61NuCard-449
61P-92
61Peters-18
61T-80
61T/St-181
62Bz
62Exh
62J-85
62P-85
62P/Can-85
62Salada-36
62Shirriff-36
62T-316IA
62T-53LL
62T-70
62T/St-76
62T/bucks
63Bz-7
63Exh
63J-5
63P-5
63T-4LL
63T-500
63T/SO
64Bz-7
64T-10LL
64T-12LL
64T-177
64T-81M
64T/Coins-112
64T/Coins-133AS
64T/S-38
64T/SU
64T/St-34
64T/tatt
64Wheat/St-25
65Bz-7
65OPC-3LL
65OPC-5LL
65OldLond-28
65T-3LL
65T-400
65T-5LL
65T/E-56
65T/trans-52
66Bz-11
66OPC-120
66T-120
66T/RO-45
66T/RO-50
67Bz-11
67CokeCap/ALAS-26
67CokeCap/AS-18
67CokeCap/Twin-6
67OPC/PI-23
67T-241LL
67T-243LL
67T-334M
67T-460
67T/PI-23
67T/Test/SU-6
68Bz-8
68Dexter-46
68OPC-4LL
68OPC-6LL
68T-220
68T-361AS
68T-490M
68T-4LL
68T-6LL
68T/ActionSt-14B
68T/ActionSt-2B
68T/ActionSt-9A
68T/G-5
68T/Post-10
69Citgo-4
69MB-145
69MLB/St-68
69MLBPA/Pin-14
69T-375
69T/S-19
69T/St-195
69T/decal
69Trans-11
70K-61
70MB-12
70MLB/St-234
70OPC-150
70OPC-64LL
70OPC-66LL
70T-150
70T-64LL
70T-66LL
70T/S-4
70T/SO
70T/Super-4
70Trans-15
71Bz
71Bz/Test-17
71K-55
71MD
71MLB/St-465
71MLB/St-566
71OPC-550
71OPC-65LL
71T-550
71T-65LL
71T/Coins-100
71T/GM-8
71T/Greatest-8
71T/S-60
71T/Super-60
71T/tatt-6
71T/tatt-6a
72MB-182
72OPC-51
72OPC-52IA
72OPC-88LL
72ProStars/PostC-28
72T-51
72T-52IA
72T-88LL
72T/Post-20
73OPC-170
73T-170
73T/Comics-9
73T/Lids-25
73T/PinUps-9
74OPC-400
74T-400
74T/St-208
75OPC-207MVP
75OPC-640
75T-207MVP
75T-640
75T/M-207MVP
75T/M-640
76Laugh/Jub-13
76SSPC-168
78TCMA-90
78Twin/Frisz-8
80Laugh/3/4/5-14
80Marchant-15
80Pac/Leg-69
80Perez/HOF-188
82CJ-5
82KMart-15
84West/1-23
85CircK-5
86BLChew-5
86Sf/Dec-48M
87KMart-4
87Nestle/DT-22
88Chatt/Team-18
88Grenada-18
88Pac/Leg-86
89Kahn/Coop-7
89Pac/Leg-163
89Swell-70
89T/LJN-49
90MSA/AGFA-3
90Pac/Legend-35
90Perez/GreatMom-48
91CollAB-34
91K/3D-6
91LineD-41
91MDA-16
91Swell/Great-49
91UD/HOF-H1
91UD/HOF-x
93AP/ASG-118
93AP/ASG24K-52G
93MCI-10
94T/Arc54-254
94TedW-49
94TedW/500-3
Exh47
PM10/Sm-88
Rawl

Killeen, Tim
92SoOreg/ClBest-12
92SoOreg/ProC-3419

Killefer, Bill
94Conlon-1178M
94Conlon-1274IA

Killefer, Wade H.
(Red)
16FleischBrd-51
94Conlon-1178

Killen, Brent
92Niagara/ClBest-23
92Niagara/ProC-3332

Killian, Ed
12Sweet/Pin-27
81Tiger/Detroit-87
E254
T201
T205
T206
T213/brown

Killifer, William
09Buster/Pin-8
14CJ-135
14Piedmont/St-30
15CJ-135
21Exh-91
BF2-86
D327
D328-93
D329-95
D350/2-93
E121/120
E121/80
E122
E135-93
E254
E286
M101/4-95
M101/5-93
M116
V100
W501-56
W514-87

Killingsworth, Kirk
83Tulsa-12
85Tulsa-32
86Tulsa-3
87OKCty-9

Killingsworth, Sam
75BurlB

Kilmer, Wilson
89KS*-90ACO

Kilner, John Steven
86Durham-16
87Greenvl/Best-14
88Greenvl/Best-20
89Greenvl/Star-11
89Richm/Ko-30
90Foil/Best-289
90Greenvl/Best-21
90Greenvl/ProC-1125
90Greenvl/Star-10

Kilroy, Mathew
N172
N284

Kim, Wendell
75Lafay
77Phoenix
78Cr/PCL-98
81Clinton-2
82Clinton/Frit-2MG
85Fresno/Pol-1MG
86Shrev-13
86Shrev-14
87Phoenix-23
88Phoenix/CMC-24
88Phoenix/ProC-65
90Mother/Giant-21M
91Mother/Giant-27CO
92Giant/PGE-22CO
92Mother/Giant-28M
93Mother/Giant-28M

Kimball, Doug
92GreatF/SportP-18

Kimball, Newt
90Target-409

Kimball, Ricky
88CapeCod/Sum-142
91SoOreg/ClBest-6
91SoOreg/ProC-3838
92ProC/Tomorrow-137

Kimball, Scott
90Beloit/Best-8
90Beloit/Star-11
90Foil/Best-124
90MidwLgAS/GS-12

Kimberlin, Keith
89Niagara/Pucko-13
90FSLAS/Star-34
90Lakeland/Star-15
90Star/ISingl-36
91AA/LineD-389
91ClBest/Singl-170
91London/LineD-389
91London/ProC-1885

Kimbler, Doug
90Niagara/Pucko-2
91Fayette/ClBest-19
91Fayette/ProC-1178

Kimbro, Henry
92Negro/RetortII-21

Kimbrough, Larry
86Negro/Frit-37
86Negro/Frit-61
92Negro/Retort-35

Kimel, Jack
94ClBest/Gold-30

Kimm, Bruce
77T-554
81F-355
81T-272
83Cedar-1
83Cedar/Frit-22
86TexGold-CO
88Kahn/Reds-CO
89VFJuice-36CO
90CedarDG/Best-27MG
92Mother/Padre-27M
92Pol/Padre-26CO
92Smok/Padre-16CO

Kimsey, Chad
92Conlon/Sport-511

Kimsey, Donna
89GA-12M

Kimsey, Keith
91Bristol/ClBest-12
91Bristol/ProC-3618
92Niagara/ClBest-22
92Niagara/ProC-3340
94B-561

Kin, Clinton
82Clinton/Frit-32

Kinard, Rudy
75Spokane/Caruso-3

Kindall, Jerry

58T-221
59T-274
60T-444
61P-199
61T-27
62AmTract-51A
62AmTract-51B
62J-191
62P-191
62P/Can-191
62Sugar-13
62T-292
63F-13
63J-68
63P-68
63Sugar-13
63T-36
78TCMA-218
78TCMA-271
78Twin/Frisz-35
84AZ/Pol-9CO
86AZ/Pol-9CO
87AZ/Pol-7CO
88AZ/Pol-6CO
90AZ/Pol-10CO
92AZ/Pol-7CO

Kinder, Ellis
50B-152
51B-128
52T-78
53T-44
54B-98
54T-47
55T-115
55T/DH-130
56T-336
57T-352
79TCMA-115
91T/Arc53-44
94T/Arc54-47
Exh47
R423-55

Kindler, Tom
92Spokane/ClBest-8
92Spokane/ProC-1289

Kindred, Curt
83Visalia/Frit-22
84Visalia-2
86Cedar/TCMA-6
87Cedar-4

Kindred, Vincent L.
87Spring/Best-23
89Savan/ProC-355
90Foil/Best-302
90Spring/Best-10

Kiner, Ralph
47HomogBond-28
47TipTop
48B-3
48L-91
49B-29
49Eureka-164
50B-33
51BR-C1
51T/CAS
51T/RB-15
52B-11
52BR
52Dix-53
52RM-NL12
52StarCal-89D
52StarCal-89DM
52StarCal/L-77B
52Wheat*
53B/Col-80
53Exh/Can-22
53RM-NL15
53T-191
54B-45
54Dix
54RH
55B-197
55Gol/Ind-13
55Salem
60F-79
61F-50
74Laugh/ASG-51
76Shakey-151
77Galasso-2
77T-437HL
79TCMA-13
80Pac/Leg-81
80Perez/HOF-151
80SSPC/HOF
82CJ-11
83D/HOF-38
85CircK-30
85West/2-36
86Sf/Dec-35
88Pac/Leg-9
89T/LJN-141
90Pac/Legend-36
90Swell/Great-80
91CollAB-12
91K/3D-15
91Swell/Great-50
91T/Arc53-191
92AP/ASG-5
92AP/ASG24K-5G
92Bz/Quadra-17M
93AP/ASGCoke/Amo-5
93TWill-127
93TWill-76
D305
Exh47
PM10/Sm-89
R302-110
R346-7
R423-58

King, Andre
94B-217
94ClBest/Gold-48
94FExcel-157
94SigRook-42
94T-752DP
94T/Gold-752DP

King, Brett
94B-603
94ClBest/Gold-62

King, Bryan
88SanBern/Best-22
88SanBern/Cal-28
89SanBern/Best-20
89SanBern/Cal-80
90Wmsprt/Best-12
90Wmsprt/ProC-1063
90Wmsprt/Star-13
91SanBern/ClBest-17
91SanBern/ProC-1994

King, Charles F.
(Silver)
N172

King, Charles G.
(Chick)
55B-133
59T-538

King, Clarence
92Negro/Retort-36

King, Clay
92Everett/ClBest-14
92Everett/ProC-1697

King, Clyde
51B-299
52B-56
52T-205
69T-274MG
70T-624MG
71Richm/Team-11
75OPC-589MG
75T-589MG
75T/M-589MG
83T-486MG
89Rini/Dodg-12
90Swell/Great-117
90Target-410
91Swell/Great-51
V362-26

King, David
90AppFox/Box-16
90AppFox/ProC-2101
91BBCity/ClBest-18
91BBCity/ProC-1404

King, Douglas
90Cedar/Best-21
90CharWh/ProC-2235
91CharWh/ClBest-5
91CharWh/ProC-2882

King, Eric
86D/Rook-27
86Sf/Rook-42
86T/Tr-53T
87Cain's-19
87D-250
87F-155
87Sf/TPrev-15M
87T-36
87T/JumboR-8
87ToysRUs-16
88D-50
88F-60
88OPC-108
88Pep/T-25
88S-471
88T-499
88T/St-271
88Toledo/CMC-5
88Toledo/ProC-592
89Coke/WS-14
89D-535
89D/Best-235
89D/Tr-37
89F-136
89F/Up-19
89S-471
89S/Tr-26
89S/YS/II-7
89T-238
89T/Tr-61T
89UD-493
90B-304
90Coke/WSox-12
90D-337
90D/BestAL-46
90F-537
90F/Can-537
90Leaf-43
90OPC-786
90PublInt/St-392
90S-28
90T-786
90UD-651
91B-63
91Classic/200-56
91D-271
91F-126
91Indian/McDon-17
91Leaf-382
91Leaf/Stud-47
91OPC-121
91S-124
91S/RookTr-60T
91StCl-328
91T-121
91UD-281
91UD/Ext-782
92B-317
92F-115
92OPC-326
92OPC/Premier-80
92Pinn-503
92S-144
92S/RookTr-42T
92StCl-125
92StCl-638
92T-326
92T/Gold-326
92T/GoldWin-326
92UD-679

King, Frank J.
T206

King, Hank
85Phill/TastyK-8CO

King, Harold 1
(Hal)
69MB-146
70OPC-327
70T-327
71MLB/St-15
71OPC-88
71T-88
72T-598
74OPC-362
74T-362
76Laugh/Clown-32
93Rang/Keeb-21

King, Harold 2
R314/Can
V355-121

King, Jake
91Clmbia/PII-18

King, James H.
(Jim)
56T-74
57T-186
58T-332
60Maple-11
61T-351
62T-42
63T-176
64T-217
65OPC-38
65T-38
65T/E-54
65T/trans-53
66T-369
67CokeCap/Senator-8
67T-509
78TCMA-207

King, Jason
90Pittsfld/Pucko-8
92StLucie/ClBest-23
92StLucie/ProC-1754

King, Jeff
87Salem-24
88EastLAS/ProC-16
88F-653R
88Harris/ProC-859
89BuffB/CMC-16
89BuffB/ProC-1671
89F/Up-114
90D-480
90F-469
90F/Can-469
90Homer/Pirate-13
90HotRook/St-25
90Leaf-163
90OPC-454
90S-549
90S/100Ris-71
90S/YS/II-16
90T-454
90T/89Debut-66
90T/Big-117
90T/JumboR-17
90UD-557
91B-520
91D-233
91F-39
91Leaf-71
91OPC-272
91Panini/FrSt-117
91S-244
91StCl-528
91T-272
91UD-687
91Ultra-280
92D-468
92F-555
92L-420
92L/BlkGold-420
92OPC-693
92Pinn-317
92Pirate/Nation-9
92S-511
92StCl-24
92T-693
92T/Gold-693
92T/GoldWin-693
92UD-111
92Ultra-553
93B-654
93D-252
93F-113
93Flair-113
93L-207
93OPC-96
93Pac/Spanish-245
93Panini-284
93Pinn-355
93Pirate/Nation-13
93S-159
93StCl-93
93StCl/1stDay-93
93Studio-102
93T-136
93T/Gold-136
93TripleP-182
93UD-240
93UD/SP-185
93Ultra-97
94B-490
94D-538
94D/MVP-11
94F-611
94L-145
94OPC-151
94Pac/Cr-499
94Panini-236
94Pinn-208
94Pinn/Artist-208
94Pinn/Museum-208
94S-382
94Select-56
94StCl-338
94StCl/1stDay-338
94StCl/Gold-338
94Studio-146
94T-44
94T/Finest-65
94T/FinestRef-65
94T/Gold-44
94TripleP-185
94UD-238
94UD/CollC-163
94UD/CollC/Gold-163
94UD/CollC/Silv-163
94UD/ElecD-238
94UD/SP-142
94Ultra-256

King, Jerome
83Tacoma-6

King, Jerry
81Bristol-13

King, Joe
82Danvl/Frit-22
83Peoria/Frit-2

King, John
90GA-14

King, Kenny
87Miami-1
88Bakers/Cal-254

King, Kevin
80Wausau-20
81Wausau-27
83Chatt-18
84Chatt-2
86MidldA-12
87Edmon-8
88CapeCod/Sum-99
88Edmon/CMC-25
88Edmon/ProC-573
89TNTech-33MG

King, Kevin Ray
88OK-20
89OK-19
90OK-13
91Penin/ClBest-6
91Penin/ProC-372
92SanBern/ClBest-22
92SanBern/ProC-
93River/Cal-9
94T-774
94T/Gold-774
94Ultra-420

King, Lee
E120
V100
V61-92
W572

King, Lynn
40Hughes-11
43Centen-16

King, Michael J.
87CharRain-4
88Charl/ProC-1202
89Watlo/ProC-1787
89Watlo/Star-15

King, Mike
81QuadC-17
84Nashvl-11

King, Nelson
55T-112
57T-349
79TCMA-247

King, Randy
85Newar-2

King, Richard 1
76Laugh/Clown-31
76Laugh/Clown-5

King, Richard 2
91Waverly/Fut-10
92SoOreg/ProC-3412

King, Ron
86Salem-14

King, Steve
86James-14
89Boise/ProC-2002
90QuadC/GS-10
91AA/LineD-439
91MidldA/LineD-439
91MidldA/OneHour-15
91MidldA/ProC-432

King, Tom
75AppFx
76Clinton

Kingery, Mike
82CharR-12
84Memphis-7
85Omaha-23
86Omaha/ProC-13

86Omaha/TCMA-4
86Sf/Rook-37
87D-424
87D/OD-119
87F-371
87F/Up-U57
87Mother/Sea-17
87T-203
87T/Tr-58T
88D-322
88F-376
88Leaf-104
88Mother/Sea-17
88OPC-119
88Panini/St-193
88S-178
88T-532
88T/Big-160
89Calgary/CMC-20
89Calgary/ProC-545
89T-413
90AAASingl/ProC-49
90D-601
90Phoenix/CMC-11
90Phoenix/ProC-23
90ProC/Singl-538
91D-573
91Leaf-224
91Mother/Giant-21
91OPC-657
91PG&E-16
91S-547
91T-657
92StCl-862
92Tacoma/ProC-2516
Kingman, Brian
77SanJose-19
79Ogden/TCMA-13
80T-671R
81D-360
81F-529
81T-284
82D-87
82F-96
82OPC-231
82T-476
82Tacoma-25
83F-522
83T-312
84Cram/PCL-15
Kingman, Dave
72OPC-147
72T-147
73K-44
73OPC-23
73T-23
74OPC-610
74T-610
74T/St-106
75Ho-85
75OPC-156
75SSPC/Sam-3
75T-156
75T/M-156
76Crane-26
76Ho-15
76Ho/Twink-15
76MSA/Disc
76OPC-193LL
76OPC-40
76SSPC-542
76SSPC/MetsY-M9
76T-193LL
76T-40
77BurgChef-141
77Ho-60
77Ho/Twink-60
77K-35
77OPC-98
77Pep-69
77T-500
77T/CS-24
77T/ClothSt-24
78Ho-26
78Pep-33
78SSPC/270-252
78T-570
78Tastee/Discs-19
78Wiffle/Discs-34
79Ho-146
79OPC-191
79T-370
79T/Comics-20
80K-6
80OPC-127
80T-202LL
80T-240
80T/S-16
80T/Super-16
81Coke
81D-553
81Drake-19
81F-291
81F/St-111
81OPC-361
81PermaGr/CC-18
81Sqt-14
81T-450
81T/HT
81T/St-151
81T/St-69
81T/Tr-781
82D-17DK
82D-182
82Drake-21
82F-530
82F/St-85
82K-19
82OPC-276
82T-690
82T/St-72
83D-301
83Drake-14
83F-548
83F/St-21M
83OPC-160
83OPC-161SV
83OPC/St-11
83OPC/St-207
83OPC/St-259
83T-160
83T-161SV
83T-702LL
83T/Fold-2M
83T/LeadS-7
83T/St-11
83T/St-207
83T/St-259
84D-360
84D/Champs-3
84F-590
84F/X-U62
84Mother/A's-15
84Nes/792-573
84Nes/792-703LL
84OPC-172
84T-573
84T-703LL
84T/Tr-63T
85CircK-26
85D-54
85D/AAS-32
85F-427
85F/LimEd-15
85F/St-14
85F/St-29
85F/St-48
85FunFoodPin-36
85Leaf-182
85Mother/A's-2
85OPC-123
85T-730
85T/3D-12
85T/Gloss40-5
85T/St-320
85T/Super-59
86D-54
86F-423
86F/St-67
86Mother/A's-2
86OPC-322
86Seven/Coin-W9M
86Sf-116
86Sf-145M
86Sf-68M
86T-410
86T/St-167
86Woolwth-16
87D-425
87F-396
87F/LL-27
87OPC-266
87RedFoley/St-115
87Sf-178
87T-709
87T/Mini-69
87T/St-173
88AlaskaAS60/Team-7
89Pac/Leg-175
89Pac/SenLg-164
89Pac/SenLg-186
89T/SenLg-101
89TM/SenLg-59
90EliteSenLg-126
90EliteSenLg-24
90Pac/Legend-87
90Smok/SoCal-7
91Swell/Great-52
91WIZMets-211
92AP/ASG-56
92MCI-7
92Yank/WIZ70-90
93TWill-57
Kingman, Eamon
88CapeCod/Sum-17
Kingsolver, Kurt
80BurlB-19
82ElPaso-4
Kingston, Mark
92Helena/ProC-1721
93Peoria/Team-13
Kingwood, Tyrone
88WPalmB/Star-14
90SanBern/Cal-102
90SanBern/ProC-2644
91AA/LineD-234
91ClBest/Singl-304
91Hagers/LineD-234
91Hagers/ProC-2467
92London/ProC-646
92London/SB-411
92Sky/AASingl-175
92UD/ML-220
Kinlaw, Jeff
92Albany/ClBest-28TR
Kinnard, Kenneth Joe
(Ken)
83Kinston/Team-9
86Ventura-10
87Greenvl/Best-27
Kinney, Brad
84Butte-13
Kinney, Dennis
75SanAn
79Hawaii-18
81D-363
81Evansvl-22
81F-505
81T-599
82Tacoma-6
Kinney, Tom
91ClBest/Singl-139
91Savan/ClBest-8
91Savan/ProC-1649
Kinnunen, Mike
81Toledo-6
83Memphis/TCMA-24
85Omaha-18
86RochR-12
88AAA/ProC-10
88Colum/CMC-9
88Colum/Pol-4
88Colum/ProC-316
89Denver/CMC-4
89Denver/ProC-33
91Crown/Orio-239
Kinsel, David
83AppFx/Frit-23
Kinsella, W.P.
90LitSun-15
Kinslow, Thomas
90Target-1000
N300/unif
Kinyoun, Tavis
89Bristol/Star-13
91BBCity/ClBest-14
91BBCity/ProC-1400
Kinzer, Matt
85Spring-14
86StPete-17
88ArkTr/GS-14
88Louisvl-24
89Louisvl-25
89Louisvl/CMC-7
89Louisvl/ProC-1255
90AAASingl/ProC-374
90F-652R
90F/Can-652
90ProC/Singl-382
90S-628RP
90SpringDG/Best-13
90T/89Debut-67
90Toledo/CMC-5
90Toledo/ProC-144
Kiper, Kory
92GulfCY/ProC-3787
Kipfer, Greg
82Wisco/Frit-2GM
Kipila, Jeff
88Bend/Legoe-2
89BendB/Legoe-18
90PalmSp/Cal-205
90PalmSp/ProC-2584
91QuadC/ClBest-18
91QuadC/ProC-2637
92MidldA/OneHour-12
92MidldA/ProC-4038
92MidldA/SB-462
92Sky/AASingl-196
93FExcel/ML-144
93Vanco/ProC-2610
Kipp, Fred
59T-258
60T-202
90Target-1001
92Yank/WIZ60-67
Kipper, Bob
83Peoria/Frit-25
83TriCit-3
86D-44RR
86D/Rook-46
86F-648R
86T/Tr-54T
87D-572
87F-612
87T-289
88D-115
88F-332
88T-723
88T/Big-141
89B-414
89D-409
89F-211
89S-354
89T-114
89UD-520
89VFJuice-16
90D-362
90F-470
90F/Can-470
90Homer/Pirate-14
90OPC-441
90T-441
90UD-560
91D-720
91F-40
91OPC-551
91S-646
91StCl-334
91T-551
91UD-407
92D-622
92F-556
92L-506
92L/BlkGold-506
92OPC-64
92Pinn-495
92S-340
92StCl-752
92T-64
92T/Gold-64
92T/GoldWin-64
Kipper, Thornton
54T-108
55T-62
55T/DH-10
94T/Arc54-108
Kiraly, Jeff
92Kingspt/ClBest-6
92Kingspt/ProC-1539
Kirby, Butch
81BurlB-18
82Beloit/Frit-15
83Beloit/Frit-1
Kirby, Chris
78Wausau
Kirby, Clay
69T-637R
70MLB/St-115
70OPC-79
70T-79
71MLB/St-230
71OPC-333
71T-333
72OPC-173
72OPC-174IA
72T-173
72T-174A
73OPC-655
73T-655
73T/Lids-26
74OPC-287
74T-287
74T/St-96
75OPC-423
75T-423
75T/M-423
76Expo/Redp-16
76OPC-579
76SSPC-28
76T-579
76T/Tr-579T
Kirby, Wayne Edward
85VeroB-8
86VeroB-14
87Bakers-23
88Bakers/Cal-249
88SanAn/Best-8
89SanAn/Best-8
90AAASingl/ProC-80
90Albuq/CMC-23
90Albuq/ProC-359
90Albuq/Trib-17
90ProC/Singl-425
91AAA/LineD-87
91ColoSp/LineD-87
91ColoSp/ProC-2197
92AAA/ASG/SB-87
92ColoSp/ProC-764
92ColoSp/SB-87
92F-670
92T/91Debut-101
93D-380RR
93F/Final-201
93Flair-193
93Indian/WUAB-14
93JDean/Rook-5
93L-528
93S-328
93Select/RookTr-56T
93StCl-35
93StCl/1stDay-35
93UD/SP-123
94D-125
94F-107
94F/RookSen-9
94Flair-40
94L-283
94OPC-219
94OPC/DiamD-3
94Pac/Cr-171
94Panini-57
94Pinn-132
94Pinn/Artist-132
94Pinn/Museum-132
94S-230
94S/GoldR-230
94StCl-43
94StCl/1stDay-43
94StCl/Gold-43
94T-508
94T/Finest-36
94T/FinestRef-36
94T/Gold-508
94TripleP-114
94UD/CollC-164
94UD/CollC/Gold-164
94UD/CollC/Silv-164
94Ultra-43
Kirby, Wayne
76Tucson-15
Kirchenwitz, Arno
78StPete
79ArkTr-1
Kirk, Chuck
90Hunting/ProC-3277
91Peoria/ClBest-6
91Peoria/ProC-1338
91Peoria/Team-9
92WinSalem/ClBest-17
92WinSalem/ProC-1205
Kirk, Thomas
52Park-79
Kirk, Tim
86Watertn-11
87Salem-8
88CLAS/Star-11
88Salem/Star-9
89Penin/Star-9
Kirke, Judson

T207
Kirkland, Willie
58SFCallB-12
58T-128
59T-484
60T-172
61Kahn
61P-146
61T-15
62J-41
62Kahn
62P-41
62P/Can-41
62Salada-61
62Shirriff-61
62Sugar-11
62T-447
63J-72
63P-72
63Sugar-11
63T-187
64T-17
65OPC-148
65T-148
66T-434
91Crown/Orio-240
Kirkpatrick, Bill
75IntAS/TCMA-14
Kirkpatrick, Ed
63T-386R
64T-296
65T-393
66OPC-102
66T-102
67CokeCap/DodgAngel-35
67T-293
68T-552
69MB-147
69MLB/St-59
69T-529
70MLB/St-223
70OPC-165
70T-165
70T/PI-19
71MLB/St-418
71OPC-299
71T-299
72MB-183
72T-569
72T-570IA
73OPC-233
73T-233
74OPC-262
74T-262
74T/St-183
74T/Tr-262T
75OPC-171
75T-171
75T/M-171
76OPC-294
76SSPC-580
76T-294
77T-582
78T-77
93Rang/Keeb-218
Kirkpatrick, Enos
90Target-411
Kirkpatrick, Jay
91GreatF/SportP-18
92VeroB/ClBest-7
92VeroB/ProC-2882
93ClBest/MLG-98
93FExcel/ML-52
Kirkpatrick, Stephen
88Clearw/Star-16
88Spartan/Star-9
89Clearw/Star-12
90Reading/Best-22
90Reading/ProC-1232
90Reading/Star-15
Kirkreit, Daron
92T/Tr-60T
92T/TrGold-60T
93StCl/MurphyS-21
94B-495
94ClBest/Gold-186
94ClBest/GoldLP-7
94FExcel-45
94Pinn-263
94Pinn/Artist-263
94Pinn/Museum-263
94S-527
94TedW-126
94UD-534TP
Kirkwood, Don
76OPC-108
76T-108
77T-519
78BJ/PostC-12
78T-251
79OPC-334
79T-632
Kirsch, Paul
82Cedar-14
84Cedar-5
85Cedar-26
86Cedar/TCMA-24
87Cedar-24
91AAA/LineD-425M
91Portl/LineD-425CO
91Portl/ProC-1584CO
92Portl/SB-425CO
92Portland/ProC-2682CO
Kirt, Tim
90Niagara/Pucko-3
Kirwin, Steve
88Bend/Legoe-8
Kiser, Bob
88CapeCod-10
88CapeCod/Sum-74
Kiser, Dan
89Modesto/Chong-4
Kiser, Garland
86Cram/NWL-154
89Watertn/Star-12
90CLAS/CL-37
90Kinston/Team-12
91AA/LineD-84
91CLAS/ProC-CAR17
91Canton/LineD-84
91Canton/ProC-976
92Canton/ProC-687
92T/91Debut-102
Kiser, Larry G.
76OkCty/Team-15
Kish, Bobby
82Spring/Frit-14
83StPete-8
84Savan-12
Kisinger, Charles S.
(Rube)
T206
Kison, Bruce
72OPC-72
72T-72
73OPC-141
73T-141
75OPC-598
75T-598
75T/M-598
76OPC-161
76SSPC-568
76T-161
77T-563
78T-223
79T-661
80T-28
81F-284
81T-340
82D-66
82F-467
82T-442
83D-267
83F-96
83F/St-13M
83F/St-23M
83T-712
84D-499
84F-523
84Nes/792-201
84OPC-201
84Smok/Cal-15
84T-201
84T/St-235
85D-377
85F-306
85F/Up-U65
85T-544
85T/Tr-67T
86D-616
86F-353
86T-117
89Pac/SenLg-136
89T/SenLg-11
89TM/SenLg-60
90EliteSenLg-37
92Pol/Royal-27M
93Pol/Royal-27M
Kissell, George
73OPC-497CO
73T-497CO
74OPC-236CO
74T-236CO
90Johnson/Star-28CO
Kissick, David
91Brisbane/Fut-7
Kissinger, John
C46-72
Kistaitis, Dale
88NE-7
90MedHat/Best-18
Kisten, Dale
88Hamil/ProC-1728
89Spring/Best-20
90ArkTr/GS-19
90Louisvl/LBC-22
90SpringDG/Best-19
91AA/LineD-36
91ArkTr/LineD-36
91ArkTr/ProC-1279
Kite, Dan
88Elmira-6
90LSUGreat-3
90WinHaven/Star-13
91WinHaven/ClBest-3
91WinHaven/ProC-483
Kitson, Frank R.
90Target-412
E107
Kittle, Hub
73OPC-624CO
73T-624C
74OPC-31CO
74T-31C
77StPete
Kittle, Ron
77Clinton
79Knoxvl/TCMA-12
81GlenF-19
82Edmon-13
83F-241
83T/Tr-55T
83TrueVal/WSox-42
84D-18DK
84D-244
84Drake-17
84F-64
84F/St-109
84F/St-22
84MiltBrad-15
84Nes/792-480
84OPC-373
84Seven-17C
84T-480
84T/RD-2M
84T/St-382YS
84T/Super-11
84TrueVal/WS-19
85Coke/WS-40
85D-180
85D/AAS-13
85D/WaxBox-PC3
85F-518
85F/LimEd-16
85FunFoodPin-53
85Leaf-210
85OPC-105
85T-105
85T/RD-2M
85T/St-232
86Coke/WS-42
86D-526
86F-210
86F/Mini-45
86F/St-68
86Jay's-11
86Leaf-257
86OPC-288
86Sf-67M
86Sf-86
86T-574
86T/St-289
86T/Tatt-6M
87D-351
87F-103
87T-584
88D-422
88F-213
88Gator-33
88Leaf-251
88S-449
88S/Tr-44T
88T-259
88T/Tr-58T
89B-69
89Coke/WS-15
89D-428
89D/Best-249
89D/Tr-51
89F/Up-20
89OPC-268
89S-96
89T-771
89T/Tr-62T
89UD-228
89UD/Ext-711
90Coke/WSox-13
90D-148
90F-538
90F/Can-538
90Kodak/WSox-4
90Leaf-405
90OPC-79
90Panini/St-51
90Publint/St-393
90RedFoley/St-54
90S-529
90T-79
90T/St-302
90UD/Ext-790
91Crown/Orio-241
91D-613
91F-480
91OPC-324A
91OPC-324B
91T-324A
91T-324B
92Yank/WIZ80-101
Kittredge, Malachi
E107
Kizer, Craig
82AubAs-14
Kizer, Hal
(Bubba)
79QuadC-15
Kizziah, Daren
89StCath/ProC-2076
90Myrtle/ProC-2772
91Dunedin/ClBest-4
91Dunedin/ProC-200
92Knoxvl/ProC-2985
92Knoxvl/SB-382
93Knoxvl/ProC-1250
Klages, Fred
67T-373R
68T-229
69MB-148
Klamm, Ted
92Welland/ClBest-14
92Welland/ProC-1317
Klancnik, Joe
88James/ProC-1919
89James/ProC-2155
91QuadC/ProC-2622
Klaus, Robert
61T/St-203
64T-524R
65OPC-227
65T-227
66OPC-108
66T-108
69T-387
91WIZMets-212
Klaus, William
(Billy)
55B-150
56T-217
57T-292
58T-89
59T-299
60T-406
61P-79
61T-187
62J-67
62P-67
62P/Can-67
62Salada-10
62Shirriff-10
62T-571
63T-551
78TCMA-19
79TCMA-251
91Crown/Orio-242
Exh47
Klavitter, Clay
91Belling/ClBest-2
91Belling/ProC-3668
91SanBern/ClBest-13
91SanBern/ProC-1989
Klawitter, Tom
84Toledo-14
85Twin/Team-25
Klebba, Rob
80WHave-6
Kleean, Tom
86Beloit-12
Klein, Bob
75AppFx
Klein, Bruce
89Augusta/ProC-513
Klein, Chuck
31Exh/4-11
33DH-26
33DL-22
33Exh/4-6
33G-128
34Exh/4-3
34G-10
35BU-185
35Exh/4-3
35G-1F
35G-3D
35G-4D
35G-5D
35Wheat
36G
38Exh/4-6
39PlayBall-82
40PlayBall-102
41PlayBall-60
49Exh
60F-30
61F-51
72F/FFeat-36
77Galasso-218
77Galasso-48
80Laugh/FFeat-6
80Pac/Leg-112
80Perez/HOF-171
80SSPC/HOF
81Conlon-88
88Conlon/NatAS-12
88Grenada-13
89HOF/St-48
90Perez/GreatMom-60
91Conlon/Sport-30
91Conlon/Sport-300
92Conlon/Sport-438
92Conlon/Sport-531
93Conlon-671
94Conlon-1095
94TedW-74
PR1-18
R300
R306
R308-157
R314
R315-A19
R315-B19
R316
R328-21
R332-17
V354-56
V355-13
W517-10
WG8-38
Klein, Gary
83Butte-6
Klein, Larry
85BurlR-3
86Tulsa-24
88OkCty/CMC-17
88OkCty/ProC-32
Klein, Lou
49Eureka-188
60T-457C
Kleinke, Norbert
40Hughes-12
Kleinow, John
(Red)
E101
E102
E105
E92
E94
E97
T204
T205
T206
T216

T3-21
W555
Klem, Bill
21Exh-92
50Callahan
50W576-46
72F/FFeat-31
76Shakey-68
77Galasso-173UMP
80Perez/HOF-67
80SSPC/HOF
86Conlon/1-5
88Conlon/4-15
89TM/Umpire-63
92Conlon/Sport-460
94Conlon-1190UMP
94Conlon/Pr-1190
R332-6
Klenoshek, Bill Jr.
88CapeCod/Sum-50
Klesko, Ryan
89LittleSun-20
90A&AASingle/ProC-106
90Foil/Best-236
90ProC/Singl-826
90Sumter/Best-9
90Sumter/ProC-2441
91AA/LineD-209
91B-590
91ClBest/Gold-15
91ClBest/Singl-388
91Classic/II-T53
91Greenvl/ClBest-17
91Greenvl/LineD-209
91Greenvl/ProC-3011
91Leaf/GRook-BC21
91UD/FinalEd-1FCL
91UD/FinalEd-8F
92B-549
92B-623FOIL
92D-13RR
92D/Preview-9
92D/RookPhen-BC15
92OPC-126
92ProC/Tomorrow-181
92Richm/Bleach-4
92Richm/Comix-8
92Richm/ProC-383
92Richm/SB-430
92Sky/AAASingl-197
92T-126M
92T/Gold-126
92T/GoldWin-126
92T/McDonB-39
92TripleP/Gal-GS10
92UD-1CL
92UD-24SR
93B-634
93Brave/LykePerf-15
93Classic/Gamel-48
93Classic/Gamel-NNO
93D-422
93F-6
93L-469
93OPC-189
93Pac/Spanish-9
93Pinn-251
93Pinn/RookTP-4
93Pinn/Team2001-27
93Richm/Bleach-1
93Richm/Pep-1
93S-294
93S/Boys-8
93S/Proctor-5
93Select-405
93StCl-541
93StCl/1stDay-541
93StCl/Brave-26
93T-423
93T/Gold-423
93ToysRUs-4
93UD-376
93Ultra-7
94B-105
94D-617
94F-362
94Finest-437
94Flair-128
94Flair/Wave-4
94L-286
94OPC-75
94OPC/HotPros-9
94Pac/Cr-12
94Pinn-157
94Pinn/Artist-157
94Pinn/Museum-157
94S-464
94S/Boys-41
94Select-197
94Select/RookSurg-3
94SelectSam-197
94Sf/2000-20
94StCl-148
94StCl/1stDay-148
94StCl/Gold-148
94StCl/Team-38
94Studio-37
94T-777M
94T/Gold-777M
94TripleP-282
94UD-64
94UD/CollC-165
94UD/CollC/Gold-165
94UD/CollC/Silv-165
94UD/ElecD-64
94UD/HoloFX-22
94UD/SP-52
94Ultra-444
94Ultra/AllRook-5
Kleven, Jay
75Tidew/Team-14
91WIZMets-213
Kleven, Mark
88Charl/ProC-1205
Kliafas, Steve
92Bakers/Cal-14
92SanAn/ProC-3984
92VeroB/ProC-2883
Klieman, Ed
44Playball-13
Klimas, Phil
77Cocoa
80Tulsa-13
81Tulsa-3
90TulsaDG/Best-22
Klimchock, Lou
60L-116
60T-137
61T-462
62T-259
63T-542
65T-542
66T-589
70OPC-247
70T-247
91WIZMets-214
Klimkowski, Ron
70T-702R
71MLB/St-492
71OPC-28
71T-28
72OPC-363
72T-363
72T/Cloth-18
73Syrac/Team-12
92Yank/WIZ60-68
92Yank/WIZ70-91
Kline, Bob
84Newar-24
Kline, Doug
88Visalia/Cal-169
88Visalia/ProC-107
89WPalmB/Star-14
90Jacks/GS-2
91AA/LineD-636
91Wmsprt/LineD-636
91Wmsprt/ProC-288
Kline, Greg
75Clinton
76Clinton
Kline, John Robert
55T-173
Kline, Kris
83Peoria/Frit-7
Kline, Ron
53T-175
56T-94
57Kahn
57T-256
58Hires-31
58Kahn
58T-82
59Kahn
59T-265
59T-428M
60Kahn
60L-105
60T-197
61T-127
61T/St-90
62T-216
63T-84
64T-358
65OPC-56
65T-56
65T/trans-54
66T-453
67CokeCap/Twin-1
67OPC-133
67T-133
68KDKA-27
68T-446
69MB-149
69T-243
69T/St-86
78TCMA-251
91T/Arc53-175
Kline, Steve
71MLB/St-493
71OPC-51
71T-51
72OPC-467
72T-467
73K-50
73OPC-172
73Syrac/Team-13
73T-172
74OPC-324
74Syrac/Team-12
74T-324
75OPC-639
75T-639
75T/M-639
76SSPC-532
92Yank/WIZ70-92
Klinefelter, David
88AubAs/ProC-1972
Kling, John
(Johnny)
11Helmar-79
61F-52
93Conlon-867
93UD/T202-3
E254
E300
E91
E96
E98
M116
S74-63
T201
T202
T205
T206
T207
T3-102
WG3-24
Klingbell, Scott
85Visalia-23
Klingenbeck, Scott
92FrRow/DP-45
92Kane/Team-17
93StCl/MurphyS-80
94B-86
94FExcel-8
Klinger, Robert
39PlayBall-90
40PlayBall-165
41DP-35
41DP-98
48Smith-25
Klink, Joe
85Lynch-13
86OrlanTw-9
87Sf/TPrev-17M
89Huntsvl/Best-27
90Classic/III-26
90Leaf-503
90Mother/A's-26
90T/Tr-51T
91D-591
91F-13
91Leaf-461
91Mother/A's-26
91OPC-553
91S-588
91T-553
91UD-468
92D-183
92OPC-678
92S-151
92StCl-326
92T-678
92T/Gold-678
92T/GoldWin-678
92UD-530
93F/Final-64
93Marlin/Publix-14
93T/Tr-95T
93UD-715
93USPlayC/Marlin-5H
93Ultra-380
94F-470
94S-283
94S/GoldR-283
94StCl-68
94StCl/1stDay-68
94StCl/Gold-68
94StCl/Team-87
94T-409
94T/Gold-409
Klippstein, John
51B-248
52T-148
53T-46
54B-29
54T-31
55B-152
56Kahn
56T-249
57Kahn
57Sohio/Reds-11
57T-296
58T-242
59T-152
60BB-12
60T-191
61T-539
61T/St-204
62T-151
63T-571
64T-533
65T-384
66T-493
67T-588
78Twin/Frisz-36
79TCMA-62
90Target-413
91T/Arc53-46
94T/Arc54-31
Klipstein, Dave
84ElPaso-18
86Vanco-16
87Denver-12
88Nashvl/CMC-20
88Nashvl/ProC-474
Kloek, Kevin
92FrRow/DP-30
Kloff, August
N172
Klonoski, Jason
87AZ/Pol-8
88AZ/Pol-7
88CapeCod/Sum-127
90Bend/Legoe-10
91ClBest/Singl-370
91Kenosha/ClBest-27
91Kenosha/ProC-2069
92OrlanSR/ProC-2843
92OrlanSR/SB-508
Klopp, Frank
85PrWill-26
Klopper, Rod
88Alaska/Team-12
Kluge, Matt
92SanBern/ClBest-5
92SanBern/ProC-
Klugman, Joe
90Target-1002
Klump, Ken
83Wisco/Frit-21
85OrlanTw-17
Klumpp, Elmer
90Target-414
Klusener, Matt
90WichSt-19
Klusman, William F.
N172
Kluss, Dennis
90Watertn/Star-12
Kluszewski, Ted
48L-38
49Eureka-87
50B-62
51B-143
51FB
51T/RB-39
52Dix-53
52T-29
53B/Col-62
53NB
53RM-NL6
53T-162
54Dix
54RH
54RM-NL6
54T-7
55Armour-11
55Kahn
55RFG-10
55RM-NL16
55T-120
55T/DH-121
55W605-10
56Kahn
56T-25
56T/Hocus-A12
56T/Hocus-B14
56T/Pin-56
56YellBase/Pin-17
57Kahn
57Sohio/Reds-12
57T-165
58Hires-67
58Kahn
58T-178
58T-321M
59Kahn
59T-17M
59T-35
60Kahn
60MacGregor-10
60NuCard-57
60T-505
61Bz-18
61NuCard-457
61P-31
61T-65
61T/St-173
62P-82
73OPC-296CO
73T-296C
74OPC-326CO
74T-326C
76SSPC-618CO
79TCMA-12
81TCMA-439
82Ohio/HOF-18
85West/2-48
86Sf/Dec-38M
88Pac/Leg-72
89Kodak/WSox-1M
91T/Arc53-162
92Bz/Quadra-17M
93AP/ASG-138
94T/Arc54-7
94TedW-22
Exh47
PM10/Sm-90
Klutts, Gene
(Mickey)
77T-490R
78SSPC/270-21
78T-707R
80T-717
81D-110
81F-584
81T-232
82F-97
82T-148
83D-465
83T-571
83T/Tr-56T
92Yank/WIZ70-93
Kluttz, Clyde
44Playball-39
52T-132
V362-41
Klvac, David
92LynchRS/ClBest-15
92LynchRS/ProC-2902
Kmak, Joe
85Everett/Cram-7
86Fresno/Smok-6
88Shrev/ProC-1280
89AS/Cal-46
89Reno/Cal-252
90ElPaso/GS-19
91AAA/LineD-144
91Denver/LineD-144

91Denver/ProC-125
92B-545
92Denver/ProC-2643
92Denver/SB-135
93B-15
93F/Final-225
93FExcel/ML-190
93Pinn-575
93Pol/Brew-14
93UD-782
93Ultra-570
Knabe, Franz Otto
(Otto)
11Helmar-144
14CJ-1
15CJ-1
D303
E101
E102
E104
E105
E106
E254
E270/2
E92
M116
T206
T207
T213/blue
T213/brown
T216
Knabenshue, Chris
85Spokane/Cram-9
86CharRain-12
87Wichita-7
88TexLgAS/GS-34
88Wichita-14
89LasVegas/CMC-23
89LasVegas/ProC-19
90AAASingl/ProC-313
90ProC/Singl-246
90ScranWB/CMC-20
90ScranWB/ProC-611
91AAA/LineD-485
91ScranWB/LineD-485
91ScranWB/ProC-2551
92Huntsvl/SB-312
Knackert, Brent
88FSLAS/Star-40
88Tampa/Star-11
89Saraso/Star-13
90D/Rook-52
90Mother/Mar-18
90T/Tr-52T
91CounHrth-17
91D-662
91OPC-563
91S-774
91T-563
91T/90Debut-78
91UD-378
92D-608
92Jaxvl/SB-372
92Sky/AASingl-153
Knapland, Greg
91Watertn/ClBest-8
91Watertn/ProC-3363
Knapp, John
87CharWh-12
88Bakers/Cal-236
89VeroB/Star-14
90VeroB/Star-17
91Adelaide/Fut-10
92GulfCD/ProC-3584
Knapp, Michael
86Cram/NWL-87
87QuadC-27
88MidldA/GS-13
88TexLgAS/GS-36
89MidldA/GS-20
90MidldA/GS-13
90TexLgAS/GS-6
91AA/LineD-136
91CharlK/LineD-136
91CharlK/ProC-1691
92Iowa/ProC-4053
92Iowa/SB-210
Knapp, Rick
86Tulsa-9B
88Gaston/ProC-1000
91GulfCR/SportP-30M
Knapp, Robert C.
(Chris)
77T-247
78SSPC/270-212
78T-361
79T-453
80T-658
81D-173
81SLCity-7
81T-557
82Iowa-18
83Kinston/Team-10
Knauss, Tom
92Classic/DP-49
92FrRow/DP-19
93StCl/MurphyS-38
Knecht, Bobby
88AppFx/ProC-161
88MidwLAS/GS-41
Knell, Phillip
N172
Knepper, Bob
75Phoenix-10
75Phoenix/Caruso-16
75Phoenix/CircleK-10
76Phoenix/Coke-12
77Phoenix
78T-589
79Ho-52
79K-35
79OPC-255
79Pol/Giants-39
79T-486
80OPC-61
80Pol/Giants-39
80T-111
81D-194
81F-447
81OPC-279
81T-279
81T/Tr-782
82D-41
82F-219
82F/St-49
82K-31
82OPC-389
82T-672
82T/St-45
82T/StVar-45
83D-92
83F-451
83T-382
84D-572
84Mother/Ast-16
84Nes/792-93
84OPC-93
84T-93
85D-476
85F-352
85Leaf-61
85Mother/Ast-20
85OPC-289
85T-455
85T-721AS
85T/St-62
86D-161
86F-304
86Leaf-90
86Mother/Ast-22
86OPC-231
86Pol/Ast-15
86T-590
87D-112
87F-61
87F/AwardWin-20
87F/GameWin-23
87F/Mini-60
87Leaf-249
87Mother/Ast-5
87OPC-129
87Pol/Ast-20
87RedFoley/St-17
87Sf-29
87Sf/TPrev-8M
87T-722
87T/Gloss60-13
87T/Mini-10
87T/St-32
88D-138
88D/Best-176
88F-451
88Mother/Ast-5
88Pol/Ast-15
88S-344
88T-151
89D-123
89D/AS-54
89F-360
89F/BBAS-25
89Lennox/Ast-10
89Mother/Ast-7
89OPC-280
89Panini/St-82
89S-273
89S/HotStar-38
89T-280
89T/St-22
89T/St/Backs-63
89UD-422
90AAASingl/ProC-33
90D-485
90OPC-104
90Phoenix/ProC-7
90PublInt/St-97
90T-104
90UD-599
Knetzer, Elmer
14CJ-84
15CJ-84
16FleischBrd-52
90Target-1003
T207
Kneuer, Frank
83Nashvl-9
Knicely, Alan
75Dubuq
76Dubuq
80T-678R
80Tucson-14
81T-82R
81Tucson-4
83D-620
83F-452
83T-117
83T/Tr-57
84F-473
84Nes/792-323
84T-323
84Wichita/Rock-18
85T/Tr-68T
86Louisvl-15
86OPC-316
86T-418
87OKCty-22
Knickerbocker, Wm.
(Bill)
35BU-58
35G-8I
35G-9I
40PlayBall-182
91Conlon/Sport-79
R313
R314
Knieper, Aaron
93James/ClBest-12
93James/ProC-3321
Kniffen, Chuck
88Wausau/GS-2
89SanBern/Best-10
89SanBern/Cal-89CO
90SanBern/Best-8CO
90SanBern/Cal-115CO
90SanBern/ProC-2650CO
91SanBern/ClBest-26CO
91SanBern/ProC-2004CO
92WPalmB/ClBest-30CO
92WPalmB/ProC-2104CO
93Harris/ProC-286CO
Knight, Brock
85Elmira-9
Knight, C. Ray
(Ray)
76Indianap-3
78Pep-16
78SSPC/270-110
78T-674
79OPC-211
79T-401
80OPC-98
80T-174
81Coke
81D-61
81F-198
81OPC-325
81T-325
81T/HT
82D-374
82F-71
82F/St-18
82OPC-319
82T-525
82T/St-39
82T/Tr-57T
83D-522
83F-453
83F/St-18M
83F/St-24M
83F/St-26M
83F/St-2M
83OPC-275
83OPC/St-238
83T-275
83T-441
83T/Gloss40-18
83T/St-238
84D-12DK
84D-232
84F-229
84F/St-10
84Mother/Ast-6
84Nes/792-660
84OPC-321
84T-660
84T/RD-3M
84T/St-68
84T/St/Box-9
85D-617
85F-86
85Indianap-28
85OPC-274
85T-590
86D-597
86F-86
86Mother/Ast-24
86OPC-27
86T-27
87D-586
87D/OD-137
87F-14
87F/AwardWin-21
87F/RecSet-18
87F/Up-U58
87F/WS-11M
87F/WS-12
87French-25
87Leaf-166
87OPC-275
87Sf-88
87Sf/TPrev-21M
87T-488
87T/HL-30
87T/HL-33
87T/St-24WS
87T/Tr-59T
87Woolwth-30
87Woolwth-33
88D-108
88F-564
88F/Up-U28
88OPC-124
88Panini/St-12
88Pep/T-22
88RedFoley/St-43
88S-96
88S/Tr-17T
88Sf-115
88T-124
88T/St-229
88T/Tr-59T
89S-135
89UD-259
91Crown/Orio-243
91WIZMets-215
93Reds/Kahn-8M
Knight, Dennis
83TriCit-5
Knight, Jack
93UD/T202-4
Knight, John
10Domino-62A
10Domino-62B
11Helmar-73
12Sweet/Pin-36A
12Sweet/Pin-36B
14Piedmont/St-31
E101
E105
E254
E90/1
E92
M116
S74-23
T202
T204
T205
T206
T216
Knight, Randy
89TNTech-12
Knight, Steve
80SanJose/JITB-12
Knight, Tim
82Nashvl-15
83Nashvl-10
84Nashvl-12
85Albany-33
85Colum-20
85Colum/Pol-15
86Portl-12
Knoblauch, Chuck
88CapeCod-15
88CapeCod/Sum-94
90A&AASingle/ProC-56
90B-415
90Foil/Best-146
90Foil/Best-322
90OrlanSR/Best-3
90OrlanSR/ProC-1090
90OrlanSR/Star-8
90ProC/Singl-807
90S-672DC
91B-330
91Classic/III-46
91D-421RR
91D/Rook-39
91F/UltraUp-U37
91F/Up-U37
91Leaf-396
91S/ASFan-10
91S/RookTr-93T
91StCl-548
91StCl/Member*-20
91T/Tr-69T
91UD-40
91Ultra-382MLP
92B-24
92CJ/DI-24
92Classic/Game200-181
92Classic/I-50
92Classic/II-T71
92Colla/ASG-10
92D-390
92D-BC5ROY
92D/BC-BC5ROY
92F-206
92F/RookSIns-10
92French-1
92Hardee-14
92JDean/18-12
92L-230
92L/BlkGold-230
92MJB/Knoblauch-Set
92MJB/Proto-R1
92Mother/Knoblauch-Set
92OPC-23
92OPC/Premier-35
92P-6
92Panini-116
92Pinn-119
92Pinn-285I
92Pinn-307SH
92Pinn/Team2000-6
92S-572
92S-792ROY
92S/100RisSt-11
92S/Impact-1
92StCl-601MC
92StCl-830
92T-23
92T/91Debut-103
92T/Gold-23
92T/GoldWin-23
92T/Kids-112
92T/McDonB-35
92TripleP-171
92UD-446
92USPlayC/Twin-12S
92USPlayC/Twin-8H
92Ultra-93
92Ultra/AwardWin-2
93B-481
93Classic/GameI-49
93Colla/DM-61
93D-415
93F-357M
93F-639
93F/Fruit-32
93Flair-237
93Ho-29

93KingB-24
93L-98
93L/Fast-6
93L/GoldAS-5
93OPC-175
93Pac/Spanish-172
93Panini-126
93Pinn-107
93Pinn/Team2001-4
93S-148
93Select-36
93StCl-314
93StCl/1stDay-314
93StCl/MurphyMP-5AS
93StCl/MurphyS-8
93Studio-109
93T-250
93T/Finest-76
93T/FinestRef-76
93T/Gold-250
93T/HolPrev-250
93ToysRUs-39
93ToysRUs/MPhoto-7
93TripleP-48
93UD-254
93UD/FunPack-193
93UD/SP-248
93Ultra-583
94B-229
94D-28
94D/Special-28
94F-210
94F-712M
94Finest-324
94L-64
94OPC-155
94Pac/Cr-357
94Panini-92
94Pinn-83
94Pinn/Artist-83
94Pinn/Museum-83
94S-89
94S/GoldR-89
94Select-29
94Sf/2000-83
94StCl-416
94StCl/1stDay-416
94StCl/Gold-416
94Studio-197
94T-555
94T/Gold-555
94TripleP-254
94UD-152
94UD/CollC-166
94UD/CollC/Gold-166
94UD/CollC/Silv-166
94UD/ElecD-152
94UD/SP-185
94Ultra-89
Knoblauh, Jay
88Oneonta/ProC-2067
89Penin/Star-10
90FSLAS/Star-35
90FtLaud/Star-11
90Star/ISingl-40
91AA/LineD-8
91Albany/LineD-8
91Albany/ProC-1019
92Albany/ProC-2238
92ColClip/SB-106
93ColClip/Pol-22
Knoop, Bobby
64T-502R
65OPC-26
65T-26
65T/trans-18
66T-280
66T/RO-46
66T/RO-81
67CokeCap/DodgAngel-28
67OPC-175
67OPC/PI-17
67T-175
67T/PI-17
68Bz-3
68T-271
69MB-150
69MLB/St-23
69T-445
69T/St-145
69Trans-17
70MLB/St-188
70T-695
71OPC-506
71T-506
72MB-184
72T-664
75QuadC
78TCMA-234
89Smok/Angels-4
90ElPasoATG/Team-44MG
93Mother/Angel-28M
Knorr, Randy
87Myrtle-12
88Myrtle/ProC-1182
89Dunedin/Star-10
90Foil/Best-273
90Knoxvl/Best-26
90Knoxvl/ProC-1248
90Knoxvl/Star-9
90ProC/Singl-813
91AA/LineD-361
91ClBest/Singl-21
91Knoxvl/LineD-361
91Knoxvl/ProC-1770
91Syrac/MerchB-10
92F/Up-65
92Sky/AAASingl-226
92Syrac/MerchB-9
92Syrac/ProC-1981
92Syrac/SB-508
92T/91Debut-104
93BJ/D/45-25
93BJ/Demp-17
93BJ/Fire-17
93D-717
93F-695
93OPC/Premier-25
93StCl-321
93StCl/1stDay-321
93T-534
93T/Gold-534
93UD-682
93Ultra-643
94F-336
94Pac/Cr-645
94StCl-174
94StCl/1stDay-174
94StCl/Gold-174
94StCl/Team-176
94T-96
94T/Gold-96
Knose, Mark
75WPalmB/Sussman-26
Knott, Jack
39PlayBall-91
40PlayBall-13
41PlayBall-68
91Conlon/Sport-178
Knott, James
92GulfCM/ProC-3475
Knott, John
93Macon/ClBest-13
93Macon/ProC-1408
Knout, Edward
(Fred)
N172
Knowles, Darold
64T-418R
65T-577R
66OPC-27R
66T-27R
67CokeCap/Senator-15
67T-362
68T-483
70OPC-106
70Pol/SenY-6
70T-106
71MLB/St-544
71OPC-261
71T-261
72T-583
73OPC-274
73T-274
74OPC-472WS
74OPC-57
74T-472WS
74T-57
75OPC-352
75T-352
75T/M-352
76OPC-617
76SSPC-307
76T-617
77T-169
78T-414
79OPC-303
79T-581
80T-286
88Louisvl-3
89Phill/TastyK-16CO
90Phill/TastyK-34CO
91Clearw/ClBest-10CO
91Clearw/ProC-1640CO
91Crown/Orio-244
92Clearw/ClBest-25CO
92Clearw/ProC-2075
93Rang/Keeb-219
Knowles, Eric
92Oneonta/ClBest-24
Knowles, Greg
91Miami/Bumble-8
92Savan/ProC-661
Knox, Jeff
86Clearw-14
87Albany-17
94B-591
Knox, John
74OPC-604R
74T-604R
75OPC-546
75T-546
75T/M-546
76Indianap-21
76OPC-218
76SSPC-361
76T-218
Knox, Kerry
89Spokane/SP-14
90Foil/Best-221
90River/Best-14
90River/ProC-2603
91AA/LineD-609
91Wichita/LineD-609
91Wichita/ProC-2594
91Wichita/Rock-4
92Beloit/ClBest-27
92Beloit/ProC-402
Knox, Mike
83Cedar-4
83Cedar/Frit-9
83Durham-8
84Durham-15
85Greenvl/Team-10
Knox, Scott
85PrWill-29
Knudsen, Kurt
89Lakeland/Star-13
90Lakeland/Star-16
91London/ProC-1874
92D/Rook-62
92F/Up-25
92Sky/AAASingl-266
92Toledo/SB-592
93D-145
93F-231
93S-264
93Select-306
93StCl-65
93StCl/1stDay-65
93T-272
93T/Gold-272
93Tiger/Gator-15
94F-136
Knudson, Mark
83DayBe-7
85Cram/PCL-60
86Tucson-10
87Denver-20
88D-495
88Denver/CMC-1
88Denver/ProC-1275
88T-61
89Pol/Brew-41
90Brewer/MillB-12
90D-575
90F-327
90F/Can-327
90Leaf-348
90OPC-566
90Pol/Brew-41
90S-539
90T-566
91Brewer/MillB-13
91D-328
91F-587
91Leaf-159
91OPC-267
91Panini/FrSt-211
91Panini/St-165
91Pol/Brew-12
91S-239
91T-267
91UD-393
91Ultra-176
92LasVegas/ProC-2793
92LasVegas/SB-233
92S-373
Knudtson, Jim
87Cedar-27
Kobbe, Eric
89GA-16
90GA-15
Kobel, Kevin
74OPC-605R
74T-605R
75OPC-337
75T-337
75T/M-337
76OPC-588
76T-588
77Spoka
79OPC-6
79T-21
80OPC-106
80T-189
91WIZMets-216
Kobernus, Jeff
82Madis/Frit-25
Kobetitsch, Kevin
91Eugene/ClBest-16
91Eugene/ProC-3721
92AppFox/ClBest-22
92BBCity/ProC-3841
Kobza, Greg
89Utica/Pucko-13
90SoBend/Best-15
90SoBend/GS-24
91ClBest/Singl-73
91Saraso/ClBest-14
91Saraso/ProC-1116
92Stockton/ClBest-10
92Stockton/ProC-36
Koch, Barney
90Target-1004
Koch, Donn
82AppFx/Frit-17
Koch, Ken
86BirmB/Team-24TR
87OrlanTw-8
Kochanski, Mark
82Idaho-9
Kocher, Bradley W.
16FleischBrd-53
C46-82
Koegel, Pete
71OPC-633R
71T-633R
72OPC-14R
72T-14R
77Jaxvl
Koehler, James
91Butte/SportP-1
93River/Cal-26
Koehnke, Odie
75AppFx
76AppFx
Koelling, Brian
91Billing/SportP-20
91Billings/ProC-3762
92B-65
92Cedar/ClBest-26
92Cedar/ProC-1079
92ClBest-49
92MidwLAS/Team-25
92UD/ML-330
93B-554
94B-542
94StCl-503
94StCl/1stDay-503
94StCl/Gold-503
94UD-217
94UD/ElecD-217
Koenecke, Leonard
(Len)
34Exh/4-2
90Target-415
Koenig, Fred
83Thorn-26CO
88Pulaski/ProC-1749
89Pulaski/ProC-1900
91Pulaski/ClBest-23CO
91Pulaski/ProC-4024CO
92Pulaski/ProC-3198CO
93Rang/Keeb-220CO
Koenig, Gary
90BBCity/Star-14
Koenig, Mark
29Exh/4-26
31Exh/4-24
32Orbit/num-30
32Orbit/un-39
33G-39
34G-56
35E-8A
35G-9A
87Conlon/2-41
88Conlon/4-16
91Conlon/Sport-125
92Mega/Ruth-154M
93Conlon-751
94Conlon-1121
94Conlon-1230
94Conlon/Pr-1230
R305
R315-A20
R315-B20
R316
V353-39
W513-83
Koenigsfeld, Ron
82ElPaso-3
84Cram/PCL-25
Koeyers, Ramsey
93James/ClBest-1
93James/ProC-3331
Koga, Hide
90Salinas/Cal-142MG
90Salinas/ProC-2735MG
91Salinas/ClBest-24MG
91Salinas/ProC-2260MG
92Salinas/ClBest-25
92Salinas/ProC-3773MG
Koh, Joe
87Idaho-20
Kohl, Jim
92FtMyr/ProC-2741
Kohli, John
88Belling/Legoe-15
88NE-23
Kohlogi, Acey
(Asst.)
89Visalia/Cal-121
Kohn, Jim
92Miracle/ClBest-25
Kohno, Takayuki
90Salinas/Cal-143CO
90Salinas/ProC-2736CO
91Salinas/ClBest-26CO
91Salinas/ProC-2262CO
92Salinas/ProC-3775CO
Koklys, Wayne
91Idaho/ProC-4322
Kokora, Pat
89Anchora-17
Kokos, Dick
49B-31
50B-50
51B-68
51T/RB-19
53T-232
54B-37
54Esskay
54T-106
91Crown/Orio-245
91T/Arc53-232
94T/Arc54-106
Kolarek, Frank
79Ogden/TCMA-19
Kolb, Gary
62Pep/Tul
63Pep/Tul
64T-119
65T-287
68KDKA-10
68T-407
69MB-151
69T-307
78TCMA-268
78TCMA-283
91WIZMets-217
Kolb, Pete
86ElPaso-15TR
87ElPaso-9
88Denver/ProC-1252
89Denver/ProC-50
Kolbe, Brian
82Jacks-7
Koller, Jerry

91Idaho/ProC-4323
92Macon/ProC-263
93Durham/Team-10
Koller, Mark
87Watertn-25
88Watertn/Pucko-7
Koller, Mike
88Bristol/ProC-1880
89Fayette/ProC-1576
90Fayette/ProC-2403
Koller, Rodney
91BurlInd/ProC-3299
92BurlInd/ClBest-7
92BurlInd/ProC-1651
Kolloway, Don
43Playball-10
49B-28
50B-133
51B-105
52B-91
52T-104
53T-97
91T/Arc53-97
Exh47
Kolodny, Mike
80Batavia-5
Kolotka, Chuck
82Madis/Frit-6
83Miami-8
84Beaum-22
Kolp, Ray
33G-150
94Conlon-1160
V100
V353-82
Kolstad, Harold
(Hal)
62T-276
63T-574
Komadina, Tony
75AppFx
Komazaki, Yukiichi
83SanJose-9
Komminsk, Brad
80Ander-28
81Durham-10
83Richm-19
84D-36RR
84F/X-U63
84Richm-10M
84Richm-11
85D-321
85F-331
85Ho/Braves-13
85Pol/Atl-36
85T-292
86F-520
86OPC-210
86Richm-11
86T-698
87Denver-6
88D-583
88Denver/CMC-21
88Denver/ProC-1263
89F/Up-28
90D-350
90F-496
90F/Can-496
90Leaf-303
90OPC-476
90Richm/25Ann-14
90Rochester/L&U-27
90S-496
90S/Tr-53T
90T-476
90T/Tr-53T
90UD-428
91AAA/LineD-540
91Crown/Orio-246
91S-259
91Tacoma/LineD-540
92S-735
Koncz, Mark
89KS*-22
Konderla, Mike
83Cedar-7
83Cedar/Frit-14
84Cedar-9
87Nashvl-12
88Denver/CMC-2
88Denver/ProC-1276
Konemann, Troy
92Spring/ClBest-12
92Spring/ProC-862
Konetchy, Ed
10Domino-63
11Helmar-172
12Sweet/Pin-150
14CJ-118
15CJ-118
16FleischBrd-54
21Exh-93
90Target-416
91Conlon/Sport-263
92Conlon/Sport-638
D328-94
D329-96
D350/2-94
E135-94
E254
E270/2
E96
M101/4-96
M101/5-94
M116
PM1-8
S74-121
T202
T204
T205
T206
T207
T213/blue
T214-16
T215/blue
T3-103
W514-93
WG5-24
WG6-23
Konieczki, Dominic
91Erie/ClBest-17
91Erie/ProC-4062
92Kenosha/ProC-599
Konieczny, Doug
75OPC-624R
75T-624R
75T/M-624R
76OPC-602
76SSPC-49
76T-602
Konopa, Bob
82OrlanTw-18/A
82OrlanTw/B-6
84CharlO-15
90HagersDG/Best-14
Konopki, Mark
91Elmira/ClBest-22
91Elmira/ProC-3268
92LynchRS/ClBest-21
92LynchRS/ProC-2903
Konstanty, Jim
44Playball-30
49Eureka-139
50B-226
51B-27
51BR-D6
51FB
51T/CAS
52T-108
53B/BW-58
55B-231
56T-321
61T-479MVP
79TCMA-53
90HOF/St-44
Exh47
PM10/Sm-91
R423-56
Rawl
Kontorinis, Andrew
92Kenosha/ProC-614
Kontos, Chris
92StCl/MemberIII*-9
Konuszewski, Dennis
92Welland/ClBest-13
93ClBest/MLG-178
Koob, Ernie
92Conlon/Sport-349
Kooiman, Bill
90Idaho/ProC-3265
Kooman, Chris
87Everett-14
Koonce, Cal
63T-31
65OPC-34
65T-34
66T-278
67CokeCap/Cub-15
67OPC-171
67T-171
68T-486
69T-303
70OPC-521
70T-521
71MLB/St-320
71OPC-254
71T-254
72MB-185
91WIZMets-218
94Mets/69-28
Koontz, Jim
81ElPaso-10
82ElPaso-20
84Cram/PCL-45
Koopman, Bob
86PrWill-14
87Salem-20
Koosman, Jerry
68OPC-177R
68T-177R
69Citgo-12
69MLB/St-168
69MLBPA/Pin-49
69OPC-90
69T-434AS
69T-90
69T/DE-25
69T/S-51
69T/St-66
69T/decal
69Trans-46
70MLB/St-79
70OPC-309WS
70OPC-468AS
70T-309WS
70T-468AS
70T-610
70Trans-5
70Trans/M-22
71MLB/St-157
71OPC-335
71T-335
71T/Coins-23
71T/tatt-3
72MB-186
72T-697
72T-698IA
73OPC-184
73T-184
74OPC-356
74T-356
74T/St-65
75OPC-19
75SSPC/42-17
75T-19
75T/M-19
76Crane-27
76Laugh/Jub-22
76MSA/Disc
76OPC-64
76SSPC-609
76SSPC/MetsY-M14
76T-64
77BurgChef-143
77Ho-77
77Ho/Twink-77
77K-29
77OPC-26
77T-300
78Ho-80
78Pep-34
78T-565
78Tastee/Discs-12
78Wiffle/Discs-35
79Ho-149
79OPC-345
79T-655
79Twin/FriszP-12
80BK/PHR-5
80OPC-144
80T-275
80T/S-38
80T/Super-38
81D-531
81F-552
81F/St-19
81OPC-298
81T-476
81T/St-104
82D-603
82F-347
82OPC-63
82T-714
83D-39
83F-242
83F/St-12M
83F/St-7M
83OPC-153
83T-153
83T/Fold-1M
83TrueVal/WSox-36
84D-501
84F-65
84F/X-64
84Nes/792-311
84Nes/792-716LL
84OPC-311
84Phill/TastyK-23
84T-311
84T-716LL
84T/Tr-64
85CIGNA-7
85D-233
85F-256
85Leaf-178
85OPC-15
85Phill/TastyK-21
85Phill/TastyK-9
85T-15
85T/St-117
86D-23DK
86D/DKsuper-23
86Leaf-23DK
86OPC-343
86Sf-64M
86T-505
88Pac/Leg-66
89Swell-109
90Pac/Legend-88
91Pittsfld/ClBest-26CO
91Pittsfld/ProC-3440CO
91WIZMets-219
92ColumMet/ClBest-27CO
92ColumMet/SAL/II-2
93AP/ASG-160
94Mets/69-37
94Mets/69-39
94Mets/69-4
94Mets/69-48
94Mets/69-54
94Mets/69Pr-2
Kopacz, George
71OPC-204R
71T-204R
Koperda, Mike
80Ander-21
Kopetsky, Brian
86Bakers-18
Kopf, Dave
86Pittsfld-11
87Iowa-10
88Pittsfld/ProC-1373
Kopf, William
88Pac/8Men-91
E120
E220
W514-118
W572
Koplitz, Howard
62T-114
63T-406
64T-372
66OPC-46
66T-46
78TCMA-221
Koppe, Joe
59T-517
60T-319
61T-179
62Salada-209
62Shirriff-209
62T-39
63J-26
63P-26
63T-396
64T-279
Kopriva, Dan
92Princet/ClBest-25
92Princet/ProC-3095
Kopyta, Jeff
86Cram/NWL-66
87Madis-18
88Modesto-12
88Modesto/Cal-63
89Modesto/Cal-272
Korcheck, Steve
58T-403
59T-284
60L-79
60T-56
Korczyk, Steve
82Toledo-3
83Toledo-5
Kordish, Steve
83TriCit-2
84Tulsa-30
86Salem-15
Korince, George
67OPC-72R
67T-526R
67T-72R
68T-447R
Korn, Ray
91Erie/ClBest-27CO
91Erie/ProC-4085CO
Korneev, Leonid
89EastLDD/ProC-DD15
Kornfeld, Craig
79QuadC-16
Korolev, Sergey
89EastLDD/ProC-DD4
Kortright, Jim
88Idaho/ProC-1858
89Idaho/ProC-2031
Korwan, Jim
90Target-1005
Kosc, Greg
88TM/Umpire-25
89TM/Umpire-23
90TM/Umpire-22
Kosco, Andrew
(Dru)
87Wausau-14
88Wausau/GS-26
89Wmsprt/ProC-626
90Wmsprt/Best-13
90Wmsprt/ProC-1068
90Wmsprt/Star-14
Kosco, Andy
66T-264R
67CokeCap/Twin-18
67T-366
68T-524
69MB-152
69OPC-139
69T-139
69T/4in1-8
69T/St-204
70OPC-535
70T-535
71MLB/St-440
71OPC-746
71T-746
72MB-187
72OPC-376
72T-376
74OPC-34
74T-34
90Target-417
92Yank/WIZ60-69
Kosco, Bryn
88James/ProC-1896
89Rockford/Team-15
90Jaxvl/Best-6
90Jaxvl/ProC-1382
91AA/LineD-259
91Harris/LineD-259
91Harris/ProC-635
92Harris/ProC-465
92Harris/SB-285
94FExcel-192
Kosenski, John
88CapeCod/Sum-108
88OK-13
89OK-20
90OK-15
91Fayette/ClBest-4
91Fayette/ProC-1165
92Lakeland/ClBest-14
92Lakeland/ProC-2273
Koshevoy, Alexei
89EastLDD/ProC-DD7
Koshorek, Clem
52T-380
53B/Col-147
53T-8
91T/Arc53-8
Koslo, George B.
(Dave)
47TipTop

48B-48
49B-34
49Eureka-114
50B-65
51B-90
52B-182
52BR
52T-336
54Esskay
55Gol/Braves-16
55JC-20
79TCMA-231
91Crown/Orio-247
Koslofski, Kevin
86FtMyr-16
87FtMyr-24
88BBCity/Star-15
89BBCity/Star-14
90Memphis/Best-10
90Memphis/ProC-1021
90Memphis/Star-12
91AA/LineD-408
91Memphis/LineD-408
91Memphis/ProC-666
92D/Rook-63
92F/Up-28
92Omaha/ProC-2975
92Omaha/SB-332
92ProC/Tomorrow-74
92Sky/AAASingl-152
93D-205
93F-240
93Pol/Royal-15
93S-226
93Select-394
93StCl-505
93StCl/1stDay-505
93T-158
93T/Gold-158
93UD-351
93USPlayC/Rook-4D
93Ultra-211
94Pac/Cr-291
Kosnik, Jim
88Belling/Legoe-16
Kostich, Billy
89LittleSun-15
91Penin/ClBest-7
91Penin/ProC-373
92Penin/ClBest-21
92Penin/ProC-2928
Kostickhka, Steve
87Beloit-6
Kostro, Frank
63T-407R
65T-459
68OPC-44
68T-44
69T-242
Kotarski, Mike
92Bend/ClBest-16
93T-621
93T/Gold-621
Kotch, Darrin
90James/Pucko-19
91Sumter/ClBest-6
91Sumter/ProC-2329
92Rockford/ClBest-5
92Rockford/ProC-2110
Kotchman, Randy
89Miami/II/Star-8
90Boise/ProC-3325
Kotchman, Tom
86PalmSp-19MG
86PalmSp/Smok-2
87Edmon-12
88Edmon/CMC-22
88Edmon/ProC-580
89AAA/ProC-28
89Edmon/CMC-25
89Edmon/ProC-549
90Boise/ProC-3331MG
91Boise/ProC-3899MG
92Boise/ProC-3646MG
Kotes, Chris
91StCath/ClBest-17
91StCath/ProC-3389
92Myrtle/ClBest-14
92Myrtle/ProC-2192
93Dunedin/ClBest-13
93Dunedin/ProC-1792
93SALAS/II-19
Kouba, Curtis
82Wausau/Frit-5
Koufax, Sandy
55Gol/Dodg-16
55T-123
56T-79
57T-302
58BB
58T-187
59Morrell
59T-163
60BB-9
60Morrell
60T-343
60Union/Dodg-10
61BB-32
61Morrell
61T-207M
61T-344
61T-49LL
61Union/Dodg-11
62BB-32
62Bz
62Exh
62J-109
62P-109
62P/Can-109
62Salada-109
62Shirriff-109
62T-5
62T-60LL
62T/St-136
62T/bucks
63Exh
63F-42
63J-121
63P-121
63Salada-4
63T-210
63T-412M
63T-5LL
63T-9LL
63T/SO
64Bz-32
64T-1LL
64T-200
64T-3LL
64T-5LL
64T/Coins-106
64T/Coins-159AS
64T/S-3
64T/SU
64T/St-91
64T/tatt
65Bz-32
65OPC-8LL
65T-300
65T-8LL
65T/E-8
65T/trans-55
66Bz-1
66OPC-100
66T-100
66T-221LL
66T-223LL
66T-225LL
66T/RO-14
66T/RO-47
67T-234LL
67T-236LL
67T-238LL
72Laugh/GF-4
75OPC-201MVP
75T-201MVP
75T/M-201MVP
76Laugh/Jub-4
76Shakey-131
77Galasso-244
78TCMA-130
79TCMA-49
80Pac/Leg-10
80Perez/HOF-131
80SSPC/HOF
81Albuq/TCMA-23B
82KMart-4
83MLBPA/Pin-24
87Smok/Dodg-16
88Smok/Dodg-4
88Smok/Dodg-6M
89HOF/St-79
89Smok/Dodg-15
90HOF/St-69
90OPC-665TBC
90Perez/GreatMom-16
90T-665TBC
90Target-418
Exh47
Koukalik, Joe
90Target-1006
Kounas, Tony
88CapeCod/Sum-144
91Penin/ClBest-14
91Penin/ProC-380
92SanBern/ClBest-8
92SanBern/ProC-
Koupal, Lou
90Target-1007
93Conlon-713
Kovach, Ty
89Watertn/Star-13
90CLAS/CL-34
90Kinston/Team-4
91AA/LineD-85
91Canton/LineD-85
91Canton/ProC-977
91ClBest/Singl-309
92Kinston/ClBest-6
92Kinston/ProC-2470
Kowalski, Wladek
(Killer)
72Dimanche*-123
Kowar, Frank
90StCath/ProC-3462
Kowitz, Brian
90A&AASingle/ProC-192
90Pulaski/Best-22
90Pulaski/ProC-3087
91ClBest/Singl-66
91Durham/ClBest-25
91Durham/ProC-1559
92Durham/ProC-1114
92Greenvl/SB-237
93ClBest/MLG-90
93FExcel/ML-4
Koy, Ernest
41DP-118
90Target-419
92TX-28
Koza, Dave
81Pawtu-16
83Pawtu-17
Kozar, Al
49B-16
50B-15
R302
Kozeniewski, Blaise
92Oneonta/ClBest-21
93Greens/ClBest-14
93Greens/ProC-894
Kozyrez, Alexander
89EastLDD/ProC-DD18
Krablin, Justin
92GulfCM/ProC-3476
Kracl, Darin
87BYU-10
89Medford/Best-13
90A&AASingle/ProC-114
90Madison/ProC-2262
90MidwLgAS/GS-55
90ProC/Singl-867
Kraeger, Don
79AppFx-23
Kraemer, Joe
85Madis-20
85Madis/Pol-17
86Modesto-18
86Peoria-13
87Iowa-9
88Iowa/CMC-7
88Iowa/ProC-549
89Iowa/CMC-3
89Iowa/ProC-1715
90D/Rook-10
90F/Up-U8
90T/89Debut-68
90T/TVCub-10
90UD/Ext-740
91AAA/LineD-207
91Iowa/LineD-207
91Iowa/ProC-1054
91S-755RP
92MidldA/OneHour-13
92MidldA/ProC-4023
92MidldA/SB-463
92Sky/AASingl-197
Kraft, Ken
86Clearw-15
Kraft, Mike
89Johnson/Star-15
90Spring/Best-11
Krafve, Keith
86Cram/NWL-24
86Everett/Pop-10
Krahenbuhl, Ken
90Hunting/ProC-3278
91Peoria/ClBest-26
91Peoria/Team-10
92Peoria/Team-10
92WinSalem/ClBest-15
Krajewski, Chris
80SanJose/JITB-13
Krakauskas, Joe
40PlayBall-188
41DP-77
47Signal
91Conlon/Sport-228
Kralick, Jack
61Clover-11
61Peters-6
61T-36
62T-346
62T/St-77
63J-11
63P-11
63Sugar-28
63T-448
64Kahn
64T-338
65Kahn
65T-535
65T/E-72
66OPC-129
66T-129
67CokeCap/Indian-14
67T-316
78TCMA-134
78Twin/Frisz-37
Kraly, Steve
54NYJour
55T-139
Kramer, John
(Jack)
41G-14
45Parade*-68
47TipTop
49B-53
50B-199
51B-200
52Wheat*
79TCMA-107
W753
Kramer, Mark
85BurlR-18
86DayBe-15
87PortChar-19
88CharlR/Star-11
89Miami/II/Star-9
Kramer, Randy
83BurlR-8
83BurlR/Frit-5
86Kinston-13
86Tulsa-23
87Vanco-16
88BuffB/CMC-5
88BuffB/ProC-1464
89D-480
89D/Best-213
89D/Rook-48
89F-647R
89F/Up-U115
89Panini/St-159
89S/HotRook-57
89T-522
90BuffB/Team-12
90D-409
90F-471
90F/Can-471
90Homer/Pirate-15
90HotRook/St-26
90OPC-126
90Panini/St-327
90S/100Ris-41
90T-126
90UD-519
91AAA/LineD-432
91Richm/Bob-8
91Richm/LineD-432
91Richm/ProC-2561
91Richm/Team-17
92B-398
92Calgary/SB-62
92Sky/AAASingl-27
93Edmon/ProC-1132
Kramer, Tom
(Tommy)
88MidwLAS/GS-22
88Watlo/ProC-689
89Kinston/Star-11
89Star/Wax-76
90CLAS/CL-38
91AA/LineD-86
91Canton/LineD-86
91Canton/ProC-978
92ColoSp/ProC-748
92ColoSp/SB-88
92Sky/AAASingl-38
92T/91Debut-105
93B-37
93F/Final-202
93Indian/WUAB-15
93Pinn-585
93Select/RookTr-73T
94D-384
94F-108
94Pac/Cr-172
94S-314
94S/GoldR-314
94T-642
94T/Gold-642
94Ultra-44
Kranepool, Ed
63T-228R
64T-393M
64T-566
65OPC-144
65T-144
65T/E-6
65T/trans-56
66Bz-9
66T-212
66T/RO-20
66T/RO-48
67CokeCap/YMet-21
67Kahn
67OPC-186M
67T-186M
67T-452
68OPC-92
68T-92
68T/ActionSt-5CM
69MB-153
69MLB/St-169
69T-381
69T/St-67
70K-1
70MLB/St-80
70T-557
70Trans/M-21
71MLB/St-158
71OPC-573
71T-573
72MB-188
72OPC-181
72OPC-182IA
72T-181
72T-182IA
73OPC-329
73T-329
74OPC-561
74T-561
75OPC-324
75T-324
75T/M-324
76OPC-314
76SSPC-533
76SSPC/MetsY-M10
76T-314
77BurgChef-136
77OPC-60
77T-201
78OPC-205
78T-49
78Wiffle/Discs-36
79OPC-265
79T-505
80OPC-336
80T-641
89Pac/Leg-114
89Swell-28
91WIZMets-220
94Mets/69-13
94Mets/69-36
Exh47
PM10/Sm-92
Kranitz, Rick
80Holyo-1
81ElPaso-17
82Vanco-19

86WinSalem-11C
88Peoria/Ko-19
89Peoria/Team-31
90CharlK/Team-25CO
91AA/LineD-150CO
91CharlK/LineD-150CO
91CharlK/ProC-1705CO
92Iowa/ProC-4066CO
92Iowa/SB-225CO
Krattli, Tom
77DaytB
Kratz, Ron
92Batavia/ClBest-15
92Batavia/ProC-3273
Kraus, Jeff
77Spartan
Kraus, Ralph
87PrWill-5
88FtLaud/Star-14
89FtLaud/Star-12
Krause, Andrew
85Madis-21
85Madis/Pol-18
Krause, Guy
75WPalmB/Sussman-28
Krause, Harry
10Domino-64
11Helmar-56
12Sweet/Pin-46
28Exh/PCL-17
E104
E90/1
E91
E95
M116
S74-32
T202
T205
T206
T207
T208
T213/blue
T215/blue
T215/brown
T3-22
WG7-25
Krause, Ron
90Rockford/ProC-2700
90Rockford/Team-13
91WPalmB/ClBest-21
92WPalmB/ClBest-2
92WPalmB/ProC-2095
93Harris/ProC-275
Krauss, Ron
82CharR-15
Krauss, Timothy
81Redwd-17
82Holyo-17
84Cram/PCL-98
85Cram/PCL-17
86BuffB-14
87Hawaii-23
Krausse, Lew
63T-104
64T-334
65T-462
66T-256
67CokeCap/A's-16
67T-565
68T-458
69MB-154
69OPC-23
69Sunoco/Pin-12
69T-23
69T/St-217
70McDon-4
70OPC-233
70T-233
71MLB/St-441
71OPC-372
71T-372
71T/Coins-20
72T-592
73OPC-566
73T-566
75OPC-603
75T-603
75T/M-603
75Tucson-20
75Tucson/Caruso-13
75Tucson/Team-7
Krauza, Ron
89BuffB/CMC-19
Kravec, Ken
77T-389
78T-439
79OPC-141
79T-283
80OPC-299
80T-575
81T-67
81T/Tr-783
82D-378
82Iowa-19
82RedLob
82T-639
87FtMyr-28
88Memphis/Best-14
89Pac/SenLg-151
91Pac/SenLg-10
Kravitz, Dan
57T-267
58T-444
59T-536
60T-238
61T-166
Krawczyk, Ray
82AlexD-4
84Cram/PCL-129
85Cram/PCL-245
86Hawaii-14
87Hawaii-17
89Denver/CMC-7
89Denver/ProC-32
Krebs, Dave
87Savan-3
88Savan/ProC-338
Kreevich, Mike
38Exh/4-10
39Exh
44Playball-3
R303/A
R303/B
R312/M
V351B-29
WG8-39
Krehmeyer, Charles
N172/PCL
Kremblas, Frank
90Cedar/ProC-2324
91AA/LineD-160
91Chatt/LineD-160
91Chatt/ProC-1966
92Chatt/ProC-3828
92Chatt/SB-188
Kremer, Ken
89Beloit/I/Star-12
89Beloit/II/Star-18
Kremer, Remy
(Ray)
25Exh-53
26Exh-53
27Exh-26
28Exh-25
29Exh/4-14
31Exh/4-14
33G-54
91Conlon/Sport-279
R306
V354-38
WG7-26
Kremers, Jimmy
89Greenvl/Best-24
89Greenvl/ProC-1163
89Greenvl/Star-12
89SLAS-8
90AAASingl/ProC-406
90Brave/Dubuq/Singl-17
90F/Up-U4
90ProC/Singl-286
90Richm/Bob-12
90Richm/CMC-10
90Richm/ProC-261
90Richm/Team-17
91AAA/LineD-187
91D-739
91F-694
91Indianap/LineD-187
91Indianap/ProC-464
91S-736RP
91T/90Debut-79
91UD-262
92Indianap/ProC-1862
92Indianap/SB-185
92Sky/AAASingl-91
Kremmel, Jim
93Rang/Keeb-221
Krenchicki, Wayne
78RochR
80RochR-16
80T-661R
82Coke/Reds
82F-168
82T-107
82T/Tr-58T
83D-314
83F-594
83F/St-4M
83T-374
84D-334
84F-83
84F/X-65
84Nes/792-223
84T-223
84T/Tr-65T
84Wichita/Rock-7
85D-140
85F-539
85T-468
86D-140
86Expo/Prov/Pan-20
86F-180
86F/Up-U60
86OPC-81
86Provigo-20
86T-777
86T/Tr-55T
87D-406
87F-322
87OPC-81
87T-774
87Tacoma-6
88Louisvl-25
88Tacoma/CMC-14
88Tacoma/ProC-635
89Pac/SenLg-157
89T/SenLg-75
90EliteSenLg-38
91Crown/Orio-248
91Pac/SenLg-42
92Beloit/ClBest-28MG
92Beloit/ProC-422
Krenke, Keith
92Bend/ClBest-17
92MN-9
Kress, Charlie
(Chuck)
54T-219
90Target-420
94T/Arc54-219
Kress, Ralph
(Red)
29Exh/4-29
31Exh/4-30
33G-33
35BU-169
35G-2C
35G-4C
35G-7C
39PlayBall-115
40PlayBall-45
54T-160CO
55Gol/Ind-14
55Salem
55T-151
60T-460C
92Conlon/Sport-383
94T/Arc54-160
PR1-19
R316
V353-33
Kretlow, Lou
52B-221
52T-42
53B/Col-50
54B-197
54Esskay
55B-108
55Esskay
57T-139
91Crown/Orio-249
Kreuter, Chad
86Salem-16
87PortChar-25
88TexLgAS/GS-3
88Tulsa-19
89Classic-27
89D-579
89F-526
89Panini/St-444
89S-638
89S/HotRook-51
89S/YS/II-40
89Sf-43
89Smok/R-17
89T-432
89UD-312
90D-520
90F-303
90F/Can-303
90OPC-562
90PublInt/St-414
90S-406
90S/100Ris-51
90T-562
90TulsaDG/Best-23
90UD-609
92B-515
92L-496
92L/BlkGold-496
92Ultra-365
93D-673
93F-607
93Flair-205
93I-463
93Pac/Spanish-444
93Rang/Keeb-222
93T-692
93T/Gold-692
93Tiger/Gator-16
93Ultra-201
94B-13
94D-224
94F-137
94Finest-388
94L-5
94Pac/Cr-223
94Pinn-125
94Pinn/Artist-125
94Pinn/Museum-125
94S-503
94StCl-411
94StCl/1stDay-411
94StCl/Gold-411
94T-257
94T/Gold-257
94UD-392
94UD/CollC-167
94UD/CollC/Gold-167
94UD/CollC/Silv-167
94Ultra-56
Kreutzer, Frank
64T-107R
65T-371
66T-211
78TCMA-116
Krevokuch, James
(Krev)
91Welland/ClBest-8
91Welland/ProC-3579
92Augusta/ClBest-3
92Augusta/ProC-246
93CaroMud/RBI-18
Krichell, Paul
E270/2
Krieg, William
N172
N284
Kries, John
89Salem/Team-14
Kripner, Mike
80Cedar-23
82Water-12
Krippner, Curt
88Beloit/GS-16
89Beloit/II/Star-19
90Stockton/Cal-185
90Stockton/ProC-2184
91ClBest/Singl-403
91Erie/ProC-4063
Krislock, Zak
92AubAs/ClBest-24
92AubAs/ProC-1351
Krist, Howie
W754
Kristan, Kevin
85Cram/PCL-124
87WPalmB-22
Krivda, Rick
91Bluefld/ClBest-18
91Bluefld/ProC-4123
92Kane/ClBest-14
92Kane/ProC-87
92Kane/Team-18
92MidwLAS/Team-26
92ProC/Tomorrow-13
93FExcel/ML-124
94B-159
94FExcel-9
94FExcel/LL-12
94Ultra-306
Krizmanich, Mike
75IntAS/TCMA-23
75IntAS/TCMA-3
Kroc, Ray
78Padre/FamFun-17OWN
Krock, August
E223
N172
N403
Kroener, Chris
86Visalia-12
Kroh, Floyd
(Rube)
12Sweet/Pin-83
E254
E97
M116
T205
T206
Krokroskia, Sean
90Bend/Legoe-3
Krol, David
88CapeCod/Sum-180
Krol, Jack
84Smok/SDP-15CO
87LasVegas-3MG
88Charl/ProC-1219MG
89CharRain/ProC-991MG
90CharRain/Best-26MG
90CharRain/ProC-2054MG
92Louisvl/ProC-1902MG
92Louisvl/SB-274MG
Kroll, Gary
65T-449R
66T-548
66T/RO-2
66T/RO-49
78TCMA-27
91WIZMets-221
Kroll, Todd
87Bakers-8
88Bakers/Cal-255
Kromy, Ted
79Wisco-19
82OrlanTw/A-19
82OrlanTw/B-19
83OrlanTw-17
Kroon, Marc
92Kingspt/ClBest-18
92Kingspt/ProC-1527
92StCl/Dome-99
Krsnich, Mike
62T-289
Krsnich, Rocco
(Rocky)
53T-229
91T/Arc53-229
Krueger, Arthur T.
E286
M116
T206
Krueger, Bill
82WHave-7
84Cram/PCL-84
84F-450
84Nes/792-178
84OPC-178
84T-178
85D-467
85F-428
85Mother/A's-21
85T-528
86D-298
86F-424
86Mother/A's-21
86T-58
87T-238
88Albuq/CMC-3
88Albuq/ProC-271
88TripleA/ASCMC-42
90Brewer/MillB-13
90F-328
90F/Can-328
90Leaf-421
90OPC-518
90Pol/Brew-47
90S-366
90T-518

90Target-421
91B-248
91D-647
91F-588
91F/UltraUp-U52
91F/Up-U54
91OPC-417
91S-598
91T-417
91T/Tr-70T
91UD/FinalEd-60F
92D-672
92D/Up-U16
92F-285
92L-477
92L/BlkGold-477
92OPC-368
92Pinn-501
92S-253
92StCl-861
92T-368
92T/Gold-368
92T/GoldWin-368
92T/Tr-61T
92T/TrGold-61T
92UD-403
92UD-781
92Ultra-397
93D-352
93F/Final-211
93L-348
93OPC/Premier-38
93Pac/Spanish-445
93Pinn-547
93Tiger/Gator-17
93UD-530
93Ultra-552
94D-252
94F-138
94Pac/Cr-222
94T-552
94T/Gold-552
Krueger, Ernie
90Target-422
Krueger, Kirby
81Wisco-6
83OrlanTw-18
Krueger, Steve
81LynnS-7
82LynnS-5
Krug, Everett B.
(Chris)
62Pep/Tul
63Pep/Tul
66OPC-166
66T-166
Krug, Martin
E120
Kruk, John
83Beaum-11
84Cram/PCL-228
84Cram/PCL-250
85Cram/PCL-103
86D/Rook-42
86F/Up-U61
86Sf/Rook-1
86T/Tr-56T
87Bohem-8
87D-328
87F-420
87Leaf-217
87Sf-61
87Sf/TPrev-16M
87Stuart-12
87T-123
87T/St-113
87ToysRUs-17
88Classic/Blue-203
88Classic/Red-162
88Coke/Padres-8
88D-205
88D/Best-245
88F-589
88F/Mini-113
88F/SS-20
88F/St-124
88KennerFig-59
88Leaf-176
88OPC-32
88OPC/WaxBox-G
88Panini/St-403
88RedFoley/St-44
88S-36
88S/YS/I-17
88Sf-64
88Smok/Padres-14
88T-596
88T/Big-60
88T/Coins-45
88T/Mini-75
88T/St-110
88T/UK-41
88T/WaxBox-G
89B-460
89D-86
89D/Best-240
89F-309
89F/Up-109
89KennerFig-77
89OPC-235
89Padre/Mag-5
89Panini/St-200
89Phill/TastyK-42
89RedFoley/St-69
89S-148
89S/Tr-70T
89Sf-184
89T-235
89T/Big-216
89T/LJN-88
89T/St-102
89T/Tr-63T
89UD-280
90B-154
90Classic/III-T3
90D-160
90D/BestNL-69
90F-565
90F/Can-565
90Leaf-284
90OPC-469
90Panini/St-310
90Phill/TastyK-18
90PublInt/St-52
90S-467
90Sf-124
90T-469
90T/Big-214
90T/St-117
90UD-668
91B-503
91Classic/III-47
91D-260
91F-402
91Leaf-278
91OPC-689
91Panini/St-107
91Phill/Medford-22
91S-94
91StCl-227
91T-689
91UD-199
91USPlayC/AS-4S
91Ultra-266
92B-541
92D-230
92D/DK-DK12
92F-537
92L-313
92L/BlkGold-313
92L/GoldPrev-8
92L/Prev-8
92OPC-30
92OPC/Premier-134
92Panini-242
92Phill/Med-17
92Pinn-147
92S-235
92StCl-209
92StCl/Dome-100
92Studio-76
92Studio/Prev-4
92T-30
92T/Gold-30
92T/GoldWin-30
92T/Kids-18
92TripleP-38
92UD-326
92UD-38TC
92UD/HRH-HR23
92UD/TmMVPHolo-28
92Ultra-246
93B-540
93Classic/GameI-50
93Colla/ASG-4
93Colla/DM-62
93D-436
93Duracel/PPII-3
93F-104
93F/Atlantic-12
93F/Fruit-33
93F/TLNL-8
93Flair-105
93Ho-4
93Kenner/Fig-18
93L-366
93L/UpGoldAS-3M
93OPC-216
93OPC/Premier-76
93P-29
93Pac/Jugador-30
93Pac/Spanish-238
93Panini-270
93Phill/Med-21
93Pinn-8
93Pinn/Slug-17
93S-79
93Select-33
93Select/StatL-53
93Select/StatL-6
93StCl-83
93StCl/1stDay-83
93StCl/MurphyS-84
93StCl/Phill-30
93Studio-183
93Studio/Her-12
93Studio/Sil-7
93T-340
93T/Finest-38
93T/FinestRef-38
93T/Gold-340
93TB/Full-16
93TripleP-139
93UD-247
93UD-485
93UD/FunPack-146
93UD/SP-14AS
93USPlayC/Ace-10D
93Ultra-90
94B-412
94D-7
94D/DK-9
94D/DomII-10
94D/Elite-41
94D/Special-7
94F-594
94F/AS-44
94Finest-416
94L-347
94L/Gamer-11
94OPC-257
94Oscar-25
94Pac/Cr-479
94Pac/Silv-32
94Panini-229
94Phill/Med-18
94Pinn-63
94Pinn/Artist-63
94Pinn/Museum-63
94Pinn/Run-25
94RedFoley-13
94S-28
94S/DT-3
94S/GoldR-28
94S/GoldS-7
94S/Tomb-12
94Select-24
94SelectSam-24
94Sf/2000-101
94StCl-361
94StCl-533QS
94StCl/1stDay-361
94StCl/1stDay-533QS
94StCl/Dugout-3
94StCl/Gold-361
94StCl/Gold-533QS
94StCl/Team-226
94Studio-142
94T-401
94T/BlkGold-37
94T/Gold-401
94TripleP-177
94UD-276HFA
94UD-410
94UD/CollC-168
94UD/CollC/Gold-168
94UD/CollC/Silv-168
94UD/ElecD-276HFA
94UD/HoloFX-23
94UD/SP-138
94Ultra-249
94Ultra/PhillFinest-10
94Ultra/PhillFinest-6
94Ultra/PhillFinest-7
94Ultra/PhillFinest-8
94Ultra/PhillFinest-9
94Ultra/Pr-249
94Ultra/Pr-249
Krukow, Mike
77T-493R
78SSPC/270-267
78T-17
79T-592
80OPC-223
80T-431
81Coke
81F-312
81OPC-176
81T-176
81T/HT
82D-351
82F-598
82F/St-92
82OPC-215
82T-215
82T/St-31
82T/Tr-59T
83D-119
83F-163
83Mother/Giants-12
83OPC-331
83T-331
83T/Tr-58T
84D-509
84F-374
84Nes/792-633
84OPC-37
84T-633
85D-630
85F-609
85Mother/Giants-11
85OPC-74
85T-74
85T/St-163
86D-143
86D/HL-49
86F-546
86Mother/Giants-11
86OPC-126
86T-752
86T/St-93
86T/Tatt-8M
87BK-12
87Classic-67
87D-609
87D/AAS-58
87D/AS/Wax-PC15
87D/OD-98
87F-275
87F-630M
87F/GameWin-24
87F/Lim-24
87F/Mini-61
87F/St-69
87Ho/St-17
87Leaf-86
87Mother/SFG-6
87OPC-241
87Sf-62
87Sf/TPrev-10M
87Smok/NL-12
87T-580
87T/Mini-36
87T/St-92
88D-116
88D/Best-50
88F-85
88Mother/Giants-6
88OPC-393
88Panini/St-417
88RedFoley/St-45
88S-185
88T-445
89Classic-114
89D-258
89D/Best-135
89F-331
89Mother/Giants-6
89OPC-125
89S-190
89T-125
89T/St-83
89UD-46
90OPC-241
90PublInt/St-72
90S-215
90T-241
90UD-639
Krum, Sandy
89Chatt/Best-24
89Chatt/GS-3
90Salem/Star-27TR
91Salem/ClBest-24
Krumback, Mark
88Boise/ProC-1625
89Greens/ProC-425
90Cedar/Best-12
90Cedar/ProC-2335
91CalLgAS-34
91Reno/Cal-2
Krume, Sandy
88Cedar/ProC-1140
Krumm, Todd
90Lakeland/Star-17
91AA/LineD-390
91London/LineD-390
91London/ProC-1875
Krupenchemkov, Alex.
89EastLDD/ProC-DD14
Kruppa, Ken
75FtLaud/Sus-15
Krusinski, Clar
89Peoria/Team-33OWN
Krusinski, Mark
91Peoria/Team-30M
Kryhoski, Dick
49B-218
49Remar
50B-242
52B-133
52T-149
53B/Col-127
54B-117
54Esskay
54T-150
79TCMA-241
91Crown/Orio-250
94T/Arc54-150
Kryka, Mark
77Clinton
78Clinton
Kryzanowski, Rusty
86AubAs-15
87Kenosha-9
88Kenosha/ProC-1383
89Kenosha/ProC-1077
89Kenosha/Star-10
Kuahn, Bill
89Welland/Pucko-33
Kubala, Brian
86SanJose-11
Kubek, Tony
57T-312
58T-393
59T-505
59YooHoo-3
60T-83
61P-9
61T-265
61T/Dice-7
61T/St-195
62J-4
62P-4
62P/Can-4
62Salada-18
62Shirriff-18
62T-311IA
62T-430
62T/St-87
63Kahn
63T-20
64T-415
65OPC-65
65T-65
65T/E-71
79TCMA-244
81TCMA-477M
88Pac/Leg-29
89Swell-68
92Yank/WIZ60-70
92Yank/WIZAS-37
Exh47
WG10-11
WG9-13
Kubiak, Ted
68OPC-79
68T-79
69Sunoco/Pin-13
69T-281
70McDon-1

70T-688
71MLB/St-442
71OPC-516
71T-516
72MB-189
72OPC-23
72T-23
73OPC-652
73T-652
74OPC-228
74T-228
75OPC-329
75T-329
75T/M-329
76OPC-578
76SSPC-129
76T-578
77T-158
89Modesto/Chong-1MG
90Modesto/Cal-171MG
90Modesto/Chong-33MG
90Modesto/ProC-2229MG
91Modesto/ClBest-17MG
91Modesto/ProC-3106MG
92AS/Cal-21
92Modesto/ClBest-25MG
92Modesto/ProC-3910MG
93Modesto/ClBest-26MG
93Modesto/ProC-815MG
93Rang/Keeb-22

Kubicki, Marc
91Utica/ClBest-1
91Utica/ProC-3237
92ProC/Tomorrow-48
92Salinas/ClBest-6

Kubiszyn, Jack
60Maple-12
77Fritsch-42

Kubit, Joe
83Visalia/Frit-17

Kuboto, Masahiro
90Salinas/Cal-148TR

Kubski, Gil
78Cr/PCL-35
79SLCity-16
80SLCity-21
81Syrac-18
81Vanco-9
82Indianap-28
91Hunting/ProC-3354CO
92Hunting/ClBest-29CO

Kucab, John
52T-358

Kucek, Jack
75OPC-614R
75T-614R
75T/M-614R
76OPC-597R
76T-597R
77T-623
79OkCty
80Syrac-11
80Syrac/Team-13
81Syrac-6
81Syrac/Team-12

Kucharski, Joe
84RochR-18
85RochR-20
87CharlO/WBTV-37
87RochR/TCMA-27

Kucks, John
56T-88
57T-185
58T-87
59T-289
60L-96
60T-177
61T-94
62Kahn/Atl
62T-241
92Yank/WIZAS-38

Kuder, Jeff
89Augusta/ProC-491
89Welland/Pucko-16

Kuecker, Mark
77Cedar
79Phoenix

Kuehl, John
88Spokane/ProC-1934
89CharRain/ProC-986
89SALAS/GS-12
91ClBest/Singl-354
91MidwLAS/ProC-30
91Waterlo/ClBest-17
91Waterlo/ProC-1264
92ClBest-130
92HighD/ClBest-15

Kuehl, Karl
75IntAS/TCMA-25MG
76Expo/Redp-17MG
76SSPC-611MG
76T-216MG
79Twin/FriszP-13CO

Kuehne, William
N172
WG1-60

Kuenn, Harvey
53Tiger/Glen-18
54B-23
54RH
54T-25
54Wilson
55Armour-12A
55Armour-12B
55B-132
56T-155
57T-88
58T-304M
58T-434
59Armour-11
59Bz
59T-70
60Bz-34
60Kahn
60NuCard-59
60T-330
60T-429M
60T/tatt-27
61Bz-15
61NuCard-459
61P-57
61T-500
61T/St-77
62J-135
62P-135
62P/Can-135
62Salada-121
62Shirriff-121
62T-480
62T/St-197
62T/bucks
63Exh
63J-105
63P-105
63T-30
64T-242
65OPC-103
65T-103
66T-372
73OPC-646CO
73T-646CO
74T-99CO
75SSPC/42-41CO
78Newar
79TCMA-104
80Pac/Leg-66
81Tiger/Detroit-96
82D-578MG
83D-608MG
83Gard-1MG
83Kaline-15M
83Kaline-16M
83Pol/Brew-32MG
83T-726MG
84Nes/792-321MG
84T-321MG
84T/Gloss22-1MG
86Tiger/Sport-11
88Pac/Leg-56
89Swell-9
91Swell/Great-114
91T/Arc53-301
92Brew/Carlson-11MG
92Bz/Quadra-20M
94T/Arc54-25
Exh47

Kuhaulua, Fred
77SLCity
79Hawaii-20
80Hawaii-25
81Hawaii-17
82Hawaii-17
82T-731R

Kuhel, Joe
33G-108
34DS-78
34Exh/4-16
34G-16
35BU-128
35BU-80
35G-8H
35G-9H
37Exh/4-16
37OPC-127
38G-243
38G-267
40PlayBall-185
41PlayBall-31
45Playball-4
47TipTop
49Exh
61F-119
88Conlon/5-18
88Conlon/AmAS-18
91Conlon/Sport-188
R310
R313
R314
V300
V351-52
V355-63

Kuhlman, Eric
88Idaho/ProC-1851
89Idaho/ProC-2028

Kuhlmann, Hank
62Pep/Tul

Kuhn, Bowie
83Kaline-64COM

Kuhn, Chad
88Spokane/ProC-1935
89Watlo/ProC-1797
89Watlo/Star-16
90Madison/Best-17
90Madison/ProC-2263
91AA/LineD-287
91Huntsvl/ClBest-13
91Huntsvl/LineD-287
91Huntsvl/Team-12
91HuntsvlProC-1790
92Huntsvl/ProC-3944

Kuhn, Ken
55Salem
57T-266

Kuhn, Todd
85Fresno/Pol-21

Kuhn, Walter
(Red)
T207

Kuhualua, Fred
81Hawaii/TCMA-17

Kuilan, Jorge
88WinHaven/Star-11

Kuiper, Duane
76OPC-508
76SSPC-522
76T-508
77BurgChef-55
77OPC-233
77Pep-19
77T-85
78Ho-34
78OPC-39
78T-332
79Ho-13
79OPC-67
79T-146
80OPC-221
80T-429
81D-319
81OPC-226
81T-612
82D-198
82F-373
82OPC-233
82T-233
82T/Tr-60T
83F-263
83F/St-10M
83F/St-16M
83Mother/Giants-11
83T-767
84D-553
84F-375
84Nes/792-542
84OPC-338
84T-542
84T/St-169
85F-610
85T-22

Kuiper, Glen
85Spokane/Cram-10
86Erie-16

Kulakov, Vadim
89EastLDD/ProC-DD5

Kuld, Pete
88Watlo/ProC-682
89Miami/I/Star-22
90Huntsvl/Best-14
91AA/LineD-610
91Wichita/LineD-610
91Wichita/ProC-2602
91Wichita/Rock-12
92Tulsa/SB-610

Kume, Mike
52Park-100
57Seattle/Pop-23

Kummerfeldt, Jason
92Billings/ProC-3348
93FExcel/ML-23

Kunkel, Jeff
84Rang-20
85D-587
85F-561
85OKCty-3
85OPC-288
85T-136FS
85T-288
85T/St-350
86OKCty-9
87Mother/Rang-24
88OkCty/CMC-18
88OkCty/ProC-30
88S-407
89B-231
89D-496
89F-527
89Mother/R-19
89S-484
89Smok/R-18
89T-92
89UD-463
90D-496
90F-304
90F/Can-304
90Mother/Rang-18
90OPC-174
90PublInt/St-415
90S-431
90T-174
90T/St-246
90UD-394
91F-292
91Leaf/Stud-126
91OPC-562
91S-783
91StCl-580
91T-562
92Denver/ProC-2648
92Denver/SB-136
93Rang/Keeb-223

Kunkel, Kevin
86Cram/NWL-70
87Madis-19

Kunkel, William
(Bill)
61T-322
62T-147
63T-523
85T-136FS
92Yank/WIZ60-71

Kuntz, Lee
86Watlo-16TR
88Wmsprt/ProC-1303
90Canton/Best-3
90Canton/Star-21TR

Kuntz, Rusty
78Knoxvl
81D-282
81T-112R
82Edmon-20
82F-348
82T-237
84F-568
84F/X-U66
84Nes/792-598
84T-598
84T/Tr-66T
84Tiger/Wave-24
85D-516
85F-14
85T-73
85Wendy-13
90Mother/Mar-27M
92Mother/Mar-27M

Kuoda, Masa
89Salinas/Cal-134
89Salinas/ProC-1804

Kupsey, John
89Pulaski/ProC-1913
90Sumter/Best-10
90Sumter/ProC-2442
92Spartan/ClBest-11
92Spartan/ProC-1270

Kurczewski, Tommy
88Watlo/ProC-665
89BurlB/ProC-1603

Kurosaki, Ryan
77ArkTr
80ArkTr-13

Kurowski, George
(Whitey)
43Playball-26
47TipTop
48L-81
62Pep/Tul
92Card/McDon/Pac-8
Exh47

Kurpiel, Ed
70Tidew

Kurri, Jari
92StCl/MemberIII*-10

Kurtz, John
89GA-17CO
90GA-16CO

Kurys, Sophie
94TedW-97

Kush, Emil
47TipTop
49Eureka-59

Kusick, Craig
74Tacoma/Caruso-3
75OPC-297
75T-297
75T/M-297
77T-38
78T-137
78Twin/FriszP-11
79T-472
79Twin/FriszP-14
80Hawaii-7
80OPC-374
80T-693
81Evansvl-16

Kusnyer, Art
72OPC-213R
72T-213R
75IntLgAS/Broder-15
75PCL/AS-15
75Sacra/Caruso-10
77Spoka
79Iowa/Pol-10
89Mother/A's-27CO
90Mother/A's-27M
91Mother/A's-28CO
92Mother/A's-28M
93D-396M
93Mother/A's-27M

Kustus, Joe
90Target-1008

Kutcher, Randy
80Clinton-14
83Phoenix/BHN-15
84Cram/PCL-18
85Cram/PCL-177
86Phoenix-13
87D-547
87F-276
87Phoenix-12
88Pawtu/CMC-11
88Pawtu/ProC-464
89T/Tr-64T
90OPC-676
90PublInt/St-459
90S-551
90T-676
90T/TVRSox-31
91F-100
91S-837

Kutina, Joe
T207

Kutner, Mike
82Miami-20

Kutsukos, Pete
84Beaum-2
85Beaum-7

Kutyna, Marty
60T-516
61T-546
62T-566

Kutzler, Jerry

88Tampa/Star-12
89BirmB/Best-15
89BirmB/ProC-117
89SLAS-15
90Coke/WSox-14
90Coke/WSox-28
90D-503
90D/Rook-25
90S/Tr-80T
91AAA/LineD-639
91S-749RP
91T/90Debut-80
91Vanco/LineD-639
91Vanco/ProC-1592
Kuykendall, Kevin
87Watlo-12
Kuzava, Robert
(Bob)
50B-5
51B-97
51T/BB-22
52B-233
52BR
52T-85
53B/BW-33
54Esskay
54NYJour
54T-230
55B-215
55Esskay
91Crown/Orio-251
94T/Arc54-230
Kuzma, Greg
88Butte-3
Kuzniar, Paul
(Kooz)
87Watlo-19
88Wmsprt/ProC-1321
89Canton/Best-20
89Canton/ProC-1305
89Canton/Star-11
90NewBrit/Star-7
Kvansnicka, Jay
89Kenosha/ProC-1063
89Kenosha/Star-11
90Visalia/ProC-2168
91AA/LineD-483
91OrlanSR/LineD-483
91OrlanSR/ProC-1862
92OrlanSR/ProC-2859
92Portl/SB-412
92Portland/ProC-2679
Kwasny, Joe
75FtLaud/Sus-18
Kwolek, Chuck
79Ashvl/TCMA-24
Kwolek, Joe
86Osceola-16
Kyles, Stan
81QuadC-19
83MidldC-19
84Albany-15
85Cram/PCL-138
87Tacoma-3
88Albuq/CMC-2
88Albuq/ProC-275
91BendB/ClBest-3CO
91BendB/ProC-3712CO
92Geneva/ClBest-27CO
92Geneva/ProC-1577CO
Kyslinger, Dan
92FrRow/DP-95
92Helena/ProC-1712
Kyte, Frank
92BBCity/ClBest-27TR
LaBare, Jay
80Elmira-39
LaCasse, Michael
79Newar-10
LaCerra, Tony
88Reno/Cal-270
LaChance, George
(Candy)
90Target-424
E107
LaChance, Vincent
(Vince)
93James/ClBest-13
93James/ProC-3338
LaCock, R. Pete
73Wichita-5
74Wichita-124
75OPC-494
75T-494
75T/M-494
76OPC-101
76SSPC-317
76T-101
77T-561
78SSPC/270-223
78T-157
79T-248
80OPC-202
80T-389
81D-344
81F-47
81T-9
89Pac/SenLg-33
89T/SenLg-99
90EliteSenLg-98
91Pac/SenLg-120
91Pac/SenLg-53
LaCorte, Frank
76OPC-597R
76SSPC-612
76T-597R
78Richm
80T-411
81D-143
81F-55
81OPC-348
81T-513
82D-270
82F-220
82T-248
83D-218
83F-454
83T-14
84D-283
84F-230
84F/X-67
84Nes/792-301
84Smok/Cal-16
84T-301
84T/Tr-68T
85OPC-153
85T-153
LaCoss, Mike
77Indianap-11
78Indianap-4
79T-717R
80OPC-111
80T-199
81D-183
81OPC-134
81T-474
82D-440
82F-72
82T-294
82T/Tr-61T
83D-344
83F-455
83T-97
84D-370
84F-231
84Mother/Ast-24
84Nes/792-507
84T-507
85D-405
85F-353
85F/Up-U66
85T-666
85T/Tr-69T
86F/Up-U62
86Mother/Giants-17
86T-359
86T/Tr-57T
87D-636
87F-277
87Mother/SFG-21
87T-151
88D-436
88F-86
88Mother/Giants-21
88Panini/St-418
88S-465
88T-754
89D-602
89F/Up-129
89Mother/Giants-21
89RedFoley/St-70
89S-500
89T-417
89UD-48
90D-652
90F-59
90F/Can-59
90Leaf-463
90Mother/Giant-11
90OPC-53
90PublInt/St-73
90S-253
90T-53
90UD-140
91F-264
91Leaf-309
91Mother/Giant-11
91OPC-242
91PG&E-17
91S-652
91SFExam/Giant-9
91StCl-479
91T-242
91UD-691
LaFever, Greg
86Watlo-17
87Wmsprt-17
88SanAn/Best-4
LaFountain, James
77Visalia
LaFrancois, Roger
81Pawtu-23
83D-534
83Pawtu-12
83T-344
84Richm-14
85Durham-27
88James/ProC-1894
89SoBend/GS-4
90AAASingl/ProC-185CO
90ProC/Singl-671CO
90Vanco/CMC-27CO
90Vanco/ProC-507CO
91AAA/LineD-650M
91Vanco/LineD-650CO
91Vanco/ProC-1611
92Vanco/ProC-2735CO
92Vanco/SB-650CO
LaGrow, Lerrin
71OPC-39R
71T-39R
73OPC-369
73T-369
74OPC-433
74T-433
75OPC-116
75T-116
75T/M-116
76OPC-138
76SSPC-356
76T-138
78OPC-152
78SSPC/270-161
78T-14
79T-527
80T-624
90Target-426
LaHonta, Ken
76Dubuq
LaMar, Danny
82Cedar-12
83Tampa-16
84Cedar-18
LaMarche, Michel
87Spartan-10
LaMarque, Jim
92Negro/Retort-37
LaMaster, Wayne
90Target-428
LaMotta, Jake
47HomogBond-29BOX
D305
LaPalme, Paul
52T-166
53B/BW-19
53T-201
54B-107
54DanDee
55B-61
55Hunter
57T-344
91T/Arc53-201
LaPlante, Michel
92Welland/ClBest-15
92Welland/ProC-1318
LaPoint, Dave
77Newar
78BurlB
79Clinton/TCMA-19
80Vanco-7
83D-544
83F-14
83T-438
84D-290
84F-328
84Nes/792-627
84T-627
84T/St-146
85D-138
85F-233
85F/Up-U68
85Mother/Giants-16
85OPC-229
85T-229
85T/St-143
85T/Tr-71T
86Cain's-10
86D-387
86F-547
86F/Up-U64
86OPC-162
86T-551
86T/Tr-61T
87D-607
87F-421
87OPC-319
87T-754
88Coke/WS-13
88D-552
88D/Best-123
88F-402
88F/BB/AS-21
88F/Slug-24
88S-589
88T-334
89B-165
89D-488
89D/Best-244
89D/Tr-27
89F-212
89OPC-89
89S-384
89S/NWest-15
89S/Tr-4
89T-89
89T/Tr-67T
89UD-600
89UD/Ext-706
90D-72
90OPC-186
90PublInt/St-539
90S-357
90S/NWest-12
90T-186
90T/TVYank-11
90UD-507
91D-481
91F-669
91OPC-484
91S-218
91T-484
91UD-483
92Yank/WIZ80-102
LaPoint, J. Anthony
(Tony)
86Geneva-15
87CharWh-19
LaPorte, Frank
10Domino-66
11Helmar-62
12Sweet/Pin-53A
12Sweet/Pin-53B
14CJ-98
14Piedmont/St-48
15CJ-98
E254
M116
T201
T202
T205
T206
T213/brown
LaRoche, Dave
71OPC-174
71T-174
72OPC-352
72T-352
73OPC-426
73T-426
74OPC-502
74T-502
74Wichita-107
75OPC-258
75T-258
75T/M-258
76OPC-21
76SSPC-510
76T-21
77BurgChef-60
77OPC-61
77Pep-15
77T-385
78SSPC/270-197
78T-454
79OPC-317
79T-601
80T-263
81F-285
81T-529
81T/Tr-789
82D-569
82T-142
83F-384
83OPC-333
83OPC-334SV
83T-333
83T-334SV
85Albany-24
86Colum-13CO
87Syrac-19
87Syrac/TCMA-24
89Pac/SenLg-97
89T/SenLg-89
89TM/SenLg-65
90Coke/WSox-30CO
90Swell/Great-108
91Kodak/WSox-x
92Mets/Kahn-28CO
LaRocque, Gary
76BurlB
77Holyo
88Bakers/Cal-262CO
LaRosa, Bill
78Ashvl
LaRosa, Mark
88CapeCod/Sum-77
91James/ClBest-15
91James/ProC-3541
91LSU/Pol-9
92Albany/ClBest-9
92Albany/ProC-2300
93WPalmB/ClBest-11
93WPalmB/ProC-1334
94FExcel-227
LaRose, Vic
69T-404
LaRussa, Tony
64T-244
68T-571
72OPC-451
72T-451
73Wichita-6
78Knoxvl
78TCMA-229
79Iowa/Pol-1MG
81D-402MG
81F-344MG
82D-319MG
83D-571MG
83T-216MG
83TrueVal/WSox-10MG
84F/St-126MG
84Nes/792-591MG
84T-591MG
84TruVl/WS-20MG
85Coke/WS-10MG
85T-466MG
86Coke/WS-MG
86T-531MG
87T-68MG
88Mother/A's-1MG
88T-344
89Mother/A's-1MG
89Pac/Leg-140
89T-224MG
89T/LJN-36
90KMart/SS-33MG
90Mother/A's-1MG
90OPC-639MG
90Pac/Legend-90
90T-639MG
90T/Gloss22-12MG
90T/TVAS-33MG M
91Leaf/Stud-263MG
91Mother/A's-1MG
91OPC-171MG
91T-171MG
92Mother/A's-1MG
92OPC-429MG
92T-429MG

92T/Gold-429MG
92T/GoldWin-429MG
93Mother/A's-1MG
93T-511MG
93T/Gold-511MG
LaValley, Todd
92Yakima/ClBest-17
92Yakima/ProC-3444
LaValliere, Mike
83Reading-12
85Louisvl-22
86D/Rook-35
86F/Up-U65
86Schnucks-14
87D-331
87F-302
87F/Up-U60
87T-162
87T/Tr-61T
87ToysRUs-19
88D-312
88D/Best-129
88F-333
88F/Slug-25
88Leaf-112
88OPC-57
88Panini/St-369
88S-421
88Sf-193
88T-539
88T/Big-61
88T/St-131
89B-417
89D-244
89D/Best-201
89F-213
89KennerFig-82
89OPC-218
89Panini/St-168
89RedFoley/St-74
89S-33
89Sf-98
89T-218
89T/Big-306
89T/LJN-12MG M
89T/St-128
89T/St/Backs-56
89UD-417
89VFJuice-12
90B-172
90Classic-42
90D-211
90D/BestNL-107
90D/Learning-43
90F-473
90F/Can-473
90Homer/Pirate-18
90Leaf-32
90OPC-478
90Panini/St-333
90PublInt/St-158
90S-116
90Sf-157
90T-478
90T/Big-104
90T/St-133
90T/TVAS-57
90UD-578
91B-514
91D-121
91F-42
91Leaf-15
91Leaf/Stud-226
91OPC-665
91Panini/FrSt-114
91S-222
91StCl-279
91T-665
91UD-129
91Ultra-282
92B-245
92D-121
92F-558
92F/ASIns-5
92L-228
92L/BlkGold-228
92OPC-312
92Panini-251
92Pinn-146
92Pirate/Nation-10
92S-38
92StCl-216
92StCl/Dome-103
92Studio-85
92T-312
92T/Gold-312
92T/GoldWin-312
92TripleP-232
92UD-113
92Ultra-254
93D-306
93F-114
93F/Final-196
93L-510
93OPC-145
93Pac/Spanish-246
93Panini-280
93Pinn-219
93S-83
93Select-203
93StCl-496
93StCl/1stDay-496
93T-54
93T/Gold-54
93TripleP-110
93UD-120
93Ultra-98
93WSox-17
94D-201
94F-87
94Pac/Cr-131
94S-181
94S/GoldR-181
94StCl-118
94StCl/1stDay-118
94StCl/Gold-118
94StCl/Team-124
94T-147
94T/Gold-147
LaVigne, Randy
82Iowa-6
83MidldC-24
Laabs, Chester
(Chet)
40PlayBall-206
43Playball-16
94Conlon-1278
V362-31
W753
Laake, Pete
91Gaston/ProC-2694
Labay, Steve
86Reading-13
Labine, Clem
52T-342
53T-14
54B-106
54NYJour
54T-121
55Gol/Dodg-17
55T-180
56T-295
57T-53
58Hires-34
58T-305
59Morrell
59T-262M
59T-403
60BB-6
60L-60
60T-29
61T-22
79TCMA-31
81TCMA-482M
89Rini/Dodg-19
89Smok/Dodg-61
90Pac/Legend-89
90Target-423
91Swell/Great-54
91T/Arc53-14
91WIZMets-222
92AP/ASG-59
94T/Arc54-121
Labossiere, Dave
80Tucson-12
81Tucson-14
82Tucson-27
83Tucson-25
90Mother/Ast-28TR
92Mother/Ast-28M
Laboy, Carlos
87AubAs-14
88Ashvl/ProC-1056
89Osceola/Star-10
91PalmSp/ProC-2029
92Salinas/ClBest-22
92Salinas/ProC-3769
Laboy, Jose A.
(Coco)
66Pep/Tul
69Expos/Pins-4
69Fud's-6
69T-524R
70Expo/PostC-8
70Expos/Pins-9
70K-66
70MLB/St-67
70OPC-238
70T-238
71Expo/ProS-12
71LaPizza-5
71MLB/St-132
71OPC-132
71T-132
72Dimanche*-24
72MB-190
72T-727
73OPC-642
73T-642
87FtLaud-20
88PrWill/Star-14
92Nabisco-9
Labozzetta, Al
86GlenF-11
Lacer, Mike
86Pittsfld-12TR
Lacey, Kerry
91Butte/SportP-14
Lacey, Robert
76Tucson-19
77SanJose-14
78T-29
79T-647
80OPC-167
80T-316
81D-240
81F-578
81T-481
81T/Tr-784
82T-103
85Cram/PCL-191
85F-611
93Rang/Keeb-224
Lach, Elmer
45Parade*-49M
Lachemann, Bill
83Clinton/Frit-29
86QuadC-18MG
87PalmSp-17
88CalLgAS-35
88PalmSp/Cal-112
88PalmSp/ProC-1436
89PalmSp/Cal-63MG
89PalmSp/ProC-489
Lachemann, Bret
91QuadC/ClBest-6
91QuadC/ProC-2623
Lachemann, Marcel
71MLB/St-518
71OPC-84
71T-84
75WPalmB/Sussman-11CO
82Danvl/Frit-14CO
93Marlin/Publix-28CO
Lachemann, Rene
65T-526R
66OPC-157
66T-157
67CokeCap/A's-10
67T-471
68T-422
77SanJose-2MG
78SanJose-2MG
79Spokane-16MG
80Spokane-18MG
81Spokane-13MG
82D-600MG
83T-336MG
84F-655M
84Gard-1MG
84Pol/Brew-9MG
84T/Tr-67T
85T-628MG
88Chatt/Team-19
88Mother/A's-27CO
89Mother/A's-27CO
90Mother/A's-27M
91Mother/A's-28CO
92Mother/A's-28M
93Marlin/Publix-15MG
93T-505M
93T/Gold-505M
Lachmann, Tom
88OK-22
89BurlInd/Star-14
Lachowetz, Anthony J.
81VeroB-8
82VeroB-23
Lachowicz, Al
82Tulsa-7
84OKCty-1
85Tulsa-36
93Rang/Keeb-225
Lackey, John
83LynnP-4
Lackey, Stephen
92GulfCM/ProC-3491
92LitSun/HSPros-23
Lacko, Rich
87Lakeland-14
88GlenF/ProC-920
Lacks, Charles K.
55Gol/Braves-17
Lacy, Kerry
92Gaston/ClBest-15
92Gaston/ProC-2250
94B-241
94ClBest/Gold-31
94FExcel-135
Lacy, Lee
73OPC-391
73T-391
74OPC-658
74T-658
75OPC-631
75T-631
75T/M-631
76OPC-99
76SSPC-78
76T-99
76T/Tr-99T
77T-272
78SSPC/270-69
78T-104
79OPC-229
79T-441
80T-536
81D-376
81F-374
81T-332
82D-276
82F-483
82F/St-80
82T-752
83D-276
83F-308
83F/St-16M
83F/St-2M
83OPC-69
83T-69
84D-479
84F-252
84Nes/792-462
84OPC-229
84T-462
84T/St-138
85D-508
85F-467
85F/St-9
85F/Up-U67
85Leaf-40
85T-669
85T/St-126
85T/Tr-70T
86D-228
86F-277
86Leaf-104
86OPC-226
86Sf-87
86T-226
86T/St-229
87D-336
87F-473
87French-27
87OPC-182
87Sf-86
87Sf/TPrev-21M
87T-182
87T/St-231
88F-565
88S-173
88T-598
89Pac/SenLg-184
89T/SenLg-72
89TM/SenLg-61
90EliteSenLg-25
90Swell/Great-94
90Target-425
91Crown/Orio-252
Lacy, Steve
76Watlo
77DaytB
Ladd, Jeff
92StCath/ClBest-18
92StCath/ProC-3389
93Hagers/ClBest-16
93Hagers/ProC-1882
Ladd, Pete
80T-678R
81Tucson-19
82Vanco-17
83F-37
83Pol/Brew-27
84D-124
84F-204
84F/St-77
84Gard-10
84Nes/792-243
84Pol/Brew-27
84T-243
85D-271
85F-585
85Gard-10
85Pol/Brew-27
85T-471
86F-492
86F/Up-U63
86Mother/Mar-17
86T-163
86T/Tr-58T
87Albuq/Pol-12
87D-660
87F-588
87T-572
92Brew/Carlson-12
Lade, Doyle
49B-168
49Eureka-60
50B-196
51B-139
Ladell, Cleveland
92Princet/ClBest-4
92Princet/ProC-3098
94B-46
94FExcel-177
Ladnier, Deric
86FtMyr-17
87AppFx-8
89Memphis/Best-11
89Memphis/ProC-1189
89Memphis/Star-13
89Star/Wax-43
91AA/LineD-409
91Memphis/LineD-409
91Memphis/ProC-662
Lafata, Joe
49Eureka-115
Lafitte, Edward
(Doc)
E254
E270/2
Lafitte, James A.
T206
Lafleur, Guy
72Dimanche*-77IA
72Dimanche*-78
Laforce, Ernest
45Parade*-29
Laga, Mike
82Evansvl-16
83Evansvl-15
84D-491
84Evansvl-16
86D-578
86T/Tr-59T
87D-293
87Louisvl-23
87Smok/Cards-15
87T-321
88Louisvl-26
89Phoenix/CMC-17
89Phoenix/ProC-1493
89S-536
90BirmDG/Best-20
90Phoenix/CMC-21
90ProC/Singl-548
Lague, Raymond
52Laval-14
Lahoud, Joe

69OPC-189R
69T-189R
69T/4in1-14M
70OPC-78
70T-78
71MLB/St-321
71OPC-622
71T-622
72MB-191
72OPC-321
72T-321
72T/Cloth-19
73OPC-212
73T-212
74OPC-512
74T-512
75Ho-10
75Ho/Twink-10
75OPC-317
75T-317
75T/M-317
76OPC-612
76SSPC-20
76T-612
78SSPC/270-226
78T-382
93Rang/Keeb-226

Lahrman, Tom
86Penin-15
87Penin-22
88Tampa/Star-13

Lahti, Jeffrey Allen
80Water-2
81Indianap-16
82Louisvl-13
83F-12
83T-284
84D-327
84F-327
84Nes/792-593
84T-593
85F-231
85T-447
86D-475
86F-40
86KAS/Disc-18
86Leaf-233
86Schnucks-12
86Seven/Coin-S12
86T-33
87D-577
87F-299
87T-367

Lain, Marty
83Beaum-9

Laird, Tony
85Nashua-13
86Nashua-14

Lairsey, Eric
91Pulaski/ClBest-24
91Pulaski/ProC-4001
92Idaho/ProC-3507

Lajeskie, Dick
48Sommer-22
49B/PCL-16
49Sommer-12

Lajoie, Napoleon
(Nap)
10Domino-65
11Diamond-17
11Helmar-24
12Sweet/Pin-18
14CJ-66
15CJ-66
33G-106
40PlayBall-173
48Exh/HDF
50Callahan
50W576-47
60F-1
61F-120
61GP-31
63Bz/ATG-8
69Bz/Sm
72F/FFeat-28
73F/Wild-35M
75F/Pion-18
76Motor-2
76Shakey-6
77Galasso-137
77Galasso-260
77Shakey-15
80Laugh/3/4/5-9
80Pac/Leg-74
80Perez/HOF-8
80SSPC/HOF
82Ohio/HOF-26
89HOF/St-10
92Conlon/Sport-528
93Conlon-837
93Conlon/MasterCol-2
93CrackJack-8
94Conlon-1218
BF2-35
D303
D304
D329-97
E101
E102
E103
E105
E106
E107
E254
E270/2
E300
E90/1
E92
E93
E94
E96
E98
L1-121
M101/4-97
M116
PM1-10
S81-96
T201
T206
T213/blue
T214-17
T215/blue
T215/brown
T216
T3-23
W514-62
W555
WG2-32
WG4-12
WG5-25
WG6-24

Lajszky, Werner
80Wausau-21

Lak, Carlos
91Clinton/ProC-842

Lake, Dan
85Anchora-18

Lake, Edward
45Playball-19
47TipTop
49B-107
50B-240
51B-140
Exh47

Lake, Fred
M116

Lake, Joe
11Helmar-61
E94
M116
T201
T206
T215/blue
W555

Lake, Ken
89James/ProC-2148
89Miami/I/Star-10
90WPalmB/Star-12
91AA/LineD-260
91Harris/LineD-260
91Harris/ProC-643

Lake, Mike
77LodiD
78LodiD

Lake, Steve
80Holyo-17
81Vanco-25
82Tucson-5
83Thorn-16
84D-198
84Nes/792-691
84T-691
85SevenUp-16
85T-98
86Gator-29
86T-588
87D-604
87F-300
87Smok/Cards-10
87T-84
88D-510
88F-38
88S-596
88Smok/Card-11
88T-208
89B-399
89F-454
89Phill/TastyK-17
89S-363
89S/Tr-12
89T-463
89T/Tr-65T
90D-431
90F-566
90F/Can-566
90Leaf-395
90OPC-183
90Phill/TastyK-19
90PublInt/St-245
90S-435
90T-183
90T/Big-191
90UD-491
91D-334
91F-403
91Leaf-385
91Leaf/Stud-216
91OPC-661
91Phill/Medford-23
91S-572
91StCl-395
91T-661
92OPC-331
92Phill/Med-18
92S-467
92StCl-54
92T-331
92T/Gold-331
92T/GoldWin-331
93Cub/Mara-12
93S-443
93StCl/Cub-10
94F-388

Lakeman, Al
49Eureka-14

Laker, Tim
88James/ProC-1904
89James/ProC-2137
90MidwLgAS/GS-13
90Rockford/ProC-2696
90Rockford/Team-14
91ClBest/Singl-205
91WPalmB/ClBest-16
91WPalmB/ProC-1232
92ClBest-125
92Harris/ProC-463
92Harris/SB-286
92Sky/AASingl-121
93B-156
93D-440RR
93F-77
93L-367
93OPC-276
93OPC/Premier-120
93Pac/Spanish-534
93Pinn-583
93StCl-18
93StCl/1stDay-18
93T-816
93T/Gold-816
93ToysRUs-7
93Ultra-416
94Pinn-465
94T-524
94T/Gold-524

Lamabe, Jack
62T-593R
63T-251
64T-305
65OPC-88
65T-88
66T-577
67T-208
68T-311
85Beaum-24C
91WIZMets-223
92CharRain/ClBest-23CO
92CharRain/ProC-136

Lamanno, Ray
49B-113

Lamanske, Frank
90Target-1009

Lamar, Bill
90Target-427
93Conlon-852

Lamar, Johnny
92Bristol/ClBest-24
92Bristol/ProC-1425

Lamb, David
94B-36

Lamb, Marty
92MissSt-49M

Lamb, Randy
77Cocoa
78Wausau

Lamb, Ray
70OPC-131R
70T-131R
71MLB/St-377
71OPC-727
71T-727
72OPC-422
72T-422
73OPC-496
73T-496
85SpokAT/Cram-11
90Target-429

Lamb, Todd
84Durham-19
85Greenvl/Team-11
86Durham-17

Lambert, Gene
82Clinton/Frit-17
83Clinton/Frit-10

Lambert, Ken
87VeroB-10

Lambert, Layne
90AubAs/ProC-3396
91BurlAs/ClBest-16
91BurlAs/ProC-2810
92Osceola/ClBest-15

Lambert, Mark
90LitSun/HSPros-17
90LitSun/HSProsG-17

Lambert, Reese
87Madis-23
88Tacoma/CMC-4
88Tacoma/ProC-631
89Tacoma/CMC-3
89Tacoma/ProC-1548
90AAASingl/ProC-134
90ProC/Singl-585
90Tacoma/CMC-8
90Tacoma/ProC-87
92Omaha/ProC-2957
92Omaha/SB-333

Lambert, Reggie
86PalmSp-20
86PalmSp/Smok-27
87PalmSp-5
88PalmSp/Cal-113
88PalmSp/ProC-1461

Lambert, Rob
87PrWill-25
88Colum/CMC-14
88Colum/ProC-319

Lambert, Tim
82Idaho-10
84Albany-17
85Cram/PCL-140
86Tacoma-11
87Memphis-13
87Memphis/Best-16
90AlbanyDG/Best-24

Lambert, Yvon
72Dimanche*-79

Lamle, Adam
88CharlR/Star-12
88FSLAS/Star-41
89Miami/II/Star-10
89Tulsa/GS-12

Lammon, John
90Elmira/Pucko-14
91Elmira/ClBest-7
91Elmira/ProC-3272

Lamonde, Larry
82AlexD-3
84Cram/PCL-124
85Nashua-14

Lamont, Gene
71OPC-39R
71T-39R
75OPC-593
75T-593
75T/M-593
84Omaha-2
85Omaha-22MG
89VFJuice-36CO
90Homer/Pirate-16CO
92T/Tr-62T
92T/TrGold-62T
92WSox-33MG
92WSox-NNO
93T-504MG
93T/Gold-504MG
93WSox-16MG
93WSox-30M

Lamoureux, Leo
45Parade*-30

Lamp, Dennis
78SSPC/270-260
78T-711R
79T-153
80OPC-129
80T-54
81D-573
81F-305
81T-331
81T/Tr-785
82D-619
82F-349
82T-216TL
82T-622
83D-165
83F-243
83OPC-26
83T-434
83TrueVal/WSox-53
84D-526
84F-66
84F/X-U68
84Nes/792-541
84T-541
84T/St-239
84T/Tr-69T
84Tor/Fire-21
85D-119
85F-111
85OPC-83
85T-774
85Tor/Fire-17
86BJ/Ault-17
86D-626
86F-64
86Leaf-244
86OPC-219
86T-219
86T/St-193
86T/Tatt-12M
86Tor/Fire-21
87F-233
87OPC-336
87T-768
88D/RedSox/Bk-NEW
88F-284
88S-616
88S/Tr-6T
89D-633
89F-92
89S-508
89T-188
89T/Big-169
89UD-503
90D-423
90F-280
90F/Can-280
90Leaf-315
90OPC-338
90Pep/RSox-12
90PublInt/St-460
90S-471
90T-338
90T/TVRSox-13
91D-138
91F-101
91OPC-14
91Pep/RSox-11
91S-612
91T-14
92F-42
92OPC-653
92S-335
92T-653
92T/Gold-653
92T/GoldWin-653
92USPlayC/RedSox-4H
92USPlayC/RedSox-7S

Lampard, C. Keith
(Keith)
70OPC-492R

70T-492R
71OPC-728R
71T-728R
72OPC-489R
72T-489R
Lampe, Ed
88Hamil/ProC-1742
Lampert, Ken
86VeroB-15
Lamphere, Lawrence
(Larry)
87PanAm/USAB-11
87PanAm/USAR-11
88AubAs/ProC-1947
89Ashvl/ProC-967
89SALAS/GS-4
90Osceola/Star-14
90TeamUSA/87-11
Lampkin, Tom
87Watlo-23
88BBAmer-7
88EastLAS/ProC-41
88Wmsprt/ProC-1304
89AAA/ProC-35
89ColoSp/ProC-254
89D-639
90AAASingl/ProC-220
90ColoSp/CMC-12
90ColoSp/ProC-39
90OPC-172
90ProC/Singl-464
90T-172
91Leaf-512
91Padre/MagRal-4
91S-720RP
91S/100RisSt-70
91StCl-530
92F-610
92LasVegas/SB-234
92Pol/Padre-12
92S-338
92Smok/Padre-15
92StCl-453
93D-654
93F/Final-226
93T-492
93T/Gold-492
94StCl-147
94StCl/1stDay-147
94StCl/Gold-147
94T-558
94T/Gold-558
Lamplugh, Ian
92AS/Cal-26
Lamson, Chuck
78Ashvl
80Tulsa-20
Lancaster, Lester
(Les)
86WinSalem-12
87D/Rook-10
88Berg/Cubs-50
88D-561
88D/Best-172
88D/Cubs/Bk-561
88F-421
88S-602
88T-112
89D-341
89F-429
89Iowa/CMC-8
89Iowa/ProC-1689
89Mara/Cubs-50
89S-60
89T-694
89UD-84
90Cub/Mara-11
90D-628
90D/BestNL-38
90F-35
90F/Can-35
90Leaf-361
90OPC-437
90S-413
90T-437
90T/TVCub-11
90UD-584
91Cub/Mara-50
91Cub/Vine-16
91D-256
91F-424
91OPC-86
91S-293A
91S-293B
91T-86
91Ultra-63
92D-296
92F-384
92L-402
92L/BlkGold-402
92OPC-213
92S-348
92StCl-88
92T-213
92T/Gold-213
92T/GoldWin-213
92UD-481
92USPlayC/Cub-12D
92USPlayC/Cub-5S
92Ultra-177
93F/Final-126
93Pac/Spanish-111
93StCl/Card-26
94F-635
94Pac/Cr-594
94S-269
94S/GoldR-269
94StCl/Team-330
Lance, Gary
75Omaha/Team-8
79Spokane-11
83Idaho-32
84Madis/Pol-2
85Huntsvl/BK-24
87CharRain-9
88Charl/ProC-1212
89AubAs/ProC-28
89Wichita/Rock-38CO
90AAASingl/ProC-26CO
90LasVegas/CMC-23CO
90LasVegas/ProC-138CO
90Martins/ProC-3191CO
90ProC/Singl-526CO
91Pac/SenLg-62
91Sumter/ClBest-27CO
91Sumter/ProC-2352CO
92Albany/ClBest-29CO
92Albany/ProC-2322CO
Lance, Mark
83Durham-19
84Durham-2
Lancellotti, Rick
78Salem
79BuffB/TCMA-3
80Port-20
81Hawaii-11
81Hawaii/TCMA-9
82Hawaii-11
84Cram/PCL-230
85Tidew-1
86Phoenix-14
89Pawtu/Dunkin-29
90AAASingl/ProC-444
90Pawtu/CMC-19
90Pawtu/ProC-472
90ProC/Singl-270
90T/TVRSox-48
91AAA/LineD-358
91Pac/SenLg-122
91Pawtu/LineD-358
91Pawtu/ProC-47
Land, David
93MissSt-48M
Landaker, Dave
92Classic/DP-26
92FrRow/DP-94
92LitSun/HSPros-19
93T-743
93T/Gold-743
Landers, Hank
83Beloit/Frit-7
Landers, Lee
78Spring/Wiener-12TR
Landestoy, Rafael
75Water
78Cr/PCL-6
78SSPC/270-74
79T-14
80T-268
81Coke
81D-19
81F-70
81OPC-326
81T-597
81T/St-168
81T/Tr-786
82Coke/Reds
82F-73
82T-361
83F-595
83T-684
83T/Tr-59
84Nes/792-477
84Pol/Dodg-17
84T-477
85Albany-17
85Cram/PCL-61
87Pocatel/Bon-2MG
89Pac/SenLg-60
89T/SenLg-5
89TM/SenLg-62
90EliteSenLg-85
90Target-430
91Pac/SenLg-24
Landinez, Carlos
90Spring/Best-12
91Savan/ClBest-18
91Savan/ProC-1659
92StPete/ProC-2035
Landis, Craig
78Cedar
81Richm-5
Landis, Jim
57T-375
58T-108
59T-493
60MacGregor-11
60T-550
61P-27
61T-271
61T/St-122
62Bz
62Exh
62P-50
62P/Can-50
62Salada-49
62Shirriff-49
62T-50
62T-540
62T/St-26
62T/bucks
63Exh
63F-10
63J-40
63P-40
63Salada-60
63T-485
64T-264
65T-376
66OPC-128
66T-128
67T-483
68CokeCap/Astro-17
89Kodak/WSox-4M
Exh47
Landis, Kenesaw M.
(Judge)
50Callahan
50W576-48
60F-64
61F-53
63Bz-30
76Shakey-28COMM
77Galasso-123COMM
80Perez/HOF-28
80SSPC/HOF
82Ohio/HOF-49
88Pac/8Men-66
88Pac/8Men-67
88Pac/8Men-79
89HOF/St-95
92Mega/Ruth-159M
Landis, William
68OPC-189
68T-189
69T-264
72MB-192
Landmark, Neil
85Visalia-20
Landphere, Ed
90Salinas/Cal-130
90Salinas/ProC-2728
Landreaux, Ken
78SSPC/270-190
79T-619
79Twin/FriszP-15
80OPC-49
80T-88
81D-565
81F-553
81F/St-46
81K-30
81OPC-219
81Pol/Dodg-44B
81T-219
81T/SO-41
81T/St-101
81T/Tr-787
82D-388
82F-11
82OPC-114
82Pol/Dodg-44
82T-114
82T/St-49
82T/StVar-49
83D-236
83F-210
83F/St-15M
83F/St-21M
83OPC/St-246
83Pol/Dodg-44
83T-376
83T/St-246
84D-470
84F-104
84F/St-2
84Nes/792-533
84OPC-216
84Pol/Dodg-44
84Smok/Dodg-1
84T-533
84T/St-76
85Coke/Dodg-17
85D-494
85F-375
85T-418
85T/St-75
86Coke/Dodg-15
86D-470
86F-134
86OPC-2
86Pol/Dodg-44
86T-782
87D-352
87D/OD-81
87F-444
87Mother/Dodg-24
87OPC-123
87Pol/Dodg-23
87T-699
88RochR/Gov-14
88S-247
88T-23
89T/SenLg-109
89TM/SenLg-63
90ElPasoATG/Team-41
90EliteSenLg-9
90Target-431
91Pac/SenLg-134
Landress, Roger
91Eugene/ClBest-24
91Eugene/ProC-3722
92AppFox/ClBest-5
92BBCity/ProC-3842
Landreth, Harry
83Chatt-25
84Chatt-15
Landreth, Larry
78T-701R
Landrith, Dave
83Butte-13
Landrith, Hobie
54B-220
55B-50
56T-314
57T-182
58T-24
59T-422
60T-42
61P-150
61T-114
61T/St-78
62Salada-181
62Shirriff-181
62T-279
62T/St-157
63T-209
81TCMA-344
91Crown/Orio-253
91WIZMets-224
Landrum
46Sunbeam
Landrum, Bill
82Water-1
83Water-5
84Wichita/Rock-17
87Kahn-43
88F-238
88Iowa/CMC-8
88Iowa/ProC-541
88T-42
89BuffB/CMC-2
89BuffB/ProC-1674
89F/Up-U116
89VFJuice-43
90B-166
90D-668
90D/BestNL-58
90F-472
90F/Can-472
90Homer/Pirate-17
90Leaf-222
90OPC-425
90Panini/St-326
90PublInt/St-157
90S-456
90T-425
90T/Big-164
90T/St-128
90UD-442
91B-523
91D-350
91F-41
91Leaf/Stud-225
91OPC-595
91S-98
91StCl-431
91T-595
91UD-614
91Ultra-281
92D-221
92Expo/D/Duri-17
92F-557
92L-333
92L/BlkGold-333
92OPC-661
92OPC/Premier-68
92Pinn-116
92S-196
92StCl-672
92T-661
92T/Gold-661
92T/GoldWin-661
92TripleP-248
92UD-636
93Reds/Kahn-12
94F-413
Landrum, Cedric
(Ced)
86Geneva-13
87WinSalem-4
88Pittsfld/ProC-1370
89CharlK-4
90AAASingl/ProC-637
90Iowa/CMC-19
90Iowa/ProC-330
90ProC/Singl-94
90T/TVCub-51
91AAA/LineD-208
91Classic/III-49
91D/Rook-11
91Iowa/LineD-208
91Iowa/ProC-1075
92D-662
92F-385
92Iowa/SB-211
92OPC-81
92S-418
92S/100RisSt-30
92StCl-334
92T-81
92T/91Debut-106
92T/Gold-81
92T/GoldWin-81
92UD-50
92USPlayC/Cub-3D
92USPlayC/Cub-5D
94Pac/Cr-409
Landrum, Darryl
86Ventura-11
87Dunedin-11
88Wmsprt/ProC-1319
Landrum, Don
58T-291
61T-338
62T-323
63T-113
64T-286
65T-596
66OPC-43

66T-43
66T/RO-50
66T/RO-99
Landrum, Terry
(Tito)
76ArkTr
77ArkTr
78StPete
79ArkTr-4
81F-539
81Louisvl-12
81T-244R
82D-292
82F-118
82T-658
83D-498
83F-13
83Louisvl/Riley-12
83T-337
84F/X-69
84T/St-14LCS
85D-168
85F-232
85OPC-33
85T-33
86D-425
86F-41
86KAS/Disc-3
86OPC-171
86Schnucks-13
86T-498
86T/St-19WS
86T/Tatt-15M
87D-386
87D/OD-66
87F-301
87OPC-288
87Smok/Cards-23
87T-288
88Pol/Dodg-21M
88RochR/CMC-22
88T-581
89Nashvl/Team-11
89Pac/SenLg-168
89T/SenLg-94
89TM/SenLg-64
90EliteSenLg-26
90Miami/I/Star-15
90Target-432
91Crown/Orio-254
91GreatF/SportP-28
91Pac/SenLg-149
92Yakima/ClBest-11
92Yakima/ProC-3462
Landry, Greg
89Beloit/I/Star-13
89Helena/SP-10
90Beloit/Best-9
Landry, Howard
89WinHaven/Star-11
90LynchRS/Team-19
Landuyt, Doug
78Cedar
81Shrev-14TR
83Phoenix/BHN-25TR
Landy, Brian
88Billings/ProC-1820
89Greens/ProC-412
Landy, Ron
89GA-18ACO
Lane, Andy
89KS*-13M
Lane, Brian
88Greens/ProC-1555
88SALAS/GS-7
89BBAmAA/BPro-AA16
89Chatt/Best-4
89Chatt/GS-14
90AAASingl/ProC-551
90B-48
90Nashvl/CMC-20
90Nashvl/ProC-239
90ProC/Singl-145
92Chatt/SB-189
92ClBest-87
92Nashvl/ProC-1839
92Sky/AASingl-84
Lane, Danny
92James/ClBest-14
92James/ProC-1507
Lane, Gene
82Durham-24
90BurlB/Best-29TR
90BurlB/Star-31TR
Lane, Heath
87AZ/Pol-9
88AZ/Pol-8
89Beloit/I/Star-14
90River/Best-26
90River/Cal-19
90River/ProC-2604
Lane, Ira
82DayBe-14
Lane, Jerald H.
(Jerry)
54T-97
94T/Arc54-97
Lane, Jerry
81ElPaso-7
Lane, Kevin
91BurlAs/ClBest-6
91BurlAs/ProC-2797
92Osceola/ClBest-25
92Osceola/ProC-2528
Lane, Marvin
77Evansvl/TCMA-17
Lane, Nolan
88CapeCod/Sum-46
89Burllnd/Star-15
89Star/IISingl-179
90CLAS/CL-42
90Kinston/Team-10
91AA/LineD-87
91Canton/LineD-87
91Canton/ProC-990
92Canton/SB-111
92Miracle/ClBest-20
92Sky/AASingl-52
Lane, Scott
88Rockford-19AGM
89Rockford-19AGM
Lane, William C.
52Park-50
Lanfair, Dave
75Water
Lanfranco, Luis
90SoOreg/Best-6
90SoOreg/ProC-3432
91Madison/ClBest-23
91Madison/ProC-2139
Lanfranco, Raphael
90Ashvl/ClBest-19
91Ashvl/ProC-571
92BurlAs/ClBest-8
92BurlAs/ProC-550
Lang, Perry
88Pac/8Men-15
Lang, Robert
(Chip)
76Expo/Redp-18
77OPC-216
77T-132
Langbehn, Gregg
89Pittsfld/Star-14
90Clmbia/PCPII-7
90Columbia/GS-16
91StLucie/ClBest-20
91StLucie/ProC-705
92Bingham/ProC-512
92Bingham/SB-64
92Sky/AASingl-29
Langdon, Ted
83Tampa-17
84Cedar-2
86Tampa-9
87Vermont-3
Langdon, Tim
91Kinston/ClBest-4
91Kinston/ProC-316
Lange, Clark
85Osceola/Team-19
87Visalia-26
Lange, Frank H.
E254
T205
T207
Lange, Fred
N172
Lange, Richard
74OPC-429
74T-429
75OPC-114
75T-114
75T/M-114
76OPC-176
76T-176
77SLCity
Langfield, Paul
80Utica-28
Langford, Rick
75Shrev/TCMA-8
78Ho-120
78OPC-33
78T-327
79T-29
80OPC-284
80T-546
81A's/Granny-22
81D-238
81F-572
81F/St-27
81K-55
81OPC-154
81T-154
81T/St-121
82D-161
82F-98
82F/St-126
82Granny-7
82OPC-43
82T-454
83D-365
83F-523
83F/St-17M
83Granny-22
83OPC/St-106
83T-286
83T-531TL
83T/St-106
84F-451
84Nes/792-629
84OPC-304
84T-629
85T-347
85ThomMc/Discs-14
86F-425
86Mother/A's-14
86T-766
88Colum/CMC-10
88Colum/Pol-5
88Colum/ProC-308
91Billing/SportP-19
91Billings/ProC-3749
91Cedar/ClBest-7
91Cedar/ProC-2715
91ClBest/Singl-347
92Billings/ProC-3349
92CharWh/ClBest-9
92CharWh/ProC-5
Langford, Sam
T3/Box-65
Langiotti, Fred
89Spring/Best-24
90Spring/Best-13
91StPete/ClBest-16
91StPete/ProC-2279
Langley, Lee
87VeroB-28
88Bakers/Cal-256
89Clearw/Star-13
90Clearw/Star-10
91Miami/ClBest-14
91Miami/ProC-404
92Clearw/ClBest-11
92Clearw/ProC-2054
Langowski, Ted
91MedHat/ProC-4107
Langston, Bruce
90MissSt-44M
Langston, Keith
88CapeCod/Sum-109
89Niagara/Pucko-14
Langston, Mark
83Chatt-11
84F/X-U70
84Mother/Mar-13
84T/Tr-70T
85D-557
85Drake-38
85F-492
85F/LimEd-17
85F/St-109
85FunFoodPin-18
85Leaf-56
85Mother/Mar-3
85OPC-259
85T-625
85T/3D-22
85T/RD-29
85T/St-281
85T/St-337
85T/St-371M
85T/Super-20
86D-118
86F-467
86Mother/Mar-3
86OPC-198
86T-495
86T/St-225
87Classic-89
87D-568
87D/HL-34
87D/OD-116
87F-589
87F/AwardWin-22
87F/Hottest-26
87F/Mini-62
87F/St-70
87Leaf-55
87Mother/Sea-5
87OPC-215
87RedFoley/St-45
87S/Test-30
87Sf-102
87Sf/TPrev-25M
87Stuart-25
87T-215
87T/Mini-71
87T/St-219
88Classic/Blue-250
88D-20DK
88D-317
88D/AS-26
88D/Best-136
88D/DKsuper-20DK
88F-377
88F/BB/AS-20
88F/BB/MVP-21
88F/Hottest-23
88F/LL-24
88F/Mini-52
88F/Slug-23
88F/St-60
88F/TL-18
88Grenada-16
88KennerFig-60
88Leaf-123
88Leaf-20DK
88Mother/Sea-5
88OPC-80
88Panini/St-181
88RedFoley/St-46
88S-30
88Sf-46
88T-80
88T/Big-176
88T/Coins-18
88T/Mini-34
88T/Revco-33
88T/St-214
88T/St/Backs-63
88T/UK-42
89B-205
89D-227
89D/Best-68
89F-551
89F/Excit-29
89F/Superstar-27
89F/Up-97
89KMart/DT-21
89KennerFig-78
89Mother/Sea-5
89OPC-355
89Panini/St-430
89RedFoley/St-71
89S-161
89S/HotStar-67
89S/Mast-13
89S/Tr-25
89Sf-159
89T-355
89T/Hills-19
89T/LJN-11
89T/Mini-73
89T/St-221
89T/Tr-66T
89T/UK-47
89UD-526
90B-284
90Classic-72
90Classic/Up-28
90D-338
90D/BestAL-17
90F-352
90F/Can-352
90F/Up-U78
90Leaf-155
90Leaf/Prev-6
90OPC-530
90Panini/St-287
90PublInt/St-179
90RedFoley/St-55
90S-401
90S-688DT
90S/100St-96
90S/Tr-11T
90Sf-110
90Smok/Angel-10
90T-530
90T/Big-232
90T/Mini-62
90T/St-70
90T/Tr-54T
90UD-647
90UD/Ext-783
91B-202
91D-190
91D-BC1M
91D/BC-BC1
91F-318
91F/WaxBox-1M
91Leaf-67
91Leaf/Stud-27
91MajorLg/Pins-25
91OPC-755
91Panini/FrSt-352
91Panini/St-1
91S-21
91S-411KM
91S-699
91Smok/Angel-8
91StCl-27
91StCl/Charter*-17
91T-755
91T/CJMini/I-17
91UD-234
91USPlayC/AS-5H
91Ultra-49
92B-520
92CJ/DII-20
92Classic/Game200-113
92Classic/II-T6
92D-531
92D/DK-DK20
92D/McDon-19
92F-63
92L-229
92L/BlkGold-229
92OPC-165
92Panini-11
92Pinn-132
92Pol/Angel-14
92S-12
92S/100SS-32
92StCl-670
92StCl/Dome-101
92Studio-148
92T-165
92T/Gold-165
92T/GoldWin-165
92T/Kids-98
92TripleP-36
92UD-305
92Ultra-327
92Ultra/AwardWin-16
93B-469
93D-593
93F-194
93Flair-175
93JDean/28-9
93L-324
93L/UpGoldAS-1
93Mother/Angel-8
93OPC-232
93Pac/Spanish-48
93Panini-2
93Pinn-56
93Pol/Angel-8
93S-66
93S/Franchise-3
93Select-52
93StCl-355
93StCl/1stDay-355
93StCl/Angel-4
93StCl/MurphyS-107
93T-210
93T/Finest-82
93T/FinestRef-82
93T/Gold-210
93TripleP-235

93UD-128
93UD-53
93UD/FunPack-40
93UD/SP-5AS
93Ultra-166
93Ultra/AwardWin-10
94B-235
94D-31
94D/Special-31
94F-61
94F/AS-14
94F/Smoke-6
94Kraft-6
94L-162
94OPC-175
94Pac/Cr-81
94Panini-38
94Pinn-311
94RedFoley-23M
94S-71
94S/GoldR-71
94St/2000-38
94StCl-442
94StCl/1stDay-442
94StCl/Gold-442
94Studio-13
94T-665
94T/Finest-24
94T/FinestRef-24
94T/Gold-665
94TripleP-17
94UD-485
94UD/CollC-169
94UD/CollC/Gold-169
94UD/CollC/Silv-169
94UD/SP-25
94Ultra-331
94Ultra/AwardWin-9
94Ultra/Strike-2

Laniauskas, Vitas
89Ashvl/ProC-941

Lanier, H. Max
50B-207
51B-230
52B-110
52T-101
92Conlon/Sport-620
W754

Lanier, Hal
65OPC-118
65T-118
66OPC-156M
66T-156M
66T-271
67CokeCap/Giant-8
67OPC-4
67T-4
68CokeCap/Giant-8
68T-436
69MB-155
69MLB/St-201
69T-316
69T/St-106
70MLB/St-126
70T-583
71MLB/St-255
71OPC-181
71T-181
72MB-193
72T-589
73OPC-479
73T-479
74OPC-588
74T-588
78StPete
86Pol/Ast-6MG
86T/Tr-60T
87Mother/Ast-1
87Pol/Ast-7MG
87T-343MG
88Mother/Ast-1MG
88Pol/Ast-25MG
88T-684MG
89T-164MG
90Phill/TastyK-34CO
91Phill/Medford-24CO
92Yank/WIZ70-94
PM10/Sm-93

Lankard, Steve
86Salem-17
87PortChar-3
88Tulsa-20
89TexLAS/GS-35
89Tulsa/GS-13
90AAASingl/ProC-674
90OkCty/CMC-2
90OkCty/ProC-428
90ProC/Singl-152

Lankford, Ray
88MidwLAS/GS-26
88Spring/Best-14
89ArkTr/GS-9
89BBAmAA/BPro-AA23
89TexLAS/GS-22
90AAASingl/ProC-530
90B-192
90Classic/Up-29
90Leaf-308
90Louisvl/CMC-14
90Louisvl/LBC-23
90Louisvl/ProC-416
90ProC/Singl-114
90S/Tr-84T
90SpringDG/Best-24
90T/TVCard-53
90UD/Ext-755
91B-388
91Classic/200-83
91Classic/III-48
91D-43RR
91D/Rook-8
91F-637
91Leaf-523
91Leaf/Prev-10
91Leaf/Stud-234
91MajorLg/Pins-50
91OPC-682
91OPC/Premier-72
91Pol/Card-16
91S-731RP
91S/ASFan-1
91S/HotRook-7
91S/Rook40-2
91Seven/3DCoin-10MW
91StCl-537
91StCl/Member*-21
91T-682
91T/90Debut-81
91UD-346
91Ultra-290
92B-643
92Classic/Game200-130
92Classic/I-51
92D-350
92F-583
92F/RookSIns-17
92L-195
92L/BlkGold-195
92OPC-292
92OPC/Premier-148
92Panini-177
92Pinn-126
92Pinn/Team2000-51
92Pol/Card-10
92S-223
92S/100RisSt-43
92S/Impact-8
92StCl-8
92T-292
92T/Gold-292
92T/GoldWin-292
92TripleP-194
92UD-262
92UD/ASFF-8
92Ultra-265
93B-404
93Cadaco-38
93Classic/Gamel-51
93D-366
93D/MVP-12
93DennyGS-7
93F-127
93F/Fruit-34
93F/TLNL-3
93Flair-122
93Ho-5
93JDean/28-20
93Kenner/Fig-19
93L-297
93L/Fast-8
93OPC-191
93OPC/Premier-44
93Pac/Spanish-296
93Panini-196
93Pinn-116
93Pinn/Team2001-19
93Pol/Card-9
93S-56
93S/Franchise-24
93Select-155
93Select/StatL-17M
93StCl-49
93StCl/1stDay-49
93StCl/Card-17
93Studio-175
93T-386
93T/BlkGold-10
93T/Finest-187
93T/FinestRef-187
93T/Gold-386
93ToysRUs-100
93TripleP-254
93UD-244
93UD-461IN
93UD-482M
93UD/Diam-7
93UD/FunPack-76
93UD/HRH-HR20
93UD/SP-76
93Ultra-108
93Ultra-298M
93Ultra/AS-7
94B-96
94D-367
94D/Special-367
94F-636
94Finest-347
94Flair-226
94L-384
94L/MVPNL-9
94OPC-251
94Panini-245
94Pinn-36
94Pinn/Artist-36
94Pinn/Museum-36
94RedFoley-14
94S-16
94S/GoldR-16
94Select-152
94St/2000-65
94StCl-353
94StCl/1stDay-353
94StCl/Gold-353
94StCl/Team-310
94Studio-52
94T-530
94T/Gold-530
94TripleP-64
94UD-446
94UD/SP-64
94Ultra-566

Lanning, David P.
81VeroB-9

Lanning, Johnny
94Conlon-1301

Lanok, Dale
85BurlR-7

Lanoux, Marty
86Kenosha-11
87Visalia-23
88CalLgAS-39
88Visalia/Cal-153
88Visalia/ProC-104
89OrlanTw/Best-26
89OrlanTw/ProC-1328
90AAASingl/ProC-256
90Portl/ProC-186

Lansford, Carney
76QuadC
78SSPC/270-207
79T-212
80OPC-177
80T-337
81Coke
81D-409
81F-270
81F/St-12
81OPC-245
81T-639
81T/HT
81T/SO-25
81T/St-43
81T/Tr-788
82Coke/BOS
82D-82
82F-298
82F/St-164
82K-41
82OPC-91
82PermaGr/CC-15
82T-161LL
82T-786TL
82T-91
82T/St-156
82T/St-2
82T/StVar-156
83D-408
83F-187
83F/St-16M
83F/St-18M
83Granny-4
83OPC-318
83OPC/St-32
83T-523
83T/St-32
83T/Tr-60T
84D-176
84D/AAS-39
84F-452
84Mother/A's-7
84Nes/792-767
84OPC-59
84T-767
84T/RD-18M
84T/St-328
85D-345
85D-8DK
85D/DKsuper-8
85F-429
85FunFoodPin-55
85Leaf-8DK
85Mother/A's-8
85OPC-347
85T-422
85T/RD-17M
85T/St-330
86D-131
86F-426
86Leaf-55
86Mother/A's-8
86OPC-134
86Seven/Coin-W10M
86Sf-75M
86T-134
86T/St-169
86T/Tatt-7M
86Woolwth-17
87D-158
87D/OD-20
87F-397
87F/BB-24
87F/Mini-63
87F/St-71
87OPC-69
87RedFoley/St-37
87Sf-138
87Sf/TPrev-23M
87Smok/A's-8
87Stuart-24M
87T-678
87T/St-171
88AP/Test-4
88D-178
88D/A's/Bk-178
88D/Best-246
88F-285
88F/Slug-C3
88F/St-55
88KennerFig-61
88Leaf-195
88Mother/A's-6
88OPC-292
88Panini/St-169
88S-253
88Sf-202
88T-292
88T/Big-221
88T/St-167
89B-198
89D-243
89D/AS-17
89D/Best-22
89F-16
89F-633M
89KMart/Lead-20
89KennerFig-79
89Mother/A's-5
89OPC-47
89Panini/St-421
89RedFoley/St-72
89S-179
89S/HotStar-12
89Sf-53
89T-47
89T/Big-57
89T/LJN-83
89T/St-170
89UD-562
90B-452
90Classic-12
90D-95
90D/BestAL-117
90ElPasoATG/Team-40
90F-14
90F/Can-14
90KMart/CBatL-12
90Leaf-213
90MLBPA/Pins-73
90Mother/A's-8
90OPC-316
90Panini/St-134
90Panini/St-184
90Publint/St-309
90RedFoley/St-56
90S-296
90S/100St-20
90Sf-84
90T-316
90T/Big-83
90T/DH-39
90T/Gloss60-6
90T/Mini-29
90T/St-183
90T/TVAS-4
90UD-253
91BBBest/HitM-12
91D-273
91F-14
91Mother/A's-8
91OPC-502
91Panini/FrSt-194
91S-630
91StCl-231
91T-502
91UD-194
91Ultra-250
92B-78
92D-775
92F-261
92L-148
92L/BlkGold-148
92Mother/A's-8
92OPC-495
92Panini-17
92Pinn-455
92S-648
92StCl-45
92Studio-225
92T-495
92T/Gold-495
92T/GoldWin-495
92UD-682
92Ultra-423
93Panini-17
93Select-156
93T-127
93T/Gold-127

Lansford, Joe
81Hawaii-6
82Hawaii-6
83LasVegas/BHN-13
84Cram/PCL-220
85Cram/PCL-146
87LasVegas-4

Lansing, Mike
90Miami/I/Star-16
90WichSt-20
91ClBest/Singl-45
91FSLAS/ProC-FSL24
91Miami/ClBest-21
91Miami/ProC-415
92Harris/ProC-466
92Harris/SB-287
92UD/ML-131
93B-184
93F/Final-95
93FExcel/ML-61
93Flair-85
93JDean/Rook-6
93L-464
93OPC/Premier-82
93Pac/Spanish-535
93Pinn-620
93Select/RT/ASRook-3
93Select/RookTr-60T
93StCl-691
93StCl/1stDay-691
93Studio-46
93T/Finest-186
93T/FinestRef-186

93T/Tr-99T
93UD-677
93UD/SP-105
93Ultra-417
93Ultra/AllRook-4
94B-228
94D-208
94F-543
94F/RookSen-10
94L-89
94OPC-218
94Pac/Cr-384
94Panini-212
94Pinn-455
94S-488
94Select-88
94T-287
94T/Finest-10
94T/FinestRef-10
94T/Gold-287
94TripleP-97
94UD-244
94UD/CollC-170
94UD/CollC/Gold-170
94UD/CollC/Silv-170
94UD/ElecD-244
94Ultra-230
Lantigua, Eduardo
92GulfCD/ProC-3573
94B-266
Lantigua, Manny
75SanAn
79Portl-16
Lantrip, Joe
92Bluefld/ClBest-16
92Bluefld/ProC-2357
Lantrip, Rick
88AZ/Pol-9
90Oneonta/ProC-3387
91Greens/ProC-3066
92Greens/ClBest-15
92Greens/ProC-788
Lantz, Tom
75Clinton
Lapchick, Joe
33SK*-32
Lapenta, Jerry
86Geneva-14
87Peoria-6
88Peoria/Ko-20
88Pittsfld/ProC-1366
Laperriere, Jacques
72Dimanche*-80IA
72Dimanche*-81
Lapointe, Guy
72Dimanche*-82IA
72Dimanche*-83
Lapp, John
BF2-13
D329-98
D350/2-96
E104
E300
M101/4-98
M101/5-96
M116
T201
T207
T208
T222
Lapple, Bob
80Cedar-10
Laprade, Edgar
45Parade*-31
Lara, Carlos
91Pulaski/ClBest-3
91Pulaski/ProC-4009
Lara, Crucito
87StPete-20
88StPete/Star-11
89StLucie/Star-12
90Jacks/GS-25
Larcom, Mark
82Wisco/Frit-22
83Wisco/Frit-12
Lardizabal, Ruben
90Modesto/Chong-17
91Modesto/ClBest-7
91Modesto/ProC-3082
Lardner, Ring
88Pac/8Men-30
88Pac/8Men-35M
88Pac/8Men-42M
Largusa, Levon
92Classic/DP-70
92StCath/ClBest-25
92StCath/ProC-3384
93Hagers/ClBest-17
93Hagers/ProC-1876
93StCl/MurphyS-23
Laribee, Russ
81Pawtu-20
Larios, John
86Cram/NWL-35
87AppFx-3
Lariviere, Chris 42
88Rockford-20
89Rockford-20
Larker, Norm
53Exh/Can-37
59Morrell
59T-107
60BB-1
60T-394
60Union/Dodg-11
61BB-5
61Bz-34
61Morrell
61P-156
61T-130
61T-41LL
61T/St-28
61Union/Dodg-12
62Bz
62J-113
62P-113
62P/Can-118
62Salada-194
62Shirriff-194
62T-23
62T/bucks
63J-188
63P-188
63T-536
89Smok/Ast-14
89Smok/Dodg-67
90Target-433
Larkin, Andy
94B-262
Larkin, Barry
86Sf/Rook-34
87Classic-18
87Classic/Up-133
87D-492
87D/OD-191
87F-204
87Kahn-15
87S/Test-72
87Sf/TPrev-4M
87T-648
87ToysRUs-18
88D-492
88D/Best-222
88F-239
88Kahn/Reds-11
88Leaf-226
88OPC-102
88Panini/St-280
88S-72
88S/YS/II-34
88T-102
88T/Big-74
88T/St-140
89B-311
89Cadaco-32
89Classic-70
89Classic/Up/2-165
89D-257
89D/AS-47
89D/Best-110
89F-164
89F/BBAS-26
89Kahn/Reds-11
89KennerFig-80
89OPC-363
89Panini/St-74
89RedFoley/St-73
89S-31
89S/HotStar-52
89S/Mast-24
89Sf-136
89T-515
89T/Big-199
89T/LJN-31
89T/Mini-11
89T/St-137
89T/St/Backs-44
89UD-270
90B-50
90Classic-48
90D-71
90D/BestNL-52
90D/Learning-51
90F-423
90F/BB-23
90F/Can-423
90F/LL-22
90F/LgStand-1
90Kahn/Reds-12
90Kenner/Fig-49
90Leaf-18
90Leaf/Prev-5
90MLBPA/Pins-21
90OPC-10
90Panini/St-253
90PublInt/St-266
90PublInt/St-33
90RedFoley/St-57
90S-155
90S-689DT
90Sf-160
90T-10
90T/Big-189
90T/Coins-51
90T/DH-40
90T/Gloss60-5
90T/St-136
90T/TVAS-36
90UD-167
90UD-99TC
90USPlayC/AS-6D
91B-379SLUG
91B-673
91BBBest/HitM-13
91Cadaco-34
91Classic/200-142
91Classic/II-T33
91CollAB-31
91D-471
91D-5DK
91D/SuperDK-5DK
91F-68
91F-711M
91F/ASIns-2
91JDean-10
91Kahn/Reds-11
91Kenner-34
91Leaf-168
91Leaf/Prev-3
91Leaf/Stud-167
91OPC-400AS
91OPC-730
91Panini/FrSt-130
91Panini/St-129
91Panini/Top15-28
91Pep/Reds-11
91Post-18
91RedFoley/St-58
91S-505
91S-666AS
91S-795WS
91S-888DT
91S/100SS-20
91S/Cooper-B2
91Seven/3DCoin-10F
91StCl-92
91Sunflower-16
91T-400AS
91T-730
91T/CJMini/II-11
91UD-353
91UD/SilSlug-SS18
91USPlayC/AS-6C
91Ultra-96
91Woolwth/HL-30
92B-353
92B-694FOIL
92CJ/DI-19
92Classic/Game200-76
92Classic/II-T74
92D-185
92D/McDon-15
92DPep/MSA-18
92F-411
92F-704M
92F/ASIns-16
92F/Performer-14
92L-73
92L/BlkGold-73
92OPC-465
92OPC/Premier-96
92P-23
92Panini-265
92Pinn-5
92Pinn/RookI-9M
92Pinn/TeamP-7M
92Reds/Kahn-11
92S-100
92S-775AS
92S/100SS-77
92S/Impact-50
92Seven/Coin-13
92StCl-100
92StCl-596MC
92StCl/Dome-102
92Studio-23
92T-389AS
92T-465
92T/DQ-4
92T/Gold-389AS
92T/Gold-465
92T/GoldWin-389AS
92T/GoldWin-465A
92T/GoldWin-465B
92T/Kids-37
92T/McDonB-21
92TripleP-31
92UD-144
92UD/ASFF-30
92UD/TmMVPHolo-29
92Ultra-191
92Ultra/AS-13
93B-470
93Classic/Gamel-52
93Colla/ASG-20
93Colla/DM-63
93D-426
93D/Elite-23
93D/EliteUp-5
93D/Prev-3
93D/Spirit-SG13M
93Duracel/PPII-17
93F-394
93F/ASNL-4
93F/Fruit-35
93Flair-27
93Ho-8
93JDean/28-2
93Kenner/Fig-20
93Kraft-25
93L-311
93L/GoldAS-14M
93L/UpGoldAS-6M
93MSA/Metz-32
93MilkBone-3
93OPC-147
93OPC/Premier-103
93P-28
93Pac/Spanish-84
93Panini-293
93Pinn-22
93Pinn-306HH
93Pinn/Cooper-26
93Post/Can-15
93Reds/Kahn-13
93S-16
93S/Franchise-17
93Select-23
93StCl-415
93StCl/1stDay-415
93Studio-43
93Studio/Her-7
93T-110
93T-404
93T/BlkGold-11
93T/Finest-114AS
93T/FinestASJ-114AS
93T/FinestRef-114AS
93T/Gold-110
93T/Gold-404
93TB/Full-17
93TripleP-31
93TripleP/Act-8
93UD-245
93UD-473M
93UD/Clutch-R13
93UD/Diam-22
93UD/FunPack-167GS
93UD/FunPack-170
93UD/Iooss-WI21
93UD/SP-15AS
93Ultra-30
93Ultra/AS-4
94B-471
94Church-12
94D-45
94D/DK-17
94D/Special-45
94F-414
94F/AS-45
94F/TL-17
94Finest-240
94Flair-146
94KingB-17
94Kraft-26
94L-126
94L/MVPNL-11
94OPC-125
94P-12
94Pac/Cr-150
94Panini-163
94Pinn-12
94Pinn/Artist-12
94Pinn/Museum-12
94RedFoley-15
94S-74
94S/DT-5
94S/GoldR-74
94S/GoldS-15
94S/HobSam-DT5
94S/Tomb-13
94Select-7
94Sf/2000-109
94StCl-414
94StCl/1stDay-414
94StCl/Gold-414
94Studio-168
94T-250
94T/Gold-250
94TripleP-214
94TripleP/Medal-8
94UD-269HFA
94UD-385
94UD/CollC-171
94UD/CollC/Gold-171
94UD/CollC/Silv-171
94UD/DColl-C3
94UD/ElecD-269HFA
94UD/HoloFX-24
94UD/SP-159
94Ultra-474
Larkin, Gene
85Visalia-14
86OrlanTw-10
87D/Rook-23
87F/Up-U59
87Portl-19
87Sf/Rook-34
87T/Tr-60T
88D-564
88D/Best-158
88F-14
88OPC-384
88Panini/St-145
88RedFoley/St-47
88S-276
88Sf-107
88Smok/Minn-5
88T-746
88T/Big-264
88T/St-279
89B-160
89D-355
89F-117
89Panini/St-388
89S-280
89S/YS/II-6
89T-318
89T/Big-226
89T/St-294
89UD-580
90Classic/III-53
90D-436
90F-379
90F/Can-379
90Leaf-215
90OPC-556
90PublInt/St-331
90S-276
90T-556
90T/Big-302
90T/St-291
90UD-471
91D-152
91F-615
91Leaf-157
91OPC-102
91Panini/FrSt-306
91Panini/St-246
91S-471

91StCl-132
91T-102
91UD-501
91Ultra-190
92B-479
92D-496
92F-207
92L-415
92L/BlkGold-415
92OPC-284
92Pinn-435
92S-272
92S/Factory-B7M
92StCl-66
92T-284
92T/Gold-284
92T/GoldWin-284
92UD-187
92USPlayC/Twin-11D
92USPlayC/Twin-7S
93D-575
93F-269
93Pac/Spanish-173
93S-444
93StCl-42
93StCl/1stDay-42
93T-61
93T/Gold-61
93UD-540
93Ultra-584
94F-211
94Pac/Cr-358
94S-288
94S/GoldR-288

Larkin, Henry
(Ted)
N172
N690

Larkin, Pat
84Evansvl-5

Larkin, Steve
34G-92

Larocque, Michel
72Dimanche*-84

Larosa, John
88Spartan/ProC-1031
88Spartan/Star-10
89Pac/SenLg-43
89Spartan/ProC-1054
89Spartan/Star-12

Larose, Claude
72Dimanche*-85IA
72Dimanche*-86

Larose, Steve
88Clmbia/GS-6
89StLucie/Star-13
90Jacks/GS-8
91AA/LineD-566
91Jacks/LineD-566
91Jacks/ProC-924
92Jacks/SB-337

Larregui, Ed
90Hunting/ProC-3300
91Geneva/ClBest-11
91Geneva/ProC-4231
92ClBest-221
92MidwLAS/Team-27
92Peoria/ClBest-13
92Peoria/Team-11
92Peoria/Team-31M

Larsen, Bill
88Rockford-21
89Rockford-21AGM

Larsen, Don
54B-101
54Esskay
55B-67
56T-332
57T-175
58T-161
59T-205
59T-383M
60NuCard-18
60T-353
61NuCard-418
61T-177
61T-402HL
62T-33
63T-163
64T-513
65T-389
72Laugh/GF-45
76Laugh/Jub-17
77Galasso-3
78TCMA-211
78TCMA-266
79TCMA-272
88Pac/Leg-42
90BBWit-7
90HOF/St-54
91Crown/Orio-255
93AP/ASG-144
Exh47

Larsen, Jim
86Cram/NWL-36

Larson, Dan
77T-641
79OkCty
81OkCty/TCMA-7
83Iowa-6
84Butte-14
84OKCty-6
86Kinston-14
86Wausau-12
87BurlEx-26

Larson, Danny
91Martins/ClBest-3
91Martins/ProC-3468

Larson, Duane
80Knoxvl/TCMA-27
82Syrac-27

Larson, Jamie
85Anchora-36bb

Larson, Joe
92Johnson/ClBest-16
92Johnson/ProC-3110

Larson, Kirk
92AubAs/ClBest-13
92AubAs/ProC-1360

Larson, Michael
(Mike)
88Boise/ProC-1620
89Boise/ProC-2003
90Erie/Star-12

Lary, Frank
55B-154
56T-191
57T-168
58T-245
59T-393
60L-3
60T-85
60T/tatt-28
61P-38
61T-243
61T-48LL
61T-50LL
61T/St-153
62J-22
62P-22
62P/Can-22
62Salada-58
62Shirriff-58
62T-474AS
62T-57LL
62T/St-48
62T/bucks
63F-14
63J-55
63P-55
63T-140
63T-218M
64Det/Lids-8
64T-197
65OPC-127
65T-127
78TCMA-253
79TCMA-183
81Tiger/Detroit-125
91WIZMets-225

Lary, Lynford H.
(Lyn)
28Exh/PCL-18
31Exh/4-26
33G-193
35G-1C
35G-2C
35G-6C
35G-7C
90Target-434
91Conlon/Sport-318
R314

Lasek, Jim
77Spartan

Laseke, Eric
85Elmira-10
86WinHaven-14
87WinHaven-7
89WinHaven/Star-12

Laseter, Tom
76Watlo

Lash, Herbie
52LaPatrie-8

Lasher, Fred
68T-447R
69T-373
70OPC-356
70T-356
71MLB/St-347
71OPC-707
71T-707
72MB-194
88Domino-10

Lashley, Mickey
77Clinton
78LodiD

Laskey, Bill
81Omaha-10
83D-424
83F-264
83F/St-12M
83F/St-13M
83Mother/Giants-15
83OPC-218
83OPC/St-325
83T-171TL
83T-518
83T/St-325
84D-358
84F-376
84Nes/792-129
84OPC-129
84T-129
84T/St-172
85D-387
85F-612
85Mother/Giants-9
85OPC-331
85T-331
86D-585
86F-251
86Mother/Giants-24
86OPC-281
86T-603
87Toledo-21
87Toledo/TCMA-4
88Gator-17
90AAASingl/ProC-399
90ProC/Singl-300
90Richm/Bob-3
90Richm/CMC-24
90Richm/ProC-254
90Richm/Team-18

Lasky, Larry
85Osceola/Team-27TR
86Ashvl-17TR
87ColAst/ProC-21TR
88ColAst/Best-15TR
89Tucson/ProC-182TR

Lasorda, Tom
52Park-58
53Exh/Can-50
54T-132
55Gol/Dodg-18
73OPC-569CO
73T-569CO
74OPC-144CO
74T-144CO
77T-504MG
78SSPC/270-63MG
78T-189MG
79T-526MG
81D-420MG
81F-116MG
81Pol/Dodg-2MG
81T-679MG
82D-110MG
82F/St-111M
82Pol/Dodg-2MG
83D-136
83Pol/Dodg-2MG
83T-306MG
84F/St-124MG
84Nes/792-681MG
84Pol/Dodg-2
84T-681MG
85Coke/Dodg-18MG
85SpokAT/Cram-12
85T-601MG
86Coke/Dodg-16MG
86Pol/Dodg-2
86T-291MG
87Mother/Dodg-1MG
87Pol/Dodg-1MG
87Smok/Dodg-17MG
87T-493MG
88Mother/Dodg-1MG
88Pol/Dodg-2MG
88Pol/Dodg-MG
88Smok/Dodg-23MG
88T-74MG
89Mother/Dodg-1MG
89OPC/BoxB-HMG
89Pol/Dodg-2MG
89Rini/Dodg-13MG
89T-254MG
89T/LJN-50
89T/WaxBox-H
90Mother/Dodg-1MG
90OPC-669MG
90OPC/BoxB-GMG
90Pol/Dodg-1MG
90Pol/Dodg-x
90T-669MG
90T/Gloss22-1MG
90T/WaxBox-G
90Target-435
91Leaf/Stud-262MG
91Mother/Dodg-1MG
91OPC-789MG
91Pol/Dodg-x
91T-789MG
92Mother/Dodg-1MG
92OPC-261MG
92Pol/Dodg-2MG
92Pol/Dodg-NNO
92T-261MG
92T/GPro-261MG
92T/Gold-261MG
92T/GoldWin-261MG
92T/Pr-261MG
93Mother/Dodg-1MG
93Pol/Dodg-14MG
93Pol/Dodg-30M
93T-507M
93T/Gold-507M
94T/Arc54-132
V362-45

Lassard, Paul
87FtLaud-14

Lata, Tim
88CapeCod/Sum-129
89Hamil/Star-20
90Foil/Best-267
90Spring/Best-16
91StPete/ClBest-29
91StPete/ProC-2273

Latham, Bill
83Lynch-3
84Tidew-6
85Tidew-10
87Portl-18
87Tidew-22
87Tidew/TCMA-28
91Clmbia/PII-2CO
91WIZMets-226
92StLucie/ClBest-28CO
92StLucie/ProC-1765
93StLucie/ProC-2938CO

Latham, Chris
91Kissim/ProC-4194
92GreatF/SportP-7

Latham, John
89Welland/Pucko-17
90Salem/Star-9
91Augusta/ClBest-9
91Augusta/ProC-801

Latham, W. Arlie
12Sweet/Pin-115
N172
N172/BC
N284
N300/unif
N338/2
N370
Scrapps
T202
T205
T206
T207
T215/brown

Lathers, Charles
M116

Latimer, Tacks
90Target-1010

Latimer, William
92Hunting/ClBest-20
92Hunting/ProC-3144

Latman, Barry
59T-477
60T-41
61T-560
61T/St-137
62Kahn
62Sugar-1
62T-145
62T-37M
62T/St-36
63Sugar-1
63T-426
64T-227
65T-307
66T-451
67OPC-28
67T-28
68CokeCap/Astro-5

Latmore, Bob
86Miami-14
87Miami-10
88Hagers/Star-10
89Hagers/Best-4
89Hagers/ProC-271
89Hagers/Star-12
90EastLAS/ProC-EL34
90Hagers/Best-7
90Hagers/ProC-1422
90Hagers/Star-12

Latta, Greg
85BuffB-3
86BuffB-15TR
87Hawaii-25
89Vanco/ProC-574

Latter, Dave
89Medford/Best-12
90Madison/Best-18
90Madison/ProC-2264
91AA/LineD-288
91Huntsvl/ClBest-14
91Huntsvl/LineD-288
91Huntsvl/Team-13
91HuntsvlProC-1791
92Huntsvl/ProC-3945
92Huntsvl/SB-313

Lattimore, William
T206

Lau, Charley
58T-448
60T-312
61T-261
62T-533
63T-41
64T-229
65OPC-94
65T-94
66T-368
67T-329
73OPC-593CO
73T-593CO
74T-166CO
91Crown/Orio-256

Lau, David
88Clmbia/GS-13
89StLucie/Star-14

Lauck, Jeff
84Savan-2

Laudenslager, Kevin
90GA-17

Laudner, Tim
80OrlanTw-12
82D-549
82OrlanTw/A-8
82T-766R
83D-177
83F-618
83OPC/St-314
83OPC/St-93
83T-529
83T/St-314
83T/St-93
83Twin/Team-10
83Twin/Team-31M
83Twin/Team-32M
84F-569
84Nes/792-363
84T-363
85D-652
85F-283
85Seven/Minn-12
85T-71
85Twin/Seven-12

85Twin/Team-11
86D-391
86F-398
86T-184
87D-320
87F-546
87OPC-392
87T-478
88D-631
88F-15
88Master/Disc-5
88OPC-78
88Panini/St-135
88S-153
88Smok/Minn-7
88T-671
88T/Big-243
88T/St-278
89B-154
89D-615
89D/AS-19
89F-118
89KennerFig-81
89OPC-239
89Panini/St-384
89S-134
89Sf-152
89T-239
89T/St-290
89UD-62
90D-419
90F-380
90F/Can-380
90OPC-777
90PublInt/St-332
90S-318
90T-777
90T/Big-218
90UD-419

Lauer, John Charles
N172

Laureano, Francisco
(Frank)
86BurlEx-13
87AppFx-7
88Virgini/Star-13
89BBCity/Star-15
90Memphis/Best-7
90Memphis/ProC-1018
90Memphis/Star-13
91AAA/LineD-338
91Omaha/LineD-338
91Omaha/ProC-1043

Laurent, Milfred
(Rick)
92Negro/RetortII-22

Lauzerique, George
69T-358R
70McDon-6
70OPC-41
70T-41
75Dubuq
76Dubuq

Lav, David
87Columbia-5

Lavagetto, Harry
(Cookie)
35BU-51
39PlayBall-74
40PlayBall-69
41DP-17
47TipTop
48Signal
49Remar
50Remar
52T-365CO
59T-74M
60T-221MG
61Peters-10
61T-226MG
81TCMA-482M
89Rini/Dodg-10
89Rini/Dodg-35
89Smok/Dodg-40
90HOF/St-43
90Target-436
R313
R314

Lavan, John
(Doc)
21Exh-94
BF2-42
D327
D328-95
D329-99
D350/2-97
E120
E121/120
E121/80
E122
E135-95
M101/4-99
M101/5-97
V100
V61-102
W501-108
W514-4
W575

Lavelle, Gary
75OPC-624R
75T-624R
75T/M-624R
76OPC-105
76SSPC-96
76T-105
77T-423
78Ho-32
78T-671
79Pol/Giants-46
79T-311
80Pol/Giants-46
80T-84
81D-314
81F-448
81OPC-62
81T-588
82D-60
82F-392
82OPC-209
82T-209
83D-60
83F-265
83F/St-4M
83F/St-7M
83Mother/Giants-14
83OPC-376
83T-791
83T/Fold-4M
84D-573
84D/AAS-1
84F-377
84Mother/Giants-10
84Nes/792-145
84OPC-145
84T-145
84T/St-164
85D-265
85F-613
85F/Up-U69
85Leaf-114
85OPC-2
85OPC/Post-24
85T-462
85T/St-159
85T/Tr-72T
85Tor/Fire-18
86BJ/Ault-18
86D-621
86F-65
86OPC-22
86T-622
86Tor/Fire-22
87Tor/Fire-17

Lavenda, John
91CalLgAS-27

Lavender, James
(Jimmy)
14CJ-105
15CJ-105
92Conlon/Sport-344
BF2-65
D328-96
D329-100
D350/2-98
E135-96
M101/4-100
M101/5-98
T206
WG4-13

Lavender, Jeff
89TNTech-13

Lavender, Robert
88Gaston/ProC-996
89CharlR/Star-11

Laviano, Frank
90Tampa/DIMD-13
91Oneonta/ProC-4151
92Greens/ClBest-6

Lavigne, Ben
92Idaho/ProC-3515

Lavigne, Martin
91Kissim/ProC-4179

Lavoie, Marc
90AZ/Pol-11

Lavrusky, Chuck
87Idaho-7
88Boise/ProC-1621

Law, Joe
83Idaho-14
85Huntsvl/BK-40
87Modesto-19
89Tacoma/CMC-6
89Tacoma/ProC-1550
90AAASingl/ProC-135
90ProC/Singl-587
90Tacoma/CMC-10
90Tacoma/ProC-88

Law, Rudy
77LodiD
78Cr/PCL-56
79Albuq-19
79T-719R
81Albuq/TCMA-20
81D-180
81F-139
81Pol/Dodg-3
81T-127
82D-582
83D-521
83F-244
83F/St-18M
83T-514
83TrueVal/WSox-11
84D-257
84F-67
84F/St-93
84Nes/792-47
84OPC-47
84T-47
84T/St-245
84TrueVal/WS-21
85Coke/WS-23
85D-244
85F-519
85Leaf-117
85OPC-286
85T-286
85T/St-241
86D-632
86F-211
86F/Up-U66
86OPC-6
86T-637
86T/St-291
86T/Tr-62T
87D-343
87F-372
87T-382
90Target-437

Law, Travis
88Butte-23
89CharlR/Star-12

Law, Vance
79Portl-5
80Port-9
81Portl-14
81T-551R
82D-582
82F-484
82T-291
83D-117
83F-245
83OPC-98
83T-98
83TrueVal/WSox-5
84D-546
84F-68
84Nes/792-667
84T-667
84T/St-249
84TrueVal/WS-22
85D-122
85Expo/PostC-10
85F-520
85F/Up-U70
85Leaf-183
85OPC-81
85T-137FS
85T-413
85T/St-242
85T/Tr-73T
86D-132
86Expo/Prov/Pan-23
86Expo/Prov/Post-12
86F-252
86GenMills/Book-6M
86Leaf-57
86OPC-99
86Provigo-23
86T-787
86T/St-81
87D-212
87D/OD-94
87Expo/PostC-2
87F-323
87GenMills/Book-4M
87OPC-127
87T-127
88Berg/Cubs-2
88D-212
88D/Best-60
88D/Cubs/Bk-NEW
88F-187
88F/Up-U79
88OPC-346
88Panini/St-324
88S-85
88S/Tr-16T
88Sf-41
88T-346
88T/Tr-60T
89B-293
89D-276
89D/AS-49
89F-430
89F/BBAS-27
89Mara/Cubs-2
89OPC-338
89Panini/St-57
89S-102
89Sf-162
89T-501
89T/Big-143
89T/St-46
89T/St/Backs-42
89UD-473
90D-629
90F-36
90F/Can-36
90OPC-287
90PublInt/St-197
90S-73
90T-287
90UD-380
91B-222
91Leaf-355
91Mother/A's-12
91UD/Ext-760

Law, Vernon
(Vern)
51B-203
52B-71
52T-81
54B-187
54T-235
55B-199
56T-252
57T-199
58Hires/T
58Kahn
58T-132
59Kahn
59T-12
59T-428M
60Kahn
60T-453
60T/tatt-29
61Kahn
61NuCard-406
61P-126
61T-250M
61T-400
61T-47LL
61T/St-66
62J-179
62P-179
62P/Can-179
62T-295
63F-58
63T-184
64T-472
65T-515
66Bz-18
66EH-32
66OPC-15
66T-15
66T-221LL
66T/RO-48
66T/RO-51
67CokeCap/Pirate-16
67T-351
67T/Test/PP-11
78TCMA-239
79TCMA-42
85T-137FS
90Pac/Legend-37
91Swell/Great-55
91T/Arc53-324
92AP/ASG-19
92Bz/Quadra-18M
93UD/ATH-81
94T/Arc54-235

Lawler, Chris
92MN-10

Lawless
N172

Lawless, Thomas
80Water-18
81Water-14
82Indianap-15
83D-400
83Indianap-12
83T-423
86Schnucks-15
86T-228
87Smok/Cards-19
87T-647
88Smok/Card-15
88T-183
88T/St-22
88Woolwth-25WS4
89B-255
89T-312
89Tor/Fire-18
90D-681
90OPC-49
90PublInt/St-519
90T-49
90Tor/BJ-18

Lawn, Mike
91Helena/SportP-4
92Salinas/ClBest-8
92Salinas/ProC-3770
92Stockton/ProC-49

Lawrence, Andy
85Lynch-22
86Jacks/TCMA-16
87Jaxvl-7
88Jaxvl/Best-19
88Jaxvl/ProC-972

Lawrence, Bill
43Centen-17

Lawrence, Brooks
55B-75
55Hunter
55RM-NL4
56Kahn
56T-305
57Kahn
57Sohio/Reds-13
57T-66
58Kahn
58T-374
59T-67
60Kahn
60L-36
60T-434
79TCMA-217

Lawrence, Matt
92Hunting/ClBest-14
92Hunting/ProC-3145

Lawrence, Randy
92Elmira/ClBest-7
92Elmira/ProC-1379

Lawrence, Scott
86Erie-17
87Savan-25
88StPete/Star-12
89Spring/Best-13
90Tidew/CMC-30TR

Lawrence, Sean
92Welland/ClBest-16
92Welland/ProC-1319

Lawrenson, Scott
87Lynch-27
90ProC/Singl-687TR

Lawson, Alfred V.
(Roxie)
38Wheat
92Conlon/Sport-513

Lawson, Cale
91BurlInd/ProC-3304
Lawson, David
92Belling/ClBest-24
92Belling/ProC-1457
Lawson, James
(Jim)
88SoOreg/ProC-1712
89Madis/Star-12
90Madison/Best-19
90Modesto/Cal-152
90Modesto/ProC-2209
Lawson, Rex
V355-104
Lawson, Steve
73OPC-612R
73T-612R
93Rang/Keeb-23
Lawton, Marcus
86Lynch-14
87Jacks/Feder-16
87TexLgAS-24
88Tidew/ProC-1591
89Tidew/CMC-23
89Tidew/ProC-1967
90AAASingl/ProC-178
90OPC-302
90ProC/Singl-643
90T-302
90T/89Debut-69
90Vanco/CMC-16
90Vanco/ProC-500
91AA/LineD-440
91MidldA/LineD-440
91MidldA/OneHour-16
91MidldA/ProC-446
92Memphis/SB-438
92MidldA/OneHour-14
92Sky/AASingl-184
92Yank/WIZ80-103
Laxamana, Brian
90AS/Cal-34UMP
91CalLgAS-50
Laxton, Brett
93LSU/McDag-15
94LSU-8
Laxton, William
75Tidew/Team-15
76SSPC-615
77T-394
Lay, Shane
92Helena/ProC-1728
Laya, Jesus
87Pocatel/Bon-28
88Pocatel/ProC-2096
89Everett/Star-19
Layana, Tim
87Albany-11
88Albany/ProC-1333
89Albany/Best-5
89Albany/ProC-329
89Albany/Star-9
89EastLgAS/ProC-14
90AlbanyDG/Best-11
90B-41
90Classic/III-46
90D/Rook-23
90F/Up-U14
90Kahn/Reds-14
90Leaf-410
90S/Tr-107T
90T/Tr-55T
90UD/Ext-717
91B-689
91D-516
91F-69
91OPC-627
91S-64
91S/100RisSt-54
91StCl-396
91T-627
91T/90Debut-82
91UD-396
92RochR/ProC-1933
92RochR/SB-460
92S-628
92StCl-419
Layne, Hillis
47Centen-15
47Signal
88Chatt/Team-21
Layne, Jerry
90TM/Umpire-58
Layton, Tom
83Kinston/Team-11
87Iowa-8
Lazar, John Dan
69T-439R
70T-669R
72MB-195
Lazor, Joe
87Cedar-5
88Chatt/Best-4
88SLAS-35
89Chatt/Best-5
89Chatt/GS-15
90Chatt/GS-18
Lazor, John Paul
45Playball-20
49B/PCL-30
Lazorko, Jack
80Tulsa-6
81Tulsa-19
83ElPaso-23
84Cram/PCL-48
85Cram/PCL-176
85T-317
86D-628
86Nashvl-15
87Edmon-2
87F/Up-U61
87T/Tr-62T
88D-160
88Edmon/CMC-3
88Edmon/ProC-556
88F-494
88S-437
88T-601
89Edmon/CMC-1
89F-482
89T-362
90TulsaDG/Best-13
91Pac/SenLg-113
Lazzeri, Anthony
(Tony)
26Exh-100
27Exh-50
28Yueng-29
29Exh/4-25
31Exh/4-25
32Orbit/num-107
33CJ/Pin-15
33Exh/4-13
33G-31
34DS-74
35BU-45
35Exh/4-13
35G-2D
35G-4D
35G-7D
36Exh/4-13
37Exh/4-13
37OPC-117
40PlayBall-238
60Exh/HOF-14
60F-31
61F-54
69Bz-3
75Shakey-16
77Galasso-116
77Galasso-191
80Laugh/FFeat-26
81Conlon-11
88Conlon/3-17
88Conlon/AmAS-19
90Target-438
91Conlon/Sport-113
91Perez/HOF-209
92Yank/WIZAS-39
92Yank/WIZHOF-20
93AP/ASG-101
93AP/ASG24K-35G
93Conlon-761
93Conlon-762
93Conlon-911
94Conlon-1053
PR1-20
R311/Leath
R315-A21
R315-B21
R328-18
V300
V353-31
W502-29
W513-79
W517-27
LeBlanc, Michael
88CapeCod/Sum-61
89Belling/Legoe-7
LeBlanc, Richie Jr.
88BBCity/Star-16
88FSLAS/Star-42
90Memphis/Best-16
90Memphis/ProC-1024
90Memphis/Star-14
LeBoeuf, Alan
85Cram/PCL-32
86Portl-13
87Maine-22
87Maine/TCMA-13
88Reading/ProC-864
90Clearw/Star-27CO
91AA/LineD-525CO
91Reading/LineD-525CO
91Reading/ProC-1386CO
92ScranWB/ProC-2463CO
92ScranWB/SB-500M
LeBron, Jose
89Watlo/ProC-1775
89Watlo/Star-17
90Foil/Best-37
90Waterlo/Best-27
90Waterlo/ProC-2375
91HighD/ClBest-6
91HighD/ProC-2389
92HighD/ClBest-22
LeClair, Morgan
90WichSt-22
LeClaire, George
(Frenchy)
C46-3
LeFlore, Ron
75OPC-628
75T-628
75T/M-628
76Greyhound-3
76Ho-69
76K-17
76OPC-61
76SSPC-363
76T-61
77BurgChef-98
77Ho-50
77Ho/Twink-50
77K-25
77OPC-167
77Pep-28
77T-240
77Tiger/BK-2
78BK/T-19
78Ho-95
78OPC-88
78T-480
78Wiffle/Discs-37
79Ho-34
79OPC-348
79T-4LL
79T-660
79T/Comics-8
80BK/PHR-27
80OPC-45
80T-80
81Coke
81D-576
81F-154
81F/St-2
81MSA/Disc-20
81OPC-104
81Sqt-26
81T-204M
81T-4LL
81T-710
81T/HT
81T/St-23
81T/Tr-791
82D-165
82F-350
82F/St-182
82OPC-140
82T-140
82T/St-172
83D-543
83F-246
83F/St-21M
83F/St-3M
83OPC-297
83T-560
83T/Fold-5M
89Pac/SenLg-4
89T/SenLg-111
89TM/SenLg-67
90EliteSenLg-39
91Pac/SenLg-63
LeJeune, Larry
90Target-1105
LeJohn, Don
(Ducky)
66OPC-41
66T-41
75Water
77Clinton
78Clinton
86Bakers-19MG
90Target-445
LeMaster, Denny
63T-74
64T-152
65Kahn
65T-441
66Kahn
66T-252
67CokeCap/Astro-16
67CokeCap/Brave-7
67T-288
68Dexter-47
68T-491
69MB-157
69OPC-96
69T-96
69T/St-34
70MLB/St-42
70OPC-178
70T-178
71MLB/St-84
71OPC-636
71T-636
72MB-197
72OPC-371
72T-371
78TCMA-17
LeMaster, Johnnie
75IntLgAS/Broder-16
75PCL/AS-16
75Phoenix-12
75Phoenix/Caruso-12
75Phoenix/CircleK-12
76OPC-596R
76Phoenix/Coke-13
76T-596R
77T-151
78T-538
79Pol/Giants-10
79T-284
80OPC-224
80Pol/Giants-10
80T-434
81D-432
81F-450
81OPC-84
81T-84
82D-524
82F-393
82T-304
82T/St-108
83D-125
83F-266
83Mother/Giants-4
83OPC-154
83OPC/St-304
83T-154
83T/St-304
84D-649
84F-378
84Nes/792-663
84OPC-107
84T-663
84T/RD-2M
84T/St-168
85D-114
85F-614
85Mother/Giants-14
85OPC-302
85T-772
85T/RD-2M
85T/St-164
85T/Tr-74T
86OPC-289
86T-289
90Swell/Great-68
LeMasters, Jim
87Sumter-20
88BurlB/ProC-13
88MidwLAS/GS-20
89Greenvl/Best-10
89Greenvl/ProC-1176
89Greenvl/Star-13
89Star/Wax-36
90AAASingl/ProC-598
90Omaha/CMC-5
90Omaha/ProC-63
90ProC/Singl-180
91AAA/LineD-339
91Omaha/LineD-339
91Omaha/ProC-1032
LeVander, Scott
84Idaho/Team-17
LeVangie, Dana
92WinHaven/ProC-1781
LeVasseur, Tom
86Cram/NWL-169
88River/Cal-223
88River/ProC-1417
89AubAs/ProC-26
89Wichita/Rock-21SS
89Wichita/Rock/HL-13
90AAASingl/ProC-17
90LasVegas/CMC-17
90LasVegas/ProC-129
90ProC/Singl-520
Lea, Charles
79Memphis
79Memphis/TCMA-8
80Memphis-2
81F-165
81OPC-293
81T-293
82D-320
82Expo/Hygrade-11
82F-193
82Hygrade
82OPC-38
82T-38
83D-414
83Expo/PostC-9
83F-286
83F/St-14M
83F/St-15M
83OPC-253
83Stuart-23
83T-629
84D-376
84Expo/PostC-16
84F-278
84Nes/792-421
84Nes/792-516TL
84OPC-142
84OPC-332TL
84Stuart-8
84T-421
84T-516TL
84T/St-98
85D-177
85D-21DK
85D/DKsuper-21
85F-401
85F-632M
85Leaf-21DK
85OPC-345
85OPC/Post-10
85T-345
85T/Gloss22-10
85T/Gloss40-30
85T/St-182
85T/St-84
86D-376
86F-253
86Leaf-172
86OPC-376
86T-526
86T/Tatt-21M
87WPalmB-17
88F/Up-U44
89D-473
89F-119
89S-501
89UD-81
93Expo/D/McDon-23
Leach, Chris
89WinHaven/Star-13
90LynchRS/Team-2
91LynchRS/ClBest-21
91LynchRS/ProC-1211
Leach, Don
80Elmira-19
Leach, Fred
28Exh-21
33G-179
94Conlon-1130
R315-A22
R315-B22

R316
Leach, Jalal
(Jay)
90A&AASingle/ProC-183
90Oneonta/ProC-3420
91ClBest/Singl-270
91FtLaud/ClBest-27
91FtLaud/ProC-2441
92PrWill/ClBest-5
92PrWill/ProC-161
Leach, Martin
82Tulsa-3
85Water-13
Leach, Rick
80Evansvl-24
82D-583
82F-272
82T-266
83D-81
83F-334
83T-147
84F-84
84F/X-U71
84Nes/792-427
84Syrac-6
84T-427
84T/Tr-71T
84Tor/Fire-22
85F-112
85IntLgAS-29
85OPC-52
85Syrac-11
85T-593
86T/Tr-63T
86Tor/Fire-23
87D-567
87F-234
87F/Up-U63
87OPC-5
87T-716
87Tor/Fire-18
88D-518
88F-115
88Leaf-247
88OPC-323
88S-258
88T-323
88Tor/Fire-9
89B-234
89D-638
89F-237
89Mother/R-16
89OPC-284
89S-540
89Smok/R-19
89T-682
89T/Tr-68T
89UD-554
90D-613
90F-305
90F/Can-305
90Leaf-436
90Mother/Giant-14
90OPC-27
90PublInt/St-416
90S-426
90T-27
90T/Tr-56T
90UD-640
93Rang/Keeb-227
Leach, Terry
76Baton
79Savan-19
81Tidew-29
82T-623R
82Tidew-14
83D-634
83T-187
83Tidew-5
84Richm-19
84Tidew-26
85Tidew-2
86F-87
86T-774
86Tidew-15
87F/Up-U62
87T/Tr-63T
88D-603
88D/Mets/Bk-603
88F-139
88Kahn/Mets-26
88OPC-391
88S-203
88Sf-139
88T-457
89D-502
89F-40
89S-431
89S/Tr-24
89T-207
89T/Big-96
89T/Tr-69T
89UD-288
90D-534
90F-111
90F/Can-111
90Leaf-360
90OPC-508
90S-502
90S/Tr-43T
90T-508
90T/Tr-57T
90UD-642
91B-340
91D-715
91F-616
91S-556
91StCl-397
91WIZMets-227
92D-484
92F-208
92L-486
92L/BlkGold-486
92OPC-644
92S-296
92StCl-778
92T-644
92T/Gold-644
92T/GoldWin-644
92UD-311
92USPlayC/Twin-5D
92USPlayC/Twin-6C
92WSox-34
93D-720
93F-585
93S-479
93StCl/WSox-29
93T-443
93T/Gold-443
93UD-418
93WSox-18
94D-441
Leach, Thomas
10Domino-67
11Helmar-161
12Sweet/Pin-138
12Sweet/Pin-138
14CJ-41
15CJ-41
D322
E103
E107
E254
E286
E90
E90/2
E91
E93
E94
E95
M116
S74-111
T201
T202
T205
T206
T207
T213/blue
T215
T222
T3-3
W555
WG3-25
Leader, Ramon
77Cocoa
78DaytB
Leahy, Pat
92Classic/DP-114
92Erie/ClBest-14
92Erie/ProC-1615
93T-641
93T/Gold-641
Leahy, Thomas
(Tom)
91Macon/ClBest-3
91Macon/ProC-857
92Durham/ClBest-18
92Durham/ProC-1095
92Durham/Team-25
93Durham/Team-11
Leake, Jon
85Miami-8
87SLCity/Taco-24
Leaks, Charles
54JC
55JC
Leal, Carlos
80Utica-27
Leal, Luis
80Syrac/Team-14
81OPC-238R
81T-577R
82D-255
82F-617
82OPC-368
82OPC/Post-9
82T-412
83D-129
83F-432
83OPC-109
83T-109
84D-485
84F-160
84Nes/792-783
84OPC-207
84T-783
84T/St-371
84Tor/Fire-23
85D-317
85F-113
85Leaf-29
85OPC-31
85T-622
85T/St-361
85Tor/Fire-19
86D-315
86OPC-365
86Syrac-16
86T-459
88Syrac/ProC-806
Leard, Bill
90Target-1011
Leary, Rob
87WPalmB-1
88Rockford-22
89Rockford-22
89WPalmB/Star-15
90LSUGreat-8
90Rockford/ProC-2697CO
90Rockford/Team-15CO
92Madis/ClBest-6
92Madis/ProC-1243
92Rockford/ClBest-28MG
92Rockford/ProC-2131MG
93WPalmB/ClBest-26MG
93WPalmB/ProC-1357MG
Leary, Timothy
82T-623R
83Tidew-9
84Jacks/Smok-7
85Cram/PCL-203
86D-577
86Pol/Brew-39
86T/Tr-64T
87D-232
87F-348
87Mother/Dodg-21
87Pol/Dodg-11
87T-32
87T/Tr-64T
88AlaskaAS70/Team-20
88F-521
88Mother/Dodg-21
88Pol/Dodg-54
88S-224
88T-367
89B-339
89D-552
89D/Best-309
89F-65
89F/Excit-30
89Mother/Dodg-21
89OPC-249
89Panini/St-99
89Pol/Dodg-28
89S-429
89S/HotStar-9
89S/Tr-52
89Sf-81
89T-249
89T/Big-17
89T/St-62
89UD-94
90B-429
90D-670
90D/BestAL-53
90F-424
90F/Can-424
90Leaf-148
90OPC-516
90PublInt/St-12
90S-504
90S/NWest-13
90S/Tr-27T
90T-516
90T/TVYank-12
90T/Tr-58T
90Target-439
90UD-662
90UD/Ext-705
91D-67
91F-670
91Leaf-206
91Leaf/Stud-95
91OPC-161
91S-631
91StCl-423
91T-161
91UD-693
91Ultra-236
91WIZMets-228
92D-433
92F-235
92OPC-778
92Pinn-349
92S-286
92StCl-291
92T-778
92T/Gold-778
92T/GoldWin-778
92Ultra-411
93D-289
93F-677
93Mother/Mar-21
93Pac/Spanish-624
94D-240
94F-291
94S-240
94S/GoldR-240
Leatherman, Jeff
91Welland/ClBest-17
91Welland/ProC-3580
92Augusta/ClBest-22
Leatherwood, Anthony
90GA-18
Leatherwood, Del
78DaytB
81Tucson-2
Leavell, Gregg
91Welland/ClBest-12
91Welland/ProC-3586
Lebak, David
91Spokane/ClBest-7
91Spokane/ProC-3960
92CharRain/ClBest-14
92CharRain/ProC-133
Lebo, Mike
78Dunedin
Lebron, David
78Newar
Leclair, Jean-Claude
72Dimanche*-138
Leclair, Keith
88Idaho/ProC-1850
Ledbetter, Gary
77Cedar
Ledbetter, Jeff
86ArkTr-11
Ledduke, Dan
79WHave-9
Ledee, Ricardo
90Tampa/DIMD-14
92GulfCY/ProC-3702
Ledesma, Aaron
90Kgsport/Best-1
90Kgsport/Star-13
91Clmbia/PCPII-6
91Clmbia/PCPII-6
91Clmbia/PII-13
92ClBest-275
92StLucie/ClBest-17
92StLucie/ProC-1755
93B-102
Ledezma, Carlos
75WPalmB/Sussman-8TR
81Buffa-8
82Portl-26
84Cram/PCL-143
86Hawaii-15TR
87Vanco-4
88AAA/ProC-48
88BuffB/ProC-1481
89BuffB/CMC-3
89BuffB/ProC-1678
90BuffB/Team-13
Ledinsky, Ray
91Miami/ClBest-22
91Miami/ProC-416
Leduc, Jean
78Charl
Ledwick, Shannon
91Idaho/ProC-4324
91Idaho/SportP-16
Lee, Anthony
92AppFox/ClBest-7
93Peoria/Team-14
Lee, Ben
87AppFx-13
Lee, Bob
85Visalia-15
86Kenosha-12
87Visalia-6
88Kenosha/ProC-1403
89Kenosha/ProC-1058
Lee, Charles
92James/ClBest-12
92James/ProC-1513
Lee, Chris
88Ashvl/ProC-1059
Lee, Derek
88Utica/Pucko-7
89SoBend/GS-27
90BirmB/Best-10
90BirmB/ProC-1118
90Foil/Best-144
90ProC/Singl-769
91AA/LineD-66
91BirmB/LineD-66
91BirmB/ProC-1466
91ClBest/Singl-272
92B-210
92Sky/AAASingl-285
92UD/ML-148
92Vanco/ProC-2733
92Vanco/SB-642
93B-335
Lee, Derrek
94B-232
94ClBest/Gold-142
94ClBest/GoldLP-8
94Pinn-438
94S-585
94UD-539TP
94UD/SP-10PP
Lee, Don
57T-379
59T-132
60T-503
61Clover-12
61Peters-9
61T-153
62T-166
63F-18
63T-372
64T-493
65T-595
Lee, Dudley
21Exh-95
28Exh/PCL-19
Lee, Eddie
79Elmira-11
Lee, Greg
88Pocatel/ProC-2086
89Salinas/Cal-141
89Salinas/ProC-1806
Lee, Hal
90Target-441
R310
V94-29
Lee, Harvey
86FtLaud-14
87SanJose-5
Lee, Jeremy
94ClBest/Gold-69
94T-206FDP
94T/Gold-206FDP
Lee, John
76Dubuq
Lee, Leron

70OPC-96R
70T-96R
71MLB/St-276
71OPC-521
71T-521
72OPC-238
72T-238
73OPC-83
73T-83
74OPC-651
74T-651
75OPC-506
75T-506
75T/M-506
76OPC-487
76T-487
90Target-442

Lee, Manny
85F/Up-U71
85Tor/Fire-20
86Knoxvl-14
86OPC-23
86Syrac-17
86T-23
87D-518
87OPC-289
87Syrac-14
87Syrac/TCMA-16
87T-574
88D-650
88F-116
88OPC-303
88S-561
88T-722
88Tor/Fire-4
89D-504
89F-238
89OPC-371
89Panini/St-468
89S-326
89T-371
89T/Big-70
89Tor/Fire-4
89UD-271
90B-512
90D-620
90F-86
90F/Can-86
90Leaf-370
90OPC-113
90Publlnt/St-520
90S-482
90T-113
90T/Big-219
90Tor/BJ-4
90UD-285
91B-21
91D-211
91F-179
91Leaf-399
91OPC-297
91Panini/FrSt-337
91S-534
91S/ToroBJ-16
91StCl-168
91T-297
91Tor/Fire-4
91UD-142
91Ultra-365
92B-421
92BJ/Fire-17
92D-499
92F-333
92L-382
92L/BlkGold-382
92OPC-634
92Panini-28
92Pinn-245
92S-518
92StCl-283
92T-634
92T/Gold-634
92T/GoldWin-634
92UD-118
92Ultra-148
93BJ/D/45-8
93D-688
93F-337
93L-381
93OPC-320
93OPC/WC-9
93Pac/Spanish-325
93Pinn-493
93Rang/Keeb-413
93S-205
93Select-380
93Select/RookTr-119T
93StCl-713
93StCl/1stDay-713
93StCl/MurphyS-118
93StCl/Rang-18
93T-488
93T/Gold-488
93UD-205
93UD-637
93Ultra-631
94F-310
94Flair-113
94L-372
94Panini-129
94StCl-423
94StCl/1stDay-423
94StCl/Gold-423
94StCl/Team-248
94T-51
94T/Finest-100
94T/FinestRef-188
94T/Gold-51
94UD-216
94UD/CollC-172
94UD/CollC/Gold-172
94UD/CollC/Silv-172
94UD/ElecD-216

Lee, Mark L.
78Padre/FamFun-18
79T-138
80Hawaii-17
80T-557
81Portl-15
82Evansvl-4

Lee, Mark
86Lakeland-8
87GlenF-15
87Lakeland-17
88Lakeland/Star-17
89Memphis/Best-4
89Memphis/ProC-1190
89Memphis/Star-14
91Brewer/MillB-14
91F/Up-U30
91Leaf-343
91OPC-721
91Pol/Brew-11
91S-372RP
91T-721
92D-313
92Denver/ProC-2637
92Denver/SB-137
92F-180
92OPC-384
92S-277
92StCl-32
92T-384
92T/Gold-384
92T/GoldWin-384
92UD-507

Lee, Michael
60T-521

Lee, Robert D.
64T-502R
65OPC-46
65T-46
66T-481
67T-313
68Kahn
68T-543
90Target-440

Lee, Ronnie
53Exh/Can-51
V362-25

Lee, Terry James
89Chatt/Best-10
89Chatt/GS-16
90Chatt/GS-19
91AAA/LineD-266
91AAAGame/ProC-23
91B-683
91D-752
91F-70
91Nashvl/LineD-266
91Nashvl/ProC-2165
91T/90Debut-83
91UD-37
92ColoSp/SB-89
92OPC-262
92T-262
92T/Gold-262
92T/GoldWin-262

Lee, Terry
75Cedar
80Holyo-21
81Vanco-14
83Cedar-19
83Cedar/Frit-13

Lee, Thomas
91Eugene/ClBest-23
91Eugene/ProC-3723

Lee, Thornton
35BU-109
47TipTop
89Pac/Leg-158
R313

Lee, Wiley
87Salem/ProC-2430
88MidwLAS/GS-24
88QuadC/GS-4
89AS/Cal-11
89PalmSp/Cal-39
89PalmSp/ProC-485
90MidldA/GS-11

Lee, William C.
35BU-140
37Exh/4-3
39Exh
39Wheat-4
41DP-103
47TipTop
92Cub/OldStyle-17
93Conlon-724
PM10/Sm-94
V355-109
WG8-40

Lee, William F.
70OPC-279
70T-279
71MLB/St-322
71OPC-58
71T-58
72Dimanche*-25
72T-636
73OPC-224
73T-224
74OPC-118
74T-118
74T/St-135
75Ho-66
75OPC-128
75T-128
75T/M-128
76K-29
76OPC-396
76SSPC-421
76T-396
77BurgChef-32
77T-503
78PapaG/Disc-9
78SSPC/270-167
78T-295
79OPC-237
79T-455
80OPC-53
80T-97
81D-211
81F-157
81OPC-371
81T-633
82D-194
82F-194
82OPC-323
82T-323
88AlaskaAS60/Team-6
89Chatt/II/Team-15GM
89Pac/SenLg-28
89T/SenLg-33
89TM/SenLg-66
90EliteSenLg-99
90Smok/SoCal-8
91Conlon/Sport-128
91Pac/SenLg-146
92Nabisco-1
93Expo/D/McDon-24

Lee, Wyatt
(Watty)
C46-71
E107
E270/2
T205

Leech, Skip
77Charl

Leek, Eugene
61T-527
62Salada-82A
62Salada-82B
62Shirriff-82

Leeper, Dave
83Omaha-22
84Omaha-22
85Omaha-24
86D-461
86Hawaii-16
87Vanco-14

Leetch, Brian
91StCl/Member*-46

Leever, Sam
10Domino-68
12Sweet/Pin-139
D322
E104
E107
E90/1
E90/2
E91
M116
T205

Lefebvre, Jim
65T-561R
66OPC-57
66T-57
67CokeCap/DodgAngel-12
67T-260
68Bz-2
68T-457
68T/ActionSt-13AM
68T/ActionSt-4AM
69MB-156
69MLB/St-149
69OPC-140
69T-140
69T/4in1-9
69T/St-46
69Trans-47
70MLB/St-52
70T-553
71MLB/St-106
71OPC-459
71T-459
71Ticket/Dodg-8
72MB-196
72OPC-369
72T-369
72T/Cloth-20
78TCMA-263
80Pol/Giants-5
85Cram/PCL-187
86Phoenix-15MG
87Smok/Dodg-18
89Mother/Sea-1
89Smok/Dodg-71
89T/Tr-70TMG
90Mother/Mar-1MG
90OPC-459MG
90T-459MG
90Target-443
91CounHrth-1MG
91OPC-699MG
91T-699MG
92Cub/Mara-5MG
92T/Tr-63T
92T/TrGold-63T
93Cub/Mara-13MG
93T-502M
93T/Gold-502M

Lefebvre, Joe
77FtLaud
79WHave-25
80Colum-26
81D-571
81F-103
81OPC-88
81T-88R
81T/Tr-790
82D-373
82F-575
82T-434
83D-523
83F-363
83T-644
83T/Tr-61T
84D-82
84F-37
84Nes/792-148
84Phill/TastyK-37
84T-148
85D-285
85F-257
85Phill/TastyK-12M
85Phill/TastyK-37M
85T-531
86Phill/TastyK-23
87Reading-3
88Maine/CMC-25
88Maine/ProC-301
89ScranWB/CMC-18CO
89ScranWB/ProC-722CO
90Albany/Best-25CO
90Albany/ProC-1181CO
90Albany/Star-25CO
92Yank/WIZ80-104

Lefebvre, Ryan
92MN-11

Lefebvre, Tip
84Cram/PCL-14

Lefferts, Craig
82Iowa-20
83Thorn-32
84D-388
84F-496
84F/X-U72
84Mother/Padres-19
84Nes/792-99
84T-99
84T/Tr-72T
85D-261
85F-38
85Mother/Padres-15
85OPC-76
85T-608
86D-307
86F-328
86OPC-244
86T-244
87Bohem-37
87D-387
87F-422
87F/RecSet-19
87F/Up-U64
87OPC-287
87Sf/TPrev-16M
87T-501
88D-515
88D/Best-330
88F-87
88Mother/Giants-24
88S-553
88T-734
89B-464
89D-59
89F-332
89Mother/Giants-24
89S-178
89T-372
89UD-541
90B-206
90Classic-109
90Coke/Padre-9
90D-376
90D/BestNL-23
90F-60
90F/Can-60
90F/Up-U57
90Leaf-339
90OPC-158
90Padre/MagUno-11
90Panini/St-362
90Publlnt/St-74
90S-209
90S/Tr-22T
90Sf-130
90T-158
90T/St-80
90T/Tr-59T
90UD-399
90UD/Ext-792
91B-650
91D-515
91F-534
91Leaf-390
91OPC-448
91Padre/Coke-4
91Padre/MagRal-21
91Panini/Top15-84
91RedFoley/St-59
91S-184
91StCl-533
91T-448
91UD-228
91Ultra-307
92B-105
92D-162
92F-611

92L-408
92L/BlkGold-408
92Mother/Padre-24
92OPC-41
92Padre/Carl-11
92Panini-239
92Pinn-478
92S-175
92Smok/Padre-17
92StCl-618
92T-41
92T/Gold-41
92T/GoldWin-41
92UD-589
92Ultra-577
93B-249
93D-1
93F-544
93L-309
93Pinn-522
93Rang/Keeb-414
93S-435
93Select-373
93Select/RookTr-112T
93T-617
93T/Gold-617
93UD-718
93Ultra-632
94D-472
94F-311
94Pac/Cr-621
94T-288
94T/Gold-288
Lefley, Chuck
72Dimanche*-87IA
72Dimanche*-88
Left, Jim
92Nashvl/SB-300M
Leftwich, Phil
90A&AASingle/ProC-158
90Boise/ProC-3306
91ClBest/Singl-247
91MidwLAS/ProC-27
91QuadC/ClBest-7
91QuadC/ProC-2624
92MidldA/ProC-4024
93Vanco/ProC-2592
94D-403
94F-62
94Finest-391
94L-132
94Pac/Cr-82
94Pinn-441
94T-471
94T/Gold-471
94UD-139
94UD/CollC-173
94UD/CollC/Gold-173
94UD/CollC/Silv-173
94UD/ElecD-139
94Ultra-23
Legault, Kevin
92Elizab/ClBest-8
92Elizab/ProC-3675
Legendre, Rob
91Yakima/ClBest-25
91Yakima/ProC-4245
92Yakima/ClBest-10
92Yakima/ProC-3445
Leger, Frank
83LynnP-24
Leger, Roger
45Parade*-32
Leger, Tim
92FrRow/DP-23
93StCl/MurphyS-67
Legg, Greg
83Reading-14
85Cram/PCL-48
87Maine-4
87Maine/TCMA-14
87Phill/TastyK-11
88Reading/ProC-882
89ScranWB/CMC-19
89ScranWB/ProC-708
90AAASingl/ProC-311
90ScranWB/ProC-609
91AAA/LineD-486
91ScranWB/LineD-486
91ScranWB/ProC-2546
92ScranWB/ProC-2452
92ScranWB/SB-486
93ScranWB/Team-12
Leggatt, Rich
82Buffa-1
83Durham-20
84Durham-18
85Greenvl/Team-12
86Toledo-13
Legree, Keith
92Elizab/ProC-3686
Legumina, Gary
83SanJose-15
85VeroB-9
Lehew, Jim
91Crown/Orio-257
Lehman, Andy
89KS*-78
Lehman, Bill
76AppFx
Lehman, Ken
55B-310
57T-366
58Hires-52
58T-141
59T-331
79TCMA-258
90Target-444
91Crown/Orio-258
Lehman, Mike
89Freder/Star-12
90Freder/Team-16
91AA/LineD-235
91Hagers/LineD-235
91Hagers/ProC-2459
92RochR/SB-455
92Sky/AAASingl-207
Lehner, Paul
47TipTop
49B-131
50B-158
51B-8
Lehnerz, Daniel
88Idaho/ProC-1857
Lehnerz, Mike
89Kingspt/Star-15
91Pittsfld/ClBest-20
91Pittsfld/ProC-3417
Leiber, Hank
38Exh/4-5
Leibert, Allen
90Canton/Star-10
90Foil/Best-188
Leibold, Harry
(Nemo)
88Pac/8Men-101
D327
D328-97
D329-101
D350/2-99
E120
E121/80
E135-97
E220
M101/4-101
M101/5-99
T222
V100
W575
94Conlon-1036
94Conlon-1042
Leibrandt, Charles
79Indianap-7
81D-421
81F-208
81Indianap-5
81OPC-126
81T-126
82Coke/Reds
82F-74
82T-169
83D-421
83F-596
83Indianap-4
83T-607
84Omaha-1
85D-399
85D/HL-4
85D/HL-46
85F-206
85Indianap-33
85T-459
86D-297
86F-13
86F/LL-21
86F/Slug-20
86F/St-69
86Kitty/Disc-10
86Leaf-171
86NatPhoto-37
86OPC-77
86Sf-159
86Sf-186M
86T-77
86T/Mini-19
86T/St-262
86T/Super-37
86T/Tatt-1M
87D-220
87F-373
87OPC-223
87Sf/TPrev-13M
87T-223
87T/St-258
88D-157
88D/Best-151
88F-263
88F/St-31
88Leaf-76
88OPC-218
88Panini/St-100
88S-61
88Sf-21
88Smok/Royals-13
88T-569
88T/St-260
89B-116
89Classic-82
89D-89
89D/Best-231
89F-286
89OPC-301
89Panini/St-351
89S-133
89T-301
89Tastee/Discs-10
89UD-637
90B-8
90Brave/Dubuq/Perf-15
90Brave/Dubuq/Singl-18
90D-208
90F-112
90F/Can-112
90Leaf-428
90MLBPA/Pins-103
90OPC-776
90PublInt/St-351
90S-82
90T-776
90T/Tr-60T
90UD-658
91B-573
91Brave/Dubuq/Perf-17
91Brave/Dubuq/Stand-22
91D-562
91F-695
91Leaf-209
91OPC-456
91Panini/FrSt-27
91Panini/St-23
91S-536
91StCl-527
91T-456
91UD-460
92Brave/LykePerf-17
92Brave/LykeStand-20
92D-84
92F-361
92L-113
92L/BlkGold-113
92OPC-152
92Pinn-423
92S-105
92StCl-366
92T-152
92T/Gold-152
92T/GoldWin-152
92UD-170
92USPlayC/Brave-13C
92USPlayC/Brave-9D
92Ultra-459
93B-433
93D-630
93F-7
93F/Final-280
93L-407
93OPC-204
93OPC/Premier-116
93Pac/Spanish-642
93Pinn-115
93Rang/Keeb-415
93S-393
93Select-209
93Select/RookTr-91T
93StCl-723
93StCl/1stDay-723
93StCl/Rang-16
93T-677
93T/Gold-677
93UD-678
94D-190
94F-312
94S-467
Leiby, Brent
90Princet/DIMD-30TR
91Spartan/ClBest-30TR
Leifield, Albert
(Lefty)
10Domino-69
11Helmar-162
12Sweet/Pin-140
D322
M116
S74-112
T201
T202
T205
T206
T207
T215/blue
T215/brown
Leighton, John
N172
Leimeister, Eric
90Niagara/Pucko-20
91Lakeland/ClBest-7
91Lakeland/ProC-263
Lein, Chris
82Nashvl-16
83AlexD-14
85PrWill-13
87Salem-28
89Harris/ProC-301
90Salem/Star-26CO
91Bluefld/ClBest-25CO
91Bluefld/ProC-4142CO
Leinen, Michael
90Wausau/Star-13
Leinen, Pat
88CapeCod/Sum-102
88NE-13
89Erie/Star-11
90Foil/Best-96
90Wausau/Best-3
90Wausau/ProC-2116
91Freder/ProC-2359
91Hagers/ProC-2452
91Perth/Fut-7
92RochR/ProC-1934
92RochR/SB-456
Leinhard, Steve
90Shrev/Star-14
Leiper, Dave
82Idaho-11
83Madis/Frit-27
86Tacoma-12
87D-472
87F-398
87T-441
88D-557
88F/Up-U123
88S-348
88Smok/Padres-15
89D-465
89F-310
89S-515
89T-82
89UD-363
90OPC-773
90PublInt/St-53
90S-212
90T-773
91AAA/LineD-166
91Edmon/LineD-166
91Edmon/ProC-1514
Leiper, Timothy
(Tim)
86FSLAS-29
86Lakeland-9
87GlenF-9
88GlenF/ProC-938
88Toledo/CMC-21
88Toledo/ProC-603
89London/ProC-1373
90EastLAS/ProC-EL5
90London/ProC-1281
90ProC/Singl-838
91AAA/LineD-561
91Tidew/LineD-561
91Tidew/ProC-2523
92Memphis/ProC-2431
92Memphis/SB-441
93CaroMud/RBI-23
Leister, John
86Pawtu-12
87Pawtu-5
87Pawtu/TCMA-26
88Pawtu/CMC-4
88Pawtu/ProC-470
89Pawtu/CMC-5
89Pawtu/Dunkin-22
89Pawtu/ProC-681
90AAASingl/ProC-431
90Pawtu/CMC-6
90Pawtu/ProC-459
90ProC/Singl-257
90T/TVRSox-49
Leiter, Al
87Colum-30
87Colum/Pol-15
88Classic/Blue-238
88D-43RR
88D/Best-132
88D/Rook-27
88D/Y/Bk-43
88F/Up-U49
88Leaf-43RR
88S/Tr-97T
88T-18
89B-170
89Classic-112
89D-315
89F-257
89F/Up-70
89KennerFig-83
89Panini/St-396
89S-580
89S/HotRook-80
89S/YS/I-17
89T-659
89T/Big-125
89T/JumboR-15
89T/Tr-71T
89ToysRUs-19
89UD-588
89UD/Ext-705
90D-543
90OPC-138
90PublInt/St-521
90T-138
90Tor/BJ-28
91D-697
91OPC-233
91S/ToroBJ-4
91T-233
91Tor/Fire-28
92F-334
92OPC-394
92Sky/AAASingl-227
92StCl-231
92Syrac/MerchB-10
92Syrac/ProC-1963
92Syrac/SB-509
92Yank/WIZ80-105
93BJ/D/45-34
93BJ/Demp-18
93BJ/Fire-18
93F/Final-294
93Pac/Spanish-652
93Pinn-568
93StCl-670
93StCl/1stDay-670
93UD-638
94D-229
94F-337
94L-95
94Pac/Cr-646
94Pinn-334
94StCl/Team-171
94T-732
94T/Gold-732
94Ultra-139
Leiter, Kurt
83SanJose-24
84CharlO-23
86Miami-15
Leiter, Mark
89Colum/CMC-29
89FtLaud/Star-13
90AAASingl/ProC-323

90ColClip/CMC-4
90ColClip/ProC-673
90Colum/Pol-11
90ProC/Singl-204
90T/TVYank-51
91AAA/LineD-588
91B-138
91CokeK/Tiger-23
91D/Rook-29
91S-727RP
91T/90Debut-84
91Toledo/LineD-588
92B-476
92Classic/I-52
92D-633
92F-140
92L-207
92L/BlkGold-207
92OPC-537
92OPC/Premier-48
92S-626
92StCl-880
92T-537
92T/Gold-537
92T/GoldWin-537
92UD-319
92Ultra-366
93D-495
93F-608
93OPC-174
93Pac/Spanish-112
93StCl-116
93StCl/1stDay-116
93T-216
93T/Gold-216
93Tiger/Gator-18
93UD-95
94Flair-24
94Pac/Cr-224
94T-133
94T/Gold-133

Leitner, Ted
90Padre/MagUno-16ANN
91Padre/Coke-5ANN

Leius, Scott
87Kenosha-21
88Visalia/Cal-154
88Visalia/ProC-102
89BBAmAA/BPro-AA18
89OrlanTw/Best-16
89OrlanTw/ProC-1332
89SLAS-6
90AAASingl/ProC-255
90B-423
90F-647R
90F/Can-647M
90Portl/CMC-16
90Portl/ProC-185
90ProC/Singl-568
91B-337
91D/Rook-4
91F/UltraUp-U38
91F/Up-U38
91Leaf/GRook-BC1
91S-370RP
91StCl-338
91T/90Debut-85
91T/Tr-71T
91UD-35
92B-209
92D-359
92F-209
92F/RookSIns-20
92L-214
92L/BlkGold-214
92OPC-74
92OPC/Premier-118
92Pinn-365
92S-320
92S/Factory-B2M
92StCl-350
92StCl/Dome-104
92Studio-206
92T-74
92T/Gold-74
92T/GoldWin-74
92UD-313
92USPlayC/Twin-11H
92USPlayC/Twin-7C
92Ultra-94
93D-369
93F-270
93L-208
93Pac/Spanish-522
93Panini-128
93Pinn-192
93S-178
93Select-251
93StCl-254
93StCl/1stDay-254
93T-146
93T/Gold-146
93TripleP-165
93UD-212
93Ultra-233
94Finest-377
94Flair-76
94L-337
94Pac/Cr-359
94S-545
94T-517
94T/Gold-517
94UD-322

Leiva, Jose
86Reading-14
87Reading-22
88Reading/ProC-884
89Canton/Best-22
89Canton/ProC-1312
89Canton/Star-24

Leix, Tom
81Wisco-2

Leja, Frank
54NYJour
54T-175
55T-99
60L-121
94T/Arc54-175

Lekang, Anton
33SK*-10

Leland, Stan
78DaytB
81Tucson-15

Lelivelt, William
E254
E270/1
T222

Lemaire, Jacques
72Dimanche*-89IA
72Dimanche*-90

Lemanczyk, Dave
75OPC-571
75T-571
75T/M-571
76OPC-409
76SSPC-355
76T-409
77OPC-229
77T-611
78BJ/PostC-13
78OPC-85
78T-33
79BJ/Bubble-15
79OPC-102
79T-207
80OPC-68
80T-124
81D-292
81T-391

Lemay, Bob
91Niagara/ClBest-27
91Niagara/ProC-3629
92Fayette/ClBest-8
92Fayette/ProC-2165

Lemay, Richard
62T-71
63T-459
66Pep/Tul

Lembo, Steve
53Exh/Can-36
90Target-446
V362-7

Lemieux, Mario
91StCl/Charter*-50
91StCl/Member*-47
91StCl/Member*-48

Lemke, Mark
86Sumter/ProC-16
87Durham-26
88BBAmer-16
88Greenvl/Best-10
88SLAS-15
89AAA/CMC-18
89AAA/ProC-55
89Classic-52
89D-523
89Richm/Bob-13
89Richm/CMC-19
89Richm/Ko-16
89Richm/ProC-830
89T-327
89UD-19
90B-11
90Brave/Dubuq/Perf-16
90Brave/Dubuq/Singl-19
90D-624
90D/Rook-43
90F-587
90F/Can-587
90OPC-451
90S-593
90S/DTRook-B5
90S/YS/II-22
90T-451
90T/Big-120
90TripleAAS/CMC-18
90UD-665
91Brave/Dubuq/Perf-18
91Brave/Dubuq/Stand-23
91D-604
91F-696
91OPC-251
91S-779
91S/100RisSt-89
91StCl-203
91T-251
91UD-419
92B-663
92Brave/LykePerf-18
92Brave/LykeStand-21
92D-606
92F-362
92L-94
92L/BlkGold-94
92OPC-689
92Panini-163
92Pinn-426
92S-386
92S/Factory-B3M
92StCl-316
92StCl/Dome-105
92Studio-6
92T-689
92T/Gold-689
92T/GoldWin-689
92UD-47
92USPlayC/Brave-2C
92USPlayC/Brave-4S
92Ultra-165
93Brave/FLAg-6
93Brave/LykePerf-16
93Brave/LykeStand-19
93D-316
93F-368
93Flair-6
93L-63
93OPC-236
93Pac/Spanish-334
93Panini-182
93Pinn-368
93S-147
93Select-161
93StCl-172
93StCl/1stDay-172
93StCl/Brave-4
93StCl/MurphyS-37
93T-116
93T/Gold-116
93TripleP-215
93UD-109
93Ultra-8
94D-147
94F-363
94L-392
94Pac/Cr-13
94Pinn-447
94S-392
94Select-60
94StCl-402
94StCl/1stDay-402
94StCl/Gold-402
94StCl/Team-46
94T-23
94T/Finest-95
94T/FinestRef-95
94T/Gold-23
94UD-489
94Ultra-153

Lemke, Steve
92SoOreg/ClBest-4
92SoOreg/ProC-3413

Lemle, Rob
88Clmbia/GS-21
89Clmbia/Best-4
89Clmbia/GS-14

Lemon, Chet
75Tucson-3
75Tucson/Team-8
76OPC-590R
76T-590R
77BurgChef-73
77OPC-195
77T-58
78Ho-124
78OPC-224
78SSPC/270-146
78T-127
79Ho-40
79OPC-169
79T-333
79T/Comics-5
80K-46
80OPC-309
80T-589
80T/S 57
80T/Super-57
81Coke
81D-281
81F-354
81K-19
81OPC-242
81Sqt-33
81T-242
81T/HT
81T/SO-34
81T/St-57
82D-291
82F-351
82F/St-191
82K-54
82OPC-13
82T-216TL
82T-493
82T/St-168
82T/Tr-62T
83D-511
83F-335
83F/St-9M
83OPC-53
83T-727
84D-171
84F-85
84Nes/792-611
84OPC-86
84T-611
84T/St-271
84Tiger/Farmer-9
84Tiger/Wave-23
85Cain's-12
85D-90
85F-15
85FunFoodPin-97
85Leaf-77
85OPC-20
85Seven-11D
85Seven-9G
85T-20
85T/Gloss22-18
85T/St-190
85T/St-21WS
85T/St-260
85Wendy-14
86Cain's-11
86D-90
86F-230
86Leaf-85
86OPC-160
86Seven/Coin-C14M
86T-160
86T/St-274
86T/Tatt-10M
87Cain's-10
87Coke/Tigers-10
87D-353
87D/OD-213
87F-156
87Leaf-227
87OPC-206
87Seven-DT6
87Sf/TPrev-15M
87T-739
87T/St-268
88D-215
88D/Best-147
88F-61
88Leaf-166
88OPC-366
88Panini/St-96
88Pep/T-34
88Pol/T-7
88S-119
88T-366
88T/Big-147
89D-209
89D/Best-69
89F-137
89KennerFig-84
89Mara/Tigers-34
89OPC-328
89Panini/St-344
89Pol/Tigers-34
89S-44
89Sf-171
89T-514
89T/Big-202
89T/St-283
89UD-128
90B-354
90CokeK/Tiger-10
90D-60
90D/BestAL-76
90F-608
90F/Can-608
90Leaf-133
90MLBPA/Pins-87
90OPC-271
90Panini/St-77
90PublInt/St-475
90S-106
90T-271
90T/Big-86
90T/St-278
90UD-348
91D-301
91F-341
91OPC-469
91Panini/FrSt-292
91S-557
91StCl-23
91T-469
91UD-389

Lemon, Don
89Idaho/ProC-2033

Lemon, Donald
(Don)
92Erie/ClBest-5
92Erie/ProC-1616
93T-441
93T/Gold-441

Lemon, Jim
54T-103
55B-262
57T-57
58T-15
59HRDerby-11
59T-215
59T-74M
60T-440
61Bz-12
61Clover-13
61P-93
61Peters-17
61T-44LL
61T-450
61T/St-182
62J-89
62P-89
62P/Can-89
62Salada-9A
62Salada-9B
62Shirriff-9
62T-510
63T-369
68T-341MG
69T-294MG
78Twin/Frisz-9
79TCMA-180
83Twin/Team-29CO
83Twin/Team-34M
90Elizab/Star-25
91Elizab/ProC-4316CO
94T/Arc54-103
PM10/Sm-97

Lemon, Leo
81Redwd-19

Lemon, Robert
(Bob)
49B-238
50B-40
50NumNum

51B-53
51BR-A2
51FB
51T/CAS
52B-23
52BR
52Dix
52NumNum-4
52StarCal-88A
52StarCal/L-74C
52T-268
52Wheat*
53B/BW-27
53Dix
53Exh/Can-31
53NB
53RM-AL17
54B-196
54DanDee
54RH
54RM-AL21
55B-191
55Gol/Ind-15
55RM-AL8
55Salem
56Carling-5
56T-255
57Sohio/Ind-7
57T-120
58T-2
60T-460C
71OPC-91MG
71T-91MG
72OPC-449MG
72T-449MG
76Rowe-5M
76Shakey-155
77T-418MG
78BK/Y-1
78SSPC/270-139MG
78T-574MG
79T-626MG
79TCMA-19
80Pac/Leg-120
80Perez/HOF-155
80SSPC/HOF
82D-635MG
82Ohio/HOF-32
83D/HOF-30
85West/2-45
86Sf/Dec-39M
88Pac/Leg-32
89HOF/St-68
90Perez/GreatMom-67
91T/Arc53-284
92Bz/Quadra-1M
93AP/ASG-113
93AP/ASG24K-47G
Exh47
PM10/Sm-95
PM10/Sm-96
R302-119
R423-59

Lemonds, Dave
71OPC-458R
71T-458R
72OPC-413R
72T-413R
73OPC-534
73T-534

Lemongello, Mark
77T-478R
78BK/Ast-9
78T-358
79T-187
80Wichita-22

Lemons, Richard
92AZ/Pol-8

Lemons, Tim
86BurlEx-14
87Spring/Best-7

Lemp, Chris
91Bluefld/ClBest-21
91Bluefld/ProC-4124
92Kane/ClBest-11
92Kane/ProC-88
92Kane/Team-19
92ProC/Tomorrow-12

Lemperle, John
86Alban/TCM-19bb

Lemuth, Steve
89Medford/Best-19

Lenderman, Dave
86Pittsfld-13

Lenhardt, Don
51T/BB-33
52T-4
53B/Col-20
54B-53
54Esskay
54T-157
73OPC-131CO
73T-131C
91Crown/Orio-259
94T/Arc54-157

Lennon, Patrick
86Cram/NWL-128
87Wausau-7
88Vermont/ProC-947
89Wmsprt/ProC-632
89Wmsprt/Star-12
90Foil/Best-153
90SanBern/Best-9
90SanBern/Cal-101
90SanBern/ProC-2645
91AAA/LineD-63
91B-250
91Calgary/LineD-63
91Calgary/ProC-528
91UD/FinalEd-43F
92B-192
92Calgary/SB-64
92Classic/Game200-172
92D-17RR
92Pinn-542
92Sky/AAASingl-28
92StCl-679
92T/91Debut-107
92UD-13SR

Lennon, Robert
55T-119
56T-104
57T-371

Lennox, James E.
(Ed)
11Helmar-97
90Target-447
M116
T202
T205
T206
T207
T213/blue
T213/brown
T214-18
T3-104

Lenti, Mike
81Clinton-23

Lentine, James
81Charl-17
81D-250
81F-476

Lentz, Harry
T206
T213/brown

Leon, Danilo
(Danny)
87James-23
88James/ProC-1913
88WPalmB/Star-15
89Jaxvl/Best-21
89Jaxvl/ProC-169
92D/Rook-64
92F/Up-61
92T/Tr-64T
92T/TrGold-64T
92Tulsa/ProC-2691
93D-387
93Rang/Keeb-228

Leon, Eduardo
(Eddie)
70OPC-292
70T-292
71MLB/St-378
71OPC-252
71T-252
72T-721
73OPC-287
73T-287
74OPC-501
74T-501
75OPC-528
75T-528
75T/M-528
92Yank/WIZ70-95

Leon, Johnny
90Tampa/DIMD-15

Leon, Jose
89Elizab/Star-14

Leon, Maximino
75OPC-442
75T-442
75T/M-442
76OPC-576
76SSPC-3
76T-576
77T-213

Leon, Michael
93James/ClBest-14
93James/ProC-3322

Leon, Mike
87AppFx-22TR
88AppFx/ProC-163TR
89Memphis/Best-27TR
89Memphis/ProC-1191TR
90Memphis/Best-27TR
90Memphis/Star-27TR

Leon, Ron
85Spring-15
87Erie-5

Leonard, Andy
86BurlEx-15

Leonard, Bernardo
78Holyo

Leonard, Dennis
75OPC-615R
75T-615R
75T/M-615R
76A&P/KC
76OPC-334
76SSPC-164
76T-334
77BurgChef-70
77Ho-72
77Ho/Twink-72
77OPC-91
77T-75
78Ho-88
78OPC-41
78OPC-5LL
78SSPC/270-220
78T-205LL
78T-665
79Ho-109
79OPC-109
79T-218
80OPC-293
80T-565
81Coke
81D-102
81F-42
81OPC-185
81Pol/Royals-5
81T-185
81T/St-87
82D-264
82F-413
82F/St-208
82OPC-369
82Sqt-10
82T-495
82T/St-191
82T/StVar-191
83D-412
83F-116
83F/St-12M
83F/St-23M
83OPC-87
83Pol/Royals-3
83T-785
84F-349
84Nes/792-375
84OPC-375
84T-375
86F/Up-U67
86NatPhoto-22
86T/Tr-65T
87F-374
87OPC-38
87RedFoley/St-33
87T-38
89Pac/SenLg-84
89T/SenLg-125
89TM/SenLg-68
90EliteSenLg-72
90Pac/Legend-91
93UD/ATH-82

Leonard, Emil
(Dutch)
39PlayBall-21
40PlayBall-23
41PlayBall-24
43Playball-4
48B-24
48L-113
49B-115
49Eureka-61
50B-170
51B-102
52B-159
52StarCal-92AM
52StarCal/L-80B
52T-110
52TipTop
53B/BW-50
53T-155
55B-247
90Target-448
91T/Arc53-155
93Conlon-712
94Conlon-1276

Leonard, Hubert
(Dutch)
16FleischBrd-56
61F-121
72F/FFeat-17
72Laugh/GF-34
79T-418M
85Woolwth-22
91Conlon/Sport-142
91Conlon/Sport-276
92Conlon/Sport-346
BF2-5
D327
D328-98
D329-102
D350/2-100
E135-98
E220
M101/4-102
M101/5-100

Leonard, Jeffery
(Jeff)
80T-106
81D-264
81F-67
81T-469
82D-438
82T-47
83D-474
83Mother/Giants-8
83T-309
84D-567
84F-379
84Nes/792-576TL
84Nes/792-748
84T-576TL
84T-748
84T/RD-29
84T/St-166
85D-358
85F-615
85F/LimEd-18
85GenMills-4
85Leaf-92
85Mother/Giants-4
85OPC-132
85Seven-14W
85T-619
85T-718AS
85T/RD-30
85T/St-161
85ThomMc/Discs-35
86D-79
86F-548
86Leaf-74
86Mother/Giants-4
86OPC-381
86T-490
86T/St-84
86T/Tatt-15M
87Classic-64
87D-391
87D/OD-103
87F-278
87F/GameWin-25
87F/Slug-23
87Mother/SFG-8
87OPC-280
87RedFoley/St-102
87Sf/TPrev-10M
87Stuart-13M
87T-280
87T/St-90
88Classic/Red-175
88D-327
88D/AS-54
88F-88
88F/Mini-117
88F/RecSet-23
88F/SS-21
88F/St-128
88F/Up-U39
88Grenada-31
88KennerFig-62
88Leaf-118
88Mother/Giants-8
88OPC-152
88Panini/St-427
88Panini/St-446
88RedFoley/St-48
88S-580
88Sf-82
88T-570
88T/Coins-46
88T/RiteAid-32
88T/St-16
88T/St-86
88T/St/Backs-17
88T/Tr-61T
88T/UK-43
88Woolwth-17
89B-218
89D-457
89D/Best-107
89D/Tr-1
89F-190
89F/Up-60
89Mother/Sea-8
89OPC-160
89S-557
89S/Tr-7
89T-160
89T/Ames-19
89T/St-199
89T/Tr-72T
89UD-263
89UD/Ext-789
90B-472
90Classic-93
90D-93
90D/BestAL-125
90D/GSlam-2
90F-519
90F/Can-519
90Leaf-219
90Mother/Mar-4
90OPC-455
90Panini/St-150
90PublInt/St-436
90RedFoley/St-58
90S-98
90S/100St-91
90Sf-20
90T-455
90T/Big-303
90T/St-223
90Target-449
90UD-331
91F-456
91OPC-55
91S-44
91T-55
91UD-107

Leonard, Kathy
81Redwd-24

Leonard, Mark
86Cram/NWL-182
86Everett/Pop-11
87Clinton-14
88CalLgAS-3
88SanJose/Cal-122
88SanJose/ProC-134
89Phoenix/CMC-5
89Phoenix/ProC-1498
90AAAGame/ProC-52
90AAASingl/ProC-50
90Phoenix/CMC-19
90Phoenix/ProC-24
90ProC/Singl-546
91B-624
91D-526
91F-265
91Leaf-369
91Mother/Giant-13
91PG&E-22
91S-719RP
91S/Rook40-18
91T/90Debut-86
91UD-557

91Ultra-322
92D-761
92Giant/PGE-23
92Giant/PGE-24
92Mother/Giant-13
92Phoenix/ProC-2833
92Pinn-233
92S-499
92S/100RisSt-62
92StCl-538
92Ultra-591
93D-288
93F-532
93Panini-241
93S-381
93StCl-497
93StCl/1stDay-497
93T-729
93T/Gold-729
Leonard, Mathew
88Geneva/ProC-1645
88Wythe/ProC-1996
89CharWh/Best-9
89CharWh/ProC-1758
Leonard, Tom
81Redwd-23
Leonard, Walter
(Buck)
74Laugh/Black-11
76Shakey-132
80Perez/HOF-132
86Negro/Frit-1
87Negro/Dixon-30
88Conlon/NegAS-7
88Negro/Duques-16
90Negro/Star-26
90Perez/GreatMom-58
91Negro/Lewis-22
92FrRow/Leonard-Set
92Negro/Kraft-16
92Negro/Lee-2
92Negro/Retort-38
92Negro/RetortII-41
93TWill-108
Leonard, Wilfred
48Sommer-20
Leonardo, Juan
75AppFx
Leonette, Mark
83Idaho-8
84Idaho/Team-16
85Madis-22
85Madis/Pol-19
87Pittsfld-16
88Pittsfld/ProC-1371
Leonhard, Dave
68OPC-56R
68T-56R
69MB-158
69T-228
70T-674
71MLB/St-302
71OPC-716
71T-716
72MB-198
72T-527
91Crown/Orio-260
Leonhardt, Dave
92Fayette/ClBest-21
92Fayette/ProC-2175
Leopold, Jim
83Beaum-6
84Beaum-14
85Cram/PCL-119
86Nashua-15
88Louisvl-27
88Louisvl/CMC-10
88Louisvl/ProC-437
Lepcio, Ted
52T-335
53T-18
54B-162
54T-66
55T-128
55T/DH-126
57T-288
58T-29
59T-348
60T-97
61T-234
91T/Arc53-18
94T/Arc54-66
Lepel, Joel
91Kenosha/ClBest-19MG
91Kenosha/ProC-2091MG
Lepley, John
88Hamil/ProC-1737
88NE-8
89ArkTr/GS-10
90ArkTr/GS-20
91AA/LineD-37
91ArkTr/LineD-37
91ArkTr/ProC-1280
Leppert, Don
62T-36
63T-243
64D-463
64Wheat/St-26
73OPC-517CO
73T-517C
74OPC-489CO
74T-489CO
77T-113CO
78BJ/PostC-14CO
78TCMA-101
78TCMA-110
86Kenosha-13MG
87Kenosha-27MG
88Kenosha/ProC-1399
89Kenosha/ProC-1070
91Crown/Orio-261
Lepson, Mark
79BurlB-11
80BurlB-4
81BurlB-9
Lerch, Randy
76OPC-595R
76OkCty/Team-16
76T-595R
77T-489R
78SSPC/270-44
78T-271
79BK/P-8
79T-52
80BK/P-18
80OPC-181
80T-344
81D-574
81F-25
81T-584
81T/Tr-792
82D-595
82F-147
82Pol/Brew-35
82T-466
83F-287
83OPC-22
83Stuart-28
83T-686
84F-380
85D-309
85F-616
85T-103
86Phill/TastyK-35
86Portl-14
89Pac/SenLg-23
89T/SenLg-23
90EliteSenLg-10
Leronix
72Dimanche*-124
Lersch, Barry
69OPC-206R
69T-206R
69T/4in1-22M
71MLB/St-183
71OPC-739
71T-739
72OPC-453
72T-453
73OPC-559
73T-559
74OPC-313
74T-313
74T/Tr-313T
75OkCty/Team-2
Lesher, Brian
92SoOreg/ClBest-6
92SoOreg/ProC-3434
Leshnock, Don
75Shrev/TCMA-9
Leshnock, Donnie
91T/Tr-72T
92Classic/DP-81
92Oneonta/ClBest-8
92StCl/Dome-106
93StCl/MurphyS-137
93T-701M
93T/Gold-701M
Leskanic, Curtis
90Kinston/Team-5
91ClBest/Singl-297
91Kinston/ClBest-5
91Kinston/ProC-317
92OrlanSR/ProC-2844
92OrlanSR/SB-509
92ProC/Tomorrow-57
92Sky/AASingl-218
93L-527
93T-774
93T/Gold-774
94D-580
94Pac/Cr-200
94StCl-507
94StCl/1stDay-507
94StCl/Gold-507
94StCl/Team-118
94T-191
94T/Gold-191
Lesley, Brad
81Cedar-3
82Indianap-5
83D-547
83Indianap-26
85Cram/PCL-202
85T-597
90CedarDG/Best-21
Leslie, Reggie
91CharWh/ClBest-6
91CharWh/ProC-2883
92Cedar/ClBest-9
92Cedar/ProC-1070
92Chatt/SB-190
Leslie, Roy Reid
E120
Leslie, Sam
34DS-68
34Exh/4-2
34G-49
35BU-46
35G-1G
35G-3E
35G-4E
35G-5E
37Exh/4-5
92Conlon/Sport-504
R314
V355-4
Lesslie, Bob
75Water
Lester, Jimmy
88Wichita-22
89CharRain/ProC-989CO
90CharRain/Best-27CO
90CharRain/ProC-2056CO
91Waterlo/ClBest-11
91Waterlo/ProC-1273CO
Letchas, Charlie
89Chatt/II/Team-16
Letendre, Mark
79Colum-11
80Colum-18
81Colum-25
91Mother/Giant-28TR
Letourneau, Jeff
91Erie/ClBest-18
91Erie/ProC-4064
Lett, Jim
80Cedar-22
82Water-23
83Water-19
84Cedar-12
86TexGold-CO
88Kahn/Reds-CO
90CharWh/Best-26MG
90CharWh/ProC-2257MG
91AAA/LineD-275M
91Nashvl/LineD-275CO
91Nashvl/ProC-2174CO
92Nashvl/ProC-1850CO
Letterio, Shane
88Greens/ProC-1556
89Miami/I/Star-11
89Miami/II/Star-11
90ProC/Singl-758
90Wmsprt/Best-14
90Wmsprt/ProC-1064
90Wmsprt/Star-15
91AAA/LineD-64
91Calgary/LineD-64
91Calgary/ProC-522
92Jacks/ProC-3716
92Jaxvl/SB-361
Levan, Jesse
88Chatt/Team-20
Levangie, Dana
91Elmira/ClBest-8
91Elmira/ProC-3273
92WinHaven/ClBest-20
Levenda, John
90AS/Cal-31ADM
Leverette, Gorham
(Dixie)
E120
W573
Levey, James
32Orbit/num-52
32Orbit/un-40
92Conlon/Sport-395
R305
Levi, Stan
80BurlB-27
83ElPaso-11
Levine, Al
91Utica/ClBest-21
91Utica/ProC-3238
92SoBend/ClBest-18
92SoBend/ProC-174
Levinson, Davis
81Redwd-25
Levinson, Steve
81Redwd-30
Levis, Jesse
88CapeCod-13
88CapeCod/Sum-116
89BurlInd/Star-16
90CLAS/CL-39
90Kinston/Team-8
91AA/LineD-88
91Canton/LineD-88
91Canton/ProC-981
92ColoSp/ProC-755
92ColoSp/SB-90
92D/Rook-65
92F/Up-16
93D-669
93F/Final-203
93F/MLPI-14
93Pinn-288
93Pinn/RookTP-3M
93S-330
93StCl-468
93StCl/1stDay-468
93T-801
93T/Gold-801
94Pac/Cr-173
Levsen, Dutch
94Conlon-1304
Lewallyn, Dennis
75Albuq/Caruso-20
78Cr/PCL-110
79Albuq-7
80Albuq-8
82T-356
82Wheat/Ind
83VeroB-29
85VeroB-25
90Target-451
90VeroB/Star-30CO
91VeroB/ProC-793CO
92VeroB/ClBest-30CO
92VeroB/ProC-2896CO
93Rang/Keeb-229
Lewandowski, John
92BurlInd/ClBest-1
92BurlInd/ProC-1659
Lewis, Alan
88Bakers/Cal-237
89VeroB/Star-15
90VeroB/Star-18
91Bakers/Cal-9
92ElPaso/ProC-3931
92ElPaso/SB-216
Lewis, Amos
79Ashvl/TCMA-17
Lewis, Anthony
90Savan/ProC-2083
91ClBest/Singl-137
91StPete/ClBest-27
91StPete/ProC-2290
92StPete/ClBest-17
92StPete/ProC-2040
93FExcel/ML-101
Lewis, Bill
81TCMA-362M
Lewis, Brett
87Pocatel/Bon-3
Lewis, Brian
92GulfCY/ProC-3703
Lewis, Chris
92Lipscomb-4M
93Lipscomb-15
Lewis, Craig
88Watertn/Pucko-8
Lewis, Curt
78OrlanTw
Lewis, Dan
87AubAs-8
88Ashvl/ProC-1061
89Osceola/Star-11
90AS/Cal-40
91AA/LineD-310
91Shrev/LineD-310
91Shrev/ProC-1830
92Phoenix/ProC-2828
92Phoenix/SB-385
Lewis, Darren
89AS/Cal-33
89Modesto/Cal-278
89Modesto/Chong-30
90B-463
90Foil/Best-22
90Huntsvl/Best-1
91AAA/LineD-384
91AAAGame/ProC-33
91Classic/II-T54
91D/Rook-35
91F-15
91OPC-239
91OPC/Premier-73
91Phoenix/LineD-384
91Phoenix/ProC-80
91S-350RP
91S/Rook40-28
91StCl-362
91T-239
91T/90Debut-87
91UD-564
91UD/FinalEd-38F
91Ultra-323
92B-683
92Classic/I-53
92D-615
92F-639
92F/RookSIns-6
92Giant/PGE-25
92L-441
92L/BlkGold-441
92Mother/Giant-11
92OPC-743
92OPC/Premier-151
92Pinn-408
92Pinn/Team2000-63
92ProC/Tomorrow-340
92S-562
92S/100RisSt-10
92StCl-31
92Studio-117
92T-743
92T/Gold-743
92T/GoldWin-743
92TripleP-111
92UD-565
92Ultra-292
93D-392
93F-157
93Flair-143
93L-369
93Mother/Giant-13
93OPC-193
93Pac/Spanish-273
93Pinn-94
93S-203
93StCl-143
93StCl/1stDay-143
93StCl/Giant-25
93T-176
93T/Gold-176
93UD-173
93UD/SP-113
93Ultra-134
94B-659
94D-424
94F-693
94Flair-244
94L-399
94OPC-132
94Pac/Cr-548
94Pinn-169
94Pinn/Artist-169
94Pinn/Museum-169

94S-480
94Sf/2000-8
94StCl-453
94StCl/1stDay-453
94StCl/Gold-453
94StCl/Team-19
94Studio-85
94T-354
94T/Finest-85
94T/FinestRef-85
94T/Gold-354
94TripleP-105
94UD-207
94UD/CollC-174
94UD/CollC/Gold-174
94UD/CollC/Silv-174
94UD/ElecD-207
94Ultra-291
Lewis, George
(Duffy)
16FleischBrd-57
55JC
81Conlon-16
87Conlon/2-36
88Conlon/4-17
91Conlon/Sport-146
BF2-6
D327
D328-99
D329-103
D350/2-101
E121/80
E122
E135-99
E254
E270/2
M101/4-103
M101/5-101
T207
W575
Lewis, Harry
T3/Box-63
Lewis, Herman
80Utica-26
Lewis, Irving
T207
Lewis, Jay
83Peoria/Frit-18
Lewis, Jerry
78Newar
Lewis, Jim L.
92Yank/WIZ80-106
Lewis, Jim M.
79Spokane-13
80Colum-16
81Colum-6
82Colum-22
82Colum/Pol-21
83Toledo-6
84Cram/PCL-180
85Cram/PCL-77
Lewis, Jim S.
86CharRain-13
88River/Cal-212
88River/ProC-1423
89Wichita/Rock-20RHP
90AAASingl/ProC-2
90LasVegas/CMC-6
90LasVegas/ProC-114
90ProC/Singl-509
91AA/LineD-611
91Wichita/LineD-611
91Wichita/Rock-5
92F-612
92RochR/ProC-1935
92RochR/SB-457
92T/91Debut-108
Lewis, Jimmy
89AubAs/ProC-14
91AubAS/ClBest-3
91AubAS/ProC-4269
91ClBest/Singl-411
91Classic/DP-44
91FrRow/DP-28
92Jacks/ProC-3999
92Osceola/ClBest-20
92Osceola/ProC-2529
92S-852
92StCl/Dome-107
Lewis, Joe
89Gaston/ProC-1007
89Gaston/Star-10
90Gaston/Best-20
90Gaston/ProC-2523
90Gaston/Star-12
Lewis, John K.
(Buddy)
37OPC-101
37Wheat-7
38ONG/Pin-17
39PlayBall-47
40PlayBall-20
41PlayBall-47
89Pac/Leg-119
Exh47
V300
Lewis, John
86Peoria-14
87WinSalem-16
88WinSalem/Star-8
Lewis, Johnny
62Kahn/Atl
62Pep/Tul
64T-479R
65OPC-277
65T-277
66T-282
66T/RO-24
66T/RO-52
67CokeCap/YMet-20
67OPC-91
67T-91
74OPC-236CO
74T-236C
91WIZMets-229
Lewis, Ken
89Bristol/Star-14
89Star/IISingl-188
Lewis, Mark
88BurlInd/ProC-1800
89B-87
89Kinston/Star-12
89Star/IISingl-168
89T-222FDP
90A&AASingle/ProC-27
90B-338
90Canton/Best-1
90Canton/ProC-1299
90Canton/Star-9
90EastLAS/ProC-EL36
90Foil/Best-320
90Foil/Best-4
90ProC/Singl-831
90Star/ISingl-13
91AAA/LineD-88
91B-70
91Classic/200-185
91Classic/I-37
91Classic/II-T11
91ColoSp/LineD-88
91ColoSp/ProC-2190
91D-29RR
91D/Rook-42
91F/Up-U19
91Leaf-289
91Leaf/Stud-48
91S/RookTr-106T
91StCl-492
91T/Tr-73T
91UD-17SR
92B-439
92Classic/Game200-48
92D-273
92F-116
92Indian/McDon-15
92L-49
92L/BlkGold-49
92OPC-446
92Panini-46
92Pinn-91
92Pinn/Team2000-57
92ProC/Tomorrow-49
92S-528
92S/100RisSt-50
92S/Impact-82
92StCl-193
92Studio-167
92T-446
92T/91Debut-109
92T/Gold-446
92T/GoldWin-446
92TripleP-205
92UD-235
92Ultra-51
93D-125
93F-216
93Indian/WUAB-16
93OPC-194
93Pac/Spanish-96
93Panini-49
93Pinn-374
93S-164
93Select-150
93StCl-337
93StCl/1stDay-337
93T-762
93T/Gold-762
93TripleP-155
93UD-88
93Ultra-186
94D-464
94F-109
94L-423
94S-483
94T-678
94T/Finest-91
94T/FinestRef-91
94T/Gold-678
94UD-381
Lewis, Mica
88AubAs/ProC-1974
89Ashvl/ProC-966
89AubAs/ProC-2186
90Osceola/Star-15
91Visalia/ClBest-16
91Visalia/ProC-1748
92ClBest-71
92OrlanSR/ProC-2858
92OrlanSR/SB-510
92Sky/AASingl-219
Lewis, Mike
92ClBest-296
92Visalia/ClBest-15
92Visalia/ProC-1009
Lewis, Phil
90Target-1012
Lewis, Richie
88Jaxvl/Best-10
88Jaxvl/ProC-992
90Jaxvl/Best-20
90WPalmB/Star-13
91Harris/ProC-623
92RochR/ProC-1936
92RochR/SB-458
92Sky/AAASingl-208
93B-502
93D-265
93F/Final-65
93Marlin/Publix-16
93Pinn-608
93Select/RookTr-139T
93StCl-619
93StCl/1stDay-619
93T/Tr-90T
93USPlayC/Marlin-13S
93USPlayC/Marlin-4D
93Ultra-381
94D-297
94F-471
94L-14
94Pac/Cr-245
94S-280
94S/GoldR-280
94StCl-427
94StCl/1stDay-427
94StCl/Gold-427
94StCl/Team-74
94T-47
94T/Gold-47
94Ultra-196
Lewis, Rufus
91Negro/Lewis-30
Lewis, Scott
89MidldA/GS-21
89TexLAS/GS-5
90AAASingl/ProC-92
90Edmon/CMC-10
90Edmon/ProC-516
90ProC/Singl-487
91B-192
91S-759RP
91S/Rook40-9
91Smok/Angel-19
91T/90Debut-88
91UD-594
92Edmon/ProC-3537
92S-165
92StCl-43
92Ultra-328
93D-167
93F-575
93Mother/Angel-19
93Pac/Spanish-49
93StCl/Angel-14
93T-668
93T/Gold-668
Lewis, Steve
83AlexD-25
84PrWill-19
85PrWill-9
Lewis, T.R.
89Bluefld/Star-13
90Foil/Best-10
90ProC/Singl-869
90Star/ISingl-32
90Wausau/Best-1
90Wausau/ProC-2133
90Wausau/Star-14
91ClBest/Singl-238
91Freder/ClBest-18
91Freder/ProC-2372
91Perth/Fut-10
92Freder/ProC-1811
92Kane/ClBest-8
92Kane/ProC-99
92UD/ML-183
93B-85
94FExcel-10
Lewis, Tim
89KS*-19
Lewis, Timothy
77WHave
79WHave-18
Lewis, Tony
87Spokane-3
88Charl/ProC-1214
89River/Best-9
89River/Cal-24
89River/ProC-1395
90Waterlo/Best-9
90Waterlo/ProC-2376
Lewis, Tyrone
92GulfCD/ProC-3574
Lewis, Willie
T3/Box-74
Lewright, Cleo
52Laval-23
Lexa, Michael
87Kenosha-10
88Kenosha/ProC-1395
Ley, Terry
72OPC-506R
72T-506R
92Yank/WIZ70-96
Leyland, Jim
75Clinton
80Evansvl-17
81Evansvl-1
86T/Tr-66T
87T-93MG
88T-624MG
89T-284MG
89VFJuice-10MG
90Homer/Pirate-19MG
90OPC-699MG
90T-699MG
91OPC-381MG
91T-381MG
92OPC-141MG
92Pirate/Nation-11MG
92T-141MG
92T/Gold-141MG
92T/GoldWin-141MG
93Pirate/Nation-14MG
93T-511M
93T/Gold-511M
Leyritz, Jim
87FtLaud-24
88Albany/ProC-1344
89Albany/Best-2
89Albany/ProC-325
89Albany/Star-10
89EastLgAS/ProC-9
90AAASingl/ProC-331
90AlbanyDG/Best-6
90Classic/III-60
90ColClip/CMC-11
90ColClip/ProC-681
90Colum/Pol-5
90F/Up-U112
90Leaf-465
90ProC/Singl-211
90S/NWest-10
90S/Tr-83T
90T/TVYank-50
90T/Tr-61T
90UD/Ext-723
91B-171
91D-219
91F-671
91OPC-202
91Panini/FrSt-326
91S-65
91S/100RisSt-29
91T-202
91T/90Debut-89
91T/JumboR-16
91UD-243
91Ultra-237
92D-649
92StCl-198
92UD-117
92Ultra-412
93D-477
93F/Final-248
93Flair-248
93L-468
93Pac/Spanish-559
93StCl-234
93StCl/1stDay-234
93T-385
93T/Gold-385
93Ultra-597
94D-146
94F-237
94Flair-83
94L-158
94Pac/Cr-428
94Pinn-517
94S-213
94S/GoldR-213
94StCl-283
94StCl/1stDay-283
94StCl/Gold-283
94StCl/Team-192
94T-728
94T/Gold-728
94Ultra-97
Leystra, Jeff
93MedHat/ProC-3732
93MedHat/SportP-18
Leyva, Damian
92BurlInd/ClBest-19
92BurlInd/ProC-1652
Leyva, Nick
77ArkTr
83ArkTr-23
89Phill/TastyK-18MG
89T-74MG
90OPC-489MG
90Phill/TastyK-20MG
90T-489MG
91OPC-141MG
91T-141MG
92Syrac/MerchB-11MG
92Syrac/ProC-1986MG
92Syrac/SB-524MG
93Syrac/ProC-1013MG
Lezcano, Carlos
81D-521
81F-307
81T-381R
82F-51
83Iowa-23
84Cram/PCL-79
91Penin/ProC-395CO
Lezcano, Sixto
74Sacra
76A&P/Milw
76OPC-353
76SSPC-241
76T-353
77BurgChef-89
77Ho-12
77Ho/Twink-12
77K-27
77OPC-71
77T-185
78Ho-35
78OPC-102
78T-595
78Wiffle/Discs-38
79Ho-136
79OPC-364
79T-685
80OPC-114
80T-215
80T/S-31
80T/Super-31
81Coke

81D-207
81F-513
81OPC-25
81T-25
81T/SO-45
81T/St-218
81T/Tr-793
82D-64
82F-119
82OPC-271
82T-727
82T/St-95
82T/Tr-63T
83D-499
83F-364
83F/St-27M
83F/St-5M
83OPC-244
83OPC/St-298
83T-455
83T/St-298
84F-38
84Nes/792-185
84OPC-185
84Phill/TastyK-38
84T-185
85D-529
85F-258
85F/Up-U72
85OPC-89
85T-556
85T/Tr-75T
86T-278
Libke, Al
44Centen-14
45Playball-40
47Signal
Liborio, Dennis
90Mother/Ast-28EQMG
92Mother/Ast-28M
Liburdi, John
84Albany-10
85Albany-34
86Albany/TCMA-13
Lich, Rod
84Cedar-23
85Cedar-29
86Tampa-10TR
87Vermont-27
92Augusta/ClBest-27
Lickert, John
83Pawtu-13
85Richm-11
Liddell, Dave
86Peoria-15
87Columbia-13
88Reno/Cal-287
89Jacks/GS-25
89Tidew/CMC-18
90AAASingl/ProC-278
90ProC/Singl-371
90T/TVMets-49
90Tidew/CMC-20
90Tidew/ProC-547
91T/90Debut-90
91WIZMets-230
92Denver/ProC-2644
92Denver/SB-138
Liddle, Don
53JC-9
53SpicSpan/3x5-15
54NYJour
54T-225
55B-146
55Gol/Giants-16
56T-325
94T/Arc54-225
Liddle, Steve
82Redwd-7
83Nashua-10
84Cram/PCL-107
85Cram/PCL-13
86Edmon-17
87Portl-10
88Portl/CMC-12
88Portl/ProC-655
89Kenosha/ProC-1084
89Kenosha/Star-25
90Kenosha/Best-27MG
90Kenosha/ProC-2310MG
90Kenosha/Star-25MG
91Visalia/ClBest-24MG
91Visalia/ProC-1757MG
92Visalia/ClBest-24MG
92Visalia/ProC-1029MG
Lidle, Cory
92Elizab/ClBest-15
92Elizab/ProC-3676
Lidle, Kevin
92Bristol/ProC-1414
Lieber, Jon
92ClBest/Up-421
92Classic/DP-29
92Eugene/ClBest-16
92Eugene/ProC-3027
92FrRow/DP-76
93StCl/MurphyS-57
94FExcel-68
Liebert, Allen
86Lakeland-10
87Fayette-15
88CLAS/Star-29
88Kinston/Star-15
89Canton/Best-21
89Canton/ProC-1314
89Canton/Star-12
90Canton/Best-6
90Canton/ProC-1294
90EastLAS/ProC-EL35
92BirmB/ProC-2586
92BirmB/SB-88
Lieberthal, Mike
90A&AASingle/ProC-193
90Classic/DP-3
90Classic/III-62
90LitSun/HSPros-2
90LitSun/HSProsG-2
90Martins/ProC-3197
91B-506
91ClBest/Singl-290
91OPC-471
91S-683FDP
91SALAS/ProC-SAL44
91Spartan/ClBest-14
91Spartan/ProC-899
91T-471
91UD-67TP
92ClBest-231
92Classic/DP-93FB
92ProC/Tomorrow-302
92Reading/ProC-578
92Reading/SB-532
92Sky/AASingl-230
92UD/ML-184
92UD/POY-PY17
93B-20
93ClBest/Fisher-11
93FExcel/ML-86
93FExcel/MLAS-4
93ScranWB/Team-13
93StCl/Phill-19
94B-112
94F/MLP-21
94FExcel-246
94StCl/Team-233
94Ultra-550
Liebhardt, Glenn
T206
Liebold, Harry
21Exh-96
21Exh-97
Liebovitz, Neil
75FtLaud/Sus-4
Lien, Al
48Sommer-7
49Sommer-5
52Mother-47
Lienhard, Steve
87Pocatel/Bon-5
88Clinton/ProC-694
89AS/Cal-47
89SanJose/Best-20
89SanJose/Cal-214
89SanJose/ProC-456
89SanJose/Star-17
90Shrev/ProC-1440
91AA/LineD-185
91ElPaso/LineD-185
91ElPaso/ProC-2745
92ElPaso/SB-217
Lieppman, Keith
75Tucson/Caruso-10
76Tucson-6
79Ogden/TCMA-26
82Idaho-30
82WHave-27
84Albany-7
85Cram/PCL-126MG
86Tacoma-13MG
87Tacoma-14MG
Lifgren, Kelly
88Spokane/ProC-1925
89River/Best-10
89River/Cal-16
89River/ProC-1392
90Foil/Best-190
90River/Best-15
90River/Cal-22
90River/ProC-2605
91ClBest/Singl-120
91HighD/ClBest-7
91HighD/ProC-2390
92HighD/ClBest-8
Liggett, Troy
89TNTech-14
Lightner, Ed
91BendB/ClBest-23
91BendB/ProC-3701
Liles, Greyson
90AR-19
Lillard, Robert E.
37Wheat
46Sunbeam
47Remar-22
47Signal
47Smith-6
48Signal
48Smith-8
Lilliquist, Derek
88Richm-24
88Richm/CMC-2
88Richm/ProC-21
89B-264
89Brave/Dubuq-15
89Classic/Up/2-172
89D-653
89D/Best-226
89D/Rook-54
89F/Up-73
89S-631
89S/HotRook-23
89T/Tr-73T
89UD/Ext-753
90B-7
90Brave/Dubuq/Perf-17
90D-286
90F-588
90F/Can-588
90HotRook/St-27
90OPC-282
90Panini/St-223
90PublInt/St-116
90S-243
90S/100Ris-19
90S/YS/I-30
90Sf-24
90T-282
90T/89Debut-70
90T/Big-192
90T/JumboR-18
90ToysRUs-17
90UD-234
91AAA/LineD-287
91D-570
91F-535
91LasVegas/LineD-287
91LasVegas/ProC-231
91OPC-683
91S-571
91StCl-268
91T-683
91UD-251
92Indian/McDon-16
92L-451
92L/BlkGold-451
92S/RookTr-44T
92StCl-864
93D-9
93F-217
93Flair-194
93Indian/WUAB-17
93L-444
93OPC-211
93Pac/Spanish-413
93S-548
93StCl-441
93StCl/1stDay-441
93T-31
93T/Gold-31
93UD-70
93Ultra-187
94D-154
94F-110
94Pinn-219
94Pinn/Artist-219
94Pinn/Museum-219
94S-194
94S/GoldR-194
94StCl-508
94StCl/1stDay-508
94StCl/Gold-508
94T-301
94T/Gold-301
94UD/CollC-175
94UD/CollC/Gold-175
94UD/CollC/Silv-175
94Ultra-344
Lillis, Bob
59DF
59T-133
60T-3
61BB-11
61T-38
62Salada-108A
62Salada-108B
62Shirriff-108
62T-74
63J-191
63P-191
63Pep
63T-119
64T-321
74OPC-31CO
74T-31C
78TCMA-42
83T-66MG
84D-84MG
84Mother/Ast-15MG
84Nes/792-441MG
84T-441MG
85Mother/Ast-1MG
85T-186MG
86T-561MG
89Smok/Ast-17
90Mother/Giant-21M
90Target-452
91Mother/Giant-27CO
92Giant/PGE-26CO
92Mother/Giant-28M
93Mother/Giant-28M
Lim, Ron
90LSUPol-12
Lima, Jose
90Bristol/ProC-3156
90Bristol/Star-14
92Lakeland/ClBest-9
92Lakeland/ProC-2274
93LimeR/Winter-143
93LimeR/Winter-87
94B-481
Limbach, Chris
86Cram/NWL-147
88Clearw/Star-17
88FSLAS/Star-10
90SALAS/Star-15
90Spartan/Best-7
90Spartan/ProC-2488
90Spartan/Star-13
91Clearw/ClBest-6
91Clearw/ProC-1617
92Reading/ProC-571
92Reading/SB-533
92Sky/AASingl-231
Limmer, Lou
52Park-86
54T-232
55B-80
55T-54
55T/DH-16
94T/Arc54-232
Limon, Vinny
88NE-24
Limoncelli, Bill
79Elmira-23
80Elmira-34
87Elmira/Black-2
87Elmira/Red-2
88Elmira-27MG
Limoncelli, Jeff
90Elmira/Pucko-7
Linares, Antonio
88Martins/Star-22
89Spartan/ProC-1046
89Spartan/Star-13
89Star/Wax-55
90Spartan/Best-20
90Spartan/ProC-2503
90Spartan/Star-14
Linares, Mario
91AubAS/ClBest-15
91AubAS/ProC-4277
92Ashvl/ClBest-22
Linares, Rich
94ClBest/Gold-185
94FExcel-217
Linares, Rufino
79Savan
81Pol/Atl-25
82BK/Lids-15
82D-310
82F-439
82Pol/Atl-25
82T-244
83D-275
83F-140
83T-467
84Richm-2
85T-167
86Edmon-18
Linarez, Jose
87Pocatel/Bon-32
Lincoln, Lance
84AZ/Pol-10
86Beloit-13
87Beloit-14
Lind, Carl
29Exh/4-21
94Conlon-1262
Lind, Jack
75Sacra/Caruso-4
83Redwd-30
87Nashvl-13MG
88Nashvl/CMC-23MG
88Nashvl/ProC-486MG
Lind, Jose
85PrWill-17
86Nashua-16
87Vanco-19
88Classic/Red-195
88D-38RR
88D/Best-145
88F-334
88Leaf-38RR
88Panini/St-371
88S-597
88S/YS/II-4
88T-767
88T/Big-106
88T/St-127
89B-421
89Bimbo/Discs-7
89Classic-20
89D-290
89D/Best-101
89F-214
89KennerFig-85
89OPC-273
89Panini/St-170
89RedFoley/St-75
89S-87
89Sf-62
89T-273
89T/Big-25
89T/St-126
89UD-334
89VFJuice-13
90B-170
90D-172
90D/BestNL-82
90F-474
90F/Can-474
90Homer/Pirate-20
90Leaf-77
90OPC-168
90Panini/St-328
90PublInt/St-159
90PublInt/St-616
90S-83
90Sf-58
90T-168
90T/Big-196
90T/St-131
90UD-424
91B-530
91D-58
91F-43
91Leaf-146
91Leaf/Stud-227
91OPC-537
91Panini/FrSt-116

91Panini/St-117
91S-461
91S/100SS-33
91StCl-233
91T-537
91UD-258
91Ultra-283
92B-351
92Classic/Game200-178
92D-189
92F-559
92L-175
92L/BlkGold-175
92OPC-43
92Panini-253
92Pinn-49
92Pinn-603SH
92Pirate/Nation-12
92S-265
92StCl-859
92Studio-86
92T-43
92T/Gold-43
92T/GoldWin-43
92UD-205
92Ultra-255
93B-153
93D-675
93F-115
93F/Final-221
93Flair-219
93L-402
93OPC-120
93OPC/Premier-42
93Pac/Beisbol-8
93Pac/Spanish-489
93Pac/SpanishP-2
93Pinn-103
93Pol/Royal-16
93S-660
93Select-105
93Select/RookTr-22T
93StCl-729
93StCl/1stDay-729
93StCl/Royal-10
93Studio-189
93T-108
93T/Gold-108
93UD-309
93UD-513
93Ultra-563
93Ultra/AwardWin-4
94B-611
94D-306
94F-163
94L-65
94OPC-68
94Pac/Cr-292
94Panini-76
94Pinn-199
94Pinn/Artist-199
94Pinn/Museum-199
94S-39
94S/GoldR-39
94Select-51
94SelectSam-51
94StCl-135
94StCl/1stDay-135
94StCl/Gold-135
94StCl/Pr-135
94StCl/PreProd-135
94T-332
94T/Finest-46
94T/FinestRef-46
94T/Gold-332
94TripleP-237
94UD-161
94UD/CollC-176
94UD/CollC/Gold-176
94UD/CollC/Silv-176
94UD/ElecD-161
94Ultra-68

Lind, Orlando
85PrWill-1
86Nashua-17
87Harris-14
88Harris/ProC-847
89Harris/ProC-300
89Harris/Star-9
90AAASingl/ProC-245
90OrlanSR/Star-9
90Portl/ProC-175
91AA/LineD-484
91OrlanSR/LineD-484
91OrlanSR/ProC-1845
92Portl/SB-413
92Portland/ProC-2663

Lind, Randy
87Everett-11

Lindaman, Vivian
T206

Lindblad, Paul
66T-568R
67T-227
68OPC-127
68T-127
69T-449
70OPC-408
70T-408
71MLB/St-519
71OPC-658
71T-658
72OPC-396
72T-396
73OPC-406
73T-406
74OPC-369
74T-369
75OPC-278
75T-278
75T/M-278
76K-52
76OPC-9
76SSPC-479
76T-9
77BurgChef-117
77T-583
78SSPC/270-85
78T-314
79T-634
87ElPaso-20CO
88ElPaso/Best-10CO
89ElPaso/GS-2CO
90ElPaso/GS-2CO
91AA/LineD-200CO
91ElPaso/LineD-200CO
91ElPaso/ProC-2763CO
92Penin/ClBest-29CO
92Penin/ProC-2950CO
92Yank/WIZ70-97
93Rang/Keeb-24

Lindell, John
43Playball-3
44Yank/St-17
47HomogBond-30
47TipTop
48B-11
48L-82
48Swell-17
49B-197
50B-209
52Mother-1
53T-230
54B-159
54T-51
91T/Arc53-230
92Yank/WIZAS-40
93Conlon-715
94T/Arc54-51
D305
Exh47
R346-5

Lindell, Rick
91Pac/SenLg-72

Lindeman, Ernest
E254
T204

Lindeman, Jim
86Louisvl-16
87Classic/Up-111
87D-37RR
87D/OD-59
87D/Rook-41
87F/Mini-64
87F/Up-U65
87Leaf-37RR
87Sf/Rook-43
87Smok/Cards-14
87T/Tr-65T
88D-540
88F-39
88Louisvl-28
88OPC-16
88S-302
88T-562
89Louisvl-26
89Smok/Cards-11
89T-791
90AAASingl/ProC-386
90ProC/Singl-392
90SpringDG/Best-29
90Toledo/CMC-15
90Toledo/ProC-156
91AAA/LineD-487
91ScranWB/LineD-487
92D-701
92F-538
92OPC-258
92Phill/Med-19
92S-321
92StCl-893
92T-258
92T/Gold-258
92T/GoldWin-258

Lindemann, Skip
89GA-19
89GA-28M

Lindemuth, John
90BBWit-87M

Linden, Mark
89Geneva/ProC-1878

Lindquist, Dan
83TriCit-11
84Visalia-25

Lindros, Eric
90S/Tr-100T
92StCl/MemberIII*-11

Lindsay, Chuck
80LynnS-5

Lindsay, Darian
90Kgsport/Best-2
90Kgsport/Star-14
91Parramatta/Fut-4
91Pittsfld/ClBest-19
91Pittsfld/ProC-3418
92ColumMet/ClBest-8
92ColumMet/ProC-290
92ColumMet/SAL/II-12

Lindsay, Jon
91GulfCR/SportP-16

Lindsay, Tim
91StCath/ClBest-21
91StCath/ProC-3390
92Myrtle/ClBest-18
92Myrtle/ProC-2193
93Dunedin/ClBest-14

Lindsey, Darrell
88Martins/Star-21
89Spartan/ProC-1040
89Spartan/Star-14
90Clearw/Star-11
91AA/LineD-511
91Reading/LineD-511
91Reading/ProC-1369
92Clearw/ProC-2055

Lindsey, Dave
75Sacra/Caruso-2

Lindsey, Don
89Eugene/Best-5

Lindsey, Douglas
(Doug)
82Danvl/Frit-12

Lindsey, Elmer
(Bee)
62Pep/Tul
63Pep/Tul

Lindsey, Jim
90Target-453

Lindsey, John
85Clovis-24

Lindsey, Jon
82Reading-16

Lindsey, Michael Douglas
(Doug)
88Spartan/ProC-1042
88Spartan/Star-11
90ProC/Singl-776
90Reading/Best-12
90Reading/ProC-1223
90Reading/Star-16
91AA/LineD-512
91ClBest/Singl-100
91Reading/LineD-512
91Reading/ProC-1372
92ScranWB/ProC-2449
92ScranWB/SB-487
92T/91Debut-110
93ScranWB/Team-14
93StCl/Phill-10

Lindsey, William D.
(Bill)
85Albany-12
86Albany/TCMA-22
87BirmB/Best-26
88F-403
88Vanco/CMC-16
88Vanco/ProC-758

Lindstrom, Fred
26Exh-36
27Exh-20
28Exh-19
29Exh/4-10
31Exh/4-9
33DL-11
33Exh/4-5
33G-133
35BU-122
36Exh/4-2
75Sheraton-23
76Rowe-9
76Shakey-156
77Galasso-127
80Pac/Leg-100
80Perez/HOF-156
80SSPC/HOF
88Conlon/NatAS-13
89Smok/Dodg-103
90Target-454
91Conlon/Sport-58
92Conlon/Sport-596
R306
R312/M
R314
R315-A23
R315-B23
R316
V354-17
V355-65
W517-24

Linduyt, Doug
79Cedar/TCMA-31

Linebarger, Keith
92Elizab/ClBest-2
92Elizab/ProC-3677

Lines, Richard
61Union
67CokeCap/Senator-10
67T-273
68T-291

Linfante, Rob
91OKSt-14
92OKSt-15

Lingerman, Nemo
78Wisco

Link, Bryan
94B-349
94FExcel-11
94FExcel/1stY-2

Link, Dave
83StPete-30

Link, Robert
86Water-14
87Wmsprt-7
88GlenF/ProC-937
89Toledo/CMC-6
89Toledo/ProC-778

Linke, Ed
93Conlon-961

Linke, Fred
M116

Linnert, Tom
75SanAn
76Wmsprt

Lino, Rivera Ortiz
87Gaston/ProC-9

Linquist, Bryan
89KS*-77

Linskey, Mike
89Freder/Star-13
90A&AASingle/ProC-1
90AAASingl/ProC-475
90Foil/Best-21
90Hagers/Best-20
90Hagers/ProC-1407
90HagersDG/Best-15
90RochR/ProC-718
90Rochester/L&U-20
91AAA/LineD-468
91B-105
91RochR/LineD-468
91RochR/ProC-1897
92F-663
92Wichita/ProC-3655
92Wichita/SB-638

Lint, Royce
54Hunter
55B-62

Linton, Dave
85Utica-3
86DayBe-16

Linton, Doug
87Myrtle-5
88Knoxvl/Best-15
90AAASingl/ProC-347
90ProC/Singl-331
90Syrac/CMC-5
90Syrac/MerchB-14
90Syrac/ProC-567
90Syrac/Team-14
91AAA/LineD-507
91Syrac/LineD-507
91Syrac/MerchB-11
91Syrac/ProC-2478
92B-277
92Sky/AAASingl-228
92Syrac/MerchB-12
92Syrac/ProC-1964
92Syrac/SB-510
93BJ/D/45-35
93D-321
93S-295
93Syrac/ProC-996
93T-159
93T/Gold-159

Lintz, Larry
72Dimanche*-26
74OPC-121
74T-121
75OPC-416
75T-416
75T/M-416
76OPC-109
76SSPC-286
76T-109
77T-323

Lintz, Ricky
81Watlo-11
82Watlo/B-6
82Watlo/Frit-5

Linz, Phil
62T-596R
63T-264
64T-344
65T-369
66T-522
67CokeCap/Phill-8
67OPC-14
67T-14
68T-594
78TCMA-97
91WIZMets-231
92Yank/WIZ60-72
Exh47
WG10-12
WG9-14

Linzy, Frank
65T-589R
66OPC-78
66T-78
67CokeCap/Giant-13
67T-279
68CokeCap/Giant-13
68Dexter-48
68OPC-147
68T-147
69MLB/St-202
69T-345
70MLB/St-127
70OPC-77
70T-77
71MLB/St-277
71OPC-551
71T-551
72MB-199
72OPC-243
72T-243
73OPC-286
73T-286
75Hawaii/Caruso-13

Lipe, Perry H.
T206

Lipon, John
51B-285
52B-163
52T-89
53B/Col-123
53T-40
54T-19
61BeeHive-12
76Shrev

78Colum
79Portl-9
81Buffa-1
81Tiger/Detroit-26
82AlexD-21
83AlexD-11
84PrWill-29
85Nashua-27
87Fayette-17
88FSLAS/Star-28
90FSLAS/Star-49
90Lakeland/Star-26MG
91Lakeland/ClBest-29MG
91Lakeland/ProC-282MG
91T/Arc53-40
92Lakeland/ClBest-27MG
92Lakeland/ProC-2293MG
94T/Arc54-19
Lipscomb, Bruce
89CharlR/Star-13
Lipski, Robert
63T-558R
Lipson, Marc
90A&AASingle/ProC-113
90Foil/Best-101
90Kenosha/Best-20
90Kenosha/ProC-2289
90Kenosha/Star-9
90MidwLgAS/GS-14
91ClBest/Singl-229
91Visalia/ClBest-4
91Visalia/ProC-1738
92OrlanSR/ProC-2845
Lipson, Stefan
83Butte-7
Lira, Felipe
90Bristol/ProC-3165
90Bristol/Star-15
92Lakeland/ClBest-16
92Lakeland/ProC-2275
93B-643
94FExcel-57
Liranzo, Rafael
78RochR
Liriano, Felix
88Fayette/ProC-1093
Liriano, Julio
88Watlo/ProC-675
Liriano, Nelson
85Kingst-13
86Knoxvl-15
87Syrac-2
87Syrac/TCMA-17
88BJ/5x7-8
88D-32RR
88F-117
88Leaf-32RR
88OPC-205
88S-621
88S/YS/I-13
88T-205
88T/Big-155
88Tor/Fire-2
89Classic/Up/2-196
89D-627
89D/Best-160
89F-239
89OPC-76
89S-577
89T-776
89T/Big-207
89Tor/Fire-2
89UD-109
90B-518
90D-267
90F-87
90F/Can-87
90OPC-543
90Panini/St-182
90PublInt/St-522
90S-77
90T-543
90T/Big-142
90T/St-197
90Tor/BJ-2
90UD-134
91D-603
91F-617
91OPC-18
91S-288
91T-18
91UD-360
92ColoSp/ProC-758
92ColoSp/SB-91
93LimeR/Winter-21
93T/Tr-53T
94StCl/Team-110
Lis, Joe Jr.
91StCath/ClBest-9
91StCath/ProC-3404
92Myrtle/ClBest-15
92Myrtle/ProC-2204
92Myrtle/ProC-2204
93ClBest/MLG-129
93Knoxvl/ProC-1260
93SALAS/II-20
Lis, Joseph
(Joe)
70OPC-56R
70T-56R
71OPC-138R
71T-138R
74OPC-659
74T-659
75OPC-86
75OkCty/Team-20
75T-86
75T/M-86
76SSPC-523
77Ho-125
77Ho/Twink-125
77T-269
Liscio, Joe
59DF
Lisenbee, Horace
(Hod)
33G-68
92Conlon/Sport-540
V354-45
Lisi, Rick
75Anderson/TCMA-13
79Tulsa-14
80CharCh-9
82RochR-14
83RochR-21
84Richm-7
93Rang/Keeb-230
Lisiecki, David
91Belling/ClBest-22
91Belling/ProC-3658
92ProC/Tomorrow-147
Liska, Ad
R316
Liss, Tom
88Belling/Legoe-17
89Belling/Legoe-8
List, Paul
87Salem/ProC-2431
88Bend/Legoe-32
91Augusta/ClBest-21
91Augusta/ProC-820
92Gaston/ProC-2264
Listach, Pat
89Stockton/Best-22
89Stockton/Cal-173
89Stockton/ProC-379
89Stockton/Star-4
90AS/Cal-36
90Stockton/Best-5
90Stockton/Cal-191
90Stockton/ProC-2190
91AA/LineD-191
91ElPaso/LineD-191
91ElPaso/ProC-2753
92B-526
92D/RookPhen-BC7
92D/Up-U1RR
92F/Up-36
92JDean/Rook-2
92L-370
92L/BlkGold-370
92Pinn-562
92Pinn/Rook-5
92Pol/Brew-13
92S/RookTr-80T
92StCl-757
92StCl/MemberIII*-5
92T/Tr-65T
92T/TrGold-65T
92UD-775DD
92UD/Scout-SR13
92Ultra-385
93B-395
93Classic/Gamel-53
93Colla/DM-64
93D-309
93D/DK-29ROY
93F-253
93F/ASAL-4
93F/Fruit-36
93F/RookSenl-3
93F/TLAL-3
93Flair-226
93Ho-32
93JDean/28-28
93L-264
93L/Fast-10
93OPC-205
93OPC/Premier/StarP-15
93Pac/Spanish-160
93Panini-163ROY
93Panini-39
93Pinn-33
93Pinn/TP-7M
93Pol/Brew-15
93S-357
93S-485AW
93Select-273
93Select/ChasRook-1
93Select/StatL-56
93StCl-293MC
93StCl-432
93StCl/1stDay-293MC
93StCl/1stDay-432
93Studio-146
93T-480
93T/BlkGold-35
93T/Finest-109AS
93T/FinestASJ-109AS
93T/FinestRef-109AS
93T/Gold-480
93ToysRUs-5
93TripleP-116
93TripleP/LL-L3M
93UD-253
93UD-43M
93UD-491AW
93UD-817TC
93UD/5thAnn-A13
93UD/FunPack-71
93UD/SP-67
93USPlayC/Ace-12H
93USPlayC/Rook-1H
93USPlayC/Rook-JK
93Ultra-571
93Ultra/AwardWin-19
93Ultra/Perf-5
94B-617
94D-148
94F-181
94L-420
94OPC-216
94Pac/Cr-332
94Panini-83
94Pinn-449
94Pol/Brew-16
94S-371
94StCl-354
94StCl/1stDay-354
94StCl/Gold-354
94T-130
94T/Finest-79
94T/Finest/PreProd-79
94T/FinestRef-79
94T/Gold-130
94TripleP-55
94UD-305
94UD/HoloFX-25
94UD/SP-59
94Ultra-374
Lister, Martin
92Billings/ProC-3350
94FExcel-178
Littell, Mark
74OPC-596R
74T-596R
75Omaha/Team-9
76OPC-593R
76SSPC-181
76T-593R
77T-141
78T-331
79T-466
80T-631
81D-580
81F-544
81T-255
82D-442
82F-120
82T-56
89Watlo/ProC-1784CO
89Watlo/Star-27CO
90CharRain/Best-25CO
90CharRain/ProC-2055CO
90Swell/Great-112
91HighD/ClBest-30CO
91HighD/ProC-2414CO
92Stockton/ClBest-24CO
92Stockton/ProC-52CO
Littimer, Dave
91CalLgAS-54
Little, Bryan
83Expo/PostC-10
83Stuart-24
83T/Tr-62T
84D-157
84Expo/PostC-17
84F-279
84Nes/792-188
84OPC-188
84Stuart-30
84T-188
85BuffB-9
85F-402
85OPC-257
85T-257
86D-452
86F-212
86T-346
87Colum-14
87Colum/Pol-16
87Colum/TCMA-14
88BuffB/CMC-16
88BuffB/Polar-3
88BuffB/ProC-1491
89AubAs/ProC-27
89Wichita/Rock-4CO
90Waterlo/Best-19MG
90Waterlo/ProC-2393MG
91Waterlo/ClBest-25MG
91Waterlo/ProC-1272MG
92HighD/ClBest-29MG
92Yank/WIZ80-107
Little, Dick
92Salinas/ClBest-27CO
92Salinas/ProC-3776CO
Little, Doug
87DayBe-8
88BirmB/Best-26
89BirmB/Best-22
89BirmB/ProC-93
Little, Grady
84CharlO-10
85Kingst-24
88BurlB/ProC-11
89Durham/Star-26MG
89Durham/Team-28MG
90Durham/Team-29MG
90HagersDG/Best-16MG
91Durham/ClBest-15MG
91Durham/ProC-1676MG
92Greenvl/ProC-1168
92Greenvl/SB-249MG
93Richm/Bleach-25MG
93Richm/Pep-25MG
93Richm/Team-1MG
Little, Jeff
75Lafay
78Cr/PCL-37
79Phoenix
82Toledo-4
83F-619
83T-499
83Toledo-7
Little, Marc
92WinSalem/ClBest-10
Little, Martin
80Wausau-5
Little, Mike
89Wythe/Star-20
90Hunting/ProC-3301
91Peoria/ClBest-21
91Peoria/ProC-1358
91Peoria/Team-27
92WinSalem/ProC-1221
Little, Randy
86Cram/NWL-119
Little, Richard
(Dick)
82Wichita-9
91Salinas/ClBest-25CO
91Salinas/ProC-2263CO
Little, Ronald
82Water-21
83Indianap-20
Little, Scott
84LitFalls-4
85Lynch-27
86Jacks/TCMA-21
88Harris/ProC-838
89BuffB/CMC-20
89BuffB/ProC-1681
90AAASingl/ProC-503
90BuffB/CMC-25
90BuffB/ProC-388
90BuffB/Team-14
90ProC/Singl-25
90T/89Debut-71
91AAA/LineD-31
91BuffB/LineD-31
91BuffB/ProC-552
92Augusta/ClBest-25
92Augusta/ProC-255
93SALAS/II-21MG
Little, Thomas
86Cram/NWL-109
Littlefield, John
77StPete
79ArkTr-6
81D-309
81F-535
81T-489
81T/Tr-794
82D-145
82F-576
82Syrac-5
82Syrac/Team-15
82T-278
Littlefield, Richard
(Dick)
52B-209
54B-213
54Esskay
55B-200
57T-346
58T-241
79TCMA-14
91Crown/Orio-262
Littlejohn, Dennis
78Cr/PCL-61
79Phoenix
80Phoenix/NBank-18
80T-686R
81D-313
81F-455
81Phoenix-18
81T-561
Littleton, Larry
79Portl-19
80Tacoma-3
82Charl-20
Littlewood, Mike
87BYU-9
Litton, Greg
84Everett/Cram-1
85Fresno/Pol-12
86Shrev-15
87Shrev-8
89F/Up-130
89S/Tr-86T
90AAASingl/ProC-46
90D-453
90F-61
90F/Can-61
90HotRook/St-28
90Leaf-331
90Mother/Giant-18
90OPC-66
90Phoenix/ProC-20
90S-497
90S/100Ris-91
90S/YS/I-33
90T-66
90T/89Debut-72
90T/Big-308
90UD-677
91B-621
91D-198
91F-266
91Mother/Giant-18
91OPC-628
91PG&E-8
91S-533
91StCl-45
91T-628
91Ultra-324
92F-640
92Mother/Giant-18
92OPC-238
92Phoenix/SB-386

92S-603
92StCl-439
92T-238
92T/Gold-238
92T/GoldWin-238
93Calgary/ProC-1171
93D-340
93F-533
93F/Final-273
93StCl/Mar-10
94F-292
94Pac/Cr-575
94T-111
94T/Gold-111
Littrell, Jack Jr.
78Clinton
79Wausau-15
Littrell, Jack Sr.
55Rodeo
Litwhiler, Dan
41DP-100
41DP-45
47TipTop
49B-97
49Eureka-88
50B-198
51B-179
Litzinger, Jeff
88CapeCod-8
88CapeCod/Sum-185
Livchak, Robert
87StPete-27
88StPete/Star-13
Lively, Everett
49Eureka-89
Lively, Henry
T207
Livengood, Wes
W711/1
Livernois, Derek
85Elmira-11
86Greens-13
87WinHaven-23
89Lynch/Star-12
90Foil/Best-307
90NewBrit/Best-24
90NewBrit/ProC-1314
90NewBrit/Star-8
90ProC/Singl-805
90T/TVRSox-50
91AAA/LineD-359
91B-123
91Pawtu/LineD-359
91Pawtu/ProC-34
92ClBest-197
92NewBrit/ProC-428
92NewBrit/SB-488
92Sky/AASingl-208
93Pawtu/Ball-13
Livesey, Jeff
87Anchora-19
88Oneonta/ProC-2052
89PrWill/Star-11
90FtLaud/Star-12
91AA/LineD-10
91Albany/LineD-10
91Albany/ProC-1011
92Albany/ProC-2229
92ColClip/SB-107
Livesey, Steve
91Oneonta/ProC-4162
92PrWill/ClBest-19
92PrWill/ProC-158
Livin, Jeff
86Osceola-17
87ColAst/ProC-20
Livingston, Bob
89SanDiegoSt/Smok-14
Livingston, Dennis
86Albuq-13
87Albuq/Pol-13
Livingston, Paddy
10Domino-70
11Helmar-25
12Sweet/Pin-47
E104
M116
T205
T206
T207
T208
Livingston, T.
(Mickey)
43Playball-42
47TipTop
90Target-1013
Livingstone, Scott
87PanAm/USAB-4
87PanAm/USAR-4
89London/ProC-1381
90AAASingl/ProC-387
90ProC/Singl-393
90TeamUSA/87-4
90Toledo/CMC-16
90Toledo/ProC-157
91AAA/LineD-589
91AAAGame/ProC-46
91Classic/III-50
91Toledo/LineD-589
91Toledo/ProC-1940
91UD/FinalEd-53F
92B-3
92Classic/I-54
92D-675
92F-141
92L-127
92L/BlkGold-127
92OPC-685
92OPC/Premier-56
92Pinn-490
92ProC/Tomorrow-64
92S-414
92S/100RisSt-57
92StCl-317
92T-685
92T/91Debut-111
92T/Gold-685
92T/GoldWin-685
92UD-538
92UD/Scout-SR14
92USPlayC/Tiger-3S
92USPlayC/Tiger-6D
92Ultra-61
93B-235
93D-409
93F-232
93F/RookSenII-6
93Flair-206
93L-375
93OPC-219
93Pac/Spanish-446
93Panini-116
93Pinn-106
93S-196
93Select-320
93StCl-328
93StCl/1stDay-328
93T-298
93T/Gold-298
93Tiger/Gator-19
93ToysRUs-71
93ToysRUs/MPhoto-8
93UD-63
93USPlayC/Rook-12H
93Ultra-202
94D-597
94F-139
94L-202
94S-171
94S/GoldR-171
94StCl-351
94StCl/1stDay-351
94StCl/Gold-351
94Studio-134
94T-19
94T/Gold-19
Livsey, Shawn
91ClBest/Singl-434
91Classic/DP-25
91FrRow/DP-38
92OPC-124
92Pinn-545
92StCl/Dome-108
92T-124
92T/Gold-124
92T/GoldWin-124
Llanes, Pedro
86Miami-16
87Savan-13
Llano, Jorge
82Miami-11
Llanos, Aurelio
88Martins/Star-23
89Martins/Star-17
90Princet/DIMD-13
Llanos, Bobby
92Belling/ClBest-29
92Belling/ProC-1453
Llenas, Winston
71OPC-152R
71T-152R
74OPC-467
74T-467
75OPC-597
75T-597
75T/M-597
76SSPC-195
83Nashua-20
85Cram/PCL-14MG
86Edmon-19MG
88Tor/Fire-57CO
Llewellyn, Paul
83Ander-28
Llodrat, Fernando
76Watlo
Lloyd, Graeme
88Myrtle/ProC-1167
91Dunedin/ClBest-5
91Dunedin/ProC-201
92Knoxvl/ProC-2986
92Knoxvl/SB-383
92Sky/AASingl-161
93B-423
93F/Final-227
93Flair-227
93L-459
93OPC/Premier-71
93Pac/Spanish-512
93Pinn-616
93Pol/Brew-16
93Select/RookTr-76T
93UD-725
93Ultra-572
94D-176
94F-182
94L-351
94Pac/Cr-333
94Pol/Brew-17
94S-284
94S/GoldR-284
94T-187
94T/Finest-48
94T/FinestRef-48
94T/Gold-187
94UD-332
94Ultra-78
Lloyd, John Henry
(Pop)
74Laugh/Black-33
80Perez/HOF-160
86Negro/Frit-16
88Conlon/NegAS-8
88Negro/Duques-6
90Negro/Star-5
93TWill-109
Lloyd, Mike
89Elizab/Star-15
90Kenosha/Best-6
90Kenosha/ProC-2301
90Kenosha/Star-10
LoDuca, Paul
94B-594
LoGrande, Angelo
78Watlo
81Charl-14
82Charl-15
83Charl-10
Loaiza, Esteban
94B-134
Loaiza, Steve
92Augusta/ClBest-4
92Augusta/ProC-233
Lobb, Dave
71Richm/Team-12
Lobe, Bill
55Gol/Ind-16
55Salem
Lobert, John
(Hans)
10Domino-71
11Helmar-145
12Sweet/Pin-127
14Piedmont/St-32
15CJ-70
40PlayBall-160
91Conlon/Sport-172
92Conlon/Sport-392
BF2-77
D303
D329-104
D350/2-102
E101
E102
E105
E106
E90/1
E92
E94
M101/4-104
M101/5-102
M116
S74-101
T201
T202
T204
T205
T206
T216
T222
T3-105
Lobozzetta, Al
87Cedar-1
Locas, Jacques
45Parade*-33
Lochner, Dave
83Cedar-3
83Cedar/Frit-8
Lock, Don
63T-47
64T-114
64T/Coins-53
64T/SU
64T/St-24
64T/tatt
65OldLond-29
65T-445
66OPC-165
66T-165
66T/RO-34
66T/RO-53
67CokeCap/Phill-18
67T-376
68OPC-59
68T-59
69MB-159
69T-229
69T/St-76
78TCMA-34
Exh47
WG10-31
Locke, Bobby
60T-44
61T-537
62T-359
65T-324
68OPC-24
68T-24
Locke, Charlie
91Crown/Orio-263
Locke, Roger Dale
88Ashvl/ProC-1064
Locke, Ron
64T-556R
65T-511
91WIZMets-232
Locke, William H.
D322
Lockenmeyer, Mark
84Jacks-3
Locker, John
89Elmira/Pucko-29
90Elmira/Pucko-18
Locker, Robert
65T-541R
66T-374
67CokeCap/WSox-16
67T-338
68OPC-51
68T-51
69T-548
70MLB/St-274
70McDon-5
70OPC-249
70T-249
71MLB/St-520
71OPC-356
71T-356
72T-537
73OPC-645
73T-645
74OPC-62
74T-62
74T/Tr-62T
75OPC-434
75T-434
75T/M-434
Lockett, Lester
91Negro/Lewis-28
92Negro/Kraft-3
93TWill-110
Lockett, Ron
90Princet/DIMD-14
91ClBest/Singl-348
91Clearw/ClBest-17
91Clearw/ProC-1628
91FSLAS/ProC-FSL7
92B-303
92ClBest-232
92Reading/ProC-588
92Reading/SB-534
92Sky/AASingl-232
92UD/ML-231
93StCl/Phill-26
Lockhart, Bruce
85Greens-6
86WinHaven-15
87WinHaven-13
Lockhart, Keith
87Cedar-13
88Chatt/Best-9
88SLAS-5
89Nashvl/CMC-16
89Nashvl/ProC-1278
89Nashvl/Team-12
90AAASingl/ProC-559
90CedarDG/Best-12
90Nashvl/CMC-19
90Nashvl/ProC-247
90ProC/Singl-144
91AAA/LineD-264
91Nashvl/LineD-264
91Nashvl/ProC-2166
92Tacoma/ProC-2510
92Tacoma/SB-538
94B-111
94Ultra-580
Lockhart, Mike
92Watertn/ClBest-19
92Watertn/ProC-3238
Lockhart, Tim
89FresnoSt/Smok-13
Lockie, Randy
83QuadC-13
Locklear, Dean
91ClBest/Singl-206
91SoBend/ClBest-18
91SoBend/ProC-2854
92Saraso/ClBest-7
92Saraso/ProC-201
Locklear, Gene
75OPC-13
75T-13
75T/M-13
76OPC-447
76T-447
92Yank/WIZ70-98
Locklear, Jeff
92Clinton/ProC-3593
Lockley, Blain
86Watertn-12
87Macon-12
Lockman, Carroll
(Whitey)
47HomogBond-31
47TipTop
48B-30
49B-2
49Eureka-116
50B-82
50Drake-8
51B-37
51T/RB-41
52B-38
52BR
52RM-NL13
52StarCal/L-78G
52TipTop
53B/Col-128
53Briggs
53RM-NL7
53SM
54B-153
54NYJour
54SM
55B-219
55Gol/Giants-17
55SM
56T-205
57T-232
58Hires-62

58SFCallB-13
58T-195
59T-411
60T-535
73OPC-81MG
73T-81MG
74OPC-354MG
74T-354MG
79TCMA-26
91Crown/Orio-264
91T/Arc53-292
D305
Exh47
PM10/Sm-98
R423-60
Lockwood, Claude
(Skip)
65T-526R
70OPC-499
70T-499
71MLB/St-443
71OPC-433
71T-433
72OPC-118
72T-118
73OPC-308
73T-308
74OPC-532
74T-532
75OPC-417
75T-417
75T/M-417
75Tucson-23
75Tucson/Caruso-16
75Tucson/Team-9
76OPC-166
76SSPC-549
76T-166
77BurgChef-139
77T-65
78T-379
79OPC-250
79T-481
80OPC-295
80T-567
81D-217
81T-233
91WIZMets-233
Lockwood, Rick
85CharlO-4
86Jacks/TCMA-18
88Louisvl-29
Lodbell, Dick
87Anchora-38
Lodding, Richard
89Belling/Legoe-9
91Penin/ClBest-8
91Penin/ProC-374
92SanBern/ClBest-6
92SanBern/ProC-
Lodes, Lance
90AR-32M
Lodgek, Scott
89Belling/Legoe-10
90Penin/Star-11
Lodigiani, Dario
41G-15
47Remar-19
47Signal
48Signal
48Smith-15
49Remar
Loe, Darin
89Belling/Legoe-11
90Penin/Star-12
91SanBern/ClBest-8
91SanBern/ProC-1984
Loeb, Marc
90MedHat/Best-24
91Myrtle/ClBest-14
91Myrtle/ProC-2948
93Dunedin/ClBest-15
93Dunedin/ProC-1799
Loehr, Ted
75AppFx
Loera, Javier
89GreatF-7
Loes, Billy
52B-240
52T-20
53B/Col-14
53T-174
54B-42
54NYJour
55B-240
55Gol/Dodg-19
56T-270
57T-244
58Hires-48
58T-359
59T-336
60T-181
61T-237
79TCMA-50
90Target-455
91Crown/Orio-265
PM10/L-18
Loewer, Carlton
92MissSt-25
93Bz-21
93MissSt-26
93T/Tr-4T
Lofthus, Kevin
90Modesto/Cal-170
90Modesto/ProC-2219
Loftin, Bo
91Billing/SportP-5
91Billings/ProC-3757
92Billings/ProC-3351
93FExcel/ML-24
Lofton, Kenneth
88AubAs/ProC-1953
89AubAs/ProC-2166
90FSLAS/Star-11
90Osceola/Star-16
90Star/ISingl-3
91AAA/LineD-614
91AAAGame/ProC-52
91B-565
91Tucson/LineD-614
91Tucson/ProC-2225
91UD/FinalEd-24F
92B-110
92Classic/Game200-177
92Classic/II-T46
92D-5RR
92D/RookPhen-BC8
92D/Up-U6RR
92F-655
92F/Up-17
92Indian/McDon-17
92JDean/Rook-8
92L/GRook-4
92OPC-69
92OPC/Premier-72
92Pinn-290SIDE
92Pinn-582
92Pinn/Rook-3
92Pinn/RookI-7
92Pinn/Team2000-35
92ProC/Tomorrow-223
92S-845
92S/HotRook-3
92S/Impact-32
92S/Rook-10
92S/RookTr-14T
92StCl-695
92Studio-168
92T-69
92T/91Debut-112
92T/Gold-69
92T/GoldWin-69
92T/Tr-66T
92T/TrGold-66T
92UD-25SR
92UD-766
92UD/Scout-SR15
92Ultra-350
92Ultra/AllRook-7
93B-417
93Classic/GameI-54
93Colla/DM-65
93D-537
93D/Spirit-SG11
93F-218
93F-346LL
93F/Fruit-37
93F/RookSenI-1
93Flair-195
93Indian/WUAB-18
93JDean/28-23
93L-40
93L/Fast-3
93OPC-251
93OPC/Premier/StarP-17
93Pac/Jugador-9
93Pac/Spanish-97
93Panini-53
93Pinn-40
93Pinn/Team2001-18
93S-58
93Select-275
93Select/ChasRook-4
93Select/StatL-55
93StCl-277
93StCl/1stDay-277
93Studio-180
93T-331
93T/BlkGold-36
93T/Finest-43
93T/FinestRef-43
93T/Gold-331
93ToysRUs-69
93TripleP-144AA
93TripleP-181
93UD-262
93UD-45M
93UD/FunPack-109
93UD/SP-122
93UD/SeasonHL-HI11
93USPlayC/Ace-13H
93USPlayC/Rook-1C
93Ultra-542
94B-195
94D-39
94D/Special-39
94F-111
94F/LL-4
94L-350
94OPC-237
94OPC/JAS-25
94Oscar-7
94Pac/Cr-174
94Pac/Silv-17
94Panini-58
94Pinn-179
94Pinn/Artist-179
94Pinn/Museum-179
94Pinn/Run-14
94S-81
94S/Cycle-2
94S/GoldR-81
94S/GoldS-41
94Sf/2000-43
94Sf/Shak-1
94StCl-301
94StCl/1stDay-301
94StCl/Gold-301
94Studio-93
94T-149
94T/BlkGold-11
94T/Finest-218
94T/FinestRef-218
94T/Gold-149
94T/Prev-331
94TripleP-115
94UD-215
94UD/CollC-315TP
94UD/CollC/Gold-315TP
94UD/CollC/Silv-315TP
94UD/ElecD-215
94UD/SP-98
94Ultra-45
94Ultra/AwardWin-7
94Ultra/LL-3
94Ultra/RisSt-7
Lofton, Rodney
89Freder/Star-14
90Hagers/Best-9
90Hagers/ProC-1423
90Hagers/Star-13
90ProC/Singl-765
91AA/LineD-236
91Hagers/LineD-236
91Hagers/ProC-2464
92Hagers/SB-262
92RochR/ProC-1946
92Sky/AASingl-107
92UD/ML-327
93B-258
Loftus, Dick
90Target-1014
Loftus, Thomas
N172
Logan, H. Dan
80RochR-4
81RochR-11
82RochR-15
83RochR-17
Logan, Joe Jr.
88CapeCod/Sum-19
89James/ProC-2158
90Rockford/ProC-2689
90Rockford/Team-16
91FSLAS/ProC-FSL44
91WPalmB/ClBest-7
91WPalmB/ProC-1223
Logan, Johnny
53JC-20
53SpicSpan/3x5-16
53SpicSpan/7x10-7
53T-158
54B-80
54JC-23
54RM-NL20
54SpicSpan/PostC-12
54T-122
55B-180
55Gol/Braves-18
55JC-23
55RM-NL5
55SpicSpan/DC-11
56T-136
56YellBase/Pin-18
57SpicSpan/4x5-11
57Swift-12
57T-4
58T-110
59T-225
60Lake
60SpicSpan-10
60T-205
61P-105
61T-524
62T-573
63T-259
79TCMA-158
91T/Arc53-158
92Bz/Quadra-3M
93UD/ATH-83
94T/Arc54-122
Exh47
Logan, Robert Dean
(Lefty Bob)
86Indianap-18
90Target-456
Logan, Todd
90Visalia/Cal-76
90Visalia/ProC-2157
92Visalia/ClBest-13
Loggins, Mike
86FtMyr-18
87Memphis-4
87Memphis/Best-18
88Omaha/CMC-13
88Omaha/ProC-1504
89Omaha/CMC-20
89Omaha/ProC-1738
90AAASingl/ProC-611
90Omaha/CMC-12
90Omaha/ProC-76
90ProC/Singl-187
91AAA/LineD-433
91Richm/Bob-26
91Richm/LineD-433
91Richm/Team-2
Logsdon, Kevin
91Watertn/ClBest-9
91Watertn/ProC-3364
92ColRS/ClBest-11
92ColRS/ProC-2387
93Kinston/Team-13
Logue, Matt
89Niagara/Pucko-15
Lohbeck
N172
Lohrke, Jack
47TipTop
48B-16
49B-59
49Eureka-117
51B-235
52B-251
53B/BW-47
57Seattle/Pop-24
Lohrman, Bill
40PlayBall-210
90Target-457
Lohry, Adin
90Oneonta/ProC-3367
92PrWill/ClBest-8
92PrWill/ProC-151
Lohsen, B.J.
89KS*-11
Lohuis, Mark
81Shrev-21
Lois, Alberto
76Shrev
78Colum
79Portl-14
80T-683R
Loiselle, Richard
92CharRain/ClBest-13
92CharRain/ProC-116
Lolich, Mickey
64T-128
65T-335
65T/E-55
66T-226LL
66T-455
66T/RO-54
66T/RO-65
67CokeCap/Tiger-14
67OPC-88
67T-88
68CokeCap/Tiger-14
68T-414
69Kelly/Pin-10
69MB-160
69MLB/St-50
69MLBPA/Pin-15
69OPC-168WS
69T-168WS
69T-270
69T/4in1-14M
69T/St-175
70K-65
70MB-13
70MLB/St-210
70OPC-72LL
70T-715
70T-72LL
71MLB/St-398
71OPC-133
71OPC-71LL
71T-133
71T-71LL
71T/Coins-106
71T/GM-23
71T/Greatest-23
71T/tatt-13
72K-38
72MB-200
72OPC-450
72OPC-94LL
72OPC-96LL
72ProStars/PostC-29
72T-450
72T-94LL
72T-96LL
72T/Post-5
73K-3
73OPC-390
73T-390
73T/Comics-10
73T/Lids-27
73T/PinUps-10
74OPC-166
74T-9
74T/St-178
75Ho-6
75Ho/Twink-6
75OPC-245
75SSPC/42-21
75T-245
75T/M-245
76Crane-28
76Laugh/Jub-3
76MSA/Disc
76OPC-385
76OPC-3RB
76SSPC-354
76T-385
76T-3RB
76T/Tr-385T
77T-565
78Padre/FamFun-19
79T-164
80T-459
81TCMA-347
81Tiger/Detroit-55
83Kaline-62M
86Tiger/Sport-20
88Domino-11
88Pac/Leg-39
89Swell-97
90Swell/Great-81
91Swell/Great-56
91WIZMets-234
92AP/ASG-36

93Metallic-11
93TWill-40
93UD/ATH-84
94TedW/54-31
Lolich, Ron
71OPC-458R
71T-458R
Lollar, Sherm
50B-142
51B-100
51T/BB-24
52B-237
52Hawth/Pin-5
52NTea
52T-117
53B/Col-157
53T-53
54B-182
54RH
54RM-AL5
54T-39
55B-174
55T-201
56T-243
57T-23
58T-267
58T-491AS
59T-385
60T-495
60T-567AS
61P-28
61T-285
61T/St-123
62J-53
62P-53
62P/Can-53
62Salada-55
62Shirriff-55
62T-514
63J-42
63P-42
63T-118
79TCMA-73
89Kodak/WSox-3M
91T/Arc53-53
94T/Arc54-39
Lollar, Tim
79WHave-20
80Colum-1
81F-108
81T-424R
82T-587
83D-61
83D/AAS-37
83F-365
83F/St-7M
83OPC-185
83OPC/St-296
83T-185
83T-742TL
83T/St-296
84D-284
84F-305
84Mother/Padres-3
84Nes/792-644
84OPC-267
84Smok/Padres-16
84T-644
85Coke/WS-46
85D-324
85F-39
85F/Up-U73
85Leaf-111
85OPC-13
85T-13
85T/St-153
85T/Tr-76T
86D-620
86F-354
86T-297
87F-38
87T-396
92Yank/WIZ80-108
Loman, Doug
78BurlB
80Holyo-15
81ElPaso-8
82Vanco-10
84Cram/PCL-28
85D-46RR
85Pol/Brew-5
Lomastro, Jerry
83OrlanTw-12
85Toledo-24
86Toledo-14
87Hagers-7
87RochR/TCMA-26
Lombardi, Al
89Penin/Star-11
Lombardi, Ernie
32Orbit/num-58
32Orbit/un-41
34DS-105
34DS-36
34Exh/4-4
34G-35
35BU-129
35Exh/4-4
36Exh/4-4
37Exh/4-4
37Wheat
38Exh/4-4
38G-246
38G-270
38Wheat
39Exh
39Wheat-1
41DP-12
47TipTop
48Signal
60F-17
61F-55
75Shakey-5
77Galasso-64
80Pac/Leg-11
80Perez/HOF-195
81Conlon-28
82Ohio/HOF-8
86D/HL-33
86Sf/Dec-23
89HOF/St-58
89Smok/Dodg-102
91Conlon/Sport-27
92Conlon/Sport-427
93Conlon-877
94Conlon-1064
R303/A
R303/B
R305
R312
R314
V351B-30
V354-82
W711/1
W711/2
Lombardi, John
91MedHat/ProC-4102
Lombardi, Phil
83Greens-15
85Albany-13
86Colum-14
86Colum/Pol-12
87Colum-16
87Colum/Pol-17
87Colum/TCMA-15
87D-401
87F-648R
87Sf-118M
87Sf/TPrev-7M
88T-283
88Tidew/CANDL-10
88Tidew/CMC-12
88Tidew/ProC-1578
89Tidew/CMC-12
89Tidew/ProC-1975
91WIZMets-235
92Yank/WIZ80-109
Lombardi, Vic
47TipTop
49Eureka-165
51B-204
52Park-7
90Target-459
Lombardo, Chris
78StPete
Lombardozzi, Chris
87PrWill-13
89Cedar/Best-28
89Cedar/ProC-935
89Chatt/Best-17
89Chatt/GS-25
90AAASingl/ProC-552
90Nashvl/ProC-240
Lombardozzi, Steve
83OrlanTw-6
84Toledo-1
85Toledo-17
86D-598
86D/Rook-18
86F/Up-U68
86Sf-178M
86Sf/Rook-17
87D-318
87D/OD-227
87F-547
87Sf/TPrev-17M
87T/Tr-66T
88D-196
88F-16
88Master/Disc-6
88Panini/St-137
88S-174
88T-697
89D-554
89F-120
89OPC-376
89S-421
89T-376
89Tucson/CMC-23
89Tucson/JP-13
89Tucson/ProC-181
89UD-179
90D-688
Lombarski, Tom
82OkCty-14
83MidldC-14
84Iowa-17
85Iowa-4
86Peoria-16
87Tidew-17
87Tidew/TCMA-14
Lomeli, Michael
87Idaho-14
88Boise/ProC-1622
89Boise/ProC-2004
90Erie/Star-13
Lomon, Kevin
92Durham/ClBest-8
92Durham/Team-14
93Durham/Team-12
94B-401
Lonborg, Jim
65T-573R
66OPC-93
66T-93
67CokeCap/RedSox-16
67T-371
67T/Test/RSox-9
67T/Test/SU-4
68Bz-11
68CokeCap/RedSox-16
68Dexter-49
68OPC-10LL
68OPC-12LL
68OPC-155WS
68T-10LL
68T-12LL
68T-155WS
68T-460
68T/3D
68T/ActionSt-15CM
68T/ActionSt-4CM
68T/G-14
68T/Post-11
69Citgo-3
69MB-161
69MLB/St-14
69MLBPA/Pin-16
69NTF
69OPC-109
69T-109
69T/St-135
70K-49
70MLB/St-159
70T-665
71MLB/St-323
71OPC-577
71T-577
72MB-201
72OPC-255
72T-255
73OPC-3
73T-3
74JP
74OPC-342
74T-342
74T/St-75
75OPC-94
75T-94
75T/M-94
76OPC-271
76SSPC-462
76T-271
77K-41
77T-569
78SSPC/270-52
78T-52
79OPC-233
79T-446
88Pac/Leg-80
89Swell-48
90Swell/Great-124
91LineD-16
91Swell/Great-57
92AP/ASG-50
93TWill-3
93UD/ATH-85
Lond, Joel
86FSLAS-30
London, Darren
90PrWill/Team-3
93ColClip/Pol-24M
Londos, Jim
33SK*-14
Long, Bob
52Laval-22
Long, Bruce
86Reading-15
87Reading-10
Long, Dale
55T-127
55T/DH-115
56T-56
56T/Pin-43
56YellBase/Pin-19
57Kahn
57Swift-3
57T-3
58T-7
59T-147M
59T-414
60T-375
61T-117
61T/St-205
62J-65
62P-65
62P/Can-65
62Salada-35
62Shirriff-35
62T-228
63T-484
72Laugh/GF-48
78TCMA-223
79TCMA-41
80Marchant-16
90HOF/St-53
90Pac/Legend-92
92Yank/WIZ60-73
Exh47
Long, Danny
N172/PCL
Long, Dennis
81Tulsa-14
82Tulsa-4
83Tulsa-8
Long, Don
87QuadC-19
88Bend/Legoe-27MG
89BendB/Legoe-26MG
89PalmSp/Cal-60CO
89PalmSp/ProC-476
90QuadC/GS-1MG
91AA/LineD-449MG
91MidldA/LineD-449MG
91MidldA/OneHour-17
91MidldA/ProC-449MG
92MidldA/ProC-4040MG
92MidldA/SB-474MG
Long, Ernest
(The Kid)
92Negro/RetortII-23
Long, Herman
(Germany)
E107
N172
N300/unif
Long, James V.
88PalmSp/Cal-89
88PalmSp/ProC-1460
Long, Jeoff
62Pep/Tul
64T-497
Long, Joe
92GulfCY/ProC-3788
93Greens/ClBest-15
93Greens/ProC-883
Long, Joey
91Spokane/ClBest-2
91Spokane/ProC-3946
Long, Kevin
88AZ/Pol-10
88CapeCod/Sum-98
89Eugene/Best-14
90BBCity/Star-15
92Omaha/ProC-2976
92Omaha/SB-334
92Sky/AAASingl-153
Long, R.D.
92Oneonta/ClBest-15
93Greens/ClBest-16
93Greens/ProC-895
Long, Richard
(Rich)
89Utica/Pucko-14
90SoBend/Best-10
90SoBend/GS-9
Long, Robert E.
(Bob)
78Salem
79BuffB/TCMA-20
80Port-21
81Portl-16
82Portl-5
82T-291R
84Cram/PCL-179
85Cram/PCL-95
86F-468
86Richm-12
87CharlO/WBTV-14
89Chatt/II/Team-17
Long, Ryan
91Classic/DP-40
91FrRow/DP-18
91LitSun/HSPros-30
91LitSun/HSProsG-30
92B-79
92Eugene/ClBest-2
92Eugene/ProC-3035
92StCl/Dome-109
93Rockford/ClBest-16
Long, Steve
90James/Pucko-20
91Sumter/ClBest-7
91Sumter/ProC-2330
92WPalmB/ClBest-11
92WPalmB/ProC-2085
Long, Thomas
D328-100
D329-105
D350/2-103
E135-100
M101/4-105
M101/5-103
Long, Tony
86Lakeland-11
90Eugene/GS-18
91BBCity/ClBest-9
91BBCity/ProC-1396
91FSLAS/ProC-FSL2
92BBCity/ProC-3843
Long, William
(Bill)
82Amari-18
83LasVegas/BHN-14
84Beaum-11
85BuffB-21
86BuffB-16
87D/Rook-48
87F/Up-U66
87Hawaii-16
87T/Tr-67T
88Coke/WS-14
88D-306
88F-404
88OPC-309
88RedFoley/St-49
88S-539
88T-309
89B-56
89Coke/WS-16
89D-573
89F-501
89OPC-133
89S-351
89T-133
89UD-499
90Cub/Mara-12
90OPC-499
90PublInt/St-394
90S-526

90S/Tr-62T
90T-499
90T/TVCub-52
91F-425
91OPC-668
91S-559
91T-668
91UD-495
Longaker, Scott
91Hamil/ClBest-9
91Hamil/ProC-4035
Longenecker, Jere
83Butte-18
86Memphis/GoldT-13
86Memphis/SilverT-13
87Memphis-9
87Memphis/Best-19
Longmire, Tony
87Macon-8
88Salem/Star-10
91AA/LineD-513
91B-489
91ClBest/Singl-98
91Reading/LineD-513
91Reading/ProC-1382
92ProC/Tomorrow-297
93B-596
93ScranWB/Team-15
94B-168
94Pac/Cr-480
94Phill/Med-19
94Pinn-528
94StCl-394
94StCl/1stDay-394
94StCl/Gold-394
94StCl/Team-213
94T-28
94T/Gold-28
94Ultra-551
Longuil, Rich
87Sumter-15
88Durham/Star-10
89BurlB/ProC-1624
89BurlB/Star-14
90Durham/Team-21
Lonigro, Greg
87Cedar-15
88Cedar/ProC-1152
88MidwLAS/GS-9
89Chatt/Best-16
89Chatt/GS-17
90Chatt/GS-20
91AA/LineD-161
91Chatt/LineD-161
91Chatt/ProC-1967
Lonnett, Joe
57T-241
58T-64
73OPC-356CO
73T-356C
74OPC-221CO
74T-221C
Lono, Joel
86Tampa-11
87Cedar-6
Look, Bruce
69T-317
Loomis, Geoff
92SoOreg/ClBest-10
92SoOreg/ProC-3425
Looney, Brian
91James/ClBest-17
91James/ProC-3542
92ProC/Tomorrow-269
92Rockford/ClBest-18
92Rockford/ProC-2111
93WPalmB/ClBest-12
93WPalmB/ProC-1335
94B-472
94F-544
94UD-125
94UD/ElecD-125
Looney, Steve
91Fayette/ClBest-24
91Fayette/ProC-1183
Looper, Eddie
87Savan-18
88Savan/ProC-350
89Spring/Best-23
Lopat, Ed
45Playball-17
47TipTop
49B-229
50B-215
51B-218
51BR-C6
51T/BB-39
52B-17
52BR
52Coke
52StarCal-84B
52StarCal/L-70B
52T-57
52TipTop
53Exh/Can-15
53T-87
54NYJour
54T-5
55T-109
55T/DH-41
56T/Hocus-A2
60T-465C
61Peters-2
63T-23MG
64T-348MG
79TCMA-91
81TCMA-345
90Pac/Legend-38
90Swell/Great-24
91Crown/Orio-266
91Swell/Great-58
91T/Arc53-87
92AP/ASG-67
92Bz/Quadra-12M
92Yank/WIZAS-41
93TWill-65
94T/Arc54-5
Exh47
PM10/L-19
R346-40
R423-61
Lopata, Stan
49B-177
49Eureka-140
50B-206
51B-76
51BR-B9
54B-207
55B-18
56T-183
57T-119
58Hires-29
58Hires/T
58T-353
59T-412
60T-515
79TCMA-151
PM10/Sm-99
Lopes, Dave
73OPC-609R
73T-609R
74Greyhound-4
74Greyhound-6M
74OPC-112
74T-112
74T/St-46
75Greyhound-2
75Greyhound-6
75Ho-67
75Ho/Twink-67
75OPC-93
75T-93
75T/M-93
76Greyhound-2
76Greyhound-6
76Ho-105
76OPC-197LL
76OPC-4RB
76OPC-660
76SSPC-79
76T-197LL
76T-4RB
76T-660
77BurgChef-145
77Ho-14
77Ho/Twink-14
77OPC-4LL
77OPC-96
77T-180
77T-4LL
78Ho-112
78OPC-222
78SSPC/270-67
78T-440
78Wiffle/Discs-39
79Ho-114
79K-52
79OPC-144
79T-290
80BK/PHR-28
80K-29
80OPC-291
80Pol/Dodg-15
80T-560
80T/S-60
80T/Super-60
81D-416
81F-114
81F/St-67
81K-29
81OPC-50
81PermaGr/AS-5
81Pol/Dodg-15
81T-50
81T/HT
81T/SO-92
81T/St-175
82D-327
82F-12
82F/St-10
82Granny-8
82OPC-218
82OPC-338AS
82OPC-85IA
82T-338AS
82T-740
82T-741A
82T/Tr-64T
83D-339
83F-524
83F/St-1M
83F/St-23M
83Granny-15
83OPC-365
83OPC/St-105
83T-365
83T/Fold-5M
83T/St-105
84D-400
84F-453
84Mother/A's-21
84Nes/792-669
84Nes/792-714LL
84OPC-17
84T-669
84T-714LL
84T/RD-19M
84T/St-331
85D-604
85F-60
85OPC-12
85SevenUp-15
85SpokAT/Cram-13
85T-12
86Cub/Unocal-11
86D-388
86D-9DK
86D/DKsuper-9
86F-372
86Gator-15
86Leaf-9DK
86OPC-125
86Sf-144M
86Sf-194
86T-125
87D-455
87F-62
87Mother/Ast-16
87OPC-311
87Pol/Ast-8
87Smok/Dodg-19
87T-445
87T-4RB
87T/St-7
88S-489
88Smok/Dodg-15M
88Smok/Dodg-18
88T-226
89Smok/Dodg-96
89Smok/R-20
90Mother/Rang-27M
90Target-460
91ClBest/Singl-62
91Mother/Rang-28CO
93Rang/Keeb-231
Lopez, Al
33DH-27
33Exh/4-2
34DS-28
34DS-97
34Exh/4-2
35BU-3
35Exh/4-2
37Exh/4-1
38G-257
38G-281
42Playball-39
51B-295MG
52NumNum-20
53B/Col-143MG
54DanDee
55B-308MG
55Gol/Ind-17MG
55Salem
60MacGregor-12
60T-222MG
61T-132MG
61T-337M
62T-286MG
63T-458MG
64T-232MG
65T-414MG
69T-527MG
76Rowe-14M
77Galasso-32
80Pac/Leg-98
80Perez/HOF-161
80SSPC/HOF
81TCMA-348MG
82Ohio/HOF-27
86Indianap-21MG
89Pac/Leg-197
89Smok/Dodg-38
89Swell-90
90Perez/GreatMom-64
90Target-461
91T/Arc53-329MG
93AP/ASG-104
93AP/ASG24K-38G
93Conlon-844
93Conlon-873
94Conlon-1010
94Conlon-1104
R312/M
R314
V355-131
Lopez, Albie
91BurlInd/ProC-3300
92ColRS/ClBest-19
92ColRS/ProC-2388
92ProC/Tomorrow-60
93B-613
93ClBest/MLG-12
93SALAS/II-22
94B-635
94D-648
94F/MLP-22
94Pinn-426
94T-178
94T/Gold-178
94UD/CollC-177
94UD/CollC/Gold-177
94UD/CollC/Silv-177
Lopez, Andres
93LimeR/Winter-115
Lopez, Antonio
79Wisco-1
Lopez, Art
65T-566R
92Yank/WIZ60-74
Lopez, Aurelio
78Sprin
78Spring/Wiener-22
79T-444
80T-101
81Coke
81OPC-291
81T-291
81Tiger/Detroit-75
82D-359
82F-273
82T-278
83T/Tr-63T
84D-516
84F-86
84Nes/792-95
84OPC-95
84T-95
84T/St-268
84Tiger/Wave-25
85Cain's-13
85D-349
85F-16
85FunFood/Pin-98
85Leaf-160
85Seven-9D
85T-539
85T/St-265
85Wendy-15
86D-293
86F-231
86F/Up-U69
86T-367
87D-629
87F-63
87Mother/Ast-18
87Pol/Ast-13
87T-659
Lopez, Carlos
77T-492R
78OPC-219
78T-166
79RochR-8
79T-568
89GA-20
90GA-19
90GA-34
91Crown/Orio-267
Lopez, Francisco
74Wichita-101
Lopez, Fred
89Idaho/ProC-2016
90Sumter/Best-19
90Sumter/ProC-2437
91Greenvl/ClBest-13
91Greenvl/ProC-3007
91MedHat/ProC-4095
91MedHat/SportP-13
Lopez, Hector
52Laval-56
55Rodeo
56Rodeo
56T-16
56T/Pin-13
57T-6
58T-155
59T-402
60T-163
61P-12
61T-28
62T-502
63T-92
64T-325
65T-532
66OPC-177
66T-177
78TCMA-272
79TCMA-195
92Yank/WIZ60-75
PM10/L-20
WG9-15
Lopez, Javier
78Cedar
Lopez, Javier Torres
89Pulaski/ProC-1892
90A&AASingle/ProC-132
90BurlB/Best-20
90BurlB/ProC-2352
90BurlB/Star-16
90Foil/Best-107
90MidwLgAS/GS-38
91B-587
91CLAS/ProC-CAR2
91Durham/ClBest-19
91Durham/ProC-1547
92B-452
92ClBest-117
92ClBest/BBonusC-10
92ClBest/RBonus-BC10
92Greenvl/ProC-1156
92Greenvl/SB-238
92ProC/Tomorrow-186
92Sky/AASingl-101
93B-343FOIL
93B-466
93Brave/Lyke/Stand-20
93D-782RR
93F/MLPII-15
93Richm/Bleach-15
93Richm/Pep-2
93StCl-630
93StCl/1stDay-630
93StCl/Brave-27
93T-811
93T/Gold-811
93ToysRUs-92
93UD-29SR
93UD/SP-281FOIL
93Ultra-9
94B-273

94D-613
94F-364
94Finest-425
94Flair-129
94Flair/Wave-5
94L/GRook-1
94OPC-162
94OPC/HotPros-7
94Pac/Cr-14
94Pinn-239
94Pinn/Artist-239
94Pinn/Museum-239
94Pinn/New-15
94Pinn/RookTPinn-1M
94S-620
94Select-188
94Select/RookSurg-9
94Sf/2000-172
94Sf/2000Sam-7
94Sf/Shak-7
94StCl/Team-52
94Studio-38
94Studio/Her-6
94T-194
94T/Gold-194
94TripleP-283
94UD-255
94UD/CollC-178
94UD/CollC/Gold-178
94UD/CollC/Silv-178
94UD/ElecD-255
94UD/SP-53
94Ultra-445
94Ultra/AllRook-6

Lopez, Jose
90Johnson/Star-17
91Savan/ClBest-9
91Savan/ProC-1650
92Johnson/ClBest-15
92Johnson/ProC-3111

Lopez, Juan
75Sacra/Caruso-22
77Spoka
78Spokane/Cramer-13
78Spokane/Team-13
79Vanco-12
80Evansvl-23
81Evansvl-17
82Evansvl-17
83Evansvl-16
83Watlo/Frit-6
84Evansvl-1
87Fayette-18
87Osceola-2
88ColAst/Best-10
89Niagara/Pucko-26
90Everett/ProC-3147CO
90Niagara/Pucko-28MG
91Bristol/ClBest-20MG
91Bristol/ProC-3622MG

Lopez, Luis Antonio
85VeroB-21
86FSLAS-31
86VeroB-16
87Bakers-10
88SanAn/Best-26
88TexLgAS/GS-37
89SanAn/Best-15
90AAASingl/ProC-81
90Albuq/CMC-21
90Albuq/ProC-360
90Albuq/Trib-18
90ProC/Singl-423
91AAA/LineD-90
91ColoSp/LineD-90
91ColoSp/ProC-2191
91S/RookTr-109T
91T/90Debut-91
92S-716
92S/100RisSt-84
92StCl-556

Lopez, Luis Santos
(Luis)
88Spokane/ProC-1930
89CharRain/ProC-984
90ProC/Singl-852
90River/Cal-5
90River/ProC-2616
91AA/LineD-612
91Wichita/LineD-612
91Wichita/ProC-2604
91Wichita/Rock-14
92LasVegas/ProC-2803
92LasVegas/SB-235

93B-250
94D-393
94Pac/Cr-529
94Pinn-259
94Pinn/Artist-259
94Pinn/Museum-259
94Sf/2000-159
94T-336
94T/Gold-336

Lopez, Marcelino
63T-549R
65T-537R
66OPC-155
66T-155
67CokeCap/ALAS-31
67CokeCap/AS-4
67CokeCap/DodgAngel-32
67T-513
70OPC-344
70T-344
71MLB/St-303
71OPC-137
71T-137
72T-652
91Crown/Orio-268

Lopez, Marcos
88CharWh/Best-16
89Peoria/Team-4

Lopez, Mike
92Niagara/ClBest-11
92Niagara/ProC-3318

Lopez, Orangel
92GulfCY/ProC-3798

Lopez, Pancho
73Cedar

Lopez, Pedro
89Watlo/ProC-1790
89Watlo/Star-18
90CharRain/Best-13
90CharRain/ProC-2043
92Wichita/SB-639

Lopez, Rob
86FSLAS-32
86Tampa-12
87Vermont-9
88Nashvl/CMC-8
88Nashvl/ProC-487
89Nashvl/CMC-6
89Nashvl/ProC-1295
89Nashvl/Team-13
90AAASingl/ProC-540
90Nashvl/CMC-8
90Nashvl/ProC-228
90ProC/Singl-133
91AAA/LineD-267
91Nashvl/LineD-267

Lopez, Robert
92OKSt-16

Lopez, Steve
88Idaho/ProC-1859
89Sumter/ProC-1096

Lora, Jose
90Elmira/Pucko-10
91Elmira/ClBest-9
91Elmira/ProC-3284
91WinHaven/ClBest-28

Lora, Ramon Antonio
80OkCty
81Syrac-10
81Syrac/Team-13
82Syrac-12

Loranger, Bob
52Laval-53

Lord, Bristol
10Domino-72
11Helmar-11
12Sweet/Pin-11A
12Sweet/Pin-11B
14Piedmont/St-33
E104
E224
E254
E270/1
M116
T205
T207
T208

Lord, Harry
11Diamond-18
14CJ-48
E103
E254
E270/1
E270/2

E91
E94
E95
M116
T201
T202
T204
T205
T206
T207
T215
T3-106

Lorenz, Joe
82Durham-4

Lorenzo, Gary
79AppFx-9

Loretta, Mark
94B-149

Lorms, John
90Watertn/Star-13
91Collnd/ClBest-20
91Collnd/ProC-1487
92Kinston/ClBest-10
92Kinston/ProC-2478

Lorraine, Andrew
94B-675

Losa, Bill
88Butte-13
88Gaston/ProC-1013
89CharlR/Star-14
90CharlR/Star-23
91Kinston/ClBest-14
91Kinston/ProC-325

Losauro, Carmelo
86DayBe-17
88Virgini/Star-14

Loscalzo, Bob
82Idaho-24
83Madis/Frit-15
84Madis/Pol-13
85Modesto/Chong-24

Loseke, Scott
84Cedar-22

Lott, Bill
(Billy)
89LittleSun-4
90Bakers/Cal-259
90Yakima/Team-18
91Bakers/Cal-15
92ClBest-357
92VeroB/ClBest-13
92VeroB/ProC-2891

Lotzar, Greg
85Elmira-12
86FSLAS-33
86WinHaven-16
87NewBrit-6

Loubier, Stephen
88River/Cal-213
88River/ProC-1432
89River/Best-11
89River/Cal-20
89River/ProC-1389
89Wichita/Rock/Up-14
90Wichita/Rock-13
91PalmSp/ProC-2008

Loucks, Scott
78DaytB
81Tucson-11
83Tucson-22
85Cram/PCL-228

Louden, William
D328-101
E135-101

Loudenslager, Charlie
90Target-1015

Loughlin, Mark
91AubAS/ClBest-1
91AubAS/ProC-4270
92Ashvl/ClBest-25
92ProC/Tomorrow-236

Louis, Joe
47HomogBond-32BOX
D305

Loun, Don
65OPC-181R
65T-181R

Lovdal, Stewart
89Martins/Star-18
90Batavia/ProC-3062

Love, Edward H.
(Slim)
16FleischBrd-58

Love, James

92Elmira/ClBest-26TR

Love, John
87Macon-6
88Salem/Star-11

Love, Sylvester
90Stockton/Best-9
90Stockton/Cal-194
90Stockton/ProC-2194

Love, William
(Will)
89Madis/Star-13
89Star/Wax-66
90Modesto/Cal-157
90Modesto/Chong-18
90Modesto/ProC-2210
91Modesto/ProC-3083
92Reno/Cal-45

Lovelace, Vance
82QuadC-10
83VeroB-7
86MidldA-13
87MidldA-24
88Edmon/CMC-4
88Edmon/ProC-557
89Edmon/ProC-559
89F-651M
90AAASingl/ProC-112
90Calgary/CMC-7
90Calgary/ProC-647
90ProC/Singl-434
91AAA/LineD-65
91Calgary/LineD-65
91Calgary/ProC-512
92Toledo/ProC-1041
92Toledo/SB-593

Lovell, Don
86Water-15
87BuffB-1
88ColoSp/CMC-15
88ColoSp/ProC-1523

Lovell, Jim
88Greenvl/Best-11
89Greenvl/Best-22
89Greenvl/ProC-1167
91Greenvl/ClBest-29TR
93Richm/Team-19

Lovett, Thomas
(Tom)
90Target-1016
N172
N300/unif

Loviglio, John
(Jay)
80OkCty
81T-526R
82Edmon-8
82T-599R
83Iowa-15
86Geneva-16MG
87WinSalem-13
89WinSalem/Star-19
90CharlK/Team-16
91AA/LineD-149MG
91CharlK/LineD-149MG
91CharlK/ProC-1704MG

Lovinger, Allan
90Penin/Star-27TR

Lovins, Steve
(Sarge)
79Memphis/TCMA-1
80Memphis-1

Lovitto, Joe
73OPC-276
73T-276
74OPC-639
74T-639
75OPC-36
75T-36
75T/M-36
76OPC-604
76SSPC-271
76T-604
93Rang/Keeb-25

Lovrich, Pete
63T-549R
64T-212

Lovullo, Torey
88EastLAS/ProC-8
88GlenF/ProC-923
89D/Rook-17
89F-648R
89Mara/Tigers-23
89Panini/St-332
89S/HotRook-17

89UD/Ext-782
90AAASingl/ProC-388
90ProC/Singl-401
90Toledo/CMC-24
90Toledo/ProC-158
90UD-332
91B-175
91ColClip/ProC-603
92ColClip/Pol-17
92ColClip/ProC-359
92ColClip/SB-108
92Sky/AAASingl-48
92StCl-809
93F/Final-184
93L-476
93Mother/Angel-18
93StCl/Angel-29
93Ultra-521
94D-612
94F-63
94L-204
94Pac/Cr-83
94Panini-39
94S-179
94S/GoldR-179
94StCl-506
94StCl/1stDay-506
94StCl/Gold-506
94T-634
94T/Gold-634
94UD/CollC-179
94UD/CollC/Gold-179
94UD/CollC/Silv-179
94Ultra-24

Lowdermilk, Grover
T207

Lowe, Chris
88Martins/Star-24
89Martins/Star-19
90Hamil/Star-14

Lowe, Derek
92B-98
92Belling/ClBest-11
92Belling/ProC-1439
92UD/ML-192
93B-107
93ClBest/MLG-213
93FExcel/ML-226
93River/Cal-2
94B-585

Lowe, Donald
79Wausau-17

Lowe, Jamie
89OrlanTw/Best-29

Lowe, Jason
92LitSun/HSPros-15

Lowe, Q.V.
82Oneonta-6
83Greens-29
86Jaxvl/TCMA-10
87James-29CO
88James/ProC-2039CO
89James/ProC-2152CO
90James/Pucko-28CO
91James/ClBest-28CO
91James/ProC-3561CO
92James/ClBest-26MG
92James/ProC-1516MG

Lowe, Robert
N172
N300/unif

Lowe, Sean
92ClBest/Up-404
92Classic/DP-11
92Classic/DPFoil-BC11
92UD/ML-119
93B-572
93ClBest/MLG-119
93Pinn-461DP
93S-493DP
93Select-356DP
93StCl/Card-27
93StCl/MurphyS-121
93T-191
93T/Gold-191
94SigRook-15

Lowe, Steve
(Doc)
76Wausau
78Wausau

Lowenstein, John
71OPC-231R
71T-231R
72OPC-486

72T-486
73OPC-327
73T-327
74OPC-176
74T-176
75OPC-424
75T-424
75T/M-424
76OPC-646
76SSPC-528
76T-646
77OPC-175
77T-393
78BK/R-21
78SSPC/270-87
78T-87
79T-173
80T-287
81D-235
81F-186
81OPC-199
81T-591
82D-599
82F-169
82T-747
82T/St-102
83D-153
83F-63
83F/St-13M
83F/St-21M
83OPC-337
83OPC/St-24
83T-473
83T/St-24
84D-228
84D/AAS-26
84F-10
84F/St-116
84Nes/792-604
84T-604
84T/St-209
84T/St-20WS
85D-245
85F-180
85OPC-316
85T-316
85T/St-206
91Crown/Orio-269
93Rang/Keeb-232
Lowery, David
91Gaston/ClBest-18
91Gaston/ProC-2695
91SALAS/ProC-SAL23
92CharlR/ClBest-1
92CharlR/ProC-2233
Lowery, John Jr.
92Clinton/ProC-3594
92MN-12
Lowery, Josh
89Batavia/ProC-1942
Lowery, Terrell
91Butte/SportP-17
92UD/ML-81
93B-373FOIL
94B-17
Lowman, Mel
77DaytB
Lown, Omar
(Turk)
52B-16
52T-330
53B/Col-154
53T-130
54B-157
57T-247
58T-261
59T-277
60T-313
60T-57M
61P-32
61T-424
61T/RO-35
62T-528
91T/Arc53-130
V362-14
Lowrey, Harry
(Peanuts)
43Playball-37
47TipTop
48L-33
49B-22
49Eureka-62
50B-172
51B-194
52B-102
52T-111
53Exh/Can-29
53Hunter
53T-16
54Hunter
54T-158
72T/Test-2
91T/Arc53-16
94T/Arc54-158
Exh47
Lowrey, Steve
82Cedar-4
Lowry, Dwight
83BirmB-4
87Cain's-5
87Coke/Tigers-11
87D-338
87F-157
87Seven-DT7
87Sf/TPrev-15M
87T-483
87Toledo/TCMA-25
89Pac/SenLg-21
89T/SenLg-2
90AAASingl/ProC-580
90Indianap/CMC-14
90Indianap/ProC-297
90ProC/Singl-64
91Fayette/ClBest-11CO
91Fayette/ProC-1188CO
92Fayette/ClBest-25CO
92Fayette/ProC-2185
Lowry, Mike
78Wausau
Loy, Darren
86Reading-16
87Maine-21
87Maine/TCMA-9
87Phill/TastyK-x
88CharlR/Star-13
89OkCty/CMC-20
89OkCty/ProC-1526
89Tulsa/Team-12
Loynd, Mike
86Rang-46
86Tulsa-8
87D-506
87F/Up-U67
87Mother/Rang-21
87Sf/TPrev-1M
87Smok/R-27
87T-126
88D-550
88F-472
88S-491
88T-319
88Tucson/CMC-3
88Tucson/ProC-185
89ColMud/ProC-147
89ColMud/Star-16
90AAASingl/ProC-348
90ProC/Singl-332
90Syrac/CMC-6
90Syrac/MerchB-15
90Syrac/ProC-568
90Syrac/Team-15
91Louisvl/Team-11
92Louisvl/ProC-1886
92Louisvl/SB-259
93Rang/Keeb-233
93Richm/Pep-13
Loyola, Juan
91Princet/ClBest-2
91Princet/ProC-3526
Lozado, Willie
79BurlB-7
81ElPaso-2
82Vanco-5
83Indianap-10
85D-595
85F-644R
85Louisvl-19
86OKCty-10
Lozano, Steve
89FresnoSt/Smok-14
Lozinski, Tony
89Batavia/ProC-1916
90Clearw/Star-12
Lubert, Dennis
83Durham-21
Lubratich, Steve
80SLCity-14
81SLCity-19
82Spokane-17
84Cram/PCL-112
84Cram/PCL-249
84D-377
84F-524
84Nes/792-266
84T-266
85Cram/PCL-106
86Beaum-14CO
86LasVegas-10
87Spokane-10
88LasVegas/ProC-243
88Spokane/ProC-1928
89River/Best-22MG
89River/Cal-25MG
89River/ProC-1411MG
90Wichita/Rock-25MG
91AA/LineD-624MG
91Wichita/LineD-624MG
91Wichita/ProC-2614MG
91Wichita/Rock-24MG
Luby, Hugh
48Sommer-23
Lucadello, John
W753
Lucarelli, Vito
79AppFx-3
Lucas, Arbrey
85Osceola/Team-8
Lucas, Brian
78Charl
Lucas, Charles Fred.
(Red)
29Exh/4-8
31Exh/4-8
32Orbit/num-40
32Orbit/un-42
33DH-28
33DH-29
33Exh/4-4
33G-137
34DS-106
34DS-46
35G-2B
35G-7B
91Conlon/Sport-190
R305
R313
R316
R332-43
V354-7
Lucas, Charles S.
R314/Can
Lucas, Gary
79Hawaii-9
81D-243
81F-502
81OPC-259
81T-436
82D-296
82F-577
82OPC-120
82T-120
83D-187
83F-366
83OPC-364
83T-761
84D-307
84Expo/PostC-18
84F-306
84F/X-U73
84Nes/792-7
84OPC-7
84Stuart-12
84T-7
84T/St-161
84T/Tr-73T
85D-498
85F-403
85OPC-297
85T-297
86D-453
86F-254
86OPC-351
86T-601
87D-618
87F-87
87OPC-382
87Smok/Cal-4
87T-696
88D-579
88F-495
88T-524
91CalLgAS-48CO
91SanJose/ClBest-24CO
91SanJose/ProC-29CO
92Clinton/ClBest-28CO
92Clinton/ProC-3614
Lucas, Ray
90Target-462
Lucas, Scott
91Helena/SportP-6
Lucca, Lou
91OKSt-15
92Erie/ClBest-16
92Erie/ProC-1631
92OKSt-17
93FExcel/ML-37
93T-494M
93T/Gold-494M
Lucchesi, Frank
70T-662MG
71OPC-119MG
71T-119MG
72OPC-188MG
72T-188MG
74OPC-379CO
74T-379C
76SSPC-272
76T-172MG
77T-428MG
88Chatt/Team-22
88Nashvl/Team-25MG
88T-564
89Nashvl/CMC-25MG
89Nashvl/ProC-1284MG
89Nashvl/Team-30MG
93Rang/Keeb-234MG
Lucchetti, Larry
92Savan/ClBest-4
92Savan/ProC-663
Luce, Roger
92CharlR/ClBest-4
92CharlR/ProC-2227
92ClBest-111
Lucero, Kevin
91Hamil/ClBest-4
91Hamil/ProC-4036
92Savan/ClBest-3
92Savan/ProC-662
Lucero, Robert
88Clinton/ProC-714
Lucia, Danny
78Green
81Durham-20
Luciani, Randy
88Fayette/ProC-1098
Luciano, Medina
89Pittsfld/Star-15
Luciano, Suliban
91Kingspt/ClBest-5
91Kingspt/ProC-3825
Luckham, Ken
89Salem/Team-15
90Osceola/Star-17
91Osceola/ClBest-7
91Osceola/ProC-679
92Jacks/SB-338
Luderus, Fred
11Helmar-146
14CJ-45
15CJ-45
16FleischBrd-55
BF2-87
D328-102
D329-106
D350/2-104
E135-102
M101/4-106
M101/5-104
Ludwick, Bob
53Exh/Can-38
Ludwick, Eric
94FExcel-236
Ludwig, Jeff
89Geneva/ProC-1869
Ludwig, William
E254
Ludy, John
85Beloit-19
86Stockton-13
87Stockton-16
Luebber, Steve
72T-678
77T-457
79Syrac/TCMA-20
79Syrac/Team-31
80RochR-15
81RochR-12
83Evansvl-5
86Beaum-15CO
87Wichita-23
88Wichita-42
89LasVegas/ProC-26
89Pac/SenLg-94
90River/Best-20CO
90River/Cal-25CO
90River/ProC-2623CO
91AA/LineD-240CO
91Crown/Orio-270
91Hagers/LineD-240CO
91Hagers/ProC-2473CO
91Pac/SenLg-7
92RochR/ProC-1956CO
92RochR/SB-475CO
Luebbers, Larry
90Billings/ProC-3217
91Cedar/ClBest-8
91Cedar/ProC-2716
91ClBest/Singl-373
91MidwLAS/ProC-22
92Cedar/ClBest-11
92Cedar/ProC-1071
92Chatt/ProC-3815
92ClBest-50
94D-192
94F-415
94Pac/Cr-151
94S-603
94StCl/Team-335
94T-221
94T/Gold-221
94Ultra-172
Luebke, Dick
91Crown/Orio-271
Luecken, Rick
84Chatt-19
85Cram/PCL-98
86Chatt-16
87Memphis-18
87Memphis/Best-22
88Memphis/Best-20
89AAA/ProC-38
89Omaha/CMC-7
89Omaha/ProC-1734
90B-5
90Brave/Dubuq/Perf-18
90D-562
90F-113
90F/Can-113
90OPC-87
90ProC/Singl-656
90Richm/CMC-26
90Richm/Team-19
90T-87
90T/89Debut-73
90UD-621
Luedtke, John
90AR-27ACO
Lugo, Angel
89Elizab/Star-16
90Miami/II/Star-14
91StCath/ClBest-23
91StCath/ProC-3391
Lugo, Rafael
(Urbano)
82Danvl/Frit-26
83Peoria/Frit-20
85Cram/PCL-9
85F/Up-U74
86D-329
86F-162
86T-373
87Smok/Cal-9
87T-92
88AAA/ProC-15
88Edmon/CMC-6
88Edmon/ProC-581
89Indianap/ProC-1232
90CokeK/Tiger-11
Luis, Joe
91LynchRS/ClBest-12
91LynchRS/ProC-1202
92WinHaven/ClBest-12
Lujack, Johnny
51Wheat
52Wheat*
Lukachyk, Rob
88Utica/Pucko-1
89SoBend/GS-22
90Saraso/Star-14
91FSLAS/ProC-FSL29

91Saraso/ClBest-23
91Saraso/ProC-1124
92Stockton/ClBest-13
92Stockton/ProC-50
93FExcel/ML-191
Lukasiewicz, Mark
92OKSt-18
Luke, Matt
92Classic/DP-115
92FrRow/DP-69
92Oneonta/ClBest-1
93Greens/ClBest-17
93Greens/ProC-899
94ClBest/Gold-85
94FExcel-109
Luketich, Stan
91Niagara/ClBest-30CO
91Niagara/ProC-3651CO
92Niagara/ClBest-29CO
92Niagara/ProC-3343CO
Lukevics, Mitch
76AppFx
78Knoxvl
79Knoxvl/TCMA-11
Lukish, Tom
80Utica-25
82Knoxvl-5
83Syrac-9
84Syrac-20
Lum, Mike
68T-579R
69MB-162
69T-514
70OPC-367
70T-367
71MLB/St-16
71OPC-194
71T-194
72T-641
73OPC-266
73T-266
74OPC-227
74T-227
74T/St-7
75Ho-33
75Ho/Twink-33
75OPC-154
75T-154
75T/M-154
76OPC-208
76SSPC-11
76T-208
76T/Tr-208T
77T-601
78Pep-17
78SSPC/270-119
78T-326
79OPC-286
79T-556
80T-7
81F-258
81T-457
81T/Tr-795
82D-300
82F-599
82T-732
Luman, Charley
83Butte-8
Lumenti, Ralph
58T-369
59T-316
60L-130
61T-469
Lumley, Harry G.
45Parade*-34
90Target-464
E90/1
T204
T206
WG3-26
Lumley, Mike
89Lakeland/Star-14
90London/ProC-1265
90ProC/Singl-837
91Lakeland/ClBest-9
91Lakeland/ProC-264
92ClBest-173
92London/ProC-630
92London/SB-412
93ClBest/MLG-63
Lumpe, Jerry
58T-193
59T-272
60L-47
60T-290
61P-81
61T-119M
61T-365
61T/St-164
62J-93
62P-93
62P/Can-93
62Salada-25
62Shirriff-25
62T-127M
62T-305
62T/St-54
62T/bucks
63F-16
63J-86
63P-86
63T-256
63T/SO
64Det/Lids-9
64T-165
64T/Coins-124AS
64T/Coins-28
64T/SU
64T/St-86S9
65T-353
66OPC-161
66T-161
67CokeCap/Tiger-3
67T-247
78TCMA-55
Luna, Alexis
92MedHat/ProC-3215
92MedHat/SportP-17
Luna, Guillermo
(Memo)
52Mother-26
54B-222
54Hunter
Luna, Rich
93Welland/ClBest-11
93Welland/ProC-3367
Lunar, Luis
76Wausau
77Wausau
79Jacks-13
Lund, Don
53T-277
53Tiger/Glen-19
54B-87
54T-167
90Target-465
91T/Arc53-277
94T/Arc54-167
Lund, Ed
90GreatF/SportP-4
91Bakers/Cal-13
92VeroB/ProC-2879
Lund, Gordon
(Gordy)
70T-642R
75AppFx
79Knoxvl/TCMA-4
82Edmon-22
Lund, Greg
89Everett/Star-27
Lundahl, Rich
86LitFalls-17
87Columbia-7
Lundblade, Rick
87Phill/TastyK-x
87Reading-13
88Maine/CMC-15
88Maine/ProC-291
89Tidew/CMC-19
89Tidew/ProC-1968
90Hagers/ProC-1424
Lundeen, Larry
88Boise/ProC-1615
Lundgren, Carl
T206
WG3-27
Lundgren, Jason
89BendB/Legoe-25BB
90Bend/Legoe-31M
Lundgren, Kurt
86Jacks/TCMA-7
87Jacks/Feder-8
Lundstedt, Thomas
73Wichita-7
74OPC-603R
74T-603R
75Tacoma/KMMO-4
Lundy, Dick
78Laugh/Black-6
86Negro/Frit-75
90Negro/Star-25
Lunetta, Dan
90Rochester/L&U-33GM
Lung, Rod
88QuadC/GS-16
Lupien, Ulysses
(Tony)
43Playball-18
47Signal
49B-141
Luplow, Al
62T-598R
63J-73
63P-73
63Sugar-19
63T-351
64T-184
66OPC-188
66T-188
67CokeCap/YMet-22
67T-433
91WIZMets-236
Luque, Adolpho
(Dolph)
21Exh-98
28Exh-15
28Yueng-18
33G-209
40PlayBall-231
61F-56
87Conlon/2-46
88Conlon/5-19
88Pac/8Men-90
90Target-466
92Conlon/Sport-413
94Conlon-1021
E120
E210-18
V61-72
V89-9
W502-18
W513-71
W514-17
Lusader, Scott
86GlenF-12
87Toledo-3
87Toledo/TCMA-8
88D-615
88F-62
88Toledo/CMC-13
88Toledo/ProC-594
89S/HotRook-15
89T-487
90AAASingl/ProC-393
90D-696
90OPC-632
90ProC/Singl-396
90S-575
90S/100Ris-42
90T-632
90Toledo/CMC-19
90Toledo/ProC-163
91B-174
91UD-241
Luse, Kelly
92Salinas/ClBest-28TR
Lush, John Charles
C46-33
E270/2
M116
T201
T204
T205
Lush, William L.
E107
Lussier, Pat
92Welland/ClBest-17
92Welland/ProC-1339
Lusted, Chuck
84Shrev/FB-10
Lutes, Brian
89SanDiegoSt/Smok-15
Luther, Brad
83StPete-18
85Spring-16
Luther, Tim
91Everett/ClBest-15
91Everett/ProC-3910
92Everett/ClBest-3
92Everett/ProC-1683
Lutt, Jeff
93Welland/ClBest-12
93Welland/ProC-3351
Lutticken, Bob
86Cram/NWL-156
87Spokane-18
88Charl/ProC-1217
89River/Best-1
89River/Cal-11
89River/ProC-1403
90Wichita/Rock-14
91HighD/ClBest-16
91HighD/ProC-2399
Luttrell, Lyle
57T-386
Luttrull, Bruce
85Bend/Cram-14
Lutz, Brent
91MedHat/ProC-4103
92Myrtle/ClBest-21
92Myrtle/ProC-2200
93Dunedin/ClBest-16
93Dunedin/ProC-1800
Lutz, Chris
88Geneva/ProC-1653
89CharWh/ProC-1760
90MidwLgAS/GS-39
90Peoria/Team-25
91WinSalem/ClBest-9
Lutz, Rollin Joseph
52Park-74
73OPC-449CO
73T-449CO
Lutzke, Walter
(Rube)
25Exh-83
26Exh-82
27Exh-42
94Conlon-1045
Luzinski, Greg
71OPC-439R
71T-439R
72OPC-112
72T-112
73OPC-189
73T-189
73T/Lids-28
74JP
74K-9
74OPC-360
74T-360
74T/DE-24
74T/St-76
75Ho-27
75Ho/Twink-27
75OPC-630
75SSPC/Puzzle-14
75T-630
75T/M-630
76Crane-29
76Ho-125
76K-18
76MSA/Disc
76OPC-193LL
76OPC-195LL
76OPC-610
76SSPC-467
76T-193LL
76T-195LL
76T-610
77BurgChef-163
77Ho-25
77Ho/Twink-25
77K-12
77OPC-118
77Pep-72
77T-30
78Ho-8
78K-33
78OPC-42
78SSPC/270-31
78T-420
78Tastee/Discs-5
78Wiffle/Discs-40
79BK/P-19
79Ho-30
79OPC-278
79T-540
80BK/P-11
80OPC-66
80T-120
81Coke
81D-175
81F-10
81F/St-75
81OPC-270
81T-270
81T/HT
81T/SO-74
81T/Tr-796
82D-193
82Drake-22
82F-352
82F/St-187
82OPC-152
82OPC-69IA
82T-720
82T-721IA
82T/St-165
83D-395
83D/AAS-4
83F-247
83F/St-13M
83F/St-2M
83K-50
83OPC-310
83OPC/St-51FOIL
83T-310
83T-591TL
83T/Fold-2M
83T/St-51
83TrueVal/WSox-19
84D-122
84D/AAS-41
84D/Champs-13
84Drake-18
84F-69
84F/St-47
84Nes/792-20
84Nes/792-712LL
84OPC-20
84Ralston-5
84T-20
84T-712LL
84T/Cereal-5
84T/RD-12M
84T/St-244
84T/St-7
84T/St-8
84TrueVal/WS-23
85D-546
85F-521
85FunFoodPin-34
85Leaf-75
85OPC-328
85T-650
85T/RD-15M
85T/St-238
89Swell-24
93Mother/A's-27M
Luzinski, Ryan
92Classic/DP-23
92Classic/DPFoil-BC16
92GreatF/SportP-1
92UD/ML-144
93StCl/MurphyS-140
93T-481
93T/Gold-481
94ClBest/Gold-197
94FExcel-218
Luzon, Bob
82Durham-5
83Durham-9
85Greenvl/Team-13
Lychak, Perry
83Kinston/Team-12
85Kingst-6
86Kinston-15
Lyden, Mitch
87Colum-9
87Colum/Pol-18
87Colum/TCMA-11
89Albany/Best-14
89Albany/ProC-320
89Albany/Star-11
89Star/Wax-98
90A&AASingle/ProC-33
90Albany/Best-11
90Albany/ProC-1037
90Albany/Star-9
90AlbanyDG/Best-34
90EastLAS/ProC-EL15
90Foil/Best-179
90Star/ISingl-52
91AAA/LineD-590
91Toledo/LineD-590
91Toledo/ProC-1935
92Tidew/ProC-
92Tidew/SB-561
93Edmon/ProC-1139

93F/Final-66
93T/Tr-61T
94Pac/Cr-246
Lydy, Scott
89Medford/Best-8
91ClBest/Singl-436
91Madison/ClBest-20
91Madison/ProC-2142
92Huntsvl/ProC-3963
92Reno/Cal-34
92UD/ML-171
92UD/POY-PY3
93B-49
93F/Final-256
93StCl/A's-24
94D-226
94F-267
94L-27
94Pac/Cr-455
94Pinn-232
94Pinn/Artist-232
94Pinn/Museum-232
94Sf/2000-175
94StCl-391
94StCl/1stDay-391
94StCl/Gold-391
94T-160
94T/Gold-160
94UD-218
94UD/CollC-180
94UD/CollC/Gold-180
94UD/CollC/Silv-180
94UD/ElecD-218
94Ultra-110
Lyle, Albert
(Sparky)
69MB-163
69T-311
70MLB/St-160
70OPC-116
70T-116
71MLB/St-324
71OPC-649
71T-649
72MB-202
72OPC-259
72T-259
73K-15
73OPC-394
73OPC-68LL
73Syrac/Team-14
73T-394
73T-68LL
74K-41
74OPC-66
74Syrac/Team-13
74T-66
74T/St-212
75Ho-134
75K-47
75OPC-485
75SSPC/42-28
75Syrac/Team-8
75Syrac/Team-9
75T-485
75T/M-485
76OPC-545
76SSPC-429
76SSPC/MetsY-Y22
76T-545
77BK/Y-10
77OPC-89
77T-598
78BK/Y-9
78Ho-68
78K-43
78OPC-214
78OPC-237RB
78SSPC/270-11
78T-2RB
78T-35
79Ho-143
79OPC-188
79T-365
80OPC-62
80T-115
81D-284
81F-17
81F/St-91
81OPC-337
81T-719
82D-189
82F-247
82OPC-285
82T-285
83OPC-208
83OPC-92SV
83T-693
83T-694SV
90Pac/Legend-93
92Yank/WIZ70-99
92Yank/WIZAS-42
93MCI-13M
93Rang/Keeb-235
94TedW-138
94TedW-60
Lyle, Don
79Indianap-15
80Indianap-24
Lyle, Jeff
90Welland/Pucko-22
91Augusta/ProC-802
Lyman, Billy
44Centen-15
45Centen-15
Lynch, Charlie
80Elmira-40
Lynch, David
89Tulsa/GS-14
90AAASingl/ProC-675
90OkCty/CMC-4
90OkCty/ProC-429
90ProC/Singl-154
90Tulsa/Team-14
90TulsaDG/Best-16
91AAA/LineD-13
91Albuq/LineD-13
91Albuq/ProC-1137
92Chatt/ProC-3816
92Chatt/SB-191
Lynch, Ed
78Ashvl
78Charl
79Tucson-20
80Tidew-21
81Tidew-16
82D-641
82F-531
82T-121
83D-308
83F-549
83T-601
84D-75
84F-591
84Nes/792-293
84T-293
85D-623
85F-87
85T-467
86D-631
86F-88
86OPC-68
86T-68
87Berg/Cubs-37
87D-516
87F-567
87OPC-16
87T-697
88D-477
88F-422
88S-506
88T-336
91WIZMets-237
Lynch, Jerry
54T-234
55T-142
55T/DH-73
56T-97
57T-358
58T-103
59Kahn
59T-97
60Kahn
60L-45
60T-198
60T-352M
61Kahn
61P-187
61T-97
61T/St-19
62J-127
62Kahn
62P-127
62P/Can-127
62Salada-198
62Shirriff-198
62T-487
63J-129
63Kahn
63P-129
63T-37
64Kahn
64T-193
65Kahn
65T-291
66EH-24
66OPC-182
66T-182
72Laugh/GF-22
94T/Arc54-234
Lynch, Joe
85Spokane/Cram-11
87TexLgAS-3
87Wichita-10
88LasVegas/CMC-9
88LasVegas/ProC-223
89LasVegas/CMC-3
89LasVegas/ProC-22
90AAASingl/ProC-3
90LasVegas/CMC-10
90LasVegas/ProC-115
90ProC/Singl-513
Lynch, John H.
N172
N172/SP
N690
Lynch, John
92ClBest/Up-434
92Classic/DP-122
92Erie/ClBest-17
92Erie/ProC-1617
92UD/ML-21
93FExcel/ML-38
Lynch, Mike
91Erie/ClBest-19
91Erie/ProC-4065
92WinHaven/ProC-1771
Lynch, Rich
80WHave-21
81WHave-22
Lynes, Mike
83Albany-6
Lynn, Chuck
86Lynch-15
Lynn, Fred
75OPC-622R
75SSPC/Puzzle-15
75T-622R
75T/M-622R
76Crane-30
76Ho-1
76Ho/Twink-1
76K-31
76MSA/Disc
76OPC-192LL
76OPC-196LL
76OPC-50
76SSPC-402
76T-192LL
76T-196LL
76T-50
77BurgChef-35
77Ho-51
77Ho/Twink-51
77OPC-163
77Pep-21
77T-210
78OPC-62
78PapaG/Disc-19
78SSPC/270-174
78T-320
78Wiffle/Discs-41
79K-30
79OPC-249
79T-480
80BK/PHR-18
80K-40
80OPC-60
80T-110
80T-201LL
80T/S-10
80T/Super-10
81D-218
81Drake-9
81F-223
81F/St-98
81K-40
81MSA/Disc-21
81OPC-313
81PermaGr/CC-20
81Sqt-25
81T-720
81T/HT
81T/SO-5
81T/St-42
81T/Tr-797
82D-367
82F-468
82F-642M
82F/St-214
82KMart-27
82OPC-251
82OPC-252IA
82PermaGr/AS-8
82T-251
82T-252IA
82T/St-161
82T/StVar-161
83D-241
83D/AAS-59
83F-97
83F/St-12M
83F/St-6M
83K-51
83OPC-182
83OPC-392AS
83OPC/St-158LCS
83OPC/St-44
83PermaGr/AS-3
83Seven-3
83T-392AS
83T-520
83T/Fold-3M
83T/St-158
83T/St-44
84D-108
84D-17DK
84D/AAS-27
84D/Champs-59
84Drake-19
84F-525
84F-626M
84Nes/792-680
84OPC-247
84Ralston-29
84Seven-16W
84Smok/Cal-18
84T-680
84T/Cereal-29
84T/Gloss22-7
84T/RD-15M
84T/St-230
84T/St-5
84T/St-6
84T/Super-23
85D-133
85F-307
85F/Up-U75
85FunFoodPin-54
85Leaf-198
85OPC-220
85Seven-9S
85T-220
85T/RD-13M
85T/St-225
85T/Tr-77T
86D-245
86F-278
86F/St-70
86Leaf-120
86OPC-55
86Seven/Coin-E16M
86Sf-137M
86Sf-145M
86Sf-38
86Sf-63M
86Sf-71M
86Sf-73M
86Sf/Rook-46M
86T-55
86T/St-228
86T/Tatt-8M
86Woolwth-18
87Classic-23
87D-108
87D-9DK
87D/DKsuper-9
87D/OD-135
87F-474
87F/BB-25
87F/Excit-32
87F/St-72
87French-19
87Leaf-83
87Leaf-9DK
87OPC-370
87Sf-198M
87Sf-49
87Sf/TPrev-21M
87Stuart-14
87T-370
87T/St-226
88D-248
88D/Best-297
88F-566
88French-19
88KennerFig-63
88Leaf-163
88Panini/St-15
88RedFoley/St-50
88S-42
88Sf-23
88T-707
88T/Big-169
89D-563
89F-138
89Mara/Tigers-9
89OPC-27
89Pol/Tigers-9
89RedFoley/St-76
89S-126
89Sf-68
89Smok/Angels-14
89T-416
89T/LJN-160
89UD/Ext-761
90B-216
90BBWit-28
90Classic/III-59
90Coke/Padre-10
90F-609
90F/Can-609
90HOF/St-83
90Leaf-188
90MLBPA/Pins-90
90OPC-107
90OPC-663TBC
90OPC/BoxB-H
90Padre/MagUno-17
90Panini/St-73
90PublInt/St-476
90S-131
90S/Tr-20T
90Smok/SoCal-9
90T-107
90T-663TBC
90T/Ames-10
90T/Big-277
90T/HillsHM-14
90T/St-279
90T/Tr-62T
90T/WaxBox-H
90UD-247
90UD/Ext-771
91Crown/Orio-272
91D-673
91F-536
91OPC-586
91S-554
91T-586
91UD-273
94TedW-4
94TedW/54-34
Lynn, Greg
83Clinton/Frit-6TR
91Mother/Giant-28TR
Lynn, Japhet
(Red)
47Signal
53Mother-58
Lynn, Ken
83Ander-11
Lynn, Thomas
83LynnP-26
Lyons, Albert
52Mother-42
Lyons, Barry
86Tidew-16
87T/Tr-68T
88D-619
88D/Mets/Bk-619
88F-140
88Kahn/Mets-33
88S-387
88T-633
89D-572
89F/Up-101
89Kahn/Mets-33
89S-456
89T-412

89UD-176
90B-139
90D-526
90F-209
90F/Can-209
90Kahn/Mets-33
90Leaf-119
90OPC-258
90S-29
90T-258
90T/Big-97
90T/TVMets-20
90UD-473
91Mother/Dodg-25
91Pol/Dodg-40
91WIZMets-238
92Tucson/ProC-490
92Tucson/SB-612
Lyons, Bobby
83AlexD-1
Lyons, Curt
92Princet/ClBest-11
92Princet/ProC-3083
Lyons, Dennis
N172
N690
Lyons, Eddie
90MissSt-23
91MissSt-30
92MissSt-26
93MissSt-27
Lyons, Harry P.
N172
Lyons, Jimmie
74Laugh/Black-14
86Negro/Frit-114
Lyons, Mario
90Bend/Legoe-23
Lyons, Stephen John
(Steve)
84Pawtu-18
85D-29RR
85F/Up-U76
86D-579
86F-355
86Seven/Coin-E9
86T-233
86T/Tr-67T
87Coke/WS-6
87D-409
87F-502
87T-511
88Coke/WS-15
88D-532
88D/Best-291
88F-405
88Panini/St-60
88T-108
89B-63
89Coke/WS-17
89D-253
89F-502
89Kodak/WSox-2M
89OPC-334
89Panini/St-308
89S-388
89T-334
89T/Big-105
89T/St-298
89UD-224
90B-321
90Coke/WSox-15
90D-651
90F-539
90F/Can-539
90OPC-751
90Panini/St-40
90PublInt/St-395
90S-88
90T-751
90T/Big-32
90T/St-301
90UD-390
91F-127
91F/UltraUp-U7
91F/Up-U6
91OPC-612
91S-269
91T-612
91UD-601
91Ultra-77
92D-758
92OPC-349
92S-294
92T-349
92T/Gold-349
92T/GoldWin-349
92USPlayC/RedSox-2D
92USPlayC/RedSox-5S
Lyons, Steve
92Classic/DP-78
93StCl/MurphyS-45
Lyons, Ted
28Exh-39
31Exh/4-19
32Orbit/un-43
33CJ/Pin-16
33DH-30
33Exh/4-10
33G-7
34DS-43
35BU-111M
35BU-119
35BU-36
35Exh/4-10
35G-8B
35G-9B
36Exh/4-10
38Exh/4-10
42Playball-18
50Callahan
50W576-49
61F-122
63Bz-38
76Rowe-1M
76Shakey-76
77Galasso-110
80Pac/Leg-77
80Perez/HOF-77
80SSPC/HOF
81Conlon-92
91Conlon/Sport-19
92Conlon/Sport-359
93Conlon-822
93Conlon-935
94Conlon-1248
PR1-21
R305
R306
R308-172
R332-33
V353-7
W517-45
Lyons, William Allen
(Bill)
81Louisvl-27
82Louisvl-14
82Spring/Frit-4
83Louisvl/Riley-27
84Louisvl-14
85Louisvl-17
86Louisvl-17
87Louisvl-24
88Louisvl-30
88Louisvl/CMC-12
88Louisvl/ProC-432
90SpringDG/Best-32
Lysander, Richard
(Rick)
76Tucson-28
79Ogden/TCMA-11
80Ogden-6
81Tacoma-23
82Tucson-16
83Twin/Team-13
84D-560
84F-570
84Nes/792-639
84T-639
84Toledo-23
85D-560
85F-284
85T-383
85Twin/Team-14
86F-399
86T-482
89Pac/SenLg-143
89T/SenLg-68
90AAASingl/ProC-349
90ProC/Singl-338
90Syrac/CMC-12
90Syrac/MerchB-16
90Syrac/ProC-569
90Syrac/Team-16
91Pac/SenLg-39
91Pac/SenLg-52
Lysgaard, Jim
77WHave
78Cr/PCL-59
Lytle, Wade
89Princet/Star-11
Lyttle, Jim
70OPC-516R
70T-516R
71OPC-234
71T-234
72T-648
74OPC-437
74T-437
76Expo/Redp-19
76SSPC-337
90Target-467
92Yank/WIZ60-76
92Yank/WIZ70-100
Maack, Mike
83Wisco/Frit-18
Maas, Duane
(Duke)
56T-57
57T-405
58T-228
59T-167
60T-421
61T-387
61T/RO-28
79TCMA-117
92Yank/WIZ60-77
Maas, Jason
86FtLaud-15
87PrWill-24
88Albany/ProC-1346
89Albany/Best-24
89Albany/ProC-334
89Albany/Star-12
90AAASingl/ProC-340
90ColClip/CMC-15
90ColClip/ProC-690
90Colum/Pol-8
90ProC/Singl-215
90T/TVYank-52
91AAA/LineD-111
91ColClip/LineD-111
91ColClip/ProC-609
Maas, Kevin
87FtLaud-19
88EastLAS/ProC-2
88PrWill/Star-15
89AAA/CMC-24
89AAA/ProC-18
89Colum/CMC-17
89Colum/Pol-12
89Colum/ProC-737
90AAASingl/ProC-341
90AlbanyDG/Best-12
90B-440
90Classic/Up-30
90ColClip/CMC-17
90ColClip/ProC-691
90Colla/Maas-Set
90Colum/Pol-4
90F-641R
90F/Can-641M
90F/Up-113
90Leaf-446
90ProC/Singl-217
90S-606RP
90S/100Ris-27
90Star/ISingl-19
90T/TVYank-53
90T/Tr-63T
90TripleAAS/CMC-24
90UD-70
91B-158
91Classic/200-130
91Classic/I-63
91Classic/I-NO
91Classic/III-51
91CollAB-21
91D-554
91F-672
91JDean-23
91Kenner-35
91KingB/Discs-3
91Leaf-393
91Leaf/Stud-96
91MajorLg/Pins-2
91OPC-435
91OPC-4RB
91OPC/Premier-74
91Panini/St-264
91Post-30
91Post/Can-20
91S-600
91S/100RisSt-40
91S/HotRook-2
91Seven/3DCoin-10NE
91StCl-282
91StCl/Charter*-18
91T-435
91T-4RB
91T/90Debut-92
91T/CJMini/I-20
91T/JumboR-17
91T/SU-22
91ToysRUs-16
91UD-375
91Ultra-238
91Woolwth/HL-13
92B-205
92Classic/Game200-55
92D-153
92F-236
92Kenner/Fig-29
92L-284
92L/BlkGold-284
92MooTown-5
92OPC-710
92Pinn-90
92S-613
92S/100SS-46
92StCl-35
92Studio-215
92T-710
92T/Gold-710
92T/GoldWin-710
92T/Kids-86
92TripleP-225
92UD-377
92UD-98
92Ultra-104
93D-635
93F-652
93L-206
93Pac/Spanish-207
93Panini-147
93Pinn-165
93S-634
93Select-142
93StCl-395
93StCl/1stDay-395
93StCl/Y-8
93T-168
93T/Gold-168
93TripleP-57
93UD-594
93Ultra-243
94F-238
94Pac/Cr-429
94S-425
Maasberg, Gary
88Spartan/ProC-1041
Mabe, Robert
(Bobby)
59T-356
60T-288
91Crown/Orio-273
Mabe, Todd
85FtMyr-2
Mabee, Vic
77Ashvl
79Wausau-6
Maberry, Louis
92Princet/ClBest-17
92Princet/ProC-3084
94ClBest/Gold-192
Mabry, John
91Hamil/ClBest-17
91Hamil/ProC-4053
92ProC/Tomorrow-331
92Spring/ClBest-19
92Spring/ProC-883
92UD/ML-234
94B-124
94FExcel-269
MacArthur, John
84AZ/Pol-11
MacArthur, Mark
90Hamil/Best-21
90Hamil/Star-15
91Savan/ClBest-19
91Savan/ProC-1660
92Visalia/ClBest-11
92Visalia/ProC-1022
MacCauley, John
92SoOreg/ClBest-21
92SoOreg/ProC-3414
MacCormack, Franc
78SanJose-4
MacDonald, Bill
51B-239
52T-138
MacDonald, Jim
81Tucson-23
82Tucson-12
MacDonald, Ken
91Brisbane/Fut-10
MacDonald, Kevin
79Newar-11
MacDonald, Robert
88Myrtle/ProC-1191
89Knoxvl/Best-13
89Knoxvl/ProC-1139
89Knoxvl/Star-11
90A&AASingle/ProC-44
90Knoxvl/ProC-1247
90Knoxvl/Star-10
91AAA/LineD-508
91D-636
91F/UltraUp-U61
91S/ToroBJ-32
91StCl-585
91Syrac/LineD-508
91Syrac/MerchB-15
91T/90Debut-93
92BJ/Fire-18
92D-588
92F-335
92OPC-87
92OPC/Premier-152
92S-405
92S/100RisSt-46
92StCl-372
92T-87
92T/Gold-87
92T/GoldWin-87
93BJ/D/45-36
93D-689
93F-696
93F/Final-212
93OPC-131
93Pac/Spanish-447
93StCl-434
93StCl/1stDay-434
93T-427
93T/Gold-427
93Tiger/Gator-20
93Ultra-289
94D-415
94F-140
94Pac/Cr-225
94S-286
94S/GoldR-286
94T-162
94T/Gold-162
94Ultra-57
MacDonald, Ronald
79Jacks-23
80Tidew-9
81Tidew-3
82Tidew-10
MacFayden, Dan
31Exh/4-18
33Exh/4-9
33G-156
35G-2F
35G-4F
35G-7F
36Exh/4-1
37Exh/4-1
38Exh/4-1
91Conlon/Sport-215
R314
V353-87
MacKanin, Pete
74OPC-597R
74T-597R
76Expo/Redp-20
76OPC-287
76SSPC-324
76T-287
77OPC-260
77T-156
78T-399
79BK/P-17
81F-565
81T-509
82D-354
82F-556
82T-438
83OKCty-12

84Iowa-12
86Peoria-17MG
88Iowa/CMC-24
88Iowa/ProC-543
88Peoria/Ko-35M
89AAA/ProC-43
89Iowa/CMC-25
89Iowa/ProC-1707
90AAASingl/ProC-561MG
90Nashvl/CMC-24MG
90Nashvl/ProC-249MG
90ProC/Singl-149MG
91AAA/LineD-274MG
91AAAGame/ProC-24MG
91Nashvl/LineD-274MG
91Nashvl/ProC-2172MG
91Pac/SenLg-66
92Nashvl/ProC-1848MG
92Nashvl/SB-299MG
93Rang/Keeb-236

MacKay, Bill
83Ander-1

MacKay, Joey
83Greens-25
84Greens-8

MacKenzie, Gordon
75WPalmB/Sussman-17MG
77Jaxvl
83Evansvl-22
84Evansvl-4
89Phoenix/CMC-25
89Phoenix/ProC-1504

MacKenzie, Kenneth P.
60T-534
61T-496
62T-421
63T-393
64T-297
81TCMA-433
91WIZMets-239

MacKenzie, Shaun
86Cram/NWL-20
86Everett/Pop-12
87Everett-20

MacKiewicz, Felix
48Sommer-16

MacKinnon, Tim
88Boise/ProC-1629

MacLeod, Kevin
88SoOreg/ProC-1709
89Modesto/Cal-273
90Huntsvl/Best-8

MacMillan, Darrell
89Boise/ProC-1986
90Erie/Star-14

MacNeil, Doug
92Elmira/ClBest-16
92Elmira/ProC-1380
92WinHaven/ClBest-11

MacNeil, Tim
88Butte-4
89Gaston/ProC-1024
89Gaston/Star-11
90Miami/II/Star-15

MacPhail, Larry
80Perez/HOF-165
82Ohio/HOF-62
89Rini/Dodg-20
92Yank/WIZHOF-21

MacPherson, Bruce
78OrlanTw
80Toledo-4
81Toledo-7
82RochR-3

MacQuarrie, Dave
75WPalmB/Sussman-24

MacWhorter, Keith
81Pawtu-4
81T-689R
83Pawtu-8
84Maine-21

Macaluso, Nick
88Martins/Star-25

Macauley, Drew
80Buffa-6
81Buffa-7

Macavage, Joe
87Watertn-26
88Augusta/ProC-372

Mace, Jeff
83BurlR-21
83BurlR/Frit-24
85Tulsa-24
88Boise/ProC-1616
89Boise/ProC-1977

Macfarlane, Mike
86Memphis/GoldT-16
86Memphis/SilverT-16
87Omaha-24
88D/Rook-55
88F/Up-U31
88S/Tr-76T
88Smok/Royals-17
88T/Tr-62T
89B-118
89D-416
89F-287
89S-319
89S/HotRook-97
89S/YS/I-13
89T-479
89T/Big-86
89UD-546
90D-498
90F-114
90F/Can-114
90Leaf-389
90OPC-202
90PublInt/St-352
90T-202
90UD-307
91B-301
91D-313
91F-562
91Leaf-30
91OPC-638
91Panini/FrSt-275
91Pol/Royal-13
91S-839
91StCl-15
91T-638
91UD-570
91Ultra-151
92B-589
92D-161
92F-161
92L-83
92L/BlkGold-83
92OPC-42
92Pinn-517
92Pol/Royal-15
92S-27
92StCl-74
92T-42
92T/Gold-42
92T/GoldWin-42
92TripleP-144
92UD-497
92Ultra-73
93B-505
93Colla/DM-66
93D-525
93F-241
93Flair-220
93L-422
93OPC-265
93Panini-102
93Pinn-332
93Pol/Royal-17
93S-323
93StCl-470
93StCl/1stDay-470
93StCl/Royal-2
93T-768
93T/Gold-768
93UD-327
93UD/HRH-HR25
93UD/SP-232
93Ultra-564
94B-227
94D-324
94F-164
94Finest-300
94Flair-61
94L-159
94OPC-154
94Pac/Cr-294
94Panini-77
94Pinn-488
94S-459
94Select-27
94StCl-250
94StCl/1stDay-250
94StCl/Gold-250
94Studio-187
94T-578
94T/Gold-578
94TripleP-239
94UD-107
94UD/CollC-181
94UD/CollC/Gold-181
94UD/CollC/Silv-181
94UD/ElecD-107
94Ultra-69

Macha, Ken
72Dimanche*-27
78Colum
78T-483
81D-540
81F-167
82F-618
82OPC-282
82T-282
86Expo/Prov/Pan-28M
86Provigo-28CO
93Mother/Angel-28M

Macha, Mike
78Richm

Machado, Julio
87Clearw-21
89AAA/CMC-28
89Jacks/GS-11
89Penin/Star-12
90Classic/Up-31
90D-47
90D/Rook-41
90F/Up-U37
90Kahn/Mets-48
90OPC-684
90S/Tr-92T
90T-684
90T/89Debut-74
90T/TVMets-14
90TripleAAS/CMC-28
90UD-93
91B-50
91Brewer/MillB-15
91D-764
91F/Up-U31
91Leaf-247
91OPC-434
91Pol/Brew-13
91S/100RisSt-87
91T-434
91UD/Ext-716
91WIZMets-240
92D-262
92F-181
92OPC-208
92S-353
92T-208
92T/Gold-208
92T/GoldWin-208
92UD-479

Machalec, Mark
84Butte-15

Machemer, Dave
77SLCity
78Cr/PCL-25
80Evansvl-16
81Toledo-13
82Toledo-14
85Beloit-26
86Stockton-14MG
87Stockton-3
88ElPaso/Best-6
89Denver/CMC-25
89Denver/ProC-37
90AAAGame/ProC-26MG
90AAASingl/ProC-666MG
90Denver/CMC-25MG
90Denver/ProC-641MG
90ProC/Singl-50MG

Machuca, Freddy
82Danvl/Frit-19

Macias, Angel
91Eugene/ClBest-19
91Eugene/ProC-3724

Macias, Bob
82Amari-6

Macias, Henry
77Cedar
78Cedar

Mack, Connie
(Cornelius McGillicuddy)
14CJ-12
15CJ-12
32Orbit/un-44
40PlayBall-132
48Exh/HOF
50Callahan
50W576-50
51T/CM
60F-14
61F-123
63Bz/ATG-18
69Bz/Sm
76Shakey-12
77Galasso-145MG
77Galasso-194MG
77Shakey-1
80Laugh/FFeat-37
80Perez/HOF-9
80SSPC/HOF
81Conlon-58
85West/2-39
86Conlon/1-18
88Conlon/HardC-4
89HOF/St-85
90BBWit-99
90HOF/St-45
91Conlon/Sport-45
91Conlon/Sport-46
91Conlon/Sport-47
92Conlon/Col-14
92Conlon/Sport-439
92Conlon/Sport-599
93Conlon-824MG
93CrackJack-10MG
94Conlon-1159MG
94Conlon-1217MG
94TedW-69
BF2-36
D329-107
D350/2-105
E104
E223
E96
E98
M101/4-107
M101/5-105
M116
N172
R305
R308-188
R311/Leath
R312/M
R423-67
T208
V100
V355-110
WG1-67
WG2-33
WG5-26
WG6-25

Mack, Earle
81Conlon-57
92Conlon/Sport-453

Mack, Henry
77Spartan

Mack, Jerry
86Kenosha-14

Mack, Joseph
N172

Mack, Quinn
88WPalmB/Star-16
89Jaxvl/Best-14
89Jaxvl/ProC-153
90AAASingl/ProC-582
90Indianap/CMC-16
90Indianap/ProC-299
90ProC/Singl-66
91AAA/LineD-188
91Indianap/LineD-188
91Indianap/ProC-475
92Indianap/ProC-1874
92Indianap/SB-186

Mack, Ray
43Playball-6

Mack, Raymond
89Wythe/Star-21
90Pulaski/ProC-3090
91Macon/ClBest-4
91Macon/ProC-858

Mack, Shane
85Beaum-4
85T-398OLY
86Beaum-16
87D/Rook-42
87LasVegas-18
87Sf/Rook-31
87Sf/TPrev-16M
87T/Tr-69T
88D-411
88F-590
88LasVegas/CMC-10
88LasVegas/ProC-233
88OPC-283
88S-414
88S/YS/II-36
88Smok/Padres-16
88T-548
89D-538
89S-270
89UD-182
90Classic/III-17
90D/BestAL-122
90Leaf-136
90T/Tr-64T
91B-326
91D-320
91F-618
91Leaf-40
91Leaf/Stud-88
91OPC-672
91S-284
91StCl-259
91T-672
91UD-188
91Ultra-191
92B-592
92Classic/I-55
92D-345
92F-210
92L-82
92L/BlkGold-82
92OPC-164
92Panini-119
92Pinn-230
92S-284
92S/Prev-6
92StCl-47
92Studio-207
92T-164
92T/DQ-8
92T/Gold-164
92T/GoldWin-164
92TripleP-197
92UD-428
92USPlayC/Twin-10D
92USPlayC/Twin-1C
92Ultra-95
93B-101
93Classic/Gamel-55
93D-395
93F-640
93F/Fruit-38
93Flair-238
93Kenner/Fig-21
93L-315
93OPC-263
93Pac/Spanish-174
93Panini-129
93Pinn-78
93S-19
93Select-104
93StCl-420
93StCl/1stDay-420
93T-282
93T/Finest-61
93T/FinestRef-61
93T/Gold-282
93TripleP-180
93UD-236
93UD-837TC
93UD/FunPack-194
93UD/SP-249
93USPlayC/Ace-5D
93Ultra-585
94D-253
94F-212
94L-435
94Pac/Cr-360
94Panini-93
94Pinn-148
94Pinn/Artist-148
94Pinn/Museum-148
94S-383
94StCl-429
94StCl/1stDay-429
94StCl/Gold-429
94Studio-198
94T-337
94T/Finest-105
94T/FinestRef-105
94T/Gold-337
94TripleP-255
94UD-197
94UD/CollC-182

94UD/CollC/Gold-182
94UD/CollC/Silv-182
94UD/ElecD-197
94Ultra-390
Mack, Tony Lynn
(Toby)
83Redwd-17
85Cram/PCL-6
86Edmon-20
87MidldA-19
88SanAn/Best-5
89Miami/II/Star-12
Mackey, Biz
74Laugh/Black-27
86Negro/Frit-91
90Negro/Star-4
Mackie, Bart
81Batavia-9
82Wausau/Frit-6
Mackie, Scott
89Miami/I/Star-12
Mackiewicz, Felix
45Playball-14
Mackin, Jeff
90MissSt-24
91MissSt-31
92MissSt-27
93MissSt-28
Macko, Joe
90Mother/Rang-28EQMG
Macko, Steve
80T-676R
80Wichita-18
81D-535
81T-381R
Maclin, Lonnie
88StPete/Star-14
89Spring/Best-25
90Louisvl/LBC-24
90StPete/Star-14
91AAA/LineD-239
91Louisvl/LineD-239
91Louisvl/ProC-2928
91Louisvl/Team-25
92Louisvl/ProC-1901
92Louisvl/SB-267
92Sky/AAASingl-127
94Pinn-407
Macon, Leland
94B-569
Macon, Max
90Target-468
Macrina, Eric
91SLCity/ProC-3218
Macu, Andres
90Kissim/DIMD-15
Macullar, James
N172
Macy, Frank
82Iowa-30
Madden, Billy
81TCMA-391
Madden, Bob
76AppFx
77AppFx
79QuadC-17
Madden, Michael
(Kid)
N172
N526
Madden, Mike
81ElPaso-14
82Vanco-14
83T/Tr-64T
84D-161
84F-232
84Mother/Ast-25
84Nes/792-127
84T-127
85T-479
86Pol/Ast-18
86T-691
Madden, Morris
83VeroB-8
86GlenF-13
87Toledo-18
87Toledo/TCMA-15
88BuffB/CMC-6
88BuffB/Polar-8
88BuffB/ProC-1466
89AAA/CMC-11
89S/HotRook-32
90AAASingl/ProC-61
90Albuq/CMC-5
90Albuq/ProC-340
90Albuq/Trib-19
90ProC/Singl-407
90TripleAAS/CMC-11
Madden, Scott
86Clearw-16
88Reno/Cal-273
Madden, Thomas
E254
E270/2
M116
Maddern, Clarence
49B-152
52Mother-44
53Mother-34
Maddon, Joe
76QuadC
85MidldA-10
86MidldA-14MG
Maddox, Elliott
71MLB/St-545
71OPC-11
71Pol/SenP-7
71T-11
72OPC-277
72T-277
72T/Cloth-21
73OPC-658
73T-658
74OPC-401
74T-401
75Ho-90
75K-9
75OPC-113
75T-113
75T/M-113
76OPC-503
76SSPC-451
76SSPC/MetsY-Y10
76T-503
77T-332
78Ho-133
78T-442
79OPC-28
79T-69
80OPC-357
80T-707
81D-397
81F-326
81OPC-299
81T-299
90Swell/Great-109
91Crown/Orio-274
91WIZMets-241
92Yank/WIZ70-101
93Rang/Keeb-26
Maddox, Garry
73OPC-322
73T-322
74OPC-178
74T-178
74T/St-107
75Ho-43
75Ho/Twink-43
75K-37
75OPC-240
75T-240
75T/M-240
76OPC-38
76T-38
77BurgChef-167
77K-37
77OPC-42
77T-520
78Ho-40
78K-28
78OPC-93
78SSPC/270-28
78T-610
78Wiffle/Discs-42
79BK/P-20
79K-16
79OPC-245
79T-470
80BK/P-10
80OPC-198
80T-380
81Coke
81D-55
81F-19
81F/St-70
81OPC-160
81T-160
81T/HT
81T/St-204
82D-315
82F-248
82F/St-57
82OPC-20
82T-20
82T/St-73
82T/StVar-73
83D-63
83F-164
83F/St-12M
83F/St-14M
83OPC-41
83T-615
83T/Fold-5M
84D-305
84F-39
84F/St-122
84Nes/792-755
84OPC-187
84Phill/TastyK-39
84T-755
84T/St-123
85CIGNA-11
85D-137
85F-259
85OPC-235
85Phill/TastyK-38
85T-235
85T/St-121
86D-407
86F-445
86OPC-362
86Phill/TastyK-31
86T-585
86T/St-117
86T/Tatt-14M
88Phill/TastyK-39ANN
90Phill/TastyK-36BC
Maddox, Jerry
78Richm
79Richm-6
Maddox, Leland
87Madis-13
Maddox, Mike
89KS*-46
Maddox, Nicholas
10Domino-73
12Sweet/Pin-141
D322
E104
E254
E270/2
E90/1
E95
M116
T205
T206
Maddux, Greg
86Pittsfld-14
87Berg/Cubs-31
87D-36RR
87D/Rook-52
87F/Up-U68
87Leaf-36RR
87Sf/TPrev-22M
87T/Tr-70T
88Berg/Cubs-31
88D-539
88D/Best-82
88D/Cubs/Bk-539
88F-423
88OPC-361
88Peoria/Ko-21
88Peoria/Ko-34M
88T-361
88T/St-59
89B-284
89Cadaco-33
89Classic-121
89D-373
89D/AS-56
89D/Best-37
89F-431
89F/BBMVP's-24
89F/Rec-5
89F/Superstar-28
89KennerFig-86
89Mara/Cubs-31
89OPC-240
89Panini/St-49
89RedFoley/St-77
89S-119
89S/HotStar-48
89S/YS/I-39
89Sf-108
89T-240
89T/Mini-4
89T/St-48
89UD-241
90B-27
90Classic/Up-32
90Cub/Mara-13
90D-158
90D/BestNL-14
90F-37
90F/Can-37
90Kenner/Fig-50
90Leaf-25
90MLBPA/Pins-49
90OPC-715
90Panini/St-237
90Peoria/Team-20M
90PublInt/St-198
90S-403
90Sf-211
90T-715
90T/Big-204
90T/DH-41
90T/Mini-50
90T/St-51
90T/TVCub-12
90UD-213
91B-426
91Classic/200-68
91Classic/III-52
91Cub/Mara-31
91Cub/Vine-17
91D-374
91F-426
91Leaf-127
91OPC-35
91Panini/FrSt-50
91Panini/St-43
91Panini/Top15-98
91S-317
91StCl-126
91T-35
91UD-115
91Ultra-64
92B-148
92Classic/Game200-30
92Cub/Mara-31
92D-520
92F-386
92L-294
92L/BlkGold-294
92OPC-580
92Panini-189
92Pinn-608GRIP
92Pinn-65
92Pinn/Team2000-32
92S-269
92S/Impact-77
92StCl-665
92StCl/MemberIII*-6
92Studio-15
92T-580
92T/Gold-580
92T/GoldWin-580
92TripleP-19
92UD-353
92UD/TmMVPHolo-30
92USPlayC/Cub-1D
92USPlayC/Cub-9S
92Ultra-178
92Ultra/AwardWin-24
93B-550
93Brave/LykePerf-17
93Brave/LykeStand-21
93Classic/GameI-56
93Classic/GameI-NNO
93D-608
93D/EliteDom-5
93Duracel/PPII-12
93F-380
93F-707LL
93F/ASNL-10
93F/Atlantic-13
93F/Final-3
93F/Fruit-39
93Flair-7
93L-326
93L/GoldAS-19M
93MSA/Ben-4
93OPC-135
93OPC/Premier-126
93OPC/Premier/StarP-19
93Pac/Spanish-335
93Panini-159M
93Panini-164CY
93Pinn-517
93Pinn/TP-1
93S-484AW
93S-527AS
93S-576
93Select-31
93Select/Ace-4
93Select/ChasS-9
93Select/RookTr-123T
93Select/StatL-66
93Select/StatL-78
93Select/StatL-84
93Select/StatL-88M
93StCl-2
93StCl-665
93StCl-750MC
93StCl/1stDay-2
93StCl/1stDay-665
93StCl/1stDay-750MC
93StCl/Brave-18
93StCl/MPhoto-27
93StCl/MurphyS-126
93Studio-196
93T-183
93T-409
93T/BlkGold-12
93T/Finest-85AS
93T/FinestASJ-85AS
93T/FinestRef-85AS
93T/Gold-183
93T/Gold-409
93T/Hill-17
93T/Hill-19
93T/Tr-54T
93TripleP/Gal-GS4
93TripleP/LL-L2
93UD-472
93UD-488AW
93UD-535
93UD/FunPack-65
93UD/SP-59
93USPlayC/Ace-13S
93Ultra-307
93Ultra/AS-9
93Ultra/AwardWin-1
93Ultra/AwardWin-22
93Ultra/Perf-6
94B-245
94Church-4
94D-380
94D/AwardWin-2CY
94D/Special-380
94F-365
94F/AwardWin-4
94F/LL-12
94F/Smoke-7
94Flair-130
94KingB-18
94L-94
94L/GoldS-8
94L/StatStand-5
94OPC-101
94OPC/JAS-22
94Oscar-26
94Pac/Cr-15
94Pac/Cr-656CY
94Pac/CrPr-5
94Pac/Silv-30
94Panini-147
94Pinn-11
94Pinn/Artist-11
94Pinn/HobSam-11
94Pinn/Museum-11
94Pinn/RetailSam-11
94Pinn/TeamP-9
94Pinn/Trib-12
94RedFoley-16
94S-524
94S-634NL CY CY
94S/Tomb-14
94Select-2
94Select/CrCon-1
94Sf/2000-193AS
94Sf/2000-53
94Sf/2000Sam-193
94StCl/Team-31
94Studio-39
94Studio/S&GStar-8
94T-392M
94T-499
94T/BlkGold-38

94T/Finest-209
94T/FinestRef-209
94T/Gold-392M
94T/Gold-499
94TripleP-46
94TripleP/Medal-14
94TripleP/Pr-10
94UD-320
94UD/CollC-183
94UD/CollC/Gold-183
94UD/CollC/Silv-183
94UD/SP-54
94Ultra-446
94Ultra/AS-20
94Ultra/AwardWin-18
94Ultra/AwardWin-23POY
94Ultra/Strike-3

Maddux, Mike
85Cram/PCL-38
85Phill/TastyK-42
86Phill/TastyK-x
86Portl 15
87D-535
87F-179
87Maine/TCMA-5
87Phill/TastyK-44
87T-553
88F-309
88Phill/TastyK-16
88T-756
89B-391
89D-487
89F-576
89OPC-39
89Phill/TastyK-19
89S-393
89T-39
89T/Big-74
89UD-338
90AAASingl/ProC-62
90Albuq/CMC-8
90Albuq/ProC-341
90Albuq/Trib-20
90D-312
90OPC-154
90ProC/Singl-410
90PublInt/St-246
90T-154
91F/UltraUp-U113
91Leaf-300
92D-450
92F-613
92L-393
92L/BlkGold-393
92Mother/Padre-26
92OPC-438
92Padre/Carl-12
92Pinn-489
92Pol/Padre-27M
92S-313
92Smok/Padre-18
92StCl-26
92T-438
92T/Gold-438
92T/GoldWin-438
92TripleP-196M
92UD-330
92Ultra-281
93D-286
93F-142
93F/Final-103
93L-305
93Mets/Kahn-51
93OPC-168
93Pac/Spanish-260
93S-451
93StCl-103
93StCl/1stDay-103
93T-329
93T/Gold-329
93UD-58
93UD-650
93Ultra-430
94D-213
94F-571
94Flair-201
94Pac/Cr-410
94StCl-33
94StCl/1stDay-33
94StCl/Gold-33
94T-217
94T/Gold-217

Mader, Chris
94ClBest/Gold-92

Mader, Perry
83Kinston/Team-13

Madison, Dave
52T-366
53T-99
53Tiger/Glen-20
91T/Arc53-99

Madison, Helene
33SK*-37

Madison, Jerry
90NE-14

Madison, Scotti
83Albuq-12
86Nashvl-16
87Omaha-17
88Smok/Royals-18
88T/Tr-63T
89AAA/ProC-2
89Nashvl/CMC-21
89Nashvl/ProC-1271
89Nashvl/Team-14

Madlock, Bill
74OPC-600R
74T-600R
75Ho-125
75Ho/Twink-125
75OPC-104
75SSPC/Puzzle-16
75T-104
75T/M-104
76Crane-31
76Ho-100
76K-20
76MSA/Disc
76OPC-191LL
76OPC-640
76SSPC-309
76T-191LL
76T-640
77BurgChef-198
77Ho-118
77Ho/Twink-118
77K-43
77OPC-1LL
77OPC-56
77T-1LL
77T-250
77T/CS-25
77T/ClothSt-25
78Ho-117
78OPC-89
78Pep-35
78T-410
78Tastee/Discs-15
79Ho-138
79OPC-96
79Pol/Giants-18
79T-195
80OPC-30
80T-55
81Coke
81D-252
81F-381
81OPC-137
81T-715
81T/St-213
82D-653
82Drake-23
82F-485
82F/St-77
82K-55
82OPC-365
82PermaGr/CC-7
82T-161LL
82T-365
82T-696TL
82T/St-1
82T/St-83
83D-311
83D/AAS-30
83Drake-15
83F-309
83F/St-12M
83F/St-18M
83K-18
83OPC-335
83OPC/St-275FOIL
83PermaGr/CC-8
83T-291TL
83T-645
83T/Fold-3M
83T/Gloss40-26
83T/St-275
84D-113
84D-20DK
84D/AAS-33
84D/Champs-22
84Drake-20
84F-253
84F/St-6
84MiltBrad-16
84Nes/792-131LL
84Nes/792-250
84Nes/792-696TL
84Nes/792-701LL
84OPC-250
84Ralston-26
84Seven-11E
84T-131LL
84T-250
84T-696TL
84T-701LL
84T/Cereal-26
84T/Gloss40-19
84T/RD-25M
84T/St-131
84T/St-99
84T/St/Box-12
84T/Super-8
85D-200
85F-468
85F/LimEd-19
85FunFoodPin-31
85Leaf-185
85OPC-157
85Seven-11E
85T-560
85T/RD-25M
85T/St-122
86Coke/Dodg-17
86D-617
86F-135
86F/Mini-29
86Leaf-238
86OPC-47
86Pol/Dodg-12
86Seven/Coin-W14M
86Sf-131M
86Sf-181M
86Sf-58M
86Sf-88
86T-470
86T/St-12NLCS
86T/St-70
86T/Tatt-19M
86TrueVal-23
86Woolwth-19
87D-155
87D/OD-78
87F-445
87F/Mini-65
87F/St-73
87F/Up-U69
87Leaf-120
87Mother/Dodg-8
87OPC-276
87Pol/Dodg-5
87RedFoley/St-109
87Sf-130
87T-734
87T/St-67
87T/Tr-71T
88D-496
88F-63
88Leaf-232
88OPC-145
88S-445
88Sf-123
88T-145
88T/St-266
89Pac/SenLg-214
89T/SenLg-71
89TM/SenLg-69
90EliteSenLg-116
90Target-469
92AP/ASG-82
92K/CornAS-7
92K/FrAS-2
92MCI-5
93Rang/Keeb-237
93TWill-77
93UD/ATH-86

Madrid, Alex
85Beloit-18
87Denver-10
88Denver/CMC-3
88Denver/ProC-1251
89D-604
89Phill/TastyK-20
89S/HotRook-58
89ScranWB/CMC-5
89ScranWB/ProC-720

Madrigal, Victor
91Butte/SportP-18
91ClBest/Singl-266
91Gaston/ClBest-8
91Gaston/ProC-2685

Madril, Bill
91Elmira/ClBest-10
91Elmira/ProC-3274
91WinHaven/ProC-494
92WinHaven/ClBest-5

Madril, Mike
83Redwd-18
85Cram/PCL-3
86MidldA-15

Madsen, Dan
92Geneva/ClBest-11
92Geneva/ProC-1573
93Peoria/Team-15

Madsen, Erik
89GreatF-24
90Yakima/Team-9

Madsen, Lance
89AubAs/ProC-2164
90Osceola/Star-18
91AA/LineD-567
91Jacks/LineD-567
91Jacks/ProC-933
92Jacks/ProC-4006
92Jacks/SB-339

Maebe, Art
80Clinton-11

Maeda, Koji
88SanJose/Cal-133
88SanJose/ProC-108

Maema, Takashi
90Gate/ProC-3358
90Gate/SportP-14

Maffett, Chris
91BurlInd/ProC-3301
92BurlInd/ClBest-12
92BurlInd/ProC-1653

Mag, Rick
88Bristol/ProC-1862

Magadan, Dave
86Tidew-17
87Classic-19
87D-575
87D/Rook-34
87F-648R
87F/Up-U70
87Sf/Rook-10
87Sf/Rook-3
87Sf/TPrev-2M
87T-512FS
87T/JumboR-9
88Classic/Blue-230
88D-323
88D/Mets/Bk-323
88F-141
88Kahn/Mets-29
88Leaf-108
88MSA/Disc-13
88OPC-58
88RedFoley/St-51
88S-41
88S/YS/I-23
88Sf-83
88T-58
88T/St-104
89B-384
89D-408
89D/Best-264
89F-41
89Kahn/Mets-29
89OPC-81
89S-312
89T-655
89T/Big-71
89UD-388
90D-383
90D/BestNL-56
90F-210
90F/Can-210
90Kahn/Mets-10
90Leaf-330
90OPC-135
90Panini/St-300
90PublInt/St-138
90S-46
90Sf-173
90T-135
90T/Big-24
90T/St-99
90T/TVMets-26
90UD-243
91B-484
91Classic/200-100
91Classic/I-67
91Classic/II-T72
91D-17DK
91D-362
91D/SuperDK-17DK
91F-153
91Kahn/Mets-10
91Kenner-36
91Leaf-20
91Leaf/Stud-208
91MajorLg/Pins-76
91MooTown-13
91OPC-480
91Panini/FrSt-79
91Panini/St-81
91Panini/Top15-3
91Post/Can-4
91S-190
91S/100SS-34
91StCl-210
91T-480
91UD-177
91Ultra-223
91WIZMets-242
92B-263
92D-45
92F-510
92L-306
92L/BlkGold-306
92Mets/Kahn-29
92OPC-745
92Panini-222
92Pinn-201
92S-201
92StCl-118
92T-745
92T/Gold-745
92T/GoldWin-745
92TripleP-82
92UD-112
92Ultra-236
93B-614
93Classic/Gamel-57
93D-486
93F-477
93L-391
93OPC-253
93OPC/Premier-61
93Pac/Jugador-31
93Pac/Spanish-466
93Panini-250
93Pinn-237
93Pinn/Expan-5
93S-631
93Select-149
93Select/RookTr-116T
93StCl-452
93StCl/1stDay-452
93StCl/Marlin-10
93Studio-154
93T-578
93T/Gold-578
93T/Tr-106T
93UD-479
93UD-528
93USPlayC/Marlin-1D
93USPlayC/Marlin-2C
93USPlayC/Marlin-4C
93Ultra-382
94B-450
94D-658
94F-293
94Flair-165
94L-386
94OPC-107
94Pac/AllLat-2
94Pac/Cr-247
94Pinn-187
94Pinn/Artist-187
94Pinn/Museum-187
94S-14
94S/GoldR-14
94Select-143
94StCl-365
94StCl/1stDay-365
94StCl/Gold-365
94StCl/Team-81

94T-347
94T/Finest-130
94T/Finest/PreProd-130
94T/FinestRef-130
94T/Gold-347
94TripleP-138
94UD-73
94UD/CollC-184
94UD/CollC/Gold-184
94UD/CollC/Silv-184
94UD/ElecD-73
94Ultra-197
Magallanes, Ever
88Kinston/Star-16
89Canton/Best-23
89Canton/ProC-1309
89Canton/Star-13
90AAASingl/ProC-223
90ColoSp/CMC-13
90ColoSp/ProC-42
90ProC/Singl-465
91AAA/LineD-91
91B-61
91ColoSp/LineD-91
91ColoSp/ProC-2192
92Sky/AAASingl-286
92T/91Debut-113
92Vanco/ProC-2731
92Vanco/SB-643
Magallanes, William
(Bobby)
86AppFx-13
90SanBern/Best-12
90SanBern/Cal-107
90SanBern/ProC-2640
91ClBest/Singl-263
91SanBern/ClBest-18
91SanBern/ProC-1995
92Penin/ProC-2939
Magallanes, Willie
88BirmB/Best-25
90BirmB/Best-11
90BirmB/ProC-1396
90Foil/Best-125
Magdaleno, Rick
92Classic/DP-36
93StCl/MurphyS-71
Mageau, Fernand
45Parade*-35
Magee, Bo
91Butte/SportP-22
92Gaston/ClBest-14
92Gaston/ProC-2251
Magee, Lee
15CJ-147
90Target-470
94Conlon-1273IA
D328-103
D329-108
D350/2-106
E135-103
M101/4-108
M101/5-106
Magee, Sherry
11Helmar-147
12Sweet/Pin-128
14CJ-108
14Piedmont/St-34
15CJ-108
92Conlon/Sport-449
93Conlon-897
94Conlon-1025
94Conlon-1267M
BF2-53
D328-104
D329-109
E101
E102
E135-104
E300
E92
E94
L1-123
M101/4-109
M116
S81-98
T202
T205
T206
T213/blue
T214-19
T215/brown
T216
T222
T3-31
Magee, Warren
87Clearw-14
88EastLAS/ProC-33
88Reading/ProC-871
89Reading/Best-2
89Reading/ProC-674
89Reading/Star-16
90Reading/Best-9
90Reading/ProC-1218
90Reading/Star-17
Maggio, Aggie
79WHave-29M
80WHave-22
Magistri, Greg
85Elmira-13
Maglie, Sal
51B-127
52B-66
52BR
52RM-NL14
52StarCal-90BM
52StarCal/L-78C
52TipTop
53B/Col-96
53RM-NL8
54B-105
54NYJour
55B-95
55Gol/Giants-18
55RM-NL6
57T-5
58T-43
59T-309
60NuCard-70
60T-456C
61NuCard-470
67T/Test/RSox-17CO
77Galasso-28
79TCMA-256
80Marchant-17
88Pac/Leg-85
89Niagara/Pucko-29
89Rini/Dodg-11
89Swell-99
90Swell/Great-38
90Target-471
91Swell/Great-59
91T/Arc53-303
92Bz/Quadra-16M
94TedW-53
94TedW/54-22
Exh47
PM10/Sm-100
Magnante, Michael
(Mike)
89Memphis/Best-21
89Memphis/ProC-1198
89Memphis/Star-15
90AAASingl/ProC-599
90Omaha/CMC-6
90Omaha/ProC-64
90ProC/Singl-181
91AAA/LineD-340
91Omaha/LineD-340
91Omaha/ProC-1033
92D-706
92OPC-597
92OPC/Premier-57
92Pol/Royal-16
92S-739
92StCl-448
92T-597
92T/91Debut-114
92T/Gold-597
92T/GoldWin-597
93F-620
93StCl-12
93StCl/1stDay-12
93StCl/Royal-13
93T-186
93T/Gold-186
93UD-180
94F-165
Magnante, Rick
89Niagara/Pucko-25
Magner, Rich
75Water
79Albuq-17
Magno, Chris
85Miami-9
Magnuson, Jim
72T-597
92Yank/WIZ70-102
Magnusson, Brett
88GreatF-3
89Star/Wax-30
89VeroB/Star-16
90AS/Cal-2
90Bakers/Cal-254
91AA/LineD-537
91Adelaide/Fut-9
91SanAn/LineD-537
91SanAn/ProC-2988
92Yakima/ClBest-25
Magoon, George
90Target-472
Magrane, Joe
84AZ/Pol-12
86ArkTr-12
87Classic/Up-117
87D/Rook-40
87F/Slug-24
87F/Up-U71
87Louisvl-25
87Sf/Rook-11
87Sf/TPrev-12M
87T/Tr-72T
88Classic/Blue-240
88D-140
88D/Best-100
88F-40
88Louisvl-31
88OPC-380
88Panini/St-385
88RedFoley/St-52
88S-94
88S/YS/I-9
88Sf-128
88Smok/Card-6
88T-380
88T/Gloss60-40
88T/JumboR-20
88T/St-51
88ToysRUs-15
89B-432
89Classic-148
89D-201
89D/Best-131
89F-455
89F/LL-24
89OPC-264
89Panini/St-178
89S-460
89Smok/Cards-12
89T-657
89T/Big-203
89T/LJN-94
89T/Mini-36
89T/Stbk-30
89UD-103
90B-183
90Classic-145
90D-13DK
90D-103
90D/BestNL-46
90D/Learning-34
90D/SuperDK-13DK
90F-252
90F/ASIns-5
90F/Can-252
90KMart/SS-12
90Kenner/Fig-51
90Leaf-11
90OPC-406AS
90OPC-578
90Panini/St-346
90PublInt/St-220
90PublInt/St-267
90S-17
90Sf-151
90Smok/Card-12
90T-406AS
90T-578
90T/Big-271
90T/Coins-52
90T/DH-42
90T/Gloss60-36
90T/Mini-76
90T/St-41
90T/TVAS-64
90T/TVCard-16
90UD-242
91Classic/200-29
91D-295
91F-638
91Leaf/Stud-235
91OPC-185
91Panini/FrSt-38
91Panini/St-31
91S-575
91StCl-85
91T-185
91UD-465
91Ultra-291
92D-767
92OPC-783
92Pinn-494
92Pol/Card-11
92StCl-622
92T-783
92T/Gold-783
92T/GoldWin-783
93D-492
93F/Final-127
93Pac/Spanish-633
93Pinn-342
93StCl-646
93StCl/1stDay-646
93StCl/Card-8
93UD-703
93Ultra-464
94F-64
94Pac/Cr-84
94Pinn-114
94Pinn/Artist-114
94Pinn/Museum-114
94StCl-509
94StCl/1stDay-509
94StCl/Gold-509
94T-27
94T/Gold-27
94UD-159
94UD/CollC-185
94UD/CollC/Gold-185
94UD/CollC/Silv-185
94UD/ElecD-159
Magrann, Tom
86Hagers-8
87Miami-24
89Canton/Best-10
89Canton/ProC-1313
89Canton/Star-14
90AAASingl/ProC-221
90ColoSp/CMC-14
90ColoSp/ProC-40
90D-374
90ProC/Singl-466
90T/89Debut-75
91AAA/LineD-32
91BuffB/LineD-32
91BuffB/ProC-545
Magria, Javier
89Welland/Pucko-18
90Miami/II/Star-16
Magrini, Paul
91Bristol/ClBest-27
91Bristol/ProC-3598
92Bristol/ClBest-4
92Bristol/ProC-1404
Magrini, Pete
66T-558R
Maguire, Chris
91Daikyo/Fut-8
Maguire, Fred
29Exh/4-2
31Exh/4-2
33Exh/4-1
93Conlon-791
R316
Maguire, Kevin
92Augusta/ClBest-20
92Augusta/ProC-242
Maguire, Mike
91Welland/ClBest-22
91Welland/ProC-3569
Mahaffey, Art
60T-138
61Bz-1
61T-433
61T/St-57
62Bz
62Exh
62J-199
62P-199
62P/Can-199
62Salada-112
62Shirriff-112
62T-550
62T/St-171
62T/bucks
63Bz-35
63Exh
63F-54
63J-183
63P-183
63Salada-10
63T-385
63T-7LL
63T/SO
64PhilBull-16
64T-104
65T-446
66T-570
Exh47
WG10-32
WG9-32
Mahaffey, Leroy
33G-196
34DS-10
35BU-15
35Exh/4-14
35G-1B
35G-2B
35G-6B
35G-7B
92Conlon/Sport-603
R308-175
Mahambitov, Igor
89EastLDD/ProC-DD20
Mahan, George
76Wmsprt
Mahan, Russ
88MissSt-16
89MissSt-23
Mahaney, Dan
N172
Mahar, Eddie
87Syrac/TCMA-32
Mahay, Ron
92WinHaven/ClBest-14
Mahlberg, Greg
77Tucson
78Cr/PCL-3
79Tucson-15
80CharCh-6
80T-673R
81Indianap-12
88CharWh/Best-3
89CharWh/Best-25
89CharWh/ProC-1755
90Peoria/Team-31MG
91Geneva/ClBest-19MG
91Geneva/ProC-4234MG
92Geneva/ClBest-26MG
93Rang/Keeb-238
Mahler, Mickey
78T-703R
79T-331
80Port-10
81SLCity-8
82Spokane-4
84Louisvl-28
85Expo/PostC-11
85F/Up-U77
85Indianap-16
86F/Up-U70
86T/Tr-68T
87Louisvl-18
89T/SenLg-82
89TM/SenLg-70
91Pac/SenLg-37
93Rang/Keeb-239
Mahler, Rick
78Richm
80Richm-11
81Pol/Atl-42
82BK/Lids-16
82D-349
82F-440
82Pol/Atl-42
82T-126TL
82T-579
83D-527
83F-141
83OPC-76
83T-76
84Pol/Atl-42
85D-385
85F-332
85Ho/Braves-14
85OPC-79
85Pol/Atl-42
85T-79
85T/St-26
86D-21DK

86D-77
86D/DKsuper-21
86F-521
86Leaf-21DK
86OPC-39
86Pol/Atl-42
86T-437
86T/St-43
86T/Tatt-11M
87D-190
87D/OD-41
87F-520
87OPC-242
87Sf/TPrev-24M
87Smok/Atl-5
87T-242
87T/St-43
88D-389
88D/Best-114
88OPC-171
88Panini/St-239
88S-319
88T-706
89B-302
89D-222
89D/Best-286
89D/Tr-24
89F-595
89F/Up-85
89Kahn/Reds-42
89OPC-393
89Panini/St-35
89S-229
89S/Tr-79
89T-621
89T/St-29
89T/Tr-74T
89UD-74
89UD/Ext-760
90D-375
90F-425
90F/Can-425
90Kahn/Reds-15
90OPC-151
90PublInt/St-34
90Richm/25Ann-15
90S-87
90T-151
90T/St-139
90UD-220
91F-71
91Leaf-284
91OPC-363
91S-464
91T-363
91UD-613

Mahomes, Pat
89Kenosha/ProC-1067
89Kenosha/Star-12
90A&AASingle/ProC-141
90ProC/Singl-861
90Visalia/Cal-60
90Visalia/ProC-2149
91AA/LineD-485
91OrlanSR/LineD-485
91OrlanSR/ProC-1846
92B-131
92Classic/II-T97
92D-403RR
92F/Up-40
92L/GRook-17
92OPC-676M
92Pinn-472
92Pinn/Rook-11
92Pinn/Team2000-80
92Portland/ProC-2664
92ProC/Tomorrow-93
92S/RookTr-102T
92Sky/AASingl-295
92Studio-208
92T-676R
92T/Gold-676M
92T/GoldWin-676M
92UD-776DD
92UD/Scout-SR16
92Ultra-398
92Ultra/AllRook-9
93B-157
93D-357
93F-271
93L-54
93Pac/Spanish-523
93Pinn-408
93S-337
93Select-324
93StCl-740
93StCl/1stDay-740
93T-684
93T/Gold-684
93ToysRUs-11
93UD-337
93USPlayC/Rook-2H
93Ultra-234
94B-160
94L-413
94T-43
94T/Gold-43

Mahon, Kent
89KS*-79

Mahoney, Jim
73OPC-356CO
73T-356CO
74OPC-221CO
74T-221CO
77Charl/MG
78Salem
80Port-6MG
81GlenF-22
88Portl/CMC-24
88Portl/ProC-650

Mahoney, Robert
52T-58

Mahony, Dan
91Erie/ClBest-7
91Erie/ProC-4072

Mahovlich, Frank
72Dimanche*-91IA
72Dimanche*-92

Mahovlich, Pete
72Dimanche*-93IA
72Dimanche*-94

Maietta, Ron
(Bub)
89Bristol/Star-15
89LittleSun-7
90Bristol/ProC-3158
90Bristol/Star-16

Mails, John
E120
E121/120
E220
V100
W501-23

Mails, Walter
(Duster)
21Exh-99
28Exh/PCL-20
90Target-473
WG7-27

Main, Forrest
52T-397
53T-198
91T/Arc53-198

Main, Kevin
87CharWh-16

Mainini, Marco
52Laval-93

Mains, Willard
N172

Mainville, Martin
94ClBest/Gold-72

Maisel, George
15CJ-158
21Exh-100
T222
WG4-14

Maitland, Bill
92Idaho/ProC-3508

Maitland, Mike
79AppFx-20
81GlenF-5
83GlenF-14

Maize, Dave
92Welland/ClBest-18
92Welland/ProC-1326

Majer, Steffen
90StPete/Star-15
91ArkTr/ProC-1281
92ArkTr/ProC-1125
92ArkTr/SB-36

Majeski, Carl
91Idaho/ProC-4325
91Idaho/SportP-22

Majeski, Hank
(Henry)
41DP-120
48L-149
49B-127
50B-92
51B-12
51T/BB-2
52B-58
52T-112
55B-127
55Gol/Ind-18
55Salem
91Crown/Orio-275
Exh47
R346-23

Majia, Alfredo
79LodiD-4

Majtyka, Roy
63Pep/Tul
77Indianap-2
78Indianap-2
79Indianap-2
82Evansvl-25MG
83BirmB-25
85IntLgAS-22
85Richm-26MG
86Richm-13MG
87/Richm/Crown-6MG
87Richm/TCMA-21
89Brave/Dubuq-16TR
90BirmDG/Best-21MG
90Brave/Dubuq/Singl-20TR
91Macon/ClBest-28MG
91Macon/ProC-881MG
91SALAS/ProC-SAL34MG
92Spartan/ClBest-22MG
92Spartan/ProC-1280MG

Makarewicz, Scott
89AubAs/ProC-2163
90FSLAS/Star-12
90Osceola/Star-19
90Star/ISingl-4
91AA/LineD-568
91Jacks/LineD-568
91Jacks/ProC-929
92Jacks/ProC-4001
92Jacks/SB-340

Makemson, Jay
87Oneonta-18
88Oneonta/ProC-2063
89Penin/Star-13

Maki, Timothy
82BurlR/Frit-29
82BurlR/TCMA-6
83BurlR-9
83BurlR/Frit-19

Maksudian, Michael
(Mike)
88MidwLAS/GS-48
89Miami/II/Star-15
89Star/IISingl-142
90Foil/Best-111
90Knoxvl/Best-11
90Knoxvl/ProC-1258
90Knoxvl/Star-11
90Star/ISingl-88
91AAA/LineD-509
91Syrac/LineD-509
91Syrac/MerchB-12
91Syrac/ProC-2494
92Syrac/MerchB-13
92Syrac/ProC-1982
92Syrac/SB-511
93B-297
93BJ/D/45-39
93F/Final-237

Malangone, John
52Laval-96

Malarcher, Dave
74Laugh/Black-20
86Negro/Frit-108
88Conlon/NegAS-9

Malarkey, William
C46-73
T206

Malave, Benito
86Wausau-13
87StPete-22
88ArkTr/GS-17

Malave, Jose
90Elmira/Pucko-11
92Elmira/ClBest-13
92Elmira/ProC-1390
93B-696FOIL
93FExcel/ML-133
94B-671

Malave, Omar
85Kingst-17
86Ventura-12
87Knoxvl-4
88Myrtle/ProC-1181
89Knoxvl/Best-14
89Knoxvl/ProC-1127
89Knoxvl/Star-13
93MedHat/ProC-3752MG
93MedHat/SportP-23MG

Malay, Charlie
90Target-1017

Malchesky, Tom
88Hamil/ProC-1741
89Spring/Best-19

Malcolm, Trevor
91Perth/Fut-12

Malden, Chris
79LodiD-18

Maldonado, Al
90Kissim/DIMD-16
91GreatF/SportP-2
92Bakers/Cal-15

Maldonado, Candy
79Clinton/TCMA-26
81Albuq/TCMA-21
82Albuq-21
83Albuq-14
83D-262
83F-212
83Pol/Dodg-20
84D-93
84Nes/792-244
84Pol/Dodg-20
84T-244
85Coke/Dodg-19
85D-250
85F-376
85T-523
85T/St-81
86F-136
86F/Up-U71
86Mother/Giants-9
86T-87
86T/Tr-69T
87D-327
87D/OD-102
87F-279
87F/AwardWin-23
87Leaf-216
87Mother/SFG-7
87OPC-335
87Sf-78
87Sf/TPrev-10M
87T-335
87T/Mini-37
87T/St-94
88D-391
88D/Best-247
88F-89
88F/BB/AS-22
88F/Mini-118
88F/St-129
88KennerFig-64
88KingB/Disc-16
88Leaf-239
88Mother/Giants-7
88OPC-190
88Panini/St-428
88S-54
88Sf-126
88T-190
88T/Big-35
88T/St-95
88T/UK-44
89B-478
89Bimbo/Discs-2
89D-177
89F-333
89KennerFig-87
89Mother/Giants-7
89OPC-269
89Panini/St-221
89RedFoley/St-78
89S-47
89T-495
89T/Big-197
89T/LJN-56
89T/St-89
89UD-502
90B-335
90Classic/III-34
90D-611
90D/BestAL-132
90D/Learning-42
90F-62
90F/Can-62
90F/Up-U93
90Leaf-338
90OPC-628
90PublInt/St-75
90S-138
90S/Tr-8T
90T-628
90T/Big-248
90T/Tr-65T
90Target-474
90UD-136
90UD/Ext-780
91Brewer/MillB-16
91D-391MVP
91D-480
91F-373
91Leaf-434
91Leaf/Stud-72
91OPC-723
91Panini/FrSt-220
91Panini/St-179
91Pol/Brew-14
91RedFoley/St-60
91S-93
91S/100SS-76
91S/RookTr-28T
91S/ToroBJ-29
91StCl-350
91T-723
91T/Tr-74T
91UD-138
91UD/Ext-739
91UD/FinalEd-28F
92BJ/Fire-19
92D-664
92F-336
92OPC-507
92Panini-31
92S-591
92StCl-179
92T-507
92T/Gold-507
92T/GoldWin-507
92TripleP-15
92UD-393
92Ultra-451
93B-312
93BJ/D/45-9
93BJ/D/McDon-13
93BJ/D/McDon-21M
93BJ/D/WS-4
93Cub/Mara-14
93D-684
93F-338
93F/Final-9
93L-329
93OPC-382
93OPC/Premier-83
93OPC/WC-10
93Pac/Beisbol-20M
93Pac/Spanish-379
93Pinn-422
93S-615
93Select-110
93StCl-669
93StCl/1stDay-669
93StCl/Cub-4
93T-213
93T/Gold-213
93UD-741
93Ultra-316
94D-659
94F-112
94Pac/Cr-175
94S-154
94S/GoldR-154
94StCl-464
94StCl/1stDay-464
94StCl/Gold-464
94T-667
94T/Gold-667

Maldonado, Carlos
88Bristol/ProC-1863
90A&AASingle/ProC-35
90Foil/Best-117
90Memphis/Best-21
90Memphis/ProC-1007
90Memphis/Star-15
90ProC/Singl-779
91AAA/LineD-341
91Fayette/ClBest-20
91Fayette/ProC-1179

91Omaha/LineD-341
91Omaha/ProC-1034
91T/90Debut-94
92Omaha/ProC-2958
92Omaha/SB-335
92Sky/AAASingl-154
92StCl-569
93F/Final-228
93Pac/Spanish-513
93Ultra-573
94Pac/Cr-334
Maldonado, Felix
87Elmira/Black-30
92WinHaven/ClBest-26
92WinHaven/ProC-1794MG
Maldonado, Jay
93StCath/ClBest-12
93StCath/ProC-3970
Maldonado, Jerry
89Reno/Cal-264AGM
90Reno/Cal-290AGM
Maldonado, Johnny
89Sumter/ProC-1105
Maldonado, Pete
87Spartan-2
88Clearw/Star-18
Maldonado, Phil
87Idaho-3
88Durham/Star-11
89Durham/Star-13
89Durham/Team-13
90Durham/Team-22
Malejko, Matt
94LSU-6
Maler, James
(Jim)
80Spokane-14
81Spokane-22
83SLCity-17
83T-54
84Nes/792-461
84T-461
85OKCty-20
86OKCty-11
Malespin, Gus
79Elmira-19
82Spring/Frit-10
83Spring/Frit-25
Maley, Dennis
83Miami-27
Malinak, Michael
(Mike)
87SLCity/Taco-2
88Cedar/ProC-1164
89Cedar/ProC-911
89Cedar/Star-29
Malinoski, Chris
91Rockford/ClBest-20
91Rockford/ProC-2055
92WPalmB/ClBest-15
92WPalmB/ProC-2096
93ClBest/MLG-47
94ClBest/Gold-95
Malinosky, Tony
90Target-475
Malkin, John
81Watlo-19
82Watlo/B-12
82Watlo/Frit-20
83BuffB-10
84Cram/PCL-145
85Cram/PCL-247
Malkmus, Robert
58T-356
59T-151
60T-251
61T-530
Mallatte, Mal
52LaPatrie-9
Mallea, Luis
88AppFx/ProC-138
Mallee, Johnny
91Martins/ClBest-8
91Martins/ProC-3463
92Spartan/ClBest-3
92Spartan/ProC-1271
Mallette, Malcolm
(Mal)
52Park-60
90Target-1018
Malley, Mike
89Greens/ProC-424
90CharWh/Best-3
90CharWh/ProC-2236
91Kinston/ClBest-6
91Kinston/ProC-318
91Watertn/ClBest-10
91Watertn/ProC-3365
Mallicoat, Rob
85Osceola/Team-9
86ColumAst-17
86Tucson-11
87ColAst/ProC-22
87SLAS-15
88F-452
88S/YS/II-10
89ColMud/ProC-131
89ColMud/Star-17
91AA/LineD-569
91Jacks/LineD-569
91Jacks/ProC-925
92D-673
92F-440
92Mother/Ast-23
92OPC-501
92S-819
92Sky/AAASingl-273
92T-501
92T/Gold-501
92T/GoldWin-501
92Tucson/SB-613
93S-253
93StCl/Ast-16
Mallinak, Mel
87Hagers-24
Mallon, Jim
90Welland/Pucko-32MG
Mallory, Sheldon
78Syrac
79Tacom-21
Mallory, Trevor
91Classic/DP-50
91FrRow/DP-53
92Myrtle/ClBest-3
92StCath/ClBest-6
92StCath/ProC-3385
92StCl/Dome-110
93Hagers/ClBest-18
93Hagers/ProC-1877
Malloy, Bob
87Gaston/ProC-11
88Tulsa-22
89TexLAS/GS-37
89Tulsa/GS-15
89Tulsa/Team-13
90Foil/Best-43
90Jaxvl/Best-19
90Jaxvl/ProC-1370
93Rang/Keeb-240
Malloy, Marty
93Macon/ClBest-14
93Macon/ProC-1409
94ClBest/Gold-114
Malmberg, Harry
60HenryH-2
61Union
Malone, Charles
(Chuck)
86Cram/NWL-136
87Clearw-4
88BBAmer-6
88EastLAS/ProC-34
88Reading/ProC-869
89Reading/Best-3
89Reading/ProC-656
89Reading/Star-17
90AAASingl/ProC-298
90B-144
90ProC/Singl-230
90ScranWB/CMC-4
90ScranWB/ProC-596
91AAA/LineD-488
91B-497
91F-404
91S-724RP
91S/Rook40-21
91ScranWB/LineD-488
91ScranWB/ProC-2534
91T/90Debut-95
91UD-649
Malone, Earl
88Boise/ProC-1617
Malone, Ed
47Signal
49B/PCL-31
50Remar
53Mother-20
Malone, Eddie
82Idaho-25
Malone, Jack
89Boise/ProC-1990
Malone, Kevin
80Batavia-19
88James/ProC-1893
Malone, Lew
90Target-476
Malone, Perce
(Pat)
32Orbit/num-13
32Orbit/un-45
33G-55
35G-2D
35G-4D
35G-7D
91Conlon/Sport-219
R305
R308-192
R316
V354-30
Malone, Rubio
79Wisco-18
Malone, Todd
89Oneonta/ProC-2122
90Foil/Best-18
90Greens/Best-1
90Greens/ProC-2659
90Greens/Star-13
90Oneonta/ProC-3368
90ProC/Singl-824
91Greens/ProC-3054
92PrWill/ClBest-23
92PrWill/ProC-142
Maloney, Chris
85Lynch-17
88Spring/Best-25
89ArkTr/GS-2CO
90Hamil/Best-4CO
90Hamil/Star-27CO
91Johnson/ClBest-29
91Johnson/ProC-3994MG
92Hamil/ClBest-30M
92Hamil/ProC-1609M
Maloney, Jim
61Kahn
61T-436
62Kahn
63FrBauer-13
63Kahn
63T-444
64Bz-19
64Kahn
64T-3LL
64T-420
64T-5LL
64T/Coins-158AS
64T/Coins-60
64T/S-34
64T/SU
64T/St-32
65Kahn
65T-530
65T/E-68
65T/trans-19
66Bz-45
66Kahn
66OPC-140
66T-140
66T/RO-55
66T/RO-93
67Bz-45
67CokeCap/Reds-7
67Kahn
67OPC-80
67T-80
68Kahn
68T-425
68T/3D
68T/ActionSt-16A
68T/ActionSt-3A
69Kahn
69MB-164
69MLB/St-130
69MLBPA/Pin-50
69T-362
69T/St-26
70K-10
70MLB/St-29
70OPC-320
70T-320
71MLB/St-348
71OPC-645
71T-645
72MB-203
72T-645
78TCMA-10
Maloney, Kevin
89Clmbia/Best-28
89Clmbia/GS-5
Maloney, Mark
88Kinston/Star-17
Maloney, Rich
87Sumter-18
88Durham/Star-12
89Durham/Star-14
89Durham/Team-14
90Greenvl/Best-14
90Greenvl/ProC-1139
90Greenvl/Star-11
91AA/LineD-210
91Greenvl/ClBest-18
91Greenvl/LineD-210
91Greenvl/ProC-3012
Maloney, Ryan
92WinHaven/ClBest-17
92WinHaven/ProC-1772
Maloney, William A.
T206
WG3-28
Maloof, Jack
77Indianap-24
83Beaum-21
85Spok/Cram-12MG
91AA/LineD-625M
91Wichita/LineD-625CO
91Wichita/ProC-2616CO
91Wichita/Rock-26CO
Malpeso, Dave
84Pawtu-17
85Pawtu-7
Malpica, Omar
91Princet/ClBest-3
91Princet/ProC-3527
Malseed, James
(Jim)
87Pocatel/Bon-10
88Fresno/Cal-12
88Fresno/ProC-1232
89SanJose/Best-22
89SanJose/Cal-223
89SanJose/ProC-437
89SanJose/Star-18
Maltzberger, Gordon
49B/PCL-12
52Laval-36
Malzone, Frank
55B-302
56T-304
57T-355
58T-260
58T-481AS
59Armour-12
59T-220
59T-519M
59T-558AS
60Armour-13A
60Armour-13B
60Bz-12
60T-310
60T-557AS
60T/tatt-30
61Bz-9
61P-48
61T-173M
61T-445
61T/St-113
62Exh
62J-58
62P-58
62P/Can-58
62Salada-14
62Shirriff-14
62T-225
62T/St-14
62T/bucks
63Exh
63J-79
63P-79
63T-232
64T-60
64T/Coins-126AS
64T/Coins-7
64T/SU
64T/St-6
64T/tatt
64Wheat/St-27
65T-315
65T/E-37
66OPC-152
66T-152
78TCMA-177
80Elmira-37C
87Elmira/Black-31
Exh47
PM10/Sm-101
PM10/Sm-102
WG10-33
WG9-33
Malzone, John
91WinHaven/ClBest-20
91WinHaven/ProC-499
92LynchRS/ClBest-22
92LynchRS/ProC-2914
93Pawtu/Ball-14
Mamaux, Albert L.
(Al)
16FleischBrd-59
90Target-477
BF2-91
D327
D328-105
D329-110
D350/2-107
E120
E121/80
E122
E135-105
M101/4-110
M101/5-107
W514-19
W515-2
W575
Mammola, Mark
91Boise/ClBest-13
91Boise/ProC-3873
92QuadC/ClBest-19
Manabe, Bullet
88Fresno/Cal-21
88Fresno/ProC-1235
Manahan, Anthony
90Foil/Best-83
91Jaxvl/ProC-158
92ClBest-329
92Jacks/ProC-3717
92Jaxvl/SB-362
92Sky/AASingl-154
93Calgary/ProC-1172
94ClBest/Gold-23
94Ultra-421
Manahan, Austin
89B-420
90A&AASingle/ProC-97
90Augusta/ProC-2473
90ProC/Singl-850
90SALAS/Star-36
91B-527
91ClBest/Singl-218
91Parramatta/Fut-20
91Salem/ClBest-6
91Salem/ProC-960
92CaroMud/ProC-1188
92CaroMud/SB-137
92ClBest-44
92Sky/AASingl-64
92UD/ML-78
93WPalmB/ClBest-13
93WPalmB/ProC-1348
Mancini, Joe
88Boise/ProC-1626
88Fresno/Cal-3
88Fresno/ProC-1247
89Boise/ProC-1991
Mancini, Pete
85Newar-21
Mancuso, August
(Gus)
33G-237
33G-41
35BU-67
35G-1K
35G-2A
35G-3B
35G-4A
35G-4B
35G-5B
35G-7A
35Wheat
36Exh/4-5
37Exh/4-5
38ONG/Pin-18

40PlayBall-207
41DP-38
90Target-478
91Conlon/Sport-129
R303/A
R303/B
R310
R332-24
V351B-31
V353-41
V355-9
V94-30
W754
Mancuso, Frank Octavius
45Playball-8
Mancuso, Frank
84Omaha-28
85Omaha-4
Mancuso, Paul
83Wisco/Frit-22
84Visalia-18
85OrlanTw-18
86Beaum-17
Mandel, Mike
75T/Photo-24
Manderbach, Gary
75Tidew/Team-16
Manderfield, Steve
77Newar
78Newar
79BurlB-25
80BurlB-8
82ElPaso-15
Mandeville, Bob
86Peoria-18
Mandia, Sam
90StCath/ProC-3459
91Myrtle/ClBest-9
91Myrtle/ProC-2943
Mandl, Steve
89James/ProC-2151CO
91LitSun/HSPros-33CO
91LitSun/HSProsG-33CO
Manering, Mark
87FtLaud-27
Maness, Don
89TNTech-15
Maness, Dwight
92Classic/DP-56
92GulfCD/ProC-3581
93ClBest/MLG-111
Manfre, Mike
83Cedar-20
83Cedar/Frit-20
84Cedar-21
86Vermont-12
87Nashvl-14
Manfred, Jim
91Pittsfld/ClBest-18
91Pittsfld/ProC-3419
92ColumMet/ClBest-6
92ColumMet/ProC-291
92ColumMet/SAL/II-26
Mangham, Eric
87Bakers-19
88VeroB/Star-13
89SanAn/Best-3
91AAA/LineD-591
91Toledo/LineD-591
91Toledo/ProC-1945
Mangham, Mark
85Osceola/Team-10
Mangiardi, Paul
83Erie-1
Mangrum, Lloyd
52Wheat*
Mangual, Angel
70T-654R
71OPC-317R
71T-317R
72OPC-62
72T-62
73OPC-625
73T-625
75OPC-452
75T-452
75T/M-452
76SSPC-503
76Tucson-8
Mangual, Jose
(Pepe)
75OPC-616R
75T-616R
75T/M-616R
76Expo/Redp-21
76OPC-164
76SSPC-335
76T-164
77T-552
78Tidew
79SLCity-22
80SLCity-22
81SLCity-22
82Spokane-22
91WIZMets-243
Mangual, Victor
87Belling/Team-8
88Belling/Legoe-18
Mangum, Leo
28LaPresse-27
33G-162
V353-92
Mangum, Wade
83Idaho-9
Maniac, Miami
91Miami/Bumble-0
Manicchia, Bryan
90Princet/DIMD-15
91Batavia/ClBest-16
91Batavia/ProC-3481
91Spartan/ClBest-8
91Spartan/ProC-893
92Spartan/ClBest-7
92Spartan/ProC-1263
Manion, Clyde
33G-80
94Conlon-1161
V354-35
Manion, George A.
T206
Mankowski, Phil
77T-477R
78BK/T-17
78T-559
79T-93
80T-216
81Tidew-6
82Tidew-9
91WIZMets-244
Manley, Greg
90GA-20
Mann, Bill
88Jaxvl/Best-15
Mann, Dave
61Union
Mann, Fred
N172
N690
Mann, Garth
(Red)
46Sunbeam
47Signal
47Sunbeam
Mann, Kelly
86Geneva-17
87Peoria-25
88CLAS/Star-30
88WinSalem/Star-9
89CharlK-9
89SLAS-4
90A&AASingle/ProC-63
90D-46RR
90F-642R
90F/Can-642
90Foil/Best-157
90Greenvl/Best-9
90Greenvl/ProC-1132
90Greenvl/Star-12
90HotRook/St-29
90OPC-744
90Richm/Bob-21
90S-627RP
90S/100Ris-56
90T-744
90T/89Debut-76
90UD-33
91AAA/LineD-434
91D-736
91Leaf/Stud-147
91Richm/Bob-3
91Richm/LineD-434
91Richm/ProC-2571
91Richm/Team-24
Mann, Les
94Conlon-1134
D328-106
D329-111
D350/2-108
E135-106
M101/4-111
M101/5-108
W514-49
Mann, Scott
86WPalmB-23
87Jaxvl-8
88Jaxvl/ProC-964
Mann, Skip
79LodiD-5
81VeroB-10
Mann, Tom
90Hunting/ProC-3279
91Peoria/ClBest-7
91Peoria/ProC-1339
91Peoria/Team-11
Manning, Dave
92Classic/DP-68
92FrRow/DP-93
93StCl/MurphyS-198
Manning, Dick
83GlenF-21
Manning, Henry
88CapeCod/Sum-150
92SoBend/ClBest-22
92SoBend/ProC-180
Manning, James
N172
N284
Manning, Max
86Negro/Frit-54
91Negro/Lewis-13
92Negro/Retort-39
93TWill-111
Manning, Melvin
(Al)
77BurlB
78BurlB
81ElPaso-3
Manning, Rick
76Ho-12
76Ho/Twink-12
76OPC-275
76SSPC-529
76T-275
77BurgChef-56
77Ho-53
77Ho/Twink-53
77K-15
77OPC-190
77Pep-12
77T-115
78Ho-91
78OPC-151
78T-11
79Ho-76
79OPC-220
79T-425
80OPC-292
80T-564
80T/S-44
80T/Super-44
81D-202
81F-403
81OPC-308
81T-308
81T/SO-19
81T/St-69
82D-85
82F-374
82F/St-195
82OPC-202
82T-202
82T/St-179
82Wheat/Ind
83D-198
83F-413
83F/St-10M
83F/St-5M
83OPC-147
83OPC/St-60
83T-757
83T/St-60
83T/Tr-65
83Wheat/Ind-20
84D-170
84F-205
84Gard-11
84Nes/792-128
84OPC-128
84Pol/Brew-28
84T-128
84T/St-299
85D-237
85F-586
85Gard-11
85OPC-389
85Pol/Brew-28
85T-603
85T/St-291
86D-368
86F-493
86OPC-49
86Pol/Brew-28
86T-49
87D-521
87F-349
87OPC-196
87Pol/Brew-28
87T-706
88D-486
88F-168
88S-593
88T-441
89Pac/SenLg-86
89T/SenLg-39
89TM/SenLg-71
90EliteSenLg-73
Manning, Rube
T204
T206
T3-107
Manning, Tony
75SanAn
Manning, Vida
81ArkTr-23M
Mannion, Greg
90Salinas/Cal-132
Manon, Ramon
87PrWill-23
89FtLaud/Star-14
90Albany/Best-3
90Albany/ProC-1175
90Albany/Star-10
90Cedar/Best-17
90Cedar/ProC-2316
90F/Up-124
91Cedar/ClBest-9
91FtLaud/ClBest-6
91FtLaud/ProC-2420
91T/90Debut-96
92PrWill/ClBest-3
92PrWill/ProC-143
93LimeR/Winter-12
93Rang/Keeb-241
Manos, Pete Charles
79OkCty
Manrique, Fred
82Syrac-18
82Syrac/Team-16
83Syrac-17
84Syrac-12
85Indianap-12
86Louisvl-18
87Coke/WS-5
87F/Up-U72
88Coke/WS-17
88D-493
88F-406
88Panini/St-57
88S-139
88T-437
88T/JumboR-6
88ToysRUs-16
89B-66
89D-489
89F-503
89OPC-108
89S-457
89T-108
89T/Big-84
89T/St-300
89UD-628
90D-165
90F-306
90F/Can-306
90Leaf-518
90OPC-242
90Panini/St-158
90PublInt/St-396
90S-166
90T-242
90T/Tr-66T
90UD-392
93Rang/Keeb-242
Manrique, Marco
92Bluefld/ClBest-19
92Bluefld/ProC-2363
Manser
C46-59
E254
Manship, Jeff
92Billings/ProC-3368
Manship, Ray
78Newar
Mansolino, Doug
85Crm/PCL-192C
89Vanco/ProC-575
92WSox-NNO
93WSox-30M
Mansur, Jeff
92Visalia/ProC-1010
Mantha, Georges
45Parade*-36
Manti, Sam
89Penin/Star-14
Mantick, Dennis
78OrlanTw
79Toledo-21
Mantilla, Felix
57SpicSpan/4x5-12
57T-188
58T-17
59T-157
60Lake
60SpicSpan-11
60T-19
61T-164
61T/St-44
62Salada-183
62Shirriff-183
62T-436
62T/St-158
62T/bucks
63J-198
63P-198
63T-447
64T-228
65OPC-29
65T-29
66T-557
66T/RO-112
66T/RO-56
67T-524
81TCMA-327
91WIZMets-245
Mantle, Mickey
51B-253
52B-101
52BR
52StarCal/L-70G
52T-311
52TipTop
53B/Col-44M
53B/Col-59
53Briggs
53SM
53T-82
54B-65
54DanDee
54NYJour
54RH
54SM
55Armour-13A
55Armour-13B
55B-202
55SM
56T-135
56YellBase/Pin-20
57T-407M
57T-95
58T-150
58T-418M
58T-487AS
59Bz
59HRDerby-12
59T-10
59T-461HL
59T-564AS
59YooHoo-4
60Armour-14
60Bz-31
60NuCard-22
60NuCard-50
60P*
60T-160M
60T-350
60T-563AS
60T/tatt-31
60T/tatt-92
61Bz-2
61NuCard-422

61NuCard-450
61P-4
61T-300
61T-406HL
61T-44LL
61T-475MVP
61T-578AS
61T/Dice-8
61T/St-196
62Bz
62Exh
62J-5
62P-5
62P/Can-5
62Salada-41
62Shirriff-41
62T-18M
62T-200
62T-318IA
62T-471AS
62T-53LL
62T/St-88
62T/bucks
63Bz-1
63Exh
63J-15
63P-15
63Salada-56
63T-173M
63T-200
63T-2LL
63T/SO
64Bz-1
64T-331M
64T-50
64T/Coins-120
64T/Coins-131AS
64T/S-25
64T/SU
64T/St-53
64T/tatt
65Bz-1
65OPC-134WS
65OPC-3LL
65OPC-5LL
65OldLond-30
65T-134WS
65T-350
65T-3LL
65T-5LL
65T/E-11
65T/trans-57
66Bz-7
66OPC-50
66T-50
66T/RO-57
66T/RO-57
67Bz-7
67CokeCap/YMet-8
67OPC-103CL
67OPC-150
67OPC/PI-6
67T-103CL
67T-150
67T/PI-6
67T/Test/SU-8
68Bz-11
68T-280
68T-490M
68T/ActionSt-10A
68T/ActionSt-7B
68T/G-2
68T/Post-18
69T-412CL
69T-500
69T/S-24
69T/St-205
69T/decal
69Trans-30
72Laugh/GF-33
73Syrac/Team-15
74Syrac/Team-14
75OPC-194MVP
75OPC-195MVP
75OPC-200MVP
75SSPC/42-37
75SSPC/Sam-4
75Syrac/Team-10
75T-194MVP
75T-195MVP
75T-200MVP
75T/M-194MVP
75T/M-195MVP
75T/M-200MVP
76Shakey-145
77Galasso-232
77Galasso-7
78TCMA-262
79TCMA-7
80Laugh/3/4/5-18
80Pac/Leg-6
80Perez/HOF-145
80SSPC/HOF
81TCMA-303M
81TCMA-474M
82CJ-6
82KMart-1
83D/HOF-43pz
83D/HOF-7
83Kaline-14M
83Kaline-16M
83Kaline-35M
83MLBPA/Pin-12
84D/Champs-50
84West/1-4
85CircK-6
85D/HOF-6
85Woolwth-23
86BLChew-6
86Sf/Dec-26
87KMart-5
87Leaf/SpecOlym-H1
87Nestle/DT-17
88Grenada-46
88Pac/Leg-7
89B/Ins-5
89B/Ins-6
89CMC/Mantle-Set
89HOF/St-40
89Kenner/BBGr-10
90BBWit-3
90HOF/St-49
90Perez/GreatMom-19
90Perez/Master-10
90Perez/Master-6
90Perez/Master-7
90Perez/Master-8
90Perez/Master-9
91S/MantleP-Set
91T/Arc53-82
92Pinn/MM-24
92Pinn/MM-26
92Pinn/MM-27
92Pinn/MM-Set
92S/Franchise-2
92S/Franchise-4M
92S/Franchise-AU2
92S/Franchise-AU4M
92Yank/WIZ60-78
92Yank/WIZAS-43
92Yank/WIZHOF-22
93Select/TCr-1
93UD/ATH-134M
93UD/ATH-135
93UD/ATH-137
93UD/ATH-140
93UD/ATH-141
93UD/ATH-165M
93UD/ATH-87
93UD/ATHPrev-1M
93UD/ATHPrev-2M
93UD/ATHPrev-4M
93UD/Then-TN17
94TedW/500-4
Exh47
PM10/L-21
PM10/Sm-103
PM10/Sm-104
PM10/Sm-105
PM10/Sm-106
PM10/Sm-107
PM10/Sm-108
PM10/Sm-109
WG10-13
WG9-16

Manto, Jeff
86QuadC-19
87PalmSp-4
88BBAmer-29
88MidldA/GS-21
88TexLgAS/GS-39
89Edmon/CMC-20
89Edmon/ProC-570
89F/Up-13
90AAASingl/ProC-224
90ColoSp/CMC-15
90ColoSp/ProC-43
90F-137
90F/Can-137
90F/Up-U94
90ProC/Singl-467
91B-75
91D-602
91Indian/McDon-18
91OPC-488
91S-337RP
91StCl-582
91T-488
91T/90Debut-97
91UD-238
92Richm/Bleach-1
92Richm/Comix-9
92Richm/ProC-384
92Richm/SB-431
92S-666
92StCl-699
93ScranWB/Team-16
94Pac/Cr-481

Mantrana, Manny
87Fayette-12
88Clmbia/GS-19
88StLucie/Star-15

Manuare, Jose
91MedHat/ProC-4096
91MedHat/SportP-3

Manuel, Barry
88CharlR/Star-14
89Tulsa/GS-16
90CharlR/Star-12
90FSLAS/Star-36
90LSUGreat-16
90Star/ISingl-24
91AA/LineD-586
91Tulsa/LineD-586
91Tulsa/ProC-2768
91Tulsa/Team-16
92D-401RR
92OkCty/ProC-1913
92ProC/Tomorrow-154
92T/91Debut-115
93Pinn-257
93Rang/Keeb-243
93S-225

Manuel, Charles
(Charlie)
70OPC-194
70T-194
71MLB/St-466
71OPC-744
71T-744
74Albuq/Team-9
76SSPC-86
83Wisco/Frit-27
85OrlanTw-22
86Toledo-15MG
87Portl-22
88Gator-9CO
90Target-479
91AAA/LineD-99MG
91ColoSp/LineD-99MG
91ColoSp/ProC-2200MG
92ColoSp/ProC-766
92ColoSp/SB-99MG

Manuel, Jerry
76OPC-596R
76T-596R
77Evansvl/TCMA-18
82F-195
83Iowa-17
87Indianap-5
89T/SenLg-90
90Jaxvl/Best-25MG
90Jaxvl/ProC-1391MG
91AAA/LineD-199MG
91Indianap/LineD-199
91Indianap/ProC-477

Manuel, Jose
88SanAn/Best-18

Manush, Heinie
29Exh/4-29
31Exh/4-31
33Exh/4-16
33G-107
33G-187
33G-47
34DS-30
34Exh/4-16
34G-18
35BU-77
35Exh/4-16
35G-1C
35G-2C
35G-6C
35G-7C
37Wheat-8
39PlayBall-94
40PlayBall-176
54T-187CO
60F-18
61F-57
76Rowe-10
76Shakey-100
77Galasso-56
80Pac/Leg-2
80Perez/HOF-100
80SSPC/HOF
81Conlon-77
81Tiger/Detroit-82A
81Tiger/Detroit-82B
86Conlon/1-19
88Conlon/AmAS-20
89HOF/St-36
89Smok/Dodg-16
90Target-480
91Conlon/Sport-270
91Conlon/Sport-63
94Conlon-1077
94T/Arc54-187
R308-178
R310
R314
R316
R337-416
V353-47
V354-68
V355-73
W517-28

Manwaring, Kirt
87Shrev-10
87TexLgAS-22
88D-39RR
88F-651R
88F/Mini-119
88Leaf-39RR
88Phoenix/CMC-12
88Phoenix/ProC-61
88S-627RP
88T/Tr-64T
89B-469
89D-494
89D/Best-330
89F-334
89Mother/Giants-23
89Panini/St-208
89S-619RP
89S/HotRook-46
89S/YS/I-22
89T-506
89UD-500
90AAASingl/ProC-40
90D-59
90F-63
90F/Can-63
90OPC-678
90Phoenix/CMC-10
90Phoenix/ProC-14
90ProC/Singl-537
90PublInt/St-76
90S-146
90T-678
90UD-457
91Mother/Giant-23
91OPC-472
91PG&E-25
91S-101
91T-472
92B-361
92D-494
92F-641
92Giant/PGE-27
92L-208
92L/BlkGold-208
92Mother/Giant-23
92OPC-726
92Pinn-181
92S-636
92StCl-271
92T-726
92T/Gold-726
92T/GoldWin-726
92TripleP-61M
92UD-740
92Ultra-293
93B-688
93D-122M
93D-364
93F-158
93Flair-144
93L-66
93Mother/Giant-9
93Pac/Spanish-612
93Panini-235
93Pinn-122
93S-179
93Select-247
93StCl-690
93StCl/1stDay-690
93StCl/Giant-6
93Studio-151
93T-337
93T/Gold-337
93UD-179
93Ultra-135
94B-275
94D-209
94F-694
94Finest-415
94Flair-245
94L-55
94OPC-2
94Pac/Cr-549
94Pinn-53
94Pinn/Artist-53
94Pinn/Museum-53
94S-344
94StCl-218
94StCl/1stDay-218
94StCl/Gold-218
94StCl/Team-3
94T-30
94T/Gold-30
94TripleP-106
94TripleP/Medal-2M
94UD-100
94UD/CollC-186
94UD/CollC/Gold-186
94UD/CollC/Silv-186
94UD/ElecD-100
94Ultra-292
94Ultra/AwardWin-10

Manz, George
74Wichita-105

Manzanillo, Josias
85Elmira-14
87NewBrit-21
89EastLgAS/ProC-17
89NewBrit/ProC-606
89NewBrit/Star-8
90Foil/Best-70
90NewBrit/Best-4
90NewBrit/ProC-1315
90NewBrit/Star-9
90ProC/Singl-879
90T/TVRSox-51
91Pawtu/ProC-35
92Memphis/SB-429
92Omaha/ProC-2959
92Omaha/SB-336
92S-838
92StCl-504
92T/91Debut-116
93LimeR/Winter-42
93Pac/Spanish-514
93Ultra-574
94Pac/Cr-411
94Ultra-239

Manzanillo, Ravelo
83AlexD-27
85Nashua-15
88FSLAS/Star-43
88Tampa/Star-14
89BirmB/Best-13
90AAASingl/ProC-164
90ProC/Singl-631
90Vanco/CMC-4
90Vanco/ProC-486
91AAA/LineD-510
91Syrac/LineD-510
91Syrac/MerchB-13
94B-302
94Ultra-556

Manzon, Howard
86Kenosha-15

Mapel, Steve
79Wisco-9
80OrlanTw-6
80Toledo-1
82OrlanTw/B-20

Mapes, Cliff
50B-218

51B-289
51BR-D1
52B-13
52T-103
R346-33
R423-64
Maples, Steve
79Clinton/TCMA-23
Maples, Tim
81Miami-18
Marabell, Scott
89Bakers/Cal-195
90VeroB/Star-19
91SanAn/ProC-2989
Marabella, Tony
90Gate/ProC-3347
90Gate/SportP-15
91Sumter/ClBest-16
91Sumter/ProC-2341
Marak, Paul
87Sumter-9
88Durham/Star-13
89Greenvl/Best-17
89Greenvl/ProC-1174
89Greenvl/Star-14
90AAASingl/ProC-400
90ProC/Singl-284
90Richm/Bob-10
90Richm/CMC-8
90Richm/ProC-255
90Richm/Team-20
91Classic/II-T52
91D-413RR
91Leaf-260
91OPC-753
91Richm/ProC-2562
91S-712RP
91S/Rook40-13
91T-753
91T/90Debut-98
92CharlK/ProC-2768
Maranda, Georges
52LaPatrie-10
52Laval-5
60T-479
61Clover-15
61Union
Maranville, Walter
(Rabbit)
14CJ-136
15CJ-136
16FleischBrd-60
21Exh-101
24Sherlock-5
25Exh-23
26Exh-15
31Exh/4-1
33CJ/Pin-17
33DL-13
33G-117
34DS-3
35BU-37
35G-1J
35G-3A
35G-4A
35G-5A
50Callahan
50W576-51
60Exh/HOF-15
60F-21
61F-124
63Bz-14
69Bz/Sm
76Rowe-14M
76Shakey-72
77Galasso-114
80Pac/Leg-3
80Perez/HOF-72
80SSPC/HOF
87Conlon/2-47
89HOF/St-17
89Smok/Dodg-18
90Target-481
91Conlon/Sport-4
93Conlon-914
93CrackJack-20
94Conlon-1060
BF2-54
D327
D328-107
D329-112
D350/2-109
E120
E121/120
E121/80
E122
E135-107
E220
M101/4-112
M101/5-109
R300
R316
R328-10
V100
V354-4
V355-129
V61-90
V89-42
W501-83
W515-50
W572
W573
W575
WG4-15
WG7-28
Marberry, Fred
(Firpo)
31Exh/4-31
33DH-31
33Exh/4-16
33G-104
34Exh/4-12
35BU-66
35G-1H
35G-3F
35G-5F
35G-6F
61F-125
91Conlon/Sport-326
R310
R313A-8
R315-A24
R315-B24
R332-47
V354-8
V355-10
Marcell, Ziggy
86Negro/Frit-56
Marcelle, Oliver
74Laugh/Black-3
90Negro/Star-17
Marcero, Doug
89Niagara/Pucko-16
90Niagara/Pucko-21
91Lakeland/ProC-265
Marchese, John
88Bend/Legoe-24
89QuadC/Best-18
89QuadC/GS-10
90QuadC/GS-15
Marchese, Joseph
(Joe)
86Elmira-11
87Greens-11
88CLAS/Star-12
88Lynch/Star-10
89NewBrit/ProC-616
89NewBrit/Star-9
91WinHaven/ClBest-26CO
91WinHaven/ProC-506CO
92WinHaven/ClBest-28
92WinHaven/ProC-1795CO
Marchesi, Jim
92Johnson/ClBest-21
92Johnson/ProC-3112
Marcheskie, Lee
82AlexD-2
83LynnP-5
85Nashua-16
Marchildon, Phil
49B-187
V351A-17
Marchio, Frank
53Exh/Can-53
Marchok, Chris
87James-28
88Rockford-23
89Jaxvl/Best-4
89Jaxvl/ProC-166
89Rockford-23
90AAASingl/ProC-583
90Indianap/CMC-5
90Indianap/ProC-300
90ProC/Singl-55
91AA/LineD-262
91Harris/LineD-262
91Harris/ProC-624
92Harris/ProC-457
92Harris/SB-288
Marcon, Dave
90StCath/ProC-3463
91SLCity/ProC-3206
91SLCity/SportP-23
Marcuci
46Sunbeam
Marcum, John
34G-69
35G-8J
35G-9J
92Conlon/Sport-574
R314
V355-58
Mardsen, Steve
84BuffB-17
Marett, John
89Bluefld/Star-14
90Wausau/ProC-2127
90Wausau/Star-15
Margenau, Eric
92ColumMet/SAL/II-340WN
Margheim, Greg
90Billings/ProC-3218
91Cedar/ClBest-10
91Cedar/ProC-2717
Margoneri, Joe
57T-191
Marguardt, Chuck
88Gaston/ProC-1023
Maria, Esteban
75BurlB
Mariano, Bob
84CharlO-12
85CharlO-18
89Albany/Best-28
89Albany/ProC-324
91AA/LineD-25M
91Albany/LineD-25M
91Albany/ProC-1025CO
92FtLaud/ProC-2630
92FtLaud/Team-20CO
Marichal, Juan
61T-417
61T/St-79
62J-140
62P-140
62P/Can-140
62T-505
62T/St-198
63J-109
63P-109
63Salada-5
63T-440
64T-280
64T-3LL
64T/Coins-157AS
64T/Coins-36
64T/S-37
64T/SU
64T/St-39S4
64Wheat/St-28
65Bz-24
65OPC-10LL
65OPC-50
65T-10LL
65T-50
65T/trans-20
66Bz-10
66T-221LL
66T-420
66T/RO-29
66T/RO-58
67Bz-10
67CokeCap/AS-14
67CokeCap/Giant-7
67CokeCap/NLAS-34
67OPC/PI-28
67T-234LL
67T-236LL
67T-500
67T/PI-28
68Bz-5
68CokeCap/Giant-7
68Dexter-50
68OPC-107CL
68T-107CL
68T-205
69Kelly/Pin-11
69MB-165
69MLB/St-203
69MLBPA/Pin-51
69NTF
69OPC-10LL
69OPC/DE-15
69T-10LL
69T-370
69T-572M
69T/DE-32
69T/S-64
69T/St-107
69Trans-32
70K-13
70MB-14
70MLB/St-128
70OPC-210
70OPC-466AS
70OPC-67LL
70OPC-69LL
70T-210
70T-466AS
70T-67LL
70T-69LL
70T/SO
70Trans-3
71Bz/Test-19
71MLB/St-256
71OPC-325
71T-325
71T/Coins-125
71T/tatt-1
71Ticket/Giant-6
72K-47
72MB-204
72ProStars/PostC-17
72T-567
72T-568IA
73OPC-480
73T-480
74OPC-330
74T-330
74T/Tr-330T
78TCMA-2
80Perez/HOF-183
83MLBPA/Pin-25
84Mother/Giants-3
86Sf/Dec-46
87KMart-6
88Pac/Leg-54
89Smok/Dodg-17
90Perez/GreatMom-56
90Target-482
93AP/ASG-124
93AP/ASG24K-58G
94TedW-54
PM10/Sm-110
WG10-34
WG9-34
Marichal, Victor
75BurlB
Marie, Larry
90Richm/25Ann-16
Marietta, Lou
78Cedar
82WHave-8
Marigny, Ron
87GlenF-11
87Lakeland-9
89Lakeland/Star-15
90Lakeland/Star-18
91Lakeland/ClBest-20
91Lakeland/ProC-273
Marin, Jose
91Elmira/ClBest-11
91Elmira/ProC-3278
92LynchRS/ClBest-4
92LynchRS/ProC-2915
Marina, Juan
87Columbia-18
88Clmbia/GS-7
89StLucie/Star-15
Marina, Vega
90StLucie/Star-14
Marinaro, Bob
90PrWill/Team-4
Marine, Del
92Bristol/ClBest-16
92Bristol/ProC-1415
Marini, Marc
92ColRS/ClBest-10
92ColRS/ProC-2406
93ClBest/MLG-16
93FExcel/ML-160
93Kinston/Team-14
93SALAS/II-23
93SALAS/IICS-11
Marino, Bob
92FtLaud/ClBest-25CO
Marino, Mark
86QuadC-20
87PalmSp-30
88Stockton/ProC-752
89Stockton/Best-31M
89Stockton/ProC-402M
89Stockton/Star-28M
Marion, Marty
39Exh
42Playball-27
47TipTop
48B-40
48L-97
49B-54
49Eureka-189
50B-88
51B-34
52B-85
53B/Col-52
60F-19
61F-58
61NuCard-473
79TCMA-99
90BBWit-47
91T/Arc53-302
92Card/McDon/Pac-6
92Conlon/Sport-626
93AP/ASG-134
Exh47
PM10/Sm-111
R346-3
W754
Maris, Roger
57Sohio/Ind-8
58T-47
59T-202
60T-377
60T-565AS
60T/tatt-32
61Bz-5
61NuCard-416
61Post-7
61T-2
61T-44LL
61T-478MVP
61T-576AS
61T/St-197
62Bz-14
62Exh
62J-6
62P-6
62P/Can-6
62Salada-23
62Shirriff-23
62T-1
62T-313IA
62T-401M
62T-53LL
62T/St-89
62T/bucks
63Exh
63J-16
63P-16
63Salada-57
63T-120
63T-4LL
64T-225
64T-331M
65OPC-155
65OldLond-31
65T-155
66T-365
67OPC-45
67T-45
68T-330
72Laugh/GF-50
75OPC-198MVP
75OPC-199MVP
75Sheraton-18
75T-198MVP
75T-199MVP
75T/M-198MVP
75T/M-199MVP
76Laugh/Jub-30
77Galasso-226
78TCMA-11
79T-413LL
79TCMA-161
80Marchant-18
80Pac/Leg-101
81TCMA-303
81TCMA-382

81TCMA-474
85Woolwth-24
86T-405TBC
87KMart-7
88Pac/Leg-89
90HOF/St-63
90MSA/AGFA-10
92Yank/WIZ60-79
92Yank/WIZAS-44
94TedW-139
94TedW/54-27
94TedW/Etch-Set
Exh47
PM10/L-22
PM10/L-23
PM10/Sm-112
PM10/Sm-113
PM10/Sm-114
WG10-14
WG9-17
Markell, Duke
52Park-19
Markert, Jim
86Penin-16
88BirmB/Best-5
Markham, Bobby
80WHave-12
Markham, Dan
92GulfCD/ProC-3562
Markiewicz, Brandon
91Boise/ClBest-18
91Boise/ProC-3887
92QuadC/ClBest-5
92QuadC/ProC-819
Markkanen, Pekka
89KS*-51
Markland, Gene
V362-37
Markle, Cliff
E120
Markley, Scot
86Ashvl-18
87Osceola-23
Marks, John
82Clinton/Frit-28AGM
83Wisco/Frit-26GM
Marks, Lance
91Pulaski/ClBest-9
91Pulaski/ProC-4015
92Macon/ClBest-3
92Macon/ProC-276
92ProC/Tomorrow-193
93Durham/Team-13
Markulike, Joe
90Idaho/ProC-3253
Marlowe, Dick
53Tiger/Glen-21
55B-91
Marois, Jean
45Parade*-37
Marone, Lou
70T-703
71MLB/St-206
Maropis, Pete
76AppFx
Marozas, Kevin
89KS*-58
Marquard, Richard
(Rube)
10Domino-75
11Helmar-130
12Sweet/Pin-116
16FleischBrd-61
72Laugh/GF-14
76Shakey-124
77Galasso-158
80Perez/HOF-124
80SSPC/HOF
81Conlon-45
82Ohio/HOF-57
86Conlon/1-27
89HOF/St-66
89Smok/Dodg-19
90BBWit-91
90Perez/GreatMom-30
90Target-483
91Conlon/Sport-252
92Conlon/Col-6
92Conlon/Sport-342
93CrackJack-9
94Conlon-1015
BF2-58
D303
D304
D328-108
D329-113
D350/2-110
E106
E120
E135-108
E224
E254
E90/1
E96
L1-111
M101/4-113
M101/5-110
S74-87
S81-86
T202
T205
T206
T207
T213/blue
T213/brown
T215/blue
T215/brown
T215/brown
T216
T222
T227
V100
W572
WG4-16
WG5-27
WG6-26
Marquardt, Chuck
89Gaston/ProC-1010
91Butte/SportP-28
Marquardt, John
84Madis/Pol-12
85Huntsvl/BK-18
86OrlanTw-11
Marquess, Mark
88T/Tr-65T
Marquez, Edgar
88Myrtle/ProC-1170
88StCath/ProC-2025
90StCath/ProC-3455
Marquez, Edwin
86QuadC-21
87MidldA-12
88Edmon/CMC-19
88Edmon/ProC-575
89Edmon/CMC-13
89Edmon/ProC-552
90AAASingl/ProC-584
90Foil/Best-109
90Indianap/CMC-12
90Indianap/ProC-301
90Jaxvl/Best-29
90ProC/Singl-62
Marquez, Gonzalo
73OPC-605R
73T-605R
74OPC-422
74T-422
Marquez, Ishovany
92Bluefld/ClBest-6
92Bluefld/ProC-2358
92Kane/ClBest-23
92Kane/ProC-89
Marquez, Isidrio
89SanAn/Best-16
90SanAn/GS-17
91SanAn/ProC-2970
Marquis, Roger
91Crown/Orio-276
Marr, Alan
83Clinton/Frit-18
85Everett/Cram-8CO
Marr, Charles
N172
Marrero, Conrado
51B-206
52T-317
53Briggs
53T-13
54B-200
91T/Arc53-13
Marrero, Kenny
91Erie/ClBest-8
91Erie/ProC-4073
92Bristol/ClBest-17
92Bristol/ProC-1416
Marrero, Oreste
89Beloit/I/Star-15
89Star/Wax-5
90Beloit/Best-18
90Beloit/Star-12
90Foil/Best-292
91ClBest/Singl-194
91Stockton/ClBest-6
91Stockton/ProC-3040
92ElPaso/SB-218
92Sky/AASingl-95
92Stockton/ProC-41
93Harris/ProC-276
94Pac/Cr-385
Marrero, Roger
89AubAs/ProC-2181
Marrero, Vilato
89Beloit/I/Star-16
89Beloit/II/Star-20
90Beloit/Best-12
90Beloit/Star-13
91Stockton/ClBest-21
91Stockton/ProC-3041
Marrett, Scott
86PalmSp-21
86PalmSp/Smok-13
87SanBern-15
Marriott, Bill
90Target-484
Marris, Mark
(Moose)
87Oneonta-26
88PrWill/Star-16
89PrWill/Star-12
91FtLaud/ClBest-7
91FtLaud/ProC-2421
Marrow, Buck
90Target-485
Marrs, Terry
87Elmira/Black-10
87Elmira/Red-10
88Elmira-22
89WinHaven/Star-14
Marsans, Armando
14CJ-134
15CJ-134
92Negro/RetortII-24
D328-109
D350/2-111
E135-109
E224
M101/5-111
T207
Marsh, Fred
(Freddie)
52T-8
53T-240
54T-218
55Esskay
55T-13
55T/DH-39
56T-23
91Crown/Orio-277
91T/Arc53-240
94T/Arc54-218
Marsh, Quinn
88Greens/ProC-1552
89Cedar/Best-4
89Cedar/ProC-929
89Cedar/Star-10
90Salinas/Cal-124
90Salinas/ProC-2721
Marsh, Randy
88TM/Umpire-43
89TM/Umpire-41
89TM/Umpire-60M
90TM/Umpire-39
Marsh, Tom
88Batavia/ProC-1676
89Spartan/ProC-1047
89Spartan/Star-15
90Reading/Best-23
90Reading/ProC-1233
90Reading/Star-18
90Spartan/Best-28
90Spartan/ProC-2495
90Spartan/Star-15
91AA/LineD-514
91Reading/LineD-514
91Reading/ProC-1383
92D/Rook-66
92Phill/Med-43
92ScranWB/SB-488
93F-494
93Pinn-256
93S-263
93ScranWB/Team-17
93StCl-466
93StCl/1stDay-466
93T-649
93T/Gold-649
94Ultra-552
Marsh, Trent
89Stockton/Star-26M
Marshall, Bret
89SoBend/GS-13
Marshall, Charlie
V362-35
Marshall, Clarence
43Centen-18
52NTea
52T-174
Marshall, Dave
69T-464
70OPC-58
70T-58
71MLB/St-159
71OPC-259
71T-259
72MB-205
72T-673
73OPC-513
73T-513
91WIZMets-247
Marshall, Jason
92Eugene/ClBest-17
92Eugene/ProC-3036
Marshall, John 1
88Martins/Star-26
89Spartan/ProC-1045
89Spartan/Star-16
89Star/Wax-56
Marshall, John 2
89SanDiegoSt/Smok-16
Marshall, Keith
75Omaha/Team-10
76Indianap-19
Marshall, Max
40Hughes-13
47Smith-22
Marshall, Mike A.
79LodiD-6
81Albuq/TCMA-16
82Albuq-22
82D-562
82F-13
82T-681R
83D-362
83F-211
83OPC-324
83Pol/Dodg-5
83T-324
84D-348
84F-105
84Nes/792-634
84OPC-52
84Pol/Dodg-5
84T-634
84T/St-85
85Coke/Dodg-20
85D-12DK
85D-296
85D/AAS-22
85D/DKsuper-12
85F-377
85FunFood/Pin-64
85Leaf-12DK
85OPC-85
85T-85
85T/St-72
86Coke/Dodg-18
86D-52
86Drake-8
86F-137
86F/Mini-30
86F/St-71
86Leaf-40
86OPC-26
86Pol/Dodg-5
86Seven/Coin-W11M
86Sf-89
86T-728
86T/St-71
86T/Tatt-17M
87D-176
87D/OD-77
87F-446
87F/Lim-25
87Mother/Dodg-5
87OPC-186
87Pol/Dodg-3
87RedFoley/St-31
87Seven-W8
87Sf-82
87Sf/TPrev-14M
87Smok/Dodg-21
87Stuart-6
87T-664
87T/St-66
88D-229
88D/Best-178
88F-522
88KennerFig-65
88Mother/Dodg-5
88OPC-249
88Panini/St-315
88Pol/Dodg-5
88S-135
88Sf-220
88Smok/Dodg-29
88T-249
88T/Big-133
88T/St-69
89B-350
89D-110
89D/Best-204
89D/GrandSlam-2
89F-66
89F/BBMVP's-25
89F/WS-7
89KennerFig-88
89Mother/Dodg-5
89OPC-323
89Panini/St-108
89Pol/Dodg-4
89S-186
89Sf-54
89Smok/Dodg-101
89T-582
89T/Big-48
89T/Coins-18
89T/LJN-60
89T/St-67
89T/UK-48
89UD-70
89Woolwth-26
90B-132
90Classic/III-57
90D-84
90F-401
90F/Can-401
90HOF/St-79
90Kahn/Mets-6
90Leaf-224
90OPC-198
90Panini/St-272
90PublInt/St-13
90S-384
90T-198
90T/St-62
90T/TVMets-27
90T/Tr-67T
90Target-486
90UD-262
90UD/Ext-781
91D-625
91F-102
91OPC-356
91S-617
91StCl-226
91T-356
91UD-681
91Ultra-35
91WIZMets-249
93Expo/D/McDon-25
Marshall, Mike G.
68CokeCap/Tiger-3
68T-201
69OPC-17
69T-17
71Expo/ProS-13
71MLB/St-133
71OPC-713
71T-713
72Dimanche*-28
72OPC-505
72T-505
73OPC-355
73T-355
73T/Lids-30
74OPC-208LL
74OPC-73
74T-208LL
74T-73
74T/St-57

74T/Tr-73T
75K-36
75OPC-313LL
75OPC-330
75OPC-6RB
75T-313LL
75T-330
75T-6M
75T/M-313LL
75T/M-330
75T/M-6M
76OPC-465
76T-465
77T-263
79Twin/FriszP-16
82F-532
87Smok/Dodg-20
88Smok/Dodg-16
89Smok/Dodg-84
90Target-487
91WIZMets-246
93Rang/Keeb-244
Marshall, R. James
(Jim)
1WIZMets-248
52Mother-9
58T-441
59T-153
60T-267
61T-188
62T-337
73Wichita-9
74OPC-354CO
74T-354C
75OPC-638MG
75T-638MG
75T/M-638MG
76SSPC-308
76T-277MG
84Nashvl-13MG
86BuffB-17MG
91Crown/Orio-278
91Pac/SenLg-127
91Pac/SenLg-133
91Pac/SenLg-54M
Marshall, Randy
89Butte/SP-20
89Fayette/ProC-1581
90A&AASingle/ProC-83
90Fayette/ProC-2404
90Gaston/Best-18
90Gaston/ProC-2528
90Gaston/Star-13
91AA/LineD-391
91Gaston/ClBest-19
91Gaston/ProC-2696
91London/LineD-391
91London/ProC-1876
92AAA/ASG/SB-562
92Tidew/ProC-
92Tidew/SB-562
Marshall, Todd
92Spokane/ClBest-6
92Spokane/ProC-1290
Marshall, Willard
42Playball-33
47HomogBond-33
47TipTop
48B-13
49B-48
49Eureka-118
49Royal-17
50B-73
50Drake-17
51B-98
52B-97
52T-96
53B/Col-58
53T-95
54B-70
55B-131
79TCMA-124
91T/Arc53-95
D305
Exh47
R423-65
Marshall, William R.
(Doc)
T206
T213/brown
Marsland, David
93MissSt-32
Marte, Alexis
83Kinston/Team-14
84Visalia-4
85OrlanTw-7
86Toledo-16
87Portl-17
89Tulsa/Team-14
Marte, Roberto
86Erie-18
87Erie-10
88Savan/ProC-341
89Spring/Best-21
91Erie/ClBest-26CO
91Erie/ProC-4086CO
Marte, Vic
78Charl
Martel, Ed
87Oneonta-30
88Oneonta/ProC-2040
89FtLaud/Star-15
90PrWill/Team-14
91AA/LineD-11
91Albany/LineD-11
91Albany/ProC-1004
92B-607
92ColClip/Pol-6
92ColClip/ProC-347
92ColClip/SB-109
92D/Rook-67
92L/GRook-14
92ProC/Tomorrow-112
92Sky/AAASingl-49
Martel, Jay
87Savan-7
Marten, Greg
93SoEastern-2CO
Marten, Tom
88Kenosha/ProC-1405
Marteniz, Ivan
88Wythe/ProC-1995
Martes, Sixto
84Everett/Cram-14
Martig, Rich
86Modesto-19
Martin, Al
86Sumter/ProC-17
87Sumter-24
88MidwLAS/GS-19
89Durham/Star-15
89Durham/Team-15
90Foil/Best-220
90Greenvl/Best-17
90Greenvl/ProC-1141
91AA/LineD-211
91Greenvl/ClBest-23
91Greenvl/LineD-211
91Greenvl/ProC-3015
91Richm/Bob-27
92BuffB/BlueS-11
92BuffB/ProC-333
92BuffB/SB-35
92D/Rook-68
92F/Up-114
93B-246
93Colla/DM-67
93D-716RR
93F/Final-113
93Flair-114
93L-189
93OPC/Premier-57
93Pac/Spanish-587
93Pinn-614
93Pirate/Nation-15
93S-322
93S/Boys-27
93Select/RookTr-47T
93StCl-579
93StCl/1stDay-579
93Studio-159
93T-623
93T/Finest-155
93T/FinestRef-155
93T/Gold-623
93TripleP-242
93UD-340
93Ultra-451
93Ultra/AllRook-5
94B-330
94D-494
94F-612
94F/RookSen-11
94Flair-217
94L-49
94OPC-241
94Pac/Cr-500
94Pinn-211
94Pinn/Artist-211
94Pinn/Museum-211
94S-546
94Select-50
94StCl-6
94StCl/1stDay-6
94StCl/Gold-6
94StCl/Pr-6
94Studio-147
94T-366
94T/Finest-11
94T/FinestRef-11
94T/Gold-366
94TripleP-186
94UD-243
94UD/CollC-187
94UD/CollC/Gold-187
94UD/CollC/Silv-187
94UD/ElecD-243
94Ultra-257
Martin, Alfred
(Billy)
48Signal
48Smith-17
49Remar
52BR
52T-175
53B/Col-118
53B/Col-93M
53T-86
54B-145
54RH
54T-13
56T-181
57T-62
58T-271
59Kahn
59T-295
60Kahn
60T-173
61T-89
61T/RO-26
61T/St-20
62J-84
62P-84
62P/Can-84
62Salada-43
62Shirriff-43
62T-208
69T-547MG
71OPC-208MG
71T-208MG
72OPC-33MG
72OPC-34IA
72T-33MG
72T-34IA
73OPC-323MG
73T-323MG
74OPC-379MG
74T-379MG
75OPC-511MG
75T-511MG
75T/M-511MG
76SSPC-453
76T-17MG
77T-387MG
78BK/Y-1
78SSPC/270-14MG
78T-721
78Twin/Frisz-10MG
79TCMA-143
81A's/Granny-1MG
81D-479
81F-581MG
81T-671MG
81TCMA-364
81Tiger/Detroit-107MG
81Tiger/Detroit-67MG
82D-491MG
82Granny-9MG
82T/St-115MG
83D-575MG
83Kaline-15M
83Kaline-16M
83Kaline-43M
83T-156MG
83T/Tr-66T
84Nes/792-81MG
84T-81
85Pol/MetYank-Y6
85T/Tr-78T
86T-651MG
87Mother/A's-23
90S/NWest-30
91T/Arc53-86
92Bz/Quadra-8M
92Pinn/MM-26M
92Yank/WIZAS-45
93AP/ASG-140
93Rang/Keeb-245MG
93UD/ATH-141M
93UD/ATH-88
94T/Arc54-13
94TedW-61
PM10/L-24
Martin, Andrew
(Andy)
92Hamil/ClBest-11
92Hamil/ProC-1601
Martin, Boris
(Babe)
49B-167
Martin, Chris
88Kenosha/ProC-1397
91AA/LineD-263
91Harris/LineD-263
91Harris/ProC-636
92B-493
92ClBest-126
92Harris/ProC-467
92Harris/SB-289
92Sky/AASingl-122
92UD/ML-235
93Harris/ProC-277
Martin, Darryl
87Fayette-10
89Fayette/ProC-1585
89SALAS/GS-39
90Lakeland/Star-19
Martin, Derrell
61Union
Martin, Doug
91Niagara/ClBest-23
91Niagara/ProC-3630
92Niagara/ProC-3319
Martin, Elwood
(Speed)
E121/120
W501-55
Martin, Fred
79TCMA-121
Martin, Gene
90Greenvl/Star-13
90Sumter/Best-11
90Sumter/ProC-2446
Martin, Gregg
89StCath/ProC-2070
90A&AASingle/ProC-91
90Myrtle/ProC-2773
91ClBest/Singl-193
91Dunedin/ClBest-6
91Dunedin/ProC-202
92Myrtle/ProC-2194
Martin, Herschel
39PlayBall-12
40PlayBall-100
44Playball-9
46Remar
47Remar-12
47Signal
Martin, Jake
56T-129
Martin, James
92GreatF/SportP-25
92OKSt-19
Martin, Jared
80Wichita-16
82Iowa-7
Martin, Jerry
76SSPC-475
77T-596
78SSPC/270-51
78T-222
79T-382
80OPC-256
80T-493
81D-555
81F-295
81OPC-103
81T-103
81T/SO-98
81T/Tr-798
82D-298
82F-394
82T-722
82T/Tr-65T
83D-138
83F-117
83OPC-309
83T-626
84F/X-74
84Nes/792-74
84T-74
84T/Tr-74
85T-517
Martin, Jim
91SLCity/ProC-3226
91SLCity/SportP-14
92Augusta/ProC-234
Martin, Joey
75Lafay
77Phoenix
Martin, John Leonard Roosevelt
(Pepper)
32Orbit/num-21
32Orbit/un-46
33DL-17
33G-62
34DS-26
34Exh/4-8
35BU-125
35BU-7
35Exh/4-8
35G-2F
35G-4F
35G-7F
35Wheat
36G
36Wheat
37Wheat
38Wheat
62Pep/Tul
63Pep/Tul
77Galasso-203
77Galasso-66
80Pac/Leg-106
81Conlon-24
86Conlon/1-22
88Conlon/3-18
88Conlon/NatAS-14
91Conlon/Sport-274
92Card/McDon/Pac-12
92Conlon/Sport-637
93AP/ASG-132
93Conlon-680
94Conlon-1108
94Conlon-991
94Conlon/Pr-991
R305
R306
R308-159
R310
R311/Gloss
R312
R313
R313A-9
R314
R332-36
V353-62
Martin, John Robert
77AppFx
80Evansvl-14
82D-343
82F-121
82Louisvl-15
82T-236
83D-617
83StPete-9
83T-721
84ArkTr-17
84Nes/792-24
84T-24
86ArkTr-13
87Louisvl-19
88Louisvl-32
88Louisvl/CMC-3
88Louisvl/ProC-423
89ScranWB/CMC-3
89ScranWB/ProC-719
90Clearw/Star-27CO
91AA/LineD-509CO
91Reading/LineD-509CO
91Reading/ProC-1387CO
92Batavia/ClBest-29M
92Batavia/ProC-3283
Martin, Jon
90Welland/Pucko-4
Martin, Joseph C.
(J.C.)
60L-92
60T-346

61T-124
61T/St-124
62T-91
62T/St-27
63T-499
64T-148
65T-382
66OPC-47
66T-47
67T-538
68T-211
69MB-166
69OPC-112
69T-112
69T/4in1-17M
70OPC-308WS
70OPC-488
70T-308WS
70T-488
71MLB/St-37
71OPC-704
71T-704
72MB-206
72T-639
73OPC-552
73T-552
73Wichita-8
74OPC-354CO
74T-354C
81TCMA-419
81TCMA-438M
89Pac/SenLg-197
89Pac/SenLg-6
89T/SenLg-14
91Pac/SenLg-14
91WIZMets-250
91WIZMets-251
94Mets/69-19
Martin, Justin
88Bend/Legoe-25
89QuadC/Best-11
90QuadC/GS-9
91QuadC/ClBest-8
91QuadC/ProC-2625
Martin, Lefty
49Eureka-40
Martin, Mark
87Idaho-4
88Oneonta/ProC-2068
Martin, Matt
91Billing/SportP-8
91Billings/ProC-3763
92Billings/ProC-3365
Martin, Mike 1
82Amari-9
83Beaum-1
84Cram/PCL-227
85Cram/PCL-217
86Pittsfld-15
88MissSt-17
Martin, Mike 2
93Bz-20
93T/Tr-128T
Martin, Morris
(Morrie)
52T-131
53B/BW-53
53T-227
54B-179
54T-168
58T-53
59T-38
90Target-488
91Crown/Orio-279
91T/Arc53-227
94T/Arc54-168
Martin, Norberto
87CharWh-25
88Tampa/Star-15
90AAASingl/ProC-173
90ProC/Singl-648
90Vanco/CMC-21
90Vanco/ProC-495
91AAA/LineD-640
91B-346
91Vanco/LineD-640
91Vanco/ProC-1603
92Sky/AAASingl-287
92Vanco/ProC-2732
92Vanco/SB-644
93LimeR/Winter-34
94Pac/Cr-132
94Pinn-228
94Pinn/Artist-228
94Pinn/Museum-228
94Sf/2000-161
94StCl/Team-139
Martin, R. Hollis
81VeroB-11
Martin, Renie
80T-667R
81D-103
81F-39
81OPC-266
81T-452
82D-238
82F-414
82T-594
82T/Tr-66T
83D-272
83F-267
83T-263
84D-445
84F-381
84Nes/792-603
84T-603
85Omaha-14
86Omaha/ProC-14
91Pac/SenLg-65
Martin, Russ
87James-1
Martin, Sam
81Batavia-17
82Watlo/B-17
82Watlo/Frit-21
83Spring/Frit-4
Martin, Steve W.
89Spokane/SP-18
90Foil/Best-209
90ProC/Singl-878
90Waterlo/Best-10
90Waterlo/ProC-2385
91B-662
91ClBest/Singl-85
91HighD/ClBest-25
91HighD/ProC-2408
92Hagers/SB-263
92Wichita/ProC-3668
Martin, Steve
82VeroB-8
85Cram/PCL-172
Martin, Stuart
37Exh/4-8
38Exh/4-8
Martin, T. Eugene
70T-599R
Martin, Thomas
(Tom)
89Bluefld/Star-15
90Foil/Best-178
90Wausau/Best-4
90Wausau/ProC-2117
90Wausau/Star-16
91Kane/ClBest-7
91Kane/ProC-2655
91Kane/Team-12
92HighD/ClBest-24
92Watlo/ProC-2140
Martin, Todd
90Utica/Pucko-2
Martin, Tony
77LodiD
Martin, Troy
91Sydney/Fut-4
Martin, Vic
83Chatt-7
86Calgary-13
Martina, Mario
89PalmSp/Cal-37
Martindale, Denzel
77StPete
Martindale, Ryan
91Watertn/ClBest-13
91Watertn/ProC-3368
92Kinston/ClBest-2
92Kinston/ProC-2479
Martineau, Paul Peter
86James-15
Martineau, Yves
92Idaho/ProC-3509
Martinez, Alfredo
(Fred)
79Jacks-24
81D-172
81F-288
81SLCity-9
81T-227
82Spokane-5
82T-659
Martinez, Angel 1
88Modesto-24
88VeroB/Star-14
89Madis/Star-14
Martinez, Angel 2
91MedHat/ProC-4104
91MedHat/SportP-2
92MedHat/ProC-3210
92MedHat/SportP-6
93Hagers/ClBest-19
93Hagers/ProC-1883
94B-141
Martinez, Art
84Memphis-4
86Memphis/GoldT-14
86Memphis/SilverT-14
Martinez, Ben
92Martins/ClBest-7
92Martins/ProC-3072
Martinez, Bert
83TriCit-20
Martinez, Bill
92Rockford/ProC-2112
Martinez, Carlos
86Albany/TCMA-9
87Hawaii-21
88BirmB/Best-16
89D/Rook-14
89S/Tr-103
89Vanco/CMC-17
89Vanco/ProC-579
90B-322
90BirmDG/Best-22
90Bz-13
90Coke/WSox-16
90D-531
90F-540
90F/Can-540
90Leaf-438
90OPC-461
90Panini/St-374
90S-314
90S/100Ris-70
90S/YS/I-35
90Sf-213
90T-461
90T/Big-116
90T/Coins-20
90T/Gloss60-9
90T/JumboR-19
90T/St-300
90T/St-325FS
90ToysRUs-18
90UD-347
91AA/LineD-89
91Canton/LineD-89
91Canton/ProC-987
91D-465
91F-128
91OPC-156
91Panini/FrSt-312
91S-274
91T-156
91UD-625
92D-521
92F-117
92OPC-280
92S-593
92S/100RisSt-71
92StCl-482
92T-280
92T/Gold-280
92T/GoldWin-280
92UD-598
92Ultra-52
93D-682
93F-595
93Flair-196
93Indian/WUAB-19
93L-347
93Pac/Beisbol-6M
93Pac/Spanish-98
93StCl-255
93StCl/1stDay-255
93Studio-125
93T-59
93T/Gold-59
93UD-520
93UD/SP-124
93Ultra-188
94Pac/Cr-176
Martinez, Carmelo
83Iowa-16
84D-623
84F-497
84F/X-U75
84Mother/Padres-20
84Nes/792-267
84T-267
84T/St-383
84T/Tr-75T
85D-478
85F-40
85Mother/Padres-24
85OPC-365
85T-558
85T/St-157
85T/St-375
86D-324
86F-329
86OPC-67
86T-67
86T/St-109
87Bohem-14
87D/OD-151
87F-423
87OPC-348
87T-348
88Coke/Padres-14
88D-287
88F-591
88Leaf-142
88OPC-148
88Panini/St-412
88S-181
88Smok/Padres-17
88T-148
88T/Big-238
88T/Coins-47
88T/St-106
89B-459
89Bimbo/Discs-1
89Coke/Padre-9
89D-601
89F-311
89OPC-332
89Padre/Mag-10
89Panini/St-204
89S-517
89T-449
89T/Big-11
89UD-365
90B-162
90Classic-56
90D-482
90F-162
90F/Can-162
90F/Up-U44
90Leaf-448
90OPC-686
90Phill/TastyK-21
90Publint/St-54
90S-114
90S/Tr-10T
90T-686
90T/Big-287
90T/Tr-68T
90UD-592
91F-44
91Leaf-160
91Leaf-467
91OPC-779
91S-792
91T-779
91UD-92
92S-686
92UD-696
93Calgary/ProC-1178
Martinez, Cesar
92Elmira/ClBest-12
92Elmira/ProC-1381
Martinez, Chito
85FtMyr-16
86Memphis/GoldT-15
86Memphis/SilverT-15
87Omaha-7
88Memphis/Best-21
89Memphis/Best-12
89Memphis/ProC-1200
89Memphis/Star-16
90AAASingl/ProC-612
90Omaha/CMC-13
90Omaha/ProC-77
90ProC/Singl-188
91AAA/LineD-458
91AAAGame/ProC-40
91D/Rook-54
91F/UltraUp-U2
91RochR/LineD-458
91RochR/ProC-1914
91UD/FinalEd-30F
92B-19
92Classic/I-56
92D-558
92F-13
92F/RookSlns-18
92L-300
92L/BlkGold-300
92OPC-479
92OPC/Premier-77
92Pinn-380
92ProC/Tomorrow-4
92S-400
92S/100RisSt-76
92StCl-438
92T-479
92T/91Debut-117
92T/Gold-479
92T/GoldWin-479
92T/McDonB-40
92TripleP-192
92UD-672
92Ultra-7
93D-221
93F-545
93L-274
93Pac/Spanish-19
93Pinn-214
93S-638
93StCl-362
93StCl/1stDay-362
93T-772
93T/Gold-772
93UD-514
93Ultra-141
Martinez, Christian
83StPete-10
Martinez, Dave
83QuadC-26
86Iowa-17
87Berg/Cubs-1
87D-488
87Sf/TPrev-22M
87T/Tr-73T
88D-438
88D/Best-149
88D/Cubs/Bk-438
88F-424
88Panini/St-266
88S-223
88T-439
89B-370
89D-102
89F-384
89OPC-395
89S-77
89T-763
89UD-444
90B-121
90D-452
90D/BestNL-79
90F-353
90F/Can-353
90Leaf-318
90OPC-228
90PalmSp/Cal-217
90PalmSp/ProC-2573
90Panini/St-293
90Publint/St-180
90S-27
90T-228
90T/St-71
90UD-470
91AAA/LineD-459
91B-455
91D-237
91F-237
91Leaf-8
91OPC-24
91Panini/FrSt-144
91Panini/St-66
91RochR/LineD-459
91RochR/ProC-1898
91S-82
91StCl-346
91T-24
91UD-186
91Ultra-205
92B-220
92D-732
92ElPaso/ProC-3916

92ElPaso/SB-219
92F-485
92L-457
92L/BlkGold-457
92OPC-309
92OPC/Premier-75
92Pinn-397
92Reds/Kahn-30
92S-501
92S/RookTr-33T
92StCl-723
92T-309
92T/Gold-309
92T/GoldWin-309
92T/Tr-67T
92T/TrGold-67T
92UD-382
92UD-784
92Ultra-484
93D-534
93F-395
93F/Final-153
93L-301
93Mother/Giant-16
93OPC-172
93OPC/Premier-22
93Pac/Spanish-613
93Pinn-132
93S-601
93Select/RookTr-126T
93StCl-640
93StCl/1stDay-640
93StCl/Giant-19
93T-671
93T/Gold-671
93UD-400
93UD-700
93Ultra-486
94D-463
94F-695
94L-15
94Pac/Cr-550
94StCl/Team-15
94T-174
94T/Gold-174
94Ultra-293

Martinez, David 1
86PalmSp-22
87MidldA-2
88MidldA/GS-20
89MidldA/GS-22

Martinez, David 2
87AZ/Pol-10

Martinez, Domingo
86Ventura-13
87Dunedin-23
88Knoxvl/Best-6
88SLAS-25
89Knoxvl/Best-15
89Knoxvl/ProC-1148
89Knoxvl/Star-12
90Knoxvl/Best-15
90Knoxvl/ProC-1254
90Knoxvl/Star-12
91AAA/LineD-511
91Syrac/LineD-511
91Syrac/MerchB-14
91Syrac/ProC-2485
92ProC/Tomorrow-160
92Sky/AAASingl-229
92Syrac/MerchB-14
92Syrac/ProC-1975
92Syrac/SB-512
93B-203
93BJ/D/45-38
93BJ/Fire-19
93D-363
93L-356
93LimeR/Winter-24
93Pac/Spanish-653
93Pinn-596
93Pinn/RookTP-6M
93S-257
93StCl-727
93StCl/1stDay-727
93Syrac/ProC-1004
93T-810
93T/Gold-810
93UD-651
93Ultra-644
94D-584
94Pac/Cr-647
94StCl/Team-157

Martinez, Edgar
86Chatt-17
87Calgary-1
88Calgary/CMC-16
88Calgary/ProC-782
88D/Rook-36UER
88F-378
88TripleA/ASCMC-34
89B-216
89D-645
89D/Rook-15
89F-552
89Mother/Sea-11
89Panini/St-428
89S-637
89S/HotRook-40
89UD/Ext-768
90Calgary/CMC-12
90Classic/III-23
90D/Learning-45
90F-520
90F/Can-520
90Leaf-299
90Mother/Mar-10
90OPC-148
90ProC/Singl-439
90PublInt/St-437
90S-324
90T-148
90UD-532
91B-243
91Classic/III-54
91CounHrth-7
91D-16DK
91D-606
91D/SuperDK-16DK
91F-457
91Leaf-477
91Leaf/Stud-117
91OPC-607
91Panini/FrSt-230
91Panini/St-187
91S-264
91S/100SS-17
91Seven/3DCoin-11NW
91StCl-47
91T-607
91UD-574
91Ultra-340
92B-33
92CJ/DII-24
92D-286
92F-286
92L-197
92L/BlkGold-197
92Mother/Mar-20
92OPC-553
92Panini-57
92Pinn-13
92S-485
92S/100SS-17
92StCl-267
92Studio-235
92T-553
92T/Gold-553
92T/GoldWin-553
92T/Kids-125
92TripleP-127
92UD-367
92UD-91TC
92Ultra-126
93B-515
93Classic/GameI-58
93Colla/DM-69
93D-421
93D/Elite-27
93D/EliteUp-9
93DennyGS-13
93Duracel/PPI-6
93F-309
93F-344LL
93F-716SS
93F/ASAL-3
93F/Fruit-41
93Flair-273
93L-386
93L/GoldAS-15
93Mar/DQ-2
93Mother/Mar-11
93OPC-164
93OPC/Premier/StarP-5
93Pac/Beisbol-1
93Pac/Beisbol-11M
93Pac/Spanish-290
93Pac/SpanishGold-16
93Pac/SpanishP-17
93Panini-155LL
93Panini-62
93Pinn-17
93Pinn/TP-6M
93S-49
93S-502AS
93Select-82
93Select/ChasS-16
93Select/StatL-1
93Select/StatL-13M
93Select/StatL-44
93StCl-331
93StCl/1stDay-331
93StCl/Mar-24
93StCl/MurphyS-159
93Studio-126
93T-315
93T-403M
93T/BlkGold-37
93T/Finest-190
93T/FinestRef-190
93T/Gold-315
93T/Gold-403M
93TripleP-20
93TripleP/LL-L6M
93UD-495AW
93UD-553
93UD/FunPack-116
93UD/SP-133
93USPlayC/Ace-1D
93Ultra-270
93Ultra/AS-15
94B-61
94Church-21
94D-268
94D/DomII-4
94F-294
94L-344
94OPC-44
94Pac/Cr-576
94Panini-121
94Pinn-302
94S-465
94Select-72
94Sf/2000-115
94StCl-364
94StCl/1stDay-364
94StCl/Gold-364
94Studio-103
94T-195
94T/Finest-154
94T/Finest/PreProd-154
94T/FinestRef-154
94T/Gold-195
94TripleP-129
94UD-424
94UD/SP-107
94Ultra-422

Martinez, Eric 1
91AubAS/ClBest-13
91AubAS/ProC-4280
92Ashvl/ClBest-9

Martinez, Eric 2
91Boise/ClBest-24
91Boise/ProC-3874
92QuadC/ClBest-9
92QuadC/ProC-804

Martinez, Ernest
92AubAs/ClBest-12
92AubAs/ProC-1361

Martinez, Felix
(Tippy)
75Syrac/Team-11
76OPC-41
76T-41
77OPC-254
77T-238
78T-393
79T-491
80T-706
81D-354
81F-179
81OPC-119
81T-119
82D-205
82F-171
82T-583
83D-357
83F-65
83F/St-11M
83F/St-16M
83OPC-263
83T-621
84D-472
84F-12
84F-635IA
84Nes/792-215
84OPC-215
84T-215
84T/St-208
85D-210
85F-182
85OPC-247
85T-445
85T/St-200
86D-514
86F-279
86OPC-82
86T-82
87OPC-269
87RedFoley/St-14
87T-728
89Pac/SenLg-144
89TM/SenLg-72
90EliteSenLg-40
91Crown/Orio-281
91Pac/SenLg-28
92Yank/WIZ70-103
93Orio/SUII-2
94B-162

Martinez, Fili
89BendB/Legoe-7
90MidwLgAS/GS-40
90QuadC/GS-25
91MidldA/OneHour-18

Martinez, Frank
92Spring/ClBest-11
92Spring/ProC-863
94FExcel-270

Martinez, Fred
85Louisvl-20
86Louisvl-19

Martinez, Gabby
92UD/ML-143
94B-317

Martinez, Gabriel
(Tony)
63T-466R
64T-404
66T-581

Martinez, Gil
87Greens-15
88Lynch/Star-11
89Lynch/Star-13

Martinez, Hector
93MedHat/ProC-3739
93MedHat/SportP-4

Martinez, J. Dennis
77T-491R
78T-119
79OPC-105
79T-211
80OPC-2
80T-10
81D-533
81F-180
81OPC-367
81T-367
82D-79
82F-170
82OPC-135
82T-165LL
82T-712
82T/St-10LL
83D-231
83F-64
83F/St-16M
83F/St-27M
83OPC-167
83T-553
84D-633
84F-11
84Nes/792-631
84T-631
85D-514
85F-181
85T-199
86D-454
86F-280
86T-416
87F-324
87Indianap-31
87OPC-252
87T-252
88D-549
88D/Best-146
88F-188
88Leaf-262
88OPC-76
88S-601
88T-76
88T/St-84
89B-359
89Classic-45
89D-106
89D/Best-90
89F-385
89OPC-313
89Panini/St-114
89S-114
89S/HotStar-13
89Sf-106
89T-313
89T/St-74
89UD-377
90B-111
90D-156
90D/BestNL-30
90F-354
90F/Can-354
90Leaf-54
90OPC-763
90Panini/St-288
90PublInt/St-181
90S-47
90Sf-53
90T-763
90T/Big-133
90T/St-68
90UD-413
90USPlayC/AS-3D
91B-434
91BBBest/Aces-11
91Classic/200-30
91Classic/III-53
91Crown/Orio-280
91D-139
91F-238
91Leaf-274
91OPC-528
91OPC/Premier-75
91Panini/FrSt-150
91Panini/St-68
91S-454
91StCl-273
91StCl/Member*-5
91T-528
91UD-385
91UD/FinalEd-50F
91USPlayC/AS-7S
91Ultra-206
92B-305
92Classic/Game200-134
92Classic/I-57
92D-276HL
92D-686
92D/DK-DK24
92D/McDon-16
92DPep/MSA-4
92Expo/D/Duri-12
92F-486
92F-683RS
92F-695LL
92L-190
92L/BlkGold-190
92OPC-15
92OPC/Premier-13
92Panini-149
92Panini-209
92Pinn-77
92Post/Can-1
92S-470
92S-783HL
92S-784
92S/100SS-97
92StCl-860
92StCl/Dome-111
92Studio-57
92T-15
92T-394AS
92T/GPro-15
92T/Gold-15
92T/Gold-394AS
92T/GoldWin-15
92T/GoldWin-394AS
92T/Kids-10
92T/Pr-273
92TripleP-92
92UD-365
92UD/TmMVPHolo-31
92USPlayC/Ace-1S

92Ultra-223
93B-480
93Colla/DM-68
93D-168
93Duracel/PPII-14
93Expo/D/McDon-10
93F-462
93F/Fruit-40
93Flair-86
93HumDum/Can-41
93L-300
93MSA/Ben-5
93OPC-300
93Pac/Beisbol-25M
93Pac/Spanish-187
93Pac/SpanishGold-5
93Pac/SpanishP-3
93Panini-228
93Pinn-291NT
93Pinn-38
93S-75
93Select-147
93Select/Ace-6
93Select/StatL-90M
93StCl-140
93StCl/1stDay-140
93StCl/MurphyS-58
93T-610
93T/Gold-610
93T/Hill-23
93TripleP-74
93UD-232
93UD-481M
93UD-821TC
93UD/FunPack-97
93UD/SP-106
93USPlayC/Ace-9S
93Ultra-418
94B-523
94D-422
94F-545
94Finest-412
94Flair-41
94L-310
94OPC-21
94Pac/AllLat-7
94Pac/Cr-386
94Pinn-516
94S-514
94StCl-187
94StCl/1stDay-187
94StCl/Gold-187
94T-440
94T/Gold-440
94UD-358
94UD/SP-99
94Ultra-345

Martinez, Javier
92Boise/ClBest-16
92Boise/ProC-3638

Martinez, Jesus
92ClBest/Up-447
92GreatF/SportP-10
92GulfCD/ProC-3563
93ClBest/MLG-133
93LimeR/Winter-118

Martinez, Joe
92Modesto/ClBest-23
92Modesto/ProC-3896

Martinez, John
90BurlInd/ProC-3012
91Pocatel/ProC-3785
91Pocatel/SportP-8

Martinez, John Albert
(Buck)
70T-609
71OPC-163
71T-163
72OPC-332
72T-332
75OPC-314
75T-314
75T/M-314
76A&P/KC
76OPC-616
76SSPC-165
76T-616
77T-46
78T-571
79Ho-32
79T-243
80T-477
81D-444
81F-526
81T-56
81T/Tr-799
82D-561
82OPC-314
82T-314
83D-178
83F-433
83OPC-308
83T-733
84D-612
84F-161
84Nes/792-179
84OPC-179
84T-179
84Tor/Fire-24
85F-114
85OPC-119
85OPC/Post-13
85T-673
85Tor/Fire-21
86BJ/Ault-19
86F-66
86OPC-363
86T-518
86Tor/Fire-24
87F-235
92Nabisco-24

Martinez, Jose
88StCath/ProC-2024

Martinez, Jose Luis
70OPC-8
70T-8
71MLB/St-207
71OPC-712
71T-712
77DaytB/MG
79OkCty
80OkCty
88Berg/Cubs-CO
90Cub/Mara-28CO
90T/TVCub-4CO
91Cub/Mara-x
91Cub/Vine-18CO
92Cub/Mara-NNO
93Cub/Mara-15CO

Martinez, Jose Miguel
91Clmbia/PCPII-6
91Clmbia/PII-28
91Clmbia/PII-31M
91SALAS/ProC-SAL17
92ClBest-276
92ColumMet/SAL/II-41FB
92ProC/Tomorrow-287
92StLucie/ClBest-14
92StLucie/ProC-1743
92UD/ML-248
93B-331
93Edmon/ProC-1133
93FExcel/ML-76
93LimeR/Winter-104
93StCl/Marlin-28
93UD-506DD

Martinez, Julian
87Savan-19
88StPete/Star-15
89ArkTr/GS-11
89TexLAS/GS-20
90AAASingl/ProC-524
90Louisvl/CMC-11
90Louisvl/LBC-25
90Louisvl/ProC-410
90ProC/Singl-111
90T/TVCard-54
91AAA/LineD-240
91Louisvl/LineD-240
91Louisvl/ProC-2929
91Louisvl/Team-26
92ArkTr/ProC-1142
92ArkTr/SB-37
93LimeR/Winter-33

Martinez, Louie
91AubAS/ClBest-6
91AubAS/ProC-4271

Martinez, Louis
(Louie)
89SanAn/Best-14
90SanAn/GS-18
91AAA/LineD-14
91Albuq/LineD-14
91Albuq/ProC-1147
92Albuq/ProC-727
92Albuq/SB-12
93ClBest/MLG-138

Martinez, Luis 1
86Cram/NWL-57
87Madis-8
88FSLAS/Star-11
88Modesto/Cal-74

Martinez, Luis 2
89Savan/ProC-350
90Foil/Best-56
90Spring/Best-14
91AA/LineD-38
91ArkTr/LineD-38
91ArkTr/ProC-1300

Martinez, Manuel
(Manny)
90SoOreg/Best-12
90SoOreg/ProC-3433
91CalLgAS-44
91ClBest/Singl-145
91Modesto/ClBest-24
91Modesto/ProC-3104
92ClBest-35
92Modesto/ClBest-17
94ClBest/Gold-149

Martinez, Martin
90Rockford/ProC-2693
90Rockford/Team-17
91ClBest/Singl-252
91Rockford/ClBest-8
91Rockford/ProC-2043

Martinez, Nicio
88Batavia/ProC-1667
90Savan/ProC-2076

Martinez, Orlando
(Marty)
61Clover-16
67T-504
68CokeCap/Brave-10
68T-578
69MB-167
69T-337
70OPC-126
70T-126
71MLB/St-85
71OPC-602
71T-602
72MB-207
72OPC-336
72T-336
72T/Cloth-22
76SanAn/Team-14
80Wausau-23
81Spokane-32MG
92Mother/Mar-27M
93Rang/Keeb-27

Martinez, Pablo
90CharRain/Best-14
90CharRain/ProC-2044
91CharRain/ClBest-19
91CharRain/ProC-104
92HighD/ClBest-5

Martinez, Pedro A.
89CharRain/ProC-992
89SALAS/GS-11
90Wichita/Rock-15
91AA/LineD-613
91Wichita/LineD-613
91Wichita/ProC-2595
91Wichita/Rock-6
92Wichita/ProC-3656
92Wichita/SB-640
94B-4
94D-526
94F-669
94OPC-26
94Pac/Cr-530
94T-676
94T/Finest-101
94T/FinestRef-101
94T/Gold-676
94TripleP-169
94UD/CollC-188
94UD/CollC/Gold-188
94UD/CollC/Silv-188
94Ultra-581

Martinez, Pedro J.
90GreatF/SportP-12
91Bakers/Cal-32
91CalLgAS-2
91ClBest/Singl-355
91Classic/III-55
91SanAn/ProC-2971
91UD/FinalEd-2F
92AAA/ASG/SB-13
92Albuq/ProC-716
92Albuq/SB-13
92B-82
92D/Rook-69
92L/GRook-3
92ProC/Tomorrow-244
92Sky/AAASingl-5
92UD-18SR
92UD-79M
93B-154
93D-326
93F-354
93F/MLPII-4
93FExcel/ML-110
93Flair-72
93L-163
93LimeR/Winter-126
93Mother/Dodg-16
93Pac/Spanish-500
93Pinn-259
93Pinn/RookTP-1
93Pinn/Team2001-14
93Pol/Dodg-15
93S-321
93S/Boys-3
93S/Proctor-2
93Select/RookTr-36T
93StCl-365
93StCl/1stDay-365
93StCl/Dodg-2
93T-557
93T/Gold-557
93UD-324
93Ultra-57
94D-179
94F-515
94Finest-362
94Flair-193
94L-367
94OPC-41
94Pac/Cr-313
94Pinn-501
94S-554
94S/Boys-49
94T-268
94T/Gold-268
94UD-318
94UD/CollC-189
94UD/CollC/Gold-189
94UD/CollC/Silv-189
94UD/SP-85
94Ultra-524

Martinez, Porfi
86Lakeland-12

Martinez, Rafael
88StCath/ProC-2026
89Myrtle/ProC-1467

Martinez, Ramiro 1
89Princet/Star-12

Martinez, Ramiro 2
93StCl/MurphyS-173

Martinez, Ramon Dario
90Augusta/ProC-2458
91Augusta/ClBest-16
91Augusta/ProC-812
92Salem/ClBest-2
92Salem/ProC-71
93B-66
93FExcel/ML-92
93StCl-322
93StCl-Marlin-17
93StCl/1stDay-322

Martinez, Ramon J.
86Bakers-20
87VeroB-7
88BBAmer-21
88SanAn/Best-1
88TexLgAS/GS-28
88TripleA/ASCMC-45
89AAA/CMC-40
89AAA/ProC-47
89Albuq/CMC-7
89Albuq/ProC-69
89Classic-130
89D-464
89D/Rook-45
89F-67
89Pol/Dodg-24
89S-635
89S/HotRook-55
89S/YS/I-40
89Sf-224R
89T-225
89UD-18
90B-88
90Classic-76
90D-685
90D/BestNL-141
90F-402
90F/Can-402
90HotRook/St-30
90Leaf-147
90Mother/Dodg-17
90OPC-62
90Panini/St-380
90S-461
90S/100Ris-59
90S/McDon-13
90Sf-68
90T-62
90T/JumboR-20
90T/St-61
90Target-489
90ToysRUs-19
90TripleAAS/CMC-40
90UD-675
90USPlayC/AS-1H
91B-610
91BBBest/RecBr-10
91Cadaco-35
91Classic/200-99
91Classic/I-52
91CollAB-18
91D-15DK
91D-557
91D/SuperDK-15DK
91F-212
91F/UltraG-7
91Kenner-37
91KingB/Discs-12
91Leaf-61
91Leaf/Prev-5
91Leaf/Stud-184
91MajorLg/Pins-52
91Mother/Dodg-10
91OPC-340
91Panini/FrSt-62
91Panini/St-50
91Panini/Top15-58
91Panini/Top15-75
91Pol/Dodg-48
91S-300
91S-408KM
91S-419HL
91S/100SS-16
91Seven/3DCoin-11F
91Seven/3DCoin-8SC
91StCl-516
91StCl/Charter*-19
91T-340
91T/CJMini/II-25
91T/SU-23
91UD-136
91UD-78TC
91Ultra-164
92B-255
92CJ/DI-30
92Classic/Game200-35
92Classic/II-T40
92D-656
92F-463
92F-706M
92F/ASIns-7
92F/Performer-21
92Kenner/Fig-30
92L-297
92L/BlkGold-297
92Mother/Dodg-7
92OPC-730
92Pinn-429
92Pinn/Team2000-49
92Pinn/TeamP-1M
92Pol/Dodg-48
92S-610
92S-780AS
92S/100SS-75
92S/Impact-75
92StCl-207
92Studio-46
92T-730
92T/Gold-730
92T/GoldWin-730
92T/Kids-48
92TripleP-55
92UD-346
92UD-79M
92UD/TmMVPHolo-32
92Ultra-213
93B-590
93Cadaco-39

93Colla/DM-70
93D-298
93F-354M
93F-65
93F/Fruit-42
93Flair-73
93L-335
93Mother/Dodg-12
93OPC-275
93Pac/Spanish-152
93Pac/SpanishP-4
93Panini-212
93Pinn-377
93Pol/Dodg-16
93S-199
93Select-213
93StCl-71
93StCl/1stDay-71
93StCl/Dodg-10
93Studio-149
93T-120
93T/Finest-29
93T/FinestRef-29
93T/Gold-120
93TripleP-161
93UD-133
93UD/FunPack-213ASA
93UD/FunPack-90
93UD/SP-95
93Ultra-401
93Vanco/ProC-2604
94B-398
94D-368
94D/Special-368
94F-516
94Finest-405
94L-303
94OPC-76
94Pac/Cr-314
94Pinn-353
94S-233
94S/GoldR-233
94Select-107
94Sf/2000-99
94StCl-276
94StCl/1stDay-276
94StCl/Gold-276
94T-545
94T/Gold-545
94TripleP-86
94UD-349
94UD/CollC-190
94UD/CollC/Gold-190
94UD/CollC/Silv-190
94Ultra-519

Martinez, Ramon
87Salem/ProC-2423
88Bend/Legoe-5
89PalmSp/Cal-38
89PalmSp/ProC-467
91PalmSp/ProC-2024
92Edmon/ProC-3546

Martinez, Randy
83Spring/Frit-19

Martinez, Ray
81Batavia-13
83Watlo/Frit-19

Martinez, Rey 1
85Lynch-23

Martinez, Rey 2
90Kgsport/Best-8
90Kgsport/Star-15
90MadiSon/ProC-2265
90QuadC/GS-23
92MidldA/OneHour-15
92MidldA/SB-464
92Sky/AASingl-198

Martinez, Rick
92Niagara/ClBest-6
92Niagara/ProC-3333

Martinez, Sandy
91Kissim/ProC-4195
92Yakima/ProC-3459

Martinez, Silvio
76Shrev
78Spring/Wiener-18
79T-609
80OPC-258
80T-496
81D-429
81F-546
81T-586
82Charl-7
82D-469
82F-122
82T-181

Martinez, Ted
71OPC-648R
71T-648R
72T-544
73OPC-161
73T-161
74OPC-487
74T-487
75OPC-637
75T-637
75T/M-637
76OPC-356
76SSPC-499
76T-356
78SSPC/270-64
78T-546
79OPC-59
79T-128
80Albuq-14
80Pol/Dodg-23
80T-191
90Target-490
91WIZMets-252

Martinez, Thomas
83AlexD-17

Martinez, Tino
87PanAm/USAB-1
87PanAm/USAR-1
88T/Tr-66T
89B-211
89BBAmAA/BPro-AA6
89EastLgAS/ProC-18
89Star/IISingl-124
89T/Big-93
89Wmsprt/ProC-635
89Wmsprt/Star-13
90AAASingl/ProC-124
90B-484
90Calgary/ProC-659
90F/Up-119
90S-596
90TeamUSA/87-1
90UD-37
91AAA/LineD-66
91AAAGame/ProC-5
91B-257
91Calgary/LineD-66
91Calgary/ProC-523
91Classic/200-150
91Classic/I-2
91CounHrth-10
91D-28RR
91D/Preview-6
91F-458
91Leaf/Prev-24
91Leaf/Stud-118
91MajorLg/Pins-7
91OPC-482
91OPC/Premier-76
91S-798
91S/Rook40-38
91Seven/3DCoin-12NW
91StCl-179
91T-482
91T/90Debut-99
91UD-553
91Ultra-341
92B-483
92B-626FOIL
92Classic/Game200-50
92Classic/II-T42
92D-410RR
92F-287
92L-329
92L/BlkGold-329
92Mother/Mar-11
92OPC-481
92OPC/Premier-64
92Pinn-123
92Pinn/Team2000-62
92ProC/Tomorrow-138
92S-596
92S/100RisSt-51
92S/HotRook-7
92StCl-573
92Studio-236
92T-481
92T/Gold-481
92T/GoldWin-481
92TripleP-259
92UD-554
92Ultra-127
93B-303
93D-217
93F-310
93Flair-274
93L-406
93Mother/Mar-17
93OPC-212
93Pac/Beisbol-11
93Pac/Spanish-289
93Panini-66
93Pinn-213
93S-76
93Select-246
93StCl-273
93StCl/1stDay-273
93StCl/Mar-18
93Studio-204
93T-232
93T/Gold-232
93TripleP-35
93UD-287
93UD/SP-134
93Ultra-623
94B-669
94D-296
94F-295
94Flair-106
94L-92
94Pac/Cr-577
94Panini-122
94Pinn-129
94Pinn/Artist-129
94Pinn/Museum-129
94S-59
94S/GoldR-59
94Select-163
94StCl-60
94StCl/1stDay-60
94StCl/Gold-60
94Studio-104
94T-693
94T/Finest-55
94T/FinestRef-55
94T/Gold-693
94TripleP-130
94UD-94
94UD/CollC-191
94UD/CollC/Gold-191
94UD/CollC/Silv-191
94UD/ElecD-94
94Ultra-121

Martinez, Wilfredo
83Erie-5

Martinez, William
90Gate/ProC-3344
91SALAS/ProC-SAL46
91Sumter/ClBest-8
91Sumter/ProC-2331
92Rockford/ClBest-19

Marting, Tim
71OPC-423R
71T-423R
90Columbia/GS-28GM

Martinson, Evon
78Clinton
79LodiD-21

Martinson, Mike
75QuadC
76QuadC

Marto, Johnny
T3/Box-61

Martorana, Dave
(Mutta)
91Utica/ClBest-12
91Utica/ProC-3249
92SoBend/ProC-186

Marty, Joe
40PlayBall-216
41PlayBall-28
46Sunbeam
47Signal
47Sunbeam
49B/PCL-26
52Mother-20
93Conlon-896

Martyn, Bob
58T-39
59T-41
79TCMA-254

Martz, Gary
75Omaha/Team-11

Martz, Randy
80Wichita-7
81F-300
81T-381R
82D-126
82F-600
82RedLob
82T-188
82T-456TL
83D-151
83F-501
83F/St-13M
83F/St-8M
83T-22
84Richm-18
85Cram/PCL-66

Marx, Bill
86CharRain-14
88River/Cal-214
88River/ProC-1424
89River/Cal-14
89River/ProC-1416
90River/Cal-20
90River/ProC-2606

Marx, Jerry
62Pep/Tul
63Pep/Tul

Marx, William
90CharRain/Best-16

Marzan, Jose
88Visalia/Cal-155
88Visalia/ProC-89
89Visalia/Cal-111
89Visalia/ProC-1443
90OrlanSR/Best-6
90OrlanSR/ProC-1091
90OrlanSR/Star-10
91AA/LineD-486
91OrlanSR/LineD-486
91OrlanSR/ProC-1857

Marzano, John
85T-399OLY
86NewBrit-16
87Pawtu-1
87Pawtu/TCMA-11
87Sf/Rook-49
88Classic/Red-189
88D-421
88D/RedSox/Bk-421
88F-357
88Leaf-245
88S-584
88T-757
88ToysRUs-17
89Pawtu/CMC-17
89Pawtu/Dunkin-20
89Pawtu/ProC-687
90AAASingl/ProC-437
90Pawtu/CMC-12
90Pawtu/ProC-465
90ProC/Singl-263
90T/TVRSox-19
90T/Tr-69T
91B-119
91D-346
91F-103
91Leaf-179
91OPC-574
91Pep/RSox-12
91S-831
91StCl-201
91T-574
92D-448
92OPC-677
92RedSox/Dunkin-18
92S-539
92StCl-424
92T-677
92T/DQ-3
92T/Gold-677
92T/GoldWin-677
92USPlayC/RedSox-12C
92USPlayC/RedSox-3H
92Ultra-316
93D-487
93StCl-73
93StCl/1stDay-73

Marze, Dickey
90BurlB/Best-15
90BurlB/ProC-2357
90BurlB/Star-17

Mashore, Clyde
71Expo/ProS-14
71OPC-376R
71T-376R
72Dimanche*-29
73OPC-401
73T-401

Mashore, Damon
90AZ/Pol-12
91SoOreg/ClBest-2
91SoOreg/ProC-3863
92AS/Cal-12
92ClBest-189
92Modesto/ClBest-4
92Modesto/ProC-3909
92UD/ML-300

Mashore, Justin
91Bristol/ClBest-3
91Bristol/ProC-3619
92Fayette/ClBest-17
92Fayette/ProC-2182
92StCl/Dome-112
92UD/ML-139
93B-447

Masi, Phil
43Playball-38
49B-153
49Eureka-15
50B-128
51B-160
51T/BB-19
52T-283
R346-12

Masino, Ron
87BYU-7

Maskery, Sam
N172

Maskovich, George
52Park-97

Mason, Don
66T-524R
69T-584
71MLB/St-231
71OPC-548
71T-548
72T-739

Mason, Glen
89KS*-19

Mason, Henry
60L-80
60T-331

Mason, Jim
72Dimanche*-30
72OPC-334R
72T-334R
73OPC-458
73T-458
74OPC-618
74T-618
74T/Tr-618T
75OPC-136
75T-136
75T/M-136
76SSPC-448
76SSPC/MetsY-Y18
77OPC-211
77T-212
78SSPC/270-94
78T-588
79T-67
80OPC-259
80T-497
92Yank/WIZ70-104
93Rang/Keeb-28

Mason, Kevin
89TNTech-16
89TNTech-35M

Mason, Larry
81TCMA-387

Mason, Martin
(Marty)
82Spring/Frit-16
83Spring/Frit-7
84ArkTr-19
86StPete-18CO
87StPete-19
88Savan/ProC-336
90ArkTr/GS-2CO
91AA/LineD-50M
91ArkTr/LineD-50CO
91ArkTr/ProC-1303CO
92ArkTr/ProC-1145
92ArkTr/SB-50CO

Mason, Mike
82Tulsa-5
83OKCty-20
84F/X-U76
84Rang-16
84T/Tr-76T
85D-281

85F-562
85OPC-144
85Rang-16
85T-464
85T/St-354
86D-422
86F-565
86OPC-189
86Rang-16
86T-189
87D-284
87F-129
87F/Up-U73
87OPC-208
87Smok/R-4
87T-646
88T-87
91AppFx/ClBest-28INS
91AppFx/ProC-1733CO
92AppFox/ClBest-28
93Rang/Keeb-246

Mason, Raymond
52Laval-69

Mason, Rob
88WPalmB/Star-17
89Rockford/Team-16
90WPalmB/Star-14

Mason, Roger
83BirmB-24
84Evansvl-21
85Cram/PCL-190
86D-633
86F/Up-U72
86Mother/Giants-23
86T/Tr-70T
87D-204
87F-280
87Mother/SFG-23
87T-526
88Phoenix/CMC-4
88Phoenix/ProC-62
89Tucson/CMC-4
89Tucson/JP-14
89Tucson/ProC-195
90BuffB/Team-15
91AAA/LineD-33
91AAAGame/ProC-3
91BuffB/LineD-33
91BuffB/ProC-536
92D-715
92F/Up-115
92L-454
92L/BlkGold-454
92Pirate/Nation-13
92S-727
92StCl-266
92Ultra-554
93D-358
93F-116
93Mother/Padre-25
93S-441
94F-595
94Phill/Med-20
94S-123
94S/GoldR-123
94StCl/Team-221
94T-533
94T/Gold-533

Masone, Tony
80Cedar-9

Massarelli, John
87AubAs-1
88AubAs/ProC-1961
89Ashvl/ProC-945
90FSLAS/Star-13
90Osceola/Star-20
91ClBest/Singl-165
91Osceola/ClBest-15
91Osceola/ProC-688
92Jacks/SB-341
92Tucson/ProC-491

Masse, Bill
(Billy)
88T/Tr-67T
89PrWill/Star-13
89Star/Wax-90
89T/Big-179
90Albany/Best-21
90Albany/ProC-1045
90Albany/Star-11
91AA/LineD-9
91Albany/LineD-9
91Albany/ProC-1020
92ColClip/Pol-23
92ColClip/ProC-364
92ColClip/SB-110
92Sky/AAASingl-50
93ColClip/Pol-23
94T-79
94T/Gold-79

Massey, Jim
86Cram/NWL-17
86Everett/Pop-13
87Everett-21

Massey, Mike
89KS*-61

Massicotte, Jeff
88Peoria/Ko-15
89Peoria/Team-5
90WinSalem/Team-20

Massie, Bret
88Spartan/Star-24
88Spartan/Star-8

Masson, Todd
93SoEastern-13

Mast, Brian
92Lipscomb-17
93Lipscomb-16

Masteller, Dan
90Visalia/Cal-67
90Visalia/ProC-2162
91AA/LineD-487
91ClBest/Singl-330
91OrlanSR/LineD-487
91OrlanSR/ProC-1858
92OrlanSR/ProC-2854
92OrlanSR/SB-511

Masters, Burke
88CapeCod/Sum-101
88MissSt-18
89MissSt-24
90MissSt-25

Masters, David
(Dave)
86WinSalem-13
87Pittsfld-14
88Iowa/CMC-9
88Iowa/ProC-533
89Iowa/CMC-6
89Iowa/ProC-1698
90AAASingl/ProC-622
90Iowa/CMC-2
90Iowa/ProC-315
90ProC/Singl-77
91AAA/LineD-189
91Indianap/LineD-189
91Indianap/ProC-458
92Phoenix/ProC-2816
92Phoenix/SB-387

Masters, Frank
86GlenF-14
88Madis-15
89Madis/Star-15

Masters, Wayne
90Augusta/ProC-2459

Masterson, Walt
49B-157
50B-153
51B-307
52B-205
52T-186
53B/BW-9
53Briggs

Mastropietro, Dave
90Niagara/Pucko-5

Masuyama, Daryl
86Shrev-16TR

Masuzawa, Hideki
90Gate/ProC-3342

Mata, Vic
83Nashvl-11
84Colum-10
84Colum/Pol-14
85Colum-1
85D-629
85F-644
86Colum-15
86Colum/Pol-13
88RochR/CMC-23
88RochR/Gov-15
88RochR/ProC-197
88RochR/Team-12
92Yank/WIZ80-110

Matachun, Paul
90Butte/SportP-11
91Gaston/ClBest-20
91Gaston/ProC-2697
92Gaston/ClBest-18
92Gaston/ProC-2261

Matas, Jim
86Geneva-18
87WinSalem-26
88WinSalem/Star-10

Matchett, Steve
89Bristol/Star-16

Matchick, J. Tom
67OPC-72R
67T-72R
68OPC-113R
68T-113R
69MB-168
69T-344
70T-647
71MLB/St-419
71OPC-321
71T-321
72MB-208
73OPC-631
73T-631
81TCMA-397
88Domino-12
91Crown/Orio-282

Mateo, Huascar
88Bend/Legoe-13

Mateo, Jose
90CharRain/Best-15
90CharRain/ProC-2047

Mateo, Luis
89Madis/Star-16

Matheny, Michael
91Helena/SportP-11
92ClBest-393
92Stockton/ClBest-15
92Stockton/ProC-37
94B-673
94FExcel-83
94Select-204
94Ultra-375

Matheson, Bill
43Centen-19
44Centen-16
45Centen-16

Mathews, Byron
90OK-11
92Classic/DP-120
93StCl/MurphyS-186
93T-612
93T/Gold-612

Mathews, Chuck
85Osceola/Team-11
86ColumAst-18

Mathews, Ed
86Sumter/ProC-18
87Durham-16
88Greenvl/Best-22
89Richm/Bob-14
89Richm/CMC-10
89Richm/Ko-26
89Richm/ProC-845
90Sumter/Best-12

Mathews, Edwin Lee
(Eddie)
52T-407
53B/Col-97
53JC-21
53SpicSpan/3x5-17
53SpicSpan/7x10-8
53T-37
54B-64
54JC-41
54RM-NL23
54SpicSpan/PostC-13
54T-30
55B-103
55Gol/Braves-19
55JC-41
55SpicSpan/DC-12
55T-155
56T-107
56T/Hocus-B21
56T/Pin-18
56YellBase/Pin-21
57SpicSpan/4x5-12
57T-250
58T-351M
58T-440
58T-480AS
59HRDerby-13
59T-212M
59T-450
60Armour-15
60P*
60SpicSpan-12
60T-420
60T-558AS
60T/tatt-33
61Bz-11
61NuCard-412
61P-106
61T-120
61T-43LL
61T/St-45
62Bz
62Exh
62J-147
62P-147
62P/Can-147
62Salada-111
62Shirriff-111
62T-30
62T/St-148
62T/bucks
63Exh
63J-151
63P-151
63T-275
64T-35
64T/Coins-33
64T/SU
64T/St-97
64T/tatt
65Salada-28
65T-500
65T/E-26
66T-200
66T/RO-118
66T/RO-59
67Ast/Team-9
67OPC-166
67T-166
68CokeCap/Astro-18
68CokeCap/Tiger-16
68OPC-58
68T-58
69MB-169
73OPC-237MG
73T-237MG
74OPC-634MG
74T-634MG
77Galasso-34
79TCMA-157
80Laugh/3/4/5-25
80Perez/HOF-166
80SSPC/HOF
82CJ-12
83MLBPA/Pin-26
84West/1-17
85CircK-11
86BLChew-10
86Sf/Dec-34
87Nestle/DT-25
88Domino-13
89HOF/St-25
89Kahn/Coop-8
89Kenner/BBGr-11
89Pac/Leg-116
89T/LJN-125
90Pac/Legend-66
90Perez/GreatMom-28
90Swell/Great-65
91LineD-40
91Swell/Great-147
91T/Arc53-37
92Bz/Quadra-3M
93AP/ASG-117
93AP/ASG24K-51G
94T/Arc54-30
94TedW-43
Exh47
WG10-35
WG9-35

Mathews, Greg
86D/Rook-26
86F/Up-U73
86Sf/Rook-41
87D-208
87F-303
87Smok/Cards-8
87T-567
87T/Gloss60-60
87ToysRUs-20
88D-84
88D/Best-324
88F-41
88Louisvl-33
88S-226
88S/YS/II-35
88Smok/Card-7
88T-133
88T/Big-177
89D-281
89F-456
89S-286
89T-97
89UD-531
90Louisvl/LBC-26
90OPC-209
90Publint/St-221
90S-537
90Smok/Card-13
90T-209
90T/TVCard-17
90UD-678
92ScranWB/ProC-2443
92ScranWB/SB-489
93F-495

Mathews, Jeremy
89Belling/Legoe-22

Mathews, Jim
78Ashvl

Mathews, Michael
92Classic/DP-27

Mathews, Nelson
63T-54R
64T-366
65OPC-87
65T-87
81TCMA-394

Mathews, Rick
81CharR-26
82FtMyr-22
84Memphis-1

Mathews, Robert
N172
N690

Mathews, T.J.
92Hamil/ClBest-19
92Hamil/ProC-1588
93ClBest/MLG-120
93FExcel/ML-102
94B-236
94ClBest/Gold-165
94FExcel-271

Mathews, Terry
88CharlR/Star-15
89Tulsa/GS-17
89Tulsa/Team-15
90Tulsa/ProC-1171
90Tulsa/Team-15
91AAA/LineD-311
91OkCty/LineD-311
91OkCty/ProC-173
92D-694
92F-310
92Mother/Rang-20
92ProC/Tomorrow-151
92S-737
92T/91Debut-118
92T/Gold-131
92T/GoldWin-131
92Ultra-135
93F-684
93Rang/Keeb-247

Mathews, Tom
86Fresno/Smok-22

Mathewson, Christy
10Domino-76
11Diamond-19
11Helmar-131
12Sweet/Pin-117A
12Sweet/Pin-117B
14CJ-88
15CJ-88
16FleischBrd-62
40PlayBall-175
48Exh/HOF
49Leaf/Prem-5
50Callahan
50W576-52
51T/CM
60Exh/HOF-16
60F-2
60NuCard-8
61F-59
61GP-24
61NuCard-477
61T-408HL
63Bz/ATG-4
69Bz/Sm
72F/FFeat-3

72Laugh/GF-25
73F/Wild-22
76Shakey-4
77Galasso-152
77Galasso-242
77Shakey-6
80Laugh/3/4/5-5
80Laugh/FFeat-22
80Pac/Leg-34
80Perez/HOF-3
80SSPC/HOF
81Conlon-9
83D/HOF-3
85Woolwth-25
86Conlon/1-23
86Conlon/1-32
86Conlon/1-46
87Conlon/2-3
89HOF/St-65
90BBWit-104
90HOF/St-10
90Perez/GreatMom-6
90Swell/Great-134
91Conlon/Proto-331
91Conlon/Sport-57
91Swell/Great-141
92Conlon/Col-9
92Conlon/Sport-331
93AP/ASG-87
93AP/ASG24K-21G
93Conlon-910
93Conlon/MasterCol-8M
93CrackJack-4
93UD/ATH-143
93UD/ATH-144M
93UD/ATH-155M
93UD/ATH-156
93UD/ATH-89
93UD/T202-1M
94Conlon-1220
D303
D304
E101
E102
E103
E105
E106
E107
E224
E286
E90/1
E91
E93
E95
E98
L1-133
M116
PM1-11
R332-10
R423-68
S74-88
S81-108
T201
T202
T205
T206
T213/blue
T213/brown
T215/brown
T215blue
T216
T3-27
W514-72
W516-24
W555
WG4-17
WG5-28
WG6-27

Mathias, Carl
60T-139
61BeeHive-13

Mathile, Michael
90James/Pucko-21
91Rockford/ClBest-9
91Rockford/ProC-2044
92ClBest-127
92Harris/ProC-458
92Harris/SB-290
92Sky/AASingl-123
93Ottawa/ProC-2432

Mathiot, Mike
89Kenosha/ProC-1059
89Kenosha/Star-13
90Kenosha/Best-7
90Kenosha/ProC-2302
90Kenosha/Star-11

Mathis, Monte
92Saraso/ClBest-23

Mathis, Ron
83Tucson-4
84Cram/PCL-72
85F/Up-U78
85Mother/Ast-26
85T/Tr-79T
86F-305
86T-476
86Tucson-12
87Tucson-14
88ColoSp/CMC-5
88ColoSp/ProC-1548

Mathis, Verdell
(Lefty)
86Negro/Frit-62
91Negro/Lewis-7
92Negro/Retort-40

Mathis, Wayne
90Kgsport/Best-4
90Kgsport/Star-16

Mathison, Chuck
84Greens-15

Matias, John
70OPC-444R
70T-444R
71OPC-546
71T-546
87Hawaii-8

Matilla, Pedro
88Elmira-14
89WinHaven/Star-15
90WinHaven/Star-14
91WinHaven/ClBest-14

Matlack, Jon
71OPC-648R
71T-648R
72OPC-141R
72T-141R
73K-12
73OPC-55
73T-55
74OPC-153
74OPC-471NLCS
74T-153
74T-471NLCS
74T/DE-44
74T/St-66
75K-10
75OPC-290
75T-290
75T/M-290
76Ho-97
76K-49
76OPC-190
76SSPC-554
76SSPC/MetsY-M21
76T-190
77BurgChef-137
77Ho-114
77Ho/Twink-114
77OPC-132
77Pep-68
77T-440
78BK/R-5
78OPC-98
78SSPC/270-99
78T-25
78Wiffle/Discs-43
79Ho-122
79K-58
79OPC-159
79T-315
80OPC-312
80T-592
81D-266
81F-621
81F/St-51
81OPC-339
81T-656
81T/HT
81T/St-135
82D-215
82F-323
82F/St-176
82OPC-239
82T-239
83D-195
83F-572
83F/St-26M
83F/St-7M
83Rang-32
83T-749
84D-378
84F-422
84Nes/792-149
84T-149
89Pac/Leg-214
89Pac/SenLg-9
89River/Best-23
89River/Cal-26CO
89River/ProC-1408
89T/SenLg-102
89TM/SenLg-73
89Tidew/Candl-3
90EliteSenLg-11
90Wichita/Rock-27CO
91AAA/LineD-300M
91LasVegas/LineD-300CO
91LasVegas/ProC-254CO
91WIZMets-253
92LasVegas/ProC-2811CO
92LasVegas/SB-250M
93Rang/Keeb-248

Matlock, Leroy
78Laugh/Black-32

Matney, Ron
74Wichita-115

Matos, Carlos
82Danvl/Frit-11

Matos, Domingo
90James/Pucko-3
91James/ClBest-14
91James/ProC-3554
92Rockford/ClBest-10
92Rockford/ProC-2125
93WPalmB/ClBest-14
93WPalmB/ProC-1349

Matos, Francisco
89Modesto/Cal-283
89Modesto/Chong-24
90Modesto/Cal-168
90Modesto/Chong-19
90Modesto/ProC-2220
91AA/LineD-289
91Huntsvl/ClBest-15
91Huntsvl/LineD-289
91HuntsvlProC-1804
92Huntsvl/SB-314
92Sky/AASingl-133

Matos, Luis
92Hunting/ProC-3146

Matos, Malvin
90Butte/SportP-12
91Gaston/ClBest-24
91Gaston/ProC-2701
92Gaston/ClBest-23
92Gaston/ProC-2265

Matos, Rafael
84Butte-16

Matouzas, Jeff
90Tampa/DIMD-16

Matranga, Dave
90NE-18

Matranga, Jeff
92Johnson/ProC-3113

Matrisciano, Ron
80Clinton-7

Matsuo, Hideharu
87Miami-22

Mattaick, Denny
90Foil/Best-256

Mattern, Al
10Domino-77
11Helmar-80
12Sweet/Pin-68A
12Sweet/Pin-68B
E254
M116
S74-45
T201
T205
T206

Matthews
E254

Matthews, Francis
(Fran)
92Negro/RetortII-25

Matthews, Gary
73OPC-606R
73T-606R
74OPC-386
74T-386
75Ho-31
75Ho/Twink-31
75OPC-79
75T-79
75T/M-79
76Ho-142
76OPC-133
76SSPC-110
76T-133
77BurgChef-210
77Ho-142
77Ho/Twink-142
77T-194
78Ho-19
78OPC-209
78T-475
78Wiffle/Discs-44
79Ho-42
79OPC-35
79T-85
80K-48
80OPC-186
80T-355
81D-306
81F-251
81OPC-186
81T-228
81T/SO-76
81T/St-144
81T/Tr-800
82D-441
82F-249
82F/St-58
82OPC-151
82T-680
82T/St-79
83D-420
83Drake-16
83F-165
83F/St-10M
83F/St-13M
83OPC-64
83OPC/St-269
83T-780
83T/St-269
84D-233
84Drake-21
84F-40
84F/St-121
84F/X-77T
84Nes/792-637TL
84Nes/792-70
84OPC-70
84Seven-23E
84SevenUp-36
84T-70
84T/RD-16M
84T/St-118
84T/St-18LCS
84T/Tr-77
85D-239
85Drake-18
85F-61
85F/St-24
85FunFoodPin-70
85Leaf-220
85OPC-210
85Seven-10S
85SevenUp-36
85T-210
85T/RD-30M
85T/St-44
85T/Super-19
86Cub/Unocal-12
86D-76
86F-373
86Gator-36
86GenMills/Book-4M
86OPC-292
86Sf-66M
86T-485
86T/St-59
86T/Tatt-5M
87Berg/Cubs-36
87F-568
87OPC-390
87Seven-C10
87T-390
87T/St-62
88OPC-156
88S-599
88T-156
88T/St-223
89Swell-118

Matthews, Jeff
78Green

Matthews, Jeremy
89Wausau/GS-15

Matthews, Joel
89MissSt-25
90MissSt-26
91MissSt-32
92MissSt-28
93MissSt-29

Matthews, Michael
92ClBest/Up-419
93B-261
93StCl/MurphyS-149
93T-787
93T/Gold-787

Matthews, Tom
90Kissim/DIMD-17

Matthews, W.C.
(Wid)
21Exh-102

Matthias, Brother
92Mega/Ruth-118

Mattick, Robert
80T-577MG
81D-570
81F-431
81T-674MG

Mattimore, Michael
N172

Mattingly, Don
81Nashvl
82Colum-21
82Colum/Pol-19
84D-248
84F-131
84Nes/792-8
84OPC-8
84T-8
84T/St-325
85D-295
85D-651M
85D-7DK
85D/AAS-48
85D/DKsuper-7
85D/HL-36
85D/HL-44
85D/HL-45
85Drake-19
85F-133
85F/LimEd-20
85F/St-37
85F/St-4
85FunFoodPin-77
85Leaf-140M
85Leaf-7DK
85OPC-324
85Seven-12E
85T-665
85T/3D-8
85T/Gloss40-27
85T/RD-22M
85T/St-171
85T/St-310
85T/Super-4
86BK/AP-19
86D-173
86D/AAS-50
86D/HL-48
86D/HL-53
86Dorman-13
86Drake-7
86F-109
86F-627M
86F-639M
86F/AS-1
86F/LL-22
86F/LimEd-27
86F/Mini-24
86F/Slug-21
86F/St-72
86GenMills/Book-1M
86Jiffy-6
86KayBee-19
86Leaf-103
86Meadow/Blank-8
86Meadow/Milk-5
86Meadow/Stat-5
86OPC-180
86OPC/WaxBox-J
86Quaker-18
86Seven/Coin-C3M
86Seven/Coin-E3M
86Seven/Coin-S3M
86Seven/Coin-W3M

86Sf-176M
86Sf-179M
86Sf-180M
86Sf-183M
86Sf-184M
86Sf-2
86Sf-54M
86Sf-75M
86Sf/Dec-65
86T-180
86T-712AS
86T/3D-15
86T/Gloss60-31
86T/Mini-28
86T/St-296
86T/Super-1
86T/Tatt-7M
86T/WaxBox-J
86TrueVal-5
86Woolwth-20
87BK-13
87Classic-10
87Classic/Up-104
87D-52
87D/AAS-33
87D/HL-17
87D/HL-23
87D/HL-48
87D/OD-241
87Drake-8
87F-104
87F-638M
87F/AS-1
87F/AwardWin-24
87F/BB-26
87F/Excit-33
87F/GameWin-26
87F/Hottest-27
87F/LL-28
87F/Lim-26
87F/Mini-66
87F/RecSet-20
87F/Slug-25
87F/St-131M
87F/St-74
87F/St-S8
87GenMills/Book-2M
87Ho/St-27
87Jiffy-6
87KMart-28
87KayBee-19
87Kraft-29
87Leaf-150
87MSA/Discs-6
87MnM's-11
87OPC-229
87Ralston-5
87RedFoley/St-106
87Seven-E12
87Sf-1
87Sf-159M
87Sf-75M
87Sf/TPrev-7M
87Sportflic/DealP-1
87Stuart-23M
87T-500
87T-606AS
87T/Board-32
87T/Coins-17
87T/Gloss60-1
87T/HL-15
87T/Mini-65
87T/St-294
87Woolwth-15
88AP/Test-5
88Bz-11
88CMC/Kit-1
88CMC/Kit-20
88ChefBoy-16
88Classic/Blue-211
88Classic/Blue-247M
88Classic/Red-151M
88Classic/Red-152
88D-217
88D-BC21
88D/AS-1
88D/Best-1
88D/PopUp-1
88D/Y/Bk-217
88Drake-1
88F-214
88F/AwardWin-23
88F/BB/AS-23
88F/BB/MVP-22
88F/Excit-25
88F/Head-1
88F/Hottest-24
88F/LL-25
88F/Mini-41
88F/RecSet-24
88F/SS-22
88F/Slug-26
88F/St-48
88F/TL-19
88FanSam-9
88Grenada-14
88KMart-15
88KayBee-16
88KennerFig-66
88KingB/Disc-15
88Leaf-177
88MSA/Disc-3
88Nestle-15
88OPC-300
88Panini/St-152
88Panini/St-227M
88Panini/St-430
88RedFoley/St-53
88S-1
88S-650M
88S-658HL
88S/WaxBox-2
88Sf-1
88Sf-222M
88Sf/Gamewin-1
88T-2RB
88T-300
88T-386AS
88T/Big-229
88T/Coins-19
88T/Gloss22-2
88T/Gloss60-11
88T/Mini-27
88T/RiteAid-22
88T/St-156
88T/St-299
88T/St-3
88T/St/Backs-35
88T/UK-45
88Woolwth-4
89B-176
89Cadaco-34
89Classic-106
89Classic-5
89D-26DK
89D-74
89D/AS-21
89D/Best-1
89D/DKsuper-26DK
89F-258
89F/BBAS-28
89F/BBMVP's-26
89F/Excit-31
89F/Heroes-26
89F/LL-25
89F/Rec-6
89F/Superstar-29
89Holsum/Discs-15
89Holsum/Discs-4
89KMart/DT-12
89KMart/Lead-3
89KayBee-20
89KennerFig-89
89MSA/Disc-1
89MSA/SS-11
89Master/Discs-6
89Nissen-4
89OPC-26
89Panini/St-404
89RedFoley/St-79
89S-100
89S/HotStar-10
89S/Mast-6
89S/NWest-1
89Sf-50
89T-397AS
89T-700
89T/Big-50
89T/Coins-43
89T/Crunch-8
89T/DH-1
89T/DHTest-14
89T/Gloss60-51
89T/HeadsUp-19
89T/LJN-163
89T/St-314
89T/St/Backs-2
89T/UK-49
89Tetley/Discs-1
89Topps/Ritz-Set
89UD-200
89UD-693TC
90B-443
90B/Ins-5
90Classic-16
90Classic/III-12
90Classic/III-NO
90CollAB-13
90Colla/Matting-Set
90D-190
90D/BestAL-38
90D/Learning-12
90F-447
90F-626M
90F-638M
90F/AwardWin-21
90F/BB-24
90F/BBMVP-23
90F/Can-447
90F/Can-626
90F/Can-638
90F/LL-23
90F/LgStand-2
90F/WaxBox-C19
90HOF/St-90
90HotPlay/St-25
90KMart/CBatL-4
90KMart/SS-17
90KayBee-18
90Kenner/Fig-52
90Kenner/Fig-53
90KingB/Discs-14
90Leaf-69
90MCA/Disc-14
90MLBPA/Pins-63
90MSA/Soda-11
90OPC-200
90Panini/St-125
90Post-1
90PublInt/St-291
90PublInt/St-540
90RedFoley/St-59
90S-1
90S/100St-10
90S/NWest-2
90Sf-150
90Starline/LJS-1
90Starline/LJS-28
90Starline/LJS-35
90Sunflower-8
90T-200
90T/Ames-18
90T/Big-85
90T/Coins-21
90T/DH-43
90T/Gloss60-11
90T/HeadsUp-19
90T/HillsHM-3
90T/Mini-24
90T/St-308
90T/TVAS-17
90T/TVYank-25
90Tetley/Discs-14
90UD-191
90WonderBrd-6
91B-178
91BBBest/HitM-14
91BBBest/RecBr-11
91Cadaco-36
91Classic/200-98
91Classic/I-33
91Classic/III-56
91Coke/Matting-Set
91Coke/Mattingly-Set
91D-107
91DennyGS-8
91F-673
91F/ProV-11
91Kenner-38
91Leaf-425
91Leaf/Prev-22
91Leaf/Stud-97
91MajorLg/Pins-1
91MooTown-15
91OPC-100
91OPC/Premier-77
91Panini/FrSt-324
91Panini/St-267
91Pep/SS-11
91Petro/SU-19
91Post-29
91RedFoley/St-61
91S-23
91S-856FRAN
91S/100SS-23
91Seven/3DCoin-11NE
91StCl-21
91T-100A
91T-100B
91T/CJMini/I-7
91T/SU-24
91UD-354
91Ultra-239
92B-340
92CJ/DI-36
92Classic/Game200-105
92Classic/I-58
92Classic/II-T49
92D-596
92F-237
92F/Performer-16
92F/TmLIns-1
92French-11
92JDean/18-8
92L-57
92L/BlkGold-57
92L/GoldPrev-22
92L/Prev-22
92MrTurkey-16
92OPC-300
92OPC/Premier-92
92P-3
92Panini-135
92Pinn-23
92Pinn-584M
92S-23
92S/100SS-23
92Seven/Coin-2
92StCl-420
92Studio-216
92Studio/Her-5
92Studio/Prev-9
92T-300
92T/Gold-300
92T/GoldWin-300
92T/Kids-84
92T/MicroG-300
92TripleP-159
92TripleP/Prev-4
92UD-356
92UD/ASFF-31
92UD/TmMVPHolo-33
92Ultra-105
92Ultra/AwardWin-19
92Yank/WIZ80-111
92Yank/WIZAS-46
93B-595
93Cadaco-40
93Classic/Gamel-59
93Colla/DM-71
93D-264M
93D-609
93D/Elite-24
93D/EliteDom-12
93D/EliteDom-12AU
93D/EliteUp-6
93D/MVP-5
93D/Prev-18
93Duracel/PPI-19
93F-281
93F/Atlantic-14
93F/Fruit-43
93Flair-249
93Ho-28
93JDean/28-6
93Kraft-9
93L-237
93L/GoldAS-2
93MSA/Metz-14
93OPC-103
93OPC/Premier-46
93P-12
93Pac/Spanish-208
93Panini-154
93Pinn-23
93Pinn-470NT
93Pinn/Cooper-14
93Pinn/Slug-23
93S-23
93S/Franchise-10
93Select-24
93Select/Pr-24
93Select/StatL-14
93StCl-557
93StCl/1stDay-557
93StCl/II/Ins-2M
93StCl/Y-1
93Studio-193
93T-32
93T/Finest-98AS
93T/FinestASJ-98AS
93T/FinestPr-98AS
93T/FinestRef-98AS
93T/Gold-32
93T/HolPrev-32
93T/MicroP-32
93TripleP-120
93TripleP/Act-19
93UD-134
93UD-47M
93UD/Clutch-R14
93UD/Diam-28
93UD/FunPack-208
93UD/looss-WI26
93UD/SP-265
93UD/Then-TN13
93Ultra-244
93Ultra/AwardWin-12
94B-25
94B-386
94D-340
94D/Ann-8
94D/DK-16
94D/MVP-24
94D/Pr-9
94D/Special-340
94D/Spirit-9
94F-239
94F/TL-10
94Finest-392
94Flair-84
94L-121
94L/Gamer-4
94L/GoldS-6
94L/Pr-5
94OPC-54
94P-2
94Pac/Cr-430
94Pac/Silv-10
94Panini-102
94Pinn-23
94Pinn/Artist-23
94Pinn/Museum-23
94RedFoley-17
94S-23
94S/GoldR-23
94S/GoldS-49
94Select-23
94Sf/2000-127
94Sf/Mov-9
94StCl-195
94StCl/1stDay-195
94StCl/Gold-195
94StCl/Team-181
94Studio-215
94Studio/Her-4
94Studio/S&GStar-10
94T-600
94T/Gold-600
94TripleP-276
94TripleP/Pr-9
94UD-290HFA
94UD-90
94UD/CollC-192
94UD/CollC/Gold-192
94UD/CollC/Silv-192
94UD/DColl-E8
94UD/ElecD-90
94UD/HoloFX-26
94UD/SP-198
94Ultra-400
94Ultra/AwardWin-2

Mattingly, Earl
90Target-491

Mattingly, Steve
89Boise/ProC-1989

Mattocks, Rich
84Greens-24

Mattox, Frank
85Beloit-11
86Stockton-18
87ElPaso-8
88ElPaso/Best-29
88TexLgAS/GS-38
89ElPaso/GS-23
90AAASingl/ProC-657
90Denver/CMC-14
90Denver/ProC-632
90ProC/Singl-39

Mattson, Don

91Macon/ClBest-5
Mattson, Kurt
83Clinton/Frit-22
84Shrev/FB-11
Mattson, Rob
91Durham/ProC-DUR3
91DurhamUp/ProC-3
91Macon/ProC-859
Mattson, Ronnie
77Spartan
Matula, Rick
80T-596
81D-317
81F-263
81T-611
82Evansvl-5
Matulevich, Jeff
92Johnson/ClBest-20
92Johnson/ProC-3114
Matusyavichus, Edmuntas
89EastLDD/ProC-DD9
Matuszak, Mick
91AubAS/ClBest-23TR
Matuszek, Len
80OkCty
81OkCty/TCMA-10
82OkCty-8
83Portl-8
83T-357
84D-549
84F-41
84Nes/792-275
84OPC-275
84Phill/TastyK-31
84T-275
85D-259
85F-260
85F/Up-U79
85OPC-226
85T-688
85T/Tr-80T
85Tor/Fire-22
86Coke/Dodg-19
86D-494
86F-138
86Pol/Dodg-17
86T-109
87D-423
87F-447
87Mother/Dodg-20
87Pol/Dodg-8
87T-457
88Pol/Dodg-17M
88S-424
88T-92
90Target-492
Matzen, Mark
82Cedar-13
Matznick, Danny
90MidwLgAS/GS-15
90SoBend/Best-20
90SoBend/GS-10
91Saraso/ClBest-7
91Saraso/ProC-1110
Mauch, Gene
49Eureka-63
51B-312
57T-342
61T-219MG
62T-374MG
63T-318MG
64PhilBull-17MG
64T-157MG
65T-489MG
66T-411MG
67Pol/Phill-8MG
67T-248MG
68OPC-122MG
68T-122MG
69Expos/Pins-5MG
69T-606
70OPC-442MG
70T-442MG
71Expo/ProS-15MG
71LaPizza-6
71OPC-59MG
71T-59MG
72Dimanche*-31MG
72OPC-276MG
72T-276MG
73OPC-377MG
73T-377MG
74OPC-531MG
74T-531MG
75OPC-101MG
75T-101MG
75T/M-101MG
76SSPC-597MG
76T-556MG
77T-228MG
78T-601MG
78Twin/Frisz-11MG
79T-41MG
79Twin/FriszP-17MG
81TCMA-359MG
82D-141MG
83T-276MG
85Smok/Cal-24MG
85T/Tr-81T
86Smok/Cal-24MG
86T-81MG
87T-518MG
88T-774MG
90Target-493
93Expo/D/McDon-30MG
Mauch, Thomas
87StPete-17
88StPete/Star-16
Maul, Al
90Target-494
N172
N690
WG1-61
Mauldin, Eric
91Martins/ClBest-2
91Martins/ProC-3469
Mauldin, Weldon
(Hunky)
62Pep/Tul
63Pep/Tul
Mauney, Terry
84CharlO-2
85CharlO-28
87CharlO/WBTV-xx
Mauramatsu, Arihito
91Salinas/ProC-2257
Maurer, Rob
88Butte-15
89CharlR/Star-15
89Star/Wax-7
90A&AASingle/ProC-69
90ProC/Singl-798
90TexLgAS/GS-20
90Tulsa/ProC-1163
90Tulsa/Team-16
91AAA/LineD-312
91AAAGame/ProC-26
91OkCty/LineD-312
91OkCty/ProC-186
92B-437
92Classic/Game200-184
92D-703
92F-659RP
92OkCty/ProC-1922
92OkCty/SB-314
92Pinn-273
92ProC/Tomorrow-149
92S-767
92Sky/AAASingl-144
92StCl-462
92T/91Debut-119
92UD-10SR
93D-584RR
93Pac/Spanish-313
93Rang/Keeb-249
93StCl/Rang-13
93T-763
93T/Gold-763
Maurer, Ron
90GreatF/SportP-27
91Bakers/Cal-2
91CalLgAS-21
92SanAn/ProC-3985
92SanAn/SB-569
92Sky/AASingl-248
Mauriello, Ralph
90Target-1019
Mauro, Carmen
52LaPatrie-11
52Park-71
53Exh/Can-47
79TCMA-109
90Target-495
Mauro, Mike
90Bristol/Star-17
Mauser, Timothy
(Tim)
88Spartan/Star-12
89Clearw/Star-14
89EastLgAS/ProC-24
89Star/Wax-13
90Foil/Best-115
90ProC/Singl-801
90Reading/Best-8
90Reading/ProC-1217
90Reading/Star-19
91AAA/LineD-489
91Phill/Medford-25
91ScranWB/LineD-489
91ScranWB/ProC-2535
92S-744
92ScranWB/ProC-2444
92ScranWB/SB-490
92Sky/AAASingl-221
92StCl-558
92T/91Debut-120
93ScranWB/Team-18
94D-215
94F-670
94StCl-200
94StCl/1stDay-200
94StCl/Gold-200
94T-99
94T/Gold-99
94Ultra-281
Max, Bill
82Beloit/Frit-21
83ElPaso-13
84Jacks-12
89River/Best-12
Maxcy, Brian
92Bristol/ClBest-5
92Bristol/ProC-1405
Maxey, Kevin
88StPete/Star-17
Maxie, Larry
64T-94R
71Richm/Team-13
78TCMA-59
Maxson, Dan
78Newar
Maxvill, Dal
62Pep/Tul
63T-49
64T-563
65OPC-78
65T-78
66T-338
67T-421
68OPC-141
68T-141
69MB-174
69MLB/St-213
69T-320
69T/St-117
70MLB/St-141
70OPC-503
70T-503
71MLB/St-278
71OPC-476
71T-476
72MB-214
72OPC-206
72T-206
73OPC-483
73T-483
74OPC-358
74T-358
78TCMA-241
82Pol/Atl-53CO
83Pol/Atl-53CO
84Pol/Atl-53CO
Maxwell, Billy
92Princet/ClBest-29TR
Maxwell, Charlie
52T-180
55B-162
55Esskay
57T-205
58T-380
59T-34M
59T-481
60L-48
60T-443
61P-37
61T-37
61T/RO-22
61T/St-154
62J-25
62P-25
62P/Can-25
62T-506
63J-41
63P-41
63T-86
64T-401
81TCMA-320
81Tiger/Detroit-76
91Crown/Orio-283
Maxwell, Jim
80Ashvl-16
Maxwell, John
90CharRain/Best-24
91CharRain/ClBest-28TR
92Watlo/ClBest-28TR
Maxwell, Marty
78OrlanTw
Maxwell, Pat
91Watertn/ClBest-20
91Watertn/ProC-3374
92ColRS/ClBest-5
92ColRS/ProC-2397
93Kinston/Team-15
94Ultra/Pr-36M
May, Carlos
69T-654R
70K-16
70OPC-18
70T-18
71K-45
71OPC-243
71T-243
71T/Coins-144
72MB-209
72OPC-525
72T-525
73K-45
73OPC-105
73T-105
74OPC-195
74T-195
74T/St-157
75Ho-44
75OPC-480
75T-480
75T/M-480
76Crane-32
76Ho-34
76Ho/Twink-34
76MSA/Disc
76OPC-110
76SSPC-148
76T-110
77BK/Y-22
77T-568
77T-633M
92Yank/WIZ70-105
94TedW-21
May, Darrell
93Macon/ClBest-15
93Macon/ProC-1396
94ClBest/Gold-115
94FExcel-158
May, Dave
68CokeCap/Orio-7
68OPC-56R
68T-56R
69OPC-113
69T-113
69T/4in1-17M
70OPC-81
70T-81
71MLB/St-444
71OPC-493
71T-493
72T-549
73OPC-152
73T-152
74K-13
74OPC-12
74T-12
74T/DE-58
74T/St-196
75OPC-650
75T-650
75T/M-650
76Ho-148
76OPC-281
76SSPC-19
76T-281
78SSPC/270-92
78T-362
81TCMA-385
83Ander-5C
91Crown/Orio-284
93Rang/Keeb-250
May, Davis
79Syrac/TCMA-16
79Syrac/Team-22
80Knoxvl/TCMA-7
May, Derrick
87Peoria-12
88Peoria/Ko-35M
88WinSalem/Star-11
89CharlK-5
90AAASingl/ProC-638
90F-645R
90F/Can-645M
90Iowa/CMC-14
90Iowa/ProC-331
90ProC/Singl-89
90T/TVCub-53
90UD/Ext-736
91AAA/LineD-209
91Classic/200-153
91Classic/I-28
91D-36RR
91F-427
91Iowa/LineD-209
91MajorLg/Pins-69
91OPC-288
91S-379RP
91S/Rook40-36
91StCl-73
91T-288
91T/90Debut-100
91UD-334
91Ultra-65
92Classic/II-T22
92Cub/Mara-27
92D/Rook-70
92F-387
92Iowa/SB-212
92Pinn-534
92Sky/AAASingl-108
92StCl-148
92T/Tr-68T
92T/TrGold-68T
93Cub/Mara-16
93D-318
93F-21
93F/RookSenl-8
93Flair-16
93L-200
93OPC-159
93Pac/Beisbol-19
93Pac/Jugador-32
93Pac/Spanish-380
93Panini-209
93Pinn-371
93S-213
93Select-402
93StCl-109
93StCl/1stDay-109
93StCl/Cub-12
93Studio-148
93T-391
93T/Gold-391
93ToysRUs-79
93UD-248
93UD/SP-85
93USPlayC/Rook-10H
93Ultra-19
94D-178
94F-389
94L-139
94OPC-40
94Pac/Cr-103
94Panini-154
94Pinn-196
94Pinn/Artist-196
94Pinn/Museum-196
94S-68
94S/GoldR-68
94Select-38
94StCl-287
94StCl/1stDay-287
94StCl/Gold-287
94StCl/Team-332
94Studio-61
94T-6
94T/Finest-162
94T/FinestRef-162
94T/Gold-6
94TripleP-74
94UD-328
94UD/CollC-193
94UD/CollC/Gold-193
94UD/CollC/Silv-193
94Ultra-461

May, Frank
E122
May, Jakie
91Conlon/Sport-319
E126-56
May, Jerry
65OPC-143R
65T-143R
66EH-12
66OPC-123R
66T-123R
67T-379
67T/Test/PP-13
68KDKA-12
68T-598
69MB-170
69MLB/St-186
69Pirate/JITB-5
69T-263
69T/St-87
70MLB/St-102
70OPC-423
70T-423
71MLB/St-420
71OPC-719
71T-719
72MB-210
72OPC-109
72T-109
73OPC-558
73T-558
91WIZMets-254
May, Larry
82OrlanTw-20
May, Lee Jr.
88LitFalls/Pucko-1
89Clmbia/Best-10
89Clmbia/GS-15
89Pittsfld/Star-16
90StLucie/Star-15
91AAA/LineD-562
91Tidew/LineD-562
91Wmsprt/ProC-307
92Sky/AAASingl-254
92Tidew/ProC-911
92Tidew/SB-563
May, Lee Sr.
66T-424R
67Kahn
67T-222R
68Kahn
68T-487
69Kahn
69MB-171
69MLB/St-131
69T-405
69T/St-27
69Trans-52
70MLB/St-30
70OPC-225
70OPC-65LL
70T-225
70T-65LL
71MLB/St-62
71OPC-40
71T-40
71T/Coins-29
71T/tatt-5
72K-37
72MB-211
72OPC-480
72OPC-89LL
72T-480
72T-89LL
73OPC-135
73T-135
73T/Lids-31
74OPC-500
74T-500
74T/St-33
75Ho-142
75OPC-25
75T-25
75T/M-25
76Ho-98
76OPC-210
76SSPC-389
76T-210
77BurgChef-45
77Ho-55
77Ho/Twink-55
77OPC-125
77OPC-3LL
77T-380
77T-3LL
77T-633M
77T/ClothSt-26
78Ho-53
78OPC-47
78T-640
78Wiffle/Discs-45
79OPC-1
79T-10
80OPC-255
80T-490
81F-183
82D-570
82F-415
82T-132
83D-538
83F-118
83OPC-377
83OPC-378SV
83OPC/St-9
83T-377
83T-378SV
83T/St-9
85CircK-34
86Mother/Ast-12
88Kahn/Reds-CO
90Pac/Legend-55
90Swell/Great-67
91Crown/Orio-285
92Pol/Royal-27M
93Pol/Royal-27M
93UD/ATH-90
May, Malcolm
91Melbourne/Fut-12
May, Merrill
(Pinky)
39Exh
39PlayBall-45
40PlayBall-98
41DP-46
41PlayBall-9
May, Milt
71OPC-343R
71T-343R
72OPC-247
72T-247
73OPC-529
73T-529
74OPC-293
74T-293
75Ho-35
75Ho/Twink-35
75OPC-279
75T-279
75T/M-279
76OPC-532
76SSPC-53
76T-532
76T/Tr-532T
77OPC-14
77T-98
78BK/T-2
78OPC-115
78T-176
79T-316
80OPC-340
80Pol/Giants-7
80T-647
81D-193
81OPC-273
81T-463
81T/St-237
82D-503
82F-395
82F/St-62
82OPC-242
82T-242
82T-576TL
82T/St-110
83D-312
83F-268
83F/St-13M
83OPC/St-301
83T-84
83T/St-301
84D-386
84F-254
84Nes/792-788
84T-788
85D-410
85T-509
89VFJuice-39CO
90Homer/Pirate-21
92Pirate/Nation-14CO
93Pirate/Nation-16CO
May, Rudy
65T-537R
69JB
70MLB/St-175
70OPC-203
70T-203
71JB
71MLB/St-349
71OPC-318
71T-318
72T-656
73OPC-102
73T-102
74OPC-302
74T-302
75OPC-321
75T-321
75T/M-321
76OPC-481
76SSPC-427
76T-481
77T-56
78Ho-115
78T-262
79OPC-318
79T-603
80OPC-281
80T-539
81F-90
81OPC-179
81T-179
81T-7LL
81T/HT
81T/St-3
82D-325
82F-41
82OPC-128
82T-735
83D-135
83F-385
83T-408
84D-626
84Nes/792-652
84T-652
91Crown/Orio-286
92Yank/WIZ70-106
92Yank/WIZ80-112
May, Scott
86Albuq-14
87SanAn-11
88OkCty/CMC-3
88OkCty/ProC-27
89D-636
89OkCty/CMC-5
89OkCty/ProC-1523
90ElPaso/GS-20
91AAA/LineD-210
91Iowa/LineD-210
91Iowa/ProC-1055
92Iowa/ProC-4049
92Iowa/SB-213
93Rang/Keeb-251
May, Ted
79QuadC-7
Mayberry, Germaine
92Burllnd/ClBest-4
92Burllnd/ProC-1671
Mayberry, Greg
85VeroB-20
88VeroB/Star-15
89SanAn/Best-19
90AAASingl/ProC-63
90Albuq/CMC-7
90Albuq/ProC-342
90Albuq/Trib-21
90ProC/Singl-409
Mayberry, John
70OPC-227R
70T-227R
71MLB/St-86
71OPC-148
71T-148
72OPC-373
72T-373
73OPC-118
73T-118
73T/Lids-32
74K-29
74OPC-150
74T-150
74T/DE-51
74T/St-184
75Ho-92
75OPC-95
75SSPC/42-31
75T-95
75T/M-95
76A&P/KC
76Crane-33
76Ho-91
76K-46
76MSA/Disc
76OPC-194LL
76OPC-196LL
76OPC-440
76SSPC-169
76T-194LL
76T-196LL
76T-440
77BurgChef-69
77Ho-56
77Ho/Twink-56
77OPC-16
77T-244
77T/CS-27
77T/ClothSt-27
78BJ/PostC-15
78OPC-168
78PapaG/Disc-40
78T-550
78Wiffle/Discs-46
79BJ/Bubble-16
79Ho-82
79OPC-199
79T-380
79T/Comics-17
80OPC-338
80T-643
81D-29
81Drake-31
81F-416
81OPC-169
81OPC/Post-13
81T-169
81T/SO-15
81T/St-139
82D-25DK
82D-306
82Drake-24
82F-619
82F/St-235
82FBI/Disc-12
82OPC-382
82OPC-53TL
82OPC/Post-1
82T-470
82T-606TL
82T/St-248
82T/Tr-677
83F-386
83OPC-45
83T-45
83T/Fold-2M
85Syrac-20
92Yank/WIZ80-113
Maye, A. Lee
(Lee)
60Lake
60SpicSpan-13
60T-246
61T-84
62J-156
62P-156
62P/Can-156
62Salada-216
62Shirriff-216
62T-518
63T-109
64T-416
65Kahn
65T-407
65T/E-62
65T/trans-21
66OPC-162
66T-162
67CokeCap/Indian-10
67T-258
68OPC-94
68T-94
69MB-172
69T-595
69T/St-165
70OPC-439
70Pol/SenY-7
70T-439
71OPC-733
71T-733
72MB-212
78TCMA-107
78TCMA-51
Maye, Stephen
(Steve)
86WinSalem-14
88Modesto-13
88Modesto/Cal-66
89Huntsvl/Best-10
90Salinas/Cal-128
91Salinas/ClBest-17
91Salinas/ProC-2238
Mayer, Ed
58T-461
Mayer, James Erskine
15CJ-172
D328-110
D329-114
D350/2-112
E135-110
M101/4-114
M101/5-112
Mayers, Jerry
52Laval-35
Mayes, Craig
92Everett/ClBest-26
92Everett/ProC-1693
Maynard, Ellerton
(Tow)
88Belling/Legoe-4
89Wausau/GS-7
90Foil/Best-84
90SanBern/Best-13
90SanBern/Cal-111
90SanBern/ProC-2646
91SanBern/ClBest-22
91SanBern/ProC-1999
92ClBest-141
92Jacks/ProC-3719
92Jaxvl/SB-363
92Sky/AASingl-155
93Calgary/ProC-1179
93FExcel/ML-227
93River/Cal-10
Mayne, Brent
90A&AASingle/ProC-52
90B-372
90Foil/Best-8
90Memphis/Best-1
90Memphis/ProC-1012
90Memphis/Star-16
90ProC/Singl-780
90S-664DC
91Classic/I-50
91D-617
91D/Rook-43
91F/Up-U28
91OPC-776
91S-765RP
91S/Rook40-8
91StCl-418
91T-776
91T/90Debut-101
91UD-72
91Ultra-150
92D-265
92F-162
92L-200
92L/BlkGold-200
92OPC-183
92OPC/Premier-40
92Pinn-469
92Pol/Royal-17
92S-84
92S/100RisSt-85
92S/Impact-18
92StCl-229
92Studio-186
92T-183
92T/Gold-183
92T/GoldWin-183
92Ultra-74
93D-261
93F-621
93L-36
93Pac/Spanish-490
93Pinn-359
93Pol/Royal-18
93StCl-25
93StCl/1stDay-25
93StCl/Royal-18
93T-294
93T/Gold-294
93TripleP-36

93UD-604
93Ultra-212
94D-511
94F-166
94Pac/Cr-293
94S-183
94S/GoldR-183
94StCl-333
94StCl/1stDay-333
94StCl/Gold-333
94T-38
94T/Gold-38
94Ultra-367
Mayo, Blake
92MissSt-29
Mayo, Edward
(Eddie)
45Playball-1
47TipTop
49B-75
54T-247
94T/Arc54-247
Exh47
Mayo, John
(Jackie)
49B-228
49Eureka-141
V362-36
Mayo, Todd
88CapeCod/Sum-119
89James/ProC-2146
90WPalmB/Star-15
91WPalmB/ClBest-26
91WPalmB/ProC-1241
92Harris/SB-291
Mays, Al
N172/ST
N690
N690/2
Mays, Carl W.
21Exh-103
28Yueng-17
77Galasso-126
87Conlon/2-48
88Conlon/4-18
91Conlon/Sport-150
E120
E121/120
E121/80
E210-17
R332-8
V100
V61-7
W501-29
W502-17
W514-103
W515-20
W573
W575
Mays, David
89TNTech-17
Mays, Henry
77StPete
Mays, Jeff
86Salem-18
87PortChar-11
88CharlR/Star-16
Mays, Willie
51B-305
52B-218
52BR
52Coke
52RM-NL15
52StarCal-90A
52StarCal/L-78E
52T-261
53Briggs
53T-244
54B-89
54NYJour
54RM-NL25
54SM
54T-90
55B-184
55Gol/Giants-20
55RFG-1
55RM-NL7
55T-194
55W605-1
56T-130
56T/Pin-41OF
57T-10
58Hires-25
58Hires/T
58PacBell-5
58SFCallB-14
58T-436M
58T-486AS
58T-5
59Bz
59HRDerby-14
59T-317M
59T-464HL
59T-50
59T-563AS
60Armour-16
60Bz-13
60MacGregor-13
60NuCard-27
60T-200
60T-564AS
60T-7M
60T/tatt-34
60T/tatt-93
61Bz-23
61NuCard-404
61NuCard-427
61P-145
61T-150
61T-41LL
61T-482MVP
61T-579AS
61T/Dice-9
61T/St-80
62Bz
62Exh
62J-142
62P-142
62P/Can-142
62Salada-149
62Shirriff-149
62T-18M
62T-300
62T-395AS
62T-54LL
62T/St-199
62T/bucks
63Bz-12
63Exh
63F-5
63J-106
63P-106
63Salada-22
63T-300
63T-3LL
63T/SO
64Bz-12
64T-150
64T-306M
64T-423M
64T-9LL
64T/Coins-151AS
64T/Coins-80
64T/S-51
64T/SU
64T/St-20S2
64T/tatt
64Wheat/St-29
65Bz-12
65MacGregor-6
65OPC-250
65OPC-4LL
65OPC-6LL
65OldLond-14
65T-250
65T-4LL
65T-6LL
65T/E-27
65T/trans-58
66Bz-16
66OPC-1
66T-1
66T-215LL
66T-217LL
66T-219LL
66T/RO-27
66T/RO-60
67Bz-16
67CokeCap/AS-10
67CokeCap/Giant-17
67OPC-191CL
67OPC/PI-12
67T-191CL
67T-200
67T-244LL
67T-423M
67T/PI-12
67T/Test/SU-19
68Bz-14
68CokeCap/Giant-17
68Dexter-51
68OPC-50
68T-490M
68T-50
68T/ActionSt-5B
68T/ActionSt-9CM
68T/G-8
68T/Post-20
69Kelly/Pin-12
69MB-173
69MLB/St-204
69MLBPA/Pin-52
69NTF
69OPC-190
69OPC/DE-16
69T-190
69T/4in1-1M
69T/DE-33
69T/S-65
69T/St-108
69T/decal
69Trans-34
70K-12
70MB-15
70MLB/St-129
70T-600
70T/CB
70T/S-18
70T/Super-18
70Trans-1
71Bz
71Bz/Test-47
71K-10
71MD
71MLB/St-257
71MLB/St-567
71OPC-600
71T-600
71T/Coins-153
71T/GM-41
71T/Greatest-41
71T/S-56
71T/Super-56
71T/tatt-16
71T/tatt-16a
71Ticket/Giant-7
72K-54
72MB-213
72OPC-49
72OPC-50IA
72ProStars/PostC-18
72T-49
72T-50IA
72T/Post-17
73OPC-1M
73OPC-305
73T-1M
73T-305
73T/Lids-33
74Laugh/ASG-60
74OPC-473WS
74T-473WS
75OPC-192MVP
75OPC-203MVP
75SSPC/42-35CO
75SSPC/Sam-5
75T-192MVP
75T-203MVP
75T/M-192MVP
75T/M-203MVP
76Laugh/Jub-18
76SSPC-616
77Galasso-245
77Galasso-8
78TCMA-280
79TCMA-6
80Laugh/3/4/5-10
80Marchant-19
80Pac/Leg-48
80Perez/HOF-168
80SSPC/HOF
82CJ-13
82KMart-8
83MLBPA/Pin-27
83OPC/St-3FOIL
83T/St-3F
84Mother/Giants-1
84West/1-13
85CircK-3
85Woolwth-26
86BLChew-3
86Sf/Dec-50
86Sf/Rook-46M
86T-403TBC*
87KMart-8
87Nestle/DT-28
88Grenada-52
88Pac/Leg-24
89B/Ins-7
89Kenner/BBGr-12
90BBWit-18
90HOF/St-65
90MSA/AGFA-1
90Perez/GreatMom-65
90Perez/Master-11
90Perez/Master-12
90Perez/Master-13
90Perez/Master-14
90Perez/Master-15
91K/3D-3
91Negro/Lewis-21
91Swell/Great-106
91T/Arc53-244
91WIZMets-255
92AP/ASG-14
92AP/ASG24K-14G
92AP/ASGProto-3
92Bz/Quadra-1M
92Ziploc-8
93AP/ASGCoke/Amo-14
93Metallic-12
93StCl/Ultra-1M
93StCl/Ultra-2
93StCl/Ultra-6
93StCl/Ultra-8M
93StCl/Ultra-9
93TWill-126
93TWill-138
93TWill-144
93TWill-55
93TWill/Locklear-3
93UD/ATH-137M
93UD/ATH-150
93UD/ATH-151M
93UD/ATH-163
93UD/ATH-164
93UD/ATH-91
93UD/Mays-Set
93UD/Then-TN18
94T/Arc54-90
94TedW-150
Exh47
PM10/L-25
PM10/L-26
PM10/Sm-115
PM10/Sm-116
PM10/Sm-117
PM10/Sm-118
PM10/Sm-119
PM10/Sm-120
PM10/Sm-121
Mayse, Gary
91Clinton/ClBest-15GM
92Clinton/ClBest-30M
Maysey, Matt
85Spokane/Cram-13
86CharRain-15
87CharRain-14
88Wichita-43
89LasVegas/CMC-6
89LasVegas/ProC-5
90AAASingl/ProC-4
90LasVegas/CMC-3
90LasVegas/ProC-116
90ProC/Singl-505
91AA/LineD-264
91Harris/LineD-264
91Harris/ProC-623
92D/Rook-71
92Indianap/ProC-1855
92Indianap/SB-187
92Sky/AAASingl-92
93S-316
94S-610
Mazeroski, Bill
57Kahn
57T-24
58Hires-36
58Kahn
58T-238
59Bz
59Kahn
59T-415
59T-555AS
60Kahn
60MacGregor-14
60T-55
61Bz-24
61Kahn
61NuCard-403
61P-128
61T-312WS
61T-430
61T-571AS
61T/Dice-10
61T/St-67
62J-170
62Kahn
62P-170
62P/Can-170
62Salada-131
62Shirriff-131
62T-353
62T-391AS
62T/St-179
63Bz-6
63Exh
63F-59
63IDL-12
63J-138
63Kahn
63P-138
63Salada-14
63T-323
63T/SO
64Kahn
64T-570
64T/Coins-143AS
64T/Coins-27
64T/SU
64T/St-40S4
64T/tatt
65Kahn
65OPC-95
65OldLond-15
65T-95
65T/E-23
65T/trans-59
66EH-9
66Kahn
66T-210
66T/RO-45
66T/RO-61
67CokeCap/AS-27
67CokeCap/NLAS-28
67CokeCap/Pirate-6
67Kahn
67T-510
67T/Test/PP-14
68Bz-7
68Dexter-52
68KDKA-9
68Kahn
68T-390
68T/ActionSt-14AM
68T/ActionSt-1AM
69Kahn
69MB-175
69MLB/St-187
69Pirate/JITB-6
69T-335
69T/St-88
69Trans-60
70MLB/St-103
70OPC-440
70T-440
71Bz/Test-3
71MLB/St-208
71OPC-110
71T-110
71T/Coins-15
71T/tatt-11
72MB-215
72T-760
73OPC-517CO
73T-517CO
74OPC-489CO
74T-489CO
76Laugh/Jub-6
77Galasso-261
78TCMA-62
88Pac/Leg-60
89Swell-67
89T/LJN-73
90HOF/St-62
90Pac/Legend-39
90Swell/Great-93
91CollAB-24
91LineD-13
91MDA-4

91Swell/Great-60
92AP/ASG-69
93TWill-78
93UD/ATH-92
94TedW-79
Exh47
WG10-36
WG9-36
Mazey, Randy
88BurlInd/ProC-1776
89Miami/I/Star-13
Mazur, Bob
77Salem
Mazurek, Danny
52Laval-18
Mazzilli, Lee
77T-488R
78OPC-26
78T-147
79Ho-7
79K-42
79OPC-183
79T-355
80K-38
80OPC-11
80T-25
80T/S-8
80T/Super-8
81Coke
81D-34
81Drake-33
81F-316
81F/St-42
81K-46
81MSA/Disc-22
81OPC-167
81Sqt-21
81T-510
81T/HT
81T/SO-75
81T/St-191
82D-49
82F-533
82F/St-90
82OPC-243
82T-465
82T/St-67
82T/Tr-68T
83D-638
83F-387
83F/St-25AM
83F/St-25BM
83F/St-3M
83OPC-306
83T-685
83T/Tr-67
84D-166
84F-255
84Jacks/Smok-8
84Nes/792-225
84OPC-225
84T-225
85D-386
85F-469
85OPC-323
85T-748
86D-288
86F-612
86OPC-373
86T-578
87D-562
87F-15
87T-198
88D-614
88D/Best-209
88D/Mets/Bk-614
88Kahn/Mets-13
88Leaf-223
88OPC-308
88S-158
88T-308
89Kahn/Mets-13
89S-217
89T-58
89UD-657
90BBWit-8
90D-584
90F-88
90F/Can-88
90OPC-721
90PublInt/St-139
90S-459
90T-721
91WIZMets-256
92Yank/WIZ80-114
93Rang/Keeb-252
Mazzone, Leo
75Tucson-18
75Tucson/Caruso-15
75Tucson/Team-10
79Savan-17
83Durham-29
84Durham-9
85Pol/Atl-52C
86Sumter/ProC-19CO
87Greenvl/Best-2C
87SLAS-25CO
88Richm/CMC-24CO
88Richm/ProC-16CO
89Richm/Bob-15CO
89Richm/CMC-24CO
89Richm/Ko-CO
89Richm/ProC-833CO
90AAASingl/ProC-421CO
90Brave/Dubuq/Singl-21CO
90ProC/Singl-278CO
90Richm/CMC-2CO
90Richm/ProC-276CO
90Richm/Team-21CO
91Brave/Dubuq/Stand-24CO
93Brave/Lyke/Stand-22CO
Mazzotti, Mauro
89Belling/Legoe-31CO
McAbee, Monte R.
82Madis/Frit-15
82WHave-15
83GlenF-4
McAfee, Bill
28LaPresse-23
McAfee, Bret
82Wausau/Frit-13
McAleer, James
M116
N172
T204
WG2-34
McAleese, John
T206
McAllister, Lewis
C46-57
E107
E270/2
T205
McAllister, Steve
83DayBe-21
85Nashua-17
86Nashua-18
McAllister, Troy
92Eugene/ClBest-18
92Eugene/ProC-3037
McAlpin, Mike
88StCath/ProC-2015CO
89StCath/ProC-2093CO
90StCath/ProC-3483CO
91AA/LineD-375M
91Knoxvl/LineD-375CO
91Knoxvl/ProC-1785CO
92Knoxvl/ProC-3007CO
92Knoxvl/SB-400M
93Knoxvl/ProC-1266CO
McAnally, Ernie
71OPC-376R
71T-376R
72Dimanche*-32
72OPC-58
72ProStars/PostC-8
72T-58
73OPC-484
73T-484
74Expo/West-7
74OPC-322
74T-322
74Weston-21
75OPC-318
75T-318
75T/M-318
McAnany, Jim
88PalmSp/Cal-104
88PalmSp/ProC-1452
McAnarney, James
88Clmbia/GS-8
McAndrew, James
(Jim)
69T-321
70OPC-246
70T-246
71MLB/St-160
71OPC-428
71T-428
72T-781
73OPC-436
73T-436
91WIZMets-257
94Mets/69-24
McAndrew, Jamie
89GreatF-5
90AS/Cal-22
90Bakers/Cal-237
91AAA/LineD-15
91Albuq/LineD-15
91Albuq/ProC-1138
91B-601
92Albuq/SB-14
92B-591
92ProC/Tomorrow-242
92SanAn/ProC-3971
92Sky/AAASingl-6
92UD/ML-197
93D-774
93T-412
93T/Gold-412
McArn, Brian
90NE-15
McAuliffe, David
89Greens/ProC-411
89SALAS/GS-32
90A&AASingle/ProC-123
90Cedar/Best-22
90Cedar/ProC-2320
90MidwLgAS/GS-41
91AA/LineD-162
91Chatt/LineD-162
91Chatt/ProC-1956
91Waverly/Fut-2
McAuliffe, Dick
62T-527
63J-48
63P-48
63T-64
64Det/Lids-10
64T-363
65OPC-53
65T-53
66T-495
66T/RO-62
66T/RO-64
67CokeCap/Tiger-6
67OPC-170
67T-170
68CokeCap/Tiger-6
68Kahn
68T-285
69MB-176
69MLB/St-51
69T-305
69T/St-176
70MLB/St-211
70OPC-475
70T-475
71MLB/St-399
71OPC-3
71T-3
71T/Coins-10
71T/tatt-9
72MB-216
72T-725
73OPC-349
73T-349
74OPC-495
74T-495
78TCMA-94
81Tiger/Detroit-134
88Domino-14
89Swell-14
McAvoy, Thomas
60L-108
McBean, Alvin
(Al)
62T-424
63IDL-13
63J-146
63P-146
63T-387
64Kahn
64T-525
64T/Coins-66
64T/St-17
65Kahn
65OPC-25
65T-25
65T/E-14
66EH-34
66T-353
67CokeCap/Pirate-1
67T-203
67T/Test/PP-12
68KDKA-34
68T-514
69MB-177
69OPC-14
69T-14
69T/St-96
70T-641
72MB-217
81TCMA-435
90Target-496
McBean, Douglas
52Laval-71
McBride, Bake
74OPC-601R
74T-601R
75Ho-41
75K-13
75OPC-174
75T-174
75T/M-174
76Crane-34
76Ho-93
76MSA/Disc
76OPC-135
76SSPC-277
76T-135
77BurgChef-17
77Ho-97
77Ho/Twink-97
77K-34
77T-516
78OPC-156
78SSPC/270-53
78T-340
78Wiffle/Discs-47
79BK/P-21
79OPC-332
79T-630
80BK/P-9
80OPC-257
80T-495
81Coke
81D-404
81F-9
81F/St-31
81OPC-90
81T-90
81T/HT
81T/SO-58
81T/St-202
82D-497
82F-250
82OPC-92
82T-745
82T/Tr-69T
82Wheat/Ind
83F-414
83OPC-248
83T-248
83T/Fold-3M
83Wheat/Ind-21
84F-547
84Nes/792-569
84OPC-81
84T-569
84T/St-256
89Pac/SenLg-19
89Pac/SenLg-201
89TM/SenLg-74
90EliteSenLg-58
92Card/McDon/Pac-44
McBride, George
10Domino-78
11Helmar-74
12Sweet/Pin-61
14Piedmont/St-35
BF2-47
D327
D328-111
D329-115
D350/2-113
E135-111
E254
E270/1
E91
M101/4-115
M101/5-113
M116
T201
T202
T205
T206
T207
T213
T222
T3-110
V100
McBride, Ivan
88Watlo/ProC-677
McBride, Ken
60T-276
61P-33
61T-209
62Bz
62Salada-91A
62Salada-91B
62Shirriff-91
62T-268
62T/St-66
62T/bucks
63Exh
63Salada-41
63T-510
64Bz-4
64T-405
64T/Coins-52
64T/SU
64T/St-89
64T/tatt
64Wheat/St-30
65OPC-268
65T-268
65T/E-30
Exh47
WG10-37
WG9-37
McBride, Loy
89Visalia/Cal-107
89Visalia/ProC-1449
90StLucie/Star-16
91AA/LineD-637
91Wmsprt/LineD-637
91Wmsprt/ProC-308
McBride, Thomas
49B-74
McCabe, Bill
90Target-1020
McCabe, James
T201
McCabe, Joseph
64T-564R
65OPC-181R
65T-181R
McCabe, Scott
89KS*-16
McCaffery, Dennis
92QuadC/ClBest-16
92QuadC/ProC-822
McCahan, Bill
48B-31
49B-80
McCain, Mike
82OrlanTw-10
83OrlanTw-7
83Toledo-27
McCall, John
(Windy)
55Gol/Giants-21
55T-42
55T/DH-88
56T-44
57T-291
79TCMA-200
McCall, Larry
78Cr/PCL-44
79Tucson-23
80Tacom-8
91Kane/ClBest-27CO
91Kane/ProC-2676CO
91Kane/Team-26M
92Kane/ClBest-27CO
92Kane/ProC-109CO
92Kane/Team-20CO
92Yank/WIZ70-107
93Rang/Keeb-253
McCall, Robert
(Dutch)
47Signal
48L-57
McCall, Rod
91ClBest/Singl-175
91Collnd/ClBest-26

91Collnd/ProC-1493
91SALAS/ProC-SAL18
92ColRS/ClBest-22
92ColRS/ProC-2398
93ClBest/MLG-13
93Kinston/Team-16
93SALAS/II-24
McCall, Trey
85Bend/Cram-15
87Spartan-14
88Clearw/Star-19
89Clearw/Star-15
McCallum, Thomas
N172
McCament, Randy
85Everett/II/Cram-9
86Fresno/Smok-11
87Shrev-16
88Phoenix/CMC-9
88Phoenix/ProC-71
89Shrev/ProC-1853
90AAASingl/ProC-34
90F-64
90F/Can-64
90OPC-361
90Phoenix/CMC-2
90Phoenix/ProC-8
90ProC/Singl-529
90S-580
90T-361
90T/89Debut-77
90UD-657
McCann, Brian
82AlexD-19
83LynnP-25
86Wausau-14TR
87Pittsfld-6
88EastLAS/ProC-49
88Pittsfld/ProC-1364
89CharlK-23
90Iowa/CMC-25TR
90ProC/Singl-100TR
McCann, Frank
77Jaxvl
82BirmB-19
McCann, Gene
90Target-1021
McCann, Joe 1
79Newar-12
McCann, Joe 2
89Pittsfld/Star-17
90Clmbia/PCPII-5
90Columbia/GS-6
91StLucie/ClBest-19
91StLucie/ProC-706
92StLucie/ClBest-9
92StLucie/ProC-1744
McCardell, Roger
52Laval-7
McCarren, Bill
90Target-497
McCarter, Edward
86SanJose-12
McCarthy, Alex
E254
E270/2
T207
McCarthy, Danny
79WHave-22M
McCarthy, Dave
75Anderson/TCMA-14
77Ashvl
McCarthy, Greg
88Spartan/ProC-1028
88Spartan/Star-13
89Spartan/ProC-1034
89Spartan/Star-17
90Clearw/Star-13
92Kinston/ClBest-21
92Kinston/ProC-2471
93Kinston/Team-17
McCarthy, Joe
30CEA/Pin-7
38ONG/Pin-19
42Playball-4MG
44Yank/St-18MG
76Shakey-83MG
77Galasso-70MG
80Laugh/FFeat-33
80Pac/Leg-58
80Perez/HOF-83
80SSPC/HOF
84Cub/Uno-8M
86Conlon/1-28
89HOF/St-87
91Conlon/Sport-28
92Conlon/Sport-589
92Yank/WIZHOF-23MG
93Conlon-823MG
R314/M
McCarthy, John A.
(Jack)
90Target-498
E107
N300/unif
McCarthy, John J.
40PlayBall-215
49B-220
93Conlon-726
V355-53
McCarthy, Shaun
76BurlB
80Knoxvl/TCMA-10
McCarthy, Steve
88Billings/ProC-1817
89Cedar/Best-10
89Cedar/ProC-914
89Cedar/Star-11
89Star/IISingl-192
90Cedar/ProC-2319
90CharWh/Best-4
91AA/LineD-163
91Chatt/LineD-163
91Chatt/ProC-1957
McCarthy, Thomas F.
50Callahan
50W576-53
75F/Pion-13
76Shakey-44
80Perez/HOF-44
80SSPC/HOF
89Smok/Dodg-20
90Target-499
N172
McCarthy, Tom
79Elmira-8
80Elmira-17
85Pawtu-17
86Tidew-19
87Jacks/Feder-5
87Tidew-13
87Tidew/TCMA-6
88Tidew/CANDL-22
88Tidew/CMC-7
88Tidew/ProC-1599
89T/Tr-75T
89Vanco/CMC-4
89Vanco/ProC-593
90F-541
90F/Can-541
90OPC-326
90S/100Ris-57
90T-326
91AAA/LineD-435
91Richm/Bob-10
91Richm/LineD-435
91Richm/ProC-2563
91Richm/Team-14
92Richm/Bleach-24
92Richm/Comix-10
92Richm/ProC-372
92Richm/SB-432
McCarty, David
91ClBest/Gold-18
91ClBest/Singl-400
91Classic/DP-3
91Visalia/ProC/Up-1
91Visalia/ProC/Up-3
92ClBest-350
92ClBest/BBonusC-17
92ClBest/RBonus-BC17
92Classic/DP-88FB
92OrlanSR/ProC-2860
92OrlanSR/SB-512
92ProC/Tomorrow-95
92Sky/AASingl-220
92UD-75TP
92UD/CollHolo-CP1
92UD/ML-255
92UD/ML-47M
92UD/ML/TPHolo-TP5
93B-369FOIL
93B-649
93ClBest/Fisher-15
93ClBest/GLP-2
93ClBest/GPr-2
93ClBest/MLG-93
93ClBest/MLGPr-2
93ClBest/MLGPrev-1
93F/Final-238
93FExcel/ML-202
93Flair-239
93Flair/Wave-9
93L/UpGRook-3
93Pac/Spanish-524
93Select/RookTr-45T
93StCl-569
93StCl/1stDay-569
93T/Tr-17T
93TB/Full-12
93UD-450M
93UD-462IN
93UD/FunPack-221CL
93UD/FunPack-5SOT
93UD/SP-250
93Ultra-586
94B-516
94D-281
94F-213
94L-78
94OPC-247
94OPC/DiamD-7
94Pac/Cr-361
94Pinn-333
94S-290
94S/GoldR-290
94Select-154
94Sf/2000-9
94StCl-134
94StCl/1stDay-134
94StCl/Gold-134
94T-156
94T/Finest-17
94T/FinestRef-17
94T/Gold-156
94UD-200
94UD/CollC-194
94UD/CollC/Gold-194
94UD/CollC/Silv-194
94UD/ElecD-200
94Ultra-391
McCarty, G. Lewis
90Target-500
94Conlon-1267IA
D328-112
E135-112
W514-37
McCarty, John
N172
McCarty, Scott
91Madison/ClBest-10
91Madison/ProC-2127
McCarty, Shane
92MN-21M
McCarty, Tom
C46-89
T201
McCarver, Tim
62Kahn/Atl
62T-167
62T/St-186
63T-394
64T-429
64T/Coins-156AS
65T-294
65T/E-7
66T-275
66T/RO-40
66T/RO-63
67T-485
67T/Test/SU-14
68Bz-3
68T-275
68T-376AS
68T/ActionSt-6CM
68T/G-18
68T/Post-19
69Kelly/Pin-13
69MB-178
69MLB/St-214
69MLBPA/Pin-53
69OPC-164WS
69T-164WS
69T-475
69T/4in1-7M
69T/S-61
69T/St-118
69T/decal
70K-34
70MLB/St-92
70OPC-90
70T-90
70T/S-23
70T/SO
70T/Super-23
71Bz/Test-1
71MLB/St-184
71OPC-465
71Phill/Arco-8
71T-465
71T/Coins-107
71T/GM-25
71T/Greatest-25
71T/S-34
71T/Super-34
72Dimanche*-33
72MB-218
72OPC-139
72T-139
73OPC-269
73T-269
74OPC-520
74T-520
74T/St-115
75OPC-586
75T-586
75T/M-586
76OPC 502
76T-502
77T-357
78SSPC/270-48
78T-235
79BK/P-3
79T-675
80T-178
81F-27
81TCMA-386
92Card/McDon/Pac-36
WG10-38
McCaskill, Kirk
83Redwd-19
85Cram/PCL-7
86D-474
86F-163
86Smok/Cal-5
86T-628
87D-381
87F-88
87F/GameWin-27
87F/Hottest-29
87F/Mini-67
87F/St-75
87GenMills/Book-3M
87Leaf-223
87OPC-194
87Seven-W5
87Sf-127
87Sf/TPrev-11M
87Smok/Cal-5
87T-194
87T/St-181
88D-381
88D/Best-83
88F-496
88Panini/St-36
88S-552
88Sf-78
88Smok/Angels-12
88T-16
88T/Big-168
89B-38
89D-136
89D/Best-83
89F-483
89OPC-348
89Panini/St-285
89S-181
89Sf-214
89T-421
89T/Big-149
89T/St-184
89UD-223
90B-283
90D-170
90F-138
90F/Can-138
90Leaf-247
90OPC-215
90Panini/St-37
90PublInt/St-373
90PublInt/St-598
90S-217
90S/100St-38
90Sf-169
90Smok/Angel-11
90T-215
90T/Mini-9
90T/St-167
90UD-506
91D-637
91F-319
91Leaf-199
91Leaf/Stud-28
91OPC-532
91S-590
91Smok/Angel-10
91StCl-313
91T-532
91UD-539
91Ultra-50
92B-2
92D-340
92F-64
92L-517
92L/BlkGold-517
92OPC-301
92OPC/Premier-60
92Pinn-391
92S-79
92S/RookTr-29T
92StCl-688
92Studio-155
92T-301
92T/Gold-301
92T/GoldWin-301
92T/Tr-69T
92T/TrGold-69T
92UD-128
92UD-722
92Ultra-338
92WSox-25
93D-227
93F-206
93L-151
93OPC-230
93Pac/Spanish-392
93Pinn-560
93S-469
93Select-387
93StCl-166
93StCl/1stDay-166
93StCl/WSox-28
93T-175
93T/Gold-175
93TripleP-82
93UD-608
93Ultra-535
93WSox-19
94D-540
94F-88
94Flair-34
94Pac/Cr-133
94StCl/Team-135
94T-724
94T/Gold-724
94Ultra-37
McCatty, Steve
78T-701R
80T-231
81A's/Granny-54
81D-478
81F-589
81OPC-59
81T-503
82D-35
82F-99
82F/St-131
82Granny-10
82OPC-113
82T-113
82T-156TL
82T-165LL
82T-167LL
82T/St-10LL
82T/St-14
82T/St-228
83D-491
83D/AAS-14
83F-525
83Granny-54
83T-493
84D-420
84F-454
84Mother/A's-8
84Nes/792-369
84OPC-369
84T-369
85D-497
85F-430
85Mother/A's-20

85T-63
85T/St-324
86BuffB-18
86F-427
86T-624
87SanJose-26
89Pac/SenLg-89
89T/SenLg-110
89TM/SenLg-75
91Pac/SenLg-16
McCauley
T206
McCauley, Drew
82Buffa-4
McCawley, Bill
52Mother-11
McCawley, James
N172
McCerod, George
86Pawtu-13
McClain, Charles
91Billing/SportP-1
91Billings/ProC-3750
92CharWh/ClBest-2
92CharWh/ProC-6
McClain, Joe Jr.
79QuadC-8
McClain, Joe Sr.
61T-488
62Salada-54
62Shirriff-54
62T-324
62T/St-98
63T-311
McClain, Michael
83Miami-2
85Beaum-12
86Beaum-18
McClain, Ron
76Indianap-25TR
77Indianap-26TR
78Indianap-26TR
79Indianap-30TR
83Expo/PostC-11TR
McClain, Scott
92Kane/ClBest-10
92Kane/ProC-100
92Kane/Team-21
94FExcel-12
McClear, Michael
86FtLaud-16
McClellan, Bobby
75AppFx
McClellan, Dan
74Laugh/Black-32
McClellan, Garth
85Clovis-25
McClellan, Harvey
E120
V100
W573
McClellan, Paul
86Cram/NWL-2
86Everett/Pop-14
87Clinton-21
88Shrev/ProC-1290
89Shrev/ProC-1850
90AAASingl/ProC-35
90Phoenix/CMC-1
90Phoenix/ProC-9
90ProC/Singl-528
91AA/LineD-311
91S-726RP
91Shrev/LineD-311
91Shrev/ProC-1817
91T/90Debut-102
92Classic/I-59
92D-700
92F-642
92OPC-424
92Phoenix/ProC-2817
92Phoenix/SB-388
92ProC/Tomorrow-344
92S-703
92Sky/AAASingl-177
92StCl-566
92T-424
92T/Gold-424
92T/GoldWin-424
92UD-563
McClellan, William
N172
N284
McClelland, Tim
88TM/Umpire-46
89TM/Umpire-44
90TM/Umpire-42
McClendon, Lloyd
82Lynch-16
83Water-9
87F/Up-U74
87Kahn-23
88Kahn/Reds-30
88T-172
89B-287
89D-595
89D/Best-228
89F/Up-77
89Iowa/CMC-12
89Iowa/ProC-1695
89Mara/Cubs-10
89S-521
89T-644
89T/Tr-76T
89UD-446
90B-36
90Cub/Mara-14
90D-341
90D/BestNL-134
90F-38
90F/Can-38
90OPC-337
90S-176
90T-337
90T/Big-5
90T/TVCub-32
90UD-398
91F/Up-U111
91StCl-385
92D-338
92F-560
92OPC-209
92Pirate/Nation-15
92S-566
92StCl-302
92T-209
92T/Gold-209
92T/GoldWin-209
92Ultra-256
93D-384
93F-502
93Pac/Spanish-247
93Pirate/Nation-17
93S-380
93StCl-66
93StCl/1stDay-66
93StCl/MurphyS-69
93T-81
93T/Gold-81
93UD-559
93Ultra-99
94F-613
94Pac/Cr-501
94StCl-511
94StCl/1stDay-511
94StCl/Gold-511
94T-518
94T/Gold-518
McClinic, Nath
92Negro/Retort-41
McClinton, Tim
89Kingspt/Star-16
90Clmbia/PCPII-7
90Columbia/GS-3
90Pittsfld/Pucko-10
91Clmbia/PCPII-1
91Clmbia/PII-21
92StLucie/ClBest-21
92StLucie/ProC-1756
93StLucie/ProC-2934
McClochlin, Mike
91Collnd/ProC-1481
McCloughan, Scot
90WichSt-23
92StCath/ClBest-20
92StCath/ProC-3398
93Hagers/ClBest-20
93Hagers/ProC-1893
McClure, Craig
94T-79M
94T/Gold-79M
McClure, Jack 1
44Centen-17
McClure, Jack 2
65T-553R
McClure, Rich
79QuadC-9
McClure, Robert
(Bob)
76OPC-599R
76SSPC-182
76T-599R
77T-472R
78T-243
79T-623
80T-357
81D-510
81F-520
81OPC-156
81T-156
82Pol/Brew-10
82T-487
83D-582
83F-38
83F/St-23M
83F/St-3M
83Gard-10
83Pol/Brew-10
83T-62
84D-359
84F-206
84Gard-12
84Nes/792-582
84Pol/Brew-10
84T-582
85D-536
85F-587
85Gard-12
85Pol/Brew-10
85T-203
86F-494
86Pol/Brew-10
86T-684
86T/Tr-71T
87F-325
87OPC-133
87T-707
88D-529
88F-189
88OPC-313
88S-381
88T-313
89B-43
89F-42
89F/Up-14
89S-572
89S/Tr-58T
89T-182
90D-470
90F-139
90F/Can-139
90OPC-458
90PublInt/St-374
90S-117
90Smok/Angel-20
90T-458
90UD-81
91OPC-84
91T-84
91WIZMets-258
92Brew/Carlson-13
92D-661
92S-717
92StCl-484
93F-128
93Pac/Spanish-467
93S-434
93StCl/Marlin-3
93USPlayC/Marlin-5C
93Ultra-383
McClure, Todd
87Ashvl-21
87AubAs-3
88FSLAS/Star-12
88Osceola/Star-17
89Kenosha/Star-14
89Star/Wax-52
89Visalia/ProC-1436
McCollom, Jim
87QuadC-21
88MidldA/GS-22
88TexLgAS/GS-27
McCollough, Mike
91GulfCR/SportP-1
92Gaston/ClBest-22
McCollum, Greg
87Elmira/Black-23
87Elmira/Red-23
88Lynch/Star-12
McCollum, Lou
47Sunbeam
McConachie, Dale
89Albany/Best-26
McConathy, Doug
91Bluefld/ClBest-15
91Bluefld/ProC-4135
92Freder/ClBest-21
92Freder/ProC-1812
McConnell, Ambrose
11Helmar-12
E254
E91
E97
M116
S74-6
T202
T204
T205
T3-29
W555
McConnell, Chad
92B-587FOIL
92Classic/DP-10
92Classic/DPFoil-BC10
92T/Tr-70T
92T/TrGold-70T
92UD/ML-8
93B-132
93StCl/MurphyS-35
93StCl/MurphyS-81
93StCl/Phill-4
93T-161
93T/Gold-161
93UD-439TP
94SigRook-16
McConnell, Tim
92Fayette/ProC-2171
McConnell, Walt
86FSLAS-34
86VeroB-17
87SanAn-14
88SanAn/Best-16
89Albuq/CMC-21
89Albuq/ProC-83
90AAASingl/ProC-74
90Albuq/CMC-28CO
90Albuq/ProC-353
90Albuq/Trib-22
90ProC/Singl-658M
91Albuq/ProC-1148
91MidldA/OneHour-19
92MidldA/ProC-4033
92MidldA/SB-465
McCool, Bill
64T-356R
65Kahn
65OPC-18
65T-18
66Kahn
66T-459
67CokeCap/Reds-14
67Kahn
67T-353
68Kahn
68T-597
69MB-179
69MLB/St-194
69OPC-129
69T-129
69T/4in1-15M
70MLB/St-116
70OPC-314
70T-314
72MB-219
81TCMA-351
McCord, Clinton
92Negro/Retort-42
McCorkle, Dave
86Wausau-15
88Vermont/ProC-963
McCormack, Brian
88AppFx/ProC-152
89BBCity/Star-16
90Memphis/Best-19
90Memphis/ProC-1009
90Memphis/Star-17
McCormack, Don R.
79OkCty
80OkCty
81OkCty/TCMA-9
82Evansvl-12
88Batavia/ProC-1664
90Reading/Best-24MG
90Reading/ProC-1234MG
90Reading/Star-26MG
91AA/LineD-524MG
91Reading/LineD-524MG
91Reading/ProC-1385MG
92Reading/ProC-591MG
92Reading/SB-549MG
McCormack, John
N172
McCormack, Mark
83Nashua-23
McCormack, Ron
83CharR-21
McCormack, Tim
86Jaxvl/TCM-26TR
87Indianap-32
88Indianap/ProC-498
89Indianap/CMC-9
89Indianap/ProC-1226
McCormick, Frank A.
(Buck)
39Exh
39PlayBall-36
40PlayBall-75
41DP-9
41PlayBall-5
41Wheat-18
42Playball-35
49B-239
91Conlon/Sport-306
W711/1
W711/2
McCormick, Glenn
90Bend/Legoe-17
90Madison/ProC-2277
McCormick, Harry
(Moose)
E254
T204
T206
McCormick, Jim
N172
N284
McCormick, John
89AppFx/ProC-873
90BBCity/Star-16
91BBCity/ClBest-10
91BBCity/ProC-1397
McCormick, Michael J.
(Kid or Dude)
90Target-501
McCormick, Mike F.
58SFCallB-15
58T-37
59T-148
60MacGregor-15
60T-530
61P-141
61T-305
61T-383M
61T-45LL
61T/St-81
62J-139
62P-139
62P/Can-139
62Salada-134
62Shirriff-134
62T-107
62T-319IA
62T-56LL
62T/St-200
62T/bucks
63T-563
64T-487
65T-343
66OPC-118
66T-118
67CokeCap/Giant-12
67OPC-86
67T-86
68Bz-12
68CokeCap/Giant-12
68Dexter-53
68OPC-9LL
68T-400
68T-9LL
68T/ActionSt-15AM
68T/ActionSt-2AM
68T/G-17
69MB-180
69MLB/St-205
69T-517
70MLB/St-130
70OPC-337
70T-337
71MLB/St-494
71OPC-438

71T-438
72MB-220
72T-682
79TCMA-245
84Mother/Giants-16
88Pac/Leg-67
91Crown/Orio-287
92Yank/WIZ70-108
McCormick, Mike
79ArkTr-14TR
80ArkTr-24TR
McCormick, Myron W.
(Mike)
41DP-116
49B-146
49Eureka-41
52Mother-57
90Target-1022
W711/2
McCormick, William J.
E107
McCosky, W. Barney
40PlayBall-201
41DP-53
41PlayBall-36
41Wheat-20
42Playball-14
48B-25
48L-63
49B-203
51B-84
52T-300
81Tiger/Detroit-114
Exh47
McCovey, Willie
60NuCard-67
60T-316
60T-554AS
61P-147
61T-517
61T/St-82
62J-131
62P-131
62P/Can-131
62Salada-142
62Shirriff-142
62T-544
63J-112
63P-112
63T-490
64Bz-21
64T-350
64T-41M
64T-9LL
64T/Coins-22
64T/SU
64T/St-94
64Wheat/St-31
65OPC-176
65T-176
66Bz-14
66T-217LL
66T-550
66T/RO-26
66T/RO-64
67Bz-14
67CokeCap/Giant-11
67OPC/PI-32
67T-423M
67T-480
67T/PI-32
68Bz-13
68CokeCap/Giant-11
68OPC-5LL
68T-290
68T-5LL
68T/ActionSt-7A
69Citgo-19
69MB-181
69MLB/St-206
69MLBPA/Pin-54
69OPC-4LL
69OPC-6LL
69OPC/DE-13
69T-416AS
69T-440
69T-4LL
69T-572M
69T-6LL
69T/DE-31
69T/S-66
69T/St-109
69T/decal
69Trans-36
70K-4
70MB-16
70MLB/St-131
70OPC-250
70OPC-450AS
70OPC-63LL
70OPC-65LL
70T-250
70T-450AS
70T-63LL
70T-65LL
70T/PI-7
70T/S-13
70T/Super-13
70Trans-2
71Bz
71Bz/Test-4
71K-33
71MD
71MLB/St-258
71OPC-50
71T-50
71T/Coins-57
71T/GM-52
71T/Greatest-52
71T/S-46
71T/Super-46
71T/tatt-13
71T/tatt-13a
71Ticket/Giant-8
72Dimanche*-61
72K-7
72MB-221
72OPC-280
72ProStars/PostC-19
72T-280
72T/Cloth-23
72T/Post-24
73OPC-410
73T-410
73T/Comics-11
73T/Lids-29
73T/PinUps-11
74Laugh/ASG-69
74McDon
74OPC-250
74T-250
74T/DE-28
74T/St-97
75Ho-19
75Ho/Twink-19
75OPC-207MVP
75OPC-450
75T-207MVP
75T-450
75T/M-207MVP
75T/M-450
76Ho-124
76OPC-520
76T-520
77Galasso-263
77T-547
78Ho-73
78K-23
78OPC-185
78OPC-238RB
78T-34
78T-3MVP
79K-17
79OPC-107
79Pol/Giants-44
79T-215
80Laugh/3/4/5-30
80OPC-176
80Perez/HOF-196
80Pol/Giants-44
80T-335
81F-434
82KMart-16
83MLBPA/Pin-28
84Mother/Giants-2
85CircK-8
85T/Gloss22-11
86D/HL-34
86Sf/Dec-48M
87Leaf/SpecOlym-H11
89HOF/St-4
89Kenner/BBGr-13
89Padre/Mag-4
89T/LJN-113
90MSA/AGFA-20
90Perez/GreatMom-22
92Ziploc-7
93AP/ASG-123
93AP/ASG24K-57G
93YooHoo-9
PM10/Sm-122
WG10-39
WG9-38
McCoy, Benjamin
41DP-130
McCoy, Brent
88Pulaski/ProC-1762
89Pulaski/ProC-1894
90A&AASingle/ProC-130
90BurlB/Best-27
90BurlB/ProC-2358
90BurlB/Star-18
90Foil/Best-59
90MidwLgAS/GS-42
90Star/ISingl-57
91Durham/ClBest-23
91Durham/ProC-1556
McCoy, Kevin
80BurlB-2
81BurlB-3
83ElPaso-20
McCoy, Larry
88TM/Umpire-10
89TM/Umpire-8
90TM/Umpire-8
McCoy, Timothy
(Tim)
86Cram/NWL-13
86Everett/Pop-15
88Shrev/ProC-1300
89PalmSp/Cal-57
89PalmSp/ProC-468
90Modesto/Cal-156
90Modesto/Chong-20
90Modesto/ProC-2208
91AAA/LineD-541
91Tacoma/LineD-541
McCoy, Trey
88Butte-18
89Gaston/ProC-1012
89Gaston/Star-12
89SALAS/GS-28
89Star/IISingl-138
90CharlR/Star-13
91AA/LineD-587
91Tulsa/LineD-587
91Tulsa/ProC-2781
91Tulsa/Team-17
92Tulsa/ProC-2702
92Tulsa/SB-611
94ClBest/Gold-182
94FExcel-136
94FExcel/LL-13
McCracken, Quinton
92Bend/ClBest-18
93B-260
93StCl/Rookie-2
93T-451M
93T/Gold-451M
94FExcel-185
McCrary, Arnold
77Ashvl
78Ashvl
79Wausau-23
80Wausau-22
McCrary, Sam
86Jacks/TCM-23TR
87Jacks/Feder-13
88Tidew/CANDL-1TR
88Tidew/ProC-1580
89Tidew/CMC-28
McCraw, Tom
64T-283
65T-586
66OPC-141
66T-141
67CokeCap/WSox-11
67OPC-29
67T-29
68T-413
69MB-182
69MLB/St-33
69T-388
70MLB/St-189
70T-561
71OPC-373
71Pol/SenP-8
71T-373
72MB-222
72T-767
73OPC-86
73T-86
74OPC-449
74T-449
75OPC-482
75T-482
75T/M-482
81TCMA-353
82BK/Indians-5CO
82BK/Indians-6CO
82BK/Indians-7CO
82Wheat/Ind
89French-40
92Mets/Kahn-27CO
McCray, Eric
89Gaston/ProC-1008
89Gaston/Star-13
90ProC/Singl-766
90Tulsa/ProC-1151
90Tulsa/Team-17
91B-281
91Tulsa/Team-18
McCray, Justin
90Ashvl/ProC-2756
91Saraso/ClBest-17
91Saraso/ProC-1119
McCray, Rodney
(Rod)
86CharRain-16
89Saraso/Star-14
90BirmB/Best-12
90BirmB/ProC-1119
90Foil/Best-204
91AAA/LineD-641
91OPC-523
91S-763RP
91T-523
91T/90Debut-103
91Vanco/LineD-641
91Vanco/ProC-1607
92S-517
92StCl-829
McCray, Todd
90Boise/ProC-3307
91Reno/Cal-18
McCreadie, Brant
89LittleSun-16
91Salinas/ClBest-8
91Salinas/ProC-2239
McCready, Jim
92ColumMet/ClBest-22
92ColumMet/ProC-292
92ColumMet/SAL/II-16
93StLucie/ProC-2919
McCreary, Bob
88CapeCod/Sum-82
89Elizab/Star-17
90Visalia/Cal-69
90Visalia/ProC-2163
91AA/LineD-488
91ClBest/Singl-308
91OrlanSR/LineD-488
91OrlanSR/ProC-1859
92AS/Cal-33
92OrlanSR/ProC-2846
92Visalia/ProC-1011
McCreedie, Judge
90Target-502
McCreery, Tom
90Target-503
McCubbin, Shane
93BurlB/ClBest-13
93BurlB/ProC-161
McCue, Deron
85Fresno/Pol-9
86Shrev-17
87Shrev-19
88Phoenix/CMC-23
88Phoenix/ProC-58
90Everett/ProC-3145MG
91Clinton/ClBest-28CO
91Clinton/ProC-852CO
McCulla, Harry
82Spring/Frit-22
83Spring/Frit-17
84Savan-16
85Spring-17
86ArkTr-14
90SpringDG/Best-3
McCullers, Lance
85Cram/PCL-109
86D-41RR
86F-330
86Sf/Rook-8
86T-44
87Bohem-41
87Classic-80
87D-237
87F-424
87F/Mini-68
87F/St-76
87OPC-71
87Sf/TPrev-16M
87T-559
87T/St-111
88Coke/Padres-41
88D-451
88D/Best-210
88F-592
88F/Mini-114
88OPC-197
88Panini/St-399
88S-150
88Sf-85
88Smok/Padres-18
88T-197
88T/Big-38
88T/St-114
89B-168
89D-129
89D/Best-220
89D/Tr-13
89F-312
89OPC-307
89S-158
89S/NWest-14
89S/Tr-63
89S/YS/II-19
89Sf-76
89T-307
89T/St-108
89T/Tr-77T
89UD-382
89UD/Ext-710
90D-433
90F-448
90F/Can-448
90Leaf-456
90OPC-259
90PublInt/St-541
90S-186
90T-259
90T/TVYank-13
90UD-615
91D-133
91F-342
91S-313
91UD-203
92OkCty/SB-315
92Yank/WIZ80-115
93Calgary/ProC-1163
93Rang/Keeb-254
McCullock, Alec
84BuffB-10
McCullough, Clyde
47TipTop
49B-163
49Eureka-166
50B-124
51B-94
52B-99
52T-218
55B-280
61Peters-21
72T/Test-8
McCune, Gary
83Knoxvl-22GM
88Knoxvl/Best-21GM
89Knoxvl/ProC-1121GM
McCurdy, Harry
28Exh-40
31Exh/4-12
33G-170
94Conlon-1242
McCurine, Jim
92Negro/RetortII-26
McCurry, Jeff
92Augusta/ClBest-17
92Augusta/ProC-235
92UD/ML-207
94FExcel-253
McCutcheon, Greg
88StCath/ProC-2020
89StCath/ProC-2094
90Erie/Star-15
McCutcheon, James
87Gaston/ProC-21
88Gaston/ProC-1004
89Gaston/ProC-1011
89Gaston/Star-14

McDaniel, Booker T.
(Cannonball)
87Negro/Dixon-40
McDaniel, Jim
59T-134
McDaniel, Joey
93Lipscomb-17
McDaniel, Lindy
57T-79
58T-180
59T-479
60T-195
61P-175
61T-266
61T-75M
61T/St-91
62J-163
62P-163
62P/Can-163
62Salada-144
62Shirriff-144
62T-306M
62T-522
62T/St-187
63J-167
63P-167
63T-329
64T-510
65OPC-244
65T-244
66T-496
67CokeCap/Giant-16
67OPC-46
67T-46
68CokeCap/Giant-16
68T-545
69MB-183
69OPC-191
69T-191
69T/4in1-10M
70OPC-493
70T-493
71MLB/St-495
71OPC-303
71T-303
72MB-223
72OPC-513
72T-513
73OPC-46
73Syrac/Team-16
73T-46
74OPC-182
74T-182
74T/Tr-182T
75OPC-652
75T-652
75T/M-652
79TCMA-280
84Cub/Uno-9M
92Yank/WIZ60-80
92Yank/WIZ70-109
Exh47
McDaniel, M. Von
58T-65
89Smok/Ast-21
McDaniel, Terry
88Clmbia/GS-22
89StLucie/Star-16
90Jacks/GS-27
90T/TVMets-50
90TexLgAS/GS-28
91Tidew/ProC-2524
92F-511
92S-765
92T/91Debut-121
92T/Gold-527
92T/GoldWin-527
McDarrah, Fred
75T/Photo-52
McDavid, Ray
91CharRain/ClBest-21
91CharRain/ProC-107
92AS/Cal-29
92ClBest-131
92HighD/ClBest-9
92UD/ML-256
92UD/ML-64DS
92UD/POY-PY16
93B-26
93B-359FOIL
93ClBest/MLG-58
93UD-438TP
93UD/SP-170
94B-260
94FExcel-285
94SigRook-43
94SigRook/Hot-6
94T-152
94T/Gold-152
94Ultra-582
McDermott, Maurice
(Mickey)
50B-97
50Drake-31
51B-16
51T/RB-43
52B-25
52T-119
53B/Col-35
53Briggs
53NB
53T-55
54B-56
55B-165
56T-340
57T-318
79TCMA-207
91T/Arc53-55
McDermott, Randall
92GulfCY/ProC-3789
McDermott, Terry
74Albuq/Team-10
75Albuq/Caruso-7
90Target-1023
McDevitt, Danny
58T-357
59T-364
60BB-3
60L-50
60T-333
61T-349
62T-493
90Target-504
92Yank/WIZ60-81
McDevitt, Terry
86Cram/NWL-170
87CharRain-12
88River/Cal-224
88River/ProC-1430
89Watlo/Star-31
90Clearw/Star-14
McDill, Allen
92GulfCM/ProC-3477
92Kingspt/ClBest-12
92Kingspt/ProC-1528
McDonald, Ben
87Anchora-20
89Star/IISingl-200
90A&AASingle/ProC-2
90AAASingl/ProC-456
90B-243
90Bz-10
90Classic-130
90D-32RR
90D/BestAL-114
90D/Preview-2
90D/Rook-30
90F-180
90F/Can-180
90Foil/Best-7
90Hagers/Best-1
90Hagers/ProC-1408
90Kenner/Fig-54
90LSUGreat-7
90Leaf-249
90OPC-774
90Panini/St-373
90ProC/Singl-302
90RochR/CMC-1
90RochR/ProC-699
90Rochester/L&U-3
90S-680DC
90S/100Ris-93
90S/YS/II-2
90Star/ISingl-28
90T-774FDP
90T/89Debut-78
90T/Big-228
90T/Tr-70T
90UD-54
91B-86
91Classic/200-132
91Classic/I-14
91CollAB-9
91Crown/Orio-288
91D-485
91F-481
91Kenner-39
91KingB/Discs-4
91Leaf-117
91Leaf/Stud-6
91MajorLg/Pins-31
91OPC-497
91Panini/FrSt-247
91Panini/St-197
91RedFoley/St-109
91S-645
91S/100RisSt-50
91Seven/3DCoin-8A
91StCl-264
91Sunflower-17
91T-497
91T/CJMini/II-6
91T/JumboR-18
91T/SU-25
91ToysRUs-17
91UD-446
91Ultra-19
92B-359
92Classic/Game200-59
92D-436
92F-14
92L-145
92L/BlkGold-145
92OPC-540
92Pinn-44
92Pinn/Team2000-41
92S-658
92S/100SS-94
92S/Impact-81
92StCl-490
92Studio-126
92T-540
92T/DQ-10
92T/Gold-540
92T/GoldWin-540
92T/Kids-64
92TripleP-105
92UD-163
92UD-93TC
92UD/CollHolo-CP3
92Ultra-303
93B-437
93Classic/GameI-60
93D-249
93F-169
93Flair-152
93L-1
93MilkBone-14
93OPC-254
93Pac/Spanish-20
93Panini-68
93Pinn-72
93S-202
93Select-224
93StCl-259
93StCl/1stDay-259
93T-218
93T/Finest-65
93T/FinestRef-65
93T/Gold-218
93TripleP-145
93UD-276
93UD/FunPack-133
93UD/SP-158
93Ultra-142
94B-459
94D-158
94F-8
94Flair-4
94L-127
94OPC-122
94Pac/Cr-35
94Pinn-184
94Pinn/Artist-184
94Pinn/Museum-184
94S-111
94S/GoldR-111
94Select-117
94Sf/2000-11
94StCl-413
94StCl/1stDay-413
94StCl/Gold-413
94StCl/Team-284
94Studio-124
94T-636
94T/Finest-161
94T/FinestRef-161
94T/Gold-636
94TripleP-155
94UD-456
94UD/CollC-195
94UD/CollC/Gold-195
94UD/CollC/Silv-195
94UD/SP-123
94Ultra-3
McDonald, Chad
91WPalmB/ClBest-22
91WPalmB/ProC-1237
92Harris/ProC-468
92Harris/SB-292
McDonald, Dave
91SanBern/ClBest-9
91SanBern/ProC-1985
McDonald, David B.
70OPC-189R
70T-189R
92Yank/WIZ60-82
McDonald, Ed
T207
McDonald, George
45Centen-17
McDonald, James
86James-16
McDonald, Jason
91T/Tr-75T
92StCl/Dome-113
McDonald, Jeff
84Chatt-28
86Chatt-18
McDonald, Jerry
77Salem
79BuffB/TCMA-6
80Port-4
McDonald, Jim 1
78DaytB
79WHave-10
80Colum-11
83ColumAst-15
McDonald, Jim 2
86AZ/Pol-10
McDonald, Jimmie LeRoy
55B-77
55Esskay
91Crown/Orio-289
McDonald, Kevin
90Helena/SportP-5
91SLCity/ProC-3207
91SLCity/SportP-5
92WPalmB/ClBest-8
92WPalmB/ProC-2086
93WPalmB/ClBest-15
93WPalmB/ProC-1336
McDonald, Kirk
86Madis/Pol-14
88Huntsvl/BK-11
89Modesto/Cal-274
89Modesto/Chong-13
McDonald, Manny
81OkCty/TCMA-12
McDonald, Mark
(Mac)
82Madis/Frit-29
McDonald, Michael
(Mike)
86Cram/NWL-103
87Wausau-20
88MidwLAS/GS-55
88Wausau/GS-11
89Everett/Star-20
89SanBern/Best-22
89SanBern/Cal-87
90Foil/Best-226
90ProC/Singl-794
90Wmsprt/Best-15
90Wmsprt/ProC-1069
90Wmsprt/Star-16
91AA/LineD-338
91Jaxvl/LineD-338
91Jaxvl/ProC-162
92Jacks/ProC-3720
92Jaxvl/SB-364
92Sky/AASingl-156
McDonald, Rob
91MissSt-54M
92MissSt-49M
McDonald, Rod
82Watlo/B-7
82Watlo/Frit-8
83BuffB-5
McDonald, Russ
83Tacom-7
McDonald, Rusty
78Clinton
McDonald, Shelby
88Spartan/ProC-1030
88Spartan/Star-14
89Clearw/Star-16
90Clearw/Star-15
McDonald, T.J.
84Everett/Cram-22B
86Fresno/Smok-24
87Shrev-18
88Shrev/ProC-1302
89SanJose/Best-25
89SanJose/Cal-224
89SanJose/ProC-436
89SanJose/Star-19
McDonald, Tony
82OkCty-15
82Reading-21
McDonald, Webster
78Laugh/Black-10
94TedW-108
McDonough, Brian
82Miami-4
83SanJose-5
McDougal, John
90Target-1024
McDougal, Julius
86WinSalem-15
87Portl-12
88EastLAS/ProC-9
88GlenF/ProC-919
89Canton/Best-2
89Canton/ProC-1321
89Canton/Star-15
90NewBrit/Best-3
90NewBrit/ProC-1326
90NewBrit/Star-10
90Pawtu/CMC-16
90ProC/Singl-267
90T/TVRSox-53
91AAA/LineD-503
91Syrac/LineD-503
91Syrac/MerchB-16
91Syrac/ProC-2486
McDougald, Gil
52B-33
52BR
52Coke
52RM-AL14
52T-372
52TipTop
53B/Col-63
53Briggs
53RM-AL23
53SM
53T-43
54B-97
54Dix
54NYJour
54RH
54RM-AL25
54SM
55B-9
55SM
56T-225
57Swift-9
57T-200
58T-20
59T-237M
59T-345
59YooHoo-5
60MacGregor-16
60T-247
61P-10
79TCMA-155
90Pac/Legend-94
91T/Arc53-43
92AP/ASG-33
92Yank/WIZ60-83
92Yank/WIZAS-47
93UD/ATH-93
Exh47
PM10/L-27
PM10/Sm-123
McDowell, Jack
88Coke/WS-16
88D-47RR
88D/Rook-40
88F-407
88F/Hottest-25
88F/Mini-16
88Leaf-47RR
88S/Tr-85T
88T/Tr-68T
89B-61
89D-531
89F-504

89OPC-143
89Panini/St-302
89S-289
89T-486
89T/St-302
89ToysRUs-20
89UD-530
89Vanco/ProC-577
90B-305
90Coke/WSox-17
90T/Tr-71T
90UD-625
91B-352
91Classic/III-66
91D-57
91F-129
91Kodak/WSox-29
91Kodak/WSox-x
91Leaf-340
91Leaf/Stud-36
91OPC-219
91S-27
91StCl-87
91T-219
91UD-323
91USPlayC/AS-3H
91Ultra-78
92B-371
92B-605FOIL
92CJ/DII-36
92Classic/II-T82
92D-352
92F-89
92F/Smoke-S2
92L-422
92L/BlkGold-422
92OPC-11
92Pinn-107
92Pinn-291SIDE
92Pinn-607GRIP
92S-62
92S/100SS-22
92S/Impact-73
92StCl-52
92StCl/Dome-114
92T-11
92T/Gold-11
92T/GoldWin-11
92TripleP-129
92UD-553
92UD/TmMVPHolo-34
92Ultra-40
92Ultra/AS-10
92WSox-29
93B-527
93Classic/Gamel-61
93D-433
93Duracel/PPII-20
93F-207
93F/ASAL-12
93F/Fruit-44
93Flair-188
93Ho-31
93Kenner/Fig-22
93L-400
93MSA/Ben-10
93MSA/Metz-15
93OPC-264
93Pac/Spanish-73
93Panini-134
93Pinn-80
93S-70
93Select-196
93Select/Ace-3
93Select/StatL-61
93Select/StatL-86
93StCl-75
93StCl/1stDay-75
93StCl/MurphyS-157
93StCl/WSox-18
93Studio-200
93T-344
93T/BlkGold-38
93T/Finest-172
93T/FinestRef-172
93T/Gold-344
93T/Hill-5
93TripleP-158
93UD-357
93UD/FunPack-200
93UD/SP-258
93Ultra-176
93WSox-20
94B-455
94D-20
94D/AwardWin-7CY
94D/Elite-47
94D/Special-20
94F-708M
94F-89
94F/AS-15
94F/AwardWin-3
94F/LL-5
94F/ProV-7
94Finest-226
94KingB-3
94L-125
94L/GoldS-15
94OPC-173
94OPC/JAS-14
94Oscar-8
94P-7
94Pac/Cr-134
94Pac/Cr-657CY
94Panini-50
94Panini-8
94Pinn-57
94Pinn/Artist-57
94Pinn/Museum-57
94Pinn/TeamP-9M
94RedFoley-25M
94S-6
94S-633AL CY CY
94S/GoldR-6
94S/GoldS-39
94S/HobSam-6
94S/Pr-6
94S/Tomb-22
94Select-97
94Sf/2000-184AS
94Sf/2000-92
94StCl-24
94StCl/1stDay-24
94StCl/Gold-24
94StCl/Team-122
94Studio-207
94T-392AS
94T-515
94T/BlkGold-12
94T/Gold-392AS
94T/Gold-515
94TripleP-267
94TripleP/Medal-13
94UD-395
94UD/CollC-306TP
94UD/CollC-309TP
94UD/CollC/Gold-306TP
94UD/CollC/Gold-309TP
94UD/CollC/Silv-306TP
94UD/CollC/Silv-309TP
94UD/SP-192
94Ultra-340
94Ultra/AS-10
94Ultra/AwardWin-22POY
94Ultra/LL-4

McDowell, Michael
(Mike)
89AubAs/ProC-2173
90Ashvl/ProC-2743
91BurlAs/ClBest-7
91BurlAs/ProC-2798

McDowell, Oddibe
85D/HL-24
85F/Up-U80
85OKCty-18
85Rang-0
85T-400OLY
85T/Tr-82T
86D-56
86F-566
86F/LL-23
86F/LimEd-28
86F/Mini-111
86F/St-73
86KayBee-20
86Leaf-46
86OPC-192
86OPC/WaxBox-K
86Rang-0
86Seven/Coin-S9M
86Sf-160
86T-480
86T/Gloss60-1
86T/St-237
86T/St-307
86T/Tatt-20M
86T/WaxBox-K
87Classic/Up-115
87D-161
87D/AwardWin-7CY
87D/OD-177
87F-130
87F/Lim-27
87F/St-77
87Leaf-51
87Mother/Rang-4
87OPC-95
87RedFoley/St-78
87Sf-131
87Sf/TPrev-1M
87Smok/R-16
87T-95
87T/St-243
88D-382
88F-473
88F/St-66
88Leaf-154
88Mother/R-4
88OPC-234
88Panini/St-208
88S-215
88S/YS/II-27
88Sf-175
88Smok/R-5
88T-617
88T/Big-198
88T/St-237
89B-90
89Brave/Dubuq-17
89D-378
89D/Tr-49
89F-528
89OPC-183
89Panini/St-456
89S-59
89S/Tr-72T
89T-183
89T/Big-245
89T/LJN-123
89T/Tr-78T
89UD-333
89UD/Ext-796
90B-13
90Brave/Dubuq/Perf-19
90Brave/Dubuq/Singl-22
90D-340
90D/BestNL-100
90F-589
90F/Can-589
90Leaf-112
90OPC-329
90Panini/St-221
90PublInt/St-563
90S-476
90Sf-207
90T-329
90T/Big-148
90T/St-32
90UD-145
91D-450
91F-697
91OPC-533
91RedFoley/St-62
91RochR/ProC-1915
91S-121
91T-533
91UD-497
91Ultra-8
92Edmon/SB-163
93Rang/Keeb-255

McDowell, Roger
85F/Up-U81
85T/Tr-83T
86D-629
86F-89
86KayBee-21
86Leaf-248
86OPC-139
86Seven/Coin-E15M
86Sf-161
86T-547
86T/Gloss60-39
86T/Mets/Fan-7
86T/St-103
86T/St-312
86T/Tatt-20M
87Classic-76
87D-241
87F-16
87F/AwardWin-25
87Leaf-49
87OPC-185
87Sf-160
87Smok/NL-6
87T-185
87T/Gloss60-8
87T/Mets/Fan-4
87T/St-104
88D-651
88D/Best-126
88D/Mets/Bk-651
88F-142
88F/BB/AS-24
88F/Mini-96
88F/St-105
88Kahn/Mets-42
88Leaf-243
88OPC-355
88S-188
88Sf-42
88T-355
88T/Big-101
88T/Mets/Fan-42
88T/Mini-62
88T/St-100
89D-265
89D/Best-16
89F-43
89F/Up-110
89OPC-296
89Panini/St-132
89Phill/TastyK-43
89S-281
89S/Tr-53
89Sf-79
89T-735
89T/LJN-43
89T/Mets/Fan-42
89T/St-92
89T/Tr-79T
89UD-296
90B-146
90Classic/III-69
90D-251
90D/BestNL-57
90F-567
90F/Can-567
90Leaf-20
90OPC-625
90Panini/St-308
90Phill/TastyK-22
90PublInt/St-140
90S-445
90Sf-75
90T-625
90T/Big-230
90T/St-121
90UD-416
91B-500
91Classic/200-80
91D-166
91F-405
91Leaf-410
91Leaf/Stud-217
91OPC-43
91Panini/FrSt-111
91Phill/Medford-26
91RedFoley/St-63
91S-537
91StCl-506
91T-43
91UD-406
91UD/FinalEd-57F
91Ultra-267
91WIZMets-259
92B-657
92D-750
92F-464
92L-58
92L/BlkGold-58
92Mother/Dodg-22
92OPC-713
92Pinn-445
92Pol/Dodg-31
92S-597
92StCl-804
92T-713
92T/Gold-713
92T/GoldWin-713
92TripleP-80
92UD-484
92Ultra-214
93D-350
93F-451
93Flair-74
93L-537
93Mother/Dodg-25
93Pac/Spanish-501
93Pinn-528
93Pol/Dodg-17
93S-605
93Select-375
93StCl-251
93StCl/1stDay-251
93StCl/Dodg-25
93T-39
93T/Gold-39
93TripleP-263
93UD-250
93Ultra-58
94D-207
94F-517
94Pac/Cr-315
94Pinn-339
94StCl-38
94StCl/1stDay-38
94StCl/Gold-38
94T-296
94T/Gold-296
94UD/CollC-196
94UD/CollC/Gold-196
94UD/CollC/Silv-196

McDowell, Sam
62T-591R
63Sugar-26
63T-317
64T-391
65Kahn
65OPC-76
65T-76
66Bz-17
66Kahn
66T-222LL
66T-226LL
66T-470
66T/RO-65
67Bz-17
67CokeCap/Indian-15
67Kahn
67OPC/PI-8
67T-237LL
67T-295
67T-463M
67T/PI-8
68Kahn
68OPC-115
68OPC-12LL
68T-115
68T-12LL
68T/ActionSt-12CM
69Kahn
69MB-184
69MLB/St-42
69MLBPA/Pin-17
69OPC-11LL
69OPC-7LL
69T-11LL
69T-220
69T-435AS
69T-7LL
69T/S-14
69T/St-166
69T/decal
70K-50
70MB-17
70MLB/St-201
70OPC-469AS
70OPC-72LL
70T-469AS
70T-650
70T-72LL
70T/S-10
70T/Super-10
70Trans-14
71Bz
71Bz/Test-11
71K-37
71MD
71MLB/St-379
71MLB/St-568
71OPC-150
71OPC-71LL
71T-150
71T-71LL
71T/Coins-86
71T/GM-50
71T/Greatest-50
71T/S-16
71T/Super-16
71T/tatt-4
71T/tatt-4a

72K-33
72MB-224
72T-720
73OPC-342KP
73OPC-511
73T-342KP
73T-511
74OPC-550
74Syrac/Team-15
74T-550
75SSPC/18-8
78TCMA-103
89Pac/Leg-155
89Swell-71
92AP/ASG-48
92Yank/WIZ70-110
93UD/ATH-94
94TedW-27
McDowell, Tim
90Salem/Star-10
91Parramatta/Fut-19
91Salem/ClBest-16
91Salem/ProC-946
McElfish, Shawn
90BurlInd/ProC-3007
McElroy, Charles
(Chuck)
87Spartan-5
88Reading/ProC-875
89Reading/Best-1
89Reading/ProC-669
89Reading/Star-18
90B-150
90F-650R
90F/Can-650
90Phill/TastyK-23
90T/89Debut-79
90UD/Ext-706
91Cub/Mara-33
91Cub/Vine-19
91D-709
91D/Rook-49
91F-406
91F/UltraUp-U71
91F/Up-U79
91S-374RP
91S/Rook40-34
91StCl-407
91UD/FinalEd-29F
92Classic/I-60
92Cub/Mara-35
92D-650
92F-388
92L-158
92L/BlkGold-158
92OPC-727
92OPC/Premier-85
92Pinn-329
92S-366
92S/100RisSt-63
92StCl-474
92Studio-16
92T-727
92T/Gold-727
92T/GoldWin-727
92TripleP-245
92UD-220
92USPlayC/Cub-13H
92USPlayC/Cub-8C
92Ultra-470
93D-236
93F-22
93Flair-17
93Pinn-341
93S-389
93StCl-472
93StCl/1stDay-472
93StCl/Cub-18
93T-346
93T/Gold-346
93UD-130
93Ultra-20
94D-639
94F-390
94T-613
94T/Gold-613
94Ultra-163
McElroy, Glen
86Penin-17
87DayBe-26
89BirmB/ProC-116
McElveen, Pryor
90Target-1025
M116
T205
T206
T213brown
McElwain, Tim
85Clovis-26
McEnaney, Will
75OPC-481
75T-481
75T/M-481
76Icee
76OPC-362
76T-362
77Expo/PostC-4
77OPC-50
77T-160
78OPC-81
78T-603
80T-563
91Miami/ClBest-2CO
91Miami/ProC-424CO
McFadden, Leon
69OPC-156R
69T-156R
69T/4in1-2M
70T-672
72MB-225
McFarland, Charles A.
(Chappie)
90Target-505
McFarland, Dustin
85Anchora-19
87Anchora-21
McFarland, Ed
E107
McFarland, Herm
E107
McFarland, Kelly
85Anchora-43
McFarland, Packey
T3/Box-58
McFarland, Steve
85Anchora-20MG
87Anchora-22MG
McFarland, Toby
92Bristol/ClBest-6
92Bristol/ProC-1406
McFarlane, Hemmy
85Newar-6
McFarlane, Orlando
62T-229
64T-509R
66T-569
67T-496
69MB-185
McFarlin, Jason
89Everett/Star-28
90Clinton/Best-13
90Clinton/ProC-2563
90ProC/Singl-845
91CalLgAS-43
91ClBest/Singl-70
91SanJose/ClBest-10
91SanJose/ProC-24
91SanJose/ProC-26M
92ClBest-249
92SanJose/ClBest-15
McFarlin, Terry
91Bakers/Cal-31
91CalLgAS-9
McGaffigan, Andy
79WHave-14
80Nashvl
81Colum-8
82Phoenix
82T-83R
83Mother/Giants-20
83T/Tr-68T
84D-309
84Expo/PostC-19
84F-382
84F/X-78
84Nes/792-31
84Stuart-34
84T-31
84T/Tr-78T
85D-646
85F-540
85T-323
86Expo/Prov/Pan-4
86Expo/Prov/Post-8
86F-181
86F/Up-U74
86Provigo-4
86T-133
86T/Tr-72T
87D-380
87F-326
87GenMills/Book-4M
87Leaf-220
87OPC-351
87T-742
88D-380
88F-190
88OPC-56
88S-366
88T-488
89B-356
89D-338
89F-386
89OPC-278
89S-138
89T-278
89T/Big-315
89T/St-75
89UD-359
90D-574
90F-355
90F/Can-355
90OPC-559
90Omaha/CMC-10
90ProC/Singl-185
90PublInt/St-182
90S-224
90T-559
90UD-597
91AAA/LineD-342
91OPC-671
91Omaha/LineD-342
91Pol/Royal-14
91S-619
91T-671
92Yank/WIZ80-116
McGaha, Mel
60Maple-13CO
62Sugar-18
62T-242MG
65T-391MG
McGann, Dan
90Target-1026
McGann, Dennis
E254
T206
WG3-29
McGann, Don
83Greens-30
84Nashvl-14TR
86Nashvl-17TR
87Toledo-23
88Toledo/ProC-606
89Edmon/ProC-560
McGannon, Paul
81Omaha-3
82Omaha-27
83Omaha-26
McGarity, Jeremy
90Johnson/Star-18
91Savan/ClBest-10
91Savan/ProC-1651
92B-26
92ClBest-280
92StPete/ClBest-16
92StPete/ProC-2025
McGarr, James
N172
McGeachy, John
(Jack)
N172
N284
McGee
10Domino-74
W555
McGee, Brian
91BendB/ClBest-22
91BendB/ProC-3697
92Peoria/ClBest-26
92Peoria/Team-12
McGee, Ron
80Spokane-6
McGee, Tim
86WinHaven-17
87Greens-16
88Lynch/Star-13
88NewBrit/ProC-901
McGee, Tony
89Spokane/SP-5
90River/Best-16
90River/Cal-4
90River/ProC-2611
McGee, Willie D.
79WHave-13
82Louisvl-16
83D-190
83F-15
83F/St-22M
83OPC-49
83OPC/St-147LCS
83OPC/St-326
83T-49
83T/St-147
83T/St-326
84D-353
84D-625M
84D/AAS-2
84F-329
84Nes/792-310
84OPC-310
84Seven-9C
84T-310
84T/St-141
84T/St/Box-8
85D-475
85D/HL-29M
85D/HL-38
85D/HL-52
85F-234
85FunFoodPin-33
85Leaf-125
85OPC-57
85T-757
85T/St-141
85ThomMc/Discs-36
86BK/AP-16
86D-109
86D-3DK
86D-651M
86D/AAS-36
86D/DKsuper-3
86Dorman-15
86Drake-23
86F-42
86F-636M
86F/LL-24
86F/LimEd-29
86F/Mini-9
86F/Slug-22
86F/St-74
86GenMills/Book-4M
86Jiffy-15
86KAS/Disc-20
86Leaf-225M
86Leaf-3DK
86Meadow/Blank-9
86Meadow/Milk-6
86Meadow/Stat-10
86OPC-117
86OPC/WaxBox-L
86Quaker-1
86Schnucks-16
86Seven/Coin-S16
86Sf-176M
86Sf-179M
86Sf-183M
86Sf-184M
86Sf-19
86T-580
86T-707AS
86T/3D-14
86T/Gloss60-9
86T/Mini-63
86T/St-144
86T/St-45
86T/Super-2
86T/Tatt-23M
86T/WaxBox-L
86Woolwth-21
87Classic-31
87D-84
87Drake-9
87F-304
87F/BB-27
87F/Hottest-30
87F/LL-29
87GenMills/Book-5M
87Leaf-113
87OPC-357
87RedFoley/St-86
87Sf-74
87Sf/TPrev-12M
87Smok/Cards-22
87T-440
87T/St-48
88Bz-12
88Classic/Red-173
88D-307
88D/AS-44
88D/Best-131
88F-42
88F/Mini-108
88F/St-118
88F/TL-20
88KayBee-17
88KennerFig-67
88Leaf-103
88OPC-160
88Panini/St-396
88S-40
88Sf-91
88Smok/Card-21
88T-160
88T/Big-79
88T/Gloss60-36
88T/Mini-71
88T/St-55
88T/UK-46
88Woolwth-26WS
89B-442
89Classic-98
89D-161
89D/AS-51
89F-457
89KMart/Lead-12
89KennerFig-90
89Louisvl-27
89OPC-225
89Panini/St-189
89S-88
89S/HotStar-93
89Sf-206
89Smok/Cards-13
89T-640
89T/Big-183
89T/LJN-84
89T/St-36
89UD-621
90B-194
90D-632
90D/BestNL-131
90F-253
90F/Can-253
90KMart/CBatL-14
90Leaf-367
90MLBPA/Pins-33
90OPC-285
90Panini/St-339
90PublInt/St-222
90S-374
90Smok/Card-14
90T-285
90T/Big-158
90T/TVCard-34
90UD-505
91B-640
91Bz-11
91Classic/200-162
91Classic/I-74
91Classic/II-T76
91D-666
91D-BC22
91D/BC-BC22
91F-16
91F/UltraUp-U118
91F/Up-U130
91KingB/Discs-1
91Leaf-360
91Leaf/Stud-256
91Mother/Giant-6
91OPC-380
91OPC/BoxB-I
91OPC/Premier-78
91PG&E-23
91Panini/Top15-1
91RedFoley/St-64
91S-597
91S/100SS-37
91S/RookTr-19T
91SFExam/Giant-10
91StCl-335
91StCl/Charter*-20
91T-380
91T/Tr-76T
91T/WaxBox-I
91UD-584
91UD/Ext-721
91Ultra-325
92B-604
92Card/McDon/Pac-43

92Classic/Game200-42
92D-60
92F-643
92Giant/PGE-28
92KingB-15
92L-47
92L/BlkGold-47
92Mother/Giant-6
92OPC-65
92Panini-217
92Pinn-7
92S-112
92S/100SS-18
92StCl-239
92Sunflower-24
92T-65
92T/Gold-65
92T/GoldWin-65
92T/Kids-61
92TripleP-101
92UD-194
92UD-34
92Ultra-294
93B-196
93D-355
93F-159
93Flair-145
93L-396
93Mother/Giant-8
93OPC-210
93Pac/Spanish-274
93Panini-240
93Pinn-39
93Pinn-490HH
93S-93
93Select-119
93StCl-91
93StCl/1stDay-91
93StCl/Giant-11
93Studio-179
93T-435
93T/Gold-435
93TripleP-227
93UD-281
93UD/SP-114
93Ultra-487
94D-238
94D/DomII-8
94F-696
94L-366
94Pac/Cr-551
94Panini-265
94Pinn-274
94S-70
94S/GoldR-70
94StCl/Team-6
94Studio-86
94T-574
94T/Finest-184
94T/FinestRef-184
94T/Gold-574
94TripleP-107
94UD-258
94UD/ElecD-258
94Ultra-589

McGeehee, Connor
82Buffa-3
83LynnP-21

McGehee, Kevin
90Everett/ProC-3123
91CalLgAS-37
91SanJose/ClBest-18
91SanJose/ProC-7
92B-616
92ClBest-256
92ProC/Tomorrow-351
92Shrev/ProC-3866
92Shrev/SB-587
92Sky/AASingl-259
92UD/ML-227
93FExcel/ML-120
94StCl/Team-281

McGhee, Warren E.
(Ed)
53T-195
54T-215
55T-32
55T/DH-78
91T/Arc53-195
94T/Arc54-215

McGilberry, Randy
77Jaxvl
78SSPC/270-222
79T-707R
80Tidew-25

McGinley, James
C46-2
E254
E270/1
T206

McGinn, Dan
69Fud's-7
69T-646R
70Expo/PostC-3
70Expos/Pins-10
70OPC-364
70T-364
71Expo/ProS-16
71MLB/St-134
71OPC-21
71T-21
72MB-226
72OPC-473
72T-473
73OPC-527
73T-527

McGinn, Mark
92GulfCM/ProC-3478

McGinn, Shaun
90NE-16

McGinness, Steve
89KS*-63

McGinnis
N284

McGinnis, Russ
86Beloit-14
87Beloit-13
89Tacoma/CMC-16
89Tacoma/ProC-1556
90AAASingl/ProC-143
90ProC/Singl-598
90Tacoma/CMC-21
90Tacoma/ProC-96
91AAA/LineD-211
91AAAGame/ProC-18
91Iowa/LineD-211
91Iowa/ProC-1063
92D/Rook-72
92OkCty/SB-316
92Sky/AAASingl-145
93Rang/Keeb-256
93T/Gold-824

McGinnity, Joe
(Iron Man)
50Callahan
50W576-54
61F-126
72F/FFeat-1
72Laugh/GF-6
76Shakey-45
80Perez/HOF-45
80SSPC/HOF
89Smok/Dodg-21
90HOF/St-11
90Target-506
94Conlon-1252
C46-77
E107
E254
E270
E91
T201
T206
WG3-30

McGivney, Tom
79Ashvl/TCMA-3

McGlone, Brian
91AubAS/ClBest-20
91AubAS/ProC-4281
92BurlAs/ClBest-16
92BurlAs/ProC-556

McGlone, John
N172

McGlothen, Lynn
73OPC-114
73T-114
75K-20
75OPC-272
75T-272
75T/M-272
76OPC-478
76SSPC-297
76T-478
77T-47
78T-478
78T-581
79T-323
80T-716
81D-562
81F-302
81T-609
82T-85
92Yank/WIZ80-117

McGlothin, Ezra
(Pat)
52Park-53
90Target-1027
V362-10

McGlothlin, Jim
66T-417R
67OPC-19
67T-19
68Bz-8
68T-493
68T/ActionSt-12AM
69JB
69MB-186
69MLB/St-24
69T-386
69T/St-146
70MLB/St-31
70OPC-132
70T-132
71MLB/St-63
71OPC-556
71T-556
71T/Coins-9
72K-36
72MB-227
72OPC-236
72T-236
73OPC-318
73T-318
74OPC-557
74T-557

McGlynn, Ulysses
T201
T206

McGonnigal, Brett
91Clinton/ClBest-4
91Everett/ClBest-5
91Everett/ProC-3932
92Clinton/ProC-3611
92SanJose/ClBest-24

McGorkle, Robbie
82DayBe-18

McGough, Greg
91Saraso/ClBest-13
91Saraso/ProC-1117
92Salinas/ClBest-14
92Salinas/ProC-3758

McGough, Keith
91Butte/SportP-24
91Gaston/ClBest-9
91Gaston/ProC-2686

McGough, Tom
75OkCty/Team-3
76Wmsprt

McGovern, Phil
T3/Box-70

McGovern, Steve
90Batavia/ProC-3063

McGowan, Bill
80Perez/HOF-213
93Conlon-737UMP
94Conlon-1212UMP

McGowan, Donnie
85Elmira-15
86Greens-14
87WinHaven-5
88WinHaven/Star-12

McGrath
T222

McGrath, Charles
(Chuck)
83Erie-15
84Savan-6
85Spring-20
86StPete-19
87ArkTr-3
89ArkTr/GS-12
89Louisvl-28
90AAASingl/ProC-647
90Denver/CMC-23
90Denver/ProC-622
90ElPaso/GS-21
90ProC/Singl-48

McGraw, Bob
90Target-507

McGraw, Frank E.
(Tug)
65T-533R
66OPC-124
66T-124
67CokeCap/YMet-33
67T-348
68T-236
69T-601
70OPC-26
70T-26
70Trans/M-24
71MLB/St-161
71OPC-618
71T-618
72MB-228
72OPC-163
72OPC-164IA
72T-163
72T-164A
73K-21
73OPC-30
73T-30
74OPC-265
74T-265
74T/St-67
75Ho-149
75OPC-67
75T-67
75T/M-67
76OPC-565
76SSPC-457
76T-565
77BurgChef-165
77OPC-142
77T-164
78SSPC/270-42
78T-446
78Wiffle/Discs-48
79BK/P-10
79OPC-176
79T-345
80BK/P-20
80OPC-346
80T-655
81Coke
81D-273
81F-657
81F-7
81F/St-83
81K-37
81T-40
81T/HT
81T/St-205
81T/St-262
82D-420
82F-251
82F/St-55
82OPC-250
82T-250
83D-371
83F-166
83F/St-22M
83F/St-2M
83OPC-166
83OPC-187SV
83T-510
83T-511SV
83T/Fold-4M
84D-547
84D/Champs-53
84F-42
84Nes/792-709LL
84Nes/792-728
84OPC-161
84Phill/TastyK-24
84T-709LL
84T-728
85F-261
85T-157
88Pac/Leg-96
89Swell-96
91WIZMets-260
92MCI-12
94Mets/69-12
94TedW-58

McGraw, Gary
82Idaho-26

McGraw, Hank
71Richm/Team-14

McGraw, John J.
10Domino-79
11Helmar-132
12Sweet/Pin-118A
12Sweet/Pin-118B
14CJ-69
14Piedmont/St-36
15CJ-69
21Exh-104
28Yueng-42
40PlayBall-235
48Exh/HOF
49Leaf/Prem-6
50W576-55
60Exh/HOF-17
60F-66
61F-60
61GP-23
63Bz/ATG-20
69Bz/Sm
72K/ATG-3
75F/Pion-15
76Shakey-11
77Galasso-215MG
77Galasso-98
77Shakey-2
80Pac/Leg-43
80Perez/HOF-10
80SSPC/HOF
81Conlon-6
83D/HOF-35
86Conlon/1-29
88Conlon/5-20
89HOF/St-89
90BBWit-59
91Conlon/Sport-65
92Conlon/Gold-820
92Conlon/Sport-584
93Conlon-820
93Conlon/MasterCol-7MG
93Conlon/MasterCol-8
93CrackJack-21
93UD/T202-5
94Conlon-1001
BF2-78
D303
D327
D328-113
D329-116
D350/2-114
E101
E104
E105
E106
E107
E121/120
E121/80
E122
E135-113
E210-42
E224
E286
E91
E92
E93
E94
E98
L1-116
M101/4-116
M101/5-114
M116
R332-41
S74-89
S81-91
T202
T205
T206
T207
T213/blue
T216
T3-26
V100
V89-40MG
W501-103
W501-73
W502-42
W514-52
W515-45
W555
W575
WG3-31
WG4-18
WG5-29
WG6-28

McGraw, Tom
90Beloit/Star-14
91AA/LineD-192
91ElPaso/LineD-192
91ElPaso/ProC-2746
92ElPaso/ProC-3917
92Stockton/ProC-32

McGreachery
N172
McGregor, Scott
75OPC-618R
75Syrac/Team-12
75Syrac/Team-9
75T-618R
75T/M-618R
77T-475R
78T-491
79OPC-206
79T-393
80T-237
81D-114
81F-174
81F/St-10
81OPC-65
81T-65
81T/St-37
82D-331
82F-172
82F/St-149
82OPC-246AS
82OPC-316
82T-555AS
82T-617
82T/St-143
82T/StVar-143
83D-483
83F-66
83F/St-24M
83F/St-6M
83OPC-216
83T-745
84D-594
84F-13
84F-646IA
84F/St-64
84Nes/792-260
84OPC-260
84T-260
84T/St-207
85D-413
85F-183
85FunFoodPin-102
85Leaf-72
85OPC-228
85T-550
85T/St-198
86D-291
86F-281
86F/St-75
86Leaf-165
86OPC-110
86T-110
86T/St-230
86T/Tatt-6M
87D-520
87F-475
87French-16
87Leaf-243
87OPC-347
87T-708
88OPC-254
88S-315
88T-419
89Swell-56
91Crown/Orio-290
McGrew, Charley
86Beloit-15
87Stockton-12
88Beloit/GS-7
89Modesto/Cal-284
McGriff, Fred
85Syrac-2
85Syrac-25M
86D-28RR
86Leaf-28RR
86Syrac-18
87D-621
87D/HL-39
87D/OD-38
87D/Rook-31
87F/Up-U75
87Sf/Rook-12
87Sf/TPrev-5M
87T/Tr-74T
87Tor/Fire-20
88D-195
88D/Best-160
88F-118
88Ho/Disc-15
88OPC-395
88RedFoley/St-54
88S-107
88S/YS/II-28
88Sf-168
88T-463
88Tor/Fire-19
88ToysRUs-18
89B-253
89Cadaco-35
89Classic-116
89D-16DK
89D-70
89D/Best-104
89D/DKsuper-16DK
89D/MVP-BC19
89F-240
89F/BBMVP's-27
89F/Heroes-27
89F/LL-26
89F/Superstar-30
89F/WaxBox-C19
89OPC-258
89Panini/St-467
89S-6
89S/HotStar-65
89Sf-14
89T-745
89T/Big-15
89T/Coins-44
89T/Hills-20
89T/Mini-77
89T/St-185
89T/UK-50
89Tor/Fire-19
89UD-572
89UD-671TC
90B-513
90BJ/HoSt-3M
90BJ/HoSt-5M
90Bz-5
90Classic-19
90D-188
90D/BestAL-56
90D/GSlam-9
90F-89
90F/AwardWin-22
90F/BBMVP-24
90F/Can-89
90F/LL-24
90Holsum/Discs-13
90HotPlay/St-26
90KMart/SS-31
90Kenner/Fig-55
90KingB/Discs-13
90Leaf-132
90OPC-295
90OPC-385AS
90Panini/St-170
90PublInt/St-523
90PublInt/St-599
90RedFoley/St-60
90S-271
90S/100St-45
90Sf-13
90T-295
90T-385AS
90T/Big-134
90T/Coins-22
90T/DH-44
90T/Gloss60-55
90T/Mini-43
90T/St-187
90T/TVAS-26
90Tor/BJ-19
90UD-108
90Victory-3
91B-659
91Cadaco-37
91Classic/200-163
91Classic/I-88
91Classic/II-T46
91D-261
91D-389MVP
91F-180
91F/Up-U125
91Leaf-342
91Leaf/Stud-247
91OPC-140
91OPC/Premier-79
91Padre/MagRal-24
91Panini/FrSt-336
91Panini/St-157
91Panini/Top15-16
91Panini/Top15-40
91RedFoley/St-65
91S-404MB
91S-480
91S/100SS-71
91S/RookTr-58T
91Seven/3DCoin-9SC
91StCl-357
91T-140
91T/Tr-77T
91UD-565
91UD/Ext-775
91Ultra-308
92B-650
92CJ/DII-12
92Classic/Game200-149
92Classic/I-61
92Colla/ASG-16
92D-283
92D/DK-DK26
92D/McDon-9
92DennyGS-3
92F-614
92Kenner/Fig-31
92L-274
92L/BlkGold-274
92L/GoldPrev-11
92L/Prev-11
92MooTown-17
92Mother/Padre-4
92OPC-660
92OPC/Premier-166
92Padre/Carl-13
92Panini-232
92Pinn-112
92Pol/Padre-13
92S-7
92S/100SS-65
92S/Impact-56
92S/Proctor-11
92Smok/Padre-19
92StCl-580
92StCl/MemberII-11M
92Studio-106
92Syrac/TallT-5
92T-660
92T/Gold-660
92T/GoldWin-660
92T/Kids-55
92TripleP-87
92UD-33TC
92UD-344
92UD/HRH-HR10
92UD/TWillB-T8
92UD/TmMVPHolo-35
92USPlayC/Ace-5C
92USPlayC/Ace-5H
92Ultra-282
93B-686
93BJ/D/McDon-3
93Brave/LykePerf-18
93Brave/LykeStand-23
93Classic/GameI-62
93Colla/DM-72
93D-390
93D/Elite-19
93D/EliteDom-13
93D/EliteUp-1
93D/LongBall-LL2
93D/Master-4
93D/Spirit-SG12M
93Duracel/PPII-9
93F-143
93F-349RT
93F/ASNL-1
93F/Atlantic-15
93F/Fruit-45
93Flair-8
93Ho-18
93HumDum/Can-48
93Kenner/Fig-23
93L-46
93L/GoldAS-2M
93Mother/Padre-4
93OPC-255
93OPC/Premier/StarP-2
93P-5
93Pac/Spanish-261
93Panini-258
93Pinn-71
93Pinn/HRC-2
93Pinn/Slug-5
93Pinn/TP-4
93S-44
93S-528AS
93Select-19
93Select/ChasS-1
93Select/RookTr-5T
93Select/StatL-28
93Select/StatL-36
93Select/StatL-48
93StCl-510
93StCl-594MC
93StCl/1stDay-510
93StCl/1stDay-594MC
93StCl/MurphyS-78
93Studio-157
93T-30
93T-401
93T/BlkGold-13
93T/Finest-106AS
93T/FinestASJ-106AS
93T/FinestRef-106AS
93T/Gold-30
93T/Gold-401
93T/Tr-88T
93TB/Full-21
93TripleP-95
93TripleP/LL-L4
93TripleP/Nick-10
93UD-474M
93UD-496AW
93UD-577
93UD/Clutch-R15
93UD/FunPack-136GS
93UD/FunPack-139
93UD/FunPackAS-AS1M
93UD/HRH-HR4
93UD/Iooss-WI16
93UD/SP-60
93UD/SPPlat-PP12
93UD/TCr-TC5
93USPlayC/Ace-11C
93Ultra-119
93Ultra/HRK-4
94B-405
94D-342
94D/DomI-3
94D/Pr-8
94D/Special-342
94F-366
94F-706
94F/GoldM-8
94F/Lumber-7
94Finest-224
94Flair-131
94Flair/Hot-4
94KingB-1
94L-345
94L/CleanUp-9
94L/GoldS-14
94L/MVPNL-10
94L/PBroker-8
94OPC-13
94OPC/JAS-13
94Pac/Cr-16
94Pac/Gold-14
94Panini-148
94Pinn-384
94Pinn/Run-26
94RedFoley-34
94S-82
94S/GoldR-82
94S/GoldS-18
94Sf/2000-185AS
94Sf/2000-32
94StCl-180
94StCl-264
94StCl/1stDay-180
94StCl/1stDay-264
94StCl/Gold-180
94StCl/Gold-264
94StCl/Team-47
94Studio-40
94T-384M
94T-565
94T/BlkGold-39
94T/Gold-384M
94T/Gold-565
94TripleP-47
94TripleP/Bomb-6
94TripleP/Medal-4M
94UD-225
94UD/CollC-197
94UD/CollC/Gold-197
94UD/CollC/Silv-197
94UD/ElecD-225
94UD/Mantle-12
94UD/SP-55
94Ultra-154
94Ultra/AS-12
94Ultra/HRK-10
McGriff, Terrence
(Terry)
83Tampa-18
87D-512
88D-556
88F-240
88Kahn/Reds-8
88Nashvl/Team-16
88S-281
88T-644
89Nashvl/Team-15
89T-151
90AAASingl/ProC-548
90Nashvl/CMC-4
90Nashvl/ProC-236
90ProC/Singl-129
91AAA/LineD-615
91Tucson/LineD-615
91Tucson/ProC-2215
93Edmon/ProC-1140
McGuire, Bill
87Chatt/Best-15
88BBAmer-10
88Vermont/ProC-943
89Calgary/CMC-21
89Calgary/ProC-533
89F-553
90AAASingl/ProC-118
90Calgary/CMC-14
90Calgary/ProC-653
90ProC/Singl-441
92Peoria/ClBest-29CO
92Peoria/Team-13
McGuire, James
(Deacon)
90Target-508
E107
E286
M116
N172
N690
WG2-35
McGuire, Mickey
91Crown/Orio-291
McGuire, Mike
87Belling/Team-22
88Wausau/GS-20
89Wausau/GS-1
McGuire, Ryan
94B-559
94FExcel-20
94T-746DP
94T/Gold-746DP
McGuire, Steve
86QuadC-22
87MidldA-26
88MidldA/GS-12
89PalmSp/Cal-54
89QuadC/Best-14
89QuadC/GS-17
McGunnigle, William
90Target-509
N172
McGwire, Mark
82Anchora-1
85T-401OLY
86SLAS-3
87Classic/Up-121
87Classic/Up-150M
87D-46RR
87D/HL-27
87D/HL-40M
87D/HL-46
87D/HL-54
87D/Rook-1
87F/Slug-26
87F/Up-U76
87Leaf-46RR
87Sf/Rook-13
87Sf/TPrev-23M
87T-366
88Bz-13
88ChefBoy-1
88Classic/Blue-212
88Classic/Blue-247M
88Classic/Red-151M
88Classic/Red-153
88Classic/Red-197M
88D-1DK
88D-256
88D-BC23
88D/A's/Bk-256

88D/AS-19
88D/Best-169
88D/DKsuper-1DK
88Drake-6
88F-286
88F-624M
88F-629M
88F-633M
88F/AwardWin-24
88F/BB/AS-25
88F/BB/MVP-23
88F/Excit-26
88F/Head-2
88F/Hottest-26
88F/LL-26
88F/Mini-46
88F/RecSet-25
88F/SS-23
88F/Slug-27
88F/St-56
88F/St-S6M
88F/TL-21
88FanSam-3
88Grenada-77
88KMart-16
88KayBee-18
88KennerFig-68
88KingB/Disc-6
88Leaf-194
88Leaf-1DK
88MSA/Disc-4
88Mother/A's-2
88Mother/McGwire-1
88Mother/McGwire-2
88Mother/McGwire-3
88Mother/McGwire-4
88Nestle-10
88OPC-394
88Panini/St-167
88Panini/St-438
88RedFoley/St-55
88S-5
88S-648M
88S-659HL
88S/YS/I-1
88Sf-100
88Sf-221
88Sf/Gamewin-2
88T-3RB
88T-580
88T/Big-179
88T/Coins-3
88T/Gloss60-39
88T/JumboR-13
88T/Mini-31
88T/Revco-17
88T/RiteAid-23
88T/St-1
88T/St-164
88T/St-309
88T/St/Backs-36
88T/UK-47
88ToysRUs-19
88Woolwth-15
89B-197
89Cadaco-36
89Classic-104
89Classic-4
89Classic/Up/2-190
89D-95
89D/AS-1
89D/Best-43
89D/GrandSlam-7
89D/PopUp-1
89F-17
89F-634M
89F/BBAS-29
89F/BBMVP's-28
89F/Excit-32
89F/Heroes-28
89F/LL-27
89F/Superstar-31
89F/WS-8
89Holsum/Discs-14
89KayBee-21
89KennerFig-91
89KingB/Discs-4
89MSA/Disc-3
89Modesto/Chong-35
89Mother/A's-2
89Mother/McGwire-Set
89Mother/ROY's-2
89Mother/ROY's-4M
89Nissen-14
89OPC-174
89OPC-70
89Panini/St-20
89Panini/St-244AS
89Panini/St-420
89Pep/McGwire-Set
89RedFoley/St-80
89S-3
89S/HotStar-25
89S/Mast-32
89Sf-200
89T-70
89T/Big-34
89T/Coins-45
89T/Crunch-22
89T/DH-12
89T/Gloss22-2
89T/Gloss60-41
89T/HeadsUp-14
89T/LJN-90
89T/Mini-70
89T/St-151
89T/St-172
89T/St/Backs-3
89T/UK-51
89Tacoma/ProC-1537
89Tetley/Discs-3
89UD-300
89Woolwth-27
90B-454
90Classic-59
90Classic/Up-33
90D-185
90D-697AS
90D/BestAL-54
90D/GSlam-4
90F-15
90F-638M
90F/BB-25
90F/BBMVP-25
90F/Can-15
90F/Can-638M
90F/LL-25
90F/WaxBox-C20
90HOF/St-91
90KMart/SS-32
90Kenner/Fig-56
90Leaf-62
90MCA/Disc-15
90MLBPA/Pins-77
90MSA/Soda-2
90Mother/A's-2
90Mother/McGwire-Set
90OPC-690
90OPC/BoxB-I
90Panini/St-132
90Panini/St-204
90Post-12
90PublInt/St-310
90PublInt/St-600
90RedFoley/St-61
90S-385
90S/100St-25
90Sf-141
90Smok/SoCal-10
90Starline/LJS-11
90Starline/LJS-27
90Starline/LJS-9
90T-690
90T/Big-28
90T/DH-45
90T/Gloss22-13
90T/Gloss60-42
90T/HeadsUp-14
90T/Mini-30
90T/St-162AS
90T/St-176
90T/TVAS-1
90T/WaxBox-I
90Tetley/Discs-15
90UD-171
90UD-36TC
90USPlayC/AS-WCM
91B-234
91Cadaco-38
91Classic/200-131
91Classic/I-73
91D-105
91D-56AS
91D-BC9
91D/BC-BC9
91D/GSlam-11
91DennyGS-10
91F-17
91F/ProV-4
91Kenner-40
91Leaf-487
91Leaf/Stud-106
91MSA/Holsum-16
91MajorLg/Pins-39
91Mother/A's-2
91OPC-270
91Panini/FrSt-167
91Panini/FrSt-192
91Panini/St-145
91Panini/Top15-110
91Panini/Top15-14
91Panini/Top15-23
91Post-2
91RedFoley/St-122
91S-324
91S/100SS-39
91SFExam/A's-8
91Seven/3DCoin-9NC
91StCl-399
91Sunflower-18
91T-270A
91T-270B
91T/CJMini/I-27
91T/SU-26
91UD-174
91UD-656HL
91Ultra-251
92B-384
92B-620FOIL
92Classic/Game200-119
92Classic/II-T10
92Colla/ASG-1
92Colla/McGwire-Set
92D-348
92D/Up-U7HL
92F-262
92L-16
92L/BlkGold-16
92L/GoldPrev-32
92Mother/A's-2
92OPC-450
92OPC/Premier-99
92Panini-15
92Pinn-217
92Pinn/Slug-2
92Pol/McGwire-Set
92S-20
92S/100SS-63
92S/Proctor-2
92StCl-475
92Studio-226
92Studio/Prev-17
92T-450
92T/DQ-1
92T/Gold-450
92T/GoldWin-450
92T/Kids-121
92TripleP-231AU
92TripleP-262
92UD-153
92UD/ASFF-32
92Ultra-115
92Ultra/AS-1
93B-161
93BJ/D/McDon-11M
93Cadaco-41
93Classic/Gamel-63
93Classic/Gamel-NNO
93Colla/ASG-23
93Colla/DM-73
93D-479
93D/DK-18
93D/Elite-33
93D/EliteUp-15
93D/LongBall-LL4
93D/MVP-19
93Duracel/PPI-9
93F-296
93F-710RT
93F/Atlantic-16
93F/Fruit-46
93F/TLAL-2
93Flair-261
93JDean/28-22
93Kenner/Fig-24
93Kraft-10
93L-323
93L/GoldAS-11
93MilkBone-4
93Mother/A's-2
93OPC-201
93OPC/Premier/StarP-16
93P-19
93Pac/Jugador-10
93Pac/Spanish-224
93Panini-15
93Pinn-58
93Pinn/Cooper-30
93Pinn/HRC-8
93Pinn/Slug-2
93S-557
93Select-16
93Select/StatL-26
93Select/StatL-43
93StCl-478
93StCl-595MC
93StCl/1stDay-478
93StCl/1stDay-595MC
93StCl/A's-7
93StCl/II/Ins-1M
93StCl/MPhoto-20MC
93StCl/MurphyS-153
93Studio-141
93Studio/Her-4
93Studio/SS-3
93T-100
93T/BlkGold-39
93T/Finest-92AS
93T/FinestASJ-92AS
93T/FinestRef-92AS
93T/Gold-100
93T/HolPrev-100
93TripleP-245LH
93TripleP-68
93TripleP-87
93TripleP/Act-23
93UD-41M
93UD-420M
93UD-493AW
93UD-49M
93UD-566
93UD/Diam-3
93UD/FunPack-17HS
93UD/FunPack-48GS
93UD/FunPack-51
93UD/FunPackAS-AS3
93UD/HRH-HR2
93UD/Iooss-WI3
93UD/OnDeck-D18
93UD/SP-41
93UD/SPPlat-PP13
93UDFutHero-60
93USPlayC/Ace-13C
93Ultra-609
93Ultra/AS-12
93Ultra/HRK-2
94B-192
94D-335
94D/DomI-10
94D/Special-335
94F-268
94F/TL-11
94Flair-94
94L-391
94OPC-74
94Pac/Cr-456
94Panini-110
94Pinn-300
94RedFoley-18
94S-550
94Select-57
94Sf/2000-4
94StCl-358
94StCl/1stDay-358
94StCl/Gold-358
94Studio-4
94T-340
94T/Finest-78
94T/Finest/PreProd-78
94T/FinestRef-78
94T/Gold-340
94TripleP-5
94TripleP/Nick-7
94UD-67
94UD/DColl-W8
94UD/ElecD-67
94UD/HoloFX-27
94UD/Mantle-13
94UD/SP-36
94Ultra-111

McHenry, Austin
E120
V100

McHenry, Vance
80Spokane-9
81Spokane-20
82SLCity-12
85Syrac-23

McHugh, Chip
86Lakeland-13
87GlenF-25

McHugh, Mike
88GreatF-6

McHugh, Scott
87James-4

McHugh, Tom
82CharR-4

McIlwain, W. Stover
60L-114

McInerney, Steve
86GlenF-15TR
87GlenF-7
89Toledo/CMC-24
89Toledo/ProC-762
90ProC/Singl-476TR
90Toledo/CMC-27TR

McInerny, Dan
83SanJose-7

McInnis, Bill
86NewBrit-17
87NewBrit-8
88Pawtu/CMC-12
88Pawtu/ProC-456

McInnis, John
(Stuffy)
14CJ-10
15CJ-10
21Exh-105
21Exh-106
25Exh-29
27Exh-22
28Yueng-60
77Galasso-180M
80Laugh/FFeat-29
88Conlon/5-21
91Conlon/Sport-191
BF2-37
D328-114
D329-117
D350/2-115
E120
E121/120
E121/80
E122
E126-41
E135-114
E210-60
E90/1
M101/4-117
M101/5-115
M116
T222
V100
W501-18
W502-60
W514-20
W575
WG4-19
WG7-29

McIntire, Harry
11Helmar-98
12Sweet/Pin-84
90Target-510
S74-64
WG3-32

McIntire, John Reed
10Domino-81
M116
T202
T205
T206
T207
T3-28

McIntosh, Joe
76OPC-497
76T-497
76T/Tr-497T

McIntosh, Tim
87Beloit-26
88CalLgAS-12
88Stockton/Cal-189
88Stockton/ProC-733
89ElPaso/GS-18
89TexLAS/GS-13
90AAAGame/ProC-24
90AAASingl/ProC-653
90B-394
90Denver/CMC-15
90Denver/ProC-628
90ElPasoATG/Team-24

90F-329
90F/Can-329
90ProC/Singl-40
91AAA/LineD-145
91AAAGame/ProC-10
91B-36
91Classic/I-55
91D-414RR
91Denver/LineD-145
91Denver/ProC-126
91F-589
91Leaf/Stud-71
91OPC-561
91S-347RP
91S/Rook40-35
91StCl-321
91T-561
91T/90Debut-104
91UD-547
91Ultra-177
92B-402
92D/Rook-73
92Pol/Brew-14
92S-469
92S/100RisSt-93
92S/Rook-20
92StCl-477
92Ultra-386
93D-367
93L-78
93Pol/Brew-17
93Select-334
93StCl-502
93StCl/1stDay-502
93T-234
93T/Gold-234
McIntyre, James J.
80ArkTr-12
McIntyre, Joseph
(Joe)
92Batavia/ClBest-19
92Batavia/ProC-3260
McIntyre, Matthew
09Buster/Pin-9
10Domino-82
11Helmar-13
12Sweet/Pin-12A
12Sweet/Pin-12B
E104
E254
E90/1
E95
E97
M116
T202
T204
T205
T206
T207
T213/brown
T3-25
McIver, Jeryl
76Wausau
McIver, Larry
82AubAs-9
McJames, Doc
90Target-1028
McKain, Archie
93Conlon-945
McKamie, Sean
91VeroB/ClBest-22
91VeroB/ProC-783
92VeroB/ClBest-10
92VeroB/ProC-2884
McKay, Alan
85Kingst-7
86Pittsfld-16
McKay, Dave
75IntLgAS/Broder-17
75PCL/AS-17
75Tacoma/KMMO-2
76OPC-592R
76T-592R
77Ho-130
77Ho/Twink-130
77OPC-40
77T-377
79OPC-322
79T-608
81A's/Granny-39
81D-350
81F-592
81T-461
82D-391
82F-100
82T-534
83D-213
83F-526
83T-47
83Tacom-29B
90Mother/A's-27M
91Mother/A's-28CO
92Mother/A's-28M
92Nabisco-12
93Mother/A's-27CO
McKay, Karl
80BurlB-28
81BurlB-26
McKay, Troy
86Jaxvl/TCMA-16
McKean, Edward
N172
McKean, Jim
88TM/Umpire-20
89TM/Umpire-16
90TM/Umpire-15
McKechnie, William B.
(Bill)
16FleischBrd-63
40PlayBall-153
76Rowe-8M
76Shakey-89
77Galasso-213CO
80Pac/Leg-86
80Perez/HOF-88
80SSPC/HOF
82Ohio/HOF-58
89HOF/St-88
91Conlon/Sport-34
92Conlon/Sport-592
93Conlon-831MG
94Conlon-1066MG
T207
V117-25
V355-108
W711/1
W711/2
McKee, Matt
89Ashvl/ProC-940
McKee, Ron
80Ashvl-9GM
88Ashvl/ProC-1077
89Ashvl/ProC-942
McKeel, Walt
92ClBest-389
92LynchRS/ClBest-9
92LynchRS/ProC-2911
McKelvey, Mitch
84PrWill-24
85Nashua-18
86FtMyr-19
86Memphis/GoldT-17
86Memphis/SilverT-17
McKelvie, Ron
83Visalia/Frit-12TR
McKenna, Kit
90Target-1029
McKenna, Sean
90NE-17
McKenzie, Don
81Wausau-10
McKenzie, Doug
83Peoria/Frit-8
85MidldA-7
McKeon, Brian
90A&AASingle/ProC-109
90Foil/Best-264
90Waterlo/Best-11
90Waterlo/ProC-2377
91HighD/ClBest-8
91HighD/ProC-2391
92HighD/ClBest-28
McKeon, Jack
73OPC-593MG
73T-593MG
74T-166MG
75OPC-72MG
75SSPC/18-7MG
75T-72MG
75T/M-72MG
77T-74MG
78T-328MG
84Smok/Padres-17MG
88Coke/Pad-15MG
88T/Tr-69MG
89Coke/Padre-10MG
89Padre/Mag-1MG
89T-624MG
90Coke/Padre-11MG
90OPC-231MG
90Padre/MagUno-25MG
90T-231MG
McKeon, Joel
83AppFx/Frit-5
85BuffB-22
86D/Rook-55
86F/Up-U75
87Coke/WS-25
87F-503
88LasVegas/CMC-4
88LasVegas/ProC-225
88T-409
89Indianap/ProC-1212
89Richm/Bob-16
90Hagers/Best-22
90Hagers/ProC-1409
90Hagers/Star-14
90Rochester/L&U-26
91AA/LineD-238
91Hagers/LineD-238
91Hagers/ProC-2453
McKeon, Kasey
89Bristol/Star-17
89SanDiegoSt/Smok-17
90Fayette/ProC-2411
McKeown, Dan
85Anchora-37bb
McKercher, Tim
88SLCity-24
McKinley, Leif
92Elmira/ClBest-14
92Elmira/ProC-1382
McKinley, Pat
88Virgini/Star-15
McKinley, Tim
88Salem/Star-12
89Harris/ProC-312
89Harris/Star-11
90Miami/II/Star-17
McKinley, W.F.
55B-226UMP
McKinley, William F.
82Ohio/HOF-19
McKinney, C. Rich
(Rich)
71OPC-37
71T-37
72T-619
73OPC-587
73T-587
75Tucson-14
75Tucson/Caruso-11
75Tucson/Team-11
76SSPC-587
76Tucson-22
92Yank/WIZ70-111
McKinney, Charlie
80Cedar-12
McKinney, Greg
81Cedar-25
McKinney, Jay
90MissSt-44M
91MissSt-55M
McKinney, John
85Bend/Cram-16
McKinney, Lynn
78Spokane/Cramer-24
78Spokane/Team-21
79Hawaii-2
McKinnis, Bo
88MissSt-39M
89MissSt-45M
McKinnis, Tim
88QuadC/GS-26
McKinnon, Alex
N172
McKinnon, Tom
91ClBest/Singl-426
91Classic/DP-24
91FrRow/DP-41
91Johnson/ClBest-28
91Johnson/ProC-3975
91LitSun/HSPros-16
91LitSun/HSProsG-16
92OPC-96
92ProC/Tomorrow-326
92StCl/Dome-115
92T-96DP
92T/Gold-96
92T/GoldWin-96
McKinzie, Phil
87AppFx-29
McKitrick, Greg
90OK-21
McKnight, Jack
83Knoxvl-5
86Phoenix-16
87Phoenix-14
McKnight, James
62Salada-199
62Shirriff-199
62T-597R
81TCMA-383
82DayBe-21
McKnight, Jeff
86Jacks/TCMA-17
87Jacks/Feder-2
87Tidew-4
87Tidew/TCMA-15
88Tidew/CANDL-16
88Tidew/CMC-19
88Tidew/ProC-1587
89Tidew/CMC-13
89Tidew/ProC-1953
90AAASingl/ProC-467
90ProC/Singl-320
90RochR/CMC-12
90RochR/ProC-710
90Rochester/L&U-7
90T/89Debut-80
90UD-162
91AAA/LineD-460
91Crown/Orio-292
91OPC-319
91RochR/LineD-460
91RochR/ProC-1909
91S-369RP
91T-319
91WIZMets-261
92StCl-633
92Tidew/ProC-
92Tidew/SB-565
93Mets/Kahn-7
93Pac/Spanish-544
94D-634
94F-572
94Pac/Cr-412
94StCl-324
94StCl/1stDay-324
94StCl/Gold-324
94T-331
94T/Gold-331
McKown, Steven
76Cedar
McKoy, Keith
90Spokane/SportP-1
91CharRain/ClBest-22
91CharRain/ProC-108
92Watlo/ClBest-20
92Watlo/ProC-2152
McKune, Jerry
81ArkTr-22
81Louisvl-3
82Louisvl-17
83Louisvl/Riley-3
84Louisvl-3
85Louisvl-4
McLain, Dennis
65OPC-236
65T-236
66T-226LL
66T-540
67Bz-24
67OPC/PI-20
67T-235LL
67T-420
67T/PI-20
68CokeCap/Tiger-15
68OPC-40
68T-40
69Citgo-1
69Kelly/Pin-14
69MB-187
69MLB/St-52
69MLBPA/Pin-18
69OPC-11LL
69OPC-150
69OPC-57CL
69OPC-9LL
69OPC/DE-14
69T-11LL
69T-150
69T-433AS
69T-57CL
69T-9LL
69T/4in1-21M
69T/DE-8
69T/S-17
69T/St-177
69T/decal
69Trans-4
70K-73
70MLB/St-212
70OPC-400
70OPC-467AS
70OPC-70LL
70T-400
70T-467AS
70T-70LL
70T/PI-24
70T/S-17
70T/Super-17
70Trans-11
71MLB/St-546
71MLB/St-569
71OPC-750
71Pol/SenP-9
71T-750
71T/GM-20
71T/Greatest-20
72MB-229
72OPC-210
72T-210
72T-753TR
73OPC-630
73T-630
75OPC-206MVP
75T-206MVP
75T/M-206MVP
77Galasso-239
78TCMA-210
81Tiger/Detroit-15
81Tiger/Detroit-79
81Tiger/Detroit-94
82KMart-13
83Kaline-39M
85West/2-43
86Tiger/Sport-21
88Domino-15
90HOF/St-72
93AP/ASG-154
94TedW-33
94TedW/54-32
McLain, Mike
92Clinton/ProC-3595
92Everett/ClBest-10
92Everett/ProC-1684
McLain, Tim
86Wausau-16
88SanBern/Cal-46
McLane, Larry
82BurlR/Frit-20
82BurlR/TCMA-7
83Tulsa-6
McLaren, John
75Dubuq
83Knoxvl-19
86Tor/Fire-25CO
87Tor/Fire-21CO
88Maine/CMC-6
88Maine/ProC-281
88Tor/Fire-7CO
89Tor/Fire-7CO
90Tor/BJ-7CO
92Reds/Kahn-NNO
93Mother/Mar-28M
McLarnan, John
87Reading-23
90Reading/Best-4
90Reading/ProC-1219
90Reading/Star-20
McLauchlin, Dick
81Albuq/TCMA-26
McLaughlin, Burke
52Park-12
McLaughlin, Byron
78SanJose-17
79T-712R
80T-197
81D-287
81T-344
84Nes/792-442
84T-442
McLaughlin, Colin
82Knoxvl-6
83Syrac-10
85Syrac-15
86Knoxvl-16
87Syrac/TCMA-6
88Syrac/CMC-3

88Syrac/ProC-823
89Calgary/CMC-3
89Calgary/ProC-532
McLaughlin, Dave
83AppFx/Frit-3
McLaughlin, Dick
(Mac)
77Clinton
78Clinton
79Clinton/TCMA-17
82Albuq-26
83Albuq-25
84Cram/PCL-169CO
85Cram/PCL-160CO
86Albuq-15CO
McLaughlin, Joey
78Richm
79Richm-1
80T-384
81D-271
81F-420
81OPC-248
81T-248
82D-507
82F-620
82OPC-376
82OPC/Post-8
82T-739
83D-255
83F-434
83F/St-9M
83OPC-9
83T-9
84D-617
84F-162
84F/X-79
84Nes/792-556
84OPC-11
84Rang-53
84T-556
85T-678
86Tacom-14
87Hawaii-19
93Rang/Keeb-257
McLaughlin, Michael
(Bo)
77T-184
78Charl
78T-437
80Richm-23
80T-326
82T-217
McLaughlin, Mike
88Belling/Legoe-5
McLaughlin, Steve
86AppFx-14TR
McLaughlin, Thomas
N172/ST
McLaughlin, Tom
81Clinton-24
McLaughlin, Wm.
40Hughes-14
McLaurine, William
(Bill)
77Spoka
78Spokane/Cramer-2
78Spokane/Team-2
McLean, Bobby
33SK*-12
McLean, John R.
(Larry)
10Domino-80
11Helmar-117
12Sweet/Pin-103A
12Sweet/Pin-103B
14Piedmont/St-37
E101
E103
E105
E254
E270/2
E300
E90/1
E92
E98
M116
T201
T202
T204
T205
T206
T207
T213/blue
T216
T222
WG5-30
McLemore, Mark
83Peoria/Frit-9
85MidldA-17
86D-35RR
86F-650R
86MidldA-16
87Classic/Up-119
87D-479
87D/OD-8
87D/Rook-7
87F/Up-U77
87Sf/Rook-14
87Smok/Cal-13
87T/Tr-75T
88D-181
88D/Best-251
88F-497
88Leaf-159
88OPC-162
88Panini/St-41
88S-152
88S/YS/II-29
88Smok/Angels-22
88T-162
89D-94
89F-484
89S-208
89T-51TL
89T-547
89T/Big-30
89UD-245
90Smok/Angel-12
90T/Big-310
91Leaf-86
91Mother/Ast-17
92B-446
92L-427
92L/BlkGold-427
92Ultra-304
93D-485
93F-546
93Flair-153
93L-512
93Pac/Spanish-344
93Pinn-184
93T-55
93T/Gold-55
93UD-801
93UD/SP-159
94D-186
94F-9
94Flair-5
94L-36
94Pac/Cr-36
94Pinn-379
94S-415
94Select-80
94StCl-342
94StCl/1stDay-342
94StCl/Gold-342
94StCl/Team-272
94T-379
94T/Finest-115
94T/FinestRef-115
94T/Gold-379
94TripleP-156
94UD-248
94UD/CollC-198
94UD/CollC/Gold-198
94UD/CollC/Silv-198
94UD/ElecD-248
94Ultra-4
McLeod, Bill
63MilSau-4
McLeod, Brian
90Everett/Best-8
90Everett/ProC-3124
91Clinton/ProC-830
92SanJose/ClBest-6
McLeod, Kevin
90Hamil/Best-6
90Hamil/Star-16
McLin, Joe Jr.
91Welland/ClBest-13
91Welland/ProC-3581
McLintock, Ron
87Pocatel/Bon-18
McLish, Cal
49Eureka-64
57T-364
58T-208
59T-445
60Kahn
60T-110
60T/tatt-35
61T-157
62T-453
63T-512
64T-365
69Fud's-8
72Dimanche*-34CO
73OPC-377CO
73T-377CO
74OPC-531CO
74T-531CO
79TCMA-221
81TCMA-411
90Target-511
92Brew/Carlson-NNO
McLish, Tom
78Newar
McLochlin, Mike
91Collnd/ClBest-14
McLoughlin, Tim
86Salem-19
McMahon, David
88MissSt-19
McMahon, Don
58T-147
59T-3
60Lake
60SpicSpan-14
60T-189
61T-278
62T-483
63Pep
63T-395
64T-122
65Kahn
65T-317
66OPC-133
66T-133
67CokeCap/RedSox-7
67OPC-7
67T-7
67T/Test/RSox-10
68T-464
69T-616
70OPC-519
70T-519
71MLB/St-259
71OPC-354
71T-354
71Ticket/Giant-9
72OPC-509
72T-509
73OPC-252CO
73T-252C
74OPC-78CO
74T-78C
80Pol/SFG-47C
83Wheat/Ind-22
85Polar/Ind-xx
88Domino-16
McMahon, Jack
83Visalia/Frit-9
McMahon, Mike
45Parade*-38
McMahon, Pat
88MissSt-20CO
89MissSt-42M
McMahon, Sadie
90Target-1030
McManaman, Steve
80OrlanTw-17
McManus, James M.
(Jim)
61Union
87Richm/TCMA-24
McManus, Martin
(Marty)
25Exh-115
26Exh-115
29Exh/4-23
31Exh/4-23
32Orbit/num-7
32Orbit/un-47
33DL-1
33G-48
34G-80
35G-1J
35G-3A
35G-4A
35G-5A
91Conlon/Sport-189
E120
E210-48
R305
V353-48
V61-41
W572
W573
WG7-30
McMath, Shelton
80Ashvl-27
McMichael, Chuck
81CharR-14
McMichael, Gregory
(Greg)
88Burllnd/ProC-1796
89Canton/Best-24
89Canton/ProC-1315
89Canton/Star-16
90AAASingl/ProC-212
90Canton/Star-11
90ColoSp/CMC-7
90ColoSp/ProC-31
90ProC/Singl-459
91Durham/ProC-DUR7
91DurhamUp/ProC-7
92Greenvl/SB-239
93B-317
93Brave/LykePerf-19
93Brave/LykeStand-24
93F/Final-4
93L-489
93OPC/Premier-127
93Select/RT/ASRook-10
93Select/RookTr-59T
93T/Tr-6T
93UD-652
93Ultra-308
94D-175
94F-367
94F/RookSen-12
94L-207
94OPC/DiamD-14
94Pac/Cr-17
94Pinn-69
94Pinn/Artist-69
94Pinn/Museum-69
94S-551
94StCl-241
94StCl/1stDay-241
94StCl/Gold-241
94StCl/Team-55
94T-81
94T/Finest-3
94T/FinestRef-3
94T/Gold-81
94UD-407
94UD/CollC-199
94UD/CollC/Gold-199
94UD/CollC/Silv-199
94Ultra-155
94Ultra/Second-8
McMillan, Roy
52B-238
52T-137
53B/Col-26
53T-259
54B-12
54RH
54T-120
54Wilson
55Kahn
55T-181
56Kahn
56T-123
56T/Pin-57SS
57Kahn
57Sohio/Reds-14
57T-69
58Kahn
58T-360
59Bz
59Kahn
59T-405
60Bz-33
60Kahn
60T-45
61P-183
61T-465
61T/St-46
62J-148
62P-148
62P/Can-148
62Salada-159
62Shirriff-159
62T-211M
62T-393AS
62T/St-149
63J-150
63P-150
63T-156
64T-238
64T/Coins-148AS
64T/S-8
65OPC-45
65T-45
65T/E-44
66Bz-13
66T-421
67CokeCap/YMet-31
70McDon-4CO
73OPC-257CO
73T-257CO
74OPC-179CO
74T-179C
77Visalia
79TCMA-154
80OrlanTw-22MG
91T/Arc53-259
91WIZMets-262
94T/Arc54-120
McMillan, Stu
90Idaho/ProC-3261
McMillan, Thomas E.
75OkCty/Team-16
77T-490R
78SanJose-18
89Pac/SenLg-40
90EliteSenLg-100
90Target-1032
McMillan, Thomas Law
M116
McMillan, Tim
86PrWill-15
87CharWh-17
88Salem/Star-13
McMillan, Tom
79BuffB/TCMA-15
McMillin, Darrell
90GA-21
92Eugene/ClBest-19
92Eugene/ProC-3043
McMillon, Billy
91T/Tr-78T
92StCl/Dome-116
McMorris, Mark
86WinSalem-16
87WinSalem-1
McMullen, Dale
78Memphis/Team-6
McMullen, Jon
92Classic/DP-116
McMullen, Ken
63T-537R
64T-214
65T-319
66T-401
66T/RO-35
66T/RO-66
67CokeCap/Senator-12
67OPC-47
67T-47
68OPC-116
68T-116
68T/ActionSt-8CM
69MB-188
69MLB/St-106
69T-319
69T/St-239
70MLB/St-284
70OPC-420
70T-420
71MLB/St-350
71OPC-485
71T-485
72MB-230
72T-756
73OPC-196
73T-196
74OPC-434
74T-434
75OPC-473
75T-473
75T/M-473
76OPC-566
76SSPC-80
76T-566
77T-181
81TCMA-338
90Target-512

McMullen, Kevin
91Greens/ProC-3063
McMullen, Rick
82Jacks-15
McMullin, Fred
88Pac/8Men-105
88Pac/8Men-15
94Conlon-1039
McMurray, Brock
88GreatF-16
89Salem/Team-16
90Bakers/Cal-250
91VeroB/ClBest-28
91VeroB/ProC-788
92Bakers/Cal-16
McMurtrie, Dan
86LitFalls-18
87Columbia-24
McMurtry, Craig
82Richm-6
83Pol/Atl-29
83T/Tr-69T
84D-599
84F-184
84F/St-105
84Nes/792-126TL
84Nes/792-543
84OPC-219
84Pol/Atl-29
84T-126TL
84T-543
84T/RD-30
84T/St-384
85D-188
85F-333
85Ho/Braves-15
85Leaf-45
85OPC-362
85Pol/Atl-29
85T-362
85T/RD-31
85T/St-28
86Pol/Atl-29
86T-194
87T-461
87Tor/Fire-22
88OkCty/CMC-4
88OkCty/ProC-44
89D-520
89Mother/R-20
89Smok/R-21
89T-779
90AAASingl/ProC-676
90OPC-294
90OkCty/ProC-430
90T-294
91S-602
92Phoenix/ProC-2818
92Phoenix/SB-389
93Rang/Keeb-258
McNabb, Buck
91ClBest/Singl-441
91Classic/DP-43
91FrRow/DP-42
92BurlAs/ClBest-25
92BurlAs/ProC-558
92MidwLAS/Team-28
92StCl/Dome-117
92UD/ML-328
McNabb, Glenn
89Augusta/ProC-508
89SALAS/GS-6
90Salem/Star-11
McNair, Bob
80Utica-24
McNair, Donald Eric
35BU-61
39PlayBall-105
40PlayBall-14
92Conlon/Sport-477
94Conlon-1144
R303/A
R314
V351B-32
McNair, Fred
92Belling/ClBest-6
92Belling/ProC-1458
93FExcel/ML-228
93River/Cal-11
McNally, Bob
86Sumter/ProC-20
87Sumter-5
McNally, Dave
63T-562R
64T-161
65OPC-249
65T-249
66OPC-193
66T-193
67CokeCap/Orio-1
67T-382
68CokeCap/Orio-1
68Dexter-54
68T-478
69Citgo-2
69MB-189
69MLB/St-5
69OPC-7LL
69OPC-9LL
69T-340
69T-532M
69T-7LL
69T-9LL
69T/S-1
69T/St-126
69T/decal
69Trans-15
70K-14
70MLB/St-151
70OPC-20
70OPC-70LL
70T-20
70T-70LL
71Bz
71Bz/Test-27
71K-59
71MD
71MLB/St-304
71OPC-196ALCS
71OPC-320
71OPC-69LL
71T-196ALCS
71T-320
71T-69LL
71T/Coins-26
71T/S
71T/Super-18
71T/tatt-12
72K-29
72MB-231
72OPC-223WS
72OPC-344KP
72OPC-490
72Pol/Orio-6
72ProStars/PostC-30
72T-223WS
72T-344KP
72T-490
72T/Post-1
73OPC-600
73T-600
74OPC-235
74T-235
74T/St-127
75Ho-150
75OPC-26
75T-26
75T/M-26
78TCMA-270
88Pac/Leg-38
91Crown/Orio-293
93AP/ASG-153
McNally, Mike
E120
E121/120
E121/80
V89-39
W501-33
W575
McNamara, Dennis
(Denny)
90Niagara/Pucko-4
91Lakeland/ClBest-25
91Lakeland/ProC-279
92ClBest-166
92Lakeland/ClBest-8
92Lakeland/ProC-2291
93ClBest/MLG-163
McNamara, James
86Cram/NWL-10
86Everett/Pop-16
87Clinton-9
88SanJose/Cal-123
88SanJose/ProC-133
89Salinas/Cal-145
89Salinas/ProC-1811
91AA/LineD-303
91AA/LineD-312
91Shrev/LineD-312
91Shrev/ProC-1824
92D/Rook-74
92Giant/PGE-29
92L-514
92L/BlkGold-514
92Mother/Giant-20
92Ultra-592
92Ultra/AllRook-5
93Pac/Spanish-275
McNamara, John
70T-706MG
73OPC-252CO
73T-252C
74McDon
74OPC-78CO
74T-78CO
75OPC-146MG
75T-146MG
75T/M-146MG
76SSPC-123MG
76T-331MG
77Padre/SchCd-18MG
77T-134MG
81T-677MG
82D-526MG
83T/Tr-70T
84Nes/792-651MG
84Smok/Cal-19MG
84T-651MG
85T-732MG
85T/Tr-84T
86T-771MG
87T-368MG
88D/AS-10MG
88D/PopUp-10MG
88T-414MG
88T/Gloss22-1MG
90T/Tr-72T
91Indian/McDon-19MG
91OPC-549MG
91T-549
McNamara, Mike
88CapeCod/Sum-85
McNamara, Reggie
33SK*-15
McNamara, Tom
88Belling/Legoe-6
McNamee, Bill
62Pep/Tul
McNaney, Scott
89Watlo/Star-32
McNary, Mike
88CapeCod/Sum-32
McNeal, Clyde
91Negro/Lewis-9
92Negro/Retort-43
McNeal, Paul
86Hagers-10CO
87Hagers-2CO
McNealy, Derwin
83Nashvl-12
85Syrac-29
86Colum-16
86Colum/Pol-14
McNealy, Rusty
82WHave-23
83Tacom-17
86Chatt-19
87SanJose-27
McNeely, Earl
25Exh-127
26Exh-127
91Conlon/Sport-177
McNeely, Jeff
89Elmira/Pucko-30
90Elmira/Pucko-12
90WinHaven/Star-15
91B-113
91CLAS/ProC-CAR23
91ClBest/Singl-169
91Classic/III-67
91LynchRS/ClBest-22
91LynchRS/ProC-1212
91UD/FinalEd-20F
92B-193
92ClBest-198
92D/Rook-75
92NewBrit/ProC-447
92NewBrit/SB-489
92OPC-618M
92ProC/Tomorrow-20
92Sky/AASingl-209
92StCl-577
92T-618R
92T/Gold-618M
92T/GoldWin-618M
92UD/ML-258
93FExcel/ML-134
93Pawtu/Ball-15
94B-175
94D-609
94F/MLP-23
94Pac/Cr-58
94Pinn-231
94Pinn/Artist-231
94Pinn/Museum-231
94Pinn/New-11
94S-646
94S/Boys-33
94Sf/2000-171
94StCl-48
94StCl/1stDay-48
94StCl/Gold-48
94TripleP-285
94UD-21
94UD/CollC-200
94UD/CollC/Gold-200
94UD/CollC/Silv-200
94UD/ElecD-21
McNees, Kevin
87Idaho-8
88Hagers/Star-11
McNell, Johnny
86Columbia-18
McNertney, Gerald
(Jerry)
64T-564R
67CokeCap/WSox-9
68OPC-14
68T-14
69MB-190
69T-534
69T/St-226
70MLB/St-275
70McDon-4
70OPC-158
70T-158
71MLB/St-279
71OPC-286
71T-286
71T/Coins-68
72MB-232
72T-584
79Colum-9
80Colum-22
81Colum-28
82Colum-24M
87Albany-10
87Colum-5
McNickle, Rusty
89MissSt-44M
McNulty, Bill
73OPC-603R
73T-603R
75Sacra/Caruso-6
McNulty, Pat
93Conlon-978
McNutt, Brent
92Lipscomb-18
92Lipscomb-23M
McNutt, Larry
83Lynch-2
McPhail, Lee
83Kaline-54PRES
McPhail, Marlin
86Tidew-18
87BirmB/Best-5
88Vanco/CMC-25
88Vanco/ProC-777
89Vanco/CMC-15
89Vanco/ProC-596
90AAASingl/ProC-179
90ProC/Singl-645
90Vanco/CMC-18
90Vanco/ProC-501
91AAA/LineD-190
91Indianap/LineD-190
91Indianap/ProC-470
92ColumMet/ClBest-28CO
92ColumMet/ProC-313
92ColumMet/SAL/II-3
McPhee, John
(Bid)
N172
McPheeters, Kourtney
87Anchora-35bb
McPherson, Barry
84Savan-3
McPherson, John
86Lipscomb-16
McQuade, James H.
N172/UMP
McQuade, John H.
N172/UMP
McQueen, Mike
70T-621R
71OPC-8
71T-8
72OPC-214
72T-214
McQuillan, George
15CJ-152
D303
E103
E106
E120
E90/1
E96
M116
T206
T213/blue
T216
McQuillan, Hugh
26Exh-37
93Conlon-807
V89-14
W515-33
McQuillen, Carl
52Laval-59
McQuinn, George
39Exh
39PlayBall-122
40PlayBall-53
41G-5
41PlayBall-23
43Playball-17
49B-232
52Laval-1
92Conlon/Sport-391
92Yank/WIZAS-48
McRae, Brian
86Cram/NWL-28
87FtMyr-26
88BBCity/Star-17
89Memphis/Best-13
89Memphis/ProC-1205
89Memphis/Star-17
89Star/Wax-44
90A&AASingle/ProC-50
90Foil/Best-276
90Memphis/Best-13
90Memphis/ProC-1022
90Memphis/Star-18
90ProC/Singl-829
90Star/ISingl-68
91B-292
91Classic/200-157
91Classic/I-49
91Classic/III-68
91D-575
91D/Rook-31
91F-563
91Leaf-235
91Leaf/Stud-68
91OPC-222
91Pol/Royal-15
91S-331RP
91StCl-478
91T-222
91T/90Debut-105
91ToysRUs-18
91UD-543
91Ultra-152
92B-66
92CJ/DI-20
92Classic/Game200-85
92Classic/II-T77
92D-387
92D/DK-DK16
92DennyGS-15
92F-163
92F/RookSIns-9
92Kenner/Fig-32
92L-123
92L/BlkGold-123
92OPC-659
92OPC/Premier-12
92Panini-99
92Pinn-117
92Pinn/Team2000-20
92Pol/Royal-18

92S-478
92StCl-270
92Studio-187
92T-659
92T/Gold-659
92T/GoldWin-659
92T/Kids-108
92TripleP-69
92UD-157
92Ultra-75
93B-589
93B-704FOIL
93Cadaco-42
93Colla/DM-74
93D-411
93F-242
93Flair-221
93Ho-12
93L-58
93OPC-287
93Pac/Spanish-139
93Panini-108
93Pinn-367
93Pol/Royal-19
93S-128
93Select-250
93StCl-33
93StCl/1stDay-33
93StCl/MPhoto-3
93StCl/Royal-25
93Studio-137
93T-49
93T/Gold-49
93TripleP-21
93UD-238
93UD/SP-233
93Ultra-213
94B-115
94Church-1
94D-43
94D/DK-12
94D/Special-43
94F-167
94F/TL-7
94Kraft-7
94L-306
94OPC-245
94Pac/Cr-295
94Panini-78
94Pinn-18
94Pinn/Artist-18
94Pinn/Museum-18
94RedFoley-19
94S-19
94S/Cycle-15M
94S/GoldR-19
94S/GoldS-60
94Select-47
94StCl-520
94StCl/1stDay-520
94StCl/Gold-520
94Studio-188
94T-425
94T/Finest-62
94T/Finest/PreProd-62
94T/FinestRef-62
94T/Gold-425
94TripleP-238
94UD-253
94UD/CollC-201
94UD/CollC/Gold-201
94UD/CollC/Silv-201
94UD/ElecD-253
94UD/SP-175
94Ultra-368

McRae, Hal
68T-384R
70T-683R
71MLB/St-64
71OPC-177
71T-177
72OPC-291
72OPC-292IA
72T-291
72T-292IA
72T/Cloth-24
73OPC-28
73T-28
74OPC-563
74T-563
75Ho-104
75K-53
75OPC-268
75T-268
75T/M-268
76A&P/KC
76Ho-135
76OPC-72
76SSPC-176
76T-72
77BurgChef-72
77Ho-17
77Ho/Twink-17
77K-10
77OPC-215
77T-340
78Ho-6
78K-20
78SSPC/270-219
78T-465
78Wiffle/Discs-49
79Ho-90
79OPC-306
79T-585
80OPC-104
80T-185
81Coke
81D-463
81F-41
81F-653M
81OPC-295
81Pol/Royals-6
81T-295
81T/St-86
82D-196
82F-416
82F/St-210
82OPC-384
82T-625
83D-238
83D/AAS-16
83Drake-17
83F-110
83F/St-16M
83F/St-20M
83F/St-9M
83K-5
83OPC-25
83OPC/St-19
83OPC/St-75
83PermaGr/CC-28
83Pol/Royals-4
83T-25
83T-703LL
83T/St-19
83T/St-75
84D-11DK
84D-297
84D/AAS-25
84D/Champs-17
84F-350
84F/St-44
84Nes/792-340
84Nes/792-96TL
84OPC-340
84T-340
84T-96TL
84T/RD-14M
84T/St-278
84T/St/Box-3
85D-588
85F-207
85FunFoodPin-63
85Leaf-34
85OPC-284
85T-773
85T/RD-12M
85T/St-270
86D-521
86F-14
86Kitty/Disc-4
86Leaf-251
86NatPhoto-11
86OPC-278
86T-415
86T-606M
86T/Tatt-15M
86Woolwth-22
87D-471
87F-375
87OPC-246
87RedFoley/St-59
87Sf/TPrev-13M
87Sf/TPrev-13M
87T-573
88Classic/Blue-235
89Pac/SenLg-133
89T/SenLg-122
89TM/SenLg-76
91T/Tr-79TMG
92Pol/Royal-19MG
92T-519MG
92T/Gold-519MG
92T/GoldWin-519MG
93B-704FOIL
93Pol/Royal-1MG
93T-507MG
93T/Gold-507MG

McRae, Norm
70OPC-207R
70T-207R
71OPC-93R
71T-93R

McReynolds, Kevin
83LasVegas/BHN-15
84D-34RR
84F-307
84Mother/SDP-13
84Smok/SDP-18
85D-139
85F-41
85Leaf-43
85Mother/SDP-3
86D-80
86F-331
86Leaf-76
87Classic/Up-126
87D-14DK
87D-451
87D/DKsuper-14
87D/OD-125
87F-425
87F/GameWin-28
87F/Up-U78
87Leaf-14DK
87Leaf-214
87RedFoley/St-35
87Sf-135
87Sf-155M
87Sf/TPrev-2M
87T/Mets/Fan-5
87T/Tr-76T
88D-617
88D/Best-153
88D/Mets/Bk-617
88F-143
88F/SS-24
88Kahn/Mets-22
88Leaf-228
88OPC-37
88Panini/St-346
88RedFoley/St-56
88S-21
88Sf-56
88Sf/Gamewin-22
88T-735
88T/Big-158
88T/St-102
89B-388
89Classic-24
89D-99
89D/Best-70
89D/GrandSlam-4
89F-44
89F/BBMVP's-29
89F/Heroes-29
89Kahn/Mets-22
89KennerFig-92
89OPC-85
89Panini/St-139
89S-93
89S/HotStar-96
89Sf-97
89T-291TL
89T-7RB
89T-85
89T/Ames-20
89T/Big-116
89T/DHTest-3
89T/Gloss60-26
89T/Mets/Fan-22
89T/Mini-27
89T/St-10
89T/St-95
89T/St/Backs-51
89T/UK-52
89UD-367
89Woolwth-15
90B-138
90Classic/III-56
90D-218
90D/BestNL-129
90F-211
90F/BB-26
90F/Can-211
90Kahn/Mets-22
90Kenner/Fig-57
90Leaf-198
90MLBPA/Pins-15
90OPC-545
90Panini/St-305
90PublInt/St-141
90PublInt/St-268
90RedFoley/St-62
90S-5
90Sf-127
90T-545
90T/Big-194
90T/DH-46
90T/St-94
90T/TVMets-31
90UD-265
91B-479
91Classic/200-31
91Classic/III-69
91D-191
91F-154
91Kahn/Mets-22
91Leaf-151
91Leaf/Stud-209
91OPC-105
91Panini/FrSt-83
91S-327
91StCl-35
91T-105
91UD-105
91Ultra-224
91WIZMets-263
92B-337
92Classic/Game200-170
92D-288
92F-512
92F/Up-29
92L-522
92L/BlkGold-522
92OPC-625
92OPC/Premier-54
92Panini-228
92Pinn-427
92Pol/Royal-20
92S-168
92S/RookTr-31T
92StCl-619
92Studio-188
92T-625
92T/Gold-625
92T/GoldWin-625
92T/Kids-15
92T/Tr-71T
92T/TrGold-71T
92UD-362
92UD-742
92Ultra-374
93B-321
93Classic/Gamel-64
93D-233
93F-622
93L-80
93OPC-359
93Pac/Spanish-491
93Panini-107
93Pinn-164
93Pol/Royal-20
93S-69
93Select-176
93StCl-348
93StCl/1stDay-348
93StCl/Royal-15
93Studio-75
93T-442
93T/Gold-442
93TripleP-104
93UD-592
93Ultra-214
94B-568
94D-565
94F-168
94Finest-334
94L-280
94Pac/Cr-296
94Panini-79
94S-487
94Studio-118
94T-218
94T/Gold-218
94UD-319
94Ultra-531

McSherry, John
88TM/Umpire-12
89TM/Umpire-10
90TM/Umpire-10

McSparron, Greg
81Clinton-25

McTammy, James
N172

McVey, George
N172

McWane, Rick
88LitFalls/Pucko-28TR
89Visalia/Cal-122TR
89Visalia/ProC-1431TR
90OrlanSR/Best-25TR
90OrlanSR/Star-27TR

McWeeny, Douglas
26Exh-13
90Target-513
R316
V100

McWhirter, Kevin
78OrlanTw
80OrlanTw-20

McWilliam, Tim
89River/Best-13
89River/Cal-2
89River/ProC-1401
90Wichita/Rock-16
91AA/LineD-614
91Wichita/LineD-614
91Wichita/ProC-2612
91Wichita/Rock-22
92Wichita/SB-641

McWilliams, Jim
79Ashvl/TCMA-13

McWilliams, Larry
79T-504
80T-309
81F-267
81Richm-14
81T-44
82BK/Lids-17
82D-527
82Pol/Atl-27
82T-733
83D-45
83F-310
83T-253
84D-566
84F-256
84F/St-58
84F/St-80
84Nes/792-668
84OPC-341
84T-668
84T/St-133
85D-78
85F-470
85Leaf-247
85OPC-183
85T-183
85T/St-132
86D-264
86F-613
86Leaf-136
86OPC-204
86T-425
87F-613
87OPC-14
87T-564
88S/Tr-23T
88Smok/Card-22
88T/Big-261
88T/Tr-70T
89B-397
89D-516
89F-458
89Phill/TastyK-21
89S-259
89T-259
89T/Tr-80T
89UD-143
90D-709
90PublInt/St-247

McWilliams, Ryan
92Batavia/ClBest-20
92Batavia/ProC-3261

Meacham, Bobby
83Colum-20
84D-336
84Nes/792-204
84T-204

85D-126
85F-134
85Leaf-147
85OPC-16
85T-16
85T/St-315
86D-638
86F-110
86OPC-379
86T-379
86T/St-304
87Colum-10
87Colum/Pol-19
87Colum/TCMA-16
87F-105
87T-62
88D-616
88D/Y/Bk-616
88F-215
88S-137
88SanDiegoSt-10
88SanDiegoSt-11
88T-659
89BuffB/CMC-17
89BuffB/ProC-1663
89S-509
89SanDiegoSt-10
89SanDiegoSt-11
89T-436
89UD-77
90AAASingl/ProC-607
90Omaha/CMC-14
90Omaha/ProC-72
90ProC/Singl-189
92Yank/WIZ80-118

Meacham, Rusty
88Bristol/ProC-1868
89Fayette/ProC-1575
90A&AASingle/ProC-17
90EastLAS/ProC-EL6
90London/ProC-1266
91AAA/LineD-592
91B-149
91D/Rook-53
91Toledo/LineD-592
91Toledo/ProC-1928
91UD/FinalEd-44F
92B-486
92D-654
92D/Rook-76
92F/Up-30
92Pinn-600
92S-395
92S/100RisSt-67
92StCl-768
92T/91Debut-122
92T/Tr-72T
92T/TrGold-72T
92UD-453
93D-439
93F-243
93L-14
93OPC-173
93Pinn-149
93Pol/Royal-21
93S-378
93Select-277
93StCl-439
93StCl/1stDay-439
93StCl/Royal-29
93T-321
93T/Gold-321
93ToysRUs-76
93UD-59
93USPlayC/Rook-12S
93Ultra-215

Mead, Timber
85Everett/II/Cram-10
86Clinton-12
87Tampa-16
88Chatt/Best-1
89Chatt/Best-13
89Chatt/GS-24
90AAASingl/ProC-36
90Phoenix/CMC-23
90Phoenix/ProC-10
90ProC/Singl-550
91CalLgAS-56

Meade, Paul
92ClRS/ClBest-12
92ClRS/ProC-2399
93Kinston/Team-18

Meador, Paul
91OKSt-16
92OKSt-20

Meadows, Chuck
83AlexD-3

Meadows, Henry
D328-115
E120
E135-115
E220
W515-23
W572
W573

Meadows, Jeff
82AubAs-7

Meadows, Jim
86DayBe-18
86FSLAS-35

Meadows, Lee
21Exh-107
88Conlon/3-19
93Conlon-697
E126-4

Meadows, Louie
83DayBe-26
86Tucson-13
87Tucson-9
88F/Up-U92
88Tucson/CMC-20
88Tucson/ProC-177
89F-361
89T-643
89Tucson/CMC-14
89Tucson/JP-15
89Tucson/ProC-191
89UD-401
90AAASingl/ProC-205
90OPC-534
90ProC/Singl-614
90T-534
90Tucson/CMC-12
90Tucson/ProC-215
90UD-160
91AAA/LineD-490
91ScranWB/LineD-490
91ScranWB/ProC-2552

Meadows, Scott
89Freder/Star-15
89Watlo/ProC-1773
89Watlo/Star-20
90A&AASingle/ProC-25
90EastLAS/ProC-EL9
90Foil/Best-294
90Hagers/Best-13
90Hagers/ProC-1428
90Hagers/Star-15
90ProC/Singl-735
90Star/ISingl-75
91AA/LineD-239
91Hagers/LineD-239
91Hagers/ProC-2468
92RochR/ProC-1951
92RochR/SB-459
92Sky/AAASingl-209

Meads, Dave
86Ashvl-19
87D/Rook-46
87F/Up-U79
87Mother/Ast-17
87Pol/Ast-9
87T/Tr-77T
88D-455
88F-453
88RedFoley/St-57
88S-243
88T-199
88Tucson/CMC-4
88Tucson/JP-16
88Tucson/ProC-183
89D-424
89F-362
89Mother/Ast-26
89S-593
89T-589
89Tucson/CMC-5
89Tucson/JP-16
89Tucson/ProC-180

Meagher, Adrian
86Albuq-16
88ElPaso/Best-24
91Daikyo/Fut-15

Meagher, Brad
77BurlB

Meagher, Tom
85Spokane/Cram-14
86CharRain-17
88SanJose/Cal-134
88SanJose/ProC-120

Mealy, Tony
87Macon-5
88Greens/ProC-1563
89Cedar/Best-21
89Cedar/ProC-926
89Cedar/Star-12

Meamber, Tim
87Erie-14
88Savan/ProC-344
89Spring/Best-22
90StPete/Star-16

Mean, Rick
79Cedar/TCMA-19

Meares, Pat
89Alaska/Team-8
90WichSt-24
91Visalia/ClBest-17
91Visalia/ProC-1749
92ClBest-201
92OrlanSR/ProC-2855
92OrlanSR/SB-513
92Sky/AASingl-221
93B-45
93F/Final-239
93L-451
93Select/RookTr-67T
93T/Tr-98T
94B-432
94D-392
94F-214
94L-157
94Pac/Cr-362
94Panini-94
94Pinn-304
94S-238
94S/GoldR-238
94Select-122
94StCl-210
94StCl/1stDay-210
94StCl/Gold-210
94Studio-199
94T-223
94T/Finest-119
94T/FinestRef-119
94T/Gold-223
94TripleP-257
94UD-501
94UD/CollC-202
94UD/CollC/Gold-202
94UD/CollC/Silv-202
94Ultra-90

Mears, Ronnie
78Wisco

Mecerod, George
80Elmira-16

Meche, Carl
75QuadC

Mecir, Jim
92SanBern/ClBest-11
92SanBern/ProC-
92StCl/Dome-118
93River/Cal-12

Meckes, Tim
83ColumAst-16
84Tulsa-24

Mecrina, Eric
91SLCity/SportP-13

Meddaugh, Dean
89Burllnd/Star-17

Mediavilla, Rick
91Hamil/ClBest-26
91Hamil/ProC-4054
92ClBest-365
92Savan/ProC-675

Medich, George
(Doc)
73OPC-608R
73Syrac/Team-17
73T-608R
74OPC-445
74Syrac/Team-16
74T-445
74T/St-213
75Ho-78
75OPC-426
75SSPC/42-25
75Syrac/Team-10
75Syrac/Team-13
75T-426
75T/M-426
76Crane-35
76MSA/Disc
76OPC-146
76SSPC-430
76SSPC/MetsY-Y15
76T-146
76T/Tr-146T
77OPC-222
77T-294
78BK/R-7
78Ho-86
78SSPC/270-102
78T-583
79OPC-347
79T-657
80T-336
81D-386
81F-627
81T-702
82D-142
82F-324
82T-36TL
82T-78
83F-39
89Swell-18
91WIZMets-264
92Brew/Carlson-14
92Yank/WIZ70-112
93Rang/Keeb-259

Medina, Facanel
89Martins/Star-20
90Martins/ProC-3180
91Batavia/ClBest-14
91Batavia/ProC-3497

Medina, Luis
86Watlo-18
87Wmsprt-24
88AAA/ProC-8
88ColoSp/CMC-21
88ColoSp/ProC-1543
88TripleA/ASCMC-38
89Classic-67
89D-36RR
89D/Rook-20
89F-411
89Panini/St-315
89S-633RP
89S/HotRook-5
89S/YS/II-26
89T-528
89UD-2SR
90AAASingl/ProC-225
90Classic-103
90ColoSp/CMC-16
90ColoSp/ProC-44
90HotRook/St-31
90ProC/Singl-468
90PublInt/St-564
91AAA/LineD-92
91AAAGame/ProC-6
91ColoSp/LineD-92
91ColoSp/ProC-2193
92Omaha/ProC-2969
92Omaha/SB-337
92Sky/AAASingl-157

Medina, Patrico
90Martins/ProC-3186

Medina, Pedro
82Oneonta-17
83Greens-20
84Greens-23

Medina, Ricardo
89Wythe/Star-22
90Geneva/ProC-3031
90Geneva/Star-17
91Geneva/ClBest-12
91Geneva/ProC-4225
92MidwLAS/Team-29
92Peoria/ClBest-12
92Peoria/Team-14
92Peoria/Team-31M
93ClBest/MLG-121
93Peoria/Team-16

Medina, Val
82DayBe-22

Medina, Victor
89Bluefld/Star-16

Medlinger, Irving
52Park-11
V362-33

Medrano, Anthony
94ClBest/Gold-70

Medrick, John
91Eugene/ClBest-18
91Eugene/ProC-3725

Medvin, Scott
86Shrev-18
87Shrev-7
88BuffB/CMC-10
88BuffB/ProC-1484
89BuffB/CMC-6
89BuffB/ProC-1680
89D-597
89Panini/St-160
89S/HotRook-38
89T-756
90AAASingl/ProC-484
90BuffB/CMC-6
90BuffB/ProC-369
90ProC/Singl-6

Medwick, Joe
(Ducky)
34DS-66
35BU-145
35Wheat
36Exh/4-8
36Wheat
37Dix
37Exh/4-8
37Wheat
38Exh/4-8
38G-262
38G-286
38ONG/Pin-20
38Wheat
39Exh
39Wheat
40Wheat
41DP-22
43Playball-44
60F-22
61F-61
74Laugh/ASG-37
76Rowe-11
76Shakey-108
77Galasso-63
80Laugh/FFeat-19
80Perez/HOF-110
80SSPC/HOF
81Conlon-84
86Sf/Dec-15M
88Conlon/NatAS-15
89Pac/Leg-160
89Smok/Dodg-22
90Target-514
91Conlon/Sport-18
92Card/McDon/Pac-9
92Conlon/Sport-629
93AP/ASG-108
93AP/ASG24K-42G
94Conlon-1094
PR1-22
R302
R313
R313A-10
R314
R326-11A
R326-11B
R342-11
R423-69
V355-75
WG8-41

Mee, Jimmy
88Greens/ProC-1571

Mee, Tommy
78Green

Meek, Darryl
92Johnson/ClBest-19
92Johnson/ProC-3115

Meek, Rich
89Erie/Star-12

Meek, Stan
88OK-5CO
89OK-2ACO
90OK-24CO

Meeks, Steve
89KS*-62

Meeks, Tim
85Cram/PCL-169
86Albuq-17
87Albuq/Pol-14
88Tacoma/CMC-5
88Tacoma/ProC-633
90PalmSp/Cal-227
91AAA/LineD-34
91BuffB/LineD-34
91BuffB/ProC-537

Meggers, Mike
92Billings/ProC-3369

Mehl, Steve

87CharWh-9
88Utica/Pucko-8
89SoBend/GS-18
Mehrtens, Pat
88Tampa/Star-16
88Utica/Pucko-21
89Utica/Pucko-15
Meier, Brian
80Batavia-14
Meier, Dave
82OrlanTw-9
83Toledo-22
85D-147
85F-285
85T-356
85Twin/Team-4
86F-400
87OKCty-6
88Iowa/CMC-20
88Iowa/ProC-536
93Rang/Keeb-260
Meier, Jeff
89Sumter/ProC-1118
Meier, Kevin
87Pocatel/Bon-6
88SanJose/Cal-135
88SanJose/ProC-132
89AS/Cal-40
89SanJose/Best-18
89SanJose/Cal-215
89SanJose/ProC-447
89SanJose/Star-20
90Shrev/ProC-1441
90Shrev/Star-15
91AA/LineD-313
91Shrev/LineD-313
91Shrev/ProC-1818
92ArkTr/ProC-1126
92ArkTr/SB-38
92ClBest/Up-440
93FExcel/ML-103
Meier, Randy
82Wausau/Frit-8
83Wausau/Frit-15
Meier, Scott
81AppFx-19
82AppFx/Frit-9
83GlenF-5
Meine, Heinie
33G-205
R332-50
Meiners, Doug
93StCath/ClBest-13
93StCath/ProC-3971
Meinershagen, Adam
92StCath/ClBest-5
92StCath/ProC-3386
93StCath/ClBest-14
93StCath/ProC-3972
94B-29
Meissner, Scooter
90Beloit/Best-22TR
90Beloit/Star-27TR
Meister, Ralph
88Sumter/ProC-418
Meizosa, Gus
87Gaston/ProC-12
88StLucie/Star-16
89Jacks/GS-9
Mejia, Cesar
88EastLAS/ProC-10
88GlenF/ProC-924
89RochR/CMC-4
89RochR/ProC-1635
90AAASingl/ProC-271
90ProC/Singl-358
90T/TVMets-51
90Tidew/CMC-7
90Tidew/ProC-540
Mejia, Delfino
91Modesto/ClBest-12
92Reno/Cal-47
Mejia, Leandro
90Madison/Best-13
90Madison/ProC-2266
91Madison/ClBest-11
91Madison/ProC-2128
Mejia, Oscar
82Tulsa-16
84Tulsa-7
85Tulsa-7
86Water-16
87Wmsprt-4
Mejia, Roberto
(Diaz)
91GreatF/SportP-7
92ClBest-355
92UD/ML-209
92VeroB/ClBest-3
92VeroB/ProC-2885
93B-692
93L/UpGRook-5
93Select/RookTr-87T
93StCl-406
93StCl/1stDay-406
93StCl/Rockie-8
93UD/SP-223
94B-638
94D-250
94F-446
94Flair-155
94L-63
94OPC-190
94OPC/DiamD-2
94Pac/Cr-201
94Panini-177
94Pinn-181
94Pinn/Artist-181
94Pinn/Museum-181
94S-615
94Select-75
94StCl-21
94StCl/1stDay-21
94StCl/Gold-21
94StCl/Team-93
94Studio-180
94T-258
94T/Finest-153
94T/FinestRef-153
94T/Gold-258
94TripleP-228
94UD-105
94UD/CollC-203
94UD/CollC/Gold-203
94UD/CollC/Silv-203
94UD/ElecD-105
94Ultra-186
Mejia, Secar
87Myrtle-14
Mejias, Fernando
91Martins/ClBest-21
91Martins/ProC-3450
92Martins/ClBest-27
92Martins/ProC-3052
Mejias, Marcos
75BurlB
Mejias, Roman
57T-362
58T-452
59T-218
60T-2
62T-354
63J-186
63P-186
63T-432
64T-186
Mejias, Sam
77T-479R
78OPC-99
78T-576
79OPC-42
79T-97
81F-219
81T-521
82D-295
82F-75
82T-228
91Princet/ClBest-28MG
91Princet/ProC-3531MG
93Mother/Mar-28M
Mejias, Simeon
87Peoria-21
Mejias, Teodulo
91Clinton/ClBest-19
91Clinton/ProC-838
Mele, Albert
(Dutch)
Exh47
V362-48
Mele, Sabath
(Sam)
49B-118
50B-52
51B-168
51T/BB-25
52B-15
52StarCal/L-73H
52T-94
54B-22
54Esskay
54RM-AL6
54T-240
55B-147
55Salem
60T-470C
61Peters-16
62T-482MG
63T-531MG
63Twin/Volpe-5MG
64T-54MG
65T-506MG
66OPC-3MG
66T-3MG
67T-418MG
78Twin/Frisz-12MG
80Elmira-36C
81TCMA-354
91Crown/Orio-294
94T/Arc54-240
Exh47
Melendez, Dan
91T/Tr-80T
92Classic/DP-41
92FrRow/DP-1
92StCl/Dome-119
92T/DQ-22
93B-562
Melendez, Diego
77Cocoa
78DaytB
Melendez, Francisco
83Reading-15
84Cram/PCL-199
85Cram/PCL-43
85Phill/TastyK-44
86Phill/TastyK-x
86Portl-16
87Phoenix-25
88Phoenix/ProC-64
88TripleA/ASCMC-32
89D-611
89French-43
89RochR/CMC-3
89RochR/ProC-1654
90Canton/Best-16
90Canton/ProC-1300
90Canton/Star-12
91Crown/Orio-295
Melendez, Jose
85PrWill-4
86PrWill-16
87Harris-5
88Harris/ProC-848
89Wmsprt/ProC-633
89Wmsprt/Star-14
90AAASingl/ProC-113
90Calgary/CMC-22
90Calgary/ProC-648
90ProC/Singl-449
91AAA/LineD-288
91D/Rook-23
91LasVegas/LineD-288
91LasVegas/ProC-232
91T/90Debut-106
92D-572
92F-615
92L-507
92L/BlkGold-507
92Mother/Padre-14
92OPC-518
92OPC/Premier-139
92Padre/Carl-14
92Pinn-536
92Pol/Padre-27M
92ProC/Tomorrow-332
92S-397
92S/100RisSt-19
92Smok/Padre-20
92StCl-342
92T-518
92T/Gold-518
92T/GoldWin-518
92UD-566
92Ultra-578
93D-626
93F-144
93F/Final-175
93L-371
93Pac/Spanish-361
93StCl-87
93StCl/1stDay-87
93T-58
93T/Gold-58
93UD-288
94Pac/Cr-59
Melendez, Luis A.
71OPC-216R
71T-216R
72T-606
73OPC-47
73T-47
74OPC-307
74T-307
75OPC-353
75T-353
75T/M-353
76OPC-399
76SSPC-282
76T-399
77Padre/SchCd-19
78Syrac
87Fayette-22
88Fayette/ProC-1083
88Hamil/ProC-1733
90Hamil/Best-27MG
90Hamil/Star-26MG
Melendez, Steve
86Geneva-19TR
88Peoria/Ko-16TR
89WinSalem/Star-21TR
90WinSalem/Team-27TR
91WinSalem/ClBest-28TR
92WinSalem/ClBest-28
Melendez, William
73Cedar
76Dubuq
Meleski, Mark
86NewBrit-18
87Pawtu/TCMA-28
88Pawtu/CMC-25
88Pawtu/ProC-454CO
89Pawtu/CMC-24CO
89Pawtu/Dunkin-5CO
89Pawtu/ProC-696CO
90AAASingl/ProC-450CO
90Pawtu/CMC-8CO
90Pawtu/ProC-478CO
90ProC/Singl-259CO
90T/TVRSox-35CO
91AAA/LineD-360
91Pawtu/LineD-360
91Pawtu/ProC-56CO
92Pawtu/ProC-940CO
92Pawtu/SB-375M
Melhuse, Adam
93StCath/ClBest-15
93StCath/ProC-3981
Melillo, Oscar
(Ski)
26Exh-116
29Exh/4-30
31Exh/4-29
33DH-32
33DL-3
33Exh/4-15
34DS-53
34Exh/4-15
34G-45
35BU-151
35Exh/4-15
35G-1F
35G-3D
35G-5D
35G-6D
55Rodeo
61F-127
91Conlon/Sport-81
93Conlon-890
R300
R309/2
R310
R313
R316
R332-39
V354-94
V94-31
Melito, Chuck
80Batavia-17
Mellix, Ralph
(Lefty)
88Negro/Duques-18
Mello, John
88MidwLAS/GS-43
88Rockford-24
89Rockford-24
89WPalmB/Star-16
90FSLAS/Star-14
90WPalmB/Star-16
Mellody, Honey
T3/Box-72
Meloan, Paul
M116
Melrose, Jeff
86DayBe-19
86Tulsa-21
88Gaston/ProC-1012
Melson, Gary
79Tacom-9
80Richm-8
Melton, Cliff
39PlayBall-125
40PlayBall-83
41DP-26
41DP-94
48Sommer-8
49Sommer-6
92Conlon/Sport-613
PM10/Sm-124
Melton, David
58T-391
Melton, Larry
86PrWill-17
87Salem-3
88EastLAS/ProC-17
88Harris/ProC-857
89BuffB/CMC-8
89BuffB/ProC-1673
Melton, Reuben
(Rube)
42Playball-45
47TipTop
90Target-515
Melton, Sam
87Elmira/Black-11
87Elmira/Red-11
Melton, William
(Bill)
69T-481
70MLB/St-190
70OPC-518
70T-518
71Bz
71Bz/Test-21
71MD
71OPC-80
71T-80
71T/Coins-76
71T/GM-33
71T/Greatest-33
71T/S-47
71T/Super-47
71T/tatt-14
72K-12
72MB-233
72OPC-183
72OPC-184IA
72OPC-495KP
72OPC-90LL
72ProStars/PostC-31
72T-183
72T-184IA
72T-495KP
72T-90LL
72T/Post-3
73OPC-455
73T-455
74OPC-170
74T-170
74T/DE-68
74T/St-158
75Ho-8
75Ho/Twink-8
75OPC-11
75SSPC/42-3
75T-11
75T/M-11
76OPC-309
76SSPC-155
76T-309
76T/Tr-309T
77T-107
Meltz, Rich
75FtLaud/Sus-6
Meluskey, Mitch
92BurlInd/ClBest-22
92BurlInd/ProC-1660
Melvin, Bill
92ChalK/SB-162
92CharlK/ProC-2769
Melvin, Bob

82BirmB-7
83BirmB-12
84Evansvl-11
86D-456
86Mother/Giants-12
86T-479
87D-239
87F-281
87Mother/SFG-12
87T-549
88D-638
88F-90
88Mother/Giants-12
88OPC-41
88S-477
88T-41
89B-8
89F-335
89French-36
89OPC-329
89S-617
89S/Tr-61
89T-329
89T-351TL
89UD-227
90BirmDG/Best-23
90D-451
90F-181
90F/Can-181
90Leaf-382
90OPC-626
90PublInt/St-579
90S-453
90T-626
90UD-644
91B-89
91Crown/Orio-296
91D-335
91F-482
91F/UltraUp-U3
91Leaf-240
91OPC-249
91StCl-312
91T-249
91UD-310
92D-231
92F-15
92OPC-733
92Pol/Royal-21CO
92S-208
92S/RookTr-73T
92StCl-642
92T-733
92T/Gold-733
92T/GoldWin-733
92UD-692
93Ultra-513
94F-36
Melvin, Doug
75FtLaud/Sus-17
77WHav
Melvin, Ken
75Shrev/TCMA-10
Melvin, Scott
86Kinston-16
87Spring/Best-24
88StPete/Star-18
89StPete/Star-20
90ArkTr/GS-21
91AA/LineD-50M
91ArkTr/LineD-50CO
91ArkTr/ProC-1295
92Hamil/ClBest-30CL
92Hamil/ProC-1609M
Melvin, William
87CharWh-1
88Peoria/Ko-17
90WinSalem/Team-5
91WinSalem/ClBest-7
91WinSalem/ProC-2826
Mena, Andres
87SanAn-2
Menard, Dyrryl
86Osceola-18
Mendazona, Mike
89Gaston/ProC-1026
89Gaston/Star-15
Mendek, William
87Chatt/Best-24
88Vermont/ProC-958
Mendenhall, Casey
90OK-22
92Niagara/ClBest-15
92Niagara/ProC-3320
Mendenhall, Kirk
90Niagara/Pucko-6
91FSLAS/ProC-FSL21
91Lakeland/ClBest-21
91Lakeland/ProC-274
92London/ProC-640
92London/SB-413
Mendenhall, Shannon
88Lynch/Star-14
Mendez, Eddie
89Myrtle/ProC-1453
Mendez, Jesus
86StPete-20
87StPete-3
88ArkTr/GS-15
90AAASingl/ProC-525
90Louisvl/CMC-18
90Louisvl/LBC-27
90Louisvl/ProC-411
90ProC/Singl-118
90T/TVCard-55
91Louisvl/ProC-2930
92ArkTr/ProC-1138
92ArkTr/SB-39
Mendez, Jose D.
74Laugh/Black-9
87Negro/Dixon-7
90Negro/Star-32
Mendez, Julio
89Savan/ProC-361
Mendez, Miguel
90Sumter/Best-13
90Sumter/ProC-2443
Mendez, Raul
86Cram/NWL-124
Mendez, Ricardo
92Madis/ClBest-10
92Madis/ProC-1244
92SoOreg/ProC-3426
Mendez, Roberto
85Tigres-2
Mendez, Sergio
93Welland/ClBest-13
93Welland/ProC-3360
Mendon, Kevin
80Memphis-14
Mendonca, Robert
89Batavia/ProC-1918
Mendoza, Dave
76Cedar
Mendoza, Francisco
92Beloit/ClBest-13
92Beloit/ProC-413
Mendoza, Jesus
88Sumter/ProC-398
89BurlB/ProC-1605
89BurlB/Star-13
Mendoza, Mario
75OPC-457
75T-457
75T/M-457
76SSPC-606
78T-383
79T-509
80OPC-344
80T-652
81D-45
81F-613
81OPC-76
81T-76
81T/Tr-801
82D-394
82F-325
82OPC-212
82T-212
91PalmSp/ProC-2035CO
92AS/Cal-49
92PalmSp/ClBest-28MG
92PalmSp/ProC-855MG
93Rang/Keeb-261
Mendoza, Mike
75Dubuq
76Dubuq
79CharCh-19
80Tucson-21
81Tidew-19
Mendoza, Minnie
80CharlO/Pol-11
80CharlO/W3TV-11
81Miami-6
88French-40CO
Mendoza, Reynol
92Erie/ClBest-10
92Erie/ProC-1618
93T-782
93T/Gold-782
94FExcel-193
Menees, Gene
80Indianap-21
81Indianap-18
82Water-5
Menefee, John
E107
Menendez, Antonio G.
(Tony)
86BirmB/Team-6
87BirmB/Best-10
88BirmB/Best-20
89BirmB/Best-3
89BirmB/ProC-103
90BirmDG/Best-24
92D/Rook-77
92Nashvl/ProC-1830
92Nashvl/SB-286
92Sky/AAASingl-133
93B-106
94StCl/Team-27
Menendez, William
86WinSalem-17
Mengel, Brad
90Myrtle/ProC-2782
91Dunedin/ClBest-17
91Dunedin/ProC-214
92Knoxvl/ProC-2997
Mengwasser, Brad
82Tulsa-2
Menhart, Paul
90StCath/ProC-3464
91Dunedin/ClBest-7
91Dunedin/ProC-203
91FSLAS/ProC-FSL9
92Knoxvl/ProC-2987
92Knoxvl/SB-384
92Sky/AASingl-162
93Syrac/ProC-997
Menke, Denis
62T-597R
63T-433
64T-53
64T/Coins-90
65Kahn
65T-327
66Kahn
66OPC-184
66T-184
66T/RO-119
66T/RO-67
67CokeCap/Astro-8
67CokeCap/Brave-6
67Kahn
67T-396M
67T-518
68CokeCap/Brave-6
68Dexter-55
68T-232
69MB-191
69MLB/St-140
69T-487
69T/St-35
70MB-18
70MLB/St-43
70OPC-155
70T-155
70T/CB
71K-8
71MLB/St-87
71OPC-130
71T-130
71T/Coins-89
72MB-234
72T-586
73OPC-52
73T-52
74OPC-134
74T-134
77BurlB
78Dunedin
78TCMA-58
82Tucson-26
86Mother/Ast-9CO
89Phill/TastyK-22CO
90Phill/TastyK-34CO
91Phill/Medford-27CO
92Phill/Med-20CO
93Phill/Med-22CO
94Phill/Med-21CO
Menosky, Mike
E120
V100
V61-46
W572
W573
Mentzer, Troy
89Everett/Star-21
90SanJose/Best-10
90SanJose/Cal-41
90SanJose/ProC-2013
90SanJose/Star-15
Meola, Mike
V351A-18
Meoli, Rudy
74OPC-188
74T-188
75OPC-533
75T-533
75T/M-533
76Indianap-10
76OPC-254
76SSPC-196
76T-254
77Indianap-18
78SSPC/270-270
78T-489
Mercado, Brian
90Butte/SportP-15
Mercado, Candy
75AppFx
76AppFx
77AppFx
77BurlB
Mercado, Manny
86Watlo-19
87Watlo-2
Mercado, Orlando
80LynnS-9
81Spokane-5
82SLCity-13
83T/Tr-71T
84D-318
84F-613
84Mother/Mar-14
84Nes/792-314
84T-314
85OKCty-1
85T-58
86OKCty-12
87Albuq/Pol-16
87D/OD-209
87T-514
88Tacoma/CMC-22
88Tacoma/ProC-624
89Portl/CMC-12
89Portl/ProC-209
89UD-624
90AAASingl/ProC-279
90Kahn/Mets-35
90ProC/Singl-372
90T/TVMets-21
90T/Tr-73T
90Target-517
90Tidew/CMC-21
90Tidew/ProC-548
91AAA/LineD-563
91Tidew/LineD-563
91Tidew/ProC-2514
91WIZMets-265
92Tidew/ProC-
92Tidew/SB-566
93Rang/Keeb-262
Mercado, Rafael
90SoOreg/ProC-3434
91Madison/ClBest-27
91Madison/ProC-2140
91MidwLAS/ProC-42
92Reno/Cal-48
Merced, Orlando
86Macon-15
88Augusta/ProC-364
89AAA/CMC-15
89Harris/ProC-299
89Harris/Star-10
90AAASingl/ProC-495
90BuffB/CMC-18
90BuffB/ProC-380
90BuffB/Team-16
90ProC/Singl-18
90TripleAAS/CMC-15
91AAA/LineD-35
91B-512
91BuffB/LineD-35
91Classic/III-57
91D/Rook-22
91F/Up-U112
91Leaf-489
91MajorLg/Pins-58
91S-747RP
91T/90Debut-107
91T/Tr-81T
91UD-84
91Ultra-284
92B-291
92Classic/Game200-154
92Classic/I-62
92D-310
92F-561
92F/RookSIns-3
92L-363
92L/BlkGold-363
92OPC-637
92OPC/Premier-22
92Panini-252
92Pinn-62
92Pirate/Nation-16
92S-153
92S/100RisSt-75
92S/Impact-7
92StCl-134
92T-637
92T/Gold-637
92T/GoldWin-637
92TripleP-16
92UD-517
92Ultra-257
93B-190
93Colla/DM-75
93D-282
93F-117
93Flair-115
93L-97
93Pac/Jugador-33
93Pac/Spanish-248
93Pac/SpanishGold-6
93Panini-281
93Pinn-160
93Pirate/Nation-18
93S-137
93Select-183
93StCl-372
93StCl/1stDay-372
93Studio-184
93T-378
93T/Gold-378
93UD-150
93UD/SP-186
93Ultra-100
94B-546
94D-334
94D/DK-19
94D/Special-334
94F-614
94Flair-218
94L-388
94OPC-48
94P-30
94Pac/AllLat-9
94Pac/Cr-502
94Pac/Silv-34
94Panini-237
94Pinn-76
94Pinn/Artist-76
94Pinn/Museum-76
94S-58
94S/GoldR-58
94S/GoldS-2
94Sf/2000-19
94StCl-277
94StCl/1stDay-277
94StCl/Gold-277
94Studio-148
94T-281
94T/Finest-61
94T/Finest/PreProd-61
94T/FinestRef-61
94T/Gold-281
94TripleP-187
94UD-182
94UD/CollC-204
94UD/CollC/Gold-204
94UD/CollC/Silv-204
94UD/ElecD-182
94UD/SP-143
94Ultra-557
94Ultra/OnBase-8
Mercedes, Feliciano
92Bluefld/ClBest-9
92Bluefld/ProC-2366

92Kane/ClBest-17
92Kane/ProC-101
Mercedes, Fernando
92BurlAs/ClBest-2
92BurlAs/ProC-539
Mercedes, Guillermo
86Macon-14
Mercedes, Hector
89StCath/ProC-2080
90Myrtle/ProC-2783
Mercedes, Henry
89Modesto/Chong-20
90Madison/ProC-2272
90MidwLgAS/GS-16
91CalLgAS-38
91ClBest/Singl-154
91Modesto/ClBest-22
91Modesto/ProC-3091
92D/Rook-78
92ProC/Tomorrow-131
92Tacoma/ProC-2507
92Ultra-424
93D-551
93F/Final-257
93F/MLPII-12
93LimeR/Winter-131
93Pinn-268
93S-290
93S/Boys-24
93StCl-733
93StCl/1stDay-733
93T-602
93T/Gold-602
94D-602
94Pac/Cr-457
Mercedes, Jose
93B-309
93LimeR/Winter-43
94Ultra-376
Mercedes, Juan
91Bluefld/ClBest-6
91Bluefld/ProC-4125
92Kane/ClBest-16
92Kane/ProC-90
92Kane/Team-22
Mercedes, Luis
89Freder/Star-16
89Star/IISingl-102
90A&AASingle/ProC-24
90EastLAS/ProC-EL44
90Foil/Best-313
90Hagers/Best-12
90Hagers/ProC-1429
90Hagers/Star-16
90Star/ISingl-76
91AAA/LineD-461
91B-94
91RochR/LineD-461
91RochR/ProC-1916
91UD/Ext-745
92B-163
92Classic/Game200-173
92Classic/I-63
92D-6RR
92F-16
92L-130
92L/BlkGold-130
92OPC-603
92Pinn-248
92Pinn/Rook-1
92Pinn/RookI-5
92Pinn/Team2000-71
92ProC/Tomorrow-2
92RochR/ProC-1952
92S-826
92StCl-242
92T-603
92T/91Debut-123
92T/Gold-603
92T/GoldWin-603
92TripleP-145
92UD-652
93D-645
93F-547
93LimeR/Winter-52
93OPC-43
93Pac/Spanish-345
93Pinn-376
93S/Boys-4
93Select-331
93StCl-391
93StCl/1stDay-391
93T-446
93T/Gold-446
93Ultra-496
94StCl/Team-24
Mercedes, Manuel
76QuadC
Mercer, Mark
78Ashvl
79Tulsa-10
80CharCh-11
83OKCty-13
93Rang/Keeb-263
Mercerod, George
85Pawtu-21
Merchant, James A.
(Andy)
76OPC-594R
76T-594R
Merchant, John
81Batavia-18
Merchant, Mark
88Augusta/ProC-1576
89AS/Cal-3
89Augusta/ProC-496
89SanBern/Best-27
89SanBern/Cal-93
90Foil/Best-277
90ProC/Singl-791
90Wmsprt/Best-16
90Wmsprt/ProC-1070
90Wmsprt/Star-17
91Penin/ClBest-24
91Penin/ProC-389
92Jacks/ProC-3721
92Jaxvl/SB-366
Mercker, Kent
87Durham-12
88CLAS/Star-31
88Durham/Star-14
89AAA/ProC-5
89Richm/Bob-17
89Richm/CMC-5
89Richm/Ko-24
89Richm/ProC-835
90B-6
90Classic-15
90D-31
90F-590
90F/Can-590
90ProC/Singl-657
90Richm/Bob-8
90Richm/CMC-27
90Richm/Team-22
90S/Tr-72T
90T/89Debut-81
90UD-63
91B-568
91Brave/Dubuq/Perf-19
91Brave/Dubuq/Stand-25
91Classic/200-67
91D-299
91F/UltraUp-U68
91F/Up-U74
91Leaf-41
91OPC-772
91S-79
91S/100RisSt-58
91StCl-341
91StCl/Member*-30
91T-772
91T/JumboR-19
91ToysRUs-19
91UD-642
92Brave/LykePerf-19
92Brave/LykeStand-22
92Classic/I-18
92D-116
92D-616M
92F-363
92F-700M
92OPC-596
92S-178
92S-787M
92StCl-147
92T-596
92T/Gold-596
92T/GoldWin-596
92UD-472
92USPlayC/Brave-4C
92USPlayC/Brave-7H
92Ultra-460
93Brave/LykePerf-20
93Brave/LykeStand-25
93D-2
93F-8
93L-521
93Pac/Spanish-336
93Pinn-418
93StCl-111
93StCl/1stDay-111
93StCl/Brave-11
93T-144
93T/Gold-144
93UD-393
93Ultra-309
94D-203
94F-368
94Flair-132
94L-410
94Pac/Cr-18
94Pinn-440
94S-126
94S/GoldR-126
94StCl-360
94StCl/1stDay-360
94StCl/Gold-360
94StCl/Team-39
94T-718
94T/Gold-718
94UD-442
94Ultra-447
Mercurio, Tony
88Tidew/CANDL-30
Meredith, Steve
90Salinas/Cal-136
Merejo, Domingo
87Watertn-13
88Watertn/Pucko-21
89Salem/Star-12
90Salem/Star-12
Merejo, Jesus
88Utica/Pucko-9
89Utica/Pucko-16
Merejo, Luis
86Cram/NWL-92
87QuadC-11
88PalmSp/Cal-90
88PalmSp/ProC-1437
89MidldA/GS-23
89TexLAS/GS-6
90MidldA/GS-23
Meridith, Ron
81Hawaii-16
81Tucson-16
82Hawaii-16
83Tucson-5
84Iowa-27
85Iowa-17
86D-533
86F-374
86Iowa-18
87Mother/Rang-16
87OKCty-13
88Louisvl-34
93Rang/Keeb-264
Merietta, Lou
79Cedar/TCMA-22
Merigliano, Frank
88Utica/Pucko-22
89SoBend/GS-8
90Saraso/Star-15
91AA/LineD-67
91BirmB/LineD-67
91BirmB/ProC-1453
92BirmB/ProC-2579
92BirmB/SB-89
Merila, Mark
92MN-13
93Bz-15
93T/Tr-70T
Merkle, Cliff
E120
W573
Merkle, Fred
10Domino-83
11Helmar-133
12Sweet/Pin-119
14CJ-78
60NuCard-17
61NuCard-417
81Conlon-27
86Conlon/1-49
88Conlon/4-19
90Target-516
94Conlon-1260
BF2-79
D304
D328-116
D329-118
D350/2-116
E135-116
E254
E270/2
E300
E95
M101/4-118
M101/5-116
M116
S74-90
T201
T202
T204
T205
T206
T213/blue
T215/brown
T3-108
W514-74
Merrifield, Bill
85MidldA-19
86MidldA-17
87Edmon-14
88OkCty/CMC-15
88OkCty/ProC-36
Merrifield, Doug
81Spokane-12
82SLCity-1
83SLCity-26
86Calgary-14TR
88Calgary/CMC-22
88Calgary/ProC-787
90Knoxvl/Best-7
Merrill, Carl
(Stump)
77WHave
79WHave-8
84Colum-23
84Colum/Pol-15MG
85Colum/Pol-16MG
89EastLDD/ProC-DD44CD
90AAASingl/ProC-343M
90ColClip/CMC-24CO
90ColClip/CMC-25MG
90ColClip/ProC-693MG
90Colum/Pol-3MG
90ProC/Singl-224M
90ProC/Singl-225MG
90S/NWest-1MG
90T/Tr-74TMG
91OPC-429MG
91T-429MG
93ColClip/Pol-14MG
93ColClip/Pol-24CO
Merrill, Durwood
88TM/Umpire-30
89TM/Umpire-28
90TM/Umpire-27
Merrill, Mike
86Durham-18TR
87Durham-17TR
Merriman, Brett
88BurlInd/ProC-1795
89Miami/I/Star-14
89Star/IISingl-182
89Watertn/Star-14
90PalmSp/ProC-2574
91PalmSp/ProC-2009
92MidldA/OneHour-16
92MidldA/ProC-4025
92MidldA/SB-466
93T-593
93T/Gold-593
Merriman, Lloyd
49Eureka-90
50B-173
51B-72
52B-78
55B-135
Merriman, Rob
89KS*-81
Merritt, George
E254
T205
T206
Merritt, Jim
66OPC-97
66T-97
67CokeCap/Twin-4
67T-523
68OPC-64
68T-64
69MLB/St-132
69T-661
70MLB/St-32
70T-616
71Bz
71Bz/Test-7
71K-25
71MD
71MLB/St-65
71OPC-420
71T-420
71T/Coins-129
71T/tatt-15
72T-738
74OPC-318
74T-318
75OPC-83
75T-83
75T/M-83
78Twin/Frisz-38
93Rang/Keeb-265
Merritt, Lloyd
58T-231
84Savan-21MG
85Spring-10
Merriweather, James
92Fayette/ClBest-10
92Fayette/ProC-2176
Mersh, Neil
78Cr/PCL-19
79WHave-30
Merson, John
52T-375
Mertens, Warren
78OrlanTw
Mertes, Sam
E107
Merullo, Lenny
45Playball-25
Merullo, Matt
87DayBe-14
88BirmB/Best-22
88SLAS-7
89D/Rook-50
89F/Up-21
90BirmB/Best-3
90BirmB/ProC-1112
90BirmDG/Best-25
90F-542
90F/Can-542
90Foil/Best-167
90ProC/Singl-819
90S-605
90T/89Debut-82
90UD-67
91F/Up-U13
91Kodak/WSox-5
91StCl-382
92D-264
92F-90
92OPC-615
92S-367
92StCl-404
92T-615
92T/Gold-615
92T/GoldWin-615
92TripleP-121AA
92Vanco/ProC-2725
92WSox-5
94StCl/Team-148
Mesa, Audy
90Bend/Legoe-29
91Pocatel/ProC-3790
91Pocatel/SportP-24
Mesa, Baltazar
90Bakers/Cal-232
Mesa, Ivan
79AppFx-12
81GlenF-13
82Toledo-15
Mesa, Jose
85Kingst-8
86Ventura-14
87Knoxvl-1
88D-601
88RochR/CMC-3
88RochR/ProC-206
88RochR/Team-13
89Hagers/Best-3
89RochR/ProC-1636
90A&AASingle/ProC-4
90Hagers/Best-28
90Hagers/ProC-1410
90Hagers/Star-17
91B-91
91Crown/Orio-297
91D-765

91F/Up-U3
91Leaf-166
91OPC-512
91StCl-380
91T-512
91UD/Ext-703
92D-773
92F-17
92L-351
92L/BlkGold-351
92OPC-310
92Pinn-496
92S-707
92StCl-888
92T-310
92T/Gold-310
92T/GoldWin-310
92Ultra-305
93D-465
93F-596
93Flair-197
93Indian/WUAB-20
93L-374
93LimeR/Winter-62
93Pac/Beisbol-6M
93Pac/Spanish-414
93Pinn-436
93S-424
93T-696
93T/Gold-696
93UD-798
94D-182
94F-113
94L-438
94Pac/Cr-177
94Pinn-337
94S-419
94T-7
94T/Finest-138
94T/FinestRef-138
94T/Gold-7
94TripleP-116
94UD/CollC-205
94UD/CollC/Gold-205
94UD/CollC/Silv-205
94Ultra-46
Mesewicz, Mark
92Welland/ProC-1320
Mesh, Mike
85Pawtu-8
86Pawtu-14
87Pawtu-18
87Pawtu/TCMA-15
88Pawtu/CMC-18
88Pawtu/ProC-463
89Omaha/CMC-16
89Omaha/ProC-1730
Mesner, Steve
46Sunbeam
47Signal
47Sunbeam
W754
Messaros, Mike
80Cedar-20
Messer, Doug
89Salinas/Cal-125
89Salinas/ProC-1817
91Reno/Cal-11
Messerly, Michael
(Mike)
88SoOreg/ProC-1704
89Madis/Star-7
90Modesto/Cal-160
90Modesto/Chong-21
90Modesto/ProC-2221
91ClBest/Singl-44
91Modesto/ClBest-20
91Modesto/ProC-3097
Messersmith, John
(Andy)
69JB
69T-296
70MLB/St-176
70OPC-430
70OPC-72LL
70T-430
70T-72LL
70T/PI-9
70T/S-25
70T/Super-25
71JB
71MD
71MLB/St-351
71OPC-15
71T-15
71T/Coins-112
72K-42
72MB-235
72OPC-160
72T-160
72T/Post-18
73OPC-515
73T-515
74OPC-267
74T-267
74T/St-47
75Ho-79
75Ho/Twink-79
75K-30
75OPC-310LL
75OPC-440
75SSPC/Puzzle-17
75T-310LL
75T-440
75T/M-310LL
75T/M-440
76Crane-36
76MSA/Disc
76OPC-199LL
76OPC-201LL
76OPC-203LL
76OPC-305
76SSPC-70
76T-199LL
76T-201LL
76T-203LL
76T-305
77BurgChef-213
77Ho-150
77Ho/Twink-150
77K-54
77OPC-155
77T-80
77T/CS-28
77T/ClothSt-28
78OPC-79
78T-156
78Wiffle/Discs-50
79OPC-139
79T-278
87Smok/Dodg-22
88AlaskaAS60/Team-5
89Smok/Dodg-85
90Target-518
92Yank/WIZ70-113
Messier, Mark
91StCl/Member*-49
Messier, Tom
84Everett/Cram-30A
86Fresno/Smok-10
Messitt, John
N172
Mestek, Barney
75Water
Metcalf, Clyde
90LitSun/HSPros-24CO
90LitSun/HSProsG-24CO
Metcalf, Scott
91Perth/Fut-16
92Bluefld/ClBest-10
92Bluefld/ProC-2367
Metcalf, Thomas
64T-281R
92Yank/WIZ60-84
WG10-15
WG9-18
Metheny, Bud
44Playball-7
44Yank/St-19
Methven, Marlin
81Watlo-23
82Chatt-12
82Watlo/Frit-18
Metil, Bill
82Cedar-18
Metkovich, George
48Signal
49B/PCL-2
49Remar
50Remar
51B-274
52B-108
52T-310
53T-58
54JC-27
55Gol/Braves-20
91T/Arc53-58
Metkovich, John
52Park-89
Metoyer, Tony
86Ashvl-20
87Osceola-12
89Miami/II/Star-13
Metro, Charles
46Remar-11
66Pep/Tul
70OPC-16MG
70T-16MG
Mettler, Bradley
85Greens-27
Metts, Carey
89Erie/Star-13
Metzger, Clarence E.
(Butch)
75Hawaii
75Hawaii/Caruso-19
76OPC-593R
76T-593
77BurgChef-127
77Ho-99
77Ho/Twink-99
77Padre/SchCd-20
77T-215
78H-85
78T-431
80Richm-13
91WIZMets-266
Metzger, Curt
86ArkTr-15TR
Metzger, Roger
71OPC-404R
71T-404
72OPC-217
72T-217
73OPC-395
73T-395
74OPC-224
74T-224
74T/St-34
75Ho-115
75OPC-541
75T-541
75T/M-541
76Ho-67
76OPC-297
76SSPC-57
76T-297
77BurgChef-5
77Ho-20
77Ho/Twink-20
77OPC-44
77T-481
78BK/Ast-15
78Ho-85
78T-697
79Pol/Giants-16
79T-167
80OPC-164
80Pol/Giants-16
80T-311
Metzler, Alex
29Exh/4-20
94Conlon-1265
Meulens, Hensley
87PrWill-1
88Albany/ProC-1349
88BBAmer-1
88EastLAS/ProC-3
89Albany/Best-17
89Albany/ProC-337
89Albany/Star-13
89Classic-110
89D-547
89F/Up-U51
89S/HotRook-12
89Star/Wax-99
89UD/Ext-746
90AAAGame/ProC-13
90AAASingl/ProC-332
90AlbanyDG/Best-23
90Classic-133
90ColClip/CMC-9
90ColClip/ProC-682
90Colum/Pol-23
90F-449
90F/Can-449
90OPC-83
90ProC/Singl-209
90S-636RP
90S/100Ris-53
90T-83
90T/89Debut-83
90T/TVYank-54
90UD-546
91B-181
91Classic/200-179
91Classic/I-69
91D-31RR
91F/Up-U47
91Leaf-349
91Leaf/Stud-98
91MajorLg/Pins-3
91OPC-259
91OPC/Premier-80
91S-828RP
91S/100RisSt-84
91S/ASFan-4
91S/Rook40-39
91StCl-503
91T-259
91UD-675
91Ultra-240
92AAA/ASG/SB-111
92B-338
92ColClip/Pol-18
92ColClip/ProC-360
92ColClip/SB-111
92D-711
92F-238
92OPC-154
92Pinn-366
92S-89
92S/100RisSt-72
92Sky/AAASingl-51
92StCl-64
92T-154
92T/Gold-154
92T/GoldWin-154
92UD-606
92Ultra-106
92Yank/WIZ80-119
93ColClip/Pol-19
93LimeR/Winter-139
93Pinn-124
93S-595
93T-549
93T/Gold-549
93Ultra-245
Meury, Bill
91ClBest/Singl-339
91Waterlo/ClBest-18
91Waterlo/ProC-1265
92HighD/ClBest-4
Meusel, Emil
(Irish)
25Exh-36
26Exh-38
81Conlon-42
87Conlon/2-22
90Target-519
E120
E121/120
E121/80
E126-34
E220
V100
V117-17
V61-55
V89-20
W501-113
W501-36
W515-21
W572
W573
W575
Meusel, Robert W.
(Bob)
21Exh-114
25Exh-98
26Exh-101
27Exh-51
28Yueng-7
77Galasso-133
81Conlon-43
86Conlon/1-34
87Conlon/2-21
88Conlon/5-22
91Conlon/Sport-122
92Mega/Ruth-159M
E126-39
E210-7
E220
V100
V89-19
W501-35
W502-7
W515-21
W517-49
W572
W575
WG7-31
Meyer, Alfred
77StPete
Meyer, Basil
88Kenosha/ProC-1404
89Visalia/Cal-94
89Visalia/ProC-1445
90OrlanSR/Best-17
90OrlanSR/ProC-1079
90OrlanSR/Star-11
90ProC/Singl-755
Meyer, Benny
90Target-520
Meyer, Bob B.
64T-488R
65OPC-219
65T-219
70McDon-2
70T-667
71MLB/St-445
71OPC-456
71T-456
92Yank/WIZ60-85
Meyer, Brad
88Gaston/ProC-1015
Meyer, Brian
86AubAs-16
87Osceola-13
88ColAst/Best-5
88SLAS-31
89B-319
89D-640
89Tucson/CMC-9
89Tucson/JP-17
89Tucson/ProC-189
90AAASingl/ProC-192
90D-648
90F-232
90F/Can-232
90OPC-766
90ProC/Singl-604
90T-766
90Tucson/CMC-2
90Tucson/ProC-202
90UD-22
91F-510
Meyer, Dan
75OPC-620R
75T-620R
75T/M-620R
76Ho-132
76OPC-242
76SSPC-365
76T-242
77Ho-135
77Ho/Twink-135
77OPC-186
77T-527
78Ho-97
78K-12
78OPC-55
78T-57
79OPC-363
79T-683
80OPC-207
80T-396
81D-43
81F-603
81OPC-143
81Pol/Mariners-5
81T-143
81T/SO-40
81T/St-125
82D-176
82F-512
82T-413
82T/Tr-70T
83D-413
83F-527
83OPC/St-110
83T-208
83T/St-110
84Cram/PCL-96
84F-455
84Nes/792-609
84T-609
85Mother/A's-23
89Pac/SenLg-155
89T/SenLg-97
89TM/SenLg-77

Meyer, Jack
56T-269
57T-162
58T-186
59T-269
60L-137
60T-64
61T-111
Meyer, Jay
91Hunting/ClBest-14
91Hunting/ProC-3330
92Peoria/ClBest-22
92Peoria/Team-15
Meyer, Joey
86Vanco-17
87D-460
87Denver-5
88D-36RR
88D/Best-239
88D/Rook-38
88F-645R
88F/Up-U40
88Leaf-36RR
88Pol/Brew-23
88S/Tr-75T
88T-312
89B-138
89Classic-10
89D-339
89F-191
89Gard-13
89OPC-136
89Panini/St-363
89Pol/Brew-23
89S-374
89S/HotRook-93
89S/YS/I-33
89Sf-135
89T-136
89T/Big-153
89UD-403
90OPC-673
90PublInt/St-498
90S-532
90T-673
91AAA/LineD-36
91BuffB/LineD-36
91BuffB/ProC-547
Meyer, Lambert
(Dutch)
No Cards.
Meyer, Lee
E254
Meyer, Paul
91Kingspt/ClBest-9
91Kingspt/ProC-3823
Meyer, Randy
81CharR-20
Meyer, Rick
89Martins/Star-21
90Martins/ProC-3178
92Clearw/ClBest-21
92Clearw/ProC-2063
Meyer, Russ
49Lummis
51B-75
51BR-D7
52B-220
52T-339
53B/Col-129
54B-186
54NYJour
55B-196
55Gol/Dodg-20
56T-227
59T-482
79TCMA-194
88FSLAS/Star-29
89Albany/Best-27CO
89Albany/ProC-322CO
90Albany/Best-6CO
90Albany/ProC-1182CO
90Target-521
91AAA/LineD-125M
91ColClip/LineD-125CO
Meyer, Scott
80WHave-9
81WHave-21
Meyer, Stephen W.
86Erie-19
87Spring/Best-4
88Spring/Best-18
Meyer, William
49Eureka-167MG
51B-272MG
52B-155MG
52T-387MG
PM10/Sm-125
Meyers
WG1-34
WG1-64
Meyers, Benny
C46-28
Meyers, Brian
88AppFx/ProC-139
Meyers, Don
90GreatF/SportP-17
91Yakima/ClBest-12
91Yakima/ProC-4251
92Bakers/Cal-17
Meyers, Glenn
86QuadC-23
Meyers, Henry W.
V100
Meyers, Jim
90Foil/Best-223
Meyers, John
(Chief)
10Domino-84
11Helmar-134
12Sweet/Pin-120
14Piedmont/St-38
16FleischBrd-64
90Target-522
91Conlon/Sport-171
92Conlon/13Nat-775
93Conlon-775
BF2-59
D304
D328-117
D329-119
D350/2-117
E135-117
E224
E254
E270/1
E286
E91
E96
E97
E98
M101/4-119
M101/5-117
S74-91
T201
T202
T205
T206
T213
T214-20
T215/brown
T3-50
W501-94
W555
WG4-20
WG5-31
WG6-29
Meyers, Paul
87Shrev-2
88Shrev/ProC-1288
89Phoenix/CMC-22
89Phoenix/ProC-1490
Meyett, Don
89Beloit/I/Star-17
89Beloit/II/Star-21
Meza, Larry
(Lorenzo)
91Hamil/ClBest-28
91Hamil/ProC-4046
92Spring/ClBest-26
92Spring/ProC-874
Mezzanotte, Tom
91Bristol/ClBest-4
91Bristol/ProC-3607
92ProC/Tomorrow-70
Miceli, Dan
91Eugene/ClBest-21
91Eugene/ProC-3726
92AppFox/ClBest-6
92Memphis/ProC-2415
92ProC/Tomorrow-77
93B-293
93StCl/Royal-30
94B-574
94F/MLP-24
94T-224
94T/Gold-224
94Ultra-258
Micelotta, Robert Peter
(Mickey)
54T-212
94T/Arc54-212
Michael, Bill
75Clinton
Michael, Gene
66EH-45
67T-428R
68T-299
69T-626
70OPC-114
70T-114
71MLB/St-496
71OPC-483
71T-483
72T-713
72T-714IA
73OPC-265
73Syrac/Team-18
73T-265
74OPC-299
74Syrac/Team-17
74T-299
74T/St-214
75OPC-608
75T-608
75T/M-608
76SSPC-369
79Colum-7
81D-500MG
81T-670MG
81TCMA-384
86Gator-4MG
86T/Tr-73T
87Berg/Cubs-4
87T-43MG
90Target-523
92Yank/WIZ60-86
92Yank/WIZ70-114
Michael, Steve
79Memphis/TCMA-2
82ElPaso-12
84ElPaso-4
87Elmira/Black-19
87Elmira/Red-19
88Elmira-3
89Elmira/Pucko-7
90WinHaven/Star-16
Michaels, Cass
47TipTop
48L-13
49B-12
50B-91
51B-132
51FB
52B-36
52T-178
53B/Col-130
54B-150
55B-85
Michalak, Chris
94T-316M
94T/Gold-316M
Michalak, Tony
87Everett-15
88Clinton/ProC-710
Michalak, Wade
94T-713M
94T/Gold-713M
Micheal, Matt
89Penin/Star-15
Michel, Domingo
86VeroB-18
87SanAn-7
88SanAn/Best-6
89Albuq/CMC-22
89Albuq/ProC-81
90AAASingl/ProC-389
90ProC/Singl-389
90Toledo/CMC-12
90Toledo/ProC-159
91AA/LineD-392
91London/LineD-392
91London/ProC-1886
93LimeR/Winter-120
Michel, John
82Idaho-19
83Madis/Frit-19
Micheu, Buddy
89Butte/SP-25
90Gaston/Best-8
90Gaston/ProC-2524
90Gaston/Star-14
Michno, Tim
88WinSalem/Star-12
Michno, Tom
89CharlK-15
91FSLAS/ProC-FSL25
91Miami/ClBest-9
91Miami/ProC-405
Mickan, Dan
84Newar-5
Mickens, Glenn
90Target-1033
Middaugh, Scott
90Saraso/Star-16
91AA/LineD-68
91BirmB/LineD-68
91BirmB/ProC-1454
Middlekauff, Craig
89Niagara/Pucko-17
Middleton, Damon
77Clinton
Mielke, Gary
88OkCty/CMC-5
88OkCty/ProC-35
89OkCty/CMC-6
89OkCty/ProC-1528
90D-679
90F/Up-125
90Mother/Rang-17
90OPC-221
90S-574
90T-221
90UD-612
91F-293
91OPC-54
91S-167
91T-54
92Gaston/ProC-2270
93Rang/Keeb-266
Mielke, Greg
75AppFx
76AppFx
Mieses, Melanio
91Elizab/ProC-4297
Mieske, Matt
90Spokane/SportP-19
91B-694
91CalLgAS-4
91ClBest/Gold-3
91ClBest/Singl-8
91HighD/ClBest-26
91HighD/ProC-2409
92B-608FOIL
92Denver/ProC-2654
92Denver/SB-139
92ProC/Tomorrow-335
92Sky/AAASingl-67
92UD/ML-113
93B-99
93F/Final-229
93FExcel/ML-192
93StCl-687
93StCl/1stDay-687
93T-616
93T/Gold-616
93T/Tr-72T
93UD-704
93Ultra-575
94B-589
94D-522
94F-183
94Finest-399
94Pinn-258
94Pinn/Artist-258
94Pinn/Museum-258
94Pol/Brew-18
94Select-206
94StCl-126
94StCl/1stDay-126
94StCl/Gold-126
94T-339
94T/Gold-339
Mifune, Hideyuki
91CalLgAS-32
91Salinas/ClBest-4
91Salinas/ProC-2252
Miggins, Larry
53B/Col-142
53Hunter
79TCMA-285
Miggins, Mark
77Cocoa
79CharCh-10
81Tucson-9
82Tucson-17
83Miami-26
Miglio, John
81QuadC-21
82Watlo/B-8
82Watlo/Frit-16
83Watlo/Frit-11
85Water-8
87ElPaso-12
87TexLgAS-20
88Denver/CMC-4
88Denver/ProC-1260
89ElPaso/GS-10
Mijares, Willie
85Everett/Cram-9
86Everett/Pop-17
87Clinton-6
88SanJose/Cal-124
88SanJose/ProC-110
Mikan, George
51Wheat
52Wheat*
Mikesell, Larry James
82Wisco/Frit-12
Mikkelsen, Lincoln
90Erie/Star-16
91Stockton/ClBest-5
91Stockton/ProC-3029
92Stockton/ClBest-9
92Stockton/ProC-33
Mikkelsen, Pete
64T-488R
65OPC-177
65T-177
66EH-19
66T-248
67CokeCap/Pirate-5
67T-425
67T/Test/PP-15
68T-516
71MLB/St-107
71Ticket/Dodg-9
81TCMA-431
90Target-524
92Yank/WIZ60-87
WG10-16
Miksis, Eddie
47TipTop
49Eureka-42
51B-117
52B-32
52StarCal-92BM
52StarCal/L-80A
52T-172
53T-39
54B-61
55B-181
56T-285
57T-350
58T-121
59T-58
89Rini/Dodg-24
90Target-525
91Crown/Orio-298
91T/Arc53-39
Mikulik, Joe
86ColumAst-19
87ColAst/ProC-15
88Tucson/CMC-18
88Tucson/JP-17
88Tucson/ProC-176
90ColMud/Best-22
90ColMud/ProC-1360
90ColMud/Star-16
91AA/LineD-570
91Jacks/LineD-570
91Jacks/ProC-939
92Jacks/ProC-4007
92Tucson/ProC-499
92Tucson/SB-614
Milacki, Bob
86Hagers-11
87CharlO/WBTV-30
88AAA/ProC-35
88RochR/Gov-16
89Classic-92
89D-651
89D/Best-254
89D/Rook-22
89F-649R
89F/Up-U6
89French-18
89Panini/St-251
89S-651RP
89Sf-224R

89T-324
89UD/Ext-735
90D-333
90D/BestAL-2
90F-182
90F/Can-182
90Leaf-402
90OPC-73
90Panini/St-6
90PublInt/St-580
90PublInt/St-601
90S-239
90S/100Ris-68
90S/YS/I-20
90T-73
90T/JumboR-21
90T/St-240
90ToysRUs-20
90UD-635
91B-101
91Crown/Orio-299
91D-69
91F-483
91Hagers/ProC-2454
91OPC-788
91S-512
91StCl/Member*-10
91T-788
91UD-328
92B-61
92D-101
92F-18
92L-262
92L/BlkGold-262
92OPC-408
92Pinn-339
92S-314
92S-427NH
92StCl-331
92T-408
92T/Gold-408
92T/GoldWin-408
92UD-480
92Ultra-306
93D-587
93F-548
93T-192
93T/Gold-192
Milan, J. Clyde
10Domino-85
11Helmar-75
12Sweet/Pin-62
14CJ-56
15CJ-56
21Exh-108
40PlayBall-130
77Galasso-141
93Conlon-806
BF2-48
D327
D328-118
D329-120
D350/2-118
E120
E121/120
E121/80
E122
E135-118
E220
E254
E91
M101/4-120
M101/5-118
M116
T202
T204
T205
T206
T207
V100
V89-34MG
W501-15
W516-25
W573
W575
WG5-32
WG6-30
Milbourne, Larry
75OPC-512
75T-512
75T/M-512
76SSPC-58
78T-366
79OPC-100
79T-199
80T-422
81D-486
81F-611
81T-583
81T/Tr-802
82D-614
82F-42
82T-669
82T/Tr-71T
83D-411
83F-415
83T-91
83T/Tr-72T
84Mother/Mar-10
84Nes/792-281
84T-281
84T/Tr-79
85F-493
85T-754
89Pac/SenLg-112
89Pac/SenLg-203
90EliteSenLg-86
91Savan/ClBest-27MG
91Savan/ProC-1668MG
92Yank/WIZ80-120
Milchin, Mike
89Hamil/Star-21
90SpringDG/Best-26
90StPete/Star-17
90T/TVCard-56
91AA/LineD-39
91ArkTr/LineD-39
91ArkTr/ProC-1282
91B-397
91ClBest/Singl-107
91Louisvl/ProC-2910
91Louisvl/Team-9
92B-567
92Louisvl/SB-273
92Sky/AAASingl-128
92UD/ML-79
93B-516
Milene, Jeff
89Elizab/Star-18
90Kenosha/Best-8
90Kenosha/ProC-2296
90Kenosha/Star-12
Miles, Don
90Target-1034
Miles, Eddie
82AppFx/Frit-20
83GlenF-6
Miles, James
69T-658R
70OPC-154R
70T-154R
Miles, John
92Negro/Retort-44
Miles, Wilson
(Dee)
40PlayBall-195
93Conlon-743
Mileur, Jerome
83Nashua-25
85Nashua-29
Miley, Dave
81Cedar-9
83Water-10
84Wichita/Rock-2
87Vermont-17
89Cedar/Best-22MG
89Cedar/ProC-927MG
89Cedar/Star-22MG
90Cedar/Best-19MG
90Cedar/ProC-2337MG
90MidwLgAS/GS-53M
91CharWh/ProC-2902MG
91SALAS/ProC-SAL8MG
92Chatt/SB-199MG
93Reds/Kahn-8M
Miley, Michael
(Mike)
75SLCity/Caruso-8
76OPC-387
76T-387
77T-257
90LSUGreat-13
Milhaven, McGraw
88NE-25
Milholland, Eric
86AppFx-15
87DayBe-3
88Tampa/Star-17
Militello, Sam Jr.
90A&AASingle/ProC-176
90Oneonta/ProC-3378
91B-693
91CLAS/ProC-CAR34
91ClBest/Gold-8
91ClBest/Singl-150
91PrWill/ClBest-7
91PrWill/ProC-1423
92AAA/ASG/SB-112
92B-21
92ColClip/Pol-7
92ColClip/ProC-348
92ColClip/SB-112
92D-407RR
92D/RookPhen-BC16
92F/Up-43
92OPC-676
92ProC/Tomorrow-122
92S/RookTr-82T
92Sky/AAASingl-52
92T-676R
92T/Gold-676
92T/GoldWin-676
93B-243
93Classic/GameI-65
93Classic/GameI-NNO
93ColClip/Pol-9
93D-371
93F-282
93F/RookSenII-7
93L-52
93OPC-127
93Pinn-225
93Pinn/Team2001-25
93S-351
93Select-315
93Select/ChasRook-8
93StCl-11
93StCl/1stDay-11
93StCl/MPhoto-4
93StCl/Y-27
93T-624
93T/Gold-624
93ToysRUs-72
93ToysRUs/MPhoto-9
93TripleP-75
93UD-383
93Ultra-246
Milius, Dennis
92Hamil/ClBest-13
92Hamil/ProC-1589
Miljus, John
90Target-526
V100
W513-65
Mill, Steve
91Pocatel/ProC-3778
91Pocatel/SportP-3
Millan, Bernie
90Kgsport/Best-5
90Kgsport/Star-17
91Clmbia/PCPII-3
91Clmbia/PII-17
91Pittsfld/ClBest-11
91Pittsfld/ProC-3430
92StLucie/ClBest-2
92StLucie/ProC-1757
93StLucie/ProC-2929
94ClBest/Gold-168
Millan, Felix
67OPC-89
67T-89
68CokeCap/Brave-7
68T-241
69MB-192
69MLB/St-115
69OPC-210
69T-210
69T/4in1-10
69T/St-7
70MLB/St-8
70OPC-452AS
70T-452AS
70T-710
71MD
71MLB/St-17
71OPC-81
71T-81
71T/Coins-5
71T/S-33
71T/Super-33
71T/tatt-12
72MB-236
72T-540
73OPC-407
73T-407
74K-53
74OPC-132
74T-132
74T/DE-26
74T/St-68
75Ho-111
75OPC-445
75T-445
75T/M-445
76Ho-120
76K-9
76OPC-245
76SSPC-536
76SSPC/MetsY-M16
76T-245
77BurgChef-138
77Ho-96
77Ho/Twink-96
77OPC-249
77T-605
78T-505
78TCMA-31
89T/SenLg-85
89TM/SenLg-78
91WIZMets-267
92GulfCM/ProC-3498
Millares, Jose
91Kane/ClBest-17
91Kane/ProC-2664
91Kane/Team-13
92Freder/ClBest-17
92Freder/ProC-1813
Millay, Gar
84AZ/Pol-13
86AZ/Pol-11
87PortChar-23
88OkCty/CMC-13
88OkCty/ProC-40
88Tulsa-21
89Tulsa/GS-18
89Tulsa/Team-16
90AAASingl/ProC-691
90OkCty/CMC-18
90OkCty/ProC-445
90ProC/Singl-168
91AAA/LineD-313
91OkCty/LineD-313
91OkCty/ProC-191
Millay, Keith
92Madis/ProC-1229
Miller, Barry
91Clinton/ClBest-21
91Clinton/ProC-843
92AS/Cal-10
92ClBest-248
92SanJose/ClBest-9
Miller, Bernie
Miller, Bill
89GreatF-31
89Idaho/ProC-2020
89Salem/Team-17
89SanDiegoSt/Smok-18
90Miami/I/Star-18
90Miami/II/Star-18
92AS/Cal-25
Miller, Brent
91Kane/ClBest-18
91Kane/ProC-2665
91Kane/Team-14
92B-150
92Hagers/ProC-2563
92Hagers/SB-264
92Sky/AASingl-108
Miller, C. Bruce
(Pic)
75OPC-606
75T-606
75T/M-606
76OPC-367
76Phoenix/Coke-14
76SSPC-102
76T-367
82Spring/Frit-3TR
Miller, Charles B.
(Molly)
T206
Miller, Damian
90Elizab/Star-13
92Kenosha/ProC-608
93FExcel/ML-203
Miller, Danny
75QuadC
Miller, Darrell
81Holyo-17
82Holyo-22
84Cram/PCL-107
85D-644
86Smok/Cal-18
86T-524
87Sf/TPrev-11M
87Sf/TPrev-11M
87Smok/Cal-11
87T-337
88D-551
88Edmon/CMC-12
88Edmon/ProC-579
88F-498
88S-463
88T-679
89Colum/CMC-19
89Colum/Pol-13
89Colum/ProC-733
89S-499
89T-68
89UD-462
90ProC/Singl-324
90RochR/CMC-23
90RochR/ProC-705
Miller, Dave 1
87Durham-11
88Greenvl/Best-14
88Richm-20
89Freder/Star-17
89OkCty/CMC-7
89OkCty/ProC-1522
89Star/IISingl-103
90AAASingl/ProC-677
90Hagers/Best-24
90Hagers/ProC-1411
90Hagers/Star-18
90OkCty/CMC-6
90OkCty/ProC-431
90ProC/Singl-156
92Hagers/ProC-2551
92Hagers/SB-265
92Sky/AASingl-109
Miller, Dave 2
79Ashvl/TCMA-11
Miller, Don
(Killer)
88Stockton/Cal-204GM
88Stockton/ProC-750GM
89Stockton/Best-27GM
89Stockton/Cal-175GM
89Stockton/ProC-397GM
89Stockton/Star-24GM
Miller, Dyar
75IntAS/TCMA-2
75OPC-614R
75T-614R
75T/M-614R
76OPC-555
76SSPC-379
76T-555
77T-77
78SSPC/270-206
78T-239
79T-313
80Tidew-10
81Louisvl-4
81T-472
82F-534
82Louisvl-18
82T-178
83Louisvl/Riley-4
84Louisvl-4
86Louisvl-2
89Pac/SenLg-211
89T/SenLg-129
90EliteSenLg-59
91CollInd/ProC-1505CO
91Crown/Orio-301
91Pac/SenLg-12
91WIZMets-270
92ColoSp/ProC-768
92ColoSp/SB-100M
Miller, Edmund
(Bing)
21Exh-109
25Exh-109
26Exh-109
31Exh/4-27
33G-59
40PlayBall-137
60F-39
61F-62

75Sheraton-14
91Conlon/Sport-192
94Conlon-1139
E120
R315-A25
R315-B25
R316
V353-59
V61-23
W517-31
W573
Miller, Edward Lee
78Richm
79Richm-24
80Richm-22
80T-675R
81Pol/Atl-45
82D-425
82F-441
82T-451
83Portl-20
85Beaum-13
93Rang/Keeb-267
Miller, Edward R.
39PlayBall-49
40PlayBall-56
41PlayBall-1
43Playball-27
48L-68
Miller, Edward S.
R314/Can
Miller, Elmer
E120
E121/120
E121/80
V100
W573
W575
Miller, Eric
92Johnson/ClBest-18
92Johnson/ProC-3116
Miller, Frank
93Richm/Team-30
Miller, Gary
91StCath/ClBest-15
91StCath/ProC-3392
92StCath/ClBest-19
92StCath/ProC-3387
Miller, George
E223
N172
N284
N29
N403
N43
Miller, Gerry
81BurlB-24
82Beloit/Frit-3
Miller, Gregg
90WichSt-43
Miller, Jeff
88Belling/Legoe-9
89Wausau/GS-23
92BurlAs/ClBest-3
92BurlAs/ProC-540
Miller, Jerry
86Miami-17C
Miller, Jessica
93Richm/Team-30M
Miller, Jim 1
77Charl
Miller, Jim 2
91Princet/ClBest-7
91Princet/ProC-3509
92Princet/ClBest-8
92Princet/ProC-3085
Miller, Joey
92Elizab/ClBest-22
92Elizab/ProC-3695
Miller, John Allen
69T-641R
81TCMA-392
92Yank/WIZ60-88
Miller, John B.
(Dots)
11Diamond-20
14CJ-49
14Piedmont/St-39
15CJ-49
D303
D322
D329-121
E102
E104
E105
E106
E254
E270/2
E90/1
E90/2
E91
E92
M101/4-121
M116
T205
T206
T207
T213/blue
Miller, John E.
63T-208R
65OPC-49R
65T-49R
66T-427
67OPC-141
67T-141
90Target-1036
91Crown/Orio-302
Miller, Joseph
N172
Miller, Keith Alan
85Lynch-18
86Jacks/TCMA-27
87Sf/Rook-50
87Tidew-10
87Tidew/TCMA-16
88D-562
88D/Mets/Bk-562
88F-144
88S-639
88Sf-225
88T-382
88Tidew/CANDL-11
88Tidew/CMC-20
88Tidew/ProC-1604
89AAA/ProC-24
89B-380
89Classic-16
89D-623
89F-45
89S-464
89S/HotRook-62
89S/YS/I-23
89T-557
89T/Mets/Fan-25
89Tidew/CMC-14
89Tidew/ProC-1948
89UD/Ext-739
90AAASingl/ProC-314
90B-136
90D-507
90Kahn/Mets-25
90Leaf-462
90Mets/Fan-25
90OPC-58
90ProC/Singl-247
90S-559
90T-58
90T/TVMets-32
90UD-190
91D-248
91F-155
91Kahn/Mets-25
91OPC-719
91S-318
91StCl-239
91T-719
91UD-196
91Ultra-225
91WIZMets-272
92B-285
92D-657
92F-513
92F/Up-31
92L-459
92L/BlkGold-459
92OPC-157
92OPC/Premier-94
92Pinn-403
92Pol/Royal-22
92S-462
92S/RookTr-50T
92StCl-786
92Studio-189
92T-157
92T/Gold-157
92T/GoldWin-157
92T/Tr-73T
92T/TrGold-73T
92UD-383
92UD-704
92Ultra-375
93B-209
93D-543
93F-244
93L-168
93Pac/Spanish-492
93Panini-109
93Pinn-384
93Pol/Royal-22
93S-96
93Select-54
93StCl-401
93StCl/1stDay-401
93StCl/Royal-7
93T-267
93T/Gold-267
93UD-302
93Ultra-565
94F-169
94Pac/Cr-297
94T-454
94T/Gold-454
Miller, Kenny
86Cram/NWL-142
87Spartan-9
Miller, Kevin
90Bristol/ProC-3151
90Bristol/Star-18
91Niagara/ClBest-11
91Niagara/ProC-3636
92Fayette/ClBest-7
92Fayette/ProC-2172
Miller, Kurt
90Classic/DP-5
90Welland/Pucko-1
91Augusta/ClBest-28
91Augusta/ProC-803
91B-521
91OPC-491FDP
91S-682FDP
91T-491FDP
91UD-68TP
92CharlR/ClBest-21
92ClBest-67
92ClBest/BBonusC-5
92ClBest/RBonus-BC5
92ProC/Tomorrow-309
92UD-70TP
92UD/ML-166
92UD/ML-42M
92UD/ML-58DS
92UD/POY-PY19
93B-53
93UD-20SR
93UD-9SR
94B-357
94B-478
94SigRook-17
94SigRook/Hot-7
Miller, Larry Don
59DF
65T-349
69T-323
81TCMA-373
90Target-528
91WIZMets-271
Miller, Lawrence H.
(Hack)
21Exh-110
90Target-1035
94Conlon-1054
E120
V61-86
W573
WG7-32
Miller, Lemmie
83Albuq-22
84Cram/PCL-150
85Cram/PCL-165
90Target-1037
Miller, Lowell
(Otto)
14CJ-53
15CJ-53
16FleischBrd-65
90Target-529
BF2-60
D121/80
D327
D328-119
D329-122
D350/2-119
E121/120
E122
E135-119
M101/4-122
M101/5-119
T207
V100
W501-95
W575
Miller, Mark
75Anderson/TCMA-15
80Cedar-16
80ElPaso-8
80Indianap-18
Miller, Michael
83Butte-19
86Clearw-17
86Memphis/GoldT-18
86Memphis/SilverT-18
86Omaha/ProC-15
87Memphis/Best-15
87Pittsfld-9
87Reading-25
87WinSalem-20
88Clmbia/GS-9
88Memphis/Best-22
88SALAS/GS-14
89StLucie/Star-17
90Jacks/GS-18
Miller, Mickey
76Baton
Miller, Mike
79Savan-25
Miller, Nancy
76Laugh/Clown-9UMP
Miller, Neal Keith
(Keith)
86Portl-17
86Reading-17
87Maine-8
87Maine/TCMA-15
88Maine/CMC-20
88Maine/ProC-290
88Phill/TastyK-27
88Phill/TastyK-36
89ScranWB/CMC-13
89ScranWB/ProC-716
89T-268
90AAAGame/ProC-7
90ScranWB/CMC-21
90ScranWB/ProC-612
91AAA/LineD-37
91BuffB/LineD-37
91BuffB/ProC-553
92OkCty/ProC-1923
Miller, Norm
67T-412R
68OPC-161
68T-161
69OPC-76
69T-76
70T-619
71MLB/St-88
71OPC-18
71T-18
72MB-237
72OPC-466
72T-466
73OPC-637
73T-637
74OPC-439
74T-439
Miller, Orlando
89Oneonta/ProC-2124
90A&AASingle/ProC-101
90Ashvl/ProC-2757
90ProC/Singl-668
90SALAS/Star-16
91AA/LineD-571
91ClBest/Singl-377
91Jacks/LineD-571
91Jacks/ProC-934
92B-555
92ClBest-140
92Jacks/SB-342
92Sky/AASingl-143
92UD/ML-237
93B-588
94B-146
94B-358
94FExcel-203
94SigRook-44
94T-158
94T/Gold-158
94Ultra-508
Miller, Pat
90Helena/SportP-7
91Beloit/ClBest-5
91Beloit/ProC-2100
92Stockton/ClBest-18
92Stockton/ProC-34
Miller, Paul
89Salem/Star-13
90CLAS/CL-26
90Salem/Star-13
91AA/LineD-112
91CaroMud/LineD-112
91CaroMud/ProC-1083
92B-686
92BuffB/BlueS-13
92BuffB/ProC-319
92D/Rook-79
92L-492
92L/BlkGold-492
92ProC/Tomorrow-307
92T/91Debut-124
92Ultra-555
93Pac/Spanish-249
93Pinn-258
93S-239
93S/Boys-29
Miller, Ralph Jr.
77StPete
78StPete
83StPete-27GM
Miller, Ralph
90Target-530
Miller, Randall
80OPC-351R
80T-680R
91Crown/Orio-303
Miller, Ray
86T-381MG
89VFJuice-31CO
90Homer/Pirate-22CO
93Pirate/Nation-19CO
Miller, Rhonda
90Miami/II/Star-30PER
Miller, Richard A.
(Rick)
72T-741R
74OPC-247
74T-247
74T/St-136
75OPC-103
75T-103
75T/M-103
76OPC-302
76SSPC-416
76T-302
77T-566
78SSPC/270-199
78T-482
79T-654
80OPC-27
80T-48
81D-294
81F-279
81OPC-239
81T-239
83OPC-188
84D-493
84F-403
84Nes/792-344
84T-344
85D-517
85F-163
85T-502
86T-424
Miller, Richard
(Rich)
76Dubuq
78Tidew
79Jacks-18
86LitFalls-19MG
88Tidew/CANDL-4C
88Tidew/CMC-26
88Tidew/ProC-1585
89Tidew/CMC-25
90AAASingl/ProC-293CO
90ProC/Singl-686CO
90Tidew/CMC-29CO
90Tidew/ProC-562CO
91Modesto/ClBest-8
92SanJose/ClBest-27CO
Miller, Robert G.
(Bob)
54T-241

55T-9
56T-263
62T-572
91WIZMets-268
94T/Arc54-241
Miller, Robert J.
(Bob)
50B-227
51B-220
52T-187
55B-110
55T-157
55T/DH-60
56T-334
57T-46
58T-326
59T-379
79TCMA-289
Miller, Robert L.
(Bob)
60T-101
61T-314
62Salada-185
62Shirriff-185
62T-293
62T/St-159
63T-261
64T-394
65OPC-98
65T-98
66T-208
67CokeCap/DodgAngel-14
67T-461
68T-534
69T-403
70OPC-47
70T-47
71MLB/St-38
71OPC-542
71T-542
72OPC-414
72T-414
73OPC-277
73T-277
74OPC-624
74T-624
75Hawaii/Caruso-21
77T-113C
78BJ/PostC-16CO
81TCMA-468
90Target-527
91WIZMets-269
Miller, Roger 1
75Sacra/Caruso-19
77Spoka
Miller, Roger 2
88CapeCod/Sum-184
90Clinton/Best-19
90Clinton/ProC-2553
90Foil/Best-120
90MidwLgAS/GS-43
91SanJose/ClBest-2
91SanJose/ProC-13
Miller, Roscoe
E107
Miller, Roy
(Doc)
10Domino-86
11Helmar-163
12Sweet/Pin-142
D303
E286
S74-113
T201
T202
T207
T215/blue
T216
Miller, Russ
90Bend/Legoe-15
Miller, Scott 1
82QuadC-23
Miller, Scott 2
88CapeCod/Sum-87
90MedHat/Best-15
90Myrtle/ProC-2784
91Myrtle/ClBest-21
91Myrtle/ProC-2955
92Dunedin/ClBest-25
92MedHat/ProC-3223CO
92MedHat/SportP-27CO
93MedHat/ProC-3754CO
93MedHat/SportP-25CO
Miller, Scott 3
92Classic/DP-66
92FrRow/DP-47
Miller, Shawn
92Elizab/ClBest-1
92Elizab/ProC-3678
92StCl/Dome-120
Miller, Steve
86Shrev-19
87Phoenix-26
Miller, Stu
53B/BW-16
53Hunter
53T-183
54B-158
54Hunter
54T-164
56T-293
58SFCallB-16
58T-111
59T-183
60T-378
61T-72
62J-143
62P-143
62P/Can-143
62Salada-205
62Shirriff-205
62T-155
62T/St-201
62T/bucks
63T-286
64T-565
65T-499
66T-265
67CokeCap/Orio-7
67T-345
78TCMA-254
84Mother/Giants-18
91Crown/Orio-304
91T/Arc53-183
94T/Arc54-164
Miller, Ted
86Kenosha-16
Miller, Terry
92BurlInd/ClBest-24
92BurlInd/ProC-1672
Miller, Todd
85Everett/Cram-10
86Clinton-13
88Clinton/ProC-706
91Elmira/ClBest-24
91Elmira/ProC-3269
92WinHaven/ClBest-24
92WinHaven/ProC-1773
Miller, Tom
82Lynch-11
Miller, Tony
91AubAS/ClBest-2
91AubAS/ProC-4272
Miller, Trever
91Bristol/ClBest-14
91Bristol/ProC-3599
91ClBest/Singl-406
91Classic/DP-37
91FrRow/DP-7
92Bristol/ClBest-7
92Bristol/ProC-1407
92OPC-684
92Pinn-579
92ProC/Tomorrow-72
92StCl/Dome-121
92T-684DP
92T/Gold-684
92T/GoldWin-684
Miller, Walt
90Target-531
Miller, Ward
14CJ-5
15CJ-5
T207
Miller, Warren
M116
Miller, Wayne
75Albuq/Caruso-21
Miller, William Paul
(Bill)
52T-403
53B/BW-54
53T-100
54NYJour
55B-245
55Esskay
79TCMA-209
91Crown/Orio-300
91T/Arc53-100
PM10/L-28
Miller-Jones, Gary
85Pawtu-9
86Pawtu-15
87Pawtu-19
87Pawtu/TCMA-16
88Pawtu/CMC-19
88Pawtu/ProC-459
89Pawtu/CMC-12
89Pawtu/Dunkin-11
89Pawtu/ProC-689
Millerick, Edwin
91Erie/ClBest-20
91Erie/ProC-4066
Milles, Rhadames G.
81ArkTr-6
Millette, Joe
89Batavia/ProC-1922
90Clearw/Star-16
90FSLAS/Star-15
90Star/ISingl-71
91Clearw/ProC-1629
91Reading/ProC-1374
92D/Rook-80
92ScranWB/ProC-2453
92ScranWB/SB-491
93ScranWB/Team-19
93StCl-360
93StCl/1stDay-360
93T-531
93T/Gold-531
Millies, Walter
40PlayBall-218
90Target-532
Milligan, John
N172
N690
Milligan, Randy
82Lynch-15
83Lynch-7
84Jacks-25
86Jacks/TCMA-26
86Tidew-20
87Tidew-28
87Tidew/TCMA-17
88D/Rook-32
88F/Up-U115
88S-623RP
89B-10
89F/Up-7
89French-15
89T/Tr-81T
89Tidew/Candl-13
89UD-559
89UD/Ext-740
90B-257
90D-519
90D/BestAL-85
90F-183
90F/Can-183
90Leaf-92
90OPC-153
90Panini/St-1
90S-252
90T-153
90T/Big-263
90T/St-233
90UD-663
91Crown/Orio-305
91D-542
91F-484
91Leaf-109
91Leaf/Stud-7
91OPC-416
91Panini/FrSt-240
91Panini/St-201
91S-86
91S/100SS-43
91Seven/3DCoin-9A
91StCl-80
91T-416
91UD-548
91Ultra-20
91WIZMets-273
92D-222
92F-19
92OPC-17
92Panini-65
92Pinn-179
92S-87
92StCl-587
92T-17
92T/Gold-17
92T/GoldWin-17
92UD-181
92Ultra-8
93D-191
93F-170
93F/Final-16
93L-513
93Pac/Spanish-402
93Panini-71
93Pinn-157
93Reds/Kahn-14
93S-112
93Select-212
93StCl-158
93StCl/1stDay-158
93Studio-105
93T-678
93T/Gold-678
93UD-228
93UD-622
93Ultra-330
94D-210
94L-343
94Pinn-485
94S-498
Milligan, William J.
T206
Milliken, Bob
53Exh/Can-44
53T-221
54T-177
55T-111
55T/DH-118
62Kahn/Atl
79TCMA-234
90Johnson/Star-28CO
90Target-533
91T/Arc53-221
94T/Arc54-177
Millner, Tim
83MidldC-9
Mills, Alan
86Cram/NWL-81
87PrWill-7
88PrWill/Star-17
89FtLaud/Star-16
90B-428
90D/Rook-44
90F/Up-114
90Leaf-491
90S/NWest-29
90S/Tr-89T
90T/TVYank-14
90T/Tr-75T
91AAA/LineD-112
91Classic/I-64
91ColClip/LineD-112
91ColClip/ProC-595
91D-338
91OPC-651
91S-73
91S/100RisSt-62
91StCl-473
91T-651
91T/90Debut-108
91UD-222
92B-342
92F/Up-2
92StCl-871
93D-691
93F-171
93L-111
93OPC-195
93Pac/Spanish-346
93S-440
93Select-367
93StCl-643
93StCl/1stDay-643
93T-137
93T/Gold-137
93UD-312
93USPlayC/Rook-11C
93Ultra-143
94D-214
94F-10
94Pac/Cr-37
94StCl/Team-277
94T-324
94T/Gold-324
94Ultra-5
Mills, Art
47TipTop
Mills, Brad
80Memphis-15
82Expo/Hygrade-12
82F-196
82Hygrade
82OPC-118R
82T-118R
83D-366
83Expo/PostC-12
83F-288
83OPC-199
83Stuart-30
83T-744
83Wichita/Dog-13
84Indianap-9
85Cram/PCL-75
86Iowa-19
88CharWh/Best-2
89Peoria/Team-30MG
90CLAS/CL-51CO
90WinSalem/Team-29CO
91CLAS/ProC-CAR44MG
91WinSalem/ClBest-12MG
91WinSalem/ProC-2845MG
92Iowa/ProC-4065MG
92Iowa/SB-224MG
Mills, Colonel
(Buster)
54T-227CO
90Target-534
94T/Arc54-227CO
Mills, Craig
86GlenF-16
87Lakeland-3
Mills, E.L.
N172
Mills, Gil
52Park-59
53Exh/Can-55
Mills, Gotay
82Louisvl-19
83ArkTr-21
84ArkTr-21
Mills, Jim
76Wausau
Mills, Ken
83Clinton/Frit-19
Mills, Lefty
93Conlon-966
Mills, Michael
85Beaum-17
86Beaum-19
88Wichita-31
89Dunedin/Star-11
89Knoxvl/Best-16
89Knoxvl/ProC-1141
89Knoxvl/Star-23
Mills, Richard Allen
71OPC-512R
71T-512R
Mills, Tony
90WichSt-25
Milnar, Al
40PlayBall-202
41PlayBall-33
Milne, Blaine
92Hamil/ClBest-4
92Hamil/ProC-1594
Milne, Darren
92Bristol/ClBest-25
92Bristol/ProC-1426
Milne, William J.
(Pete)
49Eureka-119
53Mother-28
Milner, Brian
78BJ/PostC-17
81OPC-238R
81T-577R
82Knoxvl-10
82OPC-203R
82T-203R
90Oneonta/ProC-3392CO
91Greens/ProC-3076
92Greens/ClBest-28CO
92Greens/ProC-797
Milner, Eddie
79Indianap-10
80Indianap-10
81Indianap-9
82T/Tr-72T
83D-169
83F-597
83F/St-7M

83OPC-363
83T-449
84Borden-20
84D-365
84F-474
84Nes/792-34
84OPC-34
84T-34
84T/St-60
85D-428
85F-541
85OPC-198
85T-198
85T/St-53
86D-325
86F-182
86T-544
86TexGold-20
87D-433
87F-205
87Mother/SFG-15
87OPC-253
87T-253
87T/St-144
87T/Tr-78T
88F-91
88Kahn/Reds-9
88S-548
88T-677
91Pac/SenLg-25
Milner, John
72T-741R
73OPC-4
73T-4
74OPC-234
74T-234
74T/St-69
75Ho-15
75Ho/Twink-15
75OPC-264
75T-264
75T/M-264
76OPC-517
76SSPC-547
76SSPC/MetsY-M1
76T-517
77T-172
78T-304
79T-523
80OPC-38
80T-71
81D-377
81F-386
81T-618
82D-266
82Expo/Hygrade-13
82F-197
82Hygrade
82OPC-331
82T-638
83F-311
91WIZMets-274
Milner, Ted
84Savan-9
86SanJose-13
Miloszewski, Frank
78Salem
Milstien, David
86Elmira-12
87WinHaven-14
88WinHaven/Star-13
89EastLDD/ProC-DD23
89NewBrit/ProC-621
89NewBrit/Star-10
90NewBrit/Best-5
90NewBrit/ProC-1327
90NewBrit/Star-11
91AA/LineD-466
91NewBrit/LineD-466
91NewBrit/ProC-358
92Pawtu/ProC-931
92Pawtu/SB-359
92Sky/AAASingl-163
93Pawtu/Ball-16
Milton, Herb
90AppFox/Box-17
90AppFox/ProC-2092
91AppFx/ClBest-6
91AppFx/ProC-1712
Mimbs, Mark
90GreatF/SportP-9
91Bakers/Cal-12
92Albuq/ProC-717
92Albuq/SB-15
92Sky/AAASingl-7
92UD/ML-77
Mimbs, Michael
90GreatF/SportP-10
91FSLAS/ProC-FSL40
91VeroB/ClBest-9
91VeroB/ProC-770
92ProC/Tomorrow-247
92SanAn/ProC-3972
92SanAn/SB-570
92Sky/AASingl-249
Mims, Fred
73Cedar
74Cedar
Mims, Larry
87Miami-23
88Hagers/Star-12
89AubAs/ProC-6
89Hagers/ProC-264
89Wichita/Rock/Up-13
Minarcin, John
78Wisco
79Wisco-10
Minarcin, Rudy
55T-174
56T-36
Minaya, Omar
81Wausau-22
Minaya, Robert
88Pulaski/ProC-1767
89Sumter/ProC-1111
Minch, John
87Modesto-7
88Huntsvl/BK-12
Mincher, Donald
(Don)
60T-548
61Clover-17
61Peters-5
61T-336
62T-386
63T-269
63Twin/Volpe-6
64T-542
65OPC-108
65T-108
66T-388
67CokeCap/DodgAngel-25
67T-312
68Bz-12
68OPC-75
68T-75
68T/ActionSt-8AM
69MB-193
69MLB/St-96
69T-285
69T/S-33
69T/St-227
69T/decal
70K-75
70MB-19
70MLB/St-261
70OPC-185
70T-185
70T/PI-17
71K-27
71MLB/St-521
71OPC-680
71T-680
72MB-238
72OPC-242
72T-242
78TCMA-54
78Twin/Frisz-14
89Smok/Angels-5
93Rang/Keeb-29
Minchey, Nate
88OPC-6
88Rockford-25
89Rockford-25
89Rockford/Team-17
90Durham/Team-27
91Durham/ProC-DUR5
91DurhamUp/ProC-5
91Miami/ClBest-10
91Miami/ProC-406
92Greenvl/SB-240
93B-31
93Pawtu/Ball-17
94D-484
94F/MLP-25
94Pinn-406
94T-716
94T/Gold-716
Minchk, Kevin
92Spokane/ClBest-13
92Spokane/ProC-1303
Mincho, Tom
90Miami/I/Star-17
Minear, Clint
91Kissim/ProC-4180
92Yakima/ClBest-8
92Yakima/ProC-3446
Miner, Gary
87BYU-17
Miner, J.R.
86BurlEx-16MG
87BurlEx-24MG
Miner, James
82CharR-1
84Memphis-16
85Cram/PCL-72
86Tucson-14
87Tucson-13
Minetto, Craig
80Ogden-3
80T-494
81T-316
82RochR-4
83RochR-5
84Cram/PCL-69
Mingori, Steve
69T-339R
71OPC-612R
71T-612R
72OPC-261
72T-261
73OPC-532
73T-532
74OPC-537
74T-537
75OPC-544
75T-544
75T/M-544
76OPC-541
76SSPC-161
76T-541
77T-314
78SSPC/270-242
78T-696
79T-72
80T-219
86Syrac-19CO
87Dunedin-13CO
90Myrtle/ProC-2793CO
91AA/LineD-375M
91Knoxvl/LineD-375CO
91Knoxvl/ProC-1786CO
92Knoxvl/ProC-3008CO
92Knoxvl/SB-400CO
93Knoxvl/ProC-1267CO
Minick, Jeff
86Lakeland-14
Minier, Pablo
77Spartan
Minik, Tim
91BendB/ClBest-8
91BendB/ProC-3693
92Madis/ProC-1230
Minissale, Frank
88LitFalls/Pucko-29
Minium, Matt
80Batavia-24
Minker, Al
80WHave-1
Minnehan
N172
Minnema, Dave
86Lakeland-15
Minner, Paul
49Eureka-43
52B-211
52T-127
53B/Col-71
53T-92
54B-13
54T-28
56T-182
79TCMA-163
90Target-535
91T/Arc53-92
94T/Arc54-28
Minnich, Bill
92AubAs/ClBest-5
92AubAs/ProC-1366
Minnick, Don
80LynnS-8
Minnifield, Wallace
89Kingspt/Star-17
90Pittsfld/Pucko-4
Minnis, Billy
91MidwLAS/ProC-28
91QuadC/ClBest-19
91QuadC/ProC-2638
Minor, Blas
89Salem/Star-14
90Harris/ProC-1189
90Harris/Star-11
90ProC/Singl-738
90Star/ISingl-29
91AAA/LineD-38
91BuffB/LineD-38
91BuffB/ProC-538
92BuffB/BlueS-12
92BuffB/ProC-320
92BuffB/SB-36
92D/Rook-81
92F/Up-116
92Sky/AAASingl-15
93B-486
93F/Final-114
93L-539
93Pac/Spanish-588
93Pinn-283
93Pirate/Nation-20
93S-304
93Select/RookTr-71T
93T/Tr-82T
93UD-745
93Ultra-452
94D-189
94F-615
94Pac/Cr-503
94Pinn-160
94Pinn/Artist-160
94Pinn/Museum-160
94S-211
94S/GoldR-211
94StCl-465
94StCl/1stDay-465
94StCl/Gold-465
94T-253
94T/Gold-253
94UD/CollC-206
94UD/CollC/Gold-206
94UD/CollC/Silv-206
94Ultra-259
Minoso, Orestes Jr.
77AppFx
Minoso, Orestes
(Minnie)
52B-5
52BR
52RM-AL15
52StarCal-87BM
52StarCal/L-73E
52T-195
53B/Col-36
53NB
53T-66
54B-38
54Dix
54RH
54RM-AL7
55B-25
55RM-AL24
56T-125
56YellBase/Pin-22
57T-138
58T-295
59Kahn
59T-166M
59T-80
60T-365
61Bz-7
61P-25
61T-380
61T-42LL
61T/St-125
62J-51
62P-51
62P/Can-51
62Salada-39A
62Salada-39B
62Shirriff-39
62T-28
62T/St-188
62T/bucks
63T-190
64T-538
77OPC-262RB
77T-232RB
78SSPC/270-160CO
79TCMA-286
80Marchant-20
80Pac/Leg-96
84TrueVal/WS-24
86Coke/WS-CO
87Coke/WS-29
88Coke/WS-18
88Pac/Leg-51
89Coke/WS-30
89Kodak/WSox-4M
89Swell-59
91K/Leyenda-9
91T/Arc53-66
92AP/ASG-37
92Bz/Quadra-8M
93TWill-27
93UD/ATH-153M
93UD/ATH-95
Exh47
PM10/Sm-126
Minter, Larry
91Pocatel/ProC-3797
91Pocatel/SportP-1
Minton, Greg
75Phoenix-8
75Phoenix/Caruso-15
75Phoenix/CircleK-8
77Phoenix
77T-489R
78Cr/PCL-102
78T-312
79T-84
80Pol/Giants-38
80T-588
81D-579
81F-449
81OPC-111
81T-111
81T/St-238
82D-348
82F-396
82OPC-144
82T-687
82T/St-107
83D-186
83D/AAS-10
83F-269
83F/St-23M
83F/St-5M
83K-46
83Mother/Giants-5
83OPC-107
83OPC/St-137RB
83OPC/St-138RB
83OPC/St-299
83T-3RB
83T-470
83T/Fold-4M
83T/St-137
83T/St-138
83T/St-249
84D-187
84F-383
84F/St-69
84Mother/Giants-8
84Nes/792-205
84OPC-205
84T-205
85D-143
85F-617
85Mother/Giants-8
85OPC-45
85T-45
85T/St-167
86D-480
86F-549
86Mother/Giants-8
86T-310
86T-516M
87F-282
87F/Up-U80
87Mother/SFG-9
87OPC-333
87T-724
87T/Tr-79T
88D-505
88F-499
88OPC-129
88S-176
88Smok/Angels-11
88T-129
88T/St-176
89D-490

89D/Best-283
89F-485
89OPC-306
89S-543
89T-576
89UD-635
90D-116
90F-140
90F/Can-140
90OPC-421
90PublInt/St-375
90S-48
90T-421
90UD-83
91S-823
Minton, Jesse
87Sumter-17
Mintz, Alan
80Elmira-41
Mintz, Steve
90Yakima/Team-29
91Bakers/Cal-11
92VeroB/ClBest-25
92VeroB/ProC-2871
Minutelli, Gino
86Cedar/TCMA-7
87Tampa-20
88Chatt/Best-16
90Chatt/GS-21
91AAA/LineD-268
91B-677
91Nashvl/LineD-268
91Nashvl/ProC-2153
91T/90Debut-109
92Nashvl/ProC-1831
92Nashvl/SB-287
92Pinn-261
92S-408
92Sky/AAASingl-134
92StCl-452
93Mother/Giant-27
Miquet, Felix
45Parade*-69
Mirabella, Geno
91SLCity/ProC-3208
91SLCity/SportP-17
Mirabella, Paul
78Cr/PCL-48
79Colum-26
81D-151
81OPC-11
81Syrac/Team-14
81T-382
82D-629
82OPC-163
82T-499
83D-541
83F-573
83T-12
84Mother/Mar-17
85Cram/PCL-89
85F-494
85T-766
86Mother/Mar-13
87Denver-9
88Denver/CMC-5
88Denver/ProC-1258
89D-654
89F-192
89Pac/SenLg-165
89Pol/Brew-27
89S-569
89T-192
89T/SenLg-51
89TM/SenLg-79
89UD-322
90Brewer/MillB-14
90EliteSenLg-27
90Pol/Brew-27
90PublInt/St-499
91Crown/Orio-306
91F-590
91S-558
92Yank/WIZ70-115
93Rang/Keeb-268
Mirabelli, Doug
90WichSt-26
93StCl/MurphyS-40
94ClBest/Gold-151
Mirabito, Tim
86Tampa-13
87Vermont-8
Miran, Tory
92Yakima/ClBest-13
92Yakima/ProC-3463
Miranda, Angel
88Stockton/Cal-180
88Stockton/ProC-749
89Beloit/II/Star-22
90A&AASingle/ProC-139
90AS/Cal-51
90Stockton/Best-25
90Stockton/Cal-175
90Stockton/ProC-2175
91AA/LineD-193
91B-53
91ElPaso/LineD-193
91ElPaso/ProC-2747
92B-63
92Denver/ProC-2638
92Denver/SB-140
92Sky/AAASingl-68
93F/Final-230
93Select/RookTr-72T
94D-488
94F-184
94Pac/Cr-335
94Pinn-341
94T-709
94T/Gold-709
94UD/CollC-207
94UD/CollC/Gold-207
94UD/CollC/Silv-207
94Ultra-79
Miranda, Giovanni
90AppFox/Box-18
90AppFox/ProC-2102
90Eugene/GS-19
90ProC/Singl-723
91AppFx/ClBest-19
91AppFx/ProC-1725
92BBCity/ClBest-18
92Saraso/ProC-214
Miranda, Willie
53T-278
54T-56
55B-79
55Esskay
55T-154
56T-103
56T/Pin-2SS
57T-151
58Hires-32
58T-179
59T-540
91Crown/Orio-307
91T/Arc53-278
94T/Arc54-56
Misa, Joe
91SoOreg/ClBest-28
91SoOreg/ProC-3839
92Reno/Cal-57
Miscik, Bob
82Buffa-2
84Cram/PCL-136
85Cram/PCL-239
86Hawaii-17
87Edmon-4
88Edmon/CMC-15
88Edmon/ProC-577
90Freder/Team-3
91Kane/ClBest-26MG
91Kane/ProC-2674MG
91Kane/Team-26M
92Freder/ProC-1822
Miscik, Dennis
77Cocoa
80Tucson-13
81OkCty/TCMA-11
Mishkin, Sol
28LaPresse-18
Misuraca, Mike
89Elizab/Star-19
89Kenosha/ProC-1071
89Kenosha/Star-15
89Star/IISingl-148
90Foil/Best-272
90Kenosha/Best-21
90Kenosha/ProC-2290
90Kenosha/Star-13
91Visalia/ClBest-5
91Visalia/ProC-1739
92FtMyr/ProC-2742
92Miracle/ClBest-18
Mitchell, Albert
(Roy)
E270/2
Mitchell, Antonio
(Tony)
91Welland/ClBest-5
91Welland/ProC-3587
92Augusta/ClBest-13
92Augusta/ProC-252
92ClBest-18
93B-121
93FExcel/ML-93
93Kinston/Team-19
93SALAS/II-25
Mitchell, Charlie
84Pawtu-1
85D-40RR
85IntLgAS-18
85Pawtu-20
86Toledo-17
88Nashvl/Team-17
89Nashvl/CMC-1
89Nashvl/ProC-1273
89Nashvl/Team-16
90AAASingl/ProC-541
90Nashvl/CMC-6
90Nashvl/ProC-229
90ProC/Singl-131
91AAA/LineD-260
91Nashvl/LineD-260
91Nashvl/ProC-2154
Mitchell, Clarence
10Domino-87
11Helmar-118
12Sweet/Pin-104
28Yueng-15
90Target-537
91Conlon/Sport-202
D328-120
E120
E135-120
E210-15
L1-118
S81-93
W502-15
W573
Mitchell, Craig
75Tucson-15
75Tucson/Caruso-14
75Tucson/Team-12
76OPC-591R
76T-591R
76Tucson-32
77SanJose-15
77T-491R
78T-711
79Ogden/TCMA-21
79Ogden/TCMA-5
Mitchell, David
88MissSt-21
89MissSt-26
90MissSt-27
Mitchell, Donovan
92AubAs/ClBest-6
92AubAs/ProC-1362
94FExcel-204
Mitchell, Fred F.
90Target-539
C46-47
E107
E270/2
E90/1
M116
T206
V100
W514-96
Mitchell, Glenn
88Idaho/ProC-1837
88Sumter/ProC-408
89Sumter/ProC-1116
92QuadC/ClBest-11
92QuadC/ProC-805
Mitchell, Howie
78Cr/PCL-116
Mitchell, J.W.
79QuadC-10
Mitchell, Jackie
88Chatt/Team-23
Mitchell, Joe 1
77Newar
Mitchell, Joe 2
90AAASingl/ProC-658
90ProC/Singl-37
Mitchell, John
92Negro/RetortII-27
Mitchell, John Franklin
W575
Mitchell, John Kyle
83Beloit/Frit-5
86Tidew-21
87D/Rook-37
87F/Up-U81
87Idaho-24
87T/Tr-80T
87Tidew-20
87Tidew/TCMA-7
88F-145
88S-249
88T-207
88Tidew/CANDL-23
88Tidew/CMC-8
88Tidew/ProC-1577
89Tidew/CMC-4
89Tidew/ProC-1970
90AAASingl/ProC-457
90ProC/Singl-322
90RochR/CMC-21
90RochR/ProC-700
90Target-540
91AAA/LineD-67
91Calgary/LineD-67
91Calgary/ProC-513
91Crown/Orio-308
91D-710
91F-485
91OPC-708
91S-569
91T-708
91WIZMets-275
Mitchell, Johnny
93Welland/ClBest-14
93Welland/ProC-3374
Mitchell, Jorge
87James-11
88James/ProC-1916
Mitchell, Joseph
(Joe)
85Beloit-3
86Stockton-15
87ElPaso-2
88ElPaso/Best-25
89Denver/CMC-20
89Denver/ProC-43
90Denver/CMC-12
90Denver/ProC-633
Mitchell, Keith
88Sumter/ProC-390
89BurlB/ProC-1609
89BurlB/Star-15
90CLAS/CL-29
90Durham/Team-2
91AA/LineD-212
91B-575
91Brave/Dubuq/Stand-26
91ClBest/Singl-224
91Classic/III-58
91Greenvl/ClBest-21
91Greenvl/LineD-212
91Greenvl/ProC-3016
91Richm/Bob-33
91UD/FinalEd-56F
92B-62
92D-508
92F-364
92OPC-542
92Pinn-258
92Pinn/RookI-8
92ProC/Tomorrow-182
92Richm/Bleach-10
92Richm/Comix-11
92Richm/ProC-387
92Richm/SB-433
92S-748
92Sky/AAASingl-198
92StCl-551
92T-542
92T/91Debut-125
92T/Gold-542
92T/GoldWin-542
92UD-454
92UD-80M
92UD/ML-185
93Richm/Bleach-3
93Richm/Pep-18
93Richm/Team-20
94Pinn-524
94Select-202
94Ultra-423
Mitchell, Kevin
82Lynch-6
84Tidew-23
85IntLgAS-4
85Tidew-18
86D/Rook-17
86F/Up-U76
86Sf/Rook-49
86T/Tr-74T
87Bohem-7
87D-599
87D/OD-145
87F-17
87F/RecSet-21
87F/Up-U82
87Leaf-170
87OPC-307
87Sf-144
87Sf/TPrev-16M
87T-653
87T/Gloss60-50
87T/Tr-81T
87ToysRUs-21
88D-66
88F-92
88F/Hottest-27
88F/St-S5
88Leaf-87
88Mother/Giants-3
88OPC-387
88Panini/St-424
88Panini/St-448IA
88S-481
88T-497
88T/Big-57
88T/St-88
88T/UK-48
89B-474
89Classic-31
89Classic/Up/2-198
89D-485
89D/Best-281
89F-336
89KennerFig-93
89Mother/Giants-3
89OPC-189
89Panini/St-216
89S-39
89S/Mast-12
89S/YS/II-38
89Sf-142
89T-189
89T/Big-129
89T/LJN-144
89T/St-84
89UD-163
90B-232
90B/Ins-6
90Bz-1
90Classic-150
90Classic-64
90CollAB-16
90D-11DK
90D-715AS
90D-98
90D/BestNL-85
90D/Bon/MVP-BC11
90D/Learning-2
90D/Preview-4
90D/SuperDK-11DK
90F-637M
90F-65
90F/ASIns-6
90F/AwardWin-23
90F/BB-27
90F/BBMVP-26
90F/Can-637M
90F/Can-65
90F/LL-26
90F/WS-2
90F/WaxBox-C21
90Holsum/Discs-9
90HotPlay/St-27
90KMart/SS-6
90Kenner/Fig-58
90KingB/Discs-2
90Leaf-120
90MCA/Disc-6
90MLBPA/Pins-24
90Mother/Giant-5
90OPC-401AS
90OPC-500
90Panini/St-208
90Panini/St-214
90Panini/St-361
90Post-15
90PublInt/St-617
90PublInt/St-77

90RedFoley/St-64
90S-343
90S/100St-50
90Sf-1
90Sunflower-1
90T-401AS
90T-500
90T/Big-137
90T/Coins-33
90T/DH-47
90T/Gloss22-6
90T/Gloss60-21
90T/HeadsUp-15
90T/HillsHM-5
90T/Mini-86
90T/St-148AS
90T/St-79
90T/TVAS-40
90Tetley/Discs-6
90UD-117
90UD-40TC
90USPlayC/AS-12H
90WonderBrd-7
90Woolwth/HL-2MVP
90Woolwth/HL-32
91B-636
91Cadaco-39
91Classic/200-129
91Classic/I-10
91Classic/III-59
91CollAB-6
91D-255
91D-407MVP
91D-438AS
91F-267
91JDean-13
91Kenner-41
91Leaf-85
91Leaf/Stud-257
91MSA/Holsum-4
91MajorLg/Pins-64
91MooTown-23
91Mother/Giant-5
91OPC-40
91OPC/Premier-81
91PG&E-1
91Panini/FrSt-162
91Panini/FrSt-71
91Panini/St-71
91Panini/Top15-11
91Panini/Top15-35
91Post-24
91RedFoley/St-123
91RedFoley/St-66
91S-406MB
91S-451
91S/100SS-98
91SFExam/Giant-11
91Seven/3DCoin-10NC
91StCl-250
91T-40
91T/CJMini/I-30
91T/SU-27
91UD-247
91Ultra-326
91WIZMets-276
92B-276
92Classic/Game200-165
92Classic/I-64
92Classic/II-T91
92D-583
92F-644
92F/Up-56
92L-185
92L/BlkGold-185
92Mother/Mar-4
92OPC-180
92OPC/Premier-97
92Panini-218
92Pinn-393
92S-640
92S/100SS-93
92S/RookTr-18T
92StCl-215
92StCl-765
92Studio-237
92T-180
92T/Gold-180
92T/GoldWin-180
92T/Kids-59
92T/Tr-74T
92T/TrGold-74T
92UD-266
92UD-735
92UD-80M
92Ultra-434
93B-386
93Colla/DM-76
93D-157
93F-396
93F/Final-17
93Flair-28
93L-321
93OPC-252
93Pac/Spanish-403
93Panini-296
93Pinn-551
93Pinn/HRC-23
93Pinn/Slug-21
93Reds/Kahn-15
93S-407
93Select-108
93Select/RookTr-29T
93StCl-694
93StCl/1stDay-694
93Studio-162
93T-217
93T/Finest-136
93T/FinestRef-136
93T/Gold-217
93T/Tr-112T
93UD-213
93UD-55
93UD-646
93UD/FunPack-171
93UD/SP-210
93Ultra-331
94B-514
94D-377
94D/Special-377
94F-416
94Finest-323
94L-370
94OPC-29
94Pac/Cr-152
94Panini-164
94Pinn-70
94Pinn/Artist-70
94Pinn/Museum-70
94S-24
94S/GoldR-24
94Select-112
94Sf/2000-126
94StCl-422
94StCl/1stDay-422
94StCl/Gold-422
94Studio-169
94T-335
94T/Gold-335
94TripleP-215
94UD-58
94UD/ElecD-58
94UD/SP-160
94Ultra-173

Mitchell, L. Dale
48L-165
49B-43
50B-130
50NumNum
51B-5
51T/RB-13
52B-239
52NumNum-15
52StarCal-88C
52StarCal/L-74F
52T-92
52TipTop
53B/Col-119
53RM-AL9
53T-26
54B-148
54DanDee
55B-314
55Gol/Ind-19
55Salem
56T-268
79TCMA-140
90Target-538
91T/Arc53-26
Exh47

Mitchell, Larry
92FrRow/DP-22
92Martins/ClBest-1
92Martins/ProC-3053
93StCl/MurphyS-39
94B-664

Mitchell, Mark
87Oneonta-22
88FtLaud/Star-15

Mitchell, Michael F.
14Piedmont/St-40
15CJ-62
E254
E270/2
E90/1
M116
S74-78
T202
T204
T205
T206
T207
T213/blue
T213/brown
T215/blue
T3-24

Mitchell, Parris
91Perth/Fut-13

Mitchell, Paul
76OPC-393
76T-393
77SanJose-25
77T-53
78T-558
79OPC-118
79T-233
80T-131
81D-205
81T-449
91Crown/Orio-309

Mitchell, Robert Van
(Bobby)
79Albuq-18
80Albuq-20
81Albuq/TCMA-22
82F-14
82Toledo-28
83F-620
83OPC/St-91
83T-647
83T/St-91
83Twin/Team-7
84Cram/PCL-202
84F-571
84Nes/792-307
84T-307
84Toledo-10
90Target-536

Mitchell, Robert Vance
(Bobby)
71OPC-111R
71T-111R
74OPC-497
74T-497
75OPC-468
75T-468
75T/M-468
76OPC-479
76SSPC-242
76T-479
79Hawaii-1
80Hawaii-10
81Portl-18
82Portl-15
92Yank/WIZ70-116

Mitchell, Robert
91Martins/ClBest-20
91Martins/ProC-3451
92Martins/ClBest-12
92Martins/ProC-3054

Mitchell, Ron
75Shrev/TCMA-11
76Shrev
78Colum
79Portl-8
80Buffa-2

Mitchell, Scot
82Madis/Frit-11

Mitchell, Scott
88MissSt-22
89MissSt-27
90MissSt-37

Mitchell, Thomas
90Erie/Star-17
91Reno/Cal-14

Mitchell, William
D329-123
D350/2-120
M101/4-123
M101/5-120
T207

Mitchelson, Mark
91ClBest/Singl-168
91Elmira/ClBest-25
91Elmira/ProC-3270
91WinHaven/ClBest-4
91WinHaven/ProC-484
92WinHaven/ClBest-25

Mitchener, Mike
89SoBend/GS-14
90Foil/Best-131
90SoBend/Best-17
90SoBend/GS-11

Mitta, Chris
88Pulaski/ProC-1763

Mitterwald, George
68T-301R
69T-491R
70OPC-118
70T-118
71MLB/St-467
71OPC-189
71T-189
72OPC-301
72OPC-302IA
72T-301
72T-302IA
74OPC-249
74T-249
74T/St-209
74T/Tr-249T
75OPC-411
75T-411
75T/M-411
76OPC-506
76SSPC-318
76T-506
77T-124
78SanJose-20
78T-688
85Modesto/Chong-26MG
86OrlanTw-12MG
87OrlanTw-9MG

Miyauchi, Hector
88Fresno/Cal-15
88Fresno/ProC-1233

Mize, John
38Exh/4-8
39Exh
40Wheat-6
41DP-39
41DP-99
42Playball-31
47HomogBond-34
48B-4
48L-46
49B-85
49Eureka-120
50B-139
51B-50
51BR-A7
51FB
51T/BB-50
52B-145
52BR
52T-129
53B/BW-15
53NB
53RM-AL18
53T-77
60F-38
61F-63
72Laugh/GF-17
72T/Test-3
74Laugh/ASG-47
77Shakey-B
77Shakey/WAS-B
80Pac/Leg-49
80Perez/HOF-176
83D/HOF-10
85CircK-32
85D/HOF-4
85West/2-44
86Sf/Dec-24M
88Pac/Leg-63
89HOF/St-3
89Pac/Leg-180
89Swell-55
90Perez/GreatMom-23
90Swell/Great-90
91Conlon/Sport-53
91Swell/Great-62
91T/Arc53-77
92AP/ASG-13
92AP/ASG24K-13G
92Bz/Quadra-9M
92Card/McDon/Pac-3
92Conlon/Sport-435
92Conlon/Sport-628
92Perez/Master-31
92Perez/Master-32
92Perez/Master-33
92Perez/Master-34
92Perez/Master-35
92Yank/WIZAS-49
92Yank/WIZHOF-24
93AP/ASGCoke/Amo-13
93Conlon-918
93Metallic-13
93TWill-129
93TWill-145
93TWill-66
93TWill/Locklear-4
93UD/ATH-96
94Conlon-1126
94Conlon/Col-28
D305
R302
R312
R346-30
R423-70
W754

Mize, Paul
80WHave-8
81Tacom-16
82Tacom-15
82WHave-16

Mizell, Wilmer
52T-334
53B/BW-23
53Hunters
53T-128
54T-249
56T-193
57T-113
58T-385
61Kahn
61P-140
91T/Arc53-128
91WIZMets-277
92Bz/Quadra-16M
94T/Arc54-249

Mizerock, John
84D-380
85Cram/PCL-68
86D-502
86Tucson-15
87D-653
87Richm/Bob-14
87Richm/Crown-8
87Richm/TCMA-10
87T-408
88Richm-25
88Richm/CMC-21
88Richm/ProC-19
89Richm/Bob-18
89Richm/CMC-12
89Richm/Ko-25
89Richm/ProC-827
90AAASingl/ProC-407
90ProC/Singl-297
90Richm/Bob-6
90Richm/CMC-21
90Richm/ProC-262
90Richm/Team-23

Mizusawa, Hideki
90Gate/SportP-17

Mlicki, Dave
91Collnd/ClBest-6
92B-413
92Canton/ProC-688
92Canton/SB-112
92ClBest-39
92Sky/AASingl-53
93B-451
93ClBest/MLG-6
93D-273
93F/MLPII-9
93Pinn-275
93S-285
93T-571
93T/Gold-571
93UD-17SR

Mlicki, Doug
90AR-33M
92AubAs/ClBest-18
92AubAs/ProC-1352

Mmahat, Kevin
88FSLAS/Star-44
88FtLaud/Star-16

89Albany/Best-23
89Albany/ProC-341
89Albany/Star-14
90AAAGame/ProC-15
90AAASingl/ProC-324
90AlbanyDG/Best-25
90ColClip/CMC-5
90ColClip/ProC-674
90Colum/Pol-20
90D-481
90ProC/Singl-205
90S-643
90T/89Debut-84
90T/TVYank-55
92Yank/WIZ80-121
Moates, Dave
75Spokane/Caruso-2
76OPC-327
76T-327
77T-588
77Tucson
93Rang/Keeb-269
Moberg, Mike
91ClBest/Singl-317
91Rockford/ClBest-23
91Rockford/ProC-2058
Mobilia, Bill
92MN-14
Mobley, Anton
89StCath/ProC-2084
90Myrtle/ProC-2789
90StCath/ProC-3479
Moccia, Mario
89Niagara/Pucko-18
90Niagara/Pucko-7
Moeller, Daniel
C46-76
T206
Moeller, Dennis
86Cram/NWL-50
87AppFx-26
88AppFx/ProC-160
89BBCity/Star-17
90Memphis/Star-19
92AAA/ASG/SB-338
92D/Rook-82
92Omaha/ProC-2960
92Omaha/SB-338
92Sky/AAASingl-155
93B-50
93D-648
93F/Final-115
93F/MLPII-14
93OPC/Premier-54
93Pac/Spanish-589
93Pinn-600
93Pirate/Nation-21
93UD-779
93Ultra-453
Moeller, Joe
63T-53
64T-549
65OPC-238
65T-238
66T-449
67CokeCap/DodgAngel-4
67OPC-149
67T-149
68T-359
69T-444
70OPC-97
70T-97
71MLB/St-108
71OPC-288
71T-288
71Ticket/Dodg-10
81TCMA-448
85SpokAT/Cram-14
90Target-541
Moeller, Ron
61T-466
63T-541
91Crown/Orio-310
Moen, Eric
90Yakima/Team-21TR
91BendB/ClBest-27TR
Moen, Robbie
90AZ/Pol-13
92AZ/Pol-9
Moesche, Carl
84Butte-7
Moffet, Samuel
N172
Moffitt, G. Scott
76QuadC
77QuadC
80SLCity-4
81SLCity-23
Moffitt, Randy
73OPC-43
73T-43
74OPC-156
74T-156
75OPC-132
75T-132
75T/M-132
76OPC-553
76T-553
77BurgChef-101
77T-464
78T-284
78Wiffle/Discs-51
79Pol/Giants-17
79T-62
80Pol/Giants-17
80T-359
81D-195
81F-446
81T-622
83D-545
83F-456
83T-723
83T/Fold-4M
83T/Tr-73T
84D-390
84F-163
84Nes/792-108
84OPC-108
84T-108
Moford, Herb
59T-91
91WIZMets-278
Mogridge, George
92Conlon/Sport-376
E120
T207
V100
W572
W573
Mohart, George
90Target-1038
Moharter, Dave
75Spokane/Caruso-19
77Tucson
78Cr/PCL-13
79Tucson-16
80CharCh-7
87Macon-25
88Augusta/ProC-383
Mohler, Mike
90Madison/Best-20
90Madison/ProC-2267
91CalLgAS-42
91Modesto/ClBest-9
91Modesto/ProC-3084
92ClBest-137
92Huntsvl/ProC-3946
92Huntsvl/SB-315
92Sky/AASingl-134
93B-105
93F/Final-258
93Mother/A's-23
93Pac/Spanish-570
93Pinn-592
93StCl/A's-3
93Ultra-610
94D-505
94F-269
94Pac/Cr-458
94T-282
94T/Gold-282
Mohn, Solly
52LaPatrie-12
Mohorcic, Dale
81Portl-17
83LynnP-6
85OKCty-26
86OKCty-13
86Rang-34
87D-531
87F-131
87Mother/Rang-15
87Smok/R-5
87T-497
88D-470
88D/Best-144
88F-474
88Mother/R-15
88OPC-163
88S-452
88Smok/R-6
88T-163
88T/St-242
89D-630
89F-259
89S-420
89S/NWest-16
89T-26
89UD/Ext-727
90AAASingl/ProC-581
90F-450
90F/Can-450
90Indianap/CMC-8
90Indianap/ProC-298
90ProC/Singl-58
90S-191
90UD-530
91F-239
91S-596
92Yank/WIZ80-122
93Rang/Keeb-270
Mohr, Ed
79QuadC-2
Mohr, Tommy
83Butte-25
85FtMyr-19
Moisan, William
52Mother-64
Mokan, John
25Exh-46
26Exh-46
27Exh-23
E120
Moldes, Orestes
80Batavia-11
Moler, Dick
52Laval-16
Moler, Jason
92FrRow/DP-29
92T/Tr-75T
92T/TrGold-75T
93StCl/MurphyS-36
94B-636
94ClBest/Gold-39
94FExcel-247
94FExcel/LL-14
94TedW-127
Molero, Juan
87Greens-13
88Lynch/Star-15
89Lynch/Star-14
Molesworth, Carlton
E270/2
T206
T213/brown
Molina, Albert
89Salem/Star-15
Molina, Islay
(Izzy)
91Madison/ClBest-16
91Madison/ProC-2136
91MidwLAS/ProC-43
92AS/Cal-16
92Reno/Cal-49
93Modesto/ClBest-13
93Modesto/ProC-802
93StCl/A's-17
94B-164
94ClBest/Gold-126
94FExcel-121
Molina, Mario
87Salem/ProC-2418
88QuadC/GS-18
89PalmSp/ProC-477
Molinaro, Bob
77Evansvl/TCMA-19
78SSPC/270-158
79Iowa/Pol-11
79T-88
81Coke
81F-340
81T-466
81T/HT
81T/St-61
82D-417
82F-353
82RedLob
82T-363
83D-596
83F-167
83T-664
85RochR-12
86Hagers-12MG
87RochR-27
89Canton/Best-17
89Canton/ProC-1319
89Pac/SenLg-80
89T/SenLg-118
90AAASingl/ProC-235MG
90ColoSp/CMC-24MG
90ColoSp/ProC-54MG
90EliteSenLg-87
90HagersDG/Best-17MG
90ProC/Singl-477MG
91CharlR/ClBest-27MG
91CharlR/ProC-1330MG
91Crown/Orio-311
91Pac/SenLg-13
Moline, Stan
76Cedar
Molitor, Paul
78T-707R
79K-20
79OPC-8
79T-24
80OPC-211
80T-406
81D-203
81F-515
81F/St-82
81K-53
81OPC-300
81T-300
81T/SO-35
81T/St-91
82D-78
82F-148
82F/St-136
82OPC-195
82Pol/Brew-4
82T-195
82T/St-200
83D-484
83F-40
83F/St-19AM
83F/St-19BM
83F/St-4M
83Gard-11
83OPC-371
83OPC/St-139RB
83OPC/St-140RB
83OPC/St-156LCS
83OPC/St-83
83Pol/Brew-4
83T-630
83T/St-139
83T/St-140
83T/St-156
83T/St-83
84D-107
84D/AAS-35
84D/Champs-54
84F-207
84Gard-13
84Nes/792-60
84OPC-60
84Pol/Brew-4
84Seven-18C
84T-60
84T/RD-6M
84T/St-294
85D-359
85F-588
85FunFoodPin-105
85Gard-13
85OPC-395
85Pol/Brew-4
85T-522
85T/RD-7M
86D-124
86D/AAS-39
86F-495
86F/LimEd-30
86F/Mini-101
86F/St-76
86Jay's-12
86Leaf-70
86OPC-267
86Pol/Brew-4
86Seven/Coin-C16M
86Sf-128M
86Sf-39
86T-267
86T/St-203
86T/Tatt-23M
87Classic-45
87D-117
87D/HL-29
87D/OD-54
87F-350
87F/St-78
87Leaf-71
87OPC-184
87Pol/Brew-4
87RedFoley/St-22
87Sf-54
87Sf/TPrev-19M
87Stuart-21
87T-56
87T-741
87T/St-200
88Classic/Blue-232
88D-249
88D-7DK
88D-BC3
88D/Best-165
88D/DKsuper-7DK
88Drake-11
88F-169
88F/AS-12
88F/AwardWin-25
88F/LL-27
88F/Mini-31
88F/St-38
88F/TL-22
88FanSam-5
88Grenada-29
88Jiffy-12
88KMart-17
88KayBee-19
88KennerFig-70
88KingB/Disc-23
88Leaf-168
88Leaf-7DK
88OPC-231
88Panini/St-125
88Panini/St-432
88Pol/Brew-4
88S-340
88S-660HL
88Sf-221
88Sf-79
88T-465
88T/Big-1
88T/Coins-20
88T/Gloss60-57
88T/Mini-19
88T/Revco-20
88T/RiteAid-20
88T/St-194
88T/St/Backs-42
88T/UK-49
89B-140
89Brewer/YB-4
89Cadaco-37
89Classic-12
89D-291
89D/AS-3
89D/Best-15
89D/MVP-BC9
89D/PopUp-3
89F-193
89F/AS-8
89F/BBAS-30
89Gard-1
89KMart/Lead-10
89KennerFig-94
89Master/Discs-8
89OPC-110
89Panini/St-243AS
89Panini/St-373
89Pol/Brew-4
89RedFoley/St-81
89S-565
89S/HotStar-57
89Sf-209
89T-110
89T/Big-330
89T/Coins-46
89T/Gloss22-3
89T/Gloss60-43
89T/LJN-120
89T/Mini-58
89T/St-146
89T/St-204
89T/St/Backs-9
89T/UK-53
89UD-525
89UD-673TC
90B-399

90Brewer/MillB-15
90Classic/Up-34
90D-103
90D/BestAL-64
90D/Bon/MVP-BC15
90F-330
90F/BBMVP-27
90F/Can-330
90HotPlay/St-28
90KMart/CBatL-8
90Kenner/Fig-59
90Leaf-242
90MLBPA/Pins-79
90MSA/Soda-22
90OPC-360
90Panini/St-98
90Pol/Brew-4
90PublInt/St-500
90RedFoley/St-65
90S-460
90S/100St-98
90Sf-183
90T-360
90T/Ames-14
90T/Big-103
90T/Coins-23
90T/Mini-20
90T/St-199
90T/TVAS-29
90UD-254
91B-32
91Brewer/MillB-17
91Classic/200-79
91Classic/II-T14
91Classic/III-60
91D-85
91F-591
91Leaf-302
91Leaf/Prev-20
91Leaf/Stud-73
91MajorLg/Pins-42
91OPC-95
91OPC/Premier-82
91Panini/FrSt-205
91Panini/St-168
91Petro/SU-15
91Pol/Brew-15
91S-49
91S/100SS-13
91StCl-245
91StCl/Member*-6
91T-95
91T/CJMini/I-2
91UD-324
91USPlayC/AS-8H
91Ultra-178
92B-375
92B-645FOIL
92Brew/Carlson-15
92CJ/DII-22
92Classic/Game200-21
92D-51
92D/DK-DK1
92F-182
92F-702M
92Hardee-15
92KingB-14
92L-238
92L/BlkGold-238
92MSA/Ben-8
92MooTown-14
92OPC-600
92OPC/Premier-141
92P-17
92Pinn-8
92Pol/Brew-15
92S-61
92S/100SS-8
92StCl-230
92StCl/Dome-122
92Studio-194
92Studio/Her-11
92Sunflower-13
92T-600
92T/Gold-600
92T/GoldWin-600
92T/Kids-81
92TripleP-254
92UD-423
92UD/TmMVPHolo-36
92USPlayC/Ace-10D
92Ultra-81
93B-167
93BJ/D/McDon-35
93BJ/Demp-4
93BJ/Fire-20
93Brew/Sen-1
93Classic/GameI-66
93Colla/DM-77
93D-75
93D/Elite-22
93D/EliteDom-14
93D/EliteDom-14AU
93D/EliteUp-4
93D/MVP-4
93Duracel/PPII-24
93F-254
93F/Final-295
93F/Final/DTrib-DT5
93Flair-292
93HumDum/Can-18
93L-262
93L/UpGoldAS-10
93MSA/Metz-33
93MilkBone-1
93OPC-237
93OPC/Premier-124
93P-16
93Pac/Spanish-654
93Pinn-428
93Pinn-481I
93Pinn/Cooper-23
93S-598
93Select-42
93Select/ChasS-23
93Select/RookTr-16T
93Select/StatL-9
93StCl-627
93StCl/1stDay-627
93StCl/MurphyS-131
93Studio-172
93T-207
93T/Finest-70
93T/FinestRef-70
93T/Gold-207
93T/Tr-48T
93TripleP-97LH
93TripleP/Gal-GS6
93UD-333
93UD-43
93UD-705
93UD/FunPack-58
93UD/Iooss-WI6
93UD/SP-50
93USPlayC/Ace-7D
93Ultra-645
94B-281
94D-24
94D/AwardWin-10MVP
94D/DomII-3
94D/Special-24
94F-338
94F-707M
94F/AS-16
94F/TL-14
94Finest-239
94Flair-119
94Flair/Hot-5
94KingB-2
94Kraft-8
94L-395
94L/GoldS-10
94L/MVPAL-8
94OPC-1
94OPC/BJ-3
94OPC/JAS-2
94Oscar-9
94Pac/Cr-648
94Pac/Silv-4
94Panini-140
94Pinn-27
94Pinn/Artist-27
94Pinn/HobSam-TR1TRI
94Pinn/Museum-27
94Pinn/Run-4
94Pinn/Trib-1
94S-427
94S/Cycle-3
94S/GoldS-57
94Select-3
94SelectSam-3
94Sf/2000-106
94Sf/2000-NNO
94StCl-526TA
94StCl/1stDay-526TA
94StCl/Gold-526TA
94StCl/Team-161
94Studio-29
94T-540
94T-609ST
94T/BlkGold-13
94T/Gold-540
94T/Gold-609ST
94TripleP-35
94TripleP/Medal-15
94TripleP/Pr-5
94UD-294HFA
94UD-470
94UD/CollC-208
94UD/CollC/Gold-208
94UD/CollC/Silv-208
94UD/SP-44
94Ultra-140
94Ultra/AwardWin-21MVP
94Ultra/Career-2
94Ultra/Hit-7
94Ultra/OnBase-9

Mollwitz, Fred
16FleischBrd-66
94Conlon-1271IA
D329-124
D350/2-121
M101/4-124
M101/5-121

Moloney, Bill
81Bristol-2
83Pawtu-9

Moloney, Richard
71OPC-13R
71T-13R

Mompres, Danilo
91Clmbia/PCPII-3
91Clmbia/PII-20
91Pittsfld/ClBest-10
91Pittsfld/ProC-3431
92ColumMet/ClBest-16
92ColumMet/ProC-304
92ColumMet/SAL/II-5

Monasterio, Juan
76Wausau

Monastro, Frank
90BurlInd/ProC-3015

Monbouquette, Bill
59T-173
60T-544
61T-562
61T/St-114
62Salada-99
62Shirriff-99
62T-580
62T/St-15
63Bz-21
63F-7
63Salada-35
63T-480
63T/SO
64T-25
64T/Coins-47
64T/St-19
64T/tatt
65OPC-142
65T-142
66T-429
66T/RO-114
66T/RO-68
67CokeCap/Tiger-16
67T-482
68T-234
69OPC-64
69T-64
76Wausau
78TCMA-111
86Albany/TCMA-8
89Myrtle/ProC-1466
90Dunedin/Star-27CO
90Swell/Great-106
91Dunedin/ClBest-26CO
91Dunedin/ProC-224CO
92Dunedin/ClBest-29CO
92Dunedin/ProC-2015CO
92Yank/WIZ60-89
93Dunedin/ClBest-27CO
93Dunedin/ProC-1812CO
PM10/Sm-127

Moncerratt, Pablo
84Butte-17
86Wausau-17

Monchak, Al
73OPC-356CO
73T-356CO
74OPC-221CO
74T-221CO
86Pol/Atl-52C

Moncrief, Homer
82BirmB-4
83GlenF-15

Moncrief, Tony
83Idaho-29

Monda, Greg
85Cedar-17
86Vermont-13
88Nashvl/CMC-13
88Nashvl/ProC-491

Monday, Rick
67T-542R
68A's/JITB-10
68Bz-10
68T-282
68T/ActionSt-7AM
68T/G-26
69MB-194
69MLB/St-88
69MLBPA/Pin-19
69NTF
69OPC-105
69T-105
69T/DE-14
69T/S-27
69T/St-218
69T/decal
69Trans-10
70MLB/St-262
70T-547
71K-73
71MLB/St-522
71OPC-135
71T-135
71T/Coins-40
71T/tatt-15
72MB-239
72T-730
73OPC-44
73T-44
74K-2
74OPC-295
74T-295
74T/St-17
75Ho-113
75Ho/Twink-113
75OPC-129
75T-129
75T/M-129
76Crane-37
76Ho-80
76MSA/Disc
76OPC-251
76SSPC-311
76T-251
77BurgChef-146
77Ho-30
77Ho/Twink-30
77OPC-230
77T-360
78SSPC/270-77
78T-145
79K-57
79OPC-320DP
79T-605
80OPC-243
80Pol/Dodg-16
80T-465
81F-122
81K-53
81OPC-177
81Pol/Dodg-16
81T-726
81T/HT
82D-514
82F-15
82F/St-2
82OPC-6
82Pol/Dodg-16
82T-577
83D-643
83F-213
83F/St-3M
83F/St-4M
83OPC-63
83Pol/Dodg-16
83Seven-10
83T-63
83T/Fold-2M
84F-106
84Nes/792-274
84Pol/Dodg-16
84T-274
84T/St-83
87Mother/A's-2
87Smok/Dodg-23
88AlaskaAS60/Team-1
89Smok/Dodg-90
90Pac/Legend-40
90Padre/MagUno-8ANN
90Target-542
91Padre/Coke-6ANN
91Swell/Great-65
93UD/ATH-97
94TedW-13

Mondesi, Raul
90GreatF/SportP-6
91B-593
91CalLgAS-3
92Albuq/SB-16
92B-64
92D/Rook-83
92L/GRook-16
92SanAn/ProC-3987
92Sky/AAASingl-8
92UD-60TP
92UD/ML-163
92UD/ML-32M
93B-353FOIL
93B-618
93F/Final-82
93FExcel/ML-53
93L-473
93LimeR/Winter-142
93LimeR/Winter-27
93StCl/Dodg-15
93UD/SP-96
93Ultra-402
94B-538
94D-313
94F-518
94Flair-179
94Flair/Wave-6
94L-93
94OPC-199
94OPC/HotPros-4
94Pac/Cr-316
94Pinn-242
94Pinn/Artist-242
94Pinn/Museum-242
94S-618
94S/Boys-47
94Select-183
94Sf/2000-162
94StCl-390
94StCl/1stDay-390
94StCl/Gold-390
94Studio-70
94T-783
94T/Finest-74
94T/FinestRef-74
94T/Gold-783
94TripleP-288
94UD-59
94UD/CollC-209
94UD/CollC/Gold-209
94UD/CollC/Silv-209
94UD/ElecD-59
94UD/HoloFX-28
94UD/SP-79
94Ultra-216
94Ultra/AllRook-7

Mondile, Steve
89Freder/Star-18
90Freder/Team-7

Monegro, David
88Elmira-15

Monegro, Miguel
87Elmira/Black-4
87Elmira/Red-4
88WinHaven/Star-14
90LynchRS/Team-6

Monell, Johnny
85LitFalls-26
87Columbia-9
89Jacks/GS-16

Monette, Jacques
52LaPatrie-13
52Laval-114

Money, Don
69T-454R
70T-645
71MLB/St-185
71OPC-49
71Phill/Arco-9
71T-49
71T/Coins-31

71T/tatt-7
72MB-240
72T-635
73OPC-386
73T-386
74OPC-413
74T-413
74T/St-197
75Ho-112
75Ho/Twink-112
75OPC-175
75T-175
75T/M-175
76A&P/Milw
76Ho-136
76OPC-402
76SSPC-236
76T-402
77T-79
78T-24
79OPC-133
79T-265
80OPC-313
80T-595
81D-443
81F-524
81OPC-106
81T-106
82D-384
82F-149
82OPC-294
82Pol/Brew-7
82T-709
83D-132
83F-41
83Gard-12
83OPC-259
83Pol/Brew-7
83T-608
84F-208
84Nes/792-374
84T-374
92Brew/Carlson-16
Money, Kyle
82Reading-4
83Portl-4
86Portl-18
Moneypenny, Bubba
92Lipscomb-19MG
93Lipscomb-24M
Monge, Isidro
(Sid)
75IntLgAS/Broder-18
75PCL/AS-18
75SLCity
75SLCity/Caruso-17
76OPC-595R
76T-595R
77T-282
78T-101
79T-459
80OPC-39
80T-74
81D-81
81F-395
81OPC-333
81T-333
82D-620
82F-375
82T-601
82T/Tr-73T
83D-245
83F-168
83OPC/St-274
83T-564
83T/St-274
83T/Tr-74T
84D-139
84F-308
84Mother/Padres-21
84Nes/792-224
84Smok/Padres-19
84T-224
84T/Tr-80T
84Tiger/Wave-26
85F-17
85T-408
89Pac/SenLg-180
90EliteSenLg-88
90Rockford/ProC-2711CO
90Rockford/Team-18CO
92Fayette/ClBest-26CO
92Fayette/ProC-2186
Mongiello, Michael
90Foil/Best-282
90SoBend/Best-21
90SoBend/GS-12
91Saraso/ClBest-8
91Saraso/ProC-1111
92BirmB/ProC-2580
92BirmB/SB-90
92ClBest-31
92Sky/AASingl-43
Monheimer, Len
88Augusta/ProC-389
Monico, Mario
86Stockton-16
87Stockton-7
88ElPaso/Best-26
88TexLgAS/GS-24
89ElPaso/GS-30
90AAASingl/ProC-663
90Denver/CMC-13
90Denver/ProC-638
90ProC/Singl-38
Monita, Greg
87Vermont-21
Monk, Art
91StCl/Member*-31
92StCl/MemberIII*-13
Monroe, Bill
74Laugh/Black-31
86Negro/Frit-110
Monroe, Gary
81QuadC-14
Monroe, Larry
75AppFx
78Knoxvl
79Knoxvl/TCMA-14
Monroe, Zack
59T-108
60T-329
79TCMA-219
Mons, Jeffrey
88VeroB/Star-17
Monson, Steve
(Mo)
87Beloit-5
88Stockton/Cal-175
88Stockton/ProC-722
89ElPaso/GS-11
89Stockton/Best-4
89Stockton/Cal-160
89Stockton/ProC-384
90ElPaso/GS-22
91Stockton/ClBest-3
91Stockton/ProC-3030
Montague, Ed
88TM/Umpire-27
89TM/Umpire-25
90TM/Umpire-24
Montague, John
72Dimanche*-35
75OPC-405
75T-405
75T/M-405
76OkCty/Team-17
78T-117
79OPC-172
79T-337
80T-253
81T-652
Montalvo, Rafael
83VeroB-9
85Cram/PCL-173
86Tucson-16
87Tucson-5
88Tucson/CMC-6
88Tucson/JP-18
88Tucson/ProC-170
90AAASingl/ProC-93
90Edmon/CMC-11
90Edmon/ProC-517
90ProC/Singl-488
91AAA/LineD-167
91B-189
91Edmon/LineD-167
91Edmon/ProC-1515
Montalvo, Robert
88StCath/ProC-2021
90Myrtle/ProC-2875
90StCath/ProC-3466
91Dunedin/ClBest-28
91Dunedin/ProC-215
92Knoxvl/ProC-2998
92Knoxvl/SB-385
92Syrac/ProC-1976
93Syrac/ProC-1005
Montana, Joe
91Arena*-1
Montanari, Dave
86PalmSp-23
86PalmSp/Smok-21
Montanez, Willie
71OPC-138R
71T-138R
72Dimanche*-62
72T-690
73OPC-97
73T-97
74JP
74OPC-515
74T-515
74T/St-77
75Ho-137
75K-31
75OPC-162
75T-162
75T/M-162
76OPC-181
76SSPC-103
76T-181
77BurgChef-211
77Ho-19
77Ho/Twink-19
77K-31
77OPC-79
77T-410
77T/CS-29
77T/ClothSt-29
78Ho-143
78OPC-43
78T-38
78T/Zest-4
79Ho-100
79OPC-153
79T-305
80OPC-119
80T-224
81F-506
81OPC-63
81OPC/Post-1
81T-559
82F-486
82T-458
91WIZMets-279
93Rang/Keeb-271
Montano, Francisco
85Tigres-8
Montano, Martin
85Beloit-22
86Stockton-17
87Stockton-13
88Fresno/ProC-1245
Montazvo, Rafael
91MidldA/OneHour-20
Monteagudo, Aurelio
64T-466R
65T-286R
66T-532
67T-453
71MLB/St-421
71OPC-129
71T-129
72OPC-458
72T-458
74OPC-139
74T-139
74T/Tr-139T
81TCMA-432
85MidldA-20CO
86MidldA-18CO
87Knoxvl-5CO
Monteau, Sam
75BurlB
76BurlB
Montefusco, John
76Crane-38
76Ho-41
76Ho/Twink-41
76MSA/Disc
76OPC-203LL
76OPC-30
76SSPC-97
76T-203LL
76T-30
77BurgChef-106
77Ho-31
77Ho/Twink-31
77K-5
77OPC-232
77Pep-42
77T-370
77T/CS-30
77T/ClothSt-30
78OPC-59
78T-142
79OPC-288
79Pol/Giants-26
79T-560
80OPC-109
80Pol/Giants-26
80T-195
81D-434
81F-439
81Pol/Atl-24
81T-438
81T/Tr-804
82F-442
82T-697
82T/Tr-74T
83D-313
83F-367
83F/St-14M
83F/St-1M
83OPC-223
83OPC/St-297
83T-223
83T/St-297
84D-126
84F-132
84Mother/Giants-24
84Nes/792-761
84OPC-265
84T-761
85D-580
85F-135
85OPC-301
85T-301
85T/St-319
92Yank/WIZ80-123
Monteguedo, Rene
45Playball-45
Monteiro, Dave
88Idaho/ProC-1841
Montejo, Steve
88Watertn/Pucko-22
Monteleone, Rich
86Calgary-15
87Calgary-24
87Mother/Sea-24
88Calgary/CMC-3
88Calgary/ProC-797
89Edmon/CMC-2
89Edmon/ProC-564
89S/Tr-92
90AAASingl/ProC-325
90ColClip/CMC-8
90ColClip/ProC-675
90D-462
90F-648M
90F/Can-648
90OPC-99
90ProC/Singl-208
90S-565
90T-99
90T/TVYank-56
91AAA/LineD-113
91AAAGame/ProC-7
91ColClip/LineD-113
91ColClip/ProC-596
92L-352
92L/BlkGold-352
92S-690
92StCl-157
93D-445
93F-653
93OPC-152
93StCl-493
93StCl/1stDay-493
93StCl/Y-23
93T-779
93T/Gold-779
94F-240
94StCl/Team-14
94T-326
94T/Gold-326
Montero, Alberto
90Ashvl/ClBest-15
91Ashvl/ProC-576
92BurlAs/ClBest-17
92BurlAs/ProC-557
Montero, Cesar
90Hunting/ProC-3289
Montero, Danny
92Hunting/ClBest-4
92Hunting/ProC-3151
Montero, Jorge
87Salem/ProC-2422
Montero, Sixto
89Martins/Star-22
Montes, Dan
89Everett/Star-22
Montgomery, Al
80Utica-23
Montgomery, Damin
91Billing/SportP-12
91Billings/ProC-3768
Montgomery, Dan
87Bakers-2
88Bakers/Cal-238
89VeroB/Star-17
Montgomery, Don
91Everett/ClBest-6
91Everett/ProC-3919
92SanJose/ClBest-14
Montgomery, Jeff
87Nashvl-15
88F-642R
88F/Up-U32
88Omaha/CMC-7
88Omaha/ProC-1501
88S-497
88S/Tr-71T
88T-447
89B-113
89D-440
89D/Best-319
89F-288
89S-367
89T-116
89UD-618
90B-370
90D-380
90F-115
90F/Can-115
90Leaf-520
90OPC-638
90Panini/St-85
90PublInt/St-353
90S-365
90T-638
90T/St-273
90UD-698
91B-308
91D-505
91F-564
91OPC-371
91Pol/Royal-16
91S-143
91StCl-369
91T-371
91UD-637
91Ultra-153
92B-122
92D-666
92F-164
92L-136
92L/BlkGold-136
92OPC-16
92Pinn-173
92Pol/Royal-23
92S-14
92StCl-12
92Studio-190
92T-16
92T/Gold-16
92T/GoldWin-16
92UD-627
92Ultra-76
93B-533
93Classic/Gamel-67
93D-175
93F-245
93F/Fruit-47
93Flair-222
93L-124
93OPC-261
93Pac/Spanish-140
93Pinn-336
93Pol/Royal-23
93S-212
93Select-264
93Select/StatL-69
93StCl-125
93StCl/1stDay-125
93StCl/MurphyS-184
93StCl/Royal-19
93T-130
93T/Finest-42

93T/FinestRef-42
93T/Gold-130
93TripleP-236
93UD-62
93UD/SP-234
93Ultra-566
94B-59
94D-362
94D/Special-362
94F-170
94F/AS-17
94Finest-387
94Flair-62
94L-25
94OPC-7
94Pac/Cr-298
94Panini-10
94Pinn-106
94Pinn/Artist-106
94Pinn/Museum-106
94S-155
94S/GoldR-155
94S/Tomb-23
94Select-109
94StCl-49
94StCl/1stDay-49
94StCl/Gold-49
94T-394AS
94T-535
94T/BlkGold-14
94T/Gold-394AS
94T/Gold-535
94TripleP-240
94UD-339
94UD/CollC-210
94UD/CollC/Gold-210
94UD/CollC/Silv-210
94Ultra-70
94Ultra/Fire-1
Montgomery, Larry 1
77BurlB
78BurlB
81ElPaso-12
85Cram/PCL-58
Montgomery, Larry 2
91Daikyo/Fut-2
Montgomery, Mike
90Batavia/ProC-3064
Montgomery, Monty
72OPC-372R
72T-372R
73OPC-164
73T-164
Montgomery, Ray
90AubAs/ProC-3394
91BurlAs/ClBest-21
91BurlAs/ProC-2815
92Jacks/ProC-4012
Montgomery, Reggie
85MidldA-24
86Edmon-21
88RochR/ProC-207
Montgomery, Robert
71OPC-176R
71T-176R
72OPC-411
72T-411
73OPC-491
73T-491
74OPC-301
74T-301
75OPC-559
75T-559
75T/M-559
76OPC-523
76SSPC-414
76T-523
77T-288
78PapaG/Disc-10
78T-83
79OPC-219
79T-423
80T-618
Montgomery, Steve
92Classic/DP-61
92FrRow/DP-87
93StCl/MurphyS-193
Montilla, Julio
93Rockford/ClBest-17
Montoya, Albert
91MedHat/ProC-4097
91MedHat/SportP-16
92Myrtle/ClBest-24
92Myrtle/ProC-2195
93Dunedin/ClBest-17
93Dunedin/ProC-1793
Montoya, Charlie
90TexLgAS/GS-4
Montoya, Norman
91QuadC/ClBest-9
91QuadC/ProC-2626
92PalmSp/ClBest-3
92PalmSp/ProC-835
Montoyo, Charlie
88CalLgAS-16
88Stockton/Cal-199
88Stockton/ProC-737
89AS/Cal-29
89Stockton/Best-14
89Stockton/Cal-172
89Stockton/ProC-381
89Stockton/Star-12
90ElPaso/GS-23
91AAA/LineD-146
91Denver/LineD-146
91Denver/ProC-131
92Denver/ProC-2649
92Denver/SB-141
93Ottawa/ProC-2443
Montreuil, Al
73Wichita-10
74Wichita-114
Monzant, Ray
56T-264
58SFCallB-17
58T-447
59T-332
60T-338
79TCMA79-199
Monzon, Dan
90Utica/Pucko-3
91SoBend/ClBest-3
Monzon, Daniel F.
73OPC-469
73T-469
74OPC-613
74T-613
78Wausau
82Lynch-1
Monzon, Jose
89Myrtle/ProC-1459
91AA/LineD-362
91Knoxvl/LineD-362
91Knoxvl/ProC-1771
92Knoxvl/ProC-2992
92Knoxvl/SB-386
92Syrac/ProC-1971
93Syrac/ProC-1000
Moock, Chris
92LSU/McDag-3
92Peoria/Team-16
Moock, Joe
77Fritsch-32
81TCMA-340
91WIZMets-280
Moody, James
89Oneonta/ProC-2105
90PrWill/Team-15
Moody, Kyle
91Spokane/ClBest-6
91Spokane/ProC-3957
92CharRain/ProC-127
Moody, Lee
92Negro/RetortII-28
Moody, Ritchie
91OKSt-17
92ClBest/Up-429
92Classic/DP-43
92FrRow/DP-79
92Gaston/ProC-2252
92OKSt-21
93B-377
93StCl/MurphyS-195
93StCl/Rang-2
93T-438
93T/Gold-438
94B-457
Moody, Willis
88Negro/Duques-18
Moon, Glen
80Clinton-19
Moon, Ray
92Princet/ClBest-5
92Princet/ProC-3099
Moon, Wally
54T-137
55Hunter
55T-67
55T/DH-37
56T-55
56T/Pin-48OF
57T-65
58T-210
59T-530
60Bz-3
60Morrell
60T-5
60T/tatt-36
60Union/Dodg-12
61BB-9
61P-159
61T-325
61T/St-29
61Union/Dodg-13
62BB-9
62Exh
62Salada-124
62Shirriff-124
62T-190
62T-52LL
62T/St-137
62T/bucks
63Exh
63T-279
64T-353
65OPC-247
65T-247
79TCMA-137
81TCMA-372
88Pac/Leg-81
89Smok/Dodg-65
89Swell-81
90CLAS/CL-7MG
90Freder/Team-1MG
90Target-543
91Freder/ClBest-26MG
91Freder/ProC-2381MG
91Swell/Great-64
92AP/ASG-22
93UD/ATH-98
94T/Arc54-137
Exh47
Moon, Warren
91StCl/Charter*-36
91StCl/Member*-32
Mooney, James
34G-83
Mooney, John
90MissSt-44M
91MissSt-55M
92MissSt-50M
Mooney, Troy
89Princet/Star-13
90Welland/Pucko-23
91Augusta/ClBest-10
91Augusta/ProC-804
92Salem/ClBest-22
92Salem/ProC-61
Mooneyham, Bill
81Holyo-23
82Holyo-6
83Nashua-5
84Cram/PCL-110
85Huntsvl/BK-21
86D/Rook-50
86F/Up-U77
87D-302
87F-399
87T-548
87Tacom-18
88Denver/ProC-1254
88ElPaso/Best-9
Moore, Alvin
(Junior)
78Green
78SSPC/270-159
78T-421
79T-275
80T-186
81Durham-13
Moore, Andy
92Elmira/ClBest-22
92Elmira/ProC-1391
Moore, Archie
64T-581R
81TCMA-479
92Yank/WIZ60-90
Moore, Austin
V94-32
Moore, Balor
71OPC-747R
71T-747R
72Dimanche*-36
73OPC-211
73T-211
74OPC-453
74T-453
75OPC-592
75T-592
75T/M-592
78BJ/PostC-18
78SSPC/270-202
78T-368
79BJ/Bubble-17
79OPC-122
79T-238
80OPC-6
80T-19
81Vanco-10
Moore, Bart
89Elmira/Pucko-9
90WinHaven/Star-17
Moore, Billy
86Indianap-35
87Indianap-18
88Indianap/CMC-13
88Indianap/ProC-497
88TripleA/ASCMC-6
89Indianap/CMC-13
89Indianap/ProC-1211
89RochR/ProC-1647
90AAASingl/ProC-664
90Denver/CMC-11
90Denver/ProC-639
90ProC/Singl-36
Moore, Bobby
88BBCity/Star-18
89BBCity/Star-18
90A&AASingle/ProC-51
90Foil/Best-231
90Memphis/Best-9
90Memphis/ProC-1019
90Memphis/Star-20
90Star/ISingl-86
91AAA/LineD-343
91Omaha/LineD-343
91Omaha/ProC-1047
92Richm/Bleach-9
92Richm/Comix-12
92Richm/ProC-388
92Richm/SB-434
92Sky/AAASingl-199
92T/91Debut-126
Moore, Boo
90WinHaven/Star-18
91CLAS/ProC-CAR24
91ClBest/Singl-43
91LynchRS/ClBest-23
91LynchRS/ProC-1213
92LynchRS/ClBest-19
92LynchRS/ProC-2920
92UD/ML-200
Moore, Brad
86Cram/NWL-144
87Clearw-2
88Phill/TastyK-27
88Reading/ProC-866
89OPC-202
89ScranWB/CMC-8
89ScranWB/ProC-709
89T-202
90AAASingl/ProC-299
90F/Up-U45
90ScranWB/ProC-597
91AAA/LineD-564
91Tidew/LineD-564
91Tidew/ProC-2506
92Tidew/ProC-
92Tidew/SB-567
Moore, Calvin
75Cedar
Moore, Cary
89Erie/Star-14
Moore, Charlie
74OPC-603R
74T-603R
75OPC-636
75T-636
75T/M-636
76A&P/Milw
76OPC-116
76SSPC-231
76T-116
77BurgChef-84
77T-382
78T-51
79T-408
80OPC-302
80T-579
81D-324
81F-521
81OPC-237
81T-237
82D-280
82F-150
82OPC-308
82Pol/Brew-22
82T-308
83D-206
83F-42
83Gard-13
83OPC/St-157LCS
83Pol/Brew-22
83T-659
83T/St-157
84D-292
84F-209
84Gard-14
84Nes/792-751
84OPC-138
84Pol/Brew-22
84T-751
84T/St-301
85D-351
85F-589
85Gard-14
85Pol/Brew-22
85T-83
86D-246
86F-496
86F/St-77
86OPC-137
86Pol/Brew-22
86T-137
86T-426M
86T/St-204
87D-372
87F-351
87OPC-93
87SanJose-6
87T-676
87T/Tr-82T
88S-444
92Brew/Carlson-17
Moore, Charlton
92Martins/ClBest-4
92Martins/ProC-3073
Moore, Chris
89KS*-80
Moore, Curtis
89KS*-33
Moore, Daryl
90A&AASingle/ProC-107
90Foil/Best-121
90Wausau/Best-5
90Wausau/ProC-2118
91Freder/ProC-2360
92Hagers/SB-266
92ProC/Tomorrow-8
92RochR/ProC-1937
92Sky/AASingl-110
Moore, Dave
78Indianap-11
79Indianap-4
81Albuq/TCMA-1
82Albuq-6
Moore, Dee
90Target-545
Moore, Don
81ArkTr-3
82ArkTr-17
Moore, Donnie
78SSPC/270-263
78T-523
79T-17
82Richm-7
84F-185
84Nes/792-207
84Pol/Atl-31
84T-207
85D-650
85F-334
85F/Up-U82
85OPC-61
85Smok/Cal-21
85T-699
85T/Tr-85T
86D-255
86D/AAS-46
86F-164

86Leaf-130
86OPC-345
86Seven/Coin-W15M
86Smok/Cal-21
86T-345
86T/St-182
86T/Tatt-16M
87D-110
87F-89
87F/LL-30
87OPC-115
87RedFoley/St-56
87Sf/TPrev-11M
87Smok/Cal-8
87T-115
87T/Mini-46
87T/St-177
88D-621
88F-500
88KennerFig-71
88OPC-204
88S-195
88Smok/Angels-20
88T-471
89S-535
Moore, Earl A.
11Helmar-148
14CJ-124
15CJ-124
92Conlon/Sport-373
E104
E107
E224
E94
E97
M116
T201
T207
W555
WG2-36
Moore, Ed
79QuadC-3
Moore, Euel
93Conlon-772
Moore, Eugene
(Gene)
39PlayBall-160
40PlayBall-143
41DP-122
41DP-37
41PlayBall-25
45Playball-7
90Target-547
91Conlon/Sport-77
R314
Moore, Gary D.
90Target-1039
Moore, Graham E.
(Eddie)
33G-180
90Target-546
93Conlon-850
Moore, Greg
86Knoxvl-17
Moore, J.B.
85PrWill-27
Moore, Jackie S.
65T-593R
70McDon-6
73OPC-549CO
73T-549CO
74OPC-379CO
74T-379CO
77T-113CO
84T/Tr-81T
85Mother/A's-1MG
85T-38MG
86Mother/A's-1
86T-591MG
90Kahn/Reds-27M
91Kahn/Reds-x
92Reds/Kahn-NNO
93Rang/Keeb-438CO
Moore, Jeramie
94LSU-16
Moore, Jim
85FtMyr-25
Moore, Joe G.
(Jo-Jo)
33G-126
33G-231
37Wheat
38ONG/Pin-21
41DP-30
94Conlon-1182
V355-8
Moore, Joel
94B-151
Moore, John F.
(Johnny)
30CEA/Pin-18
36Exh/4-6
37Exh/4-2
37Exh/4-6
38Wheat
94Conlon-1184
R310
Moore, John
90Wausau/Star-17
91Perth/Fut-5
Moore, Kelvin
80Ogden-20
81Tacom-18
82D-534
82T-531R
82Tacom-31
83D-87
83Tacom-32
84Cram/PCL-31
84ElPaso-13
85BuffB-10
Moore, Kerwin
89Eugene/Best-17
90AppFox/Box-19
90AppFox/ProC-2109
90ProC/Singl-873
91B-312
91BBCity/ClBest-26
91BBCity/ProC-1412
91ClBest/Singl-38
91UD/FinalEd-19F
92B-593
92BBCity/ClBest-14
92ClBest-22
92UD/ML-278
93ClBest/MLG-82
94B-319
94FExcel-194
Moore, Lloyd
(Whitey)
39PlayBall-162
40PlayBall-150
W711/1
W711/2
Moore, Marcus
89BendB/Legoe-8
90QuadC/GS-13
91Dunedin/ClBest-8
91Dunedin/ProC-204
91Melbourne/Fut-6
92ClBest-160
92Knoxvl/ProC-2988
92Knoxvl/SB-387
92Sky/AASingl-163
93B-288
94B-2
94Flair-156
94L/GRook-12
94T-186
94T/Gold-186
94UD-234
94UD/ElecD-234
94Ultra-485
Moore, Mark 1
80Cedar-1
Moore, Mark 2
89KS*-64
92SoOreg/ClBest-9
92SoOreg/ProC-3420
Moore, Meredith
89WinHaven/Star-16
Moore, Michael 1
86Penin-18
88Boise/ProC-1608
91Watertn/ClBest-14
91Watertn/ProC-3369
92Watertn/ClBest-23
92Watertn/ProC-3239
Moore, Michael 2
92ClBest/BBonusC-30
92ClBest/Up-418
92Yakima/ProC-3464
93ClBest/MLG-183
93StCl/Dodg-21
93StCl/MurphyS-26
93T-576M
93T/Gold-576M
93UD-430TP
Moore, Michael W.
(Mike)
80LynnS-1
83D-428
83F-482
83SLCity-7
83T-209
84D-634
84F-614
84Mother/Mar-5
84Nes/792-547
84T-547
85D-440
85F-495
85Mother/Mar-8
85T-279FDP
85T-373
86D-240
86F-469
86Leaf-114
86Mother/Mar-21
86Sf-162
86T-646
86T/Mini-30
86T/St-221
86T/Tatt-2M
87D-70
87F-590
87Mother/Sea-3
87OPC-102
87Sf/TPrev-25M
87Smok/AL-11
87T-727
87T/St-215
88D-75
88D/Best-192
88F-379
88Mother/Sea-3
88S-464
88T-432
88T/Big-241
89B-189
89D-448
89D/Best-246
89D/Tr-21
89F-554
89F/Up-55
89Mother/A's-12
89OPC-28
89Panini/St-431
89S-274
89S/Tr-5
89Sf-77
89T-28
89T/St-220
89T/Tr-82T
89UD-123
89UD/Ext-758
90B-445
90Classic-104
90D-214
90F-16
90F/Can-16
90F/WS-1
90Leaf-293
90Mother/A's-9
90OPC-175
90Panini/St-136
90PublInt/St-311
90S-190
90S/100St-42
90Sf-185
90T-175
90T/Big-200
90T/Mini-31
90T/St-178
90UD-275
90Woolwth/HL-27
91B-212
91D-161
91F-18
91Leaf-218
91Mother/A's-11
91OPC-294
91S-516
91SFExam/A's-9
91StCl-464
91T-294
91UD-423
91Ultra-252
92B-216
92D-337
92F-263
92L-164
92L/BlkGold-164
92Mother/A's-11
92OPC-359
92Pinn-109
92S-91
92StCl-669
92Studio-227
92T-359
92T/Gold-359
92T/GoldWin-359
92UD-661
92USPlayC/Ace-2S
92Ultra-425
93B-179
93D-683
93F-666
93F/Final-213
93L-401
93OPC-186
93OPC/Premier-110
93Pac/Spanish-448
93Pinn-202
93S-641
93Select-270
93StCl-693
93StCl/1stDay-693
93T-73
93T/Gold-73
93Tiger/Gator-21
93UD-182
93UD-512
93Ultra-553
94B-565
94D-554
94F-141
94Flair-51
94L-197
94Pac/Cr-226
94Panini-66
94Pinn-212
94Pinn/Artist-212
94Pinn/Museum-212
94S-143
94S/GoldR-143
94StCl-99
94StCl/1stDay-99
94StCl/Gold-99
94T-523
94T/Finest-83
94T/FinestRef-83
94T/Gold-523
94UD-316
94Ultra-58
Moore, Pat
87Erie-27
Moore, R. Barry
(Barry)
67OPC-11
67T-11
68T-462
69T-639
70OPC-366
70T-366
72MB-241
81TCMA-360
Moore, Randolph
(Randy)
31Exh/4-1
33G-69
35G-2E
35G-4E
35G-7E
90Target-548
93Conlon-924
R308-171
R314
V354-26
V94-33
Moore, Randy
88Beloit/GS-21
Moore, Ray
55Esskay
55T-208
56T-43
57T-106
58T-249
59T-293
60T-447
61Clover-18
61Peters-13
61T-289
61T/RO-20
62T-437
63T-26
63Twin/Volpe-7
90Target-549
91Crown/Orio-312
Moore, Rick
86Chatt-20
Moore, Robert
(Bobby)
83GlenF-16
84Shrev/FB-12
86Phoenix-17
90AAASingl/ProC-542
90Nashvl/CMC-2
90Nashvl/ProC-230
90ProC/Singl-127
Moore, Rod
90AR-29M
Moore, Ron
90AR-20
Moore, Ronald
86Cram/NWL-159
Moore, Roy Daniel
E120
Moore, Sam
86Fresno/Smok-8
87Clinton-23
Moore, Steve
82Tulsa-13
Moore, Terry
42Playball-25
49B-174
92Card/McDon/Pac-10
92Conlon/Sport-641
R314
R423-71
W754
Moore, Tim 1
90Hunting/ProC-3290
90WinSalem/Team-19
91Elizab/ProC-4312
91Geneva/ClBest-13
91Geneva/ProC-4226
91Peoria/ClBest-17
91Peoria/ProC-1350
91Peoria/Team-18
92Kenosha/ProC-618
92Peoria/ClBest-11
92Peoria/Team-17
Moore, Tim 2
92FrRow/DP-4
93StCl/MurphyS-127
Moore, Tommy J.
89Pac/SenLg-148
91WIZMets-281
93Rang/Keeb-272
Moore, Tony
90Kgsport/Best-9
90Kgsport/Star-18
Moore, Vincent
92B-443
92Macon/ClBest-18
92Macon/ProC-280
92StCl/Dome-123
93Durham/Team-14
94B-476
94FExcel-159
94TedW-128
Moore, Whitey
94Conlon-1227
Moore, William Wilcey
(Cy)
90Target-544
91Conlon/Sport-109
94Conlon-1007
W513-77
Moorhead, Bob
62T-593R
91WIZMets-282
Moose, Bob
68KDKA-38
68OPC-36R
68T-36R
69T-409
70MLB/St-104
70OPC-110
70T-110
70T/Cb
71MLB/St-209
71OPC-690
71T-690
71T/Coins-147
72MB-242
72T-647
73OPC-499
73T-499

74OPC-382
74T-382
75OPC-536
75T-536
75T/M-536
76OPC-476
76SSPC-570
76T-476
81TCMA-350
Mooty, J.T.
(Jake)
49B/PCL-23
R314/Can
Mora, Andres
77T-646
78T-517
79T-287
91Crown/Orio-313
Mora, Melvin
94ClBest/Gold-15
Morales, Armando
91Princet/ClBest-11
91Princet/ProC-3510
92CharWh/ClBest-13
92CharWh/ProC-7
Morales, Edwin
87PortChar-8
Morales, Francisco
92Hunting/ProC-3152
Morales, Heriberto
92GulfCM/ProC-3485
Morales, Joe Edwin
82Beloit/Frit-16
84ElPaso-21
Morales, Jorge
91Penin/ClBest-15
91Penin/ProC-381
92Penin/ClBest-6
92Penin/ProC-2936
Morales, Jose
76Expo/Redp-22
76OPC-418
76SSPC-323
76T-418
77OPC-263RB
77OPC-90
77T-102
77T-233RB
78OPC-63
78T-374
78Twin/FriszP-12
79T-552
79Twin/FriszP-18
80OPC-116
80T-218
81D-495
81F-571
81T-43
81T/Tr-806
82D-203
82F-173
82T-648
82T/Tr-75T
83Pol/Dodg-43
83T/Tr-75T
84D-275
84F-107
84F-498
84Nes/792-143
84Pol/Dodg-43
84T-143
89Swell-38
90Target-550
91Crown/Orio-314
91Indian/McDon-30M
92Indian/McDon-30M
Morales, Julio
(Jerry)
70OPC-262R
70T-262R
71OPC-696
71T-696
73OPC-268
73T-268
74OPC-258
74T-258
74T/St-98
75OPC-282
75T-282
75T/M-282
76Crane-39
76Ho-140
76MSA/Disc
76OPC-79
76SSPC-312
76T-79
77BurgChef-196
77Ho-49
77Ho/Twink-49
77T-639
78OPC-23
78T-175
79OPC-235
79T-452
80T-572
81F-338
81T-377
81T/Tr-805
82D-309
82F-601
82F/St-93
82RedLob
82T-33
83F-502
83T-729
83Thorn-24
91WIZMets-283
Morales, Manuel
85Tigres-20
Morales, Rich Jr.
69T-654R
70OPC-91
70T-91
71OPC-267
71T-267
72T-593
73OPC-494
73T-494
74OPC-387SD
74T-387
81QuadC-30
88Vermont/ProC-954
89Calgary/CMC-24
89Calgary/ProC-538
90SanBern/Cal-109
90Wmsprt/Best-25MG
90Wmsprt/ProC-1072MG
90Wmsprt/Star-25MG
91Pocatel/ProC-3800MG
91Pocatel/SportP-30MG
92Salinas/ClBest-30CO
92Salinas/ProC-3777CO
Morales, William
87PrWill-29
88PrWill/Star-18
Morales, Willie
92AZ/Pol-10
Moralez, Paul
86Kinston-17
87Bakers-24
Moran, Bill
(Bugs)
78Knoxvl
Moran, Charles
94Conlon-1189UMP
Moran, Dino
86Watertn-13
Moran, Frank
88Hamil/ProC-1746
Moran, Jim
53Mother-12
Moran, Joseph Herbert
16FleischBrd-67
90Target-1040
D350/2-122
M101/5-122
T206
Moran, Opie
87Erie-2
89ArkTr/GS-13
Moran, Owen
T3/Box-60
Moran, Pat J.
10Domino-88A
10Domino-88B
11Helmar-149
12Sweet/Pin-129
14Piedmont/St-41
15CJ-111
24Sherlock-6MG
88Pac/8Men-89
BF2-88
D329-125
D350/2-123
E270/2
M101/4-125
M101/5-123
M116
S74-102
T202
T204
T205
T206
T207
T3-109
W514-12
WG7-33
Moran, Richard Alan
(Al)
63T-558R
64T-288
81TCMA-430
91WIZMets-284
Moran, Steve
86AppFx-16
Moran, William Nelson
(Billy)
58T-388
59T-196
60Maple-14
61BeeHive-14
62T-539
63J-25
63P-25
63Salada-48
63T-57
64T-333
64T/St-67
65T-562
81TCMA-429
Morandini, Mickey
88T/Tr-71TOLY
89Spartan/ProC-1030
89Spartan/Star-18
89Star/IISingl-120
89Star/Wax-57
89T/Big-162
90AAASingl/ProC-308
90B-153
90ProC/Singl-240
90ScranWB/CMC-14
90ScranWB/ProC-606
91AAA/LineD-491
91B-492
91Classic/200-187
91Classic/I-79
91D-44RR
91F-407
91Leaf-383
91Leaf/Stud-218
91MajorLg/Pins-61
91OPC-342
91OPC/Premier-83
91Phill/Medford-28
91S-376RP
91S/Rook40-33
91ScranWB/LineD-491
91Seven/3DCoin-12NE
91StCl-535
91T-342
91T/90Debut-110
91UD-18
91Ultra-268
92B-628
92D-669
92F-539
92L-330
92L/BlkGold-330
92OPC-587
92Panini-243
92Phill/Med-21
92Pinn-103
92S-143
92StCl-369
92StCl/MemberII-8
92Studio-77
92T-587
92T/Gold-587
92T/GoldWin-587
92UD-449
92Ultra-247
93B-428
93D-224
93F-105
93F/GoldMI-2
93L-77
93OPC-256
93Pac/Spanish-239
93Panini-271
93Phill/Med-23
93Pinn-156
93S-415
93S-512AS
93Select-245
93StCl-449
93StCl/1stDay-449
93StCl/Phill-8
93Studio-208
93T-262
93T/Gold-262
93TripleP-53
93UD-285
93UD/SP-177
93UD/SeasonHL-HI12
93Ultra-91
94D-498
94F-596
94Finest-273
94L-424
94Pac/Cr-482
94Phill/Med-22
94Pinn-159
94Pinn/Artist-159
94Pinn/Museum-159
94S-460
94S/Cycle-15M
94StCl-120
94StCl/1stDay-120
94StCl/Gold-120
94StCl/Team-234
94T-692
94T/Gold-692
94UD-463
94UD/CollC-211
94UD/CollC/Gold-211
94UD/CollC/Silv-211
94Ultra-250
Morando, Dean
78Wisco
Moraw, Carl
86Beloit-16
87Stockton-21
88Stockton/Cal-184
88Stockton/ProC-746
89ElPaso/GS-12
89Stockton/Best-5
89Stockton/Cal-156
89Stockton/ProC-378
Mordecai, Mike
88CapeCod-17
88CapeCod/Sum-42
90CLAS/CL-28
90Durham/Team-7
91Durham/ClBest-13
91Durham/ProC-1557
92Greenvl/ProC-1161
92Greenvl/SB-241
93Richm/Bleach-6
93Richm/Pep-4
93Richm/Team-21
More, Billy
87Sf/TPrev-20M
Moreau, Guy
R314/Can
Morehart, Ray
91Conlon/Sport-102
Morehead, Dave
63T-299R
64T-376
65T-434
66OPC-135
66T-135
67T-297
67T/Test/RSox-11
68Dexter-57
68T-212
69MLB/St-60
69OPC-29
69T-29
70MLB/St-224
70OPC-495
70T-495
71MLB/St-422
71OPC-221
71T-221
72MB-243
Morehead, Seth
59T-253
60L-87
60T-504
61T-107
Morehouse, Richard
86QuadC-24
87PalmSp-28
88PalmSp/Cal-91
88PalmSp/ProC-1449
89MidldA/GS-24
Morehouse, Scott
88CapeCod/Sum-162
Morel, Ramon
93Welland/ClBest-15
93Welland/ProC-3352
Moreland, Keith
79OkCty
80BK/P-3
81D-382
81F-13
81T-131
82D-119
82F-252
82RedLob
82T-384
82T/Tr-76T
83D-309
83F-503
83F/St-1AM
83F/St-1BM
83F/St-9M
83OPC-58
83OPC/St-222
83T-619
83T/St-222
83Thorn-6
84D-483
84F-499
84Nes/792-23
84Nes/792-456TL
84OPC-23
84SevenUp-6
84T-23
84T-456TL
84T/St-39
85D-117
85F-62
85Leaf-197
85OPC-197
85SevenUp-6
85T-538
85T/St-39
86Cub/Unocal-13
86D-167
86Drake-9
86F-375
86F/LL-25
86F/Mini-79
86F/St-78
86Gator-6
86Jay's-13
86Leaf-94
86OPC-266
86Sf-90
86T-266
86T/Mini-38
86T/St-54
86T/Tatt-12M
87Berg/Cubs-6
87D-169
87D-24DK
87D/DKsuper-24
87D/OD-71
87Drake-7
87F-569
87F/LL-31
87F/Mini-69
87F/St-79
87Leaf-24DK
87Leaf-77
87OPC-177
87S/Test-71
87Seven-C12
87Seven-ME7
87Sf-122
87Sf/TPrev-22M
87T-177
87T/St-65
88Coke/Padres-7
88D-201
88D/Best-266
88F-425
88F/Up-U124
88Leaf-160
88OPC-31
88Panini/St-263
88RedFoley/St-58
88S-71
88S/Tr-9T
88Sf-164
88Smok/Padres-19
88T-416
88T/Big-207

88T/St-58
88T/Tr-72T
89B-109
89D-111
89D/Best-203
89F-313
89Mara/Tigers-10
89OPC-293
89S-42
89S/Tr-29
89Sf-141
89T-773
89T/St-105
89T/Tr-83T
89UD-361
90PublInt/St-477
90S-444
90Sf-139
90UD-401
91Crown/Orio-315
92TX-29

Moreland, Owen III
84LitFalls-11

Morelli, Frank
89Elmira/Pucko-10

Morelock, Charlie
83Ander-12
86Durham-19

Moren, Lew
E104
M116

Morena, Jamie
86CharRain-18
87CharRain-18
88Charl/ProC-1218
89Watlo/ProC-1785
89Watlo/Star-26
91CharRain/ClBest-26CO
91CharRain/ProC-111CO
92CharRain/ClBest-24CO
92CharRain/ProC-137CO

Moreno, Angel
82F-469
84Cram/PCL-99

Moreno, Armando
86Jaxvl/TCMA-4
87Jaxvl-12
88Jaxvl/Best-27
88Jaxvl/ProC-983
88SLAS-21
89Indianap/CMC-19
89Indianap/ProC-1222
90AAASingl/ProC-496
90BuffB/CMC-19
90BuffB/ProC-381
90BuffB/Team-17
90ProC/Singl-19
91AAA/LineD-39
91BuffB/LineD-39
91BuffB/ProC-548
92OPC-179M
92T-179R
92T/Gold-179M
92T/GoldWin-179M

Moreno, Carlos
82Miami-5

Moreno, Chris
89Stockton/Best-26M

Moreno, Douglas
86Macon-16
86Watertn-14

Moreno, Jorge A.
91Bristol/ClBest-13
91Bristol/ProC-3615
92Bristol/ProC-1427

Moreno, Jose D.
91Watertn/ClBest-15
91Watertn/ProC-3370

Moreno, Jose de los Santos
73Cedar
74Cedar
75Dubuq
79Tidew-3
80Tidew-2
81Hawaii/TCMA-2
91WIZMets-285

Moreno, Juan
92ColumMet/ClBest-17
92ColumMet/ProC-308
92ColumMet/SAL/II-10

Moreno, Michael
83Wisco/Frit-24
85OrlanTw-8

Moreno, Omar
77T-104
78T-283
79Ho-12
79OPC-321
79T-4LL
79T-607
80BK/PHR-29
80OPC-372
80T-165
80T-204LL
81Coke
81D-17
81F-361
81F/St-100
81OPC-213
81T-535
81T/SO-100
81T/St-211
81T/St-24
82D-347
82F-487
82F/St-79
82OPC-395
82T-395
82T/St-81
82T/StVar-81
83D-347
83F-312
83F/St-16M
83OPC-332
83OPC/St-278
83T-485
83T/Fold-5M
83T/St-278
83T/Tr-76T
84D-637
84F-133
84Nes/792-16
84Nes/792-714LL
84OPC-16
84T-16
84T-714LL
84T/St-322
85D-591
85F-136
85T-738
86F-15
86F/Up-U78
86Pol/Atl-18
86T/Tr-75T
87F-521
87T-214
87T/St-44
89Pac/SenLg-138
89TM/SenLg-80
90EliteSenLg-41
91Pac/SenLg-46
92Yank/WIZ80-124

Moreno, Ric
87Dunedin-14TR
93Modesto/ClBest-28TR

Morenz, Howie
33SK*-24

Moret, Rogelio (Roger)
71OPC-692R
71T-692R
72OPC-113
72T-113
73OPC-291
73T-291
74OPC-590
74T-590
74T/St-137
75OPC-8
75T-8
75T/M-8
76OPC-632
76SSPC-420
76T-632
76T/Tr-632T
77T-292
78SSPC/270-106
78T-462
93Rang/Keeb-273

Moreta, Manuel
76Watlo

Morfin, Arvid
84Butte-18
86Cram/NWL-116

Morgan, Bill
79QuadC-5

Morgan, Bob M.
50B-222
52T-355
53B/Col-135
53T-85
55B-81
56T-337
58T-144
79TCMA-193
90Target-551
91T/Arc53-85

Morgan, Chris
86FSLAS-36
86Lakeland-16
87GlenF-17

Morgan, Curt
86Miami-18

Morgan, David
93MedHat/ProC-3740
93MedHat/SportP-19

Morgan, Eddie
31Exh/4-21
33Exh/4-11
33G-116
35BU-60
90Target-552
93Conlon-943
V354-2

Morgan, Gary
90Batavia/ProC-3081

Morgan, Gene
86Memphis/GoldT-19
86Memphis/SilverT-19
87Memphis-16
87Memphis/Best-17

Morgan, Harry (Cy)
BF2-49
E104
E95
M116
T204
T207
T208
T222

Morgan, Jim
89Chatt/II/Team-18

Morgan, Joe L.
65OPC-16R
65T-16R
66OPC-195
66T-195
66T/RO-69
67T/RO-9
67Ast/Team-10
67CokeCap/AS-30
67CokeCap/Astro-12
67CokeCap/NLAS-24
67OPC/PI-25
67T-337
67T/PI-25
68CokeCap/Astro-12
68Dexter-56
68OPC-144
68T-144
68T-364AS
69MB-195
69MLB/St-141
69OPC-35
69T-35
69T/St-36
70K-72
70MLB/St-44
70OPC-537
70T-537
71MLB/St-89
71OPC-264
71T-264
71T/Coins-117
71T/GM-34
71T/Greatest-34
72MB-244
72OPC-132
72T-132
72T-752TR
73K-34
73OPC-230
73T-230
74Greyhound-6M
74K-36
74OPC-333AS
74OPC-85
74T-333AS
74T-85
74T/St-28
75Greyhound-4
75Ho-5
75Ho/Twink-5
75K-27
75OPC-180
75T-180
75T/M-180
76Crane-40
76Greyhound-4
76Ho-2
76Ho/Twink-2
76Icee
76K-27
76MSA/Disc
76OPC-197LL
76OPC-420
76SSPC-38
76T-197LL
76T-420
77BurgChef-207
77Ho-2
77Ho/Twink-2
77OPC-220
77Pep-46
77T-100
77T/CS-31
77T/ClothSt-31
78Ho-87
78OPC-160
78Pep-18
78SSPC/270-121
78T-300
78Wiffle/Discs-52
79Ho-61
79OPC-5
79T-20
80BK/PHR-30
80OPC-342
80T-650
81D-18
81F-78
81F/St-109
81K-22
81T-560
81T/Tr-807
82D-312
82F-397
82F/St-63
82KMart-28
82KMart-30
82OPC-146IA
82OPC-208
82T-754
82T-755IA
83D-24DK
83D-438
83D-648M
83F-270
83F/St-19AM
83F/St-19BM
83F/St-8M
83OPC-264SV
83OPC-81
83OPC/St-303
83T-171TL
83T-603
83T-604SV
83T/Fold-2M
83T/Fold-5M
83T/St-303
83T/Tr-77T
84D-355
84D/Champs-44
84F-43
84F-636IA
84F/St-100
84F/St-120
84F/X-U80
84Mother/A's-3
84Nes/792-210
84Nes/792-705LL
84OPC-210
84T-210
84T-705LL
84T/St-116
84T/Tr-82
85D-584
85F-431
85FunFoodPin-74
85Leaf-28
85OPC-352
85T-352
85T-5RB
85T/St-325
85T/St-5
85T/St-6
86Mother/Ast-3
86Sf/Dec-56
89T/LJN-109
90MSA/AGFA-11
91Perez/HOF-205
92UD/Bench-40
92UD/Bench-41
92UD/Bench-42
92UD/Bench-43M
92UD/Bench-44M
92UD/Bench-AU5M
93TWill-30
93TWill/Mem-18
93YooHoo-10

Morgan, Joe M.
60T-229
61T-511
62Kahn/Atl
81Pawtu-12MG
89T-714MG
90OPC-321MG
90T-321MG
90T/TVRSox-1MG
91OPC-21MG
91T-21MG

Morgan, Ken
87Visalia-3
88Visalia/Cal-146
88Visalia/ProC-90
89OrlanTw/Best-17
89OrlanTw/ProC-1341
90Foil/Best-30
90OrlanSR/Best-10
90OrlanSR/ProC-1096
90OrlanSR/Star-12
90ProC/Singl-751
91AAA/LineD-411
91Portl/LineD-411
91Portl/ProC-1578

Morgan, Kevin
91Niagara/ClBest-1
91Niagara/ProC-3642
92ClBest-104
92Fayette/ProC-2177

Morgan, Michael
79Ogden/TCMA-3
80T-671R
83D-108
83F-388
83T-203
83T/Tr-78
84Nes/792-423
84OPC-6
84Syrac-22
84T-423
85Mother/Mar-25
86Mother/Mar-25
86T-152
87D-366
87F-591
87Mother/Sea-8
87T-546
88D-120
88D/Best-86
88F-380
88French-12
88S-295
88T-32
88T/Big-98
88T/Tr-73T
89D-164
89D/Best-122
89F/Up-91
89Mother/Dodg-13
89Pol/Dodg-23
89T-788
89T/Tr-84T
89UD-653
90D-132
90F-403
90F/Can-403
90Leaf-358
90Mother/Dodg-21
90OPC-367
90Pol/Dodg-36
90RedFoley/St-66
90S-342
90T-367
90Target-553
90UD-317
91Crown/Orio-316
91D-182

91F-213
91Leaf-193
91Mother/Dodg-21
91OPC-631
91Panini/FrSt-63
91Panini/St-52
91Panini/Top15-89
91Pol/Dodg-36
91RedFoley/St-67
91S-276
91StCl-562
91T-631
91UD-578
91USPlayC/AS-5C
91Ultra-165
92B-647
92Cub/Mara-36
92D-200
92F-465
92F/Up-74
92L-204
92L/BlkGold-204
92OPC-289
92OPC/Premier-180
92Pinn-414
92S-171
92S/RookTr-66T
92StCl-787
92StCl/Dome-124
92Studio-17
92T-289
92T/Gold-289
92T/GoldWin-289
92T/Tr-76T
92T/TrGold-76T
92UD-513
92UD-703
92USPlayC/Ace-6S
92Ultra-471
92Yank/WIZ80-125
93B-144
93Cub/Mara-17
93D-394
93F-23
93Flair-18
93L-123
93OPC-207
93Pac/Spanish-59
93Panini-201
93Pinn-63
93S-73
93Select-145
93Select/Ace-10
93Select/StatL-90
93StCl-285
93StCl/1stDay-285
93StCl/Cub-17
93T-373
93T/Finest-188
93T/FinestRef-188
93T/Gold-373
93TripleP-76
93UD-106
93UD/FunPack-82
93UD/SP-86
93USPlayC/Ace-7S
93Ultra-21
94B-26
94D-206
94F-391
94L-192
94OPC-235
94Pac/Cr-104
94Pinn-113
94Pinn/Artist-113
94Pinn/Museum-113
94S-214
94S/GoldR-214
94Select-121
94StCl-304
94StCl/1stDay-304
94StCl/Gold-304
94StCl/Team-359
94T-479
94T/Finest-96
94T/FinestRef-96
94T/Gold-479
94TripleP-75
94UD-451
94UD/CollC-212
94UD/CollC/Gold-212
94UD/CollC/Silv-212
94Ultra-164

Morgan, Ray
D327
D328-121
D329-126
D350/2-124
E135-121
M101/4-126
M101/5-124
T207

Morgan, Rick
80Knoxvl/TCMA-26

Morgan, Scott
91Kinston/ClBest-7
91Kinston/ProC-319
92Canton/SB-113
92Kinston/ProC-2472
93Kinston/Team-20

Morgan, Tom S.
52B-109
52BR
52T-331
53T-132
54NYJour
55B-100
57T-239
58T-365
59T-545
60L-97
60T-33
61T-272
62T-11
63T-421CO
73OPC-421CO
73T-421CO
74OPC-276CO
74T-276CO
91T/Arc53-132
PM10/L-29

Morgan, Vern
73OPC-49CO
73T-49C
74OPC-447CO
74T-447C

Morhardt, Greg
85OrlanTw-9
86OrlanTw-13
87Portl-20

Morhardt, Moe
62T-309

Mori, Dan
87SanJose-12

Moriarty, Edward
R314

Moriarty, George
09Buster/Pin-10
11Helmar-34
14CJ-114
15CJ-114
21Exh-111UMP
93UD/T202-6
94Conlon-1209UMP
D329-127
D350/2-125
E104
E254
E270/1
M101/4-127
M101/5-125
M116
S74-16
T202
T205
T206
T207

Moriarty, Todd
84Everett/Cram-26

Morillo, Cesar
91BBCity/ClBest-19
91BBCity/ProC-1405
91ClBest/Singl-60
92BBCity/ClBest-12
92Eugene/ClBest-20
92Eugene/ProC-3038
93Rockford/ClBest-18

Morillo, Santiago
91SoOreg/ClBest-17
91SoOreg/ProC-3840

Morin, Pierre
(Pete)
45Parade*-25M
45Parade*-39

Moritz, Chris
85Greens-7
86WinHaven-18
87NewBrit-23
88NewBrit/ProC-907
89NewBrit/ProC-603
89NewBrit/Star-11

Moritz, Tom
86BirmB/Team-7

Morlan, John
75OPC-651
75T-651
75T/M-651

Morland, Mike
91StCath/ClBest-1
91StCath/ProC-3398
92Myrtle/ClBest-8
92Myrtle/ProC-2201
93Knoxvl/ProC-1254

Morlock, Allen
83Spring/Frit-24
84ArkTr-8
86ArkTr-16
87Edmon-9

Morman, Alvin
92Ashvl/ClBest-20
94B-314
94FExcel-205

Morman, Russ
86BuffB-19
86Sf/Rook-33
87Coke/WS-8
87D-306
87F-645R
87Hawaii-22
87Sf/TPrev-26M
87T-233
88Vanco/CMC-17
88Vanco/ProC-760
89Vanco/CMC-16
89Vanco/ProC-590
90AAASingl/ProC-608
90Omaha/CMC-15
90Omaha/ProC-73
90ProC/Singl-190
90WichSt-21
91Leaf-263
92Nashvl/ProC-1840

Morogiello, Dan
79Richm-18
80Richm-1
82Louisvl-20
83RochR-6
84Nes/792-682
84T-682
85Richm-5
91Crown/Orio-317

Morones, Geno
91Hunting/ClBest-15
91Hunting/ProC-3331
92Geneva/ClBest-10
92Geneva/ProC-1558

Moronko, Jeff
80Batavia-28
81Chatt-12
82Chatt-21
83BuffB-17
84BuffB-1
85Maine-19
85Tulsa-22
86OKCty-14
87Colum-15
87Colum/TCMA-17
88Colum/CMC-18
88Colum/Pol-20
88Colum/ProC-328
89Chatt/II/Team-19
92Yank/WIZ80-126

Morphy, Pat
90Oneonta/ProC-3379
91Greens/ProC-3055
92FtLaud/ClBest-17
92FtLaud/ProC-2609
92FtLaud/Team-21

Morrelli, Anthony
85Clovis-27

Morrill, John
E223
N172
N28
N284
N43
WG1-6

Morris, Aaron
91Watertn/ClBest-19
91Watertn/ProC-3375

Morris, Angel
81BurlB-14
82Beloit/Frit-26
85FtMyr-7
86Memphis/GoldT-20
86Memphis/SilverT-20
87FtMyr-30
88Virgini/Star-16
89Memphis/Best-14
89Memphis/ProC-1203
89Memphis/Star-18
90Miami/II/Star-19

Morris, Danny W.
69OPC-99R
69T-99R

Morris, Dave
81BurlB-1
83Ander-29
85Durham-8
85Everett/II/Cram-11
86Clinton-14

Morris, Don
80WHave-4
81WHave-16

Morris, Edward
N172

Morris, Fred
78DaytB

Morris, Frosty
57Seattle/Pop-25

Morris, Hal
87Albany-21
88Colum/CMC-20
88Colum/Pol-21
88Colum/ProC-327
89AAA/CMC-17
89AAA/ProC-20
89Classic-28
89Colum/CMC-16
89Colum/Pol-14
89Colum/ProC-743
89D-545
89F-260
89S/HotRook-8
89S/NWest-29
90AlbanyDG/Best-18
90B-57
90Classic/Up-35
90D-514
90F/Up-U15
90HotRook/St-32
90Kahn/Reds-16
90Leaf-321
90OPC-236
90S-602RP
90S/100Ris-87
90S/YS/II-37
90T-236
90T/Tr-76T
90TripleAAS/CMC-17
90UD-31
91B-691
91Bz-13
91Classic/200-178
91Classic/I-98
91Classic/III-62
91D-141
91F-72
91Kahn/Reds-23
91Leaf-51
91Leaf/Stud-168
91MajorLg/Pins-71
91OPC-642
91Pep/Reds-12
91S-647
91S/100RisSt-98
91S/HotRook-3
91StCl-339
91T-642
91T/JumboR-20
91ToysRUs-20
91UD-351
91Ultra-98
92B-468
92CJ/DI-32
92Classic/Game200-137
92Classic/I-65
92D-258
92D/DK-DK19
92F-412
92Hardee-16
92L-205
92L/BlkGold-205
92OPC-773
92Panini-262
92Pinn-22
92Reds/Kahn-23
92Rem/Pr-P7
92Rem/Pr-P8
92Rem/Pr-P9
92S-125
92S/100SS-14
92S/Impact-45
92StCl-63
92Studio-24
92T-773
92T/Gold-773
92T/GoldWin-773
92TripleP-30
92UD-121
92USPlayC/Ace-5D
92Ultra-192
92Yank/WIZ80-127
93D-294
93F-37
93Flair-29
93L-257
93OPC-197
93Pac/Spanish-85
93Panini-291
93Pinn-222
93Reds/Kahn-16
93S-38
93Select-45
93StCl-534
93StCl/1stDay-534
93T-546
93T/Gold-546
93TripleP-223
93UD-121
93UD-833TC
93UD/SP-211
93Ultra-31
94B-186
94D-221
94F-417
94Flair-147
94L-433
94OPC-153
94Panini-165
94Pinn-314
94S-526
94Select-158
94StCl-363
94StCl/1stDay-363
94StCl/Gold-363
94Studio-170
94T-126
94T/Finest-70
94T/FinestRef-70
94T/Gold-126
94TripleP-216
94UD-494
94Ultra-475

Morris, Jack
77Evansvl/TCMA-20
78BK/T-8
78T-703R
79T-251
80T-371
81Coke
81D-127
81F-475
81OPC-284
81PermaGr/AS-15
81T-572
81T/St-80
81Tiger/Detroit-128
82D-107
82F-274
82F/St-159
82K-5
82OPC-108
82OPC-47AS
82T-165LL
82T-450
82T-556AS
82T/St-10LL
82T/St-139
82T/St-183
83D-107
83D-5DK
83F-336
83F/St-17M
83K-35
83OPC-65
83OPC/St-69
83T-65
83T/St-69
84D-415

84F-87
84F/St-83
84Nes/792-136LL
84Nes/792-195
84Nes/792-666TL
84OPC-195
84T-136LL
84T-195
84T-666TL
84T/Gloss40-10
84T/RD-16M
84T/St-263
84Tiger/Farmer-10
84Tiger/Wave-27
85Cain's-14
85D-415
85F-18
85F/LimEd-21
85F/St-82
85FunFoodPin-59
85Leaf-142
85OPC-382
85Seven-12D
85T-610
85T/3D-28
85T/Gloss40-26
85T/RD-14M
85T/St-15WS
85T/St-256
85T/St-9ALCS
85T/Super-43
85ThomMc/Discs-15
85Wendy-16
86Cain's-12
86D-105
86D/AAS-18
86D/HL-27
86D/PopUp-18
86Dorman-2
86F-232
86F/Mini-48
86F/Slug-23
86F/St-79
86GenMills/Book-1M
86Leaf-38
86OPC-270
86Seven/Coin-C10M
86Sf-117
86Sf-141M
86T-270
86T/3D-17
86T/Gloss22-10
86T/Mini-14
86T/St-163FOIL
86T/St-268
86T/Super-38
86T/Tatt-11M
87Cain's-14
87Classic-90
87Coke/Tigers-7
87D-13DK
87D-173
87D/DKsuper-13
87D/OD-212
87Drake-27
87F-158
87F/BB-28
87F/Lim-28
87F/Mini-70
87F/Slug-27
87F/St-80
87GenMills/Book-2M
87Jiffy-3
87KayBee-20
87Leaf-135
87Leaf-13DK
87MnM's-6
87OPC-376
87RedFoley/St-114
87Seven-DT8
87Sf-111M
87Sf-87
87Sf/TPrev-15M
87Smok/AL-6
87Stuart-19M
87T-778
87T/Coins-18
87T/Gloss60-47
87T/Mini-55
87T/St-266
88ChefBoy-3
88Classic/Red-174
88Clinton/ProC-717
88D-127
88D/AS-24
88D/Best-181
88Drake-32
88F-626M
88F-64
88F/AwardWin-26
88F/BB/AS-26
88F/BB/MVP-24
88F/Excit-27
88F/Head-3
88F/Hottest-28
88F/LL-28
88F/Mini-22
88F/RecSet-26
88F/St-26
88F/TL-23
88Grenada-67
88KennerFig-72
88Leaf-85
88OPC-340
88Panini/St-85
88Pep/T-47
88Pol/T-8
88S-545
88Sf-176
88T-340
88T/Big-170
88T/Coins-21
88T/Gloss60-17
88T/Mini-11
88T/RiteAid-27
88T/St-268
88T/St/Backs-59
88T/UK-50
89B-93
89Clinton/ProC-901
89D-234
89F-139
89F/BBMVP's-30
89KennerFig-95
89Mara/Tigers-47
89OPC-266
89Panini/St-334
89Pol/Tigers-47
89RedFoley/St-82
89S-250
89S/Mast-8
89Sf-5
89T-645
89T/Big-61
89T/LJN-106
89T/St-277
89T/UK-54
89UD-352
90CokeK/Tiger-12
90D-639
90D/BestAL-34
90F-610
90F/Can-610
90F/LL-27
90KayBee-19
90Leaf-482
90OPC-555
90Panini/St-76
90Publint/St-478
90S-203
90T-555
90T/St-276
90UD-573
91B-319
91Classic/II-T49
91Classic/III-61
91D-492
91F-343
91F/UltraUp-U39
91F/Up-U39
91Leaf-294
91Leaf/Stud-89
91OPC-75
91OPC/Premier-84
91Panini/FrSt-296
91S-114
91S/RookTr-74T
91StCl-447
91StCl/Member*-22
91T-75
91T/Tr-82T
91UD-336
91UD-45TC
91UD/Ext-736
91UD/FinalEd-80FAS
91USPlayC/AS-1H
92B-16
92BJ/Fire-20
92Classic/Game200-199
92Classic/I-66
92D-216
92D-25AS
92D/McDon-G4
92DPep/MSA-6
92F-211
92F/Up-66
92French-18
92KingB-18
92L-425
92L/BlkGold-425
92OPC-235
92OPC/Premier-79
92Panini-122
92Panini-279AS
92Pinn-483
92Pinn-585
92S-652
92S-798HL
92S/RookTr-15T
92StCl-640
92StCl/Dome-125WS
92StCl/Dome-126AS
92StCl/MemberI-5
92Studio-257
92T-235
92T/Gold-235
92T/GoldWin-235
92T/Tr-77T
92T/TrGold-77T
92TripleP/Gal-GS3
92UD-315
92UD-732
92USPlayC/Twin-13H
92USPlayC/Twin-9C
92Ultra-452
92Ultra/AwardWin-1
93B-463
93BJ/D/45-20
93BJ/D/McDon-9
93BJ/Demp-7
93BJ/Fire-21
93Classic/GameI-68
93D-351
93F-347LL
93F-697
93HumDum/Can-21
93L-113
93MSA/Ben-3
93OPC-179
93OPC/WC-11
93Pac/Spanish-326
93Panini-24
93Pinn-472NT
93Pinn-57
93S-37
93S-508AS
93Select-158
93Select/Ace-5
93Select/StatL-85
93StCl-356
93StCl/1stDay-356
93T-185
93T/Gold-185
93TripleP-160
93UD-164
93UD/FunPack-59
93UD/SP-51
93Ultra-290
94F-339
94L-401
94Pac/Cr-649
94Pinn-532
94S-453
94UD-331
94Ultra-346

Morris, Jeff
83Tucson-6
87Everett-26
90SanJose/Best-26CO
90SanJose/Cal-54CO
90SanJose/ProC-2028CO
90SanJose/Star-29CO
92Pittsfld/ClBest-19CO
92Pittsfld/ProC-3312CO

Morris, Jim
87Stockton-23
89Saraso/Star-15

Morris, Joe
90James/Pucko-23

Morris, John Daniel
84Omaha-8
85D-32RR
85Louisvl-23
85Omaha-19
86Louisvl-20
87D-480
87F/Up-U83
87Louisvl-20
87Sf/Rook-42
87T-211
87T/JumboR-10
88D-480
88F-43
88Louisvl-35
88S-346
88T-536
89Smok/Cards-14
89T-578
90D-516
90F-254
90F/Can-254
90OPC-383
90S-134
90Smok/Card-15
90T-383
90T/TVCard-35
91Crown/Orio-318
91F/Up-U109
91Leaf-496
91Phill/Medford-29
92B-474
92D-92
92StCl-796

Morris, John W.
(Johnny)
69OPC-111
69T-111
69T/4in1-1M
70McDon-1
71MLB/St-446
71OPC-721
71T-721
75OPC-577
75T-577
75T/M-577

Morris, Ken
88AubAs/ProC-1957

Morris, Marc
91Pocatel/ProC-3786
91Pocatel/SportP-12
92Visalia/ClBest-5
92Visalia/ProC-1012

Morris, Rick
87Durham-20
88CLAS/Star-32
88Durham/Star-15
89Greenvl/Best-5
89Greenvl/ProC-1172
89Greenvl/Star-15
89Star/Wax-37
90Greenvl/Best-11
90Greenvl/ProC-1136
90Greenvl/Star-14
91AA/LineD-213
91Greenvl/ClBest-19
91Greenvl/LineD-213
91Greenvl/ProC-3013

Morris, Rod
88Butte-19
89CharlR/Star-16
89Star/Wax-8
90CharlR/Star-14
91AA/LineD-588
91Tulsa/LineD-588
91Tulsa/ProC-2786
91Tulsa/Team-19
92Tulsa/ProC-2708

Morris, Rossi
91Princet/ClBest-10
91Princet/ProC-3528
92Princet/ClBest-20
92Princet/ProC-3100

Morris, Steve 1
89Elizab/Star-20
89Kenosha/ProC-1060
89Kenosha/Star-16
89Star/Wax-53
90Foil/Best-185
90Kenosha/Best-9
90Kenosha/ProC-2308
90Kenosha/Star-14

Morris, Steve 2
87Hawaii-12

Morrisette, James
89Clmbia/Best-15
89Clmbia/GS-16
89SALAS/GS-20
90StLucie/Star-17
91Miami/ClBest-25
91StLucie/ClBest-3

Morrisey
N172
N284

Morrisey, Todd
85Clovis-28CO

Morrison, Anthony
(Red, Tony)
87Oneonta-2
88FSLAS/Star-45
88FtLaud/Star-17
89FtLaud/Star-17

Morrison, Brian
87SanBern-17
88FSLAS/Star-13
88Miami/Star-15
89Knoxvl/Best-17
89Knoxvl/ProC-1146
90Salem/Star-14

Morrison, Bruce 1
83Lynch-9

Morrison, Bruce 2
91Melbourne/Fut-14

Morrison, Dan
88TM/Umpire-47
89TM/Umpire-45
89TM/Umpire-60M
90TM/Umpire-43

Morrison, James Forrest
76OkCty/Team-18
79OkCty
79T-722R
80OPC-272
80T-522
81Coke
81D-158
81F-357
81T-323
81T/HT
81T/St-60
82D-395
82F-354
82OPC-154
82T-654
82T/Tr-77T
83D-150
83F-313
83T-173
84D-322
84F-257
84Nes/792-44
84T-44
85D-532
85F-471
85T-433
86D-386
86Elmira-13
86F-614
86OPC-56
86T-553
86T/St-133
87D-484
87D/OD-169
87F-614
87F/GameWin-29
87F/Mini-71
87F/St-81
87Greens-22
87Leaf-215
87OPC-237
87Sf/TPrev-18M
87Stuart-10
87T-237
87T/St-133
88D-543
88F-65
88OPC-288
88S-272
88T-751
88T/Big-237
88T/St-272
89Pac/SenLg-137
89T/SenLg-61
89TM/SenLg-81
89UD-568
90EliteSenLg-42

Morrison, Jeff
87Belling/Team-13

Morrison, Jim
89Elmira/Pucko-8
91WinHaven/ClBest-23

91WinHaven/ProC-502
92LynchRS/ClBest-25
92LynchRS/ProC-2921
Morrison, John
21Exh-112
90Target-554
93Conlon-794
E120
V100
V61-115
W572
W573
Morrison, Keith
90Pulaski/Best-6
90Pulaski/ProC-3104
91Macon/ClBest-6
91Macon/ProC-860
92Albany/ClBest-20
92Albany/ProC-2301
Morrison, Perry
80ElPaso-19
81Holyo-24
82Holyo-7
Morrissey, Joe
33G-97
R310
V94-34
Morrow, Ben
87Salem-9
Morrow, Brian
90WichSt-27
Morrow, Chris
88GreatF-5
89Bakers/Cal-204
89Salem/Team-18
90AS/Cal-12
90Bakers/Cal-247
91FSLAS/ProC-FSL41
91VeroB/ClBest-29
91VeroB/ProC-789
92SanAn/SB-571
92Sky/AASingl-250
Morrow, David
86James-17
87BurlEx-17
Morrow, Red
88CalLgAS-50
Morrow, Steve
82FtMyr-23
84Memphis-22
86Memphis/GoldT-21TR
86Memphis/SilverT-21TR
87Memphis-26TR
87Memphis/Best-27
88Memphis/Best-4
89Omaha/CMC-24
89Omaha/ProC-1723
Morrow, Timmie
89Butte/SP-26
90Foil/Best-284
90Gaston/Best-17
90Gaston/ProC-2533
90Gaston/Star-15
90ProC/Singl-847
91CharlR/ClBest-23
91CharlR/ProC-1327
92CharlR/ProC-2238
92ClBest-68
Morse, Jacob C.
90LitSun-3
Morse, Matt
90Elizab/Star-14
91Kenosha/ClBest-5
91Kenosha/ProC-2083
Morse, Mike
81AppFx-20
83GlenF-7
Morse, Randy
84Shrev/FB-13
Morse, Scott
87PortChar-4
89CharlR/Star-17
Mortensen, Tony
89FresnoSt/Smok-15
90Spokane/SportP-4
91Waterlo/ClBest-6
91Waterlo/ProC-1253
92HighD/ClBest-11
Mortillaro, John
83Ander-13
84Durham-24
Mortimer, Bob
86Salem-20
Morton, Carl
69Fud's-9
69T-646R
70Expos/Pins-11
70OPC-109R
70T-109R
71Expo/ProS-17
71K-23
71MLB/St-135
71OPC-515
71T-515
71T/Coins-35
71T/GM-4
71T/Greatest-4NL ROY
71T/S-28
71T/Super-28
71T/tatt-16
72OPC-134
72ProStars/PostC-9
72T-134
73OPC-331
73T-331
74OPC-244
74T-244
74T/St-8
75OPC-237
75T-237
75T/M-237
76Ho-43
76Ho/Twink-43
76OPC-328
76SSPC-4
76T-328
77T-24
Morton, Guy
BF2-23
D327
D328-122
D329-128
D350/2-126
E121/80
E122
E135-122
M101/4-128
M101/5-126
W575
WG7-34
Morton, Kevin
88CapeCod-12
88CapeCod/Sum-139
89Elmira/Pucko-27
90A&AASingle/ProC-5
90EastLAS/ProC-EL32
90Foil/Best-211
90NewBrit/Best-14
90NewBrit/ProC-1316
90NewBrit/Star-12
90T/TVRSox-52
91AAA/LineD-361
91B-130
91Classic/III-63
91D-37RR
91D/Rook-40
91Pawtu/LineD-361
91Pawtu/ProC-36
91UD/FinalEd-66F
92D-330
92OPC-724
92OPC/Premier-7
92Pawtu/ProC-919
92Pinn/Team2000-14
92ProC/Tomorrow-18
92RedSox/Dunkin-19
92S-420
92S/100RisSt-36
92StCl-115
92T-724
92T/91Debut-127
92T/Gold-724
92T/GoldWin-724
92UD-676
92USPlayC/RedSox-4S
92USPlayC/RedSox-8D
Morton, Lew
52Park-13
Morton, Maurice
85Spokane/Cram-15
Morton, Ron
88Spokane/ProC-1946
89Star/IISingl-190
89Watlo/ProC-1782
89Watlo/Star-21
90Waterlo/Best-12
90Waterlo/ProC-2378
Morton, Stan
80Clinton-22
Morton, Sydney
86Negro/Frit-36
Morton, Wycliffe
(Bubba)
62T-554
63T-164
67OPC-79
67T-79
68T-216
69MB-196
69T-342
Moryn, Walt
52Park-72
53Exh/Can-39
55B-261
57T-16
58T-122
59T-147M
59T-488
60L-17
60T-74
60T/tatt-37
61T-91
61T/RO-32
79TCMA-141
90Target-555
Mosby, Linvel
78Ashvl
79Ashvl/TCMA-4
80Ashvl-20
Moscaret, Jeff
84MidldC-11
Moscat, Frank
85Lynch-20
Moschitto, Ross
65T-566R
81TCMA-441
92Yank/WIZ60-91
Moscrey, Mike
88Cedar/ProC-1139
89Chatt/Best-19
89Chatt/GS-18
90Chatt/GS-22
Mosdell, Ken
45Parade*-40
Moseby, Lloyd
80Syrac-16
80Syrac/Team-15
81F-421
81OPC-52
81OPC/Post-24
81T-643
82D-129
82F-621
82OPC-223
82OPC/Post-4
82T-223
82T/St-246
82T/StVar-246
83D-556
83F-435
83OPC-124
83OPC/St-130
83T-452
83T/St-130
84D-363
84F-164
84Nes/792-403AS
84Nes/792-606TL
84Nes/792-92
84Nestle/DT-7
84OPC-289TL
84OPC-3AS
84OPC-92
84T-403AS
84T-606TL
84T-92
84T/RD-3M
84T/St-191
84T/St-365
84T/St/Box-4
84Tor/Fire-25
85D-437
85D/AAS-5
85F-115
85F-636IA
85FunFood/Pin-132
85Leaf-143
85OPC-77
85OPC/Post-19
85T-545
85T/RD-3M
85T/St-359
85T/Super-39
85Tor/Fire-23
86BJ/Ault-20
86D-73
86F-67
86F/LL-26
86GenMills/Book-3M
86Leaf-72
86OPC-360
86T-360
86T/St-195
86T/Tatt-21M
86Tor/Fire-26
87D-21DK
87D-74
87D/AAS-59
87D/DKsuper-21
87D/OD-36
87F-236
87F/Lim-29
87F/Mini-72
87F/RecSet-22
87GenMills/Book-1M
87Leaf-105
87Leaf-21DK
87OPC-210
87RedFoley/St-55
87Sf-96
87Sf/TPrev-5M
87Stuart-28M
87T-210
87T/St-190
87Tor/Fire-23
88BJ/5x7-9
88D-367
88D/Best-199
88F-119
88F/St-75
88Grenada-61
88Ho/Disc-20
88Leaf-140
88OPC-272
88Panini/St-225
88S-109
88Sf-74
88T-565
88T/Big-113
88T/St-189
88T/UK-51
88Tor/Fire-15
89D-231
89F-241
89OPC-113
89Panini/St-473
89RedFoley/St-83
89S-12
89T-113
89T/Big-262
89T/St-188
89Tor/Fire-15
89UD-381
90B-362
90BJ/HoSt-2M
90CokeK/Tiger-13
90D-504
90D/BestAL-62
90F-90
90F/Can-90
90F/Up-U97
90Leaf-377
90OPC-779
90PubIInt/St-524
90S-404
90S/Tr-25T
90T-779
90T/Big-305
90T/Tr-77T
90UD-421
90UD/Ext-789
91B-135
91CokeK/Tiger-15
91D-188
91F-344
91Leaf-223
91Leaf/Stud-56
91OPC-632
91Panini/FrSt-293
91Panini/St-239
91Pol/Tiger-7
91S-133
91StCl-364
91T-632
91UD-559
91Ultra-124
92D-443
92F-142
92Panini-111
92S-468
92UD-468
92USPlayC/Tiger-11H
92USPlayC/Tiger-5D
Moseley, Scott
90Helena/SportP-8
Moser, Arnold
V351A-19
Moser, Larry
83Ander-30
Moser, Ricky
90Eugene/GS-20
Moser, Steve
86Watertn-15
87Salem-13
Moses, Gerald
(Gerry)
65T-573R
69T-476R
70OPC-104
70T-104
71MLB/St-352
71OPC-205
71T-205
71T/Coins-6
72OPC-356
72T-356
73OPC-431
73T-431
74OPC-19
74T-19
75OPC-271
75T-271
75T/M-271
92Yank/WIZ70-117
Moses, John
81Wausau-25
83AppFx/Frit-24
83SLCity-19
84Chatt-24
84D-74
84Nes/792-517
84T-517
85Cram/PCL-83
86Calgary-16
87D-393
87F-592
87Mother/Sea-18
87T-284
88D-440
88F-381
88F/Up-U45
88Portl/CMC-22
88Portl/ProC-643
88S-309
88T-712
89D-626
89F-121
89S-432
89T-72
89UD-242
90D-590
90F-381
90F/Can-381
90Leaf-433
90OPC-653
90PubIInt/St-333
90S-391
90T-653
90UD-240
91ColoSp/ProC-2198
91F-619
91OPC-341
91S-429
91T-341
92Calgary/ProC-3743
92Calgary/SB-63
Moses, Mark
80Ander-13
Moses, Steve
85Cram/PCL-30
86Reading-18
87Wmsprt-6
Moses, Wallace
(Wally)
35BU-98
37Dix
37Exh/4-14
37OPC-109
38Exh/4-14
38Wheat

39PlayBall-64
40PlayBall-26
41DP-126
41PlayBall-42
51B-261
53B/Col-95
55B-294CO
60T-459C
81TCMA-481M
91Conlon/Sport-90
R313
R314
R326-5A
R326-5B
R342-5
V300
Mosher, Peyton
82VeroB-9
Mosienko, Bill
45Parade*-41
Moskau, Paul
77Indianap-9
78Indianap-3
78OPC-181
78Pep-19
78T-126
79OPC-197
79T-377
80T-258
81F-207
81OPC-358
81T-546
82D-355
82F-76
82T-97
Mosley, Reggie
83TriCit-15
Mosley, Tony
87Elmira/Black-17
87Elmira/Cain-2
87Elmira/Red-17
88WinHaven/Star-15
89Elmira/Pucko-11
90WinHaven/Star-19
91LynchRS/ClBest-5
91LynchRS/ProC-1194
92NewBrit/ProC-429
92NewBrit/SB-490
92Sky/AASingl-210
Moss, Barry
77Indianap-23
87SLCity/Taco-x
88SLCity-18
89SLCity-15
91Erie/ClBest-28MG
91Erie/ProC-4084MG
92Spokane/ClBest-29CO
92Spokane/ProC-1312CO
Moss, Darren
87Anchora-36BB
Moss, J. Lester
47TipTop
50B-251
51B-210
52T-143
54B-181
54Esskay
55Esskay
57T-213
58T-153
59T-453
77Evansvl/TCMA-21
79T-66MG
91Crown/Orio-319
Moss, Ray
90Target-556
Mosser, Todd
90NE-19
Mossi, Don
55B-259
55Gol/Ind-20
55Salem
55T-85
55T/DH-84
56T-39
56T/Pin-9P
57Sohio/Ind-9
57T-8
58T-35
59T-302
60T-418
60T/tatt-38
61P-42
61T-14
62J-23
62P-23
62P/Can-23
62T-105
62T-55LL
62T/St-49
63J-56
63P-56
63T-218M
63T-530
64T-335
66OPC-74
66T-74
79TCMA-215
81TCMA-418
81Tiger/Detroit-49
90Pac/Legend-95
Mossor, Earl
90Target-1041
Mostil, Johnny A.
21Exh-113
28Yueng-24
61F-64
93Conlon-912
E120
E121/120
E210-24
V100
V61-45
W501-40
W502-24
W572
W573
WG7-35
Mota, Andres
(Andy)
87AubAs-7
88AubAs/ProC-1966
89Osceola/Star-12
89Star/Wax-16
90ColMud/Best-2
90ColMud/ProC-1354
90ColMud/Star-17
90Foil/Best-48
90ProC/Singl-752
90Star/ISingl-17
91AAA/LineD-616
91Tucson/LineD-616
91Tucson/ProC-2220
91UD/FinalEd-22F
92D-598
92F-441
92OPC-214
92Pinn-257
92ProC/Tomorrow-222
92S-872
92S/Impact-33
92S/Rook-16
92Sky/AAASingl-274
92StCl-166
92T-214
92T/91Debut-128
92T/Gold-214
92T/GoldWin-214
92Tucson/ProC-497
92Tucson/SB-615
92UD-564
Mota, Carlos
88Burllnd/ProC-1783
89Star/IISingl-183
89Watertn/Star-15
90Reno/Cal-271
91ClBest/Singl-118
91Kinston/ClBest-13
91Kinston/ProC-326
92Canton/ProC-693
92Canton/SB-114
93LimeR/Winter-17
Mota, Domingo
90Kissim/DIMD-18
91B-696
91Bakers/Cal-10
92ClBest-182
92Memphis/ProC-2427
92Memphis/SB-439
92Sky/AASingl-185
93ClBest/MLG-127
Mota, Gary
92Ashvl/ClBest-1
92ClBest-384
92UD/ML-25M
92UD/ML-272
92UD/POY-PY2
93B-695FOIL
93ClBest/MLG-106
93SALAS/II-26
93SALAS/IICS-16
93StCl/Ast-12
94T-782
94T/Gold-782
Mota, Jose Manuel
86Tulsa-27
89Huntsvl/Best-26
89Wichita/Rock/HL-15
89Wichita/Rock/Up-11
90AAASingl/ProC-18
90LasVegas/CMC-13
90LasVegas/ProC-130
90ProC/Singl-516
91AAA/LineD-289
91F/Up-U126
91LasVegas/LineD-289
91LasVegas/ProC-243
92F-616
92Omaha/ProC-2970
92Omaha/SB-339
92S-742
92S/100RisSt-47
92S/Rook-19
92T/91Debut-129
Mota, Jose
77Cocoa
78DaytB
80Cedar-13
Mota, Manny Jr.
90AubAs/Best-1
90AubAs/ProC-3398
Mota, Manny
63T-141
64T-246
65T-463
66EH-15
66OPC-112
66T-112
67CokeCap/Pirate-8
67OPC-66
67T-66
67T/Test/PP-16
68KDKA-15
68T-325
69Fud's-10
69MB-197
69MLB/St-160
69T-236
69T/St-58
70MLB/St-53
70OPC-157
70T-157
71MLB/St-109
71OPC-112
71T-112
71Ticket/Dodg-11
72MB-245
72T-596
73OPC-412
73T-412
74K-49
74OPC-368
74T-368
75OPC-414
75T-414
75T/M-414
76OPC-548
76SSPC-87
76T-548
77T-386
78SSPC/270-79
78T-228
78T/Zest-5
79T-644
80T-3RS
81D-299
81F-141
85Coke/Dodg-21CO
86Coke/Dodg-20CO
87Smok/Dodg-24CO
88Smok/Dodg-5CO
89Smok/Dodg-80
90BBWit-25
90Mother/Dodg-28M
90Pac/Legend-41
90Pol/Dodg-x
90Swell/Great-26
90Target-557
91LineD-22
91Mother/Dodg-28CO
91Pol/Dodg-x
91Swell/Great-63
92AP/ASG-83
92Mother/Dodg-28M
92Pol/Dodg-NNO
93LimeR/Winter-121
93Mother/Dodg-28M
93Pol/Dodg-30M
93UD/ATH-99
Mota, Miguel
87Bakers-4
Mota, Santo
92Johnson/ClBest-11
92Johnson/ProC-3124
Mota, Willie
89Elizab/Star-21
89Star/IISingl-151
90Kenosha/Best-10
90Kenosha/ProC-2297
90Kenosha/Star-15
91Kenosha/ClBest-2
92ClBest-349
92FtMyr/ProC-2754
92Miracle/ClBest-10
Moten, Scott
92Elizab/ClBest-4
92Elizab/ProC-3679
Mothell, Carroll Ray
(Dink)
87Negro/Dixon-19
Motley, Darryl
81Omaha-22
82D-390
82F-417
82Omaha-19
82T-471R
83Evansvl-21
84D-344
84F/X-U81
85D-461
85F-208
85Leaf-69
85T-561
85T/St-276
86D-217
86F-16
86Kitty/Disc-14
86Leaf-95
86NatPhoto-24
86Sf-186M
86T-332
86T/St-22WS
87OPC-99
87Richm/Bob-15
87Richm/Crown-30
87Richm/TCMA-19
87T-99
89Indianap/CMC-22
89Indianap/ProC-1238
90AAASingl/ProC-560
90Nashvl/CMC-18
90Nashvl/ProC-248
90ProC/Singl-143
Mottola, Chad
92Billings/ProC-3370
92Classic/DP-5
92Classic/DPFoil-BC5
92Classic/DPPrev-BB5
92FrRow/DP-82
92UD/ML-4
93B-90
93FExcel/ML-25
93StCl/MurphyMP-6
93StCl/MurphyS-55
93T-56
93T/Gold-56
93UD-443TP
93UD/SP-282FOIL
94B-214
94ClBest/Gold-196
94FExcel-179
94FExcel/LL-15
94SigRook/Bonus-1
94TedW-129
Motton, Curt
68T-549R
69OPC-37
69T-37
70OPC-261
70T-261
71MLB/St-305
71OPC-684
71T-684
72MB-246
72OPC-393
72T-393
85Everett/II/Cram-12
86RochR-13C
87RochR-13
87RochR/TCMA-23
88RochR/CMC-25
88RochR/Gov-29
88RochR/ProC-218
88RochR/Team-14
91Crown/Orio-320
Motuzas, Jeff
92ClBest-386
92PrWill/ClBest-10
92PrWill/ProC-152
Motz, Willie
91Kenosha/ProC-2079
Moulder, Glen
49B-159
90Target-1042
Moulton, Brian
77Cedar
Moultrie, Patrick
93StCath/ClBest-16
93StCath/ProC-3987
Mount, Chuck
86Cram/NWL-42
87AppFx-1
88BirmB/Best-27
89BirmB/Best-18
89BirmB/ProC-92
90CharlK/Team-18
91AAA/LineD-212
91Iowa/LineD-212
91Iowa/ProC-1056
Mountain, Joe
92Belling/ClBest-12
92Belling/ProC-1440
Moure, Brian
88CapeCod/Sum-12
Moushon, Dan
89Spring/Best-28
Mouton, Brian
90Butte/SportP-21
Mouton, James
91AubAS/ClBest-17
91AubAS/ProC-4282
92ClBest-207
92Osceola/ClBest-21
92Osceola/ProC-2538
93B-236
93FExcel/ML-48
93StCl/Ast-3
94B-258
94B-339
94ClBest/Gold-136
94FExcel-206
94FExcel/AS-3
94Finest-421
94Flair-174
94Flair/Wave-7
94L/GRook-15
94OPC-97
94OPC/HotPros-2
94Pinn-535
94Select-184
94T-782M
94T/Gold-782M
94UD-520DD
94Ultra-509
94Ultra/AllRook-8
Mouton, Lyle
91LSU/Pol-12M
91LSU/Pol-13
91Oneonta/ProC-4166
92PrWill/ClBest-16
92PrWill/ProC-162
92ProC/Tomorrow-127
92UD/ML-194
93ClBest/MLG-3
93FExcel/ML-212
94FExcel-110
Mowrey, Harry
(Mike)
11Helmar-173
16FleischBrd-68
D328-123
D329-129
E135-123
E224
E300
E96
M101/4-129
M116
T213/blue
T213/brown

W555
Mowry, David
90LitSun/HSPros-21
90LitSun/HSProsG-21
92CharRain/ClBest-20
92CharRain/ProC-128
92ClBest-55
Mowry, Joe
34G-59
R310
V94-35
Moya, Felix
90James/Pucko-22
91WPalmB/ClBest-8
91WPalmB/ProC-1224
92WPalmB/ClBest-24
92WPalmB/ProC-2087
Moyer, Greg
81Shrev-22
Moyer, Jamie
86Gator-49
86Pittsfld-17
87Berg/Cubs-49
87D-315
87F-570
87T-227
88Berg/Cubs-49
88D-169
88D/Best-228
88D/Cubs/Bk-169
88F-426
88OPC-36
88Panini/St-255
88S-573
88T-36
88T/St-62
89B-223
89D-157
89D/Tr-39
89F-432
89F/Up-65
89Mother/R-17
89OPC-171
89S-263
89Smok/R-22
89T-549TL
89T-717
89T/St-53
89T/Tr-85T
89UD-63
89UD/Ext-791
90D-378
90F-307
90F/Can-307
90Mother/Rang-24
90OPC-412
90PublInt/St-417
90S-107
90T-412
90UD-619
91B-391
91F-294
91Louisvl/Team-8
91OPC-138
91S-437
91StCl-481
91T-138
91UD-610
92Toledo/ProC-1042
93F/Final-160
93Rang/Keeb-274
94D-547
94F-11
94Flair-6
94L-215
94Pinn-442
94S-270
94S/GoldR-270
94StCl-284
94StCl/1stDay-284
94StCl/Gold-284
94StCl/Team-287
94T-526
94T/Gold-526
94UD-147
94UD/CollC-213
94UD/CollC/Gold-213
94UD/CollC/Silv-213
94UD/ElecD-147
94Ultra-6
Moyer, Jim
71MLB/St-260
72OPC-506R
72T-506R
Moyle, Michael
91Perth/Fut-11
92BurlInd/ClBest-20
92BurlInd/ProC-1661
Mraz, Don
76QuadC
Mrowka, Jim
92Kingspt/ProC-1540
Mrozinski, Ron
55B-287
Mucerino, Greg
92CharRain/ClBest-6
92CharRain/ProC-129
Mucker, Kelcey
94ClBest/Gold-81
Mueller, Clarence F.
25Exh-62
26Exh-61
V100
Mueller, Don
49Eureka-121
50B-221
51B-268
52B-18
52BR
52Coke
52Dix
52NTea
52T-52
52TipTop
53B/Col-74
53Brigg
53Dix
53SM
54B-73
54NYJour
54RM-NL7
54SM
54T-42
55Armour-14
55Gol/Giants-22
55RFG-9
55RM-NL8
55SM
55W605-9
56T-241
57T-148
58T-253
59T-368
79TCMA-149
94T/Arc54-42
Exh47
PM10/Sm-128
Mueller, Emmett
(Heinie)
39PlayBall-63
40PlayBall-96
91Conlon/Sport-179
92Conlon/Sport-643
Mueller, Pete
86Osceola-19
Mueller, Ray
49Eureka-122
51B-313
61F-128
Mueller, Willard
75BurlB
76BurlB
76Clinton
77BurlB
78Holyo
79Vanco-23
80T-668R
80Vanco-2
81Vanco-15
82Wichita-10
Muffett, Billy
58T-143
59T-241
61T-16
62T-336
76SSPC-614CO
88Pep/T-CO
89Mara/Tigers-CO
90CokeK/Tiger-28CO
91CokeK/Tiger-x
93Tiger/Gator-28M
Muh, Steve
89Kenosha/ProC-1079
89Kenosha/Star-17
90OrlanSR/Best-20
90OrlanSR/ProC-1080
91AA/LineD-489
91OrlanSR/LineD-489
91OrlanSR/ProC-1847
Muhammad, Bob
87Hawaii-23
89Beloit/I/Star-18
Muhlethaler, Mike
90SoOreg/Best-26
90SoOreg/ProC-3448
Muir, Harry
92MedHat/ProC-3206
92MedHat/SportP-10
93StCath/ClBest-17
93StCath/ProC-3973
Muir, Joseph
52T-154
Mula, Jared
92LSU/McDag-16
Mulcahy, Hugh
39PlayBall-145
40PlayBall-95
41G-1
49Exh
52Laval-51
Mulden, Chris
78Clinton
Mulholland, Terry
84Everett/Cram-20
86Phoenix-18
87D-515
87Phoenix-5
87Sf/TPrev-10M
87T-536
88Phoenix/CMC-10
88Phoenix/ProC-77
89F/Up-U111
89Phill/TastyK-44
89Phoenix/CMC-4
89Phoenix/ProC-1480
89S-474
89T-41
90Classic-127
90D-515
90F-568
90F/Can-568
90Leaf-474
90OPC-657
90Phill/TastyK-24
90S-542
90T-657
90UD-474
91B-504
91Classic/200-78
91D-541
91D-BC14
91D/BC-BC14
91F-408
91F/WaxBox-8
91Leaf-46
91Leaf/Stud-219
91OPC-413
91Panini/FrSt-359
91Panini/St-8
91Phill/Medford-30
91S-33
91S-706NH
91StCl-58
91StCl/Charter*-21
91T-413
91UD-426
91Ultra-269
92B-39
92D-268
92F-540
92L-464
92L/BlkGold-464
92MooTown-16
92OPC-719
92Panini-249
92Phill/Med-22
92Phill/Med-44
92Pinn-199
92S-118
92StCl-98
92Studio-78
92Sunflower-4
92T-719
92T/Gold-719
92T/GoldWin-719
92TripleP-11
92UD-129
92Ultra-248
93B-484
93D-172
93F-106
93Flair-106
93L-22
93L/UpGoldAS-1M
93OPC-283
93Pac/Spanish-240
93Panini-267
93Phill/Med-24
93Pinn-73
93S-117
93Select-127
93Select/StatL-64
93StCl-716
93StCl/1stDay-716
93StCl/Phill-17
93Studio-10
93T-555
93T/Gold-555
93TripleP-170
93UD-279
93UD/SP-16AS
93Ultra-92
94B-81
94D-160
94F-597
94F/AS-46
94Finest-305
94L-373
94OPC-34
94Pac/Cr-483
94Pinn-47
94Pinn/Artist-47
94Pinn/Museum-47
94S-184
94S/GoldR-184
94Sf/2000-134
94StCl-222
94StCl/1stDay-222
94StCl/Gold-222
94StCl/Team-207
94T-170
94T/Gold-170
94TripleP-178
94UD-399
94Ultra-251
94Ultra-401
Mull, Jack
75Phoenix-2
75Phoenix/Caruso-6
75Phoenix/CircleK-2
76Phoenix/Coke-15
77Cedar
78Cedar
81Shrev-1
83Phoenix/BHN-24
84Cram/PCL-24
86Clinton-15MG
87Shrev-25MG
87TexLgAS-6
88Shrev/ProC-1279MG
88TexLgAS/GS-1MG
89Phoenix/CMC-21
89Phoenix/ProC-1503
90Clinton/Best-9MG
90Clinton/ProC-2565MG
91Clinton/ClBest-26MG
91Clinton/ProC-851MG
Mullan, Paul
92F/Clemens-1M
93Ultra/EckComm-1M
Mullane, Anthony
(Count)
N172
Mullaney, Dominic
T206
Mullaney, Jack
52Laval-20
Mulleavy, Greg
60T-463C
60Union/Dodg-23M
Mullen, Billy
90Target-1043
Mullen, Charles
14CJ-24
15CJ-24
E286
Mullen, Ford
43Centen-20
Mullen, Tom
81AppFx-5
81GlenF-6
83GlenF-17
85BuffB-23
86Omaha/ProC-16
86Omaha/TCMA-21
87Omaha-26
88Omaha/CMC-8
88Omaha/ProC-1507
Muller, Fred
37Wheat
Muller, Mike
87Memphis-22
Mulligan, Bill
86FtMyr-20
87FtMyr-1
Mulligan, Bob
82OrlanTw/A-21
83Toledo-8
84Toledo-9
85OrlanTw-19
Mulligan, Edward
E121/120
W501-45
W575
Mulligan, Sean
92ClBest-132
92HighD/ClBest-17
92StCl/Dome-127
92Watlo/ProC-2144
Mullin, George
09Buster/Pin-11
10Domino-89
11Diamond-21
11Helmar-35
12Sweet/Pin-28A
12Sweet/Pin-28B
81Tiger/Detroit-119
92Conlon/Sport-338
E104
E254
E270/1
E90/1
E96
E97
E98
M116
S74-17
T202
T205
T206
T207
T213/blue
T214-21
T215/blue
T215/brown
T3-30
W555
WG2-37
Mullin, Jay
89TNTech-18
Mullin, Pat
47TipTop
49B-56
50B-135
51B-106
52B-183
52T-275
53B/BW-4
53Tiger/Glen-22
54B-151
81Tiger/Detroit-21
83Kaline-61M
83Kaline-8M
Mulliniks, S. Rance
(Rance)
75QuadC
77SLCity
78SSPC/270-216
78T-579
79SLCity-11
81D-504
81F-48
81T-433
82D-630
82F-418
82T-104
82T/Tr-78T
83D-432
83F-436
83OPC-277
83T-277
84D-584
84F-165
84Nes/792-762
84OPC-19
84T-762
84T/St-374
84Tor/Fire-26
85D-485
85F-116

85Leaf-153
85OPC-336
85OPC/Post-17
85T-336
85Tor/Fire-24
86BJ/Ault-21
86D-606
86F-68
86GenMills/Book-3M
86OPC-74
86T-74
86Tor/Fire-27
87D-319
87D/OD-32
87F-237
87OPC-91
87T-537
87Tor/Fire-24
88D-197
88D/Best-328
88F-120
88Ho/Disc-14
88Leaf-204
88OPC-167
88S-235
88T-167
88Tor/Fire-5
89B-250
89D-87
89F-242
89OPC-111
89S-385
89T-618
89T/St-192
89Tor/Fire-5
89UD-43
90D-607
90ElPasoATG/Team-42
90F-91
90F/Can-91
90OPC-466
90PublInt/St-525
90S-204RP
90T-466
90Tor/BJ-5
90UD-132
91D-663
91F-181
91OPC-229
91S-433
91S/ToroBJ-17
91T-229
91Tor/Fire-5
91Ultra-366
92BJ/Fire-21
92D-542
92F-337
92Knoxvl/ProC-2999
92OPC-133
92S-132
92StCl-202
92T-133
92T/Gold-133
92T/GoldWin-133
92Ultra-149
93BJ/D/45-26

Mullino, Ray
87Peoria-1
88CharWh/Best-25
89WinSalem/Star-12
90CharlK/Team-15
90Peoria/Team-26
90T/TVCub-54

Mullins, Fran
80GlenF/B-23
80GlenF/C-12
81T-112R
82Edmon-9
85Cram/PCL-180
85T-283
86OhHenry-22

Mullins, Ron
87Cedar-8
88Greens/ProC-1561
88SALAS/GS-9
89Miami/II/Star-14
90Penin/Star-13

Mullins, Sam
92Princet/ClBest-7
92Princet/ProC-3086

Mulvaney, Michael
88Billings/ProC-1808
89Greens/ProC-410
89SALAS/GS-33
90Cedar/Best-7
90Cedar/ProC-2330
90MidwLgAS/GS-44

Mulvey, Joseph
(Joe)
90Target-558
N172
N28
N284
N690
WG1-53

Mulville, Duane
88Billings/ProC-1805
89Cedar/Best-11
89Cedar/ProC-924
89Cedar/Star-13
92Clearw/ClBest-20
92Clearw/ProC-2059

Mumaw, Steve
86Ventura-15
87Dunedin-10
88Dunedin/Star-11
89ArkTr/GS-14

Mummau, Rob
93StCath/ClBest-18
93StCath/ProC-3982

Mumphrey, Jerry
76SSPC-289
77T-136
78T-452
79T-32
80OPC-196
80T-378
81D-124
81Drake-26
81F-494
81OPC-196
81Sqt-23
81T-556
81T/SO-97
81T/St-227
81T/Tr-808
82D-261
82F-43
82OPC-175
82T-175
82T-486TL
82T/St-220
83D-360
83F-389
83F/St-10M
83F/St-18M
83OPC-246
83OPC/St-97
83RoyRog/Disc-6
83T-670
83T-81
83T/St-97
84D-426
84F-233
84Mother/Ast-9
84Nes/792-45
84OPC-45
84T-45
84T/St-70
85D-206
85F-354
85Leaf-124
85Mother/Ast-15
85OPC-186
85T-736
85T/St-60
86Cub/Unocal-14
86D-84
86F-306
86F/Up-U79
86Gator-22
86Mother/Ast-27
86OPC-282
86Seven/Coin-S16M
86T-282
86T/Tr-76T
87Berg/Cubs-22
87D-324
87F-571
87F/Mini-73
87F/St-82
87Sf/TPrev-22M
87T-372
87T/St-58
88Berg/Cubs-22
88D-447
88D/Cubs/Bk-447
88F-427
88F/Mini-69
88OPC-63
88Panini/St-267
88S-467
88T-466
88T/Big-70
89S-288
92Yank/WIZ80-128

Muncrief, Bob
41G-8
45Playball-9
47TipTop
49B-221
W753

Munda, Steve
91Oneonta/ProC-4152
92Greens/ClBest-22
92Greens/ProC-776

Mundroig, Jorge
79Cedar/TCMA-4

Mundy, Rick
88Geneva/ProC-1640
89Geneva/ProC-1883
89Peoria/Team-12C
90Peoria/Team-6
91Peoria/ClBest-11
91Peoria/ProC-1345
91Peoria/Team-15

Munger, George
(Red)
47TipTop
49B-40
49Eureka-190
50B-89
51B-11
51T/BB-14
52B-243
52T-115

Mungin, Mike
88SoOreg/ProC-1710

Mungo, Van Lingle
34DS-102
34DS-19
35BU-131
35BU-26
35Exh/4-2
36Exh/4-2
36Wheat
37Exh/4-2
37Wheat
38Exh/4-2
38G-254
38G-278
38Wheat
39PlayBall-111
40PlayBall-64
89Smok/Dodg-45
90Target-559
94Conlon-1107
PR1-23
R303/A
R311/Leath
R312
R313
R326-6A
R326-6B
R342-6
V351B-33
WG8-42

Munley, John
83TriCit-7

Munninghoff, Scott
80OkCty
81OkCty/TCMA-13
82Chatt-2

Munns, Les
90Target-560

Munoz, Bob
90Foil/Best-192
90Greens/Best-8
90Greens/ProC-2660
90Greens/Star-14
91FSLAS/ProC-FSL16
91FtLaud/ClBest-9
91FtLaud/ProC-2422
92Albany/ProC-2224
92Albany/SB-13
92B-523
92ClBest-6
92Sky/AASingl-8
92UD/ML-222
93B-47
93ColClip/Pol-10
93F/Final-249
93FExcel/ML-213
93Flair/Wave-10
93L-548
93Select/RookTr-32T
93T/Tr-13T
93Ultra-598
94B-56
94D-174
94F-241
94Finest-414
94Pac/Cr-431
94Phill/Med-23
94Pinn-188
94Pinn/Artist-188
94Pinn/Museum-188
94S-566
94StCl-246
94StCl/1stDay-246
94StCl/Gold-246
94StCl/Team-214
94T-144
94T/Gold-144
94UD-343
94UD/CollC-214
94UD/CollC/Gold-214
94UD/CollC/Silv-214
94Ultra-553
94Ultra-98

Munoz, J.J.
90A&AASingle/ProC-186
90Martins/ProC-3196
91Spartan/ClBest-9
91Spartan/ProC-894
92Clearw/ClBest-17
92Clearw/ProC-2056

Munoz, Jose
88Bakers/Cal-239
89VeroB/Star-18
90Bakers/Cal-258
91AA/LineD-538
91SanAn/LineD-538
91SanAn/ProC-2983
92Albuq/ProC-728
92Albuq/SB-17
92Sky/AAASingl-9

Munoz, Julio
90Ashvl/ProC-2744

Munoz, Lou
88Elmira-16
88WinHaven/Star-16
89Elmira/Pucko-12
90WinHaven/Star-20

Munoz, Michael
87Bakers-27
88BBAmer-26
88SanAn/Best-7
88TexLgAS/GS-30
89Albuq/CMC-8
89Albuq/ProC-62
90D/Rook-8
90S-653
90T/89Debut-85
90Target-561
91AAA/LineD-593
91S/100RisSt-93
91Toledo/LineD-593
91Toledo/ProC-1929
92StCl-441
92Ultra-367
93D-627
93F-609
93L-191
93Pac/Spanish-449
93S-228
93StCl-248
93StCl/1stDay-248
93T-379
93T/Gold-379
93UD-601
94StCl-492
94StCl/1stDay-492
94StCl/Gold-492
94StCl/Team-102

Munoz, Omer
87WPalmB-18
88WPalmB/Star-18
90Jaxvl/Best-7
90Jaxvl/ProC-1383
91AA/LineD-265
91Harris/LineD-265
91Harris/ProC-637
92Indianap/ProC-1868
92Indianap/SB-188

Munoz, Orlando
92PalmSp/ClBest-14
92PalmSp/ProC-848

Munoz, Oscar
90Watertn/Star-14
91ClBest/Singl-149
91Kinston/ClBest-8
91Kinston/ProC-320
92OrlanSR/ProC-2847
92OrlanSR/SB-522
92UD/ML-293
94B-597
94FExcel-96
94T-771M
94T/Gold-771M

Munoz, Pedro
87Dunedin-26
88Dunedin/Star-13
89Knoxvl/Best-18
89Knoxvl/ProC-1126
89Knoxvl/Star-14
89Star/IISingl-122
90AAASingl/ProC-365
90Syrac/MerchB-17
90Syrac/ProC-585
90Syrac/Team-17
91AAA/LineD-412
91B-336
91Classic/III-64
91D-758
91D/Rook-21
91F-620
91Leaf-186
91Portl/LineD-412
91Portl/ProC-1579
91S-332RP
91StCl-318
91T/90Debut-111
91UD-432
91Ultra-192
92D-305
92F-212
92L-53
92L/BlkGold-53
92OPC-613
92Pinn-139
92Pinn/Team2000-61
92ProC/Tomorrow-91
92S-514
92S/100RisSt-74
92StCl-541
92T-613
92T/Gold-613
92T/GoldWin-613
92UD-764
92USPlayC/Twin-5H
92USPlayC/Twin-6S
92Ultra-399
93D-311
93F-272
93Flair-240
93L-219
93OPC-289
93Pac/Spanish-175
93Panini-132
93Pinn-135
93S-130
93Select-370
93StCl-117
93StCl/1stDay-117
93Studio-166
93T-119
93T/Gold-119
93ToysRUs-26
93UD-341
93UD/SP-251
93Ultra-235
94D-55
94F-215
94Finest-338
94L-360
94Pac/Cr-363
94Panini-95
94Pinn-356
94S-435
94StCl-22
94StCl/1stDay-22
94StCl/Gold-22
94T-459
94T/Gold-459
94UD-302
94Ultra-392

Munoz, Riccardo
(Ricky)
92Bristol/ClBest-8

92Bristol/ProC-1408
Munro, Peter
91Sydney/Fut-15
Munson, Jay
83Cedar-25
83Cedar/Frit-7
Munson, Joseph M.
26Exh-24
Munson, Thurman
70OPC-189R
70T-189R
71MD
71MLB/St-497
71OPC-5
71T-5
71T/Coins-118
71T/GM-1
71T/Greatest-1AL ROY
71T/tatt-10
72OPC-441
72OPC-442IA
72T-441
72T-442IA
73OPC-142
73Syrac/Team-19
73T-142
73T/Lids-34
74OPC-340
74Syrac/Team-18
74T-340
74T/DE-7
74T/St-215
75Ho-138
75OPC-20
75SSPC/Puzzle-18
75Syrac/Team-14
75T-20
75T/M-20
76Crane-41
76Ho-16
76Ho/Twink-16
76K-53
76MSA/Disc
76OPC-192LL
76OPC-650
76SSPC-433
76SSPC/MetsY-Y5
76T-192LL
76T-650
77BK/Y-2
77BurgChef-177
77Ho-5
77Ho/Twink-5
77K-23
77OPC-30
77Pep-36
77T-170
77T/CS-32
77T/ClothSt-32
78BK/Y-2
78Ho-150
78K-30
78OPC-200
78PapaG/Disc-27
78SSPC/270-1
78T-60
78Tastee/Discs-7
78Wiffle/Discs-53
79BK/Y-2
79Ho-26
79OPC-157
79T-310
80Laugh/FFeat-13
82KMart-29
82Ohio/HOF-50
84West/1-15
86Sf/Dec-62M
88Pac/Leg-34
89S/NWest-32
91CollAB-22
91LineD-38
91Swell/Great-149
92Pinn/Rookl-10M
92Yank/WIZ60-92
92Yank/WIZ70-118
92Yank/WIZAS-50
93AP/ASG-161
94TedW-62
Mura, Steve
79T-725R
80T-491
81D-362
81F-496
81T-134
82D-523
82F-578
82T-641
82T/Tr-79T
83D-292
83F-16
83F/St-6M
83OPC-24
83T-24
84Cram/PCL-196
85Cram/PCL-147
86T-281
Murakami, Les
87Hawaii-1CO
Murakami, Masanori
65OPC-282R
65T-282R
78TCMA-182
Murakami, Seiichi
90Salinas/Cal-119
90Salinas/ProC-2717
Muramatsu, Arihito
91Salinas/ClBest-10
Muratti, Rafael
86Macon-17
87Salem-17
88Miami/Star-16
91QuadC/ClBest-26
91QuadC/ProC-2644
Murcer, Bobby
66T-469R
67CokeCap/YMet-12
67OPC-93R
67T-93R
69T-657
70K-60
70MLB/St-247
70OPC-333
70T-333
70T/CB
71Bz
71Bz/Test-9
71MLB/St-498
71OPC-635
71T-635
71T/Coins-54
71T/GM-46
71T/Greatest-46
72K-16
72MB-247
72OPC-86LL
72ProStars/PostC-32
72T-699
72T-700IA
72T-86LL
73K-19
73OPC-240
73OPC-343KP
73Syrac/Team-20
73T-240
73T-343KP
73T/Comics-12
73T/Lids-35
73T/PinUps-12
74K-22
74OPC-336AS
74OPC-90
74Syrac/Team-19
74T-336AS
74T-90
74T/DE-63
74T/Puzzles-7
74T/St-216
75Ho-141
75OPC-350
75T-350
75T/M-350
76Crane-42
76Ho-123
76K-38
76MSA/Disc
76OPC-470
76SSPC-111
76T-470
77BurgChef-105
77Ho-29
77Ho/Twink-29
77OPC-83
77T-40
77T/CS-33
77T/ClothSt-33
78Ho-90
78OPC-95
78SSPC/270-265
78T-590
79Ho-6
79OPC-63
79T-135
80OPC-190
80T-365
81D-111
81F-94
81OPC-253
81T-602
82D-486
82F-44
82T-208
83D-261
83F-390
83OPC-122
83OPC-304SV
83T-782
83T-783SV
83T/Fold-2M
84Mother/Giants-23
89Pac/Leg-196
91Swell/Great-117
92AP/ASG-32
92Pinn/Rookl-14M
92Yank/WIZ60-93
92Yank/WIZ70-119
92Yank/WIZ80-129
92Yank/WIZAS-51
93TWill-67
93UD/ATH-100
PM10/Sm-129
Murch, Simeon
(Simmy)
90Target-562
E254
Murdoch, Bob J.
72Dimanche*-95
Murdock, Joe
89CharRain/ProC-982
90CharRain/Best-17
90CharRain/ProC-2036
Murdock, Kevin
88Tampa/Star-18
Murelli, Don
81Miami-5
Murff, John
(Red)
57T-321
Murillo, Javier
89Miami/I/Star5-15
Murillo, Ray
79Knoxvl/TCMA-19
Murnane, Tim
T204
Murphy, Brian 1
88BurlB/ProC-7
Murphy, Brian 2
91Sydney/Fut-2
Murphy, C.R.
N566-134
Murphy, Chris
92Spokane/ClBest-10
92Spokane/ProC-1291
Murphy, Dale
77T-476R
78T-708R
79Ho-121
79OPC-15
79T-39
80OPC-143
80T-274
81D-437
81F-243
81F/St-119
81OPC-118
81Pol/Atl-3
81T-504
81T/SO-72
81T/St-146
82BK/Lids-18
82D-299
82F-443
82OPC-391
82PermaGr/AS-14
82Pol/Atl-3
82T-668
82T/St-19
83D-12DK
83D-47
83D/AAS-45
83Drake-18
83F-142
83F/St-13M
83F/St-19AM
83F/St-19BM
83F/St-3M
83K-52
83OPC-21AS
83OPC-23
83OPC/St-160
83OPC/St-206
83OPC/St-211FOIL
83PermaGr/AS-12
83PermaGr/CC-9
83Pol/Atl-3
83T-401AS
83T-502TL
83T-703LL
83T-760
83T/Gloss40-16
83T/St-160
83T/St-206M
83T/St-211
84D-66
84D/AAS-40
84D/Champs-49
84Drake-22
84F-186
84F/St-17
84F/St-32
84F/St-50
84MiltBrad-17
84Nes/792-126TL
84Nes/792-133LL
84Nes/792-150
84Nes/792-391AS
84Nestle/DT-18
84OPC-150
84OPC-391AS
84Pol/Atl-3
84Ralston-12
84Seven-3C
84Seven-3E
84Seven-3W
84T-126TL
84T-133LL
84T-150AS
84T-391AS
84T/Cereal-12
84T/Gloss22-19
84T/Gloss40-31
84T/RD-29M
84T/St-180FOIL
84T/St-199
84T/St-27
84T/Super-2
85D-66
85D/AAS-25
85D/HL-5
85Drake-20
85F-335
85F/LimEd-22
85F/St-18
85F/St-33
85FunFoodPin-103
85GenMills-5
85Ho/Braves-16
85Leaf-222
85OPC-320
85Pol/Atl-3
85Seven-1S
85Seven-3W
85Sportflic/Test-1
85T-320
85T-716AS
85T/3D-3
85T/Gloss22-7
85T/Gloss40-1
85T/RD-30M
85T/St-177
85T/St-22
85T/St-96
85T/Super-11
86BK/AP-11
86D-66
86D/AAS-4
86D/HL-41
86D/PopUp-4
86Dorman-10
86Drake-12
86F-522
86F-635M
86F-640M
86F/LL-27
86F/LimEd-31
86F/Mini-105
86F/Slug-24
86F/St-132CL
86F/St-80
86F/WaxBox-C4
86GenMills/Book-5M
86Jiffy-16
86Leaf-60
86Meadow/Blank-10
86Meadow/Milk-7
86Meadow/Stat-4
86OPC/WaxBox-M
86Pol/Atl-3
86Quaker-8
86Seven/Coin-C5
86Seven/Coin-E5
86Seven/Coin-S5
86Seven/Coin-W5
86Sf-183M
86Sf-5
86Sf-62M
86Sf/Dec-67
86T-456M
86T-600
86T-705AS
86T/3D-16
86T/Gloss22-18
86T/Gloss60-37
86T/Mini-37
86T/St-145
86T/St-149
86T/St-35
86T/Super-39
86T/Tatt-2M
86T/WaxBox-M
86TrueVal-10
86Woolwth-23
87Classic-37
87Classic/Up-106
87D-3DK
87D-78
87D-PC10
87D/AAS-14
87D/DKsuper-3
87D/OD-40
87D/PopUp-14
87D/WaxBox-PC10
87Drake-13
87F-522
87F/AwardWin-26
87F/BB-29
87F/GameWin-30
87F/Hottest-28
87F/Lim-30
87F/Mini-74
87F/RecSet-23
87F/Slug-28
87F/St-83
87F/WaxBox-C8
87GenMills/Book-6M
87Ho/St-7
87Jiffy-2
87KMart-29
87KayBee-21
87Kraft-2
87Leaf-141
87Leaf-3DK
87MSA/Discs-15
87MnM's-9
87OPC-359
87RedFoley/St-47
87Sf-155M
87Sf-159M
87Sf-3
87Sf/TPrev-24M
87Smok/Atl-14
87Smok/NL-2
87Sportflic/DealP-3
87Stuart-2M
87T-490
87T/Board-3
87T/Coins-37
87T/Gloss22-7
87T/Gloss60-6
87T/Mini-2
87T/St-161
87T/St-36
88ChefBoy-17
88Classic/Blue-201M
88Classic/Blue-215
88Classic/Red-156
88D-78
88D-BC14
88D/AS-46
88D/Best-113
88Drake-15

88F-544
88F-639M
88F/AwardWin-27
88F/BB/AS-27
88F/BB/MVP-25
88F/Excit-28
88F/Hottest-29
88F/LL-29
88F/Mini-65
88F/RecSet-27
88F/SS-25
88F/Slug-28
88F/St-77
88F/TL-24
88F/WaxBox-C6
88FanSam-13
88Grenada-72
88KMart-18
88KayBee-20
88KennerFig-73
88KingB/Disc-2
88Leaf-83
88MSA/Disc-14
88Nestle-2
88OPC-90
88Panini/St-251
88RedFoley/St-59
88S-450
88Sf-170
88T-549TL
88T-90
88T/Big-14
88T/Coins-48
88T/Gloss60-26
88T/Mini-41
88T/RiteAid-1
88T/St-45
88T/St/Backs-18
88T/UK-52
89B-276
89Brave/Dubuq-18
89Classic-124
89D-104
89D/Best-29
89F-596
89F/Excit-33
89F/LL-28
89KayBee-22
89KennerFig-96
89MSA/Disc-20
89OPC-210
89Panini/St-45
89RedFoley/St-84
89S-30
89S/HotStar-66
89S/Mast-15
89Sf-110
89T-210
89T/Ames-21
89T/Big-172
89T/Coins-19
89T/Crunch-11
89T/HeadsUp-23
89T/Hills-21
89T/LJN-98
89T/Mini-1
89T/St-32
89T/UK-55
89Tetley/Discs-20
89UD-357
89UD-672TC
90B-19
90BBWit-38
90Brave/Dubuq/Perf-20
90Brave/Dubuq/Singl-23
90Classic/Up-36
90D-168
90D/BestNL-62
90F-591
90F-623MVP
90F/BBMVP-28
90F/Can-591
90F/Can-623
90F/Up-U46
90HotPlay/St-29
90KayBee-20
90KingB/Discs-11
90Leaf-243
90OPC-750
90Panini/St-222
90Post-18
90PublInt/St-117
90RedFoley/St-67
90Richm/25Ann-17
90S-66
90S/100St-64
90S/Tr-31T
90Sf-189
90T-750
90T/Ames-11
90T/Big-40
90T/Coins-53
90T/HillsHM-16
90T/St-25
90UD-533
90Woolwth/HL-15
91B-486
91Classic/200-148
91Classic/I-96
91D-484
91D-744M
91F-409
91JDean-3
91Leaf-412
91Leaf/Stud-220
91MajorLg/Pins-62
91OPC-545
91OPC/BoxB-J
91OPC/Premier-85
91Panini/FrSt-109
91Panini/St-104
91Petro/SU-14
91Phill/Medford-31
91S-650
91S/100SS-35
91Seven/3DCoin-13NE
91StCl-243
91T-545
91T/WaxBox-J
91UD-447
91Ultra-270
91Woolwth/HL-14
92B-684
92Classic/Game200-65
92D-146
92DennyGS-18
92F-541
92L-527
92L/BlkGold-527
92MrTurkey-17
92OPC-680
92Panini-246
92Phill/Med-23
92Pinn-124
92Pinn-284M
92S-80
92S/100SS-40
92StCl-280
92Studio-79
92T-680
92T/Gold-680
92T/GoldWin-680
92T/McDonB-30
92TripleP-158LH
92TripleP-260
92UD-127
92UD/ASFF-33
92Ultra-249
93D-646
93F-496
93Pac/Spanish-432
93Pinn-503
93Pinn/Cooper-5
93S-597
93Select-103
93StCl-572
93StCl/1stDay-572
93T-445
93T/Gold-445
93UD-32CH
93UD-706
93USPlayC/Rockie-10S
93USPlayC/Rockie-3C
93Ultra-353

Murphy, Daniel F. 1
(Danny)
10Domino-90
11Diamond-22
11Helmar-57
12Sweet/Pin-48
14CJ-140
14Piedmont/St-42
15CJ-140
16FleischBrd-69
BF2-14
D303
E101
E102
E105
E106
E107
E254
E270
E91
E92
M116
S74-33
T202
T205
T206
T208
T213/blue
T213/brown
T215/blue

Murphy, Daniel F. 2
61T-214
62T-119
63T-272
70OPC-146
70T-146

Murphy, Daniel Jr.
82Tulsa-17
83Tulsa-21
84OKCty-23
84Tulsa-16
85MidldA-9

Murphy, Daniel Lee
86ElPaso-16
87ElPaso-22
89LasVegas/CMC-7
89LasVegas/ProC-2
90AAASingl/ProC-5
90LasVegas/CMC-8
90LasVegas/ProC-117
90OPC-649
90ProC/Singl-511
90T-649
90T/89Debut-86

Murphy, Dwayne
79T-711R
80T-461
81A's/Granny-21
81D-359
81F-590
81OPC-341
81T-341
81T/St-119
82D-239
82F-101
82F/St-122
82Granny-11
82K-57
82OPC-29
82T-29
82T/St-227
83D-161
83F-528
83F/St-5M
83F/St-7M
83Granny-21
83OPC-184
83OPC/St-107
83T-598
83T/St-107
84D-101
84D-3DK
84F-456
84Mother/A's-4
84Nes/792-103
84OPC-103
84T-103
84T/St-332
85D-420
85F-432
85F/St-30
85FunFoodPin-93
85GenMills-20
85Leaf-74
85Mother/A's-6
85T-231
85T/St-323
86D-176
86F-428
86F/Mini-90
86Mother/A's-6
86OPC-8
86T-216M
86T-8
86T/St-171
86T/Tatt-20M
86TrueVal-27
87D-379
87D/OD-27
87F-400
87OPC-121
87Sf/TPrev-23M
87Smok/A's-9
87T-743
87T/St-170
88D-405
88F-287
88OPC-334
88Panini/St-176
88S-455
88T-424
89Phill/TastyK-23
89S-545
89T-667
89T/Ames-22
90F-569
90F/Can-569

Murphy, Eddie
48Smith-24

Murphy, Gary
86Ashvl-21
88Bend/Legoe-31
89MissSt-44M
89QuadC/Best-16
89QuadC/GS-19

Murphy, James
88Geneva/ProC-1638
89CharWh/Best-10
89CharWh/ProC-1745
89Fayette/ProC-1586
90PeoriaUp/Team-U7
90WinSalem/Team-14

Murphy, Jeff 1
91Princet/ClBest-18
91Princet/ProC-3511
92Billings/ProC-3352

Murphy, Jeff 2
92Hamil/ClBest-25
92Hamil/ProC-1595

Murphy, John Edward
15CJ-165
D327
D329-130
D350/2-127
E121/80
E122
M101/4-130
M101/5-127
W575

Murphy, John J.
80ArkTr-21

Murphy, John Joseph
35BU-154
41DP-110
44Yank/St-20
88Conlon/3-20
91Conlon/Sport-84
92Yank/WIZAS-52
94Conlon-1057

Murphy, John V.
87Louisvl-21
87StPete-13
88Louisvl-36
88Louisvl/CMC-16
88Louisvl/ProC-429
88Spring/Best-22

Murphy, Kent
86Water-17
87BuffB-2
88Wmsprt/ProC-1305

Murphy, Micah
89Geneva/ProC-1880
90Hunting/ProC-3291

Murphy, Michael
86Water-18
87BuffB-17
90Martins/ProC-3198
91AubAS/ClBest-14
91AubAS/ProC-4278
91Martins/ClBest-1
91Martins/ProC-3470
92Batavia/ClBest-2
92Batavia/ProC-3278
94ClBest/Gold-164

Murphy, Miguel
87Kenosha-25
88Fayette/ProC-1100

Murphy, Mike
77ArkTr

Murphy, Morgan
N300/unif

Murphy, P.L.
N172

Murphy, Pat
92BurlAs/ClBest-21
92BurlAs/ProC-541

Murphy, Patrick J.
N172
N338/2

Murphy, Pete
87Macon-11
87Watertn-24
88Salem/Star-14
89Harris/ProC-308
89Harris/Star-12
90Harris/ProC-1190
90Harris/Star-12
91AA/LineD-113
91CaroMud/LineD-113
91CaroMud/ProC-1084

Murphy, Red
WG7-36

Murphy, Rob
82Cedar-2
83Cedar-13
83Cedar/Frit-24
87Classic-70
87D-452
87F-206
87Kahn-46
87Sf/TPrev-4M
87T-82
88D-82
88D/Best-230
88F-241
88Kahn/Reds-46
88S-559
88T-603
89B-22
89Classic/Up/2-183
89D-139
89D/Best-196
89D/Tr-15
89F-165
89F/Up-10
89OPC-182
89S-141
89S/Tr-8
89T-446
89T/Tr-86T
89UD-372
89UD/Ext-759
90B-269
90CedarDG/Best-13
90D-186
90F-281
90F/Can-281
90Leaf-183
90OPC-268
90Pep/RSox-13
90PublInt/St-461
90S-181
90T-268
90T/Big-297
90T/St-261
90T/TVRSox-14
90UD-461
91D-250
91F-104
91OPC-542
91S-183
91S/RookTr-33T
91T-542
91UD-683
91UD/Ext-707
92D-329
92F-288
92Mother/Ast-21
92OPC-706
92S-492
92StCl-663
92T-706
92T/Gold-706
92T/GoldWin-706
92UD-639
92Ultra-493
93D-588
93F-439
93F/Final-128
93Pol/Card-10
93StCl-250
93StCl/1stDay-250
93StCl/Card-21
94F-637
94StCl/Team-318

Murphy, Shaun

91MidwLAS/ProC-46
91Rockford/ClBest-24
91Rockford/ProC-2059
92WPalmB/ClBest-13
92WPalmB/ProC-2099
Murphy, Steve
91WA/Via-3
93Rockford/ClBest-20
93StCl/MurphyS-100
Murphy, Tim
74Gaston
Murphy, Tom A.
69JB
69T-474
70OPC-351
70T-351
71OPC-401
71T-401
71T/tatt-5
72MB-248
72OPC-354
72T-354
73OPC-539
73T-539
74OPC-496
74T-496
74T/Tr-496T
75OPC-28
75T-28
75T/M-28
76OPC-219
76SSPC-227
76T-219
77T-396
78BJ/PostC-19
78OPC-193
78T-103
79OPC-308
79T-588
89Pac/SenLg-122
89T/SenLg-28
Murphy, Tommy
T3/Box-59
Murphy, Wayne
87WinHaven-18
Murphy, William E.
66T-574R
91WIZMets-286
Murray, Bill
88SLCity-2
88SLCity-29
89SLCity-29OWN
90CLAS/CL-8M
91Reno/Cal-27TR
Murray, Brian
88SLCity-2
Murray, Calvin
92B-652FOIL
92T/Tr-78T
92T/TrGold-78T
93StCl/MurphyS-34
93UD-421M
93UD-432TP
94FExcel-293
Murray, Dale
75OPC-568
75T-568
75T/M-568
76Expo/Redp-23
76OPC-18
76SSPC-350
76T-18
77T-252
78Ho-31
78SSPC/270-131
78T-149
79Ho-115
79OPC-198
79T-379
80OPC-274
80T-559
81Syrac-7
81Syrac/Team-15
83D-381
83F-437
83OPC-42
83T-42
83T/Tr-79
84D-577
84F-134
84Nes/792-697
84OPC-281
84T-697
85F-137
85OKCty-27
85T-481
86OPC-197
91WIZMets-287
92Yank/WIZ80-130
93Rang/Keeb-275
Murray, Dave
86Salem-21
Murray, Eddie
78K-25
78OPC-154
78T-36
79OPC-338
79T-640
79T/Comics-1
80K-24
80OPC-88
80T-160
80T/S-28
80T/Super-28
81D-112
81Drake-6
81F-184
81F/St-117
81K-18
81MSA/Disc-23
81OPC-39
81Sqt-15
81T-490
81T/SO-9
81T/St-34
82D-483
82Drake-25
82F-174
82F/St-151
82K-64
82OPC-390
82PermaGr/CC-22
82T-162LL
82T-163LL
82T-390
82T-426TL
82T/St-145
82T/St-4LL
82T/St-6
83D-405
83D/AAS-1
83Drake-19
83F-67
83F/St-10M
83F/St-2M
83K-11
83OPC-141
83OPC/St-29
83PermaGr/CC-29
83T-21TL
83T-530
83T/Gloss40-37
83T/St-29
84D-22DK
84D-47
84D/AAS-50
84D/Champs-19
84Drake-23
84F-14
84F/St-23
84F/St-38
84Nes/792-240
84Nes/792-397AS
84Nestle/DT-1
84OPC-240
84OPC-291AS
84Ralston-1
84Seven-6C
84Seven-6E
84Seven-6W
84T-240
84T-397AS
84T/Cereal-1
84T/Gloss40-4
84T/RD-28M
84T/St-195FOIL
84T/St-203
84T/St-26WS
84T/St/Box-12
84T/Super-25
85D-47
85D/AAS-9
85D/HL-34
85Drake-21
85F-184
85F/LimEd-23
85F/St-20
85F/St-62SA
85F/St-63
85F/St-64
85F/St-65
85F/St-66
85F/St-67
85FunFoodPin-119
85GenMills-21
85Leaf-203
85OPC-221
85Seven-1E
85Seven-4G
85Seven-4W
85T-700
85T-701AS
85T/3D-2
85T/Gloss40-28
85T/RD-28M
85T/St-196
85T/Super-18
86BK/AP-14
86D-88
86D/AAS-13
86D/PopUp-13
86Dorman-12
86Drake-25
86F-282
86F/LimEd-32
86F/Mini-58
86F/Slug-25
86F/St-81
86Jiffy-10
86Leaf-83
86OPC-30
86Quaker-27
86Seven/Coin-E13M
86Sf-140M
86Sf-4
86Sf-73M
86Sf/Dec-70
86Sf/Rook-48M
86T-30
86T/3D-19
86T/Gloss22-2
86T/Gloss60-33
86T/Mini-1
86T/St-158
86T/St-227
86T/Super-40
86T/Tatt-13M
86TrueVal-3
86Woolwth-24
87Classic-51
87D-48
87D/AAS-31
87D/HL-37
87D/OD-136
87Drake-24
87F-476
87F-636M
87F/LL-32
87F/Lim-31
87F/Mini-75
87F/RecSet-24
87F/St-84
87French-33
87GenMills/Book-2M
87Ho/St-18
87KMart-30
87KayBee-22
87Kraft-1
87Leaf-110
87OPC-120
87Ralston-8
87RedFoley/St-66
87Seven-ME12
87Sf-159M
87Sf-6
87Sf-75M
87Sf/TPrev-21M
87Sportflic/DealP-2
87Stuart-14M
87T-120
87T/Board-2
87T/Coins-19
87T/Gloss60-12
87T/Mini-39
87T/St-224
88D-231
88D/Best-142
88Drake-21
88F-567
88F/BB/AS-28
88F/Mini-1
88F/St-2
88French-33
88Jiffy-13
88KennerFig-74
88Leaf-172
88OPC-4
88Panini/St-442
88Panini/St-8
88S-18
88Sf-59
88T-495
88T-4RB
88T/Big-215
88T/Coins-22
88T/St-11
88T/St-233
88T/UK-53
88Woolwth-5
89B-346
89Classic/Up/2-160
89D-96
89D/Best-92
89D/Tr-12
89F-611
89F/Up-92
89KMart/Lead-11
89KayBee-23
89KingB/Discs-2
89Mother/Dodg-2
89OPC-148
89Panini/St-260
89Pol/Dodg-21
89RedFoley/St-85
89S-94
89S/HotStar-83
89S/Tr-31
89Sf-147
89T-625
89T/Big-319
89T/Coins-20
89T/Crunch-15
89T/Hills-22
89T/LJN-27
89T/Mini-44
89T/St-238
89T/Tr-87T
89T/UK-56
89UD-275
89UD/Ext-763
90B-101
90Classic/Up-37
90D-77
90D/BestNL-78
90F-404
90F/Can-404
90HotPlay/St-30
90KMart/CBatL-17
90KayBee-21
90Kenner/Fig-60
90Leaf-181
90Mother/Dodg-5
90OPC-305
90Panini/St-273
90Pol/Dodg-33
90PublInt/St-14
90RedFoley/St-68
90S-80
90Sunflower-24
90T-305
90T/Ames-7
90T/Big-29
90T/HillsHM-13
90T/Mini-60
90T/St-57
90Target-563
90UD-277
90Woolwth/HL-16
91B-376SLUG
91B-614
91Classic/200-112
91Classic/I-51
91Classic/III-65
91Crown/Orio-321
91D-405MVP
91D-502
91D-BC18
91D/BC-BC18
91D/Preview-12
91DennyGS-15
91F-214
91Leaf-126
91Leaf/Stud-185
91MajorLg/Pins-53
91Mother/Dodg-5
91OPC-397AS
91OPC-590
91OPC/BoxB-K
91OPC/Premier-86
91Panini/FrSt-55
91Panini/St-53
91Panini/Top15-2
91Pol/Dodg-33
91Post/Can-11
91RedFoley/St-68
91S-310
91S/100SS-52
91Seven/3DCoin-10SC
91StCl-177
91T-397AS
91T-590
91T/CJMini/II-1
91T/WaxBox-K
91UD-237
91UD/SilSlug-SS6
91USPlayC/AS-2S
91Ultra-166
91Woolwth/HL-15
92B-433
92Classic/Game200-162
92D-392
92D/Up-U8HL
92F-466
92L-396
92L/BlkGold-396
92Mets/Kahn-33
92OPC-780
92OPC/Premier-193
92Panini-192
92Pinn-424
92S-195
92S/100SS-78
92S/RookTr-11T
92StCl-795
92StCl/Dome-128
92StCl/MemberI-6
92StCl/MemberII-9
92Studio-68
92T-780
92T/Gold-780
92T/GoldWin-780
92T/Kids-50
92T/Tr-79T
92T/TrGold-79T
92UD-265
92UD-32TC
92UD-728
92UD-753
92Ultra-532
93B-454
93Classic/GameI-69
93Colla/DM-78
93D-278
93D/DK-25
93D/Elite-21
93D/EliteUp-3
93D/MVP-10
93D/Prev-7
93DennyGS-15
93F-91
93F/Fruit-48
93Flair-94
93JDean/28-17
93L-167
93L/Heading-4
93Mets/Kahn-33
93OPC-280
93Pac/Spanish-545
93Panini-247
93Pinn-18
93Pinn-292NT
93Pinn/Cooper-27
93Pinn/HRC-35
93S-77
93Select-29
93StCl-50
93StCl/1stDay-50
93T-430
93T/Finest-122
93T/FinestRef-122
93T/Gold-430
93TripleP-41
93UD-115
93UD-484
93UD/FunPack-128
93UD/SP-152
93UD/SeasonHL-HI13
93UD/Then-TN14
93Ultra-78
94B-467

94D-386
94F-573
94Finest-317
94L-313
94OPC-184
94Pac/Cr-413
94Panini-221
94Pinn-495
94S-36
94S/GoldR-36
94Studio-94
94T-65
94T/Gold-65
94TripleP-117
94UD-341
94UD/SP-100
94Ultra-347

Murray, George
R314/Can

Murray, Glenn
90James/Pucko-9
91MidwLAS/ProC-47
91Rockford/ClBest-25
91Rockford/ProC-2060
92B-289
92ClBest-214
92ProC/Tomorrow-265
92UD/ML-302
92WPalmB/ClBest-19
92WPalmB/ProC-2100
93ClBest/MLG-139
93Harris/ProC-279
94FExcel-228

Murray, Jack
14Piedmont/St-43

Murray, James
C46-5

Murray, Jed
80SanJose/JITB-14
81LynnS-8
82LynnS-6
83SLCity-9
84Cram/PCL-177
86Calgary-17
87Toledo-13
87Toledo/TCMA-18

Murray, Jeremiah
N172

Murray, Jim
75Clinton

Murray, John Joseph
(Red)
10Domino-91
11Helmar-135
12Sweet/Pin-121
D350/2-128
E104
E254
E270/2
E91
E94
E96
E97
M101/5-128
M116
S74-92
T202
T205
T205
T206
T213/blue
T215/blue
T215/brown
T222
T3-48
W555
WG4-21
94Conlon-1049

Murray, Joseph
52Park-99

Murray, Keith
90Butte/SportP-16
91Gaston/ClBest-25
91Gaston/ProC-2702

Murray, Larry
76SSPC-449
80T-284
92Yank/WIZ70-120

Murray, Matt
90BurlB/Best-2
90BurlB/ProC-2346
90BurlB/Star-19
90Foil/Best-285
90MidwLgAS/GS-45
91Durham/ClBest-4
91Durham/ProC-1540

Murray, Mike
87Myrtle-8
88Myrtle/ProC-1179
89Kingspt/Star-28

Murray, Pat
91Johnson/ClBest-4
91Johnson/ProC-3985

Murray, Ray
50NumNum
52B-118
52T-299
53B/BW-6
53T-234
54B-83
54Esskay
54T-49
91Crown/Orio-322
91T/Arc53-234
94T/Arc54-49

Murray, Rich
76Cedar
77Cedar
78Cr/PCL-32
79Phoenix
80Phoenix/NBank-24
81F-452
81Phoenix-24
81T-195
82Charl-16
83Phoenix/BHN-6
84Cram/PCL-6
85Omaha-8

Murray, Richard
82Wichita-11

Murray, Scott
86StPete-21
88SanJose/Cal-125
88SanJose/ProC-113

Murray, Steve
84Beaum-7
88SanBern/Cal-29
89Wausau/GS-20
90SanBern/Best-19CO
90SanBern/Cal-113CO
90SanBern/ProC-2651CO
91SanBern/ClBest-12CO
91SanBern/ProC-2005CO

Murray, Venice
78Cedar

Murray, Zambrano
94T-616
94T/Gold-616

Murrell, Ivan
68T-569R
69T-333
70OPC-179
70T-179
71MLB/St-232
71OPC-569
71T-569
72MB-249
72T-677
73OPC-409
73T-409
74OPC-628
74T-628
87Wmsprt-11
89Pac/SenLg-131
89T/SenLg-7

Murrell, Michael
90GA-22

Murrell, Rodney
86LitFalls-20
87Columbia-22
88Clmbia/GS-17
89Penin/Star-16

Murtaugh, Danny
48L-142
49B-124
49Eureka-168
50B-203
51B-273
52NTea
59T-17MG
60T-223MG
61T-138MG
61T-567AS
62T-503MG
63IDL-14MG
63T-559MG
64T-141MG
64T-268MG
70OPC-532MG
70T-532MG
71OPC-437MG
71T-437MG
74OPC-489MG
74T-489MG
75OPC-304MG
75T-304MG
75T/M-304MG
76OPC-504MG
76SSPC-586MG
76T-504MG
81TCMA-393MG
PM10/Sm-130

Murtaugh, Tim
75Shrev/TCMA-12
76Shrev

Murtha, Brian
82Clinton/Frit-20

Muscat, Scott
89Helena/SP-24
90Beloit/Best-10
90Beloit/Star-15

Muser, Tony
73OPC-238
73T-238
74OPC-286
74T-286
75OPC-348
75SSPC/18-4
75T-348
75T/M-348
76OPC-537
76SSPC-390
76T-537
77T-251
78Spokane/Cramer-8
78Spokane/Team-8
78T-418
81ElPaso-23
82ElPaso-23
84Cram/PCL-27
86Pol/Brew-35C
90ElPasoATG/Team-17MG
91AAA/LineD-149MG
91Crown/Orio-323
91Denver/LineD-149MG
91Denver/ProC-137MG
92Denver/ProC-2655
92Denver/SB-149MG
93Cub/Mara-19CO

Musgraves, Dennis
77Fritsch-47
81TCMA-398
91WIZMets-288

Musial, Stan
42Playball-26
47HomogBond-35
48B-36
48L-4
49B-24
49Eureka-191
49Royal-1
51BR-B1
51Wheat
52B-196
52BR
52RM-NL16
52Royal
52StarCal-93A
52StarCal-93AM
52StarCal/L-81E
52StarCal/L-81F
52Wheat*
53B/Col-32
53Exh/Can-57
53Hunter
53RM-NL26
54Hunter
54RH
55Hunter
55Rawl-1
55Rawl-1A
55Rawl-2
55Rawl-2A
55Rawl-3
55Rawl-4
56YellBase/Pin-23
58T-476AS
59T-150
59T-470HL
60NuCard-21
60T-250
60T/tatt-39
60T/tatt-94
61NuCard-421
61T-290
61T/Dice-11
61T/St-92
62Exh
62T-317IA
62T-50
62T/St-189
62T/bucks
63Bz-23
63Exh
63T-138M
63T-1LL
63T-250
63T/SO
72Laugh/GF-24
74Laugh/ASG-55
76Rowe-3M
76Shakey-112
77Galasso-16
77Galasso-237
77Shakey-25
79TCMA-9
80Marchant-21
80Pac/Leg-8
80Perez/HOF-114
80SSPC/HOF
83D/HOF-32
83Kaline-67M
83MLBPA/Pin-29
85CircK-15
85D/HOF-5
85Woolwth-27
86Sf/Dec-30
87Leaf/SpecOlym-H4
87Nestle/DT-23
88D-641PUZ
88Grenada-7
88Leaf-263PUZ
88Pac/Leg-6
88T-665TBC
89HOF/St-30
89Kenner/BBGr-14
89T/LJN-27
90BBWit-36
90HOF/St-51
90Perez/GreatMom-11
92Card/McDon/Pac-22
92Pinn/MM-24M
92S/Franchise-1
92S/Franchise-4
92S/Franchise-AU1
92S/Franchise-AU4
93YooHoo-11
D305
Exh47
PM10/Sm-131
PM10/Sm-132
PM10/Sm-133
R423-72

Musolino, Mike
87Salem/ProC-2434
88PalmSp/Cal-105
88QuadC/GS-30
89QuadC/Best-20
89QuadC/GS-15
92PalmSp/ClBest-22
92PalmSp/ProC-844

Musselman, Jeff
86Ventura-16
87D-591
87D/Rook-53
87F/Up-U84
87Sf/Rook-15
87T/Tr-83T
87Tor/Fire-25
88D-630
88F-121
88Leaf-234
88OPC-229
88S-478
88S/YS/II-30
88T-229
88T/Big-69
88T/JumboR-22
88T/St-308
88Tor/Fire-13
88ToysRUs-20
89B-240
89D-656
89F-243
89OPC-362
89S-558
89T-591
89Tor/Fire-13
89UD-41
90D-623
90F-212
90F/Can-212
90Kahn/Mets-13
90OPC-382
90S-525
90T-382
90T/TVMets-15
90UD-585
91AAA/LineD-542
91S-294
91Tacoma/LineD-542
91Tacoma/ProC-2301
91WIZMets-289
92Tacoma/ProC-2498
92Tacoma/SB-540

Musselman, Ron
80LynnS-23
81Spokane-17
82SLCity-14
83OKCty-14
85F/Up-U83
85Tor/Fire-25
86Syrac-20
87Portl-21

Musselwhite, Darren
90Kenosha/Best-16
90Kenosha/Star-28
91Visalia/ClBest-6
91Visalia/ProC-1740

Musselwhite, Jim
94B-27

Musser, Andy
88Phill/TastyK-39ANN
90Phill/TastyK-35ANN

Musset, Jose
92QuadC/ClBest-12
92QuadC/ProC-806
94B-221
94FExcel-28

Mussina, Mike
90Classic/DP-20
90Rochester/L&U-12
91AAA/LineD-462
91B-97
91Classic/200-146
91Classic/I-17
91F/UltraUp-U4
91Leaf/GRook-BC12
91RochR/LineD-462
91RochR/ProC-1899
91S-383FDP
91UD-65TP
92B-612
92Classic/DP-95FB
92Classic/DPFoil-BC20FB
92Classic/Game200-148
92Classic/I-67
92Classic/II-NNO
92Classic/II-T14
92Colla/ASG-15
92D-632
92F-20
92L-13
92L/BlkGold-13
92OPC-242
92OPC/Premier-87
92Pinn-204
92Pinn/Team2000-1
92ProC/Tomorrow-1
92S-755
92S/Impact-48
92StCl-225
92Studio-127
92T-242
92T/91Debut-130
92T/Gold-242
92T/GoldWin-242
92TripleP-237
92UD-675
92Ultra-9
93B-633
93Classic/GameI-70
93Colla/ASG-17
93Colla/DM-79
93D-427
93F-172
93Flair-154
93HumDum/Can-2
93JDean/28-27

93Kenner/Fig-25
93L-343
93L/Fast-4
93MSA/Ben-13
93OPC-214
93Pac/Spanish-21
93Panini-69
93Pinn-44
93Pinn/TP-1M
93Pinn/Team2001-3
93S-27
93Select-92
93Select/Ace-20
93Select/StatL-81
93Select/StatL-87M
93StCl-77
93StCl/1stDay-77
93StCl/MurphyS-145
93Studio-202
93Studio/SS-4
93T-710
93T/Finest-157
93T/FinestRef-157
93T/Gold-710
93T/Hill-2
93ToysRUs-37
93TripleP-13
93UD-233
93UD-463IN
93UD/FunPack-134
93UD/SP-160
93USPlayC/Ace-8S
93Ultra-144
93Ultra/AS-20
94B-627
94D-331
94D/DK-26
94D/Special-331
94F-12
94F-708
94F/AS-18
94F/Smoke-8
94L-105
94OPC-82
94Pac/Cr-38
94Panini-21
94Pinn-295
94RedFoley-22M
94S-9
94S/DT-1
94S/GoldR-9
94Select-36
94Sf/2000-44
94StCl-488
94StCl/1stDay-488
94StCl/Gold-488
94StCl/Team-279
94Studio-125
94Studio/Her-8
94T-598
94T/Finest-66
94T/Finest/PreProd-66
94T/FinestRef-66
94T/Gold-598
94TripleP-157
94UD-102
94UD-44FUT
94UD/ElecD-102
94UD/ElecD-44FUT
94UD/SP-124
94Ultra-307

Mustad, Eric
80Hawaii-5
81Tacom-4
82Tacom-7
83Wichita/Dog-14
84Indianap-11

Mustari, Frank
88VeroB/Star-16

Mute, Frank
89QuadC/Best-13

Muth, Bill
77Wausau

Mutis, Jeff
87PanAm/USAB-16
87PanAm/USAR-16
88BurlInd/ProC-1792
89Kinston/Star-13
90Canton/Best-22
90Canton/ProC-1291
90Canton/Star-13
90Foil/Best-290
90ProC/Singl-834
90TeamUSA/87-16
91AA/LineD-90
91Canton/LineD-90
91Canton/ProC-979
91ClBest/Singl-24
92ColoSp/ProC-749
92ColoSp/SB-92
92D-411RR
92ProC/Tomorrow-52
92Sky/AAASingl-40
92Sky/AASingl-296
92T/91Debut-131
93B-586
93Indian/WUAB-21
93OPC/Premier-122
93Ultra-543
94F-114
94Pac/Cr-178
94StCl/Team-88

Mutrie, James
E223
N172
N338/2

Mutz, Frank
87Salem/ProC-2427
88QuadC/GS-12
88Reno/Cal-276
89QuadC/GS-22

Mutz, Tommy
77Indianap-16
78Indianap-10
79Indianap-8

Myaer, Jeff
86Cram/NWL-153

Myatt, George
60Lake
60SpicSpan-15CO
60T-464C
V353-10
V355-26

Myatt, Glenn
25Exh-84
26Exh-83
27Exh-43
28Exh-42
33G-10
34DS-58
35G-1K
35G-3B
35G-5B
35G-6B
91Conlon/Sport-187
R314/Can
R337-417

Myer, Charles M.
(Buddy)
29Exh/4-32
31Exh/4-32
33G-153
34DS-4
35BU-133
35BU-19
35Exh/4-16
35G-8H
35G-9H
36Exh/4-16
37Exh/4-16
37OPC-114
38Exh/4-16
39PlayBall-100
40PlayBall-17
41DP-73
92Conlon/Sport-503
R313
R314
V300
V353-78
V355-132

Myerchin, Mike
82Beloit/Frit-12

Myers, Al
N172
N284

Myers, Brad
88CapeCod/Sum-135

Myers, Chris
88Hagers/Star-13
89Freder/Star-19
90B-250
90Foil/Best-34
90Hagers/Best-18
90Hagers/ProC-1412
90Hagers/Star-19
90HagersDG/Best-18
90ProC/Singl-792
91AAA/LineD-463
91RochR/LineD-463
91RochR/ProC-1900
92Harris/ProC-459

Myers, Dave
77Cedar
83Wausau/Frit-12
86Chatt-21
87Chatt/Best-20
87SLAS-11
88Vermont/ProC-952
91Belling/ClBest-27MG
91Belling/ProC-3683MG
92Belling/ProC-1461MG
93River/Cal-28MG

Myers, Ed
84Albany-18
86Vanco-18

Myers, Elmer
D328-124
E120
E135-124
W573

Myers, Eric
90SoOreg/Best-27
90SoOreg/ProC-3444
91Madison/ClBest-12
91Madison/ProC-2129

Myers, George
N172
N284

Myers, Glen
87Visalia-2

Myers, Greg
86Ventura-17
87Syrac-4
87Syrac/TCMA-10
88D-624
88F-644R
88Syrac/CMC-18
88Syrac/ProC-821
89Tor/Fire-16
90B-520
90D-706
90Leaf-527
90OPC-438
90T-438
90Tor/BJ-21
90UD/Ext-718
91D-494
91F-182
91F/UltraUp-U62
91Leaf-256
91OPC-599A
91OPC-599B
91Panini/FrSt-346
91S-88
91S/100RisSt-75
91S/ToroBJ-12
91StCl-289
91T-599A
91T-599B
91Tor/Fire-21
91UD-259
92BJ/Fire-22
92D-342
92F-338
92L-192
92L/BlkGold-192
92OPC-203
92Pinn-324
92S-471
92StCl-468
92T-203
92T/Gold-203
92T/GoldWin-203
92UD-407
92Ultra-150
93BJ/D/45-42
93D-269
93F/Final-185
93L-318
93Mother/Angel-16
93OPC-241
93Pac/Spanish-370
93Pol/Angel-18
93S-468
93StCl-490
93StCl/1stDay-490
93StCl/Angel-11
93T-637
93T/Gold-637
93UD-789
94D-198
94F-65
94Flair-25
94L-33
94Pac/Cr-85
94Panini-40
94Pinn-156
94Pinn/Artist-156
94Pinn/Museum-156
94S-121
94S/GoldR-121
94StCl-468
94StCl/1stDay-468
94StCl/Gold-468
94T-171
94T/Gold-171
94UD-334

Myers, Henry
(Hy)
21Exh-115
90Target-564
D327
D328-125
D329-131
D350/2-129
E120
E121/120
E121/80
E135-125
E300
M101/4-131
M101/5-129
M116
T206
T213/brown

Myers, Jason
94B-163
94B-352
94T-754DP
94T/Gold-754DP

Myers, Jeff
92Everett/ClBest-12
92Everett/ProC-1685

Myers, Jim
87Pocatel/Bon-16
88Pocatel/ProC-2076
89Clinton/ProC-886
90A&AASingle/ProC-146
90SanJose/Best-15
90SanJose/Cal-49
90SanJose/ProC-2008
90SanJose/Star-16
91AA/LineD-314
91Shrev/LineD-314
91Shrev/ProC-1819
92Phoenix/SB-390
92Sky/AAASingl-178

Myers, Linwood
39PlayBall-133

Myers, Michael R.
(Mike)
87Spokane-24
88Charl/ProC-1199
89Cedar/Best-5
89Cedar/ProC-918
89Cedar/Star-14
90Everett/Best-9
90Everett/ProC-3125
91ClBest/Singl-323
91Clinton/ProC-831
91MidwLAS/ProC-5

Myers, Michael Stanley
88CapeCod/Sum-158
93B-150
93StCl-437
93StCl/1stDay-437
93StCl/Marlin-22
94B-488

Myers, Randy
86Tidew-22
87D-29RR
87F/Up-U85
87Leaf-29RR
87Sf/TPrev-2M
87T-213
88D-620
88D/Best-265
88D/Mets/Bk-620
88F-146
88Kahn/Mets-48
88S-336
88T-412
88T/JumboR-12
88T/Mets/Fan-48
88ToysRUs-21
89B-374
89Classic/Up/2-197
89D-336
89D/Best-153
89F-46
89Kahn/Mets-48
89KennerFig-97
89OPC-104
89Panini/St-135
89S-306
89S/YS/I-41
89T-610
89T/DHTest-9
89T/LJN-155
89T/St-97
89T/St/Backs-66
89UD-634
90B-47
90Classic-107
90Classic/III-18
90D-336
90D/BestNL-88
90F-213
90F/Can-213
90Kahn/Reds-17
90Leaf-149
90OPC-105
90Panini/St-307
90PublInt/St-142
90RedFoley/St-63
90S-351
90S/Tr-16T
90T-105
90T/St-100
90T/Tr-78T
90UD-581
90UD/Ext-797
90USPlayC/AS-WCM
91B-666
91BBBest/Aces-12
91Classic/200-114
91Classic/II-T32
91D-209
91F-73
91Kahn/Reds-28
91Leaf-504
91MSA/Holsum-8
91MajorLg/Pins-73
91OPC-780A
91OPC-780B
91Panini/FrSt-135
91Panini/St-121
91Panini/Top15-82
91Pep/Reds-13
91S-501
91S-662AS
91S-885DT
91S/100SS-79
91StCl-275
91T-780A
91T-780B
91UD-371
91Ultra-97
91WIZMets-290
91Woolwth/HL-23M
92B-154
92D-624
92F-413
92F/Up-123
92Mother/Padre-11
92OPC-24
92OPC/Premier-104
92Padre/Carl-15
92S-155
92S/RookTr-12T
92Smok/Padre-21
92StCl-805
92T-24
92T/Gold-24
92T/GoldWin-24
92T/Tr-80T
92T/TrGold-80T
92UD-278
92UD-741
92Ultra-579
93B-32
93Colla/DM-80
93Cub/Mara-18
93Cub/Rolaid-1
93F-522
93F/Final-10
93Flair-19
93L-358
93MSA/Ben-9

93OPC-215
93OPC/Premier-33
93Pinn-549
93S-607
93Select-215
93Select/RookTr-25T
93Select/StatL-71
93StCl-44
93StCl-667
93StCl/1stDay-44
93StCl/1stDay-667
93StCl/Cub-16
93T-302
93T/Finest-182
93T/FinestRef-182
93T/Gold-302
93T/Tr-65T
93TripleP-142M
93UD-283
93UD-483
93UD-667
93UD/FunPack-83
93UD/SP-87
93Ultra-317
94B-194
94D-399
94F-392
94Finest-357
94Flair-139
94L-396
94OPC-119
94Pac/Cr-105
94Panini-155
94Panini-16
94Pinn-271
94RedFoley-11M
94S-534
94Select-22
94StCl-162
94StCl/1stDay-162
94StCl/Gold-162
94StCl/Team-350
94T-394M
94T-575
94T/BlkGold-40
94T/Gold-394M
94T/Gold-575
94TripleP-76
94UD-257
94UD/CollC-308TP
94UD/CollC/Gold-308TP
94UD/CollC/Silv-308TP
94UD/ElecD-257
94UD/SP-70
94Ultra-462
94Ultra/Fire-6

Myers, Richard
52Mother-58
53Mother-15

Myers, Roderick
(Rodney)
91AppFx/ProC-1713
93Rockford/ClBest-19
93Rockford/ClBest-21

Myers, Thomas
92Madis/ClBest-21
92Madis/ProC-1231
92Reno/Cal-50
93Modesto/ClBest-14
93Modesto/ProC-796

Myers, William
35G-8D
35G-9D
39PlayBall-38
40PlayBall-80
W711/1
W711/2

Myles, Rick
81Cedar-4
82Lynch-17
84Jacks-2

Myllykangas, Lauri
R314/Can
V355-82

Myres, Doug
88StLucie/Star-17

Myrick, Robert
77T-627
78T-676
78Tidew
79Tucson-21
91WIZMets-291

Mysel, David
92FrRow/DP-32
92Niagara/ClBest-12
92Niagara/ProC-3321
93StCl/MurphyS-48
94B-537

Na'te, Jeff
(Nikko)
90Beloit/Best-21CO
90Beloit/Star-26CO

Nabekawa, Tom
87SanJose-13

Naber, Bob
83Clinton/Frit-13

Nabholz, Chris
89Rockford/Team-18
90A&AASingle/ProC-37
90F/Up-U30
90Foil/Best-300
90Jaxvl/Best-21
90Jaxvl/ProC-1371
91B-459
91Classic/200-74
91D-667
91F-240
91Leaf-416
91OPC-197
91OPC/Premier-87
91S-804
91StCl-326
91T-197
91T/90Debut-112
91T/JumboR-21
91ToysRUs-21
91UD-538
92D-170
92Expo/D/Duri-13
92F-487
92L-327
92L/BlkGold-327
92OPC-32
92OPC/Premier-26
92Pinn-360
92S-140
92StCl-318
92T-32
92T/Gold-32
92T/GoldWin-32
92UD-579
92Ultra-521
93D-114
93F-78
93HumDum/Can-40
93L-73
93OPC-315
93Pac/Spanish-536
93Pinn-373
93S-477
93StCl-469
93StCl/1stDay-469
93T-278
93T/Gold-278
93UD-404
93Ultra-69
94D-589
94F-546
94Finest-420
94Pinn-60
94Pinn/Artist-60
94Pinn/Museum-60
94StCl-31
94StCl/1stDay-31
94StCl/Gold-31
94T-656
94T/Gold-656
94UD-88
94UD/ElecD-88
94Ultra-348

Naccarato, Stan
81Tacom-30
82Tacom-22
83Tacom-19
88Tacoma/ProC-620
89Tacoma/ProC-1566

Nace, Todd
88MissSt-23
91Pittsfld/ClBest-5
91Pittsfld/ProC-3435

Naehring, Mark
78Knoxvl
79Knoxvl/TCMA-1

Naehring, Tim
88Elmira-17
89AAA/CMC-30
89Lynch/Star-15
90AAAGame/ProC-16
90AAASingl/ProC-441
90F/Up-U73
90Pawtu/CMC-17
90Pawtu/ProC-469
90ProC/Singl-268
90S/Tr-87T
90T/TVRSox-54
90T/Tr-79T
90TripleAAS/CMC-30
91B-127
91Classic/I-20
91D-367
91F-105
91Leaf-150
91Leaf/Stud-16
91OPC-702
91OPC/Premier-88
91Pep/RSox-13
91S-356RP
91S/100RisSt-77
91S/ASFan-5
91S/Rook40-30
91StCl-83
91T-702
91T/90Debut-113
91T/JumboR-22
91ToysRUs-22
91UD-527
91Ultra-36
92B-416
92D-742
92L-235
92L/BlkGold-235
92OPC-758
92OPC/Premier-37
92Pinn-242
92Pinn/Team2000-15
92RedSox/Dunkin-20
92S-259
92StCl-854
92Studio-134
92T-758
92T/Gold-758
92T/GoldWin-758
92UD-523
92Ultra-317
93D-399
93OPC-304
93Pinn-382
93S-452
93T-24
93T/Gold-24
93ToysRUs-50
93UD-583
93Ultra-153
94L-201
94Pac/Cr-60
94Pinn-65
94Pinn/Artist-65
94Pinn/Museum-65
94S-429
94Select-151
94StCl-131
94StCl/1stDay-131
94StCl/Gold-131
94T-474
94T/Gold-474
94UD-337
94Ultra-315

Nagano, Cary
87Hawaii-4

Nagashima, Kazushige
92VeroB/ClBest-28

Nagel, William T.
(Bill)
41DP-50

Nagelson, Russell C.
(Rusty)
70OPC-7R
70T-7R
71OPC-708
71T-708

Nagle, Randy
91Greenvl/LineD-225CO

Nagle, Thomas E.
(Tom)
N172

Nago, Garrett
83ElPaso-12
84ElPaso-25
85Cram/PCL-223
86ElPaso-17
87ElPaso-5
88Indianap/CMC-22
88Indianap/ProC-515
89ColMud/Best-3
89ColMud/ProC-146
89ColMud/Star-18

Nagy, Charles
88T/Tr-74T
89B-73
89Kinston/Star-14
89Star/IISingl-178
89Star/Wax-77
89T/Big-217
90A&AASingle/ProC-9
90Canton/Best-27
90Canton/ProC-1292
90Canton/Star-14
90EastLAS/ProC-EL37
90Foil/Best-244
90Foil/Best-323
90ProC/Singl-833
90S-611
91B-65
91D-592
91D/Rook-18
91F/UltraUp-U20
91F/Up-U20
91Indian/McDon-20
91OPC-466
91S-75
91S/100RisSt-47
91S/ASFan-8
91StCl-472
91T-466
91T/90Debut-114
91UD-19
92B-203
92B-566FOIL
92Classic/Game200-138
92D-315
92F-118
92Indian/McDon-18
92L-115
92L/BlkGold-115
92OPC-299
92OPC/Premier-138
92Pinn-383
92Pinn-609GRIP
92Pinn/Team2000-19
92S-330
92S/100RisSt-26
92S/Impact-19
92StCl-389
92T-299
92T/DQ-12
92T/Gold-299
92T/GoldWin-299
92UD-178
92UD/TmMVPHolo-37
92Ultra-351
93B-149
93D-141
93Duracel/PPII-11
93F-219
93F/Fruit-49
93Indian/WUAB-22
93L-171
93OPC-278
93Pac/Spanish-415
93Panini-46
93Pinn-65
93Pinn/Team2001-22
93S-29
93S-538DT
93S/GoldDT-7
93Select-70
93Select/Ace-12
93Select/StatL-63
93StCl-551
93StCl/1stDay-551
93StCl/MurphyS-88
93Studio-203
93T-730
93T/Finest-58
93T/FinestRef-58
93T/Gold-730
93T/Hill-6
93TripleP-49
93UD-243
93UD/FunPack-110
93UD/SP-125
93Ultra-189
94B-251
94D-239
94F-115
94Flair-42
94L-297
94OPC-254
94Pac/Cr-179
94Panini-59
94Pinn-385
94S-333
94Sf/2000-130
94StCl-478
94StCl/1stDay-478
94StCl/Gold-478
94T-330
94T/Finest-104
94T/FinestRef-104
94T/Gold-330
94TripleP-118
94UD-394
94Ultra-349

Nagy, Jeff
92Billings/ProC-3371

Nagy, Mike
70OPC-39
70T-39
71MLB/St-325
71OPC-363
71T-363
72OPC-488
72T-488

Nagy, Steve
49Sommer-7

Nahem, Sam
90Target-565
W754

Nahorodny, William G.
(Bill)
76OkCty/Team-19
78SSPC/270-156
78T-702R
79T-169
80OPC-286
80T-552
81F-254
81Pol/Atl-15
81T-295
82Charl-11
83F-416
83T-616
84Cram/PCL-181
85Cram/PCL-39

Nail, Charlie
82BirmB-21
83Evansvl-6
84Wichita/Rock-6

Najera, Noe
92Watertn/ClBest-12
92Watertn/ProC-3230

Nakamoto, Brian
76SanAn/Team-15

Nakamura, Hector
87SanJose-2

Nakashima, Yoshi
86SanJose-14

Nalepka, Keith
91GulfCR/SportP-3

Nalley, Jerry
81Batavia-14
82Watlo/B-21
82Watlo/Frit-6

Nallin, Dick
94Conlon-1199UMP

Nalls, Gary
86QuadC-25
87PalmSp-32
88PalmSp/Cal-106
88PalmSp/ProC-1454
89AS/Cal-36
89Reno/Cal-250
90Reno/Cal-274

Nalls, Kevin
92Idaho/ProC-3518

Namar, Robert
79WHave-29M

Nandin, Bob
83Syrac-18
84Syrac-13
86ElPaso-18

Nanni, Tito
80SanJose/JITB-15
81LynnS-23
82LynnS-15
83SLCity-13
84Cram/PCL-174
85MidldA-1

Nantel, Pierre
52Laval-97

Napier, Jim
61Union
76AppFx
79QuadC-22
82Iowa-25MG
83Iowa-26
84Iowa-11
86Maine-12MG
Napoleon, Daniel
(Danny)
65T-533R
66OPC-87
66T-87
81TCMA-472
91WIZMets-292
Napoleon, Ed
78Cr/PCL-109
79WHave-2
82Nashvl-28CO
83Wheat/Ind-23CO
85Polar/Ind-xx
90Mother/Ast-27CO
Napp, Larry
55B-250UMP
Naragon, Harold R.
(Hal)
55B-129
55Gol/Ind-21
55Salem
56T-311
57T-347
58T-22
59T-376
60T-231
61Clover-19
61Peters-8
61T-92
62T-164
Narcisse, Ron
85LitFalls-14
86LitFalls-21
Narleski, Bill
88Watlo/ProC-674
Narleski, Ray
55B-96
55Gol/Ind-22
55Salem
55T-160
56T-133
57Sohio/Ind-10
57T-144
58Hires-22
58T-439
59T-442
60T-161
Narleski, Steve
77Watlo
81Chatt-5
82Chatt-19
Narron, Jerry A.
(Jerry)
75FtLaud/Sus-30
77WHave
78Cr/PCL-54
80T-16
81D-405
81OPC-249
81Pol/Sea-12
81T-637
82D-433
82F-513
82Spokane-12
82T-719
84Smok/Cal-20
85D-643
85Smok/Cal-10
85T-234
86D-451
86Smok/Cal-10
86T-543
87Calgary-21
87D-603
87T-474
88RochR/CMC-14
88RochR/Gov-17
88RochR/ProC-216
88RochR/Team-15
89Freder/Star-25
90Hagers/Best-29MG
90Hagers/ProC-1431MG
90Hagers/Star-26MG
91AA/LineD-249MG
91Hagers/LineD-249MG
91Hagers/ProC-2471MG
92RochR/ProC-1955MG
92RochR/SB-474MG
92Yank/WIZ70-121
Narron, Johnny
75AppFx
Narron, Sam
49Eureka-44
60T-467CO
63IDL-15CO
Narum, L.F.
(Buster)
64T-418R
65OPC-86
65T-86
66T-274
78TCMA-44
91Crown/Orio-324
Nash, Charles F.
(Cotton)
71OPC-391R
71T-391R
Nash, Dave
86Cram/NWL-184
86Everett/Pop-18
88Fresno/Cal-13
88Fresno/ProC-1228
Nash, Jim
67CokeCap/A's-1
67CokeCap/ALAS-30
67CokeCap/AS-7
67OPC-90
67T-90
68T-324
69MB-198
69MLB/St-89
69T-546
69T/St-219
70MLB/St-9
70OPC-171
70T-171
71MLB/St-18
71OPC-306
71T-306
72MB-250
72OPC-401
72T-401
73OPC-509
73T-509
Nash, Macolm
89KS*-53
Nash, Rob
91Batavia/ClBest-1
91Batavia/ProC-3498
Nash, William M.
(Billy)
N142
N172
N300/unif
N403
WG1-7
Nastu, Phil
77Cedar
78Cr/PCL-27
79Phoenix
80T-686R
Natal, Bob
(Rob)
87James-18
88FSLAS/Star-14
88WPalmB/Star-19
89Jaxvl/Best-17
89Jaxvl/ProC-176
90Jaxvl/Best-2
90Jaxvl/ProC-1378
91AA/LineD-266
91Harris/LineD-266
91Harris/ProC-632
92AAA/ASG/SB-189
92D/Rook-84
92Indianap/ProC-1863
92Indianap/SB-189
92ProC/Tomorrow-261
92Sky/AAASingl-93
93B-558
93D-744
93Edmon/ProC-1141
93F-428
93F/Final-67
93Marlin/Publix-17
93Pac/Spanish-468
93StCl-737
93StCl/1stDay-737
93T/Tr-108T
93USPlayC/Marlin-10S
94F-472
94Pac/Cr-248
94Pinn-173
94Pinn/Artist-173
94Pinn/Museum-173
94StCl-291
94StCl/1stDay-291
94StCl/Gold-291
94StCl/Team-75
94T-437
94T/Gold-437
94Ultra-198
Natera, Luis
85LitFalls-20
86LitFalls-22
87Columbia-14
Nattile, Sam
85Pawtu-10
86NewBrit-19
Nattress, William W.
(Natty)
C46-8
E254
T206
Natupsky, Hal
79Elmira-20
Naughton, Danny
87Columbia-19
88Clmbia/GS-23
89StLucie/Star-18
Naulty, Dan
89Alaska/Team-2
92Kenosha/ProC-600
Naumann, Rick
81AppFx-6
Nava, Lipso
91SanBern/ClBest-19
91SanBern/ProC-1996
92Penin/ClBest-4
92Penin/ProC-2940
Nava, Marlon
92Elizab/ClBest-11
92Elizab/ProC-3687
Navarro, Jaime
88Stockton/Cal-182
88Stockton/ProC-736
89ElPaso/GS-13
89F/Up-39
90B-388
90Brewer/MillB-16
90Classic/Up-38
90D-640
90ElPasoATG/Team-23
90F-331
90F/Can-331
90Leaf-85
90Pol/Brew-31
90S-569
90T/89Debut-87
90UD-646
91B-42
91Brewer/MillB-18
91D-216
91F-592
91F/UltraUp-U31
91Leaf-409
91OPC-548
91Pol/Brew-16
91S-102
91StCl-436
91T-548
91UD-476
92B-167
92D-705
92F-183
92L-144
92L/BlkGold-144
92OPC-222
92Pinn-212
92Pol/Brew-16
92S-231
92StCl-87
92Studio-195
92T-222
92T/Gold-222
92T/GoldWin-222
92TripleP-188
92UD-633
92Ultra-82
93B-647
93D-281
93F-255
93L-296
93OPC-247
93Pac/Beisbol-10
93Pac/Beisbol-9M
93Pac/Spanish-161
93Panini-35
93Pinn-343
93Pol/Brew-18
93S-218
93Select-260
93StCl-621
93StCl/1stDay-621
93T-369
93T/Gold-369
93TripleP-233
93UD-237
93UD/SP-68
94B-121
94D-621
94F-185
94L-439
94OPC-14
94Pac/Cr-336
94Pol/Brew-19
94S-145
94S/GoldR-145
94T-679
94T/Finest-129
94T/FinestRef-129
94T/Gold-679
94TripleP-56
94UD-426
Navarro, Julio
60T-140
63T-169R
64T-489
65T-563
66T-527
Navarro, Norberto
89Pittsfld/Star-18
Navarro, Rick
89SanDiegoSt/Smok-19
92FrRow/DP-48
92Niagara/ClBest-8
Navarro, Tito
90Clmbia/PCPII-6
90Columbia/GS-13
90SALAS/Star-37
90Star/ISingl-100
91AA/LineD-639
91Clmbia/PII-32
91Wmsprt/LineD-639
91Wmsprt/ProC-302
92B-139
92ProC/Tomorrow-281
92UD/ML-91
94Pac/Cr-414
94StCl-473
94StCl/1stDay-473
94StCl/Gold-473
Naveda, Edgar
86Kenosha-17
87Kenosha-5
88Visalia/Cal-156
88Visalia/ProC-103
89OrlanTw/Best-18
89OrlanTw/ProC-1347
90AAASingl/ProC-257
90OrlanSR/Best-5
90Portl/CMC-15
90Portl/ProC-187
90ProC/Singl-567
91AAA/LineD-413
91Portl/LineD-413
91Portl/ProC-1580
92Portl/SB-414
92Portland/ProC-2680
92Sky/AAASingl-189
Navilliat, James
86Cram/NWL-157
87CharRain-11
Naworski, Andy
86Bakers-21
86Cram/NWL-187
87FtMyr-9
Naylor, Earl
90Target-566
Naylor, Roleine C.
21Exh-116
E120
W573
Nazabal, Robert
85Bend/Cram-17
Neagle, Dennis
(Denny)
88CapeCod/Sum-53
89Elizab/Star-22
90A&AASingle/ProC-142
90AS/Cal-24
90OrlanSR/Star-13
90ProC/Singl-862
90Visalia/ProC-2150
91AAA/LineD-414
91AAAGame/ProC-36
91B-323
91Leaf-466
91Portl/LineD-414
91Portl/ProC-1563
91UD/FinalEd-34F
91Ultra-383MLP
92B-485
92Classic/I-68
92Classic/II-T66
92D-605
92F-213
92L/GRook-22
92OPC-592
92OPC/Premier-165
92Pinn-556
92Pinn/Rook-19
92Pirate/Nation-17
92ProC/Tomorrow-89
92S/RookTr-89T
92StCl-724
92Studio-87
92T-592
92T/91Debut-132
92T/Gold-592
92T/GoldWin-592
92T/Tr-81T
92T/TrGold-81T
92UD-426
92UD-748
92UD/Scout-SR17
92Ultra-556
93D-226
93F-503
93L-42
93Pac/Spanish-590
93Pirate/Nation-22
93S-350
93Select-299
93StCl-241
93StCl/1stDay-241
93T-244
93T/Gold-244
93UD-415
93Ultra-454
94F-616
94Pac/Cr-504
94StCl-232
94StCl/1stDay-232
94StCl/Gold-232
94T-129
94T/Finest-195
94T/FinestRef-195
94T/Gold-129
Neal, Bob
80Penin/B-25GM
80Penin/C-9GM
88AubAs/ProC-1964
89AubAs/ProC-2178
Neal, Bryan
82Durham-6
83Durham-10
Neal, Charles Lenard
(Charlie)
55B-278
56T-299
57T-242
58Hires-54
58T-16
59Morrell
59T-427
60Morrell
60T-155
60T-385AS
60T-386AS
60T-556AS
60T/tatt-40
60Union/Dodg-13
61BB-43
61P-157
61T-423
61T/St-30
61Union/Dodg-14
62J-102
62P-102
62P/Can-102

62Salada-102A
62Salada-102B
62Shirriff-102
62T-365
63Exh
63J-195
63P-195
63T-511
64T-436
81TCMA-482M
89Smok/Dodg-66
90Target-567
91WIZMets-293
Exh47
Neal, Dave
88Bend/Legoe-19
89PalmSp/Cal-49
89PalmSp/ProC-474
90QuadC/GS-5
Neal, Earl A.
21Exh-117
Neal, Edwin
80CharlO/Pol-12
80CharlO/W3TV-12
Neal, Len
57Seattle/Pop-26
Neal, Mike
92LSU/McDag-7
93LSU/McDag-8
94FExcel-46
94FExcel/1stY-5
94T-158M
94T/Gold-158M
Neal, Scott
85PrWill-2
86Hawaii-18
87Harris-9
Neal, Willie
81CharR-25
82CharR-22
Neale, Alfred Earle
(Greasy)
81Conlon-29
88Conlon/4-20
88Pac/8Men-88
92Conlon/Sport-401
94Conlon-1028
D327
D328-126
E120
E121/120
E135-126
E220
V100
W501-51
W514-6
W575
Nealeigh, Rod
83Memphis/TCMA-13
Nebraska, David
89BurlInd/Star-18
Necciai, Ron
77Fritsch-9
93UD/ATH-101
Nedin, Tim
89Elizab/Star-23
89Star/IISingl-152
90Foil/Best-306
90Kenosha/Best-22
90Kenosha/ProC-2291
90Kenosha/Star-16
91ClBest/Singl-185
91Visalia/ClBest-7
92Miracle/ClBest-14
Nee, John
T205
Needham, Thomas J.
(Tom)
10Domino-92
11Helmar-99
12Sweet/Pin-85
14Piedmont/St-44
E286
M116
S74-65
T202
T205
T206
T207
T213/blue
T214-22
Neel, Troy
88MidwLAS/GS-21
88Watlo/ProC-681
89Canton/Best-25
89Canton/ProC-1324
89Canton/Star-17
89EastLDD/ProC-DD37
89EastLgAS/ProC-7
89Star/IISingl-155
90AAASingl/ProC-226
90ColoSp/CMC-17
90ColoSp/ProC-45
90ProC/Singl-469
91AAA/LineD-543
91Huntsvl/Team-14
91Tacoma/LineD-543
91Tacoma/ProC-2318
92D/Rook-85
92F/Up-50
92Sky/AAASingl-241
92Tacoma/ProC-2517
92Tacoma/SB-541
93B-541
93D-308RR
93F/Final-259
93F/MLPI-18
93L/GRook-9
93Mother/A's-15
93OPC/Premier-85
93Pac/Spanish-571
93Pinn-246
93S-326
93S/Boys-6
93Select/RookTr-68T
93StCl-429
93StCl/1stDay-429
93StCl/A's-28
93T-807
93T/Gold-807
93UD-767
93Ultra-260
94B-464
94D-520
94F-270
94F/RookSen-13
94Flair-95
94L-6
94OPC-249
94Pac/Cr-459
94Panini-111
94Pinn-150
94Pinn/Artist-150
94Pinn/Museum-150
94S-248
94S/GoldR-248
94Select-68
94StCl-40
94StCl/1stDay-40
94StCl/Gold-40
94Studio-5
94T-493
94T/Finest-13
94T/FinestRef-13
94T/Gold-493
94TripleP-6
94UD-391
94UD/CollC-215
94UD/CollC/Gold-215
94UD/CollC/Silv-215
94Ultra-112
Neely, Jeff
89Augusta/ProC-495
89SALAS/GS-7
91AAA/LineD-40
91BuffB/LineD-40
91BuffB/ProC-539
Neeman, Calvin A.
(Cal)
57T-353
58T-33
59T-367
60T-337
79TCMA-142
Neese, Joshua
94FExcel-58
94FExcel/1stY-10
Neff, Marty
91Welland/ClBest-16
91Welland/ProC-3588
92Augusta/ClBest-16
92Augusta/ProC-253
93B-274
93ClBest/MLG-179
93SALAS/II-27
Neff, Paul
85Fresno/Pol-28BB
Nega, Chris
93Dunedin/ClBest-30BB
Negray, Ron
56T-7
56T/Pin-20
57T-254
60Maple-15
61BeeHive-15
90Target-568
Negron, Miguel
80LynnS-10
83Chatt-10
Nehf, Art N.
16FleischBrd-70
21Exh-118
25Exh-37
28Yueng-43
61F-65
75F/Pion-28
92Conlon/Sport-492
94Conlon-1246
D327
D328-127
E120
E121/120
E121/80
E126-59
E135-127
E220
V61-93
V89-41
W502-43
W515-22
W516-17
W572
W575
Neibauer, Gary
69T-611R
70OPC-384
70T-384
71OPC-668
71Richm/Team-15
71T-668
72OPC-149
72T-149
Neidinger, Joe
89Bristol/Star-18
91Fayette/ClBest-6
91Fayette/ProC-1166
Neidlinger, Jim
85PrWill-10
86Nashua-19
87Harris-20
88Harris/ProC-842
89Albuq/CMC-9
89Albuq/ProC-71
90AAASingl/ProC-64
90Albuq/CMC-10
90Albuq/ProC-343
90Albuq/Trib-23
90Pol/Dodg-39
90ProC/Singl-412
91AAA/LineD-16
91Albuq/LineD-16
91Albuq/ProC-1139
91Classic/I-53
91D-713
91F-215
91OPC-39
91Pol/Dodg-31
91S-794
91T-39
91T/90Debut-115
91UD-632
92Albuq/ProC-718
92Albuq/SB-18
Neiger, Al
61T-202
89Chatt/II/Team-20
Neill, Mike
91ClBest/Singl-415
91FrRow/DP-9
91FrRow/DPPr-2
91SoOreg/ClBest-15
91SoOreg/ProC-3864
92AS/Cal-4
92B-266
92ProC/Tomorrow-135
92Reno/Cal-35
92StCl/Dome-129
92UD/ML-26M
92UD/ML-273
92UD/ML-52DS
93B-217
93StCl/A's-30
93UD-424TP
94SigRook/Bonus-5
Neill, Scott
89Watertn/Star-16
90Kinston/Team-24
91CLAS/ProC-CAR18
91Kinston/ClBest-9
91Kinston/ProC-321
Neilson, Mike
92Watertn/ClBest-11
92Watertn/ProC-3231
Neis, Bernard E.
(Bernie)
26Exh-6
27Exh-44
90Target-569
E220
Neitzel, R.A.
90Batavia/ProC-3073
91Clearw/ClBest-19
91Clearw/ProC-1630
92Reading/ProC-581
92Reading/SB-536
Nelloms, Skip
88Oneonta/ProC-2048
89FtLaud/Star-18
90FtLaud/Star-13
Nelson, Albert
(Red)
E254
T207
Nelson, Andre
92Hunting/ClBest-5
92Hunting/ProC-3163
Nelson, Battling
T3/Box-57
Nelson, Brian
90Niagara/Pucko-22
91Bristol/ClBest-22
91Bristol/ProC-3600
Nelson, Charlie
92MN-15
93Bz-5
93T/Tr-57T
Nelson, Chester
77Newar
Nelson, Darren
87Erie-25
88StPete/Star-19
Nelson, David Earl
(Dave)
69MB-199
69T-579
70OPC-112
70T-112
71MLB/St-547
71OPC-241
71T-241
72T-529
73OPC-111
73T-111
74Greyhound-5M
74OPC-355
74T-355
74T/DE-4
74T/St-238
75OPC-435
75SSPC/42-18
75Shrev/TCMA-13
75T-435
75T/M-435
76OPC-535
76SSPC-273
76Shrev
76T-535
92Indian/McDon-30M
93Rang/Keeb-30
Nelson, Doug P.
88AppFx/ProC-141
89BBCity/Star-19
90Memphis/Best-24
90Memphis/ProC-1004
90Memphis/Star-21
Nelson, Doug
75Shrev/TCMA-14
76Shrev
Nelson, Eric
89Welland/Pucko-19
Nelson, Frank
47Sunbeam
49Remar
50Remar
Nelson, Gene
79Ashvl/TCMA-28
81T/Tr-809
82D-513
82F-45
82T-373
82T/Tr-80T
83D-55
83T-106
85Coke/WS-30
85D-615
85F-522
85T/Tr-86T
86Coke/WS-30
86D-501
86F-213
86Leaf-245
86T-493
87D-580
87F-504
87F/Up-U86
87T-273
87T/Tr-84T
88D-133
88D/A's/Bk-133
88F-288
88Mother/A's-25
88S-588
88T-621
89B-185
89D-540
89F-18
89Mother/A's-26
89OPC-318
89S-434
89T-581
89UD-643
89Woolwth-16
90D-540
90F-17
90F/Can-17
90Leaf-477
90Mother/A's-22
90OPC-726
90S-441
90T-726
90UD-80
91D-385
91F-19
91Leaf-328
91Mother/A's-22
91OPC-316
91S-478
91SFExam/A's-10
91StCl-359
91T-316
91UD-403
92D-696
92F-264
92Mother/A's-22
92OPC-62
92Pinn-443
92S-383
92StCl-414
92T-62
92T/Gold-62
92T/GoldWin-62
92UD-508
92Ultra-426
92Yank/WIZ80-131
93F/Final-186
93Mother/Angel-17
93Rang/Keeb-416
93StCl/Angel-22
94S-274
94S/GoldR-274
Nelson, Glenn Richard
(Rocky)
52Park-61
52T-390
53Exh/Can-49
54T-199
59T-446
60L-127
60T-157
61Kahn
61P-137
61T-304
61T/St-68
82Ohio/HOF-59
90Target-570
94T/Arc54-199
Nelson, Jackson

N172/SP
N284
N690
Nelson, James Lorin
(Jim)
71OPC-298
71T-298
Nelson, Jamie
83SLCity-16
84Cram/PCL-43
84Nes/792-166
84T-166
85Cram/PCL-221
87Memphis-8
87Memphis/Best-26
88Colum/CMC-12
88Colum/Pol-23
88Colum/ProC-305
89Edmon/CMC-19
89Edmon/ProC-569
90AAASingl/ProC-250
90Portl/CMC-13
90Portl/ProC-180
90ProC/Singl-565
Nelson, Jeff
86Bakers-22
88SanBern/Best-23
88SanBern/Cal-48
89Wmsprt/ProC-637
89Wmsprt/Star-15
90Wmsprt/Best-17
90Wmsprt/ProC-1056
90Wmsprt/Star-18
91AA/LineD-339
91Jaxvl/LineD-339
91Jaxvl/ProC-147
92D-408RR
92F/Up-57
92Mother/Mar-19
93D-685
93F-311
93Mother/Mar-19
93S-272
93StCl-467
93StCl/1stDay-467
93T-493
93T/Gold-493
94D-492
94F-296
94Pac/Cr-578
94S-302
94S/GoldR-302
94T-24
94T/Gold-24
Nelson, Jerome
86Modesto-20
87Modesto-5
88Huntsvl/BK-13
89Chatt/Best-23
89Chatt/GS-19
90Chatt/GS-23
91Richm/Bob-31
92Harris/ProC-472
Nelson, Jim
81LynnS-13
82LynnS-9
Nelson, Kim
79Wisco-11
Nelson, Lynn B.
(Lynn)
34G-60
39PlayBall-118
40PlayBall-135
Nelson, Mel
60DF-11
61Union
63T-522R
64T-273
65T-564
66T-367
69OPC-181
69T-181
69T/4in1-11
81TCMA-346
Nelson, Michael
90Peoria/Team-3GM
91Peoria/Team-30M
Nelson, Pat
78Ashvl
79Ashvl/TCMA-19
Nelson, Rick
84D-636
84F-615
84Nes/792-672
84T-672
84T/St-347
85Cram/PCL-91
85Everett/Cram-11A
85Everett/Cram-11B
85T-296
86Calgary-18
86Clinton-16
87Tidew-16
88Shrev/ProC-1294
90Shrev/ProC-1455
90Shrev/Star-16
Nelson, Rob
83Idaho-22
84Madis/Pol-11
85Huntsvl/BK-41
86Tacom-15
87D-595
87D/OD-25
87F-653R
87Sf/TPrev-23M
88D-574
88LasVegas/CMC-16
88LasVegas/ProC-237
89LasVegas/CMC-16
89LasVegas/ProC-24
90B-213
90UD-51
91AAA/LineD-642
91Vanco/LineD-642
91Vanco/ProC-1604
92Portl/SB-415
Nelson, Robert S.
(Bob)
56T-169
91Crown/Orio-325
Nelson, Rod
79Clinton/TCMA-20
Nelson, Roger
68T-549R
69MLB/St-61
69T-279
69T/S-23
69T/St-186
70MLB/St-225
70T-633
71OPC-581
71T-581
73OPC-251
73T-251
74OPC-491
74T-491
75OPC-572
75T-572
75T/M-572
75Tucson-25
75Tucson/Caruso-20
75Tucson/Team-13
78Colum
81TCMA-396
91Crown/Orio-326
Nelson, Ron
87Spartan-12
Nelson, Scott
88Clinton/ProC-698
89Salinas/Cal-127
89Salinas/ProC-1824
Nelson, Spike
49Eureka-192
Nelson, Thomas C.
(Tom)
47Sunbeam
Nelson, Travion
92GulfCY/ProC-3704
Nelson, Tray
92LitSun/HSPros-21
Nemeth, Carey
86Erie-20
87Savan-16
Nemeth, Joe
79Wausau-9
80Ashvl-12
81Tulsa-11
82Reading-17
82Tulsa-24
83Tulsa-19
Nen, Richard LeRoy
(Dick)
64T-14R
65T-466R
66OPC-149
66T-149
67CokeCap/Senator-11
67T-403
68T-591
69MB-200
90Target-571
Nen, Robb
88Butte-5
88Gaston/ProC-1003
89Gaston/ProC-1003
89Gaston/Star-16
89Star/IISingl-139
90B-487
90CharlR/Star-15
91AA/LineD-589
91B-270
91ClBest/Singl-240
91Tulsa/LineD-589
91Tulsa/ProC-2769
91Tulsa/Team-20
92ClBest-288
92Sky/AASingl-271
92Tulsa/ProC-2692
92Tulsa/SB-612
92UD/ML-84
93F/Final-281
93Marlin/Publix-18
93Pac/Spanish-643
93Pinn-586
93Rang/Keeb-417
93StCl/Rang-24
93UD-687
93Ultra-633
94D-625
94L-212
94StCl-45
94StCl/1stDay-45
94StCl/Gold-45
94StCl/Team-80
94T-284
94T/Gold-284
Nenad, David
82Clinton/Frit-9
Nerat, Dan
91SoOreg/ClBest-27
91SoOreg/ProC-3841
92Modesto/ProC-3897
Neri, Frank
52Laval-4
Nerone, Phil
75AppFx
76AppFx
Nesmith, Trent
90AR-30M
Nettles, Dru
93SoEastern-14
Nettles, Graig
69OPC-99R
69T-99R
70OPC-491
70T-491
71MLB/St-380
71OPC-324
71T-324
72T-590
73OPC-498
73Syrac/Team-21
73T-498
74OPC-251
74Syrac/Team-20
74T-251
74T/St-217
75Ho-24
75Ho/Twink-24
75OPC-160
75Syrac/Team-15
75T-160
75T/M-160
76Ho-81
76OPC-169
76SSPC-437
76SSPC/MetsY-Y20
76T-169
77BK/Y-15
77BurgChef-174
77Ho-116
77Ho/Twink-116
77OPC-217
77OPC-2LL
77T-20
77T-2LL
78BK/Y-14
78Ho-132
78OPC-10
78SSPC/270-25
78T-250
78Wiffle/Discs-54
79BK/Y-15
79Ho-110
79OPC-240
79T-460
80K-18
80OPC-359
80T-710
80T/Super-21
81D-105
81F-87
81F/St-72
81OPC-365
81T-365
81T/HT
82D-335
82Drake-26
82F-46
82F/St-119
82F/St-238M
82HB/LS
82OPC-21IA
82OPC-62
82T-505
82T-506IA
82T/St-215
82T/StVar-215
83D-83
83F-391
83F/St-16M
83F/St-7M
83OPC-207SV
83OPC-293
83OPC/St-13
83RoyRog/Disc-7
83T-635
83T-636SV
83T/Fold-2M
83T/St-13
84D-518
84D/Champs-12
84F-135
84F/X-U82
84Mother/Padres-22
84Nes/792-175
84Nes/792-712LL
84Nes/792-713LL
84OPC-175
84T-175
84T-712LL
84T-713LL
84T/St-326
84T/Tr-83T
85D-234
85F-42
85FunFoodPin-66
85Leaf-177
85Mother/Padres-4
85OPC-35
85T-35
85T/St-155
86D-478
86D/AAS-6
86D/PopUp-6
86F-332
86GenMills/Book-5M
86OPC-151
86Seven/Coin-W11M
86Sf-91
86T-450
86T/Gloss22-15
86T/St-106
86T/St-151
86T/Tatt-7M
87F-426
87OPC-205
87RedFoley/St-87
87Smok/Atl-15
87T-205
87T/Tr-85T
88AlaskaAS60/Team-4
88S-440
88S/Tr-25T
88SanDiegoSt-12
88T-574
89Pac/SenLg-115
89Pac/SenLg-132
89Pac/SenLg-158
89S-277
89SanDiegoSt-12
89T/SenLg-25
89TM/SenLg-82
90EliteSenLg-43
91LineD-26
91Swell/Great-67
92Kodak-3
92MCI-6
92Yank/WIZ70-122
92Yank/WIZAS-53
93AP/ASG-162
93MCI-13
93TWill-68
93YooHoo-13
Nettles, James W.
(Jim)
71OPC-74R
71T-74R
72OPC-131
72T-131
73OPC-358
73T-358
75OPC-497
75T-497
75T/M-497
80Colum-12
81Tacom-12
82Tacom-17
83Idaho-30
83Tacom-20
84Idaho/Team-18
85Madis-23
85Madis/Pol-20
86Madis/Pol-24
87Madis-4
88Madis-16
89Madis/Star-17
89Pac/SenLg-126A
89Pac/SenLg-126B
89SanDiegoSt-13
90EliteSenLg-44
90Penin/Star-25MG
91AA/LineD-349MG
91Jaxvl/LineD-349MG
91Jaxvl/ProC-166MG
92MedHat/ProC-3222MG
92MedHat/SportP-29MG
93Hagers/ClBest-25MG
93Hagers/ProC-1895MG
Nettles, Morris Jr.
75OPC-632
75T-632
75T/M-632
76OPC-434
76SSPC-202
76T-434
76T/Tr-434T
Nettles, Robert
86Erie-21
Nettnin, Rodney
91Miami/ClBest-3
Neuendorff, Tony
83Durham-11
84Durham-16
Neuenschwander, Doug
80Water-4
81Water-5
Neufang, Gerry
82Tulsa-20
83Tulsa-23
Neun, Johnny
91Conlon/Sport-204
Neuzil, Jeff
84Memphis-10
Nevers, Ernie
92Conlon/Sport-394
Nevers, Tom
90Ashvl/ClBest-16
90Classic/DP-21
91Ashvl/ProC-577
91B-542
91ClBest/Singl-201
91S-387FDP
91SALAS/ProC-SAL2
92B-226
92ClBest-208
92Osceola/ClBest-1
92Osceola/ProC-2539
92ProC/Tomorrow-234
92UD-53TP
92UD/ML-250
93B-68
93ClBest/MLG-67
93FExcel/ML-49
Nevill, Glenn
91Batavia/ClBest-19
91Batavia/ProC-3482
92Batavia/ClBest-14
92Batavia/ProC-3262

Neville, Dan
65T-398R
Neville, David
89BendB/Legoe-13
92Bluefld/ClBest-25TR
Nevin, Phil
89KS*-30
91T/Tr-83T
92B-670FOIL
92Classic/DP-1
92Classic/DPFoil-BC1
92Classic/DPPr-2
92Classic/DPPr-2
92Classic/DPPrev-BB1
92StCl/1stDP-3
92StCl/Dome-130
92T/Tr-82T
92T/TrGold-82T
93StCl/MurphyS-83
94ClBest/GAce-4
94ClBest/Gold-16
94FExcel-207
94SigRook-18
94SigRook/Hot-8
94SigRook/Pr-2
Newberg, Tom
88Vermont/ProC-955TR
90Mother/Mar-28TR
Newbrough, Dan
89KS*-74
89KS*-9
Newby, Mike
90Hamil/Best-11
90Hamil/Star-17
Newcomb, Joe Dean
89Knoxvl/Best-19
89Knoxvl/ProC-1135
89Knoxvl/Star-15
Newcombe, Donald
(Don)
49Eureka-45
50B-23
51B-6
52B-128
52BR
52StarCal/L-79D
53Briggs
53Exh/Can-16
54B-154
54NYJour
54SM
55B-143
55Gol/Dodg-21
55RFG-21
55SM
55W605-21
56T-235
56YellBase/Pin-24
57T-130
58Hires-13
58T-340
59T-312
60Kahn
60L-19
60T-345
60T/tatt-41
61T-483MVP
75OPC-194MVP
75T-194MVP
75T/M-194MVP
77Galasso-17
79TCMA-182
86Sf/Dec-39M
88Pac/Leg-33
89Rini/Dodg-3
89Smok/Dodg-55
89Swell-122
90Pac/Legend-42
90Swell/Great-76
90Target-572
91Swell/Great-68
91T/Arc53-320
92AP/ASG-51
92Bz/Quadra-2M
93Metallic-14
93TWill-139
93TWill-15
Exh47
PM10/L-30
PM10/Sm-134
PM10/Sm-135
PM10/Sm-136
R423-74
Rawl
Newell, Paul
93MissSt-33
Newell, Tom
86Clearw-18
87Maine-20
87Maine/TCMA-6
87Phill/TastyK-50
88D-604
88F-648R
88Maine/CMC-8
88Maine/ProC-293
90Albany/Best-4
90FtLaud/Star-14
91AA/LineD-16
91Albany/LineD-16
91Albany/ProC-1005
Newfield, Marc
90Classic/DP-6
90Classic/III-89
91B-698
91CalLgAS-1
91ClBest/Gold-2
91ClBest/Pr-1
91ClBest/Singl-4
91Classic/200-62
91OPC-529FDP
91S-391FDP
91SanBern/ClBest-23
91SanBern/ProC-2000
91T-529FDP
91UD/FinalEd-18F
92B-406
92ClBest-142
92Jacks/ProC-3722
92Jaxvl/SB-365
92ProC/Tomorrow-144
92Sky/AASingl-157
92UD-64TP
92UD/ML-263
92UD/ML-36M
93B-372FOIL
93B-51
93ClBest/Fisher-7
93FExcel/ML-229
93L-490
93StCl/Mar-19
93UD-434TP
93UD/SP-283FOIL
94B-417
94D-574
94F/MLP-26
94Pac/Cr-579
94Pinn-250
94Pinn/Artist-250
94Pinn/Museum-250
94Pinn/RookTPinn-8
94S-584
94S/Boys-46
94Sf/2000-165
94StCl-357
94StCl/1stDay-357
94StCl/Gold-357
94T-262
94T/Gold-262
94TripleP-295
94UD-22
94UD/CollC-14
94UD/CollC/Gold-14
94UD/CollC/Silv-14
94UD/ElecD-22
94Ultra-122
Newhauser, Don
74OPC-33
74T-33
Newhouse, Andre
92AppFox/ClBest-3
93Rockford/ClBest-22
Newhouser, Hal
39Exh
44Playball-6
48L-98
52StarCal-86AM
52StarCal/L-72B
53Exh/Can-12
53T-228
55Salem
55T-24
55T/DH-109
60F-68
61F-66
61NuCard-446
72T/Test-7
80Perez/HOF-214
81Tiger/Detroit-116
83Kaline-31M
83Kaline-39M
86Sf/Dec-19
86Tiger/Sport-9
90HOF/St-42
91T/Arc53-228
92Bz/Quadra-8M
92Conlon/Sport-445
93AP/ASG-111
93AP/ASG24K-45G
94Conlon-1009
94Conlon/Col-24
Exh47
R423-73
Newkirk, Craig
90Foil/Best-234
90Gaston/Best-22
90Gaston/ProC-2529
90Gaston/Star-16
91CharlR/ClBest-19
91CharlR/ProC-1323
92CharlR/ClBest-6
92CharlR/ProC-2234
Newlin, Jim
90AS/Cal-23
90Foil/Best-259
90SanBern/Best-23
90SanBern/Cal-89
90SanBern/ProC-2630
91AA/LineD-340
91Jaxvl/LineD-340
91Jaxvl/ProC-148
92Calgary/ProC-3728
92Calgary/SB-72
92Sky/AAASingl-29
Newman, Al
84Beaum-4
85Expo/PostC-12
85Indianap-14
86D/Rook-9
86Expo/Prov/Pan-18
86F/Up-U80
86Provigo-18
87D-426
87F-327
87OPC-323
87T-323
87T/Tr-86T
88D-645
88F-17
88S-252
88SanDiegoSt-13
88SanDiegoSt-14
88Smok/Minn-11
88T-648
89B-156
89D-436
89F-122
89S-493
89SanDiegoSt-14
89SanDiegoSt-15
89T-503
89UD-197
90B-419
90D-506
90F-382
90F/Can-382
90Leaf-347
90OPC-19
90Panini/St-110
90PublInt/St-334
90S-128
90T-19
90T/Big-53
90T/St-293
90UD-199
91D-208
91F-621
91Leaf-446
91OPC-748
91Panini/FrSt-301
91S-424
91StCl-146
91T-748
91UD-413
91Ultra-193
91Visalia/ClBest-8
92D-339
92F-214
92L-511
92L/BlkGold-511
92Mother/Rang-25
92OPC-146
92S-357
92S/RookTr-49T
92StCl-821
92T-146
92T/Gold-146
92T/GoldWin-146
92UD-293
92USPlayC/Twin-2D
92USPlayC/Twin-3C
93F-685
93Rang/Keeb-276
Newman, Alan
90A&AASingle/ProC-112
90Foil/Best-39
90Kenosha/Best-23
90Kenosha/ProC-2292
90Kenosha/Star-17
90MidwLgAS/GS-17
90Star/ISingl-56
91CalLgAS-13
92B-221
92ClBest-202
92OrlanSR/SB-514
92Sky/AASingl-222
92UD/ML-240
93B-129
Newman, Danny
88Ashvl/ProC-1071
Newman, Doug
91MissSt-33
92MissSt-30
Newman, Fred
63T-496R
64T-569
65OPC-101
65T-101
66T-213
66T/RO-70
66T/RO-82
67CokeCap/DodgAngel-24
67T-451
69T-543
81TCMA-374
Newman, Jeff
76Tucson-12
77T-204
78T-458
79OPC-319
79T-604
80K-7
80OPC-18
80T-34
81A's/Granny-5
81D-477
81F-577
81T-587
81T/St-120
82D-517
82F-102
82Granny-12
82T-187
83D-635
83F-529
83T-784
83T/Tr-80T
84D-249
84F-404
84Nes/792-296
84T-296
85T-376
87Mother/A's-19
88Modesto-1MG
88Modesto/Cal-81MG
89Huntsvl/Best-20
89SLAS-25
90Huntsvl/Best-24MG
91AAA/LineD-549MG
91Tacoma/LineD-549MG
91Tacoma/ProC-2321MG
92Indian/McDon-30CO
Newman, Mark
82FtMyr-20
Newman, Randy
83Wausau/Frit-25
86Calgary-19
Newman, Ray
72T-667
73OPC-568
73T-568
Newman, Rob
92Idaho/ProC-3519
Newman, Todd
87AubAs-17
87BYU-2
Newman, Tom
89Idaho/ProC-2036
90Idaho/ProC-3243
90Sumter/Best-14
Newsom, Gary
83VeroB-19
85VeroB-4
86Albuq-18
87Durham-9
Newsom, Norman
(Bobo)
35Exh/4-15
36Exh/4-16
36G
36Wheat
37Exh/4-16
37OPC-139
38Exh/4-15
39Exh
41DP-51
42Playball-21
53T-15
54Esskay
55Esskay
60F-70
61F-67
81Tiger/Detroit-64
88Chatt/Team-24
88Lookout-24
90Target-573
91Conlon/Sport-230
91T/Arc53-15
92Bz/Quadra-10M
92Conlon/Sport-364
93Conlon-760
R313
R314
V300
V351B-34
V94-36
Newsome, Lamar A.
(Skeeter)
39PlayBall-84
45Playball-18
R313
Newson, Warren
86Cram/NWL-174
88CalLgAS-45
88River/Cal-225
88River/ProC-1416
89AubAs/ProC-2
89TexLAS/GS-8
89Wichita/Rock-24
89Wichita/Rock/HL-10
89Wichita/Rock/Up-7
90AAASingl/ProC-24
90LasVegas/CMC-15
90LasVegas/ProC-136
90ProC/Singl-518
91AAA/LineD-643
91D/Rook-15
91F/UltraUp-U17
91F/Up-U14
91Vanco/LineD-643
91Vanco/ProC-1608
92D-668
92F-91
92OPC-355
92OPC/Premier-76
92S-398
92StCl-512
92T-355
92T/91Debut-133
92T/Gold-355
92T/GoldWin-355
92UD-621
92WSox-24
93D-463
93StCl/WSox-7
94F-90
94StCl/Team-138
Newstrom, Doug
94FExcel-219
94FExcel/1stY-4
Newton, Eustace
(Doc)
90Target-574
T204
Newton, Marty
86Cram/NWL-15
86Everett/Pop-19
Newton, Steve
88LitFalls/Pucko-18

89Clmbia/Best-18
89Clmbia/GS-17
90StLucie/Star-18
91CharRain/ClBest-9
Newton, Warren
(Newt)
87CharRain-16
Nezelek, Andy
88Greenvl/Best-19
89D-616
89Richm/Bob-19
89Richm/CMC-6
89Richm/Ko-34
89Richm/ProC-839
90AAASingl/ProC-401
90B-3
90D-523
90ProC/Singl-281
90Richm/Bob-13
90Richm/CMC-5
90Richm/ProC-256
90Richm/Team-24
91Richm/Bob-11
92Greenvl/SB-242
93ClBest/MLG-19
Niarhos, Constantine
(Gus)
49B-181
50B-154
51B-124
52B-129
52T-121
53T-63
91T/Arc53-63
R346-25
Nicastro, Steve
79Newar-2
Nice, Bill
80Ander-14
Nicely, Roy M.
48Sommer-24
49Sommer-13
Nicely, Tony
78Charl
Nichioka, Tsuyoshi
91Salinas/ClBest-18
Nicholas, Franci
R314/Can
Nicholls, Simon B.
E104
E91
T204
T206
W555
Nichols, Brian
88Billings/ProC-1819
89Billings/ProC-2043
90Billings/ProC-3224
90Cedar/ProC-2326
90CharWh/Best-13
Nichols, Carl
83SanJose-20
85CharlO-9
87RochR-11
87RochR/TCMA-10
88D-477
88D/Rook-39
88RochR/Gov-18
89AAA/ProC-45
89F-612
89Tucson/CMC-15
89Tucson/JP-18
89Tucson/ProC-185
90AAASingl/ProC-195
90ProC/Singl-613
90Tucson/CMC-11
90Tucson/ProC-205
91Crown/Orio-327
91Leaf-217
91Mother/Ast-22
91OPC-119
91StCl-440
91T-119
Nichols, Charles A.
(Kid)
50Callahan
50W576-56
61F-129
76Shakey-58
80Perez/HOF-58
80SSPC/HOF
94Conlon-1012
E97
N172
N300/unif
WG3-33
Nichols, Chet
52B-120
52T-288
53SpicSpan/7x10-9
54JC-16
54SpicSpan/PostC-14
55B-72
55Gol/Braves-22
55JC-17
55SpicSpan/DC-13
56T-278
61T-301
62T-403
63T-307
90Wausau/ProC-2144CO
90Wausau/Star-28CO
Nichols, Dolan
59T-362
Nichols, Fred
74Gaston
Nichols, Gary
88Spring/Best-23
90Louisvl/CMC-25
90ProC/Singl-125
Nichols, Howard Jr.
86Reading-19
87Reading-14
88Phill/TastyK-27
88Reading/ProC-879
89Iowa/CMC-18
89Iowa/ProC-1712
Nichols, Kevin
87BYU-7M
Nichols, Lance
82RochR-20
83RochR-1
Nichols, Rod
86Watlo-20
87Kinston-24
89D-649
89T-443
90D-546
90F-497
90F/Can-497
90OPC-108
90T-108
90UD-572
91Indian/McDon-21
92D-194
92F-119
92Indian/McDon-19
92OPC-586
92Pinn-525
92S-559
92StCl-534
92T-586
92T/Gold-586
92T/GoldWin-586
92UD-212
92Ultra-352
93D-521
93F-597
93Pac/Spanish-99
93T-372
93T/Gold-372
Nichols, Samuel
N172
Nichols, Scott
87Savan-6
89StPete/Star-21
90AAASingl/ProC-518
90Louisvl/LBC-28
90Louisvl/ProC-404
91Louisvl/ProC-2917
91Louisvl/Team-29
Nichols, Thomas Reid
(Reid)
81T-689R
82Coke/BOS
82D-632
82F-300
82T-124
83D-460
83F-189
83T-446
84D-614
84F-405
84Nes/792-238
84T-238
85D-636
85F-164
85T-37
86Coke/WS-20
86D-574
86F-214
86Leaf-224
86T-364
87D/OD-87
87Expo/PostC-3
87F/Up-U89
87T-539
87T/Tr-87T
88F-191
88OPC-261
88T-748
Nichols, Tom
91Peoria/Team-30M
Nichols, Ty
85Newar-3
86Hagers-13
88CharlK/Pep-22
89Hagers/Best-28
89Hagers/ProC-279
89Hagers/Star-13
90Hagers/Best-8
90Hagers/ProC-1425
90Hagers/Star-20
Nicholson, Carl
78Watlo
79Tacom-18
Nicholson, David L.
(Dave)
61T-182
62T-577
63T-234
64T-31
64T/Coins-32
64T/St-26
64T/tatt
65OPC-183
65T-183
66T-576
67OPC-113
67T-113
69T-298
78TCMA-99
91Crown/Orio-328
Nicholson, J.W.
N172
Nicholson, Keith
87Lakeland-2
88Fayette/ProC-1079
Nicholson, Larry
80Buffa-14
Nicholson, Rick
77Newar
78Holyo
Nicholson, Thomas
N172
Nicholson, William B.
(Bill)
43Playball-36
49B-76
49Eureka-142
49Lummis
50B-228
51B-113
52T-185
53B/BW-14
R346-11
Nichting, Chris
87PanAm/USAB-8
87PanAm/USAR-8
88FSLAS/Star-15
88VeroB/Star-18
89SanAn/Best-22
90TeamUSA/87-8
92Albuq/ProC-719
92SanAn/SB-572
Nickell, Jackie
92Belling/ClBest-16
92Belling/ProC-1441
94FExcel-126
Nickerson, Drew
74Gaston
75Anderson/TCMA-16
77Cedar
Nickerson, Jim
77Spartan
Nicol, Hugh N.
(Hugh)
E223
N172
N172/BC
N284
N370
Scrapps
Nicolau, Travis
91Daikyo/Fut-16
Nicolosi, Chris
59DF
60DF-1
Nicolosi, Sal
85Visalia-5
86Visalia-13
Nicometi, Tony
86Jaxvl/TCMA-1
Nicosia, Steven R.
(Steve)
75Shrev/TCMA-15
78Colum
80T-519
81D-373
81F-371
81OPC-212
81T-212
82D-45
82F-488
82T-652
83D-528
83F-314
83T-462
84Nes/792-98
84T-98
85Expo/PostC-13
85F-618
85T-191
85T/Tr-87T
89Erie/Star-15
Niebrugge, Kenn
89KS*-21M
Nied, David
88Sumter/ProC-413
89Durham/Star-16
89Durham/Team-16
90Durham/Team-17
91Durham/ClBest-3
91Durham/ProC-1541
92AAA/ASG/SB-435
92B-504
92D/Rook-86
92F/Up-68
92L/GRook-10
92ProC/Tomorrow-188
92Richm/Bleach-22
92Richm/Comix-13
92Richm/ProC-373
92Richm/SB-435
92Sky/AAASingl-200
93B-148
93D-792RR
93D/DK-28
93F-9
93F/Final-36
93Flair-43
93HumDum/Can-30
93JDean/Rook-7
93L-390
93OPC-49
93OPC/Premier-107
93Pac/Spanish-433
93Pinn-238
93Pinn/Expan-1M
93S-553
93S/Boys-23
93S/Franchise-28
93S/Proctor-10
93Select/RookTr-78T
93StCl-718
93StCl/1stDay-718
93StCl/I/Ins-3
93StCl/III/Ins-1
93StCl/MPhoto-28
93StCl/Rockie-1
93Studio-74
93T-444
93T/Finest-198
93T/FinestRef-198
93T/Gold-444
93T/MicroP-444
93TripleP-105
93TripleP/Gal-GS10
93UD-27SR
93UD-478M
93UD-834TC
93UD/Diam-23
93UD/FunPack-178
93UD/SeasonHL-HI14
93USPlayC/Rockie-1S
93USPlayC/Rockie-2D
93USPlayC/Rook-6S
93Ultra-354
93Ultra/AllRook-6
93Ultra/Perf-7
94B-470
94D-106
94F-447
94Finest-282
94L-312
94OPC-208
94Pac/Cr-202
94Pinn-43
94Pinn/Artist-43
94Pinn/Museum-43
94S-528
94Select-113
94StCl-153
94StCl/1stDay-153
94StCl/Gold-153
94StCl/Team-111
94T-135
94T/Gold-135
94TripleP-229
94UD-70
94UD/ElecD-70
94UD/SP-168
94Ultra-486
Niedenfuer, Tom
82Albuq-7
82F-16
82Pol/Dodg-49
83D-536
83F-214
83Pol/Dodg-49
83T-477
84D-128
84F-108
84Nes/792-112
84Pol/Dodg-49
84Smok/Dodg-2
84T-112
85Coke/Dodg-22
85D-153
85F-378
85OPC-281
85T-782
85T/St-80
86Coke/Dodg-21
86D-397
86F-139
86Leaf-186
86Pol/Dodg-49
86T-56
87D-218
87F-448
87French-49
87Leaf-204
87Mother/Dodg-14
87OPC-43
87Pol/Dodg-26
87T-538
87T/Tr-88T
88D-294
88D/Best-321
88F-568
88French-49
88OPC-242
88S-261
88T-242
88T/St-232
89B-204
89D-282
89D/Tr-54
89F-613
89Mother/Sea-12
89OPC-14
89Panini/St-254
89S-252
89T-651
89T/St-236
89UD-488
90Louisvl/LBC-29
90OPC-306
90Publnt/St-438
90Smok/Card-16
90T-306
90Target-575
91Crown/Orio-329
91F-639
91S-217
Niehoff, John Albert
(Bert)
14CJ-125
15CJ-125

91Conlon/Sport-151
D328-128
D329-132
D350/2-130
E135-128
M101/4-132
M101/5-130
Niekro, Joe
67T-536R
68T-475
69OPC-43
69T-43
70OPC-508
70T-508
71MLB/St-400
71OPC-695
71T-695
72MB-251
72OPC-216
72T-216
73OPC-585
73T-585
74OPC-504
74T-504
75Iowa/TCMA-12
75OPC-595
75T-595
75T/M-595
76OPC-273
76SSPC-50
76T-273
77T-116
78BK/Ast-5
78T-306
80BK/PHR-6
80OPC-226
80T-205LL
80T-436
81Coke
81D-380
81F-54
81OPC-102
81T-722
81T/St-174
81T/St-26
82D-167
82F-221
82F/St-45
82OPC-74
82T-611
83D-10DK
83D-470
83D-613M
83D/AAS-51
83F-457
83F/St-12M
83F/St-20M
83OPC-221
83OPC/St-240
83T-221
83T-441TL
83T/Fold-1M
83T/St-240
84D-110
84F-234
84Mother/Ast-2
84Nes/792-586
84OPC-384
84T-586
84T/St-69
85D-182
85F-355
85F/St-88
85FunFoodPin-128
85Leaf-189
85Mother/Ast-6
85OPC-295
85T-295
85T/St-69
86D-601
86D-645M
86Leaf-243M
86Mother/Ast-17
86OPC-135
86T-135
87Classic/Up-120M
87D-217
87F-106
87F/Up-U87
87T-344
87T/Tr-89T
88F-18
88OPC-233
88S-237
88T-473
88T-5RB
92Bend/ClBest-25CO
92Yank/WIZ80-132
Niekro, Phil
64T-541R
65T-461R
66OPC-28
66T-28
67T-456
68Dexter-58
68OPC-7LL
68T-257
68T-7LL
69MB-201
69MLB/St-116
69T-355
70MB-20
70MLB/St-10
70OPC-160
70OPC-69LL
70T-160
70T-69LL
70T/PI-2
70T/S-15
70T/Super-15
71MLB/St-19
71OPC-30
71T-30
71T/Coins-37
72MB-252
72T-620
73K-29
73OPC-503
73T-503
74OPC-29
74T-29
74T/St-9
75Ho-99
75OPC-130
75OPC-310LL
75T-130
75T-310LL
75T/M-130
75T/M-310LL
76Ho-3
76Ho/Twink-3
76OPC-435
76SSPC-5
76T-435
77BurgChef-209
77Ho-111
77Ho/Twink-111
77OPC-43
77T-615
78Ho-122
78OPC-155
78OPC-6LL
78T-10
78T-206LL
79Ho-62
79K-28
79OPC-313
79T-595
79T/Comics-19
80K-51
80OPC-130
80T-205LL
80T-245
80T/Super-46
81D-328
81F-242
81F/St-23
81K-12
81OPC-201
81Pol/Atl-35
81T-387
81T/St-148
82BK/Lids-19
82D-10DK
82D-475
82F-444
82F/St-68
82K-36
82OPC-185
82Pol/Atl-35
82T-185
82T/St-20
83D-613M
83D-97
83D/AAS-12
83F-143
83F/St-12M
83F/St-1AM
83F/St-1BM
83OPC-316SV
83OPC-94
83OPC/St-218
83Pol/Atl-35
83T-410
83T-411SV
83T-502TL
83T/Fold-1M
83T/St-218
84D-188
84D/Champs-34
84F-187
84F/X-U83
84Nes/792-650
84OPC-29
84T-650
84T/St-31
84T/Tr-84T
85D-458
85D/AAS-49
85D/HL-50
85F-138
85F/St-93
85FunFoodPin-115
85Leaf-138
85OPC-40
85Pol/MetYank-Y2
85Seven-11S
85T-40
85T/Gloss40-32
85T/St-309
86D-580
86D-645M
86F-112
86F-630M
86F/LL-28
86F/St-82
86F/Up-U81
86Leaf-243M
86OPC-246
86OhHenry-35
86Quaker-28
86Sf-130M
86Sf-163
86Sf-182M
86Sf-53M
86T-204RB
86T-790
86T/St-7
86T/Tatt-8M
86T/Tr-77T
87D-465
87F-254
87F-626M
87F/RecSet-25
87Gator-35
87Leaf-181
87OPC-6
87Sf-147
87Sf/TPrev-3M
87T-694
88Classic/Red-198
88Classic/Red-199
88Classic/Red-200
88S-555
88T-5RB
89Pac/Leg-212
89Swell-22
90Brave/Dubuq/Singl-24
90Pac/Legend-96
91AAA/LineD-449MG
91Richm/Bob-38MG
91Richm/LineD-449MG
91Richm/ProC-2583MG
91Richm/Team-4MG
92K/CornAS-6
92K/FrAS-3
92Yank/WIZ80-133
92Yank/WIZAS-54
93MCI-4
93Nabisco-4
Nielsen, Dan
88Watertn/Pucko-9
Nielsen, Gerald
(Jerry)
88Oneonta/ProC-2062
89PrWill/Star-14
89Star/Wax-91
90PrWill/Team-16
91FtLaud/ClBest-10
91FtLaud/ProC-2423
92Albany/SB-14
92D/Rook-87
93D-359
93F-654
93S-268
93StCl/Angel-28
93T-594
93T/Gold-594
93Vanco/ProC-2593
Nielsen, Kevin
89SanDiegoSt/Smok-20
90SDSt-6
91Spring/ClBest-19
91Spring/ProC-740
92StPete/ClBest-13
92StPete/ProC-2026
Nielsen, Scott
84Nashvl-15
85Albany-9
87D-597
87Hawaii-15
87T-57
88AAA/ProC-11
88Colum/CMC-3
88Colum/Pol-6
88Colum/ProC-310
89Colum/CMC-2
89Colum/Pol-15
89Colum/ProC-754
89F-261
90AAASingl/ProC-272
90AlbanyDG/Best-9
90ProC/Singl-359
90T/TVMets-52
90Tidew/CMC-8
90Tidew/ProC-541
92Yank/WIZ80-134
Nielsen, Steve
78Ashvl
79Tulsa-9
80Tulsa-19
81Tulsa-9
82BurlR/Frit-30CO
82BurlR/TCMA-26CO
83Tulsa-18
85BurlR-11CO
Nielson, Gerald
92Albany/ProC-2225
Nieman, Robert C.
(Bob)
53Tiger/Glen-23
55B-145
56T-267
57T-14
58Hires-26
58T-165
59T-375
60T-149
61T-178
62Sugar-10
62T-182
79TCMA-211
91Crown/Orio-330
Niemann, Art
82AppFx/Frit-23
Niemann, Randy
80T-469
81F-77
81T-148
82D-473
82Portl-6
83T-329
85Tidew-7
86F/Up-U82
86T/Tr-78T
87F-18
87Portl-3
87T-147
88Tidew/CANDL-24
88Tidew/CMC-10
89Pac/SenLg-127
90Pittsfld/Pucko-26CO
91StLucie/ClBest-28CO
91StLucie/ProC-729CO
91WIZMets-294
92Bingham/ProC-534
92Bingham/SB-75CO
Niemann, Tom
83Butte-14
85FtMyr-6
Niemeier, Jeff
89KS*-82
Nieporte, Jay
85Spokane/Cram-16
Nieson, Chuck
77Fritsch-26
Niethammer, Darren
88CharlR/Star-17
90CharlR/Star-16
91CharlR/ClBest-13
91CharlR/ProC-1317
91FSLAS/ProC-FSL5
92Tulsa/ProC-2698
92Tulsa/SB-613
Nieto, Andy
87DayBe-23
Nieto, Roy
92Ashvl/ClBest-11
Nieto, Thomas Andrew
(Tom)
81Louisvl-9
82ArkTr-12
83Louisvl/Riley-9
84Louisvl-8
85D-596
85F-235
85OPC-294
85T-294
86D-327
86F-43
86Indianap-30
86KAS/Disc-12
86T-88
87D/OD-220
87F/Up-U88
87OPC-124
87T-416
87T/Tr-90T
88D-612
88T-317
89Phill/TastyK-24
90AAASingl/ProC-305
90ScranWB/ProC-603
92Chatt/ProC-3835
92Chatt/SB-200CO
Nieva, Wilfredo
88James/ProC-1895
Nieves, Adelberto
81Batavia-10
81Watlo-30
Nieves, Ernesto
(Ernie)
90Billings/ProC-3219
90CharWh/Best-5
90CharWh/ProC-2237
91CharWh/ClBest-7
91CharWh/ProC-2884
92CharWh/ClBest-5
92CharWh/ProC-8
93SALAS/II-28
Nieves, Fionel
90Ashvl/ClBest-7
91Ashvl/ProC-565
Nieves, Juan
86D-40RR
86D/Rook-12
86F/Up-U83
86Pol/Brew-20
86Sf/Rook-5
86T/Tr-79T
87Classic/Up-136
87D-90
87D/HL-1
87F-352
87OPC-79
87Pol/Brew-20
87Sf/TPrev-19M
87T-79
87T/JumboR-11
88D-126
88F-170
88OPC-104
88Panini/St-117
88Panini/St-431
88Pol/Brew-20
88RedFoley/St-60
88S-513
88S-655HL
88S/YS/II-33
88Sf-180
88Sf-211
88T-515
88T/Big-190
89B-131
89Bimbo/Discs-10
89Brewer/YB-20
89D-575
89Gard-10
89Pol/Brew-20

89S-410
89T-287
89UD-646
90OPC-467
90Pol/Brew-20
90PublInt/St-501
90T-467
90UD-648
93Brew/Sen-2
Nieves, Melvin
89Pulaski/ProC-1893
90A&AASingle/ProC-105
90Foil/Best-219
90Sumter/Best-15
90Sumter/ProC-2447
91Durham/ProC-1560
92B-143
92ClBest-94
92Durham/ClBest-22
92Durham/Team-21
92Greenvl/ProC-1165
93B-662
93D-320RR
93F/MLPl-1
93OPC-246
93Pac/Spanish-10
93Pinn-248
93Pinn/RookTP-10
93Pinn/Team2001-5
93Richm/Bleach-5
93Richm/Pep-21
93Richm/Team-22
93S-248
93S/Boys-7
93S/Proctor-4
93StCl-89
93StCl/1stDay-89
93StCl/Brave-28
93T-658M
93T/Gold-658M
93ToysRUs-20
93UD-21SR
94B-176
94B-365
94F-671
94Finest-432
94Pac/Cr-531
94Pinn-478
94S/Boys-40
94T-307
94T/Gold-307
94UD-256
94UD/ElecD-256
Nieves, Raul
76Dubuq
Niggeling, Johnny
93Conlon-954
W753
Niles, Harry Clyde
(Harry)
E91
M116
T204
T206
T3-111
Niles, Lance
89KS*-83
Niles, Thomas
91WinHaven/ProC-485
92Elmira/ClBest-10
92Elmira/ProC-1383
Nilsson, Bob
91Daikyo/Fut-10
91Daikyo/Fut-1M
Nilsson, Dave
88Beloit/GS-19
89Stockton/Best-1
89Stockton/Cal-162
89Stockton/ProC-374
89Stockton/Star-21
90A&AASingle/ProC-151
90Stockton/Best-2
90Stockton/Cal-187
90Stockton/ProC-2186
91AA/LineD-194
91ClBest/Gold-11
91ClBest/Singl-227
91Daikyo/Fut-19
91Daikyo/Fut-1M
91ElPaso/LineD-194
91ElPaso/ProC-2751
91UD/FinalEd-25F
92B-653
92D-4RR
92Denver/SB-142
92F/Up-37
92OPC-58M
92Pinn-568
92Pinn/Rook-27
92ProC/Tomorrow-83
92S/RookTr-94T
92Sky/AAASingl-69
92T-58R
92T/Gold-58M
92T/GoldWin-58M
92T/Tr-83T
92T/TrGold-83T
92UD-57TP
92UD/Scout-SR18
93B-591
93D-235
93F-631
93L-327
93OPC-272
93Pac/Spanish-162
93Pinn-61
93Pol/Brew-19
93S-344
93Select-283
93StCl-709
93StCl/1stDay-709
93T-316
93T/Gold-316
93ToysRUs-31
93UD-795
93Ultra-222
94D-204
94F-186
94Finest-268
94L-302
94Pac/Cr-337
94Panini-84
94Pinn-210
94Pinn/Artist-210
94Pinn/Museum-210
94Pol/Brew-20
94S-533
94StCl-376
94StCl/1stDay-376
94StCl/Gold-376
94Studio-46
94T-548
94T/Gold-548
94TripleP-57
94UD-359
94UD/CollC-216
94UD/CollC/Gold-216
94UD/CollC/Silv-216
94Ultra-80
Nilsson, Gary
91Daikyo/Fut-1M
91Daikyo/Fut-7
Nina, Robin
89Salem/Team-19
90VeroB/Star-20
Nipp, Mark
80Albuq-21
Nipper, Al
85D-614
85F-165
85T-424
86D-538
86F-356
86T-181
87D-297
87F-39
87OPC-64
87T-617
88Berg/Cubs-45
88D-523
88D/Best-250
88D/Cubs/Bk-NEW
88F-358
88S-527
88T-326
88T/Tr-75T
89D-394
89F-433
89S-532
89T-86
89UD-494
91AAA/LineD-241
91Louisvl/LineD-241
91Louisvl/ProC-2911
Nipper, Mike
85Durham-28
86Durham-20
Nipper, Ronald
87Greenvl/Best-6
Nischwitz, Ron
62T-591R
63T-152
66OPC-38
66T-38
81TCMA-380
Nishijima, Takayuki
92Salinas/ClBest-7
92Salinas/ProC-3771
Nishimura, Hioetsugu
88VeroB/Star-19
Nishioka, Tsuyoshi
91Salinas/ProC-2241
Nitcholas, Otho
90Target-576
Nitschke, David
(Buzz)
75IntLgAS/Broder-19
75PCL/AS-19
75Tucson-5
75Tucson/Caruso-5
75Tucson/Team-14
Nittoli, Mike
86SanJose-15
Nitz, Rick
74Albuq/Team-11
75Albuq/Caruso-16
75IntLgAS/Broder-20
75PCL/AS-20
Nivens, Toby
87OrlanTw-12
88OrlanTw/Best-6
89Jacks/GS-6
90Jacks/GS-17
91AA/LineD-640
91Wmsprt/LineD-640
91Wmsprt/ProC-289
Nix, Dave
81AppFx-21
82AppFx/Frit-15
83GlenF-8
86Madis/Pol-15
Nix, James
92Princet/ClBest-16
92Princet/ProC-3087
Nix, John
75Cedar
Nixon, Al
90Target-577
Nixon, Donell
81Wausau-17
82Wausau/Frit-9
84Chatt-11
87Calgary-19
87D/OD-114
87Mother/Sea-19
87Sf/TPrev-25M
88Calgary/CMC-11
88F-382
88F/Up-U129
88S-436
88T-146
89B-477
89F-337
89Mother/Giants-25
89S-481
89T-447
89T/Big-214
90AAASingl/ProC-472
90D-571
90F-66
90F/Can-66
90MLBPA/Pins-25
90OPC-658
90ProC/Singl-314
90PublInt/St-78
90RochR/CMC-11
90RochR/ProC-715
90Rochester/L&U-8
90S-538
90T-658
91Crown/Orio-331
92ColoSp/ProC-765
92ColoSp/SB-93
Nixon, Jason
90Augusta/ProC-2467
Nixon, Otis
83Colum-25
85Polar/Ind-20
86F-591
86OhHenry-20
86T/Tr-80T
87F-255
87Gator-20
87T-486
88Indianap/CMC-14
88Indianap/ProC-518
89B-366
89F-387
89OPC-54
89S-451
89T-674
89T/Big-234
89T/Mini-23
89UD-480
90D-456
90F-356
90F/Can-356
90OPC-252
90PublInt/St-183
90S-241
90T-252
90T/Big-279
90UD-379
91B-571
91Brave/Dubuq/Perf-20
91Brave/Dubuq/Stand-27
91D-626
91F-241
91F/UltraUp-U69
91F/Up-U75
91Leaf-395
91OPC-558
91OPC/Premier-89
91Panini/FrSt-152
91S-431
91S/RookTr-29T
91StCl-174
91T-558
91T/Tr-84T
91UD-520
91UD/FinalEd-58F
92B-669
92Brave/LykePerf-20
92Brave/LykeStand-23
92D-33HL
92D-41
92F/Up-69
92L-358
92L/BlkGold-358
92OPC-340
92Pinn-519
92S-429HL
92S-443
92S/100SS-73
92StCl-882
92T-340
92T/Gold-340
92T/GoldWin-340
92T/Kids-35
92T/Pr-174
92UD-451
92USPlayC/Brave-10C
92USPlayC/Brave-1H
92Ultra-461
92Yank/WIZ80-135
93B-310
93BJ/D/McDon-22M
93Brave/LykePerf-21
93Brave/LykeStand-26
93Classic/Gamel-71
93D-262
93F-10
93L-180
93OPC-271
93Pac/Spanish-337
93Panini-186
93Pinn-35
93S-87
93Select-159
93StCl-678
93StCl/1stDay-678
93StCl/Brave-16
93StCl/MurphyS-92
93Studio-216
93T-333
93T/Finest-181
93T/FinestRef-181
93T/Gold-333
93UD-292
93Ultra-310
94B-91
94D-232
94F-369
94Finest-274
94L-375
94OPC-188
94Pac/Cr-19
94Pinn-498
94S-106
94S/GoldR-106
94StCl-106
94StCl/1stDay-106
94StCl/Gold-106
94Studio-163
94T-52
94T/Gold-52
94UD-497
94Ultra-316
Nixon, Russell E.
(Russ)
57Sohio/Ind-11
58T-133
59Kahn
59T-344
60Kahn
60MacGregor-17
60T-36
61P-52
61T-53
61T/St-115
62T-523
62T/St-16
63T-168
64T-329
65OPC-162
65T-162
66T-227
67T-446
68Dexter-59
68T-515
69T-363
83T-756
84Expo/PostC-20CO
84Nes/792-351MG
84Stuart-5CO
84T-351MG
86Pol/Atl-2C
88T/Tr-76MG
89Brave/Dubuq-19MG
89T-564MG
90Brave/Dubuq/Perf-21MG
90OPC-171MG
90T-171MG
91AAA/LineD-424MG
91Portl/LineD-424MG
91Portl/ProC-1581MG
92Mother/Mar-27M
Nixon, Trot
94ClBest/Gold-3
94Pinn-270
94Pinn/Artist-270
94Pinn/Museum-270
94S-486
94UD-543TP
94UD/CollC-25
94UD/CollC/Gold-25FDP
94UD/CollC/Silv-25FDP
94UD/HoloFX-29
94UD/SP-11PP
Nixon, Willard
51B-270
52T-269
53B/BW-2
53T-30
54B-114
55B-177
56T-122
57T-189
58Hires-47
58T-395
59T-361
91T/Arc53-30
Noble, Jeff
85Clovis-29
Noble, Rafael Miguel
(Ray)
50Remar
51B-269
52BR
Noble, Ray
85Utica-20
86Tucson-17
Nobles, Jim
79LodiD-10
Noboa, Milicades A.
(Junior)
81Batavia-15

82Watlo/B-18
82Watlo/Frit-28
83Watlo/Frit-8
84BuffB-4
85Maine-20
86Maine-13
87BuffB-8
87Gator-17
88Edmon/ProC-564
88T-503
89AAA/CMC-3
89AAA/ProC-8
89Indianap/CMC-20
89Indianap/ProC-1235
90T/Tr-80T
90TripleAAS/CMC-3
91D-726
91F-242
91Leaf-255
91OPC-182
91S-423
91T-182
91Ultra-207
92D-765
92L-403
92L/BlkGold-403
92Mets/Kahn-3
92OPC/Premier-187
92StCl-709
92Ultra-533
93LimeR/Winter-22

Nocas, Luke
87AppFx-25
89AppFx/ProC-877

Nocciolo, Mark
80SLCity-5
81Holyo-18

Noce, Doug
90Gate/ProC-3356
90Gate/SportP-18
91Sumter/ClBest-14
91Sumter/ProC-2337

Noce, Paul
83Miami-17
84MidldC-21
85Iowa-5
86Iowa-20
87D/Rook-51
87Iowa-11
88D-315
88D/Cubs/Bk-315
88F-428
88Iowa/CMC-16
88Iowa/ProC-538
88RedFoley/St-61
88S-329
88T-542
89Calgary/CMC-16
89Calgary/ProC-539
90AAASingl/ProC-553
90Nashvl/CMC-14
90Nashvl/ProC-241
90ProC/Singl-139
91Phoenix/ProC-72

Noch, Douglas
88VeroB/Star-20
89VeroB/Star-19

Nodell, Ray
83Miami-12

Nodine, Robert
93River/Cal-31TR

Noel, Jay
92Pulaski/ClBest-3
92Pulaski/ProC-3192
93Macon/ClBest-16
93Macon/ProC-1414

Noel, Mike
89FresnoSt/Smok-16
91FresnoSt/Smok-8

Noelke, Michael
88LitFalls/Pucko-7
89Clmbia/Best-9
89Clmbia/GS-18

Noggle, Anne
75T/Photo-85

Nokes, David
91WA/Via-4

Nokes, Matt
82Clinton/Frit-4
84Shrev/FB-14
86Nashvl-18
87Classic/Up-129
87D/Rook-12
87F/Up-U90
87Sf/Rook-16
87T/Tr-91T
88Classic/Blue-207
88Classic/Red-166
88D-152
88D/AS-16
88D/Best-237
88F-638M
88F-66
88F/AS-1
88F/BB/AS-29
88F/Excit-29
88F/Mini-23
88F/SS-26
88F/St-27
88KennerFig-75
88Leaf-60
88MSA/Disc-5
88Nestle-41
88OPC-266
88Panini/St-88
88Pep/T-33
88Pol/T-9
88RedFoley/St-62
88S-15
88S-648M
88S/YS/I-5
88Sf-6
88Sf/Gamewin-18
88T-393AS
88T-645
88T/Big-185
88T/Gloss60-59
88T/JumboR-8
88T/St-269
88T/St-311
88T/St/Backs-56
88T/UK-54
88ToysRUs-22
89B-101
89Classic-113
89D-116
89D/Best-181
89F-140
89Holsum/Discs-13
89KennerFig-98
89Mara/Tigers-33
89Nissen-13
89OPC-116
89Panini/St-339
89Pol/Tigers-33
89RedFoley/St-86
89S-23
89Sf-203
89T-445
89T/Big-303
89T/St-280
89UD-150
90Classic-141
90Classic/III-15
90CokeK/Tiger-14
90D-178
90D/BestAL-11
90F-611
90F/Can-611
90F/Up-115
90Kenner/Fig-61
90Leaf-192
90Leaf-314
90MLBPA/Pins-86
90OPC-131
90PublInt/St-479
90RedFoley/St-69
90S-55
90S/NWest-24
90S/Tr-38T
90T-131
90T/Tr-81T
90UD-226
90UD/Ext-744
91B-164
91Classic/200-32
91D-170
91F-674
91F/UltraUp-U42
91Leaf-89
91OPC-336
91S-551
91StCl-64
91T-336
91UD-673
92B-540
92CJ/DII-34
92D-126
92DennyGS-21
92F-239
92L-102
92L/BlkGold-102
92OPC-748
92Panini-134
92Pinn-72
92S-573
92StCl-111
92Studio-217
92T-404AS
92T-748
92T/Gold-404AS
92T/Gold-748
92T/GoldWin-404AS
92T/GoldWin-748
92TripleP-178
92UD-295
92UD/HRH-HR22
92Ultra-107
93B-334
93D-239
93F-283
93Flair-250
93L-352
93OPC-177
93Pac/Spanish-209
93Panini-146
93Pinn-82
93S-192
93Select-368
93StCl-189
93StCl/1stDay-189
93StCl/Y-3
93T-561
93T/Gold-561
93UD-116
93Ultra-247
94D-564
94F-242
94Flair-85
94Pac/Cr-432
94S-196
94S/GoldR-196
94StCl-23
94StCl/1stDay-23
94StCl/Gold-23
94StCl/Team-206
94T-59
94T/Gold-59
94Ultra-402

Nolan, Bob
75Phoenix-4
75Phoenix/CircleK-4
77SLCity

Nolan, Darin
91StCath/ClBest-22
91StCath/ProC-3393
92Myrtle/ClBest-17

Nolan, Gary
68OPC-196
68T-196
69MLB/St-133
69T-581
70K-53
70MLB/St-33
70OPC-484
70T-484
71K-36
71MLB/St-66
71OPC-75
71T-75
71T/tatt-4
72MB-253
72OPC-475
72T-475
73K-30
73OPC-260
73T-260
73T/Lids-36
74OPC-277
74T-277
75OPC-562
75T-562
75T/M-562
76Icee
76OPC-444
76SSPC-29
76T-444
77BurgChef-203
77Ho-113
77Ho/Twink-113
77OPC-70
77Pep-51
77T-121

Nolan, Joseph W. Jr.
(Joe)
78T-617
79T-464
80T-64
81D-302
81F-212
81OPC-149
81T-149
81T/HT
82D-62
82F-77
82T-327
82T/Tr-81T
83D-79
83F-68
83T-242
84D-489
84F-15
84Nes/792-553
84T-553
85D-594
85F-185
85T-652
86T-781
91Crown/Orio-332
91WIZMets-295

Noland, J.D.
(James)
89Watlo/ProC-1778
89Watlo/Star-22
90Foil/Best-238
90MidwLgAS/GS-46
90ProC/Singl-700
90Waterlo/Best-13
90Waterlo/ProC-2390
91CalLgAS-18
91HighD/ClBest-27
91HighD/ProC-2410
92ClBest-311
92ProC/Tomorrow-337
92Sky/AASingl-284
92Wichita/SB-642

Nold, Dick
68OPC-96R
68T-96R

Nolen, Matt
89KS*-35

Noles, Dickie
79OkCty
80T-682R
81D-568
81F-12
81OkCty/TCMA-14
81T-406
82F-253
82RedLob
82T-530
82T/Tr-82T
83D-426
83F-504
83OPC-99
83T-99
83Thorn-48
84D-266
84F-500
84Nes/792-618
84Rang-36
84T-618
85OPC-149
85Rang-36
85T-149
86D-587
86F-567
86OhHenry-48
86T-388
87Berg/Cubs-47
87F-256
87F/Up-U91
87T-244
87T/Tr-92T
88RochR/CMC-8
88RochR/Gov-19
88RochR/ProC-219
88RochR/Team-16
88T-768
89Colum/CMC-3
89Colum/Pol-16
89Colum/ProC-749
90ProC/Singl-231
90ScranWB/CMC-5
91Crown/Orio-333
93Rang/Keeb-277

Nolte, Eric
85Spokane/Cram-17
86CharRain-19
87Wichita-12
88D-534
88F-593
88S-568
88Smok/Padres-20
88T-694
89LasVegas/CMC-8
89LasVegas/ProC-12
90AAASingl/ProC-6
90LasVegas/CMC-5
90LasVegas/ProC-118
90ProC/Singl-508
92Denver/ProC-2639
92Denver/SB-143
93Rang/Keeb-278

Nonnenkamp, Leo W.
(Red)
40PlayBall-196

Noonan, Dennis
90CLAS/CL-33TR
90Kinston/Team-29

Noonan, Jim
78Wausau

Noonan, Todd
87SLCity/Taco-10

Noore, Daryl
89Bluefld/Star-27

Nops, Jerry
90Target-578

Norbert, Ted
45Centen-18

Nordbrook, Timothy C.
(Tim)
76OPC-252
76SSPC-391
76T-252
78OPC-139
78T-369
79Vanco-6
80Vanco-10
83Beloit/Frit-16
91Crown/Orio-334

Nordhagen, Wayne O.
76OkCty/Team-20
78SSPC/270-162
78T-231
79K-4
79T-351
80OPC-253
80T-487
81Coke
81D-401
81F-348
81T-186
81T/HT
81T/St-59
82D-67
82F-355
82OPC-139
82T-597
83F-438
83OPC-47
83T-714
89Pac/SenLg-154
89T/SenLg-47
90EliteSenLg-45

Nordstrom, Carl
88Billings/ProC-1831
88Cedar/ProC-1158
89Greens/ProC-429

Nored, Mike
76AppFx

Noren, Irving Arnold
(Irv)
50B-247
51B-241
51FB
51T/BB-38
52B-63
52T-40
53B/BW-45
53T-35
54NYJour
55B-63
55RM-AL9
56T-253
57T-298
58T-114
59T-59
60L-101

60T-433
73OPC-179CO
73T-179C
90Target-579
91T/Arc53-35
92Yank/WIZAS-55
PM10/L-31
Noriega, Rey
90FtLaud/Star-15
91FSLAS/ProC-FSL17
91FtLaud/ClBest-22
91FtLaud/ProC-2435
92Albany/SB-15
92FtLaud/ProC-2628
92ProC/Tomorrow-118
92Sky/AASingl-9
Norko, Tom
80Utica-7
Norman, Bull
83Tampa-30
Norman, Daniel E.
(Dan)
77Indianap-10
78Tidew
79T-721R
79Tidew-11
80T-681R
81F-337
81Tidew-28
82Expo/Hygrade-14
82Hygrade
83F-289
83OPC-237
83T-237
84MidldC-17
89Kingspt/Star-27CO
90Kgsport/Best-27CO
91Pac/SenLg-64
91WIZMets-296
92ColRS/ClBest-28CO
93Kinston/Team-28CO
Norman, Fred
64T-469R
65T-386R
70OPC-427
70T-427
71MLB/St-280
71OPC-348
71T-348
72OPC-194
72T-194
73OPC-32
73T-32
74OPC-581
74T-581
75OPC-396
75T-396
75T/M-396
76OPC-609
76SSPC-30
76T-609
77K-8
77OPC-181
77Pep-56
77T-139
78Pep-20
78SSPC/270-109
78T-273
79OPC-20
79T-47
80OPC-362
80T-714
81D-92
81F-158
81OPC-183
81T-497
90Target-580
Norman, Greg
83BirmB-13
Norman, H. Willis
(Bill)
53T-245CO
91T/Arc53-245CO
Norman, Kenny
91Elizab/ProC-4313
92Elizab/ClBest-17
92Elizab/ProC-3696
Norman, Les
91Eugene/ClBest-13
91Eugene/ProC-3739
92AppFox/ClBest-14
92Memphis/ProC-2432
92UD/ML-100
93B-673
93FExcel/ML-176
94ClBest/Gold-121
94FExcel-69
Norman, Nelson A.
78Cr/PCL-95
80CharCh-4
80OPC-270
80T-518
81D-509
82Portl-16
83LynnP-15
84Cram/PCL-133
85RochR-7
86Jaxvl/TCMA-22
87Indianap-29
88Indianap/ProC-517
93Rang/Keeb-279
Norman, Rob
88MissSt-24
89MissSt-28
90MissSt-28
91MissSt-34
Norman, Ron
75Spokane/Caruso-21
76SanAn/Team-16
Norman, Scott 1
83Clinton/Frit-3
87Spring/Best-28
Norman, Scott 2
89TNTech-19
Norman, Terry
80Batavia-2
Normand, Guy
85Anchora-21
86AubAs-17
87Ashvl-13
88Osceola/Star-18
89Osceola/Star-13
Norrid, Tim
76Wmsprt
79T-705R
79Tacom-22
80Tacom-2
81Charl-9
82Charl-12
83Charl-14
Norris, Allen
59DF
60DF-23
Norris, Bill
91CLAS/ProC-CAR25
91LynchRS/ClBest-17
91LynchRS/ProC-1207
92NewBrit/ProC-442
92NewBrit/SB-491
92Sky/AASingl-211
Norris, David
90Johnson/Star-19
91Spring/ClBest-20
91Spring/ProC-741
Norris, James Frances
(Jim)
75OkCty/Team-17
78T-484
79T-611
80T-333
81D-388
81F-634
81T-264
93Rang/Keeb-280
Norris, Joe
91Sumter/ClBest-9
91Sumter/ProC-2332
92Rockford/ClBest-22
92Rockford/ProC-2113
93WPalmB/ClBest-16
93WPalmB/ProC-1337
Norris, Mike
76OPC-653
76SSPC-487
76T-653
77BurgChef-113
77T-284
78T-434
79T-191
80T-599
81A's/Granny-17
81D-118
81F-573
81F/St-6
81MSA/Disc-24
81OPC-55
81T-55
81T/SO-53
81T/St-122
81T/St-2M
81T/St-4
81T/St-6
82D-197
82D-19DK
82F-103
82F/St-125
82Granny-13
82K-59
82OPC-370
82T-370
82T/St-222
83D-139
83F-530
83Granny-17
83OPC-276
83T-620
84F-457
84Nes/792-493
84OPC-49
84T-493
85T-246
87Mother/A's-22
90Helena/SportP-26
90Mother/A's-19
91Pac/SenLg-107
91Reno/Cal-15
Norris, Niles
93MissSt-34
Norris, Scott
75FtLaud/Sus-1
Norris, Wade
92MedHat/ProC-3216
92MedHat/SportP-13
Norsetter, Howard
91Melbourne/Fut-16MG
North, Jay
85Spring-21
86StPete-22
87StPete-25
88StPete/Star-20
89Savan/ProC-343
90StPete/Star-26CO
91StPete/ClBest-11CO
91StPete/ProC-2293CO
North, Mark
88Peoria/Ko-22
89Kenosha/ProC-1061
89Kenosha/Star-18
North, Roy
80Ander-18
81Durham-21
North, Tim
92Erie/ClBest-6
92Erie/ProC-1632
North, William Alex
(Billy)
73OPC-234
73T-234
74Greyhound-1
74Greyhound-5M
74OPC-345
74T-345
74T/St-228
75Greyhound-5
75K-23
75OPC-121
75OPC-309LL
75T-121
75T-309LL
75T/M-121
75T/M-309LL
76Greyhound-1
76Greyhound-5
76OPC-33
76SSPC-491
76T-33
77BurgChef-116
77Ho-33
77Ho/Twink-33
77K-22
77OPC-106
77OPC-4LL
77T-4LL
77T-551
78Ho-76
78T-163
78Tastee/Discs-13
79OPC-351
79Pol/Giants-36
79T-668
80BK/PHR-31
80OPC-213
80Pol/Giants-36
80T-408
81D-76
81F-441
81OPC-47
81T-713
90Target-581
Northam, J.J.
90AZ/Pol-14
Northern, Hubbard
90Target-1144
T207
Northey, Ronald J.
(Ron)
42Playball-44
49B-79
50B-81
51B-70
52T-204
57T-31
63IDL-16CO
Exh47
Northey, Scott R.
(Scott)
70OPC-241R
70T-241R
71OPC-633R
71T-633R
Northrup, George
E270/1
Northrup, James T.
(Jim)
65OPC-259R
65T-259R
66T-554
67CokeCap/Tiger-8
67T-408
68CokeCap/Tiger-8
68OPC-78
68T-78
69MB-202
69MLB/St-53
69OPC-167WS
69OPC-3LL
69T-167WS
69T-3LL
69T-580
69T/St-178
70MLB/St-213
70OPC-177
70T-177
71K-63
71MLB/St-401
71OPC-265
71T-265
71T/Coins-82
71T/GM-21
71T/Greatest-21
71T/S-55
71T/Super-55
72MB-254
72OPC-408
72T-408
73OPC-168
73T-168
74OPC-266
74T-266
75OPC-641
75T-641
75T/M-641
76SSPC-399
81Tiger/Detroit-52
83Kaline-52M
86Tiger/Sport-16
88Domino-17
90Swell/Great-78
91Crown/Orio-335
Northrup, Kevin
92James/ClBest-24
92James/ProC-1514
93WPalmB/ClBest-17
93WPalmB/ProC-1355
Norton, Doug
83Beloit/Frit-11
86Stockton-19
Norton, Greg
94T-758DP
94T/Gold-758DP
Norton, Rick
91SoOreg/ClBest-8
91SoOreg/ProC-3856
92SoOreg/ProC-3421
93Modesto/ClBest-15
93Modesto/ProC-803
Norwood, Aaron
89Bluefld/Star-19
Norwood, Steve
78Newar
79BurlB-24
80BurlB-15
81BurlB-4
Norwood, Willie
78T-705R
78Twin/FriszP-13
79T-274
79Twin/FriszP-19
80T-432
80Toledo-10
81D-516
Nosek, Randy
88Lakeland/Star-18
89London/ProC-1377
90AAASingl/ProC-375
90ProC/Singl-383
90S-607RP
90T/89Debut-88
90Toledo/CMC-6
90Toledo/ProC-145
90UD-2SR
91AAA/LineD-594
91Toledo/LineD-594
91Toledo/ProC-1930
Nossek, Joseph R.
(Joe)
64T-532R
65T-597R
66OPC-22
66T-22
67CokeCap/A's-12
67T-209
69OPC-143
69T-143
69T/4in1-25M
73OPC-646CO
73T-646C
74T-99C
78Twin/Frisz-39
90Coke/WSox-30CO
91Kodak/WSox-x
92WSox-NNO
93WSox-30M
Nossek, Scott
84AZ/Pol-14
Nottebart, Don
60T-351
61T-29
62T-541
63T-204
64T-434
64T/Coins-119
65T-469
66OPC-21
66T-21
67T-269
68OPC-171
68T-171
69T-593
78TCMA-72
92Yank/WIZ60-94
Nottle, Ed
74Gaston
75Anderson/TCMA-9M
77Tucson
80WHave-20
81Tacom-6
82Tacom-19
84Cram/PCL-90
86Pawtu-16MG
87Pawtu-22MG
87Pawtu/TCMA-21MG
88AAA/ProC-52MG
88Pawtu/CMC-24MG
88Pawtu/ProC-469
89Pac/SenLg-51
89Pawtu/CMC-25MG
89Pawtu/Dunk-17MG
89Pawtu/ProC-678MG
90AAASingl/ProC-449MG
90Pawtu/CMC-10MG
90Pawtu/ProC-477MG
90ProC/Singl-261MG
90T/TVRSox-34MG
Novak, Dave
92Hamil/ProC-1609M
Novak, Tom
87Tampa-11
Novick, Walter

52Park-77
Novikoff, Lou
42Playball-41
43MP-18
47Centen-16
47Signal
88LitSun/Minor-4
Novoa, Rafael
88CapeCod/Sum-36
90A&AASingle/ProC-116
90Clinton/Best-24
90Clinton/ProC-2541
90Foil/Best-89
90MidwLgAS/GS-57
90ProC/Singl-843
91AAA/LineD-386
91Classic/I-9
91Phoenix/LineD-386
91Phoenix/ProC-62
91S-366RP
91T/90Debut-116
91UD-674
92ElPaso/ProC-3918
94Pac/Cr-338
94StCl/Team-343
94T-623
94T/Gold-623
Novosel, Frank
52Laval-102
Novotney, Rube
49Eureka-65
Nowak, Matt
88Hagers/Star-14
Nowak, Rick
90Myrtle/ProC-2774
Nowlan, Bill
81BurlB-28TR
82Beloit/Frit-25TR
83Beloit/Frit-13TR
Nowlin, James
(Jim)
87Sumter-25
88BurlB/ProC-15
Noworyta, Steve
83AppFx/Frit-9
Nozling, Paul
88Bristol/ProC-1890
89Fayette/ProC-1591
Nugent, Barney
86Reading-20TR
87Maine-10TR
88Maine/CMC-3TR
88Maine/ProC-299TR
89ScranWB/CMC-2TR
89ScranWB/ProC-712TR
90ProC/Singl-251TR
90ScranWB/CMC-25TR
Nuismer, Jack
81Chatt-7
82Chatt-8
Nunamaker, Leslie G.
(Les)
14CJ-132
15CJ-132
D350/2-131
E120
E121/120
M101/5-131
T207
W501-115
W514-7
W573
Nuneviller, Tom
90Batavia/ProC-3082
91Clearw/ClBest-22
91Clearw/ProC-1633
92ClBest-233
92Reading/ProC-589
92Reading/SB-537
92Sky/AASingl-233
92UD/ML-112
93FExcel/ML-87
Nunez, Alex
90Kenosha/Best-11
90Kenosha/ProC-2303
90Kenosha/Star-18
91Visalia/ClBest-18
91Visalia/ProC-1750
Nunez, Bernardino
(Bernie)
88Myrtle/ProC-1169
89Dunedin/Star-12
90Knoxvl/Best-14
90Knoxvl/ProC-1256
90Knoxvl/Star-13
90ProC/Singl-772
91AA/LineD-363
91Knoxvl/LineD-363
91Knoxvl/ProC-1781
Nunez, Clemente
92B-417
92UD-701
93T-599
93T/Gold-599
Nunez, Dario
86PalmSp-24
86PalmSp/Smok-25
87PalmSp-22
88PalmSp/ProC-1448
Nunez, Edwin
80Wausau-6
81Wausau-4
83SLCity-1
84Cram/PCL-183
84D-435
85D-484
85F-496
85Mother/Mar-24
85T-34
86D-145
86F-470
86Leaf-66
86Mother/Mar-24
86OPC-364
86Seven/Coin-W15M
86T-511
86T/St-223
86T/Tatt-8M
87D-243
87F/Up-U92
87Mother/Sea-11
87T-427
88D-445
88D/Rook-36
88F-383
88Mother/Sea-11
88OPC-258
88Panini/St-182
88T-258
88T/St-216
89Toledo/ProC-773
90CokeK/Tiger-15
90D-563
90F/Up-U98
90Leaf-397
90OPC-586
90T-586
91B-40
91Brewer/MillB-19
91D-620
91F-345
91F/Up-U32
91Leaf-352
91OPC-106
91Pol/Brew-17
91StCl-595
91T-106
91WIZMets-297
92D-541
92F-184
92OPC-352
92Pol/Brew-17
92S-676
92StCl-776
92T-352
92T/Gold-352
92T/GoldWin-352
92Ultra-387
93F-686
93F/Final-260
93Mother/A's-24
93Rang/Keeb-281
93T-19
93T/Gold-19
93Ultra-611
94F-271
94Pac/Cr-460
94S-296
94S/GoldR-296
Nunez, Jose
85FtMyr-13
87F/Up-U93
87Tor/Fire-26
88D-611
88F-122
88OPC-28
88S-312
88Syrac/CMC-4
88Syrac/ProC-820
88T-28
89Syrac/CMC-2
89Syrac/MerchB-16
89Syrac/ProC-806
89Syrac/Team-16
89Tor/Fire-45
90D-467
90T/TVCub-13
90UD/Ext-716
91Iowa/ProC-1057
92Calgary/SB-65
92Sky/AAASingl-30
93LimeR/Winter-11
Nunez, Mauricio
86StPete-23
87StPete-6
88ArkTr/GS-10
89SALAS/GS-38
89Savan/ProC-357
90AAASingl/ProC-531
90Louisvl/CMC-26
90Louisvl/LBC-30
90Louisvl/ProC-417
90ProC/Singl-669
90T/TVCard-57
91StPete/ClBest-28
93LimeR/Winter-37
Nunez, Ramon
84Idaho/Team-19
Nunez, Raymond
92Pulaski/ClBest-8
92Pulaski/ProC-3185
93Macon/ClBest-17
93Macon/ProC-1410
Nunez, Rogelio
90Utica/Pucko-4
91ClBest/Singl-277
91MidwLAS/ProC-11
91SoBend/ClBest-22
91SoBend/ProC-2859
92ClBest-150
92ProC/Tomorrow-46
92Saraso/ClBest-3
92Saraso/ProC-208
Nunley, Angelo
85Spring-22
86Tampa-14
87Vermont-13
88Chatt/Best-25
Nunn, Howard
59T-549
61T-346
62T-524
Nunn, Wally
77Spartan
Nunnally, Jonathan
92Classic/DP-51
92FrRow/DP-15
92Watertn/ClBest-17
92Watertn/ProC-3248
93FExcel/ML-161
Nurre, Peter
90Kissim/DIMD-19
Nutt, Steven
92Martins/ClBest-28
92Martins/ProC-3055
Nutting, Robert
92B-85
92Hunting/ClBest-2
92Hunting/ProC-3154
Nuttle, Jamison
93Welland/ClBest-16
93Welland/ProC-3353
Nuxhall, Joe
52T-406
53B/Col-90
53T-105
54B-76
55B-194
55Kahn
56Kahn
56T-218
57Kahn
57Sohio/Reds-15
57T-103
58Kahn
58T-63
59Kahn
59T-389
60Kahn
60T-282
61T-444
63FrBauer-14
63Kahn
63T-194
64Kahn
64T-106
65Kahn
65T-312
66Kahn
66T-485
67CokeCap/Reds-15
67OPC-44
67T-44
78TCMA-65
82Ohio/HOF-63
89Pac/Leg-161
89Swell-53
90BBWit-105
91T/Arc53-105
93Reds/Kahn-4M
Rawl
Nyce, Frederick
N172
Nye, Rich
67T-608R
68T-339
69MB-203
69OPC-88
69T-88
70OPC-139
70T-139
71LaPizza-7
72MB-255
78TCMA-281
Nyman, Christopher C.
(Chris)
78Knoxvl
79Iowa/Pol-12
80Iowa/Pol-9
82Edmon-5
84Nes/792-382
84T-382
86BuffB-20
86Nashvl-19
Nyman, Gerald
69OPC-173R
69T-173R
69T/4in1-21M
70T-644
71MLB/St-233
71OPC-656
71T-656
89Salinas/Cal-147CO
89Salinas/ProC-1820CO
90James/Pucko-10CO
90Welland/Pucko-33CO
91Welland/ProC-3592CO
Nyman, Nyls W.
(Nyls)
75OPC-619R
75T-619R
75T/M-619R
76OPC-258
76SSPC-149
76T-258
78Spring/Wiener-6
Nyquist, Mike
89SLCity-5
Nyssen, Dan
87AubAs-13
87Hawaii-14
88Osceola/Star-19
89Osceola/Star-14
90Osceola/Star-21
O'Berry, Preston M.
(Mike)
80T-662R
82Coke/Reds
82D-538
82F-78
82T-562
84Colum-20
84Colum/Pol-16
84Nes/792-184
84T-184
84T/Tr-86
85Colum-12
92Bluefld/ClBest-23
92Yank/WIZ80-137
O'Bradovich, James T.
(Jim)
78Charl
O'Brien, Charlie
83Albany-10
86Vanco-19
87Denver-24
88Denver/CMC-15
88Denver/ProC-1268
88Pol/Brew-11
88T-566
89F-194
89Pol/Brew-22
89S-606
89T-214
90Brewer/MillB-17
90D-410
90ElPasoATG/Team-30
90F-332
90F/Can-332
90Leaf-375
90OPC-106
90Pol/Brew-22
90PublInt/St-502
90T-106
90UD-650
90WichSt-28
91B-473
91D-623
91Kahn/Mets-5
91Leaf-122
91OPC-442
91S-829
91StCl-157
91T-442
91UD-420
91WIZMets-298
92D-777
92F-514
92Mets/Kahn-22
92OPC-56
92Pinn-488
92S-621
92StCl-154
92T-56
92T/Gold-56
92T/GoldWin-56
92UD-381
92Ultra-534
93D-698
93F-478
93Mets/Kahn-22
93Pac/Spanish-546
93StCl-128
93StCl/1stDay-128
93T-242
93T/Gold-242
93UD-209
93Ultra-431
94D-242
94F-574
94S-195
94S/GoldR-195
94StCl/Team-34
94T-671
94T/Gold-671
94Ultra-448
O'Brien, Dan
77StPete
80Richm-10
80T-684R
81Richm-18
O'Brien, Edward J.
(Eddie)
53T-249
54T-139M
56T-116
57T-259
91T/Arc53-249
94T/Arc54-139
O'Brien, John Joseph
(Jack)
T3/Box-75
O'Brien, John K.
(Jack)
N172
WG1-69
O'Brien, John Thomas
(Johnny)
53T-223
54T-139M
55T-135
56T-65
56T/Pin-44
58T-426
59T-499
60HenryH-4
90Target-584
91T/Arc53-223
94T/Arc54-139M

O'Brien, John
91Hamil/ClBest-18
91Hamil/ProC-4047
92Spring/ClBest-21
92Spring/ProC-875
94ClBest/Gold-159
O'Brien, Kelly
91SLCity/SportP-29TR
O'Brien, Mark
91GulfCR/SportP-8
92StCl/Dome-131
O'Brien, Peter James
(Pete)
T206
O'Brien, Peter M.
(Pete)
80Ashvl-13
81Tulsa-16
83Rang-9
83T/Tr-81T
84D-281
84F-423
84Nes/792-534
84OPC-71
84Rang-9
84T-534
84T/St-357
85D-178
85F-563
85Leaf-201
85OPC-196
85Rang-9
85T-196
85T/St-344
86D-99
86F-568
86F/Mini-112
86OPC-328
86Rang-9
86T-328
86T/St-236
86T/Tatt-19M
87Classic/Up-138
87D-259
87D/OD-174
87F-132
87F/GameWin-31
87F/Mini-76
87Ho/St-30
87Leaf-186
87Mother/Rang-9
87OPC-17
87Sf-52
87Sf/TPrev-1M
87Smok/R-12
87Stuart-26M
87T-17
87T/Mini-72
87T/St-239
88D-284
88D/Best-167
88F-475
88F/St-67
88Grenada-6
88KennerFig-76
88Leaf-132
88Mother/R-9
88OPC-381
88Panini/St-200
88RedFoley/St-63
88S-29
88Sf-145
88Smok/R-2
88T-721
88T/Big-227
88T/St-240
89B-84
89Classic/Up/2-184
89D-107
89D/Best-5
89D/Tr-16
89F-529
89F/Up-29
89OPC-314
89Panini/St-452
89RedFoley/St-87
89S-22
89S/Tr-6
89Sf-8
89T-629
89T/Big-115
89T/St-248
89T/Tr-88T
89T/UK-57
89UD-54
89UD/Ext-800
90B-475
90Classic/III-38
90D-202
90D-24DK
90D/BestAL-98
90D/SuperDK-24DK
90F-498
90F/Can-498
90Leaf-9
90Mother/Mar-17
90OPC-265
90Panini/St-55
90PublInt/St-565
90S-175
90S/Tr-23T
90Sf-92
90T-265
90T/St-218
90T/Tr-82T
90TulsaDG/Best-4
90UD-110
90UD/Ext-719
91B-259
91CounHrth-8
91D-119
91F-459
91Leaf-244
91OPC-585
91Panini/FrSt-228
91S-509
91StCl-285
91T-585
91UD-459
91Ultra-342
92B-313
92D-86
92F-289
92L-260
92L/BlkGold-260
92Mother/Mar-8
92OPC-455
92Panini-55
92Pinn-125
92S-141
92StCl-192
92Studio-238
92T-455
92T/Gold-455
92T/GoldWin-455
92UD-388
92Ultra-128
93Colla/DM-81
93D-613
93F-678
93L-412
93Mother/Mar-3
93Pac/Spanish-625
93Panini-59
93Pinn-151
93Rang/Keeb-282
93S-460
93StCl-378
93StCl/1stDay-378
93StCl/Mar-26
93T-125
93T/Gold-125
93UD-627
O'Brien, Robert
72OPC-198R
72T-198R
90Target-583
O'Brien, Sydney L.
(Sid)
69T-628R
70OPC-163
70T-163
71MLB/St-353
71OPC-561
71T-561
72OPC-289
72T-289
72T/Cloth-25
O'Brien, Thomas
T207
O'Brien, William D.
(Darby)
90Target-1104
N172
O'Brien, William S.
(Billy)
R314/Can
O'Brien, William Smith
N172
N284
O'Connell, Daniel F.
(Danny)
51B-93
53SpicSpan/3x5-18
53SpicSpan/7x10-10
53T-107
54B-160
54Dix
54JC-4
54SpicSpan/PostC-15
55B-44
55Gol/Braves-23
55JC-4
55SpicSpan/DC-14
56T-272
57SpicSpan/4x5-13
57T-271
58Hires-19
58SFCallB-18
58T-166
59T-87
60T-192
61T-318
62Salada-221
62Shirriff-221
62T-411
62T/St-99
91T/Arc53-107
PM10/Sm-137
O'Connell, James J.
(Jimmy)
W515-13
WG7-37
O'Connell, Mark
81Clinton-11
O'Connell, P.J.
N172
O'Connell, Shawn
91Bluefld/ClBest-23
91Bluefld/ProC-4126
92Kane/ClBest-19
92Kane/ProC-91
O'Conner, Tim
86Kenosha-18
87Visalia-17
88OrlanTw/Best-2
O'Connor, Ben
90Yakima/Team-16
91Yakima/ClBest-15
91Yakima/ProC-4246
O'Connor, Bill
84Shrev/FB-15
85Visalia-4
86Visalia-14
O'Connor, Bob
82Clinton/Frit-25
O'Connor, Buddy
45Parade*-21M
45Parade*-25M
45Parade*-42
O'Connor, Jack
82D-539
82F-557
82T-353
82Toledo-5
83D-51
83F-621
83F/St-6M
83T-33
83Toledo-29
83Twin/Team-22
84Nes/792-268
84T-268
84Toledo-15
85Expo/PostC-14
85Indianap-22
86Calgary-20
87RochR-20
87RochR/TCMA-7
88S-434
88Syrac/CMC-10
88Syrac/ProC-805
89Syrac/CMC-3
89Syrac/MerchB-17
89Syrac/ProC-812
89Syrac/Team-17
91Crown/Orio-336
O'Connor, James
91StCath/ClBest-14
91StCath/ProC-3394
O'Connor, John J.
(Jack)
E107
M116
N172
O'Connor, Kevin
90Idaho/ProC-3257
91Macon/ClBest-25
91Macon/ProC-878
92Durham/ClBest-14
92Durham/Team-12
O'Connor, Patrick F.
(Paddy)
D322
E90/1
M116
O'Day, Henry Francis
(Hank)
94Conlon-1201UMP
N172
O'Dea, James Kenneth
(Ken)
40PlayBall-214
45Playball-27
92Conlon/Sport-497
WG8-43
O'Dell, Bill
55T-57
55T/DH-8
57T-316
58T-84
59T-250
60T-303
61P-155
61T-383M
61T-96
61T/St-83
62T-429
63Exh
63F-66
63J-111
63P-111
63T-235
63T-7LL
63T-9LL
64T-18
64T/Coins-115
65T-476
66T-237
67OPC-162
67T-162
67T/Test/PP-17
91Crown/Orio-337
Exh47
O'Dell, James Wesley
(Jim)
85Osceola/Team-20
86ColumAst-20
87BirmB/Best-4
88CharlK/Pep-7
O'Donnell, Erik
91Belling/ClBest-10
91Belling/ProC-3659
92Penin/ClBest-5
92Penin/ProC-2929
O'Donnell, George
60DF-15
O'Donnell, Glen
86Elmira-14
O'Donnell, Stephen P.
88CapeCod-18
88CapeCod/Sum-41
89GreatF-25
90Bakers/Cal-248
91VeroB/ClBest-23
91VeroB/ProC-784
92VeroB/ClBest-19
92VeroB/ProC-2886
O'Donoghue, John Jr.
90LSUPol-15
91Freder/ClBest-6
91Freder/ProC-2361
92Freder/ProC-1824
92Hagers/ProC-2552
92Hagers/SB-267
92Sky/AASingl-111
93B-197
93F/Final-162
94Pinn-253
94Pinn/Artist-253
94Pinn/Museum-253
94S-593
94StCl-86
94StCl/1stDay-86
94StCl/Gold-86
94StCl/Team-297
94T-763
94T/Gold-763
94UD/CollC-217
94UD/CollC/Gold-217
94UD/CollC/Silv-217
O'Donoghue, John Sr.
64T-388R
65OPC-71
65T-71
66T-501
66T/RO-105
66T/RO-71
67CokeCap/Indian-5
67OPC-127
67T-127
68CokeCap/Orio-6
68T-456
70McDon-1
70OPC-441
70T-441
71Expo/ProS-18
71LaPizza-8
71MLB/St-136
71OPC-743
71T-743
72MB-257
81TCMA-377
91Crown/Orio-338
91Freder/ClBest-27CO
O'Dougherty, Pat
44Yank/St-21
O'Doul, Francis J.
(Lefty)
29Exh/4-11
31Exh/4-3
32Orbit/num-31A
32Orbit/num-31B
32Orbit/un-48
33DH-33
33DL-10
33Exh/4-2
33G-232
33G-58
48Sommer-1
49Sommer-1
53Mother-9
60F-37
61F-130
72F/FFeat-34
75Shakey-17
77Galasso-219
77Galasso-47
80Laugh/FFeat-31
80Pac/Leg-29
88Conlon/5-23
90Target-585
91Conlon/Sport-165
92Conlon/Sport-447
93Conlon-681
R300
R305
R315-A26
R315-B26
R316
R328-24
R423-75
V353-58
O'Dowd, Tom
80Utica-22
O'Farrell, Robert A.
(Bob)
26Exh-62
27Exh-31
31Exh/4-10
33Exh/4-5
33G-34
35G-2F
35G-4F
35G-7F
61F-131
91Conlon/Sport-175
91Conlon/Sport-316
92Card/McDon/Pac-13
92Conlon/Sport-621
93Conlon-862
E120
E210-12
E220
R306
R310
R315-A27

R315-B27
V100
V353-34
V355-115
V61-76
W502-12
W572
W573
O'Halloran, Greg
89StCath/ProC-2079
90Dunedin/Star-14
90FSLAS/Star-38
90Star/ISingl-66
91ClBest/Singl-30
91Dunedin/ClBest-14
91Dunedin/ProC-211
92ClBest-157
92Knoxvl/ProC-2993
92Knoxvl/SB-389
92Sky/AASingl-164
93Syrac/ProC-1001
O'Halloran, Mike
91MedHat/ProC-4098
91MedHat/SportP-23
92MedHat/ProC-3207
92MedHat/SportP-20
O'Hara, Duane
88CapeCod/Sum-73
O'Hara, Pat
82Madis/Frit-27
O'Hara, William A.
C46-1
E101
E106
E92
M116
T204
T206
T216
O'Hearn, Bob
85BurlR-16
86Salem-22
O'Keeffe, Richard
76BurlB
80Water-11
81Water-6
82Syrac-27
82Syrac/Team-17
O'Laughlin, Chad
92Beloit/ClBest-11
O'Leary, Bill
84Butte-20
O'Leary, Charles T.
(Charley)
12Sweet/Pin-29
91Conlon/Sport-116
93UD/T202-7
93UD/T202-8
E104
E90/1
M116
T202
T202
T204
T205
T206
T215/blue
T215/brown
W575
O'Leary, Mike
92Bluefld/ProC-2375
O'Leary, Troy
89Beloit/I/Star-19
89Helena/SP-11
89Star/Wax-6
90Beloit/Best-5
90Beloit/Star-16
90Foil/Best-98
91CalLgAS-36
91ClBest/Singl-160
91Daikyo/Fut-17
91Stockton/ClBest-17
91Stockton/ProC-3046
92ClBest-98
92ElPaso/ProC-3936
92ElPaso/SB-220
92Sky/AASingl-96
92UD/ML-268
92UD/POY-PY6
93B-344FOIL
93ClBest/MLG-215
93F/Final-231
93FExcel/ML-193
93T/Tr-59T
94D-459
94F-187
94Pac/Cr-339
94Pinn-424
94StCl-347
94StCl/1stDay-347
94StCl/Gold-347
94T-770M
94T/Gold-770M
94Ultra-81
O'Loughlin, Silk
94Conlon-1187UMP
O'Malley, Mike
81VeroB-12
O'Malley, Thomas P.
(Tom)
81Shrev-4
82Phoenix
83D-96
83F-271
83Mother/Giants-10
83T-663
84Cram/PCL-11
84D-601
84F-384
84Nes/792-469
84T-469
84T/St-170
86RochR-14
87F-477
87OKCty-20
87T-154
88AAA/ProC-28
88OkCty/CMC-19
88OkCty/ProC-48
88S-534
88Smok/R-1
88T-77
88TripleA/ASCMC-4
89AAA/CMC-20
89AAA/ProC-13
89Tidew/CMC-15
89Tidew/ProC-1965
90Kahn/Mets-27
90OPC-504
90T-504
90T/TVMets-28
90TripleAAS/CMC-20
91Crown/Orio-339
91F-157
91OPC-257
91S-439
91T-257
91WIZMets-299
93Rang/Keeb-284
O'Malley, Walter
89Rini/Dodg-22OWN
O'Mara, Oliver E.
(Ollie)
16FleischBrd-72
D329-134
D350/2-133
M101/4-134
M101/5-133
O'Neal, Doug
92Albany/ProC-2318
O'Neal, Kelley
89Bristol/Star-19
90Niagara/Pucko-8
91Fayette/ClBest-21
91Fayette/ProC-1180
91SALAS/ProC-SAL20
92ClBest-167
92Lakeland/ClBest-7
92Lakeland/ProC-2287
O'Neal, Mark
90Savan/ProC-2084TR
O'Neal, Randy
82BirmB-8
83Evansvl-7
84Evansvl-17
85F-645R
86Cain's-13
86D-394
86F-233
86T-73
87D-584
87F-159
87Smok/Atl-3
87T-196
88Louisvl-37
88Louisvl/CMC-4
88Louisvl/ProC-430
89Phill/TastyK-25
89ScranWB/CMC-10
89ScranWB/ProC-726
90Mother/Giant-23
91F-268
O'Neil, George M.
(Mickey)
21Exh-121
25Exh-8
26Exh-14
90Target-591
E120
V100
W573
WG3-34
O'Neil, John Jordan
(Buck)
86Negro/Frit-45
87Negro/Dixon-20
92Negro/Retort-45
92Negro/RetortII-48MG
94TedW-109
O'Neil, Johnny
47Centen-17
O'Neil, Richard
91Idaho/SportP-7
O'Neil, William John
T206
O'Neill, Dan
87Fayette-3
88Lakeland/Star-19
89Lakeland/Star-16
90A&AASingle/ProC-6
90NewBrit/ProC-1317
91AAA/LineD-362
91Pawtu/LineD-362
91Pawtu/ProC-37
O'Neill, Douglas
91James/ClBest-11
91James/ProC-3559
92Albany/ProC-2318
92Rockford/ClBest-12
93BurlB/ClBest-14
93BurlB/ProC-171
O'Neill, J.F.
21Exh-123
O'Neill, James E.
(Tip)
90HOF/St-7
E223
N172/BC
N184
N284
N370
Scrapps
O'Neill, John J.
(John)
47Signal
O'Neill, Paul
80Indianap-12
82Cedar-21
83Tampa-19
86D-37
86F-646R
87F/Up-U94
87Kahn-21
87Sf/Rook-17
87Sf/TPrev-4M
88D-433
88F/Up-U85
88Kahn/Reds-21
88RedFoley/St-64
88S-304
88T-204
89B-313
89D-360
89D/Best-230
89F-166
89Kahn/Reds-21
89OPC-187
89Panini/St-77
89S-206
89S/YS/II-5
89T-604
89T/Big-39
89UD-428
90B-49
90CedarDG/Best-5
90Classic-117
90D-198
90D/BestNL-39
90F-427
90F/Can-427
90Kahn/Reds-20
90Kenner/Fig-62
90Leaf-70
90OPC-332
90Panini/St-245
90PublInt/St-36
90RedFoley/St-71
90S-295
90S/100St-17
90Sf-4
90T-332
90T/Big-30
90T/St-141
90UD-161
91B-685
91D-583
91F-76
91Kahn/Reds-21
91Leaf-219
91Leaf/Stud-169
91OPC-122
91Panini/FrSt-133
91Panini/St-120
91Pep/Reds-15
91S-227
91StCl-218
91T-122
91UD-133
91USPlayC/AS-2C
91Ultra-100
92B-267
92D-63
92DennyGS-11
92F-415
92L-99
92L/BlkGold-99
92OPC-61
92Panini-266
92Pinn-154
92Reds/Kahn-21
92S-57
92S/100SS-58
92S/Impact-66
92StCl-175
92StCl/Dome-135
92Studio-25
92T-61
92T/Gold-61
92T/GoldWin-61
92T/Kids-41
92TripleP-162
92UD-464
92UD/HRH-HR15
92Ultra-194
93B-75
93D-696
93F-39
93F/Final-250
93Flair-251
93L-379
93OPC-218
93OPC/Premier-14
93Pac/Spanish-560
93Panini-151
93Pinn-446
93S-439
93Select-86
93Select/RookTr-21T
93StCl-717
93StCl/1stDay-717
93StCl/Y-14
93Studio-140
93T-276
93T/Finest-170
93T/FinestRef-170
93T/Gold-276
93T/Tr-84T
93UD-796
93UD/HRH-HR27
93UD/SP-266
93Ultra-599
94B-249
94D-50
94D/Special-50
94F-243
94Flair-86
94L-108
94OPC-229
94Pac/Cr-433
94Panini-103
94Pinn-280
94S-15
94S/GoldR-15
94Select-8
94Sf/2000-147
94StCl-74
94StCl/1stDay-74
94StCl/Gold-74
94StCl/Team-199
94Studio-216
94Studio/Editor-7
94T-546
94T/Finest-69
94T/FinestRef-69
94T/Gold-546
94TripleP-277
94UD-186
94UD/CollC-218
94UD/CollC/Gold-218
94UD/CollC/Silv-218
94UD/ElecD-186
94UD/SP-199
94Ultra-99
O'Neill, Steve F.
15CJ-48
21Exh-122
35BU-160
51B-201MG
54T-127MG
81Tiger/Detroit-11MG
88Conlon/3-21
91Conlon/Sport-186
91T/Arc53-307MG
93Conlon-826
93Conlon-876
94T/Arc54-127
D327
D328-129
D329-135
D350/2-134
E120
E121/120
E135-129
E220
M101/4-135
M101/5-134
R311/Leath
R312
R313
V100
V355-67
V61-22
W501-116
W514-26
W572
W573
W575
WG7-39
O'Neill, Ted
76Wausau
O'Neill, Tom
92Clinton/ProC-3605
92Everett/ClBest-19
92Everett/ProC-1698
O'Quinn, Steven
87CharWh-21
O'Rear, John
78Cr/PCL-90
79Albuq-12
80Albuq-7
O'Regan, Dan
82Oneonta-5
O'Reilly, Jim
89CharWh/Best-26
89CharWh/ProC-1746
90Peoria/Team-33TR
91Peoria/ClBest-24TR
91Peoria/Team-3TR
92Peoria/ClBest-30TR
92Peoria/Team-18TR
93Peoria/Team-18TR
O'Reilly, Tom
90James/Pucko-31
91James/ClBest-29PER
O'Riley, Don
70T-552R
71OPC-679
71T-679
O'Rourke, Francis J.
(Frank)
25Exh-93
26Exh-94
29Exh/4-30
31Exh/4-29
33G-87
90Target-594
92Conlon/Sport-604
E254
V354-43

O'Rourke, James
50Callahan
50W576-57
73F/Wild-24
76Shakey-37
80Perez/HOF-37
80SSPC/HOF
90BBWit-58
E223
N167-8
N172
N284
N403
N690
WG1-42
O'Rourke, Thomas J.
(Tom)
N172
O'Toole, Dennis
73OPC-604R
73T-604R
O'Toole, Jack
85Anchora-24
87Anchora-23CO
89Anchora-18ACO
O'Toole, Jim
59T-136
60Kahn
60T-325
60T-32M
61Kahn
61P-189
61T-328
61T/St-21
62J-126
62Kahn
62P-126
62P/Can-126
62T-450
62T-56LL
62T-58LL
62T-60LL
62T/St-118
62T/bucks
63FrBauer-16
63J-136
63Kahn
63P-136
63T-70
64T-185
64T/Coins-85
64T/SU
64T/St-55
64Wheat/St-32
65Bz-6
65Kahn
65OPC-60
65T-60
65T/trans-22
66T-389
67CokeCap/WSox-12
67T-467
78TCMA-92
89Pac/Leg-147
WG10-40
WG9-39
O'Toole, Martin J.
11Helmar-164
14CJ-54
15CJ-54
D304
E300
L1-112
S81-87
T207
WG5-33
WG6-31
Oakes, Ennis T.
(Rebel)
10Domino-93
11Helmar-174
12Sweet/Pin-151A
12Sweet/Pin-151B
14CJ-139
14Piedmont/St-45
15CJ-139
D303
E106
E254
E90/1
M116
S74-122
T202
T205
T206
T207
T213/blue
T213/brown
T214-23
T215/blue
T216
Oakes, Todd
85Fresno/Pol-26
87Clinton-18
88SanJose/Cal-143
88SanJose/ProC-122
89AS/Cal-50CO
89SanJose/Best-29
89SanJose/Cal-236
89SanJose/ProC-455
90Shrev/ProC-1460
90Shrev/Star-26
91AA/LineD-325M
91Shrev/LineD-325
91Shrev/ProC-1839
92Phoenix/ProC-2838CO
92Phoenix/SB-400M
Oakland, Mike
92Bend/ClBest-19
Oates, Johnny Lane
(Johnny)
72OPC-474R
72T-474R
73OPC-9
73T-9
74OPC-183
74T-183
74T/St-10
75OPC-319
75T-319
75T/M-319
76OPC-62
76SSPC-468
76T-62
77T-619
78SSPC/270-72
78T-508
79T-104
80Pol/Dodg-5
80T-228
81F-99
81T-303
82D-404
82F-47
82Nashvl-28MG
83Colum-1
88RochR/CMC-24
88RochR/Gov-30
88RochR/ProC-211
88RochR/Team-17
89French-46
90Target-582
91Crown/Orio-340
91T/Tr-85T
92OPC-579MG
92T-579MG
92T/Gold-579MG
92T/GoldWin-579MG
92Yank/WIZ80-136
93T-501MG
93T/Gold-501MG
Oatis, Gary
89KS*-10
Obal, Dave
76Baton
Obando, Sherman
89Oneonta/ProC-2102
90PrWill/Team-17
91ClBest/Singl-116
91PrWill/ClBest-28
91PrWill/ProC-1438
92Albany/ProC-2232
92Albany/SB-1
92Sky/AASingl-10
93B-29
93F/Final-161
93L-446
93OPC/Premier-63
93Pac/Jugador-11
93Pac/Spanish-347
93Select/RookTr-70T
93StCl-715
93StCl/1stDay-715
93T/Tr-23T
93Ultra-497
94Pac/Cr-39
94S-597
94StCl/Team-274
Obardovich, Jim
74Tacoma/Caruso-1
Oberdank, Jeff
88Bend/Legoe-33M
88Bend/Legoe-4
89QuadC/Best-5
89QuadC/GS-20
90PalmSp/Cal-206
90PalmSp/ProC-2585
91Melbourne/Fut-5
91QuadC/ClBest-20
91QuadC/ProC-2639
Oberkfell, Kenneth R.
(Ken)
76ArkTr
80T-701R
81Coke
81D-583
81F-532
81OPC-32
81T-32
81T/St-222
82D-404
82F-123
82F/St-21
82OPC-121
82T-474
82T/St-89
82T/StVar-89
83D-246
83F-17
83F/St-21M
83F/St-6M
83OPC-206
83OPC/St-287
83T-206
83T/St-287
84D-504
84F-330
84F/X-U84
84Nes/792-102
84OPC-102
84T-102
84T/St-148
84T/St/Box-2
84T/Tr-85T
85D-432
85F-336
85Ho/Braves-17
85Leaf-141
85OPC-307
85Pol/Atl-24
85T-569
85T/St-32
86D-531
86F-523
86OPC-334
86Pol/Atl-24
86T-334
86T/St-38
87D-437
87D/OD-46
87F-523
87Leaf-171
87OPC-1
87RedFoley/St-99
87Sf/TPrev-24M
87Smok/Atl-16
87T-627
87T/St-38
88D-67
88D/Best-226
88F-545
88KennerFig-77
88OPC-67
88Panini/St-244
88S-245
88Sf-165
88T-67
88T/St-37
89B-418
89D-506
89OPC-97
89S-139
89T-751
89UD-313
89VFJuice-14
90B-74
90D-494
90F-67
90F/Can-67
90Leaf-294
90Mother/Ast-16
90OPC-488
90S-422
90S/Tr-58T
90T-488
90UD-360
91D-109
91F-511
91Mother/Ast-16
91OPC-286
91S-214
91StCl-414
91T-286
92Edmon/ProC-3547
Oberlander, Hartman
N172
Oberlin, Frank
T206
Obregon, Francisco
60HenryH-3
60Union-4
Obur, Paul
79AppFx-25
Ocasio, Fredy
92OKSt-22
Ocasio, Javier
89Saraso/Star-16
90FSLAS/Star-37
90Saraso/Star-17
91AA/LineD-69
91BirmB/LineD-69
91BirmB/ProC-1463
91ClBest/Singl-234
Oceak, Frank
60T-467C
63IDL-17CO
Ochoa, Alex
91FrRow/DP-29
92B-250
92Kane/ClBest-13
92Kane/ProC-106
92Kane/Team-23
92MidwLAS/Team-30
92StCl/Dome-132
92UD/ML-254
92UD/ML-59DS
93B-521
93BurlB/ClBest-29TR
93ClBest/MLG-73
93FExcel/ML-125
94B-103
94B-367
94FExcel-13
94SigRook-45
94SigRook/Hot-9
94StCl/Team-296
94UD-538TP
94UD/SP-12PP
Ochoa, Rafael
90Utica/Pucko-5
91Utica/ClBest-29
91Utica/ProC-3254
92SoBend/ProC-190
Ochs, Kevin
84Butte-19
Ochs, Tony
89Johnson/Star-16
90ProC/Singl-841
90Savan/ProC-2070
91StPete/ClBest-22
91StPete/ProC-2285
Oddo, Ron
80Elmira-23
Odekirk, Rick
88OkCty/CMC-10
88OkCty/ProC-29
91Reno/Cal-8
Odierno, Scott
88CapeCod/Sum-60
Odle, Page
86PrWill-18
Odom, Joe
84Madis/Pol-6
85Modesto/Chong-25
Odom, John
(Blue Moon)
65T-526R
67T-282
68A's/JITB-11
68T-501
69MB-204
69MLB/St-90
69OPC-195
69T-195
69T/4in1-12
69T/St-220
69Trans-8
70K-38
70MLB/St-263
70OPC-55
70T-55
70Trans-15
71MLB/St-523
71OPC-523
71T-523
72MB-256
72T-557
72T-558IA
73OPC-207WS
73OPC-315
73T-207WS
73T-315
74OPC-461
74T-461
75OPC-69
75T-69
75T/M-69
76OPC-651
76T-651
77SanJose-3
78TCMA-68
87Mother/A's-3
Odom, Tim
87FtMyr-10
88AppFx/ProC-150
89Augusta/ProC-493
Odor, Rouglas
88BurlInd/ProC-1780
89Kinston/Star-15
89Watertn/Star-17
90CLAS/CL-41
90Kinston/Team-3
91AA/LineD-91
91Canton/LineD-91
91Canton/ProC-988
92Kinston/ClBest-9
92Kinston/ProC-2485
Odwell, Frederick W.
(Fred)
E254
T201
Oedewaldt, Larry
89Stockton/Best-15
89Stockton/Cal-167
89Stockton/ProC-375
89Stockton/Star-2
Oehrlein, David
92Hamil/ProC-1590
93FExcel/ML-104
Oelkers, Bryan
83Toledo-28
83Twin/Team-12
84D-486
86Maine-14
87BuffB-18
87D-596
87F-257
87T-77
89Louisvl-29
89Louisvl/ProC-1244
Oelschlager, Ron
92AZ/Pol-11
Oertel, Chuck
91Crown/Orio-341
Oertli, Chuck
86Geneva-20
Oeschger, Joe
21Exh-119
61T-403M
72F/FFeat-19M
72Laugh/GF-37M
90HOF/St-22
90Target-586
E120
E121/120
E220
V100
V61-98
V89-6
W501-92
W572
W575
WG7-38
Oester, Ronald John
(Ron)
77Indianap-6
78Indianap-6
79Indianap-3
79T-717R

81Coke
81D-423
81F-218
81OPC-21
81T-21
81T/HT
82Coke/Reds
82D-500
82F-79
82F/St-20
82T-427
82T/St-34
83D-526
83F-598
83OPC-269
83OPC/St-230
83T-269
83T/St-230
84Borden-16
84D-62
84D/AAS-46
84F-475
84Nes/792-526
84Nes/792-756TL
84OPC-99
84T-526
84T-756TL
84T/St-53
85D-81
85F-542
85Indianap-30
85OPC-314
85T-314
85T/St-54
86D-81
86F-183
86Leaf-78
86OPC-264
86Seven/Coin-S14M
86T-627
86T/St-138
86TexGold-16
87D-206
87D/OD-195
87F-207
87Kahn-16
87OPC-172
87T-172
87T/St-141
88D-246
88F-242
88OPC-17
88S-183
88T-17
88T/St-144
89B-310
89D-553
89Kahn/Reds-16
89S-615
89T-772
89T/Big-229
89UD-287
90D-317
90Kahn/Reds-18
90OPC-492
90Publint/St-35
90S-59
90T-492
90T/Big-55
90UD-118
91D-628
91F-74
91S-651
91UD-611
92Chatt/ProC-3833

Oestreich, Mark
89BurlInd/Star-28CO

Offerman, Jose
88GreatF-22
89AS/Cal-1
89BBAmAA/BPro-AA25
89Bakers/Cal-194
89SanAn/Best-27
90AAAGame/ProC-31
90AAASingl/ProC-75
90Albuq/CMC-19
90Albuq/ProC-354
90Albuq/Trib-24
90B-92
90Classic-45
90F/Up-U24
90Leaf-464
90ProC/Singl-421
90UD-46
91AAA/LineD-17
91Albuq/LineD-17
91Albuq/ProC-1149
91B-182
91Bz-6
91Classic/200-145
91Classic/II-T37
91D-33RR
91F-216
91Leaf/Stud-186
91MajorLg/Pins-51
91OPC-587
91OPC/Premier-90
91Pol/Dodg-30
91RedFoley/St-110
91S-343RP
91S/100RisSt-99
91S/HotRook-10
91S/Rook40-26
91Seven/3DCoin-11SC
91Seven/3DCoin-12F
91StCl-340
91StCl/Charter*-22
91T-587
91T/90Debut-117
91T/JumboR-23
91ToysRUs-23
91UD-356
91Ultra-167
92B-304
92Classic/Game200-36
92D-721
92F-467
92L-322
92L/BlkGold-322
92Mother/Dodg-8
92OPC-493
92OPC/Premier-123
92Pinn-153
92Pinn/Team2000-25
92Pol/Dodg-30
92ProC/Tomorrow-237
92S-699
92S/100RisSt-31
92StCl-378
92Studio-47
92T-493
92T/Gold-493
92T/GoldWin-493
92TripleP-153
92UD-532
92Ultra-215
93B-294
93D-376
93F-66
93L-17
93LimeR/DomPr-P1
93LimeR/Winter-77
93LimeR/Winter-P1
93Mother/Dodg-5
93OPC-299
93Pac/Spanish-153
93Panini-216
93Pinn-345
93Pol/Dodg-18
93S-129
93Select-197
93StCl-129
93StCl/1stDay-129
93StCl/Dodg-17
93Studio-182
93T-776
93T/Gold-776
93UD-225
93UD-464IN
93UD/FunPack-91
93UD/SP-97
93Ultra-59
94B-182
94D-623
94F-519
94Flair-180
94L-123
94OPC-104
94Pac/AllLat-5
94Pac/Cr-317
94Panini-202
94Pinn-190
94Pinn/Artist-190
94Pinn/Museum-190
94S-340
94StCl-282
94StCl/1stDay-282
94StCl/Gold-282
94Studio-71
94T-241
94T/Finest-23
94T/Finest/PreProd-23
94T/FinestRef-23
94T/Gold-241
94TripleP-87
94UD-236
94UD/CollC-219
94UD/CollC/Gold-219
94UD/CollC/Silv-219
94UD/ElecD-236
94Ultra-217

Office, Rowland J.
75OPC-262
75T-262
75T/M-262
76OPC-256
76SSPC-20
76T-256
77T-524
78T-632
79OPC-62
79T-132
80T-39
81D-213
81F-147
81OPC-319
81T-319
82F-198
82OPC-165
82OkCty-2
82T-479
83Colum-27
92Yank/WIZ80-138

Officer, Jim
76QuadC

Ofstun, John
90NE-20

Ogawa, Kuni
79Vanco-15
80Holyo-8

Ogden, Charles
88CLAS/Star-33
88Kinston/Star-18
89Canton/Best-27

Ogden, Jamie
92ClBest-149
92Kenosha/ProC-619

Ogden, John M.
33G-176

Ogden, Todd
89Canton/ProC-1322
89Canton/Star-18

Ogden, Warren
(Curly)
28Exh-58
33G-174

Ogea, Chad
90LSUPol-8
91LSU/Pol-15
92ClBest-154
92Kinston/ClBest-25
92Kinston/ProC-2473
92StCl/Dome-133
92UD/ML-296
92UD/POY-PY12
93B-289
93ClBest/MLG-21
93FExcel/ML-162
94B-607
94FExcel-47
94T-316
94T/Gold-316
94Ultra-350

Ogier, Moe
68T-589R

Ogiwara, Mitsuru
88Miami/Star-17

Oglesbee, Mike
85Anchora-22
86Cram/NWL-29
87Ashvl-22

Oglesby, Ron
88River/Cal-232
88River/ProC-1407
89CharRain/ProC-978
90Waterlo/Best-20CO
90Waterlo/ProC-2394CO

Ogliaruso, Mike
89Myrtle/ProC-1463
90A&AASingle/ProC-90
90Myrtle/ProC-2775
90SALAS/Star-38
91ClBest/Singl-133
91Dunedin/ClBest-9
91Dunedin/ProC-205
92Dunedin/ProC-1998
92Knoxvl/ProC-2989
92Knoxvl/SB-388

Oglivie, Benjamin A.
72T-761R
73OPC-388
73T-388
75OPC-344
75T-344
75T/M-344
76OPC-659
76SSPC-359
76T-659
77BurgChef-91
77OPC-236
77T-122
78T-286
79T-519
80T-53
81D-446
81F-508
81F/St-14
81K-20
81OPC-340
81PermaGr/CC-30
81Sqt-3
81T-2LL
81T-415
81T/SO-7
81T/St-11M
81T/St-14m
81T/St-92
82D-484
82F-151
82F/St-138
82OPC-280
82Pol/Brew-24
82T-280
82T/St-197
83D-384
83Drake-20
83F-43
83F-640M
83F/St-20M
83F/St-5M
83F/St-7M
83Gard-14
83OPC-91
83OPC/St-82
83Pol/Brew-24
83T-750
83T/St-82
84D-229
84D/Champs-6
84F-210
84Gard-15
84Nes/792-190
84OPC-190
84Pol/Brew-24
84T-190
84T/RD-31
84T/St-296
85D-333
85F-590
85FunFoodPin-67
85Gard-15
85Leaf-123
85OPC-332
85Pol/Brew-24
85T-681
85T/RD-29M
85T/St-292
86D-333
86F-497
86Leaf-199
86OPC-372
86Pol/Brew-24
86T-372
86T/St-200
86T/Tatt-24M
86Woolwth-25
87D-419
87F-353
87F/RecSet-26
87F/St-85
87RedFoley/St-100
87T-586
92Brew/Carlson-18
94TedW-44

Ogrodowski, Bruce
40Hughes-15
48Sommer-21

Ohlms, Mark
89PrWill/Star-15
89Star/Wax-92
90FtLaud/Star-16
91CLAS/ProC-CAR35
91PrWill/ClBest-8
91PrWill/ProC-1424
92Knoxvl/ProC-2990
92Knoxvl/SB-390
92Sky/AASingl-165
93Syrac/ProC-998

Ohman, Ed
89CharlR/Star-18
89Star/Wax-9

Ohnoutka, Brian
85Everett/II/Cram-13
86Shrev-20
87Shrev-12
88Phoenix/CMC-7
88Phoenix/ProC-79
90AAASingl/ProC-7
90LasVegas/CMC-21
90LasVegas/ProC-119
90ProC/Singl-524

Ohta, Katsumasa
91Salinas/ClBest-14
91Salinas/ProC-2242

Ohtsubo, Yukio
91Salinas/ClBest-16
91Salinas/ProC-2243

Ohtsuka, Kenichi
(Ken)
90Salinas/Cal-120
90Salinas/ProC-2716

Ohtsuka, Yoshiki
90Salinas/Cal-141
90Salinas/ProC-2722

Ojala, Kirt
90A&AASingle/ProC-178
90Oneonta/ProC-3380
91PrWill/ClBest-9
91PrWill/ProC-1425
92Albany/ProC-2226
93ColClip/Pol-6

Ojea, Alex
87Spring/Best-3
88Spring/Best-17

Ojeda, Bob
81Pawtu-5
82Coke/BOS
82D-540
82F-301
82T-274
83D-260
83F-190
83T-654
84D-538
84F-406
84Nes/792-162
84Nes/792-786TL
84OPC-162
84T-162
84T-786TL
85D-371
85F-166
85OPC-329
85T-477
86D-636
86F-357
86F/Up-U84
86OPC-11
86T-11
86T/Tr-81T
87Classic-73
87D-364
87D/OD-127
87F-19
87F/BB-30
87F/GameWin-32
87F/Mini-77
87F/St-86
87Leaf-94
87OPC-83
87Sf-36
87Sf/TPrev-2
87T-746
87T/Gloss60-36
87T/HL-24
87T/Mets/Fan-6
87T/Mini-25
87T/St-99
87Woolwth-24
88D-632

88D/Best-238
88D/Mets/Bk-632
88F-147
88Kahn/Mets-19
88S-563
88T-558
88T/Big-234
89B-371
89D-218
89D/Best-209
89F-47
89Kahn/Mets-19
89OPC-333
89S-116
89T-333
89UD-386
90D-117
90F-214
90F/Can-214
90Kahn/Mets-19
90OPC-207
90PublInt/St-143
90S-53
90T-207
90T/Big-131
90T/TVMets-16
90UD-204
91B-591
91D-584
91F-156
91F/UltraUp-U89
91F/Up-U95
91Leaf-476
91Leaf/Stud-187
91Mother/Dodg-13
91OPC-601
91OPC/Premier-91
91Pol/Dodg-17
91S-321
91S/RookTr-79T
91StCl-449
91T-601
91T/Tr-86T
91UD-179
91UD/Ext-715
91WIZMets-300
92B-379
92D-157
92F-468
92L-345
92L/BlkGold-345
92Mother/Dodg-23
92OPC-123
92Pinn-512
92Pol/Dodg-17
92S-527
92StCl-537
92T-123
92T/Gold-123
92T/GoldWin-123
92TripleP-21
92UD-666
92Ultra-509
93D-614
93F-452
93Indian/WUAB-23
93Pinn-537
93S-589
93Select-263
93Select/RookTr-121T
93T-338
93T/Gold-338
93UD-808
94F-116
94Pac/Cr-180
94Pinn-507
94T-93
94T/Gold-93

Ojeda, Luis
82ArkTr-16
83ArkTr-16
86Miami-19
87Miami-26

Ojeda, Ray
86Beloit-17
87Beloit-22

Oka, Yukitoshi
91Salinas/ClBest-15
91Salinas/ProC-2244

Okamoto, Yoshi
90Salinas/Cal-147OPMG

Okerlund, Ron
85Anchora-39GM

Okubo, Dave
86SanJose-16

Olah, Bob
89Clmbia/Best-7
89Clmbia/GS-19
89SALAS/GS-18
90StLucie/Star-19

Olander, Jim
85Cram/PCL-36
86Reading-21
87Maine-1
87Maine/TCMA-18
87Phill/TastyK-38
88Maine/CMC-21
88Maine/ProC-277
89ScranWB/CMC-15
89ScranWB/ProC-723
90AAASingl/ProC-206
90ProC/Singl-619
90Tucson/CMC-17
90Tucson/ProC-216
91AAA/LineD-147
91AAAGame/ProC-11
91Denver/LineD-147
91Denver/ProC-135
92B-575FOIL
92D-766
92Denver/SB-144
92OPC-7
92S-839
92Sky/AAASingl-293
92Sky/AAASingl-70
92StCl-274
92T-7
92T/91Debut-134
92T/Gold-7
92T/GoldWin-7

Olden, Paul
82Spokane-6

Oldham, J.C.
V100

Oldis, Robert Carl
(Bob)
53Briggs
53T-262
54T-91
55T-169
60T-361
61T-149
62T-269
63T-404
89Chatt/II/Team-22
91T/Arc53-262
94T/Arc54-91

Oldring, Reuben Henry
(Rube)
10Domino-94
11Helmar-58
12Sweet/Pin-49
14CJ-8
15CJ-8
16FleischBrd-71
93Conlon-788
BF2-38
D329-133
D350/2-132
E104
E286
E300
E91
M101/4-133
M101/5-132
M116
S74-34
T201
T202
T205
T206
T207
T208
T215/blue
T222

Oleksak, Mike
79Newar-8

Olerud, John
90B-510
90Classic-35
90Classic/III-96
90D-711
90D/BestAL-100
90D/Rook-2
90F/Up-U128
90Leaf-237
90S-589RP
90S/100Ris-39
90S/McDon-17
90S/YS/II-5
90T/89Debut-89
90T/Big-199
90T/Tr-83T
90Tor/BJ-9
90UD-56
91B-7
91Classic/200-116
91Classic/I-1
91Classic/II-T24
91D-530
91F-183
91KingB/Discs-7
91Leaf-125
91Leaf/Stud-136
91MajorLg/Pins-27
91OPC-168
91OPC/Premier-92
91Panini/FrSt-348
91Panini/St-159
91Post/Can-17
91S-625
91S-860FRAN
91S/100RisSt-100
91S/ToroBJ-18
91StCl-482
91T-168
91T/JumboR-24
91Tor/Fire-9
91ToysRUs-24
91UD-145
91Ultra-367
92B-644
92BJ/Fire-23
92D-98
92F-339
92L-60
92L/BlkGold-60
92OPC-777
92Panini-25
92Pinn-78
92Pinn/Team2000-65
92S-345
92S/100SS-71
92S/Impact-41
92StCl-531
92Studio-258
92T-777
92T/Gold-777
92T/GoldWin-777
92TripleP-110
92UD-375
92Ultra-151
93B-659
93BJ/D/45-10
93BJ/D/McDon-27
93BJ/D/WS-6
93BJ/Demp-10
93BJ/Fire-22
93Colla/ASG-13
93Colla/DM-82
93Colla/DMArt-5
93D-483
93D/EliteDom-3
93F-339
93Flair-293
93HumDum/Can-19
93L-47
93L/UpGoldAS-3
93OPC-188
93OPC/Premier-52
93OPC/WC-12
93Pac/Jugador-12
93Pac/Spanish-327
93Panini-26
93Pinn-86
93Pinn/HRC-29
93S-68
93Select-124
93StCl-649
93StCl/1stDay-649
93Studio-195
93T-240
93T/Finest-13
93T/FinestRef-13
93T/Gold-240
93TB/Full-10
93TripleP-222
93UD-344
93UD/FunPack-60
93UD/SP-6AS
93Ultra-291
94B-169
94D-354
94D/DK-24
94D/Elite-43
94D/MVP-28
94D/Pr-3
94D/Special-354
94D/Spirit-1
94F-340
94F-707
94F/AS-19
94F/LL-1
94F/ProV-2
94Finest-221
94Flair-120
94Flair/Hot-6
94KingB-13
94L-378
94L/GoldS-12
94OPC-130
94OPC/BJ-5
94OPC/JAS-16
94P-24
94Pac/Cr-650
94Pac/Silv-6
94Panini-141
94Panini-5
94Pinn-5
94Pinn/Artist-5
94Pinn/HobSam-5
94Pinn/Museum-5
94Pinn/RetailSam-5
94Pinn/Run-1
94RedFoley-1M
94S-2
94S/Cycle-6
94S/GoldR-2
94S/GoldS-37
94S/HobSam-2
94S/Pr-2
94S/Pr-2GR
94S/Tomb-24
94Select/CrCon-7
94Sf/2000-75
94StCl-228
94StCl/1stDay-228
94StCl/Gold-228
94StCl/Team-172
94Studio-30
94T-10
94T/BlkGold-15
94T/Gold-10
94TripleP-36
94TripleP/Medal-3M
94TripleP/Nick-5
94UD-48FUT
94UD-99
94UD/ElecD-48FUT
94UD/ElecD-99
94UD/SP-45
94Ultra-141
94Ultra/AS-9
94Ultra/Hit-8
94Ultra/LL-1
94Ultra/OnBase-10
94Ultra/RisSt-8

Olin, Steve
88MidwLAS/GS-30
88Watlo/ProC-688
89AAA/CMC-42
89AAA/ProC-34
89ColoSp/ProC-252
90B-326
90D-438
90F-499
90F/Can-499
90OPC-433
90Panini/St-375
90S-590
90S/YS/II-23
90Sf-178
90T-433
90T/89Debut-90
90TripleAAS/CMC-42
90UD-553
91D-339
91F-374
91Indian/McDon-22
91Leaf-94
91OPC-696
91S-496
91S/100RisSt-86
91StCl-336
91T-696
91UD-118
91Ultra-116
92B-236
92D-151
92F-120
92Indian/McDon-20
92L-141
92L/BlkGold-141
92OPC-559
92Pinn-120
92S-644
92StCl-169
92T-559
92T/Gold-559
92T/GoldWin-559
92TripleP-156
92UD-215
92Ultra-53
93D-567
93F-220
93OPC-349
93Pinn-410
93S-388
93Select-377
93T-167
93T/Gold-167
93TripleP-204
93UD-206

Oliva, Antonio Pedro
(Tony)
63T-228R
64T-116R
64T/S-44
65Bz-4
65MacGregor-7
65OPC-1LL
65T-1LL
65T-340
65T/trans-60
66Bz-41
66T-216LL
66T-220LL
66T-450
66T/RO-52
66T/RO-72
67Bz-41
67CokeCap/ALAS-27
67CokeCap/AS-12
67CokeCap/Twin-17
67OPC-50
67OPC/PI-18
67T-239LL
67T-50
67T/PI-18
68Bz-9
68Dexter-60
68OPC-165
68T-165
68T-371AS
68T-480M
68T/ActionSt-11A
69MB-205
69MLB/St-69
69MLBPA/Pin-20
69NTF
69OPC-1LL
69T-1LL
69T-427AS
69T-600
69T/S-20
69T/St-196
69T/decal
69Trans-7
70K-63
70MLB/St-235
70OPC-510
70OPC-62LL
70T-510
70T-62LL
70T/CB
70T/S-26
70T/Super-26
70Trans-13
71Bz/Test-36
71K-12
71MD
71MLB/St-468
71OPC-290
71OPC-61LL
71T-290
71T-61LL
71T/Coins-128
71T/GM-11

71T/Greatest-11
71T/S-11
71T/Super-11
71T/tatt-16
72K-25
72MB-258
72OPC-400
72OPC-86LL
72T-400
72T-86LL
72T/Post-7
73K-4
73OPC-80
73T-80
74OPC-190
74T-190
74T/DE-62
74T/St-210
75Ho-20
75Ho/Twink-20
75OPC-325
75SSPC/42-20
75T-325
75T/M-325
76Ho-10
76Ho/Twink-10
76OPC-35
76SSPC-217
76T-35
77Galasso-257
78TCMA-71
78Twin/Frisz-15
82CJ-7
83MLBPA/Pin-13
85Twin/Team-3CO
85West/2-41
86Sf/Dec-51M
88Pac/Leg-59
89Swell-12
89T-665TBC
92AP/ASG-60
93TWill-50

Oliva, Jose
89Butte/SP-12
90Gaston/Best-21
90Gaston/ProC-2530
90Gaston/Star-17
91CharlR/ClBest-20
91CharlR/ProC-1324
92B-55
92ClBest-289
92Sky/AASingl-272
92Tulsa/ProC-2703
92Tulsa/SB-614
92UD/ML-283
93B-282
93FExcel/ML-235
93LimeR/Winter-146
93LimeR/Winter-25
93Richm/Bleach-16
93Richm/Pep-7
93Richm/Team-23
93UD-426TP
94StCl/Team-48

Oliva, Steve
77QuadC

Olivares, Edward B.
(Ed)
62T-598R

Olivares, Jose
89Myrtle/ProC-1472
90Myrtle/ProC-2776

Olivares, Omar
87CharRain-13
88Charl/ProC-1210
88SALAS/GS-10
89AubAs/ProC-11
89TexLAS/GS-11
89Wichita/Rock-26
89Wichita/Rock/HL-4
89Wichita/Rock/Up-4
90AAASingl/ProC-514
90Louisvl/CMC-20
90Louisvl/LBC-31
90Louisvl/ProC-400
90ProC/Singl-120
90T/TVCard-58
91AAA/LineD-237
91D-503
91F/UltraUp-U108
91Louisvl/LineD-237
91Louisvl/ProC-2912
91Louisvl/Team-3
91OPC-271
91S-748RP
91S/Rook40-5
91T-271
91T/90Debut-118
91UD-463
92B-420
92Classic/Game200-22
92D-481
92F-584
92L-282
92L/BlkGold-282
92OPC-193
92OPC/Premier-38
92Pinn-186
92Pol/Card-12
92ProC/Tomorrow-316
92S-334
92StCl-386
92T-193
92T/Gold-193
92T/GoldWin-193
92UD-478
92Ultra-266
93B-432
93D-388
93F-512
93L-438
93OPC-206
93Pac/Spanish-297
93Pinn-394
93Pol/Card-11
93StCl-489
93StCl/1stDay-489
93StCl/Card-24
93T-490
93T/Gold-490
93UD-194
93Ultra-465
94D-120
94F-638
94Pac/Cr-595
94StCl-425
94StCl/1stDay-425
94StCl/Gold-425
94StCl/Team-302
94T-689
94T/Gold-689

Oliver, Albert
(Al)
69OPC-82R
69Pirate/JITB-7
69T-82R
70MLB/St-105
70OPC-166
70T-166
71MLB/St-210
71OPC-388
71T-388
72T-575
73OPC-225
73T-225
74OPC-52
74T-52
74T/St-85
75Ho-81
75K-15
75OPC-555
75T-555
75T/M-555
76Crane-43
76Ho-112
76MSA/Disc
76OPC-620
76SSPC-576
76T-620
77BurgChef-189
77Ho-45
77Ho/Twink-45
77K-46
77OPC-203
77T-130
77T/CS-34
77T/ClothSt-34
78BK/R-17
78OPC-97
78SSPC/270-108
78T-430
78Wiffle/Discs-55
79Ho-80
79OPC-204
79T-391
79T/Comics-16
80OPC-136
80T-260
80T/Super-35
81D-387
81Drake-24
81F-626
81F/St-64
81K-4
81OPC-70
81Sqt-22
81T-70
81T/HT
81T/SO-4
81T/St-131
81T/St-246
82D-116
82Expo/Hygrade-15
82F-326
82F/St-178
82FBI/Disc-13
82Hygrade
82K-61
82OPC-22IA
82OPC-326
82T-36TL
82T-590
82T-591IA
82T/St-239
82T/Tr-83T
83D-140
83D/AAS-6
83Drake-21
83F-290
83F/St-16M
83F/St-1AM
83F/St-1BM
83F/St-8M
83OPC-111TL
83OPC-311
83OPC-5SV
83OPC/St-174
83OPC/St-205
83OPC/St-206M
83OPC/St-251FOIL
83PermaGr/AS-13
83PermaGr/CC-10
83Stuart-6
83T-111TL
83T-420
83T-421SV
83T-701LL
83T-703LL
83T/Fold-3M
83T/Gloss40-30
83T/LeadS-3
83T/St-174
83T/St-205
83T/St-206M
83T/St-251
84D-177
84D-9DK
84D/Champs-30
84Drake-24
84F-280
84F-632IA
84F/St-27
84F/X-85
84MiltBrad-18
84Nes/792-516TL
84Nes/792-620
84Nes/792-704LL
84OPC-307
84OPC-332TL
84T-516TL
84T-620
84T-704LL
84T/Gloss22-13
84T/Gloss40-21
84T/St-87
84T/St/Box-1
84T/Tr-87
85Coke/Dodg-23
85D-598
85F-262
85F/Up-U84
85Leaf-67
85OPC-130
85T-130
85T/St-118
85T/Tr-88T
86D-485
86F-69
86OPC-114
86Sf-126M
86Sf-135M
86Sf-164
86T-775
86T/St-14ALCS
86Woolwth-26
89Pac/SenLg-142
89T/SenLg-36
89TM/SenLg-83
90EliteSenLg-46
90Target-587
92AP/ASG-68
92Nabisco-21
93Expo/D/McDon-16
93MCI-11
93Rang/Keeb-283
93TWill-79
93TWill/Mem-12
93UD/ATH-102

Oliver, Brent
89KS*-21M
92Lipscomb-20TR
93Lipscomb-24M

Oliver, Bruce
79Cedar/TCMA-11
81Clinton-5

Oliver, Darren
89Gaston/ProC-1021
89Gaston/Star-17
89SALAS/GS-24
90CharlR/Star-17
91CharlR/ClBest-7
91CharlR/ProC-1311
92CharlR/ClBest-19
92UD/ML-308
93Rang/Keeb-418
94B-513
94F/MLP-27
94Pinn-233
94Pinn/Artist-233
94Pinn/Museum-233
94Select-203

Oliver, David Jacob
(Dave)
78T-704R
79T-705R
79Tacom-12
80Tacom-15
81Batavia-27
83TriCit-26
85OKCty-15
86OKCty-15MG
87Smok/R-30
89Smok/R-23
90Mother/Rang-27M
91Mother/Rang-28CO
92Mother/Rang-28M
93Rang/Keeb-439CO

Oliver, Eugene George
(Gene)
59T-135
60T-307
61T-487
62T-561
63F-62
63J-164
63P-164
63T-172
64T-316
65Kahn
65OPC-106
65T-106
66T-541
67CokeCap/Brave-4
67OPC-18
67T-18
68CokeCap/RedSox-9
68T-449
69MB-206
69T-247
81QuadC-31C

Oliver, Harry
82Redwd-19

Oliver, Joe
84Cedar-14
87Vermont-19
88Nashvl/CMC-17
88Nashvl/ProC-483
89Nashvl/CMC-12
89Nashvl/ProC-1283
89Nashvl/Team-17
89S/Tr-104
90B-54
90CedarDG/Best-8
90Classic/III-98
90D-586
90D/BestNL-15
90F-426
90F/Can-426
90HotRook/St-33
90Kahn/Reds-19
90Leaf-453
90OPC-668
90Panini/St-378
90S-576
90S/100Ris-26
90S/YS/I-10
90Sf-71
90T-668
90T/89Debut-91
90T/Big-281
90UD-568
91B-671
91D-381
91F-75
91Kahn/Reds-9
91Leaf-73
91OPC-517
91Panini/FrSt-126
91Pep/Reds-14
91S-620
91StCl-68
91T-517
91UD-279
91Ultra-99
91Woolwth/HL-28
92B-594
92D-261
92F-414
92L-7
92L/BlkGold-7
92OPC-304
92Panini-261
92Pinn-331
92Reds/Kahn-9
92S-370
92StCl-306
92T-304
92T/Gold-304
92T/GoldWin-304
92UD-101
92Ultra-193
93B-6
93Cadaco-43
93D-586
93DennyGS-22
93F-38
93Flair-30
93L-263
93OPC-260
93Pac/Spanish-86
93Panini-290
93Pinn-190
93Reds/Kahn-17
93S-125
93Select-235
93StCl-96
93StCl/1stDay-96
93StCl/MPhoto-5
93Studio-187
93T-138
93T/BlkGold-14
93T/Gold-138
93TripleP-220
93UD-234
93UD/SP-212
93Ultra-32
94B-298
94D-249
94F-418
94L-146
94OPC-189
94Pac/Cr-153
94Panini-166
94Pinn-402
94S-444
94Select-149
94StCl-7
94StCl/1stDay-7
94StCl/Gold-7
94T-485
94T/Finest-37
94T/FinestRef-37
94T/Gold-485
94TripleP-217
94UD-134
94UD/CollC-220
94UD/CollC/Gold-220
94UD/CollC/Silv-220
94UD/ElecD-134
94Ultra-174

Oliver, Nathaniel
(Nate)
63T-466R
65OPC-59
65T-59
66T-364
68OPC-124
68T-124
69T-354
70OPC-223
70T-223
81TCMA-389
88Reno/Cal-291
89MidldA/GS-2
90PalmSp/Cal-228MG
90PalmSp/ProC-2594MG
90Target-588
91PalmSp/ProC-2033MG
92MidldA/OneHour-17CO
92MidldA/ProC-4041CO
92MidldA/SB-475CO
92Yank/WIZ60-95
Oliver, Rick
76Wmsprt
80SLCity-10
Oliver, Robert Lee
(Bob)
69T-662R
69T/St-187
70MLB/St-226
70T-567
71MLB/St-423
71OPC-470
71T-470
71T/Coins-48
71T/tatt-11
72MB-259
72OPC-57
72T-57
73OPC-289
73T-289
74OPC-243
74T-243
74T/St-143
75OPC-657
75SSPC/18-16
75T-657
75T/M-657
76OkCty/Team-21
79QuadC-26
91Crown/Orio-342
92Yank/WIZ70-123
Oliver, Scott
82Danvl/Frit-16
83Redwd-20
85Cram/PCL-5
Oliver, Thomas
54Esskay
54T-207
94T/Arc54-207
R314/Can
V355-119
Oliver, Warren
82FtMyr-5
Oliveras, David
88Burllnd/ProC-1789
89Kinston/Star-16
90Kinston/Team-17
Oliveras, Francisco
81Miami-10
85CharlO-15
87CharlO/WBTV-12
88OrlanTw/Best-24
89D/Rook-9
89Portl/CMC-9
89Portl/ProC-229
90AAASingl/ProC-246
90Leaf-515
90Portl/CMC-8
90Portl/ProC-176
90ProC/Singl-560
90T/89Debut-92
91AAA/LineD-387
91D-469
91OPC-52
91PG&E-24
91Phoenix/LineD-387
91Phoenix/ProC-63
91S-635
91T-52
92D-702
92F-645
92Phoenix/SB-391
92S-295
92StCl-347
92UD-49
93F-534
93Pac/Spanish-276
Oliveras, Herbie
84CharlO-27
Oliveras, Max
75Shrev/TCMA-16
86FSLAS-37CO
87MidldA-15
88MidldA/GS-1MG
89MidldA/GS-1
90AAASingl/ProC-107
90Edmon/CMC-2MG
90Edmon/ProC-531MG
90ProC/Singl-502MG
91AAA/LineD-174MG
91AAAGame/ProC-14
91Edmon/LineD-174
91Edmon/ProC-1531
92Edmon/ProC-3553MG
92Edmon/SB-174MG
93Vanco/ProC-2613MG
Oliveras, Ossie
77Salem
78Colum
79Portl-2
Oliverio, Steve
85Cedar-10
86Vermont-14
87Vermont-14
88Nashvl/CMC-9
88Nashvl/ProC-482
88Nashvl/Team-18
89Calgary/CMC-4
89Calgary/ProC-543
89ColMud/Best-24
Olivo
92Kane/Team-25
Olivo, Frederico
(Chi-Chi)
66T-578
81TCMA-349M
Olivo, Mike
70OPC-381R
70T-381R
Olker, Joe
84Everett/Cram-4
86Fresno/Smok-12
88Shrev/ProC-1282
88TexLgAS/GS-8
89Phoenix/CMC-8
89Phoenix/ProC-1497
91Reno/Cal-25
Ollar, Rick
78Clinton
Oller, Jeff
86James-18
87BurlEx-8
88WPalmB/Star-20
90CharlR/Star-18
Ollison, Ron
92Clearw/ProC-2064
Ollison, Scott
91BendB/ClBest-20
91BendB/ProC-3702
Ollom, James
67OPC-137R
67T-137R
68OPC-91
68T-91
81TCMA-378
Ollom, Mike
84AZ/Pol-15
87Penin-9
88Tampa/Star-19
89BirmB/Best-2
89BirmB/ProC-95
Olmeda, Jose
89Idaho/ProC-2015
90Foil/Best-183
90Sumter/Best-16
90Sumter/ProC-2444
91Macon/ProC-874
91SALAS/ProC-SAL35
92ClBest-95
92Durham/Team-13
92Greenvl/ProC-1162
Olmi, Pat
92MissSt-49M
Olmo, Luis
90Target-589
Olmstead, Fred
T205
Olmstead, Reed
87Erie-4
87Savan-17
88Savan/ProC-346
89Spartan/ProC-1048
89Spartan/Star-19
90Foil/Best-257
90OrlanSR/Best-7
90OrlanSR/ProC-1092
90OrlanSR/Star-14
90ProC/Singl-754
90Star/ISingl-46
91AA/LineD-490
91OrlanSR/LineD-490
91OrlanSR/ProC-1860
Olmsted, Alan
80ArkTr-11
81Hawaii/TCMA-13
81T-244R
82Louisvl-21
Olsen, Al
86Ventura-18TR
87MidldA-9
88Edmon/ProC-584TR
89PalmSp/Cal-61TR
89PalmSp/ProC-480
Olsen, John
52Laval-113
Olsen, Lefty
52Mother-23
Olsen, Lew
77Jaxvl
Olsen, Rick
78Newar
79Holyo-9
80Vanco-22
81Vanco-13
82Vanco-15
Olsen, Steve
92Saraso/ClBest-21
92Saraso/ProC-202
92UD/ML-208
93B-691
93ClBest/MLG-77
93FExcel/ML-153
Olson, Dan
89Boise/ProC-1995
Olson, Dean
77Visalia
Olson, Greg
83Lynch-8
84Jacks-xx
86Jacks/TCMA-12
87Tidew-19
87Tidew/TCMA-11
88Tidew/CANDL-6
88Tidew/CMC-13
88Tidew/ProC-1597
89Portl/CMC-13
89Portl/ProC-225
90Brave/Dubuq/Perf-22
90Brave/Dubuq/Singl-25
90Classic/III-19
90D/BestNL-25
90D/Rook-46
90F/Up-U5
90Leaf-323
90RedFoley/St-70
90S/Tr-69T
90T/Big-241
90T/Tr-84T
90USPlayC/AS-2D
91B-577
91Brave/Dubuq/Perf-21
91Brave/Dubuq/Stand-28
91D-285
91F-698
91Leaf-158
91OPC-673
91Panini/FrSt-18
91Panini/St-25
91Petro/SU-2
91S-56
91S/100RisSt-15
91StCl-288
91T-673
91UD-303
91Ultra-9
92Brave/LykePerf-21
92Brave/LykeStand-24
92D-386
92F-365
92L-226
92L/BlkGold-226
92OPC-39
92Panini-161
92Pinn-149
92S-474
92StCl-675
92StCl/Dome-134
92Studio-7
92T-39
92T/Gold-39
92T/GoldWin-39
92TripleP-54
92UD-189
92USPlayC/Brave-13D
92USPlayC/Brave-9S
92Ultra-166
93Brave/FLAg-7
93Brave/LykePerf-22
93Brave/LykeStand-27
93D-530
93F-11
93L-357
93OPC-296
93Pac/Spanish-338
93Panini-180
93Pinn-173
93S-209
93Select-233
93Select-46
93StCl-450
93StCl/1stDay-450
93StCl/Brave-7
93T-708
93T/Gold-708
93UD-187
93Ultra-10
94D-382
94F-370
94S-442
94T-346
94T/Gold-346
94UD/CollC-221
94UD/CollC/Gold-221
94UD/CollC/Silv-221
Olson, Gregg
87PanAm/USAB-12
87PanAm/USAR-12
89B-6
89Classic-132
89D-46RR
89D/Best-322
89D/Rook-35
89French-30
89S/Tr-96
89T-161FDP
89T/Tr-89T
89UD/Ext-723
90B-249
90B/Ins-7
90Bz-11
90Classic-3
90CollAB-32
90D-377
90D/BestAL-43
90D/Learning-27
90F-184
90F/AwardWin-24
90F/Can-184
90F/LL-28
90HagersDG/Best-19
90Holsum/Discs-20
90HotRook/St-34
90KingB/Discs-23
90Leaf-7
90MLBPA/Pins-114
90OPC-655
90Panini/St-2
90Publlnt/St-581
90S-63
90S/100Ris-32
90S/YS/I-4
90Sf-215
90T-655
90T/89Debut-93
90T/Coins-3
90T/DH-48
90T/Gloss60-29
90T/HeadsUp-10
90T/JumboR-22
90T/St-10HL
90T/St-238
90T/TVAS-30
90TeamUSA/87-12
90ToysRUs-21
90UD-604
90USPlayC/AS-4C
90Woolwth/HL-5ROY
91B-92
91BBBest/Aces-13
91Classic/III-70
91Crown/Orio-343
91D-111
91D-23DK
91D-393MVP
91D/SuperDK-23
91F-486
91Leaf-519
91Leaf/Stud-8
91OPC-10
91OPC/Premier-93
91Panini/FrSt-248
91Panini/St-193
91Panini/Top15-88
91RedFoley/St-69
91S-490
91S/100SS-27
91Seven/3DCoin-10A
91StCl-156
91StCl/Member*-10M
91T-10
91T/CJMini/II-22
91UD-326
91UD-47
91Ultra-21
92B-577
92B-629FOIL
92B-677
92CJ/DII-25
92D-110
92F-21
92F-701M
92L-277
92L/BlkGold-277
92OPC-350
92OPC/Premier-101
92Panini-72
92Pinn-61
92Pinn/Team2000-13
92S-427NH
92S-71
92S/100SS-91
92S/Impact-87
92StCl-293
92Studio-128
92T-350
92T/Gold-350
92T/GoldWin-350
92T/Kids-66
92TripleP-13
92UD-227
92UD/TmMVPHolo-38
92Ultra-307
93B-465
93D-117
93F-173
93Flair-155
93L-23
93MSA/Ben-17
93OPC-281
93Pac/Spanish-22
93Pinn-97
93S-80
93StCl-418
93StCl/1stDay-418
93T-246
93T/Finest-121
93T/FinestRef-121
93T/Gold-246
93TripleP-135
93UD-674
93UD/SP-161
93Ultra-145
94B-461
94D-8
94D/Special-8
94F-13
94Finest-246
94Pac/Cr-40
94Pinn-277
94S-525
94StCl-196
94StCl/1stDay-196
94StCl/Gold-196
94T-723
94T/Gold-723
94UD-393

Olson, Ivan M.
(Ollie)
21Exh-120
90Target-590
E120
E220
T207
V100
W514-70
Olson, James Vincent
87BurlEx-2
Olson, Jimmy
86AubAs-18
87Ashvl-9
Olson, Karl Arthur
(Karl)
52T-72
54T-186
55T-72
55T/DH-35
56T-322
57T-153
94T/Arc54-186
Olson, Ken
91Salinas/ProC-2240
Olson, Kurt
88CapeCod/Sum-47
90Yakima/Team-6
Olson, Mike
81CharR-4
Olson, Terry
75Anderson/TCMA-17
Olson, Warren
86Beloit-18
88WinHaven/Star-17
Olsson, Dan
86Tulsa-19
Olszta, Ed
75AppFx
77AppFx
Olwine, Ed
83Nashvl-13
84Tidew-11
85Tidew-12
86Richm-14
87D-560
87F-524
87Richm/Bob-16
87Smok/Atl-6
87T-159
88S-379
88T-353
89Omaha/CMC-8
89Omaha/ProC-1725
89UD-435
90AAASingl/ProC-402
90ProC/Singl-282
90Richm/Bob-1
90Richm/CMC-6
90Richm/ProC-257
90Richm/Team-25
Omachi, George
88Fresno/ProC-1246
Omo, Bob
78Cedar
Ongarato, Mike
81Pawtu-21
Onge, Paul S.
74Wichita-128TR
Onichuk, Sergei
89EastLDD/ProC-DD11
Onis, Curly
90Target-1045
Onslow, Eddie
82Ohio/HOF-28
Ontiveros, Steve
83Albany-7
84Cram/PCL-83
86D-589
86F-429
86Mother/A's-22
86Seven/Coin-W16M
86T-507
87D-221
87D/HL-15
87F-401
87T-161
88D-467
88D/A's/Bk-467
88F-289
88Mother/A's-13
88S-511
88T-272
89D-596
89D/Tr-11
89Phill/TastyK-26
89S-337
89T-692
89T/Tr-90T
90AlbanyDG/Best-7
90B-145
91S-832
Ontiveros, Steven Robert
(Steve)
74OPC-598R
74T-598R
75OPC-483
75T-483
75T/M-483
76OPC-284
76SSPC-104
76T-284
78K-44
78SSPC/270-250
78T-76
79OPC-150
79T-299
80OPC-268
80T-514
89T/SenLg-79
90EliteSenLg-117
Opdyke, Paul
88Idaho/ProC-1854
Opie, James
83AlexD-6
85Cram/PCL-226
86Nashua-20
87Jaxvl-13
Oppenheimer, Jose
77BurlB
Oppenheimer, Juan
78Cedar
79Cedar/TCMA-26
Opperman, Dan
88GreatF-10
89VeroB/Star-20
90SanAn/GS-19
91Albuq/ProC-1140
91B-606
91Classic/II-T83
91Ultra-384MLP
92Albuq/ProC-720
Oquendo, Ismael
84RochR-8
Oquendo, Jorge
82Idaho-27
Oquendo, Jose Manuel
(Jose)
82Tidew-15
83Tidew-29
84D-643
84F-592
84Nes/792-208
84OPC-208
84T-208
84T/St-112
85F-88
85Louisvl-15
85T-598
86Schnucks-17
86T/Tr-82T
87D-510
87F-305
87Smok/Cards-18
87T-133
88D-234
88D/Best-313
88F-44
88S-248
88Smok/Card-16
88T-83
88T/St-18
89B-438
89Bimbo/Discs-5
89D-319
89D/Best-100
89F-459
89MSA/Disc-19
89OPC-69
89Panini/St-184
89S-529
89S/YS/II-16
89Smok/Cards-15
89T-442
89T/Big-77
89T/St-45
89Tetley/Discs-19
89UD-514
90B-200
90D-161
90D/BestNL-108
90F-255
90F/Can-255
90Kenner/Fig-63
90Leaf-129
90MLBPA/Pins-59
90OPC-645
90Panini/St-341
90PublInt/St-223
90S-68
90Sf-85
90Smok/Card-17
90T-645
90T/Big-65
90T/St-44
90T/TVCard-27
90UD-319
91B-395
91D-281
91F-640
91Leaf-58
91Leaf/Stud-236
91OPC-343
91Panini/FrSt-32
91Panini/St-30
91Pol/Card-11
91S-622
91StCl-190
91T-343
91UD-193
91Ultra-292
91WIZMets-301
92D-280
92F-585
92L-289
92L/BlkGold-289
92OPC-723
92Panini-173
92Pinn-239
92Pol/Card-13
92S-305
92StCl-571
92T-723
92T/Gold-723
92T/GoldWin-723
92TripleP-118
92UD-283
92Ultra-267
93D-46
93F-513
93L-26
93Pac/Beisbol-28
93Pac/Spanish-298
93Pac/SpanishGold-7
93Pinn-316
93Pol/Card-12
93S-163
93StCl/Card-4
93T-535
93T/Gold-535
93TripleP-228
93UD-84
94F-639
94Pac/Cr-596
94StCl/Team-313
94T-406
94T/Gold-406
94Ultra-268
Oquist, Mike
89Erie/Star-16
90CLAS/CL-2
90Freder/Team-22
91AA/LineD-241
91ClBest/Singl-188
91Hagers/LineD-241
91Hagers/ProC-2455
92RochR/ProC-1938
92RochR/SB-461
92Sky/AAASingl-210
93B-74
94Pinn-224
94Pinn/Artist-224
94Pinn/Museum-224
94StCl/Team-276
94T-763M
94T/Gold-763M
Oravetz, Ernest E.
(Ernie)
56T-51
57T-179
89Chatt/II/Team-23
Ordway, Jeff
90Spokane/SportP-2
Orengo, Joseph C.
(Joe)
41DP-29
47Sunbeam
90Target-592
Orensky, Herb
80Penin/B-23
80Penin/C-15
82OkCty-20
Orhan, Hugh
47Sunbeam
Orie, Kevin
93Peoria/Team-19
94B-166
94T-762DP
94T/Gold-762DP
Orman, Richard
90MedHat/Best-7
Ormsby, Red
94Conlon-1207UMP
Oropeza, Clemente
82Idaho-20
Oropeza, Dave
89Rockford/Team-19
Orosco, Jesse
79Tidew-23
80T-681R
81Tidew-20
82D-646
83D-434
83F-550
83T-369
84D-197
84F-593
84F/St-60
84Jacks/Smok-9
84Nes/792-396AS
84Nes/792-54
84OPC-396AS
84OPC-54
84T-396AS
84T-54
84T/Gloss40-33
84T/Mets/Fan-5
84T/RD-15M
84T/St-104
85D-22DK
85D-75
85D/DKsuper-22
85F-89
85F/St-106
85Leaf-22DK
85OPC-250
85T-250
85T/Gloss40-2
85T/RD-13M
85T/St-101
85T/Super-54
85ThomMc/Discs-37
86D-646
86F-90
86OPC-182
86T-465
86T/Tatt-5M
87Classic-75
87D-439
87F-20
87F/Mini-78
87F/RecSet-27
87F/St-87
87Leaf-175
87OPC-148
87RedFoley/St-84
87Sf-76
87T-704
88D-192
88D/Best-234
88F-148
88F/Up-U96
88Mother/Dodg-13
88Pol/Dodg-47
88S-495
88S/Tr-64T
88Sf-89
88T-105
88T/Tr-77T
89B-81
89D-228
89D/Tr-26
89F-68
89S-356
89T-513
89T/Tr-91T
89UD-87
90D-154
90F-500
90F/Can-500
90Leaf-101
90OPC-636
90PublInt/St-566
90S-353
90T-636
90Target-593
90UD-588
91B-72
91D-171
91F-375
91Indian/McDon-23
91OPC-346
91S-578
91StCl-322
91T-346
91UD-240
91WIZMets-302
92D-473
92F-121
92L-524
92L/BlkGold-524
92OPC-79
92Pol/Brew-18
92S-547
92T-79
92T/Gold-79
92T/GoldWin-79
92UD-580
93F-632
93Pac/Beisbol-10M
93Pac/Spanish-163
93Pol/Brew-20
93StCl-37
93StCl/1stDay-37
93T-289
93T/Gold-289
93Ultra-223
94F-188
94Pac/Cr-340
94Pinn-473
94Pol/Brew-21
94S-299
94S/GoldR-299
94T-492
94T/Gold-492
Oroz, Felix Andres
81VeroB-13
83LasVegas/BHN-16
84Cram/PCL-233
Orphal, John
47Centen-18
Orr, David L.
N172
N172/SP
N284
N338/2
N690
Orr, Geoff
90Idaho/ProC-3252
91Macon/ClBest-22
91Macon/ProC-875
Orr, Jimmy
52Laval-42
Orr, Johnny
89TNTech-20
Orr, William
T222
Orsag, Jim
86Greens-15
87WinHaven-28
88CLAS/Star-13
88Lynch/Star-16
89NewBrit/ProC-610
89NewBrit/Star-12
89Star/IISingl-128
90Canton/Best-9
90Foil/Best-269
Orsatti, Ernesto R.
(Ernie)
33G-201
35G-1A
35G-2A
35G-6A
35G-7A
92Conlon/Sport-650
V94-37
Orsino, John Joseph
(Johnny)

61Union
62T-377
63T-418
64T-63
64T/Coins-3
65T-303
65T/E-51
66OPC-77
66T-77
66T/RO-09
66T/RO-73
67T-207
81TCMA-375
91Crown/Orio-344
Orsulak, Joe
82AlexD-22
85F/Up-U85
85T/Tr-89T
86D-444
86F-615
86F/LL-29
86F/Mini-118
86F/St-83
86Leaf-218
86Sf-177M
86T-102
86T/St-132
87D-291
87F-615
87F/RecSet-28
87Sf/TPrev-18M
87T-414
87T/St-132
88D/Best-310
88F/Up-U2
88French-6
88S/Tr-41T
88T/Tr-78T
89D-287
89D/Best-310
89F-614
89French-6
89Panini/St-263
89S-247
89T-727
89T/Big-181
89UD-429
90B-252
90Classic/III-50
90D-287
90D/BestAL-129
90F-185
90F/Can-185
90Leaf-355
90OPC-212
90Panini/St-5
90Publint/St-582
90S-41
90Sf-38
90T-212
90T/Big-318
90T/St-234
90UD-270
91B-84
91Crown/Orio-345
91D-654
91F-487
91Leaf-152
91OPC-521
91Panini/FrSt-246
91Panini/St-200
91RedFoley/St-70
91S-508
91S/100SS-8
91StCl-191
91T-521
91UD-506
91Ultra-22
92B-432
92D-475
92F-22
92L-36
92L/BlkGold-36
92OPC-325
92Panini-71
92Pinn-362
92S-551
92StCl-135
92T-325
92T/Gold-325
92T/GoldWin-325
92UD-207
93D-751
93F-549
93F/Final-104
93Flair-95
93L-337
93Mets/Kahn-6
93OPC-303
93OPC/Premier-55
93Pac/Spanish-23
93Panini-77
93Pinn-501
93S-590
93Select-234
93Select/RookTr-131T
93StCl-92
93StCl/1stDay-92
93T-28
93T/Gold-28
93UD-260
93UD-712
93Ultra-432
94B-72
94D-270
94F-575
94L-124
94Pac/Cr-415
94Pinn-92
94Pinn/Artist-92
94Pinn/Museum-92
94S-398
94Select-94
94StCl-384
94StCl/1stDay-384
94StCl/Gold-384
94T-643
94T/Finest-45
94T/FinestRef-45
94T/Gold-643
94TripleP-147
94Ultra-240
Orta, Jorge Nunez
(Jorge)
73OPC-194
73T-194
74OPC-376
74T-376
74T/St-159
75Ho-122
75Ho/Twink-122
75K-14
75OPC-184
75T-184
75T/M-184
76Ho-57
76Ho/Twink-57
76K-45
76OPC-560
76SSPC-144
76T-560
77BurgChef-74
77T-109
78Ho-105
78OPC-77
78SSPC/270-142
78T-42
78Wiffle/Discs-56
79Ho-126
79OPC-333
79T-631
80T-442
81D-439
81F-388
81OPC-222
81T-222
82D-211
82F-376
82OPC-26
82Pol/Dodg-31
82T-26
82T/St-175
82T/Tr-84T
83D-388
83F-215
83T-722
83T/Tr-82T
84D-317
84F-166
84F/X-U86
84Nes/792-312
84OPC-312
84T-312
84T/Tr-88T
85D-130
85F-209
85Leaf-226
85T-164
85T/St-273
86D-339
86F-17
86Kitty/Disc-6
86Leaf-205
86NatPhoto-3
86OPC-44
86T-541
87D-348
87F-376
87OPC-63
87T-738
90Target-595
Ortega, Dan
81AppFx-7
Ortega, Eduardo
89Batavia/ProC-1939
90Spartan/Best-17
90Spartan/ProC-2499
90Spartan/Star-16
91SLCity/ProC-3219
91SLCity/SportP-18
Ortega, Hector
90Gate/ProC-3341
91Sumter/ClBest-17
91Sumter/ProC-2342
92Rockford/ClBest-16
92Rockford/ProC-2126
Ortega, Kirk
81Clinton-16
Ortega, Phil
59DF
62T-69
63T-467
64T-291
65OPC-152
65T-152
66T-416
66T/RO-32
66T/RO-74
67CokeCap/Senator-16
67T-493
68T-595
69MB-207
69T-406
81TCMA-390
90Target-596
Ortega, Roberto
92Bristol/ClBest-19
92Bristol/ProC-1420
Ortegon, Ronnie
89PalmSp/Cal-35
89PalmSp/ProC-478
90QuadC/GS-22
Orteig, Ray
48Sommer-25
52Mother-50
53Mother-31
Ortenzio, Frank
75Omaha/Team-12
Orth, Albert Lewis
(Al)
94Conlon-1192UMP
E107
E254
T206
Ortiz, Adalberto Jr.
(Junior)
77Charl
78Charl
79Ashvl/TCMA-14
80Buffa
81Portl-19
82Portl-11
84D-319
84F-594
84Nes/792-161
84T-161
84T/St-114
85T-439
85ThomMc/Discs-38
86D-508
86T-682
87D-449
87D/OD-164
87F-616
87T-583
88D-168
88F-335
88S-404
88T-274
89AAA/ProC-46
89D-387
89D/Best-269
89F-215
89S-402
89T-769
89T/Big-66
89UD-86
89VFJuice-0
90F-475
90F/Can-475
90F/Up-108
90OPC-322
90Publint/St-160
90S-143
90S/Tr-66T
90T-322
90T/Tr-85T
90UD-389
91B-328
91D-659
91F-622
91Leaf-498
91OPC-72
91S-438
91StCl-13
91T-72
91UD-170
91Ultra-194
91WIZMets-303
92D-684
92F-215
92Indian/McDon-21
92OPC-617
92S-473
92StCl-727
92T-617
92T/Gold-617
92T/GoldWin-617
92T/Tr-84T
92T/TrGold-84T
92UD-109
92USPlayC/Twin-2H
92USPlayC/Twin-4C
92Ultra-353
93D-699
93F-598
93Indian/WUAB-24
93Pac/Beisbol-6M
93Pac/Spanish-416
93T-199
93T/Gold-199
93UD-603
93Ultra-544
93Ultra-650M
94D-425
94F-117
94Pac/Cr-181
94S-262
94S/GoldR-262
94StCl-15
94StCl/1stDay-15
94StCl/Gold-15
94StCl/Pr-15
94StCl/PreProd-15
94T-423
94T/Gold-423
Ortiz, Alfredo
86Ventura-19CO
89Johnson/Star-25CO
Ortiz, Andy
83Watlo/Frit-5
84BuffB-15
Ortiz, Angel
88Watlo/ProC-667
89Kinston/Star-17
92Clinton/ClBest-3
92Clinton/ProC-3596
Ortiz, Basilio
91Bluefld/ClBest-9
91Bluefld/ProC-4140
92Freder/ClBest-16
92Freder/ProC-1820
Ortiz, Darrell
80Tulsa-23
Ortiz, Hector Jr.
89Salem/Team-20
89VeroB/Star-21
90Yakima/Team-11
91VeroB/ClBest-16
91VeroB/ProC-777
92AS/Cal-44
92Bakers/Cal-18
Ortiz, Javier
84Tulsa-31
85Tulsa-31
86Tulsa-17
87OKCty-15
88SanAn/Best-22
89Albuq/CMC-25
89Albuq/ProC-84
90AAASingl/ProC-207
90F/Up-U16
90ProC/Singl-617
90Tucson/CMC-15
90Tucson/ProC-217
91AAA/LineD-617
91B-562
91D-643
91T/90Debut-119
91Tucson/LineD-617
91Tucson/ProC-2226
92D-551
92OPC-362
92S-403
92T-362
92T/Gold-362
92T/GoldWin-362
92UD-657
Ortiz, Joe
88Ashvl/ProC-1066
88CalLgAS-22
88Reno/Cal-285
89Beloit/I/Star-20
89Osceola/Star-15
90ColMud/Star-18
90Modesto/Cal-158
90Modesto/ProC-2216
Ortiz, Jorge
81Wisco-7
Ortiz, Jose
73Wichita-11
Ortiz, Lou
55T-114
55T/DH-91
D301
Ortiz, Luis
92B-306
92LynchRS/ClBest-11
92LynchRS/ProC-2916
92UD/ML-114
93B-523
93FExcel/ML-135
93LimeR/Winter-144
93LimeR/Winter-35
93Pawtu/Ball-18
94B-119
94F/MLP-28
94Pinn-243
94Pinn/Artist-243
94Pinn/Museum-243
94Pinn/RookTPinn-4
94S-602
94T-369
94T/Gold-369
94UD-109
94UD/CollC-15
94UD/CollC/Gold-15
94UD/CollC/Silv-15
94UD/ElecD-109
Ortiz, Miguel
80Utica-21
Ortiz, Ramon 1
89Burllnd/Star-19
90Burllnd/ProC-3022
Ortiz, Ramon 2
92Savan/ClBest-24CO
92Savan/ProC-680CO
Ortiz, Ray
90A&AASingle/ProC-153
90ProC/Singl-864
90Visalia/Cal-70
90Visalia/ProC-2169
91AA/LineD-491
91OrlanSR/LineD-491
91OrlanSR/ProC-1863
92OrlanSR/ProC-2861
92OrlanSR/SB-515
Ortman, Doug
87Madis-9
Orton, John
85Anchora-23
87Salem/ProC-2417
88PalmSp/Cal-107
88PalmSp/ProC-1433
89MidldA/GS-25
90B-298
90Classic/III-61
90D/Rook-54
90F-647
90F/Can-647

90F/Up-U79
90Leaf-511
90S-582
90S/100Ris-64
90S/YS/II-30
90Sf-132
90T/89Debut-94
90UD-672
91D-714
91F-320
91Leaf-191
91OPC-176
91S-467
91Smok/Angel-20
91StCl-591
91T-176
92Edmon/SB-155
92F-65
92OPC-398
92S-712
92StCl-263
93D-431
93F-195
93L-385
93Mother/Angel-10
93Pac/Spanish-371
93Pinn-197
93Pol/Angel-16
93S-453
93StCl-459
93StCl/1stDay-459
93StCl/Angel-17
93TripleP-131
93UD-317
93Ultra-167

Oruna, Roland
82CharR-17
83CharR-11

Osaka, Rocky
87SanJose-7

Osborn, Bob
93Conlon-947

Osborn, Dan
76OPC-282
76SSPC-135
76T-282

Osborn, Don
47Signal
74OPC-489CO
74T-489CO

Osborn, Pat
75Sacra/Caruso-21

Osborn, Wilfred
E254

Osborne, Donovan
90Classic/DP-13
90Hamil/Best-1
91AA/LineD-40
91ArkTr/LineD-40
91ArkTr/ProC-1283
91B-410
91ClBest/Singl-27
91S-677FDP
92B-96
92Classic/II-T94
92D/Rook-88
92F/Up-120
92JDean/Rook-7
92L/GRook-19
92Pinn-541
92Pinn/Rook-20
92ProC/Tomorrow-317
92S/RookTr-90T
92Studio-95
92T/Tr-85T
92T/TrGold-85T
92UD-702M
92UD-770DD CL CL
92UD-777DD
92UD/Scout-SR19
92Ultra-570
92Ultra/AllRook-10
93B-376
93Classic/GameI-72
93D-178
93F-129
93F/RookSenI-10
93Flair-123
93L-62
93OPC-248
93Pac/Spanish-634
93Panini-199
93Pinn-370
93Pol/Card-13
93S-349
93Select-276
93Select/ChasRook-7
93StCl-586
93StCl/1stDay-586
93StCl/Card-16
93T-662
93T/Gold-662
93ToysRUs-41
93UD-347
93USPlayC/Rook-11H
93Ultra-109
94D-149
94F-640
94Pac/Cr-597
94Pinn-209
94Pinn/Artist-209
94Pinn/Museum-209
94S-63
94S/GoldR-63
94StCl/Team-304
94T-501
94T/Gold-501
94UD/CollC-222
94UD/CollC/Gold-222
94UD/CollC/Silv-222
94Ultra-269

Osborne, Jeff
89Augusta/ProC-494
89SALAS/GS-46
90Harris/ProC-1200
90Harris/Star-13
90ProC/Singl-786

Osborne, Lawrence S.
(Bobo)
59T-524
60T-201
61T-208
62T-583
63T-514
81TCMA-463

Osborne, Tiny
90Target-1046

Osentowski, Jared
92Kingspt/ClBest-3
92StCl/Dome-136

Osentowski, Ozzie
92Kingspt/ProC-1541

Osik, Keith
90LSUPol-5
91Salem/ClBest-2
91Salem/ProC-956
92CaroMud/ProC-1184
92CaroMud/SB-138
93CaroMud/RBI-2

Osinski, Dan
63T-114
64T-537
65OPC-223
65T-223
66OPC-168
66T-168
67T-594
68T-331
69T-622

Osinski, Glenn
90Madison/Best-8
90SoOreg/Best-28
91Modesto/ClBest-10
91Modesto/ProC-3098

Osmon, Scott
89Idaho/ProC-2032

Osofsky, Aaron
52Laval-86

Osofsky, Alvin
75Dubuq

Osowski, Tom
83Butte-33
84Butte-6
85Everett/Cram-12
86PalmS/Smk-1GM

Osteen, Claude
59T-224
60T-206
62T-501
63J-100
63P-100
63T-374
64T-28
64T/Coins-13
64T/SU
64T/St-74
64T/tatt
65MacGregor-8
65T-570
66T-270
67CokeCap/AS-16
67CokeCap/DodgAngel-15
67CokeCap/NLAS-22
67T-330
68OPC-9LL
68T-440
68T-9LL
68T/ActionSt-16CM
68T/ActionSt-1CM
68T/G-12
69MB-208
69MLB/St-150
69T-528
69T/St-47
70MLB/St-54
70OPC-260
70T-260
70T/S-1
70T/SO
70T/Super-1
71Bz
71Bz/Test-39
71K-70
71MD
71MLB/St-110
71OPC-10
71T-10
71T/Coins-45
71T/S-27
71T/Super-27
71Ticket/Dodg-12
72K-34
72MB-260
72OPC-297
72OPC-298IA
72T-297
72T-298IA
73K-49
73OPC-490
73T-490
74OPC-42
74T-42
74T/DE-38
74T/St-48
74T/Tr-42T
75OPC-453
75T-453
75T/M-453
76OPC-488
76T-488
78TCMA-273
84Phill/TastyK-12CO
85Phill/TastyK-5CO
85Phill/TastyK-8CO
86Phill/TastyK-3CO
87Phill/TastyK-x
87Smok/Dodg-25
88Phill/TastyK-29
89Pac/Leg-132
89SanAn/Best-26
89Smok/Dodg-73
89Swell-17
90AAASingl/ProC-83CO
90Albuq/CMC-28CO
90Albuq/ProC-363CO
90Albuq/Trib-25CO
90ProC/Singl-658CO
90Target-597
91AAA/LineD-25M
91Albuq/LineD-25CO
91Albuq/ProC-1159CO
92Albuq/ProC-740
92Albuq/SB-25M
93Rang/Keeb-440CO

Osteen, Dave
87StPete-1
88ArkTr/GS-23
89ArkTr/GS-15
89TexLAS/GS-23
90AAASingl/ProC-515
90ArkTr/GS-22
90Louisvl/CMC-7
90Louisvl/LBC-32
90Louisvl/ProC-401
90ProC/Singl-107
90TexLgAS/GS-34
91AAA/LineD-242
91Louisvl/LineD-242
91Louisvl/ProC-2913

Osteen, Gavin
89Medford/Best-29
90Madison/Best-21
90Madison/ProC-2268
90ProC/Singl-692
91AA/LineD-290
91Huntsvl/ClBest-16
91Huntsvl/LineD-290
91Huntsvl/Team-15
91HuntsvlProC-1792
92Huntsvl/ProC-3947
92Sky/AAASingl-242
92Tacoma/SB-542

Osteen, M. Darrell
66T-424R
67T-222R
68T-199R

Oster, Dave
88Geneva/ProC-1659

Oster, Mike
92MN-21

Oster, Paul
88OK-18
89OK-21
89Oneonta/ProC-2127
90PrWill/Team-18
91PrWill/ClBest-21
91PrWill/ProC-1439

Ostermeyer, Bill
90Spokane/SportP-6
91CharRain/ProC-105
91ClBest/Singl-196
91SALAS/ProC-SAL5
92CharRain/ProC-130
92HighD/ClBest-19

Ostermueller, Fred
(Fritz)
34DS-73
34G-93
35G-8G
35G-9G
39PlayBall-22
40PlayBall-33
41G-12
47TipTop
49B-227
90Target-598
91Conlon/Sport-99
R314
W753

Ostopowicz, Rich
89Kingspt/Star-18

Ostrosser, Brian L.
(Brian)
75OkCty/Team-14
91WIZMets-304

Ostrowski, Joe P.
49Royal-20
52BR
52Mother-2
52T-206

Ostrowski, John T.
(John)
47Signal

Osuna, Al
87AubAs-22
88Osceola/Star-20
89Osceola/Star-16
90A&AASingle/ProC-43
90ColMud/Best-19
90ColMud/ProC-1344
90ColMud/Star-19
90Foil/Best-312
91D/Rook-52
91Leaf-492
91Mother/Ast-20
91OPC-149
91S/RookTr-89T
91T-149
91T/90Debut-120
91UD/Ext-752
92B-639
92D-318
92F-442
92L-209
92L/BlkGold-209
92Mother/Ast-20
92OPC-614
92OPC/Premier-121
92Pinn-347
92S-452
92S/100RisSt-83
92StCl-68
92T-614
92T/Gold-614
92T/GoldWin-614
92UD-259
92Ultra-207
93D-216
93F-440
93S-475
93StCl-236
93StCl/1stDay-236
93StCl/Ast-11
93T-63
93T/Gold-63
93Ultra-45
94D-541
94F-497
94Pac/Cr-271
94StCl-293
94StCl/1stDay-293
94StCl/Gold-293
94T-277
94T/Gold-277

Osuna, Antonio
91Kissim/ProC-4181
94B-678

Osuna, Pedro
92ProC/Tomorrow-252

Oswald, Steve
86BirmB/Team-1

Otanez, Willis
91GreatF/SportP-14
92ClBest-356
92UD/ML-102
92VeroB/ClBest-8
92VeroB/ProC-2887
93LimeR/Winter-76

Otero, Regino J.
(Reggie)
47Signal
60T-459C
63FrBauer-15

Otero, Ricky
91Kingspt/ClBest-8
91Kingspt/ProC-3826
92ColumMet/ClBest-12
92ColumMet/ProC-309
92ColumMet/SAL/II-24
92ColumMet/SAL/II-31M
92ProC/Tomorrow-288
92UD/ML-236
93ClBest/MLG-158
93FExcel/ML-77
93SALAS/II-29
93SALAS/IICS-9

Otey, William
T206

Otis, Amos Joseph
(Amos)
69OPC-31R
69T-31R
70OPC-354
70T-354
71Bz
71Bz/Test-42
71K-38
71MLB/St-424
71OPC-610
71T-610
71T/Coins-96
71T/S-45
71T/Super-45
71T/tatt-4
72K-2
72OPC-10
72T-10
72T/Post-6
73K-1
73OPC-510
73T-510
73T/Lids-37
74Greyhound-5M
74K-17
74OPC-337AS
74OPC-65
74T-337AS
74T-65
74T/DE-1
74T/St-185
75Ho-50
75OPC-520
75SSPC/42-22
75T-520
75T/M-520
76A&P/KC

76Ho-51
76Ho/Twink-51
76OPC-198LL
76OPC-510
76SSPC-177
76T-198LL
76T-510
77BurgChef-65
77Ho-92
77Ho/Twink-92
77OPC-141
77Pep-33
77T-290
78OPC-16
78SSPC/270-227
78T-490
79Ho-132
79OPC-185
79T-360
80OPC-72
80T-135
80T/S-50
80T/Super-50
81Coke
81D-104
81F-32
81F-483
81F/St-28
81OPC-288
81Pol/Royals-7
81T-585
82D-70
82F-419
82F/St-211
82OPC-162
82OPC-350IA
82T-725
82T-726IA
82T/St-194
83D-364
83F-120
83F/St-10M
83F/St-12M
83OPC-75
83OPC/St-72
83Pol/Royals-5
83T-75
83T/Fold-5M
83T/St-72
84F-351
84F/X-U87
84Nes/792-655
84OPC-53
84T-655
84T/Tr-89T
88Smok/Padres-21
89Pac/SenLg-83
89T/SenLg-81
89TM/SenLg-84
89Tidew/Candl-4
90EliteSenLg-74
90Padre/MagUno-22CO
91Pac/SenLg-26
91WIZMets-305
94TedW-38

Ott, Melvin Thomas
(Mel)
29Exh/4-9
31Exh/4-10
33G-127
33G-207
34DS-50
34Exh/4-5
35BU-27
35Exh/4-5
35G-2A
35G-7A
35Wheat
36Exh/4-5
36Wheat
37Exh/4-5
38Exh/4-5
38ONG/Pin-22
39Exh
39PlayBall-51
39Wheat
40PlayBall-88
40Wheat
41DP-31
41DP-89
41G-33
41PlayBall-8
42Playball-32MG
43MP-19
50Callahan
50W576-58
52Mother-53
60Exh/HOF-18
60F-36
60NuCard-58
61F-68
61GP-1
61NuCard-458
63Bz-36
69Bz/Sm
72F/FFeat-25
73F/Wild-17
76Rowe-12
76Shakey-60
77Galasso-256
77Galasso-50
80Laugh/3/4/5-12
80Laugh/FFeat-14
80Pac/Leg-35
80Perez/HOF-60
80SSPC/HOF
81Conlon-85
83D/HOF-40
85CircK-12
86BLChew-11
86Conlon/1-36
86Sf/Dec-8
88Conlon/4-21
88Grenada-58
89HOF/St-49
89Pac/Leg-189
90Swell/Great-55
91Conlon/Sport-225
91Conlon/Sport-7
91Swell/Great-144
92Conlon/Col-11
93AP/ASG-102
93AP/ASG24K-36G
93Conlon-834
93UD/ATH-103
93UD/ATH-136
94Conlon-1097
94Conlon-1254
94TedW-55
R300
R302
R309/2
R310
R316
R326-3A
R326-3B
R342-3
R346-18
V351B-35
WG8-44

Ott, Nathan Edward
(Ed)
76OPC-594R
76T-594
77T-197
78OPC-161
78T-28
79Ho-31
79OPC-289
79T-561
80OPC-200
80T-383
81Coke
81D-133
81F-365
81OPC-246
81T-246
81T/St-214
81T/Tr-810
82D-192
82F-470
82OPC-225
82T-469
83F-98
83T-131
84Cram/PCL-120CO
85PrWill-23
86Watertn-16MG
91Mother/Ast-28CO
92Mother/Ast-27M
93Mother/Ast-28M

Ott, William
65T-354R

Otten, Brian
86Geneva-21
87Peoria-15
88WinSalem/Star-13

Otten, Jim
75OPC-624R
75T-624R
75T/M-624R
77T-493R

Otto, Dave
86Madis/Pol-16
88F-652R
89S/HotRook-60
89T-131
89Tacoma/CMC-10
89Tacoma/ProC-1547
89UD-4SR
90AAASingl/ProC-136
90B-448
90ProC/Singl-584
90S/Tr-101T
90Tacoma/CMC-7
90Tacoma/ProC-89
91AAA/LineD-93
91ColoSp/LineD-93
91ColoSp/ProC-2180
91F-20
91Indian/McDon-24
92B-619
92D-730
92Indian/McDon-22
92L-218
92L/BlkGold-218
92OPC-499
92Pinn-316
92StCl-461
92T-499
92T/Gold-499
92T/GoldWin-499
92UD-698
92Ultra-354
93Pirate/Nation-23

Otto, Steve
88Eugene/Best-4
89AppFx/ProC-876
90BBCity/Star-17

Ouellette, Phil
82Clinton/Frit-5
84Cram/PCL-1
85Cram/PCL-182
86Phoenix-19
88AAA/ProC-7
88Calgary/CMC-12
88Calgary/ProC-801
90AAASingl/ProC-383
90ProC/Singl-390
90Toledo/CMC-13
90Toledo/ProC-153

Outen, Chink
90Target-1049

Outlaw, James Paulus
(Jimmy)
39PlayBall-155
44Playball-4
47TipTop

Overall, Orval
11Diamond-23
12Sweet/Pin-86
E254
E90/1
E90/3
E91
M116
S74-66
T202
T205
T206
T3-32
WG3-35

Overeem, Steve
88James/ProC-1914

Overholser, Drew
91Spokane/ClBest-14
91Spokane/ProC-3947

Overmire, Frank
(Stubby)
47TipTop
48L-17
51B-280
52T-155

Overton, Jeff
82AppFx/Frit-2

Overton, Mike
79Newar-5

Overy, Mike
77SLCity
77T-489R
78Cr/PCL-108
79SLCity-9
80SLCity-26

Oviedo, Gelso
52Laval-104

Owchinko, Bob
77Padre/SchCd-21
78Padre/FamFun-20
78T-164
79OPC-257
79T-488
80OPC-44
80T-79
81D-563
81T-536
81T/Tr-811
82D-287
82F-104
82T-243
83D-265
83F-531
83T-338
84F/X-U88
85Cram/PCL-144
85D-506
85F-543
85T-752
86Indianap-9
91Pac/SenLg-83

Owen, Arnold Malcolm
(Mickey)
38G-263
38G-287
39PlayBall-135
40PlayBall-111
41DP-15
44Playball-43
50B-78
51B-174
60NuCard-15
61NuCard-475
89Rini/Dodg-32
89Smok/Dodg-44
90Target-599

Owen, Billy
WG2-38

Owen, Dave
83Iowa-18
84Iowa-18
84SevenUp-19
85D-483
85Iowa-6
85T-642
86OKCty-16
87OKCty-3
88Omaha/CMC-16
88Omaha/ProC-1510
89Iowa/CMC-19
89Iowa/ProC-1694
89Lynch/Star-16
90A&AASingle/ProC-7
90NewBrit/Best-18
90NewBrit/ProC-1318
90NewBrit/Star-13
91B-110
92WinHaven/ProC-1774

Owen, Frank Malcomb
T206

Owen, Lawrence T.
(Larry)
79Richm-5
82Richm-11
82T-502R
83Pol/Atl-24
84Richm-8
85IntLgAS-9
85Richm-12
86Richm-15
88Omaha/CMC-18
88Omaha/ProC-1516
88S-230
89T-87
89UD-528
90Richm/25Ann-18

Owen, Marvin James
(Marv)
34DS-67
35BU-168
93Conlon-941
R314
V351B-36
V355-69

Owen, Spike D.
83SLCity-23
84D-313
84F-616
84Mother/Mar-6
84Nes/792-413
84T-413
84T/St-349
85D-435
85D/AAS-4
85F-497
85Leaf-167
85Mother/Mar-7
85T-84
85T/St-339
86D-362
86F-471
86Mother/Mar-20
86OPC-248
86T-248
86T/St-224
87D-633
87D/OD-185
87F-40
87Leaf-87
87T-591
88D-544
88D/RedSox/Bk-544
88F-359
88OPC-188
88Panini/St-30
88S-372
88T-21TL
88T-733
89B-363
89D-593
89D/Best-236
89D/Tr-14
89F-93
89F/Up-98
89S-218
89S/Tr-13
89T-123
89T/Big-221
89T/Tr-92T
89UD-161
89UD/Ext-717
90B-116
90D-102
90D/BestNL-6
90F-357
90F/Can-357
90Leaf-186
90OPC-674
90Panini/St-285
90PublInt/St-184
90S-247
90T-674
90T/Big-25
90T/St-73
90UD-291
91B-454
91D-251
91Expo/PostC-5
91F-243
91Leaf-36
91OPC-372
91Panini/FrSt-142
91Panini/St-62
91S-452
91StCl-236
91T-372
91UD-189
91Ultra-208
92B-121
92D-518
92Expo/D/Duri-14
92F-488
92L-455
92L/BlkGold-455
92OPC-443
92Panini-205
92Pinn-234
92S-323
92StCl-221
92Studio-58
92T-443
92T/Gold-443
92T/GoldWin-443
92TX-30
92UD-206
92Ultra-224
93B-483
93D-732
93F-463
93F/Final-251

93L-405
93OPC-327
93OPC/Premier-8
93Pac/Spanish-561
93Pinn-499
93S-554
93Select-239
93Select/RookTr-109T
93StCl-677
93StCl/1stDay-677
93StCl/Y-15
93Studio-79
93T-42
93T/Gold-42
93T/PreProd-8
93UD-548
93Ultra-600
94D-80
94F-244
94Finest-264
94Pac/Cr-434
94Pinn-492
94S-507
94T-297
94T/Gold-297
Owen, Tim
85BurlR-14
86DayBe-20
Owen, Tommy
90Idaho/ProC-3248
91James/ClBest-13
91James/ProC-3549
Owens, Billy
90AZ/Pol-15
92AZ/Pol-12
92Classic/DP-53
92FrRow/DP-2
92Kane/Team-24
93StCl/MurphyS-146
94ClBest/Gold-7
Owens, Brad
92Hamil/ClBest-28
92Hamil/ProC-1602
Owens, Brick
94Conlon-1211UMP
Owens, Eric
92Billings/ProC-3366
92Classic/DP-121
92FrRow/DP-88
93StCl/MurphyS-109
94FExcel-180
Owens, Frank Walter
(Frank)
14CJ-74
15CJ-74
E254
Owens, Jayhawk
(J.)
90Foil/Best-224
92OrlanSR/ProC-2849
92OrlanSR/SB-516
92Sky/AASingl-223
93F/Final-37
93L-505
93T-606
93T/Gold-606
94D-278
94F-448
94Pac/Cr-203
94Pinn-418
94StCl-512
94StCl/1stDay-512
94StCl/Gold-512
94StCl/Team-100
94UD/CollC-223
94UD/CollC/Gold-223
94UD/CollC/Silv-223
Owens, Jim
55T-202
55T/DH-122
56T-114
59T-503
60L-39
60T-185
61P-116
61T-341
62T-212
63FrBauer-17
63T-483
64T-241
65T-451
66T-297
67T-582
73OPC-624CO
73T-624CO
Owens, Larry
88CapeCod/Sum-52
90Pulaski/Best-7
90Pulaski/ProC-3102
Owens, Markus
(Mark)
87Everett-30
87Hawaii-19
88Clinton/ProC-704
88MidwLAS/GS-1
89Shrev/ProC-1849
90Shrev/ProC-1446
90Shrev/Star-17
Owens, Marty
88Geneva/ProC-1658
Owens, Michael
88Batavia/ProC-1675
89Batavia/ProC-1930
90Batavia/ProC-3074
91Spartan/ClBest-10
91Spartan/ProC-895
Owens, Paul
84F-643IA
84F/St-123MG
84Nes/792-229MG
84Phill/TastyK-8MG
84T-229MG
85T-92MG
85T/Gloss22-1MG
Owens, Steve
88CharWh/Best-8
Owens, Tom
79Wausau-25
81Watlo-12
82Chatt-9
83BuffB-6
Ownbey, Rick
82Tidew-1
83F-551
83T-739
84Louisvl-23
85Louisvl-26
86F/Up-U85
86Schnucks-18
91WIZMets-306
Oxner, Stan
83Butte-15
Oyama, Randy
87Hawaii-26
Oyas, Danny
92Princet/ClBest-26
92Princet/ProC-3101
Oyler, Raymond F.
(Ray)
65OPC-259R
65T-259R
66OPC-81
66T-81
67T-352
68CokeCap/Tiger-1
68T-399
69MB-209
69MLB/St-97
69OPC-178
69T-178
69T/4in1-13
69T/St-228
70MLB/St-264
70T-603
72MB-261
81TCMA-379
81Tiger/Detroit-30
88Domino-18
Oyster, Jeff
87ArkTr-18
88ArkTr/GS-24
88Louisvl-38
89ArkTr/GS-16
90SpringDG/Best-11
Ozario, Claudio
91Sumter/ClBest-18
91Sumter/ProC-2343
92Albany/ClBest-4
92Albany/ProC-2319
93WPalmB/ClBest-18
93WPalmB/ProC-1356
Ozark, Danny
73OPC-486MG
73T-486MG
74OPC-119MG
74T-119MG
75OPC-46MG
75T-46MG
75T/M-46MG
76SSPC-476MG
76T-384MG
77T-467MG
78BK/P-1MG
78SSPC/270-50MG
78T-631MG
79T-112MG
85T-365MG
Ozawa, Kouichi
89Visalia/Cal-114
89Visalia/ProC-1422
Ozuna, Gabriel
89SALAS/GS-37
89Savan/ProC-345
90ArkTr/GS-23
91AA/LineD-41
91ArkTr/LineD-41
91ArkTr/ProC-1284
92ArkTr/ProC-1127
92ArkTr/SB-40
92Sky/AASingl-17
93LimeR/Winter-63
Ozuna, Mateo
89Savan/ProC-359
90Savan/ProC-2077
91ClBest/Singl-244
91Spring/ClBest-21
91Spring/ProC-749
92ClBest-281
92StPete/ClBest-18
92StPete/ProC-2036
93LimeR/Winter-85
Paccito, Fred
52Laval-85
Pace, Jim
88Reno/Cal-288
Pace, Tubby
85Cedar-23
Pacella, John
78Tidew
79Tidew-2
81Colum-22
81T-414
82Colum-1
82Colum/Pol-17
83D-130
83F-622
83T-166
87Toledo-8
87Toledo/TCMA-14
91Crown/Orio-346
91WIZMets-307
92Yank/WIZ80-139
Pacheco, Al
89Johnson/Star-17
90ProC/Singl-706
90Savan/ProC-2067
Pacheco, Alex
90Welland/Pucko-24
92James/ClBest-5
92James/ProC-1499
93James/ClBest-15
93James/ProC-3323
Pacheco, Tony
74OPC-521CO
74T-521CO
Pacheco, Yogi
92Peoria/ClBest-15
Pacheo, Jose
91Hunting/ClBest-16
91Hunting/ProC-3332
92Hunting/ClBest-15
92Hunting/ProC-3147
Pacho, Juan
81Watlo-24
83Charl-11
89Greenvl/Best-8
89Greenvl/ProC-1155
89Greenvl/Star-16
Pacholec, Joe
87Watertn-23
88Augusta/ProC-373
89Salem/Star-16
Pacillo, Pat
85T-402OLY
87Kahn-35
87Nashvl-16
87T/Tr-93T
88D-536
88Nashvl/CMC-10
88Nashvl/ProC-472
88T-288
89Indianap/CMC-4
89Indianap/ProC-1236
90AAASingl/ProC-114
90Calgary/CMC-1
90Calgary/ProC-649
90ProC/Singl-428
Paciorek, Jim
83ElPaso-4
85Cram/PCL-213
86Vanco-20
87F/Up-U95
87Pol/Brew-14
90ElPasoATG/Team-11
Paciorek, Thomas M.
(Tom)
71OPC-709R
71T-709R
73OPC-606R
73T-606R
74OPC-127
74T-127
75OPC-523
75T-523
75T/M-523
76OPC-641
76SSPC-88
76T-641
77BurgChef-215
77T-48
78T-322
79OPC-65
79T-141
80T-481
81D-408
81F-614
81OPC-228
81Pol/Sea-11
81T-228
81T/SO-23
81T/St-124
82D-253
82F-514
82F/St-224
82OPC-371
82T-336TL
82T-678
82T/St-236
82T/StVar-236
82T/Tr-85T
83D-243
83F-248
83F/St-14M
83F/St-24M
83OPC-72
83OPC/St-47
83T-72
83T/St-47
83TrueVal/WSox-44
84D-282
84F-70
84Nes/792-777
84OPC-132
84T-777
84T/St-246
84TrueVal/WS-25
85Coke/WS-44
85D-488
85F-523
85OPC-381
85SpokAT/Cram-15
85T-572
86F-91
86F/Up-U86
86Rang-44
86T-362
86T/Tr-83T
87F-133
87Mother/Rang-8
87OPC-21
87Smok/R-14
87T-729
88S-531
89Pac/SenLg-204
89T/SenLg-107
89TM/SenLg-85
90EliteSenLg-60
90Pac/Legend-97
90Target-600
91WIZMets-308
93Rang/Keeb-285
Packard, Eugene
14CJ-142
15CJ-142
Packer, Bill
83Erie-6
84Savan-17
Pactwa, Joe
76OPC-589R
76T-589
81TCMA-376
Padden, Richard J.
(Dick)
E107
Padden, Thomas F.
(Tom)
35G-8K
35G-9K
92Conlon/Sport-607
R313
R314
Paddy, Marco
88Idaho/ProC-1835
Padget, Chris
86SLAS-7
87RochR-6
87RochR/TCMA-12
88RochR/CMC-13
88RochR/Gov-20
88RochR/ProC-204
88RochR/Team-18
89RochR/CMC-14
89RochR/ProC-1644
90AAASingl/ProC-473
90ProC/Singl-317
90RochR/CMC-17
90RochR/ProC-716
90Rochester/L&U-21
Padgett, Don W.
(Don)
39PlayBall-157
40PlayBall-109
49Remar
50Remar
90Target-601
93Conlon-716
W754
Padgett, Ernest
(Ernie)
21Exh-124
91Conlon/Sport-206
Padia, Steve
83Cedar-12
83Cedar/Frit-25
86OrlanTw-14
Padilla, Freddy
88Bristol/ProC-1873
89Fayette/ProC-1595
Padilla, Livio
87WinHaven-3
88FSLAS/Star-46
88WinHaven/Star-18
89NewBrit/ProC-620
89NewBrit/Star-13
Padilla, Paul
79Albuq-23TR
80Albuq-24TR
Paduano, Donato
72Dimanche*-139
Padula, Jim
78Newar
79BurlB-23
Paepke, Dennis Rae
(Dennis)
70T-552R
Paez, Raul
93Welland/ClBest-17
93Welland/ProC-3368
Pafko, Andrew
(Andy)
39Exh
47HomogBond-36
47TipTop
48L-125
49B-63
49Eureka-66
49MP-108
49Royal-6
50B-60
51B-103
51FB
51T/BB-27
52B-204
52Royal
52T-1
52TipTop
53B/BW-57
53JC-24
53SpicSpan/3x5-19
53SpicSpan/7x10-11

54B-112
54JC-48
54RM-NL8
54SpicSpan/PostC-16
54T-79
54Wilson
55B-12
55Gol/Braves-24
55JC-48
55SpicSpan/DC-15
56T-312
57SpicSpan/4x5-14
57T-143
58T-223
59T-27
60Lake
60SpicSpan-16CO
60T-464C
79TCMA-181
89Pac/Leg-123
89Rini/Dodg-16
89Swell-74
90Target-602
92Cub/OldStyle-18
94T/Arc54-79
D305
Exh47
PM10/Sm-138
R423-82
RM53-NL9

Pagan, Dave
74Syrac/Team-21
75IntAS/TCMA-9
75OPC-648
75Syrac/Team-11
75Syrac/Team-16
75T-648
75T/M-648
76SSPC-432
77Ho-132
77Ho/Twink-132
77OPC-151
77T-508
77T/CS-35
77T/ClothSt-35
78Colum
91Crown/Orio-347
92Yank/WIZ70-124

Pagan, Felix
83Idaho-23

Pagan, Jose Antonio
(Jose)
60T-67
61T-279
62J-132
62P-132
62P/Can-132
62Salada-200
62Shirriff-200
62T-565
63J-103
63P-103
63T-545
64T-123
65T-575
66EH-11
66OPC-54
66T-54
67CokeCap/Pirate-11
67T-322
67T/Test/PP-18
68KDKA-11
68T-482
69MB-210
69OPC-192
69Pirate/JITB-8
69T-192
69T/4in1-18M
70T-643
71MLB/St-211
71OPC-282
71T-282
72MB-262
72T-701
72T-702IA
73OPC-659
73T-659
78TCMA-102
79Ogden/TCMA-6
80Ogden-23

Pagano, Scott
92Niagara/ClBest-3
92Niagara/ProC-3341

Page, Greg
90Salinas/Cal-126
90Salinas/ProC-2714

Page, Joe
47TipTop
48B-29
49B-82
50B-12
50Drake-27
51B-217
51BR-C5
51FB
51T/BB-10
52T-48
79TCMA-197
92Yank/WIZAS-56
Exh47
PM10/Sm-139

Page, Kelvin
85LitFalls-7

Page, Marc J.
82Wisco/Frit-24

Page, Mike
85BurlR-2

Page, Mitchell Otis
(Mitchell)
75Shrev/TCMA-17
78Ho-38
78K-47
78OPC-75
78PapaG/Disc-39
78T-55
79Ho-17
79OPC-147
79T-295
79T/Comics-14
80OPC-307
80T-586
81A's/Granny-6
81D-480
81F-580
81T-35
82F-105
82OPC-178
82T-633
82Tacom-36
83T-737
84Nes/792-414
84T-414
85Cram/PCL-234
92Tacoma/ProC-2519CO
92Tacoma/SB-550CO

Page, Phil
49Eureka-91

Page, Phillip
91MissSt-55M
92MissSt-50M

Page, Sean
90Johnson/Star-20
91Savan/ClBest-20
91Savan/ProC-1661

Page, Ted
78Laugh/Black-16
86Negro/Frit-2
88Negro/Duques-15

Page, Thane
91Martins/ClBest-19
91Martins/ProC-3452
92Batavia/ClBest-21
92Batavia/ProC-3263

Page, Vance
41DP-2

Pagel, Dave
81QuadC-1

Pagel, Karl Douglas
(Karl)
79T-716R
80T-676R
80Wichita-1
81Charl-18
82Charl-21
83Charl-12
84Maine-16

Pages, Javier
92Albany/ClBest-11
92Albany/ProC-2310
93BurlB/ClBest-15
93BurlB/ProC-162

Pagliari, Armando
88StCath/ProC-2005
89StCath/ProC-2092
91Myrtle/ClBest-30TR

Pagliaroni, James V.
(Jim)
60DF-2
61T-519
62J-63
62P-63
62P/Can-63
62Salada-81
62Shirriff-81
62T-81
63IDL-18
63Sugar-D
63T-159
64Kahn
64T-392
64T/Coins-62
65Kahn
65OPC-265
65T-265
66EH-10
66Kahn
66OPC-33
66T-33
67CokeCap/Pirate-9
67Kahn
67OPC-183
67T-183
67T/Test/PP-19
68T-586
69MB-211
69T-302
78TCMA-91

Pagliarulo, Mike
83Nashvl-14
84Colum-1
84Colum/Pol-17
85D-539
85F-139
85T-638
85T/St-317
86D-152
86F-113
86Leaf-80
86OPC-327
86T-327
87Classic-22
87D-298
87D/OD-239
87F-107
87F/LL-33
87Leaf-189
87OPC-195
87Seven-E6
87Sf-55
87Sf/TPrev-7M
87Smok/AL-9
87T-195
87T/Gloss60-56
87T/St-300
88D-105
88D/Best-105
88D/Y/Bk-105
88F-216
88F/St-49
88OPC-109
88Panini/St-156
88S-170
88Sf-121
88Sf/Gamewin-23
88T-435
88T/Big-138
88T/St-295
89B-175
89D-127
89F-262
89KennerFig-99
89OPC-211
89Panini/St-406
89S-189
89S/NWest-13
89S/Tr-11T
89Sf-153
89T-211
89T/Big-28
89T/DHTest-20
89T/St-311
89UD-569
90B-219
90Coke/Padre-12
90D-364
90D/BestNL-137
90F-163
90F/Can-163
90Leaf-320
90OPC-63
90Padre/MagUno-3
90PublInt/St-542
90S-494
90T-63
90T/Big-226
90T/St-106
90UD-329
91B-339
91D-140
91F-537
91F/Up-U40
91Leaf-339
91OPC-547
91Panini/FrSt-93
91S-199
91S/RookTr-42T
91StCl-522
91T-547
91T/Tr-87T
91UD-206
91UD/Ext-709
92B-685
92D-62
92F-216
92L-346
92L/BlkGold-346
92OPC-721
92Panini-117
92Pinn-246
92S-173
92StCl-152
92StCl/Dome-137
92T-721
92T/Gold-721
92T/GoldWin-721
92UD-509
92USPlayC/Twin-5C
92USPlayC/Twin-6H
92Ultra-96
92Yank/WIZ80-140
93D-707
93F-641
93Flair-241
93L-474
93Pac/Spanish-176
93Pinn-508
93Select/RookTr-115T
93Studio-191
93T-336
93T/Gold-336
93UD-306
93Ultra-587
94D-243
94F-14
94Pac/Cr-41
94S-489
94UD/CollC-224
94UD/CollC/Gold-224
94UD/CollC/Silv-224

Paglino, Joseph J.
82AppFx/Frit-16

Pagnozzi, Tom
83Erie-20
86Louisvl-21
87Louisvl-22
87Smok/Cards-12
88D-577
88S-358
88Smok/Card-12
88T-689
89D-399
89S-483
89Smok/Cards-16
89T-208
89UD-602
90D-591
90Leaf-498
90OPC-509
90PublInt/St-224
90Smok/Card-18
90SpringDG/Best-35
90T-509
90T/TVCard-23
91B-389
91D-337
91F-641
91Leaf-72
91OPC-308
91Panini/FrSt-30
91Pol/Card-19
91S-797
91StCl-223
91T-308
91UD-91
91Ultra-293
92B-241
92Classic/I-69
92D-254
92F-586
92French-9M
92L-359
92L/BlkGold-359
92OPC-448
92Panini-171
92Pinn-69
92Pol/Card-14
92S-136
92StCl-162
92Studio-96
92T-448
92T/Gold-448
92T/GoldWin-448
92UD-379
92Ultra-268
92Ultra/AS-15
92Ultra/AwardWin-8
93B-220
93Colla/DM-83
93D-360
93F-130
93F/Fruit-50
93Flair-124
93L-136
93OPC-273
93Pac/Spanish-299
93Panini-191
93Pinn-62
93Pol/Card-14
93S-135
93Select-37
93StCl-399
93StCl/1stDay-399
93StCl/Card-6
93StCl/MurphyS-72
93Studio-198
93T-92
93T/Gold-92
93TripleP-194
93UD-405
93UD/SP-77
93Ultra-110
93Ultra/AwardWin-2
94B-320
94D-177
94F-641
94Finest-384
94L-7
94OPC-103
94Pac/Cr-598
94Panini-246
94Pinn-439
94S-466
94Select-98
94StCl-122
94StCl/1stDay-122
94StCl/Gold-122
94StCl/Pr-122
94StCl/PreProd-122
94StCl/Team-319
94Studio-53
94T-719
94T/Gold-719
94TripleP-65
94UD-106
94UD/ElecD-106
94Ultra-567

Paige, Carey
92Classic/DP-67
92FrRow/DP-20
92LitSun/HSPros-9

Paige, George L.
(Pat)
T206

Paige, LeRoy
(Satchel)
48L-8
49B-224
53T-220
72T/Test-1
74Laugh/Black-15
76Laugh/Clown-21
76Shakey-125
77Galasso-22
77Galasso-258
80Pac/Leg-60
80Perez/HOF-125
80SSPC/HOF
82Ohio/HOF-33

83D/HOF-11
83MLBPA/Pin-14
85West/2-37
86Negro/Frit-10
86Negro/Frit-21
86Negro/Frit-4
87Negro/Dixon-21
88Conlon/NegAS-10
88Negro/Duques-11
89B/Ins-8
90BBWit-64
90Negro/Star-20
90Perez/GreatMom-20
90Swell/Great-115
91Homer/Classic-2
91LineD-47
91Swell/Great-133
91T/Arc53-220
92Bz/Quadra-18M
92S-882
93AP/ASG-115
93AP/ASG24K-49G
93Spectrum/HOFI-3
93TWill-112
93TWill-131
93TWill/Locklear-5
93TWill/Pr-115
Exh47
PM10/Sm-140
Rawl

Paine, Phil
54JC-11
55JC-11
58T-442
59DF

Painter, Chris
89GA-21

Painter, Gary
91ClBest/Singl-129
91FSLAS/ProC-FSL45
91WinHaven/ClBest-6
91WinHaven/ProC-486
92NewBrit/ProC-430
92NewBrit/SB-492

Painter, Lance
90Spokane/SportP-21
91ClBest/Singl-352
91Waterlo/ClBest-7
91Waterlo/ProC-1254
92ClBest-313
92ProC/Tomorrow-339
92Sky/AASingl-285
92Wichita/ProC-3657
92Wichita/SB-643
93B-89
93F/Final-38
93Select/RookTr-48T
93T-738
93T/Gold-738
94D-474
94StCl-77
94StCl/1stDay-77
94StCl/Gold-77
94StCl/Team-119
94T-229
94T/Gold-229

Painton, Tim 1
80Clinton-15

Painton, Tim 2
89FresnoSt/Smok-17
91FresnoSt/Smok-16M

Paixao, Paulino
85Utica-4

Pakele, Louis
90Boise/ProC-3309
91PalmSp/ProC-2010

Palacios, Peter
85Clovis-30

Palacios, Rey
86GlenF-17
87Toledo-15
87Toledo/TCMA-1
88AAA/ProC-43
88Toledo/CMC-18
88Toledo/ProC-605
89F-648R
89UD-21SR
90B-381
91OPC-148
91T-148

Palacios, Vicente
87Vanco-22
88Classic/Red-191
88D-45RR
88F-336
88Leaf-45RR
88S-643RP
88Sf-224R
88T-322
89F-216
89S/HotRook-2
90AAASingl/ProC-485
90BuffB/CMC-7
90BuffB/ProC-370
90BuffB/Team-18
90ProC/Singl-7
91D-732
91F/Up-U113
91Leaf-442
91OPC-438
91StCl-443
91T-438
91UD/FinalEd-71F
92D-365
92OPC-582
92Pinn-386
92S-109
92StCl-486
92T-582
92T/Gold-582
92T/GoldWin-582
92Ultra-557
93Pinn-130

Palafox, Juan
85Tigres-12

Palat, Ed
74Tacoma/Caruso-26
75Tacoma/KMMO-20

Palermo, Pete
86Hagers-14
87Hagers-17
88Hagers/Star-16

Palermo, Steve
88TM/Umpire-29
89TM/Umpire-27
90TM/Umpire-26

Palica, Alex
45Centen-19

Palica, Ambrose
46Remar-22
47Remar-10
47Smith-12

Palica, Erv
51B-189
52T-273
54NYJour
55B-195
56T-206
60HenryH-21
61Union
79TCMA-233
90Target-603
91Crown/Orio-348

Palica, John
81Wisco-22
83OrlanTw-8

Pall, Donn Steven
86AppFx-17
87BirmB/Best-15
88AAA/ProC-45
88Vanco/CMC-9
88Vanco/ProC-759
89Coke/WS-18
89D/Rook-7
89F-505
89S/Tr-102
89T-458
90BirmDG/Best-26
90Coke/WSox-18
90D-606
90F-543
90F/Can-543
90Leaf-392
90OPC-219
90PublInt/St-397
90S-304
90S/100Ris-7
90T-219
90T/JumboR-23
90UD-386
91D-215
91F-130
91Kodak/WSox-22
91Leaf-468
91OPC-768
91S-132
91T-768
91UD-603
92B-380
92D-56
92F-92
92OPC-57
92S-484
92StCl-184
92T-57
92T/Gold-57
92T/GoldWin-57
92UD-592
92Ultra-41
92WSox-22
93D-667
93F-586
93Pac/Spanish-393
93StCl-240
93StCl/1stDay-240
93StCl/WSox-21
93T-707
93T/Gold-707
93WSox-21
94StCl/Team-200
94T-328
94T/Gold-328

Pallas, Ted
82Beloit/Frit-27

Pallone, Dave
88TM/Umpire-37
89TM/Umpire-35

Palma, Brian
89Reno/Cal-258
91Salinas/ClBest-12
91Salinas/ProC-2258

Palma, Jay
83Ander-22

Palmeiro, Orlando
91Boise/ClBest-9
91Boise/ProC-3895
92MidwLAS/Team-31
92QuadC/ClBest-3
92QuadC/ProC-823
93B-637
93FExcel/ML-145
94FExcel-29

Palmeiro, Rafael
86Pittsfld-18
87D-43RR
87D/Rook-47
87Iowa-24
87Leaf-43RR
87Sf-158M
87Sf/Rook-2
87Sf/Rook-32
87Sf/TPrev-22M
87T-634FS
87T/JumboR-12
88Berg/Cubs-25
88D-324
88D/Best-93
88D/Cubs/Bk-324
88F-429
88F/Slug-C4
88OPC-186
88Panini/St-268
88Peoria/Ko-23
88Peoria/Ko-34M
88S-186
88T-186
89B-237
89Classic/Up/2-163
89D-49
89D/AS-53
89D/Best-88
89D/Tr-6
89F-434
89F-631M
89F/Up-66
89Mother/R-5
89OPC-310
89Panini/St-60
89RedFoley/St-88
89S-199
89S/HotStar-56
89S/Tr-1
89S/YS/I-35
89Sf-30
89Smok/R-24
89T-310
89T/Big-257
89T/Coins-47
89T/Mini-5
89T/St-47
89T/St/Backs-52
89T/Tr-93T
89T/UK-58
89UD-235
89UD/Ext-772
90B-496
90Classic-74
90D-225
90D/BestAL-41
90F-308
90F/Can-308
90Leaf-100
90Mother/Rang-9
90OPC-755
90Panini/St-164
90PublInt/St-418
90RedFoley/St-72
90S-405
90S/100St-58
90Sf-9
90T-755
90T/Big-127
90T/HeadsUp-12
90T/St-250
90UD-335
91B-286
91Classic/200-115
91Classic/I-85
91Classic/III-71
91D-19DK
91D-394MVP
91D-521
91D/SuperDK-19
91F-295
91Leaf-347
91Leaf/Stud-127
91MissSt-35
91Mother/Rang-9
91OPC-295
91Panini/FrSt-252
91Panini/St-211
91Panini/Top15-29
91Panini/Top15-7
91Pep/SS-14
91S-216
91S/100SS-56
91Seven/3DCoin-10T
91StCl-502
91T-295
91UD-30
91UD-474
91USPlayC/AS-6D
91Ultra-350
92B-610
92Classic/Game200-69
92Classic/II-T62
92D-46
92F-311
92F/ASIns-17
92F/TmLIns-12
92Hardee-17
92L-296
92L/BlkGold-296
92Mother/Rang-9
92OPC-55
92Panini-75
92Pinn-35
92S-55
92S/100SS-27
92S/Impact-68
92StCl-516
92StCl/Dome-138
92Studio-244
92T-55
92T/Gold-55
92T/GoldWin-55
92T/Kids-130
92TripleP-183
92UD-223
92UD/ASFF-34
92USPlayC/Ace-8D
92Ultra-136
93B-137
93D-365
93F-687
93Flair-283
93KingB-20
93L-49
93MilkBone-8
93OPC-171
93Pac/Beisbol-14M
93Pac/Spanish-314
93Pac/SpanishGold-17
93Panini-81
93Pinn-220
93Rang/Keeb-419
93S-74
93Select-162
93StCl-115
93StCl/1stDay-115
93StCl/Rang-26
93Studio-185
93T-305
93T/Finest-52
93T/FinestRef-52
93T/Gold-305
93TripleP-71
93UD-52M
93UD-574
93UD/FunPack-157
93UD/SP-196
93Ultra-281
94B-515
94D-26
94D/Special-26
94F-313
94F-710
94F/LL-3
94F/Lumber-8
94Finest-227
94L-289
94L/MVPAL-9
94OPC-25
94Pac/AllLat-16
94Pac/Cr-622
94Pac/Gold-5
94Pac/Silv-3
94Panini-130
94Pinn-493
94Pinn/Run-5
94S-495
94S/GoldS-59
94Sf/2000-144
94StCl-208
94StCl-265
94StCl/1stDay-208
94StCl/1stDay-265
94StCl/Gold-208
94StCl/Gold-265
94StCl/Team-295
94Studio-126
94T-470
94T/BlkGold-16
94T/Gold-470
94TripleP-158
94TripleP/Medal-3M
94UD-340
94UD-34FT
94UD/ElecD-34FT
94UD/SP-125
94Ultra-308
94Ultra/HRK-5
94Ultra/LL-2

Palmer, Bob
75AppFx
82Holyo-11

Palmer, David
80OPC-21
80T-42
81D-451
81F-160
81OPC-243
81T-607
82F-199
82OPC-292
82T-292
83D-68
83Expo/PostC-13
83F-291
83OPC-164
83T-164
84Expo/PostC-21
84Stuart-23
85D-341
85Expo/PostC-15
85F-404
85Leaf-105
85OPC-211
85OPC/Post-3
85T-526
86D-254
86F-255
86F/Up-U87
86OPC-143
86Pol/Atl-46
86T-421
86T/Tr-84T
87D-325
87F-525
87Sf/TPrev-24M

87Smok/Atl-4
87T-324
87T/St-45
88D-266
88F-546
88F/Up-U111
88Phill/TastyK-17
88S-457
88T-732
88T/Tr-79T
89D-133
89F-577
89OPC-67
89S-544
89T-67
89Toledo/CMC-4
89Toledo/ProC-789
89UD-515

Palmer, Dean
87Gaston/ProC-8
88CharlR/Star-18
88FSLAS/Star-47
89BBAmAA/BPro-AA27
89TexLAS/GS-32
89Tulsa/GS-19
89Tulsa/Team-17
90AAASingl/ProC-687
90Classic/Up-39
90D-529
90HotRook/St-35
90OkCty/ProC-441
90S-594RP
90S/100Ris-38
90Sf-225R
90T/89Debut-95
90Tulsa/ProC-1170
90TulsaDG/Best-5
90UD-74SR
91AAA/LineD-314
91B-288
91Classic/III-72
91D/Rook-48
91F/UltraUp-U56
91F/Up-U61
91OkCty/LineD-314
91OkCty/ProC-187
91S/100RisSt-28
91T/Tr-88T
91UD/FinalEd-74F
92B-107
92D-177
92F-312
92L-225
92L/BlkGold-225
92L/GoldPrev-28
92Mother/Rang-26
92OPC-567
92OPC/Premier-112
92Panini-77
92Pinn-351
92Pinn/Team2000-64
92ProC/Tomorrow-148
92S-392
92S/100RisSt-60
92StCl-211
92Studio-245
92T-567
92T/Gold-567
92T/GoldWin-567
92UD-465
92Ultra-137
93B-81
93D-339
93F-325
93Flair-284
93Kenner/Fig-26
93L-159
93OPC-258
93Pac/Spanish-315
93Panini-84
93Pinn-161
93Pinn/HRC-25
93Pinn/Team2001-28
93Rang/Keeb-420
93S-138
93Select-248
93StCl-22
93StCl/1stDay-22
93StCl/Rang-11
93Studio-210
93T-545
93T/Finest-159
93T/FinestRef-159
93T/Gold-545
93TripleP-111
93UD-241
93UD-465IN
93UD/FunPack-158
93UD/FunPack-217FOLD
93UD/SP-197
93UD/SPPlat-PP14
93Ultra-282
94B-213
94D-355
94D/LongBall-2
94D/Special-355
94F-314
94L-311
94OPC-152
94Pac/Cr-623
94Pac/Gold-7
94Panini-131
94Pinn-101
94Pinn/Artist-101
94Pinn/Museum-101
94Pinn/Power-25
94Pinn/TeamP-3M
94S-389
94Sf/2000-85
94Sf/Shak-8
94StCl-336
94StCl/1stDay-336
94StCl/Gold-336
94StCl/Team-269
94Studio-156
94T-136
94T/Finest-177
94T/Finest/PreProd-177
94T/FinestRef-177
94T/Gold-136
94TripleP-197
94UD-180
94UD/ElecD-180
94UD/Mantle-14
94UD/SP-150
94Ultra-130

Palmer, Denzil
76Clinton

Palmer, Donald
87BuffB-28

Palmer, Doug
85Visalia-2
86OrlanTw-15
87OrlanTw-17
88NewBrit/ProC-892

Palmer, Jim
66OPC-126
66T-126
67CokeCap/Orio-5
67OPC-152WS
67T-152WS
67T-475
68CokeCap/Orio-5
68T-575
69T-573
70OPC-449
70OPC-68LL
70T-449
70T-68LL
71K-60
71MD
71MLB/St-306
71OPC-197ALCS
71OPC-570
71OPC-67LL
71T-197ALCS
71T-570
71T-67LL
71T/Coins-90
71T/tatt-3
72K-13
72MB-263
72OPC-270
72OPC-92LL
72T-270
72T-92LL
73JP
73K-17
73OPC-160
73OPC-341KP
73T-160
73T-341KP
73T/Comics-13
73T/Lids-38
73T/PinUps-13
74K-6
74OPC-206LL
74OPC-40
74T-206LL
74T-40
74T/DE-45
74T/Puzzles-8
74T/St-128
75Ho-126
75OPC-335
75SSPC/42-5
75SSPC/Puzzle-19
75T-335
75T/M-335
76Crane-44
76Ho-56
76Ho/Twink-56
76K-37
76MSA/Disc
76OPC-200LL
76OPC-202LL
76OPC-450
76SSPC-380
76T-200LL
76T-202LL
76T-450
77BurgChef-42
77Ho-1
77Ho/Twink-1
77OPC-5LL
77OPC-80
77Pep-20
77T-5LL
77T-600
77T/CS-36
77T/ClothSt-36
78Ho-116
78OPC-179
78OPC-5LL
78PapaG/Disc-31
78Pep-36
78T-160
78T-205LL
78Tastee/Discs-2
78Wiffle/Discs-57
79Ho-11
79K-5
79OPC-174
79T-340
80BK/PHR-7
80K-15
80OPC-310
80T-4M
80T-590
80T/Super-4
81D-353
81D-473
81F-169
81F/St-124
81K-2
81OPC-210
81PermaGr/CC-28
81T-210
81T/Nat/Super-9
81T/SO-50
81T/St-39
82D-231
82F-175
82F/St-143
82K-42
82OPC-80
82OPC-81IA
82T-80
82T-81IA
82T/St-146
83D-4DK
83D-77
83F-69
83F/St-23M
83F/St-8M
83K-39
83OPC-299
83OPC-328SV
83OPC/St-175
83OPC/St-23FOIL
83T-21TL
83T-490
83T-491SV
83T/Fold-1M
83T/Gloss40-19
83T/St-175
83T/St-23
83T/St/Box-5
84D-576
84D/Champs-35
84F-16
84F/St-102
84Nes/792-715LL
84Nes/792-717LL
84Nes/792-750
84OPC-194
84Ralston-23
84T-715LL
84T-717LL
84T-750
84T/Cereal-23
84T/RD-31M
84T/St-21
84T/St-211
86Sf/Dec-58
87KMart-17
89Swell-105
90BBWit-33
90MSA/AGFA-17
91Crown/Orio-349
91Perez/HOF-206
92K/CornAS-3
92K/FrAS-4
93AP/ASG-127
93AP/ASG24K-61G
93FrRowPr/Palmer-1
93FrRowPr/Palmer-2
93FrRowPr/Palmer-3
93FrRowPr/Palmer-4
93FrRowPr/Palmer-5
93Orio/SUI-2

Palmer, Ken
76Baton

Palmer, Lowell
70OPC-252
70T-252
71OPC-554
71T-554
72T-746
89Pac/SenLg-174
89TM/SenLg-86

Palmer, Mickey
82FtMyr-8

Palmer, Mike
81QuadC-33TR

Palmieri, John
82Reading-5

Palmquist, Ed
60DF-7
90Target-604

Palyan, Vince
89Everett/Star-23
90Clinton/Best-26
90Clinton/ProC-2564

Palys, Stanley F.
(Stan)
58T-126

Pancoski, Tracey
88Fresno/Cal-7
88Fresno/ProC-1240

Panetta, Mario
83QuadC-4

Paniagua, Jose
94B-32

Panick, Frank
77SLCity

Pankovits, James F.
(Jim)
77Cocoa
80Tucson-19
81Tucson-17
82Hawaii-4
83Tucson-16
84Cram/PCL-61
85D-502
85Mother/Ast-25
86D-450
86F-307
86Pol/Ast-1
86T-618
87D-605
87F-64
87Mother/Ast-22
87Pol/Ast-25
87T-249
88Mother/Ast-22
88Pol/Ast-16
88T-487
88T/Big-109
89BuffB/CMC-18
89BuffB/ProC-1664
89F-363
89S-192
89T-153
89UD-100
90AAASingl/ProC-442
90Pawtu/CMC-18
90Pawtu/ProC-470
90ProC/Singl-269
90T/TVRSox-55
91AAA/LineD-363
91Pac/SenLg-89
91Pawtu/LineD-363
91Pawtu/ProC-48
92NewBrit/ProC-449MG
92NewBrit/SB-499MG

Panther, Jim
93Rang/Keeb-31

Papa, John
91Crown/Orio-350

Papageorge, Greg
88Virgini/Star-17
89Penin/Star-17

Papai, Al
50B-245

Paparella, Joseph J.
(Joe)
55B-235UMP

Pape, Kenneth Wayne
(Ken)
75Spokane/Caruso-7
77Tucson
78Syrac
79Spokane-8
81Spokane-21
92TX-31
93Rang/Keeb-286

Pape, Lawrence
E270/1

Papi, Stanley Gerard
(Stan)
79OPC-344
79T-652
81D-246
81F-480
81T-273
82D-333
82F-280
82T-423

Papke, William
T3/Box-64

Pappageorgas, Bob
77Wausau

Pappas, Erik
86PalmSp-25
86PalmSp/Smok-6
87PalmSp-23
88MidldA/GS-14
89CharlK-12
90AAAGame/ProC-34
90AAASingl/ProC-628
90Iowa/CMC-17
90Iowa/ProC-321
90ProC/Singl-92
90T/TVCub-55
91B-432
91Cub/Vine-20
91S/RookTr-95T
92Omaha/ProC-2964
92Omaha/SB-340
92StCl-442
92T/91Debut-135
93F/Final-129
93Flair-125
93L-535
93T/Tr-5T
94D-205
94F-642
94Finest-287
94Pac/Cr-599
94S-188
94S/GoldR-188
94StCl-448
94StCl/1stDay-448
94StCl/Gold-448
94StCl/Team-323
94T-234
94T/Gold-234
94Ultra-270

Pappas, Milt
58T-457
59T-391
60Bz-5
60L-57
60T-12
60T-399M
60T/tatt-42
61P-71
61T-295
61T-48LL

61T/St-103
62Bz
62Exh
62J-34
62P-34
62P/Can-34
62Salada-98
62Shirriff-98
62T-55LL
62T-75
62T/St-7
63Exh
63F-3
63J-65
63P-65
63Salada-43
63T-358
64T-45
64T/Coins-70
64T/S-5
64T/St-4
64T/tatt
65OPC-270
65T-270
65T/E-20
65T/trans-61
66Bz-29
66Kahn
66OPC-105
66T-105
66T/RO-75
66T/RO-88
67CokeCap/Reds-15
67T-254
68OPC-74
68T-74
69MB-212
69MLB/St-117
69OPC-79
69T-79
69T/St-8
70MLB/St-11
70T-576
71MD
71MLB/St-39
71OPC-441
71T-441
72MB-264
72OPC-208
72T-208
73OPC-70
73T-70
74OPC-640
74T-640
78TCMA-56
89Pac/Leg-204
89Swell-113
90Swell/Great-107
91Crown/Orio-351
91Swell/Great-69
Exh47
WG10-41
WG9-40

Paquette, Craig
89Medford/Best-22
90Modesto/Chong-22
90Modesto/ProC-2222
90ProC/Singl-846
91B-236
91Huntsvl/Team-16
92B-94
92ClBest-138
92Huntsvl/ProC-3957
92Huntsvl/SB-316
92OPC-473M
92Sky/AASingl-135
92T-473M
92T/Gold-473M
92T/GoldWin-473M
92UD/ML-122
93B-329
93F/Final-261
93L-506
93Select/RookTr-57T
93T/Tr-38T
93UD/SP-42
94D-532
94F-272
94Pac/Cr-461
94Pinn-328
94S-567
94StCl-328
94StCl/1stDay-328
94StCl/Gold-328
94T-46
94T/Gold-46
94TripleP-7
94UD-262
94UD/CollC-225
94UD/CollC/Gold-225
94UD/CollC/Silv-225
94UD/ElecD-262
94Ultra-113

Paquette, Darryl
78Wausau

Parachke, Greg
89Utica/Pucko-17

Paragin, Billy
92Pulaski/ClBest-22
92Pulaski/ProC-3181

Paramo, Paul
91GulfCR/SportP-9

Parascand, Steve
87Fayette-4
88Fayette/ProC-1088

Pardo, Al
81Miami-2
83RochR-12
84CharlO-7
85RochR-2
86D-489
86RochR-15
86T-279
88Tidew/ProC-1594
89ScranWB/CMC-21
89ScranWB/ProC-711
90HagersDG/Best-20
91Crown/Orio-352

Pardo, Bed
89Eugene/Best-8

Pardo, Larry
86DayBe-21
87QuadC-6
88QuadC/GS-6
89QuadC/Best-12
89QuadC/GS-24
90PalmSp/ProC-2575
90ProC/Singl-710

Pardue, Roy
89KS*-20ACO
93Lipscomb-23M

Paredes, German
91Kane/ClBest-24
91Kane/ProC-2672

Paredes, Jesus
87James-6
88Rockford-26
89Rockford-26
89Rockford/Team-20
90Indianap/CMC-21
90ProC/Singl-71

Paredes, Johnny
86Jaxvl/TCMA-2
87Indianap-20
88D/Rook-29
88Indianap/CMC-11
88Indianap/ProC-516
88TripleA/ASCMC-3
89D-570
89F-388
89OPC-367
89S/HotRook-27
89T-367
89UD-477
90AAASingl/ProC-586
90Indianap/ProC-303
91AAA/LineD-595
91Toledo/LineD-595
91Toledo/ProC-1941
92Toledo/ProC-1056

Parent, Eric
82Wausau/Frit-11
83Wausau/Frit-10
84Greens-16

Parent, Frederick A.
(Freddy)
10Domino-95
11Helmar-14
12Sweet/Pin-13
14Piedmont/St-46
C46-44
E107
E254
M116
S74-7
T205
T206
WG2-39

Parent, Mark
82Amari-10
83Beaum-13
84Beaum-8
85Cram/PCL-105
86LasVegas-11
88Coke/Padres-27
88D/Rook-8
88F/Up-U125
88Smok/Padres-22
88T/Tr-80T
89Coke/Padre-11
89D-420
89F/Up-125
89S-576
89T-617
89UD-492
90Coke/Padre-13
90D-229
90F-164
90F/Can-164
90Leaf-497
90OPC-749
90Padre/MagUno-7
90PublInt/St-55
90S-119
90T-749
90UD-569
91D-506
91F-538
91OPC-358
91S-213
91T-358
91UD-470
92AAA/ASG/SB-462
92RochR/ProC-1942
92RochR/SB-462
92StCl-623
93Rang/Keeb-287
94StCl/Team-349

Parese, Billy
89StCath/ProC-2082
90Myrtle/ProC-2786
91Dunedin/ClBest-18
91Dunedin/ProC-216

Parfrey, Brian
82Redwd-26

Parham, Bill
89Bakers/Cal-191

Paris, Juan
85Spokane/Cram-18
86CharRain-20
87Greens-12
88WinHaven/Star-19
89Lynch/Star-17
90NewBrit/Best-17
90NewBrit/ProC-1331
90NewBrit/Star-14
91AA/LineD-467
91NewBrit/LineD-467
91NewBrit/ProC-366
92Pawtu/ProC-936
92Pawtu/SB-361

Paris, Kelly Jay
(Kelly)
77StPete
78StPete
80ArkTr-22
82Louisvl-22
84Cram/PCL-123
84D-384
84F-476
84Nes/792-113
84T-113
85IntLgAS-28
85RochR-8
86RochR-16
88Vanco/CMC-12
89F-506
89UD-192
89Vanco/CMC-11
89Vanco/ProC-594
91Crown/Orio-353

Paris, Zacarias
82Tucson-14
83ColumAst-17
86Ventura-20

Parish, Jack
76Clinton

Parisotto, Barry
89GreatF-20
90Bakers/Cal-242

Park, Chan Ho
94B-98
94Finest-426
94Flair-181
94Flair/Wave-8
94Pinn-527
94Select-177
94StCl-521
94StCl/1stDay-521
94StCl/Gold-521
94UD-521DD
94UD/SP-13PP
94Ultra-520
94Ultra/AllRook-9

Parke, Jim
77Charl

Parker, Bob
85Osceola/Team-21
86ColumAst-21

Parker, Brad
92ClBest-178
92Madis/ClBest-17
92Madis/ProC-1245

Parker, Carrol
86Erie-22
87Savan-14

Parker, Clay
86Wausau-18
88Colum/CMC-2
88Colum/Pol-7
88Colum/ProC-309
88F-649R
89Colum/CMC-4
89Colum/Pol-17
89Colum/ProC-751
89D/Best-164
89D/Rook-52
89S/NWest-30
89S/Tr-94
89T/Tr-94T
90D-363
90F-451
90F/Can-451
90LSUGreat-11
90OPC-511
90PublInt/St-543
90S-316
90S/100Ris-17
90S/YS/I-8
90T-511
90T/TVYank-15
91D-605
91F-346
91OPC-183
91T-183
91Tacoma/ProC-2302
92B-366
92Calgary/SB-67
92Mother/Mar-25
92StCl-631
92Ultra-435
92Yank/WIZ80-141
93StCl-45
93StCl/1stDay-45

Parker, Corey
92Niagara/ClBest-13
92Niagara/ProC-3334

Parker, Darrell
76Watlo
77Jaxvl

Parker, David Gene
(Dave)
74OPC-252
74T-252
74T/St-86
75OPC-29
75SSPC/Puzzle-20
75T-29
75T/M-29
76Crane-45
76Ho-133
76K-15
76MSA/Disc
76OPC-185
76SSPC-572
76T-185
77BurgChef-187
77K-19
77OPC-242
77T-270
78Ho-135
78K-52
78OPC-1LL
78OPC-60
78T-201LL
78T-560
78Wiffle/Discs-58
79Ho-53
79K-21
79OPC-223
79T-1LL
79T-430
79T/Comics-29
80BK/PHR-19
80K-23
80OPC-163
80T-310
80T/S-17
80T/Super-17TP
81Coke
81D-136
81Drake-4
81F-360
81F/St-26
81K-13
81MSA/Disc-25
81OPC-178
81PermaGr/AS-6
81PermaGr/CC-13
81Sqt-10
81T-640
81T/Nat/Super-10
81T/SO-59
81T/St-210
81T/St-257
82D-12DK
82D-95
82F-489
82F-638
82F/St-241M
82F/St-71
82FBI/Disc-14
82K-48
82KMart-34
82OPC-343AS
82OPC-40
82OPC-41IA
82T-343AS
82T-40
82T-41IA
82T/St-127
82T/St-87
83D-473
83F-315
83F/St-13M
83F/St-25AM
83F/St-25BM
83OPC-205
83OPC/St-280
83PermaGr/CC-11
83T-205
83T/Fold-3M
83T/St-280
84Borden-39
84D-288
84D/Champs-57
84F-258
84F/X-U89
84Nes/792-701LL
84Nes/792-775
84OPC-31
84T-701LL
84T-775
84T/St-130
84T/Tr-90T
85D-62
85D/AAS-35
85D/HL-13
85Drake-22
85F-544
85FunFoodPin-80
85Leaf-169
85OPC-175
85T-175
85T/St-47
85T/Super-42
86D-203
86D/AAS-24
86Drake-4
86F-184
86F-640M
86F/AS-6
86F/LL-30
86F/LimEd-33
86F/Mini-39
86F/St-84
86GenMills/Book-5M
86Leaf-135
86OPC-287

86Quaker-9
86Seven/Coin-C4M
86Seven/Coin-E4M
86Seven/Coin-S4M
86Seven/Coin-W4M
86Sf-181M
86Sf-183M
86Sf-23
86Sf-58M
86T-595
86T/3D-18
86T/Gloss60-13
86T/Mini-41
86T/St-135
86T/Super-41
86T/Tatt-9M
86TexGold-39
86Woolwth-27
87Classic-33
87D-388
87D/AAS-34
87D/OD-198
87Drake-18
87F-208
87F-639M
87F/AwardWin-27
87F/Mini-80
87F/Slug-29
87F/St-88
87F/WaxBox-C10
87GenMills/Book-6M
87Kahn-39
87KayBee-23
87Leaf-79
87OPC-352
87Ralston-7
87RedFoley/St-90
87Sf-117M
87Sf-35
87Sf/TPrev-4M
87Stuart-4M
87T-600AS
87T-691
87T/Board-20
87T/Coins-38
87T/Gloss60-17
87T/Mini-6
87T/St-145
88D-388
88D/A's/Bk-NEW
88D/Best-190
88F-243
88F/Mini-47
88F/Up-U55
88KayBee-21
88KennerFig-78
88Mother/A's-5
88OPC-315
88Panini/St-284
88S-17
88S/Tr-50T
88Sf-101
88T-315
88T/Big-242
88T/Gloss60-34
88T/Mini-48
88T/St-136
88T/St/Backs-19
88T/Tr-81T
88T/UK-55
89B-202
89D-150
89D/Best-336
89F-19
89KMart/Lead-13
89KennerFig-100
89Mother/A's-4
89OPC-199
89Panini/St-424
89S-108
89Sf-49
89T-475
89T/Ames-23
89T/Big-144
89T/LJN-135
89T/St-169
89UD-605
90B-398
90Brewer/MillB-18
90Classic-95
90Classic/III-10
90D-328
90D/BestAL-51
90D/Learning-33
90F-18
90F/Can-18
90F/Up-106
90F/WS-10M
90F/WS-9
90KMart/CBatL-13
90KayBee-22
90Leaf-190
90OPC-45
90OPC/BoxB-J
90Pol/Brew-39
90PublInt/St-312
90S-135
90S/Tr-12T
90T-45
90T/Ames-6
90T/Big-227
90T/HillsHM-21
90T/St-179
90T/Tr-86T
90T/WaxBox-J
90UD-192
90UD/Ext-766
90USPlayC/AS-12S
90Windwlk/Discs-1
91B-199
91B-375SLUG
91Classic/200-34
91D-142
91D-390MVP
91D-6DK
91D/SuperDK-6DK
91DennyGS-5
91F-593
91F/UltraUp-U10
91F/Up-U10
91Leaf-334
91Leaf/StudPrev-3
91OPC-235
91OPC/BoxB-L
91OPC/Premier-94
91Panini/FrSt-210
91Panini/St-171
91S-484
91S/100SS-44
91Smok/Angel-4
91StCl-75
91T-235
91T/CJMini/I-11
91T/Tr-89T
91T/WaxBox-L
91UD-274
91UD-48
91UD/Ext-733
91UD/SilSlug-SS14
91Woolwth/HL-16
92UD-522
93AP/ASG-165

Parker, Don
92AZ/Pol-13
92Kingspt/ProC-1543

Parker, Francis James
(Salty)
60T-469C
62Sugar-16
73OPC-421CO
73T-421C
74OPC-276CO
74T-276C
76Cedar
87Belling/Team-28CO

Parker, Harry
74OPC-106
74T-106
75OPC-214
75SSPC/18-1
75T-214
75T/M-214
91WIZMets-309

Parker, James 1
87Chatt/Best-4

Parker, James 2
89GA-22
90GA-23

Parker, Jarrod
89Pulaski/ProC-1906
90Clmbia/PCPII-2
90Columbia/GS-4
90Pittsfld/Pucko-7

Parker, Joel
81BurlB-27

Parker, Mark
80Wichita-4
82Iowa-21

Parker, Maurice W.
(Wes)
64T-456R
65T-344
66OPC-134
66T-134
67CokeCap/DodgAngel-13
67T-218
68T-533
69MB-213
69MLB/St-151
69T-493
70MLB/St-55
70OPC-5
70T-5
71MLB/St-111
71OPC-430
71T-430
71T/Coins-121
71T/GM-30
71T/Greatest-30
71T/S-14
71T/Super-14
71T/tatt-8
71Ticket/Dodg-13
72K-17
72MB-265
72OPC-265
72T-265
73OPC-151
73T-151
81TCMA-365
88Smok/Dodg-10
90Target-605

Parker, Mike
89Idaho/ProC-2035

Parker, Olen
87Clearw-5

Parker, Richard
85Bend/Cram-18
87Clearw-1
88Reading/ProC-878
89BendB/Legoe-14
89EastLgAS/ProC-25
89Reading/Best-9
89Reading/ProC-660
89Reading/Star-19
90AAASingl/ProC-52
90Classic/III-72
90F/Up-U63
90Leaf-398
90PalmSp/Cal-210
90PalmSp/ProC-2581
90Phoenix/ProC-26
90S/Tr-77T
90T/Tr-87T
90UD/Ext-732
91F-269
91OPC-218
91PG&E-26
91Phoenix/ProC-73
91S-58
91S/100RisSt-11
91T-218
91T/90Debut-121
92S-601
92StCl-769
92Tucson/ProC-500
92Tucson/SB-616
93Mother/Ast-13
93StCl/Ast-27
94Pac/Cr-272

Parker, Rob
87ColAst/ProC-10

Parker, Stacy
89Butte/SP-1
91BendB/ClBest-21
91BendB/ProC-3706
91Clearw/ClBest-23
91Clearw/ProC-1634

Parker, Steve
87Peoria-24
88Pittsfld/ProC-1369
89WinSalem/Star-13
90AAASingl/ProC-623
90Iowa/CMC-5
90Iowa/ProC-316
90ProC/Singl-80
90T/TVCub-56

Parker, Tim
90A&AASingle/ProC-174
90Geneva/ProC-3049
90Geneva/Star-18
91AA/LineD-137
91CharlK/LineD-137
91CharlK/ProC-1686
92ChalK/SB-163
92ClBest-62
92Sky/AASingl-75

Parker, William David
(Billy)
72OPC-213R
72T-213R
73OPC-354
73T-354
75Syrac/Team-12
75Syrac/Team-17

Parkins, Rob
86WinHaven-19
93Calgary/ProC-1164

Parkinson, Eric
89Princet/Star-14
90Augusta/ProC-2460
90ProC/Singl-726
91Salem/ClBest-17
91Salem/ProC-947
92Salem/ClBest-4
92Salem/ProC-62
93CaroMud/RBI-8

Parkinson, Frank J.
E120
V100

Parks, Art
90Target-1048

Parks, Danny
81Pawtu-6

Parks, Derek
87Kenosha-19
88BBAmer-12
88OrlanTw/Best-1
88SLAS-12
89OrlanTw/Best-19
89OrlanTw/ProC-1350
90AAASingl/ProC-251
90B-422
90Classic/Up-40
90Portl/CMC-14
90Portl/ProC-181
90ProC/Singl-566
91AA/LineD-492
91ClBest/Singl-159
91OrlanSR/LineD-492
91OrlanSR/ProC-1852
92Portl/SB-416
92Portland/ProC-2670
92Sky/AAASingl-190
93D-237
93Pinn-267
93S-245
93StCl-74
93StCl/1stDay-74
94D-477
94F-216
94Pac/Cr-364
94T-649
94T/Gold-649
94Ultra-393

Parks, Jack
55T-23
55T/DH-68

Parks, Jeff
85Spokane/Cram-19

Parmalee, LeRoy
28LaPresse-28
33G-239
35BU-94
91Conlon/Sport-85
94Conlon-1062
R312
V355-20

Parmenter, Gary
86Iowa-21
87Iowa-7
88Pittsfld/ProC-1378

Parnell, Mark
89AppFx/ProC-875
90BBCity/Star-18
90Star/ISingl-44
91AA/LineD-410
91ClBest/Singl-301
91London/LineD-410
91Memphis/ProC-648
92Memphis/ProC-2416
92Memphis/SB-440
92Sky/AASingl-186

Parnell, Mel
50B-1
51FB
51T/RB-10
52B-241
52BR
52Dix
52StarCal-85BM
52StarCal/L-71A
52T-30
53B/Col-66
53Dix
53NB
53RM-AL25
53T-19
54Dix
54RM-AL8
54T-40
55RFG-28
55T-140
55T/DH-119
55W605-28
56T/Hocus-A18
57T-313
63MilSau-5
79TCMA-58
90Pac/Legend-98
91Swell/Great-118
91T/Arc53-19
92AP/ASG-21
92Bz/Quadra-14M
93TWill-4
93UD/ATH-104
94T/Arc54-40
PM10/Sm-141
R423-77

Parra, Franklin
91Butte/SportP-20
92Gaston/ClBest-17

Parra, Jose
90Kissim/DIMD-20
91GreatF/SportP-6
92Bakers/Cal-19
93LimeR/Winter-56
94B-42

Parra, Luis
92GulfCY/ProC-3790

Parrett, Jeff
86Expo/Prov/Pan-25
86F/Up-U88
86Provigo-25
88D-406
88F/Up-U102
88OPC-144
88T-588
89B-390
89D-334
89D/Best-296
89D/Tr-55
89F-389
89F/Up-112
89OPC-176
89Phill/TastyK-27
89S-377
89S/Tr-33
89S/YS/I-18
89T-176
89T/St-73
89T/Tr-95T
89UD-398
89UD/Ext-741
90B-149
90D-369
90F-570
90F/Can-570
90Leaf-210
90OPC-439
90Panini/St-312
90Phill/TastyK-25
90PublInt/St-248
90T-439
90T/St-119
90UD-92
91Brave/Dubuq/Perf-22
91Brave/Dubuq/Stand-29
91D-660
91F-699
91OPC-56
91Richm/Bob-32
91S-565
91StCl-544
91T-56
91UD-417
92L-520
92L/BlkGold-520
92Mother/A's-16

92StCl-834
93D-241
93F-297
93F/Final-39
93Pac/Spanish-434
93Pinn-431
93S-180
93Select-396
93StCl-414
93StCl-99
93StCl/1stDay-414
93StCl/1stDay-99
93StCl/Rockie-9
93T-209
93T/Gold-209
93T/Tr-46T
93UD-311
93UD-529
93USPlayC/Rockie-12D
93USPlayC/Rockie-7S
93Ultra-261
93Ultra-355
94F-449
Parrill, Marty
78RochR
Parris, Steve
88CapeCod/Sum-43
89Batavia/ProC-1923
90Batavia/ProC-3065
91Clearw/ClBest-7
91Clearw/ProC-1618
92Reading/ProC-572
92Reading/SB-538
93ScranWB/Team-20
Parrish, Lance M.
77Evansvl/TCMA-22
78T-708R
79T-469
80K-54
80OPC-110
80T-196
81Coke
81D-366
81F-467
81OPC-8
81T-392
81T/SO-14
81T/St-73
81Tiger/Detroit-90
82D-281
82F-276
82F/St-152
82OPC-214
82T-535
82T/St-188
83D-407
83D/AAS-50
83F-337
83F/St-22M
83F/St-8M
83K-40
83OPC-285
83OPC/St-193RB
83OPC/St-194RB
83OPC/St-63FOIL
83PermaGr/CC-30
83T-285
83T-4RB
83T/Gloss40-27
83T/St-193
83T/St-194
83T/St-63
84D-15DK
84D-49
84D/AAS-34
84F-637IA
84F-88
84Nes/792-640
84Nestle/DT-8
84OPC-158
84T-640
84T/Gloss40-2
84T/RD-14M
84T/St-265
84Tiger/Farmer-11
84Tiger/Wave-28
85Cain's-15
85D-49
85D/AAS-53
85Drake-23
85F-19
85F/St-31
85FunFoodPin-2
85Leaf-41
85OPC-160
85Seven-13C
85Seven-14D
85T-160
85T-708AS
85T/Gloss22-20
85T/RD-12M
85T/St-189
85T/St-259
85T/Super-55
85Wendy-17
86Cain's-14
86D-334
86F-234
86F/LL-31
86F/Mini-49
86F/St-85
86GenMills/Book-1M
86Jiffy-3
86Leaf-201
86OPC-147
86Seven/Coin-C12M
86Sf-92
86Sf/Dec-72M
86T-36M
86T-740
86T/Gloss60-8
86T/Mini-15
86T/St-273
86T/Tatt-22M
87D-91
87D/AAS-9
87D/OD-153
87D/PopUp-9
87F-160
87F/AwardWin-28
87F/Up-U96
87Jiffy-13
87Leaf-107
87MSA/Discs-19
87OPC-374
87Phill/TastyK-13
87RedFoley/St-36
87Sf-101
87Sf-154M
87T-613AS
87T-791
87T/Board-19
87T/Gloss22-20
87T/Gloss60-58
87T/St-149
87T/St-269
87T/Tr-94T
88D-359
88D/Best-184
88F-310
88KayBee-22
88Leaf-130
88OPC-95
88Panini/St-355
88Phill/TastyK-18
88RedFoley/St-65
88S-131
88Sf-143
88T-95
88T/Big-45
88T/St-123
89B-45
89D-278
89D/AS-55
89D/Best-59
89F-578
89F/Up-15
89OPC-114
89S-95
89S/Tr-36T
89Sf-59
89T-470
89T/Big-250
89T/Tr-96T
89UD-240
89UD/Ext-775
90B-295
90D-213
90D/BestAL-59
90D/Learning-41
90F-141
90F/Can-141
90Leaf-195
90MLBPA/Pins-94
90OPC-575
90Panini/St-38
90PublInt/St-376
90RedFoley/St-73
90S-35
90Smok/Angel-13
90T-575
90T/Big-323
90T/St-170
90UD-674
90USPlayC/AS-2C
91B-188
91B-374SLUG
91Cadaco-40
91D-135
91D-388MVP
91F-321
91Leaf-368
91Leaf/Stud-29
91MooTown-20
91OPC-210
91Panini/FrSt-179
91Panini/St-133
91S-37
91Smok/Angel-5
91StCl-166
91T-210
91UD-552
91UD/SilSlug-SS11
91Ultra-51
92D-166
92F-66
92L-269
92L/BlkGold-269
92OPC-360
92Panini-4
92Pinn-105
92S-298
92StCl-94
92Studio-149
92T-360
92T/Gold-360
92T/GoldWin-360
92TripleP-169
92TripleP-234LH
92UD-431
92Ultra-28
93D-85
93F-679
93Pol/Dodg-19
93S-587
93Select-388
93StCl-252
93StCl/1stDay-252
93T-609
93T/Gold-609
93UD-117
Parrish, Larry A.
76Expo/Redp-24
76Ho-126
76OPC-141
76SSPC-326
76T-141
77BurgChef-161
77OPC-72
77T-526
78OPC-153
78T-294
79OPC-357
79T-677
80OPC-182
80T-345
80T/S-53
80T/Super-53
81D-89
81F-146
81F/St-69
81OPC-15
81OPC/Post-4
81T-15
81T/SO-89
81T/St-183
82D-466
82F-200
82F/St-34
82OPC-353
82OPC/Post-15
82T-445
82T/St-64
82T/Tr-86T
83D-467
83F-574
83F/St-7M
83F/St-9M
83OPC-2
83OPC/St-120
83Rang-15
83T-776
83T/St-120
84D-21DK
84D-422
84D/AAS-42
84F-424
84Nes/792-169
84OPC-169
84Rang-15
84T-169
84T/RD-26M
84T/St-354
85D-300
85D/AAS-29
85F-564
85F/St-38
85Leaf-96
85OPC-203
85Rang-15
85T-548
85T/RD-26M
85T/St-346
86D-178
86F-569
86F/St-86
86Leaf-110
86OPC-238
86Rang-15
86T-238
86T/St-240
86T/Tatt-19M
87Classic-25
87Classic-50
87D-469
87D/HL-10
87D/OD-173
87F-134
87F/GameWin-33
87F/LL-34
87F/Mini-81
87F/RecSet-29
87F/St-89
87GenMills/Book-3M
87Leaf-209
87Mother/Rang-5
87RedFoley/St-104
87Sf-174
87Sf/TPrev-1M
87Smok/R-18
87Stuart-26
87T-629
87T/St-234
88ChefBoy-9
88D-347
88D/AS-21
88D/Best-334
88F-476
88F/Mini-57
88F/RecSet-28
88F/St-68
88F/TL-25
88F/Up-U7
88KennerFig-79
88KingB/Disc-21
88Leaf-119
88Mother/R-5
88OPC-226
88Panini/St-205
88RedFoley/St-66
88S-191
88S/Tr-65T
88Sf-49
88Smok/R-14
88T-490
88T/St-243
88T/UK-56
89F-94
89S-495
89T-354
89UD-36
92Nabisco-17
92Niagara/ClBest-27MG
92Niagara/ProC-3342MG
93Expo/D/McDon-17
93Rang/Keeb-288
Parrot, Steve
82ElPaso-19
83ElPaso-16
Parrott, Mike
79OPC-300
79T-576
80T-443
81Pol/Mar-10
81T-187
82D-226
82T-358
83Omaha-7
84Omaha-11
85OKCty-12
86OKCty-17
88Rockford-27CO
89Rockford-27CO
89Rockford/Team-29CO
91Crown/Orio-354
91WPalmB/ProC-1246CO
92Harris/ProC-476CO
92Harris/SB-300CO
Parrotte, Brian
89Billings/ProC-2050
Parry, Bob
88Madis-17
89Modesto/Cal-286
89Modesto/Chong-31
90Modesto/Chong-23
90Modesto/ProC-2228
Parry, Dave
82Tucson-28M
Parsons, Bill
59DF
Parsons, Bob
78Salem
Parsons, Casey R.
(Casey)
78Cr/PCL-42
79Phoenix
81Spokane-26
82F-515
82SLCity-15
85Louisvl-27
86Louisvl-22
87BuffB-9
88Memphis/Best-9
90Madison/Best-25MG
90Madison/ProC-2283MG
90MidwLgAS/GS-26MG
91AA/LineD-299MG
91Huntsvl/ClBest-22MG
91Huntsvl/LineD-299MG
91Huntsvl/Team-25MG
91HuntsvlProC-1811MG
92Huntsvl/ProC-3964MG
92Huntsvl/SB-324MG
Parsons, Charles
N172
Parsons, Scott
87LasVegas-5
Parsons, Thomas
62T-326
65T-308R
91WIZMets-310
Parsons, William Raymond
72K-5
72OPC-281
72T-281
73OPC-231
73T-231
74OPC-574
74T-574
75OPC-613
75T-613
75T/M-613
Partee, Roy Robert
(Roy)
43Playball-20
47TipTop
49B-149
Partin, Billy
89Sumter/ProC-1089
Partley, Calvin
74Cedar
Partlow, Roy
87Negro/Dixon-18
Partrick, Dave
88Bend/Legoe-11
89QuadC/Best-24
89QuadC/GS-9
90Boise/ProC-3327
90PalmSp/Cal-212
90PalmSp/ProC-2591
91PalmSp/ProC-2030
92Boise/ClBest-6
92Boise/ProC-3621
Partridge, Glenn
77BurlB
Partridge, Jay
90Target-606
Pascarella, Andy
79Newar-24

Paschal, Ben
91Conlon/Sport-107
Paschall, Bill
77Jaxvl
80T-667R
81Omaha-11
Pascual, Camilo Jr.
83Idaho-10
Pascual, Camilo
55T-84
55T/DH-104
56T-98
57T-211
58T-219
59T-291
59T-413
60Bz-14
60L-4
60T-483
60T-569AS
60T/tatt-43
61Clover-20
61NuCard-411
61P-99
61Peters-23
61T-235
61T/Dice-12
61T/St-183
62J-91
62P-91
62P/Can-91
62Salada-78
62Shirriff-78
62T-230
62T-59LL
62T/St-78
62T/bucks
63Bz-13
63Exh
63J-9
63P-9
63Salada-36
63T-10LL
63T-220
63T-8LL
64Bz-13
64T-2LL
64T-4LL
64T-500
64T-6LL
64T/Coins-137AS
64T/Coins-76
64T/S-32
64T/SU
64T/St-92
64T/tatt
65OPC-11LL
65OPC-255
65T-11LL
65T-255
65T/trans-23
66T-305
67CokeCap/Senator-5
67OPC-71
67T-71
68T-395
69MB-214
69MLB/St-107
69T-513
69T/S-31
69T/St-240
69T/decal
69Trans-27
70OPC-254
70T-254
78TCMA-32
78Twin/Frisz-16
79Twin/FriszP-20CO
90Target-607
94T/Arc54-255
Exh47
Pascual, Jorge
89Salem/Team-21
90Martins/ProC-3203
90Miami/I/Star-19
90Miami/II/Star-20
Pashnick, Larry
81Evansvl-5
83D-233
83Evansvl-8
83F-338
84D-394
Pasillas, Andy
77AppFx
78Knoxvl
79Knoxvl/TCMA-20
80GlenF/B-15
80GlenF/C-6
81GlenF-10
93Conlon-922
Paskert, George H.
(Dode)
10Domino-96
11Helmar-150
12Sweet/Pin-130A
12Sweet/Pin-130B
14Piedmont/St-47
16FleischBrd-73
BF2-89
D327
D328-130
D329-136
D350/2-135
E135-130
E254
E270
M101/4-136
M101/5-135
M116
S74-103
T202
T204
T205
T206
T207
T213/blue
T213/brown
T215/blue
T215/brown
T3-112
V100
W514-55
Paskievitch, Tom
91Erie/ClBest-21
91Erie/ProC-4067
92Watlo/ClBest-13
92Watlo/ProC-2141
Pasley, Kevin P.
(Kevin)
74Albuq/Team-12
75IntLgAS/Broder-21
75PCL/AS-21
77T-476R
78T-702R
80Syrac-3
80Syrac/Team-16
81Syrac-8
82BirmB-17
90Target-608
Pasqua, Dan
84Nashvl-16
85Colum-21
85Colum/Pol-17
85D-637
85F/Up-U86
86Colum-17
86Colum/Pol-15
86D-417
86F-114
86KayBee-22
86Leaf-195
86T-259
86T/Gloss60-20
87Classic-13
87D-474
87D/OD-244
87F-108
87F/Mini-79
87OPC-74
87Sf-143
87Sf/TPrev-7M
87T-74
87T/St-297
88Coke/WS-19
88D-463
88D/Best-137
88F-217
88F/Up-U18
88OPC-207
88Panini/St-159
88S-196
88S/Tr-56T
88T-691
88T/Big-164
88T/Tr-82T
89B-67
89Coke/WS-19
89D-294
89D/Best-123
89F-507
89KennerFig-101
89OPC-31
89Panini/St-313
89S-338
89T-558
89T/Big-44
89T/St-301
89UD-204
90B-313
90Coke/WSox-19
90D-176
90F-544
90F/Can-544
90Leaf-274
90OPC-446
90PublInt/St-398
90S-306
90T-446
90T/Big-144
90T/St-306
90T/St-309
90UD-286
91B-361
91D-103
91F-131
91Kodak/WSox-44
91Leaf-428
91OPC-364
91S-85
91StCl-214
91T-364
91UD-605
91Ultra-79
92D-142
92F-93
92L-369
92L/BlkGold-369
92OPC-107
92Pinn-227
92S-237
92StCl-794
92T-107
92T/Gold-107
92T/GoldWin-107
92UD-281
92Ultra-339
92WSox-44
92Yank/WIZ80-142
93D-491
93F-587
93L-20
93Pac/Spanish-394
93Pinn-354
93S-210
93StCl-94
93StCl/1stDay-94
93StCl/WSox-11
93T-204
93T/Gold-204
93UD-649
93WSox-22
94F-91
94Pac/Cr-139
94StCl-375
94StCl/1stDay-375
94StCl/Gold-375
94StCl/Team-149
Pasquale, Jeff
91Hamil/ClBest-8
91Hamil/ProC-4037
Pasquali, Jeff
83Erie-13
Passalacqua, Ricky
76Watlo
Passeau, Claude W.
39Exh
93Conlon-720
Passero, Joe
45Centen-20
Passmore, Jay
76BurlB
77BurlB
Pastore, Frank
78Indianap-23
80T-677R
81F-204
81OPC-1
81T-499
82Coke/Reds
82D-122
82F-80
82F/St-13
82T-128
83D-62
83F-599
83OPC-119
83T-658
84D-164
84F-477
84Nes/792-87
84OPC-87
84T-87
85D-550
85F-545
85OPC-292
85T-727
86F-185
86T-314
86T/Tr-85T
87OKCty-4
87T-576
Pastorius, James
90Target-1047
E103
E90/1
E93
T206
W555
Pastornicky, Cliff
81CharR-16
82CharR-21
83Omaha-17
84Omaha-21
86Water-19
Pastors, Greg
82Buffa-5
83LynnP-16
Pastrovich, Steve
80GlenF/B-1
80GlenF/C-16
81AppFx-8
82AppFx/Frit-11
83GlenF-18
Paszek, John
52Laval-31
Patchett, Hal
45Centen-21
Patchin, Steve
75Water
80Evansvl-22
Pate, Robert Wayne
(Bobby)
81D-545
81OPC-136R
81T-479R
83Tucson-21
87BurlEx-23
Patek, Freddie Joe
69Pirate/JITB-9
69T-219
70OPC-94
70T-94
71MLB/St-425
71OPC-626
71T-626
72MB-266
72T-531
73OPC-334
73T-334
74Greyhound-5M
74OPC-88
74T-88
74T/St-186
75Ho-32
75Ho/Twink-32
75OPC-48
75T-48
75T/M-48
76A&P/KC
76OPC-167
76SSPC-170
76T-167
77BurgChef-67
77Ho-109
77Ho/Twink-109
77K-36
77OPC-244
77T-422
78Ho-48
78OPC-4LL
78OPC-91
78SSPC/270-234
78T-204LL
78T-274
79Ho-46
79K-36
79OPC-273
79T-525
80OPC-356
80T-705
81D-170
81F-283
81T-311
82D-241
82F-471
82T-602
Patenaude, Alain
85Miami-11
Paterson, Jeff
92AS/Cal-27
Paterson, Pat
78Laugh/Black-18
86Negro/Frit-106
Patino, Benny
85Clovis-31
Patonix
72Dimanche*-124M
Patrick, Bronswell
89Madis/Star-18
90Madison/Best-22
90Modesto/Cal-155
90Modesto/Chong-24
90Modesto/ProC-2211
90ProC/Singl-666
91Modesto/ClBest-11
91Modesto/ProC-3085
92Huntsvl/ProC-3948
92Huntsvl/SB-317
Patrick, Hisel
59DF
Patrick, James
85Clovis-32ACO
Patrick, Otis
87Belling/Team-17
88Belling/Legoe-27
Patrick, Ron
77Ashvl
Patrick, Tim
90VeroB/Star-21
90Yakima/Team-14
91VeroB/ClBest-10
91VeroB/ProC-771
Patrizi, Mike
91Kingspt/ClBest-4
91Kingspt/ProC-3816
92ColumMet/ClBest-4
92ColumMet/ProC-300
92ColumMet/SAL/II-23
Pattee, Harry Ernest
(Harry)
T206
Patten, Bill
75Anderson/TCMA-18
Patten, Case
WG2-40
Patten, Eric
90Helena/SportP-18
Patterson, Bob
83Beaum-7
84Cram/PCL-221
85Cram/PCL-117
86Hawaii-19
87D/OD-166
87Sf/TPrev-18M
88BuffB/CMC-7
88BuffB/ProC-1467
88F-337
88T-522
89BuffB/ProC-1684
90B-168
90F/Up-U49
90T/Tr-88T
91D-345
91F-45
91OPC-479
91S-636
91StCl-594
91T-479
92D-590
92F-562
92OPC-263
92Pirate/Nation-18
92S-548
92StCl-876
92T-263
92T/Gold-263
92T/GoldWin-263
92Ultra-558
93D-174

93F-118
93Rang/Keeb-421
93Select/RookTr-120T
93T-299
93T/Gold-299
93UD-412
94D-218
94Pac/Cr-624
94S-292
94S/GoldR-292
Patterson, Danny
91GulfCR/SportP-11
92Gaston/ClBest-24
92Gaston/ProC-2253
Patterson, Daryl
68OPC-113R
68T-113R
69OPC-101
69T-101
70T-592
71MLB/St-402
71OPC-481
71T-481
88Domino-19
Patterson, Dave
86Everett/Pop-20
87Clinton-3
88CalLgAS-1
88SanJose/Cal-126
88SanJose/ProC-111
89Shrev/ProC-1843
90A&AASingle/ProC-73
90Shrev/ProC-1453
90Shrev/Star-18
90TexLgAS/GS-22
91AA/LineD-315
91ClBest/Singl-253
91Shrev/LineD-315
91Shrev/ProC-1831
92Phoenix/ProC-2829
92Phoenix/SB-392
Patterson, David Glenn
(Dave)
77LodiD
79Albuq-6
80Albuq-10
80T-679R
81Albuq/TCMA-2
82Tacom-8
86Cram/NWL-12
90Target-609
Patterson, Gil
77T-472R
92Madis/ClBest-27CO
92Madis/ProC-1253CO
92Yank/WIZ70-125
Patterson, Glenn
87Gaston/ProC-2
88Gaston/ProC-1021
Patterson, Greg
88WinSalem/Star-14
89Geneva/ProC-1882
90LSUGreat-14
Patterson, Jeff
89Martins/Star-23
90Clearw/Star-17
91Spartan/ClBest-11
91Spartan/ProC-896
92Clearw/ClBest-7
92Reading/ProC-573
93ScranWB/Team-21
Patterson, Jim
91FresnoSt/Smok-9
92Erie/ClBest-28
92Erie/ProC-1619
Patterson, Jimmy
52Wheat*
Patterson, Joe
62Pep/Tul
63Pep/Tul
Patterson, John
90A&AASingle/ProC-155
90Foil/Best-202
90SanJose/Best-9
90SanJose/Cal-33
90SanJose/ProC-2017
90SanJose/Star-17
91AA/LineD-316
91ClBest/Singl-314
91Shrev/LineD-316
91Shrev/ProC-1832
92B-67
92D/Rook-89
92Phoenix/ProC-2830
92Phoenix/SB-379
92Pinn-532
92ProC/Tomorrow-345
92UD-778DD
92Ultra-593
93D-193RR
93F-535
93L-160
93Pinn-413
93Pinn/RookTP-5
93S-279
93S/Boys-13
93T-573
93T/Gold-573
93ToysRUs-32
93USPlayC/Rook-4C
94F-697
94Select-189
94StCl-381
94StCl/1stDay-381
94StCl/Gold-381
94StCl/Team-18
94Ultra-590
Patterson, Ken
82CharR-16
84Idaho/Team-20
86FtLaud-17
87FtLaud-30
88Vanco/CMC-6
88Vanco/ProC-757
89Coke/WS-20
89D/Rook-37
89F-508
89S/HotRook-61
89S/Tr-97
89T-434
90Coke/WSox-20
90D-371
90F-545
90F/Can-545
90OPC-156
90S-207
90S/100Ris-89
90S/YS/I-27
90T-156
91D-522
91F-132
91Kodak/WSox-34
91OPC-326
91T-326
91UD-283
92Cub/Mara-34
92D-457
92F-94
92L-509
92L/BlkGold-509
92OPC-784
92Peoria/Team-19
92S-347
92StCl-289
92T-784
92T/Gold-784
92T/GoldWin-784
92UD-440
92Ultra-472
93D-742
93F-381
93Mother/Angel-24
93StCl-162
93StCl/1stDay-162
94F-66
94Ultra-25
Patterson, Larry
80LynnS-2
81Spokane-23
82Holyo-12
83Nashua-11
Patterson, Michael L.
79Ogden/TCMA-24
80WHave-15
82Colum-20
82Colum/Pol-14
83Colum-22
92Yank/WIZ80-143
Patterson, Reggie
80GlenF/B-9
80GlenF/C-18
82Edmon-15
82T-599R
83Iowa-7
84Iowa-31
86F-376
Patterson, Rick 1
77Wausau
Patterson, Rick 2
88Utica/Pucko-26
89SoBend/GS-2
90SoBend/Best-24MG
90SoBend/GS-27MG
91Saraso/ClBest-27
91Saraso/ProC-1129
92Saraso/ClBest-27MG
92Saraso/ProC-224MG
Patterson, Rob
92MedHat/SportP-25
93MedHat/ProC-3733
93MedHat/SportP-21
Patterson, Roy
E107
Patterson, Scott
80Ander-9
81Durham-22
82Colum-19
82Colum/Pol-11
83Nashvl-15
84Colum-14
84Colum/Pol-18
85Albany-10
86Colum-18
86Colum/Pol-16
Patterson, Shane
90Butte/SportP-14
Patterson, Steve
91Pocatel/ProC-3779
91Pocatel/SportP-15
Pattin, Jon
90Clinton/Best-28
90Clinton/ProC-2552
91SanJose/ClBest-3
91SanJose/ProC-14
Pattin, Marty
69Sunoco/Pin-14
69T-563
70McDon-6
70OPC-31
70T-31
71MLB/St-447
71OPC-579
71T-579
72OPC-144
72T-144
73OPC-415
73T-415
74OPC-583
74T-583
74T/St-187
75OPC-413
75T-413
75T/M-413
76OPC-492
76SSPC-162
76T-492
77T-658
78SSPC/270-231
78T-218
79T-129
80T-26
81D-343
81F-37
81T-389
Pattison, James
90Target-1050
R314/Can
Patton, Eric
89Helena/SP-20
Patton, Jack
88Bakers/Cal-266
89Reno/Cal-263GM
90Reno/Cal-292GM
Patton, Jeff
84PrWill-17
Patton, Owen
N172
Patton, Scott
92FrRow/DP-16
92LitSun/HSPros-12
93StCl/MurphyS-16
Patton, Tom
91Crown/Orio-355
Patzke, Jeff
92LitSun/HSPros-26
92MedHat/SportP-23
93MedHat/ProC-3746
93MedHat/SportP-12
93StCl/MurphyS-104
93T-529M
93T/Gold-529M
Paul, Corey
87Belling/Team-31
89Belling/Legoe-27
90Salinas/ProC-2733
Paul, Gabe
82Ohio/HOF-51
Paul, Mike
69T-537
70T-582
71MLB/St-381
71OPC-454
71T-454
72MB-267
72T-577
73OPC-58
73T-58
74OPC-399
74T-399
85Cram/PCL-208
86Vanco-21CO
90Mother/Mar-27M
93Rang/Keeb-32
Paul, Ron
81TCMA-381
Paula, Carlos C.
(Carlos)
55T-97
56T-4
56T/Pin-58
58Union
79TCMA-205
Paulesic, David
66Pep/Tul
Paulino, Dario
91Idaho/ProC-4338
91Idaho/SportP-23
92Macon/ClBest-6
92ProC/Tomorrow-198
Paulino, Elvin
87Peoria-17
88Peoria/Ko-24
89Peoria/Team-24
90CLAS/CL-48
90WinSalem/Team-24
91AA/LineD-138
91CharlK/LineD-138
91CharlK/ProC-1697
92B-95
92Iowa/SB-214
92ProC/Tomorrow-201
92Sky/AAASingl-103
93LimeR/Winter-90
Paulino, Luis
87Hagers-14
88Hagers/Star-15
89Freder/Star-20
Paulino, Nelson
92Pulaski/ClBest-26
92Pulaski/ProC-3186
93Macon/ClBest-18
93Macon/ProC-1411
Paulino, Richard
92Macon/ProC-281
Paulino, Victor
84Savan-19
Paulis, George
89Watlo/Star-28
Paulsen, Troy
88Alaska/Team-13
91Clearw/ClBest-20
91Clearw/ProC-1631
91FSLAS/ProC-FSL8
92ProC/Tomorrow-300
92Reading/ProC-582
92Reading/SB-539
92Sky/AASingl-234
Paustian, Mike
85Clovis-33CO
Pautt, Juan
83Pawtu-23
84Pawtu-12
Paveloff, David
91Kane/ClBest-8
91Kane/ProC-2656
91Kane/Team-15
92Freder/ClBest-3
92Freder/ProC-1802
Pavlas, Dave
86WinSalem-18
87Pittsfld-15
88TexLgAS/GS-21
88Tulsa-23
89OkCty/CMC-8
89OkCty/ProC-1529
90AAASingl/ProC-624
90Iowa/CMC-6
90Iowa/ProC-317
90ProC/Singl-81
90T/TVCub-57
91AAA/LineD-213
91Iowa/LineD-213
91Iowa/ProC-1058
91S-378RP
91T/90Debut-122
Pavletich, Donald S.
(Don)
59T-494
62T-594R
63FrBauer-18
65T-472
66OPC-196
66T-196
67CokeCap/Reds-9
67Kahn
67T-292
68OPC-108
68T-108
69MB-215
69OPC-179
69T-179
69T/4in1-4M
70OPC-504
70T-504
71MLB/St-326
71OPC-409
71T-409
72OPC-359
72T-359
81TCMA-333
Pavlick, Greg
78Tidew
79Tidew-20
84Jacks-10
88Kahn/Mets-52CO
89Kahn/Mets-52CO
90Kahn/Mets-52CO
90T/TVMets-5CO
91Kahn/Mets-52CO
Pavlik, John
84PrWill-9
Pavlik, Roger
87Gaston/ProC-15
88Gaston/ProC-1020
89CharlR/Star-19
90CharlR/Star-19
90Tulsa/Team-18
91AAA/LineD-315
91OkCty/LineD-315
91OkCty/ProC-174
92D/Rook-90
92F/Up-62
92OkCty/ProC-1914
92OkCty/SB-317
93D-113
93F-688
93L-550
93Rang/Keeb-422
93S-325
93StCl-193
93StCl/1stDay-193
93StCl/Rang-5
93T-223
93T/Gold-223
93Ultra-283
94D-527
94F-315
94Pac/Cr-625
94Pinn-469
94S-365
94StCl-178
94StCl/1stDay-178
94StCl/Gold-178
94StCl/Team-263
94T-22
94T/Finest-155
94T/FinestRef-155
94T/Gold-22
94TripleP-198
94UD-418
94UD/CollC-226
94UD/CollC/Gold-226
94UD/CollC/Silv-226
94Ultra-131
Pawling, Eric
86Clinton-17
86Cram/NWL-193

Pawlowski, John
86Penin-19
87BirmB/Best-17
88Coke/WS-20
88D-457
89Vanco/CMC-7
89Vanco/ProC-595
90AAASingl/ProC-165
90ProC/Singl-637
90S-617
90Vanco/CMC-10
90Vanco/ProC-487
92Edmon/ProC-3538
92Edmon/SB-164
Paxton, Darrin
90WichSt-29
92Albany/ClBest-3
92Albany/ProC-2302
93BurlB/ClBest-16
93BurlB/ProC-153
Paxton, Greg
90Reno/Cal-282
Paxton, Mike
78T-216
79OPC-54
79T-122
80T-388
80Tacom-27
81Charl-5
81F-401
Payne, Chad
90GA-24
Payne, Frederick T.
(Fred)
E90/3
M116
S74-8
T201
T202
T205
T206
Payne, Harley
90Target-610
Payne, Jeff
90Hamil/Best-25
Payne, Jim
79Wausau-24
81Wisco-17
Payne, Joe
V362-15
Payne, Larry
76Indianap-2
77Indianap-7
78Indianap-13
Payne, Mike
80Ander-15
81Durham-23
82Durham-19
85Richm-6
87Jaxvl-16
Payne, Stan
92SoOreg/ClBest-25
92SoOreg/ProC-3415
Paynter, Billy
88Wythe/ProC-1983
89Peoria/Team-13
90Geneva/ProC-3040
90Geneva/Star-19
90Peoria/Team-5
Payton, Dave
87Erie-21
88Spring/Best-15
89Spring/Best-15
Payton, Ray
88MidwLAS/GS-49
89Saraso/Star-17
90Saraso/Star-18
Pazik, Mike
73Syrac/Team-22
74Tacoma/Caruso-8
75Tacoma/KMMO-14
76OPC-597R
76T-597R
77T-643
80GlenF/B-24MG
80GlenF/C-21MG
82AppFx/Frit-30CO
88CharlK/Pep-14
90Freder/Team-2
Pe, Bobby S.
90Butte/SportP-18
Peacock, John Gaston
(Johnny)
39PlayBall-16
40PlayBall-34
90Target-611
Pearce, Chris
94LSU-13
Pearce, Jeff
90Spokane/SportP-17
91CharRain/ClBest-23
91CharRain/ProC-109
92Watlo/ClBest-23
92Watlo/ProC-2153
Pearce, Jim
55T-170
Pearce, Steve
77Cedar
Pearlman, David
93StCath/ClBest-19
93StCath/ProC-3974
Pearn, Joe
87PortChar-27
88Gaston/ProC-1006
Pearse, Steve
88Rockford-30
89Rockford-28
Pearsey, Les
81Holyo-19
82Spokane-18
Pearson, Albert G.
(Albie)
58T-317
59T-4
60T-241
61T-288
62J-78
62P-78
62P/Can-78
62Salada-63A
62Salada-63B
62Shirriff-63
62T-343
62T/St-67
63F-19
63J-29
63P-29
63T-182
64T-110
64T/Coins-111
64T/Coins-132AS
64T/S-23
64T/SU
64T/St-42
64T/tatt
64Wheat/St-33
65T-358
66OPC-83
66T-83
78TCMA-16
91Crown/Orio-356
Exh47
Pearson, Cory
92Classic/DP-82
Pearson, Darren
85Everett/Cram-13A
85Everett/Cram-13B
86Clinton-18
Pearson, Don
77Wausau
78Wausau
Pearson, Donna
88OK-19M
Pearson, Eddie
92ClBest/Up-409
92UD/ML-15
93ClBest/MLG-200
94B-427
94ClBest/Gold-93
94UD-549TP
Pearson, Frank
92Negro/Retort-46
Pearson, George
89GA-23
89GA-28M
Pearson, Ike
47Centen-19
Pearson, Kevin
87Tampa-6
88Greens/ProC-1560
89Chatt/Best-18
89Chatt/GS-20
89Nashvl/Team-18
90AAASingl/ProC-554
90Nashvl/CMC-17
90Nashvl/ProC-242
90ProC/Singl-142
91AAA/LineD-269
91Nashvl/LineD-269
91Nashvl/ProC-2167
92FrRow/DP-31
93StCl/MurphyS-25
Pearson, Monte
37OPC-131
39PlayBall-71
40PlayBall-5
92Conlon/Sport-369
92Yank/WIZAS-57
93Conlon-748
R310
V300
V355-114
Pearson, Steve
87SLCity/Taco-14MG
88SLCity-16MG
Pechek, Wayne
76Cedar
80Phoenix/NBank-19
81Phoenix-19
Peck, Hal
45Playball-21
49B-182
90Target-612
Peck, Steve
90Madison/ProC-2269
90Modesto/Chong-25
91PalmSp/ProC-2011
92MidldA/OneHour-18
92MidldA/ProC-4026
92MidldA/SB-467
93Vanco/ProC-2594
Peckinpaugh, Roger
14CJ-91
15CJ-91
21Exh-125
21Exh-126
61F-132
77Galasso-163
82Ohio/HOF-20
86Conlon/1-37
91Conlon/Sport-308
94Conlon-1258
D327
D328-131
D329-137
D350/2-136
E120
E121/120
E121/80
E122
E135-131
E210
E220
M101/4-137
M101/5-136
V100
V117-23
W502-56
W514-44
W516-20
W575
WG7-40
Pecorilli, Aldo
92Johnson/ClBest-10
92Johnson/ProC-3119
94ClBest/Gold-172
94FExcel-272
Pecota, Bill
82FtMyr-21
84Memphis-24
85Omaha-29
86Omaha/ProC-17
86Omaha/TCMA-12
87F/Up-U97
88D-466
88F-264
88S-377
88Smok/Royals-22
88T-433
89F-289
89Omaha/CMC-15
89S-339
89T-148
89T/Big-292
89UD-507
90B-377
90Omaha/CMC-16
90ProC/Singl-191
91D-672
91F-565
91F/UltraUp-U28
91OPC-754
91Panini/FrSt-277
91Pol/Royal-17
91S-513
91T-754
92D-361
92F-165
92L-244
92L/BlkGold-244
92Mets/Kahn-32
92OPC-236
92OPC/Premier-149
92Panini-96
92Pinn-319
92S-252
92S/RookTr-52T
92StCl-811
92T-236
92T/Gold-236
92T/GoldWin-236
92T/Tr-86T
92T/TrGold-86T
92UD-240
92UD-793
92Ultra-535
93Brave/LykePerf-23
93Brave/LykeStand-28
93D-248
93F-92
93Pac/Spanish-339
93S-365
93StCl-148
93StCl/1stDay-148
93StCl/Brave-2
93T-517
93T/Gold-517
94F-371
94S-144
94S/GoldR-144
94StCl-486
94StCl/1stDay-486
94StCl/Gold-486
94StCl/Team-57
94T-414
94T/Gold-414
Peden, Les
53T-256
91T/Arc53-256
Pedersen, Don
89Niagara/Pucko-1
90Fayette/ProC-2414
Pedersen, Mark
81Wausau-6
Pederson, Stu
82VeroB-24
85Cram/PCL-167
86Albuq-19
87Albuq/Pol-29
89Syrac/CMC-16
89Syrac/MerchB-18
89Syrac/ProC-798
89Syrac/Team-18
90AAASingl/ProC-366
90ProC/Singl-349
90Syrac/CMC-23
90Syrac/MerchB-18
90Syrac/ProC-586
90Syrac/Team-18
90Target-613
91AAA/LineD-512
91Syrac/LineD-512
91Syrac/MerchB-17
91Syrac/ProC-2495
92Syrac/MerchB-15
92Syrac/ProC-1983
92Syrac/SB-513
Pedraza, Nelson
83Watlo/Frit-7
85Water-1
Pedraza, Rodney
91ClBest/Singl-425
91FrRow/DP-16
91James/ClBest-27
91James/ProC-3543
92Albany/ClBest-6
92Albany/ProC-2303
92StCl/Dome-139
Pedre, Jorge
88AppFx/ProC-137
88MidwLAS/GS-37
89BBCity/Star-20
90Foil/Best-139
90Memphis/Best-2
90Memphis/ProC-1013
90Memphis/Star-22
90Star/ISingl-87
91AA/LineD-411
91London/LineD-411
91Memphis/ProC-658
92Iowa/ProC-4054
92Iowa/SB-215
92S-844RP
92T/91Debut-136
Pedrique, Alfredo
(Al)
82Jacks-16
84Jacks-23
85IntLgAS-14
85Tidew-24
86Tidew-24
88D-361
88F-338
88Panini/St-375
88S-301
88T-294
88T/JumboR-17
88T/St-128
88T/St-304
88ToysRUs-23
89B-104
89Mara/Tigers-17
89S-614
89T-566
89T-699TL
90AAASingl/ProC-149
90ProC/Singl-596
90Tacoma/CMC-19
90Tacoma/ProC-102
91AAA/LineD-565
91Tidew/LineD-565
91Tidew/ProC-2519
91WIZMets-311
92Omaha/ProC-2971
92Omaha/SB-341
93Edmon/ProC-1144
Pedro, Blanco
92Elizab/ClBest-13
Peek, Timothy
88Spartan/ProC-1027
88Spartan/Star-15
90Madison/Best-23
91AA/LineD-291
91Huntsvl/ClBest-18
91Huntsvl/LineD-291
91Huntsvl/Team-17
91HuntsvlProC-1793
92ProC/Tomorrow-130
92Sky/AAASingl-243
92Tacoma/ProC-2499
92Tacoma/SB-543
Peel, Homer
34G-88
Peel, Jack
87CharWh-24
88Tampa/Star-20
89Saraso/Star-18
90CharlR/Star-20
Peever, Lloyd
92FrRow/DP-37
92LSU/McDag-8
93StCl/MurphyS-171
Peguero, Jerry
87Modesto-17
88Huntsvl/BK-14
90Salinas/Cal-135
Peguero, Jose
89Beloit/I/Star-21
90Salinas/ProC-2726
Peguero, Julio
87Macon-16
88CLAS/Star-14
88Salem/Star-15
89Harris/ProC-294
89Harris/Star-13
90EastLAS/ProC-EL24
90Harris/ProC-1206
90Harris/Star-14
90ProC/Singl-763
91AAA/LineD-492
91ScranWB/LineD-492
91ScranWB/ProC-2553
92ScranWB/ProC-2460
92ScranWB/SB-498
92Ultra-547
93LimeR/Winter-26
Peguero, Pablo
75Albuq/Caruso-15
77LodiD

78Cr/PCL-114
79Albuq-1
80Albuq-3
Pegues, Steve
88Fayette/ProC-1081
89Fayette/ProC-1594
90London/ProC-1282
90ProC/Singl-836
91AA/LineD-393
91ClBest/Singl-126
91London/LineD-393
91London/ProC-1891
92LasVegas/ProC-2806
92LasVegas/SB-236
92Sky/AAASingl-115
93B-166
Peitz, Henry
E107
E254
Pelka, Brian
93Welland/ClBest-18
93Welland/ProC-3354
Pellagrini, Ed
49B-172
51B-292
52T-405
53T-28
91T/Arc53-28
Pellant, Gary
80LynnS-14
82Wausau/Frit-23CO
83Wausau/Frit-3CO
Pellegrino, Tony
86Cram/NWL-172
88Charl/ProC-1194
89AubAs/ProC-3
89Wichita/Rock-12
Pelletier, Michel
72Dimanche*-125
Pells, Harry
76QuadC
77QuadC
Pelmmons, Scott
90CharWh/Best-6
Peltier, Dan
89Butte/SP-27
90A&AASingle/ProC-71
90ProC/Singl-804
90Tulsa/ProC-1168
90Tulsa/Team-19
91AAA/LineD-316
91B-266
91Classic/200-176
91Classic/II-T23
91OkCty/LineD-316
91OkCty/ProC-192
91UD-69TP
92D/Rook-91
92OPC-618M
92OkCty/ProC-1927
92OkCty/SB-318
92Sky/AAASingl-146
92T-618R
92T/Gold-618M
92T/GoldWin-618M
93D-473RR
93L-443
93Pac/Spanish-644
93Pinn-605
93Rang/Keeb-423
93S-240
93Select/RookTr-147T
93StCl-242
93StCl/1stDay-242
93StCl/Rang-30
94D-515
94F-316
94S-569
94StCl-457
94StCl/1stDay-457
94StCl/Gold-457
94StCl/Team-254
94T-441
94T/Gold-441
Pelty, Barney
10Domino-97
11Helmar-63
12Sweet/Pin-54
E286
M116
S74-35
T202
T204
T205
T206
T207
T215/blue
T215/brown
Peltz, Peter
81GlenF-14
Peltzer, Kurt
90Everett/Best-10
90Everett/ProC-3126
91Clinton/ClBest-7
91Clinton/ProC-832
92Clinton/ClBest-12
94B-107
Pemberton, Brock
75Tidew/Team-17
91WIZMets-312
Pemberton, Jose
87Elmira/Black-26
87Elmira/Red-26
Pemberton, Rudy
89Bristol/Star-20
90Fayette/ProC-2421
90SALAS/Star-17
91ClBest/Singl-181
91Lakeland/ClBest-26
91Lakeland/ProC-280
92ClBest-168
92Lakeland/ClBest-26
92Lakeland/ProC-2292
92OPC-656
92T-656M
92T/Gold-656
92T/GoldWin-656
93ClBest/MLG-164
Pena, Abelino
75BurlB
76BurlB
Pena, Adriano
81Wisco-8
Pena, Alejandro
79Clinton/TCMA-9
81Albuq/TCMA-4
82Pol/Dodg-26
83Pol/Dodg-26
83T/Tr-83T
84D-250
84F-109
84Nes/792-324
84Pol/Dodg-26
84T-324
84T/St-82
85Coke/Dodg-24
85D-337
85F-379
85F/St-94
85Leaf-64
85OPC-110
85Seven-15W
85T-110
85T/Gloss40-33
85T/St-73
85T/Super-17
86Coke/Dodg-22
86F-140
86Pol/Dodg-26
86T-665
87F-449
87Mother/Dodg-18
87OPC-363
87Pol/Dodg-13
87T-787
88D-598
88F/Up-U97
88Mother/Dodg-18
88Pol/Dodg-26
88T-277
89D-557
89F-69
89Mother/Dodg-18
89Pol/Dodg-16
89S-389
89T-57
89UD-137
90B-124
90D-664
90F-405
90F/Can-405
90F/Up-U38
90Kahn/Mets-26
90Leaf-403
90OPC-483
90PublInt/St-15
90S-39
90S/Tr-32T
90T-483
90T/TVMets-17
90T/Tr-89T
90Target-614
90UD-279
90UD/Ext-703
91D-566
91F-158
91Kahn/Mets-26
91Leaf-70
91OPC-544
91S-204
91StCl-583
91StCl/Member*-30M
91T-544
91UD-388
91WIZMets-313
92Brave/LykePerf-22
92Brave/LykeStand-25
92Classic/I-18
92D-616HL
92D-772
92F-700M
92F/Up-70
92L-489
92L/BlkGold-489
92OPC-337
92Pinn-528
92S-691
92S-787M
92StCl-833
92T-337
92T/Gold-337
92T/GoldWin-337
92UD-694
92Ultra-462
93F-369
93OPC-311
93S-625
93StCl-205
93StCl/1stDay-205
93T-198
93T/Gold-198
Pena, Antonio
91SanBern/ClBest-10
91SanBern/ProC-1986
Pena, Arturo
93LimeR/Winter-88
Pena, Bert
81Tucson-7
82Tucson-1
83Tucson-17
84Cram/PCL-67
86Tucson-18
87Mother/Ast-24
87Tucson-16
88Colum/CMC-13
88Colum/Pol-16
88Colum/ProC-322
Pena, Dan
87VeroB-4
88Bakers/Cal-257
Pena, George
73OPC-601R
73T-601R
74Tacoma/Caruso-16
75Iowa/TCMA-13
Pena, Geronimo
87Savan-4
88FSLAS/Star-16
88StPete/Star-21
90AAASingl/ProC-526
90F/Up-U52
90Louisvl/CMC-19
90Louisvl/LBC-33
90Louisvl/ProC-412
90ProC/Singl-119
90T/TVCard-59
91D-712
91F/Up-U118
91OPC-636
91Pol/Card-7
91S-717RP
91S/Rook40-17
91T-636
91T/90Debut-123
91UD-20SR
92D-533
92F-587
92OPC-166
92Pinn-487
92Pol/Card-15
92S-516
92S/100RisSt-12
92StCl-466
92T-166
92T/Gold-166
92T/GoldWin-166
92UD-596
93B-604
93D-310
93F-131
93Flair-126
93L-118
93LimeR/Winter-78
93OPC-238
93Pac/Beisbol-30
93Pac/Spanish-300
93Pac/SpanishGold-8
93Panini-193
93Pinn-174
93Pol/Card-15
93S-161
93Select-372
93StCl-215
93StCl/1stDay-215
93StCl/Card-20
93T-312
93T/Gold-312
93UD-331
93UD-466IN
93UD-482
93Ultra-466
94D-234
94F-643
94Finest-315
94L-172
94Pac/Cr-600
94Panini-247
94Pinn-214
94Pinn/Artist-214
94Pinn/Museum-214
94Select-148
94StCl-523
94StCl/1stDay-523
94StCl/Gold-523
94StCl/Team-307
94T-444
94T/Gold-444
Pena, Hipolito
86Nashua-21
87Vanco-18
88Colum/CMC-7
88Colum/Pol-8
88Colum/ProC-315
89Colum/CMC-5
89Colum/Pol-18
89Colum/ProC-744
89D-598
89F-263
89T-109
90ColClip/CMC-6
90ProC/Singl-206
91AAA/LineD-114
91ColClip/LineD-114
91ColClip/ProC-597
92Yank/WIZ80-144
93LimeR/Winter-64
Pena, Jaime
89Erie/Star-17
Pena, James
86Cram/NWL-14
86Everett/Pop-21
87Clinton-19
89SanJose/Best-16
89SanJose/Cal-216
89SanJose/ProC-445
89SanJose/Star-21
90Shrev/ProC-1442
90Shrev/Star-19
90TexLgAS/GS-35
91AA/LineD-317
91Shrev/LineD-317
91Shrev/ProC-1820
92D/Rook-92
92F/Up-129
92Phoenix/ProC-2819
92Phoenix/SB-393
93B-54
93D-628
93F-536
93S-288
Pena, Jose G.
69T-339R
70OPC-523
70T-523
71MLB/St-112
71OPC-693
71T-693
72OPC-322
72T-322
90Target-615
Pena, Jose
86Clinton-19
88Shrev/ProC-1292
88Utica/Pucko-23
89Shrev/ProC-1848
Pena, Luis
86Macon-18
Pena, Manny
83OrlanTw-13
Pena, Orlando
59T-271
63T-214
64T-124
65T-311
66T-239
67T-449
68T-471
69T/St-97
73JP
74OPC-393
74T-393
75OPC-573
75T-573
75T/M-573
75Tucson-12
75Tucson/Team-15
91Crown/Orio-357
Pena, Pedro
89Medford/Best-11
90Madison/ProC-2270
90MidwLgAS/GS-56
90Modesto/Chong-26
91SanJose/ClBest-19
91SanJose/ProC-8
Pena, Porfirio
90Batavia/ProC-3068
91Martins/ClBest-15
91Martins/ProC-3456
Pena, R. Roberto
65T-549R
66T-559
69OPC-184
69T-184
69T/4in1-15M
70OPC-44
70T-44
71MLB/St-448
71OPC-334
71T-334
Pena, Ramon
86GlenF-18
87GlenF-20
88Toledo/CMC-6
88Toledo/ProC-610
89Mara/Tigers-18
89Toledo/CMC-2
89Toledo/ProC-779
90T/89Debut-96
Pena, Tony
77Salem
79BuffB/TCMA-5
80Port-24
81T-551R
82D-124
82F-490
82F/St-72
82T-138
83D-59
83D/AAS-35
83F-316
83F/St-14M
83F/St-1AM
83F/St-1BM
83OPC-133
83OPC/St-281
83T-590
83T/St-281
84D-186
84D/AAS-3
84F-259
84Nes/792-645
84Nestle/DT-19
84OPC-152
84Seven-18E
84T-645
84T/RD-32
84T/St-129
85D-24DK
85D-64
85D/AAS-10

85D/DKsuper-24
85F-472
85F/LimEd-24
85FunFoodPin-88
85Leaf-24DK
85OPC-358
85T-358
85T/RD-32
85T/St-124
86BK/AP-1
86D-64
86D/AAS-22
86F-616
86F/LimEd-34
86F/Mini-119
86F/St-87
86Leaf-58
86OPC-260
86Seven/Coin-C12M
86Sf-165
86Sf/Dec-72M
86T-260
86T/St-125
86T/Tatt-5M
87BK-15
87Classic-34
87D-115
87D/AAS-46
87D/OD-64
87F-617
87F/BB-31
87F/LL-35
87F/Lim-32
87F/St-90
87F/Up-U98
87Ho/St-14
87Kraft-12
87Leaf-256
87MSA/Discs-5
87MnM's-2
87OPC-60
87RedFoley/St-25
87S/Test-48
87Sf-151M
87Sf-93
87Sf/TPrev-18M
87Smok/Cards-11
87T-60
87T/Coins-39
87T/St-129
87T/Tr-95T
88D-170
88D/Best-156
88F-45
88F/WS-5M
88Leaf-95
88OPC-117
88Panini/St-387
88Panini/St-447IA
88Panini/St-449IA
88RedFoley/St-67
88S-48
88Sf-142
88Smok/Card-13
88T-351TC
88T-410
88T/St-52
89B-435
89Cadaco-38
89D-163
89D/Best-299
89F-460
89KMart/DT-30
89KennerFig-102
89OPC-94
89Panini/St-180
89S-36
89Smok/Cards-17
89T-715
89T/St-38
89UD-330
90B-271
90Classic/III-67
90D-181
90D/BestAL-44
90F-256
90F/Can-256
90F/Up-U74
90Leaf-104
90MLBPA/Pins-34
90OPC-115
90Pep/RSox-14
90PubIInt/St-225
90PubIInt/St-269
90S-122
90S/Tr-7T
90T-115
90T/Big-290
90T/TVRSox-20
90T/Tr-90T
90UD-276
90UD/Ext-748
91B-124
91Cadaco-41
91D-456
91F-106
91Leaf-33
91Leaf/Stud-17
91OPC-375
91Panini/FrSt-263
91Panini/St-219
91Pep/RSox-14
91S-790
91StCl-505
91T-375
91UD-652
91Ultra-37
92B-364
92D-208
92F-43
92French-9
92L-323
92L/BlkGold-323
92OPC-569
92Panini-84
92Pinn-33
92RedSox/Dunkin-21
92S-446
92StCl-706
92Studio-135
92T-569
92T/Gold-569
92T/GoldWin-569
92TripleP-48
92UD-252
92USPlayC/RedSox-11S
92USPlayC/RedSox-6C
92Ultra-18
92Ultra/AwardWin-17
93B-439
93Cadaco-44
93D-297
93F-563
93L-43
93LimeR/Winter-105
93OPC-316
93Pac/Spanish-34
93Panini-91
93Pinn-506
93S-261
93Select-148
93StCl-164
93StCl/1stDay-164
93T-618
93T/Gold-618
93TripleP-85
93UD-185
93UD-33CH
93UD/FunPack-165
93Ultra-154
94D-191
94F-37
94Pac/Cr-61
94Panini-32
94S-363
94StCl-71
94StCl/1stDay-71
94StCl/Gold-71
94T-85
94T/Gold-85

Penafeather, Pat
88AubAs/ProC-1952

Pender, Shawn
92Watertn/ClBest-26
92Watertn/ProC-3250MG

Pendergast, Steve
W514-117

Pendleton, Jim
52Park-69
53JC-25
53SpicSpan/3x5-20
53T-185
54JC-3
54T-165
55Gol/Braves-25
55JC-2
55T-15
55T/DH-33
57T-327
58T-104
59T-174
62T-432
89Smok/Ast-25
91T/Arc53-185
94T/Arc54-165

Pendleton, Terry
83ArkTr-15
84Louisvl-15
85D-534
85F-236
85OPC-346
85T-346
86D-205
86F-44
86KAS/Disc-14
86KayBee-23
86Leaf-137
86OPC-321
86Schnucks-19
86T-528
86T/St-53
86T/Tatt-17M
87D-183
87D/OD-62
87F-306
87Leaf-124
87OPC-8
87Sf/TPrev-12
87Smok/Cards-16
87T-8
87T/St-54
88D-454
88D/Best-187
88F-46
88F/AwardWin-28
88F/SS-27
88F/St-119
88Leaf-246
88OPC-105
88Panini/St-392
88RedFoley/St-68
88S-190
88Sf-159
88Smok/Card-17
88T-635
88T/Big-53
88T/St-49
88T/St/Backs-7
89B-437
89D-230
89D/Best-156
89F-461
89KennerFig-103
89OPC-375
89Panini/St-185
89S-137
89Sf-99
89Smok/Cards-18
89T-375
89T/Big-151
89T/St-42
89UD-131
90B-197
90D-299
90D/BestNL-34
90F-257
90F/Can-257
90Leaf-260
90OPC-725
90Panini/St-337
90PubIInt/St-226
90S-208
90Sf-174
90Smok/Card-19
90T-725
90T/Big-135
90T/St-40
90T/TVCard-28
90UD-469
91B-570
91Brave/Dubuq/Perf-23
91Brave/Dubuq/Stand-30
91D-446
91F-642
91F/Up-U76
91Leaf-304
91Leaf/Stud-148
91OPC-485
91OPC/Premier-95
91S-230
91S/RookTr-50T
91StCl-327
91StCl/Member*-23
91StCl/Member*-24
91T-485
91T/Tr-90T
91UD-484
91UD/Ext-708
91Ultra-10
92B-254
92Brave/LykePerf-23
92Brave/LykeStand-26
92CJ/DI-26
92Card/McDon/Pac-40
92Classic/Game200-182
92Classic/I-70
92Colla/ASG-8
92D-237
92D-BC2MVP
92D/BC-BC2MVP
92D/Elite-E16
92F-366
92F-691LL
92F/ASIns-15
92F/Performer-15
92French-3M
92Hardee-18
92KingB-1
92L-245
92L/BlkGold-245
92MSA/Ben-14
92OPC-115
92OPC/Premier-195
92P-22
92Panini-148
92Panini-164
92Pinn-18
92S-18
92S-789MVP
92S/100SS-45
92S/Proctor-13
92StCl-510
92Studio-8
92Sunflower-7
92T-115
92T/Gold-115
92T/GoldWin-115
92T/Kids-33
92T/McDonB-7
92TripleP-139
92UD-229
92UD/TmMVPHolo-2MVP
92UD/TmMVPHolo-39
92USPlayC/Ace-7D
92USPlayC/Brave-10D
92USPlayC/Brave-1C
92Ultra-167
92Ultra/AwardWin-4
93B-254
93Brave/FLAg-8
93Brave/LykePerf-24
93Brave/LykeStand-29
93Classic/Gamel-73
93Colla/DM-84
93D-234
93D/MVP-7
93DennyGS-5
93Duracel/PPI-8
93F-12
93F/Atlantic-17
93F/Fruit-51
93F/TLNL-2
93Flair-9
93Ho-9
93Kenner/Fig-27
93Kraft-26
93L-387
93L/GoldAS-6M
93MSA/Metz-34
93OPC-322
93P-17
93Pac/Spanish-340
93Panini-184
93Pinn-473NT
93Pinn-60
93Post/Can-18
93S-36
93S/Franchise-15
93Select-17
93Select/StatL-10
93Select/StatL-18M
93Select/StatL-35
93StCl-338
93StCl/1stDay-338
93StCl/Brave-21
93StCl/MurphyS-102
93Studio-117
93T-650
93T/BlkGold-15
93T/Finest-101AS
93T/FinestASJ-101AS
93T/FinestRef-101AS
93T/Gold-650
93TripleP-147
93UD-163
93UD/Clutch-R16
93UD/Diam-5
93UD/FunPack-66
93UD/FunPackAS-AS5M
93UD/HRH-HR18
93UD/SP-61
93USPlayC/Ace-3D
93Ultra-11
93Ultra/AwardWin-5
94B-573
94D-556
94F-372
94L-189
94OPC-38
94Pac/Cr-20
94Panini-149
94Pinn-371
94S-72
94S/GoldR-72
94Select-34
94StCl-313
94StCl/1stDay-313
94StCl/Gold-313
94StCl/Team-40
94Studio-41
94T-735
94T/Finest-118
94T/FinestRef-118
94T/Gold-735
94TripleP-48
94TripleP/Medal-10
94UD-95
94UD/ElecD-95
94Ultra-449

Penigar, C.L.
86Clinton-20
88MidldA/GS-17
89BirmB/Best-23
89BirmB/ProC-115
90AAASingl/ProC-180
90ProC/Singl-636
90Vanco/CMC-9
90Vanco/ProC-502

Penix, Troy
92ClBest/Up-441
92FrRow/DP-68
92SoOreg/ClBest-1
92SoOreg/ProC-3427

Penland, Ken
88Butte-6

Penn, Shannon
90Butte/SportP-24
91Gaston/ClBest-21
91Gaston/ProC-2698
92Niagara/ClBest-16
92Niagara/ProC-3335
94FExcel-59

Penn, Trevor
88Rockford-28
89Rockford-29
89WPalmB/Star-21
90Jaxvl/Best-11
90Jaxvl/ProC-1386

Penniall, David
77StPete
80ArkTr-10

Pennington, Art
86Negro/Frit-53
92Negro/Retort-47

Pennington, Brad
89Bluefld/Star-18
90Foil/Best-65
90Wausau/Best-8
90Wausau/ProC-2121
90Wausau/Star-18
91ClBest/Singl-390
91Kane/ClBest-9
91Kane/ProC-2657
92B-136
92ClBest-108
92Freder/ClBest-20
92UD/ML-198
93B-361FOIL
93B-661
93F/Final-163

93FExcel/ML-126
93Flair/Wave-11
93L-526
93Select/RookTr-75T
93T-797
93T/Gold-797
93UD-437TP
93Ultra-498
94B-243
94D-317
94F-15
94L-177
94S-258
94S/GoldR-258
94StCl-17
94StCl/1stDay-17
94StCl/Gold-17
94StCl/Team-286
94T-271
94T/Gold-271
94UD-227
94UD/CollC-227
94UD/CollC/Gold-227
94UD/CollC/Silv-227
94UD/ElecD-227
94Ultra-7

Pennington, Ken
87Sumter-23
88Durham/Star-16
89Durham/Star-17
89Durham/Team-17
89Star/Wax-72
90EastLAS/ProC-EL16
90Foil/Best-177
90ProC/Singl-757
90Wmsprt/Best-18
90Wmsprt/ProC-1065
90Wmsprt/Star-19
91AA/LineD-341
91Jaxvl/LineD-341
91Jaxvl/ProC-159
92SanBern/ProC-

Pennock, Herb
28Yueng-8
31Exh/4-25
33Exh/4-13
33G-138
50Callahan
50W576-59
60Exh/HOF-19
60F-35
61F-133
63Bz/Sm
76Rowe-16M
76Shakey-54
77Galasso-106
80Laugh/FFeat-2
80Pac/Leg-111
80Perez/HOF-54
80SSPC/HOF
86Conlon/1-51
89HOF/St-67
90Perez/GreatMom-54
91Conlon/Sport-120
91Conlon/Sport-143
92Conlon/Sport-465
92Conlon/Sport-594
92Mega/Ruth-123M
92Yank/WIZHOF-25
E120
E210-8
E220
R315-A28
R315-B28
R316
R423-84
V100
V117-27
V354-16
V89-50
W502-8
W513-68

Pennye, Darwin
88Watertn/Pucko-23
89Augusta/ProC-504
90CLAS/CL-24
90Salem/Star-15
91AA/LineD-114
91CaroMud/LineD-114
91CaroMud/ProC-1098
92Harris/ProC-473
92Harris/SB-294
92Sky/AASingl-124

Pennyfeather, William
89Welland/Pucko-1
90Augusta/ProC-2477
90SALAS/Star-39
91B-517
91ClBest/Singl-158
91Salem/ClBest-11
91Salem/ProC-965
92B-17
92BuffB/ProC-334
92BuffB/SB-37
92D/Rook-93
92Sky/AAASingl-16
93D-702
93F/Final-116
93S-301
93StCl-447
93StCl/1stDay-447
93T-819
93T/Gold-819
94D-485
94Ultra-558

Penrod, Jack
88Pocatel/ProC-2102

Pensiero, Russ
80CharlO/Pol-13
80CharlO/W3TV-13

Penson, Paul
54T-236
94T/Arc54-236

Penton, Jack
28Exh/PCL-6

Pentz, Gene
77T-308
78BK/Ast-11
78T-64
79Portl-12
80Phoenix/NBank-20
80Port-25
81Phoenix-20

Penvose, Randy
86Geneva-22

Peoples, James
N172
N284

Peoples, Nathaniel
92Negro/Retort-48

Pepin, Robert
(Bob)
45Parade*-44

Pepitone, Joe
62T-596R
63T-183
64T-360
64T/Coins-121AS
64T/St-22
64Wheat/St-34
65OPC-245
65T-245
66OPC-79
66T-79
67CokeCap/ALAS-28
67CokeCap/AS-13
67CokeCap/YMet-13
67OPC/PI-22
67T-340
67T/PI-22
68Bz-5
68OPC-195
68T-195
68T/ActionSt-16AM
68T/ActionSt-3AM
69MB-216
69MLB/St-76
69MLBPA/Pin-21
69Sunoco/Pin-7
69T-589
69T/St-206
70K-59
70MLB/St-45
70T-598
70T-90
71MLB/St-40
71OPC-90
71T/GM-53
71T/Greatest-53
72MB-268
72OPC-303
72OPC-304IA
72T-303
72T-304IA
73OPC-580
73T-580

78TCMA-6
81TCMA-477M
92Yank/WIZ60-96
92Yank/WIZAS-58
PM10/Sm-142
WG10-17
WG9-19

Pepper, Hugh
(Laurin)
55T-147
56T-108

Pepper, Stu
91Pac/SenLg-73

Pepper, Tony
75IntLgAS/Broder-22
75PCL/AS-22
75Phoenix-18
75Phoenix/Caruso-4
75Phoenix/CircleK-18

Peppers, Devin
90Elizab/Star-15

Pequignot, Jon
86VeroB-19
87SanAn-19

Peralta, Amado
85Tigres-21

Peralta, Martin
88SLCity-22

Peraza, Luis
86AppFx-18

Peraza, Oswald
86Knoxvl-18
87Knoxvl-18
88French-23
88S/Tr-77T
89B-1
89D-524
89F-615
89S-571
89T-297
89T/Big-219
89UD-651
90Hagers/Best-27
91AA/LineD-242
91Crown/Orio-358
91Hagers/LineD-242
91Hagers/ProC-2456

Percival, Troy
90Boise/ProC-3335
91Boise/ClBest-23
91Boise/ProC-3875
92B-290
92MidldA/OneHour-19
92ProC/Tomorrow-38
92UD/ML-134
93B-363FOIL
93B-609
93F/Final-187
93StCl-681
93StCl/1stDay-681
93StCl/Angel-9
93UD-507DD
93Ultra-522
93Vanco/ProC-2595

Perconte, Jack
77LodiD
79Albuq-13
80Albuq-16
81Albuq/TCMA-17
81T-302R
82T/Tr-87T
82Wheat/Ind
83Charl-13
83D-463
83F-417
83T-569
84F/X-U90
84Mother/Mar-15
85D-74
85F-498
85Leaf-221
85Mother/Mar-11
85T-172
85T/St-341
86F-472
86T-146
86T/Tatt-1M
87Albuq/Pol-20
90Target-616

Perdomo, Felix
83Greens-21
86Columbia-19
87Lynch-12
88Jacks/GS-24

Perdue, Alphie
77Salem

Perdue, Doran
81Shrev-15

Perdue, Herbert R.
(Hub)
14CJ-121
15CJ-121
T206
T207
T213/brown
T222

Pereira, Ray
84LitFalls-8

Perez, Alex
88Kenosha/ProC-1385

Perez, Beban
89QuadC/Best-28
89QuadC/GS-23
90PalmSp/Cal-213
90PalmSp/ProC-2592
91PalmSp/ProC-2031
92Boise/ProC-3622
92QuadC/ClBest-8
92QuadC/ProC-807

Perez, Benny
75FtLaud/Sus-3
78Dunedin

Perez, Carlos 1
(Pitcher)
75QuadC
78Cr/PCL-99
79SLCity-18
80SLCity-13
81SLCity-10

Perez, Carlos 2
91ClBest/Singl-92
91Sumter/ProC-2333
92Rockford/ClBest-15
93BurlB/ClBest-17
93BurlB/ProC-154
93LimeR/Winter-57

Perez, Cesar
90Greens/Best-9
90Greens/ProC-2661
90Greens/Star-15
90Oneonta/ProC-3369
91Greens/ProC-3056
92FtLaud/ClBest-7
92FtLaud/ProC-2613
92FtLaud/Team-22
93Kinston/Team-21
94FExcel-48

Perez, Christopher
89KS*-31

Perez, Danny
91OKSt-18
92Helena/ProC-1729

Perez, Dario
91AppFx/ClBest-8
91AppFx/ProC-1714
92BBCity/ClBest-17
92BBCity/ProC-3844
93LimeR/Winter-125
94B-87

Perez, David
89Butte/SP-2
90CharlR/Star-21
90FSLAS/Star-39
90Star/ISingl-25
91AA/LineD-590
91Tulsa/LineD-590
91Tulsa/ProC-2770
91Tulsa/Team-21
92CharlR/ProC-2224
92Tulsa/SB-615

Perez, Dick
83D-654CL
85D/DKsuper-28
92D/DK-27CL

Perez, Eddie
88BurlB/ProC-23
89Sumter/ProC-1112
90Sumter/Best-17
90Sumter/ProC-2438
91Durham/ClBest-12
91Durham/ProC-1548
92Greenvl/ProC-1157
92Greenvl/SB-243

Perez, Eduardo
91Boise/ClBest-8
91Boise/ProC-3896
91ClBest/Gold-20

91ClBest/Singl-424
91Classic/DP-13
92AS/Cal-48
92ClBest-211
92MidldA/OneHour-20
92PalmSp/ClBest-1
92PalmSp/ProC-849
92ProC/Tomorrow-39
92UD-52TP
92UD/ML-24M
92UD/ML-271
93B-441
93ClBest/Fisher-10
93ClBest/MLG-32
93FExcel/ML-146
93L-483
93Select/RookTr-50T
93StCl/Angel-6
93T-494M
93T/Gold-494M
93UD-467IN
93UD/SP-284FOIL
93Vanco/ProC-2605
94B-291
94D-227
94F-67
94Flair-26
94L-341
94OPC-36
94Pac/AllLat-18
94Pac/Cr-86
94Pinn-202
94Pinn/Artist-202
94Pinn/Museum-202
94S-307
94S/GoldR-307
94Sf/2000-61
94StCl-189
94StCl/1stDay-189
94StCl/Gold-189
94Studio-14
94T-721
94T/Finest-73
94T/FinestRef-73
94T/Gold-721
94TripleP-18
94UD-124
94UD/CollC-228
94UD/CollC/Gold-228
94UD/CollC/Silv-228
94UD/ElecD-124
94Ultra-26

Perez, Eulogio
88Martins/Star-27
89Martins/Star-24
90Batavia/ProC-3075
90Spartan/ProC-2500
90Spartan/Star-17
91Spartan/ClBest-17
91Spartan/ProC-901

Perez, Francisco
86Erie-23
89Ashvl/ProC-963
89AubAs/ProC-2174
90Ashvl/ProC-2745

Perez, Fred
85Utica-21

Perez, Gil
92Welland/ClBest-19
92Welland/ProC-1321
93Welland/ClBest-19
93Welland/ProC-3355

Perez, Gorky
87Ashvl-26
87AubAs-15
88Ashvl/ProC-1062
89Osceola/Star-17

Perez, Hector
82Madis/Frit-32TR
83Madis/Frit-29TR
84LitFalls-17TR
86Lynch-16TR
87Lynch-10TR
88StLucie/Star-18
89Penin/Star-18TR

Perez, Jayson
92GulfCD/ProC-3564

Perez, Joe
90Watertn/Star-15
91Collnd/ClBest-3
91Collnd/ProC-1501

Perez, Joel
77AppFx
79Knoxvl/TCMA-16

Perez, Jose
89Salem/Team-22
90Kissim/DIMD-21
90Yakima/Team-34
Perez, Julio
75WPalmB/Sussman-1
78Memphis/Team-7
79Memphis/TCMA-4
80GlenF-16
83Reading-16
Perez, Pedro Julio
86Macon-19
87Macon-14
88Miami/Star-18
89Harris/ProC-307
89Harris/Star-14
90Harris/ProC-1201
90Harris/Star-15
Perez, Junior
90GreatF/SportP-16
Perez, Leo
89Wythe/Star-23
91Geneva/ClBest-14
91Geneva/ProC-4211
91WinSalem/ClBest-8
91WinSalem/ProC-2827
Perez, Leonardo
88Beloit/GS-18
89Stockton/Best-13
89Stockton/Cal-158
89Stockton/ProC-373
90ProC/Singl-865
90Stockton/Best-24
90Stockton/Cal-186
90Stockton/ProC-2185
Perez, Manuel R.
48Sommer-17
49Sommer-8
Perez, Mario
85Bend/Cram-19
Perez, Marty
71OPC-529R
71T-529R
72OPC-119
72T-119
73OPC-144
73T-144
74OPC-374
74T-374
75OPC-499
75T-499
75T/M-499
76Dubuq
76Ho-65
76K-26
76OPC-177
76T-177
77BurgChef-100
77OPC-183
77T-438
78Ho-4
78T-613
78Tidew
92Yank/WIZ70-126
Perez, Melido
86BurlEx-17
88Coke/WS-21
88D-589
88D/Best-179
88D/Rook-21
88F-265
88F/Up-U19
88S/Tr-108T
88T/Tr-83T
89B-59
89Classic-88
89Coke/WS-21
89D-58
89D/Best-179
89F-509
89KennerFig-104
89OPC-88
89Panini/St-300
89RedFoley/St-89
89S-386
89S/HotRook-79
89S/YS/I-7
89Sf-118
89T-786
89T/Big-235
89T/JumboR-16
89T/St-296
89ToysRUs-21
89UD-243
90B-310
90Coke/WSox-21
90D-101
90D/BestAL-18
90F-546
90F/Can-546
90Kodak/WSox-2
90Leaf-36
90OPC-621
90Panini/St-42
90PublInt/St-399
90PublInt/St-602
90S-311
90T-621
90T/Big-195
90T/St-304
90UD-525
91B-344
91D-164
91D-BC13
91D/BC-BC13
91F-133
91F/WaxBox-7
91Kodak/WSox-33
91OPC-499
91Panini/FrSt-358
91Panini/St-7
91Panini/Top15-96
91S-179
91S-705NH
91StCl-232
91StCl/Charter*-23
91T-499
91UD-623
91Ultra-80
92B-365
92D-509
92F-95
92L-479
92L/BlkGold-479
92OPC-129
92OPC/Premier-10
92Pinn-322
92S-29
92S/RookTr-36T
92StCl-869
92Studio-218
92T-129
92T/Gold-129
92T/GoldWin-129
92T/Tr-87T
92T/TrGold-87T
92UD-190
92UD-799
92Ultra-413
92Ultra-42
93B-19
93D-709
93Duracel/PPII-2
93F-284
93L-74
93LimeR/Winter-127
93OPC-231
93Pac/Spanish-210
93Pinn-109
93S-86
93Select-116
93Select/Ace-22
93Select/StatL-63M
93Select/StatL-74
93StCl-465
93StCl/1stDay-465
93StCl/Y-6
93T-304
93T/Gold-304
93T/Hill-11
93UD-326
93Ultra-248
94B-605
94D-476
94F-245
94Flair-87
94L-190
94Pac/Cr-435
94Pinn-168
94Pinn/Artist-168
94Pinn/Museum-168
94S-479
94StCl/Team-188
94T-31
94T/Gold-31
94UD-471
94Ultra-100
Perez, Michael I.
87Spring/Best-15
88ArkTr/GS-21
89ArkTr/GS-17
89TexLAS/GS-24
90AAAGame/ProC-29
90AAASingl/ProC-516
90Louisvl/CMC-8
90Louisvl/LBC-34
90Louisvl/ProC-402
90ProC/Singl-108
90SpringDG/Best-25
90T/TVCard-60
91D-615
91F-643
91Louisvl/Team-12
91OPC-205
91S-758RP
91T-205
91T/90Debut-124
91UD/Ext-728
92D/Rook-94
92F-588
92Pinn-565
92S/RookTr-95T
92StCl-798
92T/Tr-88T
92T/TrGold-88T
92Ultra-571
93D-256
93F-132
93F/RookSenl-9
93OPC-298
93Pac/Spanish-635
93Pinn-162
93Pol/Card-16
93S-345
93Select-319
93StCl-202
93StCl/1stDay-202
93StCl/Card-5
93T-229
93T/Gold-229
93ToysRUs-15
93UD-204
93Ultra-111
94D-599
94F-644
94Flair-227
94L-130
94Pac/Cr-601
94Pinn-182
94Pinn/Artist-182
94Pinn/Museum-182
94S-84
94S/GoldR-84
94Select-108
94StCl-175
94StCl/1stDay-175
94StCl/Gold-175
94StCl/Team-320
94T-567
94T/Finest-124
94T/FinestRef-124
94T/Gold-567
94UD-357
94UD/CollC-229
94UD/CollC/Gold-229
94UD/CollC/Silv-229
94Ultra-271
Perez, Neifi
94B-282
94FExcel-186
94UD-545TP
Perez, Ozzie
90Hamil/Best-18
90Hamil/Star-18
91Savan/ClBest-21
91Savan/ProC-1662
Perez, Paco
79Jacks-1
Perez, Pascual
77Charl
79Portl-20
80Port-7
81Portl-20
81T-551R
82F-491
82Portl-7
82T-383
83D-557
83F-144
83Pol/Atl-27
83T/Tr-84
84D-507
84F-188
84F/St-59
84Nes/792-675
84OPC-1
84Pol/Atl-27
84T-675
84T/St-36
85D-507
85D/AAS-18
85F-337
85Ho/Braves-18
85Leaf-55
85OPC-106
85Pol/Atl-27
85T-106
86F-524
86T-491
87D/HL-50
87Indianap-26
88D-591
88D/Best-236
88F-192
88Leaf-248
88OPC-237
88S-459
88T-647
88T/Big-196
89B-354
89Classic-85
89D-248
89D/Best-302
89F-390
89OPC-73
89Panini/St-115
89S-299
89T-73
89T/St-71
89UD-498
90B-430
90D-342
90D/BestAL-80
90F-358
90F/Can-358
90F/Up-116
90OPC-278
90Panini/St-282
90PublInt/St-185
90S-486
90S/NWest-11
90S/Tr-5T
90T-278
90T/Big-291
90T/TVYank-16
90T/Tr-91T
90UD-487
90UD/Ext-769
91F-675
91Leaf-293
91OPC-701
91StCl-485
91T-701
91UD-671
92D-695
92F-240
92OPC-503
92Pinn-182
92S-88
92T-503
92T/Gold-503
92T/GoldWin-503
Perez, Pedro
89Salem/Team-23
90VeroB/Star-22
90Yakima/Team-36
91Geneva/ClBest-15
91Geneva/ProC-4212
91Peoria/ProC-1340
92WinSalem/ProC-1206
Perez, Ralph
92Spokane/ClBest-24
92Spokane/ProC-1307
Perez, Ramon
73Cedar
74Cedar
75Iowa/TCMA-14
78Charl
79CharCh-9
Perez, Richard
91Hunting/ClBest-17
91Hunting/ProC-3342
92Hunting/ClBest-6
92Hunting/ProC-3155
93Peoria/Team-20
Perez, Robert
90StCath/ProC-3456
91Dunedin/ClBest-22
91Dunedin/ProC-220
92ClBest-161
92Knoxvl/ProC-3003
92Knoxvl/SB-391
92ProC/Tomorrow-168
92Sky/AASingl-166
93Syrac/ProC-1011
94FExcel-147
Perez, Segio
86Clearw-19
Perez, Tony
65T-581R
66OPC-72
66T-72
67CokeCap/Reds-8
67Kahn
67T-476
68Bz-12
68Kahn
68OPC-130
68T-130
68T/3D
68T/ActionSt-12CM
69Kahn
69MB-217
69MLB/St-134
69T-295
69T/St-28
70MLB/St-34
70OPC-380
70OPC-63LL
70T-380
70T-63LL
70T/SO
71K-58
71MD
71MLB/St-67
71OPC-580
71OPC-64LL
71OPC-66LL
71T-580
71T-64LL
71T-66LL
71T/Coins-105
71T/GM-14
71T/Greatest-14
71T/S-6
71T/Super-6
71T/tatt-9
72Dimanche*-37
72MB-269
72OPC-80
72T-80
73OPC-275
73T-275
74OPC-230
74T-230
74T/DE-54
74T/St-29
75Ho-127
75OPC-560
75T-560
75T/M-560
76Crane-46
76Ho-86
76Icee
76MSA/Disc
76OPC-195LL
76OPC-325
76SSPC-39
76T-195LL
76T-325
77BurgChef-160
77Expo/PostC-5
77OPC-135
77T-655
77T/CS-37
77T/ClothSt-37
78OPC-90
78T-15
78Wiffle/Discs-59
79OPC-261
79T-495
80OPC-69
80T-125
81Coke
81D-334
81F-241
81F/St-66
81K-17

81OPC-231
81T-575
81T/HT
81T/SO-8
81T/St-44
82Coke/BOS
82D-408
82F-302
82F/St-170
82OPC-255
82OPC-256IA
82T-255
82T-256IA
82T/St-152
83D-578
83F-191
83OPC-355
83OPC-74SV
83OPC/St-8
83T-715
83T-716SV
83T/Fold-2M
83T/St-8
83T/Tr-85
84Borden-24
84D-503
84D/Champs-29
84F-44
84F-636IA
84F/X-U91
84Nes/792-385
84Nes/792-702LL
84Nes/792-703LL
84Nes/792-704LL
84OPC-385
84T-385
84T-702LL
84T-703LL
84T-704LL
84T/St-126
84T/Tr-91
85CircK-28
85D/HL-9
85F-546
85FunFoodPin-99
85OPC-212
85T-675
86D-15DK
86D-428
86D/DKsuper-15
86F-186
86GenMills/Book-5M
86Leaf-15DK
86OPC-85
86Sf-138M
86T-205RB
86T-85
86T/St-143
86T/St-8
86T/Tatt-16M
86TexGold-24
87F-209
88Kahn/Reds-CO
90Kahn/Reds-27M
91Kahn/Reds-x
92K/CornAS-2
92K/FrAS-5
92Nabisco-7
92Reds/Kahn-NNO
93T-503M
93T/Gold-503M
93TWill/Mem-19
Perez, Victor
90Billings/ProC-3236
Perez, Vladimir
87Spartan-23
88LitFalls/Pucko-19
89Clmbia/Best-2
89Clmbia/GS-20
90StLucie/Star-20
92BBCity/ClBest-20
92Memphis/ProC-2417
93LimeR/Winter-65
Perez, William
89Modesto/Chong-14
Perez, Yorkis
86Kenosha-19
87WPalmB-16
88Jaxvl/Best-11
88Jaxvl/ProC-973
89WPalmB/Star-17
90Jaxvl/Best-22
90Jaxvl/ProC-1372
91AAA/LineD-436
91Richm/Bob-12
91Richm/LineD-436
91Richm/ProC-2564
91Richm/Team-16
92D-754
92T/91Debut-137
93Harris/ProC-268
93LimeR/DomPr-P4
93LimeR/Winter-68
93LimeR/Winter-P4
94B-439
94Ultra-495
Perezchica, Tony
84Everett/Cram-30B
86Fresn/Smok-20
87Shrev-6
88AAA/ProC-32
88Phoenix/CMC-16
88Phoenix/ProC-75
89F-338
89Phoenix/CMC-14
89Phoenix/ProC-1502
89S/HotRook-50
90B-235
90Phoenix/CMC-20
90ProC/Singl-547
91AAA/LineD-388
91D/Rook-10
91PG&E-30
91Phoenix/LineD-388
91Phoenix/ProC-74
91S-735RP
92ColoSp/ProC-759
92Indian/McDon-23
92S-702
92StCl-454
92T/Gold-366
92T/GoldWin-366
92Ultra-355
Perigny, Don
91SoBend/ClBest-19
91SoBend/ProC-2855
92Saraso/ClBest-12
92Saraso/ProC-203
Perisho, Matt
94B-419
Perkins, Bill
86Negro/Frit-94
Perkins, Broderick
78Padre/FamFun-21
79T-725R
80Hawaii-22
81D-525
81F-498
81T-393
81T/St-226
82D-397
82F-579
82F/St-103
82OPC-192
82T-192
82T/St-98
83D-121
83F-368
83OPC/St-292
83T-593
83T/St-292
83T/Tr-86
83Wheat/Ind-24
84D-276
84F-548
84Nes/792-212
84T-212
84Wheat/Ind-15
85T-609
Perkins, Cecil
81TCMA-471
92Yank/WIZ60-97
Perkins, Charlie
90Target-617
Perkins, Craig
75Omaha/Team-13
Perkins, Dan
94FExcel-97
Perkins, David
90MissSt-29
91MissSt-36
92MissSt-31
93MissSt-30
Perkins, Harold
82VeroB-19
83VeroB-20
89RochR/CMC-18
89RochR/ProC-1643
Perkins, Paul
91Penin/ClBest-9
91Penin/ProC-375
92SanBern/ClBest-24
92SanBern/ProC-
94B-33
Perkins, Ralph
(Cy)
21Exh-127
25Exh-110
26Exh-110
91Conlon/Sport-185
94Conlon-1157
E120
E210-29
E220
V100
V355-24
V61-11
W572
W573
Perkins, Ray
82AubAs-5
86FSLAS-38
86Miami-20
Perkins, Tom
75Clinton
Perkowski, Harry
52B-202
52T-142
53B/Col-87
53T-236
54B-44
54T-125
55T-184
91T/Arc53-236
94T/Arc54-125
Perlman, Jon
83Iowa-8
84Iowa-6
85Iowa-19
86Phoenix-20
87Phoenix-13
88ColoSp/CMC-6
88ColoSp/ProC-1542
88F-93
88F/Up-U22
89S-591
89T-476
Perlozzo, Sam
78T-704R
79Hawaii-11
79T-709R
81Tidew-22
83Lynch-11
84Jacks-16
86Tidew-23MG
88Kahn/Mets-34CO
89Kahn/Mets-34CO
90Kahn/Reds-27M
91Kahn/Reds-x
92Reds/Kahn-NNO
93Mother/Mar-28M
Perna, Bobby
90Billings/ProC-3230
91CharWh/ClBest-18
91CharWh/ProC-2895
91SALAS/ProC-SAL9
92CharWh/ClBest-21
92CharWh/ProC-16
92ClBest-56
93FExcel/ML-26
93SALAS/II-30
Perno, Donn
87Everett-23
Pernoll, H. Hub
M116
Perodin, Ron
80Clinton-21
Perona, Joe
92B-246
92ClBest-169
92Lakeland/ClBest-5
92Lakeland/ProC-2282
92UD/ML-90
94B-453
Perozo, Danny
88Billings/ProC-1813
89Billings/ProC-2058
89Greens/ProC-409
90CharWh/Best-23
90CharWh/ProC-2254
91Cedar/ClBest-23
91Cedar/ProC-2733
Perozo, Ed
89Elmira/Pucko-13
90LynchRS/Team-3
91Clmbia/PCPII-4
91Clmbia/PII-6
92ColumMet/ClBest-15
92ColumMet/ProC-310
92ColumMet/SAL/II-9
Perpetuo, Nelson
91Bristol/ClBest-28
91Bristol/ProC-3601
Perranoski, Ron
61T-525
61Union/Dodg-15
62BB-16
62T-297
63T-403
64T-30
64T/Coins-64
64T/St-46
64T/tatt
64Wheat/St-35
65T-484
66T-555
67CokeCap/DodgAngel-16
67T-197
68T-435
69OPC-77
69T-77
69T/St-197
70MLB/St-237
70OPC-226
70T-226
71MLB/St-469
71OPC-475
71T-475
71T/Coins-104
72OPC-367
72T-367
78Twin/Frisz-40
85Coke/Dodg-25CO
86Coke/Dodg-23CO
90Mother/Dodg-28M
90Pol/Dodg-xCO
90Target-618
91Mother/Dodg-28CO
91Pol/Dodg-x
92Mother/Dodg-28M
92Pol/Dodg-NNO
93Mother/Dodg-28M
93Pol/Dodg-30M
WG10-42
WG9-41
Perrier, Hip
N172/PCL
Perring, George
14CJ-119
15CJ-119
M116
T206
Perritt, William D.
(Pol)
92Conlon/Sport-488
D327
D328-132
E135-132
Perry, Alonzo
49Remar
Perry, Bob
86Kenosha-20
Perry, David
89Boise/ProC-1981
Perry, Eric
88CharWh/Best-7
88Geneva/ProC-1633
89Peoria/Team-19
Perry, Gaylord
61Union
62T-199
62T/bucks
63T-169R
64T-468
65OPC-193
65T-193
66T-598
67CokeCap/AS-26
67CokeCap/Giant-15
67CokeCap/NLAS-31
67T-236LL
67T-320
68CokeCap/Giant-15
68Dexter-61
68OPC-11LL
68OPC-85
68T-11LL
68T-85
69MB-218
69MLB/St-207
69T-485
69T/St-110
70K-20
70MLB/St-132
70T-560
71K-6
71MD
71MLB/St-261
71OPC-140
71OPC-70LL
71T-140
71T-70LL
71T/Coins-73
71T/S-2
71T/Super-2
71Ticket/Giant-10
72MB-270
72OPC-285
72T-285
73K-38
73OPC-346KP
73OPC-400
73OPC-66LL
73T-346KP
73T-400
73T-66LL
73T/Comics-14
73T/Lids-39
73T/PinUps-14
74OPC-35
74T-35
74T/St-168
75Ho-84
75K-45
75OPC-530
75SSPC/18-9
75SSPC/42-30
75T-530
75T/M-530
76Ho-4
76Ho/Twink-4
76OPC-204LL
76OPC-55
76T-204LL
76T-55
77BurgChef-20
77Ho-73
77Ho/Twink-73
77OPC-149
77T-152
78Ho-139
78Padre/FamFun-22
78T-686
78Wiffle/Discs-60
79Ho-83
79K-49
79OPC-161
79T-321
79T-5LL
80OPC-148
80T-280
81D-471
81F-91
81Pol/Atl-46
81T-582
81T/Tr-812
82D-543
82F-445
82F/St-67
82OPC-115
82T-115
82T/St-24
82T/Tr-88T
83D-307
83D/AAS-28
83F-483
83F-630M
83F/St-18M
83F/St-1M
83Nalley-1
83OPC-159SV
83OPC-96
83OPC/St-114FOIL
83T-463
83T-464IA
83T/Fold-1M
83T/St-114
84D-LLA
84D/Champs-32

84F-352
84F-638IA
84F-641
84F/St-98
84Mother/Giants-4
84Nes/792-4HL
84Nes/792-6HL
84T-4HL
84T-6HL
88Grenada-39
89Pac/Leg-152
89Padre/Mag-24
89T/LJN-69
90BBWit-40
90Pac/Legend-43
90Swell/Great-66
91K/3D-1
91Perez/HOF-210
91Swell/Great-70
91UD/HOF-H2
91UD/HOF-x
92UD/ASFF-49
92UD/HeroHL-HI6
92Yank/WIZ80-145
92Yank/WIZHOF-26
93AP/ASG-125
93AP/ASG24K-59G
93AP/ASGCoke/Amo-9
93Metallic-15
93Rang/Keeb-289
93TWill-94
93YooHoo-12
PM10/Sm-143

Perry, Gerald
82ArkTr-6
82Richm-14
83Richm-14
84D-263
84F/X-U92
84Pol/Atl-28
84T/Tr-92T
85D-443
85F-338
85Ho/Braves-19
85Pol/Atl-28
85T-219
86D-165
86F-525
86Richm-16
86T-557
87Smok/Atl-17
87T-639
88D-437
88D/Best-58
88F-547
88Leaf-216
88Panini/St-242
88S-136
88T-39
88T/Big-40
89B-273
89Brave/Dubuq-20
89Cadaco-39
89Classic-118
89D-22DK
89D-239
89D/AS-57
89D/Best-291
89D/DKsuper-22DK
89D/MVP-BC24
89F-597
89F-638M
89F/BBAS-31
89F/BBMVP's-31
89F/Heroes-30
89KennerFig-105
89OPC-130
89Panini/St-40
89RedFoley/St-90
89S-101
89S/HotStar-20
89Sf-164
89T-130
89T/Big-279
89T/Coins-21
89T/LJN-108
89T/Mini-2
89T/St-33
89T/UK-59
89UD-431
90B-383
90Classic/III-48
90D-153
90F-592
90F/Can-592
90F/Up-103
90Leaf-441
90OPC-792
90PublInt/St-118
90Richm/25Ann-19
90S-249
90S/Tr-28T
90T-792
90T/St-27
90T/Tr-92T
90UD-101
90UD/Ext-707
91B-405
91D-130
91F-566
91F/UltraUp-U109
91F/Up-U119
91Leaf-272
91OPC-384
91Panini/St-230
91Pol/Card-21
91S-286
91S/RookTr-63T
91StCl-379
91T-384
91UD-219
92D-634
92F-589
92L-122
92L/BlkGold-122
92OPC-498
92Pol/Card-16
92S-491
92StCl-338
92T-498
92T/Gold-498
92T/GoldWin-498
92UD-690
92Ultra-572
93D-468
93F-514
93Pac/Spanish-301
93Pol/Card-17
93T-597
93T/Gold-597
94F-645
94Pac/Cr-602
94S-120
94S/GoldR-120
94StCl/Team-329
94T-263
94T/Gold-263

Perry, Herbert Scott
E220
E270/1

Perry, Herbert
91ClBest/Singl-428
91FrRow/DP-51
91Watertn/ClBest-21
91Watertn/ProC-3376
92Kinston/ClBest-23
92Kinston/ProC-2486
92UD/ML-190
93FExcel/ML-163
94B-551
94SigRook-46

Perry, Jason
92Spokane/ClBest-30BB

Perry, Jeff
84Savan-14
87Visalia-7

Perry, Jim
59Kahn
59T-542
60Kahn
60L-49
60T-324
61Bz-22
61Kahn
61P-59
61T-385
61T-48LL
61T-584AS
61T/St-138
62J-43
62Kahn
62P-43
62P/Can-43
62Salada-32
62Shirriff-32
62Sugar-5
62T-37M
62T-405
62T/St-37
63Sugar-5
63T-535
64T-34
65T-351
66T-283
67CokeCap/Twin-5
67T-246
68T-393
69MB-219
69OPC-146
69T-146
69T/4in1-14
70K-64
70MLB/St-236
70OPC-70LL
70T-620
70T-70LL
71K-3
71MD
71MLB/St-470
71OPC-500
71OPC-69LL
71T-500
71T-69LL
71T/Coins-12
71T/GM-10
71T/Greatest-10AL CY CY
71T/S-24
71T/Super-24
71T/tatt-14
72MB-271
72OPC-220
72OPC-497KP
72T-220
72T-497KP
73OPC-385
73T-385
74OPC-316
74T-316
75OPC-263
75T-263
75T/M-263
78TCMA-105
78Twin/Frisz-17
81Tacom-31
88Pac/Leg-18
89Swell-37
90BBWit-44

Perry, Melvin
(Bob)
64T-48

Perry, Parnell
86Geneva-23
87Peoria-22

Perry, Pat
83ColumAst-18
84ArkTr-18
85Louisvl-18
86D-596
86F/Up-U89
86Schnucks-20
87D-430
87F-307
87Smok/Cards-4
87T-417
88Berg/Cubs-37
88D-626
88F-244
88S-557
88T-282
89D-404
89F-435
89S-364
89T-186
89T/Big-329
89UD-345
90OPC-541
90PublInt/St-199
90S-436
90SpringDG/Best-17
90T-541
91S-527

Perry, Ron
80GlenF/B-17
80GlenF/C-1
81GlenF-15

Perry, Shawn
83Tacom-33

Perry, Steve 1
79LodiD-8
81VeroB-14
83Albuq-9
84Cram/PCL-154

Perry, Steve 2
90Oneonta/ProC-3370

Perschke, Greg
89Utica/Pucko-17
90Saraso/Star-19
90Star/ISingl-59
91AAA/LineD-644
91Vanco/LineD-644
91Vanco/ProC-1593
92B-282
92Sky/AAASingl-288
92Vanco/ProC-2720
92Vanco/SB-645

Persing, Tim
90Elizab/Star-16
91ClBest/Singl-371
91Kenosha/ClBest-8
91Kenosha/ProC-2070
91MidwLAS/ProC-38
92FtMyr/ProC-2743
92Visalia/ClBest-7
92Visalia/ProC-1013

Person, Carl
75QuadC

Person, Robert
90Kinston/Team-23
91BendB/ClBest-9
91BendB/ProC-3694
91Kinston/ClBest-10
91Kinston/ProC-322
92Saraso/ProC-204

Persons, Archie
T206
T213/brown

Pertica, William
E120

Pertotti, Mike
92SoBend/ProC-170

Perzanowski, Stan
75IntLgAS/Broder-23
75PCL/AS-23
76OPC-388
76T-388
77SLCity
93Rang/Keeb-290

Pesavento, Mike
85VeroB-22

Pesavento, Patrick
90Fayette/ProC-2415
90SALAS/Star-18

Pesky, Johnny
47HomogBond-37
47TipTop
48L-121
49B-86
50B-137
50Drake-32
51B-15
51T/BB-5
52B-45
52T-15
53B/Col-134
53Tiger/Glen-24
54B-135
54T-63
55B-241
61Union
63T-343MG
64T-248MG
67T/Test/PP-20CO
76SSPC-625CO
91T/Arc53-315
92Bz/Quadra-13M
94T/Arc54-63
94TedW-5
D305
Exh47
PM10/Sm-144
R302

Pesut, Nick
47Sunbeam

Petagine, Roberto
91BurlAs/ClBest-17
91BurlAs/ProC-2811
92B-31
92ClBest-205
92Jacks/ProC-4008
92Osceola/ClBest-23
92Osceola/ProC-2540
92UD/ML-313
93B-644
94B-342
94B-530
94ClBest/Gold-100
94FExcel-208
94FExcel/AS-2
94L-365
94UD-522DD
94Ultra-510

Petcka, Joe
92FrRow/DP-91
92Pittsfld/ProC-3291
93StCl/MurphyS-59

Peter, Bill S.
91AA/LineD-143

Peterek, Jeff
86Stockton-20
87ElPaso-23
88ElPaso/Best-21
89Denver/CMC-8
89Denver/ProC-46
90AAASingl/ProC-648
90D-530
90Denver/CMC-1
90Denver/ProC-623
90F-333
90F/Can-333
90ProC/Singl-26
90T/89Debut-97

Peters, Chris
93Welland/ClBest-20
93Welland/ProC-3356

Peters, Dan
88Beloit/GS-20

Peters, Donald
90A&AASingle/ProC-161
90Classic/DP-26
90Classic/III-83
90SoOreg/Best-25
90SoOreg/ProC-3424
91AA/LineD-292
91B-224
91ClBest/Singl-288
91Classic/I-77
91Huntsvl/ClBest-19
91Huntsvl/LineD-292
91Huntsvl/Team-18
91HuntsvlProC-1794
91S-381FDP
92B-244

Peters, Doug
90Eugene/GS-22
91AA/LineD-412
91London/LineD-412
91Memphis/ProC-649

Peters, Francis
81TCMA-400
68T-409R

Peters, Gary
60T-407
61T-303
63T-522R
64Bz-27
64T-130
64T-2LL
64T/Coins-140AS
64T/Coins-71
64T/S-1
64T/SU
64T/St-56
64T/tatt
65Bz-27
65OPC-9LL
65OldLond-32
65T-430
65T-9LL
65T/E-18
65T/trans-62
66OPC-111
66T-111
67Bz-9
67CokeCap/WSox-1
67T-233LL
67T-310
67T/Test/SU-2
68Bz-14
68Kahn
68OPC-8LL
68T-210
68T-379AS
68T-8LL
68T/ActionSt-10C
68T/G-13
68T/Post-13
69Kahn
69MB-220
69MLB/St-34

69OPC-34
69T-34
69T/St-157
70MLB/St-161
70OPC-540
70T-540
71MLB/St-327
71OPC-225
71T-225
71T/tatt-10
72MB-272
72OPC-503
72T-503
78TCMA-125
89Pac/Leg-159
Exh47
Peters, Jay
79SLCity-20
80SLCity-11
Peters, Jimmy
45Parade*-45
Peters, John
(Jack)
E120
V61-63
Peters, Oscar
T207
Peters, Ray
No Cards.
Peters, Reed
87Salem/ProC-2424
88PalmSp/Cal-108
88PalmSp/ProC-1439
89MidldA/GS-26
90AAASingl/ProC-105
90Edmon/CMC-17
90Edmon/ProC-529
90ProC/Singl-494
91AAA/LineD-168
91Edmon/LineD-168
91Edmon/ProC-1529
92Phoenix/ProC-2834
92Shrev/ProC-3883
92Shrev/SB-588
Peters, Rex
89Salem/Team-24
90VeroB/Star-23
91Bakers/Cal-6
91CalLgAS-19
Peters, Richard D.
(Ricky)
81D-10
81F-470
81T-177
81T/St-77
82D-155
82F-277
82OPC-269
82T-504
83Tacom-29A
84F-458
84Nes/792-436
84T-436
85Cram/PCL-130
86Mother/A's-24
90AubAs/ProC-3417MG
91Pac/SenLg-117
92BurlAs/ClBest-28CO
Peters, Rusty
94Conlon-1296
Peters, Steve
87ArkTr-9
87TexLgAS-19
88D/Rook-22
88Louisvl-39
88Smok/Card-23
88T/Tr-84T
89F-462
89Louisvl-30
89Louisvl/CMC-9
89Louisvl/ProC-1247
89T-482
89UD/Ext-771
90AAASingl/ProC-8
90LasVegas/CMC-2
90LasVegas/ProC-120
90ProC/Singl-504
90SpringDG/Best-20
91AAA/LineD-317
91OkCty/LineD-317
91OkCty/ProC-175
Peters, Tim
87SLCity/Taco-25
88MidwLAS/GS-47
89Jaxvl/Best-13
89Jaxvl/ProC-154
90Jaxvl/ProC-1373
Peters, Tom
87Belling/Team-10
Petersen, Andy
89SanDiegoSt/Smok-21
Petersen, Chris
92FrRow/DP-58
92Geneva/ProC-1568
Petersen, Matt
92Erie/ProC-1620
93T-497
93T/Gold-497
Peterson, Adam C.
86Penin-20
87BirmB/Best-13
87SLAS-20
88F-646R
88Vanco/CMC-7
88Vanco/ProC-776
89AAA/CMC-45
89D-619
89Vanco/CMC-2
89Vanco/ProC-589
90AAASingl/ProC-166
90B-307
90BirmDG/Best-27
90OPC-299
90ProC/Singl-629
90T-299
90TripleAAS/CMC-45
90Vanco/CMC-2
90Vanco/ProC-488
91AAA/LineD-290
91F-134
91LasVegas/LineD-290
91LasVegas/ProC-233
91OPC-559
91S-604
91S/100RisSt-94
91T-559
92LasVegas/ProC-2794
92LasVegas/SB-237
92UD-602
Peterson, Bart
91Kenosha/ClBest-14
91Kenosha/ProC-2071
92FtMyr/ProC-2744
92Miracle/ClBest-17
Peterson, Brian
90Memphis/Best-28CO
90Memphis/ProC-1027CO
90Memphis/Star-26CO
91AA/LineD-425M
91London/LineD-425CO
91London/LineD-425CO
91Memphis/ProC-671CO
Peterson, Carl
(Buddy)
52Mother-29
53Mother-8
91Crown/Orio-359
Peterson, Charles Andrew
(Cap)
64T-568R
65T-512
66T-349
67T-387
68OPC-188
68T-188
69T-571
Peterson, Charles
94B-658
94ClBest/Gold-75
94ClBest/GoldLP-10
94T-207FDP
94T/Gold-207FDP
Peterson, Chris
92Geneva/ClBest-9
Peterson, D. Scott
77Ashvl
78Ashvl
Peterson, Dave
85Greens-19
86NewBrit-20
Peterson, Eric
(Ricky)
77Charl
82Buffa-17C
Peterson, Erik
82Nashvl-17
83Nashvl-16
84Nashvl-17
Peterson, Fritz
66T-584R
67CokeCap/YMet-16
67T-495
68T-246
69MLB/St-77
69OPC-46
69T-46
70MLB/St-248
70OPC-142
70T-142
71MD
71MLB/St-499
71OPC-460
71T-460
71T/Coins-138
71T/GM-44
71T/Greatest-44
71T/S-13
71T/Super-13
72ProStars/PostC-33
72T-573
72T-574IA
73OPC-82
73Syrac/Team-23
73T-82
74OPC-229
74Syrac/Team-22
74T-229
75OPC-62
75T-62
75T/M-62
76Ho-32
76Ho/Twink-32
76OPC-255
76SSPC-511
76T-255
81TCMA-450M
90Swell/Great-79
92Yank/WIZ60-98
92Yank/WIZ70-127
92Yank/WIZAS-59
93Rang/Keeb-291
Peterson, Geoff
86FtMyr-21
Peterson, Harding
58T-322
Peterson, Jerry
76Watlo
Peterson, Jim
77Clinton
90Target-619
Peterson, Kent
48L-42
49Eureka-92
51B-215
Peterson, Mark
92Everett/ClBest-15
92Everett/ProC-1686
Peterson, Matt
92Erie/ClBest-2
Peterson, Pat
75FtLaud/Sus-11
Peterson, Rick
88ColoSp/ProC-1530
89BirmB/Best-28
89BirmB/ProC-99CO
89Pac/SenLg-153
89T/SenLg-104
90BirmB/Best-25CO
91AA/LineD-75M
91BirmB/LineD-75CO
91BirmB/ProC-1471CO
91Pac/SenLg-49
Peterson, Rob
89Welland/Pucko-20
90Welland/Pucko-18
Peterson, Robert A.
E254
Peterson, Tim
76Cedar
Petestio, Doug
84MidldC-12
Petit, Doug
92Erie/ProC-1621
Petit, Ricardo
91Idaho/ProC-4326
91Pulaski/ClBest-25
91Pulaski/ProC-4002
Petitt, Steven
86StPete-24
Petkovsek, Mark
88CharlR/Star-19
89TexLAS/GS-36
89Tulsa/GS-20
89Tulsa/Team-18
90AAASingl/ProC-678
90OkCty/CMC-5
90OkCty/ProC-432
90ProC/Singl-155
91AAA/LineD-318
91OkCty/LineD-318
91OkCty/ProC-177
92BuffB/BlueS-14
92BuffB/ProC-321
92BuffB/SB-38
92Sky/AAASingl-17
92T/91Debut-138
92TX-32
93Rang/Keeb-292
94F-617
Petralli, Eugene J.
(Geno)
80Knoxvl/TCMA-2
81Syrac-9
81Syrac/Team-16
82Syrac-13
82Syrac/Team-18
83D-623
83F-439
83Syrac-15
85Maine-16
85OKCty-5
86Rang-12
86T-296
87D-619
87F-135
87Mother/Rang-20
87Smok/R-8
87T-388
88D-506
88F-477
88Leaf-241
88Mother/R-20
88S-373
88Smok/R-3
88T-589
89D-343
89D/Best-312
89F-530
89Mother/R-11
89OPC-137
89Panini/St-451
89S-526
89Smok/R-25
89T-137
89T/Big-12
89T/St/Backs-24
89UD-482
90B-495
90D-56
90D/BestAL-27
90F-309
90F/Can-309
90Leaf-73
90Mother/Rang-7
90OPC-706
90Panini/St-161
90PublInt/St-419
90S-153
90T-706
90UD-633
91B-284
91D-137
91F-296
91Leaf-148
91Mother/Rang-7
91OPC-78
91Panini/FrSt-251
91S-191
91StCl-10
91T-78
91UD-492
91Ultra-351
92D-550
92F-313
92L-357
92L/BlkGold-357
92Mother/Rang-7
92OPC-409
92S-283
92StCl-3
92T-409
92T/Gold-409
92T/GoldWin-409
92UD-599
92Ultra-138
93D-319
93F-689
93Rang/Keeb-424
93StCl-232
93StCl/1stDay-232
93StCl/Rang-22
93T-332
93T/Gold-332
93UD-83
94D-247
94F-317
94S-137
94S/GoldR-137
Petrizzo, Tom
86DayBe-22CHM
Petrocella, Chris
92Helena/ProC-1713
Petrocelli, Rico
65OPC-74R
65T-74R
66T-298
67CokeCap/RedSox-11
67T-528
67T/Test/RSox-13
68Bz-5
68CokeCap/RedSox-11
68Dexter-62
68OPC-156
68T-430
69Citgo-8
69MB-221
69MLB/St-15
69OPC-215
69T-215
69T/4in1-25M
69T/St-136
69Trans-21
70K-54
70MB-21
70MLB/St-162
70OPC-457AS
70T-457AS
70T-680
70T/CB
70T/S-14
70T/Super-14
70Trans-15
71Bz
71Bz/Test-10
71MD
71MLB/St-328
71OPC-340
71T-340
71T/Coins-30
71T/GM-39
71T/Greatest-39DP AL HR
71T/S-19
71T/Super-19
71T/tatt-11
72MB-273
72OPC-30
72T-30
73OPC-365
73T-365
74OPC-609
74T-609
75Ho-132
75OPC-356
75T-356
75T/M-356
76OPC-445
76SSPC-413
76T-445
77T-111
81TCMA-335
87BirmB/Best-1
87SLAS-23
88BirmB/Best-8
88SLAS-38
89Swell-123
90BirmDG/Best-28MG
90Pac/Legend-64
90Swell/Great-56
91LineD-31
91Swell/Great-71
92Pawtu/ProC-939MG
92Pawtu/SB-374MG
94TedW-6
94TedW/54-35
PM10/Sm-145
Petrulis, Paul
91MissSt-37
92MissSt-32
93MissSt-35

Petry, Dan
80T-373
81D-128
81F-468
81T-59
82D-133
82F-278
82T-211
82T-666TL
83D-359
83F-339
83OPC-79
83OPC/St-70
83T-261TL
83T-638
83T/St-70
84D-105
84F-89
84Nes/792-147
84OPC-147
84T-147
84T/St-269
84Tiger/Farmer-12
84Tiger/Wave-29
85Cain's-16
85D-334
85F-20
85F/St-83
85FunFoodPin-60
85Leaf-188
85OPC-392
85Seven-7D
85T-435
85T/Gloss40-25
85T/St-264
85Wendy-18
86Cain's-15
86D-212
86D/AAS-42
86F-235
86Leaf-144
86OPC-216
86T-540
86T/St-270
87Cain's-15
87Coke/Tigers-12
87D-373
87F-161
87Leaf-228
87OPC-27
87Seven-DT9
87Sf/TPrev-15M
87T-752
88D-476
88D/Best-139
88F-67
88S-461
88S/Tr-26T
88Smok/Angels-8
88T-78
88T/Tr-85T
89D-344
89F-486
89S-122
89T/Big-178
89UD-552
90CokeK/Tiger-16
90F-142
90F/Can-142
90Leaf-508
90OPC-363
90PublInt/St-377
90S-211
90S/Tr-39T
90T-363
90T/Tr-93T
90UD-690
91B-146
91CokeK/Tiger-46
91D-675
91F-347
91Panini/FrSt-295
91Panini/St-240
91Pol/Tiger-8
91RedFoley/St-71
91S-434
91UD-316
91Ultra-125
92S-705
92USPlayC/RedSox-3C
92USPlayC/RedSox-7C

Pett, Jose
93B-139

Pettaway, Ike
78Green
83Durham-22

Pettee, Patrick E.
N172

Pettengill, Tim
88NE-9
89Savan/ProC-352

Pettersen, Andy
90SDSt-7

Pettibone, Jay
80Ashvl-17
82OrlanTw/B-22
83OrlanTw-14
84Toledo-24

Pettibone, Jim
82Cedar-10
83Water-6
84Cedar-3
85Cedar-11

Pettiford, Cecil
89BurlInd/Star-20
90AS/Cal-55
90Reno/Cal-279
91Kinston/ClBest-11
91Kinston/ProC-323

Pettini, Joe
78Memphis/Team-8
80Phoenix/NBank-21
81F-453
81Phoenix-21
81T-62
82F-398
82T-568
83T-143
84Cram/PCL-13
84Nes/792-449
84T-449
85Louisvl-12
86Louisvl-23
87Louisvl-2CO
88Louisvl-2CO
88Louisvl/CMC-24
88Louisvl/ProC-435
89Hamil/Star-27
90StPete/Star-26CO
91AA/LineD-49MG
91ArkTr/LineD-49MG
91ArkTr/ProC-1302MG
92ArkTr/ProC-1144
92ArkTr/SB-49MG

Pettis, Gary
81Holyo-20
82Spokane-23
84D-647
84F-526
84Smok/Cal-21
84T/Tr-93
85D-499
85F-308
85F/St-57
85OPC-39
85Smok/Cal-9
85T-497
85T/St-226
86D-158
86F-165
86F/Mini-33
86F/St-88
86Leaf-84
86OPC-323
86Smok/Cal-9
86T-604
86T/Mini-7
87Classic/Up-134
87D-160
87D/OD-10
87F-90
87F/AwardWin-29
87Leaf-152
87OPC-278
87Seven-W7
87Sf-157M
87Sf/TPrev-11M
87Smok/Cal-20
87T-278
87T/Mini-47
87T/St-16
87T/St-175
88D-210
88D/Best-203
88F/Up-U29
88OPC-71
88Panini/St-48
88Pep/T-24
88S-255
88S/Tr-38T
88T-71
88T/St-178
88T/Tr-86T
89B-108
89D-60
89F-141
89Mara/Tigers-24
89OPC-146
89Panini/St-345
89S-26
89T-146
89T/Mini-53
89T/St-279
89UD-117
90B-498
90D-661
90D/BestAL-126
90F-612
90F/AwardWin-25
90F/Can-612
90Kenner/Fig-64
90Leaf-469
90Mother/Rang-12
90OPC-512
90Panini/St-78
90PublInt/St-480
90S-136
90S/Tr-6T
90Sf-202
90T-512
90T/Big-311
90T/Mini-14
90T/St-283
90T/Tr-94T
90UD-385
90UD/Ext-770
91B-276
91D-512
91F-297
91Leaf/StudPrev-9
91Mother/Rang-12
91OPC-314
91Panini/FrSt-256
91Panini/Top15-115
91S-182
91StCl-141
91T-314
91UD-229
91Ultra-352
92F-314
92L-466
92L/BlkGold-466
92OPC-756
92Panini-80
92S-308
92Smok/Padre-22
92StCl-548
92T-756
92T/Gold-756
92T/GoldWin-756
92UD-179
92Ultra-580
93Rang/Keeb-293
93S-442

Pettis, Stacey
84PrWill-34
86PalmSp-26

Pettit
N172
WG1-13

Pettit, Bob
60P*

Pettit, Doug
92Erie/ClBest-19

Pettit, Paul
60HenryH-15
77Fritsch-13

Pettitte, Andy
92ClBest-286
92Greens/ClBest-1
92Greens/ProC-777
93B-103
93ClBest/MLG-117
93FExcel/ML-214
93SALAS/II-31
94B-493
94FExcel-111

Petty, Brian
85Everett/Cram-14

Petty, Jesse
33G-90
90Target-620
V354-42

Petway, Bruce
78Laugh/Black-7
90Negro/Star-31

Pevey, Marty
86Louisvl-24
89Indianap/CMC-15
89Indianap/ProC-1217
90OPC-137
90T-137
90T/89Debut-98
90UD-628
91AAA/LineD-513
91Syrac/LineD-513
91Syrac/MerchB-18
91Syrac/ProC-2483
92Toledo/ProC-1046

Peyton, Byron
82Cedar-17

Peyton, Eric
82ElPaso-1
83ElPaso-2
84Cram/PCL-41

Peyton, Mickey
88Augusta/ProC-362

Pezzoni, Ron
90Penin/Star-14
91CLAS/ProC-CAR29
91Penin/ClBest-20
91Penin/ProC-390
92ClBest-247
92SanBern/ClBest-2
92SanBern/ProC-
94B-219

Pfaff, Bob
86Sumter/ProC-21
87Durham-4
89BurlB/ProC-1606
89BurlB/Star-16

Pfaff, Jason
92Lakeland/ClBest-18
92Lakeland/ProC-2276
93B-503

Pfaff, Rich
89Beloit/I/Star-22
89Beloit/II/Star-23

Pfeffer, Edward
(Jeff)
90Target-621
D327
D328-133
D350/2-137
E121/80
E122
E135-133
E220
M101/5-137
V100
W575

Pfeffer, Francis
(Big Jeff)
M116
T206
W514-58
WG3-36

Pfeffer, Kurt
90Elizab/Star-17
91Kenosha/ClBest-11
91Kenosha/ProC-2090

Pfeffer, Nathaniel F.
E223
N172
N284
N300/Unif
WG1-14

Pfeil, Bobby
66Pep/Tul
70OPC-99
70T-99
72T-681
91WIZMets-314
94Mets/69-27

Pfiester, John
12Sweet/Pin-87
E254
E96
M116
T204
T205
T206
T3-33

Pfirman, Charles
94Conlon-1204UMP

Pfister, Dan
62T-592R
63T-521
64T-302

Phanatic, Phillie
84Phill/TastyK-3
87Phill/TastyK-xx
88Phill/TastyK-30
90Phill/TastyK-33

Phelan, Art
C46-35
M116
T206
T222

Phelan, James D.
N172

Phelan, James F.
T205
T206

Phelan, John
89Spokane/SP-6

Phelps, Edward
10Domino-98
11Helmar-175
12Sweet/Pin-152
C46-36
E90/1
M116
T205
T206

Phelps, Ernest Gordon
(Babe)
37Exh/4-2
38Exh/4-2
39PlayBall-96
40PlayBall-66
89Smok/Dodg-41
90Target-622
94Conlon-1125
R313

Phelps, Ken
76Watlo
77DaytB
77Jaxvl
82F-420
82Wichita-12
82Wichita-7M
85D-318
85F-499
85Leaf-129
85Mother/Mar-18
85OPC-322
85T-582
86Mother/Mar-18
86T-34
87D-317
87D/OD-118
87F-593
87F/GameWin-34
87F/Slug-30
87Mother/Sea-7
87Sf/TPrev-25M
87T-333
87T/St-222
88D-489
88D/Best-248
88F-384
88F/Slug-29
88F/St-61
88KennerFig-80
88Mother/Sea-7
88OPC-182
88RedFoley/St-69
88S-256
88T-182
88T/Big-189
89B-177
89D-363
89D/Best-276
89F-264
89S-242
89S/NWest-10
89T-741
89T/Big-293
89T/DHTest-24
89UD-167
90B-462
90D-675
90Mother/A's-14
90OPC-411
90PublInt/St-544

90T-411
91Phoenix/ProC-75
92Yank/WIZ80-146
Phelps, Tom
93BurlB/ClBest-18
93BurlB/ProC-155
93James/ClBest-16
93James/ProC-3324
Philley, Dave
48L-85
49B-44
50B-127
51B-297
52NTea
52T-226
53T-64
54B-163
54RM-AL9
54T-159
55Gol/Ind-23
55Salem
56T-222
57T-124
58Hires-12
58T-116
59T-92
60T-52
61T-369
62T-542
72Laugh/GF-46
79TCMA-192
90HOF/St-55
91Crown/Orio-360
91T/Arc53-64
94T/Arc54-159
Exh47
R423-80
Phillip, Jim
86WinSalem-19
Phillippe, Charles
(Deacon)
10Domino-99
12Sweet/Pin-143
72F/FFeat-37
D322
E104
E107
E254
E90/1
E91
E93
M116
S74-114
T202
T205
T206
W555
WG3-37
Phillips, Adolfo
66OPC-32
66T-32
67CokeCap/Cub-8
67OPC-148
67T-148
68T-202
69MB-222
69T-372
69T/St-17
70T-666
71Expo/ProS-19
71LaPizza-9
71MLB/St-137
71OPC-418
71T-418
Phillips, Anthony
92SanBern/ProC-
Phillips, Bill
83CharR-8
86Peoria-19
Phillips, Charlie
77LodiD
80ElPaso-24
80SLCity-8
Phillips, Chris
83Knoxvl-6
Phillips, Dave
88TM/Umpire-9
89TM/Umpire-7
90TM/Umpire-7
Phillips, Eddie
93Conlon-980
Phillips, J.R.
88Bend/Legoe-35
89QuadC/Best-22
89QuadC/GS-7
90Boise/ProC-3319
90PalmSp/Cal-207
90PalmSp/ProC-2586
91PalmSp/ProC-2025
92B-59
92ClBest-342
92MidldA/OneHour-21
92MidldA/SB-468
92Sky/AASingl-199
92UD/ML-228
93StCl/Giant-7
94B-247
94D-588
94Finest-429
94OPC-148
94Pinn-419
94Pinn/New-13
94Pinn/RookTPinn-2M
94Sf/2000-164
94SigRook/Bonus-4
94StCl-158
94StCl/1stDay-158
94StCl/Gold-158
94StCl/Team-4
94T-790M
94T/Gold-790M
94TripleP-294
94UD-116
94UD/ElecD-116
Phillips, Jack Dorn
52T-240
53Mother-57
57T-307
D301
Phillips, Jack
93Welland/ClBest-21
93Welland/ProC-3357
Phillips, Jim
87Pittsfld-12
89Martins/Star-25
Phillips, John
(Bubba)
55B-228
57T-395
58T-212
59T-187
60T-243
61Kahn
61T-101
61T/St-140
62J-39
62Kahn
62P-39
62P/Can-39
62Salada-74
62Shirriff-74
62Sugar-14
62T-511
62T/St-38
63J-70
63P-70
63T-177
64Det/Lids-11
64T-143
65T-306
78TCMA-192
Phillips, Keith Anthony
(Tony)
80Memphis-16
81WHave-14
82Tacom-32
83T/Tr-87T
84D-278
84F-459
84Mother/A's-23
84Nes/792-309
84T-309
85D-101
85F-433
85T-444
85T/St-329
86D-542
86F-430
86Mother/A's-19
86T-29
87D-103
87D/OD-26
87F-402
87Sf/TPrev-23M
87Smok/A's-10
87T-188
88D-221
88D/A's/Bk-221
88F-290
88Mother/A's-12
88OPC-12
88Panini/St-168
88S-294
88T-673
88T/St-165
89D/Best-211
89F/Up-56
89Mother/A's-11
89S-156
89T-248
89UD-267
90B-359
90Classic/III-79
90CokeK/Tiger-17
90D-91
90D/BestAL-20
90F-19
90F/Can-19
90F/Up-U99
90Leaf-324
90OPC-702
90S-84
90S/Tr-14T
90T-702
90T/Big-239
90T/Tr-95T
90UD-154
90UD/Ext-768
91B-137
91Classic/III-73
91CokeK/Tiger-4
91D-286
91F-348
91Leaf-4
91OPC-583
91Panini/FrSt-290
91Pol/Tiger-9
91S-38
91StCl-41
91T-583
91UD-131
91Ultra-126
92B-272
92D-328
92D/DK-DK25
92F-143
92L-40
92L/BlkGold-40
92OPC-319
92Pinn-243
92S-453
92StCl-488
92Studio-176
92T-319
92T/DQ-29
92T/Gold-319
92T/GoldWin-319
92T/Kids-79
92TripleP-218
92TripleP-99M
92UD-184
92USPlayC/Tiger-10D
92USPlayC/Tiger-1C
92Ultra-62
93B-419
93Colla/DM-85
93D-701
93F-233
93Flair-207
93L-126
93OPC-262
93Pac/Spanish-113
93Panini-115
93Pinn-406
93S-614
93Select-218
93Select/StatL-37
93StCl-5IF
93StCl/1stDay-5IF
93Studio-213
93T-189
93T/Finest-75
93T/FinestRef-75
93T/Gold-189
93Tiger/Gator-22
93TripleP-176
93UD-195
93UD/FunPack-188
93UD/SP-239
93Ultra-203
94B-397
94D-445
94F-142
94Flair-52
94L-160
94OPC-192
94Pac/Cr-227
94Panini-67
94Pinn-330
94Pinn/Run-11
94S-103
94S/Cycle-5M
94S/GoldR-103
94S/GoldS-54
94Sf/2000-56
94Studio-192
94T-48
94T/Finest-178
94T/FinestRef-178
94T/Gold-48
94TripleP-247
94UD-56
94UD/CollC-230
94UD/CollC/Gold-230
94UD/CollC/Silv-230
94UD/ElecD-56
94UD/SP-179
94Ultra-59
94Ultra/OnBase-11
Phillips, Lanny
77Holyo
78Spokane/Cramer-6
78Spokane/Team-6
Phillips, Lefty
70OPC-376MG
70T-376MG
71JB
71OPC-279MG
71T-279MG
Phillips, Lonnie
87Everett-5
88Clinton/ProC-720
89SanJose/Best-5
89SanJose/Cal-217
89SanJose/ProC-452
91Reno/Cal-3
Phillips, Mike
74OPC-533
74T-533
75OPC-642
75T-642
75T/M-642
76OPC-93
76SSPC-540
76SSPC/MetsY-M18
76T-93
77T-532
78T-88
79T-258
80T-439
81D-188
81F-538
81T-113
82F-201
82OPC-263
82T-762
83Expo/PostC-14
91WIZMets-315
Phillips, Montie
88CalLgAS-8
89SanJose/Best-12
89SanJose/ProC-433
89SanJose/Star-22
91FSLAS/ProC-FSL26
91Osceola/ClBest-8
91Osceola/ProC-680
Phillips, Randy
90Pulaski/Best-27CO
90Pulaski/ProC-3113CO
92MedHat/ProC-3208
92MedHat/SportP-11
93Dunedin/ProC-1794
94ClBest/Gold-56
Phillips, Richard E.
(Dick)
61Union
63T-544R
64T-559
78TCMA-179
79Hawaii-6
Phillips, Robbie
84Cedar-1
Phillips, Steve 1
85Lynch-16
86Lynch-17
87Jacks/Feder-18
Phillips, Steve 2
91Oneonta/ProC-4167
92Greens/ClBest-12
92Greens/ProC-794
Phillips, Thomas G.
E120
W573
Phillips, Tony
91T/Tr-91T
92StCl/Dome-140
93River/Cal-13
Phillips, Vince
89PrWill/Star-16
90Albany/Best-22
90Albany/ProC-1046
90Albany/Star-12
90ProC/Singl-782
90T/TVYank-57
91AA/LineD-12
91Albany/LineD-12
91Albany/ProC-1021
Phillips, W. Taylor
57T-343
58T-159
59T-113
60T-211
Phillips, Wade
87Fayette-9
87Lakeland-15
88Lakeland/Star-20
Phillips, William
N172
N284
Philyaw, Dino
91Pocatel/ProC-3798
91Pocatel/SportP-25
Philyaw, Thad
75Water
Phipps, Ron
83Peor/Frit-26TR
Phoebus, Tom
67CokeCap/Orio-18
67T-204R
68CokeCap/Orio-18
68Dexter-63
68OPC-97
68T-97
68T/ActionSt-13C
68T/ActionSt-2CM
69MB-223
69MLB/St-6
69OPC-185
69T-185
69T-532M
69T/4in1-18M
69T/St-127
70MLB/St-152
70T-717
71MLB/St-234
71OPC-611
71T-611
72MB-274
72OPC-477
72T-477
91Crown/Orio-361
Phoenix, Steve
91Modesto/ProC-3086
92Huntsvl/ProC-3949
92Huntsvl/SB-318
Piatt, Bruce
83Butte-32
Piatt, Doug
88BurlInd/ProC-1790
89Kinston/Star-18
89Star/IISingl-184
89Watertn/Star-18
90WPalmB/Star-17
91AAA/LineD-191
91Indianap/LineD-191
91Indianap/ProC-459
91T/Tr-92T
92ClBest-118
92D-640
92Harris/ProC-460
92Harris/SB-295
92OPC-526
92ProC/Tomorrow-253
92S-422
92Sky/AASingl-125
92StCl-408
92T-526
92T/91Debut-139
92T/Gold-526

92T/GoldWin-526
Piatt, Wiley
E107
Piazza, Anthony
87Everett-4
Piazza, Mike
89Salem/Team-25
90VeroB/Star-24
91Bakers/Cal-7
91CalLgAS-6
92Albuq/ProC-723
92B-461
92ClBest-345
92ClBest/BBonusC-16
92ClBest/RBonus-BC16
92D/RookPhen-BC9
92F/Up-92
92SanAn/SB-573
92Sky/AASingl-251
93B-646
93Classic/Gamel-74
93Colla/ASG-24
93Colla/DM-86
93D-209RR
93D/EliteDom-15
93F/MLPI-13
93Flair-75
93Flair/Wave-12
93JDean/Rook-8
93L-35
93L/UpGRook-4
93Mother/Dodg-4
93OPC-314
93OPC/Premier-26
93Pac/Jugador-34
93Pac/Spanish-502
93Pinn-252
93Pinn/HRC-26
93Pinn/RookTP-3
93Pol/Dodg-20
93S-286
93S/Boys-5
93Select-347
93Select/RT/ASRook-5
93Select/RookTr-ROY2
93StCl-585
93StCl/1stDay-585
93StCl/Dodg-6
93Studio-201
93Studio/Sil-9
93T-701
93T/Finest-199
93T/FinestRef-199
93T/Gold-701
93T/Tr-24T
93TB/Full-6
93ToysRUs-22
93TripleP-55
93UD-2SR
93UD/Diam-34
93UD/FunPack-6SOT
93UD/SP-98
93UD/SPPlat-PP15
93Ultra-300M
93Ultra-60
93Ultra/AllRook-7
94B-387
94B-510
94Church-14
94D-2
94D/AwardWin-3ROY
94D/DK-15
94D/Elite-46
94D/LongBall-7
94D/MVP-7
94D/Pr-5
94D/Special-2
94D/Spirit-4
94F-520
94F-713
94F/AS-47
94F/AwardWin-6
94F/ProV-8
94F/RookSen-14
94F/TL-21
94Flair-182
94Flair/Hot-7
94KingB-19
94Kraft-27
94L-436
94L/Gamer-12
94L/MVPNL-12
94L/PBroker-6
94L/Pr-6
94L/Slide-2
94L/StatStand-4
94OPC-147
94OPC/DiamD-1
94OPC/JAS-9
94Oscar-27
94P-1
94Pac/Cr-318
94Pac/Cr-658ROY
94Pac/CrPr-6
94Pac/Gold-16
94Pac/Silv-29
94Panini-203
94Pinn-28
94Pinn/Artist-28
94Pinn/Museum-28
94Pinn/New-2
94Pinn/Power-17
94Pinn/Run-28
94Pinn/TeamP-5M
94Pinn/Trib-7
94RedFoley-20
94S-476
94S-636ROY
94S/GoldS-13
94S/Tomb-15
94Select-4
94Select/CrCon-8
94Sf/2000-189AS
94Sf/2000-67
94Sf/Shak-11
94StCl-140
94StCl-266
94StCl/1stDay-140
94StCl/1stDay-266
94StCl/Dugout-1
94StCl/Gold-140
94StCl/Gold-266
94Studio-72
94Studio/Editor-8
94Studio/S&GStar-6
94T-1
94T-391M
94T/BlkGold-41
94T/Finest-1
94T/FinestRef-1
94T/Gold-1
94T/Gold-391M
94TripleP-88
94TripleP/Pr-6
94UD-273HFA
94UD-33FT
94UD-47FUT
94UD-500
94UD/CollC-310TP
94UD/CollC/Gold-310TP
94UD/CollC/Silv-310TP
94UD/CollHR-8
94UD/DColl-W9
94UD/ElecD-273HFA
94UD/ElecD-33FT
94UD/ElecD-47FUT
94UD/HoloFX-30
94UD/Mantle-15
94UD/SP-80
94Ultra-218
94Ultra/AS-11
94Ultra/AwardWin-25ROY
94Ultra/HRK-12
94Ultra/Hit-9
94Ultra/RBIK-10
94Ultra/RisSt-9
94Ultra/Second-9
Picano, John
92WPalmB/ClBest-29ANN
Picciolo, Dustin
87Spokane-25
Picciolo, Rob
76Tucson-9
78T-528
79T-378
80T-158
81A's/Granny-8
81D-357
81F-582
81T-604
81T/Tr-813
82D-465
82F-106
82Granny-14
82T-293
82T/Tr-89T
83D-456
83Pol/Brew-8
83T-476
84D-455
84Nes/792-88
84Smok/Cal-22
84T-88
84T/Tr-94
85Mother/A's-13
85T-756
85T/Tr-90T
86Cram/NWL-177
86D-497
86OPC-3
86T-672
87LasVegas-26
87Spokane-26
92Mother/Padre-27M
92Pol/Padre-26M
92Smok/Padre-23CO
93Mother/Padre-28M
Pichardo, Francisco
90Elizab/Star-18
90Kenosha/Best-12
90Kenosha/ProC-2309
90Kenosha/Star-19
Pichardo, Hipolito
90BBCity/Star-19
91AA/LineD-413
91ClBest/Singl-296
91London/LineD-413
91Memphis/ProC-650
92D/Rook-95
92F/Up-32
92S/RookTr-103T
92T/Tr-89T
92T/TrGold-89T
93D-571
93F-246
93LimeR/Winter-128
93OPC-390
93Pac/Spanish-493
93Pac/SpanishP-18
93Pinn-450
93Pol/Royal-24
93S-336
93Select-312
93StCl-211
93StCl/1stDay-211
93StCl/Royal-8
93T-349
93T/Gold-349
93ToysRUs-89
93UD-72
93Ultra-567
94D-391
94F-171
94L-327
94Pac/Cr-299
94Pinn-275
94S-218
94S/GoldR-218
94StCl-223
94StCl/1stDay-223
94StCl/Gold-223
94T-482
94T/Finest-194
94T/FinestRef-194
94T/Gold-482
94UD/CollC-231
94UD/CollC/Gold-231
94UD/CollC/Silv-231
94Ultra-71
Pichardo, Nelson
77WHave
Pichardo, Sandy
92GulfCM/ProC-3492
Piche, Ron
61T-61
62T-582
63T-179
65T-464
66Pep/Tul
76Expo/Redp-25CO
Picinich, Val J.
21Exh-128
21Exh-129
25Exh-67
29Exh/4-7
33G-118
90Target-623
92Conlon/Sport-479
93Conlon-875
E120
E220
V354-3
W573
Pickens, Kevin
89BBCity/Star-21
Pickens, Ritchie
86Lipscomb-17
Pickering, Oliver
E107
E254
T206
Pickett, Antoine
88Modesto-28
Pickett, Bob
92WinHaven/ClBest-19
Pickett, Danny
90CharRain/Best-18
90CharRain/ProC-2033
Pickett, John
N172
Pickett, Rich
83Lynch-21
84Tidew-12
Pickett, Ricky
92Billings/ProC-3353
Pickett, Tony
87AppFx-23
Picketts, William
90SoOreg/Best-7
90SoOreg/ProC-3435
91Madison/ClBest-26
91Madison/ProC-2141
92Reno/Cal-51
Pickford, Kevin
94ClBest/Gold-76
Pickich, Jeff
93Welland/ClBest-22
93Welland/ProC-3358
Pickle, V.H.
89KS*-10M
Pico, Brandon
92Classic/DP-107
92FrRow/DP-14
92Hunting/ClBest-1
92Hunting/ProC-3164
Pico, Jeff
86WinSalem-20
87Pittsfld-19
88Berg/Cubs-41
88F/Up-U80
88Iowa/CMC-3
88Iowa/ProC-546
88Peoria/Ko-25
88S/Tr-94T
88T/Tr-87T
89D-513
89F-436
89Mara/Cubs-41
89Panini/St-50
89S-13
89T-262
89ToysRUs-22
89UD-491
90Cub/Mara-1541
90D-585
90F-39
90F/Can-39
90Iowa/CMC-7
90OPC-613
90Peoria/Team-20M
90ProC/Singl-82
90PublInt/St-200
90S-428
90T-613
90T/TVCub-14
91AAA/LineD-537
91F-428
91OPC-311
91S-326
91T-311
91Tacoma/LineD-537
91Tacoma/ProC-2303
Picota, Len
(Leny)
87Savan-23
88StPete/Star-22
89ArkTr/GS-18
90ArkTr/GS-24
91AAA/LineD-243
91Louisvl/LineD-243
91Louisvl/ProC-2914
92Harris/ProC-461
92Harris/SB-296
93Ottawa/ProC-2433
Piechowski, Tim
88James/ProC-1902
Piela, D.
88Pulaski/ProC-1765
Pieratt, Dan
91QuadC/ClBest-25TR
92QuadC/ClBest-30TR
Pierce, Ben
89AppFx/ProC-874
90BBCity/Star-20
Pierce, Billy
51B-196
51T/BB-45
52B-54
52Hawth/Pin-6
52RM-AL16
52StarCal-87C
52StarCal/L-73B
52T-98
53B/Col-73
53RM-AL16
53T-143
54B-102
54RH
54RM-AL10
55B-214
55RFG-27
55W605-27
56T-160
57Swift-4
57T-160
58T-334M
58T-50
59Bz
59T-156M
59T-410
59T-466HL
59T-572AS
60T-150
60T-571AS
60T/tatt-44
60T/tatt-95
61P-21
61T-205
61T/St-126
62J-54
62P-54
62P/Can-54
62Salada-2
62Shirriff-2
62T-260
63T-331M
63T-50
64T-222
77Galasso-30
79TCMA-16
80Marchant-22
88Coke/WS-22
89Pac/Leg-134
89Swell-57
90Pac/Legend-82
91T/Arc53-143
92AP/ASG-38
92Bz/Quadra-16M
Exh47
Pierce, Chris
86PrWill-19
Pierce, Dominic
88Butte-16
89Gaston/ProC-1001
89Gaston/Star-18
89Star/Wax-38
Pierce, Don Diego
82Wausau/Frit-24
Pierce, Eddie
(Ed)
89Eugene/Best-9
91AA/LineD-414
91London/LineD-414
91Memphis/ProC-651
92Memphis/ProC-2418
92Memphis/SB-442
92Sky/AASingl-187
93D-147
93F-623
93T-803
93T/Gold-803
Pierce, G.
C46-68
D350/2-138
M101/5-138
Pierce, Jeff
91Utica/ClBest-13
91Utica/ProC-3255
92MidwLAS/Team-32

92SoBend/ClBest-5
92SoBend/ProC-175
94FExcel-39
Pierce, Jim
85Clovis-34
Pierce, L. Jack
76OPC-162
76SSPC-386
76T-162
78SanJose-23
79Spokane-7
Pierce, Rob
92Madis/ClBest-22
92Madis/ProC-1232
92Reno/Cal-52
Pierce, Tony
67T-542R
68OPC-38
68T-38
81TCMA-401
Pierce, Walter
83ArkTr-5
84ArkTr-24
Piercy, Bill
21Exh-130
21Exh-131
Pieretti, Marino
(Chick)
49B-217
50B-181
50NumNum
52Mother-12
53Mother-35
Pierorazio, Wes
83Watlo/Frit-23
85Visalia-19
86Visalia-15
87OrlanTw-22
Pierre, Rogers
(Shape)
92Negro/RetortII-29
Piersall, Jim
51B-306
52B-189
53B/BW-36
54B-210
54B-66B
54RM-AL11
55B-16
55RM-AL21
56T-143
57T-75
58T-280
59T-355
60T-159
61T-345
61T/St-139
62Bz
62Salada-88A
62Salada-88B
62Shirriff-88
62T-51LL
62T-90
62T/St-100
62T/bucks
63Exh
63F-29
63T-443
64T-586
65OPC-172
65T-172
66T-565
67T-584
79TCMA-188
80Marchant-23
89Pac/Leg-182
89Swell-83
90Pac/Legend-44
90Swell/Great-92
91LineD-20
91Swell/Great-72
91T/Arc53-286
91WIZMets-316
92AP/ASG-49
93Rang/Keeb-294CO
93TWill-5
93UD/ATH-105
Exh47
PM10/Sm-146
Pierson, Larry
88StPete/Star-23
89StPete/Star-22
90ArkTr/GS-25
Piet, Tony
33G-228
34DS-72
34Exh/4-4
34G-8
35BU-142
35BU-70
35G-1H
35G-3F
35G-4F
35G-5F
88Conlon/NatAS-16
92Conlon/Sport-524
R314
V354-63
V355-95
Pietroburgo, Rob
79Spokane-18
80Tacoma
81Charl-23
82Charl-9
Pifer, Gary
87CharWh-10
88Lakeland/Star-21
Piggot, Rusty
81QuadC-4
Pignatano, Joe
58T-373
59T-16
60BB-10
60L-126
60T-292M
60T-442
61T-74
62J-97
62P-97
62P/Can-97
62Salada-45
62Shirriff-45
62T-247
73OPC-257CO
73T-257C
74OPC-179CO
74T-179C
79TCMA-204
81TCMA-407M
82Pol/Atl-52C
83Pol/Atl-52C
84Pol/Atl-52C
90Target-624
91WIZMets-317
94Mets/69-31
Pike, David
92Idaho/ProC-3510
Pike, Mark
87Watlo-6
88Watlo/ProC-683
89Kinston/Star-19
Pilarcik, Al
57T-311
58Hires-76
58Hires/T
58T-259
59T-7
60T-498
61T-62
79TCMA-212
91Crown/Orio-362
Pilkington, Eric
86Clinton-21
88SanJose/Cal-136
88SanJose/ProC-127
Pilkinton, Lem
86Elmira-15
87Greens-23
89Penin/Star-19
90CLAS/CL-44
90Penin/Star-15
91AA/LineD-350M
91Jaxvl/LineD-350CO
91Jaxvl/ProC-168CO
92Belling/ProC-1462
92SanBern/ClBest-29CO
Pill, Mike
78Charl
Pilla, Tony
82OrlanTw-11
83OrlanTw-2
Pillette, Duane
46Sunbeam
51B-316
52T-82
53B/BW-59
53T-269
54B-133
54Esskay
54T-107
55B-244
55Esskay
55T-168
79TCMA-191
91Crown/Orio-363
91T/Arc53-269
94T/Arc54-107
Pillette, Herman
21Exh-132
E120
V61-19
W572
W573
Pimentel, Ed
90FtLaud/Star-17
Pimentel, Rafael D.
81ArkTr-13
82ArkTr-5
86MidldA-19
Pimentel, Wander
90Hamil/Best-16
90Hamil/Star-19
91Savan/ClBest-22
91Savan/ProC-1663
92Spring/ClBest-8
92Spring/ProC-876
Pina, Horacio
71MLB/St-548
71OPC-497
71T-497
72T-654
73OPC-138
73T-138
74OPC-516
74T-516
74T/Tr-516T
75OPC-139
75T-139
75T/M-139
93Rang/Keeb-33
Pina, Mickey
87Elmira/Cain-3
87Elmira/Red-33
88Lynch/Star-17
89AAA/CMC-27
89NewBrit/ProC-619
89NewBrit/Star-14
89Star/IISingl-129
90AAASingl/ProC-445
90B-270
90Pawtu/CMC-20
90Pawtu/ProC-473
90ProC/Singl-271
90S/Tr-104T
90T/TVRSox-56
90TripleAAS/CMC-27
90UD/Ext-764
91AAA/LineD-364
91Pawtu/LineD-364
91Pawtu/ProC-50
Pina, Rafael
91Elizab/ProC-4298
92Elizab/ClBest-12
92Elizab/ProC-3680
Pincavitch, Kevin
92GreatF/SportP-12
Pinckes, Mike
90BurlInd/ProC-3016
91CollInd/ClBest-5
91CollInd/ProC-1494
Pinder, Chris
88Hagers/Star-17
89Hagers/Best-27
89Hagers/ProC-268
90Kinston/Team-20
Pineda, Gabriel
90Eugene/GS-21
91AppFx/ClBest-9
91AppFx/ProC-1715
Pineda, Jose
91FtLaud/ClBest-17
91FtLaud/ProC-2430
92FtLaud/ClBest-6
92FtLaud/Team-23
92Greens/ProC-781
Pineda, Rafael
87QuadC-15
87Salem/ProC-2432
Pineiro, Michael
92Boise/ClBest-8
92Boise/ProC-3632
Pinelli, Ralph
(Babe)
55B-307UMP
87Conlon/2-20
88Conlon/4-22
92Conlon/Sport-476
94Conlon-1197UMP
E120
V61-78
W572
W573
WG7-41
Pinelli, Willie
87Bakers-29
Piniella, Lou
64T-167R
68OPC-16R
68T-16R
69T-394R
70MLB/St-227
70OPC-321
70T-321
70T/S-32
70T/SO
70T/Super-32
71MLB/St-426
71OPC-35
71T-35
71T/Coins-152
71T/GM-38
71T/Greatest-38ROY
71T/S-62
71T/Super-62
71T/tatt-9
72MB-275
72OPC-491KP
72T-491KP
72T-580
73K-24
73OPC-140
73T-140
73T/Comics-15
73T/Lids-40
73T/PinUps-15
74OPC-390
74T-390
74T/St-188
74T/Tr-390T
75K-34
75OPC-217
75T-217
75T/M-217
76OPC-453
76SSPC-445
76SSPC/MetsY-Y11
76T-453
77BK/Y-23
77K-48
77T-96
78BK/Y-18
78OPC-82
78SSPC/270-3
78T-159
79BK/Y-18
79Ho-69
79OPC-342
79T-648
80OPC-120
80T-225
81D-109
81F-85
81F/St-45
81OPC-306
81T-724
82D-135
82F-48
82F/St-114
82OPC-236
82T-538
83D-335
83F-392
83F/St-14M
83F/St-8M
83OPC-307
83RoyRog/Disc-8
83T-307
84D-274
84F-136
84Nes/792-408
84OPC-351
84T-408
86T/Tr-86T
87T-168MG
88T-44MG
90Kahn/Reds-21MG
90Pac/Legend-99
90T/Tr-96TMG
91Crown/Orio-364
91Kahn/Reds-41MG
91OPC-669MG
91Pep/Reds-16MG
91T-669MG
92OPC-321MG
92Reds/Kahn-41MG
92T-321MG
92T/Gold-321MG
92T/GoldWin-321MG
92Yank/WIZ70-128
92Yank/WIZ80-147
93Mother/Mar-1MG
93T-512MG
93T/Gold-512MG
Pinkerton, Wayne
76SanAn/Team-17
77Tucson
78Cr/PCL-33
79Tucson-12
80CharCh-3
Pinkham, Bill
83Knoxvl-8
Pinkney, Alton
90Kissim/DIMD-22
91GreatF/SportP-30
92VeroB/ClBest-4
92Yakima/ClBest-3
92Yakima/ProC-3465
Pinkney, George
90Target-625
N172
Pinkston, Lal
52Laval-62
Pinkus, Jeff
77Salem
Pinnell, Lance
89SanDiegoSt/Smok-22
Pino, Rolando
83AppFx/Frit-12
86BirmB/Team-12
87BirmB/Best-19
89Kenosha/ProC-1082
89Kenosha/Star-19
90Greenvl/Best-20
92StCath/ClBest-30CO
92StCath/ProC-3402CO
93StCath/ClBest-26CO
93StCath/ProC-3990CO
Pinol, Juan
87Tampa-7
Pinon, Rudy
87BYU-7M
Pinson, Chris
90AR-32M
Pinson, Tom
92Kingspt/ClBest-1
92Kingspt/ProC-1529
Pinson, Vada
58T-420
59Kahn
59T-448
60Armour-17
60Kahn
60T-176
60T-32M
61Kahn
61P-181
61T-110
61T-25M
61T/St-22
62Bz
62Exh
62J-121
62Kahn
62P-121
62P/Can-121
62Salada-118
62Shirriff-118
62T-52LL
62T-80
62T/St-119
62T/bucks
63Exh
63F-34
63FrBauer-19
63J-130
63Kahn
63P-130
63T-265

64Kahn
64T-162M
64T-80
64T/Coins-152AS
64T/Coins-45
64T/S-56
64T/SU
64T/St-2
65Kahn
65OldLond-16
65T-355
65T/E-42
65T/trans-24
66Kahn
66OPC-180
66T-180
67CokeCap/AS-29
67CokeCap/NLAS-33
67CokeCap/Reds-11
67Kahn
67T-550
68Bz-9
68Kahn
68OPC-90
68T-90
68T/ActionSt-10AM
69Kahn
69MB-224
69OPC-160
69T-160
69T/4in1-4M
69T/St-119
70MLB/St-202
70OPC-445
70T-445
70T/CB
70T/S-31
70T/Super-31
71MLB/St-382
71OPC-275
71T-275
71T/Coins-18
71T/GM-12
71T/Greatest-12
71T/tatt-5
72MB-276
72OPC-135
72T-135
73OPC-75
73T-75
74OPC-490
74T-490
74T/St-144
75OPC-295
75SSPC/42-9
75T-295
75T/M-295
76OPC-415
76SSPC-178
76T-415
77T-597C
78TCMA-146
82D-445CO
82Ohio/HOF-52
88Pep/T-CO
89Mara/Tigers-CO
90CokeK/Tiger-28CO
91CokeK/Tiger-xCO
93Marlin/Publix-28M
94TedW-140
94TedW-23
Exh47

Pinto, Gustavo
89Niagara/Pucko-19

Piotrowicz, Brian
90GreatF/SportP-23
91Bakers/Cal-8
92VeroB/ClBest-14
92VeroB/ProC-2872

Pipgras, Ed
90Target-626

Pipgras, George
33DH-34
33G-12
61F-134
91Conlon/Sport-123
R315-A29
R315-B29
R337-404

Piphus, Ben
83Watlo/Frit-3

Pipik, Gary
89James/ProC-2138

Pipp, Wally
21Exh-133
25Exh-99
26Exh-29
27Exh-14
91Conlon/Sport-157
BF2-34
D328-134
D329-138
D350/2-139
E120
E121/120
E121/80
E122
E135-134
E220
M101/4-138
M101/5-139
V100
V61-48
V89-45
W514-84
W515-39
W572
W573
W575
WG7-42

Pippen, Henry
(Cotton)
39PlayBall-8
40PlayBall-136
46Remar
47Remar
47Signal
47Smith-9

Pippin, Craig
83LynnP-7
86Maine-15
87Omaha-15

Pirkl, Greg
88Belling/Legoe-7
89Belling/Legoe-1
90Foil/Best-233
90ProC/Singl-860
90SanBern/Best-14
90SanBern/Cal-105
90SanBern/ProC-2637
91Penin/ClBest-1
91SanBern/ClBest-14
91SanBern/ProC-1990
92B-654
92Calgary/ProC-3736
92ClBest-143
92D/Rook-96
92Jacks/ProC-3710
92Jaxvl/SB-367
92Sky/AASingl-158
93B-571
93Calgary/ProC-1173
93D-589RR
94Finest-291

Pirkl, Petagine
94T-448
94T/Gold-448

Pirruccello, Mark
83CharR-1
84Memphis-23

Pirtle, Jerry
79RochR-12
79T-720R
89Pac/SenLg-198

Pisacreta, Mike
89Pulaski/ProC-1890

Pisarkiewicz, Mike
77StPete
78StPete

Piscetta, Rob
89Bakers/Cal-187

Pisciotta, Marc
91Welland/ProC-3570
92Augusta/ProC-236
92ProC/Tomorrow-314

Pisciotta, Scott
92James/ClBest-9
92James/ProC-1500
92StCl/Dome-141
92UD/ML-149
93BurlB/ClBest-19
93BurlB/ProC-156

Pisel, Ron
78Cedar
83Phoenix/BHN-19

Pisker, Don
76Dubuq
78Charl
79Syrac/TCMA-8
79Syrac/Team-7
79T-718R
80Syrac-23
80Syrac/Team-17
81SLCity-24

Piskol, Pete
84PrWill-8

Piskor, Kirk
90AR-21

Piskor, Steve
88LitFalls/Pucko-9
89Pittsfld/Star-19

Pisoni, Jim
57T-402
59T-259
92Yank/WIZ60-99

Pitcher, Scott
88Belling/Legoe-19
89Wausau/GS-8
90SanBern/Best-17
90SanBern/Cal-95
90SanBern/ProC-2631
91SanBern/ClBest-11
91SanBern/ProC-1987
92Jacks/ProC-3706
92Penin/ClBest-9

Pitler, Jake
49Eureka-46
52T-395CO
55Gol/Dodg-22CO
79TCMA-187CO

Pitlock, Lee
(Skip)
71OPC-19
71T-19
75OPC-579
75T-579
75T/M-579
75Tucson/Caruso-19
76Tucson-44

Pittaro, Chris
85F/Up-U87
85T/Tr-91T
86D-150
86T-393
87Portl-6
88Portl/CMC-19
88Portl/ProC-653
92SoOreg/ClBest-28MG

Pittenger, Clark A.
29Exh/4-8
E120
V61-42
W573

Pittinger, Charley
WG3-38

Pittman, Charles
92Johnson/ClBest-14
92Johnson/ProC-3117

Pittman, Doug
87Salem-27
88Kenosha/ProC-1388

Pittman, James
88OrlanTw/Best-8

Pittman, Joe
76Dubuq
80Tucson-3
81Tucson-3
82D-218
82F-222
82T-119
82T/Tr-90T
83D-247
83F-369
83LasVegas/BHN-17
83T-346
89Pac/SenLg-38
89T/SenLg-19
90EliteSenLg-101
91Pac/SenLg-151

Pittman, Mike
82Spring/Frit-5
83Spring/Frit-20

Pittman, Park
87Visalia-11
89OrlanTw/Best-20
89OrlanTw/ProC-1334
90AAASingl/ProC-247
90B-408
90F/Up-109
90Portl/CMC-9
90Portl/ProC-177
90ProC/Singl-561

Pitts, Gaylen
75Tucson-16
75Tucson/Caruso-4
75Tucson/Team-16
76Tucson-42
81ArkTr-21
81Louisvl-2
82ArkTr-22MG
82Louisvl-23
83Louisvl/Riley-2
84Louisvl-2
87Spring/Best-1
89ArkTr/GS-1MG
89TexLAS/GS-19MG
90AAASingl/ProC-533MG
90Louisvl/CMC-27MG
90Louisvl/LBC-3MG
90Louisvl/ProC-419MG
90ProC/Singl-678MG
90SpringDG/Best-MG27
90T/TVCard-61MG

Pitts, Jon
91LitSun/HSPros-28
91LitSun/HSProsG-28

Pittsley, Jim
92ClBest/Up-405
92Classic/DP-80
92UD/ML-93
93ClBest/MLG-202
93Rockford/ClBest-23
94FExcel-70

Pitz, Michael
87Bakers-28
88SanAn/Best-3
89SanAn/Best-23
90SanAn/GS-20
91AA/LineD-342
91Jaxvl/LineD-342
91Jaxvl/ProC-149

Pivnick, Phil
85Albany-31

Pizarro, Germain
52Laval-78

Pizarro, Juan
57T-383
59T-188
60L-51
60Lake
60SpicSpan-17
60T-59
61P-112
61T-227
62T-255
62T-59LL
62T/St-28
62T/bucks
63J-44
63P-44
63T-10LL
63T-160
64T-2LL
64T-430
64T/Coins-14
64T/S-53
64T/SU
64T/St-31
64Wheat/St-36
65OPC-125
65OPC-9LL
65T-125
65T-9LL
65T/trans-25
66T-335
67T-602
67T/Test/PP-5
68KDKA-29
68OPC-19
68T-19
69T-498
71MLB/St-41
71OPC-647
71T-647
72OPC-18
72T-18
78TCMA-79

Pizarro, Miguel
78Ashvl

Pizzitola, Vince
52Laval-112

Place, Michael
90Pulaski/Best-8
90Pulaski/ProC-3106
91Idaho/SportP-2
92Macon/ClBest-21
92Macon/ProC-264
93Macon/ClBest-19
93Macon/ProC-1397

Placeres, Benigno
88StCath/ProC-2009

Pladson, Gordy
75Dubuq
76Dubuq
77Cocoa
79CharCh-13
80Tucson-18
81T-491
81Tucson-18
82Tucson-21
83Tucson-7

Plainte, Brandon
80Elmira-15

Plamondon, Gerry
45Parade*-43

Plamondon, Jerry
45Parade*-46

Planco, Radhames
89Clmbia/GS-21

Plank, Ed
76Phoenix/Coke-16
77Phoenix
78Cr/PCL-66
79Phoenix

Plank, Edward A.
11Diamond-24
14CJ-6
15CJ-6
48Exh/HOF
50Callahan
50W576-60
60F-46
61F-135
63Bz/ATG-9
69Bz/Sm
72F/FFeat-26
76Shakey-46
77Galasso-156
80Laugh/3/4/5-22
80Marchant-24
80Perez/HOF-46
80SSPC/HOF
81Conlon-82
87Conlon/2-49
88Conlon/3-22
89HOF/St-78
92Conlon/Sport-463
93CrackJack-19
94Conlon-1002
D303
E104
E106
E107
E224
E90/1
E91
E93
E95
M116
T204
T206
T208
T216
W555
WG2-41
WG4-22

Plante, Bill
85Elmira-16
86Greens-16

Plantenberg, Erik
89SanDiegoSt/Smok-23
90Elmira/Pucko-19
90SDSt-8
91CLAS/ProC-CAR26
91LynchRS/ClBest-6
91LynchRS/ProC-1195
92LynchRS/ClBest-13
92LynchRS/ProC-2904
94D-647
94F-297
94StCl-518
94StCl/1stDay-518
94StCl/Gold-518
94T-774M
94T/Gold-774M

Plantier, Phil
87Elmira/Red-34
88WinHaven/Star-20

89Lynch/Star-18
89Star/IISingl-170
90AAASingl/ProC-446
90Pawtu/CMC-21
90Pawtu/ProC-474
90ProC/Singl-272
90T/TVRSox-57
91AAA/LineD-365
91AAAGame/ProC-31
91B-117
91Classic/200-128
91Classic/I-22
91Classic/II-T66
91D-41RR
91F-107
91Leaf/Stud-18
91OPC-474
91Pawtu/LineD-365
91Pawtu/ProC-51
91Pep/RSox-15
91S-348RP
91StCl-459
91T-474
91T/90Debut-125
91UD-2SR
91Ultra-38
92B-459
92CJ/DII-28
92Classic/Game200-111
92Classic/I-71
92D-488
92F-44
92F/RookSIns-19
92L-50
92L/BlkGold-50
92L/GoldPrev-14
92L/Prev-14
92OPC-782
92OPC/Premier-74
92Pinn-51
92Pinn/Team2000-2
92ProC/Tomorrow-14
92RedSox/Dunkin-22
92S-406
92S/100RisSt-86
92S/Impact-20
92StCl-760
92Studio-136
92T-782
92T/Gold-782
92T/GoldWin-782
92TripleP-120
92UD-425
92UD/ASFF-7
92UD/TWillB-T18
92USPlayC/RedSox-12S
92USPlayC/RedSox-7H
92Ultra-318
93B-278
93D-3
93F-564
93F/Final-144
93Flair-136
93L-275
93Mother/Padre-8
93OPC-332
93OPC/Premier-10
93Pac/Spanish-599
93Panini-99
93Pinn-539
93S-176
93Select-242
93Select/RookTr-128T
93StCl-282
93StCl-614
93StCl/1stDay-282
93StCl/1stDay-614
93T-592
93T/Gold-592
93T/Tr-42T
93UD-274
93UD-474M
93UD-774
93UD/FunPack-140
93UD/SP-171
93Ultra-475
94B-616
94Church-22
94D-566
94F-672
94Flair-235
94L-59
94OPC-65
94Pac/Cr-532
94Pac/Gold-18
94Panini-258
94Pinn-80
94Pinn/Artist-80
94Pinn/Museum-80
94Pinn/Power-21
94S-404
94Select-120
94Sf/2000-64
94StCl-115
94StCl/1stDay-115
94StCl/Gold-115
94Studio-135
94T-13
94T/Finest-84
94T/Finest/PreProd-84
94T/FinestRef-84
94T/Gold-13
94TripleP-170
94UD-145
94UD/CollC-232
94UD/CollC/Gold-232
94UD/CollC/Silv-232
94UD/ElecD-145
94UD/SP-132
94Ultra-583

Plants, Dan
84ElPaso-17

Plaskett, Elmo
63T-549R

Plasse, Michel
72Dimanche*-96IA
72Dimanche*-97

Plaster, Allen
91Bluefld/ClBest-19
91Bluefld/ProC-4127
92Freder/ClBest-12
92Freder/ProC-1803
93Modesto/ClBest-16
93Modesto/ProC-797

Platel, Mark
79AppFx-22
80GlenF/B-5
80GlenF/C-9
81AppFx-9

Platt, Mizell
48L-159
49B-89

Platts, Jim
87Spartan-1
88Spartan/ProC-1048

Plautz, Rick
82FtMyr-9

Plaza, Ron
62Kahn/Atl

Pleasac, Joe
86CharRain-21

Pledger, Kinnis
89SoBend/GS-19
90Saraso/Star-20
91AA/LineD-70
91BirmB/LineD-70
91BirmB/ProC-1467
92BirmB/SB-91
92Saraso/ProC-221
92Sky/AASingl-44

Pleicones, Johnnie
86FtLaud-18

Pleis, Scott
83Erie-14

Pleis, William
62T-124
63T-293
64T-484
65OPC-122
65T-122
78TCMA-135
78Twin/Frisz-41

Plemel, Lee
88Hamil/ProC-1726
89Spring/Best-11
90StPete/Star-18
91AA/LineD-42
91ArkTr/LineD-42
91ArkTr/ProC-1285
92ArkTr/ProC-1128
92ArkTr/SB-41

Plemmons, Ron
89Utica/Pucko-18
90Foil/Best-36
90SoBend/Best-7
90SoBend/GS-13
91Saraso/ClBest-24
91Saraso/ProC-1125
92Saraso/ProC-222

Plemmons, Scott
90CharWh/ProC-2238
90Foil/Best-299
92Cedar/ClBest-22
92Cedar/ProC-1072

Plesac, Dan
86D/Rook-14
86F/Up-U90
86Pol/Brew-37
86Sf/Rook-10
86T/Tr-87T
87D-214
87F-354
87Pol/Brew-37
87Sf/TPrev-19M
87T-279
87T/St-201
87ToysRUs-22
88D-109
88D/AS-18
88D/Best-221
88F-171
88F-625M
88F/Mini-32
88F/St-39
88OPC-317
88Panini/St-118
88Pol/Brew-37
88RedFoley/St-70
88S-77
88S/YS/II-32
88Sf-191
88T-670
88T/Mini-20
88T/St-203
88T/St/Backs-65
89B-133
89Brewer/YB-37
89Cadaco-40
89D-382
89D/AS-22
89D/Best-165
89F-195
89F/LL-29
89F/Superstar-32
89Gard-8
89KennerFig-106
89OPC-167
89Panini/St-367
89Pol/Brew-37
89S-320
89S/HotStar-32
89Sf-128
89T-740
89T/LJN-32
89T/St-197
89UD-630
90B-386
90Brewer/MillB-19
90D-175
90D/BestAL-36
90ElPasoATG/Team-5
90F-334
90F/BB-28
90F/Can-334
90F/LL-29
90KMart/SS-30
90Leaf-216
90MLBPA/Pins-85
90OPC-490
90Panini/St-95
90Pol/Brew-37
90PublInt/St-503
90RedFoley/St-74
90S-86
90S/100St-86
90Sf-102
90T-490
90T/Big-33
90T/Mini-21
90T/St-200
90T/TVAS-31
90UD-477
91B-34
91Brewer/MillB-20
91Classic/200-33
91D-104
91F-594
91Leaf-287
91OPC-146
91Panini/FrSt-212
91Panini/St-163
91Pol/Brew-18
91RedFoley/St-72
91S-275
91StCl-7
91T-146
91UD-322
91Ultra-179
92D-682
92F-185
92OPC-303
92Pinn-162
92Pol/Brew-19
92S-567
92StCl-532
92T-303
92T/Gold-303
92T/GoldWin-303
92UD-550
92Ultra-388
93Cub/Mara-20
93D-677
93F-633
93L-388
93OPC-297
93Pac/Spanish-381
93Pinn-433
93S-456
93StCl-24
93StCl/1stDay-24
93StCl/Cub-6
93T-16
93T/Gold-16
93TripleP-142
93UD-804
93Ultra-318
94D-641
94F-393
94StCl-256
94StCl/1stDay-256
94StCl/Gold-256
94StCl/Team-355
94T-215
94T/Gold-215

Pless, Rance
56T-339
79TCMA-176

Plews, Herb
57T-169
58T-109
59T-373
60Maple-16
61BeeHive-16

Plinski, Paul
79Cedar/TCMA-17

Plitt, Norman
90Target-1051

Ploeger, Tim
91Spokane/ClBest-13
91Spokane/ProC-3948
92Spokane/ClBest-22
92Spokane/ProC-1292

Plonk, Chad
92GulfCY/ProC-3791

Plonk, Chris
92Hunting/ClBest-23
92Hunting/ProC-3156

Ploucher, George
77Cocoa

Plumb, Dave
87Sumter-13
88CLAS/Star-34
88Durham/Star-17
89Greenvl/Best-25
89Greenvl/ProC-1164
89Greenvl/Star-17
89Richm/Bob-20
90Greenvl/Best-2
90Greenvl/ProC-1133
90Greenvl/Star-15

Plummer, Bill
73OPC-177
73T-177
74OPC-524
74T-524
75OPC-656
75T-656
75T/M-656
76OPC-627
76SSPC-32
76T-627
77T-239
78SanJose-19
78T-106
79OPC-208
79Spokane-10
79T-396
80SanJose/JITB-1
81Wausau-29
84Chatt-9
86Calgary-21MG
87Calgary-4
88AAA/ProC-49
88Calgary/CMC-24
88Calgary/ProC-800
90Mother/Mar-27M
92Mother/Mar-1MG
92OPC-171MG
92T-171MG
92T/Gold-171MG
92T/GoldWin-171MG

Plummer, Dale
88LitFalls/Pucko-20
89Jacks/GS-28
89StLucie/Star-19
89Star/Wax-23
90AAASingl/ProC-273
90ProC/Singl-360
90T/TVMets-53
90Tidew/CMC-9
90Tidew/ProC-542
91AAA/LineD-566
91Tidew/LineD-566
91Tidew/ProC-2507
92Tidew/ProC-
92Tidew/SB-568

Plunk, Eric
85Huntsvl/BK-33
86D/Rook-40
86F-649R
86Tacom-16
87D-178
87F-403
87T-587
88D-503
88D/A's/Bk-503
88D/Best-267
88F-291
88Mother/A's-20
88S-614
88T-173
89B-191
89D-125
89D/Best-49
89F-20
89Mother/A's-16
89OPC-141
89S-392
89T-448
89UD-353
90D-196
90F-452
90F/Can-452
90Leaf-504
90OPC-9
90PublInt/St-313
90S/NWest-20
90T-9
90T/TVYank-17
90UD-630
91D-593
91F-676
91OPC-786
91S-428
91StCl-529
91T-786
91UD-695
91Ultra-241
92D-554
92F-241
92OPC-672
92S-379
92T-672
92T/Gold-672
92T/GoldWin-672
92UD-608
92Yank/WIZ80-148
93F-599
93Flair-198
93Indian/WUAB-25
93Pac/Spanish-417
93S-594
93StCl-486
93StCl/1stDay-486
93UD-713
94D-267
94F-118
94Pac/Cr-182
94Pinn-366
94S-131

94S/GoldR-131
94T-577
94T/Gold-577
94Ultra-47
Plunkett, Wilson
75FtLaud/Sus-23
Plympton, Jeff
88Lynch/Star-18
89NewBrit/ProC-622
89NewBrit/Star-16
90A&AASingle/ProC-8
90EastLAS/ProC-EL33
90Foil/Best-242
90NewBrit/Best-20
90NewBrit/ProC-1319
90NewBrit/Star-15
91AAA/LineD-366
91Pawtu/LineD-366
91Pawtu/ProC-38
92Pawtu/ProC-920
92Pawtu/SB-362
92ProC/Tomorrow-19
92S-823
92S/100RisSt-13
92Sky/AAASingl-164
92StCl-481
92T/91Debut-140
92UD-71TP
Poat, Ray
48B-42
Pocekay, Walter
53Mother-10
Poche, Gerry
76Baton
Pocoroba, Biff
76OPC-103
76SSPC-15
76T-103
77T-594
78Ho-99
78T-296
79OPC-285
79T-555
80OPC-73
80T-132
81F-257
81Pol/Atl-4
81T-326
82BK/Lids-20
82F-446
82Pol/Atl-4
82T-88
83D-436
83F-145
83OPC-367
83Pol/Atl-4
83T-676
84D-77
84F-189
84Nes/792-438
84T-438
Podbielan, Clarence
(Bud)
52T-188
53B/BW-21
53T-237
54T-69
55T-153
56T-224
57Seattle/Pop-27
90Target-627
91T/Arc53-237
94T/Arc54-69
V362-12
Podgajny, Johnny
93Conlon-948
Podres, Johnny
52Park-76
53T-263
54T-166
55B-97
55Gol/Dodg-23
55T-25
55T/DH-112
56T-173
57Swift-1
57T-277
58BB
58Hires-42
58T-120
59Armour-13
59Morrell
59T-262M
59T-495
60BB-19
60Morrell
60NuCard-2
60T-425
60Union/Dodg-14
61BB-22
61NuCard-474
61P-169
61T-109
61T-207M
61T/St-31
61Union/Dodg-16
62BB-22
62J-108
62P-108
62P/Can-108
62Salada-172
62Shirriff-172
62T-280
62T/St-138
62T/bucks
63Salada-9
63T-150
63T-412M
64T-580
65T-387
66T-468
67CokeCap/Tiger-15
67T-284
69T-659
73OPC-12CO
73T-12CO
78TCMA-156M
79TCMA-239M
79TCMA-267M
82D-566CO
83Twin/Team-30CO
83Twin/Team-34M
85Twin/Team-33CO
87Smok/Dodg-26
88Pac/Leg-105
89Rini/Dodg-6
89Smok/Dodg-63
90Pac/Legend-45
90Swell/Great-104
90Target-628
91Phill/Medford-32CO
91Swell/Great-73
91T/Arc53-263
92Phill/Med-24CO
93Phill/Med-26CO
93TWill/Mem-8
93UD/ATH-106
94Phill/Med-24CO
94T/Arc54-166
PM10/L-32
PM10/Sm-147
WG10-43
WG9-42
Poe, Charles
90LitSun/HSPros-6
90LitSun/HSProsG-6
91SoBend/ClBest-10
91SoBend/ProC-2870
92ClBest-261
92SoBend/ProC-191
Poe, Rick
82Jacks-13
Poehl, Michael
86Watlo-21
87Kinston-9
88EastLAS/ProC-42
88Wmsprt/ProC-1325
91AA/LineD-415
91London/LineD-415
91Memphis/ProC-652
Poepping, Mike
75Tacoma/KMMO-21
Poff, John William
79OkCty
80OkCty
Poffenberger, Boots
90Target-629
Pohle, Rich
88Idaho/ProC-1861
Pohle, Walt
85Beloit-2
86Stockton-21
87ElPaso-19
Poholsky, Tom
52T-242
54Hunter
54T-142
55B-76
55Hunter
56T-196
57T-235
94T/Arc54-142
Poindexter, Mike
81Batavia-5
83Watlo/Frit-24
Pointer, Aaron
67T-564R
68CokeCap/Astro-11
Pointer-Jones, Carl
88BurlB/ProC-2
Poissant, Rod
86Lakeland-17
87GlenF-16
89SanBern/Cal-75
90Penin/Star-16
90Star/ISingl-78
Poisson, Gilles
(The Fish)
72Dimanche*-126
Polak, Rich
90PrWill/Team-19
91FtLaud/ClBest-11
91FtLaud/ProC-2424
92PrWill/ClBest-17
92PrWill/ProC-144
Polakowski, Ted
84Idaho/Team-21
Polanco, Carlos
91Boise/ClBest-21
91Boise/ProC-3888
91QuadC/ClBest-21
91QuadC/ProC-2640
Polanco, Giovanni
91Belling/ClBest-26
91Belling/ProC-3660
Polanco, Nicholas
89Kingspt/Star-19
90Kgsport/Best-12
90Kgsport/Star-19
Polanco, Radhames
88LitFalls/Pucko-10
89Clmbia/Best-21
Polanco, Roger
75Dubuq
Poland, Philip
T206
Polasek, John
89Anchora-19
90James/Pucko-24
91WPalmB/ClBest-9
91WPalmB/ProC-1225
92Freder/ClBest-14
92Freder/ProC-1804
92Hagers/ProC-2553
Polcovich, Kevin
92Welland/ProC-1332
Poldberg, Brian
82Nashvl-18
83Omaha-11
84Omaha-23
85Omaha-31
87AppFx-17
88AppFx/ProC-162
89AppFx/ProC-872
90BBCity/Star-28MG
91AAA/LineD-350M
91Omaha/LineD-350CO
91Omaha/ProC-1051
92Memphis/ProC-2435MG
92Memphis/SB-449MG
Pole, Dick
74OPC-596R
74T-596R
74T/Tr-596T
75OPC-513
75T-513
75T/M-513
76OPC-326
76T-326
77T-187
78T-233
80Port-11
83QuadC-3
86Pittsfld-19CO
87Iowa-21CO
88Berg/Cubs-CO
90Cub/Mara-28CO
90T/TVCub-5CO
91Cub/Vine-21CO
92Pawtu/ProC-941CO
92Pawtu/SB-375CO
93Mother/Giant-28M
Poles, Spot
74Laugh/Black-21
Polese, Joe
77Newar
Polewski, Steve
90Welland/Pucko-7
91Augusta/ClBest-17
91Augusta/ProC-813
Polhemus, Mark
N284
Poli, Crip
R314/Can
V355-84
Polidor, Gus
81Holyo-21
82Holyo-18
83Nashua-14
85Cram/PCL-12
86Edmon-22
86F-650R
87D-579
87Smok/Cal-18
88D-356
88F-501
88S-341
88Smok/Angels-6
88T-708
89Pol/Brew-14
90D-412
90OPC-313
90Pol/Brew-14
90T-313
90UD-480
92Tacoma/ProC-2511
92Tacoma/SB-544
93Edmon/ProC-1145
Poling, Mark
88Clinton/ProC-699
Polinski, Bob
78Cr/PCL-82
79Colum-15
Polis, Pete
92MedHat/ProC-3211
92MedHat/SportP-16
93MedHat/ProC-3741
Polk, Riley
87Watlo-24
Polk, Ron
88MissSt-25CO
89MissSt-29CO
90MissSt-30CO
91MissSt-38CO
91T/Tr-93T
92MissSt-33CO
93MissSt-36CO
Polk, Steve
88MissSt-26
89MissSt-30
90MissSt-31
Polka, Fritz
86LitFalls-23
87Columbia-21
88FSLAS/Star-17
88StLucie/Star-19
Pollack, Chris
87James-30
88Rockford-29
89Rockford-30
90WPalmB/Star-18
91AA/LineD-267
91Harris/LineD-267
91Harris/ProC-626
92Harris/ProC-462
92Harris/SB-297
Pollack, Rick
88BirmB/Best-15
Pollard, Damon
90Eugene/GS-23
91AppFx/ClBest-10
91AppFx/ProC-1716
92BBCity/ClBest-6
92BBCity/ProC-3845
Pollard, Jim
52Wheat*
Pollard, Nathaniel
92Negro/RetortII-30
Pollet, Howard
(Howie)
39Exh
49B-95
49Eureka-193
50B-72
51B-263
51T/RB-7
52B-83
52T-63
53NB
53T-83
54T-89
55T-76
55T/DH-31
56T-262
60T-468CO
91T/Arc53-83
92Bz/Quadra-4M
92Card/McDon/Pac-49
94T/Arc54-89
R423-83
Polley, Dale
88Greenvl/Best-12
89Greenvl/Best-15
89Greenvl/ProC-1160
89Greenvl/Star-18
90AAAGame/ProC-4
90AAASingl/ProC-403
90ProC/Singl-279
90Richm/Bob-14
90Richm/CMC-3
90Richm/ProC-258
90Richm/Team-26
91AAA/LineD-437
91Richm/Bob-13
91Richm/LineD-437
91Richm/ProC-2565
91Richm/Team-23
92Richm/Bleach-17
92Richm/Comix-14
92Richm/ProC-374
92Richm/SB-436
Pollock, Syd
76Laugh/Clown-23
76Laugh/Clown-6
Pollock, Wayne
91Melbourne/Fut-17
Polly, Nick
90Target-630
Poloni, John
76SanAn/Team-18
77Tucson
80Knoxvl/TCMA-3
83Wausau/Frit-2CO
87Myrtle-17
88Knoxvl/Best-23
89Knoxvl/Best-29
89Knoxvl/ProC-1147
89Knoxvl/Star-25
90Knoxvl/Best-19CO
90Knoxvl/ProC-1261CO
90Knoxvl/Star-26CO
91AAA/LineD-522
91Syrac/LineD-522CO
91Syrac/MerchB-19CO
91Syrac/ProC-2497CO
92Syrac/MerchB-16CO
92Syrac/ProC-1987CO
92Syrac/SB-525CO
93Rang/Keeb-295
93Syrac/ProC-1014CO
Polonia, Luis
84Madis/Pol-7
85Huntsvl/BK-11
86Tacom-17
87D/Rook-25
87F/Up-U99
87Sf/Rook-18
87T/Tr-96T
88D-425
88D/A's/Bk-425
88F-292
88Leaf-256
88OPC-238
88Panini/St-177
88RedFoley/St-71
88S-64
88S/YS/I-22
88Sf-71
88T-238
88T/Big-65
88T/JumboR-14
88T/St-172
88Tacoma/CMC-16
88Tacoma/ProC-638
88ToysRUs-24
89D-386
89F-21
89Mother/A's-17
89OPC-386

89Panini/St-425
89S-380
89S/NWest-4
89S/Tr-38
89Sf-133
89T-424
89UD-162
90D-547
90D/BestAL-116
90F/Up-U80
90Leaf-295
90OPC-634
90PubInt/St-314
90S-442
90S/Tr-46T
90T-634
90T/TVYank-32
90T/Tr-97T
90UD-316
91B-209
91D-93
91D/GSlam-10
91F-322
91F/UltraUp-U11
91KingB/Discs-10
91Leaf-81
91OPC-107
91S-587
91Smok/Angel-1
91StCl-144
91T-107
91UD-187
92B-582
92D-252
92DennyGS-12
92F-67
92L-45
92L/BlkGold-45
92OPC-37
92Panini-10
92Pinn-166
92Pol/Angel-15
92S-68
92StCl-528
92T-37
92T/Gold-37
92T/GoldWin-37
92TripleP-99
92UD-147
92UD/TmMVPHolo-40
92Ultra-29
92Yank/WIZ80-149
93B-413
93D-461
93D/DK-26
93D/MVP-1
93D/Spirit-SG7M
93F-196
93Flair-176
93KingB-7
93L-399
93LimeR/Winter-111
93Mother/Angel-15
93OPC-266
93Pac/Beisbol-2
93Pac/Spanish-50
93Pac/SpanishP-19
93Panini-8
93Pinn-31
93Pol/Angel-15
93S-39
93Select-74
93StCl-100
93StCl/1stDay-100
93StCl/Angel-19
93Studio-170
93T-760
93T/Gold-760
93TripleP-12M
93TripleP-190
93UD-178
93UD/FunPack-41
93UD/SP-24
93USPlayC/Ace-10H
93Ultra-168
94B-409
94D-255
94F-68
94Finest-365
94L-390
94OPC-128
94Pac/Cr-87
94Panini-41
94Pinn-512
94S-45
94S/GoldR-45
94StCl-11
94StCl/1stDay-11
94StCl/Gold-11
94StCl/Team-208
94T-566
94T/Gold-566
94UD-496
94Ultra-403

Polverini, Steve
87AubAs-9

Pomeranz, Mike
89Kenosha/ProC-1081
89Kenosha/Star-20
90CLAS/CL-20
90Salem/Star-16

Pomierski, Joe
93ClBest/MLG-145

Pomorski
28LaPresse-13M

Pomorski, John
V355-92

Ponce, Carlos
81BurlB-22
83ElPaso-19
84Cram/PCL-34
85Cram/PCL-224
86D-595
90ElPasoATG/Team-10
91Sumter/ClBest-28INS
91Sumter/ProC-2353CO

Ponder, Charles Elmer
V100
WG7-43

Ponder, Kevin
88Clmbia/GS-10
89Miami/I/Star-16
89Miami/II/Star-16
90Miami/II/Star-21

Pone, Vince
78Newar
79BurlB-22
80BurlB-11
81BurlB-2

Ponio, Mike
89OK-22

Ponte, Edward
90Osceola/Star-22
91Osceola/ClBest-9
91Osceola/ProC-681
92Jacks/SB-344
92ProC/Tomorrow-229

Pontiff, Wally
74Gaston

Pool, Bruce
92Oneonta/ClBest-23
93Greens/ClBest-18
93Greens/ProC-884

Pool, Harlin
R314/Can

Poole, Ed
E107

Poole, James
(Jimmy)
87PanAm/USAB-13
87PanAm/USAR-13
88T/Tr-88T
89T/Big-263
89VeroB/Star-22
90SanAn/GS-21
90TeamUSA/87-13
91AAA/LineD-319
91Classic/I-54
91D-655
91F-217
91OkCty/LineD-319
91OkCty/ProC-176
91S-357RP
91T/90Debut-126
92D-600
92F-23
92OPC-683
92ProC/Tomorrow-150
92S-693
92StCl-412
92T-683
92T/Gold-683
92T/GoldWin-683
93D-295
93F/Final-164
93Pac/Spanish-348
93Rang/Keeb-296
93T-793
93T/Gold-793
94D-427
94F-16
94Flair-7
94Pac/Cr-42
94S-112
94S/GoldR-112
94StCl/Team-293
94T-449
94T/Gold-449
94Ultra-8

Poole, Mark
83Kinston/Team-15
85Syrac-17
86Syrac-21
86Tulsa-1

Poole, Stine
82Evansvl-13
83Toledo-12

Poorman, Thomas
N172

Pope, Dave
55B-198
55Gol/Ind-24
55Salem
56T-154
57T-249
61BeeHive-17
91Crown/Orio-365

Pope, Greg
81Watlo-13

Pope, Matt
85Clovis-35

Pope, Mike
78StPete

Popham, Art
80Tacom-22
81Tacom-3
82Tacom-21
83Tacom-23

Popoff, Jim
92Pittsfld/ProC-3292
93FExcel/ML-78

Popov, Andrey
89EastLDD/ProC-DD21

Popovich, Nick
77Spartan

Popovich, Paul
67T-536R
68T-266
69OPC-47
69T-47
69T/St-48
70OPC-258
70T-258
71MLB/St-42
71OPC-726
71T-726
72OPC-512
72T-512
73OPC-309
73T-309
74OPC-14
74T-14
75OPC-359
75T-359
75T/M-359
79Clinton/TCMA-8
90Target-631

Popowski, Eddie
73OPC-131CO
73T-131C
74OPC-403CO
74T-403C
87Elmira/Black-32

Popplewell, Tom
87Oneonta-9
88PrWill/Star-19
89FtLaud/Star-19
90FSLAS/Star-40
90FtLaud/Star-18
91AA/LineD-13
91Albany/LineD-13
91Albany/ProC-1006
92Albany/ProC-2227
92Albany/SB-16

Poquette, Tom
75OPC-622R
75T-622R
75T/M-622R
76A&P/KC
77BurgChef-66
77K-24
77OPC-66
77T-93
78OPC-197
78SSPC/270-239
78T-357
79T-476
80T-597
81T-153
82T-657
88Omaha/ProC-1495
89Omaha/ProC-1741
90AAASingl/ProC-616CO
90Omaha/CMC-23CO
90Omaha/ProC-81CO
90ProC/Singl-198CO
92AppFox/ClBest-27
93Rang/Keeb-297

Porcelli, Joe
90Geneva/ProC-3038
90Geneva/Star-20
91WinSalem/ClBest-10
91WinSalem/ProC-2828

Porte, Carlos
80Cedar-6
83Water-12
85Cedar-18

Porter, Andy
86Negro/Frit-15
92Negro/Kraft-14
92Negro/Retort-49

Porter, Bob
78Green
79Savan-22
81Richm-7
82Richm-21
83Richm-20
85Durham-16

Porter, Brad
84Everett/Cram-22A

Porter, Brian
89AubAs/ProC-2169
90AubAs/Best-21CO

Porter, Chuck
76QuadC
78Cr/PCL-65
79SLCity-19
81Vanco-2
82T-333R
82Vanco-21
84D-333
84F-211
84Nes/792-452
84Pol/Brew-43
84T-452
85D-115
85F-591
85Gard-16
85T-32
86T-292
86Vanco-22

Porter, Darrell
72OPC-162R
72T-162R
73OPC-582
73T-582
74OPC-194
74T-194
74T/St-198
75Ho-62
75OPC-52
75T-52
75T/M-52
76A&P/Milw
76Ho-117
76OPC-645
76SSPC-232
76T-645
77OPC-116
77T-214
78Ho-130
78OPC-66
78SSPC/270-221
78T-19
79Ho-4
79K-25
79OPC-295
79T-571
80K-12
80OPC-188
80T-360
80T/S-39
80T/Super-39
81Coke
81D-505
81F-36
81T-610
81T/St-224
81T/Tr-814
82D-498
82F-124
82F/St-29
82OPC-348IA
82OPC-98
82T-447
82T-448IA
82T/St-93
82T/StVar-93
83D-278
83F-18
83F/St-10M
83F/St-19AM
83F/St-19BM
83OPC-103
83OPC/St-148LCS
83OPC/St-149LCS
83OPC/St-182WS
83OPC/St-183WS
83PermaGr/CC-12
83T-103
83T/St-148
83T/St-149
83T/St-182
83T/St-183
84D-303
84F-331
84MiltBrad-19
84Nes/792-285
84OPC-285
84T-285
84T/RD-31M
84T/St-143
85D-353
85F-237
85Leaf-258
85OPC-246
85T-525
85T/RD-29M
85T/St-140
86D-290
86F-45
86F/Up-U91
86KAS/Disc-16
86OPC-84
86Rang-17
86Sf-148M
86T-757
86T/Tr-88T
87D-593
87F-136
87Mother/Rang-10
87OPC-213
87RedFoley/St-52
87Smok/R-10
87T-689
88S-537
93Rang/Keeb-298

Porter, Dick
32Orbit/num-36
32Orbit/un-49
34G-43
93Conlon-778
R305
V354-88

Porter, Eric 1
82Wisco/Frit-20

Porter, Eric 2
92MN-16

Porter, Griggy Jr.
73Wichita-12
74Wichita-118

Porter, Henry
E223
N172
N284

Porter, J.W.
53T-211
55T-49
55T/DH-9
58T-32
59T-246
91T/Arc53-211

Porter, Jeff
83Memphis/TCMA-22TR
84Indianap-31TR

Porter, Merle
92Negro/RetortII-31

Porter, Mike
92Bluefld/ClBest-5
92Bluefld/ProC-2359

Porterfield, Erwin
(Bob)
49B-3
50B-216
52B-194
52RM-AL17
52T-301
52TipTop
53B/Col-22
53Briggs
53RM-AL19
53T-108
54B-24
54RM-AL10
54RM-AL18
55B-104
55RFG-7
55W605-7
56T-248
56YellBase/Pin-25
57T-118
58T-344
59T-181
79TCMA-284
91T/Arc53-108
Exh47
R423-81
Porterfield, Ron
88AubAs/ProC-1954
90ColMud/Star-26TR
Portocarrero, Arnold
(Arnie)
54T-214
55Rodeo
55T-77
55T/DH-12
56T-63
58T-465
59T-98
60T-254
79TCMA-196
91Crown/Orio-366
94T/Arc54-214
Portugal, Mark
82Wisco/Frit-14
83Visalia/Frit-24
85Toledo-10
86D/Rook-44
87D-566
87F-548
87T-419
88Portl/CMC-5
88Portl/ProC-658
89B-318
89F-123
89S-482
89T-46
89Tucson/JP-19
89UD-358
90B-63
90Classic-121
90D-542
90Leaf-399
90Lennox-17
90Mother/Ast-10
90OPC-253
90S-552
90T-253
90UD-502
91B-552
91D-268
91F-512
91Leaf-63
91Mother/Ast-10
91OPC-647
91S-319
91StCl-320
91T-647
91UD-250
91Ultra-138
92B-656
92D-188
92F-443
92Mother/Ast-10
92OPC-114
92Pinn-189
92S-243
92StCl-126
92T-114
92T/Gold-114
92T/GoldWin-114
92UD-448
92Ultra-494
93D-612
93F-441
93L-467
93Mother/Ast-11
93OPC-318
93Pac/Spanish-126
93Pinn-366
93StCl-426
93StCl/1stDay-426
93StCl/Ast-30
93T-335
93T/Gold-335
93UD-99
93Ultra-394
94B-303
94D-199
94F-498
94Finest-413
94Flair-246
94L-429
94OPC-42
94Pac/Cr-273
94Pinn-506
94S-193
94S/GoldR-193
94StCl/Team-20
94T-734
94T/Gold-734
94UD-386
94Ultra-591
Portwood, Craig
89KS*-21TR
93Lipscomb-24M
Posada, Jorge
91Oneonta/ProC-4156
92Greens/ClBest-7
92Greens/ProC-782
94B-38
94FExcel-112
Posada, Leo
61T-39
62J-96
62P-96
62P/Can-96
62Salada-62
62Shirriff-62
62T-168
62T/St-55
73Cedar
74Cedar
75FtLaud/Sus-25
78DaytB/MG
Pose, Scott
89Billings/ProC-2063
90A&AASingle/ProC-103
90CharWh/Best-24
90CharWh/ProC-2255
90Foil/Best-91
90ProC/Singl-696
90SALAS/Star-19
91AA/LineD-164
91Chatt/LineD-164
91Chatt/ProC-1972
92Chatt/ProC-3831
92Chatt/SB-192
92ClBest/Up-442
92Sky/AASingl-85
92UD/ML-97
93B-318
93ClBest/MLG-54
93F/Final-68
93FExcel/ML-27
93L-272
93Pac/Spanish-469
93Pinn-576
93Pinn/Expan-8
93StCl-584
93StCl/1stDay-584
93StCl/Marlin-21
93T/Tr-113T
93UD-762
93USPlayC/Marlin-5D
93Ultra-384
Posedel, Bill
39PlayBall-121
40PlayBall-58
41G-19
41G-19
47Centen-20
49Eureka-169
52T-361CO
54Hunter
55Hunter
60T-469C
90Target-632
Posey, Bob
85Durham-29
86Durham-21
Posey, Cum
88Negro/Duques-3
Posey, Gary
90Butte/SportP-6
Posey, John
87Hagers-13
88CharlK/Pep-11
89Hagers/Best-26
89Hagers/Star-14
89RochR/CMC-12
90CharlK/Team-8
Posey, Marty
91Gaston/ClBest-26
91Gaston/ProC-2703
91SALAS/ProC-SAL24
Poss, David
87SLCity/Taco-27
Post, David
92Classic/DP-103
92FrRow/DP-70
92LitSun/HSPros-16
Post, Jeff
92SoOreg/ClBest-16
92SoOreg/ProC-3416
Post, John
88Elmira-28TR
Post, Wally
52T-151
55B-32
55Kahn
56Kahn
56T-158
57Kahn
57Sohio/Reds-16
57T-157
58Hires-14
58Kahn
58T-387
59HRDerby-15
59T-398
60T-13
61Kahn
61T-378
61T/St-23
62J-128
62Kahn
62P-128
62P/Can-128
62T-148
63T-462
64T-253
79TCMA-90
82Ohio/HOF-53
91T/Arc53-294
Postema, Andy
90Erie/Star-18
91Reno/Cal-9
Postier, Paul
87Gaston/ProC-16
88Tulsa-24
89Tulsa/GS-21
89Tulsa/Team-19
90Tulsa/ProC-1164
90Tulsa/Team-20
91AAA/LineD-320
91OkCty/LineD-320
91OkCty/ProC-188
92OkCty/SB-319
Postiff, J.P.
90Hunting/ProC-3292
91WinSalem/ProC-2838
92Peoria/ClBest-20
92Peoria/Team-20
Poston, Mark
85Beaum-16
86Beaum-20
87LasVegas-10
Pote, Lou
92Shrev/ProC-3867
92Shrev/SB-589
94B-547
Potestio, Doug
86Iowa-22
87Iowa-6
Potestio, Frank
87DayBe-17
88Spring/Best-10
89ArkTr/GS-19
89Louisvl-31
Pott, Larry
85Tulsa-17
Potter, Lonnie
90Bend/Legoe-9
Potter, Mike
78Spring/Wiener-3
79Spokane-3
Potter, Nelson
41DP-129
47TipTop
49Eureka-16
93Conlon-717
Potter, Scott
89EastLDD/ProC-48UMP
Potthoff, Michael
89GreatF-4
90Bakers/Cal-240
Pottinger, Mark
86Clearw-20
87Lakeland-20
Potts, Dave
86AubAs-19
87Osceola-16
88Osceola/Star-21
89Osceola/Star-18
Potts, Mike
92Durham/ClBest-21
92Durham/ProC-1096
92Durham/Team-5
Pough, Clyde
(Pork Chop)
89Burllnd/Star-21
90Reno/Cal-264
90Watertn/Star-16
91Kinston/ClBest-18
91Kinston/ProC-330
92Kinston/ClBest-20
92Kinston/ProC-2487
92UD/ML-199
93Kinston/Team-22
Poulin, Jim
88Beloit/GS-3
89Stockton/Best-25
89Stockton/Cal-178TR
89Stockton/ProC-387
89Stockton/Star-27
Poulis, George
90Waterlo/Best-21TR
91Waterlo/ClBest-27TR
Poulsen, Ken
77Fritsch-23
Pounders, Brad
87TexLgAS-5
87Wichita-8
88LasVegas/CMC-15
88LasVegas/ProC-247
89F-642R
Powell, Alonzo
83Clinton/Frit-14
86SLAS-15
86WPalmB-24
87D/OD-93
87Indianap-33
87Sf/Rook-8
87Sf/TPrev-20M
88Indianap/CMC-15
88Indianap/ProC-520
89Indianap/ProC-1210
89WPalmB/Star-18
90AAASingl/ProC-263
90Portl/ProC-193
91AAA/LineD-69
91Calgary/LineD-69
91Calgary/ProC-529
91F/Up-U55
91Leaf-521
92Calgary/SB-66
92D-213
92F-290
92OPC-295
92S-413
92StCl-547
92T-295
92T/Gold-295
92T/GoldWin-295
Powell, Alvin Jacob
(Jake)
38ONG/Pin-23
39PlayBall-1
40PlayBall-11
91Conlon/Sport-83
Powell, Charlie
78Charl
Powell, Colin
91B-533
Powell, Corey
91MidwLAS/ProC-48
91Rockford/ClBest-10
91Rockford/ProC-2045
92WPalmB/ClBest-17
92WPalmB/ProC-2088
93BurlB/ClBest-20
93BurlB/ProC-172
Powell, Dante
93Bz-2
93T/Tr-45T
Powell, Dennis
85Cram/PCL-154
86Coke/Dodg-24
86D-250
86Pol/Dodg-48
87Calgary-6
87D-499
87F-450
87T-47
88Calgary/CMC-4
88Calgary/ProC-796
88T-453
89F/Up-61
89T/Tr-97T
90AAASingl/ProC-649
90Brewer/MillB-20
90Denver/CMC-22
90Denver/ProC-624
90F-521
90F/Can-521
90ProC/Singl-47
90S-308
90Target-634
90UD-229
91AAA/LineD-68
91Calgary/LineD-68
91Calgary/ProC-514
92B-426
92Mother/Mar-12
93Calgary/ProC-1165
93F-312
93Mother/Mar-23
93StCl-108
93StCl/1stDay-108
Powell, Gordon Jr.
90Helena/SportP-12
91Beloit/ClBest-15
91Beloit/ProC-2111
92Beloit/ClBest-22
92Beloit/ProC-414
Powell, Grover
64T-113
91WIZMets-318
Powell, Hosken
78Twin/FriszP-14
79OPC-346
79T-656
79Twin/FriszP-21
80T-471
81D-567
81F-559
81T-137
82D-228
82F-558
82T-584
82T/StVar-206
83D-644
83F-440
83F/St-12M
83F/St-14M
83OPC-77
83T-77
84Cram/PCL-38
Powell, James E.
N172
Powell, Jay
91MissSt-39
92MissSt-34
93MissSt-31
94B-655
94ClBest/Gold-8
94ClBest/GoldLP-11
94FExcel-14
94Pinn-435
94S-575
94SigRook-19
94T-745DP
94T/Gold-745DP
Powell, John J.
11Helmar-64

E107
M116
T204
T206
Powell, John
(Boog)
62T-99
63J-62
63P-62
63T-398
64T-89
64T/Coins-104
64T/SU
64T/St-36
64T/tatt
65Bz-11
65OPC-3LL
65OldLond-33
65T-3LL
65T-560
65T/E-29
65T/trans-63
66OPC-167
66T-167
67CokeCap/Orio-11
67OPC/PI-1
67T-230
67T-241LL
67T-243LL
67T-521M
67T/PI-1
68CokeCap/Orio-11
68Dexter-64
68T-381
68T/3D
69MB-225
69MLB/St-7
69MLBPA/Pin-22
69OPC-15
69OPC/DE-17
69T-15
69T/DE-2
69T/St-128
70K-19
70MB-22
70MLB/St-153
70OPC-200ALCS
70OPC-410
70OPC-451AS
70OPC-64LL
70T-200ALCS
70T-410
70T-451AS
70T-64LL
70T/S-38
70T/SO
70T/Super-38
71K-20
71MD
71MLB/St-307
71MLB/St-570
71OPC-195ALCS
71OPC-327WS
71OPC-63LL
71OPC-700
71T-195ALCS
71T-327WS
71T-63LL
71T-700
71T/Coins-74
71T/S-5
71T/Super-5
71T/tatt-7
71T/tatt-7a
72MB-277
72OPC-250
72Pol/Orio-7
72ProStars/PostC-34
72T-250
73JP
73OPC-325
73T-325
74OPC-460
74T-460
75OPC-208MVP
75OPC-625
75T-208MVP
75T-625
75T/M-208MVP
75T/M-625
76Ho-75
76K-50
76OPC-45
76SSPC-524
76T-45
77T-206
78TCMA-80
82KMart-17
89GA-24
90BBWit-9
90Pac/Legend-46
90Swell/Great-16
90Target-633
91Crown/Orio-367
91K/3D-13
91MDA-12
91Swell/Great-74
92AP/ASG-80
93Bz-16
93Metallic-16
93T/Tr-131T
93TWill-143
93TWill-84
Exh47
Powell, Kelly
89SanDiegoSt/Smok-24
Powell, Kenny
90Foil/Best-275
90Gaston/Best-5
90Gaston/ProC-2534
90Gaston/Star-18
91CharlR/ClBest-24
91CharlR/ProC-1328
92ClBest-112
92Gaston/ProC-2266
Powell, Paul Ray
74Albuq/Team-13
76SSPC-82
90Target-635
Powell, Ray
21Exh-134
21Exh-135
E120
V100
V61-95
W572
Powell, Robert LeRoy
56T-144
Powell, Ross
89Cedar/Star-30
90CedarDG/Best-31
90Chatt/GS-24
91AAA/LineD-270
91Nashvl/LineD-270
91Nashvl/ProC-2155
94Pinn-401
94S-589
94S/Boys-56
Powell, William
92Negro/RetortII-32
Power, John
86Watlo-22
Power, Ted
80Albuq-22
81Albuq/TCMA-5
82F-17
84D-447
84F-478
84Nes/792-554
84T-554
85D-286
85F-547
85T-342
85T/St-50
86D-408
86F-187
86OPC-108
86Seven/Coin-S12M
86Sf-166
86T-108
86T/St-140
86TexGold-48
87D-536
87F-210
87Kahn-48
87T-437
88D-142
88F-245
88F/Up-U33
88OPC-236
88Panini/St-272
88S-242
88Smok/Royals-14
88T-236
88T/Tr-89T
89D-153
89F-142
89Louisvl-32
89Louisvl/CMC-10
89Louisvl/ProC-1249
89OPC-331
89S-348
89T-777
90D-653
90F-258
90F/Can-258
90F/Up-U50
90Homer/Pirate-23
90Leaf-473
90OPC-59
90T-59
90Target-636
90UD-340
91B-688
91D-608
91F-46
91F/Up-U85
91Kahn/Reds-48
91OPC-621
91S-255
91T-621
91UD-450
92D-586
92F-416
92Indian/McDon-24
92S-113
92StCl-812
92UD-680
93D-766
93F-600
93Indian/WUAB-26
93L-61
93Pac/Spanish-418
93StCl-82
93StCl/1stDay-82
94StCl-163
94StCl/1stDay-163
94StCl/Gold-163
94T-319
94T/Gold-319
94Ultra-123
Power, Vic
54T-52
55Rodeo
55T-30
55T/DH-29
56T-67
56T/Pin-14
57T-167
58T-406
59Kahn
59T-229
60Bz-16
60Kahn
60L-65
60T-75
61Clover-21
61Kahn
61P-63
61T-255
61T/St-141
62J-37
62Kahn
62P-37
62P/Can-37
62Salada-44
62Shirriff-44
62T-445
62T/St-39
62T/bucks
63F-23
63J-1
63P-1
63T-40
64PhilBull-18
64T-355
65T-442
66OPC-192
66T-192
78TCMA-196
79TCMA-147
90HOF/St-56
94T/Arc54-52
Powers, John
58Kahn
58T-432
59T-489
60T-422
91Crown/Orio-368
Powers, Larry
79LodiD-11
Powers, Michael Riley
E107
T206
Powers, Mike
82Ohio/HOF-9
Powers, Randy
90A&AASingle/ProC-159
90Boise/ProC-3305
91PalmSp/ProC-2012
92Salinas/ClBest-5
Powers, Robert
92Helena/ProC-1722
Powers, Scott
87Elmira/Black-12
87Elmira/Red-12
88Lynch/Star-19
89Lynch/Star-19
90LynchRS/Team-7
91AA/LineD-468
91NewBrit/LineD-468
91NewBrit/ProC-359
Powers, Steve 1
75QuadC
77Salem
Powers, Steve 2
90Ashvl/ClBest-8
90AubAs/Best-11
90AubAs/ProC-3407
91Ashvl/ProC-566
92BurlAs/ClBest-13
92BurlAs/ProC-542
Powers, Tad
89Penin/Star-20
90Reno/Cal-285
91SLCity/ProC-3209
91SLCity/SportP-3
91Sydney/Fut-12
Powers, Terry
91WinHaven/ClBest-7
91WinHaven/ProC-487
92ClBest-192
92WinHaven/ClBest-10
92WinHaven/ProC-1775
93WPalmB/ClBest-19
93WPalmB/ProC-1338
Powers, Thomas
N172/PCL
Powis, Carl
91Crown/Orio-369
Pozo, Arquimedez
92SanBern/ProC-
93River/Cal-14
94B-9
94UD-535TP
Prado, Jose
91Miami/Bumble-10
Prager, Howard
88CapeCod/Sum-175
89AubAs/ProC-2175
90Osceola/Star-23
91Osceola/ProC-694
92Jacks/ProC-4009
92Jacks/SB-345
92Sky/AASingl-144
Prall, Wilford
74Wichita-111
Pramesa, John
51B-324
52B-247
52T-105
PM10/Sm-148
Prappas, Jim
52Laval-99
Prather, Billy Ray
76Cedar
Prather, Mark
93TX-5
Prats, Jean
52Laval-27
Prats, Mario
91Ashvl/ProC-567
Pratt, Crestwell
(Cressy)
82Water-22
83Tampa-20
Pratt, Derrill
(Del)
14CJ-93
15CJ-93
21Exh-136
21Exh-137
91Conlon/Sport-162
D327
D328-135
D329-139
D350/2-140
E120
E121
E135-135
E220
M101/4-139
M101/5-140
V100
W501-11
Pratt, Evan
93SALAS/II-32
Pratt, Louis A.
79Savan-21
81ArkTr-20
Pratt, Steve
89Clinton/ProC-908
Pratt, Todd
85Elmira-17
86Greens-17
87WinHaven-29
88EastLAS/ProC-22
88NewBrit/ProC-906
89NewBrit/ProC-624
89NewBrit/Star-15
90NewBrit/Best-22
90NewBrit/ProC-1321
90NewBrit/Star-16
91AAA/LineD-367
91Pawtu/LineD-367
91Pawtu/ProC-41
92Reading/SB-540
92ScranWB/ProC-2450
92Sky/AASingl-235
93D-620
93F-497
93Phill/Med-27
93Pinn-598
93S-276
93T-479
93T/Gold-479
93Ultra-444
94D-188
94F-598
94Pac/Cr-484
94Phill/Med-25
94StCl-84
94StCl/1stDay-84
94StCl/Gold-84
94StCl/Team-227
94T-597
94T/Gold-597
Pratte, Evan
91Niagara/ClBest-12
91Niagara/ProC-3643
92Fayette/ClBest-22
92Fayette/ProC-2178
Pratts, Alberto
(Tato)
88Elmira-2
89WinHaven/Star-17
90LynchRS/Team-20
91Elmira/ClBest-26
91Elmira/ProC-3271
Preikszas, Dave
91Helena/SportP-14
Prendergast, Jim
V362-39
Prescott, George
61Union
Presko, Joe
52B-62
52T-220
53Hunter
54B-190
54Hunter
54T-135
79TCMA-178
94T/Arc54-135
Presley, Billy
80CharlO/Pol-14
80CharlO/W3TV-14
Presley, Jim
80Wausau-13
81Wausau-20
82LynnS-13
84Cram/PCL-184
85D-240
85F-500
85Mother/Mar-20
85T/Tr-92T
86D-313
86F-473

86F/Mini-98
86F/St-89
86KayBee-24
86Leaf-183
86Mother/Mar-7
86OPC-228
86Seven/Coin-W14M
86Sf-40
86T-598
86T/St-219
86T/Tatt-12M
87Classic-48
87D-120
87D-23DK
87D/AAS-29
87D/DKsuper-23
87D/OD-123
87F-594
87F/Lim-33
87F/Mini-82
87F/St-91
87Leaf-154
87Leaf-23DK
87Mother/Sea-4
87OPC-45
87RedFoley/St-19
87Sf-179
87Sf/TPrev-25M
87T-45
87T/St-214
88D-366
88D/Best-219
88F-385
88KennerFig-81
88Mother/Sea-4
88OPC-285
88Panini/St-189
88S-46
88Sf-54
88T-285
88T/Big-90
88T/St-217
89B-214
89Chatt/II/Team-24
89D-379
89D/Best-331
89F-555
89Mother/Sea-4
89OPC-112
89Panini/St-437
89S-73
89Sf-7
89T-112
89T/Big-75
89T/St-223
89UD-642
90B-18
90Brave/Dubuq/Perf-23
90Brave/Dubuq/Singl-26
90Classic/III-21
90D-497
90D/BestNL-37
90F-522
90F/Can-522
90F/Up-U6
90Leaf-277
90OPC-346
90PublInt/St-439
90S-34
90S/Tr-36T
90T-346
90T/Big-304
90T/St-224
90T/Tr-98T
90UD-315
90UD/Ext-760
91B-646
91D-173
91F-700
91OPC-643
91Padre/MagRal-23
91Panini/FrSt-21
91Panini/St-24
91RedFoley/St-73
91S-771
91T-643
91UD-282
91UD/Ext-791
92OkCty/ProC-1924
92OkCty/SB-320
Presley, Kirk
94B-324
94Pinn-436
94S-518
94SigRook-20
94T-740DP
94T/Gold-740DP
94UD/CollC-26
94UD/CollC/Gold-26FDP
94UD/CollC/Silv-26FDP
94UD/SP-14PP
Pressnell, Forest
(Tot)
39PlayBall-134
40PlayBall-146
90Target-637
Preston, Dayton
88ColAst/Best-24
Preston, Steve
88Eugene/Best-20
89AppFx/ProC-861
Prevost, Eric
78Wisco
Price, Al
81ElPaso-24
82ElPaso-24
83ElPaso-18
85Crm/PCL-225TR
87Denver-3
Price, Bill
81Wisco-18
Price, Bryan
85MidldA-2
86PalmSp-27
86PalmSp/Smk-15
88Vermont/ProC-940
89Calgary/CMC-9
89Calgary/ProC-540
89Wmsprt/Star-16
91Penin/ProC-396CO
92Belling/ProC-1463CO
93River/Cal-29CO
Price, Harris
75AppFx
76AppFx
Price, Jimmie
67OPC-123R
67T-123R
68T-226
69T-472
70OPC-129
70T-129
71MLB/St-403
71OPC-444
71T-444
72MB-278
88Domino-20
Price, Joe
79Nashvl
80Indianap-5
81F-210
81T-258
82Coke/Reds
82D-481
82F-81
82T-492
83D-481
83F-600
83T-191
84D-506
84F-479
84Nes/792-686
84OPC-159
84T-686
84T/St-58
85D-627
85F-548
85OPC-82
85T-82
85T/St-56
86D-506
86F-188
86T-523
86TexGold-49
87F-211
87Phoenix-17
87T-332
88D-655
88Mother/Giants-26
88T-786
89D-376
89F-339
89Mother/Giants-26
89S-444
89T-217
89UD-505
90B-245
90F-282
90F/Can-282
90OPC-473
90T-473
91AAA/LineD-464
91Crown/Orio-370
91F-488
91OPC-127
91RochR/LineD-464
91T-127
Price, John Thomas
46Remar-16
Price, Kevin
82Danvl/Frit-9
83Redwd-21
86Jaxvl/TCMA-14
86SLAS-25
87Jaxvl-20
87SLAS-17
88CharlK/Pep-4
Price, Phil
87Spartan-25
88Virgini/Star-18
Prichard, Brian
91Bristol/ClBest-8
91Bristol/ProC-3608
Pricher, John
92Boise/ClBest-18
92Boise/ProC-3623
93FExcel/ML-147
94FExcel-30
Priddy, Gerald
(Jerry)
41DP-109
48L-111
49B-4
50B-212
51B-71
51T/BB-46
52B-139
52Dix
52NTea
52T-28
53Dix
53NB
53T-113
53Tiger/Glen-25
79TCMA-213
91T/Arc53-113
R423-79
Priddy, Robert
64T-74R
65T-482
66T-572
67OPC-26
67T-26
68T-391
69T-248
70T-687
71MLB/St-20
71OPC-147
71T-147
Pride, Curtis
89Pittsfld/Star-20
91FSLAS/ProC-FSL33
91StLucie/ClBest-2
91StLucie/ProC-725
92Bingham/ProC-530
92Bingham/SB-65
92ClBest-159
92Sky/AASingl-30
93Harris/ProC-280
94D-646
94F/MLP-29
94Pac/Cr-387
94Pinn-230
94Pinn/Artist-230
94Pinn/Museum-230
94Sf/2000-167
94T-237
94T/Gold-237
94UD-250
94UD/CollC-233
94UD/CollC/Gold-233
94UD/CollC/Silv-233
94UD/ElecD-250
Pridy, Todd
92Erie/ClBest-20
92Erie/ProC-1633
93FExcel/ML-39
93T-441M
93T/Gold-441M
Pries, Jeff
86Albany/TCMA-15
86Colum-19
86Colum/Pol-17
87Albany-18
Priessman, Kraig
83SanJose-17
Priest, Jason
89KS*-15
Prieto, Arnie
88Miami/Star-19
89Miami/I/Star-23
Prieto, Pedro
(Pete)
76Dubuq
77Cocoa
Prim, Ray
47Signal
Prince, Doug
75T/Photo-119
Prince, Ray
77DaytB
Prince, Tom
86PrWill-20
87Harris-3
88AAA/ProC-5
88BuffB/CMC-19
88BuffB/ProC-1488
88D-538
89D-527
89F-217
89S-626RP
89S/HotRook-45
89T-453
89UD-311
90AAASingl/ProC-491
90B-176
90BuffB/CMC-14
90BuffB/ProC-376
90BuffB/Team-19
90ProC/Singl-14
90PublInt/St-161
92BuffB/BlueS-15
92S-618
92StCl-332
92Ultra-559
93Pac/Spanish-591
93Pirate/Nation-25
94F-618
94Pac/Cr-505
Prinz, Paul
87BYU-21
Prioleau, Laney
86Lakeland-18
Prior, Dan
82Reading-6
Pritchard, Harold
(Buddy)
58T-151
Pritchard, Kevin
89KS*-48
Pritchett, Chris
91BendB/ClBest-18
91BendB/ProC-3707
91Boise/ClBest-2
91Boise/ProC-3889
91ClBest/Singl-445
91FrRow/DP-54
92MidwLAS/Team-33
92QuadC/ClBest-26
92QuadC/ProC-820
92StCl/Dome-142
92UD/ML-152
93B-665
93FExcel/ML-148
94FExcel-31
Pritikin, James
86Cram/NWL-113
88Wausau/GS-12
89SanBern/Best-14
89SanBern/Cal-86
Probst, Alan
92AubAs/ClBest-16
92AubAs/ProC-1356
Probst, Thomas
92Bend/ClBest-27TR
Procopio, Jim
87Idaho-16
88Idaho/ProC-1853
Procter, Craig
88Spokane/ProC-1944
Proctor, Dave
88LitFalls/Pucko-21
89B-378
89StLucie/Star-20
90Jacks/GS-14
91ClBest/Singl-257
91StLucie/ProC-707
92StLucie/ProC-1745
Proctor, Jim
60T-141
Proctor, Murph
89Anchora-20
91Yakima/ClBest-5
91Yakima/ProC-4254
92AS/Cal-30
92Bakers/Cal-20
92ProC/Tomorrow-248
92UD-51
Prodanov, Peter
92OKSt-23
Proffitt, Steve
89LittleSun-9
Prohaska, Tim
89Niagara/Pucko-28
Proly, Michael
76Tulsa
79T-514
80T-399
81D-596
81F-358
81T-83
81T/Tr-815
82D-345
82F-254
82Iowa-22
82RedLob
82T-183
82T/Tr-92T
83D-225
83F-505
83T-597
83Thorn-36
84D-320
84F-501
84Nes/792-437
84Syrac-16
84T-437
Prothro, Doc
93Conlon-964
Provence, Todd
86Ventura-21
87Knoxvl-11
88Myrtle/ProC-1192
89Myrtle/ProC-1455
90Myrtle/ProC-2790
Prts, Mario
90Ashvl/ClBest-9
Prud'homme, Johnny
28LaPresse-8
Pruett, Hubert
(Hub)
87Conlon/2-50
88Conlon/5-24
93Conlon-904
Pruitt, Darrell Ray
86Penin-21
87BirmB/Best-21
88Chatt/Best-11
88SLAS-6
89Greenvl/Best-3
89Greenvl/ProC-1171
89Greenvl/Star-19
Pruitt, Donald
90Helena/SportP-20
91Beloit/ClBest-6
91Beloit/ProC-2101
91MidwLAS/ProC-34
92Beloit/ClBest-9
92Beloit/ProC-403
Pruitt, Ed
86Jacks/TCMA-8
87Jacks/Feder-14
Pruitt, Jason
91Classic/DP-26
91FrRow/DP-26
91LitSun/HSPros-31
91LitSun/HSProsG-31
92AppFox/ClBest-26
92ClBest-358
92Eugene/ClBest-21
92Eugene/ProC-3028
92OPC-246
92StCl/Dome-143
92T-246DP
92T/Gold-246
92T/GoldWin-246
Pruitt, Ron
75Spokane/Caruso-11
77T-654
78T-198

79T-226
80T-13
81T-442
82Phoenix
83Portl-21
89Pac/SenLg-103
89T/SenLg-74
93Rang/Keeb-299
Pruitt, Russell
79Elmira-12
Prusia, Greg
89AppFx/ProC-858
Prybylinski, Bruce
88Oneonta/ProC-2061
89PrWill/Star-17
90PrWill/Team-20
91FtLaud/ClBest-12
91FtLaud/ProC-2425
92PrWill/ClBest-1
92PrWill/ProC-145
92ProC/Tomorrow-117
Prybylinski, Don
91AA/LineD-43
91ArkTr/LineD-43
91ArkTr/ProC-1289
92ArkTr/ProC-1133
92ArkTr/SB-42
92ClBest-333
92Sky/AASingl-18
92StCl-748
Pryce, Ken
81QuadC-22
83MidldC-11
84Iowa-1
85Iowa-20
86Iowa-23
Pryor, Buddy
83Cedar-14
83Cedar/Frit-2
86Vermont-15
87Nashvl-17
89Tacoma/CMC-15
89Tacoma/ProC-1558
Pryor, Greg
78SSPC/270-145
79T-559
80OPC-91
80T-164
81D-278
81F-359
81T-608
82D-521
82F-356
82T-76
82T/Tr-93T
83D-264
83F-121
83T-418
84D-374
84F-353
84Nes/792-317
84T-317
85D-277
85F-210
85T-188
86D-344
86NatPhoto-4
86T-773
87D-378
87OPC-268
87T-761
93Rang/Keeb-300
Pryor, Jim
76Cedar
77Cedar
Pryor, Randy
88CapeCod/Sum-107
Przybylinski, Rodney
89TNTech-21
Psaltis, Spiro
82CharR-20
85MidldA-16
Puccinelli, George
28LaPresse-24
36Exh/4-14
38Exh/4-1
V355-127
Puchales, Javier
90Kissim/DIMD-23
91GreatF/SportP-29
Puchkov, Evgeny
89EastLDD/ProC-DD6
93T-633M
93T/Gold-633M

Puckett, Kirby
83Visalia/Frit-6
84F/X-U93
85D-438
85F-286
85F/St-122
85Leaf-107
85OPC-10
85Seven/Minn-1
85T-536
85T/St-307
85T/St-376YS
85Twin/Seven-1
85Twin/Team-24
86D-72
86D/HL-7
86F-401
86F/LL-32
86F/Mini-85
86F/Slug-M5
86F/St-90
86KayBee-25
86Leaf-69
86OPC-329
86Sf-93
86T-329
86T/St-285
86T/Tatt-13M
87Classic-55
87Classic/Up-112
87D-149
87D-19DK
87D/AAS-4
87D/DKsuper-19
87D/HL-30
87D/OD-221
87D/PopUp-4
87Drake-19
87F-549
87F-633M
87F/AS-5
87F/AwardWin-30
87F/BB-32
87F/LL-36
87F/Mini-83
87F/Slug-31
87F/St-92
87F/WaxBox-C11
87GenMills/Book-3M
87Ho/St-26
87KayBee-24
87Kraft-27
87Leaf-19DK
87Leaf-56
87MnM's-15
87OPC-82
87RedFoley/St-23
87Sf-198M
87Sf-7
87Sf/TPrev-17M
87Smok/AL-8
87Stuart-22
87T-450
87T-611AS
87T/Coins-20
87T/Gloss22-19
87T/Gloss60-57
87T/Mini-63
87T/St-146
87T/St-274
88Bz-14
88ChefBoy-13
88Classic/Red-164
88D-368
88D-BC15
88D/AS-15
88D/Best-186
88Drake-19
88F-19
88F-638M
88F/AwardWin-29
88F/BB/AS-30
88F/BB/MVP-26
88F/Excit-30
88F/Hottest-30
88F/LL-30
88F/Mini-36
88F/RecSet-29
88F/SS-28
88F/Slug-30
88F/St-45
88F/TL-26
88F/WS-8

88F/WaxBox-C7
88FanSam-1
88Grenada-43
88KayBee-23
88KennerFig-82
88KingB/Disc-3
88Leaf-144
88MSA/Disc-6
88Master/Disc-8
88Nestle-39
88OPC-120
88Panini/St-144
88Panini/St-444
88RedFoley/St-72
88S-24
88S-653HL
88Sf-180
88Sf-8
88Smok/Minn-12
88T-120
88T-391AS
88T/Big-36
88T/Coins-23
88T/Gloss60-27
88T/Mini-23
88T/Revco-21
88T/RiteAid-21
88T/St-283
88T/St/Backs-52
88T/UK-57
88Woolwth-31
89B-162
89Cadaco-41
89Classic-15
89Classic/Up/2-176
89D-182
89D/AS-23
89D/Best-130
89D/MVP-BC1
89F-124
89F-639M
89F/BBAS-32
89F/BBMVP's-32
89F/Excit-34
89F/Heroes-31
89F/LL-30
89F/Superstar-33
89F/WaxBox-C20
89Holsum/Discs-8
89KMart/DT-16
89KMart/Lead-4
89KayBee-24
89KennerFig-107
89MSA/Disc-12
89MSA/SS-8
89Master/Discs-2
89Nissen-8
89OPC-132
89Panini/St-247
89Panini/St-393
89S-20
89S/HotStar-11
89S/Mast-19
89Sf-156
89T-403AS
89T-650
89T/Ames-24
89T/Big-167
89T/Coins-48
89T/Crunch-20
89T/DH-7
89T/Gloss60-1
89T/HeadsUp-20
89T/Hills-23
89T/LJN-18
89T/Mini-62
89T/St-293
89T/St/Backs-19
89T/UK-60
89Tetley/Discs-12
89UD-376
90B-424
90Bz-7
90Classic-28
90CollAB-33
90D-269
90D-683AS
90D/BestAL-23
90D/Bon/MVP-BC8
90D/Learning-46
90D/Preview-10
90F-383
90F-635M
90F/ASIns-7

90F/AwardWin-26
90F/BB-29
90F/BBMVP-29
90F/Can-383
90F/Can-635
90F/LL-30
90F/WaxBox-C22
90Holsum/Discs-17
90HotPlay/St-31
90KMart/CBatL-3
90KMart/SS-22
90KayBee-23
90Kenner/Fig-65
90KingB/Discs-21
90Leaf-123
90MCA/Disc-13
90MLBPA/Pins-98
90MSA/Soda-12
90OPC-391AS
90OPC-700
90Panini/St-105
90Panini/St-183
90Panini/St-199M
90Post-3
90PublInt/St-292
90PublInt/St-335
90RedFoley/St-75
90S-400
90S-690DT
90S/100St-1
90Sf-11
90Sunflower-5
90T-391AS
90T-700
90T/Ames-24
90T/Big-2
90T/Coins-4
90T/DH-49
90T/Gloss22-18
90T/Gloss60-48
90T/HeadsUp-20
90T/HillsHM-27
90T/Mini-23
90T/St-157AS
90T/St-286
90T/TVAS-6
90Tetley/Discs-13
90UD-236
90UD-48TC
90USPlayC/AS-8S
90Windwlk/Discs-2
90WonderBrd-9
91B-320
91BBBest/HitM-15
91Cadaco-42
91Classic/200-111
91Classic/I-57
91Classic/III-74
91CollAB-7
91D-490
91F-623
91F/ProV-1
91F/UltraG-8
91JDean-11
91Kenner-42
91KingB/Discs-23
91Leaf-208
91Leaf/Prev-21
91Leaf/Stud-90
91MajorLg/Pins-12
91MooTown-2
91OPC-300
91OPC/Premier-96
91Panini/FrSt-305
91Panini/St-248
91Pep/SS-13
91Petro/SU-17
91Post-28
91Post/Can-30
91RedFoley/St-74
91S-200
91S-855FRAN
91S-891DT
91S/100SS-7
91Seven/3DCoin-11A
91Seven/3DCoin-13F
91StCl-110
91T-300
91T/CJMini/I-34
91UD-544
91USPlayC/AS-4D
91Ultra-195
92B-80
92CJ/DII-32

92Classic/Game200-101
92Classic/I-72
92Classic/II-T90
92Colla/ASG-9
92D-617
92D/Elite-E17
92D/McDon-21
92DPep/MSA-27
92F-217
92F-704M
92F/ASIns-22
92F/Performer-11
92F/TmLIns-5
92French-7
92Kenner/Fig-33
92KingB-20
92L-98
92L/BlkGold-98
92MSA/Ben-7
92MooTown-6
92MrTurkey-18
92OPC-575
92OPC/BoxB-4M
92OPC/Premier-102
92P-7
92Panini-120
92Pinn-20
92Pinn-289SIDE
92Pinn/Slug-13
92Post/Can-17
92S-600
92S-796HL
92S-887DT
92S/100SS-7
92S/Factory-B6M
92S/Proctor-6
92Seven/Coin-18
92StCl-500
92StCl/Dome-144WS
92StCl/Dome-145AS
92Studio-209
92Studio/Her-14
92Studio/Prev-2
92Sunflower-5
92T-575
92T/Gold-575
92T/GoldWin-575
92T/Kids-109
92T/McDonB-19
92TripleP-202
92TripleP/Prev-7
92UD-254
92UD/ASFF-35
92UD/TWillB-T9
92UD/TmMVPHolo-41
92USPlayC/Ace-6D
92USPlayC/Twin-10C
92USPlayC/Twin-1H
92Ultra-97
92Ultra/AS-8
92Ultra/AwardWin-23
93B-325
93Cadaco-45
93Classic/GameI-75
93Colla/ASG-5
93Colla/DM-87
93Colla/DMProto-6
93D-607
93D/DK-4
93D/MVP-18
93D/Master-13
93DennyGS-26
93Duracel/PPI-5
93F-273
93F-355M
93F/ASAL-9
93F/Atlantic-18
93F/Fruit-52
93F/TLAL-1
93Flair-242
93Highland-4
93HumDum/Can-11
93JDean/28-13
93Kenner/Fig-28
93Kraft-11
93L-378
93L/GoldAS-17
93L/Heading-9
93L/UpGoldAS-7
93MSA/Metz-16
93OPC-306
93OPC/Premier/StarP-11
93P-3
93Pac/Spanish-177

93Panini-130
93Pinn-426
93Pinn/Cooper-12
93Pinn/Slug-16
93Pinn/TP-9M
93Post/Can-8
93S-505AS
93S-533DT
93S-550MOY
93S-606
93S/Franchise-9
93S/GoldDT-2
93Select-4
93Select/ChasS-18
93Select/StatL-2
93Select/StatL-7
93StCl-283
93StCl-597MC
93StCl/1stDay-283
93StCl/1stDay-597MC
93StCl/MPhoto-6
93StCl/MurphyMP-7AS
93StCl/MurphyS-28
93Studio-214
93T-200
93T-406M
93T/BlkGold-40
93T/Finest-112AS
93T/FinestASJ-112AS
93T/FinestRef-112AS
93T/Gold-200
93T/Gold-406M
93T/MicroP-200
93TripleP-260
93TripleP/Act-20
93UD-34CH
93UD-50M
93UD-565
93UD/Clutch-R17
93UD/Diam-26
93UD/FunPack-191GS
93UD/FunPack-195
93UD/FunPackAS-AS9
93UD/HRH-HR24
93UD/Iooss-WI24
93UD/OnDeck-D19
93UD/SP-7AS
93UD/TCr-TC6
93UDFutHero-61
93USPlayC/Ace-12D
93Ultra-236
93Ultra/AS-18
93Ultra/AwardWin-17
94B-460
94Church-5
94D-343
94D/AwardWin-5MVP
94D/DomII-5
94D/MVP-23
94D/Special-343
94F-217
94F-712
94F/AS-20
94F/TL-9
94Flair-77
94Flair/Outfield-8
94KingB-12
94Kraft-9
94L-294
94L/Gamer-9
94L/MVPAL-10
94OPC-93
94OPC/JAS-17
94Oscar-10
94P-4
94Pac/Cr-365
94Pac/Silv-11
94Panini-96
94Pinn-21
94Pinn/Artist-21
94Pinn/Museum-21
94Pinn/Run-20
94RedFoley-21
94S-21
94S/GoldR-21
94S/GoldS-52
94S/Tomb-25
94Select-17
94SelectSam-17
94Sf/2000-42
94Sf/Mov-4
94StCl-359
94StCl/1stDay-359
94StCl/Gold-359
94Studio-200
94T-100
94T-607ST
94T/BlkGold-17
94T/Finest-204
94T/FinestRef-204
94T/Gold-100
94T/Gold-607ST
94TripleP-258
94TripleP/Medal-11M
94UD-289HFA
94UD-325
94UD/DColl-C4
94UD/HoloFX-31
94UD/SP-186
94Ultra-394
Pudlo, Scott
91Erie/ClBest-22
91Erie/ProC-4068
Pueschner, Craig
90CharRain/Best-19
90CharRain/ProC-2052
90SALAS/Star-40
91ClBest/Singl-366
91Waterlo/ClBest-22
91Waterlo/ProC-1269
92Cedar/ClBest-21
92Cedar/ProC-1086
Pugh, Scott
91Spokane/ClBest-5
91Spokane/ProC-3958
92Watlo/ClBest-4
92Watlo/ProC-2151
Pugh, Tim
89Billings/ProC-2064
90A&AASingle/ProC-92
90CharWh/Best-7
90CharWh/ProC-2239
90Foil/Best-186
90ProC/Singl-694
91AA/LineD-165
91Chatt/LineD-165
91Chatt/ProC-1958
91ClBest/Singl-299
92Martins/ClBest-17
92Martins/ProC-3056
92Nashvl/ProC-1832
92Nashvl/SB-289
92Sky/AAASingl-135
93B-442
93D-162
93F-40
93L-331
93OPC/Premier-75
93Pinn-270
93Reds/Kahn-18
93S-247
93StCl-265
93StCl/1stDay-265
93T-702
93T/Gold-702
93UD-26SR
93Ultra-332
94D-277
94F-419
94L-91
94Pac/Cr-154
94Pinn-481
94StCl-243
94StCl/1stDay-243
94StCl/Gold-243
94T-95
94T/Finest-67
94T/FinestRef-67
94T/Gold-95
94UD-481
94UD/CollC-234
94UD/CollC/Gold-234
94UD/CollC/Silv-234
Puhl, Terry
75Dubuq
78BK/Ast-19
78T-553
79K-33
79T-617
80OPC-82
80T-147
81Coke
81D-24
81F-24
81K-42
81OPC-64
81T-411
81T/HT
81T/SO-88
81T/St-171
82D-370
82F-223
82F/St-44
82OPC-277
82T-277
82T/St-42
83D-167
83F-458
83F/St-12M
83OPC-39
83OPC/St-239
83T-39
83T/S-239
84D-476
84F-235
84Mother/Ast-10
84Nes/792-383
84OPC-383
84T-383
84T/St-67
85D-426
85F-356
85GenMills-6
85Leaf-80
85Mother/Ast-7
85OPC-283
85Seven-14C
85T-613
85T/St-67
85ThomMc/Discs-39
86D-206
86F-308
86Leaf-138
86Mother/Ast-16
86OPC-161
86Pol/Ast-21
86T-763
87D-431
87F-65
87Mother/Ast-7
87OPC-227
87Pol/Ast-15
87T-693
88D-533
88F/Up-U90
88Mother/Ast-7
88Pol/Ast-17
88S-282
88T-587
89D-472
89D/Best-294
89F-364
89Lennox/Ast-22
89Mother/Ast-6
89S-567
89T-119
90D-354
90F-233
90F/Can-233
90Lennox-18
90MLBPA/Pins-60
90Mother/Ast-9
90OPC-494
90Panini/St-256
90PublInt/St-98
90S-473
90T-494
90UD-201
Puig, Ed
87Stockton-27
88ElPaso/Best-22
88TexLgAS/GS-31
89ElPaso/GS-14
90AAASingl/ProC-650
90Denver/CMC-2
90Denver/ProC-625
90ElPaso/GS-24
90ProC/Singl-27
91AAA/LineD-148
91Denver/LineD-148
91Denver/ProC-123
92Memphis/ProC-2419
92Memphis/SB-443
Puig, Rich
91WIZMets-319
Puikunas, Ed
85Fresno/Pol-15
86Shrev-21
87Shrev-15
88Phoenix/CMC-11
88Phoenix/ProC-74
88Shrev/ProC-1301
89Phoenix/CMC-2
89Phoenix/ProC-1492
Pujols, Luis
73Cedar
74Cedar
75Dubuq
78Charl
79CharCh-14
79T-139
81D-379
81F-68
81T-313
82D-576
82F-224
82T-582
83D-642
83F-459
83OPC-112
83T-752
83Tucson-13
84Cram/PCL-71
84F-236
84Nes/792-446
84T-446
85Rang-8
86OKCty-18
87Indianap-6
89Pac/SenLg-167
89T/SenLg-130
93Rang/Keeb-301
Pujols, Ruben
88Virgini/Star-19
89BBCity/Star-22
Pulchinski, Thomas
77Watlo
78Watlo
Puleo, Charles
80Knoxvl
80Knoxvl/TCMA-21
81Tidew-13
82T/Tr-94T
83D-128
83F-552
83OPC-358
83T-549
83T/Tr-88T
84D-530
84F-480
84Nes/792-273
84T-273
84Wichita/Rock-1
86Richm-17
87Smok/Atl-2
88D-537
88F-548
88S-454
88T-179
89B-263
89D-286
89F-598
89Richm/Bob-21
89S-448
89T-728
89UD-589
90PublInt/St-119
91WIZMets-320
92Bluefld/ProC-2376CO
Pulford, Don
47Centen-21
Pulido, Alfonso
84Cram/PCL-121
85Colum-12
85Colum/Pol-18
85D-34RR
86Colum-20
86Colum/Pol-18
87Colum-24
87Colum/Pol-20
87Colum/TCMA-7
87T-642
92Yank/WIZ80-150
Pulido, Carlos
90Kenosha/Best-24
90Kenosha/ProC-2293
90Kenosha/Star-20
91Visalia/ClBest-9
92OrlanSR/ProC-2848
92OrlanSR/SB-517
92Sky/AASingl-224
94B-328
Pulido, Phil
77DaytB
Pulli, Frank
88TM/Umpire-14
89TM/Umpire-12
89TM/Umpire-60M
90TM/Umpire-12
Pulliam, Harry C.
WG3-39
Pulliam, Harvey Jr.
88BBCity/Star-19
89Memphis/Best-15
89Memphis/ProC-1204
89Memphis/Star-19
89SLAS-1
90AAASingl/ProC-613
90Omaha/CMC-17
90Omaha/ProC-78
90ProC/Singl-192
91AAA/LineD-344
91B-303
91Omaha/LineD-344
91Omaha/ProC-1048
92D/Rook-97
92F-166
92OPC-687
92Omaha/SB-342
92Pinn-279
92S-761
92S/Rook-22
92Sky/AAASingl-156
92StCl-428
92T-687
92T/91Debut-141
92T/Gold-687
92T/GoldWin-687
92UD-457
93Pac/Spanish-494
93StCl/Royal-28
Pullins, Jimmie
89Idaho/ProC-2011
90Pulaski/Best-23
90Pulaski/ProC-3110
Pulsipher, Bill
92Pittsfld/ClBest-1
92Pittsfld/ProC-3293
92StCl-676
94B-212
94B-361
94FExcel-237
94T-785M
94T/Gold-785M
94Ultra-532
Purcell, William
N172
N284
Purcey, Walter
R314/Can
Purdin, John
65T-331R
68T-336
69OPC-161
69T-161
69T/4in1-9M
71OPC-748
71T-748
85SpokAT/Cram-16
90Target-638
Purdy, Alan
93Welland/ClBest-23
Purdy, Everett V.
(Pid)
29Exh/4-8
92Conlon/Sport-406
Purdy, Shawn
91Boise/ClBest-12
91Boise/ProC-3876
91ClBest/Singl-447
91Miami/Bumble-11
92ClBest-212
92PalmSp/ClBest-16
92PalmSp/ProC-836
Purkey, Bob
54T-202
55T-118
55T/DH-114
57T-368
58Kahn
58T-311
59Kahn
59T-506
60Kahn
60L-67
60T-4
61Kahn
61P-184
61T-9
62J-123

62Kahn
62P-123
62P/Can-123
62Salada-153
62Shirriff-153
62T-120
62T-263M
62T/St-120
62T/bucks
63Bz-26
63F-35
63FrBauer-20
63J-134
63Kahn
63P-134
63Salada-6
63T-350
63T-5LL
63T-7LL
63T/SO
64Kahn
64T-480
65OPC-214
65T-214
66T-551
79TCMA-260
88Pac/Leg-77
94T/Arc54-202

Purnell, Byron
76Laugh/Clown-18

Purpura, Dan
82Amari-8
83Beaum-10

Purpura, Joe
78Clinton

Pursell, Joe
83Kinston/Team-16

Purtell, William
C46-30
E254
E90/3
M116
T206
T213/blue
T215/blue

Purvis, Glenn
75Anderson/TCMA-19
77Visalia

Puryear, Nate
77Watlo
79Tacom-17
81Charl-22
82Chatt-1

Pust, John
87Visalia-21

Putman, Ed
80Evansvl-7
80T-59
81RochR-13

Putnam, Pat
77Tucson
78Cr/PCL-91
78T-706R
79T-713R
80OPC-8
80T-22
81D-265
81F-630
81OPC-302
81T-498
82D-520
82F-327
82F/St-180
82OPC-149
82T-149
82T/St-241
82T/StVar-241
83T/Tr-89
84D-145
84F-617
84Mother/Mar-16
84Nes/792-336TL
84Nes/792-636
84OPC-226
84T-636
84T/RD-23M
84T/St-339
85F-287
85Omaha-9
85T-535
89Pac/SenLg-85
89TM/SenLg-87
90EliteSenLg-75
93Rang/Keeb-302

Puttman, Ambrose
T206

Puzey, James W.
86StPete-25
87Spring/Best-5
88ArkTr/GS-22
88Louisvl-40
89Louisvl-33
89Louisvl/CMC-12
89Louisvl/ProC-1243

Pyburn, James
57T-276
91Crown/Orio-371

Pyburn, Jeff
81Hawaii-12
82Hawaii-12

Pyc, David
92GreatF/SportP-9

Pye, Eddie
88GreatF-9
89AS/Cal-19
89Bakers/Cal-198
90SanAn/GS-22
90TexLgAS/GS-2
91AAA/LineD-18
91Albuq/LineD-18
91Albuq/ProC-1150
92Albuq/ProC-729
92Albuq/SB-9

Pyfrom, Joel
82Miami-6

Pyle, Scott
81WHave-23
82WHave-28
83Tacom-26

Pytlak, Frank A.
34Exh/4-11
37Exh/4-11
38G-245
38G-269
41DP-107
91Conlon/Sport-280
R308-180
R314
V351A-20
V351B-37

Pyznarski, Tim
83Albany-13
84Cram/PCL-87
85Cram/PCL-122
86LasVegas-12
87D-654
87Denver-2
87Sf-158M
87Sf/TPrev-19M
87T-429FS
88AAA/ProC-13
88Denver/CMC-11
88Denver/ProC-1273
88RochR/Gov-21
89Omaha/ProC-1726

Quade, Mike
82AlexD-10
83AlexD-28
86Macon-20MG
87Jaxvl-27
89Rockford/Team-30MG
90Rockford/ProC-2710MG
90Rockford/Team-19MG
91AA/LineD-274MG
91Harris/LineD-274MG
91Harris/ProC-644MG
92Harris/ProC-475MG
92Harris/SB-299MG
93Ottawa/ProC-2449MG

Quade, Scott
93James/ClBest-17
93James/ProC-3335

Qualls, Jim
69T-602R
70OPC-192
70T-192
71OPC-731
71T-731
88Boise/ProC-1610

Qualters, Tom
54T-174
55T-33
55T/DH-108
58T-453
59T-341
94T/Arc54-174

Quantrill, Paul
89Elmira/Pucko-31
90WinHaven/Star-21
91AA/LineD-469
91NewBrit/LineD-469
91NewBrit/ProC-351
92B-23
92Pawtu/ProC-921
92Pawtu/SB-363
92Sky/AAASingl-165
93D-327
93F-181
93L-544
93Pac/Spanish-362
93Pinn-175
93S-221
93Select/RookTr-46T
93T-528
93T/Gold-528
93Ultra-155
94D-644
94F-38
94Pac/Cr-63
94S-583
94T-417
94T/Gold-417
94Ultra-317

Quatrine, Mike
90Elmira/Pucko-26TR

Quealey, Steve
82BirmB-20

Queen, Mel D.
64T-33R
66T-556
67T-374
68T-283
69OPC-81
69T-81
71MLB/St-354
71OPC-736
71T-736
72OPC-196
72T-196
80Tacom-7
81Charl-21
82BK/Indians-8CO
82BK/Indians-9CO
82Wheat/Ind
87Syrac/TCMA-28

Queen, Mel J.
47TipTop
51B-309
52B-171

Querecuto, Juan
90StCath/ProC-3453
92StCath/ClBest-4
92StCath/ProC-3390
93StCath/ClBest-20
93StCath/ProC-3978

Quero, Juan
91CharlR/ClBest-8
91CharlR/ProC-1312

Quesada, Ed
89Everett/Star-24

Quezada, Rafael
80Ander-29

Quezada, Silvano
75Lafay
76Phoenix/Coke-17

Quick, Gene
76Clinton

Quick, Jim
88TM/Umpire-26
89TM/Umpire-24
90TM/Umpire-23

Quick, Ron
81Shrev-17

Quigley, Ernest
94Conlon-1206UMP

Quigley, Jerry
76QuadC

Quijada, Ed
90Ashvl/ProC-2758
90ProC/Singl-662
92BurlAs/ClBest-14
92BurlAs/ProC-543

Quiles, Henry
91Bristol/ProC-3602

Quilici, Frank
66T-207
68T-557
69MB-226
69T-356
70T-572
71MLB/St-471
71OPC-141MG
71T-141
72MB-279
73OPC-49MG
73T-49MG
74OPC-447MG
74T-447MG
75OPC-443MG
75T-443MG
75T/M-443MG
78Twin/Frisz-18MG

Quillin, Lee
T206

Quillin, Ty
91Kingspt/ClBest-7
91Kingspt/ProC-3827
92Pittsfld/ClBest-4
92Pittsfld/ProC-3307

Quinlan, Craig
91StCath/ClBest-10
91StCath/ProC-3399

Quinlan, Tom
87Myrtle-11
88Knoxvl/Best-25
89Knoxvl/Best-20
89Knoxvl/ProC-1123
89Knoxvl/Star-16
90A&AASingle/ProC-62
90Foil/Best-247
90Knoxvl/Best-22
90Knoxvl/ProC-1252
90Knoxvl/Star-14
90ProC/Singl-773
91AAA/LineD-514
91Syrac/LineD-514
91Syrac/MerchB-20
91Syrac/ProC-2487
91T/90Debut-127
92Sky/AAASingl-230
92Syrac/MerchB-17
92Syrac/ProC-1977
92Syrac/SB-514
93BJ/D/45-27
93BJ/Fire-23
93D-161
93S-309
93Syrac/ProC-1006

Quinn, Bob
94Conlon-1111

Quinn, Frank W.
51B-276

Quinn, James
77Newar

Quinn, John Picus
(Jack)
10Domino-100
11Helmar-45
12Sweet/Pin-37
25Exh-68
26Exh-68
31Exh/4-4
33G-78
81Conlon-93
87Conlon/2-51
88Conlon/3-23
90Target-639
91Conlon/Sport-287
93Conlon-709
94Conlon-1148
E120
E121/80
E126-14
S74-24
T202
T205
T206
T207
T213/blue
T214-24
T215/brown
V353-53
W517-17
W572
W575

Quinn, Joseph J.
N172
N526

Quinn, Mike
92Bristol/ClBest-29TR

Quinn, Thomas G.
N172

Quinn, Tom
90MissSt-32
91MissSt-40
92MissSt-35

Quinones, Elliot
90A&AASingle/ProC-197
90Billings/ProC-3234
91CharWh/ClBest-25
91CharWh/ProC-2900
92CharWh/ClBest-11
92CharWh/ProC-22
93ClBest/MLG-188
93SALAS/II-33

Quinones, Hector
83Beloit/Frit-26
86Fresno/Smok-18

Quinones, Luis
83Albany-14
84Maine-20
85Maine-21
86F/Up-U92
86Phoenix-21
87Iowa-20
87T-362
88D-365
88Nashvl/CMC-14
88Nashvl/ProC-490
88Nashvl/Team-19
88T-667
89Nashvl/CMC-17
89Nashvl/ProC-1272
90Classic-132
90D-595
90F-428
90F/Can-428
90Kahn/Reds-22
90OPC-176
90S-499
90T-176
90UD-593
91D-459
91F-77
91F/UltraUp-U77
91Kahn/Reds-10
91Leaf-233
91OPC-581
91S-822
91T-581
92F-417
92OPC-356
92Portl/SB-405
92Portland/ProC-2676
92S-638
92StCl-151
92T-356
92T/Gold-356
92T/GoldWin-356

Quinones, Rene
77BurlB
79Holyo-1
80Vanco-16
81Vanco-18
83BuffB-18
83ElPaso-8
84BuffB-5

Quinones, Rey F.
86D/Rook-48
86F/Up-U93
86Pawtu-17
86T/Tr-89T
87D-638
87D/OD-121
87F-595
87Mother/Sea-20
87T-561
88D-198
88D/Best-275
88F-386
88Mother/Sea-20
88OPC-358
88Panini/St-190
88S-192
88T-358
88T/St-215
89B-213
89Bimbo/Discs-4
89D-330
89D/Best-185
89F-556
89KennerFig-108
89OPC-246
89Panini/St-438
89S-361

89T-246
89T/St-224
89T/Tr-98T
89UD-508
89UD/Ext-750
Quintana, Al
86Watertn-17
Quintana, Carlos
85Elmira-18
86Greens-18
87NewBrit-12
88Pawtu/CMC-20
88Pawtu/ProC-453
88TripleA/ASCMC-22
89Classic-133
89D-37RR
89F-95
89Pawtu/CMC-13
89Pawtu/Dunkin-18
89Pawtu/ProC-688
89S-623RP
89S/HotRook-13
89T-704
89T/Big-142
89UD-26SR
90Classic/III-44
90D-517
90D/BestAL-140
90F-283
90F/Can-283
90HotRook/St-36
90Leaf-394
90OPC-18
90Pep/RSox-15
90S-658
90S/100Ris-49
90S/YS/II-42
90T-18
90T/Big-273
90T/TVRSox-32
90UD-465
91B-126
91Classic/III-75
91D-568
91F-108
91Leaf-473
91OPC-206
91Panini/FrSt-264
91Panini/St-221
91Pep/RSox-16
91S-149
91StCl-12
91T-206
91UD-232
91Ultra-39
92Classic/I-73
92D-609
92F-45
92OPC-127
92Panini-85
92Pinn-358
92RedSox/Dunkin-23
92S-189
92StCl-25
92T-127
92T/Gold-127
92T/GoldWin-127
92UD-421
92USPlayC/RedSox-13S
92USPlayC/RedSox-9H
92Ultra-19
93B-227
93F/Final-176
93L-437
93Pac/Jugador-13
93Pac/Spanish-35
93Pinn-564
93StCl-605
93StCl/1stDay-605
93UD-747
93UD/SP-203
93Ultra-514
94D-219
94F-39
94Pac/Cr-62
94Pinn-175
94Pinn/Artist-175
94Pinn/Museum-175
94S-499
94StCl-290
94StCl/1stDay-290
94StCl/Gold-290
94T-349
94T/Gold-349
94T/Prev-294
Quintana, Luis
75SLCity/Caruso-16
77SLCity
80CharlO/Pol-15
80CharlO/W3TV-15
82Wichita-13
83Wichita/Dog-15
Quintell, John
91Oneonta/ProC-4157
92Albany/SB-17
92FtLaud/ProC-2615
Quintero, Frank
77Visalia
78OrlanTw
Quinzer, Paul
86Cram/NWL-165
88Wichita-23
89Wichita/Rock-27
89Wichita/Rock/Up-16
90AAASingl/ProC-9
90LasVegas/ProC-121
Quirico, Rafael
90Foil/Best-147
90Greens/Best-10
90Greens/ProC-2662
90Greens/Star-16
90Oneonta/ProC-3371
91Greens/ProC-3057
91SALAS/ProC-SAL29
92PrWill/ProC-146
92ProC/Tomorrow-126
92UD/ML-229
93LimeR/Winter-13
Quirk, Art
62T-591R
63T-522R
91Crown/Orio-372
Quirk, Jamie
75Omaha/Team-14
76OPC-598R
76T-598R
77T-463
78Spokane/Cramer-5
78Spokane/Team-5
78T-95
79T-26
80T-248
81D-341
81F-50
81T-507
82D-212
82F-421
82T-173
83T-264
83T/Tr-90T
84F-332
84Nes/792-671
84T-671
85Omaha-16
87F-377
87T-354
88D-404
88F-266
88Panini/St-103
88S-577
88Smok/Royals-19
88T-477
89B-173
89F-290
89S-461
89T-702
89UD-620
90Mother/A's-15
91Crown/Orio-373
91D-588
91F-21
91Leaf-431
91Mother/A's-15
91OPC-132
91StCl-573UER
91T-132
92D-472
92F-265
92Mother/A's-15
92OPC-19
92S-526
92StCl-83
92T-19
92T/Gold-19
92T/GoldWin-19
92Yank/WIZ80-151
93F-667
Quiros, Gus
79Vanco-11
80Vanco-4
81Vanco-11
Quisenberry, Dan
75Watlo
76Watlo
77Jaxvl
80T-667R
81Coke
81D-222
81F-31
81F/St-24
81OPC-206
81T-493
81T-8LL
81T/St-7
82D-112
82F-422
82F/St-204
82T-264
83D-70
83F-122
83F/St-14M
83F/St-2M
83K-32
83OPC-155
83OPC-396AS
83OPC/St-165
83OPC/St-22
83OPC/St-74
83Pol/Roy-6
83T-155
83T-396AS
83T-708LL
83T/Fold-4M
83T/LeadS-6
83T/St-165
83T/St-22
83T/St-74
84D-583
84D/AAS-56
84F-354
84F-635IA
84F/St-73
84Nes/792-138LL
84Nes/792-3HL
84Nes/792-407AS
84Nes/792-570
84Nes/792-718LL
84Nestle/DT-11
84OPC-273
84OPC-69AS
84Ralston-25
84Seven-24C
84T-138LL
84T-3HL
84T-407AS
84T-570
84T-718LL
84T/Cereal-25
84T/Gloss40-38
84T/RD-10M
84T/St-10
84T/St-279
84T/St-290
84T/St-9
84T/Super-9
85D-6DK
85D-95
85D/AAS-8
85D/DKsuper-6
85Drake-39
85F-211
85F/LimEd-25
85F/St-99
85FunFoodPin-25
85Leaf-6DK
85OPC-270
85Seven-15C
85T-270
85T-711AS
85T/3D-24
85T/Gloss40-35
85T/RD-10M
85T/St-173
85T/St-269
85T/Super-8
85ThomMc/Discs-16
85Woolwth-28
86D-541
86F-18
86F/AS-9
86F/Mini-2
86F/St-91
86GenMills/Book-2M
86Kitty/Disc-8
86Leaf-208
86NatPhoto-29
86OPC-50
86Quaker-29
86Seven/Coin-C7M
86Seven/Coin-E7M
86Seven/Coin-S7M
86Seven/Coin-W7M
86Sf-118
86Sf-186M
86Sf-55M
86T-50
86T-722AS
86T/3D-21
86T/Gloss60-35
86T/St-257
86T/Super-5
86T/Tatt-3M
87D-177
87F-378
87F/BB-33
87F/Mini-84
87F/St-93
87GenMills/Book-3M
87OPC-15
87RedFoley/St-7
87Sf-167
87Sf/TPrev-13M
87T-714
87T/St-257
88D-471
88F-267
88Grenada-80
88KennerFig-83
88OPC-195
88Panini/St-101
88S-290
88S/Tr-18T
88Sf-76
88Smok/Royals-15
88T-195
88T/St-256
89F/Up-120
89OPC-13
89S-520
89Smok/Cards-19
89T-612
89UD-533
90D-437
90F-259
90F/Can-259
90OPC-312
90PublInt/St-227
90S-475
90T-312
90UD-659
92K/CornAS-9
92K/FrAS-6
Raabe, Brian
91CalLgAS-8
91Visalia/ClBest-19
91Visalia/ProC-1751
92FtMyr/ProC-2755
92Miracle/ClBest-8
93ClBest/MLG-165
Raasch, Glen
91Penin/ProC-382
93Peoria/Team-21
Rabb, John
79Cedar/TCMA-5
81Shrev-2
82Phoenix
83Phoenix/BHN-1
84D-143
84Nes/792-228
84T-228
85Cram/PCL-183
85D-236
85IntLgAS-12
85Richm-22
85T-696
86Richm-18
87Richm/Bob-17
87Richm/Crown-20
87Richm/TCMA-20
91Reno/Cal-1
Rabe, Charles
57Seattle/Pop-28
58Kahn
58T-376
Rabouin, Andre
88AppFx/ProC-159
89AppFx/ProC-871
90AppFox/Box-20
90AppFox/ProC-2113CO
Rackley, Marv
45Parade*-61
47TipTop
90Target-640
Racobaldo, Mike
90Kissim/DIMD-24
Raczka, Mike
87CharlO/WBTV-10
88RochR/Gov-22
89RochR/CMC-5
89RochR/ProC-1648
92Modesto/ClBest-18
92Tacoma/ProC-2500
93D-183
93Pinn-277
Radachowsky, Gregg
90Niagara/Pucko-13
91Niagara/ProC-3637
Radar, Keith
91SLCity/SportP-1
Radatz, Dick
62T-591R
63T-363
64T-170
64T/Coins-30
64T/S-40
64T/St-41
64Wheat/St-37
65Bz-10
65OldLond-34
65T-295
65T/E-48
65T/trans-64
66T-475
66T/RO-111
66T/RO-76
67CokeCap/Indian-16
67OPC-174
67T-174
69T-663
74Laugh/ASG-63
78TCMA-76
89Pac/Leg-122
89Swell-46
PM10/Sm-149
WG10-44
WG9-43
Radbourn, Charles
(Hoss)
50Callahan
50W576-61
75F/Pion-5
76Shakey-25
80Perez/HOF-24
80SSPC/HOF
90BBWit-92
90HOF/St-2
N172
N284
N403
Radcliff, Ray
(Rip)
37OPC-125
37Wheat
38G-261
38G-285
91Conlon/Sport-98
PR1-24
R314
V300
WG8-45
Radcliffe
92Negro/Retort-50M
Radcliffe, Ernest Jr.
87Erie-9
88Virgini/Star-20
Radcliffe, Ted
(Double-Duty)
78Laugh/Black-36
86Negro/Frit-64
91Negro/Lewis-25
92Negro/Kraft-7
94TedW-110
Rader, Dave
67CokeCap/Astro-11
72OPC-232R
72T-232R
73OPC-121

73T-121
74OPC-213
74T-213
74T/St-108
75OPC-31
75T-31
75T/M-31
76Ho-21
76Ho/Twink-21
76OPC-54
76T-54
77T-427
78SSPC/270-246
78T-563
79OPC-369
79T-693
80T-296
81D-512
81OPC-359
81T-378
Rader, Doug
67T-412R
68T-332
69MB-227
69MLB/St-142
69OPC-119
69T-119
69T/4in1-15
69T/St-37
70MLB/St-46
70OPC-355
70T-355
71MLB/St-90
71OPC-425
71T-425
71T/Coins-17
72K-14
72MB-280
72T-536
73OPC-76
73T-76
74OPC-395
74T-395
74T/DE-14
74T/St-35
75Ho-89
75OPC-165
75T-165
75T/M-165
76OPC-44
76SSPC-59
76T-44
76T/Tr-44T
77BurgChef-128
77Padre/SchCd-22
77T-9
78OPC-166
78T-651
80Hawaii-2
81Hawaii-23
81Hawaii/TCMA-21
82Hawaii-23
83Rang-11MG
83T/Tr-91
84Nes/792-412MG
84Rang-11
84T-412
85T-519MG
89T/Tr-99TMG
90OPC-51MG
90T-51MG
91OPC-231MG
91T-231MG
92Mother/A's-28M
93Marlin/Publix-28M
93Rang/Keeb-303MG
Rader, Keith
91SLCity/ProC-3220
Radford, Paul
N172
Radinsky, Scott
87Penin-12
89SoBend/GS-7
90B-308
90Classic/III-T5
90Coke/WSox-22
90Coke/WSox-28
90D/Rook-40
90F/Up-U86
90Leaf-484
90S/Tr-90T
90T/Tr-99T
90UD/Ext-725
91B-365
91Bz-22
91D-332
91F-135
91F/UltraUp-U18
91Kodak/WSox-31
91Leaf-463
91OPC-299
91S-62
91S/100RisSt-83
91StCl-311
91T-299
91T/90Debut-128
91T/JumboR-25
91ToysRUs-25
91UD-621
92D-299
92F-96
92L-281
92L/BlkGold-281
92OPC-701
92Pinn-389
92Pinn/Team2000-46
92Pinn/TeamP-12
92S-444
92T-701
92T/Gold-701
92T/GoldWin-701
92UD-594
92Ultra-340
92WSox-31
93D-169
93F-208
93Pac/Spanish-74
93Pinn-451
93S-182
93StCl-275
93StCl/1stDay-275
93StCl/WSox-19
93T-550
93T/Gold-550
93UD-298
93Ultra-177
93WSox-23
94D-230
94F-92
94Pac/Cr-135
94Pinn-135
94Pinn/Artist-135
94Pinn/Museum-135
94S-276
94S/GoldR-276
94StCl-434
94StCl/1stDay-434
94StCl/Gold-434
94StCl/Team-125
94T-421
94T/Gold-421
94UD/CollC-235
94UD/CollC/Gold-235
94UD/CollC/Silv-235
Radison, Dan
88Hamil/ProC-1732
89Spring/Best-29
91AA/LineD-24MG
91Albany/LineD-24MG
91Albany/ProC-1023MG
92Albany/ProC-2348
92Albany/SB-24
93Mother/Padre-28M
Radke, Brad
92Kenosha/ProC-601
Radloff, Scott
83Cedar-15
83Cedar/Frit-21
Radovich, Robert
66Pep/Tul
Radtke, Jack
90Target-641
Radwan
28LaPresse-3M
Radziewicz, Doug
91Johnson/ClBest-8
91Johnson/ProC-3986
92Spring/ClBest-5
92Spring/ProC-877
94FExcel-273
Raeside, John
82Lynch-23
Raether, Peter
90AR-22
Raether, Richard
85Miami-12
86Tulsa-22
87PortChar-9
88Tulsa-26
90TulsaDG/Best-10
Raffensberger, Ken
49B-176
49Eureka-93
51B-48
52B-55
52T-118
52TipTop
53B/Col-106
53T-276
54B-92
54T-46
91T/Arc53-276
94T/Arc54-46
Raffo, Greg
91Bristol/ClBest-16
91Bristol/ProC-3603
92Niagara/ClBest-26
92Niagara/ProC-3322
Raffo, Thomas
88CapeCod-9
88CapeCod/Sum-79
88MissSt-27
89MissSt-31
90Miami/I/Star-20
90MissSt-33
91CharWh/ClBest-19
91CharWh/ProC-2896
91ClBest/Singl-261
91SALAS/ProC-SAL10
92Cedar/ClBest-5
92Cedar/ProC-1080
Ragan, Don C.P.
(Pat)
16FleischBrd-74
90Target-642
D329-140
M101/4-140
T207
Ragland, Tom
72OPC-334R
72T-334R
74OPC-441
74T-441
93Rang/Keeb-34
Ragland, Trace
91Welland/ClBest-14
91Welland/ProC-3589
Ragni, John
52Mother-34
Ragsdale, Jerry
83Ander-27
Rahan, Johnny
52Laval-67
Raich, Eric
76OPC-484
76T-484
77T-62
Raimondi, Bill
46Remar
47Remar-1
47Signal
47Smith-2
48Signal
48Smith-1
49B/PCL-18
49Remar
53Mother-36
Raimondo, Pasquale
81VeroB-15
Rainbolt, Ray
74Gaston
76SanAn/Team-19
79Tulsa-8
Rainer, Rick
85Tidew-28
86Tidew-25TR
87Tidew-30
87Tidew/TCMA-25
Raineri, Joe
92OKSt-24
Raines, Larry
58T-243
Raines, Mike
81Cedar-5
Raines, Ned
79Cedar/TCMA-21
Raines, Tim
(Rock)
79Memphis
79Memphis/TCMA-20
81D-538
81OPC-136R
81T-479R
81T/Tr-816
82D-214
82Expo/Hygrade-16
82F-202
82F/St-31
82FBI/Disc-15
82Hygrade
82K-53
82OPC-70
82OPC/Post-17
82PermaGr/AS-13
82PermaGr/CC-6
82T-164LL
82T-3RB
82T-70
82T/St-116
82T/St-62
82T/St-7
82Zeller-3
83D-540
83F-292
83F/St-23M
83F/St-7M
83OPC-227
83OPC-352AS
83OPC/St-210
83OPC/St-253
83PermaGr/AS-14
83Stuart-9
83T-403AS
83T-595
83T-704LL
83T/St-210
83T/St-253
84D-299
84Expo/PostC-22
84F-281
84F-631IA
84F/St-51
84F/St-88
84Nes/792-134LL
84Nes/792-370
84Nes/792-390AS
84Nestle/DT-17
84OPC-370
84OPC-390AS
84Seven-20E
84Stuart-20
84Stuart-36AS
84Stuart-37M
84T-134LL
84T-370
84T-390AS
84T/Gloss22-17
84T/Gloss40-37
84T/RD-23M
84T/St-179
84T/St-201
84T/St-91
84T/St/Box-4
85D-299
85D/AAS-1
85Drake-24
85F-405
85F/LimEd-26
85F/St-42
85F/St-58
85FunFoodPin-41
85Leaf-218
85Leaf-252CG
85OPC-277
85OPC/Post-7
85Seven-12S
85T-630
85T/3D-17
85T/RD-9M
85T/St-282
85T/St-82
85T/Super-15
86D-177
86D/AAS-20
86Drake-15
86Expo/Prov/Pan-7
86Expo/Prov/Post-1
86F-256
86F-632M
86F/LL-33
86F/Mini-54
86F/St-92
86GenMills/Book-6M
86Leaf-108
86OPC-280
86Provigo-7
86Quaker-10
86Seven/Coin-E12M
86Sf-11
86Sf-127M
86Sf-144M
86Sf/Dec-74M
86T-280
86T/Gloss60-15
86T/Mini-49
86T/St-75
86T/Super-42
86T/Tatt-17M
87Classic-29
87D-56
87D/AAS-36
87D/HL-16
87D/HL-7
87F-328
87F-642M
87F/AS-12
87F/BB-34
87F/Excit-34
87F/Mini-85
87F/RecSet-30
87F/Slug-32
87F/St-94
87GenMills/Book-5M
87KayBee-25
87Leaf-149
87OPC-30
87RedFoley/St-39
87Sf-152M
87Sf-197M
87Sf-199M
87Sf-34
87Sportflic/DealP-1
87Stuart-7M
87T-30
87T/Board-24
87T/Gloss60-48
87T/HL-11
87T/Mini-17
87T/St-85
87Woolwth-11
88Bz-15
88Classic/Red-168
88D-2DK
88D-345
88D-BC18
88D/AS-57
88D/AS-62
88D/Best-180
88D/DKsuper-2DK
88Drake-2
88F-193
88F-631M
88F/AwardWin-30
88F/BB/AS-31
88F/BB/MVP-27
88F/Excit-31
88F/Head-6
88F/Hottest-31
88F/LL-31
88F/Mini-90
88F/RecSet-30
88F/SS-29
88F/St-97
88F/TL-27
88FanSam-16
88Grenada-51
88Ho/Disc-11
88Jiffy-14
88KMart-19
88KayBee-24
88KennerFig-84
88Leaf-114
88Leaf-211MVP
88Leaf-2DK
88Nestle-31
88OPC-243
88Panini/St-330
88S-3
88S-649M
88Sf-2
88T-403AS
88T-720
88T/Big-116
88T/Coins-49
88T/Gloss60-12
88T/Mini-57
88T/Revco-5
88T/RiteAid-6
88T/St-76
88T/St/Backs-20

88T/UK-58
89B-369
89Classic-42
89D-97
89D/Best-258
89F-391
89KMart/DT-27
89KMart/Lead-7
89KayBee-25
89KennerFig-109
89MSA/SS-6
89OPC-87
89Panini/St-125
89RedFoley/St-91
89S-40
89S/HotStar-95
89Sf-150
89T-560
89T-81TL
89T/Big-73
89T/Coins-22
89T/Gloss60-53
89T/LJN-154
89T/St-77
89T/UK-61
89UD-402
90B-118
90Classic-118
90D-216
90D/BestNL-104
90D/Bon/MVP-BC7
90F-359
90F/BBMVP-30
90F/Can-359
90Holsum/Discs-2
90HotPlay/St-32
90KMart/CBatL-7
90KayBee-24
90KingB/Discs-6
90Leaf-212
90OPC-180
90Panini/St-283
90PublInt/St-186
90S-409
90S/100St-75
90Sf-69
90Starline/LJS-23
90Starline/LJS-39
90Sunflower-14
90T-180
90T/Ames-17
90T/Big-154
90T/Coins-54
90T/DH-50
90T/Gloss60-38
90T/Mini-63
90T/St-69
90T/TVAS-55
90UD-177
90UD-29TC
91B-362
91BBBest/HitM-16
91Classic/200-174
91Classic/II-T9
91D-457
91DennyGS-26
91F-244
91F/Up-U15
91Kenner-43
91Kodak/WSox-30
91Leaf-413
91Leaf/Stud-37
91Leaf/StudPrev-4
91OPC-360
91OPC/Premier-97
91Panini/FrSt-143
91Panini/St-63
91RedFoley/St-75
91S-35
91S/100SS-89
91S/RookTr-10T
91StCl-523
91T-360
91T/CJMini/I-3
91T/Tr-94T
91UD-143
91UD/Ext-773
91Ultra-81
92B-204
92Classic/Game200-99
92D-312
92F-97
92L-37
92L/BlkGold-37
92OPC-426
92Panini-131
92Pinn-178
92Pinn-605SH
92S-635
92StCl-426
92Studio-156
92T-426
92T/Gold-426
92T/GoldWin-426
92T/Kids-104
92TripleP-107
92UD-575
92Ultra-43
92WSox-30
93B-499
93D-565
93Expo/D/McDon-6
93F-209
93L-420
93OPC-290
93Pac/Spanish-75
93Panini-140
93Pinn-53
93S-658
93Select-236
93StCl-43
93StCl/1stDay-43
93StCl/WSox-5
93Studio-215
93T-675
93T/Finest-183
93T/FinestRef-183
93T/Gold-675
93TripleP-108
93UD-597
93UD/FunPack-201
93UD/SP-259
93USPlayC/Ace-6H
93Ultra-178
93WSox-24
94B-127
94D-220M
94D-258
94F-93
94Flair-35
94L-116
94OPC-228
94Pac/Cr-136
94Pinn-462
94S-379
94Select-92
94StCl-350
94StCl-525TA
94StCl/1stDay-350
94StCl/1stDay-525TA
94StCl/Gold-350
94StCl/Gold-525TA
94StCl/Team-136
94Studio-208
94T-243
94T/Finest-192
94T/FinestRef-192
94T/Gold-243
94TripleP-268
94UD-254
94UD/ElecD-254
94Ultra-341

Rainey, Chuck
80T-662R
81T-199
82Coke/BOS
82F-303
82T-522
83D-334
83F-192
83T-56
83T/Tr-92
83Thorn-30
84D-76
84F-502
84Nes/792-334
84OPC-334
84T/St-47
85D-618

Rainey, Scott
83Clinton/Frit-9
87Wichita-16

Rainout, Chief
87Peoria/PW-6

Raisanen, Keith
87Watertn-8
88Salem/Star-16
89Augusta/ProC-506
89SALAS/GS-9
90Salem/Star-17

Rajsich, Dave
78Cr/PCL-73
79T-710R
80T-548
81D-267
83OKCty-15
85RochR-21
86Louisvl-25
88Louisvl-41
88Louisvl/CMC-9
88Louisvl/ProC-443
89Pac/SenLg-3
91Beloit/ClBest-26CO
91Beloit/ProC-2120CO
91Pac/SenLg-154
91Pac/SenLg-160
92Augusta/ProC-256
92Yank/WIZ70-129
93Rang/Keeb-304

Rajsich, Gary
75FtLaud/Sus-7
77Cocoa
80Tucson-16
81Tidew-9
83D-599
83F-553
83T-317
83Tidew-8
84Louisvl-6
85Mother/Giants-24
89Pac/SenLg-7
89T/SenLg-124
90EliteSenLg-12
91Pac/SenLg-156
91Pac/SenLg-160
91WIZMets-321

Rakow, Ed
60T-551
61T-147
62T-342
63J-90
63P-90
63T-82
64Det/Lids-12
64T-491
65T-454
90Target-643

Raleigh, Matthew
92James/ClBest-23
92James/ProC-1508
93James/ClBest-18

Raley, Dan
89Lakeland/Star-17
90Lakeland/Star-20
91AA/LineD-400M
91London/LineD-400CO
91London/ProC-1894CO
92Lakeland/ClBest-29CO
92Lakeland/ProC-2295CO

Raley, Tim
88Beloit/GS-5
89Stockton/Best-20
89Stockton/Cal-169
89Stockton/ProC-401
89Stockton/Star-9
90Stockton/Best-13
90Stockton/Cal-198
90Stockton/ProC-2198
91AA/LineD-243
91Hagers/LineD-243
91Hagers/ProC-2469

Ralph, Curtis
90PrWill/Team-21
91PrWill/ClBest-10
91PrWill/ProC-1426
92FtLaud/ClBest-12
92FtLaud/Team-24
92PrWill/ClBest-25
92PrWill/ProC-147

Ralston, Bill
74Tacoma/Caruso-19
75Tacoma/KMMO-5

Ralston, Chad
89KS*-84

Ralston, Kris
94FExcel-71

Ralston, Robert
(Bobby)
84AZ/Pol-16
85OrlanTw-10
86Toledo-18
87OrlanTw-6
88Portl/CMC-21
88Portl/ProC-657
89Portl/CMC-15
89Portl/ProC-232
90Huntsvl/Best-18

Ramanouchi, Kenichi
91Salinas/ClBest-7
91Salinas/ProC-2254

Ramazzotti, Bob
49Eureka-67
51B-247
52T-184
53B/BW-41
90Target-644

Rambadt, Charles
90Helena/SportP-22

Rambo, Dan
90A&AASingle/ProC-145
90AS/Cal-53
90Foil/Best-123
90ProC/Singl-717
90SanJose/Best-23
90SanJose/Cal-44
90SanJose/ProC-2006
90SanJose/Star-18
91AA/LineD-318
91Shrev/LineD-318
91Shrev/ProC-1821
92Phoenix/ProC-2820
92Shrev/ProC-3868
92Shrev/SB-590
92Sky/AASingl-260

Rambo, Matt
88Spartan/ProC-1025
88Spartan/Star-16
89Clearw/Star-17
91ClBest/Singl-53
91Osceola/ClBest-10
91Osceola/ProC-682
92Jacks/SB-346
92Sky/AASingl-145

Rametta, Steve
75SanAn

Ramey, Jeff
92Billings/ProC-3358

Ramharter, Steve
89Anchora-21
90Butte/SportP-17

Ramie, Vern
82Knoxvl-17
83Syrac-23

Ramirez, Alex
80OrlanTw-18

Ramirez, Alexander
(Alex)
94B-335

Ramirez, Angel
93MedHat/ProC-3750
93MedHat/SportP-3

Ramirez, D. Allan
(Allan)
80CharlO/Pol-16
80CharlO/W3TV-16
82RochR-5
83RochR-7
84D-332
84Nes/792-347
84RochR-16
84T-347
85CharlO-25
91Crown/Orio-374

Ramirez, Daniel
91Kane/ClBest-19
91Kane/ProC-2666
91Kane/Team-16
92Freder/ClBest-27
92Freder/ProC-1814

Ramirez, Fausto
86Cram/NWL-125
87Belling/Team-27
88Wausau/GS-3

Ramirez, Francisco
91Elizab/ProC-4304

Ramirez, Frank
87Idaho-23

Ramirez, Hector
91Kingspt/ClBest-19
91Kingspt/ProC-3811
92ColumMet/ClBest-2
92ColumMet/ProC-293
92ColumMet/SAL/II-27

Ramirez, J.D.
89SLCity-11
90Rockford/ProC-2703
90Rockford/Team-20
91WPalmB/ClBest-23
91WPalmB/ProC-1238

Ramirez, Jack
79Tulsa-12

Ramirez, Leo
93Macon/ClBest-20
93Macon/ProC-1398

Ramirez, Luis 1
78Newar

Ramirez, Luis 2
92GulfCY/ProC-3792

Ramirez, Manny
91BurlInd/ProC-3316
91Classic/DP-10
91FrRow/DP-47
91LitSun/HSPros-7
91LitSun/HSProsG-7
92B-532
92B-676FOIL
92ClBest-155
92D/Rook-98
92Kinston/ProC-2488
92OPC-156
92Pinn-295DP
92ProC/Tomorrow-62
92S-800Draft
92StCl/Dome-146
92T-156DP
92T/Gold-156
92T/GoldWin-156
92UD-63TP
92UD/ML-146
92UD/ML-35M
92UD/ML-55DS
93B-365FOIL
93B-669
93ClBest/MLG-124
93F/Final-204
93FExcel/ML-164
93Flair/Wave-13
93UD-433TP
93UD/SP-285FOIL
93Ultra-545
94B-371
94B-55
94D-322
94F-119
94Finest-430
94Flair-43
94L/GRook-6
94OPC-121
94OPC/HotPros-6
94Pac/Cr-183
94Pinn-244
94Pinn/Artist-244
94Pinn/Museum-244
94Pinn/New-17
94Pinn/Power-13
94Pinn/RookTPinn-6
94S-645
94S/Boys-38
94Select-181
94Sf/2000-151
94Sf/Shak-12
94StCl-320
94StCl/1stDay-320
94StCl/Gold-320
94Studio-95
94T-216
94T/Gold-216
94TripleP-286
94UD-23
94UD/CollC-16
94UD/CollC/Gold-16
94UD/CollC/Silv-16
94UD/DColl-C5
94UD/ElecD-23
94UD/HoloFX-32
94UD/Mantle-16
94UD/SP-101
94Ultra-351

Ramirez, Mario
76Wausau
78Tidew
79Tidew-12
81Hawaii/TCMA-23
84F-309
84Mother/Padres-23
84Nes/792-94
84T-94
85Mother/Padres-16
85T-427

86D-568
86T-262
86Toledo-19
91WIZMets-322
Ramirez, Milt
71MLB/St-281
71OPC-702
71T-702
77SanJose-5
80Ogden-14
Ramirez, Nelson
90Hunting/ProC-3280
Ramirez, Nick
88CharWh/Best-26
88Geneva/ProC-1634
Ramirez, Omar
91Watertn/ClBest-27
91Watertn/ProC-3382
92Kinston/ClBest-4
93FExcel/ML-165
93LimeR/DomPr-P3
93LimeR/Winter-113
93LimeR/Winter-149
93LimeR/Winter-P3
94FExcel-49
Ramirez, Orlando
76SSPC-197
77T-131
Ramirez, Rafael
78Green
79Savan-23
80Richm-2
81F-266
81Pol/Atl-16
81T-192R
82BK/Lids-21
82D-546
82F-447
82Pol/Atl-16
82T-536
83D-310
83F-146
83F/St-16M
83F/St-6M
83Pol/Atl-16
83T-439
84D-589
84F-190
84F/St-26
84Nes/792-234
84OPC-234
84Pol/Atl-16
84T-234
84T/St-33
85D-141
85F-339
85Ho/Braves-20
85Leaf-86
85OPC-232
85Pol/Atl-16
85T-647
85T/St-27
86D-263
86F-526
86OPC-107
86Pol/Atl-16
86T-107
86T/St-42
86T/Tatt-11M
87D-202
87F-526
87Smok/Atl-18
87T-76
87T/St-42
88D-448
88F/Up-U91
88Mother/Ast-17
88OPC-379
88Panini/St-247
88Pol/Ast-18
88S-426
88S/Tr-12T
88T-379
88T/Tr-90T
89B-330
89D-509
89D/Best-64
89F-365
89Lennox/Ast-16
89Mother/Ast-16
89OPC-261
89Panini/St-90
89S-113
89T-749
89T/Big-268
89T/St-17
89UD-341
90D-241
90D/BestNL-77
90F-234
90F/Can-234
90Leaf-135
90Lennox-19
90Mother/Ast-19
90OPC-558
90Panini/St-266
90PublInt/St-99
90S-42
90T-558
90T/Big-183
90T/St-18
90UD-144
91B-564
91D-586
91F-513
91Mother/Ast-19
91OPC-423
91Panini/FrSt-10
91S-305
91StCl-107
91T-423
91UD-210
91Ultra-139
92Mother/Ast-19
92S-388
92StCl-451
92UD-582
92Ultra-495
93Pac/Spanish-127
Ramirez, Randy
84Chatt-21
Ramirez, Ray
86OrlanTw-16TR
87OKCty-24TR
88OkCty/ProC-51
89OkCty/ProC-1533
90OkCty/CMC-24TR
90ProC/Singl-174TR
Ramirez, Richard
87Gaston/ProC-23
Ramirez, Roberto 1
91Clinton/ProC-848
91Everett/ClBest-27
91Everett/ProC-3922
92SoOreg/ProC-3422
Ramirez, Roberto 2
91Welland/ClBest-24
91Welland/ProC-3571
Ramirez, Russell
78Newar
79BurlB-2
Ramirez, Victor
91GulfCR/SportP-30M
92Kinston/ProC-2489
Ramon, John
90Foil/Best-152
Ramon, Julio
87Oneonta-16
Ramon, Ray
86Reading-22
Ramos, Domingo
77WHave
78Cr/PCL-78
79Syrac/TCMA-6
79Syrac/Team-1
80Syrac-22
81Syrac/Team-17
82SLCity-16
84D-440
84Nes/792-194
84T-194
85Mother/Mar-12
85T-349
86Mother/Mar-12
86T-462
87Mother/Sea-21
87T-641
88ColoSp/CMC-16
88ColoSp/ProC-1534
88D-622
88F/Up-U23
88S-362
88T-206
89Mara/Cubs-15
90Cub/Mara-16
90D-491
90Leaf-440
90OPC-37
90S-489
90T-37
90T/TVCub-24
90UD-150
91F-429
91OPC-541
91T-541
91UD-85
92Yank/WIZ70-130
Ramos, Eddie
91ClBest/Singl-440
91Classic/DP-45
91FrRow/DP-33
92Ashvl/ClBest-15
92ClBest-382
92StCl/Dome-147
Ramos, George
78Green
Ramos, Jairo
91MedHat/ProC-4116
91MedHat/SportP-8
Ramos, John
87PrWill-28
88CLAS/Star-15
88PrWill/Star-20
89Albany/Best-13
89Albany/ProC-336
89Albany/Star-15
89EastLgAS/ProC-22
89Star/Wax-100
90Albany/Best-12
90Albany/ProC-1177
90Albany/Star-13
90EastLAS/ProC-EL42
91AAA/LineD-115
91Albany/ClBest-4
91ColClip/LineD-115
91ColClip/ProC-599
91Ultra-385MLP
92ColClip/Pol-14
92ColClip/ProC-356
92ColClip/SB-113
92D-15RR
92F-242
92ProC/Tomorrow-105
92S-818
92S/Rook-8
92Sky/AAASingl-53
92T/91Debut-142
92T/Gold-658
92T/GoldWin-658
Ramos, Jorge
90SoBend/Best-8
90SoBend/GS-14
91SoBend/ClBest-4
91SoBend/ProC-2864
Ramos, Jose
87Fayette-2
88Fayette/ProC-1086
89London/ProC-1387
90AAASingl/ProC-376
90ProC/Singl-384
90Toledo/CMC-7
90Toledo/ProC-146
90WichSt-30
91AA/LineD-394
91London/LineD-394
91London/ProC-1877
92London/SB-414
Ramos, Ken
88NE-14
90CLAS/CL-43
90Kinston/Team-9
91AA/LineD-97
91Canton/LineD-97
91Canton/ProC-991
92Canton/ProC-702
92Canton/SB-115
93B-473
93ClBest/MLG-7
93FExcel/ML-166
Ramos, Papo
92Everett/ClBest-17
92Everett/ProC-1704
Ramos, Pedro
56T-49
57T-326
58T-331
59T-291M
59T-78
60L-21
60T-175
61Clover-22
61P-98
61Peters-3
61T-50LL
61T-528
61T/St-184
62Sugar-19
62T-485
62T/St-79
62T/bucks
63Sugar-19
63T-14
64Kahn
64T-562
65OPC-13
65T-13
66T-439
67OPC-187
67T-187
89Pac/SenLg-217M
89Pac/SenLg-68
92Yank/WIZ60-100
WG10-18
Ramos, Richard
82Wichita-14
83Wichita/Dog-16
Ramos, Roberto
(Bobby)
75WPalmB/Sussman-7
79SLCity
81F-162
81OPC-136R
81T-479R
82Colum-18
82Colum/Pol-31
82F-203
82OPC-354
82T-354
83Stuart-20
83T/Tr-93
84D-209
84Expo/PostC-23
84F-282
84Nes/792-32
84OPC-32
84Stuart-9
84T-32
85Cram/PCL-15
85OPC-269
85T-407
86Iowa-24
87Omaha-21
88Phoenix/CMC-13
88Phoenix/ProC-69
89ColMud/Best-20
89ColMud/ProC-121
89Pac/SenLg-65
89T/SenLg-18
90Osceola/Star-29CO
91Osceola/ClBest-20CO
91Osceola/ProC-700CO
92Yank/WIZ80-152
Ramos, Wolf
80Elmira-24
Ramppen, Frank
83Visalia/Frit-7
Ramsdell, J. Willard
(Willie)
47Signal
47Sunbeam
51B-251
52B-22
52T-114
53Mother-3
79TCMA-279
90Target-645
Ramsey, Fernando
88CharWh/Best-22
89Peoria/Team-25
90WinSalem/Team-11
91AA/LineD-139
91CharlK/LineD-139
91CharlK/ProC-1701
92Iowa/ProC-4061
92Iowa/SB-216
92ProC/Tomorrow-203
92Sky/AAASingl-104
93D-539RR
93Pinn-273
93StCl/Cub-29
93UD-382
Ramsey, Jeff
90Rockford/ProC-2707
90Rockford/Team-21
Ramsey, Matthew
89MissSt-32
90MissSt-34
Ramsey, Michael James
(Mike)
87Albuq/Pol-30
87D/OD-80
87Edmon-6
87Mother/Dodg-11
88Albuq/CMC-14
88Albuq/ProC-267
88S-267
89Edmon/CMC-16
89Edmon/ProC-561
90Target-646
Ramsey, Michael Jeffery
(Mike)
76ArkTr
77ArkTr
78Spring/Wiener-5
81F-549
81T-366
82D-316
82F-125
82T-574
83D-568
83F-19
83T-128
84D-382
84F-333
84Nes/792-467
84T-467
85F-406
85OPC-62
85T-62
86Tampa-15
90Target-647
91Pac/SenLg-18
91Spring/ClBest-11MG
91Spring/ProC-759MG
92Savan/ClBest-23MG
92Savan/ProC-679MG
Ramsey, Thomas
N172
Ramstack, Curt
76AppFx
Rand, Dick
54Hunter
58T-218
Rand, Kevin
85Albany-27
87Colum-2
89EastLDD/ProC-DD49TR
Randa, Joe
91Eugene/ClBest-14
91Eugene/ProC-3736
92AppFox/ClBest-1
92B-560FOIL
92BBCity/ProC-3852
92ClBest-11
92MidwLAS/Team-34
92ProC/Tomorrow-78
92UD/ML-325
93B-237
93ClBest/MLG-5
93FExcel/ML-177
93StCl/Royal-20
94B-199
94FExcel-72
Randahl, Rick
81Tacom-2
Randall, Bob
74Albuq/Team-14
75Albuq/Caruso-6
75IntLgAS/Broder-24
75PCL/AS-24
77BurgChef-52
77T-578
78T-363
78Twin/FriszP-15
79T-58
79Twin/FriszP-22
80OPC-90
80T-162
80Toledo-2
Randall, James
(Sap)
82Redwd-8
83Nashua-18
84Cram/PCL-101
85Cram/PCL-10
86MidldA-20
87Edmon-16
88AAA/ProC-46
88Vanco/CMC-20
88Vanco/ProC-765

Randall, Mark
89Martins/Star-26
90Clearw/Star-18
91Spartan/ClBest-12
91Spartan/ProC-897
92Clearw/ProC-2057
92Spartan/ClBest-14
Randall, Mark Christopher
89KS*-45
Randall, Newton
T206
Randle, Carl
88Butte-7
89Gaston/ProC-1005
89Gaston/Star-19
90Gaston/Best-3
90Gaston/ProC-2519
90Gaston/Star-19
91CharlR/ClBest-9
91CharlR/ProC-1313
Randle, Len
72T-737
73OPC-378
73T-378
74OPC-446
74T-446
75OPC-259
75T-259
75T/M-259
76OPC-31
76SSPC-266
76T-31
77BurgChef-21
77T-196
78Ho-102
78K-22
78OPC-132
78T-544
79OPC-236
79T-454
81D-485
81F-301
81Pol/Mariners-9
81T-692
81T/TR-817
82D-307
82F-516
82OPC-312
82T-312
82T/ST-230
87Watlo-27
89Pac/SenLg-11
89T/SenLg-38
89TM/SenLg-88
90EliteSenLg-13
90Swell/Great-53
91Pac/SenLg-116
91WIZMets-323
92Yank/WIZ70-131
93Rang/Keeb-35
Randle, Michael
87Kenosha-3
88CalLgAS-37
88Visalia/Cal-147
88Visalia/ProC-85
89OrlanTw/Best-21
89OrlanTw/ProC-1339
90OrlanSR/Best-11
90OrlanSR/ProC-1097
90OrlanSR/Star-15
Randle, Randy
86Osceola-20
87Osceola-5
88Modesto/Cal-77
89NewBrit/ProC-618
89NewBrit/Star-17
90NewBrit/Best-19
90NewBrit/ProC-1328
90NewBrit/Star-17
91AA/LineD-470
91NewBrit/LineD-470
91NewBrit/ProC-360
Randolph, Bob
81LynnS-26
83Chatt-13
Randolph, Scott
87Salem/ProC-2440
Randolph, Tommy
86Lipscomb-18
Randolph, Willie
76OPC-592R
76SSPC-584
76T-592R
76T/Tr-592T
77BK/Y-13
77BurgChef-175
77OPC-110
77T-359
78BK/Y-13
78Ho-89
78OPC-228
78SSPC/270-27
78T-620
79BK/Y-13
79OPC-125
79T-250
80OPC-239
80T-460
81D-345
81F-109
81F/St-107
81OPC-60
81PermaGr/AS-16
81T-60
81T/HT
81T/So-36
81T/St-108
81T/St-242
82D-461
82F-49
82F/St-121
82OPC-159IA
82OPC-213AS
82OPC-37
82T-548AS
82T-569
82T-570IA
82T/St-219
83D-283
83F-393
83F/St-11M
83F/St-15M
83OPC-140
83OPC/St-95
83RoyRog/Disc-9
83T-140
83T/St-95
84D-417
84F-137
84Nes/792-360
84OPC-360
84T-360
84T/St-324
85D-92
85F-140
85FunFoodPin-20
85Leaf-83
85OPC-8
85Pol/MetYank-Y1
85T-765
85T/St-312
86D-16DK
86D-92
86D/DKsuper-16
86F-115
86Leaf-16DK
86OPC-332
86T-276M
86T-455
86T/St-305
86T/Tatt-15M
87D-154
87D/OD-246
87F-109
87F/BB-35
87Leaf-58
87OPC-377
87RedFoley/St-2
87Sf/TPrev-7M
87T-701
87T/St-302
88D-228
88D/AS-3
88D/Best-108
88D/PopUp-3
88D/Y/Bk-228
88Drake-18
88F-218
88F/BB/AS-32
88F/BB/MVP-28
88F/Mini-42
88F/St-50
88KennerFig-85
88Leaf-162
88Nestle-22
88OPC-210
88Panini/St-153
88Panini/St-228M
88S-266
88S/WaxBox-3
88Sf-47
88Sf/Gamewin-6
88T-210
88T-387
88T/Big-76
88T/Gloss22-3
88T/Gloss60-42
88T/Mini-28
88T/St-162
88T/St-294
88T/St/Backs-37
88T/UK-59
89B-344
89D-395
89D/Best-148
89D/Tr-8
89F-265
89F/Up-93
89Mother/Dodg-10
89OPC-244
89Panini/St-405
89Pol/Dodg-8
89RedFoley/St-92
89S-45
89S/Tr-41
89Smok/Dodg-57
89T-519TL
89T-635
89T/Big-244
89T/St-309
89T/Tr-100T
89UD-237
89UD/Ext-777
90B-90
90Classic-122
90Classic/III-71
90D-19DK
90D-250
90D/BestAL-110
90D/SuperDK-19DK
90F-406
90F/Can-406
90Kenner/Fig-66
90Leaf-345
90OPC-25
90Panini/St-279
90Pol/Dodg-12
90PublInt/St-16
90S-395
90S/100St-4
90S/Tr-51T
90Sf-175
90T-25
90T/Big-43
90T/Coins-55
90T/St-66
90T/Tr-100T
90Target-648
90UD-183
90UD/Ext-704
91B-46
91Brewer/MillB-21
91D-217
91D-766WS
91F-22
91F/UltraUp-U32
91F/Up-U33
91Leaf-419
91Leaf/Stud-74
91OPC-525
91Panini/FrSt-193
91Pol/Brew-19
91S-194
91S/RookTr-35T
91StCl-545
91T-525
91T/Tr-95T
91UD-421
91UD/Ext-720
92B-681
92Classic/Game200-169
92Classic/I-74
92D-625
92F-186
92L-240
92L/BlkGold-240
92Mets/Kahn-12
92OPC-116
92OPC/Premier-67
92Panini-36
92Pinn-382
92S-30
92S/RookTr-35T
92StCl-890
92T-116
92T/Gold-116
92T/GoldWin-116
92T/Tr-90T
92T/TrGold-90T
92UD-211
92UD-795
92USPlayC/Ace-12D
92Ultra-536
92Yank/WIZ70-132
92Yank/WIZ80-153
92Yank/WIZAS-60
93D-644
93F-479
93Pac/Spanish-200
93S-613
93Select-195
93T-324
93T/Gold-324
93UD-419
Ranew, Merritt
62T-156
64T-78
66OPC-62
66T-62
89Smok/Ast-11
Ranger, Rowdy
91Gaston/ClBest-30
Rannow, John
86Cram/NWL-19
86Everett/Pop-22
87Clinton-10
Ransom, Gene
82Madis/Frit-9
83Madis/Frit-18
Ransom, Jeff
80Phoenix/NBank-22
81Phoenix-22
83Phoenix/BHN-5
87Toledo-24
87Toledo/TCMA-11
Rantz, Mike
83Idaho-24
Raper, Ron
88CapeCod/Sum-37
Rapp, Craig
91Idaho/ProC-4327
91Idaho/SportP-20
Rapp, Earl
49Remar
50Remar
53Mother-30
Rapp, Joe
(Goldie)
21Exh-138
E120
E220
V100
V61-104
W573
Rapp, Patrick
90A&AASingle/ProC-117
90Clinton/Best-23
90Clinton/ProC-2547
91CalLgAS-39
91ClBest/Singl-275
91SanJose/ClBest-20
91SanJose/ProC-9
92D/Rook-99
92Phoenix/ProC-2821
92Phoenix/SB-394
92Sky/AAASingl-180
93Edmon/ProC-1134
93F-429
93Marlin/Publix-19
93T-791
93T/Gold-791
94F-473
94Pinn-189
94Pinn/Artist-189
94Pinn/Museum-189
94S-310
94S/GoldR-310
94StCl/Team-65
94T-227
94T/Gold-227
94UD/CollC-236
94UD/CollC/Gold-236
94UD/CollC/Silv-236
94Ultra-496
Rapp, Vern
77T-183MG
78T-324MG
83Expo/PostC-15CO
83Stuart-3CO
84T/Tr-95MG
Rappoli, Paul
91Elmira/ClBest-12
91Elmira/ProC-3285
92LynchRS/ClBest-10
92LynchRS/ProC-2922
Rariden, William A.
(Bill)
14CJ-137
15CJ-137
16FleischBrd-75
88Pac/8Men-86
94Conlon-1024
D327
D328-136
D329-141
D350/2-141
E135-136
E270
M101/4-141
M101/5-141
Raschi, Victor
(Vic)
49B-35
50B-100
51B-25
51BR-C4
52B-37
52BR
52StarCal-84AM
52StarCal/L-70D
53B/Col-27
53Exh/Can-5
54B-33
54Hunter
55B-185
55Hunter
55Rodeo
74Laugh/ASG-48
79TCMA-186
88Pac/Leg-70
90BBWit-53
92Yank/WIZAS-61
Exh47
PM10/Sm-150
R346-32
Rashid, Ralph
90Peoria/Team-3PER
91Peoria/Team-30M
Rasmus, Tony
86Cram/NWL-191
87Salem/ProC-2425
Rasmussen
T207
Rasmussen, Dennis
81Holyo-25
83Colum-8
84Colum-25
84Colum/Pol-19
84D-446
85D-518
85F-141
85Leaf-48
85T-691
86D-336
86T-301
87Classic-87
87D-175
87D/OD-247
87F-110
87F/Excit-35
87F/GameWin-35
87F/Mini-86
87F/St-95
87Leaf-260
87OPC-364
87Sf-71
87Sf/TPrev-7M
87T-555
87T/Mini-66
87T/St-303
88D-575
88F-246
88F/Up-U126
88S-560
88T-135
88T/St-145
88T/Tr-91T

89B-450
89Classic-86
89Coke/Padre-12
89D-559
89F-314
89OPC-32
89Padre/Mag-17
89Panini/St-195
89S-562
89Sf-212
89T-32
89UD-645
90B-205
90Coke/Padre-14
90D-420
90F-165
90F/Can-165
90Leaf-471
90OPC-449
90Padre/MagUno-4
90PublInt/St-56
90S-129
90T-449
90UD-594
91D-458
91F-539
91OPC-774
91Padre/MagRal-2
91S-457
91StCl-169
91T-774
91UD-230
91Ultra-309
92D-245
92F-617
92OPC-252
92RochR/SB-463
92S-536
92StCl-749
92T-252
92T/Gold-252
92T/GoldWin-252
92UD-439
92Yank/WIZ80-154
93D-778
93S-392
93StCl/Royal-12
Rasmussen, Harold
(Eric)
76OPC-182
76SSPC-296
76T-182
77T-404
78Padre/FamFun-23
78T-281
79T-57
80T-531
81D-123
81F-497
81T-342
83T-594
84Cram/PCL-49
84Nes/792-724
84OPC-377
84T-724
86Miami-21
86RochR-17
87RochR-8
87RochR/TCMA-8
88Watlo/ProC-686
89Canton/Best-11
89Canton/ProC-1308
89Pac/SenLg-107
90EliteSenLg-76
Rasmussen, Jim
81OkCty/TCMA-25
82OkCty-18
82Reading-7
84Nashvl-18
87Hawaii-11
Rasmussen, Mark
87Hawaii-3
Rasmussen, Neil
73Cedar
75BurlB
77Holyo
78Holyo
Rasp, Ronnie
88Wythe/ProC-2001
89CharWh/Best-17
89CharWh/ProC-1764
90Peoria/Team-27
90WinSalem/Team-13
Ratekin, Mark
91Boise/ClBest-28
91Boise/ProC-3877
92QuadC/ClBest-4
92QuadC/ProC-808
92StCl/Dome-148
94B-647
Rath, Fred
77Fritsch-35
Rath, Gary
92MissSt-36
93MissSt-37
Rath, Maurice
88Pac/8Men-85
E270
W514-57
Rather, Dody
86FSLAS-39
86Osceola-21
87ColAst/ProC-17
Rathjen, Dennis
80Clinton-2
Ratliff, Danny
86Stockton-22
Ratliff, Daryl
89Princet/Star-15
90Augusta/ProC-2478
90ProC/Singl-724
91CLAS/ProC-CAR36
91Salem/ClBest-12
91Salem/ProC-966
92B-71
92CaroMud/ProC-1194
92CaroMud/SB-139
92Sky/AASingl-65
93CaroMud/RBI-16
Ratliff, Jon
94B-334
94ClBest/Gold-52
94ClBest/GoldLP-12
94FExcel-166
94Pinn-437
94S-454
94T-739DP
94T/Gold-739DP
Ratliff, Kelly Eugene
65T-553R
Ratliff, Paul
63T-549R
70OPC-267R
70T-267R
71OPC-607
71T-607
Ratzer, Steve
82Tidew-21
Rau, Doug
73OPC-602R
73T-602R
74OPC-64
74T-64
75OPC-269
75T-269
75T/M-269
76OPC-124
76SSPC-71
76T-124
77BurgChef-149
77K-11
77OPC-128
77T-421
78OPC-24
78SSPC/270-78
78T-641
79K-56
79OPC-178
79T-347
80Pol/Dodg-31
80T-527
81F-133
81Redwd-9
81T-174
81T/Tr-819
90Target-649
Raubolt, Art
86Lakeland-19
Rauch, Al
(Rocky)
78Watlo
Rauch, Bob
91WIZMets-324
Rauth, Chris
85LitFalls-8
86Columbia-20
87Lynch-15
89Jacks/GS-24
90Knoxvl/Best-16
92Tidew/ProC-
92Tidew/SB-569
Rautzhan, Clarence G.
(Lance)
75Water
78T-709R
79Holyo-25
79OPC-193
79T-373
80Vanco-9
90Target-650
Raven, Luis
91Boise/ClBest-3
91Boise/ProC-3897
92PalmSp/ClBest-15
92PalmSp/ProC-850
Rawdon, Chris
86Elmira-16
Rawitzer, Kevin
94FExcel-73
Rawley, Billy
83Cedar-6
Rawley, Shane
75WPalmB
75WPalmB/Sussman-21
79OPC-30
79T-74
80OPC-368
80T-723
81D-167
81OPC-51
81Pol/Mar-16
81T-423
81T/St-129
82D-352
82F-517
82T-197
82T/Tr-95T
83D-513
83F-394
83T-592
84D-295
84F-138
84F/X-U94
84Nes/792-254
84OPC-254
84T-254
85ClGNA-15
85D-599
85D/HL-39
85F-263
85Leaf-31
85OPC-169
85Phill/TastyK-22
85Phill/TastyK-9M
85T-636
86ClGNA-6
86D-233
86F-446
86Leaf-109
86OPC-361
86Phill/TastyK-28
86T-361
86T/St-123
87D-83
87D/AAS-56
87D/OD-159
87F-180
87F/RecSet-31
87F/St-96
87Leaf-139
87OPC-239
87Phill/TastyK-28
87RedFoley/St-124
87Sf-181
87Sf/TPrev-6M
87Stuart-9M
87T-771
87T/St-120
88D-13DK
88D-83
88D/Best-240
88D/DKsuper-13DK
88F-311
88F/Hottest-32
88F/Mini-100
88F/SS-C4
88F/St-109
88F/WaxBox-C8
88KennerFig-86
88Leaf-13DK
88Leaf-92
88OPC-66
88Panini/St-352
88Phill/TastyK-19
88S-375
88Sf-51
88T-406AS
88T-66
88T/Gloss60-45
88T/Mini-65
88T/St-121
89B-151
89D-251
89F-579
89F/Up-44
89OPC-24
89S-170
89T-494
89T/St-118
89T/Tr-101T
89UD-427
89UD/Ext-786
90D-537
90F-384
90F/Can-384
90OPC-101
90PublInt/St-336
90S-71
90T-101
90UD-438
92Yank/WIZ80-155
Rawlings, John
93Conlon-699
E120
E121/120
E121/80
V100
W501-61
W573
W575
Ray
M116
Ray, Art
83AlexD-9
Ray, Bregg
84Butte-21
Ray, Glenn
81CharR-7
Ray, Jay
86Bakers-23
88VeroB/Star-21
Ray, Jim F.
68T-539R
69T-257
70OPC-113
70T-113
71MLB/St-91
71OPC-242
71T-242
72T-603
73OPC-313
73T-313
74OPC-458
74T-458
74T/Tr-458T
75Cedar
75OPC-89
75T-89
75T/M-89
Ray, Johnny
80Colum
81Tucson-10
82D-528
82F-492
82T-291R
82T/Tr-96T
83D-437
83F-317
83F/St-11M
83F/St-26M
83K-24
83OPC-149
83OPC/St-327
83T-149
83T/St-327
84D-308
84F-260
84Nes/792-387AS
84Nes/792-537
84Nestle/DT-13
84OPC-323
84OPC-387AS
84T-387AS
84T-537
84T/Gloss40-5
84T/RD-9M
84T/St-134
84T/St-186
84T/St/Box-7
85D-186
85D/AAS-50
85F-473
85F/St-43
85FunFoodPin-69
85GenMills-7
85Leaf-212
85OPC-96
85T-96
85T/RD-5M
85T/St-130
85ThomMc/Discs-40
86D-186
86D-19DK
86D/DKsuper-19
86D/HL-9
86F-617
86F/St-93
86Leaf-19DK
86OPC-37
86T-615
86T/St-124
86T/Tatt-4M
87D-144
87D/OD-162
87F-618
87F/AwardWin-31
87F/Excit-36
87F/Mini-87
87F/St-97
87Kraft-14
87Leaf-147
87OPC-291
87RedFoley/St-51
87Sf-116M
87Sf-121
87Sf/TPrev-18M
87Smok/NL-8
87Stuart-10M
87T-747
87T/Gloss60-55
87T/St-135
88D-428
88D/Best-171
88F-502
88F/Slug-31
88Leaf-260
88OPC-115
88S-254
88Sf-186
88Smok/Angels-2
88T-115
88T/Big-97
89B-49
89Cadaco-42
89D-12DK
89D-331
89D/AS-25
89D/Best-195
89D/DKsuper-12DK
89F-487
89F/BBAS-33
89F/Heroes-32
89KMart/Lead-18
89KennerFig-110
89OPC-109
89Panini/St-292
89RedFoley/St-93
89S-14
89S/HotStar-99
89Sf-195
89Smok/Angels-20
89T-455
89T/Big-7
89T/Coins-49
89T/Hills-24
89T/Mini-50
89T/St-182
89T/UK-62
89UD-481
90B-302
90CharWh/Best-8
90CharWh/ProC-2240
90D-234
90D/BestAL-73
90F-143
90F/Can-143
90KMart/CBatL-18
90Leaf-208

90OPC-334
90Panini/St-33
90PublInt/St-378
90S-293
90Sf-82
90Smok/Angel-14
90T-334
90T/Big-95
90T/St-174
90UD-509
91CharWh/ClBest-8
91CharWh/ProC-2885
91D-622
91F-323
91OPC-273
91Panini/FrSt-181
91Panini/St-138
91S-31
91T-273
91UD-678
92Cedar/ClBest-4
92Chatt/ProC-3817
92Chatt/SB-193
92Sky/AASingl-86
Ray, Larry
82Tucson-10
83Tucson-20
84Cram/PCL-70
86ColumAst-22
86SLAS-11
87Vanco-20
Ray, Rick
89Utica/Pucko-31TR
91Utica/ClBest-25TR
Ray, Steve
83Greens-11
Raybon, Shannon
86Visalia-16TR
87Visalia-27TR
88OrlanTw/Best-25TR
Raydon, Curt
59T-305
60T-49
Rayford, Floyd
78SSPC/270-200
79SLCity-20
80RochR-18
81RochR-14
81T-399R
83RochR-13
83T-192
84F-334
84F/X-U95
84Nes/792-514
84T-514
84T/Tr-96T
85D-576
85F-186
85T-341
86D-332
86F-283
86Leaf-197
86T-623
87French-6
87T-426
88S-359
88T-296
89ScranWB/CMC-22
89ScranWB/ProC-727
90ElPasoATG/Team-39
90ProC/Singl-248CO
90ScranWB/CMC-22CO
91AAA/LineD-500M
91Crown/Orio-375
91ScranWB/LineD-500CO
91ScranWB/ProC-2556CO
92Batavia/ClBest-29CO
92Batavia/ProC-3284
Raymer, Greg
83Miami-9
86Jaxvl/TCMA-12
Raymond, Arthur
(Bugs)
E254
M116
S74-93
T202
T204
T205
T206
T3-113
Raymond, Claude
63T-519
64T-504
65OPC-48
65T-48
66T-586
67T-364
68CokeCap/Astro-4
68OPC-166
68T-166
69T-446
70Expos/Pins-12
70MLB/St-68
70OPC-268
70T-268
71Expo/ProS-20
71MLB/St-138
71OPC-202
71OPC-536
71T-536
78TCMA-46
86Mother/Ast-4
92Nabisco-23
93Expo/D/McDon-26
Raynolds, Donnie
88Belling/Legoe-29CO
Raynor, Tom
92FtLaud/Team-25TR
Raziano, Barry
75IntLgAS/Broder-25
75PCL/AS-25
75SLCity/Caruso-15
Raziano, Michael S.
87Spring/Best-19
88Spring/Best-16
Razjigaev, Rudy
93T-633M
93T/Gold-633M
Razook, Mark
87Anchora-24
89Wmsprt/Star-17
90ProC/Singl-756
90Wmsprt/Best-19
90Wmsprt/ProC-1066
90Wmsprt/Star-20
Rea, Clarke
91Niagara/ClBest-8
91Niagara/ProC-3638
Rea, Shayne
90Eugene/GS-24
91AppFx/ClBest-11
91AppFx/ProC-1717
91ClBest/Singl-250
92AppFox/ClBest-17
Read, James
88Pac/8Men-11
Reade, Bill
80Utica-30
Reade, Curtis
81VeroB-16
Ready, Randy
81BurlB-17
82ElPaso-7
84Pol/Brew-2
84T/Tr-97
85F-592
85Pol/Brew-2
86D-481
86F-498
86Pol/Brew-2
86T-209
87Bohem-5
87F/Up-U100
87T/Tr-97T
88Coke/Padres-5
88D-264
88F-594
88OPC-151
88Panini/St-407
88S-512
88Smok/Padres-23
88T-426
88T/Big-102
89Coke/Padre-13
89D-365
89D/Best-215
89F-315
89OPC-82
89Panini/St-201
89Phill/TastyK-45
89S-426
89S/Tr-60
89T-551
89T/St-106
89T/Tr-102T
89UD-474
90D-396
90ElPasoATG/Team-13
90F-571
90F/Can-571
90Leaf-500
90OPC-356
90Panini/St-311
90Phill/TastyK-26
90PublInt/St-57
90S-376
90T-356
90T/Big-150
90T/St-120
90UD-404
91B-495
91D-148
91F-410A
91F-410B
91Leaf-82
91OPC-137
91Panini/FrSt-104
91Phill/Medford-33
91S-615
91StCl-265
91T-137
91UD-540
91Ultra-271
92D-179
92F-542
92L-246
92L/BlkGold-246
92Mother/A's-25
92OPC-63
92S-59
92Studio-228
92T-63
92T/Gold-63
92T/GoldWin-63
92UD-408
92Ultra-427
94F-547
Reagan, Edward
T206
T213/brown
Reagan, Kyle
89Billings/ProC-2047
Reagans, Javan
88James/ProC-1917
Reams, Ronald
90MedHat/Best-22
91Myrtle/ClBest-25
91Myrtle/ProC-2959
92Myrtle/ClBest-9
92Myrtle/ProC-2212
93Knoxvl/ProC-1264
Reardon, Beans
94Conlon-1188UMP
Reardon, Jeff
79Tidew-5
81D-156
81F-335
81OPC-79
81T-456
81T/Tr-819
82D-547
82Expo/Hygrade-17
82F-204
82F/St-37
82Hygrade
82OPC-123
82OPC/Post-23
82T-667
83D-194
83Expo/PostC-16
83F-293
83F/St-20M
83F/St-7M
83OPC-290
83OPC/St-254
83Stuart-5
83T-290
83T/St-254
84D-279
84Expo/PostC-24
84F-283
84F/St-71
84Jacks/Smok-10
84Nes/792-595
84OPC-116
84Stuart-13
84T-595
84T/St-89
85D-331
85F-407
85Leaf-126
85OPC-375
85OPC/Post-12
85T-375
85T/St-85
86D-209
86D/AAS-33
86D/HL-14
86Expo/Prov/Pan-13
86Expo/Prov/Post-11
86F-257
86F/LimEd-35
86F/Slug-26
86F/St-94
86GenMills/Book-6M
86Leaf-214
86OPC-35
86Provigo-13
86Seven/Coin-E10
86Sf-119
86T-35
86T-711AS
86T/3D-20
86T/Gloss60-55
86T/St-76
86T/Super-6
86T/Tatt-22M
87Classic-94
87D-98
87D-PC11
87D/AAS-52
87D/WaxBox-PC11
87F-329
87F/Lim-34
87F/Mini-88
87F/Slug-33
87F/St-98
87F/Up-U101
87Kraft-40
87Leaf-143
87OPC-165
87RedFoley/St-65
87Sf-77M
87Sf/TPrev-17M
87T-165
87T/Gloss60-15
87T/Mini-18
87T/St-81
87T/Tr-98T
88D-122
88D/Best-242
88F-20
88F/AwardWin-31
88F/BB/AS-33
88F/Mini-37
88F/Slug-32
88F/St-46
88F/TL-28
88KennerFig-87
88Master/Disc-4
88Nestle-27
88OPC-99
88Panini/St-133
88RedFoley/St-73
88S-91
88Sf-53
88Smok/Minn-4
88T-425
88T/Big-10
88T/Mini-24
88T/RiteAid-28
88T/St-14
88T/St-280
89B-148
89Cadaco-43
89D-155
89D/AS-24
89D/Best-242
89F-125
89F/Superstar-34
89KennerFig-111
89OPC-86
89Panini/St-382
89RedFoley/St-94
89S-305
89S/HotStar-24
89Sf-168
89T-775
89T/Gloss60-54
89T/LJN-52
89T/Mini-63
89T/St-284
89T/St-8
89T/St/Backs-33
89UD-596
89Woolwth-17
90B-265
90Classic-101
90Classic/III-55
90D-119
90D/BestAL-72
90F-385
90F/Can-385
90F/Up-U75
90Leaf-276
90OPC-235
90OPC/BoxB-K
90Panini/St-108
90Pep/RSox-16
90PublInt/St-293
90PublInt/St-337
90RedFoley/St-76
90S-522
90S/Tr-17T
90Sf-37
90T-235
90T/Big-285
90T/St-289
90T/St-6HL
90T/TVRSox-15
90T/Tr-101T
90T/WaxBox-K
90UD-417
90UD/Ext-729
90Woolwth/HL-17
91B-107
91D-369
91F-109
91Leaf-252
91Leaf/Stud-19
91OPC-605
91OPC/BoxB-M
91OPC/Premier-98
91Panini/FrSt-272
91Panini/St-218
91Pep/RSox-17
91RedFoley/St-76
91S-164
91StCl-354
91StCl/Member*-25
91T-605
91T/WaxBox-M
91UD-418
91USPlayC/AS-5D
91Ultra-40
91WIZMets-325
91Woolwth/HL-17
92B-475
92D-89
92D/Up-U9HL
92DPep/MSA-8
92F-46
92F/Up-71
92F/Up-H3
92L-151
92L/BlkGold-151
92OPC-182
92OPC-3RB
92Pinn-158
92RedSox/Dunkin-24
92S-58
92S/100SS-5
92S/RookTr-46T
92StCl-657
92StCl/Dome-149
92Studio-137
92Sunflower-1
92T-182
92T-3RB
92T/Gold-182
92T/Gold-3RB
92T/GoldWin-182
92T/GoldWin-3RB
92UD-501
92USPlayC/RedSox-10S
92USPlayC/RedSox-6H
92Ultra-20
93D-739
93Expo/D/McDon-11
93F-370
93Sf/Final-18
93L-389
93OPC-342
93Pinn-535
93Reds/Kahn-19
93S-514HL
93S-564
93Select-362
93Select/RookTr-135T

93StCl-161
93StCl-602
93StCl/1stDay-161
93StCl/1stDay-602
93T-475
93T/Gold-475
93UD-541
93UD/SeasonHL-HI15
93Ultra-333
94F-420
94Pac/Cr-155
94Pinn-521
94S-251
94S/GoldR-251
Reardon, Kenny
45Parade*-48
Reaves, Scott
88Clearw/Star-20
88Spartan/Star-17
89Clearw/Star-18
Reavis, Kelly
91OKSt-19
Reay, Billy
45Parade*-47
Reberger, Frank
69T-637R
70MLB/St-117
70OPC-103
70T-103
71MLB/St-262
71OPC-251
71T-251
72T-548
83Nashua-21
84Cram/PCL-242
85Cram/PCL-23
86Edmon-23CO
87Edmon-17CO
92SanJose/ClBest-28CO
93Marlin/Publix-28M
Reboulet, James
83Erie-4
84Savan-10
86FSLAS-40
86StPete-26
87ArkTr-23
88BuffB/CMC-17
88BuffB/Polar-7
88BuffB/ProC-1470
Reboulet, Jeff
87OrlanTw-15
88OrlanTw/Best-19
89OrlanTw/ProC-1345
90LSUGreat-4
90OrlanSR/Best-27
90OrlanSR/ProC-1093
90OrlanSR/Star-16
91AAA/LineD-415
91Portl/LineD-415
91Portl/ProC-1572
92D/Rook-100
92Portl/SB-417
93D-179
93F-642
93Pac/Spanish-525
93S-233
93StCl-146
93StCl/1stDay-146
93T-172
93T/Gold-172
93UD-733
94D-85
94F-218
94Pac/Cr-366
94StCl-183
94StCl/1stDay-183
94StCl/Gold-183
Rech, Ed
82Lynch-8
Redd, Rick R.
88Harris/ProC-840
Redd, Ricky Joe
91MissSt-41
92MissSt-37
93MissSt-38
Redd, Ulysses A.
92Negro/RetortII-33
Redding, Dick
(Cannonball)
74Laugh/Black-25
86Negro/Frit-112
90Negro/Star-3
Redding, Mike
86Kenosha-21
87Visalia-16
88Visalia/Cal-160
88Visalia/ProC-93
89OrlanTw/Best-22
89OrlanTw/ProC-1333
90OrlanSR/Best-19
90OrlanSR/ProC-1081
90OrlanSR/Star-17
90Star/ISingl-47
Reddish, Mike
83Nashvl-17
85CharlO-10
86RochR-18
Redfern, Pete
77T-249
78T-81
78Twin/FriszP-16
79T-113
79Twin/FriszP-23
80T-403
81D-548
81F-560
81T-714
82D-51
82F-559
82T-309
83D-256
83F-623
83T-559
88AlaskaAS70/Team-14
Redfield, Joe
87MidldA-13
87TexLgAS-12
88Edmon/CMC-20
88Edmon/ProC-555
89ScranWB/CMC-20
89ScranWB/ProC-731
90AAAGame/ProC-25
90AAASingl/ProC-659
90Denver/CMC-9
90Denver/ProC-634
90ProC/Singl-34
91AAA/LineD-41
91BuffB/LineD-41
91BuffB/ProC-549
92B-438
92BuffB/BlueS-16
92BuffB/ProC-335
92BuffB/SB-39
92F-563
92S-412
Redick, Kevin
86Cram/NWL-6
86Everett/Pop-23
87Clinton-13
Redington, Thomas
88Sumter/ProC-412
89BurlB/ProC-1610
89BurlB/Star-17
90Foil/Best-75
90Greenvl/Best-5
90Greenvl/ProC-1137
90Greenvl/Star-16
90Star/ISingl-95
91AA/LineD-615
91ClBest/Singl-327
91Wichita/LineD-615
91Wichita/ProC-2605
91Wichita/Rock-15
92BirmB/ProC-2593
92BirmB/SB-87
92ClBest-32
92OPC-473M
92T-473R
92T/Gold-473M
92T/GoldWin-473M
Redman, Tim
87Erie-29
88Hamil/ProC-1729
89Hamil/Star-22
90StPete/Star-19
91ArkTr/ProC-1290
92Louisvl/ProC-1890
Redmon, Glenn
75Phoenix-13
75Phoenix/Caruso-8
75Phoenix/CircleK-13
76Wmsprt
Redmond, Andre
89Princet/Star-16
90Welland/Pucko-25
91Augusta/ProC-805
Redmond, Dan
87Watlo-28
89Canton/Best-9
Redmond, H. Wayne
71OPC-728R
71T-728R
Redus, Gary
81Water-15
82Indianap-17
83T/Tr-94T
84Borden-2
84D-184
84D/AAS-16
84F-481
84Nes/792-475
84OPC-231
84T-475
84T/RD-20M
84T/St-52
85D-306
85F-549
85Indianap-34
85Leaf-47
85OPC-146
85T-146
85T/RD-20M
85T/St-49
86CIGNA-12
86D-306
86F-189
86F/Up-U94
86Keller-3
86OPC-342
86Phill/TastyK-22
86T-342
86T/Tr-90T
87Coke/WS-13
87D-288
87D/OD-229
87F-181
87F/Up-U102
87OPC-42
87T-42
87T/St-119
87T/Tr-99T
88Coke/WS-24
88D-370
88F-408
88KennerFig-88
88OPC-332
88Panini/St-64
88S-443
88T-657
88T/Mini-9
89B-425
89D-605
89F-218
89OPC-281
89S-177
89T-281
89T/Big-131
89UD-419
89VFJuice-2
90B-180
90D-597
90F-476
90F/Can-476
90Homer/Pirate-24
90Leaf-209
90OPC-507
90Panini/St-331
90PublInt/St-162
90S-14
90T-507
90T/Big-52
90T/St-127
90UD-248
91B-516
91D-587
91F-47
91Leaf-254
91OPC-771
91S-226
91StCl-486
91T-771
91UD-38
91Ultra-285
92D-67
92F-564
92L-223
92L/BlkGold-223
92OPC-453
92Pirate/Nation-19
92S-303
92StCl-524
92T-453
92T/Gold-453
92T/GoldWin-453
92UD-519
92Ultra-560
93D-516
93F-504
93L-426
93Pac/Spanish-250
93Rang/Keeb-425
93StCl/Rang-14
93Ultra-634
94D-275
94F-318
94L-387
94Pac/Cr-626
94S-191
94S/GoldR-191
94StCl-514
94StCl/1stDay-514
94StCl/Gold-514
94StCl/Team-264
94T-108
94T/Gold-108
Reece, Bob
83Wichita/Dog-17CO
Reece, Jeff
86Stockton-23
87Wichita-14
Reece, Thad
83Madis/Frit-9
84Albany-5
85Cram/PCL-135
86Tacom-18
87Tacom-10
88Memphis/Best-24
90AAASingl/ProC-609
90AlbanyDG/Best-35
90Omaha/CMC-20
90Omaha/ProC-74
90ProC/Singl-195
Reed, Billy
89LittleSun-23CO
89Watlo/ProC-1788
89Watlo/Star-23
90Foil/Best-314
90Waterlo/Best-14
90Waterlo/ProC-2379
91HighD/ClBest-9
91HighD/ProC-2392
Reed, Bob E.
70OPC-207R
70T-207R
71MLB/St-404
71OPC-732
71T-732
Reed, Bobby
88MissSt-28
89MissSt-33
90MissSt-35
91AA/LineD-591
91Tulsa/LineD-591
91Tulsa/ProC-2771
91Tulsa/Team-22
92B-522
92UD/ML-232
Reed, Chris
91Princet/ClBest-6
91Princet/ProC-3512
92Billings/ProC-3354
Reed, Curt
82AppFx/Frit-12
83GlenF-9
Reed, Curtis
81Hawaii/TCMA-10
Reed, Darren
86Albany/TCMA-23
87Albany-16
88Tidew/CANDL-17
88Tidew/CMC-16
88Tidew/ProC-1603
89Tidew/CMC-17
89Tidew/ProC-1957
90AAASingl/ProC-288
90AlbanyDG/Best-20
90F/Up-U39
90ProC/Singl-376
90T/TVMets-54
90Tidew/CMC-25
90Tidew/ProC-557
91F-159
91S-368RP
91T/90Debut-129
91WIZMets-326
92B-537
92D/Rook-101
92StCl-824
92T/Tr-91T
92T/TrGold-91T
93D-105
93Mets/Kahn-21
93T-482
93T/Gold-482
Reed, Dennis
87Anchora-25
90Ashvl/ClBest-10
91Ashvl/ProC-568
92BurlAs/ClBest-11
92BurlAs/ProC-544
Reed, Howard
60L-84
61Union
65T-544
66T-387
70T-548
71Expo/ProS-21
71LaPizza-10
71OPC-398
71T-398
90Target-651
Reed, Jack
92Yank/WIZ60-101
Reed, Jamie
84CharlO-14
85RochR-28
87RochR-22
88RochR/Gov-31
88RochR/ProC-214
Reed, Jeff
81Wisco-14
83OrlanTw-5
84Toledo-2
85D-30RR
85IntLgAS-38
85Toledo-14
85Twin/Team-7
86F/Up-U95
87D/OD-92
87F-550
87T-247
87T/Tr-100T
88D-88
88F-194
88OPC-176
88S-408
88T-176
89D-469
89F-167
89Kahn/Reds-34
89S-99
89T-626
89T/Big-158
89UD-276
90D-351
90F-429
90F/Can-429
90Kahn/Reds-23
90Leaf-505
90OPC-772
90PublInt/St-37
90S-147
90T-772
90UD-165
91D-741
91F-78
91Kahn/Reds-34
91Leaf-102
91OPC-419
91Pep/Reds-17
91StCl-534
91T-419
91Ultra-101
92D-451
92F-418
92OPC-91
92Reds/Kahn-34
92S-311
92StCl-487
92T-91
92T/Gold-91
92T/GoldWin-91
92UD-299
92Ultra-195
93F-397
93F/Final-154
93Mother/Giant-25
93Pac/Spanish-87
93StCl/Giant-13
93Ultra-488

94F-698
94Pac/Cr-552
94StCl-504
94StCl/1stDay-504
94StCl/Gold-504
94StCl/Team-17
94T-291
94T/Gold-291

Reed, Jerry M.
80OkCty
82OkCty-9
83Charl-4
84Maine-2
85Maine-8
85Polar/Ind-35
86Calgary-22
86F-592
86T-172
87Mother/Sea-22
87T-619
88D-517
88F-387
88Mother/Sea-22
88S-488
88T-332
89D-657
89F-557
89Mother/Sea-22
89S-427
89T-441
89UD-529
90D-614
90F-523
90F/Can-523
90F/Up-U76
90Leaf-368
90OPC-247
90PublInt/St-440
90S-492
90T-247
90T/TVRSox-58
90UD-210
91F-110
91Pac/SenLg-141

Reed, Jody
86NewBrit-21
87Pawtu-6
87Pawtu/TCMA-17
88D-41RR
88D/Best-196
88D/RedSox/Bk-41RR
88D/Rook-44
88F-360
88Leaf-41RR
88S-625RP
88Sf-225R
88T-152
88T/Big-202
89B-30
89D-305
89D/Best-289
89F-96
89OPC-232
89Panini/St-268
89RedFoley/St-95
89S-486
89S/HotRook-85
89S/YS/I-2
89Sf-210
89T-321TL
89T-734
89T/Big-97
89T/Gloss60-60
89ToysRUs-23
89UD-370
90B-272
90Classic/III-54
90D-398
90D/BestAL-16
90F-284
90F/Can-284
90Kenner/Fig-67
90Leaf-150
90OPC-96
90Panini/St-25
90Pep/RSox-17
90PublInt/St-462
90S-11
90T-96
90T/Big-167
90T/Mini-6
90T/TVRSox-25
90UD-321
91B-120
91D-123
91F-111
91Leaf-69
91OPC-247
91Panini/FrSt-265
91Panini/St-220
91Pep/RSox-18
91S-173
91StCl-33
91T-247
91UD-184
91Ultra-41
92B-642
92D-47
92F-47
92L-413
92L/BlkGold-413
92OPC-598
92Panini-86
92Pinn-222
92RedSox/Dunkin-25
92S-85
92StCl-816
92Studio-138
92T-598
92T/Gold-598
92T/GoldWin-598
92TripleP-25
92UD-404
92USPlayC/RedSox-13C
92USPlayC/RedSox-9D
92Ultra-21
93B-506
93D-165
93F-182
93F/Final-83
93Flair-76
93Flair/Pr-6
93L-299
93Mother/Dodg-9
93OPC-357
93OPC/Premier-115
93Pac/Spanish-503
93Pinn-519
93Pol/Dodg-21
93S-414
93Select-120
93Select/RookTr-93T
93StCl-612
93StCl/1stDay-612
93StCl/Dodg-3
93Studio-177
93T-103
93T/Gold-103
93TripleP-253M
93UD-568
93UD-96
93Ultra-403
94D-236
94F-521
94Finest-346
94L-376
94Pac/Cr-319
94Pinn-519
94Pol/Brew-22
94S-368
94StCl-13
94StCl/1stDay-13
94StCl/Gold-13
94T-325
94T/Gold-325
94UD-473
94Ultra-377

Reed, Ken
86BirmB/Team-3
87DayBe-7

Reed, Marty
86Kinston-18
87MidldA-27
87TexLgAS-15
88Edmon/CMC-9
88Edmon/ProC-562

Reed, Patrick
91GreatF/SportP-27
92Yakima/ClBest-7
92Yakima/ProC-3466
93Welland/ClBest-24
93Welland/ProC-3375

Reed, Richard
(Rick)
87Macon-10
88Salem/Star-17
88TM/Umpire-48
89BuffB/CMC-9
89BuffB/ProC-1675
89TM/Umpire-46
90AAASingl/ProC-486
90BuffB/CMC-8
90BuffB/ProC-371
90D-527
90F-477
90F/Can-477
90Leaf-427
90ProC/Singl-8
90S-544
90S/100Ris-8
90TM/Umpire-44
91AAA/LineD-42
91AAAGame/ProC-4
91BuffB/LineD-42
91BuffB/ProC-540
91S-584
92Omaha/SB-343
92S/100RisSt-73
92Sky/AAASingl-295
92StCl-434
93Rang/Keeb-426
93T-212
93T/Gold-212

Reed, Ron
68OPC-76R
68T-76R
69OPC-177
69T-177
69T/4in1-8M
69T/St-9
70MLB/St-12
70OPC-546
70T-546
71MLB/St-21
71OPC-359
71T-359
72MB-281
72T-787
73OPC-72
73T-72
74OPC-346
74T-346
75OPC-81
75T-81
75T/M-81
76OPC-58
76T-58
76T/Tr-58T
77T-243
78SSPC/270-30
78T-472
79BK/P-7
79OPC-84
79T-177
80BK/P-21
80OPC-318
80T-609
81D-44
81F-11
81T-376
82D-399
82F-255
82T-581
83D-567
83F-169
83F/St-20M
83F/St-4M
83T-728
83T/Fold-4M
84D-529
84F-45
84F/X-U96
84Nes/792-43
84T-43
84T/Tr-98T
84TrueVal/WS-26
85D-282
85F-524
85T-221
90Richm/25Ann-20

Reed, Sean
88Wythe/ProC-1981
89CharWh/Best-16
89CharWh/ProC-1762

Reed, Steve
78BurlB
80Holyo-18

Reed, Steven Vincnet
88Pocatel/ProC-2082
89Clinton/ProC-906
90Shrev/ProC-1443
90Shrev/Star-20
91AA/LineD-319
91Shrev/LineD-319
91Shrev/ProC-1822
92Phoenix/ProC-2822
92Shrev/ProC-3869
92Shrev/SB-591
92Sky/AASingl-261
93D-375RR
93F-414
93F/Final-40
93Pac/Spanish-435
93Pinn-584
93S-573
93Select-351
93StCl-674
93StCl/1stDay-674
93StCl/Rockie-26
93T-461
93T/Gold-461
93UD-752
93USPlayC/Rockie-11D
93USPlayC/Rockie-5H
93Ultra-356
94D-438
94F-450
94Pac/Cr-204
94S-170
94S/GoldR-170
94StCl-475
94StCl/1stDay-475
94StCl/Gold-475
94StCl/Team-112
94T-627
94T/Gold-627
94Ultra-187

Reed, Tom
84Visalia-13

Reed, Toncie
89AubAs/ProC-2167
90Osceola/Star-24

Reeder, Bill E.
49Eureka-194
52Mother-48

Reeder, Mike
88CharWh/Best-5

Reedy, Jerry
78Cr/PCL-101

Reelhorn, John
81OkCty/TCMA-15
82OkCty-19

Rees, Robert
90Kgsport/Best-14
90Kgsport/Star-20
91Clmbia/PCPII-4
91Clmbia/PII-8
92ColumMet/ProC-294

Rees, Sean
89Alaska/Team-11
92Penin/ClBest-7
92Penin/ProC-2930
92StCl/Dome-150
93River/Cal-15

Reese, Andrew
29Exh/4-9
R315-A30
R315-B30

Reese, Calvin
91ClBest/Singl-412
91Classic/DP-16
91FrRow/DP-23
91Princet/ClBest-15
91Princet/ProC-3523
92B-86
92CharWh/ClBest-1
92CharWh/ProC-17
92ClBest-59
92OPC-714
92ProC/Tomorrow-220
92StCl/Dome-151
92T-714
92T/Gold-714
92T/GoldWin-714
92UD/ML-226
92UD/ML-70DS
93B-146
93ClBest/MLG-189
93FExcel/ML-28
93SALAS/II-34
93SALAS/IICS-10
94B-270
94B-355
94SigRook-21
94T-278
94T/Gold-278

Reese, Chip
83Ander-10
89Boise/ProC-1979

Reese, Harold H.
(Pee Wee)
41DP-23
41PlayBall-54
41Wheat-18
42Playball-28
43MP-20
47HomogBond-38
48Swell-18
49B-36
49Eureka-47
49MP-106
49Royal-2
50B-21
50Drake-19
51B-80
52B-8
52BR
52Coke
52RM-NL17
52Royal
52StarCal-91AM
52StarCal/L-79B
52T-333
53B/Col-33
53Exh/Can-21
53RM-NL10
53T-76
54B-58
54NYJour
54RM-NL15
55Armour-15
55B-37
55Gol/Dodg-24
55RM-NL17
56T-260
56YellBase/Pin-26
57T-30
58BB
58Hires-23
58T-375
60NuCard-37
61NuCard-437
77Galasso-31
79TCMA-84
80Pac/Leg-52
80Perez/HOF-189
85West/2-34
86Sf/Dec-21
87Leaf/SpecOlym-H8
88Pac/Leg-21
89Rini/Dodg-5
89Smok/Dodg-23
90Perez/GreatMom-26
90Target-652
91T/Arc53-76
92Bz/Quadra-15M
92Ziploc-6
D305
Exh47
PM10/Sm-151
PM10/Sm-152
PM10/Sm-153
PM10/Sm-154
R302-106
R423-86

Reese, Jason
90MedHat/Best-2
91Pocatel/ProC-3780
91Pocatel/SportP-11

Reese, Jimmie
28Exh/PCL-21
31Exh/4-26
73OPC-421CO
73T-421CO
74OPC-276CO
74T-276CO
76SSPC-630CO
91B-186CO
91Leaf/Stud-21CO
93Conlon-690
93Mother/Angel-28M
93Pol/Angel-12CO

Reese, Kyle
86Erie-24
87FtMyr-27
88Virgini/Star-21
89Memphis/Best-16
89Memphis/ProC-1206
89Memphis/Star-20

90Memphis/Best-12
90Memphis/ProC-1011
90Memphis/Star-23
Reese, Marty
87Belling/Team-32M
Reese, Pokey
94UD-544TP
Reese, Rich
65T-597R
67T-486R
68OPC-111
68T-111
69MB-228
69OPC-56
69T-56
70MLB/St-238
70OPC-404
70T-404
71MLB/St-472
71OPC-349
71T-349
71T/Coins-72
72MB-282
72T-611
78Twin/Frisz-19
89Pac/Leg-112
Reese, Stan
79Ashvl/TCMA-27
Reeser, Jeffery
90Peoria/Team-3GM
Reeve, Bob
85Anchora-41
Reeves, Dave
91Billing/SportP-22
91Billings/ProC-3751
Reeves, Jim
78StPete
Reeves, Matt
79Clinton/TCMA-5
82VeroB-10
Reeves, Mel
47Smith-24
Reeves, Mickey
91Hunting/ClBest-18
91Hunting/ProC-3348
92Hunting/ClBest-12
92Hunting/ProC-3165
Reeves, Robert E.
29Exh/4-17
31Exh/4-17
31Exh/4-17
Regalado, Rudy
55B-142
60HenryH-14
Regalado, Uvaldo
82DayBe-6
83DayBe-9
Regan, Michael J.
E254
Regan, Phil
61T-439
62J-24
62P-24
62P/Can-24
62T-366
63T-494
64Det/Lids-13
64T-535
65OPC-191
65T-191
66T-347
67Bz-29
67CokeCap/DodgAngel-1
67OPC-130
67T-130
68OPC-88
68T-88
69MB-229
69MLB/St-124
69T-535
69T/St-18
70MLB/St-21
70OPC-334
70T-334
71MLB/St-43
71OPC-634
71T-634
72MB-283
72OPC-485
72T-485
84Cub/Uno-9M
87Smok/Dodg-27
88Smok/Dodg-9
89Smok/Dodg-72
90Target-653
Regan, William W.
29Exh/4-18
93Conlon-813
R316
Reger, Roy
85Clovis-36
Reggins, Mark
92Louisvl/SB-275CO
Regira, Gary
89James/ProC-2154
90Rockford/ProC-2688
90Rockford/Team-22
91WPalmB/ClBest-10
91WPalmB/ProC-1226
Rehbaum, Chris
80Batavia-27
81Batavia-23
82Watlo/B-22
82Watlo/Frit-17
Rehm, Vic
60L-61
Rehse
N172
Rehwinkel, Pat
89Helena/SP-4
Reiber, Frank
V351A-21
V355-111
Reich, Andy
89Clmbia/Best-19
89Clmbia/GS-22
89SALAS/GS-16
90StLucie/Star-21
91StLucie/ClBest-18
91StLucie/ProC-708
92Bingham/ProC-513
Reich, Frank
92StCl/MemberIV*-10
Reich, Herman
49Eureka-68
Reich, Steve
93Bz-4
93T/Tr-85T
Reichard, Clyde
(Bud)
78Wisco
85Tulsa-37
89Penin/Star-21CO
89Penin/Star-26CO
Reichardt, Kevin
87Belling/Team-5
Reichardt, Rick
65OPC-194R
65T-194R
66T-321
67Bz-1
67OPC-40
67T-40
68T-570
68T/ActionSt-14CM
68T/ActionSt-3CM
69JB
69MB-230
69MLB/St-25
69MLBPA/Pin-23
69OPC-205
69T-205
69T/4in1-7M
69T/S-8
69T/St-147
69T/decal
69Trans-18
70K-18
70MLB/St-177
70T-720
70Trans-12
71OPC-643
71T-643
71T/Coins-102
72MB-284
81TCMA-337
Reichel, Tom
87Penin-19
Reichenbach, Eric
91Pittsfld/ClBest-24
91Pittsfld/ProC-3420
92ClBest-81
92ColumMet/ClBest-23
92ColumMet/ProC-295
92ColumMet/SAL/II-17
Reichle, Darrin
87Spokane-2
88Charl/ProC-1208
88SALAS/GS-11
89River/Best-14
89River/Cal-15
89River/ProC-1393
90Foil/Best-151
90ProC/Singl-853
90River/Best-24
90River/Cal-23
90River/ProC-2607
91AA/LineD-616
91Wichita/LineD-616
91Wichita/ProC-2596
91Wichita/Rock-7
Reichler, Joe
90LitSun-7
Reid, Derek
90A&AASingle/ProC-172
90Everett/Best-26
90Everett/ProC-3142
91ClBest/Singl-273
91SanJose/ClBest-28
91SanJose/ProC-25
91SanJose/ProC-26M
92Shrev/ProC-3884
92UD/ML-87
Reid, Gregory
91Madison/ClBest-19
91Madison/ProC-2143
92Madis/ClBest-5
92Madis/ProC-1250
Reid, Jessie
84Shrev/FB-16
85Fresno/Pol-18
86Phoenix-22
87Phoenix-16
88F-643R
89Tacoma/CMC-17
89Tacoma/ProC-1549
Reid, John
91Niagara/ClBest-20
92Fayette/ClBest-4
92Fayette/ProC-2166
92Lakeland/ProC-2277
Reid, Scott D.
70OPC-56R
70T-56R
71OPC-439R
71T-439R
Reid, Terry
91Melbourne/Fut-15
Reidy, Bill
90Target-654
Reilley, John
88Sumter/ProC-394
89Wausau/GS-5
90Salinas/Cal-129
90Salinas/ProC-2720
Reilly, Charles T.
N172
Reilly, Ed
83DayBe-10
Reilly, John G.
N172
Reilly, Mike
88TM/Umpire-33
89TM/Umpire-31
90TM/Umpire-30
Reilly, Neil
85BurlR-6
Reilly, Thomas H.
E254
T204
Reimer, Kevin
86Salem-23
87PortChar-26
88Tulsa-25
89F-641R
89OkCty/CMC-19
89OkCty/ProC-1527
89S/HotRook-59
90AAASingl/ProC-692
90F-310
90F/Can-310
90OkCty/CMC-19
90OkCty/ProC-446
90ProC/Singl-169
90TulsaDG/Best-30
91D-80
91F-298
91F/UltraUp-U57
91Mother/Rang-15
91OPC-304
91S-836
91T-304
91UD-494
92B-115
92D-251
92F-315
92L-93
92L/BlkGold-93
92Mother/Rang-15
92OPC-737
92Pinn-340
92S-152
92StCl-57
92T-737
92T/Gold-737
92T/GoldWin-737
92UD-201
92Ultra-444
93B-479
93D-55
93F-326
93F/Final-232
93Flair-228
93L-377
93OPC-284
93OPC/Premier-131
93Pac/Spanish-515
93Panini-43
93Pinn-531
93Pol/Brew-21
93Rang/Keeb-305
93S-628
93Select-268
93Select/RookTr-101T
93StCl-699
93StCl/1stDay-699
93T-87
93T/Gold-87
93UD-578
93UD/SP-69
93Ultra-576
94D-233
94F-189
94Panini-85
94S-477
94T-585
94T/Gold-585
94UD/CollC-237
94UD/CollC/Gold-237
94UD/CollC/Silv-237
94Ultra-82
Reimer, Robin
86Everett/Pop-25
Reimink, Robert
90Lakeland/Star-21
91AA/LineD-395
91London/LineD-395
91London/ProC-1887
92London/ProC-641
92London/SB-415
Reimsnyder, Brian
90Erie/Star-19
Rein, Fred
77Charl
Reinbach, Mike
75IntAS/TCMA-5
91Crown/Orio-376
Reincke, Corey
91Fayette/ClBest-7
91Fayette/ProC-1167
91Niagara/ClBest-28
91Niagara/ProC-3631
Reinebold, Jim
89SoBend/GS-3
90SoBend/Best-29CO
90SoBend/GS-29CO
91SoBend/ProC-2876CO
92SoBend/ProC-196CO
Reinert, Greg
91Idaho/SportP-9
Reinhart, Art
91Conlon/Sport-242
Reinholtz, Eric
87Salem/ProC-2421
Reinisch, Paul
90Bristol/ProC-3170
90Bristol/Star-19
Reinke, Jeff
75Clinton
Reis, Dave
88Pulaski/ProC-1757
89BurlB/ProC-1619
89BurlB/Star-18
90BurlB/Best-7
90BurlB/ProC-2347
90BurlB/Star-20
90Foil/Best-195
90MidwLgAS/GS-47
Reis, Paul
88Pulaski/ProC-1759
89Sumter/ProC-1090
90BurlB/Best-17
90BurlB/ProC-2359
90BurlB/Star-21
Reis, Robert
(Bobby)
90Target-655
R314
Reis, Tom
47Centen-22
Reiser, James
86Cram/NWL-52
87Madis-10
88Madis-18
Reiser, Pete
39Exh
41DP-18
43MP-21
48B-7
48L-146
48Swell-2
49B-185
49Eureka-17
50B-193
51B-238
52T-189
60T-463C
60Union/Dodg-23M
73OPC-81CO
73T-81CO
80Marchant-25
80Pac/Leg-88
89Smok/Dodg-47
90Target-656
PM10/Sm-155
Reish, Steve
83Kinston/Team-17
84Memphis-17
Reisling, Frank
(Doc)
90Target-1052
M116
Reiter, Gary
81Durham-24
82Durham-20
83Richm-8
84Richm-15
85Richm-7
Reitmeister, Ben
87Hawaii-27
Reitz, Ken
73OPC-603R
73T-603R
74OPC-372
74T-372
75OPC-27
75T-27
75T/M-27
76OPC-158
76SSPC-280
76T-158
76T/Tr-158T
77BurgChef-13
77K-38
77T-297
78Ho-106
78T-692
79Ho-23
79OPC-307
79T-587
80OPC-103
80T-182
81Coke
81D-307
81F-530
81OPC-316
81T-441
81T/HT
81T/So-101
81T/St-158
81T/Tr-820
82D-277
82F-602
82F/St-91
82OPC-245
82T-245
82T/St-26
85Tulsa-0
86SanJose-17
87SanJose-3

89Pac/SenLg-213
89T/SenLg-35
89TM/SenLg-89
90EliteSenLg-61
91Pac/SenLg-33
91Swell/Great-119
92Card/McDon/Pac-41
Reitzel, Mark
87Hawaii-18
Reitzel, Mike
90Miami/II/Star-22
Rekar, Bryan
94B-554
94FExcel-187
Relaford, Desi
92ClBest-387
92Penin/ClBest-8
92Penin/ProC-2941
92StCl/Dome-152
93B-163
93FExcel/ML-230
93StCl/Mar-2
94B-529
Relaford, Winnie
88Sumter/ProC-400
89Sumter/ProC-1103
Relaigh, Matt
93James/ProC-3336
Relmink, Bob
89Niagara/Pucko-20
Rembielak, Rick
82Miami-16
Remlinger, Mike
87Everett-31
88Shrev/ProC-1296
89Shrev/ProC-1832
90B-227
90Shrev/ProC-1444
90Shrev/Star-21
91AAA/LineD-390
91D/Rook-37
91PG&E-27
91Phoenix/LineD-390
91Phoenix/ProC-64
91UD/FinalEd-36F
92Calgary/ProC-3729
92Calgary/SB-68
92D-336
92F-646
92S-410
92S/100RisSt-49
92Sky/AAASingl-31
92T/91Debut-143
92UD-585
93Calgary/ProC-1166
Remmerswaal, Win
81D-98
81Pawtu-7
81T-38
Remo, Bryon
91OKSt-20
Remo, Jeff
82QuadC-16
Remy, Jerry
76OPC-229
76SSPC-198
76T-229
77BurgChef-121
77K-44
77T-342
78Ho-66
78PapaG/Disc-2
78SSPC/270-186
79OPC-325
79T-618
80OPC-85
80T-155
81D-215
81F-238
81OPC-131
81T-549
82Coke/Bos
82D-156
82F-304
82F/St-171
82OPC-25
82Sqt-2
82T-25
82T/St-132
82T/St-149
83D-74
83F-193
83F/St-15M
83OPC-295
83OPC/St-33
83T-295
83T/St-33
84D-172
84F-407
84Nes/792-445
84OPC-58
84T-445
84T/RD-21M
84T/St-215
85F-167
85OPC-173
85T-761
85T/RD-21M
85T/St-218
Rende, Sal
79Tacom-11
80Tacom-14
81Chatt-17
82Chatt-11
83BuffB-13
87Chatt/Best-1MG
88Chatt/Team-25
88Lookout-25MG
88Memphis/Best-26
89AAA/ProC-37
89Omaha/CMC-23
89Omaha/ProC-1740
90AAASingl/ProC-615MG
90Fayette/ProC-2416
90Omaha/CMC-25MG
90Omaha/ProC-80MG
90ProC/Singl-200
90SALAS/Star-20
91AAA/LineD-349MG
91AAAGame/ProC-27MG
91Lakeland/ClBest-22
91Lakeland/ProC-275
91Omaha/LineD-349MG
91Omaha/ProC-1049MG
93Edmon/ProC-1152MG
Rendina, Mike
88Bristol/ProC-1877
89Bristol/Star-21
89Fayette/ProC-1584
92Lakeland/ClBest-2
92Lakeland/ProC-2288
Renfroe, Chico
92Negro/Retort-51
Renfroe, Cohen
(Laddie)
86WinSalem-21
87Pittsfld-8
88Iowa/CMC-4
88Iowa/ProC-551
89CharlK-1
90AAASingl/ProC-625
90Iowa/CMC-8
90Iowa/ProC-318
90ProC/Singl-83
90T/TVCub-58
91AAA/LineD-214
91AAAGame/ProC-19
91Iowa/LineD-214
91Iowa/ProC-1059
92Iowa/ProC-4050
92Iowa/SB-217
92S-875
92Sky/AAASingl-105
92T/91Debut-144
Renfroe, Marshall
60L-99
Renick, Rick
68T-301R
69MB-231
70OPC-93
70T-93
71MLB/St-473
71OPC-694
71T-694
72MB-285
72OPC-459
72T-459
74Tacoma/Caruso-20
75Tacoma/KMMO-8
78Twin/Frisz-42
83Memphis/TCMA-23MG
85Expo/PostC-16CO
86Expo/Prov/Pan-28CO
86Provigo-28CO
92Vanco/ProC-2734MG
92Vanco/SB-649MG
Reniff, Hal
62T-139
62T-159
63T-546
64T-36
65T-413
66OPC-68
66T-68
67CokeCap/YMet-10
67T-201
78TCMA-106
91WIZMets-327
92Yank/WIZ60-102
WG10-19
WG9-20
Renko, Steve Jr.
91WPalmB/ClBest-11
91WPalmB/ProC-1227
92WinHaven/ProC-1776
93Hagers/ClBest-21
93Hagers/ProC-1878
Renko, Steve
69Expos/Pins-6
70OPC-87
70T-87
71Expo/ProS-22
71MLB/St-139
71OPC-209
71T-209
72Dimanche*-38
72OPC-307
72OPC-308IA
72ProStars/PostC-10
72T-307
72T-308A
73OPC-623
73T-623
74Expo/West-8
74OPC-49
74T-49
74T/St-58
74Weston-18
75Ho-69
75OPC-34
75T-34
75T/M-34
76OPC-264
76T-264
77T-586
78T-493
79T-352
80T-184
81D-337
81F-231
81T-63
81T/Tr-821
82D-38
82F-472
82T-702
83D-393
83F-99
83F/St-10M
83OPC-236
83T-236
83T/Tr-95
84F-355
84Nes/792-444
84T-444
89KS*-65
93Expo/D/McDon-27
Renna, Bill
54T-112
55Rodeo
55T-121
55T/DH-99
56T-82
57Seattle/Pop-29
58T-473
59T-72
94T/Arc54-112
Renneau, Charlie
77Visalia
Rennert, Dutch
88TM/Umpire-18
89TM/Umpire-18
90TM/Umpire-16
Rennhack, Mike
92LitSun/HSPros-4
Rennicke, Dean
83Albuq-5
84Cram/PCL-160
85Cram/PCL-151
Renninger, Bob
74Cedar
Rennspies, Dustin
92GreatF/SportP-21
Rensa, Tony
93Conlon-950
Renteria, David
92GulfCY/ProC-3799
Renteria, Edgar
94B-94
Renteria, Edison
(Ed)
87AubAs-23
88Ashvl/ProC-1058
89Osceola/Star-19
90ColMud/Best-23
90ColMud/ProC-1355
90ColMud/Star-20
91Osceola/ClBest-21
91Osceola/ProC-695
Renteria, Rich
82AlexD-27
83LynnP-17
85Tigres-22
86Hawaii-20
87Mother/Sea-23
88Mother/Sea-23
89B-212
89Mother/Sea-20
89S-142
89T/Big-109
89UD-547
93B-10
93F/Final-69
93Marlin/Publix-20
93Pac/Spanish-470
93T/Tr-2T
93USPlayC/Marlin-13H
93USPlayC/Marlin-6D
93Ultra-385
94D-499
94F-474
94Panini-184
94StCl-87
94StCl/1stDay-87
94StCl/Gold-87
94StCl/Team-63
94T-681
94T/Gold-681
Rentschuler, Tom
83Peoria/Frit-16
83Redwd-22
Renz, Kevin
86Penin-22
87Penin-2
88BirmB/Best-28
Replogle, Andy
77ArkTr
79T-427
79Vanco-8
81Vanco-16
Repoz, Craig
85LitFalls-21
86Columbia-21
87Lynch-1
88StLucie/Star-20
89Jacks/GS-4
90Wichita/Rock-17
Repoz, Jeff
90Princet/DIMD-16
Repoz, Roger
66OPC-138
66T-138
67CokeCap/A's-13
67T-416
68T-587
69MB-232
69MLB/St-26
69OPC-103
69T-103
69T/St-148
70MLB/St-178
70OPC-397
70T-397
71MLB/St-355
71OPC-508
71T-508
72MB-286
72T-541
81TCMA-458
92Yank/WIZ60-103
Repulski, Rip
53T-172
54B-46
54Hunter
54RM-NL17
54T-115
55B-205
55Hunter
55T-55
55T/DH-125
56T-201
57T-245
58Hires-15
58T-14
59T-195
60BB-5
60L-86
60T-265
61T-128
90Target-657
91T/Arc53-172
94T/Arc54-115
Rescigno, Xavier
47Signal
49B/PCL-5
Resendez, Oscar
91BurlInd/ProC-3302
92ColRS/ProC-2389
92ProC/Tomorrow-61
92Watertn/ClBest-7
92Watertn/ProC-3232
Resetar, Gary
89Kenosha/ProC-1075
89Kenosha/Star-21
90Foil/Best-174
90OrlanSR/Best-12
90OrlanSR/ProC-1087
90OrlanSR/Star-18
91AA/LineD-92
91Canton/LineD-92
91Canton/ProC-982
Resinger, Grover
63Pep/Tul
Resnikoff, Bob
89Saraso/Star-19
90Saraso/Star-21
90Star/ISingl-60
91Osceola/ProC-683
Respondek, Mark
91Waverly/Fut-11
92Albany/ClBest-12
92Albany/ProC-2304
93James/ClBest-19
93James/ProC-3325
Restilli, Dino
48Sommer-12
49Sommer-17
50B-123
Restin, Eric
76BurlB
77BurlB
Retes, Lorenzo
85Tigres-10
Rettenmund, Merv
69OPC-66R
69T-66R
70T-629
71MLB/St-308
71OPC-393
71T-393
72K-11
72MB-287
72OPC-235
72OPC-86LL
72Pol/Orio-9
72ProStars/PostC-35
72T-235
72T-86LL
73JP
73OPC-56
73T-56
74OPC-585
74T-585
74T/Tr-585T
75OPC-369
75T-369
75T/M-369
76OPC-283
76SSPC-46
76T-283
77Padre/SchCd-25
77T-659
78T-566
79T-48
80T-402
90Mother/A's-27M
91Crown/Orio-377
92Mother/Padre-27M
92Pol/Padre-14CO
92Pol/Padre-26M

92Smok/Padre-24CO
93Mother/Padre-28M
93Rang/Keeb-306CO
Retzer, Ed
83Madis/Frit-10
83Tacom-31
Retzer, Ken
62T-594R
63J-94
63P-94
63T-471
64T-277
65OPC-278
65T-278
Reulbach, Ed
10Domino-101
11Helmar-100
12Sweet/Pin-88
14CJ-80
15CJ-80
69Bz-12
72F/FFeat-29
90HOF/St-12
90Target-658
92Conlon/Sport-549
E254
E286
E91
E95
M116
S74-67
T202
T204
T205
T206
T207
T213/blue
T215/blue
T215/brown
T222
WG3-40
Reuschel, Paul
73Wichita-13
74Wichita-112
77T-333
77T-634M
78SSPC/270-247
78T-663
79T-511
Reuschel, Rick
73OPC-482
73T-482
74OPC-136
74T-136
74T/St-18
75Ho-51
75OPC-153
75T-153
75T/M-153
76Ho-17
76Ho/Twink-17
76OPC-359
76SSPC-301
76T-359
77BurgChef-193
77Ho-103
77Ho/Twink-103
77OPC-214
77T-530
77T-634M
78Ho-131
78K-45
78OPC-56
78SSPC/270-245
78T-50
79Ho-67
79K-47
79OPC-123
79T-240
80OPC-99
80T-175
81Coke
81D-561
81F-293
81F/St-93
81OPC-205
81T-645
81T/HT
81T/St-157
81T/Tr-822
82D-157
82F-50
82OPC-204
82T-405
84SevenUp-47
85Cram/PCL-230
85F-63
85F/Up-U88
85OPC-306
85T-306
85T/Tr-93T
86D-532
86F-618
86F/Slug-27
86F/St-95
86Leaf-207
86T-779
86T/Mini-57
86T/St-126
86T/Tatt-7M
87D-188
87F-619
87OPC-154
87RedFoley/St-129
87T-521
87T/St-128
88D-613
88D/AS-52
88D/Best-218
88F-94
88F/LL-32
88F/St-130
88KennerFig-89
88Leaf-219
88Mother/Giants-15
88OPC-278
88S-519
88Sf-136
88T-660
88T/Big-188
88T/Mini-76
88T/Revco-13
88T/RiteAid-30
89B-466
89D-11DK
89D-335
89D/Best-162
89D/DKsuper-11DK
89F-340
89Mother/Giants-15
89OPC-65
89Panini/St-210
89S-5
89S/HotStar-22
89Sf-72
89T-65
89T/LJN-3
89T/Mini-42
89T/St-79
89T/UK-63
89UD-194
90B-223
90D-112
90D-663AS
90F-68
90F/Can-68
90KayBee-25
90Kenner/Fig-68
90MLBPA/Pins-23
90Mother/Giant-8
90OPC-190
90OPC/BoxB-L
90Panini/St-206M
90Panini/St-370
90PublInt/St-79
90RedFoley/St-77
90S-465
90S/100St-7
90Sf-161
90T-190
90T/Big-328
90T/Gloss22-10
90T/Gloss60-18
90T/Mini-87
90T/St-154AS
90T/St-89
90T/WaxBox-L
90UD-696
90Woolwth/HL-18
91D-518
91F-270
91Mother/Giant-14
91OPC-422
91S-544
91T-422
91UD-249
92Cub/OldStyle-19
92Yank/WIZ80-156
Reuss, Jerry
70OPC-96R
70T-96R
71OPC-158
71T-158
72T-775
73OPC-446
73T-446
74OPC-116
74T-116
74T/St-38
75OPC-124
75T-124
75T/M-124
76Crane-47
76Ho-29
76Ho/Twink-29
76K-43
76MSA/Disc
76OPC-60
76SSPC-562
76T-60
77BurgChef-181
77Ho-119
77Ho/Twink-119
77OPC-97
77Pep-65
77T-645
78T-255
79T-536
80Pol/Dodg-41
80T-318
81D-417
81F-118
81OPC-153
81Pol/Dodg-41
81T-440
81T/HT
81T/So-103
81T/St-181
82D-284
82F-18
82F/St-7
82OPC-278
82Pol/Dodg-41
82T-710
82T/St-259M
82T/St-56
83D-158
83F-216
83F/St-26M
83F/St-6M
83OPC-90
83OPC/St-247
83Pol/Dodg-41
83T-90
83T/Fold-1M
83T/St-247
84D-418
84F-110
84Nes/792-170
84OPC-170
84Pol/Dodg-41
84T-170
84T/St-81
85Coke/Dodg-26
85D-226
85F-380
85OPC-66
85T-680
86Coke/Dodg-25
86D-104
86F-141
86OPC-236
86Pol/Dodg-41
86Sf-53M
86T-577
86T/St-66
87F-451
87OPC-373
87Pol/Dodg-21
87Smok/Dodg-28
87T-682
88Coke/WS-23
88S-270
88S/Tr-61T
88Smok/Dodg-6M
88T-216
89B-57
89Coke/WS-22
89D-413
89D/Best-305
89F-510
89S-489
89T-357
89UD-151
90D-528
90F-335
90F/Can-335
90KayBee-26
90OPC-424
90PublInt/St-400
90T-424
90Target-659
90UD-96
Reuteman, R.C.
(AGM)
88Tidew/CANDL-26
Reutter, Derrick
83Kinston/Team-18
Revak, Ray
86Greens-19
Revelle, R.H.
(Dutch)
T206
Revenig, Todd
90SoOreg/Best-8
90SoOreg/ProC-3445
91Madison/ProC-2130
92B-198
92Huntsvl/ProC-3950
92Huntsvl/SB-319
92Sky/AASingl-136
93StCl/A's-26
93T-766
93T/Gold-766
Revering, Dave
76Indianap-7
77Indianap-4
78T-706R
79Ho-139
79OPC-113
79T-224
80OPC-227
80T-438
80T/S-58
80T/Super-58
81A's/Granny-13
81D-117
81F-576
81F/St-4
81OPC-57
81T-568
81T/So-22
81T/St-117
81T/Tr-823
82D-234
82F-51
82OPC-109
82T-109
82T/Tr-97T
83F-484
83OPC-291
83T-677
85Indianap-29
92Yank/WIZ80-157
Rex, Mike
76Cedar
79Phoenix
80Phoenix/NBank-11
81Phoenix-11
82Phoenix
Rey, Everett
81Chatt-9
82Chatt-3
83BuffB-12
Reyan, Julio
88Belling/Legoe-8
89Belling/Legoe-2
91Belling/ProC-3661
Reyes, Alberto
92Albany/ClBest-19
92Albany/ProC-2305
93BurlB/ClBest-21
93BurlB/ProC-157
93LimeR/Winter-2
Reyes, Amner
90Bend/Legoe-24
Reyes, Basilo
84Idaho/Team-22
Reyes, Carlos Alberto
92Macon/ClBest-20
92Macon/ProC-265
94B-492
94Finest-302
94L-296
94Ultra-410
Reyes, Carlos
86Ashvl-22
Reyes, Gilberto
85Cram/PCL-170
86Albuq-20
86D-581
87Albuq/Pol-17
87Pol/Dodg-7
88Albuq/CMC-21
88Albuq/ProC-257
89Indianap/CMC-11
89Indianap/ProC-1240
90Target-1053
91B-447
91F/UltraUp-U92
91F/Up-U99
91Leaf-451
92D-381
92F-489
92OPC-286
92Panini-201
92Pinn-428
92S-229
92StCl-173
92T-286
92T/Gold-286
92T/GoldWin-286
92UD-230
92Ultra-225
93LimeR/Winter-71
Reyes, Giovanny
86Cram/NWL-77
86QuadC-26
87QuadC-5
88PalmSp/Cal-109
Reyes, Jesus
73Cedar
74Cedar
Reyes, Jose 1
77Clinton
80OrlanTw-7
82OrlanTw/A-22
Reyes, Jose 2
90Bend/Legoe-13
Reyes, Joselito
84Memphis-21
85Kingst-18
86Omaha/ProC-18
Reyes, Juan
86Beloit-19
89BendB/Legoe-6
89Bristol/Star-22
91Clinton/ClBest-9
91Clinton/ProC-833
Reyes, Nap
45Playball-35
Reyes, Pablo
85Kingst-9
86Ventura-22
Reyes, Rafael
91Rockford/ClBest-11
91Rockford/ProC-2046
Reyes, Sergio
91Hunting/ClBest-19
91Hunting/ProC-3349
Reyes, Steve
88Billings/ProC-1810
Reyes, Victor
90Butte/SportP-20
Reyes, Wascar
78Charl
Reyna, Dion
88Madis-19
Reyna, Luis
86Ventura-23
87Knoxvl-9
88Syrac/CMC-12
88Syrac/ProC-810
Reyna, Paul
85Fresno/Pol-28M
Reynolds, Allie
47TipTop
48B-14
49B-114
50B-138
50Drake-28
51B-109
51BR-C3
51T/RB-6
52BR
52Dix
52StarCal-84A
52StarCal/L-70A

52T-67
52TipTop
53B/Col-68
53Dix
53NB
53T-141
54B-113
54NYJour
55Armour-16
55B-201
61F-69
75Sheraton-5
77Galasso-33
79TCMA-185
88Pac/Leg-41
89Swell-101
91Crown/Orio-378
91T/Arc53-141
92Bz/Quadra-5M
92Yank/WIZAS-62
93AP/ASG-135
PM10/L-33
R346-21
R423-89

Reynolds, Archie
71MLB/St-356
71OPC-664R
71T-664R
72T-672

Reynolds, Carl
29Exh/4-20
30CEA/Pin-19
31Exh/4-20
32Orbit/num-2
32Orbit/un-50
33CJ/Pin-18
33G-120
35BU-49
35BU-95
35G-1G
35G-3E
35G-5E
35G-6E
91Conlon/Sport-80
R300
R305
R310
R315-C4
V354-12
V94-38

Reynolds, Charles
N172

Reynolds, Craig
76OPC-596R
76SSPC-582
76T-596R
77T-474R
78T-199
79K-51
79OPC-251
79T-482
80OPC-71
80T-129
81D-378
81F-74
81OPC-12
81T-617
81T/St-46
82D-344
82F-225
82OPC-57
82T-57
83D-317
83F-460
83T-328
84D-405
84F-237
84Mother/Ast-26
84Nes/792-776
84T-776
85D-328
85F-357
85Mother/Ast-14
85OPC-156
85T-156
85T/St-65
86D-232
86F-309
86Leaf-107
86Mother/Ast-18
86OPC-298
86Pol/Ast-13
86T-298
87D-384
87D/OD-19
87F-66
87Mother/Ast-19
87OPC-298
87Pol/Ast-10
87T-779
88D-209
88F-454
88Leaf-205
88Mother/Ast-19
88OPC-18
88Panini/St-297
88Pol/Ast-19
88S-207
88T-557
88T/Big-219
89B-328
89D-477
89F-366
89Lennox/Ast-15
89Mother/Ast-18
89S-468
89T-428
89T/Big-312
89UD-284
90OPC-637
90PublInt/St-100
90T-637

Reynolds, Dave
86AppFx-19
87Penin-11
88Tampa/Star-21
89Saraso/Star-20
90BirmB/Best-21
90BirmB/ProC-1109

Reynolds, Don
78Padre/FamFun-24
79Hawaii-13
79T-292
80Hawaii-23
88SanBern/Best-28
88SanBern/Cal-55
91AA/LineD-575M
91Jacks/LineD-575CO
91Jacks/ProC-941CO
92Jacks/ProC-4016CO
92Jacks/SB-350M

Reynolds, Doug
89Erie/Star-18
90Freder/Team-9
91Freder/ClBest-14
91Freder/ProC-2368
91Kane/Team-17

Reynolds, Harold
81Wausau-18
82LynnS-17
83SLCity-22
84Cram/PCL-185
85Mother/Mar-23
86Calgary-23
86D-484
86T-769
87D-489
87D/OD-117
87F-596
87Mother/Sea-10
87T-91
87T/St-216
88D-563
88D/AS-13
88D/Best-304
88F-388
88F/AwardWin-32
88F/Mini-53
88F/RecSet-31
88F/St-62
88Leaf-227
88Mother/Sea-10
88OPC-7
88Panini/St-188
88S-277
88Sf-127
88T-485
88T/Big-142
88T/Mini-35
88T/Revco-19
88T/St-221
88T/UK-60
89B-210
89Classic-147
89D-21DK
89D-93
89D/AS-27
89D/Best-51
89D/DKsuper-21DK
89F-558
89F/BBAS-34
89F/Heroes-33
89F/LL-31
89KMart/DT-13
89KennerFig-112
89Mother/Sea-10
89OPC-208
89Panini/St-436
89RedFoley/St-96
89S-310
89S/HotStar-82
89Sf-165
89T-580
89T/Big-2
89T/LJN-80
89T/Mini-74
89T/St-226
89T/St/Backs-5
89UD-249
90B-478
90Classic-128
90D-227
90D/BestAL-138
90F-524
90F/AwardWin-27
90F/Can-524
90HotPlay/St-33
90Leaf-140
90MLBPA/Pins-118
90Mother/Mar-6
90OPC-161
90Panini/St-144
90PublInt/St-294
90PublInt/St-441
90S-167
90S/100St-43
90Sf-119
90T-161
90T/Big-321
90T/DH-51
90T/HeadsUp-17
90T/Mini-34
90T/St-221
90UD-179
91B-252
91Classic/200-47
91CounHrth-3
91D-175
91F-460
91Leaf-297
91Leaf/Stud-119
91OPC-260
91Panini/FrSt-229
91Panini/St-191
91Panini/Top15-111
91Panini/Top15-55
91S-48
91Seven/3DCoin-13NW
91StCl-217
91T-260
91UD-148
91UD-32TC
91Ultra-343
92B-503
92D-239
92F-291
92L-38
92L/BlkGold-38
92Mother/Mar-3
92OPC-670
92Panini-56
92Pinn-59
92S-250
92StCl-181
92Studio-239
92T-670
92T/Gold-670
92T/GoldWin-670
92T/Kids-123
92TripleP-203
92UD-314
92Ultra-129
93B-57
93D-639
93F-680
93F/Final-165
93Flair-156
93L-370
93OPC-279
93OPC/Premier-89
93Pac/Spanish-349
93Pinn-530
93S-559
93Select-134
93Select/RookTr-14T
93StCl-23
93StCl-668
93StCl/1stDay-23
93StCl/1stDay-668
93Studio-129
93T-757
93T/Finest-50
93T/FinestRef-50
93T/Gold-757
93UD-35CH
93UD-803
93Ultra-499
94D-271
94F-17
94L-428
94Pac/Cr-43
94Panini-22
94Pinn-475
94S-441
94T-355
94T/Gold-355
94UD-423
94Ultra-332

Reynolds, Jeff
83Syrac-19
86Jaxvl/TCMA-21
87Indianap-16
88Toledo/CMC-15
88Toledo/ProC-585
89Nashvl/Team-19

Reynolds, Ken
71OPC-664R
71T-664R
72OPC-252
72T-252
73OPC-638
73T-638
76SSPC-292
78Syrac
79Syrac/TCMA-19
79Syrac/Team-15
89Geneva/ProC-1885CO

Reynolds, Larry
80Tulsa-9
81Tulsa-7
82ArkTr-21
83ArkTr-22
84ArkTr-9

Reynolds, Mark
85Osceola/Team-14

Reynolds, Mike
79Richm-2
82Richm-18
84Richm-1
85Durham-30
86Durham-22

Reynolds, Neil
87SLCity/Taco-5

Reynolds, Robert J.
(R.J.)
81VeroB-17
84Cram/PCL-148
84F/X-U97
85Coke/Dodg-27
85D-128
85F-381
85T-369
86D-552
86F-619
86F/Mini-120
86Leaf-212
86OPC-306
86T-417
87D-65
87F-620
87GenMills/Book-5M
87OPC-109
87RedFoley/St-77
87Sf/TPrev-18M
87Stuart-10M
87T-109
87T/St-134
88D-65
88D/Best-201
88F-339
88OPC-27
88Panini/St-379
88S-34
88T-27
89D-134
89D/Best-257
89F-219
89S-91
89T-658
89UD-315
89VFJuice-23
90D-447
90F-478
90F/Can-478
90Homer/Pirate-25
90Leaf-381
90OPC-592
90PublInt/St-163
90S-469
90T-592
90T/St-126
90Target-660
90UD-540
91D-101
91F-48
91OPC-198
91S-273
91T-198
91UD-150

Reynolds, Robert
71OPC-664R
71T-664R
72OPC-162R
72T-162R
73JP
73OPC-612R
73T-612R
74OPC-259
74T-259
75OPC-142
75T-142
75T/M-142
82Iowa-28GM

Reynolds, Ronn
82Jacks-11
84Tidew-25
86F-92
86Phill/TastyK-29
86Portl-19
86T-649
87Phill/TastyK-29
87T-471
87Tucson-20
88Denver/CMC-16
88Denver/ProC-1262
90AAASingl/ProC-15
90LasVegas/CMC-12
90LasVegas/ProC-127
90ProC/Singl-515
91Pac/SenLg-109
91WIZMets-328

Reynolds, Shane
89AubAs/ProC-2161
90ColMud/Best-12
90ColMud/ProC-1345
91AA/LineD-572
91ClBest/Singl-67
91Jacks/LineD-572
91Jacks/ProC-926
92B-327
92D/Rook-102
92Sky/AAASingl-275
92Tucson/ProC-485
92Tucson/SB-617
93D-164
93Pinn-254
93S-282
93T-522
93T/Gold-522
94S-586
94Select-196
94Ultra-511

Reynolds, Thomas D.
(Tommie)
64T-528R
65T-333
67T-487
68A's/JITB-12
69T-467
70OPC-259
70T-259
71OPC-676
71T-676
75IntLgAS/Broder-26
75PCL/AS-26
75Sacra/Caruso-3
77Spoka
78Spokane/Cramer-15
78Spokane/Team-14
86Modesto-21MG

87Modesto-23MG
88Huntsvl/BK-15
89Mother/A's-27M
90Mother/A's-27M
91Mother/A's-28CO
91WIZMets-329
92Mother/A's-28M
93Mother/A's-27M
Reynolds, Tim
83Cedar-9
83Cedar/Frit-1
Reynolds, William
86Cram/NWL-56
Reynoso, Armando
91AAA/LineD-438
91AAAGame/ProC-38
91Brave/Dubuq/Stand-31
91Richm/Bob-14
91Richm/LineD-438
91Richm/ProC-2566
91Richm/Team-1
92F-367
92OPC-631
92Richm/Bleach-7
92Richm/Comix-15
92Richm/ProC-375
92Richm/SB-437
92S-877
92Sky/AAASingl-201
92Sky/AAASingl-296
92StCl-763
92T-631
92T/91Debut-145
92T/Gold-631
92T/GoldWin-631
92UD-674
92USPlayC/Brave-3C
92USPlayC/Brave-5H
93D-752
93F/Final-41
93L-454
93Pac/Jugador-35
93Pac/Spanish-436
93Select/RookTr-38T
93StCl-652
93StCl/1stDay-652
93T/Tr-116T
93UD-793
93UD/SP-224
94B-198
94D-497
94F-451
94F/RookSen-15
94Flair-157
94L-148
94OPC-114
94Pac/Cr-205
94Pinn-220
94Pinn/Artist-220
94Pinn/Museum-220
94S-227
94S/GoldR-227
94StCl-332
94StCl/1stDay-332
94StCl/Gold-332
94StCl/Team-103
94T-49
94T/Finest-14
94T/FinestRef-14
94T/Gold-49
94TripleP-230
94UD-348
94UD/CollC-238
94UD/CollC/Gold-238
94UD/CollC/Silv-238
94Ultra-188
Reynoso, Gabriel
92MedHat/ProC-3209
92MedHat/SportP-21
Reynoso, Henry
90Beloit/Best-19
90Beloit/Star-17
Rhea, Allen
90StCath/ProC-3469
Rhein, Jeff
92AubAs/ClBest-7
92AubAs/ProC-1367
Rhem, Charles
(Flint)
33DH-35
33G-136
35G-8L
35G-9L
87Conlon/2-52
88Conlon/4-23
91Conlon/Sport-325
V354-5
Rhiel, William
90Target-661
R314
R314/Can
V355-81
Rhine, Kendall
94ClBest/Gold-17
Rhinehart, Dallas
92Boise/ProC-3624
Rhoades, James
88Augusta/ProC-387
Rhoads, Robert
T206
T213/brown
T3-114
Rhodas, Kevin
83Miami-10
Rhoden, Rick
74Albuq/Team-15
75OPC-618R
75T-618R
75T/M-618R
76OPC-439
76SSPC-72
76T-439
77BurgChef-148
77OPC-57
77T-245
78OPC-159
78SSPC/270-59
78T-605
79OPC-66
79T-145
80Port-27
80T-92
81F-377
81OPC-312
81T-312
82D-423
82F-493
82T-513
82T/St-82
83D-250
83F-318
83F/St-4M
83OPC-181
83T-781
84D-552
84F-261
84Nes/792-485
84Nes/792-696TL
84OPC-46
84T-485
84T-696TL
85D-552
85F-474
85F/St-97
85Leaf-63
85OPC-53
85T-695
85T/St-127
86D-166
86D/HL-20
86F-620
86OPC-232
86T-232
86T-756M
86T/St-130
86T/Tatt-9M
87D-10DK
87D-435
87D/AAS-24
87D/DKsuper-10
87F-621
87F/Up-U103
87Leaf-10DK
87OPC-365
87RedFoley/St-103
87Sf-129
87Sf/TPrev-7M
87Smok/Dodg-29
87T-365
87T/Mini-31
87T/St-130
87T/Tr-101T
88D-128
88D/Best-161
88D/Y/Bk-128
88F-219
88F/SS-30
88F/St-51
88Leaf-98
88OPC-185
88Panini/St-149
88RedFoley/St-74
88S-74
88Sf-104
88Sf/Gamewin-16
88T-185
88T/Big-108
88T/St-298
89B-323
89D-429
89D/Tr-40
89F-266
89F/Up-89
89Lennox/Ast-3
89Mother/Ast-24
89OPC-18
89Panini/St-399
89S-317
89Smok/Dodg-87
89T-18
89T/Big-237
89T/DHTest-23
89UD-56
90F-235
90F/Can-235
90OPC-588
90PublInt/St-101
90T-588
90Target-662
90UD-504
92Yank/WIZ80-158
Rhodes, Arthur Lee
(Art)
89Erie/Star-19
90Freder/Team-29
91AA/LineD-244
91B-95
91ClBest/Gold-14
91ClBest/Singl-335
91Hagers/LineD-244
91Hagers/ProC-2457
91Leaf/GRook-BC6
91UD/FinalEd-13F
92B-631
92Classic/Game200-146
92Classic/I-75
92D-727
92F-24
92L-394
92L/BlkGold-394
92OPC-771
92Pinn-251
92ProC/Tomorrow-6
92RochR/ProC-1939
92RochR/SB-464
92S-736
92S/Impact-35
92S/Rook-7
92Sky/AAASingl-211
92StCl-641
92T-771
92T/91Debut-146
92T/Gold-771
92T/GoldWin-771
92UD-17SR
93B-169
93D-133
93F-174
93F/RookSenII-8
93L-397
93OPC-329
93Pac/Spanish-350
93Pinn-326
93S-360
93Select-300
93Select/ChasRook-14
93StCl-560
93StCl/1stDay-560
93T-554
93T/Gold-554
93ToysRUs-28
93UD-384
93USPlayC/Rook-6C
93Ultra-500
94D-299
94F-18
94Finest-335
94OPC-17
94StCl-129
94StCl/1stDay-129
94StCl/Gold-129
94StCl/Team-280
94T-477
94T/Gold-477
94Ultra-309
Rhodes, Charles
T206
Rhodes, Dusty
89Helena/SP-27
91Helena/SportP-29CO
Rhodes, Gordon
28Exh/PCL-22
Rhodes, Harry(Lefty)
92Negro/RetortII-34
Rhodes, James L.
(Dusty)
54NYJour
54T-170
55Gol/Giants-24
55RM-NL22
55SM
55T-1
55T/DH-27
56T-50
56T/Hocus-A4
56T/Hocus-B6
57T-61
61Union
79TCMA-190
91T/Arc53-299
93Conlon-983
94T/Arc54-170
94TedW/54-23
Rhodes, Jeff
83Cedar-24
83Cedar/Frit-15
Rhodes, Karl
(Tuffy)
87Ashvl-1
88FSLAS/Star-18
88Osceola/Star-22
89ColMud/Best-22
89ColMud/ProC-142
89ColMud/Star-19
90AAASingl/ProC-208
90B-79
90ProC/Singl-620
90Tucson/CMC-18
90Tucson/ProC-218
91B-544
91Classic/200-72
91D-698
91F-514
91Leaf-195
91Mother/Ast-14
91OPC-516
91S-365RP
91S/Rook40-32
91StCl-52
91T-516
91T/90Debut-130
91UD-466
91UD/Ext-702M
92StCl-241
92Tucson/SB-618
93Ultra-395
94B-222
94Finest-330
94Flair-140
94L-356
94Pac/Cr-106
94Pinn-497
94S-447
94Select-141
94StCl/Team-344
94Studio-62
94T-657
94T/Gold-657
94UD-492
94Ultra-463
Rhodes, Mike
83ArkTr-1
86ArkTr-17
89FtLaud/Star-20
89Star/Wax-79
90Greens/Best-24
90Greens/ProC-2676
90Greens/Star-17
Rhodes, Ricky
89Oneonta/ProC-2123
90A&AASingle/ProC-86
90Foil/Best-249
90Greens/Best-11
90Greens/ProC-2663
90Greens/Star-18
90ProC/Singl-823
91ClBest/Singl-235
91PrWill/ClBest-11
91PrWill/ProC-1427
92FtLaud/ClBest-22
92FtLaud/ProC-2610
92FtLaud/Team-26
Rhodriguez, Rory
91Princet/ClBest-22
91Princet/ProC-3513
Rhomberg, Kevin
78Watlo
80Tacom-20
81Chatt-23
82Charl-17
83Charl-17
85Cram/PCL-193
88Chatt/Team-26
88Lookout-26
Rhown, Bobby
52Park-4
Rhyne, Hal
28Exh/PCL-23
29Exh/4-18
31Exh/4-18
33Exh/4-9
91Conlon/Sport-195
Rial, Carey
88MissSt-39M
Rial, Cliff
89MissSt-45M
Ribant, Dennis
65OPC-73
65T-73
66T-241
67Kahn
67T-527
67T/Test/PP-3
68CokeCap/Tiger-13
68T-326
69T-463
81TCMA-443
91WIZMets-330
Ribbie
85Coke/WS
86Coke/WS
87Coke/WS-30M
Ricanelli, John
76QuadC
78Cr/PCL-69
Riccelli, Frank
74OPC-599R
74T-599R
75Lafay
76Phoenix/Coke-18
77Phoenix
78Spring/Wiener-17
80T-247
81Buffa-24
82Syrac-6
89Pac/SenLg-59
91Pac/SenLg-67
Ricci, Chuck
89Watlo/ProC-1783
89Watlo/Star-24
91Freder/ClBest-7
91Freder/ProC-2362
92Hagers/ProC-2554
Ricci, Frank
82Nashvl-19
83Beaum-17
Ricciardi, J.P.
88SoOreg/ProC-1714
Riccitant, Chuck
90Freder/Team-26
Rice, Andy
94T-208FDP
94T/Gold-208FDP
Rice, Charles
94ClBest/Gold-77
Rice, David
89BendB/Legoe-9
Rice, Del
47TipTop
49Eureka-195
50B-125
51B-156
52B-107
52T-100
53B/Col-53
53Hunter
53T-68
54B-30
54Hunter
54RM-NL9

55B-106
55Hunter
57T-193
58T-51
59T-104
60T-248
61T-448
72T-718MG
91Crown/Orio-379
91T/Arc53-68
Exh47
R302-112
R423-87
Rice, Edgar
(Sam)
21Exh-140
29Exh/4-32
31Exh/4-32
33DH-36
33G-134
34DS-32
60F-34
61F-70
76Rowe-10M
76Shakey-93
77Galasso-108
80Perez/HOF-93
80SSPC/HOF
91Conlon/Sport-54
92Conlon/Sport-436
93Conlon-887
94Conlon-1256
D327
D328-137
E120
E121/120
E121/80
E122
E126-29
E135-137
E210-3
E220
R316
V100
V354-18
W501-14
W502-36
W514-79
W572
W575
WG7-44
Rice, Gary
91Adelaide/Fut-2
Rice, Grantland
90LitSun-5
Rice, Hal
51B-300
52T-398
53T-93
54B-219
54T-95
55B-52
91T/Arc53-93
94T/Arc54-95
Rice, Harry F.
29Exh/4-23
91Conlon/Sport-216
R316
Rice, Jim
75OPC-616R
75SSPC/Puzzle-21
75T-616R
75T/M-616R
76Ho-127
76K-10
76OPC-340
76SSPC-405
76T-340
77BurgChef-29
77Ho/Twink-23
77OPC-62
77T-60
78Ho-45
78K-49
78OPC-163
78OPC-2LL
78PapaG/Disc-14
78SSPC/270-189
78T-202LL
78T-670
78Wiffle/Discs-61
79Ho-2
79K-15
79OPC-210
79T-2LL
79T-3LL
79T-400
79T/Comics-2
80BK/PHR-20
80K-46
80OPC-112
80T-200
80T/S-5
80T/Super-5
81Coke
81D-338
81Drake-8
81F-222
81F/St-53
81K-9
81OPC-68
81PermaGr/CC-23
81Sqt-7
81T-500
81T/HT
81T/Nat/Super-11
81T/So-13
81T/St-41
82Coke/Bos
82D-200
82Drake-27
82F-305
82F/St-163
82FBI/Disc-16
82KMart
82OPC-366
82T-750
82T/St-150
83D-208
83Drake-22
83F-194
83F/St-26M
83F/St-6M
83K-13
83OPC-30
83OPC/St-37
83PermaGr/AS-4
83PermaGr/CC-31
83T-30
83T-381TL
83T/Fold-2M
83T/Fold-3M
83T/St-37
84D-50
84D/AAS-52
84D/Champs-4
84Drake-25
84F-408
84F/St-20
84F/St-37
84Nes/792-132LL
84Nes/792-133LL
84Nes/792-401AS
84Nes/792-550
84Nestle/DT-5
84OPC-184AS
84OPC-364
84Ralston-9
84Seven-15E
84T-132LL
84T-133LL
84T-401
84T-550
84T/Cereal-9
84T/Gloss22-6
84T/Gloss40-22
84T/RD-16M
84T/St-102A
84T/St-189
84T/St-200B
84T/St-217
84T/Super-5
85D-15DK
85D-50
85D/AAS-27
85D/DKsuper-15
85Drake-25
85F-168
85F/LimEd-27
85F/St-13
85F/St-23
85FunFoodPin-5
85GenMills-22
85Leaf-15
85OPC-150
85Seven-2W
85Seven-4E
85Sportflic/Test-1
85T-150
85T/3D-6
85T/Gloss40-6
85T/RD-14M
85T/St-208
85T/Super-50
86BK/AP-8
86D-213
86D/AAS-16
86D/PopUp-16
86Dorman-20
86Drake-13
86F-358
86F/Mini-76
86F/St-96
86GenMills/Book-1M
86Jiffy-1
86Leaf-146
86Meadow/Stat-14
86OPC-320
86Quaker-30
86Seven/Coin-C5M
86Seven/Coin-E5M
86Seven/Coin-S5M
86Seven/Coin-W5M
86Sf-139M
86Sf-146M
86Sf-17
86Sf-52M
86Sf-61M
86Sf/Dec-57
86T-320
86T/3D-23
86T/Gloss22-6
86T/Gloss60-36
86T/St-161
86T/St-246
86T/Super-43
86T/Tatt-20M
86TrueVal-7
86Woolwth-28
87BK-16
87Classic-59
87D-92
87D/AAS-45
87D/OD-182
87Drake-15
87F-41
87F-633M
87F/Excit-37
87F/HL-6
87F/Lim-35
87F/Mini-89
87F/St-99
87Jiffy-19
87KMart-18
87KayBee-26
87Kraft-5
87Leaf-247
87OPC-146
87OPC/WaxBox-F
87RedFoley/St-44
87Seven-E14
87Seven-ME14
87Sf-80M
87Sf-97
87Sf/TPrev-9M
87Sportflic/DealP-3
87T-480
87T-610AS
87T/Board-5
87T/Coins-21
87T/Gloss60-42
87T/HL-27
87T/HL-5
87T/Mini-44
87T/St-17
87T/St-248
87T/WaxBox-F
87Woolwth-27
87Woolwth-5
88ChefBoy-21
88D-399
88D/Best-28
88D/RedSox/Bk-399
88F-361
88KennerFig-90
88Leaf-215
88OPC-61
88Panini/St-33
88S-14
88Sf-158
88T-662TBC
88T-675
88T/Big-181
88T/St-247
89B-33
89D-122
89F-97
89KMart/Lead-9
89KennerFig-113
89OPC-245
89OPC/BoxB-I
89Panini/St-281
89S-85
89Sf-173
89T-245
89T/Big-18
89T/LJN-119
89T/St-256
89T/WaxBox-I
89UD-413
90KMart/CBatL-9
90KayBee-27
90MLBPA/Pins-70
90OPC-785
90OPC/BoxB-M
90PublInt/St-463
90T-785
90T/Ames-3
90T/HillsHM-8
90T/WaxBox-M
90UD-373
91Pac/SenLg-148
92K/CornAS-8
92K/FrAS-7
93AP/ASG-166
93YooHoo-14
Rice, Lance
88GreatF-7
89AS/Cal-5
89Bakers/Cal-192
90Calgary/CMC-4
90Calgary/ProC-650
90SanAn/GS-23
91AA/LineD-539
91Calgary/LineD-70
91Calgary/ProC-515
91Classic/III-76
91SanAn/LineD-539
91SanAn/ProC-2979
92F-658
92S-423
92SanAn/ProC-3978
92T/91Debut-147
Rice, Pat
87Wausau-24
88SanBern/Best-6
88SanBern/Cal-43
89Wmsprt/ProC-646
89Wmsprt/Star-18
90AAASingl/ProC-115
90ProC/Singl-431
91AAA/LineD-70
92Calgary/ProC-3730
92Calgary/SB-69
92Sky/AAASingl-32
Rice, Pete
83AlexD-8
85Nashua-19
86Nashua-22
87Salem-7
88Toledo/CMC-23
88Toledo/ProC-598
Rice, Tim
86WinSalem-22
87Pittsfld-24
88BBCity/Star-20
Rice, Woolsey
83Beloit/Frit-2
Rich, Woody
R303/A
V351B-38
Richard, Henri
72Dimanche*-98IA
72Dimanche*-99
Richard, J.R.
72OPC-101R
72T-101R
74OPC-522
74T-522
74T/St-36
75OPC-73
75T-73
75T/M-73
76Ho-110
76OPC-625
76T-625
77BurgChef-1
77Ho-112
77Ho/Twink-112
77OPC-227
77T-260
78BK/Ast-4
78Ho-92
78OPC-149
78T-470
79Ho-29
79K-10
79OPC-310
79T-203RB
79T-590
79T-6LL
79T/Comics-23
80BK/PHR-8
80K-57
80OPC-28
80T-206LL
80T-207LL
80T-50
80T/S-25
80T/Super-25
81Coke
81D-140
81F-56
81F/St-44
81K-16
81MSA/Disc-26
81OPC-350
81T-350
82F-226
82OPC-190
82T-190
86Mother/Ast-21
Richard, Lee
(Bee Bee)
72OPC-476
72T-476
75OPC-653
75T-653
75T/M-653
76OPC-533
76SSPC-145
76T-533
Richard, Maurice
45Parade*-49
Richard, Ron
91Yakima/ClBest-4
91Yakima/ProC-4255
Richardi, Rick
85Miami-13
87Miami-8
88Miami/Star-20
Richards, Dave T.
88Fayette/ProC-1095
89Lakeland/Star-18
90London/ProC-1267
91AA/LineD-343
91Jaxvl/LineD-343
91Jaxvl/ProC-150
92ArkTr/ProC-1129
92ElPaso/ProC-3919
Richards, Dave
78LodiD
81Albuq/TCMA-8
81Hawaii-2
82Hawaii-2
Richards, Eugene
(Gene)
76Hawaii
77Padre/SchCd-23
77T-473R
78Padre/FamFun-25
78T-292
79T-364
80OPC-323
80T-616
81D-4
81F-486
81F/St-17
81OPC-171
81T-171
81T/So-86
81T/St-225
82D-499
82F-580
82F/St-104
82OPC-253
82T-708
82T/St-103
83D-271
83F-370

83OPC-7
83OPC/St-294
83T-7
83T/St-294
84D-429
84F-310
84F/X-U98
84Nes/792-594
84T-594
84T/Tr-99T
85F-619
85T-434
89Pac/SenLg-48
89T/SenLg-63
89TM/SenLg-90
90EliteSenLg-102
91AA/LineD-450M
91London/LineD-450CO
91MidldA/OneHour-21
91MidldA/ProC-450
92AS/Cal-52
92PalmSp/ClBest-29CO
92PalmSp/ProC-857CO
Richards, Fred
(Fuzzy)
53Mother-50
Richards, Kevin
81Tulsa-22
82Tulsa-8
Richards, Nicky
83CharR-2
Richards, Paul
33G-142
44Playball-5
51B-195MG
52B-93MG
52T-305MG
53B/Col-39MG
54Wilson
55B-225MG
60L-112MG
60T-224MG
61T-131MG
61T-566AS
81Tiger/Detroit-40
88Conlon/5-25
90Target-663
91T/Arc53-322MG
93Conlon-765
Richards, Rusty
87Sumter-8
89Richm/Bob-22
89Richm/CMC-7
89Richm/Ko-40
89Richm/ProC-829
90AAASingl/ProC-404
90ProC/Singl-280
90Richm/Bob-17
90Richm/CMC-4
90Richm/ProC-259
90Richm/Team-27
90T/89Debut-99
91AAA/LineD-439
91Richm/Bob-4
91Richm/LineD-439
91Richm/Team-9
92OrlanSR/SB-518
92Sky/AASingl-225
92TX-33
Richards, Ryan
91OKSt-21
Richards, Todd
80Batavia-4
81Batavia-6
Richards, Vincent
33SK*-23
Richardson, A.H.
(Hardy)
N172
N284
N526
Scrapps
WG1-23
WG1-43
Richardson, A.J.
88Visalia/Cal-157
88Visalia/ProC-87
89OrlanTw/Best-23
89OrlanTw/ProC-1346
Richardson, Bobby
57T-286
58T-101
59T-237M
59T-76
60T-405
61NuCard-415
61P-8
61T-180
61T/Dice-13
62AmTract-43A
62AmTract-43B
62AmTract-43C
62AmTract-43D
62J-2
62P-2
62P/Can-2
62Salada-64
62Shirriff-64
62T-65
62T/St-90
63F-25
63J-13
63Kahn
63P-13
63Salada-52
63T-173M
63T-420
63T/SO
64T-190
64T/Coins-123AS
64T/Coins-72
64T/SU
64T/St-12
64Wheat/St-38
65MacGregor-9
65OPC-115
65T-115
65T/E-65
65T/trans-26
66T-490
66T/RO-56
66T/RO-77
77Galasso-247
78TCMA-112
81TCMA-477M
88Pac/Leg-74
89Swell-49
90HOF/St-61
90Pac/Legend-100
91LineD-4
91Swell/Great-75
92AP/ASG-31
92Yank/WIZ60-104
92Yank/WIZAS-63
93UD/ATH-107
94TedW-63
94TedW/54-28
Exh47
WG10-20
WG9-21
Richardson, Brian
92GulfCD/ProC-3575
Richardson, C.N.
29Exh/4-24
Richardson, Daniel
(Danny)
90Target-664
E223
N167-9
N172
N284
N338/2
N690
Richardson, David
89Spring/Best-16
90Louisvl/LBC-35
90StPete/Star-20
91AAA/LineD-244
91Louisvl/LineD-244
91Louisvl/ProC-2915
Richardson, Don
86WinSalem-23
Richardson, Eric
92StCl/Dome-153
Richardson, Gordon
62Pepp/Tul
63Pep/Tul
66OPC-51
66T-51
81TCMA-460
91WIZMets-331
Richardson, James
88Kinston/Star-19
89Kinston/Star-20
Richardson, Jeffrey Scott 1
85LitFalls-9
86Lynch-18
87Lynch-24
88PalmSp/Cal-92
88PalmSp/ProC-1463
89PalmSp/Cal-51
89PalmSp/ProC-469
91B-198
91T/90Debut-131
Richardson, Jeffrey Scott 2
87Tampa-12
88Chatt/Best-22
89Nashvl/CMC-18
89Nashvl/ProC-1291
89Nashvl/Team-20
90AAASingl/ProC-497
90BuffB/CMC-12
90BuffB/ProC-382
90BuffB/Team-20
90ProC/Singl-12
90T/89Debut-100
91AAA/LineD-43
91BuffB/LineD-43
91BuffB/ProC-550
92BuffB/BlueS-17
92BuffB/ProC-328
92BuffB/SB-40
92Sky/AAASingl-18
93T/Tr-81T
Richardson, Jim
87Watlo-3
88Alaska/Team-14
Richardson, Jon
78Richm
79Richm-7
Richardson, Keith
88Watertn/Pucko-1
90Harris/ProC-1191
90Harris/Star-16
Richardson, Kenny
78Newar
Richardson, Kerry
87Kinston-23
88Wmsprt/ProC-1328
Richardson, Lenny
88CapeCod/Sum-5
Richardson, Mike
89Erie/Star-20
89Salem/Star-17
89Star/Wax-95
90Freder/Team-6
Richardson, Milt
88Eugene/Best-27
89Eugene/Best-18
Richardson, Ron
83MidldC-18
Richardson, Ronnie
87Elmira/Black-27
87Elmira/Cain-4
87Elmira/Red-27
88Lynch/Star-20
Richardson, Scott
92Helena/ProC-1723
Richardson, Tim
86Hagers-15
87Hagers-19
90HagersDG/Best-21
Richardson, Tracey
90Watertn/Star-28
Richardt, Mike
79Ashvl/TCMA-26
80CharCh-8
83D-368
83F-575
83F/St-11M
83Rang-2
83T-371
84Nes/792-641
84T-641
93Rang/Keeb-307
Richartz, Scott
75AppFx
76AppFx
Richbourg, Lance
29Exh/4-2
31Exh/4-2
33Exh/4-1
93Conlon-701
R316
Richer, Troy
92AS/Cal-35
Richert, Pete
62T-131
63T-383
64T-51
65OPC-252
65T-252
66Bz-43
66OPC-95
66T-95
66T/RO-36
66T/RO-78
67Bz-43
67CokeCap/Senator-4
67T-590
68CokeCap/Orio-12
68T-354
69MLBPA/Pin-24
69OPC-86
69T-86
70T-601
71MLB/St-311
71OPC-273
71T-273
72T-649
73OPC-239
73T-239
74OPC-348
74T-348
74T/Tr-348T
88Modesto-2CO
88Modesto/Cal-82CO
89Modesto/Cal-287CO
89Modesto/Chong-2CO
90Modesto/Cal-172CO
90Modesto/Chong-34CO
90Modesto/ProC-2230CO
90Target-665
91Crown/Orio-380
91Modesto/ClBest-18CO
91Modesto/ProC-3107CO
92AS/Cal-22
92Modesto/ProC-3911CO
93Modesto/ClBest-27CO
93Modesto/ProC-816CO
Richey, Jeff
92Everett/ClBest-20
92Everett/ProC-1687
94FExcel-294
Richey, Rodney
88Idaho/ProC-1838
89Sumter/ProC-1104
90Durham/Team-24
Richie, Bennie
83Visalia/Frit-19
84Visalia-1
Richie, Lewis
10Domino-102
11Helmar-101
12Sweet/Pin-89
E90/1
M116
T202
T204
T205
Richie, Rob
88BBAmer-3
88EastLAS/ProC-11
88GlenF/ProC-925
89AAA/CMC-29
89Toledo/ProC-765
90OPC-146
90T-146
90T/89Debut-101
90TripleAAS/CMC-29
90UD-76SR
Richmond, Bob
87Clinton-25
Richmond, Clarence
91Kissim/ProC-4203
92GulfCD/ProC-3582
Richmond, Don
51B-264
V362-43
Richmond, Ryan
89Pittsfld/Star-21
89Star/IISingl-161
90Clmbia/PCPII-3
90Columbia/GS-18
Richter
11Helmar-102
Richter, Francis C.
90LitSun-4
Rick, Dean
78Salem
Ricker, Drew
86Cram/NWL-9
86Everett/Pop-24
87Clinton-22
Ricker, Troy
85Utica-22
86James-19
87James-13
88Rockford-31
89Rockford-31
89WPalmB/Star-19
90James/Pucko-25
90Rockford/ProC-2708
90Rockford/Team-23
91WPalmB/ClBest-28
91WPalmB/ProC-1242
92ClBest-297
92Visalia/ClBest-22
92Visalia/ProC-1027
93FExcel/ML-35
Rickert, Marv
47TipTop
52T-50
Rickert, Rick
49Eureka-18
Ricketts, Dave
65T-581R
66Pep/Tul
67T-589
68OPC-46
68T-46
69MB-233
69T-232
70T-626
72MB-288
73OPC-517CO
73T-517C
90T/TVCard-4CO
Ricketts, Dick
59T-137
60T-236
Rickey, Ralph
73Wichita-14
Rickey, W. Branch
14CJ-133
15CJ-133
60F-55
76Shakey-106
77Galasso-124
80Perez/HOF-105
80SSPC/HOF
82Ohio/HOF-29
89HOF/St-91
90BBWit-101
92Yank/WIZHOF-27
93CrackJack-12
V100
W754
Rickman, Andy
88Greens/ProC-1568
89Cedar/Best-13
89Cedar/ProC-932
89Cedar/Star-15
Ricks, Ed
89Madis/Star-19
Rico, Alfredo
70T-552R
Rico, Carlos
92AZ/Pol-14
Rico, Ron
92Helena/ProC-1714
Riconda, Harry
90Target-666
Riddle, David
89Erie/Star-21
89SanDiegoSt/Smok-25
90Foil/Best-317
90ProC/Singl-693
90Wausau/Best-12
90Wausau/ProC-2125
90Wausau/Star-19
91Freder/ClBest-8
91Freder/ProC-2363
Riddle, Elmer
43Playball-28
49Eureka-170
W711/2
Riddle, John L.
(Johnny)
45Playball-42
53T-274
54Hunter
54T-147
55Hunter
55T-98
75Cedar
91T/Arc53-274
94T/Arc54-147
Riddleberger, Dennis
71OPC-93R

71T-93R
72T-642
73OPC-157
73T-157
Riddoch, Greg
88Smok/Padres-24CO
90Padre/MagUno-22CO
90T/Tr-102T
91OPC-109MG
91Padre/Coke-7MG
91Padre/MagRal-1MG
91T-109MG
92Mother/Padre-1MG
92OPC-351MG
92Padre/Carl-16MG
92Pol/Padre-15MG
92Smok/Padre-25MG
92T-351MG
92T/Gold-351MG
92T/GoldWin-351MG
Riddoch, Rory
92SanBern/ClBest-30TR
Rideau, Greg
92BurlInd/ClBest-14
92BurlInd/ProC-1654
Ridenour, Dana
87FtLaud-9
88Albany/ProC-1342
88EastLAS/ProC-4
89Wmsprt/ProC-647
90EastLAS/ProC-EL18
90Foil/Best-55
90Wmsprt/Best-20
90Wmsprt/ProC-1057
90Wmsprt/Star-21
91AAA/LineD-192
91AAAGame/ProC-16
91Indianap/LineD-192
91Indianap/ProC-460
92Indianap/ProC-1856
92Indianap/SB-190
Ridenour, Ryan
90Batavia/ProC-3069
Ridzik, Steve
53B/BW-48
54B-223
55B-111
57T-123
60Maple-17
60T-489
61BeeHive-18
64T-92
65OPC-211
65T-211
66T-294
Riechart, Pete
92Modesto/ClBest-26CO
Riel, Franich
40Hughes-16
Riemer, Matt
92Bluefld/ClBest-17
92Bluefld/ProC-2368
Riemer, Robin
86Cram/NWL-183
Riemer, Tim
89Watertn/Star-19
Riesgo, Nikco
88Spokane/ProC-1936
89CharRain/ProC-995
90FSLAS/Star-16
90StLucie/Star-22
90Star/ISingl-10
91B-536
91Reading/ProC-1375
92ProC/Tomorrow-298
92T/91Debut-148
Riewerts, Tom
82AubAs-15
Rigby, Kevin
81Durham-3
Riggar, Butch
79Holyo-18
Riggert, Joe
90Target-667
Riggins, Mark A.
81ArkTr-14
82ArkTr-7
83StPete-11
86ArkTr-18CO
87Spring/Best-2CO
89Louisvl/CMC-24CO
89Louisvl/ProC-1254
90AAASingl/ProC-534CO
90Louisvl/CMC-28CO
90Louisvl/LBC-4CO
90Louisvl/ProC-420CO
90ProC/Singl-679CO
90T/TVCard-62CO
91AAA/LineD-250CO
91Louisvl/LineD-250CO
91Louisvl/ProC-2933CO
91Louisvl/Team-31
92Louisvl/ProC-1903CO
Riggleman, James D.
75Water
77ArkTr
79ArkTr-5
80ArkTr-4
81ArkTr-19
83StPete-29
86ArkTr-19MG
87ArkTr-7MG
88ArkTr/GS-4MG
90T/TVCard-5CO
91AAA/LineD-299MG
91LasVegas/LineD-299MG
91LasVegas/ProC-253MG
92LasVegas/ProC-2809MG
92LasVegas/SB-249MG
93Mother/Padre-1MG
93T-513M
93T/Gold-513M
Riggs, Jim
82Oneonta-2
83Greens-22
85Albany-18
86Albany/TCMA-1
Riggs, Kevin
90Billings/ProC-3231
91Cedar/ClBest-19
91Cedar/ProC-2728
92Cedar/ClBest-18
92Cedar/ProC-1081
92MidwLAS/Team-35
94ClBest/Gold-176
94FExcel-84
Riggs, Lew
34DS-96
37Exh/4-4
38Exh/4-4
39PlayBall-77
40PlayBall-78
41DP-141
90Target-668
92Conlon/Sport-567
R314
W711/1
W711/2
Righetti, Dave
79WHave-21
80Colum-17
81Colum-9
82D-73
82F-52
82T-439
83D-199
83F-395
83OPC-176
83T-176
83T-81
84D-103
84D-10DK
84D/AAS-59
84F-139
84F-639IA
84F/St-86
84Nes/792-5HL
84Nes/792-635
84OPC-277
84T-5HL
84T-635
84T/Gloss40-28
84T/RD-24M
84T/St-287B
84T/St-315
85D-336
85D/HL-37
85Drake-40
85F-142
85F/St-102
85FunFoodPin-116
85Leaf-219
85OPC-260
85Pol/MetYank-Y5
85Seven-13E
85T-260
85T/RD-24M
85T/St-314
85T/Super-58
86D-214
86D/HL-52
86F-116
86F/Mini-25
86F/St-97
86GenMills/Book-1M
86Leaf-89
86OPC-34
86Seven/Coin-E10M
86Sf-141M
86Sf-41
86Sf-72M
86Sf/Rook-48M
86T-560
86T/St-303
86T/Super-44
86T/Tatt-11M
87Classic-86
87D-128
87D/AAS-55
87F-111
87F-627M
87F/AwardWin-32
87F/Hottest-31
87F/Mini-90
87F/RecSet-32
87F/Slug-34
87F/St-100
87F/WaxBox-C12
87KayBee-27
87Leaf-53
87MSA/Discs-20
87OPC-40
87Seven-E9
87Sf-119M
87Sf-194M
87Sf-57
87Sf/TPrev-7M
87T-40
87T-5RB
87T-616AS
87T/Coins-22
87T/Gloss60-24
87T/HL-14
87T/Mini-67
87T/St-299
87T/St-8
87T/St-9
87Woolwth-14
88Bz-16
88D-93
88D/AS-29
88D/Best-164
88D/Y/Bk-93
88F-220
88F-625M
88F/AwardWin-33
88F/Mini-43
88F/RecSet-32
88F/Slug-33
88F/St-52
88F/TL-29
88KMart-20
88KennerFig-91
88Leaf-57
88Nestle-28
88OPC-155
88Panini/St-150
88RedFoley/St-75
88S-351
88Sf-135
88Sf/Gamewin-19
88T-790
88T/Mini-29
88T/St-300
88T/St/Backs-66
88Woolwth-16
89B-167
89D-78
89D/Best-76
89F-267
89KennerFig-114
89OPC-335
89Panini/St-400
89RedFoley/St-97
89S-225
89S/HotStar-37
89S/NWest-6
89Sf-158
89T-335
89T/DHTest-18
89T/LJN-126
89T/St-307
89UD-59
90B-426
90Classic-41
90D-311
90D/BestAL-136
90D/Learning-14
90F-453
90F/Can-453
90Kenner/Fig-69
90OPC-160
90Panini/St-124
90PublInt/St-545
90RedFoley/St-79
90S-194
90S/100St-39
90S/NWest-16
90Sf-88
90T-160
90T/Big-102
90T/TVYank-18
90UD-479
91B-632
91BBBest/RecBr-12
91Classic/200-87
91D-21DK
91D-275
91D/SuperDK-21DK
91F-677
91F/Up-U131
91Leaf-301
91Leaf/Stud-258
91Mother/Giant-8
91OPC-410
91OPC/Premier-99
91PG&E-15
91Panini/FrSt-332
91Panini/St-266
91RedFoley/St-77
91S-24
91S/100SS-68
91S/RookTr-53T
91SFExam/Giant-12
91StCl-356
91T-410
91T/Tr-96T
91UD-448
91UD/Ext-778
92B-324
92Classic/Game200-43
92D-174
92F-647
92Giant/PGE-30
92L-135
92L/BlkGold-135
92Mother/Giant-8
92OPC-35
92Panini-219
92Pinn-82
92S-260
92StCl-107
92T-35
92T/Gold-35
92T/GoldWin-35
92T/Kids-62
92TripleP-23
92UD-171
92UD/TmMVPHolo-42
92Ultra-594
92Yank/WIZ70-133
92Yank/WIZ80-159
92Yank/WIZAS-64
93D-552
93F-537
93Mother/Giant-10
93Pac/Spanish-614
93StCl-431
93StCl/1stDay-431
93StCl/Giant-2
93T-310
93T/Gold-310
93UD-579
94Pac/Cr-553
Righetti, Lou
57Seattle/Pop-30
Righetti, Steve
78Ashvl
79Ashvl/TCMA-15
Rightnowar, Ron
87Fayette-24
88Lakeland/Star-22
89London/ProC-1369
90London/ProC-1268
91Toledo/ProC-1931
92Toledo/ProC-1043
Riginos, Tom
88CapeCod/Sum-58
Rigler, Cy
21Exh-141
94Conlon-1202UMP
Rigney, Emory E.
(Topper)
21Exh-142
25Exh-94
26Exh-69
93Conlon-728
E120
E210-38
V61-17
W573
Rigney, John D.
41DP-72
47TipTop
94Conlon-1225
Rigney, William J.
(Bill)
48B-32
49B-170
49Eureka-123
50B-117
51B-125
52BR
52NTea
52T-125
53B/BW-3
58PacBell-6MG
58SFCallB-19MG
60MacGregor-18
60T-225MG
60T-7M
61T-225MG
62T-549MG
63T-294MG
64T-383MG
65OPC-66MG
65T-66MG
66T-249MG
67T-494MG
68T-416MG
69OPC-182MG
69T-182MG
70OPC-426MG
70T-426MG
71OPC-532MG
71T-532MG
72OPC-389MG
72T-389MG
78Twin/Frisz-20MG
81TCMA-457MG
89Smok/Angels-1
91T/Arc53-328
92Bz/Quadra-19M
PM10/Sm-156
Rigoli, Joe
79Newar-3
83Erie-2
85Louisvl-2
86Erie-25MG
87Erie-3
Rigos, John
83Erie-3
85Spring-1
86StPete-27
87Salem-14
88Harris/ProC-834
Rigsby, Rickey
88Pulaski/ProC-1761
89Idaho/ProC-2013
Rigsby, Tim
90Miami/I/Star-21
90Miami/I/Star-26
91Kinston/ClBest-19
91Kinston/ProC-331
Rijo, Jose
84F/X-U99
84T/Tr-100T
85Cram/PCL-133
85D-492
85F-143
85T-238
86D-522
86D/HL-2
86F-431
86Mother/A's-13
86T-536
87D-55
87F-404

87Leaf-119
87Sf/TPrev-23M
87T-34
88D-548
88F/Up-U86
88Kahn/Reds-27
88S-392
88S/Tr-27T
88T-316
88T/Tr-92T
89B-300
89Classic-141
89D-375
89D/Best-278
89F-168
89Kahn/Reds-27
89OPC-135
89Panini/St-68
89S-552
89S/YS/I-31
89T-135
89T/Mini-12
89T/St-140
89UD-619
90B-45
90D-115
90F-430
90F/Can-430
90Kahn/Reds-24
90Leaf-282
90OPC-627
90Panini/St-243
90PublInt/St-38
90S-511
90T-627
90T/Big-257
90T/St-137
90UD-216
91B-681
91Classic/200-109
91Classic/I-97
91Classic/II-T31
91CollAB-27
91D-722
91D-742WS
91F-79
91F/WS-7
91Kahn/Reds-27
91KingB/Discs-24
91Leaf-326
91OPC-493
91Panini/FrSt-134
91Pep/Reds-18
91Pep/SS-5
91S-658
91StCl-11
91T-493
91T/CJMini/I-9
91UD-298
91Ultra-102
91Woolwth/HL-31
91Woolwth/HL-33
92B-680
92Classic/Game200-77
92D-223
92F-419
92L-139
92L/BlkGold-139
92MooTown-3
92OPC-220
92Panini-269
92Pinn-508
92Reds/Kahn-27
92S-232
92S/100SS-43
92S/Impact-83
92StCl-800
92Studio-26
92T-220
92T/Gold-220
92T/GoldWin-220
92T/Kids-42
92UD-258
92UD-712DS
92UD/TmMVPHolo-43
92USPlayC/Ace-13S
92Ultra-196
92Yank/WIZ80-160
93B-62
93Colla/DM-88
93D-454
93F-41
93F/Fruit-53
93Flair-31
93HumDum/Can-29
93KingB-8
93L-411
93MSA/Ben-15
93OPC-286
93Pac/Beisbol-21
93Pac/Spanish-88
93Pac/SpanishGold-9
93Pac/SpanishP-5
93Panini-289
93Pinn-77
93Reds/Kahn-20
93S-105
93Select-163
93StCl-233
93StCl/1stDay-233
93Studio-211
93T-165
93T/Finest-24
93T/FinestRef-24
93T/Gold-165
93T/Hill-20
93UD-226
93UD-473
93UD/SP-213
93USPlayC/Ace-6S
93Ultra-33
94B-402
94D-361
94D/MVP-3
94D/Special-361
94F-421
94F/Smoke-9
94Finest-308
94Flair-148
94L-340
94OPC-50
94Oscar-28
94Pac/AllLat-10
94Pac/Cr-156
94Panini-15
94Panini-167
94Pinn-322
94RedFoley-35
94S-52
94S/GoldR-52
94Select-40
94Sf/2000-112
94Studio-171
94T-705
94T/Gold-705
94TripleP-218
94TripleP/Medal-14M
94UD-143
94UD/CollC-239
94UD/CollC/Gold-239
94UD/CollC/Silv-239
94UD/ElecD-143
94UD/SP-161
94Ultra-476
94Ultra/LL-10
94Ultra/Strike-4

Rijo, Rafael
89Salem/Team-26
90Yakima/Team-13
91VeroB/ClBest-25
91VeroB/ProC-790
92Rockford/ClBest-27
92Rockford/ProC-2128

Riker, Robert
90Bristol/ProC-3161
90Bristol/Star-20

Riles, Earnest
83ElPaso-21
84Cram/PCL-35
85Cram/PCL-207
85F/Up-U89
86D-359
86F-499
86F/LL-34
86F/Mini-102
86F/St-98
86Jay's-14
86KayBee-26
86Leaf-161
86Pol/Brew-1
86Seven/Coin-C13M
86Sf-16
86T-398
86T/Gloss60-40
86T/St-310
87D-151
87F-355
87F/GameWin-36
87F/Mini-91
87Leaf-66
87OPC-318
87Pol/Brew-1
87Sf/TPrev-19M
87T-523
87T/St-203
88D-478
88F-172
88F/Up-U130
88Pol/Brew-1
88S-349
88S/Tr-57T
88T-88
88T/Tr-93T
89B-475
89Classic-87
89D-625
89D/Best-50
89F-341
89Gard-14
89Mother/Giants-16
89S-458
89T-676
89UD-497
90B-239
90D-131
90ElPasoATG/Team-9
90F-69
90F/Can-69
90Mother/Giant-15
90OPC-732
90PublInt/St-80
90S-447
90T-732
90T/St-81
90UD-378
91B-217
91D-461
91F-271
91F/UltraUp-U47
91F/Up-U51
91Leaf-358
91Mother/A's-16
91OPC-408
91S-626
91S/RookTr-55T
91StCl-432
91T-408
91T/Tr-97T
91UD/Ext-780
92OPC-187
92S-222
92T-187
92T/Gold-187
92T/GoldWin-187
92Tucson/ProC-498
92UD-494
94F-40

Riley, Darren
85Cedar-24
86FSLAS-41
86Tampa-16
87Vermont-25
88Chatt/Best-24
91Parramatta/Fut-5

Riley, Ed
89Elmira/Pucko-14
90WinHaven/Star-22
91LynchRS/ClBest-7
91LynchRS/ProC-1196
92NewBrit/ProC-431
92NewBrit/SB-493
92Sky/AASingl-212
93ClBest/MLG-29
93FExcel/ML-136

Riley, George
80Wichita-20
81D-588
81T-514
83Reading-8
84Cram/PCL-206

Riley, Jim
92Everett/ClBest-16
92Everett/ProC-1688

Riley, Marquis
92Boise/ClBest-1
92Boise/ProC-3644
92Classic/DP-48
92FrRow/DP-26
93StCl/MurphyS-199
94B-263
94FExcel-32

Riley, Mike
79Wisco-3
82Cedar-6

Riley, P.J.
89AubAs/ProC-2180

Riley, Randy
84Newar-1

Riley, Tim
77DaytB

Riley, Tom
83Cedar-16
83Cedar/Frit-5
84Cedar-15
85Cedar-31

Rima, Tom
74Cedar
75Dubuq

Rincon, Andrew
(Andy)
80ArkTr-9
81Louisvl-17
81T-244R
82Louisvl-24
82T-135
83Louisvl/Riley-17
89ArkTr/GS-20
90Savan/ProC-2084CO

Rincones, Hector
81Water-16
83Water-13
84Wichita/Rock-3
85Cram/PCL-157
86Memphis/GoldT-22
86Memphis/SilverT-22

Rineer, Jeff
78RochR
79RochR-16
80RochR-8
91Crown/Orio-381

Rinehart, Dallas
92Boise/ClBest-21

Rinehart, Robert Jr.
86Columbia-22

Riner, Willard
89GA-25MG
90GA-25MG

Rines, Doug
89TNTech-22

Ring, Dave
90Elmira/Pucko-20

Ring, James J.
21Exh-143
26Exh-39
28Exh-22
88Pac/8Men-87
92Conlon/Sport-614
E120
E126-24
E220
V100
V61-120
W516-11

Ringgold, Keith
90Everett/Best-27
90Everett/ProC-3143
91BendB/ClBest-19
91BendB/ProC-3708

Ringkamp, Mark
92FtMyr/ProC-2745
92Miracle/ClBest-9

Ringler, Tim
88Knoxvl/Best-22
89Knoxvl/Best-30
89Knoxvl/ProC-1122

Rings, Frank
N172

Riopelle, Howie
(Rip)
45Parade*-50

Rios, Armando
92LSU/McDag-9
93LSU/McDag-4

Rios, Carlos Rafael
78Charl
81Buffa-19
82Knoxvl-15
85IntLgAS-5
85Richm-15
86Greenvl/Team-15
87Greenvl/Best-5
88Richm-6
88Richm/CMC-18
88Richm/ProC-8
89Richm/Bob-23
89Richm/CMC-13
89Richm/Ko-6
89Richm/ProC-842

Rios, Carlos
(Coronel)
77AppFx

Rios, Enrique
87Kenosha-29
88CLAS/Star-16
88Lynch/Star-21

Rios, Jesus
85Tigres-1

Rios, Juan
69T-619R
70OPC-89
70T-89
72MB-289

Ripken, Bill
86SLAS-1
87D/Rook-16
87French-3
87RochR-12
87RochR/TCMA-13
87Sf/Rook-28
88Classic/Red-163
88D-336
88D-625M
88D/Best-254
88F-569
88F-640M
88French-7
88Leaf-134
88MSA/Disc-7
88OPC-352
88Panini/St-9
88S-200
88S/YS/I-20
88Sf-216
88T-352
88T/JumboR-1
88T/St-227
88ToysRUs-25
89B-12
89D-259
89D/Best-318
89F-616
89French-3
89OPC-22
89Panini/St-261
89RedFoley/St-98
89S-18
89T-571
89T/Big-27
89UD-283
90B-256
90D-164
90F-186
90F/Can-186
90HagersDG/Best-22
90Leaf-271
90MLBPA/Pins-113
90OPC-468
90Panini/St-3
90PublInt/St-583
90S-174
90T-468
90T/Big-244
90T/St-235
90UD-184
91B-87
91Crown/Orio-382
91D-167
91F-489
91Leaf-7
91OPC-677
91Panini/FrSt-241
91S-487
91Seven/3DCoin-12A
91StCl-222
91T-677
91UD-550
91Ultra-23
92B-373
92D-734
92F-25
92L-184
92L/BlkGold-184
92OPC-752
92Panini-66
92Pinn-336
92S-97
92StCl-533
92T-752

92T/Gold-752
92T/GoldWin-752
92UD-250
92UD-82M
92Ultra-10
93B-517
93D-59
93F-550
93F/Final-282
93L-435
93OPC/Premier-59
93Pac/Spanish-645
93Panini-72
93Pinn-153
93Rang/Keeb-427
93StCl-603
93StCl/1stDay-603
93StCl/Rang-29
93UD-181
93UD-511
93Ultra-635
94Finest-339
94StCl-369
94StCl/1stDay-369
94StCl/Gold-369
94StCl/Team-268

Ripken, Cal Jr.
80CharlO/Pol-17
80CharlO/W3TV-17
81RochR-15
82D-405
82F-176
82T-21R
82T/Tr-98T
83D-279
83D/AAS-52
83Drake-23
83F-70
83F/St-10M
83F/St-3M
83OPC-163
83OPC/St-26
83OPC/St-315
83T-163
83T/St-26
83T/St-315
84D-106
84D/AAS-20
84D/Champs-48
84Drake-26
84F-17
84F/St-15
84F/St-29
84MiltBrad-20
84Nes/792-400AS
84Nes/792-426TL
84Nes/792-490
84Nestle/DT-4
84OPC-2AS
84OPC-363
84Seven-14E
84T-400AS
84T-426TL
84T-490
84T/RD-30M
84T/St-197
84T/St-204
84T/St-24
84T/St/Box-13
84T/Super-1
85D-14DK
85D-169
85D/AAS-7
85D/DKsuper-14
85Drake-26
85F-187
85F-626IA
85F/LimEd-28
85F/St-41
85FunFoodPin-118
85Leaf-14DK
85OPC-30
85Seven-14E
85T-30
85T-704AS
85T/3D-16
85T/Gloss22-16
85T/Gloss40-24
85T/RD-31M
85T/St-185
85T/St-197
85T/Super-48
85ThomMc/Discs-17
86BK/AP-15
86D-210
86D/AAS-14
86D/PopUp-14
86Dorman-4
86Drake-11
86F-284
86F-633M
86F/AS-5
86F/LL-35
86F/LimEd-36
86F/Mini-59
86F/Slug-28
86F/St-99
86GenMills/Book-1M
86Jiffy-9
86Leaf-142
86Meadow/Blank-11
86Meadow/Milk-8
86Meadow/Stat-11
86OPC-340
86Quaker-31
86Seven/Coin-C3M
86Seven/Coin-E3M
86Seven/Coin-S3M
86Seven/Coin-W3M
86Sf-128M
86Sf-54M
86Sf-59M
86Sf-69M
86Sf-73M
86Sf-8
86Sf/Dec-73M
86Sf/Rook-48M
86T-340
86T-715AS
86T/Gloss22-5
86T/Gloss60-14
86T/Mini-2
86T/St-159
86T/St-226
86T/Super-45
86T/Tatt-4M
86TrueVal-22
87Classic-52
87D-89
87D/AAS-5
87D/HL-38
87D/OD-133
87D/PopUp-5
87Drake-6
87F-478
87F/AwardWin-33
87F/BB-36
87F/GameWin-37
87F/Mini-92
87F/Slug-35
87F/St-101
87French-8
87Jiffy-8
87Kraft-3
87Leaf-98
87MSA/Discs-14
87MnM's-13
87OPC-312
87Ralston-12
87RedFoley/St-118
87Seven-ME16
87Sf-113M
87Sf-9
87Sf/TPrev-21M
87Sportflic/DealP-49
87Stuart-14M
87T-609AS
87T-784
87T/Board-22
87T/Coins-23
87T/Gloss22-16
87T/Gloss60-37
87T/Mini-40
87T/St-151
87T/St-233
88Bz-17
88ChefBoy-7
88Classic/Red-176
88D-171
88D-26DK
88D-625M
88D-BC1
88D/AS-5
88D/Best-198
88D/DKsuper-26DK
88D/PopUp-5
88Drake-25
88F-570
88F-635M
88F-640M
88F/RecSet-33
88F/SS-31
88F/Slug-34
88F/St-3
88F/TL-30
88French-8
88Grenada-74
88KMart-21
88KayBee-25
88KennerFig-92
88KingB/Disc-24
88Leaf-100
88Leaf-26DK
88OPC-74
88Panini/St-13
88Panini/St-230M
88RedFoley/St-76
88S-550
88S-651M
88S/WaxBox-5
88Sf-152
88T-650
88T/Big-62
88T/Coins-24
88T/Gloss22-5
88T/Gloss60-6
88T/RiteAid-13
88T/St-160
88T/St-228
88T/St/Backs-44
88T/UK-61
89B-260FS
89B-9
89Cadaco-44
89Classic-56
89D-51
89D/AS-5
89D/Best-142
89D/MVP-BC15
89D/PopUp-5
89F-617
89F/BBAS-35
89F/Heroes-34
89F/LL-32
89French-8
89KMart/DT-15
89KennerFig-115
89MSA/Disc-16
89Master/Discs-12
89OPC-250
89OPC/BoxB-J
89Panini/St-241AS
89Panini/St-262
89RedFoley/St-99
89S-15
89S/HotStar-77
89S/Mast-3
89Sf-66
89T-250
89T/Big-286
89T/Coins-50
89T/Crunch-6
89T/Gloss22-5
89T/Gloss60-47
89T/LJN-142
89T/St-150
89T/St-237
89T/St/Backs-11
89T/UK-64
89T/WaxBox-J
89Tetley/Discs-16
89UD-467
89UD-682TC
90B-255
90Classic-24
90D-676AS
90D-96
90D/BestAL-57
90D/Bon/MVP-BC18
90D/Learning-19
90F-187
90F-624MVP
90F/ASIns-8
90F/BB-30
90F/BBMVP-31
90F/Can-187
90F/Can-624
90F/Can-634M
90HotPlay/St-34
90KMart/SS-20
90Kenner/Fig-70
90Leaf-197
90MLBPA/Pins-112
90MSA/Soda-4
90OPC-388AS
90OPC-570
90OPC-8RB
90OPC/BoxB-N
90Panini/St-202
90Panini/St-388
90Panini/St-7
90Post-21
90PublInt/St-584
90RedFoley/St-78
90S-2
90S/100St-66
90Sf-100
90Sunflower-23
90T-388AS
90T-570
90T-8RB
90T/Ames-15
90T/Big-327
90T/Coins-24
90T/DH-52
90T/Gloss22-16
90T/Gloss60-51
90T/HillsHM-32
90T/St-160AS
90T/St-231
90T/St-5HL
90T/TVAS-19
90T/WaxBox-N
90UD-266
90USPlayC/AS-6S
90Windwlk/Discs-9
90Woolwth/HL-19
91B-104
91BBBest/RecBr-13
91Cadaco-43
91Classic/200-110
91Classic/II-T3
91Classic/III-77
91Classic/III-xx
91CollAB-2
91Crown/Orio-383
91D-223
91D-52AS
91D-BC17
91D/BC-BC17
91DennyGS-20
91F-490
91JDean-15
91Leaf-430
91Leaf/Stud-9
91MSA/Holsum-20
91MajorLg/Pins-29
91MooTown-14
91OPC-150
91OPC-5RB
91OPC/Premier-100
91Panini/FrSt-170
91Panini/FrSt-243
91Panini/St-192
91Pep/SS-8
91Petro/SU-1
91Post-19
91Post/Can-22
91RedFoley/St-124
91RedFoley/St-78
91S-849FRAN
91S-95
91S/100SS-21
91Seven/3DCoin-13A
91SilverSt-4
91StCl-430
91StCl/Member*-26
91T-150
91T-5RB
91T/CJMini/I-13
91T/SU-28
91UD-347
91UD/FinalEd-85FAS
91USPlayC/AS-13D
91Ultra-24
91Woolwth/HL-18
92B-400
92CJ/DI-13
92Classic/Game200-190
92Classic/I-76
92Classic/II-T56
92Colla/ASG-5
92D-22AS
92D-35
92D-BC1MVP
92D/BC-BC1MVP
92D/DK-DK5
92D/Elite-S1
92D/McDon-1
92D/Preview-10
92DPep/MSA-17
92DennyGS-9
92F-26
92F-703M
92F-711PV
92F/ASIns-20
92F/Lumber-L7
92F/Performer-5
92F/TmLIns-17
92French-13
92Highland-40
92JDean/Living-5
92Kenner/Fig-34
92KingB-12
92L-199M
92L-52
92L/BlkGold-199M
92L/BlkGold-52
92L/GoldPrev-13
92L/Prev-13
92MSA/Ben-6
92MooTown-23
92MrTurkey-19
92OPC-40
92OPC/Premier-137
92P-9
92Panini-275AS
92Panini-68
92Pinn-200
92Pinn/RookI-11M
92Pinn/Slug-14
92Pinn/TeamP-7
92Post/Can-15
92S-433AS
92S-540
92S-788MVP
92S-794MOY
92S-884DT
92S/100SS-89
92S/Proctor-5
92Seven/Coin-9
92StCl-1
92StCl-595MC
92StCl/Dome-154
92StCl/MPhoto-10
92Studio-129
92Studio/Her-7
92Studio/Prev-5
92Sunflower-9
92T-40
92T-400AS
92T/GPro-40
92T/Gold-40
92T/Gold-400AS
92T/GoldWin-40
92T/GoldWin-400AS
92T/Kids-63
92T/McDonB-13
92TripleP-199
92TripleP-253LH
92TripleP/Gal-GS11
92UD-165
92UD-645DS
92UD-82M
92UD/ASFF-36
92UD/HRH-HR4
92UD/TmMVPHolo-1MVP
92UD/TmMVPHolo-44
92USPlayC/Ace-11C
92USPlayC/Ace-8H
92USPlayC/Ace-9D
92Ultra-11
92Ultra/AS-3
92Ultra/AwardWin-21A
92Ultra/AwardWin-21B
92Ultra/AwardWin-5
93B-225
93Cadaco-46
93Classic/GameI-76
93Colla/ASG-9
93Colla/DM-89
93D-559
93D/EliteDom-17
93D/MVP-14
93D/Master-6
93D/Prev-12
93DennyGS-16
93Duracel/PPII-1
93F-551
93F/Atlantic-19

93F/Fruit-54
93Flair-157
93Ho-26
93HumDum/Can-1
93JDean/28-3
93Kenner/Fig-29
93KingB-3
93Kraft-12
93L-431
93L/GoldAS-14
93L/Heading-5
93L/UpGoldAS-6
93MSA/Metz-17
93MilkBone-12
93OPC-352
93OPC/Premier-125
93Orio/SUII-3
93P-9
93Pac/Spanish-24
93Panini-73
93Pinn-20
93Pinn-305HH
93Pinn-471NT
93Pinn/Cooper-17
93Pinn/HRC-47
93Post/Can-7
93S-6
93S/Franchise-1
93Select-18
93Select/ChasS-15
93StCl-40
93StCl/1stDay-40
93StCl/MPhoto-7
93StCl/MurphyS-141
93Studio-80
93T-300
93T/Finest-96AS
93T/FinestASJ-96AS
93T/FinestRef-96AS
93T/Gold-300
93TB/Full-11
93TripleP-3
93TripleP/Act-17
93UD-36CH
93UD-44
93UD-585
93UD/Diam-16
93UD/FunPack-130GS
93UD/FunPack-135
93UD/FunPack-218FOLD
93UD/FunPack-32HERO
93UD/FunPackAS-AS6
93UD/looss-WI15
93UD/SP-8AS
93UD/TCr-TC7
93UD/Then-TN4
93USPlayC/Ace-WCO
93Ultra-501
93Ultra/AS-14
93Ultra/AwardWin-15
94B-75
94Church-7
94D-140M
94D-40
94D/Ann-6
94D/MVP-15
94D/Special-40
94F-19
94F/AS-21
94F/TL-1
94Finest-235
94Flair-8
94Flair/Hot-8
94Kraft-10
94L-1
94L/MVPAL-11
94L/Pr-7
94L/StatStand-10
94OPC-185
94OPC/JAS-15
94Oscar-11
94P-25
94Pac/Cr-44
94Pac/Silv-15
94Panini-23
94Pinn-279
94Pinn-50
94Pinn/Artist-50
94Pinn/Museum-50
94Pinn/Ripken-Set
94Pinn/TeamP-4
94Pinn/Trib-13
94RedFoley-22
94S-85
94S/GoldR-85
94S/GoldS-36
94S/Tomb-26
94Select-NNO
94Sf/2000-179AS
94Sf/2000-69
94StCl-373
94StCl/1stDay-373
94StCl/Dugout-4
94StCl/Gold-373
94StCl/Team-271
94Studio-127
94Studio/S&GStar-7
94T-200
94T-387AS
94T-604ST
94T/BlkGold-18
94T/Gold-200
94T/Gold-387AS
94T/Gold-604ST
94TripleP-159
94TripleP/Medal-7M
94TripleP/Nick-6
94UD-281HFA
94UD-425
94UD/CollC-240
94UD/CollC/Gold-240
94UD/CollC/Silv-240
94UD/DColl-E9
94UD/HoloFX-33
94UD/SP-126
94Ultra-9
94Ultra/AS-4
94Ultra/Career-3
Ripken, Cal Sr.
82D-579
87French-7MG
87T/Tr-102T
88D-625M
88F-635M
88T-444MG
89B-260FS
89French-7
90F-634M
Ripley, Allen
78PapaG/Disc-1
78SSPC/270-188
79T-702R
80T-413
81F-454
81T-144
82D-125
82F-399
82RedLob
82T-529
82T/Tr-99T
83D-57
83F-506
83T-73
Rippelmeyer, Brad
91Idaho/ProC-4333
91Idaho/SportP-3
92Durham/ClBest-13
92Durham/ProC-1105
92Durham/Team-15
Rippelmeyer, Ray
60HenryH-28
60Union-10
61T-276
62T-271
73OPC-486CO
73T-486C
74OPC-119CO
74T-119C
78SSPC/270-36CO
89Nashvl/CMC-24
89Nashvl/ProC-1280
89Nashvl/Team-29CO
90AAASingl/ProC-562CO
90Nashvl/CMC-25CO
90Nashvl/ProC-250CO
90ProC/Singl-150CO
Ripple, Charles
47Centen-23
47Signal
Ripple, Jimmy
28LaPresse-14M
28LaPresse-17
38Exh/4-5
38ONG/Pin-24
39PlayBall-66
41DP-11
41DP-95
44Centen-18
90Target-669
91Conlon/Sport-86
V355-28
Rippley, Steve
88TM/Umpire-49
89TM/Umpire-47
90TM/Umpire-45
Ripslager, Charles
N172/SP
Risberg, Charles
(Swede)
88Pac/8Men-103
88Pac/8Men-16
88Pac/8Men-26
88Pac/8Men-70
94Conlon-1032
W514-105
Riscen, Fred
88SLCity-21
Risley, William
(Bill)
88Greens/ProC-1551
89Cedar/Best-6
89Cedar/ProC-912
89Cedar/Star-16
90A&AASingle/ProC-121
90Cedar/Best-14
90Cedar/ProC-2313
91AA/LineD-166
91Chatt/LineD-166
91Chatt/ProC-1959
92D/Rook-103
92Indianap/ProC-1857
93B-44
93F/Final-96
93Ottawa/ProC-2434
Ritch, Harry
85VeroB-13
Ritchey, Claude
E107
E254
T206
WG3-41
Ritchey, Larry
86Cram/NWL-60
Ritchie, Dave
89Eugene/Best-11
Ritchie, Gregg
86Cram/NWL-5
86Everett/Pop-26
87Clinton-4
88SanJose/Cal-127
88SanJose/ProC-131
89Shrev/ProC-1841
90AAASingl/ProC-51
90Phoenix/CMC-14
90Phoenix/ProC-25
90ProC/Singl-541
91AAA/LineD-391
91Phoenix/LineD-391
91Phoenix/ProC-81
92Phoenix/ProC-2835
92Phoenix/SB-395
Ritchie, Jay
65T-494
Ritchie, Lewis
14Piedmont/St-49
Ritchie, Todd
90Classic/DP-12
90Elizab/Star-19
91B-332
91ClBest/Singl-319
91Classic/I-58
91Kenosha/ClBest-22
91Kenosha/ProC-2072
91MidwLAS/ProC-39
91S-678FDP
92B-524
92ClBest-298
92ProC/Tomorrow-99
92UD/ML-106
92Visalia/ClBest-23
92Visalia/ProC-1014
93ClBest/MLG-44
94B-272
94SigRook-47
Ritchie, Wally
86Clearw-21
87F/Up-U104
87Maine-17
87T/Tr-103T
88D-555
88F-312
88OPC-322
88Phill/TastyK-20
88S-526
88T-494
89ScranWB/CMC-9
89ScranWB/ProC-715
90AAASingl/ProC-300
90ProC/Singl-232
90ScranWB/CMC-6
90ScranWB/ProC-598
91AAA/LineD-493
91ScranWB/LineD-493
91ScranWB/ProC-2536
92D-631
92F-543
92L-443
92L/BlkGold-443
92Phill/Med-25
92S-619
92StCl-324
Ritter, Chris
86PrWill-21
87Harris-25
88Harris/ProC-845
Ritter, Darren
89Pulaski/ProC-1905
90BurlB/Best-25
90BurlB/ProC-2348
90BurlB/Star-22
90Foil/Best-47
91Durham/ProC-DUR6
91DurhamUp/ProC-6
91Macon/ClBest-7
91Macon/ProC-861
92Durham/ClBest-9
92Durham/ProC-1097
92Durham/Team-31
Ritter, Ken
89Medford/Best-15
Ritter, Lawrence
90LitSun-12
Ritter, Louis
(Lou)
90Target-670
E254
T206
Ritter, Reggie
83Watlo/Frit-15
85Water-11
86Maine-16
86OhHenry-53
87BuffB-19
88ColoSp/CMC-7
88ColoSp/ProC-1540
Ritter, William
D328-138
E135-138
Rittman, Alvin
89Belling/Legoe-24
90Spring/Best-2
Rittwage, James
65T-501R
Rittweger, Bill
82Jacks-18
Ritz, Kevin
87GlenF-6
88GlenF/ProC-926
89Toledo/CMC-7
89Toledo/ProC-786
90AAASingl/ProC-377
90B-350
90Classic-131
90CokeK/Tiger-18
90D-415
90F-613
90F/Can-613
90HotRook/St-37
90OPC-237
90ProC/Singl-385
90S-572
90S/100Ris-11
90Sf-29
90T-237
90T/89Debut-102
90Toledo/CMC-8
90Toledo/ProC-147
90UD-98
91AAA/LineD-596
91CokeK/Tiger-31
91Toledo/LineD-596
91Toledo/ProC-1932
92B-419
92L-386
92L/BlkGold-386
92StCl-337
92Ultra-368
93D-99
93F-415
93T-771
93T/Gold-771
Ritz, Trey
92Hamil/ClBest-17
92Hamil/ProC-1603
Rivard, John
89Miami/II/Star-17
Rivas, Javier
91Pulaski/ClBest-15
91Pulaski/ProC-4019
Rivas, Limbert
90Ashvl/ProC-2746
Rivas, Martin
77Charl
Rivas, Oscar
89Belling/Legoe-12
90Penin/Star-17
91SanBern/ProC-1988
Rivas, Rafael
80Utica-31
Rivas, Ralph
83Kinston/Team-19
Rivell, Robert
88CapeCod/Sum-72
91Waterlo/ClBest-19
91Waterlo/ProC-1266
Rivera, Angel
88James/ProC-1900
Rivera, Ben
88Sumter/ProC-410
89Durham/Star-18
89Durham/Team-18
90Durham/UpHer-4
90Greenvl/Best-6
90Greenvl/ProC-1126
90Greenvl/Star-17
91AA/LineD-214
91B-579
91Greenvl/ClBest-3
91Greenvl/LineD-214
91Greenvl/ProC-2997
92D/Rook-104
92F/Up-111
92Phill/Med-45
92Pinn-554
92Ultra-463
93D-412
93F-107
93L-393
93LimeR/Winter-44
93OPC-330
93Pac/Spanish-580
93Phill/Med-28
93Pinn-437
93S-242
93Select-329
93StCl-654
93StCl/1stDay-654
93StCl/Phill-20
93T-622
93T/Gold-622
93UD-389
93Ultra-93
94D-216
94F-599
94Flair-211
94L-213
94Pac/Cr-485
94Phill/Med-26
94Pinn-178
94Pinn/Artist-178
94Pinn/Museum-178
94S-293
94S/GoldR-293
94StCl-252
94StCl/1stDay-252
94StCl/Gold-252
94StCl/Team-232
94T-352
94T/Gold-352
94Ultra-252
Rivera, Carlos
87Fayette-14
88Elmira-11
88WinHaven/Star-21
89Elmira/Pucko-15
Rivera, Dave
77Ashvl
82Charl-22
Rivera, David
91Kenosha/ClBest-6

91Kenosha/ProC-2084
92Visalia/ClBest-18
92Visalia/ProC-1023
Rivera, Elvin
86QuadC-27
87QuadC-16
88Reno/Cal-269
Rivera, Ernesto
92OKSt-25
Rivera, German
78Clinton
83Albuq-17
84Pol/Dodg-25
85Cram/PCL-162
85D-638
85F-382
85T-626
86Nashvl-20
87Toledo-4
87Toledo/TCMA-3
88AAA/ProC-14
88Denver/CMC-12
88Denver/ProC-1253
88TripleA/ASCMC-9
90AAAGame/ProC-9
90AAASingl/ProC-588
90Indianap/ProC-305
90Target-671
Rivera, Hector
89WPalmB/Star-20
90Gate/ProC-3349
90Gate/SportP-20
90Jaxvl/Best-23
90Jaxvl/ProC-1374
90ProC/Singl-670
91AA/LineD-261
91B-444
91Harris/LineD-261
91Harris/ProC-625
Rivera, Jesus
(Bombo)
76Expo/Redp-26
77OPC-54
77T-178
78T-657
78Twin/FriszP-17
79T-449
79Twin/FriszP-24
80OPC-22
80T-43
81D-593
81F-556
81Omaha-23
81T-256
82Omaha-20
83Omaha-19
Rivera, Jose
83Greens-23
83QuadC-23
87Memphis-23
87Memphis/Best-4
88Memphis/Best-25
Rivera, Lino
88CharlR/Star-20
89Fayette/ProC-1573
89SALAS/GS-21
90Lakeland/Star-22
90Star/ISingl-37
91Lakeland/ClBest-11
91Lakeland/ProC-266
92ArkTr/SB-43
Rivera, Luis
83VeroB-13
86Indianap-28
87F-330
87Indianap-27
88T/Big-223
88T/Tr-94T
89B-29
89D-578
89F-392
89OPC-257
89Pawtu/CMC-20
89Pawtu/Dunkin-14
89Pawtu/ProC-697
89S-169
89T-431
89T/St-68
89UD-423
90D-421
90F-285
90F/Can-285
90Leaf-283
90OPC-601
90Pep/RSox-18
90T-601
90T/TVRSox-26
90UD-482
91D-234
91F-112
91Leaf-408
91OPC-338
91Panini/FrSt-267
91Pep/RSox-19
91S-271
91StCl-55
91T-338
91UD-182
91Ultra-42
92B-355
92D-332
92F-48
92L-355
92L/BlkGold-355
92OPC-97
92Panini-88
92Pinn-346
92RedSox/Dunkin-26
92S-159
92StCl-255
92T-97
92T/Gold-97
92T/GoldWin-97
92UD-308
92USPlayC/RedSox-11C
92USPlayC/RedSox-6D
92Ultra-22
93D-591
93F-565
93Pac/Spanish-36
93Panini-94
93Pinn-159
93StCl-533
93StCl/1stDay-533
93T-296
93T/Gold-296
93TripleP-246
93UD-602
93Ultra-515
94Pac/Cr-64
Rivera, Manuel J.
(Jim)
53T-156
54T-34
55T-58
55T/DH-90
56T-70
56T/Hocus-A11
56T/Hocus-B13
56T/Pin-35
57T-107
58T-11
59T-213
60L-55
60T-116
61P-33
61T-367
83Ander-14
84Durham-26
91T/Arc53-156
94T/Arc54-34
Rivera, Mariano
90Tampa/DIMD-17
91Greens/ProC-3058
92B-302
92FtLaud/ProC-2611
93B-327
Rivera, Maximo
93Welland/ClBest-25
93Welland/ProC-3369
Rivera, Oscar
92Belling/ClBest-15
92Belling/ProC-1442
Rivera, Pablo
89CharlK-25
Rivera, Rafael
91Salinas/ClBest-2
91Salinas/ProC-2247
92Salinas/ClBest-9
92Salinas/ProC-3759
Rivera, Ricardo
82AubAs-17
83DayBe-22
Rivera, Roberto
89Burllnd/Star-22
90Watertn/Star-17
91Collnd/ClBest-15
91Collnd/ProC-1482
92Kinston/ClBest-15
92Kinston/ProC-2474
Rivera, Rubén
92GulfCY/ProC-3705
94B-348
94FExcel-113
Rivero, Marty
88Peoria/Ko-26
89WinSalem/Star-14
Rivers, Ken
87Dunedin-27
88Knoxvl/Best-14
89Knoxvl/Best-21
89Knoxvl/ProC-1132
89Knoxvl/Star-17
90Myrtle/ProC-2779
91AA/LineD-441
91London/LineD-441
91MidldA/OneHour-22
91MidldA/ProC-437
Rivers, Mickey Jr.
88Elmira-23
89WinHaven/Star-18
90LynchRS/Team-4
91ClBest/Singl-90
91WinHaven/ClBest-24
91WinHaven/ProC-503
Rivers, Mickey Sr.
72OPC-272
72T-272
73OPC-597
73T-597
74OPC-76
74T-76
75Greyhound-1
75Ho-22
75Ho/Twink-22
75OPC-164
75T-164
75T/M-164
76Ho-102
76K-41
76OPC-198LL
76OPC-85
76SSPC-203
76T-198LL
76T-85
76T/Tr-85T
77BK/Y-18
77BurgChef-180
77K-51
77OPC-69
77T-305
78BK/Y-20
78Ho-110
78K-17
78OPC-182
78SSPC/270-13
78T-690
79BK/Y-20
79OPC-24
79T-60
80OPC-251
80T-485
81D-496
81F-617
81F/St-32
81OPC-145
81T-145
81T/HT
81T/So-31
81T/St-132
82D-242
82F-328
82F/St-174
82OPC-356
82OPC-51IA
82T-704
82T-705IA
82T/St-243
83D-394
83F-576
83OPC-224
83Rang-17
83T-224
83T/Fold-5M
84D-465
84F-425
84Nes/792-504
84OPC-269
84Rang-17
84T-504
84T/St-361
85D-465
85F-565
85Leaf-35
85OPC-371
85T-371
85T/St-355
89Pac/SenLg-163
89T/SenLg-115
89TM/SenLg-91
90EliteSenLg-28
92Yank/WIZ70-134
92Yank/WIZAS-65
93Rang/Keeb-308
Rixey, Eppa
21Exh-144
25Exh-30
26Exh-30
27Exh-15
28Yueng-16
33G-74
61F-71
76Rowe-6M
76Shakey-94
77Galasso-99
80Perez/HOF-94
80SSPC/HOF
82Ohio/HOF-41
89HOF/St-69
91Conlon/Sport-39
93Conlon-906
D327
D328-139
D329-142
D350/2-142
E120
E121/120
E121/80
E122
E135-139
E210
M101/4-142
M101/5-142
V100
V354-32
W501-54
W502-16
W572
W575
Rizza, Jerry
88SoOreg/ProC-1715
90Erie/Star-20
Rizzo, Johnny
39Exh
39PlayBall-11
40PlayBall-108
41DP-124
47Signal
47Sunbeam
90Target-672
93Conlon-944
Rizzo, Mike
83Peoria/Frit-14
Rizzo, Rick
81CharR-23
82FtMyr-1
84Memphis-3
Rizzo, Todd
92Yakima/ClBest-16
92Yakima/ProC-3447
Rizzo, Tom
88Pulaski/ProC-1754
89Sumter/ProC-1087
90Idaho/ProC-3246
Rizzuto, Phil
41DP-62
47HomogBond-39
47TipTop
48B-8
48L-11
49B-98
49Royal-11
50B-11
50Drake-25
51B-26
51BR-A3
51T/CAS
51T/RB-5
52B-52
52BR
52Royal
52StarCal-84C
52StarCal/L-70F
52T-11
52TipTop
52Wheat*
53B/Col-9
53B/Col-93M
53Briggs
53Exh/Can-25
53RM-AL10
53SM
53T-114
54B-1
54DanDee
54NYJour
54RM-AL17
54SM
54T-17
55B-10
55SM
55T-189
56T-113
56T/Pin-29
60NuCard-45
61NuCard-445
61T-471MVP
77Galasso-37
79TCMA-144
80Pac/Leg-82
80Perez/HOF-219
83MLBPA/Pin-15
86Sf/Dec-22
88Pac/Leg-10
89Swell-111
90Pac/Legend-101
91T/Arc53-114
92Bz/Quadra-2M
92Yank/WIZAS-66
93YooHoo-15
94T/Arc54-17
D305
Exh47
PM10/L-34
PM10/Sm-157
Roa, Hector
90Pulaski/Best-17
90Pulaski/ProC-3097
91Miami/ClBest-23
91Miami/ProC-417
92Durham/ClBest-5
92Durham/ProC-1110
92Durham/Team-2
93B-2
93LimeR/Winter-50
Roa, Joe
90Pulaski/Best-9
90Pulaski/ProC-3107
91Macon/ClBest-8
91Macon/ProC-862
92StLucie/ClBest-10
92StLucie/ProC-1746
Roa, Pedro
89Belling/Legoe-19
90Bend/Legoe-27
Roach, Brett
88Bristol/ProC-1884
89Fayette/ProC-1589
Roach, John
N172
Roach, Mel
54T-181
55Gol/Braves-26
55T-117
59T-54
60Lake
60SpicSpan-18
60T-491
61P-163
61T-217
62T-581
94T/Arc54-181
Roach, Petie
92Everett/ClBest-2
92Everett/ProC-1699
Roadcap, Steve
83QuadC-16
86Pittsfld-20
88Wythe/ProC-1991
89Wythe/Star-29MG
90Hunting/ProC-3303MG
91Hunting/ClBest-30MG
91Hunting/ProC-3353MG
92Peoria/ClBest-28MG
92Peoria/Team-21MG
93Peoria/Team-22MG
Roarke, Mike
61T-376
62T-87
63T-224

64T-292
74Wichita-109
83Pawtu-26
90T/TVCard-6CO
92Mother/Padre-27M
92Pol/Padre-26M
92Smok/Padre-26CO
93Mother/Padre-28M

Roarke, Tom
82AubAs-1

Robarge, Dennis
88Elmira-29ASST
89Elmira/Pucko-26

Robbe, Fletcher
53Mother-5

Robben, Roger
89KS*-2

Robbins, Bruce
80Evansvl-18
80T-666R
81D-129
81F-477
81T-79
82Evansvl-6
83BirmB-10

Robbins, Doug
88T/Tr-95T
89T/Big-49
90Foil/Best-53
90Hagers/Best-3
90Hagers/ProC-1416
90Hagers/Star-21
91AA/LineD-245
91Hagers/LineD-245
91Hagers/ProC-2460
92OPC-58M
92RochR/ProC-1943
92RochR/SB-465
92T-58R
92T/Gold-58M
92T/GoldWin-58M

Robbins, Johnny Lee
79Clinton/TCMA-3

Robbins, Leroy
80WHave-3

Robbs, Bill
92Spokane/ClBest-5
92Spokane/ProC-1308

Robbs, Don
87Hawaii-30

Roberge, Al
V362-46

Roberge, Bert
77Cocoa
80T-329
80Tucson-23
81Tucson-21
82Tucson-15
83D-496
83F-461
83T-611
83Tucson-8
85Expo/PostC-17
85F-525
85T-388
85T/Tr-94T
86D-575
86Expo/Prov/Pan-16
86F-258
86OPC-154
86Provigo-16
86T-154

Roberson, Kevin
88Wythe/ProC-1978
89CharWh/Best-7
89CharWh/ProC-1747
90WinSalem/Team-10
91AA/LineD-140
91CharlK/LineD-140
91CharlK/ProC-1702
91ClBest/Singl-2
92Iowa/ProC-4062
92Iowa/SB-218
92Sky/AAASingl-106
92UD/ML-124
93B-60
93FExcel/ML-12
93L-458
93Select/RookTr-89T
93UD/SP-88
94D-235
94F-394
94Pac/Cr-107
94S-604
94StCl-383
94StCl/1stDay-383
94StCl/Gold-383
94StCl/Team-348
94T-119
94T/Finest-77
94T/FinestRef-77
94T/Gold-119
94UD-199
94UD/CollC-241
94UD/CollC/Gold-241
94UD/CollC/Silv-241
94UD/ElecD-199
94Ultra-165

Roberson, Sid
94FExcel-85

Robert, Yvon
72Dimanche*-127
72Dimanche*-128

Roberts, Bill
76Dubuq

Roberts, Bobby
89TNTech-23

Roberts, Brent
88BurlInd/ProC-1772

Roberts, Brian
91Butte/SportP-25
92FtMyr/ProC-2750
92Miracle/ClBest-4

Roberts, Chris
91T/Tr-98T
92B-569FOIL
92Classic/DP-13
92Classic/DPFoil-BC12
92FrRow/DP-50
92StCl/Dome-155
92T/DQ-25
92T/Tr-93T
92T/TrGold-93T
93Pinn-467DP
93S-499DP
93Select-297DP
93StCl/MurphyMP-8USA
93StCl/MurphyS-170
93StCl/MurphyS-4
93StLucie/ProC-2920
94B-596
94ClBest/Gold-124
94FExcel-238

Roberts, Cliff
77DaytB

Roberts, Curt
54DanDee
54T-242
55T-107
55T/DH-11
56T-306
60DF-6
61Union
94T/Arc54-242

Roberts, Dale
72Dimanche*-129

Roberts, Dave A.
69T-536R
70OPC-151
70T-151
71MLB/St-235
71OPC-448
71T-448
72K-15
72OPC-360
72OPC-91LL
72T-360
72T-91LL
73OPC-39
73T-39
74McDon
74OPC-177
74T-177
74T/St-37
74T/St-99
75OPC-301
75T-301
75T/M-301
76OPC-649
76T-649
76T/Tr-649T
77Ho-101
77Ho/Twink-101
77OPC-38
77T-363
78SSPC/270-266
78T-501
79Pol/Giants-25
79T-473
80T-212
81D-501
81F-636
81T-431
82Phoenix
91WIZMets-332
92Yank/WIZ60-105
93Rang/Keeb-309

Roberts, Dave L.
63T-158R
66T-571

Roberts, Dave W.
73OPC-133
73T-133
74OPC-309
74T-309
75Hawaii/Caruso-5
75IntLgAS/Broder-27
75OPC-558
75PCL/AS-27
75T-558
75T/M-558
76OPC-107
76T-107
77OPC-193
77Padre/SchCd-24
77T-537
78Padre/FamFun-26
78T-501
79T-342
80T-93
81D-490
81F-607
81T-57
81T/Tr-824
82D-625
82F-227
82T-218
83D-273
83T-148

Roberts, Drex
85Kingst-20

Roberts, James Newsom
90Target-673

Roberts, James Wilfred
72Dimanche*-100IA
72Dimanche*-101

Roberts, Jay
83Ander-31

Roberts, Jeff
86Wausau-19

Roberts, John 1
86Greens-20
87Greens-8
88EastLAS/ProC-23
88NewBrit/ProC-894
89Pawtu/CMC-21
89Pawtu/Dunkin-24
89Pawtu/ProC-693

Roberts, John 2
92CharRain/ClBest-7
92CharRain/ProC-134

Roberts, Keith
90Bristol/ProC-3150
90Bristol/Star-21

Roberts, Leon K.
(Leon)
75OPC-620R
75T-620R
75T/M-620R
76OPC-292
76SSPC-362
76T-292
76T/Tr-292T
77BurgChef-3
77T-456
79Ho-37
79OPC-81
79T-166
79T/Comics-15
80OPC-266
80T-507
81D-48
81F-608
81T-368
81T/Tr-825
82D-415
82F-329
82OPC-186
82T-688
83OPC-89
83T-89
83T/Tr-96
84D-399
84F-356
84Nes/792-784
84T-784
85T-217
86Nashvl-21MG
87Toledo-20
87Toledo/TCMA-21
88Fayette/ProC-1104
89Pac/SenLg-30
89T/SenLg-113
89TM/SenLg-92
90EliteSenLg-103
91Pac/SenLg-97
92Durham/ClBest-25MG
92Durham/ProC-1115
92Durham/Team-7
93Durham/Team-15MG
93Rang/Keeb-310

Roberts, Leon
(Bip)
84PrWill-1
85Nashua-20
86D/Rook-33
86F/Up-U96
86T/Tr-91T
87D-114
87F-427
87LasVegas-23
87T-637
88LasVegas/CMC-14
88LasVegas/ProC-245
89Coke/Padre-14
89F/Up-126
89T/Tr-103T
90B-222
90Coke/Padre-15
90D-347
90D/BestNL-60
90F-166
90F/Can-166
90Leaf-233
90OPC-307
90Padre/MagUno-26
90Panini/St-359
90S-51
90S/YS/I-23
90Sf-116
90T-307
90T/Big-149
90T/St-103
90UD-303
91B-654
91D-195
91F-540
91Leaf-478
91Leaf/Stud-248
91OPC-538
91Padre/Coke-8
91Padre/MagRal-9
91Panini/FrSt-96
91Panini/St-97
91S-28
91StCl-18
91T-538
91T/CJMini/II-31
91UD-271
91Ultra-310
92B-525
92Classic/Game200-192
92D-371
92F-618
92F/Up-82
92L-252
92L/BlkGold-252
92OPC-20
92OPC/Premier-69
92Panini-233
92Pinn-404
92Reds/Kahn-10
92S-123
92S/RookTr-79T
92StCl-48
92StCl-645
92StCl/MemberII-10
92Studio-27
92T-20
92T/GPro-20
92T/Gold-20
92T/GoldWin-20
92T/Kids-56
92T/Pr-20
92T/Tr-92T
92T/TrGold-92T
92UD-141
92UD-763
92Ultra-485
93B-582
93Classic/GameI-77
93D-106
93D/DK-11
93D/MVP-23
93D/Spirit-SG9
93Duracel/PPI-18
93F-42
93F/GoldMII-2
93Flair-32
93Ho-21
93Kenner/Fig-30
93L-414
93OPC-305
93Pac/Spanish-89
93Panini-292
93Pinn-358
93Reds/Kahn-21
93S-516HL
93S-85
93Select-111
93Select/StatL-60
93StCl-30
93StCl/1stDay-30
93StCl/MPhoto-8
93StCl/MurphyS-30
93Studio-135
93T-219
93T/BlkGold-16
93T/Finest-15
93T/FinestRef-15
93T/Gold-219
93TripleP-88
93UD-112
93UD/FunPack-172
93UD/SP-214
93UD/SeasonHL-HI16
93USPlayC/Ace-4H
93USPlayC/Ace-9D
93Ultra-34
94B-64
94D-304
94F-422
94Finest-363
94L-299
94OPC-111
94Pac/Cr-157
94Pinn-500
94S-108
94S/GoldR-108
94StCl-186
94StCl/1stDay-186
94StCl/Gold-186
94T-733
94T/Gold-733
94UD-382
94UD/SP-133
94Ultra-584

Roberts, Lonell
90MedHat/Best-9
91ClBest/Singl-99
91Myrtle/ClBest-26
91Myrtle/ProC-2960
92StCath/ClBest-17
92StCath/ProC-3399
93Hagers/ClBest-22
93Hagers/ProC-1894

Roberts, Mel
88SALAS/GS-2
88Spartan/ProC-1033
88Spartan/Star-22
89Spartan/ProC-1050
90Spartan/Best-25MG
90Spartan/ProC-2508MG
90Spartan/Star-27MG
91Spartan/ClBest-28MG
91Spartan/ProC-913MG
92Phill/Med-26CO
93Phill/Med-29CO
94Phill/Med-27CO

Roberts, Mike
80Tulsa-5
81Tulsa-17

Roberts, Norman
86Hagers-16

Roberts, Pete
88LasVegas/CMC-5
88LasVegas/ProC-228
89LasVegas/CMC-9
89LasVegas/ProC-13
90AAASingl/ProC-10

90LasVegas/CMC-7
90LasVegas/ProC-122
90ProC/Singl-510
Roberts, Robin
49B-46
49Eureka-143
49Lummis
50B-32
51B-3
51BR-D8
51T/CAS
52B-4
52BR
52NTea
52RM-NL18
52T-59
52TipTop
53B/Col-65
53RM-NL11
54B-95
54RM-NL18
55B-171
56T-180
56YellBase/Pin-27
57T-15
58T-90
59T-156M
59T-352
60Bz-26
60MacGregor-19
60NuCard-44
60T-264
60T/tatt-45
61NuCard-444
61P-117
61T-20
61T/St-58
62J-198
62P-198
62P/Can-198
62T-243
63J-66
63P-66
63T-125
63T-6LL
64T-285
65OPC-15
65T-15
66T-530
76Rowe-6M
76Shakey-157
76Shakey-158
77Galasso-4
79TCMA-4
80Pac/Leg-56
80Perez/HOF-157
81TCMA-459M
82CJ-14
83D/HOF-41
83MLBPA/Pin-30
86Phill/TastyK-36
86Sf/Dec-39M
88Pac/Leg-15
89T/LJN-157
90Pac/Legend-47
90Perez/GreatMom-17
90Phill/TastyK-31
90Swell/Great-11
91Crown/Orio-384
91LineD-33
91Swell/Great-77
91T/Arc53-288
92AP/ASG-12
92AP/ASG24K-12G
92Bz/Quadra-21M
92UD/ASFF-54
92UD/HeroHL-HI7
93AP/ASGCoke/Amo-12
93TWill-73
93UD/ATH-108
Exh47
PM10/Sm-158
PM10/Sm-159
Roberts, Scott
84Cram/PCL-42
85Cram/PCL-218
86Maine-17
87BuffB-20
Roberts, Tim
91Erie/ClBest-23
91Erie/ProC-4069
Robertson, Alfred J.
(Jim)
54B-211
54T-149
55B-5
55Rodeo
55T-177
94T/Arc54-149
Robertson, Andre
81Colum-3
82Colum-17
82Colum/Pol-2
82T-83r
83D-387
83F-396
83OPC/St-316
83RoyRog/Disc-10
83T-281
83T/St-316
84Colum-9
84Colum/Pol-20
84D-347
84F-140
84Nes/792-592
84OPC-282
84T-592
84T/St-323
85F-144
85T-354
86Colum-21
86Colum/Pol-19
86D-469
86F-117
86T-738
87Chatt/Best-25
88Huntsvl/BK-16
88Tacoma/CMC-19
88Tacoma/ProC-634
89OkCty/CMC-14
89OkCty/ProC-1514
92TX-34
92Yank/WIZ80-161
Robertson, Bill
90Beloit/Best-2
90Beloit/Star-18
Robertson, Bob E.
68OPC-36R
68T-36R
69Pirate/JITB-10
69T-468R
70T-664
71K-4
71MLB/St-212
71OPC-255
71T-255
72K-45
72OPC-429
72OPC-430IA
72T-429
72T-430IA
73OPC-422
73T-422
74OPC-540
74T-540
75OPC-409
75T-409
75T/M-409
76OPC-449
76SSPC-578
76T-449
77T-176
79OPC-158
79T-312
89Swell-107
90Ashvl/C1Best-28CO
90Ashvl/ClBest-28CO
90ColMud/Star-25CO
91Ashvl/ProC-586CO
91Ashvl/ProC-586CO
92Ashvl/ClBest-27CO
Robertson, Bryant
85LitFalls-27
Robertson, Charles
21Exh-145
92Conlon/Sport-354
93Conlon-815
E120
V61-10
W573
Robertson, Dale
81Pawtu-13
84Pawtu-4
Robertson, Daryl
62Pep/Tul
77Fritsch-19
Robertson, David A.
16FleischBrd-76
D327
D328-140
D329-143
D350/2-143
E135-140
M101/4-143
M101/5-143
V100
Robertson, Doug
85Everett/II/Cram-14
86Clinton-22
87Clinton-1
88CalLgAS-6
88SanJose/Cal-137
88SanJose/ProC-115
89Shrev/ProC-1851
90AAASingl/ProC-213
90ColoSp/CMC-5
90ColoSp/ProC-32
90ProC/Singl-457
91AA/LineD-442
91London/LineD-442
91MidldA/OneHour-23
91MidldA/ProC-433
Robertson, Eugene E.
(Gene)
92Conlon/Sport-386
Robertson, Jason
89LittleSun-14
90Foil/Best-288
90Greens/Best-25
90Greens/ProC-2677
90Greens/Star-19
91PrWill/ClBest-22
91PrWill/ProC-1440
92ClBest-225
92PrWill/ClBest-24
92PrWill/ProC-163
92ProC/Tomorrow-123
Robertson, Jay
78Dunedin
80Syrac-6
80Syrac/Team-18
Robertson, Jerry L.
69T-284R
70T-661
71OPC-651
71T-651
Robertson, Michael
86James-20
87StPete-5
88ArkTr/GS-20
89ArkTr/GS-21
Robertson, Mike
92B-687
92ClBest-375
92Saraso/ClBest-20
92Saraso/ProC-215
92StCl/Dome-156
92UD/ML-156
92UD/ML-48M
93B-315
93ClBest/MLG-78
93UD-448TP
94B-43
Robertson, Rich
90Welland/Pucko-26
91Salem/ClBest-18
91Salem/ProC-948
92CaroMud/ProC-1178
93B-123
93F/Final-117
Robertson, Richard P.
69OPC-16R
69T-16R
70OPC-229
70T-229
71MLB/St-263
71OPC-443
71T-443
72T-618
Robertson, Roderick
(Rod)
86Cram/NWL-130
88Spartan/ProC-1034
88Spartan/Star-18
89Clearw/Star-19
90Reading/Best-18
90Reading/ProC-1228
90Reading/Star-21
91AA/LineD-515
91Reading/LineD-515
91Reading/ProC1376
92London/ProC-642
92London/SB-416
Robertson, Shawn
91Spokane/ClBest-10
91Spokane/ProC-3961
92Watlo/ClBest-18
92Watlo/ProC-2154
Robertson, Sherry
50B-161
51B-95
52T-245
Robertson, Stan
92Albany/ClBest-23
92Albany/ProC-2320
92James/ProC-1515
Robertson, Tommy
92SanBern/ClBest-10
92SanBern/ProC-
93River/Cal-16
Robicheaux, Randy
86Watertn-18
Robidoux, Billy Jo
83Beloit/Frit-21
86D-515
86F-652M
86F/Up-U97
86Pol/Brew-13
86Sf-178R
86Sf/Rook-28
86T/Tr-92T
87D-240
87D/OD-51
87F-356
87Pol/Brew-13
87Sf/TPrev-19M
87T-401
87T/JumboR-13
87T/St-202
88Denver/CMC-13
88Denver/ProC-1267
88S-334
89Coke/WS-23
90T/TVRSox-27
90UD/Ext-782
Robinette, Gary
81AppFx-22
Robinson, Aaron
47HomogBond-40
47TipTop
49B-133
50B-95
51B-142
53Mother-6
92Yank/WIZAS-67
D305
Robinson, Alan
92Hamil/ClBest-21
92Hamil/ProC-1608
Robinson, Bill
87Salem/ProC-2419
88QuadC/GS-8
Robinson, Bill H.
67T-442R
68T-337
68T/3D
69MB-234
69MLB/St-78
69T-313
69T/St-207
70MLB/St-249
70OPC-23
70T-23
72MB-290
73OPC-37
73T-37
74OPC-174
74T-174
74T/St-78
75OPC-501
75T-501
75T/M-501
76OPC-137
76SSPC-577
76T-137
77BurgChef-183
77T-335
78OPC-128
78T-455
79OPC-336
79T-637
80OPC-138
80T-264
81D-137
81F-373
81T-51
82D-402
82F-494
82T-543
82T/Tr-100T
83F-170
83T-754
85Pol/MetYank-M1CO
88Kahn/Mets-28CO
89Kahn/Mets-28CO
90Swell/Great-114
92Shrev/ProC-3887MG
92Shrev/SB-599MG
92Yank/WIZ60-106
Robinson, Bob
92Visalia/ClBest-10
92Visalia/ProC-1015
Robinson, Bobby
86Negro/Frit-65
91Negro/Lewis-12
92Negro/Retort-52
Robinson, Brad
88Greens/ProC-1557
Robinson, Brett
88Peoria/Ko-27
89Peoria/Team-7P
90CharlK/Team-17
Robinson, Brian
85Cedar-19
86Vermont-16
87Cedar-17
Robinson, Brooks
57T-328
58T-307
59T-439
60L-27
60T-28
61P-75
61T-10
61T-572AS
61T/Dice-14
61T/St-104
62J-29
62P-29
62P/Can-29
62Salada-40
62Shirriff-40
62T-45
62T-468AS
62T/St-8
62T/bucks
63Bz-30
63Exh
63F-4
63J-59
63P-59
63Salada-53
63T-345
63T/SO
64Bz-30
64T-230
64T/Coins-125AS
64T/Coins-18
64T/S-50
64T/SU
64T/St-21
64Wheat/St-39
65Bz-30
65OPC-150
65OPC-1LL
65OPC-5LL
65OldLond-35
65T-150
65T-1LL
65T-5LL
65T/trans-65
66Bz-34
66T-390
66T/RO-79
66T/RO-90
67Bz-34
67CokeCap/ALAS-21
67CokeCap/AS-3
67CokeCap/Orio-10
67OPC-1M
67OPC/PI-3
67T-1M
67T-531CL
67T-600
67T/PI-3
68Bz-8
68CokeCap/Orio-10
68Dexter-65
68OPC-20
68T-20

68T-365AS
68T-530M
68T/ActionSt-12C
68T/G-9
69MB-235
69MLB/St-8
69MLBPA/Pin-25
69NTF
69OPC/DE-18
69T-421AS
69T-504CL
69T-550
69T/DE-1
69T/S-3
69T/St-129
69Trans-13
70K-21
70MLB/St-154
70OPC-230
70OPC-455AS
70T-230
70T-455AS
71Bz
71Bz/Test-22
71MD
71MLB/St-309
71MLB/St-571
71OPC-300
71OPC-331WS
71T-300
71T-331WS
71T/Coins-114
71T/GM-9
71T/Greatest-9MVP
71T/S
71T/Super-59
71T/tatt-1
71T/tatt-1a
72MB-291
72OPC-222ALCS
72OPC-498KP
72Pol/Orio-8
72ProStars/PostC-36
72T-222ALCS
72T-498KP
72T-550
73JP
73OPC-90
73T-90
73T/Comics-16
73T/Lids-41
73T/PinUps-16
74Laugh/ASG-66
74OPC-160
74OPC-334AS
74T-160
74T-334AS
74T/DE-25
74T/St-129
75Ho-144
75K-18
75OPC-202MVP
75OPC-50
75SSPC/42-6
75T-202MVP
75T-50
75T/M-202MVP
75T/M-50
76Crane-48
76Ho-36
76Ho/Twink-36
76Laugh/Jub-11
76MSA/Disc
76OPC-95
76SSPC-392
76T-95
77BurgChef-43
77T-285
78OPC-239RB
78T-4RB
78TCMA-190
80Marchant-26
80Pac/Leg-54
80Perez/HOF-184
82CJ-8
82KMart-5
83Kaline-69M
83MLBPA/Pin-16
84West/1-7
86Sf/Dec-45
87KMart-9
87Leaf/SpecOlym-H9
87Nestle/DT-14
88Grenada-21
88Pac/Leg-3
89Kahn/Coop-9
89Pac/Leg-129
89Swell-134
89T/LJN-37
90BBWit-17
90MSA/AGFA-13
90Pac/Legend-102
90Perez/GreatMom-39
91Crown/Orio-385
91MDA-14
91MDA-NNO
91Swell/Great-146
92FrRow/Robinson-Set
92Kodak-4
92UD/ASFF-51
92UD/HeroHL-HI8
92Ziploc-5
93AP/ASG-120
93AP/ASG24K-54G
93Highland-5
93Nabisco-5
93Orio/SUI-3
93TWill/Robinson-Set
93YooHoo-16
94TedW-10
Exh47

Robinson, Bruce
79Colum-16
79T-711R
80Colum-15
81T-424R
84Cram/PCL-73
92Yank/WIZ70-135
92Yank/WIZ80-162

Robinson, Chris
91Boise/ClBest-27
91Boise/ProC-3878
92PalmSp/ClBest-4
92PalmSp/ProC-837

Robinson, Clyde
E254
W501-96

Robinson, Craig
74OPC-23
74T-23
74T/Tr-23T
75OPC-367
75T-367
75T/M-367
76SSPC-12
81Richm-23
82Richm-29
83Richm-24

Robinson, Daniel
93T-599M
93T/Gold-599M

Robinson, Darryl
88AppFx/ProC-144
88MidwLAS/GS-38
89AppFx/ProC-860
90BBCity/Star-21
91AA/LineD-416
91London/LineD-416
91Memphis/ProC-663
92Memphis/ProC-2428
92Memphis/SB-444

Robinson, David
88SanDiegoSt-15
89SanDiegoSt-16

Robinson, David Maurice
(Admiral)
91Arena*-5

Robinson, David T.
71OPC-262R
71T-262R

Robinson, Dewey
79Iowa/Pol-13
80Iowa/Pol-10
80T-664R
81T-487
82T-176
87Penin-7
93WSox-30M

Robinson, Don
79T-264
80T-719
81D-375
81F-366
81OPC-168
81T-168
82F-495
82OPC-332
82T-332
83D-171
83F-319
83OPC-44
83OPC/St-277
83T-44
83T/St-277
84D-532
84F-262
84Nes/792-616
84OPC-22
84T-616
85D-264
85F-475
85OPC-129
85T-537
86D-357
86F-621
86Leaf-159
86T-731
87D-608
87F-622
87OPC-387
87T-712
88D-573
88F-95
88F/Mini-120
88F/St-131
88F/TL-31
88Mother/Giants-22
88S-619
88Sf-90
88T-52
88T/St-94
89B-463
89D-571
89D/Best-191
89F-342
89F/BBAS-36
89Mother/Giants-22
89Panini/St-211
89S-440
89T-473
89T/St-86
89UD-523
90D-258
90F-70
90F/Can-70
90Leaf-267
90Mother/Giant-20
90OPC-217
90PublInt/St-81
90S-112
90T-217
90T/Big-193
90T/St-84
90UD-616
91B-384SLUG
91B-619
91D-581
91F-272
91Leaf-188
91Mother/Giant-20
91OPC-104
91PG&E-21
91Panini/FrSt-73
91Panini/St-74
91Pulaski/ClBest-13
91Pulaski/ProC-4020
91S-639
91SFExam/Giant-13
91StCl-167
91T-104
91UD-402
91UD/SilSlug-SS16
91Ultra-327
92Macon/ClBest-24
92Macon/ProC-282
92OPC-373
92Phill/Med-46
92Pinn-463
92ProC/Tomorrow-192
92StCl-729
92T-373
92T/Gold-373
92T/GoldWin-373
92Ultra-329
93Durham/Team-16

Robinson, Dwight
91Pittsfld/ClBest-3
91Pittsfld/ProC-3432
92ColumMet/ClBest-20
92ColumMet/ProC-305
92ColumMet/SAL/II-22

Robinson, Earl
60DF-20
61T-343
62T-272
78TCMA-81
90Target-674
91Crown/Orio-386

Robinson, Eli
91Princet/ClBest-17
91Princet/ProC-3524
92Princet/ClBest-2
92Princet/ProC-3096

Robinson, Emmett
86Kinston-19

Robinson, Floyd
62Salada-214
62Shirriff-214
62T-454
62T/St-29
62T/bucks
63Bz-24
63J-39
63P-39
63T-2LL
63T-405
63T/SO
64Bz-24
64T-195
64T/Coins-39
64T/SU
64T/St-18
65T-345
66OPC-8
66T-199M
66T-8
66T/RO-80
66T/RO-94
67CokeCap/Reds-1
67OPC-120
67T-120
68T-404
71T/tatt-11
Exh47

Robinson, Frank
56Kahn
57Kahn
57Sohio/Reds-17
57Swift-16
57T-35
58Kahn
58T-285
58T-386M
58T-484AS
59Armour-14
59HRDerby-16
59Kahn
59T-435
60Bz-29
60Kahn
60MacGregor-20
60T-352M
60T-490
60T/tatt-46
61Bz-31
61Kahn
61P-182
61T-25M
61T-360
61T-581AS
61T/Dice-15
61T/St-24
62Bz
62J-122
62Kahn
62P-122
62P/Can-122
62Salada-165
62Shirriff-165
62T-350
62T-396AS
62T-54LL
62T/St-121
62T/bucks
63Bz-31
63Exh
63FrBauer-22
63J-131
63Kahn
63P-131
63Salada-29
63T-1LL
63T-3LL
63T-400
63T/SO
64Bz-31
64Kahn
64T-260
64T/Coins-154AS
64T/Coins-37
64T/S-29
64T/SU
64T/St-15
64T/tatt
65Bz-31
65Kahn
65OPC-120
65OldLond-17
65T-120
65T/E-22
65T/trans-66
66Bz-32
66T-219LL
66T-310
66T/RO-3
66T/RO-81
67Bz-32
67CokeCap/ALAS-32
67CokeCap/AS-23
67CokeCap/Orio-4
67OPC-100
67OPC-1M
67OPC-62CL
67OPC/PI-19
67T-100
67T-1M
67T-239LL
67T-241LL
67T-243LL
67T-62CL
67T/PI-19
67T/Test/SU-3
68Bz-3
68CokeCap/Orio-4
68Dexter-66
68OPC-2LL
68OPC-4LL
68T-2LL
68T-373AS
68T-4LL
68T-500
68T-530M
68T/ActionSt-13A
68T/ActionSt-15B
68T/ActionSt-3B
68T/ActionSt-4A
68T/G-7
68T/Post-24
69MB-236
69MLB/St-9
69MLBPA/Pin-26
69NTF
69T-250
69T/S
69T/St-130
69T/decal
69Trans-16
70K-15
70MB-23
70MLB/St-155
70OPC-463AS
70T-463AS
70T-700
70T/PI-12
70T/S-37
70T/Super-37
70Trans-12
71Bz/Test-2
71K-15
71MD
71MLB/St-310
71MLB/St-572
71OPC-329WS
71OPC-63LL
71OPC-640
71T-329WS
71T-63LL
71T-640
71T/Coins-50WS
72MB-292
72OPC-100
72OPC-228WS
72OPC-88LL
72ProStars/PostC-20
72T-100
72T-228WS
72T-754TR
72T-88LL

73OPC-175
73T-175
73T/Lids-42
74Laugh/ASG-59
74OPC-55
74T-55
74T/DE-66
74T/St-145
75OPC-199MVP
75OPC-204MVP
75OPC-331MG
75OPC-580
75SSPC/42-8MG
75T-199MVP
75T-204MVP
75T-331MG
75T-580
75T/M-199MVP
75T/M-204MVP
75T/M-331MG
75T/M-580
76Crane-49
76Laugh/Jub-5
76MSA/Disc
76SSPC-525
76T-477MG
77T-18MG
78RochR
78TCMA-140
80Laugh/3/4/5-23
80Pac/Leg-123
80Perez/HOF-180
82D-424MG
82KMart-9
82Ohio/HOF-30
83D-564MG
83D-648M
83D/HOF-19
83Mother/Giants-1
83OPC/St-4FOIL
83T-576MG
83T/St-4
84D/Champs-43
84Nes/792-171MG
84T-171MG
85CircK-4
85D/HOF-8
85Woolwth-29
86BLChew-4
86Sf/Dec-41
86T-404TBC
87French-20CO
87KMart-10
87Nestle/DT-16
88French-20MG
88Grenada-57
88T/Tr-96MG
89French-20
89Smok/Angels-8
89Smok/Dodg-24
89T-774MG
90BBWit-48
90OPC-381MG
90T-381MG
90Target-675
91Crown/Orio-388
91OPC-639MG
91T-639MG
93Orio/SUI-4
93Select/TCr-3
Exh47

Robinson, Henry
86FtMyr-22

Robinson, Humberto
52Laval-91
55T-182
59T-366
60L-70
60T-416

Robinson, Jackie R.
47Bond/JR-1--13
47HomogBond-41
48L-79
48Swell-3
49B-50
49Eureka-48
50B-22
52BR
52StarCal-91BM
52StarCal/L-79G
52T-312
53Exh/Can-19
53T-1
54NYJour
54T-10
55Gol/Dodg-25
55T-50
55T/DH-25
56T-30
56T/Hocus-A14
56T/Pin-51
60NuCard-53
61NuCard-428
72T/Test-4
74Laugh/ASG-49
76Laugh/Jub-26
76Shakey-88
77Galasso-20
77Galasso-228
79TCMA-291
80Laugh/FFeat-18
80Pac/Leg-15
80Perez/HOF-89
80SSPC/HOF
83D/HOF-6
83MLBPA/Pin-31
84West/1-1
86Negro/Frit-11
86Negro/Frit-25
86Sf/Dec-28
87Negro/Dixon-33
87Nestle/DT-24
88Grenada-19
88Pac/Leg-40
89B/Ins-9
89HOF/St-12
89Rini/Dodg-18
89Rini/Dodg-27
89Smok/Dodg-25
89USPS-3
90BBWit-52
90Perez/GreatMom-3
90Target-676
91T/Arc53-1
92Bz/Quadra-14M
94T/Arc54-10
D302-Set
D305
Exh47
PM10/Sm-160--166
R346-36
Rawl

Robinson, Jeffrey D.
(Jeff)
84F/X-U100
84T/Tr-101T
85D-201
85F-620
85OPC-5
85T-592
86Mother/Giants-15
86T/Tr-93T
87D-559
87F-283
87Mother/SFG-25
87T-389
88D-558
88D/Best-241
88OPC-244
88S-439
88T-244
88T/Big-123
88T/St-133
89B-410
89D-370
89D/Best-129
89F-220
89F/LL-33
89OPC-351
89Panini/St-164
89S-309
89T-681
89T/Big-45
89T/St-129
89UD-332
89VFJuice-49
90B-427
90D-134
90F-479
90F/Can-479
90Leaf-412
90OPC-723
90PublInt/St-164
90S/NWest-23
90T-723
90T/TVYank-19
90T/Tr-103T
90UD-403
91B-193
91D-291
91F-678
91Leaf-307
91OPC-19
91S-192
91Smok/Angel-18
91StCl-542
91T-19
91T/Tr-99T
92Cub/Mara-38
92D-59
92Iowa/SB-219
92OPC-137
92S-274
92StCl-756
92T-137
92T/Gold-137
92T/GoldWin-137
93F-382

Robinson, Jeffrey M.
(Jeff)
85Cram/PCL-184
86Nashvl-22
87D/Rook-13
87F/Up-U105
87Sf/Rook-46
87T/Tr-104T
88D-296
88F-68
88Pep/T-44
88Pol/T-10
88S-549
88T-449
89B-97
89Classic-93
89D-18DK
89D-470
89D/DKsuper-18DK
89F-143
89Mara/Tigers-44
89OPC-267
89Panini/St-335
89Pol/Tigers-44
89S-284
89S/HotStar-34
89S/YS/II-8
89Sf-193
89T-267
89T/Big-274
89UD-472
90CokeK/Tiger-19
90D-417
90F-614
90F/Can-614
90Leaf-429
90OPC-42
90PublInt/St-481
90PublInt/St-603
90S-333
90T-42
90T/St-284
90UD-552
91B-90
91Crown/Orio-500
91D-245
91F-349
91Leaf-464
91OPC-766
91S-129
91StCl-441
91T-766
91T/Tr-100T
91UD-676
91UD/Ext-796
92D-77
92Mother/Rang-16
92Pinn-516
92S-186
92StCl-715
92UD-320
93Rang/Keeb-311

Robinson, Jerry
63T-466R

Robinson, Jim 1
78Newar
79BurlB-4

Robinson, Jim 2
88MissSt-29
89MissSt-34
90MissSt-36
90PeoriaUp/Team-U2
91Geneva/ClBest-16
91Geneva/ProC-4222
92ChalK/SB-164
92CharlK/ProC-2774
92ProC/Tomorrow-211

Robinson, Ken
91MedHat/ProC-4099
92Myrtle/ProC-2196
93Hagers/ClBest-23
93Hagers/ProC-1879

Robinson, Kevin
87Erie-20
88Hamil/ProC-1730

Robinson, Larry
72Dimanche*-102IA
72Dimanche*-103

Robinson, Lee
74Albuq/Team-16
75Albuq/Caruso-4

Robinson, Lynn
88BurlB/ProC-1

Robinson, M.C.
N172

Robinson, Marteese
88Madis-20
89Modesto/Cal-285
90Foil/Best-280

Robinson, Mike
83Erie-24
85Spring-25
86ArkTr-20
87ArkTr-2
88ArkTr/GS-19
88Louisvl-42

Robinson, Napoleon
89Salem/Team-27
90Bakers/Cal-233
91AA/LineD-215
91Greenvl/ClBest-4
91Greenvl/LineD-215
91Greenvl/ProC-2998
92B-34
92ProC/Tomorrow-184
92Richm/Bleach-20
92Richm/Comix-16
92Richm/ProC-376
92Richm/SB-438
92Sky/AAASingl-202
93FExcel/ML-5
93Richm/Bleach-4
93Richm/Pep-15
93Richm/Team-24

Robinson, Randall
87CharWh-27

Robinson, Randy
83Butte-9

Robinson, Raul
91Macon/ClBest-26
91Macon/ProC-879

Robinson, Rhett
89GA-26
89GA-28M

Robinson, Ron
81Cedar-6
82Water-9
84Wichita/Rock-8
85D-649
85F-650
86D-121
86F-190
86T-442
86TexGold-33
87D-310
87F-212
87F/GameWin-38
87F/Mini-93
87Kahn-33
87T-119
88D-166
88D/Best-308
88F-247
88F/Mini-75
88Kahn/Reds-33
88OPC-342
88S-476
88T-517
89B-303
89D-308
89F-169
89Kahn/Reds-33
89OPC-16
89S-559
89T-16
89T/Big-132
89UD-187
90Brewer/MillB-21
90CedarDG/Best-14
90D-553
90F-431
90F/Can-431
90Leaf-467
90OPC-604
90S-495
90T-604
90T/Tr-104T
91B-39
91Brewer/MillB-22
91D-254
91F-595
91Leaf-14
91Leaf/Stud-75
91OPC-313
91Pol/Brew-20
91S-517
91StCl-296
91T-313
91UD-620
92F-187
92OPC-395
92Pol/Brew-20
92StCl-739
92UD-198
93F-634

Robinson, Scott
90Billings/ProC-3220
91Cedar/ClBest-11
91Cedar/ProC-2718
92CharWh/ClBest-18
92Chatt/ProC-3818
93SALAS/II-35
93SALAS/IICS-7

Robinson, Terry
91Pocatel/ProC-3799
91Pocatel/SportP-5

Robinson, Wilbert
50Callahan
50W576-62
60F-33
63Bz-27
72F/FFeat-10
72Laugh/GF-30
76Shakey-38
77Galasso-162MG
80Perez/HOF-38
80SSPC/HOF
89HOF/St-86
89Smok/Dodg-104
90Target-677A
93Conlon-846MG
93Conlon/MasterCol-8M
D329-144
D350/2-144
E121/120
E210-43
M101/4-144
M101/5-144
N142
N172/BC
N300/SC
N690
W515-53
W575

Robinson, William E.
(Eddie)
49Royal-22
50B-18
51B-88
51T/RB-51
52B-77
52BR
52Hawth/Pin-7
52NTea
52RM-AL18
52Royal
52StarCal-87A
52StarCal-87AM
52StarCal/L-73C
52T-32
53B/BW-20
53Mother-59
53RM-AL11
53T-73
54B-193
54NYJour
54T-62
55B-153
56T-302
57T-238
60T-455C
79TCMA-283

91Crown/Orio-387
91T/Arc53-73
94T/Arc54-62
Exh47
Robinson, William H.
N172
N284
N370
Scrapps
Robitaille, Martin
88James/ProC-1921
92James/ClBest-28CO
92James/ProC-1518CO
Robledo, Nilson
91ClBest/Singl-146
91SoBend/ClBest-24
91SoBend/ProC-2860
92Saraso/ProC-209
Robles, Gabriel
(Gabby)
86Kinston-20
87WinSalem-18
Robles, Greg
82Idaho-21
83Madis/Frit-22
84Albany-25
Robles, Javier
91BurlInd/ProC-3309
Robles, Jorge
89Wausau/GS-19
90Penin/Star-18
Robles, Josman
90Durham/Team-18
Robles, Rafael
69T-592R
70T-573R
71OPC-408
71T-408
Robles, Ruben
83Tucson-26
84Cram/PCL-66
Robles, Scott
90Kenosha/Best-25
90Kenosha/ProC-2294
90Kenosha/Star-21
Robles, Sergio
73OPC-601R
73T-601R
74OPC-603R
74T-603R
90Target-678B
91Crown/Orio-389
Robles, Silvano
75AppFx
76AppFx
76Clinton
Robson, David
92Niagara/ClBest-2
92Niagara/ProC-3327
Robson, Gary
88Beloit/GS-2
89Beloit/I/Star-26M
Robson, Tom
75IntLgAS/Broder-28
75PCL/AS-28
75Spokane/Caruso-1
79Wausau-16
80Ashvl-2
87Smok/R-21CO
89Smok/R-26CO
90Mother/Rang-27M
91Mother/Rang-28CO
92Mother/Rang-28M
93Rang/Keeb-312
Roby, Ellis
86Sumter/ProC-22
87Durham-10
88Durham/Star-18
89Greenvl/Best-9
89Greenvl/ProC-1159
89Greenvl/Star-20
Roca, Gilbert
86Macon-21
87Salem-16
88Harris/ProC-851
89Jacks/GS-17
90T/TVMets-55
Rocco, Michael
(Mickey)
47Centen-24
48Sommer-26
49Sommer-14
Roche, Rod
86VeroB-20
87Bakers-17
Roche, Steve
80Wausau-7
81Chatt-8
82Chatt-15
82Watlo/Frit-10
Roche, Tim
77Clinton
78LodiD
Roche, Titi
88LitFalls/Pucko-11
89StLucie/Star-21
89Star/Wax-24
Rochelli, Lou
90Target-1055
Rochford, Mike
84Pawtu-21
86Pawtu-18
87Pawtu-9
87Pawtu/TCMA-9
88Pawtu/CMC-2
88Pawtu/ProC-447
89F-650M
89Pawtu/CMC-6
89Pawtu/Dunkin-26
89Pawtu/ProC-700
90AAASingl/ProC-432
90B-264
90Pawtu/CMC-3
90Pawtu/ProC-460
90ProC/Singl-254
90T/TVRSox-16
90UD-694
91S-739RP
Rochon, Henri
45Parade*-70
Rock, Bob
77Charl
78Salem
80Buffa-12
81Buffa-10
Rock, Royal
C46-10
E254
Rockenfeld, Isaac B.
T206
T213/brown
Rockett, Pat
78T-502
79Richm-20
80Syrac-5
80Syrac/Team-19
Rockey, Jim
86Durham-23
Rockman, Marv
88Gaston/ProC-995
89Tulsa/GS-22
89Tulsa/Team-20
90Tulsa/ProC-1152
90Tulsa/Team-21
Rockne, Knute
33SK*-35
Rockweiler, Dean
86James-21
Rodarte, Raul
92Penin/ClBest-10
92Penin/ProC-2942
93River/Cal-17
Rodas, Richard
(Rick)
82Albuq-9
83Albuq-6
84Cram/PCL-147
84Pol/Dodg-56
85Cram/PCL-174
90Target-678
Roddy, Phil
77Ashvl
Rode, Don
48Sommer-30M
Rodgers, Andre
57T-377
59T-216
60L-42
60T-431
61P-153
61T-183
62J-185
62P-185
62P/Can-185
62Salada-155A
62Salada-155B
62Shirriff-155
62T-477
63J-173
63P-173
63T-193
64T-336
65T-536
66EH-16
66T-592
67T-554
78TCMA-51
Rodgers, Charlie
91Miami/ClBest-11
Rodgers, Darrell
85Everett/II/Cram-15
86Fresno/Smok-15
88Cedar/ProC-1162
88MidwLAS/GS-13
89Chatt/Best-15
89Chatt/GS-21
92Princet/ClBest-28CO
Rodgers, Dirk
79WHave-22M
Rodgers, Doc
91Princet/ProC-3532CO
92Princet/ProC-3103CO
Rodgers, John
93Peoria/Team-23
Rodgers, Paul
87Myrtle-30
88Dunedin/Star-14
89Dunedin/Star-13
90Knoxvl/Best-12
90Knoxvl/ProC-1255
90Knoxvl/Star-15
91AA/LineD-364
91ClBest/Singl-3
91Knoxvl/LineD-364
91Knoxvl/ProC-1782
Rodgers, Robert L.
(Buck)
62T-431
62T/St-68
63Bz-2
63F-20
63J-31
63P-31
63T-280
63T/SO
64T-426
64T-61M
65T-342
65T/trans-27
66T-462
67CokeCap/DodgAngel-26
67T-281
68T-433
69MB-237
69MLB/St-27
69OPC-157
69T-157
69T/4in1-16
69T/St-149
73OPC-49CO
73T-49CO
74OPC-447CO
74T-447CO
78TCMA-63
81D-327MG
81T-668MG
82D-232MG
82Pol/Brew-37MG
84Indianap-2MG
85Expo/PostC-18MG
85Indianap-36MG
85T/Tr-95T
86Expo/Prov/Pan-3MG
86Expo/Prov/Post-4MG
86OPC-141MG
86Provigo-3MG
86T-171MG
87OPC-293MG
87T-293MG
88OPC-134MG
88T-504MG
89OPC-193MG
89T-474MG
90ElPasoATG/Team-19
90OPC-81MG
90T-81MG
91OPC-321MG
91T-321MG
92OPC-21MG
92T-21MG
92T/Gold-21MG
92T/GoldWin-21MG
93Expo/D/McDon-32MG
93Mother/Angel-1MG
93Pol/Angel-3MG
93T-503MG
93T/Gold-503MG
Exh47
Rodgers, Tim
83Kinston/Team-20
84Syrac-17
86Tulsa-7
87OKCty-17
Rodgers, William
16FleischBrd-77
Rodiles, Jose
85FtMyr-30
86Memphis/GoldT-23
86Memphis/SilverT-23
87ColAst/ProC-18
87ColumAst-18
Rodiles, Steve
85Iowa-36
Rodrigues, Cecil
93FExcel/ML-194
Rodriguez, A.
86Ashvl-23
Rodriguez, Abimael
90James/Pucko-4
91Sumter/ClBest-19
91Sumter/ProC-2344
Rodriguez, Ahmed
89Johnson/Star-18
89Savan/ProC-353
90Hamil/Best-17
90Hamil/Star-20
91Spring/ClBest-22
91Spring/ProC-750
92Spring/ProC-878
Rodriguez, Al
91Everett/ClBest-3
91Everett/ProC-3923
92Clinton/ClBest-18
Rodriguez, Alexander
75BurlB
Rodriguez, Alexander E.
94UD-24
94UD-298UDC
94UD/ElecD-24
94UD/HoloFX-34
94UD/SP-15PP
Rodriguez, Andres
90PrWill/Team-22
91FtLaud/ClBest-23
91FtLaud/ProC-2436
92FtLaud/ClBest-5
92FtLaud/ProC-2621
92FtLaud/Team-27
Rodriguez, Andy
75SanAn
Rodriguez, Angel
85Beloit-10
87Stockton-10
88ElPaso/Best-23
88Stockton/Cal-198
88Stockton/ProC-742
Rodriguez, Anthony
91Kissim/ProC-4189
92GulfCD/ProC-3569
Rodriguez, Antonio H.
(Hector)
52Hawth/Pin-8
53B/Col-98
Rodriguez, Armando
90Pulaski/Best-24
90Pulaski/ProC-3109
91Idaho/ProC-4340
91Idaho/SportP-4
Rodriguez, Aurelio
69JB
69T-653
70MLB/St-179
70OPC-228
70Pol/SenY-8
70T-228
71MLB/St-405
71OPC-464
71T-464
71T/Coins-124
72MB-293
72OPC-319
72T-319
72T/Cloth-27
73OPC-218
73T-218
74OPC-72
74T-72
74T/St-179
75OPC-221
75T-221
75T/M-221
76OPC-267
76SSPC-366
76T-267
77BurgChef-93
77Ho-120
77Ho/Twink-120
77OPC-136
77T-574
78BK/T-14
78OPC-64
78T-342
79OPC-83
79T-176
80OPC-245
80T-468
81F-105
81T-34
81Tiger/Detroit-47
82F-53
82OPC/Post-10
82T-334
82T/Tr-101T
83D-369
83F-249
83T-758
83T/Tr-97T
84Nes/792-269
84T-269
88ColoSp/CMC-25
88ColoSp/ProC-1536
90AAASingl/ProC-396CO
90ProC/Singl-402CO
90Toledo/CMC-25CO
90Toledo/ProC-166CO
91Crown/Orio-390
92Yank/WIZ80-163
Rodriguez, Beto
90Johnson/Star-21
90Rockford/Team-24
91Spring/ClBest-23
91Spring/ProC-751
Rodriguez, Buena
89James/ProC-2131
90Rockford/ProC-2705
Rodriguez, Carlos
88FtLaud/Star-18
89FtLaud/Star-21
90AAASingl/ProC-333
90Albany/ProC-1178
90Albany/Star-14
90ColClip/ProC-683
90T/TVYank-58
91AAA/LineD-116
91ColClip/LineD-116
91ColClip/ProC-604
91D/Rook-41
92Albany/ProC-2233
92Albany/SB-18
92S-411
92T/91Debut-149
92UD-77TP
93ColClip/Pol-15
Rodriguez, Chris
91Hunting/ClBest-20
91Hunting/ProC-3333
92Geneva/ClBest-8
92Geneva/ProC-1559
Rodriguez, Dave 1
83Tacom-30B
Rodriguez, Dave 2
92Bristol/ClBest-14
92Bristol/ProC-1409
Rodriguez, Eddie 1
83Peor/Frit-28C
86QuadC-28
87QuadC-1113
88QuadC/GS-1MG
89QuadC/Best-2
89QuadC/GS-1
90MidldA/GS-1MG
Rodriguez, Eddie 2
92GreatF/SportP-15
Rodriguez, Eddy Alberto
89Bristol/Star-23
90Niagara/Pucko-23
91Fayette/ClBest-8
91Fayette/ProC-1168
92Lakeland/ClBest-25
92Lakeland/ProC-2278

Rodriguez, Edgal Antonio
87Salem/ProC-2412
88QuadC/GS-7
89PalmSp/Cal-41
89PalmSp/ProC-465
90QuadC/GS-28
91PalmSp/ProC-2032
Rodriguez, Eduardo
74OPC-171
74T-171
75OPC-582
75T-582
75T/M-582
76OPC-92
76SSPC-228
76T-92
77BurgChef-86
77T-361
78T-623
79T-108
80T-273
81Holyo-1
Rodriguez, Edwin
83Colum-18
84Cram/PCL-240
85Cram/PCL-108
86LasVegas-13
87LasVegas-19
92Yank/WIZ80-164
Rodriguez, Eligio
88Geneva/ProC-1646
Rodriguez, Eliseo
(Ellie)
69OPC-49R
69T-49R
70OPC-402
70T-402
71MLB/St-449
71OPC-344
71T-344
71T/Coins-124
72MB-294
72OPC-421
72T-421
73K-2
73OPC-45
73T-45
73T/Lids-43
74OPC-405
74T-405
74T/St-146
75Ho-34
75Ho/Twink-34
75OPC-285
75T-285
75T/M-285
76OPC-512
76SSPC-193
76T-512
77T-448
81TCMA-421
90Target-679
92Yank/WIZ60-107
Rodriguez, Ernesto
91ClBest/Singl-40
91Myrtle/ClBest-22
91Myrtle/ProC-2956
91SALAS/ProC-SAL39
92Dunedin/ClBest-19
92Dunedin/ProC-2008
Rodriguez, Ernie
85Bend/Cram-20
88Butte-28
89Butte/SP-28
Rodriguez, F. Boi
87James-7
88WPalmB/Star-21
89Jaxvl/Best-16
89Jaxvl/ProC-177
90Jaxvl/Best-8
91AA/LineD-216
91Greenvl/ClBest-24
91Greenvl/LineD-216
91Richm/Bob-35
92Richm/Bleach-25
92Richm/Comix-17
92Richm/ProC-385
92Richm/SB-439
92Sky/AAASingl-203
93Richm/Bleach-24
93Richm/Pep-20
93Richm/Team-25
Rodriguez, Felix
91Kissim/ProC-4190
92GreatF/SportP-6
Rodriguez, Frankie
91ClBest/Gold-17
91ClBest/Singl-397
91Classic/DP-x
91Elmira/ClBest-14
91Elmira/ProC-3279
91FrRow/DP-1
91FrRow/DP-FR1
91FrRow/DP-FR2
91FrRow/DP-FR3
91FrRow/DP-FR4
91FrRow/DP-FR5
91FrRow/Rodriguez-1
91FrRow/Rodriguez-2
91FrRow/Rodriguez-3
91FrRow/Rodriguez-4
91UD/FinalEd-21F
92B-45
92ClBest-391
92ClBest/BBonusC-20
92ClBest/RBonus-BC20
92LynchRS/ClBest-1
92LynchRS/ProC-2905
92ProC/Tomorrow-23
92UD/ML-266
92UD/ML-43M
92UD/ML-54DS
92UD/ML/TPHolo-TP6
93B-143
93B-362FOIL
93ClBest/MLG-22
93FExcel/ML-137
93UD-442TP
94B-368
94B-615
94ClBest/GAce-5
94ClBest/Gold-112
94FExcel-21
94FExcel-21
94T-112
94T/Gold-112
Rodriguez, Gabriel
88FtLaud/Star-19
88Peoria/Ko-28
89FtLaud/Star-22
89Star/Wax-80
90Geneva/Star-21
90Osceola/Star-25
Rodriguez, Hector
91Augusta/ClBest-18
91Augusta/ProC-814
Rodriguez, Henry
89VeroB/Star-23
90SanAn/GS-24
90TexLgAS/GS-8
91AAA/LineD-19
91Albuq/LineD-19
91Albuq/ProC-1156
91B-185
91Classic/II-T51
91Leaf/GRook-BC8
91UD-21SR
91Ultra-386MLP
92AAA/ASG/SB-19
92Albuq/ProC-735
92Albuq/SB-19
92B-108
92D/Rook-105
92F-661
92OPC-656M
92ProC/Tomorrow-241
92Sky/AAASingl-10
92StCl-268
92T-656R
92T/Gold-656M
92T/GoldWin-656M
93D-218
93F-453
93LimeR/Winter-84
93Pinn-182
93Pol/Dodg-22
93S-244
93Select-404
93StCl-226
93StCl/1stDay-226
93T-284
93T/Gold-284
93ToysRUs-38
93UD-391
94D-264
94F-522
94L-385
94Pac/Cr-320
94StCl-176
94StCl/1stDay-176
94StCl/Gold-176
94T-727
94T/Gold-727
94UD-436
94Ultra-521
Rodriguez, iggy
86WPalmB-25
Rodriguez, Ivan 1
78BurlB
80Holyo-6
81Vanco-8
Rodriguez, Ivan 2
(Pudge)
89Gaston/ProC-1006
89Gaston/Star-20
89SALAS/GS-26
90CharlR/Star-22
90FSLAS/Star-41
90Star/ISingl-26
91AA/LineD-592
91B-272
91ClBest/Gold-7
91ClBest/Singl-136
91Classic/II-T82
91Classic/III-78
91D/Rook-33
91F/UltraUp-U58
91F/Up-U62
91S/RookTr-82T
91T/Tr-101T
91Tulsa/LineD-592
91Tulsa/ProC-2776
91Tulsa/Team-23
91UD/FinalEd-55F
92B-1
92CJ/DI-27
92Classic/Game200-159
92Classic/I-77
92Classic/II-T69
92Colla/ASG-23
92D-289
92F-316
92F/RookSIns-12
92L-194
92L/BlkGold-194
92Mother/Rang-5
92OPC-78
92OPC/Premier-55
92Panini-74
92Pinn-156
92Pinn/Team2000-8
92Pinn/TeamP-3
92ProC/Tomorrow-153
92S-700
92S/100RisSt-77
92S/Impact-5
92StCl-415
92Studio-246
92T-78
92T/91Debut-150
92T/Gold-78
92T/GoldWin-78
92T/McDonB-41
92TripleP-51
92UD-245
92UD/ASFF-2
92Ultra-139
93B-489
93Classic/GameI-78
93Colla/ASG-11
93Colla/DM-90
93D-187
93F-327
93F-355
93Flair-285
93HumDum/Can-17
93L-5
93L/Fast-15
93L/GoldAS-1
93L/UpGoldAS-2
93OPC-331
93Pac/Beisbol-12M
93Pac/Beisbol-16
93Pac/Beisbol-4M
93Pac/Jugador-14
93Pac/Spanish-316
93Pac/SpanishP-20
93Panini-80
93Pinn-21
93Pinn-301I
93Pinn/TP-3M
93Pinn/Team2001-29
93Rang/Keeb-428
93S-25
93S-507AS
93S-537DT
93S/GoldDT-6
93Select-136
93Select/ChasS-17
93StCl-524
93StCl-592MC
93StCl/1stDay-524
93StCl/1stDay-592MC
93StCl/MurphyS-175
93StCl/Rang-10
93Studio-133
93T-360
93T/Finest-47
93T/FinestRef-47
93T/Gold-360
93ToysRUs-33
93ToysRUs/MPhoto-10
93TripleP-16
93UD-123
93UD-450M
93UD-468IN
93UD-52M
93UD/5thAnn-A12
93UD/FunPack-159
93UD/FunPackAS-AS2
93UD/SP-9AS
93Ultra-284
93Ultra/AS-11
93Ultra/AwardWin-11
94B-101
94Church-27
94D-376
94D/DK-10
94D/Special-376
94F-319
94F/AS-22
94L-338
94OPC-87
94Pac/AllLat-13
94Pac/Cr-627
94Panini-132
94Pinn-349
94Pinn/TeamP-5
94S-31
94S/GoldR-31
94S/GoldS-58
94Sf/2000-88
94StCl-116
94StCl/1stDay-116
94StCl/Gold-116
94StCl/Team-265
94Studio-157
94T-165
94T/Finest-126
94T/Finest/PreProd-126
94T/FinestRef-126
94T/Gold-165
94TripleP-199
94UD-245
94UD/ElecD-245
94UD/SP-151
94Ultra-132
94Ultra/AwardWin-1
Rodriguez, Jonis
84Greens-20
Rodriguez, Jose
79Wisco-21
81Buffa-13
82Jacks-8
82Portl-21
83LynnP-22
83StPete-23
86ArkTr-21
86BurlEx-18
87AppFx-20
89Bristol/Star-24
89Princet/Star-17
Rodriguez, Joshua
90MidldA/GS-NNO
Rodriguez, Juan
77DaytB
Rodriguez, Luis E.
80OkCty
81OkCty/TCMA-16
82OkCty-16
Rodriguez, Manuel
90Johnson/Star-22
91Johnson/ClBest-24
91Johnson/ProC-3976
Rodriguez, Marcos
79Clinton/TCMA-15
Rodriguez, Miguel
80Utica-32
Rodriguez, Mike
79Ogden/TCMA-4
Rodriguez, Ramon
85Spokane/Cram-20
86CharRain-22
Rodriguez, Ricardo
85Modesto/Chong-18
86Tacom-19
88ColoSp/CMC-8
88ColoSp/ProC-1549
89Vanco/CMC-8
89Vanco/ProC-580
91AAA/LineD-392
91Phoenix/LineD-392
91Phoenix/ProC-65
Rodriguez, Richard 1
77Charl
Rodriguez, Richard 2
89AubAs/ProC-19
91Pocatel/ProC-3801CO
91Pocatel/SportP-29CO
Rodriguez, Richard A.
(Rich)
84LitFalls-25
86Lynch-19
87Lynch-19
88F-293
88F/Up-U24
88Jacks/GS-13
88T-166
89Wichita/Rock-29LHP
90AAASingl/ProC-11
90LasVegas/CMC-9
90LasVegas/ProC-123
90ProC/Singl-512
91D-769
91F-541
91Leaf-448
91OPC-573
91Padre/MagRal-16
91S-593
91StCl-565
91T-573
91T/90Debut-132
91UD-640
92D-388
92F-619
92L-319
92L/BlkGold-319
92Mother/Padre-22
92OPC-462
92Padre/Carl-17
92Pol/Padre-27M
92S-149
92Smok/Padre-27
92StCl-712
92T-462
92T/Gold-462
92T/GoldWin-462
92UD-568
92Ultra-581
93D-338
93F-145
93L-368
93Marlin/Publix-21
93Mother/Padre-11
93Pac/Spanish-262
93S-466
93StCl-137
93StCl/1stDay-137
93T-693
93T/Gold-693
93T/Tr-71T
93UD-330
93Ultra-120
94D-635
94F-475
94S-295
94S/GoldR-295
94StCl/Team-76
94T-312
94T/Gold-312
Rodriguez, Rigo
85Beaum-10
Rodriguez, Roberto
68T-199R
69T-358R
71MLB/St-44
71OPC-424

71T-424
74Wichita-104
Rodriguez, Roman
89Princet/Star-18
90Augusta/ProC-2474
91Salem/ClBest-7
91Salem/ProC-961
92CaroMud/SB-140
Rodriguez, Rosario
88Greens/ProC-1567
90AAASingl/ProC-543
90CedarDG/Best-24
90Chatt/GS-25
90Nashvl/ProC-231
90T/89Debut-103
91AAA/LineD-44
91BuffB/LineD-44
91BuffB/ProC-541
91OPC-688
91S-373RP
91T-688
92B-498
92BuffB/BlueS-18
92BuffB/SB-34
92D-748
92F-565
92Sky/AAASingl-19
92StCl-697
Rodriguez, Ruben
83AlexD-26
85Nashua-21
86Nashua-23
87SLCity/Taco-7CO
87Vanco-23
89Boise/ProC-1992
89Denver/CMC-18
89Denver/ProC-34
90Erie/Star-21
91AA/LineD-396
91London/LineD-396
91London/ProC-1881
92Pawtu/ProC-926
92Pawtu/SB-364
93LimeR/Winter-47
93Pawtu/Ball-19
Rodriguez, Steve
91T/Tr-102T
92Classic/DP-112
92FrRow/DP-84
92StCl/Dome-157
92T/DQ-26
92T/Tr-94T
92T/TrGold-94T
93StCl/MurphyS-10
93StCl/MurphyS-50
Rodriguez, Tomas
88Billings/ProC-1816
89Billings/ProC-2044
Rodriguez, Tony
91Elmira/ClBest-13
91Elmira/ProC-3280
92LynchRS/ClBest-7
92LynchRS/ProC-2917
Rodriguez, Victor
82RochR-16
85Cram/PCL-101
85D-535
87Louisvl-26
88Portl/CMC-20
88Portl/ProC-649
89AAA/ProC-40
89Portl/CMC-17
89Portl/ProC-210
90AAASingl/ProC-258
90Portl/CMC-12
90Portl/ProC-188
90ProC/Singl-564
91AAA/LineD-416
91Crown/Orio-391
91Portl/LineD-416
91Portl/ProC-1573
92ScranWB/ProC-2454
93ScranWB/Team-22
Rodriques, Cecil
92Helena/ProC-1730
Roe, Preacher
45Playball-32
47TipTop
49B-162
50B-167
50Drake-1
51B-118
51T/RB-16
52B-168
52BR
52Dix
52NTea
52StarCal-91CM
52StarCal/L-79F
52T-66
52Wheat*
53B/BW-26
53Dix
53Exh/Can-1
53NB
53T-254
54B-218
54Dix
54NYJour
54T-14
55B-216
79TCMA-145
79TCMA-239
89Rini/Dodg-33
89Smok/Dodg-56
90Target-680
91T/Arc53-254
92Bz/Quadra-9M
94T/Arc54-14
Exh47
PM10/Sm-167
Roe, Rocky
88TM/Umpire-42
89TM/Umpire-40
90TM/Umpire-38
Roebig, Stuart
91Brisbane/Fut-9
Roebuck, Ed
52LaPatrie-14
52Park-75
53Exh/Can-41
55Gol/Dodg-26
55T-195
56T-58
58T-435
60BB-13
60T-519
60Union/Dodg-15
61BB-37
61P-70
61T-6
61T/St-32
62BB-37
62T-535
63T-295
64PhilBull-19
64T-187
64T/Coins-20
64T/SU
64T/St-35
65OPC-52
65T-52
78TCMA-165
90Target-681
Roebuck, Joe
89Helena/SP-13
90Erie/Star-22
91Reno/Cal-13
92CharlR/ClBest-8
92CharlR/ProC-2239
Roebuck, Ron
86Ashvl-24
86AubAs-20
Roebuck, Scott
83Wausau/Frit-20
Roeder, Jack
82Wausau/Frit-3GM
Roeder, Steve
90Welland/Pucko-27
91Welland/ClBest-19
92Pulaski/ClBest-23
92Pulaski/ProC-3175
Roenicke, Gary
76SSPC-338
80T-568
81D-116
81F-187
81OPC-37
81T-37
82D-509
82F-177
82T-204
83D-27
83F-71
83OPC-382
83T-605
84D-392
84F-18
84Nes/792-372
84OPC-372
84T-372
84T/St-205
85D-123
85F-188
85OPC-109
85T-109
86D-472
86F-285
86F/Up-U98
86OPC-183
86T-494
86T/Tr-94T
87D/OD-47
87OPC-283
87Smok/Atl-23
87T-683
87T/Tr-105T
88Panini/St-252
88S-482
88T-523
91Crown/Orio-392
91Pac/SenLg-104
91Pac/SenLg-85
92Yank/WIZ80-165
Roenicke, Ron
78LodiD
80Albuq-6
81Albuq/TCMA-9
82F-19
82Pol/Dodg-40
82T-681R
83D-327
83F-217
83Pol/Dodg-40
83T-113
84Cram/PCL-237
84D-484
84F-618
84Nes/792-647
84T-647
86F/Up-U99
86T-63
87D-412
87F-182
87Phill/TastyK-17
87T-136
87T-329
88Nashvl/CMC-21
88Nashvl/ProC-475
88Nashvl/Team-20
88S-566
88T-783
89OkCty/CMC-16
89OkCty/ProC-1519
90Target-682
91Pac/SenLg-106
91Pac/SenLg-85
91SanAn/ProC-2993CO
92Mother/Dodg-28M
92Pol/Dodg-NNO
93Mother/Dodg-28M
93Pol/Dodg-30M
Roesch, John
77Newar
78Newar
Roesler, Mike
86Cedar/TCMA-8
87Tampa-5
88Nashvl/CMC-11
88Nashvl/ProC-492
89Nashvl/CMC-7
89Nashvl/ProC-1282
89Nashvl/Team-21
90BuffB/Team-21
90F-645
90F/Can-645
90OPC-203
90S-648
90T-203
90T/89Debut-104
91AA/LineD-115
91CaroMud/LineD-115
91CaroMud/ProC-1085
92BuffB/BlueS-19
92BuffB/ProC-322
92BuffB/SB-41
Roessler, Pat
90BirmB/Best-29CO
90BirmB/ProC-1399CO
91AA/LineD-75M
91BirmB/LineD-75CO
91BirmB/ProC-1472CO
92BirmB/ProC-2599
Roetter, Randy
82QuadC-28TR
88Wausau/GS-28TR
89Wmsprt/ProC-634TR
90Calgary/CMC-25TR
90ProC/Singl-452TR
Roettger, Oscar F.L.
81Conlon-94
90Target-683
Roettger, Walter H.
(Wally)
31Exh/4-8
81Conlon-95
92Conlon/Sport-653
V94-39
Rogaliner, Chris
90Niagara/Pucko-30TR
Rogalski, Wayne
86Ashvl-25
Rogan, Pat
65T-486R
Rogan, Wilbur
(Bullet)
74Laugh/Black-19
86Negro/Frit-32
87Negro/Dixon-34
90Negro/Star-29
94TedW-111
Rogascozv, Boris
89EastLDD/ProC-DD12
Rogell, William
33G-11
34DS-76
35BU-177
35G-1D
35G-2D
35G-6D
35G-7D
81Tiger/Detroit-16
83Kaline-39MII
86Tiger/Sport-7
94Conlon-1236
R313
R313A-11
R314
V353-11
V355-52
Rogers, Brad
88Batavia/ProC-1691
Rogers, Bryan
90StLucie/Star-23
91AA/LineD-641
91Wmsprt/LineD-641
91Wmsprt/ProC-290
92Bingham/ProC-514
92Bingham/SB-66
Rogers, Charlie
90Miami/I/Star-22
90Miami/I/Star-27
91ClBest/Singl-375
91Miami/ProC-407
92Stockton/ClBest-11
92Stockton/ProC-35
94FExcel-86
Rogers, Danny
87Sumter-22
90Niagara/Pucko-1
91ClBest/Singl-379
91Fayette/ClBest-22
91Fayette/ProC-1181
Rogers, Dennis
86Nashua-24MG
87Macon-24
Rogers, Doug
89Idaho/ProC-2027
Rogers, Dusty
86Tampa-17
87Cedar-11
Rogers, Jimmy
88Myrtle/ProC-1190
88SALAS/GS-22
89Knoxvl/Best-22
89Knoxvl/ProC-1133
89Knoxvl/Star-18
90Foil/Best-176
90Knoxvl/Best-2
90Knoxvl/ProC-1241
90Knoxvl/Star-16
90ProC/Singl-815
91AA/LineD-365
91Knoxvl/LineD-365
91Knoxvl/ProC-1764
Rogers, Kenny
88Tulsa-28
89D/Best-315
89D/Rook-13
89Mother/R-21
89S/Tr-107
89Smok/R-27
89T/Tr-104T
90D-283
90F-311
90F/Can-311
90Leaf-311
90Mother/Rang-22
90OPC-683
90S-301
90S/100Ris-46
90S/YS/I-21
90Sf-216
90T-683
90T/89Debut-105
90T/JumboR-24
90ToysRUs-22
90UD-606
91B-290
91D-258
91F-299
91Leaf-105
91Mother/Rang-22
91OPC-332
91S-155
91StCl-258
91T-332
91UD-606
91Ultra-353
92D-368
92F-317
92L-173
92L/BlkGold-173
92Mother/Rang-22
92OPC-511
92Pinn-482
92S-101
92StCl-311
92T-511
92T/Gold-511
92T/GoldWin-511
92UD-651
92Ultra-445
93D-509
93F-328
93L-92
93OPC-356
93Pac/Spanish-646
93Pinn-381
93Rang/Keeb-429
93S-204
93StCl-55
93StCl/1stDay-55
93StCl/Rang-19
93T-169
93T/Gold-169
93UD-92
93Ultra-285
94B-429
94D-410
94F-320
94L-293
94Pac/Cr-628
94Pinn-221
94Pinn/Artist-221
94Pinn/Museum-221
94S-212
94S/GoldR-212
94StCl-467
94StCl/1stDay-467
94StCl/Gold-467
94StCl/Team-252
94Studio-158
94T-413
94T/Finest-94
94T/FinestRef-94
94T/Gold-413
94TripleP-200
94UD-457
94UD/CollC-242
94UD/CollC/Gold-242
94UD/CollC/Silv-242
94Ultra-133
Rogers, Kevin
88Pocatel/ProC-2091
89Clinton/ProC-891
90AS/Cal-50
90Foil/Best-76

90ProC/Singl-716
90SanJose/Best-24
90SanJose/Cal-51
90SanJose/ProC-2003
90SanJose/ProC-2172M
90SanJose/Star-19
91AA/LineD-320
91B-638
91ClBest/Singl-221
91Shrev/LineD-320
91Shrev/ProC-1823
92B-415
92Shrev/ProC-3870
92Shrev/SB-593
92Sky/AASingl-262
93B-576
93F/Final-155
93F/MLPI-10
93L/GRook-11
93Mother/Giant-24
93Pac/Spanish-615
93Pinn-613
93Pinn/RookTP-2
93S-319
93Select/RookTr-64T
93StCl/Giant-8
93T-822
93T/Gold-822
93UD-8SR
93Ultra-489
94D-508
94F-699
94Pac/Cr-554
94Pinn-365
94S-581
94StCl-459
94StCl/1stDay-459
94StCl/Gold-459
94StCl/Team-23
94T-3
94T/Gold-3
94UD/CollC-243
94UD/CollC/Gold-243
94UD/CollC/Silv-243
94Ultra-592

Rogers, Lamarr
93T-746M
93T/Gold-746M

Rogers, Lee
90Target-684
V351A-22

Rogers, Mac
85Durham-9
86Durham-24

Rogers, Marte
85Elmira-19

Rogers, Packy
87Elmira/Cain-5
90Target-685

Rogers, Randy
78Tidew
83Ander-15

Rogers, Robbie
88Reno/Cal-283

Rogers, Steve
72Dimanche*-39
74OPC-169
74T-169
74T/DE-65
74T/St-59
75OPC-173
75T-173
75T/M-173
76Crane-50
76Expo/Redp-27
76MSA/Disc
76OPC-71
76SSPC-349
76T-71
77BurgChef-159
77Expo/PostC-6
77Ho-22
77Ho/Twink-22
77OPC-153
77T-316
78OPC-9DP
78T-425
78Wiffle/Discs-62
79OPC-120
79T-235
80K-8
80OPC-271
80T-520
81D-330
81F-143
81F/St-57
81OPC-344
81OPC/Post-9
81T-725
81T/So-106
81T/St-190
82D-36
82Expo/Hygrade-18
82F-205
82F/St-36
82FBI/Disc-17
82Hygrade
82OPC-52
82OPC/Post-20
82PermaGr/AS-15
82T-605
82T/St-59
82Zeller-2
83D-18DK
83D-320
83F-294
83F/St-10M
83F/St-19AM
83F/St-19BM
83OPC-106AS
83OPC-111TL
83OPC-320
83OPC/St-208
83OPC/St-256
83Stuart-10
83T-111TL
83T-320
83T-405AS
83T-707LL
83T/St-208
83T/St-256
84D-219
84D/AAS-48
84Expo/PostC-25
84F-284
84Nes/792-394AS
84Nes/792-708LL
84Nes/792-80
84OPC-394AS
84OPC-80
84Seven-20W
84Stuart-19
84Stuart-36AS
84T-394AS
84T-708LL
84T-80
84T/Gloss40-3
84T/RD-30M
84T/St-182FOIL
84T/St-88
85D-219
85F-408
85Leaf-192
85OPC-205
85OPC/Post-11
85T-205
85T/RD-31M
85T/St-89
88Grenada-34
92Nabisco-33
93Expo/D/McDon-28
94TedW-51

Rogers, Stu
85BurlR-23

Rogers, Thomas
E121/120
W501-28
W575

Roggenburk, Garry
63T-386R
64T-258
66T-582
67T-429
68T-581
81TCMA-336
91Elmira/ClBest-28CO
91Elmira/ProC-3288
92Elmira/ClBest-25CO
92Elmira/ProC-1397

Roggendorf, Kip
93StCath/ClBest-21
93StCath/ProC-3983

Rogodzinski, Mike
74OPC-492
74T-492
76SSPC-607

Rogovin, Saul
52B-165
52RM-AL19
52T-159
52TipTop
53B/Col-75
54B-140
57T-129
91Crown/Orio-393
PM10/Sm-168

Rogozenski, Karl
83StPete-28

Rohan, Tony
85Newar-7
87Miami-9
88Miami/Star-22

Rohde, Brad
86Cram/NWL-112
86Wausau-20

Rohde, Dave
86AZ/Pol-12
86AubAs-21
87Osceola-29
88ColAst/Best-11
89ColMud/Best-21
89ColMud/ProC-123
89ColMud/Star-20
89Star/Wax-2
89Tucson/JP-20
90B-75
90F/Up-U17
90Lennox-20
90ProC/Singl-621
90Tucson/CMC-19
91B-558
91D-743
91Leaf-424
91Mother/Ast-18
91OPC-531
91S/100RisSt-69
91StCl-137
91T-531
91T/90Debut-133
91UD-662
92ColoSp/ProC-760
92StCl-753
93Pac/Spanish-100

Rohde, Dr. Richard
63FrBauer-21

Rohlfing, Wayne
79QuadC-6

Rohlof, Scott
86Visalia-17

Rohm, Dave
78Dunedin

Rohn, Andy
87Everett-7

Rohn, Dan
80Wichita-6
82Iowa-8
83Iowa-19
84Iowa-8
85IntLgAS-36
85Maine-22
86OhHenry-15
87Tacom-16
88OkCty/CMC-20
88OkCty/ProC-31
89OkCty/CMC-15
89OkCty/ProC-1530
91Pac/SenLg-21
92FtMyr/ProC-2760
92Miracle/ClBest-26MG

Rohr, Les
68T-569R
91WIZMets-333

Rohr, William
67T-547R
68T-314R

Rohrmeier, Dan
88FSLAS/Star-48
88Tampa/Star-22
89Saraso/Star-21
90A&AASingle/ProC-70
90TexLgAS/GS-29
90Tulsa/ProC-1169
90Tulsa/Team-22
91AA/LineD-593
91Tulsa/LineD-593
91Tulsa/ProC-2787
91Tulsa/Team-24
92Memphis/ProC-2433
92Memphis/SB-445
93ClBest/MLG-26
93FExcel/ML-178

Rohrwild, Shawn
90Idaho/ProC-3266
91Macon/ClBest-9
91Macon/ProC-863

Roig, Tony
59DF
60DF-16
61Union
77Fritsch-12

Rois, Luis
80GlenF/B-6
80GlenF/C-17
81GlenF-20

Rojas, Cookie
63T-221
64PhilBull-20
64T-448
65T-474
66OPC-170
66T-170
66T/RO-77
66T/RO-82
67CokeCap/Phill-11
67Pol/Phill-9
67T-595
68OPC-39
68T-39
69MB-238
69MLB/St-176
69T-507
69T/S-55
69T/St-77
69Trans-55
70MLB/St-142
70T-569
71MLB/St-427
71OPC-118
71T-118
72K-39
72MB-295
72OPC-415
72T-415
73OPC-188
73T-188
74K-42
74OPC-278
74T-278
74T/St-189
75Ho-2
75Ho/Twink-2
75OPC-169
75T-169
75T/M-169
76A&P/KC
76OPC-311
76SSPC-171
76T-311
77T-509
88Smok/Angels-1MG
88T/Tr-97MG
93Marlin/Publix-28M

Rojas, Francisco
78Cedar

Rojas, Homar
85Tigres-17
87SanAn-21
88FSLAS/Star-19
88VeroB/Star-22
89SanAn/Best-21
90SanAn/GS-25

Rojas, Jeff
85Visalia-18

Rojas, Luis
82WHave-24

Rojas, Melquiades
(Mel)
87BurlEx-27
89Jaxvl/Best-28
89Jaxvl/ProC-156
89SLAS-20
90AAASingl/ProC-585
90B-108
90Indianap/ProC-302
90UD/Ext-772
91D-681
91Expo/PostC-6
91F-245
91OPC-252
91OPC/Premier-101
91S-729RP
91S/Rook40-1
91T-252
91T/90Debut-134
91UD-357
92D-435
92F-490
92Indianap/SB-191
92OPC-583
92OPC/Premier-124
92S-725
92StCl-489
92T-583
92T/Gold-583
92T/GoldWin-583
92UD-683
93D-408
93F-79
93L-364
93LimeR/Winter-14
93OPC-347
93Pac/Spanish-537
93Pinn-419
93S-363
93StCl-553
93StCl/1stDay-553
93T-341
93T/Gold-341
93UD-190
93Ultra-70
94D-491
94F-548
94L-47
94Pac/Cr-388
94Pinn-176
94Pinn/Artist-176
94Pinn/Museum-176
94S-162
94S/GoldR-162
94StCl-14
94StCl/1stDay-14
94StCl/Gold-14
94T-78
94T/Gold-78
94UD-366
94UD/CollC-244
94UD/CollC/Gold-244
94UD/CollC/Silv-244
94Ultra-525

Rojas, Mike
83Idaho-17

Rojas, Minnie
67CokeCap/DodgAngel-33
67OPC-104
67T-104
68T-305
69T-502

Rojas, Ricky
86FtMyr-23
87FtMyr-20
88EastLAS/ProC-36
88Vermont/ProC-959
89Wmsprt/Star-19
90Foil/Best-73
90Wmsprt/Best-21
90Wmsprt/ProC-1058
90Wmsprt/Star-22
91AAA/LineD-71
91Calgary/LineD-71
91Calgary/ProC-516
92London/ProC-631
92London/SB-417

Rojas, Roberto
92Bristol/ProC-1428
93LimeR/Winter-38

Rojas, Wilberto
90StCath/ProC-3478

Rojek, Stan
49B-135
49Eureka-171
49Royal-15
50B-86
51B-166
52B-137
52NTea
52T-163
90Target-686
PM10/Sm-169

Rokosz, Keith
77AppFx

Roland, James
63T-522R
64T-341
65OPC-171
65T-171
68T-276
69T-336
70T-719

71MLB/St-524
71OPC-642
71T-642
72OPC-464
72T-464
78Twin/Frisz-43
92Yank/WIZ70-136
93Rang/Keeb-36
Roland, Jason
92MN-22M
Roldan, Sal
88Miami/Star-21
88SLCity-27
Rolen, Scott
94ClBest/Gold-120
Rolen, Steve
90Clinton/Best-25
90Clinton/ProC-2559
91ClBest/Singl-112
91SanJose/ClBest-11
91SanJose/ProC-20
92SanJose/ClBest-3
Rolfe, Robert
(Red)
34DS-104
34DS-29
34G-94
35BU-181
35BU-22
35G-8E
35G-9E
41DP-65MG
51B-319MG
52T-296MG
72F/FFeat-22
92Conlon/Sport-576
92Yank/WIZAS-68
R314
V355-38
Rolland, Dave
86DayBe-23
87SanJose-15
Rollin, Rondal
82BirmB-13
84Evansvl-3
86BirmB/Team-28
87BirmB/Best-7
87SLAS-2
90BirmDG/Best-29
Rollings, Bill
79Tulsa-23OWN
Rollings, William R.
(Red)
33G-88
V354-40
Rollins, Michael
92Lipscomb-21
93Lipscomb-18
Rollins, Patrick
(Pep)
91Utica/ClBest-28
91Utica/ProC-3250
Rollins, Rich
61Clover-23
62T-596R
63F-24
63J-4
63P-4
63Salada-49
63T-110
64Bz-10
64T-270
64T-8LL
64T/Coins-51
64T/SU
64T/St-52
65OPC-90
65T-90
66T-473
67CokeCap/Twin-8
67OPC-98
67T-98
68Dexter-67
68T-243
69MB-239
69MLB/St-98
69T-451
69T/St-229
70MLB/St-276
70McDon-4
70T-652
72MB-296
78TCMA-119
89Pac/Leg-169
Exh47
WG10-45
WG9-44
Rolls, David
88Eugene/Best-12
90Eugene/GS-25
91SLCity/ProC-3213
91SLCity/SportP-9
92CharlR/ClBest-13
92CharlR/ProC-2228
Romagna, Randy
83Kinston/Team-21
85Kingst-14
86Kinston-21
Roman, Bob
77Spartan
Roman, Dan
87Oneonta-7
88FtLaud/Star-20
89FtLaud/Star-23
92Erie/ClBest-11
92Erie/ProC-1622
93T-782M
93T/Gold-782M
Roman, Jose
81Batavia-3
82Watlo/Frit-24
83Watlo/Frit-12
84BuffB-8
85F-646
85Maine-13
86Maine-18
87BuffB-21
87Tidew-23
87Tidew/TCMA-29
88Tidew/CANDL-25
88Tidew/CMC-9
88Tidew/ProC-1601
Roman, Junior
77Watlo
78Wausau
92GulfCM/ProC-3497
Roman, Miguel
81Batavia-26
83Watlo/Frit-13
86Water-20
87Wmsprt-13
88Jacks/GS-17
Roman, Ray
87Reading-11
88Reading/ProC-885
Roman, Vince
90Ashvl/ClBest-22
90AubAs/Best-10
90AubAs/ProC-3405
91Ashvl/ProC-580
92Osceola/ClBest-24
92Osceola/ProC-2544
Roman, William A.
65T-493R
Romanick, Ron
81Redwd-5
82Holyo-8
83Nashua-6
84F/X-101
84Smok/Cal-23
84T/Tr-102
85D-451
85F-309
85OPC-280
85Smok/Cal-11
85T-579
85T/St-231
86D-85
86F-166
86F/Mini-34
86F/St-100
86Leaf-81
86OPC-76
86Smok/Cal-11
86T-733
86T/St-180
87Colum-27
87Colum/Pol-21
87Colum/TCMA-8
87OPC-136
87T-136
88Stockton/Cal-176
88Stockton/ProC-731
Romano, James
52Park-73
90Target-1056
Romano, John
59T-138
60T-323
61Kahn
61T-5
61T/RO-19
61T/St-142
62Bz
62J-42
62Kahn
62P-42
62P/Can-42
62Salada-94
62Shirriff-94
62Sugar-7
62T-330
62T/St-40
62T/bucks
63Bz-18
63J-76
63P-76
63Salada-46
63Sugar-7
63T-392M
63T-72
63T/SO
64Kahn
64T-515
64T/Coins-9
64T/S-59
64T/SU
64T/St-48
64T/tatt
65OPC-17
65T-17
65T/E-10
66T-199M
66T-413
67OPC-196
67T-196
Romano, Scott
90Greens/Best-18
90Greens/ProC-2670
90Greens/Star-20
90Oneonta/ProC-3373
91Greens/ProC-3067
92FtLaud/ClBest-15
92FtLaud/ProC-2622
92FtLaud/Team-28
93Greens/ClBest-19
93Greens/ProC-896
Romano, Thomas
82Madis/Frit-28
83Albany-19
84Cram/PCL-77
85Cram/PCL-131
86Indianap-7
87Indianap-14
88BuffB/CMC-13
88BuffB/Polar-4
88BuffB/ProC-1485
89BuffB/CMC-21
89BuffB/ProC-1670
Romanoli, Paul
92Spring/ClBest-7
92Spring/ProC-864
Romanov, Vitalyi
89EastLDD/ProC-DD2
Romanovsky, Mike
86PalmSp-28
86PalmSp/Smok-10
87MidldA-22
Romay, Willie
89Belling/Legoe-28
91Penin/ClBest-17
91Penin/ProC-391
Rombard, Rich
91Fayette/ProC-1187CO
Romero, Al
83Nashua-19
85Cram/PCL-25
86Edmon-24
Romero, Brian
89Butte/SP-6
90A&AASingle/ProC-79
90Foil/Best-301
90Gaston/Best-7
90Gaston/ProC-2520
90Gaston/Star-20
90SALAS/Star-21
90Star/ISingl-97
91AA/LineD-594
91Tulsa/LineD-594
91Tulsa/ProC-2772
91Tulsa/Team-25
92Sky/AASingl-265
92Tulsa/ProC-2693
92Tulsa/SB-601
Romero, Charlie
88QuadC/GS-24
89PalmSp/Cal-36
89PalmSp/ProC-470
Romero, Ed
76BurlB
77Holyo
78Spokane/Cramer-10
78Spokane/Team-10
79T-708R
79Vanco-17
80Vanco-13
81T-659R
82D-536
82Pol/Brew-11
82T-408
83D-584
83F-44
83Gard-15
83Pol/Brew-11
83T-271
84D-89
84F-212
84Gard-16
84Nes/792-146
84Pol/Brew-11
84T-146
85D-515
85F-593
85Gard-17
85Pol/Brew-11
85T-498
85ThomMc/Discs-18
86D-455
86F-500
86OPC-317
86T-317
86T/Tr-95T
87D-606
87F-42
87OPC-158
87T-675
88D-623
88D/RedSox/Bk-623
88F-362
88S-259
88T-37
89T/Tr-105T
89UD-40
90B-361
90CokeK/Tiger-20
91AAA/LineD-291
91LasVegas/LineD-291
91LasVegas/ProC-244
92Brew/Carlson-19
92Spokane/ClBest-27MG
92Spokane/ClBest-30M
92Spokane/ProC-1310MG
Romero, Elbi
87Spartan-19
Romero, Elvis
86Cram/NWL-140
87Kenosha-23
Romero, Esmyel
82Redwd-9
Romero, Jonathan
92MidldA/ProC-4034
92PalmSp/ClBest-6
Romero, Mandy
89Augusta/ProC-498
89SALAS/GS-10
90CLAS/CL-21
90Salem/Star-18
91AA/LineD-103
91CaroMud/LineD-103
91CaroMud/ProC-1090
92CaroMud/ProC-1185
92CaroMud/SB-141
92ClBest-326
92Sky/AASingl-66
Romero, Philip
91FresnoSt/Smok-10
92Martins/ClBest-9
92Martins/ProC-3066
Romero, Ramon
78Watlo
79Wausau-14
81AppFx-23
81Watlo-14
82AppFx/Frit-6
82Watlo-9
83BuffB-9
83GlenF-10
84BuffB-16
84Maine-1
85BuffB-11
85Polar/Ind-50
86D-495
86T-208
86Toledo-20
90HagersDG/Best-23
Romero, Ronaldo
89Gaston/ProC-1016
89Gaston/Star-21
90Gaston/Best-2
90Gaston/ProC-2521
90Gaston/Star-21
Romero, Scott
90Foil/Best-270
Romero, Tony
87Elmira/Black-21
87Elmira/Cain-6
87Elmira/Red-21
Romine, Kevin
84Pawtu-13
85Pawtu-11
86Pawtu-19
87Pawtu-4
87Pawtu/TCMA-18
87T-121
88D/RedSox/Bk-NEW
88F-363
88S-644
89F-98
89Pawtu/CMC-18
89Pawtu/Dunkin-16
89Pawtu/ProC-682
89S-541
89UD-524
90B-273
90D-476
90F-286
90F/Can-286
90Leaf-414
90Pep/RSox-19
90S-458
90T/TVRSox-33
90T/Tr-105T
90UD-441
91D-290
91F-113
91OPC-652
91S-116
91T-652
Rommel, Ed
21Exh-146
25Exh-111
26Exh-111
28Yueng-55
55B-239UMP
77Galasso-196
87Conlon/2-19
94Conlon-1156
E120
E210-55
R306
R316
V100
V61-9
W501-1
W501-102
W502-55
W515-5
W572
W573
W575
WG7-45
Rommell, Rick
80ElPaso-6
81Holyo-26
Romo, Enrique
78OPC-186
78T-278
79OPC-281
79T-548
80T-332
81D-255
81F-385
81OPC-28
81T-28
82D-59
82F-496
82T-106
83F-320
83T-226

Romo, Robert
87AubAs-16
Romo, Vicente
69T-267
70MLB/St-163
70OPC-191
70T-191
71MLB/St-329
71OPC-723
71T-723
72MB-297
72OPC-499
72T-499
73OPC-381
73T-381
74OPC-197SD
74T-197
75OPC-274
75T-274
75T/M-274
83F-218
83T-633
90Target-687
Romonosky, John
59T-267
60T-87
Ronan, Kernan
82Clinton/Frit-16
83Phoenix/BHN-10
84Shrev/FB-17
89PalmSp/Cal-62CO
89PalmSp/ProC-481
90PalmSp/Cal-229CO
90PalmSp/ProC-2595CO
91AA/LineD-450M
91London/LineD-450CO
91MidldA/OneHour-24
91MidldA/ProC-451CO
92MidldA/ProC-4042CO
92MidldA/SB-475M
Ronan, Marc
88Alaska/Team-15
89Alaska/Team-15
90Hamil/Best-14
91ClBest/Singl-5
91Savan/ClBest-14
91Savan/ProC-1654
92ClBest-270
92Spring/ClBest-2
92Spring/ProC-872
Ronca, Joe
90Welland/Pucko-14
91Augusta/ClBest-22
91Augusta/ProC-821
92Salem/ProC-77
Rondon, Alberto
76Dubuq
Rondon, Alfie
89Pac/SenLg-173
91Pac/SenLg-68
91Pac/SenLg-78
Rondon, Gilbert
(Gil)
89Pac/SenLg-196
90Kgsport/Best-26CO
90Kgsport/Star-27CO
91MedHat/ProC-4118CO
91MedHat/SportP-24CO
91Pac/SenLg-11
92MedHat/SportP-28CO
Rondon, Isidro
86Tampa-18
Ronk, Jeff
82Amari-7
83Beaum-14
84Beaum-25
Ronning, Al
52Park-49
53Exh/Can-56
Ronson, Tod
86Cram/NWL-21
86Everett/Pop-27
87Clinton-8
88SanJose/Cal-128
88SanJose/ProC-126
89Salinas/Cal-143
89Salinas/ProC-1821
Roobarb
85Coke/WS
86Coke/WS
87Coke/WS-30M
Rood, Nelson
86Tucson-19
87Tucson-15
88Tucson/CMC-13
88Tucson/JP-19
88Tucson/ProC-191
90AAASingl/ProC-101
90Edmon/CMC-14
90Edmon/ProC-525
90ProC/Singl-491
92Clinton/ClBest-27CO
92Clinton/ProC-3613
Roof, Eugene L.
(Gene)
78StPete
79ArkTr-22
81Louisvl-5
82D-615
82Louisvl-25
82T-561R
83F-20
83Louisvl/Riley-5
84Louisvl-5
85Richm-20
86Nashvl-23
87Toledo-22
87Toledo/TCMA-22
88Toledo/ProC-599
89Fayette/ProC-1577
90Fayette/ProC-2423MG
90SALAS/Star-23MG
91AA/LineD-399MG
91London/LineD-399MG
91London/ProC-1892MG
93Tiger/Gator-28M
Roof, Phil
63T-324R
64T-541R
65T-537R
66T-382
67CokeCap/A's-9
67OPC-129
67T-129
68T-484
69MB-240
69Sunoco/Pin-15
69T-334
70McDon-5
70OPC-359
70T-359
71MLB/St-450
71OPC-22
71T-22
72MB-298
72OPC-201
72T-201
73OPC-598
73T-598
74OPC-388
74T-388
75OPC-576
75T-576
75T/M-576
76OPC-424
76SSPC-224
76T-424
77OPC-121
77T-392
78Padre/FamFun-27CO
83OrlanTw-1
84Mother/Mar-27CO
85Mother/Mar-27CO
86Mother/Mar-28CO
87Mother/Mar-28CO
88Mother/Mar-27CO
90Cub/Mara-28CO
90Cub/Mara-28CO
90T/TVCub-6CO
91Cub/Mara-x
91Cub/Mara-x
91Cub/Vine-22CO
92OrlanSR/ProC-2862MG
92OrlanSR/SB-524MG
Rooker, Dave
83Butte-26
86PrWill-22
87Harris-4
Rooker, Jim
69T-376R
70OPC-222
70T-222
71MLB/St-428
71OPC-730
71T-730
71T/Coins-32
72T-742
74OPC-402
74T-402
75OPC-148
75T-148
75T/M-148
76OPC-243
76SSPC-566
76T-243
77OPC-161
77T-82
78T-308
79T-584
80T-694
81F-368
93Pirate/Nation-26ANN
Rooker, Michael
88Pac/8Men-9
Rooks, George
N172
N284
Roomes, Rolando
82QuadC-24
83QuadC-27
86WinSalem-24
87Pittsfld-25
88TripleA/ASCMC-7
89D-577
89F-644R
89F/Up-86
89Kahn/Reds-36
89Nashvl/CMC-22
89Nashvl/ProC-1286
89S/HotRook-37
89S/Tr-109T
89UD-6SR
90B-56
90Classic-38
90D-360
90F-432
90F/Can-432
90OPC-364
90Panini/St-254
90S-417
90S/100Ris-92
90S/YS/I-22
90T-364
90T/Big-87
90T/St-143
90UD-170
91Denver/ProC-136
Rooney, Jim
84Newar-16
Rooney, Pat
79Memphis/TCMA-22
80Memphis-17
82Wichita-15
83Wichita/Dog-18
84Colum-3
84Colum/Pol-21
85Syrac-16
Root, Charley H.
28Exh-11
29Exh/4-6
30CEA/Pin-8
31Exh/4-6
32Orbit/un-51
33Exh/4-3
33G-226
60T-457C
77Galasso-59
88Conlon/3-24
91Conlon/Sport-93
92Cub/OldStyle-20
R303/A
R305
R306
R308-190
R316
R332-44
V351B-39
Root, Mitch
(The Rope)
91Hunting/ClBest-21
91Hunting/ProC-3343
92Hunting/ClBest-19
92Hunting/ProC-3157
Roper, Brian
89Butte/SP-3
Roper, Chad
92Classic/DP-46
92FrRow/DP-60
92LitSun/HSPros-22
93StCl/MurphyS-177
94B-572
Roper, John
91CharWh/ClBest-9
91CharWh/ProC-2886
91ClBest/Singl-276
91SALAS/ProC-SAL11
92B-528
92Chatt/ProC-3819
92Chatt/SB-194
92ClBest-72
92ProC/Tomorrow-218
92Sky/AASingl-87
92UD/ML-233
92UD/ML-44M
93B-34
93ClBest/MLG-55
93F/Final-19
93FExcel/ML-29
93Flair/Wave-14
93Select/RookTr-34T
93Ultra-334
94D-551
94F-423
94Pinn-137
94Pinn/Artist-137
94Pinn/Museum-137
94S-623
94StCl-476
94StCl/1stDay-476
94StCl/Gold-476
94T-581
94T/Gold-581
94UD-68
94UD/CollC-245
94UD/CollC/Gold-245
94UD/CollC/Silv-245
94UD/ElecD-68
94Ultra-175
Roque, Jorge
72OPC-316R
72T-316R
73OPC-606R
73T-606R
Roque, Rafael
92GulfCM/ProC-3479
Rorex, Troy
92Lipscomb-22
93Lipscomb-19
Rosa, Julio
88Bristol/ProC-1869
89Fayette/ProC-1587
Rosado, Edwin
(Ed)
88Martins/Star-28
89Batavia/ProC-1944
89Spartan/ProC-1029
89Spartan/Star-20
90Clearw/Star-19
91AA/LineD-516
91Reading/LineD-516
91Reading/ProC-1373
92Reading/ProC-579
92Reading/SB-541
Rosado, Luis
(Papo)
78Tidew
79Syrac/TCMA-18
79Syrac/Team-2
80Tidew-22
84RochR-12
85RochR-3
91WIZMets-334
Rosar, Warren
(Buddy)
41G-4
48B-10
48L-128
49B-138
50B-136
51B-236
92Yank/WIZAS-69
R346-19
Rosario, Alfonso
78Cedar
Rosario, Angel
(Jimmy)
72OPC-366
72T-366
Rosario, David
87Peoria-16
88WinSalem/Star-15
89CharlK-13
91AAA/LineD-215
91Iowa/LineD-215
91Iowa/ProC-1060
92ColClip/Pol-8
92ColClip/ProC-349
92ColClip/SB-114
92Sky/AAASingl-54
Rosario, Eliezel
90Ashvl/ProC-2747
Rosario, Francisco
88Savan/ProC-358
90Martins/ProC-3194
Rosario, Gabriel
91MedHat/ProC-4108
91MedHat/SportP-15
92Myrtle/ClBest-22
92Myrtle/ProC-2205
93Dunedin/ClBest-18
Rosario, Jimmy
75Sacra/Caruso-12
Rosario, Jose
78Dunedin
Rosario, Jossy
89CharWh/Best-8
89CharWh/ProC-1750
Rosario, Julio
86Elmira-17
87Elmira/Black-8
87Elmira/Cain-7
87Elmira/Red-8
88Elmira-18
88WinHaven/Star-22
89Elmira/Pucko-16
Rosario, Mel
86Kinston-22
87FtLaud-26
88Albany/ProC-1343
89FtLaud/Star-24
90Chatt/GS-26
92Spokane/ClBest-14
92Spokane/ProC-1297
Rosario, Sal
75BurlB
Rosario, Simon
76Dubuq
77Cocoa
78DaytB
81Tucson-8
84Durham-1
85Greenvl/Team-14
Rosario, Victor
85Elmira-20
86Greens-21
87Greens-19
88Martins/Star-29
89Reading/Star-20
89ScranWB/CMC-23
89ScranWB/ProC-710
90AAASingl/ProC-309
90ProC/Singl-241
90ScranWB/CMC-15
90ScranWB/ProC-607
91AAA/LineD-440
91F-701
91Richm/Bob-21
91Richm/LineD-440
91Richm/ProC-2577
91Richm/Team-11
91T/90Debut-135
92Sky/AAASingl-267
92Toledo/ProC-1051
92Toledo/SB-595
93LimeR/Winter-135
Roscoe, Greg
88Watlo/ProC-691
89Kinston/Star-21
89Watertn/Star-20
90Canton/Best-23
90Canton/ProC-1308
90Canton/Star-15
91AA/LineD-93
91Canton/LineD-93
91Canton/ProC-980
92ColoSp/ProC-750
92ColoSp/SB-94
Rose
53Exh/Can-42
Rose, Carl
86Watertn-19
Rose, Don
73OPC-178
73T-178
75Phoenix-7
75Phoenix/Caruso-21
75Phoenix/CircleK-7
91WIZMets-335

Rose, Guy
71Richm/Team-16
Rose, Heath
92BurlAs/ProC-545
Rose, Kevin
79Newar-20
Rose, Mark
90Tampa/DIMD-28CO
92Greens/ClBest-27CO
92Greens/ProC-798CO
93Greens/ProC-905CO
Rose, Pete Jr.
82F-640M
89Erie/Star-22
89Freder/Star-27
89Star/IISingl-175
90Classic-75
90Freder/Team-20
91Saraso/ClBest-18
91Saraso/ProC-1120
92ColRS/ClBest-1
92ColRS/ProC-2420
93Kinston/Team-23
Rose, Pete
63FrBauer-23
63T-537R
64Kahn
64T-125
64T/Coins-82
65Kahn
65OPC-207
65T-207
66Bz-38
66Kahn
66OPC-30
66T-30
66T/RO-83
66T/RO-83
67Bz-38
67CokeCap/AS-2
67CokeCap/NLAS-30
67CokeCap/Reds-13
67Kahn
67T-430
67T/Test/SU-1
68Bz-15
68Bz-6
68T-230
68T/ActionSt-5C
68T/G-30
68T/Post-23
69Citgo-14
69Kelly/Pin-15
69MB-241
69MLB/St-135
69MLBPA/Pin-55
69NTF
69OPC-120
69OPC-2LL
69T-120
69T-2LL
69T-424AS
69T/4in1-19M
69T/DE-21
69T/S-41
69T/St-29
69T/decal
69Trans-54
70K-2
70MB-24
70MLB/St-35
70OPC-458AS
70OPC-61LL
70T-458AS
70T-580
70T-61LL
70T/CB
70T/S-34
70T/Super-34
70Trans-1
71Bz
71Bz/Test-32
71K-65
71MD
71MLB/St-573
71MLB/St-68
71OPC-100
71T-100
71T/Coins-101
71T/GM-15
71T/Greatest-15
71T/S-20
71T/Super-20
71T/tatt-14
72Dimanche*-63
72K-6
72MB-299
72ProStars/PostC-21
72T-559
72T-560IA
72T/Post-11
73K-6
73OPC-130
73T-130
73T/Lids-44
74K-38
74OPC-201LL
74OPC-300
74OPC-336AS
74T-201LL
74T-300
74T-336AS
74T/DE-16
74T/St-30
75Ho-29
75Ho/Twink-29
75K-11
75OPC-211MVP
75OPC-320
75SSPC/Puzzle-22
75T-211MVP
75T-320
75T/M-211MVP
75T/M-320
76Crane-51
76Ho-66
76Icee
76K-55
76MSA/Disc
76OPC-240
76SSPC-41
76T-240
77BurgChef-204
77Ho-8
77Ho/Twink-8
77K-20
77OPC-240
77Pep-43
77T-450
77T/CS-38
77T/ClothSt-38
78Ho-128
78OPC-100DP
78OPC-240RB
78Pep-21
78SSPC/270-132
78T-20
78T-5RB
78Wiffle/Discs-63
79BK/P-13
79Ho-144
79K-22
79OPC-343
79T-204M
79T-650
79T/Comics-28
80BK/P-4
80BK/PHR-21
80K-35
80OPC-282
80T-4RB
80T-540
80T/S-19
80T/Super-19
81Coke
81D-131
81D-251
81D-371
81Drake-3
81F-1
81F-645M
81F/St-43M
81F/St-74
81K-63
81MSA/Disc-27
81OPC-180
81PermaGr/AS-7
81PermaGr/CC-5
81Sqt-11
81T-180
81T-205M
81T/HT
81T/Nat/Super-12
81T/So-62
81T/St-200
82D-168
82D-1DK
82D-585M
82Drake-28
82F-256
82F-640M
82F/St-107M
82F/St-109M
82F/St-51
82FBI/Disc-18
82K-18
82KMart-24
82KMart-44
82OPC-24IA
82OPC-337AS
82OPC-361
82PermaGr/AS-16
82PermaGr/CC-9
82Sqt-12
82T-337AS
82T-4RB
82T-636TL
82T-780
82T-781IA
82T/St-117
82T/St-121
82T/St-78
83D-42
83D/AAS-31
83Drake-24
83F-171
83F-634M
83F/St-1AM
83F/St-1BM
83F/St-24M
83F/St-3M
83F/St-5M
83K-6
83OPC-100
83OPC-101SV
83OPC-373AS
83OPC/St-272
83PermaGr/CC-13
83T-100
83T-101SV
83T-397AS
83T/Fold-3M
83T/Gloss40-14
83T/St-272
83T/St/Box-7
84D-61
84D/AAS-54
84D/Champs-27
84Drake-27
84Expo/PostC-26
84F-46
84F-636IA
84F/St-119
84F/St-99
84F/X-U102
84MiltBrad-21
84Nes/792-300
84Nes/792-701LL
84Nes/792-702LL
84OPC-300
84Ralston-4
84Seven-22C
84Stuart-17
84T-300
84T-701LL
84T-702LL
84T/Cereal-4
84T/Gloss40-1
84T/RD-24M
84T/St-115
84T/Tr-103T
85D-254
85D-641
85D/HL-10
85D/HL-40
85F-550
85F-640IA
85F/LimEd-29
85F/St-1
85F/St-2
85F/St-3
85FunFoodPin-4
85Leaf-144
85OPC-116
85Seven-10G
85Sportflic/Test-43
85T-547MG
85T-600
85T-6RB
85T/3D-5
85T/Gloss40-10
85T/RD-24M
85T/St-57
85T/Super-32
85Woolwth-30
86BK/AP-4
86D-62
86D-644IA
86D-653M
86D/AAS-34
86D/DKsuper-27
86Drake-22
86F-191
86F-628IA
86F-638M
86F/HOF-1
86F/LL-36
86F/LimEd-37
86F/Mini-40
86F/Slug-29
86F/St-101
86Jiffy-11
86Leaf-209M
86Leaf-260M
86Leaf-53
86Meadow/Blank-12
86Meadow/Milk-9
86Meadow/Stat-8
86OPC-1
86OPC/WaxBox-N
86Quaker-11
86Seven/Coin-C2M
86Seven/Coin-E2M
86Seven/Coin-S16M
86Seven/Coin-S2M
86Seven/Coin-W2M
86Sf-130M
86Sf-138M
86Sf-181M
86Sf-182M
86Sf-50
86Sf-51M
86Sf-56M
86Sf-58M
86Sf-69M
86Sf/Dec-60
86Sf/Rook-46M
86T-1
86T-206RB
86T-2M
86T-3M
86T-4M
86T-5M
86T-6M
86T-741MG
86T-7M
86T/3D-22
86T/Gloss60-51
86T/Rose-Set
86T/St-134
86T/St-1FOIL
86T/St-2
86T/Super-46
86T/Tatt-6M
86T/WaxBox-N
86TexGold-14A
86TexGold-14B
86TexGold-14C
86TrueVal-4
86Woolwth-29
87Classic-1
87Classic/Up-103
87D-186
87F-213
87F/BB-37
87F/Excit-38
87F/Hottest-32
87F/LL-37
87F/Lim-36
87F/RecSet-33
87F/St-102
87KMart-19
87Kraft-34
87Leaf-129
87OPC-200
87RedFoley/St-64
87Sf-25
87Sf/TPrev-4M
87T-200
87T-281TL
87T-393MG
87T/Gloss60-41
87T/St-139
88Classic/Blue-226
88Grenada-79
88KMart-22
88Kahn/Reds-14
88KennerFig-93
88T-475MG
89Classic-71
89Kahn/Reds-14MG
89Kenner/BBGr-15
89T-505MG
89T/LJN-133
90HOF/St-84
91T/Ruth-7
93YooHoo-17
Rose, Robert
(Bobby)
86QuadC-29
88MidwLAS/GS-23
88QuadC/GS-14
89MidldA/GS-27
89TexLAS/GS-3
90AAASingl/ProC-102
90B-293
90Classic/Up-41
90Edmon/CMC-15
90Edmon/ProC-526
90F-651R
90F/Can-651
90ProC/Singl-492
90S-604
90T/89Debut-106
90UD-77
91AAA/LineD-169
91B-206
91Edmon/LineD-169
91Edmon/ProC-1524
91F-324
92D-90
92F-68
92L-250
92L/BlkGold-250
92OPC-652
92OPC/Premier-169
92Pol/Angel-16
92S-558
92StCl-79
92T-652
92T/Gold-652
92T/GoldWin-652
92UD-611
92Ultra-330
Rose, Scott
91Modesto/ClBest-13
91Modesto/ProC-3087
91Oneonta/ProC-4169
92Madis/ClBest-23
92Madis/ProC-1233
Roseboro, Jaime
86LitFalls-24
87Columbia-6
88Clmbia/GS-24
89StLucie/Star-22
89Star/IISingl-117
90B-134
90Jacks/GS-10
90T/TVMets-56
91Tidew/ProC-2525
92Harris/ProC-474
Roseboro, Johnny
58T-42
59Morrell
59T-441
60BB-7
60MacGregor-21
60Morrell
60T-292M
60T-88
60Union/Dodg-16
61P-166
61T-363
61T/St-33
61Union/Dodg-17
62BB-8
62J-107
62P-107
62P/Can-107
62Salada-133
62Shirriff-133
62T-32
62T-397AS
62T/St-139
63J-120
63Salada-12
63T-487
64T-88
65T-405

65T/trans-28
66OPC-189
66T-189
66T/RO-15
66T/RO-84
67CokeCap/DodgAngel-9
67T-365
68Bz-7
68Dexter-68
68OPC-65
68T-65
69MB-242
69MLB/St-70
69OPC-218
69T-218
69T/4in1-9M
69T/St-198
70MLB/St-285
70Pol/SenY-9
70T-655
72MB-300
73OPC-421CO
73T-421C
74OPC-276CO
74T-276C
78TCMA-185
87Smok/Dodg-30
88Smok/Dodg-2
89Smok/Dodg-64
90Target-688
Roselli, Bob
56T-131
61T-529
62T-363
Rosello, Dave
73Wichita-15
74OPC-607R
74T-607R
76OPC-546
76T-546
77T-92
78T-423
80T-122
81D-79
82Charl-18
82D-617
82F-377
82T-724
Roseman, James
E223
N172/ST
N284
N690
N690/2
Rosen, Al
50B-232
50NumNum
51B-187
51BR-A1
51T/RB-35
52B-151
52NTea
52NumNum-10
52StarCal-88CM
52StarCal/L-74B
52T-10
53B/Col-8
53NB
53RM-AL24
53T-135
54DanDee
54RH
54RM-AL12
54T-15
55Armour-17
55Gol/Ind-25
55RM-AL11
55Salem
55T-70
55T/DH-1
56Carling-6
56T-35
56T/Hocus-A8
56T/Pin-10
61T-474MVP
72T/Test-6
74Laugh/ASG-54
75OPC-191M
75T-191MVP
75T/M-191MVP
77Galasso-35
79TCMA-175
82Ohio/HOF-60
90Pac/Legend-78
90Swell/Great-39
91Swell/Great-78
91T/Arc53-135
92AP/ASG-70
92Bz/Quadra-20M
93UD/ATH-109
94T/Arc54-15
94TedW-28
PM10/Sm-170
R423-85
Rosen, David
85Osceola/Team-30CO
Rosen, Goodwin
(Goody)
39PlayBall-76
45Playball-31
90Target-689
Rosenbalm, Marc
92SanBern/ClBest-9
Rosenberg, Steve
87Albany-1
88Vanco/CMC-3
88Vanco/ProC-754
89Coke/WS-24
89D-219
89F/Up-22
89T-616
89UD/Ext-715
90AAASingl/ProC-167
90AlbanyDG/Best-30
90D-253
90F-547
90F/Can-547
90OPC-379
90ProC/Singl-638
90S-523
90T-379
90UD-522
90Vanco/CMC-11
90Vanco/ProC-489
91AAA/LineD-292
91LasVegas/LineD-292
91LasVegas/ProC-234
Rosenbohm, Jim
92Classic/DP-30
92FrRow/DP-92
93T-667
93T/Gold-667
Rosenfeld, Max
90Target-1057
Rosenfield, Dave
88Tidew/CANDL-5GM
Rosengren, John
(Rosey)
92Bristol/ClBest-9
92Bristol/ProC-1410
94FExcel-60
Rosenthal, Larry
94Conlon-1309
Rosenthal, Wayne
87Gaston/ProC-18
88CharlR/Star-21
89CharlR/Star-20
89Tulsa/Team-21
90Tulsa/ProC-1153
91AAA/LineD-321
91OkCty/LineD-321
91OkCty/ProC-178
92F-318
92OPC-584
92OPC/Premier-30
92OkCty/ProC-1915
92OkCty/SB-304
92S-749
92Sky/AAASingl-147
92StCl-658
92T-584
92T/91Debut-151
92T/Gold-584
92T/GoldWin-584
92Ultra-446
93Rang/Keeb-313
Rosfelder, Chris
89Elmira/Pucko-17
Rosinski, Brian
80Wichita-17
Roskom, Bryan
89Kenosha/ProC-1069
89Kenosha/Star-22
90Kenosha/Best-15
90Kenosha/Star-29
Roskos, John
94ClBest/Gold-74
Roslund, John
75QuadC
Roso, James
(Jimmy)
89Bluefld/Star-17
89Star/IISingl-115
90ProC/Singl-870
90Wausau/Best-16
90Wausau/ProC-2129
90Wausau/Star-20
91Kane/ClBest-13
91Kane/ProC-2660
91Kane/Team-18
92Freder/ClBest-24
92Freder/ProC-1808
Ross, Chester
41G-31
Ross, Chuck
76BurlB
77BurlB
78Holyo
Ross, Dan
89London/ProC-1361
Ross, David
89Martins/Star-27
90Batavia/ProC-3066
91Peoria/ClBest-1
91Peoria/ProC-1341
91Peoria/Team-12
Ross, Don
45Playball-13
47Royal/Mont-3
49B/PCL-20
90Target-690
Ross, Floyd Robert
(Bob)
52T-298
54T-189
57Seattle/Pop-31
94T/Arc54-189
Ross, Gary Douglas 1
69T-404R
70T-694
71MLB/St-236
71OPC-153
71T-153
73OPC-112
73T-112
75Hawaii/Caruso-16
75IntLgAS/Broder-29
75PCL/AS-29
77T-544
78T-291
Ross, Gary Douglas 2
90Bend/Legoe-26
91Madison/ProC-2131
Ross, Jackie
92Helena/ProC-1731
Ross, Joe
89Oneonta/ProC-2125
Ross, Mark
82Tucson-3
84Cram/PCL-68
85Cram/PCL-54
86Tucson-20
87Vanco-5
88Syrac/CMC-5
88Syrac/ProC-824
89Syrac/CMC-4
89Syrac/MerchB-19
89Syrac/ProC-814
89Syrac/Team-19
90AAASingl/ProC-487
90BuffB/CMC-9
90BuffB/ProC-372
90BuffB/Team-22
90ProC/Singl-9
91AAA/LineD-441
91Richm/Bob-15
91Richm/LineD-441
91Richm/ProC-2567
91Richm/Team-28
92Greenvl/ProC-1169
92Greenvl/SB-250M
Ross, Michael
88Hamil/ProC-1727
89Spring/Best-10
90ArkTr/GS-26
91AAA/LineD-245
91Louisvl/LineD-245
91Louisvl/ProC-2931
92ArkTr/ProC-1139
92ArkTr/SB-44
Ross, Ron
89Niagara/Pucko-27
Ross, Sean
87Sumter-27
88BurlB/ProC-20
89Durham/Star-19
89Durham/Team-19
91AA/LineD-217
91ClBest/Singl-156
91Greenvl/ClBest-22
91Greenvl/LineD-217
91Greenvl/ProC-3017
92Richm/Bleach-19
92Richm/Comix-18
92Richm/ProC-389
92Richm/SB-440
93Pawtu/Ball-20
Rosselli, Joe
90A&AASingle/ProC-165
90Everett/Best-11
90Everett/ProC-3127
91Clinton/ClBest-6
92AS/Cal-17
92ClBest-250
92SanJose/ClBest-2
92UD/ML-295
92UD/POY-PY11
93B-632
93ClBest/MLG-68
94B-575
94Ultra-593
Rosser, Rex
75OkCty/Team-24
Rossi, Joe
52T-379
53T-74
91T/Arc53-74
Rossi, Tom
83Erie-21
Rossiter, Mike
91Classic/DP-34
91FrRow/DP-14
91LitSun/HSPros-21
91LitSun/HSProsG-21
92ClBest-374
92Madis/ClBest-20
92Madis/ProC-1234
92MidwLAS/Team-36
92OPC-474
92StCl/Dome-158
92T-474DP
92T/Gold-474
92T/GoldWin-474
92UD/ML-214
93Modesto/ClBest-17
93Modesto/ProC-798
Rossler, Brett
(Ross)
91Kingspt/ClBest-12
91Kingspt/ProC-3817
92Pittsfld/ClBest-9
92Pittsfld/ProC-3300
Rossman, Claude
09Buster/Pin-12
E96
E97
T206
T213/brown
Rossum, Floyd
85Bend/Cram-21
Rossy, Elem
86Miami-22
Rossy, Rico
85Newar-14
87CharlO/WBTV-5
88BuffB/CMC-18
88BuffB/ProC-1471
89Harris/ProC-289
89Harris/Star-15
90Greenvl/ProC-1138
90Richm/Bob-19
91AAA/LineD-442
91Richm/Bob-22
91Richm/LineD-442
91Richm/ProC-2578
91Richm/Team-3
92B-390
92D/Rook-106
92F-676
92Omaha/SB-344
92S-817
92StCl-629
92T/91Debut-152
92USPlayC/Brave-6C
92USPlayC/Brave-7D
92Ultra-376
93OPC/Premier-123
93Pac/Spanish-495
93StCl-106
93StCl/1stDay-106
94F-172
94Pac/Cr-300
Rostel, Bud
87Anchora-26
Rotblatt, Marv
51B-303
Roth, Bob F.
D327
D328-141
D329-145
D350/2-145
E121/80
E135-141
M101/145
M101/5-145
W514-47
W575
Roth, Greg
89SoBend/GS-26
90BirmB/Best-8
90BirmB/ProC-1115
91AA/LineD-71
91BirmB/LineD-71
91BirmB/ProC-1464
92BirmB/SB-92
92Hagers/ProC-2564
92RochR/SB-466
Roth, Kris
86Peoria-20
87WinSalem-22
88Pittsfld/ProC-1376
Rothan, Bill
78Spring/Wiener-19
Rothermal, Russ
75Iowa/TCMA-15
79CharCh-3
Rothey, Mark
81Cedar-7
82Cedar-1
83Water-7
Rothford, Jim
81Shrev-19
Rothrock, John
29Exh/4-17
31Exh/4-17
34Exh/4-8
93Conlon-851
Rothschild, Larry
77Indianap-17
79Indianap-9
80Indianap-14
81Evansvl-6
82Evansvl-7
83LasVegas/BHN-18
85Iowa-21
89Cedar/Best-26
89Cedar/ProC-933
90Kahn/Reds-27M
91Kahn/Reds-x
92Reds/Kahn-NNO
Rothstein, Arnold
88Pac/8Men-28M
Roundtree, Brian
92MissSt-38
Rounsifer, Aaron
92Classic/DP-99
Rountree, Brian
89Bristol/Star-25
90Fayette/ProC-2405
Rountree, Jerrold
91Spokane/ClBest-11
91Spokane/ProC-3962
Rountree, Mike
86Watlo-23
88Reno/Cal-284
Rouse, Chuck
77Charl
Rouse, Randy
76Dubuq
77Cocoa
78DaytB
Rousey, Steve
87WPalmB-25
Roush, Edd
15CJ-161
16FleischBrd-78
25Exh-31

26Exh-31
28Exh-20
61F-72
76Rowe-8M
76Shakey-90
77Galasso-93
80Pac/Leg-70
80Perez/HOF-90
80SSPC/HOF
82Ohio/HOF-10
87Conlon/2-54
88Pac/8Men-84
89Pac/Leg-216
89Swell-35
90Swell/Great-35
91Conlon/Sport-55
91Swell/Great-134
93AP/ASG-93
93AP/ASG24K-27G
94Conlon-1023
94Conlon-993
D327
D328-142
D329-146
D350/2-146
E120
E121/120
E121/80
E135-142
E210-53
E220
M101/4-146
M101/5-146
R316
V100
V117-28
V61-79
V89-1
W501-53
W502-53
W513-61
W514-85
W515-57
W517
W572
W575
W711/1

Rovasio, Dom
89Kenosha/ProC-1066
89Kenosha/Star-23

Rover, Vince
83Cedar-21
83Cedar/Frit-19

Rowan, John Albert
10Domino-103
11Helmar-103
12Sweet/Pin-131
14Piedmont/St-50
E154
E286
M116
S74-104
T202
T205

Rowdon, Wade
82AppFx/Frit-5
83Water-14
84Wichita/Rock-21
85D-642
87Iowa-19
87T-569
88F-430
88RochR/Gov-23
91Crown/Orio-394

Rowe, Davis E.
N172
WG1-24

Rowe, Don
57Seattle/Pop-32
63T-562R
83Redwd-28CO
84Cram/PCL-243CO
87Hawaii-10CO
91AAA/LineD-150M
91Denver/LineD-150CO
91Denver/ProC-139CO
92Pol/Brew-30M

Rowe, Harold
(Butch)
78Wisco

Rowe, Jim
85Beloit-4TR
86Beloit-20TR
87Beloit-11TR
88ElPaso/Best-11TR

Rowe, John Charles
N172
Scrapps

Rowe, Ken
63T-562R
65T-518
82RochR-22CO
87Colum-4CO
89Colum/Pol-24CO
90AAASingl/ProC-343M
90ColClip/CMC-24CO
90ColClip/ProC-693CO
90Colum/Pol-1CO
90ProC/Singl-224CO
90Target-691
91Crown/Orio-395
91WIZMets-336
92Canton/ProC-708
92Canton/SB-125CO

Rowe, Lynwood
(Schoolboy)
34DS-33
34DS-98
34Ward's/Pin-7
35BU-184
35Exh/4-12
35G-8F
35G-9F
36Exh/4-12
36Wheat
37Exh/4-12
37OPC-134
42Playball-15
49B-216
49Eureka-144
49Lummis
54T-197CO
61F-73
77Galasso-83
80Laugh/FFeat-17
81Tiger/Detroit-93
86Tiger/Sport-8
90Target-692
91Conlon/Sport-256
93Conlon-718
94T/Arc54-197
PR1-25
R309/2
R311/Gloss
R312/M
R313
R314
V300
V355-44

Rowe, Matt
86Sumter/ProC-23

Rowe, Pete
78Dunedin
80Knoxvl/TCMA-4
82AlexD-14
83LynnP-13
90Salinas/Cal-146CO
90Salinas/ProC-2737CO
91Dunedin/ClBest-27

Rowe, Ralph
73OPC-49CO
73T-49CO
74OPC-447CO
74T-447CO
76SSPC-603CO
89Sumter/ProC-1091CO
90Sumter/ProC-2453CO

Rowe, Tom A.
80RochR-9
81RochR-16
85IntLgAS-42
85Maine-9
86Maine-19

Rowell, Carvel
41DP-44
47TipTop

Rowen, Rob
87SanAn-6
88Fresno/Cal-19
88Fresno/ProC-1244

Rowland, Clarence
(Pants)
92Conlon/Sport-485
BF2-15
D328-143
D329-147
D350/2-147
E135-143
M101/4-147
M101/5-147

Rowland, Donnie
85Miami-14
86FSLAS-42
86Lakeland-20
87Lakeland-6
88Toledo/CMC-22
88Toledo/ProC-589
89London/ProC-1363

Rowland, Mike
78Cr/PCL-17
79Phoenix
80Phoenix/NBank-10
81Phoenix-10
81T-502R
82Phoenix

Rowland, Rich
88Bristol/ProC-1872
89Fayette/ProC-1578
90London/ProC-1271
91AAA/LineD-597
91Classic/II-T95
91T/90Debut-136
91Toledo/LineD-597
91Toledo/ProC-1936
92OPC-472
92Sky/AAASingl-268
92StCl-508
92T-472
92T/Gold-472
92T/GoldWin-472
92Toledo/ProC-1047
92Toledo/SB-596
93D-77RR
93F-610
93Pinn-264
93S-283
93S/Boys-30
93StCl-519
93StCl/1stDay-519
94D-645
94Pac/Cr-228
94S-228
94S/GoldR-228
94T-588
94T/Gold-588

Rowley, Bill
87Indianap-36

Rowley, Steve
89Butte/SP-10
90CharlR/Star-24
91CharlR/ClBest-10
91CharlR/ProC-1314
91Tulsa/Team-26
92Sky/AASingl-273
92Tulsa/SB-617

Roy, Jean-Pierre
45Parade*-62
52Park-90

Roy, Kevin
83Wausau/Frit-13

Roy, Luther
90Target-693

Roy, Norman
51B-278

Roy, Pat
76Cedar

Roy, Patrick
91StCl/Member*-50

Roy, Walt
90BurlB/Best-14
90BurlB/ProC-2349
90BurlB/Star-23
91Durham/ProC-1542

Royalty, Doug
87AubAs-26
88Ashvl/ProC-1065

Royer, Stan
88SoOreg/ProC-1701
89AS/Cal-31
89B-195
89Modesto/Cal-276
89Modesto/Chong-25
90Foil/Best-240
90Huntsvl/Best-19
90Louisvl/LBC-36
91AAA/LineD-246
91Louisvl/LineD-246
91Louisvl/ProC-2924
91Louisvl/Team-22
92D-602
92Louisvl/ProC-1894
92Louisvl/SB-268
92Pinn-263
92S-822
92Sky/AAASingl-129
92StCl-286
92T/91Debut-153
93D-680
93F/Final-130
93Pac/Spanish-636
93Pol/Card-18
93T-820
93T/Gold-820
94Pac/Cr-603
94StCl/Team-311

Royster, Jerry
74Albuq/Team-17
75Albuq/Caruso-3
75IntLgAS/Broder-30
75PCL/AS-30
76OPC-592R
76T-592R
77BurgChef-212
77Ho-38
77Ho/Twink-38
77OPC-251
77T-549
78T-187
79T-344
80OPC-241
80T-463
81D-339
81F-250
81Pol/Atl-1
81T-268
82BK/Lids-22
82D-555
82F-448
82Pol/Atl-1
82T-608
83D-425
83F-147
83F/St-20M
83F/St-3M
83Pol/Atl-1
83T-26
84D-531
84F-191
84Nes/792-572
84Pol/Atl-1
84T-572
84T/St-37
85F-340
85F/Up-U90
85Mother/Padres-18
85T-776
85T/Tr-96T
86D-446
86F-333
86OPC-118
86T-118
87Coke/WS-1
87D-534
87F-428
87OPC-324
87T-403
87T/Tr-106T
88D-660
88F-221
88T-257
89UD-433
90EliteSenLg-47
90Target-694
90Yakima/Team-23MG
91VeroB/ClBest-30MG
91VeroB/ProC-791MG
92SanAn/ProC-3988MG
92SanAn/SB-574MG
92Yank/WIZ80-166

Royster, Willie
79RochR-5
80CharlO/Pol-18
80CharlO/W3TV-18
82RochR-11
83Evansvl-12
91Crown/Orio-396

Rozek, Richard
52NumNum-11
52T-363

Rozema, Dave
75Clinton
77Tiger/BK-3
78BK/T-5
78Ho-36
78K-21
78OPC-38
78T-124
79OPC-12
79T-33
80OPC-151
80T-288
81D-9
81F-464
81T-614
82D-259
82F-279
82F/St-153
82T-319
83D-133
83F-340
83T-562
84D-272
84F-90
84Nes/792-457
84OPC-133
84T-457
84Tiger/Farmer-13
84Tiger/Wave-30
85D-125
85F-21
85F/Up-U91
85Rang-30
85Seven-5D
85T-47
85T/Tr-97T
86D-343
86F-570
86Leaf-154
86OPC-208
86T-739
91Pac/SenLg-135
93Rang/Keeb-314

Rozman, Richard
88SoOreg/ProC-1694

Roznovsky, Ron
75Iowa/TCMA-16

Roznovsky, Vic
65T-334
66T-467
67OPC-163
67T-163
68T-428
69T-368
91Crown/Orio-397

Rozook, Mark
89Wausau/GS-12

Rub, Jerry
88PrWill/Star-21
89Albany/Best-12
89Albany/ProC-328
89Albany/Star-16
90Albany/ProC-1035
90Albany/Star-15
90ProC/Singl-781
91AA/LineD-14
91Albany/LineD-14
91Albany/ProC-1007

Rub, Ron
87FtLaud-15

Rubel, John
83Butte-27

Rubel, Mike
82Tulsa-28
83Tulsa-15
84OKCty-14
85OKCty-22
87Phoenix-27
90TulsaDG/Best-12

Rubeling, Albert
52Park-82

Ruberto, John E.
(Sonny)
76Indianap-11
80ArkTr-5

Rubio, Jorge
77Fritsch-34

Ruby, J. Gary
87QuadC-20
88CalLgAS-36
88PalmSp/Cal-114
88PalmSp/ProC-1435
89MidldA/GS-3
90MidldA/GS-2CO
91AAA/LineD-175M
91Edmon/LineD-175CO
91Edmon/ProC-1532CO
92Edmon/ProC-3554CO
92Edmon/SB-175M
93Vanco/ProC-2614CO

Rucker, Dave
80Evansvl-9
82Evansvl-8
82T-261R
83D-641
83Evansvl-9
83F-341
83T-304
84D-260
84Nes/792-699
84T-699
85Cram/PCL-26
85D-260
85F-238
85F/Up-U92
85T-421
85T/Tr-98T
86D-448
86F-447
86Phill/TastyK-39
86T-39
87OKCty-27
88BuffB/CMC-8
88BuffB/ProC-1472
89BuffB/CMC-5
89BuffB/ProC-1662
89UD-436
Rucker, George
(Nap)
10Domino-104
11Helmar-88
12Sweet/Pin-75
12Sweet/Pin-75A
14CJ-51
15CJ-51
16FleischBrd-79
90Target-695
92Conlon/Sport-333
94Conlon-1263
BF2-61
D304
D329-148
D350/2-148
E103
E254
E300
E96
L1-117
M101/4-148
M101/5-148
M116
S74-54
S81-92
T201
T202
T204
T205
T206
T207
T213/blue
T215/blue
T215/brown
T3-34
WG4-23
WG5-34
WG6-32
Rucker, Johnny
40PlayBall-213
41DP-137
47Centen-25
49B/PCL-7
Ruckman, Scott
86Cram/NWL-133
88Spartan/ProC-1037
88Spartan/Star-19
Rudi, Joe
69T-587
70OPC-102
70T-102
71MLB/St-525
71OPC-407
71T-407
72OPC-209
72T-209
73K-36
73OPC-360
73T-360
74OPC-264
74T-264
74T/St-229
75Ho-40
75Ho/Twink-40
75K-28
75OPC-45
75OPC-465WS
75T-45
75T-465WS
75T/M-45
75T/M-465WS
76K-7
76OPC-475
76SSPC-490
76T-475
77BurgChef-125
77Ho-146
77Ho/Twink-146
77OPC-206
77T-155
77T/CS-39
77T/ClothSt-39
78Ho-114
78OPC-28
78SSPC/270-214
78T-635
78Wiffle/Discs-64
79Ho-84
79OPC-134
79T-267
80OPC-289
80T-556
81D-174
81F-272
81F/St-113
81OPC-362
81T-701
81T/Tr-826
82D-586
82F-306
82OPC-388
82T-388
82T/Tr-102T
83D-287
83F-532
83T-87
87Mother/A's-9
93MCI-7
Rudison, Karl
90Pulaski/Best-18
90Pulaski/ProC-3094
Rudolph, Blaine
88Bristol/ProC-1879
89Fayette/ProC-1579
90Dunedin/Star-15
Rudolph, F. Don
58T-347
59T-179
60HenryH-33
60Union-17
62T-224
63T-291
64T-427
Rudolph, Greg
92StPete/ClBest-25
92StPete/ProC-2037
Rudolph, Ken
70OPC-46
70T-46
71MLB/St-45
71OPC-472
71T-472
72OPC-271
72T-271
73OPC-414
73T-414
74OPC-584
74T-584
75OPC-289
75T-289
75T/M-289
76OPC-601
76SSPC-287
76T-601
78Spring/Wiener-24CO
91Crown/Orio-398
Rudolph, Mason
90Kgsport/Best-6
90Kgsport/Star-21
91Clmbia/PCPII-2
91Clmbia/PII-25
92StLucie/ClBest-16
92StLucie/ProC-1749
93StLucie/ProC-2925
Rudolph, Richard
15CJ-154
16FleischBrd-80
93Conlon-704
BF2-55
C46-22
D328-144
D329-149
D350/2-149
E135-144
E254
M101/4-149
M101/5-149
T206
T213/blue
W514-13
W516-15
Rudstrom, Tom
89BendB/Legoe-15
Ruebel, Matt
90OK-18
91Welland/ClBest-20
91Welland/ProC-3572
92Augusta/ClBest-12
92Augusta/ProC-237
92ClBest-19
93SALAS/II-36
Ruel, Harold
(Muddy)
21Exh-147
25Exh-128
26Exh-128
27Exh-63
28Exh-64
29Exh/4-31
33DH-37
33Exh/4-12
33G-18
35G-1J
35G-3A
35G-5A
35G-6A
40PlayBall-127
91Conlon/Sport-284
93Conlon-865
E120
E121/120
E126-25
R306
R316
V100
V117-24
V353-18
W501-10
W573
W575
Rueter, Kirk
92Rockford/ClBest-13
92Rockford/ProC-2114
93Harris/ProC-269
93Select/RookTr-88T
94B-60
94D-237
94F-549
94F/RookSen-16
94Flair-194
94L-8
94OPC-255
94OPC/DiamD-8
94Pac/Cr-389
94Pinn-382
94S-312
94S/GoldR-312
94Select-172
94StCl-302
94StCl/1stDay-302
94StCl/Gold-302
94T-628
94T/Finest-9
94T/FinestRef-9
94T/Gold-628
94TripleP-98
94UD-171
94UD/CollC-246
94UD/CollC/Gold-246
94UD/CollC/Silv-246
94UD/ElecD-171
94Ultra-231
94Ultra/RisSt-10
Ruether, Walter
(Dutch)
21Exh-139
28Yueng-2
88Pac/8Men-83
90Target-696
91Conlon/Sport-104
E120
E121/120
E210-2
V61-64
W501-98
W502-2
W514-108
W515-40
W573
Ruff, Dan
91Bristol/ClBest-24
91Bristol/ProC-3616
92Lakeland/ClBest-4
92Lakeland/ProC-2289
Ruffcorn, Scott
91ClBest/Singl-409
91Classic/DP-21
91FrRow/DP-4
91FrRow/DPPr-3
92B-88
92ClBest-373
92ClBest/BBonusC-18
92ClBest/RBonus-BC18
92OPC-36
92Pinn-300DP
92S-806DC
92Saraso/ClBest-1
92Saraso/ProC-205
92StCl/Dome-159
92T-36DP
92T/Gold-36
92T/GoldWin-36
92UD/ML-246
93B-443
93ClBest/Fisher-16
93ClBest/MLG-79
93F/Final-197
93FExcel/ML-154
94B-595
94D-619
94Finest-440
94L/GRook-5
94Pinn-255
94Pinn/Artist-255
94Pinn/Museum-255
94Pinn/New-16
94S-611
94Sf/2000-169
94StCl/Team-127
94T-356
94T/Gold-356
94UD-25
94UD/CollC-247
94UD/CollC/Gold-247
94UD/CollC/Silv-247
94UD/ElecD-25
Ruffin, Bruce
86Reading-23
86Sf/Rook-29
87D-555
87F-183
87F/Hottest-33
87Leaf-168
87Phill/TastyK-47
87Sf/TPrev-6M
87T-499
87T/JumboR-14
87T/St-123
87T/St-312
87ToysRUs-23
88D-165
88F-313
88OPC-268
88Panini/St-353
88Phill/TastyK-21
88S-492
88T-268
88T/St-119
89B-393
89D-515
89F-580
89OPC-222
89Panini/St-148
89Phill/TastyK-28
89S-328
89ScranWB/ProC-728
89T-518
89T/St-122
89UD-319
90F-572
90F/Can-572
90Leaf-151
90OPC-22
90Phill/TastyK-27
90T-22
90UD-580
91AAA/LineD-494
91F-411
91OPC-637
91S-524
91ScranWB/LineD-494
91ScranWB/ProC-2537
91StCl-89
91T-637
91UD-410
92B-354
92D-680
92F-544
92L-414
92L/BlkGold-414
92OPC-307
92Pol/Brew-21
92S-161
92S/RookTr-71T
92StCl-867
92T-307
92T/Gold-307
92T/GoldWin-307
92T/Tr-95T
92T/TrGold-95T
92TX-35
92UD-309
93F/Final-42
93Pac/Spanish-437
93StCl-270
93StCl/1stDay-270
93StCl/Rockie-15
93UD-670
93USPlayC/Rockie-12S
93USPlayC/Rockie-7D
93Ultra-357
94D-305
94F-452
94Flair-158
94Pac/Cr-206
94StCl/Team-101
94T-407
94T/Finest-199
94T/FinestRef-199
94T/Gold-407
94Ultra-189
Ruffin, Johnny
89Utica/Pucko-19
90SoBend/GS-15
91B-347
91ClBest/Singl-95
91Saraso/ClBest-9
91Saraso/ProC-1112
92B-451
92BirmB/SB-93
92ClBest-33
92D/Rook-107
92L/GRook-13
92ProC/Tomorrow-43
92Saraso/ProC-206
92Sky/AASingl-45
92UD/ML-224
93B-147
93StCl/WSox-26
94B-102
94D-135
94F-424
94Finest-283
94L-305
94Pinn-410
94T-779
94T/Gold-779
94UD-170
94UD/CollC-17
94UD/CollC/Gold-17
94UD/CollC/Silv-17
94UD/ElecD-170
94Ultra-176
Ruffing, Charles H.
(Red)
25Exh-69
26Exh-70
29Exh/4-17
33CJ/Pin-19
33G-56
34DS-60
35G-2D
35G-4D
35G-7D
36Exh/4-13
37OPC-136
37Wheat
38ONG/Pin-25
39PlayBall-3
40PlayBall-10
40Wheat

41DP-68
41DP-86
43MP-22
60F-63
61F-74
76Rowe-1M
76Shakey-105
77Galasso-54
80Pac/Leg-109
80Perez/HOF-106
80SSPC/HOF
82Ohio/HOF-11
83D/HOF-31
86Sf/Dec-14M
89HOF/St-83
91Conlon/Sport-13
91Conlon/Sport-227
92Yank/WIZAS-70
92Yank/WIZHOF-28
93Conlon-882
94Conlon-1078
PM10/Sm-171
R300
R310
R311/Leath
R312
R316
R328-20
V300
V354-48
V355-102
Ruffner, Mark
89Reading/Best-24
Rugg, Rusty
89Helena/SP-6
91Helena/SportP-19
Ruhle, Vern
75OPC-614R
75T-614R
75T/M-614R
76Ho-46
76Ho/Twink-46
76OPC-89
76T-89
77OPC-212
77T-311
78Charl
78T-456
79T-49
80T-234
81D-261
81F-53
81T-642
82D-293
82F-228
82T-539
83D-627
83F-462
83T-172
84D-564
84F-238
84Mother/Ast-23
84Nes/792-328
84T-328
85D-380
85F-358
85F/Up-U93
85Polar/Ind-48
85T-426
85T/Tr-99T
86F-593
86T-768
87F-91
87T-221
90Swell/Great-128
91Swell/Great-76
Ruiz, Augie
79LodiD-2
82Evansvl-9
83Richm-9
Ruiz, Benny
86GlenF-19
87GlenF-14
88Toledo/CMC-16
88Toledo/ProC-602
Ruiz, Cecilio
83LasVegas/BHN-19
Ruiz, Estuar
92Kane/Team-26
Ruiz, Hiraldo S.
(Chico)
63T-407R
64T-356R
65T-554
66OPC-159
66T-159
67CokeCap/Reds-12
67T-339
68Kahn
68T-213
69MB-243
69T-469
70T-606
71MLB/St-357
71OPC-686
71T-686
72MB-301
78TCMA-35
Ruiz, Manuel
(Chico)
78Richm
79Richm-13
81Richm-9
82Richm-15
83Richm-15
90Richm/25Ann-21
Ruiz, Nelson
80Batavia-29
Ruiz, Stewart
91Bluefld/ClBest-3
91Bluefld/ProC-4136
92Kane/ProC-102
Ruling, Stephen
77Spoka
78Spokane/Cramer-11
78Spokane/Team-11
Rumer, Tim
90Tampa/DIMD-18
91FtLaud/ClBest-13
91FtLaud/ProC-2426
92ClBest-224
92PrWill/ClBest-13
92PrWill/ProC-148
Rumfield, Toby
91ClBest/Singl-413
91FrRow/DP-35
91Princet/ClBest-13
91Princet/ProC-3518
92Billings/ProC-3359
Rumler, William G.
D328-145
E135-145
Rumsey, Dan
91Clinton/ProC-849
92MidldA/ProC-4039
92PalmSp/ClBest-26
Rumsey, Derrell
91Visalia/ClBest-23
91Visalia/ProC-1755
92ClBest-371
92FtMyr/ProC-2757
92Miracle/ClBest-12
Rundels, Matt
92James/ClBest-6
92James/ProC-1509
93BurlB/ClBest-22
93BurlB/ProC-167
Runge, Ed
55B-277UMP
90TM/Umpire-64M
Runge, Paul W.
81Richm-10
82Richm-16
83Richm-16
84Richm-24
85Pol/Atl-12
85T/Tr-100T
86Richm-19
86T-409
87Richm/Crown-12
87Richm/TCMA-14
88F/Up-U71
89LasVegas/CMC-21
89T-38
89T/Big-23
89UD-55
90AAASingl/ProC-359
90ProC/Singl-343
90Syrac/MerchB-19
90Syrac/CMC-17
90Syrac/ProC-579
90Syrac/Team-19
Runge, Paul
87Richm/Bob-18
88TM/Umpire-17
89TM/Umpire-17
90TM/Umpire-17
90TM/Umpire-64M
Runge, Scott
86Watertn-20
87Watertn-5
88Augusta/ProC-376
89SanBern/Best-19
89Wmsprt/ProC-638
Runion, Jeff
93ClBest/MLG-108
Runnells, Tom
80Phoenix/NBank-23
81Phoenix-23
82Phoenix
83Phoenix/BHN-9
84Wichita/Rock-11
86D-569
87Vermont-16
88Chatt/Best-14
89Chatt/II/Team-25MG
89Indianap/CMC-25
89Indianap/ProC-1220
91T/Tr-103T
92Expo/D/Duri-15A
92OPC-51MG
92T-51MG
92T/Gold-51MG
92T/GoldWin-51MG
Runnels, James E.
(Pete)
52T-2
53B/Col-139
53Briggs
53T-219
54T-6
55B-255
55RM-AL20
56T-234
57T-64
58Hires-38
58T-265
59T-370
59T-519M
60T-15
60T/tatt-47
61Bz-32
61NuCard-407
61P-47
61T-210
61T-42LL
61T/RO-29
61T/St-116
62J-57
62P-57
62Salada-47A
62Salada-47B
62Shirriff-47
62T-3
62T/St-17
62T/bucks
63Exh
63J-77
63P-77
63Pep
63Salada-61
63T-230
63T-2LL
64T-121
80Marchant-27
90Pac/Legend-103
91T/Arc53-219
94T/Arc54-6
Exh47
Runyan, Sean
92FrRow/DP-41
92LitSun/HSPros-14
93B-616
93ClBest/MLG-161
93StCl/MurphyS-89
Ruocchio, James
91Boise/ClBest-6
91Boise/ProC-3890
Rupcich, Mike
89FresnoSt/Smok-18
91FresnoSt/Smok-16M
Rupe, Brian
83Visalia/Frit-25
Rupkey, Rich
90Hamil/Best-12
90Hamil/Star-21
Rupp, Brian
93B-700FOIL
94ClBest/Gold-160
94FExcel-274
Rupp, Mark
89Erie/Star-23
90Helena/SportP-21
Rupp, Terry
89Spokane/SP-9
90Waterlo/Best-15
90Waterlo/ProC-2386
Ruppert, Jacob
(Colonel)
92Mega/Ruth-129M
92Mega/Ruth-131M
Rusciano, Chris
92Idaho/ProC-3511
Rush, Andy
89Elmira/Pucko-18
90Target-1058
90WinHaven/Star-23
91LynchRS/ClBest-28
91LynchRS/ProC-1197
92LynchRS/ClBest-14
92LynchRS/ProC-2906
Rush, Bob
49Eureka-69
50B-61
51B-212
52NTea
52StarCal-92C
52StarCal/L-80D
52T-153
53B/Col-110
54B-77
55B-182
55RFG-13
55W605-13
56T-214
57T-137
58T-313
59T-396
60Lake
60SpicSpan-19
60T-404
79TCMA-164
Rush, Edward
(Eddie)
88Cedar/ProC-1155
89Greens/ProC-418
90Cedar/Best-6
90Cedar/ProC-2329
91Cedar/ProC-2729
91MidwLAS/ProC-23
Rush, Larry
79Holyo-20
80Vanco-1
81Vanco-12
82Vanco-7
Rush, Rod
84Everett/Cram-13B
Rushworth, Jim
92James/ClBest-22
92James/ProC-1501
93BurlB/ClBest-23
93BurlB/ProC-158
Rusie, Amos
75F/Pion-12
80Perez/HOF-162
80SSPC/HOF
81Conlon-72
86Indianap-8
87Conlon/2-53
92Conlon/Sport-535
N172
N300/unif
N566-175
Rusin, Dave
91Perth/Fut-4
Rusk, Mike
75FtLaud/Sus-28
Rusk, Troy
90Princet/DIMD-17
91Spartan/ClBest-15
91Spartan/ProC-902
92Clearw/ProC-2065
92Spartan/ClBest-4
92Spartan/ProC-1272
Ruskin, Scott
87Macon-22
88Salem/Star-18
89Salem/Star-18
90B-167
90D/Rook-27
90Leaf-512
90T/Tr-106T
90UD/Ext-713
91D-612
91F-246
91OPC-589
91S-799
91T-589
91T/90Debut-137
91T/JumboR-26
91UD-383
91Ultra-209
92D-394
92F-491
92F/Up-83
92L-521
92L/BlkGold-521
92OPC-692
92Reds/Kahn-28
92S-121
92S/RookTr-57T
92StCl-777
92T-692
92T/Gold-692
92T/GoldWin-692
92T/Tr-96T
92T/TrGold-96T
92UD-384
93F-398
93StCl-199
93StCl/1stDay-199
93T-328
93T/Gold-328
Russ, Kevin
84Idaho/Team-23
86Madis/Pol-18
Russell, Alan
91Boise/ClBest-30TR
Russell, Bill E.
70MLB/St-56
70OPC-304
70T-304
71MLB/St-113
71OPC-226
71T-226
71Ticket/Dodg-14
72T-736
73OPC-108
73T-108
74OPC-239
74T-239
74T/DE-40
74T/St-49
75Ho-91
75OPC-23
75T-23
75T/M-23
76OPC-22
76T-22
77T-322
78SSPC/270-56
78T-128
79T-546
80OPC-40
80Pol/Dodg-18
80T-75
81D-57
81F-117
81F/St-68
81OPC-20
81Pol/Dodg-18
81T-465
81T/HT
81T/St-179
82D-453
82F-20
82F/St-8
82Pol/Dodg-18
82T-279
83D-210
83F-219
83F/St-22M
83OPC-123
83OPC/St-249
83Pol/Dodg-18
83T-661
83T/St-249
84D-587
84F-111
84Nes/792-792
84OPC-14
84Pol/Dodg-18
84T-792
84T/RD-21M
84T/St-77
85Coke/Dodg-28
85D-93
85F-383
85Leaf-232

85OPC-343
85SpokAT/Cram-17
85T-343
85T/RD-21M
85T/St-76
86Coke/Dodg-26
86D-153
86F-142
86Pol/Dodg-18
86T-506
86T-696M
87F-452
87Smok/Dodg-31
87T-116
88Smok/Dodg-13
88Smok/Dodg-15M
89Smok/Dodg-81
90Mother/Dodg-28M
90Pol/Dodg-x
90Target-697
91Mother/Dodg-28CO
91Pol/Dodg-x
92Albuq/ProC-737
92Albuq/SB-24MG
Russell, Dan
88Modesto-25
Russell, Dave
80WHave-18
Russell, Ewell A.
(Reb)
14CJ-15
15CJ-15
92Conlon/Sport-482
BF2-16
D328-146
D329-150
D350/2-150
E135-146
M101/4-150
M101/5-150
V100
WG4-24
Russell, Fred
88Eugene/Best-15
89Eugene/Best-19
90AppFox/Box-21
90AppFox/ProC-2103
90ProC/Singl-698
91BBCity/ClBest-20
91BBCity/ProC-1406
91ClBest/Singl-122
Russell, Glen David
(Rip)
39Exh
47TipTop
93Conlon-727
Russell, Jack Erwin
33G-123
33G-167
94Conlon-1048
R316
Russell, James W.
47TipTop
49B-235
49Eureka-20
50B-223
52Mother-52
52T-51
90Target-698
Russell, Jeff
82Water-8
83Indianap-14
84Borden-46
84D-569
84Nes/792-270
84T-270
85D-487
85F-551
85T-651
86OKCty-19
86Rang-40
87D-550
87F-137
87Mother/Rang-26
87Smok/R-32
87T-444
88D-531
88F-478
88Mother/R-26
88S-514
88Smok/R-17
88T-114
89B-226
89D-403
89D/AS-26
89D/Best-200
89F-531
89KennerFig-116
89Mother/R-6
89OPC-166
89Panini/St-447
89S-438
89Smok/R-28
89T-565
89T/Big-309
89T/St-243
89UD-461
90B-485
90D-284
90D/BestAL-99
90F-312
90F-633M
90F/AwardWin-28
90F/Can-312
90F/Can-633M
90Leaf-152
90Mother/Rang-8
90OPC-395AS
90OPC-80
90Panini/St-159
90PublInt/St-420
90RedFoley/St-80
90S-263
90S/100St-23
90Sf-192
90T-395AS
90T-80
90T/Big-15
90T/Mini-38
90T/St-252
90UD-638
91B-267
91D-202
91F-300
91Leaf-291
91Mother/Rang-8
91OPC-344
91S-277
91StCl-421
91T-344
91UD-648
91Ultra-354
92B-218
92D-129
92F-319
92L-90
92L/BlkGold-90
92Mother/Rang-8
92OPC-257
92Pinn-209
92S-124
92StCl-28
92Studio-247
92T-257
92T/Gold-257
92T/GoldWin-257
92UD-695
92Ultra-140
93B-115
93D-711
93F-668
93F/Final-177
93Flair-167
93L-494
93OPC/Premier-9
93Pinn-444
93Rang/Keeb-315
93S-413
93Select-365
93Select/RookTr-7T
93StCl-635
93StCl/1stDay-635
93T-736
93T/Gold-736
93T/Tr-25T
93UD-702
93UD/SP-204
93Ultra-516
94D-248
94F-41
94L-336
94OPC-113
94Pac/Cr-65
94Pinn-46
94Pinn/Artist-46
94Pinn/Museum-46
94S-529
94T-55
94T/Finest-90
94T/Finest/PreProd-90
94T/FinestRef-90
94T/Gold-55
94TripleP-206
94UD-213
94UD/ElecD-213
94Ultra-17
Russell, Jim
44Playball-27
Russell, Joe
75Anderson/TCMA-20
79Tulsa-2
81Tulsa-27
Russell, John
83Portl-17
84Cram/PCL-208
84Phill/TastyK-42
85D-648
85F-653R
85Phill/TastyK-11N
85Phill/TastyK-31
86CIGNA-14
86D-82
86F-448
86Phill/TastyK-6
86T-392
87D-207
87F-184
87Phill/TastyK-6
87T-379
88Maine/CMC-12
88Maine/ProC-285
88Phill/TastyK-37
88T-188
89Brave/Dubuq-21
89UD-532
90AAASingl/ProC-682
90D-458
90Leaf-442
90Mother/Rang-26
90OkCty/CMC-11
90OkCty/ProC-436
90ProC/Singl-161
90PublInt/St-120
90T/Tr-107T
90Target-699
91F-301
91Mother/Rang-26
91OPC-734
91S-802
91StCl-474
91T-734
91UD-191
92S-339
92StCl-846
92Tulsa/ProC-2699
92Tulsa/SB-618
93Pac/Spanish-647
93Rang/Keeb-430
93StCl/Rang-23
Russell, LaGrande
91Belling/ClBest-28
92Penin/ClBest-12
92Penin/ProC-2931
93B-403
Russell, Larry
88CapeCod/Sum-28
Russell, Leonard
91StCl/Member*-33
Russell, Matt
89BendB/Legoe-25BB
90Bend/Legoe-31BB
Russell, Richard
91Belling/ProC-3662
Russell, Rob
85PrWill-7
86PrWill-23
87Harris-12
88Harris/ProC-858
89Harris/ProC-303
89Harris/Star-16
Russell, Ron
86DayBe-24
Russell, Todd
90Bend/Legoe-14
91Madison/ClBest-1
Russell, Tony
83Greens-26
85Albany-21
86Albany/TCMA-10
87Albany-2
Russo, Marius
41DP-112
44Yank/St-22
92Yank/WIZAS-71
Russo, Pat
91Kenosha/ClBest-15
91Kenosha/ProC-2073
Russo, Paul
90Elizab/Star-20
91B-695
91ClBest/Singl-344
91Kenosha/ProC-2085
92ClBest-203
92OPC-473M
92OrlanSR/ProC-2856
92OrlanSR/SB-519
92Sky/AASingl-226
92T-473M
92T/Gold-473M
92T/GoldWin-473M
93ClBest/MLG-94
Russo, Tony
87Erie-16
88Savan/ProC-333
89StPete/Star-23
Rusteck, Dick
77Fritsch-43
81TCMA-420
91WIZMets-337
Ruth, Claire
92Mega/Ruth-121M
Ruth, Dorothy
92Mega/Ruth-151M
Ruth, George Herman
(Babe)
21Exh-148
21Exh-149
24Sherlock-7
25Exh-100
26Exh-102
27Exh-52
28Exh-51
28FrJoy-Set
28Yueng-6
29Exh/4-26
31Exh/4-26
33Exh/4-13
33G-144
33G-149
33G-181
33G-53
33SK*-2
34Exh/4-13
35Exh/4-1
35G-1J
35G-3A
35G-4A
35G-5A
48BRS-Set
48Exh/HOF
48L-3
48Swell-12
49Leaf/Prem-7
50Callahan
50W576-63
51T/CM
56T/Hocus-B1
60Exh/HOF-20
60F-3
60NuCard-1
60NuCard-16
60NuCard-47
61F-75
61GP-3
61NuCard-447
61NuCard-455
61T-401M
62T-135M
62T-136M
62T-137M
62T-138M
62T-139M
62T-140M
62T-141M
62T-142M
62T-143M
62T-144M
63Bz-17
69Bz-10
69Bz-11
69Bz-9
69Bz/Sm
72F/FFeat-20
72K/ATG-14
72K/ATG-6
72Laugh/GF-32
73F/Wild-34M
73OPC-1LL
73OPC-474LL
73Syrac/Team-24
73T-1LL
73T-474LL
74Laugh/ASG-33
74Syrac/Team-23
75Syrac/Team-13
75Syrac/Team-18
76Laugh/Jub-32
76Motor-9
76OPC-345ATG
76Rowe-16M
76Shakey-2
76T-345ATG
77Galasso-165
77Galasso-193
77Galasso-227
77Galasso-69
77Galasso-91
77Shakey-20
80Laugh/3/4/5-2
80Laugh/FFeat-16
80Pac/Leg-1
80Perez/HOF-4
80SSPC/HOF
81Conlon-4
83OPC/St-2FOIL
83T/St-2F
84D/Champs-1
85CircK-2
85D/HOF-1
85West/2-47
85Woolwth-31
86BLChew-2
86Conlon/1-13
86Conlon/1-20
86Conlon/1-48
86Conlon/1-50
86Conlon/1-54
86Sf/Dec-1
87Nestle/DT-5
88Conlon/3-25
88Conlon/AmAS-21
88Grenada-81
89CMC/Ruth-Set
89Cadaco-45
89HOF/St-47
89Kenner/BBGr-16
89Pac/Leg-176
89Smok/Dodg-26
89Swell-1
89T/LJN-77
89USPS-4
90BBWit-86
90CollAB-10
90HOF/St-25
90Perez/GreatMom-1
90Swell/Great-10
91Cadaco-44
91Conlon/Proto-145
91Conlon/Sport-110
91Conlon/Sport-145
91Homer/Classic-1
91Swell/Great-124
91T/Ruth-Set
92Conlon/13Nat-663
92Conlon/ASP-663G
92Conlon/Col-4
92Conlon/Sport-426
92GoldEnt/Ruth-Set
92Mega/Ruth-109
92Mega/Ruth-120
92Mega/Ruth-121
92Mega/Ruth-122
92Mega/Ruth-123
92Mega/Ruth-124
92Mega/Ruth-125
92Mega/Ruth-126
92Mega/Ruth-128
92Mega/Ruth-129
92Mega/Ruth-131
92Mega/Ruth-134
92Mega/Ruth-141
92Mega/Ruth-149
92Mega/Ruth-150
92Mega/Ruth-151
92Mega/Ruth-152
92Mega/Ruth-153
92Mega/Ruth-154
92Mega/Ruth-158
92Mega/Ruth-159
92Mega/Ruth-160

92Mega/Ruth-161
92Mega/Ruth-Set
92Mega/RuthProto-Set
92S-879
92Whitehall-3
92Whitehall/Proto-3
92Yank/WIZAS-72
92Yank/WIZHOF-29
93AP/ASG-94
93AP/ASG24K-28G
93Cadaco-47
93Conlon-663
93Conlon-888
93Conlon/MasterBW-2
93Conlon/MasterCol-5
93Conlon/Proto-888
93Spectrum/HOFI-1
93TWill-121
93TWill/Locklear-6
93UD/ATH-110
93UD/ATH-131
93UD/ATH-133M
93UD/ATH-134
93UD/ATH-146
93UD/ATH-149M
93UD/ATH-151
93UD/ATH-152
94Conlon-1080
94Conlon/Col-33
94Conlon/Col-35
94Mega/Ruth-Set
94TedW/500-6
94TedW/Trade-1
D327
D328-146
D329-151
D350/2-151
E120
E121/120
E121/80
E126-38
E135-146
E210-6
E220
M101/4-151
M101/5-151
PM10/Sm-172
R309/1
R310
R315-A31
R315-B31
R316
R328-32
R332-26
R332-42
R337-402
R423-92
Rawl
V100
V117-8
V353-80
V353-93
V354-28
V61-37
V89-25
W501-49
W502-6
W512-6
W514-2
W515-3
W515-47
W516-1
W517-20
W517-4
W573
W575

Ruth, Helen
92Mega/Ruth-120M

Ruth, Pat
85Clovis-37
89FresnoSt/Smok-19
91Batavia/ClBest-4
91Batavia/ProC-3486
92ClBest-265
92Spartan/ProC-1277

Rutherford, John
52T-320
53T-137
90Target-700
91T/Arc53-137

Ruthven, Dick
74OPC-47
74T-47
75OPC-267
75T-267
75T/M-267
76OPC-431
76SSPC-477
76T-431
77BurgChef-208
77Ho-74
77Ho/Twink-74
77T-575
78T-75
79BK/P-6
79T-419
80BK/P-19
80T-136
81D-153
81F-16
81OPC-285
81T-691
81T/HT
82D-525
82F-257
82F/St-52
82OPC-317
82T-317
83D-497
83F-172
83OPC-313
83T-484
83T/Tr-98
83Thorn-44
84D-510
84F-503
84Nes/792-736
84OPC-156
84SevenUp-44
84T-736
84T/St-49
85F-64
85OPC-268
85SevenUp-44
85T-563
86D-564
86F-377
86T-98

Rutkay, Gary
52Laval-38

Rutledge, Jeff
82QuadC-19
86Pittsfld-21

Rutter, Sam
92Beloit/ClBest-5
92Beloit/ProC-404

Ruyak, Craig
90Johnson/Star-23

Ruyak, Todd
92Princet/ClBest-12
92Princet/ProC-3088

Ruynon, Curt
75Anderson/TCMA-21

Ruzek, Don
77LodiD
78LodiD
83AppFx/Frit-27

Ryal, Mark
82Omaha-21
83Omaha-20
84Omaha-24
85BuffB-15
86Edmon-25
87D-583
87Smok/Cal-14
88F-503
88Louisvl-43
88T-243
90AAASingl/ProC-498
90BuffB/CMC-20
90BuffB/ProC-383
90BuffB/Team-23
90ProC/Singl-20
93Edmon/ProC-1149

Ryan, Bobby
90Watertn/Star-18
91Rockford/ClBest-12
91Rockford/ProC-2047

Ryan, Colin
88CapeCod/Sum-71
89Eugene/Best-13
90AppFox/Box-22
90AppFox/ProC-2098
91BBCity/ClBest-15
91BBCity/ProC-1401
91ClBest/Singl-130

Ryan, Connie
44Playball-40
47TipTop
49Eureka-19
51B-216
52B-164
52T-107
53B/Col-131
53NB
53T-102
54T-136
74OPC-634CO
74T-634CO
91Jesuit-3
91T/Arc53-102
93Rang/Keeb-316MG
94T/Arc54-136

Ryan, Craig
79Vanco-5
80Vanco-15

Ryan, Dan
89SLCity-8LHP

Ryan, Duffy
81Redwd-11

Ryan, Jack
90Target-1059

Ryan, James E.
E107
E223
N172
N28
N284
N300/SC
N403
N43
WG1-15

Ryan, Jody
86Cram/NWL-117
87Wausau-3
88SanBern/Best-7
88SanBern/Cal-42
89SanBern/Best-21
89SanBern/Cal-67

Ryan, John Budd
90Target-701
E254
E270/2
T207

Ryan, John C.
(Blondy)
34DS-40
34Exh/4-5
34G-32
35Exh/4-6
81Conlon-25
93Conlon-694
R310
V354-73
V94-40

Ryan, Kenny Jr.
86Elmira-18
87Greens-6
88Lynch/Star-22
89WinHaven/Star-19
90LynchRS/Team-21
91WinHaven/ClBest-8
91WinHaven/ProC-488
92NewBrit/ProC-432
92NewBrit/SB-494
92Sky/AASingl-213
93B-3
93D-383
93F/MLPII-18
93L/GRook-13
93OPC/Premier-41
93Pinn-278
93S-329
93Select/RookTr-65T
93T-786M
93T/Gold-786M
93T/Tr-103T
93UD-772
93Ultra-517
94D-276
94F-42
94S-592
94StCl-404
94StCl/1stDay-404
94StCl/Gold-404
94T-264
94T/Gold-264
94UD/CollC-248
94UD/CollC/Gold-248
94UD/CollC/Silv-248

Ryan, Kevin
85Anchora-26
91Bluefld/ClBest-17
91Bluefld/ProC-4128
92Freder/ClBest-26
92Freder/ProC-1805

Ryan, Mike
65T-573R
66T-419
67CokeCap/RedSox-9
67T-223
67T/Test/RSox-14
68T-306
69MLB/St-177
69OPC-28
69T-28
70MLB/St-93
70T-591
71MLB/St-186
71OPC-533
71T-533
72MB-302
72OPC-324
72T-324
73OPC-467
73T-467
74OPC-564
74T-564
84Phill/TastyK-13CO
85Phill/TastyK-6CO
85Phill/TastyK-8CO
86Phill/TastyK-5CO
87Phill/TastyK-x
88Phill/TastyK-29CO
89Phill/TastyK-29
89Phill/TastyK-30CO
90Phill/TastyK-34CO
92Phill/Med-27CO
93Phill/Med-30CO
94Phill/Med-28CO

Ryan, Nolan
68OPC-177R
68T-177R
69T-533
70MLB/St-81
70OPC-197NLCS
70T-197NLCS
70T-712
70Trans/M-24
71MLB/St-162
71OPC-513
71T-513
72T-595
73K-16
73OPC-220
73OPC-67LL
73T-220
73T-67LL
73T/Comics-17
73T/Lids-45
73T/PinUps-17
74K-8
74OPC-20
74OPC-207LL
74T-20
74T-207LL
74T/DE-41
74T/Puzzles-9
74T/St-147
75Ho-58
75Ho/Twink-58
75K-26
75OPC-312LL
75OPC-500
75OPC-5RB
75OPC-7M
75SSPC/42-10
75T-312LL
75T-500
75T-5RB
75T-7M
75T/M-312LL
75T/M-500
75T/M-5RB
75T/M-7M
76Crane-52
76Ho-79
76Laugh/Jub-1
76MSA/Disc
76OPC-330
76SSPC-187
76SSPC-593CL
76T-330
77BurgChef-123
77Ho-81
77Ho/Twink-81
77OPC-264RB
77OPC-65
77OPC-6LL
77Pep-24
77T-234RB
77T-650
77T-6LL
77T/CS-40
77T/ClothSt-40
78Ho-83
78K-51
78OPC-105
78OPC-241RB
78OPC-6LL
78Pep-37
78Pep-37
78SSPC/270-203
78T-206LL
78T-400
78T-6RB
78Wiffle/Discs-65
79Ho-101
79OPC-51
79T-115
79T-417LL
79T-6LL
79T/Comics-4
80BK/PHR-9
80K-20
80OPC-303
80T-206LL
80T-580
80T/S-20
80T/Super-20
81Coke-69
81D-260
81F-57
81F/St-108
81K-6
81OPC-240
81PermaGr/CC-26
81T-240
81T/HT
81T/St-173
81T/St-30
82D-13DK
82D-419
82F-229
82F/St-242M
82F/St-42
82FBI/Disc-19
82K-11
82OPC-90
82T-167LL
82T-5RB
82T-66TL
82T-90
82T/St-13
82T/St-41
82T/StVar-41
83D-118
83D/AAS-23
83F-463
83F/St-11M
83F/St-12M
83F/St-1AM
83F/St-1BM
83K-31
83OPC-360
83OPC-361SV
83OPC/St-235FOIL
83T-360
83T-361SV
83T/Fold-1M
83T/Gloss40-28
83T/St-235
84D-60
84D/AAS-14
84D/Champs-39
84F-239
84F/St-82
84Mother/Ast-1
84Nes/792-470
84Nes/792-4HL
84Nes/792-66TL
84Nes/792-707LL
84OPC-66
84Ralston-14
84Seven-13W
84T-470
84T-4HL
84T-66TL
84T-707LL
84T/Cereal-14

84T/Gloss40-15
84T/RD-26M
84T/St-66
84T/Super-28
85D-60
85D/AAS-20
85D/HL-22
85F-359
85F/LimEd-30
85F/St-115
85FunFoodPin-109
85Leaf-216
85Mother/Ast-2
85OPC-63
85Seven-1C
85Seven-3S
85T-760
85T-7RB
85T/RD-26M
85T/St-58
85T/Super-23
85Woolwth-32
86D-258
86D/AAS-21
86Drake-33
86F-310
86F/HOF-5
86F/Mini-65
86F/Slug-30
86F/St-102
86Jiffy-13
86Leaf-132
86Mother/Ast-23
86OPC-100
86Pol/Ast-2
86Quaker-12
86Seven/Coin-C8M
86Seven/Coin-E8M
86Seven/Coin-S8M
86Seven/Coin-W8M
86Sf-141M
86Sf-143M
86Sf-182M
86Sf-43
86Sf/Dec-63M
86T-100
86T/Gloss60-45
86T/Mini-43
86T/St-24
86T/St-9
86T/Super-47
86T/Tatt-24M
86TrueVal-26
87Classic-82
87D-138
87D/HL-53
87Drake-32
87F-67
87F/BB-38
87F/St-103
87KMart-20
87Kraft-48
87Leaf-257
87MnM's-22
87Mother/Ast-8
87OPC-155
87Pol/Ast-16
87Ralston-1
87RedFoley/St-121
87Sf-125
87Sf/TPrev-8M
87Stuart-5M
87T-757
87T/Coins-40
87T/St-27
88Classic/Red-179
88D-61
88D/Best-232
88F-455
88F/BB/AS-34
88F/Mini-79
88F/St-88
88Grenada-22
88KMart-23
88KennerFig-94
88Leaf-77
88Mother/Ast-8
88Nestle-43
88OPC-250
88OPC/WaxBox-N
88Panini/St-288
88Panini/St-435
88Pol/Ast-20
88S-575
88Sf-39
88T-250
88T-661TBC
88T-6RB
88T/Big-29
88T/Coins-50
88T/Mini-50
88T/Revco-8
88T/St-7
88T/UK-62
88T/WaxBox-N
88Woolwth-6
89B-225
89BestWest/Ryan-NNO
89Cadaco-46
89Classic/Up/2-164
89D-154
89D/Best-55
89D/Tr-19
89F-368
89F/Up-67
89KingB/Discs-10
89Mother/R-2
89OPC-366
89OPC/BoxB-K
89Panini/St-226
89Panini/St-83
89RedFoley/St-100
89S-300
89S/HotStar-64
89S/Mast-5
89S/Tr-2
89Sf-115
89Smok/Angels-7
89Smok/R-29
89T-530
89T/LJN-114
89T/Mini-15
89T/St-20
89T/Tr-106T
89T/WaxBox-K
89UD-145
89UD-669TC
89UD/Ext-774
90B-486
90B/Ins-8
90BBWit-55
90Classic-1
90Classic/III-84
90Classic/III-91M
90Classic/Up-26
90CollAB-14
90D-166
90D-659
90D-665K
90D/BestAL-49
90D/Learning-24
90D/Preview-7
90F-313
90F-636M
90F/AwardWin-29
90F/Can-313
90F/Can-636
90F/LL-31
90F/Up-131
90Ho/St-77
90HoPlay/St-35
90KMart/SS-25
90KayBee-28
90Kenner/Fig-71
90KingB/Discs-22
90Leaf-21
90Leaf-264CL
90Leaf-265K
90MCA/Disc-20
90MSA/Soda-16
90Mother/Rang-2
90Mother/Ryan-Set
90OPC-1
90OPC-2SA
90OPC-3SA
90OPC-4SA
90OPC-5SA
90OPC/BoxB-O
90Panini/St-160
90Panini/St-185
90Panini/St-387
90Post-11
90PublInt/St-21
90RedFoley/St-81
90S-250
90S-696HL
90S/100St-44
90S/ComRyan-xx
90Sf-8
90Starline/LJS-13
90Starline/LJS-26
90T-1
90T-2SA
90T-3SA
90T-4SA
90T-5SA
90T/Big-171
90T/Coins-25
90T/DH-53
90T/Gloss60-2
90T/Mini-39
90T/St-242
90T/St-3HL
90T/TVAS-9
90T/WaxBox-O
90Tetley/Discs-20
90UD-34HL
90UD-544
90UD/Ext-734
90WonderBrd-16
90Woolwth/HL-20
91B-280
91BBBest/RecBr-14
91Bleach/Pr-3
91Bleach/Pr-4
91Bleach/Pr-5
91Bleach/Pr-6
91Bleach/Pr-7
91Cadaco-45
91Classic/200-196
91Classic/I-86
91Classic/II-T80
91Classic/II-T97
91Classic/III-79Number 7
91Classic/III-98
91Classic/Ryan10-Set
91CollAB-3
91D-89
91D-BC15
91D-BC3
91D/BC-BC15
91D/BC-BC3
91D/Elite-L1(Legend)
91D/Preview-7
91F-302
91F/WaxBox-3
91JDean-24
91Kenner-44
91Leaf-423
91Leaf/GRook-BC25
91Leaf/Prev-25
91Leaf/Stud-128
91MSA/Holsum-19
91MajorLg/Pins-35
91Mother/Rang-2
91Mother/Ryan-Set
91OPC-1
91OPC-6RB
91OPC/BoxB-N
91OPC/Premier-102
91Pac/Ryan7NH-Set
91Pac/RyanSIns-Set
91Pac/RyanTE-Set
91Panini/FrSt-259
91Panini/FrSt-354
91Panini/St-205
91Panini/St-3
91Panini/Top15-77
91Petro/SU-25
91Post-17
91Post/Can-27
91RedFoley/St-79
91S-4
91S-417HL
91S-686KM
91S-701NH
91S/100SS-25
91S/Cooper-B7
91S/RyanL&T-Set
91Seven/3DCoin-11T
91Seven/3DCoin-12SC
91Seven/3DCoin-14A
91Seven/3DCoin-14F
91Seven/3DCoin-14NW
91Seven/3DCoin-8NC
91SilverSt-2
91StCl-200
91StCl/Charter*-24
91StCl/Charter*-25
91StCl/Member*-27
91StCl/Member*-7
91Sunflower-20
91T-1
91T-6RB
91T/CJMini/I-1
91T/SU-29
91T/WaxBox-N
91UD-345
91UD/Ext-SP2M
91UD/Nat-1
91UD/Nat-3
91UD/Ryan-Set
91Ultra-355
91Ultra-395EP
91Ultra-400CL
91WIZMets-338
91Woolwth/HL-19
92B-222
92Bleach/Ryan-1
92Bleach/Ryan-2
92Bleach/Ryan-3
92CJ/DI-15
92ClBest-1
92ClBest/BBonusC-1
92ClBest/Pr-1
92ClBest/Pr-PR1
92ClBest/RBonus-BC1
92Classic/Game200-183
92Classic/I-78
92Classic/I-xx
92Classic/II-T67
92Colla/Ryan-Set
92Conlon/Gold-934GM
92Conlon/Gold-934M
92D-154HL
92D-555M
92D-707
92D/McDon-5
92D/Preview-11
92D/RyanCoke-Set
92F-320
92F-682RS
92F-710PV
92F/Performer-1
92F/Smoke-S5
92Highland-1
92JDean/Living-6
92Kenner/Fig-35
92KingB-7
92L-133M
92L-41
92L/BlkGold-133M
92L/BlkGold-41
92L/GoldPrev-25
92L/Prev-25
92MooTown-20
92Mother/Rang-2
92Mother/Ryan7NH-Set
92MrTurkey-20
92OPC-1
92OPC-4RB
92OPC/Premier-81
92P-27
92Pac/RyanGold-Set
92Pac/RyanLtd-Set
92Pac/RyanMag6-Set
92Pac/RyanTExpII-Set
92Pac/S-82M
92Panini-82
92Pinn-281M
92Pinn-294SIDE
92Pinn-50
92Pinn-618TECH
92Pinn/RookI-12M
92S-2
92S-425NH
92S/100SS-50
92Seven/Coin-11
92StCl-605MC
92StCl-770
92StCl/MPhoto-11
92StCl/MemberIV*-3
92StCl/MemberIV*-4
92Studio-248
92T-1
92T-4RB
92T/GPro-1
92T/Gold-1
92T/Gold-4RB
92T/GoldWin-1
92T/GoldWin-4RB
92T/Kids-127
92T/McDonB-24
92T/MicroG-1
92TripleP-22
92UD-655
92UD-92HL
92UD/ASFF-37
92UD/TmMVPHolo-45
92USPlayC/Ace-3S
92Ultra-141
93B-405
93Bleach/Pr-4
93Bleach/Pr-5
93Bleach/Pr-6
93Bleach/Pr-7
93Bleach/Pr-8
93Bleach/Pr-9
93Bleach/Ryan6-1
93Bleach/Ryan6-2
93Bleach/Ryan6-3
93Bleach/Ryan6-4
93Bleach/Ryan6-5
93Bleach/Ryan6-6
93Cadaco-48
93Classic/GameI-79
93Colla/DM-91
93Colla/DMArt-6
93Conlon-928M
93Conlon-929M
93Conlon-930M
93Conlon-931M
93Conlon-932M
93Conlon-933M
93Conlon-934M
93Conlon-935M
93Conlon/MasterCol-3
93Conlon/Proto-934M
93D-423
93D/EliteDom-1
93D/EliteDom-1AU
93D/EliteUp-20
93D/Master-2
93Duracel/PPI-20
93F-690
93F/Atlantic-20
93F/Final/DTrib-DT6
93F/Fruit-55
93Flair-286
93Flair/Pr-7
93HumDum/Can-16
93JDean/28-16
93Kenner/Fig-31
93KingB-17
93Kraft-13
93L-115
93L/GoldAS-19
93L/Heading-1
93MSA/Metz-35
93Mother/RyanF-Set
93OPC-229
93OPC/Premier/StarP-20
93P-20
93Pac/Jugador-15
93Pac/Ryan27-241
93Pac/Ryan27-Set
93Pac/RyanFare-Set
93Pac/RyanLtd-Set
93Pac/RyanPrism-Set
93Pac/Spanish-317
93Panini-87
93Pinn-290NT
93Pinn-75
93Pinn/Cooper-1
93Pinn/Trib-10
93Pinn/Trib-6
93Pinn/Trib-7
93Pinn/Trib-8
93Pinn/Trib-9
93Rang/Keeb-431
93S-59
93Select-90
93Select/RookTr-NR1
93Spectrum/Ryan10-Set
93Spectrum/Ryan23-Set
93Spectrum/Ryan5-Set
93StCl-353
93StCl/1stDay-353
93StCl/MPhoto-21
93StCl/Rang-1
93Studio-71
93Studio/Sil-10
93T-700
93T/Finest-107AS
93T/FinestASJ-107AS
93T/FinestPr-107
93T/FinestRef-107AS
93T/Gold-700
93T/MicroP-700
93TripleP-96

93TripleP/Nick-7
93UD-155
93UD-37CH
93UD-SP6
93UD/5thAnn-A5
93UD/Diam-30
93UD/FunPack-160
93UD/FunPack-18HS
93UD/FunPack-214ASA
93UD/FunPack-26KS
93UD/FunPack-33HERO
93UD/Iooss-WI19
93UD/OnDeck-D20
93UD/SP-198
93UD/SeasonHL-HI17
93UD/Then-TN5
93Ultra-636
93Ultra/Strike-4
93WhatRyan-Set
94Conlon/Col-30M
94D-1
94D/Ann-5
94D/Special-1
94F-321
94F/GoldM-7
94F/Smoke-10
94Mets/69-7
94StCl-34
94StCl/1stDay-34
94StCl/Gold-34
94T-34
94T/Gold-34
94T/Prev-700
94UD/CollC-249
94UD/CollC/Gold-249
94UD/CollC/Silv-249

Ryan, Ray
T206

Ryan, Reid
90Classic/III-91M

Ryan, Sean
90Batavia/ProC-3076
91AA/LineD-517
91ClBest/Singl-117
91Reading/LineD-517
91Reading/ProC-1377
92ClBest-234
92Reading/ProC-583
92Reading/SB-542
92Sky/AASingl-236
92UD/ML-120
93ScranWB/Team-23

Ryan, Wilfred
(Rosy)
90Target-702
93Conlon-746
E121/120
E121/80
V100
W501-75
W575

Ryba, Dominic
(Mike)
44Playball-11
54Hunter
54T-237
94T/Arc54-237

Rychel, Kevin
90Augusta/ProC-2461
91Salem/ClBest-19
91Salem/ProC-949
92Augusta/ClBest-9
92Salem/ProC-63

Ryder, Brian
81Colum-14
82Indianap-11
83Indianap-11

Ryder, Scott
90Idaho/ProC-3245
91Pulaski/ClBest-26
91Pulaski/ProC-4003
92Durham/ClBest-4
92Durham/ProC-1098
92Durham/Team-26

Ryerson, Gary
75SLCity/Caruso-14

Rymer, Carlos
80Ander-16

Rypien, Mark
91StCl/Member*-34

Saa, Humberto
90Hunting/ProC-3293
91Geneva/ClBest-17
91Geneva/ProC-4227

Saatzer, Michael
82Redwd-10
83Nashua-7
86QuadC-30CO

Saavedra, Ed
81Watlo-27
82Chatt-4
83BuffB-20
84BuffB-22

Saavedra, Justo
80Batavia-23

Saberhagen, Bret
84F/X-U103
84T/Tr-104T
85D-222
85D/HL-26
85F-212
85F/St-124
85OPC-23
85T-23
86D-100
86D-11DK
86D/DKsuper-11
86Drake-29
86F-19
86F/LL-37
86F/LimEd-38
86F/Mini-3
86F/Slug-31
86F/St-103
86GenMills/Book-2M
86KayBee-27
86Kitty/Disc-3
86Leaf-11DK
86NatPhoto-31
86OPC-249
86OPC/WaxBox-O
86Quaker-19
86Seven/Coin-C6M
86Seven/Coin-E6M
86Seven/Coin-S6M
86Seven/Coin-W6M
86Sf-10
86Sf-176M
86Sf-185M
86Sf-186M
86T-487
86T-720AS
86T/3D-25
86T/Gloss60-27
86T/Mini-20
86T/St-17WS
86T/St-260
86T/Super-3
86T/Tatt-2M
86T/WaxBox-O
87Classic-88
87Classic/Up-116
87D-132
87D/HL-6
87F-379
87F/AwardWin-34
87F/LimWaxBox-C5
87F/Slug-36
87Leaf-261
87OPC-140
87Sf-145
87Sf/TPrev-13M
87Stuart-20M
87T-140
88Classic/Red-172
88D-96
88D/AS-8
88D/Best-231
88D/PopUp-8
88F-268
88F-626M
88F/LL-33
88F/Mini-26
88F/St-32
88F/TL-32
88Grenada-53
88Jiffy-15
88KennerFig-95
88Leaf-68
88Nestle-11
88OPC-5
88Panini/St-102
88Panini/St-229
88RedFoley/St-77
88S-89
88S/WaxBox-9
88S/YS/II-17
88Sf-15
88Smok/Royals-16
88T-540
88T/Big-94
88T/Coins-25
88T/Gloss22-10
88T/Mini-14
88T/St-163
88T/St-254
88T/St/Backs-60
88T/UK-63
89B-111
89Classic-62
89D-144
89D/Best-95
89F-291
89KennerFig-117
89OPC-157
89Panini/St-352
89S-251
89Sf-109
89T-750
89T/Big-6
89T/LJN-39
89T/St-263
89Tastee/Discs-11
89UD-37
90B-364
90B/Ins-9
90BBWit-21
90Bz-4
90Classic-139
90Classic/Up-NNO
90CollAB-30
90D-89
90D/BestAL-21
90F-116
90F/AwardWin-30
90F/BB-31
90F/BBMVP-32
90F/Can-116
90F/LL-32
90Holsum/Discs-5
90HotPlay/St-36
90KMart/SS-26
90Leaf-72
90MCA/Disc-17
90OPC-350
90OPC-393ASen
90Panini/St-81
90PublInt/St-354
90S-195
90Sf-94
90Starline/LJS-19
90Starline/LJS-36
90T-350
90T-393AS
90T/Big-21
90T/Coins-2
90T/DH-54
90T/Gloss60-13
90T/HeadsUp-7
90T/Mini-17
90T/St-266
90T/TVAS-15
90Tetley/Discs-17
90UD-326
90USPlayC/AS-3C
90Windwlk/Discs-4
90Woolwth/HL-3
91B-291
91BBBest/Aces-14
91Cadaco-46
91Classic/200-36
91Classic/III-80
91D-88
91F-567
91Leaf-118
91Leaf/Stud-69
91OPC-280
91Panini/FrSt-283
91Panini/St-225
91Pol/Royal-18
91RedFoley/St-80
91S-6
91S/100SS-59
91StCl-38
91StCl/Member*-28
91T-280
91T/CJMini/II-14
91UD-33TC
91UD-435
91Ultra-154
92B-586
92Classic/Game200-175
92D-128
92D-434HL
92F-167
92Kenner/Fig-36
92L-376
92L/BlkGold-376
92Mets/Kahn-18
92OPC-75
92OPC/Premier-82
92Panini-101
92Pinn-442
92S-6
92S-786HL
92S/100SS-11
92S/RookTr-20T
92StCl-755
92Studio-69
92T-75
92T/Gold-75
92T/GoldWin-75
92T/Kids-107
92T/Tr-97T
92T/TrGold-97T
92UD-233
92UD-751
92Ultra-537
93B-510
93Cadaco-49
93D-222
93F-93
93Flair-96
93L-93
93Mets/Kahn-18
93OPC-302
93Pac/Spanish-201
93Pinn-185
93S-115
93Select-123
93StCl-335
93StCl/1stDay-335
93Studio-112
93T-600
93T/Finest-53
93T/FinestRef-53
93T/Gold-600
93TripleP-124
93UD-282
93UD/FunPack-129
93UD/SP-153
93Ultra-79
94B-16
94D-298
94F-576
94Finest-419
94L-437
94OPC-46
94Pac/Cr-416
94Panini-222
94Pinn-203
94Pinn/Artist-203
94Pinn/Museum-203
94S-92
94S/GoldR-92
94Select-101
94StCl-368
94StCl/1stDay-368
94StCl/Gold-368
94Studio-119
94T-245
94T/Gold-245
94TripleP-148
94UD-428
94UD/CollC-250
94UD/CollC/Gold-250
94UD/CollC/Silv-250
94UD/SP-120
94Ultra-533

Sabino, Miguel
87Sumter-3
88Greenvl/Best-7
89Greenvl/Best-27
89Greenvl/ProC-1170
89Greenvl/Star-21
90Canton/Best-15
90Canton/ProC-1305
90Canton/Star-16
90ProC/Singl-721
91AA/LineD-94
91Canton/LineD-94
91Canton/ProC-992
93LimeR/Winter-36

Sable, Luke
88Gaston/ProC-1002
89CharlR/Star-21
90CharlR/Star-25
91AA/LineD-595
91Tulsa/LineD-595
91Tulsa/ProC-2782
91Tulsa/Team-27
92Tulsa/ProC-2704
92Tulsa/SB-619

Sabo, Chris
87Nashvl-18
88D/Best-278
88D/Rook-30
88F/Slug-35
88F/Up-U87
88Kahn/Reds-17
88S/Tr-100T
88T/Tr-98T
89B-309
89Bz-18
89Classic-53
89D-317
89D-4DK
89D/AS-59
89D/Best-222
89D/DKsuper-4DK
89F-170
89F-637M
89F/BBMVP's-33
89F/Excit-35
89F/Superstar-35
89F/WaxBox-C21
89KMart/DT-3
89Kahn/Reds-17
89KennerFig-118
89KingB/Discs-7
89OPC-156
89Panini/St-476
89Panini/St-64
89S-104
89S/HotRook-76
89S/YS/I-10
89Sf-13
89T-490
89T/Big-251
89T/Coins-3
89T/Gloss60-40
89T/JumboR-17
89T/LJN-68
89T/Mini-13
89T/St-142
89T/St-325
89T/UK-65
89ToysRUs-24
89UD-180
89UD-663ROY
89Woolwth-6
90B-53
90CedarDG/Best-4
90Classic/Up-43
90D-242
90D/BestNL-64
90F-433
90F/Can-433
90Kahn/Reds-25
90Kenner/Fig-72
90KingB/Discs-10
90Leaf-146
90MCA/Disc-3
90MLBPA/Pins-19
90OPC-737
90Panini/St-248
90PublInt/St-39
90S-70
90Starline/LJS-20
90Starline/LJS-25
90T-737
90T/Big-121
90T/St-140
90Tetley/Discs-3
90UD-181
90USPlayC/AS-5H
91B-674
91Cadaco-47
91Classic/200-108
91Classic/I-26
91D-153
91D-412MVP
91D-440AS
91F-80
91F/UltraG-9
91F/WS-5
91Kahn/Reds-17
91Kenner-45
91Leaf-65

91Leaf/Stud-170
91MooTown-21
91OPC-45
91Panini/FrSt-129
91Panini/FrSt-160
91Panini/St-127
91Pep/Reds-19
91Post-13
91Post/Can-10
91RedFoley/St-125
91RedFoley/St-81
91S-462
91S-795WS
91S/100SS-28
91StCl-165
91T-45
91T/CJMini/II-29
91UD-135
91UD-77TC
91UD/FinalEd-94F
91USPlayC/AS-12C
91Ultra-103
91Woolwth/HL-29
92B-595
92CJ/DII-16
92Classic/Game200-79
92D-424AS
92D-50
92F-420
92F/TmLIns-3
92French-14M
92JDean/18-6
92Kenner/Fig-37
92KingB-2
92L-271
92L/BlkGold-271
92L/GoldPrev-3
92L/Prev-3
92MrTurkey-21
92OPC-485
92OPC/Premier-23
92Panini-264
92Panini-283AS
92Pinn-135
92Reds/Kahn-17
92S-70
92StCl-273
92StCl/Dome-160
92Studio-28
92Sunflower-10
92T-485
92T/Gold-485
92T/GoldWin-485
92T/Kids-39
92TripleP-90
92UD-123
92UD/ASFF-38
92Ultra-197
93B-286
93Cadaco-50
93D-58
93F-43
93Flair-33
93L-418
93OPC-333
93Pac/Spanish-90
93Panini-294
93Pinn-47
93Reds/Kahn-22
93S-149
93Select-135
93StCl-286
93StCl/1stDay-286
93Studio-73
93T-245
93T/Finest-39
93T/FinestRef-39
93T/Gold-245
93TripleP-184
93UD-147
93UD/SP-215
93Ultra-35
94B-187
94D-330
94F-425
94Finest-418
94Flair-9
94L-324
94OPC-136
94Pac/Cr-158
94Panini-168
94Pinn-490
94S-360
94StCl/Team-291
94T-542
94T/Gold-542
94TripleP-160
94UD-347
94Ultra-310

Sabo, Scott
84Idaho/Team-24
85Madis-1
85Madis/Pol-21
86Madis/Pol-17
87Wmsprt-20

Sabol, Tony
46Remar-13
47Remar-15
47Signal
47Smith-13

Saccavino, Craig
92Elizab/ClBest-3
92Elizab/ProC-3681

Saccomanno, Joseph
89BurlB/ProC-1600
89BurlB/Star-19

Sacka, Frank
89Chatt/II/Team-26

Sackinsky, Brian
92ClBest/Up-420
92Classic/DP-28
93StCl/MurphyS-160
93T-647
93T/Gold-647
94FExcel-15

Sadecki, Ray
60T-327
61T-32
62T-383
62T/St-190
63T-486
64T-147
65OPC-10LL
65OPC-230
65T-10LL
65T-230
66OPC-26
66T-26
67CokeCap/Giant-14
67T-409
68CokeCap/Giant-14
68Dexter-69
68T-494
69MB-244
69OPC-125
69T-125
69T/4in1-17
70T-679
71MLB/St-163
71OPC-406
71T-406
72MB-303
72T-563
72T-564IA
73OPC-283
73T-283
74OPC-216
74T-216
75OPC-349
75SSPC/18-14
75T-349
75T/M-349
77T-26
91WIZMets-339
92Peoria/Team-22

Sadecki, Steve
92CharlR/ProC-2225
92ClBest-113
92Gaston/ClBest-2

Sadek, Mike
74OPC-577
74T-577
75Phoenix-3
75Phoenix/CircleK-3
76OPC-234
76T-234
77T-129
78T-8
79Pol/Giants-3
79T-256
80OPC-240DP
80Pol/Giants-3
80T-462
81D-498
81T-384

Sadler, Alan
85Beloit-21
86Stockton-24
87ElPaso-24
88Stockton/Cal-181
88Stockton/ProC-726
89Denver/CMC-9
89Denver/ProC-44
90AAASingl/ProC-651
90Denver/CMC-19
90Denver/ProC-626
90ProC/Singl-44

Sadler, Sean
90Niagara/Pucko-14
91Fayette/ClBest-15
91Fayette/ProC-1173

Sadowski, Ed
59T-139
60L-113
60T-403
61T-163
62T-569
63T-527
64T-61M

Sadowski, Robert F.
62Kahn/Atl
62T-595R
63T-568

Sadowski, Robert
64T-271
65OPC-156
65T-156
66T-523
78TCMA-167

Sadowski, Ted
61Clover-24
61T-254
61T/St-174

Sadowsky, Clinton
91Bristol/ClBest-17
91Bristol/ProC-3604

Saenz, Olmedo
92SoBend/ClBest-13
92SoBend/ProC-187
94FExcel-40

Saetre, Damon
90Penin/Star-19
91Penin/ClBest-16
91Penin/ProC-392

Saferight, Harry
75Shrev/TCMA-18
76Shrev
78Colum
79Portl-21
80Richm-16
80T-683R
81Richm-24
82Toledo-10

Saffell, Tom
51B-130
52Mother-36
59DF

Saffer, Jon
93ClBest/MLG-140
93James/ClBest-20
93James/ProC-3339
93StCl/MurphyS-166

Safly, Joel
92Visalia/ClBest-26TR

Sagawa, Kiyoshi
89Visalia/Cal-103
89Visalia/ProC-1434

Sage, Henry
N172

Sager, A.J.
88Spokane/ProC-1933
89CharRain/ProC-971
90Wichita/Rock-18
91AA/LineD-617
91Wichita/LineD-617
91Wichita/ProC-2597
91Wichita/Rock-8
92LasVegas/ProC-2795
92LasVegas/SB-238
94B-474

Saier, Vic
14CJ-104
15CJ-104
BF2-66
D328-148
D329-152
D350/2-152
E135-148
M101/4-152
M101/5-152
T207
T222

Sain, Joe
83Wisco/Frit-5

Sain, Johnny
47HomogBond-42
47TipTop
48B-12
49B-47
49Eureka-21
51B-314
51FB
51T/BB-9
52BR
52T-49
53B/BW-25
53T-119
54T-205
55Rodeo
55T-193
73OPC-356CO
73T-356CO
74OPC-221CO
74T-221CO
75SSPC/42-2CO
78Richm
79Richm-3CO
80Richm-9CO
81Richm-1CO
81TCMA-481M
82Richm-28CO
83Richm-25CO
84Richm-26CO
85Pol/Atl-33CO
86Pol/Atl-33CO
89Swell-121
91T/Arc53-119
92Bz/Quadra-15M
92Yank/WIZAS-73
93AP/ASG-136
94T/Arc54-205
D305
Exh47
R302-122

Sain, Tom
78OrlanTw
79Toledo-15

Saitta, Pat
87Dunedin-29

Saitz, Robbie
91FresnoSt/Smok-11
92ClBest-361
92PalmSp/ClBest-2
92PalmSp/ProC-838

Sajonia, Brian
88James/ProC-1907

Sakata, Lenn
76Spoka
77Spoka
79Vanco-22
80T-668R
81D-499
81F-194
81T-287
82D-644
82F-178
82T-136
83D-205
83F-72
83T-319
84D-620
84F-19
84Nes/792-578
84T-578
85F-189
85T-81
86T-446
86Tacom-20
88SoOreg/ProC-1717
88T-716
89Modesto/Cal-288
91AAA/LineD-175M
91Crown/Orio-399
91Edmon/LineD-175CO
91Edmon/ProC-1533CO
91Pac/SenLg-91
92Edmon/ProC-3555CO
92Edmon/SB-175CO
92Yank/WIZ80-167
93Vanco/ProC-2615CO

Sakowski, Vince
83TriCit-19

Sala, David J.
87Spring/Best-16
89Savan/ProC-367

Salaiz, David
89ColMud/Best-5
89ColMud/ProC-138

Salamon, John
91Martins/ClBest-18
91Martins/ProC-3453

Salas, Mark
82ArkTr-11
82Nashvl-20
83ArkTr-12
84Louisvl-27
85D-547
85F/Up-U94
85T/Tr-101T
85Twin/Team-9
86D-316
86F-402
86F/St-104
86KayBee-28
86Leaf-185
86OPC-43
86Sf-177M
86T-537
86T/St-278
86T/St-315
86T/Tatt-17M
87F-551
87F/Up-U106
87OPC-87
87Sf/TPrev-17M
87T-87
87T/Tr-107T
88Coke/WS-26
88S-232
88S/Tr-52T
88T/Tr-99T
89ColoSp/CMC-20
89ColoSp/ProC-240
89F-511
89S-542
89T-384
89UD-460
90CokeK/Tiger-21
91CokeK/Tiger-27
91D-65
91F-350
91OPC-498
91Pol/Tiger-10
91StCl-456
91T-498
91UD-205
91Ultra-127
92D-512
92F-144
92S-394
92Yank/WIZ80-168

Salava, Randy
82Reading-18
83Reading-19
84Cram/PCL-203
85Cram/PCL-37
85Phill/TastyK-45

Salazar, Argenis
(Angel)
83Wichita/Dog-19
84D-33RR
84Expo/PostC-27
84Stuart-31
85D-523
85OPC-154
85T-154
86F/Up-U100
86T/Tr-96T
87D-624
87F-380
87T-533
87T/St-259
88Berg/Cubs-18
88D-502
88D/Cubs/Bk-NEW
88F-269
88OPC-29
88Panini/St-109
88S-330
88T-29
89S-527
89T-642
89UD-222

Salazar, Carlos
90SoOreg/Best-19
90SoOreg/ProC-3436
91Modesto/ProC-3099
92Modesto/ClBest-19

92Modesto/ProC-3907
Salazar, Jeff
83Peoria/Frit-17
Salazar, Julian
91Beloit/ClBest-16
91Beloit/ProC-2112
92Stockton/ProC-42
Salazar, Lazerio
86Negro/Frit-93
Salazar, Luis Ernesto
77Salem
78Salem
79BuffB/TCMA-16
80Port-9
81F-501
81T-309
81T/St-228
82D-472
82F-581
82OPC-133
82T-366TL
82T-662
82T/St-101
82T/StVar-101
83D-548
83F-371
83OPC-156
83T-533
84D-356
84F-311
84Mother/Padres-24
84Nes/792-68
84OPC-68
84Smok/Padres-20
84T-68
84T/St-159
85Coke/WS-5
85D-568
85F-43
85F/Up-U95
85T-789
85T/Tr-102T
86D-302
86F-215
86T-103
87T-454
87T/Tr-108T
88F-595
88F/Up-U30
88OPC-276
88Pep/T-12
88S-284
88S/Tr-13T
88T-276
88T/Tr-100T
89Classic-72
89Coke/Padre-15
89D-352
89F-144
89KennerFig-119
89OPC-122
89Panini/St-342
89S-316
89T-553
89T/St-276
89T/Tr-107T
89UD-136
90B-40
90Cub/Mara-17
90D-513
90F/Up-U9
90Leaf-388
90OPC-378
90S-92
90T-378
90T/Big-182
90T/TVCub-25
90UD-6
91B-428
91Cub/Mara-10
91Cub/Vine-24
91D-372
91F-430
91Leaf-185
91OPC-614
91Panini/FrSt-45
91S-207
91StCl-94
91T-614
91UD-311
91Ultra-67
92Cub/Mara-10
92D-152
92OPC-67
92Panini-184
92Pinn-372
92S-508
92StCl-21
92T-67
92T/Gold-67
92T/GoldWin-67
92UD-638
92USPlayC/Cub-12S
92USPlayC/Cub-7C
92Ultra-179
93F-383
93Pac/Spanish-60
93StCl-549
93StCl/1stDay-549
93T-21
93T/Gold-21
Salazar, Terry
81Buffa-21
Salcedo, Edwin
90Tampa/DIMD-19
92PrWill/ClBest-14
92PrWill/ProC-153
Salcedo, Jose
91Kissim/ProC-4182
Salcedo, Luis
87Madis-24
Salcedo, Ron
84CharlO-4
85CharlO-11
87RochR-4
87RochR/TCMA-19
88RochR/CMC-16
88RochR/Gov-24
88RochR/ProC-200
88RochR/Team-19
89ScranWB/CMC-16
89ScranWB/ProC-707
90HagersDG/Best-24
Salee
N172
Salery, Johnny
82Wisco/Frit-9
83Wisco/Frit-13
Salfran, Francisco
52Laval-110
Salinas, Manual V.
86BirmB/Team-2
87BirmB/Best-23
88Jacks/GS-18
88TexLgAS/GS-14
89Jacks/GS-13
89Tidew/ProC-1951
Salisbury, Jim
86Sumter/ProC-24
87Durham-24
Salkeld, Bill
49B-88
49Eureka-22
50B-237
Salkeld, Roger
89Belling/Legoe-13
90A&AASingle/ProC-135
90AS/Cal-21
90B-465
90Foil/Best-14
90OPC-44FDP
90ProC/Singl-858
90S-674DC
90SanBern/Best-1
90SanBern/Cal-87
90SanBern/ProC-2632
90T-44FDP
91AA/LineD-344
91B-262
91ClBest/Singl-106
91Classic/II-T59
91Jaxvl/LineD-344
91Jaxvl/ProC-151
91Leaf/GRook-BC19
91UD-63TP
92B-369
92Calgary/SB-51
92D-7RR
92OPC-676M
92ProC/Tomorrow-140
92Sky/AAASingl-33
92T-676R
92T/Gold-676M
92T/GoldWin-676M
92UD-15SR
92UD/ML-257
94B-145
94F/MLP-30
94Finest-318
94Pac/Cr-580
94Pinn-393
94S-644
94StCl-495
94StCl/1stDay-495
94StCl/Gold-495
94T-376
94T/Gold-376
94UD-164
94UD/ElecD-164
94Ultra-424
Sallee, Andy
91Martins/ClBest-7
91Martins/ProC-3464
92Batavia/ClBest-28
92Batavia/ProC-3274
Sallee, H. Slim
11Helmar-176
14CJ-123
15CJ-123
88Conlon/4-24
88Pac/8Men-82
93Conlon-780
94Conlon-1020
BF2-94
D327
D328-149
D329-153
D350/2-153
E121/80
E122
E135-149
E254
E270/2
E300
M101/4-153
M101/5-153
M116
T204
T222
T3-37
V100
W514-86
W575
Salles, John
89Peoria/Team-8P
90CLAS/CL-47
90WinSalem/Team-3
91AA/LineD-141
91CharlK/LineD-141
91CharlK/ProC-1687
92Iowa/SB-220
92Sky/AAASingl-107
Salmon, Chico
64T-499R
65OPC-105
65T-105
66T-594
67CokeCap/Indian-11
67OPC-43
67T-43
68T-318
69MB-245
69MLB/St-99
69OPC-62
69T-62
69T/St-230
70MLB/St-156
70OPC-301
70T-301
71MLB/St-312
71OPC-249
71T-249
72MB-304
72T-646
91Crown/Orio-400
Salmon, Tim
88CapeCod/Sum-176
89BendB/Legoe-23
90PalmSp/Cal-215
90PalmSp/ProC-2593
90ProC/Singl-854
91AA/LineD-443
91B-203
91ClBest/Singl-329
91Classic/III-81
91London/LineD-443
91MidldA/OneHour-25
91MidldA/ProC-447
92AAA/ASG/SB-165
92B-259
92D/RookPhen-BC10
92Edmon/ProC-3551
92Edmon/SB-165
92F/Up-10
92ProC/Tomorrow-32
92S/RookTr-93T
92Sky/AAASingl-81
93B-229
93B-341FOIL
93Colla/DM-92
93D-176RR
93D/EliteDom-2
93F-197
93Flair-177
93Flair/Wave-15
93JDean/Rook-9
93L-445
93L/GRook-10
93Mother/Angel-7
93OPC-292
93OPC/Premier-37
93Pac/Spanish-51
93Pinn-276
93Pinn-303I
93Pinn/HRC-42
93Pinn/RookTP-8M
93Pinn/Team2001-20
93Pol/Angel-20
93S-346
93S/Boys-2
93Select-339
93Select/ChasRook-11
93Select/RT/ASRook-8
93Select/RookTr-ROY1
93StCl-249
93StCl/1stDay-249
93StCl/Angel-13
93Studio-114
93T-20
93T/Finest-163
93T/FinestRef-163
93T/Gold-20
93T/MicroP-20
93TB/Full-9
93ToysRUs-67
93TripleP-37
93UD-1CL
93UD-25SR
93UD-812TC
93UD/5thAnn-A15
93UD/Diam-1
93UD/FunPack-37GS
93UD/FunPack-7SOT
93UD/Iooss-WI1
93UD/OnDeck-D21
93UD/SP-25
93UD/SPPlat-PP16
93Ultra-523
93Ultra/AllRook-8
94B-395
94Church-9
94D-353
94D/AwardWin-8ROY
94D/DK-4
94D/Elite-39
94D/MVP-17
94D/Pr-6
94D/Special-353
94D/Spirit-7
94F-69
94F/AwardWin-5
94F/Pr-69
94F/RookSen-17
94F/Salmon-Set
94F/Salmon-Set
94F/TL-3
94Flair-27
94Flair/Outfield-9
94KingB-7
94L-109
94L/Slide-8
94L/Slide-8
94OPC-194
94OPC/DiamD-11
94OPC/JAS-10
94Oscar-12
94P-26
94Pac/Cr-659ROY
94Pac/Cr-88
94Pac/CrPr-7
94Pac/Gold-9
94Pac/Silv-12
94Panini-42
94Pinn-9
94Pinn/Artist-9
94Pinn/Museum-9
94Pinn/New-1
94Pinn/Power-4
94Pinn/Run-13
94Pinn/TeamP-8
94RedFoley-23
94S-539
94S-635ROY
94S/GoldS-44
94S/Tomb-27
94Sf/2000-89
94Sf/Shak-2
94StCl-181M
94StCl-36
94StCl/1stDay-181M
94StCl/1stDay-36
94StCl/Gold-181M
94StCl/Gold-36
94StCl/Pr-36
94Studio-15
94Studio/Editor-6
94T-397
94T/BlkGold-19
94T/Finest-18
94T/FinestRef-18
94T/Gold-397
94TedW-158
94TedW-159
94TedW-160
94TedW 161ROY
94TripleP-19
94TripleP/Pr-7
94UD-111
94UD-283HFA
94UD-54FUT
94UD/CollC-251
94UD/CollC/Gold-251
94UD/CollC/Silv-251
94UD/DColl-W10
94UD/ElecD-111
94UD/ElecD-54FUT
94UD/HoloFX-35
94UD/Mantle-17
94UD/SP-26
94Ultra-27
94Ultra/AwardWin-24ROY
94Ultra/RisSt-11
94Ultra/Second-4
Saltzgaber, Brian
90Niagara/Pucko-9
91Fayette/ClBest-16
91Fayette/ProC-1174
91SALAS/ProC-SAL21
92Lakeland/ClBest-10
92Lakeland/ProC-2283
Saltzgaver, Jack
93Conlon-972
Salva, Elias
80Wausau-8
Salveson, John
V94-41
Salvior, Troy
90Hamil/Best-10
90Hamil/Star-22
91ClBest/Singl-310
91StPete/ClBest-10
91StPete/ProC-2274
92StPete/ProC-2027
Salvo, Manny
94Conlon-1294
Salyer, Ron
75SanAn
Samaniego, Art
79Elmira-5
Sambel, Arnie
90Eugene/GS-26
Sambito, Joe
74Cedar
77T-227
78BK/Ast-10
78T-498
79T-158
80T-571
81Coke
81D-21
81F-65
81OPC-334
81T-385
81T/St-172
82D-65
82F-230
82F/St-47
82T-34
83D-244
83F-464

83OPC-296
83T-662
85D-572
85F-360
85F/Up-U96
85T-264
85T/Tr-103T
86F/Up-U101
86Mother/Ast-19
86T/Tr-97T
87D-421
87F-43
87OPC-262
87T-451
88F-364
88S-314
88T-784
88Tucson/JP-20
89Pac/SenLg-18
89T/SenLg-95
89TM/SenLg-93
91Pac/SenLg-157
91WIZMets-340
93UD/ATH-111

Sambo, Ramon
87Vermont-7
88Cedar/ProC-1149
89ElPaso/GS-28
89TexLAS/GS-15
90AAASingl/ProC-181
90ProC/Singl-642
90Vanco/CMC-15
90Vanco/ProC-503
91AA/LineD-444
91London/LineD-444
91MidldA/OneHour-26
91MidldA/ProC-448
93LimeR/Winter-122

Samboy, Alvaro
91Spokane/ClBest-25
91Spokane/ProC-3949

Samcoff, Ed
48Smith-19
49Remar

Samford, Ron
59T-242
60T-409
79TCMA-102

Sammons, Lee
90Bend/Legoe-22
91Madison/ClBest-28
91Tacoma/ProC-2319
92Jacks/ProC-4013
92Jacks/SB-347
92Sky/AASingl-146

Samonds, Shereen
89OrlanTw/Best-28

Sampen, Bill
86Watertn-21
87Salem-21
89Harris/ProC-290
89Harris/Star-17
90B-104
90D/Rook-12
90F/Up-U31
90S/Tr-79T
90Swell/Great-118
90T/Tr-108T
90UD/Ext-724
91D-351
91F-247
91Leaf-318
91Leaf/Stud-199
91OPC-649
91Panini/FrSt-149
91S-68
91S/100RisSt-64
91StCl-249
91Swell/Great-79
91T-649
91T/90Debut-138
91ToysRUs-26
91UD-661
92B-348
92D-571
92Expo/D/Duri-3
92F-492
92OPC-566
92S-166
92StCl-277
92T-566
92T/Gold-566
92T/GoldWin-566
92TripleP-221
92Ultra-522
93D-337
93F-624
93Pac/Spanish-188
93StCl/Royal-22

Sample, Billy
78Cr/PCL-72
79T-713R
80T-458
81D-268
81F-637
81OPC-283
81T-283
82D-69
82F-330
82OPC-112
82T-112
83D-242
83F-577
83F/St-4M
83Rang-5
83T-641
84D-403
84F-426
84Nes/792-12
84OPC-12
84Rang-5
84T-12
84T/St-352
85D-464
85F-566
85F/Up-U97
85T-337
85T/St-351
86D-539
86F-118
86F/Up-U102
86Pol/Atl-5
86T-533
86T/Tr-98T
87D-143
87F-527
87T-104
90Swell/Great-118
92Yank/WIZ80-169
93Rang/Keeb-317

Sample, Deron
89Kingspt/Star-20
90Clmbia/PCPII-1
90Columbia/GS-10
90SALAS/Star-41
91StLucie/ClBest-17
91StLucie/ProC-709
92Erie/ClBest-7
92Erie/ProC-1623

Sample, Frank
91Hunting/ClBest-22
91Hunting/ProC-3334

Samples, Todd
90James/Pucko-11
91SALAS/ProC-SAL47
91Sumter/ClBest-24
91Sumter/ProC-2349
92Rockford/ClBest-25
92Rockford/ProC-2129

Samplinski, Rich
88CapeCod/Sum-104
89OK-23
90OK-7

Sampson, Mark
86Cram/NWL-166

Sampson, Michael
89VeroB/Star-24
90Yakima/Team-3
91VeroB/ClBest-11
91VeroB/ProC-772

Sampson, Tommy
92Negro/Kraft-15
92Negro/Retort-53

Sams, Andre
78Green

Samson, Frederic
(Fred)
87PortChar-14
89Tulsa/GS-23
89Tulsa/Team-22
90CharlR/Star-26
90FSLAS/Star-42
90Star/ISingl-27
91AA/LineD-596
91Tulsa/LineD-596
91Tulsa/ProC-2783
91Tulsa/Team-28

Samson, William
52Park-51
53Exh/Can-54

Samuel, Amado
62T-597R
64T-129
91WIZMets-341

Samuel, Juan
83Portl-2
83Reading-17
84F-47
84Phill/TastyK-32
84T/Tr-105T
85CIGNA-1
85D-183
85D-23DK
85D/AAS-56
85D/DKsuper-23
85Drake-27
85F-264
85F-634IA
85F/St-44
85F/St-59
85FunFoodPin-68
85Leaf-23DK
85OPC-265
85Phill/TastyK-11M
85Phill/TastyK-32
85Seven-15E
85T-265
85T-8RB
85T/Gloss40-31
85T/RD-16M
85T/St-114
85T/St-369YS
85T/Super-28
86BK/AP-10
86CIGNA-1
86D-326
86D/HL-37
86F-449
86F/LL-38
86F/LimEd-39
86F/Mini-93
86F/St-105
86KayBee-29
86Keller-4
86Leaf-196
86OPC-237
86Phill/TastyK-8
86Seven/Coin-E12M
86Sf-94
86T-475
86T/Mini-54
86T/St-121
86T/Tatt-15M
87Champion-3
87D-165
87D/OD-156
87F-185
87F-642M
87F/BB-39
87F/LL-38
87F/Mini-94
87F/St-104
87Leaf-132
87OPC-255
87Phill/TastyK-8
87Sf-123
87Sf/TPrev-6M
87Stuart-9
87T-255
87T/Mini-29
87T/St-125
88Bz-18
88D-288
88D/AS-55
88D/Best-215
88Drake-20
88F-314
88F/AS-10
88F/BB/AS-35
88F/Mini-101
88F/St-110
88F/TL-33
88KayBee-26
88KennerFig-96
88Leaf-146
88Nestle-16
88OPC-19
88Panini/St-359
88Phill/TastyK-22
88S-32
88Sf-96
88Sf/Gamewin-12
88T-398AS
88T-705
88T/Big-67
88T/Coins-51
88T/Gloss60-43
88T/Mini-66
88T/Revco-7
88T/St-120
88T/St/Backs-5
88T/UK-64
89B-405
89Cadaco-47
89Classic-146
89D-76
89D/Best-238
89F-581
89F/Up-102
89Kahn/Mets-7
89KennerFig-120
89OPC-372
89Panini/St-152
89Phill/TastyK-31
89RedFoley/St-101
89S-255
89S/HotStar-26
89S/Tr-21
89Sf-17
89T-575
89T/Ames-25
89T/Big-321
89T/Coins-23
89T/Gloss60-13
89T/Hills-25
89T/LJN-51
89T/Mini-29
89T/St-117
89T/St/Backs-37
89T/Tr-108T
89T/UK-66
89UD-336
90B-91
90Classic/III-45
90D-53
90D/BestNL-29
90F-215
90F/Can-215
90F/Up-U25
90Kenner/Fig-73
90Leaf-226
90Mother/Dodg-7
90OPC-85
90Pol/Dodg-10
90PublInt/St-249
90S-198
90S/Tr-33T
90T-85
90T/Ames-25
90T/Big-283
90T/Mini-68
90T/Tr-109T
90UD-583
90UD/Ext-795
91B-596
91Classic/III-82
91D-62
91F-218
91Leaf-10
91Leaf/Stud-188
91Mother/Dodg-7
91OPC-645
91OPC/BoxB-O
91Panini/FrSt-56
91Pol/Dodg-10
91S-446
91StCl-495
91T-645
91T/WaxBox-O
91UD-117
91USPlayC/AS-8C
91Ultra-168
91WIZMets-342
92B-253
92Classic/Game200-37
92D-105
92F-469
92L-125
92L/BlkGold-125
92Mother/Dodg-24
92OPC-315
92Panini-193
92Pinn-99
92Pol/Dodg-10
92S-73
92StCl-11
92StCl/Dome-161
92T-315
92T/Gold-315
92T/GoldWin-315
92TripleP-125
92TripleP-73AA
92UD-195
92Ultra-216
93Pac/Beisbol-21M
93Pac/Spanish-404
93Reds/Kahn-23
93S-611
93Select-237
93Select/RookTr-129T
93UD-527
93Ultra-335
94F-426
94Pac/Cr-159

Samuel, Mike
81BurlB-19
82Beloit/Frit-19
84ElPaso-9
85Beloit-1

Samuels, Geoff
91BendB/ClBest-10
91BendB/ProC-3695
92Salinas/ClBest-3
92Salinas/ProC-3752

Samuels, Roger
86ColumAst-23
88F/Up-U131
88Phoenix/CMC-8
88Phoenix/ProC-70
90AAASingl/ProC-274
90ProC/Singl-370
90T/TVMets-57
90Tidew/CMC-19
90Tidew/ProC-543

Samuels, Scott
92ClBest/Up-443
92Erie/ClBest-13
92Erie/ProC-1639

Sanborn, Kyle
88CapeCod/Sum-112

Sanchez, Adam
92Peoria/Team-31M

Sanchez, Adrian
90Hunting/ProC-3281
91Hunting/ClBest-23
91Hunting/ProC-3335
92MidwLAS/Team-37
92Peoria/ClBest-18
92Peoria/Team-23
93Peoria/Team-24

Sanchez, Alejandro
82OkCty-7
83Portl-22
84Cram/PCL-8
85D-43RR
85F-648R
85F/Up-U98
86D-415
86F-236
86T-563
87Tacom-20

Sanchez, Alex
88BBAmer-13
88Knoxvl/Best-1
88OPC-194DP
88SLAS-26
88Tacoma/CMC-17
88Tacoma/ProC-637
89AAA/CMC-25
89B-245
89D-47RR
89F/Up-U71
89Syrac/CMC-10
89Syrac/MerchB-20
89Syrac/ProC-813
89Syrac/Team-20
89T/Tr-109T
90AAASingl/ProC-350
90D-45RR
90F-92
90F/Can-92
90OPC-563
90ProC/Singl-327
90Syrac/CMC-1
90Syrac/MerchB-20
90Syrac/ProC-570
90Syrac/Team-20
90T-563

90T/89Debut-107
90Tor/BJ-23
90ToysRUs-23
90TripleAAS/CMC-25
90UD/Ext-757
91AAA/LineD-515
91Syrac/Kraft-3
91Syrac/LineD-515
91Syrac/MerchB-21
91Syrac/ProC-2479
92BBCity/ProC-3846
Sanchez, Carlos
88Pocatel/ProC-2077
Sanchez, Celerino
73OPC-103
73Syrac/Team-25
73T-103
74OPC-623
74Syrac/Team-24
74T-623
92Yank/WIZ70-137
Sanchez, Daniel
90Greens/Best-19
90Greens/ProC-2671
90Greens/Star-21
91PrWill/ClBest-19
91PrWill/ProC-1436
Sanchez, Francisco
87Gaston/ProC-28
Sanchez, Frank
78Wausau
Sanchez, Geraldo
86Hagers-17
87Hagers-28
Sanchez, Gordon
92FrRow/DP-38
92Oneonta/ClBest-6
93ColClip/Pol-12
Sanchez, Israel
83CharR-22
85FtMyr-15
86Memphis/GoldT-24
86Memphis/SilverT-24
87Omaha-18
88F/Up-U34
88Omaha/CMC-11
88Omaha/ProC-1496
89D-474
89T-452
89UD-326
90UD-384
91AAA/LineD-465
91RochR/LineD-465
91RochR/ProC-1901
92RochR/SB-467
Sanchez, Juan
87Clearw-22
Sanchez, Leo
84PrWill-28
85Nashua-22
Sanchez, Luis M.
82T-653
83D-519
83F-100
83T-623
84D-597
84F-527
84Nes/792-258
84OPC-258
84Smok/Cal-24
84T-258
84T/St-233
85D-352
85F-310
85OPC-42
85Smok/Cal-16
85T-42
86T-124
Sanchez, Luis
73Cedar
74Cedar
Sanchez, Orlando
80OkCty
81Louisvl-24
82D-636
82F-126
82Louisvl-26
82T-604
83Louisvl/Riley-24
85Maine-23
91Crown/Orio-401
Sanchez, Osvaldo
(Ozzir)
87Spokane-1

88Charl/ProC-1200
89Watlo/ProC-1786
89Watlo/Star-25
90Foil/Best-281
90ProC/Singl-701
90Waterlo/Best-16
90Waterlo/ProC-2391
91HighD/ClBest-28
91HighD/ProC-2411
92Durham/ClBest-6
92Durham/ProC-1111
92Durham/Team-17
Sanchez, Pedro 1
75BurlB
Sanchez, Pedro 2
86AubAs-22
87Ashvl-27
88Osceola/Star-23
89ColMud/Best-6
89ColMud/ProC-127
89ColMud/Star-21
90AAASingl/ProC-197
90ProC/Singl-624
90Tucson/CMC-22
90Tucson/ProC-207
Sanchez, Perry
90Gate/ProC-3360
90Gate/SportP-21
91WPalmB/ClBest-17
91WPalmB/ProC-1233
Sanchez, Raul
57T-393
60T-311
61BeeHive-19
Sanchez, Rey
89OkCty/CMC-18
89OkCty/ProC-1511
91AAA/LineD-216
91AAAGame/ProC-20
91Iowa/LineD-216
91Iowa/ProC-1067
92Cub/Mara-6
92D-412RR
92F/Up-75
92Iowa/SB-221
92Pinn-550
92ProC/Tomorrow-200
92StCl-308
92T/91Debut-154
92T/Tr-98T
92T/TrGold-98T
92UD-562
92Ultra-180
93B-496
93Cub/Mara-22
93D-424
93F-24
93L-88
93Pac/Beisbol-18
93Pac/Spanish-61
93Pinn-317
93S-324
93StCl-36
93StCl/1stDay-36
93StCl/Cub-24
93T-292
93T/Gold-292
93ToysRUs-60
93UD-612
93USPlayC/Rook-8H
93Ultra-319
93Ultra-648M
94D-383
94F-395
94Finest-249
94Pac/Cr-108
94S-482
94StCl-104
94StCl/1stDay-104
94StCl/Gold-104
94StCl/Team-338
94T-422
94T/Gold-422
Sanchez, Sammye
88LitFalls/Pucko-12
Sanchez, Stan
87SanBern-6
89SanBern/Best-26
89SanBern/Cal-91CO
Sanchez, Yuri
92Bristol/ClBest-20
92Bristol/ProC-1421
92ClBest/Up-427
92Classic/DP-39

Sanchez, Zoilo
86Lynch-20
87Jacks/Feder-6
88Jacks/GS-2
89Jacks/GS-15
90AAASingl/ProC-289
90ProC/Singl-377
90T/TVMets-58
90Tidew/CMC-26
90Tidew/ProC-558
Sand, John Henry
(Heinie)
21Exh-150
25Exh-47
26Exh-47
28Exh-23
33G-85
92Conlon/Sport-615
V354-27
Sandberg, Chuck
81Bristol-11
Sandberg, Ryne
80Reading
81OkCty/TCMA-17
82RedLob
83D-277
83F-507
83OPC-83
83OPC/St-328
83T-83
83T/St-328
83Thorn-23
84Cub/Uno-12
84Cub/Uno-2M
84Cub/Uno-3M
84Cub/Uno-7M
84D-311
84D/AAS-43
84F-504
84Nes/792-596
84OPC-64
84SevenUp-23
84T-596
84T/St-45
85D-1DK
85D-67
85D/AAS-24
85D/DKsuper-1
85D/WaxBox-PC2
85Drake-28
85F-630IA
85F-65
85F/LimEd-31
85F/St-11
85F/St-45
85FunFoodPin-13
85GenMills-8
85Leaf-1DK
85OPC-296
85Seven-11G
85SevenUp-23
85T-460
85T-713AS
85T/3D-7
85T/Gloss22-3
85T/Gloss40-21
85T/RD-9M
85T/St-175FOIL
85T/St-34
85T/Super-1
85ThomMc/Discs-41
86Cub/Unocal-15
86D-67
86D/AAS-32
86Dorman-14
86Drake-19
86F-378
86F/LL-39
86F/LimEd-40
86F/Mini-80
86F/Slug-32
86F/St-106
86Gator-23
86GenMills/Book-4M
86Jay's-15
86Jiffy-12
86Leaf-62
86Meadow/Blank-13
86Meadow/Milk-10
86Meadow/Stat-12
86OPC-19
86Quaker-13
86Seven/Coin-C9M

86Sf-127M
86Sf-20
86Sf-51M
86T-690
86T/Gloss60-34
86T/Mini-39
86T/St-55
86T/Super-48
86T/Tatt-8M
86TrueVal-14
87BK-18
87Berg/Cubs-23
87Classic-35
87D-77
87D/AAS-13
87D/OD-75
87D/PopUp-13
87Drake-21
87F-572
87F-639M
87F/AwardWin-35
87F/LL-39
87F/Mini-95
87F/St-105
87F/WaxBox-C14
87GenMills/Book-5M
87Ho/St-8
87Jiffy-1
87KayBee-28
87Kraft-8
87Leaf-234
87MnM's-4
87OPC-143
87Ralston-15
87RedFoley/St-16
87Seven-C14
87Seven-ME11
87Sf-116M
87Sf-197M
87Sf-8
87Sf/TPrev-22M
87T-680
87T/Board-30
87T/Coins-41
87T/Gloss22-3
87T/St-156
87T/St-61
88Berg/Cubs-23
88Bz-19
88ChefBoy-11
88Classic/Red-169
88D-242
88D/AS-35
88D/Best-116
88D/Cubs/Bk-242
88D/PopUp-13
88F-431
88F-628M
88F/BB/MVP-29
88F/Excit-32
88F/Mini-70
88F/SS-C5
88F/St-80
88F/WaxBox-C10
88Grenada-49
88KennerFig-97
88Leaf-207
88OPC-10
88Panini/St-234M
88Panini/St-260
88S-26
88S/WaxBox-12
88Sf-12
88T-10
88T/Big-16
88T/Coins-52
88T/Gloss22-14
88T/Gloss60-14
88T/St-147
88T/St-57
88T/St/Backs-6
88T/UK-65
89B-290
89Cadaco-48
89D-105
89D/AS-35
89D/Best-26
89D/PopUp-35
89F-437
89F/Heroes-35
89KMart/DT-24
89KayBee-26
89KennerFig-121
89KingB/Discs-5

89Mara/Cubs-23
89OPC-360
89Panini/St-233AS
89Panini/St-56
89S-35
89S/HotStar-54
89S/Mast-23
89Sf-201
89T-360
89T-387AS
89T/Ames-26
89T/Big-212
89T/DH-14
89T/Gloss22-14
89T/Gloss60-34
89T/HeadsUp-9
89T/LJN-110
89T/St-155
89T/St-55
89T/St/Backs-38
89T/UK-67
89UD-120
89UD-675TC
90B-30
90Classic-27
90Classic/III-86
90CollAB-29
90Cub/Mara-18
90D-105
90D-692AS
90D/BestNL-26
90D/Bon/MVP-BC10
90D/Learning-11DK
90F-40
90F-625MVP
90F-639M
90F/ASIns-9
90F/AwardWin-31
90F/BB-32
90F/BBMVP-33
90F/Can-40
90F/Can-625
90F/Can-639M
90F/LL-33
90HotPlay/St-37
90KMart/SS-2
90Kenner/Fig-74
90Leaf-528CL
90Leaf-98
90MCA/Disc-12
90MLBPA/Pins-47
90MSA/Soda-19
90OPC-210
90OPC-398AS
90OPC/BoxB-P
90Panini/St-212
90Panini/St-231
90Post-9
90PublInt/St-201
90PublInt/St-270
90S-561HL
90S-691DT
90S-90
90S/100St-32
90S/McDon-8
90Sf-54
90Sunflower-20
90T-210
90T-398AS
90T/Big-75
90T/Coins-56
90T/DH-55
90T/Gloss22-3
90T/Gloss60-1
90T/HeadsUp-9
90T/Mini-51
90T/St-12HL
90T/St-152AS
90T/St-46
90T/TVAS-51
90T/TVCub-26
90T/WaxBox-P
90Tetley/Discs-12
90UD-324
90USPlayC/AS-4H
90WonderBrd-20
90Woolwth/HL-21
91B-377SLUG
91B-416
91BBBest/HitM-17
91BBBest/RecBr-15
91Bz-9
91Cadaco-48
91Classic/200-107

91Classic/I-29
91Classic/I-NO
91Classic/II-T67
91CollAB-15
91Colla/Sandberg-Set
91Cub/Mara-23
91Cub/Vine-23
91Cub/Vine-36MVP
91D-14DK
91D-404MVP
91D-433AS
91D-504
91D-BC7
91D/BC-BC7
91D/Elite-S1
91D/Preview-9
91D/SuperDK-14
91F-431
91F-709M
91F-713
91F/ASIns-1
91F/ProVF-3F
91F/UltraG-10
91JDean-6
91Kenner-46
91KingB/Discs-19
91Leaf-207
91Leaf/Prev-2
91Leaf/Stud-158
91LineD/Sandberg-Set
91MSA/Holsum-6
91MajorLg/Pins-68
91MooTown-5
91OPC-398AS
91OPC-740
91OPC-7RB
91OPC/Premier-103
91Panini/FrSt-159
91Panini/FrSt-44
91Panini/St-40
91Panini/Top15-101
91Panini/Top15-27
91Panini/Top15-34
91Panini/Top15-49
91Panini/Top15-9
91Pep/SS-3
91Petro/SU-4
91Post-16
91RedFoley/St-126
91RedFoley/St-82
91S-3
91S-665AS
91S-815MANYR
91S-862FRAN
91S/100SS-60
91Seven/3DCoin-11MW
91Seven/3DCoin-12T
91Seven/3DCoin-8NW
91StCl-230
91StCl/Charter*-26
91T-398AS
91T-740
91T-7RB
91T/CJMini/I-6
91T/SU-30
91UD-132
91UD/Ext-725M
91UD/FinalEd-79F
91UD/FinalEd-93F
91UD/SilSlug-SS8
91USPlayC/AS-12S
91Ultra-66
91Woolwth/HL-20
92B-300
92CJ/DI-28
92Classic/Game200-131
92Classic/I-79
92Classic/II-NNO
92Classic/II-T29
92Colla/ASG-4
92Cub/Mara-23
92D-429AS
92D-576
92D/McDon-6
92DPep/MSA-16
92DennyGS-10
92F-389
92F/ASIns-14
92F/Lumber-L4
92F/Performer-3
92French-12M
92Highland-110
92JDean/18-18
92Kenner/Fig-38
92KingB-19
92L-317
92L-331M
92L/BlkGold-317
92L/BlkGold-331M
92L/GoldPrev-2
92L/Prev-2
92MSA/Ben-19
92MrTurkey-22
92OPC-110
92OPC/Premier-34
92P-2
92Panini-183
92Panini-282AS
92Pinn-10
92Pinn-617TECH
92Pinn/RookI-13M
92Pinn/Slug-9
92Pinn/TeamP-5M
92Post/Can-4
92S-200
92S-442DT
92S-774AS
92S/100SS-85
92S/Prev-5
92S/Proctor-12
92Seven/Coin-15
92StCl-50
92StCl-600MC
92StCl/Dome-162
92Studio-18
92Studio/Her-1
92Studio/Prev-3
92T-110
92T-387AS
92T/Gold-110
92T/Gold-387AS
92T/GoldWin-110
92T/GoldWin-387AS
92T/Kids-1
92T/McDonB-5
92TripleP-229
92UD-145
92UD/ASFF-39
92UD/TmMVPHolo-46
92USPlayC/Cub-1S
92USPlayC/Cub-9H
92Ultra-181
92Ultra/AS-12
92Ultra/AwardWin-25
93B-200
93Bleach/Pr-10
93Bleach/Pr-11
93Bleach/Pr-12
93Bleach/Pr-13
93Bleach/Sandberg-1
93Bleach/Sandberg-2
93Bleach/Sandberg-3
93Cadaco-51
93Classic/GameI-80
93Colla/ASG-10
93Colla/DM-93
93Colla/DMProto-7
93Cub/Mara-21
93D-344
93D/DK-2
93D/Elite-20
93D/EliteDom-8
93D/EliteUp-2
93D/LongBall-LL15
93D/MVP-22
93D/Master-5
93D/Prev-2
93D/Spirit-SG14
93DennyGS-8
93Duracel/PPII-13
93F-25
93F-356
93F/Atlantic-21
93F/Fruit-56
93F/TLNL-6
93Flair-20
93Ho-2
93JDean/28-25
93Kenner/Fig-32
93KingB-22
93Kraft-27
93L-224
93L/GoldAS-4M
93L/Heading-8
93L/UpGoldAS-4M
93MSA/Metz-18
93OPC-274
93OPC/Premier/StarP-4
93P-13
93Pac/Spanish-62
93Panini-204
93Pinn-15
93Pinn/Cooper-8
93Pinn/HRC-12
93Pinn/Slug-27
93Post/Can-14
93S-4
93S-530AS
93S/Franchise-16
93Select-97
93Select/ChasS-2
93Select/StatL-11
93StCl-366
93StCl-600MC
93StCl/1stDay-366
93StCl/1stDay-600MC
93StCl/Cub-1
93StCl/II/Ins-3
93StCl/MurphyMP-9AS
93StCl/MurphyS-44
93Studio-176
93T-3
93T-402
93T/BlkGold-17
93T/Finest-105AS
93T/FinestASJ-105AS
93T/FinestRef-105AS
93T/Gold-3
93T/Gold-402
93TripleP-10
93TripleP/Act-4
93TripleP/Nick-3
93UD-175
93UD-38CH
93UD-483M
93UD-735M
93UD/Clutch-R18
93UD/Diam-8
93UD/FunPack-19HS
93UD/FunPack-80GS
93UD/FunPack-84
93UD/FunPackAS-AS4M
93UD/HRH-HR11
93UD/OnDeck-D22
93UD/SP-17AS
93UD/SPPlat-PP17
93UD/Then-TN6
93Ultra-320
93Ultra/AS-3
94B-250
94B-388
94Church-16
94D-110M
94D-18
94D/Ann-9
94D/Special-18
94F-396
94F/AS-48
94F/TL-16
94Flair-141
94Flair/Hot-9
94KingB-22
94L-425
94L/Pr-8
94L/Slide-4
94OPC-16
94OPC/JAS-7
94Oscar-29
94Pac/Cr-109
94Pac/Silv-26
94Panini-156
94Pinn-6
94Pinn/Artist-6
94Pinn/Museum-6
94RedFoley-36
94S-20
94S/GoldR-20
94Select-32
94Sf/2000-45
94Sf/Mov-2
94StCl-397
94StCl/1stDay-397
94StCl/Gold-397
94StCl/Team-331
94Studio-63
94Studio/Her-5
94T-300
94T-602ST
94T/Finest-210
94T/FinestRef-210
94T/Gold-300
94T/Gold-602ST
94TripleP-77
94TripleP/Medal-6
94TripleP/Nick-2
94UD-92
94UD/DColl-C6
94UD/ElecD-92
94UD/SP-71
94Ultra-166
94Ultra/AS-13
94Ultra/Career-4

Sander, Mike
88Hagers/Star-18
89EastLDD/ProC-DD40
89Hagers/Best-25
89Hagers/ProC-275
89Hagers/Star-15
90Hagers/Best-21
90Hagers/ProC-1413
90Hagers/Star-22
90HagersDG/Best-25

Sander, Rick
77LodiD

Sanderlin, Rick
77Phoenix
78Cr/PCL-12
79Phoenix

Sanders, Adam
90Utica/Pucko-6

Sanders, Al
88Elmira-10
89Elmira/Pucko-19
89WinHaven/Star-20
90Star/ISingl-5
90WinHaven/Star-24
91AA/LineD-471
91NewBrit/LineD-471
91NewBrit/ProC-352
92NewBrit/ProC-433
92NewBrit/SB-495

Sanders, Alexander
N172

Sanders, Anthony
93MedHat/ProC-3751
93MedHat/SportP-16

Sanders, Barry
91Arena*-4
91StCl/Charter*-37
91StCl/Member*-35

Sanders, Deion
89Albany/Best-1
89Albany/ProC-338
89Albany/Star-23
89Classic/Up/2-200
89D/Rook-6
89F/Up-U53
89S/NWest-22
89Star/IISingl-150
89T/Tr-110T
90AlbanyDG/Best-1
90Classic-21
90D-427
90F-454
90F/Can-454
90HotRook/St-38
90Leaf-359
90OPC-61
90S-586
90S/100Ris-40
90S/NWest-22
90S/YS/II-27
90Sf-221
90T-61
90T/89Debut-108
90T/TVYank-33
90UD-13
91B-588
91Brave/Dubuq/Perf-24
91Brave/Dubuq/Stand-32
91Leaf-436
91Richm/Bob-37
91S/100RisSt-6
91S/RookTr-34T
91StCl-442
91UD-352
91UD/Ext-743
92B-160
92Brave/LykePerf-24
92Brave/LykeStand-28
92Classic/Game200-127
92Classic/I-80
92Classic/II-T13
92D-564
92F-368
92L-448
92L/BlkGold-448
92L/GoldPrev-27
92OPC-645
92OPC/Premier-91
92Pinn-170
92Pinn/Team2000-31
92S-571
92StCl-15
92StCl/MPhoto-12
92Studio-9
92T-645
92T/Gold-645
92T/GoldWin-645
92TripleP-186
92UD-247
92UD-SP3
92USPlayC/Brave-2H
92USPlayC/Brave-3S
92Ultra-464
92Ultra/AS-17
92Yank/WIZ80-170
93B-438
93BJ/D/McDon-17M
93Brave/LykePerf-25
93Brave/LykeStand-31
93Classic/GameI-81
93Colla/DM-94
93D-158
93D/Master-16
93Duracel/PPII-7
93F-13
93Flair-10
93L-222
93OPC-372
93OPC/Premier/StarP-10
93Pac/Spanish-11
93Panini-188
93Pinn-4
93S-123
93Select-84
93Select/StatL-22
93StCl-408
93StCl/1stDay-408
93StCl/Brave-22
93T-795
93T/Finest-141
93T/FinestRef-141
93T/Gold-795
93ToysRUs-82
93TripleP-162
93TripleP/Act-9
93TripleP/Nick-8
93UD-166
93UD/FunPack-219FOLD
93UD/FunPack-34HERO
93UD/FunPack-67
93UD/SP-62
93Ultra-12
94B-301
94D-430
94F-373
94L-101
94L/MVPNL-13
94OPC-118
94Pac/Cr-21
94Panini-150
94Pinn-174
94Pinn/Artist-174
94Pinn/Museum-174
94S-496
94S/GoldS-6
94Sf/2000-108
94StCl-472
94StCl/1stDay-472
94StCl/Gold-472
94StCl/Team-54
94Studio-172
94T-375
94T/Finest-22
94T/Finest/PreProd-22
94T/FinestRef-22
94T/Gold-375
94TripleP-49
94UD-85
94UD/ElecD-85
94UD/SP-162
94Ultra-156

Sanders, Earl
87Dunedin-24
88Dunedin/Star-15
89Dunedin/Star-14
90Knoxvl/Best-23
90Knoxvl/ProC-1245
90Knoxvl/Star-17

91AA/LineD-218
91Greenvl/ClBest-5
91Greenvl/LineD-218
91Greenvl/ProC-2999
Sanders, Ken
66T-356R
69Sunoco/Pin-16
71MLB/St-451
71OPC-116
71T-116
72OPC-391
72T-391
73OPC-246
73T-246
74OPC-638
74T-638
75OPC-366
75T-366
75T/M-366
76OPC-291
76SSPC-550
76T-291
77Spoka
77T-171
91WIZMets-343
Sanders, Lance
89Utica/Pucko-20
Sanders, Matt
91Bluefld/ClBest-16
91Bluefld/ProC-4129
92Kane/ClBest-7
92Kane/ProC-92
92Kane/Team-27
Sanders, Paul
91Eugene/ClBest-8
91Eugene/ProC-3729
Sanders, Ray
44Playball-23
47TipTop
Sanders, Reginald Jerome
(Reggie)
74OPC-600R
74T-600R
75OPC-617R
75T-617R
75T/M-617R
78SSPC/270-149
Sanders, Reginald Laverne
(Reggie)
88Billings/ProC-1822
89Greens/ProC-415
89SALAS/GS-23
90A&AASingle/ProC-128
90Cedar/Best-11
90Cedar/ProC-2334
90MidwLgAS/GS-48
90ProC/Singl-655
91AA/LineD-167
91B-537
91Chatt/LineD-167
91Chatt/ProC-1973
91ClBest/Gold-4
91ClBest/Singl-41
91Classic/200-70
91Leaf/GRook-BC10
91PreRookPrev/LineD-167
91UD-71TP
91UD/FinalEd-11F
91UD/FinalEd-1FCL
92B-118
92CJ/DII-15
92Classic/Game200-141
92Classic/I-81
92Classic/II-NNO
92Classic/II-T72
92D-415RR
92F-421
92JDean/Rook-5
92L-360
92L/BlkGold-360
92L/GoldPrev-33
92OPC-283
92OPC/Premier-25
92Pinn-440
92Pinn/Rook-22
92Pinn/RookI-1
92Pinn/Team2000-70
92ProC/Tomorrow-214
92Reds/Kahn-16
92S-829
92S/Impact-76
92S/Rook-35
92StCl-865
92Studio-29
92T-283
92T/91Debut-155
92T/Gold-283
92T/GoldWin-283
92TripleP-109
92UD-27SR
92UD/Scout-SR20
92Ultra-486
92Ultra/AllRook-8
93B-666
93Classic/GameI-82
93Colla/DM-95
93D-402
93F-44
93F/RookSenI-7
93Flair-34
93L-428
93L/GoldAS-17M
93OPC-358
93Pac/Spanish-405
93Panini-298
93Pinn-158
93Pinn/Team2001-24
93Reds/Kahn-24
93S-171
93Select-274
93Select/ChasRook-3
93StCl-471
93StCl/1stDay-471
93T-83
93T/Finest-20
93T/FinestRef-20
93T/Gold-83
93ToysRUs-27
93UD-354
93UD-469IN
93UD-473M
93UD/SP-216
93USPlayC/Rook-10C
93Ultra-36
94B-242
94D-436
94F-427
94Flair-149
94L-106
94OPC-207
94Pac/Cr-160
94Panini-169
94Pinn-360
94Pinn/Power-10
94RedFoley-15M
94S-394
94Select-71
94StCl-136
94StCl/1stDay-136
94StCl/Gold-136
94Studio-173
94T-647
94T/Finest-43
94T/Finest/PreProd-43
94T/FinestRef-43
94T/Gold-647
94TripleP-219
94UD-222
94UD/CollC-252
94UD/CollC/Gold-252
94UD/CollC/Silv-252
94UD/ElecD-222
94UD/SP-163
94Ultra-177
Sanders, Rod
92Princet/ClBest-21
92Princet/ProC-3097
Sanders, Satch
81Miami-9
Sanders, Scott
90Spokane/SportP-14
91ClBest/Singl-338
91Waterlo/ClBest-8
91Waterlo/ProC-1255
92Sky/AASingl-286
92Wichita/SB-644
93B-110
93Ultra-476
94D-489
94F/MLP-31
94L-37
94Pinn-381
94T-789M
94T/Gold-789M
94UD-362
94Ultra-282
Sanders, Stan
82Oneonta-7
Sanders, Tracy
90A&AASingle/ProC-188
90BurlInd/ProC-3023
91CLAS/ProC-CAR19
91ClBest/Singl-202
91Kinston/ClBest-27
91Kinston/ProC-339
92B-42
92Canton/ProC-703
92Canton/SB-116
92ClBest-40
92ProC/Tomorrow-53
92Sky/AASingl-54
92UD/ML-127
93B-9
93FExcel/ML-167
93T-616M
93T/Gold-616M
Sanderski, John
86WinHaven-20
87Greens-24
Sanderson, Scott
79T-720R
80OPC-301
80T-578
81D-450
81F-166
81OPC-235
81OPC/Post-12
81T-235
82D-288
82Expo/Hygrade-19
82F-206
82F/St-40
82Hygrade
82OPC-7
82OPC/Post-22
82T-7
82T/St-63
82Zeller-17
83D-446
83Expo/PostC-17
83F-295
83F/St-21M
83OPC-54
83Stuart-17
83T-717
84D-341
84F-285
84F/X-U104
84Nes/792-164
84OPC-164
84SevenUp-24
84T-164
84T/Tr-106T
85D-266
85F-66
85Leaf-194
85OPC-373
85SevenUp-21
85T-616
85T/St-40
86Cub/Unocal-16
86D-442
86F-379
86Gator-21
86T-406
87Berg/Cubs-21
87D-447
87F-573
87Sf/TPrev-22M
87T-534
87T/St-60
88AlaskaAS70/Team-21
88Berg/Cubs-21
88D-646
88D/Cubs/Bk-646
88F-432
88S-544
88T-311
89D-629
89F/Up-78
89Mara/Cubs-21
89T-212
89UD-342
90B-447
90D-647
90F-41
90F/Can-41
90F/Up-118
90Leaf-194
90Mother/A's-11
90OPC-67
90PublInt/St-202
90S-488
90S/Tr-61T
90T-67
90T/Tr-110T
90UD-39
90UD/Ext-739
91B-177
91D-533
91F-23
91F/UltraUp-U43
91Leaf-169
91Leaf/Stud-99
91OPC-728
91OPC/Premier-104
91S-118
91S/RookTr-78T
91T-728
91T/Tr-104T
91UD-582
91UD/Ext-750
91USPlayC/AS-3D
92D-227
92D/DK-DK10
92F-243
92L-152
92L/BlkGold-152
92OPC-480
92Panini-142
92Pinn-337
92Pinn-587M
92S-211
92S/100SS-59
92StCl-496
92StCl/Dome-163
92Studio-219
92T-480
92T/Gold-480
92T/GoldWin-480
92TripleP-39
92TripleP-77LH
92UD-415
92UD/TmMVPHolo-47
92Ultra-414
92Yank/WIZAS-74
93D-726
93F-655
93F/Final-188
93Flair-178
93L-419
93Mother/Angel-9
93OPC/Premier-100
93Pac/Spanish-211
93Panini-145
93Pinn-574
93Pol/Angel-9
93S-618
93Select-261
93StCl-679
93StCl/1stDay-679
93StCl/Angel-7
93Studio-15
93T-525
93T/Gold-525
93UD-734
93Ultra-524
94D-266
94F-700
94L-406
94S-401
Sanderson, Shaun
89SLCity-17C
90Erie/Star-23
Sandling, Bob
80Elmira-14
Sandlock, Mike
53T-247
54T-104
90Target-703
91T/Arc53-247
94T/Arc54-104
Sandoval, Dennis
77Wausau
Sandoval, Guillermo
89Beloit/II/Star-24
90Stockton/Best-22
90Stockton/Cal-183
90Stockton/ProC-2183
91Stockton/ClBest-10
Sandoval, Jesus
86AppFx-20
Sandoval, Jose
93B-78
Sandoval, Mike
87Watertn-31TR
90Harris/Star-25TR
92BuffB/BlueS-20TR
Sandry, Bill
83AppFx/Frit-28
Sands, Charlie
72T-538
74OPC-381
74T-381
75OPC-548
75T-548
75T/M-548
75Tucson-24
75Tucson/Team-17
76Tucson-39
92Yank/WIZ60-108
Sands, Tony
89KS*-3
Sandt, Tommy
75Tucson-1
75Tucson/Caruso-2
75Tucson/Team-18
77T-616
78Syrac
79Portl-6
80Port-8
81Portl-21
82Buffa-18
83LynnP-23
84Cram/PCL-137
85Cram/PCL-233
86Hawaii-6MG
89VFJuice-31CO
90Homer/Pirate-26CO
93Pirate/Nation-27CO
Sandy, Tim
90Kgsport/Best-17
90Kgsport/Star-22
91Pittsfld/ClBest-8
91Pittsfld/ProC-3436
92StLucie/ClBest-3
92StLucie/ProC-1762
93StLucie/ProC-2935
Saneaux, Francisco
92Bluefld/ClBest-7
92Bluefld/ProC-2360
Sanford, Chance
92Welland/ClBest-20
92Welland/ProC-1333
Sanford, Ed
82ArkTr-8
Sanford, John F.
47TipTop
49B-236
50B-156
51B-145
52Mother
53Mother
Sanford, John S.
(Jack)
57T-387
58Hires-39
58T-264
59T-275
60L-54
60T-165
61P-154
61T-258
61T-383M
61T/St-84
62J-141
62P-141
62P/Can-141
62T-538
63J-110
63P-110
63T-325
63T-7LL
63T/SO
64T-414
65OPC-228
65T-228
66OPC-23
66T-23
67CokeCap/DodgAngel-27
67T-549
79TCMA-125
Sanford, Meredith Jr.
(Mo)
89Greens/ProC-423

89SALAS/GS-31
90A&AASingle/ProC-120
90Cedar/Best-23
90Cedar/ProC-2321
90MidwLgAS/GS-49
91AA/LineD-168
91Chatt/LineD-168
91Chatt/ProC-1960
91ClBest/Singl-47
91F/Up-U86
92B-281
92Classic/Game200-197
92Classic/I-82
92D-417RR
92Nashvl/SB-290
92OPC-674
92OPC/Premier-17
92Pinn-254
92Pinn/Team2000-77
92ProC/Tomorrow-215
92S-769
92S/Rook-40
92Sky/AAASingl-136
92StCl-336
92T-674
92T/91Debut-156
92T/Gold-674
92T/GoldWin-674
92UD-45
92UD/ML-253
93D-760
93Pinn-230
93Select/RookTr-33T
93T-634
93T/Gold-634
94F-453
94S-253
94S/GoldR-253
94T-343
94T/Gold-343

Sanguillen, Manny
68KDKA-35
68T-251
69Pirate/JITB-11
69T-509
70MLB/St-106
70OPC-188
70T-188
71K-13
71MD
71MLB/St-213
71OPC-480
71OPC-62LL
71T-480
71T-62LL
71T/tatt-5
72K-19
72MB-305
72OPC-225WS
72OPC-228WS
72OPC-60
72T-225WS
72T-228WS
72T-60
73K-42
73OPC-250
73T-250
73T/Lids-46
74K-15
74OPC-28
74T-28
74T/DE-22
74T/St-87
75Ho-21
75Ho/Twink-21
75OPC-515
75T-515
75T/M-515
76Crane-53
76Ho-72
76K-42
76MSA/Disc
76OPC-191LL
76OPC-220
76SSPC-571
76T-191LL
76T-220
77BurgChef-111
77OPC-231
77Pep-4
77T-61
78T-658
78Wiffle/Discs-66
79T-447
80T-148
81D-14
81F-376
81T-226
89Swell-29
90Pac/Legend-75
90Swell/Great-126
91K/Leyenda-10
91Swell/Great-80
93MCI-9
93TWill-80
93TWill/Mem-13
93UD/ATH-112

Sanjurjo, Jose
91Bristol/ClBest-11
91Bristol/ProC-3620

Sankey, Ben
R314/Can
V355-83

Sanner, Dale
75Tucson-4
75Tucson/Caruso-7
75Tucson/Team-19
76Tucson-14

Sano, Motokuni
88Miami/Star-23

Santa Maria, Silverio
92WinHaven/ClBest-13

SantaCruz, Nick
88Batavia/ProC-1678
89Spartan/ProC-1043
89Spartan/Star-21
90Spartan/Best-18
90Spartan/ProC-2501
90Spartan/Star-18

SantaMaria, Silverio
90Elmira/Pucko-21
91WinHaven/ClBest-9
91WinHaven/ProC-489

Santaella, Alexis
90Tampa/DIMD-20

Santana, Andres
87Pocatel/Bon-23
88Clinton/ProC-705
88MidwLAS/GS-2
89SanJose/Best-1
89SanJose/Cal-226
89SanJose/ProC-450
89SanJose/Star-23
89Star/Wax-87
90B-230
90Shrev/ProC-1449
90Shrev/Star-22
90TexLgAS/GS-23
91AAA/LineD-393
91AAAGame/ProC-34
91Phoenix/LineD-393
91Phoenix/ProC-76
91S-762RP
91T/90Debut-139
91UD-87
91Ultra-328
92Phoenix/ProC-2831
92S/100RisSt-32
92StCl-491

Santana, Ernesto
87Macon-1
88Watertn/Pucko-10
89StCath/ProC-2087
90Utica/Pucko-22

Santana, Jose
89AubAs/ProC-2165
90Ashvl/ProC-2763
90Boise/ProC-3318
92AubAs/ClBest-11
92AubAs/ProC-1363

Santana, Miguel
88FSLAS/Star-20
90Jaxvl/Best-12
90Jaxvl/ProC-1387
93LimeR/Winter-59

Santana, Rafael
82Louisvl-27
84Tidew-16
85D-610
85F-90
85T-67
86D-319
86F-93
86OPC-102
86T-587
86T/St-102
87D-569
87D/OD-126
87F-21
87Leaf-167
87T-378
88D-633
88D/Best-273
88D/Y/Bk-NEW
88F-149
88F/Up-U50
88Panini/St-344
88S-316
88S/Tr-54T
88T-233
88T/Big-246
88T/Tr-101T
89B-174
89D-309
89F-268
89Panini/St-407
89S-296
89S/NWest-11
89T-792
89T/Big-192
89T/DHTest-21
89T/St-313
89UD-216
90OPC-651
90PublInt/St-546
90T-651
91WIZMets-344
92BBCity/ClBest-25CO
92BBCity/ProC-3861
92Yank/WIZ80-171

Santana, Ralph
80Knoxvl/TCMA-11

Santana, Raul
91Sumter/ClBest-15
91Sumter/ProC-2338
92Rockford/ClBest-3
92Rockford/ProC-2120
93WPalmB/ClBest-20
93WPalmB/ProC-1345

Santana, Rodolfo
80Elmira-42

Santana, Ruben
90Penin/Star-20
91SanBern/ClBest-20
91SanBern/ProC-1997
92ClBest-215
92Penin/ClBest-14
92Penin/ProC-2943
93FExcel/ML-231
93LimeR/Winter-148
93LimeR/Winter-23
94ClBest/Gold-102
94FExcel-127
94T-527M
94T/Gold-527M

Santana, Simon
77Charl

Santangelo, F.P.
88CapeCod/Sum-156
89James/ProC-2132
90WPalmB/Star-19
91AA/LineD-268
91Harris/LineD-268
91Harris/ProC-638
92Indianap/ProC-1869
92Indianap/SB-192
93Ottawa/ProC-2447

Santarelli, Cal
85Water-9
86Water-21

Santiago, Angelo
90Gate/ProC-3354
90Gate/SportP-16

Santiago, Benito
83Miami-20
85Beaum-21
86F-644R
86LasVegas-14
87Bohem-9
87Classic/Up-132
87D-31RR
87D/HL-45
87D/HL-55
87D/OD-148
87D/Rook-44
87F-429
87Leaf-31
87Sf-118M
87Sf/Rook-19
87Sf/Rook-9
87Sf/TPrev-16M
87T/Tr-109T
88Bz-20
88Classic/Blue-219
88Classic/Red-160
88Coke/Padres-9
88D-114
88D-3DK
88D/Best-301
88D/DKsuper-3DK
88F-596
88F/AwardWin-34
88F/BB/MVP-30
88F/Excit-33
88F/Hottest-33
88F/LL-34
88F/Mini-115
88F/RecSet-34
88F/SS-32
88F/St-125
88Grenada-59
88KMart-24
88KennerFig-98
88Leaf-3DK
88Leaf-58
88MSA/Disc-15
88Nestle-12
88OPC-86
88Panini/St-402
88Panini/St-433
88RedFoley/St-78
88S-25
88S-654HL
88S/YS/I-2
88Sf-22
88Sf-222M
88Sf/Gamewin-10
88Smok/Padres-25
88T-404AS
88T-693
88T-699M
88T-7RB
88T/Big-12
88T/Coins-35
88T/Gloss60-30
88T/JumboR-18
88T/St-112
88T/St-2
88T/UK-66
88ToysRUs-26
88Woolwth-14
89B-453
89Bimbo/Discs-3
89Cadaco-49
89Classic-73
89Coke/Padre-16
89D-205
89F-316
89KennerFig-122
89MSA/Disc-9
89OPC-256
89Padre/Mag-11
89Panini/St-199
89RedFoley/St-102
89S-4
89S/HotStar-47
89Sf-22
89T-256
89T/Big-134
89T/Coins-24
89T/Gloss60-15
89T/LJN-100
89T/St-101
89T/St/Backs-57
89T/UK-68
89Tetley/Discs-9
89UD-165
90B-218
90Classic/Up-44
90Coke/Padre-16
90D-465
90D-708AS
90D/BestNL-121
90D/Learning-4
90F-167
90F/AwardWin-32
90F/Can-167
90HOF/St-92
90Leaf-207
90MLBPA/Pins-58
90OPC-35
90Padre/MagUno-2
90Padre/MagUno-21
90Panini/St-213
90Panini/St-358
90PublInt/St-271
90PublInt/St-58
90RedFoley/St-82
90S-454
90S/100St-63
90S/McDon-15
90Sf-115
90T-35
90T/Big-125
90T/DH-56
90T/Gloss22-9
90T/St-110
90T/St-153AS
90UD-12TC
90UD-325
90USPlayC/AS-10H
91B-383SLUG
91B-656
91Cadaco-49
91Classic/200-175
91Classic/II-T43
91D-449
91DennyGS-18
91F-542
91F/ASIns-9
91Kenner-47
91KingB/Discs-20
91Leaf-432
91Leaf/Stud-249
91OPC-760
91OPC/Premier-105
91Panini/FrSt-157
91Panini/FrSt-90
91Panini/St-93
91Panini/Top15-99
91Post/Can-13
91RedFoley/St-83
91S-416RIF
91S-663AS
91S-810
91S-870FRAN
91S-893DT
91S/100SS-61
91Seven/3DCoin-13SC
91StCl-105
91T-760
91T/CJMini/I-33
91UD-467
91UD/FinalEd-91F
91UD/SilSlug-SS17
91USPlayC/AS-11S
91Ultra-311
92B-395
92Classic/Game200-62
92Colla/ASG-14
92D-40
92D-430AS
92F-620
92French-10M
92Hardee-19
92L-321
92L/BlkGold-321
92Mother/Padre-6
92OPC-185
92OPC/Premier-154
92Padre/Carl-18
92Panini-231
92Panini-280AS
92Pinn-2
92Pinn-601
92Pinn-615TECH
92Pinn/TeamP-3M
92Pol/Padre-16
92Post/Can-2
92S-245
92S/100SS-36
92S/Impact-58
92S/Proctor-10
92Smok/Padre-28
92StCl-130
92StCl/Dome-164
92Studio-107
92T-185
92T/Gold-185
92T/GoldWin-185
92T/Kids-54
92T/McDonB-2
92TripleP-70
92UD-253
92UD/ASFF-40
92Ultra-283
93B-178
93Cadaco-52
93Colla/DM-96
93D-522

93DennyGS-14
93Duracel/PPII-10
93F-523
93F/Final-70
93Flair-53
93HumDum/Can-31
93JDean/28-21
93KingB-6
93L-410
93Marlin/Publix-22
93OPC-353
93OPC/Premier-43
93Pac/Beisbol-23M
93Pac/Spanish-263
93Pac/Spanish-471
93Pac/SpanishGold-10
93Pac/SpanishP-6
93Pinn-502
93Pinn/Expan-2
93S-591
93Select-269
93Select/RookTr-26T
93StCl-274
93StCl-319
93StCl/1stDay-274
93StCl/1stDay-319
93StCl/Marlin-12
93StCl/MurphyS-5
93StCl/MurphyS-7
93Studio-127
93T-220
93T/Finest-138
93T/FinestRef-138
93T/Gold-220
93T/Tr-44T
93TripleP-210
93TripleP/Gal-GS9
93UD-776
93UD/Diam-14
93UD/FunPack-117GS
93UD/FunPack-121
93UD/SP-142
93USPlayC/Marlin-1H
93USPlayC/Marlin-2S
93Ultra-386
94B-122
94D-348
94D/Special-348
94F-476
94Finest-366
94L-96
94OPC-150
94Pac/AllLat-1
94Pac/Cr-249
94Panini-185
94Pinn-305
94S-40
94S/GoldR-40
94Sf/2000-13
94StCl-143
94StCl/1stDay-143
94StCl/Gold-143
94StCl/Team-79
94Studio-111
94T-370
94T/Gold-370
94TripleP-139
94UD-397
94Ultra-497

Santiago, Cedric
90Elmira/Pucko-22

Santiago, Delvy
89Princet/Star-19
90Augusta/ProC-2462
91CollInd/ClBest-16
91CollInd/ProC-1483

Santiago, Gus
91Sumter/ClBest-20
91Sumter/ProC-2345

Santiago, Jorge
91BurlInd/ProC-3310

Santiago, Jose G.
56T-59

Santiago, Jose R.
65T-557
66T-203
67CokeCap/RedSox-4
67T-473
67T/Test/RSox-15
68CokeCap/RedSox-10
68OPC-123
68T-123
69MB-246
69MLB/St-16
69OPC-21
69T-21
69T/St-137
70T-708

Santiago, Mike
85Durham-11
86Jacks/TCMA-9
87Jacks/Feder-25
88Jacks/GS-9

Santiago, Norm
86FtLaud-19
87Jaxvl-3
88WPalmB/Star-22

Santiago, Rafael
90CharRain/Best-20
90CharRain/ProC-2031

Santiago, Sandi
90Tampa/DIMD-21
91Oneonta/ProC-4153
92Oneonta/ClBest-13
93Greens/ClBest-20
93Greens/ProC-885

Santo, Ron
61Bz-3
61P-196
61T-35
61T/St-9
62Bz
62J-184
62P-184
62P/Can-184
62Salada-136
62Shirriff-136
62T-170
62T/St-109
63Exh
63F-32
63J-170
63P-170
63T-252
64T-375
64T/Coins-146AS
64T/Coins-68
64T/S-58
64T/SU
64T/St-33
64Wheat/St-40
65Bz-28
65OPC-110
65OPC-6LL
65T-110
65T-6LL
65T/E-28
65T/trans-67
66Bz-39
66T-290
66T/RO-102
66T/RO-85
67Bz-39
67CokeCap/AS-6
67CokeCap/Cub-11
67CokeCap/NLAS-23
67OPC-70
67OPC/PI-26
67T-70
67T/PI-26
67T/Test/SU-22
68Bz-15
68Bz-6
68Kahn
68OPC-5LL
68T-235
68T-366AS
68T-5LL
68T/ActionSt-16B
68T/ActionSt-4B
68T/ActionSt-5AM
68T/G-19
68T/Post-21
69Citgo-13
69Kahn
69Kelly/Pin-16
69MB-247
69MLB/St-125
69MLBPA/Pin-56
69NTF
69OPC-4LL
69OPC/DE-19
69Sunoco/Pin-8
69T-420AS
69T-4LL
69T-570
69T/DE-19
69T/S-38
69T/St-19
69T/decal
69Trans-42
70Dunkin-5
70K-42
70MB-25
70MLB/St-22
70OPC-454AS
70OPC-63LL
70T-454AS
70T-63LL
70T-670
70T/PI-5
70T/S-21
70T/Super-21
70Trans-2
71MD
71MLB/St-46
71OPC-220
71T-220
71T/Coins-95
71T/S
71T/Super-35
71T/tatt-13
72MB-306
72T-555
72T-556A
73K-54
73OPC-115
73T-115
74K-7
74OPC-270
74OPC-334AS
74T-270
74T-334M
74T/St-19
74T/Tr-270T
75OPC-35
75T-35
75T/M-35
78TCMA-22
83MLBPA/Pin-32
84Cub/Uno-2M
84Cub/Uno-7M
88Pac/Leg-97
89Swell-36
90BBWit-14
90Pac/Legend-48
90Swell/Great-64
91LineD-5
91MDA-5
91Swell/Great-81
92AP/ASG-39
92Cub/OldStyle-21
93TWill-23
93UD/ATH-113
Exh47
WG10-46
WG9-45

SantoDomingo, Rafael
78Indianap-17
80Indianap-22

Santop, Louis
74Laugh/Black-16
90Negro/Star-33

Santora, Steve
85Everett/Cram-15
85Everett/II/Cram-16

Santorini, Al
69T-592R
70OPC-212
70T-212
71MLB/St-237
71OPC-467
71T-467
72T-723
73OPC-24
73T-24

Santos, Don
86Watlo-24
87Watlo-20

Santos, Ed
77LodiD

Santos, Eddie
83Kinston/Team-22

Santos, Faustoe
85Madis-2
85Madis/Pol-22

Santos, Gerald
(Jerry)
91Johnson/ClBest-21
91Johnson/ProC-3977
92Bristol/ClBest-10
92Bristol/ProC-1411
92MidwLAS/Team-38
92ProC/Tomorrow-328
92Spring/ClBest-24
92Spring/ProC-865
93FExcel/ML-105
94B-452

Santovenia, Nelson
83Memphis/TCMA-8
86Jaxvl/TCMA-8
87Jaxvl-5
87SLAS-5
88F/Up-U103
88Indianap/CMC-18
88Indianap/ProC-500
88S/Tr-96T
88T/Tr-102T
89B-361
89D-366
89D/Best-146
89F-393
89OPC-228
89Panini/St-112
89S-346
89S/HotRook-71
89T-228
89T/Big-98
89T/JumboR-18
89T/St-78
89ToysRUs-25
89UD-380
90D-224
90F-360
90F/Can-360
90Leaf-502
90OPC-614
90Panini/St-289
90PublInt/St-187
90S-451
90Sf-162
90T-614
90UD-432
91F-248
91OPC-744
91S-777
91StCl-416
91T-744
92OPC-732
92T-732
92T/Gold-732
92T/GoldWin-732
92Vanco/ProC-2726
92Vanco/SB-646

Santoya, Cristobal
91Idaho/SportP-18

Sapienza, Rich
87Tampa-29
88Cedar/ProC-1148

Sarafini, Ken
94FExcel-98

Sarazen, Gene
33SK*-22

Sarbaugh, Mike
90AS/Cal-46
91Kinston/ClBest-20
91Kinston/ProC-332
92Canton/ProC-699
92Canton/SB-117

Sarcia, Joe
91Geneva/ClBest-18
91Geneva/ProC-4228

Sardinha, Ed
86Elmira-19

Sarmiento, Danny
92GulfCD/ProC-3565

Sarmiento, Manny
76Indianap-16
77Indianap-25
77T-475R
78Pep-22
78SSPC/270-122
78T-377
79Indianap-21
79OPC-69
79T-149
80Spokane-12
80T-21
81Pawtu-10
81T-649
82Portl-8
83D-502
83F-321
83F/St-4M
83F/St-9M
83T-566
84D-200
84F-263
84Nes/792-209
84T-209
85Cram/PCL-248

Sarmiento, Wally
80Toledo-12
81Toledo-8

Sarni, Bill
54T-194
55B-30
55Hunter
55RM-NL9
56T-247
57T-86
79TCMA-106
94T/Arc54-194

Sarrett, Daniel
80Water-17

Sartain, Dave
91Elizab/ProC-4299
92ClBest-152
92Kenosha/ProC-602
92ProC/Tomorrow-100

Sasaki, Shigehi
90Salinas/Cal-118
90Salinas/ProC-2719

Sass, James
90Stockton/Best-10
90Stockton/Cal-195
90Stockton/ProC-2195
91Beloit/ClBest-9
91Beloit/ProC-2118

Sasser, Don
75Cedar
76Cedar

Sasser, Mackey
85Fresno/Pol-8
86Shrev-22
87Phoenix-20
88D-28RR
88D/Mets/Bk-NEW
88D/Rook-51
88F/Up-U106
88Kahn/Mets-2
88Leaf-28RR
88S-642RP
88S/Tr-30T
88T/Tr-103T
89Classic-26
89D-454
89F-48
89Kahn/Mets-2
89S-303
89S/HotRook-82
89S/YS/I-38
89T-457
89T/JumboR-19
89ToysRUs-26
89UD-561
90Classic-78
90D-471
90F-216
90F/Can-216
90Kahn/Mets-2
90Leaf-435
90OPC-656
90PublInt/St-144
90S-510
90T-656
90T/TVMets-22
90UD-185
91Classic/200-37
91D-136
91F-160
91Kahn/Mets-2
91Leaf-361
91OPC-382
91Panini/FrSt-78
91S-307
91S/100SS-75
91StCl-172
91T-382
91UD-103
91Ultra-226
91WIZMets-345
92D-256
92F-515
92L-108
92L/BlkGold-108
92Mets/Kahn-2
92OPC-533
92Pinn-447
92S-472

92StCl-249
92T-533
92T/Gold-533
92T/GoldWin-533
92Ultra-237
93D-512
93F-480
93F/Final-274
93Mother/Mar-22
93OPC-328
93StCl/Mar-11
93T-788
93T/Gold-788
94F-298
94Pac/Cr-581
94S-439
94StCl-510
94StCl/1stDay-510
94StCl/Gold-510
94Ultra-124

Sassone, Mike
87StPete-4
88ArkTr/GS-18

Satnat, Dave
86Salem-24

Satoh, Hiroyuki
90Gate/ProC-3340
90Gate/SportP-19

Satre, Jason
89Greens/ProC-414
90CharWh/Best-9
90CharWh/ProC-2241
90Foil/Best-42
90ProC/Singl-707
91Cedar/ClBest-12
91Cedar/ProC-2719
92Chatt/ProC-3820

Satriano, Tom
63T-548
64T-521
65OPC-124
65T-124
66T-361
67T-343
68T-238
69MB-248
69OPC-78
69T-78
69T/St-150
70MLB/St-164
70T-581
71MLB/St-330
71OPC-557
71T-557
72MB-307

Satterfield, Cory
88Hamil/ProC-1731
89Spring/Best-18
90StPete/Star-21

Sattler, Bill
82Wichita-16
83Wichita/Dog-20
84Indianap-19

Saturnino, Sherton
92Idaho/ProC-3528

Satzinger, Jeff
86Macon-22
87Kenosha-17
88OrlanTw/Best-13
89OrlanTw/Best-24
89OrlanTw/ProC-1330
90AAASingl/ProC-679
90OkCty/CMC-8
90OkCty/ProC-433
90ProC/Singl-158

Saucier, Kevin
79OkCty
80BK/P-22
80T-682R
81F-24
81T-53
81T/Tr-827
82D-485
82F-275
82F/St-158
82OPC-238
82T-238
83T-373

Sauer, Ed
47Signal
49Eureka-196

Sauer, Henry
(Hank)
48B-45
48L-20
49B-5
50B-25
51B-22
51T/BB-49
52Dix
52NTea
52StarCal-92CM
52StarCal/L-80E
52T-35
53B/Col-48
53Dix
53Exh/Can-7
53NB
53RM-NL16
53T-111
54RH
54T-4
54Wilson
55T-45
55T/DH-103
56T-41
56T/Hocus-A3
56T/Pin-6
57T-197
58Hires-49
58PacBell-7
58SFCallB-20
58T-378
59T-404
61T-481MVP
74Laugh/ASG-52
75OPC-190MVP
75T-190MVP
75T/M-190MVP
77Galasso-27
79TCMA-70
84Cub/Uno-3M
88Pac/Leg-23
91T/Arc53-111
92Bz/Quadra-2M
92Cub/OldStyle-22
94T/Arc54-4
Exh47
R302/2-113

Saugstad, Mark
92Everett/ClBest-1
92Everett/ProC-1700

Saul, Jim
62Kahn
80ElPaso-7MG
81Holyo-2
82Portl-23
82Portl-24
83Nashvl-18CO
84Nashvl-19CO
85Albany-25
86Albany/TCMA-16
89BurlB/ProC-1615
90BurlB/Best-28MG
90BurlB/ProC-2365MG
90BurlB/Star-27MG

Saulter, Kevin
91Pulaski/ClBest-29
91Pulaski/ProC-4004
92Macon/ClBest-14
92Macon/ProC-266

Saunders, Chris
92Pittsfld/ProC-3305
93ClBest/MLG-168
93StLucie/ProC-2930

Saunders, Dennis
71OPC-423R
71T-423R

Saunders, Doug
89Clmbia/Best-20
89Clmbia/GS-23
90StLucie/Star-24
91StLucie/ClBest-5
91StLucie/ProC-721
92Bingham/ProC-525
92Bingham/SB-67
93F/Final-105
93T/Tr-43T

Saunders, Mark
79Elmira-28

Saunier, Randy
82Clinton/Frit-12

Sauveur, Rich
84PrWill-23
85Nashua-23
86Nashua-25
87Harris-24
88Jaxvl/Best-3
88Jaxvl/ProC-986
89Indianap/ProC-1228
90Miami/I/Star-23
91AAA/LineD-567
91Tidew/LineD-567
91Tidew/ProC-2508
92Omaha/ProC-2962
92Omaha/SB-345

Savage, Ashleigh
89Anchora-22

Savage, Jack
86Bakers-24
87SanAn-22
87TexLgAS-34
88F-650R
88Tidew/CANDL-27
88Tidew/CMC-1
88Tidew/ProC-1583
89D-618
89Tidew/CMC-5
89Tidew/ProC-1971
90T/Tr-111T
90Target-1060
91AAA/LineD-417
91OPC-357
91Portl/LineD-417
91Portl/ProC-1564
91T-357

Savage, Jim
90Batavia/ProC-3077
91BendB/ClBest-13
91BendB/ProC-3703
91Spartan/ClBest-18
91Spartan/ProC-903

Savage, John Robert
49B-204

Savage, John
88Reno/Cal-275

Savage, Reggie
92StCl/MemberIII*-12

Savage, Ted
62T-104
63IDL-19
63T-508
64T-62
66Pep/Tul
67T-552
68OPC-119
68T-119
69Sunoco/Pin-17
69T-471
70McDon-1
70T-602
71MLB/St-434
71OPC-76
71T-76
71T/Coins-44
71T/S-3
71T/Super-3
71T/tatt-7
72MB-308
81TCMA-343
90Target-704

Savard, Serge
72Dimanche*-104IA
72Dimanche*-105

Savarino, William
(Bill)
86Cram/NWL-51
87Modesto-2
88Modesto/Cal-75
89AS/Cal-44
89Huntsvl/Best-4
89Modesto/Chong-21

Saverine, Bob
63T-158R
64T-221
65T-427
66T-312
67CokeCap/Senator-13
67OPC-27
67T-27
68OPC-149
68T-149
78TCMA-14
91Crown/Orio-402

Saverino, Mike
82Danvl/Frit-23
83Peoria/Frit-27

Savinon, Odalis
89Johnson/Star-19
91Spring/ClBest-24
91Spring/ProC-757
92StPete/ClBest-21

Sawatski, Carl
53T-202
54T-198
55T-122
55T/DH-93
58T-234
59T-56
60L-120
60T-545
61T-198
62J-162
62P-162
62P/Can-162
62Salada-119
62Shirriff-119
62T-106
63T-267
64T-24
89TexLAS/GS-40PRES
91T/Arc53-202
94T/Arc54-198
Exh47

Sawkiw, Warren
88CapeCod/Sum-3
90Niagara/Pucko-10
91Lakeland/ClBest-27
91Lakeland/ProC-276
92Lakeland/ClBest-24

Sawyer, Eddie
49Eureka-145MG
50B-225MG
51B-184MG
60T-226MG

Sawyer, Rick
75Syrac/Team-14
75Syrac/Team-19
76SSPC-426
77Padre/SchCd-26
77T-268
92Yank/WIZ70-138

Sax, Dave
79Clinton/TCMA-18
82Albuq-13
83Pol/Dodg-23
84Cram/PCL-152
84D-519
85Pawtu-15
86T-307
87D-647
87Pawtu/TCMA-25
88BuffB/CMC-22
88BuffB/ProC-1483
89Colum/CMC-26
89Colum/ProC-756
90AAASingl/ProC-330
90ColClip/CMC-19
90ColClip/ProC-680
90Colum/Pol-7
90ProC/Singl-219
90T/TVYank-59
90Target-705
91AAA/LineD-117
91ColClip/LineD-117
91ColClip/ProC-600
91Pac/SenLg-34
92ColClip/Pol-15
92ColClip/ProC-357
92ColClip/SB-115

Sax, Steve
79Clinton/TCMA-10
82D-624
82F-21
82Pol/Dodg-52
82T-681R
82T/Tr-103T
83D-336
83F-220
83F/St-10M
83F/St-25AM
83F/St-25BM
83OPC-245
83OPC/St-329
83PermaGr/AS-15
83Pol/Dodg-3
83Seven-2
83T-245
83T/St-329
84D-104
84F-112
84F-633M
84F/St-90
84MiltBrad-22
84Nes/792-610
84OPC-144
84Pol/Dodg-3
84Seven-22W
84Smok/Dodg-3
84T-610
84T/Gloss22-14
84T/RD-19M
84T/St-78
85Coke/Dodg-29
85D-418
85F-384
85F/LimEd-32
85FunFoodPin-45
85Leaf-90
85OPC-369
85T-470
85T/RD-18M
85T/St-77
86Coke/Dodg-27
86D-540
86D/HL-50
86F-143
86GenMills/Book-5M
86OPC-175
86Pol/Dodg-3
86Sf-60M
86Sf-95
86Sf/Rook-48M
86T-175
86T/St-72
86T/Tatt-21M
87Classic-20
87D-26DK
87D-278
87D/AAS-28
87D/DKsuper-26
87D/OD-85
87Drake-25
87F-453
87F/AS-4
87F/GameWin-39
87F/Hottest-34
87F/Mini-96
87F/RecSet-34
87F/St-106
87GenMills/Book-6M
87Kraft-38
87Leaf-203
87Leaf-26DK
87MnM's-21
87Mother/Dodg-3
87OPC-254
87Pol/Dodg-2
87Seven-W10
87Sf-12
87Smok/Dodg-32
87Smok/NL-1
87T-596AS
87T-769
87T/Coins-42
87T/Mini-15
87T/St-70
88D-176
88D/Best-204
88F-523
88F/Mini-85
88F/St-93
88KennerFig-99
88Leaf-185
88Mother/Dodg-3
88OPC-305
88Panini/St-311
88Pol/Dodg-3
88S-35
88Smok/Dodg-25
88T-305
88T/Big-46
88T/St-74
89B-178
89Cadaco-50
89Classic/Up/2-179
89D-84
89D/Best-20
89D/Tr-23
89F-70
89F/Up-52
89F/WS-9
89OPC-40
89Panini/St-106
89RedFoley/St-103
89S-69
89S/HotStar-33
89S/NWest-2
89S/Tr-20

89Sf-58
89Smok/Dodg-99
89T-40
89T/Big-111
89T/DHTest-19
89T/LJN-71
89T/Mini-19
89T/St-57
89T/St/Backs-39
89T/Tr-111T
89T/UK-69
89UD-53
89UD/Ext-748
90B-442
90Classic-149
90D-2DK
90D-78
90D/BestAL-24
90D/Bon/MVP-BC22
90D/SuperDK-2DK
90F-455
90F/BB-33
90F/Can-455
90F/LL-34
90Holsum/Discs-16
90HotPlay/St-38
90Kenner/Fig-75
90Leaf-96
90Leaf/Prev-1
90MCA/Disc-19
90MLBPA/Pins-62
90OPC-560
90Panini/St-129
90Publnt/St-547
90RedFoley/St-83
90S-125
90S/100St-2
90S/McDon-22
90S/NWest-3
90Sf-12
90T-560
90T/Big-141
90T/Coins-26
90T/DH-57
90T/Gloss60-8
90T/Mini-25
90T/St-310
90T/TVAS-18
90T/TVYank-26
90Target-706
90Tetley/Discs-19
90UD-172
90UD-18TC
90USPlayC/AS-4S
90Windwlk/Discs-7
91B-170
91Cadaco-50
91Classic/200-106
91Classic/II-T17
91D-163
91D-48AS
91F-679
91Kenner-48
91Leaf-220
91Leaf/Stud-100
91OPC-290
91Panini/FrSt-168
91Panini/FrSt-325
91Panini/St-271
91Panini/Top15-46
91RedFoley/St-127
91RedFoley/St-84
91S-32
91S/100SS-72
91StCl-204
91T-290
91T/CJMini/II-30
91UD-462
91Ultra-242
92B-469
92Classic/Game200-195
92F-244
92L-217
92L/BlkGold-217
92OPC-430
92OPC/Premier-43
92Panini-136
92Pinn-328
92S-475
92S/RookTr-4T
92StCl-635
92Studio-157
92T-430
92T/Gold-430
92T/GoldWin-430
92T/Kids-85
92T/Tr-99T
92T/TrGold-99T
92TripleP/Gal-GS4
92UD-358
92UD-743
92Ultra-108
92Ultra-341
92WSox-7
92Yank/WIZ80-172
92Yank/WIZAS-75
93Cadaco-53
93D-123
93F-588
93L-107
93OPC-307
93Pac/Spanish-395
93Panini-137
93Pinn-335
93S-418
93Select-160
93StCl-482
93StCl/1stDay-482
93T-367
93T/Gold-367
93TripleP-47
93UD-369
93Ultra-179
93WSox-25
94D-286
94F-94
94L-210
94Pac/Cr-137
94S-254
94S/GoldR-254
94StCl/Team-128
94T-662
94T/Gold-662

Sayler, Barry
83StPete-24

Sayles, Bill
90Target-707

Sayles, Steve
83Miami-24

Scafa, Bob
93Bz-17
93T/Tr-120T

Scaglione, Tony
88Watlo/ProC-690
89Kinston/Star-22

Scala, Jerry
V362-28

Scales, George
78Laugh/Black-26

Scalzitti, Will
92Bend/ClBest-20
93T-476M
93T/Gold-476M

Scanlan, Bob
86Clearw-22
87Phill/TastyK-39B
87Reading-20
88Maine/CMC-9
88Maine/ProC-294
89Reading/Best-8
89Reading/ProC-652
89Reading/Star-21
90AAASingl/ProC-301
90ProC/Singl-233
90ScranWB/CMC-7
90ScranWB/ProC-599
91AAA/LineD-223
91Cub/Mara-30
91Iowa/LineD-223
91Iowa/ProC-1061
91Leaf-520
91S/RookTr-102T
91T/Tr-105T
91UD/FinalEd-48F
92Cub/Mara-30
92D-454
92F/Up-76
92L-437
92L/BlkGold-437
92OPC-274
92OPC/Premier-14
92S-285
92S/100RisSt-59
92StCl-112
92T-274
92T/91Debut-157
92T/Gold-274
92T/GoldWin-274
92USPlayC/Cub-11S
92USPlayC/Cub-5H
92Ultra-473
93Cub/Mara-23
93D-292
93F-26
93L-13
93OPC-325
93Pinn-417
93S-361
93StCl-444
93StCl/1stDay-444
93StCl/Cub-22
93T-47
93T/Gold-47
93UD-617
93Ultra-22
94D-263
94F-397
94Finest-310
94Pol/Brew-23
94T-451
94T/Gold-451

Scanlan, William
(Doc)
10Domino-105A
10Domino-105B
11Helmar-151
12Sweet/Pin-76
M116
S74-55
T202
T205
T207

Scanlin, Michael
87Gaston/ProC-19
88Tulsa-1

Scanlon, James P.
(Pat)
76SSPC-332
78T-611

Scanlon, Ken
80Ander-23
81Durham-4
82Durham-7
83Durham-12

Scanlon, Steve
88Visalia/Cal-161
88Visalia/ProC-94

Scannell, Larry
87Elmira/Black-5
87Elmira/Red-5
88Elmira-24
89WinHaven/Star-21

Scantlebury, Pat
60Maple-18
61BeeHive-20
86Negro/Frit-35

Scarbery, Randy
77SanJose-18
80T-291

Scarborough, Carey
75BurlB

Scarborough, Ray
49B-140
49Royal-14
50B-108
50Drake-29
51B-39
51T/RB-42
52B-140
52Royal
52T-43
52TipTop
53T-213
79TCMA-208
91T/Arc53-213

Scarce, Mac
73OPC-6
73T-6
74OPC-149
74T-149
75OPC-527
75T-527
75T/M-527
76Indianap-22
77Indianap-15
91WIZMets-346

Scarpace, Ken
81Cedar-17
82Water-19

Scarpetta, Dan
83Beloit/Frit-25
87Denver-15
88ElPaso/Best-3
88TexLgAS/GS-6
89SanAn/Best-18

Scarsella, Les
46Remar
47Remar-2
47Signal
47Smith-3
48Signal
48Smith-6
49B/PCL-25
49Remar
R314/Can
W711/1

Scarsone, Stephen
86Cram/NWL-135
87CharWh-5
88Clearw/Star-22
89EastLDD/ProC-DD25
89Reading/Best-4
89Reading/ProC-665
89Reading/Star-22
90Clearw/Star-20
91AA/LineD-518
91AAAGame/ProC-41
91Reading/LineD-518
91ScranWB/ProC-2548
92AAA/ASG/SB-492
92D/Rook-108
92ScranWB/ProC-2455
92ScranWB/SB-492
92Sky/AAASingl-222
93D-381
93StCl/Giant-21
94F-701
94Pac/Cr-555
94S-596
94StCl-3
94StCl/1stDay-3
94StCl/Gold-3
94StCl/Team-9
94T-729
94T/Gold-729

Schaal, Paul
65T-517R
66T-376
67CokeCap/DodgAngel-21
67OPC-58
67T-58
68T-474
69MB-249
69MLB/St-62
69T-352
69T/St-188
70MLB/St-228
70OPC-338
70T-338
71MLB/St-429
71OPC-487
71T-487
72MB-309
72OPC-177
72OPC-178IA
72T-177
72T-178IA
73OPC-416
73T-416
74OPC-514
74T-514

Schacht, Al
39PlayBall-113
40PlayBall-116
87Conlon/2-9
92Conlon/Sport-559
93Conlon-920
R312/M
R314
V355-29

Schaefer, Bob
82Tidew-22
84Tidew-10
85IntLgAS-1
85Tidew-27
86GlenF-20
87Memphis-10
87Memphis/Best-1
91Pol/Royal-26CO

Schaefer, Chris
88CapeCod/Sum-31
89Eugene/Best-1
90AppFox/Box-23
90AppFox/ProC-2093

Schaefer, Doug
79Phoenix
80Phoenix/NBank-7
81Phoenix-7

Schaefer, Herman
(Germany)
09Buster/Pin-13
10Domino-106
11Helmar-76
12Sweet/Pin-63
14Piedmont/St-51
77Galasso-167
81Tiger/Detroit-102
D303
D350/2-154
E101
E102
E105
E106
E90/1
E92
M101/5-154
M116
S74-40
T204
T205
T206
T207
T213/blue
T215/blue
T215/brown
T216

Schaefer, Jeff
84RochR-10
85CharlO-12
85Utica-14
86MidldA-21
87SanAn-1
88Vanco/CMC-21
88Vanco/ProC-753
89Coke/WS-25
89Vanco/CMC-24
90AAASingl/ProC-125
90Calgary/ProC-660
90T/89Debut-109
91CounHrth-2
91F/Up-U56
91OPC-681
91T-681
92D-525
92L-513
92L/BlkGold-513
92Mother/Mar-24
92OPC-391
92S-629
92StCl-108

Schaefer, Jim
79Tulsa-13
80Ashvl-6

Schaefer, Steve
79Elmira-15

Schafer, Bill
90Sumter/Best-18
90Sumter/ProC-2430

Schafer, Dennis
81Clinton-13

Schafer, Randy
79Memphis/TCMA-11

Schaffer, Jim
89Hagers/ProC-282

Schaffer, Jimmie
61Union
62T-579
63T-81
64T-359
65T-313
68T-463
78TCMA-152
78TCMA-169
78TCMA-184
91WIZMets-347
93Rang/Keeb-318CO

Schaffernoth, Joe
61T-58
63T-463

Schaive, John Jr.
82Buffa-6
83LynnP-18

Schaive, John Sr.
61T-259
62T-529
63T-356

Schalk, Ray
14CJ-61
15CJ-61
21Exh-151

25Exh-78
26Exh-78
27Exh-40
50Callahan
50W576-64
60F-56
61F-136
75Sheraton-24
76Motor-6
76Shakey-79
77Galasso-177
80Pac/Leg-85
80Perez/HOF-78
80SSPC/HOF
87Conlon/2-55
88Pac/8Men-100
88Pac/8Men-43
88Pac/8Men-45M
88Pac/8Men-50
88Pac/8Men-51
88Pac/8Men-52
89Kodak/WSox-3M
91Conlon/Sport-48
93Conlon-879
94Conlon-1033
94Conlon/Col-38
BF2-17
D327
D328-150
D329-154
D350/2-155
E120
E121/120
E121/80
E122
E126-8
E135-150
E210-23
E254
M101/4-154
M101/5-155
V117-3
V355-124
V89-16
W501-43
W502-23
W514-60
W515-51
W516-4
W572
W573
W575

Schall, Gene
91Batavia/ClBest-2
91Batavia/ProC-3493
91FrRow/DP-6
92ClBest-266
92Spartan/ProC-1278
92StCl/Dome-165
93B-512
93StCl/Phill-18
94B-280
94FExcel-248
94T-786M
94T/Gold-786M

Schallock, Art
91Crown/Orio-403

Schammel, Bill
83MidldC-1

Schang, Walter H.
(Wally)
14CJ-58
15CJ-58
16FleischBrd-81
21Exh-152
25Exh-101
28Exh-59
29Exh/4-29
31Exh/4-24
91Conlon/Sport-249
92Conlon/Sport-448
93Conlon-872
94Conlon-1231
BF2-39
D327
D328-151
D329-155
D350/2-156
E120
E121/80
E122
E135-151
E220
M101/4-155
M101/5-156
T222
V100
V61-20
V89-11
W501-27
W514-99
W515-17
W572
W573
W575

Schanz, Charley
44Playball-44
52Mother-41
53Mother-40

Schanz, Scott
91Penin/ClBest-10
91Penin/ProC-376
92SanBern/ClBest-12
92SanBern/ProC-

Schardt, Wilbur
(Bill)
90Target-708
T207

Scharein, George
47Signal

Scharff, Tony
91SoOreg/ClBest-19
91SoOreg/ProC-3842
92Madis/ClBest-24

Schatter, Jim
89Hagers/Best-10

Schattinger, Jeff
81Omaha-12
82Edmon-25

Schatz, Dan
87Visalia-25

Schatzeder, Dan
77Expo/PostC-7
78T-709R
79OPC-56
79T-124
80OPC-140
80T-267
81D-248
81F-482
81OPC-112
81T-417
82D-385
82F-281
82OPC-106
82T-691
82T/Tr-104T
83Expo/PostC-18
83F-296
83OPC-189
83Stuart-22
83T-189
84D-132
84Expo/PostC-28
84F-286
84Nes/792-57
84OPC-57
84Stuart-7
84T-57
85D-543
85F-409
85Leaf-59
85OPC-293
85T-501
86Expo/Prov/Pan-12
86F-259
86OPC-324
86Provigo-12
86T-324
87D-482
87Expo/PostC-4
87F-186
87OPC-168
87Phill/TastyK-35
87T-789
88F-21
88Gator-31
88T-218
89F/Up-90
89Lennox/Ast-9
89Tucson/CMC-10
89Tucson/JP-21
89Tucson/ProC-198
90B-69
90D-594
90F-236
90F/Can-236
90Lennox-21
90Mother/Ast-18
90S-418
91D-497
91WIZMets-348

Schauer, A.J.
(Rube)
16FleischBrd-82

Scheckla, Roddy
88AubAs/ProC-1960
89Ashvl/ProC-946

Scheckter, Jody
72Dimanche*-142

Scheer, Ron
83Wisco/Frit-2
84Visalia-21
86Penin-23
87Penin-17

Scheetz, Brian
90Butte/SportP-19

Scheetz, Rick
82Wisco/Frit-11

Scheffing, Bob
48L-160
49B-83
49Eureka-71
50B-168
54T-76
60Lake
60SpicSpan-20CO
60T-464C
61T-223MG
62T-416MG
62T-72M
63T-134MG
94T/Arc54-76

Scheffler, Jim
90Pittsfld/Pucko-21
91Pittsfld/ClBest-17
91Pittsfld/ProC-3421

Schefsky, Steve
84Beaum-13
85Beaum-11

Scheib, Carl
49B-25
50B-213
51B-83
52B-46
52T-116
53B/Col-150
53T-57
54B-67
54T-118
91T/Arc53-57
94T/Arc54-118

Scheibe, Britton
92Spokane/ClBest-3
92Spokane/ProC-1309

Scheibeck, Frank
N172

Scheid, Rich
87FtLaud-18
88Pittsfld/ProC-1372
89Iowa/CMC-9
89Iowa/ProC-1713
90BirmB/Best-22
90BirmB/ProC-1110
91AAA/LineD-645
91Vanco/LineD-645
91Vanco/ProC-1594
92Vanco/ProC-2721
92Vanco/SB-647
93Edmon/ProC-1135
93T-646
93T/Gold-646

Scheinblum, Richie
65T-577R
68OPC-16R
68T-16R
69T-479
70OPC-161
70T-161
71OPC-326
71T-326
72OPC-468
72T-468
73OPC-78
73T-78
74OPC-323
74T-323
74T/St-148

Schell, Clyde
(Danny)
55T-79
55T/DH-81

Scheller, Rod
77LodiD
78LodiD

Schellhasse, Albert
N172

Schemer, Mike
47Sunbeam

Schenbeck, Tom
92Helena/ProC-1715

Schenck, Bruce
91Pocatel/ProC-3781
91Pocatel/SportP-6

Schenck, Larry
89GA-27
90GA-26
90GA-33

Schenkle, William
N172

Schenz, Henry
52Mother-30

Scherer, Doug
85Cram/PCL-141
85Modesto/Chong-23
88Knoxvl/Best-11

Scherger, George
73OPC-296CO
73T-296CO
74OPC-326CO
74T-326C
81Water-22MG
82Indianap-2
86TexGold-CO

Scherger, Joe
82Amari-4

Scherman, Fred
71MLB/St-406
71OPC-316
71T-316
72OPC-6
72T-6
73OPC-660
73T-660
74OPC-186
74T-186
74T/Tr-186T
75OPC-252
75SSPC/18-10
75T-252
75T/M-252
76Expo/Redp-28
76OPC-188
76SSPC-343
76T-188

Scherrer, Bill
80Water-7
81Water-7
84D-203
84F-482
84Nes/792-373
84T-373
84T/St-62
85Cain's-17
85F-22
85T-586
85Wendy-19
86D-516
86F-237
86T-217
87T-98
88RochR/CMC-9
88RochR/ProC-209
88RochR/Team-20
89OkCty/CMC-3
89Tidew/ProC-1955
91Crown/Orio-404

Schettler, Louis
M116

Scheuer, Chris
89Augusta/ProC-520

Scheznayder, Wade
81Redwd-12

Schiefelbein, Mike
92AZ/Pol-15

Schiel, Rob
90Kenosha/Best-13
90Kenosha/ProC-2304
90Kenosha/Star-22

Schildnecht
N172

Schiller, Jon
89Everett/Star-25

Schilling, Chuck
61T-499
62Bz
62J-56
62P-56
62P/Can-56
62T-345
62T-467AS
62T/St-18
63T-52
64T-182M
64T-481
64T/Coins-103
65OPC-272
65T-272
66OPC-6
66T-6
78TCMA-183
PM10/Sm-173
PM10/Sm-174

Schilling, Curt
86Elmira-20
87Greens-2
88NewBrit/ProC-908
89D-635
89RochR/CMC-7
89RochR/ProC-1655
90AAASingl/ProC-458
90B-246
90D-667
90F/Up-U68
90OPC-97
90ProC/Singl-306
90RochR/CMC-5
90RochR/ProC-701
90Rochester/L&U-14
90S-581
90S/100Ris-94
90Sf-133
90T-97
91B-560
91Crown/Orio-405
91D-556
91F-491
91Leaf-292
91Leaf/Stud-179
91Mother/Ast-15
91OPC-569
91S-788
91S/RookTr-80T
91T-569
91UD-528
92D-757
92F/Up-112
92L-516
92L/BlkGold-516
92OPC-316
92Phill/Med-28
92S-671
92S/RookTr-25T
92StCl-279
92T-316
92T/Gold-316
92T/GoldWin-316
92T/Tr-100T
92T/TrGold-100T
92Ultra-208
92Ultra-548
93B-680
93D-118
93F-108
93Flair-107
93L-4
93OPC-354
93Pac/Spanish-581
93Panini-268
93Phill/Med-31
93Pinn-402
93S-52
93Select-229
93Select/StatL-65
93StCl-422
93StCl/1stDay-422
93StCl/Phill-14
93Studio-131
93T-421
93T/Finest-10
93T/FinestRef-10
93T/Gold-421
93T/Hill-25
93TripleP-129
93TripleP-230
93UD-67
93UD/SP-178
93USPlayC/Ace-12S
93Ultra-445

94B-308
94D-577
94F-600
94F/Smoke-11
94L-320
94OPC-66
94Pac/Cr-486
94Panini-230
94Phill/Med-29
94Pinn-105
94Pinn/Artist-105
94Pinn/Museum-105
94S-88
94S/GoldR-88
94Select-161
94Sf/2000-51
94StCl-289
94StCl/1stDay-289
94StCl/Gold-289
94StCl/Team-229
94T-142
94T/Finest-150
94T/FinestRef-150
94T/Gold-142
94TripleP-179
94UD-460
94UD/CollC-253
94UD/CollC/Gold-253
94UD/CollC/Silv-253
94Ultra-554
Schilling, Jarrett
85Clovis-38
Schimdt, Eric
88Colum/CMC-8
Schimpf, Rex
82DayBe-7
83DayBe-11
Schiraldi, Calvin
84Jacks-4
85D-38RR
85F/Up-U99
85Tidew-5
86D-652
86Pawtu-20
86Sf/Rook-44
86T-210
87D-641
87F-44
87Leaf-137
87Sf/TPrev-9M
87T-94
87T/HL-20
87Woolwth-20
88Berg/Cubs-32
88D-375
88D/Best-194
88D/Cubs/Bk-NEW
88F-365
88OPC-62
88S-218
88S/Tr-39T
88T-599
88T/Tr-104T
89D-285
89D/Best-82
89F-438
89Mara/Cubs-32
89OPC-337
89S-321
89T-337
89T/St-56
89UD-82
90Coke/Padre-17
90D-672
90F-168
90F/Can-168
90OPC-693
90Padre/MagUno-13
90PublInt/St-203
90T-693
90UD-643
91AAA/LineD-610
91D-308
91F-543
91OPC-424
91S-611
91T-424
91Tucson/LineD-610
91Tucson/ProC-2212
91WIZMets-349
92TX-36
93Rang/Keeb-319
Schirm, George
C46-29
E254
T206
Schlafly, Harry
E254
T206
Schlei, George
(Admiral)
E101
E104
E105
E92
E97
M116
S74-94
T204
T205
T206
T216
T3-115
Schleighoffer, Mike
86Albuq-21
Schlesinger, Bill
65T-573R
68T-258R
Schley, Van
88SLCity-16M
89SLCity-18PPDir
Schlichting, John
85VeroB-3
86VeroB-21
Schlitzer, Victor
E90/1
Schlopy, Butch
86Watertn-22
88Augusta/ProC-374
89Salem/Star-19
90Salem/Star-19
Schmakel, Jim
84Tiger/Wave-31
Schmandt, Ray
90Target-1062
E120
E220
V100
W573
Schmees, George
52B-245
53Mother-13
V362-20
Schmelz, Al
91WIZMets-350
Schmelz, Heinrich
N172
Schmid, Michael
82BurlR/Frit-18
82BurlR/TCMA-8
Schmidt, Augie
83Knoxvl-12
84Syrac-8
85Cram/PCL-194
Schmidt, Bill 1
40Hughes-17
Schmidt, Bill 2
91Oneonta/ProC-4170CO
92Oneonta/ClBest-28CO
Schmidt, Charles John
(Butcher Boy)
C46-12
Schmidt, Charles
(Boss)
10Domino-107
11Helmar-36
12Sweet/Pin-30A
12Sweet/Pin-30B
14CJ-127
15CJ-127
D350/2-157
E101
E102
E104
E105
E92
M101/5-157
M116
T205
T206
T213/blue
T213/brown
T216
T3-116
Schmidt, Curtis
92James/ClBest-18
92James/ProC-1502
93WPalmB/ClBest-21
93WPalmB/ProC-1339
Schmidt, David F.
(Dave)
82T-381R
Schmidt, David J.
(Dave)
80Ashvl-25
80Tulsa-22
82T-418R
83D-321
83F-578
83Rang-24
83T-116
84D-586
84F-427
84Nes/792-584
84Rang-24
84T-584
85D-586
85F-567
85OPC-313
85Rang-24
85T-313
86Coke/WS-24
86D-378
86F-571
86F/Up-U103
86OPC-79
86T-79
86T/Tr-99T
87D-182
87F-505
87F/Up-U107
87French-24
87OPC-372
87T-703
87T/Tr-110T
88D-371
88D/Best-333
88F-571
88F/Mini-2
88French-24
88OPC-214
88Panini/St-6
88S-103
88T-214
88T/St-226
89B-5
89D-13DK
89D-215
89D/DKsuper-13DK
89F-618
89French-24
89OPC-231
89Panini/St-255
89S-292
89T-677
89T/Big-130
89UD-447
90B-110
90D-524
90F-188
90F/Can-188
90F/Up-U32
90Leaf-457
90OPC-497
90PublInt/St-585
90S-30
90T-497
90T/Tr-112T
90UD-641
91Crown/Orio-406
91F-249
91OPC-136
91S-156
91T-136
91UD-684
92Calgary/SB-70
93Rang/Keeb-320
Schmidt, David M.
92WinHaven/ClBest-4CO
92WinHaven/ProC-1787CO
Schmidt, Eric 1
77Clinton
78LodiD
79Clinton/TCMA-12
Schmidt, Eric 2
86Albany/TCMA-21
87Albany-4
88Colum/Pol-9
88Colum/ProC-313
Schmidt, Garry
89KS*-67
Schmidt, Gregg
86FtMyr-24
Schmidt, Henry M.
90Target-1063
Schmidt, Jason
92ClBest-260
92Macon/ClBest-25
92Macon/ProC-267
93Durham/Team-17
Schmidt, Jeff
92Boise/ClBest-27
92Boise/ProC-3625
92ClBest/Up-413
92Classic/DP-21
92FrRow/DP-57
93Pinn-469DP
93S-501DP
93StCl/MurphyS-113
Schmidt, Keith
89Bluefld/Star-20
90Wausau/Best-27
90Wausau/ProC-2141
90Wausau/Star-21
91ClBest/Singl-59
91Kane/ClBest-25
91Kane/ProC-2673
92Kane/ClBest-15
92Kane/ProC-107
92Kane/Team-28
Schmidt, Mike
73OPC-615R
73T-615R
74JP
74OPC-283
74T-283
75Ho-133
75K-56
75OPC-307LL
75OPC-70
75T-307LL
75T-70
75T/M-307LL
75T/M-70
76Crane-54
76Ho-84
76MSA/Disc
76OPC-193LL
76OPC-480
76SSPC-470
76T-193LL
76T-480
77BurgChef-168
77Ho-43
77Ho/Twink-43
77OPC-245
77OPC-2LL
77Pep-70
77T-140
77T-2LL
77T/CS-41
77T/ClothSt-41
78Ho-113
78K-3
78OPC-225
78SSPC/270-46
78T-360
78Wiffle/Discs-67
79BK/P-16
79Ho-9
79OPC-323
79T-610
80BK/P-6
80K-2
80OPC-141
80T-270
80T/S-2
80T/Super-2TP
81Coke
81D-11
81D-590MVP
81Drake-7
81F-5
81F-640M
81F-645
81F/St-43M
81F/St-9
81F/St-CL3
81K-5
81MSA/Disc-28
81OPC-207
81PermaGr/AS-8
81PermaGr/CC-2
81Sqt-8
81T-206HL
81T-2LL
81T-3LL
81T-540
81T/HT
81T/Nat/Super-13
81T/So-60
81T/St-19
81T/St-199
81T/St-21
81T/St-254
82D-294
82D-585M
82Drake-29
82F-258
82F-637M
82F-641M
82F/St-53
82FBI/Disc-20
82K-16
82KMart-39
82KMart-41
82OPC-100
82OPC-101IA
82OPC-339AS
82PermaGr/AS-17
82PermaGr/CC-3
82Sqt-14
82T-100
82T-101IA
82T-162LL
82T-163LL
82T-339AS
82T/St-123
82T/St-3
82T/St-5
82T/St-74
83D-168
83D/AAS-57
83Drake-25
83F-173
83F/St-1M
83F/St-24M
83F/St-25AM
83F/St-25BM
83K-58
83OPC-300
83OPC-301SV
83OPC-342AS
83OPC/St-10
83OPC/St-172
83OPC/St-270
83PermaGr/AS-16
83PermaGr/CC-14
83T-300
83T-301SV
83T-399AS
83T/Fold-2M
83T/Gloss40-8
83T/St-10
83T/St-172
83T/St-270
83T/St/Box-3
84D-183
84D-23DK
84D/AAS-57
84D/Champs-11
84Drake-28
84F-48
84F/St-16
84F/St-35
84F/St-48
84MiltBrad-23
84Nes/792-132LL
84Nes/792-388AS
84Nes/792-700
84Nes/792-703LL
84Nestle/DT-14
84OPC-361
84OPC-388AS
84Phill/TastyK-33
84Phill/TastyK-6HOF
84Ralston-22
84Seven-4C
84Seven-4E
84Seven-4W
84T-132LL
84T-388AS
84T-700
84T-703LL
84T/Cereal-22
84T/Gloss22-15
84T/Gloss40-39
84T/RD-23M

84T/St-101
84T/St-117
84T/St-188FOIL
84T/Super-6
85CIGNA-4
85CircK-19
85D-61
85D/AAS-17
85Drake-29
85F-265
85F-627IA
85F-630IA
85F/LimEd-33
85F/St-17
85F/St-34
85F/St-74SA
85F/St-75
85F/St-76
85F/St-77
85F/St-78
85F/St-79
85FunFoodPin-11
85GenMills-9
85Leaf-205
85OPC-67
85Phill/TastyK-11M
85Phill/TastyK-33
85Seven-16E
85Seven-1W
85Seven-4C
85Sportflic/Proto-2
85Sportflic/Test-1
85T-500
85T-714AS
85T/3D-1
85T/Gloss22-4
85T/Gloss40-23
85T/RD-9M
85T/St-111
85T/St-193
85T/St-94
85T/Super-12
85ThomMc/Discs-42
86BK/AP-5
86CIGNA-10
86D-61
86D/HL-36
86D/HL-4
86Dorman-8
86Drake-26
86F-450
86F/LimEd-41
86F/Mini-94
86F/Slug-33
86F/St-107
86GenMills/Book-4M
86Jiffy-17
86Keller-5
86Leaf-51
86Meadow/Blank-14
86Meadow/Milk-11
86Meadow/Stat-16
86OPC-200
86Phill/TastyK-20
86Quaker-14
86Seven/Coin-C5M
86Seven/Coin-E5M
86Seven/Coin-S5M
86Seven/Coin-W5M
86Sf-139M
86Sf-148M
86Sf-182M
86Sf-44
86Sf-62M
86Sf-68M
86Sf/Dec-55
86T-200
86T/3D-24
86T/Gloss60-17
86T/Mini-55
86T/St-114
86T/Super-49
86T/Tatt-7M
86TrueVal-28
86Woolwth-30
87BK-17
87Champion-4
87Classic-62
87Classic/Up-101
87D-139
87D/AAS-17
87D/HL-2
87D/OD-160
87D/PopUp-17
87Drake-23
87F-187
87F/AS-6
87F/AwardWin-36
87F/BB-40
87F/GameWin-40
87F/Hottest-35
87F/LL-40
87F/Lim-37
87F/Mini-97
87F/RecSet-35
87F/Slug-37
87F/St-107
87F/WaxBox-C15
87GenMills/Book-5M
87Ho/St-13
87Jiffy-16
87KMart-31
87KayBee-29
87Kraft-30
87Leaf-122
87MSA/Discs-11
87MnM's-3
87OPC-396
87Phill/TastyK-20
87Ralston-14
87RedFoley/St-46
87Sf-115M
87Sf-156M
87Sf-30
87Sf/TPrev-6M
87Sportflic/DealP-1
87Stuart-9M
87T-430
87T-597AS
87T/Board-1
87T/Coins-43
87T/Gloss22-4
87T/Gloss60-28
87T/HL-8
87T/Mini-30
87T/St-116
87T/St-160
87Woolwth-8
88ChefBoy-14
88Classic/Red-167
88D-330
88D-BC4
88D/AS-39
88D/Best-271
88D/PopUp-17
88Drake-8
88F-315
88F-636M
88F/AwardWin-35
88F/BB/AS-36
88F/BB/MVP-31
88F/Excit-34
88F/Hottest-34
88F/LL-35
88F/Mini-102
88F/RecSet-35
88F/SS-33
88F/Slug-36
88F/St-111
88F/TL-34
88F/WaxBox-C11
88FanSam-19
88Grenada-23
88KMart-25
88KayBee-27
88KennerFig-100
88KingB/Disc-1
88Leaf-124
88MSA/Disc-16
88Nestle-6
88OPC-321
88OPC/WaxBox-O
88Panini/St-234M
88Panini/St-360
88Panini/St-429
88Phill/TastyK-23
88RedFoley/St-79
88S-16
88S-657HL
88S/WaxBox-13
88Sf-180M
88Sf-35
88Sf/Gamewin-21
88T-600
88T/Big-88
88T/Coins-53
88T/Gloss22-15
88T/Gloss60-3
88T/Mini-67
88T/RiteAid-8
88T/St-125
88T/St-149
88T/St-9
88T/St/Backs-8
88T/UK-67
88T/WaxBox-O
88Woolwth-7
89B-402
89Cadaco-51
89Classic-48
89Classic/Up/2-153
89D-193
89F-582
89F/Superstar-36
89F/Up-U131
89KayBee-27
89KennerFig-123
89MSA/SS-4
89OPC-100
89OPC/BoxB-L
89Panini/St-153
89Panini/St-3
89Phill/TastyK-32
89RedFoley/St-104
89S-149
89S/HotStar-76
89Sf-21
89T-100
89T-489TL
89T/Ames-27
89T/Big-220
89T/Crunch-16
89T/HeadsUp-24
89T/LJN-122
89T/St-120
89T/UK-70
89T/WaxBox-L
89UD-406
89UD-684TC
90BBWit-39
90D-643
90HOF/St-94
90MSA/AGFA-21
90OPC-662TBC'80
90Phill/TastyK-32
90Phill/TastyK-36BC
90PublInt/St-250
90T-662TBC
90UD-20Special
91BBBest/RecBr-16
91Bakers/Cal-AU2100
91ClBest/Gold-1
91ClBest/Singl-1
92ClBest-100
92K/CornAS-10
92K/FrAS-8
94TedW-141
94TedW-151
94TedW-75
94TedW/500-7
94TedW/Schmidt-Set

Schmidt, Pete
88Belling/Legoe-10

Schmidt, Robert B.
(Bob)
58SFCallB-21
58T-468
59T-109
60T-501
61P-151
61T-31
62Salada-179
62Shirriff-179
62T-262
63T-94
65T-582
79TCMA-246
84Mother/Giants-14
92Yank/WIZ60-109

Schmidt, Tom
92Bend/ClBest-21
93T-433M
93T/Gold-433M
94B-114

Schmidt, Walter
92Conlon/Sport-571
E120
V61-113
W572
W573
WG7-46

Schmidt, Willard
53Hunter
53T-168
56T-323
57T-206
58T-214
59T-171
62Kahn/Atl
79TCMA-153
91T/Arc53-168

Schmitt, Todd
92Spokane/ClBest-7
92Spokane/ProC-1293

Schmittou, Larry
89Nashvl/Team-28PRES

Schmittou, Mike
89TNTech-24

Schmitz, Dan
79WHave-5
81Colum-5
82Colum-16
82Colum/Pol-6
82Nashvl-21
83Tidew-17
84Toledo-7
85Visalia-25
86Visalia-18MG

Schmitz, John
47TipTop
48L-48
49B-52
49Eureka-70
50B-24
51B-69
51T/BB-41
52B-224
52NTea
52T-136
53Briggs
54T-33
55B-105
55T-159
56T-298
56T/Hocus-A16
56T/Hocus-B18
90Target-709
91Crown/Orio-407
94T/Arc54-33
Exh47

Schmutz, Charlie
90Target-1064

Schnacke, Ken
92ColClip/Pol-1
93ColClip/Pol-25MG

Schneck, Dave
76Indianap-15
91WIZMets-351

Schneider, Dan
63T-299R
64T-351
65T-366
67T-543
68OPC-57
68T-57
69T-656

Schneider, Jeff
80RochR-10
82Spokane-7
82T-21R
83Syrac-11
90F/Up-120
91Crown/Orio-408

Schneider, Paul
83Wausau/Frit-19
86Chatt-22
86SLAS-20
87Calgary-8
88Calgary/CMC-2
88Calgary/ProC-793
88SanBern/Best-2

Schneider, Pete
16FleischBrd-83

Schneider, Tom
93James/ClBest-21
93James/ProC-3326

Schnoor, Chuck
82Lynch-14

Schnurbusch, Chris
88Fayette/ProC-1097
89Cedar/Best-16
89Cedar/ProC-934
89Cedar/Star-17

Schober, Dave
84Madis/Pol-3
85Madis-25TR
85Madis/Pol-23
86Madis/Pol-25
87Madis-2TR
89Huntsvl/Best-19

Schock, William
(Will)
88Huntsvl/BK-17
88Madis-21
88MidwLAS/GS-54
89Huntsvl/Best-2
90Foil/Best-197
90Huntsvl/Best-9
91AAA/LineD-544
91Tacoma/LineD-544
91Tacoma/ProC-2304

Schockman, Mark
85Newar-16

Schoen, Jerry
91BendB/ClBest-14
91BendB/ProC-3704

Schoendienst, Albert
(Red)
48B-38
49B-111
49Eureka-197
50B-71
51B-10
51FB
51T/BB-6
52B-30
52BR
52Dix
52RM-NL19
52StarCal-93B
52StarCal/L-81A
52T-91
52TipTop
53B/Col-101
53Dix
53Hunter
53NB
53RM-NL12
53T-78
54B-110
54DanDee
54Dix
54Hunter
54RH
54RM-NL10
55B-29
55Hunter
55RFG-3
55RM-NL18
55W605-3
56T-165
56YellBase/Pin-28
57SpicSpan/4x5-15
57T-154
58T-190
59T-480
60Lake
60MacGregor-22
60NuCard-25
60SpicSpan-21
60T-335
61NuCard-425
61P-111
61T-505
62Salada-151
62Shirriff-151
62T-575
65T-556MG
66OPC-76MG
66T-76MG
67T-512MG
68T-294MG
69T-462MG
70OPC-346MG
70T-346MG
71OPC-239MG
71T-239
72OPC-67MG
72T-67MG
73OPC-497MG
73T-497MG
74Laugh/ASG-50
74OPC-236MG
74T-236MG
75OPC-246MG
75T-246MG
75T/M-246MG
76OPC-581

76SSPC-300MG
76T-581MG
79TCMA-94
80Perez/HOF-203
81D-431MG
81TCMA-395MG
88Pac/Leg-2
90Perez/GreatMom-55
90T/Tr-113TMG
91T/Arc53-78
92Bz/Quadra-11M
92Card/McDon/Pac-21
93AP/ASG-114
93AP/ASG24K-48G
93AP/ASGCoke/Amo-4
94TedW-83
Exh47
R423-97

Schoendienst, Kevin
81QuadC-10

Schoenhaus, Ted
76Cedar

Schoenvogel, Chad
91FrRow/DP-3
91FrRow/DPPr-4
92ClBest-325
92StCl/Dome-166
92WinHaven/ClBest-16
92WinHaven/ProC-1777

Schofield, John R.
(Ducky)
54Hunter
54T-191
55Hunter
55T-143
58T-106
59T-68
60T-104
61Kahn
61T-453
62T-484
63IDL-20
63Sugar-E
63T-34
64T-284
65OPC-218
65T-218
66OPC-156M
66T-156M
66T-474
67T-381
68T-588
69OPC-18
69T-18
70OPC-251
70T-251
71MLB/St-282
71OPC-396
71T-396
72MB-310
78TCMA-199
85T-138FS
92Yank/WIZ60-110
94T/Arc54-191

Schofield, John
86Kinston-23
87PortChar-2

Schofield, Richard C.
(Dick)
82Danvl/Frit-27
84D-35RR
84F/X-U105
84Smok/Cal-25
84T/Tr-107T
85D-329
85F-311
85Smok/Cal-13
85T-138FS
85T-629
86D-133
86F-167
86OPC-311
86Smok/Cal-13
86T-311
87D-283
87D/OD-4
87F-92
87OPC-54
87Seven-W9
87Smok/Cal-15
87T-502
87T/St-176
88D-233
88D/Best-195
88F-504
88Leaf-178
88OPC-43
88Panini/St-45
88RedFoley/St-80
88S-274
88Smok/Angels-16
88T-43
88T/Big-204
88T/St-177
89B-46
89D-108
89D/Best-251
89F-488
89KennerFig-124
89OPC-286
89Panini/St-294
89S-16
89T-477
89T/Big-53
89T/St-174
89UD-201
90B-291
90D-288
90D/BestAL-131
90F-144
90F/Can-144
90Leaf-419
90OPC-189
90PublInt/St-379
90S-44
90Smok/Angel-15
90T-189
90T/Big-211
90Target-710
90UD-669
91B-191
91D-262
91F-325
91Leaf-59
91OPC-736
91Panini/FrSt-183
91S-776
91Smok/Angel-14
91StCl-59
91T-736
91UD-169
91Ultra-52
92D-44
92F-69
92F/Up-105
92L-419
92L/BlkGold-419
92Mets/Kahn-11
92OPC-230
92Panini-8
92Pinn-338
92S-552
92S/RookTr-26T
92StCl-16
92StCl-738
92T-230
92T/Gold-230
92T/GoldWin-230
92T/Tr-101T
92T/TrGold-101T
92UD-269
92UD-791
92Ultra-30
92Ultra-538
93BJ/D/McDon-30
93BJ/Demp-23
93BJ/Fire-24
93F-94
93L-382
93OPC/Premier-129
93Pac/Spanish-202
93T-79
93T/Gold-79
93UD-768
93Ultra-646
94F-341
94L-211
94StCl-234
94StCl/1stDay-234
94StCl/Gold-234
94StCl/Team-160

Scholzen, Jeffrey
91Pocatel/ProC-3791
91Pocatel/SportP-22

Schooler, Michael
86Wausau-21
87Chatt/Best-8
88Calgary/CMC-9
88Calgary/ProC-795
88S/Tr-91T
88T/Tr-105T
89Chatt/II/Team-27
89D-637
89D/Best-275
89F-559
89Mother/Sea-25
89S-528
89S/HotRook-73
89S/YS/II-34
89T-199
89ToysRUs-27
89UD-28
90B-470
90Classic-79
90D-330
90D/BestAL-82
90F-525
90F/Can-525
90Leaf-258
90Mother/Mar-21
90OPC-681
90Panini/St-151
90RedFoley/St-84
90S-149
90Sf-187
90T-681
90T/Big-235
90T/Mini-35
90T/St-228
90UD-214
91B-241
91CounHrth-25
91D-302
91F-461
91Leaf-230
91OPC-365
91Panini/FrSt-236
91Panini/St-184
91RedFoley/St-85
91S-489
91Seven/3DCoin-15NW
91StCl-508
91T-365
91UD-638
92B-336
92D-444
92F-292
92Mother/Mar-10
92OPC-28
92Pinn-171
92S-654
92StCl-313
92T-28
92T/Gold-28
92T/GoldWin-28
92UD-405
93D-449
93F-313
93OPC-350
93Rang/Keeb-432
93S-544
93Select-392
93StCl-198
93StCl/1stDay-198
93T-258
93T/Gold-258
93Ultra-271

Schoonmaker, Jerry
56T-216
57T-334

Schoonover, Gary
87BYU-19
88Idaho/ProC-1836
89BurlB/ProC-1602
89BurlB/Star-20

Schoppee, Dave
81Bristol-9
83Pawtu-10

Schorr, Bill
88Butte-8

Schorr, Bradley
91Kingspt/ClBest-22
91Kingspt/ProC-3812
92ColumMet/ClBest-5
92ColumMet/ProC-296
92ColumMet/SAL/II-20
92ColumMet/SAL/II-30M
93StLucie/ProC-2921

Schott, Arthur Eugene
R312
W711/1

Schott, Marge
93Reds/Kahn-25OWN

Schourek, Pete
88LitFalls/Pucko-22
89Clmbia/Best-14
89Clmbia/GS-24
90StLucie/Star-25
90T/TVMets-59
90TexLgAS/GS-33
91B-482
91F/Up-U104
91Kahn/Mets-48
91Leaf/GRook-BC15
91OPC/Premier-106
91S/RookTr-87T
91T/Tr-106T
91UD/Ext-766
92D-535
92F-516
92L-176
92L/BlkGold-176
92OPC-287
92OPC/Premier-58
92Pinn-141
92S-332
92S/100RisSt-20
92Sky/AAASingl-255
92StCl-521
92T-287
92T/91Debut-158
92T/Gold-287
92T/GoldWin-287
92Tidew/SB-570
92UD-673
92Ultra-539
93D-198
93F-95
93Mets/Kahn-48
93Pac/Spanish-203
93Pinn-324
93StCl-238
93StCl/1stDay-238
93T-352
93T/Gold-352
93UD-658
93Ultra-433
94D-652
94F-577
94StCl-439
94StCl/1stDay-439
94StCl/Gold-439
94T-699
94T/Gold-699
94TripleP-149

Schramka, Paul
77Fritsch-14

Schramm, Carl
91Geneva/ClBest-27
91Geneva/ProC-4213
92Peoria/ClBest-8
92Peoria/Team-24

Schrammel, Jamie
80GlenF/C-29bb

Schreckengost, Ossie
E107
E91
T206
WG2-42

Schreiber, Bruce
89Princet/Star-20
89Star/IISingl-174
90CLAS/CL-23
90Salem/Star-20
90Star/ISingl-1
91AA/LineD-116
91CaroMud/LineD-116
91CaroMud/ProC-1094
91ClBest/Singl-225
92CaroMud/ProC-1189
92Salem/ClBest-5
93CaroMud/RBI-5

Schreiber, Marty
84Durham-27
85Durham-12
86Osceola-22

Schreiber, Paul Frederick
54T-217CO
94T/Arc54-217CO

Schreiber, Paul
92AS/Cal-24

Schreiber, Ted
91WIZMets-352

Schreiner, John
91BBCity/ClBest-21
91BBCity/ProC-1407

Schreiser, Andre
52Laval-82

Schrenk, Steve
89SoBend/GS-15
90Foil/Best-104
90SoBend/Best-16
90SoBend/GS-16
92Saraso/ClBest-15
92Saraso/ProC-207
93FExcel/ML-155

Schriver, William
N172

Schroder, Bob
65T-589R

Schroeck, Bob
82ElPaso-16
83ElPaso-24
84ElPaso-3

Schroeder, Alfred W.
(Bill)
81ElPaso-13
82Vanco-3
84D-515
84Nes/792-738
84Pol/Brew-21
84T-738
85D-124
85F-594
85Gard-18
85Pol/Brew-21
85T-176
86D-211
86F-501
86Pol/Brew-21
86T-662
87D-486
87D/OD-49
87F-357
87Pol/Brew-21
87T-302
88D-419
88F-173
88Pol/Brew-21
88S-311
88T-12
89B-44
89D-644
89T-563
89UD-627
90D-567
90ElPasoATG/Team-18
90OPC-244
90S-362
90T-244
90UD-149
91OPC-452
91T-452

Schroeder, Jay
83Kinston/Team-23

Schroeder, Todd
91Welland/ClBest-3
91Welland/ProC-3582
92Augusta/ClBest-6
92Salem/ClBest-20
92Salem/ProC-72

Schroll, Al
55B-319
57Seattle/Pop-33
59T-546
60L-95
60T-357
62T-102

Schrom, Ken
77QuadC
80SLCity-7
81F-425
81OPC-238R
81Syrac-21
81Syrac/Team-18
81T-577R
82Syrac-7
82Syrac/Team-19
83Toledo-9
84D-72
84F-572
84Nes/792-11TL
84Nes/792-322
84OPC-322
84T-322
84T/St-308
85D-486
85F-288

85OPC-161
85T-161
85Twin/Team-13
86D-635
86F-403
86F/Up-U104
86OPC-71
86OhHenry-18
86T-71
86T/Tr-100T
87D-403
87D/AAS-53
87F-258
87F/Mini-98
87Gator-18
87OPC-171
87Sf-107
87Sf/TPrev-3M
87T-635
87T/St-204
88D-501
88F-614
88OPC-256
88S-574
88T-256
90ElPasoATG/Team-36
Schu, Rick
84Cram/PCL-209
85Cram/PCL-34
85D-448
85F/Up-U100
85Phill/TastyK-43
85T/Tr-104T
86D-570
86F-451
86OPC-16
86Phill/TastyK-15
86Seven/Coin-E9M
86T-16
86T/St-122
87D-509
87F-188
87Phill/TastyK-15
87T-209
88D-432
88F-316
88French-25
88S-448
88T-731
88T/Big-122
89D-406
89F-619
89Mara/Tigers-35
89OPC-352
89RedFoley/St-105
89RochR/CMC-23
89RochR/ProC-1642
89S-452
89T-352
89T/Big-164
89T/Tr-112T
89UD-490
90D-599
90OPC-498
90T-498
91AAA/LineD-495
91Crown/Orio-409
91F-326
91ScranWB/LineD-495
91ScranWB/ProC-2547
92AAA/ASG/SB-493
92ScranWB/ProC-2456
92ScranWB/SB-493
92Sky/AAASingl-223
Schubert, Brian
90Niagara/Pucko-24
Schuble, Henry
33G-4
35G-1H
35G-3F
35G-5F
35G-6F
R337-411
V353-4
Schuckert, Wayne
81AppFx-12
82AppFx/Frit-18
83GlenF-19
Schueler, Ron
73OPC-169
73T-169
74JP
74OPC-544
74T-544
74T/Tr-544T
75OPC-292
75T-292
75T/M-292
76OPC-586
76T-586
77T-337
78SSPC/270-138
78T-409
79T-686
Schueler, Russ
87BurlEx-14
Schuermann, Lance
91Butte/SportP-16
92FtMyr/ProC-2746
92Miracle/ClBest-24
Schugel, Jeff
84Visalia-14
85Visalia-6
Schula, Kevin
92Idaho/ProC-3516
Schuler, Dave
77Watlo
78Cr/PCL-103
79SLCity-17
80SLCity-6
81SLCity-11
82Omaha-8
83Omaha-9
85Richm-8
86Omaha/ProC-19
86Omaha/TCMA-18
87Denver-11
88Vermont/ProC-941
90FtLaud/Star-24CO
91PrWill/ClBest-25CO
91PrWill/ProC-1443CO
92PrWill/ProC-166CO
Schulhofer, Adam
92Geneva/ClBest-7
92Geneva/ProC-1560
Schullstrom, Erik
88Alaska/Team-16
89FresnoSt/Smok-20
92ClBest-121
92Hagers/ProC-2555
92Hagers/SB-268
92Sky/AASingl-112
Schulmerich, Wes
34Exh/4-6
34G-54
88Conlon/NatAS-17
Schult, Art
53T-167
58T-58
60L-123
60T-93
79TCMA-253
91T/Arc53-167
Schulte, Frank
10Domino-108
11Helmar-104
12Sweet/Pin-90
14CJ-101
15CJ-101
91Conlon/Sport-304
BF2-67
D328-152
D329-156
D350/2-158
E135-152
E254
E270/1
E90/3
E91
M101/4-156
M101/5-158
M116
S74-68
T202
T204
T205
T206
T207
T213/blue
T214-25
T215/blue
T215/brown
T222
T3-117
W514-10
WG4-25
Schulte, Fred
28Exh-60
29Exh/4-30
31Exh/4-29
33G-112
33G-190
35BU-50
35Exh/4-16
91Conlon/Sport-286
R316
Schulte, Joe
86Ashvl-26
87Osceola-14
Schulte, John C.
33G-186
40PlayBall-12
44Yank/St-23
94Conlon-1046
Schulte, John
90LitSun/HSPros-12
90LitSun/HSProsG-12
90Welland/Pucko-9
92Augusta/ClBest-15
92Augusta/ProC-254
Schulte, Mark
84ArkTr-13
86ArkTr-22
87FtMyr-12
Schulte, Rich
91AubAS/ClBest-10
91AubAS/ProC-4287
92BurlAs/ClBest-24
92BurlAs/ProC-559
Schulte, Todd
83BurlR-10
83BurlR/Frit-2
Schultz, Bob D.
52T-401
53T-144
54B-59
91T/Arc53-144
Schultz, Bobby
91Burllnd/ProC-3317
Schultz, Charles
(Buddy)
78T-301
79T-532
80T-601
82ArkTr-9
Schultz, George
(Barney)
62T-89
62T/St-110
63T-452
65OPC-28
65T-28
66Pep/Tul
73OPC-497CO
73T-497C
74OPC-236CO
74T-236C
78TCMA-15
Schultz, Greg
83Albuq-18
84Cram/PCL-157
85Cram/PCL-196
Schultz, Howie
90Target-711
Schultz, Joseph C. Jr.
(Dode)
47TipTop
62Kahn/Atl
69T-254MG
73OPC-323CO
73T-323CO
89Pac/Leg-162
Schultz, Joseph C. Sr.
(Germany)
90Target-1065
93Conlon-790
E120
V61-114
W572
W573
Schultz, Scott 1
87Lakeland-5
Schultz, Scott
92LSU/McDag-6
93LSU/McDag-16
94LSU-9
Schultz, Ted
76AppFx
Schulz, Harry
75Clinton
Schulz, Jeff
83Butte-28
86Omaha/ProC-20
86Omaha/TCMA-6
87Omaha-23
88Omaha/CMC-15
88Omaha/ProC-1508
89Omaha/CMC-22
89Omaha/ProC-1736
90AAASingl/ProC-614
90Omaha/CMC-18
90Omaha/ProC-79
90ProC/Singl-193
90T/89Debut-110
91AAA/LineD-45
91BuffB/LineD-45
91BuffB/ProC-554
91D-687
91F-568
91S-336RP
91S/100RisSt-25
91UD-607
92Iowa/ProC-4063
92Nashvl/SB-291
Schulze, Don
81QuadC-29
83Iowa-9
84Iowa-22
84Wheat/Ind-37
85D-639
85F-454
85T-93
86OhHenry-37
86T-542
87BuffB-22
87F-259
87T-297
87Tidew-25
87Tidew/TCMA-26
88T-131
88Toledo/CMC-3
88Toledo/ProC-604
89Colum/CMC-6
89Colum/Pol-19
89Colum/ProC-753
89Tidew/Candl-11
91WIZMets-353
92Yank/WIZ80-173
Schumacher, Hal
33G-129
33G-240
35BU-110
35BU-52
35G-1K
35G-3B
35G-4B
35G-5B
36Wheat
38ONG/Pin-26
39PlayBall-73
40PlayBall-85
48Swell-7
61F-137
77Galasso-221
88Conlon/NatAS-18
94Conlon-1127
V355-23
Schumacher, Roy
81AppFx-11
Schuman, Rich
87AZ/Pol-11
Schumate, Jack
79Wisco-22
Schunk, Jerry
87Dunedin-25
88Dunedin/Star-16
89Knoxvl/Best-23
89Knoxvl/ProC-1142
89Knoxvl/Star-19
90Knoxvl/Best-25
90Knoxvl/ProC-1250
90Knoxvl/Star-18
90Star/ISingl-89
91AAA/LineD-516
91B-20
91S/ToroBJ-34
91Syrac/LineD-516
91Syrac/MerchB-22
91Syrac/ProC-2488
92Sky/AAASingl-231
92Syrac/MerchB-18
92Syrac/ProC-1978
92Syrac/SB-515
Schupp, Ferdie
16FleischBrd-84
90Target-712
D328-153
E121/120
E121/80
E122
E135-153
W575
Schurr, Wayne
64T-548R
65OPC-149
65T-149
Schuster, Bill
47Signal
Schuster, Frank
74Tacoma/Caruso-9
Schuster, Mark
79Holyo-7
80Holyo-3
81Vanco-5
82ElPaso-8
84Cram/PCL-7
85Cram/PCL-185
Schwab, Chris
94B-556
94ClBest/Gold-73
94ClBest/GoldLP-13
Schwab, Ken
80Clinton-8
Schwabe, Mike
88GlenF/ProC-927
89F/Up-32
89London/ProC-1375
90AAASingl/ProC-378
90ProC/Singl-386
90T/89Debut-111
90Toledo/CMC-9
90Toledo/ProC-148
91F-351
92Portl/SB-418
92Portland/ProC-2665
Schwall, Don
62Bz
62J-64
62P-64
62P/Can-64
62Salada-210
62Shirriff-210
62T-35
62T/St-19
62T/bucks
63Sugar-C
63T-344
64T-558
65T-362
66OPC-144
66T-144
67CokeCap/Brave-15
67T-267
78TCMA-118
Schwaner, Tom
62Pep/Tul
Schwanke, Jim
91OKSt-22ACO
92OKSt-5M
Schwankl, Darren
92MN-17
Schwarber, Mike
80Batavia-10
81Watlo-15
82Chatt-10
Schwarber, Tom
91Bristol/ClBest-23
91Bristol/ProC-3605
92Fayette/ClBest-19
92Fayette/ProC-2167
Schwartz, Dave
91Elizab/ProC-4300
Schwartz, Randy
67OPC-33R
67T-33R
Schwarz, Jeff
88WinSalem/Star-19
89Hagers/Best-24
89Hagers/ProC-263
89Hagers/Star-16
91AA/LineD-195
91ElPaso/LineD-195
91ElPaso/ProC-2748
92BirmB/ProC-2581
92BirmB/SB-94
92Vanco/ProC-2722
93F/Final-198
93WSox-26
94F-95
94S-588

94StCl-482
94StCl/1stDay-482
94StCl/Gold-482
94StCl/Team-137
94T-33
94T/Gold-33
94Ultra-38
Schwarz, Tom
86Visalia-19
87OrlanTw-18
88Reading/ProC-863
Schweighoffer, Mike
85VeroB-18
87SanAn-13
88SanAn/Best-10
Schweitzer, Al
M116
Schweitzer, Tim
92AZ/Pol-16
Schwerman, Brian
77Charl
78Charl
Sciortino, Michael
90Pittsfld/Pucko-15
91Pittsfld/ClBest-9
91Pittsfld/ProC-3433
Scioscia, Mike
77Clinton
79Albuq-10
80Albuq-26
81F-131
81Pol/Dodg-14
81T-302R
82D-598
82F-22
82OPC-173
82Pol/Dodg-14
82T-642
83D-75
83F-221
83Pol/Dodg-14
83T-352
84F-113
84Nes/792-64
84Pol/Dodg-14
84T-64
85Coke/Dodg-30
85D-459
85F-385
85Leaf-118
85T-549
85T/St-79
86Coke/Dodg-28
86D-93
86F-144
86Leaf-87
86OPC-111
86Pol/Dodg-14
86Sf-167
86T-468
86T/St-68
86T/Tatt-19M
87D-130
87D/OD-82
87F-454
87Leaf-123
87Mother/Dodg-10
87OPC-144
87Pol/Dodg-6
87Seven-W12
87Sf-151M
87Sf-67
87Sf/TPrev-14
87T-144
87T/St-73
88D-106
88D/Best-260
88F-524
88Leaf-97
88Mother/Dodg-10
88OPC-225
88Panini/St-307
88Pol/Dodg-14
88S-53
88Sf-110
88T-225
88T/Big-72
88T/St-67
89B-342
89D-77
89D/Best-66
89F-71
89F/AS-9
89F/WS-4
89KennerFig-125
89Mother/Dodg-3
89OPC-7
89Panini/St-104
89Pol/Dodg-9
89S-121
89Sf-138
89Smok/Dodg-31
89T-669TL
89T-755
89T/Big-281
89T/St-58
89UD-116
90B-89
90D-316
90D/BestNL-5
90D/GSlam-7
90F-407
90Leaf-49
90Mother/Dodg-4
90OPC-605
90Panini/St-276
90Pol/Dodg-14
90PublInt/St-17
90S-398
90S/100St-48
90Sf-163
90T-605
90T/Big-67
90T/DH-58
90T/Gloss60-34
90T/St-64
90Target-713
90UD-298
90USPlayC/AS-2H
91B-613
91D-112
91D-436AS
91F-219
91Leaf-24
91Leaf/Stud-189
91Mother/Dodg-4
91OPC-305
91OPC-404AS
91Panini/FrSt-54
91Panini/St-57
91Pol/Dodg-14
91RedFoley/St-128
91S-520
91StCl-19
91T-305
91T-404AS
91UD-139
91Ultra-169
92B-368
92D-480
92F-470
92L-165
92L/BlkGold-165
92Mother/Dodg-9
92OPC-13
92Panini-191
92Pinn-210
92Pol/Dodg-14
92S-226
92S-782AS
92StCl-140
92Studio-48
92T-13
92T/Gold-13
92T/GoldWin-13
92TripleP-191
92UD-152
92Ultra-217
93D-508
93F-67
93Mother/Padre-23
93OPC-326
93Panini-213
93Pinn-498
93S-623
93Select-69
93StCl-46
93StCl/1stDay-46
93StCl/MPhoto-9
93T-202
93T/Gold-202
93TripleP-196AA
93UD-688
94StCl/Team-255
Scoble, Troy
91Adelaide/Fut-15
Sconiers, Daryl
80ElPaso-14
81SLCity-20
82T-653R
83D-141
83T/Tr-99
84D-451
84F-528
84F/St-112
84Nes/792-27
84Smok/Cal-26
84T-27
85D-620
85F-312
85OPC-256
85T-604
86F-168
86SanJose-18
86T-193
87SanJose-28
88Vanco/CMC-22
88Vanco/ProC-766
91AA/LineD-445
91London/LineD-445
91MidldA/ProC-443
Scoras, John
78Memphis/Team-9
79Memphis/TCMA-17
Score, Herb
55Gol/Ind-26
55Salem
56Carling-7
56T-140
57Sohio/Ind-12
57T-50
58T-352
58T-495AS
59Kahn
59T-88
60Kahn
60T-360
60T/tatt-48
61T-185
61T-337M
61Union
62T-116
79TCMA-134
80Marchant-28
86Indianap-24
89Pac/Leg-126
89Swell-114
90Pac/Legend-49
90Swell/Great-32
91Swell/Great-82
92AP/ASG-79
94T/Arc54-256
Exh47
Scott, Andrew
91Adelaide/Fut-16
Scott, Charles
86Watlo-25
88ColoSp/CMC-9
88ColoSp/ProC-1529
89ColoSp/CMC-8
90AAASingl/ProC-248
90Portl/CMC-7
90Portl/ProC-178
90ProC/Singl-559
91AAA/LineD-419
91Portl/LineD-419
91Portl/ProC-1565
Scott, Craig
89Kingspt/Star-21
Scott, Dale
88TM/Umpire-58
89TM/Umpire-56
90TM/Umpire-54
Scott, Darryl
88CapeCod/Sum-34
90Boise/ProC-3313
91QuadC/ClBest-10
91QuadC/ProC-2627
92MidldA/OneHour-22
92MidldA/ProC-4027
92MidldA/SB-469
92ProC/Tomorrow-35
92Sky/AASingl-200
93F/Final-189
93StCl/Angel-26
93Vanco/ProC-2596
94Pinn-225
94Pinn/Artist-225
94Pinn/Museum-225
Scott, Donald M.
(Donnie)
80Ashvl-21
81Tulsa-13
82Tulsa-11
83OKCty-23
84OKCty-19
84Rang-43
85Cram/PCL-81
85D-544
85F-568
85T-496
85T/Tr-105T
86F-474
86RochR-19
86T-568
87ElPaso-3
88ElPaso/Best-2
89Denver/CMC-6
89Denver/ProC-52
90AAASingl/ProC-549
90Nashvl/CMC-12
90Nashvl/ProC-237
90ProC/Singl-137
91AAA/LineD-271
91Nashvl/LineD-271
91Nashvl/ProC-2160
92Billings/ProC-3373
93Rang/Keeb-321
Scott, Floyd John
(Pete)
33G-70
92Conlon/Sport-578
V354-33
Scott, Gary
89Geneva/ProC-1877
90CLAS/CL-49
90WinSalem/Team-1
91B-535
91Classic/II-T88
91Cub/Vine-25
91F/UltraUp-U72
91F/Up-U80
91Iowa/ProC-1068
91Leaf/GRook-BC4
91Leaf/Stud-159
91OPC/Premier-107
91S/ASFan-3
91S/RookTr-90T
91StCl-596
91T/Tr-107T
91UD-58TP
92B-128
92L-6
92L/BlkGold-6
92Pinn-269
92Pinn/Rook-15
92Pinn/Team2000-73
92S/100RisSt-81
92StCl-708
92Studio-19
92T/91Debut-159
92T/Tr-102T
92T/TrGold-102T
92USPlayC/Cub-2C
92USPlayC/Cub-4D
92Ultra-474
93D-750
93S-547
93T-656
93T/Gold-656
93TripleP-84
Scott, George Charles
66T-558R
67CokeCap/ALAS-22
67CokeCap/AS-34
67CokeCap/RedSox-12
67OPC-75
67T-75
67T/Test/RSox-16
68Bz-7
68CokeCap/RedSox-12
68Dexter-70
68T-233
68T/ActionSt-13CM
68T/ActionSt-2C
68T/G-22
69MLB/St-17
69T-574
69T/St-138
70MLB/St-165
70OPC-385
70T-385
71MD
71MLB/St-331
71OPC-9
71T-9
71T/Coins-98
72MB-311
72T-585
73OPC-263
73T-263
73T/Comics-18
73T/Lids-47
73T/PinUps-18
74OPC-27
74T-27
74T/DE-30
74T/St-199
75Ho-26
75Ho/Twink-26
75OPC-360
75T-360
75T/M-360
76A&P/Milw
76Ho-54
76Ho/Twink-54
76K-21
76OPC-15
76OPC-194LL
76OPC-196LL
76SSPC-237
76T-15
76T-194LL
76T-196LL
77Ho-148
77Ho/Twink-148
77OPC-210
77T-255
78Ho-24
78OPC-12
78PapaG/Disc-15
78SSPC/270-183
78T-125
79OPC-340
79T-645
80T-414
92Yank/WIZ70-139
PM10/Sm-175
Scott, George C.
92Elmira/ClBest-1
92Elmira/ProC-1392
Scott, James
(Death Valley Jim)
11Helmar-15
14CJ-26
15CJ-26
92Conlon/Sport-341
BF2-18
D329-158
D350/2-159
M101/4-158
M101/5-159
M116
T205
T206
W501-30
WG4-26
Scott, Jeff
77Ashvl
79Ashvl/TCMA-22
Scott, Jim
86Vermont-17
Scott, Joe
86Negro/Frit-58
92Negro/Retort-54
Scott, John H.
75OPC-616R
75T-616R
75T/M-616R
76SSPC-131
77OPC-94
77T-473R
78Spring/Wiener-4
78T-547
Scott, John William
91Conlon/Sport-97
W515-25
Scott, Kelly
83Nashvl-19
84Colum-19
84Colum/Pol-22
85Colum-9
85Colum/Pol-19
Scott, Kevin
89AubAs/ProC-2183
90Ashvl/ProC-2752
91ClBest/Singl-37
91Osceola/ClBest-28
91Osceola/ProC-689
92Osceola/ClBest-14

92Osceola/ProC-2534
Scott, L. Everett
21Exh-153
21Exh-154
91Conlon/Sport-149
D327
D328-154
D329-157
D350/2-160
E120
E121/120
E121/80
E122
E135-154
E220
M101/4-157
M101/5-160
V100
W512-7
W514-90
W515-46
W575
Scott, Mark 1
59HRDerby-17ANN
Scott, Mark 2
80CharCh-2
Scott, Martin
(Marty)
79Tucson-10
81Tulsa-4
82BurlR/Frit-28MG
82BurlR/TCMA-25MG
83Tulsa-25
90TulsaDG/Best-34
Scott, Michael Warren
(Mike)
78Tidew
79Tidew-15
80T-681R
80Tidew-23
81D-37
81T-109
82D-128
82F-535
82T-246TL
82T-432
83F-554
83T-679
83T/Tr-100T
84D-136
84F-240
84Mother/Ast-14
84Nes/792-559
84T-559
85D-258
85F-361
85Mother/Ast-18
85OPC-17
85T-17
86D-476
86D/HL-46
86F-311
86F/Mini-66
86F/St-108
86Greenvl/Team-16
86Leaf-235
86Pol/Ast-3
86Seven/Coin-S11
86Sf-195
86T-268
86T/St-27
86T/Tatt-23M
87Classic-81
87Classic/Up-123
87D-163
87D-18DK
87D/AAS-32
87D/AS/Wax-PC13
87D/DKsuper-18
87D/OD-15
87Drake-33
87F-630M
87F-68
87F/AwardWin-37
87F/Lim-38
87F/Mini-99
87F/RecSet-36
87F/Slug-38
87F/St-108
87GenMills/Book-6M
87Ho/St-10
87Jiffy-18
87KayBee-30
87Kraft-4
87Leaf-18DK
87Leaf-258
87MnM's-18
87Mother/Ast-2
87OPC-330
87Pol/Ast-11
87Sf-119M
87Sf-120M
87Sf-19
87Sf/TPrev-8M
87Smok/NL-5
87Stuart-5
87T-330
87T/Coins-44
87T/HL-18
87T/Mini-11
87T/St-15LCS
87T/St-35
87Woolwth-18
88ChefBoy-19
88Classic/Blue-221
88D-112
88D-BC12
88D/AS-40
88D/Best-206
88D/PopUp-18
88F-456
88F-632M
88F/AwardWin-36
88F/BB/AS-37
88F/BB/MVP-32
88F/Excit-35
88F/Hottest-35
88F/LL-36
88F/Mini-80
88F/RecSet-36
88F/SS-34
88F/Slug-37
88F/St-89
88F/TL-35
88Grenada-50
88KMart-26
88KennerFig-101
88KingB/Disc-13
88Leaf-54
88Mother/Ast-2
88OPC-227
88Panini/St-233
88Panini/St-289
88Pol/Ast-21
88RedFoley/St-81
88S-335
88S/WaxBox-18
88Sf-66
88T-760
88T/Big-140
88T/Coins-54
88T/Gloss22-21
88T/Gloss60-5
88T/Mini-51
88T/RiteAid-4
88T/St-154FOIL
88T/St-30
88T/St/Backs-26
88T/UK-68
89B-322
89Classic-23
89D-69
89D/Best-94
89D/MVP-BC2
89F-367
89F/BBMVP's-34
89F/LL-34
89F/Superstar-37
89KennerFig-126
89Lennox/Ast-4
89Mother/Ast-2
89OPC-180
89Panini/St-84
89RedFoley/St-106
89S-550
89S/HotStar-60
89S/Mast-4
89Sf-120
89T-180
89T/Big-51
89T/LJN-34
89T/Mini-14
89T/St-15
89UD-295
90B-71
90BBWit-12
90Classic-29
90D-207
90D/BestNL-16
90D/Learning-50
90F-237
90F-636M
90F/ASIns-10
90F/AwardWin-33
90F/Can-237
90F/Can-636M
90F/LL-35
90HotPlay/St-39
90KMart/SS-9
90Kenner/Fig-76
90KingB/Discs-1
90Leaf-4
90Lennox-22
90MLBPA/Pins-43
90Mother/Ast-4
90OPC-405AS
90OPC-460
90Panini/St-262
90Post-20
90PublInt/St-102
90RedFoley/St-85
90S-40
90S-692 DT
90S/100St-97
90Sf-55
90Sunflower-22
90T-405AS
90T-460
90T/Big-249
90T/DH-59
90T/Gloss60-14
90T/Mini-56
90T/St-19
90T/TVAS-42
90UD-125
90UD-88TC
91B-546
91BBBest/Aces-15
91Classic/200-38
91D-483
91F-515
91Leaf/Stud-180
91Mother/Ast-4
91OPC-240
91Panini/FrSt-14
91Panini/St-16
91Petro/SU-8
91RedFoley/St-86
91S-46
91Seven/3DCoin-9T
91StCl-209
91T-240
91UD-531
91Ultra-140
91WIZMets-354
94TedW-36
Scott, Michael Wm.
87Greenvl/Best-28
Scott, Philip
90Pittsfld/Pucko-1
91Greens/ProC-3068
Scott, Ralph
(Mickey)
70T-669R
72T-724R
73OPC-553
73T-553
76OPC-276
76T-276
77T-401
78Colum
91Crown/Orio-410
Scott, Rennie
90LynchRS/Team-22
91LynchRS/ClBest-8
91LynchRS/ProC-1198
Scott, Richard E.
(Dick)
82Colum-15
85Albany-19
87Colum-17
88Albany/ProC-1350
89Tacoma/CMC-20
89Tacoma/ProC-1554
90ProC/Singl-601CO
90T/89Debut-112
90Tacoma/CMC-24CO
90Tacoma/ProC-103
92Madis/ProC-1252MG
Scott, Richard L.
(Dick)
77Fritsch-38
90AAASingl/ProC-150
90Target-714
92Madis/ClBest-26MG
Scott, Rodney
72Dimanche*-40
76SSPC-172
78T-191
79T-86
80OPC-360
80T-712
81D-209
81F-155
81OPC-227
81OPC/Post-2
81T-204M
81T-539
81T/St-185
82D-240
82F-207
82F/St-38
82OPC-259
82OPC/Post-14
82T-259
89Pac/SenLg-177
89T/SenLg-29
89TM/SenLg-94
90EliteSenLg-29
91Pac/SenLg-69
92Nabisco-13
92Yank/WIZ80-174
93Expo/D/McDon-18
Scott, Sean
92SoOreg/ClBest-26
92SoOreg/ProC-3435
Scott, Shawn
90StCath/ProC-3480
91Dunedin/ClBest-23
91Dunedin/ProC-221
92Knoxvl/ProC-3004
92Knoxvl/SB-392
93Syrac/ProC-1012
Scott, Steve
87SLCity/Taco-26
Scott, Tary
85Greens-3
86FSLAS-43
86WinHaven-21
87NewBrit-22
Scott, Tim
83Cedar-8
83Cedar/Frit-3
87Hawaii-14
87SanAn-4
88Bakers/Cal-258
89SanAn/Best-24
90AAASingl/ProC-65
90Albuq/CMC-9
90Albuq/ProC-344
90Albuq/Trib-26
90ProC/Singl-411
91AAA/LineD-293
91LasVegas/LineD-293
91LasVegas/ProC-235
92B-454
92Bend/ClBest-22
92D/Rook-109
92LasVegas/ProC-2796
92LasVegas/SB-239
92Pol/Padre-27M
92StCl-881
92T/91Debut-160
93D-362
93F-524
93L-174
93Mother/Padre-27
93Pac/Spanish-600
93S-251
93StCl-76
93StCl/1stDay-76
93T-166
93T/Gold-166
93UD-662
93Ultra-477
94D-265
94F-550
94L-219
94T-373
94T/Gold-373
Scott, Tony
76SSPC-339
78T-352
79T-143
80OPC-17
80T-33
81Coke
81D-191
81F-531
81T-165
81T/St-223
81T/Tr-828
82D-522
82F-231
82F/St-46
82T-698
83D-293
83F-465
83T-507
84D-527
84F-241
84Mother/Ast-20
84Nes/792-292
84T-292
85OPC-367
85T-733
89T/SenLg-91
90EliteSenLg-104
91Batavia/ProC-3502CO
91Pac/SenLg-121
92Spartan/ClBest-23CO
92Spartan/ProC-1282CO
Scott, Tyrone
90AubAs/Best-19
90AubAs/ProC-3402
91BurlAs/ClBest-8
91BurlAs/ProC-2799
92BurlAs/ClBest-9
92BurlAs/ProC-546
Scranton, Jim
84Omaha-27
85Omaha-17
86Omaha/ProC-21
86Omaha/TCMA-7
Scripture, Billy
78Charl
Scrivener, Churck
(Chuck)
77T-173
78T-94
79Syrac/Team-3
Scruggs, Ron
86AppFx-21
87Penin-25
Scruggs, Tony
88CharlR/Star-22
89Tulsa/GS-24
89Tulsa/Team-23
90A&AASingle/ProC-98
90Foil/Best-19
90Gaston/Best-1
90Gaston/ProC-2535
90Gaston/Star-22
90ProC/Singl-654
90SALAS/Star-22
90Star/ISingl-98
91AAA/LineD-304
91B-289
91OkCty/LineD-304
92OkCty/ProC-1928
92OkCty/SB-321
92T/91Debut-161
93Rang/Keeb-322
Scudder, Bill
83VeroB-10
85Cram/PCL-166
Scudder, Scott
87Cedar-7
88Cedar/ProC-1157
88MidwLAS/GS-14
89F/Up-U87
89Nashvl/CMC-8
89Nashvl/ProC-1293
89Nashvl/Team-22
89S/Tr-99
90AAASingl/ProC-544
90B-46
90CedarDG/Best-15
90D-435
90F-434
90F/Can-434
90HotRook/St-39
90Leaf-433
90Nashvl/CMC-10
90Nashvl/ProC-232
90OPC-553
90ProC/Singl-135
90S-518
90S/100Ris-65
90T-553

90T/89Debut-113
90UD-164
91D-265
91F-81
91Kahn/Reds-47
91Leaf-183
91OPC-713
91S-642
91T-713
91UD-615
92B-571
92Classic/Game200-180
92D-306
92F-422
92Indian/McDon-25
92L-429
92L/BlkGold-429
92OPC-48
92OPC/Premier-181
92Pinn-480
92S-209
92S/RookTr-67T
92StCl-644
92T-48
92T/Gold-48
92T/GoldWin-48
92UD-485
92UD-787
92Ultra-356
93D-653
93F-601
93Indian/WUAB-27
93Pac/Spanish-101
93StCl-243
93StCl/1stDay-243
93T-248
93T/Gold-248
93UD-208
93Ultra-190

Scull, Angel
53Briggs
54T-204
94T/Arc54-204

Scully, Vin
60Union/Dodg-22M
61Union/Dodg-24M
71Ticket/Dodg-20ANN

Scurry, Rod
76Shrev
78Colum
79Portl-22
81F-380
81T-194
82D-185
82F-497
82T-207
83D-376
83F-322
83T-537
84D-235
84F-264
84Nes/792-69
84T-69
85D-142
85F-476
85T-641
86T-449
87D-374
87F-113
87OPC-393
87T-665
88Calgary/CMC-10
88Calgary/ProC-779
89S-516
89UD-208
92Yank/WIZ80-175

Seabaugh
E254

Seal, Mike
88OK-23
89Myrtle/ProC-1461

Sealer, Joel
88NE-15

Seals, Joey
89GreatF-15
91GreatF/SportP-10

Sealy, Randy
75Shrev/TCMA-19
76Shrev
80WHave-23

Sealy, Scot
92Gaston/ProC-2256
93ClBest/MLG-206

Seaman, Kim
77Wausau
81Hawaii-22
81Hawaii/TCMA-16
82Hawaii-22
82Wichita-17

Seamon, Jonathan
86Lipscomb-19

Seanez, Rudy
87Watlo-18
88Watlo/ProC-692
89Kinston/Star-23
90A&AASingle/ProC-10
90Canton/Best-24
90Canton/ProC-1293
90F-640R
90F/Can-640
90Foil/Best-164
90Leaf-417
90ProC/Singl-832
90T/89Debut-114
91AAA/LineD-89
91ColoSp/LineD-89
91ColoSp/ProC-2181
91D-218
91F-376
91UD-358
92D-552
92F-122
92S-696
92SanAn/SB-575
92StCl-713
93D-758
93OPC-391
93StCl/Rockie-16
93T-676
93T/Gold-676

Searage, Ray
77StPete
79ArkTr-20
81Tidew-24
82Charl-10
82T-478
84Cram/PCL-30
85F-595
85Pol/Brew-41
86D-536
86F-502
86T-642
86Vanco-23
87Coke/WS-21
87F-506
87T-149
88Albuq/CMC-4
88Albuq/ProC-262
88D-429
88F-409
88T-788
89F/Up-94
89Mother/Dodg-22
89Pol/Dodg-30
90D-649
90F-408
90F/Can-408
90Mother/Dodg-22
90OPC-84
90Pol/Dodg-59
90T-84
90Target-1066
91AAA/LineD-496
91F-220
91ScranWB/LineD-496
91ScranWB/ProC-2538
91WIZMets-355
92Edmon/ProC-3539

Search, Michael
90Boise/ProC-3316
90PalmSp/Cal-223
90PalmSp/ProC-2576

Searcy, Steve
86GlenF-21
87Toledo-2
87Toledo/TCMA-16
88Toledo/CMC-4
88Toledo/ProC-609
88TripleA/ASCMC-25
89B-95
89Classic-78
89D-29RR
89F-145
89S-627RP
89S/HotRook-47
89S/YS/II-27
89T-167FS
89UD/Ext-764
90AAAGame/ProC-20
90AAASingl/ProC-379
90F-615
90F/Can-615
90HotRook/St-40
90OPC-487
90ProC/Singl-387
90S/100Ris-97
90T-487
90Toledo/CMC-10
90Toledo/ProC-149
90UD-575
91CokeK/Tiger-49
91D-549
91Leaf-187
91OPC-369
91S-649
91S/100RisSt-76
91StCl-352
91T-369
91UD-338
92F-545
92OPC-599
92Phill/Med-29
92S-698
92ScranWB/ProC-2445
92StCl-648
92T-599
92T/Gold-599
92T/GoldWin-599
92USPlayC/Tiger-3D
92USPlayC/Tiger-4H

Sears, Allen
83Durham-23

Sears, Jimmy
91Boise/ClBest-20
91Boise/ProC-3891

Sears, Ken
44Yank/St-24

Sears, Mike
86FSLAS-44TR
86WinHaven-22TR
87WinHaven-19

Seaton, Billy
91GulfCR/SportP-13

Seaton, Tom
14CJ-100
15CJ-100
D329-159
D350/2-161
M101/4-159
M101/5-161

Seats, Dean
81Cedar-13

Seats, Tom
49B/PCL-35
90Target-715

Seaver, Tom
67T-581R
68OPC-45
68T-45
68T/ActionSt-14CM
68T/ActionSt-3CM
69MB-250
69MLB/St-170
69NTF
69T-480
69T/S-52
69T/St-68
69T/decal
69Trans-48
70K-7
70MB-26
70MLB/St-82
70OPC-195NLCS
70OPC-300
70OPC-69LL
70T-195NLCS
70T-300
70T-69LL
70T/S-5
70T/SO
70T/Super-5
70Trans-4
70Trans/M-21
71Bz/Test-35
71K-2
71MD
71MLB/St-164
71MLB/St-574
71OPC-160
71OPC-68LL
71OPC-72LL
71T-160
71T-68LL
71T-72LL
71T/Coins-127
71T/S-53
71T/Super-53
71T/tatt-14
71T/tatt-14a
72K-1
72MB-312
72OPC-347KP
72OPC-445
72OPC-446IA
72OPC-91LL
72OPC-93LL
72OPC-95LL
72ProStars/PostC-22
72T-347KP
72T-445
72T-446IA
72T-91LL
72T-93LL
72T-95LL
72T/Post-13
73K-46
73OPC-350
73T-350
73T/Comics-19
73T/Lids-48
73T/PinUps-19
74K-52
74Laugh/ASG-68
74OPC-206LL
74OPC-207LL
74OPC-80
74T-206LL
74T-207LL
74T-80
74T/DE-9
74T/Puzzles-10
74T/St-70
75Ho-75
75OPC-370
75SSPC/42-15
75SSPC/Puzzle-23
75SSPC/Sam-6
75T-370
75T/M-370
76Crane-55
76Ho-35
76Ho/Twink-35
76K-32
76MSA/Disc
76OPC-199LL
76OPC-201LL
76OPC-203LL
76OPC-5RB
76OPC-600
76SSPC-551
76SSPC/MetsY-M12
76T-199LL
76T-201LL
76T-203LL
76T-5RB
76T-600
77BurgChef-142
77Ho-7
77Ho/Twink-7
77OPC-205
77OPC-6LL
77Pep-67
77T-150
77T-6LL
77T/CS-42
77T/ClothSt-42
78Ho-149
78K-27
78OPC-120
78Pep-23
78SSPC/270-116
78T-450
78Tastee/Discs-10
78Wiffle/Discs-68
79Ho-65
79K-29
79OPC-44DP
79T-100
79T/Comics-22
80BK/PHR-10
80K-49
80OPC-260
80Perez/HOF-215
80T-500
80T/S-15
80T/Super-15
81Coke
81D-422
81D-425
81F-200
81F/St-49
81K-38
81MSA/Disc-29
81OPC-220
81PermaGr/CC-11
81T-220
81T/HT
81T/Nat/Super-14
81T/So-107
81T/St-165
82Coke/Red
82D-148
82D-16DK
82D-628M
82F-634M
82F-645M
82F-82
82F/St-11
82K-8
82OPC-30
82OPC-31IA
82OPC-346AS
82PermaGr/CC-2
82Sqt-21
82T-165LL
82T-30
82T-31IA
82T-346AS
82T-756TL
82T/St-36
82T/St-9
83D-122
83F-601
83F/St-10M
83F/St-8M
83OPC-354SV
83OPC-52
83OPC/St-233
83T-580
83T-581SV
83T/Fold-1M
83T/St-233
83T/Tr-101T
84D-116
84D/AAS-53
84D/Champs-40
84F-595
84F/X-U106
84Nes/792-246TL
84Nes/792-706LL
84Nes/792-707LL
84Nes/792-708LL
84Nes/792-740
84OPC-261
84Ralston-8
84Seven-8E
84T-246TL
84T-706LL
84T-707LL
84T-708LL
84T-740
84T/Cereal-8
84T/RD-17M
84T/St-106
84T/Tr-108T
84TrueVal/WS-27
85Coke/WS-41
85D-424
85D/HL-1
85D/HL-30
85Drake-41
85F-526
85F/LimEd-34
85F/St-68SA
85F/St-69
85F/St-70
85F/St-71
85F/St-72
85F/St-73
85FunFoodPin-15
85Leaf-101
85OPC-1
85Seven-12G
85Sportflic/Test-45
85T-670
85T/3D-30
85T/RD-28M
85T/St-235

85T/Super-31
85ThomMc/Discs-19
86Coke/WS-41
86D-609
86F-216
86F-630M
86F/HOF-3
86F/LL-40
86F/Mini-46
86F/Slug-34
86F/St-109
86Jay's-16
86Leaf-234
86OPC-390
86Quaker-32
86Seven/Coin-C8M
86Seven/Coin-E8M
86Seven/Coin-S8M
86Seven/Coin-W8M
86Sf-130M
86Sf-134M
86Sf-142M
86Sf-182M
86Sf-25
86Sf-56M
86Sf-67M
86Sf-70M
86Sf/Dec-52
86Sf/Rook-47M
86T-390
86T-402TBC
86T/Gloss60-22
86T/St-10
86T/St-287
86T/Super-50
86T/Tatt-10M
86T/Tr-101T
86TrueVal-12
87D-375
87F-45
87KMart-21
87Leaf-263
87OPC-49
87Sf-28
87T-425
87T/St-246
88AlaskaAS60/Team-3
89T/LJN-57
90BBWit-46
90HOF/St-76
90MSA/AGFA-14
90Pac/Legend-60
90Smok/SoCal-11
90Swell/Great-1
91Swell/Great-107
91WIZMets-356
92FrRow/ATGHolo-3
92K/CornAS-5
92K/FrAS-9
92Kenner/Fig-39
92Pac/S-82
92Pac/S-Set
92Pac/SIns6-Set
93AP/ASG-129
93AP/ASG24K-63G
93AP/SeavPr-TS1
93AP/SeavPr-TS2
93AP/SeavPr-TS3
93AP/SeavPr-TS4
93AP/SeavPr-TS5
93Pac/Ryan27-241M
93YooHoo-18
94Mets/69-3
94Mets/69-42
94Mets/69-52
94Mets/69Pr-1

Seay, Dick
78Laugh/Black-14

Seay, Mark
87SanJose-16

Sebach, Kyle
92Boise/ProC-3626
92QuadC/ClBest-20
92QuadC/ProC-809

Sebra, Bob
83TriCit-1
85OKCty-19
86Indianap-23
87D-468
87Expo/PostC-5
87F-331
87Leaf-213
87OPC-314
87T-479
88AAA/ProC-17
88D-458
88F-195
88Indianap/CMC-3
88Indianap/ProC-511
88OPC-93
88S-337
88T-93
89ScranWB/CMC-4
89ScranWB/ProC-718
90AAASingl/ProC-545
90Brewer/MillB-22
90Nashvl/CMC-11
90Nashvl/ProC-233
90ProC/Singl-136
90TulsaDG/Best-8
92Iowa/ProC-4051
92OkCty/SB-322
92Sky/AAASingl-148
93Rang/Keeb-323

Sebring, James
90Target-716
T204

Secory, Frank
55B-286UMP

Secrest, Charlie
59T-140

Secrist, Don
69T-654R

Seda, Israel
91Penin/ClBest-22
91Penin/ProC-387

Sedar, Ed
83AppFx/Frit-18
86Penin-24
87DayBe-19
91Pocatel/ProC-3802CO
91Pocatel/SportP-28CO

See, Larry
82VeroB-20
84Cram/PCL-162
86Albuq-22
87Albuq/Pol-21
89Toledo/CMC-14
89Toledo/ProC-784
90Target-717
93Rang/Keeb-324

Seeburger, John
88Oneonta/ProC-2050
89FtLaud/Star-25

Seeds, Robert Ira
32Orbit/un-52
33Exh/4-10
39PlayBall-32
40PlayBall-91
R305
R314/Can
V355-27

Seefried, Tate
90Tampa/DIMD-22
91Oneonta/ProC-4163
92ClBest-307
92Greens/ClBest-25
92Greens/ProC-789
94B-661
94FExcel-114

Seeger, Mark
81AppFx-24

Seegers, Pat
78Newar
79BurlB-3

Seelbach, Christopher
92ClBest-252
92Macon/ClBest-22
92Macon/ProC-268
92StCl/Dome-167
92UD/ML-94
93Durham/Team-18

Seelbach, Chuck
73OPC-51
73T-51
74OPC-292
74T-292

Seerey, James Pat
48L-73
94TedW-152

Seery, John Emmett
N172
N284
WG1-35

Sefly, Joel
90Visalia/Cal-82TR
91Visalia/ClBest-27TR

Segelke, Herman
82Iowa-23
83Phoenix/BHN-13
84Cram/PCL-10

Segrist, Kal
58Union
91Crown/Orio-411

Segui, Daniel
89Pittsfld/Star-25
89Star/IISingl-166
90Visalia/Cal-77
90Visalia/ProC-2164

Segui, David
88Hagers/Star-19
89Freder/Star-21
90AAAGame/ProC-54
90B-251A
90B-251B
90F/Up-U69
90HagersDG/Best-26
90Rochester/L&U-2
90S/Tr-95T
90UD/Ext-773
91AAA/LineD-466
91B-102
91Classic/I-15
91Crown/Orio-412
91D-730
91F-492
91Leaf/Stud-10
91MajorLg/Pins-30
91OPC-724
91RochR/LineD-466
91RochR/ProC-1910
91S-362RP
91S/100RisSt-61
91S/Rook40-31
91Seven/3DCoin-15A
91StCl-50
91T-724
91T/90Debut-140
91UD-342
91Ultra-25
92D-321
92F-27
92OPC-447
92OPC/Premier-153
92Pinn-185
92ProC/Tomorrow-5
92S-554
92S/100RisSt-33
92StCl-783
92T-447
92T/Gold-447
92T/GoldWin-447
92UD-316
92Ultra-308
93D-397
93F-175
93L-306
93Pac/Spanish-25
93Pinn-325
93S-610
93StCl-479
93StCl/1stDay-479
93T-82
93T/Gold-82
93ToysRUs-45
93TripleP-12
93UD-792
93UD/SP-162
93Ultra-146
94D-624
94F-20
94L-352
94Pac/Cr-45
94Panini-24
94Pinn-131
94Pinn/Artist-131
94Pinn/Museum-131
94S-361
94StCl-95
94StCl/1stDay-95
94StCl/Gold-95
94StCl/Team-285
94T-571
94T/Finest-103
94T/FinestRef-103
94T/Gold-571
94UD-421
94UD/CollC-254
94UD/CollC/Gold-254
94UD/CollC/Silv-254
94Ultra-534

Segui, Diego
61Union
63T-157
64T-508
64T/Coins-24
65OPC-197
65T-197
65T/E-24
65T/trans-68
66T-309
68T-517
69T-511
70OPC-2
70T-2
71MLB/St-526
71OPC-215
71OPC-67LL
71T-215
71T-67LL
72T-735
73OPC-383
73T-383
74OPC-151
74T-151
74T/Tr-151T
75OPC-232
75T-232
75T/M-232
76SSPC-423
77T-653
87Pocatel/Bon-30CO
88Pocatel/ProC-2100
89Everett/Star-31
90Everett/ProC-3146CO
90Pac/Legend-104

Segura, Jose
85Kingst-10
86Knoxvl-19
87Syrac-9
87Syrac/TCMA-7
88Coke/WS-27
88F/Up-U20
89Vanco/CMC-6
89Vanco/ProC-591
90AAASingl/ProC-168
90ProC/Singl-639
90Vanco/CMC-12
90Vanco/ProC-490
91AAA/LineD-394
91Phoenix/LineD-394
91Phoenix/ProC-66
92Nashvl/SB-292
92S-278
93LimeR/Winter-69

Sehorn, Jason
90Hunting/ProC-3302

Seibert, Gib
85Cram/PCL-27
87Maine-15
87Maine/TCMA-16

Seibert, Kurt
80Toledo-20
81Toledo-14

Seibert, Mal
90Fayette/ProC-2406

Seibert, Rick
89Penin/Star-22

Seibold, Harry
(Socks)
33DH-38
93Conlon-975
R316

Seidel, Dick
83Greens-12

Seidensticker, Andy
88Visalia/Cal-172
88Visalia/ProC-106

Seidholz, Don
78Knoxvl
79Knoxvl/TCMA-9

Seifert, Keith
87Watlo-21
88Watlo/ProC-678
90Tampa/DIMD-23
91Greens/ProC-3059

Seiler, Keith
92PrWill/ClBest-20
92PrWill/ProC-149

Seilheimer, Rick
80GlenF/B-7
80GlenF/C-8
81GlenF-9
82Edmon-21
85BuffB-5
86BirmB/Team-14

Seirra, Ernie
89SanJose/Best-30

Seitz, Charles
T206

Seitz, David
86Sumter/ProC-25

Seitzer, Brad
91Bluefld/ClBest-8
91Bluefld/ProC-4137
91Kane/Team-19
92ClBest-146
92Freder/ClBest-11
92Freder/ProC-1815

Seitzer, Kevin
83Butte-20
85FtMyr-9
86Omaha/ProC-22
86Omaha/TCMA-3
87Classic/Up-139
87D/HL-26
87D/HL-47
87D/OD-207
87D/Rook-15
87F-652R
87F/Slug-39
87F/Up-U108
87Sf-158R
87Sf/Rook-20
87Sf/TPrev-13M
87T/Tr-111T
88Classic/Blue-218
88Classic/Red-159
88D-280
88D-BC17
88D/AS-27
88D/Best-175
88F-270
88F/AwardWin-37
88F/BB/AS-38
88F/BB/MVP-33
88F/Excit-36
88F/Hottest-36
88F/LL-37
88F/Mini-27
88F/RecSet-37
88F/SS-35
88F/Slug-38
88F/St-33
88F/TL-36
88F/WaxBox-C12
88KMart-27
88KennerFig-102
88Leaf-105
88MSA/Disc-8
88OPC-275
88Panini/St-108
88Panini/St-436
88S-6
88S/YS/I-10
88Sf-17
88Sf/Gamewin-13
88Smok/Royals-21
88T-275
88T/Big-115
88T/Gloss60-9
88T/JumboR-9
88T/Mini-15
88T/Revco-22
88T/RiteAid-19
88T/St-261
88T/St-306
88T/UK-69
88ToysRUs-27
89B-123
89Cadaco-52
89Classic-65
89D-10DK
89D-238
89D/Best-207
89D/DKsuper-10DK
89F-292
89F/Excit-36
89F/Heroes-36
89F/WaxBox-C22
89Holsum/Discs-9
89KennerFig-127
89Nissen-9
89OPC-58
89Panini/St-357
89RedFoley/St-107
89S-55
89S/HotStar-17

89Sf-55
89T-670
89T/Big-313
89T/LJN-151
89T/St-264
89Tastee/Discs-2
89UD-510
90B-380
90D-85
90D/BestAL-91
90F-117
90F/Can-117
90Leaf-230
90MLBPA/Pins-102
90OPC-435
90Panini/St-86
90PublInt/St-355
90RedFoley/St-86
90S-199
90S/100St-88
90Sf-46
90T-435
90T/Big-76
90T/Mini-18
90T/St-267
90UD-363
91B-305
91Classic/200-40
91D-73
91F-569
91KingB/Discs-2
91Leaf-133
91Leaf/StudPrev-5
91OPC-695
91Panini/FrSt-278
91Panini/St-227
91Pol/Royal-19
91S-279
91S/100SS-97
91StCl-88
91T-695
91UD-433
91Ultra-155
92B-126
92D-577
92D/Up-U15
92F-168
92F/Up-38
92L-399
92L/BlkGold-399
92OPC-577
92OPC/Premier-27
92Pinn-11
92Pol/Brew-22
92Pol/Royal-24
92S-310
92S/RookTr-2T
92StCl-285
92StCl-820
92T-577
92T/Gold-577
92T/GoldWin-577
92T/Tr-103T
92T/TrGold-103T
92UD-327
92UD-783
92Ultra-389
93B-597
93D-603
93F-256
93F/Final-262
93L-353
93Mother/A's-21
93OPC-312
93OPC/Premier-121
93Pac/Spanish-164
93Panini-40
93Pinn-117
93S-571
93Select-87
93StCl-57
93StCl-657
93StCl/1stDay-57
93StCl/1stDay-657
93StCl/A's-5
93Studio-169
93T-44
93T/Gold-44
93UD-295
93UD-616
93Ultra-612
94D-261
94F-190
94Finest-314
94Flair-70
94L-339
94Pac/Cr-341
94Panini-86
94Pol/Brew-24
94S-519
94StCl-90
94StCl/1stDay-90
94StCl/Gold-90
94Studio-47
94T-411
94T/Gold-411
94UD-378
94Ultra-378
Seja, Aaron
91Fayette/ProC-1184
91Niagara/ClBest-7
91Niagara/ProC-3648
Selak, Ron**
78Spring/Wiener-21
Selanne, Teemu
92StCl/MemberIV*-6
92StCl/MemberIV*-7
Selbach, Albert
(Kip)
E107
Selby
E254
Selby, Bill
92Elmira/ClBest-19
92Elmira/ProC-1393
92FrRow/DP-49
Sele, Aaron
91ClBest/Singl-437
91Classic/DP-19
91FrRow/DP-2
92B-311
92ClBest-175
92ClBest/BBonusC-11
92ClBest/RBonus-BC11
92LynchRS/ClBest-16
92LynchRS/ProC-2907
92OPC-504
92S-809Draft
92StCl/Dome-168
92T-504DP
92T/Gold-504
92T/GoldWin-504
92UD/ML-291
92UD/POY-PY20
93B-255
93ClBest/Fisher-8
93ClBest/MLG-23
93F/Final-178
93FExcel/ML-138
93FExcel/MLAS-7
93Flair/Wave-16
93L-518
93Pawtu/Ball-21
93Select/RookTr-86T
93T/Tr-3T
93UD/SP-205
94B-643
94D-303
94F-43
94F/RookSen-18
94Flair-15
94L-199
94OPC-89
94OPC/DiamD-17
94Pac/Cr-66
94Pinn-95
94Pinn/Artist-95
94Pinn/Museum-95
94Pinn/New-5
94S-561
94Sf/2000-37
94StCl-179
94StCl/1stDay-179
94StCl/Gold-179
94Studio-164
94T-445
94T/Finest-6
94T/FinestRef-6
94T/Gold-445
94TripleP-207
94UD-45FUT
94UD-80
94UD/CollC-255
94UD/CollC/Gold-255
94UD/CollC/Silv-255
94UD/ElecD-45FUT
94UD/ElecD-80
94UD/SP-156
94Ultra-18
94Ultra/RisSt-12
94Ultra/Second-5
Selig, Kevin
76AppFx
Selkirk, George
34DS-88
37OPC-108
38ONG/Pin-27
39PlayBall-25
40PlayBall-8
92Conlon/Sport-388
92Yank/WIZAS-76
V300
V355-11
Sellas, Marcelino
88CapeCod/Sum-91
Selleck, Tom
92UD-SP4
Sellers, Jeff
86D/Rook-29
86Pawtu-21
87D-544
87F-46
87Leaf-158
87T-12
88D-585
88D/RedSox/Bk-585
88F-366
88S-541
88T-653
89B-299
89D-517
89Nashvl/ProC-1270
89S-491
89T-544
92Tulsa/ProC-2694
Sellers, Rick
89Niagara/Pucko-21
90Fayette/ProC-2412
91Lakeland/ClBest-16
92London/ProC-637
92London/SB-418
Sellick, John
88SALAS/GS-25
88Savan/ProC-347
89Spring/Best-14
90StPete/Star-22
91AA/LineD-44
91ArkTr/LineD-44
91ArkTr/ProC-1296
92ArkTr/ProC-1140
92ArkTr/SB-45
92Sky/AASingl-19
Sellner, Scott
88Billings/ProC-1807
89Cedar/Best-17
89Cedar/ProC-925
89Cedar/Star-18
90Chatt/GS-27
91AA/LineD-169
91Chatt/LineD-169
91Chatt/ProC-1968
Sells, Dave
74OPC-37
74T-37
90Target-718
Sells, George
88CapeCod/Sum-117
90Hamil/Best-9
90Hamil/Star-23
91StPete/ProC-2275
Selma, Dick
66OPC-67R
66T-67R
67T-386
68T-556
69MLB/St-195
69OPC-197
69T-197
69T/4in1-6M
69T/S-62
69T/St-98
69T/decal
70MLB/St-23
70OPC-24
70T-24
71K-21
71MLB/St-187
71OPC-705
71Phill/Arco-10
71T-705
72T-726
73OPC-632
73T-632
75Albuq/Caruso-11
91WIZMets-357
Seltzer, Randy
76AppFx
77AppFx
Semall, Paul
79Colum-3
80Wichita-15
83OKCty-16
84Cram/PCL-125
85Cram/PCL-232
Sember, Mike
79Syrac/TCMA-10
79Syrac/Team-10
Sembera, Carroll
66T-539R
67OPC-136
67T-136
68T-207
69T-351
Sementelli, Chris
89Spartan/ProC-1049
Semerano, Bob
77Charl
Seminara, Frank
88Oneonta/ProC-2071
89Oneonta/ProC-2121
89PrWill/Star-18
90CLAS/CL-14
90PrWill/Team-23
91AA/LineD-618
91ClBest/Singl-382
91Wichita/LineD-618
91Wichita/ProC-2598
91Wichita/Rock-9
92B-561
92D-10RR
92D/RookPhen-BC17
92F/Up-124
92LasVegas/SB-240
92Pinn/Rook-25
92Pol/Padre-17
92ProC/Tomorrow-334
92S/RookTr-97T
92Sky/AAASingl-116
92Smok/Padre-29
92T/Tr-104T
92T/TrGold-104T
93B-222
93Classic/Gamel-83
93D-550
93F-146
93L-64
93Mother/Padre-16
93OPC-282
93Pac/Spanish-601
93Pinn-561
93S-342
93Select-305
93StCl-438
93StCl/1stDay-438
93T-247
93T/Gold-247
93ToysRUs-57
93UD-307
93USPlayC/Rook-10D
93Ultra-121
94F-673
94Pac/Cr-533
94Ultra-283
Seminick, Andy
45Playball-43
49B-30
49Eureka-146
49Lummis
49Royal-7
50B-121
51B-51
51BR-C7
51T/RB-45
52Dix
52Royal
52T-297
53B/BW-7
53Dix
53T-153
54B-172
55B-93
56T-296
91T/Arc53-153
Exh47
PM10/Sm-176
Semore, Enos
88OK-6CO
89OK-1CO
Semprini, John
82Jacks-9
84Chatt-12
Semproch, Roman
58T-474
59T-197
60T-286
61T-174
61T/St-206
Sempsrott, Ed
76Watlo
77DaytB
Sena, Sean
90Yakima/Team-22
Seninger, Glenn
87SLCity/Taco-14PR
Senkowitz, Mark
92Elmira/ClBest-17
92Elmira/ProC-1385
Senn, Terry
75Tidew/Team-18
Senne, Michael
86AZ/Pol-13
87StPete-9
88ArkTr/GS-25
89Shrev/ProC-1840
Senne, Tim
86Visalia-20
87Visalia-14
Senteney, Steve
82Syrac-8
82Syrac/Team-20
83D-52
83Tidew-10
Sentlinger, Rick
77QuadC
Seoane, Manuel
(Manny)
76OkCty/Team-22
80Wichita-21
81Evansvl-7
Seoane, Mitch
84Greens-25
86PalmSp/Smok-24
87MidldA-20
89QuadC/Best-25
89QuadC/GS-2
90QuadC/GS-3CO
91QuadC/ClBest-27MG
91QuadC/ProC-2645MG
92QuadC/ClBest-27MG
92QuadC/ProC-826MG
Sepanek, Rob
86FtLaud-20
87PrWill-10
88Albany/ProC-1332
89Albany/Best-9
89Albany/ProC-330
89Albany/Star-17
89EastLgAS/ProC-8
90AAASingl/ProC-334
90AlbanyDG/Best-29
90ColClip/CMC-21
90ColClip/ProC-684
90Colum/Pol-22
90ProC/Singl-221
Sepeda, Jamie
92Batavia/ClBest-1
92Batavia/ProC-3264
93ClBest/MLG-152
Sepela, Thom
86Elmira-21
87Elmira/Black-20
87Elmira/Red-20
Seppala, L.
33SK*-48
Septimo, Felix
90MedHat/Best-11
91StCath/ProC-3409
Sepulveda, Jorge
86VeroB-22
Serad, William
N172
Serafini, Dan
92ClBest/BBonusC-28
92ClBest/Up-411
92Classic/DP-20
92UD/ML-104
93B-397
93ClBest/MLG-114

93Pinn-465DP
93S-497DP
93Select-352DP
93StCl/MurphyS-43
93T-307
93T/Gold-307
94ClBest/Gold-67
94FExcel-98
Serafini, Rudy
83QuadC-14
Serbalik, Mike
92Yakima/ProC-3460
Serbin, Scott
90Saraso/Star-30BB
Serena, Bill
50B-230
51B-246
52T-325
53B/Col-122
54B-93
55B-233
Serna, Joe
93Welland/ClBest-26
Serna, Paul
81LynnS-18
82D-567
83Chatt-2
83T-492
84Chatt-13
85Cram/PCL-79
86Wausau-23
Serna, Ramon
87ElPaso-25
88ElPaso/Best-7
Serra, Armando
88StCath/ProC-2037
Serra, Jose
92Bluefld/ClBest-8
92Bluefld/ProC-2369
Serrano, Andy
79Elmira-17
Serrano, Marty
77DaytB
Serritella, John
83Butte-10
83CharR-23
Serum, Gary
78Twin/FriszP-18
79T-627
79Twin/FriszP-25
80T-61
80Toledo-5
82OrlanTw/B-23
Servais, Scott
87PanAm/USAB-3
87PanAm/USAR-3
88T/Tr-106TOLY
89Osceola/Star-20
89Star/Wax-17
89T/Big-291
90AAASingl/ProC-196
90ProC/Singl-623
90TeamUSA/87-3
90Tucson/CMC-21
90Tucson/ProC-206
91AAA/LineD-618
91Tucson/LineD-618
91Tucson/ProC-2216
91UD/FinalEd-68F
92B-463
92D-763
92F-444
92L-121
92L/BlkGold-121
92Mother/Ast-17
92OPC-437
92Pinn-255
92S-816
92S/Rook-36
92StCl-509
92T-437
92T/91Debut-162
92T/Gold-437
92T/GoldWin-437
92UD-561
92Ultra-496
93D-108
93F-442
93L-33
93Mother/Ast-6
93OPC-339
93Pac/Spanish-480
93StCl-363
93StCl/1stDay-363
93StCl/Ast-13
93T-36
93T/Gold-36
93UD-613
93USPlayC/Rook-8C
93Ultra-396
94D-381
94F-499
94Flair-175
94L-332
94Pac/Cr-274
94Pinn-134
94Pinn/Artist-134
94Pinn/Museum-134
94S-257
94S/GoldR-257
94StCl-150
94StCl/1stDay-150
94StCl/Gold-150
94T-674
94T/Finest-135
94T/FinestRef-135
94T/Gold-674
94UD-404
94UD/CollC-256
94UD/CollC/Gold-256
94UD/CollC/Silv-256
94Ultra-209
Servello, Dan
91Eugene/ClBest-12
91Eugene/ProC-3740
92AppFox/ClBest-20
Service, Scott
88Reading/ProC-868
89F-653R
89Reading/Best-6
89Reading/ProC-657
89Reading/Star-23
90AAASingl/ProC-302
90B-143
90ProC/Singl-234
90ScranWB/CMC-8
90ScranWB/ProC-600
90UD-35
91AAA/LineD-193
91Indianap/LineD-193
91Indianap/ProC-461
92Indianap/SB-193
94F-428
94T-306
94T/Gold-306
Servoss, Bob
76Wmsprt
Sevcik, John
65T-597
Severeid, Henry
21Exh-155
25Exh-116
28Exh/PCL-24
93Conlon-855
D327
D328-155
E120
E121/80
E122
E135-155
T207
V100
V61-25
W572
W573
W575
Severinsen, Al
70OPC-477R
70T-477R
71MLB/St-238
71OPC-747R
71T-747R
72OPC-274
72T-274
72T/Cloth-28
91Crown/Orio-413
Severns, Bill
77Holyo
78Spokane/Cramer-7
78Spokane/Team-7
79Vanco-21
80Vanco-8
Severson, Rich
71MLB/St-430
71OPC-103
71T-103
Sewell, Joe
91AubAS/ClBest-9
91AubAS/ProC-4273
92BurlAs/ClBest-7
92BurlAs/ProC-547
Sewell, Joseph W.
(Joe)
21Exh-156
25Exh-85
26Exh-84
28Exh-43
28Yueng-10
29Exh/4-21
32Orbit/num-116
33G-165
61F-76
72Laugh/GF-40
77Galasso-107
80Perez/HOF-163
80SSPC/HOF
81Conlon-53
82Ohio/HOF-42
89HOF/St-22
89Pac/Leg-125
90HOF/St-33
90Pac/Legend-67
90Perez/GreatMom-68
91Conlon/Sport-275
91Conlon/Sport-40
92Yank/WIZHOF-30
93Conlon-786
94Conlon-1175M
94Conlon-992
E120
E121/120
R316
V100
V117-12
V353-89
V61-12
W501-16
W502-10
W507-46
WG7-47
Sewell, Luke
29Exh/4-22
31Exh/4-22
33Exh/4-11
33G-114
33G-163
35BU-155
35G-1F
35G-2F
35G-6F
35G-7F
38Exh/4-10
39PlayBall-5
40PlayBall-48
49Eureka-94
51B-322MG
52B-94MG
61F-138
81Conlon-54
82Ohio/HOF-12
91Conlon/Sport-193
94Conlon-1175
94Conlon-996
E220
R312/M
R314
R316
V353-91
V355-62
W753
Sewell, T. Rip
43Playball-34
47TipTop
49B-234
49Eureka-172
89Pac/Leg-202
Exh47
Sexauer, Elmer
90Target-1067
Sexton, Jimmy
75Shrev/TCMA-20
76Shrev
77SanJose-22
79T-232
80T-11
80Tucson-2
81Tacom-15
82Tacom-38
83D-449
83F-533
83T-709
Sexton, Wayne
(Twink)
79Jacks-4
Seybold, Ralph
E107
E254
E91
Seyfried, Gordon
64T-499R
Seymour, Bob
82VeroB-25
Seymour, Harold
90LitSun-16
Seymour, James B.
(Cy)
C46-38
E104
E254
E91
M116
T201
T206
WG3-42
Seymour, Paul
81Batavia-29
Seymour, Steve
91Kingspt/ClBest-20
91Kingspt/ProC-3813
92Pittsfld/ClBest-7
92Pittsfld/ProC-3294
Seymour, Winston
89Salem/Star-20
89Welland/Pucko-21
90Augusta/ProC-2475
Sferrazza, Matt
86Jaxvl/TCMA-13
87GlenF-13
Sferrazza, Vince
86Fres/Smk-3TR
87Shrev-23
88Shrev/ProC-1284
89Spring/Best-26
Shaab, Doug
85Osceola/Team-12
Shabazz, Basil
91Johnson/ClBest-15
91Johnson/ProC-3990
92Johnson/ClBest-1
92Johnson/ProC-3131
92StCl/Dome-169
93B-108
93FExcel/ML-106
93StCl/Card-23
94B-292
Shabosky, Brian
88CapeCod-7
88CapeCod/Sum-186
Shackelford, Brett
93Lipscomb-25M
Shackle, Richard
89Johnson/Star-20
89Star/IISingl-167
90SALAS/Star-42
90Savan/ProC-2068
91FSLAS/ProC-FSL35
91StPete/ClBest-12
91StPete/ProC-2276
92ArkTr/ProC-1130
92ArkTr/SB-46
Shaddy, Chris
83Knoxvl-14
86Knoxvl-20
87Knoxvl-2
88Syrac/CMC-22
88Syrac/ProC-833
89Richm/Bob-24
89Richm/CMC-22
89Richm/Ko-10
89Richm/ProC-824
Shade, Mike
(Mick)
83Spring/Frit-11
85Louisvl-24
87Jaxvl-14
88Jaxvl/Best-2
88Jaxvl/ProC-985
Shade, Steve
86Erie-26
Shafer
11Helmar-136
Shafer, Bill**
92Pulaski/ClBest-24
92Pulaski/ProC-3176
Shafer, Frank T.
N172
Shafer, George
N172
Shaffer, Duane
78Knoxvl
79AppFx-21
80GlenF/C-24C
80GlenF/C-25C
Shaffer, Travis
92Kingspt/ClBest-4
92Kingspt/ProC-1530
Shambaugh, Mike
88Boise/ProC-1611
Shamblin, Bill
87Kinston-1
88Reno/Cal-272
Shamburg, Ken
90Freder/Team-17
90Rochester/L&U-31
91AA/LineD-246
91Hagers/LineD-246
91Hagers/ProC-2465
92RochR/ProC-1947
92RochR/SB-468
92Sky/AAASingl-212
Shamsky, Art
65T-398R
66OPC-119
66T-119
67CokeCap/Reds-17
67Kahn
67OPC-96
67T-96
68Kahn
68T-292
69MB-251
69T-221
69T/St-69
70OPC-137
70T-137
70Trans/M-23
71MLB/St-165
71OPC-445
71T-445
71T/Coins-43
72MB-313
72OPC-353
72T-353
72T/Cloth-29
78TCMA-278
91WIZMets-358
94Mets/69-11
Shanahan, Bill
92ColumMet/SAL/II-35MG
Shanahan, Chris
91Pittsfld/ClBest-16
91Pittsfld/ProC-3422
92StLucie/ClBest-4
92StLucie/ProC-1747
Shanahan, Paul
(Greg)
74Albuq/Team-18
74OPC-599R
74T-599R
75Albuq/Caruso-12
90Target-719
Shaner, Wally
94Conlon-1292
Shankman, Herbert
52Laval-9
Shanks, Howard S.
(Hank)
21Exh-157
93Conlon-729
D328-156
D329-160
D350/2-162
E120
E135-156
M101/4-160
M101/5-162
V100
Shanks, Willie
85Kingst-11
86Ventura-24
Shannon, Dan
89Hamil/Star-23
90Spartan/Best-21
90Spartan/ProC-2504
90Spartan/Star-19
Shannon, Daniel

N172
Shannon, Maurice J.
E220
Shannon, Mike
90LitSun-24
Shannon, Robert
86James-22
Shannon, Scott
91StCath/ClBest-24TR
92StCath/ClBest-29TR
93StCath/ClBest-29TR
Shannon, Thomas L.
88Rockford-32GM
89Rockford-32GM
Shannon, Thomas Michael
(Mike)
61Union
62Kahn/Atl
64T-262R
65OPC-43
65T-43
66T-293
67T-605
68T-445
69MB-252
69MLB/St-215
69OPC-110
69T-110
69T/4in1-18
69T/St-120
70MLB/St-143
70T-614
71MLB/St-283
71OPC-735
71T-735
72MB-314
78TCMA-275
92Card/McDon/Pac-31
Shannon, Wally
60L-93
Shannon, William P.
T206
Shannon, William
52Laval-63
Shantz, Bobby
50B-234
51B-227
52Dix-53
52RM-AL20
52StarCal/L-76C
52T-219
53B/Col-11
53NB
53RM-AL20
53T-225
54B-19
54T-21
55B-139M
55B-140
55Rodeo
56Rodeo
56T-261
57T-272
58T-289M
58T-419
59T-222
60T-315
61P-15
61T-379
61T-473MVP
61T/St-198
62Salada-188
62Shirriff-188
62T-177
62T/St-128
62T/bucks
63T-533
64PhilBull-21
64T-278
75OPC-190MVP
75T-190MVP
75T/M-190MVP
79TCMA-171
81TCMA-456
88Pac/Leg-61
89Smok/Ast-7
89Swell-131
90Pac/Legend-105
91Swell/Great-83
91T/Arc53-225
92AP/ASG-78
92Bz/Quadra-3M
92Yank/WIZ60-112
92Yank/WIZAS-77
93TWill-69
94T/Arc54-21
PM10/Sm-177
PM10/Sm-178
Rawl
Shantz, Wilmer
55B-139M
55B-175
55Rodeo
56Rodeo
92Yank/WIZ60-111
Shapley, Joe
90NE-21
Sharitt, Kelly
89Oneonta/ProC-2108
90Greens/Star-26TR
90SALAS/Star-25TR
Sharko, Gary
89Clinton/ProC-887
90SanJose/Best-19
90SanJose/Cal-46
90SanJose/ProC-2005
90SanJose/Star-20
91CalLgAS-35
91SanJose/ClBest-21
91SanJose/ProC-10
92ProC/Tomorrow-352
Sharon, Dick
74OPC-48
74T-48
75OPC-293
75T-293
75T/M-293
Sharp, Bill
74OPC-519
74T-519
75OPC-373
75T-373
75T/M-373
76A&P/Milw
76OPC-244
76SSPC-246
76T-244
77Spoka
Sharp, Gary
82BurlR/Frit-19
82BurlR/TCMA-9
Sharp, Mike
91Yakima/ClBest-26
91Yakima/ProC-4247
92AS/Cal-34
92Bakers/Cal-21
92ProC/Tomorrow-251
Sharpe, Bayard
C46-31
M116
T205
T206
Sharpe, Ken
91Parramatta/Fut-1CO
Sharperson, Mike
83Kinston/Team-24
85Syrac-19
86Syrac-22
87D-565
87D/OD-31
87Tor/Fire-27
88Albuq/CMC-16
88Albuq/ProC-253
88F-525
88Pol/Dodg-27M
89Albuq/CMC-14
89Albuq/ProC-59
89B-348
89F-72
89Pol/Dodg-17
89S-602
90D-603
90Leaf-490
90Mother/Dodg-20
90OPC-117
90Pol/Dodg-27
90T-117
90Target-720
91B-602
91D-168
91F-221
91Mother/Dodg-20
91OPC-53
91Pol/Dodg-27
91S-546
91StCl-541
91T-53
91UD-598
91Ultra-170
92D-526
92F/Up-93
92L-318
92L/BlkGold-318
92Mother/Dodg-25
92OPC-627
92Pinn-167
92Pol/Dodg-27
92S-592
92StCl-93
92Studio-49
92T-627
92T/Gold-627
92T/GoldWin-627
92Ultra-218
93D-166
93F-68
93Mother/Dodg-14
93OPC-346
93Pac/Spanish-154
93Panini-217
93Pinn-37
93Pol/Dodg-23
93S-429
93Select-157
93StCl-307
93StCl/1stDay-307
93StCl/Dodg-9
93StCl/MurphyS-164
93T-526
93T/Gold-526
93UD-316
93Ultra-404
94F-523
94S-287
94S/GoldR-287
Sharpnack, Bob
86Modesto-22
87Madis-25
88Huntsvl/BK-18
89Huntsvl/Best-11
Sharrott, George
90Target-1068
Sharsig, William J.
N172
Sharts, Scott
91Watertn/ClBest-22
91Watertn/ProC-3377
92Watertn/ClBest-4
92Watertn/ProC-3233
Sharts, Stephen
85Bend/Cram-22
87Clearw-16
88Reading/ProC-865
89Reading/Best-5
89Reading/ProC-651
90AAASingl/ProC-303
90ProC/Singl-235
90ScranWB/CMC-9
90ScranWB/ProC-601
Shaughnessy, Francis
(Shag)
R314/Can
T206
V355-78
Shaute, Joe
90Target-721
93Conlon-857
Shave, Jon
88MissSt-30
89MissSt-35
90Butte/SportP-26
90MissSt-38
91ClBest/Singl-380
91Gaston/ClBest-22
91Gaston/ProC-2699
92ClBest/Up-445
92Sky/AASingl-274
92Tulsa/ProC-2705
92Tulsa/SB-620
92UD/ML-312
93B-59
93ClBest/MLG-9
93F/Final-283
93FExcel/ML-236
93Rang/Keeb-433
93StCl-725
93StCl/1stDay-725
93T-451M
93T/Gold-451M
93T/Tr-78T
94Pac/Cr-629
94Pinn-422
94Pinn/RookTPinn-3
94StCl-199
94StCl/1stDay-199
94StCl/Gold-199
94StCl/Team-247
94T-775
94T/Gold-775
Shaver, Jeff
86Madis/Pol-18
88Tacoma/CMC-8
88Tacoma/ProC-619
89Tacoma/CMC-11
89Tacoma/ProC-1559
Shaw, Al
T206
Shaw, Bob
58T-206
59T-159
60L-83
60T-380
61P-23
61T-352
61T/St-127
62T-109
62T/St-56
63J-154
63P-154
63Salada-7
63T-255
63T-5LL
64T-328
65T-428
65T/E-57
66T-260
67CokeCap/YMet-25
67Kahn
67T-470
73OPC-646CO
73T-646C
91WIZMets-359
Shaw, Cedric
88Butte-9
89CharlR/Star-22
90A&AASingle/ProC-164
90Tulsa/ProC-1154
90Tulsa/Team-23
91AA/LineD-597
91Tulsa/LineD-597
91Tulsa/ProC-2773
91Tulsa/Team-29
92Sky/AASingl-275
92Tulsa/ProC-2695
92Tulsa/SB-621
Shaw, Don
67T-587R
68T-521
69OPC-183
69T-183
70OPC-476
70T-476
71OPC-654
71T-654
72OPC-479
72T-479
81TCMA-449M
88SanDiegoSt-16
89SanDiegoSt-17
91WIZMets-360
Shaw, Jeff
87Watlo-16
88Wmsprt/ProC-1309
89Canton/Best-3
89Canton/ProC-1298
89Canton/Star-19
90AAASingl/ProC-214
90B-329
90ColoSp/ProC-33
90D/Rook-53
91AAA/LineD-95
91ColoSp/LineD-95
91ColoSp/ProC-2182
91S-746RP
91T/90Debut-141
92B-410
92ColoSp/ProC-751
92ColoSp/SB-95
92D-595
92S-624
92Sky/AAASingl-41
92StCl-843
92UD-660
93F/Final-97
94F-551
94T-469
94T/Gold-469
Shaw, John W.
N172
Shaw, Kerry
88SLCity-17
89Salinas/Cal-144
89Salinas/ProC-1803
90SanJose/Best-2
90SanJose/Cal-29
90SanJose/ProC-2020
90SanJose/Star-21
Shaw, Kevin
88AppFx/ProC-140
89BBCity/Star-8
89Star/Wax-63
90BBCity/Star-22
91BBCity/ClBest-11
91BBCity/ProC-1398
91FSLAS/ProC-FSL3
92BBCity/ClBest-2
92BBCity/ProC-3847
Shaw, Malcolm
(Curtis)
89KS*-70
90SoOreg/Best-17
90SoOreg/ProC-3427
91Madison/ClBest-14
91Madison/ProC-2132
92AS/Cal-19
92B-174
92ClBest-190
92Modesto/ClBest-2
92Modesto/ProC-3898
93B-513
93ClBest/MLG-75
93FExcel/ML-218
94B-52
Shaw, Rick
82Amari-22
Shaw, Robert
C46-83
Shaw, Royal N.
T206
Shaw, Samuel E.
N172
Shaw, Scott
86FtLaud-21
87FtLaud-7
88Albany/ProC-1345
89Albany/Best-4
89Albany/ProC-317
89Albany/Star-18
Shaw, Shelby
92CharlR/ClBest-22
92CharlR/ProC-2226
Shaw, Theo
81CharR-8
84Omaha-17
85FtMyr-20
86Omaha/ProC-23
86Omaha/TCMA-19
87Memphis-15
87Memphis/Best-12
88Wmsprt/ProC-1318
89ColoSp/ProC-259
90Calgary/CMC-20
90ProC/Singl-447
Shawkey, J. Bob
15CJ-164
25Exh-102
26Exh-103
28LaPresse-1
61F-139
88Conlon/5-26
91Conlon/Sport-156
D327
D328-157
D329-161
D350/2-163
E120
E121/120
E121/80
E126-37
E135-157
E210-59
E220
M101/4-161
M101/5-163
R315-A32
R315-B32
V61-39
W501-31
W514-29
W515-9

W572
W573
W575
Shay, Dan
E91
Shea, Bill
90BBWit-27
Shea, Ed
87Watertn-4
Shea, Frank
(Spec)
48B-26
49B-49
50B-155
52B-230
52T-248
53B/Col-141
53Briggs
53T-164
54B-104
55B-207
91T/Arc53-164
92Yank/WIZAS-78
PM10/Sm-179
R346-13
Shea, John
87Myrtle-18
88Knoxvl/Best-3
89Knoxvl/Best-24
89Knoxvl/ProC-1140
89Knoxvl/Star-20
90AAASingl/ProC-351
90ProC/Singl-334
90Syrac/CMC-8
90Syrac/MerchB-21
90Syrac/ProC-571
90Syrac/Team-21
91AAA/LineD-517
91Syrac/LineD-517
91Syrac/MerchB-23
91Syrac/ProC-2480
92Syrac/MerchB-20
92Syrac/ProC-1965
92Syrac/SB-516
Shea, Kevin
87VeroB-29
Shea, Kurt
88Bristol/ProC-1887
89Fayette/ProC-1582
Shea, Mervyn D.J.
29Exh/4-24
90Target-722
92Conlon/Sport-412
Shea, Patrick
(Red)
E121/120
E121/80
W501-63
W575
WG7-48
Shea, Steven F.
69T-499R
Sheaffer, Danny
85Pawtu-12
86Pawtu-22
87Pawtu/TCMA-8
89ColoSp/CMC-21
89ColoSp/ProC-241
90AAASingl/ProC-492
90BuffB/CMC-15
90BuffB/ProC-377
90BuffB/Team-24
90ProC/Singl-15
91AAA/LineD-418
91Portl/LineD-418
91Portl/ProC-1568
92Portl/SB-419
92Portland/ProC-2671
92Sky/AAASingl-191
93F/Final-43
93StCl/Rockie-28
93T/Tr-39T
93USPlayC/Rockie-6C
93USPlayC/Rockie-9H
93Ultra-358
94D-610
94F-454
94S-197
94S/GoldR-197
94StCl-185
94StCl/1stDay-185
94StCl/Gold-185
94StCl/Team-96
94T-314
94T/Gold-314
Shean, David
11Helmar-105
E101
E102
E286
E90/1
E92
M116
S74-46
T202
T205
Shean, Larry
W514-116
Shearer, Ray
58T-283
Sheary, Kevin
85Miami-15
88Rockford-33
89Rockford-33
Sheckard, James
10Domino-109
11Helmar-106
12Sweet/Pin-91
90Target-723
93Conlon-900
D328-158
E107
E135-158
E254
E90/1
E90/3
E91
S74-69
T202
T204
T205
T206
T215/brown
WG3-43
Sheehan, Chris
92Eugene/ClBest-22
92Eugene/ProC-3029
93Rockford/ClBest-24
94FExcel-74
Sheehan, Jack
90Target-724
Sheehan, John
87Ashvl-28
88Osceola/Star-24
89Osceola/Star-21
90ColMud/Best-18
90ColMud/ProC-1346
90ColMud/Star-21
Sheehan, Terry
78OrlanTw
79Toledo-10
80OrlanTw-16
Sheehan, Tommy
90Target-1069
Sheehy, Mark
84Cram/PCL-246C
87Bakers-16C
88SanAn/Best-25
Sheely, Earl Homer
21Exh-158
25Exh-79
26Exh-79
28Exh/PCL-25
28Yueng-37
29Exh/4-13
31Exh/4-2
33Exh/4-1
46Sunbeam
47Centen-26
92Conlon/Sport-515
E120
E121/120
E210-37
V100
V61-34
W501-46
W502-37
W572
W573
W575
Sheen, Charlie
88Pac/8Men-10
Sheets, Andy
92LSU/McDag-10
93River/Cal-18
Sheets, Larry
84RochR-1
85D-36RR
85F/Up-U101
85T/Tr-106T
86D-350
86F-286
86Seven/Coin-E9M
86Sf-177M
86T-147
86T/Gloss60-50
86T/St-308
86T/Tatt-7M
87D-248
87F-479
87F/Hottest-36
87French-18
87Sf/TPrev-21M
87Smok/AL-10
87T-552
87T/St-229
88Classic/Red-188
88D-273
88D/Best-286
88Drake-23
88F-572
88F/AwardWin-38
88F/BB/MVP-34
88F/Excit-37
88F/Hottest-37
88F/LL-38
88F/Mini-3
88F/St-4
88French-18
88OPC-327
88Panini/St-16
88S-219
88Sf-161
88T-327
88T/Big-26
88T/St-230
88T/UK-70
89B-16
89D-333
89F-620
89French-19
89KennerFig-128
89OPC-98
89Panini/St-264
89S-81
89T-381TL
89T-98
89T/Big-113
89T/St-239
89UD-254
90CokeK/Tiger-22
90D-495
90F-189
90F/Can-189
90F/Up-100
90HagersDG/Best-27
90Leaf-350
90OPC-708
90PublInt/St-586
90S-111
90S/Tr-65T
90T-708
90UD-287
91Crown/Orio-414
91F-352
91OPC-281
91S-176
91T-281
91UD-340
Sheff, Chris
92Classic/DP-101
92FrRow/DP-59
93B-642
Sheffield, Gary
87Stockton-1
88BBAmer-22
88ElPaso/Best-1
88TexLgAS/GS-26
88TripleA/ASCMC-14
89B-142
89Brewer/YB-1
89Bz-19
89Classic-101
89D-31RR
89D/Best-113
89D/Rook-1
89F-196
89Panini/St-364
89Pol/Brew-1
89S-625RP
89S/HotRook-10
89S/YS/I-25
89Sf-223R
89Sf-41
89T-343FS
89T/Big-55
89T/HeadsUp-13
89T/JumboR-20
89ToysRUs-28
89UD-13SR
90B-391
90Brewer/MillB-23
90Bz-16
90Classic-14
90D-501
90D/BestAL-121
90ElPasoATG/Team-27
90F-336
90F/Can-336
90HotRook/St-41
90Kenner/Fig-77
90Leaf-157
90OPC-718
90Pol/Brew-11
90PublInt/St-504
90PublInt/St-604
90S-97
90S/100Ris-20
90S/McDon-12
90Sf-52
90T-718
90T/Big-163
90T/Coins-27
90T/Gloss60-10
90T/HeadsUp-13
90T/JumboR-25
90T/St-202
90T/St-326FS
90ToysRUs-24
90UD-157
91B-52
91Brewer/MillB-23
91Cadaco-51
91Classic/200-103
91Classic/II-T13
91D-751
91F-596
91JDean-7
91Leaf-173
91Leaf/Stud-76
91OPC-68
91Panini/FrSt-206
91Panini/St-170
91Pol/Brew-20
91Post-15
91S-473
91S/100SS-30
91StCl-95
91T-68
91UD-266
91Ultra-180
92B-214
92Classic/II-T59
92Colla/ASG-20
92D-192
92D/Up-U11
92F-188
92F/Up-125
92L-446
92L/BlkGold-446
92Mother/Padre-3
92OPC-695
92Padre/Carl-19
92Pinn-235
92Pinn/Team2000-59
92Pol/Padre-18
92S-589
92S/RookTr-1T
92Smok/Padre-30
92StCl-309
92StCl-766
92StCl/MemberI-10
92StCl/MemberII-11
92Studio-108
92T-695
92T/Gold-695
92T/GoldWin-695
92T/Tr-105T
92T/TrGold-105T
92TripleP-53
92UD-234
92UD-745
92UD-84M
92Ultra-582
92Ultra-83
92Ultra/AS-14
93B-490
93Cadaco-54
93ClBest/MLG-216
93Classic/GameI-84
93Colla/DM-97
93D-444
93D/DK-21
93D/Elite-28
93D/EliteUp-10
93D/LongBall-LL16
93D/MVP-26
93D/Master-3
93D/Prev-10
93D/Spirit-SG12
93DennyGS-17
93Duracel/PPII-18
93F-147
93F-351RT
93F-356M
93F-704LL
93F/ASNL-3
93F/Atlantic-22
93F/Final-71
93F/Fruit-57
93F/ProVI-3
93F/TLNL-5
93Flair-54
93Ho-6
93JDean/28-18
93Kenner/Fig-33
93Kraft-28
93L-307
93L/GoldAS-15M
93L/UpGoldAS-5M
93Marlin/Publix-23
93Mother/Padre-2
93OPC-317
93OPC/Premier/StarP-6
93P-11
93Pac/Spanish-264
93Panini-158LL
93Panini-261
93Pinn-1
93Pinn-300I
93Pinn/HRC-6
93Pinn/Slug-7
93Pinn/TP-6
93Post/Can-16
93S-2
93S-531AS
93S-534DT
93S/Franchise-25
93S/GoldDT-3
93Select-41
93Select/ChasS-4
93Select/Pr-41
93Select/RookTr-4T
93Select/StatL-30
93Select/StatL-4
93Select/StatL-47
93StCl-300MC
93StCl-618
93StCl/1stDay-300MC
93StCl/1stDay-618
93StCl/MurphyMP-10AS
93StCl/MurphyS-17
93Studio-207
93T-140
93T-403
93T/BlkGold-18
93T/Finest-31
93T/FinestRef-31
93T/Gold-140
93T/Gold-403
93T/Tr-51T
93TB/Full-18
93ToysRUs-64
93ToysRUs/MPhoto-11
93TripleP-6
93TripleP/Act-10
93TripleP/LL-L6
93UD-222
93UD-474
93UD-492AW
93UD-494AW
93UD-828TC
93UD/5thAnn-A2
93UD/FunPack-141
93UD/FunPack-20HS
93UD/FunPack-25KS
93UD/SP-18AS
93UD/SPPlat-PP18
93UD/TCr-TC8
93USPlayC/Ace-13D

93USPlayC/Ace-7C
93Ultra-122
93Ultra/AS-5
93Ultra/AwardWin-25
93Ultra/HRK-8
93Ultra/Perf-8
94B-290
94Church-18
94D-5
94D/DK-25
94D/Pr-10
94D/Special-5
94F-477
94F/AS-49
94F/TL-19
94Finest-225
94Flair-166
94Kraft-28
94L-319
94L/MVPNL-1
94OPC-45
94P-5
94Pac/Cr-250
94Panini-186
94Pinn-88
94Pinn/Artist-88
94Pinn/Museum-88
94Pinn/Power-15
94RedFoley-24
94S-100
94S/GoldR-100
94S/GoldS-20
94Sf/2000-28
94StCl-180M
94StCl-4
94StCl/1stDay-180M
94StCl/1stDay-4
94StCl/Gold-180M
94StCl/Gold-4
94StCl/Team-67
94Studio-112
94T-560
94T/Gold-560
94TripleP-140
94TripleP/Medal-10M
94TripleP/Nick-3
94UD-271HFA
94UD-475
94UD-50FUT
94UD/CollC-257
94UD/CollC/Gold-257
94UD/CollC/Silv-257
94UD/DColl-E10
94UD/ElecD-271HFA
94UD/ElecD-50FUT
94UD/HoloFX-36
94UD/SP-114
94Ultra-199

Sheffield, Tony
92ClBest/Up-428
92Classic/DP-40
92FrRow/DP-17
92LitSun/HSPros-5
93StCl/MurphyS-85
93T-687
93T/Gold-687

Sheffield, Travis
86DayBe-25

Sheffler, Jim
89Kingspt/Star-22

Shehan, Brian
88CapeCod/Sum-38

Sheid, Rich
90Foil/Best-175

Shelby, John
80CharlO/Pol-19
80CharlO/W3TV-19
82RochR-17
83T/Tr-102T
84D-291
84F-20
84F/St-114
84Nes/792-86
84T-86
85D-472
85F-190
85OPC-264
85RochR-13
85T-508
85T/St-204
86D-643
86F-287
86F/Mini-60
86T-309
87D-354
87D/OD-139
87F-480
87F/Up-U109
87T-208
87T/Tr-112T
88D-352
88D/Best-290
88F-526
88Mother/Dodg-14
88OPC-307
88Panini/St-316
88Pol/Dodg-31
88S-286
88T-428
88T/Big-218
89B-349
89D-314
89F-73
89KennerFig-129
89Mother/Dodg-14
89OPC-175
89Panini/St-109
89Pol/Dodg-20
89S-103
89T-175
89T/St-63
89UD-75
90Mother/Dodg-25
90Pol/Dodg-31
90PublInt/St-18
90Target-725
91CokeK/Tiger-25
91Crown/Orio-415
91D-563
91F-353
91OPC-746
91Pol/Tiger-11
91S-609
91T-746
91UD-201
92Pawtu/ProC-937
92Pawtu/SB-365
92USPlayC/Tiger-4S
92USPlayC/Tiger-7D

Sheldon, Bob
75OPC-623R
75Sacra/Caruso-8
75T-623R
75T/M-623R
76OPC-626
76SSPC-256
76T-626
77Spoka

Sheldon, Dave
86AppFx-22

Sheldon, Roland
61T-541
62T-185
63T-507
65OPC-254
65T-254
66OPC-18
66T-18
69T-413
92Yank/WIZ60-113

Sheldon, Scott
91SoOreg/ClBest-13
91SoOreg/ProC-3857
92ClBest-179
92Madis/ClBest-15
92Madis/ProC-1246
92MidwLAS/Team-39

Sheldon-Collins, Mathew
91Waverly/Fut-9

Shell, Scott
91Elizab/ProC-4308

Shellenback, Frank
28Exh/PCL-26
88LitSun/Minor-7

Shellenback, Jim
67T-592R
69T-567R
70OPC-389
70T-389
71MLB/St-549
71OPC-351
71T-351
74OPC-657
74T-657
75Hawaii/Caruso-14
84Toledo-21
85Toledo-27
87OrlanTw-7
88Portl/CMC-25CO
88Portl/ProC-644CO
89Portl/CMC-25CO
89Portl/ProC-226CO
90AAASingl/ProC-264MG
90Portl/CMC-21CO
90Portl/ProC-194G
90ProC/Singl-573CO
91AA/LineD-496CO
91OrlanSR/LineD-496CO
91OrlanSR/ProC-1867CO
92OrlanSR/ProC-2864CO
92OrlanSR/SB-526M
93Rang/Keeb-37

Shelton, Andrew
E270/1

Shelton, Ben
88Augusta/ProC-370
89Augusta/ProC-511
90Salem/Star-21
91Parramatta/Fut-3
91Salem/ClBest-8
91Salem/ProC-962
92B-568
92CaroMud/ProC-1190
92CaroMud/SB-142
92ClBest-45
92Sky/AASingl-67
92UD/ML-282
93F/Final-118

Shelton, Derek
92Oneonta/ClBest-10

Shelton, Harry
86Geneva-24
87Peoria-19
88CharWh/Best-21
89Peoria/Team-26
90Miami/I/Star-24
90Miami/II/Star-23

Shelton, Mike
86Reading-24
87Reading-9
88AAA/ProC-25
88Maine/CMC-7
88Maine/ProC-282

Shelton, Ron
90LitSun-17

Shepard, Jack
55T-73
55T/DH-23
79TCMA-112

Shepard, Kelvin
87James-12
89Rockford/Team-21

Shepard, Ken
88Geneva/ProC-1656

Shepard, Larry
68KDKA-7MG
68T-584
69T-384
73OPC-296CO
73T-296C
74OPC-326CO
74T-326C
79Pol/Giants-8CO

Shepherd, Keith
87Watertn-15
88Augusta/ProC-375
89BBCity/Star-23
90Reno/Cal-276
90Watertn/Star-19
91SoBend/ClBest-20
91SoBend/ProC-2856
92BirmB/ProC-2582
92BirmB/SB-95
93D-332
93F-109
93F/Final-44
93T-447
93T/Gold-447
94Pac/Cr-207

Shepherd, Mike
90Pulaski/Best-10
90Pulaski/ProC-3105

Shepherd, Ron
82Knoxvl-20
83Syrac-24
84Syrac-5
85F/Up-U102
86Syrac-23
87Indianap-12
87OPC-117
87T-643
88Indianap/CMC-16
88Indianap/ProC-524
89Louisvl-34
89Louisvl/CMC-22
89Louisvl/ProC-1261

Sheppard, Don
89LittleSun-22
91SoBend/ClBest-11
91SoBend/ProC-2871
92Salinas/ClBest-13
92Salinas/ProC-3772
93Dunedin/ClBest-19

Sheppard, Phillip
84Visalia-8

Shepperd, Richard
90Boise/ProC-3329
91Salinas/ClBest-13
91Salinas/ProC-2259

Shepston, Mike
79QuadC-24

Sherdel, Bill
25Exh-63
26Exh-63
91Conlon/Sport-194
92Conlon/Sport-619
E120
E126-12
V61-100
W517-6
W572

Sheridan, Bobby
87Spokane-13
89River/Cal-19
89River/ProC-1418
89Spokane/SP-22

Sheridan, John
94Conlon-1198UMP

Sheridan, Neil
52Park-16

Sheridan, Pat
81Omaha-24
82Omaha-22
83Omaha-21
84D-588
84F-357
84Nes/792-121
84T-121
84T/St-286
85D-339
85F-213
85T-359
85T/St-272
86D-155
86F-20
86Kitty/Disc-11
86OPC-240
86T-743
87Cain's-18
87Coke/Tigers-6
87F-162
87T-234
88D-522
88F-69
88Panini/St-97
88Pep/T-15
88S-171
88T-514
89B-107
89D-417
89F-146
89Mara/Tigers-15
89Pol/Tigers-15
89S-204
89S/Tr-71T
89T-288
89T/Big-150
89UD-652
90D-367
90F-71
90F/Can-71
90OPC-422
90PublInt/St-482
90S-509
90T-422
90UD-460
91ColClip/ProC-610

Sheridan, Shane
89Anchora-23

Sheriff, Dave
79WHave-29M
81LynnS-9
82Idaho-33
83Idaho-34
84Idaho/Team-25

Sherlock, Glenn
85Osceola/Team-15
86Osceola-23
87Colum-7
87Colum/Pol-22
87Colum/TCMA-25
88Colum/ProC-304
89Albany/Best-7
89Albany/ProC-339
90Albany/ProC-1183CO
90Albany/Star-26CO
90Tampa/DIMD-28MG
91FtLaud/ClBest-3MG
91FtLaud/ProC-2443MG

Sherlock, Vince
90Target-726

Sherman, Darrell
89Spokane/SP-26
90A&AASingle/ProC-147
90AS/Cal-10
90Foil/Best-286
90ProC/Singl-719
90River/Best-17
90River/Cal-3
90River/ProC-2620
91AA/LineD-619
91ClBest/Singl-153
91Wichita/LineD-619
91Wichita/ProC-2613
91Wichita/Rock-23
92ClBest-347
92Sky/AASingl-287
92UD/ML-249
92UD/ML-61DS
92Wichita/SB-645
93B-602
93L/GRook-20
93Mother/Padre-15
93OPC/Premier-118
93Pac/Spanish-602
93Pinn-619
93StCl-739
93StCl/1stDay-739
93T-576
93T/Gold-576
93UD-784
93Ultra-478
94S-595
94S/Boys-54
94StCl/Team-94

Sherman, Jack
47Signal

Sherman, Jim
83ColumAst-5
86Tucson-21

Sherman, Steve
76Cedar
77Cedar

Sherman, Tyril
92GulfCM/ProC-3480

Shermet, Dave
86AZ/Pol-14
87AZ/Pol-12
88AZ/Pol-11
88AubAs/ProC-1958
89Ashvl/ProC-948

Shermeyer, Keith
77Wausau
78Wausau

Sherow, Dennis
79Memphis/TCMA-19
80Memphis-18
81WHave-19
82Tacom-18
82WHave-25
83Tacom-27

Sherrill, Dennis
79Colum-19
80Colum-23
92Yank/WIZ80-176

Sherrill, Tim
88Savan/ProC-334
89StPete/Star-24
90AAASingl/ProC-517
90Louisvl/CMC-22
90Louisvl/LBC-37
90Louisvl/ProC-403
90ProC/Singl-122
90T/TVCard-63
91AAA/LineD-247
91Louisvl/LineD-247
91Louisvl/Team-6
91OPC-769

91T-769
91T/90Debut-142
92Louisvl/ProC-1887
92Louisvl/SB-269
92S-404
92S/100RisSt-90
92StCl-822
Sherry, Larry
60Bz-17
60Morrell
60T-105
60Union/Dodg-17
61BB-51
61NuCard-431
61P-161
61T-412
61T-521M
61T/St-34
61Union/Dodg-18
62BB-51
62J-111
62P-111
62P/Can-111
62T-435
63T-565
64T-474
65T-408
66T-289
67CokeCap/Tiger-1
67T-571
68T-468
90HOF/St-59
90Target-727
Sherry, Norm
59DF
60T-529
60Union/Dodg-18
61BB-34
61T-521M
61Union/Dodg-19
62BB-34
62T-238
63T-316
75IntLgAS/Broder-31
75PCL/AS-31
75SLCity/Caruso-20
77T-34MG
84Smok/SDP-21C
85Spokane/Cram-21
90Mother/Giant-21M
90Target-728
91Mother/Giant-27CO
91WIZMets-361
92Everett/ClBest-30MG
92Everett/ProC-1706
Shetrone, Barry
60T-348
63T-276
91Crown/Orio-416
Shevlin, Jim
90Salinas/Cal-138
90Salinas/ProC-2727
Shibata, Keith
88AppFx/ProC-153
88Eugene/Best-29
Shidawara, Cliff
86Phoenix-23TR
87Phoenix-19TR
88Phoenix/ProC-66TR
Shields, Doug
88CapeCod/Sum-40
90Eugene/GS-27
91BBCity/ClBest-27
91BBCity/ProC-1413
92Memphis/ProC-2434
Shields, Mike
79Savan-9
Shields, Steve
81Bristol-17
83Pawtu-11
84Richm-17
85Richm-9
86F-527
86Richm-20
87T/Tr-113T
88Colum/CMC-6
88Colum/Pol-10
88Colum/ProC-314
88D/Y/Bk-NEW
88S-396
88S/Tr-47T
88T-632
89F-269
89Portl/CMC-4
89Portl/ProC-218
89S-578
89T-484
90Publnt/St-338
92Yank/WIZ80-177
Shields, Tom
86Watertn-23
88Harris/ProC-836
89EastLDD/ProC-DD26
89Harris/ProC-298
89Harris/Star-18
89Star/Wax-20
90AAASingl/ProC-499
90BuffB/CMC-21
90BuffB/ProC-384
90BuffB/Team-25
90ProC/Singl-21
91AAA/LineD-467
91RochR/LineD-467
91RochR/ProC-1911
92RochR/ProC-1948
92RochR/SB-469
93B-228
93Pac/Spanish-382
93Ultra-321
94Pac/Cr-110
94StCl/Team-336
Shifflett, Steve
90AppFox/Box-24
90AppFox/ProC-2094
91AA/LineD-417
91London/LineD-417
91Memphis/ProC-653
92D/Rook-110
92Omaha/ProC-2961
92Omaha/SB-346
92Sky/AAASingl-158
93D-73
93F-625
93S-266
93StCl-84
93StCl/1stDay-84
93T-735
93T/Gold-735
93Ultra-216
Shiflett, Chris
88Gaston/ProC-1001
89Butte/SP-14
90Tulsa/ProC-1155
91AA/LineD-598
91Tulsa/LineD-598
91Tulsa/ProC-2774
Shiflett, Mark
83Nashvl-20
84Nashvl-20
87Memphis-6
87Memphis/Best-13
90Albany/Star-27CO
90Oneonta/ProC-3391CO
91Greens/ProC-3077CO
91SALAS/ProC-SAL30CO
92FtLaud/ClBest-24CO
92FtLaud/ProC-3010CO
92FtLaud/Team-29CO
Shiflett, Matt
87James-25
89Rockford/Team-22
91Durham/ClBest-1
91Durham/ProC-1543
Shikles, Larry
86Greens-22
87WinHaven-4
88NewBrit/ProC-899
89NewBrit/ProC-613
89NewBrit/Star-18
90AAASingl/ProC-433
90Pawtu/CMC-4
90Pawtu/ProC-461
90ProC/Singl-255
90T/TVRSox-59
91AAA/LineD-368
91Pawtu/LineD-368
91Pawtu/ProC-39
92Pawtu/ProC-922
92Pawtu/SB-366
92Sky/AAASingl-166
Shillinglaw, Dave
86Madis/Pol-26
Shimp, Tommy Joe
80Memphis-19
83Memphis/TCMA-10
84Tulsa-37
85OKCty-13
86OKCty-20
Shinall, Zakary
88Bakers/Cal-259
89VeroB/Star-25
90SanAn/GS-26
91AA/LineD-540
91B-612
91ClBest/Singl-384
91SanAn/LineD-540
91SanAn/ProC-2972
92Albuq/ProC-721
92Albuq/SB-20
Shindle, William
90Target-729
N172
N300/SC
Shines, Razor
83Memphis/TCMA-21
84Indianap-17
85D-401
85Expo/PostC-19
85Leaf-164
86OPC-132
86T-132
87Indianap-8
88Indianap/CMC-12
88Indianap/ProC-514
89Indianap/CMC-12
89Indianap/ProC-1219
91AAA/LineD-194
91Indianap/LineD-194
91Indianap/ProC-471
91Pac/SenLg-128
92Indianap/ProC-1870
92Indianap/SB-194
Shingledecker, Gary
89Erie/Star-24
90Wausau/Best-19
90Wausau/ProC-2132
Shinholster, Vince
87SanBern-12
Shinners, Ralph
E120
V100
W573
Shiozaki, Kenny
88Butte-11
Shipanoff, Dave
83Knoxvl-7
84Syrac-25
85Cram/PCL-28
86D-34RR
86F-452
86Leaf-29RR
86Phill/TastyK-33
86Portl-20
87Edmon-5
Shipke, William
T204
T206
Shipley, Craig
85Cram/PCL-155
86Albuq-23
87Albuq/Pol-22
88Jacks/GS-12
89Tidew/CMC-22
89Tidew/ProC-1961
90T/TVMets-60
90Target-730
91LasVegas/ProC-245
91WIZMets-362
92D-667
92F-621
92Mother/Padre-25
92OPC-308
92OPC/Premier-33
92Padre/Carl-20
92Pol/Padre-19
92S-856
92Smok/Padre-31
92StCl-374
92T-308
92T/Gold-308
92T/GoldWin-308
92Ultra-583
93D-206
93L-395
93Mother/Padre-20
93Pac/Spanish-603
93Panini-260
93StCl-258
93StCl/1stDay-258
93Studio-130
93T-601
93T/Gold-601
93UD-788
93Ultra-123
94D-516
94F-674
94Pac/Cr-534
94Panini-259
94StCl-460
94StCl/1stDay-460
94StCl/Gold-460
94T-184
94T/Gold-184
Shipley, Joe
59T-141
60T-239
62Pep/Tul
Shipley, Mark
91Sydney/Fut-1
Shipman, Mike
92Martins/ClBest-19
92Martins/ProC-3061
Shippy, Greg
75Clinton
Shirahata, Hiro
83SanJose-10
Shireman, Jeff
89Spring/Best-12
90StPete/Star-23
91AA/LineD-45
91ArkTr/LineD-45
91ArkTr/ProC-1297
92Louisvl/ProC-1895
92Louisvl/SB-270
Shires, Charles A.
(Art)
30CEA/Pin-20
92Conlon/Sport-608
R315-C5
R316
W517-43
Shirley, Al
91Classic/DP-14
91FrRow/DP-43
91LitSun/HSPros-2
91LitSun/HSProsG-2
92Kingspt/ClBest-9
92Kingspt/ProC-1544
92OPC-306
92Pinn-297DP
92S-802DC
92StCl/Dome-170
92T-306DP
92T/Gold-306
92T/GoldWin-306
93B-566
93FExcel/ML-79
Shirley, Bart
66T-591R
67T-287R
69T-289
90Target-731
91WIZMets-363
92TX-37
Shirley, Bob
77Padre/SchCd-27
78Padre/FamFun-28
78T-266
79T-594
80OPC-248
80T-476
81D-242
81F-495
81OPC-49
81T-49
81T/Tr-829
82D-120
82F-127
82OPC-33
82T-749
82T/Tr-105T
83F-602
83T-112
83T/Tr-103T
84D-214
84F-141
84Nes/792-684
84T-684
85D-370
85F-145
85T-328
86D-458
86F-119
86T-213
87D-463
87F-114
87T-524
88Syrac/CMC-7
88Syrac/ProC-827
89Pac/SenLg-207
89StCath/ProC-2095
89T/SenLg-6
89TM/SenLg-95
90AAASingl/ProC-369CO
90ProC/Singl-333
90Syrac/CMC-7CO
90Syrac/MerchB-22CO
90Syrac/ProC-589CO
90Syrac/Team-22CO
92Yank/WIZ80-179
Shirley, Mike
91Burllnd/ProC-3318
92FtMyr/ProC-2758
92Miracle/ClBest-7
Shirley, Steve
77LodiD
78LodiD
81Albuq/TCMA-3
82Albuq-8
85Cram/PCL-235
86Albuq-24
87Omaha-14
88Indianap/CMC-4
88Indianap/ProC-505
90Target-732
Shive, Chuck
89Martins/Star-28
Shoch, George
90Target-1071
N172
WG1-70
Shocker, Urban
21Exh-159
25Exh-103
26Exh-104
28Exh-52
91Conlon/Sport-114
93Conlon-711
E120
E121/120
E126-36
E220
V100
V61-40
W501-2
W515-48
W573
W575
Shockey, Greg
92Belling/ClBest-2
92Belling/ProC-1459
93ClBest/MLG-192
93River/Cal-19
Shockey, Richard
90Modesto/Chong-27
Shockey, Scott
88CapeCod/Sum-63
89Medford/Best-2
90Madison/ProC-2278
90ProC/Singl-659
91AA/LineD-293
91ClBest/Singl-237
91Huntsvl/ClBest-21
91Huntsvl/LineD-293
91Huntsvl/Team-19
91HuntsvlProC-1805
93Modesto/ClBest-18
93Modesto/ProC-809
Shockley, John Costen
(Costen)
65OPC-107R
65T-107R
88Chatt/Team-27
88Lookout-27
Shoebridge, Terry
77BurlB
78BurlB
80Holyo-9
81ElPaso-5
Shoemaker, John
78LodiD
81VeroB-26
82VeroB-29
83VeroB-26
85VeroB-27
86VeroB-23CO
87VeroB-30
88FSLAS/Star-1MG
89SanAn/Best-25

90SanAn/GS-1MG
91AA/LineD-549MG
91SanAn/LineD-549MG
91SanAn/ProC-2991MG
92GulfCD/ProC-3583

Shoemaker, Steve
92Madis/ClBest-12
92Madis/ProC-1235

Shoen, Gerry
77Fritsch-20

Shoeneck, Lewis
N172
WG1-36

Shoffner, Milburn
39PlayBall-87
40PlayBall-149
93Conlon-925
W711/1
W711/2

Shofner, Frank S.
48Sommer-9
49Sommer-15

Sholl, Derek
88Eugene/Best-25

Sholton, Craig
91Welland/ClBest-15

Shombert, Otto
N172
N284

Shook, Wes
94FExcel-137

Shoop, Brian
88MissSt-31CO
89MissSt-42M

Shopay, Tom
70OPC-363
70T-363
72OPC-418
72T-418
76SSPC-401
78Colum
89Pac/SenLg-71
91Crown/Orio-417
92Yank/WIZ60-114

Shore, Eddie
33SK*-19

Shore, Ernest
(Ernie)
16FleischBrd-85
73F/Wild-31
87Conlon/2-56
90HOF/St-15
91Conlon/Sport-141
92Conlon/Sport-351
D327
D328-159
D329-162
D350/2-164
E135-159
M101/4-162
M101/5-164

Shore, Jeff
89CharlR/Star-23

Shore, Ray
63FrBauer-24

Shore, Roy
52Park-18

Shores, Brad
86BurlEx-19TR
89AppFx/ProC-869
91AppFx/ClBest-21TR

Shores, William
94Conlon-1145
W517-7

Short, Ben
91Oneonta/ProC-4154
92Greens/ClBest-9
92Greens/ProC-778

Short, Bill
60T-142
61T-252
62T-221
67T-577
68T-536
69T-259
91Crown/Orio-418
91WIZMets-364
92Yank/WIZ60-115

Short, Chris
64PhilBull-22
67CokeCap/Phill-15
67Pol/Phill-10
67T-395
68OPC-139
68OPC-7LL
68T-139
68T-7LL
68T/ActionSt-9CM
69MB-253
69MLB/St-178
69T-395
69T/S-54
69T/St-78
69T/decal
70K-41
70MLB/St-94
70OPC-270
70T-270
71K-75
71MLB/St-188
71OPC-511
71Phill/Arco-11
71T-511
72MB-315
72T-665
PM10/L-35

Shorten, Charles
(Chick)
91Conlon/Sport-136
D328-160
E120
E135-160

Shotkoski, David
88Huntsvl/BK-19
88Modesto-31
88Modesto/Cal-57
89Huntsvl/Best-15
91AA/LineD-446
91London/LineD-446
91MidldA/OneHour-27
91MidldA/ProC-434

Shotton, Burt
14CJ-86
15CJ-86
49Eureka-49
90Target-733
91Conlon/Sport-152
D327
D328-161
D329-163
D350/2-165
E135-161
M101/4-163
M101/5-165
Rawl
W514-78

Shotton, Craig
91Welland/ProC-3590
92Welland/ClBest-21

Shoun, Clyde
50Remar
92Conlon/Sport-379
R423-99
W754

Shoup, Eric
88Bristol/ProC-1876

Shouppe, Jamey
83DayBe-12

Shourds, Jeff
77Cedar

Shouse, Brian
90Welland/Pucko-28
91Augusta/ClBest-11
92CaroMud/ProC-1179
92CaroMud/SB-143

Show, Eric
81Hawaii
81Hawaii/TCMA-19
82T/Tr-106T
83D-439
83F-372
83F/St-26M
83F/St-6M
83OPC-68
83OPC/St-330
83T-68
83T/St-330
84D-406
84F-312
84Mother/Padres-4
84Nes/792-532
84OPC-238
84Smok/Padres-22
84T-532
84T/RD-27M
84T/St-162
85D-202
85D/AAS-59
85F-44
85Leaf-137
85Mother/Padres-9
85OPC-118
85T-118
85T/RD-27M
85T/St-156
86D-234
86F-334
86Leaf-111
86OPC-209
86T-762
87Bohem-30
87D-164
87D/OD-149
87F-430
87F/Hottest-37
87OPC-354
87T-730
87T/St-112
88Coke/Padres-30
88D-387
88F-597
88Panini/St-400
88S-338
88Smok/Padres-26
88T-303
89B-446
89Coke/Padre-17
89D-482
89F-317
89OPC-147
89Padre/Mag-7
89Panini/St-196
89S-254
89T-427
89T/Big-35
89UD-171
90B-209
90Coke/Padre-18
90D-559
90F-169
90F/Can-169
90Leaf-115
90OPC-239
90Padre/MagUno-5
90Publint/St-59
90S-493
90T-239
90T/Big-71
90T/St-111
90UD-587
91B-223
91F-544
91Leaf-354
91Leaf/Stud-108
91Mother/A's-23
91OPC-613
91S-563
91S/RookTr-64T
91SFExam/A's-11
91StCl-138
91T-613
91UD-293
91UD/Ext-798
92OPC-132
92S-662
92T-132
92T/Gold-132
92T/GoldWin-132

Showalter, J.R.
90Boise/ProC-3326
91PalmSp/ProC-2026

Showalter, William N.
(Buck)
79WHave-7
81Colum-20
82Nashvl-22
83Nashvl-21
88FSLAS/Star-27
89Albany/Best-8
89Albany/ProC-326
89Albany/Star-22
89EastLgAS/ProC-26MG
92OPC-201MG
92T-201MG
92T/Gold-201MG
92T/GoldWin-201MG
93T-510MG
93T/Gold-510MG

Shrev, Ben
88Geneva/ProC-1652
88Wythe/ProC-1992

Shrev, Leven
N172

Shuba, George
52T-326
53B/Col-145
53T-34
54B-202
54NYJour
55B-66
55Gol/Dodg-27
79TCMA-277
89Rini/Dodg-17
90Target-734
91T/Arc53-34

Shubert, Rich
74Gaston
76SanAn/Team-20
77Holyo

Shuey, Paul
91T/Tr-108T
92ClBest/BBonusC-21
92ClBest/Up-401
92Classic/DP-2
92Classic/DPFoil-BC2
92Classic/DPPrev-BB2
92ColRS/ProC-2390
92StCl/Dome-171
92T/DQ-32
92UD/ML-142
93ClBest/Fisher-19
93ClBest/MLG-14
93FExcel/ML-168
94ClBest/Gold-107
94SigRook-23

Shuffield, Jack
83CharR-12

Shuler, Dave
92PrWill/ClBest-27CO

Shull, Mike
87PalmSp-10
90PalmSp/Cal-222

Shulleeta, Mike
82QuadC-11

Shulock, John
88TM/Umpire-39
89TM/Umpire-37
90TM/Umpire-35

Shultea, Chris
91SLCity/SportP-19

Shultis, Chris
86Cram/NWL-22
86Everett/Pop-28
88Boise/ProC-1613

Shumake, Brooks
86Vermont-18

Shumpert, Terry
88AppFx/ProC-142
89Omaha/CMC-18
89Omaha/ProC-1721
90Classic/III-65
90D/BestAL-134
90D/Rook-55
90F/Up-104
90Leaf-409
90S/Tr-110T
90T/Tr-114T
90UD/Ext-733
91B-314
91D-297
91F-570
91Leaf-104
91MajorLg/Pins-22
91OPC-322
91OPC/Premier-108
91Pol/Royal-20
91S-349RP
91S/100RisSt-3
91S/ASFan-9
91S/Rook40-27
91Seven/3DCoin-15F
91StCl-111
91T-322
91T/90Debut-143
91UD-521
91Ultra-156
92B-157
92Classic/I-83
92D-562
92F-169
92L-347
92L/BlkGold-347
92OPC-483
92Omaha/ProC-2972
92Panini-95
92Pinn-203
92Pol/Royal-25
92S-248
92S/100RisSt-44
92StCl-165
92T-483
92T/Gold-483
92T/GoldWin-483
92UD-348
93D-601
93Pac/Spanish-141

Shupe, Wilford
WG7-49

Shutt, Steve
72Dimanche*-107

Shwan, Dan
91SLCity/ProC-3229CO
91SLCity/SportP-27ACO

Siberz, Bo
90Oneonta/ProC-3381
91Greens/ProC-3060

Siblerud, Daniel
86Columbia-23

Siddall, Joe
88James/ProC-1908
89Rockford/Team-23
90WPalmB/Star-20
91AA/LineD-269
91Harris/LineD-269
91Harris/ProC-633
92Harris/ProC-464
92Harris/SB-298
93Ottawa/ProC-2439
94Pac/Cr-390

Sides, Craig
92BurlInd/ClBest-5
92BurlInd/ProC-1655

Siebern, Norm
58T-54
59T-308
60T-11
61P-82
61T-119M
61T-267
61T/Dice-16
61T/St-165
62Bz
62Exh
62J-92
62P-92
62P/Can-92
62Salada-85
62Shirriff-85
62T-127M
62T-275
62T/St-57
62T/bucks
63Bz-4
63Exh
63F-17
63J-85
63P-85
63Salada-51
63T-2LL
63T-430
63T/SO
64T-145
64T/Coins-49
64T/SU
64T/St-14
64T/tatt
64Wheat/St-41
65T-455
66OPC-14
66T-14
67T-299
68CokeCap/Giant-5
68CokeCap/RedSox-15
68T-537
79TCMA-223
91Crown/Orio-419
Exh47

Siebert, Dick
40PlayBall-192
41DP-128
43Playball-23
90Target-735
93Conlon-926

Siebert, Mac
89Bristol/Star-26

Siebert, Paul
75Iowa/TCMA-17
75OPC-614R

75T-614R
75T/M-614R
89Pac/SenLg-212
91WIZMets-365
Siebert, Rick
86Durham-25
87Durham-18
88Sumter/ProC-402
89Penin/Star-22
Siebert, Sonny
64T-552R
65OPC-96
65T-96
66Kahn
66T-197
66T-222LL
66T-226LL
67CokeCap/Indian-8
67Kahn
67OPC-95
67T-463M
67T-95
68OPC-8LL
68T-295
68T-8LL
69MLB/St-43
69T-455
69T/St-167
70MLB/St-166
70T-597
71MLB/St-332
71OPC-710
71T-710
71T/Coins-122
72K-36
72OPC-290
72T-290
73K-14
73OPC-14
73T-14
74OPC-548
74T-548
75OPC-328
75T-328
75T/M-328
76SSPC-484
85Cram/PCL-121
87LasVegas-6
88LasVegas/CMC-25
88LasVegas/ProC-248
91Waterlo/ClBest-26CO
91Waterlo/ProC-1274CO
92Wichita/SB-650CO
93Rang/Keeb-325
Siebert, Steve
90Spokane/SportP-13
91Utica/ClBest-15
91Utica/ProC-3251
Siebler, Dwight
64T-516R
65T-326
66T-546
67OPC-164
67T-164
78TCMA-126
Siegel, Bob
86Wausau-24
Siegle, John H.
E101
E105
E216
E90/1
E92
Sieradzki, Al
89Bluefld/Star-21
Sierra, Ruben
85Tulsa-12
86D/Rook-52
86F/Up-U105
86OKCty-21
86Rang-3
86Sf/Rook-16
87Classic/Up-149
87D-346
87D/OD-172
87F-138
87F/Mini-100
87Leaf-225
87Mother/Rang-13
87Sf/TPrev-1M
87Smok/R-17
87T-261
87T-6RB
87T/JumboR-15
87T/St-10
87ToysRUs-24
88Classic/Red-180
88D-223
88D-BC26
88D/Best-200
88F-479
88F/Excit-38
88F/Hottest-38
88F/LL-39
88F/Mini-58
88F/SS-36
88F/St-69
88KayBee-28
88KennerFig-103
88Leaf-206
88Mother/R-10
88OPC-319
88Panini/St-209
88S-113
88S/YS/I-36
88Sf-113
88Smok/R-9
88T-771
88T/Coins-26
88T/Gloss60-4
88T/RiteAid-25
88T/St-234
88T/UK-71
89B-235
89Bimbo/Discs-6
89Classic/Up/2-162
89D-48
89D/Best-111
89D/MVP-BC26
89F-532
89F/BBAS-37
89F/BBMVP's-35
89F/Excit-37
89F/Heroes-37
89KennerFig-130
89Mother/R-7
89OPC-53
89Panini/St-457
89RedFoley/St-108
89S-43
89S/Mast-31
89Sf-189
89Smok/R-30
89T-53
89T/Big-82
89T/Coins-51
89T/Hills-26
89T/St-242
89T/UK-71
89Tulsa/Team-27
89UD-416
89UD-686TC
90B-490
90Classic-59
90Classic-7
90Classic/III-77
90CollAB-7
90D-174
90D-3DK
90D-673AS
90D/BestAL-143
90D/SuperDK-3DK
90F-314
90F/ASIns-11
90F/AwardWin-34
90F/BB-34
90F/BBMVP-34
90F/Can-314
90F/LL-36
90F/WaxBox-C25
90HotPlay/St-40
90Leaf-257
90Mother/Rang-3
90OPC-185
90OPC-390AS
90Panini/St-162
90Panini/St-203
90PublInt/St-422
90PublInt/St-605
90S-420
90S/100St-85
90Sf-188
90Starline/LJS-33
90Starline/LJS-8
90T-185
90T-390AS
90T/Ames-32
90T/Big-175
90T/Coins-28
90T/DH-60
90T/Gloss22-19
90T/Gloss60-26
90T/HillsHM-20
90T/Mini-40
90T/St-161AS
90T/St-244
90T/TVAS-7
90TulsaDG/Best-35
90UD-355
91B-283
91Cadaco-52
91Classic/200-41
91Classic/III-83
91D-567
91DennyGS-21
91F-303
91F/ProV-3
91KingB/Discs-9
91Leaf-97
91Leaf/Stud-129
91MooTown-16
91Mother/Rang-3
91OPC-535
91OPC/Premier-109
91Panini/FrSt-257
91Panini/St-202
91RedFoley/St-87
91S-495
91S-859FRAN
91S/100SS-12
91Seven/3DCoin-13T
91StCl-123
91T-535
91T/CJMini/II-18
91UD-455
91USPlayC/AS-9H
91Ultra-356
92B-225
92CJ/DII-26
92Classic/Game200-151
92Classic/II-T65
92D-298
92DennyGS-25
92F-321
92F/Performer-18
92F/Up-51
92Kenner/Fig-40
92L-383
92L/BlkGold-383
92Mother/Rang-3
92OPC-700
92OPC/Premier-66
92Panini-79
92Pinn-14
92Pinn-616TECH
92Pinn/Slug-10
92Pinn/TeamP-10
92S-437AS
92S-490
92S/100SS-87
92S/Impact-46
92S/RookTr-63T
92StCl-387
92StCl/Dome-172
92Studio-249
92Studio/Prev-1
92T-403AS
92T-700
92T/Gold-403AS
92T/Gold-700
92T/GoldWin-403AS
92T/GoldWin-700
92T/Kids-128
92T/MicroG-403
92TripleP-238
92UD-176
92UD/ASFF-41
92UD/TWillB-T10
92UD/TmMVPHolo-48
92USPlayC/Ace-9H
92Ultra-142
93B-245
93Classic/Gamel-85
93Colla/DM-98
93D-637
93Duracel/PPII-6
93F-298
93Flair-262
93L-29
93Mother/A's-5
93OPC-243
93Pac/Spanish-225
93Pac/SpanishGold-18
93Panini-21
93Pinn-200
93Pinn/HRC-46
93Pinn/Slug-12
93Rang/Keeb-326
93S-608
93Select-366
93StCl-580
93StCl/1stDay-580
93StCl/A's-10
93StCl/MPhoto-22
93StCl/MurphyS-47
93Studio-113
93T-440
93T/Finest-158
93T/FinestRef-158
93T/Gold-440
93TripleP-60
93UD-145
93UD-49
93UD/FunPack-52
93UD/SP-43
93Ultra-613
94B-24
94Church-3
94D-33
94D/DK-18
94D/MVP-25
94D/Special-33
94F-273
94Finest-371
94L-67
94OPC-195
94Oscar-13
94Pac/AllLat-12
94Pac/Cr-462
94Panini-112
94Pinn-61
94Pinn/Artist-61
94Pinn/Museum-61
94S-409
94S/Tomb-28
94Select-45
94Sf/2000-73
94StCl-307
94StCl-536QS
94StCl/1stDay-307
94StCl/1stDay-536QS
94StCl/Gold-307
94StCl/Gold-536QS
94Studio-6
94T-680
94T/Gold-680
94TripleP-8
94UD-380
94UD/CollC-258
94UD/CollC/Gold-258
94UD/CollC/Silv-258
94UD/SP-37
94Ultra-411
Sierra, Ulises
(Candy)
85Beaum-9
86Beaum-21
87Wichita-20
88Nashvl/Team-21
89F-171
89T-711
90River/Best-23
90River/ProC-2609
Siever, Edward
E107
Sievers, Jason
90Everett/Best-15
90Everett/ProC-3131
92Everett/ProC-1694
Sievers, Roy
50B-16
51B-67
51FB
51T/RB-9
52T-64
53T-67
54T-245
55T-16
55T/DH-79
56T-75
56T/Pin-59OF
57T-89
58T-250
59Armour-15
59Bz
59T-340
59T-465HL
59T-566AS
59T-74M
60NuCard-23
60T-25
61NuCard-423
61P-26
61T-470
61T/St-128
62/Can-46
62J-46
62P-46
62Salada-66
62Shirriff-66
62T-220
62T/St-169
62T/St-58
62T/bucks
63J-177
63P-177
63T-283
64T-43
65T-574
77Galasso-43
78TCMA-242
79TCMA-206
88Pac/Leg-26
89Swell-47
91T/Arc53-67
94T/Arc54-245
Exh47
PM10/L-36
Sievert, Mark
93MedHat/ProC-3735
93MedHat/SportP-15
Sigler, Allen
85Cedar-25
86Cedar/TCMA-22
Siglin, W.
(Paddy)
WG7-50
Sigman, Lee
78BurlB
80Holyo-25
81Vanco-20
83ElPaso-25
Sikes, Bob
82Jacks-24
83Tidew-27
84Tidew-17
Silch, Edward
N172
Silcox, Rusty
90Spokane/SportP-3
91HighD/ClBest-10
91HighD/ProC-2393
92HighD/ClBest-1
Siler, Mike
87Bakers-26
Silkwood, Joe
83Spring/Frit-12
84ArkTr-20
Silton
C46-24
Silva, Freddie
82Spring/Frit-6
83StPete-12
Silva, Jose
93Hagers/ClBest-24
93Hagers/ProC-1880
94FExcel-148
94FExcel/LL-16
94TedW-130
94UD-526TP
94UD/SP-16PP
Silva, Mark
83Nashvl-22
85Colum-24
85Colum/Pol-20
86Colum-22
86Colum/Pol-20
Silva, Ryan
86Cram/NWL-149
Silvas, Brian
81Batavia-7
Silver, Chad
90Princet/DIMD-18
Silver, Keith
84Everett/Cram-10A
86Shrev-23
Silver, Larry
78StPete
Silver, Roy
86StPete-28

87ArkTr-12
87TexLgAS-2
88Louisvl-44
88Louisvl/CMC-22
88Louisvl/ProC-431
89ArkTr/GS-22
89TexLAS/GS-38
90AAASingl/ProC-532
90Louisvl/CMC-16
90Louisvl/LBC-38
90Louisvl/ProC-418
90ProC/Singl-116
90T/TVCard-64
91Savan/ClBest-2CO
91Savan/ProC-1669CO
92Spring/ClBest-28CO
92Spring/ProC-886CO
Silvera, Al
56T-137
Silvera, Charlie
52B-197
52T-168
53T-242
54T-96
55T-188
57T-255
73OPC-323CO
73T-323C
74OPC-379CO
74T-379C
79TCMA-266
91T/Arc53-242
93Rang/Keeb-327CO
94T/Arc54-96
Silverio, Francisco
86Tampa-19
87Cedar-23
Silverio, Luis
76Watlo
77Jaxvl
82Omaha-23
88FSLAS/Star-30CO
Silverio, Nelson
86Madis/Pol-19
88Charl/ProC-1220
Silverio, Tom
72OPC-213R
72T-213R
Silverio, Victor
91QuadC/ClBest-11
91QuadC/ProC-2628
92PalmSp/ClBest-5
92PalmSp/ProC-839
93LimeR/Winter-3
Silverman, Aaron
52Park-2
V362-19
Silverman, Bob
80Knoxvl/TCMA-9
Silverman, Don
85Iowa-27
Silverstein, Allan
88Myrtle/ProC-1187
89Dunedin/Star-15
90Dunedin/Star-16
Silvestri, David
87PanAm/USAB-24
87PanAm/USAR-24
88T/Tr-107TOLY
89Osceola/Star-22
89Star/Wax-18
89T/Big-141
90PrWill/Team-24
90TeamUSA/87-24
91AA/LineD-15
91Albany/LineD-15
91Albany/ProC-1016
92B-87
92Classic/II-T95
92ColClip/Pol-19
92ColClip/Pol-19
92ColClip/ProC-361
92ColClip/SB-116
92D/Rook-111
92L/GRook-20
92Pinn-531
92ProC/Tomorrow-111
92Sky/AAASingl-55
93ColClip/Pol-16
93F/Final-252
93F/MLPII-5
93Pinn-180
93S-252
93T-529
93T/Gold-529
94StCl/Team-191
Silvestri, Ken
49Eureka-147
51B-256
52B-200
60T-466CO
73OPC-237CO
73T-237CO
74OPC-634CO
74T-634CO
78Knoxvl
87Portl-23
89Watertn/Star-26
90Watertn/Star-25CO
Silvey, Jeff
90GA-27
Silvia, Brian
92Princet/ClBest-18
92Princet/ProC-3090
Sima, Al
52T-93
53T-241
54T-216
88Chatt/Team-28
88Lookout-28
91T/Arc53-241
94T/Arc54-216
Simas, Bill
92Boise/ClBest-29
92Boise/ProC-3627
Simcox, Larry
82DayBe-23
83ColumAst-7
Simmermacher, Bret
86Cram/NWL-114
Simmons
11Diamond-25
Simmons, Aloysius (Al)
21Exh-160
28Exh-56
31Exh/4-27
32Orbit/num-39
32Orbit/un-53
33CJ/Pin-20
33DH-39
33DL-2
33Exh/4-14
33G-35
34DS-2
34Exh/4-10
34Exh/4-14
35BU-34
35Exh/4-10
35G-1J
35G-3A
35G-5A
35G-6A
35Wheat
38ONG/Pin-28
50Callahn
50W576-65
60Exh/HOF-21
60F-32
61F-77
61GP-20
63Bz-22
69Bz/Sm
75Sheraton-8
76Rowe-13
76Shakey-64
77Galasso-190
77Galasso-58
80Laugh/FFeat-3
80Pac/Leg-119
80Perez/HOF-68
80SSPC/HOF
81Conlon-81
83Miami-16
86Sf/Dec-5
88Conlon/4-25
88Conlon/AmAS-22
91Conlon/Sport-311
91Conlon/Sport-49
91T/Arc53-326M
92Conlon/Col-13
92Conlon/Sport-423
92Conlon/Sport-554
93Conlon-666
94Conlon-1084
94Conlon-1136
94TedW-70
PR1-26
R300
R303/A
R303/B
R305
R306
R308-154
R310
R313
R314
R315-A33
R315-B33
R316
R328-17
R332-1
R337-415
R423-102
V351B-40
V353-35
V355-77
V94-42
W517-40
Simmons, Brad
77DaytB
Simmons, Curt
49B-14
49Eureka-148
49Lummis
50B-68
51B-111
51BR-D9
52B-184
52StarCal/L-77C
52T-203
53B/Col-64
54B-79
54RM-NL12
55Armour-18
55B-64
55RFG-6
55RM-NL24
55W605-6
56T-290
57T-158
58Hires-28
58T-404
59T-382
60T-451
61T-11
61T/St-93
62J-167
62P-167
62P/Can-167
62T-285
62T-56LL
63T-22
64T-385
65T-373
66T-489
67CokeCap/Cub-16
67OPC-39
67T-39
79TCMA-54
91T/Arc53-318
Exh47
PM10/Sm-180
Simmons, Enoch
89Medford/Best-26
90Madison/Best-10
90Madison/ProC-2281
91ClBest/Singl-256
91Modesto/ClBest-23
91Modesto/ProC-3105
92AS/Cal-11
92Reno/Cal-53
Simmons, George
C46-75
T205
Simmons, Greg
85Beloit-17
86Beloit-21
Simmons, John Earl
52Park-62
53Exh/Can-35
V362-5
Simmons, John
92Idaho/ProC-3512
93Macon/ClBest-21
93Macon/ProC-1399
Simmons, Josh
92Hunting/ClBest-10
92Hunting/ProC-3158
93Peoria/Team-25
Simmons, Mark
92Boise/ClBest-7
92Boise/ProC-3639
Simmons, Mitch
92Albany/ProC-2315
Simmons, Nelson
83BirmB-16
84Evansvl-9
85F/Up-U103
86Cain's-16
86D-272
86F-238
86RochR-21
86T-121
87RochR-18
88Calgary/CMC-19
88Calgary/ProC-802
90Huntsvl/Best-22
91AAA/LineD-545
91Crown/Orio-420
91Tacoma/LineD-545
91Tacoma/ProC-2320
Simmons, Randy
88Pulaski/ProC-1768
89SALAS/GS-44
89Sumter/ProC-1110
90BurlB/Best-24
90BurlB/ProC-2364
90BurlB/Star-24
90Foil/Best-81
91Durham/ProC-1561
Simmons, Scott
91Hamil/ProC-4038
92ClBest-271
92MidwLAS/Team-40
92Spring/ClBest-22
92Spring/ProC-866
Simmons, Ted
71OPC-117
71T-117
72OPC-154
72T-154
73OPC-85
73T-85
74K-21
74OPC-260
74T-260
74T/DE-10
74T/St-116
75Ho-95
75OPC-75
75T-75
75T/M-75
76Crane-56
76Ho-113
76K-57
76MSA/Disc
76OPC-191LL
76OPC-290
76SSPC-274
76T-191LL
76T-290
77BurgChef-16
77Ho-61
77Ho/Twink-61
77OPC-196
77T-470
77T/CS-43
77T/ClothSt-43
78Ho-65
78OPC-150
78Pep-38
78T-380
78Wiffle/Discs-69
79Ho-44
79K-2
79OPC-267
79T-510
79T/Comics-30
80K-45
80OPC-47
80T-85
80T/Super-36
80T/Super-36
81D-308
81F-528
81F/St-120
81OPC-352
81PermaGr/CC-17
81T-705
81T/Nat/Super-15
81T/So-63
81T/St-94
81T/Tr-830
82D-106
82F-152
82F/St-137
82OPC-150
82Pol/Brew-23
82T-150
82T/St-201
82T/StVar-201
83D-332
83F-45
83F/St-14M
83F/St-9M
83Gard-16
83OPC-284
83OPC-33SV
83OPC/St-85
83PermaGr/AS-5
83Pol/Brew-23
83T-450
83T-451SV
83T/St-85
84D-473
84D/AAS-58
84F-213
84Gard-17
84MiltBrad-24
84Nes/792-404AS
84Nes/792-630
84Nes/792-713LL
84Nes/792-726TL
84OPC-122
84OPC-94AS
84Pol/Brew-23
84Ralston-3
84Seven-21C
84T-404AS
84T-630
84T-713LL
84T-726TL
84T/Cereal-3
84T/Gloss22-9
84T/Gloss40-18
84T/St-193
84T/St-293
84T/St/Box-2
85D-414
85F-596
85FunFoodPin-124
85Gard-19
85Leaf-104
85OPC-318
85Pol/Brew-23
85T-318
85T/St-294
86D-292
86F-503
86F/Up-U106
86Leaf-167
86Pol/Atl-23
86Sf-196
86Sf/Dec-62M
86T-237
86T/St-199
86T/Tatt-4M
86T/Tr-102T
87D-537
87F-528
87Smok/Atl-13
87T-516
88D-560
88F-549
88Leaf-222
88S-285
88T-791
89F-599
89S-611
89UD-570
91MDA-2
92Brew/Carlson-20
92Card/McDon/Pac-35
93Pirate/Nation-28XGM
Simmons, Todd
86Beaum-22
87LasVegas-11
88F-650R
88LasVegas/CMC-6
88LasVegas/ProC-240
89Denver/CMC-10
89Denver/ProC-30
89F-318
Simms, Michael
87Ashvl-17
88FSLAS/Star-21
88Osceola/Star-25
89ColMud/Best-7
89ColMud/ProC-141

89ColMud/Star-22
89Star/Wax-3
90AAASingl/ProC-198
90ProC/Singl-622
90Tucson/CMC-20
90Tucson/ProC-208
91AAA/LineD-619
91B-551
91Classic/II-T90
91F-516
91OPC-32
91S-766
91StCl-281
91T-32
91T/90Debut-144
91Tucson/LineD-619
91Tucson/ProC-2221
91UD-664
92D-747
92F-445
92OPC-463
92Panini-156
92S-632
92Sky/AAASingl-276
92StCl-262
92T-463
92T/Gold-463
92T/GoldWin-463
92Tucson/ProC-501
92Tucson/SB-619
92UD-584
93D-32
93Pac/Spanish-128
Simon, Michael Edward
11Helmar-165
14CJ-25
15CJ-25
D322
M116
T201
T207
Simon, Michael
75T/Photo-30
Simon, Richard
(Richie)
86AubAs-23
87AubAs-25
88Ashvl/ProC-1069
89Osceola/Star-23
90ColMud/Best-13
90ColMud/ProC-1347
90ColMud/Star-22
91AA/LineD-564
91AA/LineD-573
91Jacks/LineD-573
91Jacks/ProC-927
92Jacks/ProC-4000
92Jacks/SB-343
92Sky/AASingl-147
92Tucson/ProC-486
Simon, Rick
74Gaston
Simon, Willie
76Wausau
Simond, Rob
80LynnS-6
81LynnS-10
Simonds, Dan
88Fresno/Cal-6
88Fresno/ProC-1230
89EastLDD/ProC-DD29
89Freder/Star-22
89Hagers/Best-23
90Hagers/Best-2
90Hagers/ProC-1417
91AAA/LineD-217
91Iowa/LineD-217
91Iowa/ProC-1064
93Cub/Mara-24
Simoneaux, Wayne
91Idaho/SportP-19
Simons, Doug
89AS/Cal-17
89Visalia/Cal-95
89Visalia/ProC-1435
90OrlanSR/Best-21
90OrlanSR/ProC-1082
90OrlanSR/Star-19
90ProC/Singl-749
91B-463
91Classic/II-T86
91D/Rook-26
91Kahn/Mets-43
91OPC/Premier-110
91S/RookTr-91T
91T/Tr-109T
91UD/FinalEd-63F
92D-688
92Indianap/ProC-1858
92OPC-82
92S-479
92S/100RisSt-91
92T-82
92T/91Debut-163
92T/Gold-82
92T/GoldWin-82
93D-276
93Ottawa/ProC-2435
Simons, Mitchel
91James/ClBest-12
91James/ProC-3555
91OKSt-23
92Albany/ClBest-25
92Albany/ProC-2315
93WPalmB/ClBest-22
93WPalmB/ProC-1350
Simons, Neil
82DayBe-15
Simonson, Bob
85Beloit-6
86Beloit-22
88Beloit/GS-9
Simonton, Benji
92Classic/DP-55
92Everett/ClBest-9
92Everett/ProC-1705
93B-112
93StCl/MurphyS-60
Simpson, Danny
83TriCit-22
Simpson, Dick
63T-407R
64T-127R
65T-374R
66T-311R
67CokeCap/Reds-18
67OPC-6
67T-6
68T-459
69MB-254
69T-608
92Yank/WIZ60-116
Simpson, Greg
86Cedar/TCMA-9
87Vermont-6
88Cedar/ProC-1137
Simpson, Harry
(Suitcase)
52B-223
52NumNum-17
52T-193
53B/Col-86
53T-150
55Rodeo
56Rodeo
56T-239
57T-225
58T-299
59T-333
60L-81
60T-180
61Union
79TCMA-79
86Negro/Frit-92
91T/Arc53-150
Simpson, Herb
92Negro/Retort-56
Simpson, Jay
92Boise/ClBest-10
Simpson, Joe
75Albuq/Caruso-2
75IntLgAS/Broder-32
75PCL/AS-32
78Cr/PCL-63
79T-719R
80T-637
81D-168
81F-616
81Pol/Mar-15
81T-116
82D-55
82F-518
82T-382
83F-485
83T-567
83T/Tr-104
84Cram/PCL-115
84D-496
84F-358
84Nes/792-219
84T-219
90Target-736
Simpson, Shelton
90Welland/Pucko-29
Simpson, Wayne
70T-683R
71K-1
71MD
71MLB/St-69
71OPC-339
71OPC-68LL
71T-339
71T-68LL
71T/Coins-53
72T-762
73OPC-428
73T-428
76SSPC-599
Simpson, William
77Ashvl
78Ashvl
Sims, Daniel Jr.
89Idaho/ProC-2018
90Sumter/Best-20
90Sumter/ProC-2448
Sims, Duane
(Duke)
66OPC-169
66T-169
67OPC-3
67T-3
68T-508
69MB-255
69T-414
69T/St-168
70MLB/St-203
70OPC-275
70T-275
71MLB/St-114
71OPC-172
71T-172
71T/Coins-66
71Ticket/Dodg-15
72MB-316
72OPC-63
72T-63
73OPC-304
73T-304
74OPC-398
74T-398
86AppFx-23MG
89Swell-128
90Target-737
92Yank/WIZ70-140
93Rang/Keeb-328
Sims, Greg
89Augusta/ProC-517
89SALAS/GS-5
90Salem/Star-22
91Visalia/ProC-1756
Sims, Gregory E.
66T-596R
Sims, Harry
52Laval-33
Sims, Joe Beely
86James-23
87James-8
Sims, Kinney
88Reno/Cal-278
Sims, Mark
87Spartan-6
88Clearw/Star-21
89Clearw/Star-20
90EastLAS/ProC-EL22
90Foil/Best-182
90Reading/Best-10
90Reading/ProC-1220
90Reading/Star-22
91AA/LineD-519
91Reading/LineD-519
91Reading/ProC-1370
92ScranWB/ProC-2446
92ScranWB/SB-494
Sims, Mike
83Tampa-29TR
86Vermont-19TR
Simunic, Doug
79Memphis/TCMA-7
80Memphis-22
83Charl-7
84BuffB-6
84Maine-5
89AubAs/ProC-2184
89Pac/SenLg-35
89T/SenLg-84
90EliteSenLg-105
91Kissim/ProC-4205CO
91Pac/SenLg-55
92GulfCD/ProC-3586
Sinacori, Chris
91GreatF/SportP-21
92VeroB/ClBest-16
92VeroB/ProC-2873
Sinatro, Greg
77SanJose-8
Sinatro, Matt
81Richm-20
82D-149
82Richm-12
83D-622
83Richm-11
85Greenvl/Team-15
87Tacom-9
88Tacoma/CMC-18
88Tacoma/ProC-616
89Tucson/CMC-11
89Tucson/ProC-201
90AAASingl/ProC-119
90Calgary/CMC-13
90Calgary/ProC-654
90ProC/Singl-440
90T/Tr-115T
91OPC-709
91T-709
92B-462
92Mother/Mar-18
92StCl-872
Sinclair, John
87BYU-12
Sinclair, Ken
84Savan-25
Sinclair, Steve
91MedHat/ProC-4100
91MedHat/SportP-12
93MedHat/ProC-3736
93MedHat/SportP-2
Siner, Hosea John
E254
Singer, Bill
66T-288R
67OPC-12R
67T-12R
68T-249
69MLB/St-152
69OPC-12LL
69T-12LL
69T-575
69T/St-49
70K-17
70MLB/St-57
70OPC-490
70OPC-71LL
70T-490
70T-71LL
70T/CB
71MLB/St-115
71OPC-145
71T-145
71Ticket/Dodg-16
72MB-317
72OPC-25
72T-25
73OPC-570
73T-570
74K-12
74OPC-210
74T-210
74T/St-149
75Ho-82
75Ho/Twink-82
75OPC-40
75T-40
75T/M-40
76OPC-411
76SSPC-188
76T-411
76T/Tr-411T
77Ho-139
77Ho/Twink-139
77OPC-85
77T-346
77T/CS-44
77T/ClothSt-44
87Smok/Dodg-33
88Smok/Dodg-6M
89Smok/Dodg-75
90Target-738
92Nabisco-18
93Rang/Keeb-329
Singer, Tom
90StCath/ProC-3457
91Myrtle/ClBest-10
91Myrtle/ProC-2944
92Dunedin/ClBest-16
92Dunedin/ProC-1999
93Dunedin/ClBest-20
93Dunedin/ProC-1795
Singletary, Chico
87Savan-15
Singleton, Bert Elmer
49B-147
49Sommer-25
57T-378
59T-548
63MilSau-6
Singleton, Chris
94ClBest/Gold-63
Singleton, Duane
92B-679
92ClBest-285
92Stockton/ClBest-7
92UD/ML-196
93B-43
93ClBest/MLG-100
94B-533
Singleton, Ken
71OPC-16
71T-16
72OPC-425
72OPC-426IA
72ProStars/PostC-11
72T-425
72T-426IA
73OPC-232
73T-232
74Expo/West-9
74K-48
74OPC-25
74T-25
74T/St-60
74Weston-29
75K-40
75OPC-125
75T-125
75T/M-125
76Ho-76
76K-12
76OPC-175
76SSPC-400
76T-175
77BurgChef-41
77Ho-107
77Ho/Twink-107
77OPC-19
77T-445
78Ho-75
78K-55
78OPC-80
78T-65
79Ho-135
79OPC-324
79T-615
80K-30
80OPC-178
80T-340
80T/S-11
80T/Super-11
81D-115
81Drake-12
81F-188
81F/St-103
81K-39
81OPC-281
81PermaGr/AS-17
81T-570
81T/So-17
81T/St-33
82D-105
82D-24DK
82Drake-30
82F-179
82F/St-150
82FBI/Disc-21
82K-58
82OPC-290
82OPC-2AS
82T-290
82T-552AS
82T/St-136
82T/St-144

87D/OD-240
87F-115
87Sf/TPrev-7M
87T-626
88D-474
88D/Best-300
88D/Y/Bk-474
88S-532
88T-109
89D-427
89D/Best-224
89D/Tr-22
89F-270
89OPC-127
89S-447
89S/Tr-76T
89T-536
89UD-328
90D-73
90F-501
90F/Can-501
90Leaf-286
90OPC-54
90PublInt/St-567
90T-54
90UD-369
91D-120
91F-377
91Indian/McDon-25
91Leaf-211
91OPC-783
91S-809
91StCl-561
91T-783
91UD-121
92D-99
92F-123
92Indian/McDon-26
92L-181
92L/BlkGold-181
92OPC-378
92S-227
92StCl-278
92T-378
92T/Gold-378
92T/GoldWin-378
92UD-199
92Yank/WIZ80-180
93Indian/WUAB-28

Skinner, John
82AppFx/Frit-14

Skinner, Matt
85Newar-23

Skinner, Mike
86RochR-22
87RochR-5
87RochR/TCMA-9

Skizas, Lou
57T-83
58T-319
59T-328
60Union-15

Sklar, Joel
86LitFalls-25

Skodny, Joe
86Cram/NWL-48
87AppFx-11
88BBCity/Star-21

Skoglund, Brad
83Wisco/Frit-23

Skok, Craig
79T-363
80Richm-20
93Rang/Keeb-330

Skoog, Jack
89SanDiegoSt/Smok-26

Skorochocki, John
77Newar
78BurlB
81ElPaso-4
82Vanco-6

Skowron, Bill
54T-239
55B-160
55T-22
55T/DH-21
56T-61
56T/Pin-30
57T-135
58T-240
58T-477AS
59T-554AS
59T-90
59YooHoo-6
60MacGregor-23
60T-370
60T-553AS
61P-3
61T-371
61T-42LL
61T-568AS
62J-1
62P-1
62P/Can-1
62Salada-59
62Shirriff-59
62T-110
62T/St-91
63J-12
63P-12
63T-180
64T-445
64T/S-60
65OPC-70
65T-70
65T/E-5
65T/trans-69
66Bz-33
66T-199M
66T-590
66T/RO-4
66T/RO-86
67CokeCap/WSox-13
67T-357
78TCMA-230
79TCMA-210
81TCMA-474M
83Kaline-18M
83MLBPA/Pin-17
88Pac/Leg-82
90Target-742
92AP/ASG-35
92Yank/WIZ60-117
92Yank/WIZAS-79
93Metallic-17
93UD/ATH-114
94T/Arc54-239
94TedW-64
Exh47
PM10/L-37
WG9-46

Skripko, Joseph
85Greens-8

Skripko, Scott
86WinHaven-23
87NewBrit-10
89Lynch/Star-25

Skryd, Chris
89SLCity-19

Skube, Bob
81ElPaso-15
82Vanco-1
83Pol/Brew-26
85Cram/PCL-214

Skurla, John
86Fresno/Smok-23
88Shrev/ProC-1297
88TexLgAS/GS-15
89Phoenix/CMC-23
89Phoenix/ProC-1496
90AAASingl/ProC-106
90Edmon/CMC-12
90Edmon/ProC-530
90ProC/Singl-489

Skurski, Andy
47Signal

Skyta, Damon
86Everett/Pop-29

Slack, Bill
85Greenvl/Team-16CO
86Greenvl/Team-17CO
87Durham-15
89Greenvl/Best-18
89Greenvl/ProC-1168
90Greenvl/ProC-1144CO
90Greenvl/Star-24CO
91AA/LineD-225M
91Greenvl/ClBest-26CO
91Greenvl/LineD-225CO
91Greenvl/ProC-3020CO
92Greenvl/ProC-1170CO

Slade, Gordon
28Exh/PCL-27
90Target-743

Slagle, Eric
92MN-18

Slagle, James J.
E91
T206

Slagle, Lee
91James/ClBest-28TR
91James/ProC-3561TR
92James/ClBest-29TR
93WPalmB/ClBest-28TR

Slagle, Roger
77WHave
78Cr/PCL-4
80Colum-2
82Nashvl-23
91Pac/SenLg-17
92Yank/WIZ70-141

Slater, Bob
76QuadC
79SLCity-21
79T-703R

Slater, Vernon
90Eugene/GS-28
91AppFx/ClBest-7
91Eugene/ClBest-10
91Eugene/ProC-3741

Slaton, Jim
72T-744
73OPC-628
73T-628
74OPC-371
74T-371
74T/St-200
75OPC-281
75T-281
75T/M-281
76A&P/Milw
76OPC-163
76SSPC-226
76T-163
77BurgChef-83
77Ho-105
77Ho/Twink-105
77OPC-29
77T-604
78BK/T-7
78Ho-14
78OPC-146
78T-474
79T-541
80OPC-10
80T-24
81D-447
81F-518
81T-357
82D-80
82F-153
82Pol/Brew-41
82T-221
83D-330
83F-46
83Gard-17
83OPC-114
83Pol/Brew-41
83T-114
84D-481
84F-214
84F/X-107
84Nes/792-772
84OPC-104
84Smok/Cal-27
84T-772
84T/St-302
84T/Tr-109
85D-545
85F-313
85Smok/Cal-17
85T-657
86D-402
86F-169
86Smok/Cal-17
86T-579
87F-163
87T-432
89Pac/SenLg-110
89TM/SenLg-96
91SoOreg/ProC-3867CO
92Brew/Carlson-21
92Reno/Cal-61CO
92SoOreg/ClBest-29CO

Slattery, Chris
88CapeCod/Sum-161

Slattery, Don
92Johnson/ClBest-17
92Johnson/ProC-3125

Slattery, Kevin
75Clinton

Slattery, Mike
N172
N338/2

Slaught, Don
82Omaha-12
83D-196
83F-123
84D-419
84F-359
84Nes/792-196
84T-196
85D-496
85F-214
85F/Up-U104
85OPC-159
85Rang-4
85T-542
85T/St-279
85T/Tr-107T
86D-281
86F-572
86Leaf-155
86OPC-24
86Rang-4
86T-761
86T/St-243
87D-136
87D/OD-176
87F-139
87Mother/Rang-12
87OPC-308
87Sf-154M
87Sf-32
87Sf/TPrev-1M
87Smok/R-9
87T-308
87T/St-241
88AlaskaAS70/Team-13
88D/Best-188
88D/Y/Bk-NEW
88F/Up-U51
88S-268
88S/Tr-19T
88T-462
88T/Tr-108T
89B-172
89D-190
89D/Best-105
89F-271
89KennerFig-131
89OPC-238
89Panini/St-403
89S-561
89S/NWest-12
89Sf-218
89T-611
89T/Big-138
89UD-178
90B-182
90D-277
90F-456
90F/Can-456
90F/Up-U51
90Homer/Pirate-27
90Leaf-354
90MLBPA/Pins-65
90OPC-26
90PublInt/St-548
90S-79
90S/Tr-13T
90T-26
90T/St-318
90T/Tr-116T
90UD-152
91B-532
91D-213
91F-49
91Leaf-29
91Leaf/Stud-228
91OPC-221
91S-610
91StCl-358
91T-221
91UD-181
91Ultra-286
92D-653
92F-566
92L-124
92L/BlkGold-124
92OPC-524
92Pinn-416
92Pirate/Nation-20
92S-280
92StCl-545
92T-524
92T/Gold-524
92T/GoldWin-524
92UD-540
92Ultra-258
92Yank/WIZ80-181
93B-430
93D-438
93F-119
93Flair-116
93L-6
93Pac/Spanish-251
93Pinn-188
93Pirate/Nation-29
93Rang/Keeb-331
93S-181
93Select-171
93StCl-127
93StCl/1stDay-127
93Studio-209
93T-778
93T/Gold-778
93UD-743
93UD/SP-187
93Ultra-455
94B-602
94D-217
94F-619
94Flair-219
94L-135
94Pac/Cr-506
94Panini-238
94Pinn-217
94Pinn/Artist-217
94Pinn/Museum-217
94S-86
94S/GoldR-86
94Select-65
94StCl-137
94StCl/1stDay-137
94StCl/Gold-137
94Studio-149
94T-405
94T/Finest-127
94T/FinestRef-127
94T/Gold-405
94TripleP-188
94UD-479
94UD/CollC-259
94UD/CollC/Gold-259
94UD/CollC/Silv-259
94Ultra-260

Slaughter, Enos
41DP-40
47HomogBond-43
47TipTop
48B-17
48L-127
49B-65
49Eureka-198
50B-35
50Drake-36
51B-58
51T/BB-30
52B-232
52Dix
52NTea
52RM-NL20
52StarCal-93BM
52StarCal/L-81D
52T-65
52TipTop
53B/Col-81
53Dix
53Hunter
53NB
53RM-NL13
53T-41
54B-62
54Dix
54Hunter
54RH
54RM-NL19
54Wilson
55B-60
55Rodeo
56Rodeo
56T-109
57T-215
58T-142
59T-155
74Laugh/ASG-53
77Galasso-40

79TCMA-240
80Pac/Leg-32
80Perez/HOF-191
85West/2-27
86Sf/Dec-18
88Pac/Leg-84
89Pac/Leg-137
89Swell-65
90Pac/Legend-50
90Perez/GreatMom-29
90Swell/Great-54
91Conlon/Sport-56
91Swell/Great-84
91T/Arc53-41
92AP/ASG-15
92AP/ASG24K-15G
92Bz/Quadra-13M
92Card/McDon/Pac-23
92Conlon/Sport-642
92Yank/WIZHOF-31
93AP/ASGCoke/Amo-15
93TWill-92
93TWill/Locklear-7
93UD/ATH-115
94Conlon/Col-27
D305
Exh47
PM10/L-38
PM10/Sm-181
R346-34
R423-96
W754

Slaughter, Garland
89Welland/Pucko-22

Slaughter, Sterling
64T-469R
65T-314

Slavic, Joseph
86Lakeland-21
88Lakeland/Star-23

Slavin, Dave
88Pocatel/ProC-2094
89Clinton/ProC-909

Slavin, Tim
83Wausau/Frit-8

Slayback, Bill
73OPC-537
73T-537

Slaymaker, Joe
75BurlB

Sleater, Lou
52T-306
53T-224
55Rodeo
58T-46
91Crown/Orio-424
91T/Arc53-224

Slettvet, Doug
75QuadC
76QuadC
77QuadC

Slezak, Robert
82VeroB-11
83VeroB-12

Slider, Rachel
(Rac)
61Union
85IntLgAS-45
85Pawtu-14
90T/TVRSox-6CO

Slifko, Paul
86NewBrit-22
87WinHaven-20

Sline, Fred
C46-9

Slininger, Dennis
91Johnson/ClBest-20
91Johnson/ProC-3978
92Spring/ClBest-15
92Spring/ProC-867
94ClBest/Gold-26

Sliwinski, Kevin
86Knoxvl-21
87Knoxvl-10
88Huntsvl/BK-20
88Tacoma/CMC-20
88Tacoma/ProC-626

Sloat, Dwain
(Lefty)
90Target-744

Slocum, Ron
70T-573R
71MLB/St-239
71OPC-274
71T-274

Slocumb, Heathcliff
86LitFalls-26
87WinSalem-7
88WinSalem/Star-16
89Peoria/Team-9
90CharlK/Team-6
91B-421
91Classic/III-84
91Cub/Mara-51
91Cub/Vine-26
91D/Rook-25
91F/UltraUp-U73
91F/Up-U81
91Leaf-370
91S/RookTr-84T
91UD/Ext-767
92D-334
92F-390
92OPC-576
92S-213
92S/100RisSt-28
92StCl-382
92T-576
92T/91Debut-164
92T/Gold-576
92T/GoldWin-576
92UD-569
92USPlayC/Cub-4C
92USPlayC/Cub-8S
93D-664
93T-783
93T/Gold-783
94Phill/Med-30
94StCl/Team-231

Slominski, Rich
86Wausau-22

Slomkowski, Rich
89Watlo/ProC-1798
89Watlo/Star-19
90Freder/Team-8

Sloniger, Chris
88SLCity-5
89Miami/II/Star-17

Slosson, Bill
91Sumter/ClBest-29TR

Slotnick, Joe
86BurlEx-20

Slowik, Tad
86Peoria-21
87WinSalem-11

Slusarski, Joe
87PanAm/USAB-20
87PanAm/USAR-20
88T/Tr-109TOLY
89Modesto/Cal-266
89Modesto/Chong-15
89T/Big-213
90Foil/Best-203
90Huntsvl/Best-10
90TeamUSA/87-20
91B-233
91Classic/III-85
91S/RookTr-105T
91Tacoma/ProC-2305
91UD/Ext-777
92B-58
92D-626
92F-266
92L-431
92L/BlkGold-431
92Mother/A's-19
92OPC-651
92Pinn-187
92S-309
92S/100RisSt-18
92StCl-782
92T-651
92T/91Debut-165
92T/DQ-14
92T/Gold-651
92T/GoldWin-651
92UD-663
93StCl-376
93StCl/1stDay-376

Sly, Kian
92Pulaski/ClBest-4
92Pulaski/ProC-3193
93Macon/ClBest-22
93Macon/ProC-1415

Smajstra, Craig
83AppFx/Frit-10
86Water-22
87BuffB-10
88Tucson/CMC-23
88Tucson/JP-21
88Tucson/ProC-168
89Tucson/CMC-12
89Tucson/JP-22
89Tucson/ProC-200
90AAAGame/ProC-40
90AAASingl/ProC-199
90ProC/Singl-611
90Tucson/CMC-9
90Tucson/ProC-209
91AAA/LineD-205
91Iowa/LineD-205
91Iowa/ProC-1069

Smaldone, Ed
89Geneva/ProC-1861

Small, Aaron
90Myrtle/ProC-2777
91ClBest/Singl-361
91Dunedin/ClBest-10
91Dunedin/ProC-206
92ClBest-162
92Knoxvl/ProC-2991
92Knoxvl/SB-393
92Sky/AASingl-167
93B-631
93Knoxvl/ProC-1251

Small, Chris
88AubAs/ProC-1949

Small, Hank
78Richm

Small, Jeff
86Peoria-22
87WinSalem-24
90AAAGame/ProC-35
90AAASingl/ProC-632
90Iowa/CMC-20
90Iowa/ProC-325
90ProC/Singl-95
90T/TVCub-59
91AAA/LineD-218
91Iowa/LineD-218
91Iowa/ProC-1070
92Nashvl/ProC-1841
92Nashvl/SB-293
93Edmon/ProC-1146

Small, Jim
56T-207
57T-33
61Union
D301

Small, Mark
89AubAs/ProC-2188
90Ashvl/ProC-2748
91Osceola/ClBest-11
91Osceola/ProC-684
92Osceola/ClBest-12
92Osceola/ProC-2530

Small, Nataniel
(Lefty)
76Laugh/Clown-7

Small, Robert
89James/ProC-2133

Smalley, Dave
84Greens-13

Smalley, Roy Jr.
75Spoka
75Spokane/Caruso-6
76OPC-657
76OPC-70FS
76SSPC-267
76T-657
76T-70FS
77Ho-66
77Ho/Twink-66
77T-66
78Ho-118
78T-471
78Twin/FriszP-19
79Ho-60
79OPC-110
79T-219
79Twin/FriszP-26
80K-13
80OPC-296
80T-570
80T/S-40
80T/Super-40
81D-487
81F-551
81F/St-55
81MSA/Disc-30
81OPC-115
81T-115
81T/So-43
81T/St-100
82D-22DK
82D-573
82F-560
82F/St-228
82OPC-197
82T-767
82T/St-207
82T/Tr-107T
83D-209
83F-397
83F/St-24M
83F/St-2M
83OPC-38
83OPC/St-96
83RoyRog/Disc-11
83T-460
83T/St-96
84D-225
84F-142
84Nes/792-305
84OPC-305
84T-305
85D-622
85F-527
85F/Up-U105
85OPC-26
85Seven/Minn-6
85T-140FS
85T-26
85T/St-237
85T/Tr-108T
85Twin/Seven-6
85Twin/Team-2
86D-486
86F-404
86Leaf-237
86OPC-156
86T-613
87D-443
87F-552
87OPC-47
87Sf/TPrev-17M
87T-744
87T/St-282
88D-566
88F-22
88Leaf-233
88S-606
88T-239
90Smok/SoCal-12
92Yank/WIZ80-182
93Rang/Keeb-332
PM10/Sm-182

Smalley, Roy Sr.
48L-77
49Eureka-72
50B-115
51B-44
51FB
51T/BB-17
52B-64
52T-173
53B/BW-56
54B-109
54T-231
55B-252
55JC-30
57T-397
60DF-3
76OPC-70FS
76T-70FS
85T-140FS
91T/Arc53-297
94T/Arc54-231

Smalls, Roberto
88Wythe/ProC-1986
89CharWh/Best-15
89CharWh/ProC-1761
90Geneva/ProC-3052
90Geneva/Star-22

Smallwood, DeWitt
(Woody)
92Negro/RetortII-35

Smallwood, Kevin
90AR-29M

Smay, Kevin
81Clinton-9

Smedes, Mike
89Anchora-24

Smelko, Mark
82Redwd-11
83Redwd-23

Smelser, Don
80ElPaso-15

Smiley, John
85PrWill-22
86PrWill-24
87D/Rook-39
87F/Up-U110
87Sf/Rook-21
87Sf/Rook-7
87Sf/TPrev-18M
87T/Tr-114T
88D-449
88D/Best-257
88F-340
88RedFoley/St-82
88S-287
88T-423
88ToysRUs-28
89B-413
89Classic/Up/2-191
89D-329
89D/Best-157
89F-221
89OPC-322
89Panini/St-167
89S-409
89S/YS/I-37
89T-322
89T/Big-85
89T/St-124
89UD-516
89VFJuice-57
90Classic-126
90D-17DK
90D-54
90D/BestNL-21
90D/SuperDK-17DK
90F-480
90F/Can-480
90Homer/Pirate-30
90Kenner/Fig-78
90Leaf-328
90OPC-568
90Panini/St-323
90PublInt/St-165
90S-334
90S/100St-65
90Sf-191
90T-568
90T/Big-79
90T/St-132
90UD-387
91B-509
91Classic/III-86
91D-664
91F-50
91F/UltraUp-U102
91Leaf-123
91Leaf/Stud-229
91OPC-143
91S-465
91StCl-471
91T-143
91UD-669
91USPlayC/AS-3C
92B-257
92Classic/Game200-156
92Classic/II-T88
92D-331
92F-567
92F/Up-41
92French-5M
92L-526
92L/BlkGold-526
92MooTown-12
92OPC-232
92OPC/Premier-2
92Pinn-184
92S-659
92S/100SS-3
92S/Impact-79
92S/RookTr-22T
92StCl-380
92StCl-625
92StCl/Dome-173
92Studio-210
92Sunflower-17
92T-232
92T/Gold-232
92T/GoldWin-232
92T/Tr-106T
92T/TrGold-106T
92TripleP-52

92UD-467
92UD-785
92Ultra-259
92Ultra-400
93B-230
93Classic/Gamel-86
93D-475
93F-643
93F/Final-20
93L-433
93OPC-335
93OPC/Premier-56
93Pac/Spanish-406
93Pinn-543
93Pinn/TP-2M
93Reds/Kahn-26
93S-624
93Select-75
93Select/Ace-13
93Select/Pr-75
93Select/RookTr-100T
93StCl-190
93StCl/1stDay-190
93T-363
93T/Finest-14
93T/FinestRef-14
93T/Gold-363
93T/Hill-10
93UD-268
93UD-694
93Ultra-336
94D-105
94F-429
94Flair-150
94L-24
94Pac/Cr-161
94Pinn-99
94Pinn/Artist-99
94Pinn/Museum-99
94S-424
94Select-169
94StCl-487
94StCl/1stDay-487
94StCl/Gold-487
94Studio-174
94T-12
94T/Finest-179
94T/FinestRef-179
94T/Gold-12
94TripleP-220
94UD-327
94Ultra-178

Smiley, Reuben
88Pocatel/ProC-2087
89Clinton/ProC-894
90AS/Cal-45
90Foil/Best-310
90SanJose/Best-3
90SanJose/Cal-30
90SanJose/ProC-2024
90SanJose/Star-22
90SanJose/Star-26M
91AA/LineD-321
91Shrev/LineD-321
91Shrev/ProC-1836
92Shrev/ProC-3885
92Shrev/SB-594

Smith
10Domino-110
12Sweet/Pin-77
S74-56

Smith, Ackroyd
52Laval-77

Smith, Adam
88Pocatel/ProC-2092

Smith, Alex
87Durham-14
88Richm-30
88Richm/CMC-13
88Richm/ProC-25
89Richm/Bob-25
89Richm/Ko-14
89Richm/ProC-841

Smith, Alexander B.
(Broadway Aleck)
90Target-1072

Smith, Alfred J.
(Al)
43Playball-8
46Sunbeam
47Signal
47Sunbeam
92Conlon/Sport-580
V94-43

Smith, Alphonse E.
54T-248
55B-20
55Gol/Ind-27
55Salem
55T-197
56Carling-8
56T-105
56T/Pin-11OF
57Sohio/Ind-13
57T-145
58T-177
59T-22
60T-428
61P-24
61T-170
61T-42LL
61T/St-129
62J-48
62P-48
62P/Can-48
62Salada-29
62Shirriff-29
62T-410
63J-38
63P-38
63T-16
64T-317
91Crown/Orio-425
94T/Arc54-248

Smith, Anthony
90Target-1075
T204
T205

Smith, Ben
90Kgsport/Star-30BB

Smith, Bernie
83Redwd-29

Smith, Bill 1
60Maple-19
61BeeHive-21

Smith, Bill 2
83AppFx/Frit-1GM

Smith, Billy Edward
76SSPC-199
78T-666
79T-237
80OkCty
80T-367
82F-400
82T-593
91Crown/Orio-426

Smith, Billy Lavern
78DaytB
80Tucson-11
81Tucson-24
82T-441R
82Tucson-18
84Tor/Fire-27CO
85Tor/Fire-26CO
86Tor/Fire-28CO
87Tor/Fire-28CO
88Tor/Fire-42CO

Smith, Billy
85Everett/II/Cram-17

Smith, Bob E.
33G-185
35BU-47
91Conlon/Sport-217
R316

Smith, Bob G.
58T-226
59T-83

Smith, Bob W.
58T-445

Smith, Bob
60Maple-20
61BeeHive-22

Smith, Bobby Gene
57T-384
58T-402
59T-162
60T-194
61T-316
62J-196
62P-196
62P/Can-196
62Salada-176A
62Salada-176B
62Shirriff-176
62T-531
91WIZMets-368

Smith, Bobby Glen
78BurlB
79Holyo-6
80Vanco-5
81Vanco-19

Smith, Brad
88Clearw/Star-23

Smith, Brick
84Chatt-5
86Chatt-23
86SLAS-17
87Calgary-12
87Sf/Rook-5
88Calgary/ProC-803
89Chatt/II/Team-28
89Tucson/CMC-17
89Tucson/JP-23
89Tucson/ProC-193

Smith, Bryan
86Bakers-25
87VeroB-24
90AubAs/Best-12
90AubAs/ProC-3406
91BurlAs/ClBest-22
91BurlAs/ProC-2816
91ClBest/Singl-313

Smith, Bryn
78Denver
79Memphis/TCMA-5
80Memphis-20
82Expo/Hygrade-20
82Hygrade
82OPC-118R
82T-118R
83D-88
83Expo/PostC-19
83F-297
83OPC-234
83Stuart-29
83T-447
84D-453
84Expo/PostC-29
84F-287
84Nes/792-656
84OPC-77
84Stuart-21
84T-656
85D-209
85Expo/PostC-20
85F-410
85Leaf-171
85OPC-88
85T-88
85T/St-90
86D-299
86Expo/Prov/Pan-19
86Expo/Prov/Post-2
86F-260
86F/Mini-55
86F/Slug-35
86F/St-110
86GenMills/Book-6M
86Leaf-174
86OPC-299
86Provigo-19
86Sf-120
86T-299
86T/St-79
86T/Super-51
86T/Tatt-22M
87D-159
87Expo/PostC-6
87F-332
87GenMills/Book-4M
87Leaf-60
87OPC-281
87Stuart-8
87T-505
87T/St-83
88D-335
88D/Best-202
88F-196
88Leaf-129
88OPC-161
88Panini/St-320
88S-356
88T-161
88T/Big-250
89B-353
89D-216
89D/Best-124
89F-394
89OPC-131
89Panini/St-116
89S-428
89T-464
89T/Big-47
89UD-78
90B-184
90D-106
90D-25DK
90D/BestNL-10
90D/SuperDK-25DK
90F-361
90F/Can-361
90Leaf-393
90OPC-352
90PublInt/St-188
90S-419
90S/Tr-55T
90Smok/Card-20
90T-352
90T/St-78
90T/TVCard-18
90T/Tr-117T
90UD-579
90UD/Ext-794
91B-407
91D-113
91F-644
91Leaf-226
91OPC-743
91Pol/Card-36
91S-444
91StCl-17
91T-743
91UD-307
91Ultra-294
92D-323
92F-590
92L-157
92L/BlkGold-157
92OPC-31
92Pinn-474
92Pol/Card-17
92S-529
92StCl-368
92T-31
92T/Gold-31
92T/GoldWin-31
92UD-591
92Ultra-269
93F-515
93L-409
93Pac/Spanish-438
93StCl/Rockie-4
93UD-723
93USPlayC/Rockie-5D
93USPlayC/Rockie-8H
93Ultra-359

Smith, C. Bernard
71OPC-204R
71T-204R

Smith, C.L.
90Rockford/Team-25

Smith, Calvin
91Hunting/ClBest-24
91Hunting/ProC-3344

Smith, Carl R.
(Reggie)
67T-314R
67T/Test/RSox-12
68OPC-61
68T-61
69MB-256
69MLB/St-18
69T-660
69T/St-139
70K-46
70MLB/St-167
70OPC-215
70OPC-62LL
70T-215
70T-62LL
70T/PI-20
71K-52
71MD
71MLB/St-333
71OPC-305
71T-305
71T/Coins-78
71T/S-1
71T/Super-1
71T/tatt-8
72K-35
72MB-318
72OPC-88LL
72T-565
72T-566IA
72T-88LL
73OPC-40
73T-40
74OPC-285
74T-285
74T/St-118
75Ho-59
75K-3
75OPC-490
75T-490
75T/M-490
76Crane-57
76Ho-30
76Ho/Twink-30
76MSA/Disc
76OPC-215
76SSPC-278
76T-215
77BurgChef-152
77OPC-223
77T-345
78Ho-30
78K-34
78OPC-57
78SSPC/270-58
78T-168
78Wiffle/Discs-70
79Ho-72
79OPC-243
79T-465
79T/Comics-25
80OPC-350
80Pol/Dodg-8
80T-695
81D-59
81F-111
81F/St-87
81K-36
81OPC-75
81Pol/Dodg-8
81T-75
81T/HT
81T/So-57
81T/St-178
82D-488
82F-23
82OPC-228IA
82OPC-5
82T-545
82T-546IA
82T/Tr-110T
83D-611
83F-272
83F/St-2M
83F/St-3M
83OPC-282
83OPC-283SV
83OPC/St-12
83OPC/St-302
83T-282
83T-283SV
83T/St-12
83T/St-302
87Smok/Dodg-34
88Smok/Dodg-21M
89Smok/Dodg-88
90Target-750
92Card/McDon/Pac-34
93AP/ASG-159

Smith, Carlos
T206

Smith, Chad
88BurlB/ProC-4
89Sumter/ProC-1108
90Durham/Team-23
90Miami/I/Star-25
92Hamil/ClBest-3
92Hamil/ProC-1591

Smith, Charles M.
M116
N172
N284
N300/SC
WG1-62

Smith, Charles W.
60DF-12
62Salada-135A
62Salada-135B
62Shirriff-135
62T-283
63T-424
64T-519
65OPC-22
65T-22

66T-358
67CokeCap/YMet-11
67T-257
68T-596
69T-538
78TCMA-289
90Target-745
91WIZMets-369
92Yank/WIZ60-118
Smith, Charles
(Bubba)
91Belling/ClBest-12
91Belling/ProC-3675
91ClBest/Singl-446
92ClBest-216
92Penin/ClBest-1
92Penin/ProC-2944
92UD/ML-170
93B-346FOIL
93ClBest/MLG-34
93FExcel/ML-232
93T-423M
93T/Gold-423M
94B-344
Smith, Chris W.
80Memphis-21
82Wichita-18
83Phoenix/BHN-22
84D-46RR
87Salem/ProC-2444MG
Smith, Chris
92Boise/ClBest-26
92Boise/ProC-3640
92ClBest/Up-423
92Classic/DP-33
93StCl/MurphyS-132
94B-154
Smith, Chuck
92Ashvl/ClBest-23
Smith, Clay
79Clinton/TCMA-2
Smith, Cleo
75Albuq/Caruso-9
Smith, Coleman
92Hunting/ClBest-17
92Hunting/ProC-3166
Smith, Coley
74Tacoma/Caruso-10
75Tacoma/KMMO-17
Smith, D.L.
90AAASingl/ProC-660
90ProC/Singl-35
91AAA/LineD-126
92ColoSp/SB-96
Smith, Dan 1
75Cedar
78Tidew
79Jacks-17
Smith, Dan 2
86Bakers-26
87OrlanTw-3
Smith, Dana
86Hagers-18
88CharlK/Pep-21
89Hagers/Best-21
89Hagers/ProC-286
89Hagers/Star-18
Smith, Dandy
91Rockford/ProC-2056
Smith, Daniel Scott
90Butte/SportP-7
90Classic/DP-16
91AAA/LineD-322
91B-275
91OkCty/LineD-322
91OkCty/ProC-179
91Rockford/ClBest-21
91S-384FDP
92B-391
92ClBest-291
92Sky/AASingl-276
92Tulsa/ProC-2696
92Tulsa/SB-622
93B-109
93ClBest/MLG-10
93D-374RR
93F-329
93Pac/Spanish-648
93Pinn-603
93Rang/Keeb-333
93StCl/Rang-6
93T-607
93T/Gold-607
93ToysRUs-68
93UD-7SR
93Ultra-637
94SigRook-22
Smith, Danny
85Cedar-12
86Vermont-20
Smith, Daryl
80Ashvl-19
83Tulsa-7
86Water-23
87Wmsprt-12
88BirmB/Best-19
90Memphis/Star-24
91AAA/LineD-345
91Omaha/LineD-345
91Omaha/ProC-1035
91T/90Debut-145
Smith, Dave
76BurlB
77Holyo
78Holyo
Smith, David A.
80Spokane-2
81LynnS-11
82Holyo-9
Smith, David Lee
(D.L.)
87RochR-14
87RochR/TCMA-14
88RochR/CMC-17
89ElPaso/GS-24
89TexLAS/GS-16
90Denver/CMC-10
90Denver/ProC-635
91Denver/LineD-126
91Denver/ProC-132
Smith, David S.
(Dave)
77Cocoa
79CharCh-11
81D-23
81F-71
81OPC-287
81T-534
82D-191
82F-232
82OPC-297
82T-761
83D-370
83F-466
83OPC-247
83T-247
84D-548
84F-242
84Mother/Ast-13
84Nes/792-361
84T-361
85D-548
85F-362
85Mother/Ast-21
85T-123
86D-328
86F-312
86F/St-111
86OPC-222
86Pol/Ast-11
86Seven/Coin-S12M
86T-408
86T/St-31
87Classic-66
87D-308
87D/AAS-30
87F-6
87F/Hottest-38
87F/St-109
87Leaf-224
87Mother/Ast-20
87OPC-50
87Pol/Ast-17
87Sf-94
87Sf/TPrev-8M
87T-50
87T/Mini-12
88AlaskaAS70/Team-24
88D-410
88D/Best-262
88F-457
88F/Hottest-39
88F/Mini-81
88F/St-90
88F/TL-37
88Mother/Ast-20
88OPC-73
88Panini/St-290
88Pol/Ast-22
88RochR/ProC-195
88RochR/Team-21
88S-365
88SanDiegoSt-17
88Sf-208
88T-520
88T/St-26
89B-317
89Classic-22
89D-272
89D/Best-232
89F-369
89F/BBAS-38
89KennerFig-132
89Lennox/Ast-19
89Mother/Ast-19
89OPC-305
89Panini/St-87
89S-245
89SanDiegoSt-18
89T-305
89T/St-13
89UD-302
90B-62
90Classic-94
90D-88
90D/BestNL-40
90F-238
90F/Can-238
90Leaf-122
90Lennox-23
90Mother/Ast-17
90OPC-746
90Panini/St-257
90PublInt/St-103
90RedFoley/St-87
90S-45
90S/100St-19
90Sf-140
90T-746
90T/Big-145
90T/St-16
90T/St-190
90T/TVAS-49
90UD-448
90USPlayC/AS-8D
91B-425
91Classic/III-87
91Cub/Mara-42
91Cub/Vine-27
91D-212
91F-517
91F/Up-U82
91Leaf-456
91Leaf/Stud-160
91OPC-215
91OPC/Premier-111
91Panini/St-12
91S-314
91S/RookTr-9T
91StCl-345
91T-215
91T/Tr-110T
91UD-513
91UD/Ext-704
92B-333
92Classic/Game200-31
92Cub/Mara-42
92D-53
92F-391
92L-30
92L/BlkGold-30
92OPC-601
92Pinn-94
92S-98
92StCl-219
92T-601
92T/Gold-601
92T/GoldWin-601
92UD-549
92USPlayC/Cub-10C
92USPlayC/Cub-4S
92Ultra-475
Smith, David Wayne
(D.W.)
82Holyo-10
83Nashua-8
83Wausau/Frit-27
84Cram/PCL-103
84Newar-11
85Cram/PCL-16
86Edmon-26
Smith, Demond
91Kingspt/ClBest-2
91Kingspt/ProC-3828
92Pittsfld/ClBest-2
92Pittsfld/ProC-3308
Smith, Don
84Cram/PCL-155
85Cram/PCL-171
Smith, Donald
(Snuffy)
47Smith-16
Smith, Dwight
86Peoria-23
87Pittsfld-26
88AAA/ProC-19
88Iowa/CMC-21
88Iowa/ProC-530
89B-297
89D/Best-205
89D/Rook-32
89F/Up-79
89Iowa/CMC-22
89Iowa/ProC-1708
89Mara/Cubs-18
89S-642RP
89S/HotRook-64
89T/Tr-113T
89UD/Ext-780
90B-32
90Classic-30
90Cub/Mara-19
90D-393
90D/BestNL-63
90F-42
90F/BBMVP-35
90F/Can-42
90F/SoarSt-12
90HotRook/St-42
90Leaf-255
90OPC-311
90Panini/St-235
90PublInt/St-204
90S-240
90S/100Ris-4
90S/YS/I-2
90Sf-152
90T-311
90T/89Debut-116
90T/Big-151
90T/Coins-57
90T/HeadsUp-23
90T/JumboR-26
90T/St-52
90T/TVCub-33
90ToysRUs-25
90UD-376
91Cub/Mara-18
91Cub/Vine-28
91D-559
91F-432
91OPC-463
91Panini/FrSt-47
91S-301
91StCl-181
91T-463
91UD-452
91Ultra-68
92Cub/Mara-18
92D-561
92F-392
92OPC-168
92Pinn-293SIDE
92S-612
92StCl-196
92T-168
92T/Gold-168
92T/GoldWin-168
92USPlayC/Cub-10S
92USPlayC/Cub-2H
93Cub/Mara-25
93D-476
93F-384
93Flair-21
93L-547
93Pac/Spanish-63
93S-637
93StCl-278
93StCl/1stDay-278
93StCl/Cub-11
93T-688
93T/Gold-688
93TripleP-172
93Ultra-23
94D-570
94F-398
94Pac/Cr-111
94Panini-157
94Pinn-66
94Pinn/Artist-66
94Pinn/Museum-66
94S-408
94T-536
94T/Gold-536
Smith, Earl L.
28Yueng-48
E120
V100
W573
Smith, Earl S.
21Exh-162
21Exh-163
25Exh-54
26Exh-54
27Exh-27
28Exh-26
91Conlon/Sport-74
E120
E121/120
E121/80
E220
V100
W501-71
W502-48
W572
W573
W575
Smith, Ed
89SoBend/GS-28
90Saraso/Star-22
91Saraso/ClBest-19
91Saraso/ProC-1121
92ElPaso/ProC-3932
92Stockton/ClBest-4
92Stockton/ProC-43
Smith, Edward
(Mayo)
55T-130MG
56T-60MG
56T/Hocus-A9
56T/Pin-21MG
67T-321MG
68T-544MG
69OPC-40MG
69T-40MG
70OPC-313MG
70T-313MG
81Tiger/Detroit-35MG
Smith, Elmer E.
N172
Smith, Elmer John
21Exh-164
D328-163
E120
E121/120
E135-163
W501-109
W572
W575
Smith, Emmitt
91StCl/Member*-36
92StCl/MemberIV*-11
Smith, Eric
92Batavia/ClBest-12
92Batavia/ProC-3265
Smith, F.C.
N172
Smith, Forest
(Woody)
75SanAn
77Watlo
78Watlo
81Chatt-24
Smith, Frank Elmer
(Nig)
14CJ-90
15CJ-90
D303
E101
E102
E105
E254
E270/1
E90/3
E92
M116
T206
T207

T213/blue
T215/blue
T215/brown
T3-118
Smith, Frank
90Kissim/DIMD-25
91GreatF/SportP-1
92GreatF/SportP-27
Smith, Frank T.
52B-186
52T-179
53T-116
54B-188
54T-71
55Hunter
55T-204
91T/Arc53-116
94T/Arc54-71
Smith, Fred
92Watertn/ClBest-13
92Watertn/ProC-3234
Smith, Freddie
81Miami-3
Smith, Garry J.
77WHave
79Colum-5
80Colum-5
81Colum-21
82Colum-14
82Colum/Pol-13
82Nashvl-24
Smith, Gary
78Cr/PCL-29
Smith, Gene
81BurlB-5
Smith, George A.
90Target-747
V100
Smith, George C.
65T-483
66T-542
67CokeCap/RedSox-13
67T-444
67T/Test/RSox-18
Smith, George H.
E254
T206
Smith, George J.
(Germany)
90Target-748
N172
Smith, Greg
81VeroB-18
85Beaum-6
86Erie-27
86LasVegas-16
87Erie-11
87OKCty-19
88Spokane/ProC-1932
89CharRain/ProC-979
90AAASingl/ProC-633
90F/Can-643
90ProC/Singl-88
90River/Best-18
90River/Cal-2
90River/ProC-2621
91AAA/LineD-20
92Toledo/ProC-1052
92Toledo/SB-597
Smith, Gregory A.
(Greg)
87Peoria-14
88CLAS/Star-35
88WinSalem/Star-17
89CharlK-11
89SLAS-11
90B-31
90F-643
90Iowa/CMC-13
90Iowa/ProC-326
90S-614
90T/89Debut-117
90T/TVCub-27
90UD/Ext-738
91Albuq/LineD-20
91Albuq/ProC-1151
91B-594
91D-574
91F-433
91OPC-560
91StCl-554
91T-560
Smith, Hal R.
56T-283
57T-111
58T-273
59T-497
60L-58
60L-94M
60T-84
61P-180
61T-549
61T/St-94
Smith, Hal W.
55Esskay
55T-8
55T/DH-70
56T-62
56T/Hocus-A15
56T/Pin-3C
57T-41
58T-257
59T-227
60L-119
60L-94M
60T-48
61P-139
61T-242
61T/St-70
62J-181
62Kahn
62P-181
62P/Can-181
62Salada-190
62Shirriff-190
62T-492
62T/St-129
62T/bucks
63T-153
64T-233
78TCMA-127
89Smok/Ast-12
91Crown/Orio-427
Smith, Harold 1
89TNTech-25
Smith, Harold 2
V94-44
Smith, Harry Thomas
E107
M116
Smith, Henry J.
(Hap)
90Target-1073
T206
Smith, Hilton
78Laugh/Black-34
86Negro/Frit-27
87Negro/Dixon-27
Smith, Hut
92Classic/DP-75
92LitSun/HSPros-18
93StCl/MurphyS-95
Smith, Ira
90GreatF/SportP-28
92Bakers/Cal-22
94ClBest/Gold-143
94FExcel-286
Smith, Jack 1
21Exh-165
92Conlon/Sport-507
E126-51
V61-75
WG7-53
Smith, Jack 2
82WHave-9
83ColumAst-20
Smith, Jack Everett
(Jack)
86Tampa-20
87Tampa-14
88Greens/ProC-1569
89EastLgAS/ProC-20
89Wmsprt/ProC-643
89Wmsprt/Star-20
91AA/LineD-345
91Jaxvl/LineD-345
91Jaxvl/ProC-160
92OrlanSR/SB-521
92Tacoma/ProC-2512
93Calgary/ProC-1174
Smith, Jack H.
63T-496R
64T-378R
79Knoxvl/TCMA-17
90Target-749
Smith, James C.
(Red)
16FleischBrd-86
90Target-1074
D327
D328-164
D329-165
D350/2-167
E135-164
E220
M101/4-165
M101/5-167
T222
Smith, James Lorne
(Jimmy)
77Charl
79BuffB/TCMA-17
79RochR-13
80RochR-17
80Tidew-20
81Portl-22
83D-402
83F-323
83T-122
Smith, Jason
92Elmira/ClBest-6
92Elmira/ProC-1386
Smith, Jed
81Louisvl-30
82Louisvl-28
83Louisvl/Riley-30
84Louisvl-10
85Louisvl-10
86Louisvl-29
Smith, Jeff 1
75Dubuq
76Dubuq
Smith, Jeff 2
81Redwd-6
82Redwd-12
Smith, Jeff 3
86Beloit-23
Smith, Jeff 4
91Eugene/ClBest-20
91Eugene/ProC-3727
92AppFox/ClBest-21
Smith, Jim
88Eugene/Best-8
91AA/LineD-418
91London/LineD-418
91Memphis/ProC-654
Smith, JoJo
91Yakima/ClBest-27
91Yakima/ProC-4248
Smith, Joe
87BYU-21M
92Bakers/Cal-23
Smith, Joel
88SoOreg/ProC-1697
89Rockford/Team-24
90WPalmB/Star-22
92Boise/ClBest-4
92Boise/ProC-3633
Smith, John 1
(Duke)
82Madis/Frit-5
Smith, John 2
78Cedar
Smith, John 3
89Utica/Pucko-22
90Utica/Pucko-23
92Pittsfld/ProC-3309
93StLucie/ProC-2936
Smith, John Francis
N172
Smith, John W.
E102
V100
W572
W573
Smith, Jon
62Pep/Tul
63Pep/Tul
Smith, Keith L.
74Gaston
77Tucson
78Cr/PCL-76
78T-710R
81D-539
81F-534
92Yank/WIZ80-183
93Rang/Keeb-334
Smith, Kelly
82Phoenix
Smith, Kelvin
83Clinton/Frit-20
Smith, Ken
79Savan-24
80Richm-18
81Richm-4
82BK/Lids-23
82Richm-23
83F-148
83Pol/Atl-11
84Richm-3
85Richm-16
86RochR-23
88Savan/ProC-332
89StPete/Star-25
Smith, Kevin
91Kissim/ProC-4183
92GulfCD/ProC-3566
Smith, Kielan
93MedHat/ProC-3737
Smith, Lance
90Ashvl/ClBest-20
91Ashvl/ProC-572
92BurlAs/ClBest-10
92BurlAs/ProC-551
Smith, Larry
83Idaho-11
85Huntsvl/BK-30
87SanBern-2
Smith, Lawrence
(Larry)
89Miami/I/Star-18
89Welland/Pucko-31
93Welland/ClBest-29MG
Smith, Lee
80Wichita-12
82D-252
82F-603
82RedLob
82T-452
83D-403
83F-508
83T-699
83Thorn-46
84Cub/Uno-9M
84D-289
84F-505
84F/St-67
84Nes/792-176
84OPC-176
84SevenUp-46
84T-176
84T/St-44
85D-311
85F-67
85F/St-105
85FunFoodPin-108
85Leaf-128
85OPC-43
85SevenUp-46
85T-511
85T/St-41
86Cub/Unocal-17
86D-144
86D/AS/WaxBox-PC8
86F-380
86F/LL-41
86F/LimEd-42
86Gator-46
86GenMills/Book-4M
86Jay's-17
86Leaf-64
86OPC-355
86Seven/Coin-C11M
86Sf-45
86Sf-55M
86T-355
86T-636M
86T/St-56
86T/Super-52
86T/Tatt-1M
87Berg/Cubs-46
87D-292
87F-574
87F/Excit-39
87F/Lim-39
87F/Mini-101
87F/St-110
87Leaf-80
87OPC-23
87RedFoley/St-42
87Seven-C16
87Seven-ME15
87Sf-104
87Sf-77M
87Sf/TPrev-22M
87T-23
87T/Mini-3
87T/St-56
88D-292
88D/AS-60
88D/Best-252
88D/RedSox/Bk-NEW
88F-433
88F/Mini-9
88F/Up-U8
88OPC-240
88Panini/St-256
88S-31
88S/Tr-20T
88Sf-179
88T-240
88T/Gloss60-56
88T/Mini-44
88T/St-64
88T/St/Backs-33
88T/Tr-110T
89B-19
89D-66
89D/Best-84
89F-99
89KennerFig-133
89OPC-149
89Panini/St-272
89RedFoley/St-109
89S-150
89S/HotStar-18
89Sf-148
89T-760
89T/St-251
89UD-521
90B-263
90Classic-137
90D-110
90D/BestNL-120
90F-287
90F/Can-287
90F/Up-U53
90Leaf-524
90OPC-495
90Panini/St-14
90Pep/RSox-20
90PublInt/St-464
90S-37
90S/Tr-48T
90Smok/Card-21
90T-495
90T/St-262
90T/TVRSox-17
90T/Tr-118T
90UD-393
91B-387
91D-169
91D-403MVP
91F-645
91Leaf-44
91Leaf/Stud-237
91OPC-660
91Panini/FrSt-39
91Panini/St-38
91Panini/Top15-83
91Pol/Card-47
91S-81
91StCl-42
91T-660
91UD-348
91USPlayC/AS-10C
91Ultra-295
92B-505
92CJ/DII-4
92Card/McDon/Pac-53
92Classic/Game200-23
92Classic/II-T28
92D-112
92F-591
92F-697LL
92F/ASIns-8
92F/Smoke-S1
92French-6M
92L-254
92L/BlkGold-254
92OPC-565
92OPC/Premier-190
92Panini-179
92Pinn-195
92Pol/Card-18
92S-630
92S-781AS
92S/100SS-28

92StCl-180
92StCl/Dome-174
92StCl/MemberIII*-7
92Studio-97
92T-396AS
92T-565
92T/Gold-396AS
92T/Gold-565
92T/GoldWin-396AS
92T/GoldWin-565
92T/Kids-28
92TripleP-62
92UD-376
92UD/TmMVPHolo-49
92Ultra-270
93B-600
93Classic/GameI-87
93Cub/Rolaid-2
93D-548
93F-133
93F/ASNL-12
93F/Final/DTrib-DT7
93Flair-127
93Kraft-29
93L-154
93OPC-324
93Pac/Spanish-303
93Panini-160LL
93Panini-192
93Pinn-416
93Pol/Card-19
93S-103
93S-529AS
93Select-83
93Select/ChasS-12
93Select/RookTr-31T
93Select/StatL-70
93StCl-462
93StCl/1stDay-462
93StCl/Card-13
93StCl/MurphyS-128
93Studio-147
93T-12
93T-411
93T/BlkGold-19
93T/Finest-95AS
93T/FinestASJ-95AS
93T/FinestRef-95AS
93T/Gold-12
93T/Gold-411
93TripleP-83
93UD-82
93UD/FunPack-77
93UD/SP-78
93Ultra-112
93Ultra/AS-10
94B-299
94D-650
94F-246
94Finest-351
94L-357
94Pac/Cr-436
94Pinn-499
94Pinn/Trib-18
94S-245
94S-627HL
94S/GoldR-245
94Studio-128
94T-110
94T/Gold-110
94UD-505
94UD/CollC-260
94UD/CollC/Gold-260
94UD/CollC/Silv-260
94UD/SP-127
94Ultra-311
Smith, Leslie
90Miami/II/Star-30PER
Smith, Lonnie
76OkCty/Team-23
79OkCty
79T-722R
80BK/P-14
81Coke
81D-295
81F-15
81OPC-317
81T-317
82D-606
82F-259
82F-641M
82F/St-60
82OPC-127
82T-127
82T/Tr-108T
83D-91
83D/AAS-34
83F-21
83F-636M
83F/St-15M
83F/St-23M
83K-30
83OPC-273
83OPC/St-283
83PermaGr/CC-15
83T-465
83T-561TL
83T/Fold-3M
83T/St-283
84D-231
84D-625M
84D/Champs-23
84F-335
84F/St-7
84Nes/792-186TL
84Nes/792-580
84OPC-113
84Seven-14C
84T-186TL
84T-580
84T/RD-1M
84T/St-140
84T/St/Box-5
85D-231
85F-239
85F/St-61
85F/Up-U106
85Leaf-225
85OPC-255
85T-255
85T/RD-1M
85T/St-139
85T/Tr-109T
86D-399
86F-21
86F/Mini-4
86F/St-112
86Kitty/Disc-1
86Leaf-188
86NatPhoto-21
86OPC-7
86Sf-186M
86T-617
86T/Mini-21
86T/St-264
87D-225
87F-381
87F/Lim-40
87F/St-111
87Sf/TPrev-13M
87T-69
87T/St-262
88D-527
88Panini/St-111
88Richm-5
88Richm/CMC-14
88Richm/ProC-1
88S-263
88T-777
88TripleA/ASCMC-24
89B-278
89Brave/Dubuq-22
89D/Best-114
89F/Up-74
89T/Big-242
89T/LJN-84
89T/Tr-114T
89UD/Ext-731
90B-12
90Brave/Dubuq/Perf-24
90Brave/Dubuq/Singl-28
90Classic-52
90D-222
90D/BestNL-86
90F-593
90F/AwardWin-35
90F/Can-593
90F/LL-37
90KMart/CBatL-19
90Leaf-217
90OPC-152
90Panini/St-227
90PublInt/St-121
90RedFoley/St-88
90S-399
90S/100St-82
90Sf-65
90T-152
90T/Big-7
90T/Coins-58
90T/DH-61
90T/Mini-46
90T/St-24
90UD-215
91B-567
91Brave/Dubuq/Perf-26
91Brave/Dubuq/Stand-33
91D-364
91F-702
91Leaf-13
91OPC-306
91Panini/FrSt-24
91Panini/St-22
91S-543
91StCl-97
91T-306A
91T-306B
91UD-305
91Ultra-11
92Brave/LykePerf-25
92Brave/LykeStand-29
92D-517
92F-369
92L-480
92L/BlkGold-480
92OPC-467
92Panini-168
92Pinn-465
92S-13
92S/Factory-B4M
92StCl-282
92T-467
92T/Gold-467
92T/GoldWin-467
92TripleP-40
92UD-301
92USPlayC/Brave-12S
92USPlayC/Brave-8H
92Ultra-168
93D-658
93F-371
93F/Final-119
93L-394
93Pinn-454
93Pirate/Nation-30
93S-431
93StCl-658
93StCl/1stDay-658
93StCl/MurphyS-182
93UD-716
93Ultra-456
94S-462
Smith, Mandy
81Wisco-19
Smith, Mark
83BirmB-7
83RochR-8
Smith, Mark Edward
88CapeCod/Sum-146
90Hamil/Best-7
90Hamil/Star-24
91Classic/DP-6
91StPete/ClBest-13
92B-556
92ClBest-122
92Classic/DP-91FB
92Hagers/ProC-2569
92Hagers/SB-269
92Sky/AASingl-113
92Spring/ClBest-14
92Spring/ProC-868
92UD-66TP
92UD/ML-281
92UD/ML-38M
92UD/POY-PY15
93B-253
93ClBest/MLG-59
93FExcel/ML-127
94B-47
94ClBest/Gold-145
Smith, Marvin David
(David)
88Kenosha/ProC-1391
89Belling/Legoe-29
89Visalia/Cal-117
89Visalia/ProC-1448
90SanBern/Best-20
90SanBern/Cal-99
90SanBern/ProC-2647
Smith, Michael A. 1
(Texas Mike)
86Cedar/TCMA-10
87Vermont-12
88Chatt/Best-21
89RochR/CMC-8
89RochR/CMC-9
89RochR/ProC-1634
89RochR/ProC-1637
90AAASingl/ProC-459
90OPC-249
90ProC/Singl-309
90RochR/CMC-8
90RochR/ProC-702
90Rochester/L&U-23
90T-249
90T/89Debut-118
91Crown/Orio-428
Smith, Michael A. 2
(Mississippi)
87Indianap-23
88Indianap/CMC-7
88Indianap/ProC-509
90OPC-552
90T-552
90Tampa/DIMD-24
Smith, Mike 1
76AppFx
82Richm-26
Smith, Mike 2
80GlenF/B-28bb
80GlenF/C-29bb
Smith, Mike 3
(Indiana)
92FrRow/DP-78
92Gaston/ProC-2262
93StCl/MurphyS-101
Smith, Milt
61Union
Smith, Myrl
79Tucson-2
Smith, Nate
91Crown/Orio-429
Smith, Nick
N172
Smith, Ottis
91Pittsfld/ClBest-15
91Pittsfld/ProC-3423
92ColumMet/ClBest-3
92ColumMet/SAL/II-19
93StLucie/ProC-2922
Smith, Ozzie
78Padre/FamFun-29
79Ho-102
79OPC-52
79T-116
80OPC-205
80T-393
81D-1
81F-488
81OPC-254
81T-207RB
81T-254
81T/SO-68
81T/St-230
82D-21DK
82D-94
82F-582
82F/St-101
82K-6
82OPC-95
82T-95
82T/St-104
82T/Tr-109T
83D-120
83F-22
83F-636M
83F/St-15M
83F/St-6M
83K-21
83OPC-14
83OPC/St-168
83OPC/St-180WS
83OPC/St-186WS
83OPC/St-288
83PermaGr/AS-17
83PermaGr/CC-16
83T-540
83T/St-168
83T/St-180
83T/St-186
83T/St-288
84D-59
84D-625M
84F-336
84MiltBrad-25
84Nes/792-130
84Nes/792-389AS
84Nestle/DT-15
84OPC-130
84OPC-389AS
84Ralston-2
84Seven-19C
84T-130
84T-389AS
84T/Cereal-2
84T/Gloss22-16
84T/Gloss40-17
84T/RD-28M
84T/St-144
84T/St-187
85D-59
85D/AAS-28
85F-240
85F-631IA
85F/LimEd-35
85FunFoodPin-71
85GenMills-10
85Leaf-60
85OPC-191
85Seven-16C
85T-605
85T-715AS
85T/Gloss22-5
85T/RD-28M
85T/St-137
85T/St-181
85T/Super-47
86D-59
86D/AAS-8
86D/PopUp-8
86F-46
86F/LL-42
86F/Mini-10
86F/St-113
86GenMills/Book-4M
86KAS/Disc-7
86Leaf-47
86OPC-297
86Quaker-15
86Schnucks-21
86Seven/Coin-S10M
86Sf-121
86T-704AS
86T-730
86T/Gloss22-16
86T/Gloss60-46
86T/St-11NLCS
86T/St-153
86T/St-46
86T/Super-53
86T/Tatt-16M
86TrueVal-9
87BK-14
87Classic-32
87D-5DK
87D-60
87D/AAS-15
87D/DKsuper-5
87D/OD-65
87D/PopUp-15
87F-308
87F/AwardWin-38
87F/BB-41
87F/Mini-102
87F/St-112
87GenMills/Book-5M
87Ho/St-15
87Jiffy-7
87Kraft-16
87Leaf-108
87Leaf-5DK
87MnM's-24
87OPC-107
87Ralston-13
87RedFoley/St-112
87Sf-142
87Sf-79M
87Sf/TPrev-12M
87Smok/Cards-17
87Smok/NL-9
87Stuart-11
87T-598AS
87T-749
87T/Coins-45
87T/Gloss22-5
87T/Gloss60-23
87T/St-162
87T/St-46
88AP/Test-6
88ChefBoy-5

88Classic/Blue-210
88D-263
88D-BC22
88D/AS-37
88D/AS-63
88D/Best-243
88D/PopUp-15
88F-47
88F-628M
88F/AwardWin-39
88F/BB/AS-39
88F/BB/MVP-35
88F/Hottest-40
88F/Mini-109
88F/RecSet-38
88F/St-120
88F/TL-38
88F/WS-4
88FanSam-11
88Grenada-35
88KMart-28
88KennerFig-104
88KingB/Disc-4
88Leaf-115
88Nestle-5
88OPC-39
88Panini/St-235M
88Panini/St-393
88S-12
88S/WaxBox-14
88Sf-68
88Smok/Card-18
88T-400AS
88T-460
88T/Big-228
88T/Coins-55
88T/Gloss22-16
88T/Gloss60-47
88T/Mini-72
88T/St-153
88T/St-53
88T/St/Backs-12
88T/UK-72
89B-436
89Cadaco-53
89Classic-58
89D-63
89D/AS-37
89D/AS-62
89D/Best-44
89D/MVP-BC14
89D/PopUp-37
89F-463
89F/Excit-38
89F/LL-35
89Holsum/Discs-3
89KayBee-28
89KennerFig-134
89MSA/SS-1
89OPC-230
89Panini/St-186
89Panini/St-235AS
89RedFoley/St-110
89S-80
89S/HotStar-88
89S/Mast-27
89Sf-105
89Smok-20
89T-230
89T-389AS
89T/Big-110
89T/Coins-25
89T/DH-16
89T/Gloss22-16
89T/Gloss60-42
89T/HeadsUp-17
89T/LJN-45
89T/Mini-37
89T/St-161
89T/St-44
89T/St/Backs-45
89T/UK-72
89UD-265
89UD-674TC
90B-195
90BBWit-41
90Classic-18
90CollAB-5
90D-201
90D-710AS
90D/BestNL-83
90D/Learning-9
90F-260
90F/AwardWin-36
90F/BB-35
90F/BBMVP-36
90F/Can-260
90HotPlay/St-41
90KMart/SS-4
90KayBee-29
90Kenner/Fig-79
90KingB/Discs-4
90Leaf-142
90Leaf-364CL
90Leaf/Prev-12
90MLBPA/Pins-30
90MSA/Soda-10
90OPC-400AS
90OPC-590
90Panini/St-206 M
90Panini/St-338
90Post-6
90PublInt/St-228
90PublInt/St-272
90RedFoley/St-89
90S-285
90S/100St-6
90S/McDon-24
90Sf-16
90Smok/Card-22
90T-400AS
90T-590
90T/Big-203
90T/DH-62
90T/Gloss22-5
90T/Gloss60-16
90T/St-145AS
90T/St-42
90T/TVAS-52
90T/TVCard-29
90UD-225
90USPlayC/AS-6H
90WonderBrd-5
91B-398
91BBBest/RecBr-17
91Cadaco-53
91Classic/200-39
91D-240
91D-437AS
91F-646
91JDean-20
91Leaf-80
91Leaf/Stud-238
91MajorLg/Pins-49
91MooTown-8
91OPC-130
91OPC/Premier-112
91Panini/FrSt-161
91Panini/FrSt-34
91Panini/St-39
91Panini/Top15-103
91Pep/SS-12
91Petro/SU-18
91Pol/Card-1
91Post/Can-8
91RedFoley/St-129
91S-825
91S/100SS-18
91Seven/3DCoin-12MW
91StCl-154
91Sunflower-1
91T-130
91T/CJMini/II-27
91T/Gloss 16 AS
91T/SU-31
91UD-162
91UD/FinalEd-95F
91USPlayC/AS-13S
91Ultra-296
92B-675
92CJ/DI-6
92Card/McDon/Pac-38
92Classic/Game200-24
92Classic/II-T26
92Colla/ASG-6
92D-423AS
92D-432
92D/McDon-26
92DPep/MSA-19
92F-592
92French-13M
92Hardee-20
92JDean/Living-3
92L-400
92L/BlkGold-400
92MrTurkey-23
92OPC-760
92OPC/Premier-84
92P-8
92Panini-175
92Panini-284AS
92Pinn-285M
92Pinn-6
92Pinn/RookI-15M
92Pol/Card-19
92Post/Can-6
92S-590
92S/100SS-47
92S/Factory-B9
92S/Proctor-14
92Seven/Coin-14
92StCl-680
92StCl/Dome-175
92StCl/MemberI-7
92StCl/MemberI-8
92StCl/MemberII-12
92Studio-98
92Studio/Prev-20
92T-760
92T/Gold-760
92T/GoldWin-760
92T/Kids-25
92T/McDonB-11
92TripleP-244
92UD-177
92UD-716DS
92UD/ASFF-42
92UD/TmMVPHolo-50
92Ultra-271
92Ultra/AwardWin-9
93B-460
93Cadaco-55
93Classic/GameI-88
93Colla/ASG-22
93Colla/DM-99
93D-520
93Duracel/PPI-11
93F/Final-131
93F/Final/DTrib-DT8
93Flair-128
93HumDum/Can-50
93KingB-12
93L-328
93L/Heading-10
93MSA/Metz-36
93OPC-313
93P-26
93Pac/Spanish-302
93Panini-194
93Pinn-329
93Pinn/Cooper-9
93Pinn/TP-7
93Pol/Card-20
93Post/Can-17
93S-522AS
93S-532DT
93S-562
93S/GoldDT-1
93Select-15
93Select/ChasS-3
93StCl-548
93StCl/1stDay-548
93StCl/Card-1
93StCl/MurphyS-147
93Studio-217
93Studio/Her-6
93T-40
93T/BlkGold-20
93T/Finest-28
93T/FinestRef-28
93T/Gold-40
93TripleP-122
93TripleP/Act-3
93TripleP/Nick-9
93UD-146
93UD-482M
93UD/Diam-31
93UD/FunPack-215ASA
93UD/FunPack-35HERO
93UD/FunPack-74GS
93UD/FunPack-78
93UD/FunPackAS-AS6M
93UD/looss-WI7
93UD/SP-79
93UD/Then-TN7
93USPlayC/Ace-3H
93Ultra-113
93Ultra/AwardWin-6
94B-424
94Church-26
94D-35
94D/Special-35
94F-646
94F/ProV-5
94Flair-228
94Kraft-29
94L-409
94OPC-181
94Pac/Cr-604
94Panini-248
94Pinn-389
94Pinn/Trib-10
94RedFoley-14M
94S-384
94Select-30
94Sf/2000-41
94StCl-417
94StCl/1stDay-417
94StCl/Gold-417
94StCl/Team-301
94Studio-54
94T-320
94T/Finest-136
94T/Finest/PreProd-136
94T/FinestRef-136
94T/Gold-320
94TripleP-66
94UD-278HFA
94UD-360
94UD/DColl-C7
94UD/ElecD-278HFA
94UD/HoloFX-37
94UD/SP-65
94Ultra-568

Smith, P. Keith
83Nashvl-23
84Nashvl-21
85Colum-19
85Colum/Pol-22
86Colum-23
86Colum/Pol-22
87Denver-25
88Denver/CMC-14
88Denver/ProC-1261
89Vanco/CMC-13
89Vanco/ProC-578
90AAASingl/ProC-174
90ProC/Singl-646
90Vanco/CMC-19
90Vanco/ProC-496
92Richm/Bleach-3
92Richm/Comix-20
92Richm/ProC-386
92Richm/SB-441

Smith, Paul
54DanDee
54T-11
57T-345
58T-269
63MilSau-8
94T/Arc54-11

Smith, Pete J.
86Greenvl/Team-18
87Greenvl/Best-24
88D-571
88D/Best-197
88D/Rook-10
88F-647R
88F/Up-U73
88S/Tr-84T
88T/Tr-111T
89B-269
89Brave/Dubuq-23
89D-263
89F-600
89OPC-388
89Panini/St-36
89S-207
89S/HotRook-74
89S/YS/I-19
89T-537
89T/St-31
89ToysRUs-29
89UD-412
90Brave/Dubuq/Perf-25
90Brave/Dubuq/Singl-29
90D-499
90F-594
90F/Can-594
90Leaf-144
90OPC-771
90PublInt/St-122
90S-225
90T-771
90T/Big-161
90UD-613
91Brave/Dubuq/Perf-27
91Brave/Dubuq/Stand-34
91F-703
91OPC-383
91S-205
91StCl-519
91T-383
91UD-622
92AAA/ASG/SB-442
92F-370
92OPC-226
92Richm/Bleach-18
92Richm/Comix-21
92Richm/ProC-3014
92Richm/SB-442
92S-464
92StCl-632
92T-226
92T/Gold-226
92T/GoldWin-226
92USPlayC/Brave-11C
92USPlayC/Brave-3D
93Brave/LykePerf-26
93Brave/LykeStand-32
93D-498
93F-372
93L-214
93OPC-222
93Pinn-541
93S-408
93StCl-237
93StCl/1stDay-237
93StCl/Brave-13
93T-413
93T/Gold-413
93UD-589
93Ultra-311
94B-624
94D-585
94F-374
94Finest-350
94L-419
94T-658
94T/Gold-658
94UD-419
94Ultra-535

Smith, Peter L.
63MilSau-9
64T-428R

Smith, Phil
82DayBe-24

Smith, Quintin
89KS*-21

Smith, Randy
76QuadC
90Idaho/ProC-3263CO
91Idaho/ProC-4346CO

Smith, Ray
77Visalia
78OrlanTw
79Toledo-22
80Toledo-16
82Toledo-11
83Twin/Team-3
83Twin/Team-32M
84F-573
84Nes/792-46
84T-46
84Toledo-4
85Cram/PCL-114
86Tacom-21
89Elizab/Star-29CO
90Elizab/Star-24CO
91Elizab/ProC-4315MG
92Elizab/ClBest-23MG
92Elizab/ProC-3697

Smith, Red
90LitSun-8

Smith, Rhett
89OK-24

Smith, Richard Arthur
(Dick)
64T-398R
65T-579
90Target-746
91WIZMets-370

Smith, Richard H.
53Mother-3
55B-288

Smith, Richard
90Wausau/Best-7
90Wausau/ProC-2120
90Wausau/Star-22

Smith, Rick 1
88Bakers/Cal-267
Smith, Rick 2
91CalLgAS-27M
Smith, Robbie
86OrlanTw-17
87OrlanTw-2
Smith, Robert A.
(Robbie)
91Collnd/ClBest-28
91Collnd/ProC-1495
92ColRS/ClBest-23
92ColRS/ProC-2401
Smith, Robert D.
(Rob)
88Stockton/Cal-192
88Stockton/ProC-741
89Stockton/Best-23
89Stockton/Cal-168
89Stockton/ProC-394
89Stockton/Star-18
90Beloit/Star-19
Smith, Robert Eldridge
(Bob)
21Exh-166
28Exh-3
29Exh/4-2
52Laval-13
Smith, Rogers
88MissSt-39M
89MissSt-45M
90MissSt-44M
91MissSt-55M
Smith, Ron
75BurlB
76BurlB
76Watlo
80Penin/B-20
80Penin/C-26
Smith, Ronnie
47Signal
Smith, Roosevelt
91Erie/ClBest-24
91Erie/ProC-4070
Smith, Roy
80Penin/B-12
80Penin/C-4
82Reading-8
83Charl-5
84Maine-3
84Wheat/Ind-33
85D-611
85F-455
85Maine-10
85Polar/Ind-33
85T-381
86D-468
86T-9
87Portl-8
88AAA/ProC-33
88Portl/CMC-6
88Portl/ProC-645
90D-273
90F-386
90F/Can-386
90Leaf-400
90OPC-672
90Panini/St-107
90S-568
90T-672
90UD-284
91D-470
91F-624
91OPC-503
91RochR/ProC-1902
91S-151
91T-503
91UD-490
92F-28
92S-256
Smith, Ryan
92Belling/ClBest-14
92Belling/ProC-1443
Smith, Samuel
N172
Smith, Sean
92Greens/ClBest-8
92Greens/ProC-779
93ClBest/MLG-150
93StCl/MurphyS-152
Smith, Shad
91Greens/ProC-3061
92PrWill/ClBest-18
92PrWill/ProC-150
Smith, Sherrod
(Sherry)
21Exh-167
21Exh-168
25Exh-86
26Exh-85
28Yueng-31
90Target-751
92Conlon/Sport-609
E120
E126-22
E210-31
E220
W502-31
Smith, Sloan
94T-748DP
94T/Gold-748DP
Smith, Steve 1
79Hawaii-14
80Hawaii-18
81Hawaii-3
81Hawaii/TCMA-4
82Hawaii-3
86Beaum-23MG
87TexLgAS-13
87Wichita-9
88LasVegas/CMC-24
88LasVegas/ProC-244
89AAA/ProC-50
89LasVegas/CMC-24
89LasVegas/ProC-25
90OkCty/CMC-21MG
90OkCty/ProC-448MG
90ProC/Singl-171MG
91Penin/ProC-394MG
Smith, Steve 2
90WichSt-31
Smith, Steve 3
90MissSt-41M
91MissSt-42CO
92MissSt-39CO
93MissSt-39CO
Smith, Steve 4
84Shrev/FB-18
85Fresno/Pol-23
86Fresno/Smok-17
Smith, Syd
E270/1
T206
T213/brown
Smith, Terry
86Lakeland-22TR
87Lakeland-11TR
90Lakeland/Star-28TR
90Princet/DIMD-19
Smith, Tim
84Newar-14
Smith, Timothy Christian
92Reno/Cal-54
92StCl/Dome-176
Smith, Timothy James
90Elmira/Pucko-23
91CLAS/ProC-CAR27
91LynchRS/ClBest-9
91LynchRS/ProC-1199
91SoOreg/ClBest-3
91SoOreg/ProC-3843
92NewBrit/ProC-434
92NewBrit/SB-496
92ProC/Tomorrow-22
92Sky/AASingl-214
Smith, Tobe
87Negro/Dixon-14
Smith, Todd 1
86Miami-23
87Salem-26
Smith, Todd 2
89Medford/Best-30
90Modesto/Cal-151
90Modesto/Chong-28
90Modesto/ProC-2212
91Modesto/ClBest-14
91Modesto/ProC-3088
91OKSt-24
92Huntsvl/SB-320
92ProC/Tomorrow-132
92Sky/AASingl-137
Smith, Tom 1
52Laval-70
Smith, Tom 2
81QuadC-18
83Peoria/Frit-10
Smith, Tom 3
89Salem/Star-21
91AppFx/ClBest-25
91AppFx/ProC-1730
92B-383
92BBCity/ClBest-7
92BBCity/ProC-3858
92ClBest-145
Smith, Tommy 1
75Lafay
Smith, Tommy 2
75Anderson/TCMA-22
Smith, Tommy 3
80CharlO/Pol-20
80CharlO/W3TV-20
80RochR-19
Smith, Tommy A.
74OPC-606R
74T-606R
75OPC-619R
75OkCty/Team-15
75T-619R
75T/M-619R
76SSPC-530
77OPC-92
77T-14
78Cr/PCL-31
Smith, Tony
C46-32
Smith, Tracy
88Geneva/ProC-1647
89Peoria/Team-20
90WinSalem/Team-21
Smith, Vinnie
52Mother-59
Smith, Wallace H.
T207
Smith, Ward
75Anderson/TCMA-23
Smith, William G.
(Willie)
63T-241
Smith, Willie 1
65OPC-85
65T-85
66T-438
67T-397
68T-568
69MB-257
69OPC-198
69T-198
69T/4in1-23M
70OPC-318
70T-318
71OPC-457
71T-457
72MB-319
Smith, Willie 2
88Augusta/ProC-377
90AAASingl/ProC-326
90Albany/Best-7
90B-425
90ColClip/CMC-7
90ColClip/ProC-676
90Colum/Pol-14
90ProC/Singl-207
90T/TVYank-60
91AA/LineD-17
91Albany/ClBest-5
91Albany/LineD-17
91Albany/ProC-1008
91B-160
91ClBest/Singl-332
91SLCity/ProC-3214
91SLCity/SportP-15
92Canton/ProC-689
92Canton/SB-120
92ColoSp/ProC-752
92ProC/Tomorrow-113
94B-508
Smith, Willie 3
90Batavia/ProC-3070
Smith, Woody
88Wythe/ProC-1990
89Peoria/Team-22
90Peoria/Team-13
Smith, Zane
83Durham-24
85F-651R
85Pol/Atl-34
86D-565
86F-528
86Leaf-222
86OPC-167
86Pol/Atl-34
86T-167
87D-167
87F-529
87OPC-226
87RedFoley/St-73
87Sf/TPrev-24M
87Smok/Atl-1
87T-544
88D-167
88D/Best-170
88F-550
88F/Mini-66
88F/St-78
88F/TL-39
88KennerFig-105
88OPC-297
88Panini/St-240
88S-410
88Sf-134
88T-297
88T/Big-193
88T/Mini-42
88T/St-40
88T/UK-73
89B-262
89D-499
89F-601
89F/Up-99
89KennerFig-135
89OPC-339
89RedFoley/St-111
89S-492
89S/Tr-56T
89T-688
89T/St-27
89UD-71
90D-460
90F-362
90F/Can-362
90Leaf-238
90OPC-48
90Publint/St-123
90S-477
90T-48
90UD-607
91B-524
91Classic/200-82
91D-532
91F-51
91Leaf-495
91OPC-441
91Panini/Top15-66
91S-845
91StCl-260
91T-441
91UD/Ext-759
92B-409
92D-360
92F-568
92L-96
92L/BlkGold-96
92OPC-345
92Pinn-237
92Pirate/Nation-21
92S-493
92StCl-807
92StCl/Dome-177
92T-345
92T/Gold-345
92T/GoldWin-345
92UD-486
92Ultra-260
93D-94
93F-120
93L-152
93OPC-170
93Pac/Spanish-252
93Panini-278
93Pinn-403
93Pirate/Nation-31
93S-121
93Select-231
93StCl-343
93StCl/1stDay-343
93T-560
93T/Gold-560
93UD-349
93UD/FunPack-150
93Ultra-101
94D-559
94F-620
94Finest-381
94Flair-220
94L-374
94Pac/Cr-507
94Panini-239
94S-239
94S/GoldR-239
94StCl-310
94StCl/1stDay-310
94StCl/Gold-310
94T-707
94T/Gold-707
94UD-251
94UD/ElecD-251
94Ultra-559
Smithberg, Roger
89LasVegas/ProC-17
90AAASingl/ProC-12
90B-203
90LasVegas/CMC-1
90LasVegas/ProC-124
90ProC/Singl-503
91HighD/ClBest-11
91HighD/ProC-2394
91Wichita/ProC-2599
94D-421
94T-652
94T/Gold-652
Smithson, Mike
81Pawtu-11
83Rang-48
83T/Tr-106T
84D-221
84F-428
84F/X-U108
84Nes/792-89
84T-89
84T/Tr-110T
85D-316
85F-289
85OPC-359
85Seven/Minn-11
85T-483
85T/St-301
85Twin/Seven-11
85Twin/Team-34
86D-147
86F-405
86Leaf-73
86OPC-101
86T-695
86T/Mini-24
86T/St-282
86T/Tatt-10M
87D-245
87F-553
87OPC-225
87T-225
87T/St-275
88D/RedSox/Bk-NEW
88F-23
88F/Up-U9
88OPC-389
88S/Tr-59T
88T-554
89D-628
89F-100
89S-403
89T-377
89T/Big-222
89UD-38
90D-464
90F-288
90F/Can-288
90OPC-188
90Publnt/St-465
90S-512
90T-188
90UD-610
93Rang/Keeb-335
Smock, Greg
92Reno/Cal-58
Smolen, Bruce
91Batavia/ClBest-11
91Batavia/ProC-3494
Smoll, Clyde
87Elmira/Black-1
87Elmira/Red-1
88Elmira-30GM
89Elmira/Pucko-25
Smoltz, John
86Lakeland-23
87GlenF-24
88F/Up-U74
88Richm-26

88Richm/CMC-3
88Richm/ProC-23
88TripleA/ASCMC-30
89B-266
89Brave/Dubuq-24
89Classic/Up/2-174
89D-642
89D/Best-85
89F-602
89S-616
89T-382
89T/Big-260
89UD-17
90B-10
90Brave/Dubuq/Perf-26
90Brave/Dubuq/Singl-30
90Classic-13
90D-121
90D-8DK
90D/BestNL-50
90D/Bon/MVP-BC12
90D/SuperDK-8DK
90F-595
90F/BB-36
90F/Can-595
90HotPlay/St-42
90Leaf-59
90OPC-535
90Panini/St-228
90PublInt/St-124
90RedFoley/St-90
90S-370
90S/100St-35
90S/YS/I-36
90Sf-61
90Starline/LJS-14
90Starline/LJS-34
90T-535
90T/Big-306
90T/Mini-47
90T/St-30
90UD-535
90UD-84TC
91B-580
91Brave/Dubuq/Perf-28
91Brave/Dubuq/Stand-35
91Classic/200-180
91Classic/II-T27
91D-75
91F-704
91Leaf-27
91Leaf/Stud-149
91OPC-157
91Panini/FrSt-26
91Panini/St-26
91S-208
91StCl-365
91T-157
91UD-264
91Ultra-12
92B-347
92Brave/LykePerf-26
92Brave/LykeStand-30
92Classic/Game200-18
92D-442
92F-371
92L-191
92L/BlkGold-191
92OPC-245
92Pinn-191
92Pinn/Team2000-30
92S-287
92S/Impact-30
92StCl-459
92StCl/Dome-178
92Studio-10
92T-245
92T/Gold-245
92T/GoldWin-245
92TripleP-172
92UD-322
92USPlayC/Brave-11S
92USPlayC/Brave-8D
92Ultra-169
93B-494
93Brave/LykePerf-27
93Brave/LykeStand-33
93Classic/GameI-89
93Colla/DM-100
93D-130
93F-14
93Flair-11
93HumDum/Can-27
93Kenner/Fig-34
93L-104
93MSA/Ben-8
93OPC-364
93Pac/Spanish-12
93Pinn-143
93Pinn-298I
93S-61
93Select-177
93Select/Ace-17
93Select/StatL-66M
93Select/StatL-76
93StCl-463
93StCl-599MC
93StCl/1stDay-463
93StCl/1stDay-599MC
93StCl/Brave-12
93StCl/MurphyS-135
93StCl/MurphyS-86
93Studio-61
93T-35
93T/Finest-166
93T/FinestRef-166
93T/Gold-35
93T/Hill-30
93TripleP-67
93UD-363
93UD-472M
93UD/Clutch-R19
93UD/FunPack-68
93UD/SP-63
93Ultra-312
93Ultra/Strike-5
94B-629
94D-260
94F-375
94F/AS-50
94F/Smoke-12
94L-309
94OPC-39
94Pac/Cr-22
94Panini-151
94Pinn-342
94S-366
94Select-174
94Sf/2000-136
94StCl-405
94StCl/1stDay-405
94StCl/Gold-405
94StCl/Team-35
94T-687
94T/Finest-100
94T/Finest/PreProd-100
94T/FinestRef-100
94T/Gold-687
94TripleP-50
94UD-87
94UD/ElecD-87
94Ultra-157
94Ultra/Strike-5

Smoot, Allen
82Clinton/Frit-18

Smyth, Harry
90Target-752
R314/Can
V355-79

Snaith, Andy
82AlexD-26

Snead, Jay
89Augusta/ProC-519

Snead, Sam
51Wheat
52Wheat*

Snead, Scott
91Billing/SportP-3
91Billings/ProC-3764

Snedeker, Sean
88GreatF-20
89AS/Cal-21
89Bakers/Cal-181
91VeroB/ClBest-12
91VeroB/ProC-773

Snediker, Jim
86WinHaven-24

Snell, Dave
86Wausau-25
88Vermont/ProC-956

Snell, Nate
85F/Up-U107
85T/Tr-110T
86D-367
86F-288
86Leaf-166
86T-521
87D-396
87F-481
87T-86
88F-70
91Crown/Orio-430

Snider, Duke
49B-226
49Eureka-50
50B-77
50Drake-5
51B-32
51T/RB-38
52B-116
52BR
52NTea
52RM-NL21
52StarCal-91C
52StarCal/L-79E
52T-37
52TipTop
53B/Col-117
53Briggs
53RM-NL14
53SM
54B-170
54DanDee
54NYJour
54RH
54RM-NL16
54SM
54T-32
55Armour-19
55Gol/Dodg-28
55RM-NL19
55SM
55T-210
56T-150
56T/Pin-52
56YellBase/Pin-29
57T-170
57T-400M
58BB
58Hires-61
58T-314M
58T-436M
58T-88
59Bz
59HRDerby-18
59Morrell
59T-20
59T-468HL
60BB-2
60L-37
60Morrell
60NuCard-55
60T-493
60Union/Dodg-19
61BB-4
61P-167
61T-443
61T/St-35
61Union/Dodg-20
62BB-4
62J-114
62P-114
62P/Can-114
62Salada-215
62Shirriff-215
62T-500
62T/St-140
63J-118
63P-118
63T-550
63T-68M
64T-155
64Wheat/St-42
75Shakey-12
76SSPC-351
77Galasso-24
79TCMA-43
79TCMA-72
80Pac/Leg-19
80Perez/HOF-172
80SSPC/HOF
81TCMA-363
82CJ-15
83D/HOF-14
83MLBPA/Pin-33
84D-648PUZ
84West/1-24
85CircK-20
86Sf/Dec-32
87Leaf/SpecOlym-H6
87Nestle/DT-33
88Pac/Leg-55
89B/Ins-10
89Rini/Dodg-4
89Smok/Dodg-27
89T/LJN-117
90Perez/GreatMom-33
90Perez/Master-16
90Perez/Master-17
90Perez/Master-18
90Perez/Master-19
90Perez/Master-20
90Target-753
91T/Arc53-327
91WIZMets-371
92Bz/Quadra-10M
93TWill-16
93TWill/Mem-4
93YooHoo-19
94T/Arc54-32
Exh47
PM10/L-39
PM10/Sm-183
PM10/Sm-184
PM10/Sm-185
R423-95
WG9-47

Snider, Kelly
77LodiD
79Albuq-14
80Albuq-4
81Toledo-15
82Toledo-16

Snider, Mark
89GA-29
90GA-28

Snider, Van
83CharR-13
84Memphis-9
86Memphis/GoldT-25
86Memphis/SilverT-25
87Omaha-4
88Nashvl/CMC-22
88Nashvl/ProC-473
88Nashvl/Team-22
88TripleA/ASCMC-8
89D-586
89F-172
89Nashvl/CMC-23
89Nashvl/ProC-1281
89Nashvl/Team-23
89S-640
89S/HotRook-41
89Sf-177
89UD-23
90AAASingl/ProC-342
90ColClip/CMC-16
90ColClip/ProC-692
90Colum/Pol-15
90ProC/Singl-216
90T/TVYank-61
91AAA/LineD-118
91ColClip/LineD-118
91ColClip/ProC-611
92Pawtu/ProC-938
92Pawtu/SB-367

Snitker, Brian
78Green
79Savan-5
83Durham-28
84Durham-28
86Sumter/ProC-26MG
87Durham-6
89Brave/Dubuq-25CO
90Brave/Dubuq/Singl-31CO
91Macon/ClBest-18CO
91Macon/ProC-883CO
92Macon/ClBest-26MG
92Macon/ProC-284MG

Snoddy, Chris
86Lipscomb-20TR

Snoddy, Ralph
33SK*-25

Snodgrass, Fred
11Helmar-137
16FleischBrd-87
60NuCard-54
61NuCard-454
88Conlon/3-26
91Conlon/Sport-168
D328-165
D329-166
D350/2-168
E135-165
E254
E270
M101/4-166
M101/5-168
M116
S74-95
T202
T205
T206
T207
W555

Snopek, Chris
93B-259
94B-539

Snover, Colonel L.
E120

Snover, Dan
87Hawaii-10
90Durham/UpHer-6

Snover, Don
89Pulaski/ProC-1896

Snow, J.T. Jr.
87AZ/Pol-13
88AZ/Pol-12
88CapeCod/Sum-125
89Oneonta/ProC-2112
90CLAS/CL-17
90PrWill/Team-25
91AA/LineD-18
91Albany/ProC-1017
91ClBest/Singl-279
92ColClip/Pol-20
92ColClip/Pol-20
92ColClip/ProC-362
92ColClip/SB-117
92ProC/Tomorrow-114
92Sky/AAASingl-56
93B-173
93B-340FOIL
93Colla/DM-101
93D-110RR
93F/Final-190
93F/MLPI-7
93Flair-179
93L-500
93L/GRook-17
93Mother/Angel-4
93OPC/Premier-70
93Pac/Jugador-16
93Pac/Spanish-372
93Pinn-609
93Pinn/HRC-27
93Pinn/RookTP-4M
93Pol/Angel-10
93S-260
93Select-385
93Select/RookTr-44T
93StCl-719
93StCl/1stDay-719
93StCl/Angel-1
93StCl/MPhoto-29
93Studio-58
93Studio/Her-11
93Studio/Sil-6
93T-422
93T/Finest-156
93T/FinestRef-156
93T/Gold-422
93T/Tr-62T
93TripleP/Gal-GS8
93UD-23SR
93UD-785
93UD/Diam-35
93UD/FunPack-8SOT
93UD/SP-26
93Ultra-525
93Ultra/AllRook-9
93Ultra/Perf-9
94B-11
94D-283
94F-70
94F/RookSen-19
94OPC-55
94OPC/DiamD-9
94Pac/Cr-89
94Panini-43
94Pinn-68
94Pinn/Artist-68
94Pinn/Museum-68
94Pinn/New-9
94Pinn/Power-5
94S-511
94Sf/2000-121
94Sf/Shak-10
94StCl-181

94StCl-447
94StCl/1stDay-181
94StCl/1stDay-447
94StCl/Gold-181
94StCl/Gold-447
94T-293
94T/Finest-157
94T/Finest/PreProd-157
94T/FinestRef-157
94T/Gold-293
94TripleP-20
94Ultra-28
Snuder, Kendall
87Kenosha-4
Snyder, Ben
82DayBe-8
83ColumAst-19
Snyder, Brett
90Beloit/Best-11
90Beloit/Star-20
90Foil/Best-145
Snyder, Brian
80SanJose/JITB-16
81Wausau-7
82SLCity-17
83SLCity-4
84Cram/PCL-178
84Shrev/FB-19
85Cram/PCL-92
86LasVegas-17
86T-174
87LasVegas-15
88Tacoma/CMC-9
88Tacoma/ProC-629
89Tacoma/CMC-4
89Tacoma/ProC-1545
90AAASingl/ProC-405
90ProC/Singl-301
90Richm/Bob-4
90Richm/CMC-25
90Richm/ProC-260
90Richm/Team-28
Snyder, Charles N.
N172
Snyder, Chris
88CapeCod/Sum-9
90Princet/DIMD-20
Snyder, Cory
85T-403OLY
85Water-23
86D-29RR
86D/Rook-15
86F-653R
86Maine-20
86Sf/Rook-18
87Classic/Up-110
87D-526
87D/OD-106
87F-260
87F/Excit-40
87F/Hottest-39
87F/Mini-103
87F/Slug-M5
87F/St-113
87Gator-28
87Kraft-17
87Leaf-157
87OPC-192
87Sf-24
87Sf/TPrev-3M
87T-192
87T/Coins-24
87T/Gloss60-9
87T/JumboR-16
87T/St-213
87ToysRUs-25
88Classic/Red-184
88D-350
88D/Best-224
88F-615
88F-622M
88F/SS-37
88F/St-21
88Gator-28
88KennerFig-106
88KingB/Disc-10
88Leaf-125
88OPC-169
88Panini/St-80
88RedFoley/St-83
88S-92
88S/YS/I-40
88Sf-29
88T-620
88T/Big-43
88T/Coins-27
88T/Gloss60-23
88T/St-208
88T/St/Backs-53
88T/UK-74
89B-89
89Classic-19
89D-191
89D-8DK
89D/Best-168
89D/DKsuper-8DK
89F-412
89F/Superstar-38
89KennerFig-136
89OPC-80
89Panini/St-329
89S-52
89S/HotStar-6
89Sf-196
89T-80
89T/Big-175
89T/LJN-2
89T/St-210
89T/UK-73
89UD-170
89UD-679TC
90B-336
90D-272
90D/BestAL-47
90F-502
90F/Can-502
90KingB/Discs-12
90Leaf-187
90OPC-770
90Panini/St-56
90PublInt/St-568
90RedFoley/St-91
90S-10
90S/100St-28
90Sf-3
90T-770
90T/Big-221
90T/St-211
90UD-126
91B-357
91Classic/200-188
91Classic/II-T8
91D-288
91F-378
91Kodak/WSox-28
91Leaf-506
91OPC-323
91OPC/Premier-113
91Panini/FrSt-221
91RedFoley/St-88
91S-19
91S-695RF
91S/100SS-74
91S/RookTr-61T
91StCl-488
91T-323
91T/Tr-111T
91UD-123
91UD/Ext-724
91Ultra-83
92B-492
92D/Up-U21
92F/Up-130
92Giant/PGE-31
92L-188
92L/BlkGold-188
92Mother/Giant-19
92Pinn-506
92S-598
92S/RookTr-48T
92StCl-772
92T/Tr-107T
92T/TrGold-107T
92UD-504
92Ultra-595
93D-656
93F-160
93F/Final-84
93L-436
93Mother/Dodg-20
93OPC-250
93Panini-242
93Pinn-529
93Pol/Dodg-24
93S-574
93Select-71
93Select/RookTr-111T
93StCl/Dodg-29
93T-254
93T/Gold-254
93UD-218
93UD-791
93Ultra-405
94D-535
94F-524
94Flair-183
94Pac/Cr-321
94Panini-204
94Pinn-466
94S-80
94S/GoldR-80
94Select-170
94StCl-463
94StCl/1stDay-463
94StCl/Gold-463
94T-683
94T/Gold-683
94UD-266
94UD/CollC-261
94UD/CollC/Gold-261
94UD/CollC/Silv-261
94UD/ElecD-266
94Ultra-219
Snyder, Doug
86Osceola-24
87Osceola-9
88Visalia/Cal-158
88Visalia/ProC-100
89OrlanTw/Best-25
89OrlanTw/ProC-1327
Snyder, Frank
(Pancho)
21Exh-169
25Exh-38
26Exh-35
40PlayBall-159
91Conlon/Sport-232
93Conlon-870
E120
E121/120
E121/80
E220
V61-94
V89-33
W501-66
W515-44
W575
Snyder, Gene W.
59T-522
90Target-1076
Snyder, Gerald
52B-246
54B-216
55B-74
57T-22
Snyder, Jim
76Indianap-1MG
80OkCty
81OkCty/TCMA-23
88T/Tr-112MG
89T-44MG
92Mother/Padre-27CO
92Pol/Padre-26M
92Smok/Padre-32CO
93Richm/Team-4CO
Snyder, Randy
89Stockton/Best-17
89Stockton/Cal-170
89Stockton/ProC-382
89Stockton/Star-16
90Beloit/Best-13
90Beloit/Star-21
90Foil/Best-215
90MidwLgAS/GS-18
91Stockton/ClBest-14
91Stockton/ProC-3035
Snyder, Russ
60L-102
60T-81
61T-143
62Salada-206
62Shirriff-206
62T-64
63J-63
63P-63
63T-543
64T-126
65OPC-204
65T-204
66T-562
67CokeCap/Orio-6
67T-405
68T-504
69MB-258
69OPC-201
69T-201
69T/4in1-13M
70McDon-6
70OPC-347
70T-347
71MLB/St-452
71OPC-653
71T-653
72MB-320
78TCMA-136
91Crown/Orio-431
Soar, Hank
55B-279UMP
Soares, Todd
88Jaxvl/ProC-978
91Kissim/ProC-4196
Sobbe, William
81VeroB-19
Sobczyk, Bob
88Beloit/GS-11
89Boise/ProC-1993
Sobocienski, Adam
92MN-19
Sobolewski, Mark
92SoOreg/ClBest-5
92SoOreg/ProC-3428
92SoOreg/ProC-3428M
93Modesto/ClBest-19
93Modesto/ProC-810
Sodders, Mike
82Toledo-18
83OrlanTw-9
88Geneva/ProC-1642
89Peoria/Team-10
91AA/LineD-142
91CharlK/LineD-142
91CharlK/ProC-1688
92ChalK/SB-165
92CharlK/ProC-2770
Sodders, Randy
89Wythe/Star-24
Soden, Frank
79Richm-9M
Soderholm, Dale
74Tacoma/Caruso-2
Soderholm, Eric
73OPC-577
73T-577
74OPC-503
74T-503
75OPC-54
75T-54
75T/M-54
76K-28
76OPC-214
76SSPC-223
76T-214
77T-273
78Ho-20
78K-32
78OPC-21
78SSPC/270-148
78T-602
79Ho-103
79OPC-93
79T-186
80T-441
81D-106
81F-92
81T-383
90Swell/Great-98
91LineD-6
91Swell/Great-85
92Yank/WIZ80-184
93Rang/Keeb-336
Soderstrom, Steve
91FresnoSt/Smok-12
94ClBest/Gold-161
94ClBest/GoldLP-14
94UD-533TP
94UD/CollC-24
94UD/CollC/Gold-24
94UD/CollC/Silv-24
94Ultra-594
Sodowsky, Clint
92Bristol/ClBest-11
92Bristol/ProC-1412
Soff, Ray
81QuadC-23
83MidldC-22
84MidldC-9
86ArkTr-23
86Louisvl-26
87D-631
87F-309
87Louisvl-27
87OPC-96
87Smok/Cards-1
87T-671
88Portl/CMC-7
88Portl/ProC-662
89Portl/CMC-5
89Portl/ProC-216
90AAASingl/ProC-275
90ProC/Singl-361
90T/TVMets-61
90Tidew/CMC-10
90Tidew/ProC-544
91AAA/LineD-568
91Tidew/LineD-568
91Tidew/ProC-2509
92Edmon/SB-166
Sofield, Rick
77Visalia
79T-709R
80T-669R
81D-592
81F-563
81OPC-278
81T-278
82T-42
82Toledo-21
Softy, Mark
79WHave-16
80Wausau-9
Sohn, Young Chul
91Kissim/ProC-4184
Sohns, Thomas
80Water-16
Sojo, Luis
87Myrtle-29
88Myrtle/ProC-1189
88SALAS/GS-18
89Syrac/CMC-22
89Syrac/MerchB-21
89Syrac/ProC-809
89Syrac/Team-21
90AAAGame/ProC-3
90AAASingl/ProC-360
90B-517
90F/Up-129
90Leaf-291
90OPC-594
90ProC/Singl-344
90Syrac/CMC-18
90Syrac/MerchB-23
90Syrac/ProC-580
90Syrac/Team-23
90T-594
91B-197
91D-579
91F-184
91F/UltraUp-U12
91Leaf-367
91OPC-26
91OPC/Premier-114
91S-342RP
91S/100RisSt-43
91S/RookTr-49T
91Smok/Angel-15
91StCl-507
91T-26
91T/90Debut-146
91T/Tr-112T
91UD-297
91UD/Ext-714
92B-418
92D-302
92Edmon/SB-167
92F-70
92L-5
92L/BlkGold-5
92OPC-206
92Panini-6
92Pinn-223
92S-127
92StCl-373
92T-206
92T/Gold-206
92T/GoldWin-206
92UD-149
92Ultra-31
93BJ/Demp-24
93BJ/Fire-25
93D-137

93F-198
93OPC-338
93Pac/Spanish-655
93Panini-28
93S-124
93Select-77
93StCl-27
93StCl/1stDay-27
93T-347
93T/Gold-347
93UD-802
93UD-94
Solaita, Tony
72Dimanche*-41
75OPC-389
75T-389
75T/M-389
76A&P/KC
76OPC-121
76SSPC-143
76T-121
77T-482
78SSPC/270-215
78T-557
79T-18
80OPC-212
80T-407
92Yank/WIZ60-119
Solano, Julio
83Tucson-11
84Cram/PCL-63
85F-363
85Mother/Ast-12
85T-353
86Pol/Ast-16
87Pol/Ast-18
88Mother/Sea-24
89Mother/Sea-26
Solano, Ramon
87Fayette-6
Solarte, Jose
88James/ProC-1912
Solimine, Joe
90Utica/Pucko-7
91SoBend/ProC-2861
Solis, Julio
85Miami-16
Solis, Marcelino
59T-214
Solo, Julio
89Pac/SenLg-50
Solomon, Eddie
(Buddy)
74Albuq/Team-19
75OPC-624R
75T-624R
75T/M-624R
78T-598
79OPC-74
79T-156
80T-346
81D-16
81F-384
81T-298
82D-437
82F-498
82T-696TL
82T-73
90Target-754
Solomon, Steve
92Batavia/ClBest-17
92Batavia/ProC-3279
93ClBest/MLG-153
Solseth, David
89Eugene/Best-12
90AppFox/Box-25
90AppFox/ProC-2099
91BBCity/ClBest-16
91BBCity/ProC-1402
Soltero, Saul
87Spokane-4
88Charl/ProC-1215
89AubAs/ProC-23
89River/Best-16
89River/Cal-31
89River/ProC-1406
89Wichita/Rock/Up-9
92CharRain/ClBest-19
92CharRain/ProC-120
Solters, Julius
(Moose)
34DS-85
34G-30
38G-255
38G-279
39PlayBall-78
40PlayBall-126
41DP-71
81Conlon-34
91Conlon/Sport-285
R313
R314
V354-77
Soma, Katsuya
83SanJose-18
Somers, P.T.
N172
Sommer, David
89James/ProC-2144
90WPalmB/Star-21
91AA/LineD-642
91Wmsprt/LineD-642
91Wmsprt/ProC-291
Sommer, Joseph J.
N172
Sommers, Dennis
(Denny)
75Lafay
82BK/Indians-10
82BK/Indians-11
82BK/Indians-12CO
82Wheat/Ind
83Wheat/Ind-25
85Polar/Ind-xx
88Smok/Padres-27
90Padre/MagUno-22CO
93Mother/Giant-28M
Sommers, Joseph A.
N172
Sommers, Scott
86Elmira-22
88Lynch/Star-23
89NewBrit/ProC-623
89NewBrit/Star-19
89Star/IISingl-130
Sonberg, Erik
85Cram/PCL-159
89Hagers/Best-18
89Hagers/ProC-267
Sondrini, Joe
91Augusta/ClBest-26
91Augusta/ProC-815
92B-211
92ProC/Tomorrow-310
92Salem/ClBest-16
92Salem/ProC-73
Songer, Don
94Conlon-1303
Songini, Michael
(Mike)
88Billings/ProC-1829
89Greens/ProC-421
90Erie/Star-24
91Reno/Cal-21
Sonneberger, Steve
88Hagers/Star-20
Sontag, Alan
86OrlanTw-18
87OrlanTw-23
91MidldA/OneHour-28
91PalmSp/ProC-2013
92Salinas/ClBest-11
92Salinas/ProC-3753
Soos, Charles
87Kinston-4
88Kinston/Star-20
Soper, Mike 1
83BurlR-11
86Colum-24
86Colum/Pol-23
Soper, Mike 2
90AS/Cal-52
90Reno/Cal-277
91CLAS/ProC-CAR20
91Kinston/ClBest-12
91Kinston/ProC-324
92Canton/SB-118
92ProC/Tomorrow-54
92Sky/AASingl-55
Sorce, Sam
83BurlR-22
83BurlR/Frit-3
85OrlanTw-11
86OrlanTw-19
Sorensen, Lary
77Spoka
78T-569
79T-303
80OPC-84
80T-154
81Coke
81D-325
81F-519
81T-379
81T/Tr-831
82D-246
82F-128
82OPC-136
82T-689
82T/Tr-111T
82Wheat/Ind
83D-363
83F-418
83F/St-12M
83OPC-48
83T-48
83Wheat/Ind-26
84D-635
84F-549
84F/X-U109
84Mother/A's-14
84Nes/792-286
84Nes/792-546TL
84OPC-286
84T-286
84T-546TL
84T/St-259
84T/Tr-111T
85D-131
85F-434
85F/Up-U108
85SevenUp-42
86F-381
86T-744
87F/Up-U111
88Chatt/Best-20
90Swell/Great-63
Sorey, Ron
75WPalmB/Sussman-27
78Dunedin
Soriano, Hilario
77Clinton
Soriano, Tony
47Remar-24
Soroko, Mark
77Tucson
Sorrel, Mike
81Cedar-14
82CharR-3
Sorrell, Billy
66T-254R
67T-341R
71OPC-17
71T-17
Sorrell, Vic
33G-15
92Conlon/Sport-577
V355-21
Sorrento, Paul
87PalmSp-11
88PalmSp/Cal-110
88PalmSp/ProC-1450
89BBAmAA/BPro-AA19
89OrlanTw/Best-1
89OrlanTw/ProC-1343
89SLAS-13
90AAASingl/ProC-259
90B-421
90D-626
90Portl/CMC-25
90Portl/ProC-189
90ProC/Singl-577
90S-647
90T/89Debut-119
90T/Tr-119T
90UD/Ext-784
91AAA/LineD-420
91D-745
91OPC-654
91Portl/LineD-420
91Portl/ProC-1574
91S-796
91S/100RisSt-44
91StCl-408
91T-654
91UD-680
92D-752
92F-218
92F/Up-18
92Indian/McDon-27
92L-401
92L/BlkGold-401
92OPC-546
92StCl-707
92Studio-169
92T-546
92T/Gold-546
92T/GoldWin-546
92T/Tr-108T
92T/TrGold-108T
92Ultra-357
93B-501
93D-229
93F-221
93Flair-199
93Indian/WUAB-29
93L-105
93Pac/Beisbol-6M
93Pac/Spanish-102
93Panini-55
93Pinn-320
93S-194
93Select-226
93StCl-194
93StCl/1stDay-194
93Studio-67
93T-264
93T/Gold-264
93UD-196
93UD/SP-126
93Ultra-191
94B-83
94D-536
94F-120
94Flair-44
94L-361
94Pac/Cr-184
94Panini-60
94Pinn-308
94S-473
94Studio-96
94T-358
94T/Finest-185
94T/Finest/PreProd-185
94T/FinestRef-185
94T/Gold-358
94TripleP-119
94UD-363
94UD/CollC-262
94UD/CollC/Gold-262
94UD/CollC/Silv-262
94Ultra-48
Sosa, Elias
72Dimanche*-42
74OPC-54
74T-54
74T/St-109
75OPC-398
75T-398
75T/M-398
76OPC-364
76SSPC-558
76T-364
77T-558
78T-694
79T-78
80OPC-153
80T-293
81D-599
81F-151
81OPC-181
81T-181
82D-446
82F-208
82OPC-116
82T-414
82T/Tr-112T
83D-259
83F-342
83T-753
83T/Fold-4M
83T/Tr-107T
84F-313
84Nes/792-503
84T-503
87SanJose-18
89Pac/SenLg-8
89Sumter/ProC-1093
89T/SenLg-45
89TM/SenLg-97
90EliteSenLg-14
90Target-755
91Pac/SenLg-137
92MCI-11
Sosa, Jose Y.
73Cedar
74Cedar
76OPC-591R
76T-591R
78Charl
Sosa, Jose
90Princet/DIMD-21
92Augusta/ClBest-19
92Augusta/ProC-238
Sosa, Miguel
80Ander-24
81Durham-1
82Durham-9
85IntLgAS-3
85Richm-17
86Albany/TCMA-4
86Colum-25
Sosa, Sammy
87Gaston/ProC-29
88CharlR/Star-23
89BBAmAA/BPro-AA29
89D/Best-324
89Tulsa/GS-25
89Tulsa/Team-24
90B-312
90Classic-140
90Coke/WSox-23
90D-489
90D/BestAL-104
90F-548
90F/Can-548
90HotRook/St-43
90Leaf-220
90OPC-692
90S-558
90S/100Ris-35
90S/YS/II-25
90Sf-81
90Star/ISingl-61
90T-692
90T/89Debut-120
90T/Big-286
90TulsaDG/Best-31
90UD-17
91B-350
91Classic/200-60
91D-147
91F-136
91Kodak/WSox-25
91Leaf-321
91Leaf/Stud-38
91MajorLg/Pins-16
91OPC-414
91Panini/FrSt-316
91S-256
91StCl-6
91T-414
91UD-265
91Ultra-82
92B-116
92Classic/II-T27
92Cub/Mara-21
92D-740
92F-98
92F/Up-77
92L-412
92L/BlkGold-412
92OPC-94
92OPC/Premier-120
92Panini-129
92Pinn-369
92Pinn/Team2000-55
92S-258
92S/RookTr-23T
92StCl-628
92Studio-20
92T-94
92T/Gold-94
92T/GoldWin-94
92T/Tr-109T
92T/TrGold-109T
92UD-438
92UD-723
92Ultra-476
93B-636
93Cub/Mara-26
93D-186
93F-27
93Flair-22
93Flair/Pr-8
93L-70
93LimeR/Winter-31
93Pac/Beisbol-19M
93Pac/Beisbol-20
93Pac/Spanish-383

93Panini-208
93Pinn-145
93Rang/Keeb-337
93S-143
93Select-165
93StCl-531
93StCl/1stDay-531
93StCl/Cub-2
93Studio-121
93T-156
93T/Finest-79
93T/FinestRef-79
93T/Gold-156
93TripleP-151
93UD-127
93UD-819TC
93UD/FunPack-85
93UD/SP-89
93Ultra-24
94B-82
94D-337
94D/Special-337
94F-399
94Finest-236
94L-98
94OPC-161
94Pac/Cr-112
94Pac/Gold-19
94Panini-158
94Pinn-3
94Pinn/Artist-3
94Pinn/HobSam-3
94Pinn/Museum-3
94Pinn/Power-7
94Pinn/RetailSam-3
94S-510
94Select-58
94Sf/2000-81
94Sf/Mov-7
94StCl-80
94StCl/1stDay-80
94StCl/Gold-80
94StCl/Team-347
94Studio-64
94T-725
94T/BlkGold-42
94T/Gold-725
94TripleP-78
94UD-268HFA
94UD-510
94UD/CollC-263
94UD/CollC/Gold-263
94UD/CollC/Silv-263
94UD/ElecD-268HFA
94UD/HoloFX-38
94UD/SP-72
94Ultra-464
Sosh, John
52Laval-68
Sossamon, L. Timothy
(Tim)
86Cram/NWL-148
87CharWh-23
88Reading/ProC-870
90Jaxvl/ProC-1375
Soth, Paul
77AppFx
79AppFx-1
Sothern, Denny
90Target-1077
Sothoron, Allen
21Exh-170
92Conlon/Sport-523
E120
E126-11
R312/M
W573
Soto, Ed
86DayBe-26
87Gaston/ProC-14
Soto, Emison
91Elmira/ClBest-15
91Elmira/ProC-3286
92WinHaven/ProC-1782
Soto, Jose
86Geneva-25
Soto, Mario
77Indianap-21
78Indianap-9
78SSPC/270-117
78T-427
79Indianap-28
80T-622
81Coke
81D-63
81F-214
81T-354
81T/HT
82Coke/Reds
82D-103
82F-83
82F/St-19
82T-63
83D-248
83F-603
83F/St-2M
83F/St-2M
83OPC-215
83OPC/St-234
83PermaGr/AS-18
83T-215
83T-351TL
83T/St-234
84Borden-36
84D-428
84F-483
84F/St-79
84Nes/792-160
84Nes/792-756TL
84OPC-160
84Seven-13C
84T-160
84T-756TL
84T/Gloss22-21
84T/RD-18M
84T/St-51
85D-184
85D-19DK
85D/AAS-3
85D/DKsuper-19
85F-552
85F/LimEd-36
85F/St-116
85F/St-86
85FunFoodPin-61
85GenMills-11
85Indianap-31
85Leaf-19DK
85OPC-131
85Seven-13G
85T-495
85T/Gloss40-37
85T/RD-17M
85T/St-46
85T/Super-21
86D-184
86F-192
86F/Mini-41
86F/Slug-36
86F/St-114
86Leaf-119
86OPC-28
86Seven/Coin-S11M
86Sf-168
86T-725
86T/Mini-42
86T/St-136
86T/Tatt-12M
86TexGold-36
87D-82
87F-214
87Leaf-140
87OPC-11
87T-517
88T-666
88T/Big-120
89S-588
Soto, Max
86GlenF-22
Soto, Miguel 1
84Savan-24
Soto, Miguel 2
91GulfCR/SportP-27
92Idaho/ProC-3517
93Macon/ClBest-23
93Macon/ProC-1403
Soto, Ozzie
85Cedar-13
86Tampa-21
Soto, Rafael
90Hunting/ProC-3294
91Peoria/ClBest-27
91Peoria/ProC-1351
91Peoria/Team-19
92WinSalem/ClBest-3
92WinSalem/ProC-1216
93Peoria/Team-26
Soto, Tom
78Newar
79Holyo-10
81Vanco-23
Sottile, Shaun
89Pulaski/ProC-1898
90Sumter/Best-21
90Sumter/ProC-2431
91Durham/ClBest-22
Souchock, Steve
52B-235
52T-234
53B/Col-91
53Tiger/Glen-26
54B-103
Soult, David
89KS*-85
Southland, Kip
87Everett-8
Southworth, Bill
25Exh-39
27Exh-32
47TipTop
49Eureka-24
51B-207MG
80Pac/Leg-17
91Conlon/Sport-89
92Conlon/Sport-627
93Conlon-839MG
E120
E121/120
E126-10
W501-89
W502-118
W514-16
W572
W754
Souza, Brian
90Helena/SportP-25
91Beloit/ClBest-7
91Beloit/ProC-2102
91Helena/SportP-24
92Beloit/ClBest-8
Souza, Mark
76Watlo
79Ogden/TCMA-17
80Ogden-10
81Tacom-22
Sovern, Jeff
76Indianap-8
78Indianap-25
Sowards, Van
83Clinton/Frit-21
84Shrev/FB-20
Sowders, John
N172
Sowders, William J.
E223
N172
N403/Bos
N526
Sowell, Scott
90MidldA/GS-25TR
Spaan, Tony
90Elizab/Star-21
Spade, Robert
E254
M116
T206
Spagnola, Glen
83Cedar-5
83Cedar/Frit-16
86Vermont-21
87Vermont-18
88ColAst/Best-4
89Calgary/CMC-10
89Calgary/ProC-527
89EastLDD/ProC-DD33
89Wmsprt/Star-21
Spagnuolo, Joe
87VeroB-3
Spahn, Warren E.
47TipTop
48B-18
48L-32
49B-33
49Eureka-25
49Royal-5
50B-19
50Drake-14
51B-134
51BR-B2
51T/RB-30
52B-156
52Dix
52NTea
52RM-NL22
52Royal
52T-33
52TipTop
53B/Col-99
53Dix
53Exh/Can-32
53JC-10
53NB
53RM-NL19
53SpicSpan/3x5-22
53SpicSpan/7x10-12
53T-147
54JC-21
54RH
54RM-NL11
54SpicSpan/PostC-17
54T-20
55Armour-20
55Gol/Braves-27
55JC-21
55RM-NL10
55SpicSpan/DC-16
55T-31
55T/DH-127
56T-10
56T/Hocus-A10
56T/Hocus-B12
56T/Pin-19
57SpicSpan/4x5-15
57T-90
58T-270
58T-494AS
59T-40
59T-571AS
60Bz-19
60Lake
60NuCard-63
60SpicSpan-22
60T-230M
60T-445
60T/tatt-49
61Bz-29
61NuCard-402
61NuCard-463
61P-101
61T-200
61T-47LL
61T-589AS
61T/St-47
62Bz
62Exh
62T-100
62T-312IA
62T-399AS
62T-56LL
62T-58LL
62T/St-150
62T/bucks
63Bz-5
63Exh
63F-45
63Salada-8
63T-320
63T/SO
64Bz-5
64T-3LL
64T-400
64T/Coins-160AS
64T/Coins-88
64T/S-31
64T/SU
64T/St-57
64T/tatt
64Wheat/St-43
65OPC-205
65T-205
73OPC-449CO
73T-449CO
75SSPC/42-36
76Rowe-14
76Shakey-139
77Galasso-264
77Galasso-38
79TCMA-3
80Laugh/3/4/5-15
80Marchant-29
80Pac/Leg-57
80Perez/HOF-139
80SSPC/HOF
81Redwd-22
82CJ-16
82F/St-108M
83MLBPA/Pin-34
84West/1-19
86Sf/Dec-27
87Nestle/DT-32
88Grenada-63
88Pac/Leg-109
89D-588PUZ
89HOF/St-84
90CollAB-24
90HOF/St-68
90Pac/Legend-51
90Perez/GreatMom-14
90Perez/Master-21
90Perez/Master-22
90Perez/Master-23
90Perez/Master-24
90Perez/Master-25
90Swell/Great-12
91K/3D-12
91Swell/Great-86
91T/Arc53-147
91WIZMets-372
92AP/ASG-16
92AP/ASG24K-16G
92AP/ASGProto-4
92Bz/Quadra-9M
92Ziploc-1
93AP/ASGCoke/Amo-16
93Metallic-18
93TWill-48
93UD/ATH-116
93UD/ATH-144
94T/Arc54-20
Exh47
PM10/L-40
R346-20
Spain, Dan
78OrlanTw
Spalding, Albert G.
50Callahan
50W576-67
75F/Pion-4
76Shakey-26
80Perez/HOF-26
80SSPC/HOF
Spalt, Paul
88Watertn/Pucko-24
Span, Brian
89CharRain/ProC-975
89Spokane/SP-15
Spang, R.J.
92GulfCM/ProC-3481
Spangler, Al
60L-38
60Lake
60SpicSpan-23
60T-143
61P-114
61T-73
62J-157
62P-157
62P/Can-157
62Salada-196
62Shirriff-196
62T-556
62T/St-130
63F-39
63J-185
63P-185
63Pep
63T-77
64T-406
65OPC-164
65T-164
65T/E-53
65T/trans-70
66OPC-173
66T-173
68T-451
69MB-259
69T8-268
70T-714
72MB-321
74OPC-354CO
74T-354CO
78TCMA-166
78TCMA-171
89Smok/Ast-23
Spann, Tookie
88Bristol/ProC-1891
89Lakeland/Star-19
90Lakeland/Star-23

92ClBest-133
92HighD/ClBest-13
Spanswick, Bill
63MilSau-10
64T-287R
65T-356
78TCMA-147
Sparks, Donald
89PrWill/Star-19
90Albany/Best-18
90Albany/ProC-1042
90Albany/Star-17
90EastLAS/ProC-EL2
90Foil/Best-237
90ProC/Singl-736
90Star/ISingl-53
91AAA/LineD-119
91ColClip/LineD-119
91ColClip/ProC-605
92Albany/ProC-2234
92Albany/SB-19
92ClBest-7
93ClBest/MLG-4
93ColClip/Pol-17
Sparks, Greg
86CharRain-23
88Huntsvl/BK-21
89AS/Cal-48
89Salinas/ProC-1819
90Albany/Best-19
90Albany/ProC-1043
90Albany/Star-18
90EastLAS/ProC-EL14
90Foil/Best-252
91AA/LineD-117
91CaroMud/LineD-117
91CaroMud/ProC-1095
92London/ProC-647
92London/SB-419
93Pawtu/Ball-22
Sparks, Joe
75Iowa/TCMA-18
81Omaha-1
82Omaha-25
83Omaha-24
86Indianap-3MG
87Indianap-4
88AAA/ProC-50
88Indianap/CMC-24
88Indianap/ProC-496
90T/TVYank-5CO
91AAA/LineD-599
91Toledo/LineD-599MG
91Toledo/ProC-1946MG
92Toledo/ProC-1057MG
92Toledo/SB-599MG
Sparks, Shane
92Augusta/ClBest-2
92Augusta/ProC-239
Sparks, Steve
88Beloit/GS-24
89Stockton/Best-8
89Stockton/Cal-152
89Stockton/ProC-390
89Stockton/Star-11
91AA/LineD-196
91ElPaso/LineD-196
91ElPaso/ProC-2749
91Stockton/ProC-3031
92ElPaso/ProC-3920
92ElPaso/SB-221
Sparks, Tully
E107
E254
M116
Sparling, Don
85FtMyr-5
87Memphis-19
87Memphis/Best-14
Sparma, Blase
92Durham/ProC-1099
92Macon/ClBest-13
Sparma, Joe
64T-512R
65T-587
66T-267
67CokeCap/Tiger-5
67OPC-13
67T-13
68CokeCap/Tiger-5
68T-505
69T-488
70MLB/St-69
70OPC-243
70T-243
88Domino-21
Sparrow, Chris
89Idaho/ProC-2024
90Utica/Pucko-8
Speake, Bob
56T-66
57T-339
58T-437
59T-526
Speaker, Tris
10Domino-111
11Helmar-4
12Sweet/Pin-6
12Sweet/Pin-6A
14CJ-65
14Piedmont/St-52
15CJ-65
16FleischBrd-88
21Exh-171
24Sherlock-9
25Exh-87
26Exh-86
27Exh-64
28Yung-28
33G-89
40PlayBall-170
48Exh/HOF
50Callahan
50W576-68
51T/CM
60Exh/HOF-22
60F-10
61F-79
61GP-309
63Bz-24
69Bz/Sm
72F/FFeat-32
72K/ATG-11
76Shakey-7
77Galasso-138
77Galasso-268
77Galasso-96
77Shakey-22
80Perez/HOF-11
80SSPC/HOF
81Conlon-14
82Ohio/HOF-13
85Woolwth-34
86Conlon/1-30
87Nestle/DT-6
88Conlon/3-27
89HOF/St-41
90BBWit-72
90Swell/Great-45
91Conlon/Sport-44
91Swell/Great-140
92Conlon/Col-18
92Conlon/Sport-422
92Conlon/Sport-591
93AP/ASG-91
93AP/ASG24K-25G
93Conlon-795
93Conlon-827
93Conlon/MasterBW-6
93CrackJack-6
93TWill-128
93TWill-35
93UD/ATH-117
93UD/ATH-161
93UD/T202-10M
94Conlon-1222
D303
D327
D328-166
E106
E120
E121/120
E121/80
E122
E126-27
E135-166
E210-28
E220
E224
E254
E270/1
E300
E90/1
E91
E94
L1-131
M116
PM1-12
R312/M
R423-104
S74-3
S81-106
T201
T202
T205
T206
T207
T213/blue
T215/blue
T215/brown
T216
T3-36
V100
V354-29
V89-13MG
W501-19
W502-28
W512-4
W514-102
W515-28
W516-5
W572
W573
W575
WG4-27
WG5-35
WG6-33
Speakes, Joey
88Pocatel/ProC-2097
Speakman, Tim
85Elmira-21
Speakman, Willie
91Belling/ClBest-14
91Belling/ProC-3669
92Penin/ClBest-13
Spear, Mike
88Butte-20
Spearman, Vernon
91Yakima/ClBest-1
91Yakima/ProC-4261
92ProC/Tomorrow-249
92VeroB/ClBest-12
92VeroB/ProC-2892
93ClBest/MLG-180
93FExcel/ML-54
Spearnock, Mike
86Cram/NWL-99
87PalmSp-1
Speck, R. Cliff
80OkCty
82RochR-6
83RochR-9
86Richm-21
87D-571
87Richm/Bob-19
87Richm/Crown-39
87Richm/TCMA-25
87T-269
88Colum/CMC-22
88Colum/Pol-11
88Colum/ProC-311
Speckenbach, Paul
64T-548R
Specyalski, Brian
88CapeCod/Sum-89
89BendB/Legoe-19
90Boise/ProC-3322
Speece, Byron
43Centen-22
44Centen-21
45Centen-23
Speed, Horace
75IntLgAS/Broder-33
75PCL/AS-33
75PCL/AS-34
75Phoenix-22
75Phoenix/Caruso-3
75Phoenix/CircleK-22
76Phoenix/Coke-19
76SSPC-112
77Phoenix
79T-438
80Richm-14
Speek, Frank
90Johnson/Star-24
91Savan/ClBest-11
91Savan/ProC-1652
92Spring/ClBest-3
92Spring/ProC-869
Speer, V. Floyd
46Remar-18
47Remar-14
47Signal
48Signal
48Smith-18
Spehr, Tim
90AAASingl/ProC-604
90Omaha/CMC-21
90Omaha/ProC-69
90ProC/Singl-196
91AAA/LineD-346
91AAAGame/ProC-28
91B-298
91Omaha/LineD-346
91Omaha/ProC-1038
92Classic/I-84
92D-689
92F-674
92OPC-342
92Omaha/ProC-2965
92Omaha/SB-347
92S-416
92Sky/AAASingl-159
92StCl-96
92T-342
92T/91Debut-166
92T/Gold-342
92T/GoldWin-342
93D-15
93UD-669
94F-552
94StCl-515
94StCl/1stDay-515
94StCl/Gold-515
94T-714
94T/Gold-714
Speier, Chris
72K-28
72OPC-165
72OPC-166IA
72T-165
72T-166IA
73OPC-273
73OPC-345KP
73T-273
73T-345KP
73T/Lids-49
74K-40
74OPC-129
74OPC-335AS
74T-129
74T-335AS
74T/DE-29
74T/St-110
75Ho-73
75Ho/Twink-73
75OPC-505
75SSPC/Puzzle-24
75T-505
75T/M-505
76Ho-82
76OPC-630
76SSPC-105
76T-630
77BurgChef-108
77OPC-53
77Pep-41
77T-515
78OPC-232
78T-221
79OPC-221
79T-426
80OPC-168
80T-319
81D-329
81F-153
81OPC-97
81OPC/Post-3
81T-97
81T/St-189
82D-366
82Expo/Hygrade-21
82F-209
82F/St-32
82Hygrade
82OPC-198
82T-198
82T/St-58
82Zeller-8
83D-266
83F-298
83F/St-1M
83F/St-8M
83OPC-121
83OPC/St-258
83Stuart-27
83T-768
83T/St-258
84D-523
84Expo/PostC-30
84F-288
84Mother/Giants-22
84Nes/792-678
84OPC-328
84Stuart-27
84T-678
84T/St-95
85F/Up-U109
85SevenUp-28
85T-577
85T/Tr-111T
86F-382
86Gator-28
86OPC-212
86T-212
87D-392
87F-575
87F/Up-U112
87Mother/SFG-18
87T-424
87T/Tr-115T
88D-239
88F-96
88Mother/Giants-18
88S-493
88T-329
89D-532
89F-343
89Mother/Giants-18
89S-297
89T-94
89UD-206
90F-72
90F/Can-72
90OPC-753
90Publint/St-82
90T-753
Spence, J. Bob
71OPC-186
71T-186
Spence, Samuel
77Watlo
78Watlo
Spence, Stan
43Playball-5
49B-102
Exh47
Spencer, Daryl
54B-185
56T-277
57T-49
58Hires-51
58SFCallB-22
58T-68
59T-443
60L-129
60MacGregor-24
60T-368
61P-173
61T-357
61T-451M
61T/St-95
61Union/Dodg-21
62BB-20
62J-103
62P-103
62P/Can-103
62Salada-178A
62Salada-178B
62Shirriff-178
62T-197
62T/St-141
63FrBauer-27
63J-124
63P-124
63T-502
79TCMA-226
90Target-756
Spencer, Edward
(Tubby)
C46-81
E220
E254
E96
T204
T206
W514-36
Spencer, George
52BR
52T-346

53T-115
55Gol/Giants-25
63MilSau-11
91T/Arc53-115
Spencer, Glenn Edward
33G-84
V354-37
Spencer, Jeff
89KS*-68
Spencer, Jim
70OPC-255
70T-255
71MLB/St-358
71OPC-78
71T-78
71T/Coins-4
72MB-322
72OPC-419
72T-419
73OPC-319
73T-319
74OPC-580
74T-580
74T/St-239
75OPC-387
75T-387
75T/M-387
76OPC-83
76SSPC-268
76T-83
76T/Tr-83T
77BurgChef-79
77Ho/Twink-16
77OPC-46
77T-648
78BK/Y-16
78OPC-122
78T-182
79BK/Y-17
79OPC-315
79T-599
80OPC-147
80T-278
81D-226
81F-96
81OPC-209
81T-435
81T/Tr-832
82D-265
82F-107
82F/St-127
82OPC-88
82T-729
82T/St-223
92Yank/WIZ70-142
92Yank/WIZ80-185
93Rang/Keeb-338
Spencer, John
88Elmira-25
89Elmira/Pucko-20
Spencer, Joseph B.
92Negro/RetortII-36
Spencer, Kyle
88Butte-10
89Gaston/ProC-1002
89Gaston/Star-22
90CharlR/Star-27
91CharlR/ClBest-11
91CharlR/ProC-1315
Spencer, Robert
90NewBrit/Best-27
Spencer, Roy
31Exh/4-31
33Exh/4-16
90Target-757
91Conlon/Sport-320
Spencer, Shane
90Tampa/DIMD-25
92Greens/ClBest-4
92Greens/ProC-795
93Greens/ClBest-21
93Greens/ProC-900
Spencer, Stan
91AA/LineD-270
91B-441
91ClBest/Singl-84
91Harris/LineD-270
91Harris/ProC-628
Spencer, Hubert Thomas
(Tom)
76Indianap-6
78Knoxvl
79Knoxvl/TCMA-25
80Tucson-15
81Tucson-13
86Pittsfld-22MG
88Gator-2CO
89Cedar/Best-25
89Cedar/ProC-917
89Cedar/Star-24
89Pac/SenLg-101
89T/SenLg-24
90Cedar/Best-13
90MidwLgAS/GS-53M
90SanJose/Best-29MG
90SanJose/Cal-53MG
90SanJose/ProC-2026MG
90SanJose/Star-27MG
91Kahn/Mets-51CO
92Mother/Ast-27M
93Mother/Ast-28M
Spencer, Tom
91CharWh/ClBest-24TR
92CharWh/ClBest-24TR
Spencer, Troy
52Laval-66
Sperring, Robert
74Wichita-116
76OPC-323
76SSPC-320
76T-323
77T-514
78Charl
79CharCh-16
Sperry, Chris
89Salem/Team-28
Spetter, Bryan
92Pulaski/ClBest-19
92Pulaski/ProC-3187
Spicer, Len
79Newar-22
Spicer, Robert
52Mother-61
Spiers, Bill
88Stockton/Cal-197
88Stockton/ProC-738
89D/Rook-5
89F/Up-40
89Pol/Brew-6
89S/Tr-82
89T/Tr-115T
89UD/Ext-745
90B-402
90Brewer/MillB-24
90Classic-134
90D-382
90ElPasoATG/Team-26
90F-337
90F/Can-337
90Leaf-203
90OPC-538
90Panini/St-376
90S-449
90S/100Ris-55
90S/YS/I-14
90Sf-206
90T-538
90T/89Debut-121
90T/Big-88
90T/JumboR-27
90ToysRUs-26
90UD-237
91Brewer/MillB-24
91D-310
91F-597
91Leaf-111
91OPC-284
91Panini/FrSt-207
91Panini/St-162
91Pol/Brew-21
91S-84
91StCl-360
91T-284
91UD-268
91Ultra-181
92B-536
92D-364
92F-189
92L-106
92L/BlkGold-106
92OPC-742
92Panini-38
92Pinn-177
92Pol/Brew-23
92S-218
92StCl-379
92T-742
92T/Gold-742
92T/GoldWin-742
92UD-214
92Ultra-84
93F-635
93Flair-229
93L-403
93OPC-323
93Pac/Spanish-516
93Panini-38
93Pinn-525
93Pol/Brew-22
93S-88
93Select-259
93StCl-566
93StCl/1stDay-566
93T-619
93T/Gold-619
93UD-325
93Ultra-577
94D-288
94F-191
94Pac/Cr-342
94Pinn-370
94Pol/Brew-25
94S-105
94S/GoldR-105
94T-73
94T/Gold-73
94UD/CollC-264
94UD/CollC/Gold-264
94UD/CollC/Silv-264
Spiers, Mike
90Salinas/Cal-145CO
Spiezio, Ed
65T-431R
66Pep/Tul
67OPC-128
67T-128
68T-349
69MLB/St-197
69T-249
70MLB/St-119
70T-718
71MLB/St-240
71OPC-6
71T-6
72MB-323
72OPC-504
72T-504
Spiezio, Scott
94B-413
Spikes, Charlie
73OPC-614R
73T-614R
74OPC-58
74T-58
74T/DE-33
74T/St-169
75OPC-135
75T-135
75T/M-135
76OPC-408
76SSPC-531
76T-408
77T-168
78T-459
80T-294
81F-259
92Yank/WIZ70-143
Spiller, Derron
92Savan/ClBest-22
92Savan/ProC-664
Spillner, Dan
75OPC-222
75T-222
75T/M-222
76OPC-557
76SSPC-119
76T-557
77Padre/SchCd-29
77T-182
78Padre/FamFun-30
78T-488
79T-359
80T-38
81F-392
81T-276
82D-411
82F-378
82OPC-1
82T-664
82Wheat/Ind
83D-137
83F-419
83F/St-15M
83F/St-25AM
83F/St-25BM
83OPC-278
83OPC/St-59
83T-725
83T/St-59
83Wheat/Ind-27
84D-582
84F-550
84Nes/792-91
84OPC-91
84T-91
85Coke/WS-37
85F-528
85T-169
86D-122
86F-217
86T-423
91Everett/ProC-3935CO
Spilman, Harry
78Indianap-5
79Indianap-5
79T-717R
80T-677
81D-304
81F-209
81T-94
81T/Tr-833
82F-233
82T-509
82Tucson-11
83D-65
83F-467
83T-193
84D-258
84Mother/Ast-12
84Nes/792-612
84T-612
85Mother/Ast-19
85T-482
86T-352
87F-284
87Mother/SFG-16
87T-64
88D-607
88F-97
88Mother/Giants-16
88S-618
88T-217
89Tucson/CMC-18
89Tucson/JP-24
89Tucson/ProC-199
90AAASingl/ProC-200
90ProC/Singl-616
90Tucson/CMC-14
90Tucson/ProC-210
Spink, J.G. Taylor (Mrs.)
94Conlon-1111
94Conlon-1112M
Spink, J.G. Taylor
94Conlon-1111M
94Conlon-1112
Spinks, Scipio
70OPC-492R
70T-492R
71MLB/St-92
71OPC-747R
71T-747R
72OPC-202
72T-202
73OPC-417
73T-417
74OPC-576
74T-576
74Wichita-125
75Iowa/TCMA-19
Spino, Tom
79QuadC-23
Spinosa, John
87WPalmB-28
92Indianap/ProC-NNO
Spires, Tony
90Everett/Best-19
90Everett/ProC-3135
91ClBest/Singl-113
91SanJose/ClBest-8
91SanJose/ProC-21
Spitale, Ben
87BurlEx-12
Spivey, Jim
90Johnson/Star-25
91Savan/ClBest-13
91Savan/ProC-1655
Split, Lickety
90WinSalem/Team-26
Splitt, Steve
77BurlB
78Holyo
79Holyo-19
Splittorff, Paul
71OPC-247R
71T-247R
72OPC-315
72T-315
73OPC-48
73T-48
74OPC-225
74T-225
74T/DE-56
74T/St-190
75OPC-340
75T-340
75T/M-340
76A&P/KC
76OPC-43
76SSPC-163
76T-43
77BurgChef-64
77OPC-41
77T-534
78Ho-11
78SSPC/270-230
78T-638
79K-10
79OPC-90
79T-183
80OPC-214
80T-409
81D-342
81F-30
81F/St-95
81T-218
82D-464
82F-423
82OPC-126
82T-759
83D-286
83F-124
83T-316
83T/Fold-1M
84D-521
84F-360
84Nes/792-52
84T-52
84T/St-281
Spohrer, Al
31Exh/4-1
33G-161
35G-8L
35G-9L
92Conlon/Sport-602
R310
V353-94
Spoljaric, Paul
91StCath/ClBest-20
91StCath/ProC-3395
92Myrtle/ClBest-23
92Myrtle/ProC-2197
93B-279
93ClBest/MLG-130
93Dunedin/ClBest-21
93FExcel/ML-245
94B-581
94Pinn-539
94SigRook-48
94StCl/Team-175
94T-776M
94T/Gold-776M
94UD-26
94UD/ElecD-26
94Ultra-439
Spoolstra, Scott
88Clmbia/GS-20
Spooner, Karl
55Gol/Dodg-29
55T-90
55T/DH-19
56T-83
56T/Hocus-B20
56T/Pin-53P
79TCMA-238
90Target-758
Sposito, Gus
85SpokAT/Cram-19
Spradlin, Jerry
88Billings/ProC-1821

89Greens/ProC-413
90Cedar/ProC-2322
90CharWh/Best-10
91AA/LineD-170
91Chatt/LineD-170
91Chatt/ProC-1961
92Chatt/ProC-3821
92Chatt/SB-195
93FExcel/ML-30
94D-579
94F-430
94Pac/Cr-162
94StCl-56
94StCl/1stDay-56
94StCl/Gold-56
94StCl/Pr-56
94T-779M
94T/Gold-779M
94Ultra-179

Sprague, Charles
N172

Sprague, Ed Jr.
87PanAm/USAB-22
87PanAm/USAR-22
88T/Tr-113T
89B-252
89Dunedin/Star-16
89T/Big-40
90AAASingl/ProC-361
90B-511
90ProC/Singl-345
90Syrac/CMC-19
90Syrac/MerchB-24
90Syrac/ProC-581
90Syrac/Team-24
90TeamUSA/87-22
91AAA/LineD-518
91B-26
91Classic/I-90
91Classic/III-88
91D/Rook-14
91F/UltraUp-U63
91F/Up-U66
91Leaf-485
91S/ASFan-7
91S/RookTr-101T
91S/ToroBJ-26
91StCl-387
91Syrac/Kraft-4
91Syrac/LineD-518
91Syrac/MerchB-24
91Syrac/ProC-2484
91UD/FinalEd-47F
92AAA/ASG/SB-517
92D-187
92F-340
92OPC-516
92ProC/Tomorrow-162
92S-504
92S/100RisSt-52
92Sky/AAASingl-232
92StCl-445
92Syrac/MerchB-21
92Syrac/ProC-1972
92Syrac/SB-517
92T-516
92T/91Debut-167
92T/DQ-15
92T/Gold-516
92T/GoldWin-516
92UD-242
93B-491
93BJ/D/45-11
93BJ/D/McDon-14
93BJ/D/McDon-29
93BJ/D/WS-3
93BJ/Demp-8
93BJ/Fire-26
93D-219
93F-698
93Flair-294
93L-408
93OPC-203
93OPC/WC-13
93OPC/WSHero-3
93Pac/Spanish-328
93Pinn-223
93S-214
93S-520WS
93StCl-90
93StCl/1stDay-90
93StCl/MurphyS-112
93Studio-116
93T-659
93T/Gold-659
93TripleP-238
93UD-764
93UD/SP-52
93UD/SeasonHL-HI18
93Ultra-292
94B-57
94D-84
94F-342
94L-117
94OPC-265
94OPC/BJ-7
94Pac/Cr-651
94Pinn-459
94S-399
94Select-135
94StCl-418
94StCl/1stDay-418
94StCl/Gold-418
94StCl/Team-156
94Studio-31
94T-426
94T/Finest-160
94T/FinestRef-160
94T/Gold-426
94TripleP-37
94UD-241
94UD/ElecD-241
94Ultra-142

Sprague, Ed
69T-638
72OPC-121
72T-121
75OPC-76
75T-76
75T/M-76
76SSPC-230

Spratke, Ken
87Chatt/Best-12
88Memphis/Best-23
89Omaha/CMC-9
89Omaha/ProC-1719

Spratt, Greg
91SALAS/ProC-SAL31TR

Spratt, Henry
(Jack)
T207

Sprick, Scott
91Erie/ClBest-9
91Erie/ProC-4078
91Freder/ClBest-19
91Freder/ProC-2373

Spriggs, George
67T-472R
68T-314R
69T-662R
71MLB/St-431
71OPC-411
71T-411

Spring, Jack
57Seattle/Pop-34
62T-257
63T-572
64T-71
85SpokAT/Cram-20

Springer, Billy
(Steve)
84Jacks-22
85IntLgAS-13
85Tidew-16
85Tidew-17
86Tidew-27
87Tidew-11
87Tidew/TCMA-18
88Tidew/CANDL-12
88Tidew/CMC-21
88Tidew/ProC-1598
89Vanco/CMC-12
89Vanco/ProC-592

Springer, Dennis
88Bakers/Cal-260
89SanAn/Best-20
89TexLAS/GS-18
90Albuq/CMC-12
90Albuq/Trib-27
90ProC/Singl-414
90SanAn/GS-27
90TexLgAS/GS-15
91AA/LineD-541
91SanAn/LineD-541
91SanAn/ProC-2973
92SanAn/ProC-3973
92SanAn/SB-568
92Sky/AASingl-252

Springer, Gary
83SanJose-6

Springer, Russell
87Anchora-27
88CapeCod/Sum-35
90LSUGreat-15
91FSLAS/ProC-FSL18
91FtLaud/ClBest-14
91FtLaud/ProC-2427
92B-308
92Classic/II-T93
92ColClip/Pol-9
92ColClip/ProC-350
92ColClip/SB-118
92Pinn-561
92Sky/AAASingl-57
93B-285
93D-285
93F/Final-191
93F/MLPI-8
93L-549
93S-238
93Select-337
93StCl-736
93StCl/1stDay-736
93StCl/Angel-24
93T-686
93T/Gold-686
93UD/SP-27
93Vanco/ProC-2597
94D-325
94S-562
94T-113
94T/Gold-113

Springer, Steve
90AAASingl/ProC-227
90ColoSp/CMC-18
90ColoSp/ProC-46
90ProC/Singl-470
91AAA/LineD-72
91Calgary/LineD-72
91Calgary/ProC-524
91T/90Debut-147
92Tidew/ProC-
92Tidew/SB-571

Sprinz, Joseph C.
48Sommer-28
49Sommer-22

Sproat, Ed
N172

Sproesser, Mark
81Redwd-18
82Redwd-13

Sproviero, Nick
91James/ClBest-19
91James/ProC-3544

Sprowl, Robert
(Bobby)
80Tucson-6
81T-82R
82T-441R
82Tucson-19
83ColumAst-21

Spurgeon, Fred
26Exh-87

Spurgeon, Scott
88AubAs/ProC-1948
89Ashvl/ProC-958

Spurlock, Robert
90Visalia/Cal-85BB

Spykstra, David
92Classic/DP-65
93StCl/MurphyS-150

Squires, Mike
78SSPC/270-147
79T-704R
80T-466
81D-398
81F-349
81T-292
82D-39
82F-357
82F/St-188
82T-398
83D-495
83F-250
83T-669
83TrueVal/WSox-25
84D-404
84F-71
84Nes/792-72
84T-72
84TrueVal/WS-29
85D-501
85F-529
85OPC-278
85T-543
89Tor/Fire-25CO
90Tor/BJ-25CO
91Tor/Fire-6CO
92WSox-NNO

St-Vincent, Claude
52Laval-94

St.Clair, Dan
83Omaha-8
84Omaha-18

St.Claire, Ebba
52B-172
52T-393
53B/BW-34
53JC-16
53SpicSpan/3x5-21
53T-91
54B-128
91T/Arc53-91

St.Claire, Randy
85D-575
85Indianap-19
86D-463
86F-261
86Indianap-15
86Leaf-229
86OPC-89
86T-89
87F/Up-U113
87OPC-366
87T-467
88D-426
88F-197
88OPC-279
88S-397
88T-279
89Portl/CMC-11
89Portl/ProC-213
89T-666
89UD-29
90OPC-503
90T-503
90Tucson/CMC-5
90Tucson/ProC-203
91Richm/LineD-443
91Richm/ProC-2568
92S-708

St.Claire, Steve
85Utica-23
86James-24
87BurlEx-11

St.John, Anthony
89SLCity-16

St.John, Rich
89Watertn/Star-28
90Reno/Cal-289TR

St.Laurent, Jim
85BurlR-15
86DayBe-27
87TexLgAS-17
88OkCty/CMC-23
88OkCty/ProC-39
89OkCty/CMC-17
89OkCty/ProC-1524
90TulsaDG/Best-7

St.Peter, William
(Bill)
88Geneva/ProC-1650
89CharWh/Best-6
89CharWh/ProC-1753
90Peoria/Team-12
91CharlK/LineD-143
91CharlK/ProC-1698

Staats, Todd
89GA-30

Stabile, Ed
92Watertn/ClBest-28

Stablein, George
80Hawaii-15
81Hawaii-15
81Hawaii/TCMA-14
81T-356R
82Hawaii-15

Stacey, Al
89Geneva/ProC-1874
90Erie/Star-25

Stack, William Edward
(Eddie)
80Perez/HOF-D
80Perez/HOF-FM
90Target-759
T207

Stackhouse, Brian
86Macon-23TR

Stading, Greg
86PrWill-25
87Salem-6

Stadler, Jeff
78Cedar
79Cedar/TCMA-7

Staehle, Marv
65OPC-41R
65T-41R
66OPC-164R
66T-164R
69T-394R
71LaPizza-11
71MLB/St-140
71OPC-663
71T-663

Stafford, Bill
61T-213
61T/St-199
62J-13
62P-13
62P/Can-13
62T-55LL
62T-570
63J-22
63Kahn
63P-22
63T-155
63T-331M
64T-299
65OPC-281
65T-281
92Yank/WIZ60-120
WG10-21
WG9-22

Stafford, Gil
75BurlB

Stafford, Jerry
92Erie/ClBest-26
92Erie/ProC-1624
93T-683
93T/Gold-683

Stagg, Bob
47Centen-27

Staggs, Ron
75WPalmB/Sussman-14

Staggs, Steve
75Omaha/Team-15
78OPC-94
78T-521

Stahl, Charles
(Chick)
E107

Stahl, Garland
(Jake)
E224
E254
E270/1
E90/1
E91
L1-130
M116
S74-4
S81-105
T202
T204
T205
T206
T215/blue
T215/brown
T3-38
WG2-43
WG5-36

Stahl, Larry
66OPC-107R
66T-107R
69MB-260
69MLB/St-198
69T-271
69T/St-99
70MLB/St-120
70OPC-494
70T-494
71OPC-711
71T-711
72MB-324
72T-782
73OPC-533
73T-533
74OPC-507
74T-507

91WIZMets-373
Stahlhoefer, Larry
92Welland/ClBest-22
92Welland/ProC-1327
Stahoviak, Scott
91ClBest/Singl-401
91Classic/DP-23
91FrRow/DP-25
91Visalia/ProC/Up-2
91Visalia/ProC/Up-3M
92AS/Cal-41
92B-360
92ClBest-299
92OPC-66
92ProC/Tomorrow-97
92StCl/Dome-179
92T-66DP
92T/Gold-66
92T/GoldWin-66
92UD/ML-320
92Visalia/ClBest-1
92Visalia/ProC-1024
93ClBest/MLG-45
93FExcel/ML-204
94Pinn-248
94Pinn/Artist-248
94Pinn/Museum-248
94Sf/2000-154
94StCl-51
94StCl/1stDay-51
94StCl/Gold-51
94UD-27
94UD/CollC-18
94UD/CollC/Gold-18
94UD/CollC/Silv-18
94UD/ElecD-27
Staiger, Roy
75Tidew/Team-19
76OPC-592R
76SSPC-560
76T-592R
77T-281
78Cr/PCL-113
79Colum-2
80Colum-9
89Tidew/Candl-10
91WIZMets-374
92Yank/WIZ70-144
Stainback, G. Tucker
34DS-52
44Yank/St-25
45Playball-10
47Signal
90Target-760
Stairs, Matt
89James/ProC-2141
89WPalmB/Star-22
90WPalmB/Star-23
91AA/LineD-271
91Harris/LineD-271
91Harris/ProC-639
92B-434
92B-602FOIL
92D/Rook-112
92Indianap/SB-195
92L/GRook-8
92Pinn-583
92Pinn/Rook-28
92ProC/Tomorrow-259
92Sky/AAASingl-94
92Sky/AASingl-293
92T/Tr-110T
92T/TrGold-110T
92UD-786
93D-460
93F-464
93Ottawa/ProC-2448
93S-232
93Select-327
Stajduhar, Marty
90Mother/Rang-28TR
Staley, Gerald
(Gerry)
46Sunbeam
51B-121
51T/BB-7
52B-50
52NTea
52StarCal/L-81G
52T-79
53B/Col-17
53Hunter
53RM-NL24
53T-56
54B-14
54Hunter
55B-155
57T-227
58T-412
59T-426
60T-510
60T-57M
61P-29
61T-90
61T/St-130
79TCMA-40
89Kodak/WSox-5M
91T/Arc53-56
R423-98
Staley, Henry E.
N172
Stallard, Tracy
61T-81
62T-567
63T-419
64T-176
65OldLond-18
65T-491
66OPC-7
66T-7
91WIZMets-375
Stallcup, Jeff
89TNTech-26
Stallcup, T. Virgil
49B-81
49Eureka-95
50B-116
51B-108
52B-6
52NTea
52T-69
53T-180
91T/Arc53-180
Staller, George
73OPC-136CO
73T-136CO
74OPC-306CO
74T-306CO
Stallings, George T.
15CJ-162MG
16FleischBrd-89MG
90HOF/St-21
90Target-761
D329-167
D350/2-169
M101/4-167
M101/5-169
M116
WG5-37
WG6-34
Stalp, Joe
83Cedar-10
83Cedar/Frit-4
Stampel, Eric
86Lynch-21
Stamps, Crandall
89GA-31
90GA-29
Stamps, Jerry
75Cedar
Stanage, Oscar
11Helmar-37
12Sweet/Pin-31
14Piedmont/St-53
BF2-29
D303
D328-167
D329-168
D350/2-170
E106
E135-167
E90/1
M101/4-168
M101/5-170
M116
T202
T205
T206
T207
T216
W514-115
Stancel, Mark
86Cram/NWL-54
88Modesto-14
88Modesto/Cal-65
90Huntsvl/Best-11
Standaert, Jerry
90Target-762
Standart, Rich
75Shrev/TCMA-21
76Shrev
Standiford, Mark
87Anchora-28
89Salinas/Cal-139
89Salinas/ProC-1801
Standley, Don
75Water
Stanek, Al
64T-99
65T-302
66T-437
Stanfield, Kevin
77Visalia
79T-709R
79Toledo-5
Stanfield, Mike
88Clinton/ProC-713
Stanford, Don
89PrWill/Star-20
90A&AASingle/ProC-21
90Albany/Best-8
90Albany/ProC-1036
90Albany/Star-19
90Foil/Best-92
91AA/LineD-19
91Albany/LineD-19
91Albany/ProC-1009
92ColClip/Pol-10
92ColClip/ProC-351
92ColClip/SB-119
93ColClip/Pol-7
Stanford, Larry
89Oneonta/ProC-2106
90FSLAS/Star-43
90FtLaud/Star-19
90Star/ISingl-41
91AA/LineD-20
91Albany/LineD-20
91Albany/ProC-1010
92ColClip/ProC-352
92ColClip/SB-120
92ProC/Tomorrow-116
92Sky/AAASingl-58
Stange, Albert Lee
61Clover-25
62T-321
63T-246
63Twin/Volpe-8
64T-555
65T-448
66T-371
67CokeCap/RedSox-1
67OPC-99
67T-99
67T/Test/RSox-19
68CokeCap/RedSox-1
68T-593
69MB-261
69OPC-148
69T-148
69T/4in1-19
70OPC-447
70T-447
71OPC-311
71T-311
72MB-325
73OPC-131CO
73T-131CO
74OPC-403CO
74T-403CO
78Twin/Frisz-44
89Pawtu/Dunkin-38CO
89Pawtu/ProC-692CO
90AAASingl/ProC-451CO
90Pawtu/ProC-479CO
91WinHaven/ClBest-16CO
92WinHaven/ClBest-30CL
Stange, Kurt
87SLCity/Taco-1
88MidwLAS/GS-58
88Wausau/GS-10
89SanBern/Best-13
Stange, Tim
88Elmira-9
90LynchRS/Team-23
Stangel, Chris
84Everett/Cram-18
Stanhope, Chester D.
(Chuck)
86Hagers-19
87CharlO/WBTV-31
88RochR/Gov-25
89Hagers/Best-17
89Hagers/ProC-269
89RochR/CMC-2
90HagersDG/Best-28
Stanhouse, Don
73OPC-352
73T-352
75OPC-493
75T-493
75T/M-493
76Expo/Redp-29
77K-32
77OPC-63
77T-274
78OPC-162
78T-629
79T-119
80Pol/Dodg-29
80T-517
81D-557
81F-121
81OPC-24
81Pol/Dodg-26
81T-24
90Target-763
91Crown/Orio-432
93Rang/Keeb-38
Stanicek, Pete
86Hagers-20
87CharlO/WBTV-1
88D-541
88D/Best-294
88D/Rook-15
88F-573
88French-17
88RochR/CMC-18
88RochR/ProC-205
88RochR/Team-22
88S-628
88T/Tr-114T
89B-14
89D-169
89F-622
89Hagers/Star-20
89KennerFig-137
89OPC-317
89Panini/St-265
89S-236
89T-497
89T/Coins-52
89T/St-232
89ToysRUs-30
89UD-592
90AAASingl/ProC-474
90HagersDG/Best-29
90RochR/ProC-717
91Crown/Orio-433
Stanicek, Steve
84Shrev/FB-21
86ElPaso-19
87Denver-27
88Denver/CMC-22
88Denver/ProC-1266
88F-174
89ScranWB/CMC-12
89ScranWB/ProC-717
90AAASingl/ProC-310
90ProC/Singl-242
90ProC/Singl-315
90RochR/CMC-15
90ScranWB/CMC-16
90ScranWB/ProC-608
Staniland, Steve
77ArkTr
Stanka, Joe
58Union
Stankiewicz, Andy
87FtLaud-10
88Albany/ProC-1330
88EastLAS/ProC-5
89Albany/Best-15
89Albany/ProC-333
89Albany/Star-19
89EastLgAS/ProC-2
90AAASingl/ProC-335
90AlbanyDG/Best-17
90ColClip/CMC-10
90ColClip/ProC-685
90Colum/Pol-24
90ProC/Singl-210
90T/TVYank-62
91AAA/LineD-120
91ColClip/LineD-120
91ColClip/ProC-606
92B-482
92Classic/II-T7
92D/RookPhen-BC11
92D/Up-U2RR
92F/Up-44
92JDean/Rook-1
92L-470
92L/BlkGold-470
92OPC-179M
92Pinn-564
92Pinn/Rook-6
92S/RookTr-100T
92StCl-725
92T-179R
92T/Gold-179M
92T/GoldWin-179M
92T/Tr-111T
92T/TrGold-111T
92UD-779DD
92UD/Scout-SR21
92Ultra-415
92Ultra/AllRook-2
93ColClip/Pol-18
93D-213
93F-285
93L-9
93OPC-291
93Pac/Spanish-212
93Panini-149
93Pinn-363
93S-338
93Select-279
93Select/ChasRook-17
93StCl-105
93StCl/1stDay-105
93StCl/Y-29
93T-348
93T/Gold-348
93ToysRUs-34
93TripleP-101A
93TripleP-101B
93UD-257
93USPlayC/Rook-12D
93Ultra-249
94Finest-253
94Pac/Cr-437
Stanky, Eddie
44Playball-41
49B-104
49Eureka-26
50B-29
50Drake-22
51B-13
51T/CAS
51T/RB-48
52B-160
52BR
52RM-NL23
52T-76
53B/Col-49
53Exh/Can-9
53Hunter
54Hunter
54T-38MG
55B-238MG
55Hunter
55T-191MG
66T-448MG
67OPC-81MG
67T-81MG
68T-564MG
79TCMA-108
89Smok/Dodg-53
90Target-764
91T/Arc53-300
92Bz/Quadra-17M
93Rang/Keeb-340MG
94T/Arc54-38
Exh47
R346-31
R423-105
Stanley, Bob
78PapaG/Disc-12
78SSPC/270-164
78T-186
79OPC-314
79T-597
80OPC-35
80T-63
81Coke
81D-456
81F-234
81OPC-296

81T-421
81T/HT
82Coke/Bos
82D-134
82F-307
82F/St-169
82OPC-289
82T-289
83D-386
83F-195
83F/St-10M
83F/St-19AM
83F/St-19BM
83OPC-242
83T-381TL
83T-682
84D-644
84F-409
84F/St-74
84Nes/792-320
84OPC-320
84T-320
84T/St-220
85D-91
85Drake-42
85F-169
85FunFoodPin-81
85OPC-204
85T-555
85T/St-215
86D-91
86F-359
86OPC-158
86Seven/Coin-E10M
86Sf-169
86T-785
86T/St-253
87D-216
87D/OD-180
87F-47
87OPC-175
87RedFoley/St-18
87T-175
87T/St-245
88D-92
88D/RedSox/Bk-92
88F-367
88OPC-369
88Panini/St-23
88S-300
88T-573
89B-25
89D-421
89D/Best-233
89F-101
89S-383
89T-37
89T/St-258
89UD-411
90F-289
90F/Can-289
90PublInt/St-466
90UD-654
Stanley, Carl
90Geneva/Star-23
Stanley, Derek
92Johnson/ClBest-2
92Johnson/ProC-3132
Stanley, Fred
72OPC-59
72T-59
74OPC-423
74Syrac/Team-25
74T-423
75OPC-503
75Syrac/Team-15
75Syrac/Team-20
75T-503
75T/M-503
76OPC-429
76SSPC-442
76SSPC/MetsY-Y13
76T-429
77BK/Y-16
77T-123
78BK/Y-17
78SSPC/270-12
78T-664
79BK/Y-16
79T-16
80T-387
81D-585
81F-100
81T-281
81T/Tr-834
82D-449
82F-108
82Granny-15
82T-787
83D-197
83F-534
83T-513
89TM/SenLg-98
91Brewer/MillB-32
91Pac/SenLg-133
91Pac/SenLg-6
91Pol/Brew-x
92Yank/WIZ70-145
92Yank/WIZ80-186
Stanley, Kevin
83Butte-21
Stanley, Mickey
66T-198
67T-607
68CokeCap/Tiger-4
68OPC-129
68T-129
69MB-262
69MLB/St-54
69OPC-13
69T-13
69T/St-179
70MLB/St-214
70OPC-383
70T-383
71MLB/St-407
71OPC-524
71T-524
72MB-326
72OPC-385
72T-385
73OPC-88
73T-88
74OPC-530
74T-530
74T/St-180
75OPC-141
75T-141
75T/M-141
76OPC-483
76SSPC-372
76T-483
77T-533
77Tiger/BK-4
78BK/T-21
78T-232
79OPC-368
79T-692
81Tiger/Detroit-25
86Tiger/Sport-15
88Domino-22
89Swell-104
Stanley, Mike
86Tulsa-25
87D-592
87D/Rook-28
87F-647R
87OKCty-8
87Sf/Rook-44
87Smok/R-23
87T/Tr-116T
88D-259
88D/Best-223
88F-480
88Mother/R-11
88OPC-219
88Panini/St-199
88S-47
88Smok/R-11
88T-219
88T/St-238
88ToysRUs-29
89D-166
89F-533
89Mother/R-22
89OPC-123
89S-241
89Smok/R-31
89T-587
89T/St-244
89UD-579
90D-579
90Mother/Rang-20
90OPC-92
90T-92
90TulsaDG/Best-6
91Mother/Rang-20
91OPC-409
91S-92
91StCl-526
91T-409
92B-370
92D-582
92L-367
92L/BlkGold-367
92S-549
92StCl-741
92Ultra-416
93D-718
93F-656
93Flair-252
93L-184
93Pinn-563
93Rang/Keeb-341
93StCl-323
93StCl/1stDay-323
93StCl/Y-12
93T-359
93T/Gold-359
93UD/SP-267
93Ultra-601
94B-137
94D-202
94F-247
94L-295
94OPC-95
94Pac/Cr-438
94Panini-104
94Pinn-338
94S-451
94S/DT-10
94Select-100
94Sf/2000-2
94StCl-271
94StCl/1stDay-271
94StCl/Gold-271
94StCl/Team-197
94Studio-217
94T-391AS
94T-695
94T/BlkGold-20
94T/Finest-76
94T/Finest/PreProd-76
94T/FinestRef-76
94T/Gold-391AS
94T/Gold-695
94TripleP-278
94UD-229
94UD/CollC-265
94UD/CollC/Gold-265
94UD/CollC/Silv-265
94UD/ElecD-229
94Ultra-101
Stanley, Scott
90AZ/Pol-16ACO
92AZ/Pol-17ACO
Stanley, Tim
87Anchora-29
88James/ProC-1919
Stanley, Todd
93MissSt-40
Stansberry
E254
Stantiago, Ramon
90Gaston/Best-29MG
Stanton, Gary
91Idaho/SportP-13
Stanton, Leroy
(Lee)
72OPC-141R
72T-141R
73OPC-18
73T-18
74OPC-594
74T-594
75K-12
75OPC-342
75T-342
75T/M-342
76Ho-39
76Ho/Twink-39
76OPC-152
76SSPC-204
76T-152
77T-226
78Ho-60
78OPC-123
78T-447
79OPC-275
79T-533
87Myrtle-9
88Myrtle/ProC-1180
89Myrtle/ProC-1451
90Myrtle/ProC-2794CO
91Myrtle/ClBest-29CO
91Myrtle/ProC-2963CO
91WIZMets-376
92Myrtle/ClBest-28CO
92Myrtle/ProC-2215CO
93Hagers/ClBest-26CO
93Hagers/ProC-1897CO
Stanton, Michael Thomas
(Mike)
73Cedar
75Iowa/TCMA-20
78Syrac
81F-400
82D-285
82F-379
82T-473
82T/Tr-113T
83D-433
83F-486
83T-159
84F-619
84Mother/Mar-20
84Nes/792-694
84T-694
85D-562
85F-501
85Mother/Mar-16
85T-256
85T/St-343
Stanton, William Michael
(Mike)
89Greenvl/Best-14
89Greenvl/ProC-1166
89Greenvl/Star-22
90B-4
90Brave/Dubuq/Perf-27
90Classic/Up-45
90D-508
90D/Rook-7
90F-596
90F/Can-596
90F/SoarSt-2
90OPC-694
90S-609RP
90S/100Ris-29
90S/YS/II-7
90T-694
90T/89Debut-122
90UD-61
91Brave/Dubuq/Perf-29
91Brave/Dubuq/Stand-36
91D-716
91F-705
91Leaf-491
91OPC-514
91S-468
91StCl-413
91T-514
91UD/Ext-749
92Brave/LykePerf-27
92Brave/LykeStand-31
92Classic/Game200-19
92D-780
92F-372
92L-377
92L/BlkGold-377
92OPC-788
92Pinn-350
92S-498
92StCl-344
92T-788
92T/Gold-788
92T/GoldWin-788
92UD-653
92USPlayC/Brave-3H
92USPlayC/Brave-6S
92Ultra-170
93Brave/LykePerf-28
93Brave/LykeStand-34
93D-474
93F-15
93Flair-12
93L-398
93Pac/Spanish-341
93Pinn-569
93S-317
93StCl-38
93StCl/1stDay-38
93StCl/Brave-17
93T-88
93T/Finest-176
93T/FinestRef-176
93T/Gold-88
93UD-90
93Ultra-13
94D-506
94F-376
94L-20
94Pinn-461
94S-205
94S/GoldR-205
94StCl-471
94StCl/1stDay-471
94StCl/Gold-471
94StCl/Team-58
94T-107
94T/Gold-107
94Ultra-450
Staples, Ken
81Wisco-1MG
82Wisco/Frit-3MG
Stapleton, David E.
(Dave)
86ElPaso-20
88D-521
88D/Rook-4
88Pol/Brew-43
89S-581
89UD-304
Stapleton, David L.
(Dave)
81Coke
81D-544
81F-236
81OPC-81
81T-81
81T/St-215
82D-208
82F-308
82F/St-76
82OPC-93
82T-589
82T/St-85
83D-200
83F-196
83OPC-239
83OPC/St-35
83T-239
83T/St-35
84D-273
84F-410
84Nes/792-653
84OPC-249
84T-653
84T/St-221
85T-322
86T-151
87T-507
Stargell, Tim
88Belling/Legoe-11
89Wausau/GS-26
90Foil/Best-297
90ProC/Singl-859
90SanBern/Best-24
90SanBern/Cal-108
90SanBern/ProC-2641
91AA/LineD-346
91ClBest/Singl-109
91Jaxvl/LineD-346
91Jaxvl/ProC-163
Stargell, Willie
63IDL-21
63T-553R
64T-342
65Kahn
65T-377
66EH-8
66Kahn
66OPC-99M
66T-255
66T-99M
66T/RO-44
66T/RO-87
67CokeCap/AS-11
67CokeCap/NLAS-29
67CokeCap/Pirate-12
67Kahn
67OPC-140
67T-140
67T-266M
67T/Test/PP-22
67T/Test/PP-31
68KDKA-8
68OPC-86
68T-86
69MB-263

69MLB/St-188
69Pirate/JITB-12
69T-545
69T/St-89
70K-29
70MLB/St-107
70OPC-470
70T-470
70T/S-19
70T/SO
70T/Super-19
71K-68
71MLB/St-214
71OPC-230
71T-230
71T/Coins-123
71T/S-43
71T/Super-43
71T/tatt-8
72Dimanche*-64
72K-53
72MB-327
72OPC-343KP
72OPC-447
72OPC-448IA
72OPC-87LL
72OPC-89LL
72ProStars/PostC-23
72T-343KP
72T-447IA
72T-448IA
72T-87LL
72T-89LL
72T/Post-15
73K-25
73OPC-370
73T-370
73T/Comics-20
73T/Lids-50
73T/PinUps-20
74K-37
74Laugh/ASG-65
74OPC-100
74OPC-202LL
74OPC-203LL
74T-100
74T-202LL
74T-203LL
74T/DE-31
74T/Puzzles-11
74T/St-88
75Ho-135
75OPC-100
75T-100
75T/M-100
76Crane-58
76Ho-49
76Ho/Twink-49
76K-22
76MSA/Disc
76OPC-270
76SSPC-573
76T-270
77BurgChef-186
77Ho-27
77Ho/Twink-27
77OPC-25
77Pep-64
77T-460
77T/CS-45
77T/ClothSt-45
78Ho-11
78T-510
78Tastee/Discs-11
78Wiffle/Discs-71
79Ho-104
79OPC-22
79T-55
80K-25
80OPC-319
80Perez/HOF-200
80T-610
80T/S-1
80T/Super-1
81D-12
81D-132
81F-363
81F/St-15
81K-11
81MSA/Disc-31
81OPC-127
81PermaGr/CC-14
81T-380
82D-639
82F-499
82F/St-106M
82KMart-37
82OPC-188IA
82OPC-372
82PermaGr/CC-5
82T-715
82T-716IA
82T/StVar-85
83D-610
83D-8DK
83F-324
83F-634M
83F/St-3M
83F/St-9M
84West/1-6
85CircK-16
86Pol/Atl-8CO
87KMart-22
89HOF/St-27
89Kahn/Coop-10
89Kenner/BBGr-17
89T/Gloss22-22
89T/LJN-61
90BBWit-4
90Perez/GreatMom-38
91D-702PUZ
91MDA-3
92AP/ASG-17
92AP/ASG24K-17G
92AP/ASGProto-5
92FrRow/Stargell-Set
92K/CornAS-1
92K/FrAS-10
92Perez/Master-36
92Perez/Master-37
92Perez/Master-38
92Perez/Master-39
92Perez/Master-40
92Pinn-588M
93AP/ASGCoke/Amo-17
93Metallic-19
93Nabisco-6
93TWill-81
93TWill/Mem-14
93YooHoo-20
Stark, Clinton
61Union
62Pep/Tul
66Pep/Tul
Stark, George
83Kaline-12M
Stark, Greg
92Pittsfld/ClBest-13
92Pittsfld/ProC-3295
Stark, Jeff
87Spartan-4
88Spartan/ProC-1024
Stark, Matt
86Knoxvl-22
87Tor/Fire-29
90A&AASingle/ProC-47
90BirmB/Best-4
90BirmB/ProC-1113M
90Foil/Best-99M
90ProC/Singl-746
91AAA/LineD-646
91Classic/I-30
91D-747
91S-751RP
91Vanco/LineD-646M
91Vanco/ProC-1597M
92MidldA/SB-470
Stark, Monroe
(Dolly)
39PlayBall-106
40PlayBall-117
90Target-765
94Conlon-1191UMP
T206
Starkovich, Paul
75SanAn
Starks, Bob
76QuadC
Starr, Charles
T201
T206
T213/brown
Starr, Chris
91Butte/SportP-3
Starr, Dick
50B-191
51B-137
Starrette, Herm
64T-239
65T-539
74OPC-634CO
74T-634CO
78TCMA-194
86Pol/Brew-38C
88French-31CO
91Crown/Orio-434
92Rockford/ClBest-29CO
93James/ProC-3344DIR
Statham, Cliff
52Laval-2
Staton, Dave
88CapeCod/Sum-167
89Spokane/SP-1
90A&AASingle/ProC-148
90AS/Cal-1
90Foil/Best-6
90River/Best-1
90River/Cal-1
90River/ProC-2617
91AAA/LineD-294
91B-645
91Classic/200-182
91Classic/II-T44
91LasVegas/LineD-294
91LasVegas/ProC-246
91UD-66TP
92AAA/ASG/SB-241
92B-499
92LasVegas/ProC-2807
92LasVegas/SB-241
92OPC-126M
92ProC/Tomorrow-333
92Sky/AAASingl-117
92Smok/Padre-33
92T-126R
92T/Gold-126M
92T/GoldWin-126M
92UD/ML-191
93D-325RR
93FExcel/ML-111
94B-448
94F/MLP-32
94Finest-428
94Flair-236
94Flair/Wave-9
94L-349
94OPC-83
94Pinn-396
94Select-200
94T-507
94T/Gold-507
94UD-214
94UD/CollC-266
94UD/CollC/Gold-266
94UD/CollC/Silv-266
94UD/ElecD-214
94Ultra-585
94Ultra/AllRook-10
Statz, Arnold
(Jigger)
21Exh-172
37Wheat
88LitSun/Minor-9
90Target-766
93Conlon-782
E120
E126-33
V100
V117-16
Staub, Rusty
63Pep
63T-544R
64T-109
64T/Coins-96
64T/St-88
65T-321
66OPC-106
66T-106
66T-273M
67Ast/Team-11
67CokeCap/AS-5
67CokeCap/Astro-13
67CokeCap/NLAS-32
67OPC-73
67T-73
67T/Test/SU-17
68Bz-14
68CokeCap/Astro-13
68Dexter-71
68T-300
68T/3D
68T/ActionSt-6CM
68T/G-28
68T/Post-22
69Citgo-15
69Expos/Pins-7
69Fud's-11
69MB-264
69MLB/St-161
69NTF
69OPC/DE-20
69T-230
69T/DE-22
69T/S-48
69T/St-38
69T/decal
69Trans-39
70Expo/PostC-11
70Expos/Pins-13
70MLB/St-70
70T-585
70T/CB
70T/S-41
70T/Super-41
71Bz
71Bz/Test-40
71Expo/ProS-23
71LaPizza-12
71MD
71MLB/St-141
71MLB/St-575
71OPC-289
71OPC-560
71T-560
71T/Coins-111
71T/GM-35
71T/Greatest-35
71T/S-9
71T/Super-9
71T/tatt-7
72Dimanche*-65
72MB-328
74OPC-475WS
74OPC-629
74T-475WS
74T-629
75Ho-129
75OPC-90
75T-90
75T/M-90
76Crane-59
76MSA/Disc
76OPC-120
76SSPC-537
76SSPC/MetsY-M7
76T-120
76T/Tr-120T
77BurgChef-96
77Ho-82
77Ho/Twink-82
77OPC-88
77Pep-29
77T-420
77T/CS-46
77T/ClothSt-46
78BK/T-22
78OPC-188
78T-370
78Wiffle/Discs-72
79Ho-56
79OPC-228
79T-440
79T/Comics-7
80OPC-347
80T-660
81Coke
81F-629
81T-80
81T/HT
81T/Tr-835
82D-56
82F-536
82F/St-82
82OPC-270
82T-270
83D-350
83F-555
83F/St-12M
83F/St-15M
83OPC-1
83OPC-51SV
83OPC/St-14
83T-740
83T-741SV
83T/Fold-2M
83T/St-14
84D-554
84D-6DK
84D/Champs-28
84F-597
84F/St-40
84Nes/792-430
84Nes/792-702LL
84Nes/792-704LL
84OPC-224
84T-430
84T-702LL
84T-704LL
84T/Mets/Fan-6
84T/St-287A
85F-92
85F/St-50
85FunFoodPin-84
85OPC-190
85T-190
86F-95
86Mother/Ast-6
86Sf-138M
86T-570
90Pac/Legend-52
90Swell/Great-91
91Jesuit-6
91Swell/Great-87
91WIZMets-377
92AP/ASG-81
92Nabisco-25
93Expo/D/McDon-20
93Rang/Keeb-342
94TedW-52
Staubach, Roger
92Pinn-589
Stauffacher, Stuart
86BurlEx-21
Staydohar, Dave
90Boise/ProC-3328
92QuadC/ClBest-25
92QuadC/ProC-824
Stearnes, Turkey
90Negro/Star-15
Stearns, Bill
83OKCty-1
86Tulsa-6MG
Stearns, Dan
N172
Stearns, Don
87SanBern-4
Stearns, John
75IntAS/TCMA-7
76OPC-633
76SSPC-546
76SSPC/MetsY-M8
76T-633
77BurgChef-140
77T-119
78T-334
79Ho-124
79OPC-280
79T-205RB
79T-545
80K-37
80OPC-41
80T-76
81D-35
81F-317
81OPC-255
81T-428
81T/So-96
81T/St-194
82D-434
82F-537
82F/St-89
82OPC-232
82T-743
83D-380
83D/AAS-25
83F-556
83F/St-11M
83OPC-212
83OPC/St-264
83T-212
83T/St-264
84F-598
90Knoxvl/Best-9MG
90Knoxvl/ProC-1259MG
90Knoxvl/Star-24MG
91AA/LineD-374MG
91Knoxvl/LineD-374MG
91Knoxvl/ProC-1784MG

91WIZMets-378
Stearns, Norman
(Turkey)
78Laugh/Black-4
87Negro/Dixon-35
Stearns, Randy
87SanBern-5
Steck, Dave
76QuadC
Stedman, Tom
75Lafay
Steed, Rick
90StCath/ProC-3473
91Myrtle/ClBest-11
91Myrtle/ProC-2945
91SALAS/ProC-SAL40
92Dunedin/ClBest-18
92Dunedin/ProC-2000
93Dunedin/ClBest-22
93Dunedin/ProC-1796
Steed, Scott
91Perth/Fut-19
Steel, Ed
86Negro/Frit-48
Steele, Don
75Lafay
Steele, Steve
92Kingspt/ClBest-11
92Kingspt/ProC-1535
Steele, Tim
75Water
Steele, Walt
80BurlB-20
Steele, William
(Bill)
11Helmar-177
90Target-1078
T207
Steelman, Farmer
90Target-1080
Steels, James
82Amari-11
83Beaum-20
83LasVegas/BHN-20
84Beaum-3
85Cram/PCL-125
86LasVegas-18
87Bohem-21
87D/Rook-50
88D-360
88F/Up-U64
88Mother/R-21
88OkCty/CMC-24
88OkCty/ProC-38
88T-117
90AAASingl/ProC-589
90Indianap/CMC-15
90Indianap/ProC-306
90ProC/Singl-65
93Rang/Keeb-343
Steen, Mike
76SanAn/Team-21
Steen, Scott
86Clearw-23
Steenstra, Kennie
90WichSt-32
91T/Tr-113T
92Geneva/ClBest-6
92Geneva/ProC-1561
92Peoria/Team-25
92StCl/Dome-180
92T/DQ-23
94ClBest/Gold-131
94FExcel-167
Stefan, Todd
91SLCity/ProC-3221
91SLCity/SportP-21
92Peoria/ClBest-9
92Peoria/Team-26
Stefani, Mario
89Bristol/Star-27
90Fayette/ProC-2407
Stefanski, Jim
82Durham-10
Stefanski, Mike
92Beloit/ClBest-16
92Beloit/ProC-408
92ClBest-360
92MidwLAS/Team-41
94FExcel-87
Stefaro, John
84D-622
85CharlO-5
87D-541
87Expo/PostC-8
87F-652R
87T-563
88ColoSp/CMC-11
88ColoSp/ProC-1522
90CharlK/Team-9
90HagersDG/Best-30
91Crown/Orio-435
Steffen, David
80Evansvl-4
81T-626R
Steffens, Mark
90Princet/DIMD-22
91Spartan/ClBest-27
91Spartan/ProC-912
92Clearw/ProC-2071
92Spartan/ClBest-19
92Spartan/ProC-1279
Steger, Chip
77Tucson
Steger, Kevin
80SanJose/JITB-17
81Wausau-1
83Chatt-22
Stegman, Dave
79T-706R
82Colum-13
82Colum/Pol-23
84Nes/792-664
84T-664
84TrueVal/WS-28
85Syrac-31
85T-194
86Colum/Pol-24
92Yank/WIZ80-187
Steigerwald, John
75Lafay
Stein, Bill
76OPC-131
76SSPC-146
76T-131
77Ho-136
77Ho/Twink-136
77OPC-20
77T-334
78Ho-39
78OPC-147
78T-476
79Ho-18
79OPC-372
79T-698
80OPC-121
80T-226
81D-543
81F-605
81T-532
81T/Tr-836
82D-37
82F-331
82F/St-179
82T-402
82T/St-118
83D-594
83F-579
83Rang-1
83T-64
84F-429
84Nes/792-758
84Rang-1
84T-758
85D-621
85Rang-1
85T-171
86D-403
86T-371
88LitFalls/Pucko-26
89Clmbia/Best-22
89Clmbia/GS-1
89TM/SenLg-99
90Clmbia/PCPII-1MG
90Columbia/GS-1MG
90SALAS/Star-46MG
91BendB/ClBest-28MG
91BendB/ProC-3710MG
92Clinton/ClBest-26MG
92Clinton/ProC-3612
93Rang/Keeb-344
Stein, John
86AppFx-24
87Bakers-9
Stein, Jose
91Boise/ClBest-11
Stein, W. Randy
79T-394
79Vanco-16
80Spokane-13
80T-613
81Spokane-24
82Iowa-24
83Iowa-10
Steinbach, Terry
84Madis/Pol-10
85Huntsvl/BK-16
86SLAS-10
87D-34RR
87D/Rook-26
87F-405
87Leaf-34RR
87Sf-118M
87Sf/Rook-1
87Sf/Rook-22
87Sf/TPrev-23M
87T/Tr-117T
88Classic/Red-186
88D-158
88D/A's/Bk-158
88D/Best-78
88F-294
88Mother/A's-4
88OPC-44
88Panini/St-166
88S-82
88S/YS/I-16
88Sf-174
88T-551
88T/Big-39
88T/Coins-28
88T/JumboR-15
88ToysRUs-30
89B-193
89Cadaco-54
89Classic-69
89D-268
89D/AS-31
89D/AS-9
89D/Best-323
89D/PopUp-9
89F-22
89F-634M
89KMart/DT-19
89KennerFig-138
89Mother/A's-3
89OPC-304
89Panini/St-236AS
89Panini/St-419
89S-365
89Sf-119
89T-725
89T/Big-80
89T/Gloss22-9
89T/St-152
89T/St-165
89UD-256
90B-456
90Classic/Up-46
90D-268
90D-637AS
90D/BestAL-137
90F-20
90F/BB-38
90F/Can-20
90F/WS-3
90F/WS-7
90Leaf-252
90MLBPA/Pins-115
90Mother/A's-3
90OPC-145
90Panini/St-143
90Panini/St-205
90PublInt/St-315
90S-162
90S-693DT
90S/100St-55
90Sf-33
90T-145
90T/Big-118
90T/Gloss22-20
90T/St-163AS
90T/St-186
90UD-246
90Woolwth/HL-28
91B-216
91Cadaco-54
91D-329
91F-24
91Leaf-87
91Mother/A's-3
91OPC-625
91Panini/FrSt-191
91S-780
91SFExam/A's-12
91Seven/3DCoin-11NC
91StCl-518
91T-625
91UD-153
91Ultra-253
92B-392
92D-104
92F-267
92L-501
92L/BlkGold-501
92Mother/A's-3
92OPC-234
92Panini-14
92Pinn-76
92S-440AS
92S-633
92StCl-22
92Studio-229
92T-234
92T/Gold-234
92T/GoldWin-234
92TripleP-10
92UD-473
92Ultra-116
93B-21
93Colla/DM-102
93D-505
93F-299
93Flair-263
93L-7
93Mother/A's-3
93OPC-268
93Pac/Spanish-226
93Panini-14
93Pinn-12
93S-626
93Select-132
93StCl-208
93StCl/1stDay-208
93StCl/A's-9
93Studio-57
93T-18
93T/Finest-67
93T/FinestRef-67
93T/Gold-18
93TripleP-177
93UD-278
93UD/FunPack-53
93UD/SP-44
93Ultra-262
94B-408
94D-254
94F-274
94Flair-96
94L-178
94OPC-117
94Pac/Cr-463
94Panini-113
94Pinn-120
94Pinn/Artist-120
94Pinn/Museum-120
94S-47
94S/GoldR-47
94StCl-346
94StCl/1stDay-346
94StCl/Gold-346
94Studio-7
94T-610
94T/Finest-38
94T/FinestRef-38
94T/Gold-610
94TripleP-9
94UD-291HFA
94UD-488
94UD/CollC-267
94UD/CollC/Gold-267
94UD/CollC/Silv-267
94UD/SP-38
94Ultra-412
Steinbach, Tom
85Beloit-9
Steinbacher, Hank
94Conlon-1316
Steinberg, David
83Wisco/Frit-8
Steiner, Brian
88Gaston/ProC-1018
89Butte/SP-18
90Gaston/Best-15
90Gaston/ProC-2522
90Gaston/Star-23
91CharlR/ClBest-12
91CharlR/ProC-1316
Steinert, Paul
84Butte-22
Steinert, Rob
93StCath/ClBest-22
93StCath/ProC-3975
Steinfeldt, Harry
12Sweet/Pin-92
84Cub/Uno-7M
90BBWit-57
E107
E254
E90/3
E91
E97
M116
S74-47
S74-70
T202
T204
T205
T206
T207
T215/blue
T215/brown
W555
Steinkamp, Mike
89SLCity-13RHP
Steinmetz, Earl
90Foil/Best-136
90ProC/Singl-729
90Sumter/Best-22
90Sumter/ProC-2432
91Durham/ClBest-9
91Durham/ProC-1544
92Durham/ClBest-12
92Durham/ProC-1100
92Durham/Team-23
Steinmetz, Kevin
83Tampa-21
Steirer, Ricky
80ElPaso-4
81SLCity-12
82Spokane-8
84Cram/PCL-102
Stela, Jose
91Boise/ProC-3883
91QuadC/ClBest-13
91QuadC/ProC-2631
92MidwLAS/Team-42
92QuadC/ClBest-15
92QuadC/ProC-813
Stellern, Mike
82AubAs-4
85Osceola/Team-25
Stello, Dick
88TM/Umpire-60
Stelmaszek, Rick
70T-599R
73OPC-601R
73T-601R
74OPC-611
74T-611
75OPC-338
75T-338
75T/M-338
77Tucson
78Wisco
79Wisco-23
83Twin/Team-28CO
83Twin/Team-34M
85Twin/Team-32CO
93Rang/Keeb-345
Stember, Jeff
78Cedar
79Cedar/TCMA-16
80Phoenix/NBank-5
81Phoenix-5
82Phoenix
Stemberger, Brian
82Knoxvl-9
Stemler, Andy
91Watertn/ClBest-11
91Watertn/ProC-3366
Stemmyer, William
N172
Stengel
N172
Stengel, Charles Dillon
(Casey)
16FleischBrd-90
21Exh-173
40PlayBall-142

42Playball-42MG
46Remar-10
47Remar-8
47Signal
47Smith-1
48Signal
48Smith-20
50B-217MG
51B-181MG
52B-217MG
52RM-AL1
53B/BW-39MG
53RM-AL1
58T-475AS
59T-383M
59T-552AS
60T-227MG
61NuCard-461
62T-29MG
63T-233MG
63T-43M
64T-324MG
64T-393M
65OPC-187MG
65T-187MG
72Laugh/GF-20
75Shakey-8
76Laugh/Clown-40
76Rowe-14M
76Shakey-104
77Galasso-13
77Galasso-253
80Laugh/FFeat-20
80Pac/Leg-47
80Perez/HOF-103
80SSPC/HOF
81Conlon-71
81TCMA-422MG
81TCMA-482M
83D/HOF-37
85West/2-35
86Conlon/1-33
88Conlon/HardC-5
89Pac/Leg-218
89Smok/Dodg-28
89Swell-130
90BBWit-85
90HOF/St-60
90Swell/Great-40
90Target-767
91Conlon/Sport-37
91LineD-46
91Swell/Great-136
91T/Arc53-325MG
92Bz/Quadra-21M
92Conlon/Col-5
92Conlon/Sport-558
92Pinn/MM-27M
92Yank/WIZHOF-32
93Conlon-829
93Spectrum/HOFII-5
94TedW/Lock-16
D327
D328-168
D329-169
D350/2-171
E135-168
E220
M101/4-169
M101/5-171
R312
R423-93
W514-113
W515-24
W575

Stenholm, Richard A.
77WHave
81Colum-1

Stenhouse, Dave
60HenryH-26
62T-592R
63F-30
63J-97
63P-97
63Salada-37
63T-263
63T/SO
64T-498
65T-304
78TCMA-141
84Syrac-26
85T-141FS
86Syrac-24
87Syrac-13
87Syrac/TCMA-11

Stenhouse, Michael
82Wichita-19
83Wichita/Dog-21
84D-29RR
84Expo/PostC-31
84Indianap-30
84Stuart-26
85D-376
85F-411
85F/Up-U110
85OPC-282
85T-141FS
85T-658
85T/Tr-112T
85Twin/Team-23
86F-406
86OPC-17
86Pawtu-23
86T-17
87Toledo-19
87Toledo/TCMA-5

Stennett, Matt
86AubAs-24

Stennett, Rennie
72OPC-219
72T-219
73OPC-348
73T-348
74OPC-426
74T-426
74T/St-89
75Ho-131
75OPC-336
75T-336
75T/M-336
76Crane-60
76Ho-9
76Ho/Twink-9
76MSA/Disc
76OPC-425
76OPC-6RB
76SSPC-575
76T-425
76T-6M
77BurgChef-182
77Ho-101
77Ho/Twink-100
77OPC-129
77T-35
78Ho-33
78OPC-25
78T-165
79OPC-365
79T-687
80Pol/Giants-6
80T-501
81D-72
81F-438
81OPC-257
81T-257
82D-563
82F-401
82OPC-84
82T-84
83Wichita/Dog-22
89Pac/SenLg-79
89T/SenLg-127
89TM/SenLg-100
90EliteSenLg-89
90HOF/St-82

Stenta, Jeff
91Erie/ClBest-10
91Erie/ProC-4079

Stento, Bernie
87Elmira/Black-28
87Elmira/Red-28

Stenz, Dan
90Boise/ProC-3314

Stepanov, Roman
89EastLDD/ProC-DD16

Steph, Rodney
91Princet/ClBest-9
91Princet/ProC-3514
92Cedar/ClBest-13
92Cedar/ProC-1073
94B-654

Stephan, Todd
89Penin/Star-23
90CLAS/CL-3
90Freder/Team-24
91AA/LineD-247
91Hagers/LineD-247
91Hagers/ProC-2458
91Perth/Fut-6
92RochR/ProC-1940
92RochR/SB-470
92Sky/AAASingl-213

Stephans, Russell
81CharR-13
83Omaha-12
84Omaha-26
85D-42RR
86Omaha/ProC-24
86Omaha/TCMA-10

Stephen, Louis
(Buzz)
70OPC-533
70T-533

Stephens, B.F.
N172

Stephens, Bill
91Kissim/ProC-4197
91LitSun/HSPros-17
91LitSun/HSProsG-17
92GulfCD/ProC-3567

Stephens, Brian
91Reno/Cal-24

Stephens, Bryan
46Remar-19
V362-11

Stephens, Carl Ray
(Ray)
87ArkTr-22
87TexLgAS-31
88Louisvl-45
88Louisvl/CMC-19
88Louisvl/ProC-422
89ArkTr/GS-23
89TexLAS/GS-21
90AAASingl/ProC-519
90Louisvl/CMC-13
90Louisvl/LBC-39
90Louisvl/ProC-405
90ProC/Singl-113
90T/TVCard-65
91AAA/LineD-248
91AAAGame/ProC-22
91Louisvl/LineD-248
91Louisvl/ProC-2918
91Louisvl/Team-27
91S-743RP
91T/90Debut-148
92D-764
92OkCty/ProC-1917
92ScranWB/SB-495
93Rang/Keeb-346

Stephens, Darryl
82Redwd-14
83Nashua-15

Stephens, Gene
53T-248
56T-313
57T-217
58Hires-72
58T-227
59T-261
60T-363
61T-102
61T/St-105
62J-95
62P-95
62P/Can-95
62Salada-56
62Shirriff-56
62T-38
62T/St-59
64T-308
65T-498
90HOF/St-48
91Crown/Orio-436
91T/Arc53-248

Stephens, James W.
M116
T201
T204
T206

Stephens, Mark
90Helena/SportP-14
91Beloit/ClBest-8
91Beloit/ProC-2103
91SLCity/ProC-3211
91SLCity/SportP-20
92Salinas/ProC-3754

Stephens, Reggie
91Spokane/ClBest-9
91Spokane/ProC-3963
91Waterlo/ClBest-23
91Waterlo/ProC-1270

Stephens, Ron
88Utica/Pucko-24
89Saraso/Star-22
89Star/Wax-60
90BirmB/Best-23
90BirmB/ProC-1393
90Foil/Best-50
91AAA/LineD-647
91Vanco/LineD-647
91Vanco/ProC-1595
92Sky/AAASingl-289
92Vanco/ProC-2723
92Vanco/SB-648

Stephens, Seth
91Fayette/ClBest-5

Stephens, Vern
42Playball-8
47HomogBond-44
47TipTop
48L-161
49B-71
50B-2
50Drake-34
51B-92
51T/RB-4
52B-9
52RM-AL21
52StarCal-85C
52StarCal/L-71D
52T-84
52TipTop
53T-270
54T-54
54Wilson
55B-109
56YellBase/Pin-30
91Crown/Orio-437
91T/Arc53-270
94T/Arc54-54
D305
Exh47
R423-94

Stephenson, Chester
(Earl)
72OPC-61R
72T-61R
74Tacoma/Caruso-11
75IntAS/TCMA-4
78RochR
79Tidew-25
86Hagers-21C
89Pac/SenLg-159
91Crown/Orio-438

Stephenson, Ed
76Baton

Stephenson, Garrett
92Bluefld/ClBest-1
92Bluefld/ProC-2361

Stephenson, Gene
90WichSt-44

Stephenson, J. Riggs
21Exh-174
30CEA/Pin-9
31Exh/4-5
32Orbit/num-3
32Orbit/un-54
33DL-15
33Exh/4-3
33G-204
61F-140
77Galasso-51
80Pac/Leg-95
88Conlon/4-27
88Conlon/NatAS-19
91Conlon/Sport-218
92Conlon/Sport-441
92Cub/OldStyle-23
R305
R308-170
R315-A34
R315-B34
R316
V100
V117-26

Stephenson, Jerry
65OPC-74R
65T-74R
66T-396
67T/Test/RSox-20
68T-519
69OPC-172
69T-172
71OPC-488
71T-488
90Target-768

Stephenson, John
64T-536R
66OPC-17
66T-17
67CokeCap/YMet-26
67T-522
68OPC-83
68T-83
71OPC-421
71T-421
91Kodak/WSox-xCO
91WIZMets-379
92Mets/Kahn-51CO

Stephenson, Joseph
85Greens-11

Stephenson, Phil
83Albany-15
84Cram/PCL-88
85Cram/PCL-132
86Pittsfld-23
87Iowa-18
88Iowa/CMC-17
88Iowa/ProC-540
89D/Rook-36
90AlbanyDG/Best-14
90OPC-584
90S-642RP
90T-584
90T/89Debut-123
90WichSt-35
91F-545
91OPC-726
91S-138
91StCl-420
91T-726
92LasVegas/ProC-2804
92Pol/Padre-20
92StCl-684
93T-357
93T/Gold-357

Sterling, J.C.
N172

Sterling, Randy
75Tidew/Team-20
91WIZMets-380

Stetson, Mike
91CalLgAS-52

Stevanus, Mike
86Macon-24
87Salem-22
88Salem/Star-19
88Watertn/Pucko-11
89Augusta/ProC-502

Steve, Harry
83SanJose-26GM
86SanJose-19GM
89SanJose/Cal-237GM

Stevens, Charles
52Mother-39
53Mother-17

Stevens, Dale
90Hunting/ProC-3282
91Geneva/ProC-4214
91Pocatel/ProC-3782
91Pocatel/SportP-17

Stevens, Dave
92ChalK/SB-166
93B-116

Stevens, Donald
52Laval-98

Stevens, Edward Lee
(Ed)
47TipTop
48L-43
49B-93
49Eureka-173
52Park-25
90Target-769
Exh47

Stevens, J.H.
33SK*-47

Stevens, John 1
89Johnson/Star-21

Stevens, John 2
55B-258UMP

Stevens, Julia Ruth
92Mega/Ruth-152M
92Mega/Ruth-153M

Stevens, Lee
86Cram/NWL-96
87PalmSp-12
88MidldA/GS-18

89AAA/CMC-44
89Edmon/CMC-21
89Edmon/ProC-554
89F/Up-U16
90AAAGame/ProC-42
90AAASingl/ProC-103
90B-300
90D-449
90Edmon/CMC-13
90Edmon/ProC-527
90F-145
90F/Can-145
90ProC/Singl-490
90TripleAAS/CMC-44
91AAA/LineD-170
91AAAGame/ProC-15
91Classic/I-25
91D-754
91Edmon/LineD-170
91Edmon/ProC-1530
91F-327
91MajorLg/Pins-24
91OPC-648
91S-67
91S/100RisSt-82
91StCl-293
91T-648
91T/90Debut-149
91UD-573
91Ultra-53
92B-427
92Classic/I-85
92D-460
92F-71
92L-361
92L/BlkGold-361
92L/GoldPrev-15
92L/Prev-15
92OPC-702
92Pinn-453
92Pol/Angel-17
92ProC/Tomorrow-28
92S-372
92StCl-281
92Studio-150
92T-702
92T/Gold-702
92T/GoldWin-702
92TripleP-119
92UD-634
92Ultra-331
93D-65
93F-576
93Pac/Spanish-52
93Panini-9
93Pinn-169
93StCl-219
93StCl/1stDay-219
93Syrac/ProC-1007
93T-467
93T/Gold-467

Stevens, Matt
89Batavia/ProC-1924
90Spartan/Best-8
90Spartan/ProC-2489
90Spartan/Star-20
91Clearw/ClBest-8
91Clearw/ProC-1619
92Reading/ProC-574
92Reading/SB-543
92Sky/AASingl-237

Stevens, Mike
85PrWill-24
86PrWill-26
87Salem-2

Stevens, Morris
65T-521R
78TCMA-175

Stevens, Paul
77DaytB
80WHave-7

Stevens, R.C.
58T-470
59T-282
61T-526

Stevens, Scott
89Utica/Pucko-23
90SoBend/Best-22
90SoBend/GS-17
91Saraso/ClBest-10
91Saraso/ProC-1113
92BBCity/ClBest-22

Stevens, Tony
80Elmira-22

Stevenson, Bill
85Spokane/Cram-22
86CharRain-24
88Wichita-29

Stevenson, Jeff
92AppFox/ClBest-29

Stevenson, John
78Newar
82Amari-3
84Shrev/FB-22

Stevenson, Stevie
V355-128

Stevenson, Tenoa
82Idaho-12

Steverson, Todd
89Alaska/Team-9
92ClBest/BBonusC-27
92ClBest/Up-410
92Classic/DP-19
92FrRow/DP-7
92StCath/ClBest-1
92StCath/ProC-3400
92UD/ML-16
93ClBest/MLG-177
93Dunedin/ClBest-1
93Dunedin/ProC-1810
93FExcel/ML-246
93OPC/Premier/TDP-4
93Pinn-464DP
93S-496DP
93Select-353DP
93StCl/MurphyS-129
93T-269
93T/Gold-269
93UD/SP-286FOIL
94ClBest/Gold-57

Steward, Charles
(Chuck)
88Fayette/ProC-1092
89Lakeland/Star-20

Steward, Hector
86NewBrit-23

Stewart, Andy
92BBCity/ClBest-13
92BBCity/ProC-3849

Stewart, Brady
90Eugene/GS-29
91AppFx/ClBest-20
91AppFx/ProC-1726
92BBCity/ClBest-8
92BBCity/ProC-3853

Stewart, Carl
88Billings/ProC-1826
90Billings/ProC-3221
91CharWh/ClBest-10
91CharWh/ProC-2887
92CharWh/ClBest-19

Stewart, Dave
77Clinton
79Albuq-5
80Albuq-1
81Pol/Dodg-48
82D-410
82F-24
82Pol/Dodg-48
82T-213
83D-588
83F-222
83Pol/Dodg-48
83T-532
84D-343
84F-430
84Nes/792-352
84OPC-352
84Rang-31
84T-352
84T/St-360
85D-343
85F-569
85Rang-48
85T-723
86D-619
86F-453
86Phill/TastyK-48
86T-689
87D-648
87F-406
87Smok/A's-11
87T-14
87T/St-167
88Classic/Red-196
88D-472
88D/A's/Bk-472
88D/Best-99
88F-295
88F/BB/MVP-36
88F/Mini-48
88F/Slug-39
88F/St-57
88F/WaxBox-C14
88Leaf-217
88Mother/A's-3
88OPC-353
88Panini/St-164
88S-458
88Sf-162
88T-476
88T/Gloss60-33
88T/Mini-32
88T/Revco-29
88T/St-168
88T/UK-75
89B-188
89Cadaco-55
89D-214
89D/Best-99
89F-23
89F/Excit-39
89F/LL-36
89KennerFig-139
89Mother/A's-6
89OPC-145
89Panini/St-415
89RedFoley/St-112
89S-32
89S-582M
89S/Mast-14
89Sf-23
89T-145
89T/Big-101
89T/Coins-53
89T/Gloss60-45
89T/Hills-27
89T/Mini-71
89T/St-163
89T/St/Backs-27
89T/UK-74
89UD-185
90B-449
90Classic/Up-47
90CollAB-18
90D-150
90D-6DK
90D-703AS
90D/BestAL-25
90D/Bon/MVP-BC3
90D/Learning-35
90D/Preview-5
90D/SuperDK-6DK
90F-21
90F/AwardWin-37
90F/BB-39
90F/BBMVP-38
90F/Can-21
90F/WS-8
90F/WaxBox-C26
90Holsum/Discs-14
90Kenner/Fig-80
90Leaf-81
90MLBPA/Pins-74
90Mother/A's-5
90OPC-270
90Panini/St-141
90Panini/St-198 M
90PublInt/St-295
90PublInt/St-316
90S-410
90S/100St-13
90S/McDon-23
90Sf-194
90Sunflower-16
90T-270
90T/Big-64
90T/Coins-29
90T/DH-63
90T/Gloss22-21
90T/Gloss60-4
90T/Mini-32
90T/St-164AS
90T/St-185
90T/TVAS-16
90Target-770
90UD-272
90Woolwth/HL-25
90Woolwth/HL-33
91B-225
91BBBest/Aces-16
91Cadaco-55
91Classic/200-102
91Classic/II-T89
91CollAB-32
91D-102
91D-BC4
91D/BC-BC4
91F-25
91F/ProVF-4F
91F/WS-6
91F/WaxBox-4
91Kenner-49
91Leaf-417
91Leaf/Stud-107
91Mother/A's-5
91OPC-580
91OPC/Premier-115
91Panini/FrSt-199
91Panini/FrSt-355
91Panini/St-144
91Panini/St-4
91Panini/Top15-62
91Panini/Top15-71
91Panini/Top15-93
91RedFoley/St-90
91S-150
91S-702NH
91S-883DT
91S/100SS-24
91SFExam/A's-13
91Seven/3DCoin-12NC
91StCl-1
91StCl/Charter*-27
91T-580
91T/CJMini/II-10
91T/SU-32
91UD-127
91UD-28TC
91Ultra-254
91Woolwth/HL-24
92B-280
92Classic/Game200-10
92D-225
92F-268
92L-258
92L/BlkGold-258
92Mother/A's-5
92OPC-410
92Pinn-157
92S-580
92S/100SS-60
92StCl-390
92Studio-230
92T-410
92T/Gold-410
92T/GoldWin-410
92T/Kids-117
92TripleP-88
92UD-547
92Ultra-117
93BJ/Demp-14
93BJ/Fire-27
93Cadaco-56
93Colla/DM-103
93D-611
93Duracel/PPI-10
93F-669
93F/Final-296
93Flair-295
93L-294
93OPC-294
93OPC/Premier-45
93Pac/Spanish-656
93Panini-29
93Pinn-442
93Rang/Keeb-347
93S-656
93Select-240
93Select/RookTr-24T
93StCl-629
93StCl/1stDay-629
93T-290
93T/Gold-290
93T/Hill-12
93T/Tr-114T
93UD-39CH
93UD-546
93Ultra-647
94B-113
94D-257
94F-343
94Flair-121
94L-308
94OPC-12
94Pac/Cr-652
94Pinn-374
94S-133
94S/GoldR-133
94Select-165
94StCl-317
94StCl/1stDay-317
94StCl/Gold-317
94StCl/Team-179
94T-455
94T/Finest-134
94T/FinestRef-134
94T/Gold-455
94TripleP-38
94UD-89
94UD/ElecD-89
94Ultra-143

Stewart, Denard
89KS*-86

Stewart, Duncan
87Nashvl-25M

Stewart, Ed
83Clinton/Frit-23

Stewart, Edward P.
(Bud)
48L-104
49B-173
50B-143
51B-159
52B-185
52Hawth/Pin-9
52T-279

Stewart, Gaye
45Parade*-51

Stewart, Glen
(Gabby)
43Playball-41
46Remar
47Signal

Stewart, Hector
87Pawtu-11
87Pawtu/TCMA-10
89WinHaven/Star-22

Stewart, James F.
64T-408R
65T-298
66OPC-63
66T-63
67OPC-124
67T-124
70T-636
71MLB/St-70
71OPC-644
71T-644
72MB-329
72T-747
73OPC-351
73T-351

Stewart, Jeff
87Wichita-17

Stewart, Joe
77Visalia

Stewart, John F.
(Stuffy)
90Target-771
94Conlon-1132

Stewart, John
87Cedar-21
87Durham-13
89SLCity-30
91Salinas/ClBest-19
91Salinas/ProC-2245

Stewart, Lee
89GA-32

Stewart, Riley A.
92Negro/RetortII-37

Stewart, Sammy
79T-206RB
79T-701R
80T-119
81D-474
81F-181
81OPC-262
81T-262
82D-457
82F-180
82OPC-279
82T-426TL
82T-679
83D-203
83F-74
83OPC-347
83T-347
84D-514

84F-22
84Nes/792-59
84T-59
84T/St-25WS
85D-148
85F-192
85Leaf-98
85OPC-213
85T-469
86D-270
86F-289
86F/Up-U107
86OPC-172
86T-597
86T/St-235
86T/Tr-103T
87D-658
87F-48
87T-204
88D-596
88F-616
88T-701
89Pac/SenLg-135
89Pac/SenLg-27
89TM/SenLg-101
90EliteSenLg-48
91Crown/Orio-439

Stewart, Shannon
92ClBest/BBonusC-24
92ClBest/Up-406
92Classic/DP-14
92Classic/DPFoil-BC13
92UD/ML-10
93ClBest/MLG-174
93OPC/Premier/TDP-2
93Pinn-462DP
93S-494DP
93Select-355DP
93StCath/ClBest-1
93StCath/ProC-3988
93StCl/MurphyS-180
94B-309
94ClBest/Gold-22
94FExcel-149
94UD-299UDC

Stewart, Tito
88NewBrit/ProC-905
89NewBrit/Star-5
89Star/IISingl-136
90AAASingl/ProC-434
90Pawtu/CMC-1
90Pawtu/ProC-462
90ProC/Singl-252
90T/TVRSox-60
91AAA/LineD-195
91Indianap/LineD-195
91Indianap/ProC-462

Stewart, Vernon
(Bunky)
55T-136
55T/DH-76

Stewart, Walter C.
(Lefty)
31Exh/4-30
33G-121
33G-146
35G-8I
35G-9I
91Conlon/Sport-243
R308-179
V353-75

Stiboro, Tom
80Batavia-13

Stickels, Bob
71MLB/St-527

Stidham, Phillip
90AR-23
92Lakeland/ClBest-20
92Lakeland/ProC-2279
94B-204
94FExcel-61

Stieb, Dave
80OPC-42
80T-77
81D-582
81F-414
81OPC-5
81OPC/Post-22
81T-467
81T/St-142
82D-52
82F-622
82F/St-232
82FBI/Disc-22
82OPC-380
82OPC-53TL
82OPC/Post-6
82T-380
82T-606TL
82T/St-250
83D-507
83D-9DK
83D/AAS-48
83F-441
83F/St-10M
83F/St-27M
83K-36
83OPC-130
83OPC-202TL
83OPC/St-127FOIL
83PermaGr/AS-6
83T-130
83T-202
83T/Gloss40-25
83T/St-127
84D-71
84D/AAS-19
84F-167
84F/St-85
84MiltBrad-26
84Nes/792-590
84Nes/792-606TL
84OPC-134
84OPC-289TL
84Seven-13E
84T-590
84T-606TL
84T/Gloss22-10
84T/Gloss40-24
84T/RD-8M
84T/St-368
84Tor/Fire-28
85D-193
85D/HL-12
85F-117
85F/LimEd-37
85F/St-110
85F/St-91
85FunFoodPin-75
85GenMills-23
85Leaf-251CG
85Leaf-54
85OPC-240
85OPC/Post-22
85Seven-14S
85T-240
85T/3D-20
85T/Gloss22-21
85T/Gloss40-40
85T/RD-22M
85T/St-191
85T/St-356
85T/Super-22
85Tor/Fire-27
86BJ/Ault-22
86D-146
86D/AAS-55
86Drake-34
86F-642M
86F-70
86F/LL-43
86F/Mini-16
86F/Slug-37
86F/St-115
86GenMills/Book-3M
86Leaf-68
86OPC-353
86Seven/Coin-E14M
86Sf-96
86T-650
86T/3D-27
86T/Gloss60-43
86T/Mini-36
86T/St-186
86T/Super-54
86T/Tatt-23M
86Tor/Fire-29
86TrueVal-19
87D-195
87F-238
87GenMills/Book-1M
87Leaf-72
87OPC-90
87RedFoley/St-81
87Sf/TPrev-5M
87Stuart-28M
87T-90
87Tor/Fire-30
88BJ/5x7-10
88D-148
88D/Best-284
88F-123
88Grenada-2
88Ho/Disc-17
88Leaf-80
88OPC-153
88Panini/St-215
88S-76
88T-775
88T/Big-172
88T/St-191
88Tor/Fire-37
89B-239
89Classic-49
89D-349
89D/AS-28
89D/Best-143
89F-244
89F/BBAS-40
89OPC-4
89Panini/St-463
89S-197
89Sf-35
89T-460
89T/Big-128
89T/St-194
89Tor/Fire-37
89UD-383
90B-505
90BJ/HoSt-6M
90Classic-97
90D-87
90D/BestAL-127
90F-93
90F/Can-93
90Leaf-79
90OPC-320
90Panini/St-173
90PublInt/St-526
90S-201
90S/100St-89
90Sf-26
90Sunflower-7
90T-320
90T/Big-112
90T/Mini-44
90Tor/BJ-37
90UD-605
90USPlayC/AS-10C
91B-22
91BBBest/Aces-17
91Classic/I-89
91D-1DK
91D-551
91D-BC21
91D/BC-BC21
91D/SuperDK-1DK
91F-185
91F/WaxBox-9
91Leaf-96
91Leaf/Prev-26
91Leaf/Stud-137
91MSA/Holsum-18
91MajorLg/Pins-26
91OPC-460
91OPC/Premier-116
91Panini/FrSt-344
91Panini/FrSt-360
91Panini/St-160
91Panini/St-9
91Panini/Top15-64
91Pep/SS-4
91Post/Can-16
91RedFoley/St-89
91S-30
91S-707NH
91S/100SS-93
91S/ToroBJ-5
91StCl-62
91StCl/Charter*-28
91T-460
91T/CJMini/II-32
91Tor/Fire-37
91UD-106
91Ultra-368
92B-376
92BJ/Fire-24
92Classic/Game200-13
92D-724
92F-341
92L-291
92L/BlkGold-291
92OPC-535
92Panini-32
92Pinn-108
92S-656
92S/100SS-37
92StCl-97
92T-535
92T/Gold-535
92T/GoldWin-535
92T/Kids-91
92TripleP-147
92UD-136
92UD-99CL
92Ultra-152
93BJ/D/45-29
93BJ/D/McDon-8
93D-708
93F-699
93OPC-235
93OPC/Premier-60
93Pac/Spanish-396
93Pinn-552
93S-630
93Select-386
93StCl-641
93StCl/1stDay-641
93StCl/WSox-4
93T-295
93T/Gold-295
93UD-805
93Ultra-536

Stiegele, Rob
89Bluefld/Star-22
90Freder/Team-23

Stieglitz, Al
60T-144

Stigman, Dick
59T-142
60L-85
60T-507
61Clover-26
61T-77
62T-37M
62T-532
63T-89
64T-245
64T-6LL
65T-548
66T-512
78TCMA-162
78Twin/Frisz-45

Stiles, Will
84LitFalls-1
86Columbia-24
87Lynch-16
88StLucie/Star-21

Stillman, Royle
76OPC-594R
76SSPC-393
76T-594R
78T-272
79Ogden/TCMA-14
79Spokane-2
80Ogden-18
91Crown/Orio-440

Stillman, Sam
80WHave-18

Stillwell, Kurt
84Cedar-17
86F/Up-U108
86T/Tr-104T
86TexGold-11
87Classic/Up-142
87D-123
87F-215
87Kahn-11
87T-623
87T/JumboR-17
87ToysRUs-26
88D-265
88D/Best-207
88F-248
88F/Up-U35
88Panini/St-276
88S-221
88S/Tr-4T
88Smok/Royals-23
88T-339
88T/Big-136
88T/Tr-115T
89B-120
89Classic-14
89D-322
89D/AS-29
89D/Best-63
89F-293
89KennerFig-140
89OPC-217
89S-162
89S/YS/II-42
89T-596
89T/Big-161
89T/St-266
89Tastee/Discs-8
89UD-616
90B-376
90CedarDG/Best-6
90Classic/III-29
90D-120
90D/BestAL-106
90F-118
90F/Can-118
90Leaf-256
90MLBPA/Pins-106
90OPC-222
90Panini/St-79
90PublInt/St-356
90S-96
90T-222
90T/Big-293
90T/St-269
90UD-361
91B-307
91D-24DK
91D-520
91D/SuperDK-24DK
91F-571
91Leaf-2
91Leaf/Stud-70
91OPC-478
91Panini/FrSt-279
91Pol/Royal-21
91RedFoley/St-91
91S-295
91StCl-189
91T-478
91UD-587
91Ultra-157
92B-135
92D-440
92F-170
92L-142
92L/BlkGold-142
92Mother/Padre-5
92OPC-128
92OPC/Premier-177
92Padre/Carl-21
92Panini-97
92Pinn-418
92Pol/Padre-21
92S-236
92S/RookTr-19T
92Smok/Padre-34
92StCl-650
92Studio-109
92T-128
92T/Gold-128
92T/GoldWin-128
92T/Tr-112T
92T/TrGold-112T
92UD-329
92UD-705
92Ultra-584
93B-434
93D-258
93F-148
93L-138
93Pac/Spanish-265
93Panini-259
93Pinn-154
93S-379
93Select-193
93StCl-568
93StCl/1stDay-568
93T-84
93T/Gold-84
93TripleP-69
93UD-152
93Ultra-124
94Pac/Cr-90
94T-198
94T/Gold-198

Stillwell, Rod
90AppFox/Box-26
90AppFox/ProC-2104

Stimac, Craig
79Hawaii-4
80Hawaii-6

81T-356R
82Charl-13
Stinnett, Kelly
90Watertn/Star-20
91Collnd/ClBest-21
91Collnd/ProC-1488
92Canton/ProC-694
92Canton/SB-119
92Sky/AASingl-56
94B-653
94Finest-369
94Pinn-538
94Select-195
94Ultra-536
Stinson, Gorrell R.
(Bob)
70OPC-131R
70T-131R
71MLB/St-285
71OPC-594R
71T-594R
72T-679R
74OPC-653
74T-653
75OPC-471
75T-471
75T/M-471
76OPC-466
76SSPC-166
76T-466
77T-138
78T-396
79Ho-79
79OPC-126
79T-252
80OPC-305
85SpokAT/Cram-21
90Target-772
Stipetich, Mark
75QuadC
Stirnweiss, George
(Snuffy)
39Exh
44Yank/St-26
45Playball-12
47TipTop
48B-35
48L-95
49B-165
50B-249
51B-21
52T-217
92Yank/WIZAS-80
Exh47
Stitt, Jerry
84AZ/Pol-17ACO
86AZ/Pol-15ACO
87AZ/Pol-14ACO
88AZ/Pol-13ACO
90AZ/Pol-17ACO
92AZ/Pol-18ACO
Stitz, John
88Watlo/ProC-669
Stitzel, Glenn
75IntAS/TCMA-19
Stivers, Pat
88Idaho/ProC-1849
Stobbs, Chuck
52T-62
53Briggs
53T-89
54T-185
55T-41
55T/DH-44
56T-68
56T/Pin-60P
57T-101
58T-239
59T-26
60T-432
61Clover-27
61P-94
61Peters-4
61T-431
61T/St-185
62Salada-90A
62Salada-90B
62Shirriff-90
79TCMA-101
81Chatt-19CO
82Chatt-24CO
91T/Arc53-89
94T/Arc54-185
Stober, Mark
80Knoxvl/TCMA-6
Stock, Kevin
83BurlR-23
83BurlR/Frit-22
85Modesto/Chong-1
92Belling/ClBest-13
92Belling/ProC-1444
Stock, Milt
21Exh-175
25Exh-14
52T-381CO
90Target-773
D327
D328-169
D329-170
D350/2-172
E120
E121/120
E121/80
E122
E135-169
E220
M101/4-170
M101/5-172
V100
V61-56
W501-77
W572
W575
Stock, Sterling
89StCath/ProC-2089
Stock, Wes
60T-481
61T-26
62T-442
63T-438
64T-382
65OPC-117
65T-117
67OPC-74
67T-74
70McDon-2CO
73OPC-179CO
73T-179CO
77T-597CO
78TCMA-139
78TCMA-154
91Crown/Orio-441
Stockam, Doug
88Durham/Star-19
89Greenvl/Best-16
89Greenvl/ProC-1165
89Greenvl/Star-23
90Greenvl/Best-15
90Greenvl/ProC-1127
90Greenvl/Star-18
Stocker, Bob
86Madis/Pol-20
88Madis-23
89Huntsvl/Best-8
Stocker, Kevin
91FrRow/DP-10
92ClBest-76
92Clearw/ClBest-19
92StCl/Dome-181
92UD/ML-110
93B-104
93B-356FOIL
93L-523
93ScranWB/Team-24
93Select/RT/ASRook-4
93Select/RookTr-84T
93StCl-682
93StCl/1stDay-682
93StCl/Phill-6
93UD-508DD
93UD/SP-179
94B-252
94D-245
94F-601
94F/RookSen-20
94Flair-212
94L-417
94OPC-5
94OPC/DiamD-4
94Pac/Cr-487
94Panini-231
94Phill/Med-31
94Pinn-460
94S-619
94Select-52
94StCl-444
94StCl/1stDay-444
94StCl/Gold-444
94StCl/Team-240
94Studio-143
94T-57
94T/Finest-2
94T/FinestRef-2
94T/Gold-57
94TripleP-180
94UD-84
94UD/CollC-268
94UD/CollC/Gold-268
94UD/CollC/Silv-268
94UD/ElecD-84
94UD/SP-139
94Ultra-253
94Ultra/Second-10
Stocksdale, Otis
N300/SC
Stockstill, Dave
79Wausau-5
81Tulsa-5
82Tulsa-15
83OKCty-17
84OKCty-8
85OKCty-23
Stoddard, Bob
80Spokane-1
81Spokane-18
82SLCity-18
83T-195
84D-619
84F-620
84Mother/Mar-22
84Nes/792-439
84T-439
85Cram/PCL-90
85F-502
86LasVegas-19
87F-431
87Omaha-12
88Tacoma/CMC-10
88Tacoma/ProC-628
89Denver/CMC-11
89Denver/ProC-31
Stoddard, Tim
78RochR
80T-314
81D-475
81F-176
81OPC-91DP
81T-91
82D-131
82F-181
82T-457
83D-581
83F-75
83OPC-217
83T-217
84D-245
84F-23
84F/X-110
84Nes/792-106
84SevenUp-49
84T-106
84T/Tr-112
85D-144
85F-68
85F/Up-U111
85Mother/Padres-19
85OPC-393
85T-693
85T/Tr-113T
86D-406
86F-335
86T-558
87D-497
87F-116
87OPC-321
87T-788
88D-497
88D/Y/Bk-497
88F-222
88S-258
88T-359
89Pac/SenLg-182
89T/SenLg-37
89TM/SenLg-102
90EliteSenLg-30
91Crown/Orio-442
92Yank/WIZ80-188
Stoeckel, Jim
87SanAn-3C
Stoecklin, Tony
92Idaho/ProC-3513
Stoerck, Scott
87Belling/Team-26
88Belling/Legoe-21
88Wausau/GS-23
89Wausau/GS-14
Stohr, Bill
90Princet/DIMD-23
Stojsavljevic, Paul
92Geneva/ClBest-5
92Geneva/ProC-1564
Stoker, Mike
87Ashvl-14
88Durham/Star-20
89Durham/Star-20
89Durham/Team-20
Stokes, Gus
81Clinton-15GM
82Clinton/Frit-27GM
83Clinton/Frit-1GM
Stokes, Randall
90Bristol/Star-23
91Fayette/ClBest-28
91Fayette/ProC-1169
Stokke, Doug
80Tucson-24
Stoll, Pete
83Spring/Frit-1TR
84ArkTr-23
85Spring-23
Stoll, Rich
85Indianap-4
86Indianap-4
Stoltenberg, Scott
79Wisco-12
Stone, Bill
77Visalia
Stone, Brian
87Beloit-9
88Stockton/Cal-178
88Stockton/ProC-739
90ArkTr/GS-27
91AA/LineD-46
91ArkTr/LineD-46
Stone, Dave
88Watertn/Pucko-25
Stone, Dean
54T-114
55T-60
55T/DH-17
56T-87
57T-381
59T-286
62T-574
63T-271
79TCMA-65
91Crown/Orio-443
94T/Arc54-114
Stone, Eric
89Lakeland/Star-21
90AAASingl/ProC-380
90B-348
90ProC/Singl-388
90Toledo/CMC-11
90Toledo/ProC-150
91AA/LineD-397
91London/LineD-397
91London/ProC-1878
92Kinston/ClBest-19
92Kinston/ProC-2476
Stone, Fred
WG2-44
Stone, George H.
69T-627
70OPC-122
70T-122
71MLB/St-22
71OPC-507
71T-507
72MB-330
72T-601
73OPC-647
73T-647
74OPC-397
74T-397
75OPC-239
75T-239
75T/M-239
76OPC-567
76SSPC-557
76SSPC/MetsY-M13
76T-567
91WIZMets-381
Stone, George R.
12Sweet/Pin-55
E254
E90/1
E92
M116
S74-36
T205
T206
T3-119
Stone, George
86AppFx-25
Stone, H. Ron
66T-568R
68T-409R
69T-576R
70OPC-218
70T-218
71MLB/St-189
71OPC-366
71T-366
72T-528
Stone, Jeff
83Reading-20
84Cram/PCL-197
84F/X-U111
84Phill/TastyK-43
85CIGNA-8
85D-624
85F-266
85F/St-119
85Phill/TastyK-12
85Phill/TastyK-39
85T-476
85T/St-116
86D-259
86F-454
86KayBee-30
86Phill/TastyK-14
86Portl-21
86T-686
87D-309
87F-189
87Maine-11
87Maine/TCMA-19
87Phill/TastyK-14
87T-532
88D-482
88F-317
88OPC-154
88RochR/Gov-26
88T-154
88T/Big-146
89Mother/R-26
89OkCty/ProC-1510
89UD-486
90AAASingl/ProC-447
90Pawtu/CMC-22
90Pawtu/ProC-475
90ProC/Singl-273
90T/TVRSox-61
91AAA/LineD-369
91Crown/Orio-444
91Pawtu/LineD-369
91Pawtu/ProC-52
92Nashvl/ProC-1846
92Nashvl/SB-294
93Rang/Keeb-348
Stone, John Thomas
(John)
33Exh/4-12
34G-80
35G-8H
35G-9H
37Exh/4-16
38Exh/4-16
81Tiger/Detroit-41
91Conlon/Sport-289
R314
V354-89
Stone, Marcenia
94TedW-112
Stone, Michael
77StPete
78Clinton
78LodiD
Stone, Rocky
75IntLgAS/Broder-34
75PCL/AS-35
75Tacoma/KMMO-12
Stone, Shawn
84PrWill-21

Stone, Steve
82Amari-17
Stone, Steven M.
(Steve)
72OPC-327
72T-327
72T/Cloth-30
73OPC-167
73T-167
74OPC-486
74T-486
74T/Tr-486T
75OPC-388
75T-388
75T/M-388
76OPC-378
76SSPC-302
76T-378
77T-17
78OPC-46
78T-153
79OPC-115
79T-227
80T-688
81D-476
81F-170
81F/St-104
81K-58
81OPC-101
81T-520
81T-5LL
81T/So-49
81T/St-1
81T/St-249
81T/St-40
82D-357
82F-182
82F/St-144
82T-419
90Pac/Legend-63
90Swell/Great-27
91Crown/Orio-445
Stone, Toni
76Laugh/Clown-27
Stonecipher, Eric
89KS*-69
91Everett/ClBest-23
91Everett/ProC-3911
92Clinton/ClBest-11
Stoneman, Bill
68OPC-179
68T-179
69Expos/Pins-8
69OPC-67
69T-67
70Expo/PostC-4
70MLB/St-71
70OPC-398
70T-398
71Expo/ProS-24
71MLB/St-142
71OPC-266
71T-266
72Dimanche*-43
72MB-331
72OPC-95LL
72ProStars/PostC-12
72T-610
72T-95LL
73K-23
73OPC-254
73T-254
74Expo/West-10
74OPC-352
74T-352
74Weston-26
92Nabisco-29
93Expo/D/McDon-29
Stoner, Lil
92Conlon/Sport-605
Stonikas, Bill
88AppFx/ProC-147
89BBCity/Star-24
Stoppel, Craig
89KS*-71
Storey, Harvey
49B/PCL-15
Storke, Alan
E91
Story, Jonathan
91Utica/ClBest-14
91Utica/ProC-3256
Stottlemyre, Jeff
80SanJose/JITB-18
81LynnS-27
81Wausau-2
82LynnS-7
83Chatt-16
Stottlemyre, Mel Jr.
86Osceola-25
87ColAst/ProC-6
88Memphis/Best-1
89B-110
89B-261FS
90AAASingl/ProC-601
90Leaf-310
90OPC-263
90Omaha/CMC-7
90Omaha/ProC-66
90ProC/Singl-182
90T-263
91D-257
91OPC-58
91S-361RP
91S/100RisSt-23
91T-58
91T/90Debut-150
Stottlemyre, Mel
65OPC-133WS
65T-133WS
65T-550
66Bz-5
66T-224LL
66T-350
66T/RO-58
66T/RO-88
67Bz-5
67CokeCap/YMet-1
67T-225
68OPC-120
68T-120
68T/3D
68T/ActionSt-16C
68T/ActionSt-1C
69Citgo-5
69MB-265
69MLB/St-79
69MLBPA/Pin-27
69NTF
69OPC-9LL
69OPC/DE-21
69T-470
69T-9LL
69T/DE-13
69T/S-25
69T/St-208
69T/decal
69Trans-28
70K-5
70MB-27
70MLB/St-250
70OPC-100
70OPC-70LL
70T-100
70T-70LL
70T/S-27
70T/SO
70T/Super-27
70Trans-13
71K-40
71MD
71MLB/St-500
71OPC-615
71T-615
71T/Coins-94
71T/S-10
71T/Super-10
71T/tatt-12
72K-50
72MB-332
72OPC-325
72OPC-492KP
72T-325
72T-492KP
73OPC-520
73Syrac/Team-26
73T-520
74OPC-44
74Syrac/Team-26
74T-44
74T/St-218
75OPC-183
75Syrac/Team-21
75T-183
75T/M-183
81TCMA-450M
88Kahn/Mets-30CO
88Pac/Leg-22
89B-261FS
89Kahn/Mets-30CO
90BBWit-15A
90BBWit-15B
90Kahn/Mets-30CO
90T/TVMets-6CO
91Kahn/Mets-30CO
92Mets/Kahn-30CO
92Yank/WIZ60-121
92Yank/WIZAS-81
WG10-22
Stottlemyre, Todd
86Ventura-25
87Syrac-11
87Syrac/TCMA-8
88D-658
88D/Rook-37
88F/Up-U68
88S/Tr-90T
88T/Tr-116T
88Tor/Fire-16
89B-242
89D-620
89F-245
89OPC-237
89Panini/St-460
89S-453
89S/HotRook-81
89S/YS/II-20
89T-722
89T/Big-298
89Tor/Fire-30
89UD-362
90D-669
90F-94
90F/Can-94
90Leaf-475
90OPC-591
90Panini/St-172
90PublInt/St-527
90S-554
90T-591
90T/Big-240
90Tor/BJ-30
90UD-692
91B-10
91Classic/III-89
91D-155
91F-186
91Leaf-227
91OPC-348
91Panini/FrSt-349
91S-39
91S/ToroBJ-6
91StCl-564
91T-348
91Tor/Fire-30
91UD-257
92B-18
92BJ/Fire-25
92Classic/Game200-14
92D-263
92F-342
92L-167
92L/BlkGold-167
92OPC-607
92Pinn-240
92S-74
92StCl-307
92T-607
92T/Gold-607
92T/GoldWin-607
92TripleP-58
92UD-371
92Ultra-153
93B-111
93BJ/D/45-21
93BJ/Demp-5
93BJ/Fire-28
93D-585
93F-340
93L-25
93OPC-244
93OPC/WC-14
93Pac/Spanish-329
93Pinn-311
93S-186
93StCl-409
93StCl/1stDay-409
93T-23
93T/Gold-23
93UD-413
93Ultra-293
94D-504
94F-344
94Flair-122
94L-28
94Pinn-56
94Pinn/Artist-56
94Pinn/Museum-56
94S-149
94S/GoldR-149
94StCl/Team-173
94T-155
94T/Finest-113
94T/FinestRef-113
94T/Gold-155
94UD-189
94UD/CollC-269
94UD/CollC/Gold-269
94UD/CollC/Silv-269
94UD/ElecD-189
94Ultra-440
Stotz, Carl
90BBWit-87M
Stouffer, Blair
76SanAn/Team-22
Stoughton, Mark
92Miracle/ClBest-28TR
Stout, Allyn
V94-45
Stout, Jeff
89Augusta/ProC-501
Stout, John
89TNTech-33M
Stout, Tim
82Cedar-22
Stoval, Jerry
80Clinton-5
Stovall, DaRond
91Johnson/ClBest-12
91Johnson/ProC-3991
92Savan/ClBest-11
92Savan/ProC-676
Stovall, George T.
10Domino-112
11Helmar-65
12Sweet/Pin-19A
12Sweet/Pin-19B
14CJ-11
15CJ-11
94Conlon-1259
D303
E106
E254
E90/1
M116
T201
T202
T205
T206
T207
T213/blue
T216
WG5-38
Stovey, Harry
90Target-774
N172
N693
Stowe
N690
Stowe, Harold
62T-291
92Yank/WIZ60-122
Stowell, Brad
91SoOreg/ProC-3844
92Madis/ClBest-18
92Madis/ProC-1236
Stowell, Steve
88Kenosha/ProC-1384
89Visalia/Cal-97
89Visalia/ProC-1444
90Foil/Best-304
90OrlanSR/Best-22
90OrlanSR/ProC-1083
90OrlanSR/Star-20
91AA/LineD-494
91OrlanSR/LineD-494
91OrlanSR/ProC-1848
Stoyanovich, Pete
91StCl/Charter*-38
Strahler, Mike
71MLB/St-116
71OPC-188R
71T-188R
72OPC-198R
72T-198R
73OPC-279
73T-279
74Albuq/Team-20
90Target-775
Strain, Joe
78Cr/PCL-7
79Phoenix
79T-726R
80OPC-280
80Pol/Giants-20
80T-538
81D-73
81F-458
81T-361
81T/Tr-837
82Iowa-9
82T-436
83OKCty-21
85Everett/II/Cram-18
86Cram/NWL-180
86Everett/Pop-30
87Everett-12
89Everett/Star-30
Straker, Les
80Cedar-17
81Water-8
83Water-8
84Albany-19
85OrlanTw-20
86Toledo-21
87D/Rook-21
87Sf/Rook-45
87T/Tr-118T
88D-73
88F-24
88S-108
88T-264
89Portl/CMC-10
89Portl/ProC-219
89S-244
89T-101
89T/Big-90
89UD-83
Strampe, Bob
73OPC-604R
73T-604R
75Hawaii/Caruso-17
Strand, Paul
94Conlon-1300
Strang, Sammy Nicklin
89Chatt/II/Team-21MG
90Target-776
E107
T206
Strange, Alan
W753
Strange, Don
89Pulaski/ProC-1895
90A&AASingle/ProC-94
90Foil/Best-305
90SALAS/Star-43
90Sumter/Best-24
90Sumter/ProC-2433
91Durham/ProC-1545
92Greenvl/ProC-1152
92Greenvl/SB-244
92ProC/Tomorrow-189
92Sky/AASingl-102
93Richm/Pep-10
94FExcel-160
Strange, Doug
86FSLAS-45
86Lakeland-24
87GlenF-10
88Toledo/CMC-14
88Toledo/ProC-587
89Toledo/CMC-13
89Toledo/ProC-782
90AAASingl/ProC-201
90D-535
90OPC-641
90ProC/Singl-618
90S/100Ris-63
90T-641
90T/89Debut-124
90T/TVCub-60
90Tucson/CMC-16
90Tucson/ProC-211
91AAA/LineD-219
91Iowa/LineD-219
91Iowa/ProC-1071
92B-322
92Cub/Mara-1
92Iowa/SB-222

92L-476
92L/BlkGold-476
93D-136
93F/Final-284
93L-542
93Rang/Keeb-434
93StCl-132
93StCl/1stDay-132
94D-302
94F-322
94Finest-353
94Flair-114
94L-328
94Pac/Cr-630
94Panini-133
94Pinn-376
94S-163
94S/GoldR-163
94StCl-97
94StCl/1stDay-97
94StCl/Gold-97
94StCl/Team-267
94T-591
94T/Gold-591
94UD-317
94UD/CollC-270
94UD/CollC/Gold-270
94UD/CollC/Silv-270
94Ultra-134

Strange, Keith
90Utica/Pucko-9
91SoBend/ClBest-5
91SoBend/ProC-2865
92Saraso/ClBest-5
92Saraso/ProC-210

Strange, Kurt
88Wausau/GS-10
89SanBern/Cal-69

Stranski, Scott
80SanJose/JITB-19
81Spokane-3
82LynnS-8
85BuffB-24
86Hagers-22
87Memphis-14
87Memphis/Best-10
90HagersDG/Best-31

Strathairn, David
88Pac/8Men-14

Stratton, C. Scott
N172

Stratton, Drew
88Modesto-29
88Modesto/Cal-69

Stratton, Monty
80Pac/Leg-103

Strauss, Joseph
N172
N284

Strauss, Julio
90WinSalem/Team-23
91AA/LineD-144
91CharlK/LineD-144
91CharlK/ProC-1689
92ChalK/SB-167
92Iowa/ProC-4052

Strawberry, Darryl
82Jacks-21
83T/Tr-108T
83Tidew-28
84D-68
84Drake-29
84F-599
84F/St-104
84Jacks/Smok-12
84Nes/792-182
84OPC-182
84Seven-17E
84T-182
84T/Gloss40-29
84T/Mets/Fan-7
84T/RD-7M
84T/St-385YS
84T/Super-12
85D-312
85Drake-30
85F-631M
85F-93
85F/LimEd-38
85F/St-36
85FunFoodPin-8
85Leaf-159
85OPC-126
85Pol/MetYank-M6
85Seven-13S
85T-278FDP
85T-570
85T/3D-9
85T/Gloss22-8
85T/Mets/Fan-8
85T/RD-8M
85T/St-100
85T/St-179
85T/Super-30
86D-197
86D/AAS-5
86D/HL-24
86D/PopUp-5
86Drake-16
86F-632M
86F-96
86F/Mini-21
86F/Slug-38
86F/St-116
86KayBee-31
86Leaf-131
86OPC-80
86Quaker-16
86Seven/Coin-E11M
86Sf-60M
86Sf-97
86Sf/Rook-48M
86T-80
86T/3D-26
86T/Gloss22-19
86T/Gloss60-11
86T/Mets/Fan-8
86T/St-150
86T/St-95
86T/Super-55
86T/Tatt-18M
87BK-19
87Classic-3
87Classic/Up-122
87D-118
87D-4DK
87D/AAS-12
87D/DKsuper-4
87D/HL-42
87D/HL-49
87D/OD-128
87D/PopUp-12
87Drake-1
87F-23
87F-629M
87F-638M
87F/Excit-41
87F/LL-41
87F/Slug-40
87F/St-114
87F/WS-11M
87GenMills/Book-5M
87Jiffy-17
87KMart-32
87KayBee-31
87Kraft-26
87Leaf-4DK
87Leaf-68
87MSA/Discs-1
87OPC-379
87RedFoley/St-58
87Seven-E13
87Sf-20
87Sf/TPrev-2M
87Stuart-1
87T-460
87T-601AS
87T/Board-33
87T/Coins-46
87T/Gloss22-8
87T/Gloss60-32
87T/HL-29
87T/Mets/Fan-7
87T/Mini-26
87T/St-103
87T/St-159
87Woolwth-29
88Bz-21
88Classic/Blue-209
88D-439
88D-BC20
88D/AS-34
88D/Best-182
88D/Mets/Bk-439
88D/PopUp-12
88Drake-3
88F-151
88F-637M
88F/AwardWin-40
88F/BB/AS-40
88F/BB/MVP-37
88F/Excit-39
88F/Head-4
88F/Hottest-41
88F/LL-40
88F/Mini-97
88F/RecSet-39
88F/SS-38
88F/Slug-40
88F/St-106
88F/TL-40
88FanSam-17
88Grenada-71
88KMart-29
88Kahn/Mets-18
88KayBee-29
88KennerFig-107
88KingB/Disc-8
88Leaf-220
88MSA/Disc-17
88Nestle-18
88OPC-178
88OPC/WaxBox-L
88Panini/St-236M
88Panini/St-347
88S-360
88S/WaxBox-17
88S/YS/II-20
88Sf-155
88Sf/Gamewin-15
88T-710
88T/Big-253
88T/Coins-56
88T/Gloss22-19
88T/Gloss60-22
88T/Mets/Fan-18
88T/Mini-63
88T/RiteAid-7
88T/St-151
88T/St-96
88T/St/Backs-21
88T/UK-76
88T/WaxBox-L
89B-387
89Bz-20
89Cadaco-56
89Classic-108
89Classic-150
89Classic-8
89D-147
89D/AS-34
89D/Best-40
89D/MVP-BC6
89D/PopUp-34
89F-49
89F-632M
89F/AS-10
89F/BBAS-39
89F/BBMVP's-36
89F/Excit-40
89F/Heroes-38
89F/LL-37
89F/Superstar-39
89F/WaxBox-C25
89Holsum/Discs-10
89KMart/DT-28
89Kahn/Mets-18
89KayBee-29
89KennerFig-141
89KingB/Discs-15
89MSA/Disc-5
89MSA/SS-3
89Nissen-10
89OPC-300
89Panini/St-140
89Panini/St-223
89Panini/St-231AS
89RedFoley/St-113
89S-10
89S/HotStar-50
89S/Mast-42
89Sf-205
89T-291TL
89T-300
89T-390AS
89T/Ames-28
89T/Big-139
89T/Coins-26
89T/Crunch-7
89T/DH-18
89T/DHTest-1
89T/Gloss22-19
89T/Gloss60-8
89T/HeadsUp-6
89T/Hills-28
89T/LJN-10
89T/Mets/Fan-18
89T/Mini-28
89T/St-157
89T/St-98
89T/St/Backs-53
89T/UK-75
89Tetley/Discs-5
89UD-260
89UD-681TC
90B-141
90Classic-33
90CollAB-20
90D-235
90D/BestNL-80
90F-217
90F/AwardWin-38
90F/BB-37
90F/BBMVP-37
90F/Can-217
90F/LL-38
90F/LgStand-3
90HotPlay/St-43
90Kahn/Mets-18
90Kenner/Fig-81
90Kenner/Fig-82
90Leaf-250
90MLBPA/Pins-13
90Mets/Fan-18
90OPC-600
90Panini/St-302
90Post-10
90PublInt/St-145
90PublInt/St-273
90RedFoley/St-92
90S-200
90S/100St-15
90Sf-146
90Starline/LJS-21
90Starline/LJS-37
90T-600
90T/Ames-23
90T/Big-186
90T/DH-64
90T/Gloss60-7
90T/HillsHM-4
90T/St-91
90T/TVAS-56
90T/TVMets-33
90UD-182
90USPlayC/AS-13H
90WonderBrd-10
91B-382SLUG
91B-609
91Classic/200-177
91Classic/I-68
91Classic/I-99
91Classic/II-T73
91Colla/Strawb-Set
91D-408MVP
91D-696
91D/GSlam-13
91F-161
91F/ProV-12
91F/Up-U96
91JDean-5
91Kenner-50
91Kenner-51
91Leaf-377
91Leaf-444CL
91Leaf/Stud-190
91MSA/Holsum-1
91Mother/Dodg-2
91OPC-200
91OPC-402AS
91OPC/Premier-117
91Panini/FrSt-164
91Panini/FrSt-85
91Panini/St-88
91Panini/Top15-10
91Pol/Dodg-44
91Post-7
91S-640
91S-691MB
91S-864FRAN
91S/100SS-62
91S/RookTr-16T
91Seven/3DCoin-14NE
91Seven/3DCoin-14SC
91StCl-301
91T-200
91T-402AS
91T/SU-33
91T/Tr-114T
91UD-245
91UD/SilSlug-SS9
91Ultra-171
91WIZMets-382
92B-40
92CJ/DII-7
92Classic/Game200-132
92Classic/I-86
92Classic/II-T38
92D-559
92D/McDon-7
92F-471
92F/Lumber-L3
92F/Performer-12
92F/TmLIns-16
92French-17M
92JDean/18-9
92Kenner/Fig-41
92L-29
92L/BlkGold-29
92L/GoldPrev-5
92L/Prev-5
92MooTown-11
92Mother/Dodg-10
92MrTurkey-24
92OPC-550
92OPC/Premier-179
92P-10
92Panini-196
92Pinn-308SH
92Pinn-80
92Pinn/RookI-16M
92Pol/Dodg-44
92Post/Can-7
92S-9
92S/100SS-55
92S/Impact-59
92Seven/Coin-24
92StCl-560
92StCl/MPhoto-13
92Studio-50
92Studio/Her-6
92Sunflower-20
92T-550
92T/Gold-550
92T/GoldWin-550
92T/Kids-47
92TripleP-187
92TripleP/Prev-2
92UD-174
92UD/ASFF-43
92UD/HRH-HR16
92UD/TmMVPHolo-51
92Ultra-219
92Ultra/AS-18
93B-126
93Cadaco-57
93Colla/DM-104
93D-112
93D/LongBall-LL11
93DennyGS-9
93Duracel/PPII-21
93F-454
93Ho-7
93L-210
93MSA/Metz-19
93Mother/Dodg-8
93OPC-375
93Pac/Spanish-155
93Panini-219
93Pinn-309HH
93Pinn-64
93Pinn/Slug-19
93Pol/Dodg-25
93S-42
93Select-21
93StCl-398
93StCl/1stDay-398
93StCl/Dodg-1
93StCl/II/Ins-4
93StCl/MPhoto-23
93Studio-122
93T-450
93T/Finest-89AS
93T/FinestASJ-89AS
93T/FinestRef-89AS
93T/Gold-450
93TripleP-187
93UD-477M
93UD-575
93UD-820TC

93UD/Diam-9
93UD/FunPack-220FOLD
93UD/FunPack-92
93UD/OnDeck-D23
93UD/SP-99
93UD/Then-TN8
93Ultra-406
94D-292
94F-525
94Pac/Cr-322
94Panini-205
94Pinn-294
94S-428
94Select-99
94StCl-335
94StCl/1stDay-335
94StCl/Gold-335
94T-640
94T/Finest-87
94T/FinestRef-87
94T/Gold-640
94TripleP-89
Strawn, Fla
79Tucson-13
79Tulsa-5
80CharCh-14
Strebeck, Rick
90Modesto/Chong-29
91Modesto/ClBest-15
92Huntsvl/ProC-3951
92Huntsvl/SB-321
92Sky/AASingl-138
93Modesto/ClBest-20
93Modesto/ProC-799
Street, Charles
(Gabby)
10Domino-113A
10Domino-113B
11Helmar-46
12Sweet/Pin-64
12Sweet/Pin-64A
40PlayBall-169
73F/Wild-16
77Galasso-85
88Conlon/5-27
92Conlon/Sport-652
93Conlon-833
E254
E91
M116
S74-41
T201
T202
T204
T205
T206
T207
T213/blue
T213/brown
T215/brown
T3-120
Street, Mickey
85Water-7
Streeter, Sam
88Negro/Duques-13
Strelitz, Len
79ArkTr-2
Stricek, Jim
86Modesto-23TR
90WinHaven/Star-28TR
91WinHaven/ClBest-27TR
92WinHaven/ClBest-27
Stricker, John
N172
Strickland, Bob
86Geneva-26
87CharWh-18
89WinSalem/Star-15
Strickland, Chad
91AppFx/ClBest-14
91AppFx/ProC-1720
92AppFox/ClBest-4
92MidwLAS/Team-43
Strickland, Dedrick
90Oneonta/ProC-3372
Strickland, George
52B-207
52T-197
54B-36
54DanDee
55B-192
55Gol/Ind-28
55Salem
56Carling-9
57Sohio/Ind-14
57T-263
58T-102
59Kahn
59T-207
60L-30
60T-63
63Sugar-16
Strickland, Jim
72T-778R
73OPC-122
73T-122
75OkCty/Team-9
76SSPC-512
Strickland, Rick
88CapeCod/Sum-49
89Oneonta/ProC-2116
91FtLaud/ClBest-28
91FtLaud/ProC-2442
92Albany/ProC-2239
92Albany/SB-20
Stricklett, Elmer
90Target-777
Strijek, Randy
88CLAS/Star-17
88Hagers/Star-21
89Hagers/Best-20
89Hagers/ProC-265
89Hagers/Star-19
90Shrev/ProC-1452
90Shrev/Star-23
Striker, Jake
60T-169
Strincevich, Nick
44Playball-28
47TipTop
V362-17
Stringer, Lou
47Signal
49B-183
50B-187
52Mother-38
Stringfellow, Thornton
(Bean)
86Greenvl/Team-19
87Richm/Crown-31
87Richm/TCMA-7
88Richm-19
88Richm/CMC-4
88Richm/ProC-13
Stripp, Joe
34DS-89
34G-46
35G-1G
35G-3E
35G-4E
35G-5E
90Target-778
93Conlon-809
R300
V354-91
Strittmatter, Mark
92Bend/ClBest-23
93T-746
93T/Gold-746
Strobel, Craig
86Hagers-23TR
87Hagers-8TR
90Spartan/Best-30TR
90Spartan/Star-28TR
92Clearw/ClBest-26TR
93ScranWB/Team-25TR
Strode, Lester
(Jim)
82FtMyr-19
84Memphis-14
85Omaha-7
86Omaha/ProC-25
86Omaha/TCMA-17
88Louisvl-46
89Wythe/Star-29CO
90Peoria/Team-32CO
91Peoria/ClBest-23CO
91Peoria/ProC-1360CO
91Peoria/Team-2CO
92WinSalem/ClBest-27
92WinSalem/ProC-1224CO
Strohmayer, John
71Expo/ProS-25
71OPC-232
71T-232
72Dimanche*-44
72T-631
73OPC-457
73T-457
91WIZMets-383
Strom, Brent
73OPC-612R
73T-612R
74OPC-359
74T-359
75Hawaii/Caruso-12
75OPC-643
75T-643
75T/M-643
76OPC-84
76T-84
77Padre/SchCd-30
77T-348
78T-509
80Tucson-20
81Albuq/TCMA-12
82Albuq-27
83Albuq-13
87Albuq/Pol-3CO
88AlaskaAS60/Team-11
88Albuq/ProC-251
89Albuq/ProC-60
90AAASingl/ProC-210CO
90Tucson/ProC-220CO
91AAA/LineD-622
91Tucson/LineD-622
91Tucson/ProC-2230CO
91WIZMets-384
92Tucson/ProC-506CO
92Tucson/SB-625CO
Stromer, Rick
83Peoria/Frit-11
85Huntsvl/BK-43
Strong, Garret
75Cedar
Strong, Jeff
87BYU-14M
Strong, Joe
85Modesto/Chong-9
86Modesto-24
88CalLgAS-20
88Reno/Cal-274
89AS/Cal-41
89Reno/Cal-245
Strong, Kevin
91Elizab/ProC-4314
Strong, Shannon
90Eugene/GS-30
Strong, Steve
86AZ/Pol-16
87AZ/Pol-15
89Lakeland/Star-22
Strong, Stewart
91GreatF/SportP-13
Stroth, Scott
92Everett/ClBest-8
92Everett/ProC-1689
Stroud, Derek
88Geneva/ProC-1649
89Peoria/Team-11
90WinSalem/Team-9
92PalmSp/ProC-840
Stroud, Ed
67T-598R
68OPC-31
68T-31
69MB-266
69MLB/St-108
69T-272
70MLB/St-286
70OPC-506
70Pol/SenY-10
70T-506
71MLB/St-550
71OPC-217
71T-217
72MB-333
Stroud, Ralph
16FleischBrd-91
C46-58
M116
T201
Stroughter, Steve
78Cr/PCL-45
80Spokane-23
81Toledo-22
82T/Tr-114T
Strovink, Eric
91GulfCR/SportP-5
Strube, Bob
86Kenosha-22
87Visalia-5
88Visalia/Cal-162
88Visalia/ProC-101
89Visalia/Cal-99
89Visalia/ProC-1429
Strucher, Mark
82DayBe-25
83ColumAst-6
86Richm-22
87Richm/Bob-20
87Richm/Crown-5
87Richm/TCMA-15
Struck, J.O.
N172
Struek, Randy
87Hagers-9
Strunk, Amos
14CJ-33
15CJ-33
16FleischBrd-92
D327
D328-170
D329-171
D350/2-173
E104
E120
E121/120
E121/80
E135-170
E270/1
M101/4-171
M101/5-173
M116
T207
T208
T222
W501-44
W573
W575
Stryffeler, Dan
82Spring/Frit-9
83Spring/Frit-21
84ArkTr-3
86Louisvl-27
Stryker, Dutch
90Target-1081
Stryker, Ed
90GreatF/SportP-26
91Bakers/Cal-5
92VeroB/ClBest-17
92VeroB/ProC-2874
Stuart, Marlin
52B-147
52T-208
53B/Col-120
54Esskay
66T/RO-89
81TCMA-366
91Crown/Orio-446
Stuart, Richard L.
(Dick)
59HRDerby-19
59Kahn
59T-357
60Armour-18
60Bz-6
60Kahn
60T-402
61Kahn
61NuCard-409
61P-127
61T-126
61T/St-71
62Bz
62J-169
62Kahn
62P-169
62P/Can-169
62Salada-120
62Shirriff-120
62Sugar-D
62T-160
62T/St-180
62T/bucks
63J-137
63P-137
63T-18M
63T-285
64T-10LL
64T-12LL
64T-410
64T/Coins-12
64T/Coins-122AS
64T/S-42
64T/SU
64T/St-51
64T/tatt
65OPC-280
65OPC-5LL
65T-280
65T-5LL
65T/trans-29
66T-480
66T/RO-75
90Target-779
91WIZMets-385
PM10/Sm-186
Stubberfield, Chris
86Cram/NWL-18
86Everett/Pop-31
Stubbs, Franklin
83Albuq-1
84Cram/PCL-151
85Cram/PCL-175
85D-348
85F-386
85T-506
86D-592
86Pol/Dodg-22
86T/Tr-105T
87D-299
87D/OD-83
87F-455
87Mother/Dodg-13
87OPC-292
87Pol/Dodg-10
87Seven-W14
87Sf/TPrev-14M
87T-29
87T/St-72
88D-218
88D/Best-331
88F-527
88KennerFig-108
88Leaf-182
88Mother/Dodg-11
88OPC-198
88Panini/St-308
88Pol/Dodg-22
88RedFoley/St-84
88S-147
88T-198
88T/Big-112
88T/St-66
89D-321
89D/GrandSlam-9
89F-74
89Mother/Dodg-11
89Pol/Dodg-13
89S-599
89T-697
89T/Big-32
89UD-91
90D-615
90D/BestNL-143
90Leaf-425
90Lennox-24
90Mother/Ast-14
90OPC-56
90Pol/Dodg-22
90PublInt/St-19
90S-478
90S/Tr-40T
90T-56
90T/Tr-120TUER
90Target-780
90UD-550
91B-37
91Brewer/MillB-25
91D-99
91F-518
91F/Up-U34
91Leaf-277
91Leaf/Stud-77
91OPC-732
91Panini/FrSt-13
91Pol/Brew-22
91S-308
91S/RookTr-59T
91StCl-461
91T-732
91T/Tr-115T
91UD-168
91UD/Ext-718
92B-49
92D-618
92L-328
92L/BlkGold-328

92OPC-329
92Panini-35
92Pinn-320
92Pol/Brew-24
92S-292
92StCl-189
92Studio-196
92T-329
92T/Gold-329
92T/GoldWin-329
92UD-396
92Ultra-390
93D-177
93F-636
93Panini-37
93StCl-168
93StCl/1stDay-168
93T-124
93T/Gold-124
93UD-269
Stubing, Lawrence
(Moose)
76QuadC
80SLCity-18
81SLCity-25
82Spokane-24
84Cram/PCL-97
89T-444MG
Stuckeman, Al
75Lafay
Studeman, Dennis
87FtMyr-13
89AppFx/ProC-851
Stull, Everett
92Classic/DP-52
92James/ClBest-13
92James/ProC-1503
93ClBest/MLG-123
93StCl/MurphyS-41II
Stull, Walt
86Bakers-27
87SanBern-18
Stuper, John
82Louisvl-29
83D-621
83F-23
83F/St-24M
83T-363
84D-412
84F-337
84Nes/792-186TL
84Nes/792-49
84T-186TL
84T-49
85F/Up-U112
86F-193
86T-497
91Savan/ClBest-28CO
91Savan/ProC-1669CO
92StPete/ClBest-28CO
Stupur, Dan
89Salem/Team-29
Sturdivant, Dave
88Bend/Legoe-15
89PalmSp/Cal-33
89PalmSp/ProC-486
90PalmSp/Cal-211
90PalmSp/ProC-2582
Sturdivant, Tom
57T-34
58T-127
59T-471
60T-487
61T-293
62T-179
63IDL-22
63T-281
64T-402
91WIZMets-386
Sturgeon, Bob
47TipTop
Sturm, Johnny
41DP-114
94Conlon-1312
Sturtze, Tanyon
91ClBest/Singl-439
91Madison/ClBest-2
91Madison/ProC-2133
91MidwLAS/ProC-44
92AS/Cal-8
92Modesto/ClBest-8
93B-569
Stutheit, Tim
92Hunting/ClBest-24
92Hunting/ProC-3159
Stutts, Dennis
93James/ClBest-22
93James/ProC-3327
Stutz, John
92Johnson/ProC-3126
Stutzriem, Jerry
79Wausau-2
Stynes, Chris
92Myrtle/ClBest-10
92Myrtle/ProC-2206
92StCl/Dome-182
93Dunedin/ClBest-23
93Dunedin/ProC-1805
94ClBest/Gold-58
Su'a, Murphy
81BurlB-13
Suarez, Ken
66T-588R
68T-218
69OPC-19
69T-19
70OPC-209
70T-209
71MLB/St-383
71OPC-597
71T-597
72MB-334
72OPC-483
72T-483
74OPC-39
74T-39
93Rang/Keeb-39
Suarez, Luis
81Wisco-9
Suarez, Nelson
81Wisco-23
Subbiondo, Joe
52Laval-10
Such, Dick
70T-599R
71OPC-283
71T-283
93Rang/Keeb-339CO
Sudakis, Bill
69T-552R
70OPC-341
70T-341
71MLB/St-117
71OPC-253
71T-253
71Ticket/Dodg-17
72T-722
73OPC-586
73T-586
74OPC-63
74T-63
74T/St-240
74T/Tr-63T
75OPC-291
75T-291
75T/M-291
90Target-781
91WIZMets-387
92Yank/WIZ70-146
93Rang/Keeb-349
Sudbury, Craig
90SoOreg/Best-9
90SoOreg/ProC-3430
91Madison/ClBest-3
91Modesto/ClBest-3
91Modesto/ProC-3089
92Modesto/ClBest-14
92Modesto/ProC-3899
93Modesto/ClBest-21
93Modesto/ProC-800
Suder, Pete
42Playball-24
50B-140
51B-154
52B-179
52T-256
53B/BW-8
54B-99
55B-6
R346-15
Sudhoff, John
E107
Sudhoff, William
WG2-45
Sudo, Bob
85Utica-5
86BurlEx-22
87Jaxvl-19
88Spring/Best-11
Sued, Jose
93LimeR/Winter-95
Sued, Nick
92ColRS/ClBest-17
92ColRS/ProC-2394
93Kinston/Team-24
93SALAS/II-38
Suehr, Scott
83Peoria/Frit-21
85MidldA-21
Sueme, Hal
43Centen-23
44Centen-22
45Centen-24
47Centen-28
47Signal
Suero, Williams
(William)
88Myrtle/ProC-1186
88SALAS/GS-17
89Dunedin/Star-17
90A&AASingle/ProC-61
90Foil/Best-44
90Knoxvl/Best-5
90Knoxvl/ProC-1249
90Knoxvl/Star-19
90Star/ISingl-90
91AAA/LineD-519
91B-8
91Syrac/LineD-519
91Syrac/MerchB-25
91Syrac/ProC-2489
92B-181
92D/Rook-113
92Denver/ProC-2650
92L-475
92L/BlkGold-475
92Pol/Brew-25
92Ultra-391
93LimeR/Winter-109
93Pinn-271
93Pol/Brew-23
93S-258
93StCl-377
93StCl/1stDay-377
94Pac/Cr-343
Suess, Ken
52Laval-32
Suetsugu, Toshimitsu
87Miami-25
Sugden, Joseph
93Conlon-937CO
E107
Suggs, George
10Domino-114
11Helmar-119
12Sweet/Pin-105
14CJ-113
15CJ-113
M116
T202
T205
Suhr, Gus
31Exh/4-13
33CJ/Pin-21
33Exh/4-7
33G-206
34DS-56
35BU-187
35BU-41
35G-8K
35G-9K
37Exh/4-7
38Exh/4-7
39PlayBall-83
40PlayBall-94
R310
R314
Suigiura, Mamoru
87Miami-27
Sukeforth, Clyde
52B-227
52T-364
90Target-782
Sukla, Ed
66T-417R
75Phoenix-6
Sularz, Guy
78Cr/PCL-89
79Phoenix
80Phoenix/NBank-15
81Phoenix-15
83D-605
83F-273
83Phoenix/BHN-14
83T-379
84Cram/PCL-22
91Pac/SenLg-129
Sulka, Ed
75Phoenix/Caruso-18
75Phoenix/CircleK-6
Sullivan, Adam
89KS*-23
93Lipscomb-9M
Sullivan, Brian
89Reno/Cal-246
90Johnson/Star-26
90Rockford/ProC-2690
91Niagara/ClBest-9
91Niagara/ProC-3649
92Fayette/ProC-2183
Sullivan, Carl
87DayBe-2
88FSLAS/Star-49
88Tampa/Star-23
89Saraso/Star-23
90Saraso/Star-23
91ClBest/Singl-303
91Saraso/ClBest-25
91Saraso/ProC-1126
Sullivan, Charlie
91Butte/SportP-19
Sullivan, Dan 1
86WinHaven-25
87WinHaven-9
Sullivan, Dan 2
92Penin/ClBest-22
92Penin/ProC-2932
93River/Cal-20
Sullivan, Daniel C.
Scrapps
Sullivan, Dave
87Elmira/Black-3
87Elmira/Red-3
Sullivan, Frank
55B-15
55T-106
55T/DH-22
56T-71
56T/Pin-25P
57T-21
58Hires-58
58T-18
59T-323
60T-280
61P-55
61T-281
62T-352
63T-389
79TCMA-57
Sullivan, Glenn
88WinSalem/Star-18
89CharlK-10
90AAASingl/ProC-634
90CharlK/Team-11
90Iowa/CMC-15
90Iowa/ProC-327
90ProC/Singl-90
91AAA/LineD-220
91Iowa/LineD-220
91Iowa/ProC-1072
Sullivan, Grant
91Oneonta/ProC-4155
92Greens/ClBest-19
92Greens/ProC-780
Sullivan, Haywood
57T-336
58T-197
59T-416
60T-474
61P-56
61T-212
62J-99
62P-99
62P/Can-99
62T-184
62T/St-60
63J-92
63P-92
63T-359
Sullivan, Jack
(Twin)
T3/Box-56
Sullivan, Jim
75FtLaud/Sus-12
Sullivan, Joe
41G-22
R312
R314
Sullivan, John L.
V100
Sullivan, John Paul
44Playball-21
Sullivan, John Peter
65T-593R
66T-597
67T-568
76Watlo-MG
84Tor/Fire-29CO
85Tor/Fire-28CO
86Tor/Fire-30CO
87Tor/Fire-31CO
88Tor/Fire-8CO
89Tor/Fire-8
90Tor/BJ-8CO
91Tor/Fire-8CO
91WIZMets-388
92BJ/Fire-26CO
93BJ/Fire-29CO
Sullivan, Marc
84Pawtu-20
86D-614
86T-529
87D-643
87D/OD-187
87OPC-66
87T-66
88S-271
88T-354
Sullivan, Martin J.
E223
N172
N284
N690/2
Sullivan, Michael J.
N172
Sullivan, Mike 1
81Water-9
Sullivan, Mike 2
89Batavia/ProC-1929
90Spartan/Best-9
90Spartan/ProC-2490
90Spartan/Star-21
91Clearw/ClBest-9
91Clearw/ProC-1620
92Reading/ProC-575
92Reading/SB-544
Sullivan, Russell
53Tiger/Glen-27
Sullivan, Scott
94B-598
94FExcel-181
Sullivan, Sport
88Pac/8Men-27
Sullivan, William J.
11Helmar-16
61F-141
90Target-783
D329-172
D350/2-174
E107
E254
E270/1
E270/2
E300
E97
M101/4-172
M101/5-174
M116
T206
T207
T3-121
WG1-16
Sullivan, William
92Billings/ProC-3355
Sultea, Chris
91SLCity/ProC-3210
Summa, Howard Homer
25Exh-88
26Exh-88
29Exh/4-28
81Conlon-100
91Conlon/Sport-205
94Conlon-1147
V117-6
Summers, Craig
91Parramatta/Fut-13
Summers, Jeff
83SanJose-22
84CharlO-25
85CharlO-16

Summers, John
(Champ)
76OPC-299
76T-299
78Indianap-12
78SSPC/270-125
78T-622
79T-516
80OPC-100
80T-176
81D-130
81F-466
81OPC-27
81T-27
81T/So-24
81T/St-76
82D-81
82F-282
82F/St-154
82T-369
82T/Tr-115T
83F-274
83T-428
84F/X-U112
84Mother/Padres-25
84Nes/792-768
84T-768
84T/Tr-113T
85T-208
86Indianap-32
87Colum-6
89Colum/Pol-24CO
89Pac/SenLg-96
89TM/SenLg-103
90T/TVYank-6CO
Summers, Lonnie
92Negro/Retort-57
Summers, Oron Edgar
(Ed)
09Buster/Pin-14
81Tiger/Detroit-66
E104
E254
E270/1
E90/1
M116
S74-18
T201
T202
T205
T206
T213/blue
T215/blue
T215/brown
Summers, Scott
87Greens-9
Summers, Tom
86Tampa-22
Summers, William
55B-317UMP
Summitt, Kerry
92Lipscomb-24
Sumner, Chad
92Johnson/ClBest-13
92Johnson/ProC-3127
Sunday, Billy
E223
N172
N284
N403
WG1-63
Sundberg, Jim
75Ho-100
75OPC-567
75T-567
75T/M-567
76Ho-68
76OPC-226
76SSPC-260
76T-226
77BurgChef-23
77Ho-110
77Ho/Twink-110
77OPC-185
77T-351
78BK/R-2
78Ho-79
78SSPC/270-83
78T-492
79Ho-97
79K-60
79OPC-53
79T-120
80OPC-276
80T-530
81D-385
81F-619
81OPC-95
81T-95
81T/HT
81T/St-133
82D-268
82F-332
82F/St-181
82OPC-335
82T-335
82T/St-240
83D-609
83D-7DK
83D/AAS-26
83F-580
83F/St-8M
83K-38
83OPC-158
83OPC/St-126
83Rang-10
83T-665
83T/St-126
84D-178
84F-431
84F/X-U113
84Gard-18
84Nes/792-779
84OPC-251
84Pol/Brew-8
84T-779
84T/St-355
84T/Tr-114T
85D-89
85F-597
85F/Up-U113
85Leaf-78
85OPC-102
85T-446
85T/St-286
85T/Tr-114T
86D-277
86F-22
86Kitty/Disc-18
86Leaf-149
86NatPhoto-8
86OPC-245
86Sf-186M
86T-245
86T/St-15ALCS
86T/St-259
87Berg/Cubs-11
87D-280
87F-382
87F/Up-U114
87OPC-190
87T-190
87T/St-256
87T/Tr-119T
88D-488
88D/Cubs/Bk-488
88F-434
88S-244
88T-516
88T/Big-100
89B-227
89Mother/R-24
89Smok/R-32
89T-78
89T/Big-103
89UD-331
90PublInt/St-423
93Rang/Keeb-350
94TedW-87
Sundberg, Richard
82Redwd-15
Sunderlage, Jeff
82Lynch-9
83Lynch-18
Sundgren, Scott
86BurlEx-23
Sundin, Gordie
91Crown/Orio-447
Sundra, Steve
40PlayBall-122
93Conlon-902
Sunkel, Mark
88Alaska/Team-17
Sunkel, Tom
39PlayBall-146
40PlayBall-110
90Target-784
Sunker, Steve
78Clinton
Sunnen, Gene
88Watertn/Pucko-34
Suntop, Lionel
75T/Photo-117
Suplee, Ray
92Classic/DP-113
92Oneonta/ClBest-17
93Greens/ClBest-22
93Greens/ProC-901
94B-396
94ClBest/Gold-86
Suppan, Jeff
94B-391
Surane, John
90Idaho/ProC-3250
Surhoff, B.J.
86Vanco-24
87Classic/Up-135
87D-28RR
87D/Rook-17
87F/Up-U115
87Leaf-28RR
87Pol/Brew-5
87Sf/Rook-23
87Sf/Rook-6
87Sf/TPrev-19M
87T-216
88Classic/Blue-202
88D-172
88D/Best-277
88F-175
88KennerFig-109
88Leaf-164
88OPC-174
88Panini/St-120
88Pol/Brew-5
88RedFoley/St-85
88S-22
88S/YS/I-8
88Sf-57
88T-491
88T/Big-22
88T/Gloss60-49
88T/JumboR-10
88T/St-202
88T/St/Backs-57
88ToysRUs-31
89B-137
89Brewer/YB-5
89Classic-25
89D-221
89D/Best-221
89F-197
89Gard-5
89KennerFig-142
89OPC-33
89Panini/St-368
89Pol/Brew-5
89S-154
89Sf-208
89T-33
89T/St-200
89UD-343
90B-393
90Brewer/MillB-25
90D-173
90D/BestAL-78
90F-338
90F/Can-338
90Leaf-290
90MLBPA/Pins-84
90OPC-696
90Panini/St-93
90PublInt/St-505
90S-74
90T-696
90T/Big-198
90T/St-203
90UD-159
91B-44
91Brewer/MillB-26
91D-460
91F-598
91Leaf-42
91Leaf/Stud-78
91OPC-592
91Panini/FrSt-203
91Panini/St-169
91Pol/Brew-23
91S-477
91StCl-206
91T-592
91UD-254
91Ultra-182
92B-481
92D-70
92F-190
92L-212
92L/BlkGold-212
92OPC-718
92Panini-34
92Pinn-118
92Pol/Brew-26
92S-78
92StCl-117
92Studio-197
92T-718
92T/DQ-7
92T/Gold-718
92T/GoldWin-718
92T/Kids-82
92TripleP-56
92UD-120
92Ultra-85
93B-71
93Colla/DM-105
93D-545
93F-257
93Flair-230
93L-166
93OPC-343
93Pac/Spanish-165
93Panini-36
93Pinn-87
93Pol/Brew-24
93S-33
93Select-62
93StCl-711
93StCl/1stDay-711
93Studio-174
93T-417
93T/Finest-8
93T/FinestRef-8
93T/Gold-417
93TripleP-248
93UD-102
93UD/SP-70
93Ultra-224
94D-310
94F-192
94Finest-344
94L-369
94OPC-197
94Pac/Cr-344
94Panini-87
94Pinn-152
94Pinn/Artist-152
94Pinn/Museum-152
94Pol/Brew-26
94S-77
94S/GoldR-77
94StCl-215
94StCl/1stDay-215
94StCl/Gold-215
94T/Gold-102
94TripleP-58
94UD-369
94UD/SP-60
94Ultra-379
9y4T-102
Surhoff, Rich
85Cram/PCL-49
85Phill/TastyK-46
86D-42RR
86OKCty-22
88Iowa/CMC-10
88Iowa/ProC-529
93Rang/Keeb-351
Surico, Steve
89Anchora-25
90Butte/SportP-23
Suris, Jorge
85Spokane/Cram-23
Surkont, Max
52B-12
52T-302
53B/Col-156
53JC-11
53SpicSpan/3x5-23
54B-75
54DanDee
55B-83
56T-209
57T-310
Surner, Ben
82Holyo-26
83Nashua-24
Surratt, Alfred
92Negro/Retort-58
Susce, George
55B-320
55Rodeo
56T-93
57T-229
58T-189
59T-511
93Rang/Keeb-43CO
Susce, Steve
83AlexD-21
Sutch, Ray
(Rick)
92Madis/ClBest-19
92Madis/ProC-1237
Sutcliffe, Rick
78Cr/PCL-51
80Pol/Dodg-43
80T-544
81D-418
81F-125
81OPC-191
81Pol/Dodg-43
81T-191
82F-25
82OPC-141
82T-609
82T/Tr-116T
82Wheat/Ind
83D-72
83F-420
83F/St-24M
83F/St-2M
83OPC/St-20
83OPC/St-61
83T-141
83T-497
83T-707LL
83T/St-20
83T/St-61
83Wheat/Ind-28
84Cub/Uno-12M
84Cub/Uno-14
84D-338
84F-551
84F/St-87
84F/X-114
84Nes/792-245
84OPC-245
84SevenUp-40
84T-245
84T/RD-8M
84T/St-254
84T/Tr-115
85D-433
85Drake-43
85F-69
85F/LimEd-39
85F/St-89
85FunFoodPin-32
85Leaf-139
85OPC-72
85Seven-14G
85SevenUp-40
85T-72
85T-720AS
85T/3D-29
85T/Gloss40-9
85T/RD-14M
85T/St-35
85T/St-97
85T/Super-3
85ThomMc/Discs-43
86Cub/Unocal-18
86D-189
86Dorman-17
86F-383
86F/Mini-81
86F/Slug-39
86Gator-40
86Jay's-18
86Leaf-122
86Meadow/Stat-19
86OPC-330
86Seven/Coin-C10M
86Sf-134M
86Sf-149M
86Sf-46
86Sf-56M

86Sf-70M
86Sf-72M
86T-330
86T/St-61
86T/Tatt-21M
86TrueVal-18
87Berg/Cubs-40
87D-68
87D/OD-69
87F-576
87F/Slug-41
87OPC-142
87T-142
88Berg/Cubs-40
88Classic/Blue-224
88D-68
88D/AS-43
88D/Best-138
88D/Cubs/Bk-68
88Drake-31
88F-435
88F/AwardWin-41
88F/BB/AS-41
88F/BB/MVP-38
88F/Excit-40
88F/Hottest-42
88F/LL-41
88F/Mini-71
88F/RecSet-40
88F/SS-39
88F/St-81
88F/TL-41
88KMart-30
88KennerFig-110
88Leaf-91
88OPC-372
88Panini/St-257
88RedFoley/St-86
88S-50
88Sf-27
88T-740
88T/Big-128
88T/Coins-57
88T/Mini-45
88T/Revco-9
88T/St-61
88T/St/Backs-27
88T/UK-77
89B-281
89D-223
89D/Best-138
89F-439
89KennerFig-143
89Mara/Cubs-40
89OPC-394
89Panini/St-51
89S-407
89Sf-217
89T-520
89T/LJN-136
89T/St-52
89UD-303
90B-21
90Cub/Mara-20
90D-157
90F-43
90F/Can-43
90Kenner/Fig-83
90Leaf-6
90MLBPA/Pins-53
90OPC-640
90Panini/St-233
90PublInt/St-205
90S-450
90Sf-181
90T-640
90T/Big-38
90T/St-55
90T/TVCub-15
90Target-785
90UD-109
91B-430
91Cub/Mara-40
91Cub/Vine-29
91D-462
91F-434
91OPC-415
91Peoria/Team-31
91S-785
91T-415
91UD-473
92B-106
92Classic/II-T54
92D-642
92D/Up-U13
92F-393
92F/Up-3
92L-508
92L/BlkGold-508
92OPC/Premier-98
92Pinn-398
92S-665
92S/RookTr-8T
92StCl-700
92Studio-130
92T/Tr-113T
92T/TrGold-113T
92UD-529
92UD-708
92Ultra-309
93B-113
93D-719
93F-552
93Flair-158
93L-89
93OPC-381
93Pac/Spanish-26
93Pinn-532
93S-563
93Select-182
93StCl-246
93StCl/1stDay-246
93StCl/MPhoto-10
93T-274
93T/Gold-274
93TripleP-106
93UD-80
93Ultra-502
94D-500
94F-21
94L-315
94S-497
94T-91
94T/Gold-91
94Ultra-569

Sutcliffe, Terry
81VeroB-20

Suter, Bill
80OkCty
81OkCty/TCMA-18

Sutey, John
91Bristol/ClBest-10
91Bristol/ProC-3621
92Bristol/ClBest-26
92Bristol/ProC-1429

Sutherland, Alex
92B-123
92SanBern/ProC-

Sutherland, Darrell
66OPC-191
66T-191
68T-551
69T/St-59
91WIZMets-389

Sutherland, Gary
67T-587R
68OPC-98
68T-98
69Fud's-12
69T-326
70Expo/PostC-7
70T-632
71Expo/ProS-26
71LaPizza-13
71MLB/St-143
71OPC-434
71T-434
72MB-335
72OPC-211
72T-211
73OPC-572
73T-572
74OPC-428
74T-428
74T/Tr-428T
75Ho-146
75OPC-522
75T-522
75T/M-522
76OPC-113
76SSPC-364
76T-113
77Padre/SchCd-31
77T-307

Sutherland, Harry
WG7-54

Sutherland, John
92Oneonta/ClBest-12

Sutherland, Leo
77AppFx
79Knoxvl/TCMA-7
80Iowa/Pol-11
81D-42
81T-112R
82Edmon-11
82T-599

Sutherland, Matt
79Cedar/TCMA-8

Suthers, Gregory
91Brisbane/Fut-3

Sutko, Glenn
88Billings/ProC-1806
89Greens/ProC-420
90Cedar/Best-2
91AA/LineD-171
91B-668
91Chatt/LineD-171
91Chatt/ProC-1963
91ClBest/Singl-216
91MajorLg/Pins-72
91S-767RP
91T/90Debut-151
92Chatt/ProC-3823
92Chatt/SB-196
92F-423
92S/100RisSt-98
92Sky/AASingl-88
92StCl-559

Sutryk, Tom
87Penin-15

Sutter, Bruce
77T-144
78Ho-5
78K-48
78OPC-196
78SSPC/270-254
78T-325
79Ho-130
79K-1
79OPC-238
79T-457
80BK/PHR-11
80K-10
80OPC-4
80T-17
80T/S-32
80T/Super-32
81Coke
81D-560
81F-294
81F/St-80
81K-56
81OPC-9
81PermaGr/CC-24
81T-590
81T-7LL
81T/St-221
81T/St-32
81T/Tr-838
82D-372
82F-129
82F-631M
82F/St-28
82FBI/Disc-23
82K-17
82OPC-260
82OPC-347AS
82Sqt-22
82T-168LL
82T-260
82T-347AS
82T/St-130
82T/St-15
82T/St-94
83D-40
83D/AAS-41
83F-24
83F/St-25AM
83F/St-25BM
83F/St-6M
83K-37
83OPC-150
83OPC-151SV
83OPC-266AS
83OPC/St-166
83OPC/St-187WS
83OPC/St-209
83OPC/St-284FOIL
83PermaGr/CC-17
83T-150
83T-151SV
83T-407AS
83T-708LL
83T/Fold-4M
83T/Gloss40-40
83T/LeadS-8
83T/St-166
83T/St-187
83T/St-209
83T/St-284
84Cub/Uno-9M
84D-13DK
84D-534
84F-338
84F/St-70
84Nes/792-709LL
84Nes/792-730
84OPC-243
84Ralston-24
84Seven-7C
84T-709LL
84T-730
84T/Cereal-24
84T/RD-22M
84T/St-145
85D-109
85Drake-44
85F-241
85F/St-104
85F/Up-U114
85FunFoodPin-14
85Ho/Braves-21
85Leaf-163
85OPC-370
85Pol/Atl-40
85Seven-4S
85Seven-5C
85Seven-5G
85Sportflic/Proto-3
85T-370
85T-722AS
85T-9RB
85T/3D-23
85T/Gloss40-22
85T/RD-23M
85T/St-135
85T/St-172
85T/Super-9
85T/Tr-115T
85ThomMc/Discs-44
86D-321
86F-529
86F/Mini-106
86F/St-117
86GenMills/Book-5M
86Leaf-192
86Meadow/Stat-17
86OPC-133
86Pol/Atl-40
86Seven/Coin-C7M
86Seven/Coin-E7M
86Seven/Coin-S7M
86Seven/Coin-W7M
86Sf-47
86Sf-65M
86T-620
86T/St-37
86T/Tatt-10M
86TrueVal-15
87F-530
87OPC-344
87RedFoley/St-125
87T-435
88T-155
89D-458
89F-603
89KennerFig-144
89OPC-11
89OPC/BoxB-M
89Panini/St-39
89RedFoley/St-114
89S-425
89T-11
89T/Big-64
89T/LJN-91
89T/St-25
89T/WaxBox-M
89UD-414
90MSA/AGFA-19
90PublInt/St-125
92Card/McDon/Pac-52
92Cub/OldStyle-24
93Cub/Rolaid-3
94TedW-18

Suttles, Mule
74Laugh/Black-30
86Negro/Frit-115
90Negro/Star-21

Sutton, Daron
92Boise/ClBest-22
92Boise/ProC-3628

Sutton, Don
66T-288R
67CokeCap/DodgAngel-5
67T-445
68OPC-103
68T-103
69MB-267
69MLB/St-153
69OPC-216
69T-216
69T/4in1-19M
69T/St-50
70K-8
70MLB/St-59
70T-622
71K-31
71MLB/St-118
71OPC-361
71T-361
71T/Coins-145
71Ticket/Dodg-18
72MB-336
72T-530
73K-5
73OPC-10
73T-10
73T/Comics-21
73T/Lids-51
73T/PinUps-21
74OPC-220
74T-220
74T/DE-12
74T/St-50
75Ho-7
75Ho/Twink-7
75OPC-220
75T-220
75T/M-220
76Crane-61
76K-13
76MSA/Disc
76OPC-530
76SSPC-73
76T-530
77BurgChef-147
77Ho-70
77Ho/Twink-70
77OPC-24
77Pep-62
77T-620
77T/CS-47
77T/ClothSt-47
78Ho-70
78K-57
78OPC-96
78SSPC/270-80
78T-310
79Ho-92
79OPC-80
79T-170
80OPC-228
80Pol/Dodg-20
80T-440
81Coke
81D-58
81F-112
81F/St-59
81Sqt-16
81T-605
81T-7LL
81T/HT
81T/St-27
81T/Tr-839
82D-443
82F-234
82F/St-43
82K-21
82OPC-305
82OPC-306IA
82T-305
82T-306IA
83D-531
83F-47
83F/St-27M
83F/St-4M
83Gard-18

83OPC-145
83OPC-146SV
83Pol/Brew-21
83T-145
83T-146SV
83T/Fold-1M
84D-414
84D/Champs-41
84F-215
84Gard-19
84Nes/792-35
84Nes/792-715LL
84Nes/792-716LL
84OPC-35
84Pol/Brew-20
84T-35
84T-715LL
84T-716LL
84T/St-300
85D-107
85D-16DK
85D/DKsuper-16
85F-598
85F/Up-U115
85FunFoodPin-86
85Leaf-16DK
85Mother/A's-3
85OPC-172
85T-10RB
85T-729
85T/St-290
85T/St-7
85T/St-8
85T/Tr-116T
86D-611
86D/HL-16
86F-170
86F/LimEd-43
86F/Mini-35
86Leaf-236
86OPC-335
86Sf-130M
86Sf-175
86Smok/Cal-4
86T-335
86T/Tatt-7M
87D-181
87F-626M
87F-93
87F/RecSet-37
87F/St-115
87Leaf-153
87OPC-259
87OPC/WaxBox-G
87Ralston-6
87Seven-W11
87Sf-156M
87Sf-99
87Sf/TPrev-11
87Smok/Cal-2
87Smok/Dodg-35
87T-673
87T/HL-6
87T/St-183
87T/WaxBox-G
87Woolwth-6
88D-407
88F-505
88Mother/Dodg-9
88Panini/St-37
88Pol/Dodg-20
88S-105
88Sf-213
88Smok/Dodg-30
88T-575
89OPC/BoxB-N
89S-400
89Smok/Dodg-78
89T/WaxBox-N
90Target-786
92Brew/Carlson-22

Sutton, Doug
89Bluefld/Star-23

Sutton, Ezra
E223
N172
N284
WG1-8

Sutton, Jim
82AppFx/Frit-4

Sutton, Johnny
74Gaston
79Iowa/Pol-14
79T-676
80Ogden-13

Sutton, Larry
92Eugene/ClBest-24
92Eugene/ProC-3040
93B-697FOIL
93FExcel/ML-179
93Rockford/ClBest-26
93T-423M
93T/Gold-423M

Sutton, Mark
83BurlR-24
83BurlR/Frit-21

Sutton, Phil
79Cedar/TCMA-30

Sutton, Rico
80Utica-33
83Kinston/Team-25

Suzuki, Ken
88SanJose/Cal-129
88SanJose/ProC-121

Suzuki, Makato
(Mac)
94B-313
94B-378
94FExcel-128
94TedW-131
94Ultra-425

Suzuki, Yasu
89Salinas/Cal-135
89Salinas/ProC-1814

Sveum, Dale
84ElPaso-24
85Cram/PCL-209
86D/Rook-37
86F/Up-U109
86Sf/Rook-4
86T/Tr-106T
86Vanco-25
87D-542
87D/OD-55
87F-358
87Leaf-156
87Pol/Brew-7
87Sf/TPrev-19M
87T-327
87T/JumboR-18
87T/St-309
87ToysRUs-27
88D-232
88D/Best-305
88F-176
88OPC-81
88Panini/St-126
88Pol/Brew-7
88S-120
88T-592
88T/Big-44
88T/St-199
89B-139
89Brewer/YB-7
89D-146
89F-198
89Gard-6
89OPC-12
89Panini/St-374
89Pol/Brew-7
89S-256
89S/YS/II-24
89T-12
89T/Big-126
89T/St-206
89UD-421
90Brewer/MillB-26
90ElPasoATG/Team-8
90OPC-739
90Pol/Brew-7
90PublInt/St-506
90T-739
90UD-499
91Brewer/MillB-27
91Pol/Brew-24
91S-814
92B-367
92D-452
92F-191
92L-473
92L/BlkGold-473
92OPC-478
92Phill/Med-30
92S-181
92StCl-687
92T-478
92T/Gold-478
92T/GoldWin-478
92UD-498
93Brew/Sen-3
93Mother/A's-11
93Pac/Spanish-572
93StCl/A's-29

Swacina, Harry
E270/1

Swafford, J.C.
89TNTech-27

Swaggerty, Bill
82RochR-7
83RochR-10
84RochR-17
85D-392
85F-193
85RochR-22
85T-147
86D-594
88Omaha/CMC-9
88Omaha/ProC-1498
91Crown/Orio-448

Swaggerty, Glenn
81QuadC-25

Swail, Steve
89Pulaski/ProC-1914
90BurlB/Best-9
90BurlB/ProC-2353
90BurlB/Star-25
91Durham/ClBest-11
91Durham/ProC-1549
92Durham/ProC-1106
92Macon/ClBest-7
93Durham/Team-19

Swain, Rob
86Watlo-26
87Kinston-18
88CLAS/Star-36
88Kinston/Star-21
89Canton/Best-26
89Canton/ProC-1303
89Canton/Star-20
90Canton/Best-11
90Canton/ProC-1301
92Kinston/ClBest-28CO
92Kinston/ProC-2493CO

Swain, Steve
82AubAs-16

Swain, Thayer
88Butte-21
90CharlR/Star-28

Swan, Craig
74OPC-602R
74T-602R
75Tidew/Team-21
76OPC-494
76SSPC-558
76T-494
77T-94
78T-621
79Ho-41
79OPC-170
79T-334
79T-7LL
79T/Comics-27
80OPC-1
80T-8
80T/S-41
80T/Super-41
81Coke
81D-155
81F-319
81OPC-189
81T-189
82D-589
82F-548
82T-592
83D-254
83F-557
83F/St-1M
83F/St-6M
83OPC-292
83OPC/St-262
83T-292
83T-621TL
83T/St-262
84D-441
84F-600
84F/X-U115
84Nes/792-763
84T-763
84T/Tr-116T
89Tidew/Candl-9
91WIZMets-391

Swan, Russ
86Cram/NWL-8
88SanJose/Cal-138
88SanJose/ProC-118
89Shrev/ProC-1831
90B-224
90Phoenix/CMC-5
90ProC/Singl-532
90T/89Debut-125
90T/Tr-121T
91CounHrth-22
91D-621
91F/Up-U57
91OPC-739
91StCl-577
91T-739
92B-378
92D-382
92F-293
92L-203
92L/BlkGold-203
92Mother/Mar-22
92OPC-588
92Pinn-484
92S-281
92StCl-472
92T-588
92T/Gold-588
92T/GoldWin-588
92UD-618
93D-713
93F-314
93Mother/Mar-16
93Pac/Spanish-626
93StCl-179
93StCl/1stDay-179
93StCl/Mar-14
93T-96
93T/Gold-96
93UD-624
93Ultra-272

Swank, Ken
82CharR-18

Swank, Randy
91Everett/ClBest-4
91Everett/ProC-3924

Swann, Pedro
91Idaho/ProC-4341
91Idaho/SportP-25
92Pulaski/ClBest-21
92Pulaski/ProC-3194
93Durham/Team-20

Swanson, Art
56T-204

Swanson, Chad
88Kenosha/ProC-1386
89Kenosha/ProC-1078
90Visalia/Cal-57
90Visalia/ProC-2152

Swanson, Dave
92Kingspt/ClBest-5
92Kingspt/ProC-1531

Swanson, Eric
82DayBe-16

Swanson, Evar
33G-195
34Exh/4-10
88Conlon/AmAS-23
92Conlon/Sport-393
94Conlon-1239
R308-174

Swanson, John
91OKSt-25

Swanson, Perry
82CharR-8

Swanson, Stan
72OPC-331
72T-331
72T/Cloth-31

Swartwood, Cyrus
N172

Swartz, Nick
84Omaha-7
85Omaha-3
86Omaha/ProC-26C
87Omaha-5
88Omaha/ProC-1500

Swartzbaugh, David
88CapeCod/Sum-66
89Geneva/ProC-1866
90Peoria/Team-28
91Peoria/ProC-1342
91WinSalem/ProC-2829
92ChalK/SB-168
92CharlK/ProC-2771
92ClBest-63
92Sky/AASingl-76

Swartzel, Parke
N172

Swartzlander, Keith
86Macon-25

Sweatt, George Alexander
86Negro/Frit-117
87Negro/Dixon-26

Sweeney, Bill
31Exh/4-18

Sweeney, D.B.
88Pac/8Men-13

Sweeney, Dennis
91Elizab/ProC-4301
92Kenosha/ProC-603

Sweeney, Ed
11Helmar-47
11Helmar-81
14CJ-112
15CJ-112
E106
E270/1
E286
E90/1
M116
T201
T202
T205
T206
T213/blue
T216
T222
WG5-39
WG6-35

Sweeney, Jeff
T214-26

Sweeney, Jim
89Geneva/ProC-1873
90PeoriaUp/Team-U6

Sweeney, Mark
88CapeCod/Sum-59
91Boise/ClBest-15
91Boise/ProC-3898
92ClBest-228
92ColRS/ClBest-8
92Kinston/ProC-2475
92QuadC/ClBest-21
92QuadC/ProC-825
94T-237M
94T/Gold-237M

Sweeney, Michael
89Idaho/ProC-2023
90Idaho/ProC-3258

Sweeney, Mike
91LitSun/HSPros-5
91LitSun/HSProsG-5
92Eugene/ClBest-25
92Eugene/ProC-3033

Sweeney, Peter
N172

Sweeney, Robert
90Kissim/DIMD-26
91Kissim/ProC-4185
92Bakers/Cal-24

Sweeney, Roger
91Yakima/ProC-4262
92GreatF/SportP-8

Sweeney, William John
D303
E224
E90/1
M116
T204
T206
T207
T213/blue
T213/brown
T215/brown

Sweeney, William
(Bill)
53Mother-23

Sweet, Richard
78Padre/FamFun-31
78T-702R
79Hawaii-3
79OPC-341
79T-646
80Hawaii-20
81Tidew-1
83D-352
83F-487

83Nalley-6
83T-437
84D-196
84F-621
84Nes/792-211
84T-211
87Belling/Team-24MG
88Wausau/GS-1
89Osceola/Star-27
90ColMud/ProC-1361MG
90ColMud/Star-25MG
91AA/LineD-574MG
91Jacks/LineD-574MG
91Jacks/ProC-940MG
91WIZMets-392
92Jacks/ProC-4014MG
92Jacks/SB-349MG
Sweetland, Lester L.
29Exh/4-12
Swenson, Mark
82Clinton/Frit-31
82Clinton/Frit-32M
Swenson, Mickey
82Clinton/Frit-30
82Clinton/Frit-32M
Swepson, Dobie
86Clinton-23
88Pocatel/ProC-2095
Swepson, Lyle
84Everett/Cram-2
Swetonic, Steve
94Conlon-1163
R310
Swiacki, Bill
79Albuq-4
80Albuq-5
81Albuq/TCMA-6
82Tacom-9
Swift, Bill
85T-404OLY
86D-562
86F-475
86Mother/Mar-16
86T-399
86T/Mini-46
87D-517
87F-597
87T-67
88F/Up-U61
88Mother/Sea-25
88T/Tr-117T
89F-560
89Mother/Sea-17
89OPC-198
89RedFoley/St-115
89S-219
89T-712
89T/St-228
89UD-623
90D-566
90F-526
90F/Can-526
90Mother/Mar-11
90OPC-574
90PublInt/St-442
90T-574
90Target-787
90UD-313
91CounHrth-12
91D-564
91F-462
91F/UltraUp-U53
91Leaf-380
91OPC-276
91S-123
91StCl-372
91T-276
91UD-498
92B-182
92B-611FOIL
92Classic/II-T33
92D-260
92D/Up-U22
92F-294
92F/Up-131
92Giant/PGE-32
92L-407
92L/BlkGold-407
92Mother/Giant-3
92OPC-144
92OPC/Premier-133
92Pinn-448
92S-541
92S/RookTr-32T
92StCl-243
92StCl-855
92Studio-118
92T-144
92T/Gold-144
92T/GoldWin-144
92T/Tr-114T
92T/TrGold-114T
92UD-620
92UD-736
92Ultra-596
93B-380
93D-232
93D/DK-5
93F-161
93F-708LL
93F/Fruit-58
93Flair-146
93L-194
93MilkBone-5
93Mother/Giant-5
93OPC-277
93Pac/Spanish-616
93Panini-234
93Pinn-347
93S-67
93Select-51
93Select/StatL-82
93StCl-204
93StCl/1stDay-204
93StCl/Giant-20
93T-755
93T/Gold-755
93T/Hill-29
93TripleP-262
93UD-118
93UD/FunPack-102
93UD/SP-115
93USPlayC/Ace-1S
93Ultra-136
94B-435
94D-294
94F-702
94L-288
94OPC-79
94Pac/Cr-556
94Panini-266
94Pinn-326
94S-430
94Sf/2000-54
94StCl-330
94StCl/1stDay-330
94StCl/Gold-330
94StCl/Team-16
94Studio-87
94T-639
94T/Finest-151
94T/Finest/PreProd-151
94T/FinestRef-151
94T/Gold-639
94TripleP-108
94TripleP/Medal-14M
94UD-62
94UD/CollC-271
94UD/CollC/Gold-271
94UD/CollC/Silv-271
94UD/ElecD-62
94UD/SP-93
94Ultra-294
Swift, Robert V.
(Bob)
47TipTop
49B-148
50B-149
51B-214
52B-131
52T-181
54T-65
60T-470C
81Tiger/Detroit-42
94T/Arc54-65
W753
Swift, Weldon
78BurlB
79Holyo-23
80Holyo-11
81ElPaso-19
Swift, William V.
34G-57
39PlayBall-129
R312
R313
R314
Swim, Greg
91Salinas/ClBest-29
91Salinas/ProC-2253
Swindell, Greg
86Sf/Rook-30
87D-32RR
87F-644M
87F/Up-U116
87Gator-21
87Leaf-32RR
87Sf/TPrev-3M
87T-319
88D-227
88D/Best-280
88F-617
88F/Slug-41
88Gator-21
88Leaf-158
88OPC-22
88Panini/St-70
88S-154
88S/YS/II-39
88T-22
88T/Big-156
88T/St-210
89B-76
89Classic-61
89Classic/Up/2-195
89D-232
89D/Best-112
89F-413
89F/LL-38
89KennerFig-145
89OPC-315
89Panini/St-320
89RedFoley/St-116
89S-282
89Sf-4
89T-315
89T/Big-68
89T/Coins-54
89T/Mini-52
89T/St-213
89T/UK-76
89UD-250
90B-325
90Classic/Up-48
90D-310
90D/BestAL-6
90D/Bon/MVP-BC24
90F-503
90F/AwardWin-39
90F/BBMVP-39
90F/Can-503
90HotPlay/St-44
90Leaf-206
90OPC-595
90Panini/St-59
90PublInt/St-569
90PublInt/St-606
90RedFoley/St-93
90S-230
90S/100St-11
90T-595
90T/Big-288
90T/DH-65
90T/St-214
90T/TVAS-32
90UD-574
90WonderBrd-15
91B-58
91Classic/200-101
91Classic/II-T0
91D-546
91F-379
91Indian/McDon-26
91Leaf-6
91Leaf/Stud-49
91OPC-445
91S-110
91StCl-428
91T-445
91UD-236
91Ultra-117
92B-46
92B-578FOIL
92Classic/Game200-193
92D-483
92D/DK-DK23
92F-124
92F/Up-84
92L-384
92L/BlkGold-384
92OPC-735
92OPC/Premier-44
92Panini-52
92Pinn-327
92Reds/Kahn-29
92S-371
92S/RookTr-10T
92StCl-673
92Studio-30
92T-735
92T/Gold-735
92T/GoldWin-735
92T/Kids-72
92TX-38
92UD-336
92UD-765
92UD-95
92Ultra-487
93B-320
93D-634
93F-399
93F/Final-80
93Flair-67
93L-334
93Mother/Ast-17
93OPC-392
93OPC/Premier-86
93Pac/Spanish-481
93Pinn-507
93S-566
93Select-179
93Select/Ace-18
93Select/RookTr-99T
93StCl-165
93StCl-608
93StCl/1stDay-165
93StCl/1stDay-608
93StCl/Ast-9
93Studio-59
93T-515
93T/Finest-137
93T/FinestRef-137
93T/Gold-515
93T/Tr-32T
93TripleP-232M
93UD-695
93USPlayC/Ace-4S
93Ultra-397
94B-6
94D-228
94F-500
94L-379
94OPC-157
94Pac/Cr-275
94Pinn-163
94Pinn/Artist-163
94Pinn/Museum-163
94S-502
94StCl-113
94StCl/1stDay-113
94StCl/Gold-113
94T-125
94T/Finest-99
94T/FinestRef-99
94T/Gold-125
94UD-484
94UD/SP-32
94Ultra-210
Swindle, Allen
83Tampa-22
Swingle, Paul
89BendB/Legoe-10
90Boise/ProC-3312
91PalmSp/ProC-2014
92ClBest-339
92MidldA/OneHour-23
92MidldA/ProC-4028
92MidldA/SB-471
92Sky/AASingl-201
93Vanco/ProC-2598
94T-765M
94T/Gold-765M
Swingle, Russ
52Park-94
Swinton, Jermaine
90Ashvl/ClBest-23
91Ashvl/ProC-581
91ClBest/Singl-77
92B-137
92BurlAs/ClBest-5
92BurlAs/ProC-560
92UD/ML-316
Swisher, Steve
74Wichita-123
75OPC-63
75T-63
75T/M-63
76OPC-173
76SSPC-319
76T-173
77OPC-23
77T-419
78T-252
79T-304
80T-163
81T-541
81T/Tr-840
82T-764
83D-633
83Richm-12
83T-612
86Watlo-27MG
87Wmsprt-18
88ColoSp/CMC-24
88ColoSp/ProC-1546
89Jacks/GS-20
90AAASingl/ProC-291MG
90ProC/Singl-684MG
90T/TVMets-62MG
90Tidew/CMC-27MG
90Tidew/ProC-560MG
91AAA/LineD-574MG
91AAAGame/ProC-50MG
91Tidew/LineD-574MG
91Tidew/ProC-2526MG
92Bingham/ProC-532
92Bingham/SB-74MG
Swob, Tim
87Tampa-9
Swoboda, Ron
65T-533R
66OPC-35
66T-35
66T/RO-23
66T/RO-90
67CokeCap/AS-28
67CokeCap/NLAS-26
67CokeCap/YMet-27
67OPC-186M
67T-186M
67T-264
67T/Test/SU-5
68Bz-13
68OPC-114
68T-114
68T/3D
68T/ActionSt-15AM
68T/ActionSt-2AM
68T/Post-17
69Citgo-18
69MB-268
69MLB/St-171
69MLBPA/Pin-57
69T-585
69T/St-70
69Trans-44
70MLB/St-83
70OPC-431
70T-431
70Trans/M-25
71MLB/St-166
71OPC-665
71T-665
72MB-337
72OPC-8
72T-8
73OPC-314
73T-314
81TCMA-322M
91WIZMets-390
92Yank/WIZ70-147
94Mets/69-9
Swoope, Bill
77Clinton
78Clinton
79LodiD-13
Swope, Mark
90AR-24
91ClBest/Singl-74
91Visalia/ClBest-10
91Visalia/ProC-1741
92FtMyr/ProC-2747
92Miracle/ClBest-11
Sykes, Bob
77T-491R
79T-569
80T-223
81F-533

81T-348
82Colum-12
82Colum/Pol-38
82D-640
82F-130
82Nashvl-25
82T-108
Sylvester, John
77Cedar
Sylvia, Dave
75BurlB
Sylvia, Ronald
81Redwd-7
82Redwd-16
83Nashua-9
Syverson, Dain
85Water-25
86Water-24
87Wmsprt-1
Szczechowski, Dennis
92Clinton/ProC-3597
92Everett/ClBest-22
92Everett/ProC-1690
Szczepanski, Joe
91Geneva/ClBest-20
91Geneva/ProC-4215
92WinSalem/ClBest-22
92WinSalem/ProC-1207
Szekely, Joe
83CharR-3
85VeroB-6
87SanAn-17
87TexLgAS-35
89Albuq/CMC-19
89Albuq/ProC-77
90AAASingl/ProC-354
90ProC/Singl-337
90Syrac/CMC-11
90Syrac/MerchB-25
90Syrac/ProC-574
90Syrac/Team-25
91AAA/LineD-444
91Richm/Bob-18
91Richm/LineD-444
91Richm/ProC-2572
91Richm/Team-12
92Richm/Bleach-16
92Richm/Comix-22
92Richm/ProC-381
92Richm/SB-444
93Macon/ClBest-28CO
93Macon/ProC-1419CO
Szeryk, Neil
91OKSt-26
Szotkiewicz, Ken
71OPC-749
71T-749
Szymarek, Paul
81Shrev-12
82Phoenix
Szymczak, Dave
83Nashvl-24
84BuffB-13
Szynal, Jon
89Spartan/ProC-1031
89Spartan/Star-22
Tabacheck, Marty
V362-23
Tabaka, Jeff
86James-25
87WPalmB-5
88WPalmB/Star-23
89Reading/Best-7
89Reading/ProC-663
91AA/LineD-520
91Reading/LineD-520
91Reading/ProC-1371
92ElPaso/ProC-3921
92ElPaso/SB-222
93ClBest/MLG-154
93T-586
93T/Gold-586
Tabb, Jerry
78T-224
Tabeling, Bob
86Visalia-21
Tabler, Pat
77FtLaud
81Colum-16
82D-529
82Iowa-10
83D-552
83F-509
84D-536
84F-552
84Nes/792-329
84T-329
84T/St-252
84Wheat/Ind-10
85D-460
85F-456
85Leaf-76
85OPC-158
85Polar/Ind-10
85T-158
85T/St-250
86D-129
86F-594
86Leaf-52
86OPC-66
86OhHenry-10
86T-674
86T/St-212
86T/Tatt-8M
87D-254
87D/OD-107
87F-261
87F/Slug-42
87Gator-10
87GenMills/Book-2M
87Leaf-182
87OPC-77
87Sf-66
87Sf/TPrev-3M
87Stuart-18M
87T-575
87T/Mini-52
87T/St-205
88D-219
88D/AS-17
88F-618
88F-633M
88F/Hottest-43
88F/Mini-20
88F/St-22
88F/Up-U36
88Gator-10
88KennerFig-111
88OPC-230
88Panini/St-81
88RedFoley/St-87
88S-23
88S/Tr-22T
88Sf-205
88T-230
88T/Big-173
88T/St-204
88T/Tr-118T
89B-125
89D-326
89F-294
89KMart/Lead-19
89KennerFig-146
89OPC-56
89Panini/St-359
89S-391
89Sf-172
89T-56
89T/Big-67
89T/St-6
89Tastee/Discs-3
89UD-233
89Woolwth-18
90D-444
90F-119
90F/Can-119
90OPC-727
90PublInt/St-357
90S-242
90Sf-218
90T-727
90T/Big-89
90UD-142
91B-28
91F/Up-U67
91Leaf-443
91OPC-433
91OPC/Premier-118
91S-811
91S/RookTr-22T
91S/ToroBJ-19
91T-433
91Tor/Fire-15
91WIZMets-393
92BJ/Fire-27
92OPC-333
92S-312
92StCl-333
92T-333
92T/Gold-333
92T/GoldWin-333
92UD-203
93BJ/D/45-12
93F-700
93OPC-270
93StCl-160
93StCl/1stDay-160
Tabor, Greg
82BurlR/Frit-15
82BurlR/TCMA-10
84Tulsa-19
85OKCty-28
86OKCty-23
87OKCty-21
88F-644R
88Iowa/CMC-18
88Iowa/ProC-548
93Rang/Keeb-352
Tabor, Jim
39PlayBall-14
40PlayBall-36
41DP-58
49B/PCL-33
92Conlon/Sport-542
R303/A
V351B-41
Tabor, Scott
83BirmB-15
86Omaha/ProC-27
86Omaha/TCMA-16
Taborn, Earl
92Negro/RetortII-38
Tackett, Gary
90NE-23
Tackett, Jack
(Jeff)
85Newar-5
87CharlO/WBTV-9
88CharlK/Pep-8
89RochR/CMC-17
89RochR/ProC-1645
90AAASingl/ProC-463
90ProC/Singl-310
90RochR/CMC-9
90RochR/ProC-706
90Rochester/L&U-13
91AAA/LineD-469
91B-106
91RochR/LineD-469
91RochR/ProC-1906
92D/Rook-114
92L-411
92L/BlkGold-411
92S/RookTr-86T
92StCl-383
92T/91Debut-168
92T/Tr-115T
92T/TrGold-115T
92Ultra-310
93D-529
93F-553
93Pac/Spanish-351
93S-355
93Select-294
93StCl-186
93StCl/1stDay-186
93T-6
93T/Gold-6
93UD-517
93Ultra-147
94S-136
94S/GoldR-136
94StCl/Team-294
94T-664
94T/Gold-664
94T/Prev-6
Tafoya, Dennis
88Ashvl/ProC-1070
88AubAs/ProC-1951
89Osceola/Star-24
90ColMud/Best-24
90ColMud/ProC-1348
90ColMud/Star-23
91AA/LineD-118
91CaroMud/LineD-118
91CaroMud/ProC-1086
92CaroMud/SB-144
Tafoya, Rod
89Boise/ProC-1987
90Erie/Star-26
Taft, Dennie
83Clinton/Frit-24
Taft, Steve
90AR-32M
Taft, Tim
88Bend/Legoe-14
88Clearw/Star-24
Taft, William Howard
90BBWit-107
Tagi, Anthony
88Fresno/Cal-20
88Fresno/ProC-1234
Tagle, Hank
91Utica/ClBest-26
91Utica/ProC-3239
92SoBend/ClBest-23
92SoBend/ProC-176
Tagliaferri, Gino
90Fayette/ProC-2417
90Niagara/Pucko-11
Taguchi, Dragon
89Salinas/Cal-132
89Salinas/ProC-1809
Tahan, Kevin
90ProC/Singl-664
90Savan/ProC-2078
91Spring/ClBest-25
91Spring/ProC-752
92Spring/ClBest-20
92Spring/ProC-873
Taitt, D.
29Exh/4-18
Takach, Dave
87Spring/Best-14
88Salem/Star-20
Takacs, John
77Ashvl
Takahashi, Shigeyuki
92Niagara/ClBest-28CO
92Niagara/ProC-3344CO
Takao, Scott
92SoBend/ClBest-27TR
Takara, Steven
87Hawaii-15
Talamantez, Greg
85Newar-4
86Hagers-24
87CharlO/WBTV-35
88FSLAS/Star-22
88StLucie/Star-22
89Jacks/GS-1
91AA/LineD-643
91Wmsprt/LineD-643
91Wmsprt/ProC-292
Talanoa, Scott
92Beloit/ClBest-7
92Beloit/ProC-415
92ClBest-362
92MidwLAS/Team-44
94B-505
94FExcel-88
Talbert, Louis
90AppFox/Box-27
90AppFox/ProC-2095
90ProC/Singl-699
91AA/LineD-419
91London/LineD-419
91Memphis/ProC-655
Talbot, Bob D.
52Mother-16
54T-229
55B-137
94T/Arc54-229
Talbot, Fred
65OPC-58
65T-58
66T-403
66T/RO-104
66T/RO-91
67CokeCap/YMet-5
67T-517
68T-577
69T-332
70OPC-287
70T-287
72MB-338
81TCMA-467
92Yank/WIZ60-123
Talbott, Rick
92LitSun/HSPros-17
Talbott, Shawn
86Ashvl-27
87Ashvl-18
Talford, Calvin
89Martins/Star-29
Tallent, Ron
91Boise/ClBest-16
91Boise/ProC-3892
Tallman, Troy
92Kane/ClBest-12
92Kane/ProC-94
Talton, Marion
(Tim)
67T-603R
Tam, Andy
79Ashvl/TCMA-8
Tamarez, Adame
92Clinton/ClBest-20
92Clinton/ProC-3606
Tamarez, Carlos
90Madison/ProC-2279
90SoOreg/ProC-3437
Tamargo, John
78Spring/Wiener-10
79Pol/Giants-30
79T-726R
80OPC-351R
80T-680
81D-210
81F-152
81OPC-35DP
81T-519
82Miami-22
87Lynch-22
91StLucie/ClBest-26MG
91StLucie/ProC-727MG
92StLucie/ClBest-26MG
92StLucie/ProC-1763
93StLucie/ProC-2937
Tambay, Patrick
72Dimanche*-143
Tamulis, Vito
39PlayBall-139
40PlayBall-145
41G-17
90Target-788
R309/2
R314
V355-101
Tanabe, Collin
82Beloit/Frit-13
Tanabe, Nori
86SanJose-20
Tanana, Frank
74OPC-605R
74T-605R
75OPC-16
75T-16
75T/M-16
76Ho-101
76K-30
76OPC-204LL
76OPC-490
76SSPC-189
76T-204LL
76T-490
77BurgChef-122
77Ho-63
77Ho/Twink-63
77K-45
77OPC-105
77T-200
78Ho-101
78K-54
78OPC-65
78OPC-7LL
78PapaG/Disc-33
78SSPC/270-211
78T-207LL
78T-600
78Tastee/Discs-23
78Wiffle/Discs-73
79Ho-47
79OPC-274
79T-530
80OPC-57
80T-105
81Coke
81D-171
81F-276
81OPC-369
81T-369
81T/HT
81T/St-56
81T/Tr-841
82D-326
82F-309
82OPC-4

82T-792
82T/Tr-117T
83D-447
83F-581
83Rang-28
83T-272
84D-98
84F-432
84Nes/792-479
84OPC-276
84Rang-28
84T-479
85D-220
85D-9DK
85D/DKsuper-9
85F-570
85FunFoodPin-133
85Leaf-9DK
85OPC-55
85T-55
85T/St-348
86Cain's-17
86D-491
86F-239
86Leaf-241
86OPC-124
86T-592
87Cain's-20
87Coke/Tigers-5
87D-152
87F-164
87F/Hottest-40
87OPC-231
87Seven-DT10
87Sf/TPrev-15M
87T-726
88D-461
88D/Best-259
88F-71
88F/Slug-42
88OPC-177
88Panini/St-86
88Pep/T-26
88Pol/T-11
88S-490
88Sf-133
88T-177
88T/St-264
89B-92
89D-90
89D/Best-91
89F-147
89Mara/Tigers-26
89OPC-299
89Panini/St-336
89Pol/Tigers-26
89RedFoley/St-117
89S-112
89Sf-103
89Smok/Angels-9
89T-603
89T-609TL
89T/LJN-140
89T/St-275
89UD-391
90B-343
90Classic-108
90CokeK/Tiger-23
90D-180
90D/BestAL-48
90F-616
90F/Can-616
90KayBee-30
90Leaf-87
90OPC-343
90Panini/St-72
90PublInt/St-483
90S-57
90T-343
90T/Big-119
90T/St-277
90UD-516
91CokeK/Tiger-26
91D-508
91F-354
91Leaf-497
91Leaf/Stud-57
91OPC-236A
91OPC-236B
91Pol/Tiger-12
91S-328
91StCl-158
91T-236A
91T-236B
91UD-369
91Ultra-128
92D-111
92F-145
92L-21
92L/BlkGold-21
92OPC-458
92Pinn-198
92S-271
92StCl-416
92Studio-177
92T-458
92T/Gold-458
92T/GoldWin-458
92TripleP-249
92UD-605
92USPlayC/Tiger-1S
92USPlayC/Tiger-9H
93D-599
93F-611
93F/Final-106
93L-365
93Mets/Kahn-29
93OPC-288
93Pac/Spanish-547
93Panini-120
93Pinn-542
93Rang/Keeb-353
93S-652
93Select-398
93Select/RookTr-127T
93StCl-267
93StCl/1stDay-267
93T-53
93T/Gold-53
93UD-626
93UD-68
93Ultra-434
94S-538

Tanderys, Jeff
91Hamil/ClBest-12
91Hamil/ProC-4039
92Hamil/ClBest-1
92Hamil/ProC-1592

Tanks, Talmage
76BurlB

Tanksley, Scott
93MissSt-41

Tannahill, Kevin
89Helena/SP-23
91CharlR/ClBest-14
91CharlR/ProC-1318

Tannehill, Jesse
T206

Tannehill, Lee Ford
11Helmar-17
E254
E90/1
M116
S74-9
T202
T205
T206
T207

Tanner, Bruce
85BuffB-25
85F/Up-U116
86BuffB-21
86F-218
87Tacom-8
88Huntsvl/BK-22
89Tacoma/ProC-1540
90Spokane/SportP-27CO
91CharRain/ClBest-25CO
91CharRain/ProC-112CO
91SALAS/ProC-SAL6CO
92HighD/ClBest-30CO

Tanner, Chuck
55JC-18
55T-161
56T-69
57T-392
58T-91
59T-234
60L-115
60T-279
61BeeHive-23
71OPC-661MG
71T-661MG
72OPC-98MG
72T-98MG
73OPC-356MG
73T-356MG
74OPC-221MG
74T-221MG
75OPC-276MG
75T-276MG
75T/M-276MG
76SSPC-151MG
76T-656MG
77T-354MG
78T-494MG
79T-244MG
79TCMA-63
81D-257MG
81F-367MG
81T-683R
82D-150
83D-124
83T-696
84Nes/792-291MG
84T-291MG
85T-268MG
86Pol/Atl-7MG
86T-351MG
86T/Tr-107T
87Smok/Atl-26MG
87T-593MG
88T-134MG

Tanner, Ed
(Eddie)
81Batavia-16
82Watlo/B-19
82Watlo/Frit-22
83Spring/Frit-8
84ArkTr-1
86ArkTr-24
87Nashvl-19
88Nashvl/Team-23
89Nashvl/CMC-19
89Nashvl/ProC-1287
89Nashvl/Team-24
90AAASingl/ProC-555
90Nashvl/CMC-21
90Nashvl/ProC-243
90ProC/Singl-146
90SpringDG/Best-6

Tanner, Mark
74Gaston

Tanner, Roy
76Watlo
77DaytB
82CharR-24
83CharR-24

Tanzi, Bobby
79Ashvl/TCMA-16
80Wausau-12

Tanzi, Michael
82AppFx/Frit-25
83GlenF-20

Tapais, Luis
86Kenosha-23

Tapani, Kevin
86Cram/NWL-64
87Modesto-12
88Jacks/GS-23
89Tidew/CMC-10
89Tidew/ProC-1972
90B-407
90Classic/III-16
90D-473
90D/BestAL-93
90D/Rook-35
90F/Up-110
90Leaf-269
90OPC-227
90S/Tr-82T
90S/YS/II-31
90T-227
90T/89Debut-126
90T/Big-225
90UD-87
91B-322
91Classic/200-42
91D-116
91F-625
91Leaf-128
91MajorLg/Pins-13
91OPC-633
91Panini/FrSt-307
91Panini/St-249
91S-60
91S/100RisSt-52
91StCl-161
91T-633
91T/JumboR-27
91UD-434
91Ultra-196
91WIZMets-394
92B-552
92Classic/Game200-104
92Classic/I-87
92D-236
92F-219
92L-14
92L/BlkGold-14
92OPC-313
92Pinn-176
92S-507
92StCl-433
92T-313
92T/Gold-313
92T/GoldWin-313
92TripleP-98
92UD-624
92USPlayC/Twin-13S
92USPlayC/Twin-9H
92Ultra-98
93B-269
93D-443
93F-274
93L-404
93OPC-361
93Pac/Spanish-178
93Pinn-334
93S-45
93Select-130
93Select/Ace-24
93StCl-492
93StCl/1stDay-492
93T-420
93T/Gold-420
93TripleP-240
93UD-313
93Ultra-237
94B-628
94D-115
94F-219
94L-52
94OPC-246
94Pac/Cr-367
94Pinn-54
94Pinn/Artist-54
94Pinn/Museum-54
94S-351
94Select-144
94StCl-117
94StCl/1stDay-117
94StCl/Gold-117
94T-185
94T/Finest-21
94T/FinestRef-21
94T/Gold-185
94TripleP-259
94UD-439
94UD/CollC-272
94UD/CollC/Gold-272
94UD/CollC/Silv-272
94Ultra-395

Tapia, Dagoberto
90Martins/ProC-3208

Tapia, Jose
87QuadC-7
87VeroB-2
88PalmSp/Cal-93
88PalmSp/ProC-1446

Tappe, Elvin
53Mother-48
55B-51
55T-129
55T/DH-94
58T-184
60T-457C

Tarangelo, Joseph
84Visalia-23

Tarasco, Tony
89Pulaski/ProC-1904
90Foil/Best-100
90Sumter/Best-23
90Sumter/ProC-2449
91Durham/ClBest-21
91Durham/ProC-1675
92Greenvl/ProC-1166
92Greenvl/SB-245
92Sky/AASingl-103
92UD/ML-82
93B-522
93Brave/LykePerf-29
93Brave/LykeStand-35
93F/Final-5
93FExcel/ML-6
93L-452
93Richm/Bleach-12
93Richm/Pep-11
93StCl-696
93StCl/1stDay-696
93StCl/Brave-29
93UD-623
94B-77
94D-287
94F-377
94Finest-422
94L-2
94Pac/Cr-23
94Pinn-256
94Pinn/Artist-256
94Pinn/Museum-256
94S-617
94StCl-272
94StCl/1stDay-272
94StCl/Gold-272
94StCl/Team-51
94T-442
94T/Gold-442
94UD-206
94UD/CollC-273
94UD/CollC/Gold-273
94UD/CollC/Silv-273
94UD/ElecD-206
94Ultra-451

Tarchione, Travis
88CapeCod/Sum-23
89SLCity-6OF

Tardif, Marc
72Dimanche*-108

Tarin, Fernando
77QuadC

Tarjick, Dave
90Pittsfld/Pucko-29PER

Tarnow, Greg
81QuadC-3
83AppFx/Frit-21

Tarrh, Jamey
90WichSt-33

Tarrolly, Dave
83Beloit/Frit-17GM

Tartabull, Danny
82Water-14
83Chatt-6
84Cram/PCL-170
85Cram/PCL-94
85D-27RR
85F-647R
86D-38
86D/Rook-45
86F-476
86F/Mini-99
86Mother/Mar-22
86Sf-178R
86Sf/Rook-22
86T/Tr-108T
87Classic/Up-145
87D-147
87D/OD-200
87F-598
87F/Up-U117
87Leaf-250
87OPC-332
87RedFoley/St-97
87Sf-23
87Sf/TPrev-13M
87T-476
87T/Coins-25
87T/Gloss60-19
87T/JumboR-19
87T/St-223
87T/St-306
87T/Tr-120T
87ToysRUs-28
88Classic/Blue-235
88D-177
88D-5DK
88D/Best-287
88D/DKsuper-5DK
88F-271
88F/AwardWin-42
88F/Excit-41
88F/Mini-28
88F/SS-40
88F/St-34
88KayBee-30
88KennerFig-112
88Leaf-190
88Leaf-5DK
88OPC-211
88Panini/St-112

88S-106
88S/YS/II-5
88Sf-19
88Smok/Royals-4
88T-724
88T/Big-230
88T/Coins-29
88T/Mini-16
88T/Revco-26
88T/St-257
88T/UK-78
89B-128
89Chatt/II/Team-29
89D-61
89D/Best-39
89D/GrandSlam-10
89F-295
89F/BBMVP's-37
89KennerFig-147
89OPC-275
89Panini/St-360
89RedFoley/St-118
89S-105
89S/HotStar-19
89Sf-46
89T-275
89T/Big-107
89T/Coins-55
89T/St-267
89Tastee/Discs-4
89UD-329
90B-375
90D-322
90D/BestAL-128
90F-120
90F/Can-120
90Leaf-99
90OPC-540
90Panini/St-90
90Publlnt/St-358
90S-244
90S/100St-72
90Sf-129
90T-540
90T/Ames-33
90T/Big-56
90T/HillsHM-9
90T/St-274
90UD-656
91B-294
91Classic/200-43
91D-463
91DennyGS-16
91F-572
91Leaf-147
91OPC-90
91Panini/FrSt-282
91Pol/Royal-22
91S-515
91StCl-272
91T-90
91UD-523
91UD/FinalEd-89F
91USPlayC/AS-JK
91Ultra-158
92B-550
92CJ/DII-35
92Classic/Game200-167
92Classic/I-88
92Classic/II-T98
92D-26AS
92D-676
92D/Up-U17
92F-171
92F/ASIns-12
92F/TmLIns-18
92F/Up-45
92Kenner/Fig-42
92KingB-13
92L-406
92L/BlkGold-406
92MSA/Ben-13
92OPC-145
92OPC/Premier-93
92P-30
92Panini-98
92Pinn-309SH
92Pinn-547
92Pinn/TeamP-8
92Rem/Pr-P13
92Rem/Pr-P14
92Rem/Pr-P15
92Rem/Pr-P16
92Rem/Pr-P18
92Rem/Pr-P20
92S-145
92S/100SS-90
92S/Impact-64
92S/RookTr-3T
92StCl-191
92StCl-690
92StCl/Dome-183
92StCl/MPhoto-14
92Studio-220
92T-145
92T/Gold-145
92T/GoldWin-145
92T/Kids-106
92T/McDonB-26
92T/Tr-116T
92T/TrGold-116T
92TripleP/Gal-GS5
92UD-237
92UD-746
92UD-88TC
92UD/HRH-HR11
92USPlayC/Ace-2D
92USPlayC/Ace-4C
92Ultra-417
92Ultra-77
93B-299
93Classic/Gamel-90
93Colla/DM-106
93D-549
93D/Spirit-SG16
93DennyGS-28
93F-286
93F/Fruit-59
93Flair-253
93L-119
93MSA/Metz-20
93OPC-308
93Pac/Spanish-213
93Pac/SpanishGold-19
93Panini-153
93Pinn-168
93Pinn-478I
93Pinn/HRC-33
93Pinn/Slug-10
93S-35
93S-515HL
93Select-12
93Select/StatL-50
93StCl-85
93StCl/1stDay-85
93StCl/MPhoto-11
93StCl/Y-4
93T-330
93T/Finest-167
93T/FinestRef-167
93T/Gold-330
93TripleP-207
93UD-242
93UD-839TC
93UD/FunPack-209
93UD/HRH-HR13
93UD/SP-268
93Ultra-602
94B-577
94Church-23
94D-414
94F-248
94Finest-325
94Flair-88
94Kraft-11
94L-353
94L/Clean-6
94OPC-8
94Pac/AllLat-11
94Pac/Cr-439
94Pac/Gold-10
94Panini-105
94Pinn-81
94Pinn/Artist-81
94Pinn/Museum-81
94Pinn/Run-21
94S-373
94Sf/2000-118
94StCl-410
94StCl/1stDay-410
94StCl/Gold-410
94StCl/Team-209
94Studio-218
94T-670
94T/Gold-670
94TripleP-279
94UD-212
94UD/ElecD-212
94UD/SP-200
94Ultra-102

Tartabull, Jose Jr.
86Cram/NWL-108
87Wausau-8
88RedFoley/St-88
88SanBern/Best-13
88SanBern/Cal-36
89SanBern/Best-18
89SanBern/Cal-79

Tartabull, Jose
62T-451
63T-449
64T-276
66OPC-143
66T-143
67CokeCap/RedSox-17
67OPC-56
67T-56
67T/Test/RSox-21
68T-555
69MB-269
69T-287
70OPC-481
70T-481
72MB-339
81TCMA-331

Tarumi, Kanenori
88Miami/Star-11

Tarutis, Pete
91James/CIBest-26
91James/ProC-3545

Tarver, LaSchelle
82Lynch-2
84Tidew-21
85IntLgAS-6
85Tidew-13
86Pawtu-24
87Pawtu-10
87Pawtu/TCMA-19

Tasby, Willie
59T-143
60L-100
60T-322
61P-51
61T-458
61T/St-117
62J-70
62P-70
62P/Can-70
62Salada-21
62Shirriff-21
62T-462
91Crown/Orio-449

Tata, Terry
88TM/Umpire-16
89TM/Umpire-14
89TM/Umpire-60M
90TM/Umpire-14

Tatar, Kevin
90Billings/ProC-3222
91CharWh/CIBest-11
91CharWh/ProC-2888
91CIBest/Singl-294
92B-621
92Chatt/SB-197
92CIBest-73
92Sky/AASingl-89
92UD/ML-306

Tatarian, Dean
89Utica/Pucko-24
90Utica/Pucko-10
91Saraso/CIBest-20
91Saraso/ProC-1122
92BBCity/CIBest-4
92BBCity/ProC-3854
92CIBest-139

Tate, Bennie
91Conlon/Sport-220
R314/Can
V355-80

Tate, Chuck
86Cram/NWL-16
86Everett/Pop-32

Tate, Coray
87BYU-7M

Tate, Edward
N172

Tate, Henry
31Exh/4-20

Tate, Lee W.
59T-544

Tate, Michael
88Boise/ProC-1606

Tate, Randy L.
76OPC-549
76SSPC-555
76T-549
78Colum
91WIZMets-395

Tate, Stuart
(Stu)
84Everett/Cram-12
85Fresno/Pol-19
86Shrev-24
87Shrev-20
88Shrev/ProC-1295
89AAA/ProC-52
89Phoenix/CMC-9
89Phoenix/ProC-1491
90F-643R
90F/Can-643M
90T/89Debut-127
91AAA/LineD-395
91Phoenix/LineD-395
91Phoenix/ProC-67

Tatis, Bernie
83Kinston/Team-26
86Knoxvl-23
87Knoxvl-16
87SLAS-4
88BuffB/CMC-14
88BuffB/ProC-1475
90AAASingl/ProC-693
90OkCty/CMC-20
90OkCty/ProC-447
90ProC/Singl-170
91AA/LineD-95
91Canton/LineD-95
91Canton/ProC-993
91ColoSp/ProC-2194
93LimeR/Winter-96

Tatis, Fausto
90Bakers/Cal-231
90Yakima/Team-33
91Bakers/Cal-3

Tatis, Rafael
73Cedar
74Cedar
75Dubuq

Tatis, Ramon
92GulfCM/ProC-3482

Tatsuno, Derek
82EIPaso-22
87Hawaii-5

Tatterson, Gary
91Watertn/CIBest-12
91Watertn/ProC-3367
92Kinston/CIBest-8

Tatum, Jarvis
70T-642R
71MLB/St-334
71OPC-159
71T-159

Tatum, Jim
85Spokane/Cram-24
86CharRain-25
87CharRain-19
88Wichita-18
90Canton/Best-12
90Canton/ProC-1302
90ProC/Singl-774
91AA/LineD-197
91EIPaso/LineD-197
91EIPaso/ProC-2757
92AAA/ASG/SB-145
92Denver/ProC-2651
92Denver/SB-145
92ProC/Tomorrow-86
92Sky/AAASingl-71
93B-339FOIL
93D-341RR
93F-416
93F/Final-45
93Pac/Spanish-439
93Pinn-587
93StCl-730
93StCl/1stDay-730
93StCl/Rockie-25
93T-691
93T/Gold-691
93UD-13SR
93UD-761
93USPlayC/Rockie-1C
93USPlayC/Rockie-2H
93Ultra-360
94F-455
94Pac/Cr-208
94S-311
94S/GoldR-311
94StCl/Team-120

Tatum, Ken
70MLB/St-180
70T-658
71MLB/St-335
71OPC-601
71T-601
72MB-340
72T-772
73OPC-463
73T-463

Tatum, Reece
(Goose)
76Laugh/Clown-16
86Negro/Frit-107

Tatum, Tommy
90Target-1082

Tatum, Willie
88Elmira-19
89WinHaven/Star-23
90LynchRS/Team-8
91LynchRS/CIBest-18
91LynchRS/ProC-1208
92NewBrit/ProC-443
92NewBrit/SB-497
92ProC/Tomorrow-21
92Sky/AASingl-215
93Pawtu/Ball-23

Taubensee, Edward
(Eddie)
88Greens/ProC-1558
88SALAS/GS-6
89Cedar/Best-12
89Cedar/ProC-937
89Cedar/Star-19
90Cedar/Best-3
90Cedar/ProC-2325
90CedarDG/Best-11
90Foil/Best-184
90MidwLgAS/GS-50
90ProC/Singl-876
91AAA/LineD-76
91ColoSp/LineD-76
91ColoSp/ProC-2187
92B-697
92Classic/Game200-166
92D-18RR
92D/Rook-115
92L/GRook-9
92Mother/Ast-11
92OPC-427
92OPC/Premier-136
92Pinn-538
92S-871
92S/100RisSt-29
92StCl-790
92Studio-40
92T-427
92T/91Debut-169
92T/Gold-427
92T/GoldWin-427
92T/Tr-117T
92T/TrGold-117T
92UD-757
92Ultra-497
93B-476
93D-560
93F-55
93L-362
93Mother/Ast-18
93Pac/Spanish-482
93Panini-169
93Pinn-140
93S-108
93Select-333
93StCl-329
93StCl/1stDay-329
93StCl/Ast-2
93T-117
93T/Gold-117
93TripleP-17
93UD-296
93USPlayC/Rook-9S
93Ultra-46
94D-256
94F-501
94Pac/Cr-276
94S-456
94StCl-168
94StCl/1stDay-168
94StCl/Gold-168

94T-68
94T/Gold-68
Tauken, Daniel
87Penin-5
Taussig, Don
62Salada-186
62Shirriff-186
62T-44
89Smok/Ast-22
Tavarez, Alfonso
85Utica-15
86BurlEx-24
Tavarez, Davis
83Clinton/Frit-12
84Everett/Cram-21
Tavarez, Hector
90MedHat/Best-27
91MedHat/ProC-4109
91MedHat/SportP-6
92Dunedin/ClBest-21
Tavarez, Jesus
90Penin/Star-21
91CalLgAS-11
91SanBern/ClBest-24
91SanBern/ProC-2001
92ClBest-144
92Jacks/ProC-3723
92Jaxvl/SB-368
92Sky/AASingl-159
93LimeR/Winter-30
Tavarez, Juan
93Kinston/Team-25
Tavarez, Julian
92Burllnd/ClBest-18
92Burllnd/ProC-1657
93LimeR/Winter-89
94B-279
94D-627
94Pinn-411
94StCl-128
94StCl/1stDay-128
94StCl/Gold-128
94T-767M
94T/Gold-767M
94UD/CollC-274
94UD/CollC/Gold-274
94UD/CollC/Silv-274
Tavener, Jack
28Exh-46
29Exh/4-21
92Conlon/Sport-572
Taveras, Alex
74Cedar
75Iowa/TCMA-21
77T-474R
79Albuq-15
81Albuq/TCMA-18
82Albuq-18
83Albuq-10
84Cram/PCL-153
85BuffB-12
89Beloit/I/Star-26M
89Beloit/II/Star-25MG
Taveras, Frank
74OPC-607R
74T-607R
75OPC-277
75OPC-460NLCS
75T-277
75T-460NLCS
75T/M-277
75T/M-460NLCS
76OPC-36
76SSPC-583
76T-36
77BurgChef-184
77T-538
78OPC-4LL
78T-204LL
78T-685
79OPC-79
79T-165
80BK/PHR-32
80OPC-237
80T-456
81Coke
81D-154
81F-320
81OPC-343
81T-343
81T/HT
81T/St-196
82D-98
82Expo/Hygrade-22
82F-539
82Hygrade
82OPC-351
82T-782
82T/Tr-118T
91WIZMets-396
Taveras, Marcos
88StCath/ProC-2028
89Dunedin/Star-18
90Dunedin/Star-17
Taveras, Ramon
89Salem/Team-30
90FSLAS/Star-17
90Star/ISingl-21
90VeroB/Star-25
91AA/LineD-542
91SanAn/LineD-542
Tawwater, Darren
91OKSt-27
92OKSt-26
Taylor, Aaron
89Wythe/Star-25
90Hunting/ProC-3283
91Peoria/ClBest-9
91Peoria/ProC-1343
91Peoria/Team-13
92WinSalem/ClBest-23
92WinSalem/ProC-1208
93T-786M
93T/Gold-786M
Taylor, Andrew
86LitFalls-27
88Spring/Best-8
89Savan/ProC-368
Taylor, Antonio S.
(Tony)
58T-411
59T-62
60L-44
60T-294
61P-118
61T-411
61T/St-59
62J-193
62P-193
62P/Can-193
62Salada-156
62Shirriff-156
62T-77
62T/St-170
62T/bucks
63J-178
63P-178
63T-366
64PhilBull-23
64T-585
64T/Coins-113
64T/Coins-144AS
64T/St-9
65T-296
66T-585
67CokeCap/Phill-12
67OPC-126
67T-126
68T-327
69MB-270
69MLB/St-179
69OPC-108
69T-108
70MB-28
70MLB/St-95
70OPC-324
70T-324
71K-67
71MLB/St-190
71OPC-246
71Phill/Arco-12
71T-246
72MB-341
72OPC-511
72T-511
73OPC-29
73T-29
75OPC-574
75T-574
75T/M-574
76OPC-624
76SSPC-474
76T-624
78SSPC/270-41CO
78TCMA-133
88Phill/TastyK-29CO
89Phill/TastyK-33CO
90Shrev/ProC-1459CO
90Shrev/Star-27CO
91AA/LineD-325M
91Shrev/LineD-325CO
91Shrev/ProC-1840CO
92Phoenix/SB-400CO
Taylor, Ben
78Laugh/Black-12
90Negro/Star-10
Taylor, Bob
76Baton
Taylor, Bobbie
85Anchora-45
Taylor, Brien
91Classic/DP-1
91Classic/DPPr-3
92B-124
92ClBest-300
92ClBest/BBonusC-15
92ClBest/Pr-2
92ClBest/Pr-PR2
92ClBest/RBonus-BC15
92Classic/DP-86FB
92Classic/DPFoil-BC18FB
92Classic/DPPr-3
92Classic/DPPr-3
92FtLaud/ClBest-1
92FtLaud/ProC-2612
92FtLaud/Team-30
92OPC-6
92StCl/1stDP-2
92StCl/Dome-184
92T-6DP
92T/Gold-6
92T/Gold-7931
92T/GoldWin-6
92UD/ML-265
92UD/ML-49M
92UD/ML-57DS
92UD/ML/TPHolo-TP7
92UD/POY-PY26
93B-370FOIL
93B-679
93ClBest/Fisher-14
93ClBest/GLP-3
93ClBest/GPr-3
93ClBest/MLG-17
93ClBest/MLGPr-3
93ClBest/MLGPrev-2
93FExcel/ML-215
93FExcel/MLAS-1
93StCl-689
93StCl/1stDay-689
93StCl/MPhoto-30
93StCl/Y-22
93T-742M
93T/Gold-742M
93ToysRUs-19
94B-165
94ClBest/GAce-1
94ClBest/Gold-1
94FExcel-115
94FExcel/LL-17
94T-772M
94T/Gold-772M
94TedW-132
94TedW/Gardiner-8
Taylor, Bruce
77Evansvl/TCMA-23
78T-701R
Taylor, Carl
68T-559R
69T-357
70OPC-76
70T-76
71MLB/St-286
71MLB/St-432
71OPC-353
71T-353
71T/Coins-55
73OPC-99
73T-99
74OPC-627
74T-627
89Pac/SenLg-160
Taylor, Charles Gilbert
(Chuck)
63Pep/Tul
70OPC-119
70T-119
71OPC-606
71T-606
72OPC-407
72T-407
73OPC-176
73T-176
74OPC-412
74T-412
75OPC-58
75T-58
75T/M-58
76Expo/Redp-30
76SSPC-346
91WIZMets-397
Taylor, Charles Isam
(C.I.)
87Negro/Dixon-12
Taylor, Charley
85Osceola/Team-2
86ColumAst-24C
87Ashvl-11C
88Ashvl/ProC-1067
89Ashvl/ProC-944
90ColMud/Best-21CO
90ColMud/ProC-1362CO
90ColMud/Star-25CO
91AA/LineD-575M
91Jacks/LineD-575CO
91Jacks/ProC-942CO
92Jacks/ProC-4015CO
92Jacks/SB-350CO
Taylor, Dan
35BU-108
35Exh/4-2
90Target-789
93Conlon-898
R314
V355-72
Taylor, Dave
86AZ/Pol-17
87Beloit-25
88Stockton/Cal-195
88Stockton/ProC-729
90Miami/II/Star-24
Taylor, David Michael
(Mike)
88Gaston/ProC-998
89CharlR/Star-25
90Tulsa/ProC-1156
90Tulsa/Team-24
Taylor, Dorn
83AlexD-30
84PrWill-6
85Nashua-24
86Nashua-26
87F/Up-U118
87Vanco-24
88BuffB/CMC-9
88BuffB/Polar-5
88BuffB/ProC-1468
88TripleA/ASCMC-11
89AAA/ProC-9
89VFJuice-52
90AAAGame/ProC-22
90AAASingl/ProC-488
90BuffB/CMC-10
90BuffB/ProC-373
90BuffB/Team-26
90ProC/Singl-10
91Crown/Orio-451
Taylor, Dwight
82Watlo-23
83BuffB-21
84Maine-18
85Maine-28
86Omaha/TCMA-11
87Omaha-8
89ColoSp/CMC-19
89ColoSp/ProC-234
90AAASingl/ProC-232
90ColoSp/ProC-51
92Chatt/SB-198
92Nashvl/ProC-1847
Taylor, Eddie
45Centen-25
47Centen-29
Taylor, Edward
26Exh-7
Taylor, Gary
91Hamil/ClBest-14
91Hamil/ProC-4055
92Savan/ClBest-14
92Savan/ProC-677
Taylor, Gene
91Billing/SportP-16
91Billings/ProC-3769
92Cedar/ClBest-2
92Cedar/ProC-1088
Taylor, Harry
90Target-790
92TX-39
Taylor, Herb
52Laval-24
Taylor, Jack
26Exh-8
27Exh-4
28Exh-4
90HOF/St-13
WG3-44
Taylor, James
(Zack)
33G-152
51B-315MG
90Target-791
91Conlon/Sport-210
94TedW-113
V353-79
W753
Taylor, Jamie
92FrRow/DP-27
92Watertn/ClBest-1
92Watertn/ProC-3244
93B-205
93StCl/MurphyS-165
Taylor, Jeff
83Memphis/TCMA-14
85Greenvl/Team-17
86OrlanTw-20
88NE-16
88Oneonta/ProC-2070
89Oneonta/ProC-2101
Taylor, Joe
52Laval-57
Taylor, John W.
E107
E254
E270/1
Taylor, John
81Clinton-17
82AlexD-1
82AppFx/Frit-8
83AlexD-12
Taylor, Jonathon
92VeroB/ProC-2880
Taylor, Joseph C.
(Joe)
58T-451
60HenryH-22
60Union-13
61Union
91Crown/Orio-450
Taylor, Joseph F.
54JC
55JC
Taylor, Kerry
89Elizab/Star-25
89Star/IISingl-153
91Kenosha/ClBest-16
91Kenosha/ProC-2074
92Kenosha/ProC-604
93B-63
93F/Final-145
93Mother/Padre-26
94D-244
94F-675
Taylor, Lawrence
91StCl/Charter*-39
Taylor, Luther H.
(Dummy)
C46-41
E91
T206
WG3-45
Taylor, Mark
91Savan/ClBest-15
91Savan/ProC-1656
Taylor, Michael David
(Mike)
88StCath/ProC-2032
89Myrtle/ProC-1462
90Dunedin/Star-18
91AA/LineD-366
91Knoxvl/LineD-366
91Knoxvl/ProC-1776
92Knoxvl/SB-394
Taylor, Michael Larry
(Mike)
90StCath/ProC-3474
91MedHat/ProC-4101
91MedHat/SportP-7
92MedHat/SportP-22

92Myrtle/ClBest-20
92ProC/Tomorrow-176
Taylor, Michael Patrick
91BurlInd/ProC-3305
92Erie/ClBest-24
92Erie/ProC-1628
Taylor, Mike
81Watlo-28
82Watlo-24
86BirmB/Team-13
87Hawaii-12
Taylor, Phil
86Miami-24
Taylor, Randy
77SanJose-21
Taylor, Rob
90Clinton/Best-27
90Clinton/ProC-2544
90Foil/Best-129
90MidwLgAS/GS-51
91SanJose/ClBest-22
91SanJose/ProC-11
92Shrev/ProC-3871
92Shrev/SB-595
Taylor, Robert D.
(Hawk)
58T-164
61T-446
62T-406
63T-481
64T-381
65T-329
68OPC-52
68T-52
69T-239
91WIZMets-399
Taylor, Rodney Scott
(Scott)
88Elmira-4
90LynchRS/Team-24
91AA/LineD-472
91ClBest/Singl-83
91NewBrit/LineD-472
91NewBrit/ProC-353
92B-618
92Pawtu/ProC-923
92Pawtu/SB-368
92Sky/AAASingl-167
93D-267
93F/MLPII-13
93Pawtu/Ball-24
93T-456
93T/Gold-456
Taylor, Ron
62T-591R
63T-208R
64T-183
65T-568
66OPC-174
66T-174
67T-606
68T-421
69OPC-72
69T-72
69T/St-79
70OPC-419
70T-419
71MLB/St-167
71OPC-687
71T-687
72OPC-234
72T-234
81TCMA-449
81TCMA-466
91WIZMets-398
94Mets/69-15
Taylor, Sam
88CapeCod/Sum-121
89Batavia/ProC-1937
91ClBest/Singl-349
91Clearw/ClBest-24
91Clearw/ProC-1635
92Reading/ProC-590
92Reading/SB-545
92Sky/AASingl-238
Taylor, Sammy
58T-281
59T-193
60L-131
60T-162
61P-198
61T-253
61T/St-10
62J-189
62P-189
62P/Can-189
62Salada-164
62Shirriff-164
62T-274
63T-273
91WIZMets-400
Taylor, Scott Michael 1
(Scott)
89Wausau/GS-11
90Foil/Best-246
90SanBern/Best-15
90SanBern/Cal-93
90SanBern/ProC-2633
91AA/LineD-219
91Durham/ProC-1546
91Greenvl/LineD-219
92ElPaso/ProC-3922
92Greenvl/ProC-1153
92Greenvl/SB-246
Taylor, Scott Michael 2
(Scott)
88CharWh/Best-4
88Geneva/ProC-1651
89CharWh/Best-5
89CharWh/ProC-1757
89SALAS/GS-13
90WinSalem/Team-22
91AA/LineD-145
91CharlK/LineD-145
91CharlK/ProC-1692
92WinSalem/ClBest-8
92WinSalem/ProC-1212
Taylor, Steve 1
78Cr/PCL-39
79Colum-20
Taylor, Steve 2
90Elizab/Star-22
91B-121
91CLAS/ProC-CAR3
91Kenosha/ClBest-17
91Kenosha/ProC-2075
Taylor, Terry Derrell
83Wausau/Frit-9
86Chatt-24
87Calgary-17
88Calgary/ProC-781
89F-651R
89T-597
90Calgary/CMC-5
90Calgary/ProC-651
91Memphis/LineD-420
91Memphis/ProC-656
Taylor, Terry
88CapeCod/Sum-137
89BendB/Legoe-24
90AAASingl/ProC-116
90PalmSp/Cal-208
90PalmSp/ProC-2587
90ProC/Singl-432
91AA/LineD-420
91AA/LineD-447
91ClBest/Singl-328
91Midland/LineD-447
91MidldA/OneHour-29
91MidldA/ProC-444
92MidldA/OneHour-24
92MidldA/ProC-4035
92MidldA/SB-472
Taylor, Tex
52Laval-28
Taylor, Thomas
(Tommy)
89Bluefld/Star-24
90Wausau/Best-9
90Wausau/ProC-2122
90Wausau/Star-23
91ClBest/Singl-242
91Kane/ClBest-10
91Kane/Team-20
Taylor, Todd
91T/Tr-116T
92Elizab/ProC-3683
92StCl/Dome-185
Taylor, Tom
90MidwLgAS/GS-19
90ProC/Singl-871
92Freder/ClBest-22
92Freder/ProC-1806
Taylor, Wade
87Belling/Team-14
88FtLaud/Star-21
89PrWill/Star-21
90A&AASingle/ProC-20
90Albany/Best-9
90Albany/ProC-1176
90Albany/Star-20
90EastLAS/ProC-EL12
90Foil/Best-154
90ProC/Singl-778
90T/TVYank-63
91AAA/LineD-121
91Albany/ClBest-2
91B-165
91Classic/II-T87
91ColClip/LineD-121
91ColClip/ProC-598
91D/Rook-34
91F/Up-U48
91Leaf/GRook-BC16
91OPC/Premier-119
91S/RookTr-100T
91T/Tr-117T
92Classic/Game200-56
92ColClip/Pol-12
92ColClip/ProC-353
92ColClip/SB-121
92D-527
92F-245
92OPC-562
92ProC/Tomorrow-107
92S-631
92S/100RisSt-45
92Sky/AAASingl-59
92StCl-667
92T-562
92T/91Debut-170
92T/Gold-562
92T/GoldWin-562
92TripleP-96
Taylor, William 1
(Bill)
75QuadC
76QuadC
Taylor, William 2
89Madis/Star-20
90Madison/Best-24
90Modesto/Cal-154
90Modesto/ProC-2213
Taylor, William Christopher
(Will or Ooiee)
86Cram/NWL-179
87CharRain-6
88River/Cal-227
88River/ProC-1419
89River/Best-17
89River/Cal-13
89River/ProC-1402
90Wichita/Rock-19
91AAA/LineD-295
91LasVegas/LineD-295
91LasVegas/ProC-250
92LasVegas/SB-243
92Sky/AAASingl-118
Taylor, William H.
N690
Taylor, William Howell
(Bill)
80Ashvl-18
82Wausau/Frit-26
83Tulsa-5
84Tulsa-32
85Tulsa-34
87OKCty-25
88OkCty/ProC-28
89LasVegas/CMC-10
89LasVegas/ProC-3
91Greenvl/ClBest-6
91Greenvl/ProC-3000
92Richm/Bleach-12
92Richm/Comix-23
92Richm/ProC-378
92Richm/SB-445
93Richm/Bleach-23
93Richm/Pep-17
93Richm/Team-27
94B-276
94Flair-97
94Ultra-413
Taylor, William M.
(Bill)
54T-74
55Gol/Giants-26
55T-53
55T/DH-7
58T-389
94T/Arc54-74
Tayor, Fiona
85Anchora-38BG
Teague, Scott
89Wythe/Star-26
Teahan, Jim
83Beloit/Frit-19
92Negro/RetortII-39
Teasley, Ronald
86Negro/Frit-55
Tebbetts, George
(Birdie)
47HomogBond-45
47TipTop
50Drake-30
51B-257
52B-124
52NumNum-3
52T-282
55B-232
58T-386M
62T-588MG
63Sugar-18
63T-48MG
64T-462MG
65T-301MG
66T-552MG
81Tiger/Detroit-92
82Ohio/HOF-64
D305
Exh47
Tebbetts, Steve
76QuadC
77QuadC
Tebeau, Oliver
(Patsy)
N172
Techman, Marc
90AubAs/Best-22ASST
91AubAS/ClBest-28GM
Tedder, Scott
89Saraso/Star-24
89Star/Wax-61
90FSLAS/Star-44
90Saraso/Star-24
91Saraso/ClBest-26
91Saraso/ProC-1127
92BirmB/ProC-2596
92BirmB/SB-96
Teegarden, Travis
89Billings/ProC-2040
Teel, Garett
88CapeCod/Sum-171
90Bakers/Cal-252
92VeroB/ProC-2895CO
Teeters, Brian
92Eugene/ClBest-26
92Eugene/ProC-3044
Tegtmeier, Doug
88NE-17
90NE-24
91Penin/ClBest-11
91Penin/ProC-377
Teich, Mike
91Welland/ClBest-27
91Welland/ProC-3573
92Augusta/ClBest-5
92Augusta/ProC-240
Teising, John
78Watlo
Teixeira, Joe
89Bluefld/Star-25
90Wausau/Best-11
90Wausau/ProC-2124
Teixeira, Vince
86Cram/NWL-74
87Madis-5
88Modesto/Cal-80
89Visalia/Cal-113
89Visalia/ProC-1423
Tejada, Alejandro
89James/ProC-2153
Tejada, Domingo
90Martins/ProC-3206
Tejada, Eugenio
88Utica/Pucko-10
89SoBend/GS-25
90SoBend/GS-18
Tejada, Francisco
88Martins/Star-30
90Princet/DIMD-24
92Spartan/ClBest-8
92Spartan/ProC-1266
Tejada, Joaquin
86Elmira-23
87Elmira/Black-25
87Elmira/Red-25
Tejada, Leo
90SoBend/Best-6
91Saraso/ClBest-21
91Saraso/ProC-1123
Tejada, Wilfredo
86Jaxvl/TCMA-18
87D-529
87Indianap-25
88Indianap/CMC-19
88Indianap/ProC-523
89B-468
89OPC-391
89Phoenix/CMC-12
89Phoenix/ProC-1489
89T-747
91AA/LineD-294
91Huntsvl/LineD-294
93LimeR/Winter-4
Tejcek, John
92AZ/Pol-19
Tejeda, Enrique
88Bend/Legoe-16
Tejeda, Felix
86VeroB-24
87SanAn-15
Tejero, Fausto
90Boise/ProC-3334
91QuadC/ClBest-14
91QuadC/ProC-2632
92MidldA/ProC-4031
92MidldA/SB-454
Tekulve, Kent
76OPC-112
76SSPC-561
76T-112
77T-374
78T-84
79T-223
80OPC-297
80T-573
80T/Super-45
81Coke
81D-254
81F-362
81F/St-21
81OPC-94
81T-695
82D-311
82F-500
82F/St-73
82OPC-281
82T-485
83D-297
83F-326
83F/St-2M
83F/St-8M
83OPC-17
83OPC-18SV
83T-17
83T-18SV
83T/Fold-4M
84D-410
84F-265
84Nes/792-754
84OPC-74
84T-754
84T/RD-12M
84T/St-132
85D-479
85F-477
85F/Up-U117
85FunFoodPin-12
85Leaf-119
85OPC-125
85T-125
85T/RD-15M
85T/St-129
85T/Tr-117T
86CIGNA-4
86D-111
86F-455
86OPC-326
86Phill/TastyK-27
86T-326
87D-453
87F-190
87F/Excit-42
87F/Mini-104
87F/St-116
87OPC-86
87Phill/TastyK-27

87Sf/TPrev-6M
87T-684
87T/St-118
88D-535
88D/Best-327
88F-318
88OPC/WaxBox-P
88Panini/St-354
88Phill/TastyK-24
88S-425
88T-543
88T/Revco-10
88T/WaxBox-P
89F-583
89Kahn/Reds-43
89OPC/BoxB-O
89S-287
89T/Tr-116T
89T/WaxBox-O
89UD-207
90PublInt/St-40
93AP/ASG-167
Telemaco, Amaury
92Hunting/ClBest-27
92Hunting/ProC-3148
93Peoria/Team-27
94B-49
94FExcel-168
Telford, Anthony
88Hagers/Star-22
89Freder/Star-23
90Freder/Team-11
90Hagers/Star-23
91AAA/LineD-470
91Classic/I-16
91Crown/Orio-452
91D-501
91F-493
91OPC-653
91RochR/LineD-470
91RochR/ProC-1903
91S-354RP
91StCl-330
91T-653
91T/90Debut-152
91UD-304
92D-623
92F-29
92RochR/ProC-1941
92RochR/SB-471
92S-853
92S/HotRook-8
92Sky/AAASingl-214
92StCl-557
93D-789
Telgheder, Dave
89Pittsfld/Star-22
90Clmbia/PCPII-1
90Columbia/GS-26
91AA/LineD-644
91ClBest/Singl-342
91Wmsprt/LineD-644
91Wmsprt/ProC-293
92Sky/AAASingl-256
92Tidew/ProC-
92Tidew/SB-572
93F/Final-107
93T/Tr-89T
94D-467
94F-578
94Pac/Cr-417
94S-599
94T-402
94T/Gold-402
94UD-69
94UD/ElecD-69
94Ultra-537
Tellechea, John
90LSUPol-9
91LSU/Pol-6
Tellers, David
90Welland/Pucko-30
91CLAS/ProC-CAR37
91Salem/ClBest-20
91Salem/ProC-950
92CaroMud/ProC-1180
92Salem/ClBest-7
Tellez, Alonzo
87SanAn-5
Tellgren, Scott
83Toledo-25
85Maine-32
Tellmann, Tom
79Hawaii-23
80Hawaii-14
81Hawaii/TCMA-15
81T-356R
82Hawaii-19
83Pol/Brew-42
83T/Tr-109T
84D-149
84F-216
84Gard-20
84Nes/792-476
84Pol/Brew-42
84T-476
84T/St-297
85Cram/PCL-150
85D-246
85F-599
85Gard-20
85T-112
85T/Tr-118T
86T-693
Temperly, Kevin
89Clinton/ProC-881
92Clinton/ClBest-30
Temple, Johnny
55B-31
55Kahn
56Kahn
56T-212
57Kahn
57Sohio/Reds-18
57T-9
58Kahn
58T-205
58T-478AS
59Kahn
59T-335
60Kahn
60MacGregor-25
60T-500
60T/tatt-50
61Kahn
61T-155
61T/St-143
62J-38
62P-38
62P/Can-38
62Salada-52A
62Salada-52B
62Shirriff-52
62T-34
63J-189
63P-189
63Pep
63T-576
91Crown/Orio-453
Rawl
Templeton, Chuck
79TCMA-282
90Target-793
Templeton, Garry
76Tulsa
77Ho-78
77Ho/Twink-78
77OPC-84
77T-161
78Ho-43
78K-31
78OPC-51
78T-32
79Ho-127
79OPC-181
79T-350
80OPC-308
80T-587
80T-5HL
80T/S-37
80T/Super-37
81Coke
81D-187
81F-529
81F/St-125
81K-27
81MSA/Disc-32
81OPC-144
81PermaGr/CC-10
81Sqt-12
81T-485
81T/So-82
81T/St-217
81T/St-255
82D-545
82F-131
82F/St-27
82OPC-288
82T-288
82T/St-96
82T/Tr-119T
83D-145
83F-373
83F/St-9M
83K-17
83OPC-336
83OPC/St-291
83T-505
83T/St-291
84D-185
84F-314
84Mother/Padres-8
84Nes/792-615
84OPC-173
84Smok/Padres-24
84T-615
84T/St-151
85D-356
85F-45
85Mother/Padres-7
85OPC-124
85T-735
85T/St-151
86D-202
86D/AAS-30
86F-336
86F/Mini-71
86F/St-118
86Leaf-133
86OPC-90
86Sf-170
86T-90
86T/St-110
86T/Tatt-19M
87Bohem-1
87D-141
87D/OD-150
87F-432
87Leaf-63
87OPC-325
87T-325
87T/St-110
88Coke/Padres-1
88D-649
88F-598
88OPC-264
88Panini/St-409
88RedFoley/St-89
88S-189
88Smok/Padres-28
88T-640
88T/St-113
89B-455
89Coke/Padre-18
89D-483
89D/Best-154
89F-319
89Padre/Mag-19
89Panini/St-202
89S-176
89T-121
89T/Big-328
89UD-297
90B-215
90Coke/Padre-19
90D-246
90D/BestNL-133
90F-170
90F/Can-170
90Leaf-102
90OPC-481
90Padre/MagUno-14
90Panini/St-354
90PublInt/St-60
90S-336
90T-481
90T/Big-177
90UD-288
91D-252
91F-546
91OPC-253
91Panini/FrSt-94
91S-117
91S/RookTr-38T
91StCl-72
91T-253
91T/Tr-118T
91UD-295
91Ultra-312
92OPC-772
92S-588
92T-772
92T/Gold-772
92T/GoldWin-772
92UD-411
Tena, Paulino
90Watertn/Star-21
91Kinston/ClBest-21
91Kinston/ProC-333
Tenace, Gene
70OPC-21R
70T-21R
71MLB/St-528
71OPC-338
71T-338
72OPC-189
72T-189
73OPC-203WS
73OPC-206WS
73OPC-524
73T-203WS
73T-206WS
73T-524
74OPC-79
74T-79
74T/St-230
75Ho-64
75Ho/Twink-64
75OPC-535
75T-535
75T/M-535
76Ho-122
76OPC-165
76SSPC-493
76T-165
77BurgChef-131
77Ho-141
77Ho/Twink-141
77OPC-82
77Padre/SchCd-32
77Pep-39
77T-303
78Ho-125
78OPC-35
78Padre/FamFun-32
78T-240
78Tastee/Discs-20
78Wiffle/Discs-74
79Ho-19
79OPC-226
79T-435
80OPC-355
80T-704
81D-241
81F-489
81OPC-29
81T-29
81T/Tr-842
82D-152
82F-132
82F/St-26
82OPC-166
82T-631
83D-442
83F-25
83OPC-252
83T-515
83T/Tr-110T
84D-264
84F-266
84Nes/792-729
84T-729
87Mother/A's-14
90Tor/BJ-15CO
91Tor/Fire-18CO
92BJ/Fire-28CO
93BJ/Fire-30CO
Tenacen, Francisco
86Tampa-23
87Vermont-4
88WinSalem/Star-20
89WinSalem/Star-16
Tenbarge, Jeffrey
92AubAs/ClBest-4
92AubAs/ProC-1353
Tenenini, Bob
79Memphis/TCMA-15
80Memphis-23
83Memphis/TCMA-17
Tener, John
N172
Tenhunfeld, Joe
88Batavia/ProC-1679
90Clearw/Star-21
Tennant, Mike
77LodiD
79Albuq-2
Tenney, Fred
D304
E103
E107
E90/1
E91
E98
M116
T204
T206
T3-122
WG3-46
Tenney, Mickey
81QuadC-8
Tepedino, Frank
70T-689
71OPC-342
71T-342
73Syrac/Team-27
74OPC-526
74T-526
75OPC-9
75T-9
75T/M-9
81TCMA-469
92Yank/WIZ60-124
92Yank/WIZ70-148
Tepper, Marc
89Miami/I/Star-19
89Star/IISingl-185
89Watertn/Star-21
90Kinston/Team-11
91Kinston/ClBest-22
91Kinston/ProC-334
Tepsic, Joe
90Target-1083
Terilli, Joey
91Geneva/ClBest-21
91Geneva/ProC-4232
92MidwLAS/Team-45
92Peoria/ClBest-6
92Peoria/Team-27
92Peoria/Team-31M
Terlecky, Greg
76SSPC-299
77T-487R
78Spring/Wiener-20
Terpko, Jeff
72Dimanche*-45
77T-137
93Rang/Keeb-354
Terrazas, Marc
82Holyo-24
83Redwd-31
Terrell, James
91Belling/ClBest-6
91Belling/ProC-3681
92Penin/ClBest-26
92Penin/ProC-2946
Terrell, Jerry
74OPC-481
74T-481
75OPC-654
75T-654
75T/M-654
75Tacoma/KMMO-3
76OPC-159
76SSPC-222
76T-159
77T-513
78SSPC/270-243
78T-525
79T-273
80T-98
87FtMyr-29MG
91Pac/SenLg-8
Terrell, Walt
81Tulsa-12
82Tidew-24
83Tidew-12
84D-640
84F-601
84Nes/792-549
84T-549
84T/St-110
85D-597
85F-94
85F/Up-U118
85OPC-287
85T-287
85T/St-109
85T/Tr-119T
86Cain's-18

86D-247
86F-240
86Leaf-123
86OPC-301
86T-461
86T/Mini-16
87Cain's-16
87Coke/Tigers-3
87D-275
87F-165
87Leaf-180
87OPC-72
87T-72
88D-91
88D/Best-293
88F-72
88F/Mini-24
88F/St-28
88OPC-284
88Panini/St-87
88Pep/T-35
88Pol/T-12
88RedFoley/St-90
88S-538
88T-668
89B-445
89Coke/Padre-19
89D-296
89D/Best-245
89D/Tr-28
89F-149
89S-314
89S/Tr-75
89T-127
89T/Tr-117T
89UD-475
89UD/Ext-703
90B-165
90D-309
90F-457
90F/Can-457
90Homer/Pirate-28
90OPC-611
90PublInt/St-61
90S-463
90T-611
90TulsaDG/Best-11
90UD-661
91CokeK/Tiger-35
91D-717
91OPC-328
91S-801
91StCl-315
91T-328
91UD-320
91WIZMets-401
92D-565
92F-146
92OPC-722
92Pinn-190
92S-355
92StCl-139
92T-722
92T/Gold-722
92T/GoldWin-722
92UD-520
92USPlayC/Tiger-12H
92USPlayC/Tiger-3C
92Yank/WIZ80-189
93D-772
93F-612
93StCl-223
93StCl/1stDay-223

Terrill, James
87Everett-19
88Clinton/ProC-702
89SanJose/Best-4
89SanJose/Cal-218
89SanJose/ProC-449
89SanJose/Star-24
91AA/LineD-543
91SanAn/LineD-543
91SanAn/ProC-2974

Terrio, Tim
89AS/Cal-26TR
89Bak/Cal-208TR

Terris, Adam
89Rockford/Team-25
90WPalmB/Star-24

Terry, Brent
88SLCity-6CO

Terry, Brett
88Utica/Pucko-3

Terry, Doug
89KS*-28

Terry, Ralph
57T-391
58T-169
59T-358
60T-96
61T-389
62J-10
62P-10
62P/Can-10
62Salada-77
62Shirriff-77
62T-48
63Bz-20
63F-26
63J-20
63Kahn
63P-20
63Salada-38
63T-10LL
63T-315
63T-8LL
64T-458
65Kahn
65T-406
66OPC-109
66T-109
66T/RO-69
66T/RO-92
67OPC-59
67T-59
78TCMA-168
81TCMA-480
88Pac/Leg-64
89Swell-31
91WIZMets-402
92Yank/WIZ60-125
92Yank/WIZAS-82
WG9-23

Terry, Scott
81Cedar-18
82Cedar-23
83Tampa-23
87Nashvl-20
87T-453
88D-647
88F/Up-U121
88Louisvl-47
88Smok/Card-8
88T/Tr-119T
89D-397
89F-464
89S-397
89Smok/Cards-20
89T-686
89T/Big-31
90CedarDG/Best-7
90D-418
90F-261
90F/Can-261
90Leaf-234
90OPC-82
90PublInt/St-229
90S-235
90Smok/Card-23
90T-82
90T/TVCard-19
90UD-260
91F-647
91OPC-539
91Pol/Card-37
91S-247
91StCl-469
91T-539
92D-655
92F-593
92OPC-117
92Pol/Card-20
92S-219
92StCl-522
92T-117
92T/Gold-117
92T/GoldWin-117
92UD-688

Terry, William Harold
(Bill)
25Exh-40
26Exh-40
28Yueng-46
29Exh/4-9
31Exh/4-10
33CJ/Pin-22
33DL-4
33G-125
33G-20
34DS-14
34Exh/4-5
34G-21
35BU-6
35Exh/4-5
35G-1K
35G-3B
35G-4B
35G-5B
36Exh/4-5
38ONG/Pin-29
50Callahan
50W576-69
60F-52
61F-142
61GP-5
76Rowe-12M
76Shakey-73
77Galasso-112
77Galasso-204
77Galasso-250
80Laugh/3/4/5-7
80Pac/Leg-9
80Perez/HOF-73
80SSPC/HOF
81Conlon-7
86Conlon/1-31
88Conlon/3-28
88Conlon/NatAS-20
89HOF/St-2
90Target-1084
91Conlon/Proto-661
91Conlon/Sport-64
92Conlon/ASP-661G
92Conlon/Sport-588
93Conlon-661
93Conlon-841
94Conlon-1100
E210-46
R300
R306
R311/Gloss
R315-A35
R315-B35
R316
R328-4
R337-405
V353-20
V354-53
V355-7
W502-46
W513-67
W517

Terry, William H.
(Adonis)
N172

Terry, Zeb
D327
D328-171
E121/120
E121/80
E135-171
W501-58
W575

Terwilliger, Wayne
50B-114
51B-175
51T/RB-14
52T-7
53Briggs
53T-159
54T-73
55T-34
55T/DH-132
56T-73
59T-496
60L-134
60T-26
77Ashvl
79Ashvl/TCMA-5
80Tulsa-24
90Target-794
91T/Arc53-159
93Rang/Keeb-44CO
94T/Arc54-73

Terzarial, Anthony
88Billings/ProC-1811
90Cedar/Best-10
90Cedar/ProC-2333

Teske, David
92Pittsfld/ProC-3296

Tesmer, Jim
89Pittsfld/Star-28

Tesreau, Charles
(Jeff)
14CJ-45
15CJ-45
16FleischBrd-96
81Conlon-46
88Conlon/3-29
92Conlon/Sport-340
BF2-80
D328-172
D329-173
D350/2-175
E135-172
M101/4-173
M101/5-175

Teston, Phil
80Penin/C-1

Teter, Craig
90SoBend/Best-11
90SoBend/GS-26
90Utica/Pucko-11

Tettleton, Mickey
84Albany-22
85F/Up-U119
85Mother/A's-11
85T/Tr-120T
86D-345
86F-432
86Mother/A's-11
86T-457
87D-349
87D/OD-23
87F-407
87T-649
88D-103
88French-14
88RochR/CMC-21
88RochR/ProC-202
88RochR/Team-23
88S-269
88S/Tr-31T
88T-143
88T/Tr-120T
89D-401
89D/Best-86
89F-623
89French-14
89Panini/St-259
89S-358
89T-521
89T/Big-198
89T/St-231
89UD-553
90AlbanyDG/Best-31
90B-254
90Classic-39
90D-169
90D-5DK
90D/BestAL-15
90D/SuperDK-5DK
90F-190
90F/ASIns-12
90F/Can-190
90HotPlay/St-45
90KMart/SS-24
90Kenner/Fig-84
90Leaf-65
90MLBPA/Pins-111
90OPC-275
90Panini/St-8
90PublInt/St-587
90RedFoley/St-94
90S-322
90S/100St-9
90Sf-171
90T-275
90T/Coins-30
90T/Gloss60-57
90T/St-237
90T/TVAS-24
90UD-297
90UD-60TC
91B-140
91Cadaco-56
91Classic/II-T62
91CokeK/Tiger-20
91Crown/Orio-454
91D-597
91F-494
91F/UltraUp-U24
91F/Up-U24
91Leaf-322
91Leaf/Stud-58
91OPC-385
91Panini/FrSt-239
91S-270
91S/RookTr-25T
91StCl-412
91T-385
91T/Tr-119T
91UD-296
91UD/Ext-729
92B-117
92Classic/Game200-89
92D-85
92F-147
92F/ASIns-9
92F/Lumber-L2
92L-285
92L/BlkGold-285
92OPC-29
92Panini-104
92Pinn-226
92S-134
92StCl-195
92Studio-178
92T-29
92T/Gold-29
92T/GoldWin-29
92TripleP-44
92UD-251
92USPlayC/Ace-3C
92USPlayC/Tiger-13H
92USPlayC/Tiger-9C
92Ultra-63
92Ultra/AS-5
93B-615
93Colla/DM-107
93D-13
93D/Spirit-SG10M
93F-234
93F/Fruit-60
93Flair-208
93L-213
93MSA/Metz-37
93OPC-334
93Pac/Spanish-114
93Panini-113
93Pinn-52
93Pinn/HRC-18
93Pinn/Slug-22
93S-60
93Select-60
93StCl-31
93StCl/1stDay-31
93Studio-138
93T-135
93T/BlkGold-41
93T/Finest-80
93T/FinestRef-80
93T/Gold-135
93Tiger/Gator-23
93TripleP-92
93UD-46M
93UD-86
93UD/FunPack-189
93UD/SP-240
93USPlayC/Ace-6C
93Ultra-554
94B-125
94D-44
94D/Special-44
94F-143
94Finest-281
94L-279
94OPC-32
94Pac/Cr-229
94Pac/Gold-8
94Panini-68
94Pinn-67
94Pinn/Artist-67
94Pinn/Museum-67
94Pinn/Run-19
94S-51
94S/GoldR-51
94Sf/2000-131
94StCl-192
94StCl/1stDay-192
94StCl/Gold-192
94Studio-193
94T-495
94T/Gold-495
94TripleP-248
94TripleP/Medal-1M
94UD-301

94UD/CollC-275
94UD/CollC/Gold-275
94UD/CollC/Silv-275
94UD/SP-180
94Ultra-357
Teufel, Tim
82OrlanTw/A-9
82OrlanTw/B-12
83Toledo-16
84D-37RR
84F-574
84T/Tr-117
85D-192
85F-290
85Leaf-97
85OPC-239
85Seven/Minn-10
85T-239
85T/St-303
85Twin/Seven-10
85Twin/Team-8
86D-242
86F-407
86F/Up-U110
86OPC-91
86T-667
86T/St-280
86T/Tr-109T
87D-581
87D/OD-131
87F-24
87T-158
88D-648
88D/Mets/Bk-648
88F-152
88Kahn/Mets-11
88S-128
88T-508
89B-382
89D-507
89F-50
89Kahn/Mets-11
89S-58
89T-9
89T/DHTest-11
89UD-277
90D-618
90F-218
90F/Can-218
90Kahn/Mets-11
90Leaf-383
90OPC-764
90PublInt/St-146
90S-501
90T-764
90T/TVMets-29
90UD-492
91D-370
91F-162
91F/UltraUp-U114
91F/Up-U127
91Kahn/Mets-11
91Leaf-314
91OPC-302
91S-427
91S/RookTr-67T
91StCl-43
91T-302
91T/Tr-120T
91UD-370
91WIZMets-403
92D-171
92F-622
92L-261
92L/BlkGold-261
92Mother/Padre-17
92OPC-413
92Padre/Carl-22
92Pinn-313
92Pol/Padre-22
92S-234
92Smok/Padre-35
92StCl-485
92Studio-110
92T-413
92T/Gold-413
92T/GoldWin-413
92TripleP-255
92UD-349
92Ultra-585
93D-98
93F-525
93L-10
93Mother/Padre-6
93Pac/Spanish-266
93Pinn-183
93S-480
93StCl-213
93StCl/1stDay-213
93T-636
93T/Gold-636
93TripleP-183
93UD-61
94D-272
94F-676
94Pac/Cr-535
94StCl-46
94StCl/1stDay-46
94StCl/Gold-46
94T-254
94T/Gold-254
Teutsch, Mark
79AppFx-15
80GlenF/B-13
80GlenF/C-3
Tevlin, Creighton J.
78Spokane/Cramer-12
78Spokane/Team-12
79Vanco-23
81Syrac-19
81Syrac/Team-19
82Syrac-22
82Syrac/Team-21
Tewell, Terry
90Martins/ProC-3202
91Clearw/ClBest-14
91Clearw/ProC-1625
92Clearw/ClBest-15
92Clearw/ProC-2060
Tewksbury, Bob
84Nashvl-22
85Albany-11
86D/Rook-8
86F/Up-U111
86T/Tr-110T
87Colum/TCMA-9
87D-422
87F-117
87Sf/TPrev-7
87T-254
88Iowa/CMC-5
88Iowa/ProC-534
88T-593
89Louisvl-35
89Louisvl/CMC-11
89Louisvl/ProC-1250
90AlbanyDG/Best-13
90D-714
90Leaf-406
90Louisvl/LBC-40
90T/TVCard-20
90T/Tr-122T
91B-394
91D-183
91F-648
91Leaf-460
91OPC-88
91Panini/St-36
91Pol/Card-39
91S-499
91StCl-417
91T-88
91UD-630
92D-201
92F-594
92L-95
92L/BlkGold-95
92OPC-623
92Pinn-219
92Pinn-288SIDE
92Pol/Card-21
92S-282
92StCl-258
92T-623
92T/Gold-623
92T/GoldWin-623
92UD-512
92Ultra-573
92Yank/WIZ80-190
93B-248
93Classic/GameI-91
93D-204
93D/DK-22
93F-134
93Flair-129
93L-44
93OPC-344
93Pac/Spanish-304
93Panini-190
93Pinn-13
93Pol/Card-21
93S-34
93Select-107
93Select/Ace-15
93Select/StatL-83
93Select/StatL-89M
93StCl-341
93StCl/1stDay-341
93StCl/Card-10
93StCl/MurphyS-66
93T-285
93T/Finest-193
93T/FinestRef-193
93T/Gold-285
93T/Hill-27
93TripleP-156
93UD-318
93UD/FunPack-79
93UD/SP-80
93Ultra-114
94B-264
94D-262
94F-647
94L-333
94OPC-217
94Pac/Cr-605
94Panini-249
94Pinn-452
94S-56
94S/GoldR-56
94Select-83
94StCl/Team-312
94Studio-55
94T-473
94T/Finest-42
94T/FinestRef-42
94T/Gold-473
94TripleP-67
94UD-353
94UD/SP-66
94Ultra-272
Texidor, Esteban
78Holyo
Texidor, Jose
91Butte/SportP-26
91CharlR/ClBest-25
91CharlR/ProC-1329
92Gaston/ClBest-9
92Gaston/ProC-2267
Thacker, Moe
59T-474
61T-12
62T-546
Thatcher, Aaron
92FrRow/DP-25
Thayer, Ernest
90BBWit-98
Thayer, Greg
75Tacoma/KMMO-15
78Twin/FriszP-20
79Toledo-16
Thayer, Scott
78Green
Thebo, Antonio
T206
Thees, Michael
91SoOreg/ClBest-26
91SoOreg/ProC-3845
Theilman, Harry
WG3-47
Theisen, Mike
86StPete-29
Theiss, Duane
78Richm
79Richm-16
80Ander-3
92Visalia/ClBest-9
92Visalia/ProC-1016
Thelen, Jeffrey John
90Foil/Best-149
90Kenosha/Best-26
90Kenosha/ProC-2295
90Kenosha/Star-24
91Kenosha/ClBest-18
91Kenosha/ProC-2076
Theobald, Ron
72OPC-77
72T-77
Theodore, George
74OPC-99
74T-8
75Tidew/Team-22
89Tidew/Candl-8
91WIZMets-404
Therrien, Dominic
91Idaho/ProC-4342
91Pulaski/ProC-4021
92Macon/ProC-277
93Durham/Team-22
94FExcel-161
Therrien, Ed
88CapeCod/Sum-4
Thevenow, Tom J.
31Exh/4-13
33Exh/4-7
33G-36
34Exh/4-7
35G-2B
35G-4B
35G-7B
91Conlon/Sport-69
V353-36
Thibault, Ryan
90Spokane/SportP-25
91Waterlo/ClBest-9
91Waterlo/ProC-1256
92HighD/ClBest-21
Thibert, John
90Tampa/DIMD-26
92Greens/ClBest-10
92Oneonta/ClBest-16
Thibodeau, John
69OPC-189R
69T-189R
69T/4in1-14M
Thibodeaux, Keith
82Buffa-8
83LynnP-8
Thielen, D.J.
91Everett/ClBest-1
91Everett/ProC-3925
92Clinton/ClBest-21
92Clinton/ProC-3607
93B-224
Thielker, Dave
85CharlO-6
Thielman, John
T206
Thienpont, Gregg
84Butte-23
Thies, Dave
61Union
77Fritsch-53
Thies, Vernon
(Jake)
55T-12
55T/DH-40
Thiesen, Gator
89MissSt-44M
Thiessen, Tim
86WPalmB-26
Thigpen, Arthur
90Niagara/Pucko-25
Thigpen, Bobby
86BirmB/Team-19
87Coke/WS-22
87D-370
87F-507
87Seven-C13
87Sf/TPrev-26M
87T-61
88Coke/WS-28
88D-247
88D/Best-235
88F-410
88F/St-17
88F/TL-42
88S-307
88T-613
88ToysRUs-32
89B-55
89Coke/WS-26
89D-266
89D/Best-25
89F-512
89F/BBMVP's-38
89F/Heroes-39
89F/LL-39
89KennerFig-148
89Kodak/WSox-5M
89OPC-368
89Panini/St-303
89S-399
89S/HotStar-68
89S/YS/I-29
89Sf-207
89T-762
89T/St-305
89UD-647
90B-306
90BirmDG/Best-30
90Classic/III-81
90Coke/WSox-24
90D-266
90D/BestAL-32
90F-549
90F/BB-40
90F/BBMVP-40
90F/Can-549
90F/LL-39
90Leaf-175
90OPC-255
90Panini/St-50
90PublInt/St-401
90RedFoley/St-95
90S-335
90S-694DT
90S/100St-87
90Sf-27
90T-255
90T/Big-295
90T/Mini-12
90T/St-297
90UD-269
90USPlayC/AS-9C
91B-342
91Classic/200-140
91Classic/I-31
91D-399MVP
91D-8DK
91D-90
91D-BC20
91D/BC-BC20
91D/SuperDK-8DK
91F-137
91F-712M
91Kodak/WSox-37
91Leaf-336
91Leaf/Stud-39
91MajorLg/Pins-15
91MissSt-43
91OPC-396AS
91OPC-420
91OPC-8RB
91OPC/Premier-120
91Panini/FrSt-320
91Panini/St-252
91Panini/Top15-85
91Post/Can-25
91RedFoley/St-92
91S-280
91S-401AS
91S-418HL
91S/100SS-95
91Seven/3DCoin-13MW
91StCl-256
91StCl/Charter*-29
91Sunflower-22
91T-396AS
91T-420
91T-8RB
91T/CJMini/I-32
91UD-261
91UD-93HL
91Ultra-396EP
91Ultra-84
91Woolwth/HL-21
92B-36
92Classic/Game200-100
92Classic/II-T89
92D-708
92F-99
92L-210
92L/BlkGold-210
92OPC-505
92Panini-132
92Pinn-214
92S-570
92S/100SS-54
92StCl-224
92StCl/MemberII-13
92Studio-158
92T-505
92T/Gold-505
92T/GoldWin-505
92T/Kids-101
92TripleP-32
92UD-285
92Ultra-342
92WSox-37

93B-119
93D-67
93F-589
93L-173
93OPC-336
93Pac/Spanish-76
93Pinn-452
93S-582
93Select-232
93StCl-575
93StCl/1stDay-575
93StCl/WSox-20
93T-645
93T/Gold-645
93UD-671
93Ultra-180
93WSox-27
94D-273

Thigpen, Len
89Penin/Star-24

Thobe, J.J.
94B-144
94ClBest/Gold-45
94FExcel-50

Thobe, Tom
93Macon/ClBest-24
93Macon/ProC-1400
94ClBest/Gold-117

Thoden, John
88CapeCod/Sum-106
89James/ProC-2157
90Rockford/ProC-2686
90Rockford/Team-26
91WPalmB/ClBest-12
91WPalmB/ProC-1228

Thoenen, Dick
68T-348R

Thoma, Ray
84Albany-26
85Huntsvl/BK-19
87Pittsfld-1
88Pittsfld/ProC-1358

Thomas, Alphonse (Tommy)
26Exh-76
27Exh-38
29Exh/4-20
33G-169
91Conlon/Sport-106
92Conlon/Sport-579
R316

Thomas, Andres
83Ander-23
84Durham-14
85Greenvl/Team-18
86D/Rook-10
86F/Up-U112
86Pol/Atl-14
86Sf/Rook-14
86T/Tr-111T
87Classic-7
87D-266
87D/OD-43
87F-531
87F/BB-42
87F/Mini-105
87F/St-117
87Sf/TPrev-24M
87Smok/Atl-20
87T-296
87T/JumboR-20
87T/St-305
87T/St-39
87ToysRUs-29
88D-627
88F-551
88OPC-13
88S-299
88T-13
88T/Big-68
88T/St-41
89B-272
89Brave/Dubuq-26
89Cadaco-57
89Classic-21
89D-576
89D/Best-197
89F-604
89OPC-358
89Panini/St-43
89S-406
89S/YS/II-35
89T-171TL
89T-523
89T/St-26
89UD-144
90Brave/Dubuq/Perf-28
90Brave/Dubuq/Singl-32
90D-263
90F-597
90F/Can-597
90Leaf-33
90OPC-358
90Panini/St-229
90PublInt/St-126
90S-99
90T-358
90T/St-33
90UD-212
91D-491
91F-706
91OPC-111
91S-613
91T-111
91UD-384
92Phoenix/SB-396

Thomas, Bill
83ArkTr-7

Thomas, C.L.
88Billings/ProC-1823

Thomas, Carey
91ClBest/Singl-281

Thomas, Carl
87Kenosha-18

Thomas, Carlos
91Yakima/ClBest-28
91Yakima/ProC-4249
92Yakima/ProC-3448

Thomas, Chester David
16FleischBrd-93
D327
D328-173
E121/80
E122
E135-173
T213/blue
T213/brown
W575

Thomas, Chris 1
83VeroB-11

Thomas, Chris 2
92AubAs/ClBest-3
92AubAs/ProC-1368

Thomas, Claude
T207

Thomas, Clinton
89Martins/Star-30
91SALAS/ProC-SAL45
91Spartan/ClBest-20
91Spartan/ProC-905

Thomas, Clinton Cyrus
86Negro/Frit-33

Thomas, Corey
92Clearw/ProC-2067

Thomas, Danny
77T-488R

Thomas, Dave
81Holyo-5M

Thomas, Delvin
90Penin/Star-22
91SanBern/ClBest-21
91SanBern/ProC-1998

Thomas, Dennis
82Reading-9
83Reading-9

Thomas, Deron
82Spring/Frit-21
83StPete-19
84ArkTr-4

Thomas, Derrel
72OPC-457R
72T-457R
73OPC-57
73T-57
74OPC-518
74T-518
75OPC-378
75T-378
75T/M-378
76OPC-493
76SSPC-106
76T-493
77T-266
78Padre/FamFun-33
78T-194
79OPC-359
79T-679
80OPC-9
80Pol/Dodg-30
80T-23
81D-419
81F-123
81OPC-211
81Pol/Dodg-30
81T-211
82D-537
82F-26
82Pol/Dodg-30
82T-348
83F-223
83Pol/Dodg-30
83T-748
84D-397
84Expo/PostC-32
84F-114
84F/X-116
84Nes/792-583
84Stuart-28
84T-583
84T/Tr-118
85F-314
85OPC-317
85T-448
85T/Tr-121T
86T-158
89Pac/SenLg-64
89T/SenLg-55
89TM/SenLg-104
90EliteSenLg-90
90Target-795
91Pac/SenLg-87

Thomas, Derrick
91StCl/Charter*-40

Thomas, Don G.
76SanAn/Team-23

Thomas, Don
74Gaston

Thomas, Duane
92Bluefld/ClBest-11
92Bluefld/ProC-2372

Thomas, Eric
75AppFx

Thomas, Fay
90Target-796

Thomas, Frank Edward
87PanAm/USAB-23
87PanAm/USAR-23
88CapeCod-14
88CapeCod/Sum-126
90A&AASingle/ProC-46
90B-320
90BirmB/Best-1
90BirmB/ProC-1116
90Classic/III-93
90Coke/WSox-25
90F/Up-U87
90Foil/Best-1
90Foil/Best-318BC
90Leaf-300
90OPC-414
90ProC/Singl-818
90S-663DC
90S/Tr-86T
90T-414
90TeamUSA/87-23
91Arena*-3
91B-366
91Bleach/Thomas-1
91Bleach/Thomas-2
91Bleach/Thomas-3
91Bz-7
91Classic/200-181
91Classic/I-32
91Classic/II-T28
91D-477
91F-138
91JDean-9
91Kodak/WSox-35
91Kodak/WSox-x
91Leaf-281
91Leaf/Stud-40
91MajorLg/Pins-17
91OPC-79
91OPC/Premier-121
91RedFoley/St-111
91S-840
91S-874FRAN
91S/100RisSt-78
91S/HotRook-4
91Seven/3DCoin-14MW
91StCl-57
91T-79
91T/90Debut-153
91T/CJMini/II-20
91T/JumboR-28
91ToysRUs-27
91UD-246
91Ultra-85
92AP/ASG-77
92B-114
92B-551FOIL
92CJ/DI-35
92Classic/Game200-106
92Classic/I-89
92Classic/II-T87
92Colla/Thomas-Set
92D-592
92D/DK-DK8
92D/Elite-E18
92D/McDon-2
92F-100
92F-701M
92F-712PV
92F/ASIns-11
92F/Performer-2
92F/RookSIns-1
92FrRow/Thomas-Set
92FrRow/ThomasGold-Set
92JDean/18-4
92Kenner/Fig-43
92Kenner/Fig-44
92KingB-3
92L-349
92L-67M
92L/BlkGold-349
92L/BlkGold-67M
92L/GoldPrev-16
92L/Prev-16
92MSA/Ben-11
92MTV-2
92MooTown-24
92OPC-555
92OPC/Premier-59
92P-24
92Panini-125
92Pinn-1
92Pinn/Slug-11
92Pinn/Team2000-3
92Pinn/TeamP-4
92S-505
92S-893DT
92S/100SS-51
92S/Impact-43
92Seven/Coin-16
92StCl-301
92StCl-591MC
92StCl/MPhoto-15
92Studio-159
92Studio/Prev-18
92T-555
92T/Gold-555
92T/GoldWin-555
92T/Kids-99
92T/McDonB-25
92TripleP-206
92TripleP/Gal-GS12
92TripleP/Prev-6
92UD-166
92UD-87TC
92UD-SP4M
92UD/ASFF-10
92UD/HRH-HR8
92UD/TWillB-T19
92UD/TmMVPHolo-52
92USPlayC/Ace-4D
92USPlayC/Ace-7C
92USPlayC/Ace-7H
92Ultra-44
92Ultra/AS-9
92WSox-35
93B-555
93Cadaco-58
93Classic/GameI-92
93Colla/DM-108
93Colla/DMArt-7
93Colla/DMProto-8
93D-7
93D/EliteDom-6
93D/EliteUp-19
93D/LongBall-LL10
93D/MVP-2
93D/Master-1
93D/Prev-14
93D/Spirit-SG18
93D/Spirit-SG6M
93Duracel/PPI-2
93F-210
93F-714M
93F/ASAL-1
93F/Atlantic-23
93F/Fruit-61
93F/GoldMII-3
93F/TLAL-5
93Flair-189
93Highland-6
93Ho-13
93HumDum/Can-6
93JDean/28-1
93Kenner/Fig-35
93KingB-4
93L-195
93L-FT3500
93L/Fast-1
93L/GoldAS-12
93L/Thomas-Set
93L/UpThomasJ-Set
93OPC-362
93OPC/Premier/StarP-1
93P-14
93Pac/Spanish-77
93Panini-136
93Pinn-108
93Pinn/Cooper-24
93Pinn/HRC-17
93Pinn/Slug-9
93Pinn/TP-4M
93S-3
93S-510AS
93S-541DT
93S/Franchise-4
93S/GoldDT-10
93Select-6
93Select/StatL-13
93Select/StatL-3
93Select/StatL-33
93Select/StatL-38
93Select/StatL-45
93Select/StatL-49
93StCl-200
93StCl-746MC
93StCl/1stDay-200
93StCl/1stDay-746MC
93StCl/II/Ins-3M
93StCl/WSox-1
93Studio-139
93Studio/Her-8
93Studio/SS-6
93Studio/Sil-1
93Studio/Thomas-Set
93T-150
93T-401M
93T/BlkGold-42
93T/Finest-102AS
93T/FinestASJ-102AS
93T/FinestRef-102AS
93T/Gold-150
93T/Gold-401M
93T/HolPrev-150
93T/MicroP-150
93TB/Full-1
93ToysRUs-66
93ToysRUs/MPhoto-12
93TripleP-26
93TripleP-77LH
93TripleP/Act-21
93TripleP/Nick-1
93UD-105M
93UD-51M
93UD-555
93UD/5thAnn-A14
93UD/ATH-118
93UD/Clutch-R20
93UD/Diam-27
93UD/FunPack-197GS
93UD/FunPack-202
93UD/FunPack-21HS
93UD/FunPack-225CL
93UD/FunPack-27KS
93UD/FunPack-36HERO
93UD/FunPackAS-AS1
93UD/looss-WI25
93UD/OnDeck-D24
93UD/SP-260
93UD/SPPlat-PP19
93UD/TCr-TC9
93UDFutHero-62
93USPlayC/Ace-8D
93Ultra-181
93Ultra/AS-19
93Ultra/Perf-10

93WSox-28
94B-15
94D-341
94D/AwardWin-6MVP
94D/DK-28
94D/DomII-2
94D/Elite-37
94D/LongBall-8
94D/MVP-18
94D/Pr-4
94D/Pr-4SESP
94D/Special-341
94D/Spirit-6
94F-96
94F/AS-23
94F/AwardWin-1
94F/GoldM-9
94F/Lumber-9
94F/TL-4
94Flair-36
94Flair/Hot-10
94KingB-14
94Kraft-12
94L-400
94L/Gamer-7
94L/GoldS-11
94L/MVPAL-12
94L/PBroker-1
94L-NNO
94L/Pr-9
94L/Slide-1
94L/StatStand-1
94OPC-127
94OPC/JAS-1
94Oscar-14
94P-21
94Pac/Cr-138
94Pac/Cr-660MVP
94Pac/CrPr-8
94Pac/Gold-3
94Pac/Silv-13
94Panini-51
94Pinn-1
94Pinn/Artist-1
94Pinn/Museum-1
94Pinn/Power-6
94Pinn/Run-2
94Pinn/TeamP-1M
94Pinn/Trib-14
94RedFoley-25
94S-41
94S-631MVP
94S/Cycle-18
94S/GoldR-41
94S/GoldS-45
94S/Tomb-29
94Select-6
94Select/CrCon-4
94Sf/2000-176AS
94Sf/2000-70
94StCl-267
94StCl-285
94StCl-528DL
94StCl/1stDay-267
94StCl/1stDay-285
94StCl/1stDay-528DL
94StCl/Gold-267
94StCl/Gold-285
94StCl/Gold-528DL
94StCl/Team-121
94Studio-209
94Studio/Editor-2
94Studio/Her-2
94Studio/S&GStar-3
94T-270
94T-384AS
94T-601ST
94T/BlkGold-21
94T/Finest-203
94T/FinestRef-203
94T/Gold-270
94T/Gold-384AS
94T/Gold-601ST
94TripleP-269
94TripleP/Bomb-1
94TripleP/Medal-3
94TripleP/Pr-2
94UD-284HFA
94UD-300
94UD-55FUT
94UD/DColl-C8
94UD/ElecD-55FUT
94UD/Mantle-18
94UD/HoloFX-39
94UD/SP-193
94Ultra-39
94Ultra/AS-2
94Ultra/AwardWin-19MVP
94Ultra/HRK-3
94Ultra/Hit-10
94Ultra/OnBase-12
94Ultra/RBIK-2

Thomas, Frank J.
54B-155
54DanDee
55Armour-21
55B-58
55RM-NL20
56T-153
57Kahn
57T-140
58Hires-27
58Kahn
58T-409
59Armour-17
59Kahn
59T-17M
59T-490
60Kahn
60T-95
61P-193
61T-382
62J-151
62P-151
62P/Can-151
62Salada-104
62Shirriff-104
62T-7
63J-196
63P-196
63Salada-59
63T-495
64PhilBull-24
64T-345
64T/Coins-73
65OPC-123
65T-123
79TCMA-24
89Pac/Leg-153
90Swell/Great-113
91T/Arc53-283
91WIZMets-405
Exh47

Thomas, Frank
(Frankie)
80Holyo-5
81Vanco-6
82Vanco-2
83ElPaso-22
84Cram/PCL-33

Thomas, George
61T-544
62T-525
62T/St-69
63J-34
63P-34
63T-98
64T-461
65OPC-83
65T-83
66T-277
67CokeCap/RedSox-18
67OPC-184
67T-184
67T/Test/RSox-22
69T-521
71OPC-678
71T-678
78TCMA-153

Thomas, Ira
10Domino-115
11Diamond-26
11Helmar-59
12Sweet/Pin-50A
12Sweet/Pin-50B
14CJ-34
14Piedmont/St-54
15CJ-34
E103
E104
E300
E90/1
E91
E96
M116
T201
T202
T204
T205
T206
T207
T208
T3-123
W514-97

Thomas, J. Leroy
(Lee)
61T-464
62Bz
62T-154
62T/St-70
62T/bucks
63Bz-32
63Exh
63J-30
63P-30
63T-441
63T/SO
64T-255
64T/SU
64T/St-99
64T/tatt
65OPC-111
65T-111
66T-408
67CokeCap/Astro-6
67CokeCap/Cub-12
67T-458
68T-438
78TCMA-231
92Yank/WIZ60-126
Exh47

Thomas, James Gorman
(Gorman)
74OPC-288
74Sacra
74T-288
75OPC-532
75T-532
75T/M-532
76OPC-139
76SSPC-243
76T-139
77Spoka
77T-439
79OPC-196
79T-376
80K-11
80OPC-327
80T-202TL
80T-623
80T/S-30
80T/Super-30
81D-326
81F-507
81F/St-77
81OPC-135
81PermaGr/CC-29
81T-135
81T/St-12
81T/St-96
82D-132
82D-26DK
82F-154
82F/St-134
82OPC-324
82Pol/Brew-20
82T-765
82T/St-204
83D-510
83Drake-27
83F-48
83F/St-10M
83F/St-5M
83Gard-19
83K-47
83OPC-10
83OPC/St-17M
83OPC/St-84
83PermaGr/CC-32
83Pol/Brew-20
83T-10
83T-702LL
83T/LeadS-2M
83T/St-17M
83T/St-84
83T/Tr-111T
84D-574
84D/Champs-5
84F-553
84F/X-U117
84Mother/Mar-7
84Nes/792-515
84OPC-146
84T-515
84T/St-253
84T/Tr-119T
85F-503
85FunFoodPin-56
85Mother/Mar-9
85OPC-202
85T-202
86D-440
86F-477
86F/AS-11
86F/St-119
86Leaf-213
86Mother/Mar-9
86OPC-347
86Seven/Coin-W9M
86T-750
86T/Gloss60-48
86T/Mini-31
86T/St-216
86T/Super-56
86T/Tatt-22M
86Woolwth-31
87F-359
87T-495
92Brew/Carlson-23
94TedW-45

Thomas, Jeff
85Clovis-40

Thomas, Jim 1
83DayBe-23
84Beaum-15
86Tucson-22
87ColAst/ProC-5
88MidldA/GS-23
89Edmon/CMC-22
89Edmon/ProC-550

Thomas, Jim 2
76SanAn/Team-24

Thomas, John
90Hamil/Best-24
90Hamil/Star-25
91StPete/ClBest-5
92ArkTr/SB-47
92ClBest-14
92Sky/AASingl-20

Thomas, Keith 1
53B/BW-62
53T-129
91T/Arc53-129

Thomas, Keith 2
88Greens/ProC-1554
89Modesto/Chong-32
90Madison/Best-11
90Modesto/Cal-161
90Modesto/ProC-2226
91Madison/ProC-2144
92Salem/ClBest-10
92Salem/ProC-78
93CaroMud/RBI-6
93FExcel/ML-94

Thomas, Kelvin
90Penin/Star-23
91Erie/ClBest-11
91Erie/ProC-4081
91Penin/ClBest-3
91Penin/ProC-393

Thomas, Larry Jr.
91ClBest/Singl-418
91Utica/ClBest-20
91Utica/ProC-3240
92BirmB/ProC-2583
92ClBest-323
92Saraso/ClBest-22
92StCl/Dome-186
93B-35
93FExcel/ML-156

Thomas, Luther
(Bud)
39PlayBall-158
40PlayBall-42

Thomas, Mark
87Watertn-20
89Augusta/ProC-507
89Welland/Pucko-23
90Clmbia/PCPII-4
90Columbia/GS-24
91StLucie/ClBest-1
91StLucie/ProC-726

Thomas, Mike Samuel
(Mike)
91Bluefld/ClBest-5
91Bluefld/ProC-4141
92Bluefld/ClBest-3
92Bluefld/ProC-2373

Thomas, Mike Steven
(Mike)
90Pittsfld/Pucko-18
91Clmbia/PCPII-5
91Clmbia/PII-16
91Clmbia/PII-31M
92Rockford/ClBest-1
92Rockford/ProC-2115
93WPalmB/ClBest-23
93WPalmB/ProC-1340

Thomas, Mitch
86Salem-25
87PortChar-6
88Tulsa-4
90Tulsa/ProC-1157

Thomas, Orlando
87Erie-18
89Savan/ProC-349
90Spring/Best-15
91Spring/ClBest-26
91Spring/ProC-745
92Johnson/ClBest-27CO
92Johnson/ProC-3135CO

Thomas, Randy
79ArkTr-18

Thomas, Ray
90Target-1085

Thomas, Ricky
82Idaho-28

Thomas, Rob
88Bristol/ProC-1888
89Fayette/ProC-1571

Thomas, Rodney
91Princet/ClBest-16
91Princet/ProC-3529
92Princet/ClBest-19
92Princet/ProC-3102

Thomas, Ron
88Pulaski/ProC-1769
89Pulaski/ProC-1889
90Sumter/Best-6
90Sumter/ProC-2434

Thomas, Roy Allen
E107
WG3-48

Thomas, Roy J.
78Charl
78T-711R
79T-563
80T-397
81Tacom-20
82SLCity-19
84F-622
84Mother/Mar-25
84Nes/792-181
84T-181
84T/St-348
85Cram/PCL-82
86F-478
86Mother/Mar-26
86T-626
87Calgary-13
89Pac/SenLg-124
89T/SenLg-121
90EliteSenLg-118
91Pac/SenLg-130

Thomas, Royal Jr.
88Clearw/Star-25
88Spartan/Star-20
89Clearw/Star-21
89Clearw/Star-26
90Foil/Best-248
90River/Best-25
90River/Cal-21
90River/ProC-2608
91Brisbane/Fut-18
91HighD/ClBest-12
91HighD/ProC-2395
92Wichita/ProC-3658
92Wichita/SB-646

Thomas, Skeets
91StPete/ProC-2291
92ArkTr/ProC-1143
92UD/ML-95

Thomas, Stan
76OPC-148
76T-148
77T-353
78Cr/PCL-53
92Yank/WIZ70-149
93Rang/Keeb-355

91OPC-63
91Panini/FrSt-36
91Pol/Card-25
91S-54
91StCl-66
91T-63
91UD-309A
91UD-309B
91Ultra-297
92D-513
92F-595
92L-150
92L/BlkGold-150
92OPC-323
92Pinn-345
92Pol/Card-22
92S-114
92StCl-447
92T-323
92T/Gold-323
92T/GoldWin-323
92UD-397
92Ultra-272
93D-775
93L-417
93OPC/Premier-74
93Pac/Spanish-582
93Phill/Med-32
93Pinn-516
93S-397
93Select-223
93Select/RookTr-125T
93StCl-642
93StCl/1stDay-642
93StCl/Phill-28
93UD-558
93Ultra-446
94D-301
94F-602
94Flair-213
94L-22
94Pac/Cr-488
94Phill/Med-32
94S-158
94S/GoldR-158
94StCl-355
94StCl/1stDay-355
94StCl/Gold-355
94StCl/Team-219
94T-722
94T/Finest-198
94T/FinestRef-198
94T/Gold-722
94UD-184
94UD/ElecD-184

Thompson, Mitch
91MissSt-54M
92MissSt-40CO
93MissSt-42CO

Thompson, Richard
(Rich)
81Watlo-16
82Chatt-5
83Ander-32
83BuffB-7
84BuffB-12
85F/Up-U120
85Maine-11
85Polar/Ind-41
85T/Tr-122T
86F-595
86OPC-242
86T-242
86T/St-215
86Vanco-26
88Memphis/Best-2
89Indianap/CMC-10
89Indianap/ProC-1237
90AAASingl/ProC-587
90Indianap/CMC-9
90Indianap/ProC-304
90OPC-474
90ProC/Singl-59
90T-474

Thompson, Rick
82AubAs-19

Thompson, Rob
89Utica/Pucko-25
92Albany/SB-25M

Thompson, Robby
86D/Rook-39
86F/Up-U115
86Mother/Giants-16
86Sf/Rook-25
86T/Tr-113T
87D-145
87D/OD-101
87F-285
87F/AwardWin-39
87F/Mini-106
87Leaf-64
87MSA/Discs-12
87Mother/SFG-10
87Sf-46
87Sf/TPrev-10M
87Stuart-13
87T-658
87T/Gloss60-40
87T/JumboR-21
87T/St-307
87T/St-91
87ToysRUs-30
88D-268
88D/Best-274
88F-98
88Leaf-120
88Mother/Giants-10
88OPC-208
88Panini/St-423
88S-146
88S/YS/I-28
88Sf-24
88T-472
88T/Big-83
88T/St-93
89B-473
89D-98
89D/Best-79
89F-344
89KennerFig-150
89Mother/Giants-10
89OPC-15
89Panini/St-215
89RedFoley/St-120
89S-172
89S/HotStar-84
89Sf-78
89T-15
89T/Big-163
89T/St-87
89UD-172
90B-233
90D-140
90D/BestNL-73
90F-73
90F/Can-73
90Leaf-199
90MLBPA/Pins-26
90Mother/Giant-10
90OPC-325
90Panini/St-371
90PublInt/St-83
90S-397
90S/100St-21
90Sf-60
90T-325
90T/Big-169
90T/Coins-59
90T/Mini-88
90T/St-83
90UD-169
91B-623
91Classic/200-44
91D-363
91F-273
91Leaf-107
91Mother/Giant-10
91OPC-705
91PG&E-2
91Panini/FrSt-68
91Panini/St-77
91S-26
91SFExam/Giant-14
91StCl-77
91StCl/Member*-8
91T-705
91UD-178
91Ultra-329
92B-448
92Classic/Game200-44
92D-52
92F-648
92Giant/PGE-33
92L-109
92L/BlkGold-109
92Mother/Giant-10
92OPC-475
92Panini-213
92Pinn-143
92S-247
92StCl-160
92Studio-119
92T-475
92T/Gold-475
92T/GoldWin-475
92TripleP-45
92UD-286
92Ultra-295
93B-436
93D-524
93F-538
93Flair-147
93L-30
93Mother/Giant-14
93OPC-301
93Pac/Spanish-277
93Panini-237
93Pinn-491
93S-593
93Select-139
93StCl-688
93StCl/1stDay-688
93StCl/Giant-30
93Studio-124
93T-115
93T/Gold-115
93TripleP-81
93UD-126
93UD-822TC
93UD/FunPack-103
93UD/SP-116
93Ultra-137
94B-407
94D-48
94D/Special-48
94F-703
94L-30
94OPC-20
94Pac/Cr-557
94Pac/Silv-36
94Panini-267
94Pinn-315
94Pinn/TeamP-2M
94S-406
94S/GoldS-29
94Sf/2000-186AS
94Sf/2000-46
94StCl/Team-5
94Studio-88
94T-385M
94T-505
94T/BlkGold-43
94T/Finest-68
94T/FinestRef-68
94T/Gold-385M
94T/Gold-505
94TripleP-109
94TripleP/Medal-6M
94UD-193
94UD/ElecD-193
94UD/SP-94
94Ultra-595
94Ultra/AwardWin-12

Thompson, Ryan
88StCath/ProC-2035
89StCath/ProC-2072
90Dunedin/Star-19
91AA/LineD-367
91Knoxvl/LineD-367
91Knoxvl/ProC-1783
92F/Up-106
92Syrac/MerchB-22
92Syrac/ProC-1984
92Syrac/SB-518
93B-270
93D-242RR
93F-481
93L/GRook-7
93Mets/Kahn-44
93OPC-351
93OPC/Premier-79
93Pac/Spanish-548
93Pinn-249
93Pinn/RookTP-9
93S-227
93S/Boys-9
93S/Proctor-6
93Select/RookTr-39T
93StCl-542
93StCl/1stDay-542
93T-547
93T/Gold-547
93ToysRUs-17
93UD-373
93Ultra-435
94B-240
94D-157
94F-579
94Flair-202
94L-48
94OPC-135
94Pac/Cr-418
94Panini-223
94Pinn-400
94S-576
94Select-46
94StCl-274
94StCl/1stDay-274
94StCl/Gold-274
94Studio-120
94T-98
94T/Finest-39
94T/FinestRef-39
94T/Gold-98
94TripleP-150
94UD-160
94UD/CollC-276
94UD/CollC/Gold-276
94UD/CollC/Silv-276
94UD/ElecD-160
94Ultra-241

Thompson, Sam
76Shakey-146
80Perez/HOF-146
80SSPC/HOF
E223
N172
N284
Scrapps
WG1-25

Thompson, Scot
79T-716R
80OPC-298
80T-574
81Coke
81D-519
81F-296
81T-295
82Iowa-11
82RedLob
83D-378
83T-481
84D-167
85F-621
85Mother/Giants-15
85T-646
86F-262
86Fresno/Smok-21
86OPC-93
86T-93

Thompson, Sean
88Pocatel/ProC-2079
90Salinas/Cal-137
90Salinas/ProC-2734

Thompson, Squeezer
88Spokane/ProC-1927
90CharRain/ProC-2030

Thompson, Tim
80Knoxvl/TCMA-15
82Knoxvl-12
83Syrac-20
84Syrac-30

Thompson, Timothy
84Visalia-11

Thompson, Tom
86BuffB-22
87SanBern-23

Thompson, Tommy 1
47Signal
47Sunbeam

Thompson, Tommy 2
79ArkTr-7
81Durham-5
82Durham-11
82FtMyr-3
85Greenvl/Team-19
86Jaxvl/TCMA-19C
87Hawaii-9
87Jaxvl-25
88BirmB/Best-10
88Jaxvl/Best-24
88Jaxvl/ProC-971
88SLAS-39
89BirmB/Best-27
89BirmB/ProC-104
89Tulsa/GS-1MG
89Tulsa/Team-25MG
90Tulsa/ProC-1172MG
90Tulsa/Team-25MG
90Utica/Pucko-25
91AAA/LineD-324MG
91OkCty/LineD-324MG
91OkCty/ProC-193MG
91Pac/SenLg-86
91SoBend/ClBest-27MG
91SoBend/ProC-2MG
92OkCty/ProC-1929MG
92OkCty/SB-324MG
94Conlon-1244

Thompson, Tony
86LitFalls-28

Thompson, William
90CharRain/Best-22

Thompson, Willie
78Knoxvl
79Knoxvl/TCMA-26

Thomsen, Chris
91SoOreg/ClBest-7
91SoOreg/ProC-3858
92SoOreg/ProC-3429

Thomson, Bobby
47HomogBond-46
48B-47
49B-18
49Eureka-124
49Royal-10
50B-28
50Drake-9
51B-126
52B-2
52BR
52Coke
52RM-NL24
52Royal
52StarCal-90C
52StarCal/L-78A
52T-313
53RM-NL25
53SpicSpan/3x5-24
53SpicSpan/7x10-13
54B-201
54JC-34
54SpicSpan/PostC-18
55B-102
55Gol/Braves-28
55JC-34
55RFG-23
55SpicSpan/DC-17
55W605-23
56T-257
57SpicSpan/4x5-16
57T-262
58Hires-46
58SFCallB-24
58T-430
59T-429
60NuCard-10
60T-153
61NuCard-480
76Laugh/Jub-29
77Galasso-255
77Galasso-39
79TCMA-202
80Pac/Leg-115
88Pac/Leg-45
89Swell-133
89T/LJN-45
90HOF/St-46
90Pac/Legend-106
90Swell/Great-21
91B-410M
91Crown/Orio-456
91Swell/Great-88
91T/Arc53-330
92AP/ASG-52
92Albany/ProC-2350
92Bz/Quadra-7M
93UD/ATH-119
93UD/ATH-164M
94TedW-56
D305
Exh47
PM10/Sm-188
R346-41

Thomson, Rob
88Lakeland/Star-24
89EastLDD/ProC-DD45CO
89London/ProC-1379CO
90FtLaud/Star-25CO
91PrWill/ClBest-26CO

91PrWill/ProC-1444CO
Thon, Dickie
76QuadC
78Cr/PCL-112
80T-663R
81D-290
81F-277
81T-209
81T/Tr-844
82F-235
82T-404
83D-191
83F-468
83F/St-10M
83F/St-3M
83T-558
84D-304
84D/AAS-44
84F-243
84F-634IA
84F/St-1
84Mother/Ast-7
84Nes/792-692
84OPC-344
84Seven-23W
84T-692
84T/RD-22M
84T/St-64
85F-364
85Mother/Ast-9
85OPC-44
85T-44
85T/RD-23M
85T/St-63
86D-572
86F-313
86Mother/Ast-26
86OPC-166
86Pol/Ast-17
86T-166
86T/St-33
86T/Tatt-1M
87D-261
87F-70
87Leaf-196
87Mother/Ast-25
87Pol/Ast-14
87T-386
88S/Tr-29T
88Smok/Padres-29
88T/Tr-121T
89B-400
89D-441
89F-320
89OPC-181
89Phill/TastyK-34
89S-234
89S/Tr-55
89T-726
89T/Tr-119T
89UD-258
89UD/Ext-704
90B-155
90D-549
90D/BestNL-81
90F-573
90F/Can-573
90Leaf-105
90MLBPA/Pins-4
90OPC-269
90Panini/St-318
90Phill/TastyK-28
90PublInt/St-251
90S-142
90T-269
90T/Big-115
90T/St-115
90UD-439
91B-499
91D-91
91F-412
91Leaf-60
91OPC-439
91Panini/FrSt-106
91Panini/St-106
91Phill/Medford-34
91S-103
91StCl-184
91T-439
91UD-449
91Ultra-272
92B-162
92D-510
92F-546
92L-180
92L/BlkGold-180
92Mother/Rang-12
92OPC-557
92OPC/Premier-19
92Panini-245
92Pinn-394
92S-24
92S/RookTr-41T
92StCl-868
92Studio-250
92T-557
92T/Gold-557
92T/GoldWin-557
92T/Tr-118T
92T/TrGold-118T
92UD-150
92UD-769
92Ultra-447
93L-482
93OPC/Premier-16
93Pac/Spanish-318
93Pol/Brew-25
93Rang/Keeb-358
93UD-769
93Ultra-578
94F-193
94Pac/Cr-345
94S-505
Thon, Frankie
78Cedar
80Clinton-17
Thoney, John
E107
M116
T201
Thor, Audie
80Memphis-30
Thorell, Billy
90NE-26
Thorell, Greg
90NE-25
Thorell, Mike
87AZ/Pol-16
88AZ/Pol-14
Thoren, Rick
77AppFx
Thormahlen, H.F.
90Target-801
V100
Thormahlen, Herb
28LaPresse-10
28LaPresse-13M
Thormodsgard, Paul
78OPC-73
78T-162
78Twin/FriszP-21
79T-249
79Toledo-2
80OkCty
Thorn, John
90LitSun-23
Thornton, Al
86Elmira-24
87Elmira/Black-13
87Elmira/Red-13
88Elmira-20
Thornton, Andre
74OPC-604R
74T-604R
75OPC-39
75T-39
75T/M-39
76Crane-62
76Expo/Redp-31
76MSA/Disc
76OPC-26
76T-26
78OPC-114
78T-148
79Ho-93
79OPC-140
79T-280
79T/Comics-6
80K-28
80OPC-278
80T-534
80T/S-43
80T/Super-43
81D-198
81OPC-128
81T-388
81T/St-70
82D-324
82F-380
82F/St-201
82OPC-161
82T-746
82T/St-174
82Wheat/Ind
83D-211
83F-421
83F-635M
83F/St-8M
83F/St-9M
83K-26
83OPC-344
83OPC/St-55FOIL
83T-640
83T/Gloss40-3
83T/St-55
83Wheat/Ind-29
84D-25DK
84D-94
84D/AAS-15
84F-554
84Nes/792-115
84OPC-115
84T-115
84T/RD-22M
84T/St-255
84Wheat/Ind-29
85D-468
85F-457
85F/St-32
85F/St-47
85FunFoodPin-125
85Leaf-102
85OPC-272
85Polar/Ind-29
85T-475
85T/RD-23M
85T/St-244
86D-251
86F-596
86F/St-120
86Leaf-129
86OPC-59
86OhHenry-29
86Sf-171
86T-336M
86T-59
86T/St-208
86T/Tatt-3M
87D-279
87D/OD-108
87F-262
87Gator-29
87OPC-327
87T-780
88RedFoley/St-91
88S-231
89Swell-117
90Swell/Great-47
93UD/ATH-120
Thornton, Eric
89Kingspt/Star-23
90Pittsfld/Pucko-3
Thornton, Lou
85F/Up-U121
85Tor/Fire-29
86F-71
86OPC-18
86Syrac-25
86T-488
87Syrac-3
87Syrac/TCMA-21
89BuffB/CMC-22
89BuffB/ProC-1669
89Tidew/ProC-1954
90AAASingl/ProC-290
90Kahn/Mets-1
90ProC/Singl-362
90T/TVMets-34
90Tidew/CMC-11
90Tidew/ProC-559
91WIZMets-406
Thornton, Woodie A.
T206
T213/brown
Thorp, Bradley S.
81VeroB-22
Thorpe, Benjamin R.
(Bob)
52T-367
53SpicSpan/3x5-25
57Seattle/Pop-35
77Fritsch-5
Thorpe, James F.
(Jim)
33SK*-6
73F/Wild-3
81Conlon-31
87Conlon/2-59
88Conlon/4-28
92Conlon/Col-22
92Conlon/Sport-403
93Conlon-771
D350/2-176
M101/5-176
Thorpe, Michael
86Cram/NWL-111
87Wausau-19
Thorpe, Paul
86Hagers-25
87Hagers-23
88CharlK/Pep-17
89Hagers/Best-19
89Hagers/ProC-285
89Hagers/Star-21
90EastLAS/ProC-EL10
90Hagers/Best-26
90Hagers/ProC-1414
90Hagers/Star-24
Thorson, Brian
(Doc)
79Holyo-16
80BurlB-9
81Vanco-7
82Vanco-24
84Albany-9
85Huntsvl/BK-TR
88Madis-24
90Huntsvl/Best-26
91Huntsvl/ClBest-10
92Madis/ClBest-28TR
Thorton, John
86ElPaso-21
Thoutsis, Paul
87WinHaven-27
90ArkTr/GS-28
92NewBrit/ProC-448
92NewBrit/SB-498
Thrams, Jeff
89Boise/ProC-1988
Threadgill, Chris
88Bend/Legoe-12
89PalmSp/Cal-42
89PalmSp/ProC-472
Threadgill, George
85BurlR-8
86DayBe-28
86FSLAS-46
88Tulsa-2
89Tulsa/GS-26
90Tulsa/Team-26
92Durham/ClBest-27CO
92Durham/ProC-1117
Threadgill, Henry
90QuadC/GS-20
Threatt, Tony
83Tampa-24
Thrift, Jim
87Salem-18
89Penin/Star-26MG
90Kgsport/Best-25MG
90Kgsport/Star-26MG
91Pittsfld/ClBest-25MG
91Pittsfld/ProC-3438MG
92Pittsfld/ClBest-18MG
92Pittsfld/ProC-3310MG
93Rockford/ClBest-30CO
Throneberry, M. Faye
52T-376
53T-49
55T-163
57T-356
59T-534
60L-136
60T-9
61T-282
91T/Arc53-49
Throneberry, Marv
58T-175
59T-326
60T-436
61P-85
61T-57
61T/St-166
63J-194
63P-194
63T-78
79TCMA-173
88Pac/Leg-48
90Pac/Legend-62
90Swell/Great-77
91Crown/Orio-457
91Swell/Great-89
91WIZMets-407
93UD/ATH-121
Throop, George
75Omaha/Team-16
76OPC-591R
76T-591R
Thrower, Keith
85Cram/PCL-128
86Tacom-22
Thurberg, Tom
77Wausau
81Louisvl-25
82ArkTr-10
83Louisvl/Riley-25
Thurman, Gary
85FtMyr-18
86Memphis/GoldT-26
86Memphis/SilverT-26
86SLAS-4
87Omaha-6
88D-44
88D/Rook-33
88F-272
88F/Mini-29
88Leaf-44RR
88Omaha/CMC-14
88Omaha/ProC-1521
88S-631
88S/YS/II-25
88Sf-223
88Smok/Royals-6
88T-89
89D-498
89F-296
89Panini/St-348
89S/HotRook-24
89T-323
89UD-347
90D-416
90F-121
90F/Can-121
90OPC-276
90Omaha/CMC-19
90ProC/Singl-194
90PublInt/St-359
90T-276
91B-316
91F-573
91F/UltraUp-U29
91Pol/Royal-23
91StCl-306
92D-346
92F-172
92OPC-494
92Pol/Royal-26
92S-512
92StCl-131
92T-494
92T/Gold-494
92T/GoldWin-494
92UD-629
93D-629
93F-626
93Pac/Spanish-450
93StCl-52
93StCl/1stDay-52
93Tiger/Gator-24
94S-268
94S/GoldR-268
Thurman, Robert
52Mother-49
56Kahn
57Kahn
57T-279
58T-34
59T-341
86Negro/Frit-60
87Negro/Dixon-39
92Negro/Retort-59
Thurmond, Mark
81Hawaii-21
82Hawaii-21
83LasVegas/BHN-21
84D-505
84F-315
84Mother/Padres-26
84Nes/792-481

84Smok/Padres-25
84T-481
85D-284
85F-46
85Leaf-149
85Mother/Padres-21
85OPC-236
85T-236
86D-261
86F-337
86T-37
87Cain's-17
87D-543
87F-166
87T-361
88D-599
88F-73
88S-382
88T-552
89French-21
89T-152
89UD-571
90D-612
90F-191
90F/Can-191
90OPC-758
90PubIInt/St-588
90S-350
90T-758
91AAA/LineD-389
91Crown/Orio-458
91F-274
91Phoenix/LineD-389

Thurston, Hollis
(Sloppy)
25Exh-80
26Exh-80
28Exh/PCL-28
90Target-802
92Watlo/ClBest-11
92Watlo/ProC-2145
93Conlon-735
94Conlon-1264

Thurston, Jerrey
91CharRain/ClBest-13
91CharRain/ProC-98
91ClBest/Singl-102
91Spokane/ClBest-21
91Spokane/ProC-3952

Tiant, Luis
65Kahn
65OPC-145
65T-145
65T/trans-30
66T-285
67CokeCap/Indian-1
67T-377
68Kahn
68T-532
69Kahn
69MB-271
69MLB/St-44
69MLBPA/Pin-28
69OPC-11LL
69OPC-7LL
69OPC-9LL
69OPC/DE-22
69T-11LL
69T-560
69T-7LL
69T-9LL
69T/DE-7
69T/S-13
69T/St-169
69T/decal
69Trans-3
70K-56
70MLB/St-239
70OPC-231
70T-231
71MLB/St-475
71OPC-95
71T-95
72MB-342
73OPC-270
73OPC-65LL
73T-270
73T-65LL
74OPC-167
74T-167
74T/DE-27
74T/St-138
75Ho-102
75K-49
75OPC-430
75T-430
75T/M-430
76Crane-63
76Ho-23
76Ho/Twink-23
76MSA/Disc
76OPC-130
76SSPC-424
76T-130
77BurgChef-34
77Ho-10
77Ho/Twink-10
77OPC-87
77T-258
77T/CS-48
77T/ClothSt-48
78OPC-124
78PapaG/Disc-23
78SSPC/270-176
78T-345
78Wiffle/Discs-75
79BK/Y-8
79OPC-299
79T-575
80OPC-19
80T-35
81D-231
81F-82
81Portl-23
81T-627
82OPC-160
82T-160
83D-542
83OPC-179SV
83T-178
83T-179SV
89Pac/SenLg-77
89TM/SenLg-105
89TM/SenLg-118M
90EliteSenLg-119
91LineD-11
91Swell/Great-90
92AP/ASG-46
92GulfCD/ProC-3585
92Yank/WIZ70-151
92Yank/WIZ80-191
93Metallic-20
93TWill-6
93UD/ATH-122
94TedW/54-36

Tibbs, Jay
82Lynch-19
83Lynch-16
84Tidew-15
85D-262
85F-553
85T-573
86D-262
86Expo/Prov/Pan-8
86F-194
86F/Up-U116
86Provigo-8
86T-176
86T/Tr-114T
87D-282
87Expo/PostC-9
87F-333
87Leaf-207
87OPC-9
87T-9
88French-53
88OPC-282
88RochR/CMC-10
88RochR/ProC-201
88RochR/Team-24
88S-608
88T-464
89F-624
89RochR/ProC-1633
89S-262
89T-271
89UD-655
90F-192
90F/Can-192
90OPC-677
90PubIInt/St-589
90S-480
90T-677
91Crown/Orio-459

Tiburcio, Freddy
82Durham-12
83Durham-14
85Greenvl/Team-20
86Greenvl/Team-20
87Toledo-11
87Toledo/TCMA-6

Tidrow, Dick
72OPC-506R
72T-506R
73OPC-339
73T-339
74OPC-231
74T-231
74T/St-170
75OPC-241
75T-241
75T/M-241
76OPC-248
76SSPC-428
76SSPC/MetsY-Y23
76T-248
77BK/Y-9
77OPC-235
77T-461
78BK/Y-6
78SSPC/270-10
78T-179
79OPC-37
79T-89
80T-594
81Coke
81D-551
81F-299
81T-352
82D-477
82F-604
82F/St-99
82OPC-249
82RedLob
82T-699
82T/St-27
83F-510
83F/St-11M
83F/St-2M
83OPC/St-225
83T-787
83T/St-225
83T/Tr-112T
83TrueVal/WSox-41
84F-72
84Nes/792-153
84T-153
91WIZMets-408
92Yank/WIZ70-152

Tidwell, Danny
75Anderson/TCMA-24

Tidwell, Mike
91Geneva/ClBest-22
91Geneva/ProC-4216
92Peoria/ClBest-3
92Peoria/Team-28

Tiefenauer, Bob
55Hunter
59T-501
62T-227
62T/St-131
64T-522
65OPC-23
65T-23
68T-269
80Penin/B-10C
80Penin/C-27C
83Reading-24
85Cram/PCL-47
86Portl-22C
87Spartan-22C
88Batavia/ProC-1662
92Yank/WIZ60-127

Tiernan, Mike
N172
N566-176
WG1-44

Tierney, James A.
(Cotton)
21Exh-176
21Exh-177
90Target-803
E120
V100
W572
W573
WG7-55

Tierney, Tom
91Idaho/ProC-4343

Tietje, Les
94Conlon-1283

Tijerina, Tony
91Pittsfld/ClBest-1
91Pittsfld/ProC-3426
92StLucie/ClBest-22
92StLucie/ProC-1750

Tilden, Bill
33SK*-16

Tillman, Darren
91Hunting/ClBest-25
91Hunting/ProC-3350
92Geneva/ClBest-24
92Geneva/ProC-1574
92Peoria/ClBest-2

Tillman, J. Bob
61Union
62T-368
63T-384
64T-112
65OPC-222
65T-222
66OPC-178
66T-178
67CokeCap/RedSox-10
67OPC-36
67T-36
67T/Test/RSox-23
68OPC-174
68T-174
69MB-272
69T-374
70T-668
71MLB/St-453
71OPC-244
71T-244
72MB-343
78TCMA-172
92Yank/WIZ60-128

Tillman, Ken
81Redwd-20

Tillman, Rusty
82Tidew-11
83Tidew-19
84Tidew-9
85Cram/PCL-102
86Tacom-23
88Phoenix/CMC-21
88Phoenix/ProC-59
89Phoenix/CMC-15
89Phoenix/ProC-1479
91WIZMets-409

Tillman, Tommy
(Tony)
89BurlInd/Star-23
90BurlInd/ProC-3008

Tillotson, Thad
67T-553R
81TCMA-462
92Yank/WIZ60-129

Tilma, Tommy
90WichSt-34

Tilmon, Pat
88BurlB/ProC-6
89Durham/Star-21
89Durham/Team-21
90Durham/Team-14

Timberlake, Don
83Peoria/Frit-13
85MidldA-12
86MidldA-22

Timberlake, Gary
No Cards.

Timko, Andy
81Miami-13
90HagersDG/Best-32

Timko, John
92Niagara/ClBest-20
92Niagara/ProC-3328

Timlin, Mike
88Myrtle/ProC-1184
89Dunedin/Star-19
90Dunedin/Star-20
90FSLAS/Star-45
90Star/ISingl-67
91B-15
91Classic/III-90
91D/Rook-27
91F/Up-U68
91Leaf-525
91OPC/Premier-122
91S/RookTr-85T
91S/ToroBJ-7
91T/Tr-121T
91UD/Ext-785
92BJ/Fire-29
92D-301
92F-343
92F/RookSIns-8
92OPC-108
92OPC/Premier-172
92S-214
92S/100RisSt-58
92StCl-493
92Syrac/MerchB-23
92T-108
92T/91Debut-172
92T/Gold-108
92T/GoldWin-108
92UD-409
93BJ/D/45-22
93BJ/Demp-25
93BJ/Fire-31
93D-87
93F-701
93L-465
93OPC-295
93Pac/Spanish-657
93S-410
93StCl-120
93StCl/1stDay-120
93T-564
93T/Gold-564
93ToysRUs-42
93UD-322
93Ultra-294
94F-345
94Flair-123
94S-298
94S/GoldR-298
94StCl-441
94StCl/1stDay-441
94StCl/Gold-441
94StCl/Team-180
94T-333
94T/Gold-333
94Ultra-144

Timmerman, Tom
70T-554
71MLB/St-408
71OPC-296
71T-296
72OPC-239
72T-239
73OPC-413
73T-413
74OPC-327
74T-327

Timmons, Ozzie
91Geneva/ClBest-23
91Geneva/ProC-4233
92StCl/Dome-187
92UD/ML-162
92UD/POY-PY8
93B-552
94B-466
94FExcel-169

Tincup, Frank
44Centen-23

Tingle, Darrel
87Oneonta-3
88PrWill/Star-22

Tingley, Ron
81Hawaii-1
82Hawaii-1
83LasVegas/BHN-22
85Cram/PCL-97
86Richm-23
87BuffB-11
88ColoSp/CMC-12
88ColoSp/ProC-1532
89ColoSp/CMC-11
89ColoSp/ProC-257
89F-414
89Panini/St-316
89S/HotRook-56
89T-721
89T/Big-37
90AAASingl/ProC-96
90Edmon/CMC-23
90Edmon/ProC-520
90ProC/Singl-500
91AAA/LineD-171
91Edmon/LineD-171
91Edmon/ProC-1519
92D-287
92OPC-388
92S-757
92StCl-233

92TripleP-193M
93D-621
93F-577
93Mother/Angel-25
93Pac/Spanish-373
93Panini-3
93StCl-169
93StCl/1stDay-169
93StCl/Angel-5
94F-71
94Pac/Cr-91
Tinker, Harold
88Negro/Duques-19
92Negro/Retort-60
Tinker, Joe
10Domino-116
11Diamond-27
11Helmar-107
12Sweet/Pin-93
12Sweet/Pin-93A
14CJ-3
14Piedmont/St-55
15CJ-3
48Exh/HOF
50Callahan
50W576-70
60Exh/HOF-23
60F-40
61F-143
63Bz/ATG-1
69Bz/Sm
76Shakey-47
77Galasso-160
80Marchant/HOF-29
80Pac/Leg-42
80Perez/HOF-47
80SSPC/HOF
84Cub/Uno-7M
90Perez/GreatMom-40
92Cub/OldStyle-25
93Conlon-817
93CrackJack-16
93UD/ATH-123
93UD/ATH-147
93UD/T202-9
94Conlon-1164
BF2-68
D303
D329-174
D350/2-177
E101
E102
E105
E106
E254
E270/1
E300
E90/1
E90/3
E91
E92
E93
E96
E98
L1-122
M101/4-174
M101/5-177
M116
PM1-13
S74-71
S81-97
T202
T204
T205
T206
T207
T213/blue
T214-27
T215/blue
T215/brown
T216
T3-35
W555
WG5-40
WG6-36
Tinkey, Jim
86SanJose-21
Tinkey, Robert
87Kenosha-13
88Kenosha/ProC-1379
Tinkle, David
86Cram/NWL-27
87FtMyr-5
Tinney, Roy
57Seattle/Pop-36
Tinning, Lyle
32Orbit/num-17
32Orbit/un-55
34G-71
R305
Tinsley, Lee
88SoOreg/ProC-1706
89Madis/Star-21
90Madison/Best-12
90Madison/ProC-2282
90MidwLgAS/GS-20
90ProC/Singl-868
91AA/LineD-295
91ClBest/Singl-207
91Huntsvl/ClBest-23
91Huntsvl/LineD-295
91Huntsvl/Team-20
91HuntsvlProC-1810
92Canton/ProC-704
92ColoSp/SB-97
92OPC-656M
92Sky/AAASingl-42
92T-656R
92T/Gold-656M
92T/GoldWin-656M
93F/Final-275
93Pinn-604
93StCl/Mar-12
93Ultra-624
94StCl-493
94StCl/1stDay-493
94StCl/Gold-493
Tippitt, Brad
91Kane/Team-21
92Freder/ClBest-5
92Freder/ProC-1807
Tipton, Eric
44Playball-29
Tipton, Gordon
88CapeCod/Sum-136
90GreatF/SportP-20
91Bakers/Cal-4
92Bakers/Cal-25
Tipton, Jeff
82Madis/Frit-13
Tipton, Joe
49B-103
50B-159
51B-82
52T-134
53B/BW-13
53Briggs
54B-180
Tirado, Aristarco
86Albany/TCMA-25
86FtLaud-22
87PrWill-18
88Albany/ProC-1348
89Albany/Best-18
89Albany/ProC-331
89Albany/Star-20
Tirpack, Ken
92Elizab/ClBest-9
92Elizab/ProC-3688
94FExcel-99
Tischinski, Tom
70OPC-379
70T-379
71MLB/St-476
71OPC-724
71T-724
74Albuq/Team-21
Tisdale, Freddie
79ArkTr-11
80ArkTr-18
81ArkTr-5
Tisdale, Tom
90Gaston/Best-28TR
91Gaston/ClBest-28TR
Titcomb, Ledell
N172
N338/2
Titus, John
10Domino-117
11Helmar-152
12Sweet/Pin-132A
12Sweet/Pin-132B
E254
M116
S74-105
T201
T202
T205
T206
Tjader, Jimmy
80Ashvl-11
Toale, John
85Elmira-22
86Cram/NWL-7
86Everett/Pop-33
86Greens-23
87Clinton-2
87WinHaven-16
88StLucie/Star-23
89London/ProC-1365
90EastLAS/ProC-EL3
90London/ProC-1283
90ProC/Singl-732
91AA/LineD-21
91Albany/LineD-21
91Albany/ProC-1013
94ClBest/Gold-96
94FExcel-195
Tobey, Keith
90LitSun/HSPros-10
90LitSun/HSProsG-10
Tobias, Grayling
80Memphis-24
Tobik, Dave
79T-706R
80T-269
81T-102
82D-511
82T-391
83D-385
83F-343
83OPC-186
83Rang-41
83T-691
83T/Tr-113T
84F-433
84Nes/792-341
84T-341
85Cram/PCL-87
93Rang/Keeb-359
Tobin, Dan
90LitSun/HSPros-18
90LitSun/HSProsG-18
91Billing/SportP-4
91Billings/ProC-3752
92Billings/ProC-3356
Tobin, James A.
39PlayBall-9
41G-30
43Playball-40
90HOF/St-41
92Conlon/Sport-372
94Conlon-1257
Tobin, John T.
(Jack)
21Exh-178
25Exh-118
48Sommer-16
49Sommer-27
53Mother-45
88Conlon/5-28
94Conlon-1168
E120
E126-44
E126-50
V100
V61-2
W573
Todd, Alfred
41G-28
90Target-804
91Conlon/Sport-239
Todd, Chuck
86Watlo-28
Todd, Jackson
78T-481
79Syrac/TCMA-13
79Syrac/Team-16
80Syrac-4
80Syrac/Team-20
81D-31
81OPC-142
81T-142
82D-178
82F-623
82OPC-327
82Syrac-9
82Syrac/Team-22
82T-565
86ElPaso-22CO
87Denver-21CO
88Denver/ProC-1250
89Denver/CMC-24CO
89Denver/ProC-51CO
90AAASingl/ProC-667CO
90Denver/CMC-26CO
90Denver/ProC-642CO
90ProC/Singl-672CO
91Gaston/ProC-2706CO
91WIZMets-410
92Tulsa/ProC-2711CO
92Tulsa/SB-625M
Todd, Jim
73Wichita-16
74Wichita-110
75OPC-519
75T-519
75T/M-519
76OPC-221
76SSPC-478
76T-221
77T-31
78T-333
79OPC-46
79T-103
80T-629
Todd, Kyle
86PrWill-27
87Harris-13
88ColAst/Best-9
Todd, Theron
88CLAS/Star-37
88Durham/Star-21
89Durham/Star-22
89Durham/Team-22
89Star/Wax-73
90Durham/Team-15
Todt, Phil
25Exh-70
26Exh-71
27Exh-35
28Exh-36
29Exh/4-18
33G-86
92Conlon/Sport-419
R316
V354-39
Toerner, Sean
81Clinton-20
Tofoya, Dennis
93CaroMud/RBI-13
Toft, Marv
61Union
Togher, Martin
91FresnoSt/Smok-13
Togneri, Paul
87Belling/Team-30
Tokheim, David
92ClBest-77
92Clearw/ClBest-9
92Clearw/ProC-2072
Tokunaga, Eric
87Hawaii-30M
Tolan, Bob
65OPC-116R
65T-116R
66OPC-179R
66Pep/Tul
66T-179R
67T-474
68OPC-84
68T-84
69MB-273
69T-448
69T/St-30
70MLB/St-36
70OPC-409
70T-409
71MD
71MLB/St-71
71OPC-190
71OPC-200NLCS
71T-190
71T-200NLCS
71T/Coins-81
71T/tatt-12
72MB-344
72OPC-3
72T-3
73K-32
73OPC-335
73T-335
74Greyhound-6M
74McDon
74OPC-535
74T-535
75Ho-1
75Ho/Twink-1
75OPC-402
75T-402
75T/M-402
76Ho-42
76Ho/Twink-42
76OPC-56
76T-56
77T-188
80T-708
84Beaum-21
85Beaum-25
89Erie/Star-27
89Pac/SenLg-1
89T/SenLg-59
89TM/SenLg-106
90EliteSenLg-2
91Pac/SenLg-152
Tolar, Kevin
90Utica/Pucko-24
91ClBest/Singl-114
91MidwLAS/ProC-12
91SoBend/ClBest-1
91SoBend/ProC-2857
92Salinas/ClBest-16
92SoBend/ProC-177
Tolbert, Mark
90Savan/ProC-2069
Tolentino, Jose
85Cram/PCL-127
86SLAS-6
87Tacom-17
88OkCty/CMC-14
88OkCty/ProC-41
89Tucson/CMC-13
89Tucson/JP-25
89Tucson/ProC-183
90AAASingl/ProC-202
90ProC/Singl-615
90Tucson/CMC-13
90Tucson/ProC-212
91AAA/LineD-620
91Tucson/LineD-620
91Tucson/ProC-2222
92BuffB/BlueS-21
92BuffB/ProC-329
92BuffB/SB-42
92D-589
92OPC-541
92T-541
92T/91Debut-173
92T/Gold-541
92T/GoldWin-541
Tolentino, Reynaldo
91GulfCR/SportP-25
Toler, Greg
85Cedar-15
86Cedar/TCMA-11
Toliver, Fred
82Cedar-7
83Indianap-19
84Wichita/Rock-20
86CIGNA-15
86D-612
86F-647R
86F/Up-U117
86Phill/TastyK-43
86Portl-23
87Maine-5
87Maine/TCMA-7
87Phill/TastyK-43
87T-63
88Portl/CMC-8
88Portl/ProC-664
88T-203
89B-147
89D-510
89F-126
89S-479
89T-623
89UD-64
90OPC-423
90T-423
92Salinas/ProC-3755
93CaroMud/RBI-21
93F/Final-120
Tolleson, Wayne
79Tulsa-1
80Tulsa-16
83D-573
83Rang-3

83T/Tr-114T
84D-464
84F-434
84Nes/792-557
84Rang-3
84T-557
84T/St-358
85D-378
85F-571
85Rang-3
85T-247
86Coke/WS-1
86D-134
86F-573
86F/Up-U118
86Leaf-59
86T-641
86T/Tr-115T
87D-524
87D/OD-245
87F-118
87OPC-224
87T-224
88D-154
88F-223
88OPC-133
88Panini/St-157
88S-117
88T-411
89D-659
89S/NWest-9
89T-716
90PubIInt/St-549
90S-386
90S/NWest-26
90T/TVYank-27
90T/Tr-123T
90TulsaDG/Best-3
90UD-320
92Yank/WIZ80-192
93Rang/Keeb-360

Tolliber, Jerome
92ColumMet/SAL/II-14

Tollison, Dave
88CapeCod/Sum-141
90StCath/ProC-3471
91Dunedin/ClBest-19
91Dunedin/ProC-217
92ClBest-163
92Knoxvl/ProC-3000
92Knoxvl/SB-395
93ClBest/MLG-175

Tolliver, Jerome
91Pittsfld/ClBest-7
91Pittsfld/ProC-3437
92ClBest-82
92ColumMet/ClBest-1
92ColumMet/ProC-311

Tolman, Tim
81Tucson-20
82Tucson-8
84Cram/PCL-57
85Mother/Ast-23
86Nashvl-24
86T-272
87Toledo-12
87Toledo/TCMA-23
88Tidew/CANDL-13
88Tidew/CMC-23
88Tidew/ProC-1584
89Syrac/CMC-14
89Syrac/MerchB-22
89Syrac/ProC-815
89Syrac/Team-22
90AAASingl/ProC-211CO
90Tucson/ProC-221CO
91BurlAs/ClBest-27MG
91BurlAs/ProC-2817MG
92Ashvl/ClBest-26

Toman, Tom
75AppFx
76AppFx
78Knoxvl

Tomanek, Dick
58T-123
59T-369

Tomaselli, Chuck
84Nashvl-23

Tomasello, John
92Gaston/ProC-2263

Tomberlin, Andy
86Sumter/ProC-27
88BurlB/ProC-24
89Durham/Star-23
89Durham/Team-23
89Star/Wax-74
90Foil/Best-265
90Greenvl/Best-19
90Greenvl/ProC-1142
90Greenvl/Star-19
90Richm/Bob-20
91AAA/LineD-445
91Richm/Bob-1
91Richm/LineD-445
91Richm/Team-19
92Richm/Bleach-8
92Richm/Comix-24
92Richm/ProC-390
92Richm/SB-446
94D-329
94Pinn-227
94Pinn/Artist-227
94Pinn/Museum-227
94StCl-70
94StCl/1stDay-70
94StCl/Gold-70

Tomberlin, Rob
86Sumter/ProC-28

Tomchek, Dave
93Durham/Team-21TR

Tomkins, Larry
91MissSt-44
92MissSt-41
93MissSt-43

Tomlin, Dave
75OPC-578
75T-578
75T/M-578
76OPC-398
76SSPC-627
76T-398
77Padre/SchCd-33
77T-241
78Pep-24
78T-86
79T-674
80T-126
81Syrac-22
81Syrac/Team-21
82Indianap-25
84Cram/PCL-126
85Cram/PCL-241
86Indianap-31
87Indianap-7

Tomlin, Randy Leon
88Watertn/Pucko-12
89Salem/Star-22
90A&AASingle/ProC-14
90Harris/ProC-1192
90Harris/Star-17
91B-518
91Classic/I-83
91D-725
91F-52
91F/UltraUp-U103
91Leaf-203
91OPC-167
91S-782
91StCl-178
91T-167A
91T-167B
91T/90Debut-154
91T/JumboR-29
91ToysRUs-28
91UD/FinalEd-76F
92B-495
92D-367
92F-569
92L-256
92L/BlkGold-256
92OPC-571
92Pinn-213
92Pinn-606GRIP
92Pirate/Nation-22
92S-86
92StCl-661
92Studio-88
92T-571
92T/Gold-571
92T/GoldWin-571
92UD-537
92Ultra-261
93B-213
93D-570
93F-121
93L-24
93OPC-257
93Pac/Spanish-592
93Pinn-74
93Pirate/Nation-32
93S-101
93Select-61
93StCl-104
93StCl/1stDay-104
93Studio-219
93T-416
93T/Gold-416
93TripleP-197
93UD-284
93Ultra-102
94D-274
94F-621
94Pac/Cr-508
94Pinn-49
94Pinn/Artist-49
94Pinn/Museum-49
94StCl-316
94StCl/1stDay-316
94StCl/Gold-316
94T-338
94T/Finest-156
94T/FinestRef-156
94T/Gold-338
94UD-368

Tomlin, Rick
90Elizab/Star-25
91Elizab/ProC-4317CO
92Elizab/ClBest-24CO
92Elizab/ProC-3698

Tommy, Phillip
N172

Tomori, Denny
88Butte-12

Tompkins, Ron
66OPC-107R
66T-107R
68T-247R
73Wichita-17

Toms, Tommy
75Phoenix/Caruso-17
76Phoenix/Coke-20
77Phoenix
78Spring/Wiener-14

Tomsick, Troy
85Durham-13

Tomski, Jeffery
77Watlo
81Chatt-22

Tomso, Matt
91Savan/ClBest-12
91Savan/ProC-1653

Tonascia, Bruce
78Green

Toney, Anthony
(Andy)
88Fayette/ProC-1082
88SALAS/GS-15
89Lakeland/Star-23

Toney, Chris
88Martins/Star-31

Toney, Fred
11Helmar-108
16FleischBrd-94
61F-80
69Bz-1
72F/FFeat-14M
72Laugh/GF-39M
90HOF/St-17M
92Conlon/Sport-347
D327
D328-174
D329-175
D350/2-178
E120
E121/120
E121/80
E135-174
M101/4-175
M101/5-178
W501-69
W575

Toney, Mike
93MedHat/SportP-9

Tonkin, Wyatt
(Tonk)
78Green

Tonnucci, Norm
86Knoxvl-24
87Knoxvl-25
88Syrac/CMC-6
88Syrac/ProC-809

Tooch, Chuck
91Welland/ProC-3583
92Welland/ClBest-23
92Welland/ProC-1334

Toole, Matt
90Waterlo/Best-24
90Waterlo/ProC-2387

Tooley, Albert
90Target-805
T207

Toolson, Earl
49Remar

Toporcer, George
(Specs)
21Exh-179
25Exh-64
26Exh-64
81Conlon-35
88Conlon/3-30
91Conlon/Sport-176
92Conlon/Sport-644
93Conlon-893
E120
E121/120
E126-9
V61-82
W501-79
W573
W575

Torassa, George
79Cedar/TCMA-20

Torborg, Doug
85Anchora-27
87Watertn-28
88Salem/Star-21
89Miami/II/Star-18

Torborg, Jeff
64T-337R
65T-527
66T-257
67CokeCap/DodgAngel-10
67T-398
68T-492
69MB-274
69T-353
70OPC-54
70T-54
71MLB/St-119
71OPC-314
71T-314
72MB-345
72OPC-404
72T-404
73OPC-154
73T-154
78T-351
79T-96
89Coke/WS-3
89T/Tr-120MG
90Coke/WSox-26MG
90OPC-21MG
90T-21MG
90Target-806
91Kodak/WSox-10MG
91OPC-609MG
91T-609MG
92Mets/Kahn-10MG
92OPC-759MG
92T-759MG
92T/Gold-759MG
92T/GoldWin-759MG
93T-509M
93T/Gold-509M

Torchia, Todd
87Spokane-21
88Charl/ProC-1209

Torchia, Tony
81Bristol-8
83Pawtu-25
84Pawtu-3A
84Pawtu-3B
86NewBrit-24MG
87CharRain-17
88River/Cal-229
88River/ProC-1413
89LasVegas/ProC-27
90AAASingl/ProC-27CO
90LasVegas/CMC-24CO
90LasVegas/ProC-139CO
90ProC/Singl-527CO
91AAA/LineD-300M
91LasVegas/LineD-300CO
91LasVegas/ProC-255CO
92LasVegas/ProC-2810CO
92LasVegas/SB-250CO

Torgeson, Earl
49B-17
50B-163
50Drake-3
51B-99
51T/BB-34
52B-72
52NTea
52RM-NL25
52T-97
52TipTop
54B-63
55B-210
56T-147
57T-357
58T-138
59T-351
60L-122
60T-299
61T-152
92Yank/WIZ60-130
Exh47

Torian, Van
92Idaho/ProC-3520

Tornay, Nine
53Mother-11
57Seattle/Pop-37

Torre, Frank
56T-172
57T-37
58T-117
59T-65
60Lake
60SpicSpan-24
60T-478
62T-303
63T-161
90Pac/Legend-53
90Swell/Great-74
91Swell/Great-91

Torre, Joe
62J-152
62P-152
62P/Can-152
62Salada-152
62Shirriff-152
62T-218
62T-351M
62T/St-151
63J-156
63P-156
63T-347
64T-70
64T/Coins-118
64T/Coins-155AS
64T/S-26
64T/SU
64T/St-59
64T/tatt
64Wheat/St-44
65Bz-16
65Kahn
65OPC-200
65OldLond-19
65T-200
65T/E-12
65T/trans-31
66Bz-36
66Kahn
66OPC-130
66T-130
66T/RO-120
66T/RO-93
67Bz-36
67CokeCap/AS-20
67CokeCap/Brave-9
67CokeCap/NLAS-21
67Kahn
67OPC/PI-27
67T-350
67T/PI-27
68Bz-10
68CokeCap/Brave-9
68Dexter-73
68Kahn
68OPC-30
68T-30
68T/ActionSt-12A
68T/G-31
69Citgo-11
69Kahn

69Kelly/Pin-17
69MB-275
69MLB/St-216
69MLBPA/Pin-58
69T-460
69T/S-36
69T/St-10
69Trans-49
70MLB/St-144
70OPC-190
70T-190
70Trans-3
71K-62
71MLB/St-287
71OPC-370
71OPC-62LL
71T-370
71T-62LL
71T/Coins-11
71T/S-61
71T/Super-61
71T/tatt-10
72K-10
72MB-346
72OPC-341KP
72OPC-500
72OPC-85LL
72OPC-87LL
72ProStars/PostC-24
72T-341KP
72T-500
72T-85LL
72T-87LL
72T/Post-16
73K-31
73OPC-450
73T-450
73T/Comics-22
73T/Lids-52
73T/PinUps-22
74OPC-15
74T-15
74T/St-119
75Ho-70
75OPC-209MVP
75OPC-565
75T-209MVP
75T-565
75T/M-209MVP
75T/M-565
76Crane-64
76MSA/Disc
76OPC-585
76SSPC-541
76SSPC/MetsY-M20
76T-585
77T-425
78T-109MG
78TCMA-137
79T-82MG
80T-259MG
81D-506MG
81F-325MG
81T-681MG
82KMart-20
82Pol/Atl-9MG
83D-628MG
83Pol/Atl-9
83T-126MG
84Nes/792-502MG
84Pol/Atl-9MG
84T-502MG
85T-438MG
86Sf/Dec-49M
90MSA/AGFA-4
90Pac/Legend-107
90Swell/Great-130
91Leaf/StudPrev-17MG
91LineD-2
91OPC-351MG
91Pol/Card-9MG
91Swell/Great-92
91T-351MG
91WIZMets-411
92Card/McDon/Pac-39
92OPC-549MG
92Pol/Card-23MG
92T-549MG
92T/Gold-549MG
92T/GoldWin-549MG
93AP/ASG-151
93Pol/Card-22MG
93T-512M
93T/Gold-512M
93TWill-93

Torrealba, Pablo
76OPC-589R
76T-589R
77T-499
78T-78
79T-242
90Richm/25Ann-22

Torres, Al
77Charl
78Salem
79BuffB/TCMA-18
80Buffa-13
81Portl-24
82Buffa-7
89Miami/II/Star-19

Torres, Angel
78Indianap-18
80Indianap-27

Torres, Dilson
93StCath/ClBest-23
93StCath/ProC-3976

Torres, Felix
62T-595R
63J-27
63P-27
63T-482

Torres, Freddy
89Fayette/ProC-1588
89Niagara/Pucko-22
90Fayette/ProC-2418

Torres, Hector
69T-526
70OPC-272
70T-272
71MLB/St-47
71OPC-558
71T-558
72Dimanche*-46
72T-666
76OPC-241
76SSPC-128
76T-241
78Syrac
80Utica-11
81TCMA-342
82Knoxvl-22
87Syrac-20
87Syrac/TCMA-25
88Syrac/CMC-23
88Syrac/ProC-822
89Syrac/MerchB-25M
89Syrac/ProC-801
89Syrac/Team-25CO
91Tor/Fire-56
92Dunedin/ClBest-27CO
92Dunedin/ProC-2014CO

Torres, Jaime
92GulfCY/ProC-3794
93Greens/ClBest-23
93Greens/ProC-888

Torres, Jessie
90Augusta/ProC-2468
91Augusta/ClBest-14
91Augusta/ProC-808
92CaroMud/ProC-1186
92CaroMud/SB-145

Torres, Jose
83Butte-11
89Princet/Star-21

Torres, Leonardo
(Leo)
89Fayette/ProC-1569
90Fayette/ProC-2408
91Lakeland/ClBest-12
91Lakeland/ProC-267
92London/SB-420
92Sky/AASingl-176

Torres, Martin
85Tigres-13

Torres, Miguel
88Oneonta/ProC-2054

Torres, Paul
89Wythe/Star-27
90Geneva/ProC-3048
90Geneva/Star-7
90Peoria/Team-14
91ClBest/Singl-174
91Peoria/ClBest-13
91Peoria/Team-20
91WinSalem/ClBest-26
91WinSalem/ProC-2843
92ClBest-318
92WinSalem/ClBest-7
92WinSalem/ProC-1222

Torres, Phil
87VeroB-31
88SanAn/Best-17
89ColMud/Best-27

Torres, Rafael
92Helena/ProC-1716

Torres, Ramon
89BurlInd/Star-24
90BurlInd/ProC-3024
91ColInd/ProC-1502

Torres, Ray
79Knoxvl/TCMA-23
80GlenF/B-8
80GlenF/C-27
80Iowa/Pol-12A
80Iowa/Pol-12B
81AppFx-25
81GlenF-21

Torres, Rick
(Ricky)
84Greens-17
87PrWill-4
88Albany/ProC-1338
89Albany/Best-11
89Albany/ProC-335
89Albany/Star-21
90AAASingl/ProC-327
90Albany/Best-10
90Albany/Star-21
90ColClip/CMC-18
90ColClip/ProC-677
90ProC/Singl-218
90T/TVYank-64

Torres, Rosendo
(Rusty)
72OPC-124R
72T-124R
73OPC-571
73T-571
74OPC-499
74T-499
75SLCity/Caruso-1
77T-224
78Cr/PCL-118
80T-36
81Portl-25
92Yank/WIZ70-153

Torres, Rudy
83Ander-17

Torres, Salomon
91ClBest/Singl-324
91Clinton/ClBest-8
91Clinton/ProC-834
91MidwLAS/ProC-6
92B-4
92B-584FOIL
92ClBest-257
92ClBest/BBonusC-14
92ClBest/RBonus-BC14
92D/RookPhen-BC18
92L/GRook-11
92ProC/Tomorrow-353
92Shrev/ProC-3872
92Shrev/SB-596
92Sky/AASingl-263
92UD/ML-261
92UD/ML-34M
93B-660
93ClBest/MLG-134
93FExcel/ML-121
93LimeR/Winter-147
93LimeR/Winter-66
93StCl/Giant-5
94B-366
94B-631
94D-327
94F/MLP-33
94Finest-439
94Flair-247
94L-318
94OPC-165
94OPC/HotPros-3
94Pac/Cr-558
94Pinn-261
94Pinn/Artist-261
94Pinn/Museum-261
94Pinn/New-6
94Pinn/RookTPinn-9M
94S-641
94S/Boys-39
94Select-182
94Select/RookSurg-7
94Sf/2000-156
94Sf/Shak-5
94StCl-314
94StCl/1stDay-314
94StCl/Gold-314
94StCl/Team-10
94T-298
94T/Gold-298
94TripleP-293
94UD-28
94UD/CollC-19
94UD/CollC/Gold-19
94UD/CollC/Silv-19
94UD/ElecD-28
94Ultra-295

Torres, Tony
80Holyo-24
81ElPaso-18
92Erie/ClBest-29
92Erie/ProC-1634

Torrez, Mike
68OPC-162R
68T-162R
69OPC-136R
69T-136R
69T/4in1-25M
70OPC-312
70T-312
71MLB/St-288
71OPC-531
71T-531
72Dimanche*-47
73OPC-77
73T-77
74OPC-568
74T-568
75OPC-254
75T-254
75T/M-254
76Ho-139
76OPC-25
76SSPC-381
76T-25
77BK/Y-7
77BurgChef-110
77Ho-13
77Ho/Twink-13
77OPC-144
77T-365
78Ho-127
78PapaG/Disc-21
78SSPC/270-170
78T-645
79Ho-22
79OPC-92
79T-185
80OPC-236
80T-455
81D-216
81F-233
81OPC-216
81T-525
82Coke/Bos
82D-235
82F-310
82F/St-160
82T-225
82T-786TL
82T/St-151
82T/StVar-151
83D-512
83F-197
83F/St-26M
83OPC-312
83T-743
83T/Fold-1M
83T/Tr-115
84D-556
84F-602
84Nes/792-78
84OPC-78
84T-78
84T/St-113
89Pac/Leg-168
91Crown/Orio-460
91WIZMets-412
92Yank/WIZ70-154

Torrez, Peter
80RochR-21
84CharlO-9

Torricelli, Tim
87Stockton-22
88Beloit/GS-14
89ElPaso/GS-19
90AAASingl/ProC-654
90Denver/CMC-8
90Denver/ProC-629
90ProC/Singl-33
92Rockford/ProC-3012CO
93James/ClBest-26MG
93James/ProC-3342MG

Torrienti, Christobel
74Laugh/Black-18
90Negro/Star-19

Tortorice, Mark
86Modesto-25

Torve, Kelvin
83Phoenix/BHN-12
84Shrev/FB-23
85CharlO-7
86RochR-24
87RochR-21
87RochR/TCMA-15
88Portl/CMC-15
88Portl/ProC-641
89AAA/CMC-32
89Panini/St-380
89Portl/CMC-16
89Portl/ProC-220
89UD-177
90AAAGame/ProC-5
90AAASingl/ProC-285
90F/Up-U40
90ProC/Singl-373
90T/TVMets-63
90Tidew/CMC-22
90Tidew/ProC-554
90TripleAAS/CMC-32
91AAA/LineD-569
91F-163
91S-754RP
91Tidew/LineD-569
91Tidew/ProC-2520
91WIZMets-413

Torve, Kenton Craig
87BirmB/Best-20

Tosar, Mike
91Miami/Bumble-12

Tosca, Carlos
83Greens-27
84Greens-1
91BBCity/ClBest-28MG

Tosone, Joe
93James/ClBest-24
93James/ProC-3341

Tost, Lou
49Remar
50Remar

Toth, Dave
91Idaho/ProC-4334
91Idaho/SportP-15
92Macon/ClBest-4
92Macon/ProC-271
93Macon/ClBest-25
93Macon/ProC-1404

Toth, Paul
62Kahn/Atl
63T-489
64T-309

Toth, Robert
92AppFox/ClBest-15
94B-311
94FExcel-75

Touch, Chuck
91Welland/ClBest-11

Touma, Tim
87WPalmB-2

Toups, Tony
77Watlo

Toussaint, Daris
88Pocatel/ProC-2088

Toutsis, Paul
86Greens-24

Touzzo, John
85LitFalls-10

Tovar, Cesar
65OPC-201R
65T-201R
66T-563R
67CokeCap/Twin-11
67T-317
68Dexter-72
68T-420
69MB-276
69MLB/St-71
69T-530
69T/St-199
69Trans-9
70MLB/St-240

70OPC-25
70T-25
71K-18
71MD
71MLB/St-477
71OPC-165
71T-165
71T/Coins-52
72MB-347
72OPC-275
72T-275
73OPC-405
73T-405
74OPC-538
74T-538
74T/Tr-538T
75OPC-178
75T-178
75T/M-178
76OPC-246
76T-246
77T-408
78TCMA-174
78Twin/Frisz-21
92Yank/WIZ70-155
93Rang/Keeb-361

Tovar, Edgar
92James/ClBest-21
92James/ProC-1510
93FExcel/ML-62
93Harris/ProC-278

Tovar, Raul
82Miami-18
83BirmB-1
86MidldA-23

Towers, Kevin
84Beaum-10
86CharRain-26
88LasVegas/CMC-8
88LasVegas/ProC-242
89Spokane/SP-23
90Spokane/SportP-28CO

Towey, Steve
88Myrtle/ProC-1185
89Modesto/Chong-16

Towle, Justin
92Princet/ClBest-24
92Princet/ProC-3091

Town, Randall
80Water-6
81Water-10

Townley, Jason
88Dunedin/Star-17
88StCath/ProC-2027
90Dunedin/Star-21
90FSLAS/Star-46
91AA/LineD-368
91Knoxvl/LineD-368
91Knoxvl/ProC-1772
92ClBest-330
92Knoxvl/ProC-2994
92Knoxvl/SB-396

Townsend, Chad
92Burllnd/ClBest-25
92Burllnd/ProC-1665

Townsend, George
N172
N690

Townsend, Howard
85Everett/Cram-16A
85Everett/Cram-16B
86Clinton-24
87Wausau-5
88SanBern/Cal-45
89Visalia/Cal-100
89Visalia/ProC-1421

Townsend, James
87Salem/ProC-2426
88QuadC/GS-17
89PalmSp/Cal-48
89PalmSp/ProC-463

Townsend, John
E107

Townsend, Ken
77Clinton
78LodiD

Townsend, Lee
88SanBern/Best-3

Townsend, Mike
91Martins/ClBest-30TR

Townsend, Richard
92Welland/ClBest-24
92Welland/ProC-1322

Toy, Tracy
86Watertn-24
87Macon-2
88Augusta/ProC-379

Toyotoshi, Chikada
89Salinas/Cal-131

Tozier, Pat
90OK-9

Traber, Jim
85D-45RR
85RochR-9
86RochR-25
86Sf/Rook-32
87D-477
87F-482
87RochR-26
87RochR/TCMA-20
87Sf/TPrev-21M
87T-484
87T/St-232
87ToysRUs-31
88French-28
88RochR/Team-25
88T-544
89B-13
89F-625
89French-28
89OPC-124
89S-590
89T-124
89T/St-233
89UD-294
90D-569
90F-193
90F/Can-193
90HagersDG/Best-33
90Publlnt/St-590
90UD-268
91Crown/Orio-461

Trabous, Manuel
52Laval-89

Tracewski, Dick
64T-154
65OPC-279
65T-279
66T-378
67CokeCap/Tiger-11
67T-559
68CokeCap/Tiger-11
68T-488
69MB-277
69OPC-126
69T-126
69T/4in1-20M
73OPC-323CO
73T-323CO
81TCMA-461
84Tiger/Wave-32CO
88Domino-23
88Pep/T-CO
89Mara/Tigers-CO
90CokeK/Tiger-28CO
90Target-807
91CokeK/Tiger-xCO
93Tiger/Gator-28CO

Trachsel, Steve
91Geneva/ProC-4217
92ChalK/SB-169
92CharlK/ProC-2772
92Sky/AASingl-77
92UD/ML-118
93B-172
94B-634
94D-636
94F/MLP-34
94Finest-296
94Flair-142
94L/GRook-19
94Pinn-536
94StCl-62
94StCl/1stDay-62
94StCl/Gold-62
94StCl/Team-345
94T-778
94T/Gold-778
94UD-29
94UD/ElecD-29
94UD/SP-73
94Ultra-465

Tracy, Jack
81TCMA-451

Tracy, James C.
(Jim)
87Myrtle-16
88Dunedin/Star-18
88Peoria/Ko-29
89Harris/ProC-309
89Harris/Star-19
90A&AASingle/ProC-13
90EastLAS/ProC-EL27
90Harris/ProC-1193
90Harris/Star-18
91BuffB/LineD-46
91BuffB/ProC-542
92BuffB/BlueS-22
92BuffB/ProC-323
92BuffB/SB-43

Tracy, James E.
(Jim)
80Wichita-2
81D-520
81F-308
82F-605
82F/St-97
82T-403
82Tucson-9
87Peoria-27MG
89Chatt/Best-7
89Chatt/GS-1
90Chatt/GS-1MG
91AA/LineD-174MG
91AAA/LineD-46
91Chatt/LineD-174MG
91Chatt/ProC-1974MG
91Pac/SenLg-70
93Harris/ProC-284MG

Tracy, Rich
88Batavia/ProC-1685

Tracy, Rick
87SanJose-20

Traen, Tom
86Jaxvl/TCMA-5
87WPalmB-20

Traffley, William
N172

Trafton, Todd
84AZ/Pol-18
86AZ/Pol-18
87DayBe-1
88BirmB/Best-9
89BirmB/Best-19
89BirmB/ProC-97
89SLAS-10
90AAASingl/ProC-175
90ProC/Singl-647
90Vanco/CMC-20
90Vanco/ProC-497
91AA/LineD-172
91Chatt/LineD-172
91Chatt/ProC-1969
92Chatt/ProC-3832
92Nashvl/ProC-1842
92Nashvl/SB-295

Tragresser, Walter
16FleischBrd-95

Trail, Chet
81TCMA-399

Tramble, Otis
82QuadC-20

Trammell, Alan
78BK/T-15
78T-707R
79OPC-184
79T-358
80OPC-123
80T-232
81Coke
81D-5
81F-461
81F/St-89
81K-51
81OPC-133DP
81T-709
81T/So-38
81T/St-75
81Tiger/Detroit-68
82D-5DK
82D-76
82F-283
82F/St-155
82OPC-381
82Sqt-4
82T-475
82T/St-181
82T/StVar-181
83D-207
83F-344
83F/St-21M
83OPC-95
83OPC/St-66
83T-95
83T/St-66
84D-293
84Drake-30
84F-91
84F/St-14
84Nes/792-510
84OPC-88
84T-510
84T/RD-25M
84T/St-266
84T/St/Box-9
84Tiger/Farmer-14
84Tiger/Wave-33
85Cain's-18
85D-171
85D/AAS-44
85Drake-31
85F-23
85F/LimEd-40
85FunFoodPin-40
85Leaf-158
85OPC-181
85Seven-15G
85Seven-8D
85T-690
85T/Gloss40-16
85T/RD-25M
85T/St-18WS
85T/St-20
85T/St-258
85T/Super-25
85ThomMc/Discs-20
85Wendy-20
86Cain's-19
86D-171
86D/AAS-45
86F-241
86F-633M
86F/Mini-50
86F/St-121
86Leaf-101
86OPC-130
86Sf-147M
86Sf-172
86T-130
86T/St-267
86T/Tatt-10M
87Cain's-7
87Coke/Tigers-4
87D-127
87D/HL-51
87D/OD-216
87F-167
87F/Hottest-41
87F/Mini-107
87F/RecSet-38
87F/St-118
87Leaf-126
87OPC-209
87RedFoley/St-62
87Seven-DT11
87Sf-188
87Sf/TPrev-15M
87Stuart-19M
87T-687
87T/Mini-56
87T/St-270
88Classic/Blue-231
88D-230
88D-4DK
88D-BC11
88D/AS-22
88D/Best-281
88D/DKsuper-4DK
88Drake-13
88F-635M
88F-74
88F/AS-9
88F/AwardWin-43
88F/BB/AS-42
88F/BB/MVP-39
88F/Excit-42
88F/Hottest-44
88F/LL-42
88F/Mini-25
88F/RecSet-41
88F/SS-41
88F/St-29
88F/TL-43
88FanSam-6
88Jiffy-16
88KayBee-31
88KennerFig-113
88Leaf-167
88Leaf-4DK
88Nestle-35
88OPC-320
88Panini/St-444
88Panini/St-94
88Pep/T-2
88Pol/T-13
88S-37
88S-651M
88Sf-25
88T-320
88T-389AS
88T/Big-8
88T/Coins-30
88T/Gloss60-37
88T/Mini-12
88T/RiteAid-18
88T/St-273
88T/St/Backs-45
88T/UK-79
89B-105
89Cadaco-58
89Classic-128
89D-180
89D/Best-13
89D/MVP-BC17
89F-148
89F/AS-11
89F/BBAS-41
89F/BBMVP's-39
89F/Excit-41
89F/Heroes-40
89F/LL-40
89F/Superstar-40
89F/WaxBox-C26
89KMart/Lead-22
89KayBee-30
89KennerFig-151
89KingB/Discs-9
89MSA/SS-10
89Mara/Tigers-3
89Master/Discs-4
89OPC-49
89Panini/St-343
89Pol/Tigers-3
89RedFoley/St-121
89S-110
89S/HotStar-7
89Sf-215
89T-400AS
89T-609TL
89T-770
89T/Ames-29
89T/Big-123
89T/Coins-56
89T/Crunch-12
89T/DH-4
89T/Gloss60-25
89T/Hills-29
89T/LJN-6
89T/St-281
89T/St/Backs-12
89T/UK-77
89UD-290
89UD-690TC
90B-353
90Classic-106
90CokeK/Tiger-24
90D-90
90D/BestAL-7
90D/Bon/MVP-BC26
90D/Learning-20
90F-617
90F/BB-41
90F/BBMVP-41
90F/Can-617
90HotPlay/St-46
90Kenner/Fig-85
90Leaf-218
90MLBPA/Pins-88
90OPC-440
90Panini/St-70
90Post-28
90Publlnt/St-296
90Publlnt/St-484
90RedFoley/St-96
90S-9
90S/100St-41
90Sf-154
90Starline/LJS-10

90Starline/LJS-24
90Sunflower-15
90T-440
90T/Big-190
90T/Coins-31
90T/DH-66
90T/St-281
90UD-554
90USPlayC/AS-10S
90WonderBrd-13
91B-154
91B-370SLUG
91Cadaco-57
91Classic/200-97
91Classic/II-T96
91CokeK/Tiger-3
91D-118
91F-355
91Kenner-52
91Leaf-351
91Leaf/Stud-59
91MSA/Holsum-10
91MajorLg/Pins-33
91OPC-275
91OPC-389AS
91OPC/Premier-123
91Panini/FrSt-291
91Panini/St-238
91Panini/Top15-8
91Pol/Tiger-13
91RedFoley/St-93
91S-40
91S-852FRAN
91S/100SS-63
91Seven/3DCoin-15MW
91StCl-63
91T-275
91T-389AS
91T/CJMini/II-26
91UD-223
91UD/SilSlug-SS2
91Ultra-129
92B-690
92CJ/DII-31
92Classic/Game200-90
92D-164
92F-148
92L-172
92L/BlkGold-172
92OPC-120
92OPC/Premier-31
92Panini-108
92Pinn-113
92Pinn/RookI-17M
92S-515
92StCl-850
92Studio-179
92T-120
92T/Gold-120
92T/GoldWin-120
92T/Kids-75
92TripleP-176
92UD-273
92USPlayC/Tiger-11S
92USPlayC/Tiger-8H
92Ultra-64
93B-391
93Colla/DM-109
93D-655
93F-613
93Flair-209
93L-421
93MSA/Metz-38
93OPC-360
93Pac/Spanish-115
93Pinn-353
93S-313
93Select-230
93StCl-416
93StCl/1stDay-416
93T-660
93T/Finest-18
93T/FinestRef-18
93T/Gold-660
93Tiger/Gator-25
93TripleP-191
93UD-532
93UD/SP-241
93Ultra-204
94B-509
94D-280
94F-144
94F-709M
94Flair-53
94L-120
94OPC-72
94Pac/Cr-230
94Panini-69
94Pinn-429
94S-337
94Sf/2000-93
94StCl-331
94StCl/1stDay-331
94StCl/Gold-331
94Studio-194
94T-75
94T/Finest-159
94T/Finest/PreProd-159
94T/FinestRef-159
94T/Gold-75
94TripleP-249
94TripleP/Medal-7M
94UD-201
94UD/ElecD-201
94UD/SP-181
94Ultra-358

Trammell, Marcus
88Utica/Pucko-11

Tramuta, Marc
91Yakima/ClBest-3
91Yakima/ProC-4256

Tranbarger, Mark
92Spring/ClBest-16
92Spring/ProC-870

Tranberg, Mark
92Batavia/ClBest-22
92Batavia/ProC-3266
94B-468
94FExcel-249

Trapp, Mike
87FtMyr-4

Trautman, Keith
92Yakima/ClBest-19

Trautwein, Dave
88StLucie/Star-24
89Jacks/GS-8
89TexLAS/GS-27
90AAASingl/ProC-276
90ProC/Singl-363
90T/TVMets-64
90Tidew/CMC-12
90Tidew/ProC-545
91AAA/LineD-570
91Tidew/LineD-570
91Tidew/ProC-2510
92Salinas/ClBest-4
92Salinas/ProC-3756

Trautwein, John
86Jaxvl/TCMA-7
87Jaxvl-21
87SLAS-14
88D/RedSox/Bk-NEW
88D/Rook-24
88F/Up-U10
89Pawtu/CMC-9
89Pawtu/Dunkin-40
89Pawtu/ProC-685
90AAASingl/ProC-435
90Pawtu/CMC-2
90Pawtu/ProC-463
90ProC/Singl-253
90T/TVRSox-62

Travels, Darren
85Utica-6
86James-26

Travers, Bill
75OPC-488
75Sacra/Caruso-20
75T-488
75T/M-488
76A&P/Milw
76OPC-573
76SSPC-244
76T-573
77BurgChef-90
77Ho-87
77Ho/Twink-87
77K-9
77OPC-174
77T-125
77T/CS-49
77T/ClothSt-49
78T-355
79OPC-106
79T-213
80T-109
81D-508
81F-525
81T-704
81T/Tr-845
82T-628
89Pac/SenLg-118
89T/SenLg-21
89TM/SenLg-107

Travers, Steve
82Idaho-13

Travis, Cecil
37OPC-126
37Wheat
38Wheat
39Exh
39PlayBall-114
40PlayBall-16
41DP-75
41PlayBall-48
R303/A
R313
R314
V300
V351A-23
V351B-42

Traxler, Brian
89SanAn/Best-11
90Albuq/Trib-28
90D/Rook-38
91AA/LineD-544
91SanAn/LineD-544
91SanAn/ProC-2984
91T/90Debut-155
92Albuq/ProC-730
92Albuq/SB-21

Traylor, Keith
84LitFalls-9

Traynor, Harold
(Pie)
25Exh-55
26Exh-55
27Exh-28
28Yueng-14
29Exh/4-13
31Exh/4-13
33DL-12
33G-22
34DS-27
34DS-99
34Exh/4-7
35BU-100
35BU-14
35Exh/4-7
35G-2B
35G-4B
35G-7B
36Exh/4-7
50Callahan
50W576-71
60F-77
61F-144
61F-89M
61GP-15
72K/ATG-8
76OPC-343AS
76Rowe-15
76Shakey-55
76T-343AS
77Galasso-102
77Galasso-205
77Shakey-17
80Pac/Leg-36
80Perez/HOF-55
80SSPC/HOF
81Conlon-63
86Conlon/1-38
86Sf/Dec-11
87Nestle/DT-3
88Conlon/NatAS-21
91Conlon/Sport-268
91Conlon/Sport-36
91Swell/Great-148
92Conlon/Sport-434
93AP/ASG-96
93AP/ASG24K-30G
93Conlon-670
93Conlon/MasterBW-9
94Conlon-1050
94Conlon-1093
94Conlon/Col-29
94Conlon/Pr-1050
94TedW-80
E120
E210-14
R311/Gloss
R312/M
R313
R315-A36
R315-B36
R316
R332-23
R337
V117-2
V353-22
W502-14
W513-82
W517-2
W572
WG8-46

Treadgill, Chris
90QuadC/GS-29

Treadway, Andre
82Durham-21
85Greenvl/Team-21
86Richm-24

Treadway, Doug
88WinHaven/Star-24

Treadway, George
90Target-1086

Treadway, Jeff
86Vermont-22
87Nashvl-21
88D-29RR
88D/Rook-17
88F-249
88F/Mini-76
88Kahn/Reds-15
88Leaf-29RR
88S-646RP
88S/YS/II-26
88Sf-225R
88T/Big-214
88T/Tr-122T
89Brave/Dubuq-27
89Classic-54
89D-351
89D/Best-141
89F-173
89F/Up-75
89KennerFig-152
89OPC-61
89Panini/St-73
89S-86
89S/HotRook-84
89S/Tr-18
89Sf-107
89T-685
89T/St-139
89T/Tr-121T
89ToysRUs-31
89UD-393
90Brave/Dubuq/Perf-29
90Brave/Dubuq/Singl-33
90Classic/III-25
90D-50
90D/BestNL-123
90F-598
90F/Can-598
90Leaf-455
90OPC-486
90Panini/St-218
90S-95
90Sf-219
90T-486
90T/St-29
90UD-141
91B-586
91Brave/Dubuq/Perf-30
91Brave/Dubuq/Stand-37
91D-117
91F-707
91Leaf-246
91Leaf/Stud-150
91OPC-139
91Panini/FrSt-20
91Panini/St-28
91S-219
91S/100SS-31
91StCl-497
91T-139
91UD-499
91Ultra-13
92Brave/LykePerf-28
92Brave/LykeStand-32
92D-324
92F-373
92OPC-99
92S-142
92StCl-82
92T-99
92T/Gold-99
92T/GoldWin-99
92UD-389
92USPlayC/Brave-13S
92USPlayC/Brave-9H
92Ultra-171
93D-448
93F/Final-205
93Indian/WUAB-31
93L-480
93S-461
93Ultra-546
94D-295
94F-122
94Pac/Cr-185
94Panini-61
94S-115
94S/GoldR-115
94StCl-30
94StCl/1stDay-30
94StCl/Gold-30

Treadway, Steven
88CapeCod/Sum-181

Treadwell, Jody
91AA/LineD-545
91SanAn/LineD-545
91SanAn/ProC-2975
92SanAn/ProC-3974

Treanor, Dean
88Fresno/Cal-26
88Fresno/ProC-1236
90Reno/Cal-288CO
91Reno/Cal-28CO
92Watlo/ClBest-27CO
92Watlo/ProC-2157CO

Trebelhorn, Tom
80Port-18
81Portl-2
85Cram/PCL-215
86Pol/Brew-42C
87Pol/Brew-42MG
87T/Tr-121T
88Pol/Brew-42MG
88T-224MG
89Brewer/YB-42MG
89Pol/Brew-42
89T-344MG
90Brewer/MillB-27MG
90OPC-759MG
90Pol/Brew-42MG
90T-759MG
91Brewer/MillB-28MG
91OPC-459MG
91Pol/Brew-25MG
91T-459MG
92Cub/Mara-NNO
93Cub/Mara-27CO

Trechuck, Frank
V362-6

Tredaway, Chad
92Geneva/ClBest-4
92Geneva/ProC-1569
93FExcel/ML-13

Tredway, Ed
90Madison/Best-2
90Madison/ProC-2273

Tredway, George
N172

Treece, Jack
44Centen-24

Trella, Steve
75Clinton

Tremark, Nick
90Target-808

Tremblay, Gary
86Pawtu-25
87Pawtu-20
87Pawtu/TCMA-12
88Pawtu/CMC-22
88Pawtu/ProC-450
89Pawtu/CMC-14
89Pawtu/Dunkin-32
89Pawtu/ProC-702
90AAASingl/ProC-438
90Pawtu/CMC-13
90Pawtu/ProC-466
90ProC/Singl-264
90T/TVRSox-63

Tremblay, Wayne
79Elmira-25
85Greens-12

Trembley, Dave
86Kinston-24MG
87Harris-2

88EastLAS/ProC-45
88Harris/ProC-846
89EastLDD/ProC-DD46MG
89Harris/ProC-292MG
91CharRain/ClBest-24MG
91CharRain/ProC-110MG
92CharRain/ClBest-22MG
92CharRain/ProC-135

Tremel, William
55T-52
55T/DH-102
56T-96
56T/Pin-7

Tremper, Overton
90Target-1087

Trent, Ted
(Ted)
78Laugh/Black-1
86Negro/Frit-116
87Negro/Dixon-3

Tresamer, Michael
86Cram/NWL-49
87AppFx-9
88BBCity/Star-22
89Memphis/Best-22
89Memphis/ProC-1197
89Memphis/Star-21
89Star/Wax-45
90AAASingl/ProC-600
90Omaha/ProC-65

Tresch, Dave
85Lynch-3
86Lynch-22TR

Tresh, Michael
(Mike)
41DP-69
43Playball-9
47TipTop
49B-166
50NumNum

Tresh, Mickey
87PrWill-12
88PrWill/Star-23
89Penin/Star-25
90Lakeland/Star-24
90Star/ISingl-38

Tresh, Tom
62T-31
63J-23
63P-23
63Salada-54
63T-173
63T-470
64T-395
64T/Coins-10
64Wheat/St-45
65T-440
66Bz-40
66T-205
66T/RO-59
66T/RO-94
67Bz-40
67CokeCap/YMet-17
67T-289
68OPC-69
68T-69
69MB-278
69MLB/St-80
69OPC-212
69T-212
69T/St-209
70MLB/St-215
70T-698
72MB-348
88Pac/Leg-25
89Swell-52
90Swell/Great-17
91Swell/Great-66
92Yank/WIZ60-131
92Yank/WIZAS-83
WG10-23
WG9-24

Treuel, Ralph
80Evansvl-15
91AAA/LineD-600M
91Toledo/LineD-600CO
91Toledo/ProC-1947CO
92Toledo/ProC-1059
92Toledo/SB-600M

Trevino, Alex
77Wausau
78Tidew
80T-537
81Coke
81F-318
81T-23
81T/HT
82Coke/Reds
82D-350
82F-540
82T-368
82T/Tr-120T
83D-374
83F-604
83OPC/St-232
83T-632
83T/St-232
84D-286
84F-484
84F/X-U118
84Nes/792-242
84Pol/Atl-25
84T-242
84T/Tr-120T
85D-565
85F-341
85F/Up-U122
85OPC-279
85T-747
85T/St-30
85T/Tr-123T
86Coke/Dodg-29
86F-550
86F/Up-U119
86OPC-169
86Pol/Dodg-29
86T-444
86T/Tr-116T
87D-546
87F-456
87Mother/Dodg-23
87Pol/Dodg-15
87T-173
88D-376
88Pol/Dodg-29
88S-182
88T-512
88Tucson/CMC-16
88Tucson/JP-22
89B-326
89Lennox/Ast-6
89Mother/Ast-17
89OPC-64
89S-574
89T-64
89UD-262
90D-443
90F-239
90F/Can-239
90Leaf-432
90Lennox-25
90Mother/Ast-21
90OPC-342
90PublInt/St-104
90T-342
90Target-809
90UD-205
91WIZMets-414
92Louisvl/ProC-1891
92Louisvl/SB-271

Trevino, Gerald
92Idaho/ProC-3521

Trevino, Tony
88Batavia/ProC-1665
88Spartan/ProC-1040
89Clearw/Star-22
90Clearw/Star-22
90FSLAS/Star-18
90Star/ISingl-72
91AA/LineD-521
91Reading/LineD-521
91Reading/ProC-1378
92Clearw/ClBest-16
92Reading/ProC-584

Triandos, Gus
55Esskay
55T-64
55T/DH-82
56T-80
56T/Pin-4
57Swift-2
57T-156
58T-429
59Armour-18
59Bz
59HRDerby-20
59T-330
59T-568AS
60Armour-19
60Bz-11
60T-60
60T/tatt-51
61Bz-25
61P-69
61T-140
61T/St-106
62J-33
62P-33
62P/Can-33
62Salada-93
62Shirriff-93
62T-420
62T/St-9
62T/bucks
63T-475
64PhilBull-25
64T-83
65OPC-248
65T-248
79TCMA-75
91Crown/Orio-462
Exh47
PM10/Sm-189

Tribble, Scott
93SoEastern-15

Tribolet, Scott
91MissSt-45
92MissSt-42

Trice, Robert Lee
52Laval-60
54T-148
55Rodeo
55T-132
55T/DH-124
86Negro/Frit-43
94T/Arc54-148
PM10/Sm-190

Trice, Walter
(Wally)
88AubAs/ProC-1950
89Osceola/Star-25
90ColMud/Best-15
90ColMud/ProC-1349
90ColMud/Star-24
90Foil/Best-205
91BurlAs/ClBest-9
91BurlAs/ProC-2800
91ClBest/Singl-326
91MidwLAS/ProC-18
92Canton/ProC-690
92ProC/Tomorrow-232

Triche, Bryan
91MissSt-46
92MissSt-43
93MissSt-44

Trillo, Manny
74OPC-597R
74T-597R
75OPC-617R
75T-617R
75T/M-617R
76OPC-206
76SSPC-316
76T-206
77BurgChef-191
77OPC-158
77Pep-59
77T-395
78Ho-69
78OPC-217
78T-123
78Wiffle/Discs-76
79BK/P-14
79OPC-337
79T-639
80BK/P-5
80OPC-50
80T-90
81Coke
81D-22
81F-3
81F/St-96
81OPC-368
81T-470
81T/HT
82D-245
82F-260
82F/St-59
82OPC-220
82PermaGr/AS-18
82T-220
82T/St-122
82T/St-76
83D-294
83F-174
83F-631M
83F/St-21M
83F/St-9M
83OPC-174AS
83OPC-73
83OPC/St-141RB
83OPC/St-142RB
83OPC/St-268
83PermaGr/AS-8
83T-398AS
83T-535
83T-5M
83T/St-141
83T/St-142
83T/St-268
83T/Tr-116
83Wheat/Ind-30
84D-575
84F-289
84F-627IA
84F/X-119
84Nes/792-180
84OPC-180
84T-180
84T/Gloss22-3
84T/St-93
84T/Tr-121T
85D-431
85D/AAS-31
85F-622
85FunFoodPin-57
85Mother/Giants-5
85OPC-310
85T-310
86Cub/Unocal-19
86D-201
86F-551
86F/Up-U120
86Gator-19
86OPC-142
86T-655
86T/St-88
86T/Tr-117T
87Berg/Cubs-19
87D-570
87F-577
87OPC-32
87T-732
88Berg/Cubs-19
88D-516
88D/Cubs/Bk-516
88F-436
88S-524
88T-287
89B-308
89D-608
89F-440
89S-446
89T-66
89T/Big-295
89UD-127
90PublInt/St-41

Trinidad, Hector
92Geneva/ClBest-3
92Geneva/ProC-1562
93Peoria/Team-28
94B-662
94ClBest/Gold-132
94FExcel-170

Trinkle, Ken
47TipTop
49B-193
49Eureka-150

Triplett, Antonio
82BurlR/Frit-6
82BurlR/TCMA-11
83BurlR-25
83BurlR/Frit-6
86Tulsa-2
87SanBern-21
88Fresno/Cal-1
88Fresno/ProC-1243

Triplett, Coaker
V362-16
W754

Triplett, Hunter
92OKSt-27

Tripodi, Max
89SLCity-20

Tripp, Dave
90SoOreg/Best-23
90SoOreg/ProC-3446

Trisler, John
91Helena/SportP-1
92Beloit/ProC-405

Tritonenkov, Timur
89EastLDD/ProC-DD19

Trlicek, Rick
88Batavia/ProC-1670
90Dunedin/Star-22
91AA/LineD-369
91Knoxvl/LineD-369
91Knoxvl/ProC-1765
92B-76
92D/Rook-116
92L/GRook-15
92ProC/Tomorrow-166
92Syrac/MerchB-24
92Syrac/ProC-1966
93BJ/D/45-37
93F/Final-85
93Mother/Dodg-27
93Pac/Spanish-504
93Pinn-284
93S-318
93Select/RookTr-138T
93StCl-218
93StCl/1stDay-218
93Ultra-407
94F-526
94S-600
94T-276
94T/Gold-276

Troedson, Rich
74OPC-77
74T-77

Troglin, Mike
90AR-33M

Trombley, Mike
88CapeCod/Sum-75
90Visalia/Cal-58
90Visalia/ProC-2153
91AA/LineD-495
91OrlanSR/LineD-495
91OrlanSR/ProC-1849
92B-102
92Portl/SB-420
92Portland/ProC-2666
92Sky/AAASingl-192
93B-621
93D-47
93F-644
93Pac/Spanish-526
93Pinn-578
93Pinn/RookTP-1M
93S-287
93Select/RookTr-52T
93StCl-336
93StCl/1stDay-336
93T-588
93T/Gold-588
93ToysRUs-47
93UD-28SR
93Ultra-588
94D-620
94F-220
94Pac/Cr-368
94S-591
94StCl-477
94StCl/1stDay-477
94StCl/Gold-477
94T-308
94T/Gold-308
94Ultra-91

Troncoso, Nolberton
90Yakima/Team-25

Troncoso, Roberto
91GulfCR/SportP-25M

Tronerud, Rick
80WHave-24
81WHave-15
84Albany-8
85Modesto/Chong-27CO
89Huntsvl/Best-18

Trosky, Hal
34DS-70
34G-76
35Exh/4-11
35G-1L
35G-2E
35G-6E
35G-7E

36Exh/4-11
37Exh/4-11
37OPC-113
37Wheat
38Exh/4-11
38ONG/Pin-30
40PlayBall-50
41DP-80
41DP-87
41PlayBall-16
41Wheat
61F-145
75Sheraton-4
77Fritsch-15
92Conlon/Sport-385
R303/A
R314
V300
V351A-24
V351B-43
Trott, Sam
N172
Trotter, Bill
39PlayBall-148
40PlayBall-54
W753
Troup, James
89SLCity-27OF
Trouppe, Quincy
45Playball-2
78Laugh/Black-33
91Negro/Lewis-16
92Negro/Retort-61
Trout, Jeff
85OrlanTw-12
86OrlanTw-21
Trout, Paul
(Dizzy)
39Exh
39PlayBall-153
40PlayBall-44
47TipTop
48L-10
49B-208
50B-134
51T/BB-23
52NTea
52T-39
53T-169
85T-142FS
91Crown/Orio-463
91T/Arc53-169
Trout, Steve
77AppFx
78Knoxvl
80T-83
81D-400
81F-345
81OPC-364
81T-552
82D-243
82F-358
82OPC-299
82T-299
82T/St-169
83D-417
83F-251
83T-461
83T/Tr-117
83Thorn-34
84D-533
84F-506
84Nes/792-151
84OPC-151
84SevenUp-34
84T-151
85D-198
85F-70
85Leaf-243
85OPC-139
85SevenUp-34
85T-142FS
85T-668
85T/St-43
86Cub/Unocal-20
86D-117
86F-384
86Gator-34
86OPC-384
86T-384
86T/St-57
87Berg/Cubs-34
87D-201
87F-578
87OPC-147
87T-750
88D-524
88Mother/Sea-8
88S-342
88T-584
88T/Big-107
89Mother/Sea-24
89S-522
89T-54
90Louisvl/LBC-41
90PublInt/St-443
92Yank/WIZ80-193
Troutman, Keith
92Yakima/ProC-3449
Trowbridge, Bob
57SpicSpan/4x5-16
58T-252
59T-239
60T-66
Trower, Don
48Sommer-10
Trucchio, Frank
83Madis/Frit-30C
Trucks, Phil
76Clinton
79Knoxvl/TCMA-2
Trucks, Virgil
47TipTop
48L-5
49B-219
49Royal-21
50B-96
51B-104
52Dix
52T-262
53B/BW-17
53Dix
53T-96
54B-198
55Armour-22
55B-26
56T-117
57T-187
58T-277
59T-417
63IDL-23CO
79TCMA-85
81Tiger/Detroit-111
89Pac/Leg-120
89Swell-73
91T/Arc53-96
92AP/ASG-20
94TedW-34
Exh47
R423-106
Trudeau, Kevin
86Watlo-29
87Portl-15
88OrlanTw/Best-14
89MidldA/GS-28
90MidldA/GS-19
Trudo, Glenn
86Watertn-25TR
87Macon-21
88Augusta/ProC-384
True, Bryan
86Lipscomb-21
Truesdale, Fred
C46-53
Truitt, Bill
52Laval-26
Trujillo, Jose
89Hamil/Star-24
89Star/IISingl-106
90StPete/Star-24
91StPete/ClBest-23
91StPete/ProC-2286
92Geneva/ClBest-2
92Geneva/ProC-1570
92Peoria/ClBest-5
Trujillo, Louie
83Cedar-11
83Cedar/Frit-12
Trujillo, Mike
83AppFx/Frit-2
86F-360
86Pawtu-26
86T-687
87D-613
87Mother/Sea-25
87T-402
88T-307
88Toledo/CMC-7
88Toledo/ProC-593
89AAA/ProC-25
89Toledo/CMC-3
89Toledo/ProC-776
Truschke, Mike
88CapeCod/Sum-24
Trusky, Ken
89Welland/Pucko-24
90Augusta/ProC-2479
90SALAS/Star-44
91Salem/ClBest-13
91Salem/ProC-967
Tsamis, George
88CapeCod/Sum-80
90A&AASingle/ProC-143
90AS/Cal-16
90Visalia/Cal-65
90Visalia/ProC-2154
91AAA/LineD-421
91Portl/LineD-421
91Portl/ProC-1566
92Portl/SB-421
92Portland/ProC-2667
92Sky/AAASingl-193
93B-509
93F/Final-240
94F-221
94Pac/Cr-369
94T-128
94T/Gold-128
Tschida, Tim
88TM/Umpire-59
89TM/Umpire-57
90TM/Umpire-55
Tsitouris, John
60L-63
60T-497
63FrBauer-28
63T-244
64Kahn
64T-275
65Kahn
65OPC-221
65T-221
66OPC-12
66T-12
68T-523
Tsitouris, Marc
90James/Pucko-5
91Sumter/ClBest-21
91Sumter/ProC-2346
Tsotsos, Pete
88CapeCod/Sum-26
Tsoukalas, John
91MedHat/ProC-4110
91MedHat/SportP-4
92Myrtle/ClBest-2
92Myrtle/ProC-2207
Tubbs, Gregory Alan
86Greenvl/Team-21
87Greenvl/Best-26
88Richm-15
88Richm/CMC-15
88Richm/ProC-5
89AAA/CMC-23
89Greenvl/ProC-1152
89Richm/Bob-26
89Richm/ProC-823
90TripleAAS/CMC-23
91AAA/LineD-47
91BuffB/LineD-47
91BuffB/ProC-555
91PreRookPrev/LineD-47
92BuffB/BlueS-23
92BuffB/ProC-336
92BuffB/SB-44
Tuck, Gary
82Tucson-25
83Tucson-24
84Cram/PCL-248
86Osceola-26CO
87AubAs-12
88Ashvl/ProC-1068
89Colum/Pol-24CO
Tucker, Bill
89Belling/Legoe-34OWN
Tucker, Bob
86VeroB-25
Tucker, Eddie
90Foil/Best-274
90SanJose/Best-13
90SanJose/ProC-2014
Tucker, Lanning H.
92Elizab/ClBest-25TR
Tucker, Michael
92B-682FOIL
92Classic/DP-7
92Classic/DPFoil-BC7
92FrRow/DP-39
92FrRow/DP-44
92T/Tr-119T
92T/TrGold-119T
92UD/ML-6
93Pinn-466DP
93S-498DP
93Select-291DP
93StCl/MurphyS-196
93UD-445TP
93UD/SP-287FOIL
94ClBest/Gold-122
94FExcel-76
94FExcel/LL-18
94SigRook-24
94SigRook/Hot-11
94TedW-133
94TedW/Gardiner-2
94Ultra-369
Tucker, Mike
81Shrev-8
82Phoenix
Tucker, Robert
91Helena/SportP-22
Tucker, Scooter
89Clinton/ProC-897
90AS/Cal-37
90SanJose/Cal-37
90SanJose/Star-23
91AA/LineD-322
91ClBest/Singl-315
91Shrev/LineD-322
91Shrev/ProC-1825
92D/Rook-117
92Sky/AAASingl-277
92T/Tr-120T
92T/TrGold-120T
92Tucson/ProC-492
92Tucson/SB-620
93D-60
93F/MLPII-1
93Pinn-245
93S-237
93StCl-488
93StCl/1stDay-488
93T-814
93T/Gold-814
93Ultra-47
Tucker, Stephen
(Tuck)
90Greens/Best-12
90Greens/ProC-2664
90Greens/Star-22
91PrWill/ClBest-12
91PrWill/ProC-1428
Tucker, Terry
62Pep/Tul-bb
63Pep/Tul-bb
Tucker, Thomas
90Target-810
N172
N300/unif
Tucker, Thurman
44Playball-18
47TipTop
50NumNum
51B-222
Tucker, Vance
89CharRain/ProC-972
Tucker, William
78Green
Tuckerman, William
N172
Tudor, John
81D-457
81T-14
82Coke/Bos
82D-260
82F-311
82T-558
83D-563
83F-198
83F/St-9M
83T-318
84D-416
84F-411
84F/X-U120
84Nes/792-601
84OPC-171
84T-601
84T/St-225
84T/Tr-122T
85D-235
85D/HL-20
85F-479
85F/Up-U123
85OPC-214
85T-214
85T/Tr-124T
86D-260
86Drake-30
86F-47
86F/AS-12
86F/Mini-11
86F/Slug-40
86F/St-122
86KAS/Disc-17
86Leaf-134
86OPC-227
86Schnucks-22
86Seven/Coin-S11M
86Sf-122
86Sf-184M
86Sf-185M
86T-474
86T-710AS
86T/3D-28
86T/Gloss60-53
86T/Mini-64
86T/St-20WS
86T/St-52
86T/Super-57
86T/Tatt-12M
87Classic-77
87D-170
87D/OD-63
87Drake-30
87F-310
87F/GameWin-41
87F/Mini-108
87F/RecSet-39
87F/St-119
87Kraft-22
87OPC-110
87RedFoley/St-34
87Sf-173
87Sf/TPrev-12M
87Smok/Cards-3
87T-110
87T/St-53
88D-553
88D/Best-212
88Drake-33
88F-48
88F/Mini-110
88F/St-121
88F/WS-3
88Leaf-212
88OPC-356
88S-275
88Sf-198
88Smok/Card-9
88T-792
88T/RiteAid-29
88T/St-13
88T/St-21
88Woolwth-23
89Classic-63
89D-195
89F-75
89Mother/Dodg-9
89OPC-35
89Panini/St-100
89Pol/Dodg-19
89RedFoley/St-122
89S-560
89Sf-86
89T-35
89T/LJN-118
89T/Mini-20
89T/St-64
89UD-66
90B-188
90Classic/III-T2
90F/Up-U54
90Leaf-176
90PublInt/St-20
90Smok/Card-25
90T/Big-253
90T/TVCard-21
90T/Tr-124T
90Target-811
90UD-396

91F-650
91RedFoley/St-94
91S-53
91S/100SS-47
91UD-329
92Card/McDon/Pac-50
Tudor, Mark
81Clinton-29
82Clinton/Frit-26TR
Tufts, Bob
80Phoenix/NBank-3
81Phoenix-3
82Omaha-9
82T-171R
Tuggle, Eugene
90GA-30
Tuholald, Tom
89Welland/Pucko-25
Tukes, Stan
89CharRain/ProC-977
Tulacz, Mike
77AppFx
Tuller, Brian
83QuadC-15
Tullier, Mike
86WinSalem-25
87WinSalem-19
88Pittsfld/ProC-1365
89Iowa/CMC-23
89Iowa/ProC-1701
91Bluefld/ClBest-24CO
91Bluefld/ProC-4143CO
Tullish, Bill
76Cedar
Tumbas, Dave
83AlexD-15
84PrWill-27
85Nashua-25
Tumpane, Bob
82Durham-13
83Durham-15
84Durham-12
85Greenvl/Team-22
85IntLgAS-2
86Greenvl/Team-22
87Richm/Bob-21
87Richm/Crown-9
87Richm/TCMA-16
Tunison, Rich
89Eugene/Best-16
90A&AASingle/ProC-125
90AppFox/Box-28
90AppFox/ProC-2105
90MidwLgAS/GS-21
90ProC/Singl-874
91AA/LineD-421
91ClBest/Singl-200
91London/LineD-421
91Memphis/ProC-664
92Memphis/ProC-2429
92Memphis/SB-446
92Sky/AASingl-188
Tunkin, Scott
91Parramatta/Fut-16
Tunnell, Lee
82Portl-9
83T/Tr-118T
84D-592
84F-268
84F/St-107
84Nes/792-384
84T-384
85D-288
85F-480
85F-638IA
85T-21
86F-623
86Hawaii-21
86T-161
87F/Up-U119
88F-49
88Louisvl-48
88S-587
89Portl/CMC-6
89Portl/ProC-217
90AAASingl/ProC-194
90ProC/Singl-609
90Tucson/CMC-7
90Tucson/ProC-204
91AAA/LineD-621
91Tucson/LineD-621
91Tucson/ProC-2213
Tunney, Gene
33SK*-18
Tunstall, Sean
89KS*-52
Tuozzo, John
86Columbia-25
Turang, Brian
88CapeCod-20
88CapeCod/Sum-22
89Belling/Legoe-20
90A&AASingle/ProC-149
90SanBern/Best-18
90SanBern/Cal-106
90SanBern/ProC-2642
91AA/LineD-347
91Jaxvl/LineD-347
91Jaxvl/ProC-161
92Jacks/ProC-3718
92Jaxvl/SB-358
93Calgary/ProC-1175
93FExcel/ML-233
93StCl/Mar-27
94D-314
94F-299
94Pac/Cr-582
94Pinn-377
94S-637
94S/Boys-37
94StCl-177
94StCl/1stDay-177
94StCl/Gold-177
94T-82
94T/Gold-82
Turbeville, George
93Conlon-979
Turco, Frank
91BendB/ClBest-15
91BendB/ProC-3705
91Reno/Cal-4
92CharlR/ClBest-5
92CharlR/ProC-2235
Turco, Steve F.
81ArkTr-2
83StPete-25
85Spring-18
91Hamil/ClBest-30CO
91Hamil/ProC-4057CO
92Johnson/ClBest-26MG
92Johnson/ProC-3134MG
Turek, Joseph
88Greens/ProC-1559
88SALAS/GS-8
89Cedar/Best-7
89Cedar/ProC-920
89Cedar/Star-20
90Cedar/Best-18
91Chatt/ProC-1962
92Canton/ProC-691
92Canton/SB-121
92Sky/AASingl-57
Turgeon, David
87Oneonta-12
88FtLaud/Star-22
89PrWill/Star-22
90FtLaud/Star-20
Turgeon, Mike
80Wichita-11
82Phoenix
Turgeon, Steve
83StPete-26
85Spring-19
86Erie-28CO
Turlais, John
92FrRow/DP-64
Turley, Robert
54Esskay
54T-85
55Armour-23
55T-38
55T/DH-64
56T-40
56T/Pin-31P
57T-264
58T-255
58T-493AS
59Armour-19
59Bz
59T-237M
59T-570AS
59T-60
60L-103
60NuCard-30
60T-270
61NuCard-430
61P-5
61T-40
61T/St-200
62T-589
63T-322
79TCMA-136
81TCMA-459
88Pac/Leg-52
91Crown/Orio-464
92Yank/WIZ60-132
92Yank/WIZAS-84
94T/Arc54-85
Turnbull, Keith
83Erie-8
Turner
N172
Turner, Brian
90Greens/Best-26
90Greens/ProC-2678
90Greens/Star-23
90Oneonta/ProC-3374
91Greens/ProC-3069
92FtLaud/ClBest-20
92FtLaud/ProC-2623
92FtLaud/Team-31
Turner, Chris
91Boise/ClBest-17
91Boise/ProC-3884
92QuadC/ClBest-6
92QuadC/ProC-814
93B-525
93Vanco/ProC-2602
94B-95
94D-567
94F/MLP-35
94Finest-370
94L-291
94Pac/Cr-92
94Pinn-405
94S-500
94Select-205
94StCl-92
94StCl/1stDay-92
94StCl/Gold-92
94T-322
94T/Gold-322
94UD-30
94UD/CollC-277
94UD/CollC/Gold-277
94UD/CollC/Silv-277
94UD/ElecD-30
94Ultra-29
Turner, Col. R.
33SK*-27
Turner, Gregory
91Sydney/Fut-6
Turner, Jim
44Yank/St-27
52T-373C
62T-263M
63FrBauer-29
73OPC-116CO
73T-116C
W711/2
Turner, John Webber
(Jerry)
75Hawaii/Caruso-8
75IntLgAS/Broder-35
75OPC-619R
75PCL/AS-36
75T-619R
75T/M-619R
76OPC-598R
76T-598R
77Padre/SchCd-34
77T-447
78Padre/FamFun-34
78T-364
79T-564
80T-133
81D-244
81F-504
81T-285
81T/St-229
82D-609
82T-736
82Wheat/Ind
83F-345
83T-41
Turner, John
86Peoria-24
Turner, Lloyd
78Watlo
79Wausau-10
Turner, Matt
91AAA/LineD-446
91Richm/Bob-17
91Richm/Team-25
92Tucson/ProC-487
92Tucson/SB-621
93Edmon/ProC-1136
93F/Final-72
93Marlin/Publix-24
93Pac/Spanish-472
93StCl/Marlin-27
93T/Tr-56T
94D-593
94F-478
94Pac/Cr-251
94S-306
94S/GoldR-306
94StCl-319
94StCl/1stDay-319
94StCl/Gold-319
94StCl/Team-78
94T-587
94T/Gold-587
94Ultra-200
Turner, Rick
82Danvl/Frit-7
83Redwd-24
93Mother/Angel-28M
Turner, Roy
WG2-46
Turner, Ryan
91BendB/ClBest-16
91BendB/ProC-3709
92B-346
92UD-710
92Visalia/ClBest-17
92Visalia/ProC-1028
93T-537M
93T/Gold-537M
Turner, Shane
86FSLAS-47
86FtLaud-23
87Colum-13
87Colum/Pol-24
87Colum/TCMA-18
88Maine/CMC-13
88Maine/ProC-288
88Phill/TastyK-27
89F-653M
89Reading/Best-12
89Reading/ProC-655
89Reading/Star-24
89S/HotRook-67
90AAASingl/ProC-468
90ProC/Singl-325
90RochR/CMC-24
90RochR/ProC-711
90Rochester/L&U-22
91AAA/LineD-471
91RochR/LineD-471
91RochR/ProC-1912
92Calgary/ProC-3741
92Calgary/SB-71
92D/Rook-118
92F/Up-58
93Calgary/ProC-1176
93F-681
93StCl-97
93StCl/1stDay-97
93T-694
93T/Gold-694
Turner, Terry
10Domino-118
11Helmar-26
12Sweet/Pin-20
14Piedmont/St-56
D328-175
D329-176
D350/2-179
E135-175
E254
E270/1
E94
M101/4-176
M101/5-179
M116
S74-11
T201
T202
T205
T206
T207
Turner, Trent
88CapeCod/Sum-179
Turner, William
(Matt)
87Sumter-2
88BurlB/ProC-5
89Durham/Star-24
89Durham/Team-24
90Greenvl/Best-12
90Greenvl/ProC-1128
90Greenvl/Star-20
91Richm/LineD-446
91Richm/ProC-2569
Turnes, Jose
78DaytB
Turnier, Aaron
92Pulaski/ClBest-14
92Pulaski/ProC-3177
Turpin, Hal
43Centen-24
44Centen-25
45Centen-26
Turrentine, Richard
90Tampa/DIMD-27
91Greens/ProC-3070
92Greens/ClBest-23
92Greens/ProC-790
Turri, Shawn
91Niagara/ClBest-22
91Niagara/ProC-3632
Turtletaub, Greg
88LitFalls/Pucko-13
Turvey, Joe
90Hamil/Best-15
90Savan/ProC-2071
91Hamil/ClBest-20
91Hamil/ProC-4042
92Savan/ClBest-15
92Savan/ProC-665
Tuss, Jeff
91ClBest/Singl-364
91WPalmB/ClBest-13
91WPalmB/ProC-1229
92WPalmB/ClBest-7
92WPalmB/ProC-2089
Tutt, John
84CharlO-24
85Beaum-22
86LasVegas-20
Tuttle, Bill
55B-35
56T-203
57Swift-14
57T-72
58T-23
59T-459
60L-32
60T-367
61Bz-36
61Clover-28
61P-84
61T-536
61T/St-167
62J-88
62P-88
62P/Can-88
62Salada-87A
62Salada-87B
62Shirriff-87
62T-298
62T/St-80
63T-127
79TCMA-103
Tuttle, David
91T/Tr-122T
92StCl/Dome-188
Twardoski, Michael
88CLAS/Star-38
88Kinston/Star-22
89Canton/Best-12
89Canton/ProC-1299
89Canton/Star-21
89EastLDD/ProC-DD35
90Foil/Best-155
90NewBrit/Best-9
90NewBrit/ProC-1329
90NewBrit/Star-18
90Star/ISingl-31
91AAA/LineD-357
91Pawtu/LineD-357
92AAA/ASG/SB-369
92Pawtu/ProC-932
92Pawtu/SB-369
92Sky/AAASingl-168

Twardy, Glenn
89Belling/Legoe-14
Twellman, Tom
74Cedar
75Dubuq
76Dubuq
Twitchell, Lawrence
E223
N172
WG1-26
Twitchell, Wayne
71OPC-692R
71T-692R
72OPC-14R
72T-14R
73OPC-227
73T-227
74K-26
74OPC-419
74T-419
74T/St-79
75OPC-326
75T-326
75T/M-326
76OPC-543
76T-543
77T-444
78OPC-189
78T-269
79OPC-18
79T-43
91WIZMets-415
Twitty, Doug
90Bend/Legoe-21
Twitty, Jeff
81F-49
82Richm-8
Twitty, Sean
91Belling/ClBest-7
91Belling/ProC-3682
92Penin/ClBest-15
92SanBern/ProC-
Twombly, Babe
28Exh/PCL-29
Twomey, Mike
92Niagara/ClBest-30TR
Tyler, Brad
91Kane/ClBest-20
91Kane/ProC-2667
91MidwLAS/ProC-35
92ClBest-109
92Freder/ClBest-6
92Hagers/ProC-2565
94FExcel-16
Tyler, Dave
81Bristol-19
Tyler, George
(Lefty)
15CJ-146
BF2-56
D327
D328-176
D329-177
E121/80
E122
E135-176
M101/4-177
T207
T222
W575
Tyler, Mike
76Dubuq
78Charl
79CharCh-7
80Port-1
Tyner, Matt
90HagersDG/Best-34
Tyng, James
N172
Tyrer, Jason
89KS*-17
Tyrone, Jim
74OPC-598R
74T-598R
76SSPC-604
77SanJose-7
78T-487
Tyson, Albert T.
(Ty)
90Target-1088
Tyson, Jeremy
94LSU-14
Tyson, Mike
74OPC-655
74T-655
74T/St-120
75OPC-231
75T-231
75T/M-231
76Crane-65
76MSA/Disc
76OPC-86
76SSPC-283
76T-86
77BurgChef-18
77Pep-38
77T-599
78T-111
79OPC-162
79T-324
80OPC-252
80T-486
81Coke
81F-315
81T-294
81T/HT
81T/St-155
82D-435
82F-606
82F/St-100
82T-62
Tyson, Terry
77Watlo
Ubiera, Miguel
91GulfCR/SportP-20
Ubinas, Alex
90Bristol/ProC-3157
90Bristol/Star-24
91Bristol/ClBest-9
91Bristol/ProC-3609
Ubri, Fermin
84Jacks-24
Uchinokura, Tokashi
92Salinas/ClBest-24
92Salinas/ProC-3765
Uchiyama, Kenichi
90Salinas/Cal-122
90Salinas/ProC-2713
Uecker, Bob
62T-594R
63T-126
64T-543
65T-519
66OPC-91
66T-91
67CokeCap/Phill-10
67T-326
93AP/ASG-152
Ueda, Joe
88Fresno/ProC-1238
Ueda, Sadahito
83SanJose-16
Ugueto, Jesus
91Johnson/ClBest-10
91Johnson/ProC-3987
92Johnson/ProC-3128
Uhal, Bob
88LitFalls/Pucko-8
Uhey, Jackie
76Clinton
82ElPaso-18
85Everett/II/Cram-19CO
86Everett/Pop-34
Uhlaender, Ted
66T-264R
67T-431
68Dexter-74
68OPC-28
68T-28
69MB-279
69MLB/St-72
69OPC-194
69T-194
69T/4in1-19M
69T/St-200
70MLB/St-204
70T-673
71MLB/St-384
71OPC-347
71T-347
72MB-349
72T-614
78TCMA-161
78Twin/Frisz-47
90Greens/Best-28CO
90Greens/ProC-2682CO
90Greens/Star-26CO
91FtLaud/ClBest-8CO
91FtLaud/ProC-2445CO
92ColClip/Pol-2M
92ColClip/SB-125M
93ColClip/Pol-24M
Uhle, George E.
28Exh-44
28Yueng-11
29Exh/4-24
31Exh/4-23
33Exh/4-12
33G-100
40PlayBall-239
61F-146
82Ohio/HOF-43
91Conlon/Sport-224
E120
E210-11
R306
V354-22
V61-16
W502-11
W572
W573
WG7-56
Uhrhan, Kevin
91LynchRS/ClBest-10
91LynchRS/ProC-1200
92NewBrit/ProC-435
92NewBrit/SB-479
Ujdur, Gerry
80Evansvl-10
81Evansvl-8
81T-626R
82Evansvl-10
83D-600
83F-346
83T-174
Ullger, Scott
80OrlanTw-21
82OrlanTw/A-10
82Toledo-22
83Twin/Team-4
84D-438
84Nes/792-551
84T-551
84Toledo-12
85IntLgAS-27
85Toledo-18
86Toledo-22
87RochR-7
87RochR/TCMA-21
88Visalia/Cal-170
88Visalia/ProC-99
89AS/Cal-25CO
89Visalia/Cal-118MG
89Visalia/ProC-1433
90AS/Cal-25MG
90Visalia/Cal-79MG
90Visalia/ProC-2170MG
91AA/LineD-499MG
91OrlanSR/LineD-499MG
91OrlanSR/ProC-1865MG
92Portl/SB-424MG
92Portland/ProC-2681MG
Ulrich, Dutch
94Conlon-1298
Ulrich, George
89AS/Cal-55UMP
Ulrich, Jeff
80Penin/B-22
80Penin/C-16
81OkCty/TCMA-26
82OkCty-17
Umbach, Arnie
66T-518R
Umbarger, Jim
76OPC-7
76SSPC-257
76T-7
77T-378
78SSPC/270-90
79T-518
79Tucson-24
93Rang/Keeb-362
Umbricht, Jim
60T-145
63T-99
64T-389
89Smok/Ast-9
Umdenstock, Bob
79AppFx-19
82CharR-11
Umont, Frank
55B-305UMP
Umphlett, Tom
53Briggs
54B-88
55B-45
57Seattle/Pop-38
61Union
Underhill, Pat
91GulfCR/SportP-15
Underwood, Bill
92Oneonta/ClBest-20
93Greens/ClBest-24
93Greens/ProC-886
Underwood, Bobby
88Watertn/Pucko-13
89Augusta/ProC-500
90Augusta/ProC-2463
91Salem/ClBest-15
Underwood, Curtis
92Savan/ClBest-10
92Savan/ProC-672
Underwood, Kent
93Greens/ProC-887
Underwood, Pat
80OPC-358
80T-709
81D-368
81Evansvl-9
81F-469
81T-373
82T-133
83D-29
83Evansvl-10
83F-347
83Kaline-70M
83T-588
Underwood, Tom
75OPC-615R
75T-615R
75T/M-615R
76OPC-407
76SSPC-461
76T-407
77T-217
78BJ/PostC-20
78T-531
79BJ/Bubble-18
79OPC-26
79T-64
80OPC-172
80T-324
81D-108
81F-97
81OPC-114
81T-114
81T/Tr-846
82D-323
82F-109
82T-757
83D-391
83F-535
83F/St-6M
83F/St-6M
83Granny-31
83T-466
84D-253
84F-460
84F/X-U121
84Nes/792-642
84OPC-293
84T-642
84T/St-335
84T/Tr-123T
85F-194
85T-289
89Pac/SenLg-169
89TM/SenLg-108
91Crown/Orio-465
92Yank/WIZ80-194
Undorf, Bob
92Lakeland/ClBest-1
92Lakeland/ProC-2280
92ProC/Tomorrow-68
Unglaub, Robert
90Niagara/Pucko-26
91Fayette/ClBest-27
91Fayette/ProC-1170
E254
E270/1
E90/1
E91
M116
T204
T206
Ungs, Mike
79Wisco-2
80OrlanTw-15
81Wisco-10
Unitas, John
60P*
Unrein, Todd
91Kane/ClBest-11
91Kane/ProC-2658
91Kane/Team-23
Unroe, Tim
92Helena/ProC-1724
93FExcel/ML-195
Unser, Al
47Signal
Unser, Del
69MB-280
69T-338
70MLB/St-287
70OPC-336
70T-336
71MLB/St-551
71OPC-33
71T-33
72MB-350
72T-687
73OPC-247
73T-247
74JP
74OPC-69
74T-69
74T/St-80
75OPC-138
75T-138
75T/M-138
76Expo/Redp-32
76OPC-268
76SSPC-535
76SSPC/MetsY-M4
76T-268
77BurgChef-155
77OPC-27
77T-471
78OPC-216
78T-348
79OPC-330
79T-628
80BK/P-13
80OPC-12
80T-27
81D-164
81F-26
81OPC-56
81T-566
81T/HT
82D-273
82F-261
82T-713
85Phill/TastyK-7CO
85Phill/TastyK-8CO
86Phill/TastyK-25CO
87Phill/TastyK-x
88Phill/TastyK-29CO
91WIZMets-416
Upham, John
67T-608R
81TCMA-473
Upp, George
(Jerry)
E90/1
Upshaw, Cecil
67OPC-179R
67T-179R
68CokeCap/Brave-1
68T-286
69T-568
70OPC-295
70T-295
71MLB/St-23
71OPC-223
71T-223
72OPC-74
72T-74
73OPC-359
73T-359
74OPC-579
74T-579
74T/Tr-579T
75OPC-92
75T-92
75T/M-92
76SSPC-138

92Yank/WIZ70-156
Upshaw, Lee
88Durham/Star-22
89BurlB/ProC-1598
89BurlB/Star-21
90Foil/Best-25
90Greenvl/Best-1
91AA/LineD-220
91Greenvl/ClBest-7
91Greenvl/LineD-220
91Greenvl/ProC-3001
Upshaw, Willie
76FtLaud
78BJ/PostC-21
79OPC-175
79Syrac/TCMA-4
79Syrac/Team-26
79T-341
80Syrac-21
82D-652
82F-624
82OPC-196
82T-196
83D-558
83F-442
83F/St-4M
83OPC-338
83OPC/St-128
83T-556
83T/St-128
84D-315
84F-168
84Nes/792-453
84OPC-317
84T-453
84T/RD-30M
84T/St-363
84Tor/Fire-30
85D-10DK
85D-71
85D/AAS-52
85D/DKsuper-10
85F-118
85F-635IA
85F/LimEd-41
85FunFoodPin-94
85Leaf-10DK
85OPC-75
85OPC/Post-14
85Seven-15S
85T-75
85T/RD-31M
85T/St-358
85Tor/Fire-30
86BJ/Ault-23
86D-195
86F-72
86GenMills/Book-3M
86Leaf-128
86OPC-223
86Sf-98
86T-745
86T/St-188
86Tor/Fire-31
87D-367
87D/OD-30
87F-239
87GenMills/Book-1M
87Leaf-231
87OPC-245
87RedFoley/St-107
87Sf/TPrev-5
87T-245
87T/St-186
87Tor/Fire-32
88BJ/5x7-11
88D-271
88F-124
88F/Up-U25
88Gator-20
88Leaf-131
88OPC-241
88Panini/St-217
88S-279
88S/Tr-42T
88Sf-214
88T-505
88T/St-185
88T/Tr-123T
89D-492
89F-415
89OPC-106
89Panini/St-324
89S-188
89T-106
89UD-157
92Nabisco-8
93BJ/D/McDon-1
93Rang/Keeb-441CO
Upshur, Takashi
80Wausau-11
Upton, Jack
82Iowa-12
Upton, Thomas
52T-71
Uqueto, Jesus
92Johnson/ClBest-9
Urban, Jack E.
58T-367
59T-18
Urban, Luke
92Conlon/Sport-405
Urbanek, Jason
91Martins/ClBest-6
91Martins/ProC-3465
92Martins/ClBest-11
92Martins/ProC-3067
Urbani, Tom
90Johnson/Star-27
91Spring/ClBest-27
91Spring/ProC-742
92ArkTr/SB-48
92Louisvl/ProC-1888
92Sky/AASingl-21
93B-583
93F/Final-132
93StCl/Card-15
94StCl-392
94StCl/1stDay-392
94StCl/Gold-392
94StCl/Team-321
94T-83
94T/Gold-83
Urbanski, Bill
33DL-9
33G-212
34DS-37
34Exh/4-1
35BU-59
36Exh/4-1
37Exh/4-1
92Conlon/Sport-408
R313
R314
V355-71
Urbide, Miliciades
88Wythe/ProC-1975
89CharWh/Best-3
89CharWh/ProC-1744
Urbina, Ugueth
92Albany/ClBest-21
92Albany/ProC-2306
92B-261
92ClBest-379
92UD/ML-297
93BurlB/ClBest-24
93BurlB/ProC-159
93FExcel/ML-63
94B-88
94ClBest/Gold-91
94FExcel-229
94FExcel/LL-19
Urbina, William
92LitSun/HSPros-3
Urbon, Joe
89Batavia/ProC-1933
90Spartan/Best-22
90Spartan/ProC-2505
90Spartan/Star-22
91Clearw/ClBest-25
91Clearw/ProC-1636
Urcioli, John
91Miami/ClBest-24
91Miami/ProC-418
Uremovich, Mike
75Clinton
Urena, Fausto
92GulfCD/ProC-3576
Uribe, George
84Butte-24
Uribe, Jorge
86Wausau-26
88Vermont/ProC-953
89SanBern/Best-12
89SanBern/Cal-78
Uribe, Jose
81Louisvl-13
84Louisvl-13
85F/Up-U124
85Mother/Giants-13
85T/Tr-125T
86D-236
86F-552
86Mother/Giants-13
86OPC-12
86T-12
86T/St-87
86T/Tatt-13M
87D-436
87D/OD-99
87F-286
87Mother/SFG-13
87OPC-94
87T-633
88D-559
88D/Best-303
88F-99
88Leaf-218
88Mother/Giants-13
88Nestle-13
88OPC-302
88Panini/St-425
88S-165
88T-302
88T/Big-95
88T/St-91
89B-471
89D-131
89D/Best-106
89F-345
89KennerFig-153
89Mother/Giants-13
89OPC-8
89Panini/St-217
89S-56
89Sf-61
89T-753
89T/Big-258
89T/St-82
89UD-181
90D-335
90D/BestNL-122
90F-74
90F/Can-74
90Leaf-225
90Mother/Giant-17
90OPC-472
90Panini/St-372
90PublInt/St-84
90S-455
90Sf-79
90T-472
90T/Big-213
90UD-188
91B-627
91Cadaco-58
91D-375
91F-275
91Leaf-433
91Mother/Giant-17
91OPC-158
91PG&E-12
91Panini/FrSt-70
91S-628
91SFExam/Giant-15
91StCl-267
91T-158
91UD-207
91Ultra-330
92D-453
92F-649
92Giant/PGE-34
92Mother/Giant-17
92OPC-538
92Panini-215
92S-546
92StCl-371
92T-538
92T/Gold-538
92T/GoldWin-538
92UD-270
93F-539
93Mother/Ast-12
93Pac/Spanish-483
93T-201
93T/Gold-201
93UD-729
94F-502
94Pac/Cr-277
Uribe, Juan
88Beloit/GS-8
90Stockton/Best-18
90Stockton/Cal-170
90Stockton/ProC-2179
Uribe, Relito
89Dunedin/Star-20
Urman, Mike
88Pulaski/ProC-1764
89Sumter/ProC-1109
Urrea, John
78T-587
79T-429
81D-190
81T-152
Urso, Joe
92Boise/ClBest-17
Urso, Salvy
(Sal)
91Penin/ClBest-12
91Penin/ProC-378
92SanBern/ClBest-23
92SanBern/ProC-
Usher, Bob
51B-286
52T-157
57Sohio/Ind-15
58T-124
Utecht, Tim
83Beloit/Frit-20
Utt, Jimmy
89KS*-66
Vaccaro, Sal
86James-27
87BurlEx-6
87SanJose-4
Vachon, Maurice
(Mad Dog)
72Dimanche*-133
Vachon, Viviane
72Dimanche*-135
Vagg, Richard
91Melbourne/Fut-11
Vail, Michael
75Tidew/Team-23
76Ho-55
76Ho/Twink-55
76OPC-655
76SSPC-534
76T-655
77T-246
78T-69
79T-663
80OPC-180
80T-343
81D-554
81F-311
81T-471
81T/Tr-848
82Coke/Reds
82F-84
82T-194
83D-597
83Expo/PostC-20
83F-605
83Mother/Giants-19
83T-554
83T/Tr-119T
84Expo/PostC-33
84F-290
84F/X-U122
84Nes/792-766
84OPC-143
84T-766
84T/Tr-124T
89Tidew/Candl-6
90Target-812
91WIZMets-417
Vaji, Mark
81QuadC-24
Valdes, Marc
92T/Tr-121T
92T/TrGold-121T
93StCl/MurphyS-20
94B-646
94ClBest/Gold-119
94ClBest/GoldLP-15
94Pinn-431
94S-555
94T-750DP
94T/Gold-750DP
Valdes, Ramon
88GreatF-25
Valdes, Rene
57T-337
61Union
90Target-813
Valdespino, Sandy
65OPC-201R
65T-201R
66OPC-56
66T-56
67CokeCap/Twin-12
68T-304
69MB-281
70McDon
77WHave
78Twin/Frisz-48
81TCMA-329
85RochR-25
Valdez, Amilcar
88Bakers/Cal-241
Valdez, Angel
82Miami-17
Valdez, Carlos
92Everett/ProC-1691
Valdez, Efrain
88Tulsa-5
89Canton/Best-6
89Canton/ProC-1311
89Canton/Star-22
90AAASingl/ProC-216
90ColoSp/CMC-4
90ColoSp/ProC-35
90ProC/Singl-456
91AAA/LineD-96
91B-60
91ColoSp/LineD-96
91ColoSp/ProC-2183
91OPC-692
91S-723RP
91StCl-483
91T-692A
91T-692B
91T/90Debut-156
92Denver/ProC-2640
92Denver/SB-146
92StCl-838
93LimeR/Winter-70
Valdez, Francisco
(Frank)
88Kenosha/ProC-1393
89Gaston/ProC-1020
89Gaston/Star-23
89SALAS/GS-40
89Visalia/Cal-108
89Visalia/ProC-1440
90OrlanSR/Best-14
90OrlanSR/ProC-1094
90OrlanSR/Star-21
90ProC/Singl-722
91AA/LineD-479
91OrlanSR/LineD-479
91OrlanSR/ProC-1864
Valdez, Ismael
91Kissim/ProC-4186
Valdez, Jose 1
90Kissim/DIMD-27
Valdez, Jose 2
83Peoria/Frit-12
Valdez, Julio
81Pawtu-17
82D-560
82T-381R
83F-199
83T-628
85Iowa-7
86Iowa-25
87Iowa-17
88Pittsfld/ProC-1357
88Wythe/ProC-1988
89Wythe/Star-29INS
Valdez, Ken
92Bristol/ProC-1430
Valdez, Mica
90SanAn/GS-28
Valdez, Miguel
80Elmira-43
Valdez, Pedro
91Hunting/ClBest-27
91Hunting/ProC-3351
92Geneva/ClBest-1
92Geneva/ProC-1575
92Peoria/ClBest-21
93Peoria/Team-30
94ClBest/Gold-53
Valdez, Rafael
86CharRain-27
87CharRain-15
88CharI/ProC-1201

89River/Best-18
89River/Cal-4
89River/ProC-1398
89Wichita/Rock/HL-6M
89Wichita/Rock/Up-10
90AAASingl/ProC-13
90B-210
90F/Up-U58
90LasVegas/CMC-20
90LasVegas/ProC-125
90ProC/Singl-523
90S/Tr-93T
90UD/Ext-775
91B-663
91LasVegas/ProC-236
91S-360RP
91S/100RisSt-31
91T/90Debut-157
91UD-253
92LasVegas/ProC-2797
93LimeR/Winter-67

Valdez, Ramon
89Princet/Star-22

Valdez, Sergio
85Utica-7
87Indianap-21
88Indianap/CMC-8
88Indianap/ProC-501
89Indianap/CMC-2
89Indianap/ProC-1215
90D-405
90Leaf-496
90OPC-199
90T-199
91AAA/LineD-97
91ColoSp/LineD-97
91ColoSp/ProC-2184
91D-344
91F-380
91OPC-98
91T-98
92Indianap/ProC-1859
92Indianap/SB-196
92StCl-789
93F-465
93LimeR/Winter-15
93Ottawa/ProC-2436
93StCl-171
93StCl/1stDay-171

Valdez, Sylverio
80Utica-8
83Ander-18

Valdivielso, Jose
56T-237
57T-246
60T-527
61Clover-29
61Peters-25
61T-557
62T-339

Valeandia, Jorge
92Bristol/ClBest-22

Valencia, Gil
89Martins/Star-31
90Batavia/ProC-3083
90Spartan/Best-23
90Spartan/ProC-2506
90Spartan/Star-23

Valencia, Jose
88Sumter/ProC-399

Valennia, Max
92Boise/ClBest-2

Valente, John
88CapeCod/Sum-2

Valentin, Eddy
89AubAs/ProC-2160

Valentin, John
88CapeCod-11
88CapeCod/Sum-138
89WinHaven/Star-25
90Foil/Best-283
90NewBrit/Best-21
90NewBrit/Star-19
91AA/LineD-473
91NewBrit/LineD-473
91NewBrit/ProC-361
92D/RookPhen-BC19
92F/Up-4
92Pawtu/ProC-933
92Pawtu/SB-370
92Sky/AAASingl-169
93B-690
93D-251
93DennyGS-21
93F-183
93L-87
93OPC-220
93Pac/Spanish-363
93Pinn-224
93Pinn-482I
93S-243
93Select-344
93StCl-508
93StCl/1stDay-508
93T-424
93T/Gold-424
93ToysRUs-10
93UD-387
94D-517
94F-44
94Flair-16
94L-77
94Pac/Cr-67
94Panini-33
94Pinn-126
94Pinn/Artist-126
94Pinn/Museum-126
94S-417
94Select-49
94StCl-483
94StCl/1stDay-483
94StCl/Gold-483
94Studio-165
94T-568
94T/Finest-128
94T/FinestRef-128
94T/Gold-568
94TripleP-208
94UD-373
94UD/CollC-278
94UD/CollC/Gold-278
94UD/CollC/Silv-278
94Ultra-318

Valentin, Jose
87Spokane-23
88Charl/ProC-1198
89AS/Cal-7
89River/Best-19
89River/Cal-8
89River/ProC-1415
89Wichita/Rock/Up-18
90Wichita/Rock-20
91AA/LineD-620
91ClBest/Singl-33
91Wichita/LineD-620
91Wichita/ProC-2606
91Wichita/Rock-16
92Denver/ProC-2652
92Denver/SB-147
92Sky/AAASingl-72
93T-804
93T/Gold-804
94B-93
94D-544
94F-194
94Pac/Cr-346
94Pinn-249
94Pinn/Artist-249
94Pinn/Museum-249
94Pol/Brew-27
94StCl-456
94StCl/1stDay-456
94StCl/Gold-456
94T-251
94T/Gold-251
94UD-303

Valentine, Bill
80ArkTr-23

Valentine, Bobby
71OPC-188R
71T-188R
72OPC-11
72T-11
73OPC-502
73T-502
74OPC-101
74T-101
74T/DE-11
74T/St-150
75OPC-215
75T-215
75T/M-215
76OPC-366
76T-366
77Padre/SchCd-35
77T-629
78T-712
79OPC-222
79T-428
85Rang-2MG
85SpokAT/Cram-22
85T/Tr-126T
86Rang-2MG
86T-261MG
87Mother/Rang-1
87Smok/R-19MG
87T-118MG
88Mother/R-1MG
88Smok/R-8MG
88T-594MG
89Mother/R-1MG
89Smok/R-33MG
89T-314MG
90Mother/Rang-1MG
90OPC-729MG
90T-729MG
90Target-814
91Mother/Rang-1MG
91OPC-489MG
91T-489MG
91WIZMets-418
92Mother/Rang-1MG
92OPC-789MG
92T-789MG
92T/Gold-789MG
92T/GoldWin-789MG
93Rang/Keeb-363MG
93Reds/Kahn-8M

Valentine, Ellis
76Expo/Redp-33
76OPC-590R
76SSPC-342
76T-590R
77BurgChef-158
77Expo/PostC-8
77OPC-234
77T-52
78K-19
78OPC-45
78T-185
79Ho-50
79OPC-277
79T-535
80K-21
80OPC-206
80T-395
81F-148
81OPC-244
81OPC/Post-7
81T-445
81T/So-80
81T/St-186
81T/Tr-849
82D-605
82F-541
82F/St-83
82OPC-15
82T-15
82T/St-69
82T/StVar-69
83F-558
83F/St-15M
83F/St-18M
83T-653
83T/Tr-120T
84F-529
84Nes/792-236
84OPC-236
84Smok/Cal-29
84T-236
91WIZMets-419
93Expo/D/McDon-21
93Rang/Keeb-364

Valentine, Fred
64T-483
66T-351
67CokeCap/Senator-18
67OPC-64
67T-64
68T-248
69MB-282
91Crown/Orio-466

Valentine, Harold
(Corky)
55T-44
55T/DH-46
79TCMA-61

Valentinetti, Vito
57T-74
58T-463
59T-44

Valentini, Vincent
80Wichita-19

Valenzuela, Fernando
81F-140
81PermaGr/AS-9
81Pol/Dodg-34
81T-302R
81T/Tr-850
82D-462
82F-27
82F-635M
82F-636M
82F/St-1
82F/St-108M
82F/St-111M
82K-9
82OPC-334
82OPC-345AS
82PermaGr/CC-12
82Pol/Dodg-34
82Sqt-20
82T-166LL
82T-345AS
82T-510
82T-6RB
82T/St-11
82T/St-119
82T/St-50
83D-1DK
83D-284
83D/AAS-53
83F-224
83F/St-1AM
83F/St-1BM
83F/St-3M
83K-7
83OPC-40
83OPC/St-250FOIL
83PermaGr/CC-18
83Pol/Dodg-34
83Seven-8
83T-40
83T-681TL
83T/Gloss40-10
83T/St-250
83T/St/Box-1
84D-52
84D/AAS-13
84F-115
84F/St-81
84MiltBrad-27
84Nes/792-220
84OPC-220
84Pol/Dodg-34
84Ralston-10
84Seven-9W
84T-220
84T/Cereal-10
84T/RD-32M
84T/St-16LCS
84T/St-79
84T/Super-30
85Coke/Dodg-31
85D-52
85D/AAS-37
85D/HL-28
85D/HL-6
85F-387
85F/LimEd-42
85F/St-114
85FunFoodPin-7
85GenMills-12
85Leaf-184
85OPC-357
85Seven-16W
85T-440
85T/3D-21
85T/RD-32M
85T/St-71
85T/Super-52
85ThomMc/Discs-45
86BK/AP-3
86Coke/Dodg-30
86D-215
86D/AAS-27
86D/HL-25
86Drake-36
86F-145
86F-641M
86F/Mini-31
86F/Slug-41
86F/St-123
86GenMills/Book-5M
86Jiffy-14
86Leaf-91
86Meadow/Blank-15
86Meadow/Milk-12
86Meadow/Stat-2
86OPC-178
86OPC/WaxBox-P
86Pol/Dodg-34
86Quaker-17
86Seven/Coin-C6M
86Seven/Coin-E6M
86Seven/Coin-S6M
86Seven/Coin-W6M
86Sf-12
86Sf-132M
86Sf-143M
86Sf-56M
86Sf-72M
86Sf/Dec-66
86Sf/Rook-47M
86T-207RB
86T-401TBC
86T-630
86T/3D-30
86T/Gloss60-3
86T/Mini-47
86T/St-64
86T/Super-58
86T/Tatt-24M
86T/WaxBox-P
86TrueVal-6
87BK-20
87Classic-91
87D-94
87D/AAS-54
87Drake-29
87F-457
87F-631M
87F/AS-10
87F/AwardWin-40
87F/BB-43
87F/GameWin-42
87F/Mini-109
87F/Slug-43
87F/St-120
87GenMills/Book-6M
87Ho/St-11
87Jiffy-15
87KMart-33
87KayBee-32
87Kraft-32
87Leaf-148
87MnM's-19
87Mother/Dodg-4
87OPC-273
87Pol/Dodg-17
87Ralston-11
87RedFoley/St-57
87Seven-W16
87Sf-119M
87Sf-120M
87Sf-150
87Sf/TPrev-14M
87Smok/Dodg-36
87Sportflic/DealP-2
87Stuart-6M
87T-410
87T-604AS
87T/Coins-47
87T/Gloss22-11
87T/Gloss60-53
87T/Mini-16
87T/St-75
88ChefBoy-24
88D-53
88D/Best-316
88F-528
88F/BB/MVP-40
88F/Excit-43
88F/Mini-86
88F/St-94
88Grenada-68
88KMart-31
88KennerFig-114
88KingB/Disc-19
88Leaf-61
88MSA/Disc-20
88Mother/Dodg-4
88OPC-52
88Panini/St-304
88Pol/Dodg-34
88S-600
88Sf-40
88Smok/Dodg-24

88T-489
88T-780
88T/Big-18
88T/Coins-58
88T/Mini-54
88T/Revco-14
88T/St-70
88T/St/Backs-30
88T/UK-80
89B-337
89D-250
89F-76
89KMart/DT-32
89KennerFig-154
89Mother/Dodg-4
89OPC-150
89Panini/St-103
89Pol/Dodg-22
89RedFoley/St-123
89S-437
89Sf-124
89Smok/Dodg-97
89T-150
89T/LJN-78
89T/St-60
89T/UK-78
89UD-656
90D-625
90D/BestNL-90
90D/Learning-39
90F-409
90F-622MVP
90F/Can-409
90F/Can-622
90Leaf-68
90MLBPA/Pins-7
90Mother/Dodg-2
90OPC-340
90Panini/St-269
90Pol/Dodg-34
90PublInt/St-21
90S-54
90T-340
90T/St-59
90Target-815
90UD-445
91BBBest/RecBr-18
91Classic/200-73
91D-127
91D-BC11
91D/BC-BC11
91F-222
91F/WaxBox-5
91OPC-80NH
91Panini/FrSt-356
91Panini/St-5
91Panini/St-59
91S-449
91S-703
91Seven/3DCoin-15SC
91StCl-90
91StCl/Charter*-30
91T-80A
91T-80B
91UD-175
93F/Final-166
93Flair-159
93L-472
93OPC/Premier-47
93Pac/Jugador-17
93Pac/Spanish-352
93StCl-661
93StCl/1stDay-661
93UD-550
93Ultra-503
94D-408
94F-22
94Pac/Cr-46
94Pac/Silv-14
94Panini-25
94S-190
94S/GoldR-190
94StCl-69
94StCl/1stDay-69
94StCl/Gold-69
94T-175
94T/Gold-175

Valenzuela, Guillermo
83Kinston/Team-27

Valera, Julio
87Columbia-26
88Clmbia/GS-11
89BBAmAA/BPro-AA28
89Jacks/GS-29
89StLucie/Star-23
89TexLAS/GS-26
90AAASingl/ProC-277
90B-123
90ProC/Singl-364
90T/TVMets-65
90Tidew/CMC-13
90Tidew/ProC-546
91AAA/LineD-571
91D-39RR
91F-164
91OPC-504
91S-353RP
91T-504
91T/90Debut-158
91Tidew/LineD-571
91Tidew/ProC-2511
91UD-534
91WIZMets-420
92B-422
92Classic/II-T4
92D/Rook-119
92F-517
92F/Up-11
92L-490
92L/BlkGold-490
92Pinn-267
92ProC/Tomorrow-276
92S/100RisSt-17
92Sky/AAASingl-257
92StCl-304
92StCl-646
92T/Tr-122T
92T/TrGold-122T
92Tidew/ProC-
92Tidew/SB-573
92UD-747
92UD/Scout-SR23
93D-5
93F-578
93L-430
93Mother/Angel-11
93OPC-368
93Pac/Spanish-374
93Pinn-139
93Pol/Angel-14
93S-427
93Select-288
93StCl-386
93StCl/1stDay-386
93StCl/Angel-30
93T-374
93T/Gold-374
93UD-343
93Ultra-169
94F-72
94Pac/Cr-93
94S-223
94S/GoldR-223

Valera, Wilson
83Watlo/Frit-10
85Water-2
86Lynch-23
87Lynch-26

Valette, Ramon
91Elizab/ProC-4309
92Elizab/ClBest-18

Valiente, Nestor
84Butte-25

Valla, Mike
88Watertn/Pucko-26

Vallaran, Miguel
77LodiD

Valle, Dave
80SanJose/JITB-20
81LynnS-14
82SLCity-20
83Chatt-26
84Cram/PCL-176
85F/Up-U125
85Mother/Mar-17
86Calgary-24
87D-610
87D/OD-120
87Mother/Sea-9
87Sf/TPrev-25M
87T/Tr-122T
88D-393
88F-389
88Mother/Sea-9
88OPC-83
88Panini/St-184
88S-126
88T-583
88T/Big-210
88T/St-220
89B-208
89Chatt/II/Team-30
89D-614
89D/Best-248
89F-561
89Mother/Sea-9
89RedFoley/St-124
89S-27
89T-459
89T-498
89T/Big-56
89UD-320
90B-473
90D-129
90D/BestAL-55
90F-527
90F/Can-527
90Leaf-166
90MLBPA/Pins-120
90Mother/Mar-5
90OPC-76
90Panini/St-156
90PublInt/St-444
90RedFoley/St-97
90S-109
90T-76
90T/Big-266
90UD-451
91B-251
91CounHrth-6
91D-366
91F-463
91Leaf-511
91Leaf/Stud-120
91OPC-178
91Panini/FrSt-227
91RedFoley/St-95
91S-262
91StCl-32
91T-178
91UD-595
91Ultra-344
92B-134
92D-462
92F-295
92L-170
92L/BlkGold-170
92Mother/Mar-5
92OPC-294
92Panini-54
92Pinn-232
92S-343
92StCl-56
92Studio-240
92T-294
92T/Gold-294
92T/GoldWin-294
92TripleP-5
92UD-182
92Ultra-130
93Colla/DM-110
93D-507
93F-315
93Flair-275
93L-425
93Mother/Mar-7
93Pac/Spanish-291
93Panini-58
93Pinn-179
93S-200
93StCl-483
93StCl/1stDay-483
93StCl/Mar-20
93Studio-68
93T-370
93T/Gold-370
93TripleP-152
93UD-100
93Ultra-273
94D-385
94F-300
94Finest-378
94Flair-17
94L-430
94Pac/Cr-584
94Panini-123
94Pinn-514
94S-493
94T-736
94T/Gold-736
94UD-333
94Ultra-319

Valle, Hector
65T-561R
66T-314

Valle, John A.
77Evansvl/TCMA-24
78Indianap-14
79Indianap-25
80RochR-14
81RochR-17
82RochR-18
83RochR-18
84RochR-6

Valle, Tony
89Idaho/ProC-2026
90BurlB/Best-8
90BurlB/ProC-2350
90BurlB/Star-26

Vallette, Ramon
92Elizab/ProC-3689

Valley, Chick
77Salem
78Salem
79BuffB/TCMA-14
81ElPaso-16
82Vanco-18

Vallot, Joey
91GulfCR/SportP-24

Valo, Elmer
48L-29
49B-66
50B-49
51T/RB-28
52B-206
52T-34
53T-122
54T-145
55Rodeo
55T-145
55T/DH-85
56Rodeo
56T-3
57T-54
58T-323
60L-107
60T-237
61Peters-12
61T-186
63Sugar-17
79TCMA-148
81TCMA-316
89Pac/Leg-187
90Target-816
91T/Arc53-122
92Yank/WIZ60-133
94T/Arc54-145

Valois, Frank
72Dimanche*-136

Valrie, Kerry
90Utica/Pucko-12
91ClBest/Singl-243
91SoBend/ClBest-25
91SoBend/ProC-2872
92MidwLAS/Team-46
92SoBend/ClBest-7
92SoBend/ProC-192

Valverde, Joe
89SanDiegoSt/Smok-27

Valverde, Miguel
88Augusta/ProC-361
89Salem/Star-23

Van Atta, Russ
33G-215
92Conlon/Sport-611
R312/M
R314

Van Bever, Mark
78Clinton

Van Blaricom, Mark
83Butte-22
85FtMyr-10
86FtMyr-25
87Memphis-12
87Memphis/Best-6
88Memphis/Best-3

Van Brunt, Jim
87Anchora-37BB

Van Brunt, Lefty
85Anchora-28CO
87Anchora-30CO
89Anchora-26CO

Van Burkleo, Ty
82Beloit/Frit-6
86PalmSp-29
86PalmSp/Smok-20
87MidldA-7
92Edmon/ProC-3548
92Edmon/SB-169
93B-497
93Vanco/ProC-2606

Van Cuyk, Chris
52T-53
53Mother-41
90Target-819

Van DeBrake, Kevin
91Yakima/ClBest-13
91Yakima/ProC-4257

Van DeCasteele, Mike
78Tidew
79Tidew-19

Van Der Beck, Jim
75Water

Van Duzer, Donna L.
88Fresno/ProC-1249TR
91CharlR/ClBest-26TR

Van Dyke, Rod
91Boise/ClBest-7
91Boise/ProC-3879
92PalmSp/ClBest-17
92PalmSp/ProC-841

Van Dyke, William
N172

Van Every, Jason
93MissSt-45

Van Gilder, Elam
92Conlon/Sport-569
E120
E126-47

Van Gorder, Dave
80Indianap-8
81Indianap-6
82Indianap-12
83D-188
83Indianap-27
83T-322
84Wichita/Rock-10
85D-384
86D-550
86F-195
86T-143
87RochR-2
87RochR/TCMA-11
91Crown/Orio-467

Van Graflan, Roy
94Conlon-1194UMP

Van Haltren, George
E107
E223
N172
N403
N566-180
N690/2
WG1-17

Van Heyningen, Pat
85Newar-20

Van Horn, Dave
83Ander-24

Van Houten, Jim
85Spring-4
87ColAst/ProC-11

Van Kemper, John
85Everett/II/Cram-20

Van Ornum, John
80Pol/Giants-42

Van Pelt, Mark
91Adelaide/Fut-14

Van Poppel, Todd
90A&AASingle/ProC-160
90Classic/DP-14
90Madison/Best-1
90SoOreg/Best-1
90SoOreg/ProC-3422
91AA/LineD-296
91B-218
91ClBest/Gold-6
91ClBest/Singl-386
91Classic/200-151
91Classic/I-75
91Classic/I-77
91Classic/I-NO
91Classic/II-T77
91D/Rook-7
91Huntsvl/ClBest-24
91Huntsvl/LineD-296
91HuntsvlProC-1795
91Leaf/GRook-BC9
91Leaf/Stud-109
91S-389FDP

91Seven/3DCoin-13NC
91Seven/3DCoin-14T
91UD-53TP
91UD/FinalEd-12F
92B-270
92Classic/I-91
92D-9RR
92D/Preview-12
92F-269
92F/RookSIns-2
92Kenner/Fig-45
92L-248
92L/BlkGold-248
92OPC-142
92Pinn-574
92Pinn/Rook-12
92Pinn/RookI-12
92Pinn/Team2000-72
92ProC/Tomorrow-129
92S-865
92S/HotRook-4
92S/Impact-37
92S/Rook-1
92Sky/AAASingl-244
92StCl-129
92T-142
92T/91Debut-175
92T/Gold-142
92T/GoldWin-142
92T/McDonB-44
92Tacoma/ProC-2501
92Tacoma/SB-545
92TripleP-142
92UD-22SR
92UD/ML-75
92Ultra-118
93B-371FOIL
93B-681
93FExcel/ML-219
93L-448
93Select/RookTr-79T
93StCl-48
93StCl/1stDay-48
93StCl/A's-22
93T-673
93T/Gold-673
93ToysRUs-62
93UD/SP-45
94B-548
94D-557
94F-275
94L-151
94OPC-56
94Pac/Cr-464
94Panini-114
94Pinn-357
94S-607
94Select-86
94T-559
94T/Finest-182
94T/Finest/PreProd-182
94T/FinestRef-182
94T/Gold-559
94UD-195
94UD/CollC-279
94UD/CollC/Gold-279
94UD/CollC/Silv-279
94UD/ElecD-195
94Ultra-414

Van Robays, Maurice
47Remar-18
47Signal
47Smith-7
48Signal
48Smith-9
49B/PCL-32
49Remar

Van Ryn, Ben
91ClBest/Singl-31
91Sumter/ClBest-11
91Sumter/ProC-2334
92VeroB/ClBest-26
92VeroB/ProC-2875
94FExcel-220
94FExcel/LL-20
94T-783M
94T/Gold-783M

Van Rynback, Casper
90Kgsport/Best-19
90Kgsport/Star-23
91Pittsfld/ClBest-14
91Pittsfld/ProC-3424

Van Schaack, Tom
90Watertn/Star-27GM

Van Scoyoc, Aaron
89Oneonta/ProC-2115
90Greens/Best-20
90Greens/ProC-2672
90Greens/Star-24
91FtLaud/ProC-2437

Van Scoyoc, Jim
91Niagara/ClBest-6CO
91Niagara/ProC-3652CO
92Bristol/ClBest-28CO

Van Slyke, Andy
81Louisvl-18
82ArkTr-19
83Louisvl/Riley-18
84D-83
84F-339
84Nes/792-206
84T-206
84T/St-150
85D-327
85F-242
85OPC-341
85T-551
85T/St-138
86D-412
86F-48
86KAS/Disc-19
86KayBee-32
86OPC-33
86Schnucks-23
86T-683
86T/St-51
87D-417
87D/OD-161
87F-311
87F/Up-U121
87OPC-33
87Sf/TPrev-12M
87T-33
87T/St-51
87T/Tr-124T
88D-18DK
88D-291
88D-BC8
88D/Best-157
88D/DKsuper-18DK
88F-341
88F/LL-43
88F/Mini-105
88F/St-116
88F/TL-44
88KennerFig-115
88Leaf-102
88Leaf-18DK
88OPC-142
88Panini/St-380
88RedFoley/St-92
88S-416
88Sf-109
88T-142
88T/Big-184
88T/St-126
88T/UK-81
89B-424
89Cadaco-59
89Classic-111
89D-54
89D/AS-61
89D/Best-45
89D/MVP-BC10
89F-222
89F/BBAS-42
89F/BBMVP's-40
89F/Heroes-41
89F/LL-41
89F/WaxBox-C27
89KennerFig-155
89KingB/Discs-19
89MSA/Disc-17
89OPC-350
89Panini/St-173
89S-174
89S/HotStar-92
89S/Mast-38
89Sf-166
89T-350
89T-392AS
89T/Ames-30
89T/Big-255
89T/Coins-27
89T/DH-19
89T/Gloss60-4
89T/Hills-30
89T/LJN-150
89T/Mini-32
89T/St-132
89T/St/Backs-54
89T/UK-79
89Tetley/Discs-17
89UD-537
89UD-685TC
89VFJuice-18
90B-171
90Classic/III-30
90D-244
90D/BestNL-119
90D/Learning-3
90F-481
90F/AwardWin-40
90F/Can-481
90F/LL-40
90Homer/Pirate-29
90HotPlay/St-47
90Kenner/Fig-86
90Leaf-117
90MLBPA/Pins-36
90OPC-775
90Panini/St-324
90PublInt/St-166
90RedFoley/St-98
90S-440
90S/100St-78
90Sf-101
90T-775
90T/Big-217
90T/Mini-72
90T/St-124
90UD-536
91B-529
91Classic/200-45
91D-552
91F-53
91Leaf-310
91Leaf/Stud-230
91OPC-425
91Panini/FrSt-121
91Panini/St-118
91Panini/Top15-106
91RedFoley/St-96
91S-475
91S-698RF
91S/100SS-22
91StCl-118
91T-425
91UD-256
91Ultra-287
92B-35
92Classic/Game200-153
92Classic/I-92
92Classic/II-T64
92D-383
92D/McDon-17
92F-570
92Hardee-21
92L-43
92L/BlkGold-43
92L/GoldPrev-9
92L/Prev-9
92MrTurkey-25
92OPC-545
92Panini-257
92Pinn-9
92Pirate/Nation-23
92S-655
92S/Proctor-17
92Seven/Coin-7
92StCl-232
92StCl/Dome-189
92Studio-89
92Studio/Her-10
92T-545
92T/Gold-545
92T/GoldWin-545
92T/Kids-23
92TripleP-148
92TripleP-6LH
92TripleP/Prev-3
92UD-132
92UD-711M
92UD-715DS
92Ultra-262
92Ultra/AwardWin-10
93B-218
93Classic/GameI-93
93Colla/ASG-12
93Colla/DM-111
93D-414
93D/DK-9
93D/Elite-32
93D/EliteUp-14
93D/Prev-9
93DennyGS-19
93Duracel/PPII-8
93F-122
93F/ASNL-8
93F/Atlantic-24
93F/Fruit-62
93F/ProVII-1
93F/TLNL-10
93Flair-117
93Ho-1
93HumDum/Can-46
93JDean/28-4
93Kenner/Fig-36
93Kraft-30
93L-79
93L/GoldAS-7M
93MSA/Metz-39
93OPC-355
93OPC/Premier-88
93P-27
93Pac/Spanish-253
93Panini-285
93Pinn-19
93Pinn/TP-9
93Pirate/Nation-33
93Post/Can-11
93S-12
93S-524AS
93S-535DT
93S/Franchise-23
93S/GoldDT-4
93Select-35
93Select/ChasS-6
93Select/StatL-10M
93Select/StatL-16
93Select/StatL-24
93Select/StatL-42
93Select/StatL-5
93StCl-294MC
93StCl-394
93StCl/1stDay-294MC
93StCl/1stDay-394
93StCl/MurphyS-14
93Studio-132
93T-275
93T-405
93T/BlkGold-21
93T/Finest-185
93T/FinestRef-185
93T/Gold-275
93T/Gold-405
93TripleP-8
93TripleP/Act-1
93UD-124
93UD-480M
93UD/Diam-19
93UD/FunPack-148GS
93UD/FunPack-151
93UD/Iooss-WI18
93UD/OnDeck-D25
93UD/SP-188
93USPlayC/Ace-11D
93Ultra-103
93Ultra/AwardWin-8
94B-50
94D-375
94D/Special-375
94F-622
94Finest-408
94KingB-23
94Kraft-30
94L-411
94OPC-86
94Oscar-30
94Pac/Cr-509
94Panini-240
94Pinn-16
94Pinn/Artist-16
94Pinn/Museum-16
94RedFoley-3M
94S-18
94S/DT-8
94S/GoldR-18
94S/GoldS-19
94Select-129
94Sf/2000-76
94Studio-150
94T-650
94T/Gold-650
94TripleP-189
94TripleP/Medal-12M
94UD-83
94UD/CollC-280
94UD/CollC/Gold-280
94UD/CollC/Silv-280
94UD/DColl-C9
94UD/ElecD-83
94UD/HoloFX-40
94UD/SP-144
94Ultra-560

Van Stone, Paul
85Everett/II/Cram-21
86Clinton-25

Van Tiger, Tom
91Watertn/ClBest-29
91Watertn/ProC-3384
92Kinston/ClBest-24

Van Vuren, Bob
86FtMyr-26

Van Winkle, Dave
89Utica/Pucko-1
90SoBend/Best-4
91CalLgAS-5
91PalmSp/ProC-2015

Van Wyck, Jim
74Tacoma/Caruso-21

VanBuren, Chris
87Belling/Team-32BB

VanLandingham, Bill
91Everett/ClBest-24
91Everett/ProC-3913
92ClBest-251
92ClBest-390
92Clinton/ProC-3598
92LynchRS/ClBest-23
92ProC/Tomorrow-356
92SanJose/ClBest-4
94B-491
94FExcel-295

VanRyn, Ben
94ClBest/Gold-147
94FExcel-20
94FExcel-220

Vanacore, Derek
85FtMyr-29

Vance, Clarence A.
(Dazzy)
25Exh-15
28Exh-8
29Exh/4-3
31Exh/4-3
33CJ/Pin-23
33Exh/4-2
33G-2
35G-2C
35G-4C
35G-7C
50Callahan
50W576-72
60F-51
61F-81
61GP-26
63Bz/ATG-28
72F/FFeat-4
72Laugh/GF-21
76Rowe-11M
76Shakey-77
77Galasso-104
77Galasso-266
80Perez/HOF-79
80SSPC/HOF
89HOF/St-73
89Smok/Dodg-29
90Target-817
92Conlon/Sport-377
92Yank/WIZHOF-33
93Conlon-929
94Conlon-1055
R310
R315-A37
R315-B37
R316
R332-45
R423-109
V353-2
W517-36
W572

Vance, Gene
(Sandy)
71OPC-34
71T-34
85SpokAT/Cram-23
90Target-818

Vancho, Robert
(Bob)
89Helena/SP-18
90Beloit/Best-23
90Beloit/Star-22
90MidwLgAS/GS-22
90ProC/Singl-435
91AAA/LineD-73
91Stockton/ClBest-4
91Stockton/ProC-3032
92Calgary/ProC-3731
93Rang/Keeb-365
VandeBerg, Ed
81Spokane-15
82T/Tr-122T
83D-100
83F-488
83F/St-12M
83F/St-13M
83OPC-183
83OPC/St-317
83T-183
83T/St-317
84D-604
84F-623
84Mother/Mar-8
84Nes/792-63
84OPC-63
84T-63
85D-511
85F-504
85Mother/Mar-5
85OPC-207
85T-566
85T/St-336
86Coke/Dodg-31
86D-637
86F-479
86F/Up-U121
86OPC-357
86Pol/Dodg-31
86T-357
86T/Tr-118T
87D-376
87F-458
87F/Up-U120
87Gator-36
87OPC-34
87T-717
87T/Tr-123T
88AlaskaAS70/Team-22
88F-619
88OkCty/CMC-8
88OkCty/ProC-52
88T-421
89F-534
89Iowa/CMC-4
89Iowa/ProC-1710
89T-242
90Calgary/CMC-8
90Target-820
91Calgary/LineD-73
91Calgary/ProC-517
Vandenberg, Hy
40PlayBall-209
VanderMeer, John
39Exh
41DP-6
41PlayBall-56
43MP-23
47HomogBond-47
48L-53
48Swell-10
49B-128
49Eureka-96
50B-79
51B-223
60NuCard-5
61F-147
72Laugh/GF-7
74Laugh/ASG-38
76Laugh/Jub-12
77Galasso-243
77Galasso-73
80Pac/Leg-110
82Ohio/HOF-21
88Pac/Leg-30
89Swell-11
90BBWit-80
90HOF/St-36
90Swell/Great-99
91Swell/Great-61
92Conlon/Sport-367
92Conlon/Sport-368
94Conlon-1181
94TedW-24
D305
Exh47
R346-46
W711/1
W711/2
VanderWal, John
87James-14
88FSLAS/Star-23
88WPalmB/Star-24
89Jaxvl/Best-25
89Jaxvl/ProC-161
90Foil/Best-90
90Jaxvl/Best-13
90Jaxvl/ProC-1388
91AAA/LineD-197
91AAAGame/ProC-17
91Expo/PostC-7
91Indianap/LineD-197
91Indianap/ProC-476
92B-232
92Classic/II-T32
92D-414RR
92Expo/D/Duri-16
92F/Up-99
92L-416
92L/BlkGold-416
92OPC-343
92Pinn-559
92ProC/Tomorrow-255
92S/RookTr-105T
92StCl-385
92T-343
92T/91Debut-174
92T/Gold-343
92T/GoldWin-343
92Ultra-523
93D-144
93F-80
93L-19
93OPC-376
93Pac/Spanish-189
93Panini-229
93Pinn-322
93S-359
93Select-323
93StCl-442
93StCl/1stDay-442
93T-69
93T/Gold-69
93UD-619
93USPlayC/Rook-5H
93Ultra-419
94D-571
94F-553
94Pac/Cr-391
94S-180
94S/GoldR-180
94StCl-161
94StCl/1stDay-161
94StCl/Gold-161
94T-563
94T/Gold-563
VanderWeele, Doug
91Everett/ClBest-2
91Everett/ProC-3912
92ClBest-368
92Clinton/ClBest-17
Vanderbush, Walt
83Beaum-5
84Cram/PCL-229
85Cram/PCL-111
Vandersall, Mark
92MN-22
Vanderwel, Bill
86Cram/NWL-84
87PalmSp-13
88PalmSp/Cal-94
88PalmSp/ProC-1457
89QuadC/Best-15
89QuadC/GS-16
90SoBend/Best-23
Vanegmond, Tim
92LynchRS/ProC-2908
92UD/ML-121
93ClBest/MLG-24
94B-63
94FExcel-22
Vanhof, Dave
94B-89
Vanhof, John
92FrRow/DP-85
93ClBest/MLG-146
Vann, Brandy
86Cram/NWL-80
87QuadC-12
88QuadC/GS-29
89PalmSp/Cal-53
89PalmSp/ProC-471
90PalmSp/Cal-218
90PalmSp/ProC-2577
91AA/LineD-198
91ElPaso/LineD-198
91Stockton/ProC-3033
92ElPaso/ProC-3923
92ElPaso/SB-223
Vannaman, Tim
88SoOreg/ProC-1693
89Madis/Star-22
90Modesto/Cal-159
90Modesto/ProC-2227
Vannell, Dan
90Bend/Legoe-20
Vanni, Edo
47Centen-30
57Seattle/Pop-39
Vantrease, Bob
83Idaho-12
84Idaho/Team-26
Vanwinkle, Dave
90SoBend/GS-19
Vanzytveld, Jeffrey
90FSLAS/Star-19
90VeroB/Star-26
91VeroB/ClBest-26
Vargas, Eddie
78Charl
80Buffa-15
81Buffa-23
82Portl-17
Vargas, Eric
91Butte/SportP-15
Vargas, Gonzalo
89StCath/ProC-2083
Vargas, Guillaume
52Laval-109
Vargas, Hector
87Oneonta-5
87PrWill-21
88Oneonta/ProC-2049
89PrWill/Star-23
90FtLaud/Star-21
90Star/ISingl-42
91AA/LineD-22
91Albany/LineD-22
91Albany/ProC-1018
92Albany/ProC-2235
92Albany/SB-21
93Ottawa/ProC-2444
Vargas, Hedi
85Cram/PCL-236
88Chatt/Best-8
88Nashvl/Team-24
89Chatt/II/Team-31
89MidldA/GS-29
Vargas, Jose
86Osceola-27
86Salem-26
87Osceola-15
87PortChar-17
88ColAst/Best-8
88Tulsa-7
89Osceola/Star-26
90ArkTr/GS-29
91AA/LineD-645
91Wmsprt/LineD-645
91Wmsprt/ProC-294
Vargas, Julio
89Martins/Star-32
89Star/IISingl-145
90Princet/DIMD-25
91Batavia/ClBest-5
91Batavia/ProC-3487
Vargas, Leonel
(Leo)
82Richm-20
83Richm-21
84Richm-12
85Greenvl/Team-23
Vargas, Miguel
87Reading-5
Vargas, Ramon
83Ander-19
Vargas, Roberto
53SpicSpan/3x5-26
Vargo, Ed
81TCMA-423M
Varitek, Jason
92T/Tr-123T
92T/TrGold-123T
93StCl/MurphyS-197
Varnell, Dan
90Everett/Best-2
90Everett/ProC-3144
Varner, Buck
88Chatt/Team-29
Varney, Pete
76OPC-413
76SSPC-154
76T-413
Varni, Patrick
88CapeCod/Sum-182
90Miami/II/Star-25
Varoz, Brett
85Anchora-29
Varoz, Eric
86Beaum-24
Varsho, Gary
84MidldC-23
86Pittsfld-24
87Iowa-23
88Berg/Cubs-24
88F/Up-U81
88Iowa/CMC-22
88Iowa/ProC-535
89F-441
89S-604
89T-613
89UD-321
90AAASingl/ProC-639
90Iowa/CMC-21
90Iowa/ProC-332
90ProC/Singl-96
90PublInt/St-206
90T/TVCub-61
91B-510
91D-671
91F-435
91F/UltraUp-U104
91F/Up-U114
91Leaf-500
91S/RookTr-72T
92D-644
92F-571
92L-388
92L/BlkGold-388
92OPC-122
92Pirate/Nation-24
92S-481
92StCl-568
92Studio-90
92T-122
92T/Gold-122
92T/GoldWin-122
92UD-217
92Ultra-561
93D-42
93Panini-287
93Reds/Kahn-27
93T-326
93T/Gold-326
94Pac/Cr-163
Varva, Joe
92Yakima/ClBest-24
Varverde, Miguel
86Watertn-26
Vasquez, Aguedo
88BBCity/Star-23
88FSLAS/Star-50
89Memphis/Best-5
89Memphis/ProC-1186
89Memphis/Star-22
90Jacks/GS-19
91AA/LineD-646
91Wmsprt/LineD-646
91Wmsprt/ProC-295
Vasquez, Angelo
85BurlR-13
Vasquez, Chris
90Billings/ProC-3235
91CharWh/ClBest-26
91CharWh/ProC-2901
92Cedar/ClBest-19
92Cedar/ProC-1087
Vasquez, Dennis
81GlenF-7
Vasquez, Eddy
93MedHat/ProC-3747
93MedHat/SportP-8
Vasquez, Francisco
79Elmira-18
Vasquez, George
73Cedar
75Sacra/Caruso-9
Vasquez, Jesse
80BurlB-12
85Newar-22
86Hagers-26
Vasquez, Julian
89Clmbia/GS-25
90Clmbia/PCPII-3
90Columbia/GS-15
91ClBest/Singl-359
91StLucie/ClBest-16
91StLucie/ProC-710
92B-357
92Bingham/ProC-515
92Bingham/SB-68
92ClBest-27
92ProC/Tomorrow-283
92Sky/AASingl-31
92Tidew/ProC-
92UD/ML-72
93FExcel/ML-80
93Vanco/ProC-2599
Vasquez, Julio
91Idaho/SportP-12
Vasquez, Luis
85Elmira-23
86FSLAS-48
86WinHaven-26
87NewBrit-5
88EastLAS/ProC-24
88NewBrit/ProC-889
89Nashvl/CMC-10
89Nashvl/ProC-1285
89Nashvl/Team-25
91AAA/LineD-272
91Nashvl/LineD-272
91Nashvl/ProC-2156
Vasquez, Marcos
92Durham/ClBest-19
92Durham/Team-20
92Greenvl/ProC-1154
Vasquez, Rafael
77Salem
80T-672R
80Tacom-9
81Buffa-11
Vasquez, Tony
89Cedar/Best-27
Vatcher, James
88SALAS/GS-26
88Spartan/ProC-1045
88Spartan/Star-21
89Clearw/Star-23
89Star/Wax-14
90AAASingl/ProC-315
90ProC/Singl-243
90ScranWB/CMC-17
90ScranWB/ProC-613
91AAA/LineD-296
91D-753
91F-708
91LasVegas/LineD-296
91LasVegas/ProC-251
91OPC-196
91Padre/MagRal-11
91S-341RP
91T-196
91T/90Debut-159
91UD-604
92D-563
92LasVegas/ProC-2808
92LasVegas/SB-244
92Sky/AAASingl-119
92StCl-78
Vaughan, Charles
67OPC-179R
67T-179R
Vaughan, Glenn
77Fritsch-45
Vaughan, J. Floyd
(Arky)
33G-229
34G-22
35BU-21
35Exh/4-7
36Exh/4-7
36Wheat
37Exh/4-7
37Wheat

38Exh/4-7
39Exh
39PlayBall-55
39Wheat
40PlayBall-107
41DP-34
41PlayBall-10
42Playball-29
49Sommer-18
60F-11
61F-148
74Laugh/ASG-41
75Shakey-15
77Galasso-77
80Pac/Leg-122
80Perez/HOF-192
88Conlon/NatAS-22
89HOF/St-21
89Pac/Leg-200
89Smok/Dodg-30
90Perez/GreatMom-71
90Target-821
91Conlon/Sport-38
93AP/ASG-109
93AP/ASG24K-43G
94Conlon-1102
R311/Leath
R312/M
R313
R314
V351B-44
V354-70
V355-6
WG8-47

Vaughan, Rick
88StCath/ProC-2033
89Myrtle/ProC-1629

Vaughn, Billy
76Laugh/Clown-10
76Laugh/Clown-38

Vaughn, DeWayne
82Lynch-7
84Jacks-1
86Tidew-28
87Tidew-2
87Tidew/TCMA-8
88D/Rook-25
88Mother/R-24
93Rang/Keeb-366

Vaughn, Derek
91Spokane/ClBest-8
91Spokane/ProC-3964
92Watlo/ClBest-16
92Watlo/ProC-2155

Vaughn, Fred
47Signal

Vaughn, Greg
87Beloit-2
88BBAmer-24
88ElPaso/Best-20
88TexLgAS/GS-35
89AAA/CMC-8
89AAA/ProC-42
89Denver/CMC-23
89Denver/ProC-36
89F/Up-41
90B-396
90Brewer/MillB-28
90Classic-60
90D-37
90D/BestAL-107
90D/Rook-16
90ElPasoATG/Team-25
90F-339
90F/Can-339
90HotRook/St-44
90Leaf-111
90Leaf/Prev-9
90OPC-57
90Pol/Brew-23
90S-585
90S/100Ris-30
90S/DTRook-B8
90S/YS/I-13
90Sf-135
90T-57
90T/89Debut-128
90ToysRUs-27
90TripleAAS/CMC-8
90UD-25
91B-33
91Brewer/MillB-29
91Classic/200-46
91Classic/III-91
91D-478
91F-599
91Leaf/Stud-79
91OPC-347
91Pol/Brew-26
91S-528
91S/100RisSt-65
91StCl-135
91T-347
91T/JumboR-30
91ToysRUs-29
91UD-526
91Ultra-183
92B-496
92D-224
92DennyGS-17
92F-192
92L-276
92L/BlkGold-276
92OPC-572
92Panini-41
92Pinn-92
92Pol/Brew-27
92S-639
92StCl-666
92Studio-198
92T-572
92T/Gold-572
92T/GoldWin-572
92T/Kids-83
92TripleP-122
92UD-232
92UD-97TC
92UD/HRH-HR20
92Ultra-86
93B-295
93D-103
93F-258
93Flair-231
93L-56
93OPC-373
93Pac/Spanish-166
93Panini-44
93Pinn-318
93Pinn/HRC-30
93Pol/Brew-26
93S-160
93Select-222
93StCl-122
93StCl/1stDay-122
93Studio-197
93T-153
93T/Gold-153
93TripleP-150
93UD-563
93UD/FunPack-72
93UD/HRH-HR15
93UD/SP-71
93Ultra-225
94B-449
94D-339
94D/DK-20
94D/MVP-22
94D/Special-339
94F-195
94F/AS-24
94F/TL-8
94Kraft-13
94L-321
94Oscar-15
94Pac/Cr-347
94Panini-88
94Pinn-37
94Pinn/Artist-37
94Pinn/Museum-37
94Pinn/Run-16
94Pol/Brew-28
94S-49
94S/GoldR-49
94S/GoldS-47
94Sf/2000-103
94StCl-378
94StCl/1stDay-378
94StCl/Gold-378
94Studio-48
94T-225
94T/Finest-89
94T/FinestRef-89
94T/Gold-225
94TripleP-59
94UD-288HFA
94UD-445
94UD/SP-61
94Ultra-380

Vaughn, Harry
N172

Vaughn, Heath
91GulfCR/SportP-26
92Gaston/ProC-2254

Vaughn, James
(Hippo)
11Helmar-48
14Piedmont/St-57
15CJ-176
61F-82
69Bz-1
72F/FFeat-14M
72Laugh/GF-39M
90HOF/St-17
92Conlon/13Nat-800
92Conlon/Sport-348
92Cub/OldStyle-26
93Conlon-800
BF2-69
D327
D328-177
D329-178
D350/2-180
E121/120
E121/80
E122
E135-177
E220
E300
E98
M101/4-178
M101/5-180
T202
T205
T207
V100
W514-111
W555
W575

Vaughn, Maurice
(Mo)
88CapeCod-16
88CapeCod/Sum-93
90AAASingl/ProC-443
90B-275
90Pawtu/ProC-471
90S-675DC
90T/TVRSox-64
91AAA/LineD-370
91AAAGame/ProC-32
91B-112
91Classic/200-152
91Classic/I-24
91D-430RR
91D/Rook-36
91F/Up-U7
91Leaf/GRook-BC7
91Leaf/Stud-20
91MajorLg/Pins-10
91OPC/Premier-124
91Pawtu/LineD-370
91Pawtu/ProC-49
91S-750RP
91S/Rook40-6
91StCl-543
91T/Tr-123T
91UD-5SR
91Ultra-387MLP
92B-397
92Classic/Game200-73
92D-514
92F-49
92F-705M
92L-103
92L/BlkGold-103
92OPC-59
92OPC/Premier-50
92Pawtu/ProC-934
92Pinn-205
92Pinn/Team2000-54
92ProC/Tomorrow-15
92RedSox/Dunkin-27
92S-556
92S/100RisSt-100
92S/Impact-21
92StCl-325
92Studio-139
92T-59
92T/91Debut-176
92T/Gold-59
92T/GoldWin-59
92TripleP-79
92UD-445
92USPlayC/RedSox-12D
92USPlayC/RedSox-3S
92Ultra-23
93B-536
93Classic/Gamel-94
93Colla/DM-112
93D-429
93F-184
93Flair-168
93L-432
93OPC-393
93Pac/Spanish-37
93Panini-92
93Pinn-189
93Pinn/HRC-40
93S-132
93Select-214
93StCl-334
93StCl/1stDay-334
93Studio-134
93T-51
93T/Finest-165
93T/FinestRef-165
93T/Gold-51
93ToysRUs-53
93UD-396
93UD/SP-206
93Ultra-156
94B-315
94D-42
94D/DK-2
94D/MVP-16
94D/Special-42
94F-45
94F/TL-2
94Finest-258
94Flair-18
94Kraft-14
94L-285
94L/MVPAL-13
94OPC-259
94P-8
94Pac/Cr-68
94Panini-34
94Pinn-17
94Pinn/Artist-17
94Pinn/Museum-17
94Pinn/Power-3
94Pinn/Run-12
94RedFoley-26
94S-57
94S/GoldR-57
94S/GoldS-51
94Select-116
94Sf/2000-122
94StCl-440
94StCl/1stDay-440
94StCl/Gold-440
94Studio-166
94T-690
94T/Gold-690
94TripleP-209
94UD-282HFA
94UD-71
94UD/CollC-281
94UD/CollC/Gold-281
94UD/CollC/Silv-281
94UD/ElecD-71
94UD/Mantle-19
94UD/SP-157
94Ultra-19

Vaughn, Mike
76Clinton
77Watlo

Vaughn, Randy
88Eugene/Best-10
89AppFx/ProC-850
90BBCity/Star-23

Vaughn, Ron
89Utica/Pucko-28MG

Vaughn, Tim
87Macon-9

Vaught, Craig
93StCath/ClBest-24
93StCath/ProC-3984

Vaught, Jay
93TX-6

Vavra, Joe
85Cram/PCL-153
86Albuq-25
89GreatF-9
90GreatF/SportP-30MG
91Yakima/ClBest-29MG
91Yakima/ProC-4264MG
92Yakima/ProC-3468MG

Vavrock, Rob
82Madis/Frit-24

Vavruska, Paul
76Clinton

Vazquez, Archie
92Spokane/ProC-1294

Vazquez, Armando
91Negro/Lewis-14
92Negro/Kraft-5
93TWill-113

Vazquez, Arthur
92Spokane/ClBest-21

Vazquez, Ed
89Kingspt/Star-24
90Pittsfld/Pucko-22

Vazquez, Jose
89Oneonta/ProC-2126
92Johnson/ClBest-8
92Johnson/ProC-3133

Vazquez, Marcos
88Sumter/ProC-403
89Sumter/ProC-1115
90Durham/Team-10
91Durham/ProC-DUR4
91DurhamUp/ProC-4
91Macon/ClBest-11
91Macon/ProC-864

Vazquez, Pedro
90AppFox/Box-29
90AppFox/ProC-2106
91BBCity/ClBest-22
91BBCity/ProC-1408

Veach, Robert
15CJ-174
21Exh-180
25Exh-71
81Tiger/Detroit-118
91Conlon/Sport-159
92Conlon/Sport-486
BF2-30
D327
D328-178
D329-179
D350/2-181
E120
E121/120
E121/80
E122
E135-178
E220
M101/4-179
M101/5-181
N172/PCL
V100
V61-33
W501-5
W514-88
W572
W573
W575

Veach, William
N172

Veal, Orville
(Coot)
59T-52
61T-432
62J-68
62P-68
62P/Can-68
62Salada-84
62Shirriff-84
62T-573

Veale, Bob
62T-593R
63IDL-24
63T-87
64Kahn
64T-501
65Bz-13
65Kahn
65OPC-12LL
65OPC-195
65T-12LL
65T-195
65T/trans-32SP
66EH-39
66Kahn
66T-225LL
66T-425
66T/RO-46
66T/RO-95
67CokeCap/Pirate-4

67Kahn
67T-238LL
67T-335
67T/Test/PP-23
68Bz-3
68KDKA-39
68Kahn
68OPC-70
68T-70
68T/ActionSt-11AM
69Kahn
69MB-283
69MLB/St-189
69OPC-8LL
69T-520
69T-8LL
69T/St-90
70MLB/St-108
70OPC-236
70T-236
71MLB/St-215
71OPC-368
71T-368
72MB-351
72T-729
73OPC-518
73T-518
78Green
78TCMA-114

Veeck, Bill
82Ohio/HOF-44
91Perez/HOF-211

Veeck, Michael
90Miami/I/Star-29GM

Vega, Jesus
77BurlB
78OrlanTw
79Toledo-20
80Toledo-11
81Toledo-16
83D-650
83F-624
83T-308
83Toledo-17

Vegely, Bruce
88Bend/Legoe-18
89QuadC/Best-19
90QuadC/GS-7
91PalmSp/ProC-2016

Veilleux, Brian
89Modesto/Cal-268
89Modesto/Chong-17
90Huntsvl/Best-12

Veintidos, Juan
74Tacoma/Caruso-12
75OPC-621R
75T-621R
75T/M-621R
75Tacoma/KMMO-18

Veit, Steve
90Ashvl/ClBest-17
90AubAs/Best-3
90AubAs/ProC-3400
91Ashvl/ProC-578

Velandia, Jorge
92Bristol/ProC-1423

Velarde, Randy
86AppFx-26
87Albany-7
88Colum/CMC-17
88Colum/Pol-22
88Colum/ProC-324
88F-646R
88TripleA/ASCMC-20
89AAA/CMC-19
89AAA/ProC-19
89Colum/CMC-13
89Colum/Pol-20
89Colum/ProC-741
89S/HotRook-18
89T-584
89T/Big-239
89UD-189
90AlbanyDG/Best-19
90B-434
90D-630
90OPC-23
90S-524
90S/NWest-27
90T-23
90T/Big-68
90T/TVYank-28
90TripleAAS/CMC-19
91OPC-379
91S-134
91StCl-438
91T-379
92B-207
92D-679
92F-246
92L-368
92L/BlkGold-368
92OPC-212
92S-337
92StCl-237
92T-212
92T/Gold-212
92T/GoldWin-212
92UD-399
92Yank/WIZ80-195
93D-153
93F-287
93OPC-337
93Pac/Spanish-214
93Panini-148
93Pinn-314
93S-219
93StCl-32
93StCl/1stDay-32
93StCl/Y-9
93T-174
93T/Gold-174
93UD-93
93Ultra-250
94D-439
94F-249
94Pac/Cr-440
94Pinn-383
94S-216
94S/GoldR-216
94StCl-156
94StCl/1stDay-156
94StCl/Gold-156
94StCl/Team-189
94T-461
94T/Finest-41
94T/FinestRef-41
94T/Gold-461

Velasquez, Al
82Reading-12

Velasquez, Carlos
75Sacra/Caruso-17

Velasquez, Guillermo
(Gil)
88Charl/ProC-1203
88SALAS/GS-12
89River/Best-20
89River/Cal-3
89River/ProC-1394
90Wichita/Rock-21
91AA/LineD-621
91Wichita/LineD-621
91Wichita/ProC-2607
91Wichita/Rock-17
92AAA/ASG/SB-245
92B-698
92LasVegas/ProC-2805
92LasVegas/SB-245
92Sky/AAASingl-120
93D-312
93F/Final-146
93L-471
93Mother/Padre-17
93Pac/Beisbol-23
93Pac/Spanish-604
93StCl-744
93StCl/1stDay-744
93T-724
93T/Gold-724
93Ultra-479
94D-300
94F-677
94Pac/Cr-536
94StCl-278
94StCl/1stDay-278
94StCl/Gold-278
94T-556
94T/Gold-556

Velasquez, Ray
85Visalia-16
86Visalia-23
87Clinton-26
88SanJose/Cal-139
88SanJose/ProC-116
89Salinas/Cal-123
89Salinas/ProC-1807
90Salinas/Cal-125

Velazquel, Ildefonso
85Tigres-9

Velazquez, Carlos
No Cards.

Velazquez, Fred
71Richm/Team-17

Velazquez, Juan
83QuadC-17

Velez, Jose J.
91ClBest/Singl-208
91Spring/ClBest-28
91Spring/ProC-758
92Savan/ProC-678

Velez, Jose
87Gaston/ProC-25
88Gaston/ProC-1011
89PalmSp/Cal-46
89PalmSp/ProC-484

Velez, Noel
90CharWh/Best-18
90CharWh/ProC-2248
90Foil/Best-54
91Cedar/ClBest-24
91Cedar/ProC-2734
91Erie/ClBest-12
91Erie/ProC-4082

Velez, Otto
73Syrac/Team-28
74OPC-606R
74Syrac/Team-27
74T-606R
74T/St-219
75Syrac/Team-16
75Syrac/Team-22
76SSPC-455
77OPC-13
77T-299
78BJ/PostC-22
78OPC-67
78T-59
79BJ/Bubble-19
79OPC-241
79T-462
80OPC-354
80T-703
81D-391
81F-410
81OPC-351
81OPC/Post-23
81T-351
81T/So-44
81T/St-138
82D-304
82F-625
82F/St-233
82OPC-155
82OPC/Post-11
82T-155
82T/St-249
83Charl-18
92Nabisco-26
92Yank/WIZ70-157

Vella, Greg
88Myrtle/ProC-1183
88SALAS/GS-19
89Dunedin/Star-21

Velleggia, Frank
84Newar-15

Veltman, Art
V94-47

Venable, Max
77Clinton
78LodiD
79Pol/Giants-49
80Phoenix/NBank-6
81F-443
81Phoenix-6
81T-484
83F-275
83Mother/Giants-16
83T-634
84D-323
84F-385
84Indianap-28
84Nes/792-58
84T-58
85Indianap-9
86D-650
86F-196
86T-428
86TexGold-9
87F-216
87Nashvl-22
87T-226
89Edmon/CMC-23
89Edmon/ProC-556
90Leaf-459
91D-510
92S-477

Venezia, Mike
81Redwd-8

Veneziale, Mike
93T-726
93T/Gold-726

Venger, Tad
81CharR-24

Venner, Gary
83TriCit-27

Ventress, Leroy
86Cram/NWL-145
88Batavia/ProC-1666
89SALAS/GS-41
89Spartan/ProC-1044
89Spartan/Star-23
90Clearw/Star-23
91Clearw/ClBest-26
91Clearw/ProC-1637

Ventura, Candido
77Charl

Ventura, Jose
86Beloit-24
89SoBend/GS-16
90Saraso/Star-25
91AA/LineD-73
91BirmB/LineD-73
91BirmB/ProC-1455
91ClBest/Singl-271
92BirmB/ProC-2584
92BirmB/SB-97
92Sky/AASingl-46
93LimeR/Winter-129

Ventura, Reynaldo
89BurlInd/Star-25

Ventura, Robin
88T/Tr-124TOLY
89B-65
89BBAmAA/BPro-AA21
89BirmB/Best-1
89BirmB/ProC-106
89Classic/Up/2-177
89F/Up-23
89SLAS-2
89Star/IISingl-101
89T-764
89T/Big-65
90B-311
90BirmDG/Best-1
90Classic-5
90Coke/WSox-27
90Coke/WSox-28
90D-28
90D/BestAL-60
90D/Rook-15
90F-550
90F/Can-550
90F/SoarSt-4
90HotRook/St-45
90Leaf-167
90Leaf/Prev-8
90OPC-121
90S-595
90S/100Ris-96
90S/DTRook-B6
90S/YS/II-8
90Sf-222
90T-121
90T/89Debut-129
90ToysRUs-28
90UD-21SR
91B-358
91Bz-15
91Classic/200-52
91D-315
91F-139
91Kodak/WSox-23
91Kodak/WSox-x
91Leaf-271
91OPC-461
91Panini/FrSt-314
91Panini/St-260
91RedFoley/St-97
91S-320
91S/100RisSt-48
91StCl-274
91T-461
91T/JumboR-31
91ToysRUs-30
91UD-263
91UD-677M
91Ultra-86
92B-275
92B-655FOIL
92CJ/DI-33
92Classic/Game200-49
92Classic/II-T85
92D-145
92D/Preview-6
92DennyGS-8
92F-101
92F/ASIns-19
92French-8
92L-17
92L/BlkGold-17
92OPC-255
92OPC/Premier-132
92Panini-127
92Pinn-121
92Pinn-286I
92Pinn/Team2000-43
92Pinn/TeamP-6
92S-122
92S/100SS-33
92S/Impact-42
92S/Prev-3
92StCl-70
92Studio-160
92T-255
92T/DQ-11
92T/Gold-255
92T/GoldWin-255
92T/Kids-102
92TripleP-17
92UD-263
92UD/ASFF-6
92UD/TWillB-T20
92Ultra-343
92Ultra/AwardWin-15
92WSox-23
93B-667
93Cadaco-59
93Classic/GameI-95
93Colla/DM-113
93D-535
93D/DK-10
93DennyGS-27
93F-211
93F-716M
93F/Fruit-63
93Flair-190
93HumDum/Can-7
93Kenner/Fig-37
93Kraft-14
93L-439
93L/Fast-14
93L/GoldAS-6
93OPC-387
93Pac/Spanish-78
93Panini-139
93Pinn-28
93Pinn/HRC-24
93S-41
93Select-30
93StCl-295MC
93StCl-387
93StCl/1stDay-295MC
93StCl/1stDay-387
93StCl/MurphyS-111
93StCl/WSox-13
93Studio-78
93T-770
93T/BlkGold-43
93T/Finest-93AS
93T/FinestASJ-93AS
93T/FinestRef-93AS
93T/Gold-770
93ToysRUs-58
93TripleP-179
93UD-263
93UD-51
93UD-838TC
93UD/FunPack-203
93UD/FunPackAS-AS5
93UD/SP-261
93Ultra-537
93Ultra/AwardWin-14
93WSox-29
94B-295
94Church-17
94D-23
94D/Special-23
94F-97

94KingB-21
94L-26
94OPC-33
94Pac/Cr-140
94Panini-52
94Pinn-29
94Pinn/Artist-29
94Pinn/Museum-29
94Pinn/Power-9
94S-347
94Select-41
94Sf/2000-66
94StCl-315
94StCl/1stDay-315
94StCl/Gold-315
94StCl/Team-126
94Studio-210
94T-90
94T/BlkGold-22
94T/Finest-202
94T/FinestRef-202
94T/Gold-90
94TripleP-270
94TripleP/Medal-9
94UD-263
94UD/CollC-282
94UD/CollC/Gold-282
94UD/CollC/Silv-282
94UD/ElecD-263
94UD/SP-194
94Ultra-342
94Ultra/AS-5
94Ultra/AwardWin-4
Venturini, Peter Paul
(Pete)
86Penin-25
87BirmB/Best-22
88BirmB/Best-11
Venturino, Phil
86MidldA-24
86PalmSp/Smok-18
87MidldA-29
88Edmon/CMC-8
88Edmon/ProC-566
Venuto, Nicholas
88SoOreg/ProC-1695
89Medford/Best-14
Veras, Camilo
84Idaho/Team-27
86Madis/Pol-21
87Madis-15
88Huntsvl/BK-23
Veras, Quilvio
91Kingspt/ClBest-10
91Kingspt/ProC-3824
92ClBest-83
92ColumMet/ClBest-25
92ColumMet/ProC-306
92ColumMet/SAL/II-21
92ColumMet/SAL/II-31M
92ProC/Tomorrow-289
92UD/ML-187
93B-215
93ClBest/MLG-209
93FExcel/ML-81
93LimeR/Winter-110
93SALAS/II-39
93SALAS/IICS-4
94B-428
94FExcel-239
94TedW-Gardiner-6
94Ultra-538
Verban, Emil
45Playball-26
48B-28
49B-38
49Eureka-73
Exh47
Verbanic, Joe
67T-442R
68OPC-29
68T-29
69T-541
70OPC-416
70T-416
92Yank/WIZ60-134
92Yank/WIZ70-158
Verble, Gene
88Chatt/Team-30
Verdi, Frank
78Tidew
79Tidew-4
80Tidew-24
81Colum-17
82Colum-25
82Colum/Pol-26
83SanJose-1MG
84RochR-9
85RochR-24
Verdi, Mike
86SanJose-22CO
87SanJose-19
89Elmira/Pucko-22
90Elmira/Pucko-25MG
91WinHaven/ClBest-5MG
91WinHaven/ProC-505MG
Verducci, John
85Everett/Cram-17
86Shrev-26
87Phoenix-18
Verdugo, Luis
89Miami/II/Star-20
Verdugo, Mando
88SLCity-25
89Miami/I/Star-20
90Kinston/Team-21
Verduzco, Dave
92Niagara/ClBest-25
92Niagara/ProC-3323
Veres, David
86Cram/NWL-53
87Modesto-3
88CalLgAS-10
88Huntsvl/BK-24
88Modesto-32
88Modesto/Cal-56
89Huntsvl/Best-5
90AAASingl/ProC-137
90ProC/Singl-579
90Tacoma/CMC-2
90Tacoma/ProC-90
91AAA/LineD-21
91Albuq/LineD-21
91Albuq/ProC-1141
92Tucson/ProC-488
Veres, Randy
86Beloit-25
87Beloit-1
88Stockton/Cal-179
88Stockton/ProC-730
89ElPaso/GS-17
89F/Up-42
90B-390
90Brewer/MillB-29
90T/89Debut-130
90T/Tr-125T
91Classic/I-56
91D-755
91OPC-694
91Richm/ProC-2570
91S/100RisSt-12
91T-694
92Phoenix/SB-397
94TedW/Gardiner-6
Vergez, Johnny
33G-233
34DS-21
35BU-176
93Conlon-811
R337-401
V355-5
V94-48
Verhoeff, Will
77WHave
Verhoeven, John
77T-91
78T-329
79Toledo-12
81D-564
81T-603
82F-547
82T-281
Verkuilen, Mike
85OrlanTw-13
Verna, Chris
89SanBern/Cal-92TR
90Wmsprt/Best-24
90Wmsprt/Star-27TR
Vernon, Mickey
42Playball-19
49B-94
50B-132
51B-65
51T/BB-13
52B-87
52NTea
52T-106
52TipTop
53B/Col-159
53Briggs
53Exh/Can-59
53RM-AL21
54B-152
54RM-AL13
55Armour-24
55B-46
55RM-AL12
56T-228
57T-92
58T-233
59Armour-20
59T-115
60T-467C
61T-134MG
62T-152MG
63T-402MG
72Dimanche*-48CO
76SSPC-621
77Galasso-45
79Colum-29
79TCMA-87
80Pac/Leg-78
86Sf/Dec-38M
89Swell-54
91T/Arc53-287
92Bz/Quadra-12M
Exh47
Versalles, Zoilo
61Clover-30
61Peters-1
61T-21
61T/St-186
62J-86
62P-86
62P/Can-86
62Salada-51A
62Salada-51B
62Shirriff-51
62T-499
62T/St-81
63J-3
63P-3
63T-349
64T-15
64Wheat/St-46
65MacGregor-10
65OPC-157
65T-157
65T/E-33
66T-400
67CokeCap/Twin-13
67T-270
68T-315
69MB-284
69MLB/St-45
69OPC-38
69T-38
69T/St-100
70MLB/St-288
70OPC-365
70T-365
72MB-352
75OPC-203MVP
75T-203MVP
75T/M-203MVP
78Twin/Frisz-22
81TCMA-442
82KMart-7
88Pac/Leg-107
90Target-822
Verstandig, Mark
88Spokane/ProC-1943
89CharRain/ProC-990
90Waterlo/Best-25
90Waterlo/ProC-2382
91HighD/ClBest-17
91HighD/ProC-2400
Veryzer, Thomas
75OPC-623R
75T-623R
75T/M-623R
76Ho-109
76OPC-432
76SSPC-367
76T-432
77OPC-188
77T-145
78OPC-14
78T-633
79T-537
80OPC-145
80T-276
81D-199
81F-390
81T-39
82D-450
82F-381
82OPC-387
82T-387
82T/Tr-123T
83F-559
83T-496
83T/Tr-121
83Thorn-29
84Nes/792-117
84T-117
85T-405
91WIZMets-421
Veselic, Bob
80Toledo-19
81Toledo-9
82Toledo-6
83Tucson-9
Vesely, Orece
89QuadC/GS-12
Vesling, Don
88FSLAS/Star-51
88Lakeland/Star-25
89London/ProC-1374
90AAASingl/ProC-381
90ProC/Singl-378
90Toledo/CMC-1
90Toledo/ProC-151
91AAA/LineD-598
91Toledo/LineD-598
91Toledo/ProC-1933
92London/ProC-632
92London/SB-421
Vespe, Will
88CapeCod/Sum-149
89Watertn/Star-22
90Kinston/Team-15
Vessey, Tom
81Tucson-6
Vetsch, Dave
85Visalia-13
86OrlanTw-22
87OrlanTw-27
Vezendy, Gerry
65T-509R
Viarengo, Matt
91Idaho/ProC-4328
91Pulaski/ClBest-28
91Pulaski/ProC-4005
Viau, Leon
N172
Vice, Darryl
88CapeCod/Sum-152
89Modesto/Chong-26
90Madison/ProC-2280
90Modesto/Chong-30
91AA/LineD-297
91Huntsvl/ClBest-25
91Huntsvl/LineD-297
91Huntsvl/Team-21
91HuntsvlProC-1806
92Huntsvl/ProC-3958
92Huntsvl/SB-322
Vicente, Alberto
90Martins/ProC-3419
Vick, Ernie
92Conlon/Sport-402
Vick, Scott
89TNTech-28
Vickers, Mike
78Ashvl
79Ashvl/TCMA-21
80Tulsa-25
Vickers, Rube
90Target-1089
C46-37
Vickery, Lou
62Kahn/Atl
63Pep/Tul
Vico, George
48L-47
49B-122
50B-150
53Mother-25
Vidal, Jose
67T-499R
68T-432R
69T-322
Vidmar, Donald
88Bend/Legoe-26
89PalmSp/Cal-50
89PalmSp/ProC-482
90PalmSp/Cal-225
90PalmSp/ProC-2578
91MidldA/OneHour-30
91PalmSp/ProC-2017
92Edmon/ProC-3540
92Edmon/SB-170
92MidldA/OneHour-25
92ProC/Tomorrow-36
92Sky/AAASingl-82
Vidro, Jose
93B-592
93BurlB/ClBest-25
93BurlB/ProC-168
Viebahn
E270/1
Viebrock, Alan
76Watlo
Viera, John
90PrWill/Team-26
91PrWill/ClBest-23
91PrWill/ProC-1441
92Albany/ProC-2240
92Albany/SB-22
92Sky/AASingl-11
Viera, Jose
90A&AASingle/ProC-190
90Hunting/ProC-3295
91MidwLAS/ProC-9
91Peoria/ClBest-14
91Peoria/ProC-1352
91Peoria/Team-21
92ClBest-319
92WinSalem/ClBest-4
92WinSalem/ProC-1217
93B-256
93ClBest/MLG-40
93FExcel/ML-14
Vierra, Jeff
87Hawaii-6
Vierra, Joey
87Hawaii-21
88Greens/ProC-1574
89Cedar/Best-8
89Cedar/ProC-915
89Cedar/Star-21
89Star/IISingl-189
90AAASingl/ProC-546
90Nashvl/CMC-3
90Nashvl/ProC-234
90ProC/Singl-128
91AAA/LineD-273
91Nashvl/LineD-273
91Nashvl/ProC-2157
92AAA/ASG/SB-296
92Nashvl/ProC-1833
92Nashvl/SB-296
92Sky/AAASingl-137
Viggiano, Matt
88Batavia/ProC-1683
Vike, Jim
86AubAs-27
Vila, Jesus
86VeroB-26
Vilella, Lazaro
84Butte-26
Vilet, Tom
91Batavia/ClBest-15
91Batavia/ProC-3499
92Batavia/ClBest-26
92Batavia/ProC-3280
Villa, Jose
88StCath/ProC-2008
Villa, Mike
86Fresno/Smok-9
87Tampa-30
88Clinton/ProC-719
Villaescusa, Juan
81VeroB-23
Villalobos, Gary
91LynchRS/ClBest-19
91LynchRS/ProC-1209
92WinHaven/ClBest-8
92WinHaven/ProC-1788
Villalona, Kadir
92MedHat/ProC-3221
92MedHat/SportP-19
Villaman, Rafael
82Nashvl-26
Villanueva, Gilbert
87CharWh-3
88Stockton/Cal-188
88Stockton/ProC-728

Villanueva, Hector
86WinSalem-26
87Pittsfld-3
88EastLAS/ProC-28
88Pittsfld/ProC-1355
89Iowa/CMC-13
89Iowa/ProC-1696
90AAASingl/ProC-629
90Cub/Mara-21
90F/Up-U10
90Iowa/CMC-18
90Iowa/ProC-322
90Leaf-401
90ProC/Singl-93
90S/Tr-98T
90T/TVCub-62
90T/Tr-126T
90UD/Ext-741
91Cub/Mara-19
91Cub/Vine-30
91D-296
91F-436
91Leaf-75
91OPC-362
91S-71
91S/100RisSt-51
91StCl-213
91T-362
91T/90Debut-160
91UD-171
91Ultra-69
92Cub/Mara-19
92D-725
92F-394
92OPC-181
92Panini-181
92Pinn-419
92S-677
92StCl-858
92T-181
92T/Gold-181
92T/GoldWin-181
92TripleP-28
92UD-102
92USPlayC/Cub-11C
92USPlayC/Cub-6S
92Ultra-477
93Cadaco-60
93D-80
93Pac/Spanish-637
93Pol/Card-23
93StCl/Card-28
93UD-621

Villanueva, Juan
86Lynch-24
87Lynch-2
88FSLAS/Star-24
88StLucie/Star-25
89Jacks/GS-12
90Wichita/Rock-22

Villareal, Juan
90Princet/DIMD-26

Villegas, Mike
84ElPaso-8

Villegas, Ramon
85Tigres-6

Villone, Ron
93B-223
93River/Cal-1
93StCl/MurphyS-18
94ClBest/Gold-103
94FExcel-129

Vilorio, Frank
79Toledo-19
83Nashua-16

Viltz, Corey
87James-15
88WPalmB/Star-25
89WPalmB/Star-23

Viltz, Eski
80Cedar-7
81Water-17
82Water-15
90CedarDG/Best-26

Vina, Fernando
91Clmbia/PCPII-4
91Clmbia/PII-15
92ClBest-352
92StLucie/ClBest-18
92StLucie/ProC-1758
93FExcel/ML-82
93Mother/Mar-25
93Pac/Spanish-627
93StCl/Mar-9
93Ultra-625
94Finest-341

Vinas, Julio
92SoBend/ClBest-6
92SoBend/ProC-181

Vincent, Mike
86Cedar/TCMA-12
87Cedar-19

Vines, Ellsworth
33SK*-46

Vineyard, Dave
65OPC-169
65T-169
91Crown/Orio-468

Vining, Lance
91MissSt-55M
92MissSt-50M

Vinson, Chuck
68T-328R

Vinson, Clay
89GA-34
90GA-31

Vinton, William
N172

Viola, Frank
82OrlanTw/B-24
82Toledo-7
83D-382
83F-625
83T-586
83Twin/Team-11
84D-364
84F-575
84Nes/792-28
84OPC-28
84T-28
84T/St-312
85D-17DK
85D-436
85D/DKsuper-17
85F-291
85F/St-84
85Leaf-17DK
85OPC-266
85Seven/Minn-2
85T-266
85T-710AS
85T/Gloss40-7
85T/St-300
85Twin/Seven-2
85Twin/Team-12
86D-194
86F-408
86F/St-124
86KayBee-33
86Leaf-126
86OPC-269
86Sf-99
86T-742
86T/Mini-25
86T/St-284
86T/Tatt-18M
87D-196
87D/HL-24
87F-554
87Leaf-74
87OPC-310
87RedFoley/St-127
87Sf/TPrev-17M
87T-310
87T/St-277
88ChefBoy-15
88Classic/Red-183
88D-149
88D/Best-214
88Drake-29
88F-25
88F/BB/MVP-41
88F/Mini-38
88F/RecSet-42
88F/SlugWaxBox-C5
88F/St-47
88F/WS-12
88KennerFig-116
88Leaf-94
88Master/Disc-2
88OPC-259
88Panini/St-134
88S-475
88Sf-196
88Smok/Minn-1
88T-625
88T/Big-201
88T/Mini-25
88T/RiteAid-33
88T/St-25
88T/St-282
88T/UK-82
88Woolwth-19
88Woolwth-33WSMVP
89B-150
89Bz-21
89Cadaco-60
89Classic-144
89D-237
89D-23DK
89D/AS-8
89D/Best-74
89D/DKsuper-23DK
89D/PopUp-8
89F-127
89F/AS-12
89F/BBAS-43
89F/BBMVP's-41
89F/Excit-42
89F/Heroes-42
89F/LL-42
89F/Superstar-41
89F/WaxBox-C28
89Holsum/Discs-17
89KayBee-31
89KennerFig-156
89KingB/Discs-14
89Master/Discs-1
89Nissen-17
89OPC-120
89Panini/St-237AS
89Panini/St-248
89Panini/St-383
89Panini/St-475
89RedFoley/St-125
89S-290
89S/HotStar-5
89S/Tr-67
89Sf-10
89T-120
89T-406AS
89T/Big-140
89T/Coins-30
89T/Crunch-4
89T/DH-10
89T/Gloss22-10
89T/Gloss60-18
89T/HeadsUp-7
89T/Hills-31
89T/LJN-158
89T/Mini-64
89T/St-153
89T/St-292
89T/St/Backs-30
89T/UK-80
89UD-397
89UD-658CY
89UD-691TC
89Woolwth-3
90B-122
90Classic-91
90Classic/III-37
90Classic/III-NO
90D-353
90D/BestNL-68
90F-219
90F/Can-219
90Kahn/Mets-29
90Kenner/Fig-87
90Leaf-93
90MCA/Disc-16
90Mets/Fan-29
90OPC-470
90PublInt/St-297
90PublInt/St-339
90S-500
90Sf-122
90Starline/LJS-18
90Starline/LJS-7
90T-470
90T/Big-162
90T/DH-67
90T/St-95
90T/TVMets-18
90Tetley/Discs-16
90UD-626
90USPlayC/AS-1D
91B-477
91BBBest/Aces-18
91Classic/200-1
91Classic/III-92
91D-529
91F-165
91Kahn/Mets-29
91Kenner-53
91Leaf-180
91Leaf/Stud-210
91OPC-406AS
91OPC-60
91Panini/FrSt-87
91Panini/St-84
91Panini/Top15-59
91Panini/Top15-68
91Panini/Top15-76
91RedFoley/St-98
91S-460
91S-687KM
91S-882DT
91S/100SS-70
91Seven/3DCoin-15NE
91StCl-292
91StCl/Charter*-31
91T-406AS
91T-60
91T/CJMini/I-4
91T/SU-34
91UD-122
91USPlayC/AS-7C
91Ultra-227
91WIZMets-422
92B-491
92Classic/Game200-196
92Classic/II-T80
92D-498
92D/Up-U10
92F-518
92F/Up-5
92L-221
92L/BlkGold-221
92OPC-510
92OPC/Premier-115
92Panini-229
92Pinn-407
92RedSox/Dunkin-28
92S-220
92S/100SS-62
92S/RookTr-6T
92StCl-785
92StCl/Dome-190
92Studio-140
92T-510
92T/Gold-510
92T/GoldWin-510
92T/Tr-125T
92T/TrGold-125T
92TripleP/Gal-GS6
92UD-277
92UD-733
92Ultra-319
93B-171
93D-91
93F-185
93Flair-169
93L-21
93OPC-228
93Pac/Spanish-38
93Pinn-76
93S-55
93Select-94
93StCl-147
93StCl/1stDay-147
93Studio-72
93T-270
93T/Finest-33
93T/FinestRef-33
93T/Gold-270
93TripleP-178
93UD-131
93UD-48
93UD/FunPack-166
93UD/SP-207
93Ultra-157
94B-35
94D-321
94F-46
94Finest-406
94L-60
94OPC-88
94Pac/Cr-69
94Pinn-348
94RedFoley-26M
94S-331
94Sf/2000-137
94T-140
94T/Gold-140
94TripleP-210
94UD-127
94UD/CollC-283
94UD/CollC/Gold-283
94UD/CollC/Silv-283
94UD/ElecD-127
94Ultra-320

Viola, Lance
79Newar-23

Violat, Juan
T206

Viox, James
D329-180
D350/2-182
M101/4-180
M101/5-182

Virdon, Bill
55B-296
55Hunter
56T-170
57T-110
58Hires-45
58T-198
59T-190
59T-543M
60L-40
60T-496
61P-135
61T-70
61T/St-72
62J-175
62Kahn
62P-175
62P/Can-175
62Salada-168
62Shirriff-168
62T-415
62T/St-181
63IDL-25
63J-142
63Kahn
63P-142
63T-55
64Kahn
64T-268M
64T-495
65Kahn
65OPC-69
65T-69
72T-661MG
73OPC-517MG
73T-517MG
74Syrac/Team-28
75OPC-611MG
75Syrac/Team-17MG
75Syrac/Team-23
75T-611MG
75T/M-611MG
76SSPC/MetsY-Y9MG
76T-147MG
77T-327MG
78BK/Ast-1MG
78T-279MG
79T-381MG
79TCMA-100
81D-384MG
81F-61MG
81T-678MG
82D-144MG
83OPC-6MG
83Stuart-1MG
83T-516MG
84Expo/PostC-34MG
84Nes/792-111MG
84OPC-111MG
84Stuart-2MG
84T-111MG
88Pac/Leg-49
89Swell-119
91Swell/Great-93
93Pirate/Nation-34CO
94T/Arc54-257

Virgil, Ossie Jr.
77Spartan
81OkCty/TCMA-19
82T-231R
83D-606
83F-175
83T-383
84D-326
84F-49
84Nes/792-484
84Phill/TastyK-26
84T-484

85CIGNA-3
85D-82
85F-267
85Leaf-250
85OPC-103
85Phill/TastyK-10M
85Phill/TastyK-26
85T-143FS
85T-611
85T/St-110
85ThomMc/Discs-46
86D-137
86D/AAS-26
86F-456
86F/Up-U122
86OPC-95
86Pol/Atl-9
86T-95
86T/St-115
86T/Tr-119T
87D-67
87D/OD-45
87F-532
87OPC-183
87Smok/Atl-12
87T-571
88D-143
88D/AS-50
88D/Best-85
88F-552
88Jiffy-17
88Leaf-64
88OPC-291
88Panini/St-241
88RedFoley/St-93
88S-129
88Sf-217
88T-755
88T/Big-148
88T/St-36
88T/St/Backs-24
89D-145
89F-605
89OPC-179
89RedFoley/St-126
89S-111
89Sf-94
89T-179
89T/St-28
89UD-104
90AAASingl/ProC-355
90EliteSenLg-15
90ProC/Singl-348
90Syrac/CMC-22
90Syrac/MerchB-26
90Syrac/ProC-575
90Syrac/Team-26
90Tor/BJ-26
91Crown/Orio-469
91Pac/SenLg-150
91Pac/SenLg-159M

Virgil, Ossie Sr.
57T-365
58T-107
59T-203
61T-67
62T-327
65T-571
67OPC-132
67T-132
76Expo/Redp-34CO
77Expo/PostC-9CO
81Tiger/Detroit-135
84Smok/SDP-26C
85T-143FS
88KennerFig-117
89Pac/SenLg-22
91Pac/SenLg-138MG
91Pac/SenLg-159M

Virgilio, George
90Pulaski/Best-19
90Pulaski/ProC-3089
91Pulaski/ClBest-10
91Pulaski/ProC-4016
92Macon/ClBest-5
92Macon/ProC-278

Viskas, Steve
79QuadC-25

Visner, Joseph
N172

Vitale, Tony
86Fresno/Smok-28

Vitato, Richard
82CharR-14
83CharR-9

Vitiello, Joe
91ClBest/Singl-404
91Classic/DP-5
91Eugene/ClBest-15
91Eugene/ProC-3742
92BBCity/ClBest-1
92BBCity/ProC-3855
92ClBest-24
92Classic/DP-94FB
92ProC/Tomorrow-80
92UD-73TP
92UD/ML-309
93B-13
93B-367FOIL
93ClBest/Fisher-1
93ClBest/GLP-4
93ClBest/GPr-4
93ClBest/MLG-83
93ClBest/MLGPr-4
93ClBest/MLGPrev-3
93FExcel/ML-180
93StCl-570
93StCl/1stDay-570
93StCl/Royal-14
94B-415
94ClBest/Gold-123
94SigRook-25
94T-769M
94T/Gold-769M

Vitko, Joe
90Clmbia/PCPII-3
90Columbia/GS-21
90SALAS/Star-45
91StLucie/ClBest-15
91StLucie/ProC-711
92B-516
92Bingham/ProC-516
92Bingham/SB-69
92ClBest-354
92Sky/AASingl-32
93D-354
93UD-10SR

Vito, Frank
91Pac/SenLg-158

Vitt, Oscar
(Ossie)
40PlayBall-47
92Conlon/Sport-495
D327
D328-179
D329-181
D350/2-183
E121/120
E121/80
E135-179
M101/4-181
M101/5-183
T222
W501-9
W575

Vivas, Domingo
91Billing/SportP-7
91Billings/ProC-3753

Vivenzio, Augie
92Pulaski/ClBest-18
92Pulaski/ProC-3183

Vizcaino, Jose
88Bakers/Cal-240
88CalLgAS-47
89Albuq/CMC-23
89Albuq/ProC-82
90AAASingl/ProC-76
90Albuq/CMC-20
90Albuq/ProC-355
90Albuq/Trib-29
90B-98
90Classic/Up-49
90F-410
90F/Can-410
90ProC/Singl-422
90S-613
90T/89Debut-131
90Target-1090
90UD-44
91B-427
91Cub/Mara-16
91Cub/Vine-31
91D-724
91F-223
91Leaf-323
91S-787
91S/100RisSt-88
91UD-580
92Cub/Mara-16
92D-212
92L-270
92L/BlkGold-270
92OPC-561
92S-169
92StCl-359
92T-561
92T/Gold-561
92T/GoldWin-561
92USPlayC/Cub-3C
92USPlayC/Cub-6D
92Ultra-182
93Colla/DM-114
93Cub/Mara-28
93D-582
93F-385
93Flair-23
93L-499
93OPC-345
93Pac/Beisbol-18M
93Pac/Jugador-36
93Pac/Spanish-384
93StCl-68
93StCl/1stDay-68
93StCl/Cub-20
93Studio-218
93T-237
93T/Gold-237
93UD-211
93Ultra-322
94D-291
94F-400
94Finest-312
94Flair-203
94L-68
94Pac/Cr-113
94Panini-159
94Pinn-141
94Pinn/Artist-141
94Pinn/Museum-141
94S-370
94StCl-89
94StCl/1stDay-89
94StCl/Gold-89
94StCl/Team-356
94T-638
94T/Gold-638
94TripleP-79
94UD-122
94UD-329
94UD/CollC-284
94UD/CollC/Gold-284
94UD/CollC/Silv-284
94UD/ElecD-122
94Ultra-167
94Ultra-539

Vizcaino, Junior
87Watertn-14
88CLAS/Star-18
88Salem/Star-22
89Harris/ProC-293
89Harris/Star-20
90Harris/ProC-1202
90Harris/Star-19

Vizquel, Omar
86Wausau-27
88BBAmer-4
88EastLAS/ProC-37
88Vermont/ProC-946
89Calgary/CMC-23
89Calgary/ProC-537
89D/Best-163
89D/Rook-53
89F/Up-62
89Mother/Sea-15
89S/Tr-105
89T/Tr-122T
89UD/Ext-787
90B-474
90D-483
90F-528
90F/Can-528
90Leaf-88
90Mother/Mar-12
90OPC-698
90Publlnt/St-445
90S-264
90S/100Ris-37
90S/YS/I-28
90T-698
90T/89Debut-132
90T/Big-140
90T/Gloss60-59
90T/JumboR-28
90UD-233
91B-245
91CounHrth-9
91D-231
91F-464
91Leaf-91
91OPC-298
91Panini/FrSt-231
91S-299
91StCl-195
91T-298
91UD-593
91Ultra-345
92B-423
92D-641
92F-296
92L-265
92L/BlkGold-265
92Mother/Mar-16
92OPC-101
92Panini-58
92Pinn-97
92S-162
92StCl-163
92T-101
92T/Gold-101
92T/GoldWin-101
92TripleP-137
92UD-401
92Ultra-436
93B-599
93D-25
93F-316
93Flair-276
93L-434
93Mother/Mar-14
93OPC-379
93Pac/Spanish-292
93Pac/SpanishGold-20
93Panini-61
93Pinn-95
93S-102
93S-503AS
93Select-164
93StCl-67
93StCl/1stDay-67
93StCl/Mar-25
93T-68
93T/Gold-68
93TripleP-193AA
93UD-301
93UD/SP-135
93Ultra-274
94B-579
94D-328
94F-301
94Finest-285
94L-331
94OPC-267
94Pac/AllLat-20
94Pac/Cr-583
94Panini-124
94Pinn-64
94Pinn/Artist-64
94Pinn/Museum-64
94S-87
94S/GoldR-87
94StCl-93
94StCl/1stDay-93
94StCl/Gold-93
94T-593
94T/Gold-593
94UD-486
94UD/CollC-285
94UD/CollC/Gold-285
94UD/CollC/Silv-285
94Ultra-125
94Ultra-352
94Ultra/AwardWin-5

Vizzini, Dan
90SoOreg/Best-21
90SoOreg/ProC-3447
91SoOreg/ClBest-20
91SoOreg/ProC-3846

Vlasis, Chris
91Johnson/ClBest-13
91Johnson/ProC-3992
92Spring/ClBest-13
92Spring/ProC-884

Vlcek, Jim
86Salem-27
89SanDiegoSt/Smok-28
92CharlR/ClBest-17

Vodvarka, Rob
83Butte-12

Voeltz, Bill
87FtLaud-16
87Oneonta-19
87PrWill-16
88FtLaud/Star-23

Vogel, George
84Savan-20

Vogel, Mike
92SoBend/ClBest-10

Vogelgesang, Joe
92GreatF/SportP-28
93MedHat/ProC-3738
93MedHat/SportP-10

Vogler, Peter
91Brisbane/Fut-13

Voigt, Jack
88Hagers/Star-23
89Freder/Star-24
90EastLAS/ProC-EL8
90Foil/Best-103
90Hagers/Best-15
90Hagers/ProC-1430
90Hagers/Star-25
91AA/LineD-248
91Hagers/LineD-248
91Hagers/ProC-2470
92RochR/ProC-1953
92RochR/SB-472
92Sky/AAASingl-215
93B-678
93F/Final-167
93Select/RookTr-141T
93T/Tr-27T
94F-23
94Pac/Cr-47
94S-580
94Select-105
94StCl-491
94StCl/1stDay-491
94StCl/Gold-491
94StCl/Team-292
94T-117
94T/Gold-117
94Ultra-10

Voigt, Paul
83Albuq-7

Voisard, Mark
92Bend/ClBest-3
92ClBest/Up-444
93T-476
93T/Gold-476

Voiselle, Bill
44Playball-37
47TipTop
49Eureka-27
Exh47

Voit, David
89Beloit/I/Star-23
89Helena/SP-12
90Erie/Star-30
91Reno/Cal-26
91Sydney/Fut-19

Vollmer, Clyde
50B-53
51B-91
52B-57
52T-255
53B/Col-152
53Briggs
53T-32
54B-136
55B-13
91T/Arc53-32

Vollmer, Gus
90Clinton/Best-11
90Clinton/ProC-2562

Vollmer, Robby
83Wausau/Frit-16

Voltaggio, Vic
88TM/Umpire-32
89TM/Umpire-30
90TM/Umpire-29

Von Der Ahe, Christian
90BBWit-77
N172
N284
N370

Von Hoff, Bruce
68T-529

Von Ohlen, Dave
79Jacks-15

80Tidew-1
81Louisvl-8
81Tidew-18
82Tidew-23
83Louisvl/Riley-8
84D-205
84F-340
84Louisvl-9
84Nes/792-489
84T-489
85D-412
85F-243
85F/Up-U126
85Polar/Ind-38
85T-177
85T/Tr-127T
86F-597
86Miami-25
86T-632
87F-408
87T-287
87Tacom-7
88Miami/Star-24

VonDerleith, Scott
92Beloit/ClBest-2

Vondran, Steve
89Billings/ProC-2057
89FresnoSt/Smok-21
91Cedar/ClBest-20
91Cedar/ProC-2723
91ClBest/Singl-346

Vontz, Doug
87BurlEx-29

Voorhees, Mark
77Spoka

Vorbeck, Eric
91Yakima/ClBest-2
91Yakima/ProC-4263
92Bakers/Cal-26

Vosberg, Ed
84Beaum-6
85Beaum-5
86LasVegas-21
87LasVegas-24
88LasVegas/CMC-7
88LasVegas/ProC-222
89Tucson/CMC-6
89Tucson/JP-26
89Tucson/ProC-192
90AAASingl/ProC-37
90Phoenix/CMC-6
90Phoenix/ProC-11
90ProC/Singl-533
91AAA/LineD-172
91Edmon/LineD-172
91Edmon/ProC-1516
91S-757RP
91S/100RisSt-80

Vosik, Bill
90NE-27
91Watertn/ClBest-23
91Watertn/ProC-3378

Vosmik, Joe
32Orbit/num-35
32Orbit/un-56
33DH-40
33DL-20
34DS-8
34G-77
35BU-68
35G-8I
35G-9I
36Exh/4-11
36G
36Wheat
38Exh/4-9
38G-247
38G-271
39PlayBall-107
40PlayBall-144
41DP-144
90Target-823
91Conlon/Sport-221
93Conlon-767
R305
R310
R313
R314
R326-2A
R326-2B
R342-2
V351B-45
V355-76
WG8-48

Voss, Bill
66T-529R
68OPC-142R
68T-142R
69T-621
70OPC-326
70T-326
71MLB/St-454
71OPC-671
71T-671
72T-776

Vossler, Dan
74OPC-602R
74T-602R
74Tacoma/Caruso-13

Vranjes, Sam
91SanBern/ClBest-28
91SanBern/ProC-1991

Vuchinch, Steve
90Mother/A's-28M

Vuckovich, Pete
77OPC-130
77T-517
78OPC-157
78T-241
79T-407
80OPC-31
80T-57
81D-189
81F-547
81OPC-193
81T-193
81T/Tr-851
82D-458
82F-156
82F/St-14
82OPC-132
82Pol/Brew-50
82T-165LL
82T-643
82T-703TL
82T/St-10LL
82T/St-202
83D-80
83F-49
83F/St-14M
83F/St-16M
83Gard-20
83K-19
83OPC-375
83OPC-394AS
83OPC/St-86
83Pol/Brew-50
83T-321TL
83T-375
83T-394AS
83T/St-86
84F-217
84Gard-21
84Nes/792-505
84OPC-313
84Pol/Brew-50
84T-505
85Gard-21
85Pol/Brew-50
85T-254
86D-473
86F-504
86OPC-152
86T-737
90Swell/Great-83
92Brew/Carlson-24

Vukovich, George
81F-21
81OkCty/TCMA-20
81T-598
82F-262
82T-389
83D-315
83F-176
83T-16
83T/Tr-122T
83Wheat/Ind-31
84D-468
84F-555
84Nes/792-638
84T-638
84Wheat/Ind-24
85D-276
85F-458
85Leaf-120
85Polar/Ind-24
85T-212
85T/St-249
86D-346
86F-598
86OPC-337
86T-483
86T/St-214
91Pac/SenLg-45

Vukovich, John
73OPC-451
73T-451
74OPC-349
74T-349
75OPC-602
75T-602
75T/M-602
76SSPC-43
79Ho-87
79OkCty
80BK/P-8
81F-22
83Thorn-26C
88Phill/TastyK-29CO
88Phill/TastyK-38CO
89Phill/TastyK-35CO
90Phill/TastyK-34CO
91Phill/Medford-35CO
92Phill/Med-31
93Phill/Med-33CO
94Phill/Med-33CO

Vuksan, Jeff
79AppFx-8
81Durham-12

Vuz, John
87Pocatel/Bon-14
88Clinton/ProC-693
90SanJose/Best-22
90SanJose/Cal-52
90SanJose/ProC-2001
90SanJose/Star-24

Waag, Billy
81Buffa-14

Wabeke, Doug
81Shrev-18

Wacha, Chuck
87Greens-7

Wachs, Thomas
85LitFalls-11
86Columbia-26
87Lynch-3

Wachter, Derek
92Beloit/ClBest-18
92Beloit/ProC-421
94FExcel-89

Wachter, Ed
33SK*-5

Wacker, Wade
89Elizab/Star-27

Wada, Hiromi
(Hank)
83SanJose-2C
86SanJose-23C

Waddell, George E.
(Rube)
48Exh/HOF
50Callahan
50W576-73
60F-61
61F-149
76Shakey-48
80Laugh/FFeat-11
80Perez/HOF-48
80SSPC/HOF
86Conlon/1-35
88Conlon/5-29
88Conlon/HardC-6
90Perez/GreatMom-52
93Conlon-931
E107
E254
E270/1
E91
E93
M116
T206
W555
WG2-47

Waddell, James
91Perth/Fut-17

Waddell, Tom
84F/X-U123
84T/Tr-125T
84Wheat/Ind-54
85D-582
85F-459
85Polar/Ind-54
85T-453
86D-94
86F-599
86OPC-86
86OhHenry-54
86T-86
86T/St-209
87Gator-54
87T-657

Wade, Ben
52T-389
53T-4
54T-126
59DF
61Union
90Target-824
91T/Arc53-4
94T/Arc54-126

Wade, Darrin
88Dunedin/Star-19
88StCath/ProC-2036

Wade, Gale
55T-196

Wade, Jake
V362-3

Wade, Scott
86NewBrit-25
87Pawtu-21
87Pawtu/TCMA-20
88Pawtu/CMC-23
88Pawtu/ProC-458
89Pawtu/CMC-15
89Pawtu/Dunkin-33
89Pawtu/ProC-695
90AAASingl/ProC-448
90Pawtu/CMC-23
90Pawtu/ProC-476
90ProC/Singl-274
90T/TVRSox-65
91AAA/LineD-497
91ScranWB/LineD-497
91ScranWB/ProC-2554
92Iowa/ProC-4064
92Syrac/SB-519

Wade, Terrell
92Idaho/ProC-3514
93Macon/ClBest-1
93Macon/ProC-1401
94B-329
94ClBest/Gold-118
94FExcel-162
94FExcel/AS-10
94T-316M
94T/Gold-316M
94UD-527TP
94UD/SP-17PP
94Ultra-452

Wadley, Tony
82Miami-7
83Idaho-13

Waggoner, Aubrey
86AppFx-27
87Penin-8
89BirmB/Best-8
89BirmB/ProC-114
90BirmB/Best-13
90BirmB/ProC-1120
90ProC/Singl-817
91AA/LineD-72
91BirmB/LineD-72
91BirmB/ProC-1468
92Greenvl/ProC-1167
92Greenvl/SB-247
93Calgary/ProC-1180

Waggoner, Jimmy
89Medford/Best-25
90Madison/Best-9
90Modesto/Cal-166
90Modesto/Chong-31
90Modesto/ProC-2223
91ClBest/Singl-89
91Modesto/ClBest-26
91Modesto/ProC-3100
92AS/Cal-20
92Reno/Cal-55

Wagner, Adam
90FtLaud/Star-27TR
91PrWill/ClBest-27TR
92PrWill/ClBest-29TR

Wagner, Albert
(Butts)
90Target-1092

Wagner, Bill
94B-642
94ClBest/Gold-18
94ClBest/GoldLP-16
94FExcel-209
94Pinn-264
94Pinn/Artist-264
94Pinn/Museum-264
94S-536
94SigRook-26
94T-209FDP
94T/Gold-209FDP
94TedW-134
94UD-524TP
94UD/CollC-29
94UD/CollC/Gold-29
94UD/CollC/Silv-29
94UD/SP-18PP

Wagner, Bret
93Bz-22
93T/Tr-124T

Wagner, Charles
(Heinie)
10Domino-119
11Helmar-5
12Sweet/Pin-7
14CJ-31
15CJ-31
E91
M116
T202
T204
T205
T206
T207
T213/blue
T214-28
T215/blue
T215/brown
T216

Wagner, Charlie
80Elmira-38
87Elmira/Black-33

Wagner, Dan
87Penin-29
88BirmB/Best-13
89BirmB/Best-5
89BirmB/ProC-90
90MidldA/GS-20

Wagner, Darrell
90Bend/Legoe-16

Wagner, Gary
66OPC-151
66T-151
67T-529
68T-448
69T-276
69T/St-158
70T-627
71OPC-473
71T-473
81TCMA-437

Wagner, Gerald
86Durham-26
87Sumter-28

Wagner, Harold
47TipTop

Wagner, Hector
88Eugene/Best-6
89AppFx/ProC-849
90A&AASingle/ProC-34
90Foil/Best-194
90Memphis/Best-18
90Memphis/ProC-1008
90Memphis/Star-25
91AAA/LineD-347
91B-299
91Omaha/LineD-347
91Omaha/ProC-1036
91S-730RP
91T/90Debut-161
92StCl-323

Wagner, Jeff
83Ander-33
84Durham-7
85Durham-31

Wagner, John
(Honus)
11Diamond-28
14CJ-68
15CJ-68
16FleischBrd-97
24Sherlock-10

40PlayBall-168
47TipTop
48Exh/HOF
48L-70
50Callahan
50W576-74
51T/CM
60Exh/HOF-24
60F-62
61F-150
61GP-32
63Bz/ATG-10
69Bz/Sm
72F/FFeat-21
72K/ATG-9
76Motor-1
76OPC-344AS
76Rowe-15M
76Shakey-5
76T-344AS
77Galasso-148
77Shakey-18
80Laugh/FFeat-1
80Marchant/HOF-30
80Pac/Leg-18
80Perez/HOF-5
80SSPC/HOF
81Conlon-64
83D/HOF-5
85West/2-42
86Conlon/1-55
87Nestle/DT-4
88Grenada-54
89HOF/St-14
89Pac/Leg-211
89Swell-4
90BBWit-84
90Perez/GreatMom-24
90Swell/Great-50
91Cadaco-59
91Conlon/Sport-8
91Swell/Great-126
92S-880
92Whitehall-4
92Whitehall/Proto-4
93AP/ASG-86
93AP/ASG24K-20G
93Cadaco-61
93Conlon-754
93Conlon/MasterBW-4
93CrackJack-3
93Spectrum/HOFII-3
93UD/ATH-124
93UD/ATH-139
93UD/ATH-145
94Conlon-1219
94TedW-81
94TedW/Lock-17
BF2-92
D303
D304
D322
D328-180
D329-182
D350/2-184
E101
E102
E103
E105
E106
E107
E135-180
E224
E254
E270/1
E286
E90/1
E90/2
E91
E92
E93
E94
E95
E98
M101/4-182
M101/5-184
M116
R311/Leath
R312/M
R313
T206
W555
WG3-49
WG4-28
WG5-41
WG6-37

Wagner, Kirk
89KS*-50

Wagner, Leon
59T-257
60T-383
61T-547
61T/Dice-17
62P-77
62P/Can-77
62Salada-57A
62Salada-57B
62Shirriff-57
62T-491
62T/St-71
62T/bucks
63Exh
63F-21
63J-28
63P-28
63Salada-55
63T-335
63T-4LL
64Kahn
64T-41M
64T-530
64T/Coins-130AS
64T/Coins-6
64T/S-54
64Wheat/St-47
65Kahn
65OldLond-36
65T-367
65T/E-31
65T/trans-33
66Bz-8
66OPC-65
66T-65
67Bz-8
67CokeCap/ALAS-33
67CokeCap/AS-33
67CokeCap/Indian-12
67Kahn
67OPC-109M
67OPC/PI-24
67T-109M
67T-360
67T/PI-24
68Kahn
68T-495
69OPC-187
69T-187
69T/4in1-23M
78TCMA-125
78TCMA-165
Exh47

Wagner, Mark
75Clinton
77T-490R
78T-598
80OPC-13
80T-29
81D-126
81F-478
81T-358
81T/Tr-852
82D-163
82F-333
82T-443
83D-268
83F-582
83T-144
84Cram/PCL-89
85T-581
89Pac/SenLg-170
91AAA/LineD-600M
91Pac/SenLg-112
91Toledo/LineD-600CO
91Toledo/ProC-1948CO
92Bristol/ClBest-27MG
93Rang/Keeb-367

Wagner, Paul
89Welland/Pucko-26
90Augusta/ProC-2464
91CLAS/ProC-CAR38
91Salem/ClBest-21
91Salem/ProC-951
92CaroMud/ProC-1181
92CaroMud/SB-146
92D/Rook-120
92Sky/AASingl-68
93B-458
93D-334
93F/Final-121
93F/MLPII-10
93L-466
93Pinn-282
93Pirate/Nation-35
93S-315
93Select/RookTr-148T
93StCl-710
93StCl/1stDay-710
93T/Tr-109T
93UD-643
93Ultra-457
94D-611
94F-623
94Finest-309
94L-220
94Pac/Cr-510
94S-578
94StCl-505
94StCl/1stDay-505
94StCl/Gold-505
94T-157
94T/Gold-157
94UD-383
94Ultra-261

Wagner, Steve
78OrlanTw

Wagner, William G.
(Bull)
90Target-1091

Wahl, Tim
88Beloit/GS-17
89Beloit/I/Star-24

Waid, Patrick
87AZ/Pol-17
88SLCity-1
89SLCity-1OF

Wainhouse, David
89B-358
89WPalmB/Star-24
90WPalmB/Star-25
91AA/LineD-272
91Harris/LineD-272
91Harris/ProC-627
92Indianap/ProC-1860
92Indianap/SB-197
92ProC/Tomorrow-260
92Sky/AAASingl-95
92StCl-885
92T/91Debut-177
92Ultra-524
93F/Final-276
93FExcel/ML-64
93StCl/Mar-3
93Ultra-626

Waite, Jon
92Hunting/ClBest-21
92Hunting/ProC-3149

Waite, Steve
92Fayette/ClBest-12

Waitkus, Ed
47TipTop
49B-142
49Eureka-151
49Lummis
50B-30
50Drake-12
51B-28
51BR-C9
51T/BB-51
52B-92
52T-158
52TipTop
54Esskay
55B-4
55Esskay
79TCMA-77
91Crown/Orio-470
Exh47
PM10/Sm-191

Waits, M. Rick
75OkCty/Team-10
75Spokane/Caruso-16
76OPC-433
76SSPC-513
76T-433
77BurgChef-61
77Ho-88
77Ho/Twink-88
77Pep-16
77T-306
78OPC-191
78T-37
79Ho-35
79OPC-253
79T-484
80OPC-94
80T-168
81D-201
81F-396
81OPC-258
81T-697
82D-33
82F-382
82OPC-142
82T-573
82Wheat/Ind
83D-263
83F-422
83T-779
83T/Tr-123T
83Wheat/Ind-32
84Nes/792-218
84T-218
85Cram/PCL-219
85D-368
85F-600
85T-59
86F-505
86T-614
86Vanco-27
89Pac/SenLg-91
89T/SenLg-60
89TM/SenLg-109
91Pac/SenLg-15
92MCI-10
93Rang/Keeb-368

Wakamatsu, Don
86Tampa-24
87Cedar-16
88Chatt/Best-12
89BirmB/Best-16
89BirmB/ProC-107
90AAASingl/ProC-169
90ProC/Singl-649
90Vanco/CMC-22
90Vanco/ProC-491
91AAA/LineD-648
91Vanco/LineD-648
91Vanco/ProC-1598
92Albuq/ProC-724
92Albuq/SB-22
92S-814
92T/91Debut-178

Wakana, Josh
83Tidew-25

Wakefield, Bill
62Pep/Tul
63Pep/Tul
64T-576R
65OPC-167
65T-167
66T-443
91WIZMets-423
Exh47

Wakefield, Dick
43Playball-14
47TipTop
48L-50
49B-91
50Remar
79TCMA-92

Wakefield, Tim
88Watertn/Pucko-27
89Welland/Pucko-27
90Salem/Star-23
91AA/LineD-119
91CaroMud/LineD-119
91CaroMud/ProC-1087
92BuffB/BlueS-24
92BuffB/ProC-324
92BuffB/SB-45
92D/Rook-121
92F/Up-117
92ProC/Tomorrow-308
92S/RookTr-92T
92Sky/AAASingl-20
93B-570
93Classic/Gamel-96
93D-61RR
93F-123
93F/RookSenII-9
93Flair-118
93HumDum/Can-45
93L/Fast-2
93L/GRook-8
93OPC-227
93Pac/Spanish-254
93Panini-279
93Pinn-401
93Pinn/Team2001-6
93Pirate/Nation-36
93S-347
93Select-307
93Select/ChasRook-16
93StCl-13
93StCl/1stDay-13
93StCl/MPhoto-12
93StCl/MurphyS-51
93Studio-83
93T-163
93T/Finest-37
93T/FinestRef-37
93T/Gold-163
93ToysRUs-24
93TripleP-50
93UD-480
93UD-66
93UD/FunPack-152
93USPlayC/Rook-13D
93Ultra-104
94D-471
94F-624
94L-155
94Pac/Cr-511
94Pinn-448
94S-418
94StCl-152
94StCl/1stDay-152
94StCl/Gold-152
94T-669
94T/Gold-669
94Ultra-262

Walbeck, Greg
93Pac/Spanish-385

Walbeck, Matt
88CharWh/Best-1
89Peoria/Team-15
90Hunting/ProC-3285
90PeoriaUp/Team-U4
91CLAS/ProC-CAR45
91WinSalem/ClBest-15
91WinSalem/ProC-2832
92ChalK/SB-170
92CharlK/ProC-2775
93B-384
93F/Final-11
93FExcel/ML-15
93Pinn-607
93StCl/Cub-28
93T-812
93T/Gold-812
93UD-509DD
93Ultra-323
94B-20
94Finest-436
94Flair-78
94L/GRook-14
94OPC-227
94Pinn-487
94Studio-201
94T-329
94T/Gold-329
94UD-130
94UD/ElecD-130
94Ultra-396

Walberg, Bill
82Jacks-25

Walberg, George
(Rube)
32Orbit/un-57
33G-145
33G-183
81Conlon-59
91Conlon/Sport-91
94Conlon-1151
R305
R313
V353-76
W517-41

Walbring, Larry
76Clinton

Walden, Alan
90BurlInd/ProC-3009
91CollInd/ClBest-17
91CollInd/ProC-1484
92ColRS/ClBest-21

Walden, Ron
90Classic/DP-9
90Classic/III-82
90GreatF/SportP-1
91B-615

91OPC-596DP
91S-679FDP
91T-596
Walden, Travis
88Clearw/Star-26
Waldenberger, Dave
89Idaho/ProC-2019
92SanBern/ClBest-26
92SanBern/ProC-
93River/Cal-21
Waldin, Alan
92ColRS/ProC-2391
Waldron, Joe
91CharRain/ClBest-11
91CharRain/ProC-96
92Watlo/ClBest-2
92Watlo/ProC-2142
Waldrop, Tom
92Idaho/ProC-3522
93Macon/ClBest-26
93Macon/ProC-1416
Wales, Gary
91Parramatta/Fut-11
Walewander, James
86GlenF-23
87Toledo-5
87Toledo/TCMA-7
88Pep/T-32
88S-571
88T-106
89D-415
89F-150
89S-311
89T-467
89Toledo/CMC-15
89Toledo/ProC-770
89UD-454
90AAASingl/ProC-336
90ColClip/CMC-12
90ColClip/ProC-686
90Colum/Pol-21
90ProC/Singl-212
90T/TVYank-65
91AAA/LineD-122
91ColClip/LineD-122
91ColClip/ProC-607
93Vanco/ProC-2607
Walgast, Ad
T3/Box-53
Walk, Bob
81D-393
81F-14
81T-494
81T/Tr-853
82BK/Lids-24
82Pol/Atl-43
82T-296
83D-401
83F-149
83F/St-11M
83Richm-10
83T-104
84Cram/PCL-141
85Cram/PCL-243
86D-430
86T/Tr-120T
87D-203
87F-623
87T-628
88D-514
88D/Best-269
88F-342
88S-162
88T-349
89B-409
89D-172
89D/AS-58
89D/Best-145
89F-223
89KennerFig-157
89OPC-151
89OPC-66
89S-224
89Sf-34
89T-504
89T/St-123
89UD-438
89VFJuice-17
90B-163
90D-370
90D/BestNL-94
90F-482
90F/Can-482
90Homer/Pirate-31
90Leaf-64
90OPC-754
90Publint/St-167
90S-21
90T-754
90T/Big-23
90T/St-125
90UD-596
91B-526
91D-157
91F-54
91Leaf-450
91OPC-29
91S-599
91StCl-14
91T-29
91UD-689
92B-666
92D-88
92F-572
92L-353
92L/BlkGold-353
92OPC-486
92Pinn-410
92Pirate/Nation-25
92S-54
92StCl-746
92T-486
92T/Gold-486
92T/GoldWin-486
92UD-619
93D-546
93F-505
93L-134
93Pac/Spanish-593
93Panini-286
93Pinn-380
93Pirate/Nation-37
93S-144
93StCl-421
93StCl/1stDay-421
93StCl/MurphyS-77
93T-685
93T/Gold-685
93UD-78
93Ultra-458
94D-395
94F-625
94Pac/Cr-512
94Pinn-457
94S-356
94T-434
94T/Gold-434
Walkden, Mike
91GreatF/SportP-23
91LitSun/HSPros-22
91LitSun/HSProsG-22
92Bakers/Cal-27
92StCl-852
92StCl/Dome-191
Walker, Albert
(Rube)
49Eureka-74
52T-319
53T-134
54T-153
55Gol/Dodg-30
55T-108
55T/DH-15
56T-333
57T-147
58Hires-74
58T-203
73OPC-257CO
73T-257CO
74OPC-179CO
74T-179CO
79TCMA-278
80BurlB-13
81TCMA-407M
82Pol/Atl-54CO
83Pol/Atl-54CO
84Pol/Atl-54CO
90Target-826
91T/Arc53-134
94Mets/69-32
94T/Arc54-153
Walker, Andy
79QuadC-20
Walker, Anthony
(Tony)
81Water-11
81Water-21
82Water-20
83DayBe-27
86F/Up-U123
86Pol/Ast-20
87F-71
87T-24
Walker, Bernie
87Cedar-25
88Chatt/Best-23
89Chatt/Best-20
89Chatt/GS-22
89SLAS-7
91AA/LineD-173
91Chatt/LineD-173
91Nashvl/ProC-2171
Walker, Bert
85Clovis-41
Walker, Bill
93Conlon-789
Walker, Billy
91Miami/ClBest-4
Walker, Cameron
(Cam)
84ElPaso-22
86ElPaso-23
87ElPaso-18
87Wichita-25
Walker, Chico
81Pawtu-22
83Pawtu-24
84Pawtu-16
85Iowa-11
86Iowa-26
87Berg/Cubs-29
87D-539
87OPC-58
87T-695
88Edmon/ProC-561
89Syrac/CMC-23
89Syrac/MerchB-23
89Syrac/ProC-792
89Syrac/Team-23
90CharlK/Team-7
91Classic/III-93
91Cub/Mara-24
91Cub/Vine-32
91F/UltraUp-U74
91Leaf-501
92D-439
92F-395
92F/Up-107
92OPC-439
92S-578
92StCl-564
92T-439
92T/Gold-439
92T/GoldWin-439
92UD-617
92USPlayC/Cub-12H
92USPlayC/Cub-6H
92Ultra-183
93D-410
93F-482
93L-149
93Mets/Kahn-34
93Pac/Spanish-549
93S-399
93StCl-114
93StCl/1stDay-114
93UD-727
93Ultra-80
94Pac/Cr-419
Walker, Chris
88Batavia/ProC-1677
89Clearw/Star-24
Walker, Clarence
(Tilly)
21Exh-181
91Conlon/Sport-137
D328-181
D329-183
D350/2-185
E120
E135-181
E254
M101/4-183
M101/5-185
V100
V61-6
W501-99
W515-7
W572
W575
Walker, Clifton
(Cliff)
85Bend/Cram-23
87Spartan-16
Walker, Curtis
21Exh-182
92Conlon/Sport-417
E126-58
Walker, Dane
92Madis/ClBest-4
92Madis/ProC-1251
93Modesto/ClBest-22
93Modesto/ProC-812
Walker, Darcy
86WinSalem-27
Walker, Dennis
89Utica/Pucko-26
90SoBend/Best-12
90SoBend/GS-20
91SoBend/ClBest-6
91SoBend/ProC-2866
92Saraso/ClBest-13
92Saraso/ProC-216
Walker, Doak
52Wheat*
Walker, Duane
80Indianap-26
81Indianap-21
82Indianap-6
83D-624
83F-606
83T-243
84D-325
84F-485
84F/St-41
84Nes/792-659
84T-659
85D-608
85F-554
85Leaf-52
85T-441
85T/St-52
86D-500
86F-574
86T-22
86Tucson-23
87Louisvl-28
88Bristol/ProC-1878
88Louisvl-49
88Louisvl/CMC-17
88Louisvl/ProC-425
89Miami/I/Star-24
93Rang/Keeb-369
Walker, Edsall
92Negro/Kraft-11
92Negro/Retort-62
Walker, Ewart
(Dixie)
T207
Walker, Fred
(Dixie)
34DS-12
34G-39
35G-8E
35G-9E
39Exh
41DP-21
45Playball-30
49Eureka-174
53T-190CO
55Hunter
61F-151
89Smok/Dodg-49
90Target-825
91T/Arc53-190CO
92Bz/Quadra-22M
92Conlon/Sport-506
PM10/Sm-192
R346-45
V354-86
Walker, Frederick
15CJ-173
E254
E270/1
Walker, Gerald
(Gee)
33DH-41
34G-26
35BU-118
35G-8F
35G-9F
37OPC-110
38Wheat-4
41DP-135
41Wheat-10
44Playball-31
81Conlon-99
81Tiger/Detroit-109
91Conlon/Sport-87
R309/2
R313
R314
V300
V354-81
V355-48
V94-49
Walker, Glenn
81Wausau-24
82LynnS-16
83SLCity-20
84Cram/PCL-187
86MidldA-25
Walker, Greg
80AppFx
81GlenF-16
83T/Tr-124T
84D-609
84F-73
84Nes/792-518
84T-518
84TrueVal/WS-30
85Coke/WS-29
85D-366
85F-530
85OPC-244
85T-623
85T/St-236
85ThomMc/Discs-21
86Coke/WS-29
86D-135
86F-219
86Jay's-19
86OPC-123
86Seven/Coin-C16M
86Sf-174
86T-123
86T/St-293
87Coke/WS-17
87D-25DK
87D-59
87D/DKsuper-25
87D/OD-233
87F-508
87F/LL-42
87F/Mini-110
87Leaf-25DK
87OPC-302
87Seven-C15
87Sf/TPrev-26M
87T-397
87T/St-291
88Coke/WS-29
88D-162
88D/Best-193
88F-411
88KennerFig-118
88Leaf-86
88OPC-286
88Panini/St-56
88S-93
88Sf-103
88T-764
88T/Big-105
88T/St-292
88T/UK-83
89Coke/WS-27
89D-135
89KennerFig-158
89Kodak/WSox-1M
89Panini/St-307
89S-37
89Sf-19
89T-21TL
89T-408
89T/Big-4
89UD-231
90AAASingl/ProC-469
90F-551
90F/Can-551
90OPC-33
90Panini/St-45
90ProC/Singl-318
90Publint/St-402
90RochR/CMC-18
90RochR/ProC-712
90S-354
90T-33
90UD-350
91Crown/Orio-471

Walker, Harry
48L-137
49B-130
49Eureka-75
50B-180
60T-468C
65T-438MG
66EH-3
66T-318MG
67T-448MG
67T/Test/PP-24MG
69T-633MG
70OPC-32MG
70T-32MG
71OPC-312MG
71T-312MG
72OPC-249MG
72T-249MG
79TCMA-261
89Pac/Leg-190
89Swell-34
90Swell/Great-33
91Swell/Great-94
Exh47
R346-39
Walker, Hugh
89AppFx/ProC-856
89B-127
90BBCity/Star-24
91AA/LineD-422
91B-313
91ClBest/Singl-58
91London/LineD-422
91Memphis/ProC-667
91PreRookPrev/LineD-422
92BBCity/ProC-3859
92ClBest-184
92Memphis/SB-447
92Sky/AASingl-189
93ClBest/MLG-84
Walker, J. Luke
66T-498R
67OPC-123R
67T-123R
68T-559R
69OPC-36
69T-36
70OPC-322
70T-322
71MLB/St-216
71OPC-534
71OPC-68LL
71T-534
71T-68LL
71T/S-21
71T/Super-21
72MB-353
72OPC-471
72T-471
73OPC-187
73T-187
74OPC-612
74T-612
74T/Tr-612T
75OPC-474
75T-474
75T/M-474
Walker, James
87Chatt/Best-5
88Calgary/CMC-7
88Calgary/ProC-791
Walker, Jamie
92AubAs/ClBest-17
92AubAs/ProC-1354
Walker, Jerry Allen
58T-113
59T-144
60T-399M
60T-540
60T/tatt-52
60T/tatt-96
61T-85
62T-357
62T/St-61
62T/bucks
63Sugar-5
63T-413
64T-77
91Crown/Orio-472
Walker, Jerry
89Belling/Legoe-35OWN
Walker, Jim
89KS*-87
Walker, John
78LodiD
79LodiD-12
80Toledo-9
81Toledo-17
Walker, Johnny 1
90Pulaski/ProC-3112
91Idaho/SportP-14
Walker, Johnny 2
91LitSun/HSPros-12
91LitSun/HSProsG-12
Walker, Keith
80Knoxvl/TCMA-23
82Knoxvl-7
83Syrac-12
Walker, Kurt
86BirmB/Team-22
87Visalia-8
88MidldA/GS-2
Walker, Larry
85Utica-16
86BurlEx-25
87Jaxvl-1
87SLAS-8
89AAA/CMC-7
89Indianap/CMC-23
89Indianap/ProC-1239
90B-117
90Classic/Up-16
90D-578
90D/BestNL-91
90F-363
90F/Can-363
90F/SoarSt-3
90Greens/Best-15
90Greens/ProC-2667
90Greens/Star-25
90Leaf-325
90OPC-757
90S-631
90S/YS/II-9
90T-757
90T/89Debut-133
90T/Big-296
90TripleAAS/CMC-7
90UD-466
90UD/Ext-702M
91B-442
91Bz-19
91D-359
91F-250
91F/UltraUp-U93
91FtLaud/ClBest-18
91FtLaud/ProC-2431
91Leaf-241
91MajorLg/Pins-80
91OPC-339
91Panini/FrSt-145
91Panini/St-65
91S-241
91S/100RisSt-21
91StCl-93
91T-339
91T/JumboR-32
91ToysRUs-31
91UD-536
92B-648
92Classic/II-T39
92D-259
92Expo/D/Duri-18
92F-493
92FtLaud/ClBest-16
92FtLaud/ProC-2616
92FtLaud/Team-32
92L-201
92L/BlkGold-201
92OPC-531
92Panini-206
92Pinn-194
92Pinn/Team2000-21
92S-199
92S/Impact-29
92StCl-256
92Studio-59
92T-531
92T/Gold-531
92T/GoldWin-531
92TripleP-89
92UD-249
92Ultra-525
93B-100
93Classic/Gamel-97
93Colla/DM-115
93D-540
93D/DK-6
93D/Elite-30
93D/EliteUp-12
93D/LongBall-LL18
93D/MVP-9
93D/Prev-6
93Expo/D/McDon-7
93F-715SS
93F-81
93F/ASNL-6
93F/Fruit-64
93Flair-87
93Ho-30
93HumDum/Can-42
93Kenner/Fig-38
93L-392
93MilkBone-15
93Nestle-1
93OPC-384
93OPC/Premier-39
93Pac/Spanish-190
93Panini-231
93Pinn-299I
93Pinn-3
93Pinn/HRC-14
93Pinn/Slug-13
93Pinn/TP-10
93Post/Can-13
93S-5
93S/Franchise-20
93Select-27
93StCl-299MC
93StCl-320
93StCl/1stDay-299MC
93StCl/1stDay-320
93StCl/MPhoto-24
93StCl/MurphyMP-11AS
93StCl/MurphyS-94
93Studio-123
93T-406
93T-95
93T/BlkGold-22
93T/Finest-97AS
93T/FinestASJ-97AS
93T/FinestRef-97AS
93T/Gold-406
93T/Gold-95
93T/PreProd-9
93ToysRUs-23
93TripleP-42
93TripleP/Act-6
93UD-144
93UD-481M
93UD/FunPack-98
93UD/HRH-HR16
93UD/SP-107
93UD/TCr-TC10
93Ultra-71
93Ultra/AS-8
93Ultra/AwardWin-9
94B-500
94D-371
94D/Special-371
94F-554
94L-397
94L/Clean-1
94OPC-253
94OPC/JAS-19
94Pac/Cr-392
94Panini-213
94Pinn-310
94RedFoley-27
94S-376
94S/DT-9
94S/GoldS-27
94Select-18
94Sf/2000-77
94StCl-280
94StCl/1stDay-280
94StCl/Gold-280
94Studio-80
94T-230
94T/Finest-216
94T/FinestRef-216
94T/Gold-230
94TripleP-99
94UD-274HFA
94UD-370
94UD/CollC-286
94UD/CollC/Gold-286
94UD/CollC/Silv-286
94UD/ElecD-274HFA
94UD/SP-86
94Ultra-526
94Ultra/AwardWin-17
Walker, Lonnie
88LitFalls/Pucko-14
89Clmbia/Best-27
89Clmbia/GS-26
Walker, M.J.
75T/Photo-75
Walker, Matt
86Clinton-26
86Cram/NWL-186
86Everett/Pop-35
87Everett-1
Walker, Michael Aaron
(Mike)
86Watertn-27
87Harris-23
88Harris/ProC-850
90Calgary/CMC-3
90Calgary/ProC-652
Walker, Michael Charles
(Mike)
84Idaho/Team-28
87Watlo-14
88Wmsprt/ProC-1310
89B-77
89ColoSp/ProC-239
90AAASingl/ProC-117
90AAASingl/ProC-217
90ColoSp/CMC-1
90ColoSp/ProC-36
90ProC/Singl-430
90ProC/Singl-453
91D-61
91F-381
91Indian/McDon-27
91OPC-593
91T-593
91UD-694
92Calgary/ProC-3732
92D/Rook-122
92Jaxvl/SB-370
92Toledo/ProC-1044
92Toledo/SB-594
93Calgary/ProC-1167
93T/Gold-825
Walker, Moses F.
(Fleetwood)
86Negro/Frit-28
87Negro/Dixon-22
94TedW-114
Walker, Pete
90Pittsfld/Pucko-16
91StLucie/ClBest-14
91StLucie/ProC-712
92Bingham/ProC-517
92Bingham/SB-70
94B-44
94FExcel-240
94Ultra-540
Walker, R. Tom
72Dimanche*-49
73OPC-41
73T-41
74OPC-193
74T-193
75OPC-627
75T-627
75T/M-627
76OPC-186
76T-186
77T-652
78Colum
Walker, Ray
88Martins/Star-32
Walker, Rich
88Batavia/ProC-1681
90Batavia/ProC-3084TR
Walker, Rod
89LittleSun-6
Walker, Shon
92ClBest/Up-415
92Classic/DP-24
92FrRow/DP-74
92UD/ML-83
93ClBest/MLG-196
93StCl/MurphyS-155
93T-658M
93T/Gold-658M
94ClBest/Gold-188
Walker, Steve
87SanBern-1
88BBCity/Star-24
89Memphis/Best-23
89Memphis/ProC-1196
89Memphis/Star-23
89Star/Wax-46
91Hunting/ClBest-28
91Hunting/ProC-3352
92Hunting/ClBest-18
92Hunting/ProC-3167
93Peoria/Team-31
Walker, The
90Everett/Best-7
Walker, Toby
88OK-11
Walker, Todd
92LSU/McDag-12
93Bz-6
93LSU/McDag-12
93T/Tr-79T
94LSU-2
Walker, Tom
91Hunting/ClBest-29
91Hunting/ProC-3345
Walker, Tommy
88MissSt-37M
Walker, William C.
29Exh/4-7
31Exh/4-7
E120
W575
Walker, William H.
33G-94
35BU-116
R313
V353-57
Walkup, James
39PlayBall-150
Wall, Dave
81AppFx-27
Wall, Donnie
89AubAs/ProC-2182
90Ashvl/ProC-2749
91BurlAs/ClBest-10
91BurlAs/ProC-2801
91MidwLAS/ProC-19
92Osceola/ClBest-19
92ProC/Tomorrow-233
92UD/ML-138
Wall, Jason
90LSUPol-11
Wall, Murray
53T-217
58T-410
59T-42
91T/Arc53-217
Wall, Stan
74Albuq/Team-22
75Albuq/Caruso-17
75IntLgAS/Broder-36
75PCL/AS-37
76OPC-584
76T-584
77T-88
90Target-827
Wallace, Alex
85Anchora-30
Wallace, B.J.
90MissSt-39
91MissSt-47
92B-554FOIL
92Classic/DP-3
92Classic/DPFoil-BC3
92Classic/DPPrev-BB3
92FrRow/DP-80
92MissSt-44
92T/Tr-126T
92T/TrGold-126T
92UD/ML-2
93B-676
93ClBest/MLG-109
93OPC/Premier/TDP-1
93Pinn-456DP
93S-488DP
93Select-310DP
93StCl/MurphyS-125
93StCl/MurphyS-142
93T-33
93T/Gold-33
93WPalmB/ClBest-1
93WPalmB/ProC-1341
94B-640
94ClBest/Gold-191
94FExcel-230
Wallace, Brian
92Belling/ClBest-27
92Belling/ProC-1454

Wallace, Brooks
81Tulsa-24
Wallace, Curtis
76Baton
Wallace, Dave
76OkCty/Team-24
81VeroB-25
82VeroB-28
84Cram/PCL-245
86Albuq-26CO
Wallace, David
90Ashvl/ClBest-24
91Ashvl/ProC-582
92BurlAs/ClBest-1
92BurlAs/ProC-561
Wallace, Derek
92ClBest/BBonusC-23
92ClBest/Up-403
92Classic/DP-8
92Classic/DPFoil-BC8
92Peoria/Team-29
92UD/ML-7
93B-4
93Pinn-460DP
93S-492DP
93Select-357DP
93StCl/MurphyS-124
93T-459
93T/Gold-459
93UD-429TP
94B-110
94ClBest/Gold-133
Wallace, Don
67T-367R
Wallace, Greg
86Miami-26
Wallace, Jim
49Remar
Wallace, Joe
91OKSt-28
92OKSt-28
Wallace, Kent
92Oneonta/ClBest-22
93Greens/ClBest-25
Wallace, Mike
74OPC-608R
74T-608R
75OPC-401
75SSPC/18-3
75T-401
75T/M-401
76SSPC-290
77T-539
92Yank/WIZ70-159
93Rang/Keeb-370
Wallace, Roderick
(Bobby)
10Domino-120
11Helmar-66
12Sweet/Pin-56A
12Sweet/Pin-56B
14Piedmont/St-58
50Callahan
50W576-75
76Shakey-69
80Perez/HOF-69
80SSPC/HOF
90BBWit-65
93Conlon-916
94Conlon-1017
E107
E270/1
E90/1
E92
M116
S74-37
T201
T202
T204
T205
T206
T207
WG2-48
Wallace, Tim
83StPete-15
84ArkTr-5
86ArkTr-25
86Louisvl-28
86Peoria-25
87WinSalem-15
88WinSalem/Star-21
89Boise/ProC-1994
90PalmSp/Cal-216
90PalmSp/ProC-2588
91AA/LineD-622
91Wichita/LineD-622
91Wichita/ProC-2608
91Wichita/Rock-18
Wallach, Tim
82D-140
82Expo/Hygrade-23
82F-210
82Hygrade
82OPC-191
82T-191
83D-392
83F-299
83OPC-229
83OPC/St-257
83Stuart-12
83T-552
83T/St-257
84D-421
84Expo/PostC-35
84F-291
84Nes/792-232
84OPC-232
84Stuart-14
84T-232
84T/St-94
85D-87
85F-412
85Leaf-199
85OPC-3
85OPC/Post-6
85T-473
85T/St-87
86D-219
86D/AAS-25
86Expo/Prov/Pan-11
86Expo/Prov/Post-10
86F-263
86F/Mini-56
86GenMills/Book-6M
86Leaf-97
86OPC-217
86Provigo-11
86Sf-123
86T-685
86T-703
86T/St-82
86T/Tatt-18M
87D-179
87D/OD-88
87Expo/PostC-10
87F-334
87GenMills/Book-4M
87Ho/St-5
87Leaf-61
87OPC-55
87RedFoley/St-117
87Sf-115M
87Sf-72
87Sf/TPrev-20M
87Stuart-7M
87T-55
87T/St-80
88AlaskaAS70/Team-17
88D-222
88D/AS-59
88D/Best-258
88F-198
88F/AwardWin-44
88F/BB/AS-43
88F/BB/MVP-42
88F/Mini-91
88F/St-98
88F/WaxBox-C15
88Ho/Disc-7
88Jiffy-18
88KayBee-32
88Leaf-193
88Leaf-255CG
88Nestle-23
88OPC-94
88Panini/St-327
88RedFoley/St-94
88S-70
88Sf-151
88T-399
88T-560
88T/Big-7
88T/Coins-59
88T/Gloss60-18
88T/Mini-58
88T/Revco-6
88T/St-85
88T/St/Backs-9
88T/UK-84
89B-362
89D-156
89D/Best-34
89F-395
89KMart/DT-25
89OPC-78
89Panini/St-122
89RedFoley/St-127
89S-220
89Sf-114
89T-720
89T/Big-215
89T/LJN-139
89T/St-70
89UD-102
90B-114
90D-220
90D/BestNL-55
90D/Learning-28
90F-364
90F/AwardWin-41
90F/Can-364
90F/LL-41
90Leaf-80
90OPC-370
90Panini/St-286
90PublInt/St-189
90RedFoley/St-99
90S-192
90Sf-182
90T-370
90T/Big-70
90T/Coins-60
90T/DH-68
90T/Mini-64
90T/St-74
90UD-273
90USPlayC/AS-5D
91B-437
91Classic/200-2
91D-406MVP
91D-514
91DennyGS-12
91F-251
91Leaf-388
91Leaf/Prev-6
91Leaf/Stud-200
91MSA/Holsum-3
91OPC-220
91OPC/Premier-125
91Panini/FrSt-141
91Panini/St-64
91Panini/Top15-102
91Petro/SU-10
91Post/Can-2
91RedFoley/St-99
91S-210
91S-865FRAN
91S/100SS-58
91StCl-463
91Sunflower-23
91T-220
91T/CJMini/II-21
91UD-235
91UD-96
91Ultra-210
92B-372
92B-557FOIL
92Classic/Game200-40
92D-34
92DPep/MSA-22
92Expo/D/Duri-19
92F-494
92L-298
92L/BlkGold-298
92OPC-385
92Panini-204
92Pinn-161
92Post/Can-5
92S-595
92S/100SS-70
92StCl-340
92Studio-60
92T-385
92T/Gold-385
92T/GoldWin-385
92T/Kids-6
92TripleP-224
92UD-228
92Ultra-226
93B-70
93D-36
93Expo/D/McDon-8
93F-82
93F/Final-86
93Flair-77
93HumDum/Can-33
93L-363
93Mother/Dodg-6
93OPC-225
93OPC/Premier-87
93Pac/Spanish-191
93Panini-215
93Pinn-178
93Pol/Dodg-26
93S-211
93Select-190
93Select/RookTr-27T
93StCl-686
93StCl/1stDay-686
93StCl/Dodg-11
93Studio-64
93T-570
93T/Finest-118
93T/FinestRef-118
93T/Gold-570
93T/Tr-127T
93TripleP-253
93UD-547
93Ultra-408
94D-326
94F-527
94Finest-361
94Flair-184
94L-21
94Pac/Cr-323
94Pinn-484
94S-446
94Select-139
94StCl-217
94StCl/1stDay-217
94StCl/Gold-217
94Studio-73
94T-143
94T/Gold-143
94TripleP-90
94UD-408
94UD/SP-81
94Ultra-220
Wallaesa, John
47TipTop
Wallenhaupt, Ron
85Water-16
Wallenstein, John
74Wichita-127MG
Waller, Casey Lee
88CapeCod/Sum-113
90ProC/Singl-775
90Reading/Best-19
90Reading/ProC-1229
90Reading/Star-23
91AA/LineD-522
91Reading/LineD-522
91Reading/ProC-1379
92Reading/SB-546
92ScranWB/ProC-2457
92Sky/AASingl-239
93ScranWB/Team-26
Waller, Elliott
(Ty)
78StPete
79ArkTr-9
82F-607
82Iowa-13
82T-51R
84Cram/PCL-60
85Cram/PCL-64
86Tucson-24
87Tucson-6
88River/Cal-233
88River/ProC-1414
88Spokane/ProC-1923
89River/Cal-30CO
90River/Cal-27CO
Waller, Kevin D.
80Cedar-25
82Madis/Frit-22
Waller, Reggie
89AubAs/ProC-2168
Walles, Todd
91Belling/ClBest-8
91Belling/ProC-3676
Wallgren, Chris
90Elizab/Star-23
Wallin, Craig
89SoBend/GS-1
Wallin, Leslie
(Les)
88WinHaven/Star-25
89Lynch/Star-20
90LynchRS/Team-9
91WinHaven/ClBest-21
91WinHaven/ProC-500
92WinHaven/ClBest-21
92WinHaven/ProC-1789
Walling, Denny
77SanJose-17
77T-473R
79T-553
80OPC-161
80T-306
81D-144
81F-66
81T-439
82D-496
82F-236
82T-147
83D-419
83F-469
83T-692
84D-641
84F-244
84Mother/Ast-19
84Nes/792-36
84T-36
84T/St-73
85D-527
85F-365
85Mother/Ast-5
85T-382
86D-136
86F-314
86Pol/Ast-7
86T-504
87D-554
87F-72
87Leaf-159
87Mother/Ast-13
87OPC-222
87Pol/Ast-12
87S/Test-145
87T-222
87T/St-33
88D-384
88D/Best-309
88F-458
88Leaf-224
88Mother/Ast-13
88OPC-131
88Panini/St-296
88Pol/Ast-23
88S-145
88T-719
88T/St-31
89Chatt/II/Team-32
89D-279
89F-465
89S-49
89Smok/Cards-22
89T-196
89UD-327
90D-677
90F-263
90F/Can-263
90OPC-462
90Smok/Card-26
90T-462
90T/TVCard-30
91F-651
91Mother/Rang-18
92B-530
93Rang/Keeb-371
Walling, Kendall
86Cram/NWL-192
87QuadC-25
Wallis, Joe
76OPC-598R
76T-598R
77BurgChef-190
77T-279
78SSPC/270-259
78T-614
79T-406
80T-562
Walls, Doug
94B-442
Walls, R. Lee
53Mother-56
55B-82

57Kahn
57T-52
58T-66
59T-105
60Kahn
60L-111
60T-506
61P-119
61T-78
61T/St-60
62BB-56
62T-129
62T/St-160
63J-113
63P-113
63T-11
64T-411
90Target-828
Wallwork, Dave
86Penin-26TR
87Penin-18
88BirmB/Best-6
89BirmB/Best-25
89BirmB/ProC-96
90BirmB/Best-27
Walraven, Randy
78DaytB
Walsh, Christy
92Mega/Ruth-161M
Walsh, Dave
84Syrac-21
86Knoxvl-25
87Knoxvl-19
89Albuq/CMC-10
89Albuq/ProC-70
90AAAGame/ProC-33
90AAASingl/ProC-66
90Albuq/CMC-11
90Albuq/ProC-345
90Albuq/Trib-30
90ProC/Singl-413
91AAA/LineD-22
91Albuq/LineD-22
91OPC-367
91S-351RP
91T-367
91T/90Debut-162
Walsh, Dennis
91Niagara/ClBest-21
91Niagara/ProC-3633
92Fayette/ClBest-23
92Fayette/ProC-2169
Walsh, Ed
10Domino-121
11Helmar-18
12Sweet/Pin-14
14CJ-36
14Piedmont/St-59
15CJ-36
48Exh/HOF
49Leaf/Prem-8
50Callahan
50W576-76
60F-49
61F-83
63Bz/ATG-7
69Bz/Sm
72F/FFeat-23
76Shakey-49
77Galasso-143
80Laugh/FFeat-34
80Perez/HOF-49
80SSPC/HOF
85Woolwth-35
88Utica/Pucko-25
89HOF/St-77
91Conlon/Sport-273
92Conlon/Sport-337
93Conlon-703
93CrackJack-23
94Conlon-1013
BF2-19
D329-184
D350/2-187
E224
E270/1
E286
E300
E90/1
E90/3
E98
M101/4-184
M101/5-187
M116
S81-107
T201
T202
T205
T206
WG4-29
WG5-42
WG6-38
Walsh, James C.
15CJ-144
C46-20
D327
D328-182
E135-182
Walsh, Jay
83LynnP-28
Walsh, Jim
81QuadC-11
82QuadC-25
83MidldC-4
Walsh, Joseph
N172
Walsh, Rob
89MissSt-36
Walter, Craig
85FtMyr-4
Walter, Gene
83Miami-5
84Beaum-9
85Cram/PCL-112
86D/Rook-47
86F-644R
86F/Up-U124
86T/Tr-121T
87D-511
87F-433
87T-248
87Tidew-27
87Tidew/TCMA-21
88D/Mets/Bk-NEW
88F-153
88Kahn/Mets-31
89T-758
89UD-604
91WIZMets-424
92Syrac/ProC-1967
92Syrac/SB-520
93Edmon/ProC-1137
Walterhouse, Dick
77Salem
79BuffB/TCMA-19
Walters, Alfred
D328-183
E120
E135-183
Walters, Chip
89Nashvl/Team-26COM
Walters, Dan
86Ashvl-28
87Osceola-8
88ColAst/Best-12
89Wichita/Rock-11C
90Wichita/Rock-23
91AAA/LineD-297
91LasVegas/LineD-297
91LasVegas/ProC-240
92D/RookPhen-BC12
92D/Up-U4RR
92F/Up-126
92LasVegas/SB-246
92Pol/Padre-23
92S/RookTr-109T
92Sky/AAASingl-121
92T/Tr-127T
92T/TrGold-127T
93D-48
93F-149
93L-156
93Mother/Padre-19
93OPC/Premier-5
93Pac/Spanish-605
93Panini-257
93Pinn-215
93S-332
93Select-289
93StCl-175
93StCl/1stDay-175
93Studio-81
93T-273
93T/Gold-273
93TripleP-239
93UD-172
93USPlayC/Rook-4H
93Ultra-125
Walters, Darryel
85Beloit-13
86Stockton-25
87ElPaso-21
88Denver/CMC-23
88Denver/ProC-1255
89Denver/CMC-16
89Denver/ProC-54
89ElPaso/GS-29
90AAASingl/ProC-665
90Denver/CMC-6
90Denver/ProC-640
90ProC/Singl-31
Walters, David
86Elmira-25
87Greens-26
88Lynch/Star-24
89EastLDD/ProC-DD24
89NewBrit/ProC-614
89NewBrit/Star-20
90NewBrit/Best-25
90NewBrit/ProC-1320
90NewBrit/Star-20
91AAA/LineD-371
91Pawtu/LineD-371
91Pawtu/ProC-40
92Pawtu/ProC-924
92Pawtu/SB-371
92Sky/AAASingl-170
Walters, Gene
92Syrac/MerchB-25
Walters, Ken
60T-511
61P-122
61T-394
62T-328
63FrBauer-30
63T-534
81TCMA-317
Walters, Kent
88MissSt-32
Walters, Leigh
91Melbourne/Fut-8
Walters, Mike
80ElPaso-22
81SLCity-13
82Spokane-9
82Toledo-8
83Toledo-10
84Nes/792-673
84T-673
85T-187
85Toledo-11
Walters, Scott
90MissSt-44M
Walters, Vic
79AppFx-24
Walters, William H.
(Bucky)
28LaPresse-22
37Exh/4-6
38Exh/4-6
39Exh
39PlayBall-22
40PlayBall-73
41DP-8
41DP-96
41PlayBall-3
41Wheat
43Playball-29
49Eureka-97
54JC-31CO
55Gol/Braves-29
55JC-31CO
82Ohio/HOF-34
89Pac/Leg-164
92Conlon/Sport-537
93Conlon-769
94Conlon-1118
Exh47
R314
V355-61
W711/1
W711/2
Walthour, B. Jr.
33SK*-31
Walthour, B. Sr.
33SK*-7
Walton, Bruce
86Modesto-26
87Modesto-14
88Huntsvl/BK-25
89Tacoma/CMC-8
89Tacoma/ProC-1546
90AAASingl/ProC-138
90ProC/Singl-583
90Tacoma/CMC-6
90Tacoma/ProC-91
91AAA/LineD-546
91S/RookTr-88T
91Tacoma/LineD-546
91Tacoma/ProC-2306
92D/Rook-123
92F/Up-52
92StCl-563
92T/91Debut-179
92Tacoma/ProC-2502
92Ultra-428
Walton, Carlo
91Kissim/ProC-4191
Walton, Danny
69Sunoco/Pin-18
70McDon-73
70OPC-134
70T-134
71K-22
71MLB/St-455
71OPC-281
71T-281
71T/Coins-88
73OPC-516
73T-516
74Tacoma/Caruso-27
78T-263
79Spokane-4
90Target-829
92Yank/WIZ70-160
93Rang/Keeb-372
Walton, Dave
89KS*-36
Walton, Jerome
87Peoria-20
87Peoria/PW-5
88BBAmer-5
88EastLAS/ProC-29
88Peoria/Ko-30
88Pittsfld/ProC-1374
89B-295
89Classic/Up/2-156
89D/Best-172
89D/Rook-26
89F/Up-80
89Mara/Cubs-20
89S/Mast-2
89S/Tr-85
89S/YS/II-36
89T/Tr-123T
89UD/Ext-765
90B-35
90B/Ins-10
90Bz-19
90Classic-34
90CollAB-15
90Cub/Mara-22
90D-285
90D/BestNL-124
90D/Preview-10
90F-44
90F/AwardWin-42
90F/BBMVP-42
90F/Can-44
90F/LL-42
90F/SoarSt-8
90F/WaxBox-C27
90Holsum/Discs-19
90HotRook/St-46
90KMart/SS-7
90Kenner/Fig-88
90KingB/Discs-15
90Leaf-124
90MLBPA/Pins-50
90OPC-464
90Panini/St-230
90PublInt/St-207
90RedFoley/St-100
90S-229
90S/100Ris-2
90Sf-67
90T-464
90T/89Debut-134
90T/Big-267
90T/Coins-35
90T/DH-69
90T/Gloss60-39
90T/HeadsUp-24
90T/JumboR-29
90T/St-327FS
90T/St-50
90T/TVCub-34
90ToysRUs-29
90UD-345
90WonderBrd-8
90Woolwth/HL-6ROY
91B-413
91Classic/200-95
91Classic/II-T29
91Cub/Mara-20
91Cub/Vine-33
91D-72
91F-437
91Leaf-39
91OPC-135
91Panini/FrSt-48
91Panini/St-44
91S-13
91StCl-162
91T-135
91UD-332
91Ultra-70
92B-27
92Cub/Mara-20
92D-528
92F-396
92OPC-543
92Panini-187
92Pinn-224
92S-457
92StCl-421
92T-543
92T/Gold-543
92T/GoldWin-543
92UD-463
92USPlayC/Cub-11H
92USPlayC/Cub-8D
92Ultra-184
93Pac/Spanish-64
93Ultra-526
93Vanco/ProC-2611
Walton, Jim
73OPC-646CO
73T-646CO
74T-99CO
Walton, Reggie
75Lafay
79Spokane-9
80Spokane-21
81F-609
81Spokane-14
82Portl-22
82T-711
Walton, Rob
88CharlK/Pep-6
Wambsganss, Bill
25Exh-72
26Exh-112
27Exh-55
72Laugh/GF-49
76Motor-4
77Galasso-262
81Conlon-51
88Conlon/4-29
90HOF/St-24
91Conlon/Sport-200
94Conlon-1129
D327
D328-184
D329-185
E120
E121/120
E121/80
E122
E135-184
E220
M101/4-185
V117-29
V61-31
W501-22
W575
Wandler, Mike
87Pocatel/Bon-20
Waner, Lloyd L.
28Yueng-59
29Exh/4-14
31Exh/4-14
33Exh/4-7
33G-164
34DS-16
34Exh/4-7
35BU-157
35BU-17
35G-1E

35G-3C
35G-4C
35G-5C
39PlayBall-89
40PlayBall-105
41DP-119
60F-78
61F-84
72F/FFeat-35
75Sheraton-25
76Rowe-15M
76Shakey-107
77Galasso-86
80Pac/Leg-24
80Perez/HOF-107
80SSPC/HOF
81Conlon-62
83D/HOF-22M
85Woolwth-36
86Conlon/1-58
89HOF/St-42
89Pac/Leg-128
89Smok/Dodg-32
90Perez/GreatMom-15M
90Target-830
91Conlon/Sport-265
91Conlon/Sport-6
92Conlon/Col-17
92Conlon/Sport-429
92Conlon/Sport-562
94Conlon-1006
94Conlon-1180M
PR1-27
R300
R306
R310
R312/M
R314
R316
R328-13
R332-16M
R332-2
R423-110
V353-90
W502-59
W513-73
WG8-49

Waner, Paul P.
28Exh-27
28Yueng-45
29Exh/4-14
31Exh/4-14
32Orbit/un-58
33CJ/Pin-24
33Exh/4-7
33G-25
34DS-83
34Exh/4-7
34G-11
35Exh/4-7
35G-1E
35G-3C
35G-4C
35G-5C
36Exh/4-7
36G
37Exh/4-7
38Exh/4-7
38Wheat
39PlayBall-112
40PlayBall-104
41DP-16
50Callahan
50W576-77
60F-76
61F-85
72F/FFeat-24
75Shakey-2
75Sheraton-9
76Rowe-15M
76Shakey-62
77Galasso-209
77Galasso-49
80Pac/Leg-21
80Perez/HOF-62
80SSPC/HOF
81Conlon-61
83D/HOF-22M
86Conlon/1-8
86Sf/Dec-15M
88Conlon/NatAS-23
89HOF/St-45
89Pac/Leg-127
90Perez/GreatMom-15
90Target-831
91Conlon/Sport-167
91Conlon/Sport-315
91Conlon/Sport-5
92Conlon/Sport-563
92Yank/WIZHOF-34
93Conlon-672
94Conlon-1099
94Conlon-1180
R300
R305
R306
R308-201
R310
R312/M
R314
R315-A38
R315-B38
R316
R326-10A
R326-10B
R328-2
R332-16M
R337-421
R342-10
R423-111
V353-25
V354-67
V355-2
V94-50
W502-45
W513-70
W517-34
WG8-50

Wanish, John
88Bakers/Cal-261
89StCath/ProC-2086
90Myrtle/ProC-2778
91Dunedin/ClBest-11
91Dunedin/ProC-207

Wanke, Chuck
90Bend/Legoe-19
91Everett/ClBest-25
91Everett/ProC-3914
92Clinton/ClBest-16
92Clinton/ProC-3599

Wanz, Doug
81Vanco-3

Wapnick, Steve
88Myrtle/ProC-1166
89Dunedin/Star-22
90AAASingl/ProC-352
90B-346
90ProC/Singl-663
90Syrac/CMC-27
90Syrac/MerchB-27
90Syrac/ProC-572
90Syrac/Team-27
91AAA/LineD-520
91Syrac/LineD-520
91Syrac/MerchB-26
91Syrac/ProC-2481
91T/90Debut-163
92D-743
92S-863
92StCl-554
92Vanco/ProC-2724
92Vanco/SB-627

Warburton, John
89MissSt-37
90MissSt-40
91MissSt-48

Ward, Aaron
21Exh-183
25Exh-104
93Conlon-747
E120
E121/120
E121/80
E126-7
E220
V100
W501-25
W515-20
W572

Ward, Anthony
88StCath/ProC-2034
89Myrtle/ProC-1630
90Dunedin/Star-23
90FSLAS/Star-47
90Star/ISingl-69
91AA/LineD-370
91Knoxvl/LineD-370
91Knoxvl/ProC-1766
92Syrac/MerchB-26
92Syrac/ProC-1968
92Syrac/SB-521

Ward, Chris
73Wichita-18
75OPC-587
75T-587
75T/M-587

Ward, Chuck
90Target-832

Ward, Colby
85Anchora-31
86Cram/NWL-89
87PalmSp-14
88MidldA/GS-11
89Edmon/CMC-10
89Edmon/ProC-568
90AAASingl/ProC-218
90ColoSp/CMC-2
90ColoSp/ProC-37
90ProC/Singl-454
91D-330
91F-382
91OPC-31
91T-31
91T/90Debut-164

Ward, Colin
83BirmB-19
84Cram/PCL-21
85Cram/PCL-198
86F-645R
86Shrev-27
87Phoenix-9

Ward, Dan
88PalmSp/Cal-95
88PalmSp/ProC-1442

Ward, David
87SLCity/Taco-12

Ward, Duane
83Durham-25
85Greenvl/Team-24
86F/Up-U125
86Pol/Atl-48
87D-45RR
87Leaf-45RR
87OPC-153
87T-153
87Tor/Fire-33
88D-567
88F-125
88OPC-128
88T-696
88Tor/Fire-31
89D-543
89D/Best-216
89F-246
89OPC-392
89S-359
89S/YS/II-13
89T-502
89Tor/Fire-31
89UD-551
90D-307
90F-95
90F/Can-95
90Leaf-501
90OPC-28
90Publint/St-528
90S-439
90Sf-107
90T-28
90Tor/BJ-31
90UD-653
91D-92
91F-187
91Leaf-154
91OPC-181
91S-561
91S/ToroBJ-8
91StCl-363
91T-181
91Tor/Fire-31
91UD-581
91Ultra-369
92BJ/Fire-30
92D-308
92F-344
92L-101
92L/BlkGold-101
92OPC-365
92Pinn-385
92S-48
92StCl-781
92T-365
92T/Gold-365
92T/GoldWin-365
92UD-450
92Ultra-154
93B-307
93BJ/D/45-23
93BJ/Demp-11
93BJ/Fire-32
93D-379
93F-341
93Flair-296
93L-135
93OPC-310
93OPC/WC-15
93Pac/Spanish-330
93Pinn-340
93S-436
93Select-258
93StCl-382
93StCl/1stDay-382
93T-260
93T/Finest-17
93T/FinestRef-17
93T/Gold-260
93UD-339
93UD/SP-53
93Ultra-295
94B-225
94D-379
94D/Special-379
94F-346
94F/AS-25
94Finest-375
94L-355
94OPC-160
94Pinn-143
94Pinn/Artist-143
94Pinn/Museum-143
94S-481
94Sf/2000-58
94StCl-377
94StCl/1stDay-377
94StCl/Gold-377
94StCl/Team-155
94T-483
94T/Gold-483
94TripleP-39
94UD-402
94UD/CollC-287
94UD/CollC/Gold-287
94UD/CollC/Silv-287
94Ultra-145
94Ultra/Fire-2

Ward, Gary
77Tacoma
79Toledo-1
80T-669R
81D-594
81T-328R
82D-571
82F-562
82F/St-229
82T-612
83D-429
83D/AAS-18
83F-627
83F/St-16M
83F/St-22M
83OPC/St-92
83T-517
83T/St-92
83Twin/Team-21
83Twin/Team-33M
84D-192
84F-576
84F/X-U124
84Nes/792-67
84OPC-67
84Rang-32
84T-67
84T/St-303
84T/Tr-126T
85D-342
85F-572
85FunFood/Pin-95
85Leaf-70
85OPC-84
85Rang-32
85T-414
85T/St-353
86D-20DK
86D-98
86D/AAS-51
86D/DKsuper-20
86F-575
86F/Mini-113
86F/St-125
86Leaf-20DK
86OPC-105
86Rang-32
86Sf-197
86T-105
86T/St-239
86T/Tatt-21M
87D-427
87D/OD-242
87F-140
87F/Lim-41
87F/RecSet-40
87F/Up-U122
87Leaf-177
87OPC-218
87Sf-91
87T-762
87T/St-235
87T/Tr-125T
88D-251
88D/Y/Bk-251
88F-224
88OPC-235
88Panini/St-160
88RedFoley/St-95
88S-157
88Sf-125
88T-235
88T/Big-195
88T/St-303
89F-273
89F/Up-33
89Mara/Tigers-32
89OPC-302
89S-435
89T-302
89T/Big-206
89T/Tr-124T
89UD-98
90CokeK/Tiger-25
90D-621
90F-618
90F/Can-618
90Leaf-113
90OPC-679
90Panini/St-68
90S-513
90T-679
91D-728
91F-356
91OKSt-29CO
91OPC-556
91Panini/FrSt-294
91S-637
91T-556
91UD-412
92OKSt-29CO
92Yank/WIZ80-196
93Rang/Keeb-373

Ward, Greg
87Savan-8
88Reno/Cal-286

Ward, John F.
(Jay)
61Union
64T-116R
65T-421R
85Cedar-27
86Vermont-23MG
88CLAS/Star-1
89Wmsprt/Star-24

Ward, John Mont.
(Montgomery)
76Shakey-101
80Perez/HOF-101
80SSPC/HOF
89Smok/Dodg-33
90Target-833
E223
N167-10
N172
N28
N284
N300/unif
N338/2
N566-586
N566-587
WG1-45

Ward, Joseph
C46-6
T201

Ward, Kevin
86Phill/TastyK-x
86Reading-25
87Maine/TCMA-22
87Reading-12
88Maine/CMC-22
88Maine/ProC-278
89Huntsvl/Best-22
90AAASingl/ProC-156
90ProC/Singl-602
90Tacoma/CMC-25
90Tacoma/ProC-109
91AAA/LineD-298
91AAAGame/ProC-21
91LasVegas/LineD-298
91LasVegas/ProC-252
92F-623
92L-338
92L/BlkGold-338
92Mother/Padre-19
92Padre/Carl-23
92Pol/Padre-24
92S-862
92S/100RisSt-42
92Smok/Padre-36
92StCl-853
92T/91Debut-180
Ward, Max
87FtLaud-12
88Colum/ProC-326
Ward, Pete
63T-324R
64T-85
64T/Coins-21
64T/S-33
64T/SU
64T/St-8
64T/tatt
65Bz-8
65OPC-215
65OldLond-37
65T-215
65T/E-64
65T/trans-71
66OPC-25
66T-25
66T/RO-2
66T/RO-96
67CokeCap/WSox-4
67OPC-143M
67T-143M
67T-436
68OPC-33
68T-33
68T/ActionSt-15A
68T/ActionSt-2A
69Kelly/Pin-18
69MB-285
69MLB/St-35
69MLBPA/Pin-29
69OPC-155
69T-155
69T/S-11
69T/St-159
69T/decal
69Trans-20
70MLB/St-251
70T-659
71MLB/St-501
71OPC-667
71T-667
72MB-354
78TCMA-120
80Iowa/Pol-13
81Portl-1
91Crown/Orio-473
92Yank/WIZ70-161
Exh47
WG10-47
WG9-48
Ward, Preston
50B-231
53T-173
54B-139
54T-72
55B-27
55T-95
55T/DH-97
56T-328
57T-226
58T-450
59T-176
79TCMA-111
90Target-834
91T/Arc53-173
94T/Arc54-72
Ward, Ricky
90Everett/Best-20
90Everett/ProC-3136
91Clinton/ClBest-24
91Clinton/ProC-844
92SanJose/ClBest-17
Ward, Rube
90Target-1093
Ward, Todd
89GA-35
90GA-32
90GA-33M
Ward, Turner
88Colum/CMC-19
88Colum/Pol-17
90AAASingl/ProC-233
90ColoSp/CMC-20
90ColoSp/ProC-52
90ProC/Singl-472
91B-76
91D-429RR
91F-383
91Indian/McDon-28
91Leaf-449
91Leaf/Stud-138
91OPC-555
91S-732RP
91S/Rook40-4
91StCl-593
91T-555
91T/90Debut-165
91UD/Ext-762
91Ultra-118
92BJ/Fire-31
92StCl-621
92Syrac/MerchB-27
92Syrac/ProC-1985
93BJ/D/45-31
93BJ/Demp-9
93BJ/Fire-33
93D-293
93L-427
93Pac/Spanish-658
93S-473
94F-347
94Flair-71
94Pol/Brew-29
94Studio-49
94Ultra-381
Warden, Jon
69T-632
88Domino-24
Wardle, Curt
83Visalia/Frit-18
85F/Up-U127
85Twin/Team-26
86F-600
86Maine-21
86T-303
Wardlow, Jeff
88Butte-17
Wardlow, Joe
89Gaston/ProC-998
89Gaston/Star-24
89Star/Wax-39
90Foil/Best-208
90Gaston/Best-10
90Gaston/ProC-2531
90Gaston/Star-24
91PrWill/ClBest-20
91PrWill/ProC-1437
Wardlow, Mike
77Cedar
Wardwell, Shea
90Elmira/Pucko-8
91ClBest/Singl-295
91WinHaven/ClBest-25
91WinHaven/ProC-504
Ware, Derek
87Dunedin-28
Ware, Jeff
91Classic/DP-31
91T/Tr-124T
92Dunedin/ClBest-2
92Dunedin/ProC-2001
92OPC-414
92Pinn-546
92StCl/Dome-192
92T-414
92T/Gold-414
92T/GoldWin-414
92UD/ML-323
93ClBest/MLG-88
Wareham, Ronnie
85Clovis-42
Wares, Clyde E.
(Buzzy)
86Conlon/1-14M
W754
Warfel, Brian
87Elmira/Black-9
87Elmira/Cain-8
87Elmira/Red-9
88Elmira-26
88WinHaven/Star-26
Warhop, John
10Domino-122
11Helmar-49
12Sweet/Pin-38
94Conlon-1275
T206
T207
T213/blue
T215/blue
T215/brown
Waring, Jim
91AubAS/ClBest-22
91AubAS/ProC-4274
92BurlAs/ProC-548
92MidwLAS/Team-47
93ClBest/MLG-156
93FExcel/ML-50
Warneke, Lon
32Orbit/num-4
32Orbit/un-59
33CJ/Pin-25
33DL-16
33G-203
34Exh/4-3
35BU-186
35Exh/4-3
36Exh/4-3
36Wheat
37Exh/4-8
38Exh/4-8
38Wheat
39Exh
39PlayBall-41
40PlayBall-114
55B-299UMP
77Galasso-222
88Conlon/NatAS-24
91Conlon/Sport-231
92Conlon/Sport-371
92Conlon/Sport-640
93Conlon-687
94Conlon-1106
R300
R303/A
R305
R308-194
R312/M
R314
V351B-46
V355-100
W754
WG8-51
Warner, E.H.
N172
Warner, Fred
80Penin/B-5
80Penin/C-8
Warner, Harry
77T-113C
78BJ/PostC-23CO
80Syrac-19MG
80Syrac/Team-21MG
83Visalia/Frit-13
92Brew/Carlson-NNO
Warner, Jack D.
65T-354R
Warner, Jim
47Signal
47Sunbeam
Warner, John J.
(Jackie)
65T-517R
66T-553R
Warner, John Joseph
26Exh-96
E107
Warner, John R.
(Jack)
33G-178
90Target-835
92Conlon/Sport-410
Warner, Michael
92FrRow/DP-71
92Idaho/ProC-3529
93Durham/Team-23
Warner, Randy
92GulfCM/ProC-3495
Warner, Ron
91Hamil/ClBest-21
91Hamil/ProC-4048
92Savan/ClBest-6
92Savan/ProC-673
Warrecker, William
89BendB/Legoe-11
90PalmSp/Cal-224
90PalmSp/ProC-2579
Warren, Alan
88Oneonta/ProC-2066
Warren, Brian
90Bristol/ProC-3167
91Fayette/ClBest-29
91Fayette/ProC-1171
92ClBest-170
92ClBest-174
92London/ProC-633
92London/SB-422
92ProC/Tomorrow-67
92Sky/AASingl-177
Warren, Charlie
77Wausau
Warren, DeShawn
92Classic/DP-31
93StCl/Angel-25
93StCl/MurphyS-181
93T-574
93T/Gold-574
94B-207
Warren, Derrick
92Belling/ClBest-3
92Belling/ProC-1460
Warren, Glen
89Everett/Star-29
Warren, Joe
89BendB/Legoe-12
91Reno/Cal-10
Warren, Mark
84Idaho/Team-29
Warren, Marty
86AppFx-28
Warren, Mel
91Kissim/ProC-4204
Warren, Mike
84D-631
84F-461
84F-639IA
84Mother/A's-20
84Nes/792-338
84Nes/792-5HL
84T-338
84T-5HL
84T/St-288B
85D-278
85F-435
85Mother/A's-19
85T-197
86Omaha/ProC-28
89Reno/Cal-248
Warren, Randy
88Utica/Pucko-12
89SoBend/GS-17
Warren, Raymond
82BurlR/Frit-7
82BurlR/TCMA-12
Warren, Ron
86Elmira-26
Warren, Tommy
90Target-836
Warren, Travis
87Clearw-27
Warstler, Harold
(Rabbit)
39PlayBall-120
40PlayBall-59
41G-21
91Conlon/Sport-240
R314
Warthen, Dan
72Dimanche*-50
76Expo/Redp-35
76OPC-374
76SSPC-347
76T-374
77OPC-99
77T-391
79Portl-17
80Port-26
81Buffa-12
82AlexD-20
87Chatt/Best-2
88Calgary/CMC-25
88Calgary/ProC-789
89Calgary/CMC-25
89Calgary/ProC-523
90AAASingl/ProC-130CO
90Calgary/CMC-24CO
90Calgary/ProC-665CO
90ProC/Singl-451CO
92Mother/Mar-27CO
Warwick, Carl
62J-161
62P-161
62P/Can-161
62Salada-160
62Shirriff-160
62T-202
63J-190
63P-190
63Pep
63T-333
64T-179
65T-357
66T-247
90Target-837
91Crown/Orio-474
WG9-49
Warwick, Clinton
86Geneva-11
Wasdell, James
41DP-19
90Target-838
93Conlon-714
Wasdin, John
94B-660
94ClBest/Gold-128
94ClBest/GoldLP-17
94Pinn-430
94S-571
94SigRook-27
94T-749DP
94T/Gold-749DP
Wasem, Jim
84Everett/Cram-24
85Fresno/Pol-7
86CharRain-28A
86CharRain-28B
88Charl/ProC-1195
Washburn, Greg
70OPC-74R
70T-74R
Washburn, Ray
62T-19
63J-168
63P-168
63T-206
64T-332
65T-467
66T-399
67OPC-92
67T-92
68T-388
69T-415
70OPC-22
70T-22
81TCMA-404
Washington, Claudell
75Greyhound-3
75OPC-647
75T-647
75T/M-647
76K-2
76OPC-189
76OPC-198LL
76SSPC-489
76T-189
76T-198LL
77BurgChef-115
77Ho-86
77Ho/Twink-86
77OPC-178
77T-405
77T/CS-50
77T/ClothSt-50
78BK/R-19
78SSPC/270-88
78T-67
79OPC-298
79T-574

80K-34
80OPC-171
80T-322
81F-329
81Pol/Atl-18
81T-151
81T/Tr-854
82BK/Lids-25
82D-58
82F-449
82F/St-66
82OPC-32
82Pol/Atl-15
82T-126TL
82T-758
82T/St-22
83D-249
83F-150
83F/St-13M
83F/St-22M
83OPC-235
83OPC/St-216
83Pol/Atl-15
83T-235
83T/St-216
84D-310
84F-192
84Nes/792-410
84OPC-42
84Pol/Atl-15
84T-294
84T-410
84T/St-32
85D-11
85D-310
85D/DKsuper-11
85F-342
85Ho/Braves-22
85Leaf-11DK
85OPC-166
85Pol/Atl-15
85T-540
85T/St-25
86D-287
86F-531
86F/Mini-107
86Leaf-164
86OPC-303
86Pol/Atl-15
86T-675
86T/St-39
86T/Tatt-17M
86T/Tr-122T
87F-119
87Mother/A's-15
87T-15
88D-340
88D/Best-217
88D/Y/Bk-340
88F-225
88OPC-335
88S-579
88T-335
88T/Big-178
88T/St-301
89B-52
89D-72
89D/Best-227
89D/Tr-46
89F-272
89F/Up-17
89OPC-185
89S-211
89S/Tr-10T
89Sf-75
89T-185
89T/DHTest-17
89T/Tr-125T
89T/UK-81
89UD-310
89UD/Ext-794
90B-297
90D-52
90F-146
90F/Can-146
90OPC-705
90Panini/St-30
90PubInt/St-380
90S-298
90S/NWest-8
90S/Tr-45T
90Smok/Angel-17
90T-705
90T/Big-12
90UD-395
91WIZMets-425
92Yank/WIZ80-197
93Rang/Keeb-374

Washington, Glenn
86QuadC-31
87PalmSp-15
88PalmSp/Cal-111
88PalmSp/ProC-1455

Washington, Herb
75OPC-407
75T-407
75T/M-407

Washington, Keith
80Penin/B-9
80Penin/C-18
82Reading-19
83Reading-21

Washington, Kraig
89CharWh/Best-4
89CharWh/ProC-1752
90Peoria/Team-7

Washington, Kyle
90Pittsfld/Pucko-2
91Collnd/ClBest-4
91Collnd/ProC-1503
91SALAS/ProC-SAL19
92Canton/ProC-705
92Canton/SB-122
92ClBest-41
92ProC/Tomorrow-58
92Sky/AASingl-58
93FExcel/ML-169

Washington, LaRue
77Tucson
78Cr/PCL-18
80T-233
93Rang/Keeb-375

Washington, Lozando
76Cedar

Washington, Mal
75QuadC
76Clinton

Washington, Randy
81Batavia-24
82Watlo/B-26
82Watlo/Frit-26
83Watlo/Frit-1
84BuffB-20
85Water-3
86Maine-22
87BuffB-12
88ColoSp/CMC-22
88ColoSp/ProC-1525

Washington, Ron
78Cr/PCL-16
79Tidew-9
80Toledo-6
81Toledo-18
82T/Tr-124T
83D-431
83F-626
83OPC-27
83T-458
83Twin/Team-24
84D-391
84F-577
84Nes/792-623
84OPC-268
84T-623
85D-391
85F-292
85T-329
85Twin/Team-28
86D-560
86F-409
86T-513
86Toledo-23
87RochR-19
87RochR/TCMA-16
87T-169
88Gator-15
88T/Tr-125T
89D-468
89F-416
89Pac/SenLg-178
89T/SenLg-44
89TM/SenLg-110
89Tucson/CMC-19
89Tucson/JP-27
89Tucson/ProC-190
89UD-519
90AAASingl/ProC-688
90EliteSenLg-31
90OkCty/CMC-15
90OkCty/ProC-442
90ProC/Singl-165
90Target-839
91AAA/LineD-575M
91Crown/Orio-475
91Pac/SenLg-47
91Pac/SenLg-48
91Tidew/LineD-575CO
91Tidew/ProC-2528CO
92Tidew/ProC-CO
92Tidew/SB-575CO

Washington, Tyrone
90Butte/SportP-25
91Gaston/ClBest-10
91Gaston/ProC-2687
92Miracle/ClBest-16

Washington, U.L.
75Omaha/Team-17
78SSPC/270-236
78T-707R
79T-157
80T-508
81Coke
81D-460
81F-34
81OPC-26
81Pol/Royals-8
81T-26
82D-160
82F-424
82F/St-203
82OPC-329
82T-329
83D-490
83F-125
83F/St-15M
83F/St-3M
83OPC-67
83Pol/Royals-7
83T-687
84D-543
84F-361
84Nes/792-294
84OPC-294
84T/St-282
85D-521
85Expo/PostC-22
85F-215
85F/Up-U128
85OPC/Post-4
85T-431
85T/Tr-128T
86D-498
86F-264
86OPC-113
86T-113
87Vanco-25
89Pac/SenLg-205
89T/SenLg-120
89TM/SenLg-111
89Welland/Pucko-30
90EliteSenLg-62
91Pac/SenLg-102
92Memphis/ProC-2437CO
92Memphis/SB-450CO

Washko, Patrick
77Watlo

Wasiak, Stan
74Albuq/Team-23MG
77LodiD
78LodiD
79LodiD-14MG
81VeroB-27MG
83VeroB-28MG
85VeroB-26MG
86VeroB-27MG

Wasilewski, Kevin
86AubAs-25
87Ashvl-12

Wasilewski, Tom
86Ventura-26
87Shrev-21

Wasinger, Mark
84Beaum-17
85Beaum-19
86LasVegas-22
87LasVegas-27
88F-100
88Mother/Giants-23
88Phoenix/CMC-17
88Phoenix/ProC-54
88RedFoley/St-96
88S-283
89Colum/CMC-22
89Colum/Pol-21
89Colum/ProC-738
90AAASingl/ProC-337
90ColClip/CMC-22
90ColClip/ProC-687
90Colum/Pol-25
90ProC/Singl-222
91AAA/LineD-173
91Edmon/LineD-173
91Edmon/ProC-1525
92Edmon/ProC-3549
92Edmon/SB-171

Waslewski, Gary
68CokeCap/RedSox-2
69T-438
70T-607
71MLB/St-502
71OPC-277
71T-277
72OPC-108
72T-108
92Yank/WIZ70-162

Wasley, Mel
40Hughes-18
47Sunbeam

Wassenaar, Robert
87Salem/ProC-2416
88QuadC/GS-25
89Visalia/Cal-98
89Visalia/ProC-1425
90OrlanSR/Best-18
90OrlanSR/ProC-1084
90OrlanSR/Star-22
91AA/LineD-497
91OrlanSR/LineD-497
91OrlanSR/ProC-1850
92Portl/SB-422
92Portland/ProC-2668

Waszgis, B.J.
92Kane/ClBest-1
92Kane/ProC-95
92Kane/Team-29
92MidwLAS/Team-48

Watanabe, Curt
80BurlB-26

Watanabe, Masahito
87Miami-12

Waterfield, Bob
52Wheat*

Waters, Jack
60Maple-22

Wathan, John
(Duke)
75Omaha/Team-18
77T-218
78SSPC/270-233
78T-343
79T-99
80T-547
81Coke
81D-221
81F-46
81OPC-157
81T-157
82D-86
82F-425
82OPC-383
82T-429
82T/St-192
83D-86
83F-126
83OPC-289
83OPC/St-195RB
83OPC/St-196RB
83OPC/St-78
83Pol/Royals-8
83T-6M
83T-746
83T/St-195
83T/St-196
83T/St-78
84D-466
84F-362
84Nes/792-602
84OPC-72
84T-602
84T/St-284
85D-466
85F-216
85T-308
86D-496
86F-23
86Kitty/Disc-12
86T-128
87Omaha-3
88Smok/Royals-1MG
88T-534
89T-374MG
90OPC-789MG
90T-789MG
91OPC-291
91Pol/Royal-24
91T-291
93Mother/Angel-28M

Watkins, Bob C.
70OPC-227R
70T-227R
71MLB/St-93

Watkins, Bud
58Union

Watkins, Darren
87AppFx-12
90BBCity/Star-25
91AA/LineD-423
91Durham/ProC-DUR8
91DurhamUp/ProC-8
91London/LineD-423
91Memphis/ProC-668

Watkins, Dave
70OPC-168
70T-168

Watkins, George
34G-53
35Exh/4-6
90Target-840
91Conlon/Sport-222

Watkins, Jim
81Bristol-22

Watkins, Keith
88Modesto/Cal-71

Watkins, Pat
94FExcel-182
94T-743DP
94T/Gold-743DP

Watkins, Scott
91OKSt-30
92Kenosha/ProC-605
92OKSt-30

Watkins, Tim
87Beloit-21
88Denver/CMC-6
88Denver/ProC-1265
89Denver/CMC-2
89Denver/ProC-41
89ElPaso/GS-15
90AAASingl/ProC-652
90Denver/CMC-3
90Denver/ProC-627
90ProC/Singl-28
91AA/LineD-146
91CharlK/LineD-146
91CharlK/ProC-1690

Watkins, Troy
86FtMyr-27

Watkins, William H.
N172

Watlington, Julius
52Park-83

Watson, Allen
91ClBest/Singl-427
91Classic/DP-17
91FrRow/DP-44
91Hamil/ClBest-7
91Hamil/ProC-4040
92B-634
92ClBest-282
92OPC-654
92Pinn-304DP
92ProC/Tomorrow-330
92S-799
92StCl/Dome-193
92StPete/ClBest-1
92T-654
92T/Gold-654
92T/GoldWin-654
92UD/ML-153
92UD/ML-67DS
93B-24
93B-358FOIL
93Flair/Wave-17
93L/UpGRook-1
93Select/RookTr-90T
93StCl/Card-19
93UD/SP-288FOIL
93Ultra-467
94B-480
94D-289

94F-648
94Finest-331
94L-163
94OPC-15
94OPC/DiamD-16
94Pac/Cr-606
94Pinn-145
94Pinn/Artist-145
94Pinn/Museum-145
94Pinn/New-8
94S-613
94Sf/2000-26
94StCl/Team-322
94T-196
94T/Gold-196
94TripleP-68
94UD-235
94UD/CollC-288
94UD/CollC/Gold-288
94UD/CollC/Silv-288
94UD/ElecD-235
94Ultra-570
Watson, Andy
90Butte/SportP-27
91Butte/SportP-5
Watson, Bob
69T-562
70OPC-407
70T-407
71MLB/St-94
71OPC-222
71T-222
72OPC-355
72T-355
72T/Cloth-32
73OPC-110
73T-110
74K-11
74OPC-370
74T-370
74T/DE-69
74T/St-39
75Ho-53
75K-6
75OPC-227
75T-227
75T/M-227
76Crane-66
76Ho-5
76Ho/Twink-5
76K-27
76MSA/Disc
76OPC-20
76SSPC-60
76T-20
77BurgChef-6
77Ho-39
77Ho/Twink-39
77T-540
77T/CS-51
77T/ClothSt-51
78BK/Ast-12
78Ho-28
78OPC-107
78T-330
78Tastee/Discs-18
78Wiffle/Discs-77
79OPC-60
79T-130
80OPC-250
80T-480
81D-225
81Drake-28
81F-93
81OPC-208
81T-690
81T/HT
82BK/Lids-26
82D-108
82F-54
82OPC-275
82Pol/Atl-8
82T-275
82T/Tr-125T
83D-551
83F-151
83F/St-10M
83F/St-11M
83Pol/Atl-8
83T-572
84F-193
84Nes/792-739
84Pol/Atl-8
84T-739
85OPC-51
85T-51
86Mother/Ast-13
92Yank/WIZ80-198
94TedW-37
Watson, D.J.
87AppFx-5
Watson, Dave
89Princet/Star-23
91Salem/ClBest-22
91Salem/ProC-952
92Salem/ClBest-23
92Salem/ProC-64
Watson, Dejon
86FtMyr-28
88BBCity/Star-25
Watson, Frankie
88Eugene/Best-28
Watson, John Reeves
E120
W573
Watson, John
V89-8
Watson, Marty
94B-351
Watson, Matt
89Alaska/Team-5
90StCath/ProC-3460
Watson, Milton
W514-77
Watson, Phil
77Ashvl
Watson, Philip Harvey
45Parade*-52
Watson, Preston
89BurlB/ProC-1604
89BurlB/Star-22
90Greenvl/ProC-1129
90Greenvl/Star-21
91AA/LineD-221
91Greenvl/ClBest-8
91Greenvl/LineD-221
91Greenvl/ProC-3002
92Greenvl/ProC-1155
92Greenvl/SB-248
Watson, Ron
91Boise/ClBest-22
91Boise/ProC-3880
92QuadC/ClBest-13
92QuadC/ProC-810
93B-581
Watson, Shaun
91Kingspt/ClBest-18
91Kingspt/ProC-3814
92Pittsfld/ClBest-12
92Pittsfld/ProC-3297
Watson, Steve
76Cedar
83Tampa-25
Watson, Todd
90CharWh/Best-19
90CharWh/ProC-2249
90Foil/Best-94
Watt, Eddie
66T-442R
67T-271
68OPC-186
68T-186
69T-652
70OPC-497
70T-497
71OPC-122
71T-122
72MB-355
72OPC-128
72T-128
73JP
73OPC-362
73T-362
74OPC-534
74T-534
74T/Tr-534T
75OPC-374
75T-374
75T/M-374
86Tucson-25CO
87Tucson-22
88Tucson/CMC-25
88Tucson/JP-23
88Tucson/ProC-184
89Tucson/ProC-204
90BurlB/Best-12CO
90BurlB/ProC-2367CO
90BurlB/Star-29CO
91Crown/Orio-476
Watters, Mike
86Albuq-27
87Calgary-2
88Calgary/CMC-23
88Calgary/ProC-798
Watts, Andy
86Negro/Frit-17
Watts, Bob
87Dunedin-3
88Dunedin/Star-20
89Beloit/I/Star-25
Watts, Brandon
91Kissim/ProC-4187
92GreatF/SportP-24
Watts, Brian
77Spartan
Watts, Burgess
90GreatF/SportP-11
91Yakima/ClBest-14
91Yakima/ProC-4258
92Yakima/ClBest-5
92Yakima/ProC-3450
Watts, Craig
92GreatF/SportP-13
Watts, Harry
63Pep/Tul
Watts, Len
86Reading-26
87Maine-3
87Maine/TCMA-20
87Phill/TastyK-49
Watwood, Johnny
93Conlon-963
Watychowics, Stanley
52Laval-64
Waugh, James
53T-178
91T/Arc53-178
Wauner
E254
Wawruck, Jim
92Freder/ClBest-10
92Freder/ProC-1821
92UD/ML-322
Way, Ron
89Welland/Pucko-28
90Augusta/ProC-2465
91Salem/ClBest-23
91Salem/ProC-953
Wayne, Gary
86WPalmB-27
87Jaxvl-22
88Indianap/ProC-508
89D/Rook-27
89S/Tr-91
90D-318
90F-387
90F/Can-387
90OPC-348
90PubInt/St-340
90S-527
90S/100Ris-15
90S/YS/II-26
90T-348
90T/89Debut-135
90UD-372
91AAAGame/ProC-37
91D-757
91F-626
91OPC-207
91S-283
91StCl-491
91T-207
92L-424
92L/BlkGold-424
92StCl-261
92Ultra-401
93F-645
93F/Final-46
93Pac/Spanish-179
93StCl-10
93StCl/1stDay-10
93T/Tr-16T
93USPlayC/Rockie-10D
93USPlayC/Rockie-3S
94D-323
94F-456
Waznik, Allan J.
87Idaho-13
88Sumter/ProC-407
89BurlB/ProC-1612
89BurlB/Star-23
Wearing, Melvin Jr.
89Erie/Star-25
90Foil/Best-293
90Wausau/Best-23
90Wausau/ProC-2137
90Wausau/Star-24
91CLAS/ProC-CAR9
91ClBest/Singl-383
91Freder/ClBest-20
91Freder/ProC-2374
92Hagers/ProC-2566
92Hagers/SB-270
92Sky/AASingl-114
93FExcel/ML-128
Weatherford, Brant
86Tampa-25
Weatherford, Joel
83Beloit/Frit-29
Weatherly, Roy
(Stormy)
39PlayBall-152
40PlayBall-49
41PlayBall-17
44Yank/St-28
93Conlon-942
Weathers, David
88StCath/ProC-2023
89Myrtle/ProC-1475
90Dunedin/Star-24
90EliteSenLg-91
91AA/LineD-371
91Knoxvl/LineD-371
91Knoxvl/ProC-1767
91S/ToroBJ-35
91Swell/Great-95
92D-418RR
92ProC/Tomorrow-167
92Sky/AAASingl-233
92Syrac/MerchB-28
92Syrac/ProC-1969
92Syrac/SB-522
92T/91Debut-181
93BJ/D/45-43
93D-731
93Edmon/ProC-1138
93F-430
93StCl/Marlin-26
93T-739
93T/Gold-739
94F-479
94Finest-355
94Flair-167
94Pac/Cr-252
94StCl/Team-89
94T-781M
94T/Gold-781M
94UD-447
94Ultra-498
Weathers, Steven M.
75Tucson-2
75Tucson/Caruso-6
75Tucson/Team-20
76Tucson-2
77SanJose-12
Weathersby, Earl
(Tex)
28Exh/PCL-30
Weaver, D. Floyd
65T-546R
66T-231
71OPC-227
71T-227
73Wichita-19
78TCMA-176
Weaver, Earl
69T-516MG
70OPC-148MG
70T-148MG
71OPC-477MG
71T-477MG
72OPC-323MG
72Pol/Orio-10MG
72T-323MG
73JP
73OPC-136MG
73T-136MG
74OPC-306MG
74T-306MG
75OPC-117MG
75T-117MG
75T/M-117MG
76T-73MG
77T-546MG
78T-211MG
79T-689MG
80T-404MG
81D-356MG
81F-178MG
81T-661MG
82D-27MG
83T-426MG
85T/Tr-129T
86T-321MG
87T-568MG
89Pac/Leg-179
89Pac/SenLg-219M
89Pac/SenLg-56MG
89Swell-98
89T/SenLg-76MG
89TM/SenLg-112MG
89TM/SenLg-120MG
90Pac/Legend-108MG
91LineD-12MG
92MCI-1MG
93Orio/SUII-4MG
93TWill-147MG
93TWill-85MG
Weaver, George
(Buck)
73F/Wild-11
81Conlon-40
87Conlon/2-28
88Pac/8Men-107
88Pac/8Men-12
88Pac/8Men-33
88Pac/8Men-34
88Pac/8Men-40
88Pac/8Men-48M
88Pac/8Men-63
88Pac/8Men-7
88Pac/8Men-71
94Conlon-1029
BF2-20
D328-185
D329-186
D350/2-188
E135-185
M101/4-186
M101/5-188
T207
W514-91
Weaver, James B.
(Jim)
68T-328R
69OPC-134
69T-134
69T/4in1-20
Weaver, James D.
(Jim)
92Conlon/Sport-390
R312/M
W711/1
Weaver, James
83OrlanTw-3
84Toledo-13
86Maine-23
87Calgary-3
88Tucson/CMC-21
88Tucson/JP-24
88Tucson/ProC-172
89Vanco/CMC-14
89Vanco/ProC-583
90AAASingl/ProC-128
90Calgary/CMC-17
90Calgary/ProC-663
90ProC/Singl-444
92VeroB/ProC-2876
Weaver, Monte
33G-111
35G-1C
35G-2C
35G-6C
35G-7C
93Conlon-853
Weaver, Roger
80Evansvl-1
81Evansvl-10
81T-626R
82Richm-9
Weaver, Trent
89Medford/Best-16
91Modesto/ClBest-2
Weaver, William B.
N172
Webb, Ben
87Watertn-1
88Salem/Star-23

89Harris/ProC-311
89Harris/Star-21
90Harris/ProC-1194
90Harris/Star-20
91AA/LineD-120
91CaroMud/LineD-120
91CaroMud/ProC-1088
92CaroMud/ProC-1182
92CaroMud/SB-147
Webb, Chuck
88Wausau/GS-19
Webb, Cleon Earl
D322
Webb, Dennis
81QuadC-9
Webb, William Earl
(Earl)
31Exh/4-18
33Exh/4-9
35BU-98M
85Woolwth-37
87Conlon/2-25
91Conlon/Sport-261
94Conlon-1226
Webb, Hank
73OPC-610R
73T-610R
75IntAS/TCMA-24
75OPC-615R
75T-615R
75T/M-61=R
76OPC-442
76SSPC-553
76SSPC/MetsY-M2
76T-442
78Cr/PCL-77
90Target-841
91WIZMets-426
Webb, James
(Skeeter)
No Cards.
Webb, Kevin
92Ashvl/ClBest-7
Webb, Lonnie
90GreatF/SportP-7
92Bakers/Cal-28
Webb, Marvin
75Water
Webb, Normal
(Tweed)
86Negro/Frit-39
Webb, Richmond
91StCl/Charter*-41
Webb, Sam
49Eureka-125
Webb, Spyder
87Belling/Team-16TR
88Belling/Legoe-31TR
89Belling/Legoe-33TR
91Belling/ClBest-27TR
Webber, Les
90Target-842
Weber, Ben
91StCath/ClBest-19
91StCath/ProC-3396
92Myrtle/ClBest-6
92Myrtle/ProC-2198
93Dunedin/ClBest-24
93Dunedin/ProC-1797
94ClBest/Gold-59
Weber, Brent
91Idaho/ProC-4329
Weber, Charles
(Bill)
N172
Weber, Neil
93James/ClBest-25
93James/ProC-3328
Weber, Pete
87BuffB-29
90ClintUp/Team-U8
91AA/LineD-323
91Shrev/LineD-323
91Shrev/ProC-1837
92Shrev/ProC-3886
92Shrev/SB-597
92Sky/AASingl-264
Weber, Ron
89Johnson/Star-22
90Spring/Best-24
91StPete/ClBest-14
91StPete/ProC-2277
92StPete/ClBest-9
92StPete/ProC-2028

Weber, Steve
89Bristol/Star-30
90Bristol/Star-29TR
Weber, Todd
88Ashvl/ProC-1078
Weber, Weston
(Wes)
86Cram/NWL-65
87Madis-11
88Modesto-15
89Huntsvl/Best-13
89Modesto/Chong-18
90AAASingl/ProC-139
90ProC/Singl-582
90Tacoma/CMC-5
90Tacoma/ProC-92
91Huntsvl/Team-22
91HuntsvlProC-1796
92Tacoma/ProC-2503
92Tacoma/SB-546
Webster, Casey
86Watlo-30
87Kinston-13
88EastLAS/ProC-43
88Wmsprt/ProC-1317
89Canton/Best-5
89Canton/ProC-1318
89Canton/Star-23
89EastLgAS/ProC-19
90AAASingl/ProC-228
90Canton/Star-17
90ColoSp/CMC-21
90ColoSp/ProC-47
90ProC/Singl-473
Webster, Lenny
86Kenosha-25
87Kenosha-20
88Kenosha/ProC-1392
88MidwLAS/GS-31
89Visalia/Cal-110
89Visalia/ProC-1442
90A&AASingle/ProC-55
90Foil/Best-45
90OrlanSR/Best-13
90OrlanSR/ProC-1088
90OrlanSR/Star-23
90S-638RP
90T/89Debut-136
90UD/Ext-728
91AAA/LineD-422
91F/Up-U41
91Portl/LineD-422
91Portl/ProC-1569
92D/Rook-124
92F-220
92OPC-585
92Pinn-276
92S-663
92S/Rook-17
92StCl-183
92T-585
92T/Gold-585
92T/GoldWin-585
92Ultra-402
93D-694
93F-646
93S-471
93StCl-380
93StCl/1stDay-380
93T-37
93T/Gold-37
93UD-628
93USPlayC/Rook-8D
93Ultra-238
94StCl-193
94StCl/1stDay-193
94StCl/Gold-193
94T-252
94T/Gold-252
Webster, Mike
89Eugene/Best-2
90BBCity/Star-26
Webster, Mitch
78Clinton
79Clinton/TCMA-11
80Syrac-12
80Syrac/Team-22
82Syrac-23
82Syrac/Team-23
83Syrac-25
84Tor/Fire-31
85Tor/Fire-31
86D-523

86Expo/Prov/Pan-5
86Expo/Prov/Post-5
86F-265
86GenMills/Book-6M
86Leaf-253
86OPC-218
86Provigo-5
86T-629
87D-335
87D/OD-86
87Expo/PostC-11
87F-335
87F/AwardWin-41
87F/Mini-111
87GenMills/Book-4M
87OPC-263
87Sf-177
87Sf/TPrev-20M
87Stuart-7
87T-442
87T/St-82
88Berg/Cubs-28
88D-257
88D/Best-292
88F-199
88F/St-99
88Ho/Disc-1
88Leaf-198
88OPC-138
88Panini/St-331
88RedFoley/St-97
88S-345
88Sf-105
88T-138
88T/Big-150
89B-296
89D-459
89D/Best-261
89F-442
89Mara/Cubs-33
89OPC-36
89Panini/St-61
89S-71
89Sf-67
89T-36
89UD-65
90D-137
90F-45
90F/Can-45
90Leaf-312
90OPC-502
90PublInt/St-208
90S-85
90S/Tr-4T
90T-502
90T/Big-298
90T/Tr-127T
90UD-153
90UD/Ext-730
91B-66
91D-283
91F-384
91Indian/McDon-29
91OPC-762
91Panini/St-175
91S-594
91S/RookTr-68T
91StCl-448
91T-762
91UD-120
91Ultra-119
92D-714
92Mother/Dodg-26
92OPC-233
92Pol/Dodg-20
92S-643
92StCl-403
92T-233
92T/Gold-233
92T/GoldWin-233
93D-62
93F-455
93Mother/Dodg-22
93Pac/Spanish-505
93Pol/Dodg-27
93StCl-735
93StCl/1stDay-735
93StCl/Dodg-18
94D-457
94F-528
94S-130
94S/GoldR-130
94T-382
94T/Gold-382

Webster, Ramon
67T-603R
68OPC-164
68T-164
69T-618
72MB-356
75Tucson-6
75Tucson/Caruso-3
75Tucson/Team-21
Webster, Ray G.
59T-531
60T-452
Webster, Rich
82Lynch-21
Webster, Rudy
86Cram/NWL-127
87Wausau-25
88Wausau/GS-17
Wechsberg, Von
90BurlInd/ProC-3010
91Pocatel/ProC-3783
91Pocatel/SportP-7
92Spokane/ClBest-18
92Spokane/ProC-1295
Weck, Steve
85Iowa-31
Wedell, James R.
33SK*-26
Wedge, Eric
88CapeCod/Sum-51
89Elmira/Pucko-32
90EastLAS/ProC-EL41
90Foil/Best-2
90Foil/Best-319
90NewBrit/Best-1
90NewBrit/ProC-1322
90NewBrit/Star-21
90ProC/Singl-783
90T/TVRSox-66
91AAA/LineD-372
91Pawtu/LineD-372
91Pawtu/ProC-42
92Pawtu/ProC-927
92Pawtu/SB-372
92S/Rook-38
92Sky/AAASingl-171
92T/91Debut-182
93D-44RR
93F/MLPI-12
93Pinn-239
93S-561
93S/Proctor-9
93Select-401
93StCl/Rockie-22
93T-486
93T/Gold-486
93UD-653
94S-643
94StCl/Team-113
Wedvick, Jeff
86James-28
87BurlEx-16
Weeber, Mike
75Dubuq
Weekly, Johnny
62T-204
64T-256
89Smok/Ast-26
Weeks, Ben
91Idaho/ProC-4330
91Idaho/SportP-8
92Pulaski/ClBest-12
92Pulaski/ProC-3178
Weeks, Thomas
87Oneonta-13
88FtLaud/Star-24
89PrWill/Star-24
90PrWill/Team-27
Weems, Danny
86Sumter/ProC-29
87CharWh-13
88CLAS/Star-39
88Durham/Star-23
89Greenvl/Best-13
89Greenvl/ProC-1157
89Greenvl/Star-24
90Greenvl/Best-16
90Greenvl/ProC-1130
90Greenvl/Star-22
Weese, Dean
88Hamil/ProC-1744
89Savan/ProC-348
90StPete/Star-25

91ArkTr/ProC-1286
Weese, Gary
75SanAn
76Wmsprt
Wegener, Mike
69Fud's-13
69T-284R
70Expo/PostC-5
70OPC-193
70T-193
71Expo/ProS-27
71OPC-608
71T-608
75Tidew/Team-24
76Phoenix/Coke-21
77Phoenix
Weger, Wes
92FrRow/DP-77
92Helena/ProC-1725
93FExcel/ML-196
94FExcel-90
94Ultra-382
Weglarz, John
92Eugene/ClBest-27
92Eugene/ProC-3030
93Rockford/ClBest-27
Wegman, Bill
82Beloit/Frit-4
85Cram/PCL-216
86D-490
86Pol/Brew-46
86T/Tr-123T
87D-109
87F-360
87Pol/Brew-46
87T-179
88D-151
88D/Best-320
88F-177
88OPC-84
88Panini/St-119
88Pol/Brew-46
88S-296
88T-538
88T/Big-244
88T/St-200
89B-135
89Brewer/YB-46
89D-293
89F-199
89Gard-9
89OPC-354
89Pol/Brew-46
89S-335
89S/YS/II-9
89T-768
89UD-445
90Brewer/MillB-30
90OPC-333
90Pol/Brew-46
90PublInt/St-507
90S-188
90T-333
90UD-629
91Brewer/MillB-30
91F/UltraUp-U33
91F/Up-U35
91OPC-617
91Pol/Brew-27
91S-483
91StCl-398
91T-617
91UD-292
92B-447
92D-378
92F-193
92L-196
92L/BlkGold-196
92OPC-22
92Pinn-396
92Pol/Brew-28
92S-374
92StCl-758
92Studio-199
92T-22
92T/Gold-22
92T/GoldWin-22
92TripleP-185
92UD-612
92UD/TmMVPHolo-53
92USPlayC/Ace-5S
92Ultra-392
93D-17
93F-259

80SSPC/HOF
81Conlon-73
94Conlon-1250
E223
N167-11
N172
N338/2
N403
N690/2
Welch, Mike
93B-221
94B-268
94FExcel-241
Welch, Robert
(Bob)
78Cr/PCL-26
79T-318
80Pol/Dodg-35
80T-146
81D-178
81F-120
81OPC-357
81Pol/Dodg-35
81T-624
81T/HT
82D-75
82F-28
82Pol/Dodg-35
82T-82
83D-410
83F-225
83OPC-288
83Pol/Dodg-35
83T-454
84D-153
84F-116
84Nes/792-306TL
84Nes/792-722
84OPC-227
84Pol/Dodg-35
84T-306TL
84T-722
85Coke/Dodg-32
85D-372
85F-388
85OPC-291
85T-291
86Coke/Dodg-32
86D-459
86F-146
86Leaf-223
86Pol/Dodg-35
86Sf-198
86T-549
86T/Mini-48
87D-475
87F-459
87F/LL-43
87F/St-121
87Mother/Dodg-9
87OPC-328
87Pol/Dodg-18
87Smok/Dodg-37
87T-328
88D-24DK
88D-253
88D/A's/Bk-NEW
88D/Best-134
88D/DKsuper-24DK
88F-529
88F/Mini-50
88F/Up-U57
88Leaf-24DK
88Mother/A's-9
88OPC-118
88Panini/St-305
88RedFoley/St-98
88S-510
88S/Tr-15T
88Sf-167
88T-118
88T/Mini-55
88T/Revco-15
88T/St-73
88T/Tr-127T
89B-186
89Classic-91
89D-332
89D/Best-267
89F-25
89KennerFig-160
89Mother/A's-9
89Panini/St-416
89S-308
89S/HotStar-89
89Sf-91
89Smok/Dodg-92
89T-605
89T/LJN-131
89T/St-166
89UD-191
90D-332
90D/BestAL-67
90F-23
90F/Can-23
90MLBPA/Pins-76
90Mother/A's-16
90OPC-475
90Panini/St-131
90PublInt/St-318
90S-159
90Sf-35
90T-475
90T/Big-106
90T/St-180
90Target-844
90UD-251
90USPlayC/AS-1C
90Windwlk/Discs-3
91B-215
91Bz-3
91Classic/200-199
91Classic/I-76
91CollAB-5
91D-20DK
91D-54AS
91D-645
91D-727CY
91D/Preview-5
91D/SuperDK-20DK
91F-27
91Leaf-64
91Leaf/Stud-110
91MSA/Holsum-14
91Mother/A's-9
91OPC-394AS
91OPC-50
91Panini/FrSt-174
91Panini/St-151
91Panini/Top15-61
91RedFoley/St-130
91S-311
91S-568
91S-877CY
91S/100SS-49
91SFExam/A's-15
91Seven/3DCoin-14NC
91StCl-79
91StCl/Charter*-32
91T-394AS
91T-50
91T/CJMini/II-28
91UD-425
91Ultra-256
91Woolwth/HL-4
92D-190
92F-271
92L-390
92L/BlkGold-390
92Mother/A's-9
92OPC-285
92Pinn-409
92S-300
92StCl-651
92T-285
92T/Gold-285
92T/GoldWin-285
92TripleP-124
92UD-452
92Ultra-119
93B-77
93D-579
93F-301
93Flair-264
93L-94
93Mother/A's-10
93OPC-340
93Pac/Spanish-227
93Pinn-573
93S-208
93Select-254
93StCl-546
93StCl/1stDay-546
93StCl/A's-12
93T-705
93T/Finest-151
93T/FinestRef-151
93T/Gold-705
93TripleP-192
93UD-407
93Ultra-263
94B-136
94D-282
94F-276
94L-354
94OPC-213
94Pac/Cr-465
94Panini-115
94Pinn-329
94S-547
94Select-126
94StCl-297
94StCl/1stDay-297
94StCl/Gold-297
94T-521
94T/Finest-158
94T/FinestRef-158
94T/Gold-521
94UD-429
94Ultra-114
Welch, Williams
94T-713
94T/Gold-713
Welchel, Don
80CharlO/Pol-21
80CharlO/W3TV-21
81RochR-18
82RochR-8
84RochR-14
85RochR-23
86OKCty-24
88Omaha/ProC-1511
91Crown/Orio-477
Weldin, David
89Helena/SP-21
Weldon, Paul
91Pocatel/ProC-3792
91Pocatel/SportP-21
Weleno, Doug
83MidldC-8
Welish, Scott
89CharRain/ProC-988
89Spokane/SP-16
Welke, Tim
88TM/Umpire-55
89TM/Umpire-53
90TM/Umpire-51
Wellman, Bob
52Park-95
52T-41
79Jacks-6MG
Wellman, Brad
84D-265
84F-386
84Nes/792-109
84T-109
85F-623
85Mother/Giants-26
85T-409
86D-431
86F-553
86Mother/Giants-22
86OPC-41
86T-41
87Albuq/Pol-23
88Smok/Royals-24
89D-380
89S-504
90Target-845
Wellman, Phillip
86Durham-27
87Harris-7
88Pulaski/ProC-1748CO
89Pulaski/ProC-1901
90BurlB/ProC-2368CO
90BurlB/Star-30CO
91Durham/ClBest-26CO
91Durham/ProC-1679CO
Wells
C46-56
Wells, Bob
90Spartan/Best-10
90Spartan/ProC-2491
90Spartan/Star-25
91Clearw/ProC-1621
92Clearw/ClBest-13
92Reading/ProC-576
Wells, David
83Kinston/Team-28
86Ventura-27
87Syrac/TCMA-9
88D-640
88D/Best-311
88D/Rook-26
88F/Up-U69
88T/Tr-128T
88Tor/Fire-36
89D-307
89D/Best-328
89F-247
89OPC-259
89T-567
89T/JumboR-22
89Tor/Fire-36
90D-425
90F-96
90F/Can-96
90OPC-229
90S-491
90S/YS/I-31
90T-229
90Tor/BJ-36
90UD-30
91D-473
91F-188
91Leaf-140
91OPC-619
91Panini/FrSt-350
91Panini/St-153
91S-474
91S/ToroBJ-9
91StCl-133
91T-619
91Tor/Fire-36
91UD-583
91Ultra-370
92B-352
92BJ/Fire-32
92D-620
92F-345
92L-483
92L/BlkGold-483
92OPC-54
92Pinn-431
92S-49
92StCl-721
92T-54
92T/Gold-54
92T/GoldWin-54
92UD-116
92Ultra-453
93BJ/D/45-24
93D-511
93F-702
93F/Final-214
93Flair-210
93L-484
93OPC-321
93Pac/Spanish-451
93Pinn-114
93S-648
93Select/RookTr-113T
93StCl-59
93StCl/1stDay-59
93T-458
93T/Gold-458
93T/Tr-50T
93Tiger/Gator-26
93UD-699
93UD/SP-242
93Ultra-296
94D-307
94F-145
94L-39
94Pac/Cr-231
94Pinn-464
94S-369
94T-105
94T/Finest-108
94T/FinestRef-108
94T/Gold-105
94UD-179
94UD/ElecD-179
94Ultra-359
Wells, Ed
34G-73
92Conlon/Sport-389
Wells, Frank
N172
Wells, Greg
(Boomer)
78Dunedin
79Syrac/TCMA-1
80Syrac-14
80Syrac/Team-23
81Syrac-16
81Syrac/Team-22
82OPC-203R
82T-203R
82Toledo-17
Wells, Jacob
N172
Wells, Leo
47Sunbeam
Wells, Michael
89KS*-24
Wells, Terry
86Ashvl-29
87Osceola-1
88ColAst/Best-3
89ColMud/ProC-144
89ColMud/Star-23
90AAASingl/ProC-67
90Albuq/CMC-13
90Albuq/ProC-346
90Albuq/Trib-31
90ProC/Singl-415
91AAA/LineD-323
91OkCty/LineD-323
91OkCty/ProC-180
91S-359RP
91T/90Debut-166
Wells, Tim
90Butte/SportP-28
91Gaston/ClBest-11
91Gaston/ProC-2688
Wells, Willie
(Devil)
74Laugh/Black-13
86Negro/Frit-71
87Negro/Dixon-42
88Conlon/NegAS-11
90Negro/Star-11
Welmaker, Roy
52Mother-37
53Mother-52
Welsh, Chris
79Colum-24
80Colum-3
82D-44
82F-584
82T-376
83D-94
83Expo/PostC-21
83F-374
83OPC-118
83T-118
83T/Tr-125T
84D-498
84F-292
84Indianap-4
85Rang-41
86D-464
86F-576
86T-52
86TexGold-45
87F-217
87T-592
91Brisbane/Fut-5
91Pac/SenLg-142
93Rang/Keeb-376
Welsh, Jimmy D.
29Exh/4-10
92Conlon/Sport-494
R316
Welsh, William
75WPalmB/Sussman-16
Wendell, Steven
(Turk)
88Pulaski/ProC-1755
89BurlB/ProC-1616
89BurlB/Star-24
90Foil/Best-122
90Greenvl/Best-8
90Greenvl/ProC-1131
90Greenvl/Star-23
91AA/LineD-222
91Greenvl/ClBest-9
91Greenvl/LineD-222
91Greenvl/ProC-3003
92B-693
92Iowa/SB-223
92L/GRook-5
92OPC-676M
92ProC/Tomorrow-178
92Sky/AAASingl-109
92T-676R
92T/Gold-676M
92T/GoldWin-676M
92UD-780DD

92UD/ML-85
93B-664
93F/Final-12
93T/Tr-49T
94B-550
94D-312
94Pac/Cr-114
94Pinn-254
94Pinn/Artist-254
94Pinn/Museum-254
94S-616
94Sf/2000-170
94StCl-499
94StCl/1stDay-499
94StCl/Gold-499
94StCl/Team-358
94T-778M
94T/Gold-778M
94UD/CollC-290
94UD/CollC/Gold-290
94UD/CollC/Silv-290
Wendelstedt, Harry
88TM/Umpire-6
89TM/Umpire-4
90TM/Umpire-4
Wendlandt, Terry
84Omaha-30
85Omaha-5
Wendler, Doc
55Gol/Dodg-31
Wendt, Glenn
78Watlo
Wendt, Jason
92Pulaski/ClBest-20
92Pulaski/ProC-3179
Wengert, Bill
88GreatF-17
89Bakers/Cal-188
90VeroB/Star-27
91Adelaide/Fut-8
91VeroB/ClBest-13
91VeroB/ProC-774
92SanAn/ProC-3975
92VeroB/ClBest-24
Wengert, Don
92FrRow/DP-28
92SoOreg/ClBest-22
92SoOreg/ProC-3417
93ClBest/MLG-181
93StCl/MurphyS-114
Wenrick, Bill
88Boise/ProC-1623
88SLCity-26
Wenrick, John
88LitFalls/Pucko-23
89Clmbia/Best-17
89Clmbia/GS-27
90WPalmB/Star-26
Wensloff, Charles
44Yank/St-29
47TipTop
Wenson, Paul
87Lakeland-25
88GlenF/ProC-921
89Toledo/CMC-8
89Toledo/ProC-780
Wentz, Keith
86Cram/NWL-75
Wentz, Lenny
91CharWh/ClBest-20
91CharWh/ProC-2897
92CharWh/ClBest-22
92CharWh/ProC-18
Wenz, Fred
69T-628R
71OPC-92
71T-92
Wenzell, Marge
93TWill-119
Wera, Julie
91Conlon/Sport-100
Werber, Billy
34DS-61
34G-75
35Exh/4-9
35G-8G
35G-9G
36G
37Exh/4-14
38Exh/4-14
38G-259
38G-283
41DP-10
88Conlon/5-30
R313
R314
W711/1
W711/2
Werd, Norm
75SanAn
Werhas, John
64T-456R
65T-453R
67T-514
90Target-846
Werland, Henry
(Hank)
90Pulaski/Best-11
90Pulaski/ProC-3108
91ClBest/Singl-42
91Durham/ProC-DUR2
91DurhamUp/ProC-2
91Macon/ClBest-12
91Macon/ProC-865
Werle, William
48Sommer-18
49Eureka-175
50B-87
51B-64
51FB
51T/RB-33
52B-248
52T-73
53T-170
54T-144
61Union
91T/Arc53-170
94T/Arc54-144
PM10/Sm-193
Werley, George
91Crown/Orio-478
Werley, Jamie
82Colum-10
82Colum/Pol-15
Werner, Dave
89Erie/Star-29
Werner, Don
76Indianap-17
77Indianap-8
78Pep-25
78T-702R
79Indianap-22
83D-593
83OKCty-18
83T-504
84Iowa-16
86OKCty-25
87OKCty-5
88OkCty/CMC-21
88OkCty/ProC-37
89James/ProC-2150
91Augusta/ClBest-30MG
91Augusta/ProC-822MG
92CaroMud/ProC-1195
92CaroMud/SB-149MG
93Rang/Keeb-377
Wernig, Pat
88Madis-25
88MidwLAS/GS-52
89Huntsvl/Best-23
91AAA/LineD-547
91Tacoma/LineD-547
91Tacoma/ProC-2307
92LasVegas/SB-247
Werrick, Joe
N172
Wert, Don
62T-299
64T-19
65OPC-271
65T-271
66T-253
67CokeCap/Tiger-12
67T-511
68CokeCap/Tiger-12
68OPC-178
68T-178
69MB-287
69T-443
69T/St-180
70OPC-33
70T-33
71MLB/St-552
71OPC-307
71Pol/SenP-10
71T-307
72MB-358
78TCMA-163
81Tiger/Detroit-65
88Domino-25
Werth, Dennis
75FtLaud/Sus-21
78Cr/PCL-92
79Colum-10
81D-466
81F-102
81Louisvl-22
81T-424R
82F-55
82T-154
82T/Tr-126T
83Louisvl/Riley-22
84Louisvl-30
92Yank/WIZ70-163
92Yank/WIZ80-200
Wertz, Bill
90Reno/Cal-280
90Watertn/Star-23
91ClBest/Singl-138
91Collnd/ClBest-18
91Collnd/ProC-1485
92Canton/ProC-692
92Canton/SB-123
93B-529
93ClBest/MLG-8
93F/Final-206
94D-590
94F-123
94Pac/Cr-186
94StCl-481
94StCl/1stDay-481
94StCl/Gold-481
94T-64
94T/Gold-64
94Ultra-50
Wertz, Vic
49B-164
50B-9
51B-176
51T/BB-40
52B-39
52BR
52RM-AL22
52StarCal-86BM
52StarCal/L-72D
52T-244
53B/Col-2
53T-142
54B-21
54Esskay
55B-40
55Gol/Ind-29
55RM-AL13
55Salem
56T-300
57Sohio/Ind-16
57Swift-6
57T-78
58T-170
59T-500
60T-111
61P-49
61T-173M
61T-340
61T/St-118
62Salada-60
62Shirriff-60
62T-481
63T-348
78TCMA-227
79TCMA-45
81Tiger/Detroit-123
82Ohio/HOF-54
91Crown/Orio-479
91T/Arc53-142
92Bz/Quadra-1M
Exh47
Wesley, Tom
81Cedar-15
Wesolowski, Al
78Newar
Wessel, Troy
89James/ProC-2139
90James/Pucko-26
Wessenaar, Rob
92Sky/AAASingl-194
Wessinger, Jim
79Savan-26
80Richm-21
West, Bobby
89Princet/Star-24
West, Chris
89TNTech-30
West, Dave
84LitFalls-24
86Lynch-25
87Jacks/Feder-23
87TexLgAS-29
88AAA/ProC-41
88Tidew/CANDL-28
88Tidew/CMC-2
88Tidew/ProC-1592
88TripleA/ASCMC-29
89Classic-134
89D-41RR
89F-51
89Kahn/Mets-46
89S-650
89S/YS/I-32
89Sf-45
89T-787
89Tidew/CMC-7
89Tidew/ProC-1973
89ToysRUs-33
89UD-7SR
90B-413
90Classic-68
90D-387
90F-388
90F/Can-388
90HotRook/St-47
90Leaf-387
90OPC-357
90S-573
90T-357
90T/Big-325
90T/JumboR-30
90ToysRUs-30
90UD-15
91D-264
91F-627
91OPC-578
91S-158
91StCl-34
91T-578
91UD-377
91WIZMets-428
92D-638
92OPC-442
92Pinn-333
92Portl/SB-423
92Portland/ProC-2669
92S-669
92StCl-398
92T-442
92T/Gold-442
92T/GoldWin-442
92UD-548
92USPlayC/Twin-3S
92USPlayC/Twin-4D
93D-501
93F/Final-112
93L-460
93Pac/Spanish-583
93Phill/Med-34
93StCl/Phill-12
93T-652
93T/Gold-652
93UD-710
93Ultra-447
94D-409
94F-603
94Pac/Cr-489
94Phill/Med-34
94S-156
94S/GoldR-156
94StCl-130
94StCl/1stDay-130
94StCl/Gold-130
94StCl/Team-220
94T-266
94T/Gold-266
West, Freeman
89KS*-43
West, Jim 1
91Waterlo/ClBest-13
91Waterlo/ProC-1260
West, Jim 2
90Spokane/SportP-15
West, Joe
88TM/Umpire-36
89TM/Umpire-34
90TM/Umpire-33
West, Matt
83Durham-26
85Richm-10
86Richm-25
87Richm/Bob-22
87Richm/Crown-45
87Richm/TCMA-8
88Calgary/CMC-8
88Calgary/ProC-788
89Pulaski/ProC-1902
90Sumter/ProC-2451CO
90Target-847
91Macon/ClBest-29CO
91Macon/ProC-884CO
92Durham/ClBest-26CO
92Durham/ProC-1118
92Durham/Team-30
93Durham/Team-24CO
West, Milton
N172
West, Reggie
84Cram/PCL-116
85Cram/PCL-8
West, Samuel
33G-166
35G-1F
35G-3D
35G-5D
35G-6D
36Exh/4-15
37Exh/4-15
37OPC-129
38Exh/4-15
39PlayBall-31
40PlayBall-22
74Laugh/ASG-40
77Galasso-192
91Conlon/Sport-241
93Conlon-679
94Conlon-1090
R310
R313
V300
West, Tom
86DayBe-29
86FSLAS-49
West, W. Max
39PlayBall-149
40PlayBall-57
41DP-43
41PlayBall-2
52Mother-10
53Mother-19
Westbrook, Destry
92AubAs/ClBest-21
92AubAs/ProC-1355
Westbrook, Mike
84LitFalls-3
86Lynch-26
88CLAS/Star-40
88Kinston/Star-23
89Reno/Cal-251
Westbrooks, Elanis
88Clinton/ProC-716
89SanJose/Best-13
89SanJose/Cal-225
89SanJose/ProC-435
89SanJose/Star-25
90SanJose/Best-14
90SanJose/Cal-32
90SanJose/ProC-2021
90SanJose/Star-25
Westermann, Scott
88Greens/ProC-1565
Westfall, Fred
76Wausau
Westlake, James Patrick
77Fritsch-17
Westlake, James
T206
Westlake, Wally
46Remar-8
49B-45
49Eureka-176
50B-69
51T/RB-27
52BR
52NTea
52StarCal-93CM
52StarCal/L-81B
52T-38
53T-192
54DanDee
54T-92
55Gol/Ind-30

55Salem
55T-102
55T/DH-13
56T-81
91Crown/Orio-480
91T/Arc53-192
94T/Arc54-92
Exh47
Westmoreland, Claude
78Cr/PCL-21
79Albuq-21
80Albuq-11
Westmoreland, John
85Clovis-43
Weston, Mickey
85Lynch-6
86Jacks/TCMA-10
87Jacks/Feder-11
88Jacks/GS-22
89RochR/CMC-6
89RochR/ProC-1638
90OPC-377
90ProC/Singl-304
90RochR/CMC-3
90Rochester/L&U-10
90S-616
90T-377
90T/89Debut-137
90UD-683
91AAA/LineD-521
91Crown/Orio-481
91Syrac/LineD-521
91Syrac/MerchB-27
91Syrac/ProC-2482
92ScranWB/ProC-2447
92ScranWB/SB-496
Weston, Tim
88Oneonta/ProC-2065
89Albany/Best-29
89Albany/ProC-323
90Albany/Best-17
90Albany/Star-28TR
Westrope, Jack
(Jockey)
33SK*-39
Westrum, Wes
49Eureka-126
51B-161
51FB
51T/RB-37
52B-74
52BR
52Coke
52RM-NL26
52T-75
52TipTop
53RM-NL20
54B-25
54NYJour
54T-180
55B-141
55Gol/Giants-29
56T-156
57T-323
60T-469C
66T-341MG
67T-593MG
75OPC-216MG
75T-216MG
75T/M-216MG
76SSPC-113MG
79TCMA-46
91T/Arc53-323
92Bz/Quadra-10M
94T/Arc54-180
Exh47
R423-115
Wetherby, Jeff
86Sumter/ProC-30
87Greenvl/Best-21
88Richm-22
88Richm/CMC-16
88Richm/ProC-9
89Brave/Dubuq-28
89Richm/CMC-16
89Richm/Ko-22
89Richm/ProC-840
90AAASingl/ProC-234
90ColoSp/CMC-22
90ColoSp/ProC-53
90OPC-142
90ProC/Singl-474
90S-540
90S/100Ris-44
90T-142
90T/89Debut-138
90UD-611
91AAA/LineD-472
91RochR/LineD-472
91RochR/ProC-1917
92Calgary/ProC-3744
Wetteland, John
86Bakers-28
87VeroB-1
88BBAmer-28
88SanAn/Best-21
88TexLgAS/GS-7
89Albuq/CMC-11
89Albuq/ProC-63
89S/Tr-90
90B-82
90Classic-110
90D-671
90F-411
90F/Can-411
90HotRook/St-48
90Mother/Dodg-19
90OPC-631
90Pol/Dodg-57
90S-388
90S/100Ris-25
90S/YS/I-40
90T-631
90T/89Debut-139
90T/JumboR-31
90Target-1094
90ToysRUs-31
90UD-377
91AAA/LineD-23
91Albuq/LineD-23
91Albuq/ProC-1142
91D-614
91S-267
91UD-668
92B-68
92Classic/I-94
92D-627
92Expo/D/Duri-20
92F/Up-100
92L-478
92L/BlkGold-478
92OPC/Premier-108
92Pinn-461
92Pinn-593SIDE
92S/RookTr-78T
92StCl-759
92UD-788
92Ultra-526
93B-212
93D-592
93F-83
93Flair-88
93L-183
93MSA/Ben-11
93OPC-366
93Pac/Spanish-538
93Pinn-397
93S-165
93Select-201
93Select/StatL-72
93StCl-344
93StCl/1stDay-344
93Studio-65
93T-231
93T/Finest-129
93T/FinestRef-129
93T/Gold-231
93TripleP-206
93UD-392
93UD/SP-108
93Ultra-420
94B-172
94D-293
94F-555
94L-414
94OPC-105
94Pac/Cr-393
94Panini-214
94Pinn-119
94Pinn/Artist-119
94Pinn/Museum-119
94S-390
94Select-69
94StCl-446
94StCl/1stDay-446
94StCl/Gold-446
94Studio-81
94T-497
94T/Finest-133
94T/FinestRef-133
94T/Gold-497
94TripleP-100
94UD-32FT
94UD-335
94UD/ElecD-32FT
94UD/SP-87
94Ultra-232
94Ultra/Fire-9
Wetzel, Tom
84Everett/Cram-29
Wever, Stefan
82Nashvl-27
83Colum-10
92Yank/WIZ80-201
Wex, Gary
83Albany-8
Weyer, Lee
88TM/Umpire-2
89TM/Umpire-62
Weyhing, August
90Target-848
N172
Weyhing, John
N172
Whalen, Mike
84Newar-12
Whalen, Shawn
90Waterlo/Best-17
90Waterlo/ProC-2392
91ClBest/Singl-337
91Waterlo/ClBest-24
91Waterlo/ProC-1271
92Watlo/ClBest-22
Whaley, Scott Lee
84Madis/Pol-5
85Huntsvl/BK-23
85Madis-3
85Madis/Pol-24
Whaling, Albert
15CJ-163
Whalley, Jarrell
77Spartan
Wharton, Greg
91Melbourne/Fut-1
Whatley, Fred
90ClintUp/Team-U9
Wheat, Chris
90Helena/SportP-6
91Helena/SportP-20
Wheat, Danny
76SanAn/Team-26
83OKCty-24TR
85Rang-TR
86Rang-TR
90Mother/Rang-28TR
Wheat, Leroy
54T-244
94T/Arc54-244
Wheat, Zachary D.
10Domino-123
11Helmar-89
12Sweet/Pin-78
12Sweet/Pin-78A
14CJ-52
14Piedmont/St-60
15CJ-52
16FleischBrd-99
21Exh-184
25Exh-16
26Exh-16
27Exh-56
60F-12
61F-1M
61F-86
76Shakey-84
77Galasso-101
77Galasso-151
80Perez/HOF-84
80SSPC/HOF
89Smok/Dodg-34
90BBWit-82
90Target-849
90Target-850
91Conlon/Sport-164
93CrackJack-15
D327
D328-187
D329-188
D350/2-186
E120
E121/120
E121/80
E122
E135-187
E220
E270/1
M101/4-188
M101/5-186
S74-57
T201
T202
T205
T206
T207
T213/blue
T214-29
T215/brown
V100
V61-117
V89-49
W501-97
W514-110
W515-56
W572
W573
W575
WG5-43
WG6-39
Wheatcroft, Robert
(Bob)
89Bluefld/Star-28
90Wausau/Best-10
90Wausau/ProC-2123
90Wausau/Star-25
Wheaton, James
91FresnoSt/Smok-14
Wheeler
C46-51
Wheeler, Bradley
88ElPaso/Best-18
Wheeler, Chris
88Phill/TastyK-39ANN
90Phill/TastyK-35BC
Wheeler, Dave
90Billings/ProC-3226
Wheeler, Earl
91OKSt-31
92OKSt-31
Wheeler, Edward
90Target-851
Wheeler, Ed
75AppFx
Wheeler, Kenneth Jr.
(Kenny)
90Ashvl/ProC-2750
91BurlAs/ClBest-11
91BurlAs/ProC-2802
91MidwLAS/ProC-20
92Osceola/ClBest-4
92Osceola/ProC-2531
Wheeler, Ralph
(Rocket)
78Dunedin
80Knoxvl/TCMA-24
85Kingst-25
86Syrac-26CO
87Myrtle-19CO
90AAASingl/ProC-370CO
90ProC/Singl-676CO
90Syrac/CMC-28CO
90Syrac/MerchB-28CO
90Syrac/ProC-590CO
90Syrac/Team-28CO
91AAA/LineD-525CO
91Syrac/LineD-525CO
91Syrac/MerchB-28CO
91Syrac/ProC-2498CO
92Syrac/MerchB-29CO
92Syrac/ProC-1988CO
92Syrac/SB-525M
93Syrac/ProC-1015CO
Wheeler, Rodney
86Clearw-24
Wheeler, Tim
82AlexD-18
82Buffa-9
83LynnP-9
84Cram/PCL-140
Wheeler, Winston
90Martins/ProC-3185
Wheelock, Gary
75SLCity/Caruso-12
77T-493R
78SanJose-8
78T-596
79Spokane-17
80Spokane-17
87OKCty-2
88Belling/Legoe-12CO
89Belling/Legoe-32CO
91Belling/ClBest-27CO
91Belling/ProC-3684CO
92SanBern/ClBest-28CO
Wheelock, Warren
N172
Wherry, Cliff
83Tucson-18
84OKCty-4
Whipple, Jack
45Centen-27
Whipps, Joe
90Jacks/GS-20
Whisenant, Matt
90Princet/DIMD-27
91Batavia/ClBest-17
91Batavia/ProC-3483
92Spartan/ClBest-20
92Spartan/ProC-1264
92UD/ML-211
93B-38
93ClBest/MLG-136
93FExcel/ML-88
93SALAS/II-40
93SALAS/IICS-6
94B-206
Whisenant, Pete
57T-373
58T-466
59T-14
60T-424
61Peters-11
61T-201
61T/St-187
83Albany-20
Whisenton, Larry
78Richm
79Richm-4
79T-715R
80Richm-4
81Richm-6
82BK/Lids-27
82Pol/Atl-28
83D-501
83F-152
83Richm-22
83T-544
84Richm-5
85Greenvl/Team-25
Whisler, Randy
90Gaston/Best-27CO
90Gaston/ProC-2537CO
90Gaston/Star-29CO
91Gaston/ProC-2707CO
92Tulsa/ProC-2710CO
92Tulsa/SB-625CO
Whisman, Rhett
82Wisco/Frit-27
Whisonant, John
91Batavia/ClBest-23
91Batavia/ProC-3484
Whisonant, Mike
89Anchora-27
Whistler, Randy
80Ander-19
Whitacre
N172
Whitaker, Darrell
85BurlR-24
86Salem-28
87Gaston/ProC-26
88OkCty/CMC-11
88OkCty/ProC-43
88Tulsa-6
89OkCty/CMC-10
89OkCty/ProC-1516
Whitaker, Jeff
91BurlInd/ProC-3311
92BurlInd/ClBest-2
92BurlInd/ProC-1666
Whitaker, Lou
78BK/T-13
78T-704R
79Ho-117
79OPC-55
79T-123
80OPC-187
80T-358
81Coke
81D-365
81F-463

81OPC-234
81T-234
81Tiger/Detroit-59
82D-454
82F-284
82F/St-156
82OPC-39
82T-39
82T/St-187
83D-333
83F-348
83F/St-13M
83F/St-1AM
83F/St-1BM
83OPC-66
83OPC/St-65
83T-509
83T/St-65
84D-227
84D/AAS-4
84F-92
84F/St-13
84F/St-30
84MiltBrad-28
84Nes/792-398AS
84Nes/792-666TL
84Nes/792-695
84Nestle/DT-2
84OPC-181AS
84OPC-211
84Seven-16C
84T-398AS
84T-666TL
84T-695
84T/Gloss40-30
84T/RD-18M
84T/St-196
84T/St-267
84T/St/Box-1
84Tiger/Farmer-15
84Tiger/Wave-34
85Cain's-19
85D-293
85D-5DK
85D/AAS-42
85D/DKsuper-5
85F-24
85FunFood/Pin-78
85GenMills-24
85Leaf-5DK
85OPC-108
85Seven-16S
85Seven-1D
85T-480
85T/Gloss22-14
85T/RD-17M
85T/St-183
85T/St-261
85Wendy-21
86Cain's-20
86D-49
86D/AAS-11
86D/PopUp-11
86F-242
86F/LimEd-44
86F/Mini-51
86F/St-126
86GenMills/Book-1M
86Leaf-33
86OPC-20
86Seven/Coin-S10M
86Sf-48
86Sf-74M
86Sf/Dec-73M
86Sf/Rook-48M
86T-20
86T/Gloss22-3
86T/St-156
86T/St-272
86T/Tatt-23M
86TrueVal-25
87Cain's-8
87Coke/Tigers-16
87D-107
87D/AAS-3
87D/OD-218
87D/PopUp-3
87F-168
87F/Mini-112
87F/RecSet-41
87F/St-122
87Ho/St-23
87Jiffy-11
87Leaf-78
87OPC-106
87RedFoley/St-88
87Seven-DT12
87Sf-112M
87Sf-137
87Sf/TPrev-15
87T-661
87T/Gloss22-14
87T/Gloss60-7
87T/St-153
87T/St-267
88D-173
88D/Best-315
88F-75
88KennerFig-119
88Leaf-169
88OPC-179
88Panini/St-443IA
88Panini/St-92
88Pep/T-1
88Pol/T-14
88S-56
88Sf-30
88T-770
88T/Big-99
88T/Mini-13
88T/St-270
88T/St/Backs-38
89B-103
89ClassicUp/2-188
89D-298
89D/Best-35
89F-151
89KennerFig-161
89Mara/Tigers-1
89OPC-320
89Panini/St-341
89Pol/Tigers-1
89S-230
89Sf-18
89T-320
89T/Big-22
89T/Coins-57
89T/LJN-156
89T/St-282
89T/St/Backs-6
89T/UK-83
89UD-451
90B-356
90CokeK/Tiger-26
90D-16DK
90D-298
90D/BestAL-119
90D/SuperDK-16DK
90F-619
90F/Can-619
90HotPlay/St-48
90Kenner/Fig-89
90KingB/Discs-24
90Leaf-34
90MLBPA/Pins-89
90OPC-280
90Panini/St-71
90PublInt/St-485
90RedFoley/St-101
90S-75
90S/100St-71
90Sf-103
90T-280
90T/Big-130
90T/Coins-32
90T/DH-70
90T/St-275
90UD-327
90UD-41TC
91B-150
91Cadaco-60
91Classic/200-3
91CokeK/Tiger-1
91D-174
91F-357
91Leaf-120
91Leaf/Stud-60
91OPC-145
91Panini/FrSt-289
91Panini/St-233
91Pol/Tiger-14
91S-297
91StCl-101
91T-145
91UD-367
91Ultra-130
92B-630
92Classic/Game200-91
92D-285
92F-149
92L-391
92L/BlkGold-391
92OPC-570
92Panini-106
92Pinn-29
92S-255
92StCl-550
92Studio-180
92T-570
92T/Gold-570
92T/GoldWin-570
92T/Kids-77
92TripleP-117
92UD-516
92USPlayC/Tiger-13D
92USPlayC/Tiger-9S
92Ultra-65
93B-11
93Cadaco-62
93D-686
93F-614
93Flair-211
93L-148
93OPC-389
93Pac/Spanish-116
93Pinn-509
93S-596
93Select-112
93StCl-135
93StCl/1stDay-135
93Studio-76
93T-160
93T/Finest-2
93T/FinestRef-2
93T/Gold-160
93Tiger/Gator-27
93TripleP-224
93UD-273
93UD/FunPack-190
93UD/SP-243
93Ultra-555
94B-237
94D-360
94D/Special-360
94F-146
94F-709
94Finest-364
94L-80
94OPC-172
94Pac/Cr-232
94Panini-70
94Pinn-281
94S-79
94S/GoldR-79
94StCl-443
94StCl/1stDay-443
94StCl/Gold-443
94Studio-195
94T-410
94T/Gold-410
94TripleP-250
94TripleP/Medal-5M
94UD-414
94UD/CollC-291
94UD/CollC/Gold-291
94UD/CollC/Silv-291
94Ultra-60

Whitaker, Stephen E. (Steve)
67T-277
68T-383
69MLB/St-63
69OPC-71
69T-71
69T/St-189
70OPC-496
70T-496
81TCMA-445
89Pac/SenLg-67
92Yank/WIZ60-135

Whitaker, Steve
91Classic/DP-29
91FrRow/DP-40
92OPC-369
92SanJose/ClBest-5
92StCl/Dome-194
92T-369
92T/Gold-369
92T/GoldWin-369
93ClBest/MLG-69

Whitaker, William
N172

Whitby, William
67T-486R

White, Al
80Penin/B-16
80Penin/C-22

White, Andre
91BurlInd/ProC-3319

White, Bill D.
59T-359
60T-355
60T/tatt-53
61P-176
61T-232
61T-451M
61T/Dice-18
61T/St-96
62Bz
62J-158
62P-158
62P/Can-158
62Salada-115
62Shirriff-115
62T-14
62T/St-191
62T/bucks
63Bz-28
63F-63
63J-158
63P-158
63T-1LL
63T-290
63T/SO
64T-11LL
64T-240
64T/Coins-141AS
64T/Coins-78
64T/SU
64T/St-10
64Wheat/St-48
65OPC-190
65T-190
65T/E-43
65T/trans-72
66Bz-23
66T-397
66T/RO
66T/RO-97
67Bz-23
67CokeCap/Phill-13
67Pol/Phill-11
67T-290
68Bz-4
68OPC-190
68T-190
69MB-288
69T-588
72MB-359
78TCMA-12
81TCMA-414
82Danvl/Frit-6
83VeroB-21
90Pac/Legend-56
90Swell/Great-9
91LineD-27
91Swell/Great-96
92AP/ASG-84
92Card/McDon/Pac-25
93UD/ATH-125

White, Billy
89Geneva/ProC-1884
90CLAS/CL-50
90WinSalem/Team-2
91AA/LineD-148
91CharlK/LineD-148
91CharlK/ProC-1699
91ClBest/Singl-363
91Sydney/Fut-10
92ChalK/SB-172
92CharlK/ProC-2781
92ClBest-64
92Sky/AASingl-78

White, Bob
79Clinton/TCMA-25

White, Chaney
78Laugh/Black-9

White, Charles
52Park-22
54JC-24
55Gol/Braves-30
55JC-24
55T-103
55T/DH-18

White, Charlie
89Spring/Best-17
90ArkTr/GS-30
91AA/LineD-47
91ArkTr/LineD-47
91ArkTr/ProC-1301
92BirmB/ProC-2597
92BirmB/SB-98

White, Chris
91AubAS/ClBest-5
91AubAS/ProC-4275
92Ashvl/ClBest-14

White, Clinton
89Wythe/Star-28
90Geneva/ProC-3042
90Geneva/Star-24

White, Craig
89GreatF-29
90Yakima/Team-24

White, Darren
91Adelaide/Fut-11

White, Darrin
89Helena/SP-25
90Beloit/Best-14
90Beloit/Star-23
91Beloit/ClBest-12
91Beloit/ProC-2106

White, Dave
79AppFx-5
86BirmB/Team-4
86SLAS-19
87Hawaii-4

White, Derrick
91James/ClBest-3
91James/ProC-3556
92ClBest-128
92Harris/ProC-469
92Harris/SB-293
92ProC/Tomorrow-271
92UD/ML-279
93FExcel/ML-65

White, Devon
82Danvl/Frit-21
83Peoria/Frit-22
85MidldA-8
86Edmon-27
87ClassicUp-140
87D-38RR
87D/OD-5
87D/Rook-8
87F-646R
87F/Up-U123
87Leaf-38RR
87Seven-W13
87Sf/Rook-10
87Sf/Rook-24
87Sf/TPrev-11M
87Smok/Cal-23
87T-139
88Classic/Red-178
88D-283
88D-8DK
88D/Best-227
88D/DKsuper-8DK
88F-506
88F/Excit-44
88F/Mini-12
88KennerFig-120
88Leaf-127
88Leaf-8DK
88OPC-192
88Panini/St-49
88RedFoley/St-99
88S-212
88S/YS/I-12
88Sf-99
88Smok/Angels-13
88T-192
88T/Big-145
88T/Coins-31
88T/Gloss60-29
88T/JumboR-5
88T/St-183
88T/St-313
88ToysRUs-33
89B-54
89D-213
89D/Best-27
89F-489
89KennerFig-162
89OPC-344
89Panini/St-297
89S-323
89Sf-16
89T-602

89T/Ames-31
89T/Big-122
89T/St-179
89UD-110
90B-292
90Classic-63
90D-226
90F-147
90F/BB-42
90F/Can-147
90F/LL-43
90HotPlay/St-49
90Leaf-76
90OPC-65
90Panini/St-29
90PublInt/St-381
90RedFoley/St-102
90S-312
90S/100St-68
90Sf-210
90Smok/Angel-18
90T-65
90T/Big-299
90T/Mini-10
90T/St-168
90UD-129
90UD-5TC
91B-30
91Classic/III-94
91D-150
91F-328
91F/UltraUp-U64
91F/Up-U69
91Leaf-394
91Leaf/Stud-139
91OPC-704
91OPC/Premier-126
91Panini/FrSt-185
91S-466
91S/RookTr-48T
91S/ToroBJ-23
91StCl-444
91T-704
91T/Tr-125T
91Tor/Fire-25
91UD-517
91UD/Ext-783
92B-547
92BJ/Fire-33
92Classic/Game200-120
92Classic/I-95
92D-180
92D/McDon-G6
92F-346
92Hardee-22
92L-114
92L/BlkGold-114
92MSA/Ben-4
92OPC-260
92Panini-30
92Pinn-17
92S-198
92S/Impact-67
92StCl-41
92Studio-259
92Sunflower-22
92T-260
92T/Gold-260
92T/GoldWin-260
92TripleP-240
92UD-352
92Ultra-155
92Ultra/AwardWin-18
93B-251
93BJ/D/45-13
93BJ/D/McDon-16
93BJ/D/McDon-21
93BJ/D/McDon-31
93BJ/Demp-20
93BJ/Fire-34
93D-132M
93D-29
93F-342
93Flair-297
93HumDum/Can-24
93L-69
93OPC-341
93OPC/WC-16
93Pac/Spanish-659
93Panini-30
93Pinn-138
93S-92
93Select-72
93StCl-485
93StCl/1stDay-485
93Studio-60
93T-387
93T/Gold-387
93TripleP-89
93UD-346
93UD/SP-54
93Ultra-297
93Ultra/AwardWin-18
94B-497
94D-285
94F-348
94L-129
94OPC-159
94OPC/BJ-2
94Pac/Cr-653
94Panini-142
94Pinn-85
94Pinn/Artist-85
94Pinn/Museum-85
94Pinn/Run-22
94S-97
94S/Cycle-10
94S/GoldR-97
94S/GoldS-53
94Select-21
94Sf/2000-96
94StCl-326
94StCl/1stDay-326
94StCl/Gold-326
94StCl/Team-174
94Studio-32
94T-511
94T/Finest-125
94T/Finest/PreProd-125
94T/FinestRef-125
94T/Gold-511
94TripleP-40
94UD-137
94UD/CollC-292
94UD/CollC/Gold-292
94UD/CollC/Silv-292
94UD/ElecD-137
94UD/SP-46
94Ultra-146
94Ultra/AwardWin-8

White, Donnie
92Kingspt/ProC-1545

White, Eric
92BurlInd/ClBest-29
92BurlInd/ProC-1667

White, Ernie
W754

White, Foley
T206

White, Frank
74OPC-604R
74T-604R
75OPC-569
75T-569
75T/M-569
76OPC-369
76SSPC-174
76T-369
77T-117
78SSPC/270-232
78T-248
79OPC-227
79T-439
80OPC-24
80T-45
81Coke
81D-340
81F-44
81F/St-97
81K-34
81OPC-330
81Pol/Royals-9
81T-330
81T/So-47
81T/St-83
82D-286
82F-426
82F-629M
82F/St-209
82OPC-156
82OPC-183IA
82T-645
82T-646IA
82T/St-193
83D-464
83F-127
83F/St-11M
83F/St-26M
83OPC-171
83OPC/St-169
83OPC/St-71
83Pol/Royals-9
83T-525
83T/St-169
83T/St-71
84D-222
84F-363
84Nes/792-155
84OPC-155
84T-155
84T/RD-4M
84T/St-277
85D-175
85F-217
85FunFood/Pin-44
85Leaf-148
85T-743
85T/RD-4M
85T/St-274
86D-130
86F-24
86F/St-127
86GenMills/Book-2M
86Kitty/Disc-13
86Leaf-54
86NatPhoto-20
86OPC-215
86Sf-186M
86T-215
86T/St-23WS
86T/St-263
86T/Tatt-16M
87D-255
87D/AAS-41
87D/OD-204
87F-383
87F/AwardWin-42
87F/Mini-113
87F/St-123
87Leaf-188
87OPC-101
87Sf-168
87Sf/TPrev-13M
87T-692
87T/St-260
88D-225
88D/Best-319
88F-273
88F/St-35
88Nestle-29
88OPC-326
88Panini/St-105
88RedFoley/St-100
88S-79
88Sf-149
88Smok/Royals-25
88T-595
88T/Big-75
88T/St-255
88T/St/Backs-39
89B-122
89D-85
89D/Best-175
89F-297
89OPC-25
89Panini/St-356
89S-390
89T-25
89T/Big-200
89T/LJN-76
89T/St-262
89Tastee/Discs-7
89UD-350
90B-371
90D-262
90F-122
90F/Can-122
90Leaf-204
90MLBPA/Pins-108
90OPC-479
90Panini/St-83
90PublInt/St-360
90S-372
90T-479
90T/Big-105
90UD-382
91F-574
91OPC-352
91T-352
91UD-568
94TedW-142
94TedW-39

White, Fred
88Kenosha/ProC-1382
89Visalia/Cal-102
89Visalia/ProC-1446
90Visalia/Cal-63
90Visalia/ProC-2155
91ClBest/Singl-278
91Visalia/ClBest-11
91Visalia/ProC-1742
92OrlanSR/SB-523

White, G. Harris
WG2-49

White, Gabe
90LitSun/HSPros-7
90LitSun/HSProsG-7
91ClBest/Singl-61
91Sumter/ClBest-12
91Sumter/ProC-2335
92B-279
92MidwLAS/Team-49
92ProC/Tomorrow-268
92Rockford/ClBest-11
92Rockford/ProC-2116
92UD/ML-202
93B-396
93ClBest/MLG-38
93FExcel/ML-66
93Harris/ProC-270
94B-312
94FExcel-231
94SigRook-28
94SigRook/Hot-12
94T-784
94T/Gold-784
94UD/CollC-20
94UD/CollC/Gold-20
94UD/CollC/Silv-20
94Ultra-527

White, Gary 1
87Clearw-17
88Spartan/ProC-1044

White, Gary 2
91Parramatta/Fut-8

White, Guy
(Doc)
10Domino-124
11Helmar-19
12Sweet/Pin-15
80Laugh/FFeat-15
E254
E286
M116
S74-10
S74-115
T202
T205
T206
T207
T215/blue
T215/brown

White, Harold
51B-320

White, Harry
79Newar-13

White, James
(Deacon)
N172
N284
Scrapps
WG1-27

White, Jason
92SoOreg/ClBest-11
92SoOreg/ProC-3430

White, Jerry
75IntAS/TCMA-1
75IntAS/TCMA-6
76Expo/Redp-36
76OPC-594R
76SSPC-340
76T-594R
77OPC-81
77T-557
79T-494
80OPC-369
80T-724
81D-333
81F-161
81OPC-42
81OPC/Post-11
81T-42
82D-621
82Expo/Hygrade-24
82F-211
82Hygrade
82OPC-386
82OPC/Post-24
82T-386
83D-602
83Expo/PostC-22
83F-300
83OPC-214
83Stuart-19
83T-214
89Pac/SenLg-185
89T/SenLg-8
89TM/SenLg-113
90EliteSenLg-32
91Pac/SenLg-3

White, Jimmy
90Ashvl/ClBest-25
91Ashvl/ProC-583
92BurlAs/ClBest-4
92BurlAs/ProC-562

White, Joe
87AZ/Pol-18

White, John F.
C46-4
E254
T206

White, John
82Amari-13

White, Johnny
91James/ClBest-1
91James/ProC-3560

White, Joyner C.
(Jo-Jo)
34DS-45
35Wheat
39PlayBall-79
40PlayBall-84
47Centen-31
47Signal
49B/PCL-14
60T-460C
81Tiger/Detroit-27
92Conlon/Sport-612
R312/M
R313A-12
R314
V355-74

White, Joyner M.
(Mike)
64T-492R
65OPC-31
65T-31
78TCMA-155

White, K.G.
89Bakers/Cal-199

White, Kyle
92Spokane/ClBest-4
92Spokane/ProC-1304

White, Larry
81Chatt-21
82Albuq-10
83Albuq-8
83Pol/Dodg-47
84Cram/PCL-158
85Cram/PCL-168
90Target-852

White, Logan
84Butte-27

White, Marvin
89Butte/SP-29
90Gaston/Best-26CO
90Gaston/ProC-2538CO
90Gaston/Star-27CO
91CharlR/ClBest-28CO
91CharlR/ProC-1331CO
92CharlR/ClBest-27CO
92CharlR/ProC-2242

White, Mike 1
86Bakers-29
87Bakers-12
88FSLAS/Star-25
88VeroB/Star-23
89SanAn/Best-1
90SanAn/GS-29
91AA/LineD-546
91SanAn/LineD-546
91SanAn/ProC-2990
92Bingham/ProC-531
92Bingham/SB-72
92Sky/AASingl-34

White, Mike 2
81LynnS-19

White, Myron
77LodiD

80Albuq-12
90Target-853
White, Oliver Kirby
D322
T205
White, Phil
91Adelaide/Fut-13
White, Randy
83Greens-13
89Idaho/ProC-2034
White, Rich
80Utica-2
White, Rick
91Augusta/ClBest-12
91Augusta/ProC-806
92Salem/ClBest-24
92Salem/ProC-65
94B-190
94Finest-383
94Flair-221
94Flair/Wave-10
94Pinn-533
94UD-493
94UD/SP-145
94Ultra-561
White, Rondell
90Classic/DP-24
90Classic/DP-xxCL
90Classic/III-80
91B-450
91ClBest/Singl-360
91S-390FDP
91Sumter/ClBest-25
91Sumter/ProC-2350
91UD/FinalEd-10F
92B-436
92ClBest-305
92ProC/Tomorrow-266
92UD-51CL
92UD-61TP
92UD/ML-276
92UD/ML-33M
92UD/ML-65DS
92UD/ML/TPHolo-TP8
92WPalmB/ClBest-1
92WPalmB/ProC-2102
93B-72
93ClBest/Fisher-18
93ClBest/MLG-48
93FExcel/ML-67
93FExcel/MLAS-3
93Flair/Wave-18
93Harris/ProC-281
93UD-510DD
93UD/SP-289FOIL
93Ultra-421
94B-360
94B-668
94D-320
94F-556
94Finest-424
94L/GRook-2
94OPC-60
94Pac/Cr-394
94Pinn-246
94Pinn/Artist-246
94Pinn/Museum-246
94Pinn/New-19
94Pinn/RookTPinn-6M
94S-638
94S/Boys-36
94Select-201
94Select/RookSurg-6
94Sf/2000-174
94Sf/Shak-6
94StCl-435
94StCl/1stDay-435
94StCl/Gold-435
94T-784M
94T/Gold-784M
94TripleP-290
94UD-237
94UD/CollC-293
94UD/CollC/Gold-293
94UD/CollC/Silv-293
94UD/ElecD-237
94UD/SP-88
94Ultra-233
White, Roy Hilton
66T-234R
67CokeCap/YMet-18
68T-546
69MB-289
69MLB/St-81
69OPC-25
69T-25
69T/S-26
69T/St-210
69Trans-26
70MLB/St-252
70OPC-373
70T-373
70T/PI-14
71K-43
71MD
71MLB/St-503
71OPC-395
71T-395
71T/Coins-34
71T/GM-45
71T/Greatest-45
71T/S-26
71T/Super-26
71T/tatt-13
72MB-360
72OPC-340
72T-340
72T/Cloth-33
73OPC-25
73Syrac/Team-29
73T-25
74OPC-135
74Syrac/Team-29
74T-135
74T/St-220
75K-1
75OPC-375
75Syrac/Team-24
75T-375
75T/M-375
76OPC-225
76SSPC-435
76SSPC/MetsY-Y6
76T-225
77BK/Y-19
77BurgChef-179
77OPC-182
77T-485
78BK/Y-19
78OPC-48
78SSPC/270-8
78T-16
79BK/Y-19
79OPC-75
79T-159
80OPC-341
80T-648
81TCMA-453
90Swell/Great-42
91Swell/Great-97
92AP/ASG-34
92Yank/WIZ60-136
92Yank/WIZ70-164
92Yank/WIZAS-85
White, Roy
46Sunbeam
White, Sammy
52T-345
53B/Col-41
53T-139
54B-34
54RH
54RM-AL14
54Wilson
55B-47
56T-168
57T-163
58Hires-53
58T-414
59T-486
60T-203
62T-494
79TCMA-25
91T/Arc53-139
PM10/Sm-194
White, Sherman
51BR-B11
White, Sol
78Laugh/Black-22
White, William D.
N172
Whited, Ed
86AubAs-26
87Ashvl-24
88Greenvl/Best-1
88SLAS-16
89Brave/Dubuq-29
89Richm/Bob-27
89Richm/CMC-21
89Richm/Ko-36
89Richm/ProC-837
90AAASingl/ProC-413
90OPC-111
90ProC/Singl-293
90Richm/Bob-16
90Richm/CMC-17
90Richm/ProC-268
90Richm/Team-29
90S-644RP
90S/100Ris-78
90T-111
90T/89Debut-140
90UD-447
Whitehead, Burgess
(Whitey)
34DS-51
39PlayBall-23
40PlayBall-92
41DP-90
41PlayBall-28
R314
V355-59
V94-51
Whitehead, Chris
88Elmira-21
90LynchRS/Team-10
Whitehead, John
92Conlon/Sport-568
R314
Whitehead, Steve 1
76QuadC
Whitehead, Steve 2
(Pitcher)
89James/ProC-2140
90Rockford/ProC-2687
90Rockford/Team-27
91Rockford/ClBest-28
91Rockford/ProC-2048
92MidwLAS/Team-50
92Rockford/ClBest-17
92Rockford/ProC-2117
Whitehill, Earl
28Exh-47
33G-124
35Exh/4-16
35G-8H
35G-9H
36Exh/4-16
81Tiger/Detroit-31
87Conlon/2-60
88Conlon/AmAS-24
91Conlon/Sport-127
R308-165
R310
R312/M
R314
R316
V355-60
V94-52
Whitehouse, Len
77Ashvl
78Ashvl
79Tulsa-3
83T/Tr-126T
83Twin/Team-15
84D-558
84F-578
84Nes/792-648
84T-648
85D-513
85T-406
85Toledo-12
85Twin/Team-17
93Rang/Keeb-378
Whitehurst, Todd
91BurlInd/ProC-3312
Whitehurst, Wally
86Madis/Pol-23
88Tidew/CANDL-29
88Tidew/CMC-11
88Tidew/ProC-1589
89B-373
89F/Up-U103
89Tidew/CMC-6
89Tidew/ProC-1958
89UD/Ext-737
90Kahn/Mets-47
90OPC-719
90S-599
90T-719
90T/89Debut-141
90T/TVMets-19
90UD-564
91B-470
91D-511
91F-166
91Kahn/Mets-47
91Leaf-333
91OPC-557
91S-529
91S/100RisSt-91
91StCl-458
91T-557
91ToysRUs-32
91UD-221
91WIZMets-429
92D-134
92F-519
92Mets/Kahn-47
92OPC-419
92S-299
92StCl-476
92T-419
92T/Gold-419
92T/GoldWin-419
92UD-414
93D-602
93F/Final-147
93Mother/Padre-24
93T-271
93T/Gold-271
94F-678
94Flair-237
94L-216
94Pac/Cr-537
94Pinn-109
94Pinn/Artist-109
94Pinn/Museum-109
94T-486
94T/Gold-486
94UD-129
94UD/ElecD-129
94Ultra-284
Whiteman, Charles
W514-119
Whiten, Mark
87Myrtle-24
88Dunedin/Star-21
89Knoxvl/Best-26
89Knoxvl/Star-21
90AAAGame/ProC-2
90AAASingl/ProC-367
90F/Up-130
90Leaf-396
90ProC/Singl-350
90Syrac/CMC-24
90Syrac/MerchB-29
90Syrac/ProC-587
90Syrac/Team-29
91B-13
91Classic/200-65
91D-607
91D/Rook-32
91F-189
91F/UltraUp-U21
91F/Up-U21
91Leaf-234
91Leaf/Stud-50
91MajorLg/Pins-28
91OPC-588
91OPC/Premier-127
91S-358RP
91S/100RisSt-24
91S/ASFan-6
91StCl-452
91T-588
91T/90Debut-167
91T/Tr-126T
91Tor/Fire-23
91UD-561
91UD/FinalEd-75F
91Ultra-371
92B-57
92Classic/Game200-84
92D-325
92F-126
92Indian/McDon-29
92L-334
92L/BlkGold-334
92L/GoldPrev-17
92L/Prev-17
92OPC-671
92OPC/Premier-178
92Panini-49
92Pinn-355
92S-587
92S/Impact-15
92StCl-51
92Studio-170
92T-671
92T/Gold-671
92T/GoldWin-671
92T/Kids-71
92TripleP-95
92UD-524
92Ultra-55
93D-97
93F-223
93F/Final-133
93Flair-130
93L-449
93OPC-378
93Pac/Spanish-103
93Panini-54
93Pinn-420
93S-106
93Select-146
93Select/RookTr-6T
93StCl-352
93StCl/1stDay-352
93Studio-119
93T-277
93T/Gold-277
93T/Tr-20T
93TripleP-23
93UD-227
93UD-654
93UD/SP-81
93Ultra-193
93Ultra-468
94B-40
94D-311
94F-649
94F/GoldM-1
94Flair-229
94L-29
94OPC-120
94P-19
94Pac/Cr-607
94Panini-250
94Pinn-153
94Pinn/Artist-153
94Pinn/Museum-153
94Pinn/Power-20
94Pinn/Trib-11
94S-315
94S-440
94S/GoldR-315
94Select-164
94Sf/2000-142
94StCl-37
94StCl/1stDay-37
94StCl/Gold-37
94StCl/Team-305
94Studio-56
94T-54
94T/Finest-116
94T/FinestRef-116
94T/Gold-54
94TripleP-69
94UD-150
94UD/CollC-294
94UD/CollC/Gold-294
94UD/CollC/Silv-294
94UD/ElecD-150
94UD/SP-67
94Ultra-273
Whiteside, Matt
90Butte/SportP-29
91Gaston/ClBest-12
91Gaston/ProC-2689
92ProC/Tomorrow-157
92Sky/AASingl-277
92Tulsa/ProC-2697
92Tulsa/SB-623
93B-283
93F/Final-285
93L-508
93Pac/Spanish-649
93Pinn-590
93Rang/Keeb-435
93Select/RookTr-41T
93StCl-474
93StCl/1stDay-474
93StCl/Rang-3
93T-468
93T/Gold-468
93UD-390
93Ultra-638
94D-606

94F-323
94Pac/Cr-631
94S-304
94S/GoldR-304
94StCl-502
94StCl/1stDay-502
94StCl/Gold-502
94StCl/Team-266
94T-629
94T/Gold-629
94Ultra-433

Whiteside, Sean
92Niagara/ClBest-21
92Niagara/ProC-3324

Whitfield, Cat
80CharlO/Pol-22
80CharlO/W3TV-22

Whitfield, Fred
62Kahn/Atl
63Sugar-27
63T-211
64Kahn
64T-367
65OPC-283
65T-283
66Kahn
66OPC-88
66T-88
67CokeCap/Indian-13
67Kahn
67T-275
68OPC-133
68T-133
69MB-290
69T-518

Whitfield, Ken
85Kingst-22
86Kinston-25
89Kinston/Star-24
90Reno/Cal-262
91AA/LineD-98
91Canton/LineD-98
91Canton/ProC-994

Whitfield, Terry
75OPC-622R
75Syrac/Team-18
75Syrac/Team-25
75T-622R
75T/M-622R
76OPC-590R
76SSPC-443
76T-590R
78Ho-136
78T-236
79Ho-10
79OPC-309
79Pol/Giants-45
79T-589
80OPC-361
80Pol/Giants-45
80T-713
81D-435
81F-437
81T-167
81T/So-87
81T/St-233
84F/X-U125
84Pol/Dodg-45
85Coke/Dodg-33
85D-540
85F-389
85T-31
86Coke/Dodg-33
86D-337
86F-147
86Pol/Dodg-45
86T-318
90Target-854
92Yank/WIZ70-165

Whitford, Eric
92ClBest-238
92Stockton/ClBest-17
92Stockton/ProC-44

Whitford, Larry
86Beloit-26

Whiting, Don
78Holyo
79Holyo-15
82ElPaso-9
83Beloit/Frit-14

Whiting, John
75BurlB

Whiting, Mike
86Elmira-28

Whitlock, Mike
88Beloit/GS-22
89StLucie/Star-24

Whitman, Dick
49Eureka-51
51B-221
90Target-855

Whitman, Jim
91Erie/ClBest-13
91Erie/ProC-4083

Whitman, Ryan
92Erie/ClBest-9
92Erie/ProC-1625
93T-558
93T/Gold-558

Whitmer, Dan
79SLCity-19
80SLCity-2
81Syrac/Team-23
82Knoxvl-11
82Syrac-28
82Syrac/Team-24
83Knoxvl-9
93Tiger/Gator-28M

Whitmer, Joe
83Chatt-4
84Chatt-17
85Cram/PCL-99
86Calgary-26

Whitmore, Darrell
90BurlInd/ProC-3025
91Watertn/ProC-3385
92ClBest-156
92Kinston/ClBest-22
92Kinston/ProC-2490
93B-206
93Edmon/ProC-1150
93F/Final-74
93Flair/Wave-19
93Marlin/Publix-26
93Select/RookTr-77T
93StCl-516
93StCl/1stDay-516
93StCl/Marlin-24
93T-697
93T/Gold-697
93UD/SP-144
94B-123
94D-643
94F-481
94Pac/Cr-254
94Pinn-399
94Pinn/New-25
94S-556
94S/Boys-57
94StCl/Team-77
94T-161
94T/Finest-147
94T/FinestRef-147
94T/Gold-161
94UD-233
94UD/CollC-295
94UD/CollC/Gold-295
94UD/CollC/Silv-295
94UD/ElecD-233
94Ultra-201

Whitmyer, Steve
86Water-25

Whitney, Arthur C.
(Pinky)
29Exh/4-12
31Exh/4-11
32Orbit/un-60
33DH-42
36Exh/4-1
37Exh/4-6
38Exh/4-6
38Wheat
39PlayBall-98
91Conlon/Sport-288
R305
R313
R316

Whitney, Arthur W.
N172
N284
N338/2
WG1-71

Whitney, G.
N172

Whitney, James
N172
N284
N403

Whitney, Jeff
90Reno/Cal-278

Whitshire, Vernon
R313

Whitson, Anthony
89CharWh/Best-14

Whitson, Ed
78Colum
79T-189
80Pol/Giants-32
80T-561
81D-74
81F-444
81OPC-336
81T-336
81T/St-240
82D-251
82F-402
82T-656
82T/Tr-127T
82Wheat/Ind
83D-389
83F-423
83T-429
83T/Tr-127T
84D-528
84F-316
84Mother/Giants-26
84Mother/Padres-15
84Nes/792-277
84Smok/Padres-27
84T-277
85D-446
85F-47
85F/Up-U129
85OPC-98
85T-762
85T/St-152
85T/Tr-130T
86D-225
86F-120
86OPC-15
86T-15
86T/St-301
87Bohem-31
87D-360
87F-434
87T-155
88Coke/Padres-31
88D-81
88D/Best-322
88F-599
88OPC-330
88Panini/St-401
88RedFoley/St-101
88S-167
88Smok/Padres-30
88T-330
88T/Big-186
88T/St-107
89B-449
89Coke/Padre-20
89D-229
89D/Best-210
89F-321
89OPC-21
89Padre/Mag-22
89S-329
89T-516
89T/Big-81
89UD-453
90B-204
90Coke/Padre-20
90D-205
90D-26DK
90D/BestNL-98
90D/SuperDK-26DK
90F-171
90F/Can-171
90Leaf-246
90OPC-618
90Padre/MagUno-12
90Panini/St-347
90PublInt/St-62
90S-373
90S/100St-69
90Sf-212
90T-618
90T/Big-152
90T/Mini-82
90T/St-107
90UD-308
91B-651
91D-186
91F-547
91Leaf-337
91Leaf/Stud-250
91OPC-481
91Padre/MagRal-14
91Panini/FrSt-98
91Panini/St-91
91Panini/Top15-67
91S-789
91StCl-246
91T-481
91UD-312
91Ultra-313
92D-380
92F-624
92OPC-228
92Padre/Carl-24
92Pinn-104
92S-564
92StCl-172
92T-228
92T/Gold-228
92T/GoldWin-228
92UD-103
92Yank/WIZ80-202

Whitson, Tony
88Wythe/ProC-1984
89CharWh/ProC-1763

Whitt, Ernie
78Syrac
78T-708R
79Syrac/TCMA-3
79Syrac/Team-12
79T-714R
81D-390
81F-411
81OPC-282
81OPC/Post-20
81T-407
82D-381
82F-626
82OPC-19
82OPC/Post-3
82T-19
82T/St-247
83D-304
83F-443
83OPC-302
83OPC/St-131
83T-302
83T/St-131
84D-437
84F-169
84Nes/792-506
84OPC-106
84T-506
84T/St-373
84Tor/Fire-32
85D-268
85F-119
85Leaf-181
85OPC-128
85T-128
85Tor/Fire-32
86BJ/Ault-24
86D-559
86D/AAS-48
86F-73
86GenMills/Book-3M
86Leaf-217
86OPC-136
86T-673
86Tor/Fire-32
87D-148
87D/HL-39
87D/OD-33
87F-240
87GenMills/Book-1M
87Ho/St-2
87Leaf-69
87OPC-221
87Stuart-28
87T-698
87Tor/Fire-34
88D-394
88F-126
88Ho/Disc-16
88Leaf-250
88OPC-79
88Panini/St-216
88S-168
88T-79
88T/Big-239
88T/St-187
88Tor/Fire-12
89B-248
89D-591
89D/Best-255
89F-248
89OPC-289
89S-98
89T-289
89T/Big-224
89Tor/Fire-12
89UD-118
90B-16
90BJ/HoSt-4M
90Brave/Dubuq/Perf-30
90Brave/Dubuq/Singl-34
90D-385
90F-97
90F/Can-97
90Leaf-408
90OPC-742
90PublInt/St-529
90S-433
90S/Tr-30T
90T-742
90T/St-189
90T/Tr-128T
90UD-148
91Crown/Orio-501
91Leaf-391
91OPC-492
91T-492
92Nabisco-34
93BJ/D/McDon-6

Whitt, Mike
85Everett/Cram-18
85Everett/II/Cram-22
86Clinton-27

Whittaker, Stewart
89GA-36

Whitted, George
(Possum)
15CJ-151
16FleischBrd-100
21Exh-185
90Target-856
D327
D328-188
D329-189
D350/2-190
E121/120
E121/80
E135-188
E220
M101/4-189
M101/5-190
V100
W501-81
W514-92
W575

Whittemore, Reggie
81Bristol-5
83Pawtu-19
84Pawtu-15
85Toledo-19

Whitten, Casey
94B-167
94ClBest/Gold-187
94FExcel-51
94T-756DP
94T/Gold-756DP

Whitty, Todd
91CalLgAS-51

Whitworth, Clint
90OK-17

Whitworth, Dick
87Negro/Dixon-13

Whitworth, Ken
91Miami/ClBest-12
91Miami/ProC-408

Wichman, Mike
89Stockton/Best-26M

Wick, David
82Watlo/B-10
82Watlo/Frit-13

Wickander, Kevin
87Kinston-2
88BBAmer-9
88EastLAS/ProC-44
88Wmsprt/ProC-1315
89B-75
89ColoSp/CMC-5
89ColoSp/ProC-238
90B-327

90D/Rook-36
90OPC-528
90T-528
90T/89Debut-142
91AAA/LineD-98
91ColoSp/LineD-98
91ColoSp/ProC-2185
91D-649
91F-385
91OPC-246
91S-355RP
91S/100RisSt-37
91StCl-572
91T-246
92B-430
92ColoSp/SB-98
92Sky/AAASingl-43
93D-389
93F-602
93Indian/WUAB-32
93Reds/Kahn-28
93S-358
93T-358
93T/Gold-358
93Ultra-547
94F-431
94T-41
94T/Gold-41
Wicker, Bob
WG3-51
Wicker, Floyd
69Fud's-14
69T-524R
71MLB/St-456
71OPC-97
71T-97
Wicker, Kemp
90Target-857
Wickersham, Dave
61T-381
62T-517
63T-492
64Det/Lids-14
64T-181
64T/Coins-105
64T/S-35
65Bz-25
65OPC-9LL
65OldLond-38
65T-375
65T-9LL
65T/trans-34
66OPC-58
66T-58
67CokeCap/Tiger-4
67OPC-112
67T-112
68KDKA-40
68T-288
69T-647
78TCMA-195
Wickham, Mike
89Stockton/Star-26M
Wickman, Robert
90SoBend/Best-28
91B-353
91Saraso/ClBest-11
91Saraso/ProC-1114
92ColClip/Pol-13
92ColClip/ProC-354
92D/Rook-125
92F/Up-46
92UD-76TP
93B-455
93D-417
93F-288
93Flair-254
93L-424
93Pinn-226
93S-291
93Select-343
93StCl-53
93StCl/1stDay-53
93StCl/Y-28
93T-452
93T/Gold-452
93ToysRUs-40
93TripleP-189
93UD-372
93UD/SP-269
93USPlayC/Rook-9H
93Ultra-251
94D-231
94F-250
94Finest-263
94L-206
94Pinn-273
94S-147
94S/GoldR-147
94StCl-494
94StCl/1stDay-494
94StCl/Gold-494
94StCl/Team-210
94T-173
94T/Gold-173
94UD-509
94UD/CollC-296
94UD/CollC/Gold-296
94UD/CollC/Silv-296
94Ultra-404
Wickware, Frank
78Laugh/Black-19
Widger, Chris
92Belling/ClBest-20
92Belling/ProC-1448
92Classic/DP-60
92FrRow/DP-99
93River/Cal-22
93StCl/MurphyS-130
93T-632
93T/Gold-632
Widmar, Al
51B-281
52T-133
53Mother-14
74T-99CO
84Tor/Fire-33CO
85Tor/Fire-33CO
86Tor/Fire-33CO
87Tor/Fire-35CO
88Tor/Fire-41CO
89Tor/Fire-41CO
Widmar, Tom
75Sacra/Caruso-15
Widner, Steven
77Watlo
Widner, William
N172
Wieand, F. Ted
60T-146
Wieczorek, Chet
40Hughes-19
Wiedenbauer, Tom
77Cocoa
80Tucson-8
81Tucson-26
83DayBe-13
86Osceola-28MG
87ColAst/ProC-16
88ColAst/Best-25
89ColMud/Best-8
89ColMud/ProC-130
Wiegandt, Scott
89Martins/Star-34
90Spartan/Best-11
90Spartan/ProC-2492
90Spartan/Star-26
91Clearw/ClBest-11
91Clearw/ProC-1622
92Reading/ProC-577
92Reading/SB-547
Wieghaus, Tom
80Memphis-25
83Expo/PostC-23
83Wichita/Dog-23
84Mother/Ast-18
Wieland, Robert
V94-53
Wielegman, Phil
86Miami-27
Wieligman, Rich
87Lakeland-4
88GlenF/ProC-922
89Toledo/CMC-23
89Toledo/ProC-775
Wielman, Carl
D327
D328-189
D329-190
D350/2-191
E135-189
M101/4-190
M101/5-191
Wiener, Paul
79Jacks-5
Wiens, Randy
78Dunedin
Wiese, Phil
89Elizab/Star-28
90Visalia/Cal-64
90Visalia/ProC-2156
91AA/LineD-498
91OrlanSR/LineD-498
91OrlanSR/ProC-1851
Wieser, Dan
82Omaha-18
Wieser, Tom
84AZ/Pol-19MG
Wiesler, Bob
56T-327
57T-126
79TCMA-224
Wiesmiller, Bob
77Salem
Wiesner, Doug
81AppFx-29
82AppFx/Frit-29TR
Wietelmann, William
(Whitey)
44Playball-38
52Mother-24
73OPC-12CO
73T-12CO
76SSPC-598
77Padre/SchCd-37CO
78Padre/FamFun-36CO
Wieters, Rick
78Green
79Savan-18
80GlenF/B-12
80GlenF/C-13
81GlenF-8
Wiggins, Alan
79Clinton/TCMA-6
81Hawaii/TCMA-8
83D-397
83F-375
83T-251
84D-568
84F-317
84F/St-89
84Mother/Padres-10
84Nes/792-693
84OPC-27
84Smok/Padres-28
84T-693
84T/RD-6M
84T/St-153
84T/St/Box-3
85D-80
85F-48
85F/St-60
85Leaf-68
85OPC-378
85T-378
85T/RD-7M
85T/St-150
86D-607
86F-290
86T-508
87D/OD-138
87F/Up-U124
87French-2
87T/Tr-126T
88S-291
91Crown/Orio-482
Wiggins, Dave
80Phoenix/NBank-14
81Phoenix-14
Wiggins, Jimmy
91Princet/ClBest-26
91Princet/ProC-3515
Wiggins, Kevin
86OrlanTw-23
Wiggins, Tony
89TNTech-29
Wiggs, James
E107
Wiggs, Johnny
89Belling/Legoe-15
90SanBern/Best-21
90SanBern/Cal-94
90SanBern/ProC-2634
91Penin/ClBest-13
91Penin/ProC-379
Wight, Bill
50B-38
51B-164
52B-117
52T-177
53B/Col-100
53Tiger/Glen-28
55B-312
55Gol/Ind-31
56T-286
57T-340
58T-237
79TCMA-131
91Crown/Orio-483
Wihtol, Sandy
79Tacom-16
80T-665R
80Tacom-10
81Charl-7
81T-451R
83Charl-6
Wilber, Del
52B-225
52T-383
53B/BW-24
54B-178
93Rang/Keeb-379MG
Wilbins, Mike
75Cedar
Wilborn, Ted
80OPC-329R
80T-674R
82Phoenix
83Phoenix/BHN-16
86Hagers-27
87Cedar-20
92Yank/WIZ80-203
Wilbur, Bob
80Utica-10
Wilburn, Fred
85MidldA-4
Wilburn, Trey
89Billings/ProC-2041
90CharWh/Best-11
90CharWh/ProC-2242
90Gate/ProC-3355
90Gate/SportP-8
91Billing/SportP-6
91Billings/ProC-3758
Wilcox, Milt
71OPC-164R
71T-164R
72OPC-399
72T-399
73OPC-134
73T-134
74OPC-565
74T-565
75OPC-14
75T-14
75T/M-14
76SSPC-306
77Evansvl/TCMA-25
78BK/T-11
78OPC-136
78T-151
79T-288
80OPC-204
80T-392
81D-247
81F-465
81T-658
82D-223
82F-285
82F/St-157
82T-784
82T/St-186
82T/StVar-186
83D-155
83F-349
83F/St-2M
83F/St-9M
83T-457
84D-471
84F-93
84Nes/792-588
84T-588
84Tiger/Farmer-16
84Tiger/Wave-35
85Cain's-20
85D-105
85F-25
85Leaf-227
85OPC-99
85Seven-6D
85T-99
85T/St-10ALCS
85T/St-17WS
85Wendy-22
86F-243
86Mother/Mar-11
86T-192
89Pac/SenLg-13
89T/SenLg-73
89TM/SenLg-114
90EliteSenLg-16
90MedHat/Best-8
91Pac/SenLg-140
Wilcox, Steve
82Clinton/Frit-11
Wilczewski, Frank
79Clinton/TCMA-27
Wild, Jerry
63Pep/Tul
Wilder, Bill
84Memphis-11
Wilder, Dave
82Idaho-29
83Madis/Frit-5
85Modesto/Chong-21
87Pittsfld-18
Wilder, John
91Pulaski/ClBest-27
91Pulaski/ProC-4006
92Macon/ClBest-12
92Macon/ProC-269
93Durham/Team-25
93SALAS/II-41
Wilder, Mike
83Idaho-25
84Madis/Pol-4
Wilder, Troy
78Watlo
Wilder, Willie
92Penin/ClBest-18
92Penin/ProC-2947
93River/Cal-23
Wiles, Randy
78Charl
Wiley, Charles
91Belling/ClBest-24
91Belling/ProC-3664
92Penin/ClBest-2
92Penin/ProC-2933
93River/Cal-24
Wiley, Craig
87LasVegas-21
88Wichita-12
89Niagara/Pucko-23
Wiley, Jim
90PrWill/Team-28
91ClBest/Singl-167
91FtLaud/ClBest-15
91FtLaud/ProC-2428
Wiley, Joe
92Negro/RetortII-40
Wiley, Keith
88CapeCod/Sum-11
Wiley, Mark
74Tacoma/Caruso-14
75Tacoma/KMMO-1
79Syrac/TCMA-5
79Syrac/Team-27
83RochR-25
84RochR-3
85RochR-29
87French-31CO
88Gator-35CO
91Indian/McDon-30M
Wiley, Michael
91Kane/ClBest-12
91Kane/ProC-2659
91Kane/Team-23
Wiley, Skip
90A&AASingle/ProC-108
90AppFox/Box-30
90AppFox/ProC-2096
91BBCity/ClBest-12
91BBCity/ProC-1399
92Memphis/ProC-2420
92Memphis/SB-448
92Sky/AASingl-190
Wilfong, Rob
76Tacoma
78Twin/FriszP-22
79T-633
79Twin/FriszP-27
80T-238
81D-493
81F-569
81T-453
82D-130
82F-563

82F/St-231
82T-379
82T/St-205
82T/Tr-128T
83D-612
83F-101
83T-158
84D-329
84F-530
84Nes/792-79
84Smok/Cal-30
84T-79
85D-402
85F-315
85Smok/Cal-20
85T-524
86OPC-393
86Smok/Cal-20
86T-658
87D-258
87F-94
87T-251
Wilford, Eric
91Helena/SportP-27
Wilhelm, Hoyt
52T-392
53B/BW-28
53RM-NL21
53T-151
54B-57
54NYJour
54T-36
55B-1
55Gol/Giants-30
55RM-NL12
56T-307
57T-203
58T-324
59T-349
60L-69
60T-115M
60T-395
61P-80
61T-545
61T/St-107
62J-35
62P-35
62P/Can-35
62T-423M
62T-545
62T/St-10
63Salada-39
63T-108
64T-13
65OPC-276
65T-276
66T-510
67CokeCap/WSox-5
67T-422
68T-350
69JB
69MB-291
69T-565
69T/DE-11
69T/St-190
69T/decal
70OPC-17
70T-17
71MLB/St-24
71OPC-248
71T-248
71T/GM-2
71T/Greatest-2
72MB-361
72T-777
77Galasso-23
77Galasso-248
78Cr/PCL-100
78TCMA-100
79TCMA-270
79WHave-27
80Pac/Leg-121
80Perez/HOF-193
82Nashvl-28CO
83Nashvl-25CO
84Nashvl-24CO
85West/2-26
88Pac/Leg-76
89HOF/St-81
89Kodak/WSox-5M
89Pac/Leg-171
89Smok/Dodg-35
89Swell-45
90Pac/Legend-57
90Target-858
91Crown/Orio-484
91T/Arc53-151
91T/Arc53-312
92Bz/Quadra-21M
94T/Arc54-36
Wilhelm, Irvin
(Kaiser)
14Piedmont/St-61
90Target-859
E270/1
M116
T205
T206
T213/blue
V100
Wilhelm, James W.
79Hawaii-7
80T-685R
Wilhelmi, Dave
80Clinton-1
81Clinton-4
84Shrev/FB-24
Wilhoit, Joe
D328-189
E135-189
Wilholte, Arnold
78Ashvl
79Ashvl/TCMA-18
Wilie, Denney
T207
Wilke, Matt
91MedHat/ProC-4111
91MedHat/SportP-18
92MedHat/ProC-3217
Wilkerson, Bill
89London/ProC-1360
Wilkerson, Curtis
(Curt)
82BurlR/Frit-13
82BurlR/TCMA-13
82Tulsa-25
83OKCty-19
84D-99
84F/X-U126
84Rang-19
84T/Tr-127T
85D-99
85F-573
85OPC-342
85Rang-19
85T-594
85T/St-349
86D-256
86F-577
86OPC-279
86Rang-19
86T-434
86T/St-244
87D-223
87F-141
87Mother/Rang-14
87Smok/R-28
87T-228
88D-592
88F-481
88Mother/R-14
88S-127
88Smok/R-21
88T-53
88T/Big-132
89B-292
89D-402
89D/Tr-34
89F-535
89Mara/Cubs-19
89S-518
89T-331
89T/Tr-126T
89UD-465
90Cub/Mara-23
90D-608
90F-46
90F/Can-46
90OPC-667
90Publint/St-209
90S-474
90T-667
90T/TVCub-28
90UD-147
91B-511
91F-438
91Leaf-317
91OPC-142
91S-603
91StCl-512
91T-142
92D-489
92L-387
92L/BlkGold-387
92OPC-712
92S-382
92StCl-46
92StCl-849
92T-712
92T/Gold-712
92T/GoldWin-712
92UD-490
92Ultra-377
93F-627
93Pac/Spanish-142
93Pol/Royal-25
93Rang/Keeb-380
93StCl-177
93StCl/1stDay-177
93StCl/Royal-23
94Pac/Cr-301
Wilkerson, Marty
84Omaha-12
85Omaha-20
86Omaha/ProC-29
86Omaha/TCMA-9
Wilkerson, Wayne Linwood
91Princet/ClBest-21
91Princet/ProC-3530
92Billings/ProC-3372
Wilkerson, Wayne
77Ashvl
Wilkes, Greg
80Hawaii-13
Wilkie, Aldon
47Remar-23
48Signal
Wilkie, James
91Helena/SportP-13
Wilkins, Dean
88EastLAS/ProC-30
88Pittsfld/ProC-1368
89Iowa/CMC-10
89Iowa/ProC-1690
90B-26
90F-47
90F/Can-47
90Iowa/CMC-9
90ProC/Singl-84
90S-630RP
90T/89Debut-143
90T/TVCub-16
91AAAGame/ProC-54
91Tucson/ProC-2214
Wilkins, Eric
80T-511
80Tacom-25
81Charl-6
81T-99
Wilkins, Marc
92Welland/ClBest-25
92Welland/ProC-1323
Wilkins, Mark
81QuadC-28
Wilkins, Michael
88Fayette/ProC-1103
89Lakeland/Star-24
90EastLAS/ProC-EL46
90London/ProC-1269
90ProC/Singl-767
91AA/LineD-547
91SanAn/LineD-547
91SanAn/ProC-2976
92Albuq/ProC-722
Wilkins, Rick
88Peoria/Ko-31
89WinSalem/Star-17
90T/TVCub-63
91AAA/LineD-221
91B-419
91Classic/III-96
91D/Rook-38
91F/UltraUp-U75
91F/Up-U83
91Iowa/LineD-221
91Iowa/ProC-1065
91PreRookPrev/LineD-221
91S/RookTr-103T
91UD/FinalEd-46F
92B-156
92D-249
92F-397
92L-336
92L/BlkGold-336
92OPC-348
92S-483
92S/100RisSt-16
92StCl-643
92T-348
92T/91Debut-184
92T/Gold-348
92T/GoldWin-348
92UD-373
92USPlayC/Cub-11D
92USPlayC/Cub-3H
93B-524
93Cub/Mara-29
93D-28
93F-28
93L-216
93Pac/Spanish-65
93Panini-202
93Pinn-206
93S-185
93Select-390
93StCl-228
93StCl/1stDay-228
93StCl/Cub-23
93Studio-63
93T-721
93T/Gold-721
93TripleP-19
93UD-598
93UD/SP-90
93Ultra-25
94B-306
94D-444
94D/DK-5
94F-401
94L-287
94Pac/Cr-115
94Pac/Gold-20
94Panini-160
94Pinn-84
94Pinn/Artist-84
94Pinn/Museum-84
94Pinn/Power-8
94Pinn/Run-44
94S-450
94Select-16
94Sf/2000-27
94StCl-2
94StCl/1stDay-2
94StCl/Gold-2
94StCl/Team-346
94Studio-65
94T-244
94T/Finest-86
94T/FinestRef-86
94T/Gold-244
94TripleP-80
94TripleP/Medal-2M
94UD-154
94UD/CollC-297
94UD/CollC/Gold-297
94UD/CollC/Silv-297
94UD/ElecD-154
94UD/SP-74
94Ultra-168
Wilkins, Steve
76Cedar
Wilkinson, Bill
86Calgary-25
87F/Up-U125
87Mother/Sea-26
87T/Tr-127T
88D-568
88F-390
88Mother/Sea-26
88RedFoley/St-102
88T-376
89Calgary/CMC-6
89T-636
90AAASingl/ProC-602
90Omaha/ProC-67
92Huntsvl/SB-323
92Tacoma/ProC-2504
Wilkinson, Brian
87Belling/Team-3
88Belling/Legoe-13
89Wausau/GS-13
90Rockford/ProC-2692
90Rockford/Team-28
91WPalmB/ClBest-14
91WPalmB/ProC-1230
Wilkinson, Don
81TCMA-305
Wilkinson, Ray
V100
Wilkinson, Ron
82Madis/Frit-16
82WHave-18
Wilkinson, Spencer
88Gaston/ProC-1019
89Gaston/ProC-999
89Gaston/Star-25
Wilks, Ted
44Playball-25
47TipTop
49B-137
49Eureka-199
51B-193
52B-138
52T-109
53T-101
79TCMA-218
91T/Arc53-101
Will, Bob
59T-388
60T-147
61T-512
61T/St-11
62Salada-218
62Shirriff-218
62T-47
63T-58
Willard, Jerry
82Reading-11
83Charl-8
84D-520
84Wheat/Ind-16
85D-346
85F-460
85OPC-142
85Polar/Ind-16
85T-504
86D-398
86F-601
86F/Up-U126
86OPC-273
86T-273
86Tacom-24
87D-467
87F-409
87T-137
87Tacom-19
89Vanco/CMC-19
89Vanco/ProC-587
90AAAGame/ProC-37
90AAASingl/ProC-170
90ProC/Singl-650
90Vanco/CMC-23
90Vanco/ProC-492
91D-634
91Richm/Bob-36
91Richm/ProC-2573
91Richm/Team-20
92B-470
92Brave/LykePerf-29
92Brave/LykeStand-33
92S-188
92StCl/Dome-195
93Richm/Bleach-19
93Richm/Pep-22
93Richm/Team-28
Willard, Jon
91SLCity/ProC-3212
91SLCity/SportP-10
Willeford, Jerry
76Dubuq
Willes, David
87BYU-13
Willes, Mike
87BYU-3
Willett, Robert Edgar
09Buster/Pin-15
11Helmar-38
14Piedmont/St-62
E104
E254
E95
M116
S74-19
T202
T205
T206
T213/blue
T213/brown

T215/brown
Willey, Carlton
(Carl)
58T-407
59T-95
60Lake
60SpicSpan-25
60T-107
61T-105
61T/St-48
62J-155
62P-155
62P/Can-155
62T-174
63T-528
64T-84
64T/Coins-75
64T/St-44
64T/tatt
65T-401
91WIZMets-430
Willhite, Nick
64T-14R
65T-284
66OPC-171
66T-171
67T-249
78Newar
90Target-860
91WIZMets-431
Williams
E254
E254
T201
Williams, Alberto
73Cedar
Williams, Alberto H.
(Al)
80Toledo-17
81T-569
82D-429
82F-564
82T-69
83D-508
83F-628
83F/St-14M
83F/St-26M
83T-731
83Twin/Team-20
84D-316
84F-579
84Nes/792-183
84T-183
85Colum-10
85Colum/Pol-23
85T-614
Williams, Allen
90AR-33M
Williams, Barry
90Utica/Pucko-13
Williams, Bernabe
(Bernie)
87FtLaud-21
87Oneonta-4
88CLAS/Star-19
88PrWill/Star-24
89BBAmAA/BPro-AA5
89Colum/CMC-21
89Colum/Pol-22
89Colum/ProC-736
90A&AASingle/ProC-31
90Albany/Best-1
90Albany/ProC-1179
90Albany/Star-22
90AlbanyDG/Best-33
90B-439
90Classic-10
90D-689
90EastLAS/ProC-EL45
90Foil/Best-26
90OPC-701
90ProC/Singl-789
90S-619RP
90Star/ISingl-54
90T-701
90T/TVYank-66
91AAA/LineD-123
91AAAGame/ProC-8
91Albany/ClBest-3
91B-173
91Classic/II-T61
91Classic/III-97
91ColClip/LineD-123
91ColClip/ProC-612
91F/UltraUp-U44
91F/Up-U49
91Leaf/StudPrev-7
91OPC/Premier-128
91RedFoley/St-112
91UD-11
92AAA/ASG/SB-123
92B-407
92Classic/Game200-102
92ColClip/Pol-22
92ColClip/ProC-365
92ColClip/SB-123
92D-344
92F-247
92OPC-374
92OPC/Premier-109
92Pinn-229
92Pinn/Team2000-24
92ProC/Tomorrow-106
92S-401
92S/100RisSt-34
92StCl-260
92T-374
92T/91Debut-185
92T/Gold-374
92T/GoldWin-374
92UD-556
93B-623
93D-577
93F-289
93Flair-255
93OPC-363
93Pac/Spanish-215
93Pinn-7
93Pinn/Team2001-15
93S-120
93Select-393
93StCl-364
93StCl/1stDay-364
93StCl/Y-21
93T-222
93T/Finest-30
93T/FinestRef-30
93T/Gold-222
93ToysRUs-48
93UD-332
93UD-470IN
93UD/SP-270
93Ultra-252
94B-521
94D-259
94F-251
94Finest-279
94L-4
94OPC-35
94Pac/Cr-441
94Panini-106
94Pinn-139
94Pinn/Artist-139
94Pinn/Museum-139
94S-339
94Select-140
94Sf/2000-59
94StCl/Team-198
94T-2
94T/Gold-2
94TripleP-280
94UD-86
94UD/CollC-298
94UD/CollC/Gold-298
94UD/CollC/Silv-298
94UD/ElecD-86
94Ultra-103
Williams, Bernard
(Bernie)
70OPC-401R
70T-401R
71MLB/St-264
71OPC-728R
71T-728R
72T-761R
73OPC-557
73T-557
Williams, Billy Leo
61T-141
61T/St-12
62Salada-207
62Shirriff-207
62T-288
62T/St-111
62T/bucks
63Exh
63J-172
63P-172
63Salada-30
63T-353
64Bz-17
64T-175
64T/Coins-44
64T/S-52
64T/SU
64T/St-73
64T/tatt
65Bz-17
65OPC-220
65OPC-4LL
65OldLond-20
65T-220
65T-4LL
65T/E-40
65T/trans-35
66Bz-48
66T-217LL
66T-580
66T/RO-101
66T/RO-98
67Bz-48
67CokeCap/Cub-13
67T-315
68Bz-14
68Kahn
68OPC-37
68T-37
68T/ActionSt-7CM
69Kahn
69Kelly/Pin-19
69MB-292
69MLB/St-126
69MLBPA/Pin-59
69OPC-4LL
69Sunoco/Pin-9
69T-450
69T-4LL
69T/S-39
69T/St-20
69Trans-38
70Dunkin-6
70K-37
70MLB/St-24
70OPC-170
70T-170
70T/S-40
70T/Super-40
71Bz
71Bz/Test-26
71K-61
71MLB/St-48
71OPC-350
71OPC-64LL
71OPC-66LL
71T-350
71T-64LL
71T-66LL
71T/Coins-75
71T/GM-37
71T/Greatest-37
71T/tatt-12
71T/tatt-12a
72K-46
72MB-362
72OPC-439
72OPC-440IA
72T-439
72T-440IA
72T/Post-21
73K-10
73OPC-200
73OPC-61LL
73T-200
73T-61LL
73T/Comics-23
73T/Lids-53
73T/PinUps-23
74K-32
74OPC-110
74OPC-338AS
74T-110
74T-338AS
74T/St-20
75OPC-545
75T-545
75T/M-545
76OPC-525
76SSPC-496
76T-525
80Marchant-30
80Perez/HOF-199
81TCMA-402
83MLBPA/Pin-35
84Cub/Uno-1
85CircK-18
86Sf/Dec-51M
87D/HL-20
88Pac/Leg-90
88T/Gloss22-22
89HOF/St-29
89Kenner/BBGr-18
89Pac/Leg-184
89Swell-120
89T/LJN-41
90Pac/Legend-58
90Perez/GreatMom-69
90Swell/Great-13
91CollAB-36
91Indian/McDon-30CO
91K/3D-9
91LineD-28
91MDA-9
91Swell/Great-98
92AP/ASG-18
92AP/ASG24K-18G
92Cub/Mara-NNO
92Cub/OldStyle-27
92UD/ASFF-47
92UD/HeroHL-HI9
93AP/ASGCoke/Amo-18
93Cub/Mara-30CO
93TWill-24
Exh47
Williams, Billy
88TM/Umpire-3
Williams, Bo
90SanBern/ProC-2648
Williams, Bob
86BurlEx-26
88CharlK/Pep-2
88Hagers/Star-25
Williams, Brent
91Kissim/ProC-4192
Williams, Brian
91ClBest/Singl-14
91Osceola/ClBest-12
91Osceola/ProC-685
92B-125
92Classic/Game200-112
92Classic/I-96
92D-416RR
92F/Up-88
92Pinn-540
92Pinn/Rook-23
92ProC/Tomorrow-228
92S/RookTr-108T
92Sky/AAASingl-278
92T/91Debut-186
92T/Gold-787
92T/GoldWin-787
92Tucson/ProC-489
92Tucson/SB-622
92UD-23SR
92Ultra-498
93B-414
93D-692
93F-56
93L-485
93Mother/Ast-20
93OPC-369
93Pac/Spanish-484
93Pinn-339
93S-333
93Select-287
93Select/ChasRook-6
93StCl-714
93StCl/1stDay-714
93StCl/Ast-22
93T-614
93T/Gold-614
93ToysRUs-98
93UD-286
93USPlayC/Rook-5D
93Ultra-48
94D-284
94F-503
94Pac/Cr-278
94Pinn-409
94S-150
94S/GoldR-150
94StCl-205
94StCl/1stDay-205
94StCl/Gold-205
94T-249
94T/Finest-44
94T/FinestRef-44
94T/Gold-249
94Ultra-211
Williams, Bruce
83Beloit/Frit-9
Williams, Cary
90Clearw/Star-24
91AA/LineD-523
91Reading/LineD-523
91Reading/ProC-1384
92ScranWB/ProC-2461
92ScranWB/SB-497
93ScranWB/Team-27
Williams, Charles
72OPC-388
72T-388
75OPC-449
75T-449
75T/M-449
76OPC-332
76SSPC-98
76T-332
77T-73
78T-561
79T-142
91WIZMets-432
Williams, Charlie
90Kgsport/Best-24
90Kgsport/Star-25
Williams, Charles H.
(Charlie)
88TM/Umpire-41
89TM/Umpire-39
90TM/Umpire-37
Williams, Claude
(Lefty)
88Pac/8Men-108
88Pac/8Men-11
88Pac/8Men-44
88Pac/8Men-45M
88Pac/8Men-49
88Pac/8Men-60
94Conlon-1041
D327
D328-190
E135-190
W514-35
W575
Williams, Clifford
91BendB/ClBest-17
91BendB/ProC-3698
91Reno/Cal-7
Williams, Dallas
80RochR-2
81RochR-23
82Indianap-26
83Indianap-7
84Evansvl-12
86Indianap-26
87Indianap-22
91Crown/Orio-485
Williams, Dan
83BirmB-3
88Burllnd/ProC-1799
89Star/IISingl-186
89Watertn/Star-23
90Kinston/Team-22
91Kinston/ClBest-24CO
91Kinston/ProC-342CO
Williams, Dana
86Pawtu-27
87NewBrit-16
87Pawtu-26
88Pawtu/CMC-21
88Pawtu/ProC-460
89Pawtu/CMC-16
89Pawtu/Dunkin-10
89Pawtu/ProC-690
90AAASingl/ProC-182
90F-648R
90F/Can-648M
90ProC/Singl-651
90T/89Debut-144
90T/TVCub-64
90Vanco/CMC-24
90Vanco/ProC-504
Williams, Dave
85OrlanTw-24
Williams, David Carlous
(Dave)
52B-178
52T-316
53B/Col-1
53T-120
54B-9

54NYJour
55B-138
55Gol/Giants-31
79TCMA-167
91T/Arc53-120
Williams, David
90Pulaski/Best-12
90Pulaski/ProC-3091
91Macon/ClBest-13
91Macon/ProC-866
92ColumMet/SAL/II-33C/S
92Durham/ClBest-24
92Durham/ProC-1101
92Durham/Team-35
Williams, Deb
40Hughes-20
Williams, Dick H.
52T-396
53T-125
54NYJour
57T-59
58T-79
59T-292
60T-188
61P-86
61T-8
61T/St-168
62J-32
62P-32
62P/Can-32
62Salada-48A
62Salada-48B
62Shirriff-48
62T-382
63T-328
64T-153
67OPC-161MG
67T-161MG
67T/Test/RSox-26MG
68OPC-87MG
68T-87MG
69T-349MG
71OPC-714MG
71T-714MG
72OPC-137MG
72T-137MG
73OPC-179MG
73T-179MG
75OPC-236MG
75T-236MG
75T/M-236MG
76SSPC-192MG
76T-304MG
77OPC-108MG
77T-647MG
78OPC-27MG
78T-522MG
79OPC-349MG
79T-606MG
79TCMA-227
81D-453MG
81F-149MG
81T-616MG
81T-680MG
83D-625MG
83T-366MG
84Mother/SDP-1MG
84Nes/792-742MG
84Smok/SDP-29MG
84T-742MG
85F/St-126MG
85Mother/SDP-1MG
85T-66MG
86D/AAS-38
86Mother/Mar-1
86T-681MG
86T/Gloss22-12
86T/Tr-124T
87Mother/A's-12MG
87Mother/Sea-1MG
87T-418MG
88Mother/Sea-1MG
88T-104MG
89Pac/SenLg-166MG
89Pac/SenLg-183MG
89T/SenLg-22MG
89TM/SenLg-115MG
89TM/SenLg-120MG
90EliteSenLg-33MG
90Target-861
91Crown/Orio-486
91Swell/Great-99
91T/Arc53-125
92Bz/Quadra-6M
Williams, Don
(Spin)
84PrWill-20
85Nashua-26
86Nashua-27CO
87Harris-15
88Harris/ProC-839
90EastLAS/ProC-EL28CO
90Harris/ProC-1209CO
90Harris/Star-24CO
91AA/LineD-125M
91CaroMud/LineD-125CO
91CaroMud/ProC-1102CO
92BuffB/BlueS-15CO
92BuffB/ProC-340
92BuffB/SB-50M
Williams, Donald E.
77Padre/SchCd-38CO
78Padre/FamFun-37CO
Williams, Donald Fred
60T-414
Williams, Drew
91MissSt-49
92MissSt-45
93MissSt-46
Williams, Dwayne
87Tampa-10
Williams, Earl
71OPC-52R
71T-52R
72OPC-380
72T-380
73JP
73OPC-504
73T-504
74OPC-375
74T-375
74T/St-130
75OPC-97
75T-97
75T/M-97
76Ho-108
76OPC-458
76SSPC-13
76T-458
77OPC-252
77T-223
78Ho-16
78T-604
89Bluefld/Star-29
91Crown/Orio-487
Williams, Ed
91ClBest/Singl-408
91Classic/DP-41
91Johnson/ClBest-1
91Johnson/ProC-3980
91LitSun/HSPros-32
91LitSun/HSProsG-32
92B-331
92ClBest-366
92ProC/Tomorrow-323
92Savan/ClBest-1
92Savan/ProC-666
92UD/ML-175
93FExcel/ML-107
Williams, Eddie L.
85Cedar-20
86OhHenry-24
87BuffB-13
88ColoSp/CMC-17
88ColoSp/ProC-1547
88D-46RR
88F-620
88Leaf-46RR
88T-758
89Coke/WS-28
89D/Tr-29
89S/YS/II-39
89T/Tr-127T
89UD/Ext-790
90AAAGame/ProC-28
90AAASingl/ProC-19
90CedarDG/Best-10
90LasVegas/ProC-131
90PublInt/St-403
90UD-289
91F-548
91S-552
92Richm/Comix-25
92Richm/ProC-3016
92Richm/SB-447
Williams, Edward
87Peoria-18
88Peoria/Ko-32
89Peoria/Team-18
90WinSalem/Team-25
91SanJose/ClBest-12
Williams, Edwin D.
(Dib)
33G-82
35G-1B
35G-2B
35G-6B
35G-7B
93Conlon-859
V354-36
Williams, Eric
88Geneva/ProC-1635
89CharWh/Best-2
89CharWh/ProC-1756
Williams, Flavio
88Watertn/Pucko-29
89Augusta/ProC-505
89Welland/Pucko-29
90Salem/Star-24
Williams, Frank
84F/X-U127
84T/Tr-128T
85D-323
85F-624
85Mother/Giants-12
85OPC-254
85T-487
85T/St-169
86F-554
86Phoenix-24
86T-341
87F-287
87F/Up-U127
87Kahn-47
87T-96
87T/Tr-128T
88D-512
88F-250
88Kahn/Reds-47
88S-317
88T-773
89B-100
89D-478
89D/Best-259
89F-174
89F/Up-34
89Mara/Tigers-36
89S-485
89T-172
89T/Tr-128T
89UD-449
90D-327
90F-620
90F/Can-620
90OPC-599
90PublInt/St-486
90S-341
90T-599
90UD-539
Williams, Fred 1
(Cy)
21Exh-186
25Exh-48
28Exh-24
28Yueng-52
29Exh/4-12
91Conlon/Sport-154
D327
D328-191
D329-190
D350/2-191
E120
E121/80
E122
E126-42
E135-191
E210-52
M101/4-190
M101/5-191
V100
V61-118
V89-30
W501-100
W502-52
W517-18
W572
W573
W575
Williams, Fred 2
86Stockton-26
87Stockton-26
88ElPaso/Best-19
88TexLgAS/GS-25
89Jaxvl/Best-18
89Jaxvl/ProC-172
90WPalmB/Star-27
Williams, Gary
77Jaxvl
Williams, George 1
63T-324R
64T-388R
Williams, George 2
91SoOreg/ClBest-5
91SoOreg/ProC-3851
92Madis/ClBest-16
92Madis/ProC-1239
94FExcel-122
Williams, Gerald
87Oneonta-6
88PrWill/Star-25
89PrWill/Star-25
90FtLaud/Star-22
91AA/LineD-23
91Albany/LineD-23
91Albany/ProC-1022
91B-161
91ClBest/Singl-127
91Classic/III-99
91UD/FinalEd-15F
91Ultra-388MLP
92AAA/ASG/SB-122
92B-113
92ColClip/Pol-24
92ColClip/ProC-366
92ColClip/SB-122
92D-697
92OPC-656M
92ProC/Tomorrow-115
92Sky/AAASingl-60
92T-656M
92T/Gold-656M
92T/GoldWin-656M
93B-271
93ColClip/Pol-20
93D-49
93F-657
93L-130
93L/GRook-4
93OPC-386
93Pinn-266
93Pinn/RookTP-9M
93S-298
93S/Boys-11
93Select-383
93StCl-571
93StCl/1stDay-571
93StCl/Y-26
93T-654
93T/Gold-654
93ToysRUs-36
93UD-360
94D-390
94Pac/Cr-442
94Pinn-142
94Pinn/Artist-142
94Pinn/Museum-142
94S-590
94StCl/Team-190
94T-383
94T/Gold-383
Williams, Glen
94SigRook-50
94UD/SP-19PP
Williams, Glenn
77Ashvl
Williams, Greg
88StCath/ProC-2019
Williams, Gregory Scott
(Woody)
89Dunedin/Star-23
90Foil/Best-210
90Knoxvl/Best-18
90Knoxvl/ProC-1239
90Knoxvl/Star-20
91AA/LineD-372
91Knoxvl/LineD-372
91Knoxvl/ProC-1768
92Syrac/ProC-1970
93F/Final-297
93Syrac/ProC-999
93T/Tr-118T
94F-349
94Pac/Cr-654
94StCl-513
94StCl/1stDay-513
94StCl/Gold-513
94StCl/Team-154
94T-668
94T/Gold-668
94UD/CollC-300
94UD/CollC/Gold-300
94UD/CollC/Silv-300
94Ultra-441
Williams, H.
86Nashua-28TR
Williams, Harold
80Ander-25
81Durham-8
87Salem-15
88EastLAS/ProC-46
88Harris/ProC-861
89Harris/ProC-302
Williams, Jaime
88OrlanTw/Best-10
89OrlanTw/Best-2
89OrlanTw/ProC-1354
Williams, James A.
N172
Williams, James Alfred 1
70OPC-262R
70T-262R
71OPC-262R
71T-262R
Williams, James Alfred 2
76Laugh/Clown-17
76Laugh/Clown-29
76Laugh/Clown-3
76Laugh/Clown-39
Williams, James F.
(Jimy)
66T-544R
75Phoenix-19
77SLCity
78Spring/Wiener-13MG
79SLCity-22
84Tor/Fire-34CO
85Tor/Fire-34CO
86Tor/Fire-34MG
87OPC-279MG
87T-786MG
87Tor/Fire-36MG
88BJ/5x7-12MG
88OPC-314MG
88T-314MG
88Tor/Fire-3MG
89OPC-381MG
89T-594MG
89Tor/Fire-3
90Brave/Dubuq/Singl-35CO
91Brave/Dubuq/Stand-38CO
92Brave/Lyke/Stand-34CO
93Brave/Lyke/Stand-36CO
Williams, James T.
E107
T206
Williams, James
82DayBe-19
83DayBe-16
84Cram/PCL-58
86Osceola-29
87Visalia-1
88CalLgAS-40
88Visalia/Cal-163
Williams, Jamie
90WichSt-36
Williams, Jason
91MissSt-50
93LSU/McDag-14
94LSU-4
Williams, Jay 1
88Stockton/Cal-203TR
88Stockton/ProC-744TR
89Rockford/Team-31TR
90Jaxvl/Best-28TR
Williams, Jay 2
92Harris/ProC-NNO
Williams, Jeff
81Miami-19
84CharlO-20
86RochR-26
89Reading/Best-23
89Reading/ProC-675
89Reading/Star-25
Williams, Jeffrey Jay
90WichSt-37
91ClBest/Singl-164
91Freder/ClBest-9

91Freder/ProC-2364
92B-284
92ClBest-123
92Hagers/ProC-2556
92Hagers/SB-271
92ProC/Tomorrow-10
92Sky/AASingl-115
92UD/ML-318
93ClBest/MLG-60
Williams, Jerrone
88Wythe/ProC-2002
90Peoria/Team-18
91ClBest/Singl-75
91WinSalem/ClBest-27
91WinSalem/ProC-2844
92ChalK/SB-173
92ProC/Tomorrow-207
Williams, Jessie
87Negro/Dixon-5
Williams, Jim
75Phoenix/Caruso-2
75Phoenix/CircleK-19
Williams, Jimmy
80CharlO/Pol-23
80CharlO/W3TV-23
87French-40CO
88AlaskaAS60/Team-2
90AAASingl/ProC-249
90Portl/CMC-10
90Portl/ProC-179
90ProC/Singl-562
91AAA/LineD-396
91Phoenix/LineD-396
91Phoenix/ProC-68
Williams, Jody
87Watertn-19
Williams, Joe
90Boise/ProC-3323
Williams, Joseph (Smokey)
93TWill-114
Williams, John
86BurlEx-27
Williams, Jon
86Lipscomb-22
Williams, Juan
90Pulaski/Best-25
90Pulaski/ProC-3111
91Macon/ClBest-27
91Macon/ProC-880
92Macon/ClBest-17
92Macon/ProC-283
93Durham/Team-26
Williams, Keith
94FExcel-296
94FExcel/1stY-8
Williams, Kenneth Royal
83AppFx/Frit-14
86BuffB-24
87D/Rook-11
87F/Up-U128
87Fayette-25
87Hawaii-2
87Sf/Rook-41
88Coke/WS-30
88D-334
88D/Best-249
88F-412
88F/Mini-17
88F/SS-42
88GlenF/ProC-918
88OPC-92
88Panini/St-65
88S-112
88S/YS/I-6
88Sf-69
88T-559
88T/St-287
89D-337
89D/Tr-17
89Mara/Tigers-25
89S-67
89T-34
89T/Tr-129T
89Toledo/CMC-9
89Toledo/ProC-763
89UD-506
89UD/Ext-714
90CokeK/Tiger-27
90London/ProC-1270
90OPC-327
90PublInt/St-487
90T-327
90UD-249
91F-190
91Miami/ClBest-13
91Miami/ProC-409
91OPC-274
91T-274
91Tor/Fire-13
91UD-89
92S-354
Williams, Kenneth Roy
21Exh-187
25Exh-119
26Exh-119
27Exh-58
92Conlon/Sport-442
93Conlon-940
E120
E126-48
E220
V100
V61-52
V89-37
W515-26
W572
W573
Williams, Kerman
85Elmira-24
86Elmira-29
Williams, Kevin
82OrlanTw-1
83OrlanTw-4
Williams, Landon
90Penin/Star-24
Williams, Lanny
91Butte/SportP-11
92Gaston/ClBest-20
92Gaston/ProC-2257
Williams, Leroy
90Kissim/DIMD-28
Williams, Mark 1
77SanJose-6
86BirmB/Team-21
Williams, Mark 2
92Johnson/ProC-3120
93StCl/MurphyS-11
Williams, Marvin
86Negro/Frit-87
Williams, Matt E.
82Knoxvl-8
83Syrac-13
84Syrac-11
85Syrac-12
86OKCty-26
Williams, Matt
86Cram/NWL-3
87D/Rook-45
87F/Up-U129
87Mother/SFG-22
87Phoenix-2
87Pocatel/Bon-12
87Sf/Rook-25
87T/Tr-129T
88Classic/Blue-246
88D-628
88F-101
88Phoenix/CMC-18
88Phoenix/ProC-56
88S-118
88S/YS/I-18
88T-372
89AAA/CMC-35
89AAA/ProC-51
89D-594
89F-346
89Mother/Giants-12
89Panini/St-218
89Phoenix/CMC-18
89Phoenix/ProC-1485
89S-612
89T-628
89UD-247
90B-238
90Classic-73
90Classic/Up-11
90D-348
90D/BestNL-61
90D/GSlam-1
90F-75
90F/Can-75
90Leaf-94
90Mother/Giant-9
90Mother/MWilliam-Set
90OPC-41
90Panini/St-366
90S-503
90S/McDon-6
90Sf-70
90T-41
90T/Big-96
90T/St-88
90TripleAAS/CMC-35
90UD-577
90USPlayC/AS-8H
90Woolwth/HL-30
91B-378SLUG
91B-618
91Cadaco-61
91Classic/200-158
91Classic/I-8
91Classic/III-95
91CollAB-30
91D-18DK
91D-685
91D/Elite-E8
91D/GSlam-8
91D/SuperDK-18DK
91F-276
91F/ASIns-3
91Kenner-54
91KingB/Discs-16
91Leaf-93
91Leaf/Stud-259
91MajorLg/Pins-65
91Mother/Giant-9
91OPC-190
91OPC-399AS
91PG&E-11
91Panini/FrSt-69
91Panini/St-76
91Panini/Top15-17
91RedFoley/St-100
91S-189
91S-667AS
91S-689MB
91S/100SS-77
91SFExam/Giant-16
91Seven/3DCoin-15NC
91StCl-295
91Sunflower-24
91T-190
91T-399AS
91T/CJMini/II-9
91T/SU-35
91UD-157
91UD-79
91UD/SilSlug-SS13
91Ultra-331
92B-175
92B-579FOIL
92CJ/DII-11
92Classic/DP-73
92Classic/Game200-45
92Classic/II-T31
92D-135
92F-650
92F/Lumber-L6
92FrRow/DP-53
92French-8M
92Giant/PGE-35
92Hardee-23
92Kenner/Fig-46
92L-373
92L/BlkGold-373
92Mother/Giant-9
92OPC-445
92OPC/Premier-144
92Panini-214
92Pinn-28
92Pinn/TeamP-6M
92S-230
92S/100SS-95
92S/Impact-62
92StCl-582
92Studio-120
92T-445
92T/Gold-445
92T/GoldWin-445
92T/Kids-60
92TripleP-4
92UD-154
92UD/HRH-HR5
92USPlayC/Ace-10C
92Ultra-296
92Ultra/AwardWin-13
92Watertn/ClBest-10
92Watertn/ProC-3235
93B-56
93ClBest/MLG-147
93Colla/ASG-8
93Colla/DM-117
93D-182
93F-540
93Flair-148
93Kinston/Team-27
93L-158
93Mother/Giant-3
93OPC-348
93Pac/Spanish-278
93Panini-239
93Pinn-67
93Pinn/HRC-22
93Rang/Keeb-381
93S-46
93Select-95
93StCl-287
93StCl/1stDay-287
93StCl/Giant-3
93Studio-66
93T-225
93T/Finest-25
93T/FinestRef-25
93T/Gold-225
93TripleP-171
93UD-143
93UD-476M
93UD/FunPack-104
93UD/HRH-HR21
93UD/SP-117
93UD/SPPlat-PP20
93Ultra-490
94B-79
94Church-10
94D-370
94D/DomI-4
94D/Special-370
94F-704
94F/Lumber-10
94F/ProV-3
94L-334
94L/CleanUp-10
94L/MVPNL-14
94OPC-80
94Pac/Cr-559
94Pac/Gold-13
94Panini-268
94Pinn-298
94Pinn/Run-39
94Pinn/TeamP-3
94RedFoley-9M
94S-94
94S/Cycle-20
94S/DT-6
94S/GoldR-94
94S/GoldS-10
94Sf/2000-139
94Sf/2000-187AS
94StCl-268
94StCl-419
94StCl/1stDay-268
94StCl/1stDay-419
94StCl/Gold-268
94StCl/Gold-419
94StCl/Team-22
94Studio-89
94T-386M
94T-550
94T/BlkGold-44
94T/Finest-214
94T/FinestRef-214
94T/Gold-386M
94T/Gold-550
94T/Prev-225
94TripleP-110
94TripleP/Bomb-10
94UD-36FT
94UD-490
94UD/CollC-299
94UD/CollC/Gold-299
94UD/CollC/Silv-299
94UD/ElecD-36FT
94UD/Mantle-20
94UD/SP-95
94Ultra-296
94Ultra/AS-15
94Ultra/AwardWin-13
94Ultra/HRK-9
94Ultra/RBIK-11
Williams, Matthew
87Idaho-19
88Idaho/ProC-1842
89Salinas/Cal-140
89Salinas/ProC-1825
Williams, Mel
83Reading-22
Williams, Michael Darren
90Batavia/ProC-3067
91ClBest/Singl-103
91Clearw/ClBest-12
91Clearw/ProC-1623
92B-152
92D/Rook-126
92Reading/SB-548
92ScranWB/ProC-2448
92Sky/AASingl-240
93B-568
93F/MLPII-11
93ScranWB/Team-28
93StCl-539
93StCl/1stDay-539
93T-99
93T/Gold-99
93Ultra-94
94Phill/Med-35
94StCl/Team-230
94T-447
94T/Gold-447
Williams, Michael
86Lipscomb-23
Williams, Mike 1
76Watlo
77LodiD
79Albuq-3
80Phoenix/NBank-8
81Phoenix-8
89Pac/SenLg-16
Williams, Mike 2
87Pocatel/Bon-19
Williams, Mitch
86D/Rook-19
86F/Up-U127
86Rang-28
86Sf/Rook-20
86T/Tr-125T
87D-347
87F-142
87Mother/Rang-17
87Sf/TPrev-1M
87Smok/R-7
87T-291
87ToysRUs-32
88D-161
88D/Best-279
88F-482
88F/RecSet-43
88Mother/R-17
88OPC-26
88S-339
88S/YS/II-31
88Smok/R-19
88T-26
89B-283
89D-225
89D/Best-60
89D/Tr-38
89F-536
89F/Up-81
89Mara/Cubs-28
89OPC-377
89S-301
89S/Tr-32
89S/YS/I-27
89Sf-151
89T-411
89T/St-247
89T/Tr-130T
89UD-95
89UD/Ext-778
90B-25
90Classic-23
90Cub/Mara-24
90D-275
90D/BestNL-75
90F-48
90F-631M
90F/AwardWin-43
90F/BB-43
90F/BBMVP-43
90F/Can-48
90F/Can-631M
90Kenner/Fig-90
90Leaf-156
90MLBPA/Pins-48
90OPC-520
90Panini/St-232
90PublInt/St-210

90RedFoley/St-103
90S-262
90S-695DT
90S/100St-93
90Sf-196
90T-520
90T/Big-109
90T/DH-71
90T/Gloss60-47
90T/Mini-52
90T/St-48
90T/TVAS-65
90T/TVCub-17
90UD-174
91D-312
91F-439
91F/UltraUp-U101
91F/Up-U110
91Leaf-420
91OPC-335
91RedFoley/St-101
91S-220
91S/RookTr-27T
91StCl-261
91T-335
91T/Tr-127T
91UD-173
91UD/Ext-769
91Ultra-71
92B-247
92D-353
92F-547
92L-301
92L/BlkGold-301
92OPC-633
92Phill/Med-32
92Pinn-406
92S-356
92S-892DT
92StCl-499
92Studio-80
92T-633
92T/Gold-633
92T/GoldWin-633
92T/Kids-20
92TripleP-220
92UD-410
92UD/TmMVPHolo-54
92Ultra-549
93B-328
93Cub/Rolaid-4
93D-40
93F-498
93Flair-108
93L-114
93OPC-226
93Pac/Spanish-241
93Phill/Med-35
93Pinn-565
93Rang/Keeb-382
93S-367
93Select-79
93StCl-180
93StCl/1stDay-180
93StCl/Phill-29
93Studio-82
93T-235
93T/Finest-49
93T/FinestRef-49
93T/Gold-235
93TripleP-125
93UD-113
93UD/FunPack-147
93UD/SP-180
93Ultra-448
94B-446
94D-319
94F-604
94Finest-242
94Flair-176
94L-431
94OPC-99
94Pac/Cr-490
94Panini-232
94Pinn-218
94Pinn/Artist-218
94Pinn/Museum-218
94S-217
94S/GoldR-217
94T-114
94T/Gold-114
94TripleP-30
94UD-499
94Ultra-512
94Ultra/Fire-10

Williams, Paul Jr.
86Elmira-30
88WinHaven/Star-27
90CLAS/CL-11
90LynchRS/Team-13
91AA/LineD-647
91Wmsprt/LineD-647
91Wmsprt/ProC-303
92Hagers/SB-272

Williams, Quinn
86Cram/NWL-131

Williams, Ray R.
78StPete
79ArkTr-3
80ArkTr-20

Williams, Ray
88Wausau/GS-13
90SanBern/Best-22
90SanBern/Cal-112

Williams, Reggie
83VeroB-25
86Albuq-28
86D/Rook-5
86F/Up-U128
86Pol/Dodg-51
86Sf/Rook-19
87D-341
87F-460
87F/Hottest-42
87F/Mini-114
87F/St-124
87Mother/Dodg-15
87Pol/Dodg-9
87Sf/TPrev-14M
87T-232
88ColoSp/CMC-23
88ColoSp/ProC-1524
89BuffB/CMC-23
89BuffB/ProC-1685
89Clinton/ProC-893
90QuadC/GS-26
90Target-862
91MidldA/OneHour-31
92Edmon/ProC-3552
92Edmon/SB-172
93D-253
93T-543
93T/Gold-543
93Vanco/ProC-2612

Williams, Rick
73Cedar
78Charl
78Memphis/Team-10
79Memphis/TCMA-13
79T-437
80Memphis-26
80T-69
80Tucson-4
81Toledo-10
82Toledo-9

Williams, Rob
85Utica-8
87WPalmB-6

Williams, Robert E.
T207

Williams, Roger
87Pittsfld-21
88Iowa/CMC-11
88Iowa/ProC-545
89Iowa/ProC-1691

Williams, Roy
89KS*-56CO

Williams, Scott
85Newar-1

Williams, Scottie
92Kingspt/ClBest-16
92Kingspt/ProC-1532

Williams, Shad
92MidwLAS/Team-53
92QuadC/ClBest-7
92QuadC/ProC-811

Williams, Slim
88Visalia/ProC-96

Williams, Smokey Joe
74Laugh/Black-1
86Negro/Frit-86
88Conlon/NegAS-12
88Negro/Duques-8
90Negro/Star-27

Williams, Stan
59T-53
60BB-16
60L-109
60T-278
60Union/Dodg-20
61BB-40
61P-162
61T-190
61T-45LL
61T/St-36
61Union/Dodg-22
62BB-40
62J-115
62P-115
62P/Can-115
62T-515
62T-60LL
63J-122
63P-122
63T-42
64T-505
65T-404
68OPC-54
68T-54
69OPC-118
69T-118
69T/4in1-22
69T/St-170
70OPC-353
70T-353
71MLB/St-478
71OPC-638
71T-638
72OPC-9
72T-9
79Colum-6
89Smok/Dodg-68
90Kahn/Reds-27M
90Target-863
91Kahn/Reds-x
92Yank/WIZ60-137
WG9-25

Williams, Steve 1
75Shrev/TCMA-23

Williams, Steve 2
86Clearw-25
87Reading-24
89Erie/Star-26

Williams, Sweet
72Dimanche*-116M

Williams, Teddy
86Cram/NWL-123
87Idaho-10
87Wausau-12
88CalLgAS-28
88SanBern/Best-4
88SanBern/Cal-38
88Sumter/ProC-419
89BurlB/ProC-1622
89BurlB/Star-25
89EastLDD/ProC-DD36
89Wmsprt/ProC-636
89Wmsprt/Star-22
90CollAB-23
90Foil/Best-138
90ProC/Singl-759
90Wmsprt/Best-22
90Wmsprt/ProC-1071
90Wmsprt/Star-23
91AA/LineD-348
91Jaxvl/LineD-348
91Jaxvl/ProC-164

Williams, Terrell
92Kingspt/ClBest-15
92Kingspt/ProC-1542

Williams, Theodore Samuel
(Ted)
39Exh
39PlayBall-92
40PlayBall-27
41DP-57
41DP-81
41PlayBall-14
42Playball-6
43MP-24
47HomogBond-48
48L-76
48Swell-16
50B-98
51B-165
51Wheat
52BR
52RM-AL23
52StarCal-85A
52StarCal-85AM
52StarCal/L-71B
52StarCal/L-71C
52Wheat*
53Exh/Can-30
54B-66A
54T-1
54T-250
54Wilson
55T-2
55T/DH-69
56T-5
56T/Hocus-A5
56T/Hocus-B7
56T/Pin-26
57T-1
58T-1
58T-321M
58T-485AS
59F/Set
60F-72
60NuCard-39
60NuCard-52
61F-152
61NuCard-439
61NuCard-452
69T-539M
69T-650MG
70OPC-211MG
70T-211MG
71OPC-380MG
71T-380MG
72OPC-510MG
72T-510MG
74Laugh/ASG-46
75SSPC/42-19
75SSPC/42-28M
75Shakey-10
76Laugh/Jub-27
76OPC-347AS
76Rowe-16
76Shakey-103
76T-347AS
77Galasso-10
77Galasso-230
77Shakey-23
78SSPC/270-177CO
78TCMA-260
79TCMA-10
80Laugh/3/4/5-20
80Laugh/3/4/5-6
80Marchant/HOF-31
80Pac/Leg-61
80Perez/HOF-104
80SSPC/HOF
81TCMA-444
82F/St-237M
83D/HOF-9
83Kaline-68M
83MLBPA/Pin-18
84D/Champs-14
84West/1-20
85CircK-9
85D/HOF-2
85Woolwth-38
86BLChew-8
86Sf/Dec-25
87Leaf/SpecOlym-H5
87Nestle/DT-18
88Grenada-70
88Pac/Leg-50
89B/Ins-11
89HOF/St-28
89Nissen-20
89Pac/Leg-154
89Swell-100
90BBWit-50
90HOF/St-40
90Pac/Legend-59
90Perez/GreatMom-13
90Swell/Great-125
91MDA-17
91Swell/Great-100
91T/Arc53-319
92Bz/Quadra-22M
92Perez/Master-41
92Perez/Master-42
92Perez/Master-43
92Perez/Master-44
92Perez/Master-45
92UD-HH2
92UD/ASFF-50
92UD/HeroHL-HI10
92UD/TWillH-Set
92UD/TWillWB-Set
93Rang/Keeb-1MG
93TWill-1
93TWill-148
93TWill-AU148
93TWill/Locklear-9
93TWill/POG-23M
93TWill/POG-26
93TWill/Pr-1
93UD/ATH-126
93UD/ATH-132
93UD/ATH-161M
93UD/ATH-162M
93UD/ATHPrev-1
93UD/ATHPrev-3
93UD/ATHPrev-4M
94TWill/Pr-1
94TedW-1
94TedW-143
94TedW-LP2
94TedW/500-8
D305
PM10/L-41
PM10/Sm-195
PM10/Sm-196
PM10/Sm-197
PM10/Sm-198
PM10/Sm-199
PM10/Sm-200
R302-101
R303/A
R346-44
R423-113
V351A-25
V351B-47

Williams, Tim
84Greens-14
88CapeCod/Sum-143
89Alaska/Team-14

Williams, Todd
91GreatF/SportP-25
92Bakers/Cal-29
92SanAn/ProC-3976
93B-182
93StCl/Dodg-30
94B-322
94ClBest/Gold-11
94FExcel-221

Williams, Tom
88CapeCod/Sum-118

Williams, Troy
86Cram/NWL-118
87Wausau-6

Williams, Walter E.
(Walt)
66Pep/Tul
67T-598R
68OPC-172
68T-172
68T/ActionSt-6AM
69T-309
70MLB/St-191
70OPC-395
70T-395
70T/CB
71OPC-555
71T-555
71T/Coins-36
72MB-363
72OPC-15
72T-15
73OPC-297
73T-297
74OPC-418
74T-418
76OPC-123
76SSPC-436
76SSPC/MetsY-Y21
76T-123
87Sumter-4
88Durham/Star-24
89Pac/SenLg-123
89T/SenLg-126
89TM/SenLg-116
89Tulsa/GS-2CO
89Tulsa/Team-26CO
90EliteSenLg-120
90Tulsa/ProC-1173CO
90Tulsa/Team-27CO
91CharlR/ClBest-29CO
92Gaston/ClBest-25MG
92Gaston/ProC-2268MG
92Yank/WIZ70-166

Williams, Wes
79Ashvl/TCMA-12

Williams, William
(Billy)
89Canton/Best-8
89Canton/ProC-1317
Williams, Willie D.
82Danvl/Frit-18
Williams, Woodrow Wilson
(Woody)
47Signal
90Target-864
Williamson, Bret
87Tampa-13
Williamson, Edward
N172
N284
WG1-18
Williamson, Greg
86Watlo-31
Williamson, Joel
93Welland/ProC-3361
Williamson, Kevin
87Modesto-16
88Modesto/Cal-59
Williamson, Mark
83Beaum-8
85Beaum-3
86LasVegas-23
87D/Rook-3
87French-32
88D-418
88F-574
88SanDiegoSt-18
88T-571
89F-626
89French-32
89S-592
89SanDiegoSt-20
89T-546
89T/Big-147
90B-248
90D-406
90F-194
90F/Can-194
90Leaf-461
90OPC-13
90PublInt/St-591
90S-332
90T-13
90T/St-236
90UD-173
91B-85
91Crown/Orio-488
91D-238
91F-495
91Leaf-21
91OPC-296
91S-498
91StCl-20
91StCl/Member*-10M
91T-296
91UD-510
92D-511
92F-30
92OPC-628
92S-427NH
92S-487
92StCl-177
92T-628
92T/Gold-628
92T/GoldWin-628
92UD-609
93F/Final-168
93StCl-613
93StCl/1stDay-613
93UD-722
93Ultra-504
94F-24
94S-157
94S/GoldR-157
Williamson, Mike
77Ashvl
Williamson, Ray
87Watlo-22
88Kinston/Star-24
Willis, Alan
82Watlo-11
Willis, C.H.
N172
Willis, Carl
84Evansvl-22
87F-218
87Nashvl-23
87T-101
88Vanco/CMC-4
88Vanco/ProC-762
89Edmon/CMC-3
89Edmon/ProC-567
90AAASingl/ProC-219
90ColoSp/CMC-8
90ColoSp/ProC-38
90ProC/Singl-460
91AAA/LineD-423
91Portl/LineD-423
91Portl/ProC-1567
92B-466
92D-665
92L-452
92L/BlkGold-452
92OPC-393
92Pinn-491
92S-482
92StCl-779
92USPlayC/Twin-11C
92USPlayC/Twin-7D
92Ultra-403
93F-275
93L-164
93OPC-388
93Pac/Spanish-527
93Pinn-372
93StCl-182
93StCl/1stDay-182
93T-747
93T/Gold-747
93Ultra-239
94D-581
94F-222
94L-198
94Pac/Cr-370
94Pinn-378
94StCl-484
94StCl/1stDay-484
94StCl/Gold-484
94T-621
94T/Gold-621
Willis, James
54T-67
94T/Arc54-67
Willis, Jim
87AppFx-30
Willis, Kent
87Tampa-17
88Rockford-34
88Virgini/Star-22
89Rockford-34
Willis, Marty
89Lakeland/Star-25
90Lakeland/Star-25
91AA/LineD-398
91ClBest/Singl-6
91London/LineD-398
91London/ProC-1879
92London/ProC-634
92London/SB-423
Willis, Mike
75IntAS/TCMA-18
75IntAS/TCMA-28
76SSPC-382
77OPC-103
77T-493R
78BJ/PostC-24
78OPC-227
78T-293
79OPC-366
79T-688
80Syrac-7
80Syrac/Team-24
81F-426
81OPC-324
81T-324
82OkCty-1
87Maine/TCMA-25
Willis, Ron
67T-592R
68OPC-68
68T-68
69T-273
Willis, Scott
87Cedar-3
Willis, Steve
87Anchora-31
90Wausau/Best-2
90Wausau/ProC-2115
90Wausau/Star-26
91Freder/ClBest-10
Willis, Travis
89Geneva/ProC-1867
90Peoria/Team-29
91CLAS/ProC-CAR46
91WinSalem/ClBest-11
91WinSalem/ProC-2830
92CharlK/ProC-2773
94FExcel-171
Willis, Vic
E104
E107
E90/1
E91
E95
M116
T206
WG3-52
Willoughby, Claude
93Conlon-792
R316
Willoughby, Jim
73OPC-79
73T-79
74OPC-553
74T-553
76OPC-102
76SSPC-419
76T-102
77T-532
78T-373
79T-266
89Pac/SenLg-37
89T/SenLg-70
91Pac/SenLg-88
Willoughby, Mark
86Columbia-27A
86Columbia-27B
89Pittsfld/Star-23
89Star/IISingl-165
Wills, Adrian Charles
87Greenvl/Best-8
Wills, Bump
77T-494R
78BK/R-12
78Ho-21
78OPC-208
78SSPC/270-95
78T-23
79OPC-190
79T-369
80OPC-373
80T-473
81D-25
81F-628
81OPC-173
81T-173
81T/HT
81T/St-134
82D-289
82F-334
82F/St-175
82OPC-272
82RedLob
82T-272
82T/St-244
82T/Tr-129T
83D-351
83F-511
83F/St-13M
83F/St-1M
83T-643
88Butte-29
89Butte/SP-24
91Gaston/ClBest-17
91Gaston/ProC-2704MG
92CharlR/ClBest-26MG
92CharlR/ProC-2240
93Rang/Keeb-383
Wills, Frank
82Omaha-10
84Omaha-5
85Cram/PCL-85
86F-480
86Maine-24
86T-419
87BuffB-23
87Gator-22
87T-551
88Syrac/CMC-11
88Syrac/ProC-830
89Syrac/CMC-5
89Syrac/MerchB-24
89Syrac/ProC-794
89Syrac/Team-24
89Tor/Fire-44
90F-98
90F/Can-98
90T/Tr-129T
90Tor/BJ-44
91D-691
91F-191
91OPC-213
91S-521
91S/ToroBJ-10
91Syrac/MerchB-29
91T-213
91Tor/Fire-44
Wills, Maury
60BB-20
60Union/Dodg-21
61BB-30
61Morrell
61P-164
61Union/Dodg-23
62BB-30
62J-104
62P-104
62P/Can-104
62Salada-127A
62Salada-127B
62Shirriff-127
63Exh
63F-43
63J-115
63P-115
63Salada-20
67CokeCap/Pirate-13
67T-570
68Bz-1
68Bz-4
68KDKA-30
68OPC-175
68T-175
69MB-293
69MLB/St-162
69OPC-45
69OPC/DE-23
69T-45
69T/DE-24
69T/S-49
69T/St-60
69T/decal
70MLB/St-60
70T-595
71Bz/Test-34
71MLB/St-120
71OPC-385
71T-385
71T/GM-29
71T/Greatest-29
71T/tatt-14
71Ticket/Dodg-19
72MB-364
72OPC-437
72OPC-438IA
72T-437
72T-438IA
74Greyhound-6M
75OPC-200MVP
75T-200MVP
75T/M-200MVP
77T-435HL
78TCMA-70
81F-595MG
81Pol/Mar-14MG
81T-672MG
82KMart-2
83MLBPA/Pin-36
85Woolwth-39
87Smok/Dodg-38
87T-315TBC
88Smok/Dodg-7
89Smok/Dodg-69
90HOF/St-66
90MSA/AGFA-12
90Target-865
92AP/ASG-47
93TWill-17
93TWill/Mem-9
Exh47
Wills, Shawn
92Batavia/ClBest-11
92Batavia/ProC-3281
92Classic/DP-110
Wills, Ted
60L-56
61T-548
62T-444
65T-488
78TCMA-138
Willsher, Chris
84CharlO-11
Willson, Rob
87Everett-22
Wilmet, Paul
82Lynch-10
85Spring-30
87ArkTr-10
88EastLAS/ProC-18
88Harris/ProC-852
89OkCty/CMC-9
89OkCty/ProC-1509
90AAASingl/ProC-626
90Iowa/CMC-10
90Iowa/ProC-319
90ProC/Singl-85
90SpringDG/Best-16
90T/89Debut-145
93Rang/Keeb-384
Wilmont, Walter
N172
WG1-72
Wilmore, Al
92Negro/Retort-63
Wilner, Eric
85Anchora-34
Wilridge, James
84Idaho/Team-30
Wilshere, Whitey
94Conlon-1314
Wilson, A. Parke
N566/2
Wilson, Alan
84LitFalls-20
87CharWh-4
Wilson, Archie C.
52B-210
52T-327
60Maple-23
Wilson, Arthur Earl
10Domino-126
15CJ-148
16FleischBrd-101
D328-192
D329-191
D350/2-192
E135-192
E254
M101/4-191
M101/5-192
T207
Wilson, Arthur L.
(Artie)
49Remar
50Remar
52Mother-40
92Negro/Kraft-9
92Negro/Retort-64
Wilson, Barney
75Cedar
76Cedar
Wilson, Brad
89Bristol/Star-28
90Bristol/ProC-3172
90Bristol/Star-25
91Fayette/ClBest-10
91Fayette/ProC-1175
91Lakeland/ProC-270
Wilson, Brandon
91ClBest/Singl-157
91MidwLAS/ProC-13
91SoBend/ClBest-7
91SoBend/ProC-2867
92B-632
92ClBest-321
92ProC/Tomorrow-47
92Saraso/ClBest-4
92Saraso/ProC-217
92UD/ML-251
92UD/POY-PY25
93B-7
93ClBest/MLG-80
93FExcel/ML-157
93FExcel/MLAS-10
93L/GRook-5
93StCl/WSox-9
94B-267
94FExcel-41
94T-158M
94T/Gold-158M

Wilson, Bryan
91GulfCR/SportP-28
91Peoria/ClBest-15
91Peoria/Team-22
91WinSalem/ClBest-22
91WinSalem/ProC-2839
Wilson, Bubba
77Watlo
Wilson, Charles
R314/Can
Wilson, Chaun
88Hagers/Star-24
Wilson, Craig 1
85Spring-12
87StPete-2
88Louisvl-50
88Louisvl/CMC-15
88Louisvl/ProC-439
89ArkTr/GS-25
89Louisvl-36
90AAASingl/ProC-527
90Louisvl/CMC-15
90Louisvl/LBC-42
90Louisvl/ProC-413
90ProC/Singl-115
90SpringDG/Best-2
90T/89Debut-146
90T/TVCard-66
91D-544
91F-652
91Leaf-95
91OPC-566
91Pol/Card-12
91S/100RisSt-97
91StCl-566
91T-566
91UD-390
91Ultra-298
92D-744
92OPC-646
92Pol/Card-24
92S-557
92StCl-361
92T-646
92T/Gold-646
92T/GoldWin-646
93F-516
93Pol/Royal-26
93S-476
93StCl-88
93StCl/1stDay-88
93T-366
93T/Gold-366
Wilson, Craig 2
91T/Tr-128TUSA
92StCl/Dome-196
92T/DQ-30
93StCl/MurphyS-105
94ClBest/Gold-162
Wilson, Craig Gerald
87Elmira/Black-18
87Elmira/Red-18
88Lynch/Star-26
89Lynch/Star-22
90NewBrit/Best-8
90NewBrit/ProC-1323
90NewBrit/Star-23
91LynchRS/ClBest-13
91LynchRS/ProC-1203
92Jacks/ProC-3711
92Jaxvl/SB-371
92Penin/ProC-2937
92T/Tr-128T
92T/TrGold-128T
Wilson, Dan
88CapeCod/Sum-177
90Classic/DP-7
90Foil/Best-232
91B-687
91CharWh/ClBest-14
91CharWh/ProC-2891
91ClBest/Singl-353
91OPC-767FDP
91S-681FDP
91StCl-587
91T-767FDP
91UD/FinalEd-6F
92B-471
92D-399RR
92L/GRook-18
92Nashvl/ProC-1834
92Nashvl/SB-297
92ProC/Tomorrow-217
92Sky/AAASingl-138
92TripleP-241
92UD-72TP
93B-202
93D-6
93F-400
93OPC/Premier-35
93Pac/Spanish-407
93Pinn-255
93S-229
93S/Boys-28
93Select-345
93StCl-662
93StCl/1stDay-662
93T-813
93T/Gold-813
93ToysRUs-65
93UD-6SR
93Ultra-337
94B-173
94D-388
94Finest-284
94L-329
94Pinn-515
94S-355
94T-154
94T/Gold-154
94UD-240
94UD/ElecD-240
94Ultra-426
Wilson, Danny
86Lipscomb-24
Wilson, Dave
81Clinton-21
Wilson, David
89Niagara/Pucko-24
90Ashvl/ClBest-11
90AubAs/Best-4
90AubAs/ProC-3404
91Ashvl/ProC-569
91ClBest/Singl-274
Wilson, Desi
93B-337
94T-775M
94T/Gold-775M
Wilson, Don
67CokeCap/Astro-18
68Bz-13
68OPC-77
68T-77
69MLB/St-143
69OPC-202
69T-202
69T/4in1-1M
69T/St-39
69Trans-37
70K-62
70MLB/St-47
70OPC-515
70T-515
71MLB/St-95
71OPC-484
71T-484
71T/Coins-41
72K-51
72MB-365
72OPC-20
72OPC-91LL
72T-20
72T-91LL
73OPC-217
73T-217
74OPC-304
74T-304
75OPC-455
75T-455
75T/M-455
81TCMA-326
86Mother/Ast-10
Wilson, Doyle
87Kinston-20
88Wmsprt/ProC-1324
Wilson, Earl
60T-249
61T-69
63J-83
63P-83
63T-76
64T-503
65OPC-42
65T-42
66T-575
67CokeCap/Tiger-10
67T-235LL
67T-237
67T-305
68CokeCap/Tiger-10
68Kahn
68OPC-10LL
68OPC-160
68T-10LL
68T-160
68T/ActionSt-9AM
69MB-294
69T-525
70MLB/St-216
70OPC-95
70T-95
71OPC-301
71T-301
72MB-366
78TCMA-148
81Tiger/Detroit-51
88Domino-26
91Swell/Great-120
93UD/ATH-127
Wilson, Eddie
90Target-1095
Wilson, Eric
86Penin-27
Wilson, Frank
52Laval-3
Wilson, Gary Steven
76Dubuq
79CharCh-18
80Tucson-5
Wilson, Gary 2
90ProC/Singl-737
91AAA/LineD-498
92Welland/ClBest-26
92Welland/ProC-1324
93ClBest/MLG-197
Wilson, Gary D.
88Batavia/ProC-1688
89Spartan/ProC-1036
89Spartan/Star-24
90Foil/Best-158
90Reading/Best-11
90Reading/ProC-1221
90Reading/Star-24
91ScranWB/LineD-498
91ScranWB/ProC-2539
Wilson, George H.
94TedW-115
Wilson, George Washington
79TCMA-189
Wilson, Glenn
81BirmB
83D-580
83F-350
83OPC/St-318
83T-332
83T/St-318
84D-618
84F-94
84F/X-U128
84Nes/792-563
84OPC-36
84Phill/TastyK-40
84T-563
84T/St-270
84T/Tr-129T
85CIGNA-9
85D-609
85F-268
85OPC-189
85Phill/TastyK-12M
85Phill/TastyK-40
85T-454
86BK/AP-7
86CIGNA-16
86D-285
86D/AAS-29
86F-457
86F/Mini-95
86F/St-128
86Keller-6
86Leaf-160
86OPC-318
86Phill/TastyK-12
86T-736
86T/Mini-56
86T/St-118
86T/Tatt-9M
87D-62
87D/OD-158
87F-192
87F/Mini-115
87Leaf-146
87OPC-97
87Phill/TastyK-12
87Sf-166
87Sf/TPrev-6M
87T-97
87T/St-117
88D-262
88D/Best-306
88F-320
88Mother/Sea-12
88OPC-359
88Panini/St-364
88RedFoley/St-103
88S-405
88Sf-204
88T-626
88T/Big-260
88T/St-124
88T/Tr-129T
89B-423
89D-447
89D/Best-241
89F-224
89S-106
89Sf-12
89T-293
89T/Big-284
89VFJuice-11
90BirmDG/Best-31
90D-472
90F-240
90F/Can-240
90Leaf-268
90Lennox-26
90Mother/Ast-22
90OPC-112
90PublInt/St-168
90RedFoley/St-104
90S-346
90T-112
90T/Big-320
90UD-410
91AAA/LineD-447
91D-156
91F-519
91OPC-476
91Panini/FrSt-11
91Richm/LineD-447
91Richm/ProC-2582
91Richm/Team-26
91S-298
91T-476
91UD-515
Wilson, Jack
86Phoenix-25
Wilson, James George
81Bristol-6
83BuffB-14
83Pawtu-18
85IntLgAS-25
85Maine-24
86Maine-25
88EastLAS/ProC-38
88Vermont/ProC-944
89AAA/CMC-39
89AAA/ProC-32
89Calgary/CMC-22
89Calgary/ProC-536
90TripleAAS/CMC-39
91AAA/LineD-397
91Phoenix/LineD-397
91Phoenix/ProC-77
Wilson, Jeff
83Wisco/Frit-4
86Tampa-26
Wilson, Jim
88SanDiegoSt-19
89SanDiegoSt-19
Wilson, Jim A.
52T-276
53B/Col-37
53JC-12
53SpicSpan/3x5-27
53T-208
54B-16
54JC-19
55B-253
55Gol/Braves-31
55JC-19
55SpicSpan/DC-18
56T-171
57T-330
58T-163
79TCMA-130
91Crown/Orio-489
91T/Arc53-208
92Bz/Quadra-18M
Wilson, Jimmy
28Exh-32
29Exh/4-15
31Exh/4-15
33G-37
34DS-22
34Exh/4-6
34Ward's/Pin-8
35BU-38
35Exh/4-6
35G-1E
35G-3C
35G-5C
35G-6C
36Exh/4-6
36Wheat
40PlayBall-152
61F-88
77Galasso-216
81Conlon-87
91Conlon/Sport-223
93Conlon-683
93Conlon-874
R310
R332-30
R337-422
V353-37
V355-99
V94-54
W711/2
Wilson, John F.
35BU-73
39PlayBall-29
40PlayBall-31
41PlayBall-29
Wilson, John Owen
(Chief)
10Domino-125
11Helmar-138
11Helmar-166
12Sweet/Pin-122A
12Sweet/Pin-122B
12Sweet/Pin-144
14CJ-13
14Piedmont/St-63
15CJ-13
85Woolwth-41
90HOF/St-18
91Conlon/Sport-267
D322
D329-192
D350/2-193
E104
E220
E224
E91
M101/4-192
M101/5-193
M116
S74-116
T202
T205
T206
T207
T213/blue
T213/brown
T215/brown
Wilson, Johnny
85Lynch-24
86Jacks/TCMA-22
87Jacks/Feder-17
Wilson, Jud
74Laugh/Black-12
90Negro/Star-34
94TedW-116
Wilson, Lewis R.
(Hack)
28Exh-12
28Yueng-25
29Exh/4-5
30CEA/Pin-10
31Exh/4-5
33DH-43
33G-211
35BU-73
60F-48
61F-87
72F/FFeat-9
72Laugh/GF-27

77Galasso-113
79T-412LL
80Laugh/FFeat-4
80Pac/Leg-97
80Perez/HOF-169
80SSPC/HOF
81Conlon-86
85Woolwth-40
86Conlon/1-56
89Smok/Dodg-36
90BBWit-93
90HOF/St-29
90Target-866
91Conlon/Sport-29
92Conlon/Sport-424
92Conlon/Sport-585
92Cub/OldStyle-28
93Conlon-736
94Conlon-998
E210-25
R306
R315-A39
R315-B39
R316
R332-14
W502-25
W513-74
W517-42
Wilson, Mark 1
89Hamil/Star-26
Wilson, Mark 2
92SanJose/ClBest-30MG
Wilson, Matt
89GreatF-32
90VeroB/Star-31TR
91CalLgAS-25
92Bakers/Cal-32
Wilson, Michael
(Tack)
77Clinton
80Albuq-15
81Albuq/TCMA-23A
82Albuq-23
83Toledo-18
84Toledo-22
85Cram/PCL-195
87Edmon-10
89OkCty/CMC-22
89OkCty/ProC-1534
90Huntsvl/Best-23
91Pac/SenLg-50
Wilson, Mike
87Idaho-1
Wilson, Mookie
79Tidew-7
80Tidew-17
81D-575
81T-259R
82D-175
82F-542
82F/St-86
82OPC-143
82T-143
83D-56
83D/AAS-32
83Drake-29
83F-560
83F/St-25AM
83F/St-25BM
83F/St-5M
83OPC-55
83OPC/St-266FOIL
83T-55
83T-621TL
83T/Gloss40-2
83T/St-266
84D-190
84Drake-31
84F-603
84F/St-91
84Jacks/Smok-13
84Nes/792-246TL
84Nes/792-465
84OPC-270
84T-246TL
84T-465
84T/Mets/Fan-8
84T/St-108
85D-482
85F-95
85FunFood/Pin-65
85Leaf-122
85OPC-11
85Pol/MetYank-M4
85T-775
85T/St-102
86D-604
86F-97
86Leaf-232
86OPC-315
86T-126M
86T-315
86T/Tatt-6M
87D-487
87D/OD-129
87F-25
87F/Hottest-43
87Leaf-176
87OPC-84
87T-625
87T/Mets/Fan-8
88D-652
88D/Best-208
88D/Mets/Bk-652
88F-154
88Kahn/Mets-1
88Leaf-249
88Panini/St-348
88S-474
88T-255
88T/Big-182
89B-386
89D-152
89F-52
89Kahn/Mets-1
89OPC-144
89Panini/St-141
89S-302
89S/Tr-16
89T-545
89T/Big-231
89T/DHTest-13
89UD-199
90B-516
90D-442
90D/BestAL-28
90F-99
90F/Can-99
90Leaf-263
90OPC-182
90Panini/St-174
90PublInt/St-147
90S-448
90Sf-128
90T-182
90T/Big-179
90Tor/BJ-3
90UD-481
91D-585
91F-192
91Leaf/Stud-140
91OPC-727
91Panini/FrSt-341
91S-42
91S/ToroBJ-24
91StCl-99
91T-727
91Tor/Fire-3
91UD-512
91Ultra-372
91WIZMets-433
92F-347
92OPC-436
92S-458
92T-436
92T/Gold-436
92T/GoldWin-436
92UD-391
Wilson, Murray
72Dimanche*-111IA
72Dimanche*-112
Wilson, Nigel
88StCath/ProC-2017
89StCath/ProC-2081
90Myrtle/ProC-2791
91Dunedin/ClBest-24
91Dunedin/ProC-222
91FSLAS/ProC-FSL10
92B-228
92ClBest-164
92Knoxvl/ProC-3005
92Knoxvl/SB-397
92ProC/Tomorrow-169
92Sky/AASingl-168
92UD/ML-286
93B-316
93B-351FOIL
93D-737RR
93D/DK-27
93Edmon/ProC-1151
93F-431
93F/Final-75
93FExcel/ML-247
93Flair/Wave-20
93L/GRook-16
93Marlin/Publix-27
93OPC-165
93StCl-720
93StCl/1stDay-720
93StCl/I/Ins-4
93StCl/Marlin-1
93T-426
93T/Gold-426
93T/MicroP-426
93UD-825TC
93Ultra-388
94B-590
94D-537
94L-76
94Pac/Cr-255
94Pinn-240
94Pinn/Artist-240
94Pinn/Museum-240
94Pinn/New-22
94Pinn/RookTPinn-8M
94S-639
94S/Boys-35
94Sf/2000-158
94StCl/Team-66
94T-341
94T/Gold-341
94UD-103
94UD/CollC-301
94UD/CollC/Gold-301
94UD/CollC/Silv-301
94UD/ElecD-103
Wilson, Parker
80Elmira-30
Wilson, Paul
93Bz-10
93T/Tr-107T
Wilson, Phil
82Watlo/B-13
82Watlo/Frit-7
83Watlo/Frit-14
85Visalia-1
86OrlanTw-24
87Portl-9
88Portl/CMC-23
88Portl/ProC-661
89Jaxvl/ProC-171
Wilson, Preston
92Classic/DP-117
92LitSun/HSPros-27
93B-594
93StCl/MurphyMP-12
93StCl/MurphyS-27
93T-132
93T/Gold-132
94B-484
94ClBest/Gold-106
94FExcel-242
94UD-537TP
94UD/SP-20PP
Wilson, Randy
84Newar-22
Wilson, Ric
82Wausau/Frit-27
84Chatt-22
87Wausau-27
Wilson, Rick
85Everett/II/Cram-23
Wilson, Robert
(Red)
53T-250
54T-58
56T-92
57T-19
58T-213
59T-24
60T-379
61P-66
79TCMA-281
90Target-867
91T/Arc53-250
94T/Arc54-58
Wilson, Roger
86Miami-28
87Wmsprt-21
Wilson, Ryan
92LitSun/HSPros-6
Wilson, Sam W.
V100
Wilson, Scott
89AS/Cal-51TR
89SanJose/Best-17TR
89SanJose/Cal-234
89SanJose/ProC-454
90SanJose/Best-27
90SanJose/Cal-55TR
90SanJose/Star-30TR
91CalLgAS-49
91SanJose/ClBest-30TR
Wilson, Steve
86Tulsa-10
87PortChar-10
88TexLgAS/GS-5
88Tulsa-8
89B-280
89D/Best-250
89D/Rook-10
89F-640R
89F/Up-U82
89Mara/Cubs-44
89T/Tr-131T
89UD/Ext-799
90B-23
90Cub/Mara-25
90D-394
90F-49
90F/Can-49
90Leaf-420
90OPC-741
90S-531
90S/YS/II-28
90T-741
90T/JumboR-32
90T/TVCub-18
90TulsaDG/Best-9
90UD-341
91AAA/LineD-222
91Cub/Vine-34
91D-519
91F-440
91Iowa/LineD-222
91Iowa/ProC-1062
91OPC-69
91Parramatta/Fut-14
91S-306
91T-69
91UD-493
92D-710
92L-161
92L/BlkGold-161
92Mother/Dodg-27
92OPC-751
92Pol/Dodg-38
92S-812
92StCl-626
92T-751
92T/Gold-751
92T/GoldWin-751
92Ultra-510
93D-34
93F-456
93L-145
93Mother/Dodg-23
93Pac/Spanish-506
93Pol/Dodg-28
93Rang/Keeb-385
93StCl/Dodg-27
93T-133
93T/Gold-133
94F-529
94Pac/Cr-324
94T-573
94T/Gold-573
Wilson, Terry
89Myrtle/ProC-1474
Wilson, Tex
90Target-1096
Wilson, Thomas
92Greens/ClBest-11
Wilson, Tim
89Helena/SP-5
90Helena/SportP-23
Wilson, Todd
86Cram/NWL-181
86Everett/Pop-36
90Billings/ProC-3232
91Cedar/ClBest-21
91Cedar/ProC-2730
Wilson, Tom
86Tampa-27
90Pittsfld/Pucko-17
91Oneonta/ProC-4158
92ClBest-308
92Greens/ProC-783
93Greens/ProC-889
93SALAS/II-42
94ClBest/Gold-198
Wilson, Trevor
85Everett/II/Cram-24
86Clinton-28
87Clinton-27
88BBAmer-27
88Shrev/ProC-1298
89F-347
89Phoenix/CMC-10
89Phoenix/ProC-1481
89S/HotRook-31
89T-783
89UD/Ext-733
90AAASingl/ProC-38
90D-414
90F/Up-U64
90Leaf-489
90OPC-408
90Phoenix/CMC-8
90Phoenix/ProC-12
90ProC/Singl-535
90T-408
90UD-637
91B-630
91D-263
91F-277
91F/UltraUp-U119
91Mother/Giant-22
91OPC-96
91PG&E-9
91S-657
91StCl-212
91T-96
91UD-653
92B-119
92D-575
92F-651
92Giant/PGE-36
92L-340
92L/BlkGold-340
92Mother/Giant-22
92OPC-204
92Pinn-352
92S-608
92StCl-86
92T-204
92T/Gold-204
92T/GoldWin-204
92TripleP-146
92UD-337
92Ultra-297
93D-578
93F-162
93L-477
93Mother/Giant-23
93Pac/Spanish-279
93Pinn-210
93S-401
93StCl-185
93StCl/1stDay-185
93StCl/Giant-22
93T-364
93T/Gold-364
93TripleP-186
93UD-197
93Ultra-491
94D-572
94F-705
94Pac/Cr-560
94Pinn-82
94Pinn/Artist-82
94Pinn/Museum-82
94S-140
94S/GoldR-140
94StCl/Team-21
94T-462
94T/Gold-462
Wilson, W.H.
(Chauff)
76Laugh/Clown-36
Wilson, Ward
76Clinton
Wilson, Wayne
84Newar-6
85Newar-11
86Hagers-28
87Hagers-16

Wilson, William D.
54T-222
55Rodeo
55T-86
55T/DH-101
94T/Arc54-222
Wilson, William H.
67T-402R
69T-576R
70OPC-28
70T-28
71MLB/St-192
71OPC-192
71T-192
72T-587
73OPC-619
73T-619
Wilson, Willie J.
75Watlo
78SSPC/270-241
79T-409
80BK/PHR-33
80OPC-87DP
80T-157
80T-204LL
81Coke
81D-223
81F-29
81F/St-106
81K-24
81OPC-360
81PermaGr/CC-31
81Pol/Royals-10
81T-208RB
81T-360
81T/So-20
81T/St-16
81T/St-247
81T/St-81
82D-448
82F-427
82F/St-207
82K-62
82OPC-230
82T-230
82T/St-189
83D-112
83D-15DK
83D/AAS-13
83Drake-30
83F-128
83F/St-24M
83F/St-8M
83K-23
83OPC-16
83OPC/St-15
83OPC/St-161
83OPC/St-73FOIL
83PermaGr/CC-33
83Pol/Royals-10
83T-471TL
83T-701LL
83T-710
83T/Fold-3M
83T/Fold-5M
83T/Gloss40-23
83T/LeadS-1
83T/St-15
83T/St-161
83T/St-73
84D-175
84F-364
84F/St-94
84Nes/792-525
84OPC-5
84T-525
84T/St-280
84T/St/Box-5
85D-297
85F-218
85FunFood/Pin-82
85Leaf-110
85OPC-6
85T-617
85T/St-277
85ThomMc/Discs-22
85Woolwth-42
86D-175
86F-25
86F/Mini-5
86F/St-129
86Kitty/Disc-15
86Leaf-106
86NatPhoto-6
86OPC-25
86Seven/Coin-C14M
86Sf-124
86Sf-128M
86Sf-144M
86Sf-180M
86Sf-186M
86T-25
86T/Mini-22
86T/St-258
86T/Super-59
86T/Tatt-21M
86Woolwth-32
87D-96
87D/OD-208
87F-384
87F/Excit-43
87F/Mini-116
87F/RecSet-42
87F/St-125
87Leaf-97
87OPC-367
87Sf-85
87Sf/TPrev-13M
87Stuart-20
87T-783
87T/Mini-58
87T/St-261
88D-255
88D/Best-263
88F-274
88Leaf-189
88OPC-222
88Panini/St-113
88S-102
88Sf-192
88Smok/Royals-3
88T-452
88T/Big-21
88T/Mini-17
88T/Revco-25
88T/St-263
89B-124
89D-120
89F-298
89KMart/Lead-17
89OPC-168
89Panini/St-361
89S-28
89Sf-186
89T-168
89T/Big-136
89T/Mini-56
89T/St-268
89Tastee/Discs-5
89UD-244
90D-440
90F-123
90F/Can-123
90KayBee-31
90Leaf-336
90MLBPA/Pins-109
90OPC-323
90Pac/Legend-109
90PublInt/St-361
90S-104
90T-323
90T/Big-45
90UD-349
91B-230
91F-575
91F/UltraUp-U48
91Leaf-299
91Mother/A's-17
91OPC-208
91OPC/Premier-129
91S/RookTr-15T
91StCl-378
91T-208
91T/Tr-129T
91UD-609
92F/Up-53
92Mother/A's-17
92OPC-536
92S-328
92StCl-343
92T-536
92T/Gold-536
92T/GoldWin-536
92UD-238
92Ultra-429
93B-468
93Cub/Mara-31
93F-302
93F/Final-13
93L-413
93OPC-370
93OPC/Premier-53
93Pac/Spanish-228
93Pinn-141
93S-647
93Select-395
93StCl-622
93StCl/1stDay-622
93StCl/Cub-5
93Studio-199
93T-318
93T/Gold-318
93UD-417
93UD-625
93Ultra-324
94F-402
94Pac/Cr-116
94S-134
94S/GoldR-134
94StCl-311
94StCl/1stDay-311
94StCl/Gold-311
94StCl/Team-357
94T-698
94T/Gold-698
94Ultra-169
Wilstead, Randon
(Randy)
90James/Pucko-6
91MidwLAS/ProC-50
91Rockford/ClBest-22
91Rockford/ProC-2057
92WPalmB/ClBest-22
92WPalmB/ProC-2097
93WPalmB/ClBest-25
93WPalmB/ProC-1351
Wiltbank, Ben
78Salem
79Portl-4
79T-723R
81Buffa-5
Wiltse, George R.
(Hooks)
10Domino-127
11Helmar-139
12Sweet/Pin-123
14Piedmont/St-64
92Conlon/Sport-332
D303
E106
E107
E254
E90/1
E93
E95
M116
S74-96
T201
T202
T205
T206
T207
T214-30
T215/blue
T215/brown
T216
W555
Wiltse, Hal
93Conlon-955
Wiltse, Lew
WG3-53
Wiltz, Stanley
92Welland/ClBest-27
92Welland/ProC-1335
93Welland/ClBest-27
93Welland/ProC-3370
Wimmer, Chris
90WichSt-38
91T/Tr-130T
92StCl/Dome-197
92T/DQ-28
92T/Tr-129T
92T/TrGold-129T
93StCl/MurphyS-42
94ClBest/Gold-152
94FExcel-297
Winawer, Larry
91Helena/SportP-7
Winbush, Mike
86Salem-29
Winchell, Derek
87Salem/ProC-2445
88Bend/Legoe-30TR
92AS/Cal-50
Winders, Brian
94LSU-7
Windes, Cary
89FresnoSt/Smok-22
Windes, Rodney
88AubAs/ProC-1955
89Ashvl/ProC-947
90Osceola/Star-26
91Osceola/ClBest-13
91Osceola/ProC-686
92Jacks/SB-348
Windhorn, Gordon
62T-254
90Target-868
Wine, Robbie
86Tucson-26
87Sf/TPrev-8M
87Tucson-3
88D-508
88F-459
88OkCty/CMC-22
88OkCty/ProC-42
88S-496
88T-119
89Richm/Bob-28
89Richm/CMC-11
89Richm/Ko-29
89Richm/ProC-843
90Canton/Best-17
90Canton/ProC-1295
91AAA/LineD-572
91Tidew/LineD-572
Wine, Robert
(Bobby)
63T-71
64PhilBull-26
64T-347
65OPC-36
65T-36
66T-284
67CokeCap/Phill-2
67T-466
68T-396
69Expos/Pins-9
69T-648
70Expo/PostC-9
70Expos/Pins-14
70MLB/St-72
70OPC-332
70T-332
71Expo/ProS-28
71LaPizza-14
71MLB/St-144
71OPC-171
71T-171
72Dimanche*-51
72MB-367
72T-657
73OPC-486CO
73T-486CO
74OPC-119CO
74T-119CO
78SSPC/270-32CO
78TCMA-181
85Pol/Atl-7CO
86T-57MG
89Brave/Dubuq-30CO
PM10/L-42
Winegarner, Ralph
R312
Winfield, Dave
74McDon
74OPC-456
74T-456
74T/St-100
75Ho-37
75OPC-61
75T-61
75T/M-61
76Ho-83
76OPC-160
76SSPC-133
76T-160
77BurgChef-130
77Ho-44
77Ho/Twink-44
77K-28
77OPC-156
77Padre/SchCd-39
77Padre/SchCd-40
77T-390
77T/CS-52
77T/ClothSt-52
78Ho-63
78K-11
78OPC-78
78Padre/FamFun-38
78T-530
79Ho-125
79OPC-11
79T-30
79T/Comics-31
80BK/PHR-22
80K-32
80OPC-122
80T-203LL
80T-230
80T/S-18
80T/Super-18
81D-364
81Drake-14
81F-484
81F/St-25
81K-21
81PermaGr/AS-18
81PermaGr/CC-21
81Sqt-19
81T-370
81T/HT
81T/St-111
81T/Tr-855
82D-18DK
82D-31
82D-575M
82Drake-31
82F-56
82F-646M
82F/St-110M
82F/St-113
82FBI/Disc-24
82K-12
82OPC-352
82OPC-76AS
82PermaGr/CC-14
82Sqt-7
82T-553AS
82T-600
82T/St-137
82T/St-213
83D-409
83D/AAS-36
83Drake-31
83F-398
83F-633M
83F/St-27M
83F/St-4M
83K-15
83OPC-258
83OPC/St-99FOIL
83PermaGr/AS-7
83PermaGr/CC-34
83RoyRog/Disc-12
83T-770
83T/Gloss40-7
83T/St-99
84D-51
84Drake-32
84F-143
84F/St-5
84MiltBrad-29
84Nes/792-402AS
84Nes/792-460
84Nestle/DT-6
84OPC-266AS
84OPC-378
84Ralston-7
84Seven-7E
84T-402AS
84T-460
84T/Cereal-7
84T/Gloss22-8
84T/Gloss40-16
84T/RD-29M
84T/St-190
84T/St-319
84T/Super-27
85D-51
85D-651M
85D/AAS-12
85D/HL-53
85Drake-32
85F-146
85F-629IA

85F/LimEd-43
85F/St-5
85FunFood/Pin-1
85GenMills-25
85Leaf-127
85Leaf-140M
85OPC-180
85Pol/MetYank-Y4
85Seven-3C
85Seven-3G
85Seven-5E
85Seven-5S
85Seven-5W
85Sportflic/Proto-4
85Sportflic/Proto-5
85T-180
85T-705AS
85T/3D-18
85T/Gloss22-17
85T/Gloss40-14
85T/RD-30M
85T/St-186
85T/St-308
85T/Super-60
85ThomMc/Discs-23
86BK/AP-2
86D-248
86D/AAS-15
86D/PopUp-15
86Dorman-19
86Drake-18
86F-121
86F/Mini-26
86F/St-130
86F/St-S4
86Jiffy-7
86Leaf-125
86Meadow/Blank-16
86Meadow/Stat-7
86OPC-70
86Quaker-33
86Seven/Coin-E11M
86Sf-49
86Sf/Dec-74M
86T-70
86T-717AS
86T/3D-29
86T/Gloss22-8
86T/Gloss60-42
86T/Mini-29
86T/St-160
86T/St-298
86T/Super-60
86T/Tatt-1M
86Woolwth-33
87Classic-11
87D-105
87D-20DK
87D/AAS-2
87D/DKsuper-20
87D/OD-243
87D/PopUp-2
87Drake-5
87F-120
87F/Lim-42
87F/Mini-117
87F/St-126
87GenMills/Book-2M
87KayBee-33
87Kraft-33
87Leaf-20DK
87Leaf-70
87MSA/Discs-9
87OPC-36
87OPC/WaxBox-H
87Ralston-4
87RedFoley/St-28
87Seven-E15
87Sf-153M
87Sf-41
87Sf/TPrev-7M
87Stuart-23
87T-770
87T/Board-4
87T/Coins-26
87T/Gloss22-17
87T/St-152
87T/St-298
87T/WaxBox-H
88AlaskaAS70/Team-16
88Classic/Red-170
88D-298
88D/AS-2
88D/Best-244
88D/PopUp-2
88D/Y/Bk-278
88Drake-12
88F-226
88F/BB/AS-44
88F/BB/MVP-43
88F/Mini-44
88F/Slug-43
88F/St-53
88Jiffy-19
88KayBee-33
88KennerFig-121
88Leaf-116
88Nestle-33
88OPC-89
88Panini/St-161
88Panini/St-231M
88S-55
88S/WaxBox-8
88Sf-7
88Sf/Gamewin-7
88T-392AS
88T-510
88T/Big-24
88T/Gloss22-8
88T/Gloss60-46
88T/St-159
88T/St-302
88T/St/Backs-54
88T/UK-85
89B-179
89Cadaco-61
89Classic-32
89D-159
89D/AS-6
89D/GrandSlam-6
89D/MVP-BC11
89D/PopUp-6
89F-274
89F/BBAS-44
89F/BBMVP's-43
89F/Excit-43
89F/Heroes-43
89F/LL-43
89F/Superstar-43
89KayBee-32
89KennerFig-163
89KingB/Discs-16
89MSA/Disc-13
89OPC-260
89OPC/BoxB-P
89Panini/St-240AS
89Panini/St-409
89RedFoley/St-128
89S-50
89S/HotStar-3
89S/Mast-41
89S/NWest-7
89Sf-24
89T-260
89T-407AS
89T/Ames-32
89T/Big-314
89T/Coins-58
89T/DHTest-15
89T/Gloss22-8
89T/Gloss60-21
89T/Hills-32
89T/LJN-4
89T/Mini-67
89T/St-149
89T/St-315
89T/St/Backs-20
89T/UK-84
89T/WaxBox-P
89Tetley/Discs-13
89UD-349
90B-432
90D-551
90D/BestAL-87
90F-458
90F/Can-458
90F/Up-U81
90KayBee-32
90Kenner/Fig-91
90Leaf-426
90MLBPA/Pins-64
90MSA/Soda-23
90OPC-380
90PublInt/St-298
90PublInt/St-550
90S-307
90S/Tr-1T
90Sf-87
90T-380
90T/Ames-1
90T/Big-20
90T/HillsHM-17
90T/TVYank-34
90T/Tr-130T
90UD-337
90UD/Ext-745
91B-210
91D-468
91F-329
91JDean-22
91Leaf-499
91Leaf/Stud-30
91OPC-630
91OPC/Premier-130
91Panini/FrSt-184
91Panini/St-132
91Petro/SU-5
91Post/Can-28
91RedFoley/St-102
91S-83
91S/100SS-66
91Smok/Angel-3
91StCl-263
91StCl/Member*-9
91T-630
91UD-337
91Ultra-54
92B-315
92BJ/Fire-34
92Classic/Game200-194
92D-133
92D/Up-U18
92DPep/MSA-30
92F-686RS
92F-72
92F/Up-67
92L-171
92L/BlkGold-171
92OPC-5RB
92OPC-792
92OPC/Premier-150
92Pinn-375
92Pinn/RookI-18M
92S-32
92S/100SS-9
92S/Factory-B10
92S/RookTr-7T
92StCl-745
92StCl/MemberII-14
92Studio-260
92T-5RB
92T-792
92T/Gold-5RB
92T/Gold-792
92T/GoldWin-5RB
92T/GoldWin-792
92T/Kids-96
92T/Tr-130T
92T/TrGold-130T
92UD-222
92UD-28HL
92UD-734
92UD/HRH-HR17
92Ultra-454
92Yank/WIZ80-204
92Yank/WIZAS-86
93B-565
93BJ/D/45-14
93BJ/D/WS-7
93Classic/Gamel-98
93Colla/DM-118
93D-643
93D/Elite-35
93D/EliteUp-17
93Duracel/PPI-24
93F-343
93F/Final-241
93F/Final/DTrib-DT9
93F/GoldMI-3
93Flair-243
93Highland-7
93HumDum/Can-12
93L-423
93L-DW
93MSA/Metz-40
93OPC-371
93OPC/Premier-28
93OPC/WC-17
93OPC/WSHero-4
93Pac/Jugador-18
93Pac/Spanish-528
93Pinn-295NT
93Pinn-438
93Pinn-486HH
93Pinn/Cooper-10
93Pinn/HRC-32
93Rainbow-Set
93S-521WS
93S-620
93Select-32
93Select/RookTr-9T
93StCl-206
93StCl-609
93StCl/1stDay-206
93StCl/1stDay-609
93StCl/MurphyS-1
93Studio-77
93T-131
93T/BlkGold-44
93T/Finest-162
93T/FinestRef-162
93T/Gold-131
93T/Tr-83T
93TripleP/Gal-GS5
93UD-40CH
93UD-786
93UD/FunPack-196
93UD/SP-252
93UD/SeasonHL-HI19
93UD/Then-TN9
93Ultra-589
94B-300
94D-336
94D/DK-29
94D/Special-336
94F-223
94F/GoldM-3
94Flair-79
94Flair/Outfield-10
94Kraft-15
94L-137
94L/StatStand-8
94OPC-53
94Pac/Cr-371
94Panini-97
94Pinn-332
94Pinn/Trib-3
94S-407
94S-629HL
94Select-84
94Select-NNO
94Sf/2000-63
94StCl-288
94StCl/1stDay-288
94StCl/Dugout-2
94StCl/Gold-288
94Studio-202
94T-430
94T/Finest-215
94T/FinestRef-215
94T/Gold-430
94TripleP-260
94TripleP/Medal-15M
94UD-81
94UD/CollC-302
94UD/CollC/Gold-302
94UD/CollC/Silv-302
94UD/ElecD-81
94UD/SP-187
94Ultra-92
94Ultra/Career-5

Winfield, Steven W.
80Memphis-27
82Louisvl-30
82Spring/Frit-11
83ArkTr-8

Winford, Barry
88MissSt-33
89Butte/SP-7
89MissSt-38
90Foil/Best-187
90Gaston/Best-16
90Gaston/ProC-2525
90Gaston/Star-25
91CharlR/ClBest-15
91CharlR/ProC-1319
91ClBest/Singl-25

Winford, Jim
90Target-869

Winford, Ron
88MissSt-34
89MissSt-39

Wing, Harry
79Cedar/TCMA-25

Wing, Jim
84AZ/Pol-20CO
86AZ/Pol-19CO
87AZ/Pol-19CO
88AZ/Pol-15CO
90AZ/Pol-18ACO
92AZ/Pol-20ACO

Wing, Marc
84AZ/Pol-21

Wingard, Ernest
25Exh-120
26Exh-120
27Exh-60

Wingate, Ervan
92GulfCD/ProC-3577

Wingfield, Fred
26Exh-72
27Exh-36

Wingo, Al
25Exh-95
92Conlon/Sport-458
94Conlon-1177

Wingo, Ivey B.
14CJ-130
15CJ-130
16FleischBrd-102
21Exh-188
25Exh-32
26Exh-32
27Exh-16
91Conlon/Sport-235
93Conlon-868
94Conlon-1022
94Conlon-1177M
BF2-72
C46-40
D327
D329-193
D350/2-194
E120
E121/120
E121/80
E122
E220
M101/4-193
M101/5-194
T207
T222
V100
V117-14
V61-83
W501-50
W514-73
W572
W575

Wingo, John
52LaPatrie-17
52Laval-83

Winham, Lave
90Target-870

Winiarski, Chip
91Collnd/ClBest-19
91Collnd/ProC-1486
92Kinston/ClBest-14
92Kinston/ProC-2477

Winicki, Dennis
91Kissim/ProC-4198
92GreatF/SportP-20

Winkelman, George
N172

Winkler, Brad
84Greens-3
85Albany-22

Winkles, Bobby
73OPC-421MG
73T-421MG
74OPC-276MG
74T-276MG
76SSPC-624MG
78T-378MG
86Expo/Prov/Pan-14M
86Provigo-14CO
87Expo/PostC-12CO

Winn, Jim
84Cram/PCL-138
85Cram/PCL-237
85T-69
86F-624
86T-489
87Coke/WS-23
87D-312
87F-624
87F/Up-U126
87T-262
87T/Tr-130T
88D-409

88F-413
88OPC-388
88Portl/CMC-9
88Portl/ProC-642
88S-462
88T-688
88T/St-288
Winningham, Herm
82Lynch-3
84Tidew-5
85Expo/PostC-23
85F/Up-U130
85OPC/Post-8
85T/Tr-131T
86D-279
86Expo/Prov/Pan-22
86F-266
86Leaf-153
86OPC-129
86Provigo-22
86T-448
86T/St-83
87F/Up-U130
87OPC-141
87T-141
88D-581
88F-200
88Ho/Disc-4
88Leaf-242
88OPC-216
88Panini/St-332
88S-142
88S/Tr-43T
88T-614
88T/St-83
89D-435
89F-175
89Kahn/Reds-29
89S-496
89T-366
89T/Big-94
89UD-636
90D-478
90F-435
90F/Can-435
90Kahn/Reds-26
90OPC-94
90S-38
90T-94
90UD-589
91D-695
91F-82
91F/UltraUp-U78
91Kahn/Reds-29
91Pep/Reds-20
91S-656
91StCl-546
91T-204
91WIZMets-434
92OPC-547
92S-574
92S/RookTr-43T
92StCl-205
92StCl-883
92T-547
92T/Gold-547
92T/GoldWin-547
92T/Tr-131T
92T/TrGold-131T
93F-566
93T-377
93T/Gold-377
Winsett, Tom
90Target-871
Winslett, Dax
94T-755DP
94T/Gold-755DP
Winslow, Bryant
90WichSt-39
91AubAS/ClBest-16
91AubAS/ProC-4283
92AubAs/ClBest-10
92AubAs/ProC-1364
92Osceola/ClBest-7
Winslow, Daniel
81ArkTr-15
Winston, Darrin
88James/ProC-1918
89Rockford/Team-26
90Jaxvl/Best-24
90Jaxvl/ProC-1376
91AAA/LineD-198
91Indianap/LineD-198
91Indianap/ProC-463
Winston, Hank
90Target-872
Winston, Todd
92AubAs/ClBest-14
92AubAs/ProC-1357
Winter, George
E107
Winter, Lee
53Mother-1
Winterburn, Robert
88Boise/ProC-1631
Winterfeldt, Todd
79Wausau-3
81Tidew-7
Winters, Dan
85Fresno/Pol-16
86Lynch-27
87Jacks/Feder-1
Winters, George
WG2-50
Winters, James A.
86Penin-28
87BirmB/Best-24
Winters, Matt
83Colum-23
84Colum-22
84Colum/Pol-24
85Colum-22
85Colum/Pol-24
86BuffB-25
87Memphis-7
87Memphis/Best-24
87SLAS-9
88Memphis/Best-19
88SLAS-1
89Omaha/CMC-21
89Omaha/ProC-1728
90F-124
90F/Can-124
90S/100Ris-47
90T/89Debut-147
90UD-524
Wipf, Mark
92Kingspt/ClBest-14
92Kingspt/ProC-1546
Wirsta, Mike
92MedHat/SportP-26TR
93MedHat/SportP-22TR
Wirth, Alan
79Ogden/TCMA-22
79T-711R
80Ogden-17
81Spokane-25
Wirth, Greg
84Newar-10
Wisdom, Allen
87Clearw-24
Wise, Brett Wayne
81VeroB-24
Wise, K. Casey
57T-396
58T-247
59T-204
60T-342
Wise, Rick
64PhilBull-27
64T-561R
65T-322
67OPC-37
67T-37
68T-262
69MLB/St-180
69OPC-188
69T-188
69T/4in1-5M
69T/St-80
70MLB/St-96
70T-605
70T/PI-8
71MLB/St-191
71OPC-598
71Phill/Arco-13
71T-598
71T/Coins-131
72K-23
72MB-368
72OPC-345KP
72OPC-43
72OPC-44IA
72T-345KP
72T-43
72T-44IA
72T-756TR
72T/Post-14
73OPC-364
73T-364
74OPC-339AS
74OPC-84
74T-339AS
74T-84
74T/St-139
75OPC-56
75T-56
75T/M-56
76K-35
76OPC-170
76T-170
77T-455
78T-572
79OPC-127
79T-253
80OPC-370
80T-725
81D-3
81OPC-274
81T-616
81T/St-232
82D-170
82F-585
82T-330
85Madis-24C
85Madis/Pol-25C
86Madis/Pol-27C
88AubAs/ProC-1963
89AubAs/ProC-2187
89Pac/SenLg-31
89T/SenLg-41
89TM/SenLg-117
90EliteSenLg-106
91AA/LineD-475CO
91NewBrit/LineD-475CO
91NewBrit/ProC-368CO
92NewBrit/ProC-450CO
92NewBrit/SB-500M
93Pawtu/Ball-25M
Wise, Sam
N172
N284
WG1-9
Wiseman, Dennis
89Johnson/Star-23
90Foil/Best-142
90Spring/Best-25
91AA/LineD-48
91ArkTr/LineD-48
91ArkTr/ProC-1287
92ArkTr/ProC-1131
92ArkTr/SB-35
Wiseman, Greg
91Butte/SportP-23
92FtMyr/ProC-2759
92Miracle/ClBest-23
Wiseman, Michael
88CapeCod/Sum-174
Wiseman, Tim
85OrlanTw-21
Wishnevski, Mike
86Chatt-25
87Calgary-16
88Calgary/CMC-20
88Calgary/ProC-783
Wishnevski, Robert
88Dunedin/Star-22
89Knoxvl/Best-27
89Knoxvl/ProC-1138
89Knoxvl/Star-22
89SLAS-21
90Knoxvl/Star-21
90Syrac/MerchB-30
90Syrac/Team-30
91Knoxvl/ProC-1769
92ClBest-335
92Denver/ProC-2641
92ElPaso/SB-213
93B-323
Wismer, Michael
89GreatF-12
90VeroB/Star-28
Wisnaski, Len
52Laval-44
Wissel, Dick
75IntAS/TCMA-30
75IntAS/TCMA-31
Wissler, Bill
92Kenosha/ProC-606
Wistert, Francis
R314/Can
Witasick, Gerald
94FExcel-275
Witek, Nicholas
(Mickey)
47TipTop
Withem, Shannon
90Bristol/ProC-3160
90Bristol/Star-26
91ClBest/Singl-187
91Fayette/ClBest-13
91Fayette/ProC-1172
91Niagara/ClBest-26
91Niagara/ProC-3634
92Fayette/ProC-2170
Witherspoon, Richard
89Elmira/Pucko-21
90WinHaven/Star-25
Withol, Al
77Watlo
Withrow, Mike
83GlenF-21
Witkowski, Matt
89CharRain/ProC-985
90Foil/Best-68
90MidwLgAS/GS-52
90Waterlo/Best-18
90Waterlo/ProC-2388
91HighD/ClBest-23
91HighD/ProC-2406
92Wichita/ProC-3665
92Wichita/SB-647
Witmeyer, Ronald
89Modesto/Cal-281
89Modesto/Chong-27
90AS/Cal-43
90Modesto/Cal-165
90Modesto/Chong-32
90Modesto/ProC-2224
91AAA/LineD-548
91Tacoma/LineD-548
91Tacoma/ProC-2316
92Sky/AAASingl-245
92StCl-435
92T/91Debut-187
92Tacoma/ProC-2513
92Tacoma/SB-547
Witt, Bobby
85Tulsa-18
86D/Rook-49
86F/Slug-42
86F/Up-U129
86Rang-48
86Sf/Rook-12
86T/Tr-126T
87D-99
87D/HL-25
87F-143
87F/Excit-44
87Leaf-112
87Mother/Rang-25
87Sf-39
87Sf/TPrev-1M
87Smok/R-6
87T-415
88D-101
88F-483
88Mother/R-25
88Panini/St-198
88S-149
88Smok/R-7
88T-747
89B-222
89Classic-77
89D-461
89D/Best-279
89F-537
89Mother/R-14
89OPC-38
89Panini/St-448
89S-463
89S/YS/I-8
89Sf-82
89Smok/R-34
89T-548
89T/Big-191
89UD-557
90D-292
90F-315
90F/Can-315
90Leaf-337
90Mother/Rang-15
90OPC-166
90Publint/St-424
90S-457
90T-166
90UD-636
91B-287
91Classic/200-166
91Classic/I-87
91D-249
91F-304
91Leaf-3
91Leaf/Stud-130
91Mother/Rang-6
91OPC-27
91Panini/FrSt-260
91Panini/St-203
91Panini/Top15-78
91S-410KM
91S-507
91Seven/3DCoin-15T
91StCl-96
91T-27
91UD-627
91Ultra-357
92B-230
92D-391
92L-305
92L/BlkGold-305
92Mother/Rang-6
92OPC-675
92Pinn-451
92S-381
92StCl-677
92T-675
92T/DQ-5
92T/Gold-675
92T/GoldWin-675
92TripleP-154
92UD-576
93B-301
93D-51
93F-303
93Flair-265
93L-204
93Mother/A's-14
93Pinn-365
93Rang/Keeb-386
93S-150
93Select-363
93StCl-150
93StCl/1stDay-150
93StCl/A's-16
93T-398
93T/Gold-398
93TripleP-141
93UD-87
93Ultra-264
93Ultra-299M
94B-248
94D-308
94F-277
94Finest-289
94L-102
94Pac/Cr-466
94Pinn-276
94S-437
94Select-128
94StCl-91
94StCl/1stDay-91
94StCl/Gold-91
94T-255
94T/Gold-255
94TripleP-10
94UD-120
94UD/ElecD-120
94Ultra-115
Witt, George
59Kahn
59T-110
60T-298
61T-286
62T-287
Witt, Hal
78StPete
Witt, Lawton
(Whitey)
90Target-873
D327
D328-193
E135-193
E220
V100
W515-37
Witt, Mike
82D-416
82F-473

82T-744
83D-416
83F-102
83T-53
83T-651TL
84F-531
84Nes/792-499
84Smok/Cal-31
84T-499
85D-108
85F-316
85F-643M
85F/St-111
85Leaf-46
85OPC-309
85Smok/Cal-1
85T-309
85T/St-195
85T/St-227
85T/Super-45
86D-179
86D/HL-38
86F-171
86F/Mini-36
86F/Slug-43
86Leaf-112
86Seven/Coin-W12M
86Sf-53M
86Smok/Cal-1
87D-58
87D/AAS-51
87D/OD-2
87F-641M
87F-95
87F/AwardWin-43
87F/BB-44
87F/GameWin-43
87F/Mini-118
87F/Slug-44
87F/St-127
87Kraft-47
87Leaf-111
87MnM's-17
87OPC-92
87RedFoley/St-4
87Seven-W15
87Sf-59
87Sf/TPrev-11M
87Smok/Cal-3
87Stuart-16
87T-760
87T/Gloss60-33
87T/Mini-48
87T/St-179
88D-86
88D/AS-20
88D/Best-307
88F-507
88F-626M
88F/Mini-13
88F/SS-43
88F/St-13
88Grenada-15
88KennerFig-122
88Leaf-49
88OPC-270
88Panini/St-38
88S-81
88Sf-32
88Smok/Angels-4
88T-270
88T/Big-4
88T/St-174
88T/UK-86
89B-42
89D-372
89F-490
89KennerFig-164
89OPC-190
89Panini/St-286
89RedFoley/St-129
89S-298
89Sf-197
89Smok/Angels-19
89T-190
89T/Coins-59
89T/LJN-8
89T/St-176
89T/UK-85
89UD-555
90Classic/III-49
90D-580
90ElPasoATG/Team-33
90F-148
90F/Can-148
90OPC-650
90PublInt/St-382
90S-226
90S/NWest-14
90S/Tr-50T
90Smok/Angel-16
90T-650
90UD-548
91D-282
91D-BC1M
91D/BC-BC1M
91F-680
91F/WaxBox-1M
91Leaf-74
91OPC-536
91S-430
91S-699
91StCl-466
91StCl/Charter*-17M
91T-536
91UD-429
92OPC-357
92StCl-848
92T-357
92T/Gold-357
92T/GoldWin-357
93StCl/Y-18
94Pac/Cr-443

Wittcke, Darren
91Everett/ClBest-26
91Everett/ProC-3915

Witte, Jerome
47TipTop

Witte, Trey
91Belling/ClBest-18
91Belling/ProC-3665
92SanBern/ProC-

Wittig, Paul
92GulfCD/ProC-3570

Wittmayer, Kurt
78OrlanTw

Wobken, Bruce
88NE-18

Wockenfuss, John
76OPC-13
76T-13
78BK/T-3
78T-723
79T-231
80T-338
81Coke
81D-245
81F-472
81T-468
81T/St-79
82D-459
82F-286
82OPC-46
82T-629
83D-76
83F-351
83F/St-10M
83F/St-8M
83OPC/St-64
83T-536
83T/St-64
84D-150
84F-95
84F/X-U129
84Nes/792-119
84Phill/TastyK-27
84T-119
84T/St-274
84T/Tr-130T
85D-549
85F-269
85Phill/TastyK-27
85T-39
86FSLAS-50
86Miami-29
88GlenF/ProC-917
89Toledo/CMC-25
89Toledo/ProC-771
92Salem/ClBest-26MG
92Salem/ProC-79MG

Wodraska, Todd
92OKSt-32

Wohler, Barry
85VeroB-19
87SanAn-8
88SanAn/Best-2

Wohlers, Mark
89Pulaski/ProC-1908
89Sumter/ProC-1099
90Sumter/Best-25
90Sumter/ProC-2435
91AA/LineD-223
91B-582
91ClBest/Gold-13
91ClBest/Singl-331
91Greenvl/ClBest-10
91Greenvl/LineD-223
91Greenvl/ProC-3004
91Richm/Bob-30
91StCl/Member*-30M
91UD/FinalEd-77F
92B-396
92Brave/LykePerf-30
92Brave/LykeStand-35
92Classic/I-18
92Classic/I-97
92D-1RR
92D-616M
92F-374
92F-700M
92F/RookSIns-15
92OPC-703
92Pinn-55
92Pinn/Rook-21
92Pinn/RookI-4
92ProC/Tomorrow-179
92Richm/Bleach-6
92Richm/Comix-26
92Richm/ProC-3015
92Richm/SB-448
92S-759
92S-787M
92S/Impact-38
92S/Rook-5
92Sky/AAASingl-205
92StCl-217
92T-703
92T/91Debut-188
92T/Gold-703
92T/GoldWin-703
92UD-56TP
92UD/Scout-SR24
92Ultra-465
93Brave/LykePerf-30
93Brave/LykeStand-37
93D-606
93F-16
93L-519
93OPC-7
93Pac/Spanish-13
93Pinn-379
93Richm/Bleach-20
93Richm/Team-29
93S-193
93Select-282
93StCl-130
93StCl/1stDay-130
93StCl/Brave-25
93T-8
93T/Gold-8
93ToysRUs-55
93USPlayC/Rook-3C
94D-309
94F-378
94Flair-133
94Pinn-444
94StCl-522
94StCl/1stDay-522
94StCl/Gold-522
94StCl/Team-53
94T-232
94T/Gold-232
94Ultra-158

Wohlford, Jim
73OPC-611R
73T-611R
74OPC-407
74T-407
75OPC-144
75T-144
75T/M-144
76A&P/KC
76OPC-286
76SSPC-179
76T-286
77T-622
78T-376
79T-596
80Pol/Giants-9
80T-448
81D-316
81F-440
81T-11
82F-403
82T-116
83D-524
83Expo/PostC-24
83F-276
83Stuart-21
83T-688
83T/Tr-128T
84Expo/PostC-36
84F-293
84Nes/792-253
84OPC-253
84Stuart-24
84T-253
85D-585
85F-413
85Leaf-82
85OPC-4
85T-787
86D-157
86Expo/Prov/Pan-6
86OPC-344
86Provigo-6
86T-344
87F-336
87OPC-169
87T-527

Woide, Steve
88Myrtle/ProC-1172
90Erie/Star-27

Wojciechowski, Steve
91SoOreg/ClBest-29
91SoOreg/ProC-3847
92Modesto/ClBest-6
92Modesto/ProC-3900
92StCl/Dome-198
93Modesto/ClBest-23
93Modesto/ProC-801

Wojcik, Jim
81Shrev-5

Wojcik, John
63T-253R

Wojey, Pete
90Target-874

Wojna, Ed
83Reading-10
84Cram/PCL-231
85Cram/PCL-120
86D-505
86F-338
86LasVegas-24
86T-211
87D-589
87Sf/TPrev-16M
87T-88
88Vanco/CMC-5
88Vanco/ProC-756
89ColoSp/CMC-4
89ColoSp/ProC-236
90AAASingl/ProC-140
90ProC/Singl-588
90Tacoma/CMC-11
90Tacoma/ProC-93

Wolak, Jerry
89Utica/Pucko-27
90Foil/Best-77
90MidwLgAS/GS-23
90SoBend/Best-13
90SoBend/GS-21
91Saraso/ClBest-22
91Saraso/ProC-1128
92Saraso/ClBest-14
92Saraso/ProC-223

Wolaver, Jake
93Lipscomb-25M

Wolcott, Bob
92ClBest/Up-425
92Classic/DP-37
93StCl/MurphyS-9

Wolf, Brian
92FrRow/DP-86

Wolf, Michael
92Boise/ClBest-28
92Boise/ProC-3645

Wolf, Mike
78Knoxvl
80Iowa/Pol-14

Wolf, Rick
77Wausau

Wolf, Steve
89FresnoSt/Smok-23
90Niagara/Pucko-27
91Lakeland/ClBest-13
91Lakeland/ProC-268
92London/ProC-635

Wolf, Walter
(Wally)
63T-208R
70OPC-74R
70T-74R

Wolf, William Van Winkle
N172

Wolf, William
85Fresno/Pol-27CO

Wolfe, Donn
88StCath/ProC-2013

Wolfe, Joel
91SoOreg/ClBest-1
91SoOreg/ProC-3865
92Reno/Cal-56
92StCl/Dome-199
92UD/ML-193
93Modesto/ClBest-24
93Modesto/ProC-813
94ClBest/Gold-129
94FExcel-123

Wolfe, Larry
78Twin/FriszP-23
79T-137
80T-549

Wolfe, Scott
75Lafay

Wolfenbarger, Scott
91OKSt-32

Wolfer, Jim
89Greens/ProC-419

Wolff, Jim 1
43Playball-22
45Playball-6

Wolff, Jim 2
90Hunting/ProC-3286
91Hunting/ClBest-26
91Hunting/ProC-3338
92MidwLAS/Team-51
92Peoria/ClBest-25
92Peoria/Team-30
92Peoria/Team-31M

Wolfgang, Meldon
D329-194
D350/2-195
M101/4-194
M101/5-195

Wolkoys, Rob
86Cram/NWL-26
87AppFx-21

Wollenburg, Doug
92Idaho/ProC-3523
93Durham/Team-28

Wollenburg, Jay
86Macon-26

Wollenhaupt, Ron
82Watlo/B-28
82Watlo/Frit-4TR

Wolten, Brad
87Watlo-5

Wolter, Harry
10Domino-128
11Helmar-50
12Sweet/Pin-39
M116
S74-25
T202
T205

Wolters, Mike
83ArkTr-14

Wolverton, Harry
11Helmar-51
T207

Womack, Dooley
66T-469R
67CokeCap/YMet-4
67OPC-77
67T-77
68T-431
69T-594
81TCMA-339
92Yank/WIZ60-138

Womack, Tony
91Welland/ClBest-2
91Welland/ProC-3584
92Augusta/ProC-247
92ClBest-385

Womble, Brian
92Lipscomb-25
93Lipscomb-21

Wong, Dave
81CharR-3

82FtMyr-14
Wong, Kaha
89Reno/Cal-257
90Reno/Cal-273
Wong, Kevin
91Pocatel/ProC-3793
91Pocatel/SportP-14
92Salinas/ClBest-15
92Salinas/ProC-3766
Wood, Andre
78Dunedin
80Knoxvl/TCMA-22
82Knoxvl-14
83Knoxvl-13
Wood, Bill
82Tucson-22
Wood, Brian S.
86Cram/NWL-155
88River/Cal-215
88River/ProC-1420
89SALAS/GS-8
89Wichita/Rock-23RHP
90Wichita/Rock-24
91AA/LineD-623
91Wichita/LineD-623
91Wichita/ProC-2600
91Wichita/Rock-10
92Hagers/ProC-2557
92Sky/AASingl-288
92Wichita/SB-648
Wood, Chris
75WPalmB/Sussman-18
Wood, Dave
76Clinton
Wood, George
N172
N284
N690
WG1-54
Wood, Jake
61T-514
62J-15
62P-15
62Salada-83
62Shirriff-83
62T-427
62T-72
62T/St-50
63T-453
64T-272
65T-547
66T-509
67CokeCap/Tiger-13
67T-394
78TCMA-186
Wood, Jason
89Anchora-28
91FresnoSt/Smok-15
91SoOreg/ClBest-12
91SoOreg/ProC-3859
92B-262
92ClBest-191
92Modesto/ClBest-1
92Modesto/ProC-3908
Wood, Jeff
85CharlO-17
87CharlO/WBTV-TR
88CharlK/Pep-10
90Rochester/L&U-36TR
Wood, Joe
14CJ-22
15CJ-22
16FleischBrd-103
21Exh-189
81Conlon-17
87Conlon/2-57
90HOF/St-16
91Conlon/Sport-254
92Conlon/Sport-336
93Conlon-891
93UD/ATH-128
93UD/ATH-155
93UD/ATH-157M
93UD/T202-10
BF2-7
D327
D328-194
D329-195
D350/2-196
E103
E120
E121/80
E122
E135-194
E254
E270/1
E91
M101/4-195
M101/5-196
M116
T202
T207
V100
W575
WG4-30
WG5-44
WG6-41
Wood, John
90Idaho/ProC-3249
Wood, Johnson
81BurlB-12
82Beloit/Frit-5
84ElPaso-2
Wood, Ken
50B-190
51B-209
52T-139
53B/Col-109
Wood, Mathew
91Melbourne/Fut-13
Wood, Mike
84Butte-5
Wood, Pete
N172
Wood, Peter
91Perth/Fut-15
Wood, Robert Lynn
E107
Wood, Stephen
88VeroB/Star-24
Wood, Ted
87PanAm/USAB-15
87PanAm/USAR-15
88T/Tr-130TOLY
89Shrev/ProC-1842
89T/Big-308
90Shrev/ProC-1456
90Shrev/Star-24
90TeamUSA/87-15
90TexLgAS/GS-27
91AAA/LineD-398
91Phoenix/LineD-398
91Phoenix/ProC-82
92D-681
92F-678
92OPC-358
92Phoenix/ProC-2836
92Phoenix/SB-398
92ProC/Tomorrow-341
92S-768
92S/Rook-11
92Sky/AAASingl-181
92StCl-799
92T-358
92T/91Debut-189
92T/Gold-358
92T/GoldWin-358
92UD-12SR
92Ultra-597
93D-24
93Pac/Spanish-539
93Pinn-286
93StCl-455
93StCl/1stDay-455
93T-698
93T/Gold-698
Wood, Wilbur
64T-267
65T-478
67T-391
68T-585
69MB-295
69MLB/St-36
69OPC-123
69T-123
69T/4in1-12M
69T/St-160
70MLB/St-192
70OPC-342
70T-342
71OPC-436
71T-436
72K-4
72MB-369
72OPC-342KP
72OPC-92LL
72OPC-94LL
72T-342BP
72T-553
72T-554IA
72T-92LL
72T-94LL
72T/Post-19
73K-9
73OPC-150
73OPC-66LL
73T-150
73T-66LL
73T/Lids-54
74K-34
74OPC-120
74OPC-205LL
74T-120
74T-205LL
74T/DE-13
74T/St-160
75Ho-68
75Ho/Twink-68
75OPC-110
75SSPC/42-1
75T-110
75T/M-110
76Crane-67
76Ho-99
76MSA/Disc
76OPC-368
76SSPC-139
76T-368
77T-198
78SSPC/270-143
78T-726
79OPC-108
79T-216
81TCMA-325
89Pac/Leg-124
89Swell-127
91LineD-35
91Swell/Great-121
92AP/ASG-53
Woodall, Brad
91Idaho/ProC-4331
91Idaho/SportP-26
92Durham/ClBest-23
92Durham/ProC-1102
92Durham/Team-11
92ProC/Tomorrow-196
Woodall, Charles L.
(Lawrence)
21Exh-190
25Exh-96
28Exh-48
93Conlon-784
E120
E126-53
V61-21
W573
Woodall, Kevin
91GulfCR/SportP-10
92Gaston/ClBest-13
Woodard, Darrell
82BirmB-3
Woodard, Mike
81WHave-17
82WHave-19
83Tacom-13
85Cram/PCL-181
86D-46RR
86F-645R
86Phoenix-26
87Phoenix-10
87T-286
88TripleA/ASCMC-33
88Vanco/CMC-14
88Vanco/ProC-767
89Colum/CMC-12
89Colum/Pol-23
89Colum/ProC-742
89F-513
Woodbrey, Mark
75Cedar
76Cedar
Woodburn, Eugene
T207
Wooden, Mark
86Cram/NWL-129
87Wausau-16
88Vermont/ProC-939
89Wmsprt/ProC-628
89Wmsprt/Star-23
90Wmsprt/Best-23
90Wmsprt/ProC-1059
90Wmsprt/Star-24
Woodeschick, Hal
59T-106
60T-454
61T-397
62T-526
63T-517
64T-370
64T/SU
64T/St-78
64Wheat/St-49
65OPC-179
65T-179
66T-514
67T-324
78TCMA-123
86Mother/Ast-2
89Smok/Ast-10
Woodfin, Chris
92SoBend/ClBest-17
92SoBend/ProC-178
Woodfin, Olonzo
89BurlInd/Star-26
Woodhouse, Kevin
84Everett/Cram-9
Woodland, Bob
75WPalmB/Sussman-20
Woodling, Gene
48Sommer-13
51B-219
51BR-D1
52B-177
52BR
52Dix
52T-99
53B/BW-31
53Dix
53RM-AL12
53T-264
54B-209
54Dix
54NYJour
54RM-AL15
54T-101
55Esskay
55Salem
55T-190
56T-163
56YellBase/Pin-31
57Sohio/Ind-17
57T-172
58T-398
59T-170
60T-190
60T/tatt-54
61Bz-30
61P-70
61T-275
61T/St-207
62Bz
62J-71
62P-71
62P/Can-71
62Salada-96
62Shirriff-96
62T-125
62T/St-101
62T/bucks
63T-342
63T-43M
82Ohio/HOF-65
88Pac/Leg-5
89Swell-102
91Crown/Orio-490
91Swell/Great-101
91T/Arc53-264
91WIZMets-435
92AP/ASG-23
92Bz/Quadra-4M
94T/Arc54-101
Exh47
PM10/L-43
PM10/L-44
PM10/Sm-201
R423-112
TCMA79-156
Woodmansee, Mark
83SLCity-12
Woodruff
E270/1
Woodruff, Pat
89Batavia/ProC-1936
90Clearw/Star-25
91Lakeland/ClBest-28
91Lakeland/ProC-281
Woods, Alvis
(Al)
77OPC-256
77T-479R
78BJ/PostC-25
78OPC-175
78Syrac
78T-121
79BJ/Bubble-20
79OPC-85
79T-178
80OPC-230
80T-444
81D-32
81F-422
81OPC-165
81OPC/Post-17
81T-703
81T/St-141
82D-180
82F-627
82OPC-49
82OPC/Post-5
82T-49
83F-444
83OPC-59
83T-589
84Syrac-14
85Toledo-25
86Toledo-24
92Nabisco-4
Woods, Anthony
86Wausau-28
87Wausau-13
88SanBern/Best-5
89SanBern/Best-17
89SanBern/Cal-83
Woods, Byron
92Idaho/ProC-3530
Woods, Clancy
79AppFx-7
Woods, Eric
88WinSalem/Star-22
89WinSalem/Star-18
Woods, Gary
76Tucson-3
77OPC-22
77T-492R
78OPC-13
78Syrac
78T-599
79CharCh-5
80Tucson-22
81F-75
81T-172
82F-237
82RedLob
82T-483
82T/Tr-130T
83D-631
83F-512
83T-356
83Thorn-25
84D-144
84F-507
84Nes/792-231
84SevenUp-25
84T-231
85D-555
85F-71
85Leaf-49
85SevenUp-25
85T-46
86F-385
86LasVegas-25
86T-611
Woods, George
49B/PCL-4
Woods, Jim
60L-104
61T-59
Woods, Kelly
89Princet/Star-25
89Star/IISingl-176
Woods, Kenny
92Everett/ClBest-7
92Everett/ProC-1701
Woods, Lyle
87Anchora-41ANN
89Anchora-29ANN
Woods, Parnell
49Remar

Woods, Preston
88CapeCod/Sum-54
Woods, Ron
69T-544R
70OPC-253
70T-253
71MLB/St-504
71OPC-514
71T-514
72Dimanche*-52
72OPC-82
72T-82
73OPC-531
73T-531
74OPC-377
74T-377
92Yank/WIZ60-139
92Yank/WIZ70-167
Woods, Tony
83QuadC-22
84MidldC-24
86Pittsfld-25
87Miami-5
88Tampa/Star-24
88Wausau/GS-22
Woods, Tyrone
89James/ProC-2134
90MidwLgAS/GS-24
90Rockford/ProC-2709
90Rockford/Team-29
91WPalmB/ClBest-29
91WPalmB/ProC-1243
92MidwLAS/Team-52
92Rockford/ClBest-9
92Rockford/ProC-2130
93Harris/ProC-282
Woods, Walter
E254
Woodson, Dick
70OPC-479
70T-479
71MLB/St-479
71OPC-586
71T-586
72T-634
73OPC-98
73T-98
74OPC-143
74T-143
78Twin/Frisz-49
92Yank/WIZ70-168
Woodson, George
69T-244R
Woodson, Kerry
89Belling/Legoe-16
90A&AASingle/ProC-136
90AS/Cal-19
90Foil/Best-308
90ProC/Singl-857
90SanBern/Best-25
90SanBern/Cal-90
90SanBern/ProC-2635
91B-264
92B-411
92Calgary/ProC-3733
92D/Rook-127
92Jacks/ProC-3707
92Jaxvl/SB-373
92Sky/AASingl-160
93D-748
93F/MLPII-2
93S-327
93T-539
93T/Gold-539
93UD-388
93Ultra-275
Woodson, Tracy
85VeroB-2
87Albuq/Pol-24
87Mother/Dodg-22
88AAA/ProC-3
88Albuq/CMC-17
88Albuq/ProC-256
88D-499
88F/Up-U98
89Albuq/CMC-16
89Albuq/ProC-75
89F-77
89Pol/Dodg-12
89S-586
89T-306
89T/Big-92
89UD-108
90AAASingl/ProC-176
90ProC/Singl-652
90Target-875
90Vanco/CMC-25
90Vanco/ProC-498
91AAA/LineD-448
91Richm/Bob-23
91Richm/LineD-448
91Richm/ProC-2579
91Richm/Team-15
92Louisvl/ProC-1896
92Louisvl/SB-272
92Sky/AAASingl-130
93D-652
93F-517
93Pac/Spanish-638
93Pol/Card-24
93S-465
93StCl/Card-22
93T-457
93T/Gold-457
93UD-728
94F-650
Woodward, Jim
82Jacks-17
Woodward, Rob
86D/Rook-53
86F-651R
86Pawtu-28
87Classic-69
87D-652
87Pawtu/TCMA-23
87T-632
88Pawtu/CMC-1
88Pawtu/ProC-448
88S-403
89Pawtu/CMC-10
89Pawtu/Dunkin-25
89Pawtu/ProC-699
90AAASingl/ProC-460
90ProC/Singl-303
90RochR/CMC-2
90RochR/ProC-703
90Rochester/L&U-18
91AAA/LineD-473
91RochR/LineD-473
91RochR/ProC-1904
Woodward, Vince
85Clovis-44
Woodward, William
(Woody)
64T-378R
65T-487
66OPC-49
66T-49
67CokeCap/Brave-8
67Kahn
67T-546
68CokeCap/Brave-8
68Dexter-75
68T-476
69OPC-142
69T-142
69T/4in1-3M
70OPC-296
70T-296
71MLB/St-72
71OPC-496
71T-496
72MB-370
Woodworth, John
77Fritsch-16
80Utica-9
82Knoxvl-23
83Knoxvl-21
85Syrac-10TR
86Syrac-27TR
90Dunedin/Star-28TR
91Dunedin/ClBest-30
92Dunedin/ClBest-28TR
93Dunedin/ClBest-28TR
Woolridge, Floyd
55Hunter
Wooten, Daryl
89AubAs/ProC-2189
Wooten, Earl
49B-189
Wooten, Junior
88Chatt/Team-31
Wooten, Shawn
90LitSun/HSPros-14
90LitSun/HSProsG-14
94FExcel-63
94FExcel/1stY-9
Worden, Bill
82Danvl/Frit-20
83Redwd-25
84Nashvl-25
86Water-26
Workman, Michael
86Watlo-32
87Kinston-14
Works, Ralph
E286
T207
Worley, Bob
92Belling/ClBest-17
92Belling/ProC-1445
Worrell, Tim
91Brisbane/Fut-14
91MidwLAS/ProC-31
91Waterlo/ClBest-10
91Waterlo/ProC-1257
92ClBest-314
92Sky/AASingl-289
92UD/ML-181
92Wichita/SB-631
93B-138
93ClBest/MLG-49
93F/Final-148
93FExcel/ML-112
93Ultra-480
94D-318
94F-679
94StCl-519
94StCl/1stDay-519
94StCl/Gold-519
94T-458
94T/Gold-458
Worrell, Todd
81Louisvl-26
83Louisvl/Riley-26
84ArkTr-6
85Louisvl-28
86D-43RR
86D/HL-29
86D/HL-54
86D/Rook-21
86F-49
86KAS/Disc-10
86Schnucks-24
86Seven/Coin-S15M
86Sf-179R
86Sf/Rook-35
86T/Tr-127T
87Classic-97
87D-307
87F-312
87F/AS-8
87F/AwardWin-44
87F/Hottest-44
87F/LL-44
87F/Lim-43
87F/Mini-119
87F/RecSet-43
87F/St-128
87Leaf-218
87OPC-67
87Sf-33
87Sf-77M
87Sf/TPrev-12M
87Smok/Cards-2
87T-465
87T-605AS
87T-7RB
87T/Coins-48
87T/Gloss60-10
87T/HL-13
87T/JumboR-22
87T/Mini-34
87T/St-11
87T/St-12
87T/St-310
87T/St-55
87ToysRUs-33
87Woolwth-13
88Bz-22
88ChefBoy-8
88Classic/Red-181
88D-386
88D/Best-268
88F-50
88F/LL-44
88F/Mini-111
88F/RecSet-44
88F/Slug-44
88F/St-122
88F/WS-5M
88F/WaxBox-C16
88KMart-32
88KennerFig-123
88Leaf-229
88OPC-135
88Panini/St-386
88S-202
88Sf-61
88Smok/Card-10
88T-715
88T/Big-149
88T/Coins-60
88T/Mini-73
88T/St-54
88Woolwth-24
89B-429
89Cadaco-62
89D-82
89D/AS-60
89D/Best-243
89F-466
89F/BBMVP's-44
89F/Superstar-44
89KennerFig-165
89Louisvl-37
89OPC-291
89Panini/St-179
89S-265
89S/HotStar-94
89Sf-183
89Smok/Cards-23
89T-535
89T/LJN-154
89T/Mini-38
89T/St-39
89UD-512
90B-185
90BBWit-29
90D-319
90F-264
90F/Can-264
90MLBPA/Pins-29
90OPC-95
90Panini/St-340
90PublInt/St-231
90PublInt/St-274
90S-392
90Sf-165
90T-95
90T/St-43
90T/TVCard-22
90UD-467
91F-653
91Louisvl/Team-13
91Pol/Card-38
91S-807
92Card/McDon/Pac-54
92F/Up-121
92L-436
92L/BlkGold-436
92Pinn-479
92Pol/Card-25
92StCl-703
92Studio-99
92Ultra-574
93D-72
93F-135
93F/Final-87
93L-429
93Mother/Dodg-21
93OPC-374
93OPC/Premier-62
93Pol/Dodg-29
93S-635
93StCl-728
93StCl/1stDay-728
93StCl/Dodg-16
93T-121
93T/Gold-121
93TripleP-253M
93UD-692
93Ultra-409
94D-397
94F-530
94Flair-185
94L-362
94T-611
94T/Gold-611
94Ultra-221
Worth, Mottola
94T-616M
94T/Gold-616M
Wortham, Rich
80OPC-261DP
80T-502
81D-161
81F-347
81T-107
82Reading-10
92TX-40
Worthington, Al
54NYJour
55Gol/Giants-32
57T-39
58Hires-73
58SFCallB-25
58T-427
59T-28
60T-268
62AmTract-66
63FrBauer-31
63T-556
64T-144
65OPC-216
65T-216
66OPC-181
66T-181
67CokeCap/Twin-10
67T-399
68T-473
73OPC-49CO
73T-49CO
78Twin/Frisz-23
79TCMA-269
81TCMA-405
Worthington, Bob
V94-55
Worthington, Craig
86Hagers-29
87RochR-23
87RochR/TCMA-17
88D/Rook-23
88F/Up-U4
88RochR/CMC-19
88RochR/Gov-27
88RochR/ProC-217
88RochR/Team-26
88TripleA/ASCMC-19
89D-569
89D/Best-282
89D/Rook-25
89F-627
89French-11
89Panini/St-252
89S-636
89S/HotRook-6
89S/YS/II-21
89Sf-134
89T-181
89UD/Ext-725
90B-253
90Bz-15
90Classic-31
90D-141
90D/BestAL-71
90F-195
90F/Can-195
90HagersDG/Best-35
90Leaf-170
90OPC-521
90Panini/St-11
90PublInt/St-592
90S-234
90S/100Ris-21
90Sf-117
90T-521
90T/Big-146
90T/Gloss60-49
90T/HeadsUp-22
90T/JumboR-33
90T/St-239
90T/St-328FS
90ToysRUs-32
90UD-444
91Crown/Orio-491
91D-293
91F-496
91Leaf-298
91OPC-73
91Panini/FrSt-242
91Panini/St-198
91S-503
91StCl-467
91T-73
91UD-141

91Ultra-26
92ColoSp/ProC-761
92ColoSp/SB-79
92F-31
92OPC-397
92S-724
92StCl-81

Wortman, William
(Chuck)
D328-195
E135-195

Wortmann, Russ
82Idaho-15

Wotus, Ron
82Buffa-11
84Cram/PCL-128
86Hawaii-22
87Omaha-20
89Phoenix/CMC-19
89Phoenix/ProC-1501
90Clinton/ProC-2567CO
91CalLgAS-47
91SanJose/ClBest-23MG
91SanJose/ProC-27MG
92SanJose/ClBest-26MG

Woyce, Don
86FtMyr-29

Woyt, Boris
V362-29

Wrape, Dave
87BYU-14M

Wray, David
89KS*-25

Wray, James
88GreatF-13
89AS/Cal-16
89Bakers/Cal-189
90SanAn/GS-30
91AA/LineD-550
91SanAn/LineD-550
91SanAn/ProC-2977
92VeroB/ClBest-15
92VeroB/ProC-2877

Wren, Frank
80Memphis-28

Wrenn, Luke
76Shrev

Wright, Ab
92Conlon/Sport-407

Wright, Bill
87Idaho-17

Wright, Burnis
(Bill)
91Negro/Lewis-10
92Negro/Kraft-12

Wright, Brian
89Idaho/ProC-2009

Wright, Clarence
90Target-876

Wright, Clyde
69T-583
70OPC-543
70T-543
71Bz
71Bz/Test-6
71JB
71K-28
71MLB/St-359
71OPC-240
71OPC-67LL
71T-240
71T-67LL
71T/Coins-60
71T/GM-18
71T/Greatest-18
71T/S-39
71T/Super-39
71T/tatt-14
72MB-371
72OPC-55
72T-55
73OPC-373
73T-373
74OPC-525
74T-525
75OPC-408
75T-408
75T/M-408
76OPC-559
76SSPC-258
76T-559
89Smok/Angels-6
93Rang/Keeb-387

Wright, Dave
75FtLaud/Sus-5

Wright, Don
88AppFx/ProC-146
89AppFx/ProC-855
90BBCity/Star-27

Wright, Ernie
88MissSt-35
89MissSt-40

Wright, F. Glenn
25Exh-56
26Exh-56
28Exh-28
28Yueng-47
31Exh/4-4
33Exh/4-2
33G-1453
34Exh/4-2
35G-2B
35G-4B
35G-7B
90Target-877
R306
V353-77
W502-47
W512-5

Wright, George DeWitt
78Ashvl
79Ashvl/TCMA-10
80Tulsa-10
81Tulsa-1
83D-116
83F-583
83F/St-16M
83OPC/St-124
83Rang-26
83T-299
83T/St-124
84D-525
84F-435
84Nes/792-688
84OPC-314
84Rang-26
84T-688
84T/RD-21M
84T/St-353
85D-256
85F-574
85OKCty-16
85OPC-387
85T-443
85T/RD-21M
86D-220
86F-578
86T-169
86T/Tr-128T
89HOF/St-15
89Phoenix/CMC-24
89Phoenix/ProC-1484
93Rang/Keeb-388

Wright, George
50Callahan
50W576-78
76Shakey-13
80Perez/HOF-12
80SSPC/HOF
91Conlon/Sport-208

Wright, Goldie
83Redwd-26

Wright, Henderson E.
(Ed)
47TipTop
52T-368

Wright, J.P.
89Kenosha/ProC-1072
89Kenosha/Star-24

Wright, James L.
78PapaG/Disc-18
79OPC-180
79T-722R
80OkCty
80T-524
82D-490
82T-362

Wright, James R.
79T-349
80Penin/B-13
80Penin/C-7
81Syrac/Team-24
81T-526R
82Syrac-10
86Peoria-26CO
87Pittsfld-5
87Toledo/TCMA-12
88Iowa/CMC-25
88Iowa/ProC-542
89Iowa/CMC-24
89Iowa/ProC-1697
90AAASingl/ProC-316CO
90ProC/Singl-249CO
90ScranWB/CMC-23CO
90ScranWB/ProC-614CO
91AAA/LineD-500M
91ScranWB/LineD-500CO
91ScranWB/ProC-2557CO
92ScranWB/ProC-2464CO
92ScranWB/SB-500CO
93ScranWB/Team-29CO

Wright, Jamey
94B-58
94ClBest/Gold-28
94ClBest/GoldLP-18
94Pinn-268
94Pinn/Artist-268
94Pinn/Museum-268
94S-573
94SigRook-29
94T-744DP
94T/Gold-744DP

Wright, Ken
71OPC-504
71T-504
72T-638
73OPC-578
73T-578
76QuadC
77QuadC
92Yank/WIZ70-169

Wright, Larry
78Clinton
79Clinton/TCMA-22

Wright, Mark
80Batavia-30
81Wisco-11
82Wisco/Frit-6

Wright, Mel
73OPC-517
73T-517C
83Expo/PostC-25CO
83Stuart-25CO

Wright, Mike
79QuadC-1

Wright, Mitch
79Newar-21

Wright, Paul
82Redwd-17

Wright, Richard
(Ricky)
81Albuq/TCMA-7
82Albuq-11
83F-226
83Pol/Dodg-21
85OKCty-9
86Rang-24
86T/Tr-129T
87T-202
87Toledo-6
90Target-878
92TX-41
93Rang/Keeb-389

Wright, Skipper
88Sumter/ProC-404
89BurlB/ProC-1626
89Star/IISingl-112
90CLAS/CL-27
90Durham/Team-11

Wright, Taft
40PlayBall-186
41G-10
41PlayBall-32
42Playball-17
47TipTop
49B-96
Exh47

Wright, Thomas
51B-271
54T-140
55T-141
55T/DH-75
94T/Arc54-140

Wright, W. Henry
(Harry)
50Callahan
50W576-79
75F/Pion-2
76Shakey-70
80Perez/HOF-70
80SSPC/HOF
N172
N690

Wright, William S.
T206

Wrightstone, Russell
21Exh-191
26Exh-48
27Exh-24
91Conlon/Sport-238
E120
E126-43
V61-61
W573

Wrigley, Charles
R332-9UMP

Wrigley, Zeke
90Target-1097

Wrona, Bill
86Beaum-25
88Wichita-21
89LasVegas/CMC-19
89LasVegas/ProC-18
90AAASingl/ProC-635
90Iowa/CMC-16
90Iowa/ProC-328
90ProC/Singl-91
90T/TVCub-65

Wrona, Dave
88CapeCod/Sum-39
90Beloit/Star-24
91Beloit/ClBest-23
91Beloit/ProC-2113
91ClBest/Singl-213
92AS/Cal-6
92Stockton/ClBest-8
92Stockton/ProC-45

Wrona, Rick
86WinSalem-28
87Pittsfld-17
89D/Rook-38
90D-512
90OPC-187
90S-557
90S/100Ris-73
90T-187
90T/TVCub-21
90UD-582
91S-519
92Nashvl/ProC-1835
92Nashvl/SB-298
93StCl-64
93StCl/1stDay-64

Wrona, Ron
76BurlB
77Holyo
78Spokane/Cramer-17
78Spokane/Team-15

Wuerch, Jason
92GulfCY/ProC-3800
93Greens/ClBest-26
93Greens/ProC-902

Wulfemeyer, Mark
75QuadC

Wunsch, Kelly
94ClBest/Gold-20
94ClBest/GoldLP-19
94Pol/Brew-5M
94T-210FDP
94T/Gold-210FDP

Wurm, Garry
89Boise/ProC-2005
90Erie/Star-28

Wuthrich, David
88Pocatel/ProC-2074

Wuycheck, John
89KS*-88

Wyatt, Chuck
91Billing/SportP-10
91Billings/ProC-3754

Wyatt, Dave
83Lynch-19
85Lynch-10
86Tidew-29
87Tidew-14
87Tidew/TCMA-9

Wyatt, John T.
63T-376
64T-108
65OldLond-39
65T-590
66T-521
67T-261
67T/Test/RSox-24
68Dexter-76
68T-481
78TCMA-159

Wyatt, John W.
(Whit)
39PlayBall-95
40PlayBall-67
41DP-14
41G-18
41G-18
41PlayBall-55
43Playball-30
60Lake
60SpicSpan-26CO
60T-464C
68CokeCap/RedSox-4
89Smok/Dodg-43
90Target-879
92Yank/WIZ60-140
PM10/Sm-202
R314

Wyatt, Porter
78Newar

Wyatt, Reggie
84Memphis-6

Wyczawski, Paul
91MissSt-54M
92MissSt-49M

Wyde, Rich
91Everett/ClBest-17

Wykle, David
89TNTech-31

Wylie, John
91Boise/ClBest-14
91Boise/ProC-3881
92Boise/ClBest-12
92Boise/ProC-3629
92PalmSp/ClBest-7

Wynegar, Butch
77BurgChef-53
77Ho-84
77Ho/Twink-84
77K-56
77OPC-176
77Pep-3
77T-175
78Ho-37
78OPC-104
78T-555
78Twin/FriszP-24
79Ho-141
79OPC-214DP
79T-405
79Twin/FriszP-28
80OPC-159
80T-304
81D-529
81F-558
81OPC-61
81T-61
81T/St-102
82D-508
82Drake-32
82F-565
82OPC-222
82T-222
82T/St-208
82T/Tr-131T
83D-325
83F-399
83OPC-379
83OPC/St-101
83T-617
83T/St-101
84D-458
84F-144
84Nes/792-123
84OPC-123
84T-123
84T/St-321
85D-417
85D/AAS-45
85F-147
85Leaf-165
85OPC-28
85T-585
85T/St-316
86D-274
86F-122
86Leaf-147
86OPC-235
86T-235
86T/St-299
87D/OD-6

87OPC-203
87Smok/Cal-10
87T-464
88S-355
88Smok/Angels-23
88T-737
89S-140
92Yank/WIZ80-205
Wyngarden, Brett
92AubAs/ClBest-15
92AubAs/ProC-1358
Wynn, Early
49B-110
50B-148
50NumNum
51B-78
51FB
51T/RB-8
52B-142
52RM-AL24
52T-277
53B/Col-146
53RM-AL14
53T-61
54B-164
54DanDee
55B-38
55Gol/Ind-32
55RFG-14
55RM-AL14
55Salem
55W605-14
56Carling-10
56T-187
57Sohio/Ind-18
57T-40
58T-100
59T-260
60Armour-20
60Bz-28
60NuCard-71
60T-1
60T/tatt-55
61NuCard-471
61P-22
61T-337M
61T-455
61T-50LL
61T/St-131
62J-55
62P-55
62P/Can-55
62Salada-97A
62Salada-97B
62Shirriff-97
62T-385
62T/St-30
62T/bucks
63J-43
63P-43
76Laugh/Jub-23
76Shakey-133
77Galasso-36
79TCMA-20
80Laugh/3/4/5-26
80Pac/Leg-73
80Perez/HOF-133
80SSPC/HOF
82Ohio/HOF-22
83D/HOF-42
86Sf/Dec-36
88Pac/Leg-95
89Swell-60
91T/Arc53-61
92Bz/Quadra-5M
93AP/ASG-112
93AP/ASG24K-46G
Wynn, Jim
64T-38
64T/Coins-2
65OPC-257
65T-257
66Bz-35
66T-520
66T/RO-11
66T/RO-99
67Ast/Team-12
67Bz-35
67CokeCap/Astro-17
67T-390
67T/Test/SU-24
68Bz-11
68Dexter-77
68OPC-5LL
68T-260
68T-5LL
68T/ActionSt-11CM
68T/G-24
68T/Post-8
69MLB/St-144
69MLBPA/Pin-60
69T-360
69T/DE-11
69T/S-43
69T/St-40
69T/decal
69Trans-41
70K-9
70MLB/St-48
70OPC-60
70T-60
70T/S-35
70T/SO
70T/Super-35
70Trans-4
71Bz/Test-43
71MLB/St-96
71OPC-565
71T-565
71T/Coins-69
71T/GM-31
71T/Greatest-31
72MB-372
72T-770
73OPC-185
73T-185
74OPC-43
74T-43
74T/St-40
74T/Tr-43T
75Ho-25
75Ho/Twink-25
75OPC-570
75T-570
75T/M-570
76Crane-68
76Ho-129
76MSA/Disc
76OPC-395
76SSPC-89
76T-395
77BK/Y-20
77T-165
86Mother/Ast-7
87Smok/Dodg-39
88Smok/Dodg-20
89Smok/Dodg-86
90Target-880
92Yank/WIZ70-170
93AP/ASG-156
Wynne, Billy
70T-618
71MLB/St-360
71OPC-718
71T-718
91WIZMets-436
Wynne, Jim
91James/ClBest-18
91James/ProC-3546
92Albany/ClBest-13
92Albany/ProC-2307
Wynne, Marvell
82Tidew-16
83Tidew-21
84D-508
84F-269
84Jacks/Smok-14
84Nes/792-173
84T-173
84T/St-135
85D-113
85F-481
85Leaf-233
85OPC-86
85T-615
85T/St-131
86D-113
86F-625
86F/Up-U130
86OPC-293
86T-525
86T/St-128
87Bohem-16
87D-411
87D/OD-144
87F-435
87T-37
88D-237
88OPC/WaxBox-H
88S-209
88Smok/Padres-31
88T-454
88T/WaxBox-H
89D-347
89D/Best-189
89F-322
89KennerFig-166
89Panini/St-205
89S-203
89T-353
89T/St-107
89UD-154
90Cub/Mara-26
90D-255
90Leaf-270
90OPC-256
90PublInt/St-63
90S-337
90T-256
90T/TVCub-35
90UD-14
91F-441
91OPC-714
91S-531
91T-714
Wyrostek, John
48B-44
48L-19
49B-37
49Eureka-99
50B-197
51B-107
51T/BB-44
52B-42
52NTea
52T-13
53B/BW-35
53T-79
55B-237
91T/Arc53-79
Wyse, Henry
44Playball-34
47TipTop
51B-192
Wyszynski, Dennis
80WHave-2
Xavier, Joe
88Tacoma/CMC-25
88Tacoma/ProC-613
89Denver/CMC-21
89Denver/ProC-53
90AAASingl/ProC-661
90Denver/CMC-7
90Denver/ProC-636
90ProC/Singl-32
Yacopino, Ed
87Macon-20
88Salem/Star-24
89Harris/ProC-291
89Harris/Star-22
90Harris/ProC-1207
90Harris/Star-22
91AA/LineD-122
91CaroMud/LineD-122
91CaroMud/ProC-1099
92RochR/ProC-1954
92RochR/SB-473
Yaeger, Chuck
86Albany/TCMA-20
Yaeger, Edward
52Laval-41
Yagi
72Dimanche*-137
Yagi, Richard
88Fresno/Cal-14
88Fresno/ProC-1239
Yahmann, Jim
88Jaxvl/Best-26
Yahrling, Charles
52Laval-48
Yamada, Tsutoma
92AS/Cal-13
92Salinas/ClBest-19
92Salinas/ProC-3757
Yamaguchi, Yuji
89Salinas/Cal-133
89Salinas/ProC-1813
Yamamoto, Masahiro
88FSLAS/Star-26
88SanJose/Cal-140
88SanJose/ProC-117
88VeroB/Star-25
Yamano, Mickey
86SanJose-24
87SanJose-11
Yamanouchi, Kenichi
90Salinas/Cal-140
90Salinas/ProC-2724
Yamazaki, Kazuharu
(Kazu)
92Niagara/ClBest-7
92Niagara/ProC-3325
Yampierre, Eddie
81Wausau-12
Yan, Julian
87Myrtle-1
88Dunedin/Star-23
88FSLAS/Star-52
89Dunedin/Star-24
89Star/IISingl-118
90Foil/Best-148
90Knoxvl/Best-13
90Knoxvl/ProC-1253
90Knoxvl/Star-22
91AA/LineD-373
91Knoxvl/LineD-373
91Knoxvl/ProC-1777
92Knoxvl/ProC-3001
92Knoxvl/SB-398
92Sky/AASingl-169
93LimeR/Winter-134
93Syrac/ProC-1008
Yan, Roberto
82DayBe-9
Yanagida, Shikato
90AS/Cal-44
90Salinas/Cal-139
90Salinas/ProC-2723
Yancey, William
78Laugh/Black-30
86Negro/Frit-88
Yancy, Hugh
77Indianap-22
79Tacom-10
Yandle, John
80Hawaii-12
81Holyo-6
Yandrick, Jerry
77Charl
Yanes, Eddie
86Visalia-24
87OrlanTw-19
88OrlanTw/Best-4
Yang, Charles
91Daikyo/Fut-12CO
Yanus, Bud
80Memphis-29
83Memphis/TCMA-12
86WPalmB-28CO
87WPalmB-11
Yarbrough, Buddy
77DaytB
Yaroshuk, Ernie
92Oneonta/ClBest-3
Yarrison, Rube
90Target-1099
Yaryan, Clarence
E120
V100
Yastrzemski, Carl
60T-148
61T-287
61T/St-119
62J-61
62P-61
62P/Can-61
62Salada-27
62Shirrlff-27
62T-425
62T/St-20
62T/bucks
63Bz-16
63F-8
63J-80
63P-80
63T-115
63T/SO
64Bz-16
64T-210
64T-82M
64T-8LL
64T/Coins-134AS
64T/Coins-26
64T/S-48
64T/SU
64T/St-23
64T/tatt
64Wheat/St-50
65OldLond-40
65T-385
65T/E-1
65T/trans-36SP
66Bz-22
66OPC-70
66T-216LL
66T-70
66T/RO-100
66T/RO-110
67Bz-22
67CokeCap/AS-17
67CokeCap/RedSox-2
67OPC/PI-5
67T-355
67T/PI-5
67T/Test/RSox-25
67T/Test/RSox-29
67T/Test/SU-21
68Bz-2
68OPC-152WS
68OPC-192CL
68OPC-2LL
68OPC-4LL
68OPC-6LL
68T-152WS
68T-192CL
68T-250
68T-2LL
68T-369AS
68T-4LL
68T-6LL
68T/ActionSt-13B
68T/ActionSt-1B
68T/ActionSt-6A
68T/G-3
68T/Post-16
69Kelly/Pin-20
69MLBPA/Pin-30
69OPC-130
69OPC-1LL
69OPC/DE-24
69T-130
69T-1LL
69T-425AS
69T/4in1-25
69T/DE-4
69T/S-5
69T/St-140
69T/decal
70MLB/St-168
70OPC-10
70OPC-461AS
70T-10
70T-461AS
70T/S-29
70T/SO
70T/Super-29
71Bz
71Bz/Test-5
71MLB/St-336
71MLB/St-576
71OPC-530
71OPC-61LL
71OPC-65LL
71T-530
71T-61LL
71T-65LL
71T/Coins-58
71T/GM-40
71T/Greatest-40
71T/S-49
71T/Super-49
71T/tatt-2
71T/tatt-2a
72OPC-37
72OPC-38IA
72T-37
72T-38IA
72T/Post-2
73OPC-245
73T-245
73T/Comics-24
73T/Lids-55
73T/PinUps-24
74Laugh/ASG-70
74OPC-280
74T-280
74T/DE-43
74T/Puzzles-12
74T/St-140

75Ho-48
75K-51
75OPC-205MVP
75OPC-280
75SSPC/42-23
75T-205MVP
75T-280
75T/M-205MVP
75T/M-280
76Crane-69
76Ho-149
76K-24
76Laugh/Jub-9
76MSA/Disc
76OPC-230
76SSPC-409
76T-230
77BurgChef-36
77Ho-4
77Ho/Twink-4
77OPC-37
77Pep-23
77T-434TBC
77T-480
77T/CS-53
77T/ClothSt-53
78OPC-137
78PapaG/Disc-8
78Pep-39
78SSPC/270-187
78T-40
78Tastee/Discs-16
78Wiffle/Discs-78
79K-45
79OPC-160
79T-320
79T/Comics-3
80K-27
80OPC-365
80Perez/HOF-204
80T-1M
80T-720
80T/S-22
80T/Super-22
81Coke
81D-214
81D-94
81Drake-1
81F-221
81F/St-13
81K-48
81OPC-110
81PermaGr/CC-4
81T-110
81T/HT
81T/St-45
82Coke/Bos
82D-74
82F-312
82F-633M
82F/St-162
82F/St-237M
82K-43
82KMart-11
82OPC-358IA
82OPC-72
82PermaGr/CC-13
82T-650
82T-651IA
82T/St-120
82T/St-155
83D-25DK
83D-326
83D/AAS-44
83Drake-32
83F-200
83F-629M
83F/St-17M
83F/St-5M
83K-9
83OPC-126SV
83OPC-4
83OPC/St-31FOIL
83OPC/St-6
83PermaGr/CC-35
83T-550
83T-551SV
83T/Fold-2M
83T/Gloss40-1
83T/St-31
83T/St-6
84D-660
84D-LLB
84D/Champs-10
84F-412
84F-640IA
84F/St-97
84Nes/792-6HL
84T-6HL
84T/Gloss22-11
85CircK-17
86Sf/Dec-47
87KMart-11
87T-314TBC
89Kahn/Coop-11
89Kenner/BBGr-19
89T/LJN-129
90BBWit-34
90CollAB-12
90D-588PUZ
90HOF/St-71
90MSA/AGFA-2
90Pac/Legend-61
90Perez/GreatMom-72
90Swell/Great-5
90T/Gloss22-22CAPT
91Swell/Great-108
92Perez/Master-46
92Perez/Master-47
92Perez/Master-48
92Perez/Master-49
92Perez/Master-50
92S/Factory-B15
92S/Factory-B16
92S/Factory-B17
92S/Franchise-3
92S/Franchise-4M
92S/Franchise-AU3
92S/Franchise-AU4M
92Ziploc-4
93Select/TCr-2
93TWill-7
93TWill/Locklear-8
Exh47
PM10/Sm-203
PM10/Sm-204
WG10-48
WG9-50

Yastrzemski, Mike
84Durham-3
85Durham-32
86BirmB/Team-17
86SLAS-2
87Hawaii-1
88Vanco/CMC-19
88Vanco/ProC-774
90BirmDG/Best-32

Yasuda, Hideyuki
91CalLgAS-40
91Salinas/ClBest-3
91Salinas/ProC-2248

Yates, Al
No Cards.

Yates, Lance
90OK-20

Yates, Peter
91Daikyo/Fut-9

Yaughn, Kip
91CLAS/ProC-CAR10
91Freder/ClBest-11
91Freder/ProC-2365
92Hagers/ProC-2558
92Hagers/SB-273
92Sky/AASingl-116
93T-669
93T/Gold-669

Yawkey, Tom
80Perez/HOF-173
89HOF/St-93

Yde, Emil
92Conlon/Sport-546

Yeager, Eric
85Anchora-32
87Anchora-32

Yeager, Joseph F.
(Joe)
90Target-881
C46-84
E107
E270/1

Yeager, Steve
73OPC-59
73T-59
74OPC-593
74T-593
75OPC-376
75T-376
75T/M-376
76Ho-147
76OPC-515
76SSPC-83
76T-515
77BurgChef-151
77OPC-159
77T-105
78SSPC/270-73
78T-285
79OPC-31
79T-75
80OPC-371
80Pol/Dodg-7
80T-726
81D-297
81F-129
81OPC-318
81Pol/Dodg-7
81T-318
81T/HT
82D-201
82F-29
82OPC-219
82Pol/Dodg-7
82T-477
82T/St-259M
83D-201
83F-227
83OPC-261
83Pol/Dodg-7
83T-555
84D-581
84F-117
84Nes/792-661
84OPC-252
84Pol/Dodg-7
84T-661
84T/St-86
85Coke/Dodg-34
85D-519
85F-390
85OPC-148
85T-148
86D-519
86F/Up-U131
86Mother/Mar-5
86OPC-32
86T-32
86T/Tr-130T
87F-599
87OPC-258
87T-258
90Target-882

Yearout, Mike
86Knoxvl-26
87Knoxvl-3

Yeglinski, John
75Lafay
77ArkTr

Yelding, Eric
85Kingst-23
86Ventura-28
87Knoxvl-12
88AAA/ProC-37
88Syrac/CMC-17
88Syrac/ProC-832
89D/Rook-34
89Lennox/Ast-12
89Mother/Ast-21
89S/HotRook-65
90Classic/III-58
90D-123
90D/BestNL-114
90F/Up-U18
90HotRook/St-49
90Leaf-301
90Lennox-27
90Mother/Ast-24
90OPC-309
90S-411
90S/100Ris-16
90S/YS/I-15
90T-309
90T/89Debut-148
90T/Big-317
90UD-427
91B-557
91Classic/200-71
91D-277
91F-520
91Leaf-100
91Mother/Ast-7
91OPC-59
91Panini/FrSt-12
91Panini/St-13
91Panini/Top15-42
91RedFoley/St-103
91S-329
91StCl-16
91T-59
91UD-197
91Ultra-141
92D-148
92S-197
92StCl-2
92Tucson/ProC-502
92Tucson/SB-623
92UD-394
93Cub/Mara-32
93Pac/Spanish-129
94F-403
94StCl/Team-337

Yellen, Larry
64T-226R
65T-292

Yellowhorse, Moses
21Exh-192

Yelovic, John
43Centen-25

Yelton, Rob
91Bristol/ClBest-7
91Bristol/ProC-3610
92Fayette/ClBest-15
92Fayette/ProC-2173

Yerkes, Stephen
D328-196
D329-196
D350/2-197
E135-196
E224
M101/4-196
M101/5-197
T207

Yesenchak, Ed
76AppFx
77AppFx

Yeske, Kyle
92Bluefld/ClBest-2
92Bluefld/ProC-2374

Yett, Rich
81Wisco-12
83OrlanTw-15
84Toledo-5
85F/Up-U131
85Toledo-30
85Twin/Team-27
86Maine-26
86OhHenry-42
87F-263
87Gator-42
87T-134
88F-621
88Gator-42
88S-484
88T-531
89B-79
89D-546
89F-417
89S-467
89T-363
89T/Big-290
89UD/Ext-728
90B-412
90D-509
90F-504
90F/Can-504
90OPC-689
90Portl/CMC-11
90ProC/Singl-563
90PublInt/St-570
90S-274
90T-689
90UD-595

Yingling, Earl
90Target-1100
D328-197
E135-197

Ynclan, Rocky
87Hawaii-24

Yobs, Dave
85BuffB-16
86BuffB-26

Yochim, Ray
49Eureka-200

Yockey, Mark
90Everett/Best-12
90Everett/ProC-3128
91Clinton/ClBest-10
91Clinton/ProC-835
92Shrev/ProC-3873
92Shrev/SB-598

Yoder, Kris
76Wmsprt
78Richm
79Savan-13

Yojo, Minoru
89Visalia/Cal-115
89Visalia/ProC-1424

Yokota, George
86SanJose-25

York, Anthony
47Centen-32
47Signal
49B/PCL-22

York, Charles
92Watertn/ClBest-9
92Watertn/ProC-3236
94ClBest/Gold-46

York, Jim
72OPC-68
72T-68
73OPC-546
73T-546
75OPC-383
75T-383
75T/M-383
76OPC-224
76T-224
92Yank/WIZ70-171

York, Mike
86Lakeland-25
87Macon-7
88Salem/Star-25
89Harris/ProC-310
89Harris/Star-23
89Star/Wax-21
90AAASingl/ProC-489
90BuffB/CMC-11
90BuffB/ProC-374
90BuffB/Team-27
90ProC/Singl-11
91AAA/LineD-48
91BuffB/LineD-48
91BuffB/ProC-543
91OPC-508
91S-738RP
91T-508
91T/90Debut-168
91Ultra-389MLP
92LasVegas/SB-248

York, Ronald
91Idaho/SportP-1

York, Rudy
38Exh/4-12
38G-260
38G-284
39Exh
40Wheat-6
42Playball-13
47TipTop
60T-456C
72F/FFeat-12
72Laugh/GF-3
74Laugh/ASG-42
81Tiger/Detroit-9
85Woolwth-43
90HOF/St-35
93Conlon-773
R346-27
V351B-48

Yorro, Jacinto
90StCath/ProC-3481
91StCath/ProC-3410

Yoshida, Takashi
89Visalia/Cal-120CO
89Visalia/ProC-1430

Yoshinaga, Yoshi
89Salinas/Cal-136
89Salinas/ProC-1810

Yost, Eddie
49B-32
50B-162
51B-41
51T/BB-1
52B-31
52NTea
52RM-AL25
52T-123
52TipTop
53B/Col-116
53Briggs
54B-72

54RH
55B-73
56T-128
57Swift-11
57T-177
58T-173
59T-2
60T-245
61Bz-6
61P-45
61T-413
61T/St-175
62J-76
62P-76
62P/Can-76
62T-176
73OPC-257CO
73T-257CO
74OPC-179CO
74T-179CO
79TCMA-88
81TCMA-407M
90Pac/Legend-73
91Swell/Great-122
94Mets/69-33
R423-117

Yost, Edgar
(Ned)
78Spokane/Cramer-28
78Spokane/Team-24
79T-708R
79Vanco-13
80Vanco-3
81T-659R
82Pol/Brew-5
82T-542
83D-458
83F-50
83Gard-21
83Pol/Brew-5
83T-297
84D-271
84F-218
84F/X-U130
84Jacks/Smok-15
84Nes/792-107
84Rang-7
84T-107
84T/Tr-131T
85D-221
85F-575
85T-777
87Greenvl/Best-12
88SALAS/GS-3
88Sumter/ProC-414
89Sumter/ProC-1095
90Sumter/Best-30MG
90Sumter/ProC-2450MG
91Brave/Dubuq/Stand-39CO
92Brave/Lyke/Stand-36CO
92Brew/Carlson-25
93Brave/Lyke/Stand-38CO
93Rang/Keeb-390
94TedW-90

Youmans, Floyd
84Jacks-15
86D-543
86Expo/Prov/Pan-24
86F-267
86Leaf-210
86OPC-346
86Provigo-24
86T-732
87Classic-98
87D-257
87D/HL-22
87D/OD-89
87Expo/PostC-13
87F-337
87F/Mini-120
87F/RecSet-44
87GenMills/Book-4M
87Ho/St-6
87Leaf-206
87Leaf-65CG
87OPC-105
87Sf-103
87Sf/TPrev-20M
87Stuart-8M
87T-105
87T/Mini-19
87T/St-79
88D-56
88D/Best-314
88F-201
88Ho/Disc-9
88Leaf-66
88OPC-365
88Panini/St-321
88S-327
88S/YS/II-16
88Sf-108
88T-365
88T/St-82
89B-396
89OPC-91
89Phill/TastyK-36
89T-91
89UD-459
89UD/Ext-730
90Publnt/St-252
90Reading/Star-25

Young, Anthony
88LitFalls/Pucko-24
89Clmbia/Best-16
89Clmbia/GS-28
89SALAS/GS-22
90Jacks/GS-26
90TexLgAS/GS-31
91AAA/LineD-573
91B-466
91Classic/II-T56
91Leaf/GRook-BC23
91PreRookPrev/LineD-573
91Tidew/LineD-573
91Tidew/ProC-2512
91UD/FinalEd-65F
92B-268
92Classic/Game200-144
92Classic/II-T60
92D-409RR
92F-520
92L-356
92L/BlkGold-356
92Mets/Kahn-19
92OPC-148
92Pinn-558
92ProC/Tomorrow-278
92S-756
92S/Impact-39
92S/Rook-14
92StCl-85
92Studio-70
92T-148
92T/91Debut-190
92T/Gold-148
92T/GoldWin-148
92UD-535
92UD/Scout-SR25
92Ultra-238
93D-14
93F-96
93L-545
93Mets/Kahn-19
93OPC-380
93Pac/Spanish-550
93Pinn-350
93S-113
93Select-284
93StCl-582
93StCl/1stDay-582
93T-734
93T/Gold-734
93UD-71
93USPlayC/Rook-3D
93Ultra-81
94D-405
94F-580
94L-74
94S-263
94S/GoldR-263
94StCl-28
94StCl/1stDay-28
94StCl/Gold-28
94T-359
94T/Finest-167
94T/FinestRef-167
94T/Gold-359
94UD-443
94UD/CollC-303
94UD/CollC/Gold-303
94UD/CollC/Silv-303
94Ultra-466

Young, Bob G.
52B-193
52T-147
53T-160
54B-149
54Esskay
54T-8
55Esskay
91Crown/Orio-492
91T/Arc53-160
94T/Arc54-8

Young, Bobby
71Richm/Team-18

Young, Brian
90Elmira/Pucko-24
91WinHaven/ClBest-10
91WinHaven/ProC-490
92WinHaven/ProC-1778

Young, Chris
93Lipscomb-22

Young, Cliff
86Knoxvl-27
86SLAS-24
87Knoxvl-27
88Syrac/CMC-8
88Syrac/ProC-807
89Edmon/CMC-4
89Edmon/ProC-557
90AAASingl/ProC-94
90Edmon/CMC-1
90Edmon/ProC-518
90F/Up-U82
90ProC/Singl-478
91B-204
91Edmon/ProC-1517
91F-330
91T/90Debut-169
92Edmon/SB-173
92F-73
92Sky/AAASingl-83
92StCl-562
93F/Final-207

Young, Curt
83Tacom-8
84Cram/PCL-85
85D-522
85F-436
85Mother/A's-22
85T-293
86T-84
86Tacom-25
87D-344
87D/OD-29
87F-410
87F/GameWin-44
87F/St-129
87Sf/TPrev-23M
87Smok/A's-12
87T-519
87T/St-165
88D-97
88D/A's/Bk-97
88D/Best-323
88F-296
88F/St-58
88Mother/A's-17
88OPC-103
88Panini/St-165
88RedFoley/St-104
88S-125
88Sf-209
88T-103
89B-184
89D-304
89F-26
89Mother/A's-14
89S-29
89T-641
89T/Big-254
89UD-392
90D-505
90F-24
90F/Can-24
90Leaf-424
90Mother/A's-24
90OPC-328
90Publnt/St-319
90S-533
90T-328
90UD-4
91B-220
91D-723
91Mother/A's-24
91OPC-473
91S-236
91T-473
91Ultra-257
92D-469
92F-272
92OPC-704
92Omaha/SB-348
92S-722
92T-704
92T/Gold-704
92T/GoldWin-704
93F-658

Young, Danny
92Ashvl/ClBest-16
92ClBest-381

Young, Del E.
48Sommer-27
49Sommer-21

Young, Delwyn
83Cedar-17
86Vermont-24
87BurlEx-15
87SanBern-11
88EastLAS/ProC-12
88GlenF/ProC-916
89Toledo/CMC-22
89Toledo/ProC-764
90Canton/Best-14
90Canton/ProC-1306
90Canton/Star-18
90ProC/Singl-734

Young, Denton T.
(Cy)
10Domino-129
11Diamond-29
11Helmar-20
12Sweet/Pin-21A
12Sweet/Pin-21B
48Exh/HOF
50Callahan
50W576-80
60F-47
60NuCard-48
61F-153
61GP-33
61NuCard-448
63Bz/ATG-6
69Bz/Sm
72F/FFeat-11
72K/ATG-12
72Laugh/GF-29
73OPC-477LL
73T-477LL
75F/Pion-19
76Shakey-8
77Galasso-169
77Galasso-270
77Shakey-3
79T-416LL
80Laugh/3/4/5-11
80Laugh/FFeat-30
80Marchant/HOF-32
80Pac/Leg-91
80Perez/HOF-13
80SSPC/HOF
82Ohio/HOF-14
83D/HOF-27
84D/Champs-31
85Woolwth-44
88Conlon/4-30
89HOF/St-59
89Swell-5
90BBWit-79
90HOF/St-14
90Perez/GreatMom-10
90Swell/Great-100
91Homer/Classic-5
91Swell/Great-135
92Whitehall-5
92Whitehall/Proto-5
93AP/ASG-85
93AP/ASG24K-19G
93Spectrum/HOFII-4
93UD/ATH-129
93UD/ATH-138
93UD/ATH-142
93UD/ATH-156M
93UD/ATH-157
93UD/ATH-158
93UD/ATH-159
93UD/T202-3M
94TedW-7
94TedW/Lock-18
BF2-31
D304
E101
E106
E107
E120
E121/120
E121/80
E122
E254
E270/1
E90/1
E92
E93
E94
E97
E98
M116
S74-12
T202
T205
T206
T215/brown
T216
W501-68
W555
WG2-51
WG5-45
WG6-42

Young, Derrick
89Clmbia/Best-3
89Clmbia/GS-29
90StLucie/Star-26
91SanBern/ClBest-25
91SanBern/ProC-2002

Young, Dick
90LitSun-9

Young, Dmitri
91Classic/DP-4
91Classic/DPPr-4
91Johnson/ClBest-11
91Johnson/ProC-3993
91UD/FinalEd-7F
92ClBest-272
92ClBest/BBonusC-8
92ClBest/RBonus-BC8
92Classic/DP-89FB
92MidwLAS/Team-54
92ProC/Tomorrow-322
92Spring/ClBest-1
92Spring/ProC-879
92UD-58TP
92UD/ML-274
92UD/ML-30M
92UD/ML-62DS
92UD/ML/TPHolo-TP9
92UD/POY-PY7
93ClBest/Fisher-13
93ClBest/MLG-96
93D-638RR
93FExcel/ML-108
93UD-428TP
93UD/SP-290FOIL
94B-147
94ClBest/GAce-2
94ClBest/Gold-173
94FExcel-276
94Ultra-571

Young, Donald Wayne
66OPC-139R
66T-139R
69T-602R
70OPC-117
70T-117

Young, Don
89Watertn/Star-24

Young, Eric O.
90FSLAS/Star-20
90Star/ISingl-22
90VeroB/Star-29
91AA/LineD-548
91ClBest/Singl-11
91SanAn/LineD-548
91SanAn/ProC-2985
92Albuq/ProC-736
92Albuq/SB-23
92D/Rook-128
92F/Up-94
92Sky/AAASingl-11
93B-416
93D-730
93F-69
93F/Final-47
93Flair-44
93L-415
93OPC/Premier-31
93Pac/Spanish-440
93Pinn-518

93Pinn/Expan-4M
93S-586
93Select-342
93Select/RookTr-130T
93StCl-526
93StCl/1stDay-526
93StCl/Rockie-27
93T-145
93T-551
93T/Finest-48
93T/FinestRef-48
93T/Gold-145
93T/Gold-551
93UD-521
93UD/SP-225
93USPlayC/Rockie-11S
93USPlayC/Rockie-8D
93USPlayC/Rook-5C
93Ultra-361
94D-412
94F-457
94Flair-159
94L-44
94Pac/Cr-209
94Panini-178
94Pinn-133
94Pinn/Artist-133
94Pinn/Museum-133
94S-472
94Select-145
94StCl-72
94StCl/1stDay-72
94StCl/Gold-72
94StCl/Team-104
94T-712
94T/Finest-186
94T/FinestRef-186
94T/Gold-712
94UD-252
94UD/CollC-304
94UD/CollC/Gold-304
94UD/CollC/Silv-304
94UD/ElecD-252
94Ultra-190
Young, Erik
89Watertn/Star-25
Young, Ernest Wesley
(Ernie)
90SoOreg/Best-15
90SoOreg/ProC-3438
91Madison/ClBest-18
91Madison/ProC-2145
92Modesto/ClBest-10
93Modesto/ClBest-25
93Modesto/ProC-814
94ClBest/Gold-98
94FExcel-124
Young, Ernest
75Cedar
75Lafay
76Cedar
79BuffB/TCMA-8
Young, Ernie
87Hagers-27
88Fresno/Cal-5
88Fresno/ProC-1241
Young, Floyd
WG8-52
Young, Ford
60DF-24
Young, Gary
87BYU-15
Young, Gerald
85Osceola/Team-26
86ColumAst-25
87Sf/Rook-36
87Tucson-11
88D-431
88D/Best-318
88F-460
88Leaf-210
88Mother/Ast-3
88OPC-368
88Pol/Ast-24
88S-442
88S/YS/II-11
88T-368
89B-333
89D-207
89D/Best-288
89F-370
89KennerFig-167
89Lennox/Ast-20
89Mother/Ast-3
89OPC-95
89Panini/St-93
89S-97
89S/HotStar-72
89Sf-125
89T-95
89T/Coins-28
89T/Mini-16
89T/St-23
89T/UK-86
89UD-135
90B-72
90D-325
90F-241
90F/Can-241
90Leaf-214
90Lennox-28
90MLBPA/Pins-40
90Mother/Ast-8
90OPC-196
90Panini/St-263
90PublInt/St-105
90PublInt/St-618
90S-43
90T-196
90T/Big-49
90T/St-22
90UD-196
91AAA/LineD-623
91D-689
91F-521
91OPC-626
91S-844
91StCl-494
91T-626
91Tucson/LineD-623
91Tucson/ProC-2227
91Ultra-142
92D-477
92F-446
92OPC-241
92Pinn-458
92S-346
92StCl-355
92T-241
92T/Gold-241
92T/GoldWin-241
93StCl/Rockie-14
93UD-740
93USPlayC/Rockie-6S
93USPlayC/Rockie-9D
93Ultra-362
Young, Greg
91SoBend/ClBest-21
91SoBend/ProC-2858
91Utica/ClBest-9
91Utica/ProC-3241
Young, Irving
M116
T206
WG3-54
Young, Jason
90ClintUp/Team-10
90Everett/Best-21
90Everett/ProC-3137
91Clinton/ClBest-25
91Clinton/ProC-850
Young, Jim
91Rockford/ClBest-2TR
92Rockford/ClBest-30TR
Young, John
77ArkTr
80Indianap-31TR
81Indianap-32TR
83Spring/Frit-15
84ArkTr-22
87Nashvl-24
88Nashvl/CMC-25
88Nashvl/ProC-495
88Nashvl/Team-25TR
88Watertn/Pucko-30
89Nashvl/CMC-9
89Nashvl/ProC-1276
89Nashvl/Team-29TR
90Nashvl/CMC-26TR
90ProC/Singl-673TR
90SpringDG/Best-12
92Nashvl/SB-300M
Young, Kenny
81Bristol-14
Young, Kevin
90Welland/Pucko-8
91ClBest/Singl-239
91Salem/ClBest-9
91Salem/ProC-963
92B-155
92BuffB/BlueS-26
92BuffB/ProC-331
92BuffB/SB-47
92D/Rook-129
92Sky/AAASingl-22
93B-682
93D-452RR
93F/Final-122
93F/MLPI-6
93L/GRook-1
93OPC/Premier-78
93Pac/Spanish-594
93Pinn-589
93Pinn/RookTP-6
93Pirate/Nation-39
93S-273
93S/Boys-10
93S/Proctor-7
93Select/RookTr-51T
93StCl-722
93StCl/1stDay-722
93T-494
93T/Finest-34
93T/FinestRef-34
93T/Gold-494
93T/Tr-52T
93ToysRUs-9
93TripleP-72
93UD-536
93UD/Diam-36
93UD/FunPack-9SOT
93UD/SP-189
93Ultra-459
93Ultra/AllRook-10
94B-274
94D-578
94F-626
94Finest-321
94Flair-222
94L-23
94OPC-124
94Pac/Cr-514
94Panini-241
94Pinn-186
94Pinn/Artist-186
94Pinn/Museum-186
94S-492
94Select-123
94StCl-321
94StCl/1stDay-321
94StCl/Gold-321
94T-622
94T/Gold-622
94TripleP-190
94UD-482
94Ultra-263
Young, Kip
79T-706R
80Spokane-11
80T-251
81Indianap-8
82Indianap-3
Young, Larry
88TM/Umpire-54
89TM/Umpire-52
90TM/Umpire-50
Young, Lemuel
(Pep)
35BU-102
39PlayBall-102
40PlayBall-106
92Conlon/Sport-387
D327
D328-198
D329-197
E135-198
E220
M101/4-197
R313
W514-107
W516-28
Young, Mark
88Dunedin/Star-24
89Butte/SP-22
89Dunedin/Star-25
89Myrtle/ProC-1452
90Dunedin/Star-25
90Peoria/Team-30
91AA/LineD-359
91Knoxvl/LineD-359
91Knoxvl/ProC-1778
Young, Matt J.
81LynnS-12
82SLCity-22
83T/Tr-129T
84D-16DK
84D-362
84F-624
84Mother/Mar-9
84Nes/792-235
84Nes/792-336TL
84OPC-235
84Seven-24W
84T-235
84T-336TL
84T/RD-9M
84T/St-386YS
85D-267
85F-505
85Mother/Mar-14
85OPC-136
85T-485
85T/St-340
86D-267
86F-481
86Mother/Mar-14
86OPC-274
86T-676
86T/St-220
87D-193
87F-600
87F/Up-U131
87Mother/Dodg-12
87OPC-19
87Pol/Dodg-19
87RedFoley/St-123
87Sf/TPrev-14M
87T-19
87T/St-218
87T/Tr-131T
88D-423
88D/A's/Bk-NEW
88F-530
88Mother/A's-21
88OPC-367
88Panini/St-306
88S-357
88T-736
88T/St-72
90F/Up-121
90Leaf-509
90Mother/Mar-16
90OPC-501
90T-501
90T/Tr-131T
90Target-883
90UD/Ext-787
91B-128
91D-493
91F-465
91Leaf-215
91OPC-108
91Pep/RSox-20
91S-126
91S/RookTr-54T
91StCl-426
91T-108
91UD-591
91UD/Ext-740
92D-635
92OPC-403
92Pinn-518
92RedSox/Dunkin-29
92S-668
92StCl-682
92StCl/MemberI-9M
92UD-505
92USPlayC/RedSox-2H
92USPlayC/RedSox-5D
92Ultra-320
93D-459
93F-567
93F/Final-208
93L-153
93MilkBone-9
93Pac/Spanish-39
93StCl-428
93StCl/1stDay-428
Young, Matt
81Clinton-12
Young, Michael Darren
82RochR-19
83RochR-22
84D-621
84F/X-U131
84RochR-19
85D-367
85F-195
85T-173
86D-123
86F-291
86F/Mini-61
86Sf-199
86T-548
86T/St-234
86T/Tatt-11M
87CharRain-10
87D-150
87F-483
87French-43
87T-309
88D-396
88F-575
88OPC-11
88Panini/St-17
88Phill/TastyK-26
88S-393
88S/Tr-51T
88T-11
89ColoSp/ProC-251
89D-632
89River/Best-21
89River/Cal-18
89River/ProC-1399
89S-494
89T-731
89UD-649
90PublInt/St-571
90Wausau/ProC-2143MG
90Wausau/Star-28MG
91AAA/LineD-475M
91Crown/Orio-493
91RochR/LineD-475CO
91RochR/ProC-1920CO
92RochR/ProC-1957CO
92RochR/SB-475M
Young, Michael Leslie
(Mike)
90Geneva/ProC-3046
90Geneva/Star-25
91Geneva/ClBest-26
91Geneva/ProC-4219
Young, Mike 1
86AZ/Pol-20
Young, Mike 2
91Perth/Fut-2MG
Young, Norman
(Babe)
40PlayBall-212
41DP-32
41DP-93
41G-23
41PlayBall-27
49B-240
93Conlon-814
Young, Pete
88MissSt-36
89James/ProC-2136
89MissSt-41
90FSLAS/Star-21
90WPalmB/Star-28
91AA/LineD-273
91ClBest/Singl-189
91Harris/LineD-273
91Harris/ProC-630
92D/Rook-130
92Indianap/SB-198
93D-616
93F/MLPII-17
93Ottawa/ProC-2437
93S-269
93T-432
93T/Gold-432
Young, Ralph S.
E220
V100
W575
Young, Ray
87Dunedin-18
88Modesto-16
88Modesto/Cal-58
89Huntsvl/Best-24
90AAAGame/ProC-48
90AAASingl/ProC-141
90ProC/Singl-578
90Tacoma/CMC-1
90Tacoma/ProC-94
91S-761RP

Young, Rick
75QuadC
Young, Scott
83StPete-13
86ArkTr-26
Young, Shane
84LitFalls-10
86Lynch-28
87Jacks/Feder-7
87TexLgAS-14
88MidldA/GS-5
89MidldA/GS-30
Young, Sly
83Albany-16
Young, Steve
92StCl/MemberIV*-12
Young, Ty
92GulfCM/ProC-3496
Youngbauer, Jeff
79RochR-1
91Pac/SenLg-74
Youngblood, Joel
77T-548
78T-428
79OPC-48
79T-109
80OPC-194
80T-372
81Coke
81D-277
81F-331
81OPC-58
81T-58
81T/St-195
82D-613
82F-543
82OPC-189
82T-655
82T/St-65
82T/StVar-65
83D-572
83F-301
83F-641HL
83Mother/Giants-17
83OPC-265
83OPC/St-143RB
83OPC/St-144RB
83T-265
83T/St-143
83T/St-144
83T/Tr-130T
84D-480
84F-387
84Nes/792-727
84OPC-303
84T-727
84T/St-173
85D-79
85F-625
85Leaf-152
85Mother/Giants-19
85OPC-97
85T-567
85T/St-168
86D-567
86F-555
86Mother/Giants-26
86OPC-177
86T-177
87F-288
87Mother/SFG-20
87OPC-378
87T-759
88Mother/Giants-20
88S-509
88T-418
89B-315
89Kahn/Reds-12
89S-539
89S/Tr-66T
89T-304
89UD-458
90PublInt/St-42
90S-344
91Freder/ClBest-28CO
91Pac/SenLg-131
91WIZMets-437
92Kane/ClBest-26MG
92Kane/ProC-108MG
92Kane/Team-30MG
Youngblood, Todd
91Belling/ClBest-25
91Belling/ProC-3666
92Penin/ClBest-25
92Penin/ProC-2934
93River/Cal-25
Younger, Stan
82BirmB-1
83BirmB-5
84Evansvl-7
90BirmDG/Best-33
Youngman, Pete
86Greens-25TR
87Greens-4
89NewBrit/ProC-601
89NewBrit/Star-25
Youngs, Ross M.
21Exh-193
61F-154
76Shakey-134
77Galasso-131
80Perez/HOF-134
80SSPC/HOF
91Conlon/Sport-26
V100
V61-106
W573
W575
Yount, Robin
75Ho-80
75Ho/Twink-80
75OPC-223
75T-223
75T/M-223
76A&P/Milw
76Ho-11
76Ho/Twink-11
76OPC-316
76SSPC-238
76T-316
77BurgChef-88
77Ho-34
77Ho/Twink-34
77OPC-204
77Pepsi-1
77T-635
77T/CS-54
77T/ClothSt-54
78Ho-138
78OPC-29
78T-173
79Ho-55
79OPC-41
79T-95
80OPC-139
80T-265
81D-323
81F-511
81F/St-38
81K-57
81OPC-4
81T-515
81T/So-10
81T/St-244
81T/St-95
82D-510
82F-155
82F/St-135
82K-28
82OPC-237
82PermaGr/AS-4
82Pol/Brew-19
82T-435
82T/St-203
83D-258
83D/AAS-56
83Drake-33
83F-51
83F-632M
83F/St-4M
83F/St-4M
83Gard-22
83K-14
83OPC-350
83OPC-389AS
83OPC/St-145RB
83OPC/St-146RB
83OPC/St-150LCS
83OPC/St-167
83OPC/St-81FOIL
83PermaGr/AS-9
83PermaGr/CC-36
83Pol/Brew-19
83T-321TL
83T-350
83T-389AS
83T/Gloss40-5
83T/St-145
83T/St-146
83T/St-150
83T/St-167
83T/St-81
84D-1DK
84D-48
84D/AAS-5
84D/Champs-47
84Drake-33
84F-219
84Gard-22
84MiltBrad-30
84Nes/792-10
84OPC-10
84Pol/Brew-19
84Ralston-21
84Seven-2C
84Seven-2E
84Seven-2W
84T-10
84T/Cereal-21
84T/Gloss22-5
84T/Gloss40-36
84T/RD-32M
84T/St-295
84T/St/Box-6
84T/Super-29
85D-48
85D/AAS-21
85Drake-33
85F-601
85F/LimEd-44
85FunFood/Pin-29
85Gard-22
85GenMills-26
85Leaf-44
85OPC-340
85Pol/Brew-19
85Seven-16G
85T-340
85T/RD-32M
85T/St-284
85T/Super-37
86D-48
86Dorman-16
86F-506
86F/LL-44
86F/Mini-103
86F/Slug-44
86F/St-131
86Jay's-20
86Jiffy-5
86Leaf-31
86OPC-144
86Pol/Brew-19
86Seven/Coin-C9M
86Sf-42
86Sf-54M
86Sf-63M
86Sf-71M
86Sf/Dec-73M
86T-780
86T/St-197
86T/Tatt-9M
86TrueVal-11
87Classic-44
87D-126
87D/OD-58
87F-361
87F/Lim-44
87F/St-130
87F/WaxBox-C16
87GenMills/Book-2M
87Ho/St-25
87Kraft-23
87Leaf-67
87OPC-76
87Pol/Brew-19
87RedFoley/St-126
87Sf-16
87Sf/TPrev-19M
87Stuart-21M
87T-773
87T/Board-9
87T/St-196
88D-295
88D/Best-183
88F-178
88F/BB/MVP-44
88F/Mini-33
88F/SS-44
88F/St-40
88Grenada-44
88Jiffy-20
88KMart-33
88KennerFig-124
88Leaf-106
88OPC-165
88Panini/St-129
88Pol/Brew-19
88S-160
88Sf-34
88T-165
88T/Big-66
88T/Coins-32
88T/Mini-21
88T/St-201
88T/UK-87
89B-144
89Brewer/YB-19
89Classic-83
89D-55
89D-5DK
89D/Best-53
89D/DKsuper-5DK
89F-200
89F/Excit-44
89F/Heroes-44
89F/LL-44
89Gard-2
89KMart/Lead-21
89KayBee-33
89KennerFig-168
89KingB/Discs-13
89OPC-253
89Panini/St-377
89Pol/Brew-19
89RedFoley/St-130
89S-151
89S/HotStar-28
89Sf-199
89T-615
89T/Ames-33
89T/Big-249
89T/Coins-60
89T/Crunch-21
89T/Gloss60-38
89T/Hills-33
89T/LJN-58
89T/Mini-59
89T/St-205
89T/St/Backs-21
89T/UK-87
89UD-285
90B-404
90B/Ins-11
90Brewer/MillB-31
90Bz-2
90Classic-147
90CollAB-9
90D-146
90D/BestAL-22
90D/Learning-37
90F-340
90F/AwardWin-44
90F/BB-44
90F/BBMVP-44
90F/Can-340
90F/LL-44
90F/WaxBox-C28
90Holsum/Discs-7
90HotPlay/St-50
90KMart/CBatL-15
90KayBee-33
90Kenner/Fig-92
90KingB/Discs-18
90Leaf-71
90MLBPA/Pins-82
90MSA/Soda-13
90OPC-290
90OPC-389AS
90Panini/St-92
90Pol/Brew-19
90Post-26
90PublInt/St-508
90S-320
90S/100St-92
90S/McDon-25
90Sf-18
90Sunflower-6
90T-290
90T-389AS
90T/Ames-5
90T/Big-59
90T/Coins-1
90T/DH-72
90T/Gloss60-15
90T/Mini-22
90T/St-198
90T/TVAS-23
90UD-567
90UD-91TC
90WonderBrd-11
90Woolwth/HL-1MVP
90Woolwth/HL-22
91B-55
91BBBest/HitM-18
91Brewer/MillB-31
91Cadaco-62
91Classic/200-59
91D-272
91F-601
91Leaf-116
91Leaf/Stud-80
91MajorLg/Pins-43
91MooTown-17
91OPC-575
91OPC/BoxB-P
91OPC/Premier-131
91Panini/FrSt-208
91Panini/St-166
91Panini/Top15-56
91Pol/Brew-28
91Post/Can-21
91RedFoley/St-104
91S-525
91S-854FRAN
91S/100SS-38
91StCl-509
91T-575
91T/CJMini/I-23
91T/SU-36
91T/WaxBox-P
91UD-344
91Ultra-184
91Woolwth/HL-22
92B-700
92Brew/Carlson-26
92Brew/Sen/Yount-Set
92CJ/DI-8
92Classic/Game200-128
92Classic/I-98
92Classic/II-T30
92D-173
92D/McDon-12
92F-194
92F-708PV
92F/Up-H2
92Hardee-24
92JDean/Living-4
92L-397M
92L-64
92L/BlkGold-397M
92L/BlkGold-64
92L/GoldPrev-20
92L/Prev-20
92MrTurkey-26
92OPC-90
92OPC/Premier-111
92Panini-40
92Pinn-287SIDE
92Pinn-38
92Pol/Brew-29
92S-525
92S/100SS-84
92S/Factory-B11
92Seven/Coin-17
92StCl-450
92StCl-607MC
92StCl/MemberII-15
92Studio-200
92Studio/Prev-6
92T-90
92T/Gold-90
92T/GoldWin-90
92T/Kids-80
92T/McDonB-17
92TripleP-81
92UD-456
92UD/ASFF-44
92Ultra-87
93B-535
93Brew/Sen-4
93Classic/GameI-99
93Colla/DM-119
93Colla/DMArt-8
93D-441
93D/DK-16
93D/Elite-L3
93D/Master-15
93D/Prev-17

77Ho-127
77Ho/Twink-127
77OPC-152
77Pep-27
77T-483
77T/CS-55
77T/ClothSt-55
78BK/R-20
78PapaG/Disc-30
78Pep-40
78SSPC/270-98
78T-110
78Tastee/Discs-14
78Wiffle/Discs-79
79Ho-140
79K-24
79OPC-130
79T-260
80OPC-325
80T-620
81D-28
81F-620
81F/St-105
81OPC-214
81Pol/Mar-13
81T-517
81T/So-16
81T/St-27
81T/Tr-857
82D-11DK
82D-127
82Drake-33
82F-519
82F/St-223
82K-1
82OPC-66
82T-769
82T/St-229
83D-559
83D/AAS-54
83F-489
83F/St-15M
83F/St-15M
83Nalley-3
83OPC-368
83OPC/St-116
83T-368
83T/Gloss40-21
83T/St-116
84D-69
84D/AAS-30
84F-625
84Nes/792-83
84OPC-83
84T-83
84T/St-342
90Peoria/Team-35INS
91Cub/Mara-x
93Rang/Keeb-392
93UD/ATH-130

Zitek, Jeff
79Ashvl/TCMA-9

Zitzmann, William
(Billy)
28Exh-16
92Conlon/Sport-570

Zizzo, Johnny
92Bend/ClBest-26CO

Zmudosky, Tom
84Albany-20

Zoldak, Sam
49B-78
50B-182
50NumNum
51B-114
52T-231
R423-120

Zolecki, Mike
94B-404

Zollars, Mike
91BurlInd/ProC-3313
92Watertn/ClBest-21
92Watertn/ProC-3249

Zolzer, Rick
90Spartan/Best-29MG
90Spartan/Star-29GM

Zona, Jeff
89Idaho/ProC-2029

Zosky, Eddie
89FresnoSt/Smok-24
90A&AASingle/ProC-60
90B-523
90Foil/Best-23
90Knoxvl/Best-1
90Knoxvl/ProC-1251
90Knoxvl/Star-23
90ProC/Singl-812
90S-665DC
90Star/ISingl-91
91AAA/LineD-523
91AAAGame/ProC-44
91B-17
91Classic/200-172
91Classic/II-T25
91Leaf/GRook-BC24
91S/ToroBJ-30
91Syrac/Kraft-5
91Syrac/LineD-523
91Syrac/MerchB-30
91Syrac/ProC-2490
91UD/Ext-734
91UD/FinalEd-14F
91Ultra-390MLP
92B-381
92BJ/Fire-35
92Classic/Game200-123
92Classic/I-99
92D-8RR
92F-348
92OPC-72
92Pinn/RookI-11
92ProC/Tomorrow-159
92S/Impact-72
92Sky/AAASingl-234
92StCl-873
92Syrac/MerchB-30
92Syrac/ProC-1979
92Syrac/SB-523
92T-72
92T/91Debut-191
92T/Gold-72
92T/GoldWin-72
92TripleP-190
92UD-544
92Ultra-156
93BJ/D/45-32
93BJ/Fire-35
93D-57
93F-703
93L-190
93OPC-221
93Pac/Spanish-660
93Pinn-247
93S-297
93S/Boys-15
93StCl-460
93StCl/1stDay-460
93T-689
93T/Gold-689

Zottneck, Roger
86QuadC-32
87PalmSp-16

Zuber, Jon
92Batavia/ClBest-23
92Batavia/ProC-3275
92FrRow/DP-97
93ClBest/MLG-137
93FExcel/ML-89
94ClBest/Gold-40

Zuber, William
44Yank/St-30
47TipTop

Zubiri, Jon
92BurlInd/ClBest-11
92BurlInd/ProC-1658

Zupcic, Bob
87Elmira/Cain-9
87Elmira/Red-31
88CLAS/Star-20
88Lynch/Star-27
89NewBrit/ProC-600
89NewBrit/Star-22
90Foil/Best-108
90NewBrit/Best-6
90NewBrit/ProC-1333
90NewBrit/Star-24
90ProC/Singl-880
91AAA/LineD-373
91Pawtu/LineD-373
91Pawtu/ProC-53
92D-720
92F/Up-6
92OPC-377
92Pawtu/SB-373
92Pinn-576
92S-850
92Sky/AAASingl-172
92StCl-839
92T-377
92T/91Debut-192
92T/Gold-377
92T/GoldWin-377
93D-531
93F-186
93F/RookSenII-10
93L-65
93OPC-367
93Pinn-404
93S-362
93Select-292
93Select/ChasRook-10
93StCl-563
93StCl/1stDay-563
93T-562
93T/Gold-562
93ToysRUs-99
93UD-277
93USPlayC/Rook-12C
93Ultra-158
94D-411
94F-47
94Pac/Cr-70
94S-221
94S/GoldR-221
94T-661
94T/Gold-661

Zupka, Bill
85Elmira-25
86Greens-27
87NewBrit-3

Zupo, Frank
58T-229
91Crown/Orio-494

Zurn, Rick
92Beloit/ClBest-24
92Beloit/ProC-406

Zuvella, Paul
82Richm-17
83Richm-17
84Richm-23
85F-651R
85Pol/Atl-18
86F-532
86Richm-26
86T-572
86T/Tr-131T
87T-102
88ColoSp/CMC-18
88ColoSp/ProC-1528
89AAA/CMC-34
89AAA/ProC-33
89ColoSp/CMC-17
89ColoSp/ProC-245
89S-598
89UD-236
90AAASingl/ProC-610
90Omaha/CMC-22
90Omaha/ProC-75
90ProC/Singl-197
90Richm/25Ann-23
90TripleAAS/CMC-34
91AAA/LineD-348
91Omaha/LineD-348
91Omaha/ProC-1044
92Yank/WIZ80-206

Zuverink, George
52T-199
55B-92
56T-276
57T-11
58Hires-66
58T-6
59T-219
91Crown/Orio-495

Zweig, Ivan
91T/Tr-131T
92StCl/Dome-200

Zwilling, Edward
(Dutch)
D329-200
D350/2-200
M101/4-200
M101/5-200
M116

Zwolensky, Mitch
82Wausau/Frit-19
83Tulsa-9
84OKCty-21
85OKCty-2
88Pittsfld/ProC-1356
90AS/Cal-30
90Stockton/Best-28CO
90Stockton/Cal-201
90Stockton/ProC-2201CO
91Stockton/ClBest-25CO
91Stockton/ProC-3048CO

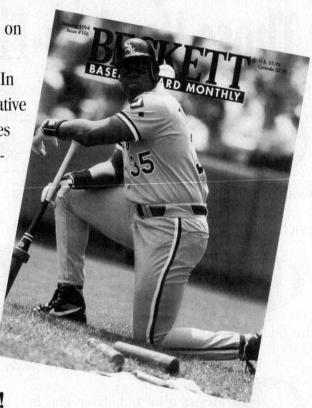